# The Elements and Dynamic Systems of Economic Growth and Trade Models

Bjarne S. Jensen

# The Elements and Dynamic Systems of Economic Growth and Trade Models

## Economic Theory and Axiomatic Analysis of Expanding Economies in Historical Perspective

Volume 1

Second Edition

palgrave
macmillan

Bjarne S. Jensen
The Faculty of Business and Social
Sciences
University of Southern Denmark (SDU)
Odense, Denmark

ISBN 978-3-031-52492-9 ISBN 978-3-031-52493-6 (eBook)
https://doi.org/10.1007/978-3-031-52493-6



This Palgrave Macmillan imprint is published by the registered company Springer Nature Switzerland AG
The registered company address is: Gewerbestrasse 11, 6330 Cham, Switzerland

# Chapters Brought with Permission

Jensen BS (2017) von Thünen: Capital, Production Functions, Marginal Productivity Wages and the Natural Wage. German Economic Review 18:51–80; here Chap. 3

Jensen BS, de Boer P, van Daal J, Jensen PS (2011) Global Restrictions on the Parameters of the CDES Indirect Utility Function. Journal of Economics 102:217–235; here Chap. 5

Jensen BS, Alsholm PK, Larsen ME, Jensen JM (2005) Dynamic Structure, Exogeneity, Phase Portraits, Growth Paths, and Scale and Substitution Elasticities. Review of International Economics 13:59–89; here Chap. 12

Jensen BS (2003) Walrasian General Equilibrium Allocations and Dynamics in Two–Sector Growth Models. German Economic Review 4:53–87; here Chap. 17

Jensen BS, Larsen ME (2005) General Equilibrium Dynamics of Multi–Sector Growth Models. Journal of Economics 10:17–56; here Chap. 18

Jensen BS, Lehmijoki U, Rovenskaya E (2015) Non–Homothetic Multisector Growth Models. Review of Development Economics 19(2):221–243; here Chap. 20

Jensen BS, Wang C (1997) General Equilibrium Dynamics of Basic Trade Models for Growing Economies. In Bjarne S. Jensen and Kar–Yiu Wong (eds.) *Dynamics, Economic Growth, and International Trade*, Ann Arbor: University of Michigan Press; here Chap. 21

Jensen BS, Richter M, Wang C, Alsholm PK (2001) Saving Rates, Trade, Technology, and Stochastic Dynamics. Review of Development Economics 5:182–204; here Chap. 22

Jensen BS, Palokangas T (2007) Stochastic Economic Dynamics. Copenhagen Business School Press, Denmark; here Chaps. 26, 32, and 33

Jensen BS, Wang C (1999) Basic Stochastic Dynamic Systems of Growth and Trade. Review of International Economics 7:378–402; here Chap. 27

# Preface to the First Edition

Two central problems in the pure theory of economic growth are analysed in this monograph: (1) the dynamic laws governing the economic growth processes, (2) the kinematic and geometric properties of the set of solutions to the dynamic systems.

With allegiance to rigor and the emphasis on the theoretical fundamentals of prototype mathematical growth models, the treatise is written in the theorem-proof style. To keep the exposition orderly and as smooth as possible, the economic analysis has been separated from the purely mathematical issues, and hence the monograph is organized in two books.

Regarding the scope and content of the two books, an "Introduction and Overview" has been prepared to offer both motivation and a brief account. The introduction is especially designed to give a recapitulation of the mathematical theory and results presented in Book II, which are used as the unifying mathematical framework in the analysis and exposition of the different economic growth models in Book I. Economists would probably prefer to go directly to Book I and proceed by consulting the mathematical theorems of Book II in confirming the economic theorems in Book I. Thereby, both the independence and interdependence of the economic and mathematical argumentations are respected.

In contrast to linear dynamics systems, which are unified by the powerful superposition principle, there is no dominant principle unifying all nonlinear dynamic systems. Hence, to analyse nonlinear dynamics successfully, it is at first necessary to specify a properly restricted class of dynamic systems. Thus, in short, the restricted class specified by the powerful homogeneity principle is the primary object for the global analyses in these two books. The homogeneity principle, encompassing the superposition principle, has indeed both mathematical and economic implications of major significance. Nevertheless, specific nonhomogeneous dynamic systems are also considered in the treatment of some basic economic growth models.

This monograph is intended for scholars in economics and applied mathematics. It can be used as a basic or supplementary curriculum text in economic and mathematical programmes.

The manuscript was, apart from the last chapter, completed by July 1992, which accordingly is reflected in the bibliographies. It was important also to include in this volume a systematic comparison of planar differential and difference equations.

Many individuals have contributed, each in an important way, to the completion of this treatise.

My interest in the problems of growth theory was inspired by Professor Ragnar Bentzel. Without his encouragement and advice at the early stage, this study would never have been undertaken. I must also acknowledge a great debt to the late Professor Herman Wold for his erudite guidance as teacher and advisor. He accentuated the need for and the importance of "hard theorems in soft sciences". His thoughts on axiomatization and empirical observation in economics remain in my memory. I am grateful to Professor Bertil Holmlund for his critique, suggestions, and helpful counsel on former versions of the text. Indeed, I am much obliged to the favourable academic environment at the University of Uppsala.

For many valuable discussions and comments through the years, I am much indebted to Mogens Esrom Larsen, University of Copenhagen. From Preben Alsholm at The Technical University of Denmark, I received constructive commentary. I am happy to express a deep-felt appreciation to my brother, Jens Martin Jensen, a physicist, who was always willing to discuss general mathematical issues and help with clarification of many intricate equations.

It is with great pleasure that I express my gratitude to Niels Henrik Börjesson, graduate student at the Copenhagen Business School, who did the final typing and endured many changes in the text. He formulated the layout, developed references, and carefully read the manuscript. Because of the technical character of the material and the size of the volume, these tasks involved great responsibility. Without his help, the text in its present form would not have been realized. Finally, I thank, Kathleen Gail Jensen for her linguistic improvements.

In closing, my sincere thanks are conveyed to the editor and staff at Kluwer Academic Publishers for their fine cooperation.

Of course, I am solely responsible for any remaining errors and omissions.

Copenhagen, Denmark
November, 1993

Bjarne S. Jensen

# Preface to the Second Edition

The additions to the 2. edition are very extensive : From two parts to six, and former two parts also include several new chapters.

To a large extent, the background for the additions of parts and topics has been the economic research program related to the international conference series with the same theme : Dynamics, Economic Growth, and International Trade, (DEGIT), held consecutively for 24 years at universities on five continents :

DEGIT I, Denmark (1996), DEGIT II, Hong Kong (1997), DEGIT III, Taiwan (1998), DEGIT IV, Tilburg (1999), DEGIT V, Rome (2000), DEGIT VI, Vienna (2001), DEGIT VII, Cologne (2002), DEGIT VIII, Helsinki (2003), DEGIT IX, Reykjavik (2004), DEGIT X, Mexico City (2005), DEGIT XI, Jerusalem (2006), DEGIT XII, Melbourne (2007), DEGIT XIII, Manila (2008), DEGIT XIV, Los Angeles (2009), DEGIT XV, Frankfurt (2010), DEGIT XVI, St. Petersburg (2011), DEGIT XVII, Milan (2012), DEGIT XVIII, Lima (2013), DEGIT XIX, Nashville (2014), DEGIT XX, Geneva (2015), DEGIT XXI, Nottingham (2016), DEGIT XXII, Paris (2017), DEGIT XXIII, Moscow (2018), DEGIT XXIV, Odense (2019).

Many individuals, colleagues, and friends have supported, each in an important way, to the completion of this volume.

It is with great pleasure that I express my gratitude to Victor Alexander Brandsen, graduate student at The Technical University of Denmark, who did the LaTeX version of the entire volume and endured many changes in the text. He formulated the layout, developed references, and carefully checked the manuscript. Because of the technical character of the material and the size of the volume, these tasks involved great responsibility. Finally, I thank my family for patience and support over the many years of writing.

In closing, my sincere thanks are conveyed to the editors and staff at Springer Nature and Palgrave Macmillan for the fine cooperation.

Of course, I am solely responsible for any remaining errors and omissions.

University of Southern Denmark (SDU) Bjarne S. Jensen
September, 2023

# Introduction and Overview

The *causes* of the *wealth* of nations and the long-term prospects of *economic evolution* have always been central topics in economics, from the writings of the classicists, neoclassicists, and into our modern epoch. Discussions on the propagation of population, capital accumulation, and income distribution were devoted to the understanding and description of the *process* (dynamics) of economic growth. In classical economics, increasing *wealth* (riches, progress of opulence, national income) originated from the *dynamic interaction* between *land, labor*, and *capital*, mostly with land (natural resources) supposed available in a fixed amount (severe restraint on states of the economy).

Macroeconomic theories of economic growth thus go far back to the beginning of the economic discipline, but the theoretical explanations and empirical results from particular growth models have, from the outset and later on, been the object of many controversies, due to the economic and *dynamic complexities* involved in any particular growth model of *continuous factor* (labor and capital) *accumulation*. Since *systems* of *nonlinear differential* equations are often the fundamentals of economic growth models, it is not surprising that the conjectured *behaviour* of *solutions* (evolutions) for the population, capital stock, wage and profit rates, income distribution have been controversial, without model solutions (conclusions) firmly and rigorously established.

On this background, the *Volume* has been divided into *six parts*. Each part treats particular elements, subjects, and growth models in separate chapters. We are now going to give a short outline of the content within the six parts and some main chapters.

*Part I : Elements of Economic Growth Models*

On some elements of economic growth models, it is instructive to compare economics with mechanics. Mechanics is divided in two parts: Statics, or the Theory of Equilibrium, and Dynamics, or the Theory of Motion.

Starting from the idea of forces as the cause of the mechanical movement of particles and bodies led to the mathematical definition of forces as a vector with components, direction and magnitude. Relating next the forces to a concept of motion as acceleration gives the *dynamic second-order* differential equation of motion to be solved for obtaining the path of the body movements. Relating the inverse square law of gravitational forces to body accelerations and solving the dynamic equations is the unique success story of body motion in celestial mechanics. Rather than using vector quantities of forces and accelerations to determine motion, *scalar quantities* as work, potential, energy, and action are used together with variational (extremal principles) methods to derive other particle and body equations of *state motions* as is now given by *dynamic first-order* differential equations to be solved.[1] Economic growth models are using economic *scalar* concepts as *state* variables that involve motion (*evolution*) obtained by the solutions of *dynamic first-order* differential equations.

The first *element* of economic growth models to consider in Part I, Chap. 1, are the first-order differential equations and the long-run properties of their solutions—stability and rapidity of growth. With the selection of *one-dimensional*, first-order, *non-linear autonomous* dynamic systems, this introductory chapter gives the possibility to illustrate the various stability properties and rapidity of growth with explicit solutions of the single dynamic (differential) equation. Readers may next go to *dynamics* in Chap. 28.

Other *elements* of economic growth models refer (as statics in mechanics) to the 'productive *forces*,' production *factors*, Labor and Capital, (L,K)—or the scalar *potentials*, production (output) *potential*, the production function, $Y = F(L, K)$, analytically representing technology and 'Division of Labor'. Mechanical equilibrium attained by balancing forces or max/min of potentials have resemblances in economic equilibrium, but economic equilibrium has a more complex structure, as elements of the economic systems are much more interrelated than those of mechanical systems. Verifying the existence or observing the equilibrium is certainly much more difficult in economics than in mechanics.

As basic *elements* of any economic growth model, Part I has chapters on *production* functions and cost functions, dealing with the historical *origin* in Chap. 3, and the merits of various functional forms and a new flexible extension of the CES function to *multi-factor* production functions with *variable* AUES (Allen-Uazwa) *substitution* elasticities in Chap. 4, which also considers the important *complementarity* elasticities of Hicks-Sato. Similarly *utility* functions are an important element of growth models, especially *optimal growth* models that will here be solved for the optimal saving rate in the Ramsey model. The flexible utility function, CDES (constant differences of elasticity of substitution), is discussed in detail, theoretically and empirically, in Chaps. 5 and 6.

With the Part I elements of *production functions*, we have also obtained and here given the analytic forms of the *factor rewards*, factor prices, factor (cost,

[1] Both Newton's and Lagrange's forms of the equations of motion may be derived from Hamilton's principle (stationary value (over path traversed) for time averages of the difference between kinetic and potential energies).

income) shares by marginal factor productivities of labor and capital, that enter all subsequent growth models. Similarly, the direct and indirect *utility functions* provide the *consumer* demand system and *budget shares* that subsequently enter as elements in growth models, especially multi-sector general equilibrium (MSG) growth models.[2]

*Part II : Basic One-Sector Growth Models*

The dynamics of economic growth models will seldom be described by either just one state variable or two independent state variables. Usually, to specify a *dynamic system* for a growing economy, we will be confronted with the necessity of using at least *two interdependent state variables.* As 'driving forces' behind the motion (output increases) of the body (economy), the *two* 'productive forces'*factors*, Labor and Capital, were considered above, together with the production (output) potential—function. The factor endowments of labor and capital, $[L(t), K(t)]$, will serve as dynamic *state variables*, i.e., their *initial values* and the *governing functions* of the *dynamic differential* equations will be able to determine all *future states* (factor endowments). But we cannot expect these two state variables to change independent of each other, i.e. the governing function of each state variable may generally have *both* state *variables* as arguments.

The crucial mathematical question is now whether we know of a *two-dimensional autonomous dynamic system* that is general enough to *encompass* essentially all the dynamic systems that usually appear in the various specifications of the basic economic growth models. In short, does there exist a *broad class* of differential equations that allows us subsequently to treat these growth models as simply special cases within such a *unifying class*? It turns out that the requirement of *homogeneous governing functions* will provide the fundamental class of differential equations—i.e., autonomous dynamic systems in normal form : $\dot{x} = F(x, y),\ \dot{y} = G(x, y),\ (x, y) \in R^2,\ F(0, 0) = 0,\ G(0, 0) = 0$, where the $C^1$-class functions, $F$ and $G$, are *homogeneous* of the same *degree*, $m \in R$.

This dynamic systems and its solution properties are established in Chap. 28—which provides an *axiomatic foundation* of many *basic economic growth models*—and it will be able to answer fundamental questions about the solutions, stability, and geometry of phase portraits raised by *classical* growth models and *neoclassical* growth models.

The main task is next to analytically describe and elucidate the properties of the actual *governing functions*, $F$ and $G$, with the specific *economic* assumptions.

[2] Our Parts I–IV correspond essentially to Book I–IV, Smith (1790, 1961), p.5, p.448, Smith (1999a), p.107, Smith (1999b), p.5, e.g., Part I as Book I : Of the Causes of Improvement in the productive Powers of Labour, and of the Order according to which its Produce is naturally distributed among different Ranks of the People.

Part II as Book II : Of the Nature, Accumulation, and the Employment of Stock.

Part III as Book III : Of the different Progress of Opulence in different Nations.

Part IV as Book IV : Of Systems of Political Economy—the Mercantile System, the Agricultural Systems.

Technology assumptions play a crucial role in economic growth models, where Chap. 2 serves as back-up. Since we will consider *homogeneous production functions* of degree $0 < m \leq 1$, all the standard descriptions of technology properties now involve intricate expressions. Generally, *scale* and *substitution* properties become intertwined, as the homogeneity parameter $m \neq 1$ also appears in every *derivative* of the production functions.

To Samuelson (1978), "A.Smith, Ricardo, Malthus, and Stuart Mill shared in common essentially one dynamic model of equilibrium, growth, and distribution—the same *canonical classical* model", which is the subject matter of Chaps. 7 and 8.

The *triple* laws of production (technology), population, and capital accumulation are the canonical elements, and they give the classical dynamic system :

$$\dot{L} = n \cdot L \cdot \frac{\partial F}{\partial L}(L, K)$$

$$\dot{K} = s_K \cdot K \cdot \frac{\partial F}{\partial L}(L, K)$$

where $s_K$ is the *saving parameter* of Total capital income—$K \cdot \frac{\partial F}{\partial K}(L, K)$—and $n$ is a *propagation parameter* to Total labor income—$L \cdot \frac{\partial F}{\partial L}(L, K)$. Economically, the methodology of homogeneous dynamics works out properly with the marginal rate of substitution, and the phase portraits are beautifully organized by the size of the substitution elasticity. The stability properties of the solutions $[L(t), K(t)]$ are described with the stability concepts, defined and demonstrated in Chap. 1. The obtained results for basic classical systems are stated in *Theorems 7.1–7.5* and *Propositions 7.1–7.4*.

The existence of positive *minimal* factor *rewards* for both factors, Labor and Capital, had the attention of the classicists, especially Ricardo and Malthus, and Chap. 8 gives the dynamic system with explicit parameters for the minimum (real) factor prices, $w_m, r_m$ :

$$\dot{L} = n \cdot L \cdot [\frac{\partial F}{\partial L}(L, K) - w_m] \quad = \quad P_1(L, K)$$

$$\dot{K} = s_K \cdot K \cdot [\frac{\partial F}{\partial L}(L, K) - r_m] \quad = \quad P_2(L, K)$$

This version of the canonical classical growth model is no longer a global homogeneous dynamic system, as there with *decreasing* returns to scale will now necessarily exist an *isolated interior* critical point, a *stationary state* solution, an attractor also called a *Malthusian* trap of stagnation.

By using Olech's theorem, the global asymptotic stability of the stationary state is proved, *Theorem 8.1*, and a phase portrait (*classical node*) of the Malthusian stagnation (trap) is shown. With *structural* parameter change such as *constant* returns to scale, the *stationary* state (equilibrium) can *bifurcate* here into [ not as Hopf into a closed curve (periodic solution) ] an always *expanding* economy converging in the long-run to steady state (balanced) growth, *Theorem 8.2.*

Replacing in the *governing functions* of the former wage- and capital incomes by *national income* in Chap. 9, the *aggregate* (macro) models have the dynamic system :

$$\dot{L} = n \cdot F(L, K)$$
$$\dot{K} = s \cdot F(L, K)$$

The results of Chaps. 7 and 8 carry over to the aggregate version. Chapter 9 ends with a *Synopsis* of the classical growth models.

The dynamic system of the seminal macro growth model, Solow (1956), was, Chap. 11:

$$\dot{L} = n \cdot L$$
$$\dot{K} = s \cdot F(L, K)$$

Labor (population) grows at an *exogenous* rate. The stability properties for the general model are discussed, complemented with explicit solutions to special cases, Cobb-Douglas and Leontief technology. It concludes with a clarification of the kinematic distinction between asymptotic ratio stability and the geometric (trajectory) convergence of the phase curves, which—together with important dynamic implications of *exogeneity* for per capita growth—are further studied with many explicit solutions in Chap. 12.

The last chapter in Part II of *one-sector* growth models studies the *optimal* growth solutions generated by the dynamics of the basic Ramsey *intertemporal* saving-consumption model. General sufficient conditions are derived for the existence of unique optimal persistent growth solutions within Ramsey models. In phase diagrams, the *optimal solution* (time paths, trajectory) is a *unique separator*. We give comprehensive quantitative applications—using CES-VES *production functions* and HARA (Hyperbolic Absolute Risk Aversion) *utility functions*, together with parametric sensitivity analyses—of these optimal time paths for observable saving and growth rates. The original Ramsey (1928) optimal saving model with *persistent growth* per capita is solved in closed form with *constant* (CEIS) and *variable* (VEIS) elasticity of *intertemporal substitution* with the *latter* to generate realistic *historically* observable evolutions of *saving rates* and economic *growth rates.* Chapter 13 is a main chapter with the old Ramsey model problems finally resolved.

*Part III : Two-Sector and Multi-Sector Growth Models*

The exposition proceeds by analyzing the economic/dynamic implications of shifting to various *two-sector* growth models that must give new focus and attention to the *output composition* and *factor allocation* issues involved in *general equilibrium* dynamics.

As to the *basic two-sector* growth models and *multi-sector* growth model Part III : *Chaps. 14–17* and *18–20*, the economy is producing a *capital good* $Y_1$ in *sector* 1 and *consumer goods* $Y_i$ in *sectors* $i > 1$. The *technologies* in each sector are described by *distinct production functions* exhibiting constant returns to scale $(m = 1)$, $Y_i = F_i(L_i, K_i) = L_i f_i(k_i) \equiv L_i y_i$, $i = 1, 2, , , , N$.

Regarding the *labor supply*, the traditional neoclassical assumption, $\dot{L} = nL$, is mainly used. The general equations of *factor* (labor and capital) *accumulation* for such *multi-sector* economies are :

$$\dot{L} = n\,L,$$
$$\dot{K} = Y_1 = F_1(L_1, K_1).$$

But these two *accumulation* equations themselves are *not* a *dynamic system* (deterministic process). The crucial question is then whether and how the accumulation equations can be transformed into *governing functions* of a homogeneous dynamic system in the *state variables*, $L$ and $K$ (*factor endowments*),

$$\dot{L} = Ln,$$
$$\dot{K} \equiv Y_1 = \mathrm{G}(L, K) = L\,\mathfrak{g}(k),$$

with $k = K/L$ and, $\mathfrak{g}(k) = Y_1/L \equiv (L_1/L)(Y_1/L_1) \equiv \lambda_{L_1} y_1 \equiv \lambda_{L_1}(k) y_1(k)$,

The standard director function, $h(k)$, becomes,

$$\dot{k} \;=\; h(k) \;=\; \mathfrak{g}(k) - n\,k,$$

Although the *one-dimensional* dynamics, $\dot{k} = h(k)$, look deceptively simple, the rather heavy task is now to *establish* the *existence* and to characterize mathematically and economically, the *global properties* of $g(k)$—in accordance with the *alternative assumptions* about sector technologies, factor allocation, saving behaviour, etc., that we adopt for the *two-sector* economy and the multi-sector economies.

In *Chap. 14*, the *sector technologies* are of *Leontief form*. Since we always want (require) that the total factor *endowments* $(L, K)$ to be *fully* and *efficiently utilized* (employed), this requirement together with Leontief ("fixed coefficients") technologies actually solves also the sectorial *factor allocation problem* $(L_1, L_2, K_1, K_2)$, and then gives the current *output composition* $(Y_1, Y_2)$ of the two-sector economy. Hence $g(k)$, is implicitly well determined.

Sorting out all the relations involved, the function $g(k)$, will here take the form,

$$g(k) = -\frac{y_1 k_2}{k_1 - k_2} + \left[\frac{y_1}{k_1 - k_2}\right] k, \quad k_1 \neq k_2.$$

where $k_1$ and $k_2$ are the *fixed* sectorial capital-labor ratios ("capital intensities") and $y_1$ is the *fixed* labor productivity of the capital good sector.

The dynamic analysis and solution methods can now follow the standard procedure of homogeneous dynamics. Since the dynamic system here is *linear*, it can of course be solved explicitly by the traditional algebraic methods, but the advantages of our calculus approach are used to give the *solutions* in more relevant economic forms in *Theorem 14.1.* The stability properties of capital-labor ratio and coordinates are given in *Corollary 14.1.* We have the global asymptotic ratio stability, if and only if,

$$\text{(i)}\ y_1 > nk_1, \quad \text{(ii)}\ k_2 > k_1 \quad \therefore \quad k_1 < \min\{y_1/n, k_2\}.$$

A unique directrix (ray, capital-labor ratio) may also exist with $k_2 > k_1$, but it will be repulsive, and the two-sector economy eventually disintegrates.

The *economic rationale* of the dynamic stability conditions called for a closer examination of the factor mobility and the implied *reallocation* of the growing factor supplies that—outside the trajectory of balanced growth—continually occur within this economy. The substance of the *sectorial capital intensity* condition is shown to be an implication of the *Rybczynski* theorem, extended to a growing two-sector economy with one of the outputs being a capital good—see *Corollary 14.3.*

For *two-sector* growth models with *flexible* sector technologies in Chaps. 15 and 16, the steps to get the function $g(k)$ is a much more complicated affair. This step cannot be accomplished just by invoking the assumptions of full employment and efficient allocation of the production factors. Demand side specifications have to be introduced, which here will be represented by either *proportional* or *classical saving* functions.

Flexible *prices* in the commodity and factor markets equilibrate supply and demand. Efficient factor allocation requires a common *wage-rental* ratio in both sectors. In short, general equilibrium values of every variable must be obtained for any given factor endowments, $(L, K)$. As to the details of our procedure for determining the *momentary general equilibrium solutions* of the two-sector economy with *proportional* and *classical* saving, we can only here refer to the relevant sections, *Chaps. The General Equilibrium Solutions* and *The General Equilibrium Model and Solutions*, where also the crucial *uniqueness* problems are considered in *Lemmas 15.1* and *16.1.*

Chapter 17 again reviews the two-sector economy, and solves the two-sector model as a miniature Walrasian general equilibrium system of momentary and moving equilibria. The Walrasian framework encompasses the fundamental neoclassical and classical two-sector growth models; the families of solutions of steady-state and persistent growth per capita in various competitive two-sector economies are parametrically characterized. The technology parameters of the capital good industry are decisive for obtaining long-run per capita growth in closed (global) economies. A review of the literature complements the theorems on the general equilibrium allocations, dynamic systems, and the time paths of Walrasian two-sector economies.

Chapter 18 analyses Walrasian general equilibrium systems and calculates the static and dynamic solutions for competitive market equilibria. The Walrasian framework encompasses the basic *multi-sector* growth (MSG) models with neoclassical production technologies in *N sectors* (industries). The endogenous behavior of all the relative prices is analyzed in detail, as are sectorial allocations of the primary factors, labor and capital. Dynamic systems of Walrasian multi-sector economies and the family of solutions (time paths) for steady-state and persistent growth per capita are parametrically characterized. The technology parameters of the capital good industry are decisive for obtaining long-run per capita growth in closed (global) economies.

Chapter 19 considers that Multisector growth (MSG) models and Computable general equilibrium (CGE) models, with their many sectors (industries and goods), are known as trying to convert Walrasian general equilibrium systems from an abstract economy representation into workable models with industrial structures changing as actually observed. Hence the main objective is to set out comparative static and dynamic systems for succinctly stating and explicitly solving MSG models. The Walrasian *general equilibrium* is completely stated by *one equation* and the *multisector dynamics* by *one differential equation*. Benchmark solutions are shown for three CES (Constant Elasticity of Substitution) parameter regimes of a *10-sector* general equilibrium model.

Chapter 20 extends the Multi-Sector Growth (MSG) models of Chap. 19, in which the CES homothetic utility functions are now replaced by *non-homothetic preferences* for the evolution of factor allocations and industrial structures in accordance with consumption expenditure patterns implied by the *non-unitary income elasticities* observed in all budget data since (Engel 1857). The comparative static general equilibrium solutions and particularly solving the dynamics of MSG models require explicit specifications of all demand and cost (price) functions. On the demand side, the CDES (constant differences of elasticity of substitution) *non-homothetic indirect utility* functions and Roy's identity provide the explicit Marshallian demand functions and budget shares. Sectorial CES cost functions and Shephard's lemma provide the explicit relative commodity price functions and the sectorial cost shares and capital-labor ratios. *Walrasian equilibria* are given by *one equation* and the *multisector dynamics* by *three differential equations*. Benchmark solutions are given for three cost regimes of a *10-sector* MSG model. History patterns of industrial/allocational evolutions are recognized.

*Part IV : International Trade and Economic Growth Models*

The reader undoubtedly feels that the transition from full-scale multi-sector growth models with non-homothetic preferences to two-sector trade models is a bit surprising. But trade models will often have to operate with *commodity prices fixed* externally, especially a *small open economy.* The fixed commodity prices imply that the two sectors are operating with fixed coefficient Leontief technologies, if they are producing both goods. Hence the growing small economy model resembles the two-sector model of Chap. 14. If specialized, we are back to the one-sector economy of Chap. 11. The *small open economies* will then be a *unified combination* of Chaps. 11 and 14.

Chapter 21 gives the Structure of Two-Sector Trade Models, and it provides a unified framework for analysing the General Equilibrium dynamics of growing two-factor—two-sector trading economies. A major distinction is international trade models for small open (fixed terms of trade) economies and large open economies (international general equilibrium prices). In terms of physical capital accumulation, savings are given by fixed saving rates of national income, or fixed proportions of capital income, or determined optimally by the Ramsey rule. There is exogenous and endogenous labor growth. The growth model for the small trading economy is explicitly solved. The main contribution of this chapter is a series of theorems, which lay down the necessary and sufficient conditions for the existence, uniqueness and asymptotic stability of the long-run capital-labor ratio in several parametric cases, with incomplete as well as complete specialization/diversification.

Chapter 22 develops a framework for analyzing the stochastic dynamics of *small growing trading* economies with CES sector technologies. The open neoclassical two-sector growth model with a *diffusion process* (uncertainty) for the aggregate saving/investment ratio is demonstrated with *sample paths* and long-run *probability distributions* of the overall factor endowment ratio. Stochastic endogenous growth and cycles require a combination of fundamental growth parameter values: saving rates, terms of trade, and sectorial substitution elasticities. It defines and demonstrates the conditions for full and partial specialization, under consideration of the factor *reversal* effects—two diversification cones—of the CES technology. With this theoretical background, it solves the same model under uncertainty, and it illustrates the regions within the parameter space that include parametric values generating non-stationary sample paths of stochastic endogenous growth and cycles. The chapter finally *compares* the results and the *expectations* of the *stochastic* model with those of its *deterministic counterpart* in Chap. 21, which serves indeed as the economic benchmark.

Production possibility curves (PPC) and five core theorems have played an important role in international trade theory. Despite the graphical appearance of PPC everywhere in the trade literature, no explicit expression has yet been obtained for *production possibility curves* (PPC).

Chapter 23 reviews Transformation Functions, Production Possibility Curves, and Factor Contract Curves, and presents *explicit formulas* of the *Transformation* Functions for *Pareto efficient* factor *allocations.* These *Production Possibility* Frontiers (Envelopes) are *explicitly* stated for any Cobb-Douglas (*CD*) sector *technology parameters* and any *factor endowments* of labor and capital. Exact *Variable Elasticity* of *Transformation* (*VET*) curves of non-joint productions are derived. *Core Theorems* of international trade are unified, extended, and economically stated explicitly with *structural parameter* formulas. Multiple output *Revenue* functions are obtained in *closed forms.*

The *output* formulas of the Transformation and Revenue functions are compared with the *autarky general equilibrium* expressions. Explicit *autarky formulas* of *comparative advantage* (price, cost) for prediction of *trade pattern* are derived and demonstrated for bilateral trading economies with *any* CD sector *technologies*, CD consumer *preferences*, and *any* country *endowment ratios* (proportions) of labor and capital.

With the background of the autarky general equilibria expressions of Chaps. 23, 24 now derives explicit *autarky formulas* of *comparative advantage* (price, cost) for prediction of trade patterns, which are demonstrated for bilateral trading economies with *any* CD sector *technologies*, CD consumer *preferences*, and *any* country *factor endowment ratios* (proportions) of labor and capital. For two trading economies, the chapter continues with the derivation and the demonstration of the *international general equilibrium* solutions, the *international terms of trade* (*world prices*) and *traded volumes.* These closed-form expressions provide a unified framework for all traditional standard trade models. They allow for international differences in country sizes, endowments, technologies and preferences, encompassing the major "pure trade theories" within a systematic analytic and historical perspective. In this unified framework, we derive the general existence conditions for the solutions under diversification and incipient country specialization.

The *agricultural sector* and agricultural cultivation systems are historically important for the populations, economic growth and international trade, especially in the eighteenth century. Chapter 25 examines the *Tellow Manor Farm* accounting records (1810–1819) for the Seven Field System of Land cultivation. The output and cost calculations with the Tellow Manor Accounts showed that the replacement of the *3-Field system* with *7-Field system* would increase *production* (output) by 83 pct. and increase *Land Rents* by 52 pct. The chapter shows the connection between cost calculations in Business Economics/Accounting and costs/prices in Macro-/Microeconomics. The Tellow quantitative agricultural model of 7-Field cultivation system serves as a benchmark for comparing/evaluating in *Denmark* and *England* the corresponding Agricultural output and Land rent increases. The agricultural cultivation *reforms*, 1760–1800, were very successful ("revolutions"), breaking economic Stagnation and the *Population* ('Malthusian') barrier.

*Part V : Stochastic Dynamic Systems*

Deterministic dynamics and stochastic dynamics *complement* each other. Basically, they contain the same theory. The governing functions of deterministic dynamics are essentially the *drift coefficients* of stochastic dynamics.

Chapter 26 extends the basic *deterministic* one-sector and two-sector growth models to a *stochastic* context in *continuous time*, using *Wiener processes* for the description of various sources of *uncertainties* in the growth rate of the *labor* force, the rate of capital *depreciation* and the *saving* rate. The *drift* and *diffusion coefficients* of the stochastic dynamic systems are *homogenous* of degree one in the two state variables, labor and capital—which allows a reduction into the stochastic dynamics of the capital-labor *ratio*. The crucial issue of hitting *absorbing boundaries* for the stochastic growth models is rigorously examined, and simple criteria (sufficient conditions) for *inaccessible* boundaries are established, a subject on which existing literature has been deficient. From the Kolmogorov forward equation is derived the *steady state probability* distribution of the capital-labor ratios. For both stochastic one- and two-sector growth models, the *sample paths*—of *transition* to *steady states* or for *persistent* endogenous growth—of particular state variables are simulated for many *parametric* specifications of the CD and CES *sector technologies* involved. Impacts of technology shocks are similarly demonstrated. All relevant sample paths are exhibited on both shorter and longer time horizons.

Uncertainties are intrinsic features of dynamic economic systems, and Chap. 27 considers the dynamic implications of factor endowment (labor, capital) uncertainties for a small growing trading economy. Our stochastic growth models extend the open neoclassical two-sector growth model of Chap. 21 to a stochastic environment in continuous time and extend the diffusion dynamics of one-sector growth models to a trading two-sector economy. We demonstrate that the basic propositions of deterministic steady-state growth and endogenous growth theory, under some specifications and certain parametric restrictions, are preserved within a stochastic framework.

*Part VI : Homogeneous Dynamic Systems*

Chapter 28 considers *autonomous dynamic* systems in the *normal* (explicit) form: $\dot{x} = F(x, y)$, $\dot{y} = G(x, y)$, $(x, y) \in R^2$, $F(0, 0) = 0, G(0, 0) = 0$, where the $C^1$-class functions, $F$ and $G$, are *homogeneous* of the same *degree*, $m \in R$. The $C^1$-class assumption about the *governing functions*, $F$, $G$, ensures everywhere the *existence* and *uniqueness* of the *coordinate solutions*: $[x, y] = [\varphi_1(t), \varphi_2(t)] = \varphi(t)$. By *homogeneity* property and by using the *ratio* variable, $r = y/x$, $x \neq 0$, we rewrite the *dynamic* system as: $\dot{x} = x|x|^{m-1} f(r)$, $\dot{y} = x|x|^{m-1} g(r)$, $x \neq 0$. The *ratio* of the individual coordinate solutions, $r = \rho(t) = \varphi_2(t)/\varphi_1(t)$, has the *time derivative* : $\dot{r} = dr/dt = |x|^{m-1} h(r)$, where, $h(r) = g(r) - rf(r)$, is called a *director function,* its roots, $h(\alpha) = 0$, are called *director roots*, and *rays*, $y = \alpha x$, are called *directrices*, and $f(\alpha)$, are called *directrix values*. A directrix reflects a *constant ratio solution*, i.e., $\rho(t) = \alpha$, $\varphi_2(t) = \alpha \varphi_1(t)$.

By $\dot{r}$ and $\dot{x}$ it is shown that *nonstationary ratio solution*, $\rho(t)$, must solve the *fundamental differential* equation : $\dot{r} = Q(r) = |k_0 \exp\{H(r)\}|^{m-1} h(r)$. Thus *dynamics* of any autonomous *system* of *two interdependent* homogeneous *differential* equations—having *same* degree of *homogeneity*—is essentially given succinctly through a *single* autonomous *differential* equation.

Having obtained, $\rho(t)$, corresponding *coordinate solutions*, $\varphi_1(t)$, $\varphi_2(t)$, are then given as : $\varphi_1(t) = k_0 \exp\{H[\rho(t)]\}$, $\varphi_2(t) = \rho(t)\,\varphi_1(t)$, and the *trajectories* as *loci* are given by the *equation* : $x - k_0 \exp\{H(y/x)\} = 0$.

Thus, we have obtained the *complete* set of *solutions* to the *homogeneous dynamic* system. Usually, the *non-stationary* ratio and coordinate *solutions cannot* be expressed in *closed form* (finite combination of elementary functions), but the fact that these *solutions* are obtained in terms of well-defined *primitives* [ integrands being determined by the *governing functions* : $f$, $g$ ], will allow us to deduce the *qualitative behaviour* of the family of solutions for *any specification* of the basic *governing functions* : $F$, $G$.

The global *asymptotic ratio stability* conditions follow from, $h(r)$, and are stated in *Theorem 28.4*, weaker *ratio* stabilities in *Theorem 28.5*. The *trajectory* geometry is given in *Theorem 28.8*. The *stability* properties of the *coordinate solutions* are summarized in *Theorems 28.9–28.12*.

Chapter 29 applies the results of the general theory of homogeneous dynamics, Chap. 28, to the special case, where $m = 1$, and the *governing functions* are *linear*. The linear system is of course well known, but our solution technique, based on calculus instead of linear algebra, is novel and helpful in obtaining relevant classification of *solutions* and the *phase portraits*. Rather than the traditional dichotomy, stable/unstable, we illustrate the use of the *kinematic* stability concepts for the *ratio* and *coordinate* solutions in *global* and *generic* versions. Bifurcation and *structural stability* are related to the regions in the parameter space, as are the kinematic stability properties. The solutions are obtained without coordinate transformations, and the main types of solutions for linear dynamics are classified directly with the *four parameters* $(a, b, c, d)$, the variation of which provides an *astoundingly* varied set of *solutions* and *phase portraits*. The parametric extension to *affine* dynamics supplements the linear dynamics.

Chapter 30 generalizes the theory of homogeneous dynamics to a wider class of differential equations. As homogeneous production functions gave the impetus to study the solutions to homogeneous dynamic systems, Chap. 28, it was also *Quasi* (also named, “Almost” or “Pseudo”)—homogeneous *production* functions that lead us to study the qualitative properties of *Quasi-homogeneous dynamics*. While the *trajectories* for homogeneous dynamics are obtained from each other by a multiplication along the *rays* through the origin, the *trajectories* for quasi-homogeneous dynamics are obtained from each other by a multiplication along the family of *power curves* $y = (\alpha x)^{\beta}$, $x > 0$. With the *class* of quasihomogeneous *governing* functions, growth models, with the total *factor endowments* $(L, K)$ as state variables, will be able to *exhibit* also a *permanent increasing* capital-labor *ratio*. Many economic (allocational, distributional, etc.) implications of the quasihomogeneous technologies need to be further and fully explored, when such technologies are admitted to enter the dynamics of *economic growth* models.

Chapter 31 extends the results of linear continuous time dynamics, Chap. 29, to observations with their solutions from *discrete time* linear dynamical system. The linear *governing functions* may belong to $C^1$-class, but continuity fails with respect to solutions (time path) of discrete time processes (difference equations). The general coordinate solution and initial value problem of the *discrete linear* dynamic systems are presented in *Propositions 31.1–31.2*. The configurations of the phase portrait for the discrete time linear system are analysed in detail. The discrete time solutions are embedded in the continuous time solution of extended linear systems by *Theorem 31.1* to which correspond exact analogue discrete system matrices.

Chapter 32 considers *continuous* differential equation growth models with a *time delay* in the productive operation of installed capital. By a local nonlinear analysis, it is demonstrated that the *equilibrium* becomes *unstable* in a Hopf *bifurcation* for sufficiently *large delays.* Periodic solutions in the form of *limit cycles* are created in the bifurcation. In a specific example with a CD production function we show the bifurcation is *supercritical* such that the limit cycles are stable and exist for delays larger than the critical value. By numerical simulations with a CES production function, we show that the model may exhibit 'square wave' solutions and 'chaos' (*aperiodic oscillations*) for our single delay differential equation, if the delay is very large. The model phase portrait integrates the phenomena of *economic growth* and *cycles.*

Chapter 33 analyses two *basic stochastic models*: The *time homogeneous* Gaussian and the geometric Wiener diffusion of *two-dimensional vector processes.* Using the theory of stochastic processes and Ito lemma, the *probability* of *distributions* of the stochastic state vectors are described by the evolution of their *moments* (*expectation* and *covariance* as *functions* of time), as these moments satisfy certain systems of ordinary (deterministic) differential equations (ODE). By solving the latter ODE, the *explicit solutions* for the first-order and second-order *moment functions* are presented. The *forward Kolmogorov* equation is used partly to derive the results by *alternative* methods and partly to gain information on the probability distributions. The general *closed form* results on the *moment evolutions* (still unavailable) have many applications in the models of linear dynamics with uncertainty.

A common procedure may be discerned in Parts I–VI of our *axiomatic analysis* of *expanding economies.* The cooperation of *mathematics* and *economic theory* has to be properly organized. The two disciplines first advance with their own subject matter and methods, and only later combine efforts in a joint endeavor.

## Bibliography

Baumol WJ (1970) Economic Dynamics, 3rd edn. MacMillan, London

Cassel G (1925) Fundamental Thoughts in Economics. T. Fisher Unwin, London

Debreu G (1986) Theoretic Models: Mathematical Form and Economic Content. Econometrica 54:1259–1270

Domar ED (1946) Capital Expansion, Rate of Growth and Employment. Econometrica 14:137–47

Engel E (1857) Die Productions- and Consumptionsverhaeltnisse des Koenigreichs Sachsen. Zeitschrift des Statistischen Bureaus des Koeniglich Saechsishen Ministerium des Inneren 8–9, reprint in: *Bulletin of the International Statistical Institute*, 9 (1895), 1–54.

Harrod RF (1939) An Essay in Dynamic Theory. Economic J 49:14–33, or Stiglitz (1969)

Jones LE, Manuelli RE (1990) A Convex Model of Equilibrium Growth: Theory and Policy Implications. Journal of Political Economy 98:1008–1038

Lucas RE (1988) On the Mechanics of Economic Development. Journal of Monetary Economics 22:3–42, Reprinted in Becker (1991)

Lundberg E (1938) Studies in the Theory of Economic Expansion. P.S. King and Sons, London

Ramsey FP (1928) A Mathematical Theory of Saving. Economic Journal 38:543–559

Rebelo S (1991) Long-Run Policy Analysis and Long-Run Growth. Journal of Political Economy 99:500–521

Romer PM (1986) Increasing Returns and Long-Run Growth. Journal of Political Economy 94:1002–1037, Reprinted in Becker (1991)

Samuelson PA (1978) The Canonical Classical Model of Political Economy. Journal of Economic Literature 16:1415–1434

Smith A (1790, 1961) An Inquiry Into The Nature and Causes of The Wealth of Nations, vol 1–2, 5th edn. Methuen, London, (ed. E. Cannan)

Smith A (1999a) The Wealth of Nations, Books I-III. Penguin Classics, London, Skinner A (ed.)

Smith A (1999b) The Wealth of Nations, Books IV-V. Penguin Classics, London, Skinner A (ed.)

Solow RM (1956) A Contribution to the Theory of Economic Growth. Quarterly Journal of Economics 70:65–94, Reprinted in Stiglitz (1969), and in Becker (1991)

Stiglitz JE, Uzawa H (1969) Readings in the Modern Theory of Economic Growth. M.I.T. Press, Cambridge, Mass

Walras L (1954) Elements of Pure Economics. George Allen and Unwin, London

Yang X, Borland J (1991) A Microeconomic Mechanism for Economic Growth. J Political Economy 99:460–82

# Contents

# List of Figures

# List of Tables

# List of Theorems

# List of Propositions

# List of Corollaries

# LIST OF LEMMAS

PART I

# Elements of Economic Growth Models

CHAPTER 1

# Growth and Long-Run Stability

## Introduction

In the development of the subject of stability theory for dynamic systems, the main endeavor has been devoted to studies of stability problems associated with admissible stationary states (stationary equilibria) of the dynamic systems. Therefore, the central issue of such stability problems is whether all the nonstationary solutions of the differential equations converge, as $t \to \infty$, to the particular stationary (constant) solutions. However, in the field of communication systems, which depend upon circuits producing stable oscillations, the stability problem is whether all the solutions of the system converge to a unique periodic solution—what is called a steady-state oscillation (see Salle 1961, p. 127).

In this chapter, we will be confined to the study of stability for ***autonomous*** (time independent) ordinary differential equations. The fundamental "laws" of the dynamic processes do not change and the evolution of the variables are fully endogenously generated.

For systems of autonomous ordinary ***linear*** differential equations with constant coefficients, the well-known necessary and sufficient conditions for global ***stability*** of admissible ***stationary*** equilibria are that the roots of the characteristic polynomial all have negative real parts—or equivalently, that the Routh-Hurwitz principal minors are all positive (cf. Samuelson 1983, p. 430). For systems of autonomous ordinary ***nonlinear*** differential equations, the stability conditions of admissible ***stationary*** equilibria are less clear-cut,

With co-author:
MOGENS ESROM LARSEN, Department of Mathematics, University of Copenhagen, Denmark.



B. S. Jensen, *The Elements and Dynamic Systems of Economic Growth and Trade Models*, https://doi.org/10.1007/978-3-031-52493-6_1

although Lyapunov has here given the necessary and sufficient conditions for *local stability*, namely, that characteristic roots of the Jacobian matrix (evaluated at the stationary values) all have negative real parts, cf. Pontryagin (1962, §26). Furthermore, a *global stability* property can also be detected by a proper application of the method of "Lyapunov functions" (see Salle 1961, (p. 33)). As is well-known, phase space analysis may be of some help here to examine the stability of simple systems.

It needs to be stressed, however, that all the stability conditions mentioned above are concerned with the stability of the stationary states (asymptotic stability). Now, if stationary solutions are inadmissible for whatever reasons, then the traditional concept of *asymptotic stability* becomes *inadequate*. In growth models with persistent growth (positive time derivatives everywhere) of all the relevant variables, we cannot, of course, apply the asymptotic stability concept to the growing variables individually.

The purpose of this chapter is to show the fundamental connections between some more general stability concepts and the admissible growth paths.

In section "Stability Criteria and Degrees of Stability", we present several *stability criteria*. Although stability, as usually understood, is a property of certain systems of differential equations, it is worthwhile first to consider stability concepts as a method of classifying families of functions of a real variable (time paths, motions). Section "Causality and Differential Equations" discusses the correspondence between stability against arbitrary initial conditions and stability against time delays that is useful in dealing with autonomous differential equations. Section "Stability Conditions for Autonomous Differential Equations" is devoted to the development of stability theorems, which give *global stability conditions* for the general first-order autonomous differential equation.

We want to emphasize that these *theorems* enable us to decide the *stability* directly from the *governing function* without any knowledge of the explicit solutions of the differential equation.

In section "Rapidity of Growth", we present a terminology for different speeds of growth. Section "Growth Versus Stability of Autonomous Differential Equations" demonstrates the basic conflict between the *rapidity* of *growth* and the *degree* of *stability*. Section "Economic Applications" shows some applications of our theorems and indicates how some assumptions of standard growth models can be weakened. Concluding comments are offered in section "Concluding Comments". An appendix treats special, but common, growth measures and their relationship to our main theorems.

## Stability Criteria and Degrees of Stability

To be *stable* means to have the ability to *recover* from a *disturbance*. To define this concept of stability precisely, one must specify both the kind of disturbance and the criterion for an adequate recovery. In this section, we deal with the problem of recovery only, postponing the discussion of the disturbance to section "Stability Conditions for Autonomous Differential Equations".

In the following, we study a motion as a real function of time, $\varphi(t)$, and a disturbed motion, $\psi(t)$. Then stability means that, in the long run, $\varphi(t)$ and $\psi(t)$ are "equivalent" in some adequate sense that must be made precise in terms of a formal criterion. We present seven *criteria* for stability, each one containing the predecessors and being contained in the successors. Hence, the criteria represent a succession from higher to lower *degrees* of stability. Usage differs among mathematicians, engineers and economists. As a standard reference and for an excellent survey, see Coddington and Levinson (1955); Kalman and Bertram (1960).

The *stability* of a motion against a *disturbance* will be called

| | | |
|---|---|---|
| 1. Asymptotic | if | $\varphi(t) = \text{const.}$ and $\psi(t) - \varphi(t) \to 0$ as $t \to \infty$. |
| 2. Strong absolute | if | $\psi(t) - \varphi(t) \to 0$ as $t \to \infty$. |
| 3. Weak absolute | if | $\lvert\psi(t) - \varphi(t)\rvert < k < \infty$ for all $t$. |
| 4. Strong relative | if | $\ln\psi(t) - \ln\varphi(t) \to 0$ as $t \to \infty$. |
| 5. Weak relative | if | $\lvert\ln\psi(t) - \ln\varphi(t)\rvert < k < \infty$ for all $t$. |
| 6. Strong logarithmic | if | $\ln\ln\psi(t) - \ln\ln\varphi(t) \to 0$ as $t \to \infty$. |
| 7. Weak logarithmic | if | $\lvert\ln\ln\psi(t) - \ln\ln\varphi(t)\rvert < k < \infty$ for all $t$. |

**Remark 1.1** The criterion 4 reflects the requirement

$$\psi(t)/\varphi(t) \to 1 \text{ as } t \to \infty \quad \text{or} \quad (\psi(t) - \varphi(t))/\varphi(t) \to 0 \text{ as } t \to \infty,$$

which justifies the name "relative stability".

Similarly, criterion 6 reflects the requirement

$$\ln\psi(t)/\ln\varphi(t) \to 1 \quad \text{as} \quad t \to \infty.$$

▽

## Causality and Differential Equations

The notion of *causality* refers in this context to systems of motions, where time paths of the variables depend only upon the *initial conditions* and the *time elapsed* since the establishment of such initial conditions, that is to say, the specification of similar given initial conditions at a later period would result in a similar evolution of the system, except at a constantly later time period (see Coddington and Levinson 1955, §15 and Samuelson 1983, p. 317). Thus, as used here, a system is said to be causal if, from an initial configuration, it determines its own behavior over time.

We now restrict ourselves to the study of a causal system in one variable. Furthermore, the variable will here—in a growth context—be required to increase monotonously in time.

Consider an increasing, differentiable function of time, $y = \varphi(t)$, moving in a range

$$-\infty \leq a < \varphi(t) < b \leq +\infty.$$

Then such a motion will be stable against delay, if there exits a transformation between the pair of functions $\varphi(t)$ and $\varphi(t+h)$ for *any* given value of $h$. This problem of the *stability* of a *motion* against *delay* can always be transformed to the corresponding problem of *stability* with respect to the *initial position* of the set of *solutions* to a first-order *autonomous* differential equation.

Such correspondence is due to the fact that the family of functions $\{\varphi(t+h) \mid h \in \mathbf{R}\}$ is a set of solutions to the equation $\dot{y} = f(y)$, $(\cdot = d/dt)$, with the function $f$ defined by

$$f(x) = \varphi'(\varphi^{-1}(x)), \quad a < x < b.$$

Hence, it is sufficient to study the stability of sets of solutions to the differential equations with respect to the disturbance of the initial position.

**Lemma 1.1** *Any solution $\varphi(t)$ to the equation $\dot{y} = f(y)$, with $f(x) > 0$ everywhere, is increasing and unbounded,*

$$\text{(i) } \varphi'(t) > 0 \quad \text{(ii) } \varphi(t) \to \infty \text{ as } t \to \infty.$$

***Proof*** Let $\varphi(t)$ be a solution. Because $\varphi'(t) = f(\varphi(t)) > 0$, the function $\varphi$ must be increasing.

Suppose $\varphi(t)$ is bounded. Then $\varphi(t) \to c$ for $t \to \infty$. Now

$$\lim_{t\to\infty} \varphi'(t) = \lim_{t\to\infty} f(\varphi(t)) = f(c) > 0.$$

Hence, $\varphi'(t) > \epsilon > 0$ for all values of $t$, and therefore

$$\varphi(t) > k + \epsilon t$$

contradicting the limit of $\varphi$. Conclusion: The function $\varphi$ must be unbounded. □

**Lemma 1.2** *Suppose the function $f(x)$ is positive and continuously differentiable everywhere. If $\varphi(t)$ is any solution to the equation $\dot{y} = f(y)$, then any other solution to this equation must take the form, $\varphi(t+h)$, for some constant $h$.*

***Proof*** Let $\psi(t)$ and $\varphi(t)$ be two solutions. Consider the time $t = 0$ and suppose $\psi(0) > \varphi(0)$. Now, as $\varphi(t) \to \infty$ for $t \to \infty$, according to Lemma 1.1, there exists $h > 0$ such that $\psi(0) = \varphi(h)$.

Since the function $f$ is continuously differentiable, it satisfies the Lipschitz condition and, hence, the solution to the initial value problem is unique, that is, $\psi(t) = \varphi(t+h)$ everywhere. □

**Corollary 1.1** *Let $\varphi(t)$ be a bijective, twice continuously differentiable function satisfying $\varphi'(t) > 0$ for all $t$. Then the family $\{\varphi(t+h) \mid h \in \mathbf{R}\}$ is equal to the whole set of solutions to the equation $\dot{y} = f(y)$, where*

$$f(x) = \varphi'(\varphi^{-1}(x)).$$

***Proof*** The function $f(x)$ is continuously differentiable and positive, so Lemma 1.2 applies. It is obvious (see above) that $\varphi(t)$ solves the equation. □

## Stability Conditions for Autonomous Differential Equations

In this section, we discuss the stability of the set of solutions to a differential equation of the form

$$\dot{y} = f(y). \tag{1.1}$$

Now we relate the different criteria of stability mentioned in section "Stability Criteria and Degrees of Stability" to the particular properties which must be satisfied by the function $f$.

*Assumption 1.1* The function $f$ is continuously differentiable everywhere.

**Theorem 1.1** *The set of solutions to Eq. (1.1) has asymptotic stability around the constant solution $y = c$, if and only if*

$$\text{(i) } f(c) = 0, \quad \text{(ii) } f(x) > 0 \textit{ for } x < c, \quad \text{(iii) } f(x) < 0 \textit{ for } x > c.$$

***Proof*** Let $\varphi(t)$ be a solution. If $\varphi(t) < c$, then $\varphi'(t) = f(\varphi(t)) > 0$ and, hence, $\varphi$ is increasing. Now, $\varphi(t) < c$ for all $t$, due to the theorem of uniqueness of solutions to differential equations. Hence, $\varphi(t) \to d \leq c$ for $t \to \infty$. Now, as $t \to \infty$:

$$f(d) = f(\lim \varphi(t)) = \lim f(\varphi(t)) = \lim \varphi'(t) \geq 0.$$

*If* $f(d) > 0$, then $\varphi'(t) > \epsilon > 0$ for all $t$ and, hence, $\varphi(t) \to \infty$ as $t \to \infty$. So $f(d) = 0$. Because $c$ is the only zero for $f$, it must be equal to $d$. Conclusion: $\varphi(t) \to c$ as $t \to \infty$.

*Only if.* Clearly $f(c) = 0$ (because $y = c$ is supposed to be a solution), and $f$ has no other zero $d$ (since then $y = d$ would be a solution not tending to $c$). □

If the function $f$ has a zero, then Theorem 1.1 applies. If the function $f$ has no zero, then following theorems shall prove useful. Hence, we shall from now on assume

*Assumption 1.2* $f(x) > 0$ everywhere.

This assumption implies that the solution must be unbounded, a fact we need in the proofs below. For each of the six criteria of stability 2–7 defined in section "Stability Criteria and Degrees of Stability", we shall state for the ***governing function*** $f$ some simple sufficient conditions that ensure the set of solutions to be either stable or unstable. The sufficient stability conditions below are also almost necessary.

**Theorem 1.2** *The set of solutions to Eq. (1.1) has strong absolute stability, if*

$$f(x) \to 0 \ \text{as} \ x \to \infty, \tag{1.2.1}$$

*and cannot have strong absolute stability, if*

$$f(x) > \epsilon > 0 \ \text{everywhere}. \tag{1.2.2}$$

***Proof*** Let $\varphi(t)$ be a solution. From Lemma 1.1 follows that $\varphi(t)$ is increasing and unbounded. From Lemma 1.2 follows that any pair of solutions can be of the form

$$\varphi(t) \ \text{and} \ \psi(t) = \varphi(t+h), \ \text{for some constant}, h > 0.$$

So we have for some $\tau = \tau(t)$, with $t < \tau < t + h$

$$\psi(t) - \varphi(t) = \varphi(t+h) - \varphi(t) = \varphi'(\tau)h = f(\varphi(\tau))h.$$

Hence, under the condition (1.2.1), we get

$$\psi(t) - \varphi(t) \to 0 \text{ as } t \to \infty,$$

because with $t$ both $\tau = \tau(t)$ and $\varphi(\tau)$ goes to infinity.

Similarly, under the condition (1.2.2), we get

$$|\psi(t) - \varphi(t)| = f(\varphi(\tau))|h| > \epsilon|h|.$$

□

**Theorem 1.3** *The set of solutions to Eq. (1.1) has weak absolute stability, if*

$$0 < f(x) < k \ \text{everywhere}, \tag{1.3.1}$$

*and cannot have weak absolute stability, if*

$$f(x) \to \infty \quad as \ x \to \infty. \tag{1.3.2}$$

***Proof*** According to Lemma 1.2, we can assume two solutions to be

$$\varphi(t) \ \text{and} \ \varphi(t+h) \text{ with } h > 0,$$

and according to Lemma 1.1, they are both increasing and unbounded.

Then for $t < \tau < t + h$, we have

$$0 < \varphi(t+h) - \varphi(t) = \varphi'(\tau)h = f(\varphi(\tau))h < kh$$

under the condition (1.3.1). This proves the weak absolute stability.

In the second case, let $K$ be any number. We can find $c$, such that

$$f(x) > K \ \text{as} \ x > c,$$

according to (1.3.2). Lemma 1.1 says that we can find $t_c$, such that for $t > t_c$, we have $\varphi(t) > c$ and hence,

$$\varphi(t+h) - \varphi(t) = \varphi'(\tau)h = f(\varphi(\tau))h > Kh,$$

because $\tau > t > t_c$ and $\varphi(\tau) > \varphi(t) > c$ and, hence, $f(\varphi(\tau)) > K$. Because $K$ was arbitrary, we cannot have weak absolute stability. □

**Theorem 1.4** *The set of solutions to Eq. (1.1) has strong relative stability, if*

$$f(x)/x \to 0 \quad as \ x \to \infty, \tag{1.4.1}$$

*and cannot have strong relative stability, if*

$$f(x)/x > \epsilon > 0 \quad as \ x > 0. \tag{1.4.2}$$

***Proof*** Let $\varphi(t)$ be a solution. Consider the function

$$\omega(t) = \ln \varphi(t).$$

We shall prove that $\omega(t)$ solves the equation

$$\dot{y} = g(y) \text{ with } g(y) = f(e^y)/e^y.$$

This follows from the straightforward computation below.

$$\omega'(t) = \varphi'(t)/\varphi(t) = f(\varphi(t))/\varphi(t) = f(e^{\omega(t)})/e^{\omega(t)} = g(\omega(t)).$$

The conditions (1.4.1) and (1.4.2) for $f$ imply that $g$ satisfies, respectively, the conditions (1.2.1) and (1.2.2) of Theorem 1.2. Hence, the pair $\omega(t)$ and $\omega(t+h)$ either have or cannot have strong absolute stability according to Theorem 1.2.

But strong *absolute* stability for $\omega(t) = \ln \varphi(t)$ and $\omega(t+h) = \ln \varphi(t+h)$ is by the definitions 2 and 4 strong *relative* stability for $\varphi(t)$ and $\varphi(t+h)$. This proves Theorem 1.4. □

**Theorem 1.5** *The set of solutions to Eq. (1.1) has weak relative stability, if*

$$0 < f(x)/x < k \quad as \ x > 0, \tag{1.5.1}$$

*and cannot have weak relative stability, if*

$$f(x)/x \to \infty \quad as \ x \to \infty. \tag{1.5.2}$$

***Proof*** As in the proof of Theorem 1.4, this theorem is easily derived from Theorem 1.3. □

**Theorem 1.6** *The set of solutions to Eq. (1.1) has strong logarithmic stability, if*

$$\frac{f(x)}{x \ln x} \to 0 \quad as \ x \to \infty \ (x > 1), \tag{1.6.1}$$

*and cannot have strong logarithmic stability, if*

$$\frac{f(x)}{x \ln x} > \epsilon > 0 \quad as \ x > 1. \tag{1.6.2}$$

***Proof*** Let $\varphi(t)$ be a solution. Then $\omega(t) = \ln \varphi(t)$ solves the equation

$$\dot{y} = g(y), \ \text{with} \ g(y) = \frac{f(e^y)}{e^y}.$$

Now the function $g$ satisfies the conditions of Theorem 1.4, as

$$\frac{g(x)}{x} = \frac{f(e^x)}{xe^x} \to 0 \text{ for } x \to \infty \quad (\text{from } (1.6.1)),$$

$$\frac{g(x)}{x} = \frac{f(e^x)}{xe^x} > \epsilon > 0 \text{ for } x > 0 \ (\text{from } (1.6.2)).$$

Hence, Theorem 1.6 follows from Theorem 1.4. □

**Table 1.1** Typical differential equations and stability properties

| Stability criteria | Differential equation | Solution | Theorem no. |
|---|---|---|---|
| 1. Asymptotic | $\dot{y} = -y$ | $\alpha e^{-t}$ | 1 |
| 2. Strong absolute | $\dot{y} = \frac{1}{y}$ | $\sqrt{2t}$ | 2 |
| 3. Weak absolute | $\dot{y} = 1$ | $t$ | 3 |
| 4. Strong relative | $\dot{y} = 2\sqrt{y}$ | $t^2$ | 4 |
| 5. Weak relative | $\dot{y} = y$ | $e^t$ | 5 |
| 6. Strong logarithmic | $\dot{y} = y\sqrt{\ln y}$ | $e^{t^2}$ | 6 |
| 7. Weak logarithmic | $\dot{y} = y \ln y$ | $e^{e^t}$ | 7 |

**Theorem 1.7** *The set of solutions to Eq. (1.1) has weak logarithmic stability, if*

$$\frac{f(x)}{x\ln(x)} < k \quad as\ x > 1, \tag{1.7.1}$$

*and cannot have weak logarithmic stability, if*

$$\frac{f(x)}{x\ln(x)} \to \infty \quad as\ x \to \infty\ (x > 1). \tag{1.7.2}$$

***Proof*** As Theorem 1.6, the theorem is easily derived from Theorem 1.5. □

We have characterized the stability properties of the solutions to (1.1) in terms of appropriate *conditions* upon the *governing function*, $f$. Typical differential equations of the form (1.1), with their explicit solutions having stability according to these theorems, are given in Table 1.1.

## Rapidity of Growth

The growth of a function is properly measured by its derivative—assuming the derivative to exist. The greater the derivative is, the faster is the growth. To distinguish different *speeds* of growth, we shall use the following terminology.

The *growth* will be called

| | | | |
|---|---|---|---|
| I. | Bounded | if | $\varphi'(t) > 0$ and $\varphi(t) < c$ everywhere. |
| II. | Unbounded | if | $\varphi'(t) > 0$ everywhere and $\varphi(t) \to \infty$ as $t \to \infty$. |
| III. | Linear | if | $\varphi'(t) > \epsilon > 0$ everywhere. |
| IV. | Polynomial | if | $\varphi'(t) \to \infty$ as $t \to \infty$. |
| V. | Exponential | if | $\varphi'(t)/\varphi(t) > \epsilon > 0$ everywhere. |
| VI. | Hyper-exponential | if | $\varphi'(t)/\varphi(t) \to \infty$ as $t \to \infty$. |
| VII. | Double-exponential | if | $\varphi'(t)/(\varphi(t) \ln \varphi(t)) > \epsilon > 0$ everywhere. |

**Remark 1.2** Of course, growth can be more rapid than here considered, for example, explosive growth means that there is a finite escape time, $a$, that is,

$$\varphi(t) \to \infty \text{ as } t \to a \ (a < \infty).$$

As examples of explosive growth, the equation $\dot{y} = y^2$, $\dot{y} = y^2 + 1$ have the respective solutions, $\varphi(t) = 1/(a - t)$, $\varphi(t) = \tan(t)$. ▽

## Growth Versus Stability of Autonomous Differential Equations

One of the main purposes of this chapter is to underline how growth prevents stability. The *more rapid* is the growth, the *less* is the *degree* of *stability*, and conversely. We prove that as the speed of growth ascends from bounded to double-exponential, the degree of stability descends from asymptotic to weak logarithmic.

Suppose we have a growing function $\varphi(t)$ and want to know the stability with respect to changes of the initial conditions or, equivalently, the stability against time delays, that is, the stability of the pair $\varphi(t + h)$ and $\varphi(t)$. For each of the situations, we have the following *complementarity* $(J, j) = (\text{II}, 2), \dots, (\text{VII}, 7)$.

**Theorem 1.8** *If the growing function $\varphi(t)$ has growth property $J \in \{II, \dots, VII\}$, then any two functions $\varphi(t + h)$ and $\varphi(t)$ for $h \neq 0$ cannot have a degree of stability stronger that $j$.*

***Proof*** The growth properties, Conditions, II–VII, imply the applicability of the Corollary 1.1 to Lemma 1.2 and Theorems 1.1–1.6, as follows:

$J = \text{II}$. The unbounded growth of $\varphi(t)$ gives $f(x) = \varphi'(\varphi^{-1}(x)) = \varphi'(t) > 0$ everywhere, preventing asymptotic stability by Theorem 1.1 (only if).

$J = \text{III}$. The linear growth of $\varphi(t)$ gives $f(x) = \varphi'(\varphi^{-1}(x)) = \varphi'(t) > \epsilon > 0$ everywhere, preventing strong absolute stability by Theorem 1.2 (1.2.2).

$J = \text{IV}$. The polynomial growth of $\varphi(t)$ gives $f(x) = \varphi'(\varphi^{-1}(x)) = \varphi'(t) \to \infty$ for $x \to \infty$, preventing weak absolute stability by Theorem 1.3 (1.3.2).

$J = \text{V}$. The exponential growth of $\varphi(t)$ gives

$$f(x)/x = \varphi'(\varphi^{-1}(x))/x = \varphi'(t)/\varphi(t) > \epsilon > 0 \text{ everywhere,}$$

preventing strong relative stability by Theorem 1.4 (1.4.2).

$J = \text{VI}$. The hyper-exponential growth of $\varphi(t)$ gives

$$f(x)/x = \varphi'(\varphi^{-1}(x))/x = \varphi'(t)/\varphi(t) \to \infty \text{ as } x \to \infty,$$

preventing weak relative stability by Theorem 1.5 (1.5.2).

**Table 1.2** Growth versus stability

| Differential equation | Solution | Growth | Instability | Stability |
|---|---|---|---|---|
| $\dot{y} = -y$ | $e^{-t}$ | Bounded | | Asymptotic |
| $\dot{y} = \frac{1}{y}$ | $\sqrt{2t}$ | Unbounded | Not asymptotic | Strong abs. |
| $\dot{y} = 1$ | $t$ | Linear | Not strong abs. | Weak abs. |
| $\dot{y} = 2\sqrt{y}$ | $t^2$ | Polynomial | Not weak abs. | Strong rel. |
| $\dot{y} = y$ | $e^t$ | Exponential | Not strong rel. | Weak rel. |
| $\dot{y} = y\sqrt{\ln y}$ | $e^{t^2}$ | Hyperexp. | Not weak rel. | Strong log. |
| $\dot{y} = y \ln y$ | $e^{e^t}$ | Doubleexp. | Not strong log. | Weak log. |
| $\dot{y} = y^2$ | $-t^{-1}$ | Explosive | Not weak log. | None |

$J =$ VII. The double-exponential growth of $\varphi(t)$ gives

$$f(x)/(x \ln(x)) = \varphi'(\varphi^{-1}(x))/(x \ln x) = \varphi'(t)/(\varphi(t) \ln \varphi(t)) > \epsilon > 0$$

everywhere, preventing strong logarithmic stability by Theorem 1.6 (1.6.2).

□

**Remark 1.3** If the growing function $\varphi(t)$ shows explosive growth, then the functions $\varphi(t)$ and $\varphi(t+h)$ cannot have any type of stability for $h \neq 0$, because $\varphi(t) \to \infty$ as $t \to a$ and $\varphi(t+h) \to \infty$ as $t \to a - h$. ▽

Using the examples and results from Table 1.1, we can give a table of behavior (Table 1.2). Some special results regarding growth and stability are given in the appendix.

## Economic Applications

Our theorems on stability and growth seem useful for the qualitative analysis of dynamic models in many fields. We can here only give a few illustrations. In this section, we demonstrate their potential applicability in the context of some basic and original prototypes of macroeconomic growth models.

### *The Multiplier-Accelerator Growth Model of Harrod*

The multiplier-accelerator model of national income growth pioneered by Harrod did provide, despite its drastic simplifications, a proper starting point for analyzing the economic growth process. Within this one-sector growth model, the time path of national income (output), $Y$, is assumed to be a *solution* of the fundamental differential equation that describes the dynamic equilibrium of investment, $I$, and saving decisions, $S$, that is,

$$\dot{K} = I = I(\dot{Y}) = S(Y), \tag{1.8}$$

where $K$ is capital stock. The original version of (1.8) (see Harrod 1939, p. 18 and Lundberg 1938, p. 185) is

$$\dot{K} = I = I(\dot{Y}) = v\dot{Y} = sY, \tag{1.9}$$

where $v$ is the constant acceleration coefficient (normal capital-output ratio) and $s$ is the constant average saving coefficient. As long as national income is positive, positive capital formation must occur, and this rules out the possibility of a Ricardo–Mill stationary state solution for $Y(t)$ in (1.9). Hence, the basic *growth* Assumption 1.2 of section "Stability Conditions for Autonomous Differential Equations" is satisfied.

The solution for $Y(t)$ and $K(t)$ from (1.9) is of course easily derived. But the effects of occasional "disturbances" upon those time paths have, ever since Harrod's contention (cf. Harrod 1939, p. 23) that "the moving (dynamic) equilibrium of advance is highly unstable", been much debated in the economic literature, see Alexander (1949, 1950), Baumol (1970), Gandolfo (1980), Hahn and Matthews (1965), Jorgenson (1960), Wan (1971). Harrod (1939, p. 22) concluded: "Thus in the dynamic field we have a condition opposite to that which holds in the static field. A departure from equilibrium, instead of being self-righting, will be self-aggravating".

Let us look at different interpretations of the Harrod instability problem. The discussion has proceeded under several handicaps.

First, "at the outset it should be noted that there is no universal agreement of the definition of stability for systems involving growth" as rightly observed by Jorgenson (1960, p. 243). The stability criteria defined in section "Introduction" hopefully go some way to meet this distinct need of properly defined stability concepts for growing economies.

Secondly, also noted in Jorgenson (1960), Harrod's nonformal presentation involves at least three different notions of stability.

(i) Instability means departure from the line of warranted advance, that is, from a particular time path of output.
(ii) Instability means that the actual rate of growth departs from the warranted rate. In particular, this alternative is referred to as "instability in the sense of Harrod".
(iii) Instability means that the actual capital-output ratio diverges from the desired (normal) capital-output ratio.

With regard to (i), Theorems 1.2 and 1.3 show that, after a "*disturbance*", the absolute deviation between any two time paths of $Y(t)$ in the simple model (1.9) will certainly not converge to zero as $t \to \infty$ or remain bounded over time. Furthermore, by Theorem 1.4, we see that neither will the relative deviation between two such time paths of $Y(t)$ converge to zero. Of course, this is not surprising, since the relative difference between two exponential solutions of (1.9) will always be the same and so can never disappear. However, any such relative deviations would not (for all $t$) get "larger' than some finite number, $k$, that is, these time paths have what is defined in section "Stability Criteria and Degrees of Stability" as *weak relative stability.*

Thus, it must be admitted that in this sense, (i), it was correctly observed by Harrod that the enunciation of a dynamic *theory* of *growth*—in contrast to the dynamics of business cycles or the short-run price dynamics around a stationary equilibrium—raises *new* stability problems beyond the traditional concepts of asymptotic and strong absolute stability, cf. section "Introduction".

With regard to (ii), it is easily seen that all solutions, in the simple version (1.9), have the same proportionate growth rate. Hence, regarding the rapidity of growth in (1.9), there is never any divergence—after a disturbance—between the actual proportional growth rate of $Y(t)$ and the "warranted rate", $s/v$, which is the rate of growth of income required to induce (or justify) enough investment expenditure to offset the savings that would be associated with the growing income, that is, a dynamic equilibrium is maintained.

To resolve the stability problem, (iii), we bring the Eqs. (1.9) into the normal form

$$\dot{K} = sY, \quad \dot{Y} = (s/v)Y. \tag{1.10}$$

Then the differential equation for the *ratio* $\rho = K/Y$ becomes

$$\dot{\rho} = -(s/v)\rho + s, \tag{1.11}$$

since, by (1.10)

$$\dot{\rho} = (K/Y)' = [Y\dot{K} - K\dot{Y}]/Y^2 = -(s/v)(K/Y) + s. \tag{1.12}$$

Hence, the stationary solution $\rho^*$ for the ratio variable $\rho(t)$ is $(K/Y)^* = \rho^* = v$, and it clearly has *asymptotic* stability. By (1.10), it is evident that the time paths of $K(t)$ and $Y(t)$ may be "disturbed" (shifted) independently over time, and so the actual ratio $K(t)/Y(t)$ may certainly at any point in time differ from its desired (normal) value, $v$. Yet, in the long run, the capital-output ratio surely reverts to $v$ in this original version, (1.9), (1.10), of the Harrod growth model.

So far we have argued on the assumption that the proportion saved out of a given income, $s$, and the amount entrepreneurs desire to invest expressed as a proportion of a given rise in income, $v$, are constant. On this basis, we did not obtain the traditional instability conclusion about the growth rate (ii) or the capital-output ratio (iii).

Evidently, $v$ and $s$ do in fact vary, and the question arises whether they are apt to do so in such a way as to uphold or even to sharpen the instability doctrine.

Consider what happens if the system (1.9) is replaced by the differential equations

$$\dot{K} = v(t)\dot{Y} = sY, \tag{1.13}$$

$$\dot{v}(t) = -\alpha(v(t) - v), \quad \alpha > 0. \tag{1.14}$$

The complete set of solutions for $v(t)$ and $Y(t)$ are

$$v_i(t) = v + a_i e^{-\alpha t}, \tag{1.15}$$

$$Y_i(t) = b_i(ve^{\alpha t} + a_i)^{s/\alpha v}, \tag{1.16}$$

where the parameters $a_i$, $b_i$, depend on the initial conditions in (1.14) and (1.13), respectively. By (1.16), we have for any pair of solutions that $Y_i(t)/Y_j(t) \to b_i/b_j$ for $t \to \infty$. Thus, the time paths of income have *weak relative* stability. Furthermore, $\dot{Y}_i/Y_i \to s/v$ as $t \to \infty$. The growth rates have *asymptotic* stability, since $s/v$ corresponds to the solutions in (1.15) and (1.16) with $a_i = 0$.

The dynamics of the capital-output ratio become, cf. (1.12)–(1.14),

$$\dot{\rho} = (s/v(t))\rho = s. \tag{1.17}$$

Let $\rho_h(t)$ solve the homogeneous part of (1.17). Due to $s/v(t) > \epsilon > 0$, which follows from (1.14) or (1.15), these solutions $\rho_h(t)$ converge to zero as $t \to \infty$. The solutions to (1.17) are given by

$$\rho(t) = \rho_h(t) \int [s/\rho_h(t)]dt = \frac{\int [s/\rho_h(t)]dt}{1/\rho_h(t)}. \tag{1.18}$$

Since both the numerator and denominator of (1.18) go to infinity as $t \to \infty$, we may use—l'Hospital—their derivatives to obtain the limit of (1.18), that is, cf. (1.17),

$$\frac{s/\rho_h(t)}{-\dot{\rho}_h(t)/[\rho_h(t)]^2} = \frac{s\rho_h(t)}{s\rho_h(t)/v(t)} = v(t). \tag{1.19}$$

Since by (1.15), $v(t) \to v$ as $t \to \infty$, then by (1.18), (1.19), $\rho(t) \to v$ as $t \to \infty$. Hence, the time paths for the capital-output ratio have *asymptotic* stability in the model (1.13), (1.14), because $\rho(t) = v$ solves (1.17) in the case of $v(t) = v$.

Also a *variation* in the average *saving ratio* may be allowed, for example, by replacing $s$ with $s(t)$ in (1.13), supplemented with an adjustment equation: $\dot{s}(t) = -\beta(s(t) - s)$, $\beta > 0$. The latter has the solutions: $s_i(t) = s + c_i e^{-\beta t}$, similar to (1.15). The *stability* properties of this extended growth model will be seen to remain *unaltered*. The same procedure (1.17), (1.19) shows that the capital-output ratio has *asymptotic* stability. As evident from (1.19), $s(t)$

does not affect this limit. As to the time path of $Y(t)$, (1.13) is now replaced by: $\dot{Y} = [s(t)/v(t)]Y = g(t)Y,\ g(t) > 0$, which gives the solutions: $Y_i(t) = b_i e^{F(t)};\ F(t) = \int g(t)dt$. Therefore, $Y_i(t)/Y_j(t) = b_i/b_j = \text{constant} \neq 1$ for all $t$, implying *weak relative* stability of $Y(t)$, independent of $g(t)$. The growth rates have *asymptotic* stability, since

$$\dot{Y}_i/Y_i = g(t) = s(t)/v(t) \to s/v \text{ as } t \to \infty.$$

(**Remark** Note that the complementarity principle does not apply to non-autonomous differential equations, for example, for $g(t) = e^t$, the growth of $Y_i(t)$ is double-exponential.) ▽

As another positive, but *nonlinear* saving function considers

$$S(Y) = s_1 Y - s_2 Y^{1-\lambda},\quad 0 < \lambda < 1,\ Y > (s_2/s_1)^{1/\lambda} \tag{1.20}$$

with $s_1 > 0$ and $s_2 > 0$, implying a rising but also the existence of a limiting saving ratio

$$s = S(Y)/Y = s_1 - s_2 Y^{-\lambda} \to s_1 \text{ as } Y \to \infty. \tag{1.21}$$

By (1.9) and (1.20), the modified growth model becomes

$$\dot{K} = v\dot{Y} = s_1 Y - s_2 Y^{1-\lambda}. \tag{1.22}$$

For the differential equation $\dot{Y} = h(Y) = (s_1/v)Y - (s_2/v)Y^{1-\lambda}$, it is seen that $h(x)/x \to s_1/v$ as $x \to \infty$, and so the time paths of $Y(t)$ have *weak relative* stability by Theorem 1.5, while the *rapidity* of growth is at most *exponential* by Theorem 1.8. The growth rates $\dot{Y}/Y$ have *strong absolute* stability, see appendix. The differential equation for $Y(t)$ (1.22) can in fact here be solved explicitly. It is a Bernoulli equation having the complete solutions ($b_i$, depending on initial conditions)

$$Y_i(t) = [b_i e^{(\lambda s_1/v)t} + s_2/s_1]^{1/\lambda}. \tag{1.23}$$

The differential equation for the capital-output ratio becomes, see (1.12), (1.21), (1.22), (1.23),

$$\dot{\rho} = s_1 - s_2 Y^{-\lambda} - 1/v(s_1 - s_2 Y^{-\lambda})\rho = s(t) - (s(t)/v)\rho. \tag{1.24}$$

The solutions to the homogeneous part of (1.24) are again converging to zero for $t \to \infty$, since $s(t)/v > \epsilon > 0$, cf. (1.23) and (1.24). Accordingly, the same procedure, (1.17)–(1.19), proves the *asymptotic* stability of the capital-output ratio.

Finally, the growth model (1.22) may be combined with (1.14). The *asymptotic* stability of $\rho(t)$ in (1.24) with (1.15) again follows from (1.17)–

(1.19). It is easily verified that the modified Bernoulli equation above will now give the solutions, cf. (1.23), (1.16).

$$Y_i(t) = [b_i(ve^{\alpha t} + a_i)^{\lambda s_1/\alpha v} + s_2/s_1]^{1/\lambda}. \tag{1.25}$$

By (1.25) we have that $Y_i(t)/Y_j(t) \to (b_i/b_j)^{1/\lambda}$ as $t \to \infty$ and that $\dot{Y}_i/Y_i \to s_1/v$ for $t \to \infty$. Thus, the time paths and growth rates of income again have, respectively, *weak relative* and *strong absolute* stability. (For $s_2 < 0$, (1.20), no change in stability properties.)

Our analysis of the Harrod growth models above has shown that the *weak relative* stability of the time paths of $Y(t)$ and the *asymptotic* stability of the capital-output ratio, $K(t)/Y(t)$, remained *unchanged* with the alternative model specifications—especially, they did not depend on particular numerical values of any of the parameters involved. Furthermore, the *growth rates* of income, $\dot{Y}(t)/Y(t)$, preserve the property of convergence. But in the more complicated models, we cannot always expect these limits to be an actual growth rate of any time path (solution) for $Y(t)$. Nevertheless, the growth rates were quite robust by preserving *strong absolute* stability. The unfortunate but well-entrenched instability doctrine associated with the Harrod growth model should clearly be revised.

### *The Neoclassical Growth Model of Solow*

In this one-sector growth model with a neoclassical production function, we consider the ratio $k = K/L$ between capital and labor as a function of time. The function $k(t)$ is assumed to *solve* the fundamental differential equation of neoclassical economic growth (see Stiglitz and Uzawa 1969, p. 69)

$$\dot{k} = h(k) = sf(k) - nk, \tag{1.26}$$

where $s$ is the constant average saving ratio, $n$ is the given proportionate growth rate of the labor force, and $y$ is the average product of labor $(Y/L)$, while $y = f(k)$ is a linear homogeneous production function in the intensive form satisfying the conditions (cf. Wan 1971, p. 37):

$$f'(k) > 0 \text{ for all } k, \tag{1.27.1}$$

$$f''(k) < 0 \text{ for all } k, \tag{1.27.2}$$

$$f'(k) \to 0 \text{ as } k \to \infty, \tag{1.27.3}$$

$$f'(k) \to \infty \text{ as } k \to 0, \tag{1.27.4}$$

$$f(0) = 0, \tag{1.27.5}$$

$$f'(k) \to \infty \text{ as } k \to \infty. \tag{1.27.6}$$

Assumptions (1.27.1–1.27.6) imply that $h(k)$ has one zero, and that $h(k)$ is decreasing through this point. Hence, Theorem 1.1 applies and gives *asymptotic stability* to the solutions for the capital-labor ratio in (1.26).

The assumptions in (1.27.1–1.27.6) may be relaxed in various ways. Instead of (1.27.3), we may suppose $sf(k)$ never crosses the line $nk$, but such that

$$h(k) = sf(k) - nk \to 0 \text{ as } k \to \infty. \tag{1.28}$$

Then Theorem 1.2 applies and ensures *strong absolute stability* of the solutions for $k(t)$. The *growth* paths of $k(t)$ are *unbounded,* but still the growth is less than "linear", see Theorem 1.8. In this case (1.28), the average product of capital (inverse capital-output ratio) must, as in the asymptotic stability case, tend toward

$$1/v = Y/K = f(k)/k \to n/s \text{ as } k \to \infty. \tag{1.29}$$

We might weaken (1.27.3) a bit more, for example, assuming

$$f'(k) > n/s \text{ for all } k; \quad f'(k) \to n/s \text{ as } k \to \infty. \tag{1.30}$$

Then we have by l'Hospital

$$\lim_{k\to\infty} \frac{h(k)}{k} = \lim_{k\to\infty} \frac{sf(k) - nk}{k} = \lim_{k\to\infty} (sf'(k) - n) = 0. \tag{1.31}$$

Hence, the growth paths of $k(t)$ have *strong relative stability* by Theorem 1.4, while the rapidity of *growth* is at most *polynomial,* according to Theorem 1.8. By (1.31), it is also seen that $Y/K$ here tends toward the same value as in (1.29).

Finally, we may allow the marginal product of capital to decline even less than indicated by (1.30), for example,

$$f'(k) \to \gamma > n/s \text{ as } k \to \infty, \tag{1.32}$$

and then

$$\lim_{k\to\infty} \frac{h(k)}{k} = \lim_{k\to\infty} \frac{sf(k) - nk}{k} = \lim_{k\to\infty} (sf'(k) - n) = s\gamma - n > 0. \tag{1.33}$$

Thus, the growth parts of $k(t)$ have *weak relative stability* by Theorem 1.5, while the *growth* is at most *exponential* by Theorem 1.8. The average product of capital here tends toward $\gamma$, since by (1.33)

$$1/v = Y/K = f(k)/k \to \gamma > n/s \text{ as } k \to \infty. \tag{1.34}$$

It follows from (1.28), (1.30), (1.32), and l'Hospital that the *rapidity* of growth of $y$ is in the long run the same as $k$.

As mentioned by Solow (1956, p. 80), we may allow for a *variable* saving ratio and a *variable* population growth, both depending directly on factor prices but indirectly on the capital-labor ratio, $k$, in the fundamental equation (1.26). With proper specifications of the behavior of $s(k)$ and $n(k)$, our theorems on growth and stability in sections "Stability Conditions for Autonomous Differential Equations–Growth Versus Stability of Autonomous Differential Equations" can be used to characterize *rigorously* the growth and stability properties of all the solutions of this modified equation (1.26), provided that the function $h(k)$ remains positive everywhere.

**Remark 1.4** Assumption (1.28) would eventually violate the concavity condition (1.27.2). However, an example of production function $f(k)$ that satisfies the conditions (1.27.1–1.27.2, 1.27.5–1.27.6) and either (1.30) or (1.32) could easily be given, for example, $y = f(k) = 1 + \gamma k - 1/(1+k)$, $\gamma \geq n/s$, which clearly has $f'(k) > 0$, $f''(k) < 0$ everywhere, and with $Y = [\gamma + 1/(1 + K/L)]K$ as the extensive form, which is clearly linearly homogeneous with convex isoquants. ▽

The basic model (1.26)—supplemented with the conditions of (1.27.1–1.27.6) or, respectively, with either (1.28), (1.30), (1.32)—has not implied any assumptions about competitive pricing or other distributional arrangements between capital and labor (cf. Solow 1956, p. 31 and Ostroy 1984). Our purpose has only been to extend and rigorously classify the growth and stability properties of the neoclassical model (1.26) under alternative *technological* assumptions about $f(k)$ and herewith to illustrate, without explicit solutions, the straightforward applications of our main theorems in sections "Stability Conditions for Autonomous Differential Equations–Growth Versus Stability of Autonomous Differential Equations".

## Concluding Comments

We have classified the concept of stability for arbitrary families of functions and the concept of growth for arbitrary functions. For solutions of first-order autonomous differential equations, we have proved a complementarity principle that—to a certain degree—growth and stability are mutually exclusive.

Out stability criteria and stability conditions in terms of properties of the governing functions were used in clarifying and extending stability propositions for the Harrod and Solow growth models. But the theorems are also applicable to other social and biological models. A subject of further mathematical research would be to extend the complementarity principle to autonomous systems of higher dimensions.

## Appendix on the Logarithmic Derivative

In economics, it is popular to consider the *logarithmic derivative* $(\ln \varphi(t))' = \varphi'(t)/\varphi(t)$, as a convenient *growth measure*. It is used in section "Rapidity of Growth" (concept V and VI for, respectively, exponential and hyper-exponential growth). Further, we have introduced the *double logarithmic derivative* $(\ln \ln \varphi(t))' = \varphi'(t)/(\varphi(t) \ln \varphi(t))$ in the definition of double-exponential growth, (VII).

If we have the situation of the differential equation

$$\dot{y} = f(y), \tag{1.35}$$

and $y = \varphi(t)$ is a solution, then the behavior of the logarithmic derivative corresponds to the satisfaction of the *stability conditions* in Theorems 1.4–1.7. This is due to the formulas

$$(\ln \varphi(t))' = \frac{\varphi'(t)}{\varphi(t)} = \frac{f(\varphi(t))}{\varphi(t)} = \frac{f(x)}{x}, \tag{1.36}$$

$$(\ln \ln \varphi(t))' = \frac{\varphi'(t)}{\varphi \ln \varphi(t)} = \frac{f(\varphi(t))}{\varphi(t) \ln \varphi(t)} = \frac{f(x)}{x \ln x}. \tag{1.37}$$

If the solution to Eq. (1.1) behaves such that the logarithmic derivative *goes to zero* in infinity,

$$(\ln \varphi(t))' \to 0 \text{ as } t \to \infty,$$

then Theorem 1.4 applies and says that the *stability* is *strongly relative,* (1.4.1), while Theorem 1.8 implies that the *growth* is at most *polynomial,* (IV).

And analogously, if the logarithmic derivative is *bounded*

$$(\ln \varphi(t))' < k < \infty \text{ for all } t,$$

then Theorem 1.5 applies and says that the *stability* is *weakly relative,* (1.5.1), while Theorem 1.8 implies that the *growth* is at most *exponential,* (V). Within the family of solutions having *weak relative* stability is included solutions, where $(\ln \varphi(t))'$ has a finite nonzero limit as $t \to \infty$—solutions that are sometimes referred to as *bounded exponential* growth. Accordingly, the *growth rates,* $\varphi'(t)/\varphi(t)$, with the same limit have *strong absolute* stability. If, furthermore, this limit is the growth rate of a solution to (1.1), then the growth rates have *asymptotic* stability.

Next, one may think of using the comparison of two logarithmic derivatives as a *criterion* of *stability,* for example, for two solutions to Eq. (1.1), we consider according to Lemma 1.2 the criterion

$$\frac{(\ln \varphi(t+h))'}{(\ln \varphi(t))'} \to 1 \text{ as } t \to \infty. \tag{1.38}$$

**Theorem 1.9** *If $\varphi(t)$ is a solution to Eq. (1.1) and the quotient (1.38) above goes to 1 as $t \to \infty$, then the solutions have strong logarithmic stability.*

***Proof*** The rule of l'Hospital ensures that

$$\lim_{t\to\infty} \frac{\ln \varphi(t+h)}{\ln \varphi(t)} = \lim_{t\to\infty} \frac{(\ln \varphi(t+h))'}{(\ln \varphi(t))'} = 1.$$

But then:

$$\ln \ln \varphi(t+h) - \ln \ln \varphi(t) \to \ln 1 = 0 \quad \text{as} \quad t \to \infty.$$

□

Of course, one might also consider as a criterion of stability the difference:

$$(\ln \varphi(t+h))' - (\ln \varphi(t))' \to 0 \quad \text{as} \quad t \to \infty. \tag{1.39}$$

But if the growth is at least exponential, this is the same as (1.38) and Theorem 1.9 applies.

**Lemma 1.3** *If $\varphi(t)$ is a solution to an equation of type (1.1), and this solution exhibits exponential growth, then*

$$(\ln \varphi(t+h))' - (\ln \varphi(t))' \to 0 \quad \textit{as} \quad t \to \infty$$

$$\Updownarrow$$

$$\frac{(\ln \varphi(t+h))'}{(\ln \varphi(t))'} \to 1 \quad \textit{as} \quad t \to \infty.$$

***Proof***

$$(\ln \varphi(t+h))' - (\ln \varphi(t))' = (\ln \varphi(t))' \left( \frac{(\ln \varphi(t+h))'}{(\ln \varphi(t))'} - 1 \right),$$

and exponential growth means that $(\ln \varphi(t))' = \varphi'(t)/\varphi(t) > \epsilon > 0$. □

These results can be weakened to

**Lemma 1.4** *If $\varphi(t)$ is a solution to an equation of type (1.1) and the quotient in (1.38) above goes to a finite limit as $t \to \infty$, then the solutions have weak logarithmic stability.*

***Proof*** As for Theorem 1.9, with 1 replaced by $K$ and 0 by $\ln K$. □

**Remark 1.5** The logarithmic derivative does not allow a distinction between the types of growth I, II, III, IV or the degrees of stability 1, 2, 3, 4. Hence, this concept does not allow the more refined analysis, which we displayed by our criteria in this chapter. ▽

## Bibliography


Alexander SS (1949) The accelerator as a generator of steady growth. Quart J Economics 63:174–197

Alexander SS (1950) Mr. Harrod's dynamic model. Economic J 60:724–739

Baumol WJ (1970) Economic Dynamics, 3rd edn. MacMillan, London

Burmeister E, Dobell AR (1970) Mathematical Theories of Economic Growth. Macmillan, London

Coddington EA, Levinson N (1955) Theory of Ordinary Differential Equation. McGraw–Hill, New York

Gandolfo G (1980) Economic Dynamics: Methods and Models, 2nd edn. North–Holland, Amsterdam

Hahn FH, Matthews RCO (1965) The theory of economic growth: a survey. Economic J 74:779–902, or in *Survey of Economic Theory,* 2, (American Economic Association/Royal Economic Society), Macmillan, London

Hamberg D (1956) Economic Growth and Instability. W.W. Norton, New York

Harrod RF (1939) An Essay in Dynamic Theory. Economic J 49:14–33, or Stiglitz (1969)

Harrod RF (1973) Economic Dynamics. MacMillan, London

Jones HG (1975) An Introduction to Modern Theories of Economic Growth. Nelson, London

Jorgenson DW (1960) On stability in the sense of Harrod. Economica 27:243–248

Kalman RE, Bertram JE (1960) Control system analysis and design via the 'second method' of Lyapunov, ASME. J Basic Eng pp 371–393

Lundberg E (1938) Studies in the Theory of Economic Expansion. P.S. King and Sons, London

Ostroy JM (1984) A reformulation of the marginal productivity theory of distribution. Econometrica 52:599–630

Pontryagin LS (1962) Ordinary Differential Equations. Addison–Wesley, Reading, Mass

Salle L (1961) J. and Lefschetz, S. Stability by Lyapunov's Direct Method, Academic Press, New York

Samuelson PA (1983) Foundations of Economic Analysis, enlarged edn. Harvard University Press, Cambridge

Solow RM (1956) A Contribution to the Theory of Economic Growth. Quarterly Journal of Economics 70:65–94, Reprinted in Stiglitz (1969), and in Becker (1991)

Stiglitz JE, Uzawa H (1969) Readings in the Modern Theory of Economic Growth. M.I.T. Press, Cambridge, Mass

Wan HY Jr (1971) Economic Growth. Harcourt Brace Jovanowich, New York

CHAPTER 2

# Basic Laws of Production

## THE PRODUCTION FUNCTION

Production is defined abstractly as an activity of converting bundles of measurable inputs into alternative bundles of measurable outputs. We will first be concerned with the activity of producing a *single output* from a combination of a finite number of inputs, subject to traditional laws of production. As to the number of *inputs* (factors of production), we only consider, as the classicists, the *triad:* land, labor, and capital.

Although *land* (natural resources) was used in production, it was mainly supposed to be available in a *fixed* nonaugmentable amount. The *abundance* or *scarcity* of the given quantity of land in existence, however, may affect the *returns* to *scale* of the production process. Returns to scale refer to the behavior of output, when all *variable* inputs are multiplied by the same positive scalar.

As keen observers, the classicists did not always assume fixed proportions between *labor* and *capital,* cf. Samuelson (1978, p. 1423). The extent of the technical *substitution* possibilities—variability of techniques (flexible capital/labor ratios)—were probably restricted, but we will not here be engaged in a textual exegesis of this matter.

Therefore, for the sake of logical completeness and mathematical convenience, the *production function,* $Y = F(L, K)$—representing *technological* alternatives (techniques) in production and showing the *maximal* output ($Y$) obtainable from any given combination of labor ($L$) and capital ($K$)—is assumed *twice* continuously differentiable on the *domain* of nonnegative real numbers:

$$Y = F(L, K), \quad F(0, 0) = 0, \quad F \in C^2\text{-class}; \qquad Y, L, K \geq 0. \tag{2.1}$$



B. S. Jensen, *The Elements and Dynamic Systems of Economic Growth and Trade Models*, https://doi.org/10.1007/978-3-031-52493-6_2

Each factor may or may not be *essential* for positive output, that is, respectively,

$$F(0, K) = F(L, 0) = 0; \tag{2.2.1}$$

$$F(0, K) > 0, \ F(L, 0) > 0. \tag{2.2.2}$$

For *positive* inputs, the *partial derivatives* of $F$ satisfy the *sign* conditions:

$$\frac{\partial F}{\partial L} = MP_L = \frac{\partial Y}{\partial L} > 0, \ \frac{\partial F}{\partial K} = MP_K = \frac{\partial Y}{\partial K} > 0; \ (L, K) \in \mathbf{R}_+^2, \tag{2.3}$$

$$\frac{\partial^2 F}{\partial L^2} < 0, \quad \frac{\partial^2 F}{\partial K^2} < 0; \qquad (L, K) \in \mathbf{R}_+^2, \tag{2.4}$$

$$\frac{\partial^2 F}{\partial L \partial K} = \frac{\partial MP_L}{\partial K} = \frac{\partial MP_K}{\partial L} = \frac{\partial^2 F}{\partial K \partial L} > 0; \ (L, K) \in \mathbf{R}_+^2, \tag{2.5}$$

that is, *both* marginal products, $MP_L$ and $MP_K$, are always *positive,* (2.3), but they fall as a *single* factor exhibits *diminishing returns,* (2.4).

As usual, increased quantities of *one* factor will be assumed to increase the marginal productivity of the other factor, (2.5), an *interacting* productivity property of the factors called *factor complementarity* (Frisch 1965, p. 60).

Formally, it is assumed that

$$\lim_{L \to 0} MP_L = \overline{B}_L \leq \infty, \qquad \lim_{K \to 0} MP_K = \overline{B}_K \leq \infty, \tag{2.6.1}$$

$$\lim_{L \to \infty} MP_L = \underline{B}_L \geq 0, \qquad \lim_{K \to \infty} MP_K = \underline{B}_K \geq 0, \tag{2.6.2}$$

that is, the marginal products start very large and diminish to very little.

Finally, a fundamental assumption is that the production function $F$ is *homogeneous* of degree, $0 < m \leq 1$, so for any positive scale factor $\lambda$,

$$F(\lambda L, \lambda K) = \lambda^m F(L, K) = \lambda^m Y; \quad \lambda > 0, \ 0 < m \leq 1. \tag{2.7}$$

For $m = 1$ and $0 < m < 1$, the production function $F$, (2.1), exhibits, respectively, *constant* and *decreasing returns* to *scale.*

## Homogeneity and the Laws of Variable Proportions

The production laws can, due to the homogeneity property, be restated in various *intensive forms.* Choosing $\lambda = 1/L$, we get from (2.7),

$$Y = F(L, K) = L^m F(1, K/L) = L^m f(K/L), \tag{2.8}$$

where the function $f$ is the intensive component of the production function $F$; $f$ is homogeneous of degree zero in $L$, $K$. Denoting per-worker quantities and *ratios* by lower case letters, we can write (2.8) as, cf. (2.2.1),

$$AP_L = y = L^{m-1} f(k), \quad f(0) = 0; \quad L \neq 0, \tag{2.9}$$

and next

$$AP_K = 1/\mathrm{v} = L^{m-1} f(k)/k, \quad k \neq 0, \quad L \neq 0, \tag{2.10}$$

where $y$ is output per worker (average labor productivity), $k$ is the capital-labor ratio (capital intensity), and v is the capital-output ratio (reciprocal of the average product of capital), that is,

$$AP_L = y = Y/L, \quad AP_K = 1/\mathrm{v} = y/k = Y/K, \quad k = K/L. \tag{2.11}$$

By assumptions (2.3–2.4), (2.6.1–2), and (2.8–2.9):

$$\forall k > 0: \; f'(k) = df(k)/dk > 0, \quad f''(k) = d^2 f(k)/dk^2 < 0; \tag{2.12}$$

$$\lim_{k \to 0} f'(k) = \overline{B} \leq \infty, \quad \lim_{k \to \infty} f'(k) = \underline{B} \geq 0; \quad f'(k) \in J = [\underline{B}, \overline{B}]. \tag{2.13}$$

Thus, the *intensive function* $f$ is a strictly concave monotonic increasing function on the nonnegative real line, with its slope decreasing from $\overline{B}$ at $k = 0$ to $\underline{B}$ at $k = +\infty$.

It follows from (2.3), (2.8–2.9), and (2.12) that the *marginal products,* which in $L, K$ are *homogeneous* functions of degree, $m - 1$, may be written as:

$$\forall k > 0: \; MP_L \quad = \quad L^{m-1}[mf(k) - kf'(k)] > 0; \; \frac{kf'(k)}{f(k)} < m, \tag{2.14.1}$$

$$\forall k > 0: \; MP_K \quad = \quad L^{m-1} f'(k). \tag{2.14.2}$$

By (2.14.1–2.14.2), (2.8) and Euler's theorem on homogeneous functions, we have

$$L \cdot MP_L + K \cdot MP_K = m \cdot Y, \tag{2.15.1}$$

$$L^m[mf(k) - kf'(k)] + L^m kf'(k) = mL^m f(k) = mY, \tag{2.15.2}$$

or in terms of *output elasticities* with respect to marginal factor variation, cf. (2.3) and (2.7–2.11),

$$\epsilon_L \equiv E(Y, L) \quad \equiv \quad \frac{\partial Y}{\partial L}\frac{L}{Y} = \frac{MP_L}{AP_L} = m - \frac{kf'(k)}{f(k)} > 0, \quad k \neq 0, \tag{2.16.1}$$

$$\epsilon_K \equiv E(Y, K) \equiv \frac{\partial Y}{\partial K}\frac{K}{Y} = \frac{MP_K}{AP_K} = \frac{kf'(k)}{f(k)} > 0, \quad k \neq 0, \tag{2.16.2}$$

$$\epsilon \equiv E(Y, \lambda) \equiv \frac{\partial Y}{\partial \lambda}\frac{\lambda}{Y} = \epsilon_L + \epsilon_K \equiv m, \tag{2.16.3}$$

where $\epsilon_L(\epsilon_K)$ is the output elasticity of labor (capital); $\epsilon$, the output elasticity with respect to scale variation is independent of $k$. The elasticities $\epsilon_L$ and $\epsilon_K$—which are of the same signs as $MP_L$ and $MP_K$ and hence are always positive—are *homogeneous* functions in $L, K$ of *degree zero,* no matter what the degree of $F(L, K)$, (2.8), is. Therefore, as to the behavior of output in response to factor variation, the *elasticities* $\epsilon_L, \epsilon_K, \epsilon$ aptly characterize the *variational* properties of the production function.

By (2.8) and Euler's theorem, the *second-order* partial derivatives (2.4–2.5) are *homogeneous* functions of degree, $m - 2$, and they have, as easily verified, the intensive forms, cf. (2.12), (2.14.1–2.14.2),

$$\partial^2 F/\partial K^2 = L^{m-2} f''(k) < 0, \tag{2.17}$$

$$\partial^2 F/\partial K \partial L = L^{m-2}\left[(m-1)f'(k) - kf''(k)\right] > 0; \quad \frac{kf''(k)}{f'(k)} < m - 1, \tag{2.18}$$

$$\begin{aligned} \partial^2 F/\partial L^2 &= L^{-1}(m-1)MP_L - k \cdot \partial^2 Y/\partial K \partial L \\ &= L^{m-2}\left[(m-1)\{mf(k) - 2kf'(k)\} + k^2 f''(k)\right] < 0. \end{aligned} \tag{2.19}$$

$$L^2 \cdot \frac{\partial^2 F}{\partial L^2} + 2LK \cdot \frac{\partial^2 F}{\partial K \partial L} + K^2 \cdot \frac{\partial^2 F}{\partial K^2} = (m-1)\, m\, Y, \tag{2.20.1}$$

$$\begin{aligned} &L^m[\,(m-1)\{mf(k) - 2kf'(k)\} + 2k^2 f''(k) + \\ &2k\{(m-1)f'(k) - kf''(k)\}\,] = (m-1)\, m\, L^m f(k) = (m-1)\, m\, Y, \end{aligned} \tag{2.20.2}$$

**Remark 2.1** In case of $m = 1$, it follows from (2.17–2.18) that $\partial^2 F/\partial K^2$ and $\partial^2 F/\partial K \partial L$ have *opposite* signs, whence *diminishing* marginal returns (2.17), (2.19), and technical *complementarity* (2.5) *must* coexist.

For $m \neq 1$, or nonhomogeneous production functions, such coexistence is no longer necessary, cf. (2.17–2.18). But since we want to keep the character of the production process as similar as possible for all values of $0 < m \leq 1$, we imposed a *positive* sign upon $\partial^2 Y/\partial K \partial L$ already in (2.5). ▽

The *Hessian determinant, D*, of the production function (2.1) is

$$D = \partial^2 F/\partial L^2 \cdot \partial^2 F/\partial K^2 - (\partial^2 F/\partial L \partial K)^2. \tag{2.21}$$

As is well-known, if $D < 0$, then $F$ is neither concave nor convex. Hence, we shall at least require that (2.21) is *nonnegative*. Then by (2.17–2.21), we obtain the condition,

$$D = L^{2(m-2)}[f'(k)]^2 m(1-m)\left[1 - 1/m - \frac{f(k)f''(k)}{[f'(k)]^2}\right] \geq 0. \tag{2.22}$$

Clearly, $m \neq 1$ is necessary for $D > 0$; further comment on (2.22) is given below, cf. end of Remark 2.2.

## Technical Substitution Possibilities

The substitution properties of the production function $Y = F(L, K)$ are characterized by the set of alternative factor combination generating the same level of output, that is, by the *shape* of the contour curves (*isoquants*):

$$I = \{L, K > 0 \mid F(L, K) = \bar{Y}\}, \quad \bar{Y} \in \mathbf{R}_+, \tag{2.23}$$

where $\bar{Y}$ is a given level of output.

At any point of the isoquants (2.23), a traditional concept and measure of the *rate* of *technical substitution* for $F \in C^2$–class is offered by the *ratio* of the marginal products of labor and capital, denoted the *marginal rate* of *substitution*, $\omega(k)$. Hence, by (2.14.1–2.14.2) and (2.16.1–2.16.3), we obtain

$$MRS = \frac{MP_L}{MP_K} = \omega = \omega(k) = \frac{\epsilon_L}{\epsilon_K}k = \frac{mf(k)}{f'(k)} - k > 0, \quad \forall k > 0. \tag{2.24}$$

Like $\epsilon_L$, and $\epsilon_K$, $MRS$ is a *homogeneous* function in $L, K$ of *degree* zero, so $MRS$ is independent of the *level* of production. But the parameter $m$ itself is involved in the *shape* of the loci (2.23) through general expression (2.24), although $m$ may drop out for special $f(k)$. As is well-known, $MRS$ is the numerical values of slopes of the negatively inclined isoquants, (2.23), in the $(L, K)$ plane.

It is commonly assumed that $MRS$, (2.24), obeys the *law* of *diminishing marginal rate* of *substitution*, which in turn is often considered equivalent to the classic *diminishing marginal returns*, (2.3–2.4). However, such equivalence does not hold generally, not even for homogeneous production functions. For later purposes, we need to elaborate a bit on this matter.

Generally, *diminishing MRS* means that (2.24) decreases monotonically as we move to the right along an isoquant (2.23) and increases monotonically as we move to left, that is, the isoquants are strictly convex to the origin. Hence by definition,

$$\text{diminishing } MRS \quad \equiv \quad dMRS/dk = \omega'(k) > 0, \quad \forall k > 0. \tag{2.25}$$

For $\omega(k)$, (2.24), to satisfy the *condition* (2.25), a *restriction* has to be imposed upon $f(k)$ beyond the property of diminishing marginal returns, (2.12).

**Lemma 2.1** *Strictly convex isoquants (2.23) is tantamount to*

$$\forall k > 0: \quad \omega'(k) > 0 \Leftrightarrow \left[\frac{f(k)f''(k)}{[f'(k)]^2} < 1 - \frac{1}{m}\right]. \tag{2.26}$$

***Proof*** By (2.24), the function $\omega(k)$ has the derivative,

$$\omega'(k) \quad = \quad m\left[1 - \frac{f(k)f''(k)}{[f'(k)]^2}\right] - 1, \tag{2.27}$$

which gives (2.26). □

**Remark 2.2** In case of $m = 1$ and given the *positivity of* $f$, (2.9), it follows from (2.26) that $\omega'(k) > 0 \Leftrightarrow f''(k) < 0$, that is, strict convexity of the isoquants (2.23), (2.25) is an implication of diminishing marginal returns, (2.3–2.4), (2.17), (2.19).

With $0 < m < 1$, the negative sign of $f''(k)$ is not enough, since now $\omega(k)$ do depend on $m$, cf. (2.24). Accordingly, the additional *inequality* (RHS), (2.26), must be satisfied by the strictly *concave* function $f(k)$, (2.12), to ensure *strictly convex* isoquants of the *positive* and *homogeneous* function $F(L, K)$.

Also with $0 < m < 1$, the inequality (2.26) ensures the *positivity* of the Hessian determinant, (2.22). Indeed, diminishing $MRS$ and $0 < m < 1$ are *sufficient* economic conditions for the *strict* concavity of $F$, (2.1). ▽

The *range* of $MRS$ may be finite or infinite. We have, cf. (2.24), (2.12–2.13)

$$\lim_{k \to 0} \omega(k) = \underline{\omega} \geq 0, \qquad \lim_{k \to \infty} \omega(k) = \overline{\omega} \leq \infty, \tag{2.28.1}$$

$$\omega(k) \in \Omega \quad = \quad [\underline{\omega}, \overline{\omega}]. \tag{2.28.2}$$

The *curvature* of the *isoquants* (2.23) is traditionally characterized by the *substitution elasticity* ($\sigma$) between $L$ and $K$, defined as, cf. (2.24–2.26), (2.16.1–2.16.3).

$$\sigma \equiv E(k, \omega) \equiv \frac{dk}{d\omega} \cdot \frac{\omega}{k} = \frac{\epsilon_L/\epsilon_K}{\omega'(k)} = \frac{m/\epsilon_K - 1}{\omega'(k)} > 0, \ \omega'(k) \neq 0, \tag{2.29}$$

that is, the percentage change in the ratio $(K/L)$ of inputs divided by the percentage change in the ratio $(MRS)$ of the marginal products of inputs. Thus, $\sigma$ is a pure number that measures the ease at which factor substitution takes place.

The inverse of (2.24), that is, $k(\omega)$, exists by (2.26). Like $\omega(k)$, the function $\sigma(k)$, (2.29), is *homogeneous* in $L, K$ of *degree* zero, cf. (2.16.1–2.16.3). Despite the latter, the actual size of $\sigma(k)$ is usually affected by the size of the degree $m$, cf. (2.29), (2.27). Thus, scale and substitution properties become intertwined with $m \neq 1$. Similarly, the size of the component, (2.18), is implicitly involved in the size of $\sigma(k)$, (2.29), that is, technical complementarity certainly does affect the shape (curvature) of the isoquants, (2.23); see Hicks (1932, 1948, p. 244), Hicks (1970), Allen (1938, p. 342), Samuelson (1968, p. 467) and also section"Iso-Marginal, Iso-Average Productivity Curves".

For later purposes, we need here—for homogeneous production functions allowing generally for a *variable elasticity* of *substitution* $(VES)$—to call attention to some, seemingly neglected, relationships between simple, qualitative properties of the $\omega(k)$ function and the *range* of the $\sigma(k)$ function.

To this end, we first state elementary properties of positive convex/concave functions in

**Lemma 2.2** *With a positive, globally increasing function, $p(x) \in C^1$-class, $x \in [0, \infty]$, the following implications hold for:* $s(x) = p'(x)/[p(x)/x]$, $\forall x > 0$,

$$p(0) = 0, \quad p(x) \text{ strictly convex} \quad \Rightarrow \forall x > 0 : \; s(x) > 1, \tag{2.30}$$

$$p(0) \geq 0, \quad p(x) \text{ strictly concave} \quad \Rightarrow \forall x > 0 : s(x) < 1, \tag{2.31}$$

$$p(0) = 0, \quad p(x) \text{ linear} \quad \Rightarrow \forall x > 0 : \; s(x) = 1. \tag{2.32}$$

***Proof*** Since at the point, $[x, p(x)]$, $s(x)$ is equal to the tangent slope divided by the slope of radius vector, properties (2.30–2.31) follow easily from standard characterizations of strict convexity/concavity, (see Rockefellar 1970, p. 242).

Property (2.32) is obvious. □

**Remark 2.3** The *reverse* implications in (2.30–2.31) can *not* hold, as the inequalities for $s(x)$ certainly do not impose global monotonicity upon $p(x)$.▽

**Lemma 2.3** *The technical substitution measures $\omega(k)$, (2.24), and $\sigma(k)$, (2.29), have systematic relationships:*

$$\omega(0) = 0, \quad \omega(k) \text{ strictly convex} \quad \Rightarrow \forall k > 0 : \sigma(k) < 1, \tag{2.33}$$

$$\omega(0) \geq 0, \quad \omega(k) \text{ strictly concave} \quad \Rightarrow \forall k > 0 : \sigma(k) > 1, \tag{2.34}$$

$$\omega(0) = 0, \quad \omega(k) \text{ linear} \quad \Leftrightarrow \forall k > 0 : \sigma(k) = 1. \tag{2.35}$$

***Proof*** By (2.29), we have

$$\forall k > 0: \quad \frac{1}{\sigma(k)} = \frac{\omega'(k)}{\omega(k)/k}. \tag{2.36}$$

Then, Lemma 2.2 and (2.36) establish Lemma 2.3. □

Thus, despite the *local* nature of the measures (2.24) and (2.29), the convexity/concavity of the $\omega(k)$ function allot important *global* properties to $\sigma(k)$.

It is apparent that a *small* value of $\sigma$ will be associated with an isoquant which is *sharply* curved, while a *large* value of $\sigma$ will be associated with an isoquant which has *little* curvature. The case (2.33) characterizes the situation with horizontal isoquants as $k$ approaches zero and vertical isoquants as $k$ approaches infinity. The case (2.34) with $\omega(0) > 0$ reflects the possibility that the isoquants cut the axis [$L$ or $K$ is not essential, cf. (2.2.1)] and that $\omega(k)$ is also bounded above. The case (2.35) evidently represents the great schism to which we occasionally shall duly return.

Notwithstanding Remark 2.3, the implications (2.33–2.34) can be reversed, if the substitutions elasticity $\sigma$ is constant.

**Lemma 2.4** *Strictly convex isoquants (2.26) and constant elasticity of substitution (CES) $\sigma$ substantiate [with $\omega(0) = 0$ in case of (2.37)]*

$$\forall k > 0: \ \sigma(k) = \sigma < 1 \quad \Leftrightarrow \quad \omega(k) \text{ strictly convex}, \tag{2.37}$$

$$\forall k > 0: \ \sigma(k) = \sigma > 1 \quad \Leftrightarrow \quad \omega(k) \text{ strictly concave}. \tag{2.38}$$

***Proof*** From (2.36) and constant $\sigma$, we have

$$\forall k > 0: \quad \omega'(k) = (1/\sigma)\omega(k)/k, \tag{2.39}$$

and next

$$\forall k > 0: \quad \omega''(k) = \frac{1}{\sigma}\frac{\omega'(k)}{k}\left(1 - \frac{\omega(k)/k}{\omega'(k)}\right) = (1/\sigma)[\omega'(k)/k](1-\sigma). \tag{2.40}$$

With $\omega'(k) > 0$, (2.25), and constant $\sigma \lesseqgtr 1$, the positive/negative sign of $\omega''(k)$ is preserved in $\mathbf{R}_+$, and so the lemma follows with the admonition $\omega(0) = 0$ in (2.37). □

## Factor Shares and Production Elasticities

Apart from some special production functions, where substitution elasticity is constant for all $k$, the general function $\sigma(k)$, (2.29), ranging in value between $0 < \sigma(k) < \infty$, will often be an unwieldy expression in $k$. However, the principal task of $\sigma(k)$ has mostly been, in case of $m \leq 1$, to provide a *distributional criterion* of change in relative *factor shares* under *competitive* factor market conditions (marginal productivity pricing of factors). Then the output elasticities, $\epsilon_L$ and $\epsilon_K$, (2.16.1–2.16.3), also represent the *factor shares* of labor and capital. In production theory, as in demand analysis by Wold and Jureen (1953, p. 98,111), elasticities (logarithmic derivatives) are often convenient variational measures.

The sensitivity of factor shares to changing factor proportions can be measured by the *distribution elasticities:*

$$E(\epsilon_L, k) \equiv \frac{d\epsilon_L}{dk} \cdot \frac{k}{\epsilon_L}; \quad E(\epsilon_K, k) \equiv \frac{d\epsilon_K}{dk} \cdot \frac{k}{\epsilon_K}, \tag{2.41.1}$$

$$\epsilon_L E(\epsilon_L, k) + \epsilon_K E(\epsilon_K, k) = 0; \quad E(\epsilon_K, k) = -\frac{\epsilon_L}{\epsilon_K} E(\epsilon_L, k), \tag{2.41.2}$$

where (2.41.2) follows immediately from (2.16.3); clearly, the distribution elasticities have opposite signs. As is well-known, the *sign* of the elasticities (2.41.1) depends on a critical value of $\sigma(k)$, viz., $\sigma(k) \gtreqless 1$.

The general relationship between the *distribution* elasticities (2.41.1) and the *substitution* elasticity (2.29) is given by the formulas

$$E(\epsilon_L, k) = \frac{\epsilon_K(1-\sigma)}{m\sigma}, \quad E(\epsilon_K, k) = \frac{\epsilon_L(\sigma - 1)}{m\sigma}. \tag{2.42}$$

The verification of (2.42) is obtained by using, cf. (2.24), (2.29),

$$\begin{aligned} \omega'(k) &= \frac{\epsilon_L}{\epsilon_K} + \frac{k}{\epsilon_K^2}\left[\epsilon_K \frac{d\epsilon_L}{dk} - \epsilon_L \frac{d\epsilon_K}{dk}\right] \\ &= \frac{\epsilon_L}{\epsilon_K}[1 + E(\epsilon_L, k) - E(\epsilon_K, k)] = \frac{\epsilon_L}{\epsilon_K} \cdot \frac{1}{\sigma}, \end{aligned} \tag{2.43}$$

together with (2.41.2), (2.16.3). Note the simple economic evaluation of (2.27) by the last expression in (2.43).

For later purposes, we state here the general expressions for the elasticity of the marginal/average products with respect to $K$ and $L$,

$$E(MP_L, K) = \epsilon_K(1 - 1/m + 1/m\sigma), \tag{2.44.1}$$

$$E(MP_K, K) = \epsilon_K(1 - 1/m) - \epsilon_L/m\sigma, \tag{2.44.2}$$

$$E(AP_L, K) = \epsilon_K, \quad E(AP_K, K) = \epsilon_K - 1, \tag{2.44.3}$$

$$E(MP_L, L) = \epsilon_L(1 - 1/m) - \epsilon_K/m\sigma, \tag{2.44.4}$$

$$E(MP_K, L) = \epsilon_L(1 - 1/m + 1/m\sigma), \tag{2.44.5}$$

$$E(AP_L, L) = \epsilon_L - 1, \quad E(AP_K, L) = \epsilon_L. \tag{2.44.6}$$

The verifications of (2.44.1–6) are straightforward, cf. (2.14.1–2.14.2), (2.16.1–2.16.3), (2.27), (2.42–2.43). Evidently (2.44.1–6) are easy to evaluate and with $m = 1$, (2.44.1–3) become the elasticities with respect to $k$.

## Iso-Marginal, Iso-Average Productivity Curves

Contour lines for marginal/average productivities, that is, curves along which the marginal/average productivity of a factor (labor or capital) is constant, are seldom discussed in production theory. But they will be useful in some of our growth models below, and we shall therefore here examine their properties for homogeneous production functions.

The definitions and notations for the *level curves* of marginal products will be

$$IMP_L = \{L, K \geq 0 \mid MP_L(L, K) = \bar{MP}_L\}, \quad \bar{MP}_L \in \mathbf{R}_+, \tag{2.45.1}$$

$$IMP_K = \{L, K \geq 0 \mid MP_K(L, K) = \bar{MP}_K\}, \quad \bar{MP}_K \in \mathbf{R}_+, \tag{2.45.2}$$

and analogously to (2.45.1–2.45.2) for the iso-average product curves, $IAP_L$ and $IAP_K$.

The $IMP$ curves (2.45.1–2.45.2) were studied in Puu (1971, p. 244-251) in connection with factor demand analysis; see also Johansen (1972, p. 77–79). Of course, with $m = 1$, the *loci* (2.45.1–2.45.2) of $IMP_L$ and $IMP_K$ are *rays* through the origin, cf. (2.14.1–2.14.2).

To examine the general *shape* of the $IMP$ curves with $0 < m < 1$, we first look at their tangent slopes, $\beta_L$ and $\beta_K$, given by expressions, cf. (2.45.1–2.45.2)

$$\beta_L = -\frac{\partial MP_L/\partial L}{\partial MP_L/\partial K} = -\frac{\partial^2 F/\partial L^2}{\partial^2 F/\partial L \partial K}, \tag{2.46.1}$$

$$\beta_K = -\frac{\partial MP_K/\partial L}{\partial MP_K/\partial K} = -\frac{\partial^2 F/\partial K \partial L}{\partial^2 F/\partial K^2}, \tag{2.46.2}$$

and hence

$$\frac{\beta_L}{\beta_K} = \frac{\partial^2 F/\partial L^2 \cdot \partial^2 F/\partial K^2}{(\partial^2 F/\partial L \partial K)^2}. \tag{2.46.3}$$

Given technical *complementarity,* (2.18), cf. Remark 2.1, it is seen from (2.17–2.22) and (2.46.1–2.46.3) that

$$0 < m < 1: \quad \beta_L > 0,\ \beta_K > 0, \quad \beta_L/\beta_K > 1, \tag{2.47}$$

that is, both $IMP$ curves are everywhere *increasing,* and at a *given* point $(L, K)$, $IMP_L$ is *steeper* than $IMP_K$ as stated in Puu (1971, p. 245).

It follows from (2.46.1–2.46.3) and (2.17–2.19) that $\beta_L$ and $\beta_K$ only depend on $k$; hence, the respective map of $IMP_L$ and $IMP_K$ curves are—like the isoquant map—"radial blow ups" of one curve (geometrical similarity). For homogeneous production functions, we further have

**Lemma 2.5** *The system of $IMP_L$ ($IMP_K$) curves, (2.45.1–2.45.2), consists—with $0 < m < 1$ and (2.18)—of increasing, strictly convex (concave) curves. An $IMP_L$ ($IMP_K$) curve is located higher (lower) for larger level values.*

***Proof*** Positive inclination was established in (2.47). The strict convexity of $IMP_L$ curves may seen by inspecting (2.14.1). Along a given ray (a constant $k$), the value of $MP_L$ falls, due to $m < 1$. Then to maintain the value of $MP_L$ a higher $k$ is required, that is, the arc of $IMP_L$ must lie above the ray mentioned. Furthermore, an $IMP_L$ cannot subsequently return to any ray, if the fixed $MP_L$ value is to be preserved in the face of $m < 1$. Hence, the slope $\beta_L$ of any $IMP_L$ curve must be continually increasing, that is, $IMP_L$ is strictly convex.

Strict concavity of an $IMP_K$ curve follows from the corresponding necessity of a declining $k$ to preserve a level value of $MP_K$. The location aspect of $IMP_L$ ($IMP_K$) curves simply follows from factor complementarity. □

The system of $IAP_L$ ($IAP_K$) curves, cf. (2.9–2.10), has analogous properties to those stated for $IMP_L$ ($IMP_K$) curves in Lemma 2.5.

## Special Production Functions

Although the *general* assumptions (2.1–2.7) and their extensions—expounded in sections "Homogeneity and the Laws of Variable Proportions–Iso-Marginal, Iso-Average Productivity Curves"—will be used in the dynamic models below, we sometimes want to illustrate the dynamic solutions by using two *specific* production functions, viz., the well-known Cobb-Douglas (CD) and CES production functions. They are given, Arrow et al. (1961), Cobb and Douglas (1928), respectively, as

$$\begin{aligned} F(L, K) &= \gamma[L^{(1-a)}K^a]^m = L^m \gamma k^{am} = L^m f(k), \\ &\quad \gamma > 0,\ 0 < a < 1,\ 0 < m \leq 1, \qquad (2.48) \\ F(L, K) &= \gamma[(1-a)L^{-b} + aK^{-b}]^{\frac{-m}{b}} \end{aligned}$$

$$= \quad L^m \gamma[(1-a) + ak^{-b}]^{\frac{-m}{b}} = L^m f(k),$$
$$\gamma > 0,\ 0 < a < 1,\ -1 \leq b < \infty, \quad 0 < m \leq 1. \tag{2.49}$$

The functions (2.48–2.49) can satisfy all the conditions (2.1–2.7).

The substitution elasticity of (2.48) and (2.49) is commonplace; clearly, their $\omega(k)$ satisfies, respectively, (2.35) and (2.37–2.38). Although (2.48–2.49) are sometimes regarded as rather restrictive production laws, $CD$ and $CES$ (that includes $CD$ as the limit function for $b \to 0$) are in fact the *only* homogeneous production functions $F(L, K)$ with a *constant* elasticity of substitution.

Thus, requiring the latter and homogeneity, one cannot at the same time complain about or argue against the actual specifications of $F(L, K)$ in (2.48–2.49). Indeed, (2.48–2.49) represent the *complete* set of solutions to the ordinary differential equations, (2.36), $\sigma(k) = \sigma$, and (2.24)—as is easily verified by the reader. Incidentally, as to explicit (closed form) nonhomogeneous production functions with constant $\sigma$, see Dickinson (1954–55) and Whitaker (1964).

Finally, to illustrate the character of the $IMP$ curves (2.45.1–2.45.2), we show these explicitly for the two production functions (2.48–2.49). In the CD-case, we immediately obtain from (2.48) and (2.14.1–2.14.2),

$$IMP_L \quad : \quad K = \left[\frac{\bar{MP}_L}{\gamma m(1-a)}\right]^{\frac{1}{am}} L^{\frac{1-m(1-a)}{am}}, \qquad \bar{MP}_L \in \mathbf{R}_+, \tag{2.50}$$

$$IMP_K \quad : \quad K = \left[\frac{\gamma ma}{\bar{MP}_K}\right]^{\frac{1}{1-am}} L^{\frac{m(1-a)}{1-am}} \quad , \qquad \bar{MP}_K \in \mathbf{R}_+. \tag{2.51}$$

Measured on logarithmic scales, the equations (2.50–2.51) are each represented by a system of parallel straight lines—with $IMP_L$ having the larger slope, cf. (2.47). This logarithmic version of (2.50–2.51) was employed in Niehans (1963, p. 352).

In the CES case, we get from (2.49), (2.14.1–2.14.2) and some manipulations,

$$IMP_L \quad : \quad K = L\left[1 - 1/a + 1/a\left(\frac{\bar{MP}_L}{\gamma m(1-a)}\right)^{\frac{-b}{b+m}} L^{\frac{-b(1-m)}{b+m}}\right]^{-\frac{1}{b}}, \tag{2.52}$$

$$IMP_K \quad : \quad L = K\left[\frac{-a}{1-a} + \frac{1}{1-a}\left(\frac{\gamma ma}{\bar{MP}_K}\right)^{\frac{b}{b+m}} K^{\frac{-b(1-m)}{b+m}}\right]^{-\frac{1}{b}}. \tag{2.53}$$

Although they exist, the inverse functions in (2.52–2.53) have no explicit (closed) forms. Evidently, the loci (2.50–2.51) and (2.52–2.53) have shape and location according to Lemma 2.5.

## Population, Division of Labor, and National Income

Population, Labor Supplies and Allocations, Wages, and National Income are subjects of classic studies in Political Economy/Economics. For our empirical and analytical economic model purposes with historical contexts, we should with public references briefly provide some *Demographic* benchmark data and related country *National Income Accounting* Statements.

The Danish *Population*, year 2010, is: $N\,(2010) = 5.551$ million. Population *age shares*, $\mathbf{n_i} = \mathbf{N_i/N}$, of *three age* groups are important: children (0–14), working age (15–69), and old age (70+). The *Labor* Force *Participation rate*, **LFP**, is defined by, $L_{15-69}/N_{15-69} = l_{15-69}$:

$$\mathbf{LFP} \equiv \frac{L_{15-69}}{N_{15-69}} \equiv l_{15-69} \tag{2.54}$$

The *Support ratio* $(L/N)$, defined as the ratio of Total **Labor** force (Labor *supply*) (**L**) (*Employment*) to Total **Population** $(N = N_{0-70+})$ and Labor Force Participation (**LFP**) rate, $l_{15-69}$, (2.54), is related to *Age* share, $n_{15-69}$, as follows:

$$\frac{L}{N} \equiv \frac{L_{15-69}}{N} = \frac{L_{15-69}}{N_{15-69}} \cdot \frac{N_{15-69}}{N} = l_{15-69} \cdot n_{15-69} \tag{2.55}$$

Hence with, **LFP** for 2010: $l_{15-69} = \mathbf{0.536}$, we get by (2.55) with *Age* share (2010), $n_{15-69} = 0.709$, the *Support* ratio in 2010: $\mathbf{L/N} = 0.536 \cdot 0.709 = \mathbf{0.38}$.

We should next explain the **Labor** *supplies* used and their associated *wages* in 2010. The *Labor age group* numbers (Labor years) $\mathbb{L}_i$ (column 3, Table 2.1) are Danish **full-time** workers (*equivalents*, **1924 hours**)—with *age distribution* ($\boldsymbol{\lambda}_i$), (col. 4), and their *average annual wages* ($\mathbf{w_i}$), (column 6). These Microlevel data (personal register) were provided by Statistics Denmark. These *Register data*, however, were excluding agriculture, fishery, and all firms with less than ten full-time employees.

The *National Accounting* data for Denmark in **2010** implies that the *sum* of $\mathbf{L_i}$ (col. 5) is equal to *aggregate employment* (Table 2.2, row 1) of **2,112,472** full-time workers (*Labor years*). We use the *age-specific* labor *fractions* ($\boldsymbol{\lambda}_i$) of *Register* data (column 4) to gross up the values of $\mathbb{L}_i$ such that the *total* of $\mathbf{L_i}$ (col. 5) is equal to: $\mathbf{L} = \mathbf{2{,}112{,}472}$. The *age-specific* wages $\mathbf{w_i}$ in Table 2.1 (col. 6) of Register data are multiplied by the adjusted (Total) Labor numbers, $\mathbf{L_i}$, (col.5), and summed to give the *aggregate Wage Bill*, which is **924.3** Billion

**Table 2.1** Age-specific data: labor groups, wages, wage shares, participation rates—Denmark 2010

| 1 | 2 | 3 | 4 | 5 | 6 | 7 | 8 | 9 | 10 |
|---|---|---|---|---|---|---|---|---|---|
| Age ($i$) | $N_i$ | $\mathbb{L}_i$ | $\boldsymbol{\lambda}_i$ | $L_i$ | $w_i$ | $w_i/w_4$ | $w_iL_i$ | $\varepsilon_i$ | $l_i = L_i/N_i$ |
| 15–19 | 353109 | 21138 | 0.0143 | 30199 | 187005 | 0.4554 | 5.647 | 0.0061 | 0.0855 |
| 20–24 | 331419 | 77504 | 0.0524 | 110731 | 273220 | 0.6653 | 30.254 | 0.0327 | 0.3341 |
| 25–29 | 310515 | 117177 | 0.0792 | 167411 | 358262 | 0.8724 | 59.977 | 0.0649 | 0.5391 |
| 30–34 | 347261 | 170826 | 0.1155 | 244059 | 410668 | 1.0000 | 100.227 | 0.1084 | 0.7028 |
| 35–39 | 388101 | 202853 | 0.1372 | 289816 | 449679 | 1.0950 | 130.324 | 0.1410 | 0.7468 |
| 40–44 | 408902 | 214618 | 0.1451 | 306624 | 471118 | 1.1472 | 144.456 | 0.1563 | 0.7499 |
| 45–49 | 405079 | 211983 | 0.1434 | 302860 | 472491 | 1.1505 | 143.099 | 0.1548 | 0.7477 |
| 50–54 | 366102 | 188472 | 0.1275 | 269270 | 471381 | 1.1478 | 126.929 | 0.1373 | 0.7355 |
| 55–59 | 350020 | 169527 | 0.1147 | 242203 | 461729 | 1.1243 | 111.832 | 0.1210 | 0.6920 |
| 60–64 | 368451 | 88874 | 0.0601 | 126974 | 478708 | 1.1657 | 60.783 | 0.0658 | 0.3446 |
| 65–69 | 309369 | 15626 | 0.0106 | 22325 | 483248 | 1.1767 | 10.789 | 0.0117 | 0.0722 |
| Total 15-69 | 3938328 | 1478598 | 1.0000 | 2112472 | 437552 | | 924.317 | 1.0000 | 0.5364 |
| 0–14 | 997084 | | | 0 | 0 | | | | 0 |
| 70+ | 615547 | | | 0 | 0 | | | | 0 |
| Total | 5550959 | | | 2112472 | 166515 | | 924.317 | | 0.3806 |

*Source*: United Nations (2015) "World Population Prospects, 2015 Revision", United Nations, New York, 2015. Total population (both sexes combined) by five-year age group
*Source*: STATISTICS DENMARK (Department of Labor and Income), Copenhagen
Column 1: **Age groups**, $i = 1, \ldots, 11; i = 1 : 15 - -19, \ldots, i = 11 : 65 - -69; i = 12 : 0 - -14, i = 13 : 70+$
Column 2: Population (totals) in age groups; UN Population Data
Column 3: ***Full-time*** workers (Annual equivalents, **1924 hours**), Labor services in **Labor years** ; *Microlevel* (personal register) ***data***
Column 4: Labor age group distribution—Fractions, $\lambda_i$, **same** in column 3 and column 5
Column 5: **Total** full-time workers in labor **age** groups, $\mathbf{L_i} = \lambda_i \mathbf{L}$, ($\mathbf{L} = \mathbf{2112472}$ = Total full-time workers) ; stat.bank, **DB07, ERHV1**
Column 6: Average annual **wages** of labor age groups (wi) in column 3 and 5; $w = \mathbf{437552} DKK = \mathbf{924.317}$ Billion DKK / **2,112,472**
Column 6: Annual wage income *per capita*, $wL/N = 924.317$ Billion / 5550959 = 166515 DKK (Danish Kingdom Kroner)
Column 7: Relative annual wages, **age** group **wage profile**—generated by the *Microlevel* (personal register) ***data*** in column 6
Column 8: Total wage incomes of **age** group, ($i$), Billion DKK; (stat.bank, **DB07**, ERHV1, **Total** wage sum : **930.286** Billion DKK)
Column 9: Age group wage income shares, $\epsilon_i$ (shares in the total wage bill, 924.317 Billion DKK)
Column 10: Labor participation rates (**LPR**) of age groups—derived from column 2 and column 5

**Table 2.2** National income accounts—data for Denmark, 2010

| | Descriptions | Symbols | Values | |
|---|---|---|---|---|
| 1 | Total (equivalent) full time workers | $L$ | 2112472 | Labor years |
| 2 | Average (aggregate) wage per labor year (man-year) | $w$ | 437552 | DKK |
| 3 | Total wage incomes | $wL$ | 924.3 | Billion DKK |
| 4 | Net capital (rental) incomes | $rK$ | 303.8 | Billion DKK |
| 5 | Net factor incomes (NFI)—net domestic value added | $Y = wL + rK$ | 1228.1 | Billion DKK |
| 6 | Capital consumption/depreciation | $\delta K$ | 318.1 | Billion DKK |
| 7 | Gross factor incomes (GFI)—gross domestic value added | $GFI$ | 1546.2 | Billion DKK |
| 8 | Net capital stock | $K$ | 5741.5 | Billion DKK |
| 9 | Net capital-output ratio | $v = K/Y$ | 4.67 | |
| 10 | Net capital-labour ratio | $k = K/L$ | 2.72 | Million DKK |
| 11 | Average labour productivity | $y = Y/L$ | 581972 | DKK |
| 12 | Depreciation rate | $\delta = \delta K/K$ | 0.055 | Percent |
| 13 | Net real interest rate | $r = rK/K$ | 0.053 | Percent |
| 14 | Gross real interest rate | $r + \delta$ | 0.108 | Percent |
| 15 | Wage share of net factor income, $w/(Y/L)$ | $\varepsilon_L = wL/Y$ | 0.752 | |
| 16 | Capital share of net factor income, $r/(Y/K)$ | $\varepsilon_K = rK/Y$ | 0.248 | |
| 17 | Factor compensation, asset income (net), to rest of world | $O$ | 29.6 | Billion DKK |
| 18 | Net national income, in factor prices | $Y + O = NNI$ | 1257.7 | Billion DKK |
| 19 | Gross national income , in factor prices | $C + Tr + S = GNI$ | 1575.8 | Billion DKK |
| 20 | Consumption ( private + public) , in factor prices | $C$ | 1104.9 | Billion DKK |
| 21 | Transfers to rest of world, net | $Tr$ | 36.6 | Billion DKK |
| 22 | Gross national saving | $S$ | 434.3 | Billion DKK |
| 23 | Gross domestic investment, in factor prices | $I$ | 331.3 | Billion DKK |
| 24 | Balance of payment, current account, Asset accumulation | $S - I = BP$ | 103.0 | Billion DKK |

(continued)

**Table 2.2** (continued)

| | Descriptions | Symbols | Values | |
|---|---|---|---|---|
| 25 | Consumption ratio, NNI | $C/NNI$ | 0.879 | |
| 26 | Consumption ratio, NFI | $C/Y$ | 0.900 | |
| 27 | Consumption per capita, in factor prices | $C/N$ | 199350 | DKK |
| 28 | Net National Income per capita, in factor prices | $NNI/N$ | 226573 | DKK |
| 29 | Annual wage income per capita, in factor prices | $wL/N$ | 166515 | DKK |
| 30 | Support Ratio | $L/N$ | 0.3806 | |
| 31 | Net factor income (NFI) per capita, Y/N = (Y/L)(L/N) | $Y/N$ | 221499 | DKK |
| 32 | Annual wage income-consumption ratio | $wL/C$ | 0.837 | |
| 33 | Gross national saving rate | $S/GNI$ | 0.276 | |
| 34 | Net national saving rate | $(S - \delta K)/NNI$ | 0.092 | |
| 35 | Gross domestic investment rate | $I/GFI$ | 0.214 | |

*Source*: **Rows** 1–3, *Microlevel* (register) data from *Table* **2.1**. **Rows** 5–9, 12, 17–26, *Macro* (aggregate) data from **NIA** (National Income Accounting): *Statistical Ten-Year Review*, (**STR**) *2015*, p. 101–102, 104–105, 120 ; STATISTICS DENMARK, Copenhagen

Row 1: Full-time **Labor years**, $L = 2.112.472 = 4064.4$ Million labor hours (1 **Labor year** = 37 hours per week × 52 = **1924 labor hours**) ; STR (2015, p. 121) gives in **NIA**: 3606.6 Million labor hours for 2010

Row 3: STR (2015, p. 104) gives in **NIA**: Wage Sum = **953.7** Billion DKK—a bit more ($\frac{1}{2}\%$) more than, **wL** = **924.3** Bill. DKK

Row 4: **rK** =Row 5 (**Y**)—Row 3 (**wL**) ; STR (2015, p. 104) gives in **NIA**: Net Capital Income = 274.4—a bit less than, **rK** = **303.8**

Rows 5–7: **STR** (2015, p. 104), with same **Y** = **1228.1**, as in Row 5. Row 8: STR (2015, p. 128). Row 17: STR (2015, p. 102). Row 18: Row 5 + Row 17

Row 19: STR (2015, p. 104 ) gives: *GNI* in market prices = *GNI* in factor prices + indirect taxes = 1578.8 + 252.5 = 1828.3 Billion DKK

Row 20: STR (2015, p. 104) gives: *C* in market prices = *C* in factor prices + indirect taxes = 1104.9 + 252.5 = 1357.4 Billion DKK. STR (2015, p. 102) gives: Indirect commodity (production) taxes/subsidies, net: 248.2 + 4.3 = 252.5 Billion DKK

Row 21: STR (2015, p. 102) ; Row 22: STR (2015, p. 104); Row 23: STR (2015, p. 103); Row 24: STR (2015, p. 106). Rows 25–26: Derived from rows above;

Row 27: $C/N = (C/Y)(L/N)(Y/L) = (0.9)(0.3806)581{,}972 =$ **199,350** DKK, cf. Table 2.1

**Table 2.3** Population age groups, labor supply, support ratios, incomes per capita: Denmark

| | | | |
|---|---|---|---|
| 2010 | 1. | $N_{15\text{-}69}$ | 3938328 |
| | 2. | $N_{0\text{-}14}$ | 997084 |
| | 3. | $N_{70+}$ | 615547 |
| | 4. | $N = Total$ | 5550959 |
| | 5. | $L = L_{15\text{-}69}$ | 2112472 |
| | 6. | $L/N_{15\text{-}69}$ | 0.5364 |
| | 7. | $L/N$ | 0.3806 |
| | 8. | *WL Bill* | 924.317 |
| | 9. | *WL/N* | 166615 |
| | 10. | $Y/N$ | 221499 |

Danish Kingdom Kroner (DKK) (col. 8). The *aggregate Annual wage*, **w**, per unit of **L** is then found by dividing the aggregate Wage Bill (col. 8) by **L**, which gives: **w (2010) = 437552** DKK $\equiv$ $\mathbf{W_A}$.
*Labor Force Participation* (**LFP**) rate, (2.54), and *Support ratio*, (2.55)—cf. Table 2.1, col.10,1—are:

$$LFP = \frac{L_{15-69}}{N_{15-69}} = l_{15-69} = 0.536 \;;\; \frac{L}{N} = \sum_{i=1}^{11} l_i \cdot n_i = l_{15-69} \cdot n_{15-69} \quad (2.56)$$

$$\frac{\mathbf{L}}{\mathbf{N}} = l_{15-69} \cdot n_{15-69} = 0.536 \cdot 0.709 = 0.38 \;;\quad \frac{\mathbf{Y}}{\mathbf{N}} = \frac{Y}{L} \cdot \frac{L}{N} \;;\; \frac{\mathbf{C}}{\mathbf{N}} = \frac{C}{Y} \cdot \frac{Y}{N} \quad (2.57)$$

*Per capita sizes* of National Income, Consumption ratios, **Y/N**, **C/N**, and *decomposition* in (2.57) are seen in National Income Product Accounting (NIPA), Table 2.2 (row 31,27)—summarized in Table 2.3.

Thus, **Micro**-based *employment*—full-time equivalents—and *wage* data in Table 2.1 (col. 5,6,8) correspond exactly to **Macro** (National Income) data in Table 2.2 (Row 1–3, 29–31), for calendar *year*, 2010. Short version of Table 2.2 is seen in Table 2.3.

### *Production and Division of Labor—National Income*

Above was demonstrated and illustrated the *ratios* (2.56–2.57) in the macro relation:

$$\frac{\mathbf{Y}}{\mathbf{N}} = \frac{Y}{L} \cdot \frac{L}{N} \;;\; \frac{\mathbf{L}}{\mathbf{N}} = l_{15-69} \cdot n_{15-69} \;;$$

$$\frac{\mathbf{W}}{\mathbf{N}} = \frac{W}{L} \cdot \frac{L}{N} = W_A \cdot \frac{L}{N} \;;\; \mathbf{W} \equiv W_A\, L \equiv \sum_{i=1}^{11} w_i L_i \quad (2.58)$$

As to *proportions* in per capita national income *identity*, (2.58), Smith (1790, 1961, p. 1) opens with the statement: "The Annual labour of every nation is the fund, which supplies it with all the necessaries and conveniences of life. - According therefore, this *produce* [ product, *output*, **Y**] bears a greater or smaller *proportion* [ $\frac{Y}{N}$ ] to number of those [ **N** ], who are to *consume* it. But this *proportion* [ $\frac{Y}{N}$ ] must in every nation be regulated by **two** different circumstances: 1. the *skill, dexterity, and judgement* with which its labour is generally applied [ *Labor productivity,* $\frac{Y}{L}$ ] 2. the *proportion* [ $\frac{L}{N}$ ] between the number of those who are employed in *useful labor* [ **L** ] and those not so employed [ **N** - **L** ]. The *abundance* or scantiness of this **supply** [ per-capita *produce,* $\frac{Y}{N}$ ] seems to depend *more* upon the *former* [ $\frac{Y}{L}$ ] of those two circumstances than upon the *latter* " [ $\frac{L}{N}$ ] (italics ours).

The **Employment / Population** [ *Support* ratio, **L/N** ], (bounded above by one) is always much *lesser* than *one*, as the *numerical size* of [ **L/N** ], (2.58), is by definition the *product* of $\mathbf{LFP} = \mathbf{l}_{15-69}$ (interval: 0.5–0.6), and Working population *share*, $\mathbf{n}_{15-69}$ (interval: 0.7–0.6), that is, $\mathbf{L/N} = l_{15-69} \cdot n_{15-69} =$ **0.38**, cf. (2.56–2.57), and Table 2.1.

As to ( **Y/L** ), Smith (1790, 1961, p. 7) says: "The greatest improvements in the **productive powers** of *labour*, and the greater part of the *skill, dexterity, and judgement* with which is anywhere directed, or applied, seems to have been the *effects* of the **division of labour**. p. 11: This great increase of the **quantity** [ Output ,**Y** ] of **work** [ Labor productivity, **Y/L** ] which, in consequence of the *division of labour*, the **same** number of people [ **L** ] are capable of performing, is owing to **three** different circumstances 1. The increase of *dexterity* in *every* particular workman 2. The *saving* of the *time* which is commonly lost in passing from one species of work to another 3. The invention of a *great number* of **machines** [ **K**, $\mathbf{K_J}$ ] which facilitate and abridge labour, and enable **one man** to do the work of *many* " (italics ours).

The **Productive** *powers* of **Labor** by the *Division of Labor* (the notion used by Smith above) are *economically* and conceptually expressed by: **Production functions,** $\mathbf{Y} = \mathbf{F(L, K)} = L \cdot f(K/L) \equiv \mathbf{L} \cdot \mathbf{f(k)}$, or $\mathbf{Y} = \mathbf{F}(\mathbf{L}_{I}, \mathbf{L}_{II}, \mathbf{K}_{III}, \mathbf{K}_{IV}, \mathbf{K}_{V})$.

*Production* ( Division of Labor ) by *different qualities* of *workers* according to skills [ education, training ], dexterity, and judgment [ age/maturity/experience ] provides the framework for analyzing **differences** in **factor prices**—the earnings *structures* by Smith (1790, 1961, p. 111):[1] "Pecuniary *wages* and *profits* [ **rentals** of machinery ], indeed, are *everywhere* in Europe extremely *different* according the *different employments* of **labor** and **stock**" (italics ours).

As to Pecuniary **wage** distributions for the complete set of *demographic* **age** groups of the *National Labor* supply—making *Total Wages* ( **W** ), (2.58), in

[1] As to *wage structure* analysis and compensating wage differentials in Smith (1790, 1961, Ch.10), see Katz and Autor (1999, p. 1464) ; Duncan and Holmlund (1983, p. 367).

the *National* income ( **Y** ), Table 2.2—it may be emphasized that we are not dealing with a Labor Economy using only distinct Labor inputs. As stressed by Smith above, *Output* (**Y**) by "Division of Labor" and *Labor productivity*, $\frac{\mathbf{Y}}{\mathbf{L}} = y$, involved "**machinery**" [ **K** ] in *Production* functions, $Y = F(L, K)$, $y = f(k)$, with $w = p\,\frac{\partial Y}{\partial L} = W_A\,(k)$:

$$w = p \cdot \frac{\partial Y}{\partial L}\ ;\ r = p \cdot \frac{\partial Y}{\partial K}\ ;\ w = p \cdot y - r \cdot k \ \equiv W_A;\quad k = 2.72\ :$$

$$W_A\,(2.72) = 582 - 0.053 \cdot 2.72 = 438\ (thousands) \tag{2.59}$$

where the *actual numbers* of Table 2.2 here are used, as seen in (2.59).

Henceforth, as seen (cited) from A. Smith above, Production ( Division of Labor, Technology) with Labor and Capital ("Machinery") will *analytically* be expressed by *Production functions*, $Y = F\,(L, K)$, specified with proper *regularity* properties.

## Literature Comments

The modern concept of a *production function* as the organizing *framework* for a description and a quantitative analysis of production activities was introduced gradually into economic theory. Many of the technological issues that faced economist in the past were mostly illustrated through tables of arithmetic, although the origin of different production functions, especially in distribution theory, goes far back, see Bentzel (1953), Bliss (1975), Cobb and Douglas (1928), Lloyd (1969), Sandelin (1976), Wicksell (1934–35, I,p. 128). The modern use of *isoquants* was introduced around 1910, see Borts and Mishan (1961–62), Johnson (1913), and technical substitution was studied extensively in the works of Carlson (1953), Frisch (1965), Schneider (1934).

Since the classical *laws of returns* in production are statements concerning *technology*, some specified properties (parameter restrictions) imposed on explicit production function expressions might be supposed to allow succinct, mathematical restatements of these older notions of quantitative production laws. However, since both *proportional* (scale properties) and *partial* (substitution properties) factor *variation* are involved in the older laws, elementary functions—given by a single analytical expression on the whole domain—are seldom flexible enough to display both properties adequately. As is well-known, nice *scale* properties (but more blurred substitution properties) are represented by homogeneous/homothetic functions, whereas the nice *substitution* properties (but more blurred scale properties) are given by concave/quasiconcave functions.

In recent years, much effort has been devoted to the description of technology by combining various generalized notions of positivity, additivity, homogeneity, and concavity, see Bentzel and Johansson (1959), Debreu (1983, 1986), Diewert et al. (1981), Färe (1975), Försund (1971, 1975), Intriligator

(1971), Newman (1962), Rockefellar (1970), Samuelson (1983b), Silberberg (1990), Varian (1992).

An axiomatic *set-theoretic* analysis of the *theory* of *production*—which seeks mathematical assumptions that are as simple and as general as possible to characterize the essential properties of the production function—is provided by Shepard (1970). Fundamentally, as mentioned by Shepard (1967, p. 211): "*Differentiability* is of no *economic* or *technological* significance. Even *continuity* is extrinsic". Moreover, in this general framework, necessary and sufficient conditions for the laws of diminishing returns to hold have been established, see Shepard and Färe (1974).

Despite such possible concessions to mathematical generality, we have *ab initio,* cf. (2.1), assumed that the production function $F$ is *twice continuously differentiable* in the input variables. This $C^2$-class property is only a matter of *mathematical* significance, which we, however, have to respect in order to avoid later on any problems with the *existence* and *uniqueness* of the *solutions* to the *dynamic* models that are our main object of study. Regarding differentiability, see Debreu (1959, 1976).

Turgot (1769) was the originator of all but the name of *diminishing returns,* cf. Brems (1986, p. 35,76). If we think of $C^2$-class, strictly concave functions, then the *classical* economists Anne R. J. Turgot, Adam Smith, David Ricardo, Thomas R. Malthus, John Stuart Mill, and J. H. von Thünen may, in retrospect, be said to have assumed that their production functions had: (i) strictly *diminishing* returns with respect to any single factor, (ii) *decreasing* returns to scale, (iii) *diminishing* marginal rate of substitution.

These *three* aspects (i)–(iii) will be referred to as the *classical regularity* properties of the *production* function, **F (L, K)**. We summarize:

$$\textit{classical regularity} \quad = \quad \{\, 0 < m < 1,\ (2.12-2.13), (2.26)\, \}. \qquad (2.60)$$

**Remark 2.4** [2] It is assumed that the economy under consideration has production possibilities restrained by a *fixed* amount of *land, A* (acreage). The latter appear formally in the aggregate production function as a parameter

$$Y = A^{1-m} F(L, K), \quad 0 < m \leq 1. \qquad (2.61)$$

Using the Ricardian terminology in (2.61), we deal only with diminishing returns for the so-called *intensive margin,* arising from applying labor and capital more intensively at a given amount of land—in contrast to the *extensive*

[2] Adam Smith was early studying the progress in natural sciences, mathematics, the new systems of Copernicus, Brahe, Kepler, Cassini, Galilei, Newton, as seen in his essay: History of Astronomy, Smith (1755, 1795, p. 92), Smith (1980). He knew mathematicians, R. Simpson of Glasgow, M. Stewart of Edinburgh. We cannot here go into the discussions of Smith's views on scientific theories and methods, and their potential influence on forming his economic systems, but may refer to Kim (2012), Fiori (2012), Montes (2008).

*margin*, where more and more land under cultivation lead to the use of land of poorer quality for production.

On occasion, we put $m = 1$ and so remove the land restraint on the scale property of the production function. Henceforth, we will not show explicitly the land parameter ($A$) in the production function, as it will be absorbed into a total productivity parameter, ($\gamma$), cf. (2.48–2.49). ▽

## Bibliography


Allen RGD (1938) Mathematical Analysis for Economists. MacMillan, London

Arrow KJ, Chenery HB, Minhas BS, Solow RM (1961) Capital–Labour Substitution and Economic Efficiency. Review of Economics and Statistics 43:225–250

Ashenfelter OC, Card D (eds) (1999) Handbook of Labor Economics, vol 3A–3C. Amsterdam, Elsevier

Bentzel R (1953) Inkomstfördelingen i Sverige. Almqvist and Wiksell, Uppsala

Bentzel R, Johansson O (1959) Om Homogenitet i Produktionsfunktioner. Ekonomisk Tidsskrift 61:146–179

Bliss C (1975) Capital Theory and the Distribution of Income. North–Holland, Amsterdam

Borts GH, Mishan EJ (1961–62) Exploring the 'Uneconomic Region' of the Production Function. Rev Econ Stud 29:300–312

Brems H (1986) Pioneering Economic Theory 1630–1980. A Mathematical Restatement. The Johns Hopkins University Press, Baltimore

Carlson S (1953) A Study on the Pure Theory of Production. In: King PS, Sons (eds) 2, London

Clemhout S (1968) The Class of Homothetic Isoquant Production Functions. The Review of Economic Studies 35(1):91–104

Cobb CW, Douglas PH (1928) A Theory of Production. American Econ Rev, Suppl Papers and Proceedings 18:139–65

Debreu G (1959) Theory of Value – An Axiomatic Analysis Of Economic Equilibrium. John Wiley and Sons, New York, Cowles Foundation Monograph No. 17, Yale University Press, New Haven

Debreu G (1976) Regular Differentiable Economies. Am Econ Rev 66:280–87, or chapter 19 in Debreu (1983)

Debreu G (1983) Mathematical Economics: Twenty papers of Gerard Debreu. Econometric Society Monographs No. 4, Cambridge University Press, Cambridge

Debreu G (1986) Theoretic Models: Mathematical Form and Economic Content. Econometrica 54:1259–1270

Dickinson HD (1954–55) A Note on Dynamic Economics. Rev Econ Stud 22:169–79

Diewert WE, Avriel M, Zang I (1981) Nine Kinds of Quasiconcavity and Concavity. Journal of Economic Theory 25:397–420

Duncan GJ, Holmlund B (1983) Was Adam Smith Right After All? Another Test of the Theory of Compensating Wage Differentials. Journal of Labor Economics 1:366–379

Färe R (1975) A Note On Ray–Homogeneous and Ray–Homothetic Production Functions. Swed Econ 77:366–72

Fiori S (2012) Adam Smith on Method: Newtonianism, History, Institutions, and the 'Invisble Hand'. Journal of History of Economic Thought 34:411–435

Försund F (1971) A Note on Technically Optimal Scale in Inhomogeneous Production Functions. Swed J Econ 73:225–240

Försund F (1975) The Homothetic Production Function. Swed J Econ 77:234–244

Frisch R (1965) Theory of Production. O. Reidel Publishing Company, Dordrecht, Holland

Hicks JR (1932, 1948) The Theory of Wages. MacMillan, London

Hicks JR (1970) Elasticities of Substitution Again: Substitutes and Complements. Oxford Economic Papers 22:289–296

Intriligator MD (1971) Mathematical Optimization and Economic Theory. Prentice-Hall, New Jersey

Johansen L (1972) Production Functions. North–Holland, Amsterdam

Johnson WE (1913) The Pure Theory of Utility Curves. Economic J 23:483–513

Katz LF, Autor DH (1999) Changes in the Wage Structure and Earnings Inequality. pp 1463–1555, in: Ashenfelter, O.C. and Card, D., Ed., (1999), Vol. 3A.

Kim K (2012) Adam Smith's 'History of Astronomy' and View of Science. Cambridge Journal of Economics 36:799–820

Lloyd PJ (1969) Elementary Geometric/Arithmetic Series and Early Production Theory. J Political Economy 77:21–34

Montes L (2008) Newton's real Influence on Adam Smith and its Context. Cambridge Journal of Economics 32:555–576

Newman P (1962) Some Properties of Concave Funtions. J of Econ Theory 1:291–314

Niehans J (1963) Economic Growth with Two Endogenous Factors. Quarterly Journal of Economics 77:349–371

Paroush J (1964) A Note on the CES Production Function. Econometrica 32(1/2):213–214

Puu T (1971) Some Comments on "Inferior" (Regressive) Inputs. Swed J Economics 73:241–251

Rockefellar RT (1970) Convex Analysis. Princeton University Press, New Jersey

Samuelson PA (1968) Two Generalizations of the Elasticity of Substitution. In: Wolfe J (ed) Value, Capital and Growth, Edinburgh University Press, Edinburgh, pp 467–81

Samuelson PA (1978) The Canonical Classical Model of Political Economy. Journal of Economic Literature 16:1415–1434

Samuelson PA (1983a) Foundations of Economic Analysis, enlarged edn. Harvard University Press, Cambridge

Samuelson PA (1983b) Thünen at Two Hundred. Journal of Economic Lite–rature 21:1468–1488

Sandelin B (1976) On the Origin of the Cobb–Douglas Production Function. Economy and History 19:117–23

Schneider E (1934) Theorie der Produktion. Springer–Verlag, Wien

Shepard RW (1967) The Notion of a Production Function. Unternehmensforschung 11:209–232

Shepard RW (1970) Theory of Cost and Production Functions. Princeton University Press, New Jersey

Shepard RW, Färe R (1974) The Law of Diminishing Returns. Zeitschrift für Nationalökonomi 34:69–90

Silberberg E (1990) The Structure of Economics, 2nd edn. McGraw–Hill, New York

Smith A (1755, 1795) The Early Writings of Adam Smith,. In: Ralph Lindgren J (ed) The Adam Smith Library, Reprints of Economic Classics, Augustus M. Kelley Publ, New York

Smith A (1790, 1961) An Inquiry Into The Nature and Causes of The Wealth of Nations, vol 1–2, 5th edn. Methuen, London, (ed. E. Cannan)
Smith A (1980) The History of Astronomy. In W.P.D.Wightman and J. C. Bryce, eds. Essays on Philosophical Subjects, pp.33–105, Clarendon Press, Oxford.
Turgot ARJ (1767) Observations sur le Mémoire de M. de Saint–Péravy. In: Daire E (ed) Oeuvres de Turgot, Paris, pp 418–433, translated as "Observations on a Paper by Saint–Péravy on the Subject of Indirect Taxation," in P. D. Groenewegen, *The Economics of A. R. J. Turgot*, The Hague, 1977, 109–122
Turgot ARJ (1769) Réflexions sur la formation et la distribution des richess. In: Ephémérides du citoyen, Paris, pp 1–71, Nov. 1769–Jan. 1770. reprinted in E. Daire (ed.), *Oeuvres de Turgot*, Paris, 1844, 1–71, translated as "Reflections on the Formation and the Distribution of Riches," New York, 1922.
Varian HR (1992) Microeconomic Analysis, 3rd edn. W.W. Norton & Company, New York
Whitaker JK (1964) A note on the CES Production Function. Rev Econ Stud 31:166–67
Wicksell K (1934–35) Lectures on Political Economy I–II. George Routledge and Sons, London, Classen, E., (trans.), and Robbins, L., (ed.)
Wold H, Jureen L (1953) Demand Analysis. John Wiley & Sons, New York

CHAPTER 3

# Production Functions, Capital, Marginal Productivity Wages, and the Natural Wage: von Thünen

## Introduction

It is well known that concepts of diminishing marginal productivity of production factors are seen, implicitly or explicitly, in Turgot, Smith, Malthus, Ricardo, and that quantitative analyses of marginal productivities for labor and capital first came by Thünen, cf. Schumpeter (1954), Lloyd (1969), Brems (1986), Streissler (1995), Blaug (2002).

von Thünen not only gave Tables of quantitative *marginal productivity* calculations, he was also the *first* to give an *algebraic formula* of a *production function* with labor and capital, Lloyd (1969, p. 31) and Lloyd (2001, p. 3). By his *natural* (normative) *wage* formula, he provided the first occurrence in the literature of models, where important results (theorems) are deduced by *maximizing* an explicit *objective* function, Dorfman (1986, p. 1774). Also von Thünen anticipated correctly the Uzawa *two-sector model* of *capital formation*, Samuelson (1983, p. 1485). All these topics are entailed in the title of this chapter.

With the range of subjects in von Thünen's great work "*The Isolated State*", it is not surprising that it was, then and now, difficult to read and comprehend. These difficulties were compounded, however, by chapter orders, as *major results* and the *basic tables* are presented *early*, his Chaps. 11–12 and *explained* and used with symbols at the *end*, his Chaps. 17–20".

Let us hear Thünen:[1]

[1] von Thünen (1990, Ch. 13, p. 531–532), von Thünen (1875, 2.I, p. 139–140), Dempsey (1960, p. 280). Always, German texts of our von Thünen references (1990, 1875) are identical. Dempsey (1960) are the English translations.



B. S. Jensen, *The Elements and Dynamic Systems of Economic Growth and Trade Models*, https://doi.org/10.1007/978-3-031-52493-6_3

" From proceeding considerations, we have shed some light on the essence of the *interest rate* [ "Zinsfuss" , **z** ] and *wages* [ "Arbeitslohn" , $\mathbf{A} = a + y$ ], realizing that,

1. (**z**) represents a relationship between the effectiveness of capital and the effectiveness of labor currently employed,
2. for wages, $\mathbf{A} = a + y$, a generally valid expression is found to be: $a + y = p/(1 + q\,z)$.

Accordingly, $(p)$, $(y)$, and, $(z)$, are *functions* of $(\mathbf{q})$. The problem therefore is to find for a *given* $(q)$, the values of $(p)$, $(y)$, and $(z)$—and the question arises, whether as many equations can be found, as are necessary for the determination of the unknowns ".

His *'interest rate'*, (**z**), [ *ratio* of marginal marginal productivity of capital, $MP_K(k)$ and labor, $MP_L(k)$] is a *marginal rate* of *substitution*, Marshall (1920, p. 522) said Thünen applied well. Using the (**z**) variable, there is *allocative efficiency* in his two-sector model.

In his generally valid wage expression, $A = a + y = p/(1 + q\,z)$, $A = a + y$, is a *budget constraint* for consumption and saving, and $A = p/(1 + q\,z)$ is a *factor income* identity with *labor, capital,* [ **p**: total product of a labor-year; **q**: capital-labor ratio ]; see (3.45–3.46). Thus income and budget restrictions are satisfied in Tables and in solving his Equations.

In accordance with the main topics above, the *first issue* and main subject in this chapter is to show *how* von Thünen coped with (resolved) problems of obtaining *production functions* in adequate *quantitative* (parametric) forms. As to getting *explicit* production functions with two variable production factors, Labor $(L)$ and real Capital $(K)$, his first problem was: *How* to describe their joint *interaction* in producing a final good $(Y)$ and express precisely the "*productivity effect*" [ "Wirksamkeit" ] of one variable (capital) upon the average productivity of the other variable (labor), i.e., how does a larger $(K)$ affect the size of the labor productivity: $AP_L = Y/L$?

He had examined separate expressions for both the marginal products of labor and capital. Then he tentatively *assumed* that the marginal product of capital $(MP_K)$ is *numerically* the *same* thing as the *rate of increase* in labor productivity $(AP_L)$ with respect to *capital.* Luckily, this *conjecture* holds for any linear homogeneous function (Euler's theorem) of two factors. With this *crucial economic* hypothesis and *mathematical* conjecture, the road was opened up to *concrete versions* of a modern *production function* (in *discrete* form) being *derived* and *tabulated*. Extensions to *smooth* production functions with *isoquants* are fully explained.

The basic questions involved have so far not received their correct answers in the economic literature.

As to the quantitative treatments of production functions (technology), a fundamental issue for any explicit production functions is: How *rapidly* does the *diminishing* marginal productivity of capital actually take place? The modern and general answer is given by the *size* of the *elasticity* of the *marginal productivity* of *capital*, $MP_K(k)$:

$$E(MP_K(k), k) = E(f'(k), k) = f''(k)\,k/f'(k) \qquad (3.1)$$

where "diminishing marginal productivity" is the *concavity* property, $f''(k) < 0$, of the production function: $f(k) = y = Y/L = AP_L$; $Y = F(L, K) = Lf(k)$; $f'(k) = MP_K(k)$.

The *reciprocal* of $E(MP_K(k), k)$ is, $E(k, MP_K)$, which is the *elasticity* of the *factor demand curve* for *capital* by cost minimizing or profit maximizing *producers*. Thus, if $E(MP_K(k), k)$ is numerically large ($>1$), i.e., $MP_K(k)$ falling rapidly, then the factor demand of capital is inelastic, $E(k, MP_K) < 1$; hence the total remuneration (return) to capital, $R(k) = MP_K(k)\,k$, declines with increasing use of capital, and so the factor cost (income) *share* of capital, $\epsilon_K(k) = R(k)/AP_L = MP_K/AP_K$, is falling.

The *factor substitution elasticity*, $\sigma(k)$, ($\lesseqgtr 1$), tells the *same* story about the directions of the *factor shares*, $\epsilon_K(k)$, $\epsilon_L(k)$, as did the *elasticity*, $E(MP_K(k), k)$. Indeed, we have,

$$\sigma(k) = -\epsilon_L(k)/E(MP_K(k), k)\,;\ \ -E(MP_K(k), k)\cdot\sigma(k) = 1-\epsilon_K(k) = \epsilon_L(k) \qquad (3.2)$$

$$E\,(AP_K, MP_K) = \frac{1}{E\,(MP_K, AP_K)} = \sigma(k) = \frac{1}{E\,(MP_L, AP_L)} = E\,(AP_L, MP_L) \qquad (3.3)$$

where (3.2) is an equivalent form of $\sigma(k)$, as defined by Hicks (1932, 1948), whereas (3.3) was used by Arrow et al. (1961) to obtain **CES**, when $\sigma(k)$ is a *constant*.

Generally (3.2–3.3) are shown and used to evaluate the *economic implications* of specific *functional forms* of $\mathbf{f(k)}$. But *how* are the relevant parametric *specifications* of production functions in (3.1–3.3) actually *obtained*? Essentially, there are *two* approaches. Either, you can experiment with plausible specifications of $f'(k)$ and integrate these expressions to get $f(k)$, or, you can try specifying functional forms of $f(k)$, and check the derivatives for economic relevance as marginal productivities. von Thünen began with the first approach, and ended with getting a relevant $f(k)$ form by the second approach. It is a fascinating story to unfold succinctly. We will proceed *axiomatically* in our exposition and sections.

**Table 3.1** Marginal productivity of labor—$MP_L$ ("Mehrertrag")—in harvesting rye

| Laborers L | | $MP_L$ | | Harvest Y | | $AP_L$ | | $\epsilon_L(L)$ |
|---|---|---|---|---|---|---|---|---|
| The 19th laborer | produces | 123 | bushels | 7114.15 | bushels | 374.4 | bushels | 0.321 |
| The 20th laborer | – | 111 | – | 7225.26 | – | 361.3 | – | 0.307 |
| The 21th laborer | – | 100 | – | 7325.26 | – | 348.8 | – | 0.287 |
| The 22th laborer | – | 90 | – | 7415.26 | – | 337.1 | – | 0.267 |
| The 23rd laborer | – | 81 | – | 7496.26 | – | 325.9 | – | 0.249 |
| The 24th laborer | – | 73 | – | 7569.16 | – | 315.4 | – | 0.230 |

*Source*: Thünen, (1990, p. 416; 1875, 2.I, p. 19), Dempsey (1960, p. 203); Hall (1966, p. 235)
Y, $AP_L$, and $\epsilon_L(L)$ were *not* shown; the rows for, $L = 19, 20$, were at the bottom

**Table 3.2** Marginal productivity of labor, $MP_L$, in harvesting (picking up) potatoes

| Number of persons employed collecting the potatoes | | Increment ("Mehrertrag") by last employed person | Labor productivity ("Arbeitsprodukt") | Relative share $\epsilon_L = MP_L/AP_L$ |
|---|---|---|---|---|
| Persons L | Harvest Y | $MP_L$ | $AP_L = Y/L$ | $\epsilon_L(L)$ |
| 4 | 80.0 bushels | – | 20.0 bushels | – |
| 5 | 86.6 bushels | 6.6 bushels | 17.3 bushels | 0.38 |
| 6 | 91.0 bushels | 4.4 bushels | 15.2 bushels | 0.29 |
| 7 | 94.0 bushels | 3.0 bushels | 13.4 bushels | 0.22 |
| 8 | 96.0 bushels | 2.0 bushels | 12.0 bushels | 0.17 |
| 9 | 97.3 bushels | 1.3 bushels | 10.8 bushels | 0.12 |
| 10 | 98.2 bushels | 0.9 bushels | 9.8 bushels | 0.09 |
| 11 | 98.8 bushels | 0.6 bushels | 9.0 bushels | 0.07 |
| 12 | 99.2 bushels | 0.4 bushels | 8.3 bushels | 0.05 |

*Source*: von Thünen (1990, Ch. 19, p. 570), von Thünen (1875, Ch. 19, 2.I, p. 179), Dempsey (1960, p. 307); Hall (1966, p. 255)
$AP_L$, $\epsilon_L(L)$ were not shown. The "harvest data" ($Y$) in Table 3.2—which are not empirical observations (data)—display minor discrepancies, but most of the "geometric series" of $MP_L(L)$ and $Y(L)$ are exact

The organization of the chapter is as follows: section "Marginal Productivities of Labor and Capital" explains the Tables 3.1 and 3.2 of one-factor (labor) marginal productivity schedules. It presents the principle of factor (capital-labor) substitution and gives his pivotal discrete formula for the marginal productivity of capital. In section "Product, Labor, Capital: $\mathbf{Y} = \mathbf{F}(\mathbf{L}, \mathbf{K}) = \mathbf{L}\mathbf{f}(\mathbf{k})$", we establish the discrete and smooth parametric production function of labor and capital, **F(L, K)**, involved in the Tables 3.3 and 3.4. Many economic implications of this production function are exhibited in von Thünen's *"Tableau Economique"* (Tables 3.3–3.4, 3.5).

Section "von Thünen's Smooth Production Function, **f(k)**" gives von Thünen's own *smooth parametric* production function, **F(L, K)**, and the *crucial* Table 3.5. Section "Natural Wages: Objective Function, Maximand" has focus on resolving the difficult model issues and debates about his normative wage calculations. In section "CES Forms and Marginal Productivity Wages", the

**Table 3.3** von Thünen's productivity calculations, cf. (3.6), (3.15), (3.19), and Wages, Rentals, Factor shares

| 1. | 2. | 3. | 4. | 5. | 6. | 7. | 8. | 9. | 10. | 11. | 12. | 13. | 14. |
|---|---|---|---|---|---|---|---|---|---|---|---|---|---|
| $K/L$ $k$ | $AP_L$ $f(k)$ | $MP_L$ $f(k) - f'(k)\,k$ | $AP_K$ $f(k)/k$ | $MP_K$ $f'(k)$ | $MP_K\,k$ $f'(k)\,k$ | $MRS$ $\frac{MP_L}{MP_K}$ | $1/MRS$ $z(k) = \frac{r}{w}$ | $\epsilon_L(k)$ $\frac{MP_L}{AP_L}$ | $\sigma(k)$ | $MP_L - 100$ $s_L(k)$ | $V(k)$ $z s_L$ | $N(k)$ $\frac{MP_L}{s_L}$ | $\sqrt{100\,AP_L}$ |
| 0 | 110 | 110 | – | – | – | – | – | 1.00 | – | 10 | – | – | 104.9 |
| 1 | 150 | 110 | 150 | 40 | 40 | 2.75 | 0.364 | 0.73 | 6.96 | 10 | 3.64 | 11.0 | 122.5 |
| 2 | 186 | 114 | 93 | 36 | 72 | 3.17 | 0.316 | 0.61 | 2.93 | 14 | 4.42 | 8.14 | 136.4 |
| 3 | 218.4 | 121.2 | 72.8 | 32.4 | 97.2 | 3.74 | 0.267 | 0.55 | 1.78 | 21.2 | 5.66 | 5.72 | 147.8 |
| 4 | 247.6 | 130.8 | 61.9 | 29.2 | 116.8 | 4.48 | 0.223 | 0.48 | 1.28 | 30.8 | 6.87 | 4.25 | 157.4 |
| 5 | 273.9 | 142.4 | 54.8 | 26.3 | 131.5 | 5.41 | 0.185 | 0.52 | 1.01 | 42.4 | 7.84 | 3.36 | 165.5 |
| 6 | 297.6 | 155.4 | 49.6 | 23.7 | 142.2 | 6.56 | 0.152 | 0.52 | 0.85 | 55.4 | 8.42 | 2.80 | 172.5 |
| 7 | 318.9 | 169.8 | 45.6 | 21.3 | 149.1 | 7.97 | 0.125 | 0.53 | 0.74 | 69.8 | 8.76 | 2.43 | 178.6 |
| 8 | 338.1 | 184.5 | 42.3 | 19.2 | 153.6 | 9.61 | 0.104 | 0.55 | 0.66 | 84.5 | 8.79 | 2.18 | 183.9 |
| 9 | 355.4 | 199.7 | 39.5 | 17.3 | 155.7 | 11.54 | 0.088 | 0.56 | 0.61 | 99.7 | 8.77 | 2.00 | 188.5 |
| 10 | 371.0 | 215.0 | 37.1 | 15.6 | 156.0 | 13.78 | 0.073 | 0.58 | 0.56 | 115 | 8.40 | 1.87 | 192.6 |

*Source*: von Thünen (1990, Ch. 11, p. 507), von Thünen (1875, Ch. 11, 2.I, p. 113), Dempsey (1960, p. 262)

**Table 3.4** von Thünen's productivity calculations, cf. Corollary 3.1, and wages, rentals, factor shares

| 1. | 2. | 3. | 4. | 5. | 6. | 7. | 8. | 9. | 10. | 11. | 12. | 13. | 14. |
|---|---|---|---|---|---|---|---|---|---|---|---|---|---|
| $K/L$ $k$ | $AP_L$ $f(k)$ | $MP_L$ $f(k)-f'(k)k$ | $AP_K$ $f(k)/k$ | $MP_K$ $f'(k)$ | $MP_K k$ $f'(k)k$ | $MRS$ $\frac{MP_L}{MP_K}$ | $1/MRS$ $z(k)=\frac{r}{w}$ | $\epsilon_L(k)$ $\frac{MP_L}{AP_L}$ | $\sigma(k)$ | $MP_L-100$ $s_L(k)$ | $V(k)$ $zs_L$ | $N(k)$ $\frac{MP_L}{s_L}$ | $\sqrt{100\,AP_L}$ |
| 5 | 205.4 | 106.8 | 41.1 | 19.7 | 98.6 | 5.41 | 0.185 | 0.52 | 1.01 | 6.8 | 1.25 | 15.7 | 143.3 |
| 6 | 223.2 | 116.4 | 37.2 | 17.8 | 106.8 | 6.56 | 0.152 | 0.52 | 0.85 | 16.4 | 2.51 | 7.10 | 149.4 |
| 7 | 239.2 | 127.2 | 34.2 | 16.0 | 112.0 | 7.97 | 0.126 | 0.53 | 0.74 | 27.2 | 3.43 | 4.67 | 154.7 |
| 8 | 253.6 | 138.4 | 31.7 | 14.4 | 115.2 | 9.61 | 0.104 | 0.55 | 0.66 | 38.4 | 3.96 | 3.60 | 159.2 |
| 9 | 266.6 | 149.6 | 29.6 | 13.0 | 117.0 | 11.54 | 0.088 | 0.56 | 0.61 | 49.6 | 4.31 | 3.02 | 163.3 |
| 10 | 278.3 | 161.3 | 27.8 | 11.7 | 117.0 | 13.78 | 0.073 | 0.58 | 0.56 | 61.3 | 4.45 | 2.63 | 166.8 |
| 11 | 288.8 | 173.3 | 26.3 | 10.5 | 115.5 | 16.50 | 0.060 | 0.60 | 0.53 | 73.3 | 4.44 | 2.36 | 169.9 |
| 12 | 298.3 | 184.3 | 24.9 | 9.5 | 114.0 | 19.40 | 0.051 | 0.62 | 0.50 | 84.3 | 4.35 | 2.18 | 172.7 |

*Source*: von Thünen (1990, Ch. 12, p. 515,562), von Thünen (1875, Ch. 12, 2.I, p. 122,170), Dempsey (1960, p. 268,302)

**Table 3.5** von Thünen : $f(k) = \gamma\,(1+k)^a$, $a = 1/2$ ; $f(0) = \gamma = 80$; cf. (3.34), (3.40)

| 1. | 2. | 3. | 4. | 5. | 6. | 7. | 8. | 9. | 10. | 11. | 12. | 13. | 14. |
|---|---|---|---|---|---|---|---|---|---|---|---|---|---|
| $\frac{K}{L}$ $k$ | $AP_L$ $y{=}f(k)$ | $MP_K$ $\Delta AP_L$ | $MP_K$ $f'(k)$ | $AP_K$ $f(k)/k$ | $MP_K k$ $f'(k)\,k$ | $MP_L$ $y - y'k$ | $MRS$ $\frac{MP_L}{MP_K}$ | $\varepsilon_L$ $\frac{MP_L}{AP_L}$ | $\sigma(k)$ | $1/MRS$ $z(k) = \frac{r}{w}$ | $MP_L - 100$ $s_L(k)$ | $V(k)$ $z s_L$ | $\sqrt{100\,AP_L}$ |
| 0 | 80.0 | – | 40.0 | – | – | 80.0 | 2.0 | 1.00 | 2.00 | 0.500 | – | – | – |
| 1 | 113.1 | 33.1 | 28.3 | 113.1 | 28.3 | 84.8 | 3.0 | 0.75 | 1.50 | 0.333 | 0.0 | 0.0 | 106.3 |
| 2 | 138.6 | 25.5 | 23.1 | 69.3 | 46.2 | 92.4 | 4.0 | 0.67 | 1.33 | 0.250 | 0.0 | 0.0 | **117.7** |
| 3 | 160.0 | 21.4 | 20.0 | 53.3 | 60.0 | 100.0 | 5.0 | 0.63 | 1.25 | 0.200 | 0.0 | 0.0 | **126.5** |
| 4 | 178.9 | 18.9 | 17.9 | 44.7 | 71.6 | 107.3 | 6.0 | 0.60 | 1.20 | 0.167 | 7.3 | 1.22 | **133.7** |
| 5 | 196.0 | 17.1 | 16.3 | 39.2 | 81.6 | 114.3 | 7.0 | 0.58 | 1.17 | 0.143 | 14.3 | 2.04 | **140.0** |
| 6 | 211.6 | 15.6 | 15.1 | 35.3 | 90.6 | 121.0 | 8.0 | 0.57 | 1.14 | 0.125 | 20.9 | 2.61 | 145.5 |
| 7 | 226.3 | 14.7 | 14.1 | 32.3 | 98.7 | 127.3 | 9.0 | 0.56 | 1.13 | 0.111 | 27.3 | 3.03 | 150.4 |
| 8 | 240.0 | 13.7 | 13.3 | 30.0 | 106.7 | 133.3 | 10.0 | 0.56 | 1.11 | 0.100 | 33.3 | 3.33 | **154.9** |
| 9 | 253.0 | 13.0 | 12.6 | 28.1 | 113.8 | 139.1 | 11.0 | 0.55 | 1.10 | 0.091 | 39.1 | 3.56 | 159.1 |
| 10 | 265.3 | 12.3 | 12.1 | 26.5 | 120.7 | 144.6 | 12.0 | 0.55 | 1.09 | 0.083 | 44.6 | 3.72 | 162.9 |
| 11 | 277.1 | 11.8 | 11.5 | 25.2 | 127.0 | 150.1 | 13.0 | 0.54 | 1.08 | 0.077 | 50.1 | 3.85 | 166.5 |
| 12 | 288.4 | 11.3 | 11.1 | 24.0 | 133.1 | 155.3 | 14.0 | 0.54 | 1.08 | 0.071 | 55.3 | 3.95 | 169.8 |

(continued)

**Table 3.5** (continued)

| 1. | 2. | 3. | 4. | 5. | 6. | 7. | 8. | 9. | 10. | 11. | 12. | 13. | 14. |
|---|---|---|---|---|---|---|---|---|---|---|---|---|---|
| $\frac{K}{L}$ $k$ | $AP_L$ $y=f(k)$ | $MP_K$ $\Delta AP_L$ | $MP_K$ $f'(k)$ | $AP_K$ $f(k)/k$ | $MP_K k$ $f'(k)k$ | $MP_L$ $y-y'k$ | $MRS$ $\frac{MP_L}{MP_K}$ | $\varepsilon_L$ $\frac{MP_L}{AP_L}$ | $\sigma(k)$ | $1/MRS$ $z(k)=\frac{r}{w}$ | $MP_L-100$ $s_L(k)$ | $V(k)$ $zs_L$ | $\sqrt{100\,AP_L}$ |
| 13 | 299.3 | 10.9 | 10.7 | 23.0 | 139.0 | 160.4 | 15.0 | 0.54 | 1.07 | 0.067 | 60.3 | 4.02 | 173.0 |
| 14 | 309.8 | 10.5 | 10.3 | 22.1 | 144.6 | 165.2 | 16.0 | 0.53 | 1.07 | 0.063 | 65.2 | 4.075 | 176.0 |
| 15 | 320.0 | 10.2 | 10.0 | 21.3 | 150.0 | 170.0 | 17.0 | 0.53 | 1.06 | 0.059 | 70.0 | 4.116 | 178.9 |
| 16 | 329.8 | 9.8 | 9.7 | 20.6 | 155.2 | 174.6 | 18.0 | 0.53 | 1.06 | 0.056 | 74.6 | 4.140 | 181.6 |
| 17 | 339.4 | 9.6 | 9.4 | 20.0 | 160.3 | 179.1 | 19.0 | 0.53 | 1.06 | 0.053 | 79.1 | 4.160 | 184.2 |
| 18 | 348.7 | 9.3 | 9.2 | 19.4 | 165.2 | 183.5 | 20.0 | 0.53 | 1.05 | 0.050 | 83.5 | 4.175 | 186.7 |
| 19 | 357.8 | 9.1 | 8.9 | 18.8 | 169.9 | 187.8 | 21.0 | 0.53 | 1.05 | 0.048 | 87.8 | 4.181 | **189.1** |
| 20 | 366.6 | 8.8 | 8.7 | 18.3 | 174.6 | 192.0 | 22.0 | 0.52 | 1.05 | 0.045 | 92.0 | 4.182 | **191.5** |
| 21 | 375.2 | 8.6 | 8.5 | 17.9 | 179.1 | 196.1 | 23.0 | 0.52 | 1.05 | 0.043 | 96.1 | 4.178 | **193.7** |
| 22 | 383.7 | 8.4 | 8.3 | 17.4 | 183.5 | 200.2 | 24.0 | 0.52 | 1.04 | 0.042 | 100.2 | 4.175 | 195.9 |
| 23 | 391.9 | 8.3 | 8.2 | 17.0 | 187.8 | 204.1 | 25.0 | 0.52 | 1.04 | 0.040 | 104.1 | 4.164 | 198.0 |
| 24 | 400.0 | 8.1 | 8.0 | 16.7 | 192.0 | 208.0 | 26.0 | 0.52 | 1.04 | 0.038 | 108.0 | 4.154 | **200.0** |

*Source*: von Thünen (1875, 2.II, p. 47), Dempsey (1960, p. 342)
Columns, (1–3, 6–7, 11–14), are his original numbers (1875), and they had proper mathematical symbols; with $a = \frac{1}{2}$, his square roots in columns (2,6,7) have nothing to do with the square root in column 14
In Dempsey, column 13 shows for, $k = 17 - 22$: $V(k) = 4.2$, missing the maximum 4.182 at $k = 20$

marginal productivity wage of the **CES** case, $\sigma = 2$, is formally restated exactly as his revered "*natural wage*" formula. It concludes and summarizes with the *properties* (3.1–3.3) of $\mathbf{f(k)}$ in review.

## Marginal Productivities of Labor and Capital

### *The Marginal Products of Labor*

On his estate *Tellow* in Mecklenburg, von Thünen was a good farmer,[2] and *accounting records* of estate costs and sales were carefully kept and studied in optimizing various economic activities. Nevertheless, what are shown throughout here are *not* empirical/harvest *data*, but his "abstract (*illustrative*) productivity numbers". The staple crops in North Germany at his time were rye and potatoes.

von Thünen points out, von Thünen (1990, p. 416), von Thünen (1875, 2.I, p. 19), Dempsey (1960, p. 203):
"It is in the *nature* of *agriculture*—and this is a circumstance that must be stressed—that the additional yield is not in direct proportion to the number of additional laborers, but every *additional laborer* brings an *additional* product *lower* than the proceeding.
For an example we show the following *schedule* [ Table 3.1,]. With this schedule and the *rye prices* per bushel and *annual wages* of workers, it turns out for obtaining *maximum profit* [ "höchsten *Reinertrag* zu erlangen" ]: the 22nd labor still shows a *profit*; when hiring the *23rd* laborer, *gain* and *cost compensate*; the addition of the 24th laborer means a *loss*":

However, von Thünen did *not* indicate any *formula* behind the $\mathbf{MP_L}$ numbers in Tables 3.1 and 3.2. With no indication of rounding errors, these numbers somehow exhibited no clear arithmetic rules. It appears that Lloyd (1969, p. 27–28) was the first to *uncover* the *geometric series* (quotient: 9/10, 2/3 ) actually involved in the Tables 3.1 and 3.2. Neither these Table numbers, nor symbols were used in von Thünen (1990), von Thünen (1875), Dempsey (1960).

Let us state these $\mathbf{MP_L}$ schedules, and calculate "missing" numbers for total product, $\mathbf{Y}$. The *marginal productivity* of one (variable) factor, labor ($\mathbf{L}$) in Table 3.1, is given by,

$$\triangle Y = MP_L\ ; \quad MP_L(L) = 100\ (0.9)^{L-21},\ L \geqslant 1;$$
$$MP_L(1) = 100\ (0.9)^{-20} = 822.5$$

[2] Adam Smith taught me political economy, Thaer scientific farming: "Adam Smith war in der Nationalökonomie, Thaer in der wissenschaftlichen Landwirtschaft mein Lehrer. Sie sind der Begründer zweier Wissenschaften, und manche ihrer Lehren werden für immer unantastbaren Grundlagen der Wissenschaft bilden", von Thünen (1990, p. 401), von Thünen (1875, 2.I, p. 3), Hall (1966, p. 225).

where $MP_L$ is *calibrated* on, $L = 21$, with $MP_L(1)$ calculated accordingly.

Thus **Y(L)** is given by the *sum* formula - [ $\lim_{L\to\infty} Y(L) = 822.5/(1-9/10) = 8225$ ] :

$$Y(L) = \sum_{i=1}^{L} MP_L(i) = MP_L(1)\,[(1-(0.9)^L)/(1-0.9)],\ L \geqslant 1;$$

$$MP_L(1) = 822.5$$

which offers the "missing" harvest data ($Y$)—conforming to the actual $MP_L$ in Table 3.1. The *average* products, $AP_L(L) = Y(L)/L$, Tables 3.1 and 3.2, are given directly by the columns.

Similarly, the marginal productivity of labor in Table 3.2 (quotient:2/3) is given by:

$$MP_L(L) = 2\,(2/3)^{L-8},\ L \geqslant 1;\quad MP_L(8) = 2\,;\quad MP_L(1) = 2\,(2/3)^{-7} = 34.2$$

where $MP_L$ is *calibrated* on the integer value of L = 8—and $MP_L(1)$ calculated as above.

$$\begin{aligned} Y(L) &= \textstyle\sum_{i=1}^{L} MP_L(i) \\ &= Y(1)[(1-(2/3)^L)/(1-2/3)],\ L \geqslant 1;\quad Y(1) = 34.2 \end{aligned}$$

Some, e.g., Frisch (1965, p. 85), see *column 2* as actual "*crop yield data*", such that $MP_L$ (column 3) are simply the *increments* from column 2. But the harvest "data" are "too good" for this arithmetic interpretation. Harvest numbers **Y**($L$) come up as in Table 3.1.

After Table 3.2 discussions, von Thünen (1990, Ch. 19, p. 576), von Thünen (1875, Ch. 19, 2.I, p. 185), Dempsey (1960, p. 312) states: "*The value of the labor of the last worker employed is also his wage* (italics original).

This proposition admits many-sided applications in social life". His marginal value product (**MVP**) *proposition* for labor values (*factor prices*, wages) become, in our symbols, ($w$: wage rate; $p$: price of product):

$$w = MVP_L = p \cdot MP_L\,;\qquad \epsilon_L = \frac{wL}{pY} = \frac{MP_L}{AP_L} \tag{3.4}$$

where ($w$) and ($p$) are given in a common *monetary* unit ["Taler" (12 Mark Silver) or any other currency ], and $\epsilon_L$ is the Labor *cost share* for the total product volume/output.

### *The Marginal Products of Capital—and Factor Substitution*

The *productive nature* and origin of *capital* is discussed in several chapters of "The Isolated State". We quote, von Thünen (1990, Ch. 17, p. 553–554), von Thünen (1875, Ch. 17, 2.I, p. 161–165), Dempsey (1960, p. 295–296): "Given that there is peat bog ["Torfmoor"] on an estate out which the water must be drained every year in order to cut this peat, and that to drain the water calls for a year's labor of a man, ("die Jahresarbeit eines Mannes", *Jahresarbeiten*, J.A).

Now, if a channel is digged by which the peat bog is drained, the annually recurring work of a man is replaced by the capital invested in digging the channel. So by means of capital, labor is directly saved. The *capital* now does the work which would otherwise be done by one man's labor. If digging the channel required, e.g. 20 J.A., the capital invested would bear a return of 5% [1/20 = 0.05]. The *capital used* [ Kapitalnutzung ] here is not expressed in bushels of rye or Talers, but in years of work" (*labor-years*, J.A).[3]

Although the *terminology* of *factor substitution* with *isoquants* is obviously *not* used, the quote clearly involves these *concepts*. Indeed the amount of capital was even *measured* by the number of *recurrent* annual *labor services* (*J.A*) that it can replace.

As to the return (yield) and factor price of capital, von Thünen (1990, Ch. 9, p. 498), von Thünen (1875, Ch. 9, 2.I, p. 103), Dempsey (1960, p. 257) says: "The *rental* ("Rente"), which capital as a whole gives when hired out, is determined by the yield ("Nutzung") of the *last unit* of *capital*. This is one of the most important *theorems* in the theory of *rental rates* ".

Although a diverse terminology is used—about units of measurements and about the advantages of optimal capital stock increases—the *marginal productivity* factor price Proposition, (3.4), is evidently involved and *extended* to the production factor, *capital*:

$$r = MVP_K = p \cdot MP_K \; ; \qquad \epsilon_K(K) = \frac{r\,K}{p\,Y} = \frac{MP_K}{AP_K} \tag{3.5}$$

[3] "Das Kapital hat einerseits die Eigenschaft, Arbeit zu ersetzen, und anderseits ist das Kapital das Erzeugnis menschlicher Arbeit. Wie ist in dieser Wechselwirkung Einheit and Klarheit zu finden? Aus 1 J.A. Kapital geht also ein Produkt ("Ertrag") von, $p/(k+q)$, Scheffel hervor. [ $k = 1/z$]

$$\triangle K = 1 : \triangle p = \triangle AP_L = \frac{p}{k+q} = \frac{AP_L}{1/z+k}$$

$$= \frac{AP_L}{MP_L/MP_K + k} = \frac{AP_L \cdot MP_K}{MP_L + MP_K\,k} = MP_K$$

Hier erscheint das Kapital selbst als Arbeiter. Indessen is das Kapital an sich ein totes und kann nur durch die Hand des Menschen wirksam werden; aber indem es die Wirksamkeit des Menschen erhöht, erscheint sie als Mitarbeiter. In diesen Sinn ist es zu nehmen, wenn hier und in der Folge von der Arbeit des Kapitals die Rede ist", von Thünen (1990, Ch. 17, p. 557), von Thünen (1875, Ch. 17, 2.I, p. 165). Instead of "capital" as "dead man working" substituting with living labor, his "capital symbol" (k) is our, MRS= $MP_L/MP_K$.

where $(r)$, the rental rate (*factor price*) of using *capital services* (input), is given in the same *monetary* unit as $(p)$, price of product; $\epsilon_K(K)$ is the capital cost share ('unit free').

Diminishing rental rates are explicitly stated, von Thünen (1990, Ch. 8, p. 494), von Thünen (1875, Ch. 8, 2.I, p. 99), Dempsey (1960, p. 255): "Every additional capital brings less rentals ("Renten") than capital previously employed".

Next, von Thünen (1990, Ch. 9, p. 495), von Thünen (1875, Ch. 9, 2.I, p. 100), Dempsey (1960, p. 255) asks: "The question is: On what *schedule* can the *decreasing effectiveness of capital* [ "abnehmende Wirksamkeit des Kapitals" ] be shown? Later on, when such required assumptions must be stated, the inquiry into the *relation* [ **f(k)** ] between *capital* [ **k** ] and the *product of labor* [ **y** ] will be subject of a special investigation[4] Here the need arises first to set up a *series*, the parts of which are *continuously smaller*, and this condition is satisfied by a *geometric series*, the *base* of which is a *fraction*, as (9/10), $(9/10)^2$, $(9/10)^3$, $(9/10)^4$.

In order to have *definite figures* for our inquiry and to be able further to develop them, I *assume* as a *preliminary* that the *product of labor* of *one* man **increases** by the application of the *first capital* of **1** J.A. by **40c**; a second capital of 1 J.A. by (9/10)40c or 36c; a third capital of 1 J.A. by (9/10)36c or 32.4c, and so forth. The continuation of that calculation gives the following schedule (italics ours)"—output (rye) *unit* (c) omitted:

$$\triangle AP_L(k) = MP_K(k) = 40\,(0.9)^{k-1}\ ;\ MP_K(1) = 40\ ;$$
$$k = K/L\ ;\ k = 1, 2, 3, .. \qquad (3.6)$$

This $\mathbf{MP_K(k)}$ *schedule* (3.6) entered—as shown in *column* (5) of—his Table 3.3 above.

The *discrete* capital input variable in (3.6) is measured by the size of capital per labor-year [ capital-labor ratio, $k = K/L$ ]. As to relations between output (Y) and inputs, crucial distinctions exist for *one-factor* $MP_L(L)$ formulas and *two-factor* $MP_K(k)$, (3.6).

[4] The inquiry of a suitable relation $y = f(k)$ took a long time. From a letter extract (to his brother, Nov.26, 1845), we read, Schneider (1934, p. 6): "*Due to my peculiar nature, I can only keep going, when I have some solid mathematical foundation.* For the natural wage rate, the *expression*, $\sqrt{ap}$, is found [found 1830 ]; it may be perfectly correct, but in order *to make a numerical application of it, the law connecting (q) and (p)—capital and product—must be found and demonstrated.* The research into such law has occupied me for 20 years, but since the real world for that hereto delivers no data, unfortunately always in vain. Although the obtained knowledge that the natural wage rate is $\sqrt{ap}$ is an important result for me, to continue working with true joy, I must know the relationship between $(q)$ and $(p)$".

## PRODUCT, LABOR, CAPITAL: $\mathbf{Y} = \mathbf{F}(\mathbf{L}, \mathbf{K}) = \mathbf{L}\,\mathbf{f}(\mathbf{k})$

The establishment of a solid economic factor price foundation for the wage rate and rental rate determination and cost minimization by using the marginal productivity principle was not the only goal of von Thünen's many inductive and deductive investigations.

His primary objective became subsequently even more ambitious: To find a clear, rational (objective) *principle* for the respective *contributions* and *shares* of labor and capital, (**L**, **K**), to the total *output*/production (**Y**), and so precisely answering the fundamental *question*: How can—for two production factors $(L, K)$—*coherent sets of numbers* be *calculated* for the *common average Labor* productivity $AP_L(L, K)$ and *joint* output (Y)? The answer relied upon his **key assumption (conjecture),**

$$\triangle AP_L(k) = MP_K(k), \ k = K/L, \ \ k = 1, 2, 3, .., \infty \tag{3.7}$$

von Thünen (1990, Ch. 9, p. 496), von Thünen (1875, Ch. 9, 2.I, p. 101), Dempsey (1960, p. 256) used (3.6–3.7) arithmetically by successively adding $MP_K(k)$ numbers (3.6) to obtain his *actual* $AP_L$ *numbers* (column 2) in Table 3.3. But the discrete *relation* (3.7) holds **generally**, without being tied to *specific* rules like the *geometric series*, $MP_K(k)$, (3.6). However, there is a critical problem for a general proceeding with (3.7). What is the *initial value* of $AP_L$? He uses:

$$K = 0, \ k = 0 \ : \ AP_L(0) = 110 \ ; \ \ k = 0 \ : \ MP_L(0) = 110 \ ; \ \ c_L = 100 \tag{3.8}$$

$AP_L(0)$: Product of a man *without* capital (Arbeitsprodukt eines Mannes ohne Kapital), $MP_L(0)$: Marginal productivity of Labor *without* capital (Arbeitslohn ohne Kapital).

The Tables 3.1 and 3.2 had production, $AP_L$, $MP_L$, *without* capital, and this should *also apply* to (3.8). We can arbitrarily fix the size of $AP_L(0)$. But we know from Tables 3.1 and 3.2 that $MP_L(0)$[5] must be much lower, and can the *limit wage*, $\mathbf{MP_L(0)}$, then be so low that even a consumption condition of "*subsistence*", ($\mathbf{c_L} = 100$), is not satisfied. To escape this dilemma, $\mathbf{MP_L(0)}$ was preliminary *fixed* also at **110**, chosen as *10 %* above ($c_L$), cf. (3.8). However, the *exogenous* sizes of ($c_L$) are clearly irrelevant for production

[5] von Thünen (1990, Ch. 12, p. 510), von Thünen (1875, Ch. 12, 2.I, p. 116), Dempsey (1960, p. 266) meets here a contradiction: Capital initially did not exist, but is created by humans without capital. But it is difficult to come up with algebraic relations that conform to any reality at *low levels* of capital, down to *zero*. [ "Das Arbeitsprodukt (p) ist eine Funktion von (q), wenn (q) die Grösse des angewandten Kapital bezeichnet; aber keine der von mir fast in allen algebraischen Formen aufgestellten Gleichungen—bis zu den niedern Graden des Kapital, oder gar bis Null, so zeigt sich derselben Widerspruch,—und das Dunkel, das hier herrscht"].

functions below; ($\mathbf{c_L}$) first becomes important for the "*natural wage rate*" calculations in section "Natural Wages: Objective Function, Maximand".

### *Homogeneous Labor Productivity Function*, $\mathbf{AP_L = f(k)}$

We must, for later use, start with the *genesis* of the rigorous establishment of the mathematical properties for some of the *general equations*—as well as for the specific parametric production functions—*implicitly* involved in his Tables 3.3 and 3.4, Chaps. 11–12), where he fully recognized the *interaction* and *joint venture of two factors*, von Thünen (1990, Ch. 19, p. 584), von Thünen (1875, Ch. 19, 2.I, p. 193), Dempsey (1960, p. 317), Samuelson (1983, p. 1469), Douglas (1934, 1957, p. 36):

**I**: "The work product ("Arbeitsprodukt") is the common product of labor and capital. How is now the *share* which both factors each has in the common product to be measured? The *effectiveness of capital* is measured by the *increment* in the *product per man*, which occurs through the increase of the capital with which a man works. Here Labor is *constant*, but capital is a *variable* quantity".

**II**: "If we retain this procedure, but conversely consider *capital* as *constant* and the quantity of *Labor* as *increasing*, then essentially the *effectiveness of labor* must also be obtained through the *increment* in the *total product* by the increase of one worker, and by which an information about the *share* of Labor in the work product can be obtained".

The *first* statement (**I**) gives—in *incremental* form—the *fundamental* and truly remarkable *relations* between,"Arbeitsprodukt" = Total product of one labor-year = Average product of labor ($\mathbf{y} = Y/L = AP_L$), and "Kapital" = capital-labor ratio ($\mathbf{k} = K/L$):

$$\triangle y = \triangle AP_L(k) = AP_L(k) - AP_L(k-1) = MP_K(k)\ ; \quad k = 1, 2, 3, ..$$
$$y = Y/L = AP_L(k) = AP_L(k-1) + MP_K(k)\ ; \quad k = 1, 2, 3, .. \tag{3.9}$$

$$y = AP_L(k) = AP_L(0) + \textstyle\sum_{i=1}^{k} \triangle AP_L(i) = AP_L(0) + \sum_{i=1}^{k} MP_K(i)\ ; \quad k = 1, 2, 3, .. \tag{3.10}$$

Thus, the *increment* in the average product of labor, $\mathbf{\Delta AP_L}$, (3.9), is explained/calculated by *effectiveness* of capital (*Wirksamkeit* des Kapitals, $\mathbf{MP_K}$)—as this term was earlier discussed and replaced by the modern term, marginal product of capital, $MP_K(k)$, (3.6).

Let us dwell a bit on the *general equations*, (3.9–3.10)—that are not tied to special $MP_K$. The conjectured *incremental* formulation (3.9) has probably more suggestive appeal for seeing the effects of larger capital, and it supports a better intuitive understanding of the mathematical *equivalence* between increases in labor productivity and the marginal products of capital than does its modern counterpart in the *differential* calculus version:

$$AP_L'(k) = \frac{d\,AP_L(k)}{d\,k} = \frac{d\,(Y/L)}{d\,(K/L)} = \frac{\partial\,[L\,f(k)]}{\partial K} = L\,f\,'(k)/L = f\,'(k)$$
$$= \partial F(L, K)/\partial K \;= MP_K(L, K) = MP_K(k) \quad (3.11)$$

where $F(L, K)$ is a nonnegative smooth function, homogeneous of degree 1, $L \neq 0$,

$$Y = F(L, K) = L\,F(1, k) = L\,AP_L(L, K) = L\;AP_L(k) = L\,f(k);\;\; F(0, 0) = 0$$

and $f(k)$ is strictly concave and monotonically increasing in $k \in [0, \infty[$, i.e.

$$\forall k > 0:\;\; f'(k) = df(k)/dk > 0, \quad f''(k) = d^2 f(k)/dk^2 < 0$$

The *second* statement (**II**) above gives in differential/incremental form these relations:

$$MP_L(L, K) = \frac{\partial F(L, K)}{\partial L} \equiv \frac{\partial\,[L\,f(k)]}{\partial L} = f(k) + L\,f'(k)\,K/L^2$$
$$= f(k) + f\,'(k)\,k = AP_L(k) \;-\; MP_K(k)\,k \;=\; MP_L(k) \quad (3.12)$$

$$MP_L'(k) \;=\; \frac{d\,MP_L(k)}{d\,k} \;=\; -\,MP_K'(k)\,k \quad (3.13)$$

$$Y/K = AP_K(k) = \frac{f(k)}{k}\,;\;\; \frac{d\,AP_K(k)}{d\,k} \;=\, -\,\frac{MP_L(k)}{k^2}\,;$$
$$\triangle\,AP_K(k) = -\frac{MP_L(k)}{k\,(k-1)} \quad (3.14)$$

Here *Incremental relations* (discrete, smooth) are a bit less "simple" than, (3.11), (3.7).

His so-called *share* of labor, in the "work product", $AP_L(k)$, mentioned in second statement (**II**), is his *effectiveness of labor*: $MP_L(k)$, (3.12)—as his *effectiveness of capital* (in the first statement) was given by: $MP_K(k)$, (3.11).

Thus, in retrospect, Thünen's *conjecture* (3.7) underlying the simple *discrete* computational formulas (3.9–3.10) had *tacit* support and rigorous *foundation* from the mathematical *homogeneity* properties ( *Euler*) displayed in (3.11–3.14) for *two factors* (L,K), *jointly* involved in determining the *product* (output), *average* products, and their *marginal* products.

***Parametric Production Functions,* F(L, K), *of Tables 3.3 and 3.4***

The *quantitative production* function with two interacting primary factors is derived by *combining* special, $\mathbf{MP_K(k)}$, (3.6)—and *general* sum (3.10), (3.8)—to *get* the explicit $\mathbf{AP_L(k)}$:

$$AP_L(k) = AP_L(0) + MP_K(1)[(1 - (0.9)^k)/(1 - 0.9)]\ ; \quad AP_L(0) = 110\ ; \quad MP_K(1) = 40$$

$$y = Y/L = AP_L(k) = f(k) = 110 + 400[1 - (0.9)^k]\ ; \quad AP_L(1) = 150\ ; \ k = 1, 2, .. \tag{3.15}$$

The *formula* (3.15) gives (directly) the Labor productivity *numbers* in *column* 2, Table 3.3, and it represents the *discrete* version of a *unique law* connecting Labor productivity and the capital/labor ratio, i.e. what today is a *production function* in the *intensive* form, $y = f(k),\ k = 1, 2, 3, ..$ Note that this $AP_L(k)$, (3.15), is bounded above: $\lim_{k\to\infty} AP_L(k) = 510 = \lim_{k\to\infty} MP_L(k)$. The relevant *closed* form (3.15) was not stated by von Thünen.

For later purposes, the **smooth** counterpart of the *discrete* function (3.15) is needed.[6] From the *marginal productivity* of capital, (3.6), (3.11), we have a *continuous derivative*:

$$MP_K = f'(k) = 40\,(0.9)^{k-1} = (40/0.9)\,e^{(\ln 0.9)k}\ ; \quad f'(1) = 40 \tag{3.16}$$

$$E(MP_K, k) = d\ln MP_K/d\ln k = (\ln 0.9)\,k = -\,0.10536\,k$$

Next (3.16) gives by integration,

$$AP_L(k) = f(k) = \int f'(k)dk = [40/(0.9\ln 0.9)]\,e^{(\ln 0.9)k} + \bar{y}\ ; \quad \bar{y} = \lim_{k\to\infty} f(k) \tag{3.17}$$

[6] An alternative production function exhibited by the columns in Table 3.4 was extensively used in some of von Thünen's "natural wage" calculations. He wanted to recognize and show that the fertility of soil and the climate would affect production, factor returns and "natural wages". He says: "If, due to lower fertility of the soil, the worker with the same amount of capital produces a product one fourth less than Table 3.3 the amounts of interest and wages fall by one fourth", von Thünen (1990, p. 508), von Thünen (1875, 2.I, p. 114), Dempsey (1960, p. 265). Hence in Table 3.4, columns are generated by, cf. (3.6), (3.15),

$$MP_K(k) = (3/4)\{40\,(0.9)^{k-1}\} = 30\,(0.9)^{k-1}\ ; \quad MP_K(1) = 30\ ; \ k = 1, 2, ..$$

$$\begin{aligned} y = AP_L(k) &= (3/4)\,\{110 + 400[1 - (0.9)^k]\}\ ; \quad k = 1, 2, 3, .. \\ &= 82.5 + 300[1 - (0.9)^k]\ ; \quad AP_L(1) = 112.5 \end{aligned}$$

This last formula of $y = AP_L(k)$ for Table 3.4 was first obtained by van Suntum (1988, p. 396).

We *calibrate* the *smooth* $AP_L(k)$, (3.17), as the *discrete* $AP_L(k)$ in (3.15) at: $\mathbf{k = 1}$, i.e.,

$$f(1) = 150 = [40/(0.9 \ln 0.9)]\, e^{(\ln 0.9)} + \bar{y} \;\Leftrightarrow$$
$$\bar{y} = 150 - (40/\ln 0.9) = 529.65 \qquad (3.18)$$

**Proposition 3.1** *The smooth*[7] *production function* $\mathbf{f(k)}$ *behind* Table 3.3 *is by (3.16–3.18)*

$$y = f(k) = 150 + (40/(0.9 \ln 0.9)\,[\,e^{(\ln 0.9)k} - 0.9\,]\,; \quad f(1) = 150\,; \; f'(1) = 40$$

$$f(k) = 529.65 - 421.83\, e^{-0.10536k}\,;$$
$$f(0) = 107.82; \; f'(0) = 40/0.9 = 44.44 \qquad (3.19)$$

*with* **isoquants, Fig. 3.1(a)**, *and derivatives having standard* **neoclassical** *properties*

$$f'(k) = 44.44 \cdot e^{-0.10536k} > 0\,, \quad f''(k) = -4.68 \cdot e^{-0.10536k} < 0\,; \quad k \geq 0$$

$$f''(k)/f'(k) = \ln 0.9 = -0.10536\,; \quad E(f'(k), k) = -0.10536\,k$$

*The explicit* **parametric** *form and qualitative type of (3.19) may be stated as,*

$$y = f(k) = \bar{y} - (\beta/\alpha)\, e^{-\alpha k} = y_{max} - [\,(y_{max} - y_{min})/\alpha\,]\, e^{-\alpha k}\,; \quad 0 < \alpha < 1$$

$$Y = F(L, K) = L\,[\,\bar{y} - (\beta/\alpha)\, e^{-\alpha k}\,]\,; \; F(0, 1) = 0\,;$$
$$F(1, 1) = 150\,, \; MP_L(1) = 110 \qquad (3.20)$$

**Corollary 3.1** *The smooth production function* $\mathbf{f(k)}$ *involved in* Table 3.4, *has the form in* Proposition 3.1 *for* Table 3.3, *but the expressions for* $f(k), f'(k), F(L, K)$, *(3.19–3.20), are multiplied by,* $A = 0.75$*; A is a TFP (total factor productivity) parameter.*

Incidentally, we may note that for $K = k = 0$, the *limit wage*: $MP_L(0) = \mathbf{f(0)} = 107.8 = AP_L(0)$, (3.19), can cover the "subsistence" consumption, ($\mathbf{c_L = 100}$) for Table 3.3, whereas low *soil* fertility in Table 3.4, with $\mathbf{f(0)} = 0.75 \cdot 107.8 = 80.9$ cannot. Smooth production functions can resolve *limit* issues that discrete functions could not, cf. Note 4 (Fig. 3.1).

[7] No (smooth) exponential function, $f(k)$, (3.19), can exactly reproduce a discrete version (3.15), (3.6). We prefer the calibration of the globally smooth $f(k)$, (3.19), at k=1; cf. (3.17–3.18).

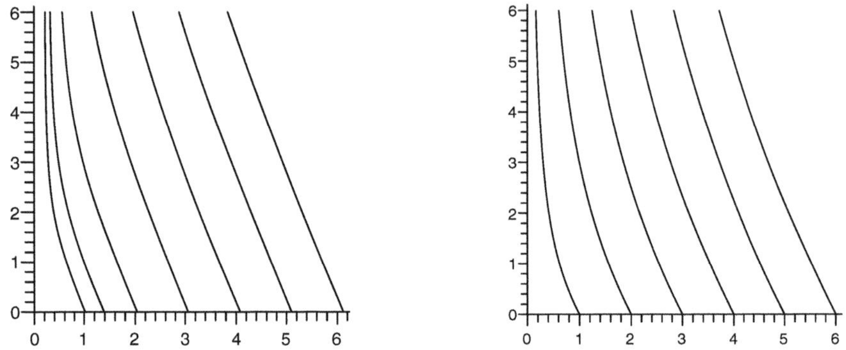


(a) (b)

**Fig. 3.1** Isoquants of: $Y = F(L, K) = L\,f(k)$. (**a**), (3.19–3.20), Y: 110, 150, 220, 330, 440, 550, 660. (**b**), (3.40), Y: 80, 160, 240, 320, 400, 480

All columns—except $AP_K$,(4); $MRS$, (7); $\varepsilon_L$,(9); $\sigma(k)$,(10); $\sqrt{100\,AP_L}$, (14);—are the original numbers from von Thünen's: Tabelle A-B, which give properties of *discrete production function*, (3.15), Table 3.3, and for Table 3.4 by Corollary 3.1. Numéraire in columns (2–5,11,12,14) is rye (in bushels); $c_L = 100$.

The "natural wage" columns (11–14) of Tables 3.3, 3.4 and 3.5 are explained in section "Natural Wages: Objective Function, Maximand".

### *Real Wage, Rental Rate, Factor Share, Substitution Elasticity*

No doubt *von Thünen* felt exalted by his Tables 3.3 and 3.4. Although he did not have our Proposition 3.1 and Corollary 3.1 behind them, all the *discrete* numbers are *correct* for all column variables. His *knowledge* of how to *calculate* the *"joint product"*, $AP_L(k)$, (*columns* 5, 2), cf. (3.6–3.8), allowed him—in many other columns, as explained below—to quantitatively solve, explain, and fully demonstrate *implications* of more *capital* (comparative statics of capital-labor ratio variations)—and hence also evaluate the plausibility of the economic results from his *"discrete implicit"* production function, (*column* 2)—our (3.15) and (3.19). The factor pricing of *capital* was earlier given by (3.5–3.6). Thus the *monetary* remuneration of total employed capital is then: $rK$, and for capital per labor: $rk$. The *"real"* compensation ("Rente", rentals) in terms of output units (rye) is, $(r/p)\,k = R(k)$,

$$R(k) \;=\; (r/p)\,k \;=\; MP_K\,k \;=\; 40\,(0.9)^{k-1}\,k \tag{3.21}$$

$$R\,(k) = f'(k)\,k = 44.44{\cdot}e^{-0.10536k}\,k\;;\;\; R'(k) = 0\;:\;k = 9.49\;;\;\; \lim_{k\to\infty} R\,(k) = 0 \tag{3.22}$$

The size of $\mathbf{R}(\mathbf{k})$, (3.21), is shown in column 6, Tables 3.3 and 3.4. Similarly, all labor units get the same factor price ($w$), according to the principle: (3.4). With capital involved in labor productivity, $AP_L(k)$, and with capital compensation by $R(k)$, the factor compensation (in rye) of a labor unit was formally obtained by a remainder calculation (residual) as,

$$w/p = MP_L = AP_L - R(k) = AP_L - MP_K\,k = f(k) - f'(k)\,k$$
$$= (AP_K - MP_K)\,k \tag{3.23}$$

tacitly justified by Euler's theorem on homogeneous functions, (3.11–3.14).

By using the discrete $AP_L$, (3.15), $MP_K$, (3.6), and inserting in (3.23), we have

$$MP_L(k) = 510 - 400\,(0.9)^k\,[1 + (1/9)k]\,; \quad k = 1, 2, 3, .. \tag{3.24}$$

which explicitly gives column 3, Table 3.3; $\lim_{k\to\infty} MP_L(k) = 510 = \lim_{k\to\infty} AP_L(k)$.

By (3.23–3.24), $\mathbf{MP_L(k)}$, is monotone increasing in the expanding use of capital ($\mathbf{k}$). Thus *"The decrease of the rentals -"Rente" $R(k)$ - with the growth of capital benefits the worker and increases the wages of his work"* (italics original), von Thünen (1990, Ch. 9, p. 499), von Thünen (1875, Ch. 9, 2.I, p. 104), Dempsey (1960, p. 258). The conclusion was: More "*machinery*" never hurts the other production factor—the "*real wage*" rates (in rye), $\mathbf{MP_L(k)}$, of the *employed* workers.

The $AP_K$ numbers of column 4 have the explicit formula (discrete), cf. (3.15),

$$AP_K(k) = AP_L(k)/k = [\,510 - 400\,(0.9)^k\,]/k\,; \quad k = 1, 2, 3, .. \tag{3.25}$$

which (as a ratio of increasing concave functions) is monotone decreasing.

When factor prices (3.4–3.5) reflect marginal factor productivities, the factor shares, $\epsilon_L, \epsilon_K$, of labor and capital are equal to product (output) elasticities, wrt. partial factor variation,

$$\epsilon_L = \frac{w\,L}{p\,Y} \equiv E(Y, L) \equiv \frac{\partial Y}{\partial L}\frac{L}{Y} = \frac{MP_L}{AP_L} = E\,(\frac{Y}{K}, \frac{L}{K}) = -E(AP_K, k) \tag{3.26}$$
$$\epsilon_K = \frac{r\,K}{p\,Y} \equiv E(Y, K) \equiv \frac{\partial Y}{\partial K}\frac{K}{Y} = \frac{MP_K}{AP_K} = \frac{f'(k)}{f(k)/k} = E(y, k) = E(AP_L, k)$$

Hence column 9, ($\epsilon_L$), is arithmetically obtained by columns 2–3 in Table 3.3.

Analytically, $(\epsilon_L, \epsilon_K)$ are explicitly given in discrete form by, cf. (3.25), (3.6),

$$\epsilon_L(k) = 1 - \epsilon_K \; ; \; \epsilon_K(k) = \frac{MP_K}{AP_K} = \frac{(1/9)\,k}{(51/40)(10/9)^k - 1} \; ;$$
$$\epsilon_K(1) = \frac{4}{15} \; ; \; k = 1, 2, 3, .. \tag{3.27}$$

$$\epsilon_K(k) = \frac{0.10536\,k}{1.26\,e^{0.10536\,k} - 1} \; ; \; \epsilon_L(0) = 1, \; \epsilon_K(0) = 0 \; ;$$
$$\lim_{k\to\infty} \epsilon_L(k) = 1 \, , \; \lim_{k\to\infty} \epsilon_K(k) = 0 \tag{3.28}$$

The factor *shares*, (3.27), are here—as observed in *column* 9—*not monotone* functions, although always being the ratio of two monotone increasing (decreasing) functions. The *share* $\epsilon_L$, (3.27–3.28), has a *minimum* at a finite size: $k = 5$, [ at $\sigma(k) = 1$], Tables 3.3 and 3.4.

As we know today, behavior of the shares (3.27) is clearer understood by values of the substitution elasticity, $\sigma(k)$. To get $\sigma(k)$, we first consider the marginal rate of substitution (**MRS**), $\omega(k)$, column 7, and given by the discrete expression, cf. (3.24), (3.6),

$$\omega(k) = \frac{w}{r} = MRS = \frac{MP_L}{MP_K} = 9\,\frac{51}{40}\,(10/9)^k \; - \; (9 + k) \; ; \; \omega(1) = \frac{11}{4} \; ;$$
$$k = 1, 2, 3, .. \tag{3.29}$$

which is monotone increasing function $\omega(k)$. Column 8 shows $z(k)$ = reciprocal of MRS.

Until (3.29), **discrete** production functions were adequate for computational purposes.

The elasticity of $\omega(k)$, (MRS), is the reciprocal of $\sigma(k)$, cf. Robinson (1965, p. 256,330)

$$\frac{1}{\sigma(k)} \equiv E(\omega(k), k) \equiv \frac{d \ln \omega}{d \ln k} = \frac{d\omega}{dk}\frac{k}{\omega} = \frac{d\omega}{dk}\frac{\epsilon_K}{\epsilon_L} \; ; \qquad E(k, \omega) = \sigma \tag{3.30}$$

But to obtain/calculate the size/values of $\sigma(k)$, (3.30), the **smooth** version of **f(k)**—in Propositions 3.1—is needed. To this end, we have, cf. (3.20), (3.16), (3.27), (3.29),

$$\omega(k) = \frac{MP_L}{MP_K} = 0.9 \left[\frac{15}{4} - \frac{1}{\ln 0.9}\right] e^{-(\ln 0.9)k} - \left[\frac{-1}{\ln 0.9} + k\right] \tag{3.31}$$

The expression for $\sigma(k)$, (3.30), of—$Y = F(L, K) = Lf(k)$—can be formulated in various *equivalent* forms as, cf. Hicks (1932, 1948, p. 117–

119,242–245),[8] and (3.26–3.27),

$$\sigma(k) \equiv \frac{\frac{\partial F}{\partial L}\frac{\partial F}{\partial K}}{\frac{\partial^2 F}{\partial L \partial K} \cdot F} = -\frac{[f(k) - f'(k)k]f'(k)}{f''(k)k f(k)}$$
$$= \frac{MP_L \, MP_K}{\partial MP_L/\partial K \cdot F} = \frac{\epsilon_K}{E(MP_L, k)}$$
$$= \frac{E(AP_L, k)}{E(MP_L, k)} = E(AP_L, MP_L) = \frac{MP_L \, MP_K}{\partial MP_K/\partial L \cdot F}$$
$$= -\frac{\epsilon_L = 1 - \epsilon_K}{E(MP_K, k)} = \frac{E(AP_K, k)}{E(MP_K, k)} = E(AP_K, MP_K) \tag{3.32}$$

The most *convenient* version in (3.32) is here the third last one, giving, cf. (3.28)

$$\sigma(k) = -\frac{1 - \epsilon_K}{E(MP_K, k)} = \frac{1}{1 - 1.26\, e^{0.10536k}} + \frac{9.491}{k} \tag{3.33}$$

$$\sigma(1) = 6.96; \quad \lim_{k \to 0} \sigma(k) = \infty; \; \lim_{k \to \infty} \sigma(k) = 0$$

The values of $\sigma(k)$ are shown in column 10, as calculated from (3.33). Although the **substitution elasticity** ($\sigma$) is *not* a *parameter* in the *production functions* above, its *implicit behavior* and our *calculated values* of $\sigma(k)$ in Tables 3.3 and 3.4, are *key* numbers in understanding the sequences of *factor shares* and the *entire pattern* for the economic variables in *all* other *columns*. It is remarkable that the full range of $\sigma(k)$ from zero to infinity (3.33) is obtained by the smooth functional forms of Proposition 3.1, (3.19–3.20). Few, if any **VES** (variable elasticity of substitution) functions have such **range** for $\sigma(k)$.

## von Thünen's Smooth Production Function, f(k)

We now come to the *apex* in his long search for a *feasible* production function. Biographic material support our exposition. In a letter (to son,1848), we read, Schneider (1934, p. 6): "*The problem to find an equation between capital and the product of labor, which I have toiled with in vain for 20 years, suddenly cleared up for me, and I have during the 3 days, January 17–19, 1848, found a schedule,*

[8] The Hicksian elasticity of factor substitution arose from the study of the elasticities of *Marshallian derived factor demands*, where it was the marginal uses and hence the changing marginal productivities of each factor that must be studied and calculated. Hicks unified the "derived factor demand" approach with the "analysis of isoquants"; on isoquants, see Frisch (1965, p. 49), Lloyd (2012, p. 4).

*which satisfies all my present requirements, if also in future I do not know"* (italics original). The **schedule** that von Thünen found—January, 1848—is given in Table 3.5, and as:

**Proposition 3.2** *von Thünen's smooth production function* **f(k)**, *in* Table 3.5, *gives*

$$y = AP_L(k) = f(k) = \gamma (1+k)^a, \quad 0 < a < 1; \quad f(0) = \gamma \ ; \quad \lim_{k\to\infty} f(k) = \infty \tag{3.34}$$

$$MP_K = f'(k) = a\gamma (1+k)^{a-1} \ ; \ E(MP_K, k) = -\frac{(1-a)\,k}{1+k} \ ; \ \lim_{k\to\infty} f'(k) = 0 \tag{3.35}$$

$$R(k) = MP_K\, k = f'(k)\, k = a\gamma(1+k)^{a-1} k \ ; \ \lim_{k\to\infty} R(k) = \infty \tag{3.36}$$

$$MP_L(k) = AP_L - MP_K\, k = \frac{\gamma (1+k)^{a-1}}{1+(1-a)\,k} \ ; \ \lim_{k\to\infty} MP_L(k) = \infty \tag{3.37}$$

$$z(k) = \frac{a}{1+(1-a)\,k} \ ; \quad z(1) = \frac{a}{2-a} \ ; \quad \lim_{k\to\infty} z(k) = 0 \tag{3.38}$$

$$\begin{gathered}
Y/K = AP_K(k) = AP_L(k)/k = \gamma (1+k)^a/k \ ; \ \lim_{k\to\infty} AP_K(k) = 0 \\
f''(k)/f'(k) = E(MP_K, k)/k = -\tfrac{1-a}{1+k} \\
\omega(k) = MP_L/MP_K = \tfrac{1}{a}[1+(1-a)\,k] \ ; \quad \omega(1) = \tfrac{2-a}{a} \\
\epsilon_K(k) = MP_K/AP_K = \tfrac{a\,k}{1+k} \ ; \quad \epsilon_K(1) = a/2 \ ; \quad \epsilon_K(0) = 0, \ \epsilon_L(0) = 1 \\
\lim_{k\to\infty} \epsilon_K(k) = a, \quad \lim_{k\to\infty} \epsilon_L(k) = 1-a
\end{gathered}$$

$$\begin{gathered}
\sigma(k) = (\epsilon_K - 1)/E(MP_K, k) = \tfrac{1+(1-a)\,k}{(1-a)(1+k)} \\
\lim_{k\to 0} \sigma(k) = \tfrac{1}{1-a} \ ; \quad \lim_{k\to\infty} \sigma(k) = 1 \ ; \sigma(1) = \tfrac{2-a}{2\,(1-a)}
\end{gathered}$$

$$V(k) = z s_L = z\,(MP_L - c_L) = a\gamma (1+k)^{a-1} - a c_L [1+(1-a)\,k]^{-1} \tag{3.39}$$

*The selected* **parameters** *of* **f(k)** *in (3.34) were:* **a = 1/2**, **$\gamma$ = 80, [isoquants, Fig. 3.1(b)]**

$$Y = L\,f(k) = L\,\gamma\,(1+k)^a = \gamma\,L^{1-a}\,(L+K)^a = L\;80\;(1+k)^{\frac{1}{2}},$$

$$f'(k) = 40\,(1+k)^{-\frac{1}{2}} \tag{3.40}$$

$$V(k) = 40\,(1+k)^{-\frac{1}{2}} - 100\,(2+k)^{-1}\;;\quad c_L = 100\;;\quad \lim_{k\to\infty} V(k) = 0 \tag{3.41}$$

The numbered *formulas* (3.34–3.41) [without the limits] are *from* von Thünen (1875, 2.II, p. 45–46), Dempsey (1960, p. 340–343) ; (3.39), (3.41), are clarified in section "Natural Wages: Objective Function, Maximand".

On Table 3.5, von Thünen (1875, 2.II, p. 47), Dempsey (1960, p. 342) says (in our notation)

"This **Table** satisfies the requirements:

1. **y** [ $\mathbf{AP_L}$, (3.40), column 2] follows from the equation [(3.34)] without, as in earlier expositions, being searched for in the summation of increments [$\Delta\,AP_L$ , (3.7), column 3].
2. For $\mathbf{k = 0 : y = \gamma}$. Its follows from the equation itself. In all the previous expositions a work product [ **y** ] had to be assumed for **k = 0**, without our being able to verify its origin.
3. Rentals [ **R(k)**, (3.36) ] rises continually with capital [column 6].
4. The workers *relative share* [ $\epsilon_L$, column 9] in the product decreases, if the capital increases, although the absolute amount of the wage continues to rise [ $\mathbf{MP_L}$, column 7 ].
5. The rentals [ **V(k)**, (3.39) ] of capital producing workers reaches the **maximum** [ column 13 ], when the *wage* [ $\mathbf{MP_L}$, column 7 ] is, $\sqrt{\mathbf{c_L\,AP_L}}$, [ column 14 ], [ $k^* = 20, k^* = 19.7$ ].

So it appears, after more than *20 years* of fruitless effort, I am finally prepared to present an Eq. (3.40), and construct a schedule [Table 3.5], satisfying all known *requirements*".

We may offer a few comments on his requirements (1–5):

Ad.(1.) The availability of a succinct *power* function (3.34) is of course for many purposes much more convenient than the fundamental discrete *summation* formula (3.10).

Ad. (2.) If *admissible* at **k = 0**, using ($\gamma$) to postpone "calibration" is often convenient.

On general calibration issues, cf. Klump and de La Grandville (2000), and see CES cases below. Ad. (3.–4.) Regarding *satisfactory* production functions for *agricultural technologies* and *factor shares*, it is true—in comparison with Tables 3.3 and 3.4—that *behavior* of total rentals **R(k)**, (3.36), and factor (cost) *shares* of *Labor* for large values of (**k**)—cf. $\epsilon_L(k)$, $\epsilon_K(k)$, a=1/2—are much more *plausible* in Table 3.5. The size of the *substitution* elasticity $\sigma(k)$ does *not* eventually fall below *one*—as in Tables 3.3 and 3.4. In Table 3.5, $\sigma(k)$ is always *above* one, but it still converges to $\sigma = 1$. The latter is a *deficiency* of Table 3.5 that he noted: "The only apparent shortcoming of this *schedule* (3.40) is that the *rentals* [column 6] can *never* increase above the *wage* [column 7], [$\epsilon_K(k) < 1/2$], however large [**k**] may become", von Thünen (1875, 2.II, p. 48), Dempsey (1960, p. 343). Clearly he foresaw that the future *wage* cost *share*, $\epsilon_L(k)$, in agriculture is *less* than (1/2).

Ad. (5). For Table 3.5, the *smooth* expression for **V(k)**, (3.39), (3.41), directly gives,

$$V'(k) = -20\,(1+k)^{-\frac{3}{2}} + 100\,(2+k)^{-2}\ ; \quad c_L = 100 \tag{3.42}$$

$$V'(k) = 0: \ -(1+k)^{-\frac{3}{2}} + 5\,(2+k)^{-2} = 0 \Leftrightarrow$$
$$k^4 - 17k^3 - 51k^2 - 43k - 9 = 0 \tag{3.43}$$

The *root* of (3.43) is: $k^* = 19.70$, i.e., the *normative* (optimal) size of (**k**), cf. section "Natural Wages: Objective Function, Maximand".

Hence his "*natural wage*" with (3.40), (3.43), cf. *underlined* numbers in Table 3.5, is,

$$MP_L(k^*) = \sqrt{c_L\,AP_L(k^*)} \quad : \quad MP_L^*(19.70) = \sqrt{100 \cdot 80\,(20.70)^{\frac{1}{2}}} = 190.8 \tag{3.44}$$

No doubt it was a *relief* for him to operate in Table 3.5 with a *smooth* parametric production function and *using* (3.42–3.44) in "natural wage" calculations, compared to the *alternative* differentiation methods/calculations shown in section "Natural Wages: Objective Function, Maximand" (although being correct, too).

Thus overall *success* of (3.40) in coping with all his *five* requirements by allowing more *plausible economic* scenarios for factor productivities, relative factor prices, distribution—compared to Table 3.3 and 3.4—was the greatest *advantage* of his *new* Table 3.5—a Table, which—paradoxically, despite its clear logic, rich economic content, and numerical *evidence* behind (3.40)—was *not* seen in *any economic journal* before Jensen (2017, p. 67); this chapter.

Some *empirical estimates* of $(a, k, \gamma)$—von Thünen (1875, 2.II, p. 58,62),[9] Dempsey (1960, p. 350,352)—and our calculations by using Proposition 3.2, (3.38–3.39), then give:

Tellow: $a = 0.425$, $k = 13.8$ : $z(13.8) = 4.8\,\%$, $\epsilon_K(13.8) = 0.40$, $\sigma(13.8) = 1.41$

The *actual wage* $(w/p)$ paid at Tellow was *not* this "natural wage", **166.5**, as $c_L \neq 100$. Tellow: $\gamma = 87$, $a = 0.43$, $k = 13.8 = k^*$ : $AP_L = 277.2 = AP_L^* = AP_L^*(13.8)$;
$\sqrt{100 \cdot AP_L^*} = 166.5 = MP_L(k^*) \neq w/p$ ; $MP_K(k^*) = 8.1$; $V(k^*) = 3.2$; $s_L^* = 66.5$

## Natural Wages: Objective Function, Maximand

### *Smooth* f(k), *Normative Capital-Labor Ratio and The Wage*

Having early completed the analysis of capital-labor ratios upon marginal productivities, factor shares and factor substitution, some *normative* accumulation and wage issues arose. Observing the *columns* (3,5,8) of Tables 3.3 and 3.4 with *numbers* of: $MP_L(k)$, $MP_K(k)$, $z(k) = MP_K(k)/MP_L(k)$, as *capital* (**k**) grows, von Thünen (1990, Ch. 10, p. 500), von Thünen (1875, Ch. 10, 2.I, p. 106), Dempsey (1960, p. 259) *noted*: "With the increase of capital, the 'rate of interest' [**z**(**k**)][10] goes down relatively much more than the decline in the rental $[MP_K]$ for the reason that wages $[MP_L]$ rises at the same time".

Hence as *real-wage* earners $(MP_L)$, *"self-interest"* of the *workers* motivates them to *promote* real-capital expansion, cf. (3.24), but as being also

[9] p. 58: Nehmen wir aber nicht, k [=1/MRS=z], sondern die zahl der J.A., i.e., q [=k], zum Masstab, so ist, da für Tellow q = 13.8 gefunden ist, und für z das Maximum der Rente stattfindet, z = 4.78; He tries next in several ways to evaluate $\gamma$. He summarizes, $[a = 0.43,\ \gamma = 87)]$ p. 62: Damit ist nun die Aufgabe gelöst, die Tellowschen Erfahrungen mit der Seite 47 mitgetheilten Skala [Table 3.5, (3.40)] in Einklang zu bringen, wenn dort $(n)$ $[a]$ statt 1/2 zu 0.43, und $(h)$ $[\gamma]$ statt 80 zum 87 angenommen wird. See also—von Thünen (1990, Ch. 23, p. 603), von Thünen (1875, Ch. 23, 2.I, p. 213), Dempsey (1960, p. 329).

[10] The "interest rate" for capital good investments is usually defined as, $\mathbf{z} = \mathbf{r}/\mathbf{P_1}$, where $P_1$ is the initial money (cost) purchase price of one unit of the capital good, sector 1. Since here only labor $(L_1)$ is used (*technology*) for the *"agricultural capital good"*, $Y_1 = F_1(L_1, 0) = L_1$, the money purchase price $P_1$ of a *capital good* (measured in J.A) is the money wage rate, i.e., here a *specific two-sector* model with:

$$P_1 = w; \quad z = r/P_1 = r/w\,; \quad r = P_2\, MP_{K_2} = p\, MP_K\,;$$

$$w = P_2\, MP_{L_2} = p\, MP_L = P_1\, MP_{L_1} = w \cdot 1$$

which Dorfman (1986, p. 1774) *identified*. Tables 3.3 and 3.4 refer to the *consumer good* (rye)—sector 2—in which both factors $(L_2, K_2)$ are used. Column 8 shows these "rates of interest" $z(k)$; $z(1) = 40/110 = 36.4$

On *general two-sector* models, Uzawa (1961), and solutions, extensions, see Jensen (2003); here Chap. 17, Jensen and Richter (2007); here Chap. 26, Jensen (2009).

an "*investor*" of a part ($\mathbf{s_L}$) of their real-wages, the "interest" series of ($\mathbf{z}$) strengthens a conjecture that real capital accumulation by investments of the worker's *own savings* should *not* go too far—and there may exist a *optimal* (normative) *level* ("natural state") of the capital variable ($k$). So von Thünen wanted with a proper *objective* function $\mathbf{V(k)}$ to *compute* a **normative** capital-labor *ratio*, ($\mathbf{k^*}$), and the associated normative (*natural*) real *wage*: $\mathbf{MP_L(k^*)}$.

Decompose wages into a *fixed* level of *consumption* ($c_L$) and saving ($s_L$), cf. (3.21–3.23),

$$(i)\ MP_L = c_L + s_L = w/p \quad (ii)\ \ p\,(c_L + s_L) = w = p\,AP_L - r\,k,\ \ pY = w\,L + r\,K \tag{3.45}$$

where (i)–(ii) are two forms of the *budget constraint* (rye, money) for consumption/savings.

Below alternative "*core relationships*" with "interest rate" ($\mathbf{z}$) are used,

$$z = \frac{r}{w} = \frac{r/p}{w/p} = \frac{MP_K}{MP_L} = \frac{AP_L - MP_L}{k\,MP_L}; \quad MP_L = \frac{AP_L}{1 + zk}, \quad MP_K = \frac{z\,AP_L}{1 + zk} \tag{3.46}$$

For ($z$) it makes no difference, whether the capital good is measured in (J.A.) or in money.

The *objective* function was the *Rentals* $V(k)$ (in rye) on worker's *real saving*, $s_L$, (saving rate, $s_W = s_L/MP_L$). By "interest rate" ($z$), Note 9, Rentals $V(k)$ are, cf. (3.45–3.46),

$$V(k) = z(k)\,s_L(k) = MP_K\,s_W = \frac{MP_K(MP_L - c_L)}{MP_L} = MP_K - c_L\frac{MP_K}{MP_L} \tag{3.47}$$

To maximize $V(k)$, the derivative $V'(k)$ is needed, and we obtain from, (3.13), (3.47),

$$\begin{aligned} V'(k) &= MP'_K - c_L\frac{MP_L MP'_K - MP_K MP'_L}{MP_L^2} \\ &= MP'_K\left[1 - c_L\frac{MP_L + MP_K\,k}{MP_L^2}\right] \\ &= MP'_K\left[1 - c_L\frac{AP_L}{MP_L^2}\right] = MP'_K\left[\frac{MP_L^2 - c_L\,AP_L}{MP_L^2}\right] \end{aligned}$$

Hence the *normative* value of the capital-labor *ratio* is a *root* of the equation above:

$$V'(k) = 0 : \; MP_L^2(k) - c_L \, AP_L(k) = 0 \;\Leftrightarrow\; [\, f(k) \; - \; f'(k)\, k\,]^2 - c_L \, f(k) = 0 \tag{3.48}$$

It follows from (3.48) that the "*Natural wage*"—$MP_L^*$ at normative $k^*$—satisfies the equality:

$$\exists k = k^* > 0 \; : \quad MP_L(k^*) = \sqrt{c_L \, AP_L(k^*)} \quad ; \qquad A \; = \; \sqrt{a\,p}\,, \;\; a = c_L \tag{3.49}$$

First, note that the succinct *square root* formulas (3.49) *need* general variables, $AP_L$ [ $p$ ] and $MP_L$ [$A$], and (3.49) *hold* for *any* parametric form of **f(k)**. Secondly, if we do not have an "exact law", $AP_L(k) = f(k)$, we cannot compute the *size* of "natural wage", $MP_L^*$, (3.49), cf. Note 3. In Table 3.5, he had $f(k)$ as (3.40), and it is "simple" to solve (3.48), which was already[11] done in (3.43–3.44) for the relevant root, $k^* > 0$ (ignoring negative $k^*$ values).

With Proposition 3.1, these *normative* ("natural wage") *calculations* can also be done for Tables 3.3 and 3.4. Thus $V(k)$, (3.47)—with $f(k)$, $f'(k)$ as in (3.19–3.20), and $c_L = 100$—is:

$$V(k) \;\; = \;\; 44.44 \cdot e^{-0.10536k} \left[ 1 - \frac{100}{529.65 - e^{-0.10536k}\,(421.83 - 44.44\,k\,)} \right] \tag{3.50}$$

For Table 3.4, $V(k)$ is (3.50) with (44.44, 529.65, 421.83) replaced by (33.33, 397.24, 316.38).

For (3.50), the *root* ($k^*$) of (3.48) is: $k^* = \mathbf{7.20}$. In Table 3.3, "The *maximum* value of $V(k)$ [ 8.79 ] is attained at $k^* =$ **8 J.A.** The rate of interest ($z^*$) is 10.4 per cent at this maximum point, where the wage ($MP_L^*$) amounts to **184.5**", von Thünen (1990, Ch. 11, p. 508), von Thünen (1875, Ch. 11, 2.I, p. 114), Dempsey (1960, p. 264), i.e., very close to the exhibited size of *natural wage* (**183.9**), (underlined column 14). Note that "*natural*" *wage* formula, (3.49) *only coincides* with a *marginal* productivity wage [here 184.5] at *level* (**k***). Column 14 was *not* shown with Tables 3.3 and 3.4—a neglect causing confusion.

For Table 3.4, we get—using Corollary 3.1 with $f(k)$, $f'(k)$, (3.19–3.20), and $c_L = 100$, the *root* ($k^*$) of (3.48) is: $\mathbf{k^*} = \mathbf{9.85}$. In *discrete* terms, Table 3.4

[11] Dorfman (1986), Samuelson (1983), Samuelson (1986) did not notice, $f(k)$, $V(k)$, (3.40–3.41), Proposition 3.2, and the related discussion of solutions of the equations (3.42–3.44), Table 3.5,—despite both using the Dempsey (1960) translation. Dorfman (1986, p. 1775) gave (3.48) in another form, as did (van Suntum 1988, p. 403). Samuelson (1986, p. 1780) essentially only (with B=1) restates (3.47) and (3.48–3.49) in "bad" notation.

gives maximum of $V(k)$: $k^* = 10$ J.A (underlined row). Hence to maintain $c_L = 100$, a higher $k^*$ is required in Table 3.4.

Thus, *summing up* and comparing the *implications* of this lower TFP *parameter* ($A = 0.8$) in Table 3.4, von Thünen (1990, Ch. 12, p. 516), von Thünen (1875, Ch. 12, 2.I, p. 123), Dempsey (1960, p. 270) writes: "At the *maximum* [ of $V(k)$] the wage in Table 3.3 is 184.5, in Table 3.4 it is 161.3; and the rate of interest in Table 3.3 is 10.4 per cent, and 7.3 per cent in Table 3.4. The *decrease* in the *fertility* of the soil therefore *implies* the following:

1. To reach the *maximum* [ of $V(k)$, (3.50)], a greater capital investment [$k^*$] is necessary
2. That [*natural* ] wages [ $MP_L(k^*)$ ] fall, as well as the interest [$z^*$], though the latter falls in much greater proportion than the former".

### *von Thünen's Natural Wage Calculations Without* f(k)

Lacking before Table 3.5 (1848) a smooth **f(k)**, von Thünen did neither get roots $k^*$ nor his natural wage formula (3.49) from (3.48). But he could see in the Tables 3.3 and 3.4, that **V(k)** had a *maximum*. Hence there are *sizes* for some *other variables* giving this *maximum* to, $V = z s_L$, (3.47). First, von Thünen eliminates the variable ($z$) in $V$ with (3.45–3.46):

$$V = z s_L = \frac{MP_K \, s_L}{MP_L} = \frac{(AP_L - MP_L)\, s_L}{k \, MP_L} = \frac{[\, AP_L - (c_L + s_L)\,]\, s_L}{k\,(c_L + s_L)} = V(s_L) \tag{3.51}$$

Treating $k, AP_L, c_L$, as *constants*,[12] variable[13] *savings* ($s_L$) maximizing[14] $V$ (3.51) imply,

$$\frac{d\,V(s_L)}{d\,s_L} = \frac{k\,(c_L + s_L)[\,AP_L - (c_L + s_L) - s_L\,] - [\,AP_L - (c_L + s_L)\,]\, s_L\, k}{[\,k\,(c_L + s_L)\,]^2} = \frac{k\,[\,c_L\, AP_L - (c_L + s_L)^2\,]}{[\,k\,(c_L + s_L)\,]^2} = \frac{c_L\, AP_L - MP_L^2}{k\, MP_L^2} \tag{3.52}$$

[12] He certainly knows, cf. Note 3, that when (k) is here being a constant, so is $AP_L$ in (3.51–3.52).

[13] In diesem für die Grösse der Rente gefundenen Ausdruck [$V(s_L)$] ist ($z$) nicht vorhanden und ($y$) [ Überschuss, surplus, saving/investment, $s_L$, (3.45 ii) ] die einzige noch unbestimmte Grösse. von Thünen (1990, Ch. 15, p. 545), von Thünen (1875, Ch. 15, 2.I, p. 154), Dempsey (1960, p. 291).

[14] On (3.53), he says: "Diesen, nicht aus dem Verhältnis zwischen Angebot und Nachfrage entspringenden, nicht nach dem Bedürfnisdes des Arbeiters abgemessenen, sondern aus der freien Selbstbestimmung der Arbeiter hervorgehenden Lohn $\sqrt{a\,p}$ nenne ich den naturgemässen oder den natürlichen Arbeitslohn". von Thünen (1990, Ch. 15, p. 549), von Thünen (1875, Ch. 15, 2.I, p. 157), Dempsey (1960, p. 292); Hall (1966, p. 251).

$$d\,V(s_L)/d\,s_L \;=\; 0\;:\; s_L^* = \sqrt{c_L\,AP_L} - c_L \quad ;\; MP_L(s_L^*) \;=\; \sqrt{c_L\,AP_L(s_L^*)} \tag{3.53}$$

The steps of reductions from (3.52) to (3.53) are obvious, using again (3.45). The *root* of (3.52) is, $s_L^* = \sqrt{c_L\,AP_L} - c_L$. Thus, from Table 3.3, $s_L^* = \sqrt{100 \cdot 338.1} - 100 = 183.9 - 100 = 83.9$, which is close to, $s_L(k) = 84.5$, with its "discrete" *maximum* of $V(k)$ and its "*natural wage*" (183.9).

Similarly for Table 3.4, $s_L^* = \sqrt{100 \cdot 278.3} - 100 = 166.8 - 100 = 66.8$, and $s_L(k) = 61.3$. Table 3.5, $s_L^* = \sqrt{100 \cdot 366.6} - 100 = 191.5 - 100 = 91.5$, and $s_L(k) = 92.0$.

This *natural wage* formula (3.53) was checked by *three* variable expressions, *equivalent* to the *variation* of $s_L$. Rewriting (3.51), as $V(z)$,[15] $V(\alpha_K)$,[16] $\alpha_K = r/p$, or $V(\alpha_L)$,[17] $\alpha_L = w/p$, cf. (3.45–3.46), we get

$$V = z\,s_L \;=\; z\left[\frac{AP_L}{1 + z\,k} \;-\; c_L\right] \;=\; V(z)$$

$$\frac{d\,V(z)}{d\,z} \;=\; \frac{AP_L}{(1 + z\,k)^2} - c_L\,, \quad z^* \;=\; \frac{(AP_L/c_L)^{\frac{1}{2}} - 1}{k}\quad ; \quad MP_L(z^*) \;=\; \sqrt{c_L\,AP_L^*} \tag{3.54}$$

$$\begin{aligned} V = z\,s_L = \left[\frac{r/p}{w/p}\right] s_L &= \frac{\frac{r}{p}\,(AP_L - \frac{r}{p}\,k - c_L)}{AP_L - \frac{r}{p}\,k} \\ &= \frac{\alpha_K\,(AP_L - \alpha_K\,k - c_L\,)}{AP_L - \alpha_K\,k} \;=\; V(\alpha_K) \end{aligned}$$

$$\begin{aligned} &\frac{d\,V(\alpha_K)}{d\,\alpha_K} = \frac{(AP_L - \alpha_K\,k)^2 - c_L AP_L}{(AP_L - \alpha_K\,k)^2},\; \alpha_K^* = \frac{AP_L - (c_L AP_L)^{\frac{1}{2}}}{k}\,; \\ &MP_L^* = (c_L AP_L^*)^{\frac{1}{2}} \end{aligned} \tag{3.55}$$

[15] von Thünen (1990, Ch. 16, p. 551), von Thünen (1875, Ch. 16, 2.I, p. 159), Dempsey (1960, p. 294).

[16] zur vollständigen Lösung gehören die Kenntnis der Gleichung zwischen $q$, $p$, und $\alpha$. In Ermanglung dieser Kenntnis können wir indessen der Lösung näher kommen, wenn wir $\alpha$ als variabel, $p$ und $q$ aber als konstant betrachten, und durch den Kalkül erforschen, in welchen Verhältnis $\alpha$ zu $q$ und $p$ stehen muss, wen die Arbeitsrente die Höchste sein soll. Bei welchem Wert von ($\alpha$) erreicht nun die Arbeitsrente [$V(\alpha_K)$], das Maximum?—von Thünen (1990, Ch. 18, p. 561), von Thünen (1875, Ch. 18, 2.I, p. 169), Dempsey (1960, p. 301).

[17] Der Arbeitslohn $\sqrt{a\,p}$ erfüllt also die Bedingung, die Rente [$V^* = z\,s_L$] mit dem Minimum von Arbeitskräften zu erzeugen—von Thünen (1990, Ch. 20, p. 593), von Thünen (1875, Ch. 20, 2.I, p. 203), Dempsey (1960, p. 322).

$$V = z s_L = \frac{(AP_L - w/p)(w/p - c_L)}{k\ (w/p)} = \frac{(AP_L - \alpha_L)(\alpha_L - c_L)}{k\,\alpha_L} = V(\alpha_L)$$

$$\frac{d\,V(\alpha_L)}{d\,\alpha_L} = \frac{c_L\,AP_L - \alpha_L^2}{(k\,\alpha_L)^2}, \quad \alpha_L^* = (c_L AP_L)^{\frac{1}{2}}; \quad MP_L^* = \sqrt{c_L AP_L^*} \tag{3.56}$$

The steps of reductions in (3.54), (3.55), (3.56), are analogous to those from (3.52) to (3.53).

The *root* of (3.54) is, $z^* = [(338.1/100)^{\frac{1}{2}} - 1]/8 = 0.1048$, cf. Table 3.3, $z(k) = 0.104$ for discrete *maximum* of $V(k)$. For Table 3.4, $z^* = [(278.3/100)^{\frac{1}{2}} - 1]/10 = 0.0668$, cf. $z(k) = 0.073$. In Table 3.5, $z^* = [(366.6/100)^{\frac{1}{2}} - 1]/20 = 0.0457$, cf. $z(k) = 0.045$.

At these "*interest numbers*", $z^* = r/P_1$, cf. Note 9, the yield $V(z)$ on *capital good investments* of the *workers* are maximized, together with $MP_L(z^*) = \sqrt{c_L\,AP_L^*}$.

The related (optimal) *normative* ($k^*$) was formally calculated by linking (3.54) with ($z$) formula (3.46), von Thünen (1990, Ch. 18, p. 559), von Thünen (1875, Ch. 18, 2.I, p. 168), Dempsey (1960, p. 300):

$$z = z^* \ : z = \frac{AP_L - \sqrt{c_L\,AP_L}}{k\,\sqrt{c_L\,AP_L}} = \frac{\sqrt{c_L\,AP_L} - c_L}{k\,c_L} \Leftrightarrow k^* = \frac{\sqrt{c_L\,AP_L} - c_L}{z^*\,c_L} \tag{3.57}$$

The size (3.57) is: $k^* = 83.88/(0.1048 \cdot 100) = 8.00$, cf. $k = 8$, Table 3.3. Thus he knew that differential procedures (3.53), (3.54), (3.57) gave same results as (3.48) with explicit $f(k)$.

Next, having obtained the normative "*interest rate*" $z^* = r/P_1$, we also know that, $z^* = r/w = 1/MRS(k) = MP_L(k)/MP_K(k)$, cf. (3.46). Hence as reciprocals, we have, $(1/z)^* = (w/r)^* = MRS(k^*)$[18] *numbers*: 9.61, 13.78, 21.9, see Tables 3.3, 3.4 and 3.5 (underlined rows). Therefore we have also solved $MRS(k^*)$ with *optimal* capital-labor substitution.

Thus for, $(1/z)^* = (w/r)^* = MRS(k^*)$, with maximum of $V(z)$ and ($MP_L$) wages equal to the "natural" wages, we have also *overall* efficient sector allocations of *labor* ($L$), and *within sector 2* optimal *substitution* of capital (K) and labor (L) at that ratio, $k = k^*$.

If $k < k^*$, some workers should be transferred from the rye fields to capital formation ("drainage, "digging canals") to improve the labor productivity of the rye field workers. Loss of rye output from departing capital producing workers is more than compensated by increased productivity and outputs of workers in the rye fields. If $k > k^*$, there should be labor adjustments with

[18] Die Frage ist, wie gross $k = 1/z$ sein muss, wenn die Ersetzung der menschlichen Arbeit durch das Kapital weder Vorteil noch Nachteil bringen soll—von Thünen (1990, Ch. 17, p. 555), von Thünen (1875, Ch. 17, 2.I, p. 163), Dempsey (1960, p. 297).

some workers leaving the *existing* estate to build up a *new* one to get maximum rentals on workers saving with its "natural wage rate" at, $k = k^*$.

The *root* of (3.55) is, $(r/p)^* = \alpha_K^* = [338.1 - (338.1/100)^{\frac{1}{2}}]/8 = 19.28$, cf. $MP_K^* = 19.2$, Table 3.3, for discrete maximum of $V(k) = 8.81$. For Table 3.4, we have, $(r/p)^* = \alpha_K^* = [278.3 - (278.3/100)^{\frac{1}{2}}]/10 = 11.25$, cf. $MP_K^* = 11.7, V(k) = 4.45$. Hence at *maximum* of $V(\alpha_K)$: $(r/p)^* = MP_K^*$—so the *rental rate condition*, (3.5), holds for minimizing the production *costs*. For Table 3.3, we see from[19] (3.55), $k^* = \frac{AP_L-(c_L AP_L)^{\frac{1}{2}}}{\alpha_K^*} = [338.1 - (338.1/100)^{\frac{1}{2}}]/19.28 = 8$—same ratio, $k^* = 8$, as with (3.57). The different ways of calculating the *normative* ($k^*$) and other variables are in harmony.

The *root* of (3.56) is, $\alpha_L^* = (w/p)^* = (100 \cdot 338.1)^{\frac{1}{2}} = 183.87$, cf. $MP_L^* = 184.4, V(k) = 8.79$, Table 3.3. Table 3.4, $\alpha_L^* = (w/p)^* = (100 \cdot 278.3)^{\frac{1}{2}} = 166.8$, cf. $MP_L^* = 161.3, V(k) = 4.45$. Thus for "natural wage", $(w/p)^* = \sqrt{c_L AP_L^*}$, we have: $(w/p)^* = MP_L(k^*)$. Hence we have shown that maximizing rentals $V = z s_L$ (3.56) wrt. (variable) wages, $(w/p)$—that satisfy budget constraint (3.45,ii) with *fixed*, $c_L$—gives "natural wage" $\sqrt{c_L AP_L^*}$, as also the wage rate: $(w/p)^* = MP_L^*$, (3.4)—the factor price for *labor input* ($L$) of minimal costs. As mentioned in Note 17, von Thünen concluded: It is in their *"own interest"* as workers that their wages are also determined by the $MP_L$ *factor price principle*, (3.4), as it is for their *cost minimizing* employer, (3.45), and here he placed Table 3.2 above as an illustration in Chap. 19, discussing both factor prices of labor $(w/p)$ and "natural wage".

von Thünen did *not* formally differentiate V wrt. $\alpha_L = w/p$ as in (3.56)—but *cheked* his normative $MP_L^*$ as: $s_L = MP_L^* - c_L = \sqrt{c_L AP_L} - c_L = c_L[(AP_L/c_L)^{\frac{1}{2}} - 1] = c_L z^* k = s_L^*$, and these equalities were satisfied by his earlier *expressions* for $s_L^*$, $z^*$, in (3.53), (3.54).

From Table 3.4, (using for $k$= 6–12, columns 2,3,5,12,14), von Thünen illustrated *convergence*[20] of wage rates to the *normative* rate, implied by a

---

[19] Erst dann, wenn $\sqrt{ap} = p - \alpha q$ , d.i, wenn $q = (p - \sqrt{ap})/\alpha$ $[q^*]$ geworden, findet das *unbedingte* Maximum statt.

Es liegt also im Interesse der Arbeiter, q genau diese Grösse zu geben, bei welcher dessen Wert $(p - \sqrt{ap})/\alpha$ ist, mithin ist diese Wert von q Bestimmungsgrund für die höhe des relativen Kapitals— von Thünen (1990, Ch. 18, p. 568), von Thünen (1875, Ch. 18, 2.I, p. 177), Dempsey (1960, p. 306).

[20] Follow-up on Note 18—von Thünen (1990, Ch. 18, p. 561), von Thünen (1875, Ch. 18, 2.I, p. 170), Dempsey (1960, p. 302):

Beim Maximum der Arbeitsrente ist also gleichzeitig der Arbeitslohn = $p - \alpha q$ und auch gleich $\sqrt{ap}$. Wie abweichend auch der Arbeitslohn = $p - \alpha q$ von dem $\sqrt{ap}$ bei verschidenen Werten von $(q)$ sein mag, so fallen sie doch zusammen, wenn $(q)$ die Höhe $[q^*]$ erlangt, bei welchem die Arbeitsrente das maximum erreicht. Beispiel in Zahlen auf Grundlage der Tabelle B.—cf. Tables 3.1 and 3.2 in Helmstädter (1995, p. 77–78).

As mentioned by van Suntum (1988, p. 396), this "Beispiel" table would have benefited from including the $\alpha_K$ column, and explaining that numbers, $\alpha_K = r/p$ (equal to $MP_K(k)$, Table 3.4) comes here from meeting budget restriction (3.45 ii) on the investments of worker's saving. The

maximum return on real savings ($s_L$): $V = zs_L$. Mathematical and economic issues involved in his "convergence" are important for the rationale and quantitative results of ***natural wage*** formulas, (3.53–3.56).

First, in Tables 3.3, 3.4 and 3.5, clearly the same values of $V(\cdot)$ are obtained by (3.45), (3.47), (3.53–3.56)

$$V(k) = V(s_L) = V(z[s_L]) = V(\alpha_K [s_L]) = V(\alpha_L [s_L]) \tag{3.58}$$

These numbers are given in our ***column*** 12—on $V(\alpha_K [s_L]) = V(\alpha_L [s_L])$, see Note 19.

Budget constraint, $w/p = AP_L - (r/p)\,k = c_L + s_L$, (3.45, ii), holds in (3.58). Restate (3.56):

$$V = zs_L = \frac{AP_L - w/p}{k}\left[1 - \frac{c_L}{w/p}\right] = V(w/p) = V(\alpha_L) = V(\alpha_L [s_L]) \tag{3.59}$$

Inseting $w/p = \sqrt{c_L AP_L(k)}$ into (3.58), the rentals on worker's real saving, ($s_L$) become

$$\begin{aligned}\widetilde{V} &= \frac{AP_L - \sqrt{c_L AP_L}}{k}\left[1 - \frac{c_L}{\sqrt{c_L AP_L}}\right] \\ &= \frac{1}{k}\,[AP_L - 2\sqrt{c_L AP_L} + c_L] = \widetilde{V}(\sqrt{c_L AP_L})\end{aligned} \tag{3.60}$$

Budget constraint (3.45, ii) also holds in (3.60), but neither $w/p$ nor $r/p$ are marginal productivity numbers, i.e (3.45, i) is violated in (3.60), whereas (3.45, i) is satisfied in (3.58–3.59).

For Table 3.4, $k$=6–12, the ***numbers*** $\widetilde{V}$ by (3.60) are: 4.07, 4.27, 4.38, 4.45, 4.47, 4.45, 4.41.

As another column to Table 3.4, the maximum 4.47 confirms (3.59–3.60) coinciding at, $k^* = 10$.

On "Natural Wage" calculations, Samuelson (1986, p. 1784) ends with a "*Moral*: Thünen should have trusted his ***arithmetical*** searching for his maximum point, as in his Tables of Chaps. 11–12. His temptation to use the fancy differentiation formulas of his elementary calculus was what did him in. Half-baked mathematics can be worse than none".

But the differentiation of the objective function in (3.56)—"critique of Schumpeter's version"—and von Thünen's own ***natural wage differentiation*** formulas, (3.53–3.55), are ***bona fide*** (mathematical correct) ***alternatives*** for deriving his natural wage ***form***: $\mathbf{MP}^*_{\mathbf{L}} = \sqrt{\mathbf{c_L AP}^*_{\mathbf{L}}}$.

last "small unit" ($dK$) of capital ("Kapitalteilchen") invested is always assumed to have the factor price, ($r/p$), (3.5).

As illustrations from Tables 3.3 and 3.4 showed, they are equivalent calculation procedures (3.58) and providing the *normative* solutions of $s_L^*$, $(r/p)^*$, $(w/p)^*$. Moreover, columns of Tables 3.3 and 3.4 were clearly *not* arbitrary numbers (*data*)—but *coherent marginal productivities* originating from a parametric *production function* $\mathbf{f}(\mathbf{k})$, Proposition 3.1—lack of which caused some mayhem in the literature, including Samuelson (1983), Samuelson (1986), Leigh (1946).

Beyond the *normative* explicit *calculations*, (3.42–3.44), (3.48–3.49) in Table 3.5, we offer von Thünen's *synopsis*[21] (our symbols) of *natural wage* calculations (3.53–3.56) for Tables 3.3 and 3.4,:

"We have determined the relationship between *wages* and *interest rates* by **four different** methods: (1) *Capital creation* by labor [ capital accumulation by labor savings, $s_L^*$; interest rate as, $z^* = r/P_1 = r/w$ ], Chaps. 15–16; (2) *Capital substitution* for labor [ interest rate as, $z^* = r/w = 1/MRS = MP_K/MP_L$ ], Chap. 17; (3) *Factor price*, rental rate, of *capital* [ rental rate as marginal product of capital, $(\boldsymbol{r}/\boldsymbol{p})^* = MP_K$ ], Chap. 18; (4) *Factor price* of *labor* [ wage rate as marginal product of labor, $(\boldsymbol{w}/\boldsymbol{p})^* = MP_L$ ], Chaps. 19–20.

As all these investigations came down to the *wage rate*: $(\boldsymbol{w}/\boldsymbol{p})^* = MP_L^* = \sqrt{c_L AP_L^*}$, I may be permitted to state the **Proposition**, the *Natural Wage* is: $\sqrt{c_L AP_L^*}$".

## CES Forms and Marginal Productivity Wages

The production functions in von Thünen's Tables 3.3, 3.4 and 3.5 implied a variable substitution elasticity, **VES**, $\sigma(k)$. Let us now consider the *isoelastic*, $\sigma(k) = \sigma$, **CES** form.

[21] Frage: Welches die Schranke für die Vermehrung des Kapitals bildet - können wir dahin beantworden.

Wir haben jezt das Verhältnis zwischen Arbeitslohn und Zinsfuss nach vier verschiedenen Methoden und Gesichtspunkten zu bestimmen gesucht; wir haben nämlich:

1. die Kapitalerzeugung durch Arbeit untersucht; dann
2. das Kapital als Arbeit ersetzend betrachtet; ferner
3. den Zinsfuss durch die Nutzung des zulezt angelegten Kapitalteilchens bestimmt; und endlich
4. das Mehrerzeugnis durch den zulezt angestellten Arbeiter als Mass für den Arbeitslohn angenommen.

Da nun aus allen diesen Untersuchungen der Arbeitslohn = $\sqrt{a\,p}$ siegreich hervorgegangen ist: so glaube ich - wenn man den, der Organisation des Menschen und der physischen Welt entsprechenden

Lohn, den naturgemässen nennt - jezt den Satz aufstellen zu dürfen:

*der naturgemässe Arbeitslohn* ist: $\sqrt{a\,p}$.

von Thünen (1990, Ch. 21, p. 596), von Thünen (1875, Ch. 21, 2.I, p. 206), Dempsey (1960, p. 324).

The **CES** expressions of $F(L, K)$ and $f(k)$, are given by, Arrow et al. (1961, p. 230):

$$Y = F(L, K) = \gamma \left[(1-a)L^{\frac{\sigma-1}{\sigma}} + aK^{\frac{\sigma-1}{\sigma}}\right]^{\frac{\sigma}{\sigma-1}} ;$$
$$F(1,1) = \gamma;\ 0 < a < 1,\ 0 < \sigma < \infty$$

$$AP_L(k) = y = f(k) = \gamma \left[1 - a + ak^{\frac{\sigma-1}{\sigma}}\right]^{\frac{\sigma}{\sigma-1}} ;$$
$$f(1) = \gamma = AP_L(1);\ f'(1) = a\gamma \tag{3.61}$$

$$MP_K(k) = f'(k) = a\gamma \left[1 - a + ak^{\frac{\sigma-1}{\sigma}}\right]^{\frac{1}{\sigma-1}} k^{\frac{-1}{\sigma}} = a\gamma \left[a + (1-a)k^{\frac{1-\sigma}{\sigma}}\right]^{\frac{1}{\sigma-1}} \tag{3.62}$$

Hence by (3.61–3.62), (3.32), we get with **CES**:

$$E\left(MP_K(k), k\right) = -\frac{1}{\sigma} \frac{1-a}{1-a+ak^{\frac{\sigma-1}{\sigma}}} = -\frac{\epsilon_L(k)}{\sigma}$$

Generally $MP_L(k)$ and $AP_L(k)$ is related to $\sigma(k)$ by core expressions (3.3), (3.32)—that as a second- differential equation was the basis for deriving, (3.61), Arrow et al. (1961, p. 229),

$$E\left(MP_L, AP_L\right) = 1/\sigma(k) = E\left(MP_K, AP_K\right) \tag{3.63}$$

Hence we see from (3.63), that any production function $\mathbf{f(k)}$ with a *constant* elasticity of substitution—$\sigma(k) = \sigma$, for ***all*** $\mathbf{k}$—must for $AP_L(k)$ allow for: The reduction of $\mathbf{MP_L(k)}$, (3.12), to a unique *proportionality* ($\beta$) relationship with $[\mathbf{AP_L(k)}]^{1/\sigma}$, i.e.

$$MP_L(k) = AP_L(k) - MP_K(k)k = \beta\, [AP_L(k)]^{1/\sigma} ;\ MP_L(1) = \gamma(1-a) \tag{3.64}$$

For several purposes, we need to calculate $\beta$ exactly ; by (3.61–3.62), and (3.64), we get:

$$\begin{aligned} MP_L &= \gamma \left[1 - a + ak^{(\sigma-1)/\sigma}\right]^{\sigma/(\sigma-1)} - a\gamma \left[1 - a + ak^{(\sigma-1)/\sigma}\right]^{1/(\sigma-1)} k^{(\sigma-1)/\sigma} \\ &= \gamma(1-a)\left[1 - a + ak^{(\sigma-1)/\sigma}\right]^{1/(\sigma-1)} = \gamma(1-a)\left[(1/\gamma)AP_L(k)\right]^{1/\sigma} \\ &= \gamma^{(\sigma-1)/\sigma}(1-a)\left[AP_L(k)\right]^{1/\sigma} = \beta\, [AP_L(k)]^{1/\sigma} ; \\ \beta &= \gamma^{\frac{\sigma-1}{\sigma}}(1-a) \end{aligned} \tag{3.65}$$

### *von Thünen's Geometric Mean Formula and CES: $\sigma = 2$*

Implications and clues for the actual size of $\sigma$ can be obtained from evaluating $f(k)$ at the lower limit value of the capital-labor ratio. We have from (3.61),

$$\sigma = 1 : f(0) = 0; \qquad \sigma < 1 : \lim_{k\to 0} f(k) = 0$$

In all his Tables 3.3, 3.4 and 3.5, von Thünen had, $\mathbf{f(0)} = \mathbf{AP_L(0)}$, *positive*, as some output in *agriculture* can be produced by labor *without* capital, i.e. capital is *not* an *essential* input. Accordingly, constant substitution elasticities, $\sigma \le 1$, are inadmissible for him.

Such calibration with, $f(0) = F(1, 0)$, for $\sigma > 1$ in (3.61), (3.64), gives:

$$\begin{aligned}\sigma > 1 :\ 0 < f(0) &= \gamma(1-a)^{\frac{\sigma}{\sigma-1}} = AP_L(0)\\ &= MP_L(0) \Leftrightarrow \gamma = (1-a)^{\frac{\sigma}{1-\sigma}}\, MP_L(0)\end{aligned}$$

Next, the *proportionality* factor $\beta$, (3.65), can be restated in the initial values of $\mathbf{MP_L(0)}$:

$$\sigma > 1 :\ \beta = \gamma^{\frac{\sigma-1}{\sigma}}(1-a) = [\,(1-a)^{\frac{\sigma}{1-\sigma}}\, MP_L(0)\,]^{\frac{\sigma-1}{\sigma}}\,(1-a) = [MP_L(0)\,]^{\frac{\sigma-1}{\sigma}} \tag{3.66}$$

The first integer value above $\sigma > 1$ is $\sigma = 2$, and we show the implications for $\mathbf{MP_L(k)}$.

**Proposition 3.3** *With* **CES**: $\sigma = 2$, *the general* $\mathbf{MP_L(k)}$ *formula becomes by (3.65–3.66),*

$$\begin{aligned}\forall k \ge 0 \quad \sigma = 2 :\ MP_L(k) &= \beta\,[AP_L(k)]^{1/\sigma} = [MP_L(0)]^{1/2}\,[AP_L(k)]^{1/2}\\ &= \sqrt{MP_L(0)\,AP_L(k)} = \sqrt{y_o\,y}\end{aligned} \tag{3.67}$$

**CES** *formula (3.67) for* $\mathbf{MP_L(k)}$ *is congruent to von Thünen's Geometric Mean formula—with the status as a positive (descriptive) marginal productivity wage rate, (3.12):*

$$\forall k \ge 0 \quad \sigma = 2 : \qquad A = \sqrt{a\,p} \tag{3.68}$$

**A**: *Wage rate (output [rye] as numéraire)—"Arbeitslohn": $w/p = MP_L(k)$, (3.4), (3.12),*
**p**: *Labor productivity—"Arbeitsprodukt": $y = AP_L(k)$, (3.10),*
**a**: *Limit wage—"Arbeitslohn ohne Kapital": $(w/p)_o = MP_L(0) = AP_L(0) = y_o$, (3.8), Labor productivity without capital, "Arbeitsprodukt eines Mannes ohne Kapital", $AP_L(0)$*

The beautifully simple formula (3.68) is engraved on a marble scroll of the gravestone for—der Gutsbesitzer Dr. Johann Heinrich v. Thünen auf Tellow, 24 Juni 1783–22 Sept.1850—in the churchyard of Belitz, Mecklenburg; see picture in Helmstädter (1995, p. 45).

His *square root formula* is now provided with a rigorous economic-mathematical foundation as a *marginal productivity wage* for ***any*** $(K/L)$ with the **CES** *parameter* value, $\boldsymbol{\sigma} = 2$, and the formulas (3.67–3.68) show correctly, how *more capital* affects labor productivities and always increase wages, as he had numerically demonstrated (3.24) in column 3, Tables 3.3 and 3.4. Indeed, the *wage rate*, $\mathbf{MP_L(k)}$, as here the *geometric mean*, (3.67–3.68), of $MP_L(0)$ and $AP_L(k)$ is always *above* $MP_L(0)$ and *below* $AP_L(k)$, (for any $k$).

**CES** *formula* (3.67) for $\boldsymbol{MP_L(k)}$ may be checked by $\boldsymbol{MP_L}(1)$, cf. (3.61–3.62), (3.64),

$$\sigma = 2: \quad MP_L(1) = \sqrt{MP_L(0)\,AP_L(1)} = \sqrt{\gamma(1-a)^2\gamma} \;=\; \gamma(1-a)$$

The tomb-stone *formula* (3.67–3.68) may *commemorate* von Thünen's fundamental **marginal productivity** (" *Wirksamkeit*") statements about *capital* and *labor*—that were expressed in the **Eqs. (3.9–3.14)** about the *partial derivatives* (discrete and continuous) of the two-factor *production function*, $\boldsymbol{Y = F(L, K)}$.

**CES** functions (3.61) may be seen as parametric *extensions* of the (3.19), (3.40), production functions. These generalization are performed by more relevant elasticity[22] properties (3.63–3.64) of the marginal productivity functions of $L$ and $K$; von Thünen's serendipity is vindicated with the *calibrated* **CES** formulas, (3.67–3.68). With *larger* values of $\boldsymbol{\sigma}$, the marginal productivities decline *less* rapidly with their *own* factor and increase *stronger* with the *other* factor. Thus $\boldsymbol{\sigma}$ is technologically also a *symmetric **total** productivity* parameter, (3.32). The economic approach of deriving **f(k)**, (3.61), was similar to that of **f(k)**, (3.32–3.33), Proposition 3.1.

[22] In Tables 3.3 and 3.4, the "exponential decay" of $\mathbf{MP_K(k)}$, (3.20), is evidently declining too fast. The elasticity $E(f'(k), k)$, (3.20), is decreasing linearly to minus infinity, implying that its reciprocal goes to zero (completely inelastic factor demand), which then gives $\sigma(k)$, (3.33), converging to zero, (Leontief). Piketty (2014, p. 221) argues that in the Twenty-First Century $\sigma$ must be larger than one, e.g., estimated on the basis of historical data: $\sigma$ between 1.3 and 1.6 .

The attention by von Thünen to *"natural wages"*, $MP_L^* = \sqrt{c_L AP_L^*}$, (3.49), was due to the *monotonic*[23] relation between wages and labor productivity at *normative*: $(k = k^*)$—as to him, the *"source of the evil"* was the *separation* of *wages* and *productivity*.

The *monotonicity* applies not only to his "natural wages", it holds *universally* to *every* marginal productivity *wage*, $MP_L$, and labor *productivity*, $AP_L$, of *any* regular production function, $f(k)$, for *all* capital-labor ratios, $(0 \leq k = K/L \leq \infty)$, cf. (3.1), (3.68).

Comparing *monotone* wage formulas, (3.68), (3.49), symbols $\forall$, $\exists$, decide a point raised by Krelle (1987, p. 6). If we want to embed one of them as a *wage* relation in *macrodynamic* models, we must *choose* (3.68), as its $\mathbf{MP_L}$ property applies to *any* capital-labor ratio (**k**). The forms of this *monotonicity* are *governed* by $\sigma(k)$, (3.2–3.3), which was implicitly behind the *production functions*, **f(k)**, *exhibited* in von Thünen's *"Tableau Economique"*, Tables 3.3, 3.4 and 3.5. Marginal productivity factor pricing (3.4–3.5) is the turning point (great achievement) in wage theory, allocative efficiency, and economic progress anywhere.

**Acknowledgments** For helpful comments on many earlier drafts, we are indebted to Peter J. Lloyd, University of Melbourne, Australia. The author alone is responsible for any errors and omissions.

## BIBLIOGRAPHY

Arrow KJ, Chenery HB, Minhas BS, Solow RM (1961) Capital–Labour Substitution and Economic Efficiency. Review of Economics and Statistics 43:225–250

Blaug M (2002) Economic Theory In Retrospect, 3rd edn. Cambridge University Press, Cambridge

Brems H (1986) Pioneering Economic Theory 1630–1980. A Mathematical Restatement. The Johns Hopkins University Press, Baltimore

Dempsey BW (1960) The Frontier Wage, Thünen. Loyola University Press, Chicago, Teil 1 (parts), Teil 2

Dorfman R (1986) 'Comment: P. A. Samuelson, Thünen at Two Hundred". Journal of Economic Literature 24:1773–1776

Douglas PH (1934, 1957) The Theory of Wages. Macmillan, New York

Frisch R (1965) Theory of Production. O. Reidel Publishing Company, Dordrecht, Holland

Hall P (ed) (1966) The Isolated State. Pergamon Press, Oxford, Wartenberg, C. M., Translation, Band 1, Band 2–3 (extracts)

[23] Alle diese Übelstände, an denen der soziale Zustand Europas erkrankt ist, fallen für den Arbeitslohn $\sqrt{a\,p}$ hinweg. In $\sqrt{a\,p}$ ist der Lohn des Arbeiters dem Wert seine Erzeugnisses proportional; in unseren gegenwärtigen Zuständen ist der Lohn des Arbeiters von seinem Arbeitsprodukt ganz unabhängig.

*In der Trennung des Arbeiters von seinem Erzeugnis liegt die Quelle des Übels* (italics original). von Thünen (1990, Ch. 22, p. 600), von Thünen (1875, Ch. 22, 2.I, p. 210), Dempsey (1960, p. 327).

Helmstädter E (1995) Wie künstlich ist von Thünens natürlicher Lohn. Schriften des Vereins für Socialpolitik Ed. H. Rieter, Duncker & Humbolt, Berlin
Hicks JR (1932, 1948) The Theory of Wages. MacMillan, London
Jensen BS (2003) Walrasian General Equilibrium Allocations and Dynamics in Two–Sector Growth Models. German Economic Review 4:53–87
Jensen BS (2009) Dynamic Extensions of the Solow Growth Model (1956), Editorial. German Economic Review 10:378–383
Jensen BS (2017) von Thünen: Capital, Production Functions, Marginal Productivity Wages and the Natural Wage. German Economic Review 18:51–80
Jensen BS, Richter M (2007) Stochastic one–sector and two–sector growth models in continuous time. In: Jensen BS, Palokangas T (eds) Stochastic Economic Dynamics, CBS Press, Copenhagen, pp 167–216
Klump R, de La Grandville O (2000) Economic Growth and the Elasticity of Substitution: Two Theorems and Some Suggestions. American Economic Review 90:282–291
Krelle W (1987) von Thünen–Vorlesung. Zeitschrift f Wirtscafts– u Sozialwiss 107:5–28
Leigh AH (1946) Von Thünen's Theory of Distribution and the Advent of Marginal Analysis. Journal of Political Economy 54:481–502
Lloyd PJ (1969) Elementary Geometric/Arithmetic Series and Early Production Theory. J Political Economy 77:21–34
Lloyd PJ (2001) The Origins of the von Thünen–Mill–Pareto–Wicksell–Cobb–Douglas Function. History of Political Economy 33:1–17
Lloyd PJ (2012) The Discovery of the Isoquant. History of Political Eco–nomy 44:619–641
Marshall A (1920) Principles of Economics, 8th edn. Macmillan, London
Piketty T (2014) Capital in The Twenty–First Century. The Bellknap Press of Harvard University Press, London
Robinson J (1965) The Economics of Imperfect Competition. Macmillan, London
Samuelson PA (1983) Thünen at Two Hundred. Journal of Economic Lite–rature 21:1468–1488
Samuelson PA (1986) Yes to Robert Dorfman's Vindication of Thünen's Natural–Wage Derivation. Journal of Economic Literature 24:1777–1785
Schneider E (1934) Johann Heinrich von Thünen. Econometrica 2:1–12
Schumpeter JA (1954) History of Economic Analysis. Oxford University Press, New York
Streissler EW (1995) Die Grenzproduktivitätstheorie der deutschen Protoklassik unter besonderer Berücksichtigung von J. H. v. Thünen. In: Rieter H (ed) Schriften des Vereins für Socialpolitik, Duncker & Humbolt, Berlin
van Suntum U (1988) Vindicating Thünen's Tombstone Formula $\sqrt{ap}$. Jahrb f Nationalöku Stat 204:393–405
von Thünen JH (1826) Der isolierte Staat in Beziehung auf Landwirtschaft und Nationalökonomie. Hamburg, Band 1 (Teil 1), 2.ed. (Rostock 1842); Band 2 (Teil 2.I), (Rostock 1850); Band 3 (Teil 2.II, Teil 3), (Rostock 1863)
von Thünen JH (1875) Der isolierte Staat in Beziehung auf Landwirtschaft und Nationalökonomie, 3rd edn. Band 1–3, (Gothic type)
von Thünen (1990) Der Isolierte Staat. Verlag Gustav Fischer, 1. Auflage, (Jena 1910); 3. Auflage, (Jena 1930); 4. Auflage, (Stuttgart 1966); 5. Auflage, Verlag Scientia, (Aalen 1990).
Uzawa H (1961) On a Two–Sector Model of Economic Growth: I. Review of Economic Studies 29:40–47

CHAPTER 4

# Flexible Regular Multi-factor Production and Cost Functions

## Introduction

The introduction by Arrow et al. (1961) of the CES production function was a major analytic advance in micro- and macroeconomic model building. The CES function was both a *globally regular* and a particular *flexible* functional form in the important *two-factor* case, where the *size* of the CES *constant* elasticity of *substitution* ($\sigma = \sigma_{12}$) could range between *zero* and *infinity*. Uzawa (1962) extended CES to *n-factors*—and shoved that if *global regularity* (e.g. concavity) was to be preserved, then *flexibility* (different *sizes*) of **constant** Allen-Uzawa *partial* elasticity of *substitution* ($\sigma_{ij}$) is **impossible**, as $\sigma_{ij}$ necessarily had to be of *same* size for[1] *all* pairs of *factors*, i.e, $\sigma_{ij} = \sigma$.

Thus, with *multiple* factors, *flexibility* in elasticities of substitution ($\sigma_{ij}$) implies that ($\sigma_{ij}$) are *changing* (at least a little bit), as a function of the variable inputs along *isoquants* (curves, surfaces, in factor space) of multi-factor production productions. However, as we keep the assumption of constant returns to scale in production (*homogeneity* of *degree* 1), all *substitution* elasticities, ($\sigma_{ij}$) [ and *complementarity* elasticities ($c_{ij}$) ] are still *constant* along a *ray* in factor space, but with *different sizes* from one ray to another ray.

With co-authors:
JENS MARTIN JENSEN, Vinci Computers, Copenhagen, Denmark.
HENNING P. JÖRGENSEN, Business and Social Sciences, University of Southern Denmark.

[1] On old problems with *different* substitution elasticities between *two* Labor categories (skilled/unskilled), and various *nonlabor* inputs such as services of *Capital*, see Berndt and Christensen (1974, p.391–392); see Goldin and Katz (1998, p. 695–696, 699–703) on the technology-skill complementarity, both today and in periods of the 19–20'th century.



B. S. Jensen, *The Elements and Dynamic Systems of Economic Growth and Trade Models*, https://doi.org/10.1007/978-3-031-52493-6_4

The suitable choice of *functional form* together with the actual *number* (M) of factors have raised many and special problems. Formally, the concept of a *flexible functional form* of the production (cost) function has, a long tradition, Diewert (1971, p. 506), Diewert (1974b, p. 133), of being tied to the ability to provide, locally, a *second-order* Taylor series *approximation* to *any* (unspecified) functional form. To satisfy such requirement with M-factors a certain *minimum* number of *free* (independent) *parameters* is needed. For a continuously differentiable *homogeneous* (degree 1) *production*, *utility* or *cost* (unit) *function*, the functional form, in order to be *flexible*, must (with **M** factors) have at least: $\mathbf{M(M+1)/2}$, *free* (independent) *parameters*. cf. Diewert (2022, p. 95–96); *Translog* unit *cost* function requires such minimal number, $M(M+1)/2$, of parameters to be flexible, Diewert (2022, p. 100). Thus, corresponding to:$M = 6, 8, 9, 11$, the minimal number of parameters, $M(M+1)/2$, are: 21, 36, 45, 60. Evidently, flexible Translog form can not go much beyond[2] $M = 6$. Labor Economics, operating with Labor market inputs of 5-year Age groups requires $M = 11$ to cover all working ages, 15–70—but a *'flexibility'* need of 60 parameters is prohibitive.

The concept of *flexible functional* forms (second-order Taylor series approximation, at initial data point) is naturally related to *flexibility* (different sizes and variation) of the, $M(M-1)/2$, Allen-Uzawa *partial* elasticities of *substitution*[3] ($\sigma_{ij}$), calculated from *bordered Hessian* matrices, Allen (1938, p. 504); cf. Perroni and Rutherford (1995, p. 337). Various *flexible* functional form, Generalized Leontief cost functions, Translog forms, Christensen et al. (1971), Christensen et al. (1973), Christensen et al. (1975), were then formed with *quadratic forms* in, respectively, the *square roots* of factor prices, or the *logarithms* of factor (commodity) prices (quantities), see Diewert (2022, p. 60). As seen, a major problem was the large number, $M(M+1)/2$, of independent *parameters*, which have to be reduced in a flexible-economic-mathematical way and sensible *parsimonious* fashion. Moreover, further *economic regularity* problems showed up in applying these flexible forms: "Translog and Generalized Leontief functional form both suffer from the same problem: In general, it is not possible to impose *concavity* on these functional forms without destroying their flexibility property ", Diewert (2022, p. 107).

Regarding *regularity* conditions, our *new Generalized* **CES** *Production* and *Cost* functions will have the properties of *Monotonicity* and *Concavity* on the *global* domain, *positive (non-negative)* orthant, i.e. *global regularity* in factor (price) space, which is important in applied equilibrium models, cf. Perroni and Rutherford (1995, p. 336).

[2] See Freeman (1979, p. 301,313) for complementarity elasticities ($c_{ij}$) with Translog.

[3] Theoretically, all $M(M-1)/2$, ($\sigma_{ij}$), can be positive, Hicks (1946, p. 311), or theoretically, $M(M-3)/2+1$, negative, and $M-1$ positive, Hicks (1946, p. 347). Empirically, ($\sigma_{ij}$) seems mostly positive (with the average, positive).

$\sigma_{ij} > 0$: Factors are called price, *p-substitutes*, larger price $W_j$ increases inputs of $X_i$ .

$\sigma_{ij} < 0$: Factors are called price, *p-complements*, larger price $W_j$ decreases inputs of $X_i$ .

As to *parsimony* of *structural* (principal economic) *parameters*, theory and empirical work of Hanoch (1971), Hanoch (1975), Jensen et al. (2011), Guest and Jensen (2016) on: *Additive Implicit* production functions, and *Additive Indirect* production (utility) functions with *multiple* factors (commodities) have aided to a structural *parsimonious* design of *parameters* for the *Generalized* **CES** functions. In such Additive, Implicit/Indirect, homogeneous (*degree* 1) functions with *multiple* (**M**) factors, (**2 M**) is the number of *free* parameters—consisting of (**M**) *intensity* (weight) parameters, and (**M**) factor *specific substitution* parameters; see Chambers and Ray (2022, p. 30–41) on various additive functions (homogeneous of degree 1).

Alike, the *Generalized* **CES** functions will have (**2 M**) *analogous* parameters, but include also **one** *general substitution* parameter, i.e. (**2 M + 1**) *free* structural parameters. Thus for, $M = 9, 11$, the required *number* of free parameters are: 19, 23—compared to: 45, 60, for '*flexible*' functional forms; so, evidently, much easier to implement. Moreover, the parametric *Generalized* **CES** *Production* and *Cost* functions are **explicit** functions (not *implicit* functions—equations)—another advantage, especially in Computable Dynamic General Equilibrium models; see Jensen et al. (2015, p. 229–230),—(Chap. 21, p. 646–647).

We will demonstrate the flexibility properties obtained by the *Generalized* **CES** *Production* and *Cost* functions—**GCES, GCESC**—by computing and showing AUES ($\sigma_{ij}$), and Hicks *Partial Complementarity* elasticities ($c_{ij}$)—for various multi-factor dimensions ($M$). The *economic* implications of the *parameters* of GCES, GCESC, are also shown by explicitly deriving and presenting the associated elasticities of their factor demand systems and inverse factor demand systems (factor price elasticities wrt. factor supplies).

The chapter is organized as follows. Section "Generalized CES Production Functions" presents and discuss the analytical function **F(X)** of **GCES**. Section "Complementarity Elasticities, Substitution Elasticities, Factor Shares" gives ($c_{ij}$) and ($\sigma_{ij}$). Section "GCES Functions and CRESH Functions, Convergence of GCES Functions" compares **F(X)** with the *implicit* function **CRESH** (Constant Ratio of Elasticity Substitution, Homothetic). Section "Generalized CES Cost Functions, GCESC" gives and discuss the analytical function **c (W)** of **GCESC** and AUES ($\sigma_{ij}$). Final remarks in section "Final Remarks". *Appendix* 1 proves concavity of GCES for a particular parameter case. *Appendix* 3 examines in detail the Regularity and Flexibility properties of the implicit CRESH production function.

## Generalized CES Production Functions

A class of *Generalized* CES (**GCES**) production functions **F(X)** is given by:

$$Y = F(X) = F(X_1, \ldots, X_M) = \gamma \left[\sum_{i=1}^{M} a_i X_i^{\rho}\right]^{\frac{1}{\rho}} \cdot \sum_{i=1}^{M} a_i \left[\frac{X_i}{\left[\sum_{i=1}^{M} a_i X_i^{\rho}\right]^{\frac{1}{\rho}}}\right]^{\rho_i} \tag{4.1}$$

$$\gamma > 0,\ -\infty < \rho \leq 1;\ \ a_i > 0,\ \sum_{i=1}^{M} a_i = 1\ ;\ \ \forall i : X_i > 0,\ \ 0 \leq \rho_i \leq 1 \tag{4.2}$$

$$\text{If } \rho = 0 : \quad Y = F(X_1, \ldots, X_M) = \gamma \prod_{i=1}^{M} X_i^{a_i} \cdot \sum_{i=1}^{M} a_i \left[\frac{X_i}{\prod_{i=1}^{M} X_i^{a_i}}\right]^{\rho_i} \tag{4.3}$$

GCES functions (4.1) are developed as *generalizations* of **CES** functions (4.4):

$$Y = F(X_1, .., X_M) = \gamma\, [\sum_{i=1}^{M} a_i\, X_i^{\rho}\,]^{\frac{1}{\rho}}\ ;\ a_i \geq 0,\ \sum_{i=1}^{M} a_i = 1,\ \ -\infty < \rho \leq 1, \sigma = \frac{1}{1-\rho} \tag{4.4}$$

All CES functions (4.4) with $0 \leq \rho \leq 1$ can be reproduced if: $\forall i$: $\rho_i = \rho$.

All CES functions (4.4) with $-\infty < \rho < 0$ can be reproduced if: $\forall i$: $\rho_i = 0$.

It is easily seen that the GCES functions (4.1) for which $\forall i$: $0 < \rho_i < 1$ are *positive, continuous* and that they are *homogeneous* of first degree (constant return to scale). We make the *conjecture* that the **GCES** functions, **F(X)**, (4.1–4.3) by **restriction,** $\forall i$: $0 < \rho_i < 1$, have the **global regularity** properties:

1. They are everywhere positive (non-negative) and continuous.
2. They have continuous first and second derivatives.
3. They are monotonically increasing (non-decreasing) in every factor.
4. They are homogeneous of first degree.
5. They are concave.

Figures 4.1 and 4.2 show typical 3-dimensional *Graphs* and *Level curves* of **GCES**, (4.1), with, $M = 5$, production factors, $X_i$, (for $\rho = 0.2$ and $\rho = -1$) indicating that they meet *regularity* properties, 1–5, especially **concavity**.

As stated, it is a presumption that GCES functions for which $\forall i$: $0 < \rho_i < 1$ have these *five global regularity* properties. **Appendix 1** provides proof that the *conjecture* is *correct* for: $\rho = 1$, where the function still has typical *general structure* of (4.1), which is why the *case* $\rho = 1$ gives *strong evidence* to regard the *conjecture* as *true* for $-\infty < \rho \leq 1$.

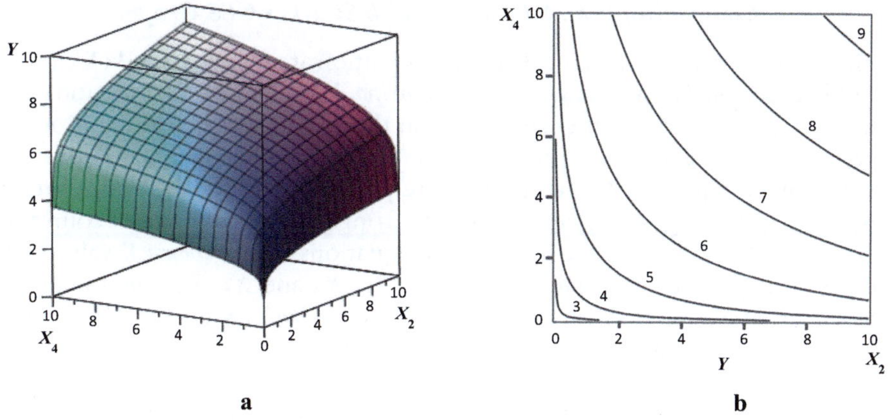


**Fig. 4.1** GCES Production function (4.1) Graph, Contour lines—$(X_2, X_4)$

$$
\begin{aligned}
&M = 5, \quad (X_1, X_2, X_3, X_4, X_5) = (4, X_2, 6, X_4, 8) \\
&\rho = 0.2, \quad (\rho_1, \rho_2, \rho_3, \rho_4, \rho_5) = (0.2, 0.3, 0.4, 0.4, 0.5) \\
&\gamma = 1.2, \quad (a_1, a_2, a_3, a_4, a_5) = (0.1, 0.2, 0.25, 0.2, 0.25)
\end{aligned}
$$

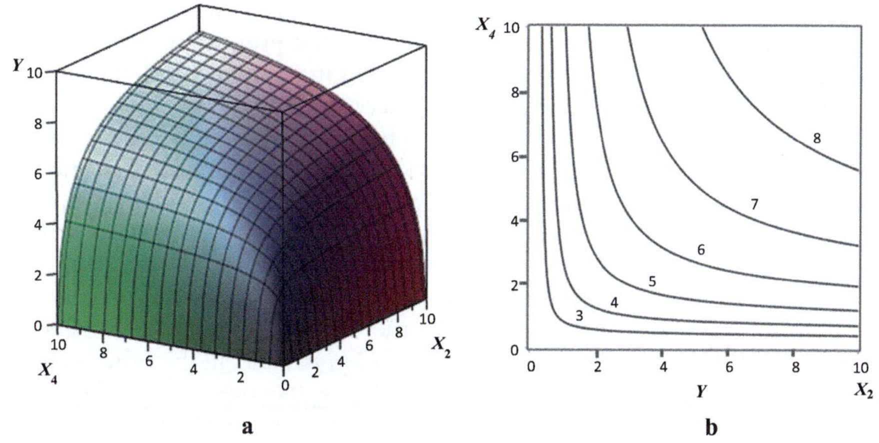


**Fig. 4.2** GCES Production function (4.1) Graph, Contour lines—$(X_2, X_4)$

$$
\begin{aligned}
&M = 5, \quad (X_1, X_2, X_3, X_4, X_5) = (4, X_2, 6, X_4, 8) \\
&\rho = -1, \quad (\rho_1, \rho_2, \rho_3, \rho_4, \rho_5) = (0.2, 0.3, 0.4, 0.4, 0.5) \\
&\gamma = 1.2, \quad (a_1, a_2, a_3, a_4, a_5) = (0.1, 0.2, 0.25, 0.2, 0.25)
\end{aligned}
$$

### *Comparing Figs. 4.1 and 4.2 with Similar CES Graphs*

When $\rho > 0$, as in Fig. 4.1, the **domain** (definition area) for GCES, **F(X)**, (4.1), could be *extended* to $X_i$—*axes*, except for *origo*. Like for the CES function (4.4) the isoquants in Fig. 4.1 then also ends on the axes. That means that if one of the variables becomes zero, the production function is still *positive*. This is also evident from Fig. 4.1a. If one wants more precise values for the **endpoints** of the isoquants in Fig. 4.1a than can be seen from a figure—one can of course set $X_4 = 0$ or $X_2 = 0$ in (4.1) and solve the equations with a *chosen* $Y$ value. The solutions depend on the *chosen values* for $X_1$, $X_3$ and $X_5$. For the important *two-factor* illustrations (with $\rho > 0$), there are for *both* GCES and CES simple expressions for the **axes endpoints** of the *isoquants*:

$$\rho > 0\,,\ \text{GCES}: \quad \bar{X}_1 = \frac{Y}{\gamma}(a_1)^{\frac{\rho_1 - 1 - \rho}{\rho}}\,,\ \text{CES}: \quad \bar{X}_1 = \frac{Y}{\gamma}(a_1)^{-\frac{1}{\rho}} \tag{4.5}$$

$$\rho > 0\,,\ \text{GCES}: \quad \bar{X}_2 = \frac{Y}{\gamma}(a_2)^{\frac{\rho_2 - 1 - \rho}{\rho}}\,,\ \text{CES}: \quad \bar{X}_2 = \frac{Y}{\gamma}(a_2)^{-\frac{1}{\rho}} \tag{4.6}$$

When $\rho < 0$, as in Fig. 4.2, the **domain** (4.2) for *both* GCES and CES does **not** include the **axes**. The CES function converges to zero (all factors are essential). This is also the case for GCES provided that in addition we assume $\forall i : \rho_i < 1$. This is obvious for CES functions. In the GCES function (4.1) the first element (CES term) will go to zero. but the second element (sum term) will go to infinity. An analysis shows that *if*, $\forall i : \rho_i < 1$, the product of the CES term with every term in the sum element to the right in function (4.1) converges to *zero*, when one or more of the $X_i$ variables converges to zero.

The *isoquants* for both GCES and CES have *horizontal* and *vertical* asymptotes, when $\rho \leq 0$. But GCES has *always* the *axis* as asymptotes. In the CES case with $\rho < 0$ every isoquant has its *own interior* pair of such asymptotes, and their intersection points can obviously be found by letting a variable go to infinity. In the two-factor CES case with $\rho < 0$ the formulas (4.5) and (4.6) are reproduced, and thus they also give the intersection coordinates of the asymptotes. These interior asymptotes in the CES case can also be understood from the fact that if *one* variable converges to *infinity* and all the other variables are kept *constant*, the CES function here with $\rho < 0$ converges to a *finite* value (output *upper bounded*). Such *finiteness* is **not** the case for the GCES function (4.1), because its second sum element will go to infinity. A product of a finite value multiplied with infinity of cause gives infinity. The consequence is that the coordinate *axes*, $X_i$, are always the *asymptotes* for any GCES isoquants, when $\rho < 0$—like in the Cobb-Douglas case. When $\rho < 0$, **domain** for GCES is the entire *non-zero orthant* and output (Y) is *not* upper bounded.

## Complementarity Elasticities, Substitution Elasticities, Factor Shares

In Figs. 4.3, 4.4, 4.5, 4.6, 4.7, 4.8, 4.9, 4.10 and 4.11, are illustrated different **GCES** functions (4.1), **F(X)**, as well as derived properties, depending on different sizes of parameters. The examined properties are AUES: Allen-Uzawa *Partial Substitution* elasticities ($\sigma_{ij}$), Hicks-Sato *Partial Complementarity* elasticities[4] ($c_{ij}$), and *Factor shares*, ($e_i$).

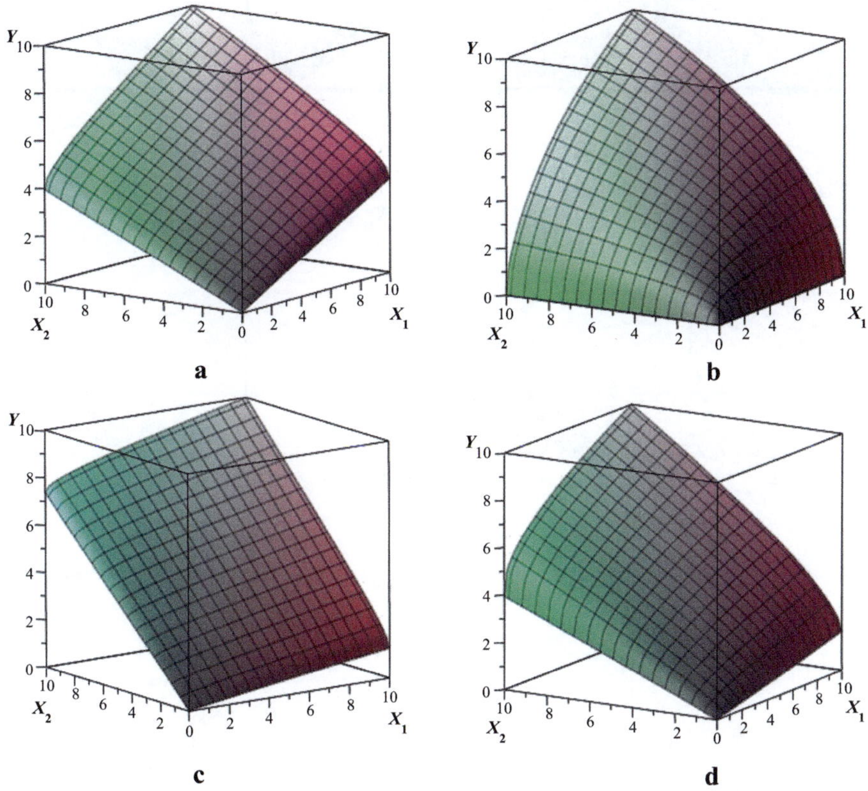


**Fig. 4.3** GCES Production functions (4.1), Graphs

$$
\begin{array}{lllll}
a: & M=2, & (a_1,a_2)=(0.2,0.8), & \rho=0.2, & (\rho_1,\rho_2)=(0.9,0.9)\\
b: & M=2, & (a_1,a_2)=(0.5,0.5), & \rho=-1, & (\rho_1,\rho_2)=(0.5,0.5)\\
c: & M=2, & (a_1,a_2)=(0.2,0.8), & \rho=0.2, & (\rho_1,\rho_2)=(0.9,0.9)\\
d: & M=2, & (a_1,a_2)=(0.5,0.5), & \rho=0.5, & (\rho_1,\rho_2)=(0.2,0.8)
\end{array}
$$

[4] $c_{ij} > 0$: Factors are quantity, *q-complements*, larger inputs $X_j$ increase price of $W_i$.
$c_{ij} < 0$: Factors are called quantity, *q-substitutes*, larger inputs $X_j$ decrease price of $W_i$.
$c_{ij} = 1 \Leftrightarrow \sigma_{ij} = 1$ (CD), $c_{ij} = 0 \Leftrightarrow \sigma_{ij} = \infty$ (Linear), $c_{ij} = \infty \Leftrightarrow \sigma_{ij} = 0$ (Leontief).

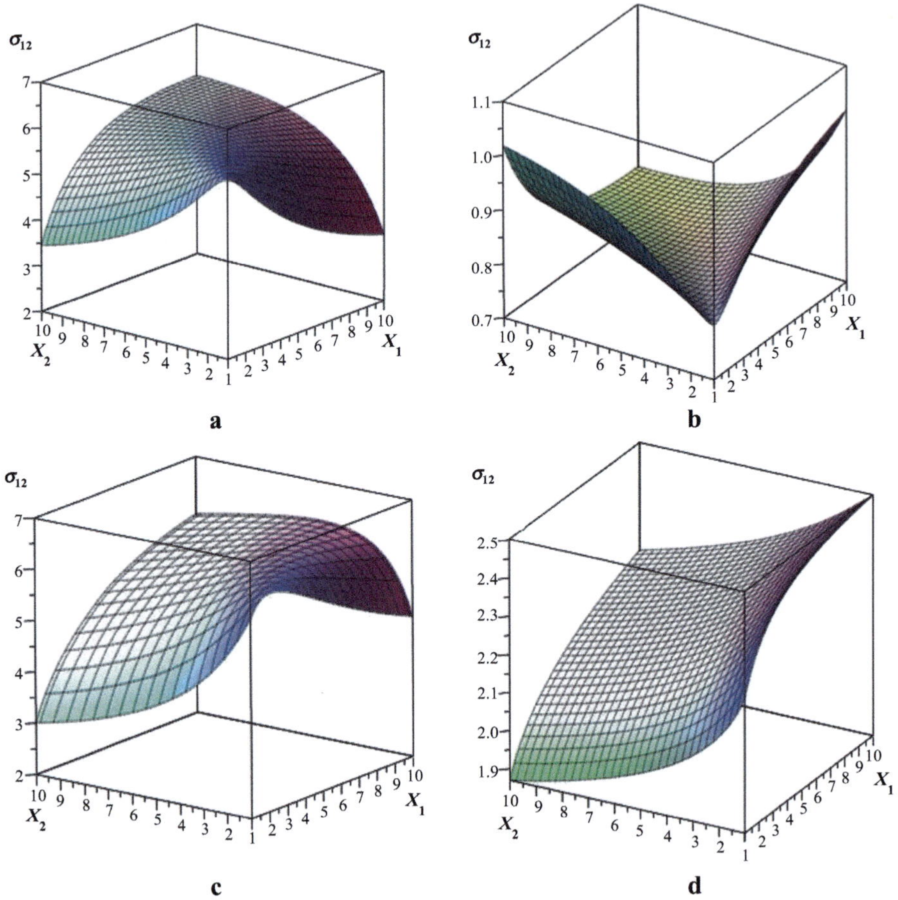


**Fig. 4.4** GCES Production functions: $\sigma_{12}\,(X_1, X_2)$, (4.15 i), (4.7)

$$\begin{array}{lllll} a: & M = 2, & (a_1, a_2) = (0.5, 0.5), & \rho = 0.2, & (\rho_1, \rho_2) = (0.9, 0.9) \\ b: & M = 2, & (a_1, a_2) = (0.5, 0.5), & \rho = -1, & (\rho_1, \rho_2) = (0.5, 0.5) \\ c: & M = 2, & (a_1, a_2) = (0.2, 0.8), & \rho = 0.2, & (\rho_1, \rho_2) = (0.9, 0.9) \\ d: & M = 2, & (a_1, a_2) = (0.5, 0.5), & \rho = 0.5, & (\rho_1, \rho_2) = (0.2, 0.8) \end{array}$$

$$\sigma_{12}\,(X_1, X_2) = \frac{\frac{\partial F\,(X_1, X_2)}{\partial X_1}\;\frac{\partial F\,(X_1, X_2)}{\partial X_2}}{F(X_1, X_2)\;\frac{\partial^2 F\,(X_1, X_2)}{\partial X_1\,\partial X_2}} \tag{4.7}$$

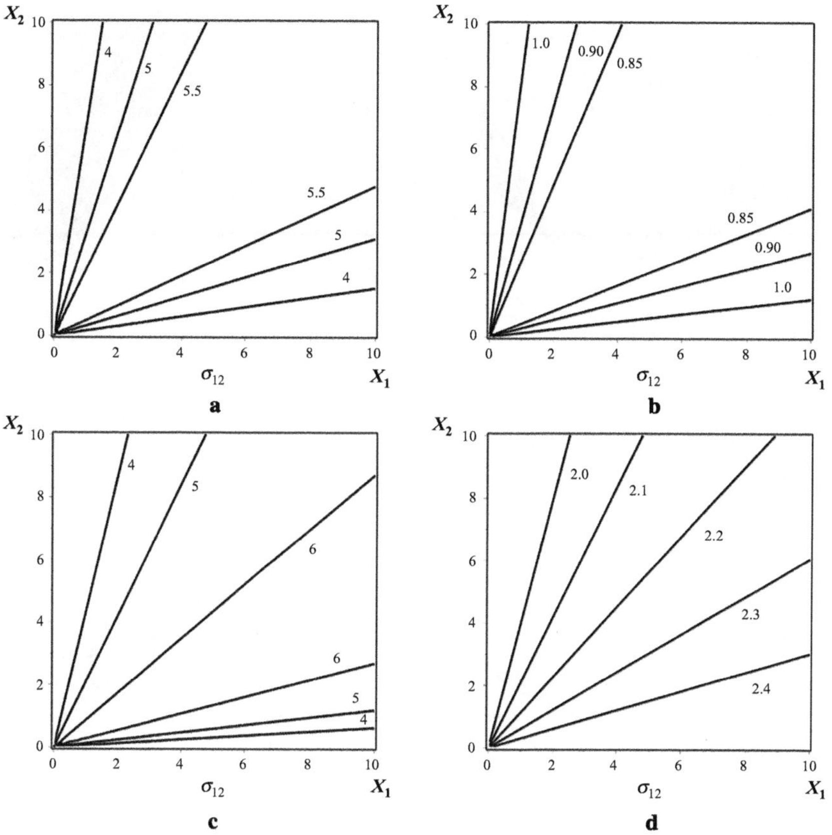


**Fig. 4.5** GCES Production functions: $\sigma_{12}$, Level curves

$$
\begin{array}{lllll}
a: & M = 2, & (a_1, a_2) = (0.2, 0.8), & \rho = 0.2, & (\rho_1, \rho_2) = (0.9, 0.9) \\
b: & M = 2, & (a_1, a_2) = (0.5, 0.5), & \rho = -1, & (\rho_1, \rho_2) = (0.5, 0.5) \\
c: & M = 2, & (a_1, a_2) = (0.2, 0.8), & \rho = 0.2, & (\rho_1, \rho_2) = (0.9, 0.9) \\
d: & M = 2, & (a_1, a_2) = (0.5, 0.5), & \rho = 0.5, & (\rho_1, \rho_2) = (0.2, 0.8)
\end{array}
$$

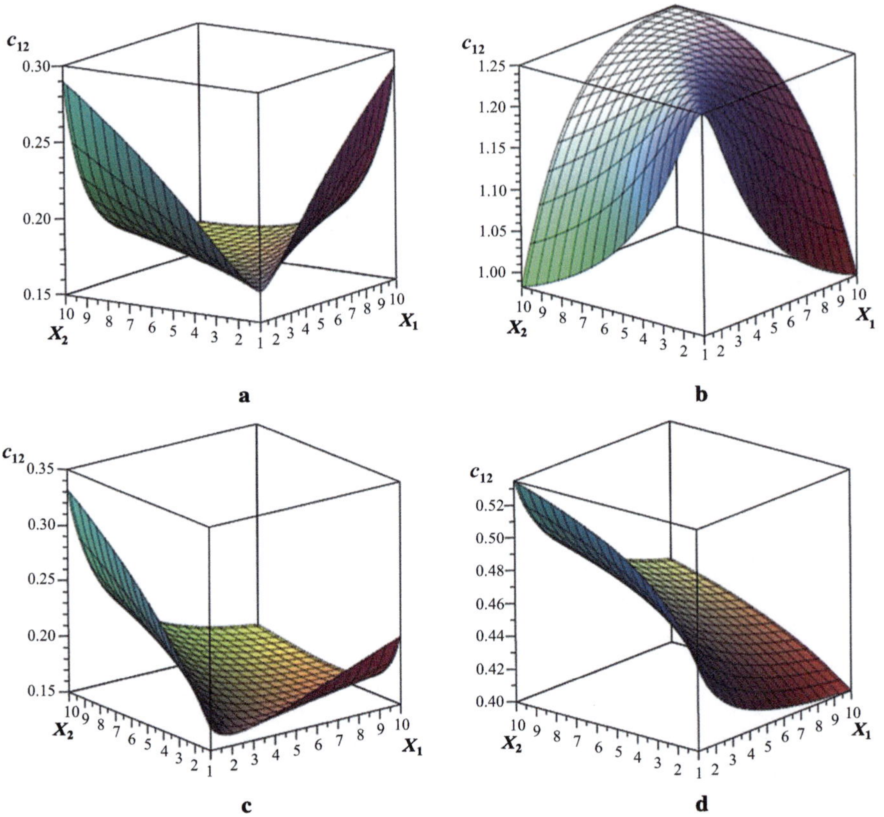


**Fig. 4.6** GCES Production functions: $c_{12}$, (4.10), (4.8)

$$
\begin{array}{lllll}
a: & M=2, & (a_1, a_2)=(0.2, 0.8), & \rho=0.2, & (\rho_1, \rho_2)=(0.9, 0.9) \\
b: & M=2, & (a_1, a_2)=(0.5, 0.5), & \rho=-1, & (\rho_1, \rho_2)=(0.5, 0.5) \\
c: & M=2, & (a_1, a_2)=(0.2, 0.8), & \rho=0.2, & (\rho_1, \rho_2)=(0.9, 0.9) \\
d: & M=2, & (a_1, a_2)=(0.5, 0.5), & \rho=0.5, & (\rho_1, \rho_2)=(0.2, 0.8)
\end{array}
$$

$$
c_{12}(X_1, X_2) = \frac{F(X)\ \frac{\partial^2 F(X)}{\partial X_1 \partial X_2}}{\frac{\partial F(X)}{\partial X_1}\ \frac{\partial F(X)}{\partial X_2}} \tag{4.8}
$$

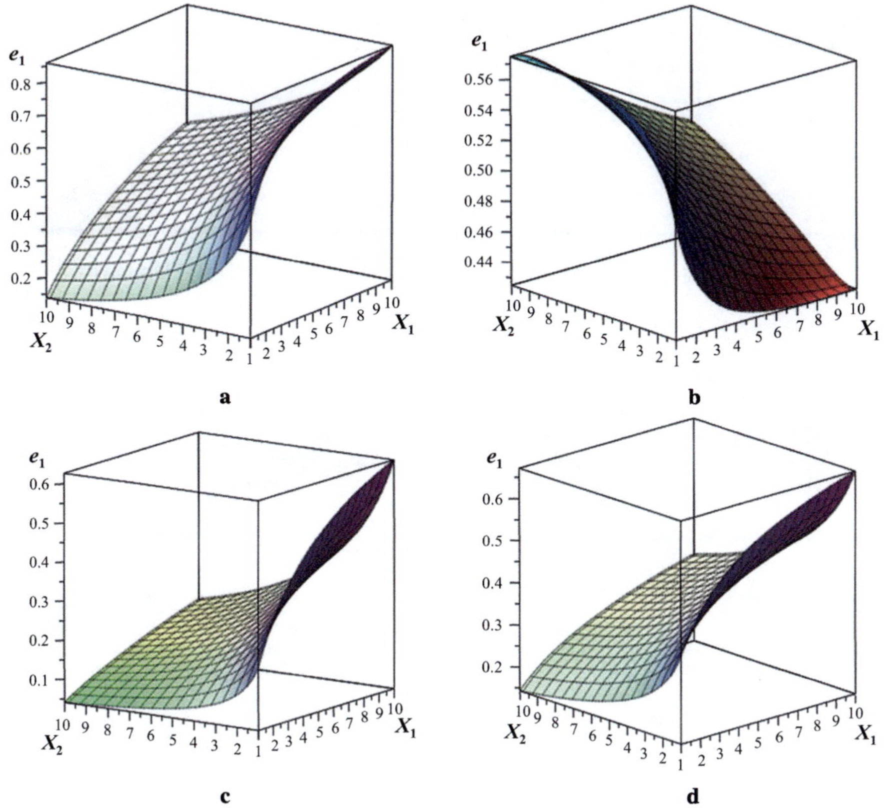


**Fig. 4.7** GCES Production functions: $e_1$, (4.10), (4.9)

$$
\begin{array}{lllll}
a: & M = 2, & (a_1, a_2) = (0.2, 0.8), & \rho = 0.2, & (\rho_1, \rho_2) = (0.9, 0.9) \\
b: & M = 2, & (a_1, a_2) = (0.5, 0.5), & \rho = -1, & (\rho_1, \rho_2) = (0.5, 0.5) \\
c: & M = 2, & (a_1, a_2) = (0.2, 0.8), & \rho = 0.2, & (\rho_1, \rho_2) = (0.9, 0.9) \\
d: & M = 2, & (a_1, a_2) = (0.5, 0.5), & \rho = 0.5, & (\rho_1, \rho_2) = (0.2, 0.8)
\end{array}
$$

$$
e_1 = \frac{\frac{\partial F,(X)}{\partial X_1} X_1}{F(X)} \tag{4.9}
$$

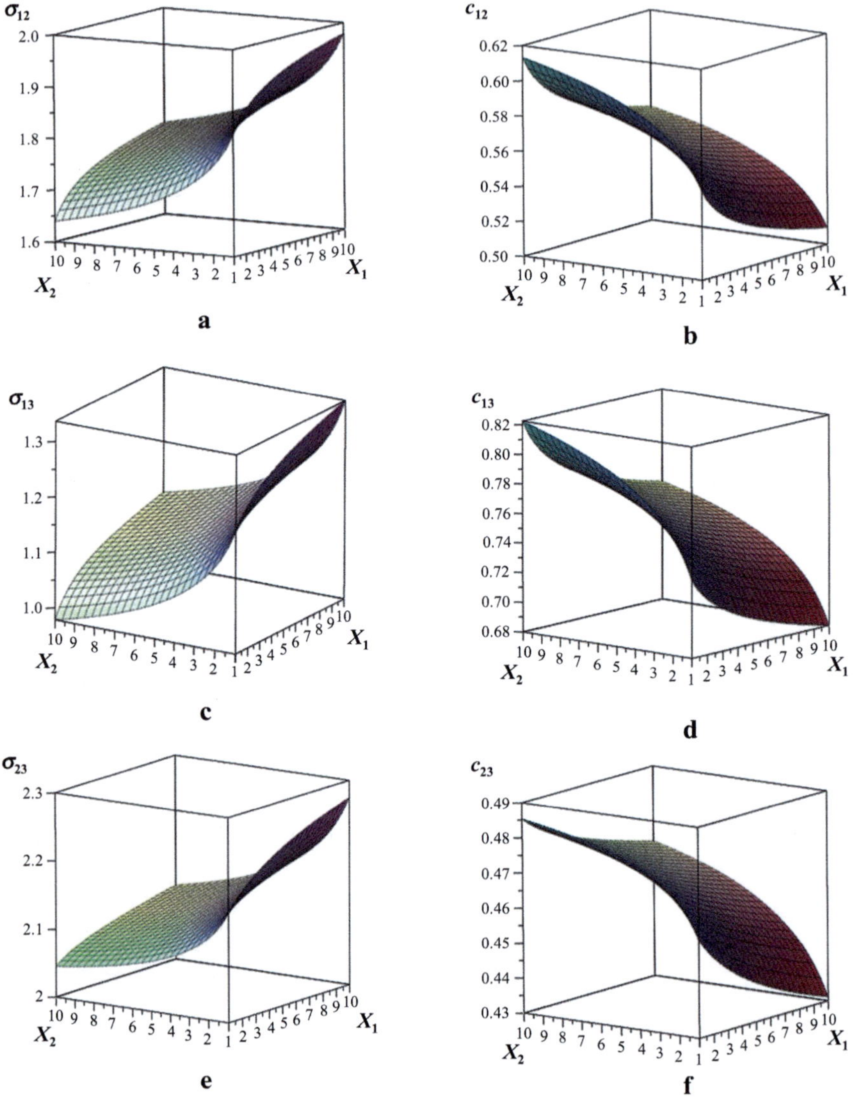


**Fig. 4.8** GCES functions: $\sigma_{ij}\,(X_1, X_2, 5), (4.15\,\text{ii}), c_{ij}\,(X_1, X_2, 5), (4.10)$

$$M = 3, \quad (X_1, X_2, 5), \quad (a_1, a_2, a_3) = (0.2, 0.7, 0.1), \quad \gamma = 1,$$
$$(\rho_1, \rho_2, \rho_3) = (0.2, 0.7, 0.5), \quad \rho = \tfrac{1}{3} \sum \rho_i = 7/15\,.$$

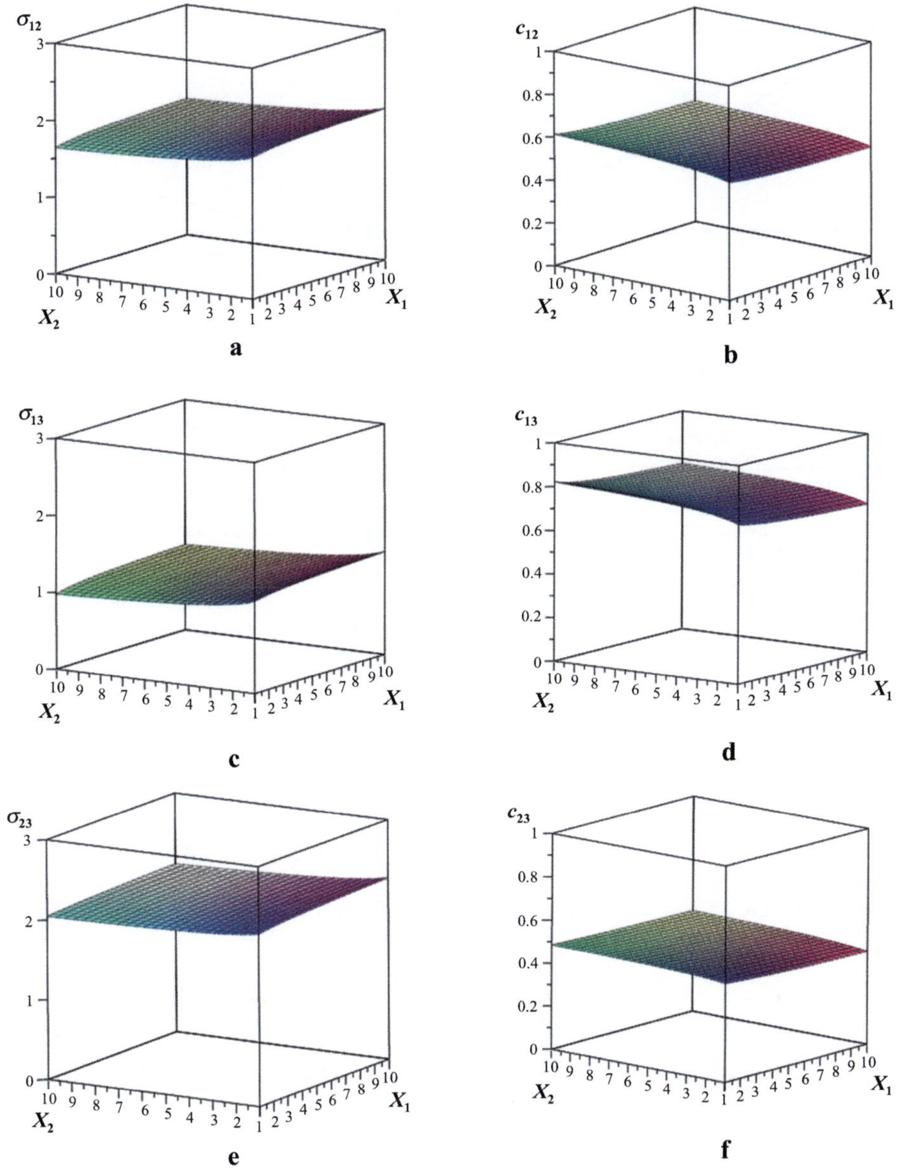


**Fig. 4.9** GCES functions: $\sigma_{ij}\,(X_1, X_2, 5), (4.15\,\text{ii})$, $c_{ij}\,(X_1, X_2, 5), (4.10)$

$$M = 3, \quad (X_1, X_2, 5), \quad (a_1, a_2, a_3) = (0.2, 0.7, 0.1), \quad \gamma = 1$$
$$(\rho_1, \rho_2, \rho_3) = (0.2, 0.7, 0.5), \quad \rho = \tfrac{1}{3}\sum \rho_i = 7/15\,.$$

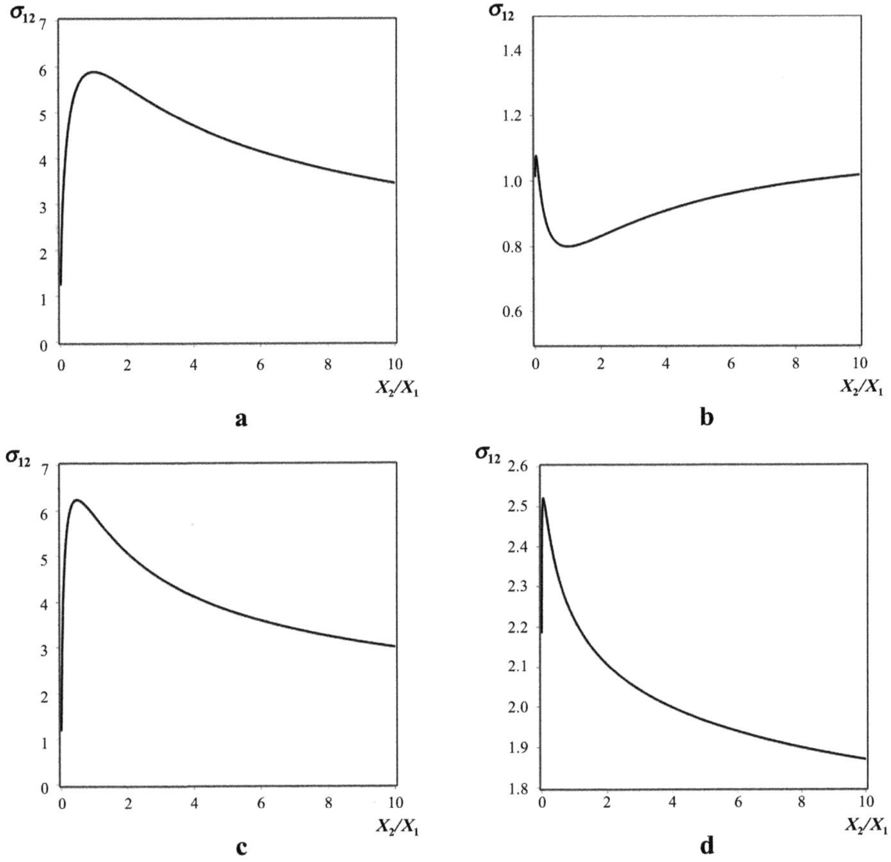


**Fig. 4.10** GCES Production functions, $\sigma_{12}\ (X_2/X_1)$, (4.15 i), (4.7)

$$
\begin{aligned}
a: &\quad M = 2, \quad (a_1, a_2) = (0.2, 0.8), \quad \rho = 0.2, \quad (\rho_1, \rho_2) = (0.9, 0.9)\\
b: &\quad M = 2, \quad (a_1, a_2) = (0.5, 0.5), \quad \rho = -1, \quad (\rho_1, \rho_2) = (0.5, 0.5)\\
c: &\quad M = 2, \quad (a_1, a_2) = (0.2, 0.8), \quad \rho = 0.2, \quad (\rho_1, \rho_2) = (0.9, 0.9)\\
d: &\quad M = 2, \quad (a_1, a_2) = (0.5, 0.5), \quad \rho = 0.5, \quad (\rho_1, \rho_2) = (0.2, 0.8)
\end{aligned}
$$

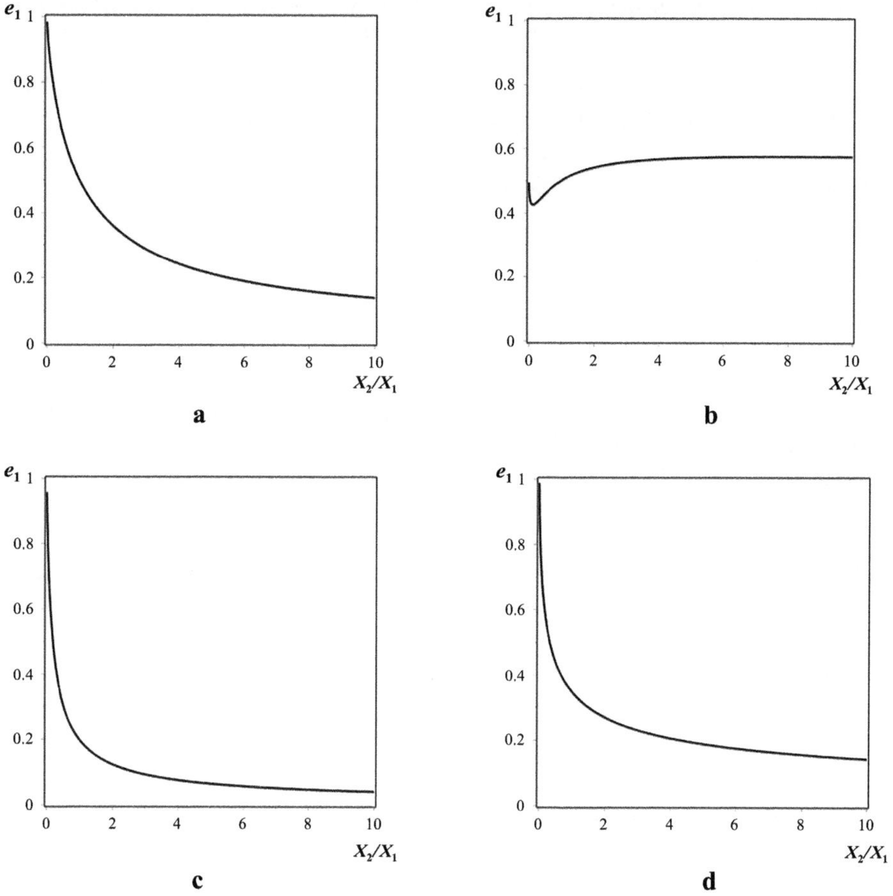


**Fig. 4.11** GCES Production functions, $e_1(X_2/X_1)$, (4.10), (4.9)

$$
\begin{array}{lllll}
a: & M=2, & (a_1,a_2)=(0.2,0.8), & \rho=0.2, & (\rho_1,\rho_2)=(0.9,0.9) \\
b: & M=2, & (a_1,a_2)=(0.5,0.5), & \rho=-1, & (\rho_1,\rho_2)=(0.5,0.5) \\
c: & M=2, & (a_1,a_2)=(0.2,0.8), & \rho=0.2, & (\rho_1,\rho_2)=(0.9,0.9) \\
d: & M=2, & (a_1,a_2)=(0.5,0.5), & \rho=0.5, & (\rho_1,\rho_2)=(0.2,0.8)
\end{array}
$$

### *Partial Complementarity Elasticities: Inverse Factor Demand and Factor Price Elasticities*

The formulas for computation of *Partial Complementarity* elasticities ($c_{ij}$), (4.10)—-Hicks (1970), Sato and Koizumi (1973a, p. 46)—and *Factor shares* ($e_i$) are simple for *any smooth* single output Production function, Y = F(X), and valid for arbitrary numbers of factors, $M$, ( $c_{ij} \gtrless 0 \equiv \frac{\partial^2 F}{\partial X_i \partial X_j} \gtrless 0$ ),

$$c_{ij} = \frac{F(X)\, \frac{\partial^2 F(X)}{\partial X_i \partial X_j}}{\frac{\partial F(X)}{\partial X_i}\, \frac{\partial F(X)}{\partial X_j}} = c_{ji}\, ; \; c_{ii} = \frac{F(X)\, \frac{\partial^2 F(X)}{\partial X_i^2}}{[\frac{\partial F(X)}{\partial X_i}]^2}\, ; \; e_i = \frac{\frac{\partial F(X)}{\partial X_i}\, X_i}{F(X)}\, ; \; i, j = 1, \ldots, M \tag{4.10}$$

Figures 4.6 and 4.7, illustrate the expressions (4.10) for computation of *Partial Complementarity* elasticities ($c_{ij}$) and *Factor shares* ($e_i$) for the two-factor case, $M = 2$, of **GCES**, $F(X)$, (4.1).

*Inverse Factor Demand and Factor Price Elasticities*
Related to the complementarity elasticities ($c_{ij}$), (4.10), are the standard factor price (*Inverse demand*) elasticity expressions (money price of output = $p$ ):

$$E(W_i, X_j) = e_j\, c_{ij} = \frac{\frac{\partial^2 F(X)}{\partial X_i \partial X_j}\, X_j}{\frac{\partial F(X)}{\partial X_i}} = \frac{\partial W_i}{\partial X_j}\, \frac{X_j}{W_i}\, ; \quad W_i = p\, \frac{\partial F(X)}{\partial X_i}; \; i, j = 1, ., M \tag{4.11}$$

$$E(W_i, X_i) = e_i\, c_{ii} = \frac{\frac{\partial^2 F(X)}{\partial X_i^2}\, X_i}{\frac{\partial F(X)}{\partial X_i}} = \frac{\partial W_i}{\partial X_i}\, \frac{X_i}{W_i}\, ; \quad W_i = p\, \frac{\partial F(X)}{\partial X_i}; \; i = 1, ., M \tag{4.12}$$

For $M = 5$, we demonstrate the formulas (4.10–4.12) for computation of *Partial Complementarity* elasticities ($c_{ij}$), *Factor shares* ($e_i$), and *Factor price* (Inverse demand ) elasticities, $E(W_i, X_j)$, $E(W_i, X_i)$—here by using the **GCES** $F(X)$, (4.1), *parameters* of Fig. 4.1, together with the chosen sizes of the 5 *inputs* ($X$), as collected in Table 4.1. Factor price, $W_i$, (4.11), is the *"shadow price"* (marginal value product: $p \cdot \frac{\partial F}{\partial X_i}$ ) of *one unit* increase of input, $X_i$.

The calculated **CGES** Partial Complementarity *elasticities* ($c_{ij}$), (4.10), are shown in Table 4.2. The symmetric *Complementarity* elasticities ($c_{ij}$) satisfy *regularity* (summation) property, Sato and Koizumi (1973a, p. 47):

$$\sum_{j=1}^{M} e_j\, c_{ji} = \sum_{j=1, j \neq i}^{M} e_j\, c_{ji} + e_i\, c_{ii} = 0 \tag{4.13}$$

which is similar to the **Hicks-Allen** summation of symmetric ($\sigma_{ij}$) in (4.29).

**Table 4.1** GCES parameters of Fig. 4.1—$M = 5$, $(X) = (4,5,6,7,8)$

| | $i = 1$ | $i = 2$ | $i = 3$ | $i = 4$ | $i = 5$ |
|---|---|---|---|---|---|
| $X_i$ | 4 | 5 | 6 | 7 | 8 |
| $\rho_i$ | 0.2 | 0.3 | 0.4 | 0.4 | 0.5 |
| $a_i$ | 0.1 | 0.2 | 0.25 | 0.2 | 0.25 |
| $e_i$ | 0.0737 | 0.1718 | 0.2480 | 0.2071 | 0.2994 |
| $\gamma = 1.2$ | | $\rho = 0.2$ | $F(X) = 7.5766$ | | |

**Table 4.2** Complementarity elasticities—$c_{ij}$ (4.10) for $(X) = (4,5,6,7,8)$

| | $j = 1$ | $j = 2$ | $j = 3$ | $j = 4$ | $j = 5$ | $\sum_{j=1}^{5} e_j c_{ij}$ |
|---|---|---|---|---|---|---|
| $i = 1$ | −9.9698 | 0.8529 | 0.8061 | 0.8054 | 0.7409 | 0 |
| $i = 2$ | 0.8529 | −3.6493 | 0.7735 | 0.7722 | 07088 | 0 |
| $i = 3$ | 0.8061 | 0.7735 | −2.1843 | 0.7255 | 0.6650 | 0 |
| $i = 4$ | 0.8054 | 0.7722 | 0.7255 | −2.7550 | 0.6633 | 0 |
| $i = 5$ | 0.7409 | 0.7088 | 0.6650 | 0.6633 | −1.5986 | 0 |
| $\sum_{i=1}^{5} e_i c_{ij}$ | 0 | 0 | 0 | 0 | 0 | – |

**Table 4.3** $E(W_i, X_j) = \frac{\partial W_i}{\partial X_j} \frac{X_j}{W_i}$, (4.11); $E(W_i, X_i) = \frac{\partial W_i}{\partial X_i} \frac{X_i}{W_i}$, (4.12); $(X) = (4,5,6,7,8)$

| | $j = 1$ | $j = 2$ | $j = 3$ | $j = 4$ | $j = 5$ | $\sum_{j=1}^{5} E(W_i, X_j)$ |
|---|---|---|---|---|---|---|
| $i = 1$ | −0.7350 | 0.1465 | 0.1999 | 0.1668 | 0.2218 | 0 |
| $i = 2$ | 0.0629 | −0.6268 | 0.1918 | 0.1599 | 0.2122 | 0 |
| $i = 3$ | 0.0594 | 0.1329 | −0.5417 | 0.1502 | 0.1991 | 0 |
| $i = 4$ | 0.0594 | 0.1326 | 0.1799 | −0.5705 | 0.1986 | 0 |
| $i = 5$ | 0.0546 | 0.1218 | 0.1649 | 0.1374 | −0.4787 | 0 |
| $\sum_{i=1}^{5} e_i E(W_i, X_j)$ | 0 | 0 | 0 | 0 | 0 | – |

The **GCES** *Factor price* (Inverse demand )—*cross-*, *own* price—elasticities, $E(W_i, X_j)$, $E(W_i, X_i)$ (4.11–4.12) are calculated from Table 4.2 and seen in Table 4.3.

These *Factor price* elasticities,[5] (4.11–4.12), generated by any and all the exogenous factor *supplies* have *summation* properties—also seen in Table 4.3:

$$(i) \sum_{j=1}^{M} E\left(W_i, X_j\right) = \sum_{j=1}^{M} e_j c_{ji} = 0 \; ; \quad (ii) \sum_{j=1}^{M} e_j E\left(W_j, X_i\right) = 0 \tag{4.14}$$

[5] Tables with *numerical estimates* of complementarity and factor price elasticities (4.10), (4.11–4.12), selected years (1948,,1987) for translog and generalized Leontief production functions on US GDP data, see Kohli (1991, p. 127–129).

### *AUES Substitution Elasticities of* F(X), *GCES*

Formula (4.15 i) and (4.7) in Fig. 4.4 for calculation of $\sigma_{12}$ is only valid for production functions, $F(X_1, \ldots, X_M)$, with $M = 2$, Allen (1938, p. 343), Uzawa (1962, p. 1).

In Figs. 4.8 and 4.9, formula for $\sigma_{ij}$, (4.15 ii), $M > 2$, is more complicated. Here $|B_{ij}|$ is a *cofactor* element in the *bordered Hessian determinant*, $|B|$, of the *bordered* Hessian matrix, $B(X)$. First-order partials, $\frac{\partial F(X)}{\partial X_i}$, border the Hessian matrix of second-order partials, $\frac{\partial^2 F(X)}{\partial X_i \partial X_j}$, see Allen (1938, p. 504).

$$(i)\ \sigma_{12} = \frac{\frac{\partial F(X_1,X_2)}{\partial X_1} \frac{\partial F(X_1,X_2)}{\partial X_2}}{F(X_1, X_2) \frac{\partial^2 F(X_1,X_2)}{\partial X_1 \partial X_2}} = \sigma_{21};\quad (ii)\ \sigma_{ij} = \frac{F(X_1, \ldots, X_M)}{X_i X_j} \cdot \frac{|B_{ij}|}{|B|} \tag{4.15}$$

Figures 4.3 and 4.4 show that **GCES** is very *flexible*, wrt. sizes of $\boldsymbol{\sigma_{12}}$. This is due to the *three* independent *structural parameters*: $\rho_1$, $\rho_2$ and $\rho$—not available/seen in other specified *two-factor* ($M = 2$) production functions.

The GCES **general** *substitution parameter* $(\rho, \sigma)$ can essentially collectively *regulate* the **level** (increase/decrease) of **all** $\sigma_{ij}$ over a great range, usually enough for practical use.

In case (a,b), we see the largest/smallest $\sigma_{ij}$ along the *diagonal* (middle) of the factor quadrant, which good sense economically with respectively large/small substitution possibilities. Similarly, the $\sigma_{ij}$ *variation* in cases (c,d) makes sense by the different *sizes* of their factor **specific** *substitution parameters*, $(\rho_i)$, and their **specific** *intensity* (weight, "distribution") *parameter*, $(a_i)$. We return to Figs. 4.3 and 4.4, case (d) in section "GCES Functions and CRESH Functions, Convergence of GCES Functions".

Figure 4.6 shows the *flexibility* of $c_{12}$. With $M = 2$, $c_{12}$ and $\sigma_{12}$ are generally just the *inverse* (reciprocal) of each other, cf. (4.7)–(4.8)—but of course, not so simple with $\mathbf{M > 2}$. But, mostly *larger* values of $\rho_i$ and $\rho_j$ give *smaller* numbers for $c_{ij}$, (4.10), together with *higher* numbers of $\sigma_{ij}$, (4.15 ii).

Figure 4.7 shows the two-factor *shares* $(e_i)$ with structural *parameter* variation.

Figures 4.8 and 4.9 show that when **M** increases ($M > 3$), the *variation* in $\sigma_{ij}$ and $c_{ij}$ as *functions* of factor *inputs*, $X = (X_1, X_2, X_3)$, seems to become *lower*, but the differences between $\sigma_{12}$, $\sigma_{13}$ and $\sigma_{23}$ at the same factor inputs do not reduce to insignificant values.

Clearly, multiplying the production function (4.1) with a factor does not change, $\sigma_{ij}$, $c_{ij}$ or $e_i$. As **GCES** is *homogeneous* (degree 1), functions (4.15–4.10) depend only on the *ratios* of the variables. *Level curves* in Fig. 4.5 are thus straight lines from origo, which is not apparent from the pictures in Figs. 4.3 and 4.4. With the homogeneity property, curves for $\sigma_{ij}$ and $e_i$ are shown as functions of factor ratios, $\frac{X_2}{X_1}$ (different rays) in Figs. 4.10 and 4.11.

## GCES Functions and CRESH Functions, Convergence of GCES Functions

For many purposes, we can specifically choose to make the *$\rho$-parameter* equal to the *arithmetic average* of *parameters* $\rho_i$, $\rho = \frac{1}{M}\sum_{i=1}^{M}\rho_i$[6] or more generally $\rho = \rho_0 + \frac{1}{M}\sum_{i=1}^{M}\rho_i$ where $-\infty < \rho_0 \le 0$. Figure 4.3d *did* show a GCES *graph*, where $\rho = \frac{1}{M}\sum_{i=1}^{M}\rho_i$ and Fig. 4.4d shows the corresponding $\sigma_{12}$ *surface*.

Alternatively, a weighted mean value of $\rho_i$ could be used for $\rho$: $\rho = \rho_0 + \sum_{i=1}^{M} a_i\rho_i$.

If $\rho = \frac{1}{M}\sum_{i=1}^{M}\rho_i$ GCES functions have significant *similarities* with an *implicit* CRESH function, when the CRESH function use the **same** $\rho_i$ values. The formula for the implicit CRESH function, $F(Y, X) = 0$, is, cf. **Appendix 2** in section "Appendix 2. The CES and CRESH Functions", (4.49):

$$F(Y, X) = 0 \;;\; F(Y, X_1, X_2, \ldots, X_M) = \sum_{i=1}^{M} a_i\left[\frac{X_i}{Y/\gamma}\right]^{\rho_i} - \delta = 0 \qquad (4.16)$$

As the formula shows, the *implicit* **CRESH** function has—like the *explicit* **GCES** function (4.1)—a *substitution* **parameter**, $\rho_i$ , associated with **each** factor, $\mathbf{X_i}$, which allows for a *variable*, $\sigma_{12}$ when $M = 2$ and *variable* and *different levels* of $\sigma_{ij}$ when $M > 2$.

For comparison of *graphs* for CRESH and GCES with the *same* $\rho_i$ values and $\rho = \frac{1}{M}\sum\rho_i$, see Figs. 4.3d and 4.12. In Fig. 4.13, and Table 4.4, *levels* and *variations* of $\sigma_{ij}$ for GCES and CRESH are compared. The CRESH $(\sigma_{ij})$ level numbers are calculated by *formula*, (4.71). The curves in Fig. 4.13, are drawn from the numbers in Table 4.4. For GCES and CRESH, the *shape* of $(\sigma_{ij})$ curves in Fig. 4.13 are almost the *same*, and the *variation* is *small* (if not observed close to the axes).

For the CRESH function, the **ratio** between different, $\sigma_{ij}$, does *not vary* with sizes of the $X_i$ variables; cf. (4.73). From Fig. 4.14, it is seen that GCES has *almost* the same property, if $\rho = \frac{1}{M}\sum\rho_i$. Then GCES in Fig. 4.15 shows that such "invariant *ratio* property" *lessen*, when its $\rho$ parameter *deviates* much from the *mean value* of the $\rho_i$'s. However, the variation with $X_i$ is still relatively small.

[6] Instead of basing $\rho$ on the mean value of the $\rho_i$'s, one could base $\rho$ on the mean value of corresponding $\sigma_i$'s:

$$\sigma_i = \frac{1}{1-\rho_i} \Leftrightarrow \rho_i = \frac{\sigma_i - 1}{\sigma_i}$$

$$m = \frac{1}{M}\sum_{i=1}^{M}\frac{1}{1-\rho_i}, \qquad \rho = \frac{m-1}{m}.$$

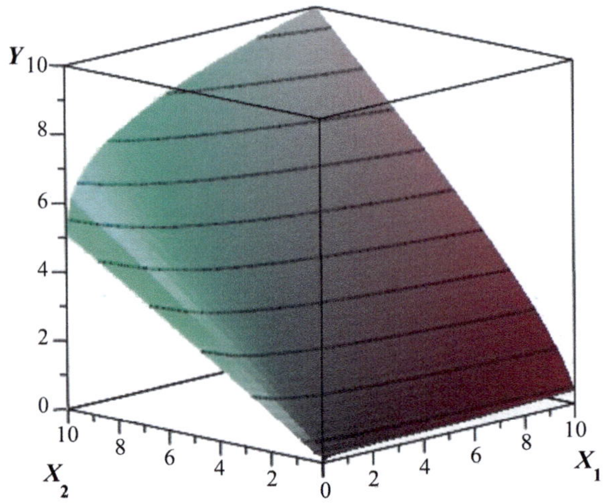


**Fig. 4.12** CRESH Production function, $F(Y, X_1, X_2) = 0$, (4.16), (4.49–4.50)

$M = 2$, $(a_1, a_2) = (0.5, 0.5)$, $(\rho_1, \rho_2) = (0.2, 0.8)$, $\delta = 1$

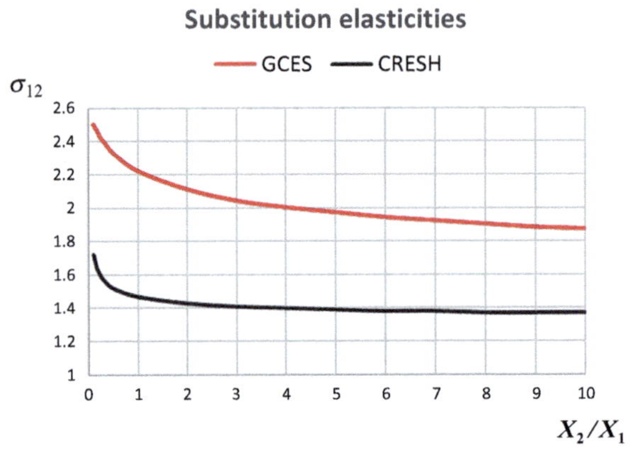


**Fig. 4.13** Substitution elasticities $\sigma_{12}$ $(X_2/X_1)$, GCES, CRESH

$M = 2$, $(a_1, a_2) = (0.5, 0.5), \rho = 0.5, (\rho_1, \rho_2) = (0.2, 0.8), X_2/X_1 \geq 0.1, \delta = 1$.

If one or more of the substitution variables $\rho_i$ is increased, the CRESH function $Y$ is not always increased. This is because the fractions in the $F$-function can be less than one. However, this has no bearing on applications. More important is whether the substitution elasticities $\sigma_{ij}$ always increase when one or more of the substitution variables $\rho_i$ increase. According to our

**Table 4.4** Partial Substitution elasticities $\sigma_{12}$

| | | $X_1 = 1$ | $X_1 = 2$ | $X_1 = 3$ | $X_1 = 4$ | $X_1 = 5$ | $X_1 = 6$ | $X_1 = 7$ | $X_1 = 8$ | $X_1 = 9$ | $X_1 = 10$ |
|---|---|---|---|---|---|---|---|---|---|---|---|
| $X_2 = 1$ | **GCES** | 2.22 | 2.33 | 2.39 | 2.42 | 2.45 | 2.47 | 2.48 | 2.49 | 2.50 | 2.50 |
| | CRESH | 1.47 | 1.52 | 1.56 | 1.59 | 1.62 | 1.64 | 1.67 | 1.69 | 1.71 | 1.72 |
| $X_2 = 2$ | **GCES** | 2.11 | 2.22 | 2.28 | 3.33 | 2.36 | 2.39 | 2.41 | 2.42 | 2.44 | 2.45 |
| | CRESH | 1.43 | 1.47 | 1.50 | 1.52 | 1.54 | 1.56 | 1.58 | 1.59 | 1.61 | 1.62 |
| $X_2 = 3$ | **GCES** | 2.04 | 2.15 | 2.22 | 2.27 | 2.30 | 2.33 | 2.35 | 2.37 | 2.39 | 2.40 |
| | CRESH | 1.41 | 1.45 | 1.47 | 1.49 | 1.51 | 1.52 | 1.54 | 1.55 | 1.56 | 1.57 |
| $X_2 = 4$ | **GCES** | 2.00 | 2.11 | 2.17 | 2.22 | 2.26 | 2.28 | 2.31 | 2.33 | 2.35 | 2.36 |
| | CRESH | 1.40 | 1.43 | 1.45 | 1.47 | 1.49 | 1.50 | 1.51 | 1.52 | 1.53 | 1.54 |
| $X_2 = 5$ | **GCES** | 1.97 | 2.07 | 2.14 | 2.18 | 2.22 | 2.25 | 2.27 | 2.29 | 2.31 | 2.33 |
| | CRESH | 1.39 | 1.42 | 1.44 | 1.46 | 1.47 | 1.48 | 1.49 | 1.50 | 1.51 | 1.52 |
| $X_2 = 6$ | **GCES** | 1.94 | 2.04 | 2.11 | 2.15 | 2.19 | 2.22 | 2.24 | 2.27 | 2.28 | 2.30 |
| | CRESH | 1.38 | 1.41 | 1.43 | 1.45 | 1.46 | 1.47 | 1.48 | 1.49 | 1.50 | 1.51 |
| $X_2 = 7$ | **GCES** | 1.92 | 2.02 | 2.08 | 2.13 | 2.16 | 2.19 | 2.22 | 2.24 | 2.26 | 2.28 |
| | CRESH | 1.38 | 1.40 | 1.42 | 1.44 | 1.45 | 1.46 | 1.47 | 1.48 | 1.49 | 1.50 |
| $X_2 = 8$ | **GCES** | 1.90 | 2.00 | 2.06 | 2.11 | 2.14 | 2.17 | 2.20 | 2.22 | 2.24 | 2.26 |
| | CRESH | 1.37 | 1.40 | 1.42 | 1.43 | 1.44 | 1.45 | 1.46 | 1.47 | 1.48 | 1.49 |
| $X_2 = 9$ | **GCES** | 1.88 | 1.98 | 2.04 | 2.09 | 2.12 | 2.15 | 2.18 | 2.20 | 2.22 | 2.24 |
| | CRESH | 1.37 | 1.39 | 1.41 | 1.42 | 1.44 | 1.45 | 1.45 | 1.46 | 1.47 | 1.48 |
| $X_2 = 10$ | **GCES** | 1.87 | 1.97 | 2.03 | 2.07 | 2.11 | 2.14 | 2.15 | 2.18 | 2.20 | 2.22 |
| | CRESH | 1.37 | 1.39 | 1.41 | 1.42 | 1.43 | 1.44 | 1.45 | 1.46 | 1.46 | 1.47 |

$\sigma_{12}(X_1, X_2)$, (4.15 i), (4.7) for GCES with $M = 2, (a_1, a_2) = (0.5, 0.5)$, $\rho = 0.5$, $(\rho_1, \rho_2) = (0.2, 0.8)$ as in Fig. 4.4d
$\sigma_{12}(X_1, X_2)$, (4.15 i), for CRESH (4.16), (4.49–4.50) with $M = 2$, $(a_1, a_2) = (0.5, 0.5)$, $(\rho_1, \rho_2) = (0.2, 0.8)$, $\delta = 1$

knowledge, this is not known for sure. However, for practical use it is only necessary that in the used area of the domain $\sigma_{ij}$ for $j = 1, \ldots, M$ increases, when $\rho_i$ increases. According to our knowledge, there have been no problems in achieving this and the CRESH function has proved to be useful in many cases.

As with the CRESH function, the GCES function does not necessarily increase if one or more of the substitution variables increase. This is because, as with the CRESH function, the last factor in the GCES function also contains fractions that can be less than one. If we set $\rho = \rho_0 + \frac{1}{M}\sum_{i=1}^{M} \rho_i$ and $\rho_0 \gtrsim -2$ the GCES function fulfils the requirement that $\sigma_{ij}$ for $j = 1, \ldots, M$, within the most relevant areas of the domain, increases when $\rho_i$ increases. The used area of the domain must not contain values of $X_i$ that are of very different orders of magnitude. Therefore, $X_i$ values must e.g. not be very close to zero. The expression for elasticity of substitution is complicated, but the fact that the $\rho$ parameter must not be constant in order to achieve the aforementioned is probably related to the fact that the first factor in the GCES function (the CES factor) must be increasing when one or more of the substitution variables increases.

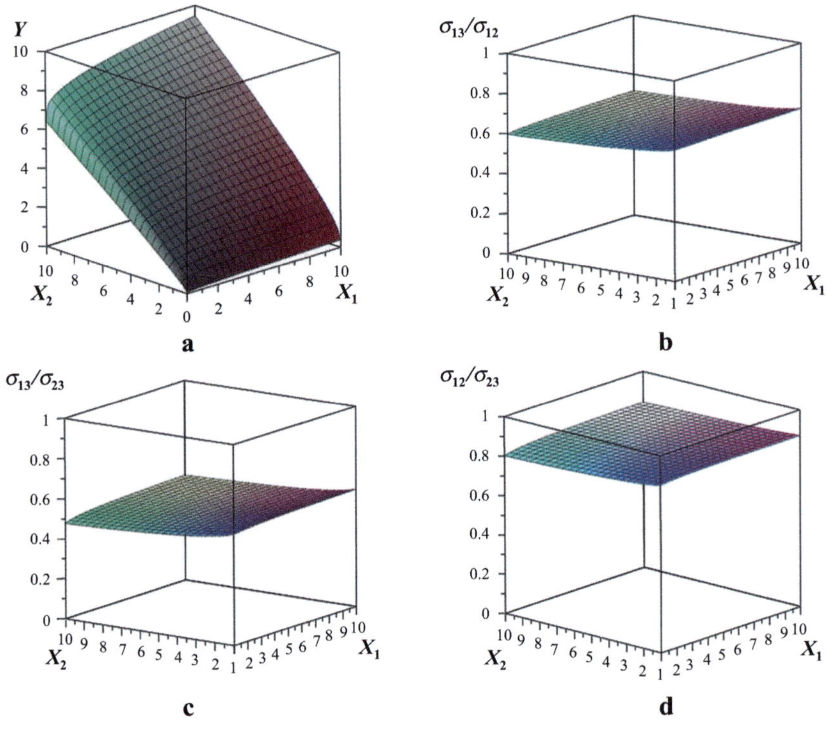


**Fig. 4.14** GCES functions, ratios of $\sigma_{ij}$ $(X_1, X_2, 5)$, (4.15 ii), with $\rho = \frac{1}{3}\sum \rho_i$

$$M = 3, \quad (X_1, X_2, X_3) = (X_1, X_2, 5), \quad (a_1, a_2, a_3) = (0.2, 0.7, 0.1)$$
$$\gamma = 1, \ (\rho_1, \rho_2, \rho_3) = (0.2, 0.7, 0.5), \quad \rho = \tfrac{1}{3}\sum \rho_i = 7/15\,.$$

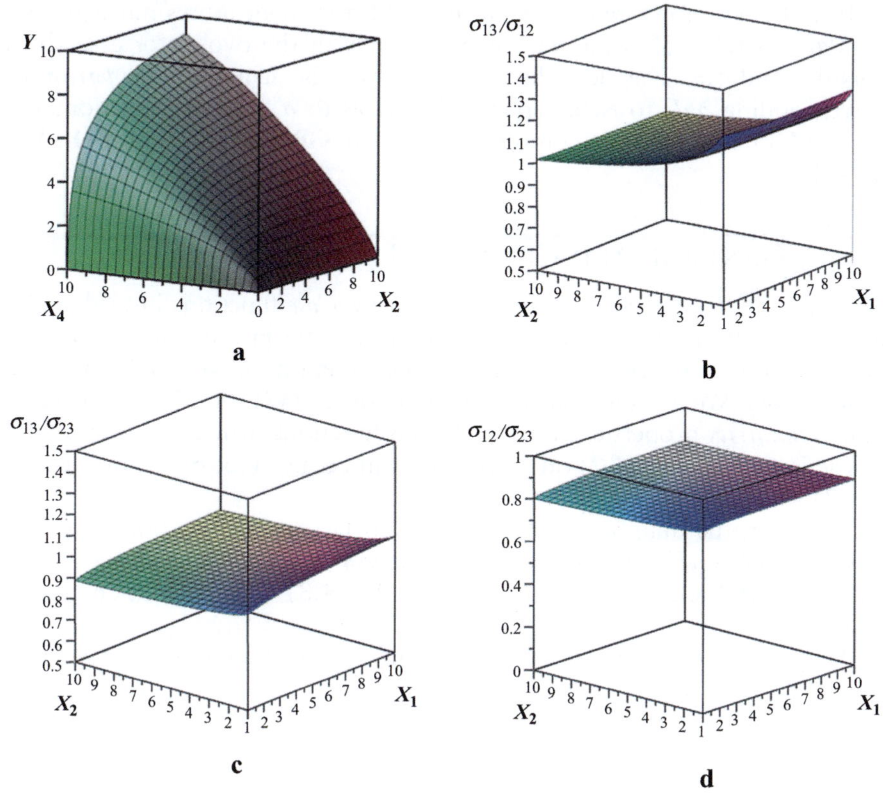


**Fig. 4.15** GCES functions, ratios of $\sigma_{ij}$ $(X_1, X_2, 5)$, (4.15 ii), with $\rho \neq \frac{1}{3}\sum \rho_i$

$$M = 3, \quad (X_1, X_2, X_3) = (X_1, X_2, 5), \quad (a_1, a_2, a_3) = (0.2, 0.7, 0.1)$$
$$\gamma = 1, \quad (\rho_1, \rho_2, \rho_3) = (0.1, 0.2, 0.3), \quad \rho = -0.5\,.$$

Another important thing about the GCES function is that if the $\rho$ parameter in the GCES function (4.1) is equal to the mean of the substitution variables, the GCES function converges to the Linear CES Function when all the $\rho_i$'s converge to one and converges to the Cobb-Douglas function if all the $\rho_i$ converge to zero.

GCES *multi -factor* production functions differ in *two* essential respects from CRESH *multi-factor* functions, (4.16): 1. GCES (4.1) is an *explicit* function 2. GCES (4.1) has an *additional substitution* **parameter**, $\rho$.

The explicit form have significance for incorporating GCES into solving the *multi-dimensional* dynamics involved in *applied general equilibrium models.* Construction of the GCES function based on observed data can also (as for CRESH functions) be done with using calibration procedures. On CRESH calibrations and applications, see Guest and Jensen (2016, p. 30).

It is the additional *parameter* $\rho$ in GCES that contributes much to extra *regular flexibility* of $\sigma_{ij}$, as was seen especially in the two-factor case above, Figs. 4.4 and 4.5. This flexibility in $\sigma_{ij}$, can *not* be achieved with *parameters* corresponding *only* to each variable $X_i$; i.e. as to $\sigma_{ij}$, **GCES** function, $Y = F(X)$, (4.1), is in this respect more *general* than **CRESH** function, $F(Y, X) = 0$, (4.16).

## Generalized CES Cost Functions, GCESC

Alternatively *Technologies* can be described by *Cost* functions instead of *Production* functions. Therefore, in the same way as for production functions we give here a *Generalization* of *unit* CES *cost* functions, **c(W)**, (4.17–4.18), cf. (4.47–4.48). We assume that the *cost* functions, **c(W)**, (4.17–4.18) have the same *regularity* properties (1–5), as GCES functions, when $\forall i : 0 < \sigma_i < 1$, restrictions similar to (4.2) on $\rho_i$. A *proof* can be given for $\sigma = 0$ by means of (4.32) with $\rho_i = 1 - \sigma_i$.

However, the unit *Generalized* CES multi-factor *Cost* functions, **GCESC**, **c(W)**, (4.17–4.18), are **not** exact *technological duals* to the specified multi-factor **GCES** Production functions, **F(X)**, (4.1–4.3)—but **c(W)** is designed as **F(X)**.

The **unit cost functions c(W)** is given in cost function *parameters*, $\sigma, \sigma_i, a_i$:

$$c(W) = c(W_1, \ldots, W_M) = \frac{1}{\gamma}\left[\sum_{i=1}^{M} a_i^{\sigma} W_i^{1-\sigma}\right]^{\frac{1}{1-\sigma}} \cdot \sum_{i=1}^{M} a_i^{\sigma_i}\left[\frac{W_i}{\left[\sum_{i=1}^{M} a_i^{\sigma} W_i^{1-\sigma}\right]^{\frac{1}{1-\sigma}}}\right]^{1-\sigma_i} \tag{4.17}$$

$$0 \leq \sigma < \infty \, ; \quad \sum_{i=1}^{M} a_i = 1; \quad \forall i : W_i > 0 \, , \; 0 \leq \sigma_i \leq 1, \; a_i > 0$$

$$\text{If } \sigma = 1 : c(W) = c(W_1, .., W_M) = \frac{1}{\gamma}\prod_{i=1}^{M}\left[\frac{W_i}{a_i}\right]^{a_i} \cdot \sum_{i=1}^{M} a_i^{\sigma_i}\left[\frac{W_i}{\prod_{i=1}^{M}\left[\frac{W_i}{a_i}\right]^{a_i}}\right]^{1-\sigma_i} \tag{4.18}$$

An example of *unit* GCES *cost* function (4.17) for $M = 2$, with $\sigma > 1$, and its corresponding, $\sigma_{12}(W_1, W_2)$, function—obtained by (4.27)—is shown in Fig. 4.16.

For similar figures of (4.17) with $M = 5$ and $\sigma < 1$, cf. Fig. 4.17, Table 4.5.

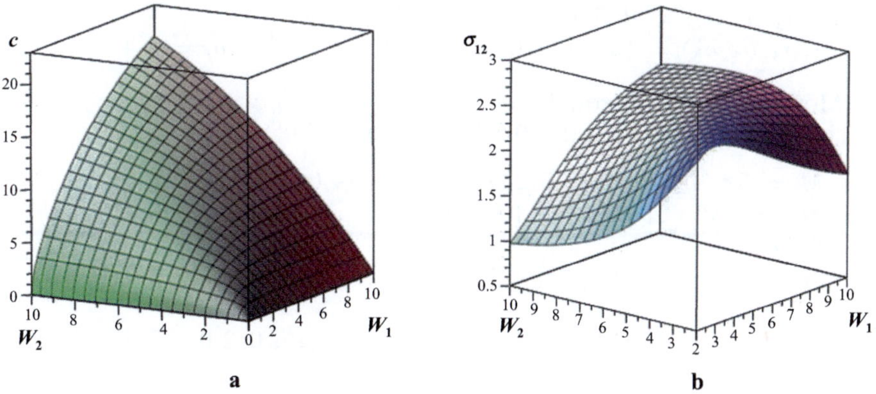


**Fig. 4.16** Unit cost function, $c\,(W_1, W_2)$, (4.17) and $\sigma_{12}\,(W_1, W_2)$. (4.27)

$\gamma = 1,\ (a_1, a_2) = (0.5, 0.5),\ \sigma = 3,\ (\sigma_1, \sigma_2) = (0.9, 0.5).$

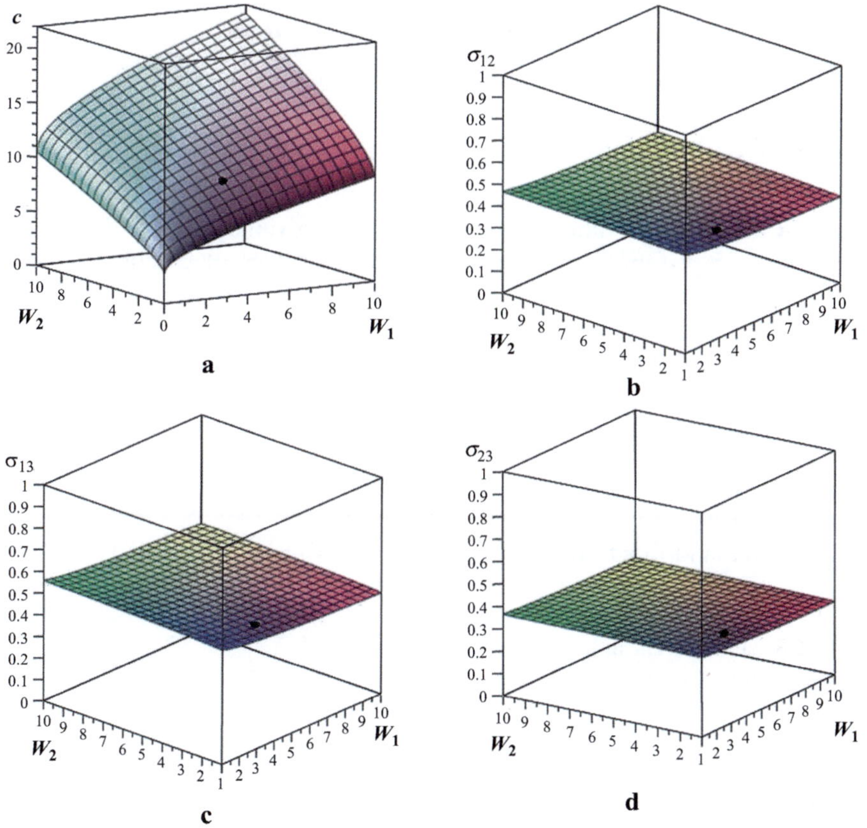


**Fig. 4.17** GCES Unit-cost function, $c(W)$, (4.17) and $\sigma_{ij}(W)$, (4.27)

$(a_1, a_2, a_3, a_4, a_5) = (0.3, 0.2, 0.15, 0.2, 0.15), \ \gamma = 1$
$(\sigma_1, \sigma_2, \sigma_3, \sigma_4, \sigma_5) = (0.6, 0.3, 0.4, 0.5, 0.2), \ \sigma = \frac{1}{5}\sum \sigma_i = 0.4$

(More generally one could set $\sigma = \sigma_0 + \frac{1}{M}\sum_{i=1}^{M} \sigma_i$ with $\sigma_0 \geq 0$)
The black spot: $W$ = (**4.0**,**2.0**,1.5,1.0,1.5)

a: $M = 5$, $c(W_1, W_2, 1.5, 1.0, 1.5)$, $c(4.0, 2.0, 1.5, 1.0, 1.5) = 9.70$
b: $M = 5$, $\sigma_{12}(W_1, W_2, 1.5, 1.0, 1.5)$, $\sigma_{12}(4.0, 2.0, 1.5, 1.0, 1.5) =$ **0.42**
c: $M = 5$, $\sigma_{13}(W_1, W_2, 1.5, 1.0, 1.5)$, $\sigma_{13}(4.0, 2.0, 1.5, 1.0, 1.5) =$ **0.50**
d: $M = 5$, $\sigma_{23}(W_1, W_2, 1.5, 1.0, 1.5)$, $\sigma_{23}(4.0, 2.0, 1.5, 1.0, 1.5) =$ **0.34**

In the corner $W$ = (**1**,**10**,1.5,1.0,1.5) we have:
$\sigma_{12} = 0.47, \quad \sigma_{13} = 0.56, \quad \sigma_{23} = 0.37$
For the black spot: $\sigma_{12} \approx \frac{\sigma_1+\sigma_2}{2} = 0.45$, $\sigma_{13} \approx \frac{\sigma_1+\sigma_3}{2} = 0.50$, $\sigma_{23} \approx \frac{\sigma_2+\sigma_3}{2} = 0.35$

### *GCESC Costs and Factor Demands*

The class of Generalized CES *Total* Cost function GCESC is:

$$C = C(W_1, \ldots, W_M, Y) = c(W_1, \ldots, W_M) \cdot Y = c(W) \cdot Y, \qquad \forall i : W_i > 0 \tag{4.19}$$

where GCES *unit* cost function, $c(W_1 \ldots W_M)$, is given by (4.17). Figure 4.17 shows $M = 5$, **GCESC** for *Parameters*, *Factor* prices, $W_i$, Table 4.5, $\sigma = \sum_{i=1}^{M} \frac{\sigma_i}{M} < 1$.

GCESC conditional (Hicksian) factor demand functions, $H_i(W, Y)$, $h_i(W)$, are (Table 4.6):

$$X_i = H_i(W, Y) = h_i(W) \cdot Y = \frac{\partial c(W)}{\partial W_i} \cdot Y \ , \quad i = 1, 2, ..5 \tag{4.20}$$

Factor demand functions for $Y = 1$: $x_i = h_i(W) = \frac{\partial c(W)}{\partial W_i}$, (4.20)

**Table 4.5** Parameters and $W_i$, GCES unit cost function, $c(W_1 \ldots W_5)$, (4.17)

| | $i = 1$ | $i = 2$ | $i = 3$ | $i = 4$ | $i = 5$ |
|---|---|---|---|---|---|
| $a_i$ | 0.30 | 0.20 | 0.15 | 0.20 | 0.15 |
| $\sigma_i$ | 0.60 | 0.30 | 0.40 | 0.50 | 0.20 |
| $W_i$ | 4.00 | 2.00 | 1.50 | 1.00 | 1.50 |
| $\gamma = 1$ | $\sigma = 0.40$ | | $c(W) = 9.6988$ | | |

**Table 4.6** *Factor demand*, $x_i = \frac{\partial c(W)}{\partial W_i}$, (4.20); *Cost shares*, $e_i(W) = \frac{\partial \ln c(W)}{\partial \ln W_i}$

| | $i = 1$ | $i = 2$ | $i = 3$ | $i = 4$ | $i = 5$ | |
|---|---|---|---|---|---|---|
| $x_i$ | 0.7103 | 1.1196 | 1.0190 | 1.2593 | 1.2205 | |
| $e_i$ | 0.2929 | 0.2309 | 0.1576 | 0.1298 | 0.1888 | $\sum_{i=1}^{5} e_i = 1.0000$ |

Factor cost shares, $e_i(W) = \frac{\partial \ln c(W)}{\partial \ln W_i} = \frac{\partial c(W)}{\partial W_i} \cdot \frac{W_i}{c(W)}$, (4.20), (4.17) (Table 4.6).

*Conditional Factor Demand Elasticities of GCESC, $c(W_1, .., W_M)$*
To cast additional light on GCESC *parameters* and *factor prices* in Table 4.5, we calculate factor price elasticities of GCESC, (4.17). The *own* price, $E(h_i, W_i)$, and *cross price* elasticities, $E(h_i, W_j)$, of *conditional* demands, $h_i(W)$, (4.20), follow simply by derivation of the explicit (parametric) formulas, $c(W)$, (4.17):

$$E(H_i, W_i) = \frac{\partial H_i}{\partial W_i}\frac{W_i}{H_i} = \frac{\partial^2 c(W)}{\partial W_i^2}\frac{W_i}{\partial c(W)/\partial W_i} = E(h_i, W_i) \quad < 0 \tag{4.21}$$

$$E(H_i, W_j) = \frac{\partial H_i}{\partial W_j}\frac{W_j}{H_i} = \frac{\partial^2 c(W)}{\partial W_i\, \partial W_j}\frac{W_j}{\partial c(W)/\partial W_i} = E(h_i, W_j), \quad i \neq j \tag{4.22}$$

$$E(H_j, W_i) = \frac{\partial H_j}{\partial W_i}\frac{W_i}{H_j} = \frac{\partial^2 c(W)}{\partial W_i\, \partial W_j}\frac{W_i}{\partial c(W)/\partial W_j} = E(h_j, W_i), \quad i \neq j \tag{4.23}$$

Conditional factor demands $H_i(W, Y)$, $h_i(W)$, are *homogeneous.* of *degree* (0) in $(W)$:

$$\sum_{j=1}^{M}\frac{\partial H_i}{\partial W_j}W_j = \sum_{j=1}^{M}\frac{\partial^2 c(W)}{\partial W_i\,\partial W_j}W_j = 0 \Leftrightarrow \sum_{j=1}^{M} E(h_i, W_j) = 0, \; h_i(W) \neq 0 \tag{4.24}$$

As an *identity*, (4.24), offers a quick and important overall *numerical check* on theoretical/empirical conditional "own price" and "in-going cross price" (4.22) factor demand *elasticity calculations*—see the *rows* in Table 4.8.

The *output* (level) *constraint* associated with conditional factor demands $H_i(W, Y)$—cf. Hicks (1946, p. 311, "third law"), Silberberg and Suen (2001,

**Table 4.7** The Hessian matrix $\frac{\partial^2 c(W)}{\partial W_i \partial W_j}$—of GCESC, $c(W)$, (4.17); Table 4.5

| | $j = 1$ | $j = 2$ | $j = 3$ | $j = 4$ | $j = 5$ | $\sum_{j=1}^{5} \frac{\partial^2 c(W)}{\partial W_i \partial W_j} W_j$ |
|---|---|---|---|---|---|---|
| $i = 1$ | −0.0556 | 0.0346 | 0.0372 | 0.0524 | 0.0301 | 0.000 |
| $i = 2$ | 0.0346 | −0.1519 | 0.0402 | 0.0567 | 0.0323 | 0.000 |
| $i = 3$ | 0.0372 | 0.0402 | −0.2285 | 0.0606 | 0.0352 | 0.000 |
| $i = 4$ | 0.0524 | 0.0567 | 0.0606 | −0.4889 | 0.0501 | 0.000 |
| $i = 5$ | 0.0301 | 0.0323 | 0.0352 | 0.0501 | −0.1920 | 0.000 |
| $\sum_{i=1}^{5} \frac{\partial^2 c(W)}{\partial W_i \partial W_j} W_i$ | 0.000 | 0.000 | 0.000 | 0.000 | 0.000 | – |

**Table 4.8** *Conditional* factor *demand elasticities*—$E(h_i, W_j)$, (4.22) Table 4.5

| | $j = 1$ | $j = 2$ | $j = 3$ | $j = 4$ | $j = 5$ | $\sum_{j=1}^{5} E(h_i, W_j)$ |
|---|---|---|---|---|---|---|
| $i = 1$ | −0.3133 | 0.0974 | 0.0786 | 0.0737 | 0.0636 | 0.000 |
| $i = 2$ | 0.1235 | −0.2713 | 0.0539 | 0.0507 | 0.0432 | 0.000 |
| $i = 3$ | 0.1461 | 0.0789 | −0.3364 | 0.0595 | 0.0519 | 0.000 |
| $i = 4$ | 0.1663 | 0.0901 | 0.0595 | −0.3883 | 0.0597 | 0.000 |
| $i = 5$ | 0.0987 | 0.0529 | 0.0433 | 0.0411 | −0.2359 | 0.000 |
| $\sum_{i=1}^{5} e_i E(h_i, W_j)$ | 0.000 | 0.000 | 0.000 | 0.0000 | 0.000 | – |

p. 295)—is satisfied by the GCESC elasticities, (4.21–4.23)—see the *columns* in Table 4.8.

$$\sum_{j=1}^{M} e_j(W)\, E(H_j, W_i) = \sum_{j=1}^{M} e_j(W)\, E(h_j, W_i) \; = \; 0 \tag{4.25}$$

The *Aggregation property* (4.25) of "own price" and "out-going cross price" elasticities, (4.23), may be called **Hicks-Shepard aggregation**, which coherently reflects *all* the *comparative static effects* of changing **one** single price.

As far as *Hicksian* price responses (4.22–4.23) are concerned, there is often in theory mentioned potential flexibility, with respect to both the *size* and *sign* (substitutes, complements), of these cross-factor price elasticities, i.e. the sign of, $\frac{\partial h_i(W)}{\partial W_j} = \frac{\partial^2 c(W)}{\partial W_i \partial W_j}$, might be positive/negative, but mostly positive, cf. Table 4.7.

### *The Allen-Uzawa Elasticities of Substitution*

The Allen-Uzawa partial elasticities of substitution (**AUES**) of factor demands, $X_i = h_i(W)$, are *not* often shown. But for our GCESC cost function a clear *parametric* connection to the non-zero Allen-Uzawa elasticities is given.

The Allen-Uzawa elasticities of substitution, $\sigma_{ij}$, can be simply obtained, cf. Frisch (1959, p. 180), by *"normalizing"* GCESC elasticities, (4.21–4.23), as:

$$\sigma_{ii}(W) = \frac{E(h_i, W_i)}{e_i(W)} = \frac{\partial^2 c(W)}{\partial W_i^2} \cdot \frac{c(W)}{[\frac{\partial c(W)}{\partial W_i}]^2} < 0 \tag{4.26}$$

$$\sigma_{ji}(W) = \frac{E(h_j, W_i)}{e_i(W)} = \frac{E(h_i, W_j)}{e_j(W)} = \sigma_{ij}(W),\ i \neq j \tag{4.27}$$

$$= \frac{\partial^2 c(W)}{\partial W_i\, \partial W_j} \cdot \frac{c(W)}{[\frac{\partial c(W)}{\partial W_i} \cdot \frac{\partial c(W)}{\partial W_j}]} = \sigma_{ij}(W),\ i \neq j \tag{4.28}$$

The elasticities $\sigma_{ii}(W)$ refer to substitution between the i'th factor and *all* others. As in (4.25), GCESC *substitution* elasticities, (4.26–4.27), meet the *output* constraint implied by *Hicksian* demands $H_i(W, Y)$, $h_i(W)$, and with (4.21–4.23), we get:

$$\sum_{j=1}^{N} e_j \sigma_{ji} = \sum_{j=1}^{N} e_j E(H_j, W_i)/e_i = 0 \tag{4.29}$$

$$\sum_{j=1}^{N} e_j \sigma_{ij} = \sum_{j=1}^{N} e_j E(H_i, W_j)/e_j = \sum_{j=1}^{N} E(H_i, W_j) = 0 \tag{4.30}$$

We call *Aggregation property*, (4.29): the **Hicks-Allen aggregation**—Hicks (1937, p. 16–17), Allen (1938, p. 504)—that is a *general* relation among factor demand elasticities that is *not tied* to GCESC substitution elasticities, (4.26–4.27). Note that **Hicks-Allen aggregation** (4.29) follows from **symmetry** and **zero**-degree *homogeneity* in (4.30).

The great mathematical-economic advantage of *any cost function* $c(W)$ is that the underlying *substitution elasticities* ($\boldsymbol{\sigma}_{ij}$) can be *explicitly* derived by the Uzawa[7] *procedure*, (4.28), and so be *studied*—as we have shown for $c(W)$, (4.17)—in terms of **basic parameters** actually *chosen* for $c(W)$ in Table 4.5.

The *sizes* of *all* substitution elasticities, (4.26–4.27), of $c(W)$, are in Table 4.9.

$\sigma_{ij}\,s$ satisfy with cost shares ($e_i$), Table 4.6, *Aggregation Conditions*, (4.29–4.30).

When $\sigma < 1$ and especially if $\sigma$ is equal to the mean value of the $\sigma_i$'s, the variation in substitution elasticities $\sigma_{ij}(W)$ as function of W is *small*, **but** the *differences* between the *different* $\sigma_{ij}$ are of the **same** order as the *differences* between the *parameters* $\sigma_i$'s—as shown at the bottom of Fig. 4.17.

[7] See Uzawa (1962, p. 293, eq.(9)), Diewert (1974b, p. 114, eq.(15)).

**Table 4.9** *Substitution elasticities—*$\sigma_{ij}$ (4.27–4.28)—by $c(W)$, (4.17); Table 4.5

| | $j = 1$ | $j = 2$ | $j = 3$ | $j = 4$ | $j = 5$ | $\sum_{j=1}^{5} e_j \sigma_{ij}$ |
|---|---|---|---|---|---|---|
| $i = 1$ | −1.0694 | 0.4217 | 0.4988 | 0.5677 | 0.3370 | 0.000 |
| $i = 2$ | 0.4217 | −1.1751 | 0.3420 | 0.3901 | 0.2289 | 0.000 |
| $i = 3$ | 0.4988 | 0.3420 | −2.1347 | 0.4583 | 0.2747 | 0.000 |
| $i = 4$ | 0.5677 | 0.3901 | 0.4583 | −2.9905 | 0.3162 | 0.000 |
| $i = 5$ | 0.3370 | 0.2289 | 0.2747 | 0.3162 | −1.2498 | 0.000 |
| $\sum_{i=1}^{5} e_i \sigma_{ij}$ | 0.000 | 0.000 | 0.000 | 0.000 | 0.000 | – |

It is not possible to construct cost functions with $\sigma_{ij}$ completely independent of $W$. The cost function $c(W)$, (4.17) comes close to having such property, if the *parameter*, $\sigma$, is either less than one or slightly bigger than one. *Variations* of $\sigma_{ij}(W)$ as function of factor prices $W$ mainly takes place close to the *axes*—and can mostly be *ignored*, cf. Fig. 4.17.

## Final Remarks

The literature on production functions, cost functions, substitution elasticities, and complementarity elasticities is extensive. In the References are listed further important contributions in this field. This chapter has focused upon obtaining *globally regular multi-factor* production and cost factor functions that can be used to enlarge the dynamic system of economic growth models and trade models—which although extended to encompass multi-sector (many industry, goods) models, have seldom included more than *two* primary *factors*, Labor and Capital. Such *low-dimensional dynamics* can generate a rich family of intricate solutions with *widely different qualitative* and *quantitative* properties. Multi-sector two-factor dynamics is seen with the two-factor CES production functions in Chaps. 19–21.

In the future, *homogeneous multi-factor* GCES production and GCESC cost functions could considerably *enlarge* the capability of *dynamic* models for *expanding* economies by computing their *general equilibrium solutions.*

**Acknowledgement:** We thank professor Christian Berg, Department of Mathematics, University of Copenhagen for the Lemma 4.1 of the concavity of (4.37) and thereby also of the concavity of (4.32) and (4.31).

## Appendix 1. Proof of Conjecture for: $\rho = 1$

With $\rho = 1$, the **GCES** function, (4.1), becomes:

$$\rho = 1: \quad F(X) \equiv F(X_1 \ldots X_M) = \gamma \left[ \sum_{i=1}^{M} a_i X_i \right] \cdot \sum_{i=1}^{M} a_i \left[ \frac{X_i}{[\sum_{i=1}^{M} a_i X_i]} \right]^{\rho_i} \tag{4.31}$$

Every *affine transformation* of the variable with *positive* real-valued elements in the transformation matrix *conserve Properties* 1–5. Therefore it is equivalent to show the properties for the following function (divide $X_i$ by $a_i$):

$$f = f(X_1 \ldots X_M) = \gamma \left[ \sum_{i=1}^{M} X_i \right] \cdot \sum_{i=1}^{M} a_i^{1-\rho_i} \left[ \frac{X_i}{[\sum_{i=1}^{M} X_i]} \right]^{\rho_i} \tag{4.32}$$

which is *continuous* and *homogeneous* of *degree*, 1, in $X$.

$$\underline{X} \equiv \sum_{i=1}^{M} X_i, \quad f = \gamma \underline{X} \cdot \sum_{i=1}^{M} a_i^{1-\rho_i} \left[ \frac{X_i}{\underline{X}} \right]^{\rho_i} = \gamma \sum_{i=1}^{M} a_i^{1-\rho_i} X_i^{\rho_i} \underline{X}^{1-\rho_i} \tag{4.33}$$

Elementary calculations leads to expressions for the derivatives:

$$\frac{\partial f(X)}{\partial X_i} = \gamma \left[ \sum_{m=1}^{M} a_m^{1-\rho_m} [1 - \rho_m] \left[ \frac{X_m}{\underline{X}} \right]^{\rho_m} + a_i^{1-\rho_i} \rho_i \left[ \frac{X_i}{\underline{X}} \right]^{\rho_i - 1} \right] > 0 \tag{4.34}$$

which is continuous, homogeneous of *degree*, 0, in $X$, and $f(X)$ is *increasing*.

$$\frac{\partial^2 f(X)}{\partial X_i \, \partial X_j} = \frac{\gamma}{\underline{X}} \left[ - \sum_{m=1}^{M} a_m^{1-\rho_m} \rho_m [1 - \rho_m] \left[ \frac{X_m}{\underline{X}} \right]^{\rho_m} \right.$$
$$\left. + a_i^{1-\rho_i} \rho_i [1 - \rho_i] \left[ \frac{X_i}{\underline{X}} \right]^{\rho_i - 1} + a_j^{1-\rho_j} \rho_j [1 - \rho_j] \left[ \frac{X_j}{\underline{X}} \right]^{\rho_j - 1} \right] \tag{4.35}$$

which is continuous and homogeneous of *degree*, −1, in $X$.

$$\frac{\partial^2 f(X)}{\partial X_i^2} = \frac{\gamma}{\underline{X}}\left[-\sum_{m=1}^{M} a_m^{1-\rho_m}\rho_m[1-\rho_m]\left[\frac{X_m}{\underline{X}}\right]^{\rho_m} + 2a_i^{1-\rho_i}\rho_i[1-\rho_i]\left[\frac{X_i}{\underline{X}}\right]^{\rho_i-1} - a_i^{1-\rho_i}\rho_i[1-\rho_i]\left[\frac{X_i}{\underline{X}}\right]^{\rho_i-2}\right] = \tag{4.36}$$

$$\frac{\gamma}{\underline{X}}\left[-\sum_{m=1,\, m\neq i}^{M} a_m^{1-\rho_m}\rho_m[1-\rho_m]\left[\frac{X_m}{\underline{X}}\right]^{\rho_m} - a_i^{1-\rho_i}\rho_i[1-\rho_i]\left[\frac{X_i}{\underline{X}}\right]^{\rho_i}\left[1-\frac{\underline{X}}{X_i}\right]^2\right] < 0$$

which is continuous and homogeneous of *degree*, −1, in $X$.

*Concavity* To verify that (4.32)–(4.33) are concave consider the functions

$$f_i(X) = X_i^{\rho_i}(X_1 + \cdots + X_M)^{1-\rho_i}, \quad i = 1, \ldots, M \tag{4.37}$$

defined on the **positive orthant**: $D = \{X_1 > 0, \ldots, X_M > 0\}$.

We claim that **each**, $f_i(X)$, is **concave**, which is proved in:

**Lemma 4.1** *For* $0 < \rho_i < 1$, **function**, $f_i(X)$, *given by (4.37) is* **concave**.

***Proof*** Let $X = (X_1, \ldots, X_M)$, $Y = (Y_1, \ldots, Y_M) \in D$ be arbitrary. Let $0 \le t \le 1$. We shall prove that the function

$$g(t) = f_i(tX + (1-t)Y), \;\; 0 \le t \le 1 \tag{4.38}$$

is concave on the unit interval. Denoting as before $\underline{X} = X_1 + \cdots + X_M$ and similarly $\underline{Y} = Y_1 + \cdots + Y_M$, we have by (4.37–4.38),

$$\begin{aligned} g(t) &= (tX_i + (1-t)Y_i)^{\rho_i}(t\underline{X} + (1-t)\underline{Y})^{1-\rho_i} \\ &= X_i^{\rho_i}\underline{X}^{1-\rho_i}\left(t + (1-t)\frac{Y_i}{X_i}\right)^{\rho_i}\left(t + (1-t)\frac{\underline{Y}}{\underline{X}}\right)^{1-\rho_i} && (4.39) \\ &= X_i^{\rho_i}\underline{X}^{1-\rho_i}\, h(t) && (4.40) \end{aligned}$$

We finally have to prove that the **auxiliary** function, $h(t)$, in (4.40):

$$h(t) = (t + (1-t)p)^{\rho_i}(t + (1-t)q)^{1-\rho_i}, \quad p = \frac{Y_i}{X_i} > 0, \; q = \frac{\underline{Y}}{\underline{X}} > 0 \qquad (4.41)$$

is concave for **t** in the ***unit interval.*** A small calculation leads to,

$$h''(t) = \rho_i(\rho_i - 1)(t + (1-t)p)^{\rho_i - 2}(t + (1-t)q)^{-1-\rho_i}[A - B]^2, \qquad (4.42)$$

where $A = (1-p)(t+(1-t)q)$, $\quad B = (1-q)(t+(1-t)p)$, Since, $\rho_i(\rho_i - 1) < 0$, we get: $h''(t) < 0$; hence, $h(t)$, (4.41)—and $f_i$, (4.37)—is concave. Finally, since cf. (4.33)

$$f = \gamma \sum_{i=1}^{M} a_i^{1-\rho_i} f_i \qquad (4.43)$$

and $a_i^{1-\rho_i} > 0$, we see that $f$ is concave, because a positive linear combination of concave functions is concave. □

## Appendix 2. The CES and CRESH Functions

The CES multi-factor production functions, homogeneous of degree 1, are (Fig. 4.18):

$$Y = F(X) = F(X_1, \ldots, X_M) = \gamma \, [ \sum_{i=1}^{M} a_i \, X_i^{\rho} \, ]^{\frac{1}{\rho}} \qquad (4.44)$$

$$a_i \geq 0, \; \sum_{i=1}^{M} a_i = 1, \; \rho \in ]-\infty, 0[ \text{ or } \rho \in ]0, 1] \qquad (4.45)$$

$$\text{If } \rho = 0 : Y = \gamma \prod_{i=1}^{M} X_i^{a_i} \quad \text{Cobb Douglas or CD} \qquad (4.46)$$

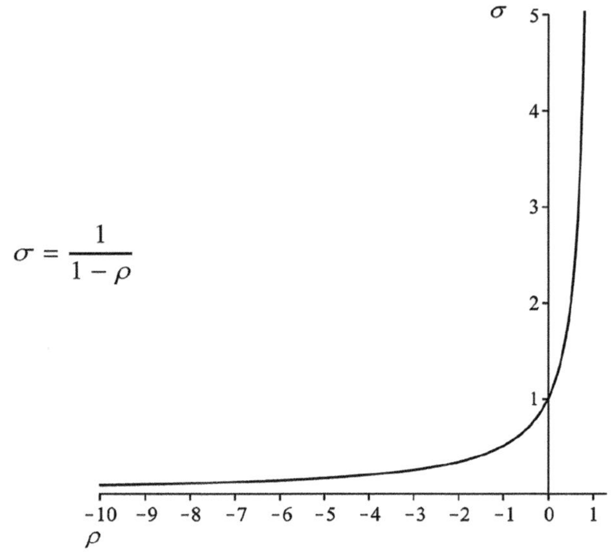


**Fig. 4.18** Elasticity of substitution for CES functions

CES functions (4.44–4.45) have an *exact dual* CES Unit ($Y = 1$) Cost function:

$$c = c(W_1, .., W_M) = \frac{1}{\gamma}\left[\sum_{i=1}^{M} a_i^{\sigma}\, W_i^{1-\sigma}\right]^{\frac{1}{1-\sigma}} \tag{4.47}$$

$$a_i \geq 0,\ \sum_{i=1}^{M} a_i = 1,\ \sigma \in [0, 1[ \text{ or } \sigma \in ]1, \infty[,\ \text{If } \sigma = 1 : c = \frac{1}{\gamma}\prod_{i=1}^{M}\left[\frac{W_i}{a_i}\right]^{a_i} \tag{4.48}$$

The CRESH *Implicit Production* functions—Hanoch (1971, p. 697)—are:

$$F(Y, X) = 0;\ F(Y, X_1, X_2, \ldots, X_M) = \sum_{i=1}^{M} a_i\left[\frac{X_i}{Y/\gamma}\right]^{\rho_i} - \delta = 0 \tag{4.49}$$

$$\gamma > 0;\ \forall i : \alpha_i > 0,\ \sum_{i=1}^{M} \alpha_i = 1;\ \forall i :\ 0 < \rho_i \leq 1 \ \textit{or}\ \rho_i < 0, \delta > 0 \tag{4.50}$$

**Remark 4.1** Since the Partial Substitution elasticities ($\sigma_{ij}$) refers to two variables, it could be of interest to have production functions, where the parameters ($\rho$) also relate to two variables instead of one variable. Such new types of production functions may be important in future work.

The following functions could be considered:
As a sum of concave functions, (4.51) is a *concave* function, but (4.51) does not reduce to the CES function, if all $\rho_{ij}$'s are equal.

$$Y = f(X_1, .., X_M) = \gamma \sum_{i=1}^{M-1} \sum_{j=i+1}^{M} \frac{a_i + a_j}{M-1} \left( \frac{a_i}{a_i + a_j} X_i^{\rho_{ij}} + \frac{a_j}{a_i + a_j} X_j^{\rho_{ij}} \right)^{\frac{1}{\rho_{ij}}} \tag{4.51}$$

$$a_i \geq 0, \ \sum_{i=1}^{M} a_i = 1, \ -\infty < \rho_{ij} \leq 1; \ \rho_{ij} = 0 : \text{use Cobb-Douglas expressions.} \tag{4.52}$$

However, if we use a mean value on the expression (4.51) either in the CES sense or in the CRESH style we can get expressions that give the CES function, if all $\rho_{ij}$'s are equal. We assume that the new functions are still *concave*.
Using CES mean value definition on (4.51) we get:

$$Y = F(X_1, .., X_M) = \gamma \left[ \sum_{i=1}^{M-1} \sum_{j=i+1}^{M} \frac{a_i + a_j}{M-1} \left( \frac{a_i}{a_i + a_j} X_i^{\rho_{ij}} + \frac{a_j}{a_i + a_j} X_j^{\rho_{ij}} \right)^{\frac{\rho}{\rho_{ij}}} \right]^{\frac{1}{\rho}} \tag{4.53}$$

$$a_i \geq 0, \ \sum_{i=1}^{M} a_i = 1, \ -\infty < \rho_{ij} \leq 1; \ \rho_{ij} = 0 : \text{ use Cobb-Douglas expressions.} \tag{4.54}$$

For CES as limit, use a mean value for $\rho$ for example: $\rho = \frac{2}{M^2 - M} \sum_{i=1}^{M-1} \sum_{j=i+1}^{M} \rho_{ij}$
Using a CRESH style mean value definition on (4.51) we get:

$$F(Y, X_1, .., X_M) = \sum_{i=1}^{M-1} \sum_{j=i+1}^{M} \frac{a_i + a_j}{M-1} \left[ \frac{\left( \frac{a_i}{a_i+a_j} X_i^{\rho_{ij}} + \frac{a_j}{a_i+a_j} X_j^{\rho_{ij}} \right)^{\frac{1}{\rho_{ij}}}}{Y/\gamma} \right]^{\rho_{ij}} - \delta = 0 \tag{4.55}$$

or

$$F(Y, X_1, .., X_M) = \sum_{i=1}^{M-1} \sum_{j=i+1}^{M} \frac{a_i}{M-1} \left( \frac{X_i}{Y/\gamma} \right)^{\rho_{ij}} + \frac{a_j}{M-1} \left( \frac{X_j}{Y/\gamma} \right)^{\rho_{ij}} - \delta = 0 \tag{4.56}$$

$$a_i \geq 0, \ \sum_{i=1}^{M} a_i = 1, \ -\infty < \rho_{ij} < 0 \text{ or } 0 < \rho_{ij} \leq 1, \delta > 0 \tag{4.57}$$

# Appendix 3. Regularity and Flexibility Properties of CRESH Functions

## *The Implicit Multi-factor Production Function, CRESH: Constant Ratio of Elasticity of Substitution, Homothetic*

As mentioned above, Hanoch (1971, p. 697) introduced an *implicit* CRESH production *function*, $F(Y, X_1, X_2, \ldots, X_M) = 0$, (4.49–4.50). A slightly parametric extended version of the *implicit* CRESH function is given by the *equation*, (4.58), and *parameter restrictions*, (4.59):

$$F\,(Y, X_1, X_2, \ldots, X_M) = \sum_{i=1}^{M} \alpha_i \left[\frac{X_i}{Y/\gamma}\right]^{\rho_i} - \delta = 0 \ ; \quad \delta > 0 \tag{4.58}$$

$$\gamma > 0; \ \ \forall i : \alpha_i > 0, \ \sum_{i=1}^{M} \alpha_i = 1; \ \forall i : \ 0 < \rho_i \leq 1 \ \ or \ \rho_i < 0 \tag{4.59}$$

**F** is *homogeneous* of degree **0**, and **F** determines **implicitly** the single *output* variable, (**Y**), from M distinct (heterogeneous) *factor inputs* (flows, services), $(X_1, X_2, \ldots, X_M)$.

If $\forall i$: $\rho_i = \rho = \frac{\sigma - 1}{\sigma}$, (4.58–4.59) give CES functions—and CD as limit function ($\rho = 0, \delta = 1$):

$$\rho_i = \rho : Y = \delta^{-\frac{1}{\rho}} \gamma \left[\sum_{i=1}^{M} \alpha_i X_i^{\rho}\right]^{\frac{1}{\rho}} ; \ \rho = 1, \ Y = \delta^{-1} \gamma \sum_{i=1}^{M} \alpha_i X_i \ ;$$

$$\rho = 0, \delta = 1, \ \ Y = \gamma \prod_{i=1}^{M} X_i^{\alpha_i} \tag{4.60}$$

Parameter *restrictions* (4.59) ensure that CRESH equation (4.58) represents a **unique** implicit *production function*, $\mathbf{Y} = \mathbf{f}\,(X_1, X_2, \ldots, X_M)$, that is *homogeneous* of degree **1**, and is **globally regular**, i.e. for all $X_i > 0$, $\mathbf{f}\,(X_1, X_2, \ldots, X_M)$ is *positive*, *non-decreasing*, *concave* (with a negative semi-definite *Hessian* matrix, $\frac{\partial^2 \mathbf{f}}{\partial \mathbf{X_i}\, \partial \mathbf{X_j}}$ ):

$$\forall X_i > 0 : \ Y = f\,(X_1, X_2, \ldots, X_M) > 0 \ ; \ \frac{\partial f}{\partial X_i} > 0 \ , \ \frac{\partial^2 f}{\partial X_i^2} < 0 \ ;$$

$$Y = \sum_{i=1}^{M} \frac{\partial f}{\partial X_i} X_i \tag{4.61}$$

The CRESH function, $F(Y, X_1, X_2, \ldots, X_M)$, (4.58), has the first-order derivatives,

$$\frac{\partial F}{\partial X_i} = \frac{\gamma^{\rho_i}\,\alpha_i\,\rho_i\,(X_i/Y)^{\rho_i-1}}{Y}, \quad i = 1, \ldots, M; \quad \frac{\partial F}{\partial Y} = -\frac{\sum_{i=1}^{M}\alpha_i\,\rho_i\left(\frac{X_i}{Y/\gamma}\right)^{\rho_i}}{Y} \tag{4.62}$$

*Marginal contributions* of $X_i$ to $Y$: $\frac{\partial Y}{\partial X_i} = \frac{\partial f}{\partial X_i}$, and *marginal* rates of *substitution* (**MRS**) are given by implicit differentiation of $F(Y, X_1, X_2, \ldots, X_M)$, i.e. we get by (4.61–4.62):

$$\frac{\partial Y}{\partial X_i} = \frac{\partial f}{\partial X_i} = -\frac{\partial F/\partial X_i}{\partial F/\partial Y} = \frac{\gamma^{\rho_i}\,\alpha_i\,\rho_i\,(X_i/Y)^{\rho_i-1}}{\sum_{i=1}^{M}\alpha_i\,\rho_i\left(\frac{X_i}{Y/\gamma}\right)^{\rho_i}} > 0, \quad i = 1, \ldots, M \tag{4.63}$$

$$\frac{dX_j}{dX_i} = MRS = \frac{\partial f/\partial X_i}{\partial f/\partial X_j} = \frac{\gamma^{\rho_i}\,\alpha_i\,\rho_i\,(X_i/Y)^{\rho_i-1}}{\gamma^{\rho_j}\alpha_j\,\rho_j\,(X_j/Y)^{\rho_j-1}}, \quad i \neq j \tag{4.64}$$

The elasticities, $E(Y, X_i)$, *shares* $(e_i)$, add up to 1 by the degree of homogeneity in (4.61),

$$e_i = E(Y, X_i) \equiv \frac{\partial Y}{\partial X_i}\frac{X_i}{Y} = \frac{\gamma^{\rho_i}\,\alpha_i\,\rho_i\,(X_i/Y)^{\rho_i}}{\sum_{i=1}^{M}\alpha_i\,\rho_i\left(\frac{X_i}{Y/\gamma}\right)^{\rho_i}}; \quad \sum_{i=1}^{M} e_i = 1 \tag{4.65}$$

**Relative** *factor prices*, (4.64)—must reflect their **MRS**. Hence CRESH relative *factor* prices, $\frac{w_i}{w_j}$, CRESH relative *factor* income *shares*, $(\frac{e_i}{e_j} = \frac{w_i X_i}{w_j X_j})$, become by (4.64–4.65):

$$\frac{w_i}{w_j} = \frac{\gamma^{\rho_i}\alpha_i\,\rho_i\,(X_i/Y)^{\rho_i-1}}{\gamma^{\rho_j}\alpha_j\,\rho_j\,(X_j/Y)^{\rho_j-1}} = \frac{\gamma^{\rho_i}\alpha_i\,\rho_i\,X_i^{\rho_i-1}}{\gamma^{\rho_j}\alpha_j\,\rho_j\,X_j^{\rho_j-1}}\,Y^{\rho_j-\rho_i}, \; i \neq j;$$

$$\frac{e_i}{e_j} = \frac{\gamma^{\rho_i}\alpha_i\,\rho_i\,(\frac{X_i}{Y})^{\rho_i}}{\gamma^{\rho_j}\alpha_j\,\rho_j\,(\frac{X_j}{Y})^{\rho_j}} \tag{4.66}$$

These CRESH expressions emphasize the *relative factor price* effects of: particular *factor supplies* (pair), $X_i, X_j$, *Substitution* parameters, $\rho_i$, $\rho_j$, and *relative Intensity* parameters, $\alpha_i$, $\alpha_j$. Via Total variable $(Y)$, *all* variables $X_i$, and *all* parameters, (4.58), *affect*, $(\frac{w_i}{w_j})$, (4.66).

The special cases of (4.66) for the CD-CES family (4.60) become ( $\rho - 1 = -\frac{1}{\sigma}$ ):

$$CD: \frac{w_i}{w_j} = \frac{\alpha_i\,X_j}{\alpha_j\,X_i}; \quad CES: \frac{w_i}{w_j} = \frac{\alpha_i}{\alpha_j}\left[\frac{X_i}{X_j}\right]^{\rho-1}; \quad Linear: \frac{w_i}{w_j} = \frac{\alpha_i}{\alpha_j}; \; i \neq j \tag{4.67}$$

If (4.60) takes the *linear* form, *relative factor prices* (4.67) depend *only* on relative intensity *parameters*, $\alpha_i$, $\alpha_j$—whereas, $X_i$, $X_j$, *also* affect CD, CES, (4.67). On CRESH aggregator, see Conlon (1993); for empirical estimation of CRESH, see Weiss (1977, p. 765).

*Changes* in relative factor prices, $\frac{w_i}{w_j}$, (4.66), are *smaller*, the *higher* is the value of $\rho_i$. Intuitively, the *more flexible* a factor flow (service) $X_i$ is (higher value of $\rho_i$), the *smaller* change in its *relative factor price* is required to *clearing* the *factor markets* (supply-demand equilibrium) for the given change in supply of this factor service ($X_i$).

The CRESH elasticity of the factor price ratio, ($\frac{w_i}{w_j}$), with respect to the factor supply ($X_i$), is simply obtained from, (4.66), (4.65), (by elasticity rules for composite functions):

$$E\left[\frac{w_i}{w_j}, X_i\right] = \rho_i - 1 + (\rho_j - \rho_i)\, e_i < 0 \ ;$$

$$E\left[\frac{w_j}{w_i}, X_i\right] = 1 - \rho_i + (\rho_i - \rho_j)\, e_i > 0 \qquad (4.68)$$

where $\varepsilon_i$ is *factor income share* of $X_i$. Thus by (4.68), *increasing* $X_i$ will always *decrease* the **CRESH** *relative factor price* of $X_i$; but the higher $\rho_i$ is, the smaller is the percentage decline in ($\frac{w_i}{w_j}$); a higher $\rho_j$ has a similar effect on diminishing the decline in ($\frac{w_i}{w_j}$) as $\rho_i$. Moreover, a larger $X_i$ will always *increase* the CRESH *relative factor prices* of $X_j$ (other factors compared to $X_i$); the higher $\rho_i$ is, the larger is the relative increase in ($\frac{w_j}{w_i}$); the effect of higher $\rho_j$ gives a smaller increase in, ($\frac{w_j}{w_i}$), as a result of larger $X_i$.

By (4.66)—and using the same elasticity rules above—we also here note that,

$$E\left[\frac{e_i}{e_j}, X_i\right] = \rho_i + (\rho_j - \rho_i)\, e_i > 0 \ ;$$

$$E\left[\frac{e_j}{e_i}, X_i\right] = -\rho_i + (\rho_i - \rho_j)\, e_i < 0 \qquad (4.69)$$

Thus, in *contrast* to their *relative factor prices* in (4.68), the *relative factor shares* of $X_i$ in (4.69) always *increases* with larger $X_i$; moreover, the **CRESH** *relative* factor *income shares* of the *other* factors $X_j$ *decline*, when $X_i$ is increased.

Since logically, $E\,(\frac{w_i}{w_j}, X_i) = E\,(w_i, X_i) - E\,(w_j, X_i)$, $E\,(\frac{e_i}{e_j}, X_i) = E\,(e_i, X_i) - E\,(e_j, X_i)$, we should **embed** pairwise CRESH *relative factor price* relations, and **ratio** elasticities (4.64–4.69) into a **complete** CRESH framework of **comparative statics** for **absolute factor price** elasticities—'*own-price*', $E\,(w_i, X_i)$, '*cross-price*', $E\,(w_j, X_i)$—factor *share* (distributional) elasticities, and to *factor substitution* elasticities, ($\sigma_{ij}$), and the *explicit* factor

**complementarity** elasticities, $(c_{ij})$—derived for the CRESH function, (4.58), (4.61), below.

### *CRESH Factor Substitution Elasticities*

From *duality theory* of production functions, $Y = F(X_1, X_2, \ldots, X_M)$, and cost functions, $C(w_1, w_2, , , w_M, Y)$, Uzawa (1962, p. 293) derived a *duality form* of Allen (1938, p. 504)'s *partial* elasticity of *substitution* $(\sigma_{ij})$—and presenting the duality expressions of $\sigma_{ij}$ as:

$$\sigma_{ij} = \frac{C \frac{\partial^2 C}{\partial w_i \partial w_j}}{\frac{\partial C}{\partial w_i} \frac{\partial C}{\partial w_j}}, \quad i \neq j \ ; \qquad \sigma_{ii} = \frac{C \frac{\partial^2 C}{\partial w_i^2}}{\left[\frac{\partial C}{\partial w_i}\right]^2} \tag{4.70}$$

But it is *impossible* to *apply* the beautiful and *simple* $\sigma_{ij}$ formulas (4.70) to get the CRESH results $(\sigma_{ij})$ by (4.70), as the relevant **dual** CRESH *Cost function*, $C(w_1, w_2, , , w_M, Y)$, has **no** *closed* form. However, such existing, but unknown *dual* CRESH *Cost* function would by $\sigma_{ij}$ (4.70) give the same CRESH *parametric substitution* elasticities (4.71–4.72), which (Hanoch 1971, p. 697–698) successfully derived from the first and second order conditions for CRESH Lagrangian cost minimization; see hereto, Chambers and Ray (2022, p. 30–32).

For **CRESH**, (4.58–4.59), Allen-Uzawa *partial substitution elasticities*, $\sigma_{ij}$, of factor pair $(X_i, X_j)$ are: Hanoch (1971, p. 699), Hanoch (1978, p. 296), Guest and Jensen (2016, p. 29):

$$\sigma_{ij} = \frac{1}{(1-\rho_i)(1-\rho_j)\bar{\rho}} = \sigma_{ji} > 0, \ i \neq j; \ \bar{\rho} = \sum_{i=1}^{M} \frac{e_i}{1-\rho_i} \tag{4.71}$$

$$\sigma_{ii} = \frac{1}{(1-\rho_i)} \left[\frac{1}{(1-\rho_i)\bar{\rho}} - \frac{1}{e_i}\right] < 0, \ \ i = 1, \ldots, M \tag{4.72}$$

where $(\sigma_{ii})$ are "*own substitution elasticity*" terms; **variable** $(\bar{\rho})$ is a weighted average of the *parameters*, $\frac{1}{(1-\rho_i)}$, with the respective wage (cost) *shares* $(e_i)$ as variable *weights*.

Usually (possibly always) *larger* sizes of $\rho_i$ and $\rho_j$ give a *larger* $\sigma_{ij}$. The *restrictions* (4.59) imply that $\boldsymbol{\sigma}_{\mathbf{ij}} > \mathbf{0}$: *All* CRESH factors/*inputs*, $X_i$, *i*=1,...,*M*, are *substitutes*. If *all* $\rho_i \gtrless 0$, then **all** $\sigma_{ij} \gtrless 1$, (4.71). Note also that **any** $\sigma_{ij}$ given by (4.71) via *shares* $e_i$, (4.65), depends on *all* the *parameters*, $\rho_i, \alpha_i$, and *all* the *factor* inputs, $X_i$, $i = 1, \ldots, M$.

It follows from (4.71) that, although *all* $(\sigma_{ij})$ are *variable* elasticities of *substitution* (**VES**), they have nevertheless an **invariant** (*constant ratio*)—**CRESH**—pattern:

$$\frac{\sigma_{ik}}{\sigma_{jk}} = \frac{(1-\rho_j)}{(1-\rho_i)} \; ; \; \rho_i > \rho_j : \sigma_{ik} > \sigma_{jk} \; ; \; \forall k \neq i, j : \; \frac{\sigma_{ij}}{\sigma_{kl}} = \frac{(1-\rho_k)(1-\rho_l)}{(1-\rho_i)(1-\rho_j)} \tag{4.73}$$

The unknown, but existing unique CRESH *minimum Cost* function, $C(w_1, w_2, , , w_M, Y)$, or *unit cost* functions, $c(w_1, w_2, , , w_M)$, may formally be expressed generally by (4.74):

$$C(w_1, w_2, , w_M, Y) = c(w_1, w_2, .., w_M)\, Y = \sum_{i=1}^{M} W_i X_i \; ;$$

$$X_i = \frac{\partial C}{\partial w_i} \; ; \; E(C, w_i) = e_i \tag{4.74}$$

as being *dual* to the **implicit** CRESH *production* function, (4.58–4.59), (4.61), $e_i = \frac{W_i X_i}{C}$, (4.65). The own-price/cross-price *factor demand* elasticities corresponding to (4.71–4.72), (4.74), are:

$$E(X_i, w_i) = e_i\, \sigma_{ii} \; ; \; E(X_i, w_j) = e_j\, \sigma_{ij} \; ;$$

$$E(X_j, w_i) = e_i\, \sigma_{ji} \; ; \quad i = 1, \ldots, M. \tag{4.75}$$

$E(X_i, w_i)$, $E(X_i, w_j)$ are *conditional* (compensated- *fixed* **Y**) factor demand elasticities. Like two-factor production/cost functions, the *changes* in factor *shares* $(\varepsilon_i)$ are ruled by,

$$\frac{\partial e_i}{\partial w_j} \gtreqless 0 \Leftrightarrow \sigma_{ij} \gtreqless 1 \Leftrightarrow E(e_i, w_j) = e_j(\sigma_{ij} - 1) \; ; \; i \neq j, \; i = 1, \ldots, M \tag{4.76}$$

The CRESH elasticities, (4.75) and (4.71–4.72), satisfy the *standard* summation properties:

$$\sum_{j=1}^{M} E(X_i, w_j) = \sum_{j=1}^{M} e_j\, \sigma_{ji} = 0 \; ; \; \sum_{j=1}^{M} e_j\, E(X_j, w_i) = 0 \tag{4.77}$$

### *CRESH Complementarity Elasticities*

As calculated in section "Complementarity Elasticities, Substitution Elasticities, Factor Shares" for the *explicit* **GCES** Production, $Y = F(X_1, X_2, \ldots, X_M)$, the *complementarity elasticities*, $c_{ij}$, $c_{ii}$, were defined as:

$$c_{ij} = \frac{F \frac{\partial^2 F}{\partial X_i \partial X_j}}{\frac{\partial F}{\partial X_i} \frac{\partial F}{\partial X_j}}, \quad c_{ii} = \frac{F \frac{\partial^2 F}{\partial X_i^2}}{\left[\frac{\partial F}{\partial X_i}\right]^2}$$

The problem with applying these, $c_{ij}$, $c_{ii}$, definitions to the *implicit* **CRESH** function, (4.58), is that CRESH, $Y = f(X_1, X_2, .., X_M)$, (4.61), does *not* exist as an *explicit* expression (function). However, we *know* (calculated), the *derivatives* of (4.61), in (4.62–4.63), from which the *new* and important formulas for the *factor* **complementarity** *elasticities* $(c_{ij})$ for for the *implicit* CRESH *Production* function, $f(X_1, X_2, \ldots, X_M)$, (4.58), (4.61) can be derived.

The *partial complementarity elasticity*, $(c_{ij})$, between any factor pair $(X_i, X_j)$ within in the *implicit* CRESH function, $\mathbf{Y = f(X_1, X_2, \ldots, X_M)}$, (4.61), is defined by, $i = 1, \ldots, M$, $j = 1, \ldots, M$:

$$c_{ij} \equiv c_{ij}(X_1, X_2, \ldots, X_M) = \frac{f \frac{\partial^2 f}{\partial X_i \partial X_j}}{\frac{\partial f}{\partial X_i} \frac{\partial f}{\partial X_j}};$$

$$c_{ii} \equiv c_{ii}(X_1, X_2, \ldots, X_M) = \frac{f \frac{\partial^2 f}{\partial X_i^2}}{\left[\frac{\partial f}{\partial X_i}\right]^2} \tag{4.78}$$

The *first-order* derivatives in (4.78) for implicit CRESH (4.58) were already given in (4.63) as,

$$\forall X_i > 0: \frac{\partial f}{\partial X_i} = -\frac{\partial F/\partial X_i}{\partial F/\partial Y} = \frac{\gamma^{\rho_i} \alpha_i \rho_i (X_i/Y)^{\rho_i - 1}}{\sum_{i=1}^{M} \alpha_i \rho_i \left(\frac{X_i}{Y/\gamma}\right)^{\rho_i}} > 0, \ i = 1, .., M \tag{4.79}$$

The *second-order* derivatives in (4.78) are derived from the *second* term (ratio) in (4.79) as,

$$\frac{\partial^2 f}{\partial X_i \partial X_j} = \frac{-1}{[\frac{\partial F}{\partial Y}]^3} \left[ \frac{\partial^2 F}{\partial X_i \partial X_j} \left[\frac{\partial F}{\partial Y}\right]^2 - \frac{\partial^2 F}{\partial X_i \partial Y} \frac{\partial F}{\partial X_j} \frac{\partial F}{\partial Y} \right.$$

$$- \frac{\partial^2 F}{\partial X_j \partial Y} \frac{\partial F}{\partial X_i} \frac{\partial F}{\partial Y} + \frac{\partial^2 F}{\partial Y^2} \frac{\partial F}{\partial X_i} \frac{\partial F}{\partial X_j} \Bigg] \tag{4.80}$$

$$\frac{\partial^2 f}{\partial X_i^2} = \frac{-1}{[\frac{\partial F}{\partial Y}]^3} \left[ \frac{\partial^2 F}{\partial X_i^2} \left[\frac{\partial F}{\partial Y}\right]^2 - 2 \frac{\partial^2 F}{\partial X_i \partial Y} \frac{\partial F}{\partial X_i} \frac{\partial F}{\partial Y} + \frac{\partial^2 F}{\partial Y^2} \left[\frac{\partial F}{\partial X_i}\right]^2 \right] \tag{4.81}$$

Insert first-order and second-order derivatives (4.79–4.81) of $\mathbf{Y} = \mathbf{f}\,(\mathbf{X_1}, \mathbf{X_2}, .., \mathbf{X_M})$ into (4.78):

$$c_{ij} = -Y \left[ \frac{\frac{\partial^2 F}{\partial X_i \partial X_j} \frac{\partial F}{\partial Y}}{\frac{\partial F}{\partial X_i} \frac{\partial F}{\partial X_j}} - \frac{\frac{\partial^2 F}{\partial X_i \partial Y}}{\frac{\partial F}{\partial X_i}} - \frac{\frac{\partial^2 F}{\partial X_j \partial Y}}{\frac{\partial F}{\partial X_j}} + \frac{\frac{\partial^2 F}{\partial Y^2}}{\frac{\partial F}{\partial Y}} \right] \tag{4.82}$$

In **CRESH** cases, we have, $\partial^2 F / \partial X_i \partial X_j = 0$, if $i \neq j$, cf. (4.85–4.86). Hence (4.82) becomes:

$$c_{ij} = -Y \left[ -\frac{\frac{\partial^2 F}{\partial X_i \partial Y}}{\frac{\partial F}{\partial X_i}} - \frac{\frac{\partial^2 F}{\partial X_j \partial Y}}{\frac{\partial F}{\partial X_j}} + \frac{\frac{\partial^2 F}{\partial Y^2}}{\frac{\partial F}{\partial Y}} \right], \quad i \neq j \tag{4.83}$$

$$c_{ii} = -Y \left[ \frac{\frac{\partial^2 F}{\partial X_i^2} \frac{\partial F}{\partial Y}}{[\frac{\partial F}{\partial X_i}]^2} - 2 \frac{\frac{\partial^2 F}{\partial X_i \partial Y}}{\frac{\partial F}{\partial X_i}} + \frac{\frac{\partial^2 F}{\partial Y^2}}{\frac{\partial F}{\partial Y}} \right], \quad i = j \tag{4.84}$$

To obtain *explicit* CRESH formulas from (4.83–4.84), the **parametric** expressions of the first-order and second-order *derivatives* of the implicit CRESH function, $F\,(Y, X_1, X_2, \ldots, X_M)$, (4.58) are now needed. We already have the *first-order* derivatives of $F$ as, cf. (4.62),

$$\frac{\partial F}{\partial X_i} = \frac{\gamma^{\rho_i}\, \alpha_i\, \rho_i\, (X_i/Y)^{\rho_i - 1}}{Y} \equiv \frac{e_i\, \beta}{X_i}\ ; \quad \frac{\partial F}{\partial Y} = - \frac{\sum_{i=1}^M \alpha_i\, \rho_i \left(\frac{X_i}{Y/\gamma}\right)^{\rho_i}}{Y} \equiv -\frac{\beta}{Y} \tag{4.85}$$

where, $\beta \equiv \sum_{i=1}^M \alpha_i\, \rho_i \left(\frac{X_i}{Y/\gamma}\right)^{\rho_i}$ ; $e_i = \gamma^{\rho_i}\, \alpha_i\, \rho_i\, (X_i/Y)^{\rho_i} / \beta$, $i = 1, \ldots, M$, cf. (4.65). The *second-order* derivatives of $F$ are derived from the second terms (ratios) in (4.85) as,

$$\frac{\partial^2 F}{\partial X_i \partial X_j} = 0\ ; \quad \frac{\partial^2 F}{\partial X_i \partial Y} = -\gamma^{\rho_i}\, \alpha_i \rho_i^2 X_i^{\rho_i - 1} Y^{-1-\rho_i} = -\frac{\rho_i\, e_i\, \beta}{X_i Y} \tag{4.86}$$

$$\frac{\partial^2 F}{\partial X_j \partial Y} = -\frac{\rho_j\, e_j\, \beta}{X_j Y} \tag{4.87}$$

$$\frac{\partial^2 F}{\partial X_i^2} = \frac{1}{Y}\gamma^{\rho_i}\alpha_i\rho_i(\rho_i - 1)(X_i/Y)^{\rho_i-2}\frac{1}{Y} = \frac{(\rho_i - 1)\, e_i\, \beta}{X_i^2} \tag{4.88}$$

$$\frac{\partial^2 F}{\partial Y^2} = \sum_{i=1}^{M}\gamma^{\rho_i}\alpha_i\rho_i(1+\rho_i)X_i^{\rho_i}Y^{-2-\rho_i} = \frac{\beta}{Y^2}\left[\sum_{i=1}^{M}(1+\rho_i)\, e_i\right] = \frac{\beta}{Y^2}(1+\tilde{\rho}) \tag{4.89}$$

where: $\tilde{\rho} = \sum_{i=1}^{M} e_i\,\rho_i$—with, $e_i$ , as stated above, (4.85).

Finally, inserting (4.85–4.89) into (4.83–4.84) give,

$$c_{ij} = -Y\left[-\frac{\frac{-\rho_i\, e_i\, \beta}{X_i Y}}{\frac{e_i\,\beta}{X_i}} - \frac{\frac{-\rho_j\, e_j\, \beta}{X_j Y}}{\frac{e_j\,\beta}{X_j}} + \frac{\frac{\beta}{Y^2}(1+\tilde{\rho})}{-\frac{\beta}{Y}}\right] \tag{4.90}$$

$$= -\rho_i - \rho_j + 1 + \tilde{\rho} \;;\quad \tilde{\rho} = \sum_{i=1}^{M} e_i\,\rho_i \tag{4.91}$$

$$c_{ii} = -Y\left[\frac{\frac{(\rho_i-1)\, e_i\, \beta}{X_i^2}\left[-\frac{\beta}{Y}\right]}{\left[\frac{e_i\,\beta}{X_i}\right]^2} - 2\frac{\frac{-\rho_i\, e_i\, \beta}{X_i Y}}{\frac{e_i\,\beta}{X_i}} + \frac{\frac{\beta}{Y^2}(1+\tilde{\rho})}{-\frac{\beta}{Y}}\right] \tag{4.92}$$

$$= \frac{\rho_i - 1}{e_i} - 2\rho_i + 1 + \tilde{\rho} \;;\quad \tilde{\rho} = \sum_{i=1}^{M} e_i\,\rho_i \tag{4.93}$$

Factor *complementarity elasticities*, $c_{ij}$, (4.90–4.92), satisfy *regularity* (summation) property, cf. (4.13):

$$\begin{aligned}
\sum_{j=1}^{M} e_j c_{ji} &= \sum_{j=1, j\neq i}^{M} e_j c_{ji} + e_i c_{ii} \\
&= \sum_{j=1, j\neq i}^{M} e_j(1-\rho_i-\rho_j+\tilde{\rho}) + e_i\left(1 - 2\rho_i + \frac{\rho_i - 1}{e_i} + \tilde{\rho}\right) \\
&= -\sum_{j\neq i}^{M} e_j\rho_j - \rho_i\sum_{j\neq i}^{M} e_j - 2\rho_i e_i + \rho_i + \tilde{\rho} \\
&= -\sum_{j=1}^{M} e_j\rho_j + \tilde{\rho} = -\tilde{\rho} + \tilde{\rho} = 0
\end{aligned} \tag{4.94}$$

It follows from (4.91) that, although **all** CRESH (4.58) *complementarity* elasticities $(c_{ij})$ are *variable* elasticities of *complementarity* (**VEC**), they nevertheless have an **invariant** ( *constant difference* ) pattern:

$$c_{ik} - c_{jk} = \rho_j - \rho_i \;;\quad c_{ij} - c_{kl} = (\rho_k + \rho_l) - (\rho_i + \rho_j) \tag{4.95}$$

Thus the *implicit* production function, CRESH (4.58), has both a *constant ratio* pattern for the *substitution* elasticities, $\sigma_{ij}$, (4.73), and a *constant difference* pattern for its *complementarity* elasticities, $c_{ij}$, (4.95).

Such CRESH **invariance** relations among ($\sigma_{ij}$), and ($c_{ij}$), do *not*, of course, exist among the CRESH, (4.58),*factor demand elasticities*, (4.75), or the CRESH, (4.58), *factor price* (Inverse demand ) *elasticities*, cf. (4.11–4.12), which here simply follow from (4.91), (4.93), and, $e_i = \frac{W_i X_i}{pY}$, i.e.:

$$E(W_i, X_j) = e_j\, c_{ij} \ , \quad i, j = 1, ., M \ ; \qquad E(W_i, X_i) = e_i\, c_{ii} \ , \quad i = 1, ., M \tag{4.96}$$

The *analytic-parametric* content of the *implicit* **CRESH** function (4.58) *factor price elasticities* (4.96), showing the impact of various factor supplies came afar along the road of the CRESH formulas (4.83–4.84), (4.90–4.93), (4.95).

The *explicit* **GCES** function (4.1) gives (calculate) *factor price elasticities* (4.96) simply (directly) from the formulas, (4.10–4.12), as is shown in Tables 4.2 and 4.3.

## Bibliography

Acemoglu D, Restrepo P (2020) Robots and Jobs: Evidence from US Labor Markets. Journal of Political Economy, 128:2188–2244

Allen RGD (1938) Mathematical Analysis for Economists. MacMillan, London

Arrow KJ, Chenery HB, Minhas BS, Solow RM (1961) Capital–Labour Substitution and Economic Efficiency. Review of Economics and Statistics 43:225–250

Berndt ER, Christensen LR (1973) The Internal Structure of Functional Relationships: Separability, Substitution, and Aggregation. Review of Economic Studies 40:403–410

Berndt ER, Christensen LR (1974) Testing the Existence of a Consistent Aggregate Index of Labor Inputs. American Economic Review 64:391–404

Bertoletti P (2005) Elasticities of Substitution and Complementarity: A Synthesis. Journal of Productivity Analysis 24:183–196

Blackorby C, Russell RR (1989) Will the real elasticity of substitution please stand up? – A comparison of the Allen/Uzawa and Morishima elasticities. American Economic Review 79:882–894

Borjas GJ (1986) The Sensitivity of Labor Demand Functions to Choice of Dependent Variable. Review of Economics and Statistics 68:58–66

Borjas GJ (2003) The Labor Demand Curve is Downward Sloping: Reexamining the Impact of Immigration on the Labor Market. Quarterly Journal of Economics 118:1335–1374

Borjas GJ (2020) Labor Economics, 8th edn. McGraw–Hill, New York

Chambers RG, Färe R (2022) Distance Functions in Production Economics. Springer Nature, Singapore, pp 295–329, in Ray et al., Eds. (2022), Vol.1, Springer Nature, Singapore.

Chambers RG, Ray SC (2022) Neoclassical Production Economics: An Introduction. Springer Nature, Singapore, in Ray. et al., Eds. (2022), Springer Nature, Singapore.

Christensen LR, Jorgensen DW, Lau LJ (1971) Conjugate Duality and the Transcendental Logarithmic Production Function. Econometrica 39:255–256
Christensen LR, Jorgenson DW, Lau LJ (1973) Transcendental Logarithmic Production Frontiers. Review of Economics and Statistics 55:256–285
Christensen LR, Jorgenson DW, Lau LJ (1975) Transcendental Logarithmic Utility Functions. American Economic Review 65:367–383
Conlon JR (1993) Separability and Separability Flexibility of the CRESH Function. The Journal of Productivity Analysis 4:371–377
Cornes R (1992) Duality and Modern Economics. Cambridge University Press, Cambridge
Denny M (1974) The Relationship between Functional Forms for the Production System. Canadian Journal of Economics 7:21–31
Diewert WE (1971) An Application of the Shephard Duality Theorem: A Leontief Production Function. Journal of Political Economy, 79:481–507
Diewert WE (1974a) A Note on Aggregation and Elasticities of Substitution. Canadian Journal of Economics 7:12–20
Diewert WE (1974b) Applications of Duality Theory. pp 106–171, In: Intriligator MD, Kendrick DA (eds) *Frontiers of Quantitative Economics*, Vol.2, North–Holland, Amsterdam
Diewert WE (2022) Duality in Production. pp 57–168, in Ray et al., Eds. (2022), Vol.1, Springer Nature, Singapore.
Freeman RB (1979) The Effect of Demographic Factors on Age–Earnings Profiles. Journal of Human Resources 14:289–318
Frisch R (1959) A Complete Scheme for Computing All Direct and Cross Demand Elasticities in a Model with Many Sectors. Econometrica 27:177–196
Goldin C, Katz LF (1998) The Origins of Technology–Skill Complementarity. Quarterly Journal of Economics 113:693–732
Guest R, Jensen BS (2016) Applying a CRESH aggregate labour index to generate age–wage profiles. Applied Economics Letters 23:27–33
Hamermesh DS (1993) Labor Demand. Princeton University Press, Princeton
Hanoch G (1967) An Economic Analysis of Earnings and Schooling. Journal of Human Resources 2:310–329
Hanoch G (1971) CRESH Production Functions. Econometrica 39:695–712
Hanoch G (1975) Production and Demand Models with Direct and Indirect Implicit Additivity. Econometrica 43:395–419
Hanoch G (1978) Polar Functions with Constant Two Factors–One Price Elasticities. pp 287–309, in: Fuss, M. and McFadden, D., (Eds), *Production Economics: A Dual Approach to Theory and Applications*, Vol.1, North–Holland, Amsterdam.
Hicks JR (1937) Theorie Mathematique de la Valeur en Regime de la Libre Concurrence. Hermann, Editeurs, Paris
Hicks JR (1946) Value and Capital, 2nd edn. Clarendon Press, Oxford
Hicks JR (1970) Elasticities of Substitution Again: Substitutes and Complements. Oxford Economic Papers 22:289–296
Hotelling H (1935) Demand Functions with Limited Budgets. Econometrica 3:66–78
Jensen BS, de Boer P, van Daal J, Jensen PS (2011) Global Restrictions on the Parameters of the CDES Indirect Utility Function. Journal of Economics 102:217–235
Jensen BS, Lehmijoki U, Rovenskaya E (2015) Non–Homothetic Multisector Growth Models. Review of Development Economics 19(2):221–243

Jensen BS, Pedersen PJ, Guest R (2022) Demographic Changes, Labor Supplies, Labor Complementarities, Calendar Annual Wages, and Cohort Life Wage Incomes, IZA Working Paper

Kim HY (2000) The Antonelli versus Hicks Elasticity of Complementarity and Inverse Input Demand Systems. Australian Economic Papers 39:245–261

Kohli U (1991) Technology, Duality, and Foreign Trade: The GNP Function Approach to Modelling Imports and Exports. UMP Press, Ann Arbor ; Harvester Wheatsheaf, London

Kumbhakar SC (2022) Modeling Technical Change: Theory and Practice. pp 872–923, in Ray et al., Eds. (2022), Vol.2, Springer Nature, Singapore.

McFadden D (1978) Cost, Revenue, and Profit Functions. Chapter I.1, in: Fuss, M. and D. McFadden, D., (Eds), *Production Economics: A Dual Approach to Theory and Applications*, Vol.1, (Amsterdam: North–Holland,),

Perroni C, Rutherford TF (1995) Regular flexibility of nested CES functions. European Economic Review 39:335–343

Podinovski VV, Försund FR (2022) Scale Elasticity and Returns to Scale. pp 682–719, in Ray et al., Eds. (2022), Vol.2, Springer Nature, Singapore.

Ray SC, Chambers RG, Kumbhakar SC (2022) Handbook of Production Economics, vol 1–3. Springer Nature, Singapore

Russell RR (1975) Functional Separability and Partial Elasticities of Substitution. Review of Economic Studies 42:79–83

Russell RR (2022) Elasticities of Substitution. pp 259–294, in Ray et al., Eds. (2022), Vol.1, Springer Nature, Singapore.

Sato K (1967) A Two–Level Constant–Elasticity–of–Substitution Production Function. Review of Economic Studies 34:201–218

Sato R, Koizumi T (1970) Substitutability, Complementarity and the Theory of Derived Demand. Review of Economic Studies 37:107–118

Sato R, Koizumi T (1973a) On the Elasticities of Substitution and Complementarity. Oxford Economic Papers 25:44–56

Sato R, Koizumi T (1973b) The Production Function and the Theory of Distributive Shares. American Economic Review 63:484–489

Silberberg E, Suen W (2001) The Structure of Economics, A Mathematical Analysis, 3rd edn. McGraw–Hill, Singapore

Stern DI (2011) Elasticities of Substitution and Complementarity. Journal of Productivity Analysis 36:79–89

ten Raa T (2022) Activity Analysis in Production Economics. pp 471–482, in Ray et al., Eds. (2022), Vol.1, Springer Nature, Singapore.

Uzawa H (1962) Production Functions with Constant Elasticities of Substitution. Review of Economic Studies 29:291–299

Weiss RD (1977) Elasticities of Substitution Among Capital and Occupations in U.S. Manufacturing. Journal of the American Statistical Association 72:746–771

Wold H (1943, 1944) A Synthesis of Pure Demand Analysis: Part I–III. Skandinavisk Aktuarietidsskrift 26, 27:69–120, 85–144, 220–275

Wold H, Jureen L (1953) Demand Analysis. John Wiley & Sons, New York

World KLEMS (2022) World KLEMS Data. URL http://www.worldklems.net

CHAPTER 5

# Utility Functions, Consumer Preferences: Global Restrictions on the Parameters of the CDES Indirect Utility Function

## Introduction

The *concept* of *indirect utility* function is due to Hotelling (1932, p. 594–595), Roy (1942, p. 19), and Roy (1947, p. 214)—the *term* to Houthakker (1952, p. 157). For a particular mathematical form of additive indirect utility functions, Houthakker (1960a, p. 252) used the "barbaric" name: "indirect addilog preference ordering". We propose a *parametric Box-Cox transform* of Houthakker's *specification* of the *basic indirect* utility function, which—since the seminal contribution of Hanoch (1975)—is known as the constant differences of elasticities of substitution (CDES) *indirect utility* function.

In the literature, there has been *no consensus* about the theoretical correct *restrictions* upon the CDES *indirect* utility function. The restrictions most widely cited are those given by Hanoch (1975). He imposed such restrictions that *all* the reaction *parameters* are *positive*, which empirically is too restrictive, as it *prevents* own-price elasticities of being absolutely less than one (*inelastic* Marshallian demand curves).

Several authors have suggested alternative restrictions. However, they have failed to give any proof of their actual parameter restrictions. This chapter proves rigorously that the parameter restrictions given by Murty (1982) are theoretically correct. Moreover, the proof of these restrictions implies that the CDES model is *globally* much more flexible than commonly presented in the economic literature.

With co-authors:
PAUL DE BOER, Econometric Institute, Erasmus University Rotterdam, The Netherlands.
JAN VAN DAAL, TrianGle, Universite de Lyon-2, France.
PETER SANDHOLT JENSEN, Business and Economics, University of Southern Denmark.



B. S. Jensen, *The Elements and Dynamic Systems of Economic Growth and Trade Models*, https://doi.org/10.1007/978-3-031-52493-6_5

For the specification of consumer demands in applied (computable) *general equilibrium* (**CGE**) models, constant elasticity of substitution (CES) is among the commonly used functional forms, Shoven and Whalley (1992, p. 95). A nesting structure for homothetic CES preferences can increase the scope for price elasticities, but *not* at all for the *unitary* income elasticities. For several purposes (theory, interpretability, tractability), the more *general* CDES demand system has certainly merits vis-â-vis alternative specifications, currently used in restricting the *parameter space* in **CGE** models, see **CDES** in Hertel et al. (1991), Rimmer and Powell (1996), Hertel and Tsigas (1997). Our parametrically corrected CDES form can be aptly used to enlarge the scope of *general equilibrium dynamics* (multi-sector growth (MSG) models), cf. Jensen and Larsen (2005), here Chap. 18.

The chapter is organized as follows. Section "Parameter Restrictions of CDES in the Literature" reviews the parameter restrictions presented in literature, and it is devoted to the *rigorous proof* of the CDES *parameter restrictions* and *global regularity* properties. Section "CDES Parameters and Analytic Elasticity Formulas" shows a *complete* set of *parametric elasticity* expressions and *unified aggregations* for the CDES demand system that can be applied to any demand system. Final comments are given in section "Final Comments".

## Parameter Restrictions of CDES in the Literature

Let $\mathbf{Y}_\mathrm{i}$ denote the quantity that a consumer buys of *commodity i* (1, ..., N), and $\mathbf{P}_\mathrm{i}$ its price; **P** denotes the *price* vector $(P_1, \ldots, P_N)$. We assume that the consumer maximizes utility subject to the *budget constraint*: $C = \sum_{i=1}^{N} P_i Y_i$, where **C** denotes total expenditures.

Houthakker (1960a, p. 252,256) defined and specified the so-called *indirect addilog* utility function, cf. Houthakker (1961, p. 721), as given by the expression:

$$V^*(P, C) = \sum_{i=1}^{N} \alpha_i^* \, (C/P_i)^{\beta_i} \,; \quad \alpha_i^* < 0, \ -1 < \beta_i < 0 \tag{5.1}$$

The theoretical and empirical background for adopting the *specification* (5.1) is outlined in Houthakker (1960b), Roy (1942, p. 19)'s "*indirect utility* function concept"—as a representation of consumer indifference surfaces "in *tangential* coordinates" (prices, income)—and Roy (1947, p. 214)'s *identity*: $Y_i = -(\partial V^*/\partial P_i)/(\partial V^*/\partial C)$, were his motivations to derive an *explicit indirect* utility function from the specified *demand equations*, proposed by Leser (1941). The integration of partial differential equations into the explicit "indirect addilog" function, (5.1), was not demonstrated, but feasible procedures required that certain relations between the parameters must be satisfied,

Houthakker (1960b, p. 13), and such *simplifying* assumptions lead to imposing the "addilog" parameter *restrictions* in (5.1).

Originally, without specifying any direct or indirect utility functions, Leser (1941, p. 49), Somermeyer and Langhout (1972, p. 351), started directly from the *functional forms* of the "addilog" demand equations, cf. Somermeyer (1974), Gamaletsos (1973), Gamaletsos (1974). Their conditions of constrained utility maximization imposed the *restriction*: $\boldsymbol{\beta_i > -1}$.

Later, Hanoch (1975, p. 411) obtained the *indirect* utility function (5.1) as a particular case embedded in a general *class* of *implicit indirect* additive utility functions, called the **CDE** model (constant differences of elasticities of substitution, **CDES**). For the specialized and *explicit* CDES model that corresponds exactly to Houthakker, (5.1), he imposed as *restrictions*: $\alpha_i^* > 0$, Hanoch (1975, p. 411, his $B_i$ is our $\alpha_i^*$), and $\beta_i > 0$, Hanoch (1975, p. 416, his $b_i$ is equivalent to our $-\beta_i$), that is, his *standard parameter* restrictions were:

$$\alpha_i^* > 0, \quad \beta_i > 0, \quad \sum_{i=1}^{N} \alpha_i^* = 1 \tag{5.2}$$

These parameter *restrictions* (5.2) are also mentioned, in Deaton and Muellbauer (1980b, p. 84), Chung (1994, p. 42), Jensen and Larsen (2005, p. 36); here page 536 in Chap. 18, and Hertel et al. (1991, p. 267).

The *demand equations* from (5.1), as obtained by using Roy's identity, are:

$$Y_i = D_i(P, C) = -\frac{\partial V^*(P, C)/\partial P_i}{\partial V^*(P, C)/\partial C} = \frac{\alpha_i^* \beta_i (C/P_i)^{\beta_i+1}}{\sum_{j=1}^{N} \alpha_j^* \beta_j (C/P_j)^{\beta_i}} \tag{5.3}$$

Inspecting (5.3) and the *positivity* condition, $\mathbf{Y_i > 0}$, Akin and Stewart (1979) naturally introduced as parameter restrictions: ($\alpha_i^* > 0$, $\beta_i > 0$); or ($\alpha_i^* < 0$, $\beta_i < 0$); Their argumentation for these restrictions also followed from theoretical monotonicity properties of $V^*(P, C)$ in $(C/P_i)$, Akin and Stewart (1979, p. 779). Moreover, due to second-order conditions, they argued that no more than one $\beta_i$ was permitted a value less than $-1$.

Murty (1982) correctly points out that the *confusion* about the *signs* of the parameters, $\beta_i$, had arisen from the particular way of specifying the indirect utility function, (5.1). He proposes the *reparametrization*, $\alpha_i = \alpha_i^* \beta_i$, cf. (5.2), so that his specification reads:

$$V(P, C) = \sum_{i=1}^{N} \frac{\alpha_i (C/P_i)^{\beta_i}}{\beta_i} \tag{5.4}$$

Murty (1982, p. 226) states, *without proof*, that the necessary and sufficient *conditions* for (5.4) to represent a *normal* preference function are: $\alpha_i \geq 0$ and

$\beta_i \geq -1$, for *all* $(i)$—but the *equality* for $\alpha_i$ holding for at *most* N-1 items, and the *equality* for $\beta_i$ holding for at most *one* commodity. Yoshihara (1969, p. 264) used the form (5.4), with $\alpha_i > 0$, but adhered to Houthakker's interval for $\beta_i$, (5.1), cf. Yoshihara (1969, p. 265).

We *generalize* the form (5.4) to include *all* **CES** *indirect* utility functions as *special* cases. We call this *extended* specification as the *CDES indirect utility* function of (5.1), in accordance with Hanoch (1975). Our main results with proof are stated in:

**Proposition 5.1** *The* **CDES** *Indirect Utility Function,* **U** $=$ **V(P, C)**, *is given by:*

$$V(P, C) = \sum_{i=1}^{N} \alpha_i \left[ \frac{(C/P_i)^{\beta_i} - 1}{\beta_i} \right]; \; \alpha_i > 0, \; \sum_{i=1}^{N} \alpha_i = 1, \; \beta_i \geq -1 \, ;$$

$$P_i > 0, \; C > 0 \tag{5.5}$$

*where the last equality sign for $\beta_i$ may apply for at most* **one** *commodity index (i).*

*The Indirect Utility Function* **V(P,C)**, *(5.5), satisfies the well-behaved* **regularity** *properties:*

*Homogeneity of degree zero, Continuity/Differentiability, Strict Monotonicity, and Strict Quasiconvexity on the global domain (positive orthant, open convex set):* $\mathbf{P_i > 0, C > 0}$

***Proof*** The Box-Cox transformation of the variables $(C/P_i)$ in (5.4) and its inclusion of CES indirect utility functions are shown in Appendix A, section. Appendix A. The Box-Cox Transformation.

The formula (5.5) can be obtained by *subtracting* the constant, $\sum_{i=1}^{N} \alpha_i/\beta_i = \sum_{i=1}^{N} \alpha_i^*$, from (5.1) and (5.4). As utility is *ordinal*, (5.1), (5.4), and (5.5) represent the *same* preference ordering.

Any *regular indirect* utility function, cf. Diewert (1974, p. 121), Diewert (1982, p. 557), Katzner (1968), Varian (1992, p. 102), Mas-Colell et al. (1995, p. 56), Gravelle and Rees (2004, p. 53), is:

- **(i)** Homogeneous of degree zero in prices $(P_i)$ and total expenditure $(C)$.
- **(ii)** Continuous in all prices $P_i > 0$ and in $C > 0$.
- **(iii)** Nonincreasing in prices $(P_i)$ and non-decreasing in total expenditure $(C)$.
- **(iv)** Quasiconvex in prices $(P_i)$ and total expenditure $(C)$.
(strict quasiconvexity is necessary to get unique demand solutions from (5.5))

Ad (**i**): It is straightforward to observe from (5.5) that (i) is met.
Ad (**ii**): It is easily seen from the power expressions of (5.5) that (ii) is satisfied.

Clearly, **V(P,C)**, (5.5), is also globally differentiable for $P_i > 0$ and $C > 0$.
Ad (**iii**): To verify (iii), we first take the derivative of (5.5) with respect to C:

$$\frac{\partial V(P, C)}{\partial C} = \sum_{i=1}^{N} \alpha_i P_i^{-\beta_i} C^{\beta_i - 1} = \sum_{i=1}^{N} \alpha_i (C/P_i)^{\beta_i} C^{-1} > 0 \tag{5.6}$$

that is, $V(P, C)$ is *increasing* in total *expenditure* $C$ for *all*, $P_i > 0$, *if and only if*

$$\alpha_i > 0 \tag{5.7}$$

As to the restriction: $\sum_{i=1}^{N} \alpha_i = 1$, on $V(P, C)$, (5.5), see below (5.22).

Secondly, the derivative of (5.5) with respect to $(P_i)$ becomes, with using (5.7):

$$\frac{\partial V(P, C)}{\partial P_i} = -\alpha_i \; P_i^{-\beta_i - 1} \, C^{\beta_i} = -\alpha_i \, (C/P_i)^{\beta_i} \, P_i^{-1} < 0 \tag{5.8}$$

that is, the CDES indirect utility function $V(P, C)$ is *decreasing* in every *price*.

Ad (**iv**): With homogeneity (i) and the monotonicities (iii) established, the proof of strict *quasiconvexity* in prices and expenditure can, without loss of generality, be given *jointly* in terms of "*normalized price*" variables $(C/P_i)$.

Geometrically, the $(C/P_i)$ are distances between the origin of the commodity space and the intersection of the budget plane, $C = \sum_{i=1}^{N} P_i Y_i$, with each of the axes. With such symmetric "price normalization", there is *no specific* (commodity) numeraire. A change in **C** is represented by a proportional change in *all* the $(\mathbf{C}/\mathbf{P_i})$. To alleviate notation in the proof, we put $\mathbf{C} = \mathbf{1}$, so that the indirect utility function (5.5) becomes:

$$V(P, 1) = V(P) = \sum_{i=1}^{n} \alpha_i \frac{P_i^{-\beta_i} - 1}{\beta_i} \tag{5.9}$$

We give the *proof* of the *strict quasiconvexity* of (5.9) [ *equivalently*, semi-negative definiteness of the Slutsky matrix or Allen partial substitution elasticity matrix ] in three steps:

(**a**) if all $\beta_i > -1$, then $V(P)$, (5.9), is strictly convex;
(**b**) if one $\beta_i = -1$ and $\beta_j > -1$ for all $j \neq i$, then V (P), (5.9), is strictly quasiconvex;
(**c**) if two (or more) $\beta_i = -1$, then V (P), (5.9), is not strictly quasiconvex.

Ad (**a**). From (5.8) and (5.9), we derive:

$$\frac{\partial^2 V(P)}{\partial P_i \partial P_j} = \begin{cases} (\beta_i + 1)\,\alpha_i\, P_i^{-\beta_i - 2} > 0 & i = j \\ 0 & i \neq j \end{cases} \tag{5.10}$$

Thus, with all, $\beta_i > -1$, V(P) is by (5.10) strictly convex, hence strictly quasiconvex.

Ad (**b**). Without loss of generality, we consider the case with *commodity* 1, having the beta value equal to minus one:

$$\beta_1 = -1, \quad \text{and } \beta_i > -1, \quad i = 2, \ldots, N. \tag{5.11}$$

We partition the price vector $P$ as:

$$P = \begin{bmatrix} P_1 \\ P_{(-1)} \end{bmatrix}, \text{ where } P_{(-1)} = \begin{bmatrix} P_2 \\ \cdot \\ \cdot \\ P_N \end{bmatrix} \tag{5.12}$$

Using (5.11) in (5.9), our *indirect* utility function V(P) can also be *decomposed* as:

$$V(P) = -\alpha_1 (P_1 - 1) + \sum_{i=2}^{N} \alpha_i \frac{P_i^{-\beta_i} - 1}{\beta_i} \equiv \alpha_1 - \alpha_1 P_1 + Q(P_{(-1)}) \tag{5.13}$$

With $\beta_i > -1, i = 2, \ldots, N$, the *function* $Q(P_{(-1)})$ in (5.13) is *strictly convex*, see (a) above.

Let two price vectors $P^A$ and $P^B$, ($P^A \neq P^B$), be partitioned as in (5.12), and let $\lambda$ be any scalar, $0 < \lambda < 1$. Inserting the convex combination, $\lambda P^A + (1 - \lambda)P^B$, of these two price vectors into **V(P)**, (5.13), we have:

$$\begin{aligned} V[\lambda P^A + (1-\lambda)P^B] &= \alpha_1 - \alpha_1[\lambda P_1^A + (1-\lambda)P_1^B] \\ &\quad + Q[\lambda P_{(-1)}^A + (1-\lambda)P_{(-1)}^B] \end{aligned} \tag{5.14}$$

Since $P^A \neq P^B$, we have to consider *two cases*:

(**b1**) $P_{(-1)}^A \neq P_{(-1)}^B$

(**b2**) $P_{(-1)}^A = P_{(-1)}^B$, but $P_1^A \neq P_1^B$, (and here without loss of generality: $P_1^A > P_1^B$)

Ad (**b1**). *Strict convexity* of $Q(P_{(-1)})$ implies the *inequality*, cf. Ginsberg (1973, p. 596):

$$Q[\lambda P_{(-1)}^A + (1-\lambda)P_{(-1)}^B] < \lambda\, Q(P_{(-1)}^A) + (1-\lambda)\, Q(P_{(-1)}^B) \tag{5.15}$$

Combining (5.14) and (5.15), and by noting (5.13), we get the expressions and evaluations:

$$V[\lambda P^A+(1-\lambda)P^B] < \lambda[\alpha_1-\alpha_1 P_1^A+Q(P^A_{(-1)})]+(1-\lambda)[\alpha_1-\alpha_1 P_1^B+Q(P^B_{(-1)})]$$

$$= \lambda V(P^A)+(1-\lambda)V(P^B) \le \max\left\{V(P^A), V(P^B)\right\}. \tag{5.16}$$

Hence by (5.16), **V(P)**, (5.9), is a *strictly quasiconvex* by satisfying the *criterion*: $P^A \neq P^B$,

$$V(P^A) \le V(P^B) \;:\; V[\lambda P^A+(1-\lambda)P^B] < \lambda V(P^A)+(1-\lambda)V(P^B) < V(P^B) \tag{5.17}$$

Ad (**b2**). With here $P^A_{(-1)} = P^B_{(-1)}$, we first get:

$$\lambda Q(P^A_{(-1)})+(1-\lambda)Q(P^B_{(-1)}) = Q(P^A_{(-1)}) = Q(P^B_{(-1)}). \tag{5.18}$$

Thus with (5.18), $V[\lambda P^A+(1-\lambda)P^B]$, (5.16), becomes:

$$V[\lambda P^A+(1-\lambda)P^B] = \alpha_1-\alpha_1[\lambda P_1^A+(1-\lambda)P_1^B]+Q\left(P^B_{(-1)}\right) \tag{5.19}$$

By (5.7), $\alpha_1 > 0$, and $P_1^A > P_1^B$, we obtain:

$$-\lambda\alpha_1 P_1^A-(1-\lambda)\alpha_1 P_1^B < -\alpha_1 P_1^B \tag{5.20}$$

Inserting (5.18) and (5.20) into (5.14), and using $P_1^A > P_1^B$ (and $P^A_{(-1)} = P^B_{(-1)}$), we get:

$$V[\lambda P^A+(1-\lambda)P^B] < \alpha_1-\alpha_1 P_1^B+Q(P^B_{(-1)})$$

$$= V(P^B) = \max\left\{V(P^A), V(P^B)\right\} \tag{5.21}$$

that is, by (5.21), **V(P)**, (5.9), is *strictly quasiconvex*, cf. (5.17); see Diewert et al. (1981, p. 398,405).

Ad (**c**). Suppose, without loss of generality that items 1 and 2 have: $\beta_1 = \beta_2 = -1$.

Let $P^C$ and $P^D$ be two price vectors which *only differ* in the *first two elements*, that is, $P_1^C \neq P_1^D$, $P_2^C \neq P_2^D$, $P_i^C = P_i^D$, $i > 2$, and which yield the same value of indirect utility. Assume that $V(P^C) = V(P^D)$, then any convex combination of such price vectors $P^C$ and $P^D$ gives the *same* value of **V(P)**, that is, *violating* (5.17)—$V(P)$ is *not* strictly quasiconvex.

This *completes* the proof of property (**iv**) and Proposition 5.1. □

It is noteworthy that the *monotonicities* (iii) of **V(P,C)**, (5.5), are established, *exclusively*, by only the *positivity requirements* for, $\alpha_i$, (5.7), in contrast to (5.1). *Strict monotonicity* of *indirect* utility functions, such as (5.5), is very important, as it ensures the *global positivity* of demanded *quantities* $\mathbf{D_i}$ and budget *shares* $\mathbf{e_i}$, for *all* prices and incomes, cf. (5.22). On strict monotonicity requirements and nonnegativity constraints, see Lee and Pitt (1986, p. 1237), Pollak (1969, p. 61), Tobin and Houthakker (1950–51, p. 146).

We may note that *quasiconvexity* of (5.5) can be examined *algebraically* by checking that its Hessian matrix has at least N-1 nonnegative eigenvalues, cf. Diewert et al. (1981, p. 401), Lau (1978, p. 417). With (5.5), (5.9), being additive, the associated Hessian matrix (5.10) is diagonal and it shows the eigenvalues. Thus by using (5.7), (5.11), we have N-1 positive eigenvalues in (5.10) and hence global quasiconvexity (for all positive prices).

But we have with (5.11) and by applying the basic *geometric*, (5.17), criterion (necessary and sufficient condition) actually proved that **CDES**, (5.5), is strictly quasiconvex on its *global domain* for *prices* and *income*: $P_i > 0, C > 0$. Indeed, its *global neoclassical* regularity properties of *strict monotonicity* and *strict quasiconvexity* may be the greatest *merit* of (5.5) in comparisons with many "*flexible functional forms*" of indirect utility and/or consumer demand systems. More on this below.

Applying Roy's *identity* with Proposition 5.1 to **CDES**, (5.5) gives *Marshallian demand functions*, $\mathbf{Y_i} = \mathbf{D_i(P, C)}$, and budget *expenditure share* forms, $\mathbf{e_i} = \frac{P_i Y_i}{C} = \mathbf{e_i(P, C)}$, as:

$$D_i(P,C) = -\frac{\partial V(P,C)/\partial P_i}{\partial V(P,C)/\partial C} = \frac{\alpha_i\,(C/P_i)^{\beta_i+1}}{\sum_{j=1}^{N}\alpha_j\,(C/P_j)^{\beta_j}} > 0\ ;$$

$$e_i(P,C) = \frac{\alpha_i\,(C/P_i)^{\beta_i}}{\sum_{j=1}^{N}\alpha_j\,(C/P_j)^{\beta_j}} > 0 \qquad (5.22)$$

It follows from (5.22) that the *parameters*, $\alpha_i$, are *not* identified: multiplication with the same scalar leads to the same demand equations. Hence, we *imposed* the *identifying* restriction: $\sum_{i=1}^{N}\alpha_i = 1$, on **V(P,C)**, (5.5)—originally *not* imposed upon (5.1). Yoshihara (1969, p. 267–268) did not indicate how his positive $(\alpha_i)$ are estimated, without using any normalization.

## CDES Parameters and Analytic Elasticity Formulas

The economic interpretation and implications of the *individual* parameters involved in any multi-dimensional indirect utility function $V(P,C)$) are not straightforward to see or provide. However, for economic purposes and intuition, it is useful to demonstrate the implications of V(P,C) *parameters* for the *size* and *signs* of various well-defined *demand* and *substitution elasticities* at any $(P, C)$ . This task is now done for our $V(P, C)$, (5.5). The underlying *derivatives* of all our dimensionless *elasticity* expressions (pure numbers) are given in Appendix B, section "Appendix B. Derivation of Marshallian and Hicksian Demand Derivatives".

### *Marshallian and Hicksian Demand Elasticities of CDES*

From **CDES** *Marshallian demand* functions, $\mathbf{Y_i} = \mathbf{D_i(P, C)}$, (5.22), we find—after some manipulations, (Appendix B)—the *expenditure* ("income") elasticity, $E(D_i, C) = (\partial D_i/\partial C)(C/D_i)$, the own *price*, $E(D_i, P_i) = (\partial D_i/\partial P_i)(P_i/D_i)$, and cross-price *elasticities*, $E(D_i, P_j) = (\partial D_i/\partial P_j)(P_j/D_i)$, expressed by their **CDES** expenditure ("Engel") and price elasticities, (5.23–5.25), cf. Houthakker (1960b, p. 14–15), Somermeyer and Langhout (1972, p. 352–353):

$$E(D_i, C) = 1 + \beta_i - \bar{\beta}\ , \quad \left[ \bar{\beta} = \bar{\beta}(P, C) = \sum_{j=1}^{N} e_j\, \beta_j \right] \ : \ \begin{cases} > 0 \\ < 0 \end{cases} \tag{5.23}$$

$$E(D_i, P_i) = -1 - \beta_i\,(1 - e_i)\ , \ [\ \beta_i \geq -1\ ,\ e_i > 0\ ] \ : \ < 0 \tag{5.24}$$

$$E(D_j, P_i) = \beta_i\, e_i > -1\ ; \quad E(D_i, P_j) = \beta_j\, e_j > -1 \tag{5.25}$$

*Expenditure* (income, Engel) elasticities of goods satisfy numerically the **Engel** *aggregation*:

$$\sum_{j=1}^{N} e_j\, E(D_j, C) = \sum_{j=1}^{N} e_j\,(1 + \beta_j - \bar{\beta}) = 1 + \sum_{j=1}^{N} e_j\, \beta_j - \sum_{j=1}^{N} e_j\, \bar{\beta} = 1 \tag{5.26}$$

and all the *price* elasticities for any good satisfy numerically the **Cournot** *aggregation*:

$$\sum_{j=1}^{N} e_j\, E(D_j, P_i) = e_i\,[-(1 + \beta_i) + \beta_i\, e_i\,] + \sum_{j \neq i}^{N} e_j\, \beta_i\, e_i = -\,e_i \tag{5.27}$$

The *higher* $\beta_i$ is, the *higher* is $\mathbf{E(D_i, C)}$, (5.23). It follows from formula (5.23) that a *normal* commodity, $E(D_i, C) > 0$, is a *necessity* (inelastic), when $\beta_i < \bar{\beta}$, and a *luxury* (elastic), whenever $\beta_i > \bar{\beta}$. By economically permitting *some* $\beta_i$—within the interval (-1,0), cf. (5.5)—**CDES** expression (5.23) more easily *allows* for some *inferior* goods, $E(D_i, C) < 0$, than the earlier restriction, $\beta_i > 0$, (5.2).

Although *every* elasticity, $\mathbf{E(D_i, C)}$—as $\mathbf{e_i}$ (5.22) and $\bar{\beta}$ (5.23)—is *varying* with **C** [ changing between income groups (rich/poor) and changing over time ], we note from (5.23) that

$$E(D_i, C) - E(D_j, C) \;=\; \beta_i - \beta_j \tag{5.28}$$

that is, the **differences** between the **CDES** *income* elasticities of *various commodities* are *constant*. In other words, a stable *hierarchy* exists between all the commodity groups. Ranking of *income elasticities* is robust and corresponds to *ranking* of their $\beta_i$, cf. (5.28).

It is evident from, $\mathbf{E\,(D_i, P_i)}$, (5.24) that with CDES, (5.5), goods with ($\beta_i > 0$) are *price elastic*, and those with ($\beta_i < 0$) are *price inelastic*. Thus, earlier parameter restrictions, (5.2), *precluded* any price *inelastic* goods, while Houthakker, (5.1), implied that all goods have *inelastic* own-price elasticities. Note that *all* $E(D_i, P_i)$, (5.24), are *negative*, which *exclude* "Giffen goods". Our *global* quasiconvexity properly prevents Giffen's paradox, which occurs only in a *local* domain of (P,C) vectors (or local area of commodity space), cf. Wold and Jureen (1953, p. 103). Thus, formulas with $E(D_i, P_i) > 0$ indicate the V(P,C) as *lacking* global regularity.

Moreover, with all $\beta_i > 0$, (5.2), only *gross—Marshallian—substitutes* (5.25) occur; in contrast with all $\beta_i < 0$, (5.25), Houthakker found that "indirect addilog" (5.1) accordingly entails *"universal gross complementarity"* (Houthakker 1961, p. 721). A very unfortunate consequence of the two extremes of either gross substitutes or gross complements has been the advice in empirical demand analysis, Houthakker (1960b, p. 14), to only include *broad* (few) groups (food, clothing, housing,..), because—among more *narrowly* specified (many) items of expenditures—the substitution and complementarity may be of *any* nature. But fortunately, the *extremes* of gross substitutes/complements are *avoided* with our CDES version, (5.5), and its demand system, (5.22), is tractable econometrically for any size of N.

To cast additional light on the CDES *parameters* (5.5), the *price* (Slutsky) elasticities of **CDES** *Hicksian demand* ("compensated") *functions*, $\mathbf{Y_i} = \mathbf{H_i(P, U)}$, will be useful. Although the Hicksian demands, $Y_i = H_i(P, U)$, implied by the CDES indirect utility function can *not* be obtained in closed form, the *own*-price, $E(H_i, P_i) = (\partial H_i/\partial P_i)(P_i/H_i)$ and *cross*-price *elasticities*, $E(H_i, P_j) = (\partial H_i/\partial P_j)(P_j/H_i)$, of Hicksian demands $H_i(P, U)$ can be presented by *explicit* (parametric) formulas. The key is the standard *Slutsky equations* of the *derivatives (elasticities)* connecting *Marshallian* and *Hicksian* demands. Thus, by the *Slutsky equations*, cf. Appendix B, section "Appendix

B. Derivation of Marshallian and Hicksian Demand Derivatives", and (5.23), (5.24–5.25), we get:

$$E(H_i, P_i) = [\frac{P_i}{D_i}] S_{ii} = E(D_i, P_i) + e_i E(D_i, C) = -(1+\beta_i) + (1+2\beta_i - \bar{\beta})e_i < 0 \tag{5.29}$$

$$E(H_j, P_i) = [\frac{P_i}{D_j}] S_{ji} = E(D_j, P_i) + e_i E(D_j, C) = (1+\beta_i+\beta_j-\bar{\beta})e_i = \begin{cases} > 0 \\ < 0 \end{cases} \tag{5.30}$$

As far as *"pure"* (Hicksian) price responses (5.30) are concerned, there is considerable flexibility, both with respect to the *signs* (complementarity, indifference, substitutability) and the *numerical* sizes of these "pure" cross-price elasticities. Behind the *gross* price elasticity values (5.24–5.25) above, there clearly exists *freedom* for distinct "*income effects*" and "*substitution effects*", (5.29–5.30), of any *price changes* within the CDES demand/expenditure/budget system, (5.22). Marshall (gross) complements (5.25) may be Hicksian substitutes (5.30).

The *utility-level constraint* associated with Hicksian demands $\mathbf{H_i(P, U)}$—Hicks (1946, p. 310,3.law), Silberberg and Suen (2001, p. 295)—is satisfied by **CDES** elasticities, (5.29–5.30):

$$\sum_{j=1}^{N} e_j E(H_j, P_i) = -e_i(1+\beta_i) + e_i(1+2\beta_i - \bar{\beta})e_i + \sum_{j \neq i}^{N} e_j(1+\beta_i+\beta_j-\bar{\beta})e_i = 0 \tag{5.31}$$

The basic aggregation property (5.31) of *Slutsky elasticities*, (5.29–5.30), will be called the **Hicks-Slutsky** *aggregation*, which—like the **Cournot** *aggregation* (5.27)—coherently reflects *all* the comparative static *effects* of changing *one* single *price*; moreover, as an identity, aggregation (5.31) offers an important *numerical* check on *empirical* Slutsky elasticity calculations.

### *The Allen Elasticities of Substitution*

The *Allen partial* elasticities of *substitution* of *Hicksian* demands, $\mathbf{Y_i} = \mathbf{H_i(P, U)}$, are *not* usually shown, and they were *neither* analyzed by Houthakker for $V^*(P, C)$, (5.1), *nor* by Leser (1941), Somermeyer and Langhout (1972), for their empirical demand equations. Moreover, Chung (1994, p. 44–45) incorrectly states that the "indirect addilog" implies: "The Allen-Uzawa cross-partial elasticities of substitution are zero. This result is a severe restriction." But certainly for our CDES, $V(P, C)$, (5.5), a clear parametric connection to the *nonzero* Allen elasticities will exist.

The *Allen partial* elasticities of *substitution*, $(\sigma_{ij})$, can be simply obtained, cf. Frisch (1959, p. 180), by *"normalizing"* the **CDES** *Slutsky elasticities*, (5.29–5.30), as:

$$\sigma_{ii} = \left[\frac{C}{D_i D_i}\right] S_{ii} = \frac{E(H_i, P_i)}{e_i} = -\left[\frac{1+\beta_i}{e_i}\right] + 1 + 2\beta_i - \bar{\beta} < 0 \qquad (5.32)$$

$$\begin{aligned} \sigma_{ji} &= \left[\frac{C}{D_i D_j}\right] S_{ji} = \frac{E(H_j, P_i)}{e_i} = 1 + \beta_i + \beta_j - \bar{\beta} \\ &= \frac{E(H_i, P_j)}{e_j} = \sigma_{ij} = \begin{cases} > 0 \\ < 0 \end{cases} \end{aligned} \qquad (5.33)$$

The elasticities $(\sigma_{ii})$ refer to the substitution between the i'th good and *all* the others. The *higher* $\beta_i$, the *higher* are *all* $\sigma_{ji}$ $(i \neq j)$. The **CDES** *substitution elasticities* (5.32–5.33) are *variable*, changing with utility (income) levels and prices via $\bar{\beta}$ and $e_i$. Like $E(H_j, P_i)$, the *sign* of $\sigma_{ji}$ decides whether a particular pair of goods are Hicksian substitutes or complements. Notably, Frisch (1959, p. 180) wrote: "The elasticity of substitution has the great practical *disadvantage* of often tending towards infinity for goods that make up a small fraction of the total budget. The Slutsky elasticity *retains* 'normal proportions'...". Such *conjecture* may be suggested from the *formal* expression of $\sigma_{ji}$ on LHS/RHS of (5.33), but as a counter example, our *explicit* **CDES** parametric expression for $\sigma_{ji}$, in (5.33), shows that it does *not* always [ in fact, *never*, cf. the *middle* expression in (5.33) ] happen.

It has been argued by Deaton and Muellbauer (1980a, p. 316), Deaton and Muellbauer (1980b, p. 68–69,76), that in practice, it is easier not to use the Slutsky equation terms, $\mathbf{S_{ij}}$, but use $c_{ij} = (P_i P_j / C)\, S_{ij}$—which in terms of the elasticity expressions, (5.33), is equivalent to:

$$c_{ij} = e_i\, e_j\, \sigma_{ij} = e_i\, E(H_i, P_j) = e_j\, E(H_j, P_i) = e_j\, e_i\, \sigma_{ji} = c_{ji} \qquad (5.34)$$

Evidently, in contrast to CDES values $\boldsymbol{\sigma_{ji}}$, (5.33), the corresponding CDES values $\mathbf{c_{ji}}$, (5.34), would be much smaller by the effect of *small* budget shares with a large number of commodities. We know the *range* of the *parametric* $\beta_i$ values, (5.5), and they *dominate* the *range* of the *Allen* elasticities, (5.33), rather than the intervals of (5.34) or (5.25), (5.30).

As in (5.31), **CDES** *substitution* elasticities, (5.32–5.33), meet the *utility-level* constraint implied by the Hicksian demands $\mathbf{H_i}\,(\mathbf{P}, \mathbf{U})$, and together with (5.29–5.30), (5.27–5.26), we get:

$$\sum_{j=1}^{N} e_j\, \sigma_{ji} = \sum_{j=1}^{N} e_j\, E(H_j, P_i)/e_i = \sum_{j=1}^{N} e_j\, [\, E(D_j, P_i)/e_i + E(D_j, C)\, ] \qquad (5.35)$$

$$= (1/e_i)\sum_{j=1}^{N} e_j\, E(D_j, P_i) + \sum_{j=1}^{N} e_j\, E(D_j, C) = -1 + 1 = 0 \tag{5.36}$$

We call aggregation property, (5.35–5.36), $\sum_{j=1}^{N} e_j \sigma_{ji} = 0$: the **Hicks-Allen** *aggregation*—Hicks (1937, p. 16–17), Allen (1938, p. 504). As demonstrated in (5.36), the **Hicks-Allen** *aggregation* formula is a *combination* of the **Cournot** *aggregation* (5.27) and **Engel** *aggregation* (5.26)—a *general relation* among demand elasticities that is *not tied* to just our CDES elasticities.

The property that the **differences** of the *elasticities* of partial *substitution* are *constant*—hence the proper Hanoch name to (5.1), (5.4), (5.5) as **CDES**—follows directly from (5.33),

$$\sigma_{ik} - \sigma_{jk} = \beta_i - \beta_j\ ; \quad \sigma_{ij} - \sigma_{kl} = (\beta_i + \beta_j) - (\beta_k + \beta_l) \tag{5.37}$$

Such revealing *invariance* relations among the *Allen* elasticities, $\sigma_{ji}$, (5.37), do *not* exist at all among the corresponding *Slutsky* elasticities, $E(H_j, P_i)$, (5.30).

The *great* mathematical-economic *advantage* of *any* **indirect** utility function $U = V(P, C)$ is that the underlying *substitution* elasticities ($\sigma_{ji}$) can be *explicitly* derived by the procedure in Appendix B, section "Appendix B. Derivation of Marshallian and Hicksian Demand Derivatives", and be studied—as we have shown for CDES—-in terms of the *parameters* of the actually chosen **V(P, C)**.

The *constant differences*, (5.37), of **CDES** are *zero* in the *special* **CES** cases, (5.46–5.47),

$$\forall_i\ \beta_i = \beta = \sigma - 1 \tag{5.38}$$

Indeed with **CES**, (5.38), CDES formulas, (5.32–5.33), (5.29–5.30), (5.24–5.25), (5.23), are reduced to:

$$\sigma_{ii} = -\sigma(1 - e_i)/e_i\ ; \quad \sigma_{ji} = \sigma \tag{5.39}$$

$$E(H_i, P_i) = -\sigma(1-e_i)\ ; \quad E(H_j, P_i) = \sigma\, e_i\ ; \quad E(H_i, P_j) = \sigma\, e_j \tag{5.40}$$

$$E(D_i, P_i) = -\sigma(1-e_i) - e_i\ ; \quad E(D_j, P_i) = (\sigma-1)e_i\ ; \quad E(D_i, P_j) = (\sigma-1)e_j \tag{5.41}$$

$$E(D_i, C) = 1 \tag{5.42}$$

Incidentally to underline the seminal and *benchmark* role that **CDES** does possess in the theory of utility/production function studies, we note that a **CES** *form* of the direct/indirect utility functions [ both functions complying with the CES, (5.38), (5.39)] is the *only* functional form with the property of *self-duality*, that is, the dual can be expressed exactly with the *same parameters*, cf. Samuelson (1965), Samuelson (1969), Houthakker (1965), Hicks (1969). Moreover, for the *global* satisfaction of the *regularity condition* (**i–iv**) on consumer behavior, it is revealing to recall the issues and proof involved in the CES extension of the *two-factor* version, Arrow et al. (1961), to the *multi-factor* case (N-goods) by Uzawa (1962), who characterized the class of *strictly quasiconcave* production (utility) functions, where the Allen elasticities ($\sigma_{ij}$), Uzawa (1962, p. 292), are *constant* for *all pairs* of factors (goods), *regardless* of factor prices (i.e., globally for any positive prices). Uzawa (1962, p. 296) proved that if *all*, ($\sigma_{ij}$), had to be *constant* at *all* price points, then these, ($\sigma_{ij}$), must be *identical*—as seen in (5.38–5.39). Hence, if they are *not* identical, these ($\sigma_{ij}$) are *foreordained* to *change* (vary) with different *prices*—as they also did in, (5.33), by the $\bar{\beta}$ term, (5.23–5.22). In this way, the **CDES** demand system with its *global regularity* can actually be regarded as a successful, *more flexible global* extension of the **CES** system, (5.38–5.42).

### *Global Regularity Restrictions*

From *any* specific real, continuous *function* $V(P, C)$ of prices and income, which is *homogeneous* of degree zero, and *differentiable* with continuous first partial derivatives of (P,C), we can immediately derive the corresponding Marshallian demand functions $D_i(P, C)$ by Roy's identity, cf. (5.22). Next, the analytic expressions for the Engel (income) elasticities $E(D_i, C)$ and the Allen (substitution) elasticities $\sigma_{ij}$ can with some efforts also be derived, and they can be studied to see how the various parameters affect the elasticities and how much *flexibility* (number of *independent* utility *parameters*) such elasticities will possess, cf. (5.23), (5.33), (5.37). However, *if* such specific $V(P, C)$ does *not* have strict *monotonicity* in (P,C) everywhere, then for particular prices, some of demanded quantities might turn negative, (budget shares straying *outside* the [ 0,1 ] interval), cf. (5.8), (5.22), rendering all such point elasticities meaningless. Similarly, *if* $V(P, C)$ does *not* have **strict** *quasiconvexity* in (P,C) everywhere, then a local optimum is *not* always at the same time a *global optimum*, hence $D_i(P, C)$ *not* being true demand functions. If such $V(P, C)$ is *not* even *quasiconvex*, the own- and cross-price elasticities of $D_i(P, C)$ (by Roy's identity) will *not* have the theoretically expected *signs* and magnitudes . *Non-quasiconvex* indirect utility functions are *inconsistent* with utility maximization, cf. Lau (1978, p. 411). But as the proof of Proposition 5.1 showed, it needs careful examinations to sort out the *combinations* of individual *parameter intervals* (exact *parameter region*) that *preserve* strict quasiconvexity *globally* (for any positive price vector).

The family of *monotonic strictly quasiconvex* functions suitable for imposing *global regularity* restrictions is *large*; many different parametric classes of algebraic functions could be suitable candidates for $V(P, C)$. Somehow research into the global regularity restrictions for such $V(P, C)$ has been rather neglected, as it was from the beginning, (5.1).

However, *local domain* problems for many "flexible functional forms" have been raised and clearly illustrated, see Caves and Christensen (1980, p. 422), Barnett and Lee (1985, p. 1421,1435), Fisher et al. (2001, p. 63); for other experiments, cf. Guilkey and Knox Lovell (1980), Guilkey et al. (1983), Chung (1987). Procedures for imposing local quasiconvexity restrictions—via reparametrizations and the Slutsky matrix—on some flexible demand system have been devised with good results, see Ryan and Wales (1998, p. 333), Moschini (1999). But with many commodities desirable, local flexibility comes at the sacrifice of global regularity.

For the specification of a *consumer demand sector* in applied *computable general equilibrium* (**CGE**) models, several functional forms, including **CES**, are commonly used, cf. Shoven and Whalley (1992, p. 95). A *nesting* structure for CES preferences can increase the *scope* for *elasticities* (5.39–5.41), but *not* at all the inadequate *unitary* income elasticities (5.42), contradicting Engel's legacy, Houthakker (1957), Chai and Moneta (2010, p. 232). The **CDES** *demand system* has *nonlinear* and fairly flexible *Engel curve patterns* and elasticities, cf. (5.23), and it has certainly *merits* vis-à-vis *alternative* specifications, currently used in restricting the parameter space in **CGE** models, cf. Hertel et al. (1991), Rimmer and Powell (1996), Yu et al. (2003), and particularly, Hertel and Tsigas (1997, p. 49), de Boer and Paap (2009), where implicit/explicit CDES are applied. However, as stressed by Diewert and Wales (1987, p. 43), it is *necessary* that *functional forms* for production and utility functions in applied general equilibrium models should satisfy *curvature conditions globally*, and this necessity offers the *main rationale* for using the **CDES** in solving various **CGE** models and especially for solving general equilibrium *dynamics* such as *multi-sector growth* (**MSG**) models. Thus, our Proposition 5.1 for CDES would clarify and significantly *improve* the "Indirect Addilog" *version* (5.2) used in Jensen and Larsen (2005, p. 36,39,47), here Chap. 18, for calculating Walrasian equilibrium states with sectoral CES production functions and non-homothetic consumer preferences. Dynamic solutions of parametrically well-specified growth models beyond current one-sector and two-sector models are urgently needed, and hereto the *globally* well-behaved **CDES** system $\mathbf{V(P, C)}$, (5.5), for the consumer sector will be very helpful for computing and analyzing alternative *evolutions*[1] of growing multi-sector economies.

## Final Comments

Houthakker mentioned a paradox in his concluding remarks on the *state* of *consumption theory*, Houthakker (1961, p. 735): "It is nevertheless pertinent to point out - without further elaborations - that the theory of consumer's

[1] See Jensen et al. (2015), cf. Chap. 20.

choice may historically have had more influence as a *prototype* to other branches of economics than as a guide to consumption research". However, his fundamental and extensive studies of demand models are a valuable *legacy*, and his seminal work on *indirect* utility functions and in particular his *original*, $V^*(P, C)$, (5.1) can—rigorously parametrically extended—once again bring new progress to the field of consumer demand models. Moreover, the *explicit* **CDES** models for household consumption patterns can be given a much *wider* empirical scope by the *richer* parameter set of Hanoch's *implicit* CDES form. But the *explicit* CDES form **V(P, C)**, (5.5), with its *parsimonous* parameter set, is suitable for new efforts in general equilibrium dynamics and **MSG** models by sectoral allowing for proper expansions as the observable Engel curves. Finally, our analytic framework for the generation of *parametric Allen substitution elasticities* and aggregations, as inspired by CDES, can also contribute to a renewed search for new indirect utility functions *parametrically* satisfying the *global regularity* properties.

## Appendix A. The Box-Cox Transformation

In econometrics, see Heij et al. (2004, p. 297–301), the Box-Cox transformation of a variable $(x)$ is defined as:

$$x(\lambda) = \frac{x^{\lambda} - 1}{\lambda} \tag{5.43}$$

If $\lambda = 1$, then (apart from the constant -1) the variable is linear.

If $\lambda \to 0$, the limits of the numerator and the denominator are equal to zero.

Hence, we apply de l'Hôpital's rule. We first take the derivative of numerator and denominator with respect to $\lambda$, and take the limit again:

$$\lim_{\lambda \to 0} \frac{x^{\lambda} - 1}{\lambda} = \lim_{\lambda \to 0} \frac{x^{\lambda} \log(x)}{1} = \log(x) \tag{5.44}$$

where $\log(x)$ denotes the natural logarithm.

In the context of economic theory, the Box-Cox transformation can also advantageously be used in the definition of the indirect utility function of the **CDES** specification (5.5):

$$V(P, C) = \sum_{i=1}^{N} \alpha_i \frac{(C/P_i)^{\beta_i} - 1}{\beta_i} \tag{5.45}$$

If a particular $\beta_i = 0$, then the term, $\frac{(C/P_i)^{\beta_i} - 1}{\beta_i}$, has to be replaced by: $\log(C/P_i)$.

If all $\beta_i = 0$, then CDES (5.45) can be reduced to,

$$V(P, C) = \sum_{i=1}^{N} \alpha_i \log(C/P_i) \tag{5.46}$$

that is, to the indirect utility function of the Cobb-Douglas transform.

If all $\beta_i = \sigma - 1 \neq 0$, then CDES becomes the **CES** indirect utility function,

$$V(P, C) = \sum_{i=1}^{N} \alpha_i \frac{(C/P_i)^{\sigma-1} - 1}{\sigma - 1} \tag{5.47}$$

The Box-Cox representation (5.47) of the CES indirect utility function is for many purposes more practical to apply, cf. (5.1), (5.3), (5.22), than the usual CES forms of $V(P, C)$; see Samuelson (1965, p. 788,795), Samuelson (1969, p. 358), Samuelson (1974, p. 1267), Varian (1992, p. 112), Silberberg and Suen (2001, p. 359), Jensen and Larsen (2005, p. 34), here page 534 in Chap. 18.

## Appendix B. Derivation of Marshallian and Hicksian Demand Derivatives

Applying Roy's identity to CDES (5.5) gave—using (5.6), (5.8)—the Marshallian demand functions, $D_i(P, C)$, and the budget share forms, $e_i(P, C)$, in (5.22). The next step to obtain the *Marshallian demand derivatives* from the $\mathbf{D_i(P, C)}$ formula (5.22) is more cumbersome, as it requires *collection* of many terms into *relevant compact* expressions.

Let $\bar{\beta}$ denote the budget-weighted $(e_j)$ sum of the parameters $(\beta_j)$ in (5.23). Differentiation of the *Marshallian demand* relation (5.22)—fraction—with respect to $C$ gives,

$$\frac{\partial D_i}{\partial C} = \frac{\partial\left(\alpha_i (C/P_i)^{\beta_i+1}\right)/\partial C}{\sum \alpha_j (C/P_j)^{\beta_j}} - \frac{\alpha_i (C/P_i)^{\beta_i+1}\, \partial\left(\sum \alpha_j (C/P_j)^{\beta_j}\right)/\partial C}{\left[\sum \alpha_j (C/P_j)^{\beta_j}\right]^2} \tag{5.48}$$

$$= (1 + \beta_i)\frac{D_i}{C} - D_i \frac{\partial\left(\sum \alpha_j (C/P_j)^{\beta_j}\right)/\partial C}{\sum \alpha_j (C/P_j)^{\beta_j}} \tag{5.49}$$

$$= (1 + \beta_i)\frac{D_i}{C} - \frac{D_i}{C}\sum \beta_j e_j = (1 + \beta_i - \bar{\beta})\frac{D_i}{C} \tag{5.50}$$

where $D_i$ , $e_j$, (5.22), have again been repeatedly used. Hence (5.50) establishes (5.23).

Regarding price derivatives, we first consider the case, $i \neq j$. Then, $P_i$ only appears in the denominator of $D_j$, and the derivative of (5.22) with respect to

$P_i$ becomes [ similar result with interchanging the index $(j)$ and $(i)$ ],

$$\frac{\partial D_j}{\partial P_i} = \alpha_j (C/P_j)^{\beta_j+1} \partial \left( \left[ \sum \alpha_j (C/P_j)^{\beta_j} \right]^{-1} \right) / \partial P_i \tag{5.51}$$

$$= - \frac{\alpha_j (C/P_j)^{\beta_j+1}}{\sum \alpha_j (C/P_j)^{\beta_j}} \times \frac{\partial (\alpha_j (C/P_j)^{\beta_j})/\partial P_i}{\sum \alpha_j (C/P_j)^{\beta_j}} = \beta_i \left( \frac{D_j D_i}{C} \right) \tag{5.52}$$

Secondly, we consider the case, $i = j$ . Then, the term $P_i$ appears in the numerator as well as in the denominator of (5.22). Differentiation with respect to $P_i$ gives, after reduction,

$$\frac{\partial D_i}{\partial P_i} = \frac{\partial (\alpha_i (C/P_i)^{\beta_i+1})/\partial P_i}{\sum \alpha_j (C/P_j)^{\beta_j}} + \beta_i \frac{(D_i)^2}{C} = -(1+\beta_i)\frac{D_i}{P_i} + \beta_i \frac{(D_i)^2}{C} \tag{5.53}$$

Hence, (5.52) and (5.53) establish (5.24), (5.25).

We collect the basic *Marshallian* first-order derivatives [Barten and Boehm 1982, p. 415], from (5.50) to (5.53) for **CDES** as:

$$\frac{\partial D_i}{\partial C} = (1 + \beta_i - \bar{\beta})(D_i/C) \tag{5.54}$$

$$\frac{\partial D_i}{\partial P_i} = -(1+\beta_i)(D_i/P_i) + \beta_i (D_i D_i/C) \tag{5.55}$$

$$\frac{\partial D_j}{\partial P_i} = \beta_i (D_i D_j/C) \; ; \qquad \frac{\partial D_i}{\partial P_j} = \beta_j (D_i D_j/C) \tag{5.56}$$

By (5.54) to (5.56), the *typical* **CDES** derivatives—$\mathbf{S_{ji}}$—in the *Slutsky matrix*, **S (P, C)**, are:

$$S_{ii}(P, C) = \frac{\partial D_i}{\partial P_i} + \frac{\partial D_i}{\partial C} D_i = -(1+\beta_i)(D_i/P_i) + (1 + 2\beta_i - \bar{\beta})(D_i D_i/C) \tag{5.57}$$

$$S_{ji}(P, C) = \frac{\partial D_j}{\partial P_i} + \frac{\partial D_j}{\partial C} D_i = (1 + \beta_i + \beta_j - \bar{\beta})(D_i D_j/C) = S_{ij} \tag{5.58}$$

that is, the Slutsky matrix is *symmetric*, as it should be. The Slutsky (1915) Eqs. (5.57–5.58) were called the "*Fundamental Equation of Value Theory*" by Hicks (1946, p. 309).

Moreover, the Slutsky ("substitution") *matrix* represents the actual size of *price* (own and cross) *derivatives* of the *Hicksian demand* functions, evaluated at the particular ( *common*, optimal) point, $\mathbf{Y_i} = \mathbf{H_i}(\mathbf{P}, \mathbf{U}) \equiv \mathbf{D_i}(\mathbf{P}, \mathbf{C})$, that is,

$$\frac{\partial H_i(P, U)}{\partial P_i} = S_{ii}(P, C)\ ; \quad \frac{\partial H_j(P, U)}{\partial P_i} = S_{ji}(P, C)\ ; \tag{5.59}$$

$$Y_i = H_i(P, U) \equiv D_i(P, C) \tag{5.60}$$

Hence, (5.57–5.60) establish (5.29–5.30) and (5.32–5.33) [ by alternative normalization of (5.57–5.58) ].

## Bibliography


Akin JS, Stewart JF (1979) Theoretical Restrictions on the Parameters of Indirect Addilog Demand Equations. Econometrica 47:779–780

Allen RGD (1938) Mathematical Analysis for Economists. MacMillan, London

Arrow KJ, Chenery HB, Minhas BS, Solow RM (1961) Capital–Labour Substitution and Economic Efficiency. Review of Economics and Statistics 43:225–250

Barnett WA, Lee YW (1985) The Global Properties of the Miniflex Laurent, Generalized Leontief, and Translog Flexible Functional Forms. Econometrica 53:1421–1437

Barten AP, Boehm V (1982) Consumer theory. pp 381–429, In: Arrow, K. J. and Intriligator, M. D. (eds), *Handbook of mathematical economics*, vol 2. North–Holland, Amsterdam.

de Boer PMC, Paap R (2009) Testing non–nested demand relations: linear expenditure systems versus indirect addilog. Stat Neerlandica 63:368–384

Caves DW, Christensen LR (1980) Global Properties of Flexible Functional Forms. American Economic Review 70:422–432

Chai A, Moneta A (2010) Retrospectives: Engel Curves. Journal of Economic Perspectives 24:225–240

Chung JW (1987) On the Estimation of Factor Substitution in the Translog Model. Review of Economics and Statistics 69:409–417

Chung JW (1994) Utility and Production Functions. Blackwell, Oxford

Deaton AS, Muellbauer J (1980a) An Almost Ideal Demand System. American Economic Review 70:312–326

Deaton AS, Muellbauer J (1980b) Economics and Consumer Behavior. Cambridge University Press, Cambridge

Diewert WE (1974) Applications of Duality Theory. pp 106–171, In: Intriligator MD, Kendrick DA (eds) *Frontiers of Quantitative Economics*, Vol.2, North–Holland, Amsterdam

Diewert WE (1982) Duality Approaches to Microeconomic Theory. In: Arrow KJ, Intriligator MD (eds) *Handbook of Mathematical Economics*, Vol.2, North–Holland, Amsterdam

Diewert WE, Wales TJ (1987) Flexible Functional Forms and Global Curvature Conditions. Econometrica 37:43–68

Diewert WE, Avriel M, Zang I (1981) Nine Kinds of Quasiconcavity and Concavity. Journal of Economic Theory 25:397–420

Fisher D, Fleissig AR, Serletis A (2001) An Empirical Comparison of Flexible Demand System Functional Forms. Journal of Applied Econometrics 16:59–80

Frisch R (1959) A Complete Scheme for Computing All Direct and Cross Demand Elasticities in a Model with Many Sectors. Econometrica 27:177–196

Gamaletsos T (1973) Further Analysis of Cross–country Comparison of Consumer Expenditure Patterns. European Economic Review 4:1–20
Gamaletsos T (1974) Reply – Further analysis of cross–country comparison of consumer expenditure patterns. European Economic Review 5:307
Ginsberg W (1973) Concavity and Quasiconcavity in Economics. Journal of Economic Theory 6:596–605
Gravelle H, Rees R (2004) Microeconomics, 3rd edn. Prentice Hall, Harlow
Guilkey DK, Knox Lovell CA (1980) On the Flexibility of the Translog Approximation. International Economic Review 21:137–147
Guilkey DK, Knox Lovell C, Sickles R (1983) A Comparison of the Performance of Three Flexible Functional Forms. International Economic Review 24:591–616
Hanoch G (1975) Production and Demand Models with Direct and Indirect Implicit Additivity. Econometrica 43:395–419
Heij C, de Boer PMC, Franses PH, Kloek T, van Dijk HK (2004) Econometric Methods with Applications in Business and Economics. Oxford University Press, Oxford
Hertel TW, Tsigas ME (1997) Structure of GTAP, In Hertel, TW. pp 13–73, In Hertel, TW *Global Trade Analysis: Modelling and Applications*, Cambridge University Press, Cambridge
Hertel TW, Preckel PV, Tsigas ME, Peterson EB, Surry Y (1991) Implicit Additivity as a Strategy for Restricting the Parameter Space in Computable General Equilibrium Models. Economic and Financial Computing 1:265–289
Hicks JR (1937) Theorie Mathematique de la Valeur en Regime de la Libre Concurrence. Hermann, Editeurs, Paris
Hicks JR (1946) Value and Capital, 2nd edn. Clarendon Press, Oxford
Hicks JR (1969) Direct and Indirect Additivity. Econometrica 37:353–354
Hotelling H (1932) Edgeworth's Taxation Paradox and the Nature of Demand and Supply Functions. Journal of Political Economy 40:577–616
Houthakker HS (1952) Compensated Changes in Quantities and Qualities Consumed. Review of Economic Studies 19:155–64
Houthakker HS (1957) An International Comparison of Household Expenditure Patterns, Commemorating the Centenary of Engel's law. Econometrica 25:532–551
Houthakker HS (1960a) Additive Preferences. Econometrica 28:244–257
Houthakker HS (1960b) The Influence of Prices and Income on Household Expenditures. Bulletin of the International Institute of Statistics 37:9–22
Houthakker HS (1961) The Present State of Consumption Theory. Econometrica 29:704–740
Houthakker HS (1965) A Note on Self–Dual Preferences. Econometrica 33:797–801
Jensen BS, Larsen ME (2005) General Equilibrium Dynamics of Multi–Sector Growth Models. Journal of Economics 10:17–56
Jensen BS, Lehmijoki U, Rovenskaya E (2015) Non–Homothetic Multisector Growth Models. Review of Development Economics 19(2):221–243
Katzner DW (1968) A Note on the Differentiability of Consumer Demand Equations. Econometrica 36:415–418
Lau LJ (1978) Testing and Imposing Monotonicity, Convexity and Quasi–Convexity Constraints. pp 409–453, In: Fuss M, McFadden D (eds) *Production Economics: A Dual Approach to Theory and Applications*, Vol.1, North–Holland, Amsterdam
Lee LF, Pitt MM (1986) Microeconometric Demand System with Binding Nonnegativity Constraints: The Dual Approach. Econometrica 54:1237–1242

Leser CEV (1941) Family Budget Data and Price Elasticities of Demand. Review of Economic Studies 9:40–57
Mas-Colell A, Whinston MD, Green JR (1995) Microeconomic Theory. Oxford University Press, New York
Moschini G (1999) Imposing Local Curvature Conditions in Flexible Demand Systems. Journal of Business and Economics 17:487–490
Murty KN (1982) Theoretical Restrictions on the Parameters of Indirect Addilog Demand Equations – A Comment. Econometrica 50:225–227
Pollak RA (1969) Conditional Demand Functions and Consumption Theory. Quarterly Journal of Economics 83:60–78
Rimmer MT, Powell AA (1996) An Implicitly Additive Demand System. Applied Economics 28:1613–1622
Roy R (1942) De l'Utilite, Contribution a la Theorie des Choix. Hermann, Paris
Roy R (1947) La Distribution du Revenue entre les Divers Biens. Econometrica 15:205–225
Ryan DL, Wales TJ (1998) A Simple Method for Imposing Local Curvature in Some Flexible Demand Systems. Journal of Business and Economics 16:331–338
Samuelson PA (1965) Using Full Duality to Show that Simultaneously Additive Direct and Indirect Utilities implies Unitary Price Elasticity of Demand. Econometrica 33:781–796
Samuelson PA (1969) Corrected Formulation of Direct and Indirect Additivity. Econometrica 37:355–359
Samuelson PA (1974) Complementarity: An Essay on The 40th Anniversary of The Hicks–Allen Revolution in Demand Theory. Journal of Economic Literature 12:1255–1289
Shoven JB, Whalley J (1992) Applying General Equilibrium. Cambridge University Press, Cambridge, UK
Silberberg E, Suen W (2001) The Structure of Economics, A Mathematical Analysis, 3rd edn. McGraw–Hill, Singapore
Slutsky EE (1915) Sulla teoria del bilancio del consumatore. Giornale degli Economisti 51:1–26, translation: "on the theory of the budget of the consumer", In: *AEA series, readings in price theory*, 1953, George Allen and Unwin, London, pp 27–56
Somermeyer WH (1974) Further analysis of cross–country comparison of consumer expenditure patterns–comment. European Economic Review 5:303–306
Somermeyer WH, Langhout A (1972) Shapes of Engel Curves and Demand Curves: Implications of the Expenditure Allocation Model, Applied to Dutch Data. European Economic Review 3:351–386
Tobin J, Houthakker HS (1950–51) The Effects of Rationing on Demand Elasticities. Review of Economic Studies 18:140–153
Uzawa H (1962) Production Functions with Constant Elasticities of Substitution. Review of Economic Studies 29:291–299
Varian HR (1992) Microeconomic Analysis, 3rd edn. W.W. Norton & Company, New York
Wold H, Jureen L (1953) Demand Analysis. John Wiley & Sons, New York
Yoshihara K (1969) Demand Functions: An Application to the Japanese Expenditure Pattern. Econometrica 37:257–274
Yu W, Hertel TW, Preckel PV, Eales JS (2003) Projecting world food demand using alternative demand systems. Economic Modelling 21:99–129

CHAPTER 6

# Properties of the CDES Indirect Utility Functions and Demand Systems: Estimated by Survey Budget Data

## Introduction

Indirect utility functions as a tool for generating consumer demand systems is due Roy (1942, p. 19) and Roy (1947, p. 214)—the term to Houthakker (1952, p. 157). Roy's identity gives a painless procedure for deriving the functional forms of consumer demand functions. A particular mathematical form of additive indirect utility functions, studied by Houthakker (1960a, p. 252, 256) constitutes an indirect utility function, which—since the seminal paper of Hanoch (1975, p. 399)—is known as the CDES *indirect utility* function.

In the subsequent literature, however, there was no consensus about the theoretical correct restrictions upon the CDES parameters. Various proposed restrictions were empirically much too restrictive, as e.g. they implied all own-price elasticities being larger than one in absolute value (preventing any inelastic Marshallian demand curves). Review of the literature and studies of the global regularity properties as well as rigorous proofs of the *global* CDES *parameter restrictions* are given in Jensen et al. (2011); Chap. 5. Moreover, the proof of these restrictions implies that the CDES model is much more flexible than conventionally considered in the economic and econometric literature.

We proceed quickly with presentation of the theory and discussions of the empirical results.

The chapter is organized as follows. Section "CDES Indirect Utility Function" summarizes the economic theory and the mathematical properties of the CDES indirect utility function. It gives a *complete* set of *parametric elasticity* expressions and *unified aggregations* for the CDES demand system that can be applied to any demand system. It also investigates the *Cardinal properties* of CDES and especially examine the *elasticity* of the *Lagrangian multiplier*—marginal utility of income. Section "Empirics: CDES Utility and



B. S. Jensen, *The Elements and Dynamic Systems of Economic Growth and Trade Models*, https://doi.org/10.1007/978-3-031-52493-6_6

Demand Systems" uses budget data to obtain the *empirical* CDES utility-demand system, Engel curves, and *Income elasticities* of 41 goods and services. Section "CDES Parameters and the Price and Substitution Elasticities" gives the Marshallian and Slutsky *Price elasticities* for all 41 goods, and their *Allen partial substitution elasticities*, which with the CDES system preserve *constant differences.* Final comments are given in section "Final Comments".

## CDES Indirect Utility Function

Let $Y_i$ denote the quantity that a consumer buys of commodity i (1,..., N) and $P_i$ its price; **Y** denotes the quantity vector $(Y_1, \ldots, Y_N)$, **P** is the price vector $(P_1, \ldots, P_N)$, and **C** denotes the **Total** expenditures. The consumer maximizes *Utility*, $\mathbf{u} = \mathbf{U}(\mathbf{Y})$, subject to the budget constraint: $C = \sum_{i=1}^{N} P_i Y_i = PY$. A dual *globally regular* **CDES** *Indirect Utility Function*, $\mathbf{U} = \mathbf{V}(\mathbf{P}, \mathbf{C})$, was stated in Proposition 5.1, Chap. 5, Eq. (5.5), as:

$$V(P, C) = \sum_{i=1}^{N} \alpha_i \left[ \frac{(C/P_i)^{\beta_i} - 1}{\beta_i} \right];$$

$$\alpha_i > 0, \ \sum_{i=1}^{N} \alpha_i = 1, \ \beta_i \geq -1; \ P_i > 0, \ C > 0 \tag{6.1}$$

where the last equality sign for $\beta_i$ may apply for *at most* one commodity index (i).

The first-order derivative of (6.1) with respect to C and $P_i$ are:

$$\frac{\partial V(P, C)}{\partial C} = \sum_{i=1}^{N} \alpha_i P_i^{-\beta_i} C^{\beta_i - 1} > 0 \ ; \quad \frac{\partial V(P, C)}{\partial P_i} = -\alpha_i \ P_i^{-\beta_i - 1} C^{\beta_i} < 0 \tag{6.2}$$

Thus with $\alpha_i > 0$, (6.1), **V(P, C)** is *increasing* in total *expenditure* $C$ for *all*, $P_i > 0$, and the **CDES** Indirect utility function $V(P, C)$ is *decreasing* in every *price*, $P_i > 0$.

Applying Roy's identity to CDES (6.1) with (6.2) gives the *Marshallian demand functions*, $\mathbf{Y_i} = \mathbf{D_i}(\mathbf{P}, \mathbf{C})$, and the *budget shares*, $e_i = P_i Y_i / C = \mathbf{e_i}(\mathbf{P}, \mathbf{C})$, in CDES forms as:

$$Y_i = D_i(P, C) = -\frac{\partial V(P, C)/\partial P_i}{\partial V(P, C)/\partial C}$$

$$= -\frac{-\alpha_i (C/P_i)^{\beta_i} P_i^{-1}}{\sum_{i=1}^{N} \alpha_i (C/P_i)^{\beta_i} C^{-1}} = \frac{\alpha_i (C/P_i)^{\beta_i + 1}}{\sum_{j=1}^{N} \alpha_j (C/P_j)^{\beta_j}} \tag{6.3}$$

$$e_i = \frac{P_i Y_i}{C} = e_i(P, C) = \frac{\alpha_i (C/P_i)^{\beta_i}}{\sum_{j=1}^{N} \alpha_j (C/P_j)^{\beta_j}} > 0 \; ; \quad \sum_{i=1}^{N} e_i(P, C) = 1 \tag{6.4}$$

By the properties (6.2), the ***quantities demanded***, $\mathbf{Y_i}$, (6.3), are well-defined (exist) for *all* positive income ($C$) and prices ($P_i$). All the *Engel curves*, $\mathbf{P_i Y_i} = e_i(P, C)\, C$, (6.4), are *nonlinear* in income ($C$).

### *Marshallian Demand, Hicksian Demand Elasticities of CDES*

From the CDES Marshallian demand function $D_i(P, C)$, (6.3), we find after some manipulations, the *expenditure* ("income") elasticity, $E(D_i, C) = (\partial D_i/\partial C)(C/D_i)$, the own *price*—, $E(D_i, P_i) = (\partial D_i/\partial P_i)(P_i/D_i)$ and cross-price *elasticities*, $E(D_i, P_j) = (\partial D_i/\partial P_j)(P_j/D_i)$, to be expressed by their following CDES formulas, cf. Houthakker (1960b, p. 14–15), Somermeyer and Langhout (1972, p. 352–353), Jensen et al. (2011, p. 220),

$$E\,(D_i, C) = 1 + \beta_i - \bar{\beta} \; , \quad \left[ \bar{\beta} = \bar{\beta}\,(P, C) = \sum_{j=1}^{N} e_j\, \beta_j \right] \; : \; \begin{cases} > 0 \\ < 0 \end{cases} \tag{6.5}$$

$$E\,(e_i, C) = \beta_i - \bar{\beta} \; : \; \gtrless 0 \; ; \quad \bar{\beta} = \bar{\beta}\,(P, C) > -1 \tag{6.6}$$

$$E\,(D_i, P_i) = -1 - \beta_i\,(1 - e_i)\, , \; [\; \beta_i \geq -1\, , \; e_i > 0 \;] \; : \; < 0 \tag{6.7}$$

$$E\,(P_i\, Y_i, P_i) = E\,(e_i, P_i) = -\,\beta_i\,(1 - e_i) \; : \; \gtrless 0 \tag{6.8}$$

$$E\,(D_j, P_i) = \beta_i\, e_i > -1 \; ; \quad E\,(D_i, P_j) = \beta_j\, e_j > -1 \tag{6.9}$$

Evidently, demand functions $\mathbf{D_i\,(P, C)}$ (6.3), are *homogeneous* degree 0 in prices and income, and **CDES** price and income *elasticities*, (6.7–6.9), (6.5), satisfy the *restriction* of Marshallian demand (6.3) being homogeneous of **degree 0** in prices and income:

$$\sum_{j=1}^{N} E(D_i, P_j) + E(D_i, C) = 0 \; \Leftrightarrow \; \sum_{j=1}^{N} E(D_i, P_j) = -\, E(D_i, C) \tag{6.10}$$

$$-\,(1 + \beta_i) + \beta_i e_i + \sum_{j \neq i} \beta_j e_j = -\,(\,1 + \beta_i - \bar{\beta}\,) \tag{6.11}$$

*Expenditure* (income, Engel) elasticities of goods satisfy numerically the **Engel** *aggregation*:

$$\sum_{j=1}^{N} e_j \, E(D_j, C) = \sum_{j=1}^{N} e_j \, (1 + \beta_j - \bar{\beta}) = 1 + \sum_{j=1}^{N} e_j \, \beta_j - \sum_{j=1}^{N} e_j \, \bar{\beta} = 1 \tag{6.12}$$

and all the *price* elasticities for any good satisfy numerically the **Cournot** *aggregation*:

$$\sum_{j=1}^{N} e_j \, E(D_j, P_i) = e_i \, [-(1 + \beta_i) + \beta_i \, e_i\,] + \sum_{j \neq i}^{N} e_j \, \beta_i \, e_i = -e_i \tag{6.13}$$

The **CDES** *Hicksian demands*, $\mathbf{Y_i} = \mathbf{H_i(P, U)}$, implied by the CDES Indirect utility function (6.1) can *not* be obtained in *closed* form. However, the *own* price elasticities, $E(H_i, P_i) = (\partial H_i / \partial P_i)(P_i / H_i)$, and *cross* price elasticities, $E(H_i, P_j) = (\partial H_i / \partial P_j)(P_j / H_i)$, of Hicksian demands $H_i(P, U)$ can nevertheless be expressed by *explicit* (parametric) formulas, cf. Chap. 5, section "Marshallian and Hicksian Demand Elasticities of CDES", as:

$$E(H_i, P_i) = E(D_i, P_i) + e_i E(D_i, C) = -(1+\beta_i) + (1+2\beta_i - \bar{\beta}) e_i < 0 \tag{6.14}$$

$$E(H_j, P_i) = E(D_j, P_i) + e_i E(D_j, C) = (1 + \beta_i + \beta_j - \bar{\beta}) e_i \; : \; \begin{cases} > 0 \\ < 0 \end{cases} \tag{6.15}$$

$$E(H_i, P_j) = E(D_i, P_j) + e_j E(D_i, C) = (1 + \beta_j + \beta_i - \bar{\beta}) e_j \; : \; \begin{cases} > 0 \\ < 0 \end{cases} \tag{6.16}$$

The **CDES** system (6.1) allows for flexibility, both wrt. *signs* (complementarity, indifference, substitutability), and the numerical *size* of these "pure/net" cross-price elasticities of CDES, (6.14–6.16).

*Homogeneity* of degree 0 in prices for Hicksian demands $\mathbf{H_i(P, U)}$ is met by CDES elasticities:

$$\sum_{j=1}^{N} E(H_i, P_j) = E(H_i, P_i) + \sum_{j \neq i}^{N} E(H_i, P_j) = 0 \tag{6.17}$$

$$-(1 + \beta_i) + (1 + 2\beta_i - \bar{\beta}) e_i + \sum_{j \neq i}^{N} (1 + \beta_i + \beta_j - \bar{\beta}) e_j = 0 \tag{6.18}$$

The *utility level constraint* associated with Hicksian demands $\mathbf{H_i(P, U)}$ is satisfied by **CDES** elasticities, (6.14–6.15):

$$\sum_{j=1}^{N} e_j E(H_j, P_i) = -e_i(1+\beta_i) + e_i(1+2\beta_i - \bar{\beta})e_i$$

$$+\sum_{j\neq i}^{N} e_j(1+\beta_i+\beta_j-\bar{\beta})e_i = 0 \qquad (6.19)$$

Aggregation property (6.19) of *Slutsky elasticities*, (6.14–6.15), is called the **Hicks-Slutsky** *aggregation.*

### *Allen Elasticities of Substitution for CDES Demand*

The Allen *elasticities of substitution*, $(\sigma_{ij})$, are obtained by normalizing the CDES Slutsky elasticities, (6.14–6.16), as:

$$\sigma_{ii} = E(H_i, P_i)/e_i = -(1+\beta_i)(1/e_i - 1) + \beta_i - \bar{\beta} < 0 \qquad (6.20)$$

$$\sigma_{ji} = E(H_j, P_i)/e_i = 1+\beta_i+\beta_j-\bar{\beta} = E(H_i, P_j)/e_j = \sigma_{ij} : \begin{cases} > 0 \\ < 0 \end{cases} \qquad (6.21)$$

The elasticities $(\sigma_{ii})$ refer to the substitution between the i'th good and *all* the others.

The CDES substitution elasticities (6.20–6.21) are not constant, but *variable*, changing with utility (income) levels and prices via $\bar{\beta}$ (6.5) and $e_i$ (6.4). The property that *differences* of these *partial elasticities* of *substitution* are *constant* follows directly from (6.21),

$$\sigma_{ik} - \sigma_{jk} = \beta_i - \beta_j \ ; \quad \sigma_{ij} - \sigma_{kl} = (\beta_i + \beta_j) - (\beta_k + \beta_l) \qquad (6.22)$$

Such *invariance* relations among the *Allen* elasticities, $\sigma_{ji}$, (6.22), do not exist at all among the corresponding *Slutsky* elasticities, $E(H_j, P_i)$, (6.15–6.16).

Similar to (6.19), the Allen substitution elasticities (6.20–6.21) satisfy a zero restriction, since together with (6.14–6.15), (6.13–6.12), we have:

$$\sum_{j=1}^{N} e_j\sigma_{ji} = \sum_{j=1}^{N} e_j E(H_j, P_i)/e_i = \sum_{j=1}^{N} e_j\,[E(D_j, P_i)/e_i + E(D_j, C)] \qquad (6.23)$$

$$= (1/e_i)\sum_{j=1}^{N} e_j\, E(D_j, P_i) + \sum_{j=1}^{N} e_j E(D_j, C) = -1 + 1 = 0$$

We call the aggregation property, $\sum_{j=1}^{N} e_j \sigma_{ji} = 0$: the *Hicks-Allen aggregation.*

Using the *symmetry* of $(\sigma_{ij})$, we derive from (6.20–6.21) another "aggregation" (restriction):

$$\sum_{j=1}^{N} e_j \sigma_{ij} = \sum_{j=1}^{N} E(H_i, P_j) = \sum_{j=1}^{N} E(D_i, P_j) + E(D_i, C) = 0 \qquad (6.24)$$

Restrictions (6.23–6.24) are in accordance with (imply) *homogeneity* conditions, (6.17), (6.10).

The great mathematical-economic *advantage* of *any globally regular* **Indirect** utility function $U = V(P, C)$ is—besides the explicit Marshallian demand functions by Roy's identity (6.3)—that the underlying globally valid *substitution elasticity* formulas $(\sigma_{ji})$, (6.20–6.22), can be *explicitly* derived via the Slutsky relations and be studied—as shown here for **CDES**—in terms of relevant *preference parameters* of *specified* $\mathbf{V(P, C)}$, (6.1).

### *Cardinal CDES and Elasticity of Marginal Utility of Income*

*Sizes and Variability of Elasticity of Marginal Utility of Income*

The *consumer preferences* of the Marshallian demand and expenditure (budget share) functions, (6.3–6.4), are usually interpreted as an *ordinal* indirect utility function $V(P, C)$, and any *monotonic* increasing transformation of $V(P, C)$ would leave the Marshallian demand functions unchanged. However, if $\mathbf{V(P, C)}$ is considered *cardinal*, then some further properties of $V(P, C)$, (6.1), can be used in extracting some relevant information from survey budget data. Especially, **MU(C)**—the *Marginal utility* of **C** (total expenditure (C), "income", "money"), the Lagrangian multiplier $(\boldsymbol{\lambda})$—and its elasticity wrt. **C**—$\mathbf{E}\,(\lambda, \mathbf{C})$—may offer crucial help in estimating and *calibrating* the *parameters* of Marshallian demands,[1] $\mathbf{D_i(P, C)}$—and hence parameters of **CDES** Indirect utility function $\mathbf{V(P, C)}$. *Elasticity* numbers [ for *given* prices (**P**) ], of $\mathbf{E}\,(\mathbf{MU(P, C)}, \mathbf{C})$ is written shortly as, $\mathbf{R_R(c)} = \theta_r(c)$, in (6.26), (6.27), (6.34), (6.37).

The Arrow-Pratt *measures* of **Absolute** risk aversion $\mathbf{R_A(c)}$ and **Relative** risk aversion $\mathbf{R_R(c)}$ are given as, Pratt (1964, p. 122, p. 130, p. 134), Varian (1992, p. 178, p. 189):

$$R_A(c) = -\frac{u''(c)}{u'(c)} = -\frac{d \ln u'(c)}{dc} = -\frac{E(MU(c), c)}{c} > 0 \qquad (6.25)$$

[1] The *explicit form* of the Marshallian demand functions, $D_i(P, C)$, could seldom be given, as $D_i(P, C)$ were only *implicitly* determined by solving the set of *Lagrangian first-order conditions* of consumer direct utility maximization under budget constraint. Historically, on measurable utility (cardinal utility), see Schumpeter (1949, p. 161).

$$R_R(c) = R_A(c)\,c = -\frac{u''(c)\,c}{u'(c)} = -\frac{d\ln u'(c)}{d\ln c} = -E(MU(c), c) > 0 \tag{6.26}$$

The ***risk aversion*** measures (functions) defined in (6.25–6.26) have been important in analyses of choice under ***uncertainty*** (maximizing expected utility), where ***cardinal utility*** **u(c)** is a function of wealth (amounts of ***money***, **c**, payoff) alone, or **u(c)** deals with ***one commodity*** (macro) economies.

It is convenient, like $\mathbf{R_R(c)}$, to have a '***relative risk*** aversion ***parameter***', $\theta_r(c)$, given by a non-negative (***positive***) number. In macroeconomics and growth literature,[2] such convenient parametric form of **u(c)** with, $\theta_r(c) = \theta > 0$, was the **CRRA** power form:

$$\theta_r(c) > 0;\ \theta_r(c) = \theta\ :\ u(c) = \frac{c^{1-\theta} - 1}{1-\theta},\ \theta > 0,\ \eta(c) = \frac{1}{\theta}\ ;$$
$$\theta = 1\ :\ u(c) = ln\,(c) \tag{6.27}$$

As to the 'parameter', $\theta(c) = R_r(c)$, Arrow (1971, p. 99) noted that " broadly speaking, the relative risk aversion must hover around 1". Browning et al. (1999, p. 552) argue that if ***constancy*** across the population is ***imposed***, "there is no strong evidence against $-\eta$ being slightly above - 1", (i.e., $\eta < 1$ or $\theta$ slightly above 1).

For **CDES**, $\boldsymbol{\lambda}$ **(P, C) = MU(P, C)**, we have from (6.2),

$$\lambda\,(P, C) = MU(P, C) = \frac{\partial V(P, C)}{\partial C} = \sum_{i=1}^{N} \alpha_i\, P_i^{-\beta_i}\, C^{\beta_i - 1} > 0 \tag{6.28}$$

$$= \sum_{i=1}^{N} \alpha_i\, (C/P_i)^{\beta_i}\, C^{-1} \tag{6.29}$$

Hence from (6.28),

$$\frac{\partial \lambda\,(P, C)}{\partial C} = \frac{\partial MU(P, C)}{\partial C} = \frac{\partial^2 V(P, C)}{\partial^2 C}$$
$$= \sum_{i=1}^{N} (\beta_i - 1)\,\alpha_i\, P_i^{-\beta_i}\, C^{\beta_i - 2}$$
$$= \sum_{i=1}^{N} (\beta_i - 1)\,\alpha_i\, (C/P_i)^{\beta_i}\, C^{-2} \tag{6.30}$$

[2] Barro and Sala-i-Martin (2004, p. 141), Solow (2000, p. 114).

and accordingly by, (6.29), (6.30), (6.5),

$$E(\lambda(P,C),C) = \frac{\partial\lambda(P,C)}{\partial C}\frac{C}{\lambda(P,C)} = \sum_{i=1}^{N}(\beta_i - 1)\cdot\frac{\alpha_i\,(C/P_i)^{\beta_i}}{\sum_{i=1}^{N}\alpha_i\,(C/P_i)^{\beta_i}} \tag{6.31}$$

$$= \sum_{i=1}^{N}(\beta_i - 1)\cdot e_i = \bar{\beta}(P,C) - 1\ ; \tag{6.32}$$

$$\bar{\beta}(P,C) = \sum_{i=1}^{N} e_i\,\beta_i \tag{6.33}$$

By (6.31–6.33), (6.26–6.27), **CDES** (6.1) elasticities, $\mathbf{E}(\lambda(\mathbf{P},\mathbf{C}),\mathbf{C}) = \mathbf{E}(\mathbf{MU}(\mathbf{P},\mathbf{C}),\ \mathbf{C})$, are :

$$\bar{\beta}(P,C) > -1 : E(\lambda(P,C),C) = \bar{\beta}(P,C) - 1 > -2 \Leftrightarrow 0 < \theta_r(c) < 2 \tag{6.34}$$

$$\mu(P,C) = \lambda(P,C)\cdot C : E(\mu(P,C),C) = \bar{\beta}(P,C) > -1 \tag{6.35}$$

**CDES** (6.1) special cases: *Homothetic* **CES-CD** *Indirect* utility functions are instructive:

$$\begin{aligned} &\forall i\ \beta_i = \beta = \bar{\beta} = \sigma - 1 > -1,\ \sigma \geqq 0\ ; \\ &\beta = -\frac{1}{2} : \sigma = \frac{1}{2};\ \beta = 0 : \sigma = 1 \end{aligned} \tag{6.36}$$

$$\begin{aligned} &E(\lambda(P,C),C) = \bar{\beta} - 1 > -2 \Leftrightarrow \sigma - 2 < 0\ ; \\ &0 \leqq \sigma < 2 \Leftrightarrow 0 \leqq \theta_r(c) = \theta < 2 \end{aligned} \tag{6.37}$$

**CDES** (6.36) includes the **CRRA** power form (6.27) with $\theta$—restricted to the *range*, (6.37).

As actual observable numbers (*range*) of **Elasticities** of **Marginal Utility** of **Income**,

$$\mathbf{E}(\lambda(\mathbf{P},\mathbf{C}),\mathbf{C}) = \mathbf{E}(\mathbf{MU}(\mathbf{P},\mathbf{C}),\ \mathbf{C}) = -R_R(c) = -\theta_r(c) \tag{6.38}$$

$$-\frac{1}{\mathbf{EIS}} = -\frac{1}{\eta(c)} = \bar{\beta}(P,C) - 1 \tag{6.39}$$

[reciprocal, $\frac{-1}{E(MU(c),c)} = \eta\,(c)$, **Elasticity** of **Intertemporal Substitution, EIS**], let us consider the **sizes**[3] of $\theta_{\mathbf{r}}\,(\mathbf{c})$, $\eta\,(\mathbf{c})$, suggested by Frisch (1959, p. 188):

$$
\begin{array}{lllllllll}
0.10 & = & \eta\,(c) & = & \frac{1}{\theta_r\,(c)} & \Leftrightarrow & \theta_r\,(c) & = & 10\ ; & \text{extremely low income} \\
0.25 & = & \eta\,(c) & = & \frac{1}{\theta_r\,(c)} & \Leftrightarrow & \theta_r\,(c) & = & 4\ ; & \text{low income} \\
0.50 & = & \eta\,(c) & = & \frac{1}{\theta_r\,(c)} & \Leftrightarrow & \theta_r\,(c) & = & 2\ ; & \text{middle income} \\
1.43 & = & \eta\,(c) & = & \frac{1}{\theta_r\,(c)} & \Leftrightarrow & \theta_r\,(c) & = & 0.7\ ; & \text{high income} \\
10 & = & \eta\,(c) & = & \frac{1}{\theta_r\,(c)} & \Leftrightarrow & \theta_r\,(c) & = & 0.1\ ; & \text{very high income}
\end{array}
$$

**CDES** (6.1) with *range*, (6.34), (6.37), corresponds to those above for *middle-higher* incomes. The *range*, $\theta_{\mathbf{r}}\,(\mathbf{c})\ :\ (\mathbf{2} - \mathbf{0.5}) \Leftrightarrow\ \eta\,(\mathbf{c})\ :\ (\mathbf{0.5} - \mathbf{2.0})$, accord with estimated results from many consumer *budget studies*—including those '*classical*' numbers mentioned above by Arrow (1971), Bernoulli (1738, 1954), Browning et al. (1999).

The empirical **CDES** estimates (6.5–6.6) of, $\bar{\beta} = \bar{\beta}\,(\mathbf{P}, \mathbf{C})$, in Table 6.9—for *Junior* and *Senior* families—are, respectively:

$$
\begin{aligned}
&\bar{\beta} = 0.18 : \bar{\beta} - 1 = -0.72\ ; \\
&\theta_r\,(c) = 0.72 \qquad\qquad \Leftrightarrow \eta\,(c) = 1.39\ ;\ C = 42557 \qquad (6.40)
\end{aligned}
$$

$$
\begin{aligned}
&\bar{\beta} = 0.09 : \bar{\beta} - 1 = -0.91\ ; \\
&\theta_r\,(c) = 0.91 \qquad\qquad \Leftrightarrow \eta\,(c) = 1.10\ ;\ C = 40831 \qquad (6.41)
\end{aligned}
$$

The results for $\theta_{\mathbf{r}}\,(\mathbf{c})$ in (6.40–6.41) are within the **CDES** *interval* for $\theta_{\mathbf{r}}\,(\mathbf{c})$, stated in (6.34).

Finally, we should note here that *Non-Homothetic* **CDES** (6.1), as characterized by the *General* expressions, (6.38–6.39) have the *same* limits (*range*) for, $\theta_r\,(c), \eta\,(c)$, seen in (6.34)—as *Homothetic* **CES-CD** functions, (6.36), with *range* of constants $(\theta_r, \eta)$ in (6.37).

*Variations in the Elasticity of Marginal Utility of Income and EIS*

We must now examine how *elasticity*, $\mathbf{E}\,(\lambda\,(\mathbf{P}, \mathbf{C}), \mathbf{C}) = \mathbf{E}\,(\mathbf{MU}(\mathbf{P}, \mathbf{C}), \mathbf{C})$, and *Income* elasticities $\mathbf{E}\,(\mathbf{D_i}, \mathbf{C})$ of $\mathbf{V}(\mathbf{P}, \mathbf{C})$, (6.1), are *changing* with income ($\mathbf{C}$) and prices ($\mathbf{P}$).

[3] Mehra and Prescott (1985, p. 154) mention that Kydland and Prescott needed: $1 < \theta_r(c) = \theta < 2$, (used $\theta = 1.5$) to mimic observed variability of consumption and investment; Tobin and Dolde used $\theta = 1.5$ to fit the observed life cycle savings patterns.

The CDES term $\bar{\beta}(P, C)$, (6.5)—with $e_j$, (6.4)—increases *monotonically* with larger **C**, see *Income derivative* of $\bar{\beta}(P, C)$, (6.43) - **Appendix A**, (6.70)—hence by (6.5), (6.31–6.33), we have,

$$\frac{\partial E(D_i, C)}{\partial C} = -\frac{\partial \bar{\beta}(P, C)}{\partial C} = -\frac{1}{C}\sum_{j=1}^{N} e_j\,[\beta_j - \bar{\beta}(P, C)]^2 < 0 \quad (6.42)$$

$$\frac{\partial E(\lambda(P, C), C)}{\partial C} = \frac{\partial \bar{\beta}(P, C)}{\partial C} = \frac{1}{C}\sum_{j=1}^{N} e_j\,[\beta_j - \bar{\beta}(P, C)]^2 > 0 \quad (6.43)$$

Thus (6.42) demonstrates that for **all** goods, CDES Income elasticities, **E (D**$_i$**, C)**, (6.5), *decline* with *larger* $(C)$. This *uniform* CDES property of **E (D**$_i$**, C)**, (6.5), goes together with *increasing* elasticity of, **E (λ (P, C), C) = E ( MU(P, C), C )**, (6.31–6.33) with *larger* $(C)$.

CDES *Price derivative* of $\bar{\beta}(P, C)$, (6.5), with $e_j$, (6.4), is (6.45)—derived in **Appendix B**, (6.72)—hence by (6.5), (6.31–6.33), we have,

$$\frac{\partial E(D_i, C)}{\partial P_j} = -\frac{\partial \bar{\beta}(P, C)}{\partial P_j} = \frac{e_j}{P_j}[\beta_j^2 - \beta_j\,\bar{\beta}(P, C)]\,e_j \gtrless 0 \Leftrightarrow \beta_j^2 \gtrless \beta_j\,\bar{\beta} \quad (6.44)$$

$$\frac{\partial E(\lambda(P, C), C)}{\partial P_j} = \frac{\partial \bar{\beta}(P, C)}{\partial P_j} = \frac{e_j}{P_j}[-\beta_j^2 + \beta_j\,\bar{\beta}(P, C)]\,e_j \gtrless 0 \Leftrightarrow \beta_j^2 \lessgtr \beta_j\,\bar{\beta} \quad (6.45)$$

Thus (6.44) demonstrates how larger *Prices*, $(P_j)$ (*own* price and *cross* prices) *affect*—will increase or diminish, depending on their *parameters*, $\beta_j$, and $\bar{\beta}(P, C)$—the CDES *Income* elasticities, **E (D**$_i$**, C)**, (6.5). Again this property in (6.44) goes together with *changing* the *Income* elasticity (6.45) of the Lagrangian multiplier,[4] **E ( λ (P, C), C)**, (6.31–6.33).

[4] Hanoch (1977, p. 418) has given eleven alternative expression for the Elasticity of Marginal Utility of Income, (relative risk aversion): $E(\lambda(P, C), C) = E(MU(P, C), C)$. On relative risk aversion and prices, cf. Deschamps (1973, p. 457), Epstein (1975, p. 882).

The *variability* of the elasticities in (6.43), (6.45) demonstrate that the CDES elasticities, (6.38–6.39) are **not** constant elasticities, and so are **neither** *income* elasticities, (6.42), (6.44), *nor* intertemporal substitution, **EIS**, (6.39)—in contrast to the special *isoelastic* (**CRRA**) cases of **homothetic** *utility* functions (6.36–6.37), which always imply **unit** income elasticities, **E ($D_i$, C)**—that **violates Engel's** *law*. "The supposition that there are neither *luxuries* nor *necessities* contradicts both common sense and more than hundred years of empirical research", Deaton (1992, p. 9). "Luxuries have *higher* **EIS** and are easier to postpone", Browning and Crossley (2000, p. 1025).

The consequences for modeling dynamic multi-sector *general equilibrium* (**GE**) allocations with **homothetic** (CES) Indirect utility (6.36–6.37) are calculated and shown in Chap. 19, section "Solving the Multi-Sector Growth—(2 × 10)—Model"—to be *compared* with dynamic multi-sector **GE** allocations with **non-homothetic** (CDES) Indirect utility, (6.38–6.39), as demonstrated in Chap. 20, section "Solving the Multi-Sector Growth—(2 × 10)—Model".

*One Good: Macro—and the Elasticity of Marginal Utility of Income*

As noted above, when, $\forall i$, $\beta_i = \beta$, then *Non-Homothetic* **CDES** (6.1) becomes the *Homothetic* **CES-CD** functions (6.36). It requires at least *two different* $\beta_i$ to preserve the Non-Homothetic property. With only a *single* consumption *good*, ($\beta$), **CDES** (6.1) is *always* reduced to become *Homothetic* **CES-CD** forms—with CRRA property, (6.27):

$$\alpha > 0,\ \beta \geq -1 \ :\ V(P, C) = \alpha \left[ \frac{(C/P)^{\beta} - 1}{\beta} \right],\ C > 0 \tag{6.46}$$

$$\alpha > 0,\ \beta = 0 \ :\ V(P, C) = \alpha\, ln\,(C/P),\ C > 0 \tag{6.47}$$

Thus *Bernoulli Utility* function,[5] (6.47), with, $\theta_r = 1$, is included in CDES family (6.1).

The *single good* **CDES** homothetic utility functions (6.46–6.47) violates Engel's *law*, as explained above. One way to comply with Engel's *law*, is to introduce a *minimal* ('subsistence') consumption, $(C_0/P_0)$, and extend $V(P, C)$ above as follows:

$$\alpha > 0,\ \beta \geq -1 \ :\ V(P, C) = \alpha \left[ \frac{(C/P - C_0/P_0)^{\beta} - 1}{\beta} \right],\quad C_0/P_0 > 0 \tag{6.48}$$

$$\alpha > 0,\ \beta = 0 \ :\ V(P, C) = \alpha\, ln\,(C/P - C_0/P_0),\quad C_0/P_0 > 0 \tag{6.49}$$

[5] Utility function (6.47) is derived and discussed in Bernoulli (1738, 1954, p. 28), Stiglitz (1969, p. 664), Brems (1986, p. 28).

The deficiency of traditional choice of *homothetic* **CRRA-CEIS** forms, (6.27), (6.36–6.37), (6.46–6.47), in *Ramsey optimal* intertemporal *saving* (growth) models is finally remedied by using the *non-homothetic* **VEIS** forms (6.48–6.49), with their *variable* **E (MU(P,C)**, and **EIS**, $\eta$ (**c**), in Chap. 13.

## EMPIRICS: CDES UTILITY AND DEMAND SYSTEMS

### *Estimation of CDES Parameters from Budget Data*

In *survey* budget *data* of consumer expenditures, the consumer *prices* do *not* vary within a *year*, and they are the *same* for **all** households. With an *index* $(h = 1, \cdots H)$ to denote *households*, the **CDES** *budget share* equations, $\mathbf{e}_i$, (6.4), of the *households* are:

$$e_{ih} = \frac{\alpha_i (C_h/P_i)^{\beta_i}}{\sum_{j=1}^{N} \alpha_j (C_h/P_j)^{\beta_j}} \tag{6.50}$$

Selecting a *reference commodity* (which without loss of generality is here the commodity number one), and using the following transformation (ratios) of (6.50), we get:

$$\log\left[\frac{e_{ih}}{e_{1h}}\right] = \log e_{ih} - \log e_{1h} = \gamma_i + (\beta_i - \beta_1)\log(C_h) + \varepsilon_{ih} \quad i = 2, \ldots, N \tag{6.51}$$

where $\varepsilon_{ih}$ is the *disturbance* term, and where the *constant* term, $\gamma_i$ is,

$$\gamma_i = \log \alpha_i - \log \alpha_1 - (\beta_i \log P_i - \beta_1 \log P_1) \tag{6.52}$$

It follows from (6.51–6.52) that with this '*log-ratio*' procedure we can only *estimate* the *differences* of the utility-preference (demand) *parameters*, $\beta_i - \beta_1$.

By defining,

$$y_i = \begin{bmatrix} (\log e_{i1} - \log e_{11}) \\ \vdots \\ (\log e_{iH} - \log e_{1H}) \end{bmatrix}; \; X = \begin{bmatrix} 1 \; \log C_1 \\ \vdots \;\; \vdots \\ 1 \; \log C_H \end{bmatrix}; \tag{6.53}$$

$$\beta_i^* = \begin{bmatrix} \gamma_i \\ \beta_i - \beta_1 \end{bmatrix}; \; \varepsilon_i = \begin{bmatrix} \varepsilon_{i1} \\ \vdots \\ \varepsilon_{iH} \end{bmatrix}$$

we can rewrite (6.51) as:

$$y_i = X\beta_i^* + \varepsilon_i \quad i = 2, \ldots, N \tag{6.54}$$

i.e. to a *seemingly unrelated regression* (SUR) model with *identical explanatory variables*—for which it is known that ordinary least squares (applied to each equation separately) is efficient, Heij et al. (2004, p. 687), cf. de Boer et al. (2023, p. 16).

Due to problems of data availability, the reference commodity will vary between countries (and periods); but irrespective of the particular choice of reference commodity, comparison of results is simple, as each set of parameter estimates can consistently be transformed to another reference by,

$$(\beta_i - \beta_1) - (\beta_m - \beta_1) = \beta_i - \beta_m \tag{6.55}$$

Hence the actual choice of *reference commodity* does neither affect the calculation of *income (C) elasticities.* Moreover, if just *one* estimated *price elasticity* was *known* from other sources, then we can calculate the *corresponding* $\beta_i$—parameter estimate from (6.7–6.9)—which together with the estimated differences (6.54) will give us the *absolute values* of *all* $\beta_i$, $i = 1, \ldots, N$. Thereby, the *complete set* of CDES *price* and *substitution elasticities* can be derived, as we shall demonstrate.

## *Data, Budget Shares, and Expenditure Elasticities*

*Classification of Consumer Goods (Services) and Social Strata*

The human wants (needs) have, in various amounts, included at least three main categories of consumer goods: *1. Food, 2. Clothing, 3. Shelter.*

As to the provision for other wants and fancies, Smith (1776, 1961, p. 34) says: "Every man is rich or poor according to the degree in which he can afford to enjoy the *necessaries, conveniences,* and *amusements* of human life".

In more detail on these wants and fancies, Smith (1776, 1961, p. 182–183) continues: "Clothing and lodging, household furniture, and what is called equipage, are the principal objects of the greater part of those wants and fancies. The rich man consumes no more food than his poor neighbour. In quality it may be very different, and to select and prepare it may require more labor and art; but in quantity it is very nearly the same.

But compare the spacious palace and great wardrobe of the one, with the hovel and the few rags of the other, and you will be sensible that the difference between their clothing, lodging, and household furniture, is almost as great in quantity as it is in quality. The desire for *food* is *limited* in every man by the narrow capacity of the human stomach; but the desire of the *conveniences* and *ornaments* of building, dress, equipage, and the household furniture, seems to have *no limit* or certain *boundary*".

Evidently, aspects of **Engel** *curve flexibility* were observed long ago. **Budget surveys** have until 1970s often exclusively focused on the *expenditure patterns* ("standard of living costs") of *employee* households (wage and salary earners), since a subsidiary purpose was to obtain " *weights*" ($e_i$) for the calculation of various official *price indexes* that regulated nominal wage contracts. Hence, less variation in ornaments of lodging and dress, etc., ("life styles") are expected for such households than those quoted from Adam Smith. But his classification of goods into: *necessaries, conveniences*, and *amusements* resembles modern measurements by *income elasticities*, $E(D_i, C)$: below, around, larger than unity, as the budget constraint (Engel aggregation) implies.

The *classification* of *consumer goods and services* that was used in the *Danish Consumer Survey (employee households)* of 1971, is shown in Table 6.1. It covers *seven* main categories: (1) Food and Beverages (2) Clothing and Footwear (3) Housing (4) Dwelling Operations (5) Medical Care and Health (6) Leisure (7) Transport.

Each category consists of a varied set of sub-items; the complete expenditure pattern is described by a total number ($N$) of *41 items*. The corresponding 41 *budget shares*, ($e_i$), for two life-cycle groups (junior-/senior families), is seen in Table 6.1.

The sampling design and *random selection* of around 1000 household in the 1971 survey from 1 million *employee* households may briefly be described. The households were interviewed, made detailed expenditure accounting for one month, and they were successively chosen throughout the year to offset seasonal influence on spending patterns. The stratifications of household units were based on several criteria: geography (metropolitan, provincial), age of members and number of children, social groupings (occupational status in private and public sector). We have here chosen to use the budget shares from a *demographic* type of the household stratification into 8 life-cycles groups; but only *two* groups are shown in Table 6.1. The **junior** families have only children below *7 years*. The **senior** families include no longer any children and the house wife is above *45 years*—these senior households are not retired (pensioners), as at least 50% of the total income of any household in this consumer survey must be *Factor* (wage, salary) *income*. Factor Income and Transfers (welfare, children allowances, unemployment benefits) gives *Gross Income*. The latter with deductions of Direct Taxes (income, real estate, social insurance) gives *Disposable Income*, which is split between *Total Consumption* (**C**) and *Gross Saving* (S). The published budget shares of various consumer expenditure usually have *disposable* income as the denominator. Since the relationship between Disposable Income and Gross Saving varies across life-cycle groups, the differences in consumer expenditure patterns are, theoretically and empirically, more adequately described (and *recalculated* by us) as *budget shares* with the *total consumption* (C) as *denominator*.

Table 6.1 shows the *average* budget *shares* ($\mathbf{e}_i$) of the life-cycle groups with their respective *average* (yearly) *totals* (**C**): **42557** DKK and **40831** DKK.

Regarding the *expenditure pattern* of the *junior* and *senior* families in Table 6.1, we cannot be surprised to see that budget shares of (milk products) and (beer,wine) are significantly higher (lower) for the junior families; the seniors enjoys higher quality foods at home (meat,9) and outside (restaurants,

**Table 6.1** Classification of consumer goods and services and budget shares ($100e_i, i = 1, \ldots 41$) of social strata

| | | Junior families | Senior families |
|---|---|---|---|
| *1. Food and beveaages* | | | |
| 1 | Bread (cereals) | 2.44 | 2.39 |
| 2 | Butter | 0.64 | 0.76 |
| 3 | Margarine (fats, oils) | 0.64 | 0.65 |
| 4 | Sugar (confectionary) | 0.85 | 0.98 |
| 5 | Milk (cream, yoghurt) | 2.23 | 1.63 |
| 6 | Cheese (curd) | 0.64 | 0.76 |
| 7 | Other foods | 1.81 | 2.17 |
| 8 | Vegetables (fruits) | 3.08 | 3.04 |
| 9 | Meat | 5.63 | 7.27 |
| 10 | Fish | 0.64 | 0.98 |
| 11 | Coffee (tea, cocoa) | 1.38 | 1.95 |
| 12 | Soft drinks (mineral water) | 0.53 | 0.76 |
| 13 | Beer | 1.27 | 1.84 |
| 14 | Wine and spirits | 0.96 | 1.74 |
| 15 | Tobacco products | 3.50 | 3.80 |
| | Sum 1–15: | **26.24** | **30.72** |
| *2. Clothing and footwear* | | | |
| 16 | Clothing | 5.73 | 5.86 |
| 17 | Footwear (shoes, boots) | 1.38 | 0.98 |
| | Sum 16–17: | **7.11** | **6.84** |
| *3. Housing* | | | |
| 18 | Fuel (gas, liquids) and light | 4.25 | 4.45 |
| 19 | Gross rents (water rates, mortgage) | 17.62 | 12.04 |
| | Sum 18–19: | **21.87** | **16.49** |
| *4. Dwelling operations* | | | |
| 20 | Glassware (tableware, utensils) | 0.96 | 0.76 |
| 21 | Household textiles (furnishings) | 0.85 | 0.98 |
| 22 | Household machines (appliances) | 1.70 | 1.08 |
| 23 | Furniture (fixtures, carpets) | 3.61 | 3.47 |
| 24 | Non-durable household goods | 2.12 | 2.17 |
| 25 | Household services (domestic services) | 0.85 | 0.54 |
| 26 | Communication (post, telephone) | 0.96 | 1.41 |
| 27 | Radio and television sets | 1.17 | 1.74 |
| 28 | Miscellaneous (services n.e.c.) | 4.46 | 2.82 |
| | Sum 20–28: | **16.68** | **14.97** |
| *5. Medical care and health* | | | |
| 29 | Medical and pharmaceutical products | 0.53 | 1.08 |
| 30 | Medical services (physicians, nurses) | 0.85 | 0.87 |
| 31 | Personal care (barber, beauty shops) | 1.27 | 1.63 |
| | Sum 29–31: | **2.65** | **3.58** |

(continued)

**Table 6.1** (continued)

| | | Junior families | Senior families |
|---|---|---|---|
| *6. Leisure* | | | |
| 32 | Personal goods (jewellery, watches, rings) | 0.96 | 0.87 |
| 33 | Leisure equipment (camera, musical, boats) | 2.65 | 3.15 |
| 34 | Entertainment (comfort, cultural services) | 2.23 | 3.15 |
| 35 | Restaurants (cafes, hotels, lodging services) | 1.49 | 3.80 |
| 36 | Books and papers (magazines) | 2.12 | 1.95 |
| | Sum 32–36: | **9.45** | **12.92** |
| *7. Transport* | | | |
| 37 | Gasoline (oil) | 3.61 | 3.15 |
| 38 | Auto repairs (transport equipment) | 2.55 | 2.17 |
| 39 | Other transport expenses (insurance, taxes) | 2.44 | 2.17 |
| 40 | Transport services (bus, train, taxi, rent) | 1.70 | 1.95 |
| 41 | Transport equipment (vehicle purchases) | 5.73 | 5.10 |
| | Sum 37–41: | **16.03** | **14.54** |
| Sum 1–41: | | **100.00** | **100.00** |
| Total consumption expenditures (average) DDK | | **42557** | **40831** |

*Source:* SU Nr. 34 (1977, p. 238–45)

35). The housing cost (gross rents, 17) takes a higher toll on the young families. Health expenditures (medical products, 29) are slightly higher for the seniors. Apart from the items mentioned, the average *budget shares* of the two life-cycles groups are overall remarkably *similar*. Cars (transport equipment,insurance, auto repairs, gasoline, 41, 39–37) became significant budget items for both the juniors and seniors in the years around 1971. The expenditures on transport equipment (41) [like housing, (19)] refer "user cost" of these physical assets [i.e., not to their asset (purchase) price]. The "user costs" are not calculated as "imputed rents (services)", but made up of cash payments on down-payments, consumer credit, mortgage interest that are recorded with renting (owning) these durable assets.

Within the *two life-cycle* groups, several sampling units will have *zero expenditures* on a number of the items listed in Table 6.1; there are non-smokers, some are vegetarians, other eschew alcoholic beverages, and many have no automobiles. In terms of consumer modelling, the nonzero budget shares in Table 6.1 each refer to budget shares of a *representative consumer*, evaluated at, respectively, ($\mathbf{C} = 42557, \mathbf{C} = 40831$). The main categories (subtotals, Table 6.1) in the Danish expenditure pattern for *employee household* in 1971 are similar to those for employees in other Scandinavian countries at that time (Sweden, 1969, Norway, 1973), cf. SU Nr. 34 (1977, p. 226).

**Remark 6.1 (Former Budget Studies)** Sampling surveys of budget data from employee household have been collected and compared by government agencies for a long time. A single table of budget shares from the first and

**Table 6.2** Budget shares of social strata: Saxony 1857

| Items of expenditure | Proportions of the expenditure of the family of- Workman with an yearly income of 45–60 £ | Workman with an yearly income of 90–120 £ | Workman with an yearly income of 150–200 £ |
|---|---|---|---|
| 1 Food (beverage, tobacco, taverns) | 62.0 | 55.0 | 50.0 |
| 2 Clothing (footwear, jewellery) | 16.0 | 18.0 | 18.0 |
| 3 Lodging (rent, utensils, furniture) | 12.0 | 12.0 | 12.0 |
| 4 Light and Fuel (wood,coal, gas,oil) | 5.0 | 5.0 | 5.0 |
| 5 Education (culture, church) | 2.0 | 3.5 | 5.5 |
| 6 Public Protection (taxes) | 1.0 | 2.0 | 3.0 |
| 7 Care of Health (medical, pharma) | 1.0 | 2.0 | 3.0 |
| 8 Personal Services | 1.0 | 2.5 | 3.5 |
| Totals | 100.0 | 100.0 | 100.0 |

*Source:* Marshall (1920, p. 115), Engel (1895b, p. 30)

most *famous*, Engel (1895b), of all family expenditure studies is quoted here in Table 6.2, because it has acted as *benchmark* for later inquiries, and because it is seldom seen anywhere in the literature, except in Marshall (1920). We have changed Marshall's item descriptions a little bit—in accordance with Engel's original expenditure classification; cf. Stigler (1954, p. 98) on the origin of the Engel data and the early collections of budgetary data in Europe and USA. By induction and the evidence of Table 6.2, Engel (1895b, p. 28) felt justified to state as a general *empirical law*: " The poorer a family is, the larger share of the total expenditures must be allotted to the provision of nourishment (nahrung, food)". Engel's law has never been refuted anywhere, and is confirmed in all subsequent surveys, Houthakker (1957), irrespective of climatic or cultural conditions. As stressed by Engel (1895b, p. 33), the general law refers to the budget *shares*,[6] ($\mathbf{e}_i$), (6.6), and *not* to the **level** (absolute size) of the *food expenditures*—which in fact were 66% higher for family type (150–200£) than the level in family type (45–60£).

The variations of the *budget shares* with income for other items in Table 6.2 also reflect some *basic patterns* and historical *tendencies* (with exceptions and gradual shifts) observed ever since in many empirical consumer demand studies. The structural consistency exhibited by consumption patterns is of great importance from the viewpoints of demand theory, empirical methods, and applications. In accordance with these assumptions, a thorough investigation of family budget data and market statistics was carried out by Wold and Jureen (1953) so as to obtain a unified *historical description* of the **demand** *structure* in *Sweden*; one picture of their budget shares is shown in Table 6.3. Finally,

[6] See especially about Engel here, Chai and Moneta (2010, p. 231).

**Table 6.3** Budget shares of social strata: Sweden 1913–1933

| | Item group | Industrial worker families 1913 | 1923 | 1933 | Middle class families 1923 | 1933 |
|---|---|---|---|---|---|---|
| 1 | Nourishment | 50.4 | 47.8 | 40.0 | 31.5 | 28.5 |
| 2 | Clothing | 14.2 | 16.0 | 14.6 | 14.5 | 14.4 |
| 3 | Fuel, Light, Laundry | 6.4 | 6.5 | 6.1 | 6.2 | 6.0 |
| 4 | Housing | 13.3 | 11.6 | 16.9 | 13.5 | 18.2 |
| 5 | Furniture (furnishings) | 4.7 | 4.8 | 5.2 | 7.1 | 6.4 |
| 6 | Personal services (domestic) | 1.0 | 0.5 | 0.4 | 4.2 | 3.3 |
| 7 | Hygiene (medical care) | 1.8 | 2.3 | 3.2 | 2.8 | 3.3 |
| 8 | Education (culture, travel) | 5.0 | 6.2 | 7.0 | 9.2 | 9.7 |
| 9 | Other expenditures | 3.1 | 4.2 | 6.6 | 11.0 | 10.2 |
| | All expenditures | 100.0 | 100.0 | 100.0 | 100.0 | 100.0 |

*Source:* Wold and Jureen (1953, p. 20), Recalculation with all expenditures = $C$

**Table 6.4** Budget shares: families in the U.S.A. 1918–19

| | Item group | $100\ e_i$ |
|---|---|---|
| 1 | Food | 38.9 |
| 2 | Clothing | 16.2 |
| 3 | Fuel, Light | 5.4 |
| 4 | Rent | 13.6 |
| 5 | Furnishings | 5.0 |
| 6 | Miscellaneous | 20.9 |
| | Total | 100.0 |

*Source:* Leser (1941, p. 53)

the average budget shares of US income groups from Leser (1941)'s *original* empirical **CDES** paper are given in Table 6.4.

A remarkable feature of Tables 6.1, 6.2, 6.3 and 6.4 is the stability of the budget share for, *Fuel and Light*, in 150 years. The budget shares of Clothing in Tables 6.2 and 6.3 imply over time an income elasticity slightly below one. High income elasticity of housing follows from budget shares of Table 6.3.

The budget shares of Table 6.5, 1998, 2001, 2004, is only shown here as an "*update*" on, Table 6.1—with their similar goods and service classification. Engel's *law* is still seen to hold in Table 6.5. The same COICOP (*Classification Of Individual Consumption* by *Purpose*) in Table 6.5 is used in other EU countries. International comparisons of consumer demand and utility *parameters* is a worthy objective of future research that the CDES system with further extensions may serve.

**Table 6.5** Budget shares for junior, senior, and all families, 1998, 2001, 2004

| | | Junior households | | | Senior households | | | All households | | |
|---|---|---|---|---|---|---|---|---|---|---|
| | | 1998 | 2001 | 2004 | 1998 | 2001 | 2004 | 1998 | 2001 | 2004 |
| | *01.–02. Food and beverages* | | | | | | | | | |
| 1 | Bread | 1.51 | 1.54 | 1.35 | 1.28 | 1.23 | 1.20 | 1.33 | 1.33 | 1.19 |
| 2 | Cerials | 0.89 | 0.90 | 0.81 | 0.57 | 0.48 | 0.50 | 0.75 | 0.71 | 0.65 |
| 3 | Meat | 2.68 | 2.82 | 2.69 | 2.93 | 2.74 | 2.84 | 2.65 | 2.64 | 2.49 |
| 4 | Fish | 0.46 | 0.42 | 0.41 | 0.81 | 0.81 | 0.69 | 0.54 | 0.52 | 0.49 |
| 5 | Milk | 1.20 | 1.15 | 1.01 | 0.77 | 0.73 | 0.72 | 0.92 | 0.92 | 0.83 |
| 6 | Cheese | 0.67 | 0.63 | 0.59 | 0.80 | 0.67 | 0.68 | 0.66 | 0.63 | 0.59 |
| 7 | Other food | 0.49 | 0.52 | 0.55 | 0.49 | 0.53 | 0.51 | 0.47 | 0.52 | 0.51 |
| 8 | Butter | 0.25 | 0.21 | 0.19 | 0.25 | 0.20 | 0.18 | 0.22 | 0.19 | 0.17 |
| 9 | Margarine, oils | 0.13 | 0.09 | 0.08 | 0.17 | 0.13 | 0.12 | 0.12 | 0.09 | 0.09 |
| 10 | Fruits, vegtables | 2.03 | 2.23 | 2.25 | 2.01 | 2.08 | 2.22 | 1.93 | 2.05 | 2.10 |
| 11 | Sugar products | 1.84 | 1.81 | 1.63 | 1.20 | 1.06 | 1.08 | 1.45 | 1.42 | 1.32 |
| 12 | Cofee, tea | 0.41 | 0.35 | 0.25 | 0.67 | 0.50 | 0.45 | 0.51 | 0.39 | 0.32 |
| 13 | Soft drinks | 0.98 | 0.98 | 0.86 | 0.58 | 0.52 | 0.46 | 0.91 | 0.86 | 0.73 |
| 14 | Wine, spirits | 1.06 | 1.03 | 0.99 | 1.92 | 2.15 | 1.93 | 1.39 | 1.40 | 1.29 |
| 15 | Beer | 0.53 | 0.47 | 0.34 | 0.81 | 0.67 | 0.56 | 0.77 | 0.61 | 0.46 |
| 16 | Tobacco products | 1.23 | 1.20 | 0.98 | 1.77 | 1.83 | 1.22 | 1.79 | 1.78 | 1.33 |
| | *03. Clothing and footware* | | | | | | | | | |
| 17 | Clothing | 4.65 | 5.01 | 4.48 | 3.74 | 3.81 | 3.42 | 4.44 | 4.34 | 4.06 |
| 18 | Footware | 1.22 | 1.16 | 1.26 | 0.68 | 0.62 | 0.55 | 0.99 | 0.98 | 0.98 |
| | *04. Housing* | | | | | | | | | |
| 19 | Gross rents | 18.86 | 19.25 | 18.71 | 23.16 | 23.85 | 24.35 | 20.96 | 21.62 | 21.59 |
| 20 | Electricity, beating | 5.64 | 6.19 | 6.22 | 7.14 | 7.39 | 7.81 | 6.26 | 6.98 | 6.91 |
| | *05. Furnishings and household equipment* | | | | | | | | | |
| 21 | Furnitures | 3.07 | 2.52 | 1.90 | 1.99 | 2.36 | 2.38 | 2.45 | 2.10 | 2.19 |
| 22 | Household textiles | 0.59 | 0.48 | 0.41 | 0.47 | 0.84 | 0.65 | 0.44 | 0.55 | 0.49 |

(continued)

**Table 6.5** (continued)

| | Junior households 1998 | 2001 | 2004 | Senior households 1998 | 2001 | 2004 | All households 1998 | 2001 | 2004 |
|---|---|---|---|---|---|---|---|---|---|
| 23 Appliances | 1.54 | 1.70 | 1.56 | 1.65 | 1.86 | 1.67 | 1.43 | 1.55 | 1.51 |
| 24 Household utensils | 0.42 | 0.44 | 0.46 | 0.50 | 0.56 | 0.65 | 0.52 | 0.53 | 0.53 |
| 25 Household goods | 0.83 | 0.82 | 0.78 | 0.94 | 0.83 | 0.81 | 0.80 | 0.76 | 0.71 |
| 26 Household services | 0.60 | 0.59 | 0.55 | 0.42 | 0.57 | 0.38 | 0.43 | 0.45 | 0.42 |
| *06. Health* | | | | | | | | | |
| 27 Medical products | 0.84 | 0.76 | 0.65 | 2.01 | 1.59 | 2.02 | 1.24 | 1.10 | 1.09 |
| 28 Medical services | 0.82 | 0.95 | t.00 | 1.46 | 1.63 | 1.91 | 1.03 | 1.20 | 1.32 |
| *07. Transport* | | | | | | | | | |
| 29 Vehicles | 7.95 | 6.43 | 8.93 | 8.37 | 5.70 | 5.59 | 8.55 | 5.81 | 7.74 |
| 30 Transport equipment operations | 4.66 | 4.38 | 4.26 | 4.24 | 4.28 | 4.02 | 3.88 | 4.07 | 3.82 |
| 31 Gasolin, lubricants | 2.87 | 3.57 | 3.17 | 2.73 | 3.36 | 3.11 | 2.66 | 3.23 | 2.93 |
| 32 Transport services | 1.28 | 1.37 | 1.34 | 1.03 | 1.27 | 1.09 | 1.62 | 1.86 | 1.88 |
| *08.–11. Communication, recreation, edu* | | | | | | | | | |
| 33 Communication | 1.70 | 1.79 | 2.00 | 1.71 | 1.61 | 1.74 | 2.01 | 2.19 | 2.33 |
| 34 Audio-visual and it equipment | 2.36 | 2.18 | 2.37 | 1.65 | 1.63 | 1.43 | 2.37 | 2.40 | 2.39 |
| 35 Major durables | 1.09 | 0.53 | 1.61 | 0.36 | 0.73 | 0.51 | 0.57 | 0.44 | 0.92 |
| 36 Recreational equipment and services | 5.05 | 5.58 | 5.22 | 4.80 | 4.75 | 4.89 | 5.17 | 5.48 | 5.12 |
| 37 Education, books, newspapers | 1.79 | 1.81 | 1.53 | 1.84 | 1.62 | 1.82 | 2.04 | 1.93 | 1.79 |
| 38 Restaurants, hotels | 4.64 | 5.41 | 5.13 | 4.89 | 5.92 | 6.12 | 5.47 | 6.14 | 5.86 |
| *12. Miscellaneous* | | | | | | | | | |
| 39 Personal care | 2.36 | 2.28 | 2.14 | 1.98 | 1.85 | 2.00 | 2.23 | 2.25 | 2.14 |
| 40 Personal effects | 0.59 | 0.80 | 0.64 | 0.58 | 0.37 | 0.55 | 0.76 | 0.59 | 0.77 |
| 41 Social protection, insurance | 7.56 | 7.28 | 8.17 | 4.26 | 4.20 | 4.76 | 4.66 | 4.57 | 5.37 |
| 42 Financial services | 0.60 | 0.40 | 0.47 | 0.34 | 0.46 | 0.43 | 0.60 | 0.50 | 0.56 |
| Sum 1–42 | **100.00** | **100.00** | **100.00** | **100.00** | **100.00** | **100.00** | **100.00** | **100.00** | **100.00** |
| Total consumption expenditures | **320,019** | **344,073** | **389,182** | **240.661** | **271,032** | **286,774** | **225,904** | **239,561** | **269,015** |
| Number of households | **500** | **516** | **481** | **501** | **449** | **488** | **2,727** | **2,639** | **2,449** |

*CDES Parameter Estimates of* $\beta_i - \beta_2$, *and the CDES Income elasticities:* $E(D_i, C)$

The entire *sample* of the respective *Junior* and *Senior families* are now used to *estimate* the **CDES** *parameters*, cf. (6.51), with here *butter* ($i = 2$) as *reference* commodity. The *estimated parameters*, $\beta_i - \beta_2$, ranked according to *size*[7] for both life-cycle groups, are shown in Table 6.6.

The CDES **Income** expenditure *elasticities* of all the **41** *consumer goods, services*—satisfying *Engel aggregation*, (6.12)—are shown in Table 6.7.

The *procedure* employed in calculating the $\mathbf{E(D_i, C)}$ elasticities in Table 6.7—from the budget *shares*, $\mathbf{e_i}$, Table 6.1, and parameter *estimates* in Table 6.6—can be explained as follows. First, we note from the income elasticity *formula*, (6.5), that the *higher* $\beta_i$ is, the *higher* is $E(D_i, C)$ —and secondly that,

$$E(D_i, C) - E(D_j, C) = \beta_i - \beta_j \Leftrightarrow E(D_i, C) = E(D_j, C) + \beta_i - \beta_j \qquad (6.56)$$

i.e., although every income elasticity, $\mathbf{E(D_i, C)}$, is *varying* with (C), the *differences* between the CDES *income elasticities* of various commodities (items) are invariant (*constant*). In other words, a **stable** hierarchy (**ranking**) exists between all the item groups in the income (**C**) *sensitivity* of their Marshallian demand. Ranking of income elasticities is robust and corresponds to *ranking* of their CDES, $\beta_i$, $\beta_j$, *parameters*, cf. (6.56). The elasticity formula, $\mathbf{E(D_i, C)}$, (6.5) can decomposed as:

$$E(D_j, C) = 1 + \beta_j - \bar{\beta} = 1 - \sum_{i=1}^{N} e_i\,(\beta_i - \beta_j) \equiv 1 - \bar{\beta}_j \qquad (6.57)$$

Hence with butter (item 2) used as the reference commodity in Table 6.6, we get $\mathbf{E(D_2, C)}$—by (6.57)—for the *Junior* families:

$$E(D_2, C) = 1 - \sum_{i=1}^{41} e_i(\beta_i - \beta_2) = 1 - \bar{\beta}_2 = 1 - 0.48614 = 0.51386 \qquad (6.58)$$

[7] We have given the parameter estimates without indicating the standard errors (or t-values) in Table 6.6; they are available in Jensen (1980, p. 283–85), but omitted here as such standard deviations carry little weight as economic-statistical significance indicators, on grounds explained by Wold and Jureen (1953, p. 260). Statistically *estimates* that are closer to zero (middle of Table 6.6) are less *'significant'* than large negative (positive) parameter estimates at the end of the rankings. Economically, the range of the *parameters* ($\beta_i$), (6.1), place many of their item *sizes*, clustering meaningful close to *zero*, cf. Table 6.9. In judging the *validity* and *reliability* of the, $\beta_i$ , $\beta_i - \beta_2$, parameter *estimates*, a main criterion will the *overall consistency* obtained for the different budget items—within and between social strata—and proper comparisons and checks with specific evidence from other sources and periods. Looking at the *point estimates* in Table 6.6 for the two family types, a main feature of the results is that a *stable hierarchy* exists between the item groups in *preference* and *demand sensitivity*, as was evident in *budget shares* of Table 6.1 discussed above.

**Table 6.6** Ranking of the reaction parameter estimates: $(\beta_i - \beta_2)$

| Junior families Rank | Commodity class | $\beta_i - \beta_2$ | Senior families Rank | Commodity Class | $\beta_i - \beta_2$ |
|---|---|---|---|---|---|
| 1 | Bread | −0.29404 | 1 | Margarine | −0.56234 |
| 2 | Margarine | −0.25465 | 2 | Bread | −0.39438 |
| 3 | Sugar | −0.24830 | 3 | Coffee | −0.33723 |
| 4 | Coffee | −0.21253 | 4 | Miscellaneous | −0.25552 |
| 5 | Tobacco | −0.20813 | 5 | Fuel and light | −0.23122 |
| 6 | Milk | −0.12385 | 6 | Tobacco | −0.24924 |
| 7 | Fuel and light | −0.06171 | 7 | Soft drinks | −0.23892 |
| 8 | Butter | – | 8 | Personal goods | −0.18789 |
| 9 | Radio, tv sets | 0.01635 | 9 | Meat | −0.18665 |
| 10 | Medical products | 0.04118 | 10 | Medical products | −0.10276 |
| 11 | Other nondurable goods | 0.09349 | 11 | Other nondurable goods | −0.09355 |
| 12 | Cheese | 0.09450 | 12 | Household machines | −0.07920 |
| 13 | Household textiles | 0.10560 | 13 | Milk | −0.05749 |
| 14 | Vegetables | 0.11840 | 14 | Medical services | −0.04911 |
| 15 | Meat | 0.12885 | 15 | Beer | −0.04888 |
| 16 | Household machines | 0.15462 | 16 | Books and papers | −0.02345 |
| 17 | Glassware | 0.20301 | 17 | Fish | −0.00829 |
| 18 | Fish | 0.23152 | 18 | Butter | – |
| 19 | Soft drinks | 0.27881 | 19 | Cheese | 0.03200 |
| 20 | Leisure equipment | 0.34423 | 20 | Entertainment | 0.06120 |
| 21 | Beer | 0.34631 | 21 | Household textiles | 0.07244 |
| 22 | Entertainment | 0.37195 | 22 | Personal care | 0.08888 |
| 23 | Auto repairs | 0.37212 | 23 | Furniture | 0.09684 |
| 24 | Clothing | 0.38976 | 24 | Sugar | 0.09990 |
| 25 | Gasoline | 0.42036 | 25 | Auto repairs | 0.12164 |
| 26 | Footwear | 0.43999 | 26 | Vegetables | 0.12429 |
| 27 | Personal goods | 0.54508 | 27 | Glassware | 0.13912 |
| 28 | Medical services | 0.58257 | 28 | Gross rents | 0.17936 |
| 29 | Wine and spirits | 0.58607 | 29 | Footwear | 0.24733 |
| 30 | Personal care | 0.60113 | 30 | Other transport | 0.29736 |
| 31 | Other foods | 0.64302 | 31 | Transport services | 0.34186 |
| 32 | Other transport | 0.66149 | 32 | Clothing | 0.37099 |
| 33 | Books and papers | 0.68632 | 33 | Radio, tv sets | 0.39254 |
| 34 | Gross rents | 0.71112 | 34 | Gasoline | 0.42218 |
| 35 | Restaurants | 0.74708 | 35 | Other foods | 0.45335 |
| 36 | Household services | 0.78325 | 36 | Wine and spirits | 0.64572 |
| 37 | Miscellaneous | 0.86186 | 37 | Leisure equipment | 0.69500 |
| 38 | Transport services | 0.91800 | 38 | Household services | 0.70973 |
| 39 | Furniture | 1.04451 | 39 | Communication | 0.89911 |
| 40 | Communication | 1.33410 | 40 | Restaurants | 1.02420 |
| 41 | Transport equipment | 1.78225 | 41 | Transport equipment | 1.32967 |
| | $\overline{\beta}_2 = \sum_{i=1}^{41} e_i(\beta_i - \beta_2)$ | 0.48614 | | $\overline{\beta}_2 = \sum_{i=1}^{41} e_i(\beta_i - \beta_2)$ | 0.19075 |

and for the *Senior* families:

$$E(D_2, C) = 1 - \sum_{i=1}^{41} e_i(\beta_i - \beta_2) = 1 - \bar{\beta}_2 = 1 - 0.19075 = 0.80925 \quad (6.59)$$

- as evaluated at, respectively, $(\mathbf{C} = 42557, \mathbf{C} = 40831)$, cf. Table 6.1.

All the other commodity ***income elasticities*** in Table 6.7 are then calculated by (6.56), (6.58), (6.59), and with $\beta_i - \beta_2$ from Table 6.6 for Junior and Senior families as, respectively,

$$E(D_i, C) = E(D_2, C) + \beta_i - \beta_2 = 0.51386 + \beta_i - \beta_2 \quad (6.60)$$

$$E(D_i, C) = E(D_2, C) + \beta_i - \beta_2 = 0.80925 + \beta_i - \beta_2 \quad (6.61)$$

The main feature of the results obtained in Table 6.7 (with the same ranking as in Table 6.6) is the overall ***similarity*** that subsists between the commodity classes in their 'income' sensitivity for the two life-cycle groups (apart from some obvious differences already mentioned, cf. Table 6.1). Since the *sample average* of **C** was *higher* for the *Junior* groupe, the ***item elasticities*** $\mathbf{E(D_i, C)}$ should ceteris paribus be *smaller* for the *Junior* families, cf. (6.42), (6.57), and their sizes in Table 6.7 comply with such tendency.

Several food items are among the *necessities* with the lowest elasticities, although fancy food also exists among the *luxuries* for both groups (rank 31, 35). Clothing, footwear, and goods and services associated with dwelling operations have elasticities around one. Housing, furniture, and cars are the high elasticity goods for Juniors, and latter good also tops the list for the Senior families.

The **CDES** ***income elasticities***, $\mathbf{E(D_i, C)}$, in Table 6.7 display ***pattern*** and ***numerical values*** that ***conform*** with the general picture of ***abundant empirical*** demand studies.

### *CDES Parameters and the Price and Substitution Elasticities*

The information about the estimated differences $(\beta_i - \beta_2)$ in Table 6.6 were sufficient for calculating income elasticities, (6.60), (6.61), of CDES demand, (6.5); adding an arbitrary constant to all the $\beta_i$—parameters would not change the *elasticity* with the respect to **C** in (6.5)—whereas any particular *price* elasticity, (6.7–6.9), would clearly be affected by such additive constant in every $\beta_i$. Thus **CDES** ***price elasticities*** can ***not*** be calculated from Table 6.6. Moreover, the actual ***parameters*** $\beta_i$ cannot be fully recovered from budget surveys (expenditure data). The set $\beta_i$ are as '**invariances**' (basic parameters) [in contrast to continuously *changing* elasticities] the ultimate ***empirical objective*** for establishing the ***parametric*** CDES indirect utility function (6.1) and demand system (6.3).

**Table 6.7** Estimates of expenditure ("income") elasticities goods and services: $E(D_i, C) = E(P_i D_i, C)$

| Junior families Rank | Commodity class | $E(D_i, C)$ | Senior families Rank | Commodity class | $E(D_i, C)$ |
|---|---|---|---|---|---|
| 1 | Bread | 0.21982 | 1 | Margarine | 0.24691 |
| 2 | Margarine | 0.25921 | 2 | Bread | 0.41487 |
| 3 | Sugar | 0.26556 | 3 | Coffee | 0.47202 |
| 4 | Coffee | 0.30133 | 4 | Miscellaneous | 0.55373 |
| 5 | Tobacco | 0.30573 | 5 | Fuel and light | 0.57803 |
| 6 | Milk | 0.39001 | 6 | Tobacco | 0.56001 |
| 7 | Fuel and light | 0.45215 | 7 | Soft drinks | 0.57033 |
| 8 | Butter | 0.51386 | 8 | Personal goods | 0.62136 |
| 9 | Radio, tv sets | 0.53021 | 9 | Meat | 0.62260 |
| 10 | Medical products | 0.55504 | 10 | Medical products | 0.70649 |
| 11 | Non-durable goods | 0.60735 | 11 | Non-durable goods | 0.71570 |
| 12 | Cheese | 0.60836 | 12 | Household machines | 0.73005 |
| 13 | Household textiles | 0.61946 | 13 | Milk | 0.75176 |
| 14 | Vegetables | 0.63226 | 14 | Medical services | 0.76014 |
| 15 | Meat | 0.64271 | 15 | Beer | 0.76037 |
| 16 | Household machines | 0.66848 | 16 | Books and papers | 0.78580 |
| 17 | Glassware | 0.71687 | 17 | Fish | 0.80096 |
| 18 | Fish | 0.74538 | 18 | Butter | 0.80925 |
| 19 | Soft drinks | 0.79267 | 19 | Cheese | 0.84125 |
| 20 | Leisure equipment | 0.85809 | 20 | Entertainment | 0.87045 |
| 21 | Beer | 0.86017 | 21 | Household textiles | 0.88169 |
| 22 | Entertainment | 0.88581 | 22 | Personal care | 0.89813 |
| 23 | Auto repairs | 0.88598 | 23 | Furniture | 0.90609 |
| 24 | Clothing | 0.90362 | 24 | Sugar | 0.90915 |
| 25 | Gasoline | 0.93422 | 25 | Auto repairs | 0.93089 |
| 26 | Footwear | 0.95385 | 26 | Vegetables | 0.93354 |
| 27 | Personal goods | 1.05894 | 27 | Glassware | 0.94837 |
| 28 | Medical services | 1.09643 | 28 | Gross rents | 0.98861 |
| 29 | Wine and spirits | 1.09993 | 29 | Footwear | 1.05658 |
| 30 | Personal care | 1.11499 | 30 | Other transport | 1.10661 |
| 31 | Other foods | 1.15688 | 31 | Transport services | 1.15111 |
| 32 | Other transport | 1.17535 | 32 | Clothing | 1.18024 |
| 33 | Books and papers | 1.20018 | 33 | Radio„ tv sets | 1.20179 |
| 34 | Gross rents | 1.22498 | 34 | Gasoline | 1.23143 |
| 35 | Restaurants | 1.26094 | 35 | Other foods | 1.26260 |
| 36 | Household services | 1.29711 | 36 | Wine and spirits | 1.45497 |
| 37 | Miscellaneous | 1.37572 | 37 | Leisure equipment | 1.50425 |
| 38 | Transport services | 1.43186 | 38 | Household services | 1.51898 |
| 39 | Furniture | 1.55837 | 39 | Communication | 1.70836 |
| 40 | Communication | 1.84796 | 40 | Restaurants | 1.83345 |
| 41 | Transport equipment | 2.29611 | 41 | Transport equipment | 2.13892 |
| | $\sum_{i=1}^{41} e_i E(D_i, C)$ | 1.00000 | | $\sum_{i=1}^{41} e_i E(D_i, C)$ | 1.00000 |

As mentioned at the end of section "Estimation of CDES Parameters from Budget Data", *extraneous information* (literature surveys, benchmark observations, calibration procedures) on any **single** price elasticity will together with Table 6.6 allow full *identification* and estimation of *all* the parameters, $(\beta_i)$. Our *parameter calibrations* will be based on the **price elasticity** of *butter* that is a well-defined homogeneous good and a classic article of many demand studies—convenient also as being our reference commodity in Table 6.6.

Hence by (6.7), the parameter $(\beta_2)$ for butter will be *calibrated* as,

$$\beta_2 = [\,E(D_2, P_2) - 1\,] / (1 - e_2) \tag{6.62}$$

Market statistics in the form of time series are often seen as the principal material for the estimation of direct price and cross-price elasticities. However, our elasticity and parameter in (6.62) do *not* refer to *total* butter market demand, but instead to butter demand elasticities *segmented* to two *life-cycle* groups. Thus information from specialized demand studies are called for; such food demand analyses are available, since our life cycle categories have been standard in many countries.

Calculations of $\beta_2$ by (6.62)—for different butter price elasticities, $\mathbf{E(D_2, P_2)}$ and with the budget share, $\mathbf{e_2}$, from Table 6.1—are collected in, Table 6.8. The *starred* **price** elasticities appear as the most *plausible* ones for several reasons. They are in line with butter elasticities seen for our family types in Wold and Jureen (1953, p. 266–69, 285–88), and conform properly with the income elasticities, $\mathbf{E(D_2, C)}$, (6.58), (6.59), and also fit the wider *implications* of the sizes of $\beta_2$—and $\overline{\beta}$, (6.5)—upon the size of *all other* price elasticities below.

This starred *selection* of $(\beta_2)$ from Table 6.8 and the parameter*estimates* in Table 6.6 finally give us the *complete set* of (reaction) *parameter* values $(\beta_i)$, listed in Table 6.9. Overall the $(\beta_i)$ numbers in Table 6.9 look *similar* (minimum, range) for the *two family types*, although natural differences in their preferences still exist. As to *Junior* families, the six items at the top of Table 6.9 are more 'urgent necessities' than the six top items of the *Seniors*. However, the *average* level $(\overline{\beta})$, (6.5), is somewhat lower for Seniors. The location and different sizes of their item specific reaction parameters $(\beta_i)$ will affect the pattern of price elasticities for the two family types.

**Table 6.8** Reaction parameter $\beta_2, \overline{\beta}$, and $E(D_2, P_2)$

| Junior families | | | Senior families | | |
|---|---|---|---|---|---|
| $E(D_2, P_2)$ | $\beta_2$ | $\overline{\beta}$ | $E(D_2, P_2)$ | $\beta_2$ | $\overline{\beta}$ |
| −0.9 | −0.10064 | 0.38550 | −0.9* | −0.10066 | 0.09009 |
| −0.8 | −0.20128 | 0.28486 | −0.8 | −0.20131 | −0.01056 |
| −0.7* | −0.30192 | 0.18422 | | | |
| −0.6 | −0.40256 | 0.08358 | | | |

The **own-price** *elasticities*, Marshallian $\mathbf{E(D_i, P_i)}$, and Slutsky $\mathbf{E(H_i, P_i)}$, as well as the **overall** *substitution* term, $\sigma_{ii}$—*calculated* according to their respective *formulas* (6.7), (6.14), (6.20), with the parameters in Table 6.9, and budget shares of Table 6.1—are [ with their income elasticities $\mathbf{E(D_i, C)}$ of Table 6.7 and Engel aggregation, (6.12)] *exhibited* for the *two* life-cycle groups in Tables 6.10 and 6.11.

As seen from the listed **own-price** *elasticities* of commodities in Tables 6.10, 6.11, the Marshallian and Slutsky own-price elasticities have *nearly* the *same size* (differing mostly only on second decimals). The *"income effect"* of *own-price* changes upon Marshallian price elasticities are very *small*, when a *large number* of goods (hence small budget shares, $\mathbf{e_i}$) are involved, cf. (6.14). Since **no** *inferior* goods were estimated for Junior or Senior families in Table 6.7, *all* the Marshallian price elasticities in Tables 6.10, 6.11 are absolutely **larger** than the corresponding Slutsky ('compensated') elasticities.

The *size* and *pattern* of the calculated *own-price elasticities* for the 41 commodities in Tables 6.10, 6.11, comply with common perceptions and normal experience: "Necessities" [low $E(D_i, C)$] are price *inelastic* and "luxuries" [high $E(D_i, C)$] are *price elastic.*

But with $\bar{\beta} = 0.18422$, $\bar{\beta} = 0.09009$ , cf. Table 6.8, the actual *exhibited* values for CDES income and price elasticities in Tables 6.10, 6.11, are limited by restrictions, cf. (6.5), (6.7),

$$E(D_i, C) + E(D_i, P_i) = -\bar{\beta} + \beta_i e_i \tag{6.63}$$

$$E(D_i, P_i) - E(D_j, P_j) = -(\beta_i - \beta_j) + \beta_i e_i - \beta_j e_j \tag{6.64}$$

Compared to (6.56), the *sum/differences* in (6.63), (6.64), are *not* exactly *constant*, but *nearly* so, when *large number* of commodities are involved (small $\mathbf{e_i}$).

For the differences between CDES own Slutsky price elasticities, (6.14), we get

$$E(H_i, P_i)-E(H_j, P_j) = -(\beta_i-\beta_j)+(1-\bar{\beta})(e_i-e_j)+2(\beta_i e_i-\beta_j e_j) \tag{6.65}$$

Thus, the actual *differences* among the Marshallian and Hicksian own-price elasticities are confined by the relations, (6.64), (6.65), respectively.

The elasticities in Tables 6.10, 6.11, represent comparative static results of computing the *effects* on demands of an increase in **one variable**: income (**C**) or price ($\mathbf{P_i}$). An increase in (**C**) affects **all** Marshallian demands ($\mathbf{D_i}$), ($i$ = 1, ..41), and to ensure that **all** these income effects, $\mathbf{E(D_i, C)}$,($i$ = 1, ..41), are numerically correct, the **Engel aggregation**, (6.12) is included (bottom line).

An increase in **one** (own) price ($\mathbf{P_i}$) has similarly effects on demands of **all** goods, but the intuitive/numerical overall check on any of the own-price elasticity are not seen in Tables 6.10, 6.11. Space allows us only to show all the

**Table 6.9** Ranking and size of reaction parameter estimates: ($\beta_i$)

| Junior families Rank | Commodity class | $\beta_i$ | Senior families Rank | Commodity class | $\beta_i$ |
|---|---|---|---|---|---|
| 1 | Bread | −0.59596 | 1 | Margarine | −0.66300 |
| 2 | Margarine | −0.55657 | 2 | Bread | −0.49504 |
| 3 | Sugar | −0.55022 | 3 | Coffee | −0.43789 |
| 4 | Coffee | −0.51445 | 4 | Miscellaneous | −0.35618 |
| 5 | Tobacco | −0.51005 | 5 | Fuel and light | −0.33188 |
| 6 | Milk | −0.42577 | 6 | Tobacco | −0.34990 |
| 7 | Fuel and light | −0.36363 | 7 | Soft drinks | −0.33958 |
| 8 | Butter | −0.30192 | 8 | Personal goods | −0.28855 |
| 9 | Radio, tv sets | −0.28557 | 9 | Meat | −0.28731 |
| 10 | Medical products | −0.26074 | 10 | Medical products | −0.20342 |
| 11 | Non-durable goods | −0.20843 | 11 | Non-durable goods | −0.19421 |
| 12 | Cheese | −0.20742 | 12 | Household machines | −0.17986 |
| 13 | Household textiles | −0.19632 | 13 | Milk | −0.15815 |
| 14 | Vegetables | −0.18352 | 14 | Medical services | −0.14977 |
| 15 | Meat | −0.17307 | 15 | Beer | −0.14954 |
| 16 | Household machines | −0.14730 | 16 | Books and papers | −0.12411 |
| 17 | Glassware | −0.09891 | 17 | Fish | −0.10895 |
| 18 | Fish | −0.07040 | 18 | Butter | −0.10066 |
| 19 | Soft drinks | −0.02311 | 19 | Cheese | −0.06866 |
| 20 | Leisure equipment | 0.04231 | 20 | Entertainment | −0.03946 |
| 21 | Beer | 0.04439 | 21 | Household textiles | −0.02822 |
| 22 | Entertainment | 0.07003 | 22 | Personal care | −0.01178 |
| 23 | Auto repairs | 0.07020 | 23 | Furniture | −0.00382 |
| 24 | Clothing | 0.08784 | 24 | Sugar | −0.00076 |
| 25 | Gasoline | 0.11844 | 25 | Auto repairs | 0.02098 |
| 26 | Footwear | 0.13807 | 26 | Vegetables | 0.02363 |
| 27 | Personal goods | 0.24316 | 27 | Glassware | 0.03846 |
| 28 | Medical services | 0.28065 | 28 | Gross rents | 0.07870 |
| 29 | Wine and spirits | 0.28415 | 29 | Footwear | 0.14667 |
| 30 | Personal care | 0.29921 | 30 | Other transport | 0.19670 |
| 31 | Other foods | 0.34110 | 31 | Transport services | 0.24120 |
| 32 | Other transport | 0.35957 | 32 | Clothing | 0.27033 |
| 33 | Books and papers | 0.38440 | 33 | Radio,, tv sets | 0.29188 |
| 34 | Gross rents | 0.40920 | 34 | Gasoline | 0.32152 |
| 35 | Restaurants | 0.44516 | 35 | Other foods | 0.35269 |
| 36 | Household services | 0.48133 | 36 | Wine and spirits | 0.54506 |
| 37 | Miscellaneous | 0.55994 | 37 | Leisure equipment | 0.59434 |
| 38 | Transport services | 0.61608 | 38 | Household services | 0.60907 |
| 39 | Furniture | 0.74259 | 39 | Communication | 0.79845 |
| 40 | Communication | 1.03218 | 40 | Restaurants | 0.92354 |
| 41 | Transport equipment | 1.48033 | 41 | Transport equipment | 1.22901 |
| | $\overline{\beta} = \sum_{i=1}^{41} e_i \beta_i$ | 0.18422 | | $\overline{\beta} = \sum_{i=1}^{41} e_i \beta_i$ | 0.09009 |

**Table 6.10** Junior families: income- and own-price elasticities

| R | Commodity class | $100e_i$ | $E(D_i, C)$ | $E(D_i, P_i)$ | $E(H_i, P_i)$ | $\sigma_{ii}$ |
|---|---|---|---|---|---|---|
| 1 | Bread | 2.44161 | 0.21982 | −0.41859 | −0.41322 | −16.92409 |
| 2 | Margarine | 0.63694 | 0.25921 | −0.44697 | −0.44532 | −69.91539 |
| 3 | Sugar | 0.84926 | 0.26556 | −0.45445 | −0.45219 | −53.24590 |
| 4 | Coffee | 1.38004 | 0.30133 | −0.49265 | −0.48849 | −35.39660 |
| 5 | Tobacco | 3.50318 | 0.30573 | −0.50782 | −0.49710 | −14.19008 |
| 6 | Milk | 2.22930 | 0.39001 | −0.58372 | −0.57502 | −25.79394 |
| 7 | Fuel and light | 4.24628 | 0.45215 | −0.65181 | −0.63261 | −14.89792 |
| 8 | Butter | 0.63694 | 0.51386 | −0.70000 | −0.69673 | −109.38614 |
| 9 | Radio, tv sets | 1.16773 | 0.53021 | −0.71776 | −0.71157 | −60.93629 |
| 10 | Medical products | 0.53079 | 0.55504 | −0.74064 | −0.73769 | −138.98171 |
| 11 | Non-durable goods | 2.12314 | 0.60735 | −0.79599 | −0.78310 | −36.88389 |
| 12 | Cheese | 0.63694 | 0.60836 | −0.79390 | −0.79002 | −124.03364 |
| 13 | Household textiles | 0.84926 | 0.61946 | −0.80534 | −0.80008 | −94.20982 |
| 14 | Vegetables | 3.07856 | 0.63226 | −0.82213 | −0.80266 | −26.07269 |
| 15 | Meat | 5.62633 | 0.64271 | −0.83666 | −0.80050 | −14.22782 |
| 16 | Household machines | 1.69851 | 0.66848 | −0.85520 | −0.84384 | −49.68135 |
| 17 | Glassware | 0.95541 | 0.71687 | −0.90203 | −0.89518 | −93.69581 |
| 18 | Fish | 0.63694 | 0.74538 | −0.93005 | −0.92530 | −145.27174 |
| 19 | Soft drinks | 0.53079 | 0.79267 | −0.97701 | −0.97280 | −183.27594 |
| 20 | Leisure equipment | 2.65393 | 0.85809 | −1.04118 | −1.01841 | −38.37373 |
| 21 | Beer | 1.27389 | 0.86017 | −1.04382 | −1.03286 | −81.07982 |
| 22 | Entertainment | 2.22930 | 0.88581 | −1.06847 | −1.04872 | −47.04251 |
| 23 | Auto repairs | 2.54777 | 0.88598 | −1.06841 | −1.04584 | −41.04905 |
| 24 | Clothing | 5.73248 | 0.90362 | −1.08280 | −1.03100 | −17.98525 |
| 25 | Gasoline | 3.60934 | 0.93422 | −1.11416 | −1.08044 | −29.93462 |
| 26 | Footwear | 1.38004 | 0.95385 | −1.13616 | −1.12300 | −81.37416 |
| 27 | Personal goods | 0.95541 | 1.05894 | −1.24083 | −1.23072 | −128.81499 |
| 28 | Medical services | 0.84926 | 1.09643 | −1.27826 | −1.26895 | −149.41910 |
| 29 | Wine and spirits | 0.95541 | 1.09993 | −1.28143 | −1.27092 | −133.02330 |
| 30 | Personal care | 1.27389 | 1.11499 | −1.29540 | −1.28119 | −100.57355 |
| 31 | Other foods | 1.80467 | 1.15688 | −1.33494 | −1.31406 | −72.81457 |
| 32 | Other transport | 2.44161 | 1.17535 | −1.35079 | −1.32209 | −54.14822 |
| 33 | Books and papers | 2.12314 | 1.20018 | −1.37624 | −1.35075 | −63.62052 |
| 34 | Gross rents | 17.62208 | 1.22498 | −1.33709 | −1.12122 | −6.36259 |
| 35 | Restaurants | 1.48620 | 1.26094 | −1.43854 | −1.41980 | −95.53232 |
| 36 | Household services | 0.84926 | 1.29711 | −1.47724 | −1.46622 | −172.64781 |
| 37 | Miscellaneous | 4.45860 | 1.37572 | −1.53497 | −1.47363 | −33.05150 |
| 38 | Transport services | 1.69851 | 1.43186 | −1.60561 | −1.58129 | −93.09859 |
| 39 | Furniture | 3.60934 | 1.55837 | −1.71578 | −1.65954 | −45.97895 |
| 40 | Communication | 0.95541 | 1.84796 | −2.02232 | −2.00466 | −209.82105 |
| 41 | Transport equipment | 5.73248 | 2.29611 | −2.39547 | −2.26384 | −39.49149 |
| | | 100.00000 | 1.00000 | | | |
| | | $100\sum e_i$ | $\sum e_i E(D_i, C)$ | | | |

**Table 6.11** Senior families: income- and own-price elasticities

| R | Commodity class | $100e_i$ | $E(D_i, C)$ | $E(D_i, P_i)$ | $E(H_i, P_i)$ | $\sigma_{ii}$ |
|---|---|---|---|---|---|---|
| 1 | Margarine | 0.65076 | 0.24691 | −0.34132 | −0.33971 | −52.20252 |
| 2 | Bread | 2.38612 | 0.41487 | −0.51678 | −0.50688 | −21.24279 |
| 3 | Coffee | 1.95228 | 0.47202 | −0.57066 | −0.56145 | −28.75864 |
| 4 | Miscellaneous | 2.81996 | 0.55373 | −0.65387 | −0.63825 | −22.63347 |
| 5 | Fuel and light | 4.44685 | 0.57803 | −0.68288 | −0.65718 | −14.77844 |
| 6 | Tobacco | 3.79610 | 0.56001 | −0.66339 | −0.64213 | −16.91551 |
| 7 | Soft drinks | 0.75922 | 0.57033 | −0.66300 | −0.65867 | −86.75665 |
| 8 | Personal goods | 0.86768 | 0.62136 | −0.71396 | −0.70857 | −81.66237 |
| 9 | Meat | 7.26681 | 0.62260 | −0.73357 | −0.68833 | −9.47224 |
| 10 | Medical products | 1.08460 | 0.70649 | −0.79879 | −0.79113 | −72.94206 |
| 11 | Non-durable goods | 2.16920 | 0.71570 | −0.81001 | −0.79448 | −36.62565 |
| 12 | Household machines | 1.08460 | 0.73005 | −0.82210 | −0.81418 | −75.06717 |
| 13 | Milk | 1.62690 | 0.75176 | −0.84443 | −0.83220 | −51.15240 |
| 14 | Medical services | 0.86768 | 0.76014 | −0.85153 | −0.84494 | −97.37921 |
| 15 | Beer | 1.84382 | 0.76037 | −0.85322 | −0.83920 | −45.51438 |
| 16 | Books and papers | 1.95228 | 0.78580 | −0.87832 | −0.86298 | −44.20359 |
| 17 | Fish | 0.97614 | 0.80096 | −0.89212 | −0.88430 | −90.59162 |
| 18 | Butter | 0.75922 | 0.80925 | −0.90000 | −0.89397 | −117.74799 |
| 19 | Cheese | 0.75922 | 0.84125 | −0.93187 | −0.92548 | −121.89884 |
| 20 | Entertainment | 3.14534 | 0.87045 | −0.96179 | −0.93441 | −29.70771 |
| 21 | Household textiles | 0.97614 | 0.88169 | −0.97206 | −0.96345 | −98.70050 |
| 22 | Personal care | 1.62690 | 0.89813 | −0.98842 | −0.97380 | −59.85654 |
| 23 | Furniture | 3.47072 | 0.90609 | −0.99632 | −0.96487 | −27.80030 |
| 24 | Sugar | 0.97614 | 0.90915 | −0.99925 | −0.99038 | −101.45870 |
| 25 | Auto repairs | 2.16920 | 0.93089 | −1.02053 | −1.00034 | −46.11553 |
| 26 | Vegetables | 3.03688 | 0.93354 | −1.02292 | −0.99457 | −32.74966 |
| 27 | Glassware | 0.75922 | 0.94837 | −1.03817 | −1.03097 | −135.79384 |
| 28 | Gross rents | 12.03905 | 0.98861 | −1.06923 | −0.95021 | −7.89274 |
| 29 | Footwear | 0.97614 | 1.05658 | −1.14524 | −1.13493 | −116.26723 |
| 30 | Other transport | 2.16920 | 1.10661 | −1.19244 | −1.16843 | −53.86478 |
| 31 | Transport services | 1.95228 | 1.15111 | −1.23650 | −1.21402 | −62.18496 |
| 32 | Clothing | 5.85683 | 1.18024 | −1.25450 | −1.18538 | −20.23922 |
| 33 | Radio,, tv sets | 1.73536 | 1.20179 | −1.28682 | −1.26596 | −72.95120 |
| 34 | Gasoline | 3.14534 | 1.23143 | −1.31141 | −1.27268 | −40.46243 |
| 35 | Other foods | 2.16920 | 1.26260 | −1.34504 | −1.31766 | −60.74394 |
| 36 | Wine and spirits | 1.73536 | 1.45497 | −1.53561 | −1.51036 | −87.03433 |
| 37 | Leisure equipment | 3.14534 | 1.50425 | −1.57565 | −1.52834 | −48.59058 |
| 38 | Household services | 0.54230 | 1.51898 | −1.60577 | −1.59753 | −294.58537 |
| 39 | Communication | 1.40998 | 1.70836 | −1.78720 | −1.76311 | −125.04515 |
| 40 | Restaurants | 3.79610 | 1.83345 | −1.88849 | −1.81889 | −47.91468 |
| 41 | Transport equipment | 5.09761 | 2.13892 | −2.16636 | −2.05733 | −40.35870 |
| | | 100.00000 | 1.00000 | | | |
| | | $100\sum e_i$ | $\sum e_i E(D_i, C)$ | | | |

relevant checks (price elasticity aggregations) for a **single** price: ($P_1$) of bread ($Y_1$) in Table 6.1. All **cross**-*price elasticities*, Marshallian $\mathbf{E(D_j, P_1)}$, Slutsky $\mathbf{E(H_j, P_1)}$, and Allen substitution elasticities, $\sigma_{j1}$—calculated, respectively, by formulas (6.9), (6.15), (6.21) from the parameters in Table 6.9, budget *shares*, $e_i$, in Table 6.1—are shown [with the *own-price* (**bold line**) elasticities of Tables 6.10, 6.11 included] for the *two* life-cycle groups in Tables 6.12 and 6.13.

For the *bread price* elasticities, the *Cournot aggregation* of $E(D_j, P_1)$, (6.13), *Hicks-Slutsky aggregation* of $\mathbf{E(H_j, P_1)}$, (6.19) and *Hicks-Allen aggregation*, (6.23), of $\sigma_{j1}$, are verified as seen in the bottom line.

As all goods are related through the budget equation, *Cournot aggregations* (6.13) in Tables 6.12, 6.13, and *Hicks-Slutsky aggregation* of $E(H_j, P_1)$, (6.19), show how the CDES readjustments are made for all goods to comply with the value of $\mathbf{E(D_1, P_1)}$. To see the "*fine structure*" of CDES readjustments into Hicksian complements/substitutes, the *Hicks-Slutsky aggregations* in Tables 6.12, 6.13 check the size of such components behind the numerical value of $\mathbf{E(H_1, P_1)}$. *Hicks-Allen aggregations* in Tables 6.12, 6.13 serve similar purposes for checking the numerical value of the diagonal term: $\sigma_{11}$.

Which cross elasticities and aggregations are most useful for confirming the size of $\mathbf{E(H_1, P_1)}$? It has often been suggested that "The elasticity of substitution has the great practical disadvantage of often tending towards infinity for goods that make up a small fraction of the total budget. The Slutsky elasticity retains 'normal proportions"'. Such impression may follow from the general theoretical expression $\sigma_{ij}$, (6.20–6.21), and Slutsky elasticity, (6.14–6.15). However, calculations with CDES formula for $\sigma_{ij}$, (6.20–6.21) shows that it is generally *unlikely* to happen—as the numbers of $\sigma_{j1}$ in Tables 6.12, 6.13 illustrate, where the Slutsky elasticities $\mathbf{E(H_j, P_1)}$ appear more "erratic" than the systematic (monotone) sequence of the Allen substitution elasticities, $\sigma_{j1}$.

Moreover, the *symmetry* $\sigma_{j1} = \sigma_{1j}$ can be utilized for a fruitful economic *reinterpretation* of the *numerical values* of $\sigma_{11}$ and $\mathbf{E(H_1, P_1)}$. As explained above, cf. (6.23–6.24), the *Hicks-Allen aggregation* (6.23) (seldom seen) is here equivalent to the **homogeneity** of Hicksian demands, $\mathbf{Y_1 = H_1(P, U)}$, shown in the last column of Tables 6.12, 6.13. For sake of completeness, the *homogeneity* (6.10) of Marshallian demands, $\mathbf{Y_1 = D_1(P, C)}$, is included (besides last column) in Tables 6.12, 6.13. All the calculations of the *cross-price elasticities* $\mathbf{E(D_1, P_j)}$ and $\mathbf{E(H_1, P_j)}$, are done as above by formulas (6.9), (6.15). The sequence of the *Slutsky elasticities* $\mathbf{E(H_1, P_j)}$ (last column) still appear 'erratic' compared to the *Allen elasticities*, $\sigma_{1j}$, (6.20–6.21).

But any 'dilemma' of choice between the columns of $\sigma_{1j}$ and $\mathbf{E(H_1, P_j)}$ is resolved, as any calculated $\mathbf{E(H_1, P_j)}$ can simply be verified in Tables 6.12, 6.13 as the product of the *systematic* (parametric determinants) column of $\sigma_{1j}$ and the column of the *empirical* (sample point influence) budget shares $e_j$. Thus, the *item* (19) gross rents is largest budget share and hence (together with

**Table 6.12** Junior families: own price and cross price elasticities: bread ($Y_1$)

| R | Commodity class (j) | $100e_j$ | $E(D_j, P_1)$ | $E(H_j, P_1)$ | $\sigma_{j1} = \sigma_{1j}$ | $E(D_1, P_j)$ | $E(H_1, P_j)$ |
|---|---|---|---|---|---|---|---|
| **1** | Bread | **2.44161** | **−0.41859** | **−0.41322** | **−16.92409** | **−0.41859** | **−0.41322** |
| 2 | Margarine | 0.63694 | −0.01455 | −0.00822 | −0.33675 | −0.00355 | −0.00214 |
| 3 | Sugar | 0.84926 | −0.01455 | −0.00807 | −0.33040 | −0.00467 | −0.00281 |
| 4 | Coffee | 1.38004 | −0.01455 | −0.00719 | −0.29463 | −0.00710 | −0.00407 |
| 5 | Tobacco | 3.50318 | −0.01455 | −0.00709 | −0.29023 | −0.01787 | −0.01017 |
| 6 | Milk | 2.22930 | −0.01455 | −0.00503 | −0.20595 | −0.00949 | −0.00459 |
| 7 | Fuel and light | 4.24628 | −0.01455 | −0.00351 | −0.14381 | −0.01544 | −0.00611 |
| 8 | Butter | 0.63694 | −0.01455 | −0.00200 | −0.08210 | −0.00192 | −0.00052 |
| 9 | Radio, tv sets | 1.16773 | −0.01455 | −0.00161 | −0.06575 | −0.00333 | −0.00077 |
| 10 | Medical products | 0.53079 | −0.01455 | −0.00100 | −0.04092 | −0.00138 | −0.00022 |
| 11 | Non-durable goods | 2.12314 | −0.01455 | 0.00028 | 0.01139 | −0.00443 | 0.00024 |
| 12 | Cheese | 0.63694 | −0.01455 | 0.00030 | 0.01240 | −0.00132 | 0.00008 |
| 13 | Household textiles | 0.84926 | −0.01455 | 0.00057 | 0.02350 | −0.00167 | 0.00020 |
| 14 | Vegetables | 3.07856 | −0.01455 | 0.00089 | 0.03630 | −0.00565 | 0.00112 |
| 15 | Meat | 5.62633 | −0.01455 | 0.00114 | 0.04675 | −0.00974 | 0.00263 |
| 16 | Household machines | 1.69851 | −0.01455 | 0.00177 | 0.07252 | −0.00250 | 0.00123 |
| 17 | Glassware | 0.95541 | −0.01455 | 0.00295 | 0.12091 | −0.00095 | 0.00116 |
| 18 | Fish | 0.63694 | −0.01455 | 0.00365 | 0.14942 | −0.00045 | 0.00095 |
| 19 | Soft drinks | 0.53079 | −0.01455 | 0.00480 | 0.19671 | −0.00012 | 0.00104 |
| 20 | Leisure equipment | 2.65393 | −0.01455 | 0.00640 | 0.26213 | 0.00112 | 0.00696 |
| 21 | Beer | 1.27389 | −0.01455 | 0.00645 | 0.26421 | 0.00057 | 0.00337 |
| 22 | Entertainment | 2.22930 | −0.01455 | 0.00708 | 0.28985 | 0.00156 | 0.00646 |
| 23 | Auto repairs | 2.54777 | −0.01455 | 0.00708 | 0.29002 | 0.00179 | 0.00739 |
| 24 | Clothing | 5.73248 | −0.01455 | 0.00751 | 0.30766 | 0.00504 | 0.01764 |
| 25 | Gasoline | 3.60934 | −0.01455 | 0.00826 | 0.33826 | 0.00427 | 0.01221 |
| 26 | Footwear | 1.38004 | −0.01455 | 0.00874 | 0.35789 | 0.00191 | 0.00494 |
| 27 | Personal goods | 0.95541 | −0.01455 | 0.01130 | 0.46298 | 0.00232 | 0.00442 |

(continued)

**Table 6.12** (continued)

| R | Commodity class (j) | $100e_j$ | $E(D_j, P_1)$ | $E(H_j, P_1)$ | $\sigma_{j1} = \sigma_{1j}$ | $E(D_1, P_j)$ | $E(H_1, P_j)$ |
|---|---|---|---|---|---|---|---|
| 28 | Medical services | 0.84926 | −0.01455 | 0.01222 | 0.50047 | 0.00238 | 0.00425 |
| 29 | Wine and spirits | 0.95541 | −0.01455 | 0.01230 | 0.50397 | 0.00271 | 0.00481 |
| 30 | Personal care | 1.27389 | −0.01455 | 0.01267 | 0.51903 | 0.00381 | 0.00661 |
| 31 | Other foods | 1.80467 | −0.01455 | 0.01370 | 0.56092 | 0.00616 | 0.01012 |
| 32 | Other transport | 2.44161 | −0.01455 | 0.01415 | 0.57939 | 0.00878 | 0.01415 |
| 33 | Books and papers | 2.12314 | −0.01455 | 0.01475 | 0.60422 | 0.00816 | 0.01283 |
| 34 | Gross rents | 17.62208 | −0.01455 | 0.01536 | 0.62902 | 0.07211 | 0.11085 |
| 35 | Restaurant | 1.48620 | −0.01455 | 0.01624 | 0.66498 | 0.00662 | 0.00988 |
| 36 | Household services | 0.84926 | −0.01455 | 0.01712 | 0.70115 | 0.00409 | 0.00595 |
| 37 | Miscellaneous | 4.45860 | −0.01455 | 0.01904 | 0.77976 | 0.02497 | 0.03477 |
| 38 | Purchased transport | 1.69851 | −0.01455 | 0.02041 | 0.83590 | 0.01046 | 0.01420 |
| 39 | Furniture | 3.60934 | −0.01455 | 0.02350 | 0.96241 | 0.02680 | 0.03474 |
| 40 | Communication | 0.95541 | −0.01455 | 0.03057 | 1.25200 | 0.00986 | 0.01196 |
| 41 | Transport equipment | 5.73248 | −0.01455 | 0.04151 | 1.70015 | 0.08486 | 0.09746 |
| | | 100.00000 | −0.02442 | 0.00000 | 0.00000 | −0.21982 | 0.00000 |
| | | $100 \sum e_j$ | $\sum e_j E(D_j, P_1)$ | $\sum e_j E(H_j, P_1)$ | $\sum e_j \sigma_{j1}$ | $\sum E(D_1, P_j)$ | $\sum E(H_1, P_j)$ |
| | | | $= -e_1$ | | $\sum e_j \sigma_{1j}$ | $= -E(D_1, C)$ | |

**Table 6.13** Senior families: own price and cross price elasticities: bread ($Y_1$)

| R | Commodity class (j) | $100e_j$ | $E(D_j, P_1)$ | $E(H_j, P_1)$ | $\sigma_{j1} = \sigma_{1j}$ | $E(D_1, P_j)$ | $E(H_1, P_j)$ |
|---|---|---|---|---|---|---|---|
| 1 | Margarine | 0.65076 | −0.01181 | −0.00592 | −0.24813 | −0.00431 | −0.00161 |
| 2 | Bread | **2.38612** | **−0.51678** | **−0.50688** | **−21.24279** | **−0.51678** | **−0.50688** |
| 3 | Coffee | 1.95228 | −0.01181 | −0.00055 | −0.02302 | −0.00855 | −0.00045 |
| 4 | Miscellaneous | 2.81996 | −0.01181 | 0.00140 | 0.05869 | −0.01004 | 0.00166 |
| 5 | Fuel and light | 4.44685 | −0.01181 | 0.00198 | 0.08299 | −0.01476 | 0.00369 |
| 6 | Tobacco | 3.79610 | −0.01181 | 0.00155 | 0.06497 | −0.01328 | 0.00247 |
| 7 | Soft drinks | 0.75922 | −0.01181 | 0.00180 | 0.07529 | −0.00258 | 0.00057 |
| 8 | Personal goods | 0.86768 | −0.01181 | 0.00301 | 0.12632 | −0.00250 | 0.00110 |
| 9 | Meat | 7.26681 | −0.01181 | 0.00304 | 0.12756 | −0.02088 | 0.00927 |
| 10 | Medical products | 1.08460 | −0.01181 | 0.00505 | 0.21145 | −0.00221 | 0.00229 |
| 11 | Non-durable goods | 2.16920 | −0.01181 | 0.00527 | 0.22066 | −0.00421 | 0.00479 |
| 12 | Household machines | 1.08460 | −0.01181 | 0.00561 | 0.23501 | −0.00195 | 0.00255 |
| 13 | Milk | 1.62690 | −0.01181 | 0.00613 | 0.25672 | −0.00257 | 0.00418 |
| 14 | Medical services | 0.86768 | −0.01181 | 0.00633 | 0.26510 | −0.00130 | 0.00230 |
| 15 | Beer | 1.84382 | −0.01181 | 0.00633 | 0.26533 | −0.00276 | 0.00489 |
| 16 | Books and papers | 1.95228 | −0.01181 | 0.00694 | 0.29076 | −0.00242 | 0.00568 |
| 17 | Fish | 0.97614 | −0.01181 | 0.00730 | 0.30592 | −0.00106 | 0.00299 |
| 18 | Butter | 0.75922 | −0.01181 | 0.00750 | 0.31421 | −0.00076 | 0.00239 |
| 19 | Cheese | 0.75922 | −0.01181 | 0.00826 | 0.34621 | −0.00052 | 0.00263 |
| 20 | Entertainment | 3.14534 | −0.01181 | 0.00896 | 0.37541 | −0.00124 | 0.01181 |
| 21 | Household textiles | 0.97614 | −0.01181 | 0.00923 | 0.38665 | −0.00028 | 0.00377 |
| 22 | Personal care | 1.62690 | −0.01181 | 0.00962 | 0.40309 | −0.00019 | 0.00656 |
| 23 | Furniture | 3.47072 | −0.01181 | 0.00981 | 0.41105 | −0.00013 | 0.01427 |
| 24 | Sugar | 0.97614 | −0.01181 | 0.00988 | 0.41411 | −0.00001 | 0.00404 |
| 25 | Auto repairs | 2.16920 | −0.01181 | 0.01040 | 0.43585 | 0.00046 | 0.00945 |
| 26 | Vegetables | 3.03688 | −0.01181 | 0.01046 | 0.43850 | 0.00072 | 0.01332 |
| 27 | Glassware | 0.75922 | −0.01181 | 0.01082 | 0.45333 | 0.00029 | 0.00344 |

(continued)

**Table 6.13** (continued)

| R | Commodity class (j) | $100e_j$ | $E(D_j, P_1)$ | $E(H_j, P_1)$ | $\sigma_{j1} = \sigma_{1j}$ | $E(D_1, P_j)$ | $E(H_1, P_j)$ |
|---|---|---|---|---|---|---|---|
| 28 | Gross rents | 12.03905 | −0.01181 | 0.01178 | 0.49357 | 0.00948 | 0.05942 |
| 29 | Footwear | 0.97614 | −0.01181 | 0.01340 | 0.56154 | 0.00143 | 0.00548 |
| 30 | Other transport | 2.16920 | −0.01181 | 0.01459 | 0.61157 | 0.00427 | 0.01327 |
| 31 | Purchased transport | 1.95228 | −0.01181 | 0.01565 | 0.65607 | 0.00471 | 0.01281 |
| 32 | Clothing | 5.85683 | −0.01181 | 0.01635 | 0.68520 | 0.01583 | 0.04013 |
| 33 | Radio, tv sets | 1.73536 | −0.01181 | 0.01686 | 0.70675 | 0.00507 | 0.01226 |
| 34 | Gasoline | 3.14534 | −0.01181 | 0.01757 | 0.73639 | 0.01011 | 0.02316 |
| 35 | Other foods | 2.16920 | −0.01181 | 0.01831 | 0.76756 | 0.00765 | 0.01665 |
| 36 | Wine and spirits | 1.73536 | −0.01181 | 0.02291 | 0.95993 | 0.00946 | 0.01666 |
| 37 | Leisure equipment | 3.14534 | −0.01181 | 0.02408 | 1.00921 | 0.01869 | 0.03174 |
| 38 | Household services | 0.54230 | −0.01181 | 0.02443 | 1.02394 | 0.00330 | 0.00555 |
| 39 | Communication | 1.40998 | −0.01181 | 0.02895 | 1.21332 | 0.01126 | 0.01711 |
| 40 | Restaurant | 3.79610 | −0.01181 | 0.03194 | 1.33841 | 0.03506 | 0.05081 |
| 41 | Transport equipment | 5.09761 | −0.01181 | 0.03923 | 1.64388 | 0.06265 | 0.08380 |
| | | 100.00000 | −0.02386 | 0.00000 | 0.00000 | −0.41487 | 0.00000 |
| | | $100\sum e_j$ | $\sum e_j E(D_j, P_1) = -e_1$ | $\sum e_j E(H_j, P_1)$ | $\sum e_j \sigma_{j1} = \sum e_j \sigma_{1j}$ | $\sum E(D_1, P_j) = -E(D_1, C)$ | $\sum E(H_1, P_j)$ |

$\sigma_{1j}$) *item* (19) exerts *largest cross* influence—(0.11085), (0.05942)—upon $\mathbf{E}(\mathbf{H}_1, \mathbf{P}_1)$ for both family types, and more so for Junior families.

Every calculated **price** (own) *elasticity* $\mathbf{E}(\mathbf{H}_i, \mathbf{P}_i)$ (6.14) in the columns of Tables 6.10, 6.11, is also the product of its mainly *'systematic'* (parametric) component $\sigma_{ii}$, (6.20) and its *empirical* (sample point) budget share $\mathbf{e}_i$. Housing (gross rents), has despite *high* $\mathbf{e}_i$, *not* a very large *Slutsky elasticity* $\mathbf{E}(\mathbf{H}_i, \mathbf{P}_i)$, because the (parametric) *substitution* component $\sigma_{ii}$ is very *small.* The last column with $\sigma_{ii}$ looks 'erratic', but *each element* of this column has economic sense in understanding the *size* of $\mathbf{E}(\mathbf{H}_i, \mathbf{P}_i)$.

## Final Comments

Consumer demand analysis was once a lively subject of progress and debate in economics. The literature debate appears to have petered out in the late 1980s for many reasons, suspension of consumer surveys and other data problems, but also from a neglect of working out precisely *variable substitution* elasticities and *aggregation* properties implied by the 'fundamental equation of value theory', Hicks (1946, p. 309). We have followed up and gone back to basics on *ordinal* and *cardinal* utility, *theoretically* and in *empirical* applications. In both areas, the *Demand/Expenditure* system (6.3), (6.4), of the **CDES** *Indirect utility* function (6.1) has a long history and proud record in economics.

Panel micro data of consumers and associated price series on disaggregated levels are becoming available in many countries. Natural subjects of further research would be extension to a richer parametric family of indirect utility functions that generate demand functions within the framework here demonstrated for the CDES specification.

## Appendix

### A. Variable Lagrangian Multiplier Elasticities, E (λ (P, C), C)

We collect here the first-order derivatives of the **CDES** *Marshallian* demand functions, $\mathbf{D}_i(\mathbf{P}, \mathbf{C})$, (20.20), from Chap. 5, Eqs. (5.54–5.56) as:

$$\frac{\partial D_i}{\partial C} = (1 + \beta_i - \bar{\beta})\,(D_i/C) \tag{6.66}$$

$$\frac{\partial D_i}{\partial P_i} = -(1 + \beta_i)\,(D_i/P_i) + \beta_i\,(D_i D_i/C) \tag{6.67}$$

$$\frac{\partial D_j}{\partial P_i} = \beta_i\,(D_i D_j/C)\ ; \qquad \frac{\partial D_i}{\partial P_j} = \beta_j\,(D_i D_j/C) \tag{6.68}$$

Regarding the **proof** of the *derivative*, (6.42), of $\bar{\beta}(P, C)$, (6.5), we have,

$$\frac{\partial \bar{\beta}(P, C)}{\partial C} = \sum \frac{\partial e_j}{\partial C} \cdot \beta_j = \sum \left[ \frac{\partial (P_j D_j C^{-1})}{\partial C} \right] \beta_j$$
$$= \sum \left[ P_j C^{-1} \frac{\partial D_j}{\partial C} - C^{-2} P_j D_j \right] \beta_j$$
$$= C^{-1} \sum \left[ P_j \frac{\partial D_j}{\partial C} - e_j \right] \beta_j \tag{6.69}$$

The expression (6.69) can, using (6.66), be rewritten as:

$$\frac{\partial \bar{\beta}(P, C)}{\partial C} = \frac{1}{C} \cdot \sum e_j (\beta_j - \bar{\beta}) \beta_j = \frac{1}{C} \cdot \sum e_j (\beta_j - \bar{\beta})^2 > 0 \tag{6.70}$$

where the last equality is obtained, using: $\sum e_j(\beta_j - \bar{\beta}) = 0$.
Hence (6.70) *establishes* (6.42).

### *B. Variable Lagrangian Multiplier Elasticities,* E ($\lambda$ (P, C), $P_j$)

As to the *Price derivative* of $\bar{\beta}(P, C)$, (6.5), we get, using (6.67) and (6.68):

$$\frac{\partial \bar{\beta}(P, C)}{\partial P_j} = \sum_i \beta_i \frac{\partial e_i}{\partial P_j}$$
$$= \sum_i \beta_i \frac{\partial (P_i D_i / C)}{\partial P_j}$$
$$= \frac{D_j \beta_j}{C} + \sum_i \frac{P_i \beta_i}{C} \left[ \beta_j \frac{D_i D_j}{C} - (1 + \beta_i) \frac{D_i}{P_i} \delta_{ij} \right]$$
$$= -\frac{D_j \beta_j^2}{C} + \frac{D_j \beta_j}{C} \sum_i \frac{P_i D_i}{C} \beta_i = -\beta_j [\beta_j - \bar{\beta}(P, C)] \frac{D_j}{C} \tag{6.71}$$
$$= \frac{e_j}{P_j} [-\beta_j^2 + \beta_j \bar{\beta}(P, C)] e_j \gtrless 0 \Leftrightarrow \beta_j^2 \lessgtr \beta_j \bar{\beta}(P, C) \tag{6.72}$$

Hence (6.71–6.72) *establish* (6.44).

## Bibliography


Akin JS, Stewart JF (1979) Theoretical Restrictions on the Parameters of Indirect Addilog Demand Equations. Econometrica 47:779–780

Allen RGD (1938) Mathematical Analysis for Economists. MacMillan, London

Antony A (2010) A Class of Changing Elasticity of Substitution Production Functions. Journal of Economics 100:165–183

Arrow KJ (1961) Additive Logarithmic Demand Functions and the Slutsky Relations. Review of Economic Studies 28:176–181

Arrow KJ (1971) Essays in The Theory of Risk–Bearing. North–Holland

Arrow KJ, Chenery HB, Minhas BS, Solow RM (1961) Capital–Labour Substitution and Economic Efficiency. Review of Economics and Statistics 43:225–250

Barnett WA, Lee YW (1985) The Global Properties of the Miniflex Laurent, Generalized Leontief, and Translog Flexible Functional Forms. Econometrica 53:1421–1437

Barro RJ, Sala-i-Martin X (2004) Economic Growth Theory, 2nd edn. M.I.T. Press, Cambridge, Mass

Barten AP, Boehm V (1982) Consumer theory. pp 381–429, In: Arrow, K. J. and Intriligator, M. D. (eds), *Handbook of mathematical economics*, vol 2. North–Holland, Amsterdam.

Bernoulli D (1738, 1954) Exposition of a New Theory on the Measurement of Risk. Econometrica 22:23–36

Brems H (1986) Pioneering Economic Theory 1630–1980. A Mathematical Restatement. The Johns Hopkins University Press, Baltimore

Browning M, Crossley TF (2000) Luxuries are Easier to Postpone: A Proof. Journal of Political Economy 108:1022–1026

Browning M, Hansen LP, Heckman JJ (1999) Micro Data and General Equilibrium Models. In: Taylor & Woodford (ed) Handbook of Macroecon.1, Elsevier, pp 543–633

Burk A (1936) Real Income, Expenditure Proportionality, and Frisch's "New Methods of Measuring Marginal Utility';'. Review of Economic Studies 4:33–52

Caves DW, Christensen LR (1980) Global Properties of Flexible Functional Forms. American Economic Review 70:422–432

Chai A, Moneta A (2010) Retrospectives: Engel Curves. Journal of Economic Perspectives 24:225–240

Chung JW (1987) On the Estimation of Factor Substitution in the Translog Model. Review of Economics and Statistics 69:409–417

Chung JW (1994) Utility and Production Functions. Blackwell, Oxford

Clark C (1973) The Marginal Utility of Income. Oxford Economic Papers 25:145–159

Deaton A (1992) Understanding Consumption. Clarendon Press, Oxford

Deaton AS (1986) Demand Theory. pp 1768–1839, in Griliches, Z. and M.D. Intriligator, (eds), *Handbook of Econometrics*, Vol. 3, Amsterdam, North–Holland.

Deaton AS, Muellbauer J (1980a) An Almost Ideal Demand System. American Economic Review 70:312–326

Deaton AS, Muellbauer J (1980b) Economics and Consumer Behavior. Cambridge University Press, Cambridge

de Boer PMC, Paap R (2009) Testing non–nested demand relations: linear expenditure systems versus indirect addilog. Stat Neerlandica 63:368–384

de Boer P, van Daal J, Rodrigues JFD (2023) Consumer preferences in CGE models, when data are scarce: Comparing the linear expenditure and the indirect addilog systems. Economic Systems Research 35:1–29
de La Grandville O (1989) In Quest of the Slutsky Diamond. American Economic Review 79:468–481
Deschamps R (1973) Risk Aversion and Demand Functions. Econometrica 41:455–465
Diewert WE (1974) Applications of Duality Theory. pp 106–171, In: Intriligator MD, Kendrick DA (eds) *Frontiers of Quantitative Economics*, Vol.2, North–Holland, Amsterdam
Diewert WE (1982) Duality Approaches to Microeconomic Theory. In: Arrow KJ, Intriligator MD (eds) *Handbook of Mathematical Economics*, Vol.2, North–Holland, Amsterdam
Diewert WE, Wales TJ (1987) Flexible Functional Forms and Global Curvature Conditions. Econometrica 37:43–68
Diewert WE, Avriel M, Zang I (1981) Nine Kinds of Quasiconcavity and Concavity. Journal of Economic Theory 25:397–420
Dybvig P (1981) Recovering Cardinal Utility. Review of Economic Studies 48:159–166
Engel E (1895a) Die Lebenshaltung belgischer Arbeiterfamilien frueher und jetzt. Bulletin of the International Statistical Institute 9:1–124, with an Appendix, 1–54
Engel E (1895b) Die Productions– und Consumptionsverhaeltnisse des Koenigreichs Sachsen. Zeitschrift des Statistischen Bureaus des Koeniglich Saechsishen Ministerium des Inneren 8–9(22), reprint in, *Bulletin of the International Statistical Institute*, 9 (1895), 1–54
Epstein L (1975) A Disaggregated Analysis of Consumer Choice Under Uncertainty. Econometrica 45:877–892
Fisher FM (1972) Gross Substitutes and The Utility Function. Journal of Economic Theory 4:82–87
Fisher D, Fleissig AR, Serletis A (2001) An Empirical Comparison of Flexible Demand System Functional Forms. Journal of Applied Econometrics 16:59–80
Frisch R (1959) A Complete Scheme for Computing All Direct and Cross Demand Elasticities in a Model with Many Sectors. Econometrica 27:177–196
Gamaletsos T (1973) Further Analysis of Cross–country Comparison of Consumer Expenditure Patterns. European Economic Review 4:1–20
Gamaletsos T (1974) Reply – Further analysis of cross–country comparison of consumer expenditure patterns. European Economic Review 5:307
Geary RC (1950–1951) A Note on “A Constant–Utility Index of the Cost of Living”. Review of Economic Studies 18:65–66
Ginsberg W (1973) Concavity and Quasiconcavity in Economics. Journal of Economic Theory 6:596–605
Gravelle H, Rees R (2004) Microeconomics, 3rd edn. Prentice Hall, Harlow
Guilkey DK, Knox Lovell CA (1980) On the Flexibility of the Translog Approximation. International Economic Review 21:137–147
Guilkey DK, Knox Lovell C, Sickles R (1983) A Comparison of the Performance of Three Flexible Functional Forms. International Economic Review 24:591–616
Hanoch G (1975) Production and Demand Models with Direct and Indirect Implicit Additivity. Econometrica 43:395–419
Hanoch G (1977) Risk Aversion and Consumer Preferences. Econometrica 45:413–426
Heij C, de Boer PMC, Franses PH, Kloek T, van Dijk HK (2004) Econometric Methods with Applications in Business and Economics. Oxford University Press, Oxford

Hertel TW, Tsigas ME (1997) Structure of GTAP, In Hertel, TW. pp 13–73, In Hertel, TW *Global Trade Analysis: Modelling and Applications*, Cambridge University Press, Cambridge

Hertel TW, Preckel PV, Tsigas ME, Peterson EB, Surry Y (1991) Implicit Additivity as a Strategy for Restricting the Parameter Space in Computable General Equilibrium Models. Economic and Financial Computing 1:265–289

Hicks JR (1937) Theorie Mathematique de la Valeur en Regime de la Libre Concurrence. Hermann, Editeurs, Paris

Hicks JR (1946) Value and Capital, 2nd edn. Clarendon Press, Oxford

Hicks JR (1969) Direct and Indirect Additivity. Econometrica 37:353–354

Hillinger C (1969) The Measurement of Utility. Review of Economic Studies 36:111–116

Hotelling H (1932) Edgeworth's Taxation Paradox and the Nature of Demand and Supply Functions. Journal of Political Economy 40:577–616

Houthakker HS (1952) Compensated Changes in Quantities and Qualities Consumed. Review of Economic Studies 19:155–64

Houthakker HS (1957) An International Comparison of Household Expenditure Patterns, Commemorating the Centenary of Engel's law. Econometrica 25:532–551

Houthakker HS (1960a) Additive Preferences. Econometrica 28:244–257

Houthakker HS (1960b) The Influence of Prices and Income on Household Expenditures. Bulletin of the International Institute of Statistics 37:9–22

Houthakker HS (1961) The Present State of Consumption Theory. Econometrica 29:704–740

Houthakker HS (1965) A Note on Self–Dual Preferences. Econometrica 33:797–801

Jensen BS (1980) Expenditure System for the Danish Household Sector. In *Symposium i Anvendt Statistik*, (Lyngby: NEUCC, Denmark)

Jensen BS, Larsen ME (2005) General Equilibrium Dynamics of Multi–Sector Growth Models. Journal of Economics 10:17–56

Jensen BS, Lehmijoki U (2011) Homothetic Multisector Growth Models. pp 289–318, in: Frontiers of Economics and Globalization, 11, La Grandville, O. de, (Ed.), Emerald, United Kingdom.

Jensen BS, de Boer P, van Daal J, Jensen PS (2011) Global Restrictions on the Parameters of the CDES Indirect Utility Function. Journal of Economics 102:217–235

Jensen BS, Lehmijoki U, Rovenskaya E (2015) Non–Homothetic Multisector Growth Models. Review of Development Economics 19(2):221–243

Jörgensen E (1965) Income–Expenditure Relations of Danish Wage and Salary Earners. (Copenhagen: Statistical Inquires No. 14, Statistical Department)

Katzner DW (1968) A Note on the Differentiability of Consumer Demand Equations. Econometrica 36:415–418

Klein LR, Rubin H (1947–1948) A Constant–Utility Index of the Cost of Living. Review of Economic Studies 15:84–87

Lau LJ (1978) Testing and Imposing Monotonicity, Convexity and Quasi–Convexity Constraints. pp 409–453, In: Fuss M, McFadden D (eds) *Production Economics: A Dual Approach to Theory and Applications*, Vol.1, North–Holland, Amsterdam

Lee LF, Pitt MM (1986) Microeconometric Demand System with Binding Nonnegativity Constraints: The Dual Approach. Econometrica 54:1237–1242

Leser CEV (1941) Family Budget Data and Price Elasticities of Demand. Review of Economic Studies 9:40–57

Marshall A (1920) Principles of Economics, 8th edn. Macmillan, London
Mas-Colell A, Whinston MD, Green JR (1995) Microeconomic Theory. Oxford University Press, New York
Matsuyama K (2023) Non-CES Aggregators: A Guided Tour. Annual Review of Economics 15(1):235–265
Mehra R, Prescott EC (1985) The Equity Premium, a Puzzle. Journal of Monetary Economics 15:145–161
Moschini G (1999) Imposing Local Curvature Conditions in Flexible Demand Systems. Journal of Business and Economics 17:487–490
Murty KN (1982) Theoretical Restrictions on the Parameters of Indirect Addilog Demand Equations – A Comment. Econometrica 50:225–227
Pollak RA (1969) Conditional Demand Functions and Consumption Theory. Quarterly Journal of Economics 83:60–78
Prais JS, Houthakker HS (1971) Analysis of Family Budgets, 2nd edn. Cambridge University Press, London
Pratt JW (1964) Risk Aversion in the Small and in the Large. Econometrica 32:122–136
Rimmer MT, Powell AA (1996) An Implicitly Additive Demand System. Applied Economics 28:1613–1622
Roy R (1942) De l'Utilite, Contribution a la Theorie des Choix. Hermann, Paris
Roy R (1947) La Distribution du Revenue entre les Divers Biens. Econometrica 15:205–225
Ryan DL, Wales TJ (1998) A Simple Method for Imposing Local Curvature in Some Flexible Demand Systems. Journal of Business and Economics 16:331–338
Samuelson PA (1947–1948) Some Implications of Linearity. Review of Economic Studies 15:88–90
Samuelson PA (1950) The Problem of Integrability in Utility Theory. Economica 17:355–385
Samuelson PA (1965) Using Full Duality to Show that Simultaneously Additive Direct and Indirect Utilities implies Unitary Price Elasticity of Demand. Econometrica 33:781–796
Samuelson PA (1969) Corrected Formulation of Direct and Indirect Additivity. Econometrica 37:355–359
Samuelson PA (1974) Complementarity: An Essay on The 40th Anniversary of The Hicks–Allen Revolution in Demand Theory. Journal of Economic Literature 12:1255–1289
Schumpeter JA (1949) Vilfredo Pareto (1848–1923). The Quarterly Journal of Economics 63(2):147–173
Shoven JB, Whalley J (1992) Applying General Equilibrium. Cambridge University Press, Cambridge, UK
Silberberg E, Suen W (2001) The Structure of Economics, A Mathematical Analysis, 3rd edn. McGraw–Hill, Singapore
Slutsky EE (1915) Sulla teoria del bilancio del consumatore. Giornale degli Economisti 51:1–26, translation: "on the theory of the budget of the consumer", In: *AEA series, readings in price theory*, 1953, George Allen and Unwin, London, pp 27–56
Smith A (1776, 1961) The Wealth of Nations I–II. Methuen University Paperbacks, London
Solow RM (2000) Growth Theory: An Exposition, 2nd edn. Oxford University Press, Oxford

Somermeyer WH (1974) Further analysis of cross–country comparison of consumer expenditure patterns–comment. European Economic Review 5:303–306

Somermeyer WH, Langhout A (1972) Shapes of Engel Curves and Demand Curves: Implications of the Expenditure Allocation Model, Applied to Dutch Data. European Economic Review 3:351–386

Stigler GJ (1954) The Early History of Empirical Studies of Consumer Behaviour. Journal of Political Economy 69:95–113

Stiglitz JE (1969) Behavior Towards Risk with Many Commodities. Econometrica 37:660–667

SU Nr 34 (1977) Økonomiske Forhold i Lønmodtagerhusstande: Forbrugsundersøgelsen 1971. Danmarks Statistik, København

Tobin J, Houthakker HS (1950–51) The Effects of Rationing on Demand Elasticities. Review of Economic Studies 18:140–153

Uzawa H (1962) Production Functions with Constant Elasticities of Substitution. Review of Economic Studies 29:291–299

Varian HR (1992) Microeconomic Analysis, 3rd edn. W.W. Norton & Company, New York

Wold H, Jureen L (1953) Demand Analysis. John Wiley & Sons, New York

Yaari ME (1973) A Note on Separability and Quasiconcavity. Econometrica 45:1183–1186

Yoshihara K (1969) Demand Functions: An Application to the Japanese Expenditure Pattern. Econometrica 37:257–274

PART II

# Basic One-Sector Growth Models

CHAPTER 7

# Canonical Classical Growth Models and Homogeneity

## Introduction

In classical economics,[1] growth originated from the *dynamic interaction* between land, labor, and capital—but mostly with land (natural resources) supposed to be available in a fixed nonaugmentable amount. A complete *macrodynamic model* for the *evolution* of the labor force, $L(t)$, and the capital stock, $K(t)$, must now be constructed.

A sufficiently *general* classical dynamic model should, with respect to the *laws* of *production* (technology), impose no further restrictions upon the production function than the conditions (2.1–2.7) and their proper amendments in Chap. 2.

The labor force will be assumed to constitute a *fixed* proportion of the total population, that is, labor market issues such as participation rates and demographic issues such as family size, age composition, etc., are ignored. Hence, the classical "*law* of *population* growth" is below applied directly to the propagation of the labor force. To complete the dynamic model, an *accumulation law* of *capital* must be specified for the *classical growth* models. The *triple* of the laws of production, population, and accumulation is the quintessence of macroeconomic growth models.

## The Dynamic System

On the propagation of the *labor* force, the classicists shared the view that its alterations depended on the *level* of the *real wage* rate $w$. This idea may formally be expressed in various ways. The *proportional* rate of growth of labor is

[1] Samuelson (1978, p. 1415): "A. Smith, Ricardo, Malthus, and Stuart Mill shared in common essentially one dynamic model of equilibrium, growth and distribution - the same canonical model."



B. S. Jensen, *The Elements and Dynamic Systems of Economic Growth and Trade Models*, https://doi.org/10.1007/978-3-031-52493-6_7

supposed to be an *increasing* function of the wage rate, for example, the linear relation,

$$\hat{L} = \dot{L}/L = (dL/dt)/L = nw, \quad n > 0, \tag{7.1}$$

where the *parameter* $n$ is identified as a "natural propensity to proliferate".

On the process of *capital* accumulation, a similar rule operated. The *proportional* rate of growth of the capital stock is supposed to be an *increasing* function of the *real rental* (interest) rate $r$, for example, the linear relation,

$$\hat{K} = \dot{K}/K = (dK/dt)/K = s_K r, \quad 0 < s_K \leq 1, \tag{7.2}$$

where the *parameter* $s_K$ is the "propensity to save" out of total capital income.

**Remark 7.1** A distinctive feature of the classical writers is the ostensible admonition of the existence of some conventional *positive minimal factor rewards* at which, respectively, $\hat{L}$ and $\hat{K}$ have a *zero* value. Hence, (7.1–7.2) would be replaced by the equations:

$$\hat{L} = n(w - w_m), \; w_m > 0, \quad \hat{K} = s_K(r - r_m), \; r_m > 0,$$

where $w_m$ is the *subsistence* (natural) real wage rate, and $r_m$ is the *abstinence* (effective) interest rate for employing capital in production rather than consumption.

At this early stage of our theoretical work, we should avoid complicating our dynamic system with *isolated* critical points in the *interior* domain. The dynamic implications of minimal factor rewards will be explored in Chap. 8. ▽

Regarding the wage and rental rates in (7.1–7.2), they are assumed to be determined in *competitive* factor markets, that is, their market returns are forced to be equal to their marginal factor productivities.

Then, by (2.3) and (7.1–7.2), we obtain the *system* of *homogeneous autonomous nonlinear* differential equations,

$$\dot{L} = n\, MP_L \cdot L = \mathcal{F}(L, K); \quad L, K \geq 0, \tag{7.3.1}$$

$$\dot{K} = s_K\, MP_K \cdot K = \mathcal{G}(L, K); \quad L, K \geq 0, \tag{7.3.2}$$

which, by using (2.14.1–2), are homogeneous of *degree*, $0 < m \leq 1$,

$$\dot{L} = L^m\, n\, [\, m\, f(k) - k\, f'(k)\,] = L^m\, \mathfrak{f}(k), \quad L \neq 0, \tag{7.4.1}$$

$$\dot{K} = L^m\, s_K\, k\, f'(k) = L^m\, \mathfrak{g}(k), \quad L \neq 0. \tag{7.4.2}$$

**Remark 7.2** With decreasing return to scale ($m < 1$), not all income will be distributed by marginal productivities to labor and capital, cf. (2.15.1–2). The *residual*, $R = (1 - m)Y = (1 - m)L^m f(k)$, may be allowed to go to a *fixed* factor, for example, land. Usually, it is tacitly assumed that this residual *(rent)* $R$ is entirely *consumed* by proprietors (landlords), and hence that $R$ has no influence, cf. (7.3.2), upon capital accumulation. Such an assumption may be deemed unsatisfactory. Combining capital income, $\Pi$, and rents, $R$, cf. (2.15.1–2), (7.3.1), (7.4.1),

$$\Pi + R = Y - MP_L \cdot L = L^m[(1-m)f(k) + kf'(k)],$$

the saving/accumulation process, (7.4.2), might be replaced by

$$\dot{K} = L^m s_K[(1-m)f(k) + kf'(k)] = L^m \, \mathfrak{g}(k). \tag{7.5}$$

The *consolidation* of capital and propriety (rent) incomes, however, is not of principal importance for the process of economic growth, as seen in Chap. 9. ▽

## Ratio and Coordinate Solutions

The *growth model* (7.3.1–7.4.2) represents a plane *homogeneous dynamic* system with the *domain* restricted to the first quadrant. The general homogeneous system is studied in Chap. 28, upon which we now draw heavily in our qualitative analysis of the behavior of the *solutions,* $[L(t), K(t)]$, to (7.3.1–7.4.2).

### *Axes Solutions*

For the *solutions* upon the *boundary* of the *domain,* we have:

**Lemma 7.1** *The* solutions, $[L(t), K(t)]$, *to (7.3.1–2)—with* initial values, $(L_0, K_0) = [L(0), K(0)]$ *upon the coordinate* axes—*are* stationary, *viz.,*

$$[K(0), L(0)] = (0,0) \quad \Rightarrow \quad \forall t \quad [L(t), K(t)] \quad = \quad (0,0), \tag{7.6.1}$$

$$L(0) = 0 \quad \Rightarrow \quad \forall t \quad [L(t), K(t)] \quad = \quad [0, K(0)], \tag{7.6.2}$$

$$K(0) = 0 \quad \Rightarrow \quad \forall t \quad [L(t), K(t)] \quad = \quad [L(0), 0]. \tag{7.6.3}$$

***Proof*** Lemma 7.1 is confirmed by (7.3.1–2), (2.15.1–2), and (2.2.1). □

**Remark 7.3** The *critical* points (7.6.1–3) assign every point of the $K$- and $L$-axes as a *trajectory* of (7.3.1–2). Since the system (7.3.1–2) is of $C^1$-class and is autonomous, no trajectories of (7.3.1–2) will intersect each other. Hence, for any initial values in the first quadrant, the *solutions,* $[L(t), K(t)]$ to (7.3.1–2), *cannot* at any time *leave* this quadrant. ▽

### *Directrix Solutions*

To study the behavior of the solutions in the *interior* of the domain, that is, $\mathbf{R}^2_+$, we introduce the *director function,* $h(k)$, for the homogeneous dynamic system

(7.3.1–2). This function $h$ is discussed in Chap. 28, section "Basic Framework, Assumptions, and Definitions", and here it is given as, cf. (7.4.1–2),

$$\begin{aligned} h(k) &= \mathfrak{g}(k) - k\mathfrak{f}(k) \\ &= s_K k f'(k) - nk[mf(k) - kf'(k)] \\ &= k[(s_K + nk)f'(k) - mnf(k)]. \end{aligned} \tag{7.7}$$

The *time derivative,* $\dot{k} = dk/dt$, of the *ratio* variable, $k = K/L,\ L \neq 0$, obeys the equation, cf. Chap. 28, section "Basic Framework, Assumptions, and Definitions" and (7.7),

$$\dot{k} = dk/dt = L^{m-1}h(k), \quad L \neq 0. \tag{7.8}$$

The director function (7.7) with its *director roots* $\mathcal{K}$ and $\complement\mathcal{K}$, defined by

$$\mathcal{K} = \{\kappa \in \mathbf{R}_+ \mid h(\kappa) = 0\}, \quad \complement\mathcal{K} = \{k \in \mathbf{R}_+ \mid h(k) \neq 0\}, \tag{7.9}$$

gives a *partition* of $\mathbf{R}_+ = \mathcal{K} \bigcup \complement\mathcal{K}$. Corresponding to $\mathcal{K}$ and $\complement\mathcal{K}$ of (7.9), we have a complete *decomposition* of the *interior domain,* $L, K > 0$, into *rays (directrices)* and *open cones,* see Chap. 28, section "Basic Framework, Assumptions, and Definitions".

To obtain and better interpret the actual values of the director roots, (7.9), we rewrite the director function (7.7) in more convenient economic terms as, cf. (2.24),

$$\begin{aligned} h(k) &= nkf'(k)\left[\frac{s_K}{n} + k - \frac{mf(k)}{f'(k)}\right] \\ &= nkf'(k)[s_K/n - \omega(k)]. \end{aligned} \tag{7.10}$$

Similarly, in order to properly interpret the *directrix values,* $\mathfrak{f}(\kappa)$, $\kappa \in \mathcal{K}$, (28.24), we rewrite the governing function $\mathfrak{f}(k)$, (7.4.1), as, cf. (2.24)

$$\mathfrak{f}(k) = n[mf(k) - kf'(k)] = nf'(k)\omega(k). \tag{7.11}$$

For the dynamic system (7.3.1–7.4.2), we are now ready to determine the *stationary solutions* of the capital-labor *ratio* $k(t)$ and the associated *coordinate solutions* $[L(t), K(t)]$ with initial values along the directrices.

**Theorem 7.1** *The classical growth model (7.1–7.4.2) has—under the classical regularity conditions (2.60) and* $(s_K/n) \in \Omega$, *(2.28.1–2)—one and only one stationary ratio solution*

$$\forall t,\ k(t) = \kappa = K_0/L_0 = k_0, \quad \kappa = \mathcal{K} \in \mathbf{R}_+, \tag{7.12}$$

*where the positive director root $\kappa$ is uniquely determined by the equation*

$$\omega(\kappa) = s_K/n. \tag{7.13}$$

*The coordinate solutions $[L(t), K(t)]$—with initial values $(L_0, K_0)$ upon the directrix (trajectory), $K = \kappa L$—have the form,*

$$L(t) = [L_0^{1-m} + (1-m)\mathfrak{f}(\kappa)t]^{\frac{1}{1-m}}, \tag{7.14.1}$$

$$K(t) = \kappa L(t), \tag{7.14.2}$$

*with the directrix value $\mathfrak{f}(\kappa)$ given as*

$$\mathfrak{f}(\kappa) = n[mf(\kappa) - \kappa f'(\kappa)] = s_K f'(\kappa). \tag{7.15}$$

***Proof*** For all $k > 0$, it follows from (7.7 to 7.10) that any director root $\kappa$ must solve the Eq. (7.13).

Given $(s_K/n) \in \Omega$, (2.28.1–2), the positivity and monotonicity of $\omega(k)$, cf. (2.24–2.26), ensure the existence and uniqueness of $\kappa$ in (7.13) for all positive values of the parameters, $n$ and $s_K$, cf. (7.1–7.2).

By (7.8), the stationary ratio solution $k(t) = \kappa$, (7.12), follows immediately.

For $0 < m < 1$, the polynomial form of the coordinate solutions (7.14.1–2) is obtained from Theorem 28.2 in section "The Ratio and Coordinate Solutions on Directrices".

The directrix value (7.15) follows from (7.11) and (7.13). □

**Remark 7.4** Although not at all necessary, a *sufficient* condition for $s_K/n \in \Omega$, (2.28.1–2), is that $\omega(k)$, (2.24), has the properties (2.33), since then $\Omega = [0, \infty]$. ▽

### *Non-directrix Solutions*

To obtain the ratio and coordinate solutions to (7.4.1–2) outside the directrix (7.12) and the axes (7.6.1–3), we need to introduce a function $H \in C^2$-class, defined by, cf. (7.10–7.11)

$$\frac{dH}{dk} = H'(k) = \frac{\mathfrak{f}(k)}{h(k)} = \frac{nf'(k)\omega(k)}{nkf'(k)[s_K/n - \omega(k)]} = \frac{\omega(k)}{k[s_K/n - \omega(k)]}$$
$$= \frac{\epsilon_L(k)/\epsilon_K(k)}{s_K/n - \omega(k)}, \quad k \in ]0, \kappa[ \vee ]\kappa, +\infty[. \tag{7.16}$$

**Theorem 7.2** *The growth model (7.1–7.4.2) has—apart from the particular solutions described by* Theorem 7.1 *and* Lemma 7.1*—the family of nonstationary ratio solutions* $k(t)$ *that solves the autonomous differential equation, $Q \in C^1$-class,*

$$\dot{k} = Q(k) = [c_0 \exp\{H(k)\}]^{m-1} h(k), \quad k \in ]0, \kappa[ \vee ]\kappa, +\infty[, \tag{7.17.1}$$

*where the constant* $c_0$ *is*

$$c_0 = L_0 \exp\{-H(k_0)\}, \quad k_0 = K_0/L_0 \in ]0, \kappa[ \vee ]\kappa, +\infty[. \tag{7.17.2}$$

*The general solution to (7.17.1–2) is given the formula,*

$$k(t) = I^{-1}(t + t_0), \quad t + t_0 \in T = ]-\infty, +\infty[, \tag{7.18}$$

*where the invertible function* $I \in C^2$*-class is the primitive*

$$I(k) = \int \frac{dk}{Q(k)} = t + t_0, \; t_0 = I(k_0), \quad k, k_0 \in ]0, \kappa[ \vee ]\kappa, +\infty[. \tag{7.19}$$

*The coordinate solutions, the history, and phase curves are given with* $k(t)$, $c_0$, *from respectively (7.18), (7.17.2), by*

$$L(t) = c_0 \exp\{H[k(t)]\}, \tag{7.20.1}$$

$$K(t) = k(t)L(t). \tag{7.20.2}$$

*The trajectories, as loci, are given by the equation [with* $c_0$ *of (7.17.2)],*

$$l(L, K) = 0 \;\; with \;\; l(L, K) = L \exp\{-H(k)\} - c_0. \tag{7.21}$$

***Proof*** This theorem follows directly from Theorem 28.1 in section "Ratio Solutions, Coordinate Solutions, and Trajectories", (7.8–7.9) and (7.6.1–3). The time interval $T$, (7.18), is infinite, due to $m < 1$, see Chap. 28, section "On Solutions and Their Maximal Time Interval of Existence". □

## Stability of Ratio and Coordinate Solutions

Leaving aside the axes solutions (7.6.1–3), the complete set of solutions to (7.3.1–7.4.2) on the interior domain has the *qualitative* properties stated in the stability theorems below.

**Theorem 7.3** *For any initial values* $k_0 = K_0/L_0 \in ]0, +\infty[$, *the set of ratio solutions* $k(t) = K(t)/L(t)$ *to the growth model (7.3.1–7.4.2) has—under the classical regularity conditions (2.60) and* $(n/s_K) \in \Omega$, *(2.28.1–2)—global asymptotic ratio stability, that is,*

$$\exists k_0 = \kappa > 0 \;\; : \; k(t) = \kappa \quad \forall t, \tag{7.22.1}$$

$$\forall k_0 \in \mathbf{R}_+/\{\kappa\} \; : \; k(t) \to \kappa \;\; as \, t \to \infty. \tag{7.22.2}$$

***Proof*** By definition, global asymptotic stability requires the existence of one and only one *stationary* solution, and that *any* nonstationary solution converges to the stationary one in finite or infinite time.

Here, the existence and uniqueness of the stationary ratio solution (7.22.1) was established in Theorem 7.1. The convergence of all the nonstationary *ratio solutions* (7.22.2)—given by (7.18–7.19) in Theorem 7.2—to the stationary one (7.22.1) in infinite time follows immediately from (7.17.1–2), the director function (7.10), and Theorem 28.4 in section "Global Asymptotic Ratio Stability", since $\omega(k)$ is monotonically increasing, cf. (2.25),

$$h(\kappa) = 0 \quad \Leftrightarrow \quad \exists k = \kappa,\ \omega(\kappa) = s_K/n, \tag{7.23.1}$$

$$h(k) > 0 \quad \Leftrightarrow \quad \forall k < \kappa,\ \omega(k) < s_K/n, \tag{7.23.2}$$

$$h(k) < 0 \quad \Leftrightarrow \quad \forall k > \kappa,\ \omega(k) > s_K/n. \tag{7.23.3}$$

**Theorem 7.4** *For any initial values* $(L_0, K_0) \in \mathbf{R}^2_+$, *the family of nonstationary coordinate solutions,* $[L(t), K(t)]$, *to the growth model, (7.3.1–7.4.2), has—under the classical regularity conditions (2.60) and* $(n/s_K) \in \Omega$, *(2.28.1–2)—strong relative stability, that is, let* $[L(t), K(t)]$ *and* $[L^*(t), K^*(t)]$ *be any pair coordinate solutions to (7.4.1–2), then*

$$\forall (L_0, K_0) \in \mathbf{R}^2_+ \quad : \quad L(t)/L^*(t) \to 1 \ as\ t \to \infty, \tag{7.24.1}$$

$$\forall (L_0, K_0) \in \mathbf{R}^2_+ \quad : \quad K(t)/K^*(t) \to 1 \ as\ t \to \infty. \tag{7.24.2}$$

***Proof*** To establish the global strong relative stability property of *coordinate solutions,* the arbitrary pair of coordinate solutions has in the proof to be properly chosen, viz., $[L^*(t), K^*(t)]$ as a directrix solution (7.14.1–2) and $[L(t), K(t)]$ as a non-directrix solution, given by the general formula (7.20.1–2). Such a pair of coordinate solutions encompasses the whole family of solutions to (7.3.1–7.4.2). The proof of (7.24.1–2) with $\mathfrak{f}(\kappa) > 0$, cf. (7.15), and $0 < m < 1$, cf. (2.60), is provided in Theorem 28.9 in section "Global Asymptotic Ratio Stability and Global Stabilities of Coordinate Solutions". □

## The Geometry of the Phase Portrait

Perhaps at first surprisingly, the *global stability properties* demonstrated in Theorems 7.3–7.4, for the ratio solutions, $k(t)$, and coordinate solutions, $[L(t), K(t)]$ of Theorems 7.1–7.2, do *not* necessarily imply that the *phase portrait*—described by (7.14.1–2), (7.20.1–2), and (7.21)—displays a geometric pattern with the *attractive directrix,* (7.12), (7.14.1–2) as an *asymptote* to the trajectories, (7.20.1–7.21).

The main structures of the trajectory geometry are given by

**Theorem 7.5** *The phase portrait (7.14.1–2), (7.20.1–7.21) of the classical growth model (7.3.1–7.4.2) can be categorized—by* Theorem 7.3, *(7.22.1–2) and the substitution elasticity (2.29)—into three geometric forms, viz.,*

$$\forall k > 0 : \sigma(k) < 1 \Rightarrow \textit{hyperbolic trajectories}, \tag{7.25}$$

$$\forall k > 0 : \sigma(k) > 1 \Rightarrow \textit{parabolic trajectories}, \tag{7.26}$$

$$\forall k > 0 : \sigma(k) = 1 \Rightarrow \textit{linear trajectories}. \tag{7.27}$$

***Proof*** By (7.3.1–7.4.2), we have, cf. (2.24)

$$\frac{dK}{dL} \equiv \frac{\dot{K}}{\dot{L}} \equiv q(k) \equiv \frac{\mathfrak{g}(k)}{\mathfrak{f}(k)} = \frac{s_K}{n} \cdot \frac{k}{\omega(k)} > 0. \tag{7.28}$$

Next, (7.28) gives, cf. (2.29),

$$q'(k) = \frac{s_K}{n} \cdot \frac{1}{\omega(k)} \left[ 1 - \frac{\omega'(k)}{\omega(k)/k} \right] = \frac{s_K}{n} \cdot \frac{1}{\omega(k)} \left[ 1 - \frac{1}{\sigma(k)} \right], \tag{7.29.1}$$

$$\therefore \qquad E(q,k) \equiv \frac{dq}{dk}\frac{k}{q} = 1 - 1/\sigma(k), \tag{7.29.2}$$

$$\forall k > 0 : \quad q'(k) \lesseqqgtr 0 \quad \Leftrightarrow \quad \forall k > 0 : \quad \sigma(k) \lesseqqgtr 1. \tag{7.29.3}$$

Then, (7.28), (7.29.3), and Theorem 28.8 in section "Asymptotic Ratio Stability and Trajectory Geometry" establish (7.25–7.27). □

The phase portrait according to Theorem 7.5 is depicted in Fig. 7.1.

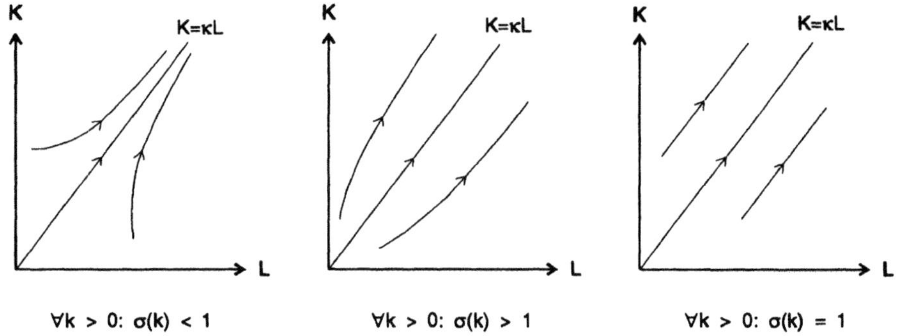


**Fig. 7.1** Phase portrait of the classical growth model, (7.3.1–7.4.2)

## Output, Distribution, and Factor Prices

Equipped with Theorems 7.1–7.4 for the family of *solutions* to (7.4.1–2), we can examine other qualitative properties of the growing economy just by utilizing various implications of the production laws, stated in Chap. 2.

The evolution (time paths, history curves) of *total output* from model (7.4.1–2) is described by, cf. (2.8),

$$Y(t) = [L(t)]^m f[k(t)], \tag{7.30}$$

where the history curves $L(t)$ and $k(t)$ are given by (7.12), (7.14.1), and (7.18), (7.20.1).

Along the *directrix* (7.14.1–2), output (7.30) has the power (polynomial/rational) form,

$$Y(t) = f(\kappa)[L_0^{1-m} + s_K f'(\kappa)(1-m)t]^{\frac{m}{1-m}}. \tag{7.31}$$

For the family of growth paths (7.30)—represented by an arbitrary pair, $Y(t)$ and $Y^*(t)$—it follows immediately from (7.22.1–2), (7.24.1), (7.30) that

$$\forall (L_0, K_0) \in \mathbf{R}_+^2 \quad : \quad Y(t)/Y^*(t) \to 1 \text{ as } t \to \infty. \tag{7.32}$$

Like (7.24.1–2), the global stability property (7.32) implies that although the *difference,* between any two paths, $[Y(t) - Y^*(t)]$, from model (7.4.1–2) will be unbounded as $t \to \infty$, their *relative difference,* $[Y(t) - Y^*(t)]/Y^*(t)$, approaches zero as $t \to \infty$.

In the model (7.4.1–2), the *distribution* of total output between labor and capital will in the *long run* be characterized by *constant factor shares,* since, cf. (2.16.1–3) and (7.22.1–2),

$$\forall k_0 \in \mathbf{R}_+ \quad : \quad \epsilon_L[k(t)] \to \epsilon_L(\kappa) \text{ as } t \to \infty, \tag{7.33.1}$$

$$\forall k_0 \in \mathbf{R}_+ \quad : \quad \epsilon_K[k(t)] \to \epsilon_K(\kappa) \text{ as } t \to \infty. \tag{7.33.2}$$

Thus, the evolution of the factor shares, $\epsilon_L(t)$ and $\epsilon_K(t)$, displays global asymptotic stability. The rent share, $1 - m$, $(m < 1)$, cf. (2.15.1–2.16.3), is obviously invariant through time.

The history curves of the *factor prices,* $w(t)$ and $r(t)$, become, cf. (7.1–7.3.2), (2.14.1–2), and (2.24)

$$w(t) = [L(t)]^{m-1} f'[k(t)]\, \omega[k(t)], \tag{7.34.1}$$

$$r(t) = [L(t)]^{m-1} f'[k(t)]. \tag{7.34.2}$$

Along the *directrix* (7.14.1–2), the evolution of the factor prices (7.34.1–2) have the form, cf. (7.13), (7.15)

$$w(t)/r(t) = s_K/n, \tag{7.35}$$

$$r(t) = \frac{1}{L_0^{1-m}/f'(\kappa) + s_K(1-m)t}, \tag{7.36.1}$$

$$w(t) = \frac{s_K/n}{L_0^{1-m}/f'(\kappa) + s_K(1-m)t}. \tag{7.36.2}$$

Hence, the history curves (7.36.1–2) are rectangular *hyperbolas,* implying that both factor prices steadily decline and approach zero as time goes to infinity.

Although history curves (7.34.1–2), apart from (7.36.1–2), are generally not hyperbolas, the factor prices (7.34.1–2) from the model (7.3.1–7.4.2) do in the long run converge to zero, that is,

$$\forall k_0 \in \mathbf{R}_+ \quad : \quad w(t) \to 0 \text{ as } t \to \infty, \tag{7.37.1}$$

$$\forall k_0 \in \mathbf{R}_+ \quad : \quad r(t) \to 0 \text{ as } t \to \infty, \tag{7.37.2}$$

which follow from pulling together (7.22.1–2), (7.24.1–2), (7.14.1–2), (7.34.1–2), (7.36.1–2).

To also convince ourselves intuitively that the dismal prospects are not intrinsically in conflict with an economy displaying *persistent* and *unbounded growth* of $L(t)$, $K(t)$, and $Y(t)$, we should verify that the *rapidity* (speeds of change) of the various *time paths* (solutions) form a *coherent* pattern, mathematically and economically. Due to the stability properties, (7.22.1–2), (7.24.1–2), we can simply use the *directrix* solutions (7.14.1–2) as a *benchmark* to settle the issue of rapidity coherency.

It is seen from Table 7.1 that *factor growth* (7.14.1–2) always exceeds *linear* growth, and for $m > 1/2$, it will take on *polynomial* growth of high order. The growth of *output* (7.31) is of course due to decreasing returns to scale, slower than factor growth. But output growth is *unbounded,* and for $m > 1/2$, it also expands *polynomially* of some high order.

Since *factor prices* (7.36.1–2) decrease as $t^{-1}$, and the factors of production (7.14.1–2) increase as $t^{\frac{1}{1-m}}$, then total *labor income* and total *capital income*

**Table 7.1** The degree of homogeneity and the rapidity of growth, (7.14.1–2), (7.31)

| $m$ | 0 | 1/10 | 1/5 | 1/4 | 1/3 | 1/2 | 2/3 | 3/4 | 4/5 | 9/10 |
|---|---|---|---|---|---|---|---|---|---|---|
| $1/1-m$ | 1 | 1 1/9 | 1 1/4 | 1 1/3 | 1 1/2 | 2 | 3 | 4 | 5 | 10 |
| $m/1-m$ | 0 | 1/9 | 1/4 | 1/3 | 1/2 | 1 | 2 | 3 | 4 | 9 |

will increase as $t^{-1+\frac{1}{1-m}} = t^{\frac{m}{1-m}}$, that is, evolve with the *same rapidity* as total *output* (7.31). Accordingly, the *factor shares* (7.33.1–2) remain unchanged in the long run.

Thus, the *rapidity* of the evolution of output, labor, capital, factor income, and factor prices display a *coherent* pattern.

Although the prospective real wages (7.37.1–2) of labor looks bleak, the blame cannot be attributed to the *marginal* product remuneration of *labor*, since the time path of the *average* product of labor evolves in the same manner as the marginal product, cf. (7.34.1), (7.24.1), (7.22.1–2), (7.20.1–2), (2.14.1), (2.9). In short, no scheme of income *redistribution* can abolish the consequences of *decreasing returns* to *scale* ($m < 1$) for the expanding economy evolving from the classical growth model (7.1–7.4.2), (2.26).

An escape route by violating (2.26) will be discussed below, cf. section "Linear Isoquants" below.

## CD and CES Technologies

The application of our general Theorems 7.1–7.5 may be illustrated with the specific production functions, (2.48–2.49).

### *CD*

In the Cobb-Douglas (CD) case, we have that, cf. (2.24), (2.48),

$$\omega(k) = \frac{1-a}{a}k. \tag{7.38}$$

By (7.13) and (7.38), the *directrix* and the *director root* are seen here to be

$$K = \kappa L, \quad \kappa = \frac{s_K a}{n(1-a)}, \tag{7.39}$$

and the *directrix value* becomes, cf. (7.15), (2.48), (7.39),

$$\mathfrak{f}(\kappa) = s_K f'(\kappa) = nm\gamma(1-a)\kappa^{am}. \tag{7.40}$$

Hence, all the *directrix solutions* $[L(t), K(t)]$ are given by (7.14.1–2), (7.39–7.40).

Outside the directrix (7.39), we have that, cf. (7.16), (7.38–7.39),

$$H'(k) = \left[\frac{s_K a}{n(1-a)} - k\right]^{-1} = (\kappa - k)^{-1}, \; k \neq \kappa, \tag{7.41}$$

and next, apart from a constant,

$$H(k) = -\ln(\kappa - k), \quad \exp\{H(k)\} = (\kappa - k)^{-1}, \; k \neq \kappa. \tag{7.42}$$

Hence, by (7.17.2), (7.21), (7.42)

$$\begin{aligned} L &= c_0 \exp\{H(k)\} = L_0 \exp\{-H(k_0)\} \exp\{H(k)\} \\ &= L_0 \frac{\kappa - k_0}{\kappa - k}; \quad k_0 \neq \kappa, \; k \neq \kappa, \end{aligned} \tag{7.43}$$

which gives

$$K = L_0(k_0 - \kappa) + \kappa L, \quad k_0 \neq \kappa. \tag{7.44}$$

Thus, with a CD technology, the *trajectories* of all the *non-directrix solutions* (7.20.1–2) are simply *straight lines,* parallel to the directrix (7.39).

To display the *kinematics* (7.18) in terms of elementary functions is not easily accomplished, if possible at all. To see the difficulties, we may look at the constituent elements of the differential equation (7.17.1).

The director function $h(k)$ is here, cf. (7.10), (7.38)

$$\begin{aligned} h(k) &= nk\gamma amk^{am-1}\left[s_K/n - \frac{1-a}{a}k\right] \\ &= nm\gamma(1-a)k^{am}(\kappa - k). \end{aligned} \tag{7.45}$$

The governing function $Q(k)$ of the ratio solutions becomes, cf. (7.17.1–2), (7.42), (7.43), (7.45)

$$\dot{k} = Q(k) = [L_0(\kappa - k_0)]^{m-1} nm\gamma(1-a)k^{am}(\kappa - k)^{2-m}; \quad k, k_0 \neq \kappa. \tag{7.46}$$

To obtain the *ratio solutions* $k(t)$ from (7.46) in closed form, we must first be able to recover in closed form the primitive $I(k)$ defined by, cf. (7.19), (7.46)

$$I(k) = C \int k^{-am}(\kappa - k)^{m-2} dk, \; C = \frac{[L_0(\kappa - k_0)]^{1-m}}{[nm\gamma(1-a)]}, \; k \neq \kappa. \tag{7.47}$$

As far as we know, $I(k)$ cannot be expressed in terms of a finite combination of elementary functions. Furthermore, although the function $I(k)$ is invertible, its inverse $I^{-1}(k)$ may still not have a closed form, even if $I(k)$ might happen to have such form.

Thus, there is little hope for ever seeing the *ratio solutions,* $k(t)$, to (7.46) in closed form, cf. (7.18). The same applies to the non-directrix *coordinate solutions* $[L(t), K(t)]$, cf. (7.20.1–2).

One might perhaps still surmise that the utmost *simplicity* of the *trajectories* in the CD-case could be utilized in deriving somehow the non-directrix solutions $[L(t), K(t)]$ from (7.4.1–2) and (7.44). Then we would have, cf. (7.4.2), (2.48),

$$\begin{aligned}\dot{K} &= L^m s_K k f'(k) = L^m s_K \gamma a m k^{am} \\ &= s_K \gamma a m L^{m(1-a)} K^{am},\end{aligned} \tag{7.48}$$

and from (7.44) and (7.48)

$$\begin{aligned}\dot{K} &= s_K \gamma a m[L_0(\kappa - k_0)/\kappa + (1/\kappa)K]^{m(1-a)} K^{am} \\ &\equiv c_1[c_2 + c_3 K]^{m(1-a)} K^{am}.\end{aligned} \tag{7.49}$$

Again, we know of no method of solving (7.49) in closed form, whenever $c_2 \neq 0$. Thus, the non-directrix *solutions* $[L(t), K(t)]$ along the trajectories (7.44) seemingly resist any attempt of being written as explicit formulas in time.

However, such formulas are of course neither particularly needed, since the *qualitative* properties of the whole family of solutions to (7.49) and (7.46) are described by Theorems 7.3–7.4.

### *CES*

In this case (2.49), we now proceed analogously to (7.38–7.44). Thus, we have, cf. (2.49), (2.24)

$$\omega(k) = \frac{1-a}{a} k^{1+b} = \frac{1-a}{a} k^{1/\sigma}, \qquad k \neq 0, \tag{7.50}$$

where $\sigma = 1/(1+b)$ is the substitution elasticity, cf. (2.29).

Hence, the *directrix* and the *director root* become, cf. (7.13), (7.50),

$$K = \kappa L, \qquad \kappa = \left[\frac{s_K a}{n(1-a)}\right]^{\sigma}, \tag{7.51}$$

and the *directrix value*, cf. (7.15), (2.49), (7.51),

$$\mathfrak{f}(\kappa) = s_K f'(\kappa) = nm\gamma(1-a)[1 - a + a\kappa^{-b}]^{-(\frac{m}{b}+1)} \tag{7.52.1}$$

$$= \gamma mn(1-a)^{-\frac{m\sigma}{1-\sigma}} \left[1 + \left(\frac{a}{1-a}\right)^{\sigma} \left(\frac{s_K}{n}\right)^{\sigma-1}\right]^{-(\frac{m\sigma}{1-\sigma}+1)}. \tag{7.52.2}$$

Thus, the family of *directrix solutions,* $[L(t), K(t)]$, is given by (7.14.1–2) and (7.52.1–2).

Corresponding to (7.41), we now get

$$H'(k) = \frac{\frac{1-a}{a}k^{1/\sigma}}{k[s_K/n - \frac{1-a}{a}k^{1/\sigma}]} = \frac{1}{k[\kappa^{1/\sigma}k^{-1/\sigma} - 1]}, \quad k \neq \kappa. \tag{7.53}$$

The primitive of (7.53) is easily found, see Selby (1973, p. 417),

$$H(k) = \sigma \ln\left[\frac{k^{-1/\sigma}}{\kappa^{1/\sigma}k^{-1/\sigma} - 1}\right] = \ln(\kappa^{1/\sigma} - k^{1/\sigma})^{-\sigma}, \tag{7.54}$$

and so analogously to (7.43), we get from (7.54)

$$L = L_0\left[\frac{\kappa^{1/\sigma} - k_0^{1/\sigma}}{\kappa^{1/\sigma} - k^{1/\sigma}}\right]^{\sigma}; \; k_0 \neq \kappa, \; k \neq \kappa, \tag{7.55}$$

which gives,

$$K = [L_0(k_0^{1/\sigma} - \kappa^{1/\sigma}) + (\kappa L)^{1/\sigma}]^{\sigma}; \quad k_0 = K_0/L_0 \neq \kappa. \tag{7.56}$$

Thus, with a constant elasticity of substitution (CES) technology, the *trajectories* of all the *non-directrix* solutions (7.20.1–2) have the geometric form (7.56), which represents graphs of monotonic functions being *convex* or *concave*.

The latter can be verified by deriving $d^2K/dL^2$, viz,

$$\frac{d^2K}{dL^2} = K^{1/\sigma}L_0(\frac{1}{\sigma} - 1)(k_0^{1/\sigma} - \kappa^{1/\sigma})[L_0(k_0^{1/\sigma} - \kappa^{1/\sigma}) + (\kappa L)^{1/\sigma}]^{\sigma-2}L^{1/\sigma-2}. \tag{7.57}$$

Since only the third and the fourth term in (7.57) affect the sign, we have:

$$0 < \sigma < 1, \;\; \forall k_0 \lesseqgtr \kappa \Rightarrow d^2K/dL^2 \lesseqgtr 0, \tag{7.58.1}$$

$$1 < \sigma < \infty, \forall k_0 \lesseqgtr \kappa \Rightarrow d^2K/dL^2 \gtreqless 0. \tag{7.58.2}$$

The *phase portraits* of (7.3.1–7.4.2) with the special CD and the CES technologies, cf. (7.44), (7.56), are shown in Fig. 7.2—which is accordance with the *general* result (including variable elasticity of substitution (VES) technologies) in Theorem 7.5.

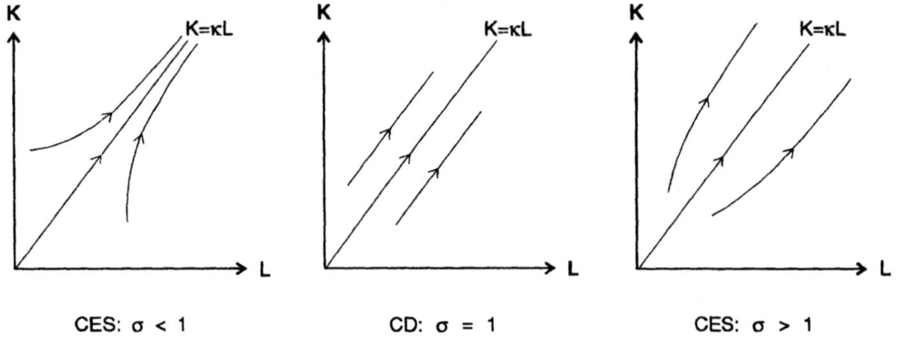


**Fig. 7.2** The trajectory systems (7.56), (7.44)

### *Linear Isoquants*

An *extreme* case of the CES technology occurs with $b = -1$, $(\sigma = \infty)$, implying *linear isoquants*. Such technology is not admitted by Theorems 7.1–7.5, since it *violates* the *classical regularity* condition (2.60), cf. (2.26). It will be instructive briefly to consider the implications of linear isoquants for the growth model (7.3.1–7.4.2).

With $b = -1$, we get from (7.50) and (7.53),

$$\forall k \quad \omega(k) = (1-a)/a, \tag{7.59}$$

$$H'(k) = \left[\left(\frac{s_K}{n}\frac{a}{1-a} - 1\right)k\right]^{-1} \equiv [(\beta - 1)k]^{-1},\ \beta > 0,\ \beta \neq 1, \tag{7.60}$$

$$H(k) = \ln k^{\frac{1}{\beta-1}}, \quad \exp\{H(k)\} = k^{\frac{1}{\beta-1}},\ \beta \neq 1, \tag{7.61}$$

where

$$s_K/n \gtrless (1-a)/a \quad \Leftrightarrow \quad \beta \gtrless 1. \tag{7.62}$$

Then we obtain from (7.61) and (7.43), $L = L_0(k_0/k)^{\frac{1}{1-\beta}}$, which gives

$$K = (K_0/L_0^{\beta})L^{\beta}, \quad (L_0, K_0) \in \mathbf{R}_+^2. \tag{7.63}$$

Thus, with linear isoquants ($b = -1$), the *trajectories* (7.63) of *all* the *solutions* to (7.4.1–2) are, depending on the inequalities (7.62), either *convex* or *concave* curves, which at infinity are parallel to, respectively, the $K$, $L$-axis.

The director function $h(k)$ is here, cf. (2.49), (7.10), (7.59–7.60)

$$\begin{aligned} h(k) &= nk\gamma am(1-a+ak)^{m-1}[s_K/n-(1-a)/a] \\ &= nm\gamma(1-a)k(1-a+ak)^{m-1}(\beta-1), \quad k>0. \end{aligned} \tag{7.64}$$

Whenever (7.62) applies ($\beta \neq 1$), there is of course *no positive* director *root* $\kappa$ of $h(k) = 0$, cf. (7.64), and so obviously no directrix (ray trajectory) exists.

**Remark 7.5** With $s_K/n = (1-a)/a$, that is, $\beta = 1$, there is an *infinite* number of *positive* roots to (7.64), that is, $\mathcal{K} = \mathbf{R}_+^2$, cf. (7.9), and the phase portrait consists entirely of rays (a *star* in $\mathbf{R}_+^2$), cf. (7.8). So, (7.63) may formally be extended to $\beta = 1$ as $K = k_0 L,\ k_0 \in \mathbf{R}_+$. Along all these star rays, it is easily verified from (7.4.1–2) that $L(t)$ and $K(t)$ evolve polynomially as $t^{\frac{1}{1-m}}$. ▽

With $b = -1,\ \beta \neq 1$, the governing function $Q(k)$ of ratio solutions becomes, cf. (7.17.1–2), (7.61), (7.64),

$$\dot{k} = Q(k) = [L_0 k_0^{\frac{1}{1-\beta}}]^{m-1} k^{\frac{m-1}{\beta-1}} nm\gamma(1-a)k(1-a+ak)^{m-1}(\beta-1). \tag{7.65}$$

**Lemma 7.2** *The qualitative properties of the family of ratio solutions to (7.65), represented by the arbitrary pair, $k(t),\ k^*(t)$, are given by,*

$$\forall k_0 \in \mathbf{R}_+,\ \beta < 1 \quad : \quad k(t) \to 0 \text{ as } t \to \infty, \tag{7.66}$$

$$\forall k_0 \in \mathbf{R}_+,\ \beta > 1 \quad : \quad k(t) - k^*(t) \to \infty \text{ as } t \to \infty, \tag{7.67}$$

$$\forall k_0 \in \mathbf{R}_+,\ \beta > 1 \quad : \quad k(t)/k^*(t) \to 1 \text{ as } t \to \infty. \tag{7.68}$$

***Proof*** For $\beta \lesseqgtr 1$, it is seen from (7.65) that $Q(k) \lesseqgtr 0,\ \forall k \in \mathbf{R}_+$. Hence, (7.66) follows immediately, and (7.67) is due to $Q(k)$ being unbounded for $\beta > 1$. The *strong relative* stability of the family of ratio solutions (7.68) follows from the property, $Q(k)/k \to 0$ as $k \to \infty$, cf. (7.65), $\beta > 1,\ m < 1$. The latter implies (7.68), see Theorem 28.5 in section "Global Asymptotic Ratio Stability.1". □

From the CES exercise with $b = -1$, (7.59–7.68), we should recognize the crucial importance of *diminishing* marginal rates of substitution (MRS) (2.25) for the very *existence* of a unique directrix (7.12–7.13) in the dynamic model (7.4.1–2); furthermore, diminishing MRS then *ensured* the *asymptotic stability* of *ratio* solutions $k(t)$, cf. (7.22.1–7.23.3). The latter was, in turn, a prerequisite to *establishing* (for $m < 1$) the *strong relative* stability of the *coordinate* solutions, $[L(t), K(t)]$, (7.24.1–2).

Thus, although the right-hand side of (2.26) has little intuitive merit, the dynamic significance of diminishing MRS (left-hand side) for the growth model (7.4.1–2) is not intuitively surprising. In short, with $0 < m < 1$,

Theorems 7.1–7.5 essentially hinge on diminishing MRS, as distinct from diminishing marginal productivity, cf. Remark 2.2.

## Constant Returns to Scale

Within the model (7.3.1–7.4.2), the culprit of the dismal prospects for the standard of living, cf. (7.37.1–2), is land scarcity, with its grim implication of decreasing returns to scale ($m < 1$) in the growing economy.

We shall now let the model (7.3.1–7.4.2) operate under technological conditions of constant return to scale. The solutions of this *extended* growth model ($m = 1$)—retaining the *classical* assumption of *endogenous* factor supply of both labor and capital—will later on be compared with the solutions of modern (neoclassical) growth models.

The modifications of Theorems 7.1–7.5 to $m = 1$ in (7.4.1–2) are briefly stated.

**Proposition 7.1** Theorems 7.1–7.3 *and* 7.5 *are unchanged with* $m = 1$, *except for the directrix solutions (7.14.1–2), (7.15) now becoming*

$$L(t) = L_0 \exp\{\mathfrak{f}(\kappa)t\}, \quad K(t) = \kappa L(t), \tag{7.69.1}$$

$$\mathfrak{f}(\kappa) = nMP_L(\kappa) = s_K MP_K(\kappa), \tag{7.69.2}$$

*and the differential equation (7.17.1–2) being reduced to*

$$\dot{k} = Q(k) = h(k) = k[s_K MP_K(k) - nMP_L(k)]. \tag{7.70}$$

***Proof*** The exponential form (7.69.1) of the directrix solutions follows from Theorem 28.2 in section "The Ratio and Coordinate Solutions on Directrices", and now $m = 1$ permits the marginal product expressions (7.69.2), cf. (7.13), (7.15), (7.11), (2.14.1–2).

Although the actual values of the director root, $\kappa$, (7.13), and the directrix value $\mathfrak{f}(\kappa)$, (7.15), may be affected by the value of $0 < m \leq 1$, the proofs of Theorems 7.1–7.3 and 7.5 were unaffected by the actual degree of homogeneity. This establishes Proposition 7.1. □

The stability properties of Theorem 7.4, however, are now replaced by

**Proposition 7.2** *For any initial values* $(L_0, K_0) \in \mathbf{R}^2_+$, *the family of non-stationary coordinate solutions,* $[L(t), K(t)]$, *to the growth model (7.3.1–7.4.2) has—under the conditions,* $m = 1$, *(2.12), and* $(n/s_K) \in \Omega$, *(2.28.1–2)—weak relative stability, that is, let* $[L(t), K(t)]$ *and* $[L^*(t), K^*(t)]$ *be any pair of coordinate solutions to (7.4.1–2), then*

$$\forall (L_0, K_0) \in \mathbf{R}^2_+ \quad : \quad L(t)/L^*(t) \ \text{are bounded as } t \to \infty, \tag{7.71.1}$$

$$\forall (L_0, K_0) \in \mathbf{R}^2_+ \quad : \quad K(t)/K^*(t) \text{ are bounded as } t \to \infty. \tag{7.71.2}$$

***Proof*** With $m = 1$, (2.26) is implied by (2.12). The stability properties (7.71.1–2) follows from Theorem 28.10 in section "Global Asymptotic Ratio Stability and Global Stabilities of Coordinate Solutions". □

Other economic aspects of the growth model (7.4.1–2) with $m = 1$ are immediately obtained from Propositions 7.1–7.2.

**Proposition 7.3** *The family of time paths for output—implied by (7.4.1–2), $m = 1$, and* Propositions 7.1–7.2*—has global weak relative stability, that is,*

$$\forall (L_0, K_0) \in \mathbf{R}^2_+ : Y(t)/Y^*(t) \text{ are bounded as } t \to \infty. \tag{7.72}$$

*The families of time paths for factor shares and factor prices—implied by (7.4.1–2), $m = 1$, and* Propositions 7.1–7.2*—have global asymptotic stability toward unique positive values, that is,*

$$\forall\, k_0 \in \mathbf{R}_+ \quad : \quad \epsilon_L[k(t)] \to \epsilon_L(\kappa) \text{ as } t \to \infty, \tag{7.73.1}$$

$$\forall\, k_0 \in \mathbf{R}_+ \quad : \quad \epsilon_K[k(t)] \to \epsilon_K(\kappa) \text{ as } t \to \infty, \tag{7.73.2}$$

$$\forall\, k_0 \in \mathbf{R}_+ \quad : \quad w[k(t)] \to MP_L(\kappa) = (s_K/n) f'(\kappa) \text{ as } t \to \infty, \tag{7.74.1}$$

$$\forall\, k_0 \in \mathbf{R}_+ \quad : \quad r[k(t)] \to MP_K(\kappa) = f'(\kappa) \text{ as } t \to \infty. \tag{7.74.2}$$

***Proof*** Property (7.72) follows from (7.30) with $m = 1$ and (7.71.1).
Properties (7.73.1–2) are due to (7.22.1–2), cf. (7.33.1–2).
Properties (7.74.1–2) follow from (7.34.1–2) with $m = 1$ and (7.13). □

**Proposition 7.4** *The phase portraits of (7.3.1–7.4.2) are in case of CD and CES technologies with $0 < m \leq 1$, exactly as given, respectively, in (7.39), (7.44) and (7.51), (7.56).*

***Proof*** For the CD and CES technologies, the degree of homogeneity $m$ is not actually involved the MRS expressions, cf. (7.38), (7.50), and hence neither in $H'(k)$, cf. (7.16), (7.41), (7.53). □

Despite (7.70), the *kinematics* of the non-directrix solutions, $[L(t), K(t)]$, *cannot,* either for CD and CES technologies with $m = 1$, be written in *closed* form, cf. (7.46), (7.49).

However, Propositions 7.1–7.4 suffice for describing the *qualitative* properties of the solutions to (7.4.1–2) with $m = 1$. In particular, $m = 1$ *abolished* the "dismal dynamics", cf. (7.37.1–2) and (7.74.1–2), and, moreover, *raised* the *rapidity* of evolution from *polynomial* growth to *exponential* growth, cf. (7.14.1–2) and (7.69.1–2), and, thereby, *lowered* the kinematic *stability* properties of the *coordinate (state) solutions* from *strong* relative to *weak* relative, cf. (7.24.1–2) and (7.71.1–2).

## Directrix Solutions, Steady States, and Constant Ratios

Our stability theorems and propositions and the three geometric configurations of the phase portrait in Figs. 7.1 and 7.2 instigate us to review the notion of *steady-state growth* that has been a key concept in modern growth theory.

Let us quote extensively from the monumental survey by Hahn and Matthews (1964, p. 3):

> The concept in growth theory that is the counterpart of long-period equilibrium in static theory is *steady-state growth*. In steady-state growth (steady-state for short) the rate of growth of all the relevant variables remains constant over time (here and generally, unless otherwise stated, the rate of growth should be taken to mean the proportional rate of growth).- - -
> It is necessary to bear firmly in mind the distinction between the following questions that may be asked about the steady-state properties of any given model:
>
> (1) Is a steady-state solution possible? In other words, given that the structure of the model, its parameters, etc., do not change, is there any set of economically meaningful values of the relevant variables that will permit the system to grow along a steady-state path without any tendency to diverge from it. This is the question of *existence*.
> (2) Assuming that a steady-state solution does exist, what are its properties? What must the value of the variables be if steady-state equilibrium is to be achieved, and how are the values affected by the values of the parameters? (For example, how is the level of the capital output ratio required for steady-state growth affected by the rate of population growth?) These are questions of *comparative dynamics,* similar to the questions of comparative statics in static equilibrium theory. - - -
> (3) Does the system tend towards the steady-state path if it is initially off it? This is the question of *stability*. - - -
> One sense in which a steady-state growth path may be said to be stable is that, when the system is initially off it, the ensuing equilibrium path tends to return to it (p. 4); - - -
> The stability of the steady-state solution means that the system will *in the long run* tend approach the steady-state path and to revert to it after any disturbance (p. 32); - - -
> A path is said to be *relatively stable* if the difference between any actual *ratio* of two variables and the ratio in the given path approaches zero as time approaches infinity (p. 27).

On the basic issues, we may also read from Stiglitz and Uzawa (1969, p. 6):

> In a sense, steady-states are the generalization to economics with growing population of the equilibrium analysis of stationary states. In a steady-state, output, population, capital stock, consumption, and investment are all growing exponentially, while the capital-output ratio, interest rate, and consumption-investment ratio are constant. Because the proportions in which the different commodities are produced are constant (the consumption-investment goods ratio), steady-states are often referred to as *balanced growth paths.*

From these quotations—which should represent the prevalent perceptions in the literature of economic growth theory—it appears that the *attributes* of *steady-state growth* paths are:

(i) the *preservation* over time of *constant ratios* among relevant variables.
(ii) *constant proportional* (exponential) *growth* of the relevant variables (coordinate solutions).

Obviously, if the relevant state variables grow at the same exponential rate, then their ratios remain constant. But, conversely, will the stipulation of a constant ratio imply a constant proportional growth of two state variables? Clearly, the answer will be negative, as is seen from,

$$[\forall t: \quad K(t)/L(t) \equiv k(t) = \kappa] \quad \Leftrightarrow \quad [\forall t: \quad \dot{K}(t)/K(t) = \dot{L}(t)/L(t)], \tag{7.75}$$

that is, the preservation of a *constant* ratio $\kappa$ is only equivalent to a *common proportional* growth rate, *not* necessarily a *constant* (exponential) one. The proportional growth rate may increase or decrease through time and still satisfy (7.75). In fact, illustration of such situations has already been given, cf. (7.12–7.15), where, notwithstanding a constant ratio, the common proportional growth rate—due to the polynomial growth of $K(t)$ and $L(t)$—always declines and converges to zero as $t \to \infty$. Indeed, *any common speed* of growth (cf. Chap. 1, section "Rapidity of Growth") of the variables $L$ and $K$ conforms with (7.75).

Therefore, preservation of *ratios* and the *rapidity* of motion should *not* be *confounded,* as is usually done, by the standard concept/definition of *steady-state paths.* Accordingly, the question of *existence* of the latter, cf. the quotation above, should only refer to the possible existence of *ray trajectories* (*maintaining* a *constant ratio* between the *coordinate solutions*), which we have called *directrices.* Under appropriate conditions, there may be only *one* directrix, for example, in homogeneous dynamics, as we have seen when the *director function* has only *one* (director) root, cf. (7.7), (7.9), (7.12–7.13).

Naturally much attention will be bestowed upon a *unique directrix,* since if also *attractive,* it may be expected (like any other *global attractive singularity,*, e.g., a stationary state, a limit cycle) to provide insight into the *long-run* properties of the solutions emanating from initial values *off* the directrix.

Next, the matter at issue for growth models is then the proper interpretation of the inherent stability properties of the dynamic systems. Economic growth theory has suffered from terminological ambiguity and misinterpretation of various stability notions. Of course, one should not quarrel about semantics, but what in the quotation above (Hahn and Matthews 1964, p. 27) was called *"relative stability"* corresponds in mathematical terms to the property of *asymptotic ratio stability* (ratio differences converging to zero as $t \to \infty$, and the existence of a unique stationary ratio solution), cf. (7.22.1–2).

The quotations on stability also show that *"relative" (asymptotic ratio)* stability of the dynamic system is somehow interpreted to mean that all the nonsteady-state paths will in the long run *return to* (approach) the steady-state path (directrix), that is, the *distance* from the steady-state path to a point on a nonsteady-state path approaches zero as $t \to \infty$, that is, the nonsteady-state path is supposed *geometrically* to have the *steady-state path* (ray, directrix) as an *asymptote*.

But such *hyperbolic configuration* of phase portrait is *not* an imperative consequence of the *asymptotic ratio* stability of a dynamic system—as Theorem 7.5 and Figs. 7.1 and 7.2 demonstrated, where the *parallel* and *parabolic* phase curves were also consonant with asymptotic ratio stability. This is very important from an economic point of view. It means that economies can over time *restore* ratios and proportions among its variables *without* being forced—by the dynamic process in the transition period—to exhibit undue *conformity* in their observed pattern of evolution (phase portraits).

Maybe the intuitive association with the *global stability* of a *stationary state* or of a *limit cycle* and possibly the association with the so-called *long-period equilibrium* concept (a formal analytical device treating all variables as *endogenously* determined in the long run) in static theory have lead to the prevalent misinterpretation in the economic growth literature (cf. the quotations above), that the global "relative" (asymptotic ratio) stability property is tantamount to the convergence ("return") of all the nonsteady-state paths toward a unique steady-state path (directrix). These misleading analogies, of stability of *closed trajectory attractors* (stationary state, limit cycles) and to analytical concepts in *static* theory, have in *growth* theory blurred and distorted the true nature of the stability and the phase portraits of *open trajectory attractors* (steady-state paths, directrices).

Incidentally, it may be noted that the classical economists in their theories on the long-period movements of population and accumulation had no perception of *steady-state* (exponential, balanced) growth paths for labor, capital, and output, because with their outlook (decreasing returns to scale in agriculture), the emergence or, at least, the more or less distant possibility of the *stationary state* obviously captured their main attention, cf. Chap. 8.

By the economic-analytical conception of a *"uniformly progressive economy"*, Cassel (1925, p. 28) and Cassel (1934, p. 29) introduced into economic theory the notion of steady-state (exponential, balanced) growth. However, Cassel's framework was still "quasi-static" economic analysis without connection to the actual behavior (*solutions*) of specified *dynamic systems* (differential/ difference equations).

First, von Neumann (1945–46) and then Solow and Samuelson (1953) demonstrated—for some *special homogeneous* dynamic systems of *degree one*—the existence, the uniqueness, and stability of steady-state (exponential, balanced) growth paths. Also with regard to families of the individual *coordinate* solutions, the concept of *relative* stability (essentially our *weak relative* stability criterion) was introduced in (Solow and Samuelson 1953, p. 419). But, their dynamic systems had homogeneous governing functions that were assumed to be *strictly* monotonically increasing in *every* argument, that is, their governing functions had *positive partial derivatives* everywhere, cf. Solow and Samuelson (1953, p. 413,422). For $m = 1$, a positive sign for these partial derivatives does *not* hold *generally* for the governing functions $\mathcal{F}, \mathcal{G}$, (7.3.1–2), and neither for the governing function $\mathcal{F}, \mathcal{G}$, (11.1.1–2) below, cf. Solow (1956, p. 72). Therefore, as a background and a prerequisite for a unified treatment and systematic discussion of the growth models in Parts 2–4, it was necessary to investigate general properties of plane homogeneous dynamic systems, where the *governing functions* were *homogeneous* of *arbitrary* degree and only restricted by belonging to the $C^1$-*class*, see Chap. 28, section "Basic Framework, Assumptions, and Definitions".

Methodologically, questions of *comparative dynamics*, cf. quotation above, deal in our terminology with the examination of alternative *directrix solutions* through essentially a *comparison* of their *director roots* ($\kappa$) and *directrix values*, $f(\kappa)$, and their *explanation* in terms of underlying *economic* and *technological* parameters. We shall now perform such analysis for the classical growth model (7.1–7.4.2).

## Classical Comparative Dynamics

The wide differences, as observed both across countries and over time, in the *levels* of per capita income and the *rates* of *growth* of national income, are truly astounding; see Barro (1991), Kuznets (1966), Lucas (1988). The ability to explain such *sustained dissimilarity* (rather than convergence to a sort of common economic growth performance) has long been regarded as a serious challenge to mathematical growth models. Of course, one-sector growth models without technical progress will not be supposed to account for much of the empirical diversity in growth performance. Nevertheless, the classical growth model (7.1–7.4.2)—with entirely endogenous factor growth and allowing for considerable quantitative variety of the production functions—is *versatile* enough to able to account for considerable long-term disparity in the *levels* and *rates* of growth of relevant economic variables.

With asymptotic ratio stability, our *formulas* of the *director roots* and the *directrix values* furnish the clues to identifying and appraising *quantitatively* some *determinants* of the *long-term disparity* in economic evolution.

### *Accumulation and Propagation Parameters*

As to the long-run implications of different magnitudes of the parameters $s_K$ and $n$, we always have within the model (7.3.1–7.4.2) that:

$$\text{larger } s_K \rightarrow \text{ larger } \kappa \wedge \text{larger } \mathfrak{f}(\kappa), \tag{7.76}$$

$$\text{larger } n \rightarrow \text{ smaller } \kappa \wedge \text{larger } \mathfrak{f}(\kappa). \tag{7.77}$$

The verification of (7.76–7.77) is obtained directly from (7.13), (2.25) and (7.15), (2.12), (2.14.1–2), (2.18).

For the family of the *directrix solutions*, we immediately have from (7.14.1–2) and (7.69.1–2),

$$0 < m < 1: \quad \dot{L}(t)/L(t) = \dot{K}(t)/K(t) = 1/[(L_0^{1-m}/\mathfrak{f}(\kappa)) + (1-m)t], \tag{7.78}$$

$$m = 1: \quad \dot{L}(t)/L(t) = \dot{K}(t)/K(t) = \mathfrak{f}(\kappa). \tag{7.79}$$

Although economic *growth* is generally considered to be the *increase* in the *output* of the economy over time, there is in economics a long tradition of regarding the *logarithmic* time *derivative* as the standard *representation* of the *rates* of growth. Obviously, this representation has the convenience of being unaffected by units of measurements and, of course, is the relevant growth representation for exponential time paths. But for other time paths, we have elsewhere and in Chap. 1 offered more *refined* distinctions (and a terminology) for the rapidity (speeds) of growth, and we shall not pursue this matter further here. Only we want to emphasize that a faster *polynomial* growth in (7.14.1–2), due to a larger directrix value $\mathfrak{f}(\kappa)$, and also represented by a larger logarithmic derivative in (7.78), should inherently be recognized as an *increase* in the long-run *rate* of *growth* (*rapidity* of evolution)—despite the formal convergence to zero of the RHS expression in (7.78) as time goes to infinity.

Thus, whether $0 < m < 1$ or $m = 1$, we are entitled in (7.3.1–7.4.2) to uphold the claim of the classical writers that *generally* a larger *saving rate*, $s_K$, does imply a *larger* long-run *growth rate* of the economy, cf. (7.76), (7.78–7.79).

Let us, in the midst of mathematical arguments, listen to the virtues and benefits of saving/accumulation (Smith 1776, 1961, p. 358,362,367):

> "Capitals are increased by parsimony and diminished by prodigality and misconduct". - - - "Every prodigal appears to be a public enemy, and every frugal man a public benefactor". - - - "But though the profusion of government must, undoubtedly, have retarded the natural progress of England towards wealth and improvement, it has not been able to stop it". - - - "In the midst of all the exactions of government, this capital has been silently and gradually accumulated by the private frugality and good conduct of individuals". - - - "It is this effort - which has maintained the progress of England towards opulence and improvements in almost all former times, and which, it is to be hoped, will do so in all future times".

The crucial role played by the propensity to save ($s_K$) for the *rapidity* of evolution in Adam Smith's system is broadly accepted.

A corresponding role for propensity to proliferate ($n$) is not usually acknowledged. However, (7.77–7.79) similarly show that in the dynamic system (7.3.1–7.4.2), the overall *rapidity* of evolution for the state variables is increased by a higher proliferation rate ($n$).

But in both cases and particularly with $m = 1$, the gain in overall rapidity is accompanied in the long run by a *lower (higher)* factor *remuneration* of the *factor,* whose *supply parameter* has (has not) increased, cf. (7.76–7.77) and (7.69.2), (2.14.1–2), (2.12). Thus, for the *labor* population and so for the *general public,* the faster economic evolution afforded by (7.76) is preferable to that of (7.77).

Let us again listen to some passages from the *Wealth of Nations* (Smith 1776, 1961, p. 90–91)::

> "The liberal reward of labour, therefore, as it is the effect of increasing wealth, so it is the cause of increasing population. To complain of it, is to lament over the necessary effect and cause of greatest public prosperity. It deserves to be remarked, perhaps, that it is the progressive state, while the society is advancing to the further acquisition, rather than when it has acquired its full complement of riches, that the condition of the labouring poor, of the great body of the people, seems to be the happiest and the most comfortable. It is hard in the stationary, and miserably in the declining state. The progressive state is in reality the cheerful and the hearty state to all the different orders of the society. The stationary is dull; the declining melancholy". - - - "What takes place among labourers in a particular workhouse, takes place, for the same reasons, among those of a great society. The greater their number, the more they naturally divide themselves into different classes and subdivisions of employment. More heads are occupied in inventing the most proper machinery for executing the work of each, and it is, more likely to be invented (Smith 1776, 1961, p. 97)". - - - "As riches, improvement, and population have increased, interest has declined. The wages of labour do not sink with the profits of stock. The demand for labour increases with the increase of stock whatever be its profits; and after these are diminished, stock may not only continue to increase, but to increase much faster than before. It is with industrious nations who are advancing in the acquisition of riches, as with industrious individuals. A great stock, though with small profits, generally increases faster than a small stock with great profits". (Smith 1776, 1961, p.104).

This impressive comparative analysis of the growing (progressive) economy, with a larger long-run capital-labor ratio (increasing wealth, further acquisition), gives the finishing touch to (7.76).

### *Technology Parameters*

In as much as the dynamic system (7.3.1–7.4.2) is founded upon very general technology assumptions, it offers rich opportunities for comparative analysis of the long-term economic disparities that arise from a host of alternative production functions. For each such function, one can derive the director root and directrix value associated with (7.3.1–7.4.2).

In the CD and CES cases they were shown in (7.39–7.40) and (7.51–7.52.2), and they will now be used to illustrate the long-term implications of some technology parameters.

Regarding the *scale parameter*, $0 < m \leq 1$, it is clear from (7.39–7.40) and (7.51–7.52.2) that

$$\text{CD and CES:} \quad \text{larger } m \;\rightarrow\; \text{same } \kappa \;\wedge\; \text{larger } \mathfrak{f}(\kappa). \tag{7.80}$$

As to the *intensity* (distribution) *parameter*, $0 < a < 1$, we have that

$$\text{CD and CES}: \quad \text{larger } a \;\rightarrow\; \text{larger } \kappa, \tag{7.81}$$

$$\text{CD}: \quad \text{larger } a \;\rightarrow\; \text{larger } \mathfrak{f}(\kappa), \;\text{ if } \ln\kappa > \frac{1-m}{m(1-a)}. \tag{7.82}$$

The latter follows by partial derivation of (7.40), viz,

$$\frac{\partial \mathfrak{f}(\kappa)}{\partial a} = nm\gamma\kappa^{am}[-1 + m + m(1-a)\ln\kappa]. \tag{7.83}$$

Simple criteria for the sign of the partial derivative, $\partial\mathfrak{f}(\kappa)/\partial a$, of (7.52.1–2) are more difficult to establish. However, for the CES technology, we usually see with larger $a$ also larger directrix values.

For the *substitution parameter*, $0 < \sigma < \infty$, we get from (7.51) that

$$CES: \; \text{larger } \sigma \;\rightarrow\; \text{larger } \kappa. \tag{7.84}$$

Also larger directrix values normally follow from larger $\sigma$.

Numerical illustrations of the influence of the *accumulation*, *propagation*, and *technology* parameters upon the *director roots* and the *directrix values* are shown in Fig. 7.3. They are all based upon CES technologies and calculated from (7.51–7.52.2) with parameters listed in Table 7.2.
Since most of the illustrations are given for $m = 1$, the *directrix values* illustrate the comparative values of (7.79).

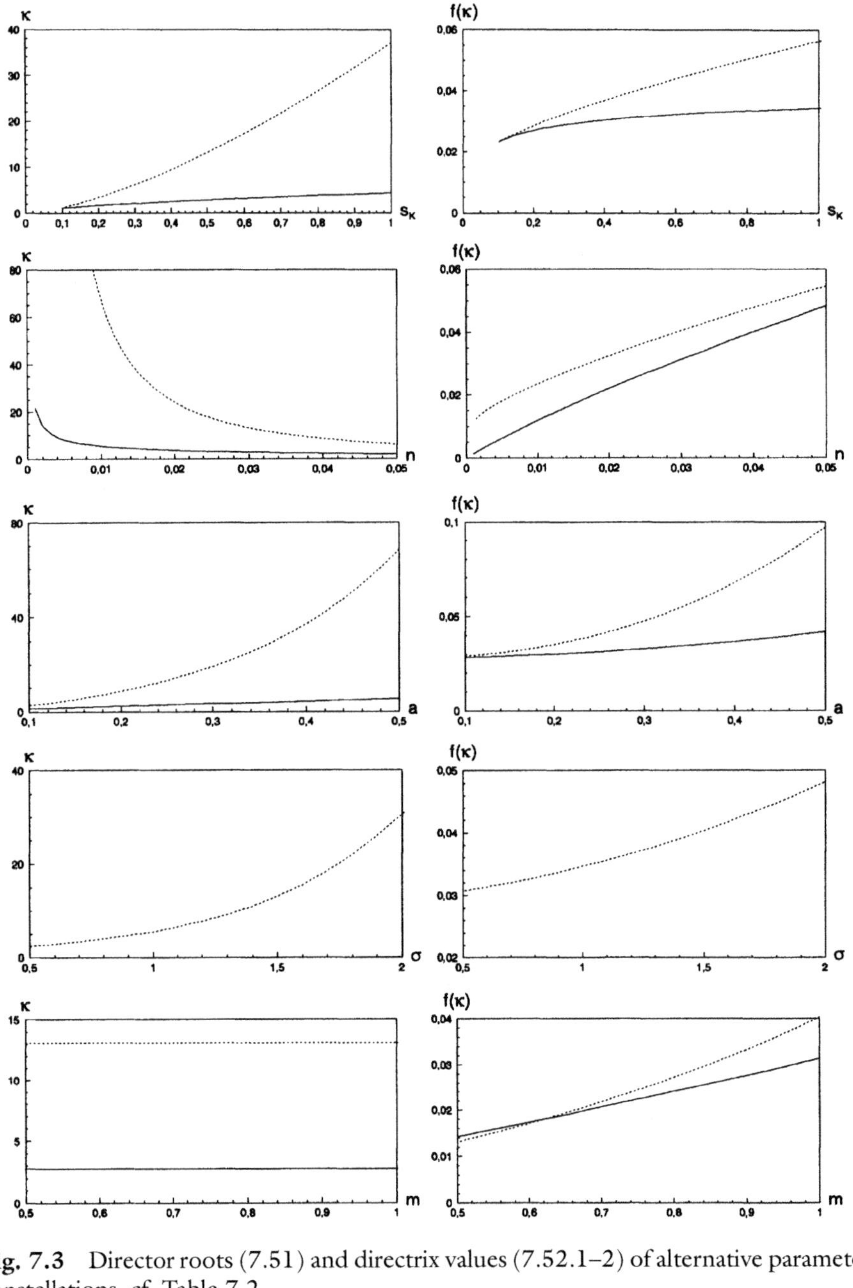


**Fig. 7.3** Director roots (7.51) and directrix values (7.52.1–2) of alternative parameter constellations, cf. Table 7.2

**Table 7.2** Parameter constellations for partial variation and range in Fig. 7.3

| Solid line | Dashed line | Range of parameters |
|---|---|---|
| $s_K = 0.50$ | $s_K = 0.50$ | $s_K$ : 0.10 – 1.00 |
| $n = 0.03$ | $n = 0.03$ | $n$ : 0.01 – 0.05 |
| $a = 0.25$ | $a = 0.25$ | $a$ : 0.10 – 0.50 |
| $\sigma = 0.60$ | $\sigma = 1.50$ | $\sigma$ : 0.50 – 2.00 |
| $m = 1.00$ | $m = 1.00$ | $m$ : 0.50 – 1.00 |

## Bibliography

Barro RJ (1991) Economic Growth in a Cross–Section of Countries. Quarterly Journal of Economics 106:407–443

Cassel G (1925) Fundamental Thoughts in Economics. T. Fisher Unwin, London

Cassel G (1934) Teoretisk Socialekonomi. Kooperative Förbundets Bokförlag, Stockholm

Hahn FH, Matthews RCO (1964) The Theory of Economic Growth: A Survey. Economic Journal 74:779–902

Kuznets S (1966) Modern Economic Growth. Rate, Structure and Spread. Yale University Press, New Haven

Lucas RE (1988) On the Mechanics of Economic Development. Journal of Monetary Economics 22:3–42, Reprinted in Becker (1991)

von Neumann J (1945–46) A Model of General Economic Equilibrium. Rev Econ Stud 13:1–9

Samuelson PA (1978) The Canonical Classical Model of Political Economy. Journal of Economic Literature 16:1415–1434

Selby SM (1973) Standard Mathematical Tables, 21st edn. The Chemical Rubber Co, Cleveland, Ohio

Smith A (1776, 1961) The Wealth of Nations I–II. Methuen University Paperbacks, London

Solow RM (1956) A Contribution to the Theory of Economic Growth. Quarterly Journal of Economics 70:65–94, Reprinted in Stiglitz (1969), and in Becker (1991)

Solow RM, Samuelson PA (1953) Balanced Growth under Constant Returns to Scale. Econometrica 21:412–424

Stiglitz JE, Uzawa H (1969) Readings in the Modern Theory of Economic Growth. M.I.T. Press, Cambridge, Mass

CHAPTER 8

# Canonical Classical Models and Minimal Factor Rewards

In Chap. 7, we encountered no stationary solutions for labor, capital, and output, except for the trivial axes solutions. However, the inevitable tendency of the economy to approach in the long run a *stationary state* was the prevalent vision of the classical writers. From an intuitive economic point of view, we are not, on the background of Chap. 7, surprised to learn that the classical vision will be confirmed when the growth model of Chap. 7, sections "The Dynamic System–The Geometry of the Phase Portrait", with *decreasing returning* to scale, is also supplemented with the *existence* of some *positive minimal* factor rewards. The latter eventually halts the steady decline of factor prices, which, in turn, terminates also the process of factor growth and hence output growth.

Nevertheless, from a mathematical point of view, the task of generally proving, rigorously, within the framework of a general classical growth model, the *existence,* the *uniqueness,* and the *global asymptotic stability* of a *stationary state* remains to be done.

## The Dynamic System

Introducing positive minimal factor rewards at which the growth rates, $\hat{L}$ and $\hat{K}$, have zero values, we have to replace (7.1–7.2) by

$$\hat{L} = \dot{L}/L = n(w - w_m), \quad n > 0, \ w_m > 0, \tag{8.1}$$

$$\hat{K} = \dot{K}/K = s_K(r - r_m), \quad 0 < s_K \leq 1, \ r_m > 0, \tag{8.2}$$

where $w_m$ is the subsistence (natural) real wage rate, and $r_m$ is the abstinence (effective) interest rate for employing capital in production rather than consumption. Ricardo's definitions were, $w_m$ (Ricardo 1965, p. 52): "The natural price of labour is that price which is necessary to enable the labourers, one with another, to subsist and to perpetuate their race, without either increase or



B. S. Jensen, *The Elements and Dynamic Systems of Economic Growth and Trade Models*, https://doi.org/10.1007/978-3-031-52493-6_8

diminution"; $r_m$ (Ricardo 1965, p. 73): "The minimum profit (rental) rate to afford them adequate compensation for their trouble and the risk which they must necessarily encounter in employing their capital productively".

As in Chap. 7, $w$ and $r$ are the *market prices*, which are again assumed to be determined in competitive markets and hence equal to the marginal productivities of the production factors.

Corresponding to (7.3.1–7.4.2), we now have, cf. (8.1–8.2)

$$\dot{L} = n\, MP_L \cdot L - n\, w_m L = P_1(L, K), \quad L, K \geq 0, \tag{8.3.1}$$

$$\dot{K} = s_K\, MP_K \cdot K - s_K\, r_m\, K = P_2(L, K), \quad L, K \geq 0, \tag{8.3.2}$$

and

$$\dot{L} = L^m\, n[\, m\, f(k) - k\, f'(k)\, ] - n\, w_m L = P_1(L, K), \quad L \neq 0, \tag{8.4.1}$$

$$\dot{K} = L^m\, s_K\, k\, f'(k) - s_K\, r_m\, K = P_2(L, K), \quad L \neq 0. \tag{8.4.2}$$

As is evident by (8.4.1–2), this system of *autonomous nonlinear* differential equations no longer represents a homogeneous dynamic system, since the *governing functions* $P_1$ and $P_2$ are not homogeneous functions, when $m \neq 1$.

Consequently, for $m \neq 1$ and initial values $L_0, K_0 > 0$, the family of *solutions* $[L(t), K(t)]$ to (8.3.1–8.4.2) does not as before consist of directrix solutions (with ray trajectories) and non-directrix solutions, cf. Theorems 7.1–7.2.

Incidentally, a homogeneous dynamic system would *never* allow the existence of an *isolated* stationary state (critical point), located in the *interior* of the domain: $L, K \geq 0$, cf. Chap. 28, section "Basic Framework, Assumptions, and Definitions" (stationary directrix). Hence, homogeneous dynamic systems in the plane can *not* corroborate mathematically, the vision of an unique isolated classical stationary state, $(\bar{L}, \bar{K} \in \mathbf{R}_+^2)$.

## Decreasing Returns to Scale and Minimal Factor Rewards

General closed form *solutions* cannot be established for the *nonhomogeneous* system (8.3.1–8.4.2), $0 < m < 1$, but their *qualitative* properties can be completely described. Here the theorems by Olech (1963) and Ito (1978) can and will be used to prove global asymptotic stability.

**Theorem 8.1** *The growth model (8.3.1–8.4.2) has—under the classical regularity conditions (2.60) and factor complementarity (2.5)—one and only stationary solution,*

$$\forall t \quad [L(t), K(t)] = (\bar{L}, \bar{K}) \in \mathbf{R}_+^2, \tag{8.5.1}$$

*with* $(\bar{L}, \bar{K})$ *determined by*

$$MP_L(\bar{L}, \bar{K}) = w_m, \qquad MP_K(\bar{L}, \bar{K}) = r_m. \tag{8.5.2}$$

*The unique stationary solution* $(\bar{L}, \bar{K})$*, (8.5.1–2), is the global attractor of all the nonstationary solutions,* $[L(t), K(t)]$*, with initial values* $(L_0, K_0) \in \mathbf{R}_+^2$*, that is,*

$$\forall (L_0, K_0) \in \mathbf{R}_+^2 / \{(\bar{L}, \bar{K})\} \quad : \quad [L(t), K(t)] \to (\bar{L}, \bar{K}) \text{ as } t \to \infty. \tag{8.6}$$

*Under the stated conditions, (2.60), (2.5), the complete set of phase curves (8.6) is entirely contained within the positive quadrant.*

***Proof*** The existence and the uniqueness of a stationary solution to (8.3.1–8.4.2) in $\mathbf{R}_+^2$ follow from the monotonicity and the convexity/concavity properties of the iso-marginal product curves, $IMP_L(L, K)$ and $IMP_K(L, K)$, (2.45.1–2), as expounded in Lemma 2.5.

Thus, the unique intersection point of the level curves, $IMP_L = w_m > 0$ and $IMP_K = r_m > 0$, is the unique critical point

$$\dot{L} = P_1(\bar{L}, \bar{K}) = 0, \quad \dot{K} = P_2(\bar{K}, \bar{L}) = 0, \tag{8.7.1}$$

of the dynamic system (8.3.1–2) outside the origin—establishing (8.5.1–2).

The sufficient conditions for the global asymptotic stability (8.6) are that the governing functions $P_1, P_2 \in C^2$-class satisfy the following conditions, see Ito (1978, p. 313),

$$\partial P_1/\partial L - P_1/L + \partial P_2/\partial K - P_2/K < 0, \tag{8.7.2}$$

$$[\partial P_1/\partial L - P_1/L][\partial P_2/\partial K - P_2/K] - \partial P_1/\partial K \cdot \partial P_2/\partial L > 0, \tag{8.7.3}$$

$$[\partial P_1/\partial L - P_1/L][\partial P_2/\partial K - P_2/K] \neq 0. \tag{8.7.4}$$

From (8.3.1–2), we get:

$$\partial P_1/\partial L = n(MP_L - w_m) + nL \cdot \partial MP_L/\partial L, \tag{8.8.1}$$

$$\partial P_1/\partial K = nL \cdot \partial MP_L/\partial K, \tag{8.8.2}$$

$$\partial P_2/\partial K = s_K(MP_K - r_m) + s_K K \cdot \partial MP_K/\partial K, \tag{8.8.3}$$

$$\partial P_2/\partial L = s_K K \cdot \partial MP_K/\partial L, \tag{8.8.4}$$

$$P_1/L = n(MP_L - w_m), \tag{8.8.5}$$

$$P_2/K = s_K(MP_K - r_m). \tag{8.8.6}$$

Inserting (8.8.1–6) into (8.7.2) gives, cf. (2.4):

$$nL \cdot \partial MP_L/\partial L + s_K K \cdot \partial MP_K/\partial K < 0, \quad \forall (L, K) \in \mathbf{R}_+^2. \tag{8.9.1}$$

Inserting (8.8.1–6) into (8.7.3) gives, cf. (2.4–2.5):

$$\begin{aligned} & ns_K LK \cdot \partial MP_L/\partial L \cdot \partial MP_K/\partial K - ns_K LK \cdot \partial MP_L/\partial K \cdot \partial MP_K/\partial L \\ = \quad & ns_K LK \left[ \frac{\partial^2 Y}{\partial L^2} \cdot \frac{\partial^2 Y}{\partial K^2} - \left( \frac{\partial^2 Y}{\partial K \partial L} \right)^2 \right] > 0, \quad \forall (L, K) \in \mathbf{R}_+^2, \end{aligned} \tag{8.9.2}$$

since the latter bracket is always positive, due to *strict concavity* of the homogeneous production function $Y = F(L, K)$, satisfying (2.21–2.22) with $D > 0$, cf. Remark 2.2. Thus, the crucial requirements for (8.9.2) are, $0 < m < 1$, and (2.26).

Inserting (8.8.1–6) into (8.7.4) gives, cf. (2.4):

$$ns_K LK \cdot \partial MP_L/\partial L \cdot \partial MP_K/\partial K \neq 0, \quad \forall (L, K) \in \mathbf{R}_+^2. \tag{8.9.3}$$

Thus, (8.5.1–2), (8.7.2–3), and (8.9.1–3) establish (8.6).

It follows immediately from (8.1–8.3.2) and (8.6) that

$$\forall (L_0, K_0) \neq (\bar{L}, \bar{K}) : \; w(t) \to w_m, \quad r(t) \to r_m \quad \text{as } t \to \infty. \tag{8.10}$$

Complementary to the proof of Theorem 8.1, we give the phase diagram of (8.3.1–2) in Fig. 8.1, where the isoclines of vertical and horizontal slope of the field vectors are, respectively, the iso-marginal product curves, $IMP_L = w_m$ and $IMP_K = r_m$.

By the disposition of the vector field in Fig. 8.1, *spiralling* trajectories toward $(\bar{L}, \bar{K})$ are clearly *ruled out,* since the trajectories cannot, after entering, again leave regions I and II.

Furthermore, in regions I–II, the *ray* determined by the unique critical point (8.5.2),

$$K = (\overline{K}/\overline{L})\, L \equiv \bar{k}\, L, \tag{8.11}$$

represents trajectories of solutions to the nonhomogeneous dynamic system (8.3.1–8.4.2). To confirm this, we note from (8.3.1–2) that

$$\frac{dK}{dL} = \frac{K}{L} \left[ \frac{s_K \, (MP_K - r_m)}{n \, (MP_L - w_m)} \right]. \tag{8.12}$$

Hence, the ray (8.11) fits the tangent field (8.12), if and only if

$$\frac{s_K \, (MP_K - r_m)}{n \, (MP_L - w_m)} = 1 \tag{8.13}$$

is always satisfied along (8.11). By (8.3.1–2), it is seen that (8.13) is equivalent to satisfying the condition,

$$\forall t \quad \hat{K}(t) = \dot{K}/K(t) = \dot{L}/L(t) = \hat{L}(t), \tag{8.14}$$

which always holds along (8.11), whatever the solutions $[L(t), K(t)]$ are, cf. (7.75).

Since (8.3.1–8.4.2) is autonomous, the ray (8.11) *decomposes* regions I–II into two parts with solutions $[L(t), K(t)]$ displaying either increasing or decreasing capital-labor ratios. Also within regions III–IV, only one trajectory leads directly to the critical point $[\overline{L}, \overline{K}]$; these particular trajectories accordingly *decompose* regions III–IV into two parts, as exhibited in Fig. 8.1, where they are drawn as convex curves converging to the axes cf. below. As vertical (horizontal) trajectory tangents *only* occur at the isoclines, $\dot{L} = 0$ ($\dot{K} = 0$), the trajectories cannot locally elsewhere in $\mathbf{R}^2_+$ have vertical or horizontal tangents.

To evaluate the trajectorial slopes near the axes, we have from (8.18.1–2), (8.4.1–2)

$$\frac{dK}{dL} = \frac{s_K}{n} \frac{L^{m-1}kf'(k) - r_m k}{L^{m-1}[mf(k) - kf'(k)] - w_m} \tag{8.15.1}$$

$$= \frac{s_k}{n} \frac{\left(k\frac{f'(k)}{f(k)}\right) - \frac{K}{L^m}\left(\frac{r_m}{f(k)}\right)}{\left(m - k\frac{f'(k)}{f(k)}\right) - L^{1-m}\left(\frac{w_m}{f(k)}\right)}. \tag{8.15.2}$$

By (2.14.1) we have that $kf'(k) < mf(k)$, and by assuming $F(L, 0) = 0$, cf. (2.2.1), that is, $f(k) \to 0$ as $k \to 0$, we obtain (8.16.1) from (8.15.1).

$$\frac{dK}{dL} \to -0 \quad \text{as} \quad K \to 0, \quad (L > \varepsilon > 0), \tag{8.16.1}$$

$$\frac{dK}{dL} \to -\infty \quad \text{as} \quad L \to 0, \quad (K > \varepsilon > 0). \tag{8.16.2}$$

As the first term in numerator (denominator) of (8.15.2) is less than $m$ (positive), cf. (2.14.1–2), and as $1/f(k)$, $k \neq 0$ is always positive and bounded, we get (8.16.2) from (8.15.2).

Thus, in Fig. 8.1, every trajectory, including the "separating trajectory" in regions III–IV, must near the axes conform to (8.16.1–2). The latter and the location of the isoclines will imply that trajectories—below the "separating trajectory" in region III–IV—typically are convex curves. Above the separating trajectories, however, the isoclines and (8.16.1–2) will imply trajectories having an inflection point, that is, concave-convex curves.

Important from an economic point of view, the conditions (8.7.2–8.7.4) guarantee—besides (8.6)—that the complete phase portrait of the dynamic system (8.3.1–8.4.2) belongs entirely to the first quadrant in Fig. 8.1, cf. Ito

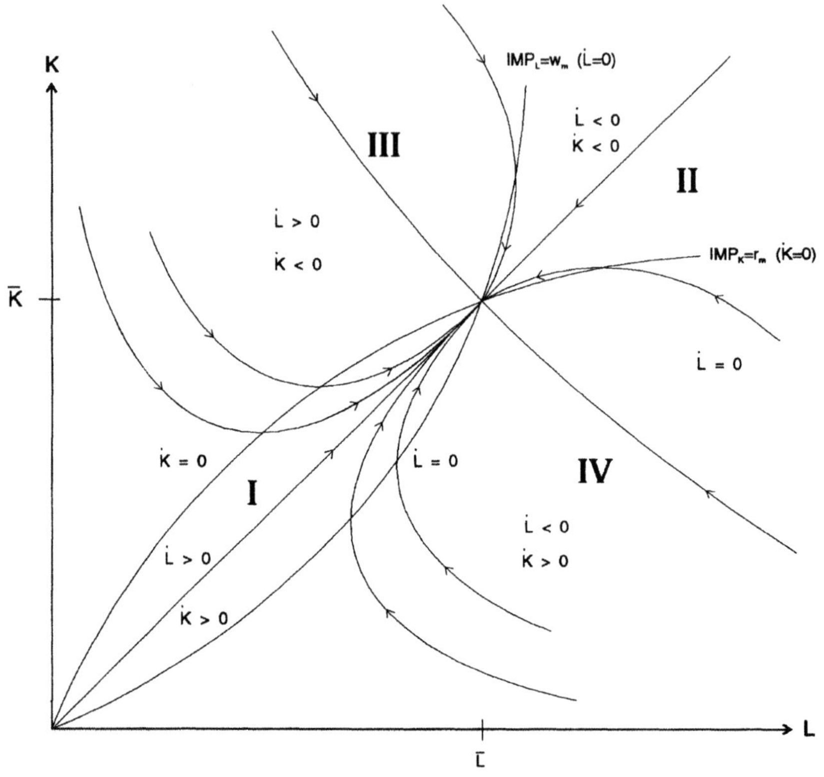


**Fig. 8.1** Phase portrait of the classical system, (8.3.1–8.4.2): "*The classical node*"

(1978). Since the conditions (8.7.2–8.7.4) imply that the Jacobian matrix of (8.3.1), cf. (8.8.1–6), evaluated at (8.5.1), have negative eigenvalues, we have in Fig. 8.1 used the term: "*The classical node*". □

With CD and CES technologies, the respective stationary state values $(\bar{L}, \bar{K})$, (8.5.1–2), become, cf. (2.48–2.49),

$$\bar{L} = [(m\gamma(1-a)/w_m)\bar{k}^{am}]^{\frac{1}{1-m}}, \quad \bar{K} = \bar{k}\bar{L}, \tag{8.17.1}$$

$$\bar{k} = (aw_m)/(1-a)r_m, \tag{8.17.2}$$

$$\bar{L} = [(m\gamma(1-a)/w_m)(1-a+a\bar{k}^{-b})^{-\frac{m}{b}-1}]^{\frac{1}{1-m}}, \quad \bar{K} = \bar{k}\bar{L}, \tag{8.18.1}$$

$$\bar{k} = (aw_m/(1-a)r_m)^{\frac{1}{1+b}}. \tag{8.18.2}$$

We see from (8.17.1) to (8.18.2) that

$$\partial \bar{L}/\partial w_m < 0, \quad \partial \bar{L}/\partial r_m < 0, \quad \partial \bar{L}/\partial m > 0, \tag{8.19.1}$$

$$\partial \bar{K}/\partial w_m < 0, \quad \partial \bar{K}/\partial r_m < 0, \quad \partial \bar{K}/\partial m > 0. \tag{8.19.2}$$

Thus, increases in the minimal factor rewards, $w_m$ and $r_m$, ***reduce*** the *sustainable* values of $\bar{L}$ and $\bar{K}$. This fact holds generally, as may be confirmed by shifting the convex/concave $IMP_L/IMP_K$ curves in Fig 8.1. Note that the stationary capital-labor ratio, $\bar{k} = \bar{K}/\bar{L}$, is optimal in the sense of satisfying $\omega(\bar{k}) = w_m/r_m$. Higher values of $m$ naturally allow larger values of both $\bar{L}$ and $\bar{K}$.

Finally, it is worth noting that generally the ***stationary state*** values $\bar{L}$ and $\bar{K}$, (8.5.1–2), are ***unaffected*** by the ***parameters*** $n$ and $s_K$. The latter affect only the ***rapidity*** of the evolution of $L(t)$ and $K(t)$, (8.6), toward the stationary state values, cf. (8.1–8.4.2). $\bar{L}$ and $\bar{K}$ depend ***only*** on the character of the ***technology*** (production functions) and the preordained ***natural prices,*** $w_m$ and $r_m$.

**Remark 8.1** The so-called Ricardian *"short-circuited"* version of classical dynamics, see Samuelson (1978, p. 1421–1422), with $L(t)$ instantaneously adjusting to maintain, $\forall t \; : \; w(t) = w_m$, may here be identified with movements along the isocline $\dot{L} = 0$, in Fig. 8.1. But evidently, the *isocline* $\dot{L} = 0$ does ***not*** represent a *trajectory* of any *solution* (8.6) to (8.3.1–8.4.2). ▽

## Constant Returns to Scale and Minimal Factor Rewards

As in Chap. 7, section "Constant Returns to Scale", we next let the model (8.1–8.4.2) operate under the conditions of constant returns to scale. Then with $m = 1$, the differential equations (8.3.1–8.4.2) constitute a ***homogeneous*** dynamic system, viz.,

$$\dot{L} \;=\; L\, n\, [\, MP_L(k) - w_m \,] \;=\; L\, \mathfrak{f}(k), \quad L \neq 0, \tag{8.20.1}$$

$$\dot{K} \;=\; L\, s_K\, k\, [\, MP_K(k) - r_m \,] \;=\; L\, \mathfrak{g}(k), \quad L \neq 0. \tag{8.20.2}$$

The ***director function*** $h(k)$ becomes, cf. (7.7), (8.20.1–2),

$$\begin{aligned} h(k) &= \mathfrak{g}(k) - k\, \mathfrak{f}(k) \\ &= n\, k\, [\, (s_K/n)(MP_K(k) - r_m) - (MP_L(k) - w_m)\, ]. \end{aligned} \tag{8.21}$$

**Theorem 8.2** *The growth model (8.20.1–2) has—under the conditions (2.12), (2.14.1–2),* $m = 1$ *and* $w_m \in [\underline{B}_L, \overline{B}_L]$, $r_m \in [\underline{B}_K, \overline{B}_K]$, *(2.6.1–2)—one and only one stationary ratio solution*

$$k(t) = \kappa = K_0/L_0 = k_0, \ \forall t, \quad \kappa \in \mathbf{R}_+, \tag{8.22}$$

*where the positive director root* $\kappa$ *is uniquely determined by the equation*

$$MP_L(\kappa) - w_m = (s_K/n)[MP_K(\kappa) - r_m]. \tag{8.23}$$

*The coordinate solutions* $[L(t), K(t)]$*—with initial values* $(L_0, K_0)$ *upon the directrix,* $K = \kappa L$*—have the form*

$$L(t) = L_0 \exp\{\mathfrak{f}(\kappa)t\}, \tag{8.24.1}$$

$$K(t) = \kappa \ L(t), \tag{8.24.2}$$

*with the directrix value given by*

$$\mathfrak{f}(\kappa) = n(MP_L(\kappa) - w_m) = s_K(MP_K(\kappa) - r_m) \gtrless 0. \tag{8.25}$$

*The non-directrix ratio and coordinate solutions to (8.20.1–2) will have the forms (7.18) and (7.20.1–2), with* $H(k)$ *and* $Q(k)$ *now derived from (8.21), cf. (7.16–7.17.2), (7.70).*

***Proof*** With $m = 1$, $MP_K(k)$ is monotonically decreasing for $k > 0$, whereas $MP_L(k)$ is monotonically increasing for $k > 0$. Then, assuming that $w_m$ and $r_m$, respectively, belong to the *range* of $MP_L(k)$ and $MP_K(k)$, cf. (2.6.1–2), (2.14.1–2), it follows that (8.21) has a unique, positive root $\kappa$, obtained by solving (8.23).

The positive or negative directrix value (8.25) follows immediately from (8.20.1) and (8.23). The exponential forms (8.24.1–2) follow from Theorem 28.2 in section "The Ratio and Coordinate Solutions on Directrices", cf. (7.69.1–2). □

A graphical illustration of the root determination (8.23) is shown in Fig. 8.2. This figure also demonstrates that if the intersection point of the curves at $\kappa$, cf. (8.23), is above/below the $k$-axis, then the directrix value (8.25) will be positive/negative. Clearly, small/large values of $w_m$ and $r_m$ are conducive to positive/negative values of (8.25). Furthermore, it is seen from Fig. 8.2 that $MP_L(\kappa) \gtrless w_m$ always *concurs* with $MP_K(\kappa) \gtrless r_m$ and vice versa. Hence, a directrix (8.22) with a *positive (negative)* directrix value (8.25) is always associated with both factor rewards $(w, r)$ being *above (below)* the minimal rewards $(w_m, r_m)$.

If a figure like Fig. 8.2 were drawn with $r_m > w_m$, then the statements above carry over unchanged; only $\kappa$ would naturally have a lower value than in Fig. 8.2.

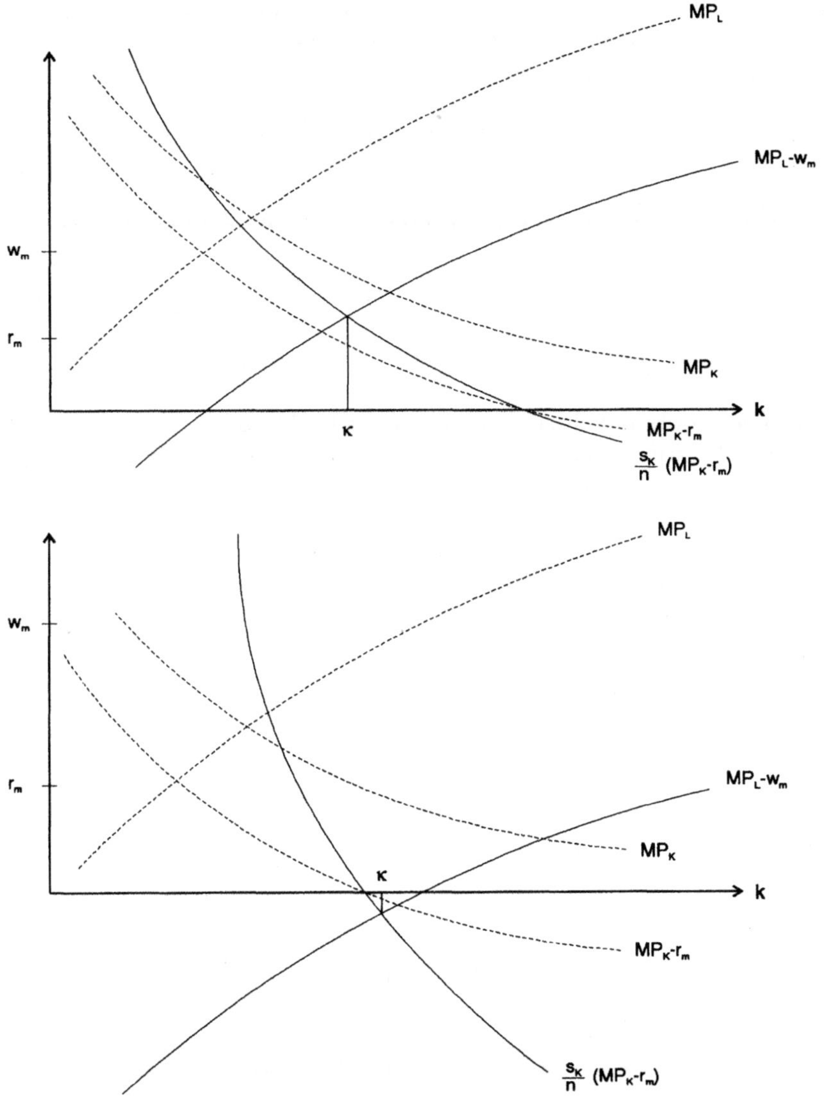


**Fig. 8.2** Director roots and directrix values of the classical system, (8.20.1–2)

The qualitative properties of the solutions may briefly be stated:

**Corollary 8.1** *The family of ratio solutions* $k(t)$ *to (8.20.1–2) has—under the conditions of* Theorem 8.2—*global asymptotic stability, that is,*

$$\exists\, k_0 = \kappa > 0 : \quad k(t) = \kappa, \qquad \forall t, \tag{8.26.1}$$

$$\forall\, k_0 \in \mathbf{R}_+/\{\kappa\} : \quad k(t) \to \kappa, \quad as\, t \to \infty. \tag{8.26.2}$$

*The family of coordinate solutions,* $[L(t), K(t)]$ *to (8.20.1–2), has—with (8.26.1–2)—respectively, global weak relative stability and global asymptotic stability for positive and negative directrix values, (8.25), that is,*

$$\forall\,(L_0, K_0) \in \mathbf{R}^2_+,\ \mathfrak{f}(\kappa) > 0 : L(t)/L^*(t) \quad \textit{are bounded as } t \to \infty, \tag{8.27.1}$$

$$\forall\,(L_0, K_0) \in \mathbf{R}^2_+,\ \mathfrak{f}(\kappa) > 0 : K(t)/K^*(t) \quad \textit{are bounded as } t \to \infty, \tag{8.27.2}$$

$$\forall\,(L_0, K_0) \in \mathbf{R}^2_+,\ \mathfrak{f}(\kappa) < 0 : L(t) \to 0 \quad \textit{as } t \to \infty, \tag{8.28.1}$$

$$\forall\,(L_0, K_0) \in \mathbf{R}^2_+,\ \mathfrak{f}(\kappa) < 0 : K(t) \to 0 \quad \textit{as } t \to \infty. \tag{8.28.2}$$

***Proof*** The proof of (8.26.1–2) is analogous to that of Theorem 7.3, (7.22.1–2). It is easily verified that $h(k)$, (8.21), decreases through $\kappa$, (8.23), cf. Fig. 8.2.

The proof of (8.27.1–2) is the same as for Proposition 7.2, cf. (7.71.1–2).

With $\mathfrak{f}(\kappa) < 0$, the global asymptotic stability (8.28.1–2) with (0, 0) as the attractor follows from the global asymptotic stability of $k(t)$, (8.26.1–2), and Theorem 28.12 in section "Global Asymptotic Ratio Stability and Global Stabilities of Coordinate Solutions". □

The *phase portraits* of (8.20.1–2) with positive and negative directrix values are shown in Fig. 8.3. The location of the isoclines, $\dot{L} = 0$ and $\dot{K} = 0$, is given

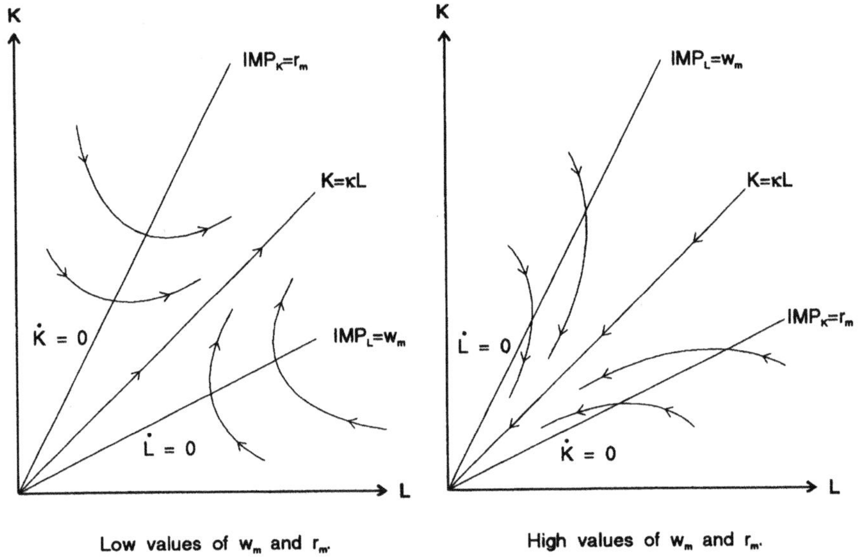


**Fig. 8.3** Phase portrait of the classical system, (8.20.1–2)

by the iso-marginal product curves, $IMP_L(k) = w_m$ and $IMP_K(k) = r_m$, which with $m = 1$ are *rays*, cf. (2.14.1–2). The slopes of the latter and of the directrix follow easily from an inspection of the curves in Fig. 8.2.

To improve its long-run factor reward $MP(\kappa)$, it is clearly advantageous in the context of (8.20.1–2) to slow its supply response to factor price increases, for example, for labor to decrease $n$ and increase $w_m$—as long as $w_m$ is not fixed so high as being beyond the feasible opportunities offered by the technology and competitive factor markets.

## Bibliography


Ito T (1978) A Note on the Positivity Constraint in Olech's Theorem. J Economic Theory 17:312–18

Nelson RR (1956) A Theory of the Low-Level Equilibrium Trap in Underdeveloped Economies. The American Economic Review 46(5):894–908

Olech C (1963) On the Global Stability of an Autonomous System on the Plane. pp 389–400, in *Contributions to Differential Equations,* Lasalle, J.P. and Diaz, J.B. (ed.), **1** (1963), Interscience, John Wiley and Sons, New York.

Ricardo D (1965) The Principles of Political Economy and Taxation, 3rd edn. J. M. Dent & Sons, London

Samuelson PA (1978) The Canonical Classical Model of Political Economy. Journal of Economic Literature 16:1415–1434

CHAPTER 9

# Canonical Classical Aggregate Growth Models

## THE AGGREGATE HOMOGENEOUS DYNAMIC SYSTEM

The aggregate analogue of the dynamic system (7.3.1–7.4.2) is given by, cf. (2.8–2.10)

$$\dot{L} = n\, AP_L \cdot L = n\, Y = n\, F(L,K) = \mathcal{F}(L,K), \quad L, K \geq 0, \tag{9.1.1}$$

$$\dot{K} = s\, AP_K \cdot K = s\, Y = s\, F(L,K) = \mathcal{G}(L,K), \quad L, K \geq 0, \tag{9.1.2}$$

or, equivalently,

$$\dot{L} = L^m\, n\, f(k) = L^m\, \mathfrak{f}(k), \qquad n > 0, \quad L \neq 0, \tag{9.2.1}$$

$$\dot{K} = L^m\, s\, f(k) = L^m\, \mathfrak{g}(k), \quad 0 < s < 1, \quad L \neq 0, \tag{9.2.2}$$

where the parameter $n$ now measures the *sensitivity* with which *population* (hence *labor* supply, still a constant fraction of total population) reacts to *income* changes, and where the parameter $s$ is now the *propensity* to *save* out of *total* income. The distinctive classical feature of (9.1.1–9.2.2) is the *endogenous* factor supply of both labor and capital. On canonical classical models, see Niehans (1990, p. 459).

The system of autonomous differential equations (9.1.1–9.2.2) again forms a homogeneous dynamic system. The *director function* $h(k)$ now becomes, cf. (7.7), (9.1.1–9.2.2)

$$\begin{aligned} h(k) &= \mathfrak{g}(k) - k\, \mathfrak{f}(k) \\ &= s\, f(k) - n\, k\, f(k) = f(k)(s - n\, k). \end{aligned} \tag{9.3}$$





B. S. Jensen, *The Elements and Dynamic Systems of Economic Growth and Trade Models*, https://doi.org/10.1007/978-3-031-52493-6_9

**Theorem 9.1** *The growth model (9.1.1–9.2.2) has—under the conditions (2.1–2.2.1), (2.8)—one and only one stationary ratio solution*

$$\forall t \quad k(t) = \kappa = K_0/L_0 = k_0, \quad \kappa \in \mathbf{R}_+, \tag{9.4}$$

*where the positive director root* $\kappa$ *is*

$$\kappa = s/n. \tag{9.5}$$

*The coordinate solutions* $[L(t), K(t)]$*—with initial values* $(L_0, K_0)$ *upon the directrix* $K = \kappa L$*—are*

$$0 < m < 1 \quad : \quad L(t) = [L_0^{1-m} + \mathfrak{f}(\kappa)(1-m)t]^{\frac{1}{1-m}}, \quad K(t) = \kappa L(t), \tag{9.6}$$

$$m = 1 \quad : \quad L(t) = L_0 \exp\{\mathfrak{f}(\kappa)t\}, \qquad K(t) = \kappa L(t), \tag{9.7}$$

*with the directrix value given by*

$$\mathfrak{f}(\kappa) = nf(\kappa) = sf(\kappa)/\kappa. \tag{9.8}$$

*The trajectories of all the non-directrix solutions* $[L(t), K(t)]$ *to (9.1.1–9.2.2) are straight lines, parallel to the directrix, viz.,*

$$K = L_0\,(k_0 - \kappa) + \kappa L, \quad k_0 = K_0/L_0 \neq \kappa. \tag{9.9}$$

***Proof*** The proofs of (9.4–9.8) are analogous to proofs of Theorem 7.1, cf. (7.12–7.15) and Proposition 7.1, cf. (7.69.1–2).

Here, the positive director root $\kappa$ (9.5) follows immediately from (9.3), and the forms of the directrix solutions (9.6–9.9) with, respectively, $0 < m < 1$ and $m = 1$ are by now standard knowledge.

To prove (9.9), we note, cf. (9.2.1–9.3) that

$$H'(k) = \frac{\mathfrak{f}(k)}{h(k)} = \frac{\mathfrak{f}(k)}{f(k)(s - nk)} = \frac{n}{s - nk} = \frac{1}{\kappa - k}, \quad k \neq \kappa. \tag{9.10}$$

Then, the juxtaposition of (9.10) to (7.41) establishes the trajectory system (9.9), cf. (7.42–7.44). Alternatively, the trajectories may here, of course, just be derived from (9.2.1–2) and (9.5), viz.,

$$dK/dL \equiv \dot{K}/\dot{L} = s/n = \kappa, \tag{9.11}$$

which gives (9.9). □

Despite the simplicity of the *phase portrait* (9.9) of (9.1.1–9.2.2), the non-directrix *solutions,* $[L(t), K(t)]$, can neither with the general production function $f(k)$ nor with the specific Cobb-Douglas function, (2.48), be written in closed forms. But their qualitative properties are, as usual, dictated by homogeneous dynamics. Hence, we have

**Corollary 9.1** *The family of ratio solutions $k(t)$ to (9.1.1–9.2.2) has global asymptotic stability, as stated in (7.22.1–2).*

*The family of coordinate solutions $[L(t), K(t)]$ to (9.1.1–9.2.2) has for $0 < m < 1$ and $m = 1$, respectively, strong relative and weak relative stability, as stated in (7.24.1–2) and (7.71.1–2).*

***Proof*** Global asymptotic ratio stability follows the fact that the director function (9.3) decreases through $\kappa$, (9.5).

The coordinate stabilities for $0 < m < 1$ and $m = 1$ follow from Theorem 28.9 in section "Global Asymptotic Ratio Stability and Global Stabilities of Coordinate Solutions" and Theorem 28.10. □

Other qualitative properties of the growing economy, as shown in Chap. 28, section "Ratio and Coordinate Solutions" and "Constant Returns to Scale", can now be derived from Theorem 9.1, Corollary 9.1, and the production laws; for example, the long-run trends of the average products of labor and capital are, $\forall(L_0, K_0) \in \mathbf{R}^2_+$,

$$0 < m < 1 \quad : \quad AP_L(t) \to 0, \qquad AP_K(t) \to 0 \qquad \text{as} \quad t \to \infty, \tag{9.12}$$

$$m = 1 \quad : \quad AP_L(t) \to f(\kappa), \qquad AP_K(t) \to (n/s) f(\kappa) \qquad \text{as} \quad t \to \infty, \tag{9.13}$$

which follow from (2.9–2.10) and Corollary 9.1.

Thus, the dismal prospects for the standard of living (measured by $AP_L$) in classical growth models with decreasing returns to scale, cf. (9.12), do *not* at all rest on the assumptions of "two classes", "marginal productivity remuneration of production factors", or the institution of "competitive factor markets".

The "*aggregate classical*" growth model (9.1.1–9.2.2) has *qualitatively* the *same* dynamic properties as the growth model (7.1–7.4.2), cf. Remark 7.2.

## Aggregate Growth and Critical Factor Productivities

For the sake of completeness, we examine the aggregate analogue of (8.1–8.3.2),

$$\hat{L} = \dot{L}/L = n\ (AP_L - a_L),\ n > 0, \tag{9.14}$$

$$\hat{K} = \dot{K}/K = s\ (AP_K - a_K),\ 0 < s < 1, \tag{9.15}$$

where the parameters $a_L$ and $a_K$ are some *critical* values of the average factor productivities. Hence, from (9.14–9.15), we have, cf. (9.1.1–9.2.2)

$$\dot{L} = n\ AP_L\ L - n\ a_L\ L = nY - na_L\ L = P_1(L, K), \quad L, K > 0, \tag{9.16.1}$$

$$\dot{K} = s\ AP_K\ K - s\ a_K\ K = sY - sa_K\ K = P_2(L, K), \quad L, K > 0, \tag{9.16.2}$$

or, equivalently, cf. (2.8),

$$\dot{L} = L^m\ n\ f(k) - n\ a_L\ L \quad = \quad P_1(L, K), \quad L \neq 0, \tag{9.17.1}$$

$$\dot{K} = L^m\ s\ f(k) - s\ a_K\ K \quad = \quad P_2(L, K), \quad L \neq 0. \tag{9.17.2}$$

### *Decreasing Returns to Scale*

With $0 < m < 1$, (9.16.1–9.17.2) is a *nonhomogeneous* dynamic system. The family of solutions has the properties given by

**Theorem 9.2** *The growth model (9.16.1–9.17.2) has—under the conditions (2.1–2.5), (2.8), $0 < m < 1$—one and only one stationary solution,*

$$\forall t \quad [L(t), K(t)] = (\bar{L}, \bar{K}) \in \mathbf{R}^2_+, \tag{9.18.1}$$

*with $(\bar{L}, \bar{K})$ determined by*

$$AP_L(\bar{L}, \bar{K}) = a_L, \qquad AP_K(\bar{L}, \bar{K}) = a_K. \tag{9.18.2}$$

*The unique stationary solution $(\bar{L}, \bar{K})$, (9.18.1–2), is the global attractor of all the nonstationary solutions with initial values $(L_0, K_0) \in \mathbf{R}^2_+$, that is,*

$$\forall (L_0, K_0) \in \mathbf{R}^2_+/\{(\bar{L}, \bar{K})\} \quad : \quad [L(t), K(t)] \to (\bar{L}, \bar{K}) \quad \textit{as} \quad t \to \infty. \tag{9.19}$$

*Under the stated conditions above, the complete set of phase curves (9.19) is entirely contained within the positive quadrant.*

***Proof*** The proof of Theorem 9.2 proceeds rather analogously to the proof of Theorem 8.1. Here, the stationary solution (9.18.1–2) is determined by the unique intersection point $(\bar{L}, \bar{K}) \in \mathbf{R}^2_+$ of the iso-average product curves: $IAP_L = a_L > 0$ and $IAP_K = a_K > 0$, cf. Chap. 2, section "Iso-Marginal, Iso-Average Productivity Curves".

The global asymptotic stability property (9.19) follows from applying the sufficient conditions (8.7.2–3) together with (9.16.1–9.17.2). From (9.16.1–2), we have

$$\partial P_1/\partial L = n(AP_L - a_L) + nL \cdot \partial AP_L/\partial L, \qquad (9.20.1)$$

$$\partial P_1/\partial K = nL \cdot \partial AP_L/\partial K, \qquad (9.20.2)$$

$$\partial P_2/\partial K = s(AP_K - a_K) + sK \cdot \partial AP_K/\partial K, \qquad (9.20.3)$$

$$\partial P_2/\partial L = sK \cdot \partial AP_K/\partial L, \qquad (9.20.4)$$

$$P_1/L = n(AP_L - a_L), \qquad (9.20.5)$$

$$P_2/K = s(AP_K - a_K). \qquad (9.20.6)$$

Inserting (9.20.1–6) into (8.7.2) gives

$$nL \cdot \partial AP_L/\partial L + sK \cdot \partial AP_K/\partial K. \qquad (9.21)$$

As $\partial(Y/L)/\partial L = L^{-1}MP_L - L^{-2}Y$, the latter, (2.9) and (2.14.1), imply that

$$nL \cdot \partial AP_L/\partial L = nL^{m-1}[(m-1)f(k) - kf'(k)] < 0, \qquad (9.22)$$

where the inequality is due to $m < 1$ and the positiveness of $f(k),\ f'(k)$, for all $k > 0$, cf. (2.9), (2.12).

As $\partial(Y/K)/\partial K = K^{-1}MP_K - K^{-2}Y$, the latter, (2.10) and (2.14.2), imply that

$$sK \cdot \partial AP_K/\partial K = sL^{m-1}[f'(k) - f(k)/k] < 0, \qquad (9.23)$$

where the inequality is due to the strict concavity of $f(k)$, cf. (2.9), (2.12), (2.31).

Inserting (9.20.1–6) into (8.7.3) gives, cf. above and (2.11),

$$\begin{aligned} & nsLK\left[\frac{\partial AP_L}{\partial L} \cdot \frac{\partial AP_K}{\partial K} - \frac{\partial AP_L}{\partial K} \cdot \frac{\partial AP_K}{\partial L}\right] \\ = \ & nsLK[(L^{-1}MP_L - L^{-2}Y)(K^{-1}MP_K - K^{-2}Y) - (L^{-1}MP_K \cdot K^{-1}MP_L)] \\ = \ & nsL^{-1}K^{-1}Y[-L \cdot MP_L - K \cdot MP_K + Y] \\ = \ & nsL^{-1}K^{-1}Y(1-m)Y > 0, \end{aligned} \qquad (9.24)$$

where the inequality is due to the Euler's relation (2.15.1) and $m < 1$.

With (9.20.1–6), the condition (8.7.4) is satisfied, since both (9.22) and (9.23) differ from zero. Thus, (9.21–9.23) and (9.24) establish (9.19). □

Similar *phase portraits* as in Fig. 8.1 will be obtained for the dynamic system (9.16.1–9.17.2).

### *Constant Returns to Scale*

With $m = 1$, (9.16.1–9.17.2) is a homogeneous dynamic system, viz.,

$$\dot{L} = L\, n\, [\, AP_L(k) - a_L\, ] \quad = L\, \mathfrak{f}(k), \tag{9.25.1}$$

$$\dot{K} = L\, s\, k\, [\, AP_K(k) - a_K\, ] = L\, \mathfrak{g}(k). \tag{9.25.2}$$

The *director function* $h(k)$ becomes, cf. (7.7), (9.25.1–2)

$$\begin{aligned} h(k) &= \mathfrak{g}(k) - k\, \mathfrak{f}(k) \\ &= n\, k\, [\, (s/n)(AP_K(k) - a_K) - (AP_L(k) - a_L)\, ]. \end{aligned} \tag{9.26}$$

The qualitative properties of the solutions to (9.25.1–2) are the same as those stated in Theorem 8.2 and Corollary 8.1, of section "Constant Returns to Scale and Minimal Factor Rewards". There is no need here to repeat the analogous proofs for (9.25.1–2), since we would just have to substitute $AP$ for $MP$ and $a_L, a_K$ for $w_m, r_m$, and the stability properties of the solutions to homogeneous dynamic systems are by now familiar matters. Similar phase portraits as in Fig. 8.3 can be drawn for (9.25.1–2).

### *One-Class Versus Two-Class Models*

In a bold and important paper, Niehans (1963, p. 365) concluded that there is "a remarkable difference between the implications of the one-class and the two-class model". Such a point of view sharply contrasts with the outcome of our investigations.

Evidently, with either $0 < m < 1$ or $m = 1$, the *family* of *solutions* (time paths) to the *"one-class"* growth models (9.1.1–9.2.2) and (9.16.1–9.17.2) are *qualitatively* equivalent (with respect to ratio and coordinate stabilities) to the *family* of *solutions* to the corresponding *"two-class"* growth models (7.3.1–7.4.2) and (8.3.1–8.4.2). Hence, to us, the evolutionary implications are, in the long run, the same for both types of growth models.

The contentious issue appears to be resolved by a scrutiny of the *governing functions* for capital accumulation. Instead of our "one-class" component, cf. (9.16.2)

$$\dot{K} = sY - sa_K K = s(AP_K - a_K)K, \tag{9.27}$$

the "one-class" counterpart in Niehans (1963, p. 358) is formulated as (in our notation):

$$\dot{K} = s\, Y - s\, a_K\, L. \tag{9.28}$$

For the *two-class* model, we both use the *same* governing function for capital accumulation, viz., cf. (8.3.2) and Niehans (1963, p. 352),

$$\dot{K} = s_K(MP_K - r_m)K. \tag{9.29}$$

Although the subsequent dynamic analysis in Niehans (1963) uses the specific Cobb-Douglas production function (2.48), whereas our analysis is conducted with the general production function (2.1–2.7), the dispute really hinges on the discrepancy between the dynamics engendered by adopting, respectively, (9.27) or (9.28).

First of all, we think that the *proper* one-class (aggregate) *analogue* of (9.29) *is* (9.27) rather than (9.28), cf. (7.2), (7.3.2), (8.2) and (9.15). Furthermore, the *economic rationale* of (9.28) seems much weaker than that of (9.27). Ceteris paribus, *low* values of $K$ and *high* values of $L$ would very likely be conducive to *rapid* capital accumulation (large positive values of $\dot{K}$), which (9.27) consents to. Hence, we admit the differential equation (9.27) into our "one class" growth model, whereas (9.28) postulates the opposite.

The queer results for one-class classical growth models in Niehans (1963, pp. 358–369) are due to the frail economic rationale and fatal dynamic consequences of endorsing (9.28) instead of (9.27).

Hopefully, by our exposition and theorems in this chapter, any lingering suspicion of dramatic differences between *two-class* and *one-class* (aggregate) classical growth models has been effectively quelled.

## Synopsis of Classical Growth Models

As a prelude to subsequent investigations of neoclassical, Keynesian, and two-sector growth models, we briefly recapitulate the main results of our inquiries into endogenous growth models, classical and their extensions. The contention of classical economics that economic welfare (the wealth of nations) depends on capital accumulation and population growth is never seriously disputed.

The elements of our growth models have been:

(i) a positive relationship between labor productivity ($MP_L$ or $AP_L$) and the growth of labor supply.
(ii) a positive relationship between capital productivity ($MP_K$ or $AP_K$) and the rate of capital accumulation.
(iii) homogeneity ($0 < m < 1$ or $m = 1$) of the production functions.

These three elements (i–iii)—restated in succinct modern usage within the context of one-sector growth models with two production factors, labor and capital—are believed to reflect essential aspects of the *classical theory* of *canonical economic growth*. Of course, the classical debate also involved broader economic aspects, cf. Bentzel and Hansen (1954), Blaug (1985), Brems (1970), Brems (1986), Eltis (1984), Hollander (1980), Hollander (1987),

Johansen (1969), Marshall (1947), Mill (1973), Peart (1990), Samuelson (1978), Wan (1971), Wold (1959).

Evidently, maintaining $m = 1$ is an extension of the standard classical assumption, $0 < m < 1$. Also, the specification of the governing functions in terms of average productivities (aggregate production) is, strictly speaking, an extension of standard classical exegesis. However, dealing with homogeneous dynamics, these two extensions were natural for us to consider, and imperative for dealing with the factor pricing and the "one-two" class issues, cf. Remark 7.2 and Chap. 9. But the extensions were also examined all along with the objective to unify or, at any rate, to build bridges between classical and neoclassical growth models, cf. Chap. 11 below.

The classical insistence of some conventional exogenous *minimal* returns ($w_m$ and $r_m$ or $a_L$ and $a_K$) for actual reproduction of labor and capital presented, together with $m < 1$, dynamic problems of some complexity to be resolved, if economic-technological generality and mathematical perfection are to be attained. The economic literature has abounded in intuitive arguments and heuristic graphical vindications of the stationary state as the ultimate destiny of the evolution on classical premises. Mathematical proofs, however, can only be established by rigorous deductive reasoning; that is, to guarantee the acceptance of the conclusion, the mathematical argumentation must proceed by logical steps from an agreed starting point. Such deductive procedure was used in the proofs of Theorems 8.1 and 9.2, where the conditions (8.7.2–3) guarantee the crucial economic *positivity* property of the variables along the solution path in addition to the *global* asymptotic stability property, whenever the stationary state and the initial values are in the positive quadrant. To our knowledge, no general and rigorous proof, as here given in Theorems 8.1 and 9.2 of the global asymptotic stability of the solutions to the classical growth model with $0 < m < 1$, is yet available in literature.

Next, with $m = 1$, a decisive change in *technology* has obviously occurred, and the family of solutions to the growth models must accordingly be expected to show an entirely different behavior than global asymptotic stability. Certainly, our mathematical analysis of the corresponding differential equations has established quite different qualitative (stability) properties, as shown in Propositions 7.1–7.3 and Theorem 8.2 (with Corollary).

Finally, we should make the following observation. Whether $0 < m < 1$ or $m = 1$, the *qualitative* (but not the quantitative) results in all our theorems and propositions *never* depended—apart from the stipulation, $(s_K/n) \in \Omega$, (2.28.1–2), in Theorems 7.1–7.5—on critical *numerical values* of the *parameters* $n$, $s_K$, and $s$. Thus, the obtained *qualitative* results for the growth models with endogenous factor supplies are robust and insensitive to the magnitude of the proliferation and saving propensities.

## Bibliography


Bentzel R, Hansen B (1954) On Recursiveness and Interdependency in Economic Models. Rev Econ Stud 22:153–168

Blaug M (1985) Economic Theory in Retrospect, 4th edn. Cambridge University Press, Cambridge

Brems H (1970) Ricardo's Long-Run Equilibrium. History of Political Economy 2:225–245

Brems H (1986) Pioneering Economic Theory 1630–1980. A Mathematical Restatement. The Johns Hopkins University Press, Baltimore

Eltis V (1984) The Classical Theory of Economic Growth. MacMillan, London

Hollander S (1980) On Professor Samuelson's Canonical Classical Model of Political Economy. J Econ Lit 18:559–74

Hollander S (1987) Classical Economics. Basil Blackwell, Oxford

Johansen L (1969) A Classical Model of Economic Growth. In *Socialism, Capitalism and Economic Growth, Essays in Honour of M. Dobb,* Feinstein, C.H. (ed.), Cambridge University Press, Cambridge.

Marshall A (1947) Principles of Economics, 8th edn. MacMillan, London

Mill JS (1973) Principles of Political Economy. A.M. Kelley Publishers, New Jersey

Niehans J (1963) Economic Growth with Two Endogenous Factors. Quarterly Journal of Economics 77:349–371

Niehans J (1990) A History of Economic Theory, Classic Contributions 1720–1980. The Johns Hopkins University Press, Baltimore

Peart S (1990) The Population Mechanism in W. S. Jevon's Applied Economics. The Manchester School of Economic and Social Studies 58:32–53

Samuelson PA (1978) The Canonical Classical Model of Political Economy. Journal of Economic Literature 16:1415–1434

Wan HY Jr (1971) Economic Growth. Harcourt Brace Jovanowich, New York

Wold H (1959) Ends and Means in Econometric Model Building. pp 355–434, in *Probability and Statistics: The Harold Cramér Volume,* Grenander, U. (ed.), John Wiley and Sons, New York.

CHAPTER 10

# Keynesian Macro Growth and Cycle Models

## Introduction

As is well-known, the work of Harrod (1939) stemmed from the desire to extend Keynes (1936)'s *aggregate demand theory* for the *short period* into the *long period*. Harrod addressed himself especially to the problems of *sustaining investment demand* and thereby bringing more into focus the trend movements of the capital stock and national income rather than the prevalent elaborations on their cyclical movements.

Harrod (1939, p. 14) wrote:

> The axiomatic basis of the theory which I propose to develop consist of three propositions – namely, (1) that the level of a community's income is the most important determinant of its supply of saving; (2) that the rate of increase of its income is an important determinant of its demand for saving, and (3) that demand is equal to supply. It thus consists in a marriage of the acceleration principle and the multiplier theory.

Harrod (1939, p. 26) modified the influence of the acceleration principle by subsequent including into investment demand other components that have no direct relation to the current increase of output.

The literature on the theory of economic growth, especially textbooks and survey-articles (Hahn and Matthews 1964), have emphasized technology assumptions as the fundamental difference between the Harrod growth model and the neoclassical growth model expounded below. However, we are not here to be bogged down in lengthy textual exegesis. Rather, the exposition below will take up some of the factual and more relevant distinctions involved, mathematically and economically.

At first, we will as hitherto be able to conduct the analysis of the Harrod growth model within the framework of homogeneous dynamic systems, but



B. S. Jensen, *The Elements and Dynamic Systems of Economic Growth and Trade Models*, https://doi.org/10.1007/978-3-031-52493-6_10

later an affine dynamic system has to be used. To facilitate an orderly discussion, we first start with a mathematical presentation and solution of the relevant, dynamic models, and then we address the economic issues involved in the final section.

## Harrodian Growth Models

In its most simple version, the Harrod model can be restated—from the quotation above—as (in obvious notation),

$$S = S(Y) = sY, \quad 0 < s < 1, \tag{10.1}$$

$$I = I(\dot{Y}) = \beta \dot{Y}, \quad \beta > 0, \tag{10.2}$$

$$S = I, \tag{10.3}$$

where the *parameters* $s$ and $\beta$ are, respectively, the constant *propensity* to *save* and the constant *acceleration* coefficient.

Equations (10.1–10.3) may, of course, be written as a single differential equation

$$\dot{Y} = (s/\beta)Y. \tag{10.4}$$

But since, besides the evolution of $Y(t)$, we are also much concerned with evolution of the capital stock $K(t)$ and in particular with *long-run* behavior of *capital-output ratio* $\mathrm{v} = K/Y$ it is convenient at the outset to regard the Harrod growth model (10.1–10.3), due to $I = S = \dot{K}$, as in fact a homogeneous dynamic *system* (with = 1) in the plane, viz.,

$$\dot{Y} = \mathcal{F}(Y, K) = (s/\beta)Y = Y\,\mathfrak{f}(\mathrm{v}), \tag{10.5.1}$$

$$\dot{K} = \mathcal{G}(Y, K) = sY = Y\,\mathfrak{g}(\mathrm{v}). \tag{10.5.2}$$

Then the *director function* $h(\mathrm{v})$ of this simple, linear system becomes

$$h(\mathrm{v}) = \mathfrak{g}(\mathrm{v}) - \mathrm{v}\,\mathfrak{f}(\mathrm{v}) = s - (s/\beta)\mathrm{v}. \tag{10.6}$$

With $m = 1$, we find, as usual, from (10.6), cf. (7.8), (7.70),

$$\dot{\mathrm{v}} = h(\mathrm{v}) = Q(\mathrm{v}) = s - (s/\beta)\mathrm{v}, \tag{10.7}$$

and, furthermore, cf. (7.16)

$$H'(\mathrm{v}) = \frac{\mathfrak{f}(\mathrm{v})}{h(\mathrm{v})} = \frac{s/\beta}{s - (s/\beta)\mathrm{v}}, \quad h(\mathrm{v}) \neq 0. \tag{10.8}$$

**Theorem 10.1** *The growth model (10.1–10.3), (10.5.1–2), has in* $\mathbf{R}_+^2$ *one and only one stationary ratio solution*

$$\forall t \quad v(t) = v = \beta = K_0/Y_0 = v_0, \qquad v \in \mathbf{R}_+. \tag{10.9}$$

*The directrix solutions,* $[Y(t), K(t)]$*, have the form*

$$Y(t) = Y_0 e^{(s/\beta)t}, \quad K(t) = Y_0 \beta e^{(s/\beta)t}, \qquad K = \beta Y, \tag{10.10.1}$$

*with the directrix value* $\mathfrak{f}(v)$*—"warranted rate of growth"—being*

$$\mathfrak{f}(v) = s/\beta = s/v. \tag{10.10.2}$$

*The family of ratio solutions* $v(t)$ *to (10.5.1–2), (10.7)—with initial values* $(Y_0, K_0)$ *outside the directrix* $K = \beta Y$*—is given by*

$$v(t) = \beta + (v_0 - \beta)e^{-(s/\beta)t}, \quad v_0 \neq \beta. \tag{10.11}$$

*The family of coordinate solutions* $[Y(t), K(t)]$*, with initial values* $(Y_0, K_0)$ *outside the directrix (10.10.1–2), is given by*

$$Y(t) = Y_0 e^{(s/\beta)t}, \tag{10.12.1}$$

$$K(t) = Y_0 \beta [v_0/\beta - 1 + e^{(s/\beta)t}], \quad v_0 = K_0/Y_0 \neq \beta. \tag{10.12.2}$$

*The system of trajectories (10.12.1–2) is, as loci, represented by the equation*

$$K = Y_0(v_0 - \beta) + \beta Y. \tag{10.13}$$

***Proof*** As we have elsewhere, Chap. 29, set out in a thorough and almost pedantic way, an alternative calculus approach—contrasting the traditional algebraic eigenvalue/eigenvector approach—to the solution of the general linear planar system, the proof of Theorem 10.1 requires only a few comments here, see (29.64–29.68).

From (10.6), we get the *director root* $v$ as

$$h(v) = 0 \Leftrightarrow v = \beta. \tag{10.14}$$

Then (10.14) and (10.5.1–2) give (10.9–10.10.2).

The formulas (10.11–10.12.2) are simply derived from, respectively, (10.7) and (10.5.1), together with $K(t) \equiv \mathrm{v}(t)Y(t)$. By (10.8), we have

$$H'(\mathrm{v}) = 1/(\beta - \mathrm{v}), \qquad H(\mathrm{v}) = -\ln(\beta - \mathrm{v}). \tag{10.15}$$

Next, (10.15) establish (10.13); cf. (10.5.1–2), $dK/dY \equiv \dot{K}/\dot{Y} = \beta$, hence (10.13). □

**Remark 10.1** We may note that the standard algebraic transformation into eigenvectors does not work for the system (10.5.1–2), since the determinant is zero. The latter, however, is immaterial to the calculus approach. Technicalities on bifurcation of the phase portrait (10.13) will here be spared, see Chap. 29, sections "Structural Stability and Bifurcations"–"Parameter Space and Kinematic Stability Properties". ▽

**Theorem 10.2** *The family of ratio solutions $v(t)$ and the family of coordinate solutions $[Y(t), K(t)]$ to the growth model (10.5.1–2) have, respectively, global asymptotic stability and global weak relative stability, that is,*

$$\exists v_0 = \beta \quad : \quad v(t) = v = \beta \quad \forall t, \tag{10.16.1}$$

$$\forall v_0 \in \mathbf{R}_+/\{v\} \quad : \quad v(t) \to v = \beta \text{ as } t \to \infty, \tag{10.16.2}$$

$$\forall (Y_0, K_0) \in \mathbf{R}_+^2 \quad : \quad Y(t)/Y^*(t) \text{ are bounded as } t \to \infty, \tag{10.16.3}$$

$$\forall (Y_0, K_0) \in \mathbf{R}_+^2 \quad : \quad K(t)/K^*(t) \text{ are bounded as } t \to \infty. \tag{10.16.4}$$

***Proof*** Since $h$(v), (10.6), decreases through $\beta$, (10.9), the proof is analogous to that of Theorem 11.2 in section "The Dynamic System, Solutions, and Stability". □

**Remark 10.2** As with the neoclassical system, cf. section "The Phase Portrait and the Steady-State Path: Theorem 11.3, the asymptotic stability property (10.16.1–2) certainly does not imply that the trajectories (10.13) have the *directrix* (10.9) as an asymptote.

Incidently, note how often a phase portrait of parallel straight lines occurs under the most disparate mathematical and economic circumstances, cf. Theorem 7.5 in section "The Geometry of the Phase Portrait, (7.44), (9.9), and (10.13). ▽

Before entering discussions of the literature about Harrodian dynamics, it will be expedient to introduce *Harrod's modifications* of the *acceleration principle*. Some investments may be conceived to vary with the current level of income, as distinct from its rate of growth. As mentioned by Harrod (1939, p. 27): "Long-period anticipations are bound to be influenced by the present state of prosperity or adversity: even public authorities are apt to reduce the volume of public works in a slump".

Accordingly, (10.2) is replaced by

$$I = \beta_1 \dot{Y} + \beta_2 Y, \quad \beta_1 > 0, \ 0 < \beta_2 < 1. \tag{10.17}$$

Hence, (10.1), (10.3), and (10.17) give the system, cf. (10.5.1–2)

$$\dot{Y} = \frac{s-\beta_2}{\beta_1}Y = Y\mathfrak{f}(v), \quad s > \beta_2, \tag{10.18.1}$$

$$\dot{K} = sY = Y\mathfrak{g}(v). \tag{10.18.2}$$

Clearly, Theorems 10.1–10.2 apply to (10.18.1–2) with just the positive director root and the directrix value, cf. (10.6), (10.9), (10.10.2), now becoming

$$h(v) = 0 \Leftrightarrow v = \beta_1/(1-\beta_2/s), \tag{10.19.1}$$

$$\mathfrak{f}(v) = (s-\beta_2)/\beta_1 = s/v; \quad s > \beta_2. \tag{10.19.2}$$

Evidently, the economic ***parameter condition*** $s > \beta_2$ in (10.18.1–10.19.2) is required for a ***viable*** dynamic model with ***growing*** solutions, $Y(t)$ and $K(t)$, along the system of linear trajectories, (10.13), with $\beta$ here replaced by the director root $v$, (10.19.1–2), cf. Fig. 10.1.

A further modification of (10.17) is to conceive of some investments that are quite independent of both the current level of income ($Y$) and its rate of increase ($\dot{Y}$). Technical progress such as new methods for producing existing output and numerous other factors are often made allowance for by introducing an ***autonomous*** (exogenous) component ($\bar{I}$) in the aggregate investment demand function, viz.,

$$I = \bar{I} + \beta_1\dot{Y} + \beta_2 Y; \qquad \beta_1 > 0,\ 0 < \beta_2 < 1,\ \bar{I} > 0. \tag{10.20}$$

The contingent effect of the interest rate may also be absorbed in the term $\bar{I}$, since no interaction between the commodity market and financial markets or endogenous interest determination is considered here.

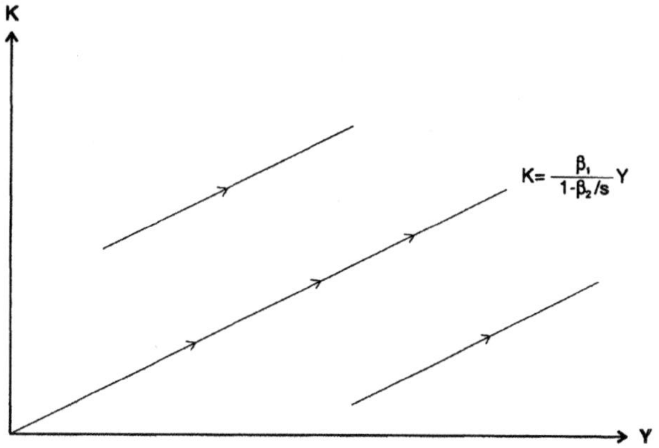


**Fig. 10.1** Phase portrait of the *Harrodian growth model*, (10.18.1–2)

The aggregate savings function (10.1) may also be modified by including an *autonomous* element, due to a *minimal* consumption *level* $\bar{C}$, that is,

$$S = -\bar{C} + sY; \quad 0 < s < 1, \ \bar{C} > 0. \tag{10.21}$$

From (10.3), (10.20), and (10.21) we now obtain the dynamic system,

$$\dot{Y} = -\bar{A}/\beta_1 + [(s - \beta_2)/\beta_1]Y; \quad \bar{A} = \bar{C} + \bar{I} > 0, \ s > \beta_2, \tag{10.22.1}$$

$$\dot{K} = -\bar{C} + sY; \quad \bar{C} > 0. \tag{10.22.2}$$

Clearly, (10.22.1–2) is not homogeneous dynamics; it is *affine dynamics*, and furthermore its *singularity* (zero determinant) *precludes* any *stationary* solutions. We should for the sake of completeness give the *family* set of *solutions* to (10.22.1–2) *explicitly* in parameters of (10.22.1–2) and the initial values $(Y_0, K_0)$, and state their stability properties.

**Proposition 10.1** *The family of coordinate solutions,* $[Y(t), K(t)]$, *to the growth model (10.22.1–2) is given by*

$$Y(t) = \frac{\bar{A}}{s-\beta_2} + \left[Y_0 - \frac{\bar{A}}{s-\beta_2}\right] e^{(\frac{s-\beta_2}{\beta_1})t}, \quad s > \beta_2, \tag{10.23.1}$$

$$\begin{aligned} K(t) &= K_0 + \left[\frac{\bar{A}}{1-\beta_2/s} - \bar{C}\right] t \\ &\quad + \left[Y_0 - \frac{\bar{A}}{s-\beta_2}\right]\left[\frac{\beta_1}{1-\beta_2/s}\right]\left[e^{(\frac{s-\beta_2}{\beta_1})t} - 1\right], \end{aligned} \tag{10.23.2}$$

*which includes the particular solutions,*

$$Y(t) = Y_0 = \bar{A}/(s - \beta_2), \quad s > \beta_2, \tag{10.24.1}$$

$$K(t) = K_0 + \left[\bar{A}/(1 - \beta_2/s) - \bar{C}\right] t. \tag{10.24.2}$$

*The system of trajectories (10.23.1–10.24.2) is, as loci, represented by*

$$K = K_0 + \frac{\beta_1}{1-\beta_2/s}\left[Y - Y_0 + \frac{\bar{A}}{s-\beta_2} - \frac{\bar{C}}{s}\right] \ln\left|\frac{Y - \bar{A}/(s-\beta_2)}{Y_0 - \bar{A}/(s-\beta_2)}\right|,$$

$$\textit{with} \ \ Y \wedge Y_0 \neq \frac{\bar{A}}{s-\beta_2}, \tag{10.25}$$

$$Y = \bar{A}/(s - \beta_2). \tag{10.26}$$

*The coordinate solutions (10.23.1–2)—excluding (10.24.1–2)—have global weak relative stability, and their ratios* $v(t) = K(t)/Y(t)$ *have global strong absolute stability, that is,*

$$\forall\,(Y_0, K_0) \in \mathbf{R}^2_+/\{\frac{\bar{A}}{s-\beta_2}, K_0\} \quad : \quad Y(t)/Y^*(t) \textit{ are bounded as } t \to \infty, \tag{10.27.1}$$

$$\forall\,(Y_0, K_0) \in \mathbf{R}^2_+/\{\frac{\bar{A}}{s-\beta_2}, K_0\} \quad : \quad K(t)/K^*(t) \textit{ are bounded as } t \to \infty, \tag{10.27.2}$$

$$\forall\,(Y_0, K_0) \in \mathbf{R}^2_+/\{\frac{\bar{A}}{s-\beta_2}, K_0\} \quad : \quad \begin{cases} v(t) \to \beta_1/(1-\beta_2/s) \textit{ as } t \to \infty, \\ v(t) - v^*(t) \to 0 \textit{ as } t \to \infty. \end{cases} \tag{10.28}$$

*Along the trajectory (10.26), the subfamily of solutions (10.24.2) and the ratios* $v(t) = K(t)/Y(t)$ *have both global strong relative stability, that is,*

$$\forall\{Y_0 = \bar{A}/(s-\beta_2),\ K_0\} \in \mathbf{R}^2_+ \quad : \quad K(t)/K^*(t) \to 1 \textit{ as } t \to \infty, \tag{10.29}$$

$$\forall\{Y_0 = \bar{A}/(s-\beta_2),\ K_0\} \in \mathbf{R}^2_+ \quad : \quad \begin{cases} v(t) \to \infty \textit{ as } t \to \infty, \\ v(t)/v^*(t) \to 1 \textit{ as } t \to \infty. \end{cases} \tag{10.30}$$

***Proof*** The general solution (10.23.1) and the particular solution (10.24.1) of (10.22.1) are obvious. Inserting (10.23.1) into (10.22.2), then elementary integration and a simple calculation with initial values gives (10.23.2).

From (10.22.1–2), we obtain

$$\begin{aligned} \frac{dK}{dY} \quad &\equiv \quad \frac{\dot{K}}{\dot{Y}} = \frac{sY - \bar{C}}{[(s-\beta_2)/\beta_1]Y - \bar{A}/\beta_1}, \qquad Y \neq \bar{A}/(s-\beta_2) \\ &= \quad \frac{\beta_1}{1-\beta_2/s}\left[1 + \frac{\bar{A} - [(s-\beta_2)/s]\bar{C}}{(s-\beta_2)Y - \bar{A}}\right], \end{aligned} \tag{10.31}$$

whence

$$K \quad = \quad \mu + \frac{\beta_1}{1-\beta_2/s}\left[Y + (\frac{\bar{A}}{s-\beta_2} - \frac{\bar{C}}{s})\ln|(s-\beta_2)Y - \bar{A}|\right]. \tag{10.32}$$

By calculating $\mu$ from $(Y_0, K_0)$ and (10.32), (10.25) is established.

From (10.23.1), we obtain, by multiplying with $\exp\left\{-\frac{s-\beta_2}{\beta_1}t\right\}$, that

$$\lim_{t\to\infty}\frac{|Y(t)|}{|Y^*(t)|} = \lim_{t\to\infty}\frac{|\frac{\bar{A}}{s-\beta_2}e^{-(\frac{(s-\beta_2)}{\beta_1})t}+Y_0-\frac{\bar{A}}{s-\beta_2}|}{|\frac{\bar{A}}{s-\beta_2}e^{-(\frac{s-\beta_2}{\beta_1})t}+Y_0^*-\frac{\bar{A}}{s-\beta_2}|}$$

$$= \frac{|Y_0-\bar{A}/(s-\beta_2)|}{|Y_0^*-\bar{A}/(s-\beta_2)|} = \mathcal{M} < \infty, \tag{10.33}$$

which establishes (10.27.1).

From (10.23.2), we see by a similar procedure as in (10.33) that $\lim_{t\to\infty}|K(t)/K^*(t)| = \mathcal{M}$; hence (10.27.2).

From (10.23.1–2), it follows that

$$\lim_{t\to\infty} \mathrm{v}(t) = \lim_{t\to\infty}\frac{K(t)}{Y(t)} = \frac{[Y_0-\bar{A}/(s-\beta_2)]\cdot[\frac{\beta_1}{1-\beta_2/s}]}{Y_0-\bar{A}/(s-\beta_2)} = \frac{\beta_1}{1-\beta_2/s}, \tag{10.34}$$

that is, a limit which is independent of the initial values $(Y_0, K_0)$.

But since the set of solutions the model (10.22.1–2) does not include the constant ratio solution $\mathrm{v}(t) = v = \beta_1/(1-\beta_2/s)$, we have in (10.22.1–2) only global *strong absolute* ratio stability (10.28) rather than global *asymptotic* ratio stability, cf. (10.16.1–2), (10.19.1).

From linear solutions (10.24.2) with a common coefficient of $t$, the stability property (10.29) is easily verified, as is (10.30). □

The *trajectories* (10.25) look at infinity like the linear trajectories of (10.18.1–2), as the trajectories (10.25) are at infinity *parallel* to the ray $K = vY$, cf. (10.19.1), (10.28) and the dotted line in Fig. 10.2.

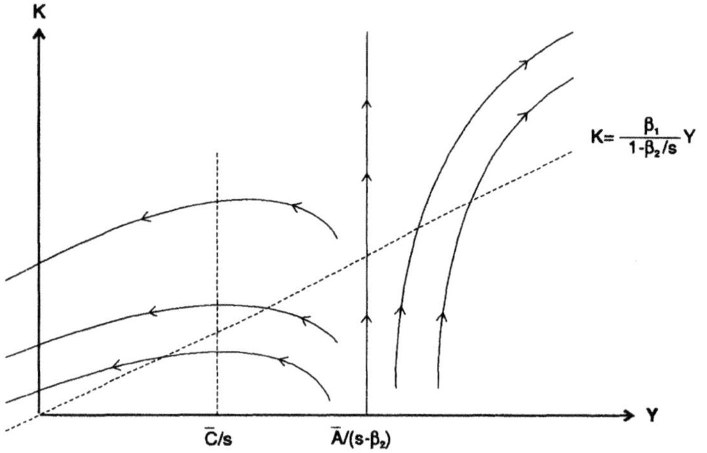


**Fig. 10.2** Phase portrait of the Harrodian growth model, (10.22.1–2)

The model (10.20–10.22.2) can be extended by including proportional income taxes, government expenditures ($\bar{G}$), imports ($M = \bar{M} + mY$), exports ($\bar{X}$), as done by Harrod (1939, p. 28). However, the distinction between private saving and private investment has now to be taken into account, and the relationship between saving and the capital stock needs to be carefully considered.

## Economic Aspects and Stability Issues

The economic rationale of Harrodian macrodynamics has been interpreted in many different ways. The application of the "acceleration principle" in the simplest version (10.1–10.3) has been construed as implicitly postulating: A *fixed-coefficient technology* with the constant accelerator coefficient $\beta$ of (10.2) representing the parameter $\beta_K$ of production function (11.28). According to this view (Solow (1956, p. 73)) the Harrod model is just the special case of (11.1.1–11.2.2) spelled out in Proposition 11.2.

The Domar model (see Domar 1946, p. 137)—dealing with the problems of maintaining long-run equilibrium between the productive *capacity (potential output)* of the economy and its national income *(actual output)*—did implicitly assume the production function of the form (11.28) with either factor being *limitational* upon maximal output. Otherwise, with continuous substitution possibilities between capital and labor, cf. (2.3), the *notion* of *capacity* (finite limits to output, due to a single fixed factor) would have *lost* its meaning, cf. Färe (1984, p. 367).

However, the Harrod model (10.1–10.3) did not, as mentioned by Harrod himself (see Harrod 1939, p. 17; Harrod 1973, p. 73) and others (Eisner 1958, p. 708; Cornwall 1970, p. 69), implicitly assume the *technology* (11.28). The *parameter* $\beta$, (10.2), is here more appropriately interpreted as a *normal* (optimal) *capital-output* ratio geared—with standard convexity assumptions about the isoquants, cf. Remark 2.3, and $m = 1$—to the assumption of *fixed* ("sticky") input *prices.* Of course, such reading of the $\beta$-value (10.2) must *not* be confounded with the *ratio* of the *state variables* in the system (10.5.1–10.6), that is, the size of the actual capital-output ratio $v(t) = K(t)/Y(t)$. The latter may fortuitously be and remain equal to $\beta$, cf. (10.9); but whenever $v(t)$ differs from $\beta$, the return to normalcy, cf. (10.16.1–2), is not foreclosed, as feared by Harrod. However, normalcy is regained in the subtle way of rendering *initial discrepancies* between $v(t)$ and $\beta$ *imperceptible* in the *long run*, cf. (10.11) and (10.13).

But, the failure to notice this submerging of the ratio discrepancies also appeared in the improper monotonicity interpretation of the ratio solutions in the neoclassical model, cf. (11.11.1–2), Theorem 11.3, and Figs. 11.1 and 11.2.

It is also worth noticing that the *labor* force (employment) is *not* a *state variable* in any of the Harrod models, and therefore, no conclusions can be formally derived about the labor market; nor does the latter formally affect the time paths of output and capital, since the Harrod models are *deterministic* dynamic systems. The economic subject matter of the Harrod and the neoclassical growth models is indeed very different. The Solow model explores the dynamic implications of full employment in the factor markets, emphasizing the *supply side* of the economy, whereas the dynamics of the Harrod model deals with the *aggregate demand side* of the economy.

All the Harrodian growth models above preserved *continuous* aggregate demand equilibrium. Hence, the *coordination* problem, arising from *independent* saving (consumption) and investment decisions, is *solved* in the Harrod model by properly determining (selecting) consistent time paths of income $Y(t)$.

With the simple model (10.1–10.3), (10.5.1–2), the problem of aggregate demand equilibrium problem is easily resolved, irrespective of the size of the positive parameters $\beta$ and s. Consequently, from any initial values, $(Y_0, K_0)$, the economy must grow in accordance with the solutions (10.10.1–2) and (10.12.1–2).

With the modified model (10.1), (10.3), (10.17), (10.18.1–2) and the parameter restriction $s > \beta_2$, aggregate demand equilibrium will also be maintained by *growing solutions* from any initial values, $(Y_0, K_0)$. Let us articulate the economic working of this model, with $s > \beta_2$. At any given income level, the output $(sY)$ released by saving (10.2) exceeds the investment component $(\beta_2 Y)$, (10.17), and so inventories would tend to *increase* by $(s - \beta_2)Y$. To avoid the latter and maintain the aggregate demand equilibrium $(S = I)$, (10.3), the investment component $\beta_1 \dot{Y}$, (10.17), has to be *positive* and absorb the "slack" $(s - \beta_2)Y$, cf. (10.18.1). Hence, *total investment* demand is actually *sustained* at the level equal to *total saving*, as evidenced by the stock increases (10.18.2).

**Remark 10.3** Although the model (10.18.1–2) with $\beta_2 > s$ represents an artificial economic situation, it is for later purposes worthwhile to examine the paradoxical nature of the *solutions*, $Y(t)$ and $K(t)$, moving here in *opposite* directions. When $\beta_2 > s$, the investment component $(\beta_2 Y)$ *exceeds* the output $(sY)$ released by saving, and so inventories *tend* to *decrease* by $(\beta_2 - s)Y$. To avoid the latter and to maintain aggregate demand equilibrium $(S = I)$, a *disinvestment* component $\beta_1 \dot{Y} < 0$ has to temper investment demand by $(\beta_2 - s)Y$. But to accommodate such disinvestment component, *income* (output) must be *decreasing*. However, total (net) invest demand remain positive throughout and equal to saving; hence, the capital stock increases, (10.18.2), whereas income decreases, (10.18.1). The phase portrait of (10.18.1–10.19.2) with $\beta_2 > s$ is parallel straight lines with a negative slope, and the $K$-axis is the attractor set. ▽

The Harrodian model (10.20–10.22.2) will only be discussed in the parameter case of economic interest, $s > \beta_2$, cf. Fig. 10.2. First, we note that the particular *solutions* (10.24.1–2) and their trajectory, $Y = \bar{A}/(s - \beta_2)$, (10.26), correspond to the traditional *short-run*, comparative *static* solutions of (10.3), (10.20–10.21) with $\beta_1 = 0$, that is, the standard Keynesian "multiplier effects" of $\bar{A}$. Evidently, the *long-run* implications (10.30) of the simple *comparative static solutions* (10.24.1–2) are untenable. Accordingly, the *long run* calls for other models, for example, the model (10.22.1–2) with $\beta_1 > 0$.

Secondly, on each side of *Keynesian trajectory* (10.26), *two* very *different subfamilies* of solutions evolve from (10.22.1–2). The economic rationale of these two subfamilies deserves a closer look.

Consider initial national income (output) values, such as

$$\bar{C}/s < Y_0 = \lambda\bar{A}/(s - \beta_2), \quad 0 \leq \lambda < 1, \ s > \beta_2, \tag{10.35}$$

$$Y_0 \geq \bar{A}/(s - \beta_2), \quad s > \beta_2. \tag{10.36}$$

Then, it is easily verified from (10.20–10.21) and (10.35) that

$$[\bar{I} + \beta_2 Y_0 > \bar{C} + sY_0 = S(Y_0)] \Leftrightarrow (1 - \lambda)\bar{A} > 0, \tag{10.37}$$

that is, inventories *tend* to *decrease* by $(1 - \lambda)\bar{A}$. To counteract this and to maintain aggregate demand equilibrium ($S = I$), the *investment* component $\beta_1\dot{Y}$, (10.20), has to temper investment demand by $(1 - \lambda)\bar{A}$. The accommodation of such disinvestment is tantamount to $\dot{Y} < 0$, cf. Remark 10.2. Although income $Y(t)$ continues to fall, the capital stock $K(t)$ nevertheless increases, as long as saving remain positive, cf. (10.21), (10.22.2). Only when income (output) has decreased so much that $Y(t)$ cannot even cover the consumption expenditure $\bar{C}/s$ will also the capital stock $K(t)$ start declining, cf. (10.35), (10.22.2), and inexorably the economy then sinks into oblivion or rather that the model ceases to operate, see Fig. 10.2.

For any value $Y_0$ satisfying (10.36), the corresponding inequality (10.37) is reversed, and consequently, aggregate demand equilibrium ($S = I$) implies $\dot{Y} > 0$. Hence, the solutions, $Y(t)$ and $K(t)$, cf. (10.23.1–2), always increase as depicted in Fig. 10.2.

Although the equilibrium dynamics of (10.20–10.22.2) can be shocked, by low initial income values (10.35), into generating a *subfamily* of economic solutions with *gloomy* prospects, the *subfamily* of *growing* solutions is obviously of much *more* practical and theoretical interest.

We have dwelt on mathematical and economic aspects of *dynamic aggregate demand equilibrium models,* based upon the simple and modified version of the acceleration principle of investment demand as contemplated by Harrod. These dynamic equilibrium *demand-side* growth models had essentially the *same ratio* and *coordinate* stability properties as the dynamic equilibrium *supply side* growth models of neoclassical kind, cf. (10.27.1–10.29), (10.16.1–10.16.4), and (11.11.1–11.12.2). With *flexible parameters,* similar results are obtained for non-autonomous *Keynesian growth models* in Chap. 1, section "The Multiplier-Accelerator Growth Model of Harrod".

## BIBLIOGRAPHY

Cornwall J (1970) The Role of Demand and Investment in Long–Term Growth. Quart J Economics 84:48–69

Domar ED (1946) Capital Expansion, Rate of Growth and Employment. Econometrica 14:137–47

Eisner R (1958) On Growth Models and the Neoclassical Resurgence. Economic J 68:707–21

Färe R (1984) The Existence of Plant Capacity. Int Econ Rev 25:209–213

Gandolfo G (1980) Economic Dynamics: Methods and Models, 2nd edn. North–Holland, Amsterdam

Hacche G (1985) The Theory of Economic Growth, An Introduction. MacMillan, London

Hahn FH, Matthews RCO (1964) The Theory of Economic Growth: A Survey. Economic Journal 74:779–902

Harrod RF (1939) An Essay in Dynamic Theory. Economic J 49:14–33, or Stiglitz (1969)

Harrod RF (1973) Economic Dynamics. MacMillan, London

Keynes JM (1936) The General Theory of Employment, Interest and Money. MacMillan, London

Solow RM (1956) A Contribution to the Theory of Economic Growth. Quarterly Journal of Economics 70:65–94, Reprinted in Stiglitz (1969), and in Becker (1991)

Stiglitz JE, Uzawa H (1969) Readings in the Modern Theory of Economic Growth. M.I.T. Press, Cambridge, Mass

Wan HY Jr (1971) Economic Growth. Harcourt Brace Jovanowich, New York

CHAPTER 11

# Neoclassical Dynamics and Solow Growth Models

## THE DYNAMIC SYSTEM, SOLUTIONS, AND STABILITY

As given by Solow (1956, p. 66–67), the neoclassical growth model consists of the dynamic system,

$$\dot{L} = n\,L \qquad\qquad = \quad \mathcal{F}(L, K), \qquad L, K \geq 0, \tag{11.1.1}$$

$$\dot{K} = s\,Y = s\,F(L, K) \quad = \quad \mathcal{G}(L, K), \qquad L, K \geq 0. \tag{11.1.2}$$

With the standard neoclassical assumption of *constant returns* ($m = 1$) to *scale* in production, (11.1.1–2) represents a *homogeneous dynamic system* of degree, $m = 1$, (but nonhomogeneous dynamics with $m \neq 1$ in production), viz., cf. (2.8),

$$\dot{L} = L\,n \qquad = \quad L\,\mathfrak{f}(k), \quad n > 0, \qquad L \neq 0, \tag{11.2.1}$$

$$\dot{K} = L\,s\,f(k) \quad = \quad L\,\mathfrak{g}(k), \quad 0 < s < 1, \qquad L \neq 0. \tag{11.2.2}$$

In contrast to the "classical" system (9.1.1–2), where the growth of the labor supply is partly linked to economic conditions (per-capita income), the natural growth rate of neoclassical labor supply (11.1.1) is *independent* of economic and social conditions, i.e., now *unrestrained* by "positive" and "preventive" checks, Malthus (1803, 1958, p. 12). Hence, (11.1.1) may in fact be said to correspond to the Malthusian view of the *power* of *procreation* only: "It may safely be pronounced, therefore, that population, when unchecked, increases in a geometrical ratio", Malthus (1803, 1958, I, p. 8).

Solow (1956, p. 67): "As a result of exogenous population growth the Labour force increases at a constant relative rate, n", (11.2.1).



B. S. Jensen, *The Elements and Dynamic Systems of Economic Growth and Trade Models*, https://doi.org/10.1007/978-3-031-52493-6_11

The neoclassical system (11.1.1–11.2.2) has been expounded in vast literature, journals, and textbooks over the last 70 years. However, from the beginning, uncertainties about the behavior of the solutions to this standard neoclassical growth model persist in the literature. Before we comment on these matters, the *qualitative* properties of the *solutions* to (11.1.1–11.2.2) are *summarized* in Theorems 11.1–11.3.

The *director function* $h(k)$ of the homogeneous dynamic system (11.2.1–2) is, cf. (7.7),

$$\begin{aligned} h(k) &= \mathfrak{g}(k) - k\,\mathfrak{f}(k) \\ &= s\,f(k) - n\,k, \end{aligned} \tag{11.3}$$

and the function $H'(k)$ becomes, cf. (7.16), (11.3)

$$H'(k) = \frac{\mathfrak{f}(k)}{h(k)} = \frac{n}{s\,f(k) - n\,k}, \qquad h(k) \neq 0. \tag{11.4}$$

Due to $m = 1$, the *governing function* $Q(r)$ of the *ratio* solutions $k(t)$ coincides with the *director function*, i.e, cf. (7.17.1–2), (7.70), (11.3)

$$\dot{k} = Q(k) = h(k) = s\,f(k) - n\,k. \tag{11.5}$$

**Theorem 11.1** *The growth model (11.1.1–11.2.2) has—under the regularity conditions (2.12) and $n/s \in J$, (2.13)—one and only one stationary ratio solution*

$$\forall t \quad k(t) = \kappa = K_0/L_0 = k_0, \quad \kappa \in \mathbf{R}_+, \tag{11.6.1}$$

*where the positive* ***director root*** $\kappa$ *is uniquely determined by the equation, cf. (2.10)*

$$AP_K(\kappa) = \frac{f(\kappa)}{\kappa} = \frac{n}{s}; \quad v(\kappa) = \kappa/f(\kappa) = s/n. \tag{11.6.2}$$

*The coordinate solutions $[L(t), K(t)]$—with initial values $L_0$, $K_0$ upon the directrix $K = \kappa L$—have the form*

$$L(t) = L_0\,e^{nt}, \quad K(t) = L_0\,\kappa\,e^{nt}, \tag{11.7.1}$$

*with the* ***directrix value*** $\mathfrak{f}(\kappa)$ *being,*

$$\mathfrak{f}(\kappa) = n. \tag{11.7.2}$$

*The family of ratio solutions $k(t)$ to (11.5)—with initial values $(L_0, K_0)$ outside the* ***directrix*** *$K = \kappa L$—is given by*

$$k(t) = I^{-1}(t + t_0), \quad t + t_0 \in T = ]-\infty, +\infty[, \tag{11.8}$$

*where the invertible function $I \in C^2$-class is the primitive*

$$I(k) = \int \frac{dk}{h(k)} = t + t_0, \; t_0 = I(k_0); \; k, k_0 \neq \kappa. \tag{11.9}$$

*The family of coordinate solutions to (11.2.1–2)—with initial values $(L_0, K_0)$ outside the directrix $K = \kappa L$—are given [with $k(t)$ from (11.8)] by*

$$L(t) = L_0 \, e^{nt}, \tag{11.10.1}$$

$$K(t) = k(t)\, L(t) = L_0 \, k(t) \, e^{nt}. \tag{11.10.2}$$

***Proof*** As usual, cf. Theorems 7.1–7.2 and Proposition 7.1 in Chap. 7, Theorem 11.1 follows from the application of Theorems 28.1–28.2 in section "Ratio Solutions, Coordinate Solutions, and Trajectories"–"The Ratio and Coordinate Solutions on Directrices", together with, (11.2.1–11.3) and (11.5).

The existence and uniqueness of the director root $\kappa$, (11.6.1–2), solving $h(k) = 0$, (11.3), follow from the strict concavity of $f(k)$, (2.12), and the condition $n/s \in J$, (2.13). The latter ensures the existence of $\kappa$, satisfying (11.6.2), since for either $k \to 0$ or $k \to \infty$, L' Hospital gives: $\lim f(k)/k = \lim f'(k)$.

The simplicity of $f(k)$, (11.2.1), gives (11.7.2) and accounts here for the simplicity of (11.10.1). □

**Theorem 11.2** *The family of ratio solution $k(t)$ to (11.5) and the family of coordinate solutions $[L(t), K(t)]$ to (11.2.1–2) have—under the regularity conditions (2.12) and $n/s \in J$, (2.13)—respectively, global asymptotic stability and global weak relative stability, i.e.,*

$$\exists k_0 = \kappa > 0 \quad : \quad k(t) = \kappa \qquad \forall t, \tag{11.11.1}$$

$$\forall k_0 \in \mathbf{R}_+/\{\kappa\} \quad : \quad k(t) \to \kappa \text{ as } t \to \infty, \tag{11.11.2}$$

$$\forall (L_0, K_0) \in \mathbf{R}^2_+ \quad : \quad L(t)/L^*(t) \text{ are bounded as } t \to \infty, \tag{11.12.1}$$

$$\forall (L_0, K_0) \in \mathbf{R}^2_+ \quad : \quad K(t)/K^*(t) \text{ are bounded as } t \to \infty. \tag{11.12.2}$$

***Proof*** The proof is analogous to that of Proposition 7.2, in ssection "Constant Returns to Scale". As $h(k)$, (11.3), decreases through $\kappa$, (11.6.2), property (11.11.2) follows from Theorem 28.4 in subsection "Global Asymptotic Ratio Stability".

Property (11.12.1–2) follows from (11.11.1–2) and Theorem 28.10 in section "Global Asymptotic Ratio Stability and Global Stabilities of Coordinate Solutions". □

## The Phase Portrait and the Steady-State Path

The *phase portrait* of (11.2.1–2), traced out by the *phase curves* (11.7.1–2) and (11.10.1–2), can be outlined via a representation of the *trajectories* as *plane loci.* Obviously, in the $(L, K)$ plane, the trajectory of (11.7.1–2) is a ray with the slope $\kappa$, and the trajectories of (11.10.1–2) can as usual be represented the equation, cf. (7.21), (11.4)

$$L - c_0 \exp\{H(k)\} = 0, \quad c_0 = L_0 \exp\{-H(k_0)\}, \quad k, k_0 \neq \kappa. \tag{11.13}$$

Then the general shape of the loci (11.13) is to be examined. On this matter, let us first consult and present the general viewpoint of Solow that permeated the subsequent literature of economic growth.

We quote Solow (1956, p. 81–82):

> Suppose there is a stable asymptotic ratio $r^*$; then all growth paths issuing from arbitrary initial conditions *approach* the ray in the limit. Two such paths are shown, issuing from initial points $P_1$ and $P_2$. Since back in Figure I the approach of $r$ to $r^*$ was *monotonic,* the paths must look as shown in figure VI (italics ours).

His Figure I shows (11.5) in a $(k, \dot{k})$ diagram, and his Figure VI shows that the plane curves (11.10.1–2), (11.13) will, in the $(L, K)$ plane, have the ray $K = \kappa L$ as an *asymptote.* The well-known survey of growth theories, (see Hahn and Matthews 1964, p. 31), concurs with this phase portrait of the neoclassical growth model.

The quotations disclose the still common misperception that the *monotonicity* of $k(t)$, (11.8), together with global *asymptotic* ratio *stability,* (11.11.1–2), necessarily implies that the *trajectories* (11.10.1–2), (11.13) have the directrix (11.7.1) as an *asymptote.*

Of course, at this stage of our exposition and application of homogeneous dynamics, the reader will know that the monotonic behavior of $\mathbf{k(t)}$ and the *property* (11.11.1–2) is certainly *not* tantamount to the corresponding system of trajectories having the directrix as an asymptote, cf. Theorem 7.5, (7.42), (7.54), Proposition 7.4, and Theorem 9.1.

But the question remains, what does the phase portrait of the general neoclassical growth model (11.2.1–2) actually look like, i.e., what is after all the shape of the trajectories, (11.10.1–2), (11.13)? The general answer is stated in

**Theorem 11.3** *The phase portrait of the growth model (11.1.1–11.2.2) is—under the assumptions (2.12) and $n/s \in J$, (2.13)—parabolic. The trajectories (11.13) are below (above) the directrix $K = \kappa L$, convex (concave) curves that are, at infinity, parallel to the directrix.*

***Proof*** The assumptions ensure for the model (11.1.1–11.2.2), the existence and the uniqueness of a ray trajectory (directrix) in the interior of the phase plane, cf. Theorem 11.1.

At any point $(L, K)$ in the phase plane, the trajectories (11.10.1–2), (11.13), have a tangent with a slope, $dK/dL$, given by, cf. (11.2.1–2)

$$dK/dL \equiv \dot{K}/\dot{L} \equiv q(k) = \mathfrak{g}(k)/\mathfrak{f}(k) = (s/n)f(k). \tag{11.14}$$

Next, we get from (11.14) and (2.9), $m = 1$, (2.12), (2.16.2), (2.44.3), cf. (7.29.1–3),

$$\forall k > 0 \quad : \quad q(k) \quad = \quad (s/n)f(k) > 0, \tag{11.15.1}$$

$$\forall k > 0 \quad : \quad q'(k) \quad = \quad (s/n)f'(k) > 0, \tag{11.15.2}$$

$$\forall k > 0 \quad : \quad E(q,k) \quad = \quad E(y,k) = \epsilon_K > 0. \tag{11.15.3}$$

Then (11.15.1–11.15.3) and (11.11.1–2) substantiate the parabolic form, see Theorem 28.8 in section "Asymptotic Ratio Stability and Trajectory Geometry", and evidently, they establish as well the convexity/concavity of the trajectories, cf. (11.15.2), and the parallelism at infinity; see Fig. 11.1a–b. □

Whereas some *classical* growth models, depending on the substitution elasticity, admitted *three* configuration types of the phase portrait, cf. Theorem 7.5 and Proposition 7.1, the general *neoclassical* growth model (11.2.1–2), *irrespective* of substitution elasticity, *admits* geometrically—like the *aggregate classical* growth model (9.2.1–2), cf. Theorem 9.1—only *one configuration* type of the phase portrait, as just seen in Theorem 11.3. Thus, contrary to the traditional perception, the directrix is *never* an asymptote for the trajectories of the *general* neoclassical system (11.1.1–11.2.2). We return to this and related matters in section "Trajectory Geometry and Kinematics" below.

## Neoclassical Growth and Special Technologies

### *CD Technology*

The dearth of closed form solutions to nonlinear dynamic systems also applies to the neoclassical system (11.2.1–2). However, it can be solved in case of a CD technology. To illustrate Theorem 11.1 and Theorem 11.3, we give

**Proposition 11.1** *The growth model (11.1.1–11.2.2) has—with the CD technology, (2.48)—one and only one stationary ratio solution*

$$\forall t \quad k(t) = \kappa = (\gamma s/n)^{\frac{1}{1-a}}. \tag{11.16}$$

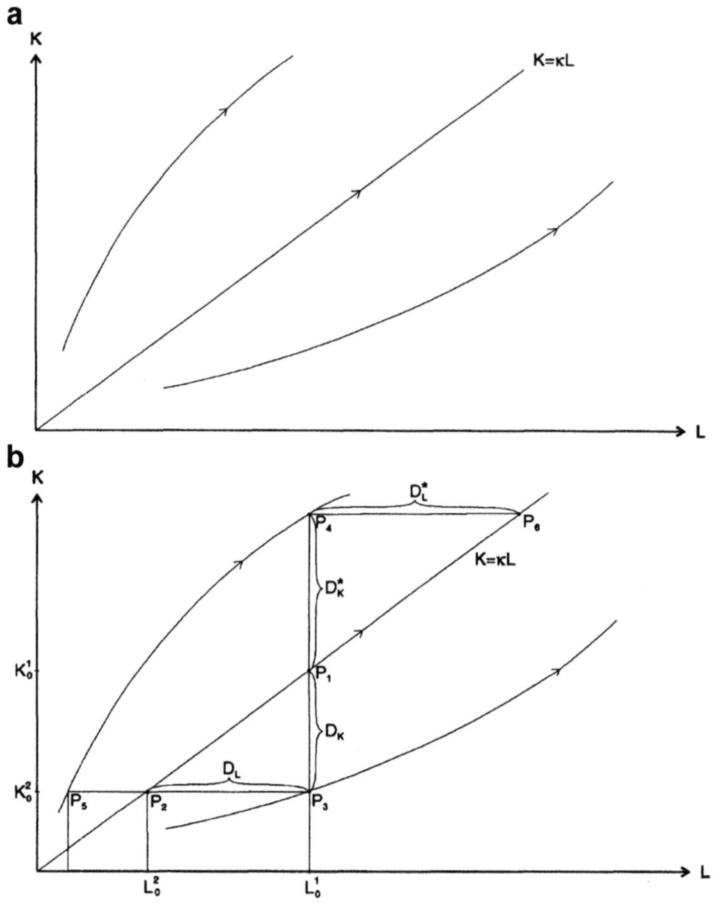


**Fig. 11.1** (**a**) Phase portrait of the neoclassical growth model, (11.1.1–11.2.2). (**b**) The CD trajectories, (11.18.1–11.19)

*The family of nonstationary ratio solutions is given by*

$$k(t) = \left[\frac{\gamma s}{n}\{1 - e^{-n(1-a)(t+t_0)}\}\right]^{\frac{1}{1-a}} \tag{11.17.1}$$

$$= \kappa\left[1 - \{1 - (k_0/\kappa)^{1-a}\}e^{-n(1-a)t}\right]^{\frac{1}{1-a}}. \tag{11.17.2}$$

*The directrix solutions* $[L(t), K(t)]$ *are given by (11.7.1–2), with* $\kappa$ *from (11.16).*

*The family of non-directrix solutions* $[L(t), K(t)]$ *are given by*

$$L(t) = L_0 e^{nt}, \tag{11.18.1}$$

$$K(t) = L_0 \kappa [(k_0/\kappa)^{1-a} - 1 + e^{n(1-a)t}]^{\frac{1}{1-a}}, \quad k_0 \neq \kappa. \tag{11.18.2}$$

*The system of trajectories, (11.18.1–2), are as loci, represented by the equation*

$$K = \kappa [\, L_0^{1-a}\{(\, k_0/\kappa \,)^{1-a} - 1\} + L^{1-a} \,]^{\frac{1}{1-a}} > 0. \tag{11.19}$$

***Proof*** From (2.48) and (11.3), we have

$$h(k) = s\,\gamma\, k^a - n\, k, \tag{11.20}$$

which gives the positive director root $\kappa$, (11.16).

From (11.9) and (11.20), we get

$$I(k) = \int \frac{dk}{h(k)} = \int \frac{dk}{s\gamma k(k^{a-1} - n/s\gamma)}, \quad k \neq \kappa \wedge 0, \tag{11.21}$$

which is a standard integral with the primitive, see Selby (1973, p. 417),

$$I(k) = \frac{-1}{n(1-a)} \ln\{1 - (n/\gamma s)k^{1-a}\}. \tag{11.22}$$

Then (11.22) and $I(k) = t + t_0$ imply (11.17.1), cf. (11.9).

By $I(k_0) = t_0$ and (11.22), we obtain, cf. (11.16)

$$e^{-n(1-a)t_0} = 1 - (n/\gamma s)k_0^{1-a} = 1 - (k_0/\kappa)^{1-a}, \tag{11.23}$$

which then gives the second formula (11.17.2).

The coordinate solutions (11.18.1–2) follow from (11.10.1–2) and (11.17.2).

By (11.4) and (11.20–11.23), we get

$$H(k) = nI(k) = -\frac{1}{1-a} \ln\{1 - (k/\kappa)^{1-a}\}, \tag{11.24}$$

and hence, cf. (11.13), (11.24), the loci of (11.18.1–2) are described by

$$L = L_0 \left[ \frac{1 - (k_0/\kappa)^{1-a}}{1 - (k/\kappa)^{1-a}} \right]^{\frac{1}{1-a}}. \tag{11.25}$$

Finally, replacing $k$ in (11.25) with $K/L$ and collecting, the loci attain the explicit form (11.19). □

**Remark 11.1** To display the trajectory geometry of Theorem 11.3, we calculate from (11.19)

$$\frac{d^2K}{dL^2} = \kappa a L_0^{1-a} L^{-1-a} \left[ L_0^{1-a} \{ \left( \frac{k_0}{\kappa} \right)^{1-a} - 1 \} + L^{1-a} \right]^{\frac{2a-1}{1-a}} \left[ 1 - (\frac{k_0}{\kappa})^{1-a} \right]. \tag{11.26}$$

As only the last bracket may be negative, this implies

$$0 < a < 1; \quad \forall k_0 \lesseqgtr \kappa \quad \Rightarrow \quad d^2K/dL^2 \gtreqless 0, \tag{11.27}$$

which complies with the convexity/concavity properties of Theorem 11.3. ▽

### *Leontief Technology*

Another *technology* worth examining is the case of *fixed proportions* (fixed coefficients). The Harrod-Domar growth model is often interpreted as being just an extreme version of (11.1.1–11.2.2), with a production function $F(L, K)$ of the *fixed-coefficient* type. We earlier discussed the Harrod model from an entirely different point of view; but here let us consider the Leontief production function

$$\begin{aligned} Y = F(L, K) &= \min \{L/\beta_L, \ K/\beta_K\}; \quad \beta_L, \beta_K > 0; \quad L, K > 0, \\ &= L \min \{1/\beta_L, \ (1/\beta_K)k\} = Lf(k). \end{aligned} \tag{11.28}$$

where the *parameters* $\beta_L$ and $\beta_K$ are the *fixed* unit requirements (input-output coefficients) of labor and capital, and where $f(k)$ is

$$f(k) = \begin{cases} (1/\beta_K)k, & 0 < k \leq \beta_K/\beta_L, \\ 1/\beta_L, & k > \beta_K/\beta_L. \end{cases} \tag{11.29}$$

Obviously, the standard assumptions (2.3–2.5), (2.12–2.13) do *not* apply to (11.28–11.29). Thus, the latter precludes the straightforward application of previous theorems that relied upon continuous substitution possibilities between labor and capital in production of a single output.

Hence, before proceeding with issues of dynamic models, we should recall the most important properties of production functions, symbolized by $Y = F(L, K)$. First of all, it gives the *maximum* output ($Y$) that can be obtained from any given factor combination ($L, K$). This maximum output property still holds for (11.28). But the well-known right-angled *isoquants* of (11.28) *no longer* retain the traditional property, cf. (2.3) and (2.23), of representing *technical efficient factor* combinations in the sense that reducing one input (without increasing the other one) always gives a smaller output (a lower isoquant). In short, until now, our growth models and their solutions and trajectories always bear the imprint of *efficient factor utilization* (minimal input sets). But with (11.29), only the corners of the isoquant are minimal input combinations, i.e.,

$$\text{efficient factor combinations: } \{L, K > 0 \mid K/L = k = \beta_K/\beta_L\}. \tag{11.30}$$

Furthermore, the growth models hitherto considered represent *full employment economics.* Initially and later on along any of the trajectories, all available quantities of labor and capital were fully employed. But, of course, state values of $L$ and $K$ outside the ray (11.30) cannot *simultaneously* reflect efficiency and full employment.

For a *neoclassical* growth model (11.1.1–11.2.2) with the production function (11.28–11.29), we should *retain* the assumption of permanent *full employment* of labor and capital. Then, what is the phase portrait of such a model, and what are the stability properties of its ratio and coordinate solutions? Our answers can still be organized within the general framework of homogeneous dynamics, with $m = 1$.

With the production function (11.29), the *director function* (11.3) becomes

$$h(k) = sf(k) - n\,k = \begin{cases} (s/\beta_K - n)k, & 0 < k \le \beta_K/\beta_L, \\ s/\beta_L - nk, & k > \beta_K/\beta_L. \end{cases} \tag{11.31}$$

The shape of $h(k)$ has, depending on the parameters $(s, \beta_K, n)$, three forms, as depicted in Fig. 11.2.

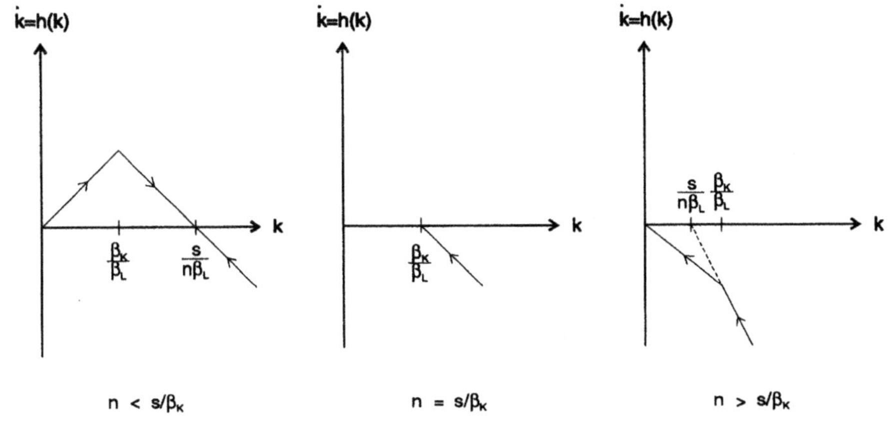


**Fig. 11.2** The director function $h(k)$, (11.31)

**Proposition 11.2** *The growth model (11.1.1–11.2.2) has—with the Leontief technology (11.28–11.29) and respectively,* $n < s/\beta_K, n = s/\beta_K, n > s/\beta_K$*—the ratio solutions* $k(t)$ *and trajectory systems:*

*(i)* $n < s/\beta_K$

$$k(t) = \begin{cases} k_0\, e^{(\frac{s}{\beta_K}-n)t}, & 0 \le k_0 < \beta_K/\beta_L,\ k(\bar{t}) = \beta_K/\beta_L, \\ \kappa + (\,k_0 - \kappa\,)\, e^{-nt}, & k_0 \ge \beta_K/\beta_L,\ \kappa = s/n\beta_L, \end{cases} \tag{11.32}$$

$$K = \begin{cases} k_0\, L_0^{1-\frac{s/\beta_K}{n}}\, L^{\frac{s/\beta_K}{n}}, & 0 \le k_0 < \beta_K/\beta_L, \\ L_0\,(\,k_0 - \kappa\,) + \kappa L, & k_0 \ge \beta_K/\beta_L,\ \kappa = s/n\beta_L. \end{cases} \tag{11.33}$$

*(ii)* $n = s/\beta_K$

$$k(t) = \begin{cases} k_0, & 0 \le k_0 < \beta_K/\beta_L,\ k_0 = \kappa, \\ \kappa + (k_0 - \kappa)e^{-nt}, & k_0 \ge \beta_K/\beta_L,\ \kappa = \beta_K/\beta_L, \end{cases} \tag{11.34}$$

$$K = \begin{cases} k_0 L, & 0 < k_0 < \beta_K/\beta_L, \\ L_0(k_0 - \kappa) + \kappa L, & k_0 \ge \beta_K/\beta_L, \kappa = \beta_K/\beta_L. \end{cases} \tag{11.35}$$

*(iii)* $n > s/\beta_K$

$$k(t) = \begin{cases} k_0\, e^{(\frac{s}{\beta_K}-n)t}, & 0 \le k_0 \le \frac{\beta_K}{\beta_L}, \\ \frac{s}{n\beta_L} + (k_0 - \frac{s}{n\beta_L})\, e^{-nt}, & k_0 > \frac{\beta_K}{\beta_L},\ k(\bar{t}) = \beta_K/\beta_L, \end{cases} \tag{11.36}$$

$$K = \begin{cases} k_0\, L_0^{1-\frac{s/\beta_K}{n}}\, L^{\frac{s/\beta_K}{n}}, & 0 \le k_0 \le \frac{\beta_K}{\beta_L}, \\ L_0\,(\,k_0 - \frac{s}{n\beta_L}\,) + (\,\frac{s}{n\beta_L}\,)L, & k_0 > \frac{\beta_K}{\beta_L}. \end{cases} \tag{11.37}$$

*The coordinate solutions* $[L(t), K(t)]$ *in case (i–iii) are given by*

$$L(t) = L_0 e^{nt}, \quad t \in [0, +\infty[, \tag{11.38}$$

$$K(t) = \begin{cases} L_0\, k_0\, e^{(\,s/\beta_K\,)\,t}, & 0 \le k_0 < \beta_K/\beta_L, \\ L_0\,[\,k_0 - s/n\beta_L + (\,s/n\beta_L\,)\, e^{nt}\,], & k_0 \ge \beta_K/\beta_L. \end{cases} \tag{11.39}$$

*Corresponding to (11.38–11.39), the time paths* $Y(t)$ *of output (11.28) become*

$$Y(t) = \begin{cases} (K_0/\beta_K)\, e^{(s/\beta_K)\,t}, & 0 \le k_0 < \beta_K/\beta_L, \\ (L_0/\beta_L)\, e^{n\,t}, & k_0 \ge \beta_K/\beta_L. \end{cases} \tag{11.40}$$

*The time interval of* $K(t)$ *and* $Y(t)$ *is infinite, but the respective time intervals of the component functions (11.39), (11.40) follow from, (11.32), (11.34) and (11.36), cf. Fig. 11.2.*

***Proof*** We shall prove the case (i) in detail; the cases (ii–iii) follow analogously with minor modifications.

*ad (i)*. By (11.31), we get the director roots

$$h(\kappa) = 0 \Leftrightarrow \kappa = s/n\beta_L \wedge 0. \tag{11.41}$$

From (11.9) and (11.31), we have, cf. (11.41)

$$I(k) = \int \frac{dk}{h(k)} = \begin{cases} \int \frac{dk}{(s/\beta_K - n)k}, & 0 < k < \beta_K/\beta_L, \\ \int \frac{dk}{n(\kappa - k)}, & k \ge \beta_K/\beta_L,\ \kappa \ne k, \end{cases} \tag{11.42}$$

which gives the primitives

$$I(k) = \begin{cases} \frac{1}{s/\beta_K - n} \ln k & 0 < k < \beta_K/\beta_L, \\ -\frac{1}{n} \ln(\kappa - k), & k \ge \beta_K/\beta_L,\ \kappa \ne k. \end{cases} \tag{11.43}$$

Using (11.8–11.9) and (11.43), the ratio solutions (11.32) are easily derived. The stationary ratio solutions, $k(t) = \kappa \wedge 0$, (11.41), are formally included in (11.32).

From (11.4) and (11.42), we have

$$H(k) = nI(k). \tag{11.44}$$

Hence, (11.44) and (11.43) give

$$\exp\{H(k)\} = \begin{cases} k^{1/[\frac{s/\beta_K}{n} - 1]}, & 0 < k < \frac{\beta_K}{\beta_L}, \\ (k - \kappa)^{-1} & k \ge \frac{\beta_K}{\beta_L}, \quad \kappa \ne k. \end{cases} \tag{11.45}$$

Finally, by (11.13) and (11.45), we easily obtain the trajectory system (11.33), where the directrix $K = \kappa L$ is formally included in (11.33).

*ad. (ii)*. By (11.31), we now get, cf. Fig. 11.2,

$$h(\kappa) = 0 \Leftrightarrow \kappa \in \mathcal{K} = [0, \beta_K/\beta_L] \in \mathbf{R}, \tag{11.46}$$

i.e., the directrices are not isolated, as the set of director roots, $\mathcal{K}$ is an interval. In accordance with (11.46), then (11.34–11.35) replace (11.32–11.33).

*ad. (iii)*. By (11.31), we see that, cf. Fig. 11.2,

$$h(\kappa) = 0 \Leftrightarrow \kappa = 0, \tag{11.47}$$

i.e, only the $L$-axis is a directrix. The procedure for deriving (11.36–11.37) is exactly the same as in case (i), since only the numerical values of the parameters have changed; but $\kappa$ is replaced by $s/n\beta_L$ in (11.42).

The general solution (11.38) is obvious.

By $K(t) \equiv L(t)k(t)$, (11.39) is obtained directly from (11.38) and (11.32), (11.34), (11.36).

Finally, (11.40) follows immediately from (11.28–11.29), (11.38) and, e.g., (11.36). □

**Remark 11.2** Incidentally, we observe that, cf. (2.9–2.10) and $m = 1$, (11.29), (11.32), (11.34), (11.36), (11.38–11.40),

$$\mathrm{v}(t) = \frac{k(t)}{f[k(t)]} = \begin{cases} \beta_K, & 0 \le k_0 < \beta_K/\beta_L, \\ \beta_L k(t) = s/n + (k_0\beta_L - s/n)e^{-nt}, & k_0 \ge \beta_K/\beta_L, \end{cases} \tag{11.48}$$

$$y(t) = f[k(t)] = \begin{cases} (1/\beta_K)k(t) = (\frac{k_0}{\beta_K})e^{(s/\beta_K - n)t}, & 0 \le k_0 < \beta_K/\beta_L, \\ 1/\beta_L, & k_0 \ge \beta_K/\beta_L. \end{cases} \tag{11.49}$$

Within the growth model of Proposition 11.2, the input-output coefficients, cf. (11.28), must clearly not be interpreted as, respectively, the capital-output ratio $\mathrm{v}(t)$ and the reciprocal of the labor productivity $y(t)$. Of course, the *parameters* $\beta_K$ and $\beta_L$ must not be confused with *ratios* of dynamic (*state*) variables, $\mathrm{v}(t)$ and $y(t)$.

Regarding the *long run* behavior of the two ratios, it is seen from (11.48–11.49) and Fig. 11.2 that $\mathrm{v}(t)$ converges as $t \to \infty$, to either $\beta_K$ or $s/n$, and that $y(t)$ converges as $t \to \infty$, to either $1/\beta_L$ or zero. The latter zero limit, which occurs with $s/\beta_K < n$, evidently renders the assumption of full employment of the labor force untenable in the long run. ▽

The *phase portrait* of the *growth model* codified in Proposition 11.2, is shown in Fig. 11.3. Note that whenever the $k(t) \to \kappa$ for $t \to \infty$, cf. Fig. 11.2,

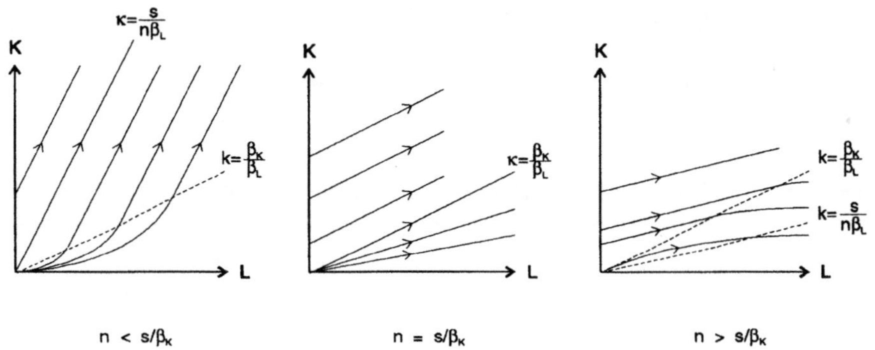


**Fig. 11.3** The phase portrait, (11.32–11.37)

the corresponding trajectories in Fig. 11.3 will *not* have the directrix as an asymptote. Except for $\mathcal{K} = [0, \beta_K/\beta_L]$, cf. (11.46), the geometry of the phase portrait in Fig. 11.3 conforms pretty well to Theorem 11.3.

## Trajectory Geometry and Kinematics

The properties of the solutions to (11.2.1–2) and the phase portraits, as stated in Theorems 11.2–11.3, need some further comments, since ***kinematic*** and ***geometric*** aspects of the ***phase curves***, (11.7.1–2), (11.10.1–2), have been confused in the economic literature. We saw above that the ray (directrix), $K = \kappa L$, (11.7.1–2), cannot be an asymptote for the trajectories of neoclassical model (11.2.1–2); a fact that has been noticed, see Deardorff (1970), Takayama (1985, p. 438). But the treatment of stability issues in Deardorff (1970) is a bit unclear, as geometric and kinematic properties are confounded. We shall here take the opportunity of using the neoclassical growth model to accentuate the fundamental distinctions involved.

As the distances between trajectories have been adduced in Deardorff (1970), we have shown the $CD$ trajectory system (11.18.1–11.19) in Fig. 11.1b, where $D_K(D_K^*)$ and $D_L(D_L^*)$ are, respectively, the vertical and the horizontal distance of a trajectory from the directrix, $K = \kappa L$. Regarding the magnitudes of these vertical/horizontal distances, we give

**Proposition 11.3** *For the growth model (11.1.1–11.2.2) with $CD$ technology (2.48), the vertical ($D_K$, $D_K^*$) and horizontal ($D_L$, $D_L^*$) distances (lengths) from the directrix in Fig. 11.1b are unbounded, i.e.,*

$$D_K \to \infty \quad \wedge \quad D_K^* \to \infty, \qquad as\ L \to \infty, \qquad (11.50.1)$$

$$D_L \to \infty \quad \wedge \quad D_L^* \to \infty, \qquad as\ K \to \infty. \qquad (11.50.2)$$

*The corresponding ratios,* $D_K/K$, $D_K^*/K$, $D_L/L$, $D_L^*/L$ *converge to zero, i.e.,*

$$D_K/K \to 0 \quad \wedge \quad D_K^*/K \to 0, \qquad \textit{as } L \to \infty, \tag{11.51.1}$$

$$D_L/L \to 0 \quad \wedge \quad D_L^*/L \to 0, \qquad \textit{as } K \to \infty. \tag{11.51.2}$$

***Proof*** From (11.7.1) and (11.19), we have, cf. Fig. 11.1b,

$$D_K = D_K(L) = \kappa L - \kappa \left[b + L^{1-a}\right]^{\frac{1}{1-a}}, \quad 0 < a < 1, \tag{11.52.1}$$

where

$$b = L_0^{1-a}\left\{(k_0/\kappa)^{1-a} - 1\right\} \lesseqgtr 0 \Leftrightarrow k_0 \lesseqgtr \kappa. \tag{11.52.2}$$

To evaluate (11.52.1–2) for $L \to \infty$, let $L = 1/x$, $x > 0$, i.e.,

$$D_K(1/x) = \kappa\left[1/x - (b + x^{a-1})^{\frac{1}{1-a}}\right] = \kappa\left[\frac{1 - (1 + bx^{1-a})^{\frac{1}{1-a}}}{x}\right]. \tag{11.53}$$

Applying L'Hospital's rule to (11.53) gives

$$\begin{aligned}\lim_{x\to 0} D_K(1/x) &= \lim_{x\to 0}\left[-b(1 + bx^{1-a})^{\frac{a}{1-a}}x^{-a}\right] \\ &= \lim_{x\to 0} -bx^{-a} = \pm\infty, \text{ for } b \gtrless 0.\end{aligned} \tag{11.54}$$

Thus, (11.54) and (11.52.1–2) establish (11.50.1).

With $D_K = \kappa D_L$, $D_K^* = \kappa D_L^*$, cf. Fig. 11.1b, the latter and (11.50.1) immediately establish (11.50.2).

Next we get from (11.52.1–2) that

$$D_K/K = D_K(L)/\kappa L = 1 - (1 + bL^{a-1})^{\frac{1}{1-a}}, \quad 0 < a < 1. \tag{11.55}$$

Since $L^{a-1}$ converges to zero, as $L \to \infty$, then (11.51.1) follows from (11.55) and (11.52.2).

As is easily verified, we similarly obtain from (11.19), cf. Fig. 11.1b, that

$$D_L/L = D_L(K)/(1/\kappa)K = (1 - b\kappa^{1-a}K^{a-1})^{\frac{1}{1-a}} - 1, \quad 0 < a < 1, \tag{11.56}$$

which converges to zero, as $K \to \infty$; hence (11.51.2). □

The parabolic configuration of neoclassical phase portrait, cf. Theorem 11.3, does not itself imply (11.50.1–2) or (11.51.1–2). For some particular production functions, one might get parabolic trajectories having asymptote (location depending on initial values) parallel to the directrix. With such trajectory configurations, (11.50.1–2) does not hold since then, of course, $D_K$ (and $D_L$) would remain finite as $L$ (and $K$) goes to infinity.

What needs to be clearly recognized, however, is that the limiting behavior of ***geometric*** concepts such as the ***distances*** (11.50.1–2) or the ***ratios*** (11.51.1–2) have inherently nothing to do with the ***kinematic*** stability properties of the ***ratio*** solutions and ***coordinate*** solutions in Theorem 11.2, cf. (11.11.1–11.12.2). Indeed, the configurations of the phase portraits are irrelevant to (11.11.1–11.12.2), as the latter also applied to the hyperbolic and linear phase portraits, cf. Propositions 7.1–7.2 and Theorem 9.1 with Corollary 9.1, but where clearly the distances such as (11.50.1–2) would go zero or remain constant.

To clinch the matter and illustrate the distinction between geometric and kinematic properties of phase portraits, we shall here dismiss the thought of a contradiction between (11.51.1–2) and (11.12.1–2). The simplicity of the neoclassical system (11.2.1–2) allows us to verify (11.12.1–2) directly from (11.10.1–11.11.2).

For the coordinate solutions of capital and labor with the initial values of $P_1$, $P_2$ and $P_3$, cf. Fig. 11.1b, we see from (11.10.2) and (11.11.2) that

$$\lim_{t\to\infty}\frac{K_3(t)}{K_2(t)} = \lim_{t\to\infty}\frac{L_0^1\,k(t)\,e^{nt}}{L_0^2\,\kappa\,e^{nt}} = L_0^1\,/\,L_0^2 > 1, \tag{11.57}$$

$$\lim_{t\to\infty}\frac{K_3(t)}{K_1(t)} = \lim_{t\to\infty}\frac{L_0^1\,k(t)\,e^{nt}}{L_0^1\,\kappa\,e^{nt}} = 1; \quad \lim_{t\to\infty}\frac{K_1(t)-K_3(t)}{K_1(t)} = 0, \tag{11.58}$$

$$\forall t:\frac{L_3(t)}{L_2(t)} = \frac{L_0^1\,e^{nt}}{L_0^2\,e^{nt}} = L_0^1\,/\,L_0^2 > 1; \quad \frac{L_3(t)-L_2(t)}{L_2(t)} = L_0^1\,/\,L_0^2 - 1 > 0. \tag{11.59}$$

Obviously, the ratio and the relative difference between the exponential solutions (11.59) will always be the same. Since the relative difference in (11.59) never disappears, (11.59) certainly does not represent the ratio (11.51.2) as $t \to \infty$.

Solutions $[L(t), K(t)]$ starting from $P_2$ and $P_3$, cf. Fig. 11.1b, will for $t > 0$ ***not*** be displayed by trajectorial points lying on the ***same*** horizontal line. The solution from $P_3$ moves faster than the solution from $P_2$, and accordingly, the solution from $P_3$ will later be located above that from $P_2$. Thus, there is no contradiction between the geometric property (11.51.2) and the kinematic property (11.59).

Since labor (11.10.1) evolves independent of capital, it follows that solutions $[L(t), K(t)]$ starting from $P_1$ and $P_3$, cf. Fig. 11.1b will for $t > 0$ *always* be described by trajectorial points lying on the *same* vertical line. Hence (11.51.1) and (11.58) have here the limit, zero. However, although some *subfamilies* of neoclassical solutions $K(t)$, (11.10.2), (with the same $L_0$) thus have *strong* relative stability, cf. (11.58), the *entire* family of $K(t)$, (11.10.2), will only have *weak* relative stability, as stated in (11.12.2) and illustrated here by (11.57), cf. Chap. 1, section "The Neoclassical Growth Model of Solow".

With reference to the discussion above and here to put things straight, we quote Deardorff (1970, p. 139)

> What, then, can we conclude about the stability of the equilibrium ray in this model? In relative terms, that is, in terms of the capital-labor ratio $r$ (or in terms of the *percentage* distance from equilibrium, $\pi/K$, if one wishes to compute it), the equilibrium is definitely stable. But in absolute terms, since the absolute distance from equilibrium does grow, it is unstable. This paradoxical result reflects the contradiction of trying to speak of stability in a growing economy, where change is the rule rather than the exception, and it points up the danger in ever speaking of, or even drawing pictures of, absolute magnitudes in such a context.

As to the traditional economic interpretation of the directrix, (11.6.1–11.7.2), as an equilibrium ray, we here just refer to Chap. 7, section "Directrix Solutions, Steady States, and Constant Ratios". But the asymptotic stability (11.11.1–2) is not tied at all to the convergence to zero of, e.g., the "percentage distance", (11.51.1), or (11.58), $\pi/K$. There is a minor slip in the formula Deardorff (1970, p. 138) for $k(t)$, (11.17.2). Moreover, the distinction between trajectory geometry and kinematics is missing as elsewhere in the economic literature on growing economies. The last paragraphs of the quotation above show the need for a rigorous mathematical treatment of dynamic systems with growing solutions and the study of the relevant long-run stability properties of such families.

In fact, the basic neoclassical growth model of Solow was our point of departure in undertaking this task of providing a general framework for analyzing any planar homogeneous dynamic system, as done in Chap. 28.

## BIBLIOGRAPHY

Deardorff AV (1970) Growth Paths in the Solow Neoclassical Growth Model. Quarterly J of Economics 85:134–139

Hahn FH, Matthews RCO (1964) The Theory of Economic Growth: A Survey. Economic Journal 74:779–902

Malthus TR (1803, 1958) An Essay on Population I–II, 2nd edn. J.M. Dent & Sons, London

Meade JE (1962) A Neo-Classical Theory of Economic Growth, 2nd edn. Allan and Unwin, London

Selby SM (1973) Standard Mathematical Tables, 21st edn. The Chemical Rubber Co, Cleveland, Ohio

Solow RM (1956) A Contribution to the Theory of Economic Growth. Quarterly Journal of Economics 70:65–94, Reprinted in Stiglitz & Uzawa (1969), and in Becker & Burmeister (1991)

Stiglitz JE, Uzawa H (1969) Readings in the Modern Theory of Economic Growth. M.I.T. Press, Cambridge, Mass

Swan TW (1956) Economic Growth and Capital Accumulation. Economic Record 32:334–361, Reprinted in Stiglitz (1969)

Takayama A (1985) Mathematical Economics, 2nd edn. Cambridge University Press, Cambridge

CHAPTER 12

# Dynamic Structure, Exogeneity—Time Paths, Phase Portraits for Two-Factor and Multi-Factor Macro Growth Models

## INTRODUCTION

Economic models are created to study multi-dimensional economic *systems* and are formally given by a multitude of *direct* and *indirect* relations among the relevant variables. The aim is to arrange the description of the economic *interdependences* in such a way that we get a consistent and complete explanation. Economic *theory* and *assumptions* underlying *growth models* tend to emphasize some positive and negative *feedback* elements between dynamic *state variables.* Factual *dynamic* models, specified by the *governing functions* (differential equations in continuous time), are meant to generate intuition and actual understanding, that is, besides describing *what* happens (from any initial state), we also want to know *why* things happen.

It requires us to recognize what leads to what and to stress which assumptions drive the conclusions (*solutions* and *geometry* of *phase portraits*). Evidently, the larger and the more complex dynamic models are, the harder it is to achieve that sort of overview and comprehension. However, a *qualitative* and *quantitative* (parametric) analysis and understanding of the solutions to fundamental growth models are the objects of this chapter, (Jensen et al. 2005).

The purpose is here further to search for economic *dynamic systems* that may allow for the existence of *increasing returns* to scale in production *without* dynamically generating *explosive* solutions (infinite *state* variables in

With co-authors:
PREBEN K. ALSHOLM, Department of Mathematics and Computer Science, Technical University of Denmark, Denmark
MOGENS ESROM LARSEN, Department of Mathematics, University of Copenhagen, Denmark
JENS MARTIN JENSEN, Vinci Computers, Copenhagen, Denmark



B. S. Jensen, *The Elements and Dynamic Systems of Economic Growth and Trade Models*, https://doi.org/10.1007/978-3-031-52493-6_12

finite time). Moreover, the *necessity* of seeing in growth models some *exogenous state* variables—for the *existence* of economic *growth per capita*—will be demonstrated within homogeneous dynamic systems that are widely used in the growth literature. An *autonomous*, *purely endogenous*—indecomposable, complete set of mutually interdependent *state* variables—*dynamic system* of positive *homogeneous differential equations* can in fact *never exhibit increasing per capita* solutions. Although *exogeneity* (unilateral linkages) and hence some *"block triangularity"* of *dynamic systems* are *necessary structural* ingredients of fundamental *per capita growth* models, it is a judicious concrete specification (selection) of the relevant exogenous state variables that matters in successful economic growth models.

On a methodological grand tour, we shall *revisit* the *seminal* contributions of Solow and Samuelson (1953), Solow (1956), Phelps (1966), Romer (1986), Romer (1990), Lucas (1988), Rebelo (1991), Mankiw et al. (1992), Aghion and Howitt (1992), Romer (2019), and *demonstrate* our methodological *Propositions* on homogeneous dynamics by *explicitly solving* several versions of the *basic* two-factor Solow and various *augmented/multi-factor* forms of *neoclassical* **one-sector** growth models, also extended, whenever possible, to any *degree* ($m \neq 1$) of *homogeneity* of the *production functions* involved.

The *organization* of the chapter is as follows. First, solutions to complete endogenous dynamic systems are discussed, and their steady-state properties and time domain are examined. Then, we analyze the implications of exogeneity (decomposability) and its proper treatment in *solving two-* and *three-dimensional* dynamics. The latter serve as general background for the analytical treatment of specific neoclassical growth models with emphasis on the *dynamic implications* of the economic *substitution* and *scale parameters* (elasticities). The consequences of the rapidity of exogenous labor growth and depreciation are given due attention, as these elements have been rather neglected in the literature and have complicated the relevant geometric phase portraits of even standard growth models. Finally, the general augmented (multi-factor) Solow model completes some long traditions of aggregate (one-sector) neoclassical growth models.

## Homogeneous Indecomposable Dynamics in the Domain: Real Nonnegative Octant, $\mathbf{R}_+^n$

Paradoxically, studies of the solutions to *multi-sectoral* growth models precede the path-breaking article, Solow (1956), on aggregate neoclassical growth. But much of the multi-sectoral dynamics was *linear* dynamics, as it was based on the *fixed* proportion (Leontief, input-output) production functions.

However, in a seminal paper, Solow and Samuelson (1953) retained the assumption of *constant* return to *scale* but permitted *continuous substitution* of *inputs* in making *single* or *joint outputs.* Accordingly, their dynamic systems in discrete and continuous time became *nonlinear* difference (differential) equations. We study some aspects of their *dynamic system* in continuous time that are described by *homogeneous* **governing** functions, $\mathbf{F_i}(\mathbf{x_1}, \mathbf{x_2}, \ldots, \mathbf{x_n})$, on the nonnegative octant, $\mathbf{R}_+^n$, or in vector notation,

$$\dot{\mathbf{x}} = \mathbf{F}(\mathbf{x}), \quad \mathbf{x} \in \mathbf{R}_+^n, \quad \mathbf{F} \in \mathbf{C}^1 - \text{Class on } \mathbf{R}_+^n \setminus \{0\} \tag{12.1}$$

$$\dot{\mathbf{x}}_\mathbf{i} = dx_i/dt = \mathbf{F_i}(\mathbf{x_1}, \mathbf{x_2}, \ldots, \mathbf{x_n}), \quad i = 1, 2, \ldots, n \tag{12.2}$$

*Assumption 12.1 (Solow and Samuelson) The governing functions* $\mathbf{F_i}(\mathbf{x})$, (12.1–12.2), are all **homogeneous** of degree, **m=1**, that is, $\lambda \in \mathbf{R}$,

$$m = 1: \qquad \mathbf{F}(\lambda\,\mathbf{x}) = \lambda\,\mathbf{F}(\mathbf{x}), \qquad \mathbf{F}(0) = \mathbf{0} \tag{12.3}$$

All $\mathbf{F_i}(\mathbf{x})$ *are* ***positive****, and all their* ***partial*** *derivatives are* ***positive***:

$$(i) \quad F_i(\mathbf{x}) > \mathbf{0}; \; (ii) \quad \partial F_i/\partial x_j > 0; \; i = 1, 2, \ldots, n \quad j = 1, 2, \ldots, n \tag{12.4}$$

The *purpose* of (12.4) is to ensure that with *positive* amounts of *any* commodity, then *all other* commodities may be produced from it in *nonzero* amounts. Otherwise, further considerations and results may apply only to one or more positive *subsets* of the commodities.

The *governing* functions (12.2) are not always to be regarded as genuine production functions. All optimization and general equilibrium problems have tacitly been solved. Thus, the functions $\mathbf{F_i}$, (12.2), are implicitly *reflecting* the properties of *production-*, *allocation-*, and *distribution* functions.

The properties (12.3) may intuitively, however, still be interpreted as reflecting assumptions about the underlying *marginal* productivities of a *joint* production process with continuously *variable* proportions.

**Theorem 12.1 (Solow and Samuelson)** *For the homogeneous dynamic system (12.1), there will—under the two conditions (12.4)—exist only* ***one*** *solution* $\mathbf{x} = \boldsymbol{\varphi}(\mathbf{t})$ *with a* ***ray trajectory****, along which* ***each*** *coordinate,* $\mathbf{x_i} = \varphi_\mathbf{i}(\mathbf{t})$*, evolves with the* ***same*** *(balanced) and unique* ***exponential*** *growth rate.*

**Corollary 12.1** *The family of* ***solutions*** *to (12.1–12.4), represented by (12.6), has global* ***relative stability****, that is, (12.5):*

$$\forall t: \quad \psi_i(t)/\varphi_i(t) < k < \infty \;, \; i = 1, 2, \ldots, n \tag{12.5}$$

*Consider any pair of solutions to (12.1) –(12.4),*

$$\boldsymbol{\varphi}(t) = [\varphi_1(t), \varphi_2(t), \ldots, \varphi_n(t)], \quad \boldsymbol{\psi}(t) = [\psi_1(t), \psi_2(t), \ldots, \psi_n(t)] \tag{12.6}$$

*where $\varphi(t)$ may be (although not necessarily) chosen as the particular ray solution of Theorem 12.1. The whole family solutions—by solving (12.1)–(12.4) from any initial values, $\mathbf{x}_o > \mathbf{0}$—share a common property, viz., (12.5).*

***Proof*** Solow and Samuelson (1953, p. 422)'s proof of Theorem 12.1 shows that the *existence* of a *ray* solution/trajectory [ "*eigenvector*" of the *mapping* **F**, (1–2) ] only requires the **positivity** of the *governing* functions $\mathbf{F}_i$, that is, (12.4i) is *sufficient* for the *existence* of at least *one* ray trajectory. The existence of *only one* (uniqueness) ray trajectory and the *uniqueness* of the *exponential growth rate*, however, depend on the **monotonicity** properties (12.4ii) in *each* argument. Their proof of the important *solution* **stability** property (12.5) also used the *monotonicity* stipulations (12.4ii). See hereto, Nikaido (1964, p. 34–36). □

### *Time Domain and the Degree of Homogeneity*

We must now explore the dynamic implications of generalizing the condition (12.3) to **any degree** of homogeneity, cf. Muth (1954), Suits (1954),

$$m \in \mathbf{R}: \qquad \mathbf{F}(\lambda\, \mathbf{x}) \;=\; \lambda^m\, \mathbf{F}(\mathbf{x}) \tag{12.7}$$

With (12.7), the critical issue is the ***maximal*** *time interval*, $T \subseteq \mathbf{R}$, for which *solutions* will *exist* to the system (12.1). To resolve this problem of *time domain*, it is convenient to introduce *polar coordinates* for the Cartesian coordinates (**x**) of the homogeneous differential equations (12.1), (12.7). As we are particularly concerned about *potential explosion* (solutions reaching *infinity* in *finite time*) of (12.1) with $m > 1$, we are especially interested in examining the behavior of **polar radius** ( *elongation*, $\eta$ ) **solutions**, $\eta\,(\mathbf{t})$, corresponding to (12.7)—whereas the corresponding *polar angle* solutions are *not* needed here.

With the *polar radius:* $\eta = dist(\mathbf{x}, \mathbf{0})$, we have—$(\mathbf{u}) = (u_1, u_2, \ldots, u_n)$ is a **unit vector** in the *direction* of (**x**)—as follows:

$$x_i = \eta\, u_i \quad , \quad \eta^2 = \sum_{i=1}^{n} x_i^2 \; , \; \eta > 0 \, , \quad \sum_{i=1}^{n} u_i^2 = 1 \tag{12.8}$$

$$\mathbf{x} = \eta\, \mathbf{u} \quad , \quad |\mathbf{u}| = 1 \quad , \quad \mathbf{u} \in \mathbf{S}^{n-1} \subset \mathbf{R}^n \tag{12.9}$$

Then (12.8) gives,

$$d\eta^2/dt \;=\; 2\,\eta\,\dot{\eta} \quad , \quad d\eta^2/dt \;=\; 2\,\sum_{i=1}^{n} x_i \dot{x}_i \tag{12.10}$$

which, together with (12.7), (12.8), (12.9), (12.2), (12.1), imply:

$$\dot{\eta} = \sum_{i=1}^{n} u_i\ F_i\ \equiv\ \mathbf{u}\cdot\mathbf{F}(\mathbf{x}) = \mathbf{u}\cdot\mathbf{F}(\eta\,\mathbf{u}) = \eta^m\ \mathbf{u}\cdot\mathbf{F}(\mathbf{u})\ \equiv\ \eta^m\ P\,(\mathbf{u}) \tag{12.11}$$

We next assume that $P(\mathbf{u})$, (12.11), satisfies:

*Assumption 12.2*

$$\min\,(\,P\,(\mathbf{u}) : |\mathbf{u}| = 1)\ \equiv\ \min\,(\,\{\mathbf{u}\cdot\mathbf{F}(\mathbf{u}) : \mathbf{u}\in\mathbf{S}^{n-1}\}) > 0 \tag{12.12}$$

The ***minimum*** in (12.12) is taken over the whole ***unit sphere*** $\mathbf{S}^{n-1}$, (12.9), but if some cone is invariant, then (12.12) can be restricted to that part of unit sphere lying inside the cone. When the *governing* functions $\mathbf{F}_i$ are all *positive* (4i) in the *closed* octant $\mathbf{R}^n_+$, then $\mathbf{R}^n_+$ is ***invariant***, and hence, $\mathbf{u}\cdot\mathbf{F}(\mathbf{u})$ has automatically a positive ***minimum*** value. Accordingly, (12.12) is a much ***weaker*** assumption than (**4i**), as ***scalar product*** (12.12) certainly does ***not*** require: $\forall_i$, $\mathbf{F}_i > \mathbf{0}$. But Assumption 12.2 is ***sufficient*** for our immediate purpose of evaluating the ***long-run*** behavior of the ***polar*** radius ***solution***, $\eta\,(\mathbf{t})$, to (12.11) and the corresponding Cartesian ***state variables***, $\mathbf{x}\,(\mathbf{t})$, (12.9).

**Theorem 12.2** *Any increasing maximal solution,* $\mathbf{x} = \varphi\,(t)$*—tending toward infinity—of the homogeneous dynamic system, (12.2–12.4), has the property:*
***(i)*** *If* $m \le 1$*, the solution* $\boldsymbol{\varphi}(\mathbf{t})$ *does* ***not*** *reach infinity in finite time.*
***(ii)*** *If* $m > 1$*, and if (12.12) is satisfied, the solution* $\boldsymbol{\varphi}(t)$ *reaches* ***infinity*** *in* ***finite*** *time.*

***Proof*** Ad (i), $m < 1$. With m $< 1$, we get using (12.11) that

$$d\,(\eta^{1-m})/dt\ =\ (1-m)\,\eta^{-m}\,\dot{\eta}\ =\ (1-m)\,P\,(\mathbf{u})\ \le\ B,\ \ (constant) \tag{12.13}$$

since $P(\mathbf{u})$ is continuous, cf. (12.1), on a ***compact*** set, $\mathbf{S}^{n-1}$, (12.9), and hence is ***bounded*** above.

For $t > 0$ ( $\eta = \eta_0$ for $t = 0$ ), we immediately have from (12.13):

$$\eta\,(t)^{1-m} - \eta_0^{1-m}\ \le\ B\,t\,;\qquad \eta(t)\ \le\ (\,\eta_0^{1-m} + B\,t\,)^{\frac{1}{1-m}} \tag{12.14}$$

which proves (**i**) for $\mathbf{m} < \mathbf{1}$.

Ad (i), $m\ = 1$. With $m = 1$, we similarly get from (12.11):

$$d\,(\ln\,\eta)/dt\ =\ \eta^{-1}\,\dot{\eta}\ =\ P\,(\mathbf{u})\ \le\ B \tag{12.15}$$

and then

$$\ln \eta(t) - \ln \eta_0 < Bt; \qquad \eta(t) \leq \eta_0 e^{Bt} \tag{12.16}$$

which proves (**i**) for $\mathbf{m} = 1$.

Ad (ii), $m > 1$. With $m > 1$ and, Min $P(\mathbf{u}) > 0$, (12.12), we get, cf. (12.13),

$$d(\eta^{1-m})/dt = (1-m)P(\mathbf{u}) \leq -B, \quad (B > 0) \tag{12.17}$$

and hence

$$\eta(t)^{1-m} \leq \eta_0^{1-m} - Bt \tag{12.18}$$

Thus, with $\mathbf{m} > \mathbf{1}$

$$\eta(t) \geq (\eta_0^{1-m} - Bt)^{\frac{-1}{m-1}} \tag{12.19}$$

and hence, it follows that $\eta(t) \to \infty$, as $t \to t_1$, where $\mathbf{t_1} = 1/(B\,\eta_0^{m-1})$.

Hence, $\boldsymbol{\eta}(\mathbf{t})$ reaches *infinity* in *finite* time, as stated in (**ii**). □

The most important message of Theorem 12.2 is that *purely endogenously* generated (**every** state variable depends on **all** the other state variables) *solutions* of *homogeneous dynamics* will be *incompatible* (cannot avoid *explosive* solutions) with the *existence* of any *increasing* return to *scale* ($\mathbf{m} > \mathbf{1}$).

Furthermore, in ***two-dimensional*** systems, the general *existence* of a **ray** solution **prevents** any other solution in the family (12.6) from displaying (as $t \to \infty$) *increasing ratios* among the two *state* variables. Hence, if *Labor* is one of *state* variables $\mathbf{x_i}$ in (12.1)–(12.3), then increasing *ratios* (per *capita* growth) is mathematically *impossible* with the **Assumptions** in (12.4).

Thus, we evidently have reached an economic-dynamic *deadlock* in ***two-dimensional*** systems with *complete endogeneity* (12.4). We shall now see that introducing some **exogeneity** is the *key* to breaking both dynamic deadlocks of *allowing*, $\mathbf{m} > \mathbf{1}$, and/or admitting *increasing ratios* among state variables.

## Decomposability, Exogeneity, and Dynamic Subsystems

### *Homogeneous Dynamics on* $\mathbf{R}_+^2$*—with Existence of Persistent Increasing Ratios*

To see clearly the mathematical basis for the necessity of some *exogeneity* in economic growth models, it will be instructive to analyze here the *two-dimensional* version of (12.2–12.3), ($x_1 = x$, $x_2 = y$; $F_1 = F$, $F_2 = G$; $r = y/x$):

$$\dot{x} = F(x, y) = x\,F(1, \; y/x) \equiv x\,f(r), \tag{12.20}$$

$$\dot{y} = G(x, y) = x\,G(1, \; y/x) \equiv x\,g(r), \tag{12.21}$$

Regarding the mathematical-economic possibility of per capita (ratio) growth, we have to simply ask and answer the crucial question: What are the *functional forms* of **F** and **G** that are able to generate *persistently* increasing ratios, ( $\forall t$ , $\dot{\mathbf{r}} > 0$ ). To this end, we obtain, cf. (12.20–12.21),

$$\dot{r} = d(y/x)/dt = (x\dot{y} - y\dot{x})/x^2 = [x\,G(x, y) - y\,F(x, y)]/x^2 \quad (12.22)$$

$$= h(r) \equiv g(r) - r\,f(r) \quad (12.23)$$

Permanently increasing ratios, $r(t) \to \infty$ as $t \to \infty$, are equivalent to

$$\dot{r} = h(r) > 0 \quad , \quad \forall r \geq r_0 > 0 \quad (12.24)$$

which in terms of $G$ and $H$ is equivalent to ( $x^2 > 0$ ), cf. (12.22), (12.24)

$$\forall t, \quad \dot{r} > 0 \quad \Leftrightarrow \quad x\,G(x, y) > y\,F(x, y) \quad , \quad \forall\, y \geq r_0 x \quad (12.25)$$

To satisfy (12.25) everywhere, a *necessary* condition must be that

$$F(0, y) \leq 0 \quad , \quad \forall\, y \geq 0 \quad (12.26)$$

as is easily seen by considering the point $(x, y)$=$(0, y)$, y>0, where (12.25) can only be satisfied by requirement (12.26). The *stipulation* (12.26) on $\mathbf{F(x, y)}$ clearly *violates* the Assumption 12.1 on governing functions (12.4). The strict monotonicity, positive cross-partial derivatives (4 ii) is *anathema* to (12.26).

The simplest and most robust way to satisfy (12.26) is having the state variable ($x$) growing *exogenously*, which, with $\boldsymbol{m} = \mathbf{1}$, implies, cf. (12.20)

$$F(x, y) = x\,F(1, 0) = x\,c_0 \quad , \quad c_0 > 0 \quad (12.27)$$

Clearly (12.27) complies with (12.26). But (12.26) is obviously not enough to guarantee the *inequality* of (12.25) *everywhere*. But using the exogeneity (12.27), the inequality (12.25) is reduced to

$$\forall t \quad \dot{r} > 0 \quad : \quad G(x, y) > y\,c_0 \quad ; \quad \forall y \geq r_0\,x \quad (12.28)$$

The **persistent growth** condition (12.28) can then *only* be satisfied, *if*

$$\forall\, y > 0 \quad , \quad G(0, y) > 0 \quad (12.29)$$

Accordingly, (12.29), (12.27), (12.20–12.21) imply that the $y$-axis is a *trajectory* with growing solutions, that is, the state variable $x$ is in principle not needed, as the system can still grow without it at all. If $G$ instead had property, $\mathbf{G(0, y) = 0}$, then (12.28) is *violated*, and *permanent* growth of $r(t)$ *impossible*.

Note that (12.29) earlier ensured the existence of a *steady-state trajectory* (ray) for *indecomposable* dynamic systems, (12.4), (12.5).

The *governing* function $G(x, y)$ corresponds—in the Solow (1956) growth model—to the *governing* function of *capital accumulation*, $\dot{K} = s\,F(L, K)$, and the crucial *per capita growth condition* (12.29) says:

$$\forall y > 0, \quad G(0, y) > 0 \quad \Leftrightarrow \quad \forall K > 0, \quad F(0, K) > 0 \tag{12.30}$$

that is, *first*, **Labor** is here an *inessential* input, and *secondly*, the *Marginal* product of **Capital** always remains *positive* for $K/L \rightarrow \infty$. Such a *lower boundary* for the *marginal product* of *capital* has since 1990 become a hallmark of new *endogenous per capita growth* literature. But it should always be kept in mind that *exogeneity* of labor is a *necessary* condition for having any *persistent* per capita *growth* with $\mathbf{F(0, K) > 0}$. We summarize as follows:

**Proposition 12.1** *With* ***exogeneity*** *of the first state variable, (x), persistently increasing ratios,* $\mathbf{r = y/x}$, *(per capita growth) are decided entirely by* $\mathbf{G(0, y)}$, *being either* ***positive*** *or* ***zero****.*

*For* $\mathbf{G(0, y) = 0}$*—hence* ***no*** *permanent per capita growth—the distinction between* ***parabolic*** *or* ***hyperbolic*** *phase portraits depends on the particular parametric form of* $\mathbf{G(x, y)}$*; cf. Fig. 12.1, Case 1.1–1.2, Fig. 12.2, Case 2.2, and below, Fig. 12.5, Case 1, 3, Fig. 12.6, Case 1, 3.*

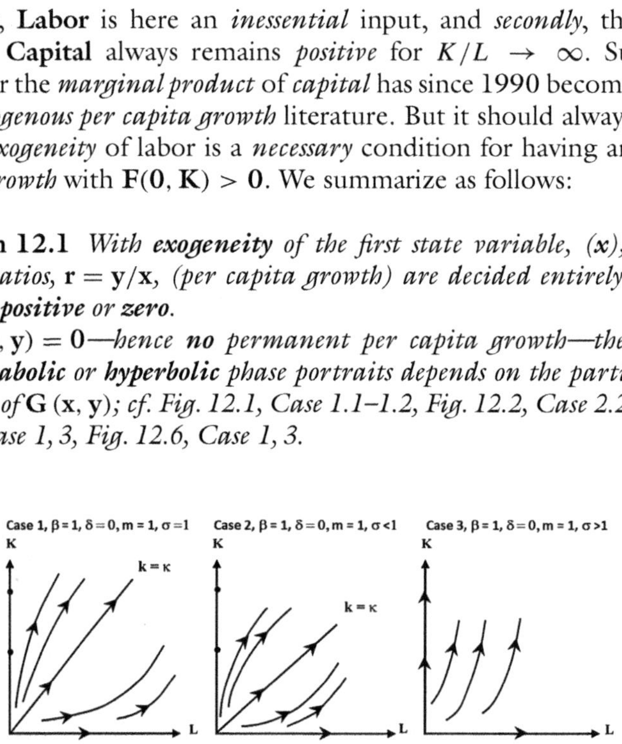


**Fig. 12.1** Phase portraits, $\beta = 1$, $m = 1$, $\delta = 0$: CD-CES solutions, $[\,L(t), K(t)\,]$, (12.71–12.79), (12.127), (12.130)

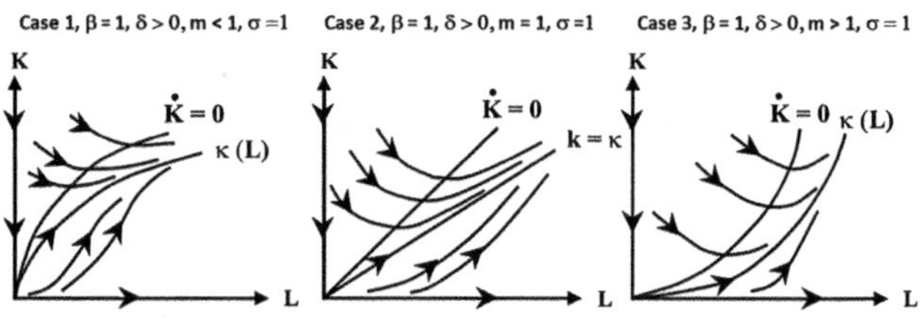


**Fig. 12.2** Phase portraits, $\beta = 1$, $\sigma = 1$: CD solutions, $[\,L(t), K(t)\,]$, (12.81–12.97)

Compared to *canonical classical* systems of Chaps. 7–9, *exogeneity* assumptions of **L(t)**, *Labor/Population*, were a *new*, decisive feature in Solow systems (1956):

> I presume that this difference in *theoretical strategy* reflects a genuine historical change in the *sensitivity* of *population* growth to economic factors, Solow (2000, p. 12).

Roughly speaking, it is *also* the *particular assumptions* about **partial factor** variation (**substitution**), such as *marginal productivity* of *capital* being *bounded below*—or combining both *knowledge* and *physical* capital, Romer (1986)—which has been *determinants* of *per capita growth* in *"endogenous"* growth models; cf. Jensen and Larsen (1987), [here (1.32) ], Rebelo (1991).

*Proportional* factor variation (**Scale** properties) has been less in focus as a *determinant* of per capita growth. The formal *dynamic problem* has been: To *deal* with *proportional* variation of at least **two** *endogenous* state variables and at least **one** *exogenous* state variable, cf. Theorems 12.1–12.2, we then need to study relevant *specifications* of $\mathbf{F_i}$ (**x**), in **three**-*dimensional* dynamics.

### *Exogeneity and Solving Subsystems in* $\mathbf{R}^3_+$, m ≠ 1

Consider the *autonomous* dynamic system, cf. (12.1–12.2), (12.7), (12.20), (12.21),

$$\dot{x} = F_1(x, y, z) = z^{m-\mu}\ F(x, y) = z^{m-\mu}\ x^{\mu}\ f(r) \tag{12.31}$$

$$\dot{y} = F_2(x, y, z) = z^{m-\mu}\ G(x, y) = z^{m-\mu}\ x^{\mu}\ g(r) \tag{12.32}$$

$$\dot{z} = F_3(z) \tag{12.33}$$

where $\mathbf{F_1}$ and $\mathbf{F_2}$ are *homogeneous* of degree $m \geq 1$, and here also assumed *separable* in the *exogenous* argument (**z**); the functions **F** and **G** are both *homogeneous* of degree $\mu \leq 1$. The function $\mathbf{F_3}$ need not be homogeneous at all, but if it is, its degree must be at most *one* to avoid explosion.

Complete generality of $\mathbf{F_1}$ and $\mathbf{F_2}$ would prevent us from succinctly obtaining the basic message of dynamic implications of $m > 1$. The analytically convenient *functional forms* of $\mathbf{F_1}$ and $\mathbf{F_2}$ are those *requiring* only *separability* (*decomposability*) in the **exogenous state** variable (**z**), growing as (12.33).

Let the *general solution* of the dynamics (12.33) be: $\varphi_3(t)$,, that is, we have,

$$z = \varphi_3(t) \quad ; \quad z^{m-\mu} = [\,\varphi_3(t)\,]^{m-\mu} \equiv e(t) \tag{12.34}$$

Hence, (12.31–12.32) show *non-autonomous homogeneous* dynamics, $0 < \mu \leq 1$:

$$\dot{x} = dx/dt = e(t)\, F(x, y) = e(t)\, x^{\mu}\, f(r) \tag{12.35}$$

$$\dot{y} = dy/dt = e(t)\, G(x, y) = e(t)\, x^{\mu}\, g(r) \tag{12.36}$$

*Assumption 12.3* The positive **exogenous**—external forcing—function, $\mathbf{e\,(t)} > 0$, $\forall t \geq 0$, (12.34–12.36), is continuous on the time interval $[0, \infty[$, and let the monotone function $\mathbf{E\,(t)}$ be:

$$\tau \equiv E\,(t) = \int_0^t e(t)\, dt \tag{12.37}$$

$$\int_0^{\infty} e\,(t)\, dt = \infty, \quad i.e.\ \ \tau = E(t) \to \infty \ \ as \ \ t \to \infty, \ and\ vice\ versa. \tag{12.38}$$

**Theorem 12.3** *The non-autonomous homogeneous dynamic system (12.35–12.36) can—under Assumption 12.3, (12.37–12.38)—be transformed to an* ***autonomous*** *homogeneous system of degree,* $\mu \leq 1$*:*

$$x' \equiv dx/d\tau = F(x, y) = x^{\mu}\, f(r) \tag{12.39}$$

$$y' \equiv dy/d\tau = G(x, y) = x^{\mu}\, g(r) \tag{12.40}$$

*The* **two***-dimensional system (12.39–12.40) is well-known and can be completely and explicitly solved in terms of primitives (integrals) with their integrands being defined by expressions of the governing functions,* **f** *and* **g***, (12.39–12.40); see Jensen (1994, p. 170); here Chap. 28, p. 1009.*

*The* **solutions** $[x(t), y(t)]$ *generated by the* **three***-dimensional system (12.31–12.33) are derived simply by using the* **solutions** $[x(\tau), y(\tau)]$ *of (12.39–12.40) together with* ***reparametrization****:* $\tau = E(t)$*, (12.37).*

***Proof*** With the *monotone* function, $\tau = E(t)$, (12.37), we can represent the values of the basic state variables, $x$ and $y$, by two (topologically equivalent) parameter representations, that is,

$$x(t) = x(\tau) \quad , \quad y(t) = y(\tau) \tag{12.41}$$

$$r(t) = y(t)/x(t) = y(\tau)/x(\tau) = r(\tau) \tag{12.42}$$

Hence, by (12.41–12.42), (12.37), we have

$$\dot{x} = dx(t)/dt = d\,[\,x(\tau)\,]/dt = (dx(\tau)/d\tau)(d\tau/dt)$$

$$= x'(\tau)(dE(t)/dt \equiv x'(\tau)\; e(t) \tag{12.43}$$

$$\dot{y} = dy(t)/dt = d\,[\,y(\tau)\,]/dt = (dy(\tau)/d\tau)(d\tau/dt)$$

$$= y'(\tau)(dE(t)/dt) \equiv y'(\tau)\; e(t) \tag{12.44}$$

By comparing $\dot{x}$ in (12.35) and (12.43), we get, cf. (12.41–12.42)

$$x'(\tau) = x(t)^{\mu}\, f[r(t)] = x(\tau)^{\mu}\, f[\,r(\tau)\,] \tag{12.45}$$

and by similarly comparing $\dot{y}$ in (12.36) and (12.44),

$$y'(\tau) = x(t)^{\mu}\, g[r(t)] = x(\tau)^{\mu}\, g[\,r(\tau)\,] \tag{12.46}$$

Thus, (12.45–12.46) establish (12.39–12.40) □

The *interacting* dynamic system, (12.39–12.40), will undoubtedly have an *inner ray* solution, as **F(x, y)**, (12.39), is unlikely to satisfy the *condition* (12.26). As this *inner ray* solution really serves as the *benchmark* for whole *family* of solutions to (12.39–12.40) and (12.5), we want to present the *closed form* (finite combination of elementary functions) of the **ray** *solutions* $[\,x(\tau), y(\tau)\,]$ in the *original time* parameter of **(t)**, $[\,\mathbf{x(t)}, \mathbf{y(t)}\,]$ solving (12.34–12.36), (12.31–12.33). To this end, we give:

**Corollary 12.2** *The inner **ray** trajectory of (12.39–12.40), (12.34–12.36), (12.31–12.33) is:* $\mathbf{y} = \alpha\,\mathbf{x}$, *with **slope*** $\boldsymbol{\alpha}$ *as the **root** of* $h(r) = 0$, *where* $h(r)$ *was defined by (12.23), (12.39–12.40). Coordinate—state—**solutions** of (12.31–12.33) along this **ray** are:*

$$\varphi_2(t) = \alpha\,\varphi_1(t) \;\; ; \quad y = \alpha\, x \tag{12.47}$$

*where **first coordinate** solutions* $\varphi_1(t)$ *have the **explicit** forms, cf. (12.35), (12.37)*

$$(i) \quad \mu = 1, \quad x = \varphi_1(t) = x_0 \exp\{f(\alpha)\, E(t)\} \tag{12.48}$$

$$(ii) \quad \mu < 1, \quad x = \varphi_1(t) = [\,x_0^{1-\mu} + (1-\mu)\, f(\alpha)\, E(t)\,]^{\frac{1}{1-\mu}} \tag{12.49}$$

***Proof*** With $r = y/x = \alpha$, $[\,h(\alpha) = 0\,]$, we get from (12.39),

$$dx/d\tau = x^{\mu}\, f(\alpha) \tag{12.50}$$

Solving the *differential* equation (12.50), for respectively $\mu = 1$ and $\mu \leq 1$, and next inserting, $\tau = E(t)$, (12.37), gives *solutions* in time (**t**), $\varphi_1(t)$, (12.48–12.49). □

The *long-run* (asymptotic) properties—such as *stability* properties (12.5)—are the *same* for the solutions of the systems (12.39–12.40) and (12.34–12.36).

Let the *family* of solutions to (12.34–12.36) be represented by an *arbitrary pair* of coordinate solutions, cf. (12.6)

$$\boldsymbol{\varphi}(t) = [\,\varphi_1(t), \varphi_2(t)\,], \quad \boldsymbol{\psi}(t) = [\,\psi_1(t), \psi_2(t)\,] \tag{12.51}$$

**Theorem 12.4** *The family of nonstationary coordinate solutions to (12.34–12.36) has—with a* ***positive*** $f(\alpha)$, *(12.50), (12.31), and either* $\mu = 1$, *or* $0 < \mu < 1$*—respectively, weak and strong relative stability, that is,*

$$f(\alpha) > 0, \quad \mu = 1: \ \psi_i(t)/\varphi_i(t) < k < \infty, \ \forall t, i = 1, 2 \tag{12.52}$$

$$f(\alpha) > 0, \quad \mu < 1: \ \psi_i(t)/\varphi_i(t) \to 1 \ as \ t \to \infty, i = 1, 2 \tag{12.53}$$

***Proof*** The properties (12.52–12.53) follow from similar properties of (12.39–12.40), as proved in Theorem 6–7, Jensen (1994, p. 201–202); here Theorem 28.12–28.13 in Chap. 28.

Strictly speaking, (12.52) also requires that $\mathbf{h}(\mathbf{r})$, in Corollary 12.2, has no inflection point at the *root*, $\mathbf{r} = \alpha$. Property (12.52), (12.5), is here called weak relative stability, to distinguish it from the stronger stability property (12.53). □

The dynamic system, (12.31–12.32), (12.35–12.36), is *topologically equivalent* to (12.39–12.40)—*geometrically*, their **phase portraits** are exactly the **same**. But the **rapidity** of *motion* (solutions and their *growth* measures) along the trajectories are **different**. With their *different rapidity* of motion, their solutions have the *distinct stability* properties. Full *knowledge* of the properties of *dynamic systems*, (12.39–12.40), (12.35–12.36), gives full description of the **quantitative** behavior of *solutions* (time paths) to the **basic three**-dimensional *dynamic system*, (12.31–12.33)

## Parameters and Explicit Solutions of Simple Two-Factor Macro Growth Models

Consider dynamic systems with **exogenous** (*neoclassical*) *Labor* growth:

$$\dot{L} = n\,L^{\beta}, \qquad n \geq 0, \ \beta \leq 1 \tag{12.54}$$

$$\dot{K} = s\,F(L, K) - \delta\,K = s\,L^m\,f(k) - \delta\,K, \quad 0 < s \leq 1, \ 0 \leq \delta \leq 1 \tag{12.55}$$

where the production function $\mathbf{f(k)}$ is strictly concave and monotonically increasing in the capital-labor ratio, $\mathbf{k} \in [0, \infty[$, that is, $\mathbf{f}$ has the properties

$$\forall k > 0: \ f'(k) = df(k)/dk > 0, \quad f''(k) = d^2 f(k)/dk^2 < 0 \qquad (12.56)$$

The *general solution*, $\mathbf{L(t)}$, of (12.54) is easily obtained as,

$$\beta = 1: \ L(t) = L_0 e^{nt}; \ \beta \neq 1: \ L(t) = \left[ L_0^{1-\beta} + (1-\beta)\, n\, t \right]^{\frac{1}{1-\beta}} \qquad (12.57)$$

$$\beta = 1: \ \widehat{L} = \dot{L}/L = n, \quad \beta < 1: \ \widehat{L} = n\, L^{\beta-1} \to 0 \text{ for } L \to \infty \qquad (12.58)$$

Clearly, solutions $\mathbf{L(t)}$ (12.57), $\beta \neq 1$, **explode** (infinite in finite time) for $\beta > 1$.

For time paths of any variable, for example, $\mathbf{L(t)}$, in any *period*, $[\,0, t\,]$, we may always calculate an ***average exponential growth rate***, $\mathbf{g_L}$, by its definition:

$$g_L \equiv \ln\, [\; L(t)/L(0) \;] \,/\, t \qquad (12.59)$$

Evidently, the calculated $\mathbf{g_L}$ numbers will usually depend on *length* of the time *period* and the ***initial*** values. Only in the case of *exponential* solutions, that is, linear differential equations, is $\mathbf{g_L}$ independent of length and starting value, $\mathbf{L_0}$. Only with *exponential* solutions, $\beta = 1$, does it make sense to distinguish between *level effects* (dependent on $L_0$) and *growth rate effects* ($\widehat{L}$ or $g_L$, ***independent*** of $L_0$), that is,

$$\beta = 1: \quad g_L = n; \quad \beta \neq 1: \quad g_L = \ln\, [\, 1 + \frac{(1-\beta)\, n\, t}{L_0^{1-\beta}} \,] \,/\, t \qquad (12.60)$$

The sensitivity of the growth rate numbers $\mathbf{g_L}$ upon $\mathbf{L_0}$ is often called "*scale effects*", but we prefer the term "**level effect**"—not to confuse dependence on small/large $\mathbf{L_0}$ with the *effects* of increasing/decreasing *returns to scale* in *production*, characterized by the **parameter**, $m \neq 1$.

A few observations on the *parameters* and evolutions of the *Labor force*, $\mathbf{L(t)}$, (12.54), (12.57–12.60), seem appropriate before proceeding with the qualitative and quantitative study of the solutions to (12.54–12.55) and (12.61–12.62). Even though the assumption of $\beta = 1$ is relevant and convenient in many contexts, the *long-run empirical realism* of $\beta < 1$ is by no means less important. For a *grotesque* example of the implications of $\beta = 1$ for $\mathbf{t} \to \infty$, is given in Sydsæter (1981, p. 207), where an illustration is that even if the universe expands spatially with the velocity of light, there will not in the long run be room enough for a population which expands with exponential growth, $\beta = 1$.

With *standard* assumptions, $\mathbf{m} = \mathbf{1}, \boldsymbol{\beta} = \mathbf{1}$, the usual *dynamic system* is:

$$m = 1: \qquad \dot{K} = s\, L\, f(k) - \delta\, K, \tag{12.61}$$

$$m = 1,\ \beta = 1: \quad \dot{k} \equiv h(k) = s\, f(k) - (n + \delta)\, k \tag{12.62}$$

The basic *parametric* forms of the *two-factor technologies,* **F(L, K)**, are:

$$\mathbf{CD}: Y = \gamma \left[L^{1-a} K^{a}\right]^{m} = L^{m}\, f(k) = L^{m}\, \gamma\, k^{am},\ \ f'(k) = \gamma\, a\, m\, k^{am-1} \tag{12.63}$$

$$\mathbf{CES}: \quad Y = \gamma \left[(1-a)L^{\frac{\sigma-1}{\sigma}} + aK^{\frac{\sigma-1}{\sigma}}\right]^{\frac{m\sigma}{\sigma-1}} \tag{12.64}$$

$$= L^{m} f(k) = L^{m} \gamma \left[(1-a) + a\, k^{\frac{\sigma-1}{\sigma}}\right]^{\frac{m\,\sigma}{\sigma-1}} \tag{12.65}$$

$$f'(k) = \gamma\, a\, m \left[a + (1-a)\, k^{-\frac{\sigma-1}{\sigma}}\right]^{\frac{m\sigma}{\sigma-1}-1} k^{m-1} \tag{12.66}$$

$$m = 1\ :\ f'(k) = \gamma\, a \left[a + (1-a)\, k^{-\frac{\sigma-1}{\sigma}}\right]^{\frac{1}{\sigma-1}} \tag{12.67}$$

$$m = 1\ :\ \epsilon_{K}(k) = \frac{k\, f'(k)}{f(k)} = \left[1 + \frac{1-a}{a} k^{\frac{1-\sigma}{\sigma}}\right]^{-1} = E\,(\,f(k), k)\,) \tag{12.68}$$

The constant elasticity of substitution(**CES**) **limits** of $f(k)$ and $f'(k)$ become, $(\sigma \gtrless 1 \Rightarrow a^{\frac{\sigma}{\sigma-1}} \lesseqgtr 1)$:

$$\sigma < 1: \begin{cases} \forall m: & \lim\limits_{k\to 0} f(k) = \lim\limits_{k\to 0} \gamma a^{\frac{m\sigma}{\sigma-1}} k^{m} = 0, \ \lim\limits_{k\to\infty} f(k) = \gamma\,(1-a)^{\frac{m\sigma}{\sigma-1}} \\ m < 1: & \lim\limits_{k\to 0} f'(k) = \infty, \qquad \lim\limits_{k\to\infty} f'(k) = 0 \\ m = 1: & \lim\limits_{k\to 0} f'(k) = \gamma\, a^{\frac{\sigma}{\sigma-1}}, \qquad \lim\limits_{k\to\infty} f'(k) = 0 \\ m > 1: & \lim\limits_{k\to 0} f'(k) = 0, \qquad \lim\limits_{k\to\infty} f'(k) = 0 \end{cases} \tag{12.69}$$

$$\sigma > 1: \begin{cases} \forall m & \lim\limits_{k\to 0} f(k) = \gamma\,(1-a)^{\frac{m\sigma}{\sigma-1}}, \lim\limits_{k\to\infty} f(k) = \infty \\ m < 1: & \lim\limits_{k\to 0} f'(k) = \infty, \qquad \lim\limits_{k\to\infty} f'(k) = 0 \\ m = 1 & \lim\limits_{k\to 0} f'(k) = \infty, \qquad \lim\limits_{k\to\infty} f'(k) = \gamma\, a^{\frac{\sigma}{\sigma-1}} \\ m > 1 & \lim\limits_{k\to 0} f'(k) = \infty, \qquad \lim\limits_{k\to\infty} f'(k) = \infty \end{cases} \tag{12.70}$$

The **Solow** growth model (Solow (1956, p. 69)) operated on the assumptions: $m = 1, \beta = 1, \delta = 0, \sigma \gtreqless 1$, that is, *technologically*, it was quite *general*, but the actual *solutions* were designed to the *simplest* cases with $\boldsymbol{\delta} = \mathbf{0}$, (12.55), which blurred the trajectorial *phase portrait* of the model (Solow (1956)) and standard model, (12.62). See, Deardorff (1970), Jensen (1994); here

Theorem 11.3 and Proposition 11.3 in Chap. 11; cf. section "Trajectory of Phase Portraits—Convergence and Divergence".

### *Family of Neoclassical Solutions for CD Technologies*

*CD Dynamics with* $\mathbf{m} = \mathbf{1}$ *and* $\boldsymbol{\beta} = \mathbf{1}$
With the differential equation (12.62) and the **CD** function (12.63), we have:

$$m = 1,\ \beta = 1: \quad \dot{k} = h(k) = s\,\gamma\,k^a - (n+\delta)\,k \tag{12.71}$$

The *steady-state* trajectory for (12.61), (12.71) is the *ray* with the *slope*, $\kappa$:

$$\dot{k} = 0 \quad \Leftrightarrow \quad k = \kappa = \left[\frac{s\,\gamma}{n+\delta}\right]^{\frac{1}{1-a}} \tag{12.72}$$

The economic dynamics[1] (12.71) has the **general solution** for the *capital-labor* ratio, $\mathbf{k(t)}$, given by, cf. (11.17.1–11.17.2):

$$k(t) = \left[\frac{s\,\gamma}{n+\delta} + \frac{1}{n+\delta}\,e^{-(n+\delta)(1-a)\,(t+t_0)}\right]^{\frac{1}{1-a}} \tag{12.73}$$

$$= \kappa\left[1 + \left\{(k_0/\kappa)^{1-a} - 1\right\} e^{-(n+\delta)(1-a)\,t}\right]^{\frac{1}{1-a}} \tag{12.74}$$

Hence by (12.61), (12.74), the evolution of the state variable capital, $\mathbf{K(t)}$, is,

$$K(t) = L(t)\,k(t) = L_0\,e^{nt}\,\kappa\left[1 + \left\{(k_0/\kappa)^{1-a} - 1\right\} e^{-(n+\delta)(1-a)t}\right]^{\frac{1}{1-a}} \tag{12.75}$$

Elimination of ($\mathbf{t}$) in (12.75)—by (12.57)—gives a **phase portrait** of (12.71) as **loci**:

$$K = K(L) = \kappa\,L\left[1 + b\cdot L^{-(1+\frac{\delta}{n})(1-a)}\right]^{\frac{1}{1-a}} \tag{12.76}$$

$$\text{where} \qquad b = L_0^{(1+\frac{\delta}{n})(1-a)}\left[\left[\frac{k_0}{\kappa}\right]^{1-a} - 1\right] \gtreqless 0 \Leftrightarrow \mathbf{k_0} \gtreqless \kappa \tag{12.77}$$

The **isocline** of *horizontal tangent* slope ($dK/dL = 0$) is a **ray**, cf. (12.61,12.63)

$$m = 1,\ \text{isocline: } \dot{K} = 0 \quad \Leftrightarrow \quad k = k^* = \left[\frac{s\,\gamma}{\delta}\right]^{\frac{1}{1-a}} > \kappa \tag{12.78}$$

[1] The nonlinear differential equation (12.71) was posed by *Jakob Bernoulli*, and its solution was obtained by *G. Leibniz* (1696); see Gandolfo (2010, p. 197,431), Simmons (1972, p. 49).

The *phase portrait* of the trajectories (12.76–12.77) has **only** the steady-state **ray**, $\mathbf{K} = \kappa\,\mathbf{L}$, (12.72), as **asymptote**—cf. Fig. 12.2, *case 2*, that is, vertical *distances* $\mathbf{D_K}$ of $\mathbf{K}(\text{L})$, (12.76), from the **CD** $\kappa$*-ray*, (12.72), converge to **zero**—**if** $a < \frac{\delta}{n+\delta}$ :

$$D_K = D_K(L) \;=\; \kappa L - \kappa L \left[1 + b\,L^{-\frac{n+\delta}{n}(1-a)}\right]^{\frac{1}{1-a}} \;\rightarrow\; 0\,,\;\; \text{as } L \rightarrow \infty \qquad (12.79)$$

***Proof*** From (12.79), we have and find, as $L \rightarrow \infty$, that

$$D_K = \kappa\,L \left[1 - \left[1 + b\,L^{-\frac{n+\delta}{n}(1-a)}\right]^{\frac{1}{1-a}}\right] \rightarrow \kappa\,L \cdot 0 \rightarrow \text{"}\infty\text{"} \cdot 0 \rightarrow 0 \qquad (12.80)$$

*only if*: $1 - \frac{n+\delta}{n}(1-a) \;<\; 0 \Leftrightarrow a < \frac{\delta}{n+\delta}$; cf. Pampel (2009, p. 390).
See hereto Proposition 12.3, $\sigma \;=\; 1$, in section "Trajectory of Phase Portraits—Convergence and Divergence". □

For demonstrations of Theorem 12.5, Proposition 12.3 on the *phase portraits* with *convergence-divergence*, $D_K(t)$, (12.137), for the **CD** system, see (12.71–12.75), (12.78), see Pampel (2009, p. 396–397).

*CD Dynamics, Returns to Scale,* $\mathbf{m} \neq \mathbf{1}$*, and* $\boldsymbol{\beta} = \mathbf{1}$
With $m \neq 1$, then (12.61), (12.62), (12.71) no longer apply. The *condition* for *non-explosive solutions* of $\mathbf{K(t)}$ from (12.55) requires with **CD**, (12.63), that $\mathbf{a\,m \leq 1}$. So for *increasing* return to *scale*, $\mathbf{m > 1}$, the *limiting* case of $\dot{\mathbf{K}}$, (12.55), is:

$$m > 1\,,\; a\,m = 1\,,\; m = 1/a : \quad \dot{K} = (\,s\gamma\, L^{(m-1)} - \delta\,)\,K \qquad (12.81)$$

**General solutions,** $\mathbf{K(t)}$ of (12.81) and $\mathbf{k(t)}$, (12.57) are, $\mathbf{m > 1,\; a\,m = 1}$, $\beta =$ 1:

$$K(t) = K_0 \,\exp\left\{L_0^{m-1}\,[\,\frac{s\,\gamma}{n\,(m-1)}\,]\,[\,e^{n\,(m-1)\,t} - 1\,] - \delta\,t\right\} \qquad (12.82)$$

$$k(t) = k_0 \exp\left\{L_0^{m-1}\,[\,\frac{s\,\gamma}{n\,(m-1)}\,]\,[\,e^{n\,(m-1)\,t} - 1\,] - (\delta + n)\,t\right\} \qquad (12.83)$$

as is simply obtained by integration. **CD** *families*, $K(t)$, (12.82), and $k(t)$, (12.83) have **double-exponential** *growth*, cf. Jensen and Larsen (1987, p. 226); here Chap. 1 section "Rapidity of Growth".
With $m \neq 1$ and $a\,m < 1$, then the differential equation (12.81) changes to

$$m \neq 1\,,\; a\,m < 1 : \;\; \dot{K} \;=\; s\,\gamma\; L^{m(1-a)} K^{am} \;-\; \delta K \qquad (12.84)$$

The **isocline** of horizontal tangents, **K*(L)**, analogous to (12.78), is:

$$am < 1 : \dot{K} = 0 \Leftrightarrow K = K^{\star}(L) = \left[\frac{s\,\gamma}{\delta}\right]^{\frac{1}{1-am}} L^{1+\frac{m-1}{1-am}} \equiv k^{\star\star} L^{1+\frac{m-1}{1-am}} \tag{12.85}$$

**CD isoclines** (12.85) are *concave* or *convex* for, respectively, **m < 1** or **m > 1**, see Fig. 12.2, *case 1, and case 3.*

The **CD time paths** (*solutions*) **K(t)** of (12.84) with (12.57), $\boldsymbol{\beta} = \mathbf{1}$, become:

$$K(t) = \left[e^{-(1-am)\delta t}(1-am)\,s\,\gamma \int_0^t L(t)^{m(1-a)} e^{(1-am)\delta t}\,dt\right]^{\frac{1}{1-am}} \tag{12.86}$$

$$= \left[e^{-(1-am)\delta t}(1-am)\,s\,\gamma \int_0^t L_0^{m(1-a)} e^{n\,m(1-a)\,t} e^{(1-am)\delta t}\,dt\right]^{\frac{1}{1-am}} \tag{12.87}$$

$$= \alpha\, L_0^{\frac{m-am}{1-am}}\, e^{\frac{nm(1-a)}{1-am}\,t}\,[\,1+\chi(t)\,]^{\frac{1}{1-am}} \tag{12.88}$$

$$\text{where} \quad \boldsymbol{\alpha} = \left[\frac{s\,\gamma}{\delta + nm(1-a)/(1-am)}\right]^{\frac{1}{1-am}} \;;\; \alpha < k^{\star\star} = \left[\frac{s\,\gamma}{\delta}\right]^{\frac{1}{1-am}} \tag{12.89}$$

$$\chi(t) = \left[L_0^{1-m}\,(k_0/\alpha)^{1-am} - 1\right] e^{-[nm(1-a)+\delta(1-am)]\,t} \rightarrow 0\,, \text{ as } t \rightarrow \infty \tag{12.90}$$

Hence, we get from (12.88–12.89) and (12.57), $\boldsymbol{\beta} = \mathbf{1}$, that

$$\beta = 1\,; \quad k(t) = K(t)/L(t) = \alpha\, L_0^{\frac{m-1}{1-am}}\, e^{\frac{n(m-1)}{1-am}\,t}\,[\,1+\chi(t)\,]^{\frac{1}{1-am}} \tag{12.91}$$

The consequences of the *scale elasticity* (**m**) are seen *explicitly* from (12.90 to 12.91),

$$m < 1 : \quad k(t) \rightarrow 0 \quad \text{as } t \rightarrow \infty \tag{12.92}$$

$$m = 1 : \quad k(t) \rightarrow \left[\frac{s\,\gamma}{n+\delta}\right]^{\frac{1}{1-a}} = \kappa \quad \text{as } t \rightarrow \infty \tag{12.93}$$

$$1/a > m > 1 : \quad k(t) \rightarrow \infty\,, \quad \text{as } t \rightarrow \infty\;; \quad \widehat{k} = \frac{\dot{k}}{k} \sim \frac{n\,(m-1)}{1-a\,m} \tag{12.94}$$

Thus, with (**m**) as in (12.94), the **CD** *family* of solutions, **K(t)**, to (12.84) in (12.88), and the *family* **k(t)**, (12.91), have in the *long run* an **exponential** *growth* rate, (12.94), *larger* than the *exogenous* growth rate of $\frac{\dot{L}}{L} = n$ ($\beta = 1$), that is, **CD**, gives *per capita* growth, $\hat{\mathbf{y}} = \hat{\mathbf{k}}$, (12.94), cf. (12.98), with (**m** > **1**)—but not as (12.83).

Elimination of (**t**) in (12.88–12.90)—by (12.57)—gives the **phase portrait** as **loci**:

$$K(L) = \alpha\, L^{1+\frac{m-1}{1-am}} \left[1 + \{L_0^{1-m} \left[\frac{k_0}{\alpha}\right]^{1-am} - 1\}\left[\frac{L}{L_0}\right]^{-[m(1-a)+\frac{\delta}{n}(1-am)]}\right]^{\frac{1}{1-am}} \tag{12.95}$$

$$\equiv \alpha\, L^{1+\frac{m-1}{1-am}} \left[1 + b^{\star} L^{-[m(1-a)+\frac{\delta}{n}(1-am)]}\right]^{\frac{1}{1-am}} \tag{12.96}$$

where $b^{\star}$ is analogous to $b$, (12.77). Hence, **k(t)** *solutions* (12.91) **converge** along **K**(L) *trajectory*, (12.96)— as $L \to \infty$—to **curves**, $\kappa$ (L) - with $b^{\star} = 0$ in (12.96):

$$m \neq 1,\ am < 1: \qquad K = \kappa\,(L) = \alpha\, L^{1+\frac{m-1}{1-am}} \tag{12.97}$$

*Attractors*, $\kappa$ (L) (12.97), Fig. 12.2, are below *isocline* (12.85), as $\boldsymbol{\alpha} < \mathbf{k}^{**}$, cf. (12.89).

Clearly, the *scale elasticity* (**m**) is the *dominating parameter* of the *solutions*, **k(t)**, and *phase portraits*, **K** (L). For **CD**, with *depreciation*, $\boldsymbol{\delta} > \mathbf{0}$, we can get non-explosive, **exponential per capita** growth of **y(t)**, by moderate *increasing* return to *scale*, **m** > **1**, **am** < **1**, cf. (12.63), (12.90–12.91), (12.94):

$$\beta = 1:\ y(t) = L(t)^{m-1}\, \gamma\, k(t)^{am} \sim e^{n(m-1)t} \cdot e^{\frac{n(m-1)am}{1-am}t} = e^{\frac{n(m-1)}{1-am}t} \tag{12.98}$$

The *marginal* product of *Labor* (**wages**) evolves *exponentially* as (12.98).

As to the *marginal* product of *Capital*, we get from (12.63), (12.89–12.91), (12.94):

$$\frac{\partial Y}{\partial K}(L, K) = MP_K(t) = L(t)^{m-1}\gamma amk(t)^{am-1} \to \frac{am}{s}\left[\delta + \frac{n(1-a)}{1-am}\right] \tag{12.99}$$

Thus, despite $f'(k)$, (12.63), going to zero, the size of *crucial* $\mathbf{MP_K(t)}$, (12.99), remains *bounded below*—due to the impact of the *scale elasticity*, **m** > **1**.

*CD Economic Evolutions with* $\boldsymbol{\beta} < \mathbf{1}$ *and* $\mathbf{m} \neq \mathbf{1}$
Recalling (12.84), (12.86), we get with *slower* evolution of Labor, (12.54), $\beta < 1$,

$$\beta < 1,\ m \neq 1,\ am < 1: \quad \dot{K} = s\,\gamma\, L^{m(1-a)}\, K^{am} - \delta\, K \tag{12.100}$$

$$K(t) = \left[ e^{-(1-am)\delta\, t} (1-am)\, s\, \gamma \int L(t)^{m(1-a)} e^{(1-am)\,\delta\, t} dt \right]^{\frac{1}{1-am}} \tag{12.101}$$

and then from rearranging (12.101),

$$k(t) = \frac{K(t)}{L(t)} = \left[ \frac{(1-am)\, s\, \gamma \int L(t)^{m(1-a)} e^{(1-am)\delta t} dt}{e^{(1-am)\delta t} L(t)^{1-am}} \right]^{\frac{1}{1-am}} = \left[ \frac{T(t)}{N(t)} \right]^{\frac{1}{1-am}} \tag{12.102}$$

**Proposition 12.2** *The limits of the* **CD** *capital-labor* ***ratio***, $\mathbf{k(t)}$, *(12.102), for* $t \to \infty$, *are with the parameters,* $\beta < 1,\ n > 0,\ \delta > 0$,*:*

$$m < 1:\ k(t) \to 0\ ;\ m = 1:\ k(t) \to \alpha\ = \left[\frac{s\,\gamma}{\delta}\right]^{\frac{1}{1-a}} = k^{\star}\ ;\ m > 1:\ k(t) \to \infty \tag{12.103}$$

***CD phase portraits*** *are seen in Fig. 12.3—no* ***ray*** *solution for* $k(t)$ *exists.*

***Proof*** We eventually obtain, using l'Hospital's rule,

$$\lim_{t\to\infty} \frac{T(t)}{N(t)} = \lim_{t\to\infty} \frac{dT/dt}{dN/dt} = \tag{12.104}$$

$$\lim_{t\to\infty} \frac{s\,\gamma L(t)^m}{nL(t)^{\beta} + \delta L(t)} = \lim_{t\to\infty} \frac{s\gamma}{nL(t)^{\beta-m} + \delta L(t)^{1-m}} \tag{12.105}$$

From (12.105) and (12.102), the *limits* (12.103) follow. □

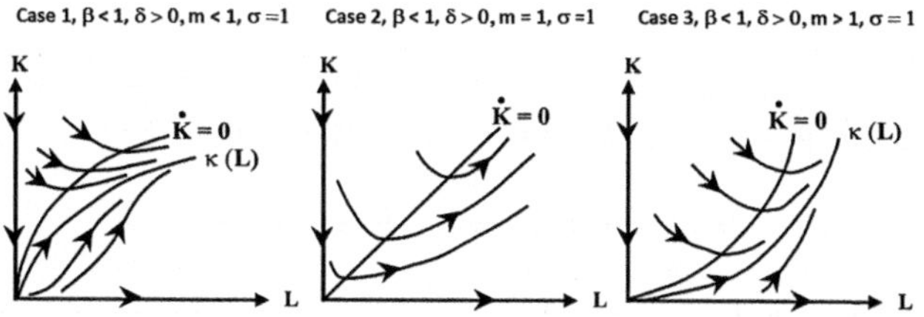


**Fig. 12.3** Phase portraits, $\beta < 1,\ \sigma = 1$: CD solutions, $[\,L(t), K(t)\,]$, (12.100–12.124)

Note that with *sub-exponential* (polynomial) *Labor growth*, the *size* of *parameters*, $\boldsymbol{\beta} < \mathbf{1}$ and $\mathbf{n}$, does not at all affect the *limiting* levels of the capital-labor *ratios*, (12.103), which for $m \neq 1$ are the *same* as (12.92), (12.94).

The *approximations* of $K(t)$, (12.101), and $k(t)$, (12.102), are, with (12.57),

$$\beta < 1, n > 0, \delta > 0: \quad K(t) \sim \left[(s\gamma/\delta)\,([1-\beta]nt)^{\frac{m(1-a)}{(1-\beta)}}\right]^{\frac{1}{1-am}} \tag{12.106}$$

$$\beta < 1, n > 0, \delta > 0: \; k(t) \sim \left[(s\gamma/\delta)([1-\beta]nt)^{\frac{m-1}{1-\beta}}\right]^{\frac{1}{1-am}} \tag{12.107}$$

From (12.107) we again get—with $\mathbf{m} = \mathbf{1}$—the particular limit in (12.103) as:

$$\beta < 1, n > 0, \delta > 0, m = 1: \quad k(t) \to \left[\frac{s\,\gamma}{\delta}\right]^{\frac{1}{1-a}} = k^{\star} \tag{12.108}$$

Next by (12.107) and (12.63), we obtain

$$\beta < 1, n > 0, \delta > 0: y(t) = L^{m-1}\gamma k^{am} \sim \gamma\left[\left(\frac{s\gamma}{\delta}\right)^{am}[(1-\beta)\,n\,t\,]^{\frac{m-1}{1-\beta}}\right]^{\frac{1}{(1-am)}} \tag{12.109}$$

$$\beta < 1, n > 0, \delta > 0, m > 1: MP_K(t) = L^{m-1}\gamma\, a\, m\, k^{am-1} \to \frac{a\,m\,\delta}{s} \tag{12.110}$$

With $\delta > 0$, *only* $\mathbf{m} > \mathbf{1}$ will create (sustain) *persistent per capita growth* (*polynomial*) of $k(t)$, $y(t)$, cf. (12.107), (12.109). The latter expressions also clearly demonstrate that any *solutions* for $k(t)$, $y(t)$ (Labor productivity) are, ceteris paribus, affected in any *finite* time by *both parameters*, ($\beta$) and ($n$). Thus, with $\beta < 1$, the *asymptotics* (limits), (12.103), can inadvertently be misleading by *disguising* the importance of significant parameters, affecting *finite time* observations. However, with $\mathbf{m} > \mathbf{1}$, note that a *slower* population/labor evolution, $\beta < 1$, reduces the *rapidity* of per *capita growth*, cf. (12.109), (12.98), and similarly *reduces* the *long-run* return to capital ($MP_K$), cf. (12.110), (12.99).

Solving (12.57) in ($\mathbf{t}$) and substituting in (12.106), the **trajectories** as **loci** are:

$$\beta < 1, n > 0, \delta > 0: \; K(L) \sim \left[[\tfrac{s\gamma}{\delta}][(1-\beta)n]^{\frac{m-1}{1-\beta}}\right]^{\frac{1}{1-am}} L^{1+\frac{m-1}{1-am}} \tag{12.111}$$

$$\beta < 1, n > 0, \delta > 0, \; m = 1: \quad K(L) \to [\tfrac{s\gamma}{\delta}]^{\frac{1}{1-a}} L \tag{12.112}$$

The *geometry* implied by (12.111–12.112) confirms the *behavior* of $\mathbf{k(t)}$, (12.107–12.108). *Trajectories* (12.112) are in long run *parallel* to *isocline*, (12.103), see Fig. 12.3, *case 2*.

With **n = 0**—a **stationary** *Labor* force—the **capital** *accumulation* is:

$$n = 0: \quad \dot{K} = s\,\gamma\, L_0^{m(1-a)}\, K^{am} - \delta\, K \tag{12.113}$$

and hence the **time paths** (*solutions*), **K(t)**, of (12.113), cf. (12.57), are:

$$n = 0, \delta > 0 : K(t) = \left[ \frac{s\,\gamma}{\delta} L_0^m + \left[ K_0^{1-am} - \frac{s\,\gamma}{\delta} L_0^m \right] e^{-(1-a)\delta\, t} \right]^{\frac{1}{1-am}} \tag{12.114}$$

$$n = 0, \delta > 0 : k(t) = K(t)/L_0 \rightarrow \left[ \frac{s\,\gamma}{\delta} \right]^{\frac{1}{1-am}} L_0^{\frac{m}{1-am}} \tag{12.115}$$

The long-run behavior (*asymptotic*), limit of **k(t)**, (12.115), is (with stationary Labor) seen affected by *initial* values, $\mathbf{L_0}$, that is, so-called *size effects* occur. The long-run *capital-labor ratio shifts* with the sizes of *parameters* in (12.115).

*The Critical Role of the Depreciation Parameter* **δ** *and* **β < 1**
Returning to the Solow (1956) models, originally without *depreciation*, then, for example, the *capital* stock of $\dot{\mathbf{K}}$, (12.100), *never* decreases:

$$m \neq 1,\ am < 1,\ \beta < 1,\ n > 0,\ \delta = 0 : \dot{K} = s\,\gamma\, L^{m(1-a)}\, K^{am} \tag{12.116}$$

The *solution*, **K(t)**, of (12.116) is (after some manipulations),

$$\beta < 1,\ n > 0,\ \delta = 0 :\ K(t) = \left[ \frac{(s\gamma/n)(1-am)}{1-\beta+m(1-a)} \cdot L(t)^{m(1-a)+1-\beta} \right]^{\frac{1}{1-am}} \tag{12.117}$$

$$\equiv \left[ \nu \cdot L(t)^{m(1-a)+1-\beta} \right]^{\frac{1}{1-am}} \tag{12.118}$$

The solution **K(t)**, (12.118), together with (12.57) is approximately,

$$\beta < 1, n > 0, \delta = 0 :\ K(t) \sim \left[ \nu \cdot [(1-\beta)n]^{\frac{m(1-a)+1-\beta}{1-\beta}} \right]^{\frac{1}{1-am}} t^{\frac{m(1-a)+1-\beta}{(1-\beta)(1-am)}} \tag{12.119}$$

and hence, by (12.119) and again (12.57), we get successively, $k(t)$, $y(t)$, $MP_K(t)$:

$$\beta < 1, n > 0, \delta = 0 :\ k(t) \sim \left[ \nu \cdot [(1-\beta)n]^{\frac{m-\beta}{1-\beta}} \right]^{\frac{1}{1-am}} t^{\frac{m-\beta}{(1-\beta)(1-am)}} \tag{12.120}$$

$$\beta < 1, n > 0, \delta = 0 : y = L^{m-1}\gamma k^{am} \sim \gamma\, \nu^{\frac{am}{1-am}} \, [(1-\beta)\, n\, t\,]^{\frac{m-1+a\,m(1-\beta)}{(1-\beta)(1-am)}} \tag{12.121}$$

$$\beta < 1, n > 0, \delta = 0 : MP_K(t) = L(t)^{m-1}\,\gamma\, a\, m\; k(t)^{\,am-1} \tag{12.122}$$

$$\sim \frac{\gamma\, a\, m}{\nu \cdot (1-\beta)n}\, t^{-1} = \frac{am\,[1-\beta+m(1-a)]}{s(1-\beta)(1-am)} \cdot t^{-1} \tag{12.123}$$

Finally, *solving* (12.57) in (**t**) and substituting in (12.120), the **trajectories** are:

$$\beta < 1,\ n > 0,\ \delta = 0\ :\ K(L) \sim \left[\nu \cdot [\,(1-\beta)\, n\,]^{\frac{m-\beta}{1-\beta}}\right]^{\frac{1}{1-am}} L^{1+\frac{m-\beta}{1-am}} \tag{12.124}$$

With $\beta < 1, \delta = 0$, we **can** here have *persistent* per capita *growth without* the *condition*: $\mathbf{m} > \mathbf{1}$. But we *need* at least, $\mathbf{m} > \boldsymbol{\beta}$. With, for example, $\mathbf{m} = \mathbf{1}$, the capital increases faster than labor, as **k**(**t**), (12.120), *grows polynomially*, and we have *polynomial per capita* growth, **y**(**t**), (12.121)—even *without* a positive *lower limit* to $\mathbf{MP_K}$, $\mathbf{MP_K}$, (12.123).

But, *with* any depreciation ($\delta$), however, small, *every polynomial* per capita *growth*, **y**(**t**), *disappears* with $m \leq 1$, cf.(12.107), (12.109). *Sic transit gloria mundi*. The physical **depreciation** ("*creative destruction*") *parameter* ($\boldsymbol{\delta}$) is **powerful**, compared to Labor and Capital *accumulation* parameters: $\beta < 1$, $s < 1$.

### *Neoclassical Growth Solutions: CES Technologies*

By $\beta = 1$, (12.54), $\dot{\mathbf{K}}$, (12.55), $\dot{\mathbf{k}}$, (12.62), and **CES** technology, (12.64–12.65), we have:

$$m \neq 1 :\ \dot{K} = s\,\gamma \left[(1-a)L^{\frac{\sigma-1}{\sigma}} + aK^{\frac{\sigma-1}{\sigma}}\right]^{\frac{\sigma m}{\sigma-1}} - \delta\, K \tag{12.125}$$

$$m > 1 :\ \dot{K} \sim s\,\gamma\, a^{\frac{\sigma m}{\sigma-1}}\, K^m - \delta\, K \tag{12.126}$$

$$\boldsymbol{\beta} = \mathbf{1},\ \mathbf{m} = \mathbf{1} :\ \dot{k} = h(k) = s\,\gamma \left[(1-a) + a\,k^{\frac{\sigma-1}{\sigma}}\right]^{\frac{\sigma}{\sigma-1}} - (n+\delta)\,k \tag{12.127}$$

$$\boldsymbol{\beta} = \mathbf{1},\ \mathbf{m} = \mathbf{1} : h(k) = 0 \equiv k = \kappa = \left[\frac{1}{1-a}\left(\left[\frac{s\,\gamma}{n+\delta}\right]^{\frac{1-\sigma}{\sigma}} - a\right)\right]^{\frac{\sigma}{1-\sigma}} \tag{12.128}$$

For **m > 1**, we have approximately $\dot{\mathbf{K}} \sim K^m$, yielding *explosive* solutions. Thus, by (12.125–12.126), solutions $K(t)$ **"explode"** with $m > 1$ for **every $\sigma \neq 1$**.

Hence, in *contrast* to $\dot{\mathbf{K}}$ of **CD** technologies (12.81), the *neoclassical* growth model (12.54–12.55) with *any* two-factor **CES** *technology* $\sigma \neq 1$, (12.126), is "*incompatible*" with any (even moderate) *increasing* returns to *scale*, **m > 1**.

To outline the **phase portrait**, we obtain the **isoclines** from (12.125) as,

$$m \neq 1 : \dot{K} = 0 : L = K\left[\frac{1}{1-a}\left(\left[\frac{s\gamma}{\delta}\right]^{\frac{1-\sigma}{\sigma m}} K^{\frac{(\sigma-1)(1-m)}{\sigma m}} - a\right)\right]^{\frac{\sigma}{\sigma-1}} \qquad (12.129)$$

$$m = 1 : \dot{K} = 0 \quad \Leftrightarrow \quad k = k^{\star} = \left[\frac{1}{1-a}\left(\left[\frac{s\gamma}{\delta}\right]^{\frac{1-\sigma}{\sigma}} - a\right)\right]^{\frac{\sigma}{1-\sigma}} \qquad (12.130)$$

The **isoclines** are depicted in Fig. 12.4, *case 1-4*. Their shapes *concave/convex* follow from the *exponents* in (12.125), due to the change of signs for $m$ passing, $m = 1$, (12.129–12.130).

Regarding (12.125) and $m > 1,\ \sigma > 1,\ L = 0 :\ K^{\star} = \left[a^{\frac{1}{1-m}} \frac{s\gamma}{\delta}\right]^{\frac{\sigma m}{\sigma-1}}$ is the K-axis *intercept*. For $m < 1$ or $\sigma < 1$, there is no K-axis intercept, except $K = 0$ for $L = 0$.

For $m < 1$ and $\sigma < 1$, it follows from (12.125) that $\boldsymbol{\delta}\mathbf{K}$ is growing *faster* than *new* additions to capital and hence terminating the solutions $\mathbf{K(t)}$ by an upper boundary. Hence, *trajectories* in *Case 1* are *bounded* from above.

For $m > 1$, the *explosive* part of the solutions is depicted by trajectories above the convex isocline curves, $\dot{\mathbf{K}} = 0$, in Fig. 12.4, *Case 3–4*.

For **m = 1**, **$\beta$ = 1**, **CES** *steady-state ray*, if it exists, was given as, (12.128):

$$\dot{k} = 0 \Leftrightarrow k = \kappa = \left[\frac{1}{1-a}\left(\left[\frac{s\gamma}{n+\delta}\right]^{\frac{1-\sigma}{\sigma}} - a\right)\right]^{\frac{\sigma}{1-\sigma}} \qquad (12.131)$$

Hence, **existence** of *steady* states—*positive* $\kappa$, (12.131)—requires parametrically:

$$\sigma < 1 : \left[\frac{s\gamma}{n+\delta}\right]^{\frac{1-\sigma}{\sigma}} > a \quad \Leftrightarrow \quad \gamma a^{\frac{\sigma}{\sigma-1}} > \frac{n+\delta}{s} \quad \Leftrightarrow s > \frac{n+\delta}{\gamma a^{\frac{\sigma}{\sigma-1}}} = \underline{s} \qquad (12.132)$$

$$\sigma > 1 : \left[\frac{s\gamma}{n+\delta}\right]^{\frac{1-\sigma}{\sigma}} > a \quad \Leftrightarrow \quad \gamma a^{\frac{\sigma}{\sigma-1}} < \frac{n+\delta}{s} \quad \Leftrightarrow s < \frac{n+\delta}{\gamma a^{\frac{\sigma}{\sigma-1}}} = \bar{s} \qquad (12.133)$$

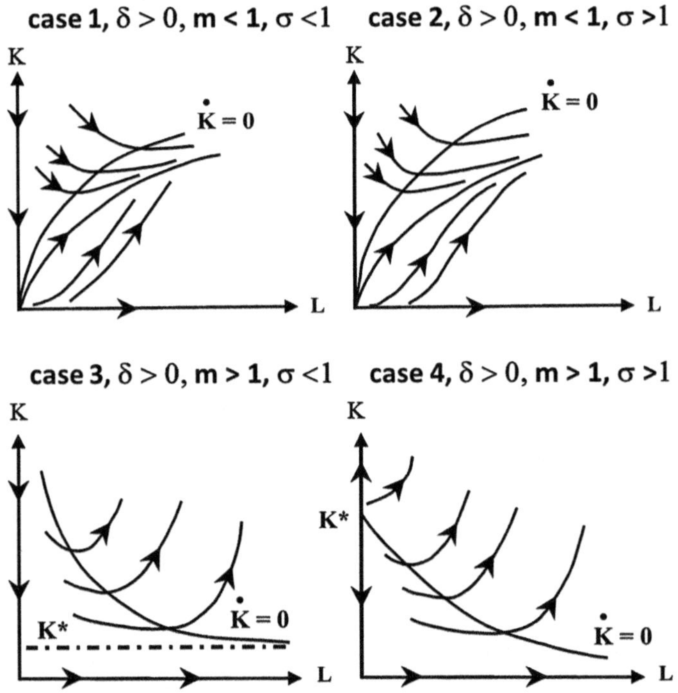


**Fig. 12.4** Phase portraits, $m \neq 1$, $\sigma \neq 1$: CES solutions, $[\,L(t), K(t)\,]$, (12.125–12.126), (12.129)

From, $\epsilon_K(k) = \left[1 + \frac{1-a}{a} k^{\frac{1-\sigma}{\sigma}}\right]^{-1}$, (12.68), and $\kappa$, (12.131), we have:

$$\epsilon_K(\kappa) = \left[1 + \frac{1}{a}\left[\left[\frac{s\gamma}{n+\delta}\right]^{\frac{1-\sigma}{\sigma}} - a\right]\right]^{-1} = a\left[\frac{s\gamma}{n+\delta}\right]^{\frac{\sigma-1}{\sigma}} \tag{12.134}$$

The general **phase portrait** of the state space *solutions* [ **L(t), K(t)** ] with **CES**, (12.127), (12.130)–12.134), is discussed below.

*Trajectory of Phase Portraits—Convergence and Divergence*
The discussion of phase portraits and trajectory geometry will, for $m = 1$, $\beta = 1$, be guided by the following theorem:

**Theorem 12.5 (Pampel)** *The standard macro (one-sector) neoclassical (Solow) dynamic system—*$\mathbf{m} = \mathbf{1}$, $\beta = \mathbf{1}$*—is given by, (12.61–12.62):*

$$\dot{K} = s\,f(k) - \delta K \;;\quad \dot{L} = n L \tag{12.135}$$

$$\dot{k} = h(k) = s\,f(k) - (n+\delta)k \;;\quad h(k) = 0 \equiv k = \kappa \tag{12.136}$$

*The steady state:* $k = \kappa$*, (12.136), is the unique asymptotic stable capital-labor ratio associated with solutions along ray:* $\forall t \; [L(t),\; K(t)] = [\; L(t),\; \kappa\, L(t)\; ]$.

*For any,* $k(0) = k_0 \neq \kappa$*, the distance,* $D_K(t)$*, to the* ***ray****,* $K(t) = \kappa\, L(t)$*, is*

$$D_K(t) = K(t) \; - \; \kappa\, L(t) \tag{12.137}$$

*The distance,* $\mathbf{D_K(t)}$*, (12.137), will for all solutions—*$[L(t), K(t)]$ *of (12.135–12.136)—converge to zero or infinity, depending on the elasticity:* $\epsilon_K(k) = \frac{k\, f'(k)}{f(k)} = E\,(\, f(k), k)\,)$ *of the production function,* $f(k)$*, (12.136), at* $k = \kappa : \epsilon_K(\kappa)$.

*There is* ***convergence*** *of* $D_K(t)$*, (12.137), to zero, if size of* $\epsilon_K(\kappa)$ *satisfies:*

$$\lim_{t\to\infty} |D_K(t)| = 0, \quad if \;\; \epsilon_K(\kappa) < \frac{\delta}{n+\delta} \quad \Leftrightarrow \quad h'(\kappa) < -n \tag{12.138}$$

*There is* ***divergence*** *of* $D_K(t)$*, (12.137), to infinity, if size of* $\epsilon_K(\kappa)$ *satisfies:*

$$\lim_{t\to\infty} |D_K(t)| = \infty, \quad if \;\; \epsilon_K(\kappa) > \frac{\delta}{n+\delta} \quad \Leftrightarrow \quad 0 > h'(\kappa) > -n \tag{12.139}$$

***Proof*** See Pampel (2009, p. 388, equations (8–11) of Theorem 1). □

Note again that $\delta = 0$ *always* imply *divergent phase portraits*, as convergence *condition* (12.138) can **never** be satisfied with $\delta = 0$.

**Proposition 12.3** ***Phase portraits*** *of the solutions* $[L(t), K(t)]$ *to neoclassical (Solow) dynamic system, m=1, (12.135–12.139)—applied to* ***CES****, (12.127–12.134)—have the convergence-divergence properties,* $\mathbf{D_K(t)}$*, (12.138–12.139), given by the following* ***CES parameter*** *conditions and* ***saving rates****,* ($\mathbf{s}$)*, restrictions:*

$\sigma < 1$*: Existence of* $\kappa$*-ray with* $\kappa$*, (12.131), requires:* $s > \frac{n+\delta}{\gamma\, a^{\frac{\sigma}{\sigma-1}}} \equiv \underline{s} > 0$

$\sigma < 1$: $\lim_{t\to\infty} |D_K(t)| = 0 : a\left[\frac{s\gamma}{n+\delta}\right]^{\frac{\sigma-1}{\sigma}} < \frac{\delta}{n+\delta} \Leftrightarrow s > \frac{1}{\gamma}\,[\,(\frac{a}{\delta})^{\sigma}\,(n+\delta)\,]^{\frac{1}{1-\sigma}}$

$\sigma < 1$: $\lim_{t\to\infty} |D_K(t)| = \infty : \;\underline{s} < s < \frac{1}{\gamma}\,[\,(\frac{a}{\delta})^{\sigma}\,(n+\delta)\,]^{\frac{1}{1-\sigma}}$

*With* $s < \underline{s}$*, there is no steady-state solution—ray,* $\kappa$*, (12.131).*

$\sigma > 1$*: Existence of* $\kappa$*-ray with* $\kappa$*, (12.131), requires:* $0 < s < \frac{n+\delta}{\gamma\, a^{\frac{\sigma}{\sigma-1}}} \equiv \bar{s}$

$\sigma > 1$: $\lim_{t\to\infty} |D_K(t)| = 0 : a\left[\frac{s\gamma}{n+\delta}\right]^{\frac{\sigma-1}{\sigma}} < \frac{\delta}{n+\delta} \Leftrightarrow s < \frac{1}{\gamma}\,[\,(\frac{a}{\delta})^{\sigma}\,(n+\delta)\,]^{\frac{1}{1-\sigma}}$

$\sigma > 1$: $\lim_{t\to\infty} |D_K(t)| = \infty : \bar{s} > s > \frac{1}{\gamma}\,[\,(\frac{a}{\delta})^{\sigma}\,(n+\delta)\,]^{\frac{1}{1-\sigma}}$

*With* $s > \bar{s}$*, there is no steady-state solution—ray,* $\kappa$*, (12.131).*

***Phase portraits*** *of dynamic system, m=1, (12.135–12.139)—for* **CD**, *(12.71–12.75), (12.134)—have convergence-divergence properties,* $\mathbf{D_K(t)}$, *(12.138–12.139), given as:*
$\sigma = 1$: $\lim_{t\to\infty} |D_K(t)| = 0 : a < \frac{\delta}{n+\delta}$ ; $\lim_{t\to\infty} |D_K(t)| = \infty : a > \frac{\delta}{n+\delta}$

***Proof*** The saving rate sizes, $s > \underline{s}$, $s < \bar{s}$, for existence of steady states (balanced growth) follow from equivalents of (12.131). The convergence-divergence **CES** parameter conditions follow from applying the *general requirements* (12.138–12.139), together with **CES** *formula* for $\epsilon_K(\kappa)$, (12.68), (12.128), (12.134). The **CD** conditions follow immediately with parameter restriction to $\sigma = 1$. □

We will give benchmark examples of $\mathbf{k(t)}$ solutions for $\boldsymbol{\sigma} = \frac{1}{2}$ and $\boldsymbol{\sigma} = \mathbf{2}$, together with applying Proposition 12.3 on phase portraits to the **CES** cases. Besides *parametric* solution formulas of $\mathbf{k(t)}$, we also *calculate* selected **solutions** of $[\,\mathbf{L(t), K(t)}\,]$ and $\mathbf{D_K(t)}$, (12.137)—as shown in Figs. 12.5 and 12.6; as to $D_K$, $D_K^*$, cf. Fig. 11.1, and Chap. 11 section "Trajectory Geometry and Kinematics".

**Remark 12.1** By using computational programs like *Maple*, which can calculate with an *accuracy* of 100 *digits*, we can without problems solve *ordinary differential* equations, $\dot{x} = F(x)$, using **Euler's method**:

$$x(t_n + \Delta t) \approx x(t_n) + \dot{x}(t_n) \cdot \Delta t = x(t_n) + F(x(t_n)) \cdot \Delta t$$

Thus, in **CES** cases, Figs. 12.5 and 12.6: $\dot{\mathbf{L}}$, $\dot{\mathbf{K}}$, are in (12.135) and (12.136), (12.127–12.128),

$$L(t_n + \Delta t) = L(t_n) + \dot{L}(t_n) \cdot \Delta t \tag{12.140}$$

$$K(t_n + \Delta t) = K(t_n) + \dot{K}(t_n) \cdot \Delta t \tag{12.141}$$

The smaller the $\Delta t$, the higher the accuracy if one can neglect *rounding errors.* Even repeating (12.140)–(12.141) *many* times, there is *no* appreciable rounding errors, when calculating with 100 *digits* of accuracy; $t_1 = 0$, $\Delta t = \frac{1}{100}$.

On **Euler's method**, see Arnold (1973, p. 109,222), Birkhoff and Rota (1989, p. 21), Simmons (1972, p. 66). ▽

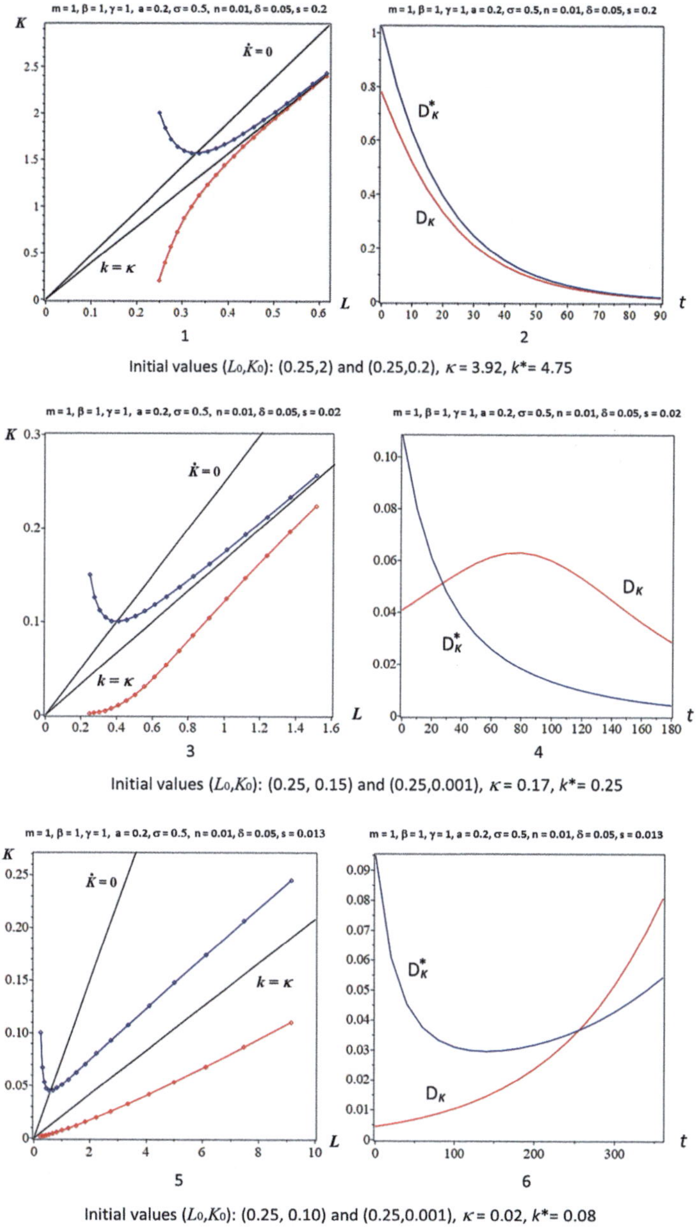


**Fig. 12.5** Phase Portraits, $m = 1$, $\beta = 1$, $\sigma = \frac{1}{2}$: CES solutions, $[\,\mathbf{L(t)}, \mathbf{K(t)}\,]$, and distance, $\mathbf{D_K(t)}$ from: (12.135–12.136), (12.137), (12.127–12.128), (12.130), (12.147–12.148)

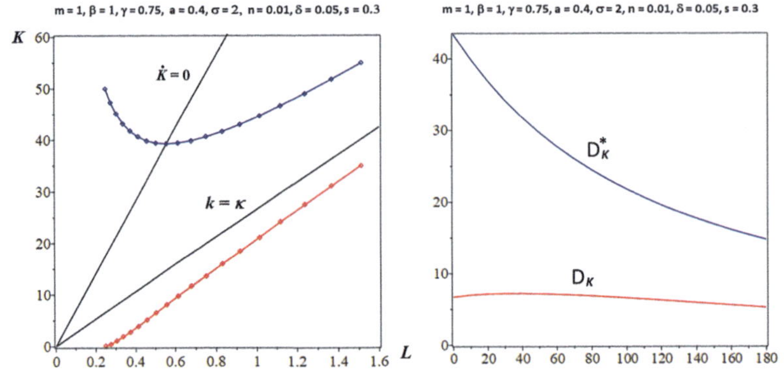


1 2

Initial values ($L_0$,$K_0$): (0.25, 50) and (0.25,0.001), $\kappa$ =26.57, $k^*$= 70.61

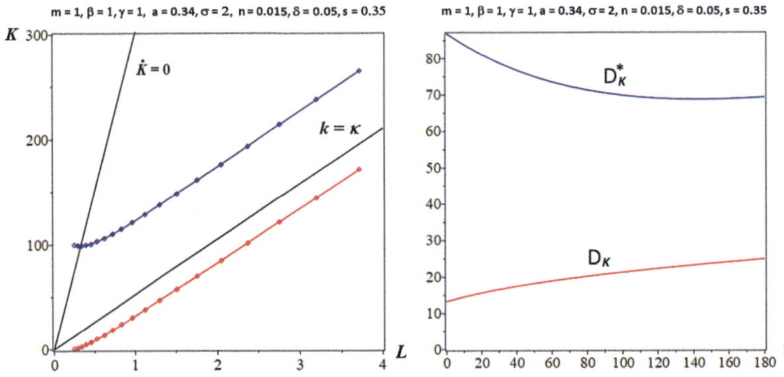


3 4

Initial values ($L_0$,$K_0$): (0.25, 100) and (0.25,0.001), $\kappa$ =52.67, $k^*$= 302.23

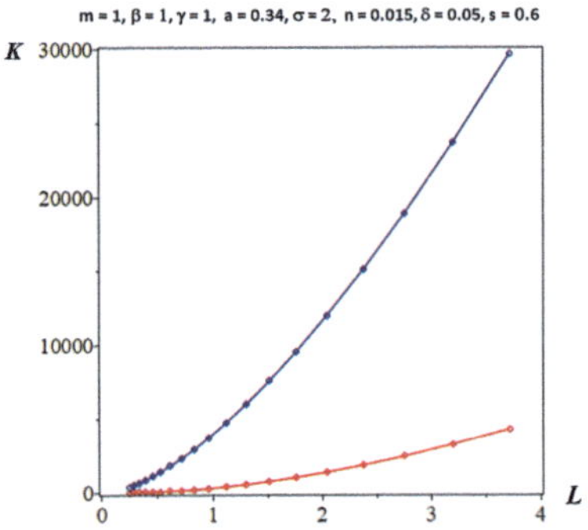


5

Initial values ($L_0$,$K_0$): (0.25, 400) and (0.25,0.001)

**Fig. 12.6** Phase Portraits, $m = 1$, $\beta = 1$, $\sigma = 2$: CES solutions, $[\,\mathbf{L(t)}, \mathbf{K(t)}\,]$ and distance, $\mathbf{D_K(t)}$ from: (12.135–12.136), (12.137), (12.127–12.128), (12.130), (12.160), (12.162)

*CES Dynamics with* $\mathbf{m} = \mathbf{1}$, $\boldsymbol{\beta} = \mathbf{1}$, *and* $\boldsymbol{\sigma} = \frac{1}{2}$

**Case 1.** With $\mathbf{m} = \mathbf{1}$, $\sigma = \frac{1}{2}$, the *governing* function $\mathbf{h(k)}$, (12.127), is:

$$\dot{k} = h(k) = s\,\gamma\,\frac{1}{1 - a + \frac{a}{k}} - (n + \delta)\,k = \frac{s\,\gamma\,k}{(1 - a)\,k + a} - (n + \delta)\,k \tag{12.142}$$

$$= k \cdot \frac{s\,\gamma\, - a\,(n + \delta) - (n + \delta)(1 - a)\,k}{(1 - a)\,k + a} \tag{12.143}$$

With $\boldsymbol{\sigma} = \frac{1}{2}$, solutions $k(t)$ to (12.142–12.143)—with the attractor, $k\,(t) \equiv \kappa$, (12.131–12.132)—have **approximate** local solutions around ( $\kappa$ ) as:

$$k(t) \sim \kappa + (\,k(0) - \kappa\,)\;e^{-\frac{n+\delta}{s\gamma}\,[\,s\,\gamma - a(n+\delta)\,]\,t}\;;\;\; s > \frac{1}{\gamma}\,a\,\delta\,(\,1 + \frac{n}{\delta}\,) \equiv \underline{s} \tag{12.144}$$

**Exact** solutions $\mathbf{k(t)}$ of (12.142–12.143) are implicitly given by the expression:

$$\sigma = \tfrac{1}{2} : k^{-a}|\,k - \kappa\,|^{\frac{s\gamma}{n+\delta}} = C_0\,e^{-[s\gamma - a(n+\delta)]\,t},\;\; C_0{=}k(0)^{-a}|k(0) - \kappa|^{\frac{s\gamma}{n+\delta}} \tag{12.145}$$

$$[\,L(t),\; K(t)\,] \;\equiv\; [\,L(t),\; k(t) \cdot L(t)\,] \;=\; L(t)\,[\,1 \,+\, k(t)\,] \tag{12.146}$$

The **trajectories** of solutions—time paths—$k(t)$, (12.145), become the **loci**:

$$k^{-a}\,|\,k - \kappa\,|^{\frac{s\gamma}{n+\delta}} \;=\; C_0\left[\frac{L}{L_0}\right]^{-\frac{s\gamma - a\,(n+\delta)}{n}}, \quad \kappa \;=\; \frac{1}{1 - a}\left[\frac{s\,\gamma}{n + \delta} - a\right] \tag{12.147}$$

Convergence of **phase portrait** of solutions (12.146) to $\kappa$, (12.147), requires:

$$\epsilon_K\,(\kappa) \;=\; a\left[\frac{s\,\gamma}{n + \delta}\right]^{-1} \;<\; \frac{\delta}{n + \delta} \;\;\Leftrightarrow\;\; s > \frac{1}{\gamma}\;a\,\delta\,(\,1{+}n/\delta\,)^2 \;>\; \underline{s} \tag{12.148}$$

according to Proposition 12.3 for: $\sigma = \frac{1}{2}$—seen in Fig. 12.5, *case 1, 3*; critical size of $s$ is, $s > 0.0144$; divergence: case 5 with, $s = 0.013$.

***Proof*** The derivatives in the roots of $h(k)$, (12.143), are positive and negative, respectively, cf. (12.133)

$$h(0) = 0, \quad h(\kappa) = 0, \quad \kappa = \frac{1}{1 - a}\left[\frac{s\gamma}{n + \delta} - a\right] \tag{12.149}$$

$$h'(k) = \frac{s\,\gamma\,a}{[\,(1 - a)\,k + a\,]^2} - (n + \delta) \tag{12.150}$$

$$h'(0) = s\gamma/a - (n+\delta) > 0 \tag{12.151}$$

$$h'(\kappa) = s\gamma a\left[\frac{s\gamma}{n+\delta}\right]^{-2} - (n+\delta) = -\frac{n+\delta}{s\gamma}[s\gamma - a(n+\delta)] < 0 \tag{12.152}$$

that is, the *root* $\kappa$ is an **attractor** of $k(t)$ with approximate **exponential** attraction. Hence, (12.152) gives (12.144).

The exact solution of (12.143) is given implicitly as,

$$\int_{k_0}^{k} \frac{(1-a)k + a}{[s\gamma - a(n+\delta) - (n+\delta)(1-a)k]k}\, dk = t + t_0 \tag{12.153}$$

$$\Leftrightarrow \frac{s\gamma(1-a)}{s\gamma - a(n+\delta)} \int_{k_0}^{k} \frac{dk}{s\gamma - a(n+\delta) - (n+\delta)(1-a)k} + \tag{12.154}$$

$$+ \frac{a}{s\gamma - a(n+\delta)} \int_{k_0}^{k} \frac{dk}{k} = t + t_0\,; \quad C_0 = e^{-[s\gamma - a(n+\delta)]t_0} \tag{12.155}$$

$$\Leftrightarrow k^{-a}|k-\kappa|^{\frac{s\gamma}{n+\delta}} = C_0\, e^{-[s\gamma - a(n+\delta)]t}\,; \quad C_0 = k(0)^{-a}\,[k(0)-\kappa]^{\frac{s\gamma}{n+\delta}} \tag{12.156}$$

Substitution of $L/L_0 = e^{nt}$ in (12.156) yields (12.147). □

*CES Dynamics with* $\mathbf{m = 1}$, $\boldsymbol{\beta} = \mathbf{1}$, *and* $\boldsymbol{\sigma} = \mathbf{2}$

An early CES growth model with $\sigma = 2$ is seen in Solow (1956, p. 77, Ex.3).

**Case 2.** With $m = 1$, $\sigma = 2$, the *governing* function, $h(k)$ of $\dot{\mathbf{k}}$, (12.127), is:

$$\dot{k} = h(k) = s\gamma(1 - a + a k^{\frac{1}{2}})^2 - (n+\delta)k \tag{12.157}$$

$$= [s\gamma a^2 - (n+\delta)]\,k + 2 s\gamma a(1-a)\, k^{\frac{1}{2}} + s\gamma(1-a)^2 \tag{12.158}$$

For $\sigma = 2$, *existence* of a *steady*- state—*positive* $\boldsymbol{\kappa}$, (12.131)—requires by (12.133):

$$\sigma = 2 : \left[\frac{s\gamma}{n+\delta}\right]^{-\frac{1}{2}} > a \Leftrightarrow a^2 < \frac{n+\delta}{s\gamma} \quad \Leftrightarrow \quad s < \frac{n+\delta}{\gamma a^2} \equiv \bar{s} \tag{12.159}$$

For $\sigma = 2$, *explicit* steady-state formula, $k = \kappa$, to (12.158–12.159), is by (12.131):

$$\sigma = 2 : \ \kappa = \left[\frac{1}{1-a}\left(\left[\frac{s\gamma}{n+\delta}\right]^{-\frac{1}{2}} - a\right)\right]^{-2} = \left[\frac{1-a}{(\frac{n+\delta}{s\gamma})^{\frac{1}{2}} - a}\right]^2 \tag{12.160}$$

The **k(t)** *solutions* of (12.158–12.160) form with, $L(t) = L_0 e^{nt}$, the *phase curves*:

$$[L(t),\ K(t)] \equiv [L(t),\ k(t) \cdot L(t)] = L(t)[1 + k(t)] \tag{12.161}$$

**Convergence** of **phase portrait** of solutions (12.161) to $\kappa$, (12.160), requires:

$$\epsilon_K(\kappa) = a\left[\frac{s\,\gamma}{n+\delta}\right]^{\frac{1}{2}} < \frac{\delta}{n+\delta} \Leftrightarrow s < \frac{\delta}{\gamma\, a^2\,(1 + n/\delta)} < \bar{s} \tag{12.162}$$

according to Proposition 12.3 for: $\sigma = 2$—such phase portraits are seen in Fig. 12.6, *case 1–2*. **Divergence** of **phase portrait** is shown in *case 3–4*, where the critical interval of $s$ for seeing Divergence is: $0.562 > s > 0.333$.

For large $\sigma$, **no** *steady state*, $\forall\, t,\ k(t) = \kappa$, exists—which is equivalent to the condition (12.133) *reversed*, that is, we have the *parameter* requirements:

$$\sigma > 1: \left[\frac{s\,\gamma}{n+\delta}\right]^{\frac{1-\sigma}{\sigma}} < a \Leftrightarrow \gamma\, a^{\frac{\sigma}{\sigma-1}} > \frac{n+\delta}{s} \Leftrightarrow s > \frac{n+\delta}{\gamma\, a^{\frac{\sigma}{\sigma-1}}} \equiv \bar{s} \tag{12.163}$$

With (12.163), **persistent** per capita growth, $y(t) = f[k(t)]$, occurs from (12.158).

A *benchmark analytic* illustration of **k(t)** for $\sigma = 2$ is:
With $\boldsymbol{\sigma} = \mathbf{2}$ : $\gamma\, a^2 > (n+\delta)/s \Leftrightarrow s > \bar{s}$, satisfying (12.163), the **solution** of **k(t)** to (12.158) is implicitly given by the expression:

$$\left[k^{\frac{1}{2}} + \frac{1-a}{a+d}\right]^{\frac{1}{a-d}} \left[k^{\frac{1}{2}} + \frac{1-a}{a-d}\right]^{-\frac{1}{a+d}} = C_0\, e^{(s\,\gamma\, d)\,t},\quad d = \left[\frac{s\gamma}{n+\delta}\right]^{-\frac{1}{2}} \tag{12.164}$$

where $C_0 = \left[k_0^{\frac{1}{2}} + \frac{1-a}{a+d}\right]^{\frac{1}{a-d}} \left[k_0^{\frac{1}{2}} + \frac{1-a}{a-d}\right]^{-\frac{1}{a+d}}$

The **trajectories** of the **k(t)** solutions (12.164) become the **loci**:

$$\left[k^{\frac{1}{2}} + \frac{1-a}{a+d}\right]^{\frac{1}{a-d}} \left[k^{\frac{1}{2}} + \frac{1-a}{a-d}\right]^{-\frac{1}{a+d}} = C_0\, L^{\frac{s\,\gamma\, d}{n}} \tag{12.165}$$

$$\Leftrightarrow \left[K^{\frac{1}{2}} + \frac{1-a}{a+d}\, L^{\frac{1}{2}}\right]^{\frac{1}{a-d}} \left[K^{\frac{1}{2}} + \frac{1-a}{a-d}\, L^{\frac{1}{2}}\right]^{-\frac{1}{a+d}} = C_0\, L^{[s\,\gamma\,(n+\delta)]^{\frac{1}{2}} \cdot \frac{s\,\gamma\, a^2 - \delta}{n\left(s\,\gamma\, a^2 - (n+\delta)\right)}} \tag{12.166}$$

The geometric *trajectories* of (12.166) are seen by the *phase portrait* in Fig. 12.6, *case 5*—and with $\delta = 0$, (no depreciation), indicated in Fig. 12.1, *case 3*.

***Proof*** Introducing, $\mathbf{k} = \mathbf{z}^2$, into (12.158), we get in $\mathbf{z}$:

$$2\,z\,\dot{z} = \left[s\gamma a^2 - (n+\delta)\right] z^2 + 2\,s\,\gamma\,a\,(1-a)\,z + s\,\gamma\,(1-a)^2 \tag{12.167}$$

Separation of variables gives,

$$\frac{2}{s\,\gamma\,a^2 - (n+\delta)} \int \frac{z\dot{z}}{z^2 + \frac{2s\gamma a(1-a)}{s\gamma a^2-(n+\delta)} z + \frac{s\gamma(1-a)^2}{s\gamma a^2-(n+\delta)}} dt = t + t_0 \tag{12.168}$$

The denominator of the fraction in (12.168) has two negative roots:

$$\rho_1 = -\frac{1-a}{a+d} < 0, \qquad \rho_2 = -\frac{1-a}{a-d} < 0; \quad d = \left[\frac{s\gamma}{n+\delta}\right]^{-\frac{1}{2}} \tag{12.169}$$

Hence, we may write the integral (12.168) as,

$$\frac{2}{s\gamma a^2 - (n+\delta)} \left( \int \frac{\frac{1}{2}\left(1+\frac{a}{d}\right)}{z-\rho_1} dz + \int \frac{\frac{1}{2}\left(1-\frac{a}{d}\right)}{z-\rho_2} dz \right) \tag{12.170}$$

The equation (12.168), (12.170) may be manipulated to

$$\frac{d+a}{ds\gamma\,(a^2-d^2)} \ln(z-\rho_1) + \frac{d-a}{ds\gamma\,(a^2-d^2)} \ln(z-\rho_2) = t + t_0 \tag{12.171}$$

$$\text{or} \qquad (z-\rho_1)^{\frac{1}{a-d}}\,(z-\rho_2)^{-\frac{1}{a+d}} = e^{s\gamma d(t+t_0)} = C\,e^{s\gamma d\,t}; \; C = e^{s\gamma d\,t_0} \tag{12.172}$$

The latter and $\mathbf{k} = \mathbf{z}^2$ give the $\mathbf{k(t)}$ *solution* wanted as:

$$\left[k^{\frac{1}{2}} - \rho_1\right]^{\frac{1}{a-d}} \left[k^{\frac{1}{2}} - \rho_2\right]^{-\frac{1}{a+d}} = C\,e^{\,s\,\gamma\,d\,(t+t_0)} \tag{12.173}$$

With $k = K/L$ and using $L = L_0\,e^{\,nt}$, we obtain the **trajectory** in the $(\mathbf{L}, \mathbf{K})$—plane of the *solution* (12.173) by eliminating $(\mathbf{t})$:

$$\left[K^{\frac{1}{2}} - \rho_1 L^{\frac{1}{2}}\right]^{\frac{1}{a-d}} \left[K^{\frac{1}{2}} - \rho_2 L^{\frac{1}{2}}\right]^{-\frac{1}{a+d}} = C_0\,L^{\,[s\gamma(n+\delta)]^{\frac{1}{2}}\,\frac{s\gamma a^2-\delta}{n\left(s\gamma a^2-(n+\delta)\right)}} \tag{12.174}$$

where $L^{\frac{d}{a^2-d^2}+\frac{s\gamma d}{n}}$, $\mathbf{d}$ (12.169), and $C_0 = C L_0^{-\frac{s\gamma d}{n}}$ give the **RHS** of (12.174). □

# Solving Multi-Factor Macro Growth Models

### *Multiple Capital Factors and Steady-State Ratios*

The **multi-factor CD** and **CES** *technologies*—$\alpha = \sum_{j=1}^{M} \alpha_j$—are:

$$\textbf{CD}: Y = \gamma\, L^{m-\alpha} K_1^{\alpha_1} \cdots K_M^{\alpha_M} = \gamma\, L^{m-\alpha} \prod_{j=1}^{M} K_j^{\alpha_j} = L^m \gamma \prod_{j=1}^{M} k_j^{\alpha_j} \quad (12.175)$$

$$m = 1: \quad Y/L = y = \gamma\, k_1^{\alpha_1} \cdots k_M^{\alpha_M} = \gamma \prod_{j=1}^{M} k_j^{\alpha_j} \quad (12.176)$$

$$\textbf{CES}: Y = \gamma \left[ (1-\alpha) L^{\frac{\sigma-1}{\sigma}} + \sum_{j=1}^{M} \alpha_j K_j^{\frac{\sigma-1}{\sigma}} \right]^{\frac{m\sigma}{\sigma-1}} \quad (12.177)$$

$$m = 1: \quad Y/L = y = \gamma \left[ 1 - \alpha + \sum_{j=1}^{M} \alpha_j k_j^{\frac{\sigma-1}{\sigma}} \right]^{\frac{\sigma}{\sigma-1}} \quad (12.178)$$

The analogous *dynamic system*—with *multiple capital factors* and proportional gross **savings** ($\mathbf{s_i}$) and **depreciation** rates ($\boldsymbol{\delta}_\mathbf{i}$)—is, cf. (12.62), (12.71),

$$\dot{K}_i = s_i\, Y - \delta_i\, K_i, \quad i = 1, \cdots, M \quad (12.179)$$

$$\dot{k}_i = s_i\, y - (n + \delta_i)\, k_i, \quad i = 1, \cdots, M \quad (12.180)$$

**CD**: Capital-labor ratios of the *steady-state rays* are given by, cf. (12.72),

$$\forall i \quad \dot{k}_i = 0 \;\Leftrightarrow\; k_i = \frac{s_i}{n+\delta_i}\, y = \frac{s_i}{n+\delta_i}\, \gamma \prod_{j=1}^{M} k_j^{\alpha_j} \;\Leftrightarrow \quad (12.181)$$

$$\forall i \quad \ln k_i = \alpha_1 \ln k_1 + \cdots + \alpha_M \ln k_M + \ln \frac{s_i\, \gamma}{n+\delta_i} \quad (12.182)$$

or in matrix form (**I**: Identity matrix, and $(\mathbf{x_i})_|$: *column vector* of entries, $(\mathbf{x_1}, \mathbf{x_2}, .., \mathbf{x_n})$),

$$(\mathbf{I} - \mathbf{A})\, (\ln \mathbf{k_i})_| = \left( \ln \frac{s_i\, \gamma}{n+\delta_i} \right)_| \quad (12.183)$$

where **A** is a *matrix* with *identical rows* of the $(\boldsymbol{\alpha}_\mathbf{i})$ elements, (12.176), (12.178).

**Proposition 12.4** *With CD technology and,* $\mathbf{m} = \mathbf{1}$*, (12.176), the* ***steady-state*** *capital labor* ***ratios****,* $\kappa_i$*, solving (12.181–12.183), are*

$$\kappa_i = \frac{s_i\, \gamma}{n+\delta_i} \prod_{j=1}^{M} \left( \frac{s_j\, \gamma}{n+\delta_j} \right)^{\frac{\alpha_j}{1-\alpha}}, \qquad \alpha = \sum_{j=1}^{M} \alpha_j \quad (12.184)$$

$$= \frac{s_i}{n+\delta_i} \left[ \gamma \prod_{j=1}^{M} \left( \frac{s_j}{n+\delta_j} \right)^{\alpha_j} \right]^{\frac{1}{1-\alpha}} \qquad i = 1, \cdots, M \quad (12.185)$$

*The **steady-state** per capita **income**, $\bar{\mathbf{y}}$, (12.176), is given by*

$$\bar{y} = y(\kappa_1, \cdots, \kappa_M) = \gamma \prod_{j=1}^{M} \kappa_j^{\alpha_j} = \left[\gamma \prod_{j=1}^{M} \left(\tfrac{s_j}{n+\delta_j}\right)^{\alpha_j}\right]^{\frac{1}{1-\alpha}} = \tag{12.186}$$

$$\bar{y} = \kappa_i (n + \delta_i)/s_i \quad \Leftrightarrow \quad \kappa_i = [\, s_i/(n + \delta_i)\,]\,\bar{y} \quad \forall i \tag{12.187}$$

*The **relative** steady-state capital-labor ratios and associated relative capital stocks are simply related to the respective saving and depreciation parameters:*

$$\kappa_i/\kappa_j = \bar{K}_i/\bar{K}_j = \frac{s_i/(n + \delta_i)}{s_j/(n + \delta_j)}; \qquad \kappa_i = \frac{s_i/(n + \delta_i)}{s_1/(n + \delta_1)}\,\kappa_1 \tag{12.188}$$

***Proof*** The steady-state capital-labor ratios solve the matrix equation:

$$(\ln \kappa_i)_| = (\mathbf{I} - \mathbf{A})^{-1}\left(\ln \frac{s_i \gamma}{n + \delta_i}\right)_| = \left(\mathbf{I} + \frac{1}{1-\alpha}\mathbf{A}\right)\left(\ln \frac{s_i \gamma}{n + \delta_i}\right)_| \tag{12.189}$$

where the column *elements* of (12.189) are seen to become,

$$\ln \kappa_i = \ln \frac{s_i \gamma}{n + \delta_i} + \frac{1}{1-\alpha}\sum_{j=1}^{M} \alpha_j \ln \frac{s_j \gamma}{n + \delta_j} \quad i = 1, \cdots, M \tag{12.190}$$

Thus, the *anti-log* of (12.190) establishes (12.184). Next, the proof of (12.187) is:

$$\bar{y} = \gamma \prod_{j=1}^{M} \kappa_j^{\alpha_j} = \gamma \prod_{j=1}^{M} \left(\tfrac{s_j}{n+\delta_j}\right)^{\alpha_j} \left[\gamma \prod_{j=1}^{M} \left(\tfrac{s_j}{n+\delta_j}\right)^{\alpha_j}\right]^{\frac{\sum_i \alpha_i}{1-\alpha}} \tag{12.191}$$

$$= \gamma^{1+\frac{\alpha}{1-\alpha}} \prod_{j=1}^{M} \left(\tfrac{s_j}{n+\delta_j}\right)^{(1+\frac{\alpha}{1-\alpha})\alpha_j} = \left[\gamma \prod_{j=1}^{M} \left(\tfrac{s_j}{n+\delta_j}\right)^{\alpha_j}\right]^{\frac{1}{1-\alpha}} \tag{12.192}$$

□

**CES**: Capital-labor ratios of steady-state *rays* are given by, cf. (12.178–12.180),

$$\dot{k}_i = 0 \Leftrightarrow 1 - \alpha + \sum_{j=1}^{M} \alpha_j k_j^{\frac{\sigma-1}{\sigma}} = \left[\frac{s_i \gamma}{n + \delta_i}\right]^{\frac{1-\sigma}{\sigma}} k_i^{\frac{\sigma-1}{\sigma}} \tag{12.193}$$

or equivalently in matrix form:

$$\forall\, i:\ \dot{k}_i = 0 \Leftrightarrow (\mathbf{D} - \mathbf{A})\left(k_i^{\frac{\sigma-1}{\sigma}}\right)_| = (1-\alpha)\iota \quad \iota = (1)_| \tag{12.194}$$

where **A** is as above, and **D** is a diagonal matrix with elements, $(d_i)$, as

$$d_i = \left[\frac{s_i \gamma}{n+\delta_i}\right]^{\frac{1-\sigma}{\sigma}}, \quad \mathbf{D} = (d_i)_| \tag{12.195}$$

**Proposition 12.5** *With CES technology and, $m = 1$, (12.178), the **steady-state** capital-labor **ratios**, $\kappa_i$, solving (12.193– 12.194), are*

$$\left(\kappa_i^{\frac{\sigma-1}{\sigma}}\right)_| = (1-\alpha)(\mathbf{D}-\mathbf{A})^{-1}\iota \tag{12.196}$$

*If the particular saving rates and depreciation rates are the same, that is,*

$$\forall\, i:\ s_i = s, \quad \delta_i = \delta; \quad d_i = d = \left[\frac{s\gamma}{n+\delta}\right]^{\frac{1-\sigma}{\sigma}}; \quad d > \alpha \tag{12.197}$$

*then (12.196) reduces to a vector of the same elements, and $\kappa_i$ is, cf. (12.131),*

$$\forall\, i:\ \kappa_i = \kappa = \left[\frac{1-\alpha}{d-\alpha}\right]^{\frac{1-\sigma}{\sigma}} = \left[\frac{1}{1-\alpha}\left(\left[\frac{s\gamma}{n+\delta}\right]^{\frac{1-\sigma}{\sigma}} - \alpha\right)\right]^{\frac{\sigma}{1-\sigma}} \tag{12.198}$$

$$\bar{y} = \gamma\left[1-\alpha+\alpha\kappa^{\frac{\sigma-1}{\sigma}}\right]^{\frac{\sigma}{\sigma-1}} \tag{12.199}$$

***Proof*** As the matrix $\mathbf{D}-\mathbf{A}$ is nonsingular, (12.196) follows from (12.194). □

Especially inspiring for Proposition 12.4 was the paper of Nonneman and Vanhoudt (1996) on several types of *capital* goods. We have here been focused on the theoretical issues and more so on succinct *analytical* expressions for the capital-labor ratios, $\kappa_i$, and we have also extended this analysis to include **CES** technologies in our Proposition 12.5. Here no *solutions* (time paths) are given for the **M**-dimensional dynamic system (12.179), (12.180), with (12.176), (12.178), but *three-factor* (**M=3**) dynamics with **exogeneity** is solved below.

### *Human Capital Augmented Macro Growth Models*

*Technology* of the *augmented* Solow model, Mankiw et al. (1992), Romer (2019, p. 101), is described by the **CD** *production* function, $\mathbf{m} \geq \mathbf{1}$:

$$Y = F(L, H, K) = \gamma\, L^{\alpha_1} H^{\alpha_2} K^{\alpha_3}, \quad m = \alpha_1 + \alpha_2 + \alpha_3 \geq 1, \tag{12.200}$$

$$= \gamma\, L^m (H/L)^{\alpha_2} (K/L)^{\alpha_3} \equiv \gamma\, L^m\, h^{\alpha_2}\, k^{\alpha_3} \tag{12.201}$$

$$= \gamma\, L^{m-\mu}\, H^{\mu}\, (K/H)^{\alpha_3} \equiv \gamma\, L^{m-\mu}\, H^{\mu}\, q^{\alpha_3}, \quad \mu = \alpha_2 + \alpha_3 \leq 1 \tag{12.202}$$

Model (12.203–12.204) assumes constant fractions, $\mathbf{s_H}$, $\mathbf{s_K}$, of *Output* (12.200) are saved/invested in *Human* Capital and *Physical* Capital. *Labor* grows *exogenously* as (12.33) and grows here *parametrically* as (12.54).

With $\mathbf{m} = \mathbf{1}$, $\beta = \mathbf{1}$, it is common in analyzing augmented growth models to use *per capita ratios*, $\mathbf{h} = \mathbf{H}/\mathbf{L}$, $\mathbf{k} = \mathbf{K}/\mathbf{L}$, and then study the differential equations of $\dot{\mathbf{h}}$ and $\dot{\mathbf{k}}$, see Mankiw et al. (1992, p. 416), cf. (12.200–12.201, 12.179–12.180),

$$m = 1 \; : \dot{h} = s_H \; y - (n + \delta_H) \; h \; = \; s_H \, \gamma \, h^{\alpha_2} \, k^{\alpha_3} - (n + \delta_H) \; h \tag{12.203}$$

$$m = 1 \; : \dot{k} = s_K \; y - (n + \delta_K) \; k \; = \; s_K \, \gamma \, h^{\alpha_2} \, k^{\alpha_3} - (n + \delta_K) \; k \tag{12.204}$$

We analyzed system, (12.180), (12.203–12.204), in Proposition 12.4. *Steady-state* sizes of the *ratios*, $\kappa_i$, $i = H, K$, (12.184), and per capita *income*, $\bar{\mathbf{y}}$, (12.187), are:

$$\kappa_H = \frac{s_H \, \gamma}{n + \delta_H} \left[ \gamma \left[ \frac{s_H \, \gamma}{n + \delta_H} \right]^{\alpha_2} \left[ \frac{s_K \, \gamma}{n + \delta_K} \right]^{\alpha_3} \right]^{\frac{1}{1-\mu}} \tag{12.205}$$

$$= \left[ \frac{s_H \, \gamma}{n + \delta_H} \left[ \frac{s_K/(n + \delta_K)}{s_H/(n + \delta_H)} \right]^{\alpha_3} \right]^{\frac{1}{1-\mu}} \tag{12.206}$$

$$\kappa_K = \frac{s_K \, \gamma}{n + \delta_K} \left[ \gamma \left[ \frac{s_H \, \gamma}{n + \delta_H} \right]^{\alpha_2} \left[ \frac{s_K \, \gamma}{n + \delta_K} \right]^{\alpha_3} \right]^{\frac{1}{1-\mu}} \tag{12.207}$$

$$= \left[ \frac{s_K \, \gamma}{n + \delta_K} \left[ \frac{s_H/(n + \delta_H)}{s_K/(n + \delta_K)} \right]^{\alpha_2} \right]^{\frac{1}{1-\mu}} \tag{12.208}$$

$$\frac{\kappa_K}{\kappa_H} = \frac{\bar{K}}{\bar{H}} = \frac{s_K/(n + \delta_K)}{s_H/(n + \delta_H)}; \quad \bar{y} = \frac{\kappa_H (n + \delta_H)}{s_H} = \frac{\kappa_K (n + \delta_K)}{s_K} \tag{12.209}$$

$$\delta = \delta_H = \delta_K : \kappa_H = \left[ \frac{s_H \, \gamma}{n + \delta} \left( \frac{s_K}{s_H} \right)^{\alpha_3} \right]^{\frac{1}{1-\mu}} \kappa_K = \left[ \frac{s_K \, \gamma}{n + \delta} \left( \frac{s_H}{s_K} \right)^{\alpha_2} \right]^{\frac{1}{1-\mu}} \tag{12.210}$$

With a **CES** technology *augmented* model, (12.178), (12.179–12.180), (12.200–12.201), the *steady-state* capital-labor *ratios* from Proposition 12.5 are, cf. (12.196):

$$\kappa_H^{\frac{\sigma-1}{\sigma}} = \frac{(1 - \mu) \, d_K}{d_H d_K - \alpha_2 d_K - \alpha_3 d_H} \quad \kappa_K^{\frac{\sigma-1}{\sigma}} = \frac{(1 - \mu) \, d_H}{d_H d_K - \alpha_2 d_K - \alpha_3 d_H} \tag{12.211}$$

where $\mathbf{d_H}$, $\mathbf{d_K}$ are given by (12.195). Evidently, we get by (12.211):

$$\left.\begin{aligned} \kappa_H &= \tfrac{n+\delta_K}{\gamma\, s_K}\left[\tfrac{1-\mu}{d_H d_K-\alpha_2 d_K-\alpha_3 d_H}\right]^{\frac{\sigma}{\sigma-1}} \\ \kappa_K &= \tfrac{n+\delta_H}{\gamma\, s_H}\left[\tfrac{1-\mu}{d_H d_K-\alpha_2 d_K-\alpha_3 d_H}\right]^{\frac{\sigma}{\sigma-1}} \end{aligned}\right\} \frac{\kappa_K}{\kappa_H} = \frac{\bar{K}}{\bar{H}} = \frac{s_K/(n+\delta_K)}{s_H/(n+\delta_H)} \tag{12.212}$$

Thus, **ratio $\bar{\mathbf{K}}/\bar{\mathbf{H}}$** in (12.212) is the **same** as (12.209), **independent** of technology.

*Growth Paths and Increasing Returns to Scale*
With $\mathbf{m} > \mathbf{1}$, the per capita "***normalization***" with $\mathbf{L(t)}$ is **not** helpful. For the *qualitative* solutions with $\mathbf{m} > \mathbf{1}$, ***depreciation*** will be *ignored*: $\delta_H = \delta_K = 0$.

Hence, we can proceed using, (12.31–12.37), (12.39–12.40), with r = $\mathbf{q}$ = $K/H$:

$$m > 1 \;:\; \dot{H} = s_H\, Y \;=\; L^{m-\mu}\, H^{\mu}\, s_H\, \gamma\, q^{\alpha_3} \tag{12.213}$$

$$m > 1 \;:\; \dot{K} = s_K\, Y \;=\; L^{m-\mu}\, H^{\mu}\, s_K\, \gamma\, q^{\alpha_3} \tag{12.214}$$

$$\dot{L} = n\, L \tag{12.215}$$

*Slope* ($\alpha$) of ***ray trajectory*** (12.47) is a root $\bar{\mathbf{q}}$ of $\mathbf{h}(q)$, cf. (12.22), (12.39–12.40), (12.188):

$$\dot{q} \equiv h(q) = \gamma\, H^{\mu-1} q^{\alpha_3}(s_K - s_H\, q) = 0 \;:\; \bar{q} = \frac{\bar{K}}{\bar{H}} = \frac{\kappa_K}{\kappa_H} = \frac{s_K}{s_H} = \alpha \tag{12.216}$$

It follows immediately from (12.213 to 12.214) that

$$dK/dH = \dot{K}/\dot{H} = s_K/s_H = \alpha \tag{12.217}$$

Thus, the *phase portrait* of the *augmented* Solow growth model (12.213–12.215) consists of *parallel* **straight lines** in a $(\mathbf{H}, \mathbf{K}) \in \mathbf{R}^2_+$ subspace *diagram*. We use Corollary 12.2, (12.47–12.49), to state explicitly the *coordinate solutions* [ $\mathbf{H(t)}, \mathbf{K(t)}$ ] of (12.213–12.215) along $\bar{q}$-***ray***, (12.216). Hence, by (12.215), (12.34), (12.37),

$$L(t) = L_0\, e^{n\,t} \quad ; \quad e(t) = [L_0 e^{n\,t})]^{m-\mu} \;\equiv\; L_0^{m-\mu}\, e^{(m-\mu)n\,t} \tag{12.218}$$

$$E(t) = \int_0^t e(t)\, dt = \int_0^t L_0^{m-\mu}\, e^{(m-\mu)n\,t}\, dt \;=\; \frac{L_0^{m-\mu}}{(m-\mu)\, n}\, [\, e^{(m-\mu)n\,t} - 1\,] \tag{12.219}$$

By (12.219), (12.216), and (12.47–12.49), we have explicit **time paths** along the $\bar{\mathbf{q}}$- *ray*,

$$K(t) = \frac{s_K}{s_H} H(t) \tag{12.220}$$

$$\mu = 1 : H(t) = H_0 \exp\{ s_H \gamma \, (\frac{s_K}{s_H})^{\alpha_3} \frac{L_0^{m-1}}{(m-1)\,n} [e^{(m-1)nt} - 1 ]\} \tag{12.221}$$

$$\mu < 1 : H(t) = \left[ H_0^{1-\mu} + (1-\mu)\, s_H \gamma \, (\frac{s_K}{s_H})^{\alpha_3} \frac{L_0^{m-\mu}}{(m-\mu)\,n} [e^{(m-\mu)nt} - 1 ] \right]^{\frac{1}{1-\mu}} \tag{12.222}$$

The combination with **m > 1** and $\boldsymbol{\mu} = \mathbf{1}$ gives **double-exponential** growth ($\sim \mathbf{A} \exp\{\mathbf{e}^{(\mathbf{m}-1)\mathbf{n}t}\}$), (12.221), of *factors*, output, and *output per capita*, when *Labor* grows exponentially, (12.218). The *scenario* (12.221) was also seen *above*, (12.82–12.83).

With **m > 1** and $\boldsymbol{\mu} < \mathbf{1}$, *human* and *physical* capitals evolve (for large t) with **exponential** growth rates, cf. (12.222), (12.220), (12.200):

$$\widehat{H}(t) \sim \frac{(m-\mu)\,n}{1-\mu} = \frac{\alpha_1 n}{1-\mu} \sim \widehat{K}(t) \tag{12.223}$$

*Per Capita Growth Paths on Steady-State Ray:* **m > 1,** $\boldsymbol{\mu} < \mathbf{1}$

Let us outline the *long-run* implications of the more important case: **m > 1** and $\mu < 1$. All *per capita ratios* will exhibit ***persistent*** (permanent) *growth*.

From (12.200), (12.218), (12.220), (12.222), we get,

$$k(t) = \frac{s_K}{s_H} \cdot \frac{H(t)}{L(t)} \equiv \frac{s_K}{s_H} \cdot h(t) \tag{12.224}$$

$$h(t) = \left[ H_0^{1-\mu} + (1-\mu)\, s_H \gamma \, (\frac{s_K}{s_H})^{\alpha_3} \frac{L_0^{m-\mu}}{(m-\mu)n} [e^{(m-\mu)nt} - 1] \right]^{\frac{1}{1-\mu}} / [L_0 \, e^{nt}]$$

$$\sim e^{(\frac{(m-\mu)\,n}{1-\mu})t} \cdot e^{-nt} = e^{\frac{(m-1)nt}{1-\mu}} \tag{12.225}$$

Per capita *income* **y(t)** evolves as, cf. (12.200), (12.218), (12.222):

$$y(t) = \gamma L^{m-\mu-1} H^{\mu} \left[ \frac{K}{H} \right]^{\alpha_3} \sim e^{(m-\mu-1)nt} \cdot e^{\frac{(m-\mu)n}{1-\mu}\mu, t} = e^{\frac{(m-1)nt}{1-\mu}} \tag{12.226}$$

Thus, along the **q̄-ray**, (12.220), the *long-run* **exponential** *growth rates* of per capita *ratios* are the **same**, cf. (12.224–12.226), (12.94):

$$\lim_{t\to\infty}[\widehat{k(t)}] = \lim_{t\to\infty}[\widehat{h(t)}] = \lim_{t\to\infty}[\widehat{y(t)}] = \frac{(m-1)\,n}{1-\mu} \tag{12.227}$$

The **capital-output** ratios, $K/Y$, $H/Y$—or equivalently, *factor productivities*, $Y/K$, $Y/H$—*converge* to positive **limit values**, as cf. (12.200), (12.222),

$$\frac{Y(t)}{H(t)} = L^{m-\mu}\, H^{\mu-1}\,\gamma\left[\frac{K}{H}\right]^{\alpha_3}$$

$$= \frac{L_0^{m-\mu}\, e^{(m-\mu)n\,t}\,\gamma\,(s_K/s_H)^{\alpha_3}}{H_0^{1-\mu} + (1-\mu)\,s_H\,\gamma\,(s_K/s_H)^{\alpha_3}\,[\,L_0^{m-\mu}/(m-\mu)\,n\,][\,e^{(m-\mu)n\,t}-1\,]}$$

$$\to \frac{(m-\mu)\,n}{(1-\mu)\,s_H}\quad,\quad as\quad t\to\infty \tag{12.228}$$

Since Y/K = (Y/H) (H/K), we get from (12.228), (12.220),

$$\frac{Y(t)}{K(t)} \to \frac{(m-\mu)\,n}{(1-\mu)\,s_K}\quad,\quad as\quad t\to\infty \tag{12.229}$$

As *ray* and *non-ray* coordinate *solutions*, [ **H(t),K(t)** ] of (12.213–12.214) have the *same stability* properties, cf. (12.53); hence, the *long-run* properties (12.227–12.229) also *apply* to all coordinate *solutions* [ **H(t),K(t)** ] along *any* trajectory.

However, *unlike* (12.220–12.222), the **non-ray** solutions [ **H(t),K(t)** ] can*not* be expressed in *closed form*, despite the *geometric simplicity* of the phase portrait, (12.217).

We note from (12.227) that with *increasing return to scale*, **m > 1**, and *exogenous* Labor growth, there is *no conflict* between high *Labor growth* and high *per capita growth*, cf. (12.226). ***Large*** communities (**size, $L_0$**) do **not** have higher per *capita growth rates* than *small* ones. But economies with ***rapid*** *growing* populations/labor force (**n**) **do** also have **rapid** per *capita growth* (**ŷ**). Simply, any *scale economies* are *unleashed* only by actual growth.

The three *technology parameters*, $(m, \mu, \gamma)$, include *externality effects* associated with the three-*factor* markets. Externalities ("spill-over") may *contribute* to making, **m > 1**, in the *augmented* Solow growth models, (12.200–12.217).

Marshall has long ago examined these very important "*external economies*", which can often be secured by the *concentration* of many small businesses of similar character in particular localities, or, as commonly said, by the "*localization*" of industry (Marshall 1920, p. 266).

Lucas (1988)'s comments on *growth* of *cities* are in the same vein; see also David (1992), Krugman (1991). With little doubt, *new cities* such as Manchester, New York, Chicago, Shanghai, Singapore grew at *certain stages* by some *economies of scale* ($m > 1$), and where high *Labor growth* (**n**) was due to inflow by migrations.

If we *replaced* the **CD** technology in (12.213–12.214) by a **CES** variant:

$$Y = F(L, H, K) = \gamma\, L^{\alpha_1} \left[\alpha_H H^{\frac{\sigma-1}{\sigma}} + \alpha_K K^{\frac{\sigma-1}{\sigma}}\right]^{\frac{\mu\sigma}{\sigma-1}}, \quad m = \alpha_1 + \mu$$

$$= \gamma L^{m-\mu} H^{\mu} \left[\alpha_H + \alpha_K q^{\frac{\sigma-1}{\sigma}}\right]^{\frac{\mu\sigma}{\sigma-1}}, \quad \mu < 1, \quad \alpha_H + \alpha_K = 1 \quad (12.230)$$

then the **phase portrait**, (12.216–12.217), (12.212), is **unchanged**—as are the **time paths**, (12.221–12.222), [apart from a proper *constant*, cf. $\mathbf{f}(\alpha)$, cf. (12.48–12.49)].

*Non-Exponential Evolution of Population and Labor Force*

The assumption of *exponential* evolution of **L(t)** in (12.218) is evidently rather *extreme* for later economic regimes; see Galor and Weil (2000). Less rapid evolution of **L(t)** is (12.54), $\boldsymbol{\beta} < \mathbf{1}$. Hence with *polynomial Labor growth*, we have, cf. e(t), E(t), (12.218–12.219):

$$E(t) = \int_0^t e(t)\, dt = \int_0^t [L_0^{1-\beta} + (1-\beta)\, n\, t]^{\frac{m-\mu}{1-\beta}}\, dt \quad (12.231)$$

$$= (1/(1 + m - \mu - \beta))\, [\, L_0^{1-\beta} + (1-\beta)\, n\, t\,]^{\frac{1+m-\mu-\beta}{1-\beta}} \quad (12.232)$$

The polynomial expression (12.231–12.232) then *replaces* (12.219) in (12.221–12.222), cf. Corollary 12.2, (12.48–12.49). Other evolutions of **L(t)** could be *logistic* growth or other forms of *bounded growth*. The extreme is here a *constant* Labor force, $\mathbf{L(t)} = \mathbf{L_0}$, which gives, cf. (12.34), (12.37),

$$E(t) = \int_0^t e(t)\, dt = \int_0^t L_0^{m-\mu}\, dt \;=\; L_0^{m-\mu}\, t \quad (12.233)$$

Thus, the *linear* **E(t)**, (12.233), *replaces* (12.219) in (12.221–12.222). Thus, when $\mathbf{m} > \mathbf{1}$ and $\boldsymbol{\mu} = \mathbf{1}$, (12.222), we can still have **exponential** per *capita growth* with **E(t)**, (12.233), and **polynomial** per *capita growth* if $\boldsymbol{\mu} < \mathbf{1}$, (12.222).

In short, *increasing returns* to scale ($\mathbf{m} > \mathbf{1}$) can be a *crucial determinant* in generating *per capita* growth—*even* with an upper bounded or a *stationary Labor* force. With $\mathbf{m} > \mathbf{1}$, a **variety** ("inequality") of per *capita growth patterns* across *industrialized* (local, regional, national) *economies* can occur; Solow (1994), van de Klundert (2001).

As classic and neoclassical economists, Smith (1776, 1961), cf. Young (1928), Wan (1971), and Alfred Marshall never doubted some importance of *aggregate economies of scale* (spatial agglomeration). A main distinction between them was the *growth process* of *Population* (Labor). Marshall in his time regarded economically the *evolution* of Labor force as mainly an *exogenous* variable, as Solow later assumed.

With ***exogeneity*** of **Labor**, the *Human* capital (and *multi-factor*) augmented models, (12.202), (12.213–12.215), may ***unify*** some **classical** and **neoclassical** growth models within a *homogeneous dynamic system* of **any degree** of homogeneity (**m**), including *increasing* return to scale.

## Dynamic Structure, Technology, Persistent Growth

With $\mathbf{m} = \mathbf{1}, \beta = 1$, and *parametric distinct* **CD** *technologies* for (**H**), (**K**), the dynamics of $\dot{\mathbf{h}}$, $\dot{\mathbf{k}}$, (12.180), (12.201), (12.203), (12.204) are analogously *replaced* by:

$$m = 1 \ : \dot{h} = s_H^* \, \gamma_H \, h^{\alpha_2} \, k^{\alpha_3} - (n + \delta_H)\, h \tag{12.234}$$

$$m = 1 \ : \dot{k} = s_K^* \, \gamma_K \, h^{\alpha_5} \, k^{\alpha_6} - (n + \delta_K)\, k \tag{12.235}$$

with

$$s_H^* = \lambda_{L_H}^{\alpha_1} \lambda_{H_H}^{\alpha_2} \lambda_{K_H}^{\alpha_3}, \quad s_K^* = \lambda_{L_K}^{\alpha_4} \lambda_{H_K}^{\alpha_5} \lambda_{K_K}^{\alpha_6} \tag{12.236}$$

and where $\lambda_{L_i}, \lambda_{H_i}, \lambda_{K_i}$ are the **fractions** of the *three* factors $L, H, K$ that are here **exogenously** *allocated* to producing the "malleable" *good*: $Y, H, K$.

Accordingly, the *output* (**Y**) is here produced by another **CD** *technology*,

$$Y = \gamma_Y \, [(1-\lambda_{L_H}-\lambda_{L_K})\, L\,]^{\alpha_7} \, [(1-\lambda_{H_H}-\lambda_{H_K})\, H\,]^{\alpha_8} \, [(1-\lambda_{K_H}-\lambda_{K_K})\, K\,]^{\alpha_9} \tag{12.237}$$

The **steady-state** sizes of $\kappa_i$, $i = H,K$, in *two*-dimensional system (12.234–12.235) can be calculated by taking logarithms and using Cramers's rule as:

$$\kappa_H = \bar{h} = \left[ \left[ \frac{s_H^* \gamma_H}{n + \delta_H} \right]^{1-\alpha_6} \left[ \frac{s_K^* \gamma_K}{n + \delta_K} \right]^{\alpha_3} \right]^{\frac{1}{(1-\alpha_2)(1-\alpha_6)-\alpha_3\alpha_5}} \tag{12.238}$$

$$\kappa_K = \bar{k} = \left[ \left[ \frac{s_H^* \gamma_H}{n + \delta_H} \right]^{\alpha_5} \left[ \frac{s_K^* \gamma_K}{n + \delta_K} \right]^{1-\alpha_2} \right]^{\frac{1}{(1-\alpha_2)(1-\alpha_6)-\alpha_3\alpha_5}} \tag{12.239}$$

### *Dynamics, Substitution, Growth Paths, and* m > 1

With **m > 1** and ignoring *depreciation*, we proceed with now *distinct* **CD** technologies as above, cf. (12.213–12.214), $\mathbf{q} = K/H$,

$$m > 1 \ : \ \dot{H} = L^{m-\mu}\, H^{\mu}\, s_H^*\, \gamma_H\, q^{\alpha_3}, \qquad \mu = \alpha_2 + \alpha_3 \tag{12.240}$$

$$m > 1 \ : \ \dot{K} = L^{m-\mu}\, H^{\mu}\, s_K^*\, \gamma_K\, q^{\alpha_6}, \qquad \mu = \alpha_5 + \alpha_6 \tag{12.241}$$

where $\mathbf{s_H^*}$ and $\mathbf{s_K^*}$ were given in (12.236). Like (12.216), we have by, (12.240–12.241),

$$\dot{q} = H^{\mu-1}\,(s_K^* \gamma_K\, q^{\alpha_6} - s_H^* \gamma_H\, q^{\alpha_3+1}) \tag{12.242}$$

Hence, the *steady-state* ratio (**ray slope** - $\alpha$) is:

$$\dot{q} = 0 \Leftrightarrow \bar{q} = \left[\frac{s_K^* \gamma_K}{s_H^* \gamma_H}\right]^{\frac{1}{1+\alpha_3-\alpha_6}} \tag{12.243}$$

The *tangent* slopes of *other* trajectories are changing, cf. (12.240–12.241),

$$\frac{dK}{dH} = \frac{\dot{K}}{\dot{H}} = \frac{s_K^* \gamma_K}{s_H^* \gamma_H}\, q^{\alpha_6-\alpha_3} = \frac{s_K^* \gamma_K}{s_H^* \gamma_H}\left[\frac{K}{H}\right]^{\alpha_6-\alpha_3} \tag{12.244}$$

By separation of variables, the entire set of *trajectories* is obtained as

$$\int K^{\alpha_3-\alpha_6} dK = \frac{s_K^* \gamma_K}{s_H^* \gamma_H} \int H^{\alpha_3-\alpha_6} dH \tag{12.245}$$

$$K = \left[\frac{s_K^* \gamma_K}{s_H^* \gamma_H} H^{1+\alpha_3-\alpha_6} + C_0\right]^{\frac{1}{1+\alpha_3-\alpha_6}} \tag{12.246}$$

where $C_0$ is an arbitrary constant (dependent on initial values $H_0, K_0$); $\bar{\mathbf{q}}$, (12.243) corresponds to $C_0 = 0$.

*Ray coordinate solutions* similar to (12.221–12.222) are easily obtained. Since ray and non-ray solutions, [ **H(t),K(t)** ], along (12.246) have the *same* long-run (stability) properties, the per capita *growth paths* of (12.240–12.241) evolve with the *long-run growth rates*, stated in (12.225–12.227).

A *distinct* **CES** variant of (12.240–12.241) is the dynamic system,

$$\dot{H} = \gamma_H(\lambda_{L_H} L)^{m-\mu}\left[\alpha_H^H(\lambda_{H_H} H)^{\frac{\sigma_H-1}{\sigma_H}} + \alpha_K^H(\lambda_{K_H} K)^{\frac{\sigma_H-1}{\sigma_H}}\right]^{\frac{\mu\sigma_H}{\sigma_H-1}} \quad (12.247)$$

$$\dot{K} = \gamma_K(\lambda_{L_K} L)^{m-\mu}\left[\alpha_H^K(\lambda_{H_K} H)^{\frac{\sigma_K-1}{\sigma_K}} + \alpha_K^K(\lambda_{K_K} K)^{\frac{\sigma_K-1}{\sigma_K}}\right]^{\frac{\mu\sigma_K}{\sigma_K-1}} \quad (12.248)$$

which can be rewritten and analyzed with **same** implications as (12.230).

An **endogenous** (indecomposable) *dynamic structure* as (12.247–12.248) does **not** allow the two **substitution elasticities**, $\sigma_H, \sigma_K$, to significantly *affect* the possibilities for *persistent* growth *per capita*.

However, if (12.247–12.248) is *decomposed*, for example, $\alpha_K^H = 0$, that is, **H** is an **exogenous** *state* variable in (12.247–12.248), then $\sigma_K > 1$ can play a role as growth determinant as $\sigma > 1$ did above, (12.163). As **parameters** $\sigma_K > 1$ and **m > 1** ($\mu < 1$) can, in (12.248), (12.237), **both**, contribute to **non-explosive** *per capita* growth—*contrasting* **two-dimensional** dynamics (12.125–12.126).

### *Homogeneous Subsystems, Growth Paths,* $\mathbf{m_H \neq m_K}$

*Relaxation* of *common* degrees of homogeneity ($m$, $\mu$) in (12.240–12.241) gives:

$$\dot{H} = s_H^* \gamma_H L^{\alpha_1} H^{\alpha_2} K^{\alpha_3} \equiv s_H^* \gamma_H L^{m_H-\mu_H} H^{\mu_H}[\frac{K}{H}]^{\alpha_3}, \ m_H = \mu_H + \alpha_1 \quad (12.249)$$

$$\dot{K} = s_K^* \gamma_K L^{\alpha_4} H^{\alpha_5} K^{\alpha_6} \equiv s_K^* \gamma_K L^{m_K-\mu_K} H^{\mu_K}[\frac{K}{H}]^{\alpha_6}, \ m_K = \mu_K + \alpha_4 \quad (12.250)$$

or

$$\widehat{H} \equiv \dot{H}/H = s_H^* \gamma_H L^{\alpha_1} H^{\alpha_2-1} K^{\alpha_3}, \quad \mu_H = \alpha_2 + \alpha_3 < 1 \quad (12.251)$$

$$\widehat{K} \equiv \dot{K}/K = s_K^* \gamma_K L^{\alpha_4} H^{\alpha_5} K^{\alpha_6-1}, \quad \mu_K = \alpha_5 + \alpha_6 = 1 \quad (12.252)$$

It may be *impossible* to find *exact solutions* to the homogeneous dynamic subsystem, (12.249–12.252). However, a *qualitative* analysis (*critical points*) (long-run behavior, t-large, infinity) enables us to obtain simple mathematical expressions (containing adjustable parameters), which give *approximate solutions* to the *long-run evolution* of the dynamic system.

The *polynomials* (12.251–12.252), (12.215) give *linear forms* of relative changes:

$$\widehat{\widehat{H}} \equiv \dot{\widehat{H}}/\widehat{H} = \alpha_1 n + (\alpha_2 - 1)\widehat{H} + (\alpha_3)\widehat{K} \tag{12.253}$$

$$\widehat{\widehat{K}} \equiv \dot{\widehat{K}}/\widehat{K} = \alpha_4 n + \alpha_5 \widehat{H} + (\alpha_6 - 1)\widehat{K} \tag{12.254}$$

Hence, *existence* and *location* (size) of *critical points* are important, that is, solving

$$\forall t : \dot{\widehat{H}}(t) = 0 \Leftrightarrow \widehat{H}(t) = \widehat{H}^* ; \; \dot{\widehat{K}} = 0 \Leftrightarrow \widehat{K}(t) = \widehat{K}(t)^* \tag{12.255}$$

Assuming nonsingularity, the *constant growth rates* (**critical points**) of (12.253–12.255) are obtained by Cramers's rule as,

$$\widehat{H}^* = \frac{[\alpha_3 \alpha_4 + \alpha_1(1-\alpha_6)]\,n}{(1-\alpha_2)(1-\alpha_6) - \alpha_3 \alpha_5} \tag{12.256}$$

$$\widehat{K}^* = \frac{[\alpha_1 \alpha_5 + \alpha_4(1-\alpha_2)]\,n}{(1-\alpha_2)(1-\alpha_6) - \alpha_3 \alpha_5} \tag{12.257}$$

The *constant* **growth rates**, (12.256–12.257), are also the **long-run** (asymptotic) growth rates for the *family* of *solutions* [ **H(t), K(t)** ] to (12.249–12.252).

Special *parametric* cases of the **dynamic system** (12.249–12.252) are widely used in *endogenous growth* theory, see references in Romer (2019, p. 101). For ease of comparison with expressions, (12.256–12.257), we relate the relevant set of our **general parameters** to those of Romer (2019, p. 109–113; **A** = **H**), that is,

$$\alpha_1 = \gamma,\; \alpha_2 = \theta,\; \alpha_3 = \beta,\; \alpha_4 = 1-\alpha,\; \alpha_5 = 1-\alpha,\; \alpha_6 = \alpha \tag{12.258}$$

$$m_H = \gamma+\theta+\beta,\; \mu_H = \theta+\beta < 1,\; m_K = 1+\alpha_4 = 2-\alpha,\; \mu_K = 1 \tag{12.259}$$

$$\widehat{H}^* = \frac{[\beta(1-\alpha) + \gamma(1-\alpha)]\,n}{(1-\theta)(1-\alpha) - \beta(1-\alpha)} = \frac{(\beta+\gamma)\,n}{1-\theta-\beta} \tag{12.260}$$

$$\widehat{K}^* = \frac{[\gamma(1-\alpha) + (1-\alpha)(1-\theta)]\,n}{(1-\theta)(1-\alpha) - \beta(1-\alpha)} = n + \frac{(\beta+\gamma)\,n}{1-\theta-\beta} \tag{12.261}$$

The **growth rate**, $\widehat{H}^*$ = (12.256) = (12.260), Romer (2019, p. 112), corresponds to the *homogeneous* dynamics (12.223). It is seen from (12.261) that the *capital-labor* ratio $\mathbf{k} = \mathbf{K}/\mathbf{L}$ is *growing*. It follows from (12.237), (12.256–12.257), (12.260–12.261):

$$\widehat{Y} = \alpha_1 \, \widehat{L} + \alpha_8 \, \widehat{H}^* + \alpha_9 \, \widehat{K}^* \; = \; (\alpha_1 + \alpha_9) \, n + (\alpha_8 + \alpha_9) \, \widehat{H}^* \qquad (12.262)$$

(12.260) and (12.262) give a **constant** *growth rate* of per **capita** income, $\mathbf{y} = \mathbf{Y}/\mathbf{L}$.

**CES** variants of, also, (12.249–12.250) are not given in this chapter. But generally, as *growth determinants*, "Endogenous Growth" theory has paid *less* attention to **substitution elasticities** than **scale elasticities**. But *both* elasticities are *needed* in accounting for the *historical record* of economic growth.

## Final Comment

This chapter has considered a wide range of subjects and does not lend itself to any succinct summary. But coming a long way, we have proved and richly demonstrated that *low-dimensional dynamics* can generate a rich family of intricate solutions with *widely different qualitative* and *quantitative* properties. Having reached a higher vantage point should now give a clear picture and overall *economic* understanding of the *homogeneous dynamic systems* involved in fundamental *macro growth* models and the *general* (complete set of) *solutions* (time paths and trajectories, phase portraits)—depending on the **dynamic structure, exogeneity**, and **specifications, parameters** for their **governing** functions to the ordinary first-order differential equations.

## Bibliography


Aghion P, Howitt P (1992) A Model of Growth through Creative Destruction. Econometrica 60:323–351

Arnold VI (1973) Ordinary Differential Equations. MIT Press, Mass

Birkhoff G, Rota G (1989) Ordinary Differential Equations, 4th edn. John Wiley & Sons, New York

David P (1992) The Marshallian Dynamics of Industrialization: Chicago, 1850–1890. Unpublished

Deardorff AV (1970) Growth Paths in the Solow Neoclassical Growth Model. Quarterly J of Economics 85:134–139

Galor O, Weil DN (2000) Population, Technology, and Growth: From the Malthusian Regime to the Demographic Transition. American Econ Rev 90:806–828

Gandolfo G (2010) Economic Dynamics: Methods and Models, 4th edn. Springer–Verlag, Berlin

Jensen BS (1994) The Dynamic Systems of Basic Economic Growth Models. Kluwer Academic Publishers, Dordrecht

Jensen BS, Larsen ME (1987) Growth and Long–Run Stability. Acta Applicandae Mathematicae 9:219–237, Reprinted in Jensen (1994)

Jensen BS, Alsholm PK, Larsen ME, Jensen JM (2005) Dynamic Structure, Exogeneity, Phase Portraits, Growth Paths, and Scale and Substitution Elasticities. Review of International Economics 13:59–89

van de Klundert TC (2001) Growth Theory in Historical Perspective. No. 2357 in Books, Edward Elgar Publishing

Krugman P (1991) Increasing Returns and Geography. Jour of Pol Econ 99:483–499

Lucas RE (1988) On the Mechanics of Economic Development. Journal of Monetary Economics 22:3–42, Reprinted in Becker (1991)

Mankiw NG, Romer D, Weil DN (1992) A Contribution to the Empirics of Economic Growth. Quarterly Journal of Economics 107:407–437

Marshall A (1920) Principles of Economics, 8th edn. Macmillan, London

Muth JF (1954) A Note on Balanced Growth. Econometrica 22:493–495

Nikaido H (1964) Balanced Growth in Multi–sectoral Income Progagation under Autonomous Expenditure Schemes. Review of Econ Stud 31:25–42

Nonneman W, Vanhoudt P (1996) A further Augmentation of the Solow model and the Empirics of Economic Growth for OECD countries. Quarterly Journal of Economics 111:943–953

Pampel T (2009) On the Dynamics of Basic Growth Models: Ratio Stability vs. Convergence and Divergence in State Space. German Economic Review 10:384–400

Phelps ES (1966) Models of Technical Progress and the Golden Rule of Research. Review of Economic Studies 33:133–146

Rebelo S (1991) Long–Run Policy Analysis and Long–Run Growth. Journal of Political Economy 99:500–521

Romer D (2019) Advanced Macroeconomics, 5th edn. McGraw–Hill, N.Y

Romer PM (1986) Increasing Returns and Long–Run Growth. Journal of Political Economy 94:1002–1037, Reprinted in Becker (1991)

Romer PM (1990) Endogenous Technological Change. Journal of Political Economy 98:S71–S102

Simmons GF (1972) Differential Equations – with applications and historical notes. McGraw–Hill, New York

Smith A (1776, 1961) The Wealth of Nations I–II. Methuen University Paperbacks, London

Solow RM (2000) Growth Theory, 2nd edn. Oxford

Solow RM (1956) A Contribution to the Theory of Economic Growth. Quarterly Journal of Economics 70:65–94, Reprinted in Stiglitz (1969), and in Becker (1991)

Solow RM (1994) Perspectives on Growth Theory. Journal of Economic Perspectives 8:45–54

Solow RM, Samuelson PA (1953) Balanced Growth under Constant Returns to Scale. Econometrica 21:412–424

Suits DB (1954) Dynamic Growth under Diminishing Returns to Scale. Econometrica 22:496–503

Sydsæter K (1981) Matematisk Analyse,I–II. SUB, Oslo

Wan HY Jr (1971) Economic Growth. Harcourt Brace Jovanowich, New York

Young AA (1928) Increasing Returns and Economic Progress. Economic Journal 38:527–542

CHAPTER 13

# Ramsey Optimal Saving: Growth Models with Constant and Variable Elasticity of Intertemporal Substitution

## INTRODUCTION

An important goal in economic models of micro agents or nations is to determine the *optimal size* and *time path* of the *saving rate*, **s(t)**—the **share** of *income* to be devoted to *investment* and hence not available for *current consumption*. In this chapter, we study the optimal saving issues within *optimal* economic *growth* models, as outlined for optimal saving-consumption by Ramsey (1928).

Ramsey (1928, p. 543) asked: "How much of its income should a nation save?" On Ramsey (1928), Keynes (1933, 1963, p. 240) wrote: "It is, I think, one of the most remarkable contributions to mathematical economics ever made, both in respect of intrinsic importance and difficulty of its subject, the power and elegance of the technical methods employed, and the clear purity of illumination with which the writer's mind is felt by the reader to play about its subject". But the Ramsey (1928) paper had to be "rediscovered", Newbery (2008), and used by growth theorists after Solow (1956, p. 60), where the *saving rate* was a given *parameter* ($s$) and *population* (Labor) growing at *exogenous* rate ($n$). The extension and new start of **optimal** *saving* (*growth*) models came with the seminal paper of Cass (1965, p. 236–237), where **existence** of a unique *optimal growth path* from an **initial** *capital-labor* ratio to a *unique* positive **steady-state ratio** was mathematically demonstrated, replacing convergence and stability issues of *stationary* states of Ramsey (1928, p. 556). The **optimal** growth model is now one of the most important

With co-author:
ULLA LEHMIJOKI, Helsinki Center of Economic Research (HECER), University of Helsinki, Finland





B. S. Jensen, *The Elements and Dynamic Systems of Economic Growth and Trade Models*, https://doi.org/10.1007/978-3-031-52493-6_13

theoretical *paradigms* for *dynamic macroeconomic* models. However, besides *qualitative* properties of such dynamic models, we need to study them also from a **quantitative** standpoint before we can claim to have *explained* and *parametrically* accounted for *major differences* in economic growth *over time* and *across counties*—or to offer empirical policy analysis and sound advice.

Beyond initial conditions, solutions of optimal growth models (control problems) depend critically on several important *parameters* involved in the *technology* and *preference assumptions.* Several choices of *functional forms* of production and utility functions have been theoretically elaborated but seldom have actual *optimal solutions* been performed (calculated) within a range of any realistic empirical parameterizations.

Recently we read from a prominent quantitative growth economist—calculating many *time paths*—for the basic Ramsey model *growth rates* and the *optimal saving* rates: "*Optimal growth* theory, as it stands today, *does* **not** work. Using strictly concave *utility functions* systematically *inflicts* on the economy *distortions* that are either *historically unobserved* or *unacceptable* by society", de La Grandville (2018, p. 77)—a serious **challenge**.

No doubt, economists need a much better *understanding* of the Euler and Pontryagin *dynamic* equations, from an *economic, intuitive, analytical,* and *computational* point of view—all contributing to resolving the difficult and very long-standing conundrums.

So the **purpose** is rigorously and *quantitatively* to *solve* the dynamics of the optimal growth and saving model with **general** *production*—$\mathbf{f}(\mathbf{k})$, and *utility* functions, $\mathbf{u}(\mathbf{c})$. The main **new** Economic Theoretical Results are the **General Existence** *Theorem* on *Persistent Growth* solutions, the **Separator** in Theorem 13.2, and the **Explicit** closed forms of **Affine Dynamics**—*Economic Evolutions* in Proposition 13.1 and the **General Asymptotics** by Corollary 13.1.

All results are amply exhibited in Figs. 13.1, 13.2, 13.3, 13.4, 13.5, 13.6, 13.7, 13.8, 13.9, 13.10, 13.11, 13.12, 13.13, 13.14, 13.15, 13.16, 13.17, 13.18, and 13.19.

Optimal **Nonlinear Dynamics** with *non-homothetic* utility are exhibited in Figs. 13.23, 13.24, 13.25, 13.26, 13.27, 13.28, 13.29, 13.30, and 13.31.

All implications and the time paths are demonstrated—with constant elasticity of substitution **(CES)** variable elasticity of substitution **(VES)** technologies, and *constant elasticity of intertemporal substitution* **(CEIS)**, *variable elasticity of intertemporal substitution* **(VEIS)** preferences—by *quantitative parametric solutions* of their **optimal control dynamic** systems. The intertemporal Ramsey saving model is capable of generating *persistent endogenous* growth. Hence we provide in Theorem 13.2 simple **sufficient** *conditions* for general **existence** of **optimal persistent** *growth paths* and apply these sufficient conditions to the original and several extensions of the Ramsey saving model.

Let us briefly state the sufficient optimal *existence conditions* by *boundaries,* $\underline{\mathbf{b}}, \overline{\eta}$:

1. *Positive* **lower** bound: $\underline{\mathbf{b}} > \rho + \delta$, [ $\lim_{k \to \infty} f'(k) \equiv \underline{b}$ ], for the **Marginal productivity** of **capital**, [ $f'(k) = MP_K(k), k = K/L$ ].
2. *Positive* **upper** bound: $\overline{\eta} < \frac{\rho - n}{(\underline{b} - \delta) - \rho}$, [ $\sup_{c>0} \eta(c) \equiv \overline{\eta}$ ], for the Elasticity of intertemporal substitution, **EIS**, [ $\eta(c) = \frac{-u'(c)}{u''(c)\,c} > 0$ ],

where $\boldsymbol{\rho}$ is the *rate of time preference* **RTP** [ constant subjective *utility discount rate* ], $\boldsymbol{n}$ is a constant *population* (labor) *growth rate*, and $\boldsymbol{\delta}$ is a constant *capital depreciation rate.*

We show that in cases of **persistent growth**, much of standard phase diagrams can be preserved, even though the **steady-state** (saddle **point**) structure **disappears**, because the *optimal persistent growth* **path** does **not** reach a **point** but instead becomes a **separator** ( *curve*) in the standard phase portrait. *Below* the separator, *over-saving* diminishes consumption, ultimately leading to a sub-optimal situation with all incomes saved. *Above* the separator the economy *implodes*, as by under-saving its productive capital vanishes. Parametric *sensitivity* analyses of *optimal* solutions are provided. The *Ramsey* intertemporal *optimal* saving-growth *model* **does** work.

The chapter is *organized* as follows: section "Normative Capital Accumulation: Optimal Saving" presents the general framework of the *standard optimal* saving model with **steady states**. Section "Persistent Growth: Optimal Solution—Separator" gives the sufficient existence and uniqueness conditions for *optimal* **persistent growth** solutions. Section "Applications: Optimal Solutions with CEIS Utility Functions and CES Production Functions" provides with phase portraits and time paths *Quantitative* demonstrations of Theorem 13.2 for **CES** technologies and **CEIS** preferences. Sections "Ramsey (1928): Affine Dynamics with CEIS Utility"–"Affine Dynamics, Minimal States, and Evolutions" *solve explicitly* the *original* **Ramsey** models of **Affine Dynamics**, first with **CEIS**—next extended as exhibited in Proposition 13.1 to **VEIS** *preferences*, Hyperbolic Absolute Risk Aversion (**HARA**), with richer *parametric functional* forms—to generate the needed and actual observational *diversity* for the **evolutions** of *growth* and *saving* rates. Section "Nonlinear Dynamics, Optimal Growth, and Saving" *extends* the Ramsey results with **VEIS** preferences to optimal **Nonlinear Dynamics** (flexible **VES, CES** technologies). Section "Conclusions and Final Comments" concludes. *Appendix* **A** gives the rigorous *proof* of Theorem 13.2—Existence and Uniqueness of the **Separator** (*optimal solutions*)—by Lemmas 13.2–13.3 and Corollary 13.2.

## Normative Capital Accumulation: Optimal Saving

We will briefly recapitulate the Theory of *Normative Capital Accumulation* (Saving, Investment) by reviewing the *standard optimal saving model* in a *historical perspective.*

Consider "infinitely lived" consumers ("dynasty") maximizing total "infinite lifetime" utility. The *representative consumer* has in continuous time a *time additive* (separable) intertemporal *cardinal utility* function, $\mathbf{u}[\mathbf{c(t)}]\mathbf{e}^{-\rho \mathbf{t}} \equiv \mathbf{I(t)}$, (Integrand), *summed* for, $\forall t \in \Re$:

$$U = U[\widetilde{c(t)}] = \int_0^\infty u[c(t)]e^{-\rho t}dt, \quad c \geq 0,\ \rho > 0\ ;$$

$$U = U(\infty) \equiv \int_0^\infty I(t)\,dt \tag{13.1}$$

where the *decision* variable $\mathbf{c(t)}$ is consumption per person at time $(t)$, and $\rho$ is a constant subjective *utility discount rate*, **RTP** (*rate of time preference*). The entire *time path* (*profile*) of *consumption* from *initial* date to *infinity* is denoted: $\widetilde{\mathbf{c(t)}} = [c(t), \forall t \in [0, \infty)]$.

The **utility** (objective) **functional** is: $\mathbf{U} = \mathbf{U}[\widetilde{\mathbf{c(t)}}]$, relating time *profile* $\widetilde{c(t)}$ to the variable **U** (finite number of total life time utility). The goal is maximizing *utility functional*, $U[\widetilde{c(t)}]$, by finding the particular (*optimal*) time *profile*, $\widetilde{\mathbf{c}^*(\mathbf{t})} = [c^*(t), \forall t \in [0, \infty)]$, making **max** $U[\widetilde{c(t)}] = U[\widetilde{c^*(t)}] = \mathbf{U}^*$, i.e., our *optimal* consumption (*control*) problem is,

$$U^* = U[\widetilde{c^*(t)}] = \max\ U[\widetilde{c(t)}]$$

$$= \max_{c(t)} \int_0^\infty u[c(t)]e^{-\rho t}dt, \quad c \geq 0, \quad \rho > 0 \tag{13.2}$$

For the economy with *exogenous population* (labor) *growth*, $\mathbf{L(t)} = \mathbf{L_0\,e^{nt}}$, the "social representative (planner)" may similarly *maximize* the *normative* (objective, welfare) utility **functional**, $\mathbf{V}[\widetilde{\mathbf{c(t)}}]$, *sum* of individual utilities, with $\mathbf{c} = \mathbf{C/L}$, *per capita consumption*:

$$V = V[\widetilde{c(t)}] = \int_0^\infty u[c(t)]e^{-\rho t}\,L(t)\,dt$$

$$= L_0 \int_0^\infty u[c(t)]e^{-(\rho-n)t}dt\ ;\ \rho - n > 0 \tag{13.3}$$

There is no "essential" difference between the objective of an "individual", ("dynasty"), (13.1), or a *society*, (13.3). By using (13.3), all $\mathbf{C(t)}$ paths are *nonstationary*, as in Cass (1965, p. 234).

The selection of *feasible* consumption *time profile* $\widetilde{\mathbf{c(t)}}$ in (13.1–13.3) is *constrained* by the *output* (production) provided at any time by the *amounts* of the *production factors*, labor and capital, available at time (t): $[\mathbf{L(t)}, \mathbf{K(t)}]$, *initially* and in the *future*, $\forall t \in [0, \infty)]$, as well as on all *current consumption* decisions, $\mathbf{c(t)}$. These *constraints* can be expressed by a proper *specification* of the **governing function, h(k, c)**, of a *differential equation* for the continuous-time changes in the continuous *capital-labor* ratio (state (phase) variable):

$$dk/dt \;=\; \dot{k} \;=\; h(k, c), \qquad k(t) \;=\; K(t)/L(t) \tag{13.4}$$

The function, $h(k, c)$, reflects that the *rate* of capital stock increases, $(\dot{\mathbf{k}})$, is not only affected by **k(t)** but that the current size of the decision variable **c(t)** affects the rate at which the capital stock increases. Hence by controlling the time path of **c(t)**, we can solve, (13.2), (13.3), and find (*compute*) the whole *path*, $\widetilde{c^*(t)}$= $\mathbf{c}^*(\mathbf{t})$, *exactly* [together with its $\mathbf{k}^*(\mathbf{t})$], as will be shown in section "Applications: Optimal Solutions with CEIS Utility Functions and CES Production Functions" for *persistent* endogenous *growth* models. To do this, we must of course describe carefully the *two fundamental* functions: **u(c)**, **h(k, c)**.

The *contemporaneous*—current period $u(c\,[t])$—*utility* function, **u(c)**, of momentary *consumption* levels (**c**) is concave, increasing, and satisfies the Inada conditions,

$$\begin{aligned} &c \geq 0: \quad u(c) \gtrless 0\,, \quad u'(c) > 0\,, \quad u''(c) < 0\,, \\ &\lim_{c\to 0} u'(c) = \infty, \qquad \lim_{c\to\infty} u'(c) = 0. \end{aligned} \tag{13.5}$$

If $\boldsymbol{u}(\mathbf{c})$ with properties (13.5) is *also upper bounded*, then the (*discounted*) total utility, (*improper integrals*) $\boldsymbol{U}$, (13.1), and $\boldsymbol{V}$, (13.3), are *always* bounded (finite, *exist*), too. But an **upper bound** imposed on the *cardinal* **u(c)** is a **restrictive** assumption (theoretically and empirically) to be **dispensed** with and elaborated on in Theorem 13.2 of section "Persistent Growth: Optimal Solution—Separator".

The **technology** is described by a smooth *concave* homogeneous *production function*, **F(L, K)**, with constant returns to scale in *Labor* input (L), (services) and *Capital* input (K), (services) of durable producer capital, in producing a *single* (good) *output* (**Y**),

$$\begin{aligned} &Y = F(L, K) = Lf(k) \equiv Ly\,, \;\; L \neq 0\,, \;\; k \in [0, \infty[\;; \\ &F(0, 0) = 0\;, \;\; f(0) \geq 0 \end{aligned} \tag{13.6}$$

where the function, **f(k)**, is concave and monotonically increasing in the *capital-labor ratio*, (*k*), i.e., $f(k)$ has the properties [ the **limits** (13.8) are essential numbers in Theorem 13.2 ],

$$\forall k > 0: \;\; f'(k) > 0, \quad f''(k) \leq 0; \quad k \in [0, \infty[ \tag{13.7}$$

$$\lim_{k\to 0} f'(k) \;\equiv\; \bar{b} \;\leq \infty, \;\; \lim_{k\to\infty} f'(k) \;\equiv\; \underline{b} \;\geq\; 0; \;\; f'(k) \in \left[\underline{b}\,,\; \bar{b}\right] \tag{13.8}$$

*Net Factor accumulation* in *one-sector, two-factor* macro models becomes, cf. (13.3–13.4), (13.6),

$$dK/dt = \dot{K} = S - \delta K = Y - C - \delta K = L\,[f(k) - \delta\,k - c]\,;$$
$$dL/dt = \dot{L} = nL \tag{13.9}$$

$$dk/dt = \dot{k} = f(k) - (n+\delta)k - c = h(k,c). \tag{13.10}$$

Thus the **Ramsey** optimization (**control, maximum**) problem (13.3) is—with $\mathbf{L_0 = 1}$:

$$\max\ V = \max\ V[\widetilde{c(t)}] = \max_{c(t)} \int_0^{\infty} u\,[\,c(t)\,]\,e^{-(\rho-n)t}\,dt \tag{13.11}$$

$$\text{s.t.}\quad \dot{k} = f(k) - c - (n+\delta)k = h(k,c), \quad c \geq 0, \quad k \geq 0 \tag{13.12}$$

which is equivalent to *maximizing* the *current* utility **Hamiltonian** function, $\mathcal{H}(c, k, \lambda)$,

$$\mathcal{H}(c,k,\lambda) = u\,(c) + \lambda(t)\cdot h(k,c)\,;$$
$$\mathcal{H}(c,k,\lambda) = u\,(c) + \lambda(t)\,[\,f(k) - (n+\delta)k - c\,] \tag{13.13}$$

with, $\boldsymbol{\lambda}(\mathbf{t})$, **Lagrange** *multiplier* (*costate, adjoint*) variable, and *transversality* condition:

$$k(0) = k_0\,, \quad \lim_{t\to\infty} \lambda(t)\cdot k(t)\cdot e^{-(\rho-n)t} = 0\ ;\ \rho > n \tag{13.14}$$

First-order (necessary) conditions by the **maximum principle** are, cf. (13.13), (13.10), (13.14)

$$\frac{\partial \mathcal{H}}{\partial c} = 0\ ; \quad \frac{\partial \mathcal{H}}{\partial c} = \frac{\partial u}{\partial c} + \lambda(t)\frac{\partial h}{\partial c} = u'(c) - \lambda(t) = 0\ ; \quad \lambda(t) = u'(c) \tag{13.15}$$

$$\frac{\partial \mathcal{H}}{\partial \lambda} = \frac{dk}{dt}\ ;$$
$$\frac{\partial \mathcal{H}}{\partial \lambda} = h(k,c) = f(k) - (n+\delta)k - c = \frac{dk}{dt} \equiv \dot{k} \tag{13.16}$$

and the necessary ("*Euler*") condition is—a costate (adjoint) *equation* of *motion* for $\lambda(t)$:

$$\frac{\partial \mathcal{H}}{\partial k} = -\frac{d\lambda}{dt} + (\rho - n)\lambda(t) \; ;$$

$$\frac{\partial \mathcal{H}}{\partial k} = \lambda(t)\left[f'(k) - (n+\delta)\right] = -\dot{\lambda}(t) + (\rho - n)\lambda(t) \qquad (13.17)$$

Besides the *necessity* of (13.15–13.17), *sufficiency* of (13.14–13.17) can be proved simply. It is observed that the *objective* function $\mathbf{u}[\mathbf{c}(\mathbf{t})]\mathbf{e}^{-(\rho-\mathbf{n})}\mathbf{t}$ is a *concave* function in $(k, c)$-space, cf. (13.5).

Also it can be shown by using (13.5), (13.7) that *Marginal utility* of consumption, $\mathbf{u}'(\mathbf{c}) = \lambda(\mathbf{t})$, (13.15), and $\mathbf{h}(\mathbf{k}, \mathbf{c})$ in (13.16), are *concave* functions in $(\mathbf{c}, \mathbf{k})$. Thus *necessary* conditions (13.15–13.17) given by the *maximum principle* are with (13.14) **sufficient** for **existence** of an **optimal solution** to—$\mathbf{k}(\mathbf{t})$, $\lambda(\mathbf{t})$, $\mathbf{c}(\mathbf{t})$—by (13.13–13.17), cf. *Pontryagin* et al. (1962, p. 78).

Economic *intuition* about the implications of the necessary conditions (13.15 -13.17) are well known and easily provided. Time derivation of (13.15) gives *costate* derivative $\dot{\boldsymbol{\lambda}}(t)$ as,

$$\dot{\lambda}(t) = u''(c)\,\dot{c}(t) \; ;$$

$$\widehat{\lambda} = \frac{\dot{\lambda}}{\lambda} = \frac{du'(c)/dt}{u'(c)} = \widehat{u'(c)} = \frac{u''(c)\,c}{u'(c)}\left[\frac{\dot{c}}{c}\right] = E(u'(c), c)\,\widehat{c} \qquad (13.18)$$

Thus if $\mathbf{c}(\mathbf{t})$ along the optimal solution is, e.g., *growing*, $\dot{\mathbf{c}}(t) > 0$, then the *concavity*, $u''(c) < 0$, *ensures* that the **Marginal utility** of *consumption*,[1] $\mathbf{u}'(\mathbf{c}) = \boldsymbol{\lambda}(\mathbf{t}) > 0$—*positive* "**shadow price**" ($\boldsymbol{\lambda}$) ["opportunity costs" (utility loss) of postponing some consumption by instead *saving* (capital *accumulation*, $\dot{\mathbf{k}}$) at time (t)]—is *falling*, $\dot{\lambda}(t) < 0$, $\widehat{\boldsymbol{\lambda}}(\mathbf{t}) < \mathbf{0}$.

The necessary (*Euler*) condition (13.17) offers further insight on *optimal* time *paths* of *shadow prices* $\lambda(t)$ of *saving* (future *utility gain* by consumption "*abstinence*"); (13.17) gives

$$\dot{\lambda}(t) = -\lambda(t)\left[f'(k) - \delta - \rho\right] \; ; \quad \widehat{\lambda}(t) = -\left[f'(k) - \delta - \rho\right] \qquad (13.19)$$

Hence along the *optimal consumption solution* (path), the *relative change* (fall /increase) in the "shadow price", $\widehat{\lambda}$—equivalent to $\widehat{u'(c)}$—must always be equal to the *net return* (positive/negative) on *capital in excess* of the time preference (discount) rate, $\rho$. This necessary optimality *condition* (13.19) is

[1] As to the *numerical* size of $E(u'(c), c) = E(MU(c), c) < 0$, see Evans (2005, p. 211), and footnote 6.

*"Ramsey's rule"*, cf. Ramsey (1928, p. 546, eq.(3), $\delta = 0, \rho = 0$; p. 554, eq.(9), $\delta = 0, \rho > 0$); see section "Ramsey (1928): Affine Dynamics with CEIS Utility". Regarding analyzing a general *dynamic system* of ($\dot{\mathbf{k}}$, $\dot{\boldsymbol{\lambda}}$), see Arrow and Kurz (1970, p. 66), Cass (1965, p. 237), Romer (1989, p. 86), Barro (1989).

An akin "Keynes-Ramsey" rule relates changes in the expression, $[\lambda(t)\,\dot{k}\,]$, to the attained levels of utility, but this stated rule relies on an *upper bounded* utility function u(c), (*bliss point*), Ramsey (1928, p. 547), Wan (1971, p. 315), Brems (1986, p. 168).

The **two** characterizations of *optimal changes* in the "*unobservable*" shadow price, $\dot{\boldsymbol{\lambda}}(t)$, in (13.18–13.19), can be *combined* to **one** differential equation for *optimal* changes in "*observable*" per capita *consumption*, $\dot{\mathbf{c}}(\mathbf{t})$,—giving alternatively *Euler-Ramsey* condition/rule (13.17) as:

$$\widehat{c} = \frac{\dot{c}}{c} = \frac{\dot{\lambda}/\lambda}{E(u'(c), c)}$$
$$= -\frac{u'(c)}{u''(c)\,c}\left[f'(k) - \delta - \rho\right] \equiv \eta(c)\left[(f'(k) - \delta) - \rho)\right] \qquad (13.20)$$

with *instantaneous* **EIS** (*elasticity of intertemporal substitution*): $\eta = \boldsymbol{\eta}\,(\mathbf{c}) = \frac{-u'(c)}{u''(c)\,c} > 0$, or *reciprocal*: $\frac{1}{\eta} = \frac{1}{\eta\,(c)} = -E(u'(c), c) = -\frac{d\ln u'c}{d\ln c} = -\mathbf{E}(\mathbf{MU}(\mathbf{c}), \mathbf{c}) = -\mathbf{E}(\boldsymbol{\lambda}(\mathbf{c}), \mathbf{c}) > 0$, being the *numerical* **size** of the **elasticity** of *cardinal* **Marginal utility** of consumption.

The *Euler-Ramsey rule* (13.20) is an *ordinary autonomous differential* equation—$\dot{\mathbf{c}}$—in (**k**, **c**):

$$\dot{c} = c\,\eta(c)\left[f'(k) - \delta - \rho\right] \equiv g(k, c)\,; \quad \forall c > 0 : \eta(c) > 0 \qquad (13.21)$$

The *dynamic role* of the actual *size* and *shape* of **EIS**, $\boldsymbol{\eta}\,(\mathbf{c})$, in (13.21) is demonstrated later; we are dealing with fundamental principles in "*Interest Theory*" and "*Capital Theory*".

We may here also rewrite the "*Euler-Ramsey rule*" of *consumption-saving*, (13.20–13.21), as,

$$\left[\rho - \widehat{u'(c)} = \rho - E(MU(c), c)\,\widehat{c} = \rho - \widehat{\lambda} = \rho + \frac{\widehat{c}}{\eta\,(c)}\right]$$
$$= \left[f'(k) - \delta = MP_K(k) - \delta\right] \qquad (13.22)$$

The *fundamental optimality* (normative) *equality* of (13.22) holds at *any point in time* : for *transitions* toward or in the *steady states*—or upon the *persistent growth paths* with *positive* asymptotic ('long-run') economic *growth rates*, as seen in sections "Persistent Growth: Optimal Solution—Separator"–"The Affine Dynamics with VEIS Utility Functions".

The *Equality* (13.22) summarizes mathematically **three causes**, given verbally by Böhm-Bawerk (1921, 318-339), for the *existence* of a positive "*interest* *(growth) rate*" that is equal to the *agio* (*premium*) attached to *present* goods in exchange with *future* goods.

The **first** cause is, $-\widehat{u'(c)} = \frac{\widehat{c}}{\eta(c)}$: The **proportional** rate of *fall* in classical *marginal utilities* from a *larger* future *consumption*, [ or *reciprocal* of the *Elasticity* of *Intertemporal Substitution*, **EIS**, $\eta(c) = \frac{-1}{E(MU(c),c)}$, *multiplied* with the growth rate, $\widehat{\mathbf{c}}$ ].

The **second** cause is the general **discount rate**, (*rate of time preference*) **RTP**, $\rho$, due to a systematic ("*impatience of waiting*", partly irrational, partly due to shortness and the uncertainty of life) underestimation of the importance of future wants/utilities. The first and second causes were "**subjective** reasons" behind a *positive* "interest rate".

The **third** cause, $\mathbf{MP_K(k)}$ in (13.22), was the "**objective/technological**" element in a determination of a *positive "interest rate"*. In his terminology, the third cause was based on the technical superiority of more "*roundabout*" (lengthy capital using processes, longer *average period* ) production methods. But with **K** in (13.6), (13.9), as a single (malleable) good, the *greater* **Labor** *productivity*, **dy** ($y = Y/L$), of *more* "roundabout" technologies is a consequence of the **increase** in capital-labor ratio, **dk**, i.e., **marginal productivity** of **capital**, $dy/dk = \mathbf{f'(k)} = \mathbf{MP_K(k)}$.

As $\mathbf{c(t)}$ is an *observable control* variable in (13.11–13.12), it is more convenient to use (13.21) instead of the *unobservable costate* variable $\boldsymbol{\lambda}(\mathbf{t})$ in (13.15–13.17)—as eliminated in (13.21). Thus the differential equations of *optimal* (normative) capital accumulation, (13.16), (13.10), and *optimal* (normative) consumption, (13.21), define a **dynamic system** in the *plane* (**k**, **c**) with the **governing** functions, **h(k, c)**, **g(k, c)**, on the **closed set** (first quadrant), $\overline{\Re}^2_+$:

$$\dot{k} = h(k, c) = f(k) - (n+\delta)k - c\,, \tag{13.23}$$

$$\dot{c} = g(k, c) = c\,\eta(c)\left[\,f'(k) - \delta - \rho\,\right]. \tag{13.24}$$

Dynamic system (13.23–13.24) and hence the *solutions* are *invariant* to *affine transformations* of cardinal **u(c)** in integrand of utility functional (13.11)—see *invariance* of $\eta(c)$, (13.20), (13.24).

By (13.15), the *transversality* condition (13.14) is accordingly replaced by,

$$\lim_{t\to\infty} u'\left[\,c(t)\,\right]k(t)\,e^{-(\rho-n)t} = 0 \;\; ; \;\; \rho > n \tag{13.25}$$

With solutions, **k(t)**, **c(t)**, of (13.23–13.24), we can give other ("*performance* indicators") *endogenous* time paths, e.g., *gross* **saving rate**, $\mathbf{s(t)} = S(t)/Y(t)$, cf.(13.6), (13.9)—$\mathbf{s_n}$(net rate),

$$s(t) = 1 - C(t)/\,Y(t) = 1 - c(t)/\,y(t) = 1 - \frac{c(t)}{f(k(t))}\;;\; s_n = s - \frac{\delta}{Y/K} \tag{13.26}$$

Indeed, since *optimal growth* theory is the theory of *optimal saving* (capital accumulation, investment) over time, the **actual** behavior ( *solution*) for the **optimal, s(t)**, (13.26), is often a **test** and hallmark for evaluating the **concrete specifications** of the *optimal* production and consumption *dynamics*, (13.23–13.25).

The *observed values* (ranges) of *saving rates*, **s(t)**, and producer *capital-output ratios* in Obstfeld and Rogoff (1995), Summers and Heston (1991), Simon (1990) [Piketty (2014, p. 164), $K/Y \in 4-7$ ] are $2 \leq K/Y \leq 6$, ( $0.17 \leq Y/K \leq 0.50$)—and **s(t)**, (fraction of GNP),

$$\begin{array}{ccc} 1885\text{–}1913 & 1921\text{–}1939 & 1973\text{–}1991 \\ 0.1 \leq s \leq 0.2 & 0.15 \leq s \leq 0.2 & 0.15 \leq s \leq 0.3 \end{array} \tag{13.27}$$

### *Steady States Within the Standard Optimal Saving Model*

This chapter will in all sections provide an *exact analytical* and *quantitative* approach. Consider the **CES** production function, **Y = F(L, K)**, Arrow et al. (1961, p. 230), Pitchford (1960), and the associated average and marginal products of Labor and durable producer Capital:

$$Y = F(L, K) = \gamma \left[ (1-a)L^{\frac{\sigma-1}{\sigma}} + aK^{\frac{\sigma-1}{\sigma}} \right]^{\frac{\sigma}{\sigma-1}} \quad ; \quad 0 < \sigma \leq \infty \tag{13.28}$$

$$AP_L(k) = Y/L = y = f(k) = \gamma \left[ (1-a) + ak^{\frac{\sigma-1}{\sigma}} \right]^{\frac{\sigma}{\sigma-1}} \tag{13.29}$$

$$MP_L(k) = f(k) - f'(k)\,k \ ;$$

$$MP_L(k) = (1-a)\,\gamma^{\frac{\sigma-1}{\sigma}}\ [AP_L(k)]^{\frac{1}{\sigma}} = w/P \tag{13.30}$$

$$MP_K(k) = f'(k) = a\gamma \left[ a + (1-a)k^{\frac{1-\sigma}{\sigma}} \right]^{\frac{1}{\sigma-1}}$$

$$= r/P \ ; \ \sigma > 1 : \ \underline{b} = \gamma\, a^{\frac{\sigma}{\sigma-1}} \tag{13.31}$$

$$AP_K(k) = Y/K = f(k)/k \ ; \qquad MP_K(k) = a\,\gamma^{\frac{\sigma-1}{\sigma}}\ [AP_K(k)]^{\frac{1}{\sigma}} \tag{13.32}$$

$$\epsilon_K(k) = MP_K/AP_K = \left[ 1 + [(1-a)/a]\,k^{\frac{1-\sigma}{\sigma}} \right]^{-1} \ ; \quad \epsilon_L = 1 - \epsilon_K \tag{13.33}$$

$\gamma$ is an overall (total) efficiency (productivity) parameter (TFP), $\mathbf{0 < a < 1}$, factor *intensity parameter*, $\sigma$ is the substitution elasticity parameter; $\lim_{k\to\infty} \mathbf{f'(k)} \equiv \underline{\mathbf{b}}$, (13.31).

The $MP_L, AP_L, MP_K, AP_K$ expressions, (13.29–13.32), and factor prices, $\frac{w}{P}, \frac{r}{P}$, follow from basic elasticity relations, cf. Arrow et al. (1961, p. 229), Jensen (2017, p. 53, p. 76), here Chap. 3, Eqs. (3.3), (3.63):

$$E\,(MP_L, AP_L) \;=\; 1/\sigma \;=\; E\,(MP_K, AP_K) \tag{13.34}$$

In the **CES** case (13.29), (13.31), the two-dimensional **dynamic system** (13.23–13.24) becomes:

$$\dot{k} = \gamma\left[(1-a) + ak^{\frac{\sigma-1}{\sigma}}\right]^{\frac{\sigma}{\sigma-1}} - (n+\delta)k - c \tag{13.35}$$

$$\dot{c} = c\,\eta(c)\left[\gamma a\left[a + (1-a)k^{\frac{-(\sigma-1)}{\sigma}}\right]^{\frac{1}{\sigma-1}} - \delta - \rho\right] \tag{13.36}$$

From (13.29) (13.31–13.33), we have the *growth rate* of *per capita income*, $\widehat{\mathbf{y}}\,(\mathbf{t})$, as

$$\widehat{y}\,(t) \;\equiv\; \dot{y}/y = E\,(f(k), k)\,(\dot{k}/k) = \epsilon_K(k)\,(\dot{k}/k) = \epsilon_K(k[t])\,\widehat{k}\,(t) \tag{13.37}$$

If they exist, *steady-state* values of capital-labor ratios and per capita consumptions in optimal one-sector growth models are *singular/critical points* of (13.23–13.24),

$$[\,\dot{c} = 0 \Leftrightarrow k(t) = \kappa\,] \Leftrightarrow [\,MP_K(\kappa) = f'(\kappa) = \rho + \delta\,] \tag{13.38}$$

$$[\,\dot{k} = 0 \Leftrightarrow c(t) = c(\kappa)\,] \Leftrightarrow [\,c(\kappa) \;=\; f(\kappa) - (n+\delta)\kappa\,] \tag{13.39}$$

Usually the optimal control motions in economics have the saddle-point property, Samuelson (1972, p. 104). The *steady-state* (saddle-point) expressions, (13.38–13.39), hold for *any* production function, $\mathbf{f(k)}$. Note that actual *sizes* of $\mathbf{MP_K}(\kappa)$ do not depend on any parameters of $f(k)$. Moreover, **saddle points,** $[\,\kappa\,,\, c(\kappa)\,]$—hence **steady state,** $\mathbf{s}(\kappa)$, cf. (13.26)—are **not** affected by concrete specification of $\mathbf{u(c)}$, (13.5), (13.13), **if** $\boldsymbol{\eta}$ **(c)** is **constant,** (13.36).

The **saddle points** of (13.38–13.39) are for an *extensive set* of CES *parameter cases*—including, CD: $\sigma = 1$: $f(k) = \gamma k^a$, $f'(k) = \gamma a k^{a-1}$—of (13.35–13.36) shown in Table 13.1, together with their *steady-state values* of, (13.29–13.33), (13.26). The size of the *six parameters* in Table 13.1 will serve also as backdrop for parametric *sensitivity analyses* of the *optimal paths,* $[\,\boldsymbol{k^*(t)},\, \boldsymbol{c^*(t)}\,]$, that ultimately *reach* $[\boldsymbol{\kappa}\,,\, \mathbf{c}(\boldsymbol{\kappa})]$; tacitly $\boldsymbol{\eta}$ **(c)** is **constant** in Table 13.1.

Note that in Table 13.1 the *optimal steady-state saving* rates, $\mathbf{s}\,(\boldsymbol{\kappa})$, are always less than $\boldsymbol{\epsilon_K(\kappa)}$ ("golden rule" saving rate). $\boldsymbol{s}\,(\boldsymbol{\kappa})$ is given by (13.26), (13.39), (13.32); $\boldsymbol{\epsilon_K(\kappa)}$ by (13.38), (13.33):

$$s(\kappa) \;=\; 1 - \frac{c(\kappa)}{f(\kappa)} \;=\; \frac{(n+\delta)\,\kappa}{f(\kappa)} \;=\; \frac{n+\delta}{AP_K(\kappa)} \;<\; \epsilon_K(\kappa) \;=\; \frac{\rho+\delta}{AP_K(\kappa)}\;\;;\;\; \rho > n \tag{13.40}$$

**Table 13.1** Parameters for optimal growth models: CES cases with steady states or asymptotics

| Parameters: steady-state models | | | | | | | Model characteristics | | | | | | | | | |
|---|---|---|---|---|---|---|---|---|---|---|---|---|---|---|---|---|
| Case | $\rho$ | n | $\delta$ | $\gamma$ | a | $\sigma$ | $\kappa$ | $c(\kappa)$ | $f(\kappa)$ | $MP_L(\kappa)$ | $f(\kappa)/\kappa$ | $MP_K(\kappa)$ | $\epsilon_K(\kappa)$ | K/Y | $s(\kappa)$ | $\rho+\delta$ |
| 1 | 0.050 | 0.02 | 0.05 | 1.0 | 0.20 | 1.0 | 2.378 | 1.023 | 1.189 | 0.951 | 0.500 | 0.100 | 0.200 | 2.000 | 0.140 | 0.100 |
| 2 | 0.050 | 0.02 | 0.05 | 1.0 | 0.25 | 1.0 | 3.393 | 1.119 | 1.357 | 1.018 | 0.400 | 0.100 | 0.250 | 2.500 | 0.175 | 0.100 |
| 3 | 0.050 | 0.02 | 0.05 | 1.0 | 0.40 | 1.0 | 10.079 | 1.814 | 2.520 | 1.512 | 0.250 | 0.100 | 0.400 | 4.000 | 0.280 | 0.100 |
| 4 | 0.050 | 0.02 | 0.05 | 3.0 | 0.40 | 1.0 | 62.898 | 11.321 | 15.724 | 9.435 | 0.250 | 0.100 | 0.400 | 4.000 | 0.280 | 0.100 |
| 5 | 0.070 | 0.02 | 0.05 | 1.0 | 0.40 | 1.0 | 7.438 | 1.710 | 2.231 | 1.339 | 0.300 | 0.120 | 0.400 | 3.333 | 0.233 | 0.120 |
| 6 | 0.075 | 0.02 | 0.08 | 1.0 | 0.40 | 1.0 | 4.855 | 1.396 | 1.881 | 1.129 | 0.388 | 0.155 | 0.400 | 2.581 | 0.258 | 0.155 |
| 7 | 0.100 | 0.02 | 0.08 | 1.0 | 0.40 | 1.0 | 3.784 | 1.325 | 1.703 | 1.022 | 0.450 | 0.180 | 0.400 | 2.222 | 0.222 | 0.180 |
| 8 | 0.120 | 0.02 | 0.08 | 1.0 | 0.40 | 1.0 | 3.175 | 1.270 | 1.587 | 0.952 | 0.500 | 0.200 | 0.400 | 2.000 | 0.200 | 0.200 |
| 9 | 0.100 | 0.02 | 0.08 | 2.0 | 0.40 | 1.0 | 12.014 | 4.205 | 5.406 | 3.244 | 0.450 | 0.180 | 0.400 | 2.222 | 0.222 | 0.180 |
| 10 | 0.050 | 0.02 | 0.08 | 0.3 | 0.40 | 1.0 | 0.875 | 0.197 | 0.284 | 0.171 | 0.325 | 0.130 | 0.400 | 3.077 | 0.308 | 0.130 |
| 11 | 0.050 | 0.02 | 0.08 | 1.0 | 0.60 | 1.0 | 45.764 | 5.339 | 9.915 | 3.966 | 0.217 | 0.130 | 0.600 | 4.615 | 0.461 | 0.130 |
| 12 | 0.050 | 0.02 | 0.08 | 1.0 | 0.40 | 1.0 | 6.509 | 1.464 | 2.115 | 1.269 | 0.325 | 0.130 | 0.400 | 3.077 | 0.308 | 0.130 |
| 13 | 0.150 | 0.02 | 0.05 | 1.0 | 0.60 | 1.0 | 15.588 | 4.105 | 5.196 | 2.078 | 0.333 | 0.200 | 0.600 | 3.000 | 0.210 | 0.200 |
| 1 | 0.050 | 0.02 | 0.05 | 1.0 | 0.25 | 0.5 | 1.775 | 0.999 | 1.123 | 0.945 | 0.632 | 0.100 | 0.158 | 1.581 | 0.111 | 0.100 |
| 2 | 0.050 | 0.02 | 0.05 | 1.0 | 0.40 | 0.5 | 2.667 | 1.146 | 1.333 | 1.067 | 0.500 | 0.100 | 0.200 | 2.000 | 0.140 | 0.100 |
| 3 | 0.050 | 0.02 | 0.05 | 1.0 | 0.60 | 0.5 | 4.624 | 1.564 | 1.888 | 1.425 | 0.408 | 0.100 | 0.245 | 2.449 | 0.172 | 0.100 |
| 4 | 0.050 | 0.02 | 0.05 | 3.0 | 0.60 | 0.5 | 9.107 | 5.802 | 6.439 | 5.529 | 0.707 | 0.100 | 0.141 | 1.414 | 0.099 | 0.100 |
| 5 | 0.075 | 0.02 | 0.05 | 1.0 | 0.40 | 1.5 | 53.718 | 5.624 | 9.384 | 2.669 | 0.175 | 0.125 | 0.716 | 5.724 | 0.400 | 0.125 |
| 6 | 0.075 | 0.02 | 0.05 | 1.0 | 0.60 | 1.2 | 820.88 | 67.504 | 124.9 | 22.356 | 0.152 | 0.125 | 0.821 | 6.569 | 0.461 | 0.125 |
| 7 | 0.100 | 0.02 | 0.08 | 0.3 | 0.40 | 1.5 | 0.385 | 0.174 | 0.212 | 0.143 | 0.551 | 0.180 | 0.327 | 1.814 | 0.181 | 0.180 |
| 8 | 0.100 | 0.02 | 0.08 | 0.2 | 0.40 | 1.5 | 0.162 | 0.094 | 0.110 | 0.080 | 0.675 | 0.180 | 0.267 | 1.481 | 0.148 | 0.180 |
| 9 | 0.060 | 0.02 | 0.05 | 1.0 | 0.40 | 1.7 | 108201 | 4478 | 12053 | 150.93 | 0.111 | 0.110 | 0.987 | 8.977 | 0.631 | 0.110 |

(continued)

**Table 13.1** (continued)

| Parameters: steady-state models | | | | | | | Model characteristics | | | | | | | | | |
|---|---|---|---|---|---|---|---|---|---|---|---|---|---|---|---|---|
| Case | $\rho$ | n | $\delta$ | $\gamma$ | a | $\sigma$ | $\kappa$ | $c(\kappa)$ | $f(\kappa)$ | $MP_L(\kappa)$ | $f(\kappa)/\kappa$ | $MP_K(\kappa)$ | $\epsilon_K(\kappa)$ | K/Y | $s(\kappa)$ | $\rho+\delta$ |
| Parameters: persistent growth models | | | | | | | Limits for $k \to \infty$ | | | | | | | | | |
| 1 | 0.100 | 0.02 | 0.05 | 1.0 | 0.60 | 1.5 | $\infty$ | $\infty$ | $\infty$ | $\infty$ | 0.216 | 0.216 | 1.000 | 4.630 | 0.630 | 0.150 |
| 2 | 0.100 | 0.02 | 0.05 | 1.0 | 0.40 | 2.0 | $\infty$ | $\infty$ | $\infty$ | $\infty$ | 0.160 | 0.160 | 1.000 | 6.250 | 0.500 | 0.150 |
| 3 | 0.060 | 0.02 | 0.08 | 1.0 | 0.40 | 3.0 | $\infty$ | $\infty$ | $\infty$ | $\infty$ | 0.253 | 0.253 | 1.000 | 3.952 | 0.842 | 0.140 |
| 4 | 0.070 | 0.02 | 0.08 | 1.0 | 0.40 | 7.0 | $\infty$ | $\infty$ | $\infty$ | $\infty$ | 0.343 | 0.343 | 1.000 | 2.915 | 0.854 | 0.150 |
| 5 | 0.080 | 0.02 | 0.05 | 1.0 | 0.40 | 3.0 | $\infty$ | $\infty$ | $\infty$ | $\infty$ | 0.253 | 0.253 | 1.000 | 3.952 | 0.763 | 0.130 |

The **steady-state** values of the **optimal saving** rate $s(\kappa)$ and other steady-state characteristics in Table 13.1 can—for the *same parametric* **CD** and **CES** technologies as in Table 13.1—be compared with the **exogenous saving** rates (**s**) and other steady-state values in *deterministic* or certainty equivalents of *stochastic* Solow (one-sector), Uzawa (two-sector) growth models, see Jensen and Richter (2007, p. 195, p. 211), Chap. 26, Merton (1975, p. 382).

Table 13.1 (*bottom*) has few numbers for *optimal asymptotic* saving rates $\mathbf{s}^*$ for, $\boldsymbol{\eta} = 1 = \boldsymbol{\theta}$, cf. parameters, (13.20), (13.79), (13.88), (13.100), below; $\boldsymbol{\rho}$ is indeed in Table 13.1 *too low* for (13.62):

$$s^* = [\,\underline{b} - \delta - \rho + n + \delta\,] / \underline{b} \quad ; \qquad \underline{b} = \gamma\, a^{\frac{\sigma}{\sigma-1}} = \lim_{k\to\infty} MP_K(k) \tag{13.41}$$

Parameter **n** (population/labor growth), observed (year 1996) *capital-output ratios*, $(K/Y)$, and *cost* (factor) *shares*, (13.33), $\epsilon_K$, Caselli and Feyrer (2007, p. 549), range over:

$$0.005 \le n \le 0.3\,,\ 1 \le K/Y \le 4\,,\ 0.25 \le Y/K \le 1\,,\ 0.15 \le \epsilon_K \le 0.5. \tag{13.42}$$

## *Transitional Dynamics in Standard Optimal Saving Model*

Through a *saddle point* of Table 13.1, as depicted in Figs. 13.1a, pass two curves, which are asymptotes to all the other curves (paths). The *optimal path*, $[\,\boldsymbol{k}^*(t),\ \boldsymbol{c}^*(t)\,]$, the asymptote ("*stable arm*") that ultimately reaches $[\boldsymbol{\kappa}\ ,\ \boldsymbol{c}(\boldsymbol{\kappa})]$, clearly satisfies the *transversality* condition, (13.38), (13.39), (13.25),

$$\begin{aligned} \lim_{t\to\infty} u'[\,c^*(t)\,]\,k^*(t)\,e^{-(\rho-n)t} &= \lim_{t\to\infty} u'[\,c(\kappa)\,]\,\kappa\,e^{-(\rho-n)t} \\ &= 0; \quad \rho > n \end{aligned} \tag{13.43}$$

As depicted in standard expositions, Blanchard and Fischer (1992, p. 46), Romer (2019, p. 69), and Barro and Sala-i-Martin (2004, p. 100), the points on this *optimal path* represent a "*razor's edge*", underscored by the dire implication that *all* the *other* (non-optimal, "inefficient") paths of (13.35–13.36) ultimately approach the *axes*, i.e., economic collapse [vanishing $\mathbf{k(t)}$ or zero $\mathbf{c(t)}$ ]. Thus the "*stable arm*" *path* (13.43) requires extreme precision in fixing the size of the *control* variable: *optimal* choice of the *initial value*, $\mathbf{c}\,(\mathbf{0})$, for any *given* $\mathbf{k}\,(\mathbf{0})$. But some feedback control rules are available, cf. Gandolfo (2010, p. 653). We return to "*razor's edge*", Akerlof and Nordhaus (1967, p. 52), "infeasible or wildly unstable paths", Arrow and Kurz (1970, p. 62), and robustness issues below with *persistent* growth [ dynamics of Fig. 13.1a is very different from the dynamics in Fig. 13.1b ].

The *shape* of the *stable arm* and the optimal solutions ("*transition paths*") from (13.35–13.36) depend on the *six parameters* in Table 13.1, and the *particular* **u(c)** and *its* $\eta$ **(c)**. Available textbook examples use parameters of **CD** functions and the *isoelastic* **u(c)**, (13.79) [with e.g. $\boldsymbol{\theta} = 3$], as seen in Barro and Sala-i-Martin (2004, p. 117), Maussner and Klump (1996, p. 129). de La Grandville (2017, p. 279) also offer **CES** illustrations of steady-state *transition paths*; Turnovsky and Garcia-Penalosa (2008, p. 1419) show CES parametric simulation experiments. For similar parametric CD and CES technologies and discount rates ($\rho$) as in Table 13.1, further tables of steady-state characteristics and rate of convergence of extended neoclassical growth models are seen in Turnovsky (2002, p. 1776), Garcia-Penalosa and Turnovsky (2005, p. 191).

It is beyond space available for us here to quantitatively demonstrate or discuss the problems associated with the *optimal* Ramsey saving *transition* paths to **steady states** $[\boldsymbol{\kappa}\,,\ \mathbf{c}(\boldsymbol{\kappa})\,]$, (13.38–13.39)—our main *object* is *optimal* saving with **persistent** growth solutions.

*Trajectory of Phase Portraits: Convergence and Divergence*
The *phase portraits* and trajectory geometry associated with the *optimal path*, $[\,k^*(t),\ c^*(t)\,]$, (13.43), Fig. 13.1a, will briefly be discussed—by here using the following theorem:

**Theorem 13.1 (Pampel)** *The dynamic system of the standard optimal growth model with* **CEIS**, $\boldsymbol{u}\,(c)$, *(13.79),—*$\eta\,(c) = 1/\theta$ *—is given by, (13.9), (13.23–13.24):*

$$\dot{K} = L\,[\,f(k) - \delta\,k - c\,]\ ; \quad \dot{L} = nL\,, \tag{13.44}$$

$$\dot{k} = h(k,c) = f(k) - (n+\delta)k - c\,, \tag{13.45}$$

$$\dot{c} = g(k,c) = c\,/\theta\left[\,f'(k) - \delta - \rho\,\right]. \tag{13.46}$$

*The steady-state* ***(saddle point)****,* $[\,\kappa\,,\ c(\kappa)\,]$, *of (13.45–13.46)—Fig. 13.1a, point A—is given by:*

$$[\,\dot{c} = 0 \Leftrightarrow k(t) = \kappa\,] \Leftrightarrow [\,f'(\kappa) = \rho + \delta\,] \Leftrightarrow \kappa = (f')^{-1}\,(\rho + \delta) \tag{13.47}$$

$$[\,\dot{k} = 0 \Leftrightarrow c(t) = c(\kappa)\,] \Leftrightarrow [\,c(\kappa) = f(\kappa) - (n+\delta)\kappa\,] \tag{13.48}$$

*The steady-state size of* $K/L = k = \kappa$, *(13.47) is a unique asymptotic stable capital-labor ratio and ray slope of optimal balanced growth paths:* $\forall t\ [\,L(t),\ K^*(t)\,] = [\,L(t),\ \kappa\,L(t)\,]$.

*In (**L**,**K**) plane, for any,* $k(0) = k_0 \neq \kappa$, *the distance,* $\mathbf{D_K(t)}$, *to **ray**,* $K(t) = \kappa L(t)$, *is*

$$D_K(t) = K^*(t) - K(t) = K^*(t) - \kappa L(t) \tag{13.49}$$

*The distance,* $\mathbf{D_K(t)}$, *(13.49), will for all optimal solutions,* $[k^*(t), c^*(t)]$, $[L(t), K^*(t)]$ *converge to zero or infinity, depending on the function,* $f(k)$, *and parameters of (13.44), (13.45–13.46).*

*There is **convergence** of* $D_K(t)$, *(13.49), to zero:*

$$\lim_{t\to\infty} |D_K(t)| = 0, \quad if \quad \theta < -\frac{f''(\kappa)\, c(\kappa)}{n\,\rho}\; ; \; n > 0,\, \rho > 0,\, f''(\kappa) < 0 \tag{13.50}$$

*There is **divergence** of* $D_K(t)$, *(13.49), to infinity :*

$$\lim_{t\to\infty} |D_K(t)| = \infty, \quad if \quad \theta > -\frac{f''(\kappa)\, c(\kappa)}{n\,\rho}\; ; \; n > 0,\, \rho > 0,\, f''(\kappa) < 0 \tag{13.51}$$

***Proof*** See Pampel (2009, p. 394, equations (39–44) of Theorem 3). □

As noted above (13.38–13.39), the **saddle point**, $[\,\boldsymbol{\kappa}\,,\, \boldsymbol{c(\kappa)}\,]$, (13.47–13.48), is seen *not* to be affected by the *size* $\boldsymbol{\theta}$ in (13.46) and so is *neither* $f''(\kappa)$ in the RHS of (13.50–13.51). Accordingly, we can have two economies with *same saddle point* and *same* RHS of (13.50–13.51), but having in (**L**,**K**) *plane* totally *different phase-portrait*—$D_K(t)$, converging or diverging, (13.50–13.51)—depending on the actual (selected) *size* of $\boldsymbol{\theta}$. Let us illustrate the application of (13.50–13.51) with a **CD** $f(k) = \gamma k^a$ in (13.45–13.46). We have,

$$f'(k) = \gamma a k^{a-1},\; f''(k) = -\gamma a(1-a)k^{a-2}\,;$$

$$\kappa = \left[\frac{\gamma\, a}{\rho + \delta}\right]^{\frac{1}{1-a}}\,;\; f''(\kappa) = -\gamma\, a(1-a)\,\kappa^{a-2} < 0 \tag{13.52}$$

$$\begin{aligned} c(\kappa) &= [\gamma\,\kappa^{a-1} - (n+\delta)\,]\,\kappa\;;\; - f''(\kappa)\, c(\kappa) \\ &= \gamma\, a(1-a)\,\kappa^{a-1}\,[\gamma\,\kappa^{a-1} - (n+\delta)\,] \end{aligned} \tag{13.53}$$

**Phase portraits** of dynamic system, (13.45–13.46), have in (**L**,**K**) plane—with **CD**, (13.52–13.53)—*convergence-divergence* properties, $\mathbf{D_K(t)}$, (13.50–13.51), as follows:

$$\lim_{t\to\infty} |D_K(t)| = 0\,[\,\infty\,]:$$

$$\theta \lessgtr \frac{\gamma\, a\,(1-a)\,[\,\gamma\,\kappa^{a-1} - n - \delta)\,]}{n\,\rho\,\kappa^{1-a}} = \frac{\gamma\, a\,(1-a)\,[\,\gamma\,\frac{\rho+\delta}{\gamma\, a} - n - \delta)\,]}{n\,\rho\,\frac{\gamma\, a}{\rho+\delta}} \tag{13.54}$$

$$\lim_{t\to\infty} |D_K(t)| = 0\,[\,\infty\,]: \quad \theta \lessgtr \frac{1-a}{n\,a}\,(\,1+\frac{\delta}{\rho})\,[\,\rho+\delta - a\,(n+\delta)\,] \tag{13.55}$$

We can illustrate (13.55) by using the ***parameters***—listed in Table 13.1—for the RHS of (13.55). Thus for the **CD** *cases*: 2, 3, 7, and 11, the RHS (13.55) gives the following results:

*Case* 2: $\theta \lessgtr 24.8$; *Case* 3: $\theta \lessgtr 10.8$; *Case* 7: $\theta \lessgtr 18.9$; *Case* 11: $\theta \lessgtr 6.1$. For all these CD *cases*, the RHS numbers above are clearly outside (far beyond) the usual range for $\theta$, cf. Table 2, note 6. Thus in all these CD *cases*, we will with usual $\theta$ have **convergence**, (13.50), (13.55), in (**L,K**) state space.

If we ignore depreciation, i.e., $\boldsymbol{\delta} = 0$, then (13.55) becomes:

$$\delta = 0: \quad \lim_{t\to\infty} |D_K(t)| = 0\,[\,\infty\,]: \quad \theta \lessgtr (1-a)\,[\,\frac{\rho}{n\,a} - 1\,]\,; \ \rho > n \tag{13.56}$$

With (13.56), CD for $a = 0.4$ or $a = 0.6$—and $\rho = 0.05, n = 0.02$— give ***divergence***, (13.51), (13.56), for respectively, $\theta = 3.2$, $\theta = 1.4$. Such divergence (13.51), (13.56), of the phase portrait in (L,K) is similar to that seen for the Solow growth model, without depreciation, in Chap. 12, section "Trajectory of Phase Portraits—Convergence and Divergence", Fig. 12.1.

**Remark 13.1** As ***convergence*** condition, (13.50), is equivalent to $n\,\rho\,\theta < -\,f''(\kappa)\,c\,(\kappa)$, it follows that $\mathbf{n} = \mathbf{0}$ always implies a phase portrait with ***convergence*** (RHS is positive) in (L,K) space to the Ramsey ***Stationary State***, $(\,\overline{L},\,\overline{K}\,)$, $\overline{K}/\overline{L} = \kappa$, (13.52).

## Persistent Growth: Optimal Solution—Separator

With **no critical points** of (13.23–13.24), (13.35–13.36), and ($\dot{\mathbf{c}} > 0$) ***everywhere***, persistent consumption growth per capita will prevail. With regard to Ramsey (optimal) saving, it has been incumbent on us to obtain **sufficient conditions**—applicable to a ***general GNP-function***, $\mathbf{f}(\mathbf{k})$, and a ***general utility function*** $\mathbf{u}(\mathbf{c})$ with $\mathbf{u}'(\mathbf{c})$ satisfying (13.5)—ensuring **persistent optimal** consumption growth per capita. [ No **CD** $\boldsymbol{f}(\boldsymbol{k})$ can satisfy, (13.60); but, see $\boldsymbol{f}(\boldsymbol{k})$ of ***extended*** **CD** below, (13.165) ].

*Assumption 13.1 (Technology)* The per capita production function, $\mathbf{f(k)}$, (13.6–13.7), in (13.23–13.24) has **continuity**, $C^0([0, \infty[)$, and **differentiability** properties, $C^1(]0, \infty[)$, i.e.,

$$(i) \quad f(k) \in C^0([0, \infty[) \cap C^1(]0, \infty[), \qquad (ii) \quad f(0) \geq 0 \tag{13.57}$$

It is further assumed that $\dot{\boldsymbol{c}} = \boldsymbol{g(k, c) > 0}$, (13.24)—hence $\mathbf{f'(k)}$, $\boldsymbol{\eta}(\mathbf{c})$, satisfy, $(iii)$ or $(\widetilde{iii})$:

$$\begin{aligned} &(iii)\ \forall k > 0 : f'(k) > \delta + \rho\ , \\ &\qquad \forall c \geq 0 : c\,\eta(c) \geq 0 \Rightarrow c = 0 : \dot{c} = 0\,,\ \forall c > 0 : \dot{c} > 0 \end{aligned} \tag{13.58}$$

$$\begin{aligned} &(\widetilde{iii})\ \forall k > \tilde{k} : f'(k) > \delta + \rho\ , \\ &\qquad \forall c \geq \tilde{c} : c\,\eta(c) \geq 0 \Rightarrow c = \tilde{c} : \dot{c} = 0\,,\ \forall c > \tilde{c} : \dot{c} > 0 \end{aligned} \tag{13.59}$$

For a **concave** production function with $\mathbf{f(k)} \to \infty$ as $k \to \infty$, (13.58–13.59) become, cf. (13.8),

$$(iv) \quad \lim_{k \to \infty} f'(k) \ \equiv \ \underline{b} \ > \ \delta + \rho. \tag{13.60}$$

It follows from (13.57–13.58), (13.60) that the *dynamic system* (13.23–13.24) has *no stationary solutions* in *closed* first quadrant, $\overline{\Re}^2_+$, [except possibly for $(0, 0)$], and that the *positive k-axis*, $c(t) = 0$, is a *solution* (trajectory) of (13.23–13.24). The *point* $(\tilde{\mathbf{k}}, \tilde{\mathbf{c}})$ replaces $(\mathbf{0}, \mathbf{0})$ with (13.59).

To characterize the **phase portrait**, as depicted in Fig. 13.1b, we give the following.

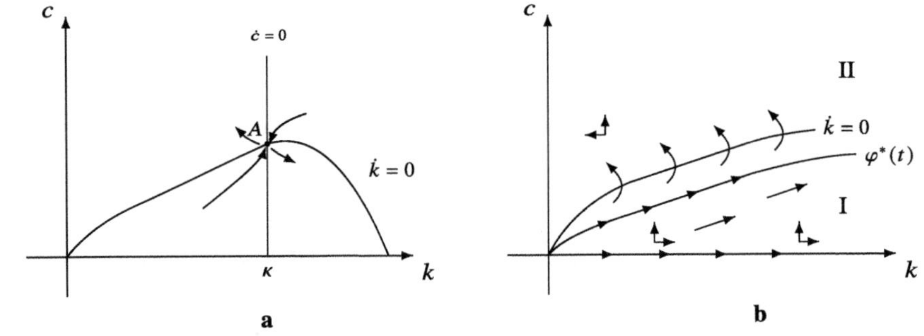


**Fig. 13.1** Dynamics with optimal saving

**Theorem 13.2** *With optimal (**Ramsey**) saving, persistent (**endogenous**) growth of per capita consumption is obtained if the concave **production** function* $\mathbf{f(k)}$ *satisfies (13.61), and the **elasticity of intertemporal substitution** of consumption, **EIS**,* $\boldsymbol{\eta}(\mathbf{c})$ *of* $\boldsymbol{u(c)}$*, **or** alternatively constant **RTP**,* $\boldsymbol{\rho}$*—in (13.1–13.3), (13.21)—satisfy **inequalities** (13.62–13.63):*

$$\textit{persistent growth } (\dot{c} > 0): \lim_{k\to\infty} f'(k) \equiv \underline{b} > \rho + \delta \Leftrightarrow \rho < \underline{b} - \delta \tag{13.61}$$

$$\exists\, \varphi^*(t) : \sup_{c>0} \eta(c) \equiv \overline{\eta} < \frac{\underline{b} - (n+\delta)}{\underline{b} - (\rho+\delta)} \Leftrightarrow \rho > \frac{(\underline{b} - \delta)(\overline{\eta} - 1) + n}{\overline{\eta}} \tag{13.62}$$

$$\exists\, V : \sup_{c>0} \eta(c) \equiv \overline{\eta} < \frac{\rho - n}{(\underline{b} - \delta) - \rho} \Leftrightarrow \rho > \frac{(\underline{b} - \delta)\overline{\eta} + n}{1 + \overline{\eta}} \; ; \; \rho > n \tag{13.63}$$

*The two **sufficient** conditions, (13.61–13.62), ensure **existence**—below the **isocline**,* $\dot{k} = 0$*:* $c = f(k) - (n+\delta)k$*, cf. (13.23)—of **separator**, (13.64),* $\boldsymbol{\varphi^*(t)}$*,* $t \in \Re$*—the particular solution, time path,* $\varphi^*(t)$*, (curve) in* $\Re^2_+$ *of vector function,* $\varphi^* = [k^*, c^*]$*, seen in Fig. 13.2b,*

$$\varphi^*(t) \equiv [k^*(t), c^*(t)], \quad t \in \Re \tag{13.64}$$

*The **existence** of this **separator**, (trajectory, locus), (13.64), depicted in Figs. 13.1b and 13.2b, is required for any viable long-run (**persistent**) economic growth per capita.*

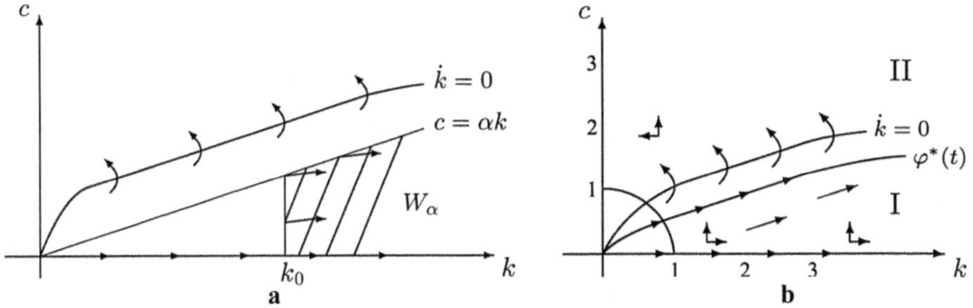


**Fig. 13.2** Dynamics with optimal saving and persistent growth (**a**) The positive invariant region $W_\alpha$, with endogenous (persistent) per capita growth. (**b**) Curve $C = C_I \cup C_{II} \cup \{(1,0),(0,1)\}$ (*closed set*), $C_{II}$ must be an *open* and *connected set* of $C$. $C_I \cup \{(1,0)\}$ must be a *closed* set *with the endpoint* $[\bar{k}^*, \bar{c}^*]$ *of curve* $C_I$*, where* $\varphi^*(t)$ *passes*

*For any concave monotone non-decreasing* ***utility*** *function* $\mathbf{u}(\mathbf{c})$*—****satisfying*** *(13.63)—****separator*** *(13.64) is a* ***unique optimal*** *solution* $[k^*(t), c^*(t)]$ *to* ***control*** *system: (13.11–13.17, 13.23–13.25).*

***Proof*** The *existence* and *uniqueness* of the optimal path (13.64) by (13.61–13.63) in Theorem 13.2 is proved by Lemmas 13.2–13.3 and Corollary 13.2 in **Appendix A**, where Fig. 13.2 is explained and extensively used. Critical point $(\tilde{\mathbf{k}}, \tilde{\mathbf{c}})$, (13.59), can replace (13.58): $(\mathbf{0}, \mathbf{0})$, Fig. 13.2. □

### *Calculating Optimal Solutions: Coordinate Transformations*

We can change the **state** variables (coordinates) from $(\mathbf{k}, \mathbf{c})$ to *new coordinates* $(\mathbf{z}, \mathbf{x})$ as:

$$z = Y/K = y/k = f(k)/k = \zeta(k)\,; \quad k = \zeta^{-1}(z) \tag{13.65}$$

$$x = C/K = c/k\,; \quad c = kx = \zeta^{-1}(z)\,x\,; \quad s = 1 - c/y = 1 - x/z \tag{13.66}$$

By *L'Hospital* and (13.65), (13.60): $\lim_{k\to\infty} z(k) = \lim_{k\to\infty} \zeta(k) = \lim_{k\to\infty} f'(k) \equiv \underline{b}$.

**Lemma 13.1** *Coordinate transformations and the Dynamic Systems. With the* ***state*** *variables (coordinates),* $(\mathbf{z}, \mathbf{x})$*, (13.65–13.66), the dynamic system, (13.23–13.24)—vector field,* $(\mathbf{h}, \mathbf{g})$*—****is transformed*** *to the* ***dynamic system****—vector field,* $(\boldsymbol{\phi}, \boldsymbol{\psi})$*:*

$$\dot{z} = \phi(z, x) = z[f'(\zeta^{-1}(z))/z - 1](z - x - n - \delta) \tag{13.67}$$

$$\dot{x} = \psi(z, x) = x[\eta(\zeta^{-1}(z)x)[f'(\zeta^{-1}(z)) - \delta - \rho] - z + x + n + \delta] \tag{13.68}$$

*Vertical and straight lines are* ***isoclines*** *of (13.67) and the* ***isocline*** *of (13.68) is curved,*

$$\dot{z} = 0 : z = \underline{b} \quad ; \quad x = z - n - \delta \tag{13.69}$$

$$\dot{x} = 0 : x + \eta(\zeta^{-1}(z)x)[f'(\zeta^{-1}(z)) - \delta - \rho] - z + n + \delta = 0 \tag{13.70}$$

*The long-term (asymptotic)* ***growth rates*** *and their parametric determinants are,*

$$\lim_{t\to\infty} \widehat{k}(t) = \lim_{t\to\infty} \widehat{c}(t) = \lim_{t\to\infty} \widehat{y}(t) = \underline{\widehat{y}} = \overline{\eta}(\underline{b} - \delta - \rho) \tag{13.71}$$

***Proof*** From (13.23–13.24) and (13.65–13.66), we have,

$$\widehat{k}(t) = \dot{k}/k = h(k,c)/k = z - x - (n+\delta), \tag{13.72}$$

$$\widehat{c}(t) = \dot{c}/c = g(k,c)/c = \eta(\zeta^{-1}(z)\,x)\left[\,f'(\zeta^{-1}(z)) - (\delta+\rho)\right] \tag{13.73}$$

By time differentiation of (13.65 – 13.66), we obtain,

$$\dot{z} = \zeta'(k)\dot{k} = [\,f'(k) - \zeta(k)\,](\dot{k}/k) = [\,f'(\zeta^{-1}(z)) - z\,](\dot{k}/k) \tag{13.74}$$

$$\dot{x} = x[\,\dot{c}/c - \dot{k}/k\,] \tag{13.75}$$

Inserting (13.72–13.73) into (13.74–13.75), we get,

$$\dot{z} = z[\,f'(\zeta^{-1}(z))/z - 1\,](z - x - n - \delta) \tag{13.76}$$

$$\dot{x} = x\,[\,\eta(\zeta^{-1}(z)\,x)\left[f'(\zeta^{-1}(z)) - \delta - \rho\right] - z + x + n + \delta\,] \tag{13.77}$$

which is (13.67–13.68); (13.67–13.68) and (13.65–13.66) give (13.69–13.70); (13.71) is verified by (13.65–13.66), (13.72–13.73).

One **critical** point of the economic optimal control system (13.67–13.68) will be a **saddle** point, $(z^*, x^*)$. The **separator** in Fig. 13.2b as the *optimal solution* $[\,k^*(t), c^*(t)\,]$, (13.64), satisfying the transversality condition, (13.25), will in the **transformed** system (13.67–13.68) be the **"stable arm"** ultimately *reaching* the stationary **saddle** point, $(z^*, x^*)$, where the *transversality* condition can easily be checked, cf. (13.43),

$$\lim_{t\to\infty} u'[\,c^*(t)\,]\,k^*(t)\,e^{-(\rho-n)t} = \lim_{t\to\infty} u'[\,\zeta^{-1}(z^*)\,x^*\,]\,\zeta^{-1}(z^*)\,e^{-(\rho-n)t}$$
$$= 0 \;\;;\;\; \rho > n \tag{13.78}$$

All *orbits*, $\varphi(t) = [k(t), c(t)]$, $t \in \Re$, *below* the separator (optimal solution) in Fig. 13.2b will in the *transformed* system (13.67–13.68) ultimately reach the *critical*, (node) point on the **z**-axis: $[\,z(t=\infty) = \underline{b},\;\; x(t=\infty) = 0\,]$. Even though at the node point, we have: $x(t=\infty) = 0$, this **node** does **correspond** to: $c\,(t=\infty) = \infty$, in Figs. 13.1b and 13.2b.

All *orbits*, $\varphi(t) = [k(t), c(t)]$, $t \in \Re$, *above* the separator (optimal solution) in Fig. 13.2b (terminating in *finite* time on *c-axis*) will in the *transformed* system (13.67–13.68) ultimately be *increasing* in $z(t)$ and $x(t)$, before **terminating** in **finite** time. □

Beyond our *sufficient* conditions—Theorem 13.2, (13.61–13.63), Lemma 13.1, (13.67–13.70), (13.78)—for the *existence* of a unique *optimal trajectory* (with *persistent growth*)—we *find* (calculate) *optimal solution* by the methods in footnote 5. The needed *optimal initial control value* $\mathbf{c^*(0)}$ for any *chosen* $\boldsymbol{k}(0)$—*point* [ k(0), c*(0) ] to (13.35–13.36) on (13.64)—comes by calculating backward from $(\boldsymbol{z}^*, \boldsymbol{x}^*)$, (13.65–13.68), cf. below (13.91–13.96); see also Newbery (1972, p. 28,39).

### *The CEIS Utility Function and VEIS Utility Functions*

For a *parametric* utility function of $\mathbf{u}(\mathbf{c})$, we first use throughout section "Applications: Optimal Solutions with CEIS Utility Functions and CES Production Functions" the *isoelastic utility* function, *constant* **EIS** (CEIS), Barro and Sala-i-Martin (2004, p. 91), Solow (2000, p. 114), Lawrance (1991, p. 57), King and Rebelo (1993, p. 911), de La Grandville (2018, p. 83):

$$u(c) = \frac{c^{1-\theta} - 1}{1-\theta}, \; u'(c) = c^{-\theta},$$

$$- \; E(MU(c), c) = \frac{1}{\eta(c)} = \theta \geq 0; \; \theta = 1 : u(c) = ln \; c \tag{13.79}$$

With **CEIS**, (13.79), and **VEIS** of HARA, (13.81), the Theorem 13.2 *conditions* (13.61), (13.63), required of $\boldsymbol{\rho}$, **RTP**—for the **existence** of both **persistent** growth and *unique* **optimal** solutions [*finite integral* of **V** (13.11) along *separator* (13.64)]—can be *summarized* as, cf. (13.86):

$$\underline{b} - \delta > \rho > \frac{\underline{b} - \delta + n\,\theta}{1+\theta} > n;$$

$$\textbf{CEIS} : \eta(c) = \overline{\eta} = \frac{1}{\theta}, \; \textbf{HARA} : \sup_{c>0} \eta(c) = \overline{\eta} = \frac{1}{\theta} \tag{13.80}$$

Sections "The Affine Dynamics with VEIS Utility Functions"–"Affine Dynamics, Minimal States, and Evolutions" show $\mathbf{u}(\mathbf{c})$ with *variable* elasticity of *intertemporal* substitution (**VEIS**), $\boldsymbol{\eta}(\mathbf{c})$, by using the **Hyperbolic** Absolute Risk Aversion (**HARA**) family[2] of **concave** utility functions, Merton (1971), Merton (1992, p. 137–138)—here in our notation—with **domains** as:

$$u(c) = \frac{\theta}{1-\theta}\left[\frac{\beta c}{\theta} - \nu\right]^{1-\theta}, \; \theta \neq 1, \; \beta > 0, \; \frac{\beta c}{\theta} - \nu > 0;$$

$$\theta \gtrless 0, \; \nu \gtrless 0; \; \theta = \infty, \nu = -1 \tag{13.81}$$

$$\theta > 0, \; \nu > 0 : c \geq \underline{c} = \frac{\nu}{\beta}\theta > 0;$$

[2] HARA family is *subsistence extended* ($\nu \neq 0$) versions of the non-homothetic *direct addilog utility* functions, Houthakker (1960), see Atkeson and Ogaki (1996), cf. footnote 15. On extensions of Houthakker-Hanoch *non-homothetic* additive *indirect utility* functions, see Jensen et al. (2011). Here Chap. 5.

$$\theta > 0,\ \nu < 0 : c \geqslant 0\ ;\ \ \theta < 0,\ \nu < 0 : c \leqslant \frac{\nu}{\beta}\theta \tag{13.82}$$

$$u'(c) = \beta\,[\,\frac{\beta c}{\theta} - \nu\,]^{-\theta} > 0\,,\ \ u''(c) = -\,\beta^2\,[\,\frac{\beta c}{\theta} - \nu\,]^{-\theta-1} < 0 \tag{13.83}$$

$0 < \theta < 1$: $u(c)$ is *unbounded*;[3] $\theta > 1, \theta < 0 : u(c)$ is negative, upper *bounded* by zero.

Important properties of the *increasing concave* HARA utility $u(c)$, (13.81–13.83), are given by the well-known Arrow-Pratt measures of *absolute* risk aversion, $R_A(c)$, and *relative* risk aversion, $R_R(c)$, cf. Pratt (1964, p. 122, p. 130, p. 134), Varian (1992, p. 178, p. 189):

$$\begin{aligned} R_A(c) &= -\frac{u''(c)}{u'(c)} = [\,c/\theta - \nu/\beta\,]^{-1} > 0\,; \\ R_R(c) &= -\frac{u''(c)\,c}{u'(c)} = \frac{c}{c/\theta - \nu/\beta} > 0 \end{aligned} \tag{13.84}$$

$$\begin{aligned} R'_A(c) &= \frac{-1}{\theta}[\,c/\theta - \nu/\beta\,]^{-2} \gtrless 0\,; \\ R'_R(c) &= \frac{-\,\nu/\beta}{(\,c/\theta - \nu/\beta\,)^2}\,;\ R''_R(c) = \frac{2\,\nu/\beta}{(\,c/\theta - \nu/\beta\,)^3} \end{aligned} \tag{13.85}$$

Thus, $R_A(c)$ and $R_R(c)$, (13.84), can both be increasing, decreasing, (13.85), or constant, for selected parameter values of $\theta \gtrless 0,\ \nu/\beta \gtrless 0, \nu = 0$; the latter $\nu = 0$ gives **CEIS**, (13.79). In Back et al. (2019, p. 302), Calvet and Paoli (2014, p. 868), $R'_R(c) \gtrless 0$ is called IRRA (DRRA) risk preferences, each with some merits in finance theory and portfolio selection.

By (13.84), (13.20–13.21), the *variable* EIS (**VEIS**), $\eta = \eta(c)$, becomes on the *domains*, (13.82):

$$\begin{aligned} \eta(c) &= \frac{1}{R_R(c)} = \frac{c/\theta - \nu/\beta}{c} = \frac{1}{\theta} - \frac{\nu/\beta}{c} > 0\,; \\ \eta'(c) &= \frac{\nu/\beta}{c^2}\,,\ \ \eta''(c) = \frac{-2\,\nu/\beta}{c^3} \end{aligned} \tag{13.86}$$

i.e., $\eta = \eta(c)$ is **hyperbolic** *increasing* (decreasing) **EIS**—DRRA (IRRA)—for, $\boldsymbol{\nu/\beta} \gtrless 0$.

With *persistent* growth, we shall see that **u(c)**, (13.81), with IRRA, (13.86), offers *new perspectives* for obtaining *empirically sensible optimal* solutions (time

[3] See *Samuelson* (1969, p. 243): "I have no particular interest in *boundedness* of utility and consider **log (c)** to be interesting and *admissible.*" cf. footnote 6.

paths) for the *Ramsey saving rates* **with** $\theta \gtreqless 1, \nu/\beta > 0$—which gives in (13.86): $\sup_{c>0} \eta(c) = \bar{\eta} = 1/\theta$.

Thus to **VEIS** (13.81), (13.86), Theorem 13.2 conditions on $\rho$, (13.61), (13.63), for the *existence* of persistent growth and *optimal* solutions along **separator** (13.64) are still **summarized** in (13.80).

## Applications: Optimal Solutions with CEIS Utility Functions and CES Production Functions

In this section, we provide *calculated phase paths* (orbits), $\boldsymbol{\varphi}(\mathbf{t}) = [\mathbf{k}(\mathbf{t}), \mathbf{c}(\mathbf{t})]$, $t \in \Re$, to *confirm* and show the **solutions** of **optimal** system **dynamics** (13.23–13.24) and Theorem 13.2.

The **quantitative** demonstrations of these endogenous **persistent** *growth paths*—unavailable in a vast literature, which is mainly *qualitative*—are here first provided with *parametric* CES production functions.

### *The CEIS–CES Solutions and Their Seven Parameters*

In **CES** cases, the *two-dimensional* dynamic system, (13.35 – 13.36), *with* **u(c)**, (13.79) becomes:

$$\dot{k} = \gamma \left[ (1-a) + ak^{\frac{(\sigma-1)}{\sigma}} \right]^{\frac{\sigma}{(\sigma-1)}} - c - (n+\delta)k \tag{13.87}$$

$$\dot{c} = (c/\theta)\left[ \gamma a \left[ a + (1-a)k^{\frac{-(\sigma-1)}{\sigma}} \right]^{\frac{1}{(\sigma-1)}} - \delta - \rho \right] \tag{13.88}$$

Isocline, $\dot{k} = 0$, of the **nonlinear** first-order *autonomous* system (13.87–13.88) is,

$$\dot{k} = 0 \Leftrightarrow c = \gamma \left[ (1-a) + ak^{\frac{(\sigma-1)}{\sigma}} \right]^{\frac{\sigma}{(\sigma-1)}} - (n+\delta)k. \tag{13.89}$$

Consider the **CES-baseline** case, defined by the **seven parameters**:

$$\begin{aligned} &\gamma = 0.661157, \ a = 0.55, \ \sigma = 2.0, \ \delta = 0.03, \ n = 0.01, \\ &\theta = 1 = \eta, \ \rho = 0.16 \end{aligned} \tag{13.90}$$

The **selected** $\boldsymbol{\rho} = \mathbf{0.16}$ satisfies Theorem 13.2 requirements[4] (13.80): $\mathbf{0.17} > \boldsymbol{\rho} > \mathbf{0.09}$.

[4] Lawrance (1991, p. 54, 69) estimates the *rate of time preference* (discount rate) as $\mathbf{0.19} > \boldsymbol{\rho} > \mathbf{0.10}$.

The seven *parameters* imply, $\underline{b} = \gamma a^{\frac{\sigma}{\sigma-1}} = 0.20$, $\widehat{\underline{y}} = (\underline{b} - \delta - \rho)/\theta = 0.01$, cf. (13.61), (13.31), (13.71). The asymptotic *saving rate* becomes $s^* = 0.25$, cf. (13.97).

The **transformed** dynamic system[5] of (13.87–13.88) is by Lemma 13.1 and (13.31–13.32),

$$\dot{z} = \phi(z, x) = z[a\gamma^{\frac{\sigma-1}{\sigma}} z^{\frac{1-\sigma}{\sigma}} - 1][z - x - n - \delta] \tag{13.91}$$

$$\dot{x} = \psi(z, x) = x[x - z(1 - \frac{1}{\theta}\gamma^{\frac{\sigma-1}{\sigma}} a z^{\frac{1-\sigma}{\sigma}}) - \frac{\delta+\rho}{\theta} + n + \delta] \tag{13.92}$$

The isoclines of (13.91–13.92) are,

$$\dot{z} = 0 \Leftrightarrow z = \gamma a^{\frac{\sigma}{\sigma-1}} = \underline{b} \quad ; \quad x = z - n - \delta \tag{13.93}$$

$$\dot{x} = 0 \Leftrightarrow x = 0 \; ; \; x = \gamma^{\frac{\sigma-1}{\sigma}} a(1 - 1/\theta) z^{\frac{1}{\sigma}} + (\delta + \rho)/\theta - n - \delta \tag{13.94}$$

The *critical* points (*saddle* and *node* points) of (13.91–13.92) in Fig. 13.4 become, cf. (13.93–13.94),

$$z^* = \gamma a^{\frac{\sigma}{\sigma-1}} = \underline{b} \; ; \quad node : (\tilde{z} = z^*, \tilde{x} = 0) \tag{13.95}$$

$$x^* = z^*(1 - 1/\theta) + (\delta + \rho)/\theta - n - \delta \tag{13.96}$$

Hence the long-run (asymptotic) saving rate, ($s^*$), and growth rate $\widehat{\underline{y}}$, (13.71), are given by,

$$s^* = 1 - \frac{x^*}{z^*} = \frac{\underline{b} - \delta - \rho + \theta(n+\delta)}{\underline{b}\,\theta} = \frac{(\underline{b} - \delta - \rho)/\theta + n + \delta}{\underline{b}};$$

$$\widehat{\underline{y}} = \frac{\underline{b} - \delta - \rho}{\theta} \tag{13.97}$$

CES-*baseline parameters* give *exactly*: $z^* = \underline{b} = 0.20$, $x^* = 0.15$, $s^* = 0.25$, $\widehat{\underline{y}} = 0.01$.

We selected in Figs. 13.3, 13.4, 13.5, and 13.6 the **initial value** of the *capital-labor* as: $\boldsymbol{k(0) = 100}$.

Figure 13.3 illustrates the *CES-baseline solutions* of the system (13.87–13.88) with isocline (13.89) in the $(\mathbf{k}, \mathbf{c})$-space by *showing* the computed

[5] We calculate the parametric time paths by the time elimination method suggested by Mulligan and Sala-i-Martin (1993). This method takes the (known) steady state as its fixed point and proceeds backward in the time along the stable saddle path to discover the route from the initial and to the asymptotic state. In system (13.87–13.90), however, the asymptotic growth rate is positive, indicating that the necessary fixed point is not available in Fig. 13.3; the required (necessary) fixed point is seen in Fig. 13.4.

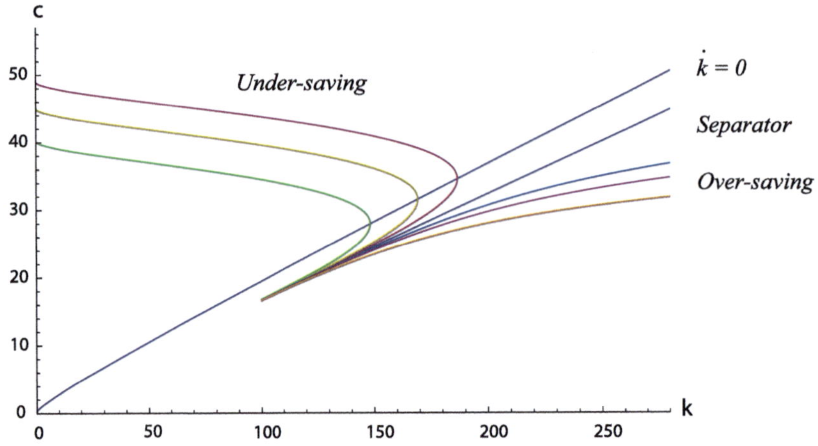


**Fig. 13.3 Phase portrait of** (13.87–13.88) in state (**k**, **c**) space; $k(0) = 100$. **CES-baseline**

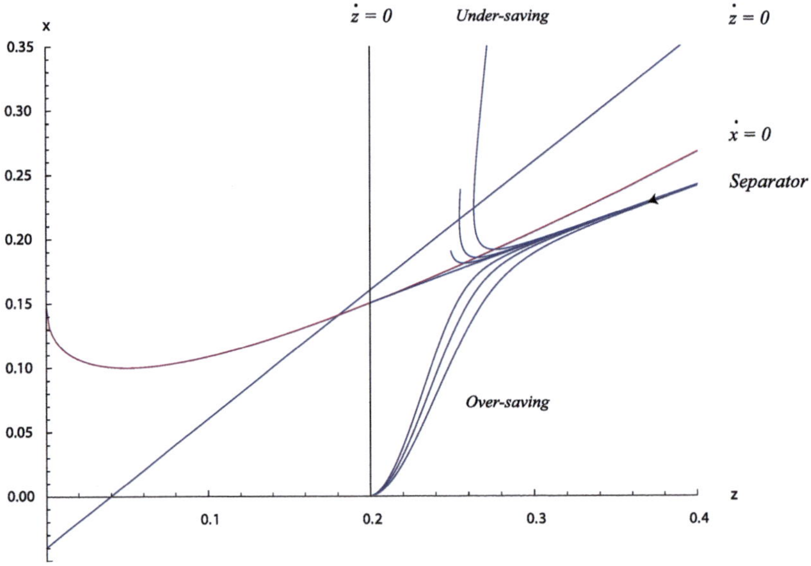


**Fig. 13.4 Transformed phase portrait** by (13.91–13.92) in $(z, x)$ space. **CES-baseline**

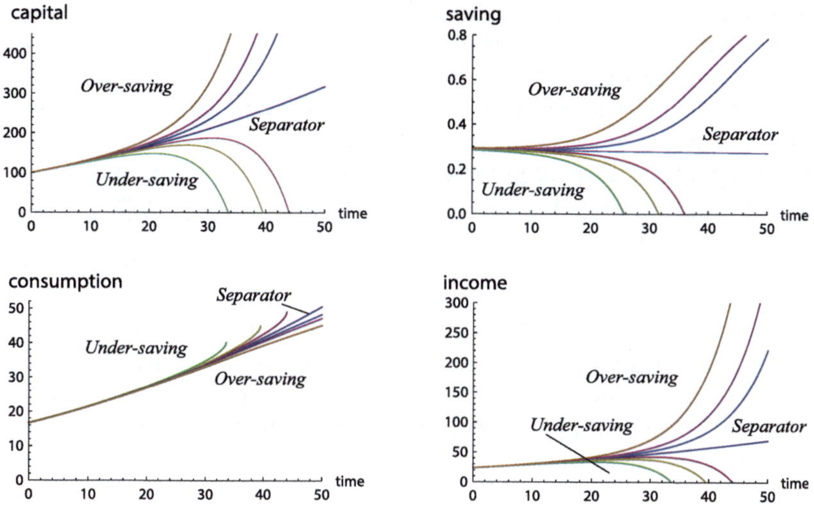


**Fig. 13.5** Time paths for (13.87–13.88), (13.29), (13.26): $k(t)$, $c(t)$, $y(t)$, and $s(t)$. **CES-baseline**

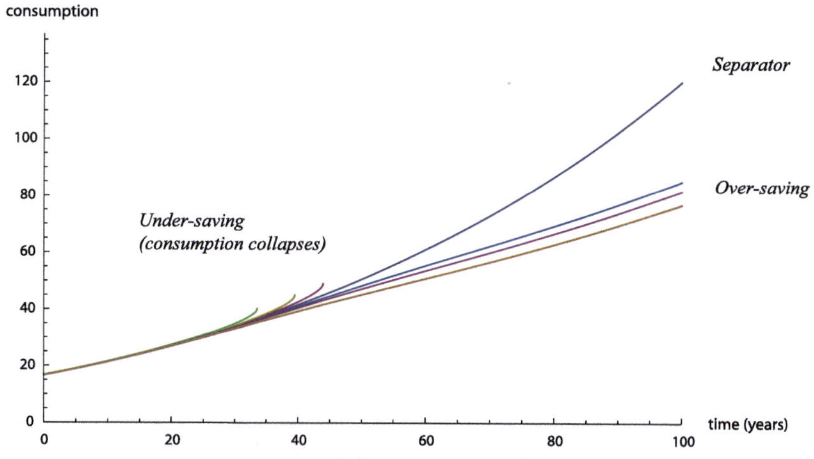


**Fig. 13.6** The **time paths** (13.87–13.88) for: $c(t)$, short run and long run. **CES-baseline**

**separator** (starting with **optimal** (calculated) **initial,** $\mathbf{c_0^* = 15}$), and *six non-optimal paths* for which the *initial values* **c(0)** are **0.1**, **0.2**, and **0.5** per cent *higher* (under-saving) or *lower* (over-saving) than $c_0^*$. In Fig. 13.3, the *computed* **separator,** $\varphi^*(t) \equiv [k^*(t), c^*(t)]$, (13.64), appears exactly as the theoretical *separator* $\varphi^*(t)$, in Fig. 13.2b.

As seen in Fig. 13.4, *over-saving* paths exist on an *infinite time domain* in reaching **node** $(\tilde{z}, \tilde{x}) = (0.2, 0.0)$ on z-axis, Fig. 13.4; $\tilde{z} = z^* = 0.20 \Leftrightarrow (K/Y) = 5$, cf. (13.65), (13.27).

Figure 13.5 illustrates seven *time paths* for **k(t)**, **c(t)**, **y(t)**, and **s(t)**, showing how over-saving soon wedges the capital stock above its *optimal (separator)* path and capital starts to accumulate very fast as almost all output is devoted to saving. On the other hand, under-saving dilutes the capital stock close to zero in some 35 – 50 years.

Figure 13.6 illustrates for consumption that even though *under-saving collapses* consumption in 35–50 years (i.e., in *finite time*), *over-saving* causes only minor deviations from the optimal path in the short run. In the long run, however, *over-saving* starts to bite; Fig. 13.6 shows that consumption which initially lies only 0.1–0.5 per cent below its optimal level causes consumption to fall some 50 per cent below its optimum in hundred years. Nevertheless, the interesting conclusion is that there exist ($\forall t > 0$) paths below the separator which generate (in terms of *short-run consumption*) very *similar* outcomes as the *optimal* path. However, all the **non-optimal** paths in Fig. 13.5 have *unrealistic time paths* for $s(t)$—compared with "**historical**" saving rates $s(t)$, cf. (13.27).

**Remark 13.2** A slip, or printing error, for the *transformed* **CES** dynamic system in Barro and Sala-i-Martin (2004, p. 231) should here be noticed and rectified.

Our Eq. (13.92), cf. (13.95), can be restated as,

$$\dot{x}/x = x - z[1 - \frac{1}{\theta}(z/A)^{\frac{1-\sigma}{\sigma}}] + n + \delta - \frac{\delta + \rho}{\theta}; \quad A = \gamma a^{\frac{\sigma}{\sigma-1}} = \underline{b} \qquad (13.98)$$

For $\dot{x}/x$, Barro and Sala-i-Martin (2004, p. 231, eq. 4.66) with $(-\psi = (1-\sigma)/\sigma)$ give,

$$\dot{x}/x = (A/\theta)[(z/A)^{\frac{1-\sigma}{\sigma}} - 1] - (z - A) + x - \varphi; \; \varphi = (A - \delta)(1 - \frac{1}{\theta}) + \frac{\rho}{\theta} - n$$
$$= x - z[1 - \frac{1}{\theta}(z/A)^{\frac{1-2\sigma}{\sigma}}] + n + \delta - \frac{\delta + \rho}{\theta} \qquad (13.99)$$

which differs from (13.98) by the *exponent* of $(z/A)$. Clearly, the real number: $z \cdot (z/A)^{\frac{1-2\sigma}{\sigma}}$, (13.99), is with $(A > 0, \sigma > 1)$ not defined for: $z = 0$; hence a computer (using any software program) refuses to solve differential equations involving (13.99)—on either form.

A problem also in their deriving of (13.99) was that it lacked the general outline of *transformations* in Lemma 13.1, which here with **CEIS**: $\eta(\zeta^{-1}(z)x) = 1/\theta$, and **CES**: $f'(\zeta^{-1}(z)) = a\gamma^{\frac{\sigma-1}{\sigma}} z^{\frac{1}{\sigma}}$, cf. (13.32), easily *gives* (13.91–13.92) and (13.98).

But even without the slip, the exposition and "*diagrams*" of the transitional dynamics in Barro and Sala-i-Martin (2004, p. 231) are *not* based on any attempt of *solving* their (eq.4.66) dynamic system—in contrast to *the solutions with phase portraits* in Figs. 13.3 and 13.4, which are not just "well-drawn diagrams" but exhibit *genuine* indisputable *solutions, phase paths*, $\varphi(t) = [k(t), c(t)], t \in \Re$, of system (13.87–13.88)—with their *corresponding solutions, paths*, $[z(t), x(t)], t \in \Re$, of system (13.91–13.92).

Incidentally, dynamic expressions in "the $\dot{x}/x$ style" of (13.98) and (13.99) are apt to miss the *attracting node* on the z-axis, $(\tilde{z}, \tilde{x}) = (A, 0)$, in Fig. 13.4. That this node is indeed attracting under our conditions may be verified by calculating the negative eigenvalues, but the latter calculation is not needed, as the *genuine solutions* below the separator in Fig. 13.4 also *prove* the character of this node on the z-axis. The *qualitative* (arrow) diagram in Barro and Sala-i-Martin (2004, Figure 4.3, p. 231) misses this *attractive node* $(\tilde{z}, \tilde{x})$ in Fig. 13.4 entirely.

### *Parameter Sensitivity of the Separator: Optimal Time Paths*

The *elasticity of intertemporal substitution* ($\boldsymbol{\eta = 1/\theta}$) and the *elasticity of factor substitution* ($\boldsymbol{\sigma}$) are the *key parameters* of (13.87–13.88). As to risk parameter, $\theta = R_r(c)$, Arrow (1971, p. 99) noted that "broadly speaking, the *relative risk aversion* must hover around $\boldsymbol{\theta = 1}$". Browning et al. (1999, p. 552) argue that if constancy across the population is imposed, "there is no strong evidence against $-\eta$ being slightly above - 1", i.e., $\eta < 1$, $\theta$ slightly above 1. On the other hand, Hall (1988) estimated $\eta$ to be far below unity: $0.1 < \eta < 0.4 \Leftrightarrow 10 > \theta > 2.5$.[6] As to $\sigma$, Solow (1956, p. 77) used $\boldsymbol{\sigma = 2}$ for **persistent** growth. Thus, **CES**-*baseline parameters*, (13.90), are: $\boldsymbol{\theta = 1, \sigma = 2}$.

Consider now variations in the CES-baseline parameter set. Several types of sensitivity analysis are possible, starting from a variation of one parameter at a time to simultaneous variations of several parameters. The best *comparability* of *separator* trajectories (with *optimal time paths)* is reached if every *new* parameter

[6] Hall (1988, p. 352) obtained his *interval* of $\eta$ values by directly estimating the Euler-Ramsey equation, (13.20), cf. (13.130), on time series data for consumption growth and asset returns. But his results were based on returns from *financial assets*, which in fact were both positive and negative with an average close to zero; see also Varian (1988). The *parameter* $\theta$ of the *power utility* function (13.79) measures the "degree of concavity" of **u(c)**—with the extreme, $\theta = 0$, (linear), cf. (13.204), and with more concavity for larger $\theta$. It is unbounded for $\theta \leq 1$. The *Bernoulli* (1738, 1954, p. 25), $\boldsymbol{\theta = 1}$, $\boldsymbol{u'(c) = 1/c}$, is the *baseline choice*.

For $\theta > 1 : \lim_{t\to\infty} u(c) = 1/(\theta - 1) = \overline{u}$, and hence $\overline{u}$ is zero for $\theta = \infty$. Let us give sizes of $\overline{u}$ and $u(2)$: $\theta = 5 : \overline{u} = 0.25$ , $u(2) = 0.234$; $\theta = 4 : \overline{u} = 0.33$ , $u(2) = 0.29$; $\theta = 3 : \overline{u} = 0.5$ , $u(2) = 0.375$; $\theta = 2 : \overline{u} = 1.0$ , $u(2) = 0.5$ . Thus for $\theta > 3$, **u(c)** is close to being horizontal after $c = 2$ and seemingly with hardly any purpose ("welfare gain") for **c(t)** going to infinity (persistent growth), see de La Grandville (2017, p. 280). We give cases with $\theta$ in the range of Hall (1988); on $\theta$ estimates closer to 1.4, see Evans (2005, p. 211), Creedy and Guest (2008, p. 124). On $\eta$(**c**), see section "The Affine Dynamics with VEIS Utility Functions".

**Table 13.2** The parameter sets used in the separator sensitivity analyses

| Parameter sets | CES-baseline | High $\theta$ | Low $\theta$ | High $\sigma$ | Low $\sigma$ |
|---|---|---|---|---|---|
| $\theta$ | 1.000 | 3.000 | 0.750 | 1.000 | 1.000 |
| $\rho$ | 0.160 | 0.140 | 0.163 | 0.160 | 0.160 |
| $\sigma$ | 2.000 | 2.000 | 2.000 | 2.500 | 1.500 |
| $\gamma$ | 0.661 | 0.661 | 0.661 | 0.540 | 1.200 |

set generates—e.g.—the *same constant (asymptotic) saving* and *growth* rates, $s^* = 0.25$, $\underline{\widehat{y}} = 0.01$, (lower boundary, limit), as the *CES-baseline* set. To this end we *vary*, $\theta$ but **preserve**, $s^* = 0.25$, $\underline{\widehat{y}} = 0.01$, by allowing another "preference" parameter, namely, $\rho$, to *vary* accordingly. Analogously, when we vary $\sigma$, we adjust another production parameter, namely, $\gamma$. All other parameters are maintained as (13.90) in the CES-*baseline separator* solution (optimal time paths).

To investigate the *sensitivity* of *optimal*—**separator**—time paths to the parameter $\theta$, we select $\theta = 3$ in the range of Hall (1988). But we also take $\theta = 0.75$, as suggested in Andersen et al. (2008, p. 590–601). To reach the constant asymptotic outcome $s^* = 0.25$, $\underline{\widehat{y}} = 0.01$, the necessary values for $\rho$ are: $\rho = 0.140$ and $\rho = 0.163$, respectively; both of them satisfy the requirements of (13.80). To investigate the sensitivity of the optimal time paths to the parameter $\sigma$, we select: $\sigma = 2.5$ and $\sigma = 1.5$. The necessary adaptive values for $\gamma$ (TFP) are: $\gamma = 0.54$ and $\gamma = 1.2$. Table 13.2 summarizes these parameter sets.

Figure 13.7 concentrates on the *variation* in $\theta$ (with adaptive $\rho$), illustrating the **optimal saving rates** and **growth rates** for high and low values of $\theta$. Furthermore, the optimal time paths are shown both for "*primitive/poor*", $\mathbf{k}(0) = \mathbf{100}$, and for " *mature/rich*", $\mathbf{k}(0) = \mathbf{1000}$, economies. Figure 13.7 shows that considerable differences exist in poor economies, as high $\theta$/low $\rho$ generates low and stable saving and growth rates, while low $\theta$/high $\rho$ generates excessive and unstable ones—with those for the CES-baseline lying between these two extremes. These differences are also present in rich economies, even though they are much less prominent. Furthermore, both the *saving and growth rates* are relatively **constant** in "*mature/rich*" economies.

Figure 13.8 concentrates on *variation* in $\sigma$ (with adaptive $\gamma$), illustrating the optimal saving and economic growth rates for primitive, $k(0) = 100$, and mature, $k(0) = 1000$, economies. For **high $\gamma$ / low $\sigma$**, for example, **excessive** saving and growth rates appear initially. Later, both rates level off but still **exceed** in Figure 13.8 those of the CES-baseline and the **low $\theta$/high $\rho$** in Fig. 13.7—even in comparing the mature economies.

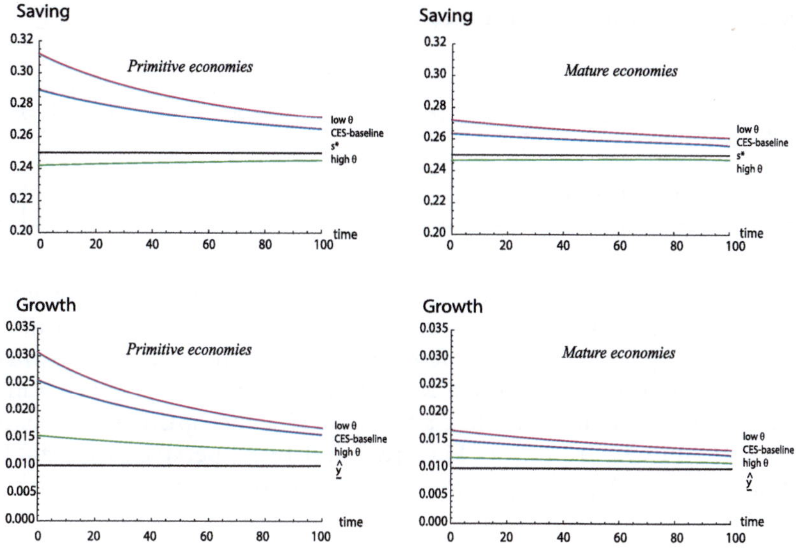


**Fig. 13.7** Low $\theta$/high $\rho$, Table 13.2. **Optimal time paths** for $\mathbf{s(t)}$, (13.26), (13.87–13.88), and $\widehat{\mathbf{y}}(\mathbf{t})$, (13.37), (13.71–13.72), (13.87–13.88), in primitive, $k(0) = 100$, and mature, $k(0) = 1000$, economies

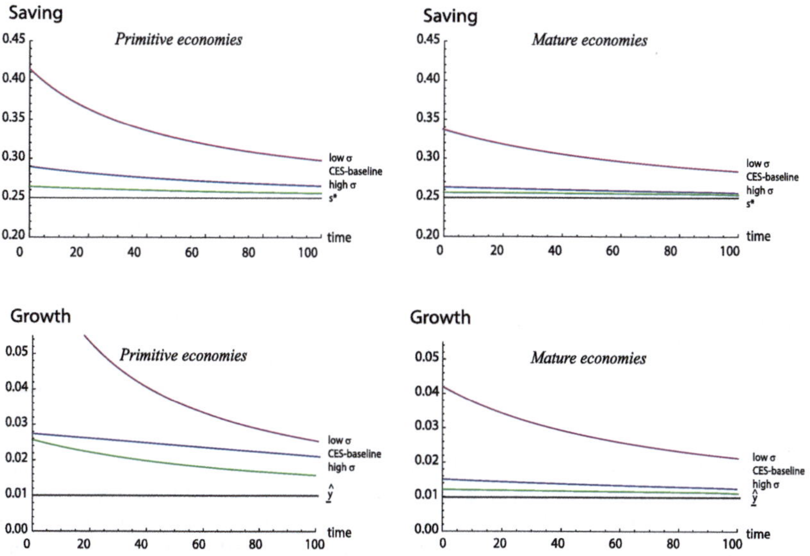


**Fig. 13.8** High $\gamma$/low $\sigma$, Table 13.2. **Optimal time paths** for $\mathbf{s(t)}$, (13.26), (13.87–13.88), and $\widehat{\mathbf{y}}(\mathbf{t})$, (13.37), (13.71–13.72), (13.87–13.88), in primitive, $k(0) = 100$, and mature, $k(0) = 1000$, economies

Despite **asymptotic equivalence** ($t = \infty$), cf. (13.71), (13.97)—$\underline{b} = 0.2$, $\widehat{\underline{y}} = 0.01$, $s^* = 0.25$:

$$\underline{b} = \gamma\, a^{\frac{\sigma}{\sigma-1}} \; ; \; \widehat{\underline{y}} = \frac{\underline{b} - \delta - \rho}{\theta} \; ; \; s^* = \frac{(\underline{b} - \delta - \rho)/\theta + n + \delta}{\underline{b}} \equiv \frac{\widehat{\underline{y}} + n + \delta}{\underline{b}} \tag{13.100}$$

different *parameter* sets can produce very *different optimal time paths* in *primitive economies* . On the other hand, the *sensitivity* to both consumption and production parameters is *restricted* (reduced) in the *mature economies*.[7]

In contrast to the saving rates in *transitions* to *steady states*, de La Grandville (2018, p. 88), King and Rebelo (1993, p. 917), the **optimal** time paths of **s(t)**, (13.26), (13.87–13.88), in Figs. 13.7 and 13.8 [ **persistent** *growth* ] with **CEIS** utility, (13.79), belong to *narrow bands* [ except, high $\gamma$/low $\sigma$ ].

## Ramsey (1928): Affine Dynamics with CEIS Utility

It is seldom recognized that the Ramsey article devoted most pages to model illustrations for a **CES** function of $\sigma = \infty$, *Ramsey* (1928, p. 549), [as *von Neumann* (1945–46, p. 2) adopting as well-known, additive, and linear production processes for each good]: i.e., devoted to determining the *optimal* solutions with **Affine** *Technologies*, **f(k)**, cf. (13.29),

$$Y = F(L, K) = \gamma\,[(1-a)L + aK] \; ; \; y = f(k) = \gamma(1-a) + \gamma a k \tag{13.101}$$

with *constant* **marginal** *productivities*—enabling him to discuss *qualitative solutions* by diagrams. *Ramsey* neither reckoned *future* utilities as equal to *present* ones and *discounted* them at a **constant** *rate* $\boldsymbol{\rho}$, Ramsey (1928, p. 553). Moreover, he also used **CEIS** *utility* function (13.79) with **marginal** *utility*: $u'(c) = c^{-\theta}$, cf. Ramsey (1928, p. 555).

[7] In Caselli and Feyrer (2007, p. 549), detailed GDP accounting calculations gave tables with estimated marginal products of capital, $\mathbf{MP_K}$, in the interval: **0.07–0.11**, for OECD economies and within the range: **0.12–0.17**, for poor countries. Real capital formation (investment projects) probably requires "*real interest*" rates, $MP_K$, hovering around **0.10**, in order to be implemented in uncertain world.

Consider as above and in Table 13.1 again a case for $\sigma = 1.5$, with the values of the seven parameters: $\gamma = 0.88$, $a = 0.5$, $\sigma = 1.5$, $\delta = 0.01$, $n = 0.01$, ($\theta = 5 \Leftrightarrow \eta = 0.2$), $\rho = 0.09$; $\underline{b} = \gamma\, a^{\frac{\sigma}{\sigma-1}} = 0.11$, $\widehat{\underline{y}} = (\underline{b} - \delta - \rho)/\theta = 0.002$, cf. (13.31), (13.71), $s^* = 0.20$, (13.97). The selected $\rho = 0.09$ satisfies the requirements of (13.80): $0.10 > \rho > 0.025$. If $\theta = 1$ here was used, we get, $\widehat{\underline{y}} = (\underline{b} - \delta - \rho)/\theta = 0.01$, cf. (13.31), (13.71), $s^* = 0.27$, (13.97), with the interval (13.80), for $\rho$: $0.10 > \rho > 0.055$..

Thus, by (13.101), (13.23–13.24), (13.87–13.88), the *optimal control* system is **Affine Dynamics**:

$$\dot{k} = \gamma\,[\,1 - a + ak\,] - (n+\delta)\,k - c \;=\; \gamma(1-a) + (\gamma a - \delta - n)\,k - c \tag{13.102}$$

$$\dot{c} = \frac{1}{\theta}\,[\,\gamma a - \delta - \rho\,]\,c\,;\;\; \dot{c} = 0 : c = 0\,,\; \dot{k} = 0 : \; c = \gamma(1-a) + (\gamma a - \delta - n)\,k \tag{13.103}$$

The *transformed* **nonlinear** dynamic system of **Affine** system (13.102–13.103), cf. (13.91–13.92), is,

$$\dot{z} = [\,a\,\gamma\; - z\,]\,[\,z\, - \,x\, - \,n\, - \delta\,] \tag{13.104}$$

$$\dot{x} = x\,[\,x\; - z + \frac{\gamma\,a\, - \delta - \rho}{\theta} + n + \delta\,]; \quad node\,:\,(z^*, x^* \;=\; 0) \tag{13.105}$$

The **saddle** point of (13.104–13.105) and **asymptotic** *saving/growth rates* are, cf. (13.95), (13.100),

$$\begin{aligned} z^* \;&=\; \underline{b} \;=\; \gamma\,a\;;\;\; x^* = z^*\,[\frac{\theta - 1}{\theta}] + \frac{\delta + \rho}{\theta} \; - n - \delta \\ &= [\,\gamma\,a - \,\delta\,]\,[1 - \frac{1}{\theta}] + \frac{\rho}{\theta} \; - \,n \end{aligned} \tag{13.106}$$

$$s^* \;=\; 1 \; - \; \frac{x^*}{z^*} \;=\; \frac{(\gamma\,a\; - \;\delta\; - \;\rho\,)/\theta\; + \;n\; + \;\delta}{\gamma\,a} \;=\; \frac{\widehat{\underline{y}} + n + \delta}{\gamma\,a} \tag{13.107}$$

Thus the *equations* (13.101–13.107) **are** (our notation) the **Ramsey Saving** model of *infinite time*—with or without discounting—that Ramsey (1928, p. 550, p. 553–554) examined for the actual *solutions*. He also—"instead of community, which lives forever"—examined finite time implications, involving issues of sizes of terminal capital, bequest, Ramsey (1928, p. 552), which we, for the sake of getting clear succinct analytical results, have completely avoided.

Let us first take his saving model cases with *discounting*, (**$\rho >$ 0**). He gives **qualitative** solutions (rules) of how much should be saved, distinguishes between labor (earned) and capital (unearned) incomes, uses diagrams of marginal utility curves of capital income, upon which a particular slope geometrically determines the optimal saving rate for a given capital income. But certainly **no dynamic solutions** (or asymptotic numbers) are given by Ramsey for the *saving rates*, incomes, or other variables. That is, however, what Eqs. (13.102–13.107) can now provide with his technology assumption (13.101).

We will here first relate Ramsey *model solutions* of (13.102–13.107) to our former asymptotic equivalence requirement, cf. (13.100), Table 13.2, of the solutions in Figs. 13.3, 13.4, 13.5, 13.6, 13.7, and 13.8, by adapting (calibrating) the size of: $\underline{b} = z^* = (Y/K)^*$, (13.60), (13.65), (13.95), to the size: $\underline{b} = \gamma a$ in (13.106). Ramsey did not offer numbers for the long-run capital-output ratio, or reciprocal $z^*$; hence we may select $z^* = \gamma a = 0.20$, implying the same asymptotic equivalence as (13.100). With *CES-baseline*, (13.90), ($\delta = 0.03$, $\rho = 0.16$, $n = 0.01$, $\theta = 1$) and $\gamma a = 0.20$, we also need in (13.102–13.103)—but not (13.104–13.105)—a splitting $\gamma a$ into a size of $\gamma$ (TFP) and **a** (capital intensity); we choose for (13.102–13.103): $\gamma = 1, a = 0.2$.

Despite **solutions** of now fully specified (13.102–13.107) have *asymptotic equivalence* with the *solutions* shown in Figs. 13.3, 13.4, 13.5, 13.6, 13.7, and 13.8, $\underline{b} = \gamma a = 0.2$, $s^* = 0.25$, $\underline{\hat{y}} = 0.01$—they are *not* the *same* as those depicted in Figs. 13.3, 13.5, 13.6, 13.7, and 13.8, especially not for *non-optimal* time paths. But **optimal** time of paths of (13.102–13.107)—not shown—*resemble* those with high $\sigma$ (2.5) in Fig. 13.8.

Keeping $\gamma a = 0.20 = z^* = (K/Y)^* = 5$, we want to see "*Ramsey*" *model* (13.101–13.107) results *deviating* from the CES-baseline parameters ($\delta = 0.03, \rho = 0.16, n = 0.01, \theta = 1$).

If we instead use $\boldsymbol{\theta} = \mathbf{2}$, then we now get by (13.107): $s^* = 0.225$, $\underline{\hat{y}} = 0.0050$—i.e., a 10 percent reduction in $s^* = 0.25$ has *halved* the long-run (asymptotic) growth rate. If we take $\boldsymbol{\theta} = \mathbf{0.75}$, then we get the larger numbers: $s^* = 0.267$, $\underline{\hat{y}} = 0.0133$—that are still economically sensible and in observable intervals, cf. (13.27)—demonstrating that in Ramsey saving models rather *small absolute increases* in asymptotic *saving* rate $s^*$ indeed *significantly enhance* the asymptotic *growth* rate, $\underline{\hat{y}}$.

As to the *size* in (13.103) of the *time preference* (discount rate) parameter, $\rho < \gamma a - \delta$, Ramsey (1928, p. 553) envisioned small numbers: $\rho \approx 3/4$ percent $= 0.0075$, and in special cases, $\rho = 0$. Let us examine Ramsey model *implications* of *assumption*: $\rho = 0$. With $\underline{b} = \gamma a$ and $\rho = 0$, the sufficient existence condition (13.62) for a *separator* becomes:

$$1/\theta = \overline{\eta} < (\gamma a - \delta - n)/(\gamma a - \delta) = 1 - 0.01/0.17 = 0.941 \Leftrightarrow \theta > 1.063 \tag{13.108}$$

But sufficient optimality condition (13.63) cannot be satisfied with $\rho = 0$. However, (13.63) may here not be necessary, as $\theta > 1.063$ implies that the *isoelastic* $u(c)$ is *bounded above*, such that *convergence* of $\boldsymbol{U^*}$, (13.2), is ensured for an "individual"—as original in Ramsey (1928). But we are in (13.102–13.103) and (13.104–13.105) dealing with **V**, (13.3), of a *society* with *increasing* population and *persistent* growing solutions, [ **k(t)**, **c(t)** ], where the optimal solution has to satisfy the *transversality* condition (13.78) that does require: $\boldsymbol{\rho > n > 0}$. Using the numbers in (13.108), we find from (13.107) and $\rho = 0$ exorbitant growth and saving rates: $\widehat{y} = 0.17/1.063 = 0.16$, $s^* = (0.16+0.04)/0.20 = 1$—certainly **not** optimal, i.e., $\boldsymbol{\rho} = \mathbf{0}$ must be **ruled out** in (13.102–13.105). Any $\boldsymbol{\rho}$ must always satisfy the **constraint** (13.80).

The *Affine* dynamic system (13.102–13.103) is solved **explicitly** below in (13.124) by combining a *particular* solution of (13.102–13.103), (13.120–13.121), with the *general* solution of the *linear* system.

General **closed-form solutions** for *affine systems* will enable us to see *non-optimal* and *optimal* time paths directly as **parametric time functions**, including **initial values** of the **control** variable, **c(0)**—instead of the **computer solutions** shown in Figs. 13.3, 13.4, 13.5, 13.6, 13.7, and 13.8.

### *Linear Dynamics in Economic State Space: (k, c)-Plane*

The *linear* dynamics—with, $y = f(k) = \gamma a k$, (13.101–13.103); **AK**-model, $B = 0$, (13.165)—is,

$$\dot{k} = (\gamma a - \delta - n)k - c \equiv a_{11} k + a_{12} c \; ; \quad a_{11} = 0.16, \quad a_{12} = -1 \tag{13.109}$$

$$\dot{c} = (1/\theta)[\gamma a - \delta - \rho]c \equiv a_{22} c \; ; \quad a_{21} = 0, \quad a_{22} = 0.01 \tag{13.110}$$

and CES-baseline parameters, (13.90): $\underline{b} = \gamma a = 0.20$, $\delta = 0.03$, $n = 0.01$, $\rho = 0.16$, $\theta = 1$. As (13.102–13.103), the system (13.109–13.110) has a *triangular coefficient* matrix, implying that,

$$\forall t \; : \frac{\dot{c}(t)}{c(t)} = \widehat{c(t)} = \frac{1}{\theta}[\gamma a - \delta - \rho] = a_{22} = \underline{\widehat{y}} \; ; \quad a_{22} = 0.01 \tag{13.111}$$

For outlining the phase portrait, we have here the *isocline*, $\dot{k} = 0$, as a *straight* line:

$$\dot{k} = 0 : \; c = (\gamma a - \delta - n)k = a_{11} k \; ; \quad a_{11} = 0.16 \tag{13.112}$$

Solving *linear autonomous* systems as (13.109–13.110) is described in expositions of standard textbooks, e.g., Pontryagin (1962, p. 115), Birkhoff and Rota (1989, p. 141), Gandolfo (2010, p. 263). Jensen (1994, p. 212), here Chap. 29, section "The Linear System, Director Function, and Directrices" complements results in Pontryagin (1962), Birkhoff and Rota (1989) with "translating" their coordinate solutions into the *economic state space*, $(k, c)$.

Hence we can be brief. System matrix of (13.109–13.110) has determinant, $|A| = a_{11} a_{22} \neq 0$, and thus two linearly independent *eigenvector*, e.g., represented by $(1, \alpha_1)$, $(1, \alpha_2)$, or *rays* with *slopes*, $\alpha_1$ and $\alpha_2$, where here,

$\alpha_1 = a_{11} - a_{22}$ and $\alpha_2 = 0$. The *real eigenvalues* are here, $\boldsymbol{\lambda_1 = a_{22}}, \boldsymbol{\lambda_2 = a_{11}}$; cf. Chap. 29, Eq. (29.14.1) . **Ray** with **slope** $\boldsymbol{\alpha_1}$ is trajectory for the **separator** of Ramsey dynamics (13.109–13.110); for selected $k_0$, **optimal** $\mathbf{c_0^*}$ is given by:

$$\frac{c^*}{k^*} = \alpha_1 = a_{11} - a_{22} = [\gamma a - \delta][1 - \frac{1}{\theta}] + \frac{\rho}{\theta} - n$$
$$= \frac{c_0^*}{k_0} = \frac{15}{100} = 0.15 = x^* \tag{13.113}$$

The unique **optimal time paths** $\boldsymbol{\varphi^*(t)}$, (13.64), along *trajectory* (13.113), are expressed by:

$$\forall t \;\; \varphi^*(t) \equiv [k^*(t), c^*(t)] = e^{a_{22}t}[k_0, c_0^*] = k_0 e^{a_{22}t}[1, \alpha_1];$$
$$a_{22} = \frac{\gamma a - \delta - \rho}{\theta} \tag{13.114}$$

and shown in Fig. 13.9a for the *coefficients* of (13.109–13.110) with: $\boldsymbol{k_0 = 100}, \mathbf{c_0^* = 15}$. The **constant** (time-invariant) **optimal** saving rate $\mathbf{s^*(t)}$ along **separator** (13.114) is:

$$s^*(t) = 1 - \frac{c^*(t)}{y^*(t)} = 1 - \frac{\alpha_1 k^*(t)}{\gamma a k^*(t)} = 1 - \frac{\alpha_1}{\gamma a}$$
$$= \frac{[\gamma a - \delta - \rho]/\theta + n + \delta}{\gamma a} = 1 - \frac{x^*}{z^*} = 0.25 \tag{13.115}$$

In Fig. 13.9d, $\mathbf{s^*}$ formulas, (13.107), (13.100), are here **actual** (not only asymptotic) numbers. All time paths $\varphi(t)$—*General Solution* $[k(t), c(t)]$ of (13.109–13.110)—have the *closed form*:

$$\varphi(t) : k(t) = k_0 e^{a_{11}t} + \frac{c_0}{a_{11} - a_{22}}(e^{a_{22}t} - e^{a_{11}t}) \; ; \; c(t) = c_0 e^{a_{22}t} \; ; \; k_0 = 100 \tag{13.116}$$

These simple parametric *initial value problem solutions* for the *coordinates*, $\mathbf{k(t)}$ and $\mathbf{c(t)}$, (13.116) were derived[8] in Chap. 29, Eq. (29.59–29.60), partly by *calculus* methods, **not** by the reduction of a *coefficient matrix* to *Jordan form*. Inserting $\mathbf{c_0^*} = \boldsymbol{k_0\,(a_{11} - a_{22})}$ into (13.116) gives (13.114).

[8] In eigen-vector space, the *phase portraits* of the *general solution* (13.116) is called an *unstable node*, Pontryagin (1962, p. 117), Birkhoff and Rota (1989, p. 148); cf. Arnold (1973, p. 118).

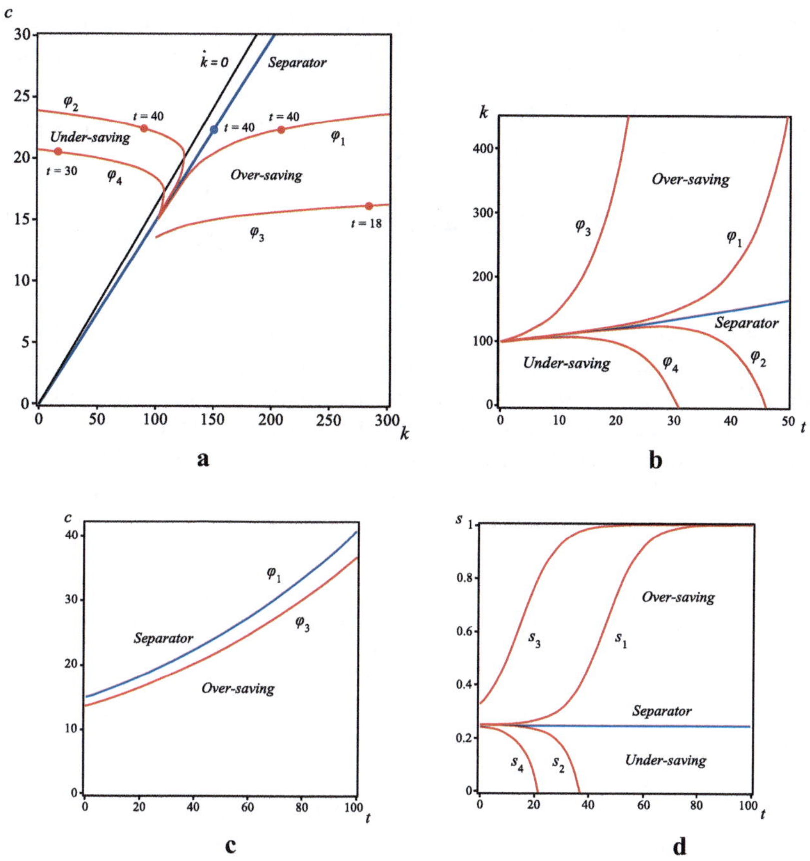


**Fig. 13.9** (**a**) The **phase portrait**—$\varphi(t)$—(13.116), in the **state** $(k, c)$ **space**; $k(0) = 100$ with **initial** (control) values: $c_0^* = 15$, **separator**; $c_0 = 15{\cdot}0.999 = 14.985$, $\varphi_1(t)$; $c_0 = 15 \cdot 0.9 = 13.5$, $\varphi_3(t)$; $c_0 = 15 \cdot 1.001 = 15.015$, $\varphi_2(t)$; $c_0 = 15 \cdot 1.01 = 15.15$, $\varphi_4(t)$. (**b**) *Time paths* for: $k(t)$—of $\varphi(t)$, (13.116)—short run. (**c**) *Time paths* for: $c(t)$—of $\varphi(t)$, (13.116)—long run. (**d**) *Time paths* for: $s(t)$, (13.119), (13.113)-along $\varphi(t)$, (13.116)

The *k-axis* **is** a solution (non-optimal) of (13.109–13.110) with $c_0 = 0$ in (13.116), cf. Fig. 13.1b,

$$\alpha_2 = 0 \;:\; \varphi(t) \;\equiv\; [\,k(t),\, c(t)\,] \;=\; e^{a_{11}t}\,[\,k_0, 0\,]\,; \qquad k_0 = 100 \qquad (13.117)$$

For various $c_0$, other non-optimal $\varphi(t)$, (13.116), are seen of *each* coordinate: Fig. 13.9b–c.

From (13.116), we directly get time paths for $k(t)/c(t)$ as (13.118), and next some *non-optimal* saving paths $s(t)$, (13.119), *depicted* in Fig. 13.9d, too.

$$k(t)/c(t) = \frac{1}{a_{11} - a_{22}} + [\frac{k_0}{c_0} - \frac{1}{a_{11} - a_{22}}]\, e^{(a_{11} - a_{22})t} \; ; \quad k_0 = 100 \qquad (13.118)$$

$$s(t) = 1 - c(t)/y(t) = 1 - c(t)/\gamma\, a\, k(t) = 1 - \frac{1}{\gamma\, a} \frac{c(t)}{k(t)} \; ; \quad k_0 = 100 \qquad (13.119)$$

In the (k,c) plane, Fig. 13.9a, all **over-saving** paths of (13.116) always remain above the k-axis and end as transformed for the **(z,x)** plane in the attractive **node** point: $(z^*, x^* = 0)$. All **under-saving** paths of (13.116) end in finite time in both spaces, cf. Figs. 13.3 and 13.4, where the isocline of vertical tangents, $\dot{k} = 0$, corresponds to an isocline, $\dot{x} = 0$, of horizontal tangents. The **optimal control** path (*separator*) of Ramsey *initial value solutions* (13.116) with *optimal* $\mathbf{c}_0^*$ (13.113) ends transformed for the **(z,x)** plane in the **saddle** point, $(\mathbf{z}^*, \mathbf{x}^*)$.

The *geometric* phase portrait in Fig. 13.9a may *exaggerate* the *time* path *differences* between the **separator** and the other $\varphi_i(t)$ solutions—especially between the optimal (separator) solution and over-saving solutions, $\varphi_1(t)$ and $\varphi_3(t)$; for particular time values (t), **dot** points in Fig. 13.9a give sizes of $k(t)$ and $c(t)$. For $t = 40$, there is almost no difference between the *size* of **c(t)** upon the *separator* and $\varphi_1(t)$. In fact, they "coincide" for 100 years, cf. **c(t)** paths in Fig. 13.9c. Their time paths of **k(t)** differ in larger absolute sizes after 20 years as seen in Fig. 13.9b. Similarly, their actual *saving rates* **s(t)**, (13.119), start to deviate absolutely after 20 years in Fig. 13.9d. Evidently, the consequences of larger differences in initial values **c(0)** away from $\mathbf{c}_0^*$ increase *exponentially* over time for our *explicit solutions*: **c(t)**, **k(t)**, and **s(t)**, of the Ramsey model (13.109–13.110).[9]

### *The Affine Dynamic System with CEIS Utility*

The Ramsey *optimal control* system was **Affine Dynamics**, (13.101–13.103), cf. (13.109–13.110):

$$\dot{k} = \gamma(1 - a) + (\gamma a - \delta - n)\, k - c \equiv \mu_1 + a_{11}\, k + a_{12}\, c \qquad (13.120)$$

$$\dot{c} = (1/\theta)\, [\, \gamma a - \delta - \rho\, ]\, c \equiv a_{22}\, c \qquad (13.121)$$

[9] With *linear* technology, $f(k) = rk = \gamma a\, k$, CEIS, $u(c)$, (13.79), and exponential discounting, $e^{-\rho t}$, (13.2), Romer (1986a, p. 903) gives restriction: $\rho > (1 - \theta)\, r$, for *convergence* of the integral $U^*$ (13.2). With $r = \gamma a = \underline{b}$, $n = \delta = 0$, $\overline{\eta} = 1/\theta$, the *condition* (13.62) for a *separator* (13.114) is: $\rho > r\,(1 - \theta)$; more on convergence and separator conditions, see footnote 30.

with $\mu_1 = \gamma(1-a) = 1(1-0.2) = 0.8$, $a_{11} = 0.16$, $a_{12} = -1$, $a_{22} = 0.01$; $\theta = 1$.

The isoclines of system (13.120–13.121), $\dot{k} = 0, \dot{c} = 0$, are straight and horizontal lines:

$$\dot{k} = 0 : \ c = \gamma(1-a) + (\gamma a - \delta - n) k = \mu_1 + a_{11} k \ ; \quad \dot{c} = 0 : c = 0 \tag{13.122}$$

The affine system (13.120–13.121) is *nonsingular*, and it has a unique *critical point*, $(\tilde{\mathbf{k}}, \tilde{\mathbf{c}})$, as:

$$\dot{k} = 0, \dot{c} = 0 : \ \tilde{k} = -\mu_1/a_{11} = -0.8/0.16 = -5.00, \quad \tilde{c} = 0 \tag{13.123}$$

The **explicit general** solution, $\psi(t) = [\,\mathbf{k(t)}, \ \mathbf{c(t)}\,]$ of (13.120–13.123) is, cf. Chap. 29, Eq. (29.197.1–29.197.2):

$$\psi(t) \ : \ k(t) = \tilde{k} + (k_0 - \tilde{k})\, e^{a_{11} t} + \frac{c_0}{a_{11} - a_{22}} (\, e^{a_{22} t} - e^{a_{11} t}\,) \ ; \ c(t) = c_0\, e^{a_{22} t} \tag{13.124}$$

The time paths for $k(t)/c(t)$ follow from (13.124) and become, with parameter values above,

$$\frac{k(t)}{c(t)} = [\,\tilde{k} + (k_0 - \tilde{k})\, e^{a_{11} t} + \frac{c_0}{a_{11} - a_{22}} (\, e^{a_{22} t} - e^{a_{11} t}\,] / c_0\, e^{a_{22} t} \tag{13.125}$$

$$= \frac{1}{a_{11} - a_{22}} + \frac{\tilde{k}}{c_0} e^{-a_{22} t} + (\frac{k_0 - \tilde{k}}{c_0} - \frac{1}{a_{11} - a_{22}})\, e^{(a_{11} - a_{22}) t} \tag{13.126}$$

$$= \frac{1}{0.15} - \frac{5}{c_0} e^{-0.01 t} + (\frac{k_0 + 5}{c_0} - \frac{1}{0.15})\, e^{0.15 t} \tag{13.127}$$

The time paths of the saving rates $\mathbf{s(t)}$ come from (13.101), $\mu_1 = \gamma(1-a)$, and (13.124), as

$$s(t) = 1 - c(t)/y(t) = 1 - \frac{c(t)}{\mu_1 + \gamma\, a\, k(t)} \ ; \ \lim_{t\to\infty} s^*(t) = 1 - \frac{0.15}{\gamma a} = 0.25 \tag{13.128}$$

Note that with $\mu_1 = 0$, and $\tilde{k} = 0$, then (13.128) is reduced to (13.119), and (13.126) to (13.118).

Selected initial values, $(k_0, c_0)$, give the solutions (time paths) to the *affine* dynamics in Fig. 13.10a–d. Our initial value of $k(0)$ is: $k(0) = 100$. The corresponding *optimal initial value* of control variable, $\mathbf{c}^*(\mathbf{0})$, comes from the

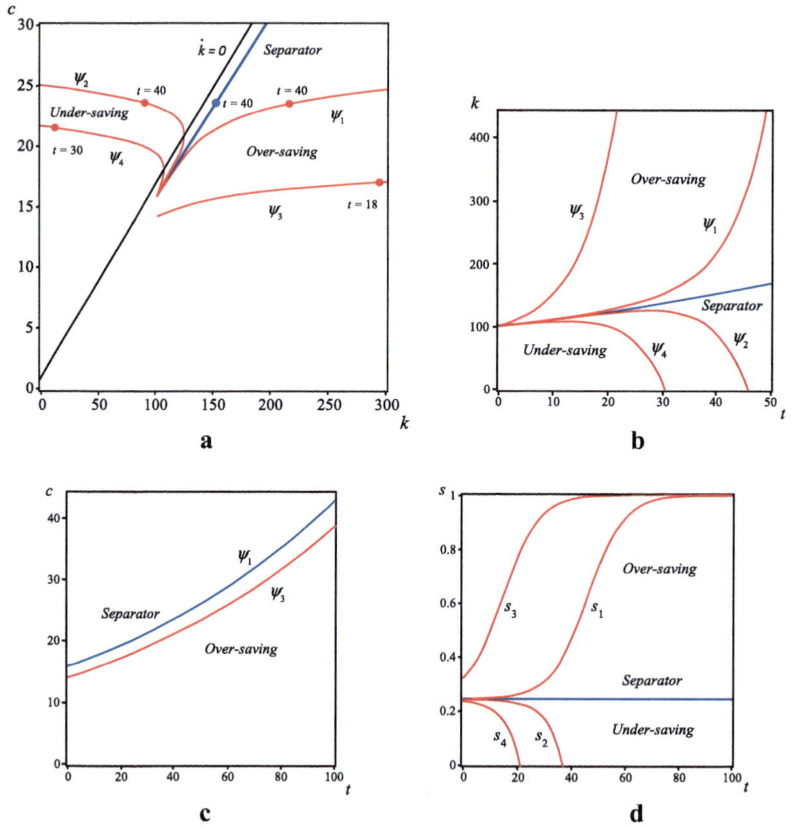


**Fig. 13.10** (**a**) The **phase portrait**—$\psi(t)$—(13.124), in the **state** $(k, c)$ **space**; $k(0) = 100$ with **initial** (control) values: $c_0^* = 15.75$, **separator**; $c_0 = 15.75 \cdot 0.999 = 15.734$, $\psi_1(t)$; $c_0 = 15.75 \cdot 0.9 = 13.275$, $\psi_3(t)$; $c_0 = 15.75 \cdot 1.001 = 15.766$, $\psi_2(t)$; $c_0 = 15.75{\cdot}1.01 = 15.908$, $\psi_4(t)$. (**b**) *Time paths* for: $k(t)$—of $\psi(t)$, (13.124)—short run. (**c**) *Time paths* for: $c(t)$—$\psi(t)$, (13.124)—long run. (**d**) Fig. 13.10d. *Time paths* for: $s(t)$, (13.128–13.129)—along $\psi(t)$, (13.124)

*dominating* (separating) *term* in (13.127) as,

$$\frac{100+5}{c_0} - \frac{1}{0.15} = 0 \Leftrightarrow c^*(0) = 15.75 \quad ; \; s^*(0)$$

$$= 1 - \frac{15.75}{0.8 + 0.2 \cdot 100} = 0.2428 \qquad (13.129)$$

Point: $\mathbf{k}^*(\mathbf{0}), \mathbf{c}^*(\mathbf{0}) = (100, 15.75)$ is *optimal initial values* to (13.124): *separator*, Fig. 13.10a, and (100, 15.75) also *represents* the **endpoint**, $[\bar{k}^*, \bar{c}^*]$, shown in Fig. 13.2b of Theorem 13.2.

A large empirical literature has for decades been devoted to estimating **EIS** elasticities, mostly by adopting **CRRA** preferences (**CEIS** utility) and using the Euler equation (13.20):

$$\widehat{c} = \eta\,(r-\rho) = -\eta\,\rho + \eta\, r = a + \eta\, r \;; \quad r = f'(k) - \delta\;; \quad r = r_i \tag{13.130}$$

to be estimated with $(r)$ as a real interest rate, or some portfolio asset returns, $(r_i)$. There is no consensus on the magnitude of estimated coefficients $\eta$ in (13.130), cf. footnote 6, but micro data (household expenditure surveys) provides estimates[10] of $\eta$ "around 0.3–0.4 for stockholders and around 0.8–1.0 for bondholders, and they are larger for households with larger asset holdings within these two groups", Vissing-Jorgensen (2002, p. 852).

The *elasticity* of *substitution* for the *consumption* between *two* points in *time* $(t, s)$ is,

$$\eta\,[\,c(s), c(t)\,] = -\frac{d\ln[\,c(s)/c(t)\,]}{d\ln[\,u'c(s)/u'c(t)\,]} \tag{13.131}$$

$$\lim_{s\to t}\eta\,[\,c(s), c(t)\,] = -\frac{d\ln c}{d\ln\, u'(c)} = -\,E\,(c, u'(c)) = \eta\,(c) \tag{13.132}$$

that as $s$ converges to $t$, (13.132), has *instantaneous* **EIS** (13.20) as *limit*:[11] $\eta\,(c) = \frac{-\,u'(c)}{u''(c)\,c} > 0$.

Throughout, the *time additive* intertemporal *utility* function, $u\,[c(t)]\,e^{-\rho t} \equiv I(t),\ \forall t \in [0,\infty)]$, (13.1), guides *optimal* time paths of *saving* rates. But the common **CEIS** utility assumption of $\eta\,[c(s), c(t)]$ being a **constant** (*homothetic* preferences)—hence $\boldsymbol{\eta}$ **(c)** *not* depending on consumption level (**c**) in (13.131)—is *unduly* restrictive.[12]

[10] Similar results from *micro data* on $\eta$ are reported by Attanasio and Weber (1989), (1995, p. 1150).

[11] See, e.g., Blanchard and Fischer (1992, p. 40), and Maussner and Klump (1996, p. 121).

[12] Let us briefly return to the problem in Table 13.1 of getting unreasonable high saving rates in models with optimal saving—as especially emphasized by de La Grandville (2018, p. 79) and hereto referring to former difficulties in Ramsey (1928), Goodwin (1961), King and Rebelo (1993).

Ramsey (1928, p. 548) met some difficulties with maximum utility calculations, discounting, proportion of income/saving. However, he did not stop using a production function (CES), utility functions, and a discount rate. The actual *economic relevance* of the **optimal control** path of the Ramsey model depends essentially on the *quantitative size* of the selected *parameters*—coefficients in (13.109–13.110).

But Goodwin (1961, p. 770,774) used: $n = 0.01$, $K/Y = 4 = \underline{b} = \gamma\, a = 0.25$, $\theta = 0.2$, $\rho = 0$, $\delta = 0.03$ (not given). By (13.62): $5 = 1/0.2 < (0.25 - 0.04)(0.25 - 0.03) = 0.95$, i.e., the *separator* does *not* even *exist*—and by (13.107): $\widehat{\underline{y}} = (0.25 - 0.03)/0.2 = 1.1$ ; $s^* = 1.14/0.25 = 4.6$. Evidently, his parameter values have *no relevance* for Ramsey models on infinite time. His model horizon was ten years (plans).

In order to obtain *dynamic numerical* results, however, we must *specify*, **u**(**c**), properly and precisely. Fortunately, we can assume that **u**(**c**) *obeys* the *three-parameter* specification of the *non-homothetic* **HARA** *utility* function (13.81)—which must next be used and demonstrated.

## THE AFFINE DYNAMICS WITH VEIS UTILITY FUNCTIONS

The *affine* dynamic system (13.120–13.121) of *Ramsey* (1928) can easily be *extended* to all members of the Hyperbolic Absolute Risk Aversion (**HARA**) family of *utility* functions.

Using *hyperbolic* **VEIS** *elasticity*, $\eta = \eta(\mathbf{c})$ formula, (13.86), it is seen by (13.23–13.24), (13.101), that Ramsey affine dynamics (13.120–13.121) is now changed to a more *general affine* system,

$$\dot{k} = \gamma(1-a) + (\gamma a - \delta - n)\,k - c \qquad \equiv \mu_1 + a_{11}\,k + a_{12}\,c \tag{13.133}$$

$$\dot{c} = -\nu/\beta\,[\gamma a - \delta - \rho] + 1/\theta\,[\gamma a - \delta - \rho]\,c \qquad \equiv \mu_2 + a_{22}\,c \tag{13.134}$$

with the *parameters*: $\mu_1 = \gamma(1-a) = 1(1-0.2) = 0.8$, $a_{11} = 0.16$, $a_{12} = -1$; $\nu/\beta = 16$, $\mu_2 = -\nu/\beta\,[\gamma a - \delta - \rho] = -16\,(0.01) = -0.16$, $\theta = 0.98$, $a_{22} = (\frac{1}{0.98})\,(0.01) = 0.0102$.

The **isoclines** of system (13.133–13.134), $\dot{k} = 0$, $\dot{c} = 0$, are straight and horizontal lines:

$$\dot{k} = 0 : \; c = \mu_1 + a_{11}\,k > 0 \; ; \qquad \dot{c} = 0 : \; c = -(\mu_2/a_{22}) = (\nu/\beta)\,\theta > 0 \tag{13.135}$$

The *affine* system (13.133–13.134) is *nonsingular* and has the unique *critical point*,[13] ($\tilde{\mathbf{k}}, \tilde{\mathbf{c}}$):

$$\tilde{k} = -\frac{\mu_1}{a_{11}} - \frac{\mu_2}{a_{22}\,a_{11}} = -\frac{\mu_1}{a_{11}} + \frac{\nu}{\beta}\frac{\theta}{a_{11}} = -5 + 98 = 93\;;$$
$$\tilde{c} = -\frac{\mu_2}{a_{22}} = \frac{\nu}{\beta}\theta = 15.68 \tag{13.136}$$

The **explicit general** solution, $\boldsymbol{\psi}(t) = [\,\boldsymbol{k}(t), \boldsymbol{c}(t)\,]$ of (13.133–13.136) is, cf. Chap. 29, Eqs. (29.194–29.197):

$$k(t) = \tilde{k} + (k_0 - \tilde{k})\,e^{a_{11}t} + \frac{c_0 - \tilde{c}}{a_{11} - a_{22}}(\,e^{a_{22}t} - e^{a_{11}t}\,)\;;\quad c(t) = \tilde{c} + (c_0 - \tilde{c})\,e^{a_{22}t} \tag{13.137}$$

[13] Note that critical point (13.136)—in contrast to (13.123)—also depends on the parameters of $\eta(c)$, (13.86).

The time paths for $\boldsymbol{k(t)/c(t)}$ follow from (13.137) and become, with *parameter* values (13.136),

$$\frac{k(t)}{c(t)} = [\tilde{k} + (k_0 - \tilde{k})\, e^{a_{11}t} + \frac{c_0 - \tilde{c}}{a_{11} - a_{22}}(e^{a_{22}t} - e^{a_{11}t}]/[\tilde{c} + (c_0 - \tilde{c})\, e^{a_{22}t}] = \tag{13.138}$$

$$\frac{1}{a_{11} - a_{22}}[\frac{c_0 - \tilde{c}}{c_0 - \tilde{c} + \tilde{c}\, e^{-a_{22}t}}] + \frac{\tilde{k}}{\tilde{c} + (c_0 - \tilde{c})\, e^{a_{22}t}} + \frac{[k_0 - \tilde{k} - \frac{c_0 - \tilde{c}}{a_{11} - a_{22}}]\, e^{(a_{11} - a_{22})t}}{c_0 - \tilde{c} + \tilde{c}\, e^{-a_{22}t}} = \tag{13.139}$$

$$\frac{1}{0.1498}[\frac{1}{1 + e^{-0.0102\,t}/[\frac{c_0}{15.68} - 1]}] + \frac{93}{15.68 + (c_0 - 15.68)\, e^{0.0102\,t}} + \frac{[k_0 - 93 - \frac{c_0 - 15.68}{0.1498}]\, e^{0.1498\,t}}{c_0 - 15.68 + 15.68\, e^{-0.0102\,t}} \tag{13.140}$$

We select here *initial value* of $\mathbf{k(0)}$ as: $\boldsymbol{k(0)} = \mathbf{150}$. The corresponding *optimal initial value* of *control variable*, $\mathbf{c^*(0)}$,[14] comes from the last *dominating* term of (13.140), cf. (13.129):

$$150 - 93 - \frac{c_0 - 15.68}{0.1498} = 0 \Leftrightarrow c^*(0) = 24.218 \tag{13.141}$$

$$s^*(0) = 1 - \frac{24.218}{0.8 + 0.2 \cdot 150} = 0.2137 \tag{13.142}$$

The *explicit general* solution (13.124) to the affine dynamics of the *original Ramsey* model, (13.102–13.103), (13.120–13.121), allowed us in (13.125–13.127) to isolate the dominating (critical) terms that *identify* the *optimal solution (separator)* from non-optimal solutions, i.e., to obtain *exactly* the optimal size of, $\mathbf{c^*(0)} = \mathbf{15.75}$, in (13.129)—that together with other non-optimal values of $\mathbf{c(0)}$ generated the *explicit solutions* (time paths) in Fig. 13.10a–d.

The **crucial** HARA *utility extension* (13.133–13.134) of Ramsey (1928)—shown in Fig. 13.11, cf. Fig. 13.12b—is similarly obtained by using the *explicit general solution*, (13.137), together with, (13.141–13.142).

The *parameter*,[15] $\mathbf{0 < \nu < c}$, can represent a *subsistence minimum requirement* of per capita consumption. The *parameter* $\theta$ essentially retains its role as *elasticity* of *marginal utility* wrt. to *excess* consumption $(\boldsymbol{c - \nu})$, cf. (13.83). With

[14] Numerical precision requires more than 20 digits to obtain this initial value $\mathbf{c^*(0)}$ for the separator.

[15] Positive $\nu$, $\theta$ imply *domains* with *minimum* consumption ($c \geqslant \underline{c} = \frac{\nu}{\beta}\theta > 0$), cf. (13.82).

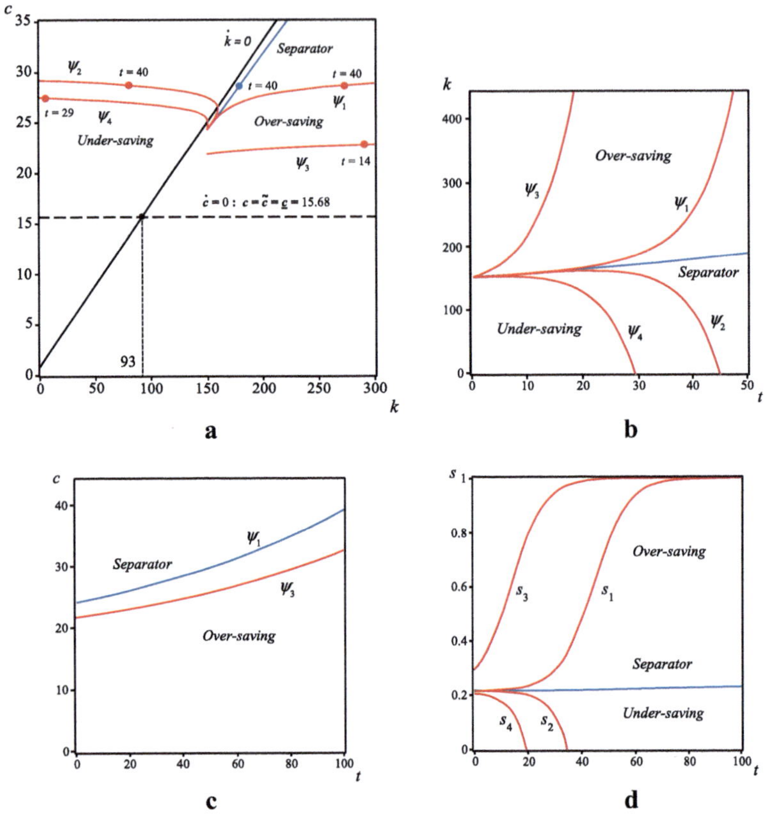


**Fig. 13.11** (**a**) The **phase portrait**—$\psi$(t)—(13.137), in the **state** $(k, c)$**space**; $k(0) = 150$ with **initial** (control) values: $c_0^* = 24.218$, **separator**; $c_0 = 24.218 \cdot 0.999 = 24.194$, $\psi_1(t)$; $c_0 = 24.218 \cdot 0.9 = 21.796$, $\psi_3(t)$; $c_0 = 24.218 \cdot 1.001 = 24.242$, $\psi_2(t)$; $c_0 = 24.218 \cdot 1.01 = 24.460$, $\psi_4(t)$. (**b**) *Time paths* for: $k(t)$—of $\psi(t)$, (13.137)—short run. (**c**) *Time paths* for: $c(t)$—of $\psi(t)$, (13.137)—long run. (**d**) *Time paths* for: $s(t)$, (13.128), (13.141)—along $\psi(t)$, (13.137)

*positive* **v**, **VEIS** of HARA,[16] $\boldsymbol{\eta}$**(c)**, is always an *increasing* concave function, $\eta'(c) > 0$, $\eta''(c) < 0$, cf. (13.86).

[16] For $0 < \nu < c$, $\beta = \theta > 0$, **HARA** (13.81) includes the *quasi-homothetic* Geary-Stone utility function: $u(c) = \frac{\beta}{1-\theta}[(c-\nu)^{1-\theta} - 1]$, $\eta(c) = \frac{1}{\theta}(1 - \frac{\nu}{c}) > 0$, (13.86)—estimated by Ogaki and Atkeson (1997, p. 569).

By using (with $\mathbf{v_i} > \mathbf{0}$) an *extended* **non-homothetic** *addilog utility* function [ *multi-good* $(i = 1 \ldots n)$]—a special multi-good HARA utility function, cf. (13.81)—as *period utility* function: $u(c_1 \ldots c_n) = \sum_{i=1}^{n} \frac{\beta_i}{1-\theta_i}[(c_i - \nu_i)^{1-\theta_i} - 1]$ across Indian households, Atkeson and Ogaki (1996, p. 511, p. 527) obtained for **Total** expenditures, *Intertemporal* elasticities of substitution (**VEIS**): $\eta(c) = 0.5$ (poorest households), $\eta(c) = 0.8$ (richest household)—p. 530, for Country Aggregate data: $\eta(c) = 0.4$ (US), $\eta(c) = 0.3$ (India). [As to **VEIS**, $\eta[c^*(t)]$, *see* Figs. 13.13, 13.16, 13.18b].

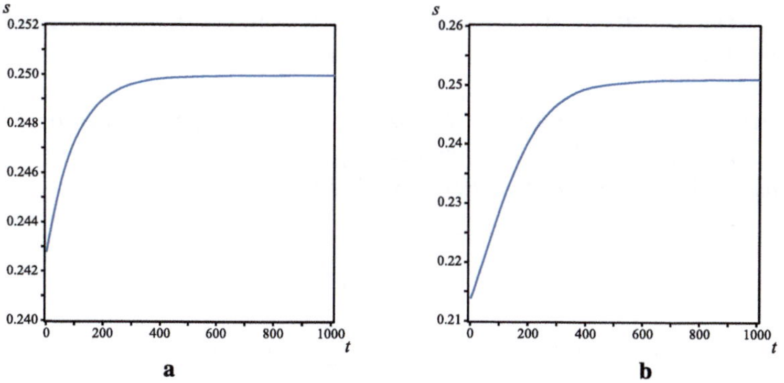


**Fig. 13.12** **Optimal saving rates** $s^*(t)$—shown in Fig. 13.10d (13.128) and 13.11d, (13.147)—exhibited in Figs. 13.12a and b with *finer (decimal) scaling* of the vertical axes

**Fig. 13.13** The *endogenous* **VEIS**, $\eta\,(c^*(t)) = \frac{1}{\theta}\,[\,1 - \frac{(\nu/\beta)\,\theta}{c^*(t)}\,]$, of **HARA**, (13.86), (13.136), (13.151)

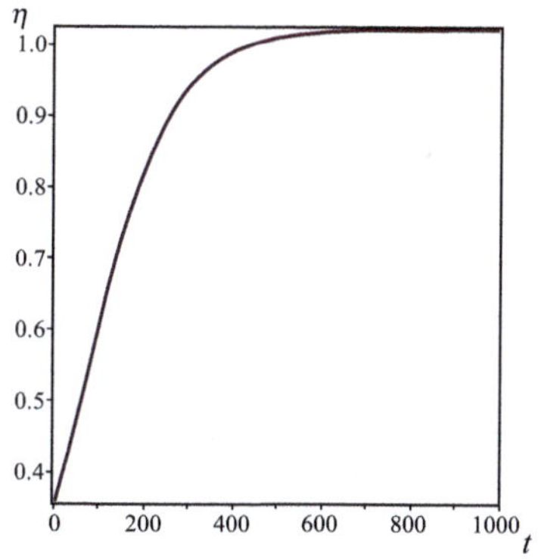


Moreover, with **VEIS/HARA**, we have a fully *endogenously* determined *elasticity* of *intertemporal substitution*, $\boldsymbol{\eta}(\mathbf{c})$, as $\mathbf{c(t)}$ and $\mathbf{k(t)}$ *interact* in **optimal** (Ramsey) dynamics.

The *relation* between the *optimal* value of the *control* variable, $\mathbf{c}^*(\mathbf{0})$, and the *state* variable, $\mathbf{k(0)}$, are called a **policy function**, see Barro and Sala-i-Martin (2004, p. 105).

It will be instructive to see the **precise formula** of this **policy function** for the **general affine** *Ramsey dynamics*, (13.133–13.134)—a formula that here follows directly from the **bracket** of last term, (13.139–13.141):

$$\forall k_0 \;\; \mathbf{c}_0^* \;=\; \tilde{c} + (a_{11} - a_{22})(k_0 - \tilde{k}) \;=\; \tilde{\mathbf{c}} + \alpha_1 (k_0 - \tilde{k}) \;=\; \mathbf{v}\,(\,\mathbf{k}_0\,)\;, \quad \boldsymbol{\alpha}_1 = \mathbf{a}_{11} - \mathbf{a}_{22} \tag{13.143}$$

The parameters $\nu_i > 0$ were referred to as *subsistence* parameters, and the parameters $\theta_i > 0$ as *curvature* parameters, $\beta_i > 0$. If $\theta_i = 1$, $(i = 1 \ldots n)$, then $u(c_1 \ldots c_n) = \sum_{i=1}^{n} \beta_i \, ln\,(c_i - \nu_i\,)$, **LES**—restrictions rejected by time series and panel evidence, (p. 526).

*Summarizing* on *affine* dynamics, *policy* function $v(k_0)$, (13.143), *separator* $\varphi^*(t)$, we state:

**Proposition 13.1** *The general solution (13.137) of **affine** dynamics (13.133–13.134) for $(\tilde{k}, \tilde{c})$, (13.136) gives **explicit** optimal (13.80) solutions for Ramsey technology (13.101), **HARA** utility (13.81–13.83):*

$$a_{11} = \gamma a - \delta - n \ , \ a_{22} = \frac{1}{\theta} [\gamma a - \delta - \rho],$$

$$0 < \alpha_1 = [\gamma a - \delta][1 - \frac{1}{\theta}] + \frac{\rho}{\theta} - n < a_{11} \tag{13.144}$$

$$\forall t \ k^*(t) = \tilde{k} + (k_0 - \tilde{k})\, e^{a_{22}\, t}, \ c^*(t) = \tilde{c} + \alpha_1 (k_0 - \tilde{k})\, e^{a_{22}\, t};$$

$$\tilde{k} = -\frac{\mu_1}{a_{11}} + \frac{\tilde{c}}{a_{11}}, \ \tilde{c} = \frac{\nu\, \theta}{\beta} \tag{13.145}$$

$$\forall t \ \varphi^*(t) \equiv [k^*(t), c^*(t)] = [\tilde{k}, \tilde{c}] + (k_0 - \tilde{k})\, e^{a_{22}\, t} [1, \alpha_1];$$

$$a_{11} > \rho - n > \frac{a_{11}}{1+\theta} \tag{13.146}$$

***Separator***, $\forall t$ $\boldsymbol{\varphi^*(t)}$, *(13.146), represents **geometrically** as a locus (trajectory) the **same curve** as the **policy function**,* $\forall k_0$ $\mathbf{c_0^*} = \mathbf{v(k_0)}$, *(13.143); optimal control function (time path)* $\mathbf{c^*(t)}$*—of* $\boldsymbol{\varphi^*(t)}$ *(13.145)—is "**rectilinear motion**' on optimal straight lines,* $c_0^* = v(k)$, *(13.143), (13.113).*

*Optimal solutions (13.145–13.146) for* $k_0 = 150$ *are illustrated with blue color in Fig. 13.11. Special cases of (13.145–13.146), without **HARA**, are:* $\tilde{c} = 0$, *and* $\tilde{k} = 0, \tilde{c} = 0$*—Figs. 13.10, 13.9.*

*The crucial economic difference between optimal solutions in Figs. 13.10 and 13.11 is better realized by calculating and demonstrating optimal time paths of endogenous **saving** rates,* $\mathbf{s^*(t)}$, *which follow directly from (13.145), (13.143), (13.128), (13.101), and (13.123), (13.136) as:*

$$s^*(t) = 1 - \frac{c^*(t)}{y^*(t)} = 1 - \frac{\tilde{c} + \alpha_1 (k_0 - \tilde{k})\, e^{a_{22}\, t}}{\mu_1 + \gamma\, a\, [\tilde{k} + (k_0 - \tilde{k})\, e^{a_{22}\, t}]};$$

$$[\tilde{k}, \tilde{c}] : [-5, 0], \ [93, 15.68] \tag{13.147}$$

$$s^*(k_0) = 1 - \frac{c^*(k_0)}{y^*(k_0)} = 1 - \frac{\tilde{c} + \alpha_1 (k_0 - \tilde{k})}{\mu_1 + \gamma\, a\, k_0} = \frac{[\gamma a - \alpha_1] k_0 - a_{22} \tilde{k}}{\mu_1 + \gamma\, a\, k_0};$$

$$[-5, 0], [93, 15.68] \tag{13.148}$$

*Curves $s^*(k_0)$, (13.148), are rectangular hyperbolas with asymptote:* $\lim_{k_0 \to \infty} s^*(k_0) = 1 - \frac{\alpha_1}{\gamma a}$. *The time paths (13.147) are monotonic increasing ("generalized logistic") curves, restated as:*

$$s^*(t) = \frac{d_1 + (1 - \alpha_1/\gamma a)\, e^{a_{22} t}}{d_2 + e^{a_{22} t}}, \quad d_1 = \frac{(n+\delta)/\gamma a}{k_0/\tilde{k} - 1},$$

$$d_2 = \frac{1 + \mu_1/\gamma a \tilde{k}}{k_0/\tilde{k} - 1}; \quad \lim_{t \to \infty} s^*(t) = 1 - \frac{\alpha_1}{\gamma a} \tag{13.149}$$

*Optimal saving rates* $\mathbf{s^*(t)}$, *(13.147), with $k_0 = 150$, were seen (blue) in Figs. 13.10d and 13.11d, exhibited with a suitable scaling on the vertical axis in Fig. 13.12a and b; the latter demonstrates much more empirically relevant* ***historical*** *time paths, cf. (13.27). The differences between* $\mathbf{s^*(t)}$ *in Fig. 13.12a and b are solely due to endogenous* ***VEIS***, $\eta\,[c^*(t)] = \frac{1}{\theta} - \frac{\nu/\beta}{c^*(t)}$, *of* ***HARA***, *(13.86), (13.134), calculated by (13.151) and seen in Fig. 13.13.*

*Another empirically important performance criterion is* ***optimal time paths*** *for growth rates,* $\widehat{\mathbf{y^*(t)}}$, *of the endogenous GDP per capita [here given by the denominator of (13.147)],*

$$\widehat{y^*}(t) = \frac{\dot{y}^*(t)}{y^*(t)} = \frac{a_{22}\, \gamma\, a\, (k_0 - \tilde{k})\, e^{a_{22} t}}{\mu_1 + \gamma\, a\, [\tilde{k} + (k_0 - \tilde{k})\, e^{a_{22} t}]}, \quad \tilde{k} : -5,\, 93;$$

$$\lim_{t \to \infty} \widehat{y^*}(t) = a_{22} = \frac{1}{\theta}[\gamma a - \delta - \rho] \tag{13.150}$$

$$\eta\,[c^*(t)] = \frac{1}{\theta}\,[\,1 - \frac{(\nu/\beta)\,\theta}{c^*(t)}\,] = \frac{1}{\theta}\,[\,1 - \frac{(\nu/\beta)\,\theta}{\tilde{c} + \alpha_1 (k_0 - \tilde{k})\, e^{a_{22} t}}\,],$$

$$\tilde{k} : -5,\, 93\,;\ \eta^* = \frac{1}{\theta} = \overline{\eta} \tag{13.151}$$

*With $k_0 = 150$,* ***time paths*** *of (13.150) for Figs. 13.10 and 13.11 are seen in Fig. 13.14a–b, where the differences between* $\widehat{\mathbf{y^*}}\mathbf{(t)}$ *are only due to: CEIS* $= \frac{1}{\theta}$, *VEIS, (13.151), in Fig. 13.13.*

***Proof*** Insert (13.143) into *general* solution, (13.137)—then simple reductions gives (13.145) as *optimal* solution of $k^*(t)$ and $c^*(t)$ with parameters, (13.144). All is in equations cited. □

As mentioned in Fig. 13.11 with HARA, the **isocline** of $\dot{c} = 0$, was no longer the horizontal axis, $c = 0$ (13.58), but now the *horizontal line*: $c = \tilde{c} = \frac{\nu}{\beta}\theta$, (13.59), which in fact—with HARA and persistent growth assumption (13.59)—holds generally for the *nonlinear* dynamic system, (13.23–

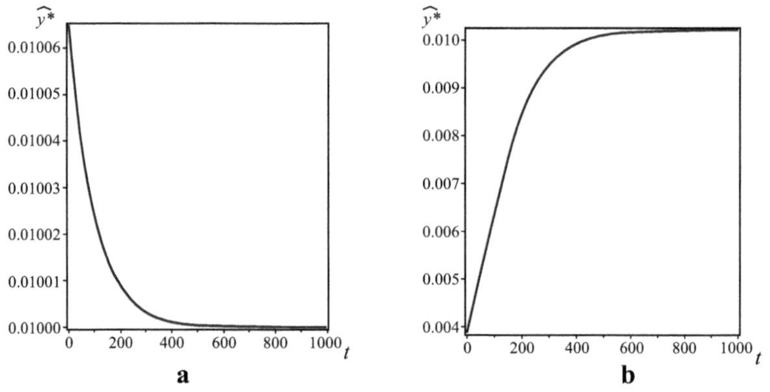


**Fig. 13.14** **Growth rates,** $\widehat{y^*(t)}$, (13.150), of **optimal** GDP *per capita*. (**a**) For **CEIS**, $\eta = \frac{1}{\theta}$, of Fig. 13.10 (**b**) For **HARA**, $\eta\,(c^*(t))$, of Figs. 13.11 as 13.13

13.24), (13.86), that simply gives this *general isocline* as:

$$\dot{c} = 0 \Leftrightarrow c\,\eta(c) = 0 \Leftrightarrow c\,[\frac{1}{\theta} - \frac{\nu/\beta}{c}] = 0 \Leftrightarrow c = \tilde{c} = \frac{\nu}{\beta}\theta \qquad (13.152)$$

The corresponding $\tilde{\mathbf{k}}$ of critical point, $(\tilde{\mathbf{k}}, \tilde{\mathbf{c}})$, is the root $(\tilde{k})$ of (13.23): $f(k) - (n+\delta)k - \tilde{c} = 0$. The $\dot{c} = 0$ isocline and critical point $(\tilde{k}, \tilde{c})$ procedure (13.152) of using HARA, (13.86), can similarly be extended to the CES system, (13.87–13.88), and to the parameters of Fig. 13.3.

The location *critical point*, $(\tilde{\mathbf{k}}, \tilde{\mathbf{c}})$, however, does *not* affect the *validity* of the conditions (13.61–13.63) of Theorem 13.2 that was derived[17] with a **general** $\boldsymbol{\eta}(\mathbf{c})$, including **HARA**, (13.86).

Neither is the general asymptotic growth rate expression (13.71) nor is particular asymptotic saddle-point expression, (13.95–13.96), Fig. 13.4, affected by **HARA** locations of $(\tilde{\mathbf{k}}, \tilde{\mathbf{c}})$ in $\Re^2_+$.

The **asymptotic** results (solutions) are—with our selected (baseline) parameters—given by the *same* formulas for **Affine dynamics**, (13.133–13.134), and the **Nonlinear CES dynamics**, (13.87–13.88), as summarized and collected in:

**Corollary 13.1** *The* ***asymptotic*** *size of* ***ratios****,* $z = Y/K = y/k$, $x = C/K = c/k$, *is:*

$$\frac{y^*}{k^*} = z^* = \underline{b} = \gamma\, a^{\frac{\sigma}{\sigma-1}}\;; \qquad \sigma = \infty:\; z^* = \underline{b} = \gamma\, a = A \qquad (13.153)$$

[17] Condition (13.199) and invariant region $W_\alpha$ are just translated to: $k \geq k_0 > \tilde{k}$, $c > \tilde{c}$ : $R(k) \geq d > 0$.

$$\frac{c^*}{k^*} = x^* = \underline{b}[1 - \frac{1}{\theta}] + \frac{\delta + \rho}{\theta} - n - \delta\,;$$

$$\sigma = \infty : x^* = [\gamma a - \delta][1 - \frac{1}{\theta}] + \frac{\rho}{\theta} - n = \alpha_1 \qquad (13.154)$$

*The limits,* $\mathbf{z}^*, \mathbf{x}^*$, *are asymptotic* ***slopes*** *of* $\mathbf{f}(\mathbf{k})$, *(13.60), and* ***separator*** $\boldsymbol{\varphi}^*(\mathbf{t})$, *(13.64), (13.146).*

***Asymptotic*** *saving rate,* $s^*$, *and per capita* ***asymptotic*** *growth rates,* $\widehat{y^*} = \widehat{c^*} = \widehat{k^*}$, *are:*

$$s^* = 1 - \frac{x^*}{z^*} = \frac{[\underline{b} - \delta - \rho]/\theta + n + \delta}{\underline{b}}\,;$$

$$\sigma = \infty : s^* = \frac{[\gamma\, a - \delta - \rho]/\theta + n + \delta}{\gamma\, a} \qquad (13.155)$$

$$\widehat{y^*} = \overline{\eta}[\underline{b} - \delta - \rho] \equiv \overline{\eta}\, i_p^*\,;\quad \widehat{y^*} = \frac{1}{\theta}[\underline{b} - \delta - \rho]\,;$$

$$\sigma = \infty : \widehat{y^*} = \frac{1}{\theta}[\gamma\, a - \delta - \rho] \qquad (13.156)$$

***Proof*** The expressions of (13.153) were given in (13.65), (13.31), (13.41), (13.61), (13.95), (13.176), (13.101). The expressions of (13.154) were stated in (13.66), (13.96), (13.177), (13.106), (13.113), (13.143), (13.146).

The expressions of (13.155) were presented in (13.41), (13.97), (13.100), (13.107), (13.115), (13.148), (13.149).

The expressions of (13.156) were obtained in (13.71), (13.97), (13.100), (13.107), (13.150).

The parameter, $i_p^*$, (13.156), may be called **saving** (investment) **premium**—in *growing economies* of substituting (adjusting) present consumption ($c_0$) to its optimal level $c_0^*$ and always moving on (13.64). In *asymptotic* state $(\mathbf{z}^*, \mathbf{x}^*)$ of (13.22):[18] $i_p^* = \underline{b} - \delta - \rho$, i.e., $i_p = f'(k) - \delta - \rho = \widehat{c}/\eta\,(c)$, with the limits of $f'(k)$ as $\underline{b}$, and $\widehat{c}/\eta\,(c)$ as $\widehat{c^*}/\overline{\eta} = \widehat{y^*}/\overline{\eta}$. □

The economic implications of the general **asymptotic** $(\mathbf{z}^*, \mathbf{x}^*)$ *saddle point* in **parametric form,** (13.153–13.154), are very **different** from the content of general **steady-state** $[\,\kappa\,,\ \mathbf{c}(\kappa)\,]$ *saddle points,* (13.38–13.39), Table 13.1—as a

[18] We remark that there is no common *interest rate* ($i$) for borrowing or lending sums of money involved in the optimal growth model or (13.22). We can write, $i_p = f'(k) - \delta - \rho = i_K - \delta - \rho$, where $i_K$ in a one-sector model, cf. (13.31), may be called a real "interest rate" of capital. But $\rho$ is the rate of discounting future *utilities* in (13.1) and must be distinguished from discounting future sums of money with *interest rate,* ($i$), as stressed by Ramsey (1928, p. 553). On consistent evaluation of assets with an imposed (exogenous) interest rate, ($i$), in asset price calculations from assets yields, cf. Dhrymes (1962, p. 275).

comparison of *steady state*, $\mathbf{s}(\kappa)$, and *asymptotic* ($\mathbf{s}^*$) in (13.40–13.41) showed, and of course, (13.38–13.39) had **no** *asymptotic* growth rate, ($\widehat{\mathbf{y}^*}$), (13.156), as $\mathbf{i}_{\mathbf{p}}^*$ was *zero.*

Theorem 13.2 and the **closed-** *form solutions* of **General Affine** dynamics, Proposition 13.1 with **HARA** utility,[19] (13.81), **VEIS**, (13.86), can fruitfully be used to economically *study optimal* paths, $\forall t\ \varphi^*(t) \equiv [k^*(t), c^*(t)]$, for many *persistent growth models* with *asymptotic limits*, $\mathbf{z}^*$, $\mathbf{x}^*$, as given in (13.153–13.154).

## Affine Dynamics, Minimal States, and Evolutions

We give *evolutions* of the affine dynamics (13.133–13.134) with new *parameters*[20] and *three* $k_0$:

$$\dot{k} = \gamma(1-a) + (\gamma a - \delta - n)k - c \equiv \mu_1 + a_{11}k + a_{12}c \tag{13.157}$$

$$\dot{c} = -\underline{c}/\theta\,[\gamma a - \delta - \rho] + 1/\theta\,[\gamma a - \delta - \rho]c \equiv \mu_2 + a_{22}c \tag{13.158}$$

$$\gamma a = A = 0.1,\ \delta = 0.01,\ \rho = 0.031,\ n = 0.01,\ \theta = 3,\ \underline{c} = 2;$$

$$\mu_1 = 0,\ \mu_2 = -0.039 \tag{13.159}$$

$$a_{11} = 0.08,\ a_{22} = 0.0197,\ \alpha_1 = 0.0603;\ \tilde{c} = -\frac{\mu_2}{a_{22}} = \underline{c} = 2,$$

$$\tilde{k} = \frac{\tilde{c}}{a_{11}} = 25 \tag{13.160}$$

$$k_0 = \frac{\tilde{k}}{0.70} = 35.7143,\ k_0 = \frac{\tilde{k}}{0.90} = 27.7778,$$

$$k_0 = \frac{\tilde{k}}{0.9991} = 25.0225 \tag{13.161}$$

[19] As mentioned in footnote 12, de La Grandville (2017, p. 280) was critical of maximizing *upper bounded* CEIS cases ($\theta \gg 1$) of $u[c(t)]$. The optimal growth calculations by de La Grandville (2018, p. 89) see any parametric CEIS choice for concave $u[c(t)]$ as incompatible with getting sensible (observable) saving rates (CEIS is "A Disaster in the Making"). *Any* **CEIS** is better replaced by **VEIS**—evident in Figs. 13.12, 13.14.

[20] Steger (2000, p. 350) parameters were: $\gamma a = A = 0.1$, $\delta = 0.02$, $\rho = 0.01$, $n = 0.03$, $\theta = 3$, $\underline{c} = 2$.

He refers this size of $A = 0.1$ to an average return ($Y/K$) on capital for the UK (1870–1914) of 10.5 %. His parameters imply: $a_{11} = 0.05$, $a_{22} = 0.0233$, $\boldsymbol{\alpha}_1 = \mathbf{0.0267}$; $\tilde{\mathbf{c}} = \mathbf{2}$, $\tilde{\boldsymbol{k}} = 40$; $\overline{\eta} = 1/\theta = 1/3$. Steger (2000, eq.6, p. 349) does correspond to the *policy function* $\boldsymbol{v}(\boldsymbol{k}_0)$, stated in our notation, (13.143).

Separator existence condition (13.62) is certainly met by these parameters, as $\rho > -0.07$. But the existence condition $\exists\,\mathbf{V}$, (13.63), (13.80), is *not* met, as, $\rho > 0.0425$, **violates,** $\rho = 0.01$. With here, $n > \rho$, $\theta > 1$, we have bounded utility, $u[\widetilde{c(t)}]$, of individuals together with unbounded welfare of society, utility functional, $\boldsymbol{V}[\widetilde{\boldsymbol{c}(\boldsymbol{t})}]$, (13.3), along the *straight line (separator)* with the slope, $\boldsymbol{\alpha}_1 = \mathbf{0.0267}$.

Proposition 13.1 indicated that—first, deep-rooted determinants (*structural parameters*) shown[21] in[22] (13.159)[23]—second, "*minimum* existence requirements" (*state conditions*) for $(\tilde{k}, \tilde{c})$ in (13.160)—third, *initial values* of endowments $k_0$ in (13.161)—are *always* involved in **evolutions** [actual optimal solution], $\forall t \ \varphi^*(t) \equiv [k^*(t), c^*(t)]$, generated by (13.157–13.158), and all *evolutions* were *explicitly* described by the *closed-form* expressions in (13.145–13.146).

Only the size of the **structural** ("deep") *parameters*: $\gamma\, a\, (A)^{24}\, \delta,\ \rho,\ n,\ \theta,$ (13.159), are involved/determine the **asymptotic** size of any variable—the closed forms given in Corollary 13.1. Note that $(\nu/\beta)$, (13.86), does **not** affect asymptotic sizes of $\overline{\eta}$, (13.80); hence $(\boldsymbol{\nu}/\boldsymbol{\beta})$, (13.145), was **not** in Corollary 13.1. Note that **n** affects: $\alpha_1$, $\mathbf{s}^*$, but *not*: $\widehat{y^*} = \widehat{c^*} = \widehat{k^*}$.

Although sizes of the **minimal states** ("existence requirements"), $(\tilde{\mathbf{k}}, \tilde{\mathbf{c}})$, in (13.160) do **not** affect *asymptotic* numbers in Corollary 13.1, these $(\tilde{\mathbf{k}}, \tilde{\mathbf{c}})$ are *crucial* for understanding the *historical* **diversity** of observed **evolutions** (*optimal paths*) for **any** variable. There have always been *minimum* ("subsistence") *levels* of consumption (food, clothing, shelter, fuel). These components differ between societies, and geographical and historical circumstances; cf. Dalgaard and Strulik (2015, p. 51). The absolute *minimal* ("necessity") consumption is: $\underline{c} = \nu = 2 = \tilde{c}$. The per capita *state* $(\tilde{\mathbf{c}})$ requires the *critical point* $(\tilde{k})$—*minimal resources* depending on *technology* and *population parameters*: $\tilde{\mathbf{k}} = \frac{\tilde{c}}{a_{11}} = \mathbf{25}$.

The three **initial values** $(k_0)$ of the endowments in (13.161) reflect *distinct* relative *initial deviations* (30, 10, 0.0009 percent) of these $(k_0)$ from its *minimal state* $\tilde{k} = 25$. *Sizes* of the absolute and relative *deviations*: $(k_0 - \tilde{k})$, $(\tilde{k}/k_0)$, are crucial and explicit elements in optimal solutions (time paths) for *all* variables—cf. Proposition 13.1, (13.145–13.151)—describing their **evolution**

[21] Our population parameter, $n = 0.01$, approximates UK 1820–1913 population growth rate: 0.009, cf. Lewis (1983), Hansen and Prescott (2002, p. 1208), and growth rate of GDP per capita, UK 1870–1913: $\widehat{y} = 0.012$.

[22] Implications of CEIS, $\theta = 3$, $\theta = 0.75$, were seen with CES technologies in Fig. 13.7. In footnote 6, the range of empirical estimates of $\theta$ was large. In Galor (2010, p. 10), variable *labor* (quality, human capital) *supply* is included in CEIS *utility* functions of each generation with weights, $1 - \theta$, $\theta$—and size, $\theta = 0.225$ in Lagerlöf (2006, p. 128); Galor (2010) OLG model gives: $\widehat{y} = 0.023$, Lagerlöf (2006, p. 130).

Within a Geary-Stone version of **HARA**, cf. footnote 15, we may (as Steger above) use the parameter, $\theta = 3$, [with a different meaning than in CEIS].

[23] The *separator existence condition* is met by the *numerical parameters*, (13.159), as $\rho = 0.031$ clearly satisfies, (13.62): $\rho > -0.03$. Also, $\rho = 0.031$ meets *existence condition* $\exists$ V, (13.63), (13.80): $\rho > 0.12/4 = 0.03$.

[24] Although (13.144–13.146) refer the general affine system (13.133–13.134), we used, $\mu_1 = 0$, in (13.159), as Steger (2000) and Strulik (2010, p. 765: $\delta = 0, n = 0$, A = 0.0067—"a real return on capital around 7 percent that accords with the average return on stock markets for the last century"). $\mu_1 = 0$: $\tilde{c} > 0 \Rightarrow \forall \tilde{k} > 0$, (13.123).

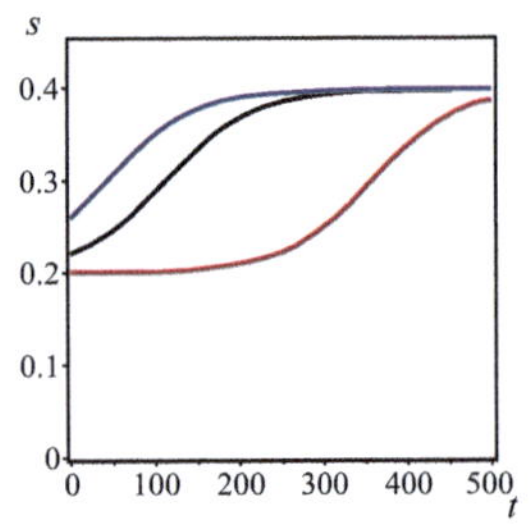


**Fig. 13.15** *Optimal saving rates* $s^*(t)$, (13.147), with *parameters* (13.159–13.160) and *initial values*, (13.161), $k_0$, respectively, (30, 10, 0.0009 percent) above the *minimal state*, (13.160), $\tilde{k} = 25$. *Initial sizes* of $s^*(0)$ are respectively, (0.26, 0.22, 0.20); *asymptotic* limit, $s^* = 0.397$

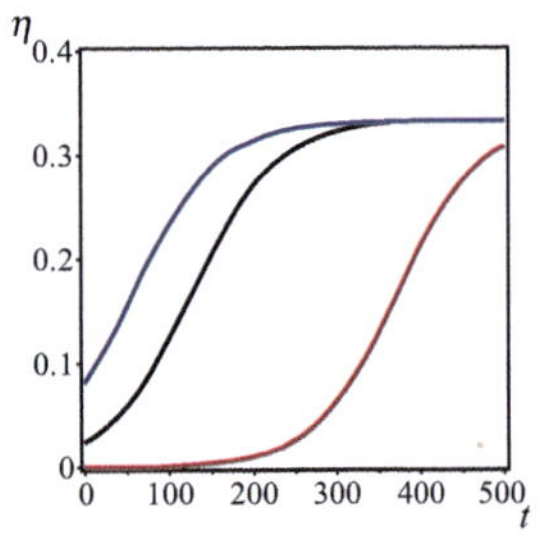


**Fig. 13.16** *The endogenous*, $\eta\,[c^*(t)] = \frac{1}{\theta}(1 - \frac{c}{c^*(t)})$, **VEIS** of **HARA**, (13.151), and (13.159–13.161). *Initial sizes* of $\eta\,[c^*(0)]$ are respectively (0.0814, 0.0258, 0.0002); *asymptotic* limit, $\eta^* = \frac{1}{3}$

("transition") from the *initial* states to infinity—or toward the asymptotic (long-run) *limits*, as was explained above and seen in Corollary 13.1.

All three **phase portraits** behind Figs. 13.15, 13.16, and 13.17 of affine dynamics (13.157–13.161) are similar to Fig. 13.11a (and not repeated here), and they have the *same* straight line *separator* (13.146), *same* critical point $[\,\tilde{\mathbf{k}},\ \tilde{\mathbf{c}}\,]$, (13.160)—but they just **start** at *three* initial values ($k_0$), (13.161).

Thus the dramatic **disparity** between the *three time paths*—optimal **evolutions** of *saving rates* $\mathbf{s}^*(\mathbf{t})$, (13.147), *growth rates* $\widehat{\mathbf{y}^*(\mathbf{t})}$, (13.150), **VEIS**, $\eta\,[c^*(t)]$, (13.151)—in Figs. 13.15, 13.16, and 13.17 is only *due* to the **three** *different initial values* of *factor endowments* ($\mathbf{k}_0$), (13.161)—the asymptotic numbers and the sizes of the three variables at t=0 are given in the captions.

Similar great *disparities* will arise if, for the **same** endowments ($k_0$), three **different minimal states** ($\tilde{\mathbf{c}}$) and hence adjusted ($\tilde{k}$) (13.145) are chosen—which (in contrast to $k_0$) imply three different *locations* of **critical point** $[\,\tilde{k},\ \tilde{c}\,]$ (but same $\alpha_1$) in (13.146). Although such *evolutions* ("transition paths") of

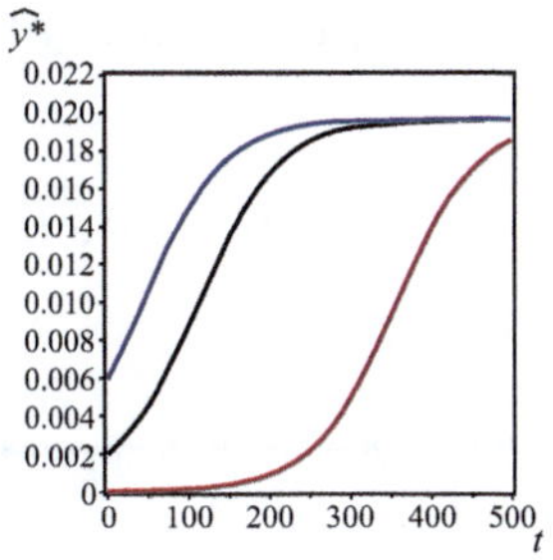


**Fig. 13.17** *Growth rates*, $\widehat{y^*(t)}$, (13.150), of *optimal* GDP per capita with $\eta^*(t)$, as Fig. 13.16. *Initial sizes* of $\widehat{y^*(0)}$ are respectively, (0.006, 0.002, 0.00002); *asymptotic*, $\widehat{y^*} = 0.0197$

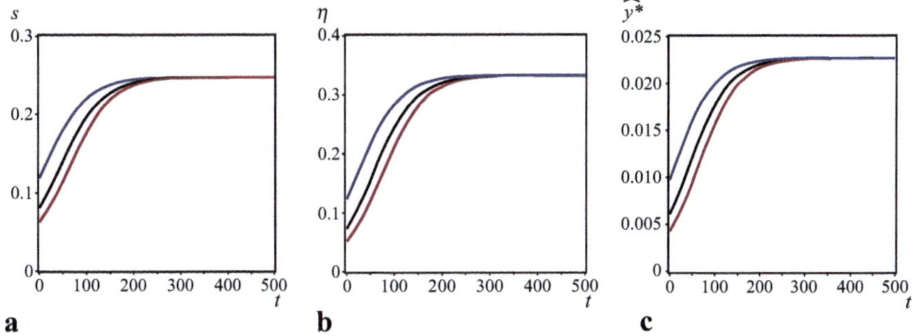


**Fig. 13.18** Optimal **saving** rates $s^*(t)$, (13.147), **VEIS,** $\eta\,(c^*(t))$, (13.151), *growth,* $\widehat{y^*(t)}$, (13.150). *Premises* (13.159–13.160): $A = 0.1$, $\delta = 0.001$, $\rho = 0.031$, $n = 0.001$, $\theta = 3$, $\bar{c} = 2$; $\mu_1 = 0$, $\mu_2 = -0.0454$, $a_{11} = 0.098$, $a_{22} = 0.0227$, $\alpha_1 = 0.0753$, $\tilde{c} = 2$, $\tilde{k} = \frac{\tilde{c}}{a_{11}} = 20.4082$. **Initial values,** (13.161): $k_0 = 35.7143$, $k_0 = 27.7778$, $k_0 = 25.0225$. **Asymptotic** limit: $s^* = 0.247$, initial $s^*(0)$: 0.117, 0.080, 0.062; limit, $\eta^* = 1/3$, initial $\eta\,[c^*(0)]$: 0.1218, 0.0724, 0.0493; limit, $\widehat{y^*} = 0.0227$, initial $\widehat{y^*(0)}$: 0.0097, 0.0060, 0.0042

$s^*(t)$, $\widehat{y^*(t)}$, $\eta\,[c^*(t)]$, *differ* from Figs. 13.15, 13.16, and 13.17, their *asymptotic* ("long-run") numbers would be the *same*—as given in the captions above.

If two **structural parameters** (13.159) are *changed* to: $n = \delta = 0.001$, then critical *point* $[\,\tilde{k},\ \tilde{c}\,]$ and *slope* $(\alpha_1)$ are changed in (13.146). With *same* endowments, optimal evolutions in Fig. 13.18 of $s^*(t)$, $\widehat{y^*(t)}$, $\eta^*(t)$ *differ* much from Figs. 13.15, 13.16, and 13.17; *asymptotic* numbers are changed, too, and also the *initials* at $t = 0$: $s^*(0)$, $\widehat{y^*(0)}$, $\eta\,[c^*(0)]$, see captions, Fig. 13.18.

However, whatever changes are made in structural parameters, minimal states, $(\tilde{k}, \tilde{c})$, initial endowments $(k_0)$, *all optimal time paths* $\boldsymbol{\varphi}^*(\mathbf{t})$, (13.146), are *geometrically* always placed on the **optimal straight lines**, $c^* = v(k)$, (13.143), here rewritten by (13.145) as,

$$\mathbf{c}^* = \mathbf{v}(\mathbf{k}_0) = \tilde{c} - \alpha_1 \tilde{k} + \alpha_1 \mathbf{k}_0 = \mu_1 + a_{11}\tilde{k} - \alpha_1 \tilde{k} + \alpha_1 \mathbf{k}_0$$
$$= \mu_1 + a_{22}\tilde{k} + \alpha_1 \mathbf{k}_0 \; ; \; k_0 \geqq \tilde{k} \qquad (13.162)$$

This simple function (*intercept*, *slope*) unifies **separators** of Figs. 13.9a, 13.10a, 13.11a, and *any* separator of **affine dynamics** (13.133–13.134). It is a **synthesizing function**[25] of *optimal controls.* Fundamentally, optimal control problems were solved in their general form by finding the *required* optimal[26] *initial controls*: $\mathbf{c}^*(\mathbf{0})$, e.g., (13.129), Figs. 13.9a, 13.3.

But instead of a function giving the *control* at an *instant*, $c^*(0)$, it is sometimes possible to give the optimal control variable for *each* possible *state* of the system—a function $c = v(k_0)$, here (13.162). By such optimal *synthesizing* function, other optimal synthesizing relations can be derived for *summarizing* essential properties/results of *affine dynamics.*

The *optimal* per capita *time paths* of GDP, $\mathbf{y}^*(\mathbf{t})$, (13.147), [denominator], and consumption, $\mathbf{c}^*(\mathbf{t})$, (13.145) from Figs. 13.11, 13.12b, 13.14b, are exhibited in Fig. 13.19. Similar curves as in Fig. 13.19 would be obtained for the $y^*(t)$ and $c^*(t)$ paths that belong to Fig. 13.15, 13.16, and 13.17.

Such *exponential* divergence shown in Fig. 13.19 between $y^*(t)$ evolutions or $c^*(t)$ paths are in the growth literature described as the **"great divergence"** in

[25] See Pontryagin et al. (1962, p. 43), Hadley and Kemp (1971, p. 272), Leonard and Long (1992).

[26] Since our treatment of the affine system is general and complete, we can clarify, reproduce, and rectify previous literature discussions with the case: $\mu_1 = 0, \delta = n = 0$, [cf. footnote 23 (Strulik) ] of (13.157–13.159)—which has its so-called direction (tangent) field [at every state point (k,c)] described as:
$\frac{dc}{dk}(k,c) = \frac{\dot{c}}{\dot{k}} = \frac{\mu_2 + a_{22}c}{a_{11}k + a_{12}c} = \frac{1}{\theta}\frac{(A-\rho)(c-\bar{c})}{Ak-c}$; $\quad a_{11} = A$, $a_{22} = \frac{1}{\theta}(A-\rho)$, $\mu_2 = -\frac{\bar{c}}{\theta}(A-\rho)$.
The kinematics (motion, speed of motion) along these trajectories is irretrievably lost, i.e., time paths are entirely missed by this $\frac{dc}{dk}(k,c)$ equation. But this particular equation can in fact with some dexterity be solved explicitly by the method of undetermined coefficients. The result is the curve shown above for the control variable relation to the state $k(0)$: policy function $c_0^* = v(k_0)$, (13.143), here restated as:
$c = \tilde{c} + (a_{11} - a_{22})(k - \tilde{k}) = \tilde{c} - \alpha_1\tilde{k} + \alpha_1 k = \frac{A-\rho}{A\theta}\bar{c} + [\,A\,(1 - \frac{1}{\theta}) + \frac{\rho}{\theta}\,]k$; $\alpha_1 = a_{11} - a_{22}$, $\tilde{k} = \frac{\bar{c}}{a_{11}}$
Strulik (2010, p. 765, eq.3) has this expression (policy function). Next, to get the dynamics (velocity) of the economy, the consumption/capital ratio is used, $x = C/K = c/k$, which has time derivative: $\dot{x} = \frac{(\dot{c}k - c\dot{k})}{k^2} = \frac{\dot{k}[\frac{dc}{dk} - \frac{c}{k}]}{k} = \frac{(Ak-c)[\frac{dc}{dk} - x]}{k} = (A-x)[\frac{dc}{dk} - x] = (A-x)[\,A\,(1-\frac{1}{\theta}) + \frac{\rho}{\theta} - x\,]$. Strulik (2010, p. 765, eq.4) gives this single differential equation in $x$, which (in notation above) is: $\dot{x} = (A-x)[\,\alpha_1 - x\,]$. It has two critical points, $x = A$ and $x = \alpha_1$, and the phase diagram shows that all solutions, $x(t)$, with, $\alpha_1 < x(0) < A$, converge to $\alpha_1$ and diverge outside this interval. Solving for the time paths of the nonlinear equation $\dot{x}(t)$ is hard—but we can give them *explicitly* from (13.145) as: $x^*(t) = c^*(t)/k^*(t) = \frac{[(\mu_1/\tilde{k}) + a_{11}]/[k_0/\tilde{k} - 1] + \alpha_1 e^{a_{22}t}}{1/[k_0/\tilde{k} - 1] + e^{a_{22}t}}$.
The *optimal* evolution of $s^*(t)$ is given by (13.149) with here: $d_1 = 0$, $d_2 = 1/(k_0/\tilde{k} - 1)$. Thus, with $\delta = n = d_1 = 0$, optimal $s^*(t)$ is the *logistic* curve.

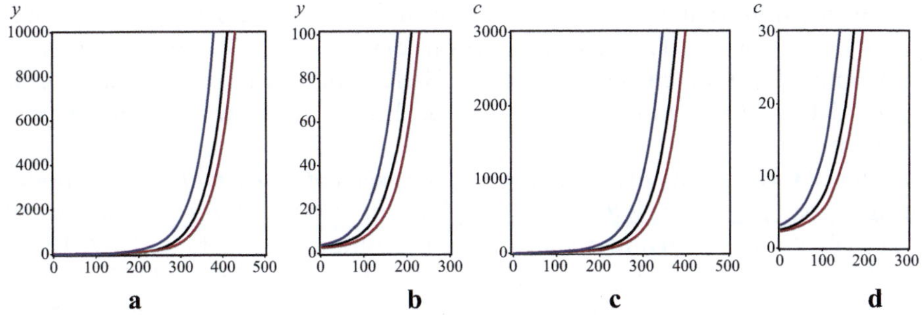


**Fig. 13.19** **Per capita**: GDP, $y^*(t)$, (13.147), and **consumption** per capita, $c^*(t)$, (13.145). *Parameters* (13.159), *premises* (13.160), and *initial values* (13.161) of $y^*(t)$ and $c^*(t)$ as in Fig. 13.18. *Initial* $y^*(0)$, (13.147): 3.571, 2.778, 2.502; *Initial* $c^*(0)$, (13.145): 3.153, 2.555, 2.347

per capita income since a take-off from stagnation to diverse growth paths across countries, see *Galor* (2005, p. 218), Ashraf and Galor (2011, 2013), Galor (2011). Behind such observable *monotonic increasing* time paths in Fig. 13.19, however, is, as we now know, a distinct pattern of *large* evolutionary *disparities* in the *optimal timing* (transitions, evolution) of *saving rates*, $\mathbf{s^*(t)}$, $\boldsymbol{\eta^*(t)}$, and *growth rates*, $\widehat{\mathbf{y^*(t)}}$, in Fig. 13.18 and Figs. 13.15, 13.16, and 13.17. On divergence, see Romer (1986b), Barro (1991), Barro, Sala-i-Martin (1992), Durlauf (1996), Grossman and Rogoff (1995), Lucas Jr. (1998; 2002), Aghion and Howitt (1998), O' Rourke and Williamson (2000), Aghion and Durlauf (2005).

The *transitions* in Figs. 13.15, 13.16, 13.17, 13.18, and 13.19, cf. (13.162), $y = \mu_1 + \gamma a\, k$, (13.148), are **synthesized** by $\mathbf{c\,(y_0)}$:

$$\begin{aligned} c^* &= \tilde{c} - \alpha_1 \tilde{k} + \alpha_1 k_0 = c\,(y_0) \\ &= \mu_1 [\,1 - \frac{\alpha_1}{\gamma a}\,] + a_{22}\,\tilde{k} + [\frac{\alpha_1}{\gamma a}\,]\,y_0 \;\equiv\; \breve{C} \,+\, [\frac{\alpha_1}{\gamma a}]\,y_0 \;\;;\;\; y_0 \geqq \tilde{y} \end{aligned} \qquad (13.163)$$

or by a **synthesized** saving rate: $s\,(y_0) = 1 - c\,(y_0)/y_0 \,=\, [1\,- \alpha_1/\gamma a\,] - \breve{C}/y_0$.

The **affine** function $\mathbf{c(y_0)}$, (13.163), or **hyperbolic** function $\mathbf{s(y_0)}$, is the *synthesized* affine dynamics of Proposition 13.1 for *optimal* growth with Ramsey *technology* (13.101), **HARA** utility (13.81–13.83). The **slope** of $\mathbf{c(y_0)}$ depends on **all** structural *parameters*, cf. (13.144). Note that **intercept** $\breve{\mathbf{C}}$ includes $\tilde{\mathbf{k}}$, (13.145), i.e., for every $\tilde{\mathbf{c}}$, there is a distinct $\breve{\mathbf{C}}$, and hence a particular synthesized $\mathbf{c\,(y_0)}$ *line* (13.163) of transitions; similarly, for every $\tilde{c}$, there will be a particular synthesized $\mathbf{s(y_0)}$ *hyperbola* (13.163) of transitions. Hence $\tilde{\mathbf{c}}$ also affects any transitions described by time paths of $\mathbf{c(t)}$ and $\mathbf{s(t)}$.

Finally, note that $\check{\mathbf{C}}$ can *never* be *zero* with *non-homothetic* (Geary-Stone) *utility* functions.[27] The **affine** function $\mathbf{c}(\mathbf{y}_0)$, (13.163), may be seen as the optimal **Engel curve** implied by HARA for both *cross-section* or *time series* data.[28] *Empirical* evidence *against* Engel curves with *no intercept* is overwhelming.

Hence **CEIS** utility (13.79) *must* also be *replaced* in *optimal* growth models if the goal is to see *historical* evolutions of $c^*(t)$ and $s^*(t)$. The *explicit* optimal *solutions* of **affine dynamics** in Proposition 13.1 and Fig. 13.9, 13.10, 13.11, 13.12, 13.13, 13.14, 13.15, 13.16, 13.17, 13.18, and 13.19, with their **synthesized** functions (13.162–13.163), have amply *demonstrated* and rigorously *proved* this basic economic conclusion.

This conclusion should be *extended* and can be verified generally (with little doubt) by solving the **nonlinear** dynamic system (13.23–13.24) of the standard Ramsey model with **CES** production functions (13.35–13.36) or **VES** (extended CD) functions (13.169–13.170), and **HARA** utility u(c), (13.80–13.83). Already indicated in (13.152–13.185), $\eta(c)$ of HARA, (13.86), implies a *critical point*, $(\tilde{k}, \tilde{c})$—to be next *inserted* in the *earlier* phase diagrams, Figs. 13.3 and 13.20. Such **points**, $(\tilde{k}, \tilde{c})$, will affect the **optimal** (transition) solutions for all the endogenous variables. Our *conjecture* is that HARA with these $(\tilde{k}, \tilde{c})$ included will greatly improve—*historically*—the optimal time path of $s^*(t)$ and $\widehat{y^*(t)}$ of Figs. 13.7 and 13.8 for the parameter set of Table 13.2. Their *asymptotic* numbers, $s^*$ and $\widehat{y}^*$, are already in Corollary 13.1, (13.155–13.156). Optimal CES paths, however, belong to the future, as we have *no explicit separator* **CES** solutions, $\forall t \ \ \varphi^*(t) \ \equiv \ [k^*(t),\ c^*(t)]$, as (13.146), *nor* a *synthesizing function*, $c^* \ = \ v(k)$, as (13.162). To get the separator curve, $\varphi^*(t)$, we need [ without new computational progress, see below) again to **find** the required optimal **initial** control **value** of $\mathbf{c}^*(\mathbf{0})$, via a *detour* from a properly **modified** version of the **transformed** dynamic system (13.91–13.96).

## NONLINEAR DYNAMICS, OPTIMAL GROWTH, AND SAVING

### *Phase Portraits with Extended CD Functions and CEIS*

Linear technologies with constant returns to a tangible and human "capital aggregate" were related to optimal growth by Rebelo (1991), and Jones and

[27] Tinbergen (1960, p. 482) used the Geary-Stone utility function for optimal (Ramsey) saving calculations, applying $\eta(c)$ [ reciprocal flexibility of marginal utility, wrt.$(c)$] as: $\eta(c) = \frac{1}{\theta}(1 - \frac{\bar{c}}{c})$, cf. note 15. Based on 1931 estimates by Frisch: $\eta(2\,c_f) = 1$, (US), $\eta(c_f) = \frac{1}{3.5}$, (French) workers, *same*: $\bar{c}, \theta$, he got: $\frac{\bar{c}}{c_f} = 0.8, \theta = 0.6$. HARA: $\overline{\eta} = \frac{1}{0.6} = 1.67$; but his: $\rho = \delta = n = 0$, $\frac{Y}{K}$=A=$\frac{1}{3}$, *violate* **RTP**, (13.80), (13.146).

[28] Ogaki (1992, p. 1044) finds that preference *parameters* are *not* systematically different between the rich and the poor, but *consumption* (budget shares) is *different* due to their *different incomes*, $y_0$. Ogaki and Qiang (2001, p. 515, p. 524) test **HARA** utility in various contexts, where **CRRA** (CEIS) is **rejected** and **DRRA** (VEIS) [ increasing $\eta(\mathbf{c})$] is **supported** by tests with their database on Indian households.

Manuelli (1990) combined **linear** and **CD** technologies, which satisfy the **persistent** growth condition: $\mathbf{MP_K(k)}$ is *bounded below*, (13.58–13.60)—see Jensen and Larsen (1987, p. 234), here Chap. 1, Eqs. (1.30, 1.32, 1.34), Jensen et al. (2005, p. 69).

The **extended CD** technologies have some merits of their own and are now included in standard textbooks, Barro and Sala-i-Martin (2004, p. 226), Gandolfo (2010, p. 659). We will here briefly apply Theorem 13.2 to solve and illustrate with $(\mathbf{k}, \mathbf{c})$ phase portraits some parametric values for the **extended CD**-case and **CEIS** utility.

Consider the **extended** *Cobb-Douglas* production function $Y = F(L, K)$ and its associated average and marginal products of capital, and its *variable* (**VES**), $\boldsymbol{\sigma(k)}$:

$$Y = F(L, K) = AK + BK^{\alpha} L^{1-\alpha}\,; \; A,\, B, > 0\,,\, 0 < \alpha < 1 \tag{13.164}$$

$$AP_L(k) = Y/L \; = \; y \; = \; f(k) = Ak + Bk^{\alpha} \;\; ; \;\; \widehat{y}\,(t) = \frac{\dot{y}\,(t)}{y\,(t)} \tag{13.165}$$

$$MP_K(k) = f'(k) = A + \alpha B k^{\alpha-1}\,, \quad \lim_{k\to\infty} MP_K(k) = A \tag{13.166}$$

$$\sigma(k) \;\equiv\; -\frac{[\,f(k) \;-\; f'(k)\,k\,]\,f'(k)}{f''(k)\,k\,f(k)} \;=\; \frac{\alpha\,B + A\,k^{1-\alpha}}{\alpha\,B + \alpha\,A\,k^{1-\alpha}} \tag{13.167}$$

$$\lim_{k\to 0} \sigma(k) = 1\,; \qquad \lim_{k\to\infty} \sigma(k) = 1/\alpha \tag{13.168}$$

The Ramsay *dynamic* system (13.23–13.24) becomes, by **VES** (13.164–13.165) and **CEIS** utility, (13.79),

$$\dot{k} = Ak + Bk^{\alpha} - c - (n+\delta)k \;=\; (A - \delta - n)\,k + B\,k^{\alpha} - c \tag{13.169}$$

$$\dot{c} = (c/\theta)[\,A + \alpha\,B\,k^{\alpha-1} - \delta - \rho\,] \tag{13.170}$$

The isocline for $\dot{k}$ is:

$$\dot{k} = 0 \;\;\Leftrightarrow\;\; c \,=\, (A - \delta - n)\,k + B\,k^{\alpha} \tag{13.171}$$

The *transformed* system of (13.169–13.170) becomes, cf. Lemma 13.1,

$$\dot{z} = z\,(1-\alpha)(A/z \;-\; 1)(z - x - n - \delta)\,, \tag{13.172}$$

$$\dot{x} = x\,[\,x - D - \frac{\theta - \alpha}{\theta}\cdot(z - A)\,] \tag{13.173}$$

where, $D = (A - \delta)\cdot(\theta - 1)/\theta + \rho/\theta - n$.

The isoclines and the *steady state* of the *transformed* system are:

$$\dot{z} = 0 \quad \Leftrightarrow \quad x = z - n - \delta \tag{13.174}$$

$$\dot{x} = 0 \quad \Leftrightarrow \quad x = D + (\frac{\theta - \alpha}{\theta})\,(z - A) \tag{13.175}$$

$$z^* = \underline{b} \; = \; A \tag{13.176}$$

$$x^* = D \; = \; (A - \delta) \cdot (\theta - 1)/\theta + \rho/\theta - n \; ; \quad node \, : \, \tilde{z} = z^*, \, \tilde{x} \; = \; 0 \tag{13.177}$$

To *compare* **CES** and *extended* **CD** *results*, consider the *parameters* $A = 0.20$, $B = 1$, and $\alpha = 0.35$ ($\lim_{k \to \infty} \sigma(k) = 1/\alpha = 2.86$) and keep other parameters as in **CES**-baseline, (13.90), ($\delta = 0.03$, $\rho = 0.16$, $n = 0.01$, and $\theta = 1$). This *parameter* set generates exactly the *same asymptotic numbers*, $\mathbf{x}^* = 0.15$, $\mathbf{z}^* = 0.20$, and $\mathbf{s}^* = 0.25$, as **CES**-baseline, (13.97).

Furthermore, Fig. 13.20 shows that the *extended* **CD** *phase portrait* is practically *identical* to its **CES** counterpart in Fig. 13.3—and the seven *time paths* for capital and consumption in Fig. 13.21 closely resemble those in Fig. 13.5, indicating that, for suitable parameter sets, one can generate *similar results* for these *two production* functions, VES, (13.165), and CES, (13.29).

### *The Phase Portraits with VES Technology and CEIS*

Before we show the Ramsey model solutions with the *extended* **CD**-**VES**-function (13.165–13.166), and **VEIS** utility, we recalculate the *phase-portrait* (solutions) with **CEIS** in Fig. 13.20. Instead of first making and solving the

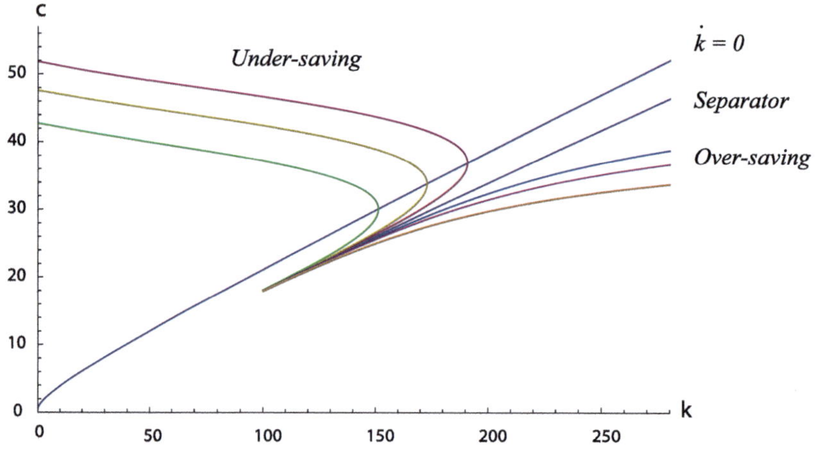


**Fig. 13.20** **Phase portrait** of (13.169–13.173) in state (**k**, **c**) space; $k(0) = 100$. *Extended* **CD**

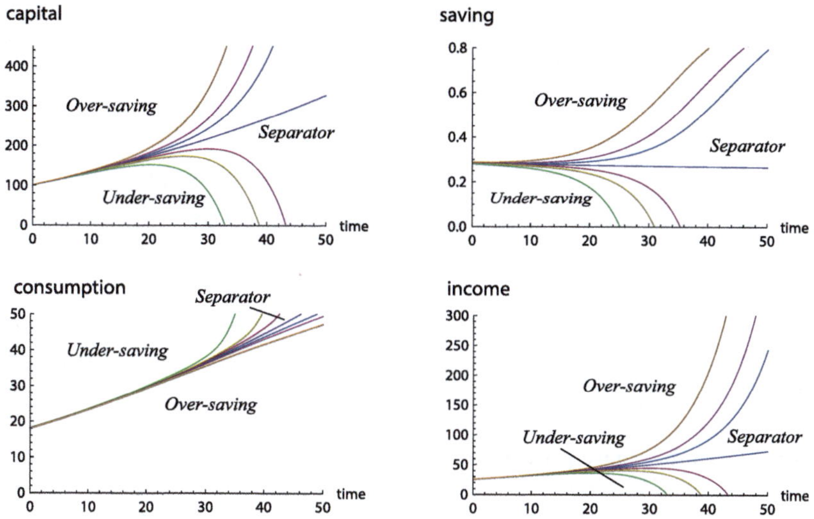


**Fig. 13.21 Time paths** for (13.169–13.170), (13.29), (13.26): **k(t)**, **c(t)**, **y(t)**, **s(t)**. *Extended* CD

*transformed* system, (13.172–13.177), and then [ as mentioned in note 5 ] going backward in time to obtain *exact initial values* to the *optimal* solution (path, separator) in Fig. 13.20, we will use an alternative method. It is easily seen from the *graph* of a *solution* if it corresponds to over-saving or under-saving. We start with initial values of, **c(0)**, corresponding to *over*- and *under*-saving. We then have an *interval*, which contains the initial value corresponding to the *separator* solution. It is possible to narrow down this interval by inspecting solutions until we have a starting value for **c(0)**, which gives the separator solution or a solution that is sufficiently close to the separator for the time period of interest. The *recalculated solutions*, corresponding to Fig. 13.20, are *shown* in Fig. 13.22a, b for comparison. The recalculated solutions have been obtained by *Euler's method*; see **Remark** on calculation.

The *method*, cf. note 29, of *interval narrowing* for $\mathbf{c}^*(0)$ will now be used to demonstrate *optimal time paths* for relevant variables in the Ramsey model with **VEIS** utility.

**Remark** regarding calculation:[29]

[29] Change in *hardware* and access to *newer math programs* such as *Maple* can have the result that solving problems that previously required the use of sophisticated methods now can use simpler and easily transparent methods. An example of this is the use of Euler's simple method for solving differential equations. *Euler's method* can be stated as follows: $\mathbf{x}(\mathbf{t_n} + \triangle\,\mathbf{t}) \approx \mathbf{x}(\mathbf{t_n}) + \dot{\mathbf{x}}(\mathbf{t_n})\,\triangle\,\mathbf{t}$. The method has *previously* mostly been used for *theoretical* considerations and has been considered almost unusable for *practical* solutions. $\triangle\,\mathbf{t}$ must be small to achieve good accuracy, which then

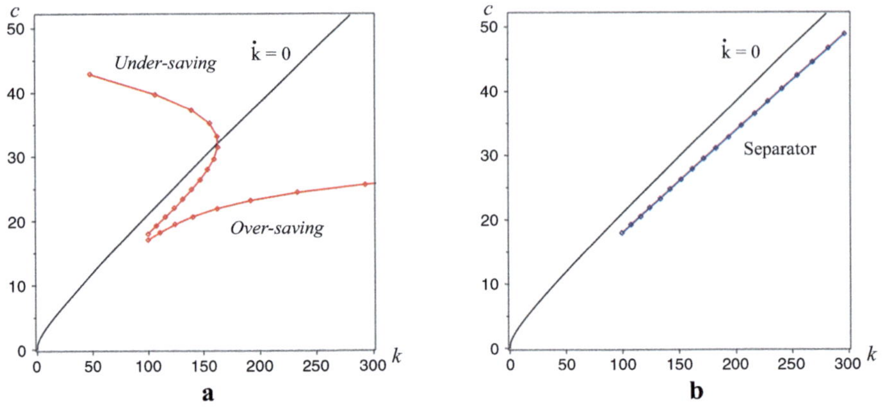


**Fig. 13.22** (**a, b**) **Phase portrait** of (13.169–13.170) in the state space: (**k, c**), with **CEIS** utility, (13.79), and *Extended* **CD**, (13.164–13.165)—same as Fig. 13.20—by solving (13.169–13.170) with *Euler method*—for **k**(0) = 100 and *three* **c**(0). (**b**) Initial values: **k**(0), **c***(0) = (100, 17.947)

### *Ramsey Saving: VEIS Utility—Non-homothetic Preferences*

As illustrative **VEIS** *utility* function **u** (**c**), we here again use the *quasi-homothetic* Geary-Stone utility function,[30] **u** (**c**), and its ***η*** (**c**), (13.178)—with[31]

requires many Euler cycles with associated rounding errors. A *math program* can now perform 1000 Euler cycles in a few seconds and can calculate with an *accuracy* corresponding to *100 digits* or more. Therefore, Euler's method for solving both linear and nonlinear differential equations is sufficient in many cases. It can here be used to find the curve for optimal saving including the *initial value* for the *separator*. Here $\triangle t = 0.0025$ is used. A *point* is marked for every 1000 cycles. The curve that solves *differential equations* (13.169–13.170) is then illustrated by drawing straight lines from each of the mentioned points to the next. The *initial value* for the **separator** can be found in the following way: we can easily find two consecutive whole numbers (here 17 and 18), where the smallest gives over-saving and the largest gives under-saving. Instead of narrowing successive intervals by halving, it is faster to judge by inspection of figures whether the sought initial value is closer to one of the interval boundaries than the other and then proceed to adjust this. If the result is over-saving, it is adjusted up a little, and conversely, it is adjusted down a little if the result is under-sawing. Fig. 13.22a shows solution curves with *initial values* of (100,17) and (100,18). The time period is shown up to a value corresponding to a **k-size** of approximately **300**, which is similar to that in Fig. 13.20. See corresponding time in Fig. 13.22a. It can be seen that the curve for *over-saving* leaves the area after much *fewer* time periods than the curve for *under-saving*. This means that the *initial value* for the **separator** in Fig. 13.22b is closer to (100,18) than to (100,17). Therefore (100,17.9) is tried. One continues to *adjust* the lower *c-value* slightly up if the result is over-saving and slightly down if the result is under-saving until a final result for the **separator**, **c***(0) = **17.947**, as shown in Fig. 13.22b, is reached.

[30] See hereto footnote 15, 25, 26.

[31] Clearly, $\theta = 1$ in VEIS (13.178–13.179) has *not* the *same* ***η***(**c**) interpretation, as $\theta = 1$ in CEIS, $u(c)$, (13.79). Certainly (13.178) is evidently not an affine transformation of (13.79), and neither is (13.179) an affine transformation of *Bernoulli*, **u**(**c**) = **ln**(**c**), cf. note 6.

$\theta = 1$ is **VEIS** version (13.179):

$$u(c) = \frac{\beta}{1-\theta}\,[\,(c-\nu)^{1-\theta} - 1\,]\,, \quad \eta(c) = \frac{1}{\theta}\,(1 - \frac{\nu}{c})\,;\ 0 < \nu/c \leqslant 1 \tag{13.178}$$

$$\theta = 1: \quad u(c) = \beta\, ln\,(c-\nu)\,, \quad \eta(c) = 1 - \frac{\nu}{c} \tag{13.179}$$

The *Ramsay dynamic system* (13.23–13.24) becomes, by **VES** (13.164–13.165) and **VEIS** (13.178–13.179):

$$\dot{c} = c\ \eta(c)\,[\,A + \alpha B\, k^{\alpha-1} - \delta - \rho\,] = \frac{1}{\theta}\,(c - \nu)\,[\,A + \alpha B\, k^{\alpha-1} - \delta - \rho\,] \tag{13.180}$$

$$\dot{k} = Ak + Bk^{\alpha} - c - (n+\delta)k = (A - \delta - n)\,k + B\,k^{\alpha} - c \tag{13.181}$$

$$\dot{c} = (\,c - \nu\,)\,[\,A + \alpha\, B\, k^{\alpha-1} - \delta - \rho\,]\,,\ 0 < \nu \leqslant c \tag{13.182}$$

The *isocline*, for $\dot{\mathbf{k}} = 0$, is seen in Figs. 13.20, 13.22a, 13.22b, 13.23a, and 13.27

$$\dot{k} = 0 \iff c = (A - \delta - n)\,k + B\,k^{\alpha} \tag{13.183}$$

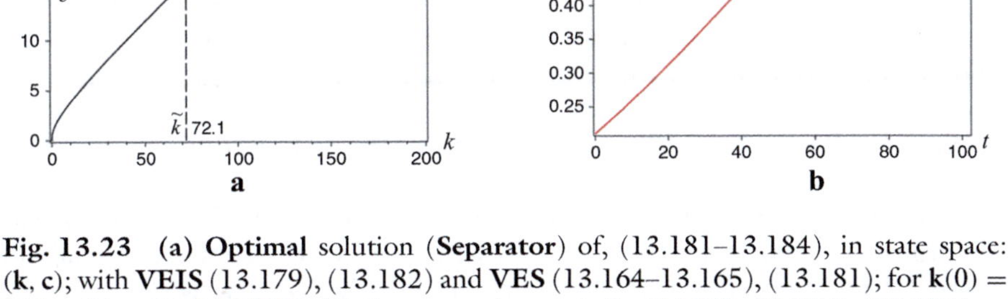


**Fig. 13.23** (**a**) **Optimal** solution (**Separator**) of, (13.181–13.184), in state space: (**k**, **c**); with **VEIS** (13.179), (13.182) and **VES** (13.164–13.165), (13.181); for $\mathbf{k}(0) = 100$, $\mathbf{c}(0) = \mathbf{20.2491732}$. (**b**) *Separator time paths* for (13.181–13.184), (13.179) to: $\eta\,[\,\mathbf{c(t)}\,]$; **VEIS** (13.182), **VES** (13.181), with $\lim_{t\to\infty} \eta[\mathbf{c^*(t)}] = 1$, (13.179)

and with the *parameters*, (13.184), this *isocline* curve is: $c = 0.16k + k^{0.35}$.

$$A = 0.20,\ B = 1,\ \alpha = 0.35,\ \delta = 0.03,\ n = 0.01,\ \rho = 0.16,$$
$$\nu = 16,\ \theta = 1;\ \theta = 0.9 \tag{13.184}$$

The critical point, $(\tilde{\mathbf{k}}, \tilde{\mathbf{c}})$, Fig. 13.23a, of the dynamic systems (13.180–13.182) with (13.184) is: $\tilde{\mathbf{c}} = \nu = 16$, and hence $\tilde{\mathbf{k}}$ in Fig. 13.23a given as,

$$(A - \delta - n)\,k + Bk^{\alpha} - \tilde{c} = 0.16k + k^{0.35} - 16 = 0 \Leftrightarrow \tilde{k} = 72.1 \tag{13.185}$$

From the dynamic system, (13.181–13.184), with *initial* value $\mathbf{c}^*(0) =$ **20.249** on the **separator** in Fig. 13.23a, are calculated (shown) the **optimal solutions** (*time paths*) for $\mathbf{k}^*(\mathbf{t})$, $\mathbf{c}^*(\mathbf{t})$, $\eta\,[\,\mathbf{c}^*(\mathbf{t})\,]$, $\mathbf{s}^*(\mathbf{t})$, $\widehat{\mathbf{y}}^*(\mathbf{t})$, $\mathbf{MP_K}[\,\mathbf{k}^*(\mathbf{t})\,]$—in the RHS (*right-hand side*) of Figs. 13.23, 13.24, 13.25. For comparisons are shown—in the LHS (*left-hand side*) of Figs. 13.24, 13.25—the corresponding **optimal solutions** (*time paths*) from the dynamic system (13.169–13.170) in Figs. 13.20, 13.21, 13.22. It is *only* **ln (c)**, **CEIS**, $\eta = 1$, and **ln (c** $-\ \nu$**)**, **VEIS**, $\eta\,(c)$, (13.179), that make all the *dramatic differences* to the **optimal solutions** in RHS and LHS of Figs. 13.24 and 13.25.

In Fig. 13.24 (LHS), the optimal solutions—$\mathbf{k}^*(\mathbf{t})$, $\mathbf{c}^*(\mathbf{t})$—have initial values, $\mathbf{k}(\mathbf{0}) = 100, \mathbf{c}^*(0) = 17.947$, Figs. 13.22b. 13.24 (RHS), initial values are, $\mathbf{k}(\mathbf{0}) = 100, \mathbf{c}^*(0) = 20.249$, Fig. 13.23a. The optimal solutions, $\mathbf{k}^*(\mathbf{t})$, $\mathbf{c}^*(\mathbf{t})$, Fig. 13.24 are unbounded (persistent growth) and grow *asymptotically* with same *growth rate*: **0.01**, cf. (13.71), $\overline{\eta} = 1$—but initially the LHS **CEIS** optimal solutions grow clearly much faster than RHS in Fig. 13.24 with **VEIS** utility, $\eta\,[\,\mathbf{c}^*(\mathbf{t})\,]$, version $\theta = 1$, *increasing* with income, consumption, as seen in Fig. 13.23b. Further consequences of **VEIS** are calculated and shown in Fig. 13.25.

The corresponding *time paths* (optimal solutions)—LHS, RHS—in Fig. 13.25 have the *same* asymptotic *limits*—but they are in (Fig. 13.25a–d), respectively, *lower* (LHS), *upper* (RHS) limits. In LHS, the **CEIS** utility with $(\eta = 1)$ starts at low initial value, $\mathbf{k(0) = 100}$, by selecting, $\mathbf{c}^*(0) = \mathbf{17.947}$, (Fig. 13.22b) as optimal *initial* consumption, which gives a *high* optimal *initial* saving rate: $\mathbf{s}^*(\mathbf{0}) = 1 - c(0)/y(0) = 0.283$, Fig. 13.25A, which makes good sense, as $\mathbf{MP_K}[\,k(0) = 100\,]$ is *high*, Fig. 13.25e, and accordingly is, $\widehat{\mathbf{y}}^*(\mathbf{0})$, Fig. 13.25c.

The *shape*—from start to lower limits of LHS *time paths* of the *optimal* solutions for saving rates, $\mathbf{s(t)}$, and growth rates, $\widehat{\mathbf{y}}^*(\mathbf{t})$—comes essentially by using **CEIS** utility, $(\eta = 1)$. This same LHS *shape* of *time paths* for saving rates, $\mathbf{s}^*(\mathbf{t})$, and growth rates, $\widehat{\mathbf{y}}^*(\mathbf{t})$ with **CEIS** utility, $(\eta = 1)$, was seen in CES-baseline case, Figs. 13.7, 13.8, where also **CEIS** utility, $(\eta = 1/\theta)$ cases, (13.79), Table 13.2, display similar *shape* as LHS, Fig. 13.25—and a similar *shape* again in Figs. 13.9, 13.10.

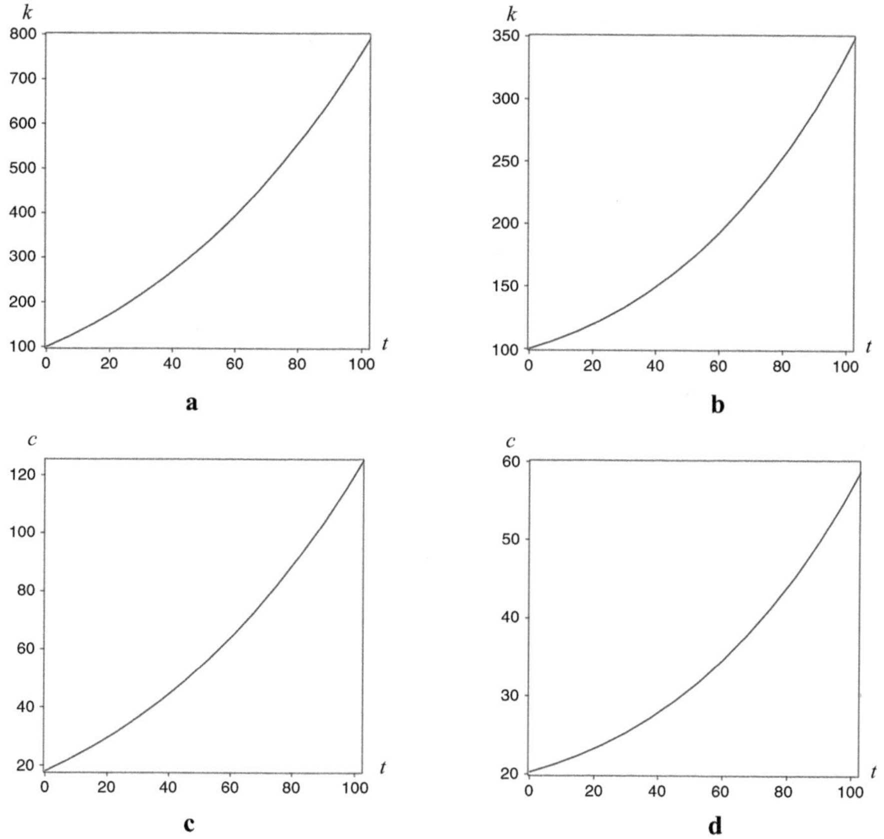


**Fig. 13.24** (**a, c**) *Separator time paths* for (13.169–13.170) to: **k(t)**, **c(t)**; **CEIS**/$\eta = 1-$**VES** (13.181) (**b, d**) *Separator time paths* for (13.181–13.184) to: **k(t)**, **c(t)**; **VEIS** (13.182)–**VES** (13.181)

In RHS, Fig. 13.25, the **VEIS** utility with $\boldsymbol{\eta}$ **(c)** starts at low initial value, **k(0)** = **100**, by selecting—despite *high* $\mathbf{MP_K}[\,k(0) = 100\,]$, Fig. 13.25f—a *high* **c***(0) = **20.249**, (Fig. 13.23a) as optimal *initial* consumption, which gives a *low* optimal *initial* saving rate: $\mathbf{s}^*(\mathbf{0})$ = 1- $c^*(0)/y^*(0 = 0.191)$, Fig. 13.25b, and accordingly is $\widehat{\mathbf{y}^*}(\mathbf{0})$, Fig. 13.25d. The *shape*—from start to higher limits of RHS *time paths* of the *optimal* solutions for saving rates, $\mathbf{s}^*(\mathbf{t})$, and growth rates, $\widehat{\mathbf{y}^*}(\mathbf{t})$—comes essentially by using **VEIS** utility, $[\,\eta\,(c^*)$, version $\theta = 1\,]$. This same RHS *shape* of *time paths* for saving rates, $\mathbf{s}^*(\mathbf{t})$, and growth rates, $\widehat{\mathbf{y}^*}(\mathbf{t})$ with **VEIS** utility, $[\,\eta\,(c^*)$, version $\theta = 0.98\,]$ was seen for *Affine* technology in Figs. 13.12b, 13.13, 13.14b. The **VEIS** utility, $[\,\eta\,(c^*)$, version $\theta = 3\,]$, was seen with *explicit* solutions of *Affine* dynamics to display similar *shape* as RHS, Fig. 13.25, in the Figs. 13.15, 13.16, 13.17, 13.18. Evidently, it is the RHS *shape* of time path for $\mathbf{s}^*(\mathbf{t})$, and $\widehat{\mathbf{y}^*}(\mathbf{t})$, and hence a

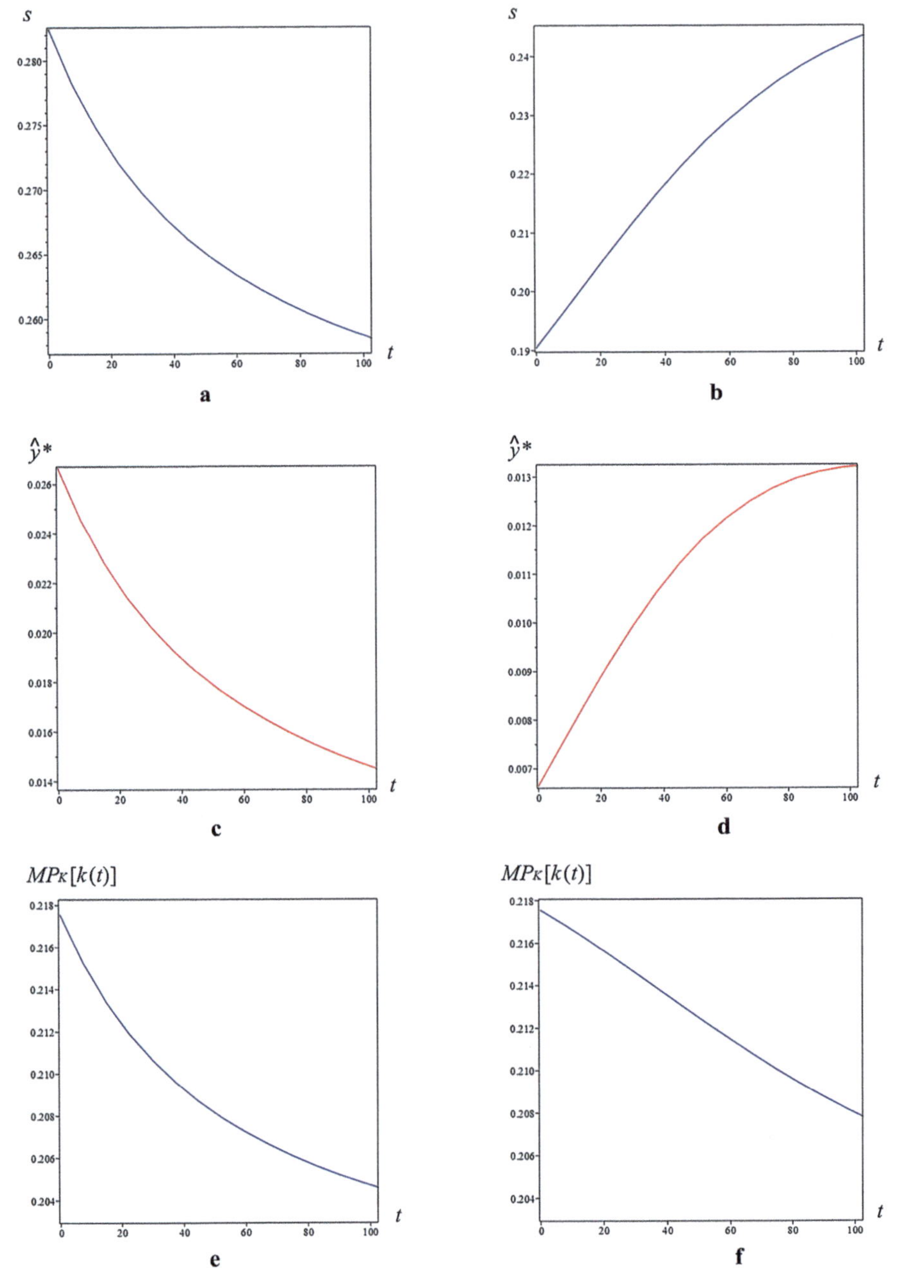


**Fig. 13.25** (**a**, **c**, **e**) *Optimal paths* for (13.169–13.170), (13.26), (13.165–13.166), (13.71), (13.100) to: $\mathbf{s(t)}$, $\widehat{\mathbf{y}^*}(\mathbf{t}) = \frac{\dot{\mathbf{y}}^*(\mathbf{t})}{\mathbf{y}^*(\mathbf{t})}$, $\mathbf{MP_K[\,k(t)\,]}$. **CEIS**, $(\eta = 1)$, and **VES** (13.181)—with $\lim_{t\to\infty} s^*(t) = 0.25$, $\lim_{t\to\infty} \hat{y}^*(t) = 0.01$, $\lim_{t\to\infty} MP_K[k^*(t)] = 0.2$. (**b**, **d**, **f**) *Optimal paths* for (13.181–13.184), (13.26), (13.165–13.166), (13.71), (13.100) to: $\mathbf{s(t)}$, $\widehat{\mathbf{y}^*}(\mathbf{t}) = \frac{\dot{\mathbf{y}}^*(\mathbf{t})}{\mathbf{y}^*(\mathbf{t})}$, $\mathbf{MP_K[\,k(t)\,]}$. **VEIS**, $\eta(c)$, (179), and **VES** (13.181)—with $\lim_{t\to\infty} s^*(t) = 0.25$, $\lim_{t\to\infty} \hat{y}^*(t) = 0.01$, $\lim_{t\to\infty} MP_K[k^*(t)] = 0.2$

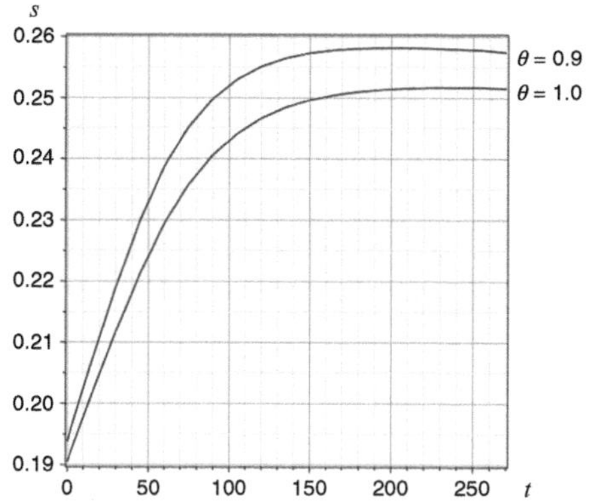


**Fig. 13.26** Case, $\theta$ = 1.0: *Optimal paths* for (13.181–13.184), (13.26), (13.100), to: $\mathbf{s^*(t)}$: **VEIS** (13.182), **VES** (13.181). $\lim_{t\to\infty} s^*(t) = 0.25$ (max. value is slightly larger than, 0.25). Case, $\theta$ = 0.9: *Optimal paths* for (13.181–13.180), (13.184), (13.26), (13.100), to: $\mathbf{s^*(t)}$: **VEIS** (13.180), **VES** (13.181). $\lim_{t\to\infty} s^*(t) = 0.256$. (max. value is larger than, 0.256)

**VEIS** *utility* with an *elasticity*, [$\eta$ (**c**)], *increasing* with income, Fig. 13.23b, that *replicate observed* $\mathbf{s^*(t)}$ and $\widehat{\mathbf{y}^*}(\mathbf{t})$ in selected periods of recorded country economic *history*, e.g., (13.27).

In Fig. 13.26, the **VEIS** ($\theta = 1$) *time path* of $\mathbf{s^*}$ (**t**), Fig. 13.25b, has been *prolonged* to $\mathbf{t} > \mathbf{250}$, where it is now clearly seen that from $t > 150$, **s**(**t**) has risen above its asymptotic limit, $\mathbf{s}^* = \frac{0.01+0.04}{0.20} = \mathbf{0.25}$, (13.100). Similarly, with **VEIS** version ($\theta = 0.9$, $\overline{\eta} = 1.11$), (13.180), and **VES** (13.181), the time path of $\mathbf{s}^*$ (**t**) is at $\mathbf{t} > \mathbf{150}$, above its asymptotic limit: $\mathbf{s}^* = \frac{0.0111+0.04}{0.20} = \mathbf{0.256}$, cf. (13.100), (13.71). Thus, the **VEIS** saving *paths* $\mathbf{s}^*$ (**t**) in Fig. 13.26 has a *hump-shaped* pattern. In Fig. 13.27, the **VEIS** ($\theta = 1$) time path of $\widehat{\mathbf{y}^*}(\mathbf{t})$, Fig. 13.25e, has also been *prolonged* to $\mathbf{t} > \mathbf{250}$, where it appears clearly that from $t > 100$, the sizes of the growth rates $\widehat{\mathbf{y}^*}(\mathbf{t})$ enter a stage (period) of *maximum* growth, after which $\widehat{\mathbf{y}^*}(\mathbf{t})$ declines toward its asymptotic limit: **0.010**. Similarly, with **VEIS** version ($\theta = 0.9$, $\overline{\eta} = 1.11$), (13.180), the time path of the growth rates $\widehat{\mathbf{y}^*}(\mathbf{t})$ have a *maximum* above ("overshooting") the *asymptotic* limit: $\overline{\eta}\cdot 0.01 = \mathbf{0.011}$. The **hump-shaped** ("overshooting") pattern of $\widehat{\mathbf{y}^*}(\mathbf{t})$ in Fig. 13.27 is indeed *stronger*[32] than that seen for the saving rates $\mathbf{s}^*(\mathbf{t})$ in Fig. 13.26.

[32] Steger (2000, p. 357, Fig. 5) has solved another parametric version of the dynamic systems (13.180–13.182), with *parameters*: $A = 0.1$, $B = 0.1$, $\alpha = 0.8$, $\delta = 0.02$, $n = 0.03$, $\rho = 0.05$, $\nu = 2$, $\theta = 1$, and a $\tau = 0.1$, that gives: $\tilde{A} = (1-\tau)A = 0.09$, $\tilde{B} = (1-\tau)B = 0.09$, such that $\tilde{A}$, $\tilde{B}$, replace A, B, in (13.180–13.182). His *time paths*, Fig. 5, for $\eta^*$ (**t**), $\mathbf{s}^*(\mathbf{t})$, $\widehat{\mathbf{y}^*}(\mathbf{t})$, $\mathbf{MP_K}[\mathbf{k}^*(\mathbf{t})]$ correspond to RHS, Fig. 13.25, *humps*: Figs. 13.26 and 13.27; the asymptotic limit of $MP_K$ is $\tilde{A} = 0.09$ and is for $\widehat{y^*} = \tilde{A} - \delta - \rho = 0.02$.

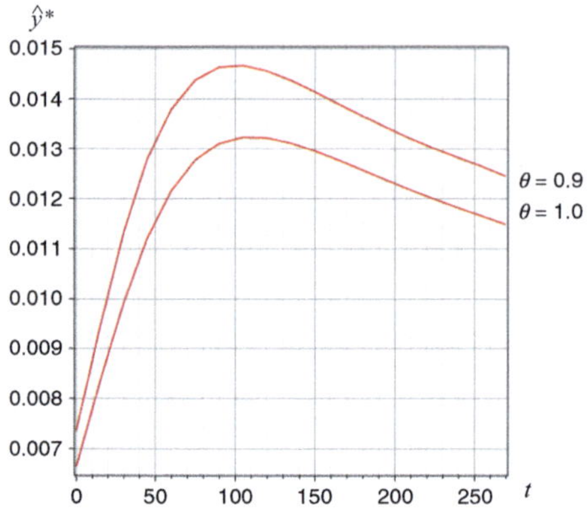


**Fig. 13.27** Case, $\theta = 1.0$: *Optimal paths* for (13.181–13.184), (13.165–13.166), (13.71), to: $\widehat{\mathbf{y}}^*(\mathbf{t})$: **VEIS** (13.182), **VES** (13.181). $\lim_{t\to\infty} \widehat{\mathbf{y}}^*(\mathbf{t}) = 0.010$. Case, $\theta = 0.9$: *Optimal paths* for (13.181–13.180), (13.184), (13.165–13.166), (13.71), to: $\widehat{\mathbf{y}}^*(\mathbf{t})$: **VEIS** (13.180), **VES** (13.181). $\lim_{t\to\infty} \widehat{\mathbf{y}}^*(\mathbf{t}) = 0.011$

In contrast to *"counter-factual"* **CEIS** utility[33] pattern of initially optimal *high* and monotonic *decreasing*, $\mathbf{s}^*(\mathbf{t})$, $\widehat{\mathbf{y}}^*(\mathbf{t})$, in LHS, Fig. 13.25, the **VEIS** utility pattern of initially optimal *low* and next, $\mathbf{s}^*(\mathbf{t})$, $\widehat{\mathbf{y}}^*(\mathbf{t})$, evolving with *increasing* a la *hump*-shaped form as in Figs. 13.26 and 13.27 is *consistent* with empirical *country studies* of long-run saving/domestic investments and growth rates in *historical periods* with significant economic development—Kuznets (1966, p. 248), Maddison (1992, p. 185,194), Easterly (1994, p. 528), Barro and Sala-i-Martin (2004, p. 561–566)—and **VEIS** utility respects Engel's law and complies with the fundamental requirement of *non-homothetic preferences*, as shown below.

The **Separators**, $[\,\mathbf{k}^*(\mathbf{t}), \mathbf{c}^*(\mathbf{t})\,]$, *Optimal* solution,[34] (13.180–13.184), corresponding to Figs. 13.26 and 13.27, are shown in Figs. 13.28 and 13.29.

[33] Cass (1965, p. 239) noted that with Cobb-Douglas and CEIS utility functions: "The optimum gross saving rate may increase steadily, remain constant, or decrease steadily, depending on the particular parameter values chosen"; see CD *transition* proof & illustration, Barro and Sala-i-Martin (2004, p. 136, Fig. 2.3), and for *persistent* growth with CES Technology in Fig. 13.7. For all technologies, however, to obtain an increasing saving rate, the required risk aversion parameter $\theta$ must be considerably larger than one (e.g., Fig. 13.7, $\theta = 3$). **CEIS** utility functions are applied *everywhere*—high $\theta$ is partly involved in puzzles and in many discussions, see Mehra and Prescott (1985, p. 150,158); Mehra and Prescott (1988, p. 135).

[34] The *two* differential equations, (13.180–13.181), and the *single* differential equation:

$$\frac{dc}{dk}(k, c) = \frac{\dot{c}}{\dot{k}} = \frac{\frac{1}{\theta}\,(c - \nu)\,[\,A + \alpha B\, k^{\alpha-1} - \delta - \rho\,]}{(A - \delta - n)\,k + B\,k^{\alpha} - c} = \frac{1}{\theta} \cdot \frac{(c - 16)\,[\,0.01 + \alpha\, k^{\alpha-1}\,]}{0.16\,k + k^{\alpha} - c}\,;$$

$\alpha = 0.35\,,\ \theta = 1\,;\ \theta = 0.9$

give the same *results* in Figs. 13.28 and 13.29 with the *Initial values* on the Separator.

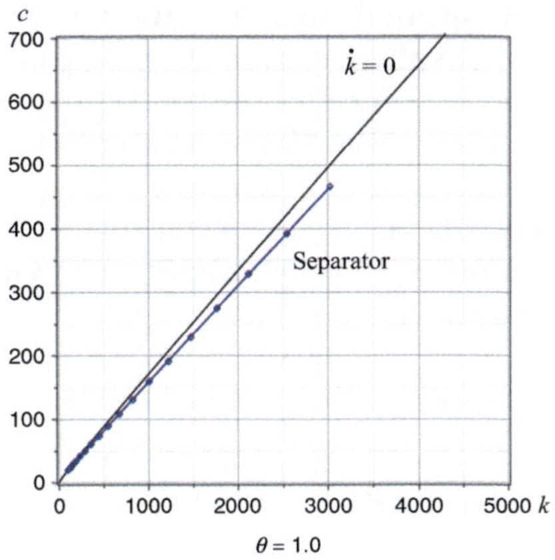


**Fig. 13.28 Optimal** solution—**Separator,** $\varphi^*(t)$ = $[\mathbf{k}^*(t), \mathbf{c}^*(t)]$—of (13.181–13.184) with **VEIS** (13.179), (13.180) (13.182) and **VES** (13.181) for: $\mathbf{k(0) = 100}$, $\mathbf{c^*(0)}$ = 20.2491731554490422465 83

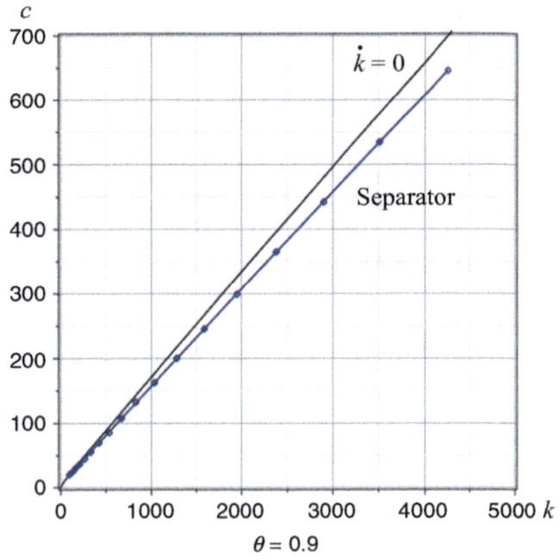


**Fig. 13.29 Optimal** solution—**Separator,** $\varphi^*(t)$ = $[\mathbf{k}^*(t), \mathbf{c}^*(t)]$—of (13.181–13.180), (13.184) with **VEIS** (13.178), (13.180) and **VES** (13.181) for: $\mathbf{k(0) = 100}$, $\mathbf{c^*(0)}$ = 20.16668204590084868 2902

Calculation[35]

The **Separators**[36] in Figs. 13.28 and 13.29 may seem as straight lines—but they are not, and although being unique *optimal solutions* and *policy functions* (curves), they have **no explicit** analytic expressions. However, for Affine technology, $\mathbf{f(k)}$, with CEIS and VEIS utility, $\mathbf{u(c)}$—in sections "Ramsey (1928): Affine Dynamics with CEIS Utility"–"Affine Dynamics, Minimal States, and Evolutions"—the *Affine* dynamics always placed $\boldsymbol{\varphi}^*(\mathbf{t})$ *geometrically*

[35] Euler step length: $\Delta t$ = 0.0025, time between points: 0.0025 · 6000 = 15, number of time intervals: 18, total time: 270, calculation accuracy: 100 digits. The accuracy required to the ***initial value***, $c^*(0)$—for growing optimally along the separator—seems overwhelming [ "knife/razor edge", Akerlof and Nordhaus (1967, p. 52)]. However, e.g., if at regular time intervals, initial optimal values $c^*(0)$ are ***updated*** by the method used in note 29, the initial values $c^*(0)$ need not be given with such high precision as stated in Figs. 13.28 and 13.29.

[36] The Separator in Fig. 13.29 is always below the Separator in Fig. 13.28, cf. respective Initial values, $c^*(0)$. The isoclines are here (13.184) the same in both in Figures.

on **optimal straight lines**, policy function, $\mathbf{c}^*(\mathbf{0}) = \mathbf{v}(\mathbf{k_0})$, (13.143), with **explicit** *parametric* time path, $\boldsymbol{\varphi}^*(\mathbf{t})$, (13.145–13.146)—and all **explicit** implications: Proposition 13.1.

For CES and VES technologies with CEIS and VEIS utility—sections "Phase Portraits with Extended CD Functions and CEIS" and —*Nonlinear* dynamics gives $\boldsymbol{\varphi}^*(\mathbf{t})$, as in Figs. 13.3, 13.20, 13.22, 13.23, 13.28, 13.29. We here summarize **Persistent** per capita **Growth** from Affine and Nonlinear dynamics as follows.

The basic Assumption 13.1, (13.60), (13.58–13.59), (13.8), implied a **concave** production function $AP_L = Y/L = y = f(k)$ with the properties:

$$\lim_{k\to\infty} [\, AP_L = y = \mathbf{f}(\mathbf{k})\,] = \infty : \lim_{k\to\infty} [\, AP_K = \mathbf{z}(\mathbf{k}) = \frac{f(k)}{k}\,] = \tag{13.186}$$

$$\lim_{k\to\infty} f'(k) \equiv \lim_{k\to\infty} \mathbf{MP_K} \equiv \underline{\mathbf{b}} = \mathbf{z}^* > 0 \tag{13.187}$$

Production function, $\mathbf{f}(\mathbf{k})$, (13.186), has by *L'Hospital* the asymptotic slope $\underline{\mathbf{b}}$, (13.187); $\mathbf{f}(\mathbf{k})$ might be shown as *curve* in Figs. 13.28 and 13.29. Below $\mathbf{f}(\mathbf{k})$ is always an *isocline*, $\dot{\mathbf{k}} = 0$, e.g.(13.183):

$$\dot{\mathbf{k}} = 0 \;\Leftrightarrow\; \mathbf{c} = (A - \delta - n)\,k + B\,k^{\alpha} \equiv \mathbf{O}(\mathbf{k}) \;; \tag{13.188}$$

$$\lim_{k\to\infty} \mathbf{O}'(\mathbf{k}) \equiv \boldsymbol{\alpha}_\mathbf{o} = \underline{\mathbf{b}} - (\mathbf{n} + \boldsymbol{\delta}) > \mathbf{0} \tag{13.189}$$

*Isoclines*, $\mathbf{c} = \mathbf{O}(\mathbf{k})$, as (13.188), have always the asymptotic *slope*, $\boldsymbol{\alpha}_\mathbf{o}$, (13.189), (here $A = \underline{b}$). Below the *Isocline*, (13.189), is always located the ***unique*** path (curve) of the *Separator*:

$$\forall t \;\; \boldsymbol{\varphi}^*(\mathbf{t}) = [\,\mathbf{k}^*(\mathbf{t}), \mathbf{c}^*(\mathbf{t})\,] \equiv \forall k_0 > \tilde{k} \quad \mathbf{c}^*(0) = \mathbf{v}(\mathbf{k_0}) \tag{13.190}$$

$$\lim_{t\to\infty} \boldsymbol{\varphi}^{*\prime}(\mathbf{t}) = \lim_{t\to\infty} \frac{c^*(t)}{k^*(t)} = \mathbf{x}^* \equiv \lim_{k_0\to\infty} \mathbf{v}'(\mathbf{k_0}) \equiv \boldsymbol{\alpha}_\mathbf{s} < \boldsymbol{\alpha}_\mathbf{o} = \underline{b} - (n + \delta) \tag{13.191}$$

The *asymptotic slope* of the Separator is always given as: $\boldsymbol{\alpha}_\mathbf{s} = \mathbf{x}^* < \boldsymbol{\alpha}_\mathbf{o}$, (13.191), where expression, $\boldsymbol{\alpha}_\mathbf{s} = \mathbf{x}^*$, includes utility parameters and the discount rate, see, e.g., (13.177). Finally, the *asymptotic saving* rate, $\mathbf{s}^*$, (13.192), is the **ratio** of the *asymptotic slope* of Separator, $\boldsymbol{\alpha}_\mathbf{s}$, (13.191), and *asymptotic slope* of $\mathbf{f}(\mathbf{k})$, (13.187), $\underline{\mathbf{b}}$—in Fig. 13.4, the *saddle points*, (13.95–13.96), (13.176–13.177), in transformed variables, $z = Y/K = y/k$, $x = C/K = c/k$, cf. (13.67–13.71).

$$\mathbf{s}^* = 1 - \frac{x^*}{z^*} = 1 - \frac{\boldsymbol{\alpha}_\mathbf{s}}{\underline{\mathbf{b}}} < 1 \;; \quad \widehat{\mathbf{y}^*} = \widehat{\mathbf{c}^*} = \widehat{\mathbf{k}^*} = \bar{\eta}\,[\,\underline{\mathbf{b}} - \delta - \rho\,] \tag{13.192}$$

The transformed dynamic systems, $(\dot{\mathbf{x}}, \dot{\mathbf{z}})$, for CES and VES technologies with saddle points as Fig. 13.4, were always based on the **CEIS** utility functions, (13.79). Extensions that include **VEIS** utility (13.178–13.179) have so far *not* been seen for various versions of the system $(\dot{\mathbf{x}}, \dot{\mathbf{z}})$. A **VEIS** utility (13.178–13.179) extension, according to (13.76–13.77), with CES or VES, e.g., the system $(\dot{\mathbf{x}}, \dot{\mathbf{z}})$, (13.172–13.173), could be worked out. But there is no need nor any advantage to use such transformed system in $(\dot{\mathbf{x}}, \dot{\mathbf{z}})$. We can with **VES** and **VEIS** here keep the original *dynamic* system, (13.180–13.181), and solve this *basic* dynamic system, [see note 34], as done and shown in Figs. 13.23, 13.24, 13.25, 13.26, 13.27, 13.28, and 13.29 with the *separators* and *optimal time paths* of various *economic variables* that are determined from the optimal solutions $\boldsymbol{\varphi}^*(\mathbf{t})$ along the separators in Fig. 13.28 and 13.29. However, to see and use the *connection* between the *dynamic system*, (13.180–13.181), and the *optimal* $\boldsymbol{\varphi}^*(\mathbf{t})$ in Figs. 13.28 and 13.29 required the rigorous mathematical *foundation* that is provided by the *conditions* (13.61–13.63) of Theorem 13.2.

The *parameter* set (13.184), ($A = \underline{b} = 0.2$), with VEIS, $\theta = 1$, clearly satisfies (13.61–13.63), equivalently (13.80)—and so does also, (13.184), with VEIS, $\theta = 0.9$. Alternatively, using (13.63) with (13.184), requirement (13.63) is: $\overline{\eta} < \frac{0.15}{0.01} = 1.5$—which is satisfied with VEIS, $\theta = 0.9$: $\overline{\eta} = 1/0.9 = 1.11$. But in (13.184), we cannot allow VEIS, $\theta = 0.5 \Leftrightarrow \overline{\eta} = 2$. Thus to satisfy: $\overline{\eta} < 1.5$, we must in (13.184) require VEIS: $\theta > 2/3$. With $\theta = 0.9$: $\overline{\eta} = 1.11$, **VEIS** utility (13.178) is *unbounded* along the *separator* in Fig. 13.29, but $\mathbf{V}[\widetilde{\mathbf{c}^*(\mathbf{t})}]$, (13.3), is *finite* (exist).

There is long-standing concern about the evolution of *factor shares* from *persistent growth* models, associated with the asymptotic properties (13.186–13.187)—implying that *capital's* shares converge to *1*, e.g., Barro and Sala-i-Martin (2004, p. 229). Let us briefly look at Affine technologies, (13.101), and VES technology, (13.165–13.166).

The factor share of capital, $\epsilon_K(k) = MP_K/AP_K$, and share of labor, $\epsilon_L(k) = MP_L/AP_L$, cf. (13.29–13.33), with **Affine** (13.101) and **VES** (13.165–13.166) are shown in (13.193) and (13.194):

$$(i) \quad \epsilon_K(\mathbf{k}) = \frac{f'(k)}{f(k)/k} = \frac{\gamma a}{\gamma a + \gamma(1-a)/k} \quad ;$$

$$\epsilon_L(\mathbf{k}) = \frac{f(k) - f'(k)\,k}{f(k)} = \frac{\gamma(1-a)}{\gamma(1-a) + \gamma a k} \tag{13.193}$$

$$(ii) \quad \mathbf{MP_L} = B(1-\alpha)\,k^{\alpha} \to \infty \ ; \quad \epsilon_L(\mathbf{k}) = \frac{\mathbf{MP_L}}{\mathbf{AP_L}} = \frac{B(1-\alpha)\,k^{\alpha}}{Ak + B\,k^{\alpha}} \to \mathbf{0} \tag{13.194}$$

As factor prices—marginal products of Labor and Capital—are *constant* in (13.193), Factor accumulation of Capital is faster than Labor, and capital-labor ratio is always increasing, the *factor shares* in (13.193) converge *1* and *0*, as $k(t) \rightarrow \infty$. With VES technology in (13.194), the persistent growth of per capita output, labor productivity, $y(t)$, goes together with the wages, Marginal products of Labor, increasing to *infinity* with **VES** (13.165–13.166) and capital accumulation, $k(t) \rightarrow \infty$. Although wages of fully employed labor are unbounded with accumulation, $k(t) \rightarrow \infty$, the *wage share*, (13.194), converges by *L'Hospital* to *0* in (13.194). Such *asymptotic factor shares* are always implied for one-*sector*, two-*factor* models, with *technology* assumptions, $\mathbf{f(k)}$, (13.186–13.187), which as properly maintained then need *inclusion* of more *factors* and additional *sectors*.

These *persistent* growth conditions are used again in the context of Chap. 12, subsections "Per Capita Growth Paths on Steady-State Ray: $\mathbf{m} > \mathbf{1}$, $\boldsymbol{\mu} < \mathbf{1}$, Homogeneous Subsystems, Growth Paths, $m_H \neq m_K$", Chap. 17, subsection "Persistent Growth and Asymptotic Growth Rates", Chap. 18, subsection "Dynamic Systems and Evolution of Multi-sector Economies", Chap. 19, subsection "Solving the Multi-Sector Growth—(2 × 10)—Model", Chap. 20, subsection "Solving the Multi-Sector Growth—(2 × 10)—Model".

Studies of technology implications of more *factors* for persistent growth and factor shares in *optimal* (intertemporal) *planning* models are provided in Jones and Manuelli (1997, p. 84), Baldwin (1992, p. 260), Grossmann (2005, p. 123), Strulik (2005, p. 132), Zeira (2006, p. 11), Grossmann et al. (2013, p. 520), Acemoglu and Restrepo (2018, p. 1503), Irmen (2020, p. 109), Afonso et al. (2023, p. 2).

*Lagrange Multiplier, VEIS, and Non-homothetic Cardinal Utility*

The *Lagrange* multiplier $\boldsymbol{\lambda}(\mathbf{t})$ of the *Hamiltonian*, $\mathcal{H}(c, k, \lambda)$, (13.13), represents here by (13.15) the *cardinal* **Marginal utility** of [ income, expenditure (budget) constraint ] current consumption, $\mathbf{c(t)}$, i.e., $u'(c) = MU(c) = \boldsymbol{\lambda}(c)$, and the **size** of instantaneous elasticity of *intertemporal substitution*, **EIS**, was, $\eta = \boldsymbol{\eta}\,(\mathbf{c}) = \frac{-\,u'(c)}{u''(c)\,c} > 0$, and *reciprocal*, i.e.,

$$\mathbf{u}'(\mathbf{c}) = \mathbf{MU}(\mathbf{c}) = \boldsymbol{\lambda}(\mathbf{c})\ ; \quad 0 < -\,\mathbf{E}\,(\boldsymbol{\lambda}(\mathbf{c}), \mathbf{c}) = \frac{\mathbf{1}}{\boldsymbol{\eta}\,(\mathbf{c})} = -\,\mathbf{E}\,(\mathbf{MU}(\mathbf{c}), \mathbf{c}) > 0 \tag{13.195}$$

The possibility of measuring ***marginal utility*** of consumption (income), **MU(c)**, has a long history of discussions on **cardinal**[37] and **ordinal**[38] utilities. Here for *Ramsey* optimal (intertemporal substitution) ***macro***[39] saving and growth, the crucial issue is whether, **E (λ(c), c)**, (13.195), is ***constant***, **CEIS**, or ***not***, **VEIS**. We have shown the optimal solutions (***time paths***) of several economic variables with **VEIS**, (13.178), in Figs. 13.23, 13.24, 13.25, 13.26, 13.27, 13.28, and 13.29. The corresponding ***optimal time paths*** of their dynamic ***Lagrange multiplier***[40] values, **λ*(t)**, (13.13), (13.15), and **VEIS** values, **η*(t)**, (13.178), are shown in Figs. 13.30 and 13.31.

[37] Once, Samuelson (1937, p. 156) stated "four assumptions to make it possible to arrive, theoretically, at a ***precise*** for ***utility*** of ***money income*** of an individual with, U(c), ***unique measurable*** utility (U) of income (c)". Using Lagrange multiplier $\lambda(c) = U'(c)$ in maximizing his Utility functional, using Euler necessary conditions for a maximum, he (p. 158, eq.11) obtains the elasticity expression: $\mathbf{E}(\boldsymbol{\lambda}(\mathbf{c}), \mathbf{c}) = [\rho - \mathbf{r(t)}] / \widehat{\mathbf{c(t)}}$, $\rho \neq r(t)$,—[ Euler-Ramsey rule, (13.22), $r(t) \approx f'(k) - \delta$ ] as the most convenient form of the relation to hold consistent with the four assumptions; see Samuelson's elasticity in Hillinger (1969, p. 116), too.

[38] Marshallian **Demand** functions, $\mathbf{Y_i} = \mathbf{D_i(P, C)}$, $\mathbf{P} = (P_1, P_2, ..., P_N)$, i=1,2,..,N, derived from the maximization of the *Direct Utility* function, $\mathbf{u} = \mathbf{U}(Y_1, Y_2, ..., Y_N)$, under budget (income) ***constraint*** (**C**) [or by *Roy's* Identity from *Indirect Utility* function, $\mathbf{u} = \mathbf{V(P, C)}$ ] are, as well known, **invariant** under any ***monotone transformation*** of the selected ***direct-indirect*** Utility functions. Accordingly, also **all** derived (calculated) income-, price *elasticities* of Marshallian Demand, Slutsky price *elasticities*, and Hicks-Allen ***substitution elasticities***, are **invariant** to ***monotone transformation*** of the underlying Ordinal Direct or Indirect utility functions. On invariance properties, see Allen (1932, p. 224). On ordinal/cardinal utility, see Schumpeter (1949, p. 161); Frisch (1964).

The income *elasticity*, **E (λ (P, C), C)**, of the *Lagrange* multiplier, **λ (P, C)** [ coming directly from, $\boldsymbol{\lambda}(\mathbf{P}, \mathbf{C}) = \frac{\partial \mathbf{V(P,C)}}{\partial \mathbf{C}}$ expression ] has seen much less attention—but the range of numbers, $E(\lambda(P, C), C)$, is useful to characterize/evaluate various utility functions, $V(P, C)$ or $U(Y_1, Y_2, ..., Y_N)$; cf. $E(\lambda(P, C), C)$ of **CDES** Indirect utility, section "Sizes and Variability of Elasticity of Marginal Utility of Income", (6.28–6.36). On the history of **E (λ (P, C), C)**, see Samuelson (1942), Samuelson (1966), Zeuthen (1937), Koopmans (1960), Koopmans et al. (1960), Yaari (1964), Yaari (1965), Rader (1981), Neumann and Morgenstern (1953, 2007), Karlin (1959).

[39] Confined to ***one good*** (Macro-One Sector) model, Non-homothetic multigood utility functions may obtain *Homothetic* functional form, e.g., CES-CD forms with ***constant***, E(MU(c),c). To restore *Non-homothetic* utility (*Engel's* Law) in one-good (macro) models, the introduction of proper ***minimal*** (subsistence) consumption in utility functions is convenient and effective; see Chap. 6, subsection "One Good: Macro—and the Elasticity of Marginal Utility of Income".

[40] In the Preface to *Analytical Mechanics*, Lagrange (1811, 1997, p. 8) says: "No figures will be found in this work. The methods I present require neither constructions nor geometrical or mechanical arguments, but solely algebraic operations subject to a regular and uniform procedure ". Besides the algebraic formulas, however, the dynamic ***Lagrange multiplier*** values, **λ*(t)**, may here be shown in Fig. 13.30; many algebraic expressions and verbal names to **λ*(t)** were stated above, cf. (13.18).

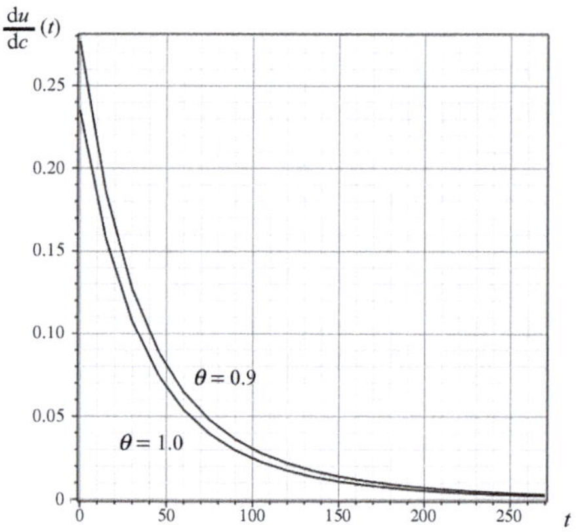


**Fig. 13.30** **Optimal** time paths of **VEIS**—$\frac{\mathbf{du(c^*)}}{\mathbf{dc^*}}(\mathbf{t}) = \mathbf{MU}[\mathbf{c^*(t)}] = \boldsymbol{\lambda}[\mathbf{c^*(t)}]$— (13.178–13.179), (13.15)—with $\varphi^*(\mathbf{t}) = [\mathbf{k^*(t)}, \mathbf{c^*(t)}]$ *solutions* to (13.180–13.184) along the **Separators** in Figs. 13.28 and 13.29: $\lim_{t\to\infty} \mathbf{MU}[\mathbf{c^*(t)}] = 0$, (13.179)—$\lim_{t\to\infty} \mathbf{MU}[\mathbf{c^*(t)}] = 0$, (13.178)

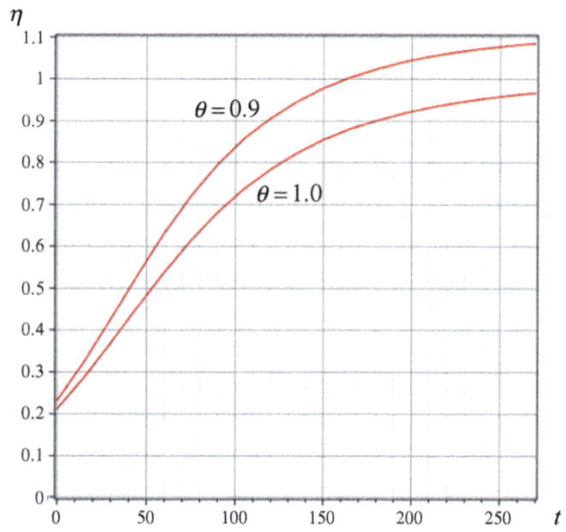


**Fig. 13.31** **Optimal** time paths of **VEIS**—$\eta[\mathbf{c^*(t)}]$—(13.178–13.179)—with $\varphi^*(\mathbf{t}) = [\mathbf{k^*(t)}, \mathbf{c^*(t)}]$ *solutions* to (13.180-13.184) along the **Separators** in Figs. 13.28 and 13.29: $\lim_{t\to\infty} \eta[\mathbf{c^*(t)}] = 1$, (13.179)—$\lim_{t\to\infty} \eta[\mathbf{c^*(t)}] = 1.11$, (13.178)

For any *common* initial value of $\mathbf{k(0)}$, the *economy* with VEIS utility *parameter*, $\theta = 0.9$, will start with a *lower* $\mathbf{c^*(0)}$ (lower located *separator*) in Figs. 13.28 and 13.29, but all its *curves* (time path) for saving, growth, MU(c), EIS $\eta$ (c) are *above* those of the economy with $\theta = 1.0$. Thus, along a *lower* separator (policy function), the economy *grows faster*. The location of the *Separator* (13.190) depended on **all** utility and production function *parameters*, whereas only *technology* parameters affected the location of the *isocline*, **c=O (k)**. The patterns of *optimal* persistent growth solutions and their long-run (*asymptotic*) properties can be obtained from $\varphi^*(\mathbf{t})$, (13.190–13.191), from which the *optimal* time paths of other model variables, as illustrated above, will be derived.

### *Further Extensions of Ramsey Optimal Growth Models*

We have *abstracted* from some observable complications in using the optimal growth model, e.g., ignoring *wealth distribution* and *heterogeneity* in optimal *household* consumption/saving plans with *different time preference* (discount) rates for *present* over *future utility* (consumption, income)—studied by

Sorger (1989), Sorger (2002), Mitra and Sorger (2013). For issues of wealth distributions and exhaustible resources, see Katayama and Long (2010).

Moreover, the ***discount rate*** $\boldsymbol{\rho}$ is *not* and should neither in optimal growth models be a *constant parameter* over time, cf. Olsen and Bailey (1981), Nairay (1984), Laibson (1997), Barro (1999), Shane et al. (2002), Galor (2016), Pignalosa (2019); our *constant* $\boldsymbol{\rho}$ did put *severe restrictions* upon choices of our other *structural* (technology, preferences) *parameters* in (13.80), cf. Table 13.2. Thus, a *flexible rate* of time preference (*discount*), determined *endogenously* by the underlying *time path* (profile) of *consumption*, $\boldsymbol{\rho}\,[\widetilde{c(t)}]$, $\widetilde{c(t)} = [c(t), \forall t \in [0, \infty)]$, should permit *better* empirical and a more comprehensive theory of *Ramsey* optimal growth models. The works on recursive utility functions, Joshi (1995, p. 602), Becker et al. (1989), Heer and Maussner (2009), Heijdra (2017), and multiattribute utility theory, Andersen et al. (2018), offer opportunities for greater *flexibility* in *time preferences.*

With suitable sizes of **technology parameters** $(\boldsymbol{\gamma}, \boldsymbol{a}, \boldsymbol{\sigma}, \boldsymbol{\delta})$, *persistent* income, and consumption, capital growth per capita was generated by **two-dimensional dynamics**: (13.23–13.24), (13.35–13.36), (13.87–13.88), (13.109–13.110), (13.120–13.121), (13.133–13.134), (13.157–13.158), (13.169–13.170), (13.180–13.182). Such *sustained*—**persistent**—economic *growth per capita* is often accomplished in growth models by using the Cobb-Douglas *technology*, including the growth rate of a *Total Factor Productivity* **TFP** ($\gamma$-variable), *endogenously* determined as Galor (2010, p. 13), or *exogenously* given by a time (trend) *parameter* as Prescott (1998, p. 536) and Solow (2000, p. 111,116).[41]

We saw above an *extended* **CD** production function used to generate sustained per capita growth by the endogenous determination of a *variable substitution* elasticity (**VES**), $\sigma(k)$, (13.167), which depended on underlying **technology parameters** and the **evolution** of $\mathbf{k(t)}$. Alternative **CES** technology specifications with *endogenous*, $\boldsymbol{\sigma}(\boldsymbol{k})$, e.g., S-shaped forms, de La Grandville (2018, p. 97), could—with proper horizontal *asymptotes* for $\boldsymbol{\sigma}(\boldsymbol{k})$—dynamically **unify** the *two regimes* of *steady-state* growth and *persistent* growth, cf. Tables 13.1 and 13.2; cf. de La Grandville (1997), Klump and de La Grandville (2000).

Thus, richer **parametric** functional forms, **VES** of $\mathbf{f(k)}$, **VEIS** forms of $\mathbf{u(c)}$, $\boldsymbol{\eta}(\mathbf{c})$, and *Variable Rate of Time Preferences*, **VRTP**, $\boldsymbol{\rho} = \boldsymbol{\rho}\,[\widetilde{\mathbf{c(t)}}]$, have potentials to offer—within the **general** and **robust** continuous-time **Dynamic System** (13.23–13.24)—much larger *scope* to a **Unified Standard Model** of Optimal Saving and Optimal Economic Growth—an object for further theoretical and quantitative economic research.

[41] By using "normalized" Labor variables (measuring *labor-augmenting* technological change), "efficiency units", $\widetilde{L}(t) = e^{\mu t}L(t)$, $\tilde{k}(t) = K(t)/\widetilde{L}(t) = k(t)\,e^{-\mu t}$, $\tilde{c}(t) = C(t)/\widetilde{L}(t) = c(t)\,e^{-\mu t}$, in (13.35–13.36), Smetters (2003, p. 699) has derived and demonstrated properties (including *saving rates*) of the optimal solutions of the Ramsey growth model with **CES** technology and **CEIS** utility.

## Conclusions and Final Comments

This chapter has dealt with a wide range of subjects: optimal control dynamics, general sufficient conditions for the existence of a trajectory (separator) with optimal time path, production functions allowing for persistent growth per capita, non-homothetic utility functions with variable intertemporal elasticity of substitution (VEIS). Since the chapter does not lend itself to a detailed summary, we only offer brief comments on some of our findings and main results.

The *Ramsey* (1928) optimal growth model was finally *parametrically* solved (*explicit* time path) by *Affine Dynamics* with Affine technology and CEIS and **VEIS** utility functions. The Affine dynamics identified the clue to generating historically observed *saving rates* in the *range*: 0.05–0.35—Variable income elasticity of the Lagrange multiplier (Cardinal Marginal utility of consumption)—corresponding to the Micro foundation of "Engel's law of Budgets" by *non-homothetic* utility functions. VEIS utility functions combined with nonlinear technologies, VES, CES, further improved the performance of the Ramsey saving-growth model. *The Macro Optimal Growth model does work.* The core theorems on the existence and uniqueness of optimal control solutions were established/proved in the main text and Appendix.

## Appendix A: Proof of Theorem 13.2 by Lemmas 13.2–13.3

**Lemma 13.2** ***Separator Existence****. If there exist numbers* $d > 0, k_0 > 0$ *such that*

$$\forall k \geq k_0 > 0,\ \forall c > 0: \quad f(k)/k - (n+\delta) - \eta(c)\left[\, f'(k) - (\delta+\rho)\right] \geq d > 0 \tag{13.196}$$

*then there* ***exists*** *to the system (13.23–13.24) a* ***solution*** *(phase path)* $-\boldsymbol{\varphi}^*(\mathbf{t}) \equiv [\mathbf{k}^*(\mathbf{t}), \mathbf{c}^*(\mathbf{t})]$, $t \in \Re$, *such that* $k^*(t) \to \infty$, $c^*(t) \to \infty$, *as* $t \to \infty$. *Such solution* $\varphi^*(t)$ *will—by the existence and uniqueness theorem for the ordinary differential equations (13.23–13.24), [through every point* $[k^*(0), c^*(0)]$ *of* $\varphi^*(t)$ *passes one and only one phase curve (trajectory)]—****separate*** *the entire first quadrant into the* ***two regions*** *I and II of Fig. 13.2b.*

*Phase paths (solutions)* $\varphi(t) = [k(t), c(t)]$, $t \in \Re$, ***starting*** *(with initial values) in the* ***lower*** *region I have the same behavior as* $\varphi^*(t)$ *(13.64) for* $t \to \infty$*—whereas paths,* $\varphi(t) = [k(t), c(t)]$, $t \in \Re$, ***starting*** *in the* ***upper*** *region II eventually* ***meet*** *the c-axis,* $k = 0$.

***Proof*** Consider the **region** $W_\alpha = \{(k, c) \mid 0 \le c \le \alpha k \wedge k \ge k_0\}$, where $\alpha$ is a *positive constant*—chosen such that $W_\alpha$ becomes *positively invariant*; see Fig. 13.2a above—the **region** $W_\alpha$ is located below the **socline,** $\dot{k} = h(k, c) = 0$: $c = f(k) - (n + \delta)k$, (13.23).

Since the *vector field*, $(h, g)$, (13.23–13.24), is directed *inward* on the *line* $k = k_0$, and as the *positive k-axis is a solution (trajectory)*, the **region** $W_\alpha$ in Fig. 13.2a is positive *invariant iff* the vector field, $(h, g)$, points *inward* on the *line* $c = \alpha k$, $(k > k_0)$.

Since the inward-pointing normal to the line $c = \alpha k$ is $(\alpha, -1)$, we require that the inner product of vector, $(h, g)$, and vector, $(\alpha, -1)$, is positive:

$$\alpha\, h(k, \alpha k) \; - \; g(k, \alpha k) \; > \; 0, \quad \text{for } k \ge k_0. \tag{13.197}$$

Inserting the expressions for vector field, $(h, g)$, (13.23–13.24), into (13.197), and next simplifying the expressions, we obtain from (13.197) the *requirement*:

$$0 < \alpha \; < \; f(k)/k \; - (n + \delta) - \eta(\alpha k)\left[f'(k) - (\delta + \rho)\right] \; \equiv \; R(k)\,, \quad \text{for } k \ge k_0. \tag{13.198}$$

A positively invariant region $W_\alpha$ (with some $\alpha > 0$) exists iff $R(k)$, (13.198), is bounded from below by a positive constant. Condition (13.196) stated that $R(k)$ satisfies for $k \ge k_0, c > 0$

$$k \ge k_0 > 0\,,\; c > 0 \;: \quad R(k) \; \ge \; d \; > \; 0. \tag{13.199}$$

*Choose* $\alpha$ in (13.198) to be any positive constant, $0 < \alpha < d$, *such that* in addition: $\alpha < \rho - n$, for $f(0) > 0$; (also $\alpha = \rho - n$ is permissible for $f(0) = 0$). Then $W_\alpha$ *is positively* invariant, and $k(t) \to \infty$ as $t \to \infty$ for any solution starting in $W_\alpha$.

For *any solution* (phase path) $\varphi(t) = [k(t), c(t)]$, $t \in \Re$, in the *open first quadrant*, $\Re^2_+$, we know by assumption (13.58) that $\dot{c}(t) > 0$. It follows by (13.60), (13.23–13.24), that any solution, $\varphi(t) = [k(t), c(t)], t \in \Re$, *starting* in $\mathbf{W}_\alpha$ must *satisfy*: $k(t) \to \infty$, $c(t) \to \infty$, as $t \to \infty$.

Any *phase path*, $\varphi(t) = [k(t), c(t)]$, $t \in \Re$, starting in open $\Re^2_+$ must **either** behave as described for region $W_\alpha$ (called **class I**, Fig. 13.2), **or** cross the $\dot{k} = 0$ nullcline (**class II**).

In the *class II* case, the phase path, $\varphi(t) = [k(t), c(t)]$, $t \in \Re$, will *meet* the *c-axis* (k=0) eventually—since otherwise $c(t) \to \infty$ and $k(t) \to k_\varepsilon$ as $t \to \infty$, for some $k_\varepsilon \ge 0$.

For $t$ sufficiently large, i.e., $k$ sufficiently small, say $\mathbf{0} < \mathbf{k} \leq \mathbf{k}_\varepsilon$, we get from dynamic system (13.23–13.24) [ *above* isocline, $\dot{\mathbf{k}} = 0$: $c > f(k) - (n+\delta)k$ ] the expression and evaluation:

$$-\frac{dc}{dk} = -\frac{\dot{c}}{\dot{k}} = -\frac{g(k,c)}{h(k,c)} = \frac{-\eta(c)\,[\,f'(k) - \rho - \delta\,]}{(1/c)\,[\,f(k) - (n+\delta)k\,] - 1}$$

$$\leq \frac{\bar{\eta}\, f'(k)}{1/2} \equiv a\, f'(k) \tag{13.200}$$

with $\bar{\eta}$ as an *upper bound* for $\eta = \eta(c)$. The result (13.200) directly rules out $k_\varepsilon > 0$, as $-\frac{dc}{dk}$ would then be bounded above by a constant. If $k_\varepsilon = 0$, we get by integrating (13.200) to $k_\varepsilon$:

$$c(k) \leq c(k_\varepsilon) + a\, f(k_\varepsilon), \quad 0 < k \leq k_\varepsilon, \tag{13.201}$$

Hence (13.201) contradicts that $c(k) \to \infty$ as $k \to 0^+$.

To get the *separating phase path*, $\varphi^*(t)$, (13.64), consider a *curve* $C$ (like a circle), Fig. 13.2b, *connecting* $(k,c) = (1,0)$ with $(k,c) = (0,1)$, and *intersecting* the nullcline $\dot{k} = 0$ *once*. We can write the curve C as: $C = C_I \cup C_{II} \cup \{(1,0),(0,1)\}$ (*closed set*), where *curves* $C_I$ and $C_{II}$ consist of the *points through* which *pass* solutions (*phase paths*) of **classes** I and II.

$C_{II}$ must be an *open* and *connected set* of $C$. Since $C_I$ and $C_{II}$ are both *non-empty*, $C_I \cup \{(1,0)\}$ must be a *closed set*. The **separating phase path** $\boldsymbol{\varphi}^*(\mathbf{t})$, (13.64), goes *through* the **endpoint** [ $\bar{k}^*, \bar{c}^*$ ] of curve $C_I$—which is for $\varphi^*(t)$, (13.64) an upper *boundary point* [$\bar{k}^* > 0, \bar{c}^* > 0$] of **positive invariant region I**, Fig. 13.2b (analogous to region, $\mathbf{W}_\alpha$, Fig. 13.2a). It is the *phase path* (solution) $\boldsymbol{\varphi}^*(\mathbf{t}) \equiv [\mathbf{k}^*(\mathbf{t}), \mathbf{c}^*(\mathbf{t})]$, $\forall t \in \Re$, (13.64) through $[\bar{\mathbf{k}}^*, \bar{\mathbf{c}}^*]$ that *traces out* entirely the upper **boundary curve** of Region I, which **separates** the *closed* domain, $\overline{\Re}^2_+$, of (13.23–13.24) into **Regions** I-II, left **boundary**, $k = 0$—of Fig. 13.2b. Application of the existence and uniqueness *theorem*, Pontryagin (1962, p. 20), to (13.64) and Lemma 13.1 for any initial values is ensured by the continuity-differentiability properties (13.57). □

A powerful and more useful extension of the necessary and sufficient condition (13.196) in Lemma 13.2 is the much *simpler sufficient* separator *existence* condition, stated in:

**Corollary 13.2** ***Separator****, Sufficient Condition. With assumptions (13.57) and (13.60), the sufficient conditions for the* ***existence*** *of* ***separator****,* $\boldsymbol{\varphi}^*(\mathbf{t})$*, (13.64), are given by the restriction:*

$$\sup_{c>0} \eta(c) \equiv \bar{\eta} < \frac{\underline{b} - (n+\delta)}{\underline{b} - (\rho+\delta)} \tag{13.202}$$

*$\overline{\eta}$ is upper bound, **supremum**, of intertemporal substitution elasticity, $\eta(c)$;* $\underline{\mathbf{b}}$ *is (13.60).*

***Proof*** Since $f(k) \to \infty$ as $k \to \infty$, it follows from (13.60) and L'Hospital that $f(k)/k \to \underline{b}$ as $k \to \infty$. Thus for any $\varepsilon > 0$, there exists a $k_\varepsilon$, such that for $k > k_\varepsilon$, we have, cf. (13.196),

$$\begin{aligned} & f(k)/k - (n+\delta) - \eta(c)\left[f'(k) - (\delta+\rho)\right] \\ & \geq \underline{b} - \varepsilon - (n+\delta) - \sup_{c>0} \eta(c)\left[\underline{b} + \varepsilon - (\delta+\rho)\right] \\ & = \underline{b} - (n+\delta) - \overline{\eta}\left[\underline{b} - (\delta+\rho)\right] - \varepsilon(1+\overline{\eta}) \equiv d. \end{aligned} \tag{13.203}$$

By *assumptions* (13.60) and (13.202), the *sum* of the first *three terms* of the expression for $d$ (13.203) is *positive*. Thus, by choosing $\varepsilon > 0$ sufficiently small, also the number $d$ is *positive*.

Hence the requirements for **d** in (13.196) [or $\alpha$ in (13.198)] of Lemma 13.2 are satisfied, and the **separating phase path** (solution), $\boldsymbol{\varphi}^*(\mathbf{t})$, (13.64), **exists** by (13.202)—which is (13.62). □

**Lemma 13.3** ***Convergence.*** *If any chosen utility function* $\mathbf{u(c)}$ *is assumed to satisfy:*

$$\forall c \geq c_0 \geq 0: \quad 0 \leq u(c) \leq A\,c\,; \;\; A > 0 \tag{13.204}$$

*then the **convergence** of the **integral**, (13.3):* $V = \int_0^\infty u[\,c(t)\,]\,e^{-(\rho-n)t}dt$, *for **solutions*** $[\mathbf{k(t)}, \mathbf{c(t)}]$ *to the dynamic system (13.23–13.24)—**is assured**, if — with* $\underline{\mathbf{b}}$ *as given in (13.60)*

$$\sup_{c>0} \eta(c) \equiv \overline{\eta} < \frac{\rho - n}{(\underline{b} - \delta) - \rho} \tag{13.205}$$

***Proof*** Let $\varepsilon > 0$. Choose $k_\varepsilon$ such that $f'(k) < \underline{b} + \varepsilon$ for $k \geq k_\varepsilon$. Choose $t_\varepsilon$ such that $k(t) > k_\varepsilon$ for $t > t_\varepsilon$. Then from (13.24) and (13.61), we find that

$$\forall t \geq t_\varepsilon: \quad \dot{c} < c \sup_{c>0} \eta(c)\left[(\underline{b} + \varepsilon) - (\delta+\rho)\right] \equiv \beta\,c \tag{13.206}$$

It follows from (13.206) that, $c(t) \leq c(t_\varepsilon)\,e^{\beta(t-t_\varepsilon)}$, which implies together with (13.204) that

$$u[\,c(t)\,]\,e^{-(\rho-n)t} \leq A\,c(t)\,e^{-(\rho-n)t} \leq A\,c(t_\varepsilon)\,e^{-\beta t_\varepsilon}\,e^{-(\rho-n-\beta)\,t}. \tag{13.207}$$

**Convergence** of the **integral** $V$, (13.3) with (13.204), is assured by (13.207), if $\beta < \rho - n$.

Using $\beta < \rho - n$ together with (13.206) gives the convergence *requirement*:

$$\sup_{c>0} \eta(c) \equiv \overline{\eta} < \frac{\rho - n}{\underline{b} + \varepsilon - (\delta + \rho)} \tag{13.208}$$

With $\varepsilon > 0$ small enough, stipulation (13.208) is met by *condition* (13.205)—which is (13.63)[42] □

**Remark 13.3** Condition (13.63) is analogous to a low $\rho$—taking over the role of a large parameter, $\underline{b}$. The condition (13.205) of Lemma 13.3, cf. (13.62–13.63), is stronger than that (13.202) of Corollary 13.2, since by assumption: $\rho < \underline{b} - \delta$, (13.60), we then have,

$$\overline{\eta} < \frac{\rho - n}{\underline{b} - (\rho + \delta)} < \frac{\underline{b} - (n + \delta)}{\underline{b} - (\rho + \delta)}; \quad \rho > n : \quad \frac{\underline{b} - (n + \delta)}{\underline{b} - (\rho + \delta)} > 1 \tag{13.209}$$

The *existence* of *separator* $\varphi^*(t)$ (13.64) is *assured* by $\overline{\eta} < 1$, cf. (13.62), (13.209); thus, if $u(c)$ always has, $\eta(c) \leq 1$, $\forall c > 0$, then (13.62) is automatically satisfied.[43] If $\eta(c) > 1$, $\forall c > 0$, then $\rho$ must be large enough to satisfy separator existence condition (13.62).

The ***separating phase path*** in Fig. 13.2b is the **optimal solution** $[\mathbf{k}^*(\mathbf{t}), \mathbf{c}^*(\mathbf{t})]$, (13.64), satisfying the *transversality condition*, (13.25), as **proved** above, (13.78).

[42] See more in footnote 31 on isoelastic (CEIS) separator condition, (13.62), as enough for finite **V**, (13.3). Barro and Sala-i-Martin (2004, eq.4.12, p. 207) gives for **CEIS**: $\underline{b} - \delta > \rho > (\underline{b} - \delta)(1 - \theta) + n\theta > n$ as a condition for finite V (13.3). However, this expression here seems only to work for $\theta > 1$.

[43] Note that supremum $\overline{\eta} < 1$ does *not* itself ensure *convergence* of $V$, (13.63), (13.3). However, for isoelastic $u(c)$, with, $\forall c$, $\eta(c) = \eta$ (constant), it can be verified that the convergence of $V$, (13.3), is in fact also ensured with the existence condition (13.62) of the separator, (13.64), satisfying the transversality condition, (13.78); see Gandolfo (2010, p. 660). Evidently, if $\eta < 1$, $(\theta > 1)$, in CEIS $u(c)$, (13.79), (bounded above), then $V$, (13.3), always exists (finite), when $\rho > n$. But also for $\eta > 1$, $(\theta < 1)$, in $u(c)$, (13.79), (now unbounded), then $V$, (13.3), still exists (finite), if and only if the separator condition (13.62) is satisfied and always $\rho > n$.

It remains to be seen how the **sufficient** supremum **condition**, (13.205), (13.63), may be relaxed for general non-isoelastic, **VEIS**, **u(c)**, in Ramsey problems. For $\rho > n$, a *conjecture* is as follows: with $\eta(c) = \frac{1}{\theta}(1 - \frac{\nu}{c}) > 0$, (13.86) of *Geary-Stone* utility function [ cf. footnote 16, Fig. 13.16, and (13.178)], the *condition*: $(\theta > 1,\ \overline{\eta} = 1/\theta < 1)$ with $\forall c > 0,\ \eta(c) < 1$, Fig. 13.16, will ensure *convergence* of **V**, (13.63), (13.3).

# Bibliography


Acemoglu D, Restrepo P (2018) The Race between Man and Machine: Implications of Technology for Growth, Factor Shares, and Employment. American Economic Review 108(6):1488–1542

Afonso O, Sequeira T, Almelda D (2023) Technological Knowledge and Wages: From Skill Premium to Wage Polarization. Journal of Economics 2023:1–17, DOI 10.1007/s00712-023-00833-y

Aghion P, Durlauf S (eds) (2005) Handbook of Economic Growth, 1st edn. Elsevier, Amsterdam, North–Holland

Aghion P, Howitt P (1998) Endogenous Growth Theory. The MIT Press, Cambridge, MA and London, England

Akerlof G, Nordhaus WD (1967) Balanced Growth – A Razor's Edge. International Economic Review 8:343–348

Allen RGD (1932) The Foundations of a Mathematical Theory of Exchange. Economica 36:197–226

Andersen S, Harrison GW, Lau MI, Rutstrom EE (2008) Eliciting Risk and Time Preferences. Econometrica 76:583–618

Andersen S, Harrison GW, Lau MI, Rutstrom EE (2018) Multiattribute Utility Theory, Intertemporal Utility, and Correlation Aversion. International Economic Review 59:537–555

Arnold VI (1973) Ordinary Differential Equations. MIT Press, Mass

Arrow KJ (1971) Essays in The Theory of Risk–Bearing. North–Holland

Arrow KJ, Kurz M (1970) Public Investment, The Rate of Return, and Optimal Fiscal Policy. The Johns Hopkins Press, Baltimore

Arrow KJ, Chenery HB, Minhas BS, Solow RM (1961) Capital–Labour Substitution and Economic Efficiency. Review of Economics and Statistics 43:225–250

Ashraf Q, Galor O (2011) Dynamics and Stagnation in the Malthusian Epoch. American Economic Review 101:2003–2041

Ashraf Q, Galor O (2013) The "Out of Africa" Hypothesis, Human Genetic Diversity, and Comparative Economic Development. American Economic Review 103:1–46

Atkeson A, Ogaki M (1996) Wealth–varying Intertemporal Elasticities of Substitution: Evidence from Panel and Aggregate Data. Journal of Monetary Economics 38:507–534

Attanasio OP, Weber G (1989) Intertemporal Substitution, Risk Aversion, and the Euler Equation for Consumption. Economic Journal 99:59–73

Attanasio OP, Weber G (1995) Is Consumption Growth Consistent with Intertemporal Optimization ? Evidence from the Consumer Expenditure Survey. Journal of Political Economy 103:1121–1157

Back K, Liu R, Teguia A (2019) Increasing Risk Aversion and Life Cycle Investing. Mathematics and Financial Economics 13:287–302

Baldwin R (1992) The Growth Effects of 1992. Economic Policy 4(9):247–281

Barro RJ (ed) (1989) Modern Business Cycle Theory. Basil Blackwell, Oxford

Barro RJ (1991) Economic Growth in a Cross–Section of Countries. Quarterly Journal of Economics 106:407–443

Barro RJ (1999) Ramsey Meets Laibson in the Neoclassical Growth Model. Quarterly Journal of Economics 114:1125–1152

Barro RJ, Sala-i-Martin X (1992) Convergence. Journal of Political Economy 100:223–251

Barro RJ, Sala-i-Martin X (2004) Economic Growth Theory, 2nd edn. M.I.T. Press, Cambridge, Mass

Becker RA, Boyd JH, Sung BY (1989) Recursive Utility and Optimal Capital Accumulation. I. Existence. Journal of Economic Theory 47:76–100

Bernoulli D (1738, 1954) Exposition of a New Theory on the Measurement of Risk. Econometrica 22:23–36

Birkhoff G, Rota G (1989) Ordinary Differential Equations, 4th edn. John Wiley & Sons, New York

Blanchard OJ, Fischer S (1992) Lectures on Macroeconomics. MIT Press

Böhm-Bawerk Ev (1921) Positive Theorie des Kapitales. Vierte Auflage, Gustav Fischer Verlag, Jena; transl. W. Smart, (1923) *Positive Theory of Capital*, Books for Libraries Press, New York.

Brems H (1986) Pioneering Economic Theory 1630–1980. A Mathematical Restatement. The Johns Hopkins University Press, Baltimore

Browning M, Hansen LP, Heckman JJ (1999) Micro Data and General Equilibrium Models. In: Taylor & Woodford (ed) Handbook of Macroecon.1, Elsevier, pp 543–633

Calvet LE, Paoli S (2014) Twin Picks: Disentangling the Determinants of Risk–Taking in Household Portfolios. Journal of Finance 69:867–906

Caselli F, Feyrer J (2007) The Marginal Product of Capital. Quarterly Journal of Economics 122:535–568

Cass D (1965) Optimum Growth in an Aggregative Model of Capital Accumulation. Review of Economic Studies 32:233–240, Reprinted in Becker (1991)

Creedy J, Guest R (2008) Discounting and the Rate of Time Preference Rate. The Economic Record 84:109–127

Dalgaard CJ, Strulik H (2015) The Physiological Foundations of the Wealth of Nations. Journal of Economic Growth 20:37–73

Dhrymes PJ (1962) A Multisectoral Model of Growth. Quarterly Journal of Economics 76:264–278

Durlauf SN (1996) On the and Divergence of Growth Rates. Economic Journal 106:1016–1018

Easterly W (1994) Economic Stagnation, Fixed Factors, and Policy Thresholds. Journal of Monetary Economics 33:525–557

Evans DJ (2005) The Elasticity of Marginal Utility of Consumption: Estimates for 20 OECD Countries. Fiscal Studies 26:197–224

Frisch R (1964) Dynamic Utility. Econometrica 32:418–424

Galor O (2005) From Stagnation To Growth: Unified Growth Theory. pp 172–293, in *Handbook 1A* Aghion & Durlauf, (eds.) (2005).

Galor O (2010) The 2008 Lawrence R. Klein Lecture – Comparative Economic Development: Insights From Unified Growth Theory. International Economic Review 51:1–44

Galor O (2011) Unified Growth Theory. Princeton University Press, Princeton and Oxford

Galor O (2016) The Agricultural Origin of Time Preference. American Economic Review 106:3064–3103

Gandolfo G (2010) Economic Dynamics: Methods and Models, 4th edn. Springer–Verlag, Berlin

Garcia-Penalosa C, Turnovsky SJ (2005) Production Risk of the Functional Distribution of Income in a Developing Economy: Tradeoffs and Policy Responses. Journal of Development Economics 76:175–208

Goodwin RM (1961) The Optimal Growth Path for an Underdeveloped Economy. The Economic Journal 71:756–774

Grossman GM, Rogoff K (1995) Handbook of International Economics, vol III. Elsevier, Amsterdam

Grossmann V (2005) White–Collar Employment, Inequality, and Technological Change. Journal of Economics 10:119–142

Grossmann V, Steger T, Trimborn T (2013) Dynamically optimal R/D subsidization. Journal of Economic Dynamics and Control 37:516–534

Hadley G, Kemp MC (1971) Variational Methods In Economics. Amsterdam, North–Holland Publ

Hall RE (1988) Intertemporal Substitution in Consumption. Journal of Political Economy 96:339–357

Hansen GD, Prescott EC (2002) Malthus to Solow. American Economic Review 92:1205–1217

Heer B, Maussner A (2009) Dynamic General Equilibrium Modeling, 2nd edn. Springer, Dordrecht Heidelberg

Heijdra BJ (2017) Foundations of Modern Macroeconomics, 3rd edn. Oxford University Press, Oxford

Hillinger C (1969) The Measurement of Utility. Review of Economic Studies 36:111–116

Houthakker HS (1960) Additive Preferences. Econometrica 28:244–257

Irmen A (2020) Tasks, Technology in the Neoclassical Production Sector. Journal of Economics 131:101–121

Jensen BS (1994) The Dynamic Systems of Basic Economic Growth Models. Kluwer Academic Publishers, Dordrecht

Jensen BS (2017) von Thünen: Capital, Production Functions, Marginal Productivity Wages and the Natural Wage. German Economic Review 18:51–80

Jensen BS, Larsen ME (1987) Growth and Long–Run Stability. Acta Applicandae Mathematicae 9:219–237, Reprinted in Jensen (1994)

Jensen BS, Palokangas T (2007) Stochastic Economic Dynamics. Copenhagen Business School Press, Denmark

Jensen BS, Alsholm PK, Larsen ME, Jensen JM (2005) Dynamic Structure, Exogeneity, Phase Portraits, Growth Paths, and Scale and Substitution Elasticities. Review of International Economics 13:59–89

Jensen BS, Richter M (2007) Stochastic one–sector and two–sector growth models in continuous time. In: Jensen BS, Palokangas T (2007) (eds) Stochastic Economic Dynamics, CBS Press, Copenhagen, pp 167–216

Jensen BS, de Boer P, van Daal J, Jensen PS (2011) Global Restrictions on the Parameters of the CDES Indirect Utility Function. Journal of Economics 102:217–235

Jones LE, Manuelli RE (1990) A Convex Model of Equilibrium Growth: Theory and Policy Implications. Journal of Political Economy 98:1008–1038

Jones LE, Manuelli RE (1997) The Sources of Growth. Journal of Economic Dynamics and Control 98:75–114

Joshi S (1995) Recursive Utility and Optimal Growth under Uncertainty. Journal of Mathematical Economics 24:601–617

Karlin S (1959) Mathematical Methods and Theory in Games, Programming and Economics. Addison–Wesley Publishing Co, Boston, Mass
Katayama S, Long NV (2010) A Dynamic Game of Status–seeking with Public Capital and an Exhaustible Resource. Optimal Control, Applications and Methods 31:43–53
Keynes JM (1933, 1963) Essays in Biography. Norton & Company, N.Y
King RG, Rebelo ST (1993) Transitional Dynamics and Economic Growth in the Neoclassical Model. American Economic Review 83:908–931
Klump R, de La Grandville O (2000) Economic Growth and the Elasticity of Substitution: Two Theorems and Some Suggestions. American Economic Review 90:282–291
Koopmans TC (1960) Stationary Ordinal Utility and Impatience. Econometrica 28:287–309
Koopmans TC, Diamond PA, Williamson RE (1960) Stationary Utility and Time Perspective. Econometrica 32:82–100
Kuznets S (1966) Modern Economic Growth. Rate, Structure and Spread. Yale University Press, New Haven
de La Grandville O (1997) Curvature and the Elasticity of Substitution: Straightening It Out. Journal of Economics 66:23–34
de La Grandville O (2017) Economic Growth – A Unified Approach, 2nd edn. Cambridge University Press, Cambridge
de La Grandville O (2018) Why is Optimal Growth Theory Mute ? Restoring its Rightful Voice. Macroeconomic Dynamics 22:77–100
Lagerlöf NP (2006) The Galor–Weil model revisited: A quantitative exercise. Review of Economic Dynamics 9:116–142
Lagrange JL (1811, 1997) Analytical Mechanics – Mecanique Analytique, vol 1–2. Translated by A. Boissonnade and V.N. Vagliente, Springer–Science+Business Media, B.V., Dordrecht
Laibson D (1997) Golden Eggs and Hyperbolic Discounting. Quarterly Journal of Economics 112:443–477
Lawrance EC (1991) Poverty and the Rate of Time Preference: Evidence from Panel Data. Journal of Political Economy 99:54–77
Leonard D, Long NV (1992) Optimal Control Theory and Static Optimization in Economics. Cambridge University Press
Lewis FD (1983) Fertility and Savings in the United States: 1830–1900. Journal of Political Economy 91:825–839
Lucas Jr RE (1998) On the Mechanics of Economic Development. Journal of Monetary Economics 22:3–42
Lucas Jr RE (2002) Lectures on Economic Growth. Harvard University Press, Cambridge, Mass
Maddison A (1992) A Long–Run Perspective on Saving. Scandinavian Journal of Economics 94:181–196
Maussner A, Klump R (1996) Wachstumstheorie. Springer, Berlin
Mehra R, Prescott EC (1985) The Equity Premium, a Puzzle. Journal of Monetary Economics 15:145–161
Mehra R, Prescott EC (1988) The Equity Premium, A Solution ? Journal of Monetary Economics 15:145–161
Merton RC (1971) Optimum Consumption and Portfolio Rules in a Continuous–Time Model. Journal of Econ Theory 3:373–413, Ch.5, Merton (1990)

Merton RC (1975) An Asymptotic Theory of Growth under Uncertainty. Review of Economic Studies 42:375–393, Ch.17 in Merton (1990)
Merton RC (1992) Continuous–Time Finance. Blackwell, Cambridge MA
Mitra T, Sorger G (2013) On Ramsey's Conjecture. Journal of Economic Theory 148:1953–1976
Mulligan C, Sala-i-Martin X (1993) A Note on the Time–Elimination Method For Solving Recursive Dynamic Economic Models. NBER WP (0116)
Nairay A (1984) Asymptotic Behavior and Optimal Propensities of a Consumption–Investment Model with Variable Time Preference. Journal of Economic Dynamics and Control 7:283–313
von Neumann J (1945–46) A Model of General Economic Equilibrium. Rev Econ Stud 13:1–9
Neumann Jv, Morgenstern O (1953, 2007) Theory of Games and Economic Behavior, 3rd edn. Princeton University Press, Princeton and Oxford
Newbery D (1972) The Importance of Malleable Capital in Optimal Growth Models. Journal of Economic Theory 5:21–41
Newbery D (2008) The Ramsey Model. The New Palgrave. McMillan, London
Obstfeld M, Rogoff K (1995) The Intertemporal Approach to the Current Account. Chapt. 34 in Grossman & Rogoff (1995).
Ogaki M (1992) Engel's Law and Cointegration. Journal of Political Economy 100:1027–1046
Ogaki M, Atkeson A (1997) Rate of Time Preference, Intertemporal Elasticity of Substitution, and Level of Wealth. Review of Economics and Statistics 79:564–572
Ogaki M, Qiang Z (2001) Decreasing Relative Risk Aversion and Tests of Risk Sharing. Econometrica 69:515–626
Olsen M, Bailey MJ (1981) Positive Time Preference. Journal of Political Economy 89:1–25
O'Rourke KH, Williamson JG (2000) Globalization and History. MIT Press, Cambridge, Mass
Pampel T (2009) On the Dynamics of Basic Growth Models: Ratio Stability vs. Convergence and Divergence in State Space. German Economic Review 10:384–400
Pignalosa D (2019) On the role of the utility function in the estimation of preference parameters. Metroeconomica pp 1–28
Piketty T (2014) Capital in The Twenty–First Century. The Belknap Press of Harvard University Press, London
Pitchford JD (1960) Growth and the Elasticity of Factor Substitution. Economic Record 36:491–504
Pontryagin LS (1962) Ordinary Differential Equations. Addison–Wesley, Reading, Mass
Pontryagin LS, Boltyanskii VG, Gamkrelidze RV, Mishchenko EF (1962) The Mathematical Theory of Optimal Processes. Pergamon Press, Wiley, New York
Pratt JW (1964) Risk Aversion in the Small and in the Large. Econometrica 32:122–136
Prescott EC (1998) Lawrence R. Klein Lecture 1997, Needed: A Theory of Total Factor Productivity. International Economic Review 39:525–551
Rader T (1981) Utility over Time: The Homothetic Case. Journal of Economic Theory 25:219–236
Ramsey FP (1928) A Mathematical Theory of Saving. Economic Journal 38:543–559
Rebelo S (1991) Long–Run Policy Analysis and Long–Run Growth. Journal of Political Economy 99:500–521

Romer D (2019) Advanced Macroeconomics, 5th edn. McGraw–Hill, N.Y
Romer P (1986a) Cake Eating, Chattering, and Jumps: Existence Results for Variational Problems. Econometrica 54:897–908
Romer PM (1986b) Increasing Returns and Long–Run Growth. Journal of Political Economy 94:1002–1037, Reprinted in Becker (1991)
Romer PM (1989) Capital Accumulation in the Theory of Long–Run Growth. Ch. 2 in Barro, Robert J., ed. (1989).
Samuelson PA (1937) A Note on Measurement of Utility. Review of Economic Studies 4:135–161, *The Collected Scientific Papers*, Vol. 1, p.212–216.
Samuelson PA (1942) Constancy of the Marginal Utility of Income. Chicago University Press. The Collected Scientific Papers 1:37–53
Samuelson PA (1966) The Collected Scientific Papers of Paul A. Samuelson. MIT Press, Mass
Samuelson PA (1969) Lifetime Portfolio Selection by Dynamic Stochastic Programming. Review of Economics and Statistics 51:239–246
Samuelson PA (1972) The General Saddlepoint Property of Optimal Control–Motions. Journal of Economic Theory 50:102–120
Schumpeter JA (1949) Vilfredo Pareto (1848–1923). The Quarterly Journal of Economics 63(2):147–173
Shane F, Loewenstein G, O'Donoghue T (2002) Time Discounting and Time Preference: A Critical Review. Journal of Economic Literature 40:351–401
Simon JL (1990) Great and Almost–Great Magnitudes in Economics. Journal of Economic Perspectives 4:149–156
Smetters K (2003) The (interesting) Dynamic Properties of the Neoclassical Growth Model with CES Production. Review of Economic Dynamics 6:697–707
Solow RM (1956) A Contribution to the Theory of Economic Growth. Quarterly Journal of Economics 70:65–94, Reprinted in Stiglitz (1969), and in Becker (1991)
Solow RM (2000) Growth Theory: An Exposition, 2nd edn. Oxford University Press, Oxford
Sorger G (1989) On the Optimality and Stability of Competitive Paths in Continuous Time Growth Models. Journal of Economic Theory 48:526–547
Sorger G (2002) On the Long–Run Distribution of Capital in the Ramsey Model. Journal of Economic Theory 105:226–243
Steger TM (2000) Economic Growth with Subsistence Consumption. Journal of Development Economics 62:343–361
Strulik H (2005) The Role of Human Capital and Population Growth in R/D–based Models of Economic Growth. Review of International Economics 13:129–145
Strulik H (2010) A Note On Economic Growth With Subsistence Consumption. Macroeconomic Dynamics 14:763–771
Summers R, Heston A (1991) The Penn World Table (Mark 5): An Expanded Set of International Comparisons, 1950–1988. Quarterly Journal of Economics 106:327–368
Tinbergen J (1960) Optimum Savings and Utility Maximization Over Time. Econometrica 28:481–489
Turnovsky SJ (2002) Intertemporal and Intratemporal Substitution, and the Speed of Convergence in the Neoclassical Growth Model. Journal of Economic Dynamics and Control 26:1765–1785

Turnovsky SJ, Garcia-Penalosa C (2008) Distributional Dynamics in a Neoclassical Growth Model: The Role of Elastic Labor Supply. Journal of Economic Dynamics and Control 32:1399–1431

Varian HR (1988) Estimating Risk Aversion from Arrow–Debreu Portfolio Choice. Econometrica 56:973–979

Varian HR (1992) Microeconomic Analysis, 3rd edn. W.W. Norton & Company, New York

Vissing-Jorgensen A (2002) Limited Asset Market Participation and the Elasticity of Intertemporal Substitution. Journal of Political Economy 110:825–853

Wan HY Jr (1971) Economic Growth. Harcourt Brace Jovanovich, New York

Yaari ME (1964) On the Existence of an Optimal Plan in a Continuous–Time Allocation Process. Econometrica 32:576–590

Yaari ME (1965) Convexity in the Theory of Choice Under Risk. Quarterly Journal of Economics 79:278–290

Zeira J (2006) Machines as Engines of Growth. Dynamics, Economic Growth, and International Trade Conference (2006) Paper 011059

Zeuthen F (1937) On the Determinateness of the Utility Function. Review of Economic Studies 4:236–239

PART III

# Two-Sector and Multi-Sector Growth Models

CHAPTER 14

# Leontief Technology and Efficient Factor Utilization

## ASSUMPTIONS AND STRUCTURE OF THE TWO-SECTOR ECONOMY

Consider an economy consisting of a *capital* good sector and a *consumer* good sector, labeled 1 and 2, respectively. This economy will be characterized by the following assumptions.

The *technology* in each sector is described by the production functions, cf. (11.28–11.29),

$$\begin{aligned} Y_i &= F_i(L_i, K_i) = \min\{L_i/\beta_{L_i}, K_i/\beta_{K_i}\}, \quad i = 1, 2 \\ &= L_i \min\{1/\beta_{L_i}, (1/\beta_{K_i})k_i\} = L_i f_i(k_i), \end{aligned} \tag{14.1.1}$$

where $f_i(k_i), i = 1, 2$, are

$$f_i(k_i) = \begin{cases} (1/\beta_{K_i})k_i, & 0 < k_i \leq \beta_{K_i}/\beta_{L_i}, \\ 1/\beta_{L_i} & k_i > \beta_{K_i}/\beta_{L_i}. \end{cases} \tag{14.1.2}$$

The *production factors*—total labor force ($L$) and the total capital stock ($K$)—are assumed *fully employed* (utilized), i.e.,

$$L = L_1 + L_2, \quad L > 0;\ L_1, L_2 \geq 0, \tag{14.2.1}$$

$$K = K_1 + K_2, \quad K > 0;\ K_1, K_2 \geq 0. \tag{14.2.2}$$



B. S. Jensen, *The Elements and Dynamic Systems of Economic Growth and Trade Models*, https://doi.org/10.1007/978-3-031-52493-6_14

The factor *allocation fractions* of labor and capital follow by *definition* from (14.2.1–2) as

$$L_1/L + L_2/L \equiv \lambda_{L_1} + \lambda_{L_2} \equiv 1, \tag{14.3.1}$$

$$K_1/K + K_2/K \equiv \lambda_{K_1} + \lambda_{K_2} \equiv 1. \tag{14.3.2}$$

Then the full employment assumption (14.2.1–2) may be rewritten as, cf. (14.3.1),

$$\begin{aligned} k \equiv \frac{K}{L} &\equiv \frac{K_1 + K_2}{L_1 + L_2} \equiv \frac{L_1}{L_1 + L_2}\left(\frac{K_1}{L_1}\right) + \frac{L_2}{L_1 + L_2}\left(\frac{K_2}{L_2}\right) \\ &\equiv \lambda_{L_1} k_1 + \lambda_{L_2} k_2 \\ &\equiv k_2 + (k_1 - k_2)\lambda_{L_1}. \end{aligned} \tag{14.4}$$

Thus, the *overall* capital-labor ratio $k$ is the weighted average of the *sectorial* capital-labor ratios, $k_1$ and $k_2$, with the labor allocation fractions as weights.

For later reference, we note that, cf. (14.3.1–14.4)

$$\lambda_{L_1} = \frac{k - k_2}{k_1 - k_2}, \quad \lambda_{L_2} = \frac{k_1 - k}{k_1 - k_2}; \quad k_1 \neq k_2, \tag{14.5}$$

and next from (14.2.1–14.5),

$$\begin{aligned} \lambda_{K_1} &= K_1/K = \frac{(K_1/L_1)(L_1/L)}{K/L} = \frac{k_1}{k}\lambda_{L_1} \\ &= \frac{k_1(k - k_2)}{k(k_1 - k_2)} = \frac{k_1 \lambda_{L_1}}{k_2 + (k_1 - k_2)\lambda_{L_1}}, \end{aligned} \tag{14.6.1}$$

$$\lambda_{K_2} = \frac{k_2}{k}\lambda_{L_2} = \frac{k_2(k_1 - k)}{k(k_1 - k_2)}. \tag{14.6.2}$$

Clearly, the expressions (14.5–14.6.2) and $k_1 \neq k_2$ dictate that

$$[0 < \lambda_{L_1} < 1] \Leftrightarrow [0 < \lambda_{K_1} < 1], \tag{14.7}$$

$$[k_1 > k > k_2] \Leftrightarrow [\lambda_{K_1} > \lambda_{L_1}] \Leftrightarrow [\lambda_{K_2} < \lambda_{L_2}], \tag{14.8}$$

$$[k_1 < k < k_2] \Leftrightarrow [\lambda_{K_1} < \lambda_{L_1}] \Leftrightarrow [\lambda_{K_2} > \lambda_{L_2}]. \tag{14.9}$$

Of course, the *accounting identities* (14.3.1–14.9) for a two-sector economy hold, independent of any sectorial technology assumptions; but they do assume *full employment* (14.2.1–2).

As we saw in Chap. 11, section "Leontief Technology", a Leontief technology and full employment of arbitrary factor endowments $(L, K)$ were, within a one-sector economy, incompatible with *technical efficiency* (minimal input sets) in production, cf. (11.30). However, for a *two-sector* economy with the Leontief technologies (14.1.1–2), overall and sectorial technical efficiency are *not*—due to the *variability* of the *allocation fractions* (14.3.1–2)—*incompatible* with the full employment condition (14.2.1–2).

Thus, we shall henceforth assume *efficient factor allocation* in the two-sector economy, i.e., cf. (11.30), (14.1.1),

$$\text{efficient factor allocation: } \{L_i, K_i \mid K_i/L_i = k_i = \beta_{K_i}/\beta_{L_i}\},\ i = 1, 2, \tag{14.10}$$

which implies that the *sectorial* capital-labor *ratios* $k_i$ become *fixed* numbers.

Then (14.10) and (14.1.1–2) give

$$f_i(k_i) = 1/\beta_{L_i}, \quad i = 1, 2, \tag{14.11.1}$$

$$Y_i = L_i/\beta_{L_i} = K_i/\beta_{K_i}, \quad i = 1, 2. \tag{14.11.2}$$

The production of the two outputs may now simply be given as, cf. (14.11.2), (14.3.1),

$$Y_i = L_i y_i = L y_i \lambda_{L_i}, \quad y_i = 1/\beta_{L_i}; \quad i = 1, 2, \tag{14.12}$$

where the sectorial *labor productivities* $y_i$ are *fixed* numbers.

Then the *composition* (ratio) of outputs is given as, cf. (14.12), (14.5)

$$\frac{Y_1}{Y_2} = \frac{y_1 \lambda_{L_1}}{y_2(1 - \lambda_{L_1})} = \frac{y_1(k - k_2)}{y_2(k_1 - k)}. \tag{14.13}$$

To maintain the assumption (14.10) through a proper variability of allocation ratios (14.3.1–2), we have implicitly assumed *full* (free) *factor mobility* between the sectors, i.e.,

$$\dot{L}_i \equiv dL_i/dt \gtreqless 0, \quad i = 1, 2, \tag{14.14.1}$$

$$\dot{K}_i \equiv dK_i/dt \gtreqless 0, \quad i = 1, 2. \tag{14.14.2}$$

Occasionally, only new workers and new capital are considered free or able to move into either sector, whereas older workers and older capital equipment are not transferable (shiftable) between the sectors. Such restricted factor mobility would imply that time derivatives (14.14.1–2) are required to be nonnegative. But we shall henceforth adopt the full (unfettered) factor mobility assumption (14.14.1–2).

The equations (14.1.1–14.6.2), (14.10–14.12) of a two-sector economy—characterized by *Leontief technologies* and *fully* and *efficient* utilization of the production factors—specify an *equilibrium model,* which for any given factor endowments $(L, K)$, can be solved uniquely with *positive* equilibrium values of all the variables, $L_1, L_2, K_1, K_2, \lambda_{L_1}, \lambda_{K_1}, Y_1, Y_2$, provided that the *factor endowments* belong to the *diversification cone,* $C_K \subset \mathbf{R}^2_+$, given as

$$C_K = \{(L, K) \in \mathbf{R}^2_+ \mid k_1 < K/L < k_2 \vee k_2 < K/L < k_1\}. \tag{14.15}$$

The *boundary rays* $(k_1, k_2)$ of the *open* cone $C_K$, (14.15), represent complete *specialization* (one sector operates). Only the factor endowments $(L, K)$ belonging to $C_K$ are compatible with *efficient* and *diversified* production. Outside the boundaries of $C_K$, full and efficient factor utilization is impossible.

Hence the domain of (14.5–14.6.2) is restricted to factor endowments within $C_K$, (14.15), as shown in Fig. 14.1, cf. (14.7–14.9). The curves of (14.6.1) are rectangular hyperbolas (center: $[0, k_1/(k_1 - k_2)]$; constant:

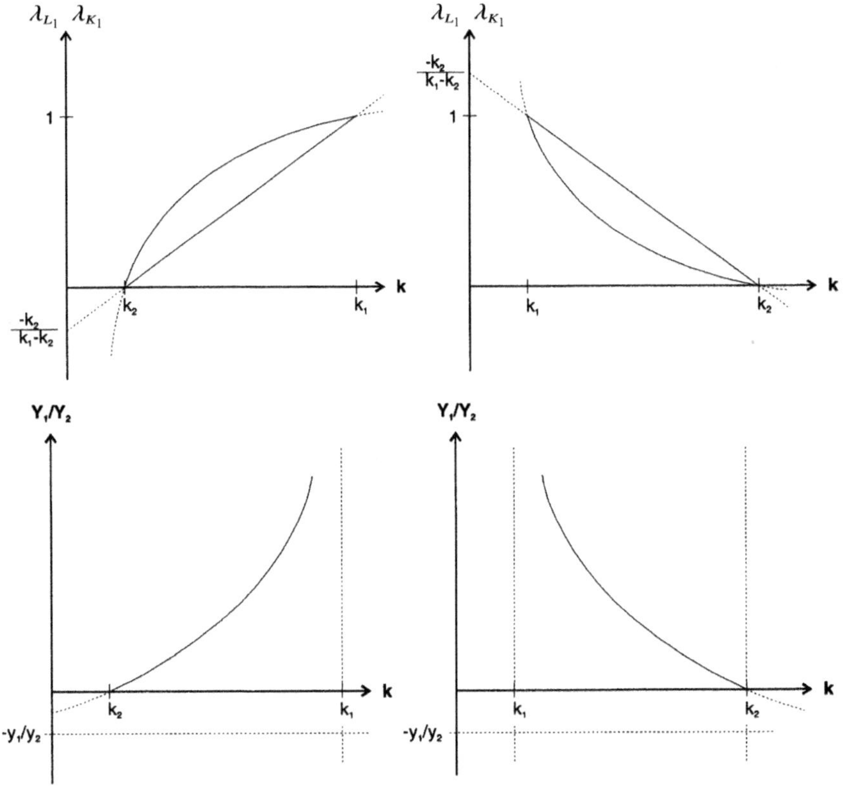


**Fig. 14.1** Allocation ratios (14.5–14.6.2) and output ratio (14.13)

$[-k_1 \cdot k_2/(k_1 - k_2)]$). The curves of (14.13) are rectangular hyperbolas (center: $[k_1, -y_1/y_2]$; constant: $[(y_1/y_2)(k_2 - k_1)]$).

It follows from the last expression in (14.6.1) that, cf. (14.10–14.11.2),

$$d\lambda_{K_1}/d\lambda_{L_1} \;=\; k_1 k_2/[k_2 + (k_1 - k_2)\lambda_{L_1}]^2 > 0 \quad \text{everywhere,} \tag{14.16}$$

i.e., $\lambda_{K_1}$ and $\lambda_{L_1}$ always rise (or fall) together, cf. Fig. 14.1.

Hence, with efficient factor utilization (14.11.2), the Leontief technologies (14.1.1–2) and the full employment assumption (14.2.1–2) impose upon the two-sector economy this very rigid scheme of factor allocation (14.16). Thus, as is evident from Fig. 14.1, a *larger* value of $K/L$ here always results in a *larger* allocation of *both labor* and *capital* to the sector that is most *capital intensive*.

Finally, we need to specify the equations of *factor accumulation*. Regarding *capital* accumulation, ignoring depreciation, we immediately have, for such a two-sector economy, that *increases* in the *total* capital *stock* are endogenously determined by the *output* of capital good sector, i.e., cf. (14.12), (14.2.2)

$$\dot{K} = \dot{K}_1 + \dot{K}_2 = Y_1 = L y_1 \lambda_{L_1}, \quad Y_1 \geq 0. \tag{14.17}$$

The growth of the *total labor force* is assumed exogenously determined, as in the neoclassical model, cf. (11.1.1), (14.2.1),

$$\dot{L} = \dot{L}_1 + \dot{L}_2 = nL. \tag{14.18}$$

Although the accumulation equations (14.17–14.18) do not by themselves represent a dynamic (deterministic) system, we have enough *mathematical information* to turn (14.17–14.18) into an *autonomous* set of differential equations.

## The Dynamic System, Solutions, Stability, and Trajectory Geometry

To obtain an explicit dynamic description of the growth process in the two-sector economy with Leontief technologies and factor accumulation, we have to find some *state variables* (of the economy), whose *present state* completely determines the entire future course (and the entire past) of the economy. We shall find it both possible and most convenient to use $L$ and $K$ as such state variables.

It appears from (14.17) and (14.5) that

$$\begin{aligned}\dot{K} &= L y_1 \lambda_{L_1} = L y_1[(k - k_2)/(k_1 - k_2)] \\ &= \frac{y_1}{k_1 - k_2} K - \frac{y_1 k_2}{k_1 - k_2} L, \quad k_1 \neq k_2.\end{aligned} \tag{14.19}$$

So (14.19) and (14.18) give us a *homogeneous dynamic system* with $m = 1$,

$$\dot{L} = nL = \mathcal{F}(L, K); \quad L, K \geq 0, \tag{14.20.1}$$

$$\dot{K} = -\frac{y_1 k_2}{k_1 - k_2} L + \frac{y_1}{k_1 - k_2} K = \mathcal{G}(L, K); \quad L, K \geq 0, \tag{14.20.2}$$

or, equivalently,

$$\dot{L} = Ln = L\,\mathfrak{f}(k); \quad L \neq 0, \tag{14.21.1}$$

$$\dot{K} = L\left(-\frac{y_1 k_2}{k_1 - k_2} + \frac{y_1}{k_1 - k_2} k\right) = L\,\mathfrak{g}(k); \quad L \neq 0. \tag{14.21.2}$$

Dynamic analysis can now proceed as usual with our mathematical apparatus of homogeneous dynamics. Of course, the linearity of (14.20.1–2) allows general closed form solutions. The latter will here be obtained immediately from Chap. 29.

The *director function* $h(k)$ of (14.21.1–2) is, cf. (7.7), (11.3), (14.19), (14.21.1–2),

$$\begin{aligned} h(k) &= \mathfrak{g}(k) - k\mathfrak{f}(k) = y_1 \lambda_{L_1}(k) - nk \\ &= -\frac{y_1 k_2}{k_1 - k_2} + \left(\frac{y_1}{k_1 - k_2} - n\right) k; \quad k_1 \neq k_2. \end{aligned} \tag{14.22}$$

For $m = 1$, we have as usual, cf. (11.5),

$$\dot{k} = Q(k) = h(k), \tag{14.23}$$

with $h(k)$ as in (14.22).

**Theorem 14.1** *The two-sector growth model (14.20.1–14.21.2) has in $C_K$, (14.15),—under the parametric feasibility condition, $y_1 > nk_1$—one and only one stationary ratio solution*

$$\forall t \quad k(t) = \kappa = K_0/L_0 = k_0; \quad K_0/L_0 \in C_K, \tag{14.24.1}$$

*where the positive director root $\kappa$ is given by*

$$\kappa = \frac{y_1 k_2}{y_1 - n(k_1 - k_2)}; \quad y_1 > nk_1. \tag{14.24.2}$$

*The factor allocation ratios,* $\lambda_{L_i}, \lambda_{K_i}$, *(14.5–14.6.2), corresponding to* $k = \kappa$, *(14.24.1–2), are*

$$\lambda_{L_1}(\kappa) = \frac{nk_2}{y_1 - n(k_1 - k_2)}, \quad \lambda_{L_2}(\kappa) = \frac{y_1 - nk_1}{y_1 - n(k_1 - k_2)}, \tag{14.25.1}$$

$$\lambda_{K_1}(\kappa) = nk_1/y_1, \qquad \lambda_{K_2}(\kappa) = 1 - nk_1/y_1. \tag{14.25.2}$$

*The coordinate solutions* $[L(t), K(t)]$*—with initial values* $(L_0, K_0)$ *upon the directrix* $K = \kappa L$*—have the form*

$$L(t) = L_0 e^{nt}, \quad K(t) = L_0 \kappa e^{nt}, \tag{14.26.1}$$

*with the directrix value* $\mathfrak{f}(\kappa)$ *being,*

$$\mathfrak{f}(\kappa) = n. \tag{14.26.2}$$

*The family of ratio solutions* $k(t)$ *to (14.22–14.23)—with initial values* $(L_0, K_0)$ *outside the directrix* $K = \kappa L$*—is given by*

$$k(t) = \kappa + (k_0 - \kappa) e^{\left(\frac{y_1}{k_1 - k_2} - n\right)t}, \quad k_0 \neq \kappa. \tag{14.27}$$

*The time paths of the factor allocation ratios* $\lambda_{L_1}(t), \lambda_{K_1}(t)$*, (14.5–14.6.2), corresponding to* $k(t)$*, (14.27), are*

$$\lambda_{L_1}(t) = \frac{nk_2}{y_1 - n(k_1 - k_2)} + \left(\frac{k_0 - \kappa}{k_1 - k_2}\right) e^{\left(\frac{y_1}{k_1 - k_2} - n\right)t}, \tag{14.28.1}$$

$$\lambda_{K_1}(t) = \frac{nk_1}{y_1} \left[ \frac{1 + \left(\frac{k_0 - \kappa}{\kappa - k_2}\right) e^{\left(\frac{y_1}{k_1 - k_2} - n\right)t}}{1 + \left(\frac{k_0}{\kappa} - 1\right) e^{\left(\frac{y_1}{k_1 - k_2} - n\right)t}} \right]. \tag{14.28.2}$$

*The family of coordinate solutions to (14.21.1–2)—with initial values* $(L_0, K_0)$ *outside the directrix* $K = \kappa L$*—are given by*

$$L(t) = L_0 e^{nt}, \tag{14.29.1}$$

$$K(t) \equiv k(t)L(t) = L_0 \left[ \kappa e^{nt} + (k_0 - \kappa) e^{\left(\frac{y_1}{k_1 - k_2}\right)t} \right], \quad k_0 \neq \kappa. \tag{14.29.2}$$

*The trajectories of the coordinate solutions (14.29.1–2) are, as loci, given by the equation*

$$K = \kappa L + \beta L^{\frac{y_1}{n(k_1 - k_2)}}, \tag{14.30.1}$$

*where*

$$\beta = (k_0 - \kappa) L_0^{\left(1 - \frac{y_1}{n(k_1 - k_2)}\right)}, \quad k_0 \neq \kappa. \tag{14.30.2}$$

*The time paths of the sector outputs* $[Y_1(t), Y_2(t)]$, *(14.12), corresponding to (14.26.1–14.29.2), are*

$$Y_1(t) = L_1(t) y_1 = L_0 y_1 \left[ \left( \frac{nk_2}{y_1 - n(k_1 - k_2)} \right) e^{nt} + \left( \frac{k_0 - \kappa}{k_1 - k_2} \right) e^{\left(\frac{y_1}{k_1 - k_2}\right)t} \right], \tag{14.31.1}$$

$$Y_2(t) = L_2(t) y_2 = L_0 y_2 \left[ \left( \frac{y_1 - nk_1}{y_1 - n(k_1 - k_2)} \right) e^{nt} - \left( \frac{k_0 - \kappa}{k_1 - k_2} \right) e^{\left(\frac{y_1}{k_1 - k_2}\right)t} \right]. \tag{14.31.2}$$

***Proof*** The expression for the director root $\kappa$ (14.24.2) follows immediately from (14.22). For this $\kappa$, however, to represent a *feasible* stationary capital-labor ratio *solution* for the two-sector economy, it is necessary that the factor proportion $\kappa = K/L$ belongs to the diversification cone $C_\kappa$, (14.15), i.e., $k_1 < \kappa < k_2$ or $k_2 < \kappa < k_1$. The latter inequalities are satisfied by (14.24.2)—as may be verified by straightforward manipulations—if and only if

$$y_1 > nk_1 \Leftrightarrow nk_1/y_1 \equiv nv_1 \equiv n\beta_{K_1} < 1. \tag{14.32}$$

A more revealing and direct way to obtain the parametric feasibility condition (14.32) is to look at the allocation ratios, (14.5–14.6.2), together with (14.24.2). Then we get

$$\lambda_{L_1}(\kappa) = \frac{\kappa - k_2}{k_1 - k_2} = \frac{y_1 k_2 - k_2[y_1 - n(k_2 - k_1)]}{(k_1 - k_2)[y_1 - n(k_1 - k_2)]} = \frac{nk_2}{y_1 - n(k_1 - k_2)}, \tag{14.33}$$

$$\lambda_{K_1}(\kappa) = \frac{k_1 \lambda_{L_1}(\kappa)}{\kappa} = \frac{nk_1 k_2 [y_1 - n(k_1 - k_2)]}{[y_1 - n(k_1 - k_2)] y_1 k_2} = nk_1/y_1. \tag{14.34}$$

A two-sector (diversified) economy requires that $0 < \lambda_{K_1}(\kappa) < 1$, cf. (14.7). Hence (14.33–14.34) impose the parameter restriction (14.32) upon the expression (14.24.2), and they establish (14.25.1–2).

The directrix solutions (14.26.1–2) follow from (14.24.1–2) and (14.21.1).

The ratio solutions (14.27) follow from the formulas (29.67) and (14.24.2); or else, (14.27) is easily derived from (14.22–14.23), and (14.24.2).

From (14.5) and (14.27), we have, cf. (14.33),

$$\lambda_{L_1}(t) = \lambda_{L_1}(\kappa) + [\lambda_{L_1}(k_0) - \lambda_{L_1}(\kappa)] e^{\left(\frac{y_1}{k_1 - k_2} - n\right)t}, \tag{14.35}$$

which is (14.28.1).

From (14.5), (14.6.1), and (14.27), we have, cf. (14.33–14.35),

$$\lambda_{K_1}(t) \quad = \quad \frac{k_1\lambda_{L_1}(\kappa)}{\kappa}\left[\frac{1+\left(\frac{\lambda_{L_1}(k_0)}{\lambda_{L_1}(\kappa)}-1\right)e^{\left(\frac{y_1}{k_1-k_2}-n\right)t}}{1+(k_0/\kappa-1)e^{\left(\frac{y_1}{k_1-k_2}-n\right)t}}\right], \tag{14.36}$$

which is (14.28.2).

The coordinate solutions (14.29.1–2) follow immediately from (14.21.1) and (14.27).

The equational form (14.30.1–2) of the trajectories may be obtained by straightforward elimination of $t$ in (14.29.1–2), or see (29.173).

The time paths (14.31.1–2) follow from (14.12), (14.28.1), and (14.3.1).

□

**Corollary 14.1** *The family of ratio solutions $k(t)$ to (14.22–14.23) and the family of coordinate solutions $[L(t), K(t)]$ to (14.21.1–2) have—within the diversification cone $C_K$, (14.15)—respectively, global asymptotic stability and global weak relative stability, if and only if*

$$(i)\quad y_1 > nk_1 \quad (ii)\quad k_2 > k_1 \quad \therefore \quad k_1 < min\{y_1/n,\ k_2\}. \tag{14.37}$$

**Corollary 14.2** *The phase portrait of the growth model (14.21.1–14.22) in $C_K$, (14.15), is hyperbolic under the conditions (14.37).*

***Proof*** It was shown above that the existence of a feasible stationary ratio solution (14.24.1–2) required that

$$y_1 > nk_1 \quad \Leftrightarrow \quad n/y_1 < 1/k_1. \tag{14.38}$$

For the unique stationary solution (14.24.1–2) to be a global attractor, the director function $h(k)$ must decrease through $\kappa$, requiring that, cf. (14.22)

$$y_1/(k_1-k_2)-n<0 \quad \Leftrightarrow \quad n/y_1 > 1/(k_1-k_2). \tag{14.39}$$

When $k_2 > k_1$, (14.39) is obviously satisfied. If $k_1 > k_2$, then (14.39) itself is not necessarily violated; but $k_1 > k_2$ is inconsistent with (14.38–14.39) for positive values of $y_1, n, k_1$ and $k_2$. Hence, (14.38–14.39) together establish (14.37) as the necessary and sufficient conditions for the asymptotic stability of the ratio solutions. Weak relative stability of the coordinate solutions follow from asymptotic ratio stability (14.37) and $m = 1$, (14.21.1–2), cf. proof of Theorem 11.2 in section "The Dynamic System, Solutions, and Stability".

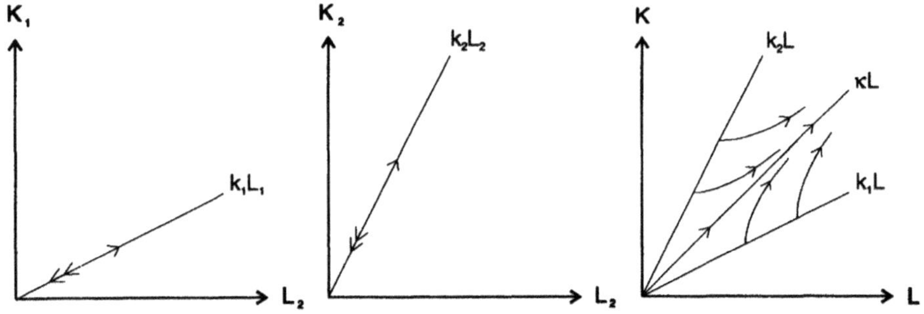


**Fig. 14.2** Phase portrait of (14.20.1–14.21.2), (14.37)

As to the geometry of the trajectory system, we consider the direction field given by $q(k)$, cf. (11.14), (14.21.1–2),

$$q(k) = \mathfrak{g}(k)/\mathfrak{f}(k) \quad = \quad \frac{-y_1 k_2}{n(k_1 - k_2)} + \frac{y_1}{n(k_1 - k_2)} k. \tag{14.40}$$

Next, we get from (14.40) and (14.37)

$$\forall k \in ]k_1, k_2[ \quad : \quad q(k) > 0, \tag{14.41}$$

$$\forall k \in ]k_1, k_2[ \quad : \quad q'(k) = \frac{y_1}{n(k_1 - k_2)} < 0. \tag{14.42}$$

Then (14.42) and the asymptotic ratio stability from Corollary 14.1 together establish the hyperbolic form of the phase portrait, see Theorem 28.8 in section "Asymptotic Ratio Stability and Trajectory Geometry". □

The stability properties and the geometric properties, stated in Corollaries 14.1–14.2, can alternatively be verified by examining here the closed form solutions stated in Theorem 14.1, cf. (14.24.1–2), (14.27), (14.29.1–2), (14.30.1–2).

The phase portrait of the two-sector growth model (14.20.1–14.21.2) with (14.37) is depicted in Fig. 14.2. The double arrows indicate that a *transitional* backward motion, cf. (14.31.1–2), may occur in one sector, as explained further below. The phase portrait (not drawn) corresponding to the unstable case 4 follows from (14.29.1–14.30.2) with $k_1 > k_2$.

## The Economic Rationale of the Stability Conditions

Although Theorem 14.1 with Corollaries 14.1–14.2 completely describes the qualitative properties and the quantitative solutions for the variables of a

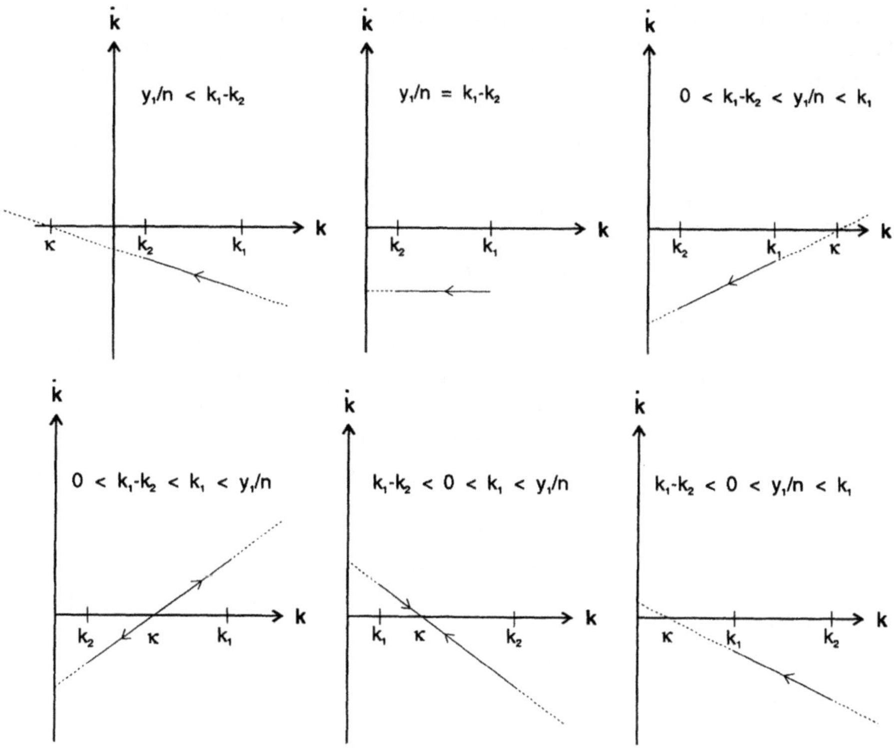


**Fig. 14.3** Phase diagrams of (14.22–14.23)

growing two-sector economy with Leontief sector technologies and overall efficient factor allocation, we should examine in more detail the economic rationale of the stability conditions (14.37). To appreciate the implications of (14.37), we show the director function and the dynamics of the capital-labor ratio (14.22–14.23) for alternative parameter constellations in Fig. 14.3.

Cases 1–3 and case 6 exhibit the situations with $y_1 < nk_1$—a parameter constellation precluding the existence of a steady-state path (directrix solutions).

Since labor increases at the exponential rate $n$, this would in sector 1 call for a steady-state investment level per worker at $nk_1$ to keep the capital-labor ratio $k_1$ constant. But as the current output of capital goods per worker in sector 1—$Y_1/L_1 = 1/\beta_L = y_1$—is fixed and below the steady-state *capital requirement* $nk_1$, the *labor productivity* ($y_1$) of the capital good sector cannot in steady state even sustain its own sector and hence of course is neither able to satisfy a steady-state *capital requirement* in the consumer good sector. Although the two-sector economy cannot sustain a steady-state path with $y_1 < nk_1$, the Leontief economy can, due to factor mobility, operate for a while with full and efficient factor utilization.

But with fixed labor (factor) productivities and exogenous labor supply, factor reallocation can not stop the decline of overall capital-labor ratio, $k$. Accordingly, from (14.17) and (14.5)

$$\hat{K} \equiv \dot{K}/K = y_1 \lambda_{L_1}/k = (y_1/k_1)\lambda_{K_1}, \tag{14.43}$$

and by (14.43), (14.3.1–2), and (14.18)

$$[y_1 < nk_1] \Rightarrow \hat{K} < n\lambda_{K_1} < n = \hat{L}, \tag{14.44}$$

i.e., $\hat{k}, \dot{k} < 0$, cf. Fig. 14.3, case 1–3, 6. Eventually, all the production factors are transferred to the sector with the lower $k_i$, $i = 1, 2$, and then the two-sector economy and the growth model (14.19–14.20.2) cease to operate.

Cases 4–5 in Fig. 14.3 reflect the situation, $y_1 > nk_1$. The capital goods sector has now the potential to supply the growing labor force with the required capital equipment in both sectors to maintain for the two-sector economy a steady-state growth path given by (14.24.1–14.26.2).

Given $y_1 > nk_1$, the economic rationale of the stability condition $k_2 > k_1$, cf. (14.37) and Fig. 14.3, is connected with the behavior of the allocation ratios (14.5–14.6.2) and the output ratio (14.13), cf. Fig. 14.1. The magnitude of these allocation and output ratios was enforced upon the two-sector economy solely by *full* and *efficient factor utilization,* (14.2.1–14.3.2), (14.10). But only for the picture in Fig. 14.1 with $k_2 > k_1$ do we obtain *momentary factor allocations* and *output compositions* of capital/consumer goods that are favorable to *restore* over time the overall capital-labor ratio $k(t)$ to its steady-state value $\kappa$, cf. case 5 in Fig. 14.3 and hereto Fig. 14.2.

A noteworthy feature of the two-sector growth model expounded in this chapter—in contrast to all one-sector models above and the two-sector model with flexible technology below—is that *no saving functions* formally appear among the structural or dynamic equations. There was here neither need for nor place for independent savings behavior, as the Leontief *technology* (14.1.1–2), together with the assumptions of *full* (14.2.1–2) and *efficient* factor utilization (14.10) of the factor endowments in $C_K$, (14.15) uniquely determined the output of the capital good sector and hence capital accumulation (saving in real/physical terms) (14.17). Thus, the latter and (14.18) established a *deterministic dynamic* system (14.20.1–2) of $C^1$-class that would run its course, unaffected by any further introduction of nominal income (product/factor price) equations into this two-sector economy.

As we have seen, the long-run *viability* of the two-sector economy imposed a *productivity* requirement upon the *capital good* sector (14.37, i), and the *consumer good* sector had to absorb/release resources (14.37, ii), cf. Fig. 14.1, to enable the capital good sector to *equilibrate* the growth rate of the capital stock to the growth rate of the labor force.

However, for later purposes and complementary to our discussion above, we must here ponder still more on the economic fundamentals embodied in the stability condition $k_2 > k_1$. The latter does neither here nor later in Chap. 15 just reflect a "casual property of the technology", Solow (1961, p.48). We shall see that it is the Leontief technology assumptions (14.1.1–2), full employment (10.4) and the extension and *application* of the *Rybczynski Theorem*—producer equilibrium under constant product/factor prices (hence fixed (optimal) values of $k_1$ and $k_2$) with full and efficient factor allocation, where a *larger* one-factor *endowment increases* the output of the factor *intensive* sector and *reduces* the output of the other sector, Rybczynski (1955)—to a *dynamic* system that gives the economic clues to the stability condition, $k_2 > k_1$.

First, we shall see that the substance of the Rybczynski Theorem follows from an inspection of the sector output elasticities with respect to the *one-factor* endowments, $K$ or $L$.

We immediately have that, cf. (14.5)

$$E(\lambda_{L_1}, k) = \frac{d\lambda_{L_1}}{dk} \cdot \frac{k}{\lambda_{L_1}} = \frac{k}{k - k_2}, \tag{14.45.1}$$

$$E(\lambda_{L_2}, k) = \frac{d\lambda_{L_2}}{dk} \cdot \frac{k}{\lambda_{L_2}} = \frac{k}{k - k_1}, \tag{14.45.2}$$

and, obviously,

$$E(\lambda_i, K) = E(\lambda_i, k), \quad E(\lambda_i, L) = -E(\lambda_i, k); \; i = 1, 2. \tag{14.46}$$

Then by (14.12) and (14.45.1–14.46), we get

$$E(Y_i, K) = E(\lambda_i, k) = \frac{k}{k - k_j}, \qquad i = 1, 2; \; j = 1, 2; \quad i \neq j, \tag{14.47}$$

$$E(Y_i, L) = 1 - E(\lambda_i, k) = -\frac{k_j}{k - k_j}, \quad i = 1, 2; \; j = 1, 2; \quad i \neq j, \tag{14.48}$$

and hence from (14.47–14.48)

$$k_i > k > k_j \;\Rightarrow\; E(Y_i, K) > 1 \;\wedge\; E(Y_j, K) < 0, \tag{14.49}$$

$$k_i > k > k_j \;\Rightarrow\; E(Y_i, L) < 0 \;\wedge\; E(Y_j, L) > 1. \tag{14.50}$$

These succinct elasticity formulas (14.47–14.50) express the Rybczynski Theorem on the changes in the two-sector outputs resulting from *one-factor* endowment changes.

Furthermore, when *both* factor endowments change, then the effects upon the sector outputs will now simply be given by (hat symbols indicate the relative change in the variables, e.g., $\hat{L} = dL/L$):

$$\begin{aligned} \hat{Y}_i &= \hat{L} + E(\lambda_i, k)\hat{k} \\ &= [1 - E(\lambda_i, k)]\hat{L} + E(\lambda_i, k)\hat{K}, \quad i = 1, 2, \end{aligned} \tag{14.51}$$

which follow directly from (14.12) with $E(\lambda_i, k)$ as in (14.45.1–2).

Hence (14.51) and the values of $E(\lambda_i, k)$, cf. (14.47), (14.49) immediately establish the following implications

$$k_i > k > k_j, \ \hat{K} = \hat{L} \quad \Rightarrow \quad \hat{Y}_i = \hat{K} = \hat{L} = \hat{Y}_j, \tag{14.52}$$

$$k_i > k > k_j, \ \hat{K} > \hat{L} \quad \Rightarrow \quad \hat{Y}_i > \hat{K} > \hat{L} > \hat{Y}_j, \tag{14.53}$$

$$k_i > k > k_j, \ \hat{K} < \hat{L} \quad \Rightarrow \quad \hat{Y}_i < \hat{K} < \hat{L} < \hat{Y}_j. \tag{14.54}$$

In a seminal article on two-sector economics, Jones (1965, p.35) wrote:

> If both endowments expand at the same rate, both commodity outputs expand at identical rates. But if factor endowments expand at different rates, the commodity intensive in the use of the fastest growing factor expands at a greater rate than either factor, and the other commodity grows (if at all) at a slower rate than either factor.

He called this the *"magnification effect"* of factor endowments on commodity outputs at unchanged commodity prices.

Regarding (14.52–14.54), our demonstration above came about as simple corollaries of (14.51) and (14.47)—a straightforward, explicit, and more concise demonstration than the proofs elsewhere, see Jones (1965), Takayama (1972, p.52–59).

Thus, it is easily seen from (14.51), (14.47), (14.49) that—even with $\hat{K} > 0$, $\hat{L} > 0$—the relative change of the last output in (14.53–14.54) may be negative, when the spread of $\hat{K}$ and $\hat{L}$ is sufficiently large.

However, it should be clearly recognized that *neither* the equation of (relative) change (14.51) *nor* the order relations (14.52–14.54) are per se *kinematic* relations involving time. Just like (14.12), (14.51–14.54) display the intrinsic *structural* relations of a two-sector economy that hold for any variation in the factor endowments—assumed *fully employed* and *efficiently allocated*—whenever the sector capital-labor ratios are fixed by either Leontief technologies (14.10–14.11.2) or implicitly optimally fixed by the given output/factor prices. Of course, it is immaterial to (14.51–14.54) whether the two outputs are consumer goods or one of them is a producer (capital) good.

Thus, although no *dynamic* model was involved in deriving (14.51–14.54), the *kinematic solutions* $[L(t), K(t), Y_1(t), Y_2(t)]$ of any two-sector growth (dynamic) model with fixed sectorial capital-labor ratios must exhibit proportional rates of change (logarithmic time derivatives, i.e., in hat symbols: $\hat{L}(t) \equiv \dot{L}/L$, $\hat{K}(t) = \dot{K}/K$, $\hat{Y}_1(t) = \dot{Y}_1/Y_1$, $\hat{Y}_2(t) = \dot{Y}_2/Y_2$) in accordance with the pattern of (14.52–14.54), since the latter by their timeless nature, eo ipso, hold at any and every point in time.

Therefore, the kinematic properties of solutions stated in Theorem 14.1 will comply with (14.52–14.54). To confirm this and to embed the Rybczynski-Jones Theorems into the framework of the dynamic model (14.20.1–14.21.2), we give

**Corollary 14.3** *In the two-sector economy of* Theorem 14.1, *the relationship between the proportional rate of change of, respectively, labor,* $\hat{L}(t)$, *capital,* $\hat{K}(t)$, *sector outputs,* $\hat{Y}_i(t)$, $i = 1, 2$, *and the momentary factor endowment ratio,* $k(t) = K(t)/L(t)$, *are given by*

$$\hat{L} = n, \quad \forall k, \tag{14.55}$$

$$\hat{K} = \frac{y_1 k - y_1 k_2}{(k_1 - k_2)k}, \tag{14.56}$$

$$\hat{Y}_1 = \hat{L}_1 = \hat{K}_1 = \frac{y_1 k - k_2[y_1 + n(k_1 - k_2)]}{(k_1 - k_2)(k - k_2)}, \tag{14.57}$$

$$\hat{Y}_2 = \hat{L}_2 = \hat{K}_2 = \frac{y_1 k - y_1 k_2 - n k_1 (k_1 - k_2)}{(k_1 - k_2)(k - k_1)}, \tag{14.58}$$

*where the curves (14.56–14.58) are rectangular hyperbolas with, respectively, centres and constants as*

$$\hat{K} : \textit{centre} \left(0, \frac{y_1}{k_1 - k_2}\right); \quad \textit{constant}: \frac{-y_1 k_2}{k_1 - k_2}, \tag{14.59}$$

$$\hat{Y}_1 : \textit{centre} \left(k_2, \frac{y_1}{k_1 - k_2}\right); \quad \textit{constant}: -n k_2, \tag{14.60}$$

$$\hat{Y}_2 : \textit{centre} \left(k_1, \frac{y_1}{k_1 - k_2}\right); \quad \textit{constant}: y_1 - n k_1. \tag{14.61}$$

*It follows from (14.56–14.61) that*

$$k = k_1 : \hat{K} = \frac{y_1}{k_1}, \quad \hat{Y}_1 = \frac{y_1 - n k_2}{k_1 - k_2}, \quad \hat{Y}_2 = \pm \infty, \tag{14.62}$$

$$k = k_2 : \hat{K} = 0, \quad \hat{Y}_1 = \pm \infty, \quad \hat{Y}_2 = \frac{n k_1}{k_1 - k_2}, \tag{14.63}$$

$$\hat{Y}_1 = 0: \qquad k = k_2[1 + n(k_1 - k_2)/y_1], \tag{14.64}$$

$$\hat{Y}_2 = 0: \qquad k = k_2 + nk_1(k_1 - k_2)/y_1. \tag{14.65}$$

*The graphs of (14.55–14.58) are with* $y_1 > nk_1$, *cf. (14.24.1–2), shown for either* $k_1 > k_2$ *or* $k_2 > k_1$ *in* Fig. 14.4a.

***Proof*** The proportional rates of change (14.55–14.56) follow directly from (14.20.1–2).

By (14.12) and (14.55), we have

$$\hat{Y}_i = \hat{L}_i = \hat{L} + \hat{\lambda}_{L_i} = n + \dot{\lambda}_{L_i}/\lambda_{L_i}, \quad i = 1, 2. \tag{14.66}$$

Next (14.5) and (14.22–14.23) give

$$\dot{\lambda}_{L_1} = \frac{\dot{k}}{k_1 - k_2}, \qquad \dot{\lambda}_{L_2} = \frac{-\dot{k}}{k_1 - k_2}, \tag{14.67}$$

$$\frac{\dot{\lambda}_{L_1}}{\lambda_{L_1}} = \frac{\dot{k}}{\lambda_{L_1}(k_1 - k_2)} = \frac{y_1\lambda_{L_1} - nk}{\lambda_{L_1}(k_1 - k_2)} = \frac{y_1}{k_1 - k_2} - \frac{nk}{k - k_2}, \tag{14.68.1}$$

$$\frac{\dot{\lambda}_{L_2}}{\lambda_{L_2}} = \frac{-\dot{k}}{\lambda_{L_2}(k_1 - k_2)} = \frac{-y_1\lambda_{L_1} + nk}{\lambda_{L_2}(k_1 - k_2)} = \frac{y_1(k - k_2)}{(k_1 - k_2)(k - k_1)} - \frac{nk}{k - k_1}. \tag{14.68.2}$$

Hence, by (14.66), (14.68.1–2) and consolidating, we obtain (14.57–14.58), where $\hat{L}_i = \hat{K}_i$, $i = 1, 2$, follow immediately from the fixed sectorial capital-labor ratios.

The equations (14.56–14.58)—by giving $\hat{K}$, $\hat{Y}_1$, and $\hat{Y}_2$ as a ***ratio*** of ***linear*** expressions in $k$—are from elementary analytical geometry recognized as representing ***rectangular*** hyperbolas with asymptotes parallel to the coordinate axes and with centres and constants of the curves as shown in (14.59–14.61).

To obtain (14.59–14.61) from (14.56–14.58), one first uses the rectangular hyperbola formula, see Allen (1938, p.74), $a_2 \neq 0$

$$y = \frac{a_1 x + b_1}{a_2 x + b_2}; \quad \text{centre: } \left(-\frac{b_2}{a_2}, \frac{a_1}{a_2}\right), \quad \text{constant} = \frac{a_2 b_1 - a_1 b_2}{a_2^2}. \tag{14.69}$$

Curve points at the boundary of $C_K$, (14.15), as well as the intercepts upon the $k$-axis are shown in (14.62–14.65).

The intersection of the curves (14.55–14.56) in Fig. 14.4a at $k = \kappa$, (14.24.1–2), is verified by substitution. □

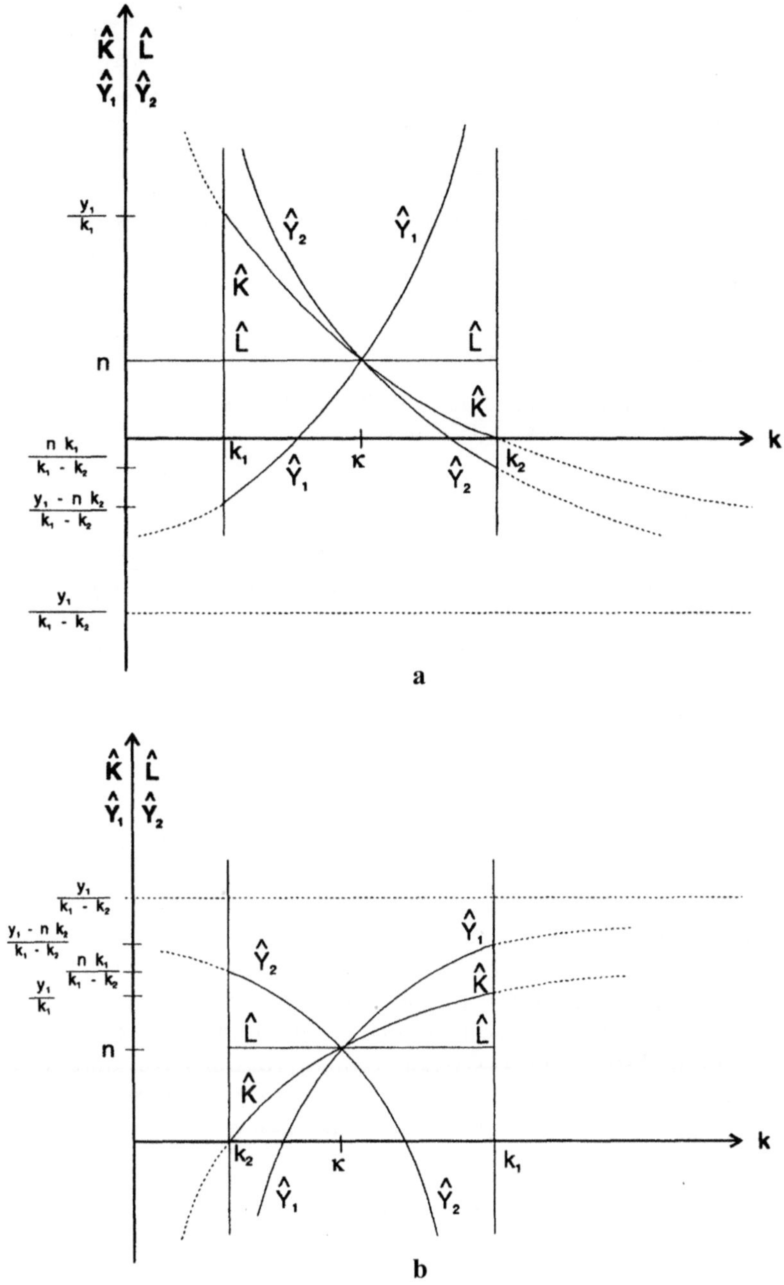


**Fig. 14.4** (**a**) Graphs of (14.55–14.58), with $k_2 > k_1$. (**b**) Graphs of (14.55–14.58), with $k_1 > k_2$

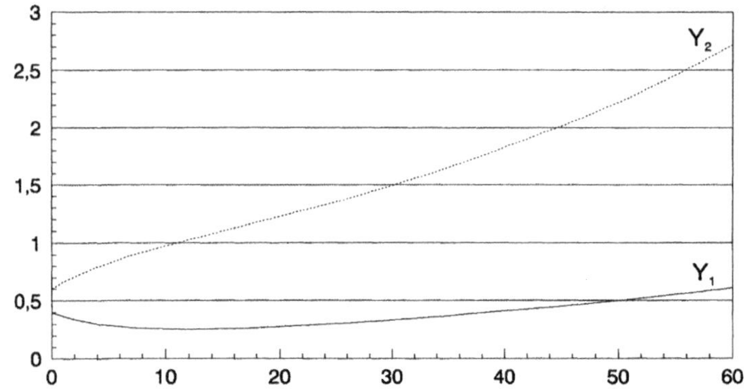


**Fig. 14.5** The solutions (14.31.1–2) with: $k_2 = 10, k_1 = 5, n = 0.02, y_1 = y_2 = 1$; $L_0 = 1, k_0 = 8, Y_1(0) = 0.4, Y_2(0) = 0.6$

Evidently, the graphs of (14.55–14.58), depicted in Fig. 14.4a–b, show the properties stated in (14.52–14.54). However, the existence of and the actual condition ($y_1 > nk_1$) for a steady state (14.52) can, of course, only be obtained from an examination of the dynamic model involved, here (14.20.1–2).

Thus, Fig. 14.4b supplements Fig. 14.2; also Fig. 14.4b clearly shows a significant feature of the solutions (14.31.1–2), viz. that with initial values $k_0$ deviating strongly from $\kappa$, one of the sectors may preliminarily decline, cf. (14.14.1–2) and Fig. 14.2, before both sectors eventually expand and ultimately grow at the common rate $n$.

Let us finish our subject with an example: For $L_0 = 1, k_0 = 8, n = 0.02, y_1 = y_2 = 1, k_1 = 5, k_2 = 10$ and so $\lambda_{L_1}(0) = 0.4$, (14.5), $\lambda_{K_1}(0) = 0.25$, (14.6.1–2), and $\kappa = 9.0909$, (14.24.1–2), $\lambda_{L_1}(\kappa) = 0.18, \lambda_{K_1}(\kappa) = 0.1$, (14.25.1–2), we have illustrated the solutions (14.31.1–2) in Fig. 14.5. Thus, until $k(t)$, (14.27), at about $t = 11$ attains the value $k = 9$, (14.64), the *entire* current output of *newly* produced capital goods $Y_1(t)$ as well as *part* of the *older* capital stock $K_1(t)$ are transferred into the consumer good sector. Transferring capital between sectors does not itself affect the size of $K(t)$. As $\dot{K}(t)$ is given by $Y_1(t)$ and not $\dot{Y}_1(t)$, a declining (but positive) output of $Y_1(t)$ does not prevent the stock $K(t)$ from growing fast in the time period $]0, 11[$. The capital good sector had initially abundant resources.

## Endogenous Labor Supply

The assumption of an exogenous labor supply, growing at a constant rate, $\dot{L}/L = n$, cf. (14.18), may easily be replaced by an endogeneity assumption, analogous to the classical or aggregate version, cf. (7.3.1), (9.1.1). Accordingly, for a two-sector economy the former one-sector analysis is properly modified by allowing the growth rate of the labor force to depend on the level of consumption per capita ("standard of living"), i.e., $\dot{L}/L = n \cdot Y_2/L$, which gives, cf. (9.1.1), (14.12),

$$\dot{L} = nY_2 = nL_2 y_2 = Lny_2\lambda_{L_2}. \tag{14.70}$$

Thus, by (14.70) and (14.5)

$$\dot{L} = Lny_2 \frac{k_1 - k}{k_1 - k_2} = L\,\mathfrak{f}(k) \tag{14.71}$$

$$= \frac{ny_2k_1}{k_1 - k_2} L - \frac{ny_2}{k_1 - k_2} K = \mathcal{F}(L, K). \tag{14.72}$$

The governing function of capital accumulation remains, of course, the same cf. (14.19), (14.20.2)

$$\dot{K} = Ly_2\lambda_{L_1} = Ly_1 \frac{k - k_2}{k_1 - k_2} = L\mathfrak{g}(k) \tag{14.73}$$

$$= -\frac{y_1k_2}{k_1 - k_2} L + \frac{y_1}{k_1 - k_2} K = \mathcal{G}(L, K). \tag{14.74}$$

Hence, the *director function* $h(k)$ of (14.71–14.74) becomes, cf. (14.22–14.23)

$$\begin{aligned} \dot{k} = h(k) &= \mathfrak{g}(k) - k\mathfrak{f}(h) = y_1\lambda_{L_1}(k) - kny_2\lambda_{L_2}(k) \\ &= \frac{y_1(k - k_2)}{k_1 - k_2} - kny_2\frac{k_1 - k}{k_1 - k_2} \\ &= \frac{1}{k_1 - k_2}\left[ny_2k^2 + (y_1 - ny_2k_1)k - y_1k_2\right]. \end{aligned} \tag{14.75}$$

The ***discriminant*** of the linear dynamic system (14.71–14.74) and the parabola (14.75) are, cf. (29.3–29.4)

$$\Delta^2 = -\frac{\frac{1}{4}(y_1 - ny_2k_1)^2 + ny_1y_2k_2}{(k_1 - k_2)^2} > 0. \tag{14.76}$$

With a positive discriminant (14.76), the two real roots of (14.75) are, cf. (29.5–29.6.1)

$$\kappa_1 = -\frac{y_1 - ny_2k_1}{2ny_2} - \frac{(k_1 - k_2)\Delta}{ny_2} = \frac{k_1}{2} - \left[\frac{y_1 + 2(k_1 - k_2)\Delta}{2ny_2}\right], \tag{14.77}$$

$$\kappa_2 = \frac{k_1}{2} - \left[\frac{y_1 - 2(k_1 - k_2)\Delta}{2ny_2}\right]. \tag{14.78}$$

From (14.75), we note that, cf. (29.6.2),

$$\kappa_1 \cdot \kappa_2 = -\frac{y_1 k_2}{n y_2} < 0, \tag{14.79}$$

and by (14.79), the roots (14.77–2) will always have opposite signs, irrespective of $k_1 \gtrless k_2$. As only positive roots of (14.75) have economic meaning, the relevant director roots from (14.77–2) are then

$$(i) \quad k_2 > k_1 : \kappa = \kappa_1, \qquad (ii) \quad k_1 > k_2 : \kappa = \kappa_2. \tag{14.80}$$

Accordingly, the parabola (14.75) has the form depicted in Chap. 29: Figs. 29.1a and d.

Compared to the results (14.24.1–2), (14.37) and Fig. 14.3, the two-sector growth model with *endogenous* labor supply (14.71–2) *always* admits the *existence* of a stationary capital-labor ratio solution, $\forall t \quad k(t) = \kappa$, (14.80). The former parametric feasibility (existence) condition, $y_1 > nk_1$, (14.24.2), (14.25.2), is no longer necessary for obtaining (14.80). But evidently global *asymptotic stability* of the ratio solutions $k(t)$ to (14.75) still holds, if and only if the *capital intensity* condition, $k_2 > k_1$, is satisfied, and then the global attractor is the *director root* $\kappa = \kappa_1$, (14.77), which becomes

$$\begin{aligned} k_2 > k_1 : \quad \kappa &= \frac{1}{2}\left(k_1 - \frac{y_1}{ny_2}\right) + \left[\frac{1}{4}\left(k_1 - \frac{y_1}{ny_2}\right)^2 + \frac{y_1 k_2}{ny_2}\right]^{1/2} \\ &= \frac{1}{2}\left|k_1 - \frac{y_1}{ny_2}\right| \left\{1 + \left|1 + \frac{4k_2}{k_1 |y_1 - y_1| ny_2}\right|^{1/2}\right\}. \end{aligned} \tag{14.81}$$

The *directrix value* $\mathfrak{f}(\kappa)$ is, cf. (14.71),

$$k_2 > k_1 : \quad \mathfrak{f}(\kappa) = \frac{ny_2}{k_2 - k_1}(\kappa - k_1), \tag{14.82}$$

with $\kappa$ given by (14.81).

Compared to (14.24.2) and (14.26.2), the expressions (14.81–14.82) certainly indicate that endogeneity of the labor supply again opens up for a quantitative *diversified* growth pattern, as it did in classical growth models, see Fig. 7.3 in section "Classical Comparative Dynamics".

As in Theorem 14.1 above, the evolution at the linear dynamic system (14.71–14.74) can be described explicitly. Only a few comments are needed here. The expression for the family of *ratio* solutions (14.27) is now replaced by

$$k(t) = \begin{cases} \frac{k_1}{2} - \frac{y_1}{2ny_2} - \frac{(k_1-k_2)\Delta}{ny_2} \tanh[\Delta(t+t_0)], & k_0 \in ]k_1, k_2[ \ \vee \ k_0 \in ]\kappa_1, \kappa_2[, \\ \frac{k_1}{2} - \frac{y_1}{2ny_2} - \frac{(k_1-k_2)\Delta}{ny_2} \coth[\Delta(t+t_0)], & k_0 \in ]k_1, k_2[ \ \vee \ k_0 \notin [\kappa_1, \kappa_2], \end{cases} \tag{14.83}$$

which are the complete set of solutions to (14.75); cf. (14.76–14.78) and (29.6.1), (29.28).

The time paths of the factor *allocation* fractions $\lambda_{L_1}(t)$, $\lambda_{K_1}(t)$ are determined by (14.83) and (14.5–14.6.1). The *general* solution for the *state* variables, $[L(t), K(t)]$ in terms of the structural parameters of the endogenous model (14.71–14.74) may be given by using the formula (29.93) of Chap. 29—which in the exogenous case gives the simple expressions (14.29.1–2). The time paths of *sector outputs* $[Y_1, Y_2(t)]$, (14.12), can also here be derived, but they will not be nice as in (14.31.1–2). Evidently, the ***kinematics*** (time paths) of the endogenous model has formally become rather more intricate that displayed with exogeneity (unilateral dynamic couplings, cf. Chap. 29, sections "The Calculus Approach and Techniques of Integration" and "Affine Dynamics in the Plane").

As to the *geometry* of the phase portrait, we have, cf. (14.71–14.74), (14.40), (14.42),

$$q(k) = \frac{\mathfrak{g}(k)}{\mathfrak{f}(k)} = \frac{y_1(k-k_2)}{ny_2(k_1-k)}, \tag{14.84}$$

$$q'(k) = \frac{ny_1y_2(k_1-k_2)}{[ny_2(k_1-k)]^2}. \tag{14.85}$$

Thus, in the case of asymptotic ratio stability (14.81), the phase portrait of the endogenous system is *hyperbolic,* as depicted in Fig. 14.2.

The *economic rationale* of the stability condition $k_2 > k_1$, cf. (14.81), is the same as before, namely, the Rybczynski-Jones relations, (14.52–14.54), which still holds, of course, in the economy described by the endogenous growth model (14.71–14.74).

Despite the complications seemingly arising from the quadratic director function (14.75), the stated qualitative results in Corollary 14.3 carry over to the endogenous model with only slight modifications. The latter are easily obtained. From (14.71), we immediately get the linear relation in $k$

$$\hat{L} = \frac{ny_2k_1}{k_1-k_2} - \frac{ny_2k}{k_1-k_2}, \tag{14.86}$$

and the hyperbola (14.56), (14.59) is unaffected, cf. (14.74)

$$\hat{K} = \frac{y_1k - y_1k_2}{(k_1-k_2)k}. \tag{14.87}$$

The proportional growth rates of the sector outputs (and sector inputs) are given by the rectangular hyperbolas

$$\hat{Y}_1 = \hat{L}_1 = \hat{K}_1 = \frac{(y_1 + ny_2k_2)k - k_2(y_1 + ny_2k_1)}{(k_1 - k_2)(k - k_2)}, \tag{14.88}$$

$$\hat{Y}_2 = \hat{L}_2 = \hat{K}_2 = \frac{(y_1 + ny_2k_1)k - y_1k_2 + ny_2k_1^2}{(k_1 - k_2)(k - k_1)}, \tag{14.89}$$

with

$$\hat{Y}_1 \text{ :centre } \left(k_2, \frac{y_1 + ny_2k_2}{k_1 - k_2}\right); \qquad \text{constant: } -ny_2k_2, \tag{14.90}$$

$$\hat{Y}_2 \text{ :centre } \left(k_1, \frac{y_1 + ny_2k_1}{k_1 - k_2}\right); \qquad \text{constant: } \quad y_1, \tag{14.91}$$

and the boundary values and intercepts

$$\hat{Y}_1(k = k_1) = \frac{y_1}{k_1 - k_2}, \qquad \hat{Y}_2(k = k_2) = \frac{ny_2k_1}{k_1 - k_2}, \tag{14.92}$$

$$\hat{Y}_1 = 0: \qquad k = \frac{k_2(y_1 + ny_2k_1)}{y_1 + ny_2k_2}, \tag{14.93}$$

$$\hat{Y}_2 = 0: \qquad k = \frac{y_1k_2 - ny_2k_1^2}{y_1 + ny_2k_1}. \tag{14.94}$$

***Proof*** By (14.75), (14.68.1), and (14.5), we have

$$\begin{aligned} \frac{\dot{\lambda}_{L_1}}{\lambda_{L_1}} &= \frac{\dot{k}}{\lambda_{L_1}(k_1 - k_2)} = \frac{y_1\lambda_{L_1} - ny_2\lambda_{L_2}k}{\lambda_{L_1}(k_1 - k_2)} \\ &= \frac{y_1}{k_1 - k_2} + \frac{ny_2k}{k_1 - k_2} - \frac{ny_2k}{k - k_2}. \end{aligned} \tag{14.95}$$

Next (14.66), (14.86), and (14.95) give

$$\hat{Y}_1 = \hat{L}_1 = \frac{y_1 + ny_2k_1}{k_1 - k_2} - \frac{ny_2k}{k - k_2}, \tag{14.96}$$

which in consolidated form becomes (14.88).

By (14.75), (14.68.2), and (14.5), we have

$$\begin{aligned} \frac{\dot{\lambda}_{L_2}}{\lambda_{L_2}} &= \frac{-\dot{k}}{\lambda_{L_2}(k_1 - k_2)} = \frac{-y_1\lambda_{L_2} + ny_2\lambda_{L_2}k}{\lambda_{L_2}(k_1 - k_2)} \\ &= \frac{y_1}{k_1 - k_2} + \frac{ny_2k}{k_1 - k_2} + \frac{y_1}{k - k_1}. \end{aligned} \tag{14.97}$$

Next (14.66), (14.86), and (14.97) give

$$\hat{Y}_2 = \hat{L}_2 = \frac{y_1 + ny_2k_1}{k_1 - k_2} + \frac{y_1}{k - k_1}, \tag{14.98}$$

which in consolidated form becomes (14.89). Applying (14.69) to (14.88–14.89) gives (14.90–14.91). □

By drawing the graphs from (14.86–14.94), we would then obtain a similar picture as displayed in Fig. 14.4a, except for horizontal line, ($\hat{L} = n$) being replaced by the straight line (14.86) with the boundary values, $\hat{L}(k = k_1) = 0$ and $\hat{L}(k = k_2) = ny_2$. All these graphs will intersect at $k = \kappa$, (14.80), (14.81).

Having now completed our treatment of two-sector growth models with Leontief technologies, a few final remarks on the various time paths and growth rates from these models seem appropriate. As is evident from Fig. 14.4a–b and (14.86–14.87), the time paths of $L(t)$ and $K(t)$ are always monotonically increasing, whereas their respective growth rate, $\hat{L}(t)$ and $\hat{K}(t)$ is either, depending on the initial factor endowment ratio ($k_0$), monotonically increasing or decreasing. The time paths of sector outputs (and inputs), $Y_1(t)$ and $Y_2(t)$, are not always monotonic as one of them may temporarily decline in absolute terms and accordingly display negative growth rates, if the initial factor endowment ratio ($k_0$) of the two-sector economy differed too much from $k = \kappa$, the "steady state" factor endowment ratio: (14.24.2), (14.77).

Owing to the progressive complexity of the kinematic expressions for $L(t)$, $K(t)$, $Y_1(t)$, and $Y_2(t)$—as discussed above in the endogenous model (14.71–14.74) and as also seen in Theorem 14.1—the evolution and the mutual size of growth rates $\hat{L}(t)$, $\hat{K}(t)$, $\hat{Y}_1(t)$, $Y_2(t)$ are not immediately apparent from the traditional coordinate solution formulas of linear dynamic systems.

But the formulas (14.56–14.57) and (14.86–14.89) will in fact also represent give kinematics (time paths), when the factor endowment ratio $k$ actually follows the time paths of the *ratio* solutions $k(t)$ from the respective dynamic models, as stated in (14.27) and (14.83).

Since the **ratio** solutions in **homogeneous dynamic systems** cf. Chap. 28, section "Ratio Solutions, Coordinate Solutions, and Trajectories", are always monotonic (increasing/decreasing), the formulas (14.27) and (14.83) indeed allow us to calculate also the exact point in time at which, e.g. the horizontal intercept values of **k**, (14.64–14.65) and (14.93–14.94) will be attained.

In short, **dynamics**, **kinematics**, and **economics** (structure, inner working of the two-sector economy) raise separate issues, but the answers must supplement and reinforce each other, if full understanding of the *accumulation* and *factor allocation* in a particular growth model is to be attained.

## Literature Comments

The first published mathematical treatment of the two-sector growth model with sectorial fixed coefficient (Leontief) technologies is due to Shinkai (1960)—oddly enough, not mentioned in Hahn (1965), who also first derived the conditions (14.37). Shinkai used the labor variables $L_1$ and $L_2$ as *state variables* for the dynamics of the two-sector economy. In these state variables, his dynamic system is also a *linear system* (see Shinkai (1960, p.109), Gandolfo (1980, p.351–57)), whose explicit *solutions* for $L_1(t)$ and $L_2(t)$ were then given in the standard form of a linear combination of "exponential basis solutions" (eigenvector/eigenvalues). The issue of the existence and stability of a steady-state growth is then pursued in the traditional way of examining the conditions under which all the explicit solutions of $L_1(t)$ and $L_2(t)$, (depending on the different assumptions about initial values) will converge, as $t \to \infty$, toward the "dominant" exponential solution associated with largest eigenvalue of the coefficient matrix. Such examination of the family of solutions $[L_1(t), L_2(t)]$ leads Shinkai to the coefficient restrictions equivalent to the parameter restrictions (14.37). We have given an alternative dynamic analysis of the two-sector economy in terms of labor variables $L_1$ and $L$ in Jensen and Larsen (1986, p.25–39).

However, it was here incumbent on us to present both the economic and dynamic aspects of the two-sector economy in more transparent forms. To this end, the structure in Chap. 15, section "The Two-Sector Economy with Proportional Saving", and the dynamic processes in Chap. 15, section "The Dynamic System, Solutions, Stability, and Trajectory Geometry" were described in terms of the state variables, $L$ and $K$. That also facilitates a comparison of this basic two-sector growth model (14.20.1–14.21.2) with, e.g., the neoclassical growth models in Chap. 11 and especially, as we shall see, with the neoclassical two-sector growth models in Chap. 16. The demonstration of Theorem 14.1 utilized the methodology of homogeneous dynamics as applied to linear plane systems in Chap. 29.

Saving aspects of the Shinkai paper Shinkai (1960) were discussed in Neisser (1962) and Shinkai (1962). But, as mentioned above, saving plays no independent role in this growth model. Complications arising from production *delays* (lags) in the capital good sector are examined in Furuno (1965); such lags do not affect the stability conditions (14.37), but they put a certain lower bound restriction upon $C_K$, (14.15): For the growth model to operate, the diversification cone must not be too narrow (Furuno (1965, p.243)). Geometric methods of comparative general equilibrium analysis were used in Corden (1966) and Findlay (1967) to investigate the factor allocations and the output compositions compatible with different assumptions about sectorial factor intensities. But the results of such qualitative geometric analysis are succinctly expressed by the equations/inequalities (14.5–14.9), (14.13), cf. Fig. 14.1.

## Bibliography

Allen RGD (1938) Mathematical Analysis for Economists. MacMillan, London

Bhagwati JN (1981) International Trade: Selected Readings, 2nd edn. MIT Press, Cambridge, MA

Corden WM (1966) The Two–Sector Growth Model with Fixed Coefficients. Review of Economic Studies 33:253–262

Findlay R (1967) Neutral Technical Progress and the Relative Stability of Two–Sector Growth Models. Int Econ Rev 8:109–15

Furuno Y (1965) The Period of Production in Two–Sector Models of Economic Growth. Int Econ Rev 6:240–44

Gandolfo G (1980) Economic Dynamics: Methods and Models, 2nd edn. North–Holland, Amsterdam

Hahn FH (1965) On Two–Sector Growth Models. Rev Econ Stud 32:339–46, or Sen (1970)

Jensen BS, Larsen ME (1986) Growth and Long–Run Stability. Tech. rep., Department of Mathematics, University of Copenhagen, Preprint series, No. 3

Jones RW (1965) The Structure of Simple General Equilibrium Models. J Political Economy 73:557–72, or Bhagwati (1981)

Neisser H (1962) On Equilibrium Growth of Capital and Labor. Int Econ Rev 3:136–37

Rybczynski TM (1955) Factor Endowments and Relative Commodity Prices. Economica 22:336–341

Sen A (1970) Growth Economics, Selected Readings. Penguin Books, London

Shinkai Y (1960) On the Equilibrium Growth of Capital and Labor. International Economic Review 1:107–111

Shinkai Y (1962) Balanced Growth and a Constant Degree of Employment of Labor: Reply to Professor Neisser. Int Econ Rev 3:138–44

Solow RM (1961) Note on Uzawa's Two–Sector Model of Economic Growth. Rev Econ Stud 29:48–50, or Stiglitz (1969)

Stiglitz JE, Uzawa H (1969) Readings in the Modern Theory of Economic Growth. M.I.T. Press, Cambridge, Mass

Takayama A (1972) International Trade. Holt, Rinehart, and Winston, New York

CHAPTER 15

# Flexible Technologies and Proportional Saving

We shall now move on to a *two-sector economy* with flexible technologies in both the capital good and the consumption good sectors. For such an economy, the assumptions of full employment and efficient allocation of the production factors (labor and capital) no longer (as in Chap. 14) suffice to establish a deterministic dynamic system. A macro savings function, as in Chaps. 8–12, is again needed to determine the part of aggregate income assigned to asset accumulation. However, as there are two commodities, and the *price mechanism* (flexible commodity and factor prices) is instrumental to determining factor allocation and output composition, *aggregate income* and savings necessarily become *monetary* (value) *concepts*. Although savings, with no financial assets, correspond to the monetary value of the new capital good output, it is not the quantitative increase in the capital stock (physical size of the production factor, capital). Evidently, in contrast to one-sector growth models, a new feature of *two-sector growth* models with flexible technologies and efficient factor allocation is the intrinsic influence of the *price mechanism*, operating to give existence to *momentary* and *moving general* equilibria in the *commodity* and *factor markets*—"miniature Walrasian general equilibrium systems", see Solow (1961), Zeuthen (1955, p.42,58).

Nevertheless, for such two-sector growth models, we should also like to emphasize that the *state variables* of the dynamic systems will throughout be the *factor endowments* $(L, K)$, and that the dynamic analysis may still be carried out within our framework of *homogeneous dynamics*.

We shall examine two-sector growth models with, respectively, proportional and classical saving functions (Chap. 16).



B. S. Jensen, *The Elements and Dynamic Systems of Economic Growth and Trade Models*, https://doi.org/10.1007/978-3-031-52493-6_15

## THE TWO-SECTOR ECONOMY WITH PROPORTIONAL SAVING

### *The General Equilibrium Model*

The two-sector general equilibrium model consists of the following *structural* equations. The sector *technologies* are described by production functions exhibiting constant returns to scale ($m = 1$),

$$Y_i = F_i(L_i, K_i) = L_i f_i(k_i), \quad i = 1, 2, \tag{15.1}$$

where $f_i(k_i)$, $i = 1, 2$, have the properties (2.12–2.13).

*Full employment* of the production factors, $L$ and $K$, is expressed alternatively by, cf. (14.2.1–14.4),

$$k = k_2 + (k_1 - k_2)\lambda_{L_1}, \tag{15.2}$$

$$\lambda_{L_1} = (k - k_2)/(k_1 - k_2), \quad \lambda_{L_2} = (k_1 - k)/(k_1 - k_2); \quad k_1 \neq k_2, \tag{15.3}$$

$$\lambda_{K_1} = k_1\lambda_{L_1}/k, \quad \lambda_{K_2} = k_2\lambda_{L_2}/k, \quad k_1 \neq k_2; \quad \lambda_{K_1} = \lambda_{L_1}, \quad k_1 = k_2. \tag{15.4}$$

*Efficient factor allocation* in the two-sector economy imposes the marginal rate of substitution (MRS) *conditions*, cf. (2.24),

$$\omega = \omega_1 = MRS_1(k_1) = \omega_1(k_1) = \omega_2 = MRS_2(k_2) = \omega_2(k_2), \tag{15.5}$$

or, equivalently, expressed by the factor prices determined in *competitive factor markets* (available factor endowments are inelastically supplied, and there is free factor mobility between the sectors),

$$w = P_1 \cdot MP_{L_1} = P_2 \cdot MP_{L_2}, \tag{15.6.1}$$

$$r = P_1 \cdot MP_{K_1} = P_2 \cdot MP_{K_2}, \tag{15.6.2}$$

$$\omega = w/r, \tag{15.6.3}$$

where the *factor prices* $(w, r)$ and the *commodity prices* $(P_1, P_2)$ are measured in terms of a *monetary* unit. The model will have no money circulation, so money only serves as a *numeraire*. Of course, only *relative money prices* matter in the model here, but we prefer to retain money prices rather than use one of the commodities as the numeraire.

*Aggregate income* $(Y)$ is the *monetary value* of *outputs* from both sectors,

$$Y \equiv P_1Y_1 + P_2Y_2, \tag{15.7}$$

and due to $m = 1$, cf. (15.1), (15.6.1–3), equal to the *factor incomes*

$$Y = rK + wL, \tag{15.8.1}$$

which defines the factor income ***distribution***, $\delta_K, \delta_L$,

$$\delta_K + \delta_L = 1; \quad \delta_K \equiv rK/Y, \quad \delta_L \equiv wL/Y; \quad \delta_K/\delta_L = k/\omega. \tag{15.8.2}$$

*Savings* are assumed to be a *constant proportion* of aggregate income,

$$S = sY, \quad 0 < s < 1. \tag{15.9}$$

*Market equilibrium* for *commodity 1* (newly produced capital goods) is expressed by condition, cf. (15.7)

$$P_1 Y_1 \quad = \quad sY. \tag{15.10}$$

Market equilibrium for commodity 2 follows from (15.7), (15.10) that obviously imply the equivalence of the value of the consumer good production and consumption expenditures, $P_2 Y_2 = (1 - s)Y$.

The *structural* equations (15.1–15.10) will characterize the *general equilibrium solutions* of the two-sector economy. Their *existence* and *uniqueness*, however, is a matter that need particular attention before proceeding any further.

As is well-known, various geometric techniques, see Johnson (1971, p.16–32), have been used to explore the issue of existence and uniqueness as well as to explore, for given factor endowments, the relationships between the production pattern, commodity prices, factor prices, and the factor income distribution. But the illustrative methods of "production possibility curves", "contract curves", etc. are inadequate for our purpose, which is to describe *qualitatively*, but precisely, the general equilibrium *solutions* to (15.1–15.10) corresponding to *variations* in the factor endowments.

Since the sectors of the two-sector economy operate under the conditions of constant return to scale, we need only, from the equations (15.1–15.10), to study the behavior of the *output ratio* $Y_1/Y_2$, *relative* prices $P_1/P_2$, *relative* factor prices $w/r$, the *allocation ratios* $\lambda_{L_1}$ and $\lambda_{K_1}$ and the *factor shares* $\delta_L$ and $\delta_K$ as functions of the overall *capital-labor ratio* $\mathbf{k}$—the fundamental ratio that will later on also govern the relevant *homogeneous dynamic* system.

### *The General Equilibrium Solutions*

Boundary (corner) solutions with only one sector producing (complete specialization) are improper and extraneous to our subject of a genuine two-sector economy. Similarly, the occurrence of a free factor (slack) invalidates the structural equations (15.5–15.6.3). To avoid these "nuisance" problems, further aspects of the underlying assumptions and certain *range* and *domain* issues for the structural relations need brief discussion.

To have efficient factor allocation, that is, for $k_1$ and $k_2$ to comply with the condition (15.5), sector production functions (15.1) with *linear isoquants*, cf. (7.59), of different slopes must clearly be *ruled out*. With $m = 1$, such sector production functions with $\sigma_i = \infty$ are indeed ruled out by the *strict convexity* property of the sector isoquants, implied by imposing (2.12–2.13) upon (15.1), cf. (2.26) and Remark 2.2. But still, for the variables $k_1$ and $k_2$ to satisfy (15.5), it is, despite (2.12–2.13), further required that the *intersection* of the *range* for, respectively, $\omega_1(k_1)$ and $\omega_2(k_2)$ is not empty, which may be formalized as follows, cf. (2.28.1–2):

$$\omega_1(k_1) \in \Omega_1 = [\underline{\omega}_1, \overline{\omega}_1], \quad \Omega_1 \subseteq \mathbf{R}_+, \tag{15.11.1}$$

$$\omega_2(k_2) \in \Omega_2 = [\underline{\omega}_2, \overline{\omega}_2], \quad \Omega_2 \subseteq \mathbf{R}_+, \tag{15.11.2}$$

$$\omega \in \Omega \equiv \Omega_1 \cup \Omega_2 = [\underline{\omega}, \overline{\omega}] \neq \emptyset, \tag{15.11.3}$$

where $\omega$ is the *common wage-rental* ratio, (15.5–15.6.3).

Regarding the *domain* of admissible factor proportions $K/L$ in the general equilibrium model (15.1–15.10), this domain is given by the *diversification* cone, cf. (14.15), which with variable sector capital-labor ratios, $k_1(\omega), k_2(\omega)$, here becomes, cf. (15.11.3)

$$C_K = \{(L, K) \in \mathbf{R}_+^2 \mid k_1(\omega) < k < k_2(\omega) \vee k_2(\omega) < k < k_1(\omega);\ \forall \omega \in \Omega\}. \tag{15.12}$$

As is well-known, even if $\Omega \subset \mathbf{R}_+$, (15.11.3), we may still have $C_K = \mathbf{R}_+^2$, for example, in case of two constant elasticity of substitution (CES) functions, (2.49), with substitution elasticities larger than one.

**Remark 15.1** As sectorial capital-labor ratios ("capital intensities") and/or sectorial substitution elasticities play important roles in the discussion of two-sector models, we may show their connection for two CES functions. We have, cf. (7.50), (15.5), (15.11.3)

$$\ln k_1 = \sigma_1 \ln \frac{a_1}{1 - a_1} + \sigma_1 \ln \omega; \quad \ln k_2 = \sigma_2 \ln \frac{a_2}{1 - a_2} + \sigma_2 \ln \omega. \tag{15.13}$$

If no uniform capital intensity property holds globally for either sector, then "reswitching" occurs at some value of $\omega = \omega^*$, which is here, cf. (15.13)

$$k^* = \left[\frac{(1 - a_2)/a_2}{(1 - a_1)/a_1}\right]^{\frac{\sigma_1\sigma_2}{\sigma_2 - \sigma_1}}, \quad \omega^* = \left[\frac{[(1 - a_2)/a_2]^{\sigma_2}}{[(1 - a_1)/a_1]^{\sigma_1}}\right]^{\frac{1}{\sigma_2 - \sigma_1}} \tag{15.14}$$

▽

The *output elasticities* of sectorial production functions are denoted by $\epsilon_{L_i}, \epsilon_{K_i}$, which are also sectorial *factor shares,* cf. (2.16.1–3), (2.24), Chap. 2. section "Factor Shares and Production Elasticities", (15.1), (15.6.1–15.8.2), that is,

$$\epsilon_{L_i} = \frac{MP_{L_i}}{AP_{L_i}} = \frac{wL_i}{P_i Y_i}, \quad \epsilon_{K_i} = \frac{MP_{K_i}}{AP_{K_i}} = \frac{rK_i}{P_i Y_i}; \quad i = 1, 2, \tag{15.15}$$

$$\epsilon_{L_i} + \epsilon_{K_i} = 1, \quad \epsilon_{K_i}/\epsilon_{L_i} = k_i/\omega; \quad i = 1, 2. \tag{15.16}$$

The *general equilibrium solutions* of the two-sector economy are obtained as follows. The *relative* commodity prices are equal to the *ratio* of *minimal* unit cost, which with common factor prices are equal to the *ratio* of marginal products, that is, cf. (15.5–15.6.3),

$$\frac{P_1}{P_2} = \frac{MP_{K_2}[k_2(\omega)]}{MP_{K_1}[k_1(\omega)]}. \tag{15.17}$$

From (15.7) and (15.10), we have

$$\frac{P_1 Y_1}{P_2 Y_2} = \frac{s}{1-s}, \tag{15.18}$$

which characterizes the "demand side" of the economy.

From (15.15), we get

$$\frac{P_1 Y_1}{P_2 Y_2} = \frac{L_1 \epsilon_{L_2}}{L_2 \epsilon_{L_1}} = \frac{\lambda_{L_1} \epsilon_{L_2}}{(1-\lambda_{L_1})\epsilon_{L_1}} \tag{15.19.1}$$

$$= \frac{K_1 \epsilon_{K_2}}{K_2 \epsilon_{K_1}} = \frac{\lambda_{K_1} \epsilon_{K_2}}{(1-\lambda_{K_1})\epsilon_{K_1}}, \tag{15.19.2}$$

which characterize the "supply side" of the economy, operating under constant returns to scale and with *full,* (15.2–15.4), and *efficient,* (15.5–15.6.3), factor utilization.

*Equilibrium* on the *commodity markets* requires by (15.18–15.19.2) that

$$\frac{s}{1-s} = \frac{\lambda_{L_1} \epsilon_{L_2}}{(1-\lambda_{L_1})\epsilon_{L_1}} = \frac{\lambda_{K_1} \epsilon_{K_2}}{(1-\lambda_{K_1})\epsilon_{K_1}}, \tag{15.20}$$

which gives

$$\lambda_{L_1} = \frac{s\epsilon_{L_1}}{s\epsilon_{L_1} + (1-s)\epsilon_{L_2}}, \quad \lambda_{L_2} = \frac{(1-s)\epsilon_{L_2}}{s\epsilon_{L_1} + (1-s)\epsilon_{L_2}}, \tag{15.21}$$

$$\lambda_{K_1} = \frac{s\epsilon_{K_1}}{s\epsilon_{K_1} + (1-s)\epsilon_{K_2}}, \quad \lambda_{K_2} = \frac{(1-s)\epsilon_{K_2}}{s\epsilon_{K_1} + (1-s)\epsilon_{K_2}}. \tag{15.22}$$

Next from (15.8.1) and (15.10), we have, cf. (15.15)

$$s/\delta_L = P_1 Y_1 / wL = \lambda_{L_1} / \epsilon_{L_1}, \tag{15.23}$$

which together with (15.21) give, cf. (15.16), (15.8.2),

$$\delta_L = s\epsilon_{L_1} + (1-s)\epsilon_{L_2}, \tag{15.24}$$

$$\delta_K = s\epsilon_{K_1} + (1-s)\epsilon_{K_2}. \tag{15.25}$$

Finally, from (15.8.2) and (15.24–15.25), we get

$$k = \omega(\delta_K/\delta_L) = \frac{\omega[s\epsilon_{K_1} + (1-s)\epsilon_{K_2}]}{s\epsilon_{L_1} + (1-s)\epsilon_{L_2}} = \Psi(\omega), \tag{15.26.1}$$

where, cf. (15.11.3–15.12)

$$k \in C_K \quad \Leftrightarrow \quad \omega \in \Omega. \tag{15.26.2}$$

Then, for example, the equations (15.26.1–2), (15.1), (15.5), (15.16), (15.17–15.18), (15.21–15.22), (15.24–15.25) give the *general equilibrium solutions* of $\omega$, $k_i$, $y_i$, $\epsilon_{L_i}$, $\epsilon_{K_i}$, $P_1/P_2$, $Y_1/Y_2$, $\lambda_{L_1}$, $\lambda_{K_1}$, $\delta_L$, $\delta_K$, corresponding to any given factor endowment ratio, $K/L = k$.

However, for these general equilibrium solutions to be *unique* at every $k \in C_K$, it is required that $\Psi(\omega)$, (15.26.1–2), is a strictly monotonic function so that the inverse $\Psi^{-1}(k)$ exists for every $k \in C_K$.

**Lemma 15.1** *The function $\Psi(\omega)$, (15.26.1–2), is monotonically increasing, and its elasticity, $E(k,\omega) = (d\Psi/d\omega)(\omega/\Psi)$, $\forall \omega \in \Omega$, is given by*

$$E(k,\omega) = \frac{1}{\delta_L}\left[\frac{s}{\delta_K}(1-s)(\epsilon_{K_1} - \epsilon_{K_2})^2 + \lambda_{L_1}\epsilon_{K_1}\sigma_1 + \lambda_{L_2}\epsilon_{K_2}\sigma_2\right] > 0, \tag{15.27.1}$$

$$E(k,\omega) = \frac{1}{\delta_K}\left[\frac{s}{\delta_L}(1-s)(\epsilon_{L_1} - \epsilon_{L_2})^2 + \lambda_{K_1}\epsilon_{L_1}\sigma_1 + \lambda_{K_2}\epsilon_{L_2}\sigma_2\right] > 0. \tag{15.27.2}$$

*Hence, in the two-sector equilibrium model (15.1–15.10), factor endowments with a higher capital-labor ratio $k$ are always accompanied by a unique and higher equilibrium value of the wage-rental ratio $\omega$, and vice versa, that is,*

$$\forall k \in C_K \quad : \quad E(\omega,k) = 1/E(k,\omega) > 0. \tag{15.28}$$

*The sign of the elasticities (15.27.1–15.28) is unaffected by the size of the substitution elasticities $\sigma_1(\omega), \sigma_2(\omega)$ and by any reswitching between the "capital intensities", $k_1(\omega)$ and $k_2(\omega)$.*

***Proof*** From (15.26.1–2), we immediately have

$$E(k, \omega) \quad = \quad 1 + E(\delta_K, \omega) - E(\delta_L, \omega). \tag{15.29}$$

It follows from (15.8.2) that

$$\delta_K E(\delta_K, \omega) + \delta_L E(\delta_L, \omega) = 0 \quad \therefore \quad E(\delta_L, \omega) = -\frac{\delta_K}{\delta_L} E(\delta_K, \omega). \tag{15.30}$$

Hence, by (15.29–15.30)

$$E(k, \omega) \quad = \quad 1 + E(\delta_K, \omega)/\delta_L. \tag{15.31}$$

Then (15.25) gives

$$E(\delta_K, \omega) \quad = \quad (1/\delta_K)[s\epsilon_{K_1} E(\epsilon_{K_1}, \omega) + (1-s)\epsilon_{K_2} E(\epsilon_{K_2}, \omega)]. \tag{15.32}$$

Recalling that, cf. (2.42), $m = 1$, (2.29)

$$E(\epsilon_{K_i}, \omega) \quad = \quad \epsilon_{L_i}(\sigma_i - 1), \quad i = 1, 2, \tag{15.33.1}$$

$$E(\epsilon_{L_i}, \omega) \quad = \quad \epsilon_{K_i}(1 - \sigma_i), \quad i = 1, 2, \tag{15.33.2}$$

we get from (15.31–15.32) and (15.33.1)

$$E(k, \omega) \quad = \quad 1 + \frac{1}{\delta_K \delta_L}[s\epsilon_{K_1}\epsilon_{L_1}(\sigma_1 - 1) + (1-s)\epsilon_{K_2}\epsilon_{L_2}(\sigma_2 - 1)], \tag{15.34}$$

which, using (15.21–15.22), (15.24–15.25), and $\epsilon_{L_i} = 1 - \epsilon_{K_i}$, reduces after some manipulation to (15.27.1–2). By the global positivity of $E(k, \omega)$, (15.27.1–2), the lemma is established. □

### *Comparative General Equilibrium Analysis*

By $\omega(k) = \Psi^{-1}(k)$, (15.26.1–15.27.2), all other equilibrium quantities and prices are determined for every $k \in C_K$. To understand the inner working of the two-sector economy, it will be instructive to see how the other general equilibrium solutions react to changes in the equilibrium values of $\omega(k)$—*comparative general equilibrium analysis.* The responses will here be stated in terms of elasticities with respect to the wage-rental ratio, $\omega$. Due to (15.28), the *sign* of the elasticities below will, of course, be the *same* with respect to $k$ as to $\omega$.

With a common wage-rental ratio in both sectors, (15.5–15.6.3), it is clear that, cf. (15.16)

$$k_2(\omega) \gtreqless k_1(\omega) \quad \Leftrightarrow \quad \epsilon_{K_2}(\omega) \gtreqless \epsilon_{K_1}(\omega) \quad \Leftrightarrow \quad \epsilon_{L_1}(\omega) \gtreqless \epsilon_{L_2}(\omega). \tag{15.35}$$

From (15.17), we get by the elasticity rule of composite functions, cf. Chap. 2. section "Factor Shares and Production Elasticities",

$$E(P_1/P_2, \omega) \quad = \quad \epsilon_{K_2} - \epsilon_{K_1}, \tag{15.36}$$

which is positive/negative according to (15.35).

Then by (15.18) and (15.36), it follows that

$$E(Y_1/Y_2, \omega) = -E(P_1/P_2, \omega) = \epsilon_{K_1} - \epsilon_{K_2}. \tag{15.37}$$

Regarding the factor income *distribution*, we already have, cf. (15.22), (15.31), (15.33.1)

$$E(\delta_K, \omega) \quad = \quad \lambda_{K_1}\epsilon_{L_1}(\sigma_1 - 1) + \lambda_{K_2}\epsilon_{L_2}(\sigma_2 - 1), \tag{15.38}$$

and analogously from (15.21), (15.24), (15.33.2),

$$E(\delta_L, \omega) \quad = \quad \lambda_{L_1}\epsilon_{K_1}(1 - \sigma_1) + \lambda_{L_2}\epsilon_{K_2}(1 - \sigma_2). \tag{15.39}$$

Obviously, a sufficient condition for $E(\delta_K, \omega) > 0$ is that both $\sigma_1$ and $\sigma_2$ are larger than one.

As to the *allocation* ratios, we find that, cf. (15.21), (15.24), (15.33.2), (15.39)

$$E(\lambda_{L_1}, \omega) \quad = \quad E(\epsilon_{L_1}, \omega) - E(\delta_L, \omega) \quad = \quad \lambda_{L_2}[\epsilon_{K_1}(1 - \sigma_1) - \epsilon_{K_2}(1 - \sigma_2)], \tag{15.40.1}$$

$$E(\lambda_{L_2}, \omega) \quad = \quad -(\lambda_{L_1}/\lambda_{L_2})E(\lambda_{L_1}, \omega), \tag{15.40.2}$$

and then by (15.22), (15.25), (15.33.1)

$$E(\lambda_{K_1}, \omega) \quad = \quad E(\epsilon_{K_1}, \omega) - E(\delta_K, \omega) \quad = \lambda_{K_2}[\epsilon_{L_1}(\sigma_1 - 1) - \epsilon_{L_2}(\sigma_2 - 1)], \tag{15.41.1}$$

$$E(\lambda_{K_2}, \omega) \quad = \quad -(\lambda_{K_1}/\lambda_{K_2})E(\lambda_{K_1}, \omega). \tag{15.41.2}$$

Further, we obtain from (15.40.1–15.41.1), [with reverse signs for $E(\lambda_{L_2}, \omega)$, $E(\lambda_{K_2}, \omega)$], that

$$\forall \omega \in \Omega \quad : \quad [\sigma_1(\omega) < 1 \ \wedge \sigma_2(\omega) > 1] \quad \Rightarrow E(\lambda_{L_1}, \omega) > 0, \tag{15.42.1}$$

$$\forall \omega \in \Omega \quad : \quad [k_1(\omega) < k_2(\omega) \wedge \sigma_2(\omega) > 1] \ \Rightarrow E(\lambda_{L_1}, \omega) > 0, \tag{15.42.2}$$

$$\forall \omega \in \Omega \quad : \quad [k_1(\omega) > k_2(\omega) \ \wedge \sigma_1(\omega) > 1] \ \Rightarrow E(\lambda_{L_1}, \omega) < 0, \tag{15.42.3}$$

$$\forall \omega \in \Omega \quad : \quad [\sigma_1(\omega) > 1 \ \wedge \sigma_2(\omega)0, \tag{15.43.1}$$

$$\forall \omega \in \Omega \quad : \quad [k_1(\omega) > k_2(\omega) \ \wedge \sigma_2(\omega)0, \tag{15.43.2}$$

$$\forall \omega \in \Omega \quad : \quad [k_1(\omega) < k_2(\omega) \ \wedge \sigma_1(\omega) < 1] \ \Rightarrow \ E(\lambda_{K_1}, \omega) < 0. \tag{15.43.3}$$

The implications (15.42.1–15.43.3) follow by using (15.35).

Thus, as appears from (15.42.1–15.43.3), general equilibria of a two-sector economy with flexible technologies are—in *contrast* to (14.16)—much *less prone* to reallocate both more capital and labor into one sector.

Besides the output *ratio* (15.37), we also want to know and *compare* the general equilibrium *level* values of $Y_1$ and $Y_2$ that correspond to alternative values of $\omega$ (and $k$), for example, whether, despite (15.37), *both* $Y_1$ and $Y_2$ may be higher or *one* of them ($Y_1$ or $Y_2$) is lower, when $\omega$ (and $k$) is altered. To examine these issues, we calculate elasticities below.

As $Y_i/L = y_i\lambda_{L_i}$, $i = 1, 2$ we get, cf. (15.40.1–2)

$$\begin{aligned} E(Y_1/L, \omega) &= E(y_1, \omega) + E(\lambda_{L_1}, \omega) \\ &= \epsilon_{K_1}\sigma_1 + \lambda_{L_2}[\epsilon_{K_1}(1 - \sigma_1) - \epsilon_{K_2}(1 - \sigma_2)] \\ &= \lambda_{L_1}\epsilon_{K_1}\sigma_1 + \lambda_{L_2}[\epsilon_{K_1} - \epsilon_{K_2}(1 - \sigma_2)], \end{aligned} \tag{15.44}$$

$$\begin{aligned} E(Y_2/L, \omega) &= E(y_2, \omega) + E(\lambda_{L_2}, \omega) \\ &= \epsilon_{K_2}\sigma_2 - \lambda_{L_1}[\epsilon_{K_1}(1 - \sigma_1) - \epsilon_{K_2}(1 - \sigma_2)] \\ &= \lambda_{L_2}\epsilon_{K_2}\sigma_2 + \lambda_{L_1}[\epsilon_{K_2} - \epsilon_{K_1}(1 - \sigma_1)]. \end{aligned} \tag{15.45}$$

Hence, by (15.44–15.45) and (15.35)

$$\forall \omega \in \Omega \quad : \quad \sigma_2(\omega) \geq 1 \quad \Rightarrow \quad E(Y_1/L, \omega) > 0, \tag{15.46.1}$$

$$\forall \omega \in \Omega \quad : \quad k_1(\omega) > k_2(\omega) \quad \Rightarrow \quad E(Y_1/L, \omega) > 0, \tag{15.46.2}$$

$$\forall \omega \in \Omega \quad : \quad \sigma_1(\omega) \geq 1 \quad \Rightarrow \quad E(Y_2/L, \omega) > 0, \tag{15.47.1}$$

$$\forall \omega \in \Omega \quad : \quad k_2(\omega) > k_1(\omega) \quad \Rightarrow \quad E(Y_2/L, \omega) > 0. \tag{15.47.2}$$

As $Y_i/K = (y_i/k_i)\lambda_{K_i}$, $i = 1, 2$, we get, cf. (15.41.1–2)

$$\begin{aligned} E(Y_1/K, \omega) &= E(y_1/k_1, \omega) + E(\lambda_{K_1}, \omega) \\ &= -\epsilon_{L_1}\sigma_1 + \lambda_{K_2}[\epsilon_{L_1}(\sigma_1 - 1) - \epsilon_{L_2}(\sigma_2 - 1)] \\ &= -\lambda_{K_1}\epsilon_{L_1}\sigma_1 - \lambda_{K_2}[\epsilon_{L_1} + \epsilon_{L_2}(\sigma_2 - 1)], \end{aligned} \tag{15.48}$$

$$\begin{aligned} E(Y_2/K, \omega) &= E(y_2/k_2, \omega) + E(\lambda_{K_2}, \omega) \\ &= -\epsilon_{L_2}\sigma_2 - \lambda_{K_1}[\epsilon_{L_1}(\sigma_1 - 1) - \epsilon_{L_2}(\sigma_2 - 1)] \\ &= -\lambda_{K_2}\epsilon_{L_2}\sigma_2 - \lambda_{K_1}[\epsilon_{L_2} + \epsilon_{L_1}(\sigma_1 - 1)]. \end{aligned} \tag{15.49}$$

Hence, by (15.48–15.49) and (15.35)

$$\forall \omega \in \Omega \quad : \quad \sigma_2(\omega) \geq 1 \quad \Rightarrow \quad E(Y_1/K, \omega) < 0, \tag{15.50.1}$$

$$\forall \omega \in \Omega \quad : \quad k_1(\omega) < k_2(\omega) \quad \Rightarrow \quad E(Y_1/K, \omega) < 0, \tag{15.50.2}$$

$$\forall \omega \in \Omega \quad : \quad \sigma_1(\omega) > 1 \quad \Rightarrow \quad E(Y_2/K, \omega) < 0, \tag{15.51.1}$$

$$\forall \omega \in \Omega \quad : \quad k_2(\omega) < k_1(\omega) \quad \Rightarrow \quad E(Y_2/K, \omega) < 0. \tag{15.51.2}$$

Elementary rules of elasticities give

$$E(Y_i/L, k) = E(Y_i/L, \omega)E(\omega, k), \qquad i = 1, 2, \tag{15.52}$$

$$E(Y_i/K, k) = E(Y_i/K, \omega)E(\omega, k), \qquad i = 1, 2, \tag{15.53}$$

$$E(Y_i, K) = E(Y_i/L, k), \qquad i = 1, 2, \tag{15.54}$$

$$E(Y_i, L) = -E(Y_i/K, k), \qquad i = 1, 2. \tag{15.55}$$

Now, we are able to state a general equilibrium theorem for the *sign* of the *elasticities* of $Y_1$ and $Y_2$ with respect to one-factor endowments.

**Theorem 15.1** *In the two-sector general equilibrium model (15.1–15.10) with sector technologies and total factor endowments satisfying, respectively, (15.11.3) and (15.12)—where the proportional savings assumption (15.9) might alternatively in case of two consumer goods* $Y_1$ *and* $Y_2$ *be replaced by the consumer demand (expenditure) system that arises from a budget-restrained utility maximization of a homothetic Cobb-Douglas utility function (substitution elasticity in consumption equal to one)—an increase in the one-factor endowment will increase the output of the sector (good) intensive in that factor, and the output of the other sector (good) will not necessarily decrease.*

*If a sector has a substitution elasticity larger than one, then the output of the other sector will increase, when one factor endowment is increased.*

*If both sectors have substitution elasticities larger than one, then the output of both sectors will increase, when one factor endowment is increased.*

*In short,* $\forall k \in C_K$, *(15.12), the output elasticities (15.54–15.55) from the general equilibrium model (15.1–15.10) have positive signs under the following conditions:*

$$E(Y_1, K) > 0, \quad \textit{if} \quad k_1(\omega) > k_2(\omega) \ \textit{or} \ \sigma_2(\omega) > 1; \quad \forall\omega \in \Omega, \tag{15.56.1}$$

$$E(Y_2, K) > 0, \quad \textit{if} \quad k_2(\omega) > k_1(\omega) \ \textit{or} \ \sigma_1(\omega) > 1; \quad \forall\omega \in \Omega, \tag{15.56.2}$$

$$E(Y_1, L) > 0, \quad \textit{if} \quad k_1(\omega) < k_2(\omega) \ \textit{or} \ \sigma_2(\omega) > 1; \quad \forall\omega \in \Omega, \tag{15.58.1}$$

$$E(Y_2, L) > 0, \quad \textit{if} \quad k_2(\omega) < k_1(\omega) \ \textit{or} \ \sigma_1(\omega) > 1; \quad \forall\omega \in \Omega, \tag{15.58.2}$$

$$\forall E(Y_i, K) > 0 \quad \textit{if} \quad \forall\sigma_i(\omega) > 1, \quad i = 1, 2; \quad \forall\omega \in \Omega, \tag{15.59.1}$$

$$\forall E(Y_i, L) > 0 \quad \textit{if} \quad \forall\sigma_i(\omega) > 1, \quad i = 1, 2; \quad \forall\omega \in \Omega. \tag{15.59.2}$$

***Proof*** The positivity of the elasticities $E(Y_i, K)$, (15.56.1–2)—under the stated conditions—follows from (15.54), (15.52), (15.46.1–15.47.2), and (15.28).

The positivity of the elasticities $E(Y_i, L)$, (15.58.1–2)—under the stated conditions—follows from (15.55), (15.53), (15.50.1–15.51.2), and (15.28).

Hence, (15.56.1–15.59.2) give the output changes for one-factor endowment variations. □

Compared to the Rybczynski *producer* (partial) equilibrium theorem, cf. Chap. 14. section "The Economic Rationale of the Stability Conditions", this *general equilibrium* theorem only *upholds* the output *increase* of the intensive sector, but *not* necessarily the *fall* of the other sector output.

For the intensive sector, Theorem 15.1 *neither* necessarily gives *magnified* output changes, since the output elasticities (15.56.1–15.58.2) are not necessarily larger than one, cf. (14.49–14.50), (14.53–14.54). In fact, the possibility of *magnification effects* upon a particular sector output—as the result of changes in the one-factor endowment—is here ruled out, if the substitution elasticity of the other sector is larger than one. We may summarize all this in a corollary to Theorem 15.1.

**Corollary 15.1** *The size of general equilibrium elasticities, (15.56.1–15.58.2),* $\forall k \in C_K$, *(15.12), is restricted by substitution elasticities as follows:*

$$\forall\omega \in \Omega \quad : \quad \sigma_2(\omega) > 1 \quad \Rightarrow \quad 0 < E(Y_1, K) < 1, \tag{15.60.1}$$

$$\forall\omega \in \Omega \quad : \quad \sigma_1(\omega) > 1 \quad \Rightarrow \quad 0 < E(Y_2, K) < 1, \tag{15.60.2}$$

$$\forall\omega \in \Omega \quad : \quad \sigma_2(\omega) > 1 \quad \Rightarrow \quad 0 < E(Y_1, L) < 1, \tag{15.61.1}$$

$$\forall\omega \in \Omega \quad : \quad \sigma_1(\omega) > 1 \quad \Rightarrow \quad 0 < E(Y_2, L) < 1. \tag{15.61.2}$$

*When both $\sigma_1(\omega)$ and $\sigma_2(\omega)$ are larger than one, it follows from (15.60.1–15.61.2) that none of the elasticities—$E(Y_i, K)$, $E(Y_i, L)$, $i = 1, 2$—are larger than one, which then in turn conform with them all being positive, (15.59.1–2).*

*For the sake of completeness, it is noted that*

$$\forall\omega \in \Omega \quad : \quad \sigma_2(\omega) > 1 \quad \Rightarrow \quad 0 < E(Y_1/L, k) < 1, \tag{15.62.1}$$

$$\forall\omega \in \Omega \quad : \quad \sigma_1(\omega) > 1 \quad \Rightarrow \quad 0 < E(Y_2/L, k) < 1. \tag{15.62.2}$$

***Proof*** In (15.60.1–15.62.2), only the upper bound of the interval, ]0, 1[, remains to be proved.

Obviously, we may write

$$E(Y_i, K) = E(Y_i/K, k) + 1, \quad i = 1, 2. \tag{15.63}$$

Then (15.60.1–2) follows from (15.50.1), (15.51.1), (15.53), and (15.63).

Similarly, we have,

$$E(Y_i, L) = E(Y_i/L, L) + 1, \quad i = 1, 2, \tag{15.64}$$

and by (15.55),

$$E(Y_i, L) = E(Y_i/K, L) = -E(Y_i/K, k), \quad i = 1, 2. \tag{15.65}$$

Hence, (15.64–15.65) give

$$E(Y_i/L, L) = -E(Y_i/K, k) - 1, \quad i = 1, 2. \tag{15.66}$$

Now (15.60.1–2) and (15.63) imply that $E(Y_i/L, L)$, $i = 1, 2$, (15.66), are negative under the respective substitution elasticity conditions stated in (15.60.1–2).

Thus, (15.60.1–2), (15.66), and (15.65) establish (15.61.1–2).

As $Y_i/K \equiv (Y_i/L)/(K/L)$, this gives immediately

$$E(Y_i/K, k) = E(Y_i/L, k) - 1, \quad i = 1, 2, \tag{15.67}$$

which together with (15.60.1–2) establish (15.62.1–2); cf. (15.46.1), (15.47.1), (15.50.1), (15.51.1), (15.52–15.53), and (15.28). □

**Remark 15.2** At the very beginning, we chose to express prices and incomes in some monetary unit, cf. (15.6.1–15.8.2). However, it has been customary in the literature on two-sector models to use the *consumption good* as the *numeraire*.

Accordingly, by using price measurements in terms of the consumer good, the *national* (aggregate) *income* $Y$, (15.7), corresponds, of course, to a *"national product"* (real national income) measured as

$$X \equiv Y/P_2 \equiv (P_1/P_2)Y_1 + Y_2 \equiv PY_1 + Y_2, \tag{15.68}$$

and a national product per capita ($L$) as

$$y \equiv \frac{X}{L} \equiv \frac{Y/P_2}{L} = (P_1/P_2)\frac{Y_1}{L} + \frac{Y_2}{L} = \left[\frac{P_1 Y_1}{P_2 Y_2} + 1\right]\frac{Y_2}{L}. \tag{15.69}$$

The *general equilibrium solution* $y(\omega)$—or $y(k)$—is now simply given by (15.69), (15.18–15.20), (15.26.1–2) as

$$y = \frac{1}{1-s} \cdot \frac{Y_2}{L} = \frac{\lambda_{L_2} y_2}{1-s}, \tag{15.70}$$

and hence, for comparative general equilibrium analysis, we have immediately from (15.70)

$$E(y, \omega) \quad = \quad E(Y_2/L, \omega), \tag{15.71}$$

where $E(Y_2/L, \omega)$ was given in (15.45), cf. (15.47.1–2).
Also, $E(y, k)$ comes directly from (15.52) and (15.71). ▽

The rather detailed, but indispensable, *examination* of the *general equilibrium solutions* to the two-sector model (15.1–15.10) is now finished. A clear understanding of the *"comparative static"* properties of an economic model is a prerequisite (necessary, but not sufficient) for also a genuine economic comprehension of the *kinematic* properties of the model in a *dynamic* setting—where the state variables, for example, the endowments $[L(t), K(t)]$, change from their initial values according to differential equations.

### *Literature Comments*

The *seminal* work on two-sector growth models with flexible sector technologies is that of Uzawa (1961) and Uzawa (1963). Before we discuss the dynamics of these growth models, we should review some of his results for the two-sector model of section "The Two-Sector Economy with Proportional Saving".

Let us first compare his analysis of a change in the wage-rentals ratio upon national product per capita with that given in (15.71), (15.45). To this end, we rewrite (15.70) in his form. Using (15.15), (15.21), (15.24), we obtain from (15.70),

$$y = y_2 \epsilon_{L_2}/\delta_L = MP_{L_2}/\delta_L. \tag{15.72}$$

With, cf. (15.8.1–2), (15.6.1–3),

$$\delta_L = \omega/(\omega + k), \qquad \omega = MP_{L_2}/MP_{K_2}, \tag{15.73}$$

we also have that, cf. (15.1), (15.72–15.73)

$$y = MP_{K_2} \cdot (\omega + k) = f_2'(k_2)(\omega + k), \tag{15.74}$$

as presented in Uzawa (1963, p.109).

Differentiating (15.74) logarithmically with respect to $\omega$, we get, using $m = 1$, (2.27), (2.24), (15.5),

$$\begin{aligned} \frac{1}{y} \cdot \frac{dy}{d\omega} &= \frac{f_2''(k_2)}{f_2'(k_2)} \frac{dk_2}{d\omega} + \frac{1 + dk(\omega)/d\omega}{\omega + k} \\ &= -\frac{1}{\omega + k_2(\omega)} + \frac{1}{\omega + k} + \frac{dk(\omega)/d\omega}{\omega + k}. \end{aligned} \tag{15.75}$$

Seemingly, by putting $dk(\omega)/d\omega = 0$—perhaps stemming from his notion of a "short-run equilibrium" (with fixed $L$ and $K$)—the logarithmic derivative of (15.74) is presented by Uzawa as

$$\frac{1}{y} \cdot \frac{dy}{d\omega} = -\frac{1}{\omega + k_2(\omega)} + \frac{1}{\omega + k}, \tag{15.76}$$

which we may write equivalently as, cf. (15.72–15.73), (15.16), (15.24),

$$E^*(y, \omega) = \frac{\omega}{y} \cdot \frac{dy}{d\omega} = -\epsilon_{L_2}(\omega) - \delta_L(\omega) = s(\epsilon_{K_2} - \epsilon_{K_1}). \tag{15.77}$$

From (15.76–15.77), Uzawa concludes that "national product per capita is an increasing function of the wage-rentals ratio *if* and *only if* the capital intensity hypothesis [$k_2(\omega) > k_1(\omega)$] is satisfied", Uzawa (1963, p.110).

By (15.35), this if and only if statement about $y$ would follow from the expressions (15.76–15.77), provided that (15.76–15.77) were valid results of the model (15.1–15.10), which Uzawa studies.

From our comparative general equilibrium analysis, we have already seen that $k_2(\omega) > k_1(\omega)$ is a sufficient condition for a positive value of the elasticity (15.71), cf. (15.47.2), but it was certainly not a necessary one, cf. (15.45), (15.47.1).

In fact, the formulas (15.76–15.77) are *invalid* and lack economic content within the context of the general equilibrium model (15.1–15.10), since $k$ cannot meaningfully be kept constant when $\omega$ changes, cf. (15.26.1–15.27.2). Otherwise, full employment or equilibrium in the commodity markets must be abandoned. In short, the formulas (15.76–15.77) do not—in contrast to (15.71), (15.45)—reflect true variational (comparative) properties of the *solutions* to (15.1–15.10).

Uzawa also examined the effect of a change in the wage-rentals ratio on the quantities of capital goods ($Y_1/L$) corresponding to full employment of labor and capital. His deductions start from, cf. (15.1–15.2)

$$Y_1/L = y_1\lambda_{L_1} = f_1(k_1)\cdot\frac{k_2-k}{k_2-k_1}. \tag{15.78}$$

Differentiating (15.78) logarithmically with respect to $\omega$, we get [using $f_1(k_1)/f_1'(k_1) = \omega + k_1$, cf. (2.24), $m = 1$, (15.5)],

$$\begin{aligned}\frac{1}{Y_1/L}\cdot\frac{d(Y_1/L)}{d\omega} &= \frac{dk_1/d\omega}{\omega+k_1} + \frac{dk_2/d\omega - dk/dw}{k_2-k} - \frac{dk_2/d\omega - dk_1/d\omega}{k_2-k_1}\\ &= \left(\frac{1}{\omega+k_1}+\frac{1}{k_2-k_1}\right)\frac{dk_1}{d\omega} + \left(\frac{1}{k_2-k}-\frac{1}{k_2-k_1}\right)\frac{dk_2}{d\omega} - \frac{1}{k_2-k}\cdot\frac{dk}{d\omega}.\end{aligned} \tag{15.79}$$

Seemingly, again by putting $dk/d\omega = 0$ and hence ignoring the last term in (15.79), Uzawa then concludes from (15.79) that "if the capital intensity hypothesis [$k_2(\omega) > k_1(\omega)$] is satisfied, the higher the wage-rentals ratio $\omega$, the larger the amount of new capital goods $Y_1/L$", Uzawa (1963, p.110), that is,

$$\forall\omega\in\Omega \quad : \quad k_2(\omega) > k_1(\omega) \quad\Rightarrow\quad d(Y_1/L)/d\omega > 0. \tag{15.80}$$

Clearly, with $dk/d\omega = 0$, the implication (15.80) follows from (15.79). But (15.80) is a peculiar result; it somewhat looks like the Rybczynski Theorem in reverse—a higher $k$ (or $\omega$) leading to output increases of the *labor*-intensive sector (good). In fact, (15.80) underscores the misleading nature of these so-called short-term equilibrium analyses.

We know from our comparative general equilibrium analysis above that (15.80) *may* occur in general equilibrium, cf. (15.44), but to *ensure* a positive value of $d(Y_1/L)/d\omega$ would require the intensities in (15.80) to be *reversed,* that is, $k_1(\omega) > k_2(\omega)$, cf. (15.46.2).

In short, although (15.78) stipulates full employment, it only reflects equilibrium in commodity markets, when $k$ of (15.78) also satisfies (15.26.1–2). It is *incoherent* to put $dk/d\omega = 0$ in (15.79), when full (general) equilibrium is to be preserved.

The rectification of (15.76–15.77) and (15.80) was necessary before we can approach properly the economic *dynamics* of the two-sector economy—which has been seriously hampered by undue emphasis upon the capital intensity hypothesis, $k_2 > k_1$.

Our *method* (15.15–15.27.2) of solving the *system* (15.1–15.10) has differed from Uzawa's, and our procedure seems more amenable to facilitate the comparative general equilibrium analysis, (15.36–15.51.2). With some dexterity, the elasticity (15.44) could alternatively have been derived from (15.79) and (15.27.1–2).

## The Dynamic System, Solutions, Stability, and Trajectory Geometry

The equations of *factor accumulation* for the two-sector economy with flexible sector technologies are similar to those with Leontief technologies, cf. (14.17–14.18), (15.1),

$$\dot{L} = nL, \tag{15.81}$$

$$\dot{K} = Y_1 = Ly_1\lambda_{L_1} = Lf_1(k_1)\lambda_{L_1}. \tag{15.82}$$

Since $k_1$ and $\lambda_{L_1}$—in our general equilibrium model of the two-sector economy in section "The Two-Sector Economy with Proportional Saving"—are through $\omega$, cf. (15.5), (15.21), ***uniquely*** determined by the ***aggregate*** capital-labor ***ratio*** $k$, cf. (15.26.1–15.28), the equations (15.81–15.82) thus represent a ***homogeneous dynamic system*** in $L$ and $K$, that is, in standard form, we have

$$\dot{L} = Ln = L\mathfrak{f}(k), \tag{15.83.1}$$

$$\dot{K} = Lf_1(k_1[\omega(k)])\lambda_{L_1}[\omega(k)] = L\mathfrak{g}(k). \tag{15.83.2}$$

The ***director function*** $h(k)$ of (15.83.1–2) is, cf. (15.82), (14.22),

$$h(k) = \mathfrak{g}(k) - k\mathfrak{f}(k) = y_1(k)\lambda_{L_1}(k) - nk, \tag{15.84}$$

and so with $m = 1$, cf. (14.23),

$$\dot{k} = Q(k) = h(k). \tag{15.85}$$

As $h(k)$, (15.84), is an intricate function of $k$, it will be helpful in deriving and interpreting the director roots to rewrite $h(k)$ in alternative forms.

By (15.82), (15.83.2), (15.4), (2.10), $m = 1$, (15.15), (15.22), and (15.25), we obtain

$$\begin{aligned} \mathfrak{g}(k) &= y_1\lambda_{L_1} = \frac{y_1}{k_1}\lambda_{K_1}k = AP_{K_1}\lambda_{K_1}k = \frac{MP_{K_1}}{\epsilon_{K_1}}\lambda_{K_1}k \\ &= \frac{s}{\delta_K}MP_{K_1}k = \frac{s}{\delta_K}f_1'(k_1)k. \end{aligned} \tag{15.86}$$

Hence, (15.84) and (15.86) give

$$h(k) = \left[\frac{y_1(k)}{k_1(k)}\right] k \left[\lambda_{K_1}(k) - \frac{nk_1(k)}{y_1(k)}\right], \tag{15.87}$$

or, equivalently,

$$h(k) = \frac{sk}{\delta_K(k)}[f_1'[k_1(k)] - \frac{n}{s}\delta_K(k)], \quad \delta_K \neq 0. \tag{15.88}$$

**Theorem 15.2** *The two-sector growth model (15.81–15.83.2) has in $C_K$, (15.12)—under the regularity conditions (2.12) for $f_i$, $i = 1, 2$, (15.1), and with $(n/s)\delta_K(k) \in J_1$ [the range of $f_1'$ (15.88) in $C_K$, cf. (2.13)] and $\delta_K(k)$, (15.25), monotone—one and only one stationary ratio solution*

$$\forall t \quad k(t) = \kappa = K_0/L_0 = k_0; \quad k_0 \in C_K, \tag{15.89}$$

*where the positive director root $\kappa$ is given by the equation*

$$f_1'[k_1(\kappa)] = (n/s)\delta_K(\kappa), \quad \kappa \in C_K, \tag{15.90.1}$$

*or else*

$$\lambda_{K_1}(\kappa) = nk_1(\kappa)/y_1(\kappa) < 1. \tag{15.90.2}$$

*The coordinate solutions along the directrix (15.89) are*

$$L(t) = L_0 \exp\{\mathfrak{f}(\kappa)t\}\, K(t) = \kappa L(t); \quad \mathfrak{f}(\kappa) = n. \tag{15.91}$$

*The family of ratio solutions $k(t)$ to (15.85) and the family of coordinate solutions $[L(t), K(t)]$ to (15.83.1–2) have in $C_K$, (15.12)—under the uniqueness conditions mentioned above for $k(t) = \kappa$, (15.89)—respectively, global asymptotic stability and global weak relative stability, if and only if*

$$f_1'[k_1(k)] \text{ cuts } (n/s)\delta_K(k) \text{ from above, at } k = \kappa. \tag{15.92}$$

*Given the uniqueness conditions for $k(t) = \kappa$, (15.89), in $C_K$, (15.12), some weak sufficient conditions—for having stability properties referred to in (15.92)—are, cf. (15.38), (15.27.1–2), (15.48),*

$$\forall \omega \in \Omega \quad : \quad E(\delta_K, \omega) \geq 0, \tag{15.93}$$

$$\forall \omega \in \Omega \quad : \quad E(k, \omega) \geq 1, \tag{15.94}$$

$$\forall\omega \in \Omega \quad : \quad E(Y_1/K, \omega) = -\lambda_{K_1}\epsilon_{L_1}\sigma_1 - \lambda_{K_2}[\epsilon_{L_1} + \epsilon_{L_2}(\sigma_2 - 1)] < 0. \tag{15.95}$$

*Given the uniqueness for $k(t) = \kappa$, (15.89), in $C_K$ (15.12), strong sufficient conditions—for having the stability properties referred to in (15.92)—are,*

$$\forall\omega \in \Omega \quad : \quad \sigma_2(\omega) \geq 1, \tag{15.96}$$

$$\forall\omega \in \Omega \quad : \quad k_2(\omega) > k_1(\omega). \tag{15.97}$$

***Proof*** Given the stated regularity and range conditions, the existence and uniqueness of the director root $\kappa$, solving (15.90.1), rely on the monotonicity properties of $f_1'(k)$ and $\delta_K(k)$, where the former (monotonically decreasing) is due to the standard concavity property of $f_1$ and where the latter is a specific (necessary and sufficient) assumption imposed upon $\delta_K(k)$, (15.25–15.28).

The expressions (15.90.1–2) follow directly from (15.87–15.88). The feasibility condition $\lambda_{K_1}(\kappa) < 1$, (15.90.2), is equivalent to $\kappa \in C_K$, (15.12), cf. (14.24.1–14.25.2), (14.34) and hence is always satisfied by $\kappa$ (15.90.1).

The necessary and sufficient global stability condition (15.92) follows from (15.83.1–2), (15.85), (15.88–15.90.1), and Theorems 28.4 and 28.10 in Chap. 28, cf. the proof of Theorems 11.1–11.2 in Chap. 11.

The sufficient condition (15.93), that is, $\delta_K(k)$, (15.25), monotonically increasing or constant, is a special way of satisfying the criterion (15.92).

The condition (15.94) is an alternative version of (15.93), since, cf. (15.31),

$$E(\delta_K, \omega) \geq 0 \Leftrightarrow E(k, \omega) \geq 1. \tag{15.98}$$

By (15.81–15.85), (15.87), we get, $K \neq 0,\ L \neq 0$,

$$\frac{\dot{k}}{k} = h(k)/k = \dot{K}/K - \dot{L}/L = Y_1/K - n = \frac{y_1(k)}{k_1(k)}\lambda_{K_1}(k) - n. \tag{15.99}$$

Given the existence conditions for $\kappa$ in (15.89–15.90.2), then the property of $Y_1/K$, (15.99), being monotonically decreasing in $k$ [or $\omega$, cf. (15.53), (15.27.1–2)] is clearly sufficient for stability. Hence, (15.99) and (15.48) establish the condition (15.95).

The overly strong conditions (15.96–15.97) are special cases of (15.95), cf. (15.50.1–2). □

**Remark 15.3** The capital intensity condition (15.97) was proved in Uzawa (1963, p.112); and the substitution elasticity condition (15.96) was proved in Drandakis (1963, p.225). The elasticity condition (15.94) was given in Burmeister (1968, p.199), Burmeister and Dobell (1970, p.122).

The expression of the *elasticity condition* (15.95) is new and represents a more general (weaker) stability condition than (15.93–15.94), as from (15.48), (15.41.1), and (15.33.1), we see that

$$\begin{aligned} E(Y_1/K,\omega) &= E(y_1/k_1,\omega) + E(\lambda_{K_1},\omega) \\ &= E(y_1/k_1,\omega) + E(\epsilon_{K_1},\omega) - E(\delta_K,\omega) \\ &= -\epsilon_{L_1} - E(\delta_K,\omega), \end{aligned} \tag{15.100}$$

and by (15.100),

$$E(Y_1/K,\omega) < 0 \quad \Rightarrow \quad E(\delta_K,\omega) > -\epsilon_{L_1}, \tag{15.101}$$

that is, (15.95) does not tacitly require (15.93) or (15.94) to be satisfied, cf. (15.98); but (15.95) encompasses (15.93–15.94).

Note that neither (15.96) nor (15.88) implies (15.93–15.94), cf. (15.38), (15.35), (15.27.1–2). However, the *expression* (15.95) *unifies* all known stability criteria of two-sector growth models with proportional saving. ▽

**Corollary 15.2** *The phase portrait of the growth model (15.83.1–2) in $C_K$, (15.12), may be* ***hyperbolic*** *or* ***parabolic*** *under the conditions (15.92) or (15.95).*

*Sufficient conditions for a* ***parabolic*** *phase portrait are given by (15.93–15.94).*

*Necessary, but not sufficient, conditions for a* ***hyperbolic*** *phase portrait are given by*

$$\forall \omega \in \Omega \quad : \quad \epsilon_{L_1} < -E(\delta_K,\omega) < 0 \quad \wedge \quad k_2(\omega) > k_1(\omega). \tag{15.102}$$

***Proof*** The direction field of the dynamic system (15.83.1–2) is given by, cf. (15.86)

$$dK/dL = q(k) = \mathfrak{g}(k)/\mathfrak{f}(k) = \frac{1}{n}\frac{y_1(k)}{k_1(k)}\lambda_{K_1}(k)k. \tag{15.103}$$

Hence,

$$\forall k \in C_K \quad : \quad q(k) > 0. \tag{15.104}$$

We will here examine the elasticity of $q(k)$, $E(q(k),k)$, rather than the derivative $q'(k)$. From (15.103), we get, cf. (15.100), (15.53),

$$E(q,k) \quad = \quad [-\epsilon_{L_1} - E(\delta_K,\omega)]E(\omega,k) + 1. \tag{15.105}$$

Now, we know that, cf. (15.31), (15.28),

$$E(\omega, k) \quad = \quad \delta_L/[\delta_L + E(\delta_K, \omega)] > 0, \tag{15.106}$$

and then (15.105–15.106) give

$$E(q, k) \quad = \quad \frac{\delta_L(1-\epsilon_{L_1}) + (1-\delta_L)E(\delta_K, \omega)}{\delta_L + E(\delta_K, \omega)}. \tag{15.107}$$

As the denominator of (15.107) is always positive, cf. (15.106), we get

$$\forall k \in C_K \quad : \quad E(\delta_K, \omega) \geq 0 \quad \Rightarrow \quad E(q, k) > 0. \tag{15.108}$$

Thus, (15.104) and (15.108) establish the ***parabolic*** phase portrait under the conditions (15.93–15.94), cf. (15.98) and Theorem 28.8 in section "Asymptotic Ratio Stability and Trajectory Geometry".

A negative value of $E(q, k)$, (15.107), at least requires that $E(\delta_K, \omega) < 0$. Since (15.92) and (15.95) must be satisfied, the ***admissible minimum*** value of $E(\delta_K, \omega)$ is close to: $-\epsilon_{L_1}$, cf. (15.100–15.101), that is,

$$E(\delta_K, \omega) \quad = \quad -E(Y_1/K, \omega) - \epsilon_{L_1} \quad \equiv \quad \beta(\omega) - \epsilon_{L_1}(\omega), \quad \beta \in \mathbf{R}_+. \tag{15.109}$$

With (15.109), we have from (15.107), cf. (15.24)

$$E(q, k) \quad = \quad \frac{\delta_L - \epsilon_{L_1} + \beta(1-\delta_L)}{\delta_L - \epsilon_{L_1} + \beta} \quad = \quad \frac{(1-s)(\epsilon_{L_2} - \epsilon_{L_1}) + \beta(1-\delta_L)}{(1-s)(\epsilon_{L_2} - \epsilon_{L_1}) + \beta}, \tag{15.110}$$

where the denominator is positive and numerator becomes negative whenever $k_2(\omega) > k_1(\omega)$, cf. (15.35), and $\beta$ is close to zero, that is,

$$\forall k \in C_K \quad : \quad \beta(\omega) \approx 0 \quad \wedge \quad k_2(\omega) > k_1(\omega) \quad \Rightarrow \quad E(q, k) < 0. \tag{15.111}$$

The conditions of (15.111) are stronger than the simpler necessary ones of (15.102), cf. (15.109).

The *hyperbolic* trajectory configuration of (15.104), (15.111) is consonant with the limiting case, $\sigma_1 = \sigma_2 = 0$, studied in Chap. 14, cf. (15.109), (15.38), (14.41–14.42). □

## The Economic Rationale of the Stability Conditions

As we have seen, the capital intensity hypothesis $k_2 > k_1$ was in the growth models with *fixed* and *flexible* sector technologies, respectively, a *necessary* and *sufficient* stability condition, cf. (14.37), (15.97). The economic rationale of the former was examined in Chap. 14. section "The Economic Rationale of the Stability Conditions", and we should now in economic terms briefly recapitulate the influence of the size of capital-labor ratios upon the inner working of the two-sector economy, set forth in the section "The Two-Sector Economy with Proportional Saving".

The implications of sectorial capital intensities upon the output ratio $Y_1/Y_2$, cf. (15.35–15.37), are shown in Fig. 15.1, which displays similar monotonicity properties as Fig. 14.1. However, the economic explanations behind the curves of $Y_1/Y_2$ are here quite different. Whereas the hyperbolas of $Y_1/Y_2$ in Fig. 14.1 originated from stipulations on the *supply side* of the economy, their pendants in Fig. 15.1 acquire their form from *price* and *demand side* conditions, cf. (15.17–15.18), (15.37), and furthermore, the monotonicities arise here from the absence of factor intensity reversals between the sectors.

That $k_2(\omega) > k_1(\omega)$, $\forall \omega \in \Omega$, is a *sufficient* stability condition for $k(t) \rightarrow \kappa$, as $t \rightarrow \infty$, cf. (15.97), is not surprising, since then for any $k(t) \neq \kappa$, cf. Fig. 15.1, the *output composition* (ratio, $Y_1/Y_2$) is clearly conducive to redress (relative to the steady state) a surplus/shortage in the stock of capital.

But it must be clearly recognized that $k_2 > k_1$ is only a sufficient *not* a *necessary* stability condition, that is, the alternative output composition (ratio, $Y_1/Y_2$) implied by $k_1 > k_2$, cf. Fig. 15.1, is also compatible, under some proper restrictions, with $k(t)$ approaching $\kappa$ over time. Indeed, this convergence depends on the proper behavior of the ratio $Y_1/K$ rather than the ratio

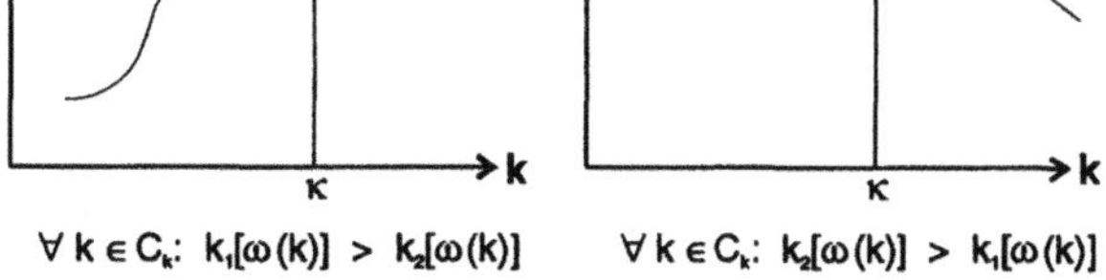


**Fig. 15.1** The output ratio $Y_1/Y_2$, (15.37), and the endowment ratio $k$, (15.27.1–15.28), no reswitching

$Y_1/Y_2$—as demonstrated in Theorem 15.2, where (15.95) *allows* the *rising* ratio of $Y_1/Y_2$ with $k$ in Fig. 15.1, but the *sign* of (15.95) effectively *curbs* any *"magnification"* effect of the endogenous capital endowment changes upon the output of the capital good sector. That is, the changes in the *general equilibrium composition* of outputs—engendered by growing factor endowments and implemented through the price mechanism, cf. (15.17), (15.36–15.37), (15.28)—are sufficiently dampened to still allow evolution toward balanced growth, despite the fact that the capital good sector always uses more capital-intensive techniques.

It should also be stressed that Theorem 15.2 does not presume, as in Fig. 15.1, that one sector is always more capital intensive than the other one. Thus, Theorem 15.2 allows for *"reswitching"* in the growth model (15.83.1–2). As an illustration, Fig. 15.2 gives the output ratio $Y_1/Y_2$ in case of CES production functions with $\sigma_1 < \sigma_2$ and, cf. Remark 15.1, which implies *"reswitching"* at $\omega^*(k^*)$, cf. (15.14), (15.28).

The technologies of capital (investment) goods are usually purported to allow rather small substitution possibilities, for example, $\sigma_1 < 1$, whereas consumer good technologies are considered more flexible, that is, at least $\sigma_2 > \sigma_1$. Regarding the technology parameters, $a_i$, $i = 1, 2$, cf. (2.49), we have assumed, not only $a_1 > a_2$, but strengthened it more so that the capital-labor ratio $k_1(\omega)$ is larger than $k_2(\omega)$ at low values of $\boldsymbol{\omega}$ or $\mathbf{k}$. Moreover, the parameters of the CES functions and the parameter $\mathbf{n}$ and $\mathbf{s}$ of (15.88) are here assumed to have such values that the director root $\kappa$ (15.90.1) is larger than $k^*(\omega^*)$, cf. Fig. 15.2.

Now, whenever (15.95) is also satisfied, $\kappa$ in Fig. 15.2 will be the global attractor of the ratio solutions $\mathbf{k(t)}$ to (15.85). The solutions of the two-sector model evolving from *small* initial values $(K_0/L_0)$ in Fig. 15.2—*first* exhibiting a *stage* of rapid expansion of the output of a provisional relatively capital-intensive investment good sector and a *second stage* with a predominant consumption good sector—reflect at least—together with the steadily *rising* wage/rental

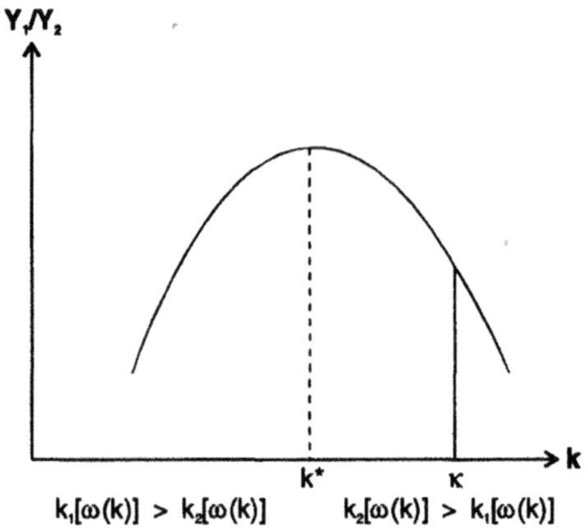


**Fig. 15.2** The output ratio $Y_1/Y_2$, (15.37), and the factor endowment ratio $k$, (15.27.1–15.28)

ratio and hence increasing capital-labor ratios in both sectors—some salient aspects of the narratives from the history of growing economies.

Finally, within the *scope* of Theorem 15.2, numerous ***simulation*** studies (with variable elasticity of substitution [VES] and not just CES sector technologies) may be performed.

## Bibliography


Burmeister E (1968) The Role of the Jacobian Determinant in the Two–Sector Model. Internt Econ Rev 9:195–203

Burmeister E, Dobell AR (1970) Mathematical Theories of Economic Growth. Macmillan, London

Drandakis EM (1963) Factor Substitution in the Two–Sector Growth Model. Rev Econ Stud 30:217–28

Johnson HG (1971) The Two–Sector Model of General Equilibrium. George Allen and Unwin, London

Solow RM (1961) Note on Uzawa's Two–Sector Model of Economic Growth. Rev Econ Stud 29:48–50, or Stiglitz (1969)

Stiglitz JE, Uzawa H (1969) Readings in the Modern Theory of Economic Growth. M.I.T. Press, Cambridge, Mass

Uzawa H (1961) On a Two–Sector Model of Economic Growth: I. Review of Economic Studies 29:40–47

Uzawa H (1963) On a Two–Sector Model of Economic Growth: II. Review of Economic Studies 30:105–18, Also in: Stiglitz and Uzawa (1969)

Zeuthen F (1955) Economic Theory and Method. Longmans, London

CHAPTER 16

# Flexible Technologies and Classical Saving

The supply side (sector technologies, full employment, allocation efficiency) specification of the two-sector economy was very general in Chap. 15, whereas the demand side (expenditure system) was based upon the particular specification of proportional saving. An interesting alternative to the latter is the classical saving hypothesis with only saving out of capital income, and hence with aggregate saving depending on the *factor income* distribution.

The case of different saving propensities for "capitalists" and "workers" will not be considered here, as we should then have to introduce, besides the factor income distribution, also the *wealth* (asset) distribution and the *personal income* distribution. To ignore the wealth distribution and to just consider different saving propensities for the capital and labor components of the factor income distribution easily creates problems and paradoxes, see Pasinetti (1962), Samuelson (1966), that we shall avoid here. Without any of these problems, the classical saving hypothesis fulfills our object of seeing the implications of an alternative demand-side specification for the two-sector economy. We will then also be able to compare this two-sector growth model to the canonical classical one-sector growth models in Chap. 7.

## The Two-Sector Economy with Classical Saving

### *The General Equilibrium Model and Solutions*

Having laid the groundwork of the two-sector general equilibrium model in Chap. 15. section "The General Equilibrium Model", the structural equations (15.1–15.8.2) carry over unchanged to the two-sector economy with



B. S. Jensen, *The Elements and Dynamic Systems of Economic Growth and Trade Models*, https://doi.org/10.1007/978-3-031-52493-6_16

classical saving, where (15.9) is replaced by

$$S = s_K \delta_K Y, \quad 0 < s_K \leq 1, \tag{16.1}$$

and (15.10) with

$$P_1 Y_1 = s_K \delta_K Y, \tag{16.2}$$

and then, cf. (15.7),

$$P_2 Y_2 = (1 - s_K \delta_K) Y. \tag{16.3}$$

Accordingly, the "demand side" of the economy is here characterized by, cf. (15.18)

$$\frac{P_1 Y_1}{P_2 Y_2} = \frac{s_K \delta_K}{1 - s_K \delta_K}. \tag{16.4}$$

The "supply side" of the economy may—with full and efficient use of factor endowments—still be characterized in the same way as in Chap. 15, that is, cf. (15.19.1–2)

$$\frac{P_1 Y_1}{P_2 Y_2} = \frac{\lambda_{L_1} \epsilon_{L_2}}{(1 - \lambda_{L_1}) \epsilon_{L_1}} = \frac{\lambda_{K_1} \epsilon_{K_2}}{(1 - \lambda_{K_1}) \epsilon_{K_1}}. \tag{16.5}$$

Thus, *equilibrium* on the *commodity markets* requires by (16.4–16.5) that

$$\frac{s_K \delta_K}{1 - s_K \delta_K} = \frac{\lambda_{L_1} \epsilon_{L_2}}{(1 - \lambda_{L_1}) \epsilon_{L_1}} = \frac{\lambda_{K_1} \epsilon_{K_2}}{(1 - \lambda_{K_1}) \epsilon_{K_1}}. \tag{16.6}$$

*Alternatively*, a general equilibrium (equilibrium of commodity markets and full and efficient factor utilization) of the two-sector economy may here also be characterized by the *conditions*, cf. (16.2), (15.5–15.8.2),

$$P_1 Y_1 = s_K r K \Leftrightarrow Y_1 = s_K M P_{K_1} K, \tag{16.7}$$

or, equivalently, by using, $Y_1 \equiv K_1 A P_{K_1}$, $\lambda_{K_1} \equiv K_1 / K$, (15.15), and (16.7)

$$\lambda_{K_1} = s_K \epsilon_{K_1}, \quad \lambda_{K_2} = 1 - s_K \epsilon_{K_1}. \tag{16.8}$$

Then (16.8) and (16.6) give, after reductions, cf. (15.16)

$$\lambda_{L_1} = \frac{s_K \epsilon_{L_1} (1 - \epsilon_{L_2})}{s_K \epsilon_{L_1} + (1 - s_K) \epsilon_{L_2}}, \quad \lambda_{L_2} = \frac{(1 - s_K + s_K \epsilon_{L_1}) \epsilon_{L_2}}{s_K \epsilon_{L_1} + (1 - s_K) \epsilon_{K_2}}, \tag{16.9}$$

$$\delta_K = \frac{\epsilon_{K_2}}{1 + s_K (\epsilon_{K_2} - \epsilon_{K_1})}, \quad \delta_L = \frac{s_K \epsilon_{L_1} + (1 - s_K) \epsilon_{L_2}}{1 + s_K (\epsilon_{L_1} - \epsilon_{L_2})}. \tag{16.10}$$

Hence for (16.10–16.11.2), we get, cf. (15.26.1–2),

$$k = \omega(\delta_K/\delta_L) = \frac{\omega\, \epsilon_{K_2}}{s_K\epsilon_{L_1} + (1-s_K)\epsilon_{L_2}} = \Psi(\omega), \tag{16.11.1}$$

where, cf. (15.11.3–15.12),

$$k \in C_K \Leftrightarrow \omega \in \Omega. \tag{16.11.2}$$

In the *extreme case*, $s_K = 1$ Uzawa (1961, p.41), we may note from (16.8–16.11.2) that *general equilibrium* implies:

$$\lambda_{K_1} = \epsilon_{K_1}, \qquad \lambda_{K_2} = \epsilon_{L_1}, \tag{16.12.1}$$

$$\lambda_{L_1} = \epsilon_{K_2}, \qquad \lambda_{L_2} = \epsilon_{L_2}, \tag{16.12.2}$$

$$\delta_K = \frac{\epsilon_{K_2}}{\epsilon_{L_1} + \epsilon_{K_2}}, \qquad \delta_L = \frac{\epsilon_{L_1}}{\epsilon_{L_1} + \epsilon_{K_2}}, \tag{16.12.3}$$

$$k = \omega(\epsilon_{K_2}/\epsilon_{L_1}) = \Psi(\omega). \tag{16.12.4}$$

As in Chap. 15, the *monotonicity* (invertibility) of $\Psi$, (16.11.1–2), is critical to the uniqueness of a general equilibrium at any given factor endowment ratio, $K/L$. To this issue, we state

**Lemma 16.1** *The elasticity, $E(k,\omega)$, of the function $\Psi(\omega)$, (16.11.1–2), is given by:*

$$E(k,\omega) = \frac{s_K\epsilon_{L_1}(\epsilon_{K_2} - \epsilon_{K_1} + \epsilon_{K_1}\sigma_1) + (1 - s_K\epsilon_{K_1})\epsilon_{L_2}\sigma_2}{s_K\epsilon_{L_1} + (1-s_K)\epsilon_{L_2}}. \tag{16.13}$$

*Hence, $\Psi(\omega)$, (16.11.1–2), is monotonically increasing, if and only if $\forall\omega \in \Omega$:*

$$E(k,\omega) > 0 \Leftrightarrow s_K\epsilon_{L_1}(\epsilon_{K_2} - \epsilon_{K_1} + \epsilon_{K_1}\sigma_1) + (1 - s_K\epsilon_{K_1})\epsilon_{L_2}\sigma_2 > 0. \tag{16.14}$$

*Sufficient conditions for $E(k,\omega) > 0$, $\forall\omega \in \Omega$, are*

$$\forall\omega \in \Omega \quad : \quad k_2(\omega) > k_1(\omega), \tag{16.15}$$

$$\forall\omega \in \Omega \quad : \quad \sigma_1(\omega) + \sigma_2(\omega) \geq 1. \tag{16.16}$$

*The special case (16.12.4), $s_K = 1$, has*

$$E(k,\omega) = \epsilon_{K_2} - \epsilon_{K_1} + \epsilon_{K_1}\sigma_1 + \epsilon_{L_2}\sigma_2. \tag{16.17}$$

***Proof*** From (16.11.1–2) and (15.16), we get

$$k = \frac{\omega \cdot \epsilon_{K_2}}{s_K \epsilon_{L_1} + (1 - s_K)\epsilon_{L_2}} = \frac{k_2}{1 - s_K + s_K(\epsilon_{L_1}/\epsilon_{L_2})} \equiv \frac{k_2(\omega)}{d(\omega)}. \tag{16.18}$$

By standard rules, the elasticity of $d(\omega)$ becomes, cf. (15.33.1–2),

$$E(d(\omega), \omega) = \frac{s_K(\epsilon_{L_1}/\epsilon_{L_2})}{1 - s_K + s_K(\epsilon_{L_1}/\epsilon_{L_2})}[\epsilon_{K_1}(1 - \sigma_1) - \epsilon_{K_2}(1 - \sigma_2)]. \tag{16.19}$$

Then from (16.18–16.19), we have

$$E(k, \omega) = \sigma_2 + \frac{s_K \epsilon_{L_1}[\epsilon_{K_2}(1 - \sigma_2) - \epsilon_{K_1}(1 - \sigma_1)]}{s_K \epsilon_{L_1} + (1 - s_K)\epsilon_{L_2}}, \tag{16.20}$$

which, by using $\epsilon_{K_i} = 1 - \epsilon_{L_i}$, $i = 1, 2$, and collecting similar terms, gives (16.13).

As the denominator of (16.13) is always positive, (16.14) is obvious.

The overly strong sufficient condition (16.15) follows immediately from (16.14) and (15.35).

The sufficiency of (16.16) may be verified as follows. First note that, ceteris paribus, the larger $s_K$ is, the "easier" it becomes to violate (16.14). Hence, to put most strain upon (16.14), set $s_K = 1$. As $\sigma_1$ and $\sigma_2$ are nonnegative, we can replace (16.16) with: $\sigma_1 = 1 - \sigma_2 + \beta$, $\beta \in [0, +\infty]$. Next substitute this expression for $\sigma_1$ and $s_K = 1$ into (16.14), which then after reduction will be seen to consist of only nonnegative terms. Hence, with (16.16), the RHS of (16.14) always remains positive, that is (16.16) is a special way of satisfying (16.14). But certainly (16.16) is not necessary for having (16.14); for example, $\sigma_1 = 0.2, \sigma_2 = 0.1$, clearly violates (16.16), but they and $\epsilon_{K_1} = 0.3, \epsilon_{K_2} = 0.2, s_K = 1$ still satisfy (16.14).

The elasticity (16.17) follows from (16.19) and $s_K = 1$, or from (16.12.4) and (15.33.1–2). □

**Remark 16.1** For every $k \in C_K$, (16.11.1–2), the ***uniqueness*** of the general equilibrium solutions for the two-sector economy is insured by (16.14), tantamount to the global ***positivity*** of (16.13). Of course, a global negativity of (16.13) would also give uniqueness, but as seen from (16.14), this possibility of $E(k, \omega) < 0$ is very unlikely and certainly does not follow from just reversing the sign of (16.15). Henceforth, we exclusively rely on the condition (16.14), describing an economy with the reasonable general equilibrium property,

$$\forall k \in C_K \quad : \quad E(\omega, k) = 1/E(k, \omega) > 0, \tag{16.21}$$

which hitherto was satisfied unconditionally, cf. (15.28), and, of course, throughout one-sector models.

The capital intensity (16.15) was given in Uzawa (1961, p.43) for the special case $s_K = 1$, (16.12.2–4). The substitution elasticity condition (16.16) was derived in Drandakis (1963, p.222). The generalized uniqueness condition given here (16.14) is very little restrictive. ▽

## *Comparative General Equilibrium Analyses*

The inner working of the two-sector economy with classical saving will now be examined analogously to the procedure in Chap. 15. section "Comparative General Equilibrium Analysis". We need not here be as detailed as in section "Comparative General Equilibrium Analysis", since the latter, cf. Theorem 15.1, had to resolve some principal questions in comparative general equilibrium analysis with flexible technologies and competitive pricing in factor and commodity markets. We shall below concentrate upon those qualitative properties of the general equilibrium solutions that are important for understanding the behavior and the dynamic stability properties of the solutions to the growth model in Chap. 28. section "Ratio Solutions, Coordinate Solutions, and Trajectories".

Due to (16.13–16.14), (16.21), we need only, as in Chap. 15. section "Comparative General Equilibrium Analysis", to study the impacts of alternative wage-rental ratios upon the general equilibrium solutions to the model with classical saving. The responses will be described by appropriate elasticity expressions.

Since the price mechanism still works in the same way as with proportional saving, we immediately have, cf. (15.17), (15.36),

$$E(P_1/P_2, \omega) \quad = \quad \epsilon_{K_2} - \epsilon_{K_1}. \tag{16.22}$$

The general equilibrium *output composition* (ratio) $Y_1/Y_2$ does not here follow the simple (symmetric) pattern of (15.37). Instead, by (16.4) and (16.10), the ratios $Y_1/Y_2$ satisfy the equation,

$$\frac{Y_1}{Y_2} = \frac{s_K \delta_K}{1 - s_K \delta_K} \cdot \frac{P_2}{P_1} = \frac{s_K \epsilon_{K_2}}{1 - s_K \epsilon_{K_1}} \cdot \frac{P_2}{P_1}. \tag{16.23}$$

Then, using (15.33.1–2) and (16.2), it may be verified, cf. (16.19), that the elasticity of (16.23) becomes

$$E(Y_1/Y_2, \omega) \quad = \quad \epsilon_{L_2}\sigma_2 - \frac{(1 - s_K \epsilon_{K_1} \sigma_1)\epsilon_{L_1}}{1 - s_K \epsilon_{K_1}}, \tag{16.24}$$

which is quite sophisticated compared to (15.37).

Thus, a *demand-side* specification of the two-sector economy by the *classical* saving and consumption hypothesis has rather *intricate* implications for the *general equilibrium composition* of outputs in the face of varying wage-rental ratios, $\omega$ [or factor endowments, $K/L$, still obeying (16.21)]. This fact also helps to explain why a uniqueness *problem* for the general equilibrium solutions may occur without some minimal restrictions, (16.14).

As to the variability of the factor *income distribution,* we obtain from (16.13), (15.30), (16.8–16.10), after some manipulations,

$$\begin{aligned} E(\delta_K, \omega) &= \frac{s_K \epsilon_{K_1} \epsilon_{L_1}(\sigma_1 - 1) + (1 - s_K \epsilon_{K_1}) \epsilon_{L_2}(\sigma_2 - 1)}{1 + s_K(\epsilon_{K_2} - \epsilon_{K_1})} \\ &= \frac{\delta_K}{\epsilon_{K_2}} [\lambda_{K_1} \epsilon_{L_1}(\sigma_1 - 1) + \lambda_{K_2} \epsilon_{L_2}(\sigma_2 - 1)], \end{aligned} \tag{16.25}$$

and next from (16.25), (15.30), (16.8–16.10), that

$$E(\delta_L, \omega) = -\frac{\delta_L}{\delta_K} E(\delta_K, \omega) = \left(\frac{\epsilon_{K_2}}{\delta_K}\right)^2 [\lambda_{L_1} \epsilon_{K_1}(1 - \sigma_1) + \lambda_{L_2} \epsilon_{K_2}(1 - \sigma_2)]. \tag{16.26}$$

These expressions (16.25–16.26) are similar to (15.38–15.39).

Regarding the *allocation* ratios, it is immediately seen from (16.8) that, cf. (15.33.1–2),

$$E(\lambda_{K_1}, \omega) = \epsilon_{L_1}(\sigma_1 - 1), \tag{16.27.1}$$

$$E(\lambda_{K_2}, \omega) = -\frac{\lambda_{K_1}}{\lambda_{K_2}} E(\lambda_{K_1}, \omega) = [(s_K \epsilon_{K_1})/(1 - s_K \epsilon_{K_1})] \epsilon_{L_1}(1 - \sigma_1), \tag{16.27.2}$$

which are much *simpler* than in Chap. 15. Note especially that values of the capital intensity in the consumer good sector $k_2(\omega)$ have no bearing on (16.8) and hence neither upon (16.27.1–2)—in contrast to (15.41.1–2), cf. (15.43.1–2).

For the *labor ratios* (16.9), we obtain, after straightforward calculations, cf. (15.33.1–2),

$$E(\lambda_{L_1}, \omega) = \frac{[-\epsilon_{L_1} - (1 - s_K) \epsilon_{K_1} \sigma_1 + (1 - s_K \epsilon_{K_1}) \sigma_2] \epsilon_{L_2}}{s \epsilon_{L_1} + (1 - s_K) \epsilon_{L_2}}, \tag{16.28.1}$$

$$E(\lambda_{L_2}, \omega) = -(\lambda_{L_1}/\lambda_{L_2}) E(\lambda_{L_1}, \omega), \tag{16.28.2}$$

which may also be verified by using the full employment identity (15.4) and (16.27.1–2), that is,

$$E(\lambda_{L_1}, \omega) = E(\lambda_{K_1}, \omega) - E(k_1, \omega) + E(k, \omega) = -\epsilon_{L_1} - \epsilon_{K_1} \sigma_1 + E(k, \omega), \tag{16.29}$$

where the general equilibrium *expression* for $E(k, \omega)$ was given in (16.13).

Incidentally, it follows from (16.29) that (16.14) is equivalent to the *requirement:*

$$\forall \omega \in \Omega \quad : \quad E(\lambda_{L_1}, \omega) > -\epsilon_{L_1} - \epsilon_{K_1}\sigma_1 = -1 + \epsilon_{K_1}(1 - \sigma_1). \tag{16.30}$$

Next, for $Y_1/L = y_1\lambda_{L_1}$, we get, cf. (16.29), (15.44),

$$E(Y_1/L, \omega) = -\epsilon_{L_1} + E(k, \omega). \tag{16.31}$$

Finally, for $Y_i/K = (y_i/k_i)\lambda_{K_i}$, $i = 1, 2$, we get, cf. (16.27.1–2), (16.8), (15.48–15.49),

$$E(Y_1/K, \omega) = -\epsilon_{L_1}, \tag{16.32}$$

$$E(Y_2/K, \omega) = -\epsilon_{L_2}\sigma_2 - \frac{s_K\epsilon_{K_1}\epsilon_{L_1}(\sigma_1 - 1)}{1 - s_K\epsilon_{K_1}}. \tag{16.33}$$

Evidently, the implication (15.51.1) carries over to (16.33). But certainly, the *negative* sign of $E(Y_1/K, \omega)$, (16.32)—irrespective of any values of the sector capital intensities, $k_1(\omega)$, $k_2(\omega)$ or substitution elasticities, $\sigma_1(\omega)$, $\sigma_2(\omega)$—*contrasts* sharply with (15.50.1–2).

To see the consequences of (16.32) in relation to *factor endowment* changes, we bring together from (15.63), (15.52–15.53), (16.31–16.32), (16.21),

$$\begin{aligned} E(Y_1/K, k) &= E(Y_1, K) - 1 = E(Y_1/K, K) \\ &= E(Y_1/K, \omega)E(\omega, k) = -\epsilon_{L_1}E(\omega, k), && (16.34) \\ E(Y_1/L, k) &= E(Y_1/L, \omega)E(\omega, k) = -\epsilon_{L_1}E(\omega, k) + 1. && (16.35) \end{aligned}$$

**Lemma 16.2** *In the two-sector economy with flexible technologies and classical saving, the general equilibrium elasticities,* $E(Y_i, K)$, $E(Y_i, L)$, $i = 1, 2$, *have—under the conditions (16.14), (16.21)—the following properties*

$$\forall k \in C_K \quad : \quad E(Y_1, K) = 1 - \epsilon_{L_1}E(\omega, k) < 1, \tag{16.36.1}$$

$$\forall k \in C_K \quad : \quad E(Y_1, K) \gtreqless 0 \quad \Leftrightarrow \quad E(\omega, k) \gtreqless 1/\epsilon_{L_1}, \tag{16.36.2}$$

$$\forall k \in C_K \quad : \quad E(Y_1, L) = \epsilon_{L_1}E(\omega, k) > 0, \tag{16.37}$$

$$\forall k \in C_K \quad : \quad E(Y_2, K) < 1, \quad \textit{if } \sigma_1(\omega) > 1, \quad \forall \omega \in \Omega, \tag{16.38.1}$$

$$\forall k \in C_K \quad : \quad E(Y_2, L) > 0, \quad \textit{if } \sigma_1(\omega) > 1, \quad \forall \omega \in \Omega. \tag{16.38.2}$$

***Proof*** The expressions (16.36.1–16.37) follow from (16.34–16.35), cf. (15.54, 15.55). The properties (16.38.1–2) are confirmed by inspecting together (16.33), (15.53), (15.55), (15.63). □

Thus, given (16.14), (16.21), the general equilibrium elasticities (16.36.1–16.37) demonstrate that, for sector 1, *magnified* output changes from capital endowment changes *never occur*, irrespective of the values $k_1(\omega)$, $k_2(\omega)$, $\sigma_1(\omega)$, $\sigma_2(\omega)$, and increasing *labor* supplies will *never reduce* the output of sector 1. All this (16.36.1–16.37) is in contrast to the potential responses of sector 1 output, shown in Theorem 15.1 and Corollary 15.1 in section "Comparative General Equilibrium Analysis".

Regarding the general equilibrium output of sector 2, no similar results to (16.36.1–16.37) prevail. Neither will the capital intensities $k_1(\omega)$ and $k_2(\omega)$ give sign restrictions as in (15.56.2), (15.58.2). However, a portion of (15.60.2) and (15.61.2) still hold, $\forall k \in C_K$, cf. (16.38.1–2).

Economic *intuition* is not at a loss or contradicted by *general equilibrium properties* (16.36.1–16.38.2) of the two-sector economy here considered. In fact, the results (16.36.1–16.37) may be obtained directly from the second equality of (16.7)—taking the uniqueness of general equilibrium for granted and also assuming $E(\omega, k) > 0, \ \forall k$.

Since (16.1) must then hold everywhere in $C_K$, we can on both sides take the derivative (or equivalently the elasticity) with respect to the capital endowment $K$. Accordingly, we get, using the elasticity rule of a composite function, immediately from (16.7), cf. section "The Two-Sector Economy with Classical Saving".

$$\begin{aligned} E(Y_1, K) &= E(MP_{K_1}[k_1(\omega[k(K)])], K) + 1 \\ &= (-\epsilon_{L_1}/\sigma_1) \cdot \sigma_1 \cdot E(\omega, k) \cdot 1 + 1 \quad = \quad -\epsilon_{L_1} E(\omega, k) + 1, \end{aligned} \tag{16.39}$$

which is (16.36.1). Thus, given (16.21), then (16.39) shows the economic linkages preventing a magnified general equilibrium value of $Y_1$, that is, $E(Y_1, K) < 1$. The crux of the matter is that $MP_{K_1}$ is bound to decline with a higher capital endowment $K$, whenever (16.21), (16.14) hold.

Similarly to (16.39), we may derive (16.37) directly from (16.7), viz.,

$$\begin{aligned} E(Y_1, L) &= E(MP_{K_1}[k_1(\omega[k(L)])], L) \\ &= (-\epsilon_{L_1}/\sigma_1) \cdot \sigma_1 \cdot E(\omega, k) \cdot -1 \quad = \quad \epsilon_{L_1} E(\omega, k), \end{aligned} \tag{16.40}$$

that is, with (16.21), $MP_{K_1}$ is bound to increase with a larger labor endowment.

The intuitive explanation of (16.38.1–2) hinges ultimately on (16.27.1–2) and (16.21).

The *reactions* (16.36.1) of the capital good sector to capital endowment changes are *crucial* to understanding the *dynamics* and the *stability* properties of the two-sector growth model with *capital accumulation*.

## Dynamics, Solutions, Stability, and Trajectory Geometry

### *Exogenous Labor Supply*

Factor accumulation and the dynamic system of the two-sector economy with classical saving are still formally expressed by the equations (15.81–15.85),

$$\dot{L} \;=\; L\,n \;=\; L\,\mathfrak{f}(k), \tag{16.41.1}$$

$$\dot{K} \;=\; L f_1(k_1[\omega(k)])\,\lambda_{L_1}[\omega(k)] \;=\; L\,\mathfrak{g}(k). \tag{16.41.2}$$

The governing function $\mathfrak{g}(k)$, (16.41.2), may here alternatively be written as, cf. (15.86), (16.8),

$$\begin{aligned}\mathfrak{g}(k) &= y_1\lambda_{L_1} = \frac{y_1}{k_1}\lambda_{K_1}k = AP_{K_1}\lambda_{K_1}k = \frac{MP_{K_1}}{\epsilon_{K_1}}\lambda_{K_1}k \\ &= s_K\,MP_{K_1}k = s_K\,f_1'(k_1)\,k.\end{aligned} \tag{16.42}$$

The *director function* $h(k)$ of (16.41.1–2) then becomes, cf. (16.42),

$$h(k) = \mathfrak{g}(k) - k\,\mathfrak{f}(k) = \left[\frac{y_1(k)}{k_1(k)}\right] k \left[\lambda_{K_1}(k) - \frac{n\,k_1(k)}{y_1(k)}\right], \tag{16.43}$$

or, equivalently,

$$h(k) \;=\; s_K k[f_1'[k_1(\omega(k))] - n/s_K]. \tag{16.44}$$

Hence, with $m = 1$,

$$\dot{k} \;=\; Q(k) \;=\; h(k). \tag{16.45}$$

**Theorem 16.1** *The two-sector growth model (16.41.1–16.44) has in $C_K$, (15.12)—under the regularity conditions (2.12) for $f_i$, $i = 1, 2$, (15.1), and $(n/s_K) \in J_1$ [the range of $f_1'$ (16.44) in $C_K$, cf. (2.13)] and given the uniqueness conditions of general equilibrium rendered by $E(\omega, k) > 0$, (16.21), (16.14)—one and only one stationary ratio solution*

$$\forall t \quad k(t) = \kappa = K_0/L_0 = k_0, \quad k_0 \in C_K, \tag{16.46}$$

*where the positive director root $\kappa$ is given by the equation*

$$f_1'[k_1(\kappa)] = n/s_K, \quad \kappa \in C_K, \tag{16.47}$$

*or else*

$$\lambda_{K_1}(\kappa) \;=\; n\,k_1(\kappa)/y_1(\kappa) = s_K\,\epsilon_{K_1}(\kappa) < 1. \tag{16.48}$$

*The coordinate solutions along the directrix (16.46) are,*

$$L(t) = L_0 \exp\{\mathfrak{f}(\kappa)t\},\, K(t) \;=\; \kappa\, L(t); \quad \mathfrak{f}(\kappa) = n. \tag{16.49}$$

*The family of ratio solutions* $\mathbf{k(t)}$ *to (16.45) and the family of coordinate solutions* $[\mathbf{L(t)}, \mathbf{K(t)}]$ *to (16.41.1–16.42) have in* $C_K$*, (15.12)—under the uniqueness conditions mentioned above for* $\mathbf{k(t)} = \boldsymbol{\kappa}$*, (16.46)—respectively, global asymptotic stability and global weak relative stability.*

***Proof*** Given the stated regularity and range conditions and given the restrictions imposed to ensure uniqueness of general equilibrium, then the existence and uniqueness of the director root $\kappa$, solving (16.44), follow immediately from concavity of $f_1$ in the argument $k_1[\omega(k)]$, which gives a well-defined monotonically decreasing function $f_1'$ in $k$, due to (16.21), (16.14).

The expressions (16.47–16.48) follow directly from (16.43–16.45).

The stated stability properties of the ratio and coordinate solutions simply follow from the property of $f_1$ mentioned above, $m = 1$, and Theorem 28.10 in section "Global Asymptotic Ratio Stability and Global Stabilities of Coordinate Solutions".

An alternative proof of Theorem 16.1 could proceed like (15.99) with here the relevant behavior of $Y_1/K$ already given in (16.34). □

**Remark 16.2** Given the regularity and appropriate range of $f_2'(k_1)$, the existence and the uniqueness of a director $k = \kappa$, solving $h(k) = 0$, (16.44), would also concur with the general equilibrium property: $E(k, \omega) < 0, \forall\omega \in \Omega$, (16.13). But the latter is a remote possibility, as argued in Remark 16.1. However, regarding stability, we should stress that (16.21), as stated in Theorem 16.1, is indeed a *necessary* and *sufficient* condition for $\kappa$ (16.46) being the *attractor*—rather than a repeller with opposite sign of (16.21)—of the solutions to (16.45). Hence, the ratio and coordinate stability properties in Theorem 16.1 hold, *if* and *only if* the condition (16.14) is satisfied, which fortunately posed no serious problem to comply with, cf. Remark 16.1. ▽

**Corollary 16.1** *The phase portrait in* $C_K$*, (15.12), of the solutions* $[L(t), K(t)]$ *described by* Theorem 16.1, *is **parabolic**, if*

$$\forall k \in C_K \quad : \quad E(\omega, k) < 1/\epsilon_{L_1}, \tag{16.50}$$

*and **hyperbolic**, if*

$$\forall k \in C_K \quad : \quad E(\omega, k) > 1/\epsilon_{L_1}. \tag{16.51}$$

***Proof*** The direction field of the dynamic system (16.41.1–16.45) is given by,

$$dK/dL = q(k) = \mathfrak{g}(k)/\mathfrak{f}(k) = (s_K/n)MP_{K_1}[k_1(\omega[k])] \cdot k. \tag{16.52}$$

Hence by (2.12) and (16.52)

$$\forall k \in C_K \quad : \quad q(k) > 0. \tag{16.53}$$

Rather than the derivative $q'(k)$, we examine the elasticity, $E(q,k)$, which from (16.52) and by using the analogous procedure in (16.39) then becomes

$$E(q,k) \quad = \quad -\epsilon_{L_1} E(\omega,k) + 1. \tag{16.54}$$

Hence, $E(q,k)$, (16.54), is *positive* or *negative,* in accordance with the conditions (16.50) and (16.51). Thus, (16.21), (16.53), and (16.54) establish, respectively, the parabolic (16.50) and the hyperbolic (16.51) phase portrait, see Theorem 28.8 in section "Asymptotic Ratio Stability and Trajectory Geometry". The economic evidence of (16.50–16.51) is supported by their implications in (16.36.2). □

### *Endogenous Labor Supply*

With a classical saving function solely sustaining the demand for the output of capital goods, cf. (16.39–16.40), it seems natural, cf. Chap. 7, also to oblige the classical view that alterations in the population (labor force) depend on the "real wage rate"—here measured by the purchasing power of money wages in terms of the consumer good, that is, $w/P_2 = MP_{L_2}$, cf. (15.6.1–3).

Accordingly, still maintaining (16.14), (16.21), the dynamic system of the two-sector economy (16.39–16.40) would then be replaced by

$$\dot{L} \quad = \quad L\, n\, MP_{L_2}[k_2(\omega(k))] \quad = \quad L\, \mathfrak{f}(k), \tag{16.55}$$

$$\dot{K} \quad = \quad L\, s_K\, MP_{K_1}\, [k_1(\omega(k))]\, k \quad = \quad L\, \mathfrak{g}(k), \tag{16.56}$$

and instead of (16.43–16.44), the *director function* **h(k)** now becomes,

$$h(k) \quad = \quad \mathfrak{g}(k) - k\, \mathfrak{f}(k) \quad = \quad k\, [s_K\, MP_{K_1}[k_1(k)] - n\, MP_{L_2}[k_2(k)]], \tag{16.57}$$

and thus with $m = 1$,

$$\dot{k} \quad = \quad Q(k) = h(k). \tag{16.58}$$

**Theorem 16.2** *The two-sector growth model (16.55–16.58) has in $C_K$, (15.12)—under the regularity conditions (2.12) and appropriate range conditions (2.13)* *for $f_i, i = 1, 2$ in $C_K$, and further the uniqueness conditions of general equilibrium rendered by $E(\omega, k) > 0$, (16.14), (16.21)—one and only one stationary ratio solution*

$$\forall t \quad k(t) = \kappa = K_0/L_0 = k_0, \quad k_0 \in C_K, \tag{16.59}$$

*where the positive director root $\kappa$ is determined by the equation*

$$s_K MP_{K_1}[k_1(\kappa)] \quad = \quad nMP_{L_2}[k_2(\kappa)]. \tag{16.60}$$

*The coordinate solutions along the directrix (16.59) are*

$$L(t) = L_0 \exp\{\mathfrak{f}(\kappa)t\}, \quad K(t) = \kappa L(t), \tag{16.61.1}$$

*where the directrix value $\mathfrak{f}(\kappa)$ is*

$$\mathfrak{f}(\kappa) = nMP_{L_2}[k_2(\kappa)] = s_K MP_{K_1}[k_1(\kappa)]. \tag{16.61.2}$$

*The family of ratio solutions $k(t)$ to (16.58) and the family of coordinate solutions $[L(t), K(t)]$ to (16.55–16.56) have in $C_K$, (15.12)—under the uniqueness conditions mentioned above for $k(t) = \kappa$, (16.59)—respectively, global asymptotic stability and global weak relative stability.*

***Proof*** Given the properties (2.12) of $f_i$, $i = 1, 2$, (15.1), property (16.21), and $m = 1$, then $MP_{K_1}[k_1(\omega(k))]$ and $MP_{L_2}[k_2(\omega(k))]$ are, respectively, monotonically *decreasing* and monotonically *increasing* in *k*, cf. (2.14.1–2), (2.17–2.18). Hence, the director root $\kappa \neq 0$, solving (16.57), (16.60), is unique and will, given the appropriate range of $MP_{K_1}$ and $MP_{L_2}$ in $C_K$, exist for every $n$ and $s_K$. The exponential form of directrix solutions (16.61.1) follows from $m = 1$ and Theorem 28.2 in section "The Ratio and Coordinate Solutions on Directrices". The directrix value (16.61.2) follows from (16.55) and $h(\kappa) = 0$, (16.57).

As usual, the stated stability properties are obtained from $m = 1$ and section "Global Asymptotic Ratio Stability and Global Stabilities of Coordinate Solutions": Theorem 28.10. □

**Corollary 16.2** *The phase portrait in $C_K$, (15.12), of the solution $[L(t), K(t)]$ described by Theorem 16.2 is* ***parabolic****, if $E(\omega, k)$, (16.21), (16.13) satisfy*

$$\forall k \in C_K \quad : \quad E(\omega, k) < 1/(\epsilon_{L_1} + \epsilon_{K_2}), \tag{16.62}$$

*and* ***hyperbolic****, if*

$$\forall k \in C_K \quad : \quad E(\omega, k) > 1/(\epsilon_{L_1} + \epsilon_{K_2}). \tag{16.63}$$

***Proof*** The direction field of the dynamic system (16.55–16.56) is given by

$$dK/dL = q(k) = \frac{\mathfrak{g}(k)}{\mathfrak{f}(k)} = \frac{s_K MP_{K_1}[k_1(\omega(k))] \cdot k}{nMP_{L_2}[k_2(\omega(k))]}. \tag{16.64}$$

Hence by (2.3), (15.1), and (16.64)

$$\forall k \in C_K \quad : \quad q(k) > 0. \tag{16.65}$$

Next, the elasticity $E(q, k)$ is obtained from (16.64) as

$$E(q,k) \quad = \quad E(MP_{K_1}, k) + 1 - E(MP_{L_2}, k), \tag{16.66}$$

which becomes, cf. (16.54), (2.44.1–6),

$$\begin{aligned} E(q,k) &= -\epsilon_{L_1} E(\omega, k) + 1 - [\epsilon_{K_2} E(\omega, k)] \\ &= 1 - (\epsilon_{L_1} + \epsilon_{K_2}) E(\omega, k). \end{aligned} \tag{16.67}$$

Thus, (16.21), (16.66), and (16.67) establish, respectively, the parabolic (16.62) and the hyperbolic (16.63) phase portrait, see Theorem 28.8 in section "Asymptotic Ratio Stability and Trajectory Geometry". □

## Comparative Two-Sector Dynamics

Theorem 16.2 provides the extension (analogue) of Propositions 7.1–7.3 in section "Constant Returns to Scale" to a general two-sector endogenous growth model that uses the *price mechanism* in the pivotal role of allocating resources (regulating efficiently the distribution of the growing factor endowments into sectors) and equilibrating supply and demand in the factor and commodity markets.

Although the expressions for the *long-run growth rate*, $\mathfrak{f}(\kappa)$, (7.69.2) and (16.61.2), look similar, it has to be kept in mind that one-sector endogenous growth models obviously had no mechanism for allocating factors and had just a simple rule of dividing income (output) between consumption and saving (capital accumulation) and furthermore, that the *long-run* aggregate *capital-labor ratio* $\kappa$ now certainly depends on the technologies (production functions) of *both* sectors, cf. (16.60), (7.13). Even though it may be gratifying to see some of the principal results in Propositions 7.1–7.3 carried over to Theorem 16.2, the complex *interactions* of the two-sector economy—embedded in the general equilibrium model (section "The Two-Sector Economy with Classical Saving"), which serves as the economic underpinning of the general equilibrium dynamics (16.55–16.56)—are the hallmarks of Theorem 16.2.

As in Chap. 7. section "Classical Comparative Dynamics" we may now—with the stability properties of Theorem 16.2—use the *directrix solutions* (16.61.1–2) as a benchmark in *comparative* two-sector *dynamics*,, that is, using the *director roots* (16.60) and the *directrix values* (16.61.2) to evaluate the long-term implications of alternative parameter values and sector specifications.

The consequences of a larger propagation *parameter* $n$ is easily seen to be, cf. (16.60), (16.61.2),

$$\text{larger } n \quad \rightarrow \quad \text{smaller } \kappa \quad \wedge \quad \text{larger } \mathfrak{f}(\kappa), \tag{16.68}$$

that is, a qualitative result that holds independent of the sector technologies. Thus, (16.68) is analogous to (7.77).

The effects of larger saving *parameter* $s_K$, however, is not for a two-sector economy as simple as (7.76). The problem is here that the parameter $s_K$ (in contrast to propagation parameter $n$) is also involved in the determination of $\omega(k) = \Psi^{-1}(k)$, cf. (16.11.1–2), and hence, alternative $s_K$ will alter the sectorial marginal products, $MP_{L_2}, MP_{K_1}$, that stipulate the size of director root and directrix value, cf. (16.60), (16.61.2). Thus, as to the comparison of director roots, we would have to consider the solutions of the equation, cf. (16.60),

$$s_K MP_{K_1}[k_1(\omega(\kappa; s_K))] \quad = \quad nMP_{L_2}[k_2(\omega(\kappa; s_K))] \tag{16.69}$$

for alternative values of $s_K$. One way to proceed could be to calculate the total derivative on both sides in (16.69) and then come up with an evaluation for the sign/size of $d\kappa/ds_K$. However, the whole subject of comparative two-sector dynamics is an area pertinent to simulation studies. The latter might moreover compare the long-run consequences of different sector technologies, for example, by variation of substitution elasticities, $\sigma_1$ and $\sigma_2$. Again, such simulation experiments would be more complicated than those exhibited in Fig. 7.3, section "Classical Comparative Dynamics".

The task of two-sector *comparative dynamics* with an *exogenous* labor supply may briefly be compared to the endogenous case above. Clearly, given the asymptotic stability of the capital-labor ratio, the common long-run growth rate of labor and capital is, of course, already given by the exogenous growth rate of the labor, cf. (16.49), $\mathfrak{f}(\kappa) = n$, which holds irrespective of saving parameters and sector technologies. Hence, it only remains to examine the size of the director root $\kappa$ implicitly given by (16.47). Thus, regarding $n$, we again have (16.68). As to the effect of $s_K$ upon $\kappa$, we should have to examine the solutions of (16.69), but here without the term $MP_{L_2}$, cf. (16.47). Otherwise, this matter of evaluating or simulating $\kappa$ is analogous to the endogenous case above.

We shall end the discussion of comparative two-sector dynamics by considering briefly another issue that has often been raised for the two-sector growth model with *classical* saving and *exogenous* (exponential) labor growth, namely, that the *profit rate*, $rK/P_1K = MP_{K_1}[k_1(\omega(k))]$, cf. (15.6.2), in the *long run* is determined only by $s_K$ and $n$, and hence is *independent* of the sector *technologies* (production functions). Such characterization of the long-run magnitude of $MP_{K_1}[k_1(\omega(k))]$ is confirmed directly from (16.47). But the independence of the long-term profit rate from the sector technologies does certainly *not* carry over to the situation with classical saving and endogenous labor supply, cf. (16.60), and *neither* to the situation with exogenous labor growth and proportional saving, cf. (15.90.1–2), (15.25).

## Synopsis of Two-Sector Growth Models

The central issues concerning two-sector growth models were sector *technologies,* factor *allocation,* output *composition,* and factor *accumulation*—issues that are highly interrelated. Regarding technologies, as described by production functions, the central issue was the extent of the admissible factor substitution within each sector.

When technical efficiency admitted only one capital-labor ratio in each sector, we had the case of *fixed coefficients* (Leontief technologies). Such sector technologies and the requirement of full employment of the available factor endowments will then completely *lock* the factor allocation and the output composition of the two-sector economy. Further, the factor *allocation* and the output *compositions* corresponding to *alternative* factor endowments (varying endowment ratios) follow a pattern that is entirely determined by the sector technologies, viz., the *relative* capital *intensities* (capital-labor ratios) of the outputs/sectors. Moreover, the necessary factor reallocations caused by changing factor endowments lead to *magnified output* changes in one of the sectors. The latter naturally become of critical importance, when *factor accumulation* is an ongoing process, where the changes in one of the factors are actually determined by the output from one of the sectors. Accordingly, the dynamic *stability properties* of the two-sector economy with *full* and *efficient* factor utilization are inevitably tied to the *specific* sectorial capital *intensity* and *productivity* conditions, as stated in (14.37) and examined in Chap. 14. section "The Economic Rationale of the Stability Conditions".

When technical efficiency admits many capital-labor ratios in each sector, we had the case of *flexible* coefficients (smooth $C^2$-class technologies). With such sector technologies, the factor allocation and the output composition *cannot* be established from the *supply side* alone. To close the two-sector model, the *demand side* of the commodity markets must be introduced. Then, a coherent treatment of supply and demand naturally called for prices as the mutual regulator and equilibrating mechanism. Thus, factor allocation and output composition for the two-sector economy became a general equilibrium problem.

The existence and *uniqueness* of a *general equilibrium* solution—clearing the commodity and factor markets—was now an important problem to be resolved. With cost minimization and competitive factor pricing, the uniqueness of a general equilibrium solution hinges on whether the factor-price ratio (wage-rental ratio) is uniquely determined for all factor endowment constellations (every factor endowment ratio), belonging to the diversification cone. This uniqueness issue posed *no* problem with *proportional* saving, cf. (15.27.1–2), Lemma 15.1, and *neither* any *serious* trouble with *classical* saving, cf. (16.14), Lemma 16.1, and Remark 16.1.

Our procedure for *resolving* the *uniqueness* issue above introduced clear-cut formulas for the sectorial labor and capital allocation ratios, factor income distribution, commodity-price ratios, and sector output ratios, all neatly expressed in terms of *sectorial output elasticities* of *labor* and *capital* (sectorial cost shares of labor and capital). These sectorial output elasticities describe crucial properties of sector technologies; furthermore, they are uniquely related to the common wage-rental ratio and also to the overall factor endowment ratio, whenever the general equilibrium is unique. By these sectorial output elasticities—whose elasticities themselves with respect to the wage-rental ratio or endowment ratio were easy to evaluate, cf. (15.33.1–2)—the *inner clockwork* of the two-sector economy could be followed, especially the general equilibrium changes in allocation ratios and sector outputs that would be the consequences of factor endowment variations.

Some of the results of the *comparative* general equilibrium analysis with proportional and classical saving were, respectively, stated in Theorem 15.1, Corollary 15.1, and Lemma 16.2. The crucial point is that our two-sector economies do not now display such extreme sector output changes as seen before in (14.49–14.50). The factor allocation ratios seldom move in the same direction, and the direction of either is accordingly not exclusively determined by the sectorial capital intensities, cf. (15.42.1–15.43.3).

Having laid bare the structural properties of the general equilibrium system and unravelled the complexities of the static and comparative static solutions for two-sector economies with either proportional or classical saving, we were next able to derive in a straightforward way the kinematics (coherent time paths) of cumulating factor endowments, that is, unravel the complexity of the complete set of solutions to the homogeneous dynamic system of factor accumulation.

Given standard regularity conditions, the main outcome of the dynamic analysis was that the *uniqueness* and the global asymptotic *stability* of a long-run capital-labor ratio ($\kappa$) is *always ensured* in the *classical* case, cf. Theorem 16.1, and is also ensured under very *mild restriction* in the proportional case, cf. (15.95), Theorem 15.2. Thus, continuous factor reallocations in these growing two-sector economies will in the *long run* lead to a *common* (balanced) *growth rate* of inputs and sector outputs—whether the labor supply is exogenous or endogenous and irrespective of any reswitching of sectorial capital intensities.

Such *robustness* of *general equilibrium dynamics* with proportional and classical saving is an *encouraging* result boding well for the future progress of dynamic model building that uses the price mechanism in the central role of allocating the growing factor endowments efficiently and in accordance with more generalized stipulations for the demand side (expenditure systems) of the economy.

A similar message, however, does *not* come out of the present literature on two-sector growth models. From the very beginning, Uzawa (1961, 1963), Hahn and Matthews (1964), Inada (1963, 1964), there has been a tendency to exaggerate both the *uniqueness* problem of general equilibrium and the *uniqueness* and *stability* problems of balanced growth. Especially the capital intensity assumption, $k_2 > k_1$, has played a prominent role as a sufficient condition in both problems. An important step forward came with Drandakis (1963) and hereto Amano (1964), Burmeister (1967, 1968), Takayama (1963), where the sectorial substitution elasticities, $\sigma_1$ and $\sigma_2$, when sufficiently large individually or combined, would take care of either or both problems. As to the stability problem, an array of overlapping and overly strong sufficient conditions are collected in standard textbooks (Burmeister and Dobell (1970, p.120–122); Wan (1971, p.121–128)), and we have placed them, for ease of comparison, together with our *generalized conditions* in Theorem 15.2 and Lemma 16.1.

As mentioned in Burmeister and Dobell (1970, p.121), it has been difficult to articulate the economic content of all these uniqueness or stability conditions. The economic rationale of our results, however, followed directly in Chaps. 15–16 from a detailed and rigorous analysis of the structure and inner working of the basic two-sector models in question. In the wake of these results, we await further progress in this field and economic dynamics in general.

## Bibliography


Amano A (1964) A further note on Professor Uzawa's Two–Sector Model of Economic Growth. Rev Econ Stud 31:97–101

Burmeister E (1967) The Existence of Golden Ages and Stability in the Two–Sector Model. Quart J Economics 81:146–154

Burmeister E (1968) The Role of the Jacobian Determinant in the Two–Sector Model. Internt Econ Rev 9:195–203

Burmeister E, Dobell AR (1970) Mathematical Theories of Economic Growth. Macmillan, London

Drandakis EM (1963) Factor Substitution in the Two–Sector Growth Model. Rev Econ Stud 30:217–28

Hahn FH, Matthews RCO (1964) The Theory of Economic Growth: A Survey. Economic Journal 74:779–902

Inada K (1963) On a Two–Sector Model of Economic Growth: Comments and a Generalization. Rev Econ Stud 30:119–27

Inada K (1964) On the Stability of Growth Equilibria in Two–Sector Models. Rev Econ Stud 31:127–42

Pasinetti L (1962) Rate of Profit and Income Distribution in Relation to the Rate of Economic Growth. Rev Econ Stud 29:267–79, or Sen (1970)

Samuelson PA (1966) The Collected Scientific Papers of Paul A. Samuelson. MIT Press, Mass

Sen A (1970) Growth Economics, Selected Readings. Penguin Books, London

Stiglitz JE, Uzawa H (1969) Readings in the Modern Theory of Economic Growth. M.I.T. Press, Cambridge, Mass

Takayama A (1963) On a Two–Sector Model of Economic Growth: A Comparative Static Analysis. Rev Econ Stud 30:95–104

Uzawa H (1961) On a Two–Sector Model of Economic Growth: I. Review of Economic Studies 29:40–47

Uzawa H (1963) On a Two–Sector Model of Economic Growth: II. Review of Economic Studies 30:105–18, Also in: Stiglitz and Uzawa (1969)

Wan HY Jr (1971) Economic Growth. Harcourt Brace Jovanowich, New York

CHAPTER 17

# Walrasian General Equilibrium Allocations and Dynamics in Two-Sector Growth Models

## Introduction

The aim of pure theory and models is to deduce definite conclusions from explicit premises. In terms of theory construction, assumptions should be fundamental (general), and from a technical (mathematical) point of view, they should be tractable. The concepts (terms and parameters) used in the theory must be capable of exact interpretation and refer to observable facts as closely as possible. Simplicity in the sense of generality and tractability has also motivated the research in economic growth theory. Great emphasis was naturally first given to labor and capital accumulation in *aggregate* (one-sector) *growth* models. In the endogenous growth literature, the scope of aggregate models has recently been enlarged by increasing the *number* of primary *factors*, such as human and intangible capital (education, useable knowledge, learning by doing) as well as the number and quality of *intermediate* inputs, through innovations. Although the *new aggregate* growth models in the last decade (1990s) have made valuable contributions in the theory of economic development, it has to be recognized that: "the *importance* of *disaggregation* calls into question the utility of research programs directed at spelling out alternative *mechanisms* driving all of *aggregate* growth in *single-good* models, as if *relative prices* and relative quantities of *different products* did not matter. Economists' emphasis on single-good models is odd given that these models offer almost no scope for the relative price effects economists stress in most contexts", De Long and Summers (1991, p.486), (italics ours).

An extensive literature on two (multi)-sector growth models, however, began in the 1960s, but debate and controversy reigned and still linger. The *seminal* work on *two-sector growth* models with flexible sector technologies was done by Drandakis (1963), Inada (1963), and Uzawa (1961, 1963). A framework for *efficient* factor *allocation* by using the *price mechanism* was established





B. S. Jensen, *The Elements and Dynamic Systems of Economic Growth and Trade Models*, https://doi.org/10.1007/978-3-031-52493-6_17

in a "*miniature Walrasian general equilibrium system*", Solow (1961). But the theoretical and empirical relevance of various sufficient conditions for stability of steady states was deemed to be of modest value, cf. Hahn and Matthews (1964). In contrast to growth theory, the main interest of *international trade theory* is directed to factor *allocation*, output *composition*, and their dualities for *commodity* and *factor prices*, Dixit and Norman (1980), Jensen et al. (2001); here Chap. 22, Jones (1956), and Kemp (1969). A systematic and elegant treatment of the basic two-factor, two-sector general equilibrium model was given by Jones (1965), and the static general equilibrium analysis was extended to growing two-sector economies, where some conditions for convergence to balanced growth were also examined.

Reference Hahn (1965, p.339) soon returned to the two-sector growth story and noted that its connection with ordinary *general equilibrium analysis* had not been given the prominence it deserved; then he stated: "The story starts with a given stock of capital inherited from the past. Since there are constant returns to scale we might just as well start with a *given capital-labor ratio*. The *first* question, familiar to general equilibrium theorists, is: does there *exist* a *momentary equilibrium* for any given capital-labor ratio? The *second* question asks: is such an equilibrium *unique*? The answer to this is important for the simple reason that *multiple* momentary equilibria would make it *impossible* without further postulates to *predict* the subsequent *development* of the system from the *initial conditions*. Supposing momentary equilibrium to be uniquely determined by the capital-labor ratio we now ask: Where is the system going? Here we want to know whether a *steady state* is approached or not. Answering this question involves an examination of the *existence* of a steady-state solution, possibly also the *uniqueness* of this and of course rather straight-forward *stability* analysis. The questions asked may be answered in varying degrees of generality" (italics ours).

Though these questions and the answers to them could seem straight-forward, the truth is that the issues indicated have dominated subsequent research and are still (2001) not resolved. Our *purpose* is now to provide *definite answers* to these *static* and *dynamic* issues of *existence, uniqueness,* and *stability*. As we shall see, in solving even standard two-sector growth models, the *uniqueness* concept of *static* general equilibria is blurred and *confounded* with the *uniqueness* of general equilibrium *dynamics* (initial value problems). An inconvenient or *intractable* choice of the *state variable* in general equilibrium dynamics has created profound *delusions* (including artifacts of limit cycles) about the solutions to basic neoclassical and classical two-sector growth models. We shall mathematically eliminate the "*causal indeterminancy*" problem.

As to both steady-state convergence or persistent (endogenous) per capita growth, the *critical* importance of *technology parameters* for the *capital good* (rather than consumer good) *industry* has been routinely *missed*. Moreover, the technological lack of generality in the widely adopted Inada (1963, 1964) *conditions* eventually impeded further advances in pure theory and reduced the observable relevance of neoclassical and other growth models, cf. Aghion and Howitt (1998, p.11). The main expositions and references to the early two-sector growth literature are: Burmeister and Dobell (1970), Gandolfo (1980), Stiglitz and Uzawa (1969), and Wan (1971). A newer treatment with an alternative population structure is Galor (1992). In this chapter, the size of sectorial *substitution elasticities* and *total factor productivity* (TFP) coefficients are among the *key* technology *parameters*.

The chapter is organized such that section "General Equilibrium of Two–Sector Economies" presents the structural equations for supply and demand and derives the *timeless* (static and comparative static) *competitive general equilibrium solutions* for all the variables as composite functions of the factor endowments. Section "The Dynamic Systems and the Evolution of Two-Sector Economies" analyzes the *dynamic* system and alternative *evolutions* of the two-sector *general equilibria*.

## General Equilibrium of Two-Sector Economies

### *Supply Side*

Consider an *economy* consisting of a *capital good* industry (sector) and a *consumer good* industry, labeled 1 and 2, respectively. Sector *technologies*, $F_i(L_i, K_i)$, $i = 1, 2$, are described by nonnegative smooth concave homogeneous production functions with *constant returns* to scale in labor and capital

$$Y_i = F_i(L_i, K_i) = L_i F_i(1, k_i) \equiv L_i f_i(k_i) \equiv L_i y_i, L_i \neq 0;\; F_i(0, 0) = 0, \tag{17.1}$$

where the function $f_i(k_i)$ is strictly concave and monotonically increasing in the capital-labor ratio $k_i \in [0, \infty[$, that is, $f_i(k_i)$ has the *properties*:

$$\forall k_i > 0:\; f_i'(k_i) = df_i(k_i)/dk_i > 0, \quad f_i''(k_i) = d^2 f_i(k_i)/dk_i^2 < 0 \tag{17.2}$$

$$\lim_{k_i \to 0} f_i'(k_i) \equiv \bar{\beta}_i \leq \infty,\; \lim_{k_i \to \infty} f_i'(k_i) \equiv \underline{\beta}_i \geq 0,\; f_i'(k_i) \in J_i \equiv \left[\underline{\beta}_i, \bar{\beta}_i\right] \tag{17.3}$$

The *sectorial output elasticities*, $\epsilon_{L_i}, \epsilon_{K_i}, \epsilon_i$, with respect to marginal and proportional factor variation are, cf. (17.1),

$$\epsilon_{L_i} \equiv E(Y_i, L_i) \equiv \frac{\partial Y_i}{\partial L_i}\frac{L_i}{Y_i} = \frac{MP_{L_i}}{AP_{L_i}} = 1 - \frac{k_i f_i'(k_i)}{f_i(k_i)} > 0, \quad k_i \neq 0, \tag{17.4}$$

$$\epsilon_{K_i} \equiv E(Y_i, K_i) \equiv \frac{\partial Y_i}{\partial K_i}\frac{K_i}{Y_i} = \frac{MP_{K_i}}{AP_{K_i}} = \frac{k_i f_i'(k_i)}{f_i(k_i)} = E(y_i, k_i) > 0, \tag{17.5}$$

$$\epsilon_i \equiv \epsilon_{L_i} + \epsilon_{K_i} = 1, \tag{17.6}$$

The *factor endowments*, total labor force ($L$) and the total capital stock ($K$), are inelastically supplied and are *fully employed* (utilized), that is,

$$L = L_1 + L_2, \qquad L_1/L + L_2/L \equiv \lambda_{L_1} + \lambda_{L_2} \equiv 1 \tag{17.7}$$

$$K = K_1 + K_2, \qquad K_1/K + K_2/K \equiv \lambda_{K_1} + \lambda_{K_2} \equiv 1, \tag{17.8}$$

$$k \equiv K/L \equiv \lambda_{L_1} k_1 + \lambda_{L_2} k_2 \equiv k_2 + (k_1 - k_2)\lambda_{L_1}, \tag{17.9}$$

$$\lambda_{L_1} \equiv (k - k_2)\,/\,(k_1 - k_2), \qquad \lambda_{K_i} \equiv (k_i/k)\,\lambda_{L_i}, \; k_1 \neq k_2, \tag{17.10}$$

The factor *allocation fractions* $\lambda_{L_i}$, $\lambda_{K_i}$, (17.7–17.8), are related, cf. (17.10).

At any point of the isoquants (17.1), the *marginal rates* of *technical substitution*, (MRS), $\omega_i(k_i)$, are by, (17.2), positive *monotonic* functions,

$$\omega_i(k_i) = \frac{MP_{L_i}}{MP_{K_i}} = \frac{f_i(k_i)}{f_i'(k_i)} - k_i = \frac{\epsilon_{L_i}}{\epsilon_{K_i}} k_i > 0, \quad \forall k_i > 0. \tag{17.11}$$

The general relation between the *sectorial factor output* elasticities, (17.4–17.5), and the *sectorial substitution* elasticities between labor and capital, $\sigma_i$, is:

$$E(\epsilon_{K_i}, k_i) \equiv \frac{\partial \epsilon_{K_i}}{\partial k_i}\frac{k_i}{\epsilon_{K_i}} = \frac{\epsilon_{L_i}(\sigma_i - 1)}{\sigma_i}, \quad E(\epsilon_{L_i}, k_i) \equiv \frac{\partial \epsilon_{L_i}}{\partial k_i}\frac{k_i}{\epsilon_{L_i}} = \frac{\epsilon_{K_i}(1 - \sigma_i)}{\sigma_i} \tag{17.12}$$

Free *factor mobility* between the two industries and *efficient* factor *allocation* impose the *common* MRS *condition*, cf. (17.11):

$$\omega = \omega_1(k_1) = \omega_2(k_2), \tag{17.13}$$

For the variables $k_1$ and $k_2$ to satisfy (17.13), it is, beyond (17.2), further required that the *intersection* of the sectorial *range* for $\omega_1(k_1)$ and $\omega_2(k_2)$ is not empty,

$$\omega_i(k_i) \in \Omega_i = [\underline{\omega}_i, \overline{\omega}_i] \subseteq \mathbf{R}_+, \; i = 1, 2; \; \omega \in \Omega \equiv \Omega_1 \cap \Omega_2 = [\underline{\omega}, \overline{\omega}] \neq \emptyset, \tag{17.14}$$

The *two industries* are assumed to operate under *perfect competition* (zero excess profit); absolute money *input* (factor) *prices* ($\mathbf{w}, \mathbf{r}$) are the *same* in both industries; and absolute money *output* (product, commodity) *prices* ($\mathbf{P}_1, \mathbf{P}_2$) represent *unit cost*. We prefer to retain money prices rather than use one of the commodities as the numeraire.

Hence, we have the *competitive producer equilibrium* equations,

$$w = P_i \cdot MP_{L_i}\,, \quad r = P_i \cdot MP_{K_i}\,; \quad \omega = \frac{w}{r}\,, \qquad P_i \neq 0 \tag{17.15}$$

$$Y_i = Ly_i\lambda_{L_i}\,,\; P_iY_i = wL_i + rK_i\,,\; \epsilon_{L_i} = \frac{wL_i}{P_iY_i},\; \epsilon_{K_i} = \frac{rK_i}{P_iY_i} \tag{17.16}$$

or

$$\frac{w}{P_i} = y_i\epsilon_{L_i},\; \frac{r}{P_i} = \frac{y_i\epsilon_{L_i}}{\omega} = f_i'(k_i)\;;\; \epsilon_{L_i} = \frac{\omega}{k_i+\omega},\; \epsilon_{K_i} = \frac{k_i}{k_i+\omega} \tag{17.17}$$

$$p \equiv \frac{P_1}{P_2} = \frac{MP_{K_2}}{MP_{K_1}} = \frac{f_2'(k_2)}{f_1'(k_1)} = \frac{y_2\epsilon_{L_2}}{y_1\epsilon_{L_1}} = \frac{f_2(k_2) - k_2 f_2'(k_2)}{f_1(k_1) - k_1 f_1'(k_1)} = \frac{MP_{L_2}}{MP_{L_1}} \tag{17.18}$$

**Remark 17.1** As our object is indeed miniature Walrasian *general equilibrium* economies, we may for (17.15) here quote, Walras (1954, p.385):

1. Free competition brings the cost of production down to a minimum.
2. In a state of equilibrium, when cost of production and selling price are equal, the prices of the services are proportional to their marginal productivities, i.e., to the partial derivatives of the production function.

These *two propositions* taken together constitute the theory of marginal productivity. This is a *cardinal theory* in pure economics. (italics ours) ▽

*Gross domestic product* (GDP), $Y$, is the monetary value of sector outputs,

$$Y \equiv P_1Y_1 + P_2Y_2 = L(P_1y_1\lambda_{L_1} + P_2y_2\lambda_{L_2}) \equiv Ly \tag{17.19}$$

and is, with (17.15–17.18), equal to the total *factor income*:

$$Y = wL + rK = L(w + rk) = L(\omega + k)P_i f_i'(k_i) = Ly \tag{17.20}$$

which defines the factor income *macro distribution shares*, $\delta_K + \delta_L = 1$:

$$\delta_K \equiv rK/Y = rk/y\,,\; \delta_L \equiv wL/Y = w/y\;;\; \frac{\delta_K}{\delta_L} = \frac{k}{\omega},\; \delta_K = \frac{k}{\omega + k} \tag{17.21}$$

*CES Sector Technologies, Boundary Values, Inada Conditions*

The general constant elasticity of substitution (CES) forms of $F_i(L_i, K_i)$, (17.1), $\gamma_i > 0$, $0 < a_i < 1$, $\sigma_i > 0$, are

$$Y_i \;=\; F_i(L_i, K_i) = \gamma_i L_i^{1-a_i} K_i^{a_i} = L_i\gamma_i k_i^{a_i} \equiv L_i f_i(k_i) \tag{17.22}$$

$$Y_i = F_i(L_i, K_i) = \gamma_i \left[ (1 - a_i) L_i^{\frac{\sigma_i - 1}{\sigma_i}} + a_i K_i^{\frac{\sigma_i - 1}{\sigma_i}} \right]^{\frac{\sigma_i}{\sigma_i - 1}} \qquad (17.23)$$

$$= L_i \gamma_i \left[ (1 - a_i) + a_i k_i^{(\sigma_i - 1)/\sigma_i} \right]^{\sigma_i/(\sigma_i - 1)} \equiv L_i f_i(k_i) \qquad (17.24)$$

$$f_i'(k_i) = \gamma_i a_i k_i^{a_i - 1}, \quad f_i'(k_i) = \gamma_i a_i \left[ a_i + (1 - a_i) k_i^{-(\sigma_i - 1)/\sigma_i} \right]^{1/(\sigma_i - 1)} \qquad (17.25)$$

By evaluating (17.22–17.25), the limits of $f_i(k_i)$ and $f_i'(k_i)$ become, ($\forall i$ : $\sigma_i \gtrless 1 \Rightarrow a_i^{\sigma_i/(\sigma_i - 1)} \lessgtr 1$),

$$\sigma_i < 1 \quad : \quad \begin{cases} \lim_{k_i \to 0} f_i(k_i) = \lim_{k_i \to 0} \gamma_i a_i^{\frac{\sigma_i}{\sigma_i - 1}} k_i = 0, & \lim_{k_i \to \infty} f_i(k_i) = \gamma_i (1 - a_i)^{\frac{\sigma_i}{\sigma_i - 1}} \\ \lim_{k_i \to 0} f_i'(k_i) = \gamma_i a_i^{\frac{\sigma_i}{\sigma_i - 1}}, & \lim_{k_i \to \infty} f_i'(k_i) = 0 \end{cases} \qquad (17.26)$$

$$\sigma_i > 1 \quad : \quad \begin{cases} \lim_{k_i \to 0} f_i(k_i) = \gamma_i (1 - a_i)^{\frac{\sigma_i}{\sigma_i - 1}}, & \lim_{k_i \to \infty} f_i(k_i) = \lim_{k_i \to \infty} \gamma_i a_i^{\frac{\sigma_i}{\sigma_i - 1}} k_i = \infty \\ \lim_{k_i \to 0} f_i'(k_i) = \infty, & \lim_{k_i \to \infty} f_i'(k_i) = \gamma_i a_i^{\frac{\sigma_i}{\sigma_i - 1}} \end{cases} \qquad (17.27)$$

A major problem in both one- and two-sector growth models has been a clear delineation of the class (parametric family) of technologies $F_i$ that comply with the Inada (1963, p.120), Uzawa (1961, p.108) *boundary conditions*:

$$f_i(0) = 0, \qquad f_i(\infty) = \infty, \qquad i = 1, 2 \qquad (17.28)$$

$$f_i'(0) = \infty, \qquad f_i'(\infty) = 0, \qquad i = 1, 2 \qquad (17.29)$$

It is a *paradox* that regularity properties of *neoclassical* production functions are often *codified* by combining the *concavity* properties (17.2) with the *boundary* (limit) values in (17.28–17.29), because—as the comparison with (17.26–17.27) shows—*neither* (17.28) *nor* (17.29) are satisfied by the *general* CES family, $\sigma_i \neq 1$. Although Drandakis (1963, p.27) and especially Wan (1971, p.37–40, p.118) noted that the Cobb-Douglas (**CD**) form (17.22) is the only CES member that fulfills the Inada-Uzawa conditions (17.28–17.29), the latter acquired a prominent role in the growth literature, where they were relied on to guarantee the *existence* of at least one balanced growth path. Relevant sufficient *stability* conditions, however, usually involved sectorial *substitution* elasticities *larger* or *smaller* than one, ($\sigma_i \lessgtr 1$), which with CES technologies is *inconsistent* with the use of (17.28–17.29) as the *existence* condition. Latent contradictions thus pervade much of the standard dynamic analysis of *neoclassical* and *classical* two-sector growth models. Moreover, the possibility of persistent ("endogenous") *growth per capita* is inherently precluded, since the limit $f_i'(\infty)$ in (17.29) must be relaxed, as generally demonstrated for the Solow model in Jensen and Larsen (1987); here Chap. 1.

The generality problem with (17.28–17.29) appears in various versions. Caballé and Santos (1993, p.1046), Ladrón-de-Guevara et al. (1999, p.612) impose—to guarantee interiority conditions in intertemporal optimization—the *unbounded marginal* productivity conditions at the *lower* boundary, and also required that *both factors* are *essential*: that is,

$$\lim_{L \to 0} MP_L(L, \bar{K}) = \infty, \qquad \lim_{K \to 0} MP_K(\bar{L}, K) = \infty, \tag{17.30}$$

$$F(\bar{L}, 0) = 0, \qquad F(0, \bar{K}) = 0 \tag{17.31}$$

For *general* CES functions with $\sigma_i \neq 1$, equations (17.30) and (17.31) are also *contradictory,* as the derivative limit (17.30) requires $\sigma_i > 1$, which implies that each production *factor* is *inessential*, that is, nonzero limits in (17.31), cf. (17.23). But when factors are essential (17.31), marginal products cannot intuitively be expected to become infinitely large, no matter how little of the factor is employed (17.30). Accordingly, as CES with $\sigma_i > 1$ demonstrates, assumptions (17.30–17.31) cannot be maintained simultaneously.

*Product Price-Factor Price Correspondence: CES Technology*

For the CES technologies, the *monotonic* relations between marginal rates of substitution, factor proportions, and output elasticities are, cf. (17.23–17.25)

$$\omega_i = \frac{1 - a_i}{a_i} k_i^{1/\sigma_i}, \qquad k_i = \frac{1}{c_i} [\omega_i]^{\sigma_i}, \quad c_i = \left[\frac{1 - a_i}{a_i}\right]^{\sigma_i} \qquad i = 1, 2. \tag{17.32}$$

$$\epsilon_{K_i} = \left[1 + \frac{1 - a_i}{a_i} k_i^{\frac{1-\sigma_i}{\sigma_i}}\right]^{-1} = \frac{1}{1 + c_i \omega^{1-\sigma_i}}, \qquad \epsilon_{L_i} = \frac{c_i \omega^{1-\sigma_i}}{1 + c_i \omega^{1-\sigma_i}} \tag{17.33}$$

With two-sector models and CES technologies, it is apparent from (17.32) that sectorial *factor* ratio ("intensity") *reversals* can only be avoided if and only if $\sigma_1 = \sigma_2$ and $a_1 \neq a_2$. Hence, with $\sigma_1 \neq \sigma_2$, there will be a *reversal* point, $(k_i, \omega_i) = (\bar{k}, \bar{\omega})$:

$$\bar{k} = \left[\frac{a_1(1 - a_2)}{a_2(1 - a_1)}\right]^{\frac{\sigma_1 \sigma_2}{\sigma_2 - \sigma_1}} = \left[\frac{c_2^{\sigma_1}}{c_1^{\sigma_2}}\right]^{\frac{1}{\sigma_2 - \sigma_1}}, \qquad \bar{\omega} = \left[\frac{c_2}{c_1}\right]^{\frac{1}{\sigma_2 - \sigma_1}} \tag{17.34}$$

The *connection* between relative *factor* (service) prices and relative *commodity* prices follows from (17.11, 17.13, 17.15, 17.18),

$$p(\omega) = \frac{P_1}{P_2}(\omega) = \frac{MP_{K_2}[k_2(\omega)]}{MP_{K_1}[k_1(\omega)]} = \frac{f_2'[k_2(\omega)]}{f_1'[k_1(\omega)]}, \quad \omega = w/r. \tag{17.35}$$

The elasticity of (17.35) is generally, by the composite rule:

$$E(P_1/P_2, \omega) = E\left(MP_{K_2}, k_2\right) E(k_2, \omega) - E\left(MP_{K_1}, k_1\right) E(k_1, \omega) \tag{17.36}$$

$$= (-\epsilon_{L_2}/\sigma_2)\sigma_2 - (-\epsilon_{L_1}/\sigma_1)\sigma_1 = \epsilon_{L_1} - \epsilon_{L_2} = \epsilon_{K_2} - \epsilon_{K_1} \tag{17.37}$$

Evidently, $p(\omega)$ is always *inelastic*, as (17.37) is numerically less than unity.

The exact form of the function (17.35) needs particular attention. With (17.25) and (17.32), the *relative commodity* prices (comparative costs) (17.35) become, with $\sigma_i = 1$, $\sigma_i \neq 1$, and $\sigma_1 = \sigma_2 = \sigma$, respectively,

$$p(\omega) = \frac{f_2'[k_2(\omega)]}{f_1'[k_1(\omega)]} = \frac{\gamma_2 a_2 k_2(\omega)^{a_2-1}}{\gamma_1 a_1 k_1(\omega)^{a_1-1}} = \frac{\gamma_2 a_2^{a_2}(1-a_2)^{1-a_2}}{\gamma_1 a_1^{a_1}(1-a_1)^{1-a_1}}\,\omega^{a_2-a_1} \tag{17.38}$$

$$p(\omega) = \frac{f_2'[k_2(\omega)]}{f_1'[k_1(\omega)]} = \frac{\gamma_2 a_2\left[a_2 + (1-a_2)k_2(\omega)^{-(\sigma_2-1)/\sigma_2}\right]^{1/(\sigma_2-1)}}{\gamma_1 a_1\left[a_1 + (1-a_1)k_1(\omega)^{-(\sigma_1-1)/\sigma_1}\right]^{1/(\sigma_1-1)}} \tag{17.39}$$

$$= \frac{\gamma_2 a_2^{\sigma_2/(\sigma_2-1)}\left(1 + c_2\omega^{1-\sigma_2}\right)^{1/(\sigma_2-1)}}{\gamma_1 a_1^{\sigma_1/(\sigma_1-1)}\left(1 + c_1\omega^{1-\sigma_1}\right)^{1/(\sigma_1-1)}} \tag{17.40}$$

$$p(\omega) = \frac{\gamma_2}{\gamma_1}\left[\left[\frac{a_2}{a_1}\right]^{\sigma}\frac{1 + c_2\omega^{1-\sigma}}{1 + c_1\omega^{1-\sigma}}\right]^{1/(\sigma-1)}, \quad c_i = \left[\frac{1-a_i}{a_i}\right]^{\sigma} \tag{17.41}$$

Hence, with $\sigma_1 \neq \sigma_2$, and (17.34),

$$\bar{p} = p(\bar{\omega}) = \frac{\gamma_2 a_2^{\sigma_2/(\sigma_2-1)}\left[1 + c_2\left(c_2/c_1\right)^{\frac{1-\sigma_2}{\sigma_2-\sigma_1}}\right]^{\frac{1}{\sigma_2-1}}}{\gamma_1 a_1^{\sigma_1/\sigma_1-1}\left[1 + c_1\left(c_2/c_1\right)^{\frac{1-\sigma_1}{\sigma_2-\sigma_1}}\right]^{\frac{1}{\sigma_1-1}}} \tag{17.42}$$

Since the CES marginal rate of substitution $\omega_i$, (17.32), always has the limit values zero and infinity, we need, for precise geometry and intuition, to know the limits of the relative prices $p(\omega)$, (17.40), for $\omega$ going to zero and to infinity. To this end, let

$$p^* \equiv \frac{\gamma_2\, a_2^{\sigma_2/(\sigma_2-1)}}{\gamma_1\, a_1^{\sigma_1/(\sigma_1-1)}}, \qquad p^{**} \equiv \frac{\gamma_2\, (1-a_2)^{\sigma_2/(\sigma_2-1)}}{\gamma_1\, (1-a_1)^{\sigma_1/(\sigma_1-1)}} \tag{17.43}$$

**Lemma 17.1** *The graph of* $p(\omega)$, *(17.40)—the* **CES** *factor price-commodity price,* **FPCP** *correspondence—has limits, classified by* $\sigma_i$, *as follows:*

$$\sigma_1 < 1, \quad \sigma_2 < 1: \qquad \lim_{\omega\to 0} p = p^* \quad \lim_{\omega\to\infty} p = p^{**} \tag{17.44}$$

$$\sigma_1 > 1, \quad \sigma_2 > 1: \qquad \lim_{\omega\to 0} p = p^{**} \quad \lim_{\omega\to\infty} p = p^* \tag{17.45}$$

$$\sigma_1 > 1, \quad \sigma_2 < 1: \qquad \lim_{\omega\to 0} p = 0 \quad \lim_{\omega\to\infty} p = 0 \tag{17.46}$$

$$\sigma_1 < 1, \quad \sigma_2 > 1: \qquad \lim_{\omega\to 0} p = \infty \quad \lim_{\omega\to\infty} p = \infty \tag{17.47}$$

*The reversal price ratio,* $P_1/P_2 = \bar{p} \equiv p(\bar{\omega})$, *is always a maximum (iff* $\sigma_1 > \sigma_2$*) or a minimum (iff* $\sigma_2 > \sigma_1$*), cf.* Fig. 17.1. *For the substitution elasticities (17.44)–(17.46), the range of* $p(\omega)$, *(17.40), is bounded. With* $\gamma_1 = \gamma_2$ *and both substitutions elasticities, either small (17.44) or large (17.45), the range of* $p(\omega)$ *becomes a narrow interval, and there will be only small differences between the values of* $p^*$ *and* $p^{**}$ *(17.43)—especially when* $a_i$, $i = 1, 2$ *have similar size, cf. (17.40)*

*Iff* $\sigma_1 = \sigma_2 \neq 1$, *the functions,* $p(\omega)$, *(17.41), are always monotonic, bounded, and increasing between* $p^*$ *and* $p^{**}$, *iff* $a_2 > a_1$. *Only the CD relative prices,* $p(\omega)$, *(17.38), are both monotonic and unbounded.*

***Proof*** Proof is given in Jensen et al. (2001, p.188); here, proof of Theorem 22.1, Chap. 22. □

### *Demand Side*

As to aggregate demand (expenditure shares) decomposition between consumption and investment (saving), we shall employ two macro-saving relations, viz., "neoclassical" saving and "classical" saving, which have been the standard opposites in much of the growth and trade literature.

Through history and across countries, households, businesses, and government have contributed in different proportions to national saving. It is immaterial for our purposes whether investment is controlled by owners or managers. The classical assumption with saving only out of capital income

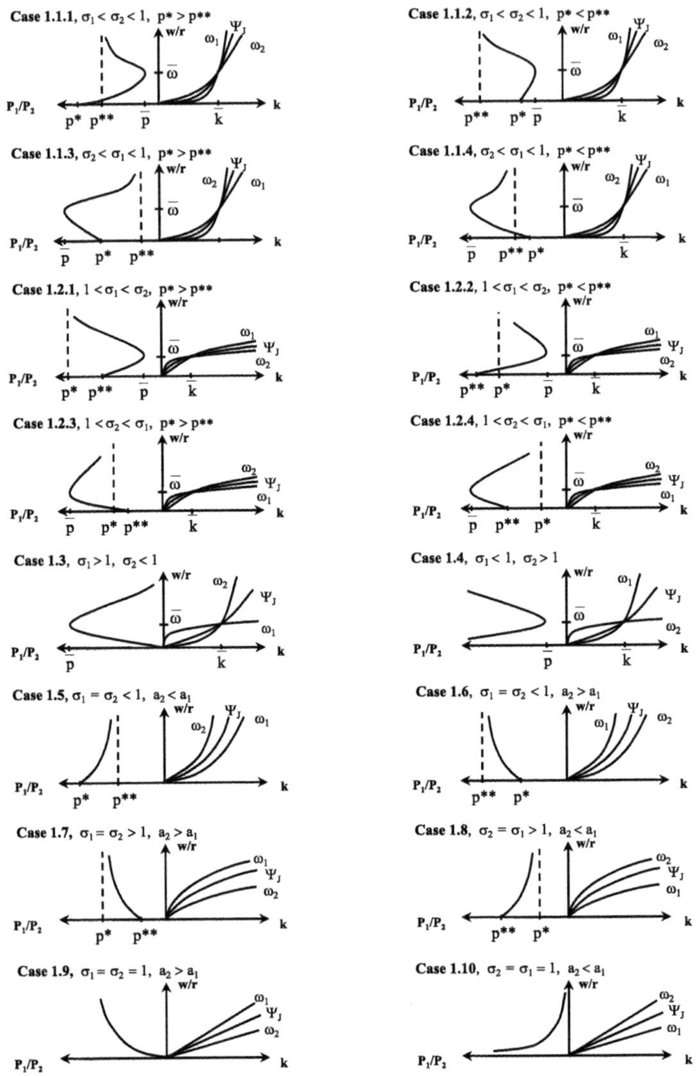


**Fig. 17.1** The **FPCP** correspondence $\mathbf{p}(\boldsymbol{\omega})$, (17.40), and the **Walrasian kernels FEFP** correspondence $\mathbf{k} = \boldsymbol{\Psi}_{\mathbf{J}}(\omega)$, (17.61–17.62, 17.82–17.83)

allows us to study the consequences of various demand-side specifications for the character of the momentary general equilibrium solutions and the evolution of two distinct macrodynamic systems. Intertemporal optimization should not be allowed to obscure and burden the analysis in this chapter on basic two-sector dynamics.

Hence, we use the "neoclassical/classical" monetary saving functions:

$$(I) \quad S = sY, \quad 0 < s < 1; \qquad (II) \quad S = s_K \delta_K Y = s_K r K, \quad 0 < s_K \leq 1 \tag{17.48}$$

The saving assumptions are alternatively expressed by the expenditure condition for commodity 1 (newly produced capital goods), cf. (17.19)

$$(I) \quad P_1 Y_1 = sY; \; y/P_1 = \lambda_{L_1} y_1/s, \; y/P_2 = \lambda_{L_2} y_2/(1-s) \tag{17.49}$$

$$(II) \quad P_1 Y_1 = s_K \delta_K Y, \quad y/P_1 = \lambda_{L_1} y_1 / s_K \delta_K, \quad \delta_K \neq 0 \tag{17.50}$$

and the equivalence of the value of consumer good production and consumption expenditures, $P_2 Y_2 = (1-s)Y$, $P_2 Y_2 = (1 - s_K \delta_K)Y$, follows obviously from (17.19), (17.49–17.50). Using (17.49–17.50), (17.21), (17.15), (17.7–17.8), (17.4–17.5), the *saving ratios*, $s$ and $s_K$, can alternatively be *decomposed* as,

$$(I) \quad s = P_1 Y_1 / Y = \delta_K \lambda_{K_1} / \epsilon_{K_1} = \delta_L \lambda_{L_1} / \epsilon_{L_1} \tag{17.51}$$

$$(II) \quad s_K = P_1 Y_1 / (rK) = s / \delta_K = \lambda_{K_1} / \epsilon_{K_1} \tag{17.52}$$

### *General Equilibrium*

The *demand side* of the economy is summarized by, respectively,

$$(I) \quad \frac{P_1 Y_1}{P_2 Y_2} = \frac{s}{1-s}, \qquad (II) \quad \frac{P_1 Y_1}{P_2 Y_2} = \frac{s_K \delta_K}{1 - s_K \delta_K}. \tag{17.53}$$

The *supply side* of the economy—operating under constant returns to scale with full, (17.7–17.8), efficient factor utilization (17.13–17.17)—is always summarized by

$$\frac{P_1 Y_1}{P_2 Y_2} = \frac{P_1 L_1 y_1}{P_2 L_2 y_2} = \frac{L_1 \epsilon_{L_2}}{L_2 \epsilon_{L_1}} = \frac{\lambda_{L_1} \epsilon_{L_2}}{\lambda_{L_2} \epsilon_{L_1}} = \frac{K_1 \epsilon_{K_2}}{K_2 \epsilon_{K_1}} = \frac{\lambda_{K_1} \epsilon_{K_2}}{\lambda_{K_2} \epsilon_{K_1}} \tag{17.54}$$

Hence, *competitive general equilibrium* (**CGE**) states (*Walrasian* equilibria), with market clearing prices on the commodity/factor markets and Pareto efficient endowments allocation, require, respectively,

$$(I) \quad \frac{s}{1-s} = \frac{\lambda_{L_1} \epsilon_{L_2}}{(1 - \lambda_{L_1}) \epsilon_{L_1}} = \frac{\lambda_{K_1} \epsilon_{K_2}}{(1 - \lambda_{K_1}) \epsilon_{K_1}}, \tag{17.55}$$

$$(II) \quad \frac{s_K \delta_K}{1 - s_K \delta_K} = \frac{\lambda_{L_1} \epsilon_{L_2}}{(1 - \lambda_{L_1}) \epsilon_{L_1}} = \frac{\lambda_{K_1} \epsilon_{K_2}}{(1 - \lambda_{K_1}) \epsilon_{K_1}}. \tag{17.56}$$

From (17.55–17.56), we have, cf. (17.51–17.52),

$$(I) \quad \lambda_{L_1} = \frac{s\,\epsilon_{L_1}}{s\,\epsilon_{L_1} + (1-s)\epsilon_{L_2}}, \quad \lambda_{K_1} = \frac{s\,\epsilon_{K_1}}{s\,\epsilon_{K_1} + (1-s)\epsilon_{K_2}} \tag{17.57}$$

$$(II) \quad \lambda_{L_1} = \frac{s_K \epsilon_{L_1}(1-\epsilon_{L_2})}{s_K \epsilon_{L_1} + (1-s_K)\epsilon_{L_2}}, \quad \lambda_{K_1} = s_K \epsilon_{K_1} \tag{17.58}$$

Next, from (17.57–17.58) and (17.51–17.52), we get,

$$(I) \quad \delta_L = s\,\epsilon_{L_1} + (1-s)\,\epsilon_{L_2}, \quad \delta_K = s\,\epsilon_{K_1} + (1-s)\,\epsilon_{K_2} \tag{17.59}$$

$$(II) \quad \delta_L = \frac{s_K \epsilon_{L_1} + (1-s_K)\epsilon_{L_2}}{1 + s_K(\epsilon_{L_1} - \epsilon_{L_2})}, \quad \delta_K = \frac{\epsilon_{K_2}}{1 + s_K(\epsilon_{K_2} - \epsilon_{K_1})} \tag{17.60}$$

Finally, by (17.21) and (17.59–17.60), we obtain, $\forall k \in R_+$, $\forall \omega \in \Omega$, (17.14)

$$(I) \quad k = \frac{\omega\,\delta_K}{\delta_L} = \frac{\omega[s\,\epsilon_{K_1} + (1-s)\,\epsilon_{K_2}]}{s\,\epsilon_{L_1} + (1-s)\,\epsilon_{L_2}} = \Psi_I(\omega) \tag{17.61}$$

$$(II) \quad k = \frac{\omega\,\delta_K}{\delta_L} = \frac{\omega\,\epsilon_{K_2}}{s_K\,\epsilon_{L_1} + (1-s_K)\,\epsilon_{L_2}} = \Psi_{II}(\omega) \tag{17.62}$$

The *formulas* of $\mathbf{\Psi}_J$ (17.61–17.62) are "*reduced form*" expressions derived from the "*structural equations*" of the respective systems, $J = I, II$, which *relate* the *endogenous* two-sector **general equilibrium** *values* (solutions) of the *wage-rental ratio*, $\boldsymbol{\omega} = \boldsymbol{w}/\boldsymbol{r}$, to the exogenous *factor endowments* (aggregate capital-labor) *ratio*, $\mathbf{k} = \mathbf{K}/\mathbf{L}$. Then, having obtained ($\boldsymbol{\omega}$) from (17.61–17.62), we can go back through (17.57–17.60), (17.18) to get the associated *general equilibrium* values of *all other* endogenous variables (sector outputs, allocation fractions of inputs, income shares, relative commodity prices).

The "reduced form" expressions (17.61–17.62) were represented in equivalent forms, Uzawa (1961, p.43), Uzawa (1963, p.108), Drandakis (1963, p.220), Inada (1963, p.124), Burmeister and Dobell (1970, p.123), Gandolfo (1980, p.487). However, the technology representation in (17.61–17.62) by the *bounded* output elasticities $\epsilon_{L_i}(\epsilon_{K_i})$ is intuitively and mathematically convenient in further economic analysis of $\Psi_J$. Incidentally, let it here be noted that our *two-sector framework* fully *encompasses one-sector* growth models. If the two industries have the same production function, $f_1 = f_2$, then the Walrasian **kernels**, $\mathbf{\Psi}_J$, (17.61–17.62) coincide with the last expression for the wage-rental curves (17.11).

*General Equilibria and the Factor Endowment-Factor Price Correspondence*

The *competitive general equilibrium* (**CGE**) *functions*, $\mathbf{\Psi}_J(\boldsymbol{\omega})$, $J = I, II$—and their *graphs*, as loci of timeless general equilibrium values and as trajectories of motion—are of paramount importance for inquiring into the statics, comparative statics, and dynamics of two-sector economies, and they will be called the *factor endowment-factor price* (**FEFP**) *correspondence*. Alternatively, a CGE function $\boldsymbol{\Psi}_J$ may be dubbed the *Walrasian kernel*, since it selects in the Edgeworth box diagram the relevant *Walrasian equilibrium allocation* as a specific allocation (*point*) within the *core* of the *contract curve*, cf. Mas-Colell et al. (1995, p.654). The graph of a Walrasian *kernel* $\boldsymbol{\Psi}_J$ constitutes the seed/nucleus elements of Walrasian allocations, since the *subset* of CGE components $(\boldsymbol{\omega}, \boldsymbol{k})$ *generates* the remaining components of Walrasian allocations (product prices and sectorial factor allocation and production). The *locus* of the Walrasian kernel, $\mathbf{k} = \boldsymbol{\Psi}_J(\boldsymbol{\omega})$, effectively *links* the *Pareto optimal allocations* [changing contract curves of expanding Edgeworth boxes] to the relevant *Walrasian* equilibrium *price vector*, $(p, \omega)$ [on the locus of the **FPCP** *correspondence* $p(\omega)$]. Regarding the *shape* of the graphs of $\Psi_J$, it is evident that if *both* substitution elasticities are *larger* than one, $\sigma_i > 1,\ i = 1, 2$, then the numerator (denominator) expression in (17.61–17.62) will increase (decrease), cf. $\epsilon_{K_i}, \epsilon_{L_i}$ (17.12), which always ensures that the two CGE (Walrasian) **kernels** $\boldsymbol{\Psi}_J$ are *monotonically* increasing. When one or both $\sigma_i$ are *less* than one, $\sigma_i < 1$, only a detailed examination will reveal the *global* and *local* shape of the graphs. To this end, we calculate **CGE** *elasticities* and summarize results in:

**Lemma 17.2** *The elasticity,* $E_I(k, \omega) = (d\Psi_I/d\omega)(\omega/\Psi_I),\ \forall \omega \in \Omega$, *of the* **CGE** *function* $\Psi_I(\omega)$, *(17.61), is given by*

$$E_I(k, \omega) = 1 + (1/\delta_L)\left[\lambda_{L_1}\epsilon_{K_1}(\sigma_1 - 1) + \lambda_{L_2}\epsilon_{K_2}(\sigma_2 - 1)\right] \tag{17.63}$$

$$= \frac{1}{\delta_L}\left[\frac{s}{\delta_K}(1-s)(\epsilon_{K_1} - \epsilon_{K_2})^2 + \lambda_{L_1}\epsilon_{K_1}\sigma_1 + \lambda_{L_2}\epsilon_{K_2}\sigma_2\right] > 0 \tag{17.64}$$

*By the global positivity (17.64),* $\boldsymbol{\Psi}_I(\boldsymbol{\omega})$ *is monotonic, and the inverse* $\boldsymbol{\omega}(\boldsymbol{k}) = \boldsymbol{\Psi}_I^{-1}(\boldsymbol{k})$ *exists (not necessarily in closed form) for every* $k \in [0, \infty]$.

*The elasticity,* $E_{II}(k, \omega)$*, of the CGE function* $\boldsymbol{\Psi}_{II}(\boldsymbol{\omega})$*, (17.62), is given by*

$$E_{II}(k, \omega) = \sigma_2 + \frac{s_K\epsilon_{L_1}[\epsilon_{K_2}(1-\sigma_2) - \epsilon_{K_1}(1-\sigma_1)]}{s_K\epsilon_{L_1} + (1-s_K)\epsilon_{L_2}} \tag{17.65}$$

$$= \frac{s_K\epsilon_{L_1}(\epsilon_{K_2} - \epsilon_{K_1} + \epsilon_{K_1}\sigma_1) + (1 - s_K\epsilon_{K_1})\epsilon_{L_2}\sigma_2}{s_K\epsilon_{L_1} + (1-s_K)\epsilon_{L_2}} \gtrless 0 \tag{17.66}$$

*By (17.66),* $\Psi_{II}(\omega)$ *is not unfailingly monotonic, and* $\boldsymbol{\Psi}_{II}^{-1}(\boldsymbol{k})$ *will not always exist as a single-valued inverse mapping, but the necessary and sufficient condition for a monotonic* $\Psi_{II}(\omega)$ *is a positive numerator of (17.66). The latter is ensured by the traditional global sectorial capital intensity ranking, cf. (17.66).*

$$\forall \omega \in \Omega:\ k_2(\omega) > k_1(\omega) \Leftrightarrow \epsilon_{K_2} > \epsilon_{K_1} \Leftrightarrow \epsilon_{L_1} > \epsilon_{L_2}. \tag{17.67}$$

*A sufficient condition for* $E_{II}(k, \omega) > 0$ *is, cf. (17.65–17.66),*

$$\forall \omega \in \Omega : \quad \sigma_1(\omega) + \sigma_2(\omega) \geq 1. \tag{17.68}$$

***Proof*** The capital intensity (17.67) was given in Uzawa (1961, p.44) for the special case $s_K = 1$. The substitution elasticity conditions (17.68) were derived in Drandakis (1963, p.222). The generalized conditions (17.66), (17.64) were proved in Jensen (1994, p.128, p.144); here proof of Lemma 16.1 in Chap. 16; see Gandolfo (1980, p.488). □

The CGE elasticity of $\Psi_{II}$ (17.62) was introduced by Drandakis (1963, p.221).

The elasticity (17.63) is always *positive*, cf. (17.10), that is, the Walrasian kernel (17.64) is monotonic increasing with any common, strictly quasiconcave homogeneous utility function for all economic agents, Hahn (1965, p.343).

*Multiple Walrasian Equilibria and Shape of Walrasian Kernels*

By admitting "*paradoxical*", cases of *negative elasticity* of the CGE function $\Psi_{II}$ (17.62), the demand pattern (expenditure shares), (17.53, *II*), creates an analog to the Giffen paradox of a positive price elasticity for a demand function of a budget-constrained utility-maximizing consumer. However, the general equilibrium paradox is more difficult to "decompose" and to formulate succinctly than the partial (consumer) equilibrium paradox, because both supply side (with two industries) and demand-side effects determine the sign of the CGE elasticities. The latter can sometimes be positive even with zero intrasectorial substitution elasticities $\sigma_i = 0$, cf. (17.64), while the ranking (17.67) is decisive for the sign of (17.66) with $\sigma_i = 0$. The paradoxical sign of price elasticities in the Giffen and the CGE case are only *local* properties, restricted to a finite part of endowment space, cf. Lemma 17.3 and Wold (1952, p.100–103).

But a local region with *negative* sign of (17.66) and *positive* sign elsewhere implies that at least *three* CGE values of the *wage-rental* ratio $w/r$ in this *local* region can coexist with a *constant* (exogenous) factor *endowment* ratio $K/L$. This phenomenon has been *interpreted* as creating both a CGE "uniqueness" problem and a "dynamic causality" problem, cf. "multiple equilibria" in Burmeister and Dobell (1970, p.113): "*uniqueness of static (momentary) equilibrium at all times* and *causality* are equivalent concepts in two-sector models".

As the circumstances of *multiple* wage-rental ratios are elusive, the subject matter is carefully explained for the classical case to eliminate these purported problems from two-sector growth models. The possibilities for the coexistence of two CGE values of $\omega$ with the same $k$ must involve the following conditions. Raising the common $\omega$ will certainly increase both sectorial capital-labor ratios $k_i$ ("intrasectorial substitution effect"). Hence, the two $k_i$ must differ, and the allocation fractions $\lambda_{L_i}$ must be distinct for $k$ to remain unchanged, cf. (17.9). As the supply side is the same for (17.64) and (17.66), the demand side and hence output composition are crucial for the actual local multiplicity of $\omega$ in the classical case (17.62, 17.66).

With unchanged $k$, a larger $w/r$ evidently implies a smaller (larger) factor income share of capital $\delta_K$ (labor, $\delta_L$), cf. hyperbola (17.21), which reduces (increases) the demand for capital good $Y_1$ (consumer good $Y_2$). We have already mentioned that negative CGE elasticity is only possible with both $\sigma_i$ less than one. The latter implies that the *intrasectorial* substitution effects may be *small* and that changes in output composition will be accomplished by *intersectorial* substitution (factor reallocations, factor mobility).

With $\sigma_1 < 1$, it is seen from (17.58), (17.12) that $\lambda_{K_1}$ decreases and so does $\lambda_{L_1} = (k/k_1)\lambda_{K_1}$, (17.10), for constant $k$. Thus, sector 1 loses both factors, and its production declines, as did its demand, whereas sector 2 expands. Accordingly, the *output* composition (ratio) $Y_1/Y_2$ *falls.*

With the sectorial "capital intensity" assumption, $k_1 > k_2$, and larger $w/r$, the *price* ratio $(P_1/P_2)$ *falls*, cf. (17.36). With both $(Y_1/Y_2)$ and $(P_1/P_2)$ reduced, the expenditure *share* $(P_1Y_1)/(P_2Y_2)$ *falls,* as it also must as a consequence of a smaller $\delta_K$, cf. hyperbola (17.53, *II*); thus, with $k_1 > k_2$ and small $\sigma_i$, it is consistent with CGE to have both *lower* and *higher* wage-rental ratios for a *constant* overall capital-labor ratio. [Incidentally, constant overall saving ratios do not allow for such necessary change in expenditure shares, cf. (17.53, *I*), hence the sign in (17.64)].

Now if we keep the small $\sigma_i$ and just change the sectorial ranking $k_2 > k_1$, then all the implications of a larger $w/r$ will again be those mentioned above, except that here the *price* ratio $(P_1/P_2)$ will *increase*. But with *constant* endowments $K/L$, the output ratio $(Y_1/Y_2)$ and the price ratio $(P_1/P_2)$ *cannot* move in *opposite* directions and preserve competitive general equilibrium states. It violates profit maximization (Pareto efficiency in production), cf. Arrow (1971, p.260); or just consider tangents to the transformation curve in a diagram of two outputs with the concavity assumptions, (17.2); see also Wan (1971, p.124–127).

The large shifts to another Walrasian equilibrium allocation can be associated with "*big push*" and coordinated investments as a basis for industrialization, as done by, for example, Murphy et al. (1989a, p.540, 1989b, p.1004): "we chiefly associate the big push with multiple equilibria of the economy and interpret it as a switch from the cottage production equilibrium to industrial equilibrium". Although the *static big push* (factor reallocation with constant endowment) and the *dynamic big push* (pace of factor endowment accumulation) are related phenomena, they are distinct, as seen below in section "The Dynamic Systems and the Evolution of Two-Sector Economies". The big-push ("*take-off*") issues are mentioned here to indicate the theoretical/empirical scope of the Walrasian kernel in the abstract CGE two-sector growth model. For extensive treatment of CGE locus, see Balasko (1988).

**Example 17.1** The widely used numerical case of multiple wage-rental ratios has been the special classical case of $s_K = 1$ and the CES sector technologies, cf. Uzawa (1961, p.45), Burmeister (1968, p.198), Burmeister and Dobell (1970, p.127):

$$y_1 = f_1(k_1) = 0.001(k_1^3 + 7^{-4})^{1/3}; \quad y_2 = f_2(k_2) = (k_2^3 + 1)^{1/3}$$

The CES parameter values of $a_i$, $\sigma_i$, $\gamma_i$ can be retrieved, (17.24), as

$$a_1 = 0.9996, \quad a_2 = 0.5 \quad \sigma_1 = \sigma_2 = 0.25 \quad \gamma_1 = 0.001 \quad \gamma_2 = 1.26$$

Although $a_1$ is extreme, other values might do as well; what matters is that both $\sigma_i$ are much less than 0.5, cf. (17.68). Note that multiple CGE values of $\omega$ for a given $k$ have nothing to do with factor intensity reversals, cf. (17.34), as the sectorial $\sigma_i$ are here identical, cf. Fig. 17.1, Case 1.5. *Multiple* CGE with $\Psi_{II}$ may occur on both sides of the *reversal point* in Cases 1.1.1–1.1.4, but only where $k_1 > k_2$. ▽

From the discussion above and the quoted literature on two-sector growth models, a *cardinal* methodological *issue* becomes manifest: Is *non-monotonicity* (allowing *multiple* values of $w/r$ for any locally given range of $K/L$) of the *CGE functions* $\Psi_J$ an insuperable *dilemma* for economic *disaggregation*, rigorous mathematical construction, and *solution* of *static* and *dynamic* competitive *general equilibrium* models?

In theoretical and empirical scientific work, it often happens that instead of deducing "effects from causes", we wish to find the "causes from the effects". Thus, despite multiple Walrasian equilibria occurring locally with a non-monotonic Walrasian kernel $\Psi_{II}$, the latter as an FEFP correspondence, $k = \Psi_{II}(\omega)$, always allows us to go back from any observed wage-rental ratio to a *unique* capital-labor ratio. That three different $\omega$-values can be related by $\Psi_{II}(\omega)$ to the same $k$, is no problem, as each $\omega$ determines other *distinct* properties (output prices, etc.) of *each* CGE allocation. But evidently, an "exogenous" (endowment) variable like $(k)$ is *not* necessarily a convenient "*state*" variable in solving the static or dynamic equations of a Walrasian two-sector economy. To insist on always using $(k)$ as a state variable is just defective mathematical procedure, and the purported "causality" problem (in the literature quoted above and in the introduction) mathematically disappears by *adopting* the *wage-rental ratio* $\omega$ as a substitute state variable. "Keine Hexerei, nur Behendigkeit" (no black magic, only cunning).

Moreover, by observing the **FEFP** and **FPCP** correspondences in Fig. 17.1, it is intuitively not surprising that the *wage-rental ratio*, $(\omega)$, turns out to be the *key variable* ("parametrization") to *describe* and unlock the *dynamics* in two-sector growth models: the *factor price ratio* $(\omega)$ is the critical *intrinsic* link (variable) connecting *factor markets* (endowments) and *commodity markets*.

Indeed, as we will see, even with a monotonic $\Psi_I(\omega)$, (17.64), the endowment ratio ($k$) will in most cases be an intractable dynamic state variable.

*General Equilibrium Allocations with CES Technologies*
***CD-case*** From (17.32) with $\sigma_i = 1$ and (17.57–17.60), we get

$$(I) \quad \delta_K = a_2 - s\,(a_2 - a_1)\,, \qquad \delta_L = 1 - a_2 + s\,(a_2 - a_1) \tag{17.69}$$

$$(II) \quad \delta_K = \frac{a_2}{1 + s_K(a_2 - a_1)}, \qquad \delta_L = \frac{1 - a_2 + s_K(a_2 - a_1)}{1 + s_K(a_2 - a_1)} \tag{17.70}$$

$$(I) \quad \lambda_{L_1} = \frac{s(1 - a_1)}{1 - a_2 + s(a_2 - a_1)}, \qquad \lambda_{K_1} = \frac{s a_1}{a_2 - s(a_2 - a_1)} \tag{17.71}$$

$$(II) \quad \lambda_{L_1} = \frac{s_K(1 - a_1)a_2}{1 - a_2 + s_K(a_2 - a_1)}, \qquad \lambda_{K_1} = s_K a_1, \tag{17.72}$$

Then, (17.61–17.62) and (17.69–17.70) give linear *competitive general equilibrium* (CGE) relations between the factor endowment ratio and the wage-rental ratio:

$$(I) \qquad k = \Psi_I(\omega) = \frac{\omega \delta_K}{\delta_L} = \omega \cdot \frac{a_2 - s\,(a_2 - a_1)}{1 - a_2 + s\,(a_2 - a_1)} = \nu_I\,\omega \tag{17.73}$$

$$(II) \qquad k = \Psi_{II}(\omega) = \frac{\omega \delta_K}{\delta_L} = \frac{\omega a_2}{1 - a_2 + s_K\,(a_2 - a_1)} = \nu_{II}\,\omega \tag{17.74}$$

The Walrasian **kernels** $\boldsymbol{\Psi_J}$ (17.73–17.74) are located *between* **CD** $\omega_i$-lines, (17.32). From (17.16), (17.37), (17.22), (17.73–17.74), we get, with $\omega(k) = \Psi_J^{-1}(k)$, $J = I, II$,

$$k_i\,[\omega(k)] = \frac{a_i \nu_J}{1 - a_i} \cdot k; \quad y_i = f_i\,(k_i\,[\omega(k)]) = \gamma_i \left[\frac{a_i \nu_J}{1 - a_i}\right]^{a_i} k^{a_i} \tag{17.75}$$

$$(I - II) : E\,(Y_1/Y_2, k) = E\,(y_1/y_2, k) = a_1 - a_2;\; E\,(P_1/P_2, k) = a_2 - a_1 \tag{17.76}$$

To recapitulate, our Walrasian—or Menger/Wieser, Brems (1986, p.190–193)—*general equilibria* of two-sector economies with CD technologies display (irrespective of the demand side) *constancy* of sectorial output elasticities (cost shares), factor allocation fractions, and factor income distributions.

Certainly, the distributional outcomes (17.69–17.70) are no surprise with $\sigma_i = 1$, but *global invariance* (17.71–17.72) of *sectorial factor allocation* fractions emphasizes the bifurcation ("knife edge") status of the CD functional form. Although the sectorial capital-labor ratios (17.75), wage-rental ratios (17.32), and the factor endowment ratio $k$ are changing, they all change at the same rate and the allocation fractions are unchanged, cf. (17.71–17.72). The general equilibrium ***invariance*** of the "occupational industrial structure", $\lambda_{L_i}(k)$, is evidently ***counterfactual*** consequences of CD sector technology assumptions. The allocation fraction invariances (irrespective of steady states or not) apply to other general equilibrium systems of multisectorial ($J = I, ., N$) economies with CD technologies, see Dhrymes (1962, p.268). CD assumptions serve us mainly in providing an important benchmark case within the CES family.

***CES case*** From (17.57–17.60), (17.33), we get

$$(I)\ \delta_K = s\left(1 + c_1\omega^{1-\sigma_1}\right)^{-1} + (1-s)\left(1 + c_2\omega^{1-\sigma_2}\right)^{-1} \tag{17.77}$$

$$= \frac{1 + (1-s)c_1\omega^{1-\sigma_1} + sc_2\omega^{1-\sigma_2}}{1 + c_1\omega^{1-\sigma_1} + c_2\omega^{1-\sigma_2} + c_1c_2\omega^{2-\sigma_1-\sigma_2}}, \qquad \delta_L = 1 - \delta_K \tag{17.78}$$

$$(II)\ \delta_K = \frac{1 + c_1\omega^{1-\sigma_1}}{1 + (1+s_K)c_1\omega^{1-\sigma_1} + (1-s_K)c_2\omega^{1-\sigma_2} + c_1c_2\omega^{2-\sigma_1-\sigma_2}}, \tag{17.79}$$

$$(I)\ \lambda_{L_1} = \frac{1 + c_2\omega^{1-\sigma_2}}{1 + \frac{1-s}{s}\frac{c_2}{c_1}\omega^{\sigma_1-\sigma_2} + \frac{c_2}{s}\omega^{1-\sigma_2}}, \qquad \lambda_{K_1} = \frac{1 + c_2\omega^{1-\sigma_2}}{\frac{1}{s} + \frac{1-s}{s}c_1\omega^{1-\sigma_1} + c_2\omega^{1-\sigma_2}} \tag{17.80}$$

$$(II)\ \lambda_{L_1} = \frac{1}{1 + \frac{1-s_K}{s_K}\frac{c_2}{c_1}\omega^{\sigma_1-\sigma_2} + \frac{c_2}{s_K}\omega^{1-\sigma_2}}, \qquad \lambda_{K_1} = \frac{s_K}{1 + c_1\omega^{1-\sigma_1}} \tag{17.81}$$

and hence finally by (17.77–17.79)

$$(I) \quad k = \Psi_I(\omega) = \frac{\omega\delta_K}{\delta_L} = \frac{\omega^{\sigma_1+\sigma_2} + sc_2\omega^{1+\sigma_1} + (1-s)c_1\omega^{1+\sigma_2}}{sc_1\omega^{\sigma_2} + (1-s)c_2\omega^{\sigma_1} + c_1c_2\omega} \tag{17.82}$$

$$(II) \quad k = \Psi_{II}(\omega) = \frac{\omega\delta_K}{\delta_L} = \frac{\omega^{\sigma_1+\sigma_2} + c_1\omega^{1+\sigma_2}}{s_Kc_1\omega^{\sigma_2} + (1-s_K)c_2\omega^{\sigma_1} + c_1c_2\omega} \tag{17.83}$$

**Lemma 17.3** *The **CES** graphs of the **Walrasian kernels**, $\boldsymbol{\Psi}_J$, $J = I, II$, (17.82–17.83), are located between the monotonic CES $\omega_i$-curves, (17.32), and for any value of the saving ratios, $s$ and $s_K$, the graphs of $\Psi_J$ pass through the intersection (reversal) point, (17.34), which is entirely determined by the technology parameters. For any size of the sectorial substitution elasticities, $\sigma_i, i = 1, 2$, the CGE functions, $\boldsymbol{\Psi}_J$, have the limit properties:*

$$\lim_{\omega\to 0} \Psi_J(\omega) = 0, \ \lim_{\omega\to\infty} \Psi_J(\omega) = \infty; \quad J = I, II \tag{17.84}$$

$$\lim_{\omega\to 0} \Psi_J(\omega)/\Psi_J'(\omega) = 0, \ \lim_{\omega\to\infty} \Psi_J(\omega)/\Psi_J'(\omega) = \infty \tag{17.85}$$

*With (17.82–17.83), the **CGE** elasticities (17.64), (17.66) have finite limits as follows:*

$$\sigma_1 < 1,\ \sigma_2 < 1 \quad : \quad \lim_{\omega \to 0} E_J(k, \omega) = \lim_{\omega \to \infty} E_J(k, \omega) = \max\{\sigma_1, \sigma_2\} \tag{17.86}$$

$$\sigma_1 > 1,\ \sigma_2 > 1 \quad : \quad \lim_{\omega \to 0} E_J(k, \omega) = \lim_{\omega \to \infty} E_J(k, \omega) = \min\{\sigma_1, \sigma_2\} \tag{17.87}$$

$$\sigma_i > 1 > \sigma_j \quad : \quad \lim_{\omega \to 0} E_I(k, \omega) = \lim_{\omega \to \infty} E_I(k, \omega) = 1 \tag{17.88}$$

$$\sigma_1 > 1 > \sigma_2 \quad : \quad \lim_{\omega \to 0} E_{II}(k, \omega) = 1, \quad \lim_{\omega \to \infty} E_{II}(k, \omega) = \sigma_2 \tag{17.89}$$

$$\sigma_2 > 1 > \sigma_1 \quad : \quad \lim_{\omega \to 0} E_{II}(k, \omega) = \sigma_2, \quad \lim_{\omega \to \infty} E_{II}(k, \omega) = 1 \tag{17.90}$$

***Proof*** The verification of the logical economic test (for any $s$ and $s_K$) of the passage of $\Psi_J(\omega)$ through the reversal point follows by inserting $\bar{\omega}$, (17.34), into (17.82–17.83), which gives $\bar{k}$ (17.34) identically. The limits (17.84–17.85) are seen immediately from (17.82–17.83). The limits (17.86–17.90) follow from the formula, $E_J(k, \omega) = \Psi_J'(\omega)\omega/\Psi_J(\omega)$, by straightforward calculations. These finite limits are due to the same exponents in the *dominating* polynomials of the numerator and the denominator. For $\sigma_i = 1$, formulas (17.77–17.83) are reduced to (17.69–17.74). □

Without technical progress, the "*conditions of economic progress* are self-evident" to Walras (1954, p.386). Besides additional labor services, "*capital goods* must evidently be created out of savings before their services can become available for use" (p.387). Saving (investment) rates, labor supplies, and the *macrodynamic* role of the *capital* good (*machinery*) in the *two industries* now need to be carefully examined.

## The Dynamic Systems and the Evolution of Two-Sector Economies

The equations of *factor accumulation* for neoclassical and classical two-sector growth models with flexible sector technologies are formally given, Uzawa (1963, p.106), by ($\delta$ is the depreciation rate of capital),

$$dL/dt \equiv \dot{L} = nL, \tag{17.91}$$

$$dK/dt \equiv \dot{K} = Y_1 - \delta K = Ly_1\lambda_{L_1} - \delta K = L\left\{f_1(k_1)\lambda_{L_1} - \delta k\right\}. \tag{17.92}$$

In the general equilibrium models of two-sector economies, $k_1$ and $\lambda_{L_1}$ are, with (17.64) through $\omega$ (17.13), ***uniquely*** determined by the ***factor*** endowments ***ratio*** $k$, cf. (17.61), (17.62). Hence, the accumulation equations (17.91–17.92) become genuine ***autonomous*** (time invariant) ***differential equations*** in the state variables $L$ and $K$ and represent a standard ***homogeneous dynamic system***,

$$\dot{L} = Ln \equiv L\,\mathfrak{f}(k), \tag{17.93}$$

$$\dot{K} = L\left\{f_1(k_1[\Psi_J^{-1}(k)])\lambda_{L_1}[\Psi_J^{-1}(k)] - \delta k\right\} \equiv L\,\mathfrak{g}_J(k); \quad J = I, II. \tag{17.94}$$

As $\mathfrak{g}_J(k)$, (17.94), are intricate functions of $k$, we rewrite $\mathfrak{g}_J(k)$ in alternative forms by (17.92), (17.48–17.50), (17.20–17.21), cf. Burmeister and Dobell (1970, p.111), Wan (1971, p.119), Gandolfo (1980, p.490),

$$\dot{K} = sY/P_1 - \delta K = Ls(\omega + k)f_1'(k_1) - \delta K = L\,k\left\{\frac{sf_1'(k_1)}{\delta_K} - \delta\right\} = L\,\mathfrak{g}_I(k) \tag{17.95}$$

$$\dot{K} = s_K\delta_K Y/P_1 - \delta K = s_K Kr/P_1 - \delta K = L\,k\{s_K f_1'(k_1) - \delta\} = L\,\mathfrak{g}_{II}(k) \tag{17.96}$$

From the ***governing*** functions $\mathfrak{g}_J(k)$, (17.95–17.96), $J = I, II$, the ***director*** functions, $h_J(k) \equiv \mathfrak{g}_J(k) - k\,\mathfrak{f}(k)$, of (17.93–17.94) that control $dk/dt \equiv \dot{k}$ become,

$$\dot{k} = h_I(k) = k\left[\frac{sf_1'\left(k_1[\omega(k)]\right)}{\delta_K[\omega(k)]} - (n+\delta)\right]; \quad \omega(k) = \Psi_I^{-1}(k) \tag{17.97}$$

$$\dot{k} = h_{II}(k) = k\left[s_K f_1'\left(k_1[\omega(k)]\right) - (n+\delta)\right]; \quad \omega(k) = \Psi_{II}^{-1}(k) \tag{17.98}$$

The neoclassical demand side (savings) was not affected by factor income distribution, cf. (17.48). However, to succinctly express and decompose the governing functions of capital accumulation (17.95), the bounded variable $\delta_K(k)$ is mainly a formal auxiliary term helpful in evaluating concrete cases.

The ***dynamic systems*** (17.97–17.98) in $k$ are difficult to evaluate ***quantitatively*** and are generally intractable; for example, if $\sigma_1 \neq \sigma_2$, then, $k = \Psi_I(\omega)$, (17.82) cannot be inverted in closed form (although $\Psi_I^{-1}$ exists). But $k = \Psi_J(\omega)$, (17.61–17.62), are ***continuously differentiable*** functions of ($\omega$), and ***dynamics*** in ($k$) can, whenever convenient, be ***converted*** into ***dual autonomous dynamics*** in ($\omega$):

$$\dot{\omega} = \frac{\dot{k}}{dk/d\omega} = \frac{h_J(k)}{dk/d\omega} = \frac{h_J(\Psi_J[\omega])}{\Psi_J'(\omega)} \equiv \boldsymbol{\hbar}_J(\omega) \tag{17.99}$$

Hence, we get, cf. (17.97–17.98),

$$\hbar_I(\omega)=\frac{\Psi_I(\omega)}{\Psi_I'(\omega)}\left[\frac{sf_1'[k_1(\omega)]}{\delta_K(\omega)}-n-\delta\right]=\frac{\omega}{E_I(k,\omega)}\left[\frac{sf_1'[k_1(\omega)]}{\delta_K(\omega)}-n-\delta\right] \tag{17.100}$$

$$\hbar_{II}(\omega)=\frac{\Psi_{II}(\omega)}{\Psi_{II}'(\omega)}\left[s_K f_1'[k_1(\omega)]-n-\delta\right]=\frac{\omega}{E_{II}(k,\omega)}\left[s_K f_1'[k_1(\omega)]-n-\delta\right] \tag{17.101}$$

With **CES** technologies, we have, from (17.100–17.101), (17.77), (17.40),

$$\hbar_I(\omega)=\frac{\Psi_I(\omega)}{\Psi_I'(\omega)}\left[\frac{s\gamma_1 a_1^{\sigma_1/(\sigma_1-1)}\left(1+c_1\omega^{1-\sigma_1}\right)^{1/(\sigma_1-1)}}{s\left(1+c_1\omega^{1-\sigma_1}\right)^{-1}+(1-s)\left(1+c_2\omega^{1-\sigma_2}\right)^{-1}}-(n+\delta)\right] \tag{17.102}$$

$$\hbar_{II}(\omega)=\frac{\Psi_{II}(\omega)}{\Psi_{II}'(\omega)}\left[s\gamma_1 a_1^{\sigma_1/(\sigma_1-1)}\left(1+c_1\omega^{1-\sigma_1}\right)^{1/(\sigma_1-1)}-(n+\delta)\right] \tag{17.103}$$

with $\Psi_I(\omega)$ and $\Psi_{II}(\omega)$ given in (17.82–17.83).

### *Existence and Uniqueness of the Steady States—Or Persistent Economic Growth Per Capita*

The complete set (family) of $k(t)$ solutions to the dynamic systems (17.97–17.98) is *qualitatively* described and classified in:

**Theorem 17.1** *The neoclassical and classical two-sector growth models (17.91–17.98) have no positive, stationary* $k(t)$*-solution* [$k(t)=0$ *is attractor*], *iff*

$$\forall k>0:\ (I)\quad \bar{\beta}_1<([n+\delta]/s)\delta_K(k),\qquad (II)\quad \bar{\beta}_1<(n+\delta)/s_K \tag{17.104}$$

*and have at least one steady state [ray path in* $(L,K)$*-space], iff, cf. (17.3)*

$$\exists k>0:\ (I)\ ([n+\delta]/s)\delta_K(k)\in J_1,\ (II)\ (n+\delta)/s_K\in J_1,\ J_1=\left[\underline{\beta}_1,\bar{\beta}_1\right] \tag{17.105}$$

*The stationary capital-labor ratios* $\forall t: k(t)=\kappa$ *are obtained by*

$$(I)\quad f_1'[k_1(\kappa)]=([n+\delta]/s)\delta_K(\kappa),\qquad (II)\quad f_1'[k_1(\kappa)]=(n+\delta)/s_K \tag{17.106}$$

*With positive (17.66) and (17.105), the root of* $h_{II}(k)$ *(17.106) is a unique attractor. With existence (17.105), a sufficient condition for a unique root of* $h_I(k)$ *is*

$$\forall k > 0 : E(h_I(k)/k, k) < 0 \Leftrightarrow -\lambda_{K_1}\epsilon_{L_1}\sigma_1 - \lambda_{K_2}[\epsilon_{L_1} + \epsilon_{L_2}(\sigma_2 - 1)] < 0 \tag{17.107}$$

*With existence assured (17.105), a weak sufficient condition for a unique neoclassical attractor by (17.106) is*

$$\forall \omega \in \Omega : E_I(\delta_K, \omega) \geq 0 \quad \Leftrightarrow \quad \forall \omega \in \Omega : E_I(k, \omega) \geq 1, \tag{17.108}$$

*and strong sufficient conditions for satisfying (17.107) are*

$$\forall \omega \in \Omega : \quad \sigma_2(\omega) \geq 1, \tag{17.109}$$

$$\forall \omega \in \Omega : \sigma_1(\omega) = \sigma_2(\omega) \wedge \epsilon_{L_1} > \epsilon_{L_2} \Leftrightarrow k_2(\omega) > k_1(\omega) \tag{17.110}$$

*The time paths of the growth model solutions,* $k(t)$*, display persistent growth—* $\lim_{t\to\infty} k(t) = \infty$*—if and only if*

$$\forall k > 0 \ : \ (I) \ \ \underline{\beta}_1 > ([n+\delta]/s)\,\delta_K(k), \ (II) \ \ \underline{\beta}_1 > (n+\delta)/s_K \tag{17.111}$$

***Proof*** The family of solutions to (17.97–17.98) depends entirely on the *shape* of the *director* function, $h(k)$, and the *number* of roots of $h(k)$. The existence of nonzero roots requires that, respectively, $([n+\delta]/s)\delta_K(k)$ and $[n+\delta]/s_K$ belong to the range of $f_1'$ as stated in (17.105). If no root exists, we have either the case (17.104) with origo as attractor or the case (17.111) with persistent growth.

If it exists, a unique attractor in the interval stated in (17.105) always occurs with a global negative sign of the elasticity, $E(h(k)/k, k) < 0$, that can be derived from (17.97); the necessary and sufficient condition for such a negative sign is shown explicitly in (17.107); cf. Jensen (1994, p.138, p.129); here Remark 15.3 in Chap. 15. A bit stronger, sufficient condition (17.108) is that $\delta_K(k)$ is monotonically increasing or constant, which is a special way of satisfying the criterion (17.107). The elasticity conditions in (17.108) are equivalent by $k = \omega\delta_K/(1-\delta_K)$, cf. (17.61).

The size of the CGE elasticity $E_I(k, \omega)$, (17.108), implies that the monotonic Walrasian kernel $\Psi_I(\omega)$, (17.61), is concave in the *diagrams* of Fig. 17.1. Similarly, the parameter condition $\sigma_2 \geq 1$, (17.109), implies that the CGE two-sector dynamics operates (through sector output and allocation of factors) such that the consumer good industry will release/absorb resources conducive to reaching and maintaining the steady state $k = \kappa$, if $\kappa > 0$ exists. □

***CES case*** The *qualitative* properties of the family of *solutions* $k(t)$ in the *Walrasian general equilibrium* growth models with CES sector technologies are summarized in:

**Proposition 17.1** *For the two-sector growth models (17.91–17.94) with CES sector technologies, the sufficient conditions for the existence of at least one positive steady-state solution are [no positive, attractive, steady-state solution* $\kappa$ *(17.106) exists with the RHS inequalities of (17.112–17.114) reversed]:*

$$(I) \qquad \sigma_1 < 1,\ \sigma_2 < 1: \qquad \bar{\beta}_1 = \gamma_1 a_1^{\frac{\sigma_1}{\sigma_1 - 1}} > (n+\delta)/s \tag{17.112}$$

$$(I) \qquad \sigma_1 < 1,\ \sigma_2 > 1: \qquad \bar{\beta}_1 = \gamma_1 a_1^{\frac{\sigma_1}{\sigma_1 - 1}} > (n+\delta) \tag{17.113}$$

$$(II) \qquad \sigma_1 < 1: \qquad \bar{\beta}_1 = \gamma_1 a_1^{\frac{\sigma_1}{\sigma_1 - 1}} > (n+\delta)/s_K \tag{17.114}$$

*With* $\sigma_1 \leq 1$ *(sufficient condition), persistent growth of* $k(t)$ *is impossible.*

*With* $\sigma_1 > 1$*, necessary and sufficient conditions for* $\lim_{t\to\infty} k(t) = \infty$ *are:*

$$(I) \qquad \sigma_1 > 1,\ \sigma_2 > 1: \qquad \underline{\beta}_1 = \gamma_1 a_1^{\frac{\sigma_1}{\sigma_1 - 1}} > (n+\delta)/s \tag{17.115}$$

$$(I) \qquad \sigma_1 > 1,\ \sigma_2 < 1: \qquad \underline{\beta}_1 = \gamma_1 a_1^{\frac{\sigma_1}{\sigma_1 - 1}} > (n+\delta) \tag{17.116}$$

$$(II) \qquad \sigma_1 > 1: \qquad \underline{\beta}_1 = \gamma_1 a_1^{\frac{\sigma_1}{\sigma_1 - 1}} > (n+\delta)/s_K \tag{17.117}$$

*except that (17.116) is occasionally not sufficient for small initial values.*

***Proof*** The proof proceeds with the dual version, $\hbar_J(\omega)$. The term $\Psi_J(\omega)/\Psi_J'(\omega)$ has no influence on these limit analyses, cf. Lemma 17.3.

Ad $\sigma_1 < 1$: The large fraction in the bracket (17.102) goes to zero for $\omega \to \infty$; hence, there are no permanent increasing solutions of $\omega(t)$. If (17.112–17.113) are satisfied, then the large fraction passes at least once monotonically through the constant when $\omega$ goes from zero to infinity. The difference $s$ in the constant comes from the denominator taking values 1 or $s$ for $\omega \to 0$, depending on the size of $\sigma_2$. If the inequalities are reversed, then $\hbar_I(\omega)$ is negative.

Ad $\sigma_1 > 1$: The large fraction in the bracket (17.102) goes to infinity for $\omega \to 0$. If and only if (17.115–17.116) are satisfied, then the large fraction eventually remains above the constant when $\omega$ goes from zero to infinity. The difference $s$ in the constant comes from the denominator going toward the values 1 or $s$ for $\omega \to \infty$, depending on the size of $\sigma_2$. Hence, $\hbar_I(\omega)$ is positive for large values of $k$. If the inequalities are reversed, then $\hbar_I(\omega)$ eventually becomes negative. The necessary conditions (17.115), (17.117) are also sufficient, as $k_I(k)$ and $k_{II}(k)$ are, with respectively $\sigma_2 > 1$ and $\sigma_1 > 1$, monotonically decreasing, cf. (17.109), (17.68), but remain above RHS values in (17.115), (17.117).

The conditions (17.114), (17.117) follow from (17.103), (17.26–17.27), cf. (17.104), (17.111). □

Proposition 17.1 shows explicitly that the *global existence issues* of any *steady-state* or *persistent* growth depend on the *size* of the *key parameters*: $\sigma_i$, $a_1$, $\gamma_1$, $s$, $s_K$, $n$, $\delta$. While the *accumulation* parameters ($s$, $s_K$, $n$, $\delta$) play some roles, the *fundamental* role of the *technology* parameters in the *capital* good sector ($\sigma_1$, $\gamma_1$, $a_1$) for deciding the types of the long-run *evolution* in the **CGE** growth models *complies* somehow with *observation* and economic *intuition*, as well as confirms the strategic importance ascribed to *capital good industries* by economic historians and the general public, cf. Mahalanobis (1955) and Rosenberg (1963).

The most important parameter in Proposition 17.1 is the *substitution elasticity* in the *capital good* sector, $\sigma_1$—with the CD technology as the critical bifurcation value. The "*total productivity*" parameter $\gamma_1$ in the *capital good* sector matters in all the stated conditions (17.112–17.117), and they can all be violated by giving $\gamma_1$ any value between 0 and $\infty$. It is beyond the scope of this chapter to enter a discussion about the dispersion of $\sigma_1$ and $\gamma_1$, cf. Easterly and Fischer (1995) and Prescott (1998). But if we restrict $\gamma_1 = 1$ and if $\sigma_1 \simeq 2$, then (17.115) will usually be satisfied for other relevant parameters, in particular with high saving rates. Note that when *persistent* growth conditions (17.115–17.117) hold, then multiple Walrasian equilibria are *ruled out*, since then classical $\Psi_{II}$ is [by $\sigma_1 > 1$, cf. (17.66), (17.68)] also monotonic in Fig. 17.1. Evidently, the critical role in Proposition 17.1 is played by $\sigma_1$ rather than $\sigma_2$. Nevertheless, the conclusions in Proposition 17.1 contrast sharply with the early standard literature on two-sector growth models.

This key role played by the *technology* of the *capital good* industry has failed to be properly recognized in the "mainstream" literature of the two-sector growth models. In an extensive summary of results, Stiglitz and Uzawa (1969, p.407) reported, (e.g., in the case of neoclassical saving) that *sufficient conditions* for *uniqueness* and *stability* of (convergence to) balanced (*steady-state*) growth paths are: "1. substitution elasticity in each sector greater than or equal to one; 2. capital intensity in capital goods sector ≤ capital intensity in consumption goods sector".

These *two* conditions are *neither necessary nor sufficient* for the long-run steady-state family. Indeed, a very high value of $\sigma_1$ would *preclude* the *existence* of steady-state growth, cf. (17.115–17.116); the "capital intensity condition" cannot be maintained when $\sigma_1 \neq \sigma_2$, cf. (17.34), and does not address the global (rather than local stability and uniqueness) issue of existence of a steady-state or persistent growth of $k(t)$. In fact, *none* of the *standard uniqueness* conditions (17.108–17.110)—or even (17.107)—*ensures existence* of a steady state. A high $\sigma_1$ as well as a high $\sigma_2$ contributes to satisfying the *monotonicity* properties (17.107), but if $\sigma_1$ is high enough ($\sigma_1 \simeq 2$), then *no* steady state exists, and we have *persistent* growth (17.115–17.116) in neoclassical/classical growth models.

It is evident from a comparison of the conditions (17.115–17.116) that (17.116) is easier to satisfy. In this situation, with $\sigma_2 < 1$, persistent growth of $k(t)$ goes together with a long-run declining *relative price* of the capital good, cf. (17.46), Fig. 17.1, Case 1.3. The persistent growth of (17.115), (17.117), however, can be accompanied by either relatively rising or relatively falling capital good prices, cf. Fig. 17.1, Case 1.2.1–1.2.4; see *motion* along the *trajectories* $\boldsymbol{\Psi}_J$ in Fig. 17.4.

### *Singularities, Multiple Equilibria: Phase Portraits*

It has been maintained that two-sector growth models occasionally have $k(t)$ solutions asymptotically approaching a limit cycle, with perpetual oscillations in the capital-labor ratio, cf. Inada (1963, p.112). Burmeister and Dobell (1970, p.131) followed up on this possibility in the classical growth model with CES technologies. We will briefly show that such dynamic anomalies are not consequences of multiple Walrasian equilibria.

If the *classical* (always monotonic) function $h_{II}(k)$ does not locally exist, [which can only occur for: $\sigma_1 < 1$, (17.68), and $E_{II}(k, \omega) < 0$, (17.66)], the *dual* (which always exists) director function $\hbar_{II}(\omega)$ must *take over* the dynamic control of the classical solutions, $\omega(t)$ and $k(t)$, and outline the motions on the CGE trajectories $\Psi_{II}$. However, the *dual* function $\hbar_{II}(\omega)$ has *singularities* of its own that need concise explanation.

The diagrammatic exposition in Fig. 17.2 gives the relevant *graphs* of $\hbar_{II}(\omega)$, (17.101), (17.103) for the *three* possible cases. The Walrasian kernel $\Psi_{II}$ in *local* regions with the multiple Walrasian equilibria is shown at the top of Fig. 17.2. The derivatives $\Psi'_{II}(\omega)$ and $f'_1(\omega)$ follow next; the three possible locations of the steady-state value, $\omega_\kappa$ (compared with $\omega^*$ and $\omega^{**}$), and their associated *sign* of the *bracket* expression (17.101) give—combined with the *sign* of $\Psi'_{II}$—the actual *sign* of $\dot{\omega}$ along the $\omega$-axis, cf. (17.101, 17.99). Such *collection* of sign *information* makes the Cases 1–3 on the left side of Fig. 17.2, which represents the *complete* description of possible graphs for the *dual* $\hbar_{II}(\omega)$. These three *phase diagrams* of $\dot{\omega}$ immediately give the corresponding solutions $\omega(t)$ on the right side of Fig. 17.2.

Note that in contrast to the *critical* values, $\omega_\kappa$, one of the *singularities* of $\hbar_{II}(\omega)$ [with vertical tangents at $\omega^*$ or $\omega^{**}$] will be approached with *infinite* speed and reached in finite time, as illustrated in Fig. 17.2. Note also that solutions starting between $\omega^*$ and $\omega^{**}$ cannot leave this interval, and solutions outside cannot enter it. Accordingly, no time path connects the multiple Walrasian equilibria allowed for in the classical growth model; that is, these *three* different momentary (static) general equilibrium states (for a given $k$) remain *isolated* from each other over time.

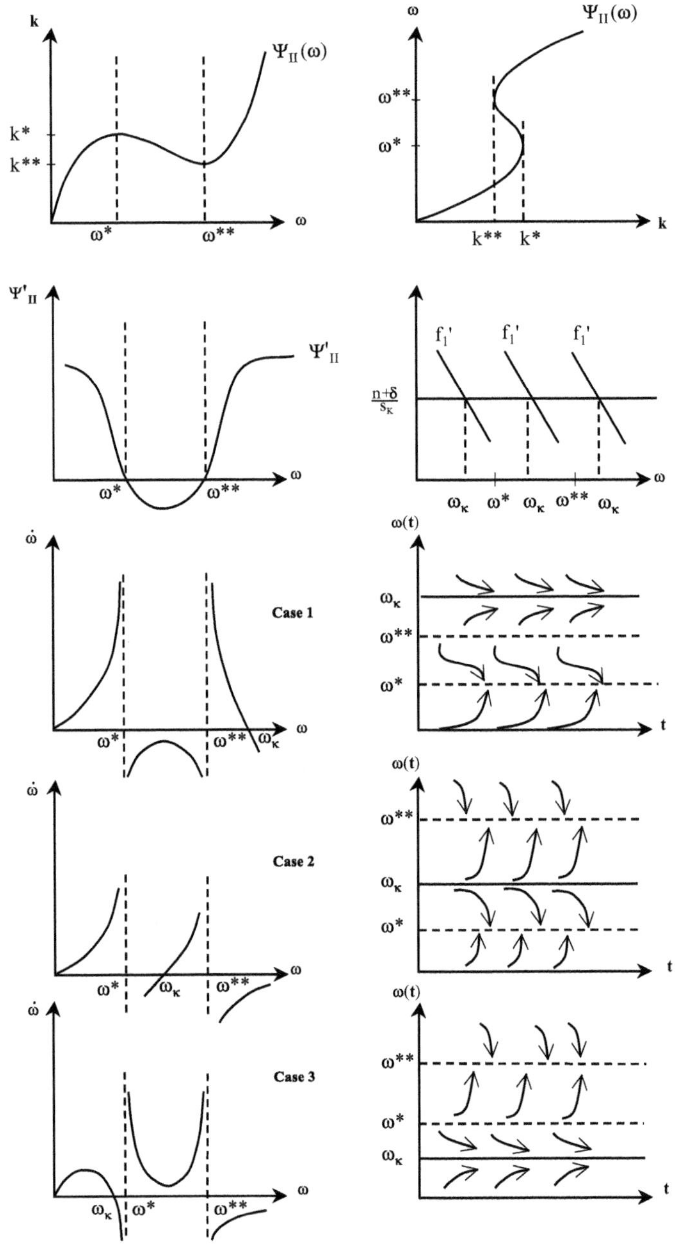


**Fig. 17.2** Dual dynamics and singularities of the classical dual director function, $\hbar_{II}(\omega)$, (17.101), of $\dot{\omega}$, cf. (17.99)

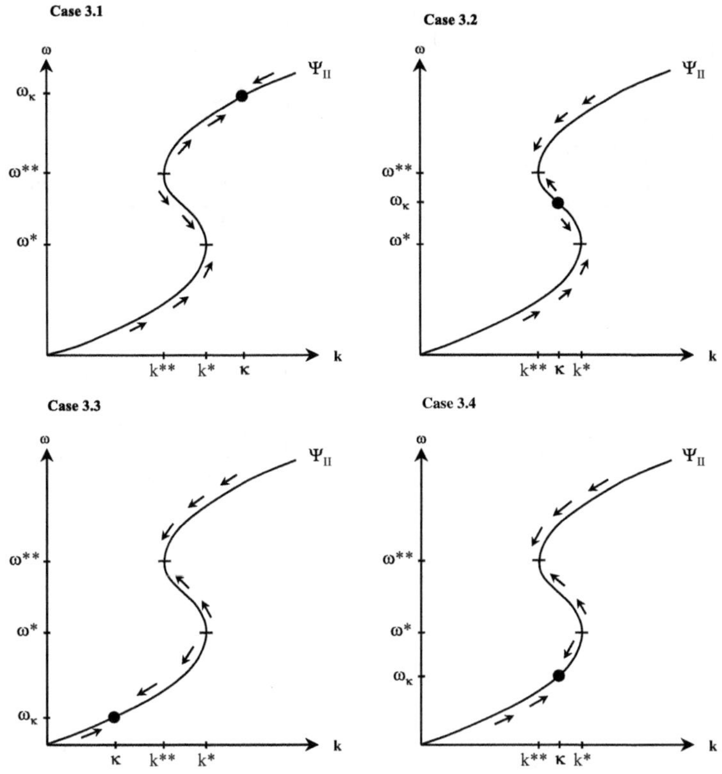


**Fig. 17.3** The Walrasian kernel, $\Psi_{II}$, (17.62), with trajectories of, $[k(t), \omega(t)]$, as given by the dual director function : $\hbar_{II}$, (17.101)

The *trajectories* of the family of solutions $\omega(t)$, as well as the attractors/repellers from Cases 1–3, Fig. 17.2, are depicted on their *Walrasian kernels* $\Psi_{II}$ in Fig. 17.3, Cases 3.1–3.3. The associated time paths and attractors of $k(t)$ are indicated in Fig. 17.3. Case 3.4 compared with Case 3.2 shows very different $k(t)$ solutions with similar initial $k(0)$ but distinct initial $\omega(0)$ values.

The *conclusion* from analyzing the graphs of the dual functions $\hbar_{II}(\omega)$ is evidently that *limit cycles* of $\omega(t)$ [and $k(t)$] as well as instantaneous *jumps* (discontinuous trajectories) for the *sectorial* capital-labor ratios $k_i(t)$, Burmeister and Dobell (1970, p.135), do *not occur* at all in a *classical* growth model with *multiple* CGE, given the assumptions hitherto upheld.

### *Neoclassical Steady States and Development Traps*

Let us again consider the *neoclassical* (proportional) saving case with a monotonic Walrasian kernel, $\Psi_I$. The shape of $h_I$ (17.97), $\hbar_I$ (17.100), (17.102) and

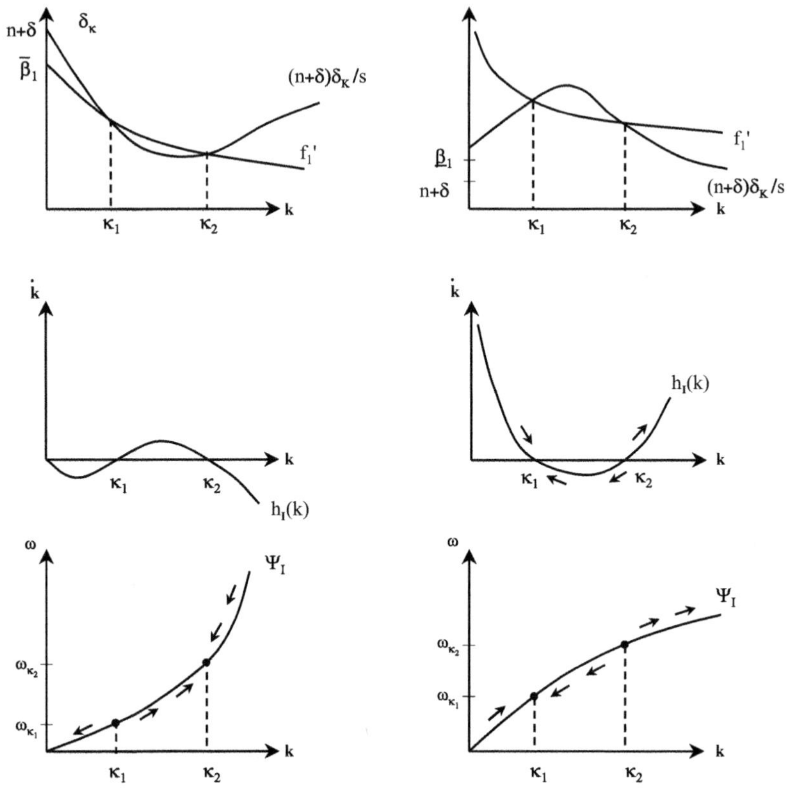


**Fig. 17.4** Singularities of neoclassical director function, $h_I(k)$, (17.97), and with the conditions: (17.113) and (17.116)

the character of its ***singularities*** critically depend on the respective ***locations*** of the graphs of the ***bounded*** function $\delta_K$ and the ***monotonically*** decreasing $f_1'$.

With $\sigma_1 < 1$, a constellation of $\delta_K(k)$ and $f_1'(k)$ (and associated $h_I$) is shown on the left side of Fig. 17.4, which give two steady states, of which the lower one is a repeller. This case [with intercepts relaxing the inequality, e.g. (17.113), cf. (17.136)], giving an ***implosion*** interval below $\kappa_1$, is hardly of much practical interest. The conditions for a ***unique*** positive attractive root $h_I$—either with $\sigma_1 < 1$ (17.132–17.133) or otherwise not satisfying the inequalities (17.115–17.116)—were already given above (17.107), (17.108), (17.110).

With $\sigma_1 > 1$ and satisfying the necessary condition (17.116), persistent growth may yet fail (when also multiple small roots of $h_I$ exist) for a range of ***initial values*** around a lower attractor. Cases like (17.116) and (17.135) are illustrated on the right side of Fig. 17.4. Thus, with current factor allocation and initial endowments below $\kappa_2$, a take-off into persistent growth is impossible, even though the necessary technological opportunities for sustaining the growth process are available in the capital good sector. The present trap problem is *not* caused by *multiple* Walrasian equilibria, cf. (17.66).

To avoid the stalemate of the *development trap* (initial values between $\kappa_1$ and $\kappa_2$), the remedy is to transfer adequate resources to the capital good sector, either by increasing (at least temporarily) the overall saving (investment) rate $s$ ("forced saving") and/or by imposing restraints on population growth, both of which contribute to lifting $h_I$ above the axis, see right side of Fig. 17.4. A larger TFP parameter of the capital good sector $\gamma_1$ may give a similar "big push" upward of $h_I$ in Fig. 17.4; cf. Murphy et al. (1989b), Parente and Prescott (1994), and Prescott (1998).

### *Persistent Growth and Asymptotic Growth Rates*

To complement the *persistent growth solutions* of the *state* variable $k(t)$ or $\omega(t)$ with *disaggregate* information about the general equilibrium *evolution* for *sectorial* and other endogenous per capita variables, we characterize the respective time paths by their *asymptotic growth rates* $[\hat{\omega}(t) \equiv \dot{\omega}/\omega(t)$, etc.]:

**Proposition 17.2** *With (17.115–17.117), the long-run growth rates of $k(t)$ and $\omega(t)$ in Walrasian two-sector growth models (17.91–17.103) with CES technologies are:*

$$(I) \quad \sigma_i > 1 \quad : \quad \lim_{t\to\infty} \hat{\omega} = \frac{s\underline{\beta}_1 - (n+\delta)}{\min\{\sigma_1, \sigma_2\}}; \qquad \lim_{t\to\infty} \hat{k} = s\underline{\beta}_1 - (n+\delta) \tag{17.118}$$

$$(II) \quad \sigma_i > 1 \quad : \quad \lim_{t\to\infty} \hat{\omega} = \frac{s_K\underline{\beta}_1 - (n+\delta)}{\min\{\sigma_1, \sigma_2\}}; \qquad \lim_{t\to\infty} \hat{k} = s_K\underline{\beta}_1 - (n+\delta) \tag{17.119}$$

*With (17.118–17.119), the long-run sectorial and per capita growth rates are:*

$$\lim_{t\to\infty} \hat{k}_i = \lim_{t\to\infty} \hat{y}_i = \lim_{t\to\infty} (w\hat{/}P_i) = \lim_{t\to\infty} (y\hat{/}P_i), \; i = 1, 2 \tag{17.120}$$

*where*

$$(I) \quad \sigma_1 > \sigma_2 > 1: \quad \lim_{t\to\infty} \hat{k}_1 = \frac{\sigma_1}{\sigma_2}[s\underline{\beta}_1 - (n+\delta)]; \qquad \lim_{t\to\infty} \hat{k}_2 = s\underline{\beta}_1 - (n+\delta) \tag{17.121}$$

$$(I) \quad 1 < \sigma_1 < \sigma_2: \quad \lim_{t\to\infty} \hat{k}_1 = s\underline{\beta}_1 - (n+\delta); \qquad \lim_{t\to\infty} \hat{k}_2 = \frac{\sigma_2}{\sigma_1}[s\underline{\beta}_1 - (n+\delta)] \tag{17.122}$$

$$(II) \quad \sigma_i > 1: \quad \lim_{t\to\infty} \hat{k}_1 = \frac{\sigma_1}{\sigma_2}[s_K\underline{\beta}_1 - (n+\delta)]; \qquad \lim_{t\to\infty} \hat{k}_2 = s_K\underline{\beta}_1 - (n+\delta) \tag{17.123}$$

*If only the capital good sector has a high substitution elasticity, we have*

$$(I)\ \sigma_1 > 1, \sigma_2 < 1: \quad \lim_{t\to\infty} \hat{\omega} = \lim_{t\to\infty} \hat{k} = \underline{\beta}_1 - (n+\delta) \tag{17.124}$$

$$(II)\ \sigma_1 > 1, \sigma_2 < 1: \quad \lim_{t\to\infty} \hat{\omega} = \frac{s_K\underline{\beta}_1 - (n+\delta)}{\sigma_2}; \qquad \lim_{t\to\infty} \hat{k} = s_K\underline{\beta}_1 - (n+\delta) \tag{17.125}$$

*With (17.124–17.125), the long-run sectorial and per capita growth rates are*

$$(I-II) \quad \lim_{t\to\infty} \hat{k}_1 = \lim_{t\to\infty} \hat{y}_1 = \lim_{t\to\infty} (\widehat{w/P_1}) = \lim_{t\to\infty} (\widehat{y/P_1}), \tag{17.126}$$

$$(I-II) \quad \lim_{t\to\infty} \hat{y}_2 = \lim_{t\to\infty} (\widehat{w/P_2}) = \lim_{t\to\infty} (\widehat{y/P_2}) = 0, \tag{17.127}$$

*where*

$$(I) \quad \lim_{t\to\infty} \hat{k_1} = \sigma_1[\underline{\beta}_1 - (n+\delta)]; \qquad \lim_{t\to\infty} \hat{k}_2 = \sigma_2[\underline{\beta}_1 - (n+\delta)] \tag{17.128}$$

$$(II) \quad \lim_{t\to\infty} \hat{k_1} = \sigma_1/\sigma_2\left[s_K\underline{\beta}_1 - (n+\delta)\right]; \quad \lim_{t\to\infty} \hat{k}_2 = s_K\underline{\beta}_1 - (n+\delta) \tag{17.129}$$

***Proof*** Proposition 17.2 follows immediately from Proposition 17.1: (17.115–17.117), combined with (17.100–17.101), (17.87–17.90), and next using (17.49–17.50), (17.32–17.33), (17.27), (17.19), and (17.13). Thus, by (17.100–17.101):

$$\lim_{t\to\infty} \hat{\omega} = [\lim_{\omega\to\infty} E_J(k,\omega)]^{-1}[s_J\underline{\beta}_1 - (n+\delta)]\ ;\ s_I = s,\ \ s_{II} = s_K$$

The **FEFP** correspondence $k = \Psi_J(\omega)$ next gives $\hat{k} = E_J(k,\omega)\hat{\omega}$; $\hat{k}_i = \sigma_i\hat{\omega}$ and $\hat{y}_i = \epsilon_{k_i}\hat{k}_i$ holds generally with **CES**. These relations and *limits* establish the relevant *asymptotic* (long-run) *growth rates* in Proposition 17.2. □

With both $\sigma_i > 1$, and $\sigma_1 \neq \sigma_2$, cf. Fig. 17.1, Cases 1.2.1–1.2.4, Cases 1.7.–1.8, the sectorial ranking of $\sigma_i$ is not critically important for the evolution of the "standard of living" (consumption per capita). The latter will continue to grow either way. The long-run growth rates of $\hat{k}$ and $\hat{k}_i$ in the classical model are the same, irrespective of $\sigma_2$. But if *maximum* growth of per *capita consumption* is the goal, then the *ranking* $\sigma_2 > \sigma_1 > 1$, cf. (17.121–17.122), with the highest $\hat{k}_2$ will be preferred—which contributes to mechanizing and maintaining the growth rate of the consumer goods and thereby increases the welfare per capita (17.120).

The growth scenario (17.124), (17.126–17.128) offers the most rapid [even unaffected by the saving parameter ($s$) ] expansion of the capital good industry and the overall capital-labor ratio. The relative prices of capital goods are declining, cf. Fig. 17.1, Case 1.3., and the capital stock will eventually be used in the production of machinery, but per capita consumption is bounded. Thus, an abnormal growth scenario with a neglected modernization of the consumer good industry evolving together with an "advanced" (highly mechanized) capital good industry is nevertheless within the scope of the neoclassical/classical two-sector growth model with **CES** parameters (17.124–17.125).

Some of our results resemble Rebelo (1991), but our capital good sector also employs *Labor*, and the class of persistent/endogenous growth solutions does *not* assume a *linear technology* for the core or *composite* capital good.

As to *empirical evidence*, the theoretical general equilibrium *predictions* of Proposition 17.2 tally with some observations and studies of *long-run growth* conducted by De Long and Summers (1991) and Jones (1994). In particular, high rates of *equipment* investment ("mechanization") are prime determinants for national growth performance (productivity, per capita growth).

We may tentatively use the sample statistics on growth and relative price series as evidence for regarding the Cases 1.2.3–1.2.4 in Fig. 17.1 as perhaps the most relevant overall choice for exhibiting the *historical record* of sectorial (industrial) *growth paths*. The parametric range of Case 1.8 is too narrow. *Cases* 1.2.3–1.2.4 imply (for smaller initial values) sectorial *reversals* of *capital-labor ratios* and *relative output prices*. Such *reversals* seem rather common and fit *historical descriptions* of the capital good industry as having the largest potential for increasing its capital-labor ratio. The production of *machinery* may *initially* be rather labor-intensive, but *eventually* becomes highly *mechanized* by making various *engines* (steam, combustion, electric) "*cheap* as well as *good*", cf. Mokyr (1990, p.87) ; on mechanization of the production processes, see Aghion and Howitt (1998, p.700). This supports *factor substitution* and mechanization subsequently in the consumer good industry.

In this way, the *capital good* (multi-purpose machinery/equipment) is a "*Lever of Riches*" (productivity and per capita growth) in *both sectors* with the *capital good industry* itself and its *technology parameters* being naturally of *primary importance* for the economic growth process.

The *Walrasian* two-sector growth models and Proposition 17.2 *confirm* this logic and demonstrate economically these *mutual* relations between *man* (Labor) and *machinery* (Capital) in the proper setting of a Walrasian *general equilibrium* framework.

## Final Comments

*Decentralization* with dispersion of factor endowment and decision-making authority is the main principle underlying the economic *assumption* of *competitive markets* with *individual* (profit, utility) *maximizing agents*. Some may find it regrettable that it is not always benevolent intentions that deliver good results. But one can argue, as did Adam Smith, that it is very important to understand that *private* interests may guide market processes and nevertheless lead to *social* good.

However, the competitive markets and the resource allocation were not yet explicitly *governed* by commodity and factor *prices*. The full recognition of a **price system**—and *several primary factors* rather than only *one* (land or labor)—as well as the concept of a **general competitive market equilibrium**, can be ascribed to Leon Walras. Momentary and moving equilibria of commodity and factor markets in "miniature *Walrasian* general equilibrium systems" have been the subject matter of our analyses of two-sector *growth models* and their *solutions*.

Walras completed his work in June 1900 with the vision that sometime "mathematical economics will rank with the mathematical sciences of astronomy and mechanics; and on that day justice will be done to our work", Walras (1954, p.48). The catching-up remains to be seen. However, several critical problems in basic *two-sector general equilibrium dynamics* have been resolved. Subjects of further research would be extensions of the *competitive* (Pareto efficient) *general equilibrium* (**CGE**) *dynamics* to *higher dimensions*.

**Acknowledgments** For many invaluable discussions and comments on an earlier draft, I am deeply indebted to Mogens Esrom Larsen, Institute for Mathematical Sciences, University of Copenhagen.

## Appendix: Asymptotic CGE Allocations

The *comparative static analysis* of exogenous factor endowment variations for *Walrasian equilibria* with CES technologies is helpful for the economic understanding of the stock evolution of the primary factors, when one of the outputs is a capital good. The economic understanding of static, comparative static, and dynamic analysis of Walrasian equilibria is inherently related.

The asymptotic factor allocations of two-sector general equilibrium economies with neoclassical/classical savings are calculated in Lemma 17.4:

**Lemma 17.4** *For the CES two-sector competitive general equilibrium economy, the limits of the factor allocation fractions and factor income shares are, with a demand-side specification according to* ***proportional*** *saving:*

$$\sigma_i \qquad k \to 0 \qquad\qquad k \to \infty \tag{17.130}$$

$$\sigma_1 < \sigma_2 < 1: \ \lambda_{L_1} \to 0\ \lambda_{K_1} \to s \quad \delta_K \to 1 \qquad \lambda_{L_1} \to s\ \lambda_{K_1} \to 0 \quad \delta_K \to 0 \tag{17.131}$$

$$1 > \sigma_1 > \sigma_2: \ \lambda_{L_1} \to 1\ \lambda_{K_1} \to s \quad \delta_K \to 1 \qquad \lambda_{L_1} \to s\ \lambda_{K_1} \to 1 \quad \delta_K \to 0 \tag{17.132}$$

$$\sigma_1 > \sigma_2 > 1: \ \lambda_{L_1} \to s\ \lambda_{K_1} \to 0 \quad \delta_K \to 0 \qquad \lambda_{L_1} \to 0\ \lambda_{K_1} \to s \quad \delta_K \to 1 \tag{17.133}$$

$$1 < \sigma_1 < \sigma_2: \ \lambda_{L_1} \to s\ \lambda_{K_1} \to 1 \quad \delta_K \to 0 \qquad \lambda_{L_1} \to 1\ \lambda_{K_1} \to s \quad \delta_K \to 1 \tag{17.134}$$

$$\sigma_1 > 1 > \sigma_2 : \quad \lambda_{L_1} \to 1 \; \lambda_{K_1} \to 0 \quad \delta_K \to 1\text{–}s \qquad \lambda_{L_1} \to 0 \; \lambda_{K_1} \to 1 \quad \delta_K \to s \tag{17.135}$$

$$\sigma_1 < 1 < \sigma_2 : \quad \lambda_{L_1} \to 0 \; \lambda_{K_1} \to 1 \quad \delta_K \to s \qquad \lambda_{L_1} \to 1 \; \lambda_{K_1} \to 0 \quad \delta_K \to 1\text{–}s \tag{17.136}$$

*and are, with* ***classical*** *saving,* $[\bar{\delta}_K \equiv 1/(1+s_K)]$*:*

$$\sigma_i \qquad k \to 0 \qquad k \to \infty \tag{17.137}$$

$$\sigma_1 < \sigma_2 < 1 : \quad \lambda_{L_1} \to 0 \; \lambda_{K_1} \to s_K \; \delta_K \to 1 \qquad \lambda_{L_1} \to 0 \; \lambda_{K_1} \to 0 \quad \delta_K \to 0 \tag{17.138}$$

$$1 > \sigma_1 > \sigma_2 : \quad \lambda_{L_1} \to 1 \; \lambda_{K_1} \to s_K \; \delta_K \to 1 \qquad \lambda_{L_1} \to 0 \; \lambda_{K_1} \to 0 \quad \delta_K \to 0 \tag{17.139}$$

$$\sigma_1 > \sigma_2 > 1 : \quad \lambda_{L_1} \to 0 \; \lambda_{K_1} \to 0 \quad \delta_K \to 0 \qquad \lambda_{L_1} \to 0 \; \lambda_{K_1} \to s_K \; \delta_K \to 1 \tag{17.140}$$

$$1 < \sigma_1 < \sigma_2 : \quad \lambda_{L_1} \to 0 \; \lambda_{K_1} \to 0 \quad \delta_K \to 0 \qquad \lambda_{L_1} \to 1 \; \lambda_{K_1} \to s_K \; \delta_K \to 1 \tag{17.141}$$

$$\sigma_1 > 1 > \sigma_2 : \quad \lambda_{L_1} \to 1 \; \lambda_{K_1} \to 0 \quad \delta_K \to \bar{\delta}_K \qquad \lambda_{L_1} \to 0 \; \lambda_{K_1} \to s_K \; \delta_K \to 0 \tag{17.142}$$

$$\sigma_1 < 1 < \sigma_2 : \quad \lambda_{L_1} \to 0 \; \lambda_{K_1} \to s_K \; \delta_K \to 0 \qquad \lambda_{L_1} \to 1 \; \lambda_{K_1} \to 0 \quad \delta_K \to \bar{\delta}_K \tag{17.143}$$

*If sector technologies have the same* $\sigma_i$*,* $i = 1, 2$*, then the limits of (17.131–17.136) become,* $[\overline{\lambda}_{L_1} \equiv sc_1/(sc_1 + (1-s)c_2), \overline{\lambda}_{K_1} \equiv sc_2/(sc_2 + (1-s)c_1)]$*:*

$$\sigma_i \qquad k \to 0 \qquad k \to \infty \tag{17.144}$$

$$\sigma_1 = \sigma_2 < 1 : \quad \lambda_{L_1} \to \overline{\lambda}_{L_1} \; \lambda_{K_1} \to s \quad \delta_K \to 1 \qquad \lambda_{L_1} \to s \; \lambda_{K_1} \to \overline{\lambda}_{K_1} \delta_K \to 0 \tag{17.145}$$

$$\sigma_1 = \sigma_2 > 1 : \quad \lambda_{L_1} \to s \; \lambda_{K_1} \to \overline{\lambda}_{K_1} \quad \delta_K \to 0 \qquad \lambda_{L_1} \to \overline{\lambda}_{L_1} \; \lambda_{K_1} \to s \; \delta_K \to 1 \tag{17.146}$$

*and (17.138–17.143) become* $[\widehat{\lambda_{L_1}} \equiv s_K c_1 / s_K c_1 + (1-s_K)c_2]$*:*

$$\sigma_i \qquad k \to 0 \qquad k \to \infty \tag{17.147}$$

$$\sigma_1 = \sigma_2 < 1 : \quad \lambda_{L_1} \to \widehat{\lambda_{L_1}} \; \lambda_{K_1} \to s_K \quad \delta_K \to 1 \qquad \lambda_{L_1} \to 0 \; \lambda_{K_1} \to 0 \; \delta_K \to 0 \tag{17.148}$$

$$\sigma_1 = \sigma_2 > 1 : \quad \lambda_{L_1} \to 0 \; \lambda_{K_1} \to 0 \quad \delta_K \to 0 \; \lambda_{L_1} \to \widehat{\lambda_{L_1}} \; \lambda_{K_1} \to s_K \; \delta_K \to 1 \tag{17.149}$$

***Proof*** Using (17.57–17.60, 17.77–17.81), most of the formulas follow directly from (17.33) and the rest via l'Hospital. □

The CGE implications of sectorial substitution elasticities (parameters) $\sigma_i$ by Lemma 17.4 can intuitively and succinctly be stated in words as:

**Proposition 17.3** *If both* $\sigma_i < 1$, *then the industry with the highest* $\sigma_i$ *will (asymptotically) completely absorb the abundant factor, but it will not necessarily entirely dispense with the relatively scarce factor.*

*If both* $\sigma_i > 1$, *then the industry with the highest* $\sigma_i$ *will (asymptotically) completely dispense with the scarce factor, but it will not necessarily entirely absorb the relatively abundant factor.*

*If* $\sigma_i > 1 > \sigma_j$, *then the industry with the higher* $\sigma_i$ *will (asymptotically) fully absorb the abundant factor and entirely dispense with the scarce factor.*

*If and only if* $\sigma_1 = \sigma_2$ *will the two industries asymptotically employ a fraction of both factors.*

## Bibliography


Aghion P, Howitt P (1998) Endogenous Growth Theory. The MIT Press, Cambridge, MA and London, England

Arrow KJ (1971) Essays in The Theory of Risk–Bearing. North–Holland

Arrow KJ, Chenery HB, Minhas BS, Solow RM (1961) Capital–Labour Substitution and Economic Efficiency. Review of Economics and Statistics 43:225–250

Balasko Y (1988) Foundations of the Theory of General Equilibrium. Academic Press Inc., New York

Brems H (1986) Pioneering Economic Theory 1630–1980. A Mathematical Restatement. The Johns Hopkins University Press, Baltimore

Burmeister E (1968) The Role of the Jacobian Determinant in the Two–Sector Model. Internt Econ Rev 9:195–203

Burmeister E, Dobell AR (1970) Mathematical Theories of Economic Growth. Macmillan, London

Caballé J, Santos MS (1993) On Endogenous Growth with Physical and Human Capital. J Political Economy 101:1042–67

De Long JB, Summers LH (1991) Equipment Investment and Economic Growth. Quarterly Journal of Economics 106:445–502

Dhrymes PJ (1962) A Multisectoral Model of Growth. Quarterly Journal of Economics 76:264–278

Dixit AK (1976) The Theory of Equilibrium Growth. Oxford University Press, Oxford

Dixit AK, Norman V (1980) Theory of International Trade: A Dual, General Equilibrium Approach. Cambridge University Press, U.K

Drandakis EM (1963) Factor Substitution in the Two–Sector Growth Model. Rev Econ Stud 30:217–28

Easterly W, Fischer S (1995) The Soviet Economic Decline. World Bank Economic Review 9:341–71

Galor O (1992) A Two–Sector Overlapping–Generations Model: A Global Characterization of the Dynamic System. Econometrica 60:351–386

Gandolfo G (1980) Economic Dynamics: Methods and Models, 2nd edn. North–Holland, Amsterdam

Gandolfo G (1997) Economic Dynamics. Springer Verlag, Berlin/New York

Goldin C, Katz LF (1998) The Origins of Technology–Skill Complementarity. Quarterly Journal of Economics 113:693–732

Hahn FH (1965) On Two–Sector Growth Models. Rev Econ Stud 32:339–46, or Sen (1970)

Hahn FH, Matthews RCO (1964) The Theory of Economic Growth: A Survey. Economic Journal 74:779–902

Inada K (1963) On a Two–Sector Model of Economic Growth: Comments and a Generalization. Rev Econ Stud 30:119–27

Inada K (1964) On the Stability of Growth Equilibria in Two–Sector Models. Rev Econ Stud 31:127–42

Jensen BS (1994) The Dynamic Systems of Basic Economic Growth Models. Kluwer Academic Publishers, Dordrecht

Jensen BS, Larsen ME (1987) Growth and Long–Run Stability. Acta Applicandae Mathematicae 9:219–237, Reprinted in Jensen (1994); here Chap. 1

Jensen BS, Wang C (1999) Basic Stochastic Dynamic Systems of Growth and Trade. Review of International Economics 7:378–402, here Chap. 27

Jensen BS, Richter M, Wang C, Alsholm PK (2001) Saving Rates, Trade, Technology, and Stochastic Dynamics. Review of Development Economics 5:182–204; here Chap. 22

Jones CI (1994) Economic growth and the relative price of capital. J Monetary Economics 34:359–82

Jones RW (1956) Factor Proportions and the Heckscher–Ohlin Theorem. Review of Economic Studies 24:1–10

Jones RW (1965) The Structure of Simple General Equilibrium Models. J Political Economy 73:557–72, or Bhagwati (1981)

Kemp MC (1969) The Pure Theory of International Trade and Investment. Prentice–Hall, New Jersey

Ladrón-de-Guevara A, Ortigueira S, Santos MS (1999) A Two–Sector Model of Endogenous Growth with Leisure. Review of Economic Studies 66:609–31

Mahalanobis PC (1955) The approach of operational research to planning in India. Sankhya: Indian Journal of Statistics 16:3–62

Mas-Colell A, Whinston MD, Green JR (1995) Microeconomic Theory. Oxford University Press, New York

Minhas BS (1962) The Homohypallagic Production Function, Factor Intensity Reversals, and the Heckscher–Ohlin Theorem. The Journal of Political Economy 70:138–156

Mokyr J (1990) The Lever of Riches: Technological Creativity and Economic Progress. Oxford University Press, New York

Murphy KM, Shleifer A, Vishny R (1989a) Income Distribution, Market Size, and Industrialization. Quarterly Journal of Economics 104:537–564

Murphy KM, Shleifer A, Vishny RW (1989b) Industrialization and the Big Push. The Journal of Political Economy 97:1003–1026

Parente SL, Prescott EC (1994) Barriers to Technology Adoption and Development. The Journal of Political Economy 102(2):298–321

Prescott EC (1998) Lawrence R. Klein Lecture 1997, Needed: A Theory of Total Factor Productivity. International Economic Review 39:525–551

Rebelo S (1991) Long–Run Policy Analysis and Long–Run Growth. Journal of Political Economy 99:500–521
Rosenberg N (1963) Capital Goods, Technology, and Economic Growth. Oxford Economic Papers 15:217–27
Solow RM (1961) Note on Uzawa's Two–Sector Model of Economic Growth. Rev Econ Stud 29:48–50, or Stiglitz (1969)
Stiglitz JE, Uzawa H (1969) Readings in the Modern Theory of Economic Growth. M.I.T. Press, Cambridge, Mass
Uzawa H (1961) On a Two–Sector Model of Economic Growth: I. Review of Economic Studies 29:40–47
Uzawa H (1963) On a Two–Sector Model of Economic Growth: II. Review of Economic Studies 30:105–18, Also in: Stiglitz and Uzawa (1969)
Walras L (1954) Elements of Pure Economics. George Allen and Unwin, London
Wan HY Jr (1971) Economic Growth. Harcourt Brace Jovanowich, New York
Wold H (1952) Demand Analysis. Almquist & Wiksell, Uppsala, or J. Wiley and Sons, N.Y., 1953

CHAPTER 18

# General Equilibrium Dynamics of Multi-sector Growth Models

## Introduction

Dynamics is concerned with calculating the motions of the widest variety of objects, and with deriving (computing) the implications (effects) of these motions. Its basic principles and logical structure have long been a model for other scientific disciplines. The domain of dynamics in physics (mechanics) have been extended tremendously on both macro- and microscopic scales, Pais (1986). In the discipline of economics, dynamics began in macroeconomics, in particular with business cycle and the basic one- and two-sector growth models. However, standard *microeconomic* (producer/consumer) theory is more naturally involved with decentralized mechanisms for resource allocation in static *multi-sector* modeling and *general equilibrium* dynamics. We may briefly refer to passages from important theoretical and empirical contributions to multi-sectoral model building.

Regarding the character of works in *applied general equilibrium analysis* (AGE-modelling), we quote Shoven and Whalley (1992, p.1):

> The central idea underlying this work is to convert the *Walrasian general equilibrium structure* (formalized in the 1950s by Arrow, Debreu, and others) from an abstract representation of an economy into realistic models of actual economies. Numerical, empirically based general equilibrium can then be used to evaluate concrete policy options by *specifying production and demand parameters* and incorporating data reflective of real economies.

With co-author:
MOGENS ESROM LARSEN, Department of Mathematics, University of Copenhagen, Denmark



B. S. Jensen, *The Elements and Dynamic Systems of Economic Growth and Trade Models*, https://doi.org/10.1007/978-3-031-52493-6_18

—and

> Most contemporary applied *general models* are *numerical analogs* of traditional *two-sector general equilibrium models* popularized by James Meade, Harry Johnson, Arnold Harberger, and others in the 1950s and 1960s. Earlier analytic work with these models has examined the distortionary effects of taxes, tariffs, and other policies, along with functional incidence questions.

Computation of general equilibria usually involves solving systems of nonlinear equations. Thus, according to Judd (1998, p.147,3):

> The Arrow-Debreu concept of general equilibrium reduces to finding a *price vector* at which *excess demand* is zero; it is the most famous nonlinear equation problem in economics.

—and

> The *computational general equilibrium* (CGE) literature is the most mature computational literature in economics.

Much of the *numerical* (algorithmic) methodology derives from the work of Scarf (1967), Scarf and Hansen (1973). Numerical approaches give *approximate solutions*; many papers on numerical methods offer little in the way of showing the qualitative dependence of the solutions upon critical parameter values. Obtaining analytical solutions in theorem-proof style is preferable wherever this is possible.

The *emphasis* in this chapter will be to provide a *conceptual framework* that supports *economic intuition* and offer a general and *unified analytical approach* to the mathematical procedures of obtaining the *static, comparative static* and *dynamic general equilibrium solutions* of an N-sector economy.

We extend the methodology and mathematical-economic analysis of two-sector dynamics, Jensen (2003); here Chap. 17, to the multi-sectorial dynamics of temporal *Pareto-efficient* labor and capital allocation/accumulation.

An important contributor to multi-sector generalizations of various macrodynamic models was Jorgenson (1961), who extended the input-output methods of Leontief to *dynamic input-output analysis*. In the *macro-planning* and *development* literature, our topic of multi-sector economies had another important contributor in Johansen (1974, p.1):

> It is a well-known fact that the *various sectors* of an economy do *not expand* in the *same proportion* in a process of economic growth. The flows of investment and new labor are not allocated proportionately to all production sectors. Existing quantities of *capital* and *labor* may be *reallocated* during the growth process. *Terms of trade* between the production sectors may *change* in a systematic way, and so on. Such considerations illustrate aspects of the economic growth process

which we shall attempt to explain and analyze within the framework of a *multi-sectoral growth model.*

Regarding structural analysis and *sectorial developments*, the three categories of Colin Clark were dealing with the reallocation of the labor force over the groups of industries: *primary* industries (agriculture, fisheries and forestry), *secondary* industries (manufacturing, handicraft, building and construction, mining, electric power production), *tertiary* industries (wholesale and retail commerce, transport, financial services and public administration), and globally observing, Clark (1951, p.365) that:

> by careful generalization of available facts to be the most important concomitant of economic progress, namely the movement of working population from agriculture to manufacture and from manufacture to commerce and services.

Concomitant *changes* in the *composition* of *demand*, e.g., the budget share of food (*Engel's law*, 1857) is confirmed by all surveys, Houthakker (1957).

Controversies related to "convergence" and "balanced growth" models as being incompatible with *structural change* and the process of economic development were given renewed attention in both the empirical and theoretical growth literature, Pasinetti (1981), Islam (1995), Echevarria (1997), Laitner (2000), Kongsamut et al. (2001), Meckl (2002). Patterns of sectorial industrial growth will here be obtained and shortly discussed.

As we consider the relationship between *resources, technology*, and *economic evolution*, we finally quote the historian Usher (1954, p.1):

> Economic history is concerned with the description and the analysis of the mutual transformations taking place between human societies and their environment. The *study* of *costs* and *prices* is *important*, and the *institutional structure* of organized social life demands careful *attention*, but the *basic problems* of *economic history* lie in the field of the *management* of *resources.* - The *quantitative* analysis of economic activities requires *study* of the processes and accomplishments of the *system* of *production* in *physical units* as well as in *value units.*

The chapter deals with *dynamic foundations* of multi-sector growth (MSG) models for closed (global) economies. We explain well-known empirical facts by modeling in terms of *basic microeconomic principles.* Section "Analytical Framework for Multi-sector Economies" presents an analytical framework with concepts, definitions, and various micro- and macroeconomic equivalence relations. Section "Relative Prices in Multi-sector Economies with CES Sector Technologies" studies the relationships between *factor prices* and *relative commodity prices.* In section "Preferences, Demand, and Expenditure Compositions of GDP", we analyze and derive GDP expenditure shares from some specific parametrizations of utility functions. Section "Walrasian General Equilibrium of Multi-sector Economies" uses a proper NIPA version of *Walras's law* to obtain the *Walrasian equilibrium* of the multi-sector economy, and we derive the *timeless* (static and comparative static) *competitive general equilibrium solutions* for all the variables as *distinct composite functions* of the *factor endowments.* In section "Dynamic Systems and Evolution of Multi-sector Economies", we analyze the *dynamic systems* and alternative *evolutions* of multi-sector *general equilibria.* Section "Persistent Growth and Asymptotic Growth Rates" gives various asymptotic sectorial growth rates of persistently growing multi-sector economies. Our final comments are found in section "Final Comments".

## Analytical Framework for Multi-sector Economies

### *The Supply Side, Technology, and Efficient Factor Allocation*

Consider an economy consisting of $N$ *industries* (sectors), and let *sector 1* be a capital good industry. Sector *technologies*, $F_i(L_i, K_i)$, are described by nonnegative smooth concave homogeneous production functions with *constant returns* to scale in labor and capital, $i = 1, \cdots, N$,

$$Y_i = F_i(L_i, K_i) = L_i F_i(1, k_i) \equiv L_i f_i(k_i) \equiv L_i y_i, \; L_i \neq 0; \; F_i(0, 0) = 0 \tag{18.1}$$

where the function $f_i(k_i)$, is strictly concave and monotonically increasing in the capital-labor ratio $k_i \in [0, \infty[$, i.e., $f_i$ has the properties

$$\forall k_i > 0: \; f_i'(k_i) = df_i(k_i)/dk_i > 0, \quad f_i''(k_i) = d^2 f_i(k_i)/dk_i^2 < 0 \tag{18.2}$$

$$\lim_{k_i \to 0} f_i'(k_i) \equiv \bar{\mathfrak{b}}_i \leq \infty, \; \lim_{k_i \to \infty} f_i'(k_i) \equiv \underline{\mathfrak{b}}_i \geq 0, \; f_i'(k_i) \in J_i \equiv \left[\underline{\mathfrak{b}}_i, \bar{\mathfrak{b}}_i\right] \tag{18.3}$$

Let us note that if our $F_i$ is defined and continuous on the *axes*, then

$$F_i(0, 1) \geq 0, \quad F_i(1, 0) \equiv f_i(0) \geq 0 \tag{18.4}$$

$$F_i(0, K_i) = K_i F_i(0, 1), \quad F_i(L_i, 0) = L_i F_i(1, 0) = L_i f_i(0) \tag{18.5}$$

where *positivity* in (18.4) says that a factor is *non-essential.* Further, note that

$$\lim_{k_i \to 0} f_i'(k_i) = \frac{\partial F_i}{\partial K_i}(1, 0), \; \lim_{k_i \to \infty} f_i'(k_i) = F_i(0, 1), \; \frac{\partial F_i}{\partial L_i}(1, 0) = F_i(1, 0) \tag{18.6}$$

The *sectorial output elasticities*, $\epsilon_{L_i}, \epsilon_{K_i}, \epsilon_i$, with respect to marginal and proportional factor variation are, cf. (18.1),

$$\epsilon_{L_i} \equiv \frac{\partial \ln Y_i}{\partial \ln L_i} \equiv \frac{\partial Y_i}{\partial L_i} \frac{L_i}{Y_i} = \frac{MP_{L_i}}{AP_{L_i}} = 1 - \frac{k_i f_i'(k_i)}{f_i(k_i)} > 0, \quad k_i \neq 0, \tag{18.7}$$

$$\epsilon_{K_i} \equiv \frac{\partial \ln Y_i}{\partial \ln K_i} \equiv \frac{\partial Y_i}{\partial K_i}\frac{K_i}{Y_i} = \frac{MP_{K_i}}{AP_{K_i}} = \frac{k_i f_i'(k_i)}{f_i(k_i)} = \frac{d \ln y_i}{d \ln k_i} > 0, \tag{18.8}$$

$$\epsilon_i \equiv \epsilon_{L_i} + \epsilon_{K_i} = 1 \tag{18.9}$$

The *factor endowments,* total labor force $(L)$ and the total capital stock $(K)$, are inelastically supplied and are fully employed (utilized), i.e.,

$$L = \textstyle\sum_{i=1}^{N} L_i, \quad \sum_{i=1}^{N} L_i/L \equiv \sum_{i=1}^{N} \lambda_{L_i} = 1 \tag{18.10}$$

$$K = \textstyle\sum_{i=1}^{N} K_i, \quad \sum_{i=1}^{N} K_i/K \equiv \sum_{i=1}^{N} \lambda_{K_i} \equiv 1 \tag{18.11}$$

$$K/L \equiv k \equiv \textstyle\sum_{i=1}^{N} \lambda_{L_i} k_i \tag{18.12}$$

where $\lambda_{L_i}, \lambda_{K_i}$, (18.10–18.11) are the *factor allocation fractions.*

At any point of the isoquants (18.1), the *marginal rates* of technical *substitution* (MRS), $\omega_i(k_i)$ are, by (18.2), positive *monotonic* functions,

$$\omega_i = \omega_i(k_i) = \frac{MP_{L_i}}{MP_{K_i}} = \frac{f_i(k_i)}{f_i'(k_i)} - k_i = \frac{\epsilon_{L_i}}{\epsilon_{K_i}} k_i > 0, \quad \forall k_i > 0 \tag{18.13}$$

and the *substitution elasticities,* $\sigma_i$ between labor and capital is the proportionate change in the ratio $(K_i/L_i)$ of inputs divided by the proportionate change in the ratio $(\omega_i)$ of the marginal products of inputs, cf. (18.13), (18.7–18.8),

$$\sigma_i \equiv \frac{d \ln k_i}{d \ln \omega_i} \equiv E(k_i, \omega_i) \equiv \frac{dk_i}{d\omega_i}\frac{\omega_i}{k_i} = \frac{dk_i}{d\omega_i}\frac{\epsilon_{L_i}}{\epsilon_{K_i}} = \frac{d \ln AP_{L_i}}{d \ln MP_{L_i}} = \frac{d \ln AP_{K_i}}{d \ln MP_{K_i}} > 0 \tag{18.14}$$

The general connection between the sectoral factor output elasticities, (18.7–18.8), ('factor shares') and the sectorial substitution elasticities, $\sigma_i$, is:

$$\frac{d \ln \epsilon_{K_i}}{d \ln k_i} \equiv \frac{d\epsilon_{K_i}}{dk_i}\frac{k_i}{\epsilon_{K_i}} = \frac{\epsilon_{L_i}(\sigma_i - 1)}{\sigma_i}; \quad \frac{d \ln \epsilon_{L_i}}{d \ln k_i} \equiv \frac{d\epsilon_{L_i}}{dk_i}\frac{k_i}{\epsilon_{L_i}} = \frac{\epsilon_{K_i}(1 - \sigma_i)}{\sigma_i} \tag{18.15}$$

Free *factor mobility* between the multiple industries and also *efficient* factor *allocation* impose the *common* MRS condition, cf. (18.13),

$$\omega = \omega_i = \omega_i(k_i) \quad \forall i = 1, \cdots, N \tag{18.16}$$

For the variables $(k_i)$ to satisfy (18.16), it is, beyond (18.2), further required that the intersection of the sectorial range for $\omega_i(k_i)$ is not empty,

$$\omega_i(k_i) \in \Omega_i = [\underline{\omega}_i, \overline{\omega}_i] \subseteq \mathbf{R}_+, \quad \omega \in \Omega \equiv \cap \Omega_i = [\underline{\omega}, \overline{\omega}] \neq \emptyset, \tag{18.17}$$

### *Efficient Factor Allocation, Costs, Price Systems, Relative Prices*

All industries are assumed to operate under *perfect competition* (zero excess profit); absolute (*money*) input (factor) *prices* (**w**, **r**) are the *same* in every sector (industry); and absolute (*money*) output (product, commodity) *prices* ($\mathbf{P_i}$) represent *unit cost*. Thus, in *each* sector (industry), we have the *competitive producer equilibrium* (Pareto efficiency) equations:

$$w = P_i \cdot MP_{L_i}, \quad r = P_i \cdot MP_{K_i}; \quad \omega = w/r, \qquad P_i \neq 0 \tag{18.18}$$

$$P_i Y_i = wL_i + rK_i, \quad \epsilon_{L_i} = wL_i/P_iY_i, \quad \epsilon_{K_i} = rK_i/P_iY_i \tag{18.19}$$

$$P_i = \frac{w + rk_i}{y_i} = \frac{w}{y_i} \cdot \frac{1}{\epsilon_{L_i}}, \quad \widehat{P_i} = \epsilon_{L_i}\hat{w} + \epsilon_{K_i}\hat{r}, \quad \left(\widehat{P_i} \equiv \frac{dP_i}{P_i}\right) \tag{18.20}$$

Thus the proportional change, $\widehat{P_i}$ , is a *convex combination*, (18.9), of $\hat{w}$ and $\hat{r}$.

Next, (18.7–18.8), (18.18), (18.20), give any *relative commodity prices*, $P_i/P_j$, as:

$$p_{ij} \equiv \frac{P_i}{P_j} = \frac{MP_{K_j}}{MP_{K_i}} = \frac{f_j'(k_j)}{f_i'(k_i)} = \frac{f_j(k_j) - k_j f_j'(k_j)}{f_i(k_i) - k_i f_i'(k_i)} = \frac{MP_{L_j}}{MP_{L_i}} = \frac{y_j \epsilon_{L_j}}{y_i \epsilon_{L_i}} \tag{18.21}$$

The quantitative *connection* (composite function) between *relative factor* (service) prices and *relative commodity* prices follows from (18.16, 18.18, 18.21),

$$p_{ij}(\omega) = \frac{P_i}{P_j}(\omega) = \frac{MP_{K_j}[k_j(\omega)]}{MP_{K_i}[k_i(\omega)]} = \frac{f_j'[k_j(\omega)]}{f_i'[k_i(\omega)]} = \left[\frac{f_i'[k_i(\omega)]}{f_j'[k_j(\omega)]}\right]^{-1}; \quad \omega = \frac{w}{r} \tag{18.22}$$

With a common wage-rental ratio, (18.16), in all sectors it is clear that, (18.19),

$$\epsilon_{L_i}(\omega) \gtreqless \epsilon_{L_j}(\omega) \;\Leftrightarrow\; \epsilon_{K_j}(\omega) \gtreqless \epsilon_{K_i}(\omega) \;\Leftrightarrow\; k_j(\omega) \gtreqless k_i(\omega) \tag{18.23}$$

Average and marginal productivities were objects of pioneering theoretical and empirical studies by von Thünen. In Table 18.1, the factor K is non-essential, cf. (18.4); accordingly, the substitution elasticity is larger than one. Hence $\epsilon_L$, (18.7, 18.15, 18.18, 18.19), is here falling with mechanization, $k = K/L$. Evidently, for $\sigma > 1$, $AP_L$ increases more than $MP_L$, (18.14). This table serves as a relevant (simple) illustration of key sectorial productivity growth numbers.

**Table 18.1** von Thünen's Productivity Calculations

| $K/L$ | $AP_L$ | $AP_K$ | $MP_K$ | $MP_L$ | $\omega$ | $\frac{1}{\omega} = \frac{r}{w}$ | $MP_K \cdot k$ | $\varepsilon_L$ |
|---|---|---|---|---|---|---|---|---|
| 0 | 110 | – | – | 110 | – | – | – | 1.00 |
| 1 | 150 | 150 | 40 | 110 | 2.75 | 0.364 | 40 | 0.73 |
| 2 | 186 | 93 | 36 | 114 | 3.17 | 0.315 | 72 | 0.61 |
| 3 | 218.4 | 72.8 | 32.4 | 121.2 | 3.74 | 0.267 | 97.2 | 0.55 |

Source: von Thünen (1850, 1930, p.507); Brems (1986, p.86)

### *Macro-equivalence Relations of Supply-Demand Sides in Multi-sector Economies*

*Gross domestic product* (GDP), national income, $Y$, is the *total* of sectoral *producer revenues* [ monetary *value* of sector *outputs*, (18.1) ]

$$Y_i = L\, y_i\, \lambda_{L_i}\,, \qquad Y \equiv \sum_{i=1}^{N} P_i Y_i = L\left[\sum_{i=1}^{N} P_i\, y_i\, \lambda_{L_i}\right] \equiv L\, y \tag{18.24}$$

and is equivalent with *competition*, (18.18–18.19), to total *factor income*,

$$Y = wL + rK = L\,(w + rk) = L\,(\omega + k)\, P_i\, f_i'\,(k_i) = L\, y \tag{18.25}$$

Hence the factor income *distribution shares* $\delta_K + \delta_L = 1$, become

$$\delta_K \equiv rK/Y = \frac{rk}{y},\ \delta_L \equiv wL/Y = \frac{w}{y};\ \delta_K = \frac{k}{\omega + k},\ \frac{\delta_K}{\delta_L} = \frac{k}{\omega} \tag{18.26}$$

The "final demand" decomposition of GDP (Y) into the aggregate expenditures on investment (I) and consumption (C) is

$$I = P_1 Y_1,\quad C = \sum_{i=2}^{N} P_i Y_i,\quad Y = C + I \tag{18.27}$$

and the *composition* of GDP (18.24) final *expenditure shares*, $s_i$, is

$$s_i = P_i Y_i / Y,\quad \sum_{i=1}^{N} s_i \equiv \sum_{i=1}^{N} P_i Y_i / Y = 1 \tag{18.28}$$

Budget studies and consumption (demand) *theory* mostly normalize the *budget shares* with the total *expenditure constraint*, $C$, i.e., the consumer expenditure *shares*, $(e_i)$, as:

$$e_i = \frac{P_i Y_i}{C},\quad \sum_{i=2}^{N} e_i = 1;\quad \underline{e} = \sum_{\sigma_i < 1} e_i,\ \bar{e} = \sum_{\sigma_i > 1} e_i,\ \underline{e} + \bar{e} = 1 \tag{18.29}$$

Evidently, the connection between the GDP *shares* (18.28) and $(e_i)$ is:

$$s_i = \quad e_i\,(1 - s_1)\,, \quad i = 2, \cdots, N \tag{18.30}$$

For later purposes, we introduce the notation, cf. (18.29),

$$\underline{s} = (1 - s_1)\,\underline{e}\,, \qquad \bar{s} = (1 - s_1)\,\bar{e}\,, \quad \bar{s} + \underline{s} + s_1 = 1 \tag{18.31}$$

**Lemma 18.1** *The macro-factor income shares, $\delta_L$, $\delta_K$, (18.26), are GDP expenditure-weighted combinations of the sectoral factor (cost) shares, $\epsilon_{L_i}$, $\epsilon_{K_i}$,*

$$\delta_L = \textstyle\sum_{i=1}^{N} s_i\,\epsilon_{L_i}, \qquad \delta_K = \sum_{i=1}^{N} s_i\,\epsilon_{K_i}, \quad \delta_K + \delta_L = 1 \tag{18.32}$$

*The factor allocation fractions (18.10–18.11) are obtained by*

$$L_i/L = \lambda_{L_i} = s_i\,\epsilon_{L_i}/\delta_L \qquad K_i/K = \lambda_{K_i} = s_i\,\epsilon_{K_i}/\delta_K \tag{18.33}$$

*The total factor endowment ratio, $K/L$, satisfies the identity, cf. (18.12), (18.26), (18.32):*

$$K/L = k = \textstyle\sum_{i=1}^{N} \lambda_{L_i}\,k_i = \dfrac{\omega\,\delta_K}{\delta_L} = \dfrac{\omega\,\sum_{i=1}^{N} s_i\,\epsilon_{K_i}}{\sum_{i=1}^{N} s_i\,\epsilon_{L_i}} \tag{18.34}$$

*which is a convenient representation of* **Walras's law** *(identity).*

***Proof*** By definition, we have

$$\delta_L = wL/Y = [\,wL_1 + wL_2 + \cdots wL_N\,]/Y \tag{18.35}$$

$$\delta_K = rK/Y = [\,rK_1 + rK_2 + \cdots rK_N\,]/Y \tag{18.36}$$

From (18.19) and (18.28), we get

$$wL_i = \epsilon_{L_i}\,P_iY_i = s_i\,\epsilon_{L_i}Y, \qquad rK_i = \epsilon_{K_i}\,P_iY_i = s_i\,\epsilon_{K_i}Y \tag{18.37}$$

Hence, by (18.35–18.36) and (18.37), we obtain (18.32). Next, as stated in (18.33),

$$\lambda_{L_i} = \frac{L_i}{L} = \frac{wL_i}{wL} = \frac{s_i\,\epsilon_{L_i}Y}{\delta_L Y} = \frac{s_i\,\epsilon_{L_i}}{\delta_L} \tag{18.38}$$

$$\lambda_{K_i} = \frac{K_i}{K} = \frac{rK_i}{rK} = \frac{s_i\,\epsilon_{K_i}Y}{\delta_K Y} = \frac{s_i\,\epsilon_{K_i}}{\delta_K} \tag{18.39}$$

□

## Relative Prices in Multi-sector Economies with CES Sector Technologies

The general CES forms of $F_i(L_i, K_i)$, (18.1), $\gamma_i > 0$, $0 < a_i < 1$, $\sigma_i > 0$, are:

$$Y_i = F_i(L_i, K_i) = \gamma_i L_i^{1-a_i} K_i^{a_i} = L_i\, \gamma_i k_i^{a_i} \equiv L_i\, f_i(k_i) \tag{18.40}$$

$$Y_i = F_i(L_i, K_i) = \gamma_i \left[(1-a_i) L_i^{\frac{\sigma_i - 1}{\sigma_i}} + a_i K_i^{\frac{\sigma_i - 1}{\sigma_i}}\right]^{\frac{\sigma_i}{\sigma_i - 1}} \tag{18.41}$$

$$= L_i\, \gamma_i \left[(1-a_i) + a_i k_i^{(\sigma_i - 1)/\sigma_i}\right]^{\frac{\sigma_i}{\sigma_i - 1}} \equiv L_i\, f_i(k_i) \tag{18.42}$$

$$f_i'(k_i) = \gamma_i a_i k_i^{a_i - 1}, \quad f_i'(k_i) = \gamma_i a_i \left[a_i + (1-a_i) k_i^{-(\sigma_i - 1)/\sigma_i}\right]^{\frac{1}{\sigma_i - 1}} \tag{18.43}$$

By evaluating (18.40–18.43), the limits of $f_i(k_i)$ and $f_i'(k_i)$ become, ($\forall i$ : $\sigma_i \gtrless 1 \Rightarrow a_i^{\sigma_i/(\sigma_i - 1)} \lessgtr 1$),

$$\sigma_i < 1: \begin{cases} \lim\limits_{k_i \to 0} f_i(k_i) = \lim\limits_{k_i \to 0} \gamma_i a_i^{\frac{\sigma_i}{\sigma_i - 1}} k_i = 0, & \lim\limits_{k_i \to \infty} f_i(k_i) = \gamma_i (1-a_i)^{\frac{\sigma_i}{\sigma_i - 1}} \\ \lim\limits_{k_i \to 0} f_i'(k_i) = \gamma_i a_i^{\frac{\sigma_i}{\sigma_i - 1}}, & \lim\limits_{k_i \to \infty} f_i'(k_i) = 0 \end{cases} \tag{18.44}$$

$$\sigma_i > 1: \begin{cases} \lim\limits_{k_i \to 0} f_i(k_i) = \gamma_i (1-a_i)^{\frac{\sigma_i}{\sigma_i - 1}}, & \lim\limits_{k_i \to \infty} f_i(k_i) = \lim\limits_{k_i \to \infty} \gamma_i a_i^{\frac{\sigma_i}{\sigma_i - 1}} k_i = \infty \\ \lim\limits_{k_i \to 0} f_i'(k_i) = \infty, & \lim\limits_{k_i \to \infty} f_i'(k_i) = \gamma_i a_i^{\frac{\sigma_i}{\sigma_i - 1}} \end{cases} \tag{18.45}$$

For the CES technologies, the *monotonic* relations between marginal rates of substitution, factor proportions, and output elasticities are, cf. (18.41–18.43),

$$\omega_i = \frac{1-a_i}{a_i} k_i^{1/\sigma_i}, \qquad k_i = \frac{1}{c_i} (\omega_i)^{\sigma_i}, \quad c_i = \left[\frac{1-a_i}{a_i}\right]^{\sigma_i}, \; i = 1, \cdots, N. \tag{18.46}$$

$$\epsilon_{K_i} = \left[1 + \frac{1-a_i}{a_i} k_i^{\frac{1-\sigma_i}{\sigma_i}}\right]^{-1} = \frac{1}{1 + c_i\, \omega^{1-\sigma_i}}, \quad \epsilon_{L_i} = \frac{c_i\, \omega^{1-\sigma_i}}{1 + c_i\, \omega^{1-\sigma_i}} \tag{18.47}$$

With multi-sector models and CES technologies, it is apparent from (18.46) that sectorial *factor* ratio ("intensity") *reversals* can only be avoided, if and only if $\sigma_i = \sigma_j$ and $a_i \neq a_j$. Hence, with $\sigma_i \neq \sigma_j$, there will be a *reversal* point, $(k_i, \omega_i) = (\bar{k}, \bar{\omega})$:

$$\bar{k} = \left[\frac{a_i(1-a_j)}{a_j(1-a_i)}\right]^{\frac{\sigma_i\sigma_j}{\sigma_j-\sigma_i}} = \left[\frac{c_j^{\sigma_i}}{c_i^{\sigma_j}}\right]^{\frac{1}{\sigma_j-\sigma_i}}, \quad \bar{\omega} = \left[\frac{c_j}{c_i}\right]^{\frac{1}{\sigma_j-\sigma_i}} \tag{18.48}$$

### *Product Price and Factor Price Correspondence with CES Technologies*

The exact form of the relative price function (18.22) needs particular attention.

With (18.43) and (18.46), the *relative commodity* prices (comparative costs) (18.22) become, with $\sigma_i = 1$, $\sigma_i \neq 1$, and $\sigma_i = \sigma$, respectively,

$$p_{ij}(\omega) = \frac{f_j'\,[k_j(\omega)]}{f_i'\,[k_i(\omega)]} = \frac{\gamma_j a_j k_j(\omega)^{a_j-1}}{\gamma_i a_i k_i(\omega)^{a_i-1}} = \frac{\gamma_j a_j^{a_j}(1-a_j)^{1-a_j}}{\gamma_i a_i^{a_i}(1-a_i)^{1-a_i}}\,\omega^{a_j-a_i} \tag{18.49}$$

$$p_{ij}(\omega) = \frac{f_j'\,[k_j(\omega)]}{f_i'\,[k_i(\omega)]} = \frac{\gamma_j a_j\left[a_j + (1-a_j)\,k_j(\omega)^{-(\sigma_j-1)/\sigma_j}\right]^{\frac{1}{\sigma_j-1}}}{\gamma_i a_i\left[a_i + (1-a_i)\,k_i(\omega)^{-(\sigma_i-1)/\sigma_i}\right]^{\frac{1}{\sigma_i-1}}} \tag{18.50}$$

$$= \frac{\gamma_j a_j^{\sigma_j/(\sigma_j-1)}\left[1 + c_j\,\omega^{1-\sigma_j}\right]^{\frac{1}{\sigma_j-1}}}{\gamma_i a_i^{\sigma_i/(\sigma_i-1)}\left[1 + c_i\,\omega^{1-\sigma_i}\right]^{\frac{1}{\sigma_i-1}}} \tag{18.51}$$

$$p_{ij}(\omega) = \frac{f_j'\,[k_j(\omega)]}{f_i'\,[k_i(\omega)]} = \frac{\gamma_j}{\gamma_i}\left[\left[\frac{a_j}{a_i}\right]^{\sigma}\frac{1 + c_j\,\omega^{1-\sigma}}{1 + c_i\,\omega^{1-\sigma}}\right]^{\frac{1}{\sigma-1}}, \quad c_i = \left[\frac{1-a_i}{a_i}\right]^{\sigma} \tag{18.52}$$

The elasticity of the functions (18.22, 18.49, 18.50, 18.51, 18.52) can generally by the composite rule be expressed as follows:

$$E\left[p_{ij}, \omega\right] = E\left[MP_{K_j}, k_j\right]E(k_j, \omega) - E\left[MP_{K_i}, k_i\right]E(k_i, \omega) = \tag{18.53}$$

$$(-\epsilon_{L_j}/\sigma_j)\,\sigma_j \; - \; (-\epsilon_{L_i}/\sigma_i)\,\sigma_i \; = \; \epsilon_{L_i} - \epsilon_{L_j} \; = \; \epsilon_{K_j} - \epsilon_{K_i} \tag{18.54}$$

Evidently, $p_{ij}(\omega)$ is always *inelastic*, as (18.54) is numerically *less* than unity—this fact is *not directly* seen from the *explicit* CES expressions (18.50, 18.51, 18.52).

The Stolper-Samuelson theorem and the "magnification effects" of price changes, Jones (1965), are implications of the Factor Price-Commodity Price **FPCP** *elasticity*, (18.53–18.54), which can be rewritten as:

$$\left(\widehat{P}_i - \widehat{P}_j\right)/\left(\widehat{w} - \widehat{r}\right) \; = \; \epsilon_{L_i} - \epsilon_{L_j} \; = \; \epsilon_{K_j} - \epsilon_{K_i} \tag{18.55}$$

Since $\widehat{P}_i$ and $\widehat{P}_j$ both lie between $\hat{w}$ and $\hat{r}$, cf. (18.20), we obviously have that

$$|\left(\widehat{P}_i - \widehat{P}_j\right)/\left(\hat{w} - \hat{r}\right)| < 1 \tag{18.56}$$

Combining (18.53–18.55), (18.56), with (18.23), we immediately obtain the following *inequalities*, ("magnification relations"):

$$k_i(\omega) < k_j(\omega), \widehat{P}_i > \widehat{P}_j : \hat{w} > \widehat{P}_i > \widehat{P}_j > \hat{r}; \quad \widehat{P}_j > \widehat{P}_i : \hat{r} > \widehat{P}_j > \widehat{P}_i > \hat{w} \tag{18.57}$$

$$k_i(\omega) > k_j(\omega), \widehat{P}_i > \widehat{P}_j : \hat{r} > \widehat{P}_i > \widehat{P}_j > \hat{w}; \quad \widehat{P}_j > \widehat{P}_i : \hat{w} > \widehat{P}_j > \widehat{P}_i > \hat{r} \tag{18.58}$$

Since the **CES** marginal rate of substitution $(\omega_i)$, (18.46), always has the limit values zero and infinity, we need, for precise *geometry* and *intuition*, to know the *limits* of the *relative prices*, $p_{ij}(\omega)$, (18.51), for $(\omega)$ going to *zero* and *infinity.*

To this end, let

$$p_{ij}^{*} \equiv \frac{\gamma_j \, a_j^{\sigma_j/(\sigma_j-1)}}{\gamma_i \, a_i^{\sigma_i/(\sigma_i-1)}}, \qquad p_{ij}^{**} \equiv \frac{\gamma_j \, (1-a_j)^{\sigma_j/(\sigma_j-1)}}{\gamma_i \, (1-a_i)^{\sigma_i/(\sigma_i-1)}} \tag{18.59}$$

With $\sigma_i \neq \sigma_j$, (18.51), (18.48), any relative price has a unique *reversal* price ratio:

$$\bar{p}_{ij} = p_{ij}(\bar{\omega}) = \frac{\gamma_j a_j^{\sigma_j/(\sigma_j-1)} \left[1 + c_j \left[\frac{c_j}{c_i}\right]^{\frac{1-\sigma_j}{\sigma_j-\sigma_i}}\right]^{\frac{1}{\sigma_j-1}}}{\gamma_i a_i^{\sigma_i/\sigma_i-1} \left[1 + c_i \left[\frac{c_j}{c_i}\right]^{\frac{1-\sigma_i}{\sigma_j-\sigma_i}}\right]^{\frac{1}{\sigma_i-1}}}; \quad a_i = a_j : \bar{p}_{ij} = \frac{\gamma_j}{\gamma_i} \tag{18.60}$$

**Proposition 18.1** *The graphs of the* ***relative prices,*** $p_{ij}(\omega)$, *(18.51)—the* **CES** *factor price-commodity price,* **FPCP**, *correspondence—have limits, classified by* $\sigma_i$, *as follows:*

$$\sigma_i < 1, \quad \sigma_j < 1: \qquad \lim_{\omega\to 0} p_{ij} = p_{ij}^{*} \quad \lim_{\omega\to\infty} p_{ij} = p_{ij}^{**} \tag{18.61}$$

$$\sigma_i > 1, \quad \sigma_j > 1: \qquad \lim_{\omega\to 0} p_{ij} = p_{ij}^{**} \quad \lim_{\omega\to\infty} p_{ij} = p_{ij}^{*} \tag{18.62}$$

$$\sigma_i > 1, \quad \sigma_j < 1: \qquad \lim_{\omega\to 0} p_{ij} = 0 \quad \lim_{\omega\to\infty} p_{ij} = 0 \tag{18.63}$$

$$\sigma_i < 1, \quad \sigma_j > 1: \qquad \lim_{\omega\to 0} p_{ij} = \infty \quad \lim_{\omega\to\infty} p_{ij} = \infty \tag{18.64}$$

*The reversal price ratio, $\bar{p}_{ij} \equiv p_{ij}(\bar{\omega})$, (18.60), is always a maximum (iff $\sigma_i > \sigma_j$) or a minimum (iff $\sigma_j > \sigma_i$), cf.* Fig. 18.0. *For the substitution elasticities (18.61)–(18.63), the* ***range*** *of* $\mathbf{p}_{ij}(\boldsymbol{\omega})$*, (18.51) is* ***bounded****. With $\gamma_i = \gamma_j$, and both substitutions elasticities, either small (18.61) or large (18.62), the range of $p_{ij}(\omega)$ becomes a narrow interval, and there will be only* **small differences** *between the values of $p^*_{ij}$ and $p^{**}_{ij}$, (18.59), if $a_i$, $a_j$, have similar size, cf.* Table 18.4.

*Iff $\sigma_i = \sigma_j \neq 1$, the functions, $p_{ij}(\omega)$, (18.52), are always monotonic, bounded, and increasing between $p^*_{ij}$ and $p^{**}_{ij}$, iff $a_j > a_i$. Only the* **CD** *relative prices, $p_{ij}(\omega)$, (18.49), are both monotonic and unbounded, cf.* Fig. 18.0.

***Proof*** Ad (18.61)–(18.62): With $\sigma_i < 1$ and $\sigma_j < 1$, the brackets in (18.51) converge to one at $\omega = 0$, which establishes the limiting $p = p^*$. For large $\omega$, the numerator and denominator in (18.51) are approximately proportional to $\omega^{-1}$ with coefficients equal to the numerator and the denominator of $p^{**}$, (18.59). Similar arguments as above establish (18.62).

Ad (18.63)–(18.64): With $\sigma_i > 1$ and $\sigma_j < 1$, the numerator in (18.51) converges to a constant and the denominator converges to infinity at $\omega = 0$, which establish the limiting value of $p = 0$. For large $\omega$, the numerator of (18.51) converges to zero, whereas the denominator converges to a non-zero constant. Hence the limiting value of $p$ is zero. Similar arguments as above establish (18.64). □

The concrete values of, $p^*_{ij}$, $p^{**}_{ij}$, $\bar{p}_{ij}$ can be calculated for any size of the CES parameters; however, for a clear *quantitative* understanding of the relevant *interval* for any *relative price*, we examine the *quotients*, cf. (18.59), (18.60),

$$q^* = \frac{p^{**}_{ij}}{p^*_{ij}} = \frac{\left[\frac{1-a_j}{a_j}\right]^{\frac{\sigma_j}{\sigma_j-1}}}{\left[\frac{1-a_i}{a_i}\right]^{\frac{\sigma_i}{\sigma_i-1}}} = \frac{c_j^{\frac{1}{\sigma_j-1}}}{c_i^{\frac{1}{\sigma_i-1}}}, \qquad \frac{\bar{p}_{ij}}{p^{**}_{ij}} = \frac{\bar{q}}{q^*} \tag{18.65}$$

$$\bar{q} = \frac{\bar{p}_{ij}}{p^*_{ij}} = \frac{\left[1 + c_j\left[\frac{c_j}{c_i}\right]^{\frac{1-\sigma_j}{\sigma_j-\sigma_i}}\right]^{\frac{1}{\sigma_j-1}}}{\left[1 + c_i\left[\frac{c_j}{c_i}\right]^{\frac{1-\sigma_i}{\sigma_j-\sigma_i}}\right]^{\frac{1}{\sigma_i-1}}}. \tag{18.66}$$

$$a_i = a_j = a : \; \bar{q} = a^{\frac{\sigma_j-\sigma_i}{(\sigma_i-1)(\sigma_j-1)}} \tag{18.67}$$

If $a_j = a_i = \frac{1}{2}$, then $q^* = 1$; and $\bar{q}$ is: *interval* (ratio scale) of *relative prices.*

Although the numerical value of $\boldsymbol{q^*}$ is sensitive to its many parameter combinations, the *dominating* influences on the *deviation* of this interval *from*

$q^* = 1$ are the *extent* to which both, $a_j$, $a_i$, *differ* from the *critical value*: $\frac{1}{2}$, and the extent to which both, $\sigma_i, \sigma_j$, *differ* from the *critical value*: 1.

To elaborate on the *size* of the *interval* (ratio scale), $q^*$, let $\delta_l$ and $d_l$ be:

$$A_{ji} = \frac{(1 - a_j)/a_j}{(1 - a_i)/a_i}, \ \delta_l = \left[A_{ji}\right]^{\frac{\sigma_l}{\sigma_l - 1}}, \ d_l = \left[\frac{1 - a_l}{a_l}\right]^{\frac{\sigma_i - \sigma_j}{(\sigma_i - 1)(\sigma_j - 1)}}, \ l = i, j \tag{18.68}$$

**Lemma 18.2** *Exact decompositions of the size of the interval,* ***q*****, (18.65), are:*

$$q^* = \delta_j \, d_i = \delta_i \, d_j \tag{18.69}$$

***Proof*** With $q^*$ from (18.65) and $d_l$ from (18.68), we get (after reductions),

$$q^* = \left[\, A_{ji} \,\right]^{\frac{\sigma_j}{\sigma_j - 1}} d_i \; = \; \left[\, A_{ji} \,\right]^{\frac{\sigma_i}{\sigma_i - 1}} d_j \tag{18.70}$$

which is (18.69). □

From (18.65–18.70), it follows that

$$\lim_{\sigma_i, \sigma_j \to \infty} q^* = A_{ji} \ ; \qquad \lim_{\sigma_i, \sigma_j \to 0} q^* = 1 \tag{18.71}$$

We illustrate Lemma 18.2 in Tables 18.2, 18.3, and 18.4.

Due to (18.9), the relation between *relative product* (cost) *prices* and *factor prices* is—within product *diversification cone* limits—*not* affected by *factor endowments*, or by any *demand* or any taxation/tariff system, specified in CGE models. Thus, as an *invariance*, this **FPCP**, $p_{ij}(\omega)$, (18.51), is *implicitly* embedded in several *applied* CGE models—with (18.9) and CES technologies—and hence (18.51) can also be *retrieved* explicitly from presentations (and can be used as computational *checks*) of the complete general equilibrium *solution*.

**Table 18.2** Evaluations of $\delta_l$, as determined by (18.68), used in (18.69), and with sizes shown in Table 18.4

| | $a_i \geq a_j$<br>$A_{ji} \geq 1$ | $a_i \leq a_j$<br>$A_{ji} \leq 1$ |
|---|---|---|
| $\sigma_l > 1$ | $\delta_l \geq 1$ | $\delta_l \leq 1$ |
| $\sigma_l < 1$ | $\delta_l \leq 1$ | $\delta_l \geq 1$ |

**Table 18.3** Evaluations of $d_l$ as determined by (18.68), used in (18.69), and with sizes shown in Table 18.4

| | $a_l \leq \frac{1}{2}$ | $\frac{1}{2} \leq a_l$ |
|---|---|---|
| $\sigma_i \leq \sigma_j$ | $d_l \geq 1$ | $d_l \leq 1$ |
| $\sigma_i \geq \sigma_j$ | $d_l \leq 1$ | $d_l \geq 1$ |

**Table 18.4** Numerical illustrations of some benchmark cases ($\gamma_i = \gamma_j = 1$)

| $a_i$ | $a_j$ | $\sigma_i$ | $\sigma_j$ | $A_{ji}$ | $\delta_i$ | $\delta_j$ | $d_i$ | $d_j$ | $q^*$ | $p^*_{ij}$ | $p^{**}_{ij}$ | $\bar{p}_{ij}$ | $\bar{q}$ |
|---|---|---|---|---|---|---|---|---|---|---|---|---|---|
| 0.3 | 0.25 | 0.1 | 0.1 | 1.29 | 0.97 | 0.97 | 1.00 | 1.00 | 0.97 | 1.02 | 0.99 | – | – |
| 0.3 | 0.25 | 0.4 | 0.3 | 1.29 | 0.85 | 0.90 | 1.22 | 1.30 | 1.10 | 0.81 | 0.89 | 1.01 | 1.24 |
| 0.8 | 0.25 | 0.3 | 0.2 | 12.0 | 0.34 | 0.54 | 0.78 | 1.22 | 0.42 | 1.29 | 0.54 | 1.29 | 1.00 |
| 0.3 | 0.40 | 0.6 | 0.7 | 0.64 | 1.94 | 2.80 | 0.49 | 0.71 | 1.38 | 1.39 | 1.93 | 0.91 | 0.65 |
| 0.3 | 0.30 | 0.6 | 0.7 | 1.00 | 1.00 | 1.00 | 0.49 | 0.49 | 0.49 | 2.73 | 1.35 | 1.00 | 0.37 |
| 0.4 | 0.30 | 0.6 | 0.7 | 1.56 | 0.52 | 0.36 | 0.71 | 0.49 | 0.25 | 4.20 | 1.07 | 0.92 | 0.22 |
| 0.3 | 0.25 | 1.6 | 1.5 | 1.29 | 1.95 | 2.13 | 1.33 | 1.44 | 2.82 | 0.39 | 1.09 | 1.11 | 2.86 |
| 0.3 | 0.25 | 2.0 | 1.9 | 1.29 | 1.65 | 1.70 | 1.10 | 1.13 | 1.87 | 0.60 | 1.11 | 1.11 | 1.87 |
| 0.3 | 0.25 | 4.0 | 4.0 | 1.29 | 1.40 | 1.40 | 1.00 | 1.00 | 1.40 | 0.78 | 1.10 | – | – |

**Table 18.5** Computational General Equilibrium *solutions*—Shoven and Whalley (1992, Tables 3.1–3.7)—and the **FPCP** correspondence, $p_{ij}(\omega)$, (18.51)

| $w$ | $r$ | $\omega = w/r$ | $p_{ij}(\omega)$ | $P_i$ | $P_j$ | $P_i/P_j$ |
|---|---|---|---|---|---|---|
| 1.00 | 1.373 | 0.728 | 1.280 | 1.399 | 1.093 | 1.280 |
| 1.00 | 1.426 | 0.701 | 1.271 | 1.412 | 1.111 | 1.271 |
| 1.00 | 1.393 | 0.718 | 1.277 | 1.404 | 1.100 | 1.276 |
| 1.00 | 1.372 | 0.729 | 1.280 | 1.399 | 1.092 | 1.281 |
| 1.00 | 1.438 | 0.695 | 1.268 | 1.415 | 1.115 | 1.269 |

The well-known **CGE** calculations in Table 18.5 use **CES** parameters:

$$\gamma_i = 1.5, \ \gamma_j = 2.0, \ a_i = 0.4, \ a_j = 0.3, \ \sigma_i = 2.0, \ \sigma_j = 0.50 \qquad (18.72)$$

i.e., refers to *Case 1.9*, Fig. 18.0, with ***maximum*** here, $\bar{p}_{ij} = 1.35$, cf. (18.60).

## Preferences, Demand, and Expenditure Compositions of GDP

### *Consumption and Saving*

On the demand side of the economy, the actual division of national income between saving and consumption is our first problem, posing major issues of long theoretical and empirical standing. However, attention here will only be given—as in National Income Product Accounting (**NIPA**)—to the accumulation of ***new*** productive capital (***tangible*** assets), ***excluding*** intangibles such as all services, education (human capital), and portfolio & wealth evaluations ("capital gains") from entering NIPA saving accounts. Hence, only the newly produced final goods of a few manufacturing, construction, and building industries will enter the **NIPA** saving/investment *share* ($s$) of GDP. Thus, with

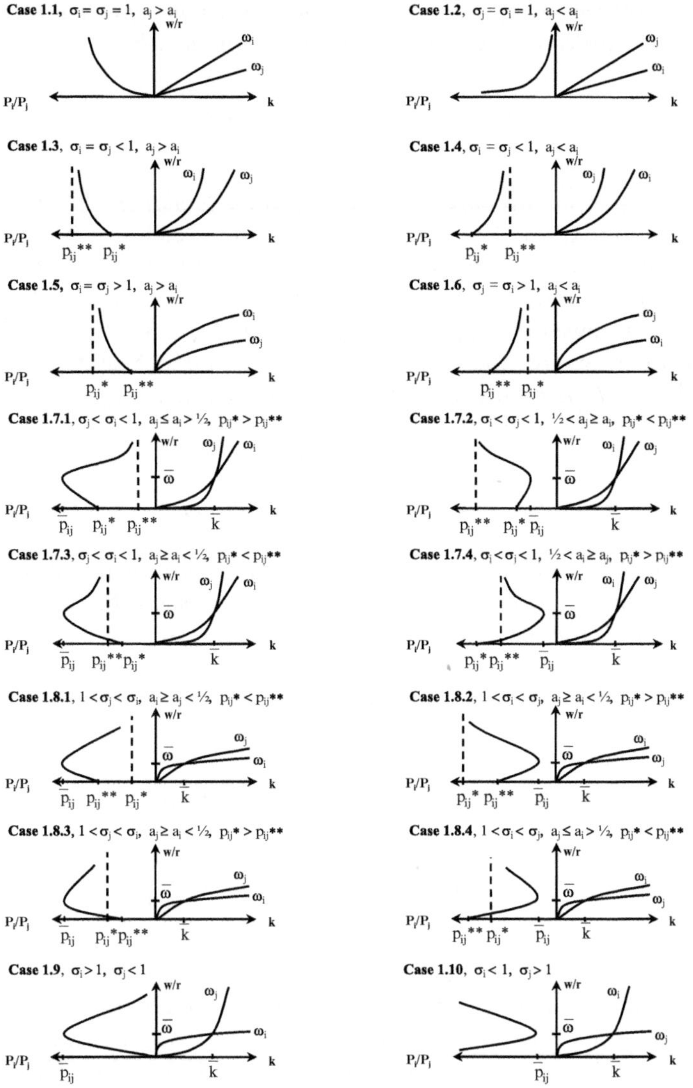


**Fig. 18.0** FPCP correspondence $p_{ij}(\omega)$, (18.49,18.51,18.52)

only *one* capital *good* ("equipment") industry, we have,

$$Y = C + S; \quad s = S/Y = I/Y = P_1 Y_1 / Y = s_1 \ ; \quad y = c_L + s_L \tag{18.73}$$

Per capita saving/consumption, in *any* numeraire, are denoted, $s_L/P_i$, $c_L/P_i$,

$$s = S/Y = (S/L)/(Y/L) = s_L/y = (s_L/P_i)/(y/P_i) \tag{18.74}$$

Optimum paths for savings and consumption by a *representative* agent may be described in terms of the *intertemporal utility functional*:

$$U = \int_0^{\infty} u\left[\frac{c_L}{P_i}(t)\right] e^{-R[u(t)]}dt \tag{18.75}$$

where $R[u(t)]$ is an *accumulated rate of time preference* by which future utility is discounted—and which summarizes the preference structure of the agent regarding the time profile of the continuous utility stream from present and future consumption, see Uzawa (1969, p.630), Uzawa (1968, p.488). According to Uzawa (1969, p.634), Uzawa (1973, p.58), if the *intertemporal preference* orderings are **homothetic**, then the *optimal* per capita *saving* $(s_L/P_i)$ is separable and *linear* with respect *income*, $(y/P_i)$, i.e.,

$$s_L/P_i = s_L(r, w, y) = s_L(r/P_i, w/P_i, y/P_i) \tag{18.76}$$

$$s_L/P_i = s_L(r/P_i, w/P_i, y/P_i) = s_L^*[r/P_i, w/P_i] \cdot (y/P_i) \tag{18.77}$$

Thus with, (18.77) and (18.74), the overall *homothetic* saving ratio $(s)$ (*share*) is solely determined by the "real“ factor prices, and such that the saving *ratio* $(s)$ *increases* with the real rental rate and *decreases* in the real wages, i.e.,

$$s = s_L^*[r/P_i, w/P_i]\ ; \qquad \partial s_L^*/\partial(r/P_i) > 0,\ \ \partial s_L^*/\partial(w/P_i) < 0 \tag{18.78}$$

A further reduction in the arguments of saving function (18.78) may occur in general equilibrium context with Pareto optimality, using $(\omega)$, cf. (18.16,18.18,18.22),

$$s = s_L^*\left[\frac{r}{P_i}(\omega), \frac{w}{P_i}(\omega)\right] = s_L^{**}(\omega) \tag{18.79}$$

which might allow the budget *share* $(s)$ to be also formally handled by *homothetic* utility functions, applied to genuine *consumer goods* below.

In the tradition of the Böhm-Bawerk & Fisherian theory of time preference, Koopmans (1960), Tinbergen (1960), Uzawa (1973, p.59), Uzawa (1968, p.494), Uzawa (1969, p.630,637), the *optimal* saving rate is essentially dependent on (increasing with) the *expected real rate of interest*, $\mathbf{i}_r^e$, with its size $\mathbf{i}_r^e$ being equal to the *marginal rate of time preference*, $\rho[u(t)]$, i.e., in short,

$$s = s(i_r^e)\ ; \qquad (r/P_1)^e = i_r^e = \rho[u(t)] \tag{18.80}$$

A serious *problem* is, however, that the homothetic saving *functions* (18.76–18.80) have *not* so far obtained generally accepted *functional forms*, and even less, been *examined* for critical *values* of fundamental *parameters*. Furthermore, the saving/investment *share* of GDP is not just a matter of optimizing *consumer preferences* (temporal/intertemporal). Actually, it needs to be based on *joint* considerations of the *producer-consumer* agent.

Hence, with some empirical support, we adopt a *provisional* assumption of mathematically treating the saving ratio as a parametric ('fixed') *constant*:

$$s = s_1 = \text{constant (parametric variation)} \tag{18.81}$$

This assumption does not preclude seeing positive *effects* of relatively declining capital good *prices* on investment (capital stock accumulation), cf. (18.73). As to the observed *long-run* constancy of the gross *private* (household and business combined) saving rate, see Denison (1958, p.267), David and Scadding (1974, p.238), Tobin (1980). The *constancy* of the total *private saving* rate (18.81) may be interpreted, Tobin (1980, p.65), as an extension of the Modigliani-Miller theorem beyond *finance* to *real capital* accumulation.

### *Consumer Expenditure Systems and CES-Class Utility Functions*

The purpose of budget (expenditure) systems is to describe mathematically how in a certain period a given money amount of total consumption expenditures is allocated to item-specific expenditure categories. The key elements determining this budget allocation are, as usual, assumed to be consumer preferences, prices of consumer goods & services, and the given size of the total budget (expenditures). Rather than giving Marshallian demand or Hicks/Slutsky (compensated) demand functions for various preference functions, we need *explicit* analytical *expressions* of the *budget shares,* $e_i$ (18.29–18.30), for here actually *solving* the *static* and *dynamic* general equilibrium *systems.*

We shall make use of a few benchmark specifications of preference (utility) functions—*direct,* $U(.)$, and *indirect utility,* $V(.)$—cf. Mas-Colell et al. (1995, p.56), Deaton and Muelbauer (1992, p.38). Among many other references, we refer to, Silberberg and Suen (2001), Chung (1994), Wold (1952).

Introducing the *notation* of *expenditure* ('income') and *price elasticities* as, $\partial \ln Y_i/\partial \ln C \equiv \mathbf{E(Y_i, C)}$, $\partial \ln Y_i/\partial \ln P_j \equiv \mathbf{E(Y_i, P_j)}$, then demand (expenditure) systems must *satisfy four* basic, well-known, Frisch (1959, p.180), *restrictions*—which also must be met by our general equilibrium solutions:

$$\text{Homogeneity:} \quad \textstyle\sum_{j=2}^{N} E(Y_i, P_j) + E(Y_i, C) = 0 \tag{18.82}$$

$$\text{Engel Aggregation:} \quad \textstyle\sum_{j=2}^{N} e_j \cdot E(Y_j, C) = 1 \tag{18.83}$$

$$\text{Cournot Aggregation:} \quad \textstyle\sum_{j=2}^{N} e_j \cdot E(Y_j, P_i) = -e_i < 0 \tag{18.84}$$

$$\text{Symmetry:} \quad E(Y_i, P_j)/e_j + E(Y_i, C) = E(Y_j, P_i)/e_i + E(Y_j, C) \tag{18.85}$$

Incidentally, note that any demand (expenditure) functions with *constant* non-unitary price and income elasticities *cannot* satisfy (18.83), except for a narrow range of the price and income variables involved, Wold (1952, p.106).

The CES form of the direct/indirect utility functions is the only functional form with the property of *self-duality*, i.e., the dual can be expressed exactly with same parameters; see, Samuelson (1965), Houthakker (1965).

We have, Silberberg and Suen (2001, p.359), Chung (1994, p.58), Shoven and Whalley (1992, p.45,96):

$$\textbf{CES}: \quad U(Y_2, \cdots, Y_N) = \gamma_u \left[ \sum_{i=2}^N \alpha_i Y_i^{\frac{\sigma_u - 1}{\sigma_u}} \right]^{\frac{\sigma_u}{\sigma_u - 1}}, \quad \alpha_i > 0, \quad \sum_{i=2}^N \alpha_i = 1 \tag{18.86}$$

$$V(P_2, \cdot, P_N, C) = \frac{1}{\gamma_u} \left[ \sum_{i=2}^N \alpha_j^{\sigma_u} \left[ \frac{C}{P_j} \right]^{\sigma_u - 1} \right]^{\frac{1}{\sigma_u - 1}} = \frac{1}{\gamma_u} \left[ \sum_{i=2}^N \alpha_j^{\sigma_u} p_{ij}^{\sigma_u - 1} \right]^{\frac{1}{\sigma_u - 1}} \frac{C}{P_i} \tag{18.87}$$

$$e_i = \frac{P_i Y_i}{C} = \frac{\alpha_i^{\sigma_u} P_i^{1-\sigma_u}}{\sum_{j=2}^N \alpha_j^{\sigma_u} P_j^{1-\sigma_u}} = \left[ \sum_{j=2}^N \left[ \frac{\alpha_j}{\alpha_i} \right]^{\sigma_u} p_{ij}^{\sigma_u - 1} \right]^{-1} \tag{18.88}$$

$$e_i = e_i(p_{i2}, \cdots, p_{iN}) = \left[ 1 + \sum_{j=2, j \neq i}^N \left[ \frac{\alpha_j}{\alpha_i} \right]^{\sigma_u} p_{ij}^{\sigma_u - 1} \right]^{-1} \quad i = 2, \cdots, N \tag{18.89}$$

Linking the relative *consumer prices* of $e_i$, (18.89), to *cost prices*, (18.22), and (18.51), we get

$$e_i(\omega) = \left[ 1 + \sum_{j=2, j \neq i}^N \left[ \frac{\alpha_j}{\alpha_i} \right]^{\sigma_u} p_{ij}(\omega)^{\sigma_u - 1} \right]^{-1}, \ i > 1, \quad 0 < e_i(\omega) < 1 \tag{18.90}$$

**Lemma 18.3** *The* **limiting** *consumer expenditure shares—with* **CES** *technologies (18.41–18.43) and* **CES** *utility functions (18.86)—are given by:*

$$\sigma_u \neq 1: \quad \forall i \ \sigma_i < 1: \qquad \lim_{\omega \to 0} e_i(\omega) = e_i^* \ \lim_{\omega \to \infty} e_i(\omega) = e_i^{**} \tag{18.91}$$

$$\sigma_u \neq 1: \quad \forall i \ \sigma_i > 1: \qquad \lim_{\omega \to 0} e_i(\omega) = e_i^{**} \ \lim_{\omega \to \infty} e_i(\omega) = e_i^* \tag{18.92}$$

*where*

$$e_i^* = \left[1 + \sum_{j=2, j\neq i}^{N} \left[\frac{\alpha_j}{\alpha_i}\right]^{\sigma_u} p_{ij}^{*\,\sigma_u - 1}\right]^{-1}, \; i > 1, \; \textstyle\sum_{i=2}^{N} e_i^* = 1 \quad (18.93)$$

$$e_i^{**} = \left[1 + \sum_{j=2, j\neq i}^{N} \left[\frac{\alpha_j}{\alpha_i}\right]^{\sigma_u} p_{ij}^{**\sigma_u - 1}\right]^{-1}, \; i > 1, \; \textstyle\sum_{i=2}^{N} e_i^{**} = 1 \quad (18.94)$$

*and* $p_{ij}^*$, $p_{ij}^{**}$ *are given by (18.59), cf.* Proposition 18.1.

*When some of the industries have* **CES** *substitution elasticities larger and smaller than one, then the* **limiting GDP** *expenditure shares become:*

$$\sigma_u < 1 : \sigma_i > 1 > \sigma_j : \lim_{\omega \to 0,\infty} e_i(\omega) = 0, \; \lim_{\omega \to 0} e_j(\omega) = \underline{e}_j^*, \; \lim_{\omega \to \infty} e_j(\omega) = \underline{e}_j^{**} \quad (18.95)$$

$$\sigma_u > 1 : \sigma_i > 1 > \sigma_j : \lim_{\omega \to 0} e_i(\omega) = \bar{e}_i^{**}, \; \lim_{\omega \to \infty} e_i(\omega) = \bar{e}_i^*, \; \lim_{\omega \to 0,\infty} e_j(\omega) = 0 \quad (18.96)$$

*where*

$$\bar{e}_j^* = \left[1 + \sum_{j\neq i, \sigma_i > 1} \left[\frac{\alpha_j}{\alpha_i}\right]^{\sigma_u} p_{ij}^{*\sigma_u - 1}\right]^{-1}, \; j > 1, \; \bar{e}^* = \sum_{j=2}^{N} \bar{e}_j^* \le 1 \quad (18.97)$$

$$\bar{e}_j^{**} = \left[1 + \sum_{j\neq i, \sigma_i > 1} \left[\frac{\alpha_j}{\alpha_i}\right]^{\sigma_u} p_{ij}^{**\sigma_u - 1}\right]^{-1}, \; j > 1, \; \bar{e}^{**} = \sum_{j=2}^{N} \bar{e}_j^{**} \le 1 \quad (18.98)$$

$$\underline{e}_i^* = \left[1 + \sum_{j\neq i, \sigma_j < 1} \left[\frac{\alpha_j}{\alpha_i}\right]^{\sigma_u} p_{ij}^{*\sigma_u - 1}\right]^{-1}, \; i > 1, \; \underline{e}^* = \sum_{i=2}^{N} \underline{e}_i^* \le 1 \quad (18.99)$$

$$\underline{e}_i^{**} = \left[1 + \sum_{j\neq i, \sigma_j < 1} \left[\frac{\alpha_j}{\alpha_i}\right]^{\sigma_u} p_{ij}^{**\sigma_u - 1}\right]^{-1}, \; i > 1, \; \underline{e}^{**} = \sum_{i=2}^{N} \underline{e}_i^{**} \le 1 \quad (18.100)$$

$$\bar{e}^* + \underline{e}^* = 1; \quad \bar{e}^{**} + \underline{e}^{**} = 1 \quad (18.101)$$

***Proof*** The *limiting* shares (18.91–18.94) follow from (18.90) and (18.61–18.62). The *limiting* shares (18.95–18.100) follow from (18.90) and (18.63–18.64). □

### *Homothetic and Non-homothetic Preferences*

The main *deficiency* of many conventional and in fact any *homothetic* direct utility function is that all the consumer goods have an "income (C)" *elasticity* of *one*. Hence, the class of indirect utility functions attracts more attention. A *flexible* expenditure system satisfying (18.83) was first proposed by Leser (1941), and it was related to the *indirect "addilog"* by Houthakker (1960). We have, cf. Silberberg and Suen (2001, p.360), Chung (1994, p.42):

**Indirect "Addilog" Utility:**

$\alpha_i > 0,\ \sum_{i=2}^{N} \alpha_i = 1,\ 0 < \beta_i < 1,$

$$V(P_2, \cdots, P_N, C) = \gamma_v \sum_{i=2}^{N} \alpha_i \left[\frac{C}{P_i}\right]^{\beta_i} = \gamma_v \sum_{j=2}^{N} \alpha_j\, p_{ij}^{\beta_j} \left[\frac{C}{P_i}\right]^{\beta_j} \tag{18.102}$$

$$e_i = \frac{\alpha_i \beta_i \left[\dfrac{C}{P_i}\right]^{\beta_i}}{\displaystyle\sum_{j=2}^{N} \alpha_j \beta_j \left[\dfrac{C}{P_j}\right]^{\beta_j}} = \left[\sum_{j=2}^{N} \frac{\alpha_j \beta_j}{\alpha_i \beta_i} \left[\frac{P_i^{\beta_i}}{P_j^{\beta_j}}\right] C^{\beta_j - \beta_i}\right]^{-1}$$

$$= \left[\sum_{j=2}^{N} \frac{\alpha_j \beta_j}{\alpha_i \beta_i}\, p_{ij}^{\beta_j} \left[\frac{C}{P_i}\right]^{\beta_j - \beta_i}\right]^{-1} \tag{18.103}$$

$$\forall j \quad \beta_j = \beta : \quad e_i(\omega) = \left[1 + \sum_{j=2, j\neq i}^{N} \left[\frac{\alpha_j}{\alpha_i}\right] p_{ij}(\omega)^{\beta}\right]^{-1} \tag{18.104}$$

$$e_i\,(\omega, L, K) = \left[1 + \sum_{j=2, j\neq i}^{N} \frac{\alpha_j\, \beta_j}{\alpha_i\, \beta_i}\, p_{ij}(\omega)^{\beta_j} \left[\frac{C}{P_i}(\omega, L, K)\right]^{\beta_j - \beta_i}\right]^{-1} \tag{18.105}$$

The budget *system* (18.104), with $\beta = \sigma_u - 1 > 0$, is seen to be a subsystem of the *homothetic* CES system (18.90) already characterized in Lemma 18.3.

With $\beta_i \neq \beta_j$ the *non-homothetic indirect addilog* utility function has budget *shares* (18.105) with terms, $C/P_i = (1-s)Y/P_i$, cf. (18.73), where $Y/P_i$ is well-defined in terms of $\omega$, $L$, $K$, see (18.25). With the *positivity* restrictions above on $\alpha_i$, $\beta_i$, the budget shares (18.104–18.105), *always* satisfies: $0 < e_i < 1$.

*Without* imposing *positivity* restrictions on *all*, $\beta_i$, but just *assuming*:

$$\alpha_i^{\star} > 0, \quad \sum_{i=2}^{N} \alpha_i^{\star} = 1, \quad \beta_i < 1 \tag{18.106}$$

then the Houthakker (Addilog) expenditure *system* (18.105) is *generalized* to:

$$e_i\,(\omega, L, K) = \left[1 + \sum_{j=2, j\neq i}^{N} [\,\tfrac{\alpha_j^\star}{\alpha_i^\star}\,]\, p_{ij}(\omega)^{\beta_j} \left[\tfrac{C}{P_i}(\omega, L, K)\right]^{\beta_j - \beta_i}\right]^{-1} \tag{18.107}$$

Still, (18.106–18.107) satisfies: $0 < e_i\,(\omega, L, K) < 1$. The *indirect* utility function of this generalized budget system is *unknown* (and may never be given in closed form).[1] But the empirical application of (18.107), e.g., Somermeyer and Langhout (1972), Jensen (1980), works reasonably well; its *Engel curve patterns* allows negative, zero, and positive "income elasticities" (the upper bound may be greater than two), and collectively, restrictions (18.82–18.85) are satisfied by (18.107).

Finally, consider the

**Translog Indirect Utility:** $\alpha_j > 0,\ \sum_{j=2}^{N} \alpha_j = 1,\ \beta_{ij} = \beta_{ji}$

$$\ln V(P_2, \cdots, P_N, C) = \ln \alpha_0 + \sum_{j=2}^{N} \alpha_j \ln \frac{C}{P_j} + \frac{1}{2} \sum_{i=2}^{N} \sum_{j=2}^{N} \beta_{ij} \ln \frac{C}{P_i} \ln \frac{C}{P_j} \tag{18.108}$$

$$e_i = \frac{P_i Y_i}{C} = \frac{\alpha_i + \sum_{j=2}^{N} \beta_{ij} \ln\left(C/P_j\right)}{1 + \sum_{k=2}^{N} \sum_{j=2}^{N} \beta_{kj} \ln\left(C/P_j\right)} \tag{18.109}$$

$$e_i = \frac{\alpha_i + \sum_{j=2}^{N} \beta_{ij} \ln(C/P_j)}{\alpha_i + \sum_{j=2}^{N} \beta_{ij} \ln(C/P_j) + \sum_{i\neq k=2}^{N} \left[\alpha_k + \sum_{j=2}^{N} \beta_{kj} \ln(C/P_j)\right]} \tag{18.110}$$

This *translog* indirect utility function, Christensen et al. (1971, 1975), Silberberg and Suen (2001, p.361), Chung (1994, p.68), is one of the most widely used flexible functional forms in empirical demand analysis. It may be interpreted as a second-order local approximation to an arbitrary indirect utility function. Its budget share is here presented in a proper explicit forms for our purposes.

The usual *monotonicity* property of *preferences* is satisfied by imposing on (18.108) the *condition* (18.111), (LHS); see Chung (1994, p.69):

$$\forall k:\quad \alpha_k + \sum_{j=2}^{N} \beta_{kj} \ln(C/P_j) > 0 \;\Rightarrow\; \forall i : 0 < e_i < 1 \tag{18.111}$$

[1] Later the explicit parametric form of the Indirect utility function, (18.102), (18.106), was exactly stated (with $\forall\, \beta_i \geqq -1$) in Jensen et al. (2011, p.220), here Chap. 5. Non-homothetic CDES and $e_i\,(\omega, L, K)$, (18.107), are applied in Jensen et al. (2015, p.227); here Chap. 20.

which is a *sufficient* condition, cf. (18.110), for relevant shares, $e_i$, too, (RHS).

Rewriting $\ln(C/P_j) = \ln[C/P_i \cdot P_i/P_j] = \ln(C/P_i \cdot p_{ij}) = \ln(C/P_i) + \ln p_{ij}$, then we get (18.110) restated (dividing by its numerator) conveniently as,

$$e_i(\omega, L, K) = \left[ 1 + \frac{\sum_{i \neq k=2}^{N} \left[ \alpha_k + \sum_{j=2}^{N} \beta_{kj} \ln p_{ij} + \ln(C/P_i) \sum_{j=2}^{N} \beta_{kj} \right]}{\alpha_i + \ln(C/P_i) \sum_{j=2}^{N} \beta_{ij}} \right]^{-1} \tag{18.112}$$

In the *non-homothetic* case, the terms, $C/P_i$, (18.112) are—as mentioned above for the non-homothetic addilog—well-defined in the arguments of $e_i$, (18.112).

By direct inspection of the budget share, (18.109), a more *tractable* and simpler *sufficient* condition than, (18.111), for always having, $0 < e_i < 1$, is:

$$\forall i : [\, \forall k : \quad P_k \leq C, \quad \wedge \quad \beta_{ik} \leq \sum_{j=2}^{N} \beta_{kj} \;\Rightarrow\; 0 < e_i < 1 \,] \tag{18.113}$$

The *implication*, (18.113), follows here from using, $\ln C/P_k > 0$, and the *symmetry*, $\beta_{ij} = \beta_{ji}$, in (18.109). Thus, (18.113) also applies to budget *shares*, (18.112).

Requiring in, (18.113), that all *unit prices*, $\mathbf{P_k}$, are *less* than *total* expenditure, **C**, is hardly any practical restriction at all; such luxury goods are ignored.

For the *homothetic* translog with the restrictions,

$$\sum_{j=2}^{N} \beta_{kj} = 0, \quad k = 2, \cdots, N \tag{18.114}$$

the budget shares ($e_i$) become, (18.112):

$$e_i(\omega) = \frac{\alpha_i}{1 - \sum_{j=2}^{N} \beta_{ij} \ln p_{ij}(\omega)} \qquad i = 2, \cdots, N \tag{18.115}$$

Besides (18.114), we must evidently impose *further* parameter restrictions on $\beta_{ij}$, or somehow upon sizes of the relative prices, $p_{ij}$—for $0 < e_i < 1$ in (18.115):

$$0 < e_i(\omega) < 1 : \quad \sum_{j=2}^{N} \beta_{kj} = 0, \quad 1 - \sum_{j=2}^{N} \beta_{ij} \ln p_{ij}(\omega) > \alpha_i > 0$$

However, we shall not pursue such restrictions, since the homothetic translog has little factual application. With translog, it is the *non-homothetic* version and its richer *Engel curve patterns* that makes it attractive/useful.

## Walrasian General Equilibrium of Multi-sector Economies

The ***demand side*** of the multi-sector economy is expressed by the respective GDP expenditure shares, $s_i$, derived from the consumer budget shares, $e_i$, in section "Preferences, Demand, and Expenditure Compositions of GDP". The *supply side* of the economy—operating under constant returns to scale and with full (18.10–18.11) and Pareto-efficient factor utilization, (18.16)—is always summarized by sectorial factor allocation fractions $\lambda_{L_i}$, $\lambda_{K_i}$, which in turn are determined by $(s_i)$, (18.28), and the sectoral cost shares, $\epsilon_{L_i}$, $\epsilon_{K_i}$, (18.33).

**Theorem 18.1** *The* **Walrasian** *equilibrium (competitive general equilibrium) states,—by market clearing prices on the commodity/factor markets and Pareto-efficient endowments allocations—are, with* **homogeneous** *production functions of degree 1, and with any* **homothetic** *preferences, given by:* $\forall k \in R_+$, $\forall \omega \in \Omega$, *(18.34), (18.28), (18.30), (18.90), (18.104), (18.115),*

$$k = \frac{\omega\,\delta_K(\omega)}{\delta_L(\omega)} = \frac{\omega \sum_{i=1}^{N} s_i(\omega)\,\epsilon_{K_i}(\omega)}{\sum_{i=1}^{N} s_i(\omega)\,\epsilon_{L_i}(\omega)} = \Psi(\omega) \tag{18.116}$$

**Corollary 18.1** *With* **CES** *sector technologies and any* **homothetic** *utility function, the* **Walrasian** *equilibrium* $k = \Psi(\omega)$ *becomes by (18.116) and (18.47):*

$$k = \frac{\omega \sum_{i=1}^{N} s_i(\omega)\,(1 + c_i\,\omega^{1-\sigma_i})^{-1}}{1 - \sum_{i=1}^{N} s_i(\omega)\,(1 + c_i\,\omega^{1-\sigma_i})^{-1}} = \Psi(\omega) \tag{18.117}$$

**Theorem 18.2** *For sector technologies with constant returns to scale, and* **non-homothetic** *utility functions,* **Walrasian** *equilibrium states are given by: (18.34), (18.28), (18.30), (18.105), (18.107) and (18.112),*

$$K/L = \frac{\omega\,\delta_K\,(\omega, L, K)}{\delta_L\,(\omega, L, K)} = \frac{\omega \sum_{i=1}^{N} s_i\,(\omega, L, K)\,\epsilon_{K_i}(\omega)}{\sum_{i=1}^{N} s_i\,(\omega, L, K)\,\epsilon_{L_i}(\omega)} = \Upsilon\,(\omega, L, K) \tag{18.118}$$

**Corollary 18.2** *With* **CES** *sector technologies, the* **Walrasian** *equilibrium, by the* **explicit** *function,* $\Upsilon\,(\omega, L, K)$*, (18.118), becomes with (18.47):*

$$K/L = \frac{\omega \sum_{i=1}^{N} s_i\,(\omega, L, K)\,(1 + c_i\,\omega^{1-\sigma_i})^{-1}}{1 - \sum_{i=1}^{N}, s_i\,(\omega, L, K)\,(1 + c_i\,\omega^{1-\sigma_i})^{-1}} = \Upsilon\,(\omega, L, K) \tag{18.119}$$

*Locus expressions (18.118), (18.119), give* $(\boldsymbol{\omega})$ **implicitly** *as a function of (L,K):*

$$\omega = \Lambda\,(L, K) \tag{18.120}$$

***Proof*** The theorems and corollaries are obtained by turning Walras's law (identity), (18.34), into the respective Walrasian equilibrium conditions, (18.116–18.119). Rather than relying on *fixed-point methods* for searching (iteration) the equilibrium prices (vector) of numerous supply and demand equations of goods and factor markets, the general equilibrium *solution procedure* of Theorems 18.1–18.2 are formulated in variables (*shares*), having simple economic and observable NIPA counterparts. Since relative *commodity prices* are *endogenous* variables, they are by construction properly eliminated from our "*structural*" general equilibrium equations. Hence, we end up with a "*reduced*" form of just ***one equation*** (explicit or implicit) between the remaining endogenous *relative factor prices* in general equilibrium and the exogenous (given) *factor endowments*. □

The competitive *general equilibrium functions*, $k = \Psi(\omega)$, $\omega = \Lambda(L, K)$, are crucial for inquiring into *statics*, the *comparative statics*, and *dynamics* of *multi-sector* economies, and they are called the *Factor Endowment-Factor Price* (**FEFP**) *correspondence*. Having obtained ($\omega$) from (18.116), we can go back through (18.22), (18.51), (18.90) (18.47), (18.32), (18.33), (18.24) to get the associated general equilibrium values of all other endogenous variables (sector outputs, allocation fractions of inputs, income shares, relative commodity prices).

Regarding the **shape** of the graph of $\Psi$, (18.117), it is evident that, if **all** substitution elasticities are *larger* than one, $\sigma_i > 1$, $i = 2, \cdots, N$, then the numerator (denominator) expression in (18.117) will increase (decrease), cf. $\epsilon_{K_i}, \epsilon_{L_i}$ (18.15), which always ensures that the Walrasian *locus* $\Psi(\omega)$, (18.117), is *monotonically increasing*. When *all* $\sigma_i$ are *less* than one, $\sigma_i < 1$, only a detailed examination will reveal the *global* and *local* shape of the graph.

**Proposition 18.2** *The graphs of the* **Walrasian** *equilibrium, $\Psi(\omega)$, (18.117), are in* Fig. 18.0, *to be located between the extreme monotonic* **CES**, *$\omega_i$-curves, (18.46). For any value of the GDP shares, $s_i$, and for any size of the sectorial substitution elasticities, $\sigma_i, i = 1, \cdots, N$, the functions, $\Psi(\omega)$, have the limit properties:*

$$\lim_{\omega\to 0} \Psi(\omega) = 0, \quad \lim_{\omega\to\infty} \Psi(\omega) = \infty; \tag{18.121}$$

$$\lim_{\omega\to 0} \Psi(\omega)/\Psi'(\omega) = 0, \quad \lim_{\omega\to\infty} \Psi(\omega)/\Psi'(\omega) = \infty \tag{18.122}$$

*With (18.117), the elasticities, $E(k, \omega)$, of $\Psi(\omega)$ have finite limits as follows:*

$$\forall i : \sigma_i < 1 : \qquad \lim_{\omega\to 0} E(k, \omega) = \lim_{\omega\to\infty} E(k, \omega) = \max_i \sigma_i \tag{18.123}$$

$$\forall i : \sigma_i > 1 : \qquad \lim_{\omega\to 0} E(k, \omega) = \lim_{\omega\to\infty} E(k, \omega) = \min_i \sigma_i \tag{18.124}$$

$$\exists i, j : \sigma_i > 1 > \sigma_j : \qquad \lim_{\omega\to 0} E(k, \omega) = \lim_{\omega\to\infty} E(k, \omega) = 1 \tag{18.125}$$

***Proof*** The limits (18.121–18.122) are seen immediately from (18.117). The limits (18.123–18.125) follow from the formula, cf., (18.116), (18.117)

$$E\,(k,\omega) = \Psi'(\omega)\,\omega/\Psi(\omega) = 1 + E(\delta_K,\omega) - E(1-\delta_K,\omega) \tag{18.126}$$

$$E\,(\delta_{K,}\omega) = \delta_K'\,(\omega)\,\omega/\delta_K, \quad E(1-\delta_K,\omega) = -\delta_K'(\omega)\,\omega/(1-\delta_K) \tag{18.127}$$

In case of ***constant*** $s_i$, the numerators of (18.127), $\pm\delta_K'(\omega)\,\omega$, go to zero for both $\omega \to 0$ and $\omega \to \infty$, as is seen by simple calculations. The denominators of (18.127), $\delta_K$, $1-\delta_K$, go to $\bar{s}$ or $\underline{s}$ for $\omega \to 0$ and $\omega \to \infty$ in accordance with (18.161–18.164). Hence in case of, $0 < \bar{s} < 1$, cf. (18.161), (18.163), the last two terms of (18.126) go to zero—giving (18.125). In case of, $\bar{s} = 0, 1$, one term of (18.126) goes to zero, while the other goes to the dominating power, in some cases seen by use of l'Hospital. This proves (18.123–18.124).

In the case of ***variable*** $s_i(\omega)$, we just have to correct the proof above by adding the limits of $s_i'(\omega)\,\omega/s_i(\omega)$, which, however, are both zero, since the budget *shares* $e_i(\omega)$ have specific *limits*, $e_i^*$ and $e_i^{**}$, for the respective CES parametric utility functions, cf. (18.91–18.99), (18.104), and (18.115). □

## Dynamic Systems and Evolution of Multi-sector Economies

In the multi-sectoral planning literature, we often read statements like that of, e.g., Johansen (1974, p.22):

"The *growth process* is generated by the following *factors*, all of which are considered to be *exogenously* determined: (a) Total investment, (b) Growth in population/working and total, (c) Growth in productivity/shifts in production functions over time, (d) Changes in exogenous demand/mainly government and net foreign demand". This broad view of the exogeneity concept refers to exogeneity (separability) assumptions of very diverse nature. Let us consider those above in reverse order.

Some "applied/planning" growth models may include a ***public sector*** with government expenditure and taxation assumptions/specifications, but this sector can properly be ***excluded*** for other theoretical/analytical purposes. Similarly, some growth models may include ***international*** trade and international factor mobility. Certainly, open and in particular small open economies operate differently from closed economies, but for obtaining some actual insights about economic evolution, a relevant *closed* (global) economy growth model may suffice. Next, "shifts" in production (or utility) functions refer to "***parametric***" changes. Since most economic parameters are not "natural constants" and occasionally undergo critical changes, an important objective of growth models is to qualitatively understand and ***identify*** the crucial ***parameters*** involved and their critical ***numerical*** values. Regarding *labor endowments* (population), no attention has so far been directed to its exogenously given size. As a state variable in a dynamic model, it may still be treated, without violating the general equilibrium model above, as *evolving exogenously* with specified parameters.

On the contrary, however, the time paths of total investments and *capital endowments* cannot be *extrapolated exogenously* without *violating the general equilibrium solutions* of Theorems 18.1–18.2. A coherent general equilibrium *evolution* for the *capital endowments* in continuous time can only be derived from consistently integrating the *endogenous output* paths of our **sector 1**.

Thus, the *macrodynamic* role of the *capital good* industry (*machinery*) in growth models of *multi-industry* economies needs to be carefully studied. The equations of *factor accumulation* for multi-sector growth models—with two primary factors and flexible constant return-to-scale sector technologies—are formally given, by ($\delta$ is the depreciation rate of capital),

$$dL/dt \equiv \dot{L} = nL, \tag{18.128}$$

$$dK/dt \equiv \dot{K} = Y_1 - \delta K = L\, y_1\, \lambda_{L_1} - \delta K = L[\, f_1(k_1)\, \lambda_{L_1} - \delta k\,] \tag{18.129}$$

### *General Equilibrium Dynamics with Homothetic Preferences*

In the general equilibrium models of multi-sector economies, $\mathbf{k_1}$ and $\lambda_{L_1}$ in (18.129) are through common ($\omega$), (18.16), and (18.116–18.117), *uniquely* determined by the *factor* endowments *ratio* **k**. Hence, the accumulation equations (18.128–18.129) become *autonomous* (time invariant) *differential equations* in the state variables, $L$ and $K$—representing a standard *homogeneous dynamic system*,

$$\dot{L} = L n \equiv L\, \mathfrak{f}(k), \tag{18.130}$$

$$\dot{K} = L[\, f_1\, (k_1[\, \Psi^{-1}(k)\,])\, \lambda_{L_1}[\, \Psi^{-1}(k)\,] - \delta k\,] \equiv L\, \mathfrak{g}(k), \;\; L \neq 0. \tag{18.131}$$

As $\mathfrak{g}(k)$, (18.131), are intricate functions of $(k)$, we rewrite $\mathfrak{g}(k)$ in *alternative* forms by (18.129), (18.25–18.26):

$$\dot{K} = s_1\, (Y/P_1) - \delta K = L\, s_1\, (\omega + k)\, f_1'(k_1) - \delta K \tag{18.132}$$

$$= L\, k \left[ \frac{s_1\, f_1'(k_1)}{\delta_K} - \delta \right] = L\, \mathfrak{g}(k); \quad L\, k = K \tag{18.133}$$

where—to succinctly express and decompose the governing functions of capital accumulation (18.132)—the bounded variable $\delta_K$ (18.25–18.26) is formally an auxiliary term helpful in evaluating concrete cases.

From the *governing* functions $\mathfrak{g}(k)$, $\mathfrak{f}(k)$, (18.130–18.133), the *director* function, $h(k)$, that controls, $dk/dt \equiv \dot{k}$, takes the form, $h(k) \equiv \mathfrak{g}(k) - k\, \mathfrak{f}(k)$, i.e.,

$$\dot{k} = h(k) = k \left[ \frac{s_1\, f_1'\,[\, k_1[\, \omega(k)\,]\,]}{\delta_K[\, \omega(k)\,]} - (n + \delta) \right]; \quad \omega(k) = \Psi^{-1}(k) \tag{18.134}$$

The dynamic system (18.134) in (**k**) is difficult to evaluate ***quantitatively*** and generally analytically intractable; e.g., if $\sigma_i \neq \sigma_j$, then, $k = \Psi(\omega)$, (18.116) can not be inverted (although $\Psi^{-1}$ exists) in closed form. But $k = \Psi(\omega)$, (18.116), are ***continuously differentiable*** functions of $(\omega)$, and dynamics in $(k)$ can, whenever convenient, be converted into ***dual autonomous dynamics*** in $(\boldsymbol{\omega})$:

$$\dot{\omega} = \frac{\dot{k}}{dk/d\omega} = \frac{h(k)}{dk/d\omega} = \frac{h(\Psi[\omega])}{\Psi'(\omega)} \equiv \boldsymbol{\hbar}(\boldsymbol{\omega}) \tag{18.135}$$

Hence we get, cf. (18.134),

$$\hbar(\omega) = \frac{\Psi(\omega)}{\Psi'(\omega)}\left[\frac{s_1 f_1'[k_1(\omega)]}{\delta_K(\omega)} - (n+\delta)\right] \tag{18.136}$$

$$= \frac{\omega}{E(k,\omega)}\left[\frac{s_1 f_1'[k_1(\omega)]}{\delta_K(\omega)} - (n+\delta)\right] \tag{18.137}$$

With **CES** technologies, we have from (18.136), (18.32), (18.30), (18.47), (18.81):

$$\hbar(\omega) = \frac{\Psi(\omega)}{\Psi'(\omega)}\left[\frac{s_1 \gamma_1 a_1^{\frac{\sigma_1}{\sigma_1-1}}\left[1 + c_1 \omega^{1-\sigma_1}\right]^{1/(\sigma_1-1)}}{\sum_{i=1}^{N} s_i(\omega)\left[1 + c_i \omega^{1-\sigma_i}\right]^{-1}} - (n+\delta)\right] \tag{18.138}$$

with $\Psi(\omega)$ given in (18.117).

### *Existence and Uniqueness of Steady States or Persistent Growth*

The complete set (family) of $k(t)$ solutions to the dynamic systems (18.134) is *qualitatively* described and classified by

**Theorem 18.3** *The multi-sector growth models (18.134) have no positive, stationary $k(t)$-solution [$k(t) = 0$ is attractor], iff, [cf. $\bar{\mathfrak{b}}_1$, (18.3), $\delta_K$, (18.26), (18.18)],*

$$\forall k > 0: \ \bar{\mathfrak{b}}_1 < \left[\frac{n+\delta}{s_1}\right] \delta_K(k) \tag{18.139}$$

*and have at least one steady state [ray path in $(L, K)$-space], iff,*

$$\exists k > 0: \ \left[\frac{n+\delta}{s_1}\right] \delta_K(k) \in J_1 \tag{18.140}$$

*The steady state capital-labor ratio,* $\forall t\,:\,k(t)=\kappa$ *, are obtained by:*

$$f_1'\left[k_1(\kappa)\right]=\left[\frac{n+\delta}{s_1}\right]\delta_K(\kappa)\;\Leftrightarrow\;\frac{n+\delta}{s_1}=\frac{f_1'\left[k_1(\kappa)\right]}{r\kappa/y}=\frac{y/P_1\left[\kappa\right]}{\kappa}\tag{18.141}$$

*With existence (18.140), a sufficient condition for a unique* $\kappa$*, (18.141), of* $h(k)$ *is*

$$\forall k>0:E\left(h(k)/k,k\right)<0\;\Leftrightarrow\;\forall\omega\in\Omega:E\left(k,\omega\right)\geq 1,\tag{18.142}$$

*The time paths of the growth model solutions,* $k(t)$*, display persistent growth—* $\lim_{t\to\infty}k(t)=\infty$*—if and only if*

$$\forall k>0\;:\quad \underline{\mathfrak{b}}_1>\left[\frac{n+\delta}{s_1}\right]\delta_K(k)\tag{18.143}$$

***Proof*** The set of solutions to (18.134) depends entirely on the *shape* of the *director* function, $h(k)$, and the *number* of roots of $h(k)$. The existence of nonzero roots requires that—$[\,\frac{n+\delta}{s_1}\,]\,\delta_K(k)$—belongs to the *range* of $f_1'$ as stated in (18.140). If no positive root exists, we have either the case (18.139) with origo as attractor or the case (18.143) with persistent growth.

If a root of (18.141) exists, a unique attractor in the interval stated in (18.140) always occurs with a global negative sign of the elasticity, $E\,(h(k)/k,k)<0$, which can be derived from (18.134); cf. (18.142, 18.123–18.125), and Jensen (1994, p.137,129); here Chap. 15, and in Jensen (2003, p.73); here Chap. 17. □

### *Dynamics of Multi-sector Growth Models with CES Technologies*

*Qualitative* properties of the family of *Walrasian general equilibrium solutions* $k(t)$ in multi-sector growth models with CES technologies are summarized by

**Theorem 18.4** *For the multi-sector growth models (18.128–18.131) with CES sector technologies, the sufficient conditions for the existence of at least one positive* **steady-state** *solution* $\kappa$ *are [no positive, attractive, steady-state solution* $\kappa$ *(18.141) exists with the inequalities of (18.144–18.145), RHS, reversed]:*

$$\forall i:\sigma_i<1\;\;\bar{\mathfrak{b}}_1=\gamma_1 a_1^{\frac{\sigma_1}{\sigma_1-1}}>(n+\delta)/s_1\qquad\underline{\beta}=1+\tfrac{1-s_1}{s_1}\underline{e}^*:\tag{18.144}$$

$$\sigma_1<1\;\;\bar{\mathfrak{b}}_1=\gamma_1 a_1^{\frac{\sigma_1}{\sigma_1-1}}>\frac{(n+\delta)(\underline{s}+s_1)}{s_1}=\begin{cases}(n+\delta)\underline{\beta} & \textit{for}\ \sigma_u<1\\ n+\delta & \textit{for}\ \sigma_u>1\end{cases}\tag{18.145}$$

*If* $\sigma_1\leq 1$ *(sufficient condition), persistent growth of* $k(t)$ *is impossible.*

*If* $\sigma_1 > 1$, *necessary and sufficient conditions for* $\lim_{t\to\infty} k(t) = \infty$ *are:*

$$\forall i : \sigma_i > 1 \ \ \underline{\mathfrak{b}}_1 = \gamma_1 a_1^{\frac{\sigma_1}{\sigma_1 - 1}} > (n+\delta)/s_1. \qquad \bar{\beta} = 1 + \tfrac{1-s_1}{s_1}\bar{e}^* : \tag{18.146}$$

$$\sigma_1 > 1 \ \ \underline{\mathfrak{b}}_1 = \gamma_1 a_1^{\frac{\sigma_1}{\sigma_1 - 1}} > \frac{(n+\delta)(\bar{s}+s_1)}{s_1} = \begin{cases} (n+\delta)\bar{\beta} & \text{for } \sigma_u > 1 \\ n+\delta & \text{for } \sigma_u < 1 \end{cases} \tag{18.147}$$

*except that (18.147) is occasionally not sufficient for small initial values.*

***Proof*** The proof proceeds with the *dual version*, $\hbar(\omega)$. The term $\Psi(\omega)/\Psi'(\omega)$ has no influence on these limit analyses, cf. Proposition 18.2.

Ad $\sigma_1 < 1$: The fraction in the large bracket (18.138) goes to zero for $\omega \to \infty$; hence, there are no permanent increasing solutions of $\omega(t)$. If (18.144–18.145) are satisfied, then this fraction passes at least once monotonically through the constant, when $\omega$ goes from zero to infinity. The difference $\underline{s}$ in the constant comes from the denominator taking values 1 or $\underline{s}$ for $\omega \to 0$, depending on the size of other $\sigma_i$. If the inequalities are reversed, then $\hbar(\omega)$ is negative. The role of $\underline{s}$ in (18.145) follows from (18.138), (18.31), (18.91–18.101).

Ad $\sigma_1 > 1$: The fraction in the large bracket (18.138) goes to infinity for $\omega \to 0$. If and only if (18.146–18.147) are satisfied, then this fraction eventually remains above the constant, when $\omega$ goes from zero to infinity. The difference $s_1$ in the constant comes from the denominator taking values 1 or $\bar{s}$ for $\omega \to \infty$, depending on the size of other $\sigma_i$. Hence $\hbar(\omega)$ is positive for large values of $k$. If the inequalities are reversed, then $\hbar(\omega)$ eventually becomes negative. The necessary conditions (18.146) are also sufficient, as $h(k)$ is, with respectively $\sigma_i > 1$ and $\sigma_1 > 1$, monotonically decreasing, but remain above RHS values, (18.146). The role of $\bar{s}$ in (18.147) follows from (18.31), (18.138), (18.91–18.101). □

Theorem 18.4 shows clearly that the *global existence* problem of *steady states* ($\kappa$)—or *persistent* growth of $k(t)$ depends on the *size* of the *key parameters*: $\sigma_i$, $a_1$, $\gamma_1$, $s_1$, $n$, $\delta$, $\bar{s}$. The *accumulation* parameters ($s_1$, $\bar{s}$, $n$, $\delta$) play some roles; but the *fundamental* role of the *technology* parameters in the *capital* good industry ($\sigma_1$, $\gamma_1$, $a_1$)—altering the long-run $k(t)$ *solutions* of multi-sectoral general equilibrium growth models—*complies* with *observation* and *intuition*. Evidently, the strategic importance ascribed to the capital good industries by economic historians and the general public, makes good economic sense, at least for the closed (global) economy.

The single most important parameter in Theorem 18.4 is the *substitution elasticity* in the capital good sector, $\sigma_1$. It must clearly be larger than one for persistent growth to take place. However, the "*total productivity*" parameter $\gamma_1$ in the capital good sector affects all the stated conditions (18.144–18.147), and they can all be violated by giving $\gamma_1$ any value between 0 and $\infty$.

A larger TFP parameter of the capital good sector $\gamma_1$ may give a "big push", cf. Murphy et al. (1989), Parente and Prescott (1994), Prescott (1998). But if we restrict $\gamma_1 = 1$ and if $\sigma_1 \simeq 2$, then (18.146) will usually be satisfied with the other parameters, in particular, with high saving rates. The key role of the *technology* in the *capital good* industry had escaped the "mainstream" literature on two- and multi-sector growth models, cf. Jensen (2003, p.75); here Chap. 17. As to *empirical evidence*, the theoretical general equilibrium predictions of Theorem 18.4 tally with studies of long-run growth conducted by, Rosenberg (1963), De Long and Summers (1991), Rebelo (1991), and Jones (1995). In particular, high rates of *equipment* investment ("mechanization") are prime determinants for national growth performance (per capita growth).

Furthermore, the making of various equipments become eventually highly mechanized by making various engines (steam, combustion, electric) "*cheap* as well as *good*," cf. Mokyr (1990, p.87). This supports factor substitution and mechanization subsequently in the consumer good industries. In this way, the *capital good* (multi-purpose machinery/equipment) is a "Lever of Riches" (productivity and per capita growth) in *several sectors* with the capital good industry itself and its technology parameters being naturally of primary importance for sustaining the economic growth process—as here mathematically demonstrated in a Walrasian general equilibrium framework.

On the advances in technology and economic evolution, Usher (1954, p.10) writes: "It is important *not* to presume a continuous *development* of *technology* at a *constant rate*, but it is important, also, to recognize that the process of social *evolution* consists in part in the *cumulative* development of science and technology. We *need* both a *general understanding* of the process or processes, and, when records make it possible, a *documented account* of the history of *particular periods* and *particular achievements*"– and (p. 380): "The *technique* of *interchangeable -part manufacture* was thus established in general outline before the invention of the sewing machine or *harvesting machinery.* The new technique was a fundamental condition of the great achievements realized by inventors and manufacturers in those fields. It made it possible to place the sewing machine in the home and it generalized the use of harvesting machinery of McCormick and Deere with astonishing rapidity. American *engineering and manufacturing firms* took the lead in this general development, achieving distinctive results over an important field that was steadily enlarged decade after decade. The group of *machine tools* became more and more *automatic,* and it became possible to build highly specialized *machinery* for *manufacturing firms.* Great refinements of execution were achieved with the *simplest labor* of attendance. These highly developed machine tools are the most distinguished "iron men" of the modern *industrial world,* for they make possible that *substitution* of *machinery* for *labor* that is so happily described as effecting a transfer of skill".

Can *historical stages* (parametric changes) of *increasing substitution elasticities* in several consumer and especially capital goods be better and more eloquently described? Multi-sectoral *dynamics* offer the same economic message about *key parameters* behind the patterns of *industrial evolution*.

### *General Equilibrium Dynamics with Non-homothetic Preferences*

The *qualitative* insight gained from Theorem 18.4 and the discussion about the dynamic role of critical parameter values is *not* confined to economies of homothetic consumer preferences. Evidently, with **non-homothetic** preferences, the factor *accumulation equations*—(18.128, 18.129, 18.132, 18.133)—still apply,

$$\dot{L} = n\,L,\ \ \dot{K} = Y_1 - \delta K = K\left[\frac{s_1\, f_1'\,(k_1\,[\omega\,(\Lambda\,[\,L, K\,])\,])}{\delta_K\,(L, K)} - \delta\right] \tag{18.148}$$

Although the equations, (18.148), cannot be reduced to a single equation in the capital-labor ratio, $(k)$, and certainly neither in the wage-rental ratio $(\omega)$, (18.135–18.138), the accumulation equations, (18.148), still represent a well-defined *dynamic system* in the state variable, $(L, K)$, by which, without explicit solutions, the logarithmic time derivative of $k(t)$ is easily obtained, cf. (18.134)

$$\widehat{K} - \widehat{L} = \hat{k} = \frac{d\ln k}{dt} = \frac{\dot{k}}{k} = \frac{s_1\, f_1'\,(k_1\,[\omega\,(\Lambda\,[\,L, K\,])\,])}{\delta_K\,(L, K)} - (n+\delta) \tag{18.149}$$

Thus the *qualitative* question of steady state or persistent growth of $k(t)$ from, (18.148), similarly depends, cf. (18.143), on the condition:

$$\forall\, L, K > 0: \quad \underline{b}_1 > \frac{n+\delta}{s_1}\,\delta_K\,(L, K) \tag{18.150}$$

The *conditions* of (18.147) still applies, but now here with $(\bar{s})$ dependent of $(L, K)$, cf. (18.105), (18.107), (18.112).

Although there are obviously **quantitatively** great differences for economies with *non-homothetic* preferences (income elasticities different from *one*, Engel's law), it is seen from (18.149–18.150) that the *critical* role of the capital good industry and its *substitution elasticity* carry over from Theorem 18.4.

## Persistent Growth and Asymptotic Growth Rates

To complement the persistent growth solutions of the *state* variable $k(t)$ or $\omega(t)$ with *disaggregate* information about the general equilibrium *evolution* for *sectoral* and other endogenous per capita variables, we characterize the respective time paths by their asymptotic growth rates [ $\hat{\omega}(t) \equiv \dot{\omega}/\omega(t)$, etc.]:

**Theorem 18.5** *With (18.146–18.147), the long-run growth rates of $k(t)$ and $\omega(t)$ in Walrasian multi-sector growth models (18.128) with* **CES** *technologies are:*

$$\forall i : \sigma_i > 1 : \lim_{t\to\infty} \hat{\omega} = \frac{s_1\underline{\mathfrak{b}}_1 - (n+\delta)}{\min\{\sigma_i\}}; \quad \lim_{t\to\infty} \hat{k} = s_1\underline{\mathfrak{b}}_1 - (n+\delta) \quad (18.151)$$

$$\sigma_1 > 1, \ \exists i : \sigma_i < 1 : \lim_{t\to\infty} \hat{\omega} = \lim_{t\to\infty} \hat{k} = \frac{s_1}{\bar{s}}\underline{\mathfrak{b}}_1 - (n+\delta) \quad (18.152)$$

*With (18.151), the long-run sectorial and per capita growth rates are*

$$\lim_{t\to\infty} \hat{k}_i = \lim_{t\to\infty} \hat{y}_i = \lim_{t\to\infty} \widehat{(w/P_i)} = \lim_{t\to\infty} \widehat{(y/P_i)} \quad (18.153)$$

*where*

$$\forall i : \sigma_i > 1 : \lim_{t\to\infty} \hat{k}_i = \frac{\sigma_i}{\min\{\sigma_j\}}[s_1\underline{\mathfrak{b}}_1 - (n+\delta)] \quad (18.154)$$

*With (18.152), some long-run sectorial and per capita growth rates are*

$$\sigma_1 > 1, \ \sigma_i > 1 : \exists j : \sigma_j < 1 : \lim_{t\to\infty} \hat{k}_i = \sigma_i\left(\frac{s_i}{\bar{s}}\underline{\mathfrak{b}}_1 - (n+\delta)\right) \quad (18.155)$$

*If only the capital good sector has a high substitution elasticity, then we have, $\sigma_1 > 1, \ \forall i : \sigma_i < 1 :$*

$$\hat{k} \to \underline{\mathfrak{b}}_1 - (n+\delta), \quad \hat{k}_1 \to \sigma_1[\underline{\mathfrak{b}}_1 - (n+\delta)], \quad \hat{k}_i \to \sigma_i[\underline{\mathfrak{b}}_1 - (n+\delta)] \quad (18.156)$$

$$\lim_{t\to\infty} \hat{k}_1 = \lim_{t\to\infty} \hat{y}_1 = \lim_{t\to\infty} \widehat{(w/P_1)} = \lim_{t\to\infty} \widehat{(y/P_1)} \quad (18.157)$$

*whereas the output of all other sectors will ultimately stagnate,*

$$\lim_{t\to\infty} \hat{y}_i = 0; \quad \lim_{t\to\infty} y_i = \gamma_i(1-a_i)^{\frac{\sigma_i}{\sigma_i-1}}, \ i \neq 1 \quad (18.158)$$

***Proof*** Theorem 18.5 follows immediately from Theorem 18.3, (18.146), combined with (18.136), (18.124), and next using, (18.46–18.47), (18.45), (18.24), (18.16). Thus, by (18.136):

$$\lim_{t\to\infty} \hat{\omega} = [\lim_{\omega\to\infty} E(k,\omega)]^{-1}[s_1\underline{\mathfrak{b}}_1 - (n+\delta)] \quad (18.159)$$

The general equilibrium **FEFP** correspondence $k = \Psi(\omega)$ next gives

$$\hat{k} = E\,(k,\omega)\,\hat{\omega}\,; \quad \hat{k}_i = \sigma_i\hat{\ }\omega, \quad \hat{y}_i = \epsilon_{k_i}\hat{k}_i \quad (18.160)$$

which holds generally with CES. These relations and limits establish the relevant *asymptotic* growth rates in Theorem 18.5. □

As Theorem 18.5 supplements Theorem 18.3 and Proposition 18.2, only a few remarks are needed. The asymptotic growth rates of $(\hat{k})$, (18.151), (18.152) correspond, respectively, to those implied by (18.146), (18.147). Evidently, with more industries to be highly mechanized ($\sigma_i > 1$) and hence larger $\overline{s}$, the slower will be the *overall* accumulation rate, $(\hat{k})$. The same applies to the *sectoral* $(\hat{k}_i)$, (18.154–18.155); but for $(\hat{k}_i)$, what also matters is the *elasticity* of $\Psi$ and its own substitution elasticity, $\sigma_i$, cf. (18.160).

If *maximum* growth of per *capita consumption* is the goal, then the *ranking* with, all $\sigma_j > \sigma_1 > 1$, is preferred—which contributes to mechanizing and maintaining the growth rate of all consumer goods and thereby increases the welfare per capita in any numeraire (sectoral) good, (18.153). The other extreme is capital accumulation for its own sake (18.156–18.158); capital accumulation, causing increasing wage-rental rates, makes it impossible to avoid increasing sectoral $(k_i)$ anywhere, even though diminishing returns (with $\sigma_i < 1$) eventually terminate increases in sectoral labor productivity.

Thus, even with *homothetic* preferences and only *price elasticities* involved on the demand side, diverse patterns of industrial growth may emerge with different **CES** technologies on the supply side of a multi-sector economy.

## Final Comments

The opinion of Ricardo (1965, p.263–269) on capital goods (machinery) was the following:

> Ever since I first turned my attention to questions of political economy, I have been of opinion that such an application of machinery to any branch of production as should have the effect of saving labour was a general good, accompanied only with that portion of inconvenience which in most cases attends the removal of capital and labour from one employment to another.
> - These were my opinions, and they continue unaltered, as far as regards the landlord and the capitalist; but I am convinced that the substitution of machinery for human labour is often very injurious to the interests of the class of laborers.
> - The statements which I have made will not, I hope, lead to the inference that machinery should not be encouraged. To elucidate the principle, I have been supposing that improved machinery is suddenly discovered and extensively used; but the truth is that these discoveries are gradual, and rather operate in determining the employment of the capital which is saved and accumulated than in diverting capital from its actual employment.

His contemporary von Thünen (1850, 1930, p.499) had similar opinion:

> Während man in Europa den gedrückten Zustand der arbeitenden Klasse so haüfig der zunehmenden Anwendung von Maschinen zuschreibt, wird in dem gesellschaftlichen Zustand, den wir hier vor Augen haben, die Lage der Arbeiter immer blühender and glänzender, je ausgedehnter beim Anwachsen des Kapitals die Anwendung von Maschinen wird.

Both issues—factor *reallocations* and capital *accumulation* combined with the GDP growth per capita of multi-sector economies—are still with us and will continue to be so, in Europe and globally. In such historical and future human circumstances, it may help (as in natural sciences)—our spirit, knowledge, daily problems and nerves—being able to basically understand the logic and to formally describe the economic laws of motion (change). Mathematical models of *general equilibrium dynamics* for growing economies serve such purposes, as elaborated in this chapter.

It was and still is a widely held *didactic* view that, Myrdal (1973, p.182):

> The emergence and triumph, about a hundred years ago, of the theory of marginal utility and its embodiment in the static equilibrium conception marked an end to the interest the classical authors, and, of course, Marx, had shown in the long-term problems of growth and development. The focus was put on problems about static efficiency and static allocation of resources, relative to given consumer preferences as expressed by aggregate demand.

As quotations above show, we do not disparage insights of classical economic writings; but some of their modes of analysis have little in common with neoclassical or modern equilibrium methodology. The significance of any *equilibrium* ("static") analysis is that it provides a *solution principle* for the economic variables that are involved with the interrelated commodity and factor markets. Moreover, "static efficiency" in allocation is not a rather trivial matter, economically or mathematically. In fact, allocative (Pareto) *efficiency* implemented by a common *marginal rate of substitution* (MRS), $\boldsymbol{\omega} = \mathbf{w}/\mathbf{r}$, gave us the *basic* economic *variable* to reduce the dimension of the solution space for multi-sector economies. The FPCP correspondence, $p_{ij}(\omega)$, consistently linked the interrelated goods and factor markets. Total factor endowments and the parameters of production and utility functions ultimately determined the set (locus) of Walrasian (general) equilibria.

In general equilibrium *dynamics*, we similarly solve for *equilibrium time paths*. As was seen in section "Dynamic Systems and Evolution of Multi-sector Economies", the dynamic system could certainly never be solved without first having obtained the *Walrasian equilibrium solutions*, $\boldsymbol{k} = \boldsymbol{\Psi}(\boldsymbol{\omega})$, or, $\boldsymbol{\omega} = \boldsymbol{\Lambda}(\boldsymbol{L}, \boldsymbol{K})$. In economics, as in physics (mechanics), there was never any progress in *dynamics* before the basic problems of *static* were resolved. No economic growth models or any "magnificent dynamics" (in mathematical sense) were ever analyzed in the classical period.

We have come a long way and reached a higher vantage point, which offer a better view and overall understanding of the roads passed. In closing, let us observe that the dynamics of growing economies is now a worldwide field of study; extensions of this chapter on both the demand/consumer and supply/producer side of multi-sector growth models should be straightforward.

**Acknowledgments** For valuable comments, we are indebted to anonymous referees and to participants at the DEGIT VIII conference, Helsinki, May, 2003—and at Seminars: WiSo, University of Rostock, October, 2003; WIF/ETH,Zürich, December, 2003; School of Mathematical Sciences, Peking University, December, 2003; School of Management and Engineering, Nanjing University, December, 2003; SIPEB, Aoyama Gakuin University, Tokyo, March, 2004; RIEB, Kobe University, March, 2004; IEAS, Academia Sinica, Taiwan, March, 2004; Dept. of Econ., National University of Singapore, March, 2004.

## Appendix A: Asymptotic Walrasian GDP and Factor Allocations

The *comparative static analysis* of exogenous factor endowment, $(L, K)$, variations for *Walrasian equilibria* with CES sector technologies is helpful for the economic understanding of the sectorial allocation implications of critical parameter values. As benchmarks, the asymptotic factor allocations of multi-sector general equilibrium economies with various GDP income shares, $\delta_K$ and sectorial factor allocations, $\lambda_{K_i}, \lambda_{L_i}$, are calculated in Lemma 18.4:

**Lemma 18.4** *For the* **CES** *multi-sector competitive general equilibrium economy, the limits of the factor allocation fractions and factor income shares—for a demand-side specification with constant $e_i$, $(\sigma_u = 1)$, (18.86), (18.89)—are:*

| $\sigma_i$ | $k \to 0$ | | $k \to \infty$ | | |
|---|---|---|---|---|---|
| $1 > \sigma_i \neq \sigma_{max}$ : | $\lambda_{L_i} \to 0 \; \lambda_{K_i} \to \frac{s_i}{\underline{s}}$ | $\delta_K \to \underline{s}$ | $\lambda_{L_i} \to \frac{s_i}{\underline{s}} \; \lambda_{K_i} \to 0$ | $\delta_K \to \bar{s}$ | (18.161) |
| $1 > \sigma_i = \sigma_{max}$ : | $\lambda_{L_i} \to 1 \; \lambda_{K_i} \to s_i$ | $\delta_K \to 1$ | $\lambda_{L_i} \to s_i \; \lambda_{K_i} \to 1$ | $\delta_K \to 0$ | (18.162) |
| $1 < \sigma_i \neq \sigma_{min}$ : | $\lambda_{L_i} \to \frac{s_i}{\bar{s}} \; \lambda_{K_i} \to 0$ | $\delta_K \to \underline{s}$ | $\lambda_{L_i} \to 0 \; \lambda_{K_i} \to \frac{s_i}{\bar{s}}$ | $\delta_K \to \bar{s}$ | (18.163) |
| $1 < \sigma_i = \sigma_{min}$ : | $\lambda_{L_i} \to s_i \; \lambda_{K_i} \to 1$ | $\delta_K \to 0$ | $\lambda_{L_i} \to 1 \; \lambda_{K_i} \to s_i$ | $\delta_K \to 1$ | (18.164) |

*where $\underline{s}$ and $\bar{s}$ are given by (18.31).*

*If the sector technologies have the same* $\sigma_i = \sigma, \forall i$, *then the limits of (18.161–18.164) become,* $[\bar{\lambda}_{L_i} \equiv s_i c_i / \sum s_j c_j, \bar{\lambda}_{K_i} \equiv (s_i/c_i)/\sum s_j/c_j]$:

| $\sigma_i$ | $k \to 0$ | | $k \to \infty$ | |
|---|---|---|---|---|
| $\sigma_i = \sigma < 1$ : | $\lambda_{L_i} \to \bar{\lambda}_{L_i}$ $\lambda_{K_i} \to s_i$ | $\delta_K \to 1$ | $\lambda_{L_i} \to s_i$ $\lambda_{K_i} \to \bar{\lambda}_{K_i}$ | $\delta_K \to 0$ (18.165) |
| $\sigma_i = \sigma > 1$ : | $\lambda_{L_i} \to s_i$ $\lambda_{K_i} \to \bar{\lambda}_{K_i}$ | $\delta_K \to 0$ | $\lambda_{L_i} \to \bar{\lambda}_{L_i}$ $\lambda_{K_i} \to s_i$ | $\delta_K \to 1$ (18.166) |

**Corollary 18.3** *In the case of the* **CES**, *(18.88), and the* **Indirect Addilog** *utility functions, (18.103), with GDP shares,* $s_i(\omega)$, *(18.29), depending on* $\omega$, *the same conclusions (18.161–18.166) hold with limits,* $\bar{e}_i^*, \underline{e}_i^{**}, \bar{e}, \underline{e}$, *given by (18.97–18.101).*

***Proof*** From Lemma 18.1, (18.31), (18.32), (18.47), we get,

$$\delta_K = \sum_{\sigma_i<1} \frac{s_i}{1 + c_i\omega^{1-\sigma_i}} + \sum_{\sigma_i>1} \frac{s_i}{1 + c_i\omega^{1-\sigma_i}} \tag{18.167}$$

For $\omega \to \infty$, the first sum goes to 0, and the second goes to $\bar{s}$.

For $\omega \to 0$, the second sum goes to zero, and the first goes to $\underline{s}$.

From (18.47), we get $\epsilon_{K_i} \to 0$ for $\omega \to \infty$ and $\sigma_i < 1$, and for $\omega \to 0$ and $\sigma_i > 1$. Furthermore, we get $\epsilon_{K_i} \to 1$ for $\omega \to \infty$ and $\sigma_i > 1$, and for $\omega \to 0$ and $\sigma_i < 1$. Together with (18.39), we get the limits for $\lambda_{K_i}$, and together with (18.38), we get the limits for $\lambda_{L_i}$. □

## BIBLIOGRAPHY


Aghion P, Howitt P (1998) Endogenous Growth Theory. The MIT Press, Cambridge, MA and London, England

Arrow KJ, Debreu G (1954) Existence of an Equilibrium for an Competitive Economy. Econometrica 22:265–90

Arrow KJ, Chenery HB, Minhas BS, Solow RM (1961) Capital–Labour Substitution and Economic Efficiency. Review of Economics and Statistics 43:225–250

Brems H (1986) Pioneering Economic Theory 1630–1980. A Mathematical Restatement. The Johns Hopkins University Press, Baltimore

Chenery HB (1960) Patterns of Industrial Growth. American Economic Review 50:624–654

Christensen LR, Jorgensen DW, Lau LJ (1971) Conjugate Duality and the Transcendental Logarithmic Production Function. Econometrica 39:255–256

Christensen LR, Jorgenson DW, Lau LJ (1975) Transcendental Logarithmic Utility Functions. American Economic Review 65:367–383

Chung JW (1994) Utility and Production Functions. Blackwell, Oxford

Clark C (1951) The Conditions of Economic Progress, 2nd edn. MacMillan, London

Clark C (1957) The Conditions of Economic Progress, 3rd edn. MacMillan, London

David PA, Scadding JL (1974) Private Savings: Ultrarationality, Aggregation, and "Denison's Law". Journal of Political Economy 82:225–249
De Long JB, Summers LH (1991) Equipment Investment and Economic Growth. Quarterly Journal of Economics 106:445–502
Deaton A, Muelbauer J (1992) Economics and Consumer Behavior. Cambridge University Press, Cambridge
Debreu G (1959) Theory of Value—An Axiomatic Analysis Of Economic Equilibrium. John Wiley and Sons, New York, Cowles Foundation Monograph No. 17, Yale University Press, New Haven
Denison EF (1958) A Note on Private Saving. Review of Economics and Statistics 40:261–267
Dhrymes PJ (1962) A Multisectoral Model of Growth. Quarterly Journal of Economics 76:264–278
Echevarria C (1997) Changes in Sectoral Composition Associated with Economic Growth. International Economic Review 38:431–452
Frisch R (1959) A Complete Scheme for Computing All Direct and Cross Demand Elasticities in a Model with Many Sectors. Econometrica 27:177–196
Frisch R (1965) Theory of Production. O. Reidel Publishing Company, Dordrecht, Holland
Gravelle H, Rees R (2004) Microeconomics, 3rd edn. Prentice Hall, Harlow
Harberger AC (1962) The Incidence of the Corporation Income Tax. Jour Pol Econ 70:215–240
Houthakker HS (1957) An International Comparison of Household Expenditure Patterns, Commemorating the Centenary of Engel's law. Econometrica 25:532–551
Houthakker HS (1960) Additive Preferences. Econometrica 28:244–257
Houthakker HS (1965) A Note on Self–Dual Preferences. Econometrica 33:797–801
Inada K (1963) On a Two–Sector Model of Economic Growth: Comments and a Generalization. Rev Econ Stud 30:119–27
Islam N (1995) Growth Empirics: A Panel Data Approach. Quarterly Journal of Economics 110:1127–1170
Jensen BS (1980) Expenditure System for the Danish Household Sector. In *Symposium i Anvendt Statistik*, (Lyngby: NEUCC, Denmark)
Jensen BS (1994) The Dynamic Systems of Basic Economic Growth Models. Kluwer Academic Publishers, Dordrecht
Jensen BS (2003) Walrasian General Equilibrium Allocations and Dynamics in Two–Sector Growth Models. German Economic Review 4:53–87
Jensen BS, Larsen ME (1987) Growth and Long–Run Stability. Acta Applicandae Mathematicae 9:219–237, Reprinted in Jensen (1994)
Jensen BS, Wang C (1999) Basic Stochastic Dynamic Systems of Growth and Trade. Review of International Economics 7:378–402; here, Chap. 27
Jensen BS, Richter M, Wang C, Alsholm PK (2001) Saving Rates, Trade, Technology, and Stochastic Dynamics. Review of Development Economics 5:182–204
Jensen BS, de Boer P, van Daal J, Jensen PS (2011) Global Restrictions on the Parameters of the CDES Indirect Utility Function. Journal of Economics 102:217–235
Jensen BS, Lehmijoki U, Rovenskaya E (2015) Non–Homothetic Multisector Growth Models. Review of Development Economics 19(2):221–243
Johansen L (1974) A Multi–Sectorial Study of Economic Growth, 2nd edn. North–Holland, Amsterdam

Jones RW (1965) The Structure of Simple General Equilibrium Models. J Political Economy 73:557–72, or Bhagwati (1981)
Jones RW (1995) R & D–Based Models of Economic Growth. J Political Economy 103:759–784
Jorgenson DW (1961) The Structure of Multi–Sector Dynamic Models. International Economic Review 2:276–293
Judd KL (1998) Numerical Methods in Economics. MIT Press, Mass
Kongsamut P, Rebelo S, Xie D (2001) Beyond Balanced Growth. Review of Economic Studies 68:869–882
Koopmans TC (1960) Stationary Ordinal Utility and Impatience. Econometrica 28:287–309
Laitner J (2000) Structural Change and Economic Growth. Review of Economic Studies 67:545–561
Leser CEV (1941) Family Budget Data and Price Elasticities of Demand. Review of Economic Studies 9:40–57
Mas-Colell A, Whinston MD, Green JR (1995) Microeconomic Theory. Oxford University Press, New York
Meckl J (2002) Structural Change and Generalized Balanced Growth. Journal of Economics 77:241–266
Mokyr J (1990) The Lever of Riches: Technological Creativity and Economic Progress. Oxford University Press, New York
Murphy KM, Shleifer A, Vishny RW (1989) Industrialization and the Big Push. The Journal of Political Economy 97:1003–1026
Myrdal G (1973) Against the Stream. Critical Essays on Economics. Pantheon Books, N.Y
Pais A (1986) Inward Bound. Of Matter and Forces in the Physical World. Oxford University Press
Parente SL, Prescott EC (1994) Barriers to Technology Adoption and Development. The Journal of Political Economy 102(2):298–321
Pasinetti LL (1981) Structural change and Economic Growth. Cambridge University Press
Prescott EC (1998) Lawrence R. Klein Lecture 1997, Needed: A Theory of Total Factor Productivity. International Economic Review 39:525–551
Rebelo S (1991) Long–Run Policy Analysis and Long–Run Growth. Journal of Political Economy 99:500–521
Ricardo D (1965) The Principles of Political Economy and Taxation, 3rd edn. J. M. Dent & Sons, London
Rosenberg N (1963) Technological Change in the Machine Tool Industry, 1840–1910. The J Economic History 23:414–443
Samuelson PA (1953) Prices of Factors and Goods in General Equilibrium. Review of Economic Studies 21:1–20
Samuelson PA (1965) Using Full Duality to Show that Simultaneously Additive Direct and Indirect Utilities implies Unitary Price Elasticity of Demand. Econometrica 33:781–796
Scarf HE (1967) The Approximation of Fixed Points of a Continnuous Mapping. SIAM Jour Appl Math 15:1328–43
Scarf HE, Hansen T (1973) The Computation of Economic Equilibria. Yale University Press

Shoven JB, Whalley J (1984) Applied General–Equilibrium Models of Taxation and International Trade: An Introduction and Survey. Journal of Economic Literature 22:1007–1051

Shoven JB, Whalley J (1992) Applying General Equilibrium. Cambridge University Press, Cambridge, UK

Silberberg E, Suen W (2001) The Structure of Economics, A Mathematical Analysis, 3rd edn. McGraw–Hill, Singapore

Somermeyer WH, Langhout A (1972) Shapes of Engel Curves and Demand Curves: Implications of the Expenditure Allocation Model, Applied to Dutch Data. European Economic Review 3:351–386

Stiglitz JE, Uzawa H (1969) Readings in the Modern Theory of Economic Growth. M.I.T. Press, Cambridge, Mass

Stolper WF, Samuelson PA (1941) Protection and Real Wages. Review of Economic Studies 9:58–73

von Thünen JH (1850) Der isolierte Staat in Beziehung auf Landwirtschaft und Nationalökonomie, 2nd edn. Hamburg, Band 1: Rostock, 1842, Band 2: Rostock, 1850. *Der isolierte Staat* (Band 1–2): Sammlung sozialwissenschaftlicher Meister, Waentig, H., ed. Verlag Gustav Fischer, Jena, 1930. Trans. Wartenberg, C. M.: *Von Thünen's Isolated State*, Oxford, 1966. Dempsey, B. W.: *The Frontier Wage, Jesuit Studies*, Chicago, 1960.

Tinbergen J (1960) Optimum Savings and Utility Maximization Over Time. Econometrica 28:481–489

Tobin J (1980) Asset Accumulation and Economic Activity. Basil Blackwell Publishers, Oxford, Yrjö Jahnsson Lectures

Usher AP (1954) A History of Mechanical Inventions, Revised edn. Dover Pub, New York

Uzawa H (1968) Time Preference, the Consumption Function, and Optimum Asset Holdings. pp 485–504, in Wolfe, J. N.: *Papers in Honour of Sir John Hicks: Value, Capital, and Growth*, University Press, Edinburgh.

Uzawa H (1969) Time Preference and the Penrose Effect in a Two–Class Model of Economic Growth. Journal of Political Economy 77:628–652

Uzawa H (1973) Towards a Keynesian Model of Monetary Growth. pp 53–74, in Mirrlees, J. A. & Stern, N. H.: *Models of Economic Growth*, Macmillan, London.

Varian HR (1992) Microeconomic Analysis, 3rd edn. W.W. Norton & Company, New York

Walras L (1954) Elements of Pure Economics. George Allen and Unwin, London

Wan HY Jr (1971) Economic Growth. Harcourt Brace Jovanowich, New York

Wold H (1952) Demand Analysis. Almquist & Wiksell, Uppsala, or J. Wiley and Sons, N.Y., 1953

CHAPTER 19

# Homothetic Multi-Sector Growth Models

## Introduction

Naturally, through more than 50 years the basic one-sector growth model of Solow (1956) has been extended in many directions, see Solow (1999), Solow (2000). Earlier, there were explorations to equip the macro model with an industrial structure by including more sectors (goods and industries).

The seminal work on two-sector growth models with flexible sector technologies was done by Uzawa (1961, 1963). In this work, a framework for efficient factor allocation using the price mechanism is set up—referred to as a "miniature Walrasian general equilibrium system" (Solow 1961, p. 49); (Walras 1954). However, in contrast to Solow (1956)—where the benchmark examples of the explicit solutions of the basic dynamic model were rigorously established for the constant elasticity of substitution (CES) technology parameter values of the factor substitution elasticity, $\sigma = 0, 1, 2$, allowing alternatively for steady-state growth or persistent growth per capita—there was no ***explicit (parametric) sectorial*** production functions used in these two-sector growth models (Uzawa 1961, 1963), cf. Jensen (1994); here Chaps. 1–2, 7–11, 14–16, and 28–31, except Chap. 17, Jensen (2003). The qualitative analysis and the subsequent focus on various sufficient conditions for the stability of the steady states (Inada 1964) hampered further progress and extensions toward multi-sector growth (MSG) models. But the allocation aspects of two-factor, two-sector general equilibrium (GE) model were given due to attention in

With co-author:
ULLA LEHMIJOKI, Helsinki Center of Economic Research (HECER), University of Helsinki, Finland



B. S. Jensen, *The Elements and Dynamic Systems of Economic Growth and Trade Models*, https://doi.org/10.1007/978-3-031-52493-6_19

trade theory by Jones (1965). The implications of heterogeneous capital in a two-sector neoclassical vintage growth model with embodied Harrod-neutral technological progress and with a constant saving rate were investigated by Stiglitz (1969). It was shown that the labor-intensive sector would attract all the newer (better) machines. However, the analysis was qualitative with emphasis on the existence and uniqueness of momentary equilibrium and steady states, using the Inada restrictions upon the sectorial production functions.

So far, most extensions of Solow (1956) have dealt with the multi-factor elaborations of the aggregate growth model, Taylor and Woodford (1999), cf. Jensen (2009). The human capital augmented macro model with the Cobb-Douglas (CD) technology was studied in Mankiw et al. (1992); it is with constant and/or optimal saving rates included in the standard textbooks of growth theory and macroeconomics (Barro and Sala-i-Martin 2004; Romer 2001). On schooling and externalities, see Carstensen et al. (2009). Further augmentation with several types of capital goods was analyzed by Nonneman and Vanhoudt (1996). Parametric solutions with multi-factor CD and CES technologies were examined in Jensen et al. (2005), particularly related to the exposition in Romer (2001).

Much of the endogenous growth theory with emphasis on innovation-driven growth and modeling technological progress—R&D (human capital) producing new (better) varieties (or larger numbers) of intermediate goods for the production function of the final output—can be seen as the particular multiple input extensions of the one-sector two-factor growth model. Thus, the textbooks of Barro and Sala-i-Martin (2004) and Aghion and Howitt (1998) do not go beyond two final goods (industries).

The handbook on economic growth, Aghion and Durlauf (2005), can neither report on much attention to multi-sectorial growth patterns. Regarding territories into which growth theory has not expanded, Solow (2005, p. 4) noted, "I suspect that early on one would have expected much more work on multi-sector growth models than there has been". Long ago, Kuznets (1966, p. 1) wrote, "We identify the economic growth of a nation as a sustained increase in per capita or per worker product, most often accompanied by an increase in population and usually by sweeping structural changes".

The economic literature contains an early genuine N-sector extension of Solow (1956), that of Dhrymes (1962). This MSG model used CD sectoral production functions, and the demand functions employed were of the Graham type—that had long been used in trade models (McKenzie 1954, p. 149). The "Graham type" demand functions imply that a constant proportion (share) of total income (consumer expenditures) is devoted to each final good regardless of its price. In other words, the price and income elasticities of consumer demand (Marshallian) are unity; hence, the implied preferences are given by the ordinal utility function of CD form. Thus, Dhrymes (1962) is a fully fledged MSG model parameterized by CD specifications. The CD assumptions have always been used first in obtaining explicit static and dynamic model solutions. Although the sectorial capital-labor ratios, the wage-rental ratio, and the overall factor endowment (capital-labor) ratio are changing in this multi-sector CD economy, they all change at the same rate and leave the sectoral allocation fractions of labor and capital unchanged. This invariance of the occupational industrial structure is evidently counterfactual consequences of the CD assumptions.

The CD growth model of Dhrymes (1962) serves us mainly as the simplest benchmark case within the economically much richer CES parameter family of consumer preferences and sector technologies. Thus, our main objective is to establish the comparative static and dynamic systems for explicitly solving the CES MSG model. Numerical illustrations are shown for three CES parameter regimes of a ten-sector general equilibrium model—continuing the seminal work within the traditions of the Solow-Uzawa legacy.

Attention to dynamic general equilibrium models with the industrial patterns of structural change is given in Echevarria (1997) and Kongsamut et al. (2001); both papers study three-sector growth models. But the sectorial production functions in Kongsamut et al. (2001) are identical up to proportionality constant, and hence, the relative prices of three different goods are not affected by factor prices, factor allocations, or change over time. The factor reallocations and sectorial changes in output composition are entirely driven by differences in the income elasticities of demand (here the linear expenditure system and its non-homothetic preferences are used in an intertemporal optimization). Echevarria (1997) uses three CD technologies and non-homothetic preferences that converge to CD preferences. The time paths in this three-sector model are asymptotically equivalent to the steady-state values in the CD growth model of Dhrymes (1962) with unitary demand elasticities.

Our *analytic* N-sector- and *simulated* ten-sector CES growth models intend to fully show how—in the short and long run—the *time paths* of the CES solutions for relative prices as the *invisible hand* (the general equilibrium prices of commodities and factors) performs its *allocative* and market clearing role (Arrow 1974, p. 253) on the tendency of goods and factor markets to balance. "When all due allowances are made, the coherence of individual economic decisions is remarkable. As income rise and demand shifts, for example from food to clothes and housing, the labor force and productive facilities follow suit. Similarly, even more surprising to the layman, there is mutual interaction between shifts in technology and the allocation of the labor force. As technology improves exogenously, through innovations, the labor made redundant does not become permanently unemployed, but find its place in the economy. It is truly amazing that the lessons of both theory and over a century of history are still so misunderstood. On the other hand, a growing accumulation of the instruments of production raises real wages and in turn induces a rise in the prices of labor intensive commodities relative to those which use little labor. All these phenomena show that by and large and in the long view of history, the economic system adjusts with a considerable degree of smoothness and indeed of rationality to changes in the fundamental facts within which it operates".

The chapter is organized as follows. Section "Structure of Homothetic Multi-Sector Economies" starts with the central theoretical core of the growth theory consisting of production-, cost-, and utility functions. The national income and product accounting of a multi-sector economy and resource accounting must next be carefully integrated to satisfy Walras's law and general equilibrium conditions. In Sect. "Walrasian Equilibrium of Two-Factor Multi-Sector Economies", the general equilibrium of the homothetic multi-sector economy with two primary factors (labor and capital) is expressed compactly by just one equation. The operating invisible hand—the correspondence between relative commodity prices and relative factor prices—is parametrically fully illustrated. Section "Dynamics and Evolution of Homothetic Multi-Sector Economies" introduces the equations of factor accumulations, which give the laws of motions that must be solved. The dynamics of our homothetic multi-sector economy can be expressed by one differential equation. Section "Solving the Multi-Sector Growth—(2 × 10)—Model" presents in detail the benchmark solutions of the general equilibrium dynamics for the CES ten-sector economy with three different parameter regimes. Section "Final Comments" offers final comments.

## Structure of Homothetic Multi-Sector Economies

### *CES Sector Technologies and Cost Functions*

Consider an economy consisting of $N$ industries (sectors). Sectoral technologies, $F_i(L_i, K_i)$, are described by nonnegative, smooth, concave homogeneous production functions with constant returns to scale in labor and capital,

$$Y_i = F_i(L_i, K_i) \equiv L_i f_i(k_i) \equiv L_i y_i; \; L_i \neq 0; \quad F_i(0,0) = 0; \; i = 1, \ldots, N, \tag{19.1}$$

$$Y_i = F_i(L_i, K_i) = \gamma_i L_i^{1-a_i} K_i^{a_i} \equiv L_i f_i(k_i) \equiv L_i y_i, \tag{19.2}$$

$$Y_i = F_i(L_i, K_i) = \gamma_i \left[ (1-a_i) L_i^{\frac{\sigma_i - 1}{\sigma_i}} + a_i K_i^{\frac{\sigma_i - 1}{\sigma_i}} \right]^{\frac{\sigma_i}{\sigma_i - 1}} \equiv L_i f_i(k_i) \equiv L_i y_i, \tag{19.3}$$

where the CES forms of $f_i(k_i)$ and $f_i'(k_i)$ are

$$\sigma_i = 1, \quad f_i(k_i) = \gamma_i k_i^{a_i}, \quad f_i'(k_i) = \gamma_i a_i k_i^{a_i - 1}, \tag{19.4}$$

$$\sigma_i \neq 1, \quad f_i(k_i) = \gamma_i \left[ (1-a_i) + a_i k_i^{(\sigma_i - 1)/\sigma_i} \right]^{\sigma_i/(\sigma_i - 1)}, \tag{19.5}$$

$$\sigma_i \neq 1, \quad f_i'(k_i) = \gamma_i a_i \left[ a_i + (1-a_i) k_i^{-(\sigma_i - 1)/\sigma_i} \right]^{1/(\sigma_i - 1)}. \tag{19.6}$$

By evaluating (19.5–19.6), the limits of $f_i(k_i)$ , $f_i'(k_i)$ are [$\sigma \gtrless 1 \Rightarrow a^{\sigma/(\sigma-1)} \lessgtr 1$]:

$$\sigma_i < 1 \ : \ \lim_{k_i \to \infty} f_i(k_i) = \gamma_i(1-a_i)^{\frac{\sigma_i}{\sigma_i-1}} \ ; \ \lim_{k_i \to \infty} f_i'(k_i) = 0, \tag{19.7}$$

$$\sigma_i > 1 \ : \ \lim_{k_i \to \infty} f_i(k_i) = \infty \ ; \ \lim_{k_i \to \infty} f_i'(k_i) = \gamma_i a_i^{\frac{\sigma_i}{\sigma_i-1}}. \tag{19.8}$$

In each sector, we have the competitive producer equilibrium equations,

$$w = P_i \cdot MP_{L_i} = P_i \cdot [f_i(k_i) - k_i f_i'(k_i)] \ ; \ r = P_i \cdot MP_{K_i} = P_i \cdot f_i'(k_i), \tag{19.9}$$

$$P_i Y_i = wL_i + rK_i \ ; \ P_i = \ (w + rk_i)/y_i \ = \ r(\omega + k_i)/y_i \ ; \ \omega = w/r, \tag{19.10}$$

$$\epsilon_{L_i} = \frac{wL_i}{P_i Y_i} = \frac{\omega}{\omega + k_i} \ ; \ \epsilon_{K_i} = \frac{rK_i}{P_i Y_i} = \frac{f_i'(k_i)}{f_i(k_i)/k_i} = \frac{k_i}{\omega + k_i} \ ; \ \epsilon_{K_i} + \epsilon_{L_i} = 1. \tag{19.11}$$

The marginal rates of technical substitution (MRTS)—$\omega_i(k_i)$—are monotone increasing functions,

$$(w/r)_i = \omega_i = \omega_i(k_i) = \frac{MP_{L_i}}{MP_{K_i}} = \frac{f_i(k_i)}{f_i'(k_i)} - k_i. \tag{19.12}$$

With the CES technologies (19.4–19.6), the monotone relations between $(\omega_i)$, (19.12), and the sectorial factor ratios $(k_i)$ and $\epsilon_{K_i}$, (19.11), have the parametric forms:

$$\omega_i = \frac{1-a_i}{a_i} k_i^{1/\sigma_i} \ ; \ k_i = \frac{1}{c_i}(\omega_i)^{\sigma_i} \ ; \ c_i = \left[\frac{1-a_i}{a_i}\right]^{\sigma_i} \ ; \quad \omega_i \, , \, k_i \in [0, \infty), \tag{19.13}$$

$$\epsilon_{K_i} = \left[1 + \frac{1-a_i}{a_i} k_i^{\frac{1-\sigma_i}{\sigma_i}}\right]^{-1} = \frac{1}{1 + c_i \omega^{1-\sigma_i}} \ ; \ \epsilon_{L_i} = \frac{c_i \omega^{1-\sigma_i}}{1 + c_i \omega^{1-\sigma_i}}. \tag{19.14}$$

The dual CES cost function $C_i(w, r, Y_i)$ to CES technology $F_i(L_i, K_i)$, (19.3) is,

$$C_i(w, r, Y_i) \ = \ r/\gamma_i \left[a_i^{\sigma_i} + (1-a_i)^{\sigma_i} (w/r)^{1-\sigma_i}\right]^{\frac{1}{1-\sigma_i}} \ Y_i. \tag{19.15}$$

Hence, the unit (average/marginal) cost (commodity price) functions are:

$$P_i = AC_i(w, r) = MC_i(w, r) = r/\gamma_i \left[a_i^{\sigma_i} + (1 - a_i)^{\sigma_i} (w/r)^{1-\sigma_i}\right]^{\frac{1}{1-\sigma_i}}, \tag{19.16}$$

$$MC_i(w/r) = (1/\gamma_i)\, a_i^{\sigma_i/(1-\sigma_i)} \left[1 + c_i (w/r)^{1-\sigma_i}\right]^{\frac{1}{1-\sigma_i}} ; \; c_i = \left[\frac{1 - a_i}{a_i}\right]^{\sigma_i}. \tag{19.17}$$

By (19.15–19.17), the relative CES cost functions (relative commodity prices) are:

$$p_{ij} = \frac{P_i}{P_j} = \frac{MC_i(w/r)}{MC_j(w/r)} = \frac{(1/\gamma_i)\, a_i^{\sigma_i/(1-\sigma_i)} \left[1 + c_i (w/r)^{1-\sigma_i}\right]^{\frac{1}{1-\sigma_i}}}{(1/\gamma_j)\, a_j^{\sigma_j/(1-\sigma_j)} \left[1 + c_j (w/r)^{1-\sigma_j}\right]^{\frac{1}{1-\sigma_j}}} \tag{19.18}$$

$$= \frac{\gamma_j a_j^{\sigma_j/(\sigma_j-1)} \left[1 + c_j (w/r)^{1-\sigma_j}\right]^{1/(\sigma_j-1)}}{\gamma_i a_i^{\sigma_i/(\sigma_i-1)} \left[1 + c_i (w/r)^{1-\sigma_i}\right]^{1/(\sigma_i-1)}} = \Phi\left[\frac{w}{r}\right] ; \; \frac{w}{r} = \omega \in [0, \infty). \tag{19.19}$$

With $\sigma_i = \sigma_j = \sigma$, we get, cf. (19.19),

$$p_{ij} = \Phi(w/r) = \frac{\gamma_j}{\gamma_i} \left[\left[\frac{a_j}{a_i}\right]^{\sigma} \frac{1 + c_j (w/r)^{1-\sigma}}{1 + c_i (w/r)^{1-\sigma}}\right]^{\frac{1}{\sigma-1}}_{;} \; ; \; c_i = \left[\frac{1 - a_i}{a_i}\right]^{\sigma}. \tag{19.20}$$

In the limit case of (19.20) with $\sigma = 1$ (Cobb-Douglas), we obtain:

$$p_{ij} = \Phi(w/r) = \frac{\gamma_j\, a_j^{a_j} (1 - a_j)^{1-a_j}}{\gamma_i\, a_i^{a_i} (1 - a_i)^{1-a_i}} \left[\frac{w}{r}\right]^{a_j - a_i} ; \; w/r = \omega \in [0, \infty). \tag{19.21}$$

### *CES Preferences and Consumer Demands*

As we are setting up a multi-sector (N) growth model with sector technologies using *two primary* factors, Labor and Capital (physical), we need at least one capital good sector. Let *sector* 1 be the *capital good* industry.

The consumer demand in the multi-sector economy is here governed by homothetic preferences, and they are expressed by parametric ordinal utility functions. We use the *expenditure shares*, $(e_i)$, derived from the CES class, (19.3):

$$U\,(Y_2,\ldots,Y_N\,) \;=\; \gamma_u\,;\; \sum_{i=2}^{N} \alpha_i\, Y_i^{\frac{\sigma_u-1}{\sigma_u}}\;\; ;\; \alpha_i > 0,\; \sum_{i=2}^{N} \alpha_i = 1\;;\; \sigma_u > 0, \tag{19.22}$$

$$e_i = \frac{P_i Y_i}{\sum_{i=2}^{N} P_i Y_i} = \frac{\alpha_i^{\sigma_u} P_i^{1-\sigma_u}}{\sum_{j=2}^{N} \alpha_j^{\sigma_u} P_j^{1-\sigma_u}} = \left[\sum_{j=2}^{N}\left[\frac{\alpha_j}{\alpha_i}\right]^{\sigma_u} p_{ij}^{\sigma_u-1}\right]^{-1};\; i = 2,\ldots,N, \tag{19.23}$$

$$e_i = e_i\,(p_{i2},\ldots,p_{iN}) = \left[1 + \sum_{j=2,\,j\neq i}^{N} \left[\alpha_j/\alpha_i\right]^{\sigma_u} p_{ij}^{\sigma_u-1}\right]^{-1};\; i = 2,\ldots,N. \tag{19.24}$$

Linking the *relative consumer prices* in $e_i$, (19.24), to the *cost prices*, (19.18–19.19), we get

$$e_i(\omega) = \left[1 + \sum_{j=2,\,j\neq i}^{N} \left[\alpha_j/\alpha_i\right]^{\sigma_u} p_{ij}\,(\omega)^{\sigma_u-1}\right]^{-1};\; i = 2,\ldots,N;\; \sum_{i=2}^{N} e_i(\omega) \;=\; 1 \tag{19.25}$$

for $\alpha_i = 1/N$ and equal $e_i$, (19.25), Dixit and Stiglitz (1977, p. 298). Price- and income (expenditure) elasticities of the CES system of the Marshallian demands (19.22–19.24) are Chung (1994, p. 58), Shoven and Whalley (1992, p. 96),

$$E(Y_i, P_i) = -\sigma_u(1 - e_i) - e_i\;;\; E(Y_i, P_j) \;=\; (\sigma_u - 1)e_j\;;\; E(Y_i, C) \;=\; 1. \tag{19.26}$$

Although there are only N-1 relative commodity prices involved in a N-sector economy, we need, in a multi-sectorial setting, to be careful about including all the relevant *cross-* (relative) *price ratios* from (19.19) into the respective budget shares in (19.24–19.25).

Thus, for the *nine* budget shares used in our *ten-sector* model below, we state:

$$e_2 = e_2\,(p_{22},\ldots,p_{2\,10}) = \left[1 + \sum_{j=2,\,j\neq i}^{10} \left[\alpha_j/\alpha_2\right]^{\sigma_u} p_{2j}^{\sigma_u-1}\right]^{-1}, \tag{19.27}$$

$$e_3 = e_3\left(p_{32}, \ldots, p_{310}\right) = \left[1 + \sum_{j=2, j \neq i}^{10} \left[\alpha_j/\alpha_3\right]^{\sigma_u} p_{3j}^{\sigma_u - 1}\right]^{-1}, \tag{19.28}$$

..........

$$e_{10} = e_{10}\left(p_{102}, \ldots, p_{1010}\right) = \left[1 + \sum_{j=2, j \neq i}^{10} \left[\alpha_j/\alpha_{10}\right]^{\sigma_u} p_{10j}^{\sigma_u - 1}\right]^{-1}. \tag{19.29}$$

### *Factor Endowments, Allocation Fractions, and GDP*

The factor endowments, total labor force ($L$) and the total capital stock ($K$), are inelastically supplied and are fully employed, that is,

$$L = \sum_{i=1}^{N} L_i \; ; \; \sum_{i=1}^{N} L_i/L \equiv \sum_{i=1}^{N} \lambda_{L_i} = 1, \tag{19.30}$$

$$K = \sum_{i=1}^{N} K_i \; ; \; \sum_{i=1}^{N} K_i/K \equiv \sum_{i=1}^{N} \lambda_{K_i} \equiv 1, \tag{19.31}$$

$$K/L \equiv k \equiv \sum_{i=1}^{N} \lambda_{L_i} k_i, \tag{19.32}$$

where $\lambda_{L_i}, \lambda_{K_i}$, (19.30–19.31) are the factor *allocation fractions.*

Free factor mobility between multiple sectors (industries) and efficient factor allocation impose the common MRTS condition, cf. (19.12), (19.9),

$$\omega = \omega_i = \omega_i(k_i) \; ; \; i = 1, \ldots, N, \tag{19.33}$$

Gross domestic product (GDP), $Y$, is the total of sectorial producer revenues [monetary value of sector outputs, $Y_i = F_i(L_i.K_i) = L_i y_i$, (19.3)],

$$Y_i = L\lambda_{L_i} y_i \; ; \; Y \equiv \sum_{i=1}^{N} P_i Y_i = L\left[\sum_{i=1}^{N} P_i \lambda_{L_i} y_i\right] \equiv Ly. \tag{19.34}$$

With perfect competition (19.9–19.10), $Y$ is equal to the total factor income

$$Y = wL + rK = L(w + rk) = Lr(\omega + k) = Ly. \tag{19.35}$$

The factor income distribution shares, $\delta_K + \delta_L = 1$, become, cf. (19.35), (19.11),

$$\delta_K \equiv rK/Y = rk/y = k/(\omega + k) \; ; \; \delta_L \equiv wL/Y = w/y = \omega/(\omega + k). \tag{19.36}$$

Thus, by (19.36),

$$\delta_K/\delta_L \equiv k/\omega \iff k \equiv \frac{\omega\,\delta_K}{\delta_L}. \tag{19.37}$$

The composition of GDP, (19.34), as final expenditure shares, $s_i$, are

$$s_i = P_iY_i/Y\ ; \quad \textstyle\sum_{i=1}^N s_i \equiv \sum_{i=1}^N P_iY_i/Y = 1. \tag{19.38}$$

**Lemma 19.1** *The macro factor income shares $\delta_L$, $\delta_K$, (19.36), are final expenditure-weighted, (19.38), combinations of the sectorial factor (cost) shares, $\epsilon_{L_i}$, $\epsilon_{K_i}$,*

$$\delta_L = \textstyle\sum_{i=1}^N s_i\,\epsilon_{L_i}\ ;\ \delta_K = \sum_{i=1}^N s_i\,\epsilon_{K_i}\ ;\ \delta_K + \delta_L = 1. \tag{19.39}$$

*The factor allocation fractions (19.30–19.31) are obtained by*

$$L_i/L = \lambda_{L_i} = s_i\,\epsilon_{L_i}/\delta_L\ ;\ K_i/K = \lambda_{K_i} = s_i\,\epsilon_{K_i}/\delta_K. \tag{19.40}$$

*The total factor endowment ratio, $K/L$, satisfies the identity, cf. (19.37), (19.39):*

$$K/L = k = \frac{\omega\,\delta_K}{\delta_L} = \omega\ \textstyle\sum_{i=1}^N s_i\,\epsilon_{K_i} \Big/ \sum_{i=1}^N s_i\,\epsilon_{L_i}, \tag{19.41}$$

*which is a convenient representation of the Walras's law (identity) and (19.32).*

***Proof*** By definition, we have

$$\delta_L = wL/Y = [wL_1 + wL_2 + \cdots wL_N]/Y, \tag{19.42}$$

$$\delta_K = rK/Y = [rK_1 + rK_2 + \cdots rK_N]/Y. \tag{19.43}$$

From (19.10) and (19.38), we get

$$wL_i = \epsilon_{L_i}P_iY_i = s_i\,\epsilon_{L_i}Y,\ ;\ rK_i = \epsilon_{K_i}P_iY_i = s_i\,\epsilon_{K_i}Y. \tag{19.44}$$

Hence, by (19.42–19.43) and (19.44), we obtain (19.39). Next, as stated in (19.40), we have

$$\lambda_{L_i} = \frac{L_i}{L} = \frac{wL_i}{wL} = \frac{s_i\,\epsilon_{L_i}Y}{\delta_L Y} = \frac{s_i\,\epsilon_{L_i}}{\delta_L}, \tag{19.45}$$

$$\lambda_{K_i} = \frac{K_i}{K} = \frac{rK_i}{rK} = \frac{s_i\,\epsilon_{K_i}Y}{\delta_K Y} = \frac{s_i\,\epsilon_{K_i}}{\delta_K}, \tag{19.46}$$

as in Jensen and Larsen (2005, p. 24); here (18.33) in Lemma 18.1 in Chap. 18.

With one capital good industry (sector 1), the final demand decomposition of the aggregate expenditures, GDP (Y), into gross investment expenditures (I) and total consumption expenditures (C) becomes,

$$I = P_1 Y_1 \; ; \; C = \textstyle\sum_{i=2}^{N} P_i Y_i \; ; \; Y = C + I \; ; \; s_1 = I/Y. \qquad (19.47)$$

□

Evidently, the connection between the GDP shares (19.38), (19.47), and (19.23–19.25) is

$$s_i(\omega) = (1 - s_1)\, e_i(\omega) \; ; \; i = 2, \ldots, N. \qquad (19.48)$$

## WALRASIAN EQUILIBRIUM OF TWO-FACTOR MULTI-SECTOR ECONOMIES

The *demand* side of the multi-sector economy is expressed by the GDP expenditure shares, $\mathbf{s_i}$: (19.38), (19.47–19.48), (19.25). The *supply* side of the economy—operating with full (19.30–19.31) and efficient factor utilization, (19.33)—is always summarized by the sectoral factor allocation fractions $\boldsymbol{\lambda}_{\mathbf{L_i}}$, $\boldsymbol{\lambda}_{\mathbf{K_i}}$, (19.40) which, in turn, are determined by $s_i(\omega)$ (19.47–19.48), (19.25), and the sectorial cost shares $\epsilon_{L_i}(\omega)$, $\epsilon_{K_i}(\omega)$, (19.14). Thus, we have established:

**Theorem 19.1** *The Walrasian equilibrium (competitive general equilibrium) states—by market clearing prices on the commodity and factor markets and Pareto efficient endowments allocations—are—with homogeneous production functions of degree one, and with any homothetic preferences—given by:* $\forall \; k, \; \omega \in R_+$,

$$k = \frac{\omega\, \delta_K(\omega)}{\delta_L(\omega)} = \frac{\omega \sum_{i=1}^{N} s_i(\omega)\, \epsilon_{K_i}(\omega)}{\sum_{i=1}^{N} s_i(\omega)\, \epsilon_{L_i}(\omega)} = \Psi(\omega) \qquad (19.49)$$

**Corollary 19.1** *With CES sector technologies and any homothetic utility function, the Walrasian equilibrium* $k = \Psi(\omega)$ *becomes by (19.49) and (19.14):*

$$k = \frac{\omega \sum_{i=1}^{N} s_i(\omega)(1 + c_i \omega^{1-\sigma_i})^{-1}}{1 - \sum_{i=1}^{N} s_i(\omega)(1 + c_i \omega^{1-\sigma_i})^{-1}} = \Psi(\omega) \; ; \; \lim_{\omega \to 0} \Psi(\omega) = 0; \; \lim_{\omega \to \infty} \Psi(\omega) = \infty. \qquad (19.50)$$

By (19.49–19.50), the competitive *general equilibrium* (GE) of the two-factor and N-sector (**2** × **N**) economy is by *composite* functions reduced to a **single** *equation* (link) between the *factor endowment* ratio (**k**) and the *factor price* ratio (**ω**). Experiments in comparative statics are straightforward.

But having obtained (ω) from (19.50), we can go back through (19.19), (19.25), (19.14), (19.39), (19.40), (19.34) to get the associated general equilibrium values of all other variables—the relative commodity prices, factor allocation fractions, income shares, sectorial capital-labor ratios, and the outputs.

The *relative* CES *commodity* prices, $p_{ij} = \Phi(w/r)$, (19.19), together with their CES pairs: $\omega_i(k_i)$, $\omega_j(k_j)$, (19.13), are shown in Fig. 19.1. With $\sigma_i \neq \sigma_j$, there will be one (and only one) intersection point of (19.13), $(k_i, \omega_i) = (k_j, \omega_j) = (\bar{k}_{ij}, \bar{\omega}_{ij})$, $[a_i = a_j = a : (\bar{k}_{ij}, \bar{\omega}_{ij}) = (1, (1-a)/a\,]$:

$$\sigma_i \neq \sigma_j \; ; \; \bar{k}_{ij} = \left[\frac{a_i(1-a_j)}{a_j(1-a_i)}\right]^{\frac{\sigma_i\sigma_j}{\sigma_j-\sigma_i}} = \left[\frac{c_j^{\sigma_i}}{c_i^{\sigma_j}}\right]^{\frac{1}{\sigma_j-\sigma_i}} \; ; \; \bar{\omega}_{ij} = \left[\frac{c_j}{c_i}\right]^{\frac{1}{\sigma_j-\sigma_i}}. \tag{19.51}$$

With (19.51), $p_{ij}(\omega) = \Phi(w/r)$, (19.19), has a unique *reversal price ratio*:

$$\bar{p}_{ij} = p_{ij}(\bar{\omega}_{ij}) = \frac{\gamma_j a_j^{\sigma_j/(\sigma_j-1)}\left[1 + c_j\left[c_j/c_i\right]^{\frac{1-\sigma_j}{\sigma_j-\sigma_i}}\right]^{\frac{1}{\sigma_j-1}}}{\gamma_i a_i^{\sigma_i/\sigma_i-1}\left[1 + c_i\left[c_j/c_i\right]^{\frac{1-\sigma_i}{\sigma_j-\sigma_i}}\right]^{\frac{1}{\sigma_i-1}}}; \; a_i = a_j : \bar{p}_{ij} = \frac{\gamma_j}{\gamma_i}. \tag{19.52}$$

The *limits*—for $\omega = w/r$, going to zero and infinity—of the relative price (cost) *functions*, $p_{ij} = \Phi(w/r)$, (19.19) become either

$$p^{*}_{ij} \equiv \frac{\gamma_j\, a_j^{\sigma_j/(\sigma_j-1)}}{\gamma_i\, a_i^{\sigma_i/(\sigma_i-1)}} \; ; \; p^{**}_{ij} \equiv \frac{\gamma_j\,(1-a_j)^{\sigma_j/(\sigma_j-1)}}{\gamma_i\,(1-a_i)^{\sigma_i/(\sigma_i-1)}}. \tag{19.53}$$

and (19.51–19.53) are depicted in Fig. 19.1.

The proper literature reference to interpreting the correspondence between the relative commodity prices and relative factor prices, $\mathbf{p_{ij}} = \boldsymbol{\Phi}\,(\mathbf{w/r})$, (19.19), as the *Invisible Hand* is: Samuelson (1949, p. 186), where the idea of the left/right panels in Fig. 19.1 was first explained.

The *graphs* of the Walrasian equilibrium, $k = \Psi(\omega)$, (19.49–19.50), could be depicted in the right panels of Fig. 19.1. Only in two-sector models will $k = \Psi(\omega)$ *pass* through the *intersection* points, (19.51), when the latter exists; see Jensen (2003, p. 61); here Fig. 17.1 in Chap. 17. These *graphs* of the Walrasian equilibria, $\mathbf{k} = \boldsymbol{\Psi}(\boldsymbol{\omega})$, (19.49–19.50), will geometrically be *trajectories* of the Walrasian multi-sector *general equilibrium dynamics* with *factor* (labor and capital) *accumulation*.

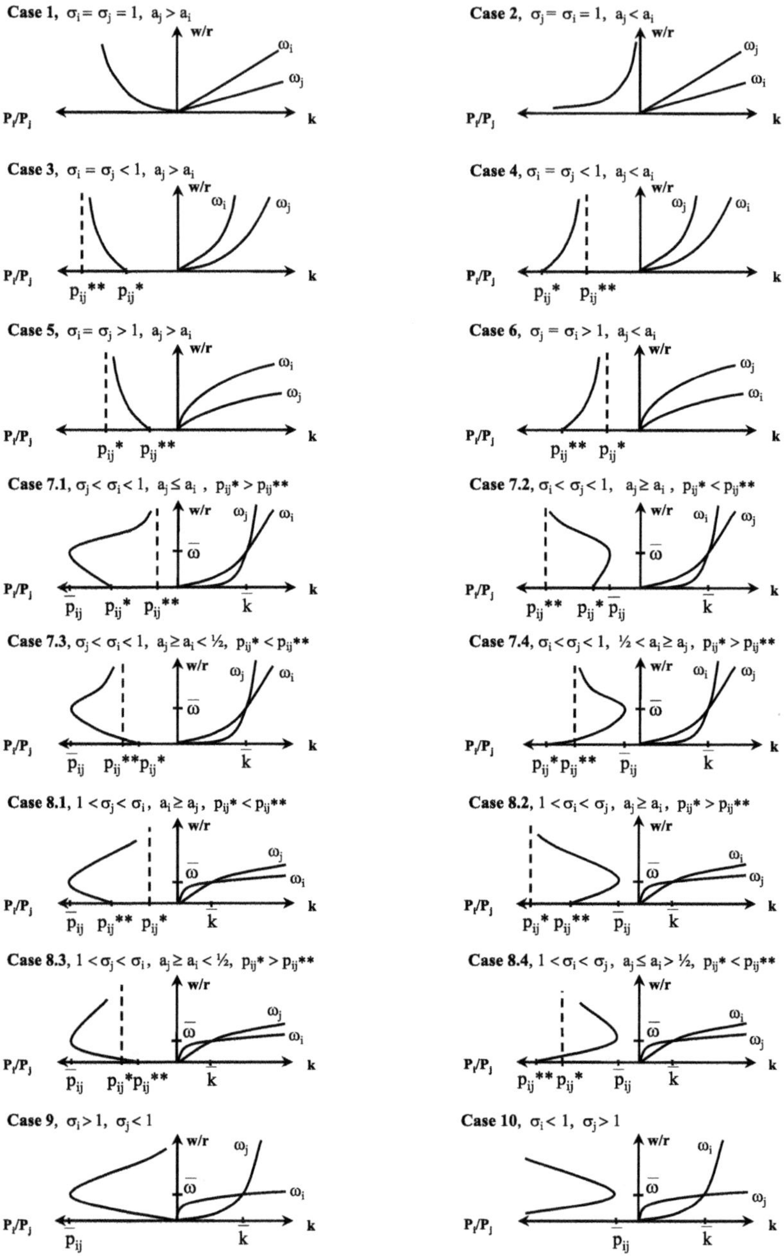


**Fig. 19.1** The relative prices $P_i/P_j = p_{ij} = \Phi(w/r)$ with CES: (19.19–19.21), and the isoelastic pair $\omega_i(k_i)$, $\omega_j(k_j)$, and (19.13)

## Dynamics and Evolution of Homothetic Multi-Sector Economies

The *equations* of factor *accumulation* for multi-sector growth models—with two primary factors and flexible constant return-to-scale sector technologies—are *formally* given by:

$$dL/dt \equiv \dot{L} = nL, \tag{19.54}$$

$$dK/dt \equiv \dot{K} = Y_1 - \delta K = Ly_1\lambda_{L_1} - \delta K = L\left\{f_1(k_1)\lambda_{L_1} - \delta k\right\}, \tag{19.55}$$

where $\mathbf{Y_1}$ is the output of *capital good* sector 1, $\delta$ the depreciation rate of capital, and $n$ the growth rate of labor. The variables $\mathbf{k_1}$ and $\boldsymbol{\lambda}_{\mathbf{L_1}}$ in (19.55) are through ($\omega$), (19.33), and (19.49), uniquely determined by the factor endowment ratio ($\mathbf{k}$): $\omega(k) = \Psi^{-1}(k)$. Hence, the accumulation Eq. (19.55) becomes an *autonomous differential* equations in the *state* variables $L$ and $K$,

$$\dot{K} = L\,\left\{\,f_1\,(k_1\,[\,\omega(k)]\,)\,\lambda_{L_1}[\,\omega(k)] - \delta\,k\,\right\} \equiv L\,\mathfrak{g}(k)\,;\;\; L \neq 0. \tag{19.56}$$

As (19.56) is an *intricate* function of $\mathbf{k}$, we rewrite $\mathfrak{g}(k)$ by (19.47), (19.35–19.36), (19.9), as

$$\dot{K} \;=\; I/P_1 - \delta K = s_1\,(Y/P_1) - \delta\,K = L\,s_1\,(\omega + k)\,f_1'(k_1) - \delta K \tag{19.57}$$

$$= L\,k\left\{\frac{s_1\,f_1'(k_1)}{\delta_K} - \delta\right\} = L\,\mathfrak{g}(k)\,;\;\; L\,k = K. \tag{19.58}$$

From the *governing* functions, (19.58) and (19.54), the *director* function, $\mathbf{h(k)}$, that controls for $dk/dt \equiv \dot{k}$ is: $h(k) \equiv \mathfrak{g}(k) - nk$, and hence $h(k)$ becomes:

$$\dot{k} = h(k) = k\left[\frac{s_1\,f_1'\,[k_1\,[\,\omega(k)]\,]}{\delta_K[\,\omega(k)]} - (n+\delta)\right];\quad \omega\,(k) = \Psi^{-1}(k). \tag{19.59}$$

The dynamic system (19.59) in ($k$) is difficult to evaluate quantitatively and analytically intractable; for example, if $\sigma_i \neq \sigma_j$, then, $k = \Psi(\omega)$, (19.50), can*not* be inverted (although $\Psi^{-1}$ exists) in a *closed* form.

But $k = \Psi(\omega)$, (19.49), is a continuously *differentiable* function of ($\omega$), and the *dynamics* of ($k$) can be converted into the *dual* autonomous *dynamics* in ($\omega$):

$$\dot{\omega} \;=\; \frac{\dot{k}}{dk/d\omega} = \frac{h\,(k)}{dk/d\omega} = \frac{h\,(\Psi[\omega])}{\Psi'(\omega)} \equiv \hbar\,(\omega) \tag{19.60}$$

Hence, we get, cf. (19.59),

$$\hbar\,(\omega) = \frac{\Psi(\omega)}{\Psi'(\omega)}\left[\frac{s_1\, f_1'\,[k_1(\omega)]}{\delta_K(\omega)} - (n+\delta)\right] \tag{19.61}$$

Thus, with **CES** *preferences* and *technologies*, we get from (19.61), (19.48), (19.39), (19.13–19.14), and (19.6)

$$\dot{\omega} = \hbar\,(\omega) = \frac{\Psi(\omega)}{\Psi'(\omega)}\left[\frac{s_1\,\gamma_1\,a_1^{\frac{\sigma_1}{\sigma_1-1}}\,\left[1+c_1\,\omega^{1-\sigma_1}\right]^{1/(\sigma_1-1)}}{\sum_{i=1}^{N} s_i\,(\omega)\left[1+c_i\,\omega^{1-\sigma_i}\right]^{-1}} - (n+\delta)\right] \tag{19.62}$$

with the **CES** expression for $\Psi(\omega)$ as given in (19.50).

Although the *pair* of time paths, $k(t)$, $\omega(t) = \Psi^{-1}[k(t)]$, obtained from (19.59) is the same as the *pair*, $\omega(t)$, $k(t) = \Psi[\omega(t)]$, given by the solution of (19.62), the *latter* (19.62) turns out to be computationally more convenient, because the *numerical calculation* of the *derivative* $\Psi'(\omega)$ in (19.62) is much quicker than getting the *inverse* function values in (19.59). Moreover, most of our variables are given *directly* in the factor price *ratio* ($\omega$) rather than in the factor endowment *ratio* ($k$). Thus, the **solution $\omega$(t)** of (19.62) is what is needed to get *all* other *time paths* of the multi-sector economy.

## Solving the Multi-Sector Growth—(2 × 10)—Model

To provide the concrete benchmark solutions of the general equilibrium dynamics, (19.62), we use a ten-sector model, in which sector 1 produces the capital good and sectors 2–10 produce consumption goods.

### *CES Parameter Sets of $U$ ($Y_2$, .., $Y_{10}$) and $F_i$ ($L_i$, $K_i$)*

For the CES utility function we use the substitution elasticity, $\sigma_u = 0.8$ (price inelastic), and the *commodity parameters* $\alpha_i$ in column 1, Table 19.1. With $\sigma_u < 1$, *all* sectoral outputs $\mathbf{Y}_i$, goods (19.22–19.23) will be strictly *positive*, cf. isoquant map in Appendix section "Appendix: CES Isoquant Map". About $\sigma_u$ for CES demands, see de La Grandville (1989, p. 473). As to the other model parameters, we adopt a fixed *saving rate*, $s_1 = 0.2$, a depreciation $\delta = 0.04$, and a population (labor) growth rate $n = 0.01$, that is,

$$\sigma_u = 0.8\,,\; s_1 = 0.2\,,\; \delta = 0.04\,,\; n = 0.01\,;\quad \gamma_i = 1\,,\; i = 1,\ldots,10. \tag{19.63}$$

**Table 19.1** The CES parameters of $U\ (Y_2, \ldots, Y_{10})$ and $F_i(L_i, K_i)$, Cases I–III

| $i$ | $\alpha_i$ | $a_i$ | $\sigma_i$ I | $\sigma_i$ II | $\sigma_i$ III |
|---|---|---|---|---|---|
| 1 | – | 0.5 | 0.8 | 1.2 | 2.0 |
| 2 | 0.15 | 0.3 | 0.9 | 1.5 | 2.5 |
| 3 | 0.10 | 0.4 | 0.7 | 1.1 | 1.5 |
| 4 | 0.20 | 0.5 | 0.9 | 0.9 | 0.8 |
| 5 | 0.10 | 0.2 | 0.8 | 0.8 | 0.8 |
| 6 | 0.15 | 0.4 | 0.6 | 1.3 | 1.3 |
| 7 | 0.10 | 0.7 | 0.7 | 0.7 | 0.7 |
| 8 | 0.10 | 0.6 | 0.5 | 0.7 | 1.1 |
| 9 | 0.05 | 0.2 | 0.5 | 1.5 | 2.5 |
| 10 | 0.05 | 0.6 | 0.6 | 1.1 | 1.5 |

The CES technology is applied in each sector ($\gamma_i$, (19.63)) with some variation in CES *parameters*, $a_i$ and $\sigma_i$, as seen in Table 19.1 for the *three Cases* I–III.

Only few comments are needed upon the CES technology parameters and the three technology regimes given by Cases I–III. The CES parameter, ($a_i$), (19.13) is traditionally referred to as a "distribution parameter", technologically a misnomer. The effect of an increase in $a_i$ is seen from (19.13) as a rightward *shift* of the $\omega_i$-curve in Fig. 19.1, right panels (or all isoquant tangents, $\omega = |dK/dL|$, smaller/flatter), that is, a higher capital-labor ratio $k_i$ for any factor price ratio. Hence, $\mathbf{a_i}$ is aptly characterized as a *capital intensity* parameter (Uzawa (1959, p. 459)). A high capital-labor ratio can alternatively be due to a movement along the $\omega_i$-curve [ or isoquants, cf. Appendix section "Appendix: CES Isoquant Map" ] the effect of which is determined by the substitution (flexibility) parameter $\sigma_i$, cf. de La Grandville (1997). As to obtaining high $k_i$ over time, the effect of $\sigma_i$ will eventually dominate the effect of $a_i$. The main parameter (determinant) of economic growth is $\sigma_i$, and its size characterizes the three technological regimes in Table 19.1.

With, $0 \leq \sigma_1 \leq 1$, all transition paths will eventually reach the steady state. If some, $\sigma_i \geq 1$, (including $\sigma_1$), *persistent* "endogenous" growth may occur, depending on the mixture of $a_i$ and $\sigma_i$. The threshold parameter values for *persistent* growth are satisfied with *Case* **III**, Table 19.1, cf. (19.8)

### *MSG Time Paths of the CES Ten-Sector Growth Model*

Corresponding to the selected *parameter* values in Table 19.1, Cases I–III and (19.63), the **solutions**, $\omega(t)$ of (19.62), are shown in Fig. 19.2 up to $t = 100$—together with $k(t) = \Psi[\,\omega(t)\,]$—as well as their respective *growth rates*, looking fairly reasonable. The actual picture displayed in Fig. 19.2 contains no surprises. With factor accumulation, rising $\boldsymbol{k(t)}$ and increasing wage-rental ratios $\boldsymbol{\omega(t)}$ go together in a *ten-sector* economy as well. For the *parameters* in *Cases* I–II,

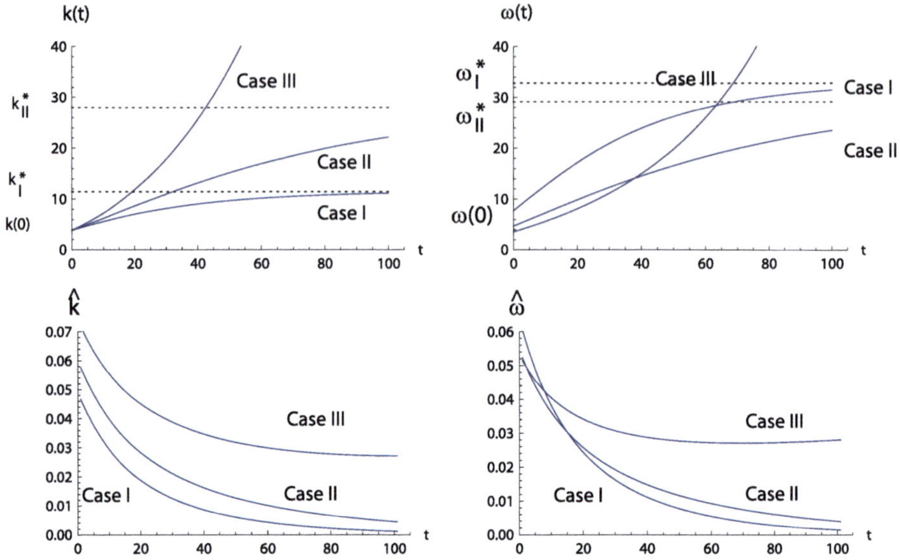


**Fig. 19.2** Time paths and growth rates of $\omega(t)$, $k(t)$ by (19.62–19.63) and Table 19.1

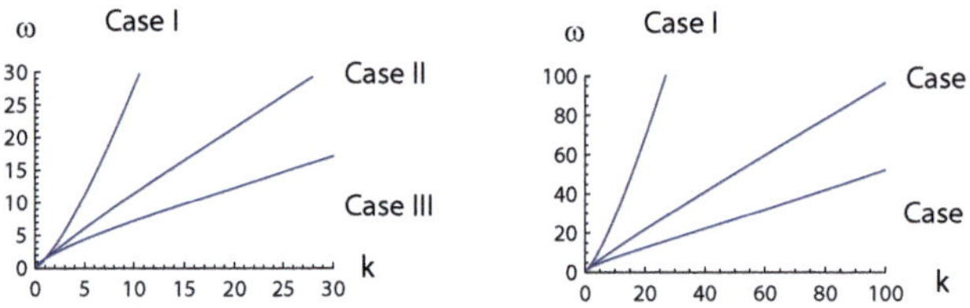


**Fig. 19.3** Left: The $(\omega, k)$ locus of Fig. 19.2. Right: $k = \Psi(\omega)$ by (19.50), Table 19.1

(19.62) has a *critical point*—a unique *steady state*—which is, respectively,

$$\omega_I^* = 32.83, \quad k_I^* = 11.46\,; \quad \omega_{II}^* = 29.17\,, \quad k_{II}^* = 27.98 \tag{19.64}$$

In *Case* III, *no* steady state exists, and *persistent* economic growth takes place, as seen below, when the solution of (19.62) is extended beyond the time horizon of Fig. 19.2. The *trajectories*—$(k, \omega)$ locus—of the time paths in Fig. 19.1 are shown in the left panel of Fig. 19.3. The right panel of Fig. 19.3 exhibits the locus of the Walrasian equilibria (comparative statics independent of time).

All the *solutions* in Figs. 19.2, 19.4, 19.5, 19.6, 19.7, 19.8, 19.9, 19.10, and 19.11 start from the *initial* time value: $K(0)/L(0 = \boldsymbol{k}(0) = 3.82 = k_I^*/3$, cf. (19.64). The corresponding *three initial* time values of $\boldsymbol{\omega}(\mathbf{0})$ for all solutions in Figs. 19.4, 19.5, 19.6, 19.7, 19.8, 19.9, 19.10, and 19.11 are *depicted* in Fig. 19.2. The absolute size of $K(0)$ and $L(0)$ can be arbitrarily chosen; all

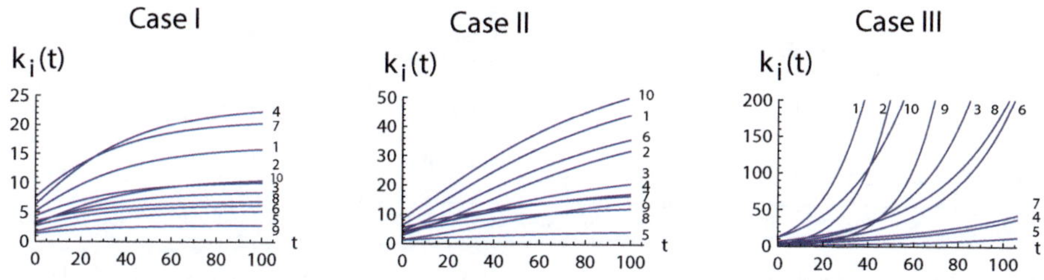


**Fig. 19.4** The sectorial $k_i(t)$ by (19.13) and $\omega(t)$, (19.62–19.63), Table 19.1, Fig. 19.2

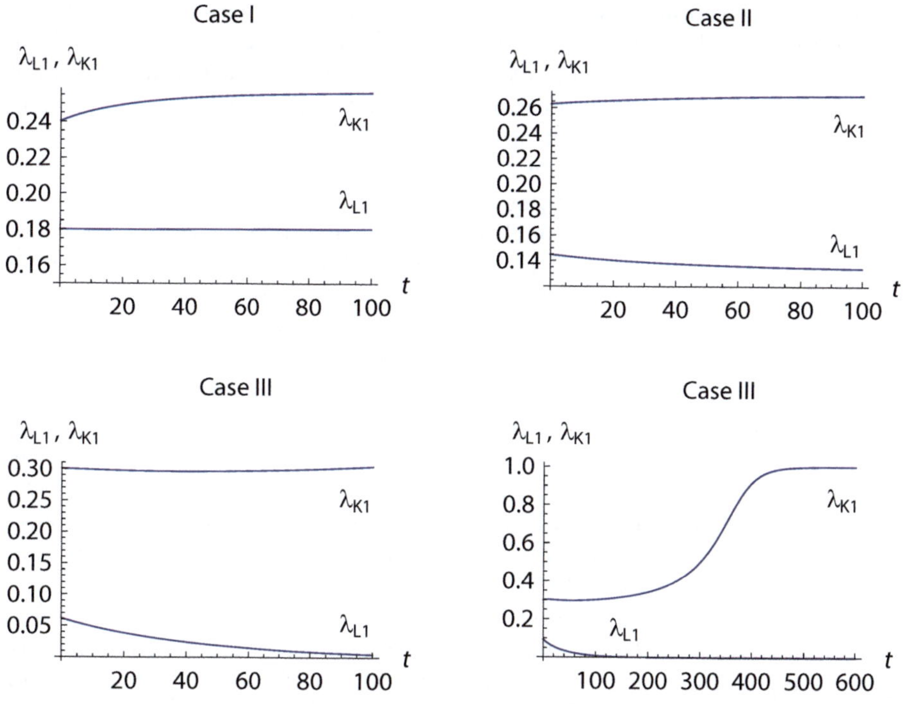


**Fig. 19.5** Allocations $\lambda_{L_1}(t)$, $\lambda_{K_1}(t)$ by (19.40) and $\omega(t)$, (19.62–19.63), Table 19.1, Fig. 19.2

solutions apply for small and large economies. With our $\gamma_i = 1$: $y_i = f_i(1) = 1$, (19.5).

The *time paths* of the sectoral capital-labor ratios, $\mathbf{k_i(t)}$, are exhibited in Fig. 19.4. Obviously, with a *rising* $\omega(t)$, *all ten* $k_i(t)$ are increasing, too, but an underlying distinct sectorial pattern evidently appears, calling for attention. However, essentially a common economic mechanism is involved behind the pattern in Fig. 19.4. In Table 19.1, the *ranking* order of the *substitution*

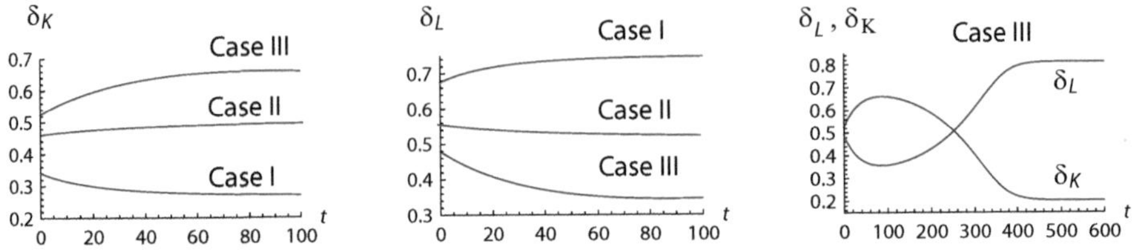


**Fig. 19.6** Factor shares $\delta_L(t)$, $\delta_K(t)$ by (19.39) and $\omega(t)$, (19.62–19.63), Table 19.1, Fig. 19.2

*elasticities* $\sigma_i$ (combined with a similar ranking of the intensity parameters $a_i$) corresponds to the *vertical* orders of $k_i(t)$ in Fig. 19.4 for $t > 50$. Thus, in Table 19.1, Case I, the sectors 4, 7, 1 have high $\sigma_i$ (backed up with high $a_i$) corresponding to the vertical order in Case I, Fig. 19.4. For Case II, an analogous ranking and vertical order occurs with sectors 10, 1, 6, 2. In Case III, this ranking/order pattern is repeated with sectors 1, 2, 10, 9, 3. In short, the sectors with high $\sigma_i$ (and high $a_i$) become *mechanized*—thus increasing $\mathbf{k_i(t)}$ by attracting both new capital and capital from other sectors with lower $\sigma_i$ (and $a_i$). This sectoral order of attraction and reallocation of capital—as evident in Fig. 19.4—will also be reflected in the *time paths* of the *allocation fractions*, $\lambda_{K_i}(t)$, of capital in Fig. 19.7. But these sectoral evolutions of $\lambda_{K_i}(t)$ in Fig. 19.7 are partly modified by their respective magnitudes of $\alpha_i$ (Table 19.1) from the demand side of the multi-sector economy. The *demand-side composition* of the economy exerts a particular powerful influence on the time paths of the allocation fraction of capital in sector 1, $\lambda_{K_1}(t)$, as shown for Cases I–III in Fig. 19.5. Below, we return to the paths of Fig. 19.5, and the sizes of the *factor income shares* exhibited in Fig. 19.6. Evidently, the allocation fractions of labor in Fig. 19.7 reflect *reallocation* of labor toward the labor-intensive sectors, cf. their parameters in Table 19.1.

With *commodity* 2 as the *numeraire*, the time paths of our nine *relative prices*: $p_{i2}(t)$, $i = 1, 3, \ldots, 10$, are seen in Fig. 19.8, Cases I–III. As these relative general equilibrium prices play the fundamental allocative role ("invisible hand") in multi-sector economies, it is important that the sizes and the overall picture for all these price numbers (rising/falling) can be checked easily, which is seldom offered for the users of the computable general equilibrium (CGE) models. Here, **Fig. 19.1** can serve as a *road map* for checking the *direction* and the *turning points* of the *nine prices* in Cases I–III, Fig. 19.8.

Hence, we *calibrate* Fig. 19.1 with the intersection/reversal points according to the parameters in *Table 19.1. Only the technology parameters affect the price reversals or limits* for Cases I–III in Table 19.2. In Fig. 19.8, we note reversals for $p_{32}(t)$, $p_{82}(t)$ in Case I; by Table 19.2, the reversal prices are: $\bar{p}_{32} = 0.935$, $\bar{p}_{82} = 0.816$, confirming *the time paths in Fig. 19.8 by Fig. 19.1, Case 7.4.*

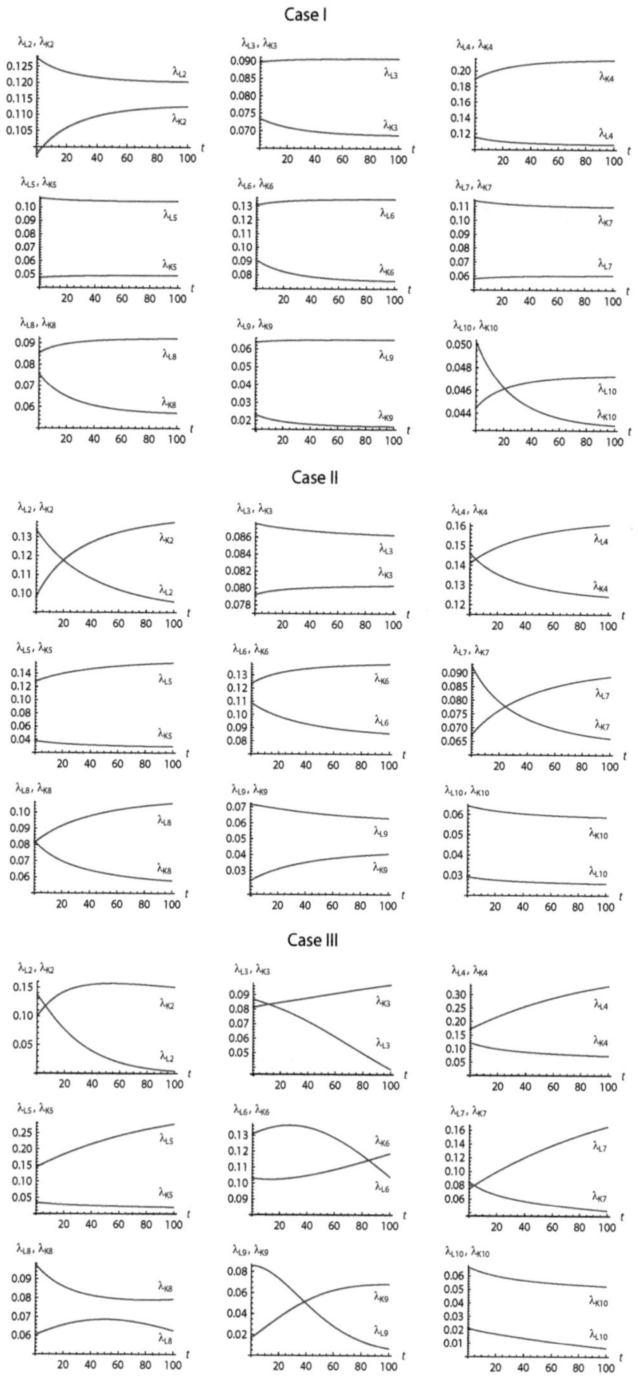


**Fig. 19.7** Allocations $\lambda_{L_i}(t)$, $\lambda_{K_i}(t)$ by (19.40) and $\omega(t)$, (19.62–19.63), Table 19.1

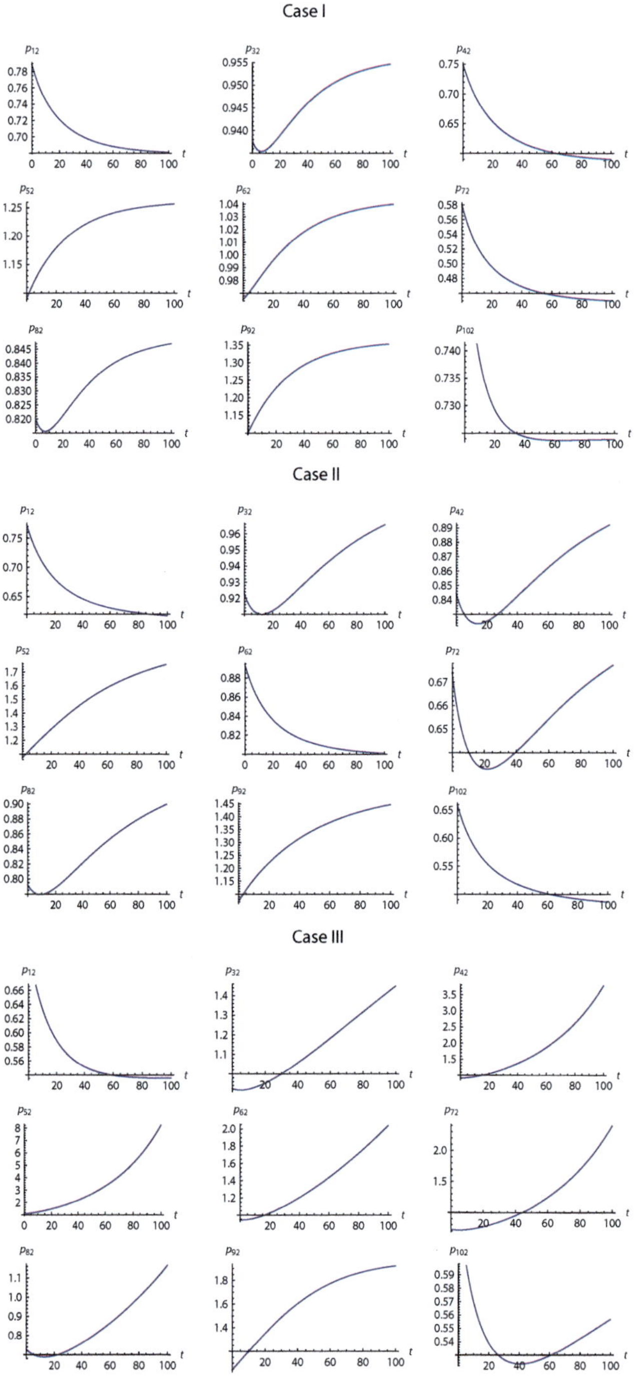


**Fig. 19.8** Relative prices $p_{i2}(t)$ by (19.19), $\omega(t)$, (19.62–19.63), Tables 19.1 and 19.2, Figs. 19.1 and 19.2

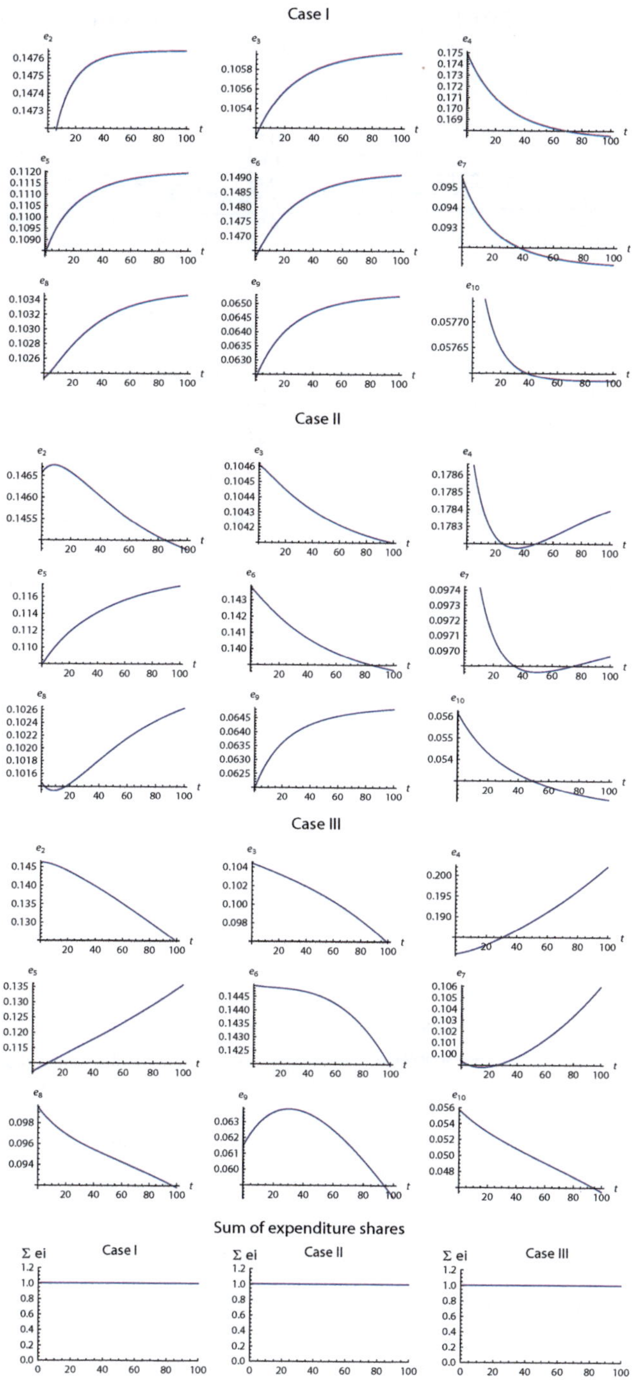


**Fig. 19.9** Budget shares $e_i(t)$ by (19.25) and $\omega(t)$, (19.62–19.63), Table 19.1, Fig. 19.8

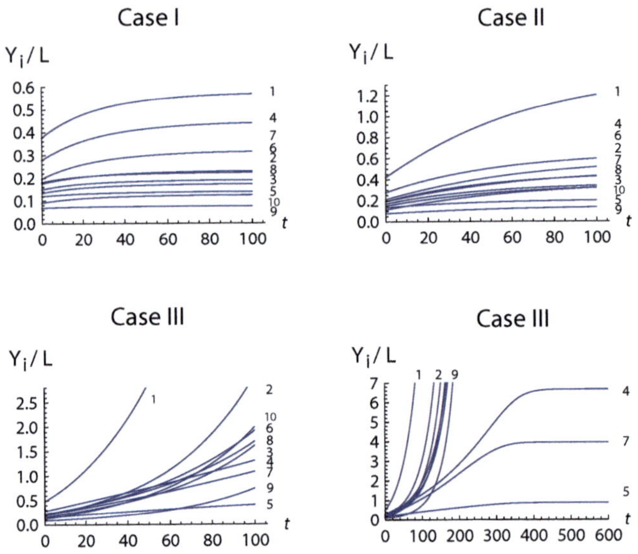


**Fig. 19.10** Per capita outputs $Y_i/L\,(t)$ by (19.34) and $\omega(t)$, (19.62–19.63), Figs. 19.4, 19.5, 19.6, and 19.7

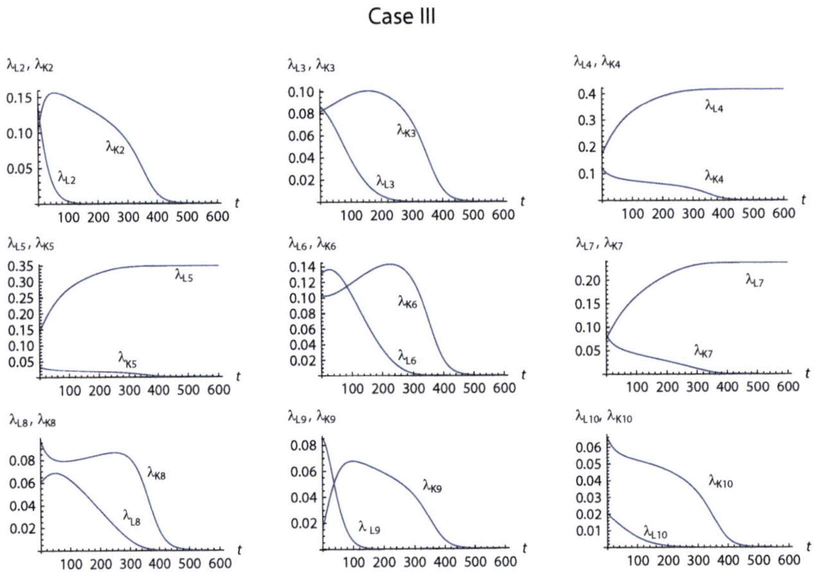


**Fig. 19.11** Long-run allocations $\lambda_{L_i}(t)$, $\lambda_{K_i}(t)$ by (19.40) and $\omega(t)$, Figs. 19.5, 19.7, and 19.10

**Table 19.2** Points of intersection/reversal $(\bar{k}_{i2}, \bar{\omega}_{i2})$, (19.51), $(\bar{p}_{i2})$, (19.52), limits, $(p^*_{i2}, p^{**}_{i2})$, (19.53), by Table 19.1, $\gamma_i = 1$

| $i$ | $\bar{k}_{i2}$ | | | $\bar{\omega}_{i2}$ | | | $\bar{p}_{i2}$ | | | $p^*_{i2}$ | | | $p^{**}_{i2}$ | | |
|---|---|---|---|---|---|---|---|---|---|---|---|---|---|---|---|
| | I | II | III | I | II | III | I | II | III | I | II | III | I | II | III |
| 1 | 446 | 161 | 4783 | 2050 | 69 | 69 | 0.578 | 0.593 | 0.535 | 3175 | 1.73 | 0.54 | 1.55 | 21.95 | 2.21 |
| 2 | | | | | | | | | | | | | | | |
| 3 | 4.02 | 6.19 | 5.24 | 10.95 | 7.86 | 4.52 | 0.935 | 0.910 | 0.916 | 5989 | 644 | 2.10 | 7.52 | 95 | 2.55 |
| 4 | – | 6.73 | 2.71 | – | 8.32 | 3.48 | – | 0.823 | 0.724 | 99.2 | – | – | 0.05 | – | – |
| 5 | 0.02 | 0.40 | 0.53 | 0.03 | 1.26 | 1.81 | 0.806 | 0.955 | 0.969 | 81.3 | – | – | 10.15 | – | – |
| 6 | 2.22 | 74.3 | 3.31 | 5.65 | 41.2 | 3.77 | 0.962 | 0.795 | 0.939 | 12852 | 1.43 | 7.13 | 11.52 | 3.14 | 5.05 |
| 7 | 208 | 9.25 | 5.19 | 879 | 10.28 | 4.51 | 0.362 | 0.632 | 0.712 | 22104 | – | – | 1.49 | – | – |
| 8 | 4.09 | 5.18 | 11.71 | 11.17 | 6.98 | 6.24 | 0.816 | 0.779 | 0.687 | 30483 | – | 37.05 | 9.91 | – | 13157 |
| 9 | 0.55 | – | – | 1.19 | – | – | 0.968 | – | – | 10161 | 3.38 | 1.97 | 19.82 | 0.67 | 0.80 |
| 10 | 9.54 | 175 | 110 | 28.6 | 73 | 15.3 | 0.724 | 0.458 | 0.523 | 23612 | 7.44 | 0.62 | 6.27 | 8178 | 8.62 |

Some reversal points occur either for lower $\omega(0)$ or higher $t$ than shown here. All the *paths* $p_{i2}(t)$ seen in Fig. 19.8 can be checked with Fig. 19.1 and Table 19.2.

All calculations of the time paths are performed by Mathematica (version 7.0) and are available on request.

The time paths of the nine *budget shares* $\mathbf{e_i(t)}$ are shown in Fig. 19.9. The evolution of $e_i\ (t)$ depends on the evolution of own- and cross prices. Since the numeraire commodity 2 is produced by a technology with a relative high $\sigma_2$ (especially in Cases I and III), its costs (price) will, with increased $\omega(t)$ and *mechanization*, become relatively *cheap*, or equivalently, the other commodities become more expensive in terms of commodity 2. Accordingly, many time paths for $p_{i2}(t)$, $i > 2$, in Fig. 19.8, are *rising*, especially in *Case* III.

With generally inelastic demand curves due to $\sigma_u = 0.8$, the higher (lower) own price $p_{i2}(t)$, implies a higher (lower) budget share $e_i(t)$. Hence, we have roughly the connection between rising consumption prices $p_{i2}(t)$, $i > 2$ in Fig. 19.8 and rising $e_i(t)$ in Fig. 19.9. The *budget shares* are *not* changing much (three-four decimals) in Fig. 19.9. With $\sigma_u = 0.8$, all consumer goods are net (Hicksian) substitutes $[E(H_i, P_i) = -\sigma_u(1 - e_i),\ E(H_i, P_j) = \sigma_u e_j]$, but they are also gross complements, cf. (19.26), which stabilizes the budget shares to cross-price changes. At the ***bottom*** of Fig. 19.9, it is seen that all the calculated paths of the budget shares $e_i(t)$ do ***add up*** to one, anytime.

Besides prices, $p_{i2}(t)$, and the shares, $e_i(t)$, it is instructive to check and examine the *time paths* of the "*real consumption*" (demand=output) of various goods in the multi-sector economy. The time paths of the *per capita outputs* of the nine *consumer goods* and the *capital good* are seen in Fig. 19.10.

In Table 19.1, the CES preference parameters ($\alpha_i$, weights) are largest for $i = 4, 6, 2$. In Cases I–II, these consumer goods are also in Fig. 19.10 among the major outputs on the whole time horizon toward the steady state. In Cases I–II, the price- and budget changes cause minor structural changes in factor allocations, Fig. 19.7—hence neither much in structure of outputs, Fig. 19.10.

In Case III, even on a *short horizon* ($t < 100$), we see considerable changes in the relative prices, Fig. 19.8, and factor reallocations, Fig. 19.7—hence also in the output compositions, Fig. 19.10, where it is already seen ($t < 100$) that the output (consumption) per capita, $Y_i/L\ (t)$, for those industries where $\sigma_i < 1$, ($i = 4, 7, 5$), are stagnating—and which is evident for $t > 100$, Fig. 19.10. The sectorial labor productivities $y_i(t)$ are bounded above for $\sigma_i < 1$, see (19.7).

For *parameter Case* III, these *structural output changes* for $t > 100$, Fig. 19.10, are dramatically underscored by the concomitant *evolution* of the *occupational structure*, $\lambda_{L_i}(t)$, as seen by the factor allocations in Fig. 19.11; the three industries with $\sigma_i < 1$, ($i = 4, 7, 5$), employ almost the entire labor force ("service industries", without much mechanization, Fig. 19.4, Case III).

The complement to the allocations for the consumer goods in Fig. 19.11 is the allocation fractions to the *capital good sector*, shown in Fig. 19.5, Case III.

The anomalous time paths of $\lambda_{K_1}(t)$ and $\delta_K(t)$ in Figs. 19.5 and 19.6, Case III, require a mathematical-economic justification, and they pose the question: what are the asymptotic limits $[k(t) \to \infty]$ for: $\delta_K(t)$ (19.39), $\lambda_{K_1}(t)$ (19.40)?

Although analytic expressions for these limits are hard to establish, some approximate answers are available, Jensen et al. (2005, p. 51), here, Chap. 18, viz.,

$$\lim_{k(t)\to\infty} \delta_K(t) \approx s_1 + \epsilon_\delta \quad \lim_{k(t)\to\infty} \lambda_{K_1}(t) \approx s_1/(s_1 + \epsilon_\lambda), \tag{19.65}$$

with, $\epsilon_\delta$, $\epsilon_\lambda$, as infinitesimals. Thus with, $s_1$ (19.63) and (19.65), we get

$$\lim_{k(t)\to\infty} \delta_K(t) \approx 0.2\,, \qquad \lim_{k(t)\to\infty} \lambda_{K_1}(t) \approx 1, \tag{19.66}$$

which is in line with: $\delta_K(t)$ and $\lambda_{K_1}(t)$ in Figs. 19.5 and 19.6, Case III, $t = 600$.

But obviously the limits (19.65) required persistent growth of $k(t)$, that is, no critical (steady-state) point in (19.59). The necessary and sufficient parametric conditions for absence of critical points in (19.59), (19.62) are:

$$\forall i \ \sigma_i > 1: \ \gamma_1 a_1^{\frac{\sigma_1}{\sigma_1-1}} > (n+\delta)/s_1\,; \quad only \ \sigma_1 > 1: \ \gamma_1 a_1^{\frac{\sigma_1}{\sigma_1-1}} > n+\delta \tag{19.67}$$

cf. the large bracket (19.62). The distinction in (19.67) derives from the bracket denominator of (19.62), which takes the values 1 or $s_1$ for $\omega \to \infty$, depending on the size of all $\sigma_i$; see Jensen et al. (2005, p. 44).

Then, from Table 19.1, (19.63), (19.67), and (19.8), we obtain

$$\gamma_1 a_1^{\frac{\sigma_1}{\sigma_1-1}} = 0.25\,; \quad (n+\delta)/s_1 = 0.25\,; \quad n+\delta = 0.05. \tag{19.68}$$

By inspecting (19.67–19.68), it is clear that, if we had, $\sigma_i > 1$, for *all* ten sectors in Table 19.1, then the strict inequality (19.67) is violated, and we could not have obtained the persistent multi-sector growth solutions for Case III, Fig. 19.2, 19.3, 19.4, 19.5, 19.6, 19.7, 19.8, 19.9, 19.10, and 19.11. If we *only* had $\sigma_1 > 1$, then inequality, (19.67–19.68), is easily satisfied, but the time paths for the *levels* of *consumer goods per capita* would be *bounded*, as in Fig. 19.10 for sectors 4, 7, 5.

It is noteworthy that the, $\forall i \ \sigma_i > 1$, *condition* in (19.67) corresponds to the macro CES threshold condition. For the combinations of the CES parameters satisfying the macro threshold values, see de La Grandville (1989, p. 479), de La Grandville (2009, p. 125), Klump and de La Grandville (2000, p. 282), Jensen and Larsen (1987, p. 234); here p. 20 in Chap. 1, Jensen et al. (2005, p. 78)).

Thus, we see by (19.67–19.68) that it is "*easier*" to generate *persistent* growth *within* CES *ten-sector* models *than* within CES *one-* to *two-* sector models. The main economic and dynamic reason for this paradoxical result is that the *occupational structure* by $\lambda_{L_1}(t)$, (19.55–19.56), and hence all the *sectoral allocations* $\lambda_{L_i}(t)$, $\lambda_{K_i}(t)$ are *endogenous* variables, and this continuous factor *reallocation* as implemented by the time paths of the *relative factor- and commodity prices* reinforces—as we have seen with our solutions of (19.62–19.63)—*capital allocation* toward the *capital good sector*.

Especially, regarding changes in the prices of the capital good and consumer goods, we note that the relative price of the capital good, $p_{12}(t)$, is declining in Fig. 19.8 for all three Cases I–III. For $p_{12}(t)$, the Case I, Table 19.1, corresponds to Case 7.4, Fig. 19.1; Cases II–III correspond to Case 8.4, Fig. 19.1.

Since $\omega_I^* = 32.83, \omega_{II}^* = 29.17$, cf. (19.64), are far below the reversal points, $\bar{\omega}_{12}$: (2050, 69), Table 19.2, any rising values of $p_{12}(t)$ will not be observed before the steady states in Cases I–II.

We get in Case III: $\bar{\omega}_{12} = 69$, Table 19.2 (exactly as Case II, with any decimals). In Table 19.2, Case III, we see that $\bar{p}_{12} = 0.535$ is very close to $p_{12}^* = 0.54$; thus, the rising part in Case 8.4, Fig. 19.1, is very short, and $p_{12}(t)$ reaches this lower zone already at $t = 60$, in Fig. 19.8. A glimpse of the role for the *capital good price* $P_1$ in obtaining persistent growth is evident in (19.57). For *empirical evidence* on the relative *price decline* of capital goods (equipment), see the pioneering study of Greenwood et al. (1997, p. 343).

The evolution of *relative shares* of capital and labor in Case III, Fig. 19.6, deserves special attention. With *mechanization* of this ten-sector CES economy, we see an initial stage with a rising *capital share*, $\delta_K(t)$; economic history has adduced to such initial phase for $\delta_K(t)$. In (19.59) with $N = 1$ and $\delta_K = \epsilon_{K_1}$, (19.11), the *share* $\epsilon_{K_1}(t)$, (19.14,) rises toward one with $\sigma_1 = \sigma > 1$. But with the *extension* to $N = 10$, the *evolution* and the convergence value of $\boldsymbol{\delta_K(t)}$, Case III, Fig. 19.6, are much *closer* to the *recorded* economic time series.

## Final Comments

Decentralization with dispersion of factor endowment and decision-making authority is the main principle underlying the general economic assumption of competitive markets with individual maximizing agents. Momentary and moving general equilibria of commodity and factor markets have been involved in the parametric solutions of the CES ten-sector growth model and in the analytical system for the N-dimensional homothetic economy.

A natural topic for future research on the multi-sector growth models is extensions to include non-homothetic preferences, allowing for nonunitary income elasticities of demand for the different goods. Constant differences of elasticity of substitution (CDES) preferences generalize CES, cf. Jensen et al. (2011).

Other extensions of general equilibrium dynamics could include financial assets, portfolio analysis, and stochastic dynamics. Stochastic and deterministic multi-sector growth models should together contribute to a better under-

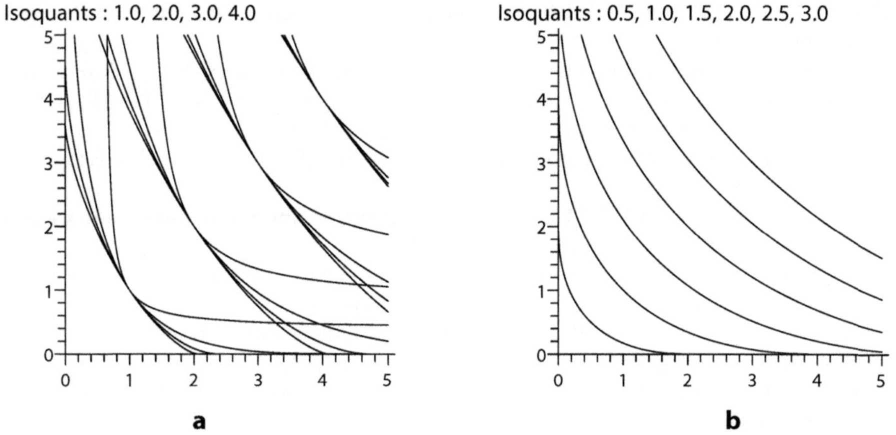


**Fig. 19.12** (**a**) CES isoquants. $\gamma_i = 1, a_i = 0.4, \sigma_i = 0.5, 1.5, 2.5, 3.5$. (**b**) CES isoquants. $\gamma_i = 1, a_i = 0.5, \sigma_i = 2.0$

standing of the historical time series in economics and other disciplines, cf. de La Grandville (2001), Jensen and Palokangas (2007); here Chap. 26.

## Appendix: CES Isoquant Map

If $\sigma > 1$, the isoquants of (19.3) reach the axes, and the interception points $(\bar{L}, 0)$ and $(0, \bar{K})$ are given by:

$$\bar{L} = (Y/\gamma)(1-a)^{\frac{\sigma}{1-\sigma}} \; ; \quad \bar{K} = (Y/\gamma)(a)^{\frac{\sigma}{1-\sigma}} \tag{19.69}$$

that is, for the unit isoquant in Fig. 19.12b, $Y = 1$: $\bar{L} = 4, \bar{K} = 4$.

If $\sigma < 1$, the CES isoquants have vertical and horizontal asymptotes. Their intersection point, $(\bar{L}, \bar{K})$, is formally given by the same expressions (19.69).

The slopes of all CES isoquants, $\omega = |dK/dL|$, range from zero to infinity, neither of which are reached in finite time for $\omega(t)$ solutions in Figs. 19.2, 19.3, 19.4, 19.5, 19.6, 19.7, 19.8, 19.9, 19.10, and 19.11.

## Bibliography

Aghion P, Durlauf S (eds) (2005) Handbook of Economic Growth, 1st edn. Elsevier, Amsterdam, North–Holland

Aghion P, Howitt P (1998) Endogenous Growth Theory. The MIT Press, Cambridge, MA and London, England

Arrow KJ (1974) General Economic Equilibrium: Purpose, Analytic Techniques, Collective Choice. American Economic Review 64:253–272

Arrow KJ, Chenery HB, Minhas BS, Solow RM (1961) Capital–Labour Substitution and Economic Efficiency. Review of Economics and Statistics 43:225–250

Barro RJ, Sala-i-Martin X (2004) Economic Growth Theory, 2nd edn. M.I.T. Press, Cambridge, Mass

Carstensen K, Gundlach E, Hartman S (2009) The Augmented Solow Model with Mincerian Schooling and Externalities. German Economic Review 10:448–463

Chung JW (1994) Utility and Production Functions. Blackwell, Oxford

Dhrymes PJ (1962) A Multisectoral Model of Growth. Quarterly Journal of Economics 76:264–278

Dixit AK, Stiglitz JE (1977) Monopolistic Competition and Optimum Product Diversity. American Economic Review 67:297–308

Echevarria C (1997) Changes in Sectoral Composition Associated with Economic Growth. International Economic Review 38:431–452

Greenwood J, Hercowitz Z, Krusell P (1997) Long–Run Implications of Investment–Specific Technological Change. American Economic Review 87:342–362

Inada K (1964) On the Stability of Growth Equilibria in Two–Sector Models. Rev Econ Stud 31:127–42

Jensen BS (1994) The Dynamic Systems of Basic Economic Growth Models. Kluwer Academic Publishers, Dordrecht

Jensen BS (2003) Walrasian General Equilibrium Allocations and Dynamics in Two–Sector Growth Models. German Economic Review 4:53–87

Jensen BS (2009) Dynamic Extensions of the Solow Growth Model (1956), Editorial. German Economic Review 10:378–383

Jensen BS, Larsen ME (1987) Growth and Long–Run Stability. Acta Applicandae Mathematicae 9:219–237, Reprinted in Jensen (1994)

Jensen BS, Larsen ME (2005) General Equilibrium Dynamics of Multi–Sector Growth Models. Journal of Economics 10:17–56

Jensen BS, Palokangas T (2007) Stochastic Economic Dynamics. Copenhagen Business School Press, Denmark

Jensen BS, Alsholm PK, Larsen ME, Jensen JM (2005) Dynamic Structure, Exogeneity, Phase Portraits, Growth Paths, and Scale and Substitution Elasticities. Review of International Economics 13:59–89

Jensen BS, de Boer P, van Daal J, Jensen PS (2011) Global Restrictions on the Parameters of the CDES Indirect Utility Function. Journal of Economics 102:217–235

Jones RW (1965) The Structure of Simple General Equilibrium Models. J Political Economy 73:557–72, or Bhagwati (1981)

Klump R, de La Grandville O (2000) Economic Growth and the Elasticity of Substitution: Two Theorems and Some Suggestions. American Economic Review 90:282–291

Kongsamut P, Rebelo S, Xie D (2001) Beyond Balanced Growth. Review of Economic Studies 68:869–882

Kuznets S (1966) Modern Economic Growth. Rate, Structure and Spread. Yale University Press, New Haven

de La Grandville O (1989) In Quest of the Slutsky Diamond. American Economic Review 79:468–481

de La Grandville O (1997) Curvature and the Elasticity of Substitution: Straightening It Out. Journal of Economics 66:23–34

de La Grandville O (2001) Bond Pricing and Portfolio Analysis. MIT Press, Cambridge, Mass.

de La Grandville O (2009) Economic Growth—a Unified Approach. Cambridge University Press, Cambridge
Mankiw NG, Romer D, Weil DN (1992) A Contribution to the Empirics of Economic Growth. Quarterly Journal of Economics 107:407–437
McKenzie L (1954) On Equilibrium in Grahamic Model of World Trade and Other Competitive Sytems. Econometrica 22:147–161
Nonneman W, Vanhoudt P (1996) A further Augmentation of the Solow model and the Empirics of Economic Growth for OECD countries. Quarterly Journal of Economics 111:943–953
Romer D (2001) Advanced Macroeconomics, 2nd edn. McGraw–Hill, Boston
Rosenberg N (1963) Capital Goods, Technology, and Economic Growth. Oxford Economic Papers 15:217–27
Samuelson PA (1949) International Factor Price Equalisation Once Again. Economic Journal 59:181–197
Shoven JB, Whalley J (1992) Applying General Equilibrium. Cambridge University Press, Cambridge, UK
Solow RM (1956) A Contribution to the Theory of Economic Growth. Quarterly Journal of Economics 70:65–94, Reprinted in Stiglitz (1969), and in Becker (1991)
Solow RM (1961) Note on Uzawa's Two–Sector Model of Economic Growth. Rev Econ Stud 29:48–50, or Stiglitz (1969)
Solow RM (1999) Neoclassical Growth Theory. Chapter 9 in Taylor (1999), *Handbook of Macroeconomics,* 1, North–Holland: Elsevier, Amsterdam.
Solow RM (2000) Growth Theory: An Exposition, 2nd edn. Oxford University Press, Oxford
Solow RM (2005) Reflections on Growth Theory. pp 3–10, Introduction, in: Aghion and Durlauf, (Eds).
Stiglitz JE (1969) Allocation of Heterogeneous Capital Goods in a Two–Sector Economy. International Economic Review 10:379–390
Taylor JB, Woodford M (1999) Handbook of Macroeconomics. Elsevier, Amsterdam, 1, North–Holland
Uzawa H (1959) Prices of the Factors of Production in International Trade. Econometrica 27:448–68
Uzawa H (1961) On a Two–Sector Model of Economic Growth: I. Review of Economic Studies 29:40–47
Uzawa H (1963) On a Two–Sector Model of Economic Growth: II. Review of Economic Studies 30:105–18, Also in: Stiglitz and Uzawa (1969)
Walras L (1954) Elements of Pure Economics. George Allen and Unwin, London

CHAPTER 20

# Non-Homothetic Multi-Sector Growth Models

## Introduction

"Early on one would have expected much more work on multi-sector growth models than there has been", Solow (2005, p. 4). Long ago Kuznets (1966, p. 1) wrote: "We identify the economic growth of a nation as a sustained increase in per capita or per worker product, most often accompanied by an increase in population and usually by sweeping structural changes". A standard textbook such as Barro and Sala-i-Martin (2004) does not go beyond two final goods.

The economic literature has paid some attention to dynamic general equilibrium models with the industrial patterns of structural change, e.g., Echevarria (1997) and Kongsamut et al. (2001) that study three-sector growth models. But the sectorial production functions in Kongsamut et al. (2001) are identical up to proportionality constant and hence the relative prices of three different goods are not affected by factor prices, factor allocations, or change over time. The factor reallocations and sectorial changes in output composition are entirely driven by differences in the income elasticities of demand (here the linear expenditure system (LES) and its non-homothetic preferences are used in an intertemporal optimization). Echevarria (1997) uses three Cobb-Douglas (CD) technologies and non-homothetic preferences that converge to CD preferences. The time paths in this three-sector model are asymptotically equivalent to the steady-state values in the CD growth model with unitary

With co-authors:
ULLA LEHMIJOKI, Helsinki Center of Economic Research (HECER), University of Helsinki, Finland
ELENA ROVENSKAYA, Faculty of Compuational Mathematics and Cybernetices, Lomonosov Moscow State University, Moscow, Russia



B. S. Jensen, *The Elements and Dynamic Systems of Economic Growth and Trade Models*, https://doi.org/10.1007/978-3-031-52493-6_20

demand elasticities. Echevarria (2010) extends this three-sector model in modified forms to include international trade. Buera and Kaboski (2009) analyze further the balanced growth paths of Kongsamut et al. (2001) and the biased productivity growth story of Ngai and Pissarides (2007). Bonatti and Felice (2008) study the transformation of a two-sector economy with a technologically progressive and stagnant industry. Buera and Kaboski (2012) examine the role of high-skilled labor behind the growth of the service sector.

Jensen and Lehmijoki (2011); here Chap. 19, studied *N-sector growth models* with *homothetic* consumer *preferences* and simulated a growing *ten-sector* CES economy. Our objective is to equip multi-sector growth models with *non-homothetic* preferences such that its consumer budget shares can actually be sensibly related to *observed Engel curve patterns.* Our outlook is much in accordance with the perspectives in Herrendorf and Valentinyi (2012), Herrendorf et al. (2013) of combining both the *evolution* of *price* and *income elasticities* as determinants of *structural transformations.* Instead of their three-sector model and non-homothetic LES demand, we apply the *non-homothetic* **CDES** demand system of Houthakker (1960), Jensen et al. (2011), here Chap. 5, to an MSG ( *ten-sector*) model. A richer system than LES is needed, as LES only allows for price inelastic demands.

As to strategy and methodology, we use *Shephard's Lemma* and *Roy's Identity* to combine the *supply* and *demand* sides of *general equilibrium* models. In this way the *Walras-Pareto* general equilibrium is *parametrically* specified. Hence the *multi-sector equilibrium dynamics* can be *explicitly* derived and *solved* (Pareto 1971; Walras 1954).

The chapter is organized as follows. Section "Structure of Non-Homothetic N-sector General Equilibrium Model" starts with the central theoretical core of the growth theory consisting of cost/production and utility functions. As is well-known from duality theory, there are two approaches to the deriving systems of optimal consumer and factor demand functions. One procedure starts from functional forms of direct utility and production functions (satisfying proper regularity properties) and then use Lagrangian techniques to solve the optimization problem. The second procedure begins with differentiable functional forms of indirect utility and cost functions to obtain consumer and factor demands by differentiation. The difficulty with the *first* methodology is that it is usually *impossible* to obtain the consumer- and factor demands as *explicit functions* expressed in the *parameters* of direct utility-/ production functions. Hence we proceed with the second method. National income accounting of a multi-sector economy is integrated with Walras law and general equilibrium conditions.

In Sect. "Walrasian Equilibrium of Two-Factor-Multi-Sector Economies", the *general equilibrium* of the non-homothetic multi-sector economy with two primary factors (labor and capital) is expressed compactly by just *one equation.* Section "Dynamics and Time Paths of Non-Homothetic MSG Models" introduces the equations of factor accumulations, which give the laws of motions that must be solved. The *dynamics* of our non-homothetic multi-sector economy can be expressed by ***three differential equations.*** Section "Solving the Multi-Sector Growth—(2 × 10)—Model" presents in detail the benchmark ***solutions*** of the general equilibrium ***dynamics*** for the CDES ***ten-sector*** economy with three different ***parameter*** regimes. Section "Conclusions" concludes.

## Structure of Non-Homothetic N-sector General Equilibrium Model

### *CES Sectoral Cost Functions and Relative Price functions*

Consider an economy consisting of $N$ industries (sectors) and two primary factors, labor ($L$) and capital ($K$) with, $(w, r)$, as the factor prices of labor and capital services. $Y_i$ is the total output of sector (commodity), $i = 1, \ldots, N$.

Our industry (sector) *cost function*, $C_i\,(w, r, Y_i)$, must be a *smooth regular* cost function, cf. Diewert (1974, p. 111), McFadden (1978, p. 13), Lehmijoki (1984, p. 386), Varian (1992, p. 72), Silberberg and Suen (2001, p. 205), i.e: (i) homogeneous of degree one in the absolute (money) factor prices $w, r$; (ii) continuously differentiable in the factor prices $w > 0, r > 0$, and in $Y_i > 0$; (iii) non-decreasing in factor prices $w, r$, and strictly increasing in $Y_i$; (iv) concave in the factor prices $w, r$; (v) constant returns to scale.

The *CES total cost functions* with two-factor prices $C_i(w, r, Y_i)$ is, cf. Varian (1992, p. 56), Silberberg and Suen (2001, p. 248), Jensen and Lehmijoki (2011); here Chap. 19,

$$C_i(w, r, Y_i) = 1/\gamma_i \left[(1 - a_i)^{\sigma_i} w^{1-\sigma_i} + a_i^{\sigma_i} r^{1-\sigma_i}\right]^{\frac{1}{1-\sigma_i}} Y_i. \tag{20.1}$$

By the homogeneity property (i) in factor prices, we get from (20.1),

$$C_i(w, r, Y_i) = r\,(1/\gamma_i)\, a_i^{\frac{\sigma_i}{1-\sigma_i}} \left[1 + b_i\,(w/r)^{1-\sigma_i}\right]^{\frac{1}{1-\sigma_i}} Y_i\,; \quad b_i = \left[\frac{1 - a_i}{a_i}\right]^{\sigma_i} \tag{20.2}$$

The average—$AC_i = C_i/Y_i$, marginal: $MC_i = dC_i/dY_i$—cost functions are:

$$AC_i(w, r) = MC_i(w, r) = (r/\gamma_i)\, a_i^{\frac{\sigma_i}{1-\sigma_i}} \left[1 + b_i \left[\frac{w}{r}\right]^{1-\sigma_i}\right]^{\frac{1}{1-\sigma_i}} = r\, c_i \left[\frac{w}{r}\right] \tag{20.3}$$

$$c_i\,(w/r) = (1/\gamma_i)\, a_i^{\frac{\sigma_i}{1-\sigma_i}} \left[1 + b_i\,(w/r)^{1-\sigma_i}\right]^{\frac{1}{1-\sigma_i}}; \quad b_i = \left[\frac{1 - a_i}{a_i}\right]^{\sigma_i} \tag{20.4}$$

Cost minimization, competitive producer equilibrium pricing, profit maximization, "zero profit condition", and Pareto optimality are equivalent to the condition: Price $(P_i)$ = Marginal Cost $(MC_i)$, $i = 1, \ldots, N$. Thus, by (20.3–20.4):

$$P_i = MC_i(w, r) = r\, c_i\,(w/r) = w\, c_i\,(r/w) \qquad (20.5)$$

where the last term follows from the homogeneity property (i) in factor prices. Then CES *relative marginal* cost functions (*relative* commodity *prices*) are:

$$p_{ij} = \frac{P_i}{P_j} = \frac{MC_i(w,r)}{MC_j(w,r)} = \frac{c_i\,(w/r)}{c_j\,(w/r)} = \frac{(1/\gamma_i)\, a_i^{\sigma_i/(1-\sigma_i)} \left[1 + b_i\,(w/r)^{1-\sigma_i}\right]^{\frac{1}{1-\sigma_i}}}{(1/\gamma_j)\, a_j^{\sigma_j/(1-\sigma_j)} \left[1 + b_j\,(w/r)^{1-\sigma_j}\right]^{\frac{1}{1-\sigma_j}}} \qquad (20.6)$$

$$= \frac{\gamma_j a_j^{\sigma_j/(\sigma_j-1)} \left[1 + b_j (w/r)^{1-\sigma_j}\right]^{1/(\sigma_j-1)}}{\gamma_i a_i^{\sigma_i/(\sigma_i-1)} \left[1 + b_i (w/r)^{1-\sigma_i}\right]^{1/(\sigma_i-1)}} = c_{ij}\left[\frac{w}{r}\right];\ \frac{w}{r} = \omega \in [0, \infty). \qquad (20.7)$$

With $\sigma_i = \sigma_j = \sigma$, we get, cf. (20.7),

$$p_{ij} = c_{ij}\,(w/r) = \frac{\gamma_j}{\gamma_i}\left[\left[\frac{a_j}{a_i}\right]^{\sigma} \frac{1 + b_j\,(w/r)^{1-\sigma}}{1 + b_i\,(w/r)^{1-\sigma}}\right]^{\frac{1}{\sigma-1}};\quad b_i = \left[\frac{1-a_i}{a_i}\right]^{\sigma}. \qquad (20.8)$$

In the limit case of (20.8) with $\sigma = 1$ (Cobb-Douglas), we obtain:

$$p_{ij} = c_{ij}\,(w/r) = \frac{\gamma_j\, a_j^{a_j}\,(1-a_j)^{1-a_j}}{\gamma_i\, a_i^{a_i}\,(1-a_i)^{1-a_i}} \left[\frac{w}{r}\right]^{a_j - a_i};\quad w/r = \omega \in [0, \infty). \qquad (20.9)$$

Relative CES commodity prices, $p_{ij} = c_{ij}\,(w/r)$, (20.7), with their CES pairs: $(w/r)_i = \omega_i = \frac{1-a_i}{a_i} k_i^{1/\sigma_i}$, $\omega_j = \frac{1-a_j}{a_j} k_j^{1/\sigma_j}$, cf. (20.14), are shown in Fig. 20.1.

For $(w/r)$ going to zero and infinity, the limits of the relative price (cost) functions, $p_{ij} = c_{ij}\,(w/r)$, (20.7) become either:

$$p^{*}_{ij} \equiv \frac{\gamma_j\, a_j^{\sigma_j/(\sigma_j-1)}}{\gamma_i\, a_i^{\sigma_i/(\sigma_i-1)}};\quad p^{**}_{ij} \equiv \frac{\gamma_j\,(1-a_j)^{\sigma_j/(\sigma_j-1)}}{\gamma_i\,(1-a_i)^{\sigma_i/(\sigma_i-1)}}. \qquad (20.10)$$

with (20.10) depicted in Fig. 20.1.

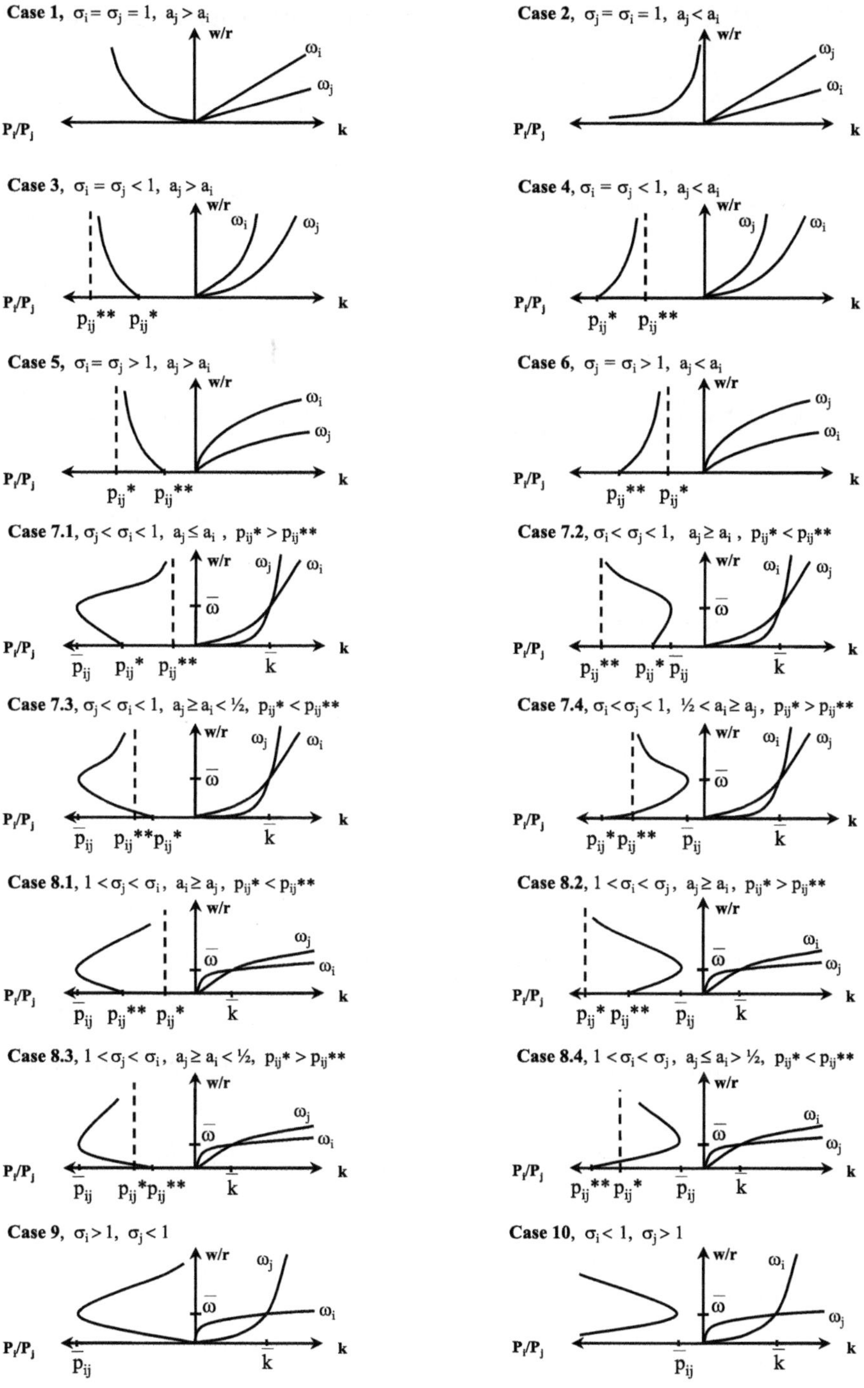


**Fig. 20.1** The relative prices $P_i/P_j = p_{ij} = c_{ij}(w/r)$ with CES: (20.7–20.9), and the isoelastic pair: $\omega_i(k_i)$, $\omega_j(k_j)$, (20.14)

*Shephard's Lemma* gives sectoral factor demand of capital $K_i$ and labor $L_i$:

$$K_i\,(w, r, Y_i) = \frac{\partial C_i}{\partial r} = \frac{Y_i}{\gamma_i}\, a_i^{\frac{\sigma_i}{1-\sigma_i}} \left[1 + b_i\,(w/r)^{1-\sigma_i}\right]^{\frac{1}{1-\sigma_i}} +$$

$$\frac{r}{1-\sigma_i}\,\frac{Y_i}{\gamma_i}\, a_i^{\frac{\sigma_i}{1-\sigma_i}} \left[1 + b_i\,(w/r)^{1-\sigma_i}\right]^{\frac{\sigma_i}{1-\sigma_i}} b_i\, w^{1-\sigma_i}(\sigma_i - 1)\, r^{\,\sigma_i - 2}$$

$$= \frac{Y_i}{\gamma_i}\, a_i^{\frac{\sigma_i}{1-\sigma_i}} \left[1 + b_i\,(w/r)^{1-\sigma_i}\right]^{\frac{1}{1-\sigma_i}} \frac{1}{1 + b_i\,(w/r)^{1-\sigma_i}} \tag{20.11}$$

$$L_i\,(w, r, Y_i) = \frac{\partial C_i}{\partial w} = \frac{r}{1-\sigma_i}\,\frac{Y_i}{\gamma_i}\, a_i^{\frac{\sigma_i}{1-\sigma_i}} \left[1 + b_i\,(w/r)^{1-\sigma_i}\right]^{\frac{\sigma_i}{1-\sigma_i}} b_i(1-\sigma_i)\frac{w^{-\sigma_i}}{r^{\,1-\sigma_i}}$$

$$= \frac{Y_i}{\gamma_i}\, a_i^{\frac{\sigma_i}{1-\sigma_i}} \left[1 + b_i\,(w/r)^{1-\sigma_i}\right]^{\frac{1}{1-\sigma_i}} \frac{b_i\,(w/r)^{-\sigma_i}}{1 + b_i\,(w/r)^{1-\sigma_i}} \tag{20.12}$$

and CES sectoral factor cost shares, $\epsilon_{K_i} + \epsilon_{L_i} = 1$, as, cf. (20.11–20.12), $w/r = \omega$,

$$\epsilon_{K_i} = \frac{\partial\, ln\, C_i}{\partial\, ln\, r} = \frac{\partial C_i}{\partial r}\,\frac{r}{C_i} = \frac{1}{1 + b_i\,\omega^{1-\sigma_i}}\,;\ \epsilon_{L_i} = \frac{\partial\, ln\, C_i}{\partial\, ln\, w} = \frac{b_i\,\omega^{1-\sigma_i}}{1 + b_i\,\omega^{1-\sigma_i}} \tag{20.13}$$

The CES sectoral capital-labor ratios, $k_i = K_i/\,L_i$, become, cf. (20.11–20.12), (20.34),

$$k_i = K_i\,(w, r, Y_i)/\,L_i\,(w, r, Y_i) = \frac{1}{b_i}\left[\frac{w}{r}\right]^{\sigma_i};\ \frac{w}{r} = \omega;\quad b_i = \left[\frac{1-a_i}{a_i}\right]^{\sigma_i} \tag{20.14}$$

Sectorial identities ("zero profit" conditions) are restated in alternative forms,

$$P_i Y_i = wL_i + rK_i;\ P_i = \frac{w + rk_i}{y_i} = \frac{r(\omega + k_i)}{y_i};\ \ y_i = Y_i/L_i\ ;\ w/r = \omega \tag{20.15}$$

By (20.15–20.14), (20.5–20.4), the CES sectoral labor productivities, $(y_i)$, become in $(\omega)$:

$$y_i = \frac{r(\omega + k_i)}{P_i} = \frac{\omega + k_i}{c_i\,(\omega)} = \gamma_i\, a_i^{\frac{\sigma_i}{\sigma_i - 1}} \left[\omega + \left[\frac{a_i\,\omega}{1-a_i}\right]^{\sigma_i}\right] \left[1 + b_i\,\omega^{1-\sigma_i}\right]^{\frac{1}{\sigma_i - 1}} \tag{20.16}$$

### *CDES Indirect Utility and the Marshallian Demands (Budget System)*

As we are setting up a *multi-sector* (N) growth model with sector technologies using *two primary* factors, *Labor* and *Capital* (physical), we need at least one capital good sector. Let sector 1 be the capital good industry.

With one *capital good* industry (sector 1), the *final demand* decomposition of the aggregate expenditures, GDP (**Y**, total factor income), into gross investment expenditures (**I**), total consumption expenditures (**C**), and final demand (expenditure) *shares* ($s_i$) become,

$$I = P_1 Y_1 \ ; \ C = \textstyle\sum_{i=2}^{N} P_i Y_i \ ; \ Y = C + I = wL + rK \ ; \ s_1 = I/Y \tag{20.17}$$

$$s_i = P_i Y_i / Y \ ; \quad \textstyle\sum_{i=1}^{N} s_i \equiv \sum_{i=1}^{N} P_i Y_i / Y = 1. \tag{20.18}$$

Just as Shephard's lemma was used above to derive sectorial systems of cost minimizing factor demands and cost shares, Roy's identity will be used to derive utility maximizing commodity demand functions and budget shares.

Our consumer demands will be governed by *non-homothetic preferences,* and specified by the **CDES** (constant differences of elasticities of substitution) class of indirect utility (ordinal) functions, cf. Jensen et al. (2011), here Chap. 5.

This CDES Indirect Utility Function **V(P,C)** is given by ($P_i > 0, \ C > 0$)

$$V(P, C) = \sum_{i=2}^{N} \alpha_i \left[ \frac{(C/P_i)^{\beta_i} - 1}{\beta_i} \right]; \ \alpha_i > 0, \ \sum_{i=2}^{N} \alpha_i = 1, \ \beta_i \geq -1 \ ; \tag{20.19}$$

where the last equality sign for $\beta_i$ may apply for at most one item index (i).

Applying *Roy's identity* to (20.19), gives the *Marshallian demand functions,* $Y_i = D_i(P, C)$, and in logarithmic form *budget shares*, $P_i Y_i / C = e_i(P, C)$, as

$$D_i(P, C) = -\frac{\partial V(P, C)/\partial P_i}{\partial V(P, C)/\partial C} = \frac{\alpha_i (C/P_i)^{\beta_i + 1}}{\sum_{j=2}^{N} \alpha_j (C/P_j)^{\beta_j}} > 0 \ ; \ i = 2, \ldots, N, \tag{20.20}$$

$$e_i(P, C) = -\frac{\partial \ln V(P, C)/\partial \ln P_i}{\partial \ln V(P, C)/\partial \ln C} = \frac{\alpha_i (C/P_i)^{\beta_i}}{\sum_{j=2}^{N} \alpha_j (C/P_j)^{\beta_j}} \ ; \ i = 2, \ldots, N, \tag{20.21}$$

Direct (own) price- and income (expenditure) elasticities for the CDES system of the Marshallian demands (20.20) are, cf. Jensen et al. (2011, p. 224),

$$E(D_i, P_i) = -1 - \beta_i(1 - e_i)\ ;\quad E(D_i, C) = 1 + \beta_i - \bar{\beta}\ ;\quad \bar{\beta} = \sum_{j=2}^{N} e_j\beta_j \tag{20.22}$$

All CDES demand curves [partial $D_i(P_i)$] of (20.20) are downward sloping throughout their domain and have the axes as asymptotes; they are convex to the origin, except for inflexion (convexity/concavity) points for very luxurious goods (very large $\beta_i$). Most price elasticities, $E(D_i, P_i)$, (20.22), numerically increase with larger $P_i$, and most $E(D_i, P_i)$ decline numerically with larger $C$. All income elasticities, $E(D_i, C)$, (20.22), *decline* with larger $C$.

The CDES *Engel curves* [budget shares, (20.21)] are of *three* main *types*: (1) Unlimited monotonic increase (2) Monotonic increase toward a maximum (saturation) level (3) Decrease toward zero, after having reached a maximum.

In any consumer demand system, e.g. (20.20–20.21), all prices and total income/expenditure $(P, C)$ are *exogenous* variables. But in *general equilibrium* (Walrasian) models, prices and total income become *endogenous* variables. To facilitate this transition, we rewrite (20.21) in the following way:

$$e_i(P, C) = \frac{P_i Y_i}{C} = \frac{\alpha_i (C/P_i)^{\beta_i}}{\sum_{j=2}^{N} \alpha_j (C/P_j)^{\beta_j}} = \left[\sum_{j=2}^{N} \frac{\alpha_j}{\alpha_i}\left[\frac{P_i^{\beta_i}}{P_j^{\beta_j}}\right] C^{\beta_j - \beta_i}\right]^{-1}$$
$$= \left[\sum_{j=2}^{N} \frac{\alpha_j}{\alpha_i}\, p_{ij}^{\beta_j}\left[\frac{C}{P_i}\right]^{\beta_j - \beta_i}\right]^{-1} = \left[1 + \sum_{j=2, j\neq i}^{N} \frac{\alpha_j}{\alpha_i}\, p_{ij}^{\beta_j}\left[\frac{C}{P_i}\right]^{\beta_j - \beta_i}\right]^{-1} \tag{20.23}$$

Linking the relative *consumer* prices in $e_i$, (20.23), to *cost* prices, (20.6–20.7), we get

$$e_i(\omega, L, K) = \left[1 + \sum_{j=2, j\neq i}^{N} \frac{\alpha_j}{\alpha_i}\, [p_{ij}(\omega)]^{\beta_j}\left[\frac{C}{P_i}(\omega, L, K)\right]^{\beta_j - \beta_i}\right]^{-1} \tag{20.24}$$

The budget shares (20.24) are well-defined in terms of $\omega$, $L$, $K$, cf. (20.17), (20.5):

$$C/P_i = (1-s_1)Y/P_i = (1-s_1)L\,(\omega+k)(r/P_i) = (1-s_1)L\,(\omega+k)\,/c_i(\omega) \tag{20.25}$$

$$(p_{ij})^{\beta_j} = \left[\frac{P_i}{P_j} = \frac{MC_i}{MC_j} = \frac{c_i(\omega)}{c_j(\omega)}\right]^{\beta_j} \tag{20.26}$$

Hence by (20.24–20.26), (20.6–20.7), we obtain the *explicit parametric* expressions,

$$e_i(\omega, L, K) = \left[1 + [\,c_i(\omega)\,]^{\beta_i} \sum_{j=2, j\neq i}^{N} \frac{(\alpha_j/\alpha_i)\,[\,c_j(\omega)\,]^{-\beta_j}}{[(1-s_1)\,L\,(\omega+k)]^{\beta_i-\beta_j}}\right]^{-1} =$$

$$\left[1 + [\frac{a_i^{\frac{\sigma_i}{1-\sigma_i}}}{\gamma_i}\,[1+b_i\,\omega^{1-\sigma_i}]^{\frac{1}{1-\sigma_i}}]^{\beta_i} \sum_{j=2, j\neq i}^{N} \frac{\frac{\alpha_j}{\alpha_i}\,[\frac{1}{\gamma_j} a_j^{\frac{\sigma_j}{1-\sigma_j}}\,[1+b_j\,\omega^{1-\sigma_j}]^{\frac{1}{1-\sigma_j}}\,]^{-\beta_j}}{[(1-s_1)\,L\,(\omega+K/L)]^{\beta_i-\beta_j}}\right]^{-1} \tag{20.27}$$

Clearly the connection between the GDP *shares*, (20.17–20.18), and (20.23), (20.27) is

$$s_i(\omega, L, K) \;=\; (1-s_1)\,e_i(\omega, L, K)\,; \quad i = 2, \ldots, N \tag{20.28}$$

Only N-1 *relative* commodity prices—with e.g. $P_2$ as numeraire, Fig. 20.8—are involved in a N-sector economy; but we must be careful of including all the relevant relative *price ratios* from (20.7) into the respective budget *shares*, (20.23).

Thus for the nine budget *time paths* in our ten-sector model below, we state:

$$e_2(P, C) = \left[1 + \sum_{j=2, j\neq i}^{N} \frac{\alpha_j}{\alpha_2}\, p_{2j}^{\beta_j} \left[\frac{C}{P_2}\right]^{\beta_j-\beta_2}\right]^{-1} \tag{20.29}$$

$$e_{10}(P, C) = \left[1 + \sum_{j=2, j\neq i}^{N} \frac{\alpha_j}{\alpha_{10}}\, p_{10j}^{\beta_j} \left[\frac{C}{P_{10}}\right]^{\beta_j-\beta_{10}}\right]^{-1}. \tag{20.30}$$

***Factor Endowments, Factor Allocation, and Factor Income Distribution***

The factor endowments, total labor force ($L$), and the total capital stock ($K$), are inelastically supplied and fully employed, i.e.,

$$L = \sum_{i=1}^{N} L_i \; ; \quad \sum_{i=1}^{N} L_i/L \equiv \sum_{i=1}^{N} \lambda_{L_i} = 1, \tag{20.31}$$

$$K = \sum_{i=1}^{N} K_i \; ; \quad \sum_{i=1}^{N} K_i/K \equiv \sum_{i=1}^{N} \lambda_{K_i} = 1, \tag{20.32}$$

$$K/L \equiv k \equiv \sum_{i=1}^{N} \lambda_{L_i} k_i , \tag{20.33}$$

where $\lambda_{L_i}$, $\lambda_{K_i}$, (20.31–20.32) are called the *factor allocation fractions.*

Free factor mobility between multiple sectors (industries) and efficient factor allocation impose the *Pareto* (common MRS) *condition*, cf. (20.14)

$$\omega = \omega_i = \omega_i(k_i) \; ; \; i = 1, \ldots, N, \tag{20.34}$$

Gross domestic product (GDP), $\mathbf{Y}$, is the total of sectorial producer revenues [ monetary value of sector outputs, $Y_i = L_i\, y_i$ ], cf. (20.15–20.16), (20.18),

$$Y_i = L\,\lambda_{L_i}\, y_i \; ; \; Y \equiv \sum_{i=1}^{N} P_i\, Y_i = L\left[\sum_{i=1}^{N} P_i\, \lambda_{L_i}\, y_i\right] \equiv Ly. \tag{20.35}$$

With cost minimization (perfect competition), $Y$ is total factor income, (20.17),

$$Y = wL + rK = L\,(w + rk) = L\,r\,(\omega + k) = L\,y. \tag{20.36}$$

The *macro* factor income *distribution* shares, $\delta_K + \delta_L = 1$, become, cf. (20.36),

$$\delta_K \equiv rK/Y = rk/y = k/(\omega + k) \; ; \; \delta_L \equiv wL/Y = w/y = \omega/(\omega + k). \tag{20.37}$$

Thus, by (20.37),

$$\delta_K/\delta_L \equiv k/\omega \iff k \equiv \frac{\omega\,\delta_K}{\delta_L}. \tag{20.38}$$

**Lemma 20.1** *The factor income shares, $\delta_L$, $\delta_K$, (20.37), are final demand weighted, $s_i$, (20.17–20.18), (20.28), combinations of sectorial factor cost shares, $\epsilon_{L_i}$, $\epsilon_{K_i}$, (20.13),*

$$\delta_L = \sum_{i=1}^{N} s_i\, \epsilon_{L_i} \; ; \; \delta_K = \sum_{i=1}^{N} s_i\, \epsilon_{K_i} \; ; \; \delta_K + \delta_L = 1. \tag{20.39}$$

*The factor allocation fractions (20.31–20.32) are obtained by, cf. (20.39),*

$$L_i/L = \lambda_{L_i} = s_i\, \epsilon_{L_i}/\delta_L \; ; \quad K_i/K = \lambda_{K_i} = s_i\, \epsilon_{K_i}/\delta_K. \tag{20.40}$$

*The total factor endowment ratio, K/L, satisfies the identity, cf. (20.38), (20.39):*

$$K/L = k = \frac{\omega\,\delta_K}{\delta_L} = \omega \sum_{i=1}^{N} s_i\,\epsilon_{K_i} \Big/ \sum_{i=1}^{N} s_i\,\epsilon_{L_i}, \qquad (20.41)$$

*which is a convenient representation of the Walras's law (identity) and (20.33).*

***Proof*** See Jensen and Lehmijoki (2011, p. 297); here page 565, Chap. 19. □

## Walrasian Equilibrium of Two-Factor-Multi-Sector Economies

The demand side of the multi-sector economy is expressed by the GDP expenditure shares, $s_i$: (20.17–20.18). The supply side of the economy [operating with full (20.31–20.32) and efficient factor utilization, (20.34)] is always summarized by the sectorial factor allocation fractions, $\lambda_{L_i}$, $\lambda_{K_i}$: (20.40)—which, in turn, are determined jointly by the final demand shares, $s_i(\omega, L, K)$: (20.17), (20.28), and the sectorial cost shares, $\epsilon_{L_i}(\omega)$, $\epsilon_{K_i}(\omega)$: (20.13). Thus, we have established:

**Theorem 20.1** *For sector cost functions with constant returns to scale, and non-homothetic utility functions, general equilibrium states (20.41) are given by:*

$$K/L = \frac{\omega\,\delta_K(\omega, L, K)}{\delta_L(\omega, L, K)} = \frac{\omega \sum_{i=1}^{N} s_i(\omega, L, K)\,\epsilon_{K_i}(\omega)}{\sum_{i=1}^{N} s_i(\omega, L, K)\,\epsilon_{L_i}(\omega)} = \Lambda\,(\omega, L, K) \qquad (20.42)$$

**Corollary 20.1** *With* ***CES*** *sector cost functions and* ***CDES*** *indirect utility functions, the Walrasian equilibria,* ***GE*** *(20.42), become by (20.13), (20.17), (20.28):*

$$K/L = k = \omega \cdot \frac{\sum_{i=1}^{N} s_i(\omega, L, K)\,(1 + b_i\,\omega^{1-\sigma_i})^{-1}}{1 - \sum_{i=1}^{N} s_i(\omega, L, K)\,(1 + b_i\,\omega^{1-\sigma_i})^{-1}} = \Lambda\,(\omega, L, K) \qquad (20.43)$$

*Locus expressions (20.42, 20.43) give (**ω**) implicitly as a function of (L,K):*

$$\omega = w/r = \Upsilon(L, K) \qquad (20.44)$$

By (20.42–20.44), the Walrasian *general equilibrium* of the *two-factor* and *N-sector* economy ($2 \times N$) is by several *composite* functions reduced to a *single equation* in the *exogenous factor endowments* $(L, K)$ and **GE** *factor price ratio* $(\omega)$.

Having obtained $(\omega)$ from (20.44) and then using $(\omega)$ itself and/or $(\omega, L, K)$, we can go back through, (20.7), (20.13), (20.14), (20.16), (20.28), (20.35), (20.39), (20.40), to get the associated *comparative static* general equilibrium *solution* (size)) of *all* other *endogenous* variables: the relative commodity prices, sectorial cost shares, sectorial capital-labor ratios and labor productivities, consumer budget shares, factor allocation fractions, sectorial outputs, and macro factor income shares.

## Dynamics and Time Paths of Non-Homothetic MSG Models

The equations of *factor accumulation* for multi-sector growth models, with two primary factors and flexible sector cost functions, are formally given by,

$$dL/dt \equiv \dot{L} = nL, \tag{20.45}$$

$$dK/dt \equiv \dot{K} = Y_1 - \delta K = Ly_1\lambda_{L_1} - \delta K = L\left\{y_1\lambda_{L_1} - \delta k\right\}, \tag{20.46}$$

where $Y_1$ is the output of capital good sector 1, $\delta$ the depreciation rate of capital, and $n$ the growth rate of labor. The variables $y_1$ and $\lambda_{L_1}$ in (20.46) are through (20.44) uniquely determined by the factor endowments $(L, K)$. Hence, the *accumulation* Eq. (20.46) becomes an *autonomous differential* equation

$$\dot{K} = L\left\{\, y_1\,[\,\Upsilon(L, K)\,]\;\lambda_{L_1}(L, K)\; - \;\delta\, k\,\right\};\; L \neq 0. \tag{20.47}$$

As (20.47) is an intricate function of $k$, we rewrite it as, cf. (20.17), (20.36–20.37), (20.4),

$$\dot{K} \;=\; I/P_1 - \delta K = s_1\,(Y/P_1) - \delta K = L\; s_1\;(\omega + k)\,/\,c_1\,(\omega)\; - \delta\, K \tag{20.48}$$

$$= L\, s_1\, \frac{\Upsilon(L, K) + k}{c_1\,(\Upsilon(L, K))} \;\; - \delta\, K \tag{20.49}$$

$$\textbf{CES}:\; c_1\,(\Upsilon(L, K)) \;=\; \frac{1}{\gamma_1}\, a_1^{\frac{\sigma_1}{1-\sigma_1}}\, \left[\,1 + b_1\,[\,\Upsilon(L, K)\,]^{1-\sigma_1}\,\right]^{\frac{1}{1-\sigma_1}} \tag{20.50}$$

The expressions (20.49) and (20.45) represent autonomous (time-invariant) differential equations in the state variables $L$ and $K$. Theoretically, solutions of (20.49), (20.45) *exist*, but the *time paths* can *not* be given by *functional* integration, as $\Upsilon(L, K)$ is only an *implicit* function. Thus *non-homothetic* MSG models require a *new* general *approach* for solving the dynamics of factor accumulation, cf. Jensen and Lehmijoki (2011, p. 301); here p. 569

in Chap. 19. Hence for the non-homothetic multi-sectoral growth (MSG) models, we give:

**Proposition 20.1** *The governing functions $h_1, h_2, h_3$, (20.51–20.53) give an autonomous dynamic system in state variables $L, K, \omega$, that generate time* ***paths*** *of the* ***non-homothetic*** *MSG model—with initial values, $L(0), K(0), \omega(0)$, obtained from* ***solving*** *the Walrasian equilibrium condition (20.43):*

$$\dot{L} = n\,L \;=\; h_1\,(L) \tag{20.51}$$

$$\dot{K} = L\;s_1\;\frac{\omega + K/L}{c_1(\omega)} \;-\; \delta\,K \;=\; h_2\,(\omega, L, K) \tag{20.52}$$

$$\dot{\omega} = \frac{1}{\frac{\partial \Lambda(\omega, L, K)}{\partial \omega}} \left[ \dot{k} - \frac{\partial \Lambda\,(\omega, L, K)}{\partial L}\,\dot{L} - \frac{\partial \Lambda\,(\omega, L, K)}{\partial K}\,\dot{K} \right]$$

$$= h_3\,(\omega, L, K) \tag{20.53}$$

$$\dot{k} = s_1\;\frac{\omega + K/L}{c_1\,(\omega)} \;-\; (n+\delta)\,(K/L) \;=\; h_4\,(\omega, L, K) \tag{20.54}$$

*The governing function $h_3\,(\omega, L, K)$, (20.53)—although complicated—has a* ***closed form*** *by the* ***explicit parametric*** *expressions involved in (20.51–20.54). The governing functions $h_1, h_2, h_3$, (20.51–20.53) are continuously differentiable on their domain, ensuring the existence and the uniqueness everywhere of the solutions (time paths) from any initial values.*

***Proof*** The differential equations (20.51–20.52) are: (20.45) and (20.48). By using the Walrasian *equilibrium equation*, (20.43), we get an expression for $\dot{k}$:

$$\dot{k} \;=\; \frac{\partial \Lambda\,(\omega, L, K)}{\partial \omega}\,\dot{\omega} \;+\; \frac{\partial \Lambda\,(\omega, L, K)}{\partial L}\,\dot{L} \;+\; \frac{\partial \Lambda\,(\omega, L, K)}{\partial K}\,\dot{K} \tag{20.55}$$

which is *equivalent* to the differential equation for $\dot{\omega}$, (20.53). By (20.51–20.52) and $\dot{k} = (L\dot{K} - K\dot{L})/L^2) = \dot{K}/L - nk$, we obtain the function $h_4\,(\omega, L, K)$, (20.54). □

## Solving the Multi-Sector Growth—(2 × 10)—Model

To provide concrete benchmark solutions of the general equilibrium dynamics by Proposition 20.1, we use a ten-sector model, in which *sector* 1 produces the capital good and *sectors* 2–10 produce the consumption goods.

### *CDES Parameters of $V(P, C)$, CES Parameters of $c_i\,(w/r)$*

For the CDES non-homothetic indirect utility function $V(P, C)$, (20.19), we use as parameters: $\beta_i$, seen in column 1, and $\alpha_i$, given in column 2, Table 20.1.

**Table 20.1** Parameters: CDES, $V(P, C)$, (20.19), and CES, $c_i\ (w/r)$, (20.4)

| $i$ | $\beta_i$ | $\alpha_i$ | $a_i$ | $\sigma_i$ I | $\sigma_i$ II | $\sigma_i$ III |
|---|---|---|---|---|---|---|
| 1 | – | – | 0.5 | 0.8 | 1.2 | 2.0 |
| 2 | −0.3 | 0.60 | 0.3 | 0.9 | 1.5 | 2.5 |
| 3 | −0.2 | 0.16 | 0.4 | 0.7 | 1.1 | 1.5 |
| 4 | −0.1 | 0.12 | 0.5 | 0.9 | 0.9 | 0.8 |
| 5 | 0.0 | 0.05 | 0.2 | 0.8 | 0.8 | 0.8 |
| 6 | 0.1 | 0.02 | 0.4 | 0.6 | 1.3 | 1.3 |
| 7 | 0.2 | 0.02 | 0.7 | 0.7 | 0.7 | 0.7 |
| 8 | 0.3 | 0.01 | 0.6 | 0.5 | 0.7 | 1.1 |
| 9 | 0.4 | 0.01 | 0.2 | 0.5 | 1.5 | 2.5 |
| 10 | 0.5 | 0.01 | 0.6 | 0.6 | 1.1 | 1.5 |

As to the other model parameters, we adopt a fixed *saving* rate, $s_1 = 0.2$, a depreciation, $\delta = 0.04$, a population (labor) growth rate, $n = 0.01$, and a common, $\gamma_i = 1$, of CES, i.e.,

$$s_1 = 0.2\,,\ \delta = 0.04\,,\ n = 0.01\,;\quad \gamma_i = 1\,,\ i = 1, \ldots, 10. \tag{20.56}$$

The CES cost function is applied in each sector with some variation in the CES *parameters*, $a_i$ and $\sigma_i$, as seen in Table 20.1 for the Cases I–III. Only few comments are needed upon the CES cost (technology) parameters and the three technology regimes given by Cases I–III—the same as in Jensen and Lehmijoki (2011, p. 302); here Table 19.1, Chap. 19. The effect of an increase in the capital-intensity parameter $a_i$ is seen from (20.14) as a rightward *shift* of the $\omega_i$-curve in Fig. 20.1, right panels—a higher capital-labor ratio $k_i$ for any factor price ratio. A high capital-labor ratio can alternatively be due to a movement along the $\omega_i$-curve, the effect of which is determined by the substitution (flexibility) parameter $\sigma_i$. As to obtaining high $k_i$ over time, the *effect* of $\sigma_i$ will eventually *dominate* the *effect* of $a_i$.

A crucial technology parameter of economic growth is the *substitution elasticity* of the *capital good sector*, $\sigma_1$—its size typifies the *three technology—cost regimes* in Table 20.1. With, $0 \leq \sigma_1 \leq 1$, all transition paths will eventually reach a *steady state*. If some, $\sigma_i \geq 1$, (including $\sigma_1$), *persistent* ("endogenous") growth may occur, depending on the mixture of $a_i$ and $\sigma_i$. The usual *threshold* condition for persistent growth, $\gamma_1 a_1^{\frac{\sigma_1}{\sigma_1 - 1}} \gtrless (n + \delta)/s_1$, is met in Case III.

Moreover, let us take the sectorial *cost* (*technology*) parameters of *Case I*, Table 20.1, to indicate the technology regime (stage) around **1860–1870**; let the sectoral cost (technology) parameters of *Case II* and *Case III* indicate technology *regimes* reached around, respectively, **1890–1900**, **1960–1970**.

Technical progress has partly been accompanied by rising capital-labor ratios, which can be identified with *larger values* in Table 20.1 of the ($a_i$) and/or substitution ($\sigma_i$) parameters, cf. Jensen and Larsen (2005); here Chap. 18.

Finally, let us in Table 20.1 call the *consumer good sectors*, items (i): 2. Food, 3. Clothing, 4. Housing, 5. Fuel, light, 6. Furniture, furnishings, 7. Personal services, 8. Personal goods, pharma, 9. Leisure goods, travel, culture, 10. Miscellaneous. Item, $i = 10$, may refer to vehicles (Case III, automotive industry).

A single table with *budget shares* from the *first* and most famous, Engel (1857), *family expenditure study* is presented in Table 20.2, since it acted as *benchmark* for all later inquiries, and it is seldom seen anywhere in the literature, except Marshall (1920). We have changed Marshall's item descriptions a little bit—in accordance with *Engel's* original expenditure classification.

A similar investigation of *budget data* was done by Wold and Jureen (1953) to obtain a unified *historical description* of the demand patterns in Sweden—one outline of his budget data (*shares*) is shown in Table 20.3 for the period **1913–1933**. The item groups in Tables 20.2 and 20.3 are very *similar*, and correspond essentially to *items* (i): **2–10**, described and adopted for consumer goods, Table 20.1.

The variations of the *budget shares* with (C) in Tables 20.2 and 20.3, and the consistency in observed consumption patterns everywhere are of great importance and the main *challenges* to the *solutions* of *non-homothetic* MSG models.

### *MSG Solutions: Time Paths—of CES-CDES Ten-Sector Growth Model*

Corresponding to the selected parameter values in Table 20.1, *Cases* I–III, and, (20.56), the *solutions*, $[\, k(t) = K(t)/L(t),\ \omega(t)\, ]$, of the dynamic system, (20.51–20.53) are shown in Fig. 20.2—as well as their respective *growth rates*. The actual time paths displayed in Fig. 20.2 contain no surprises. With factor accumulation, *rising* $k(t)$ and *increasing* wage-rental ratios $\omega(t)$ go together also in a ten-sector economy. For the parameters in *Cases* I–II, the dynamic system, (20.51–20.53) has *asymptotic limits* for $k(t)$ and $\omega(t)$, proximate *steady states*—which are, respectively,

$$k_I^* = 11.49, \quad \omega_I^* = 33.30\ ; \quad k_{II}^* = 24.48\,, \quad \omega_{II}^* = 12.73 \tag{20.57}$$

It is seen from Fig. 20.2 that the *states* (20.57) are attained closely with: $t = 100$. In *Case* III, *no* asymptotic steady state exists and *persistent* economic growth takes place—as seen when the solutions of (20.51–20.53) are extended up to a time horizon of $t = 600$ in Fig. 20.2. The *phase portrait*—trajectories, $(k, \omega)$ *locus*—of the solutions (time paths) in Fig. 20.2 are shown in Fig. 20.3.

All the solutions in Figs. 20.2, 20.3, 20.4, 20.5, 20.6, 20.7, 20.8, 20.9, 20.10, and 20.11 start from the *initial* time *value*: $K(0) = 1, L(0) = 1,$

**Table 20.2** Budget Shares of Social Strata: Saxony 1857

| Items of Expenditure | | Proportions of the Expenditure of the Family of: Workman with an yearly income of 45–60 $ | Workman with an yearly income of 90–120 $ | Workman with an yearly income of 150–200 $ |
|---|---|---|---|---|
| 1 | Food (beverage, tobacco) | 62.0 | 55.0 | 50.0 |
| 2 | Clothing (footwear, jewelry) | 16.0 | 18.0 | 18.0 |
| 3 | Lodging (rent, utensils, furniture) | 12.0 | 12.0 | 12.0 |
| 4 | Light, Fuel (wood, coal, gas, oil) | 5.0 | 5.0 | 5.0 |
| 5 | Education (culture, church) | 2.0 | 3.5 | 5.5 |
| 6 | Public Protection (taxes) | 1.0 | 2.0 | 3.0 |
| 7 | Care of Health (medical, pharma) | 1.0 | 2.0 | 3.0 |
| 8 | Personal Services | 1.0 | 2.5 | 3.5 |
| *Totals* | | 100.0 | 100.0 | 100.0 |

*Source*: Marshall (1920, p. 115); Engel (1857, p. 30)

**Table 20.3** Budget Shares of Social Strata: Sweden 1913–1933

| | | Industrial worker families | | | Middle-class families | |
|---|---|---|---|---|---|---|
| | | 1913 | 1923 | 1933 | 1923 | 1933 |
| 1 | Nourishment | 50.4 | 47.8 | 40.0 | 31.5 | 28.5 |
| 2 | Clothing | 14.2 | 16.0 | 14.6 | 14.5 | 14.4 |
| 3 | Fuel, Light, Laundry | 6.4 | 6.5 | 6.1 | 6.2 | 6.0 |
| 4 | Housing | 13.3 | 11.6 | 16.9 | 13.5 | 18.2 |
| 5 | Furniture (furnishings) | 4.7 | 4.8 | 5.2 | 7.1 | 6.4 |
| 6 | Personal Services (domestic) | 1.0 | 0.5 | 0.4 | 4.2 | 3.3 |
| 7 | Hygiene (medical care) | 1.8 | 2.3 | 3.2 | 2.8 | 3.3 |
| 8 | Education (culture, travel) | 5.0 | 6.2 | 7.0 | 9.2 | 9.7 |
| 9 | Other Expenditures | 3.1 | 4.2 | 6.6 | 11.0 | 10.2 |
| *All expenditures* | | 100.0 | 100.0 | 100.0 | 100.0 | 100.0 |

*Source*: Wold and Jureen (1953, p. 20); Recalculated as expenditure ($C$) shares

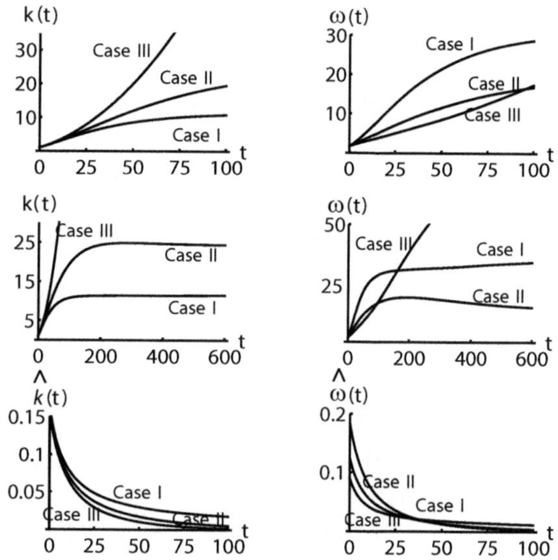


**Fig. 20.2** Time paths and growth rates: $\omega(t)$, $k(t)$ by, (20.51–20.52), (20.53); Table 20.1

$k(0) = \mathbf{1}$, with the corresponding *three initial* time *values* of $\boldsymbol{\omega}$ **(0)** from (20.43) as: $\omega_I(0) = 1.60042$, $\omega_{II}(0) = 1.67347$, $\omega_{III}(0) = 1.69222$. The absolute size of $K(0)$ and $L(0)$ can be arbitrarily chosen. All calculations of the time paths are performed by Mathematica (version7.0) and are available on request.

The time paths of the *sectoral* capital-labor ratios, $\boldsymbol{k_i(t)}$, are exhibited in Fig. 20.4. Obviously, with a rising $\omega(t)$, all $k_i(t)$ are increasing, but a distinct sectoral pattern evidently appears. Essentially a common economic mechanism is involved behind the $k_i(t)$ pattern in Fig. 20.4. In Table 20.1, the *ranking* order of the *substitution elasticities* $\sigma_i$ (combined with a similar ranking of the intensity parameters $a_i$) *corresponds* to the *vertical* orders of $\boldsymbol{k_i(t)}$ in Fig. 20.4

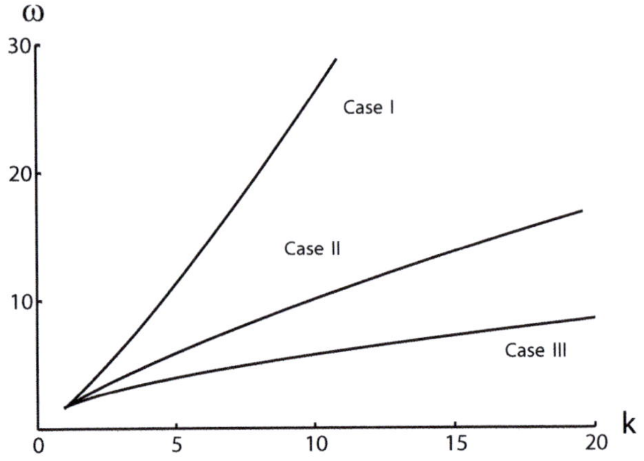


**Fig. 20.3** The $(\omega, k)$ locus of Fig. 20.2

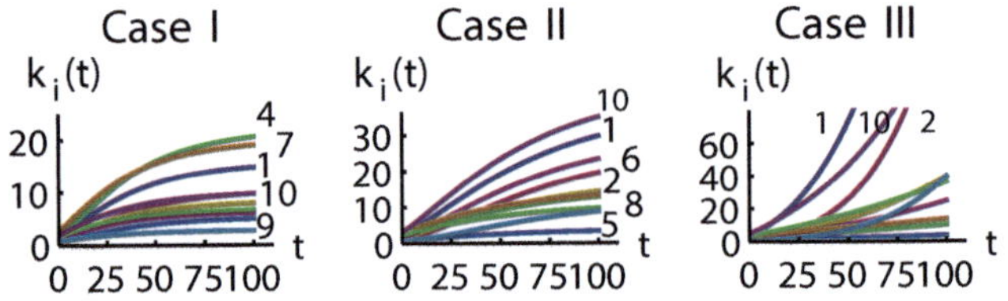


**Fig. 20.4** The sectorial $k_i(t)$ by (20.14) and $[\,\omega(t), k(t)\,]$ as in Fig. 20.2

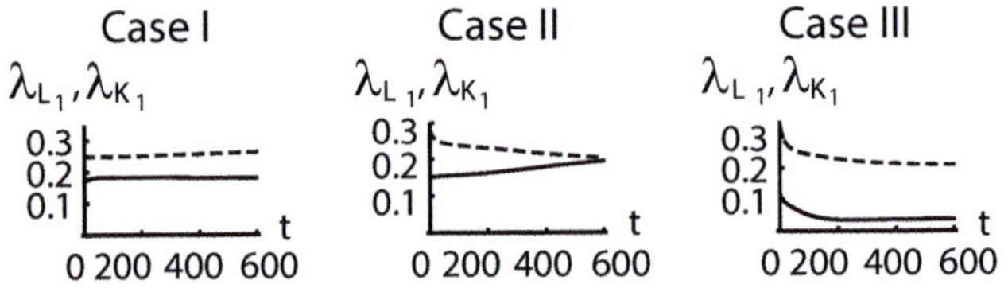


**Fig. 20.5** Allocations $\lambda_{L_1}(t)$ (solid line), $\lambda_{K_1}(t)$ (dashed line) by (20.40) and $[\,\omega(t), k(t)\,]$ as in Fig. 20.2

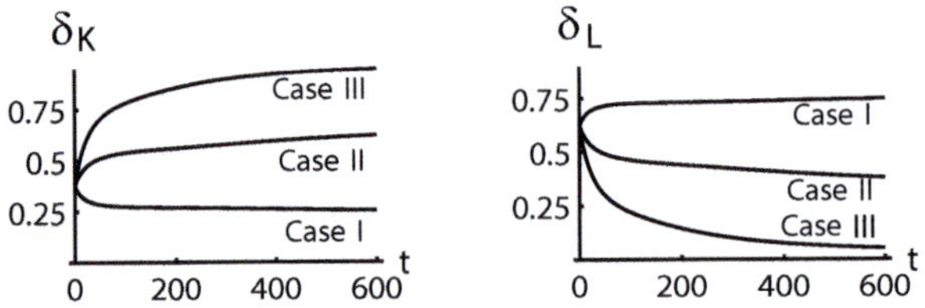


**Fig. 20.6** Factor shares $\delta_L(t)$, $\delta_K(t)$ by (20.39) and $[\,\omega(t), k(t)\,]$ as in Fig. 20.2

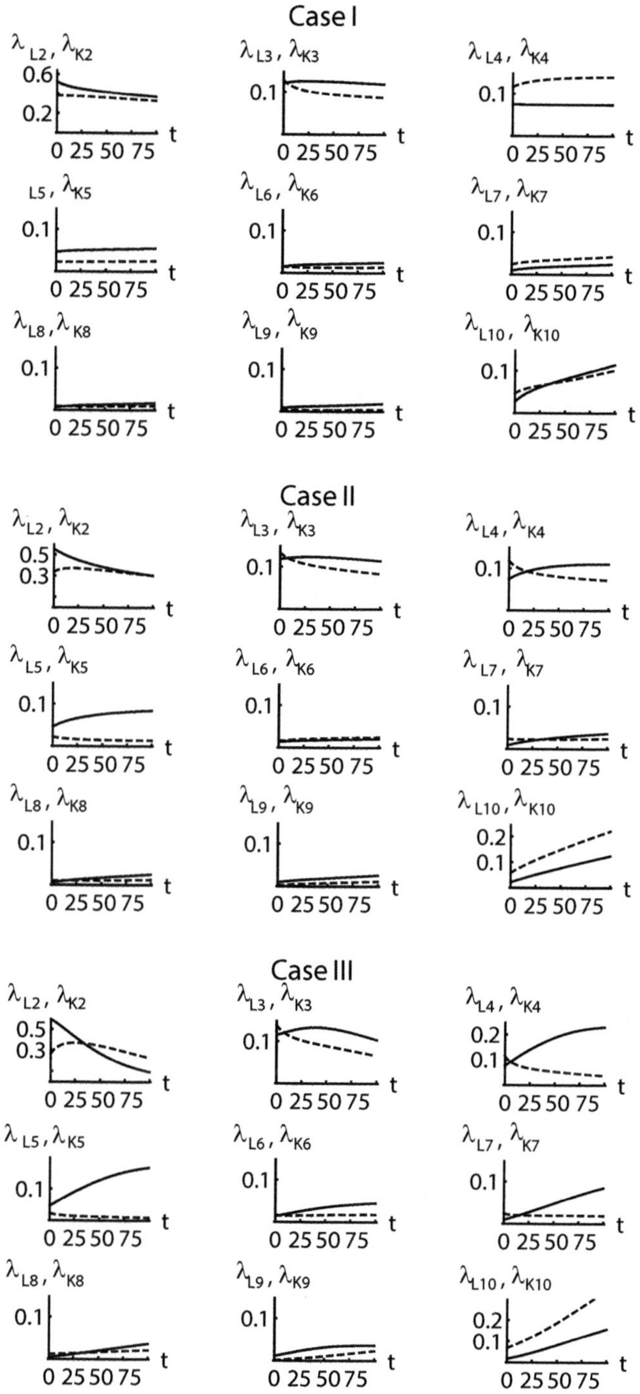


**Fig. 20.7** Allocations $\lambda_{L_i}(t)$ (solid line), $\lambda_{K_i}(t)$ (dashed line) by (20.40) and $[\,\omega(t), k(t)\,]$ as in Fig. 20.2

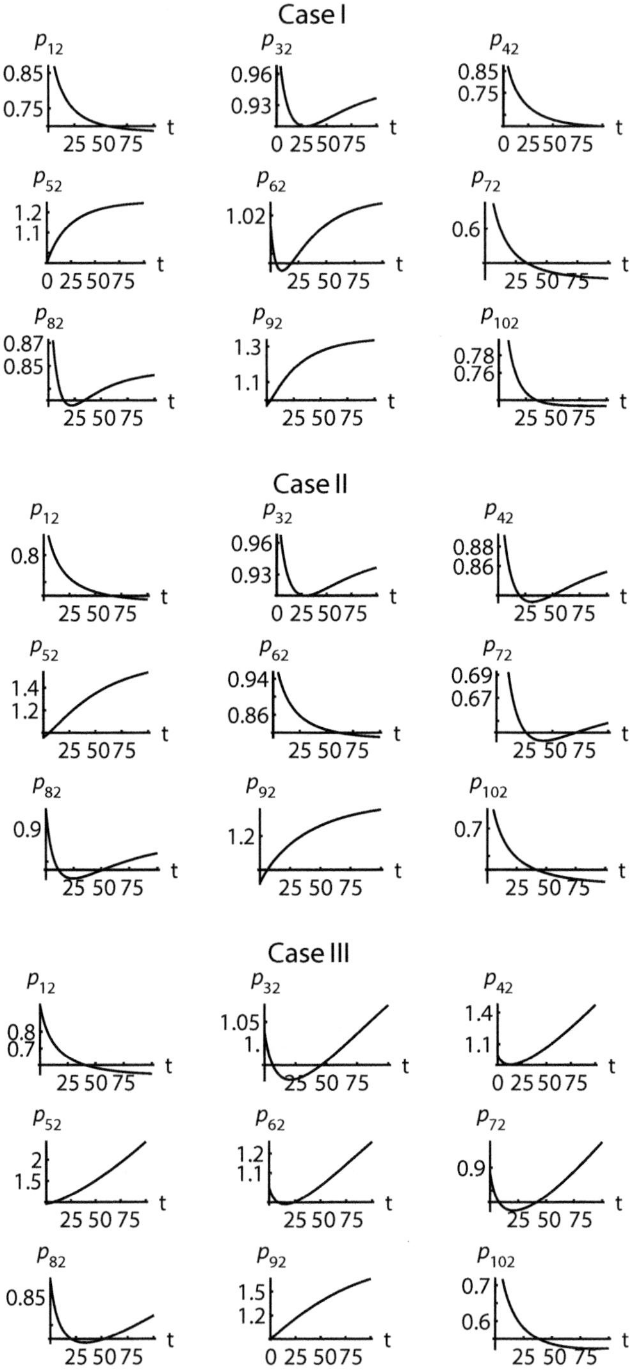


**Fig. 20.8** Relative prices $p_{i2}(t)$ by (20.7), and $[\,\omega(t), k(t)\,]$ as in Fig. 20.2

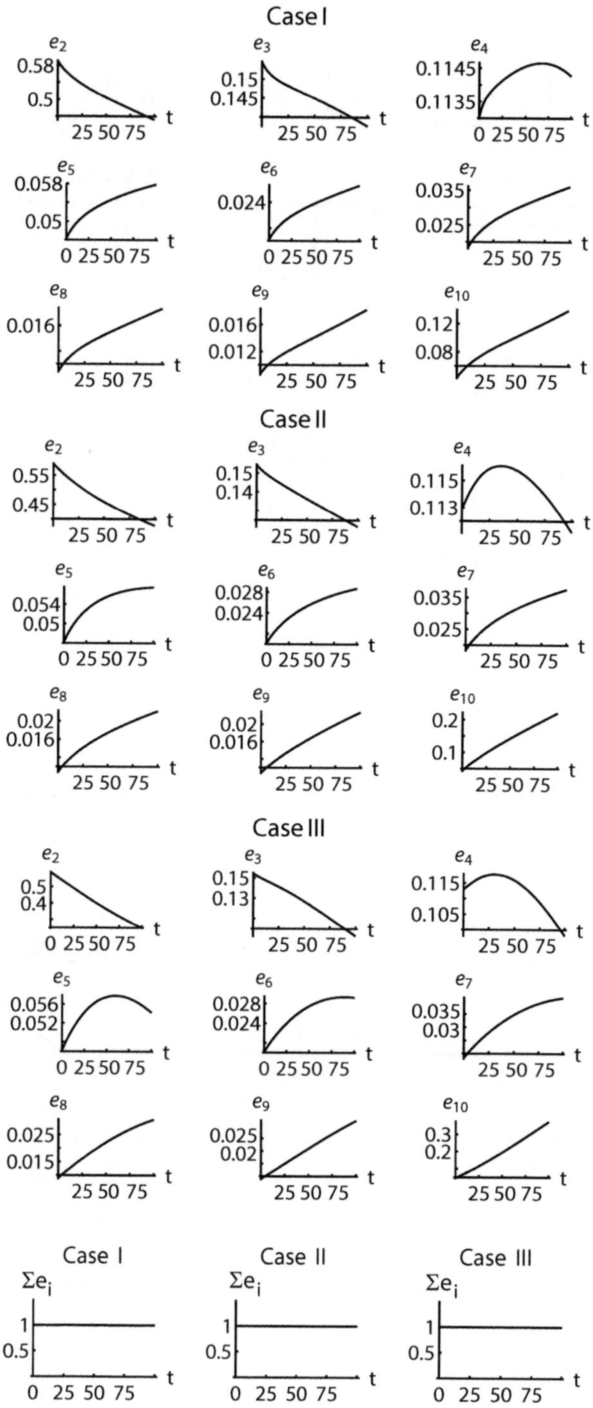


**Fig. 20.9** Budget shares $e_i(t)$ by (20.23), (20.27) and $[\,\omega(t), k(t)\,]$ as in Fig. 20.2

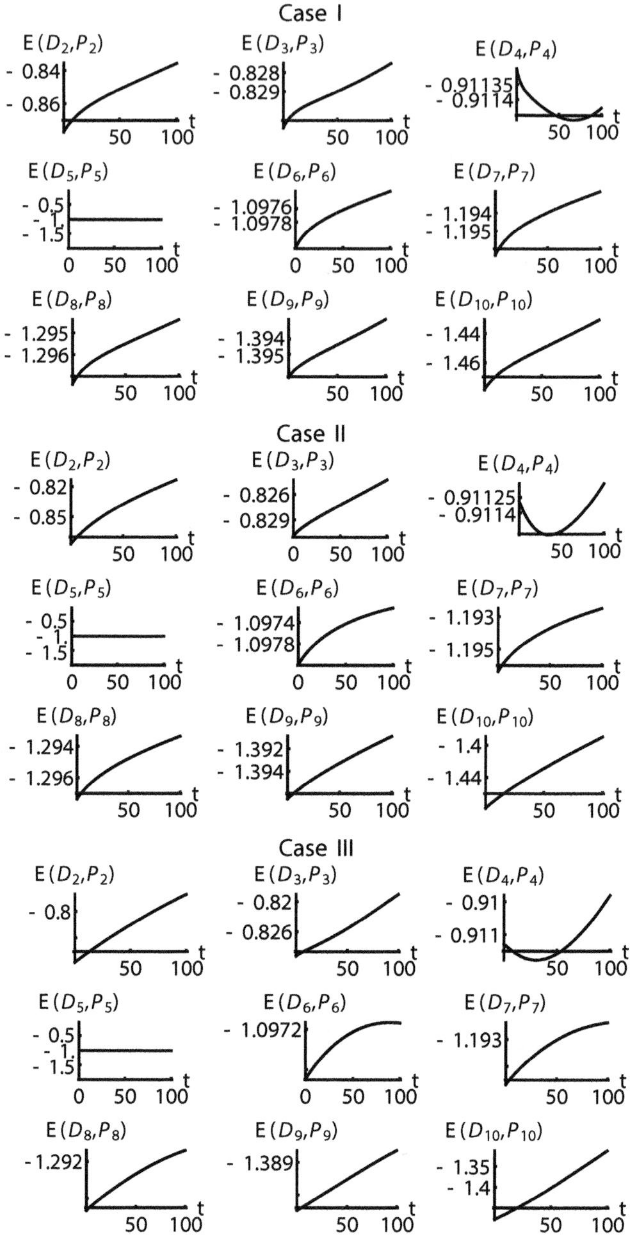


**Fig. 20.10** Price elasticities by (20.22), (20.27) and [ $\omega(t)$, $k(t)$ ] as in Fig. 20.2

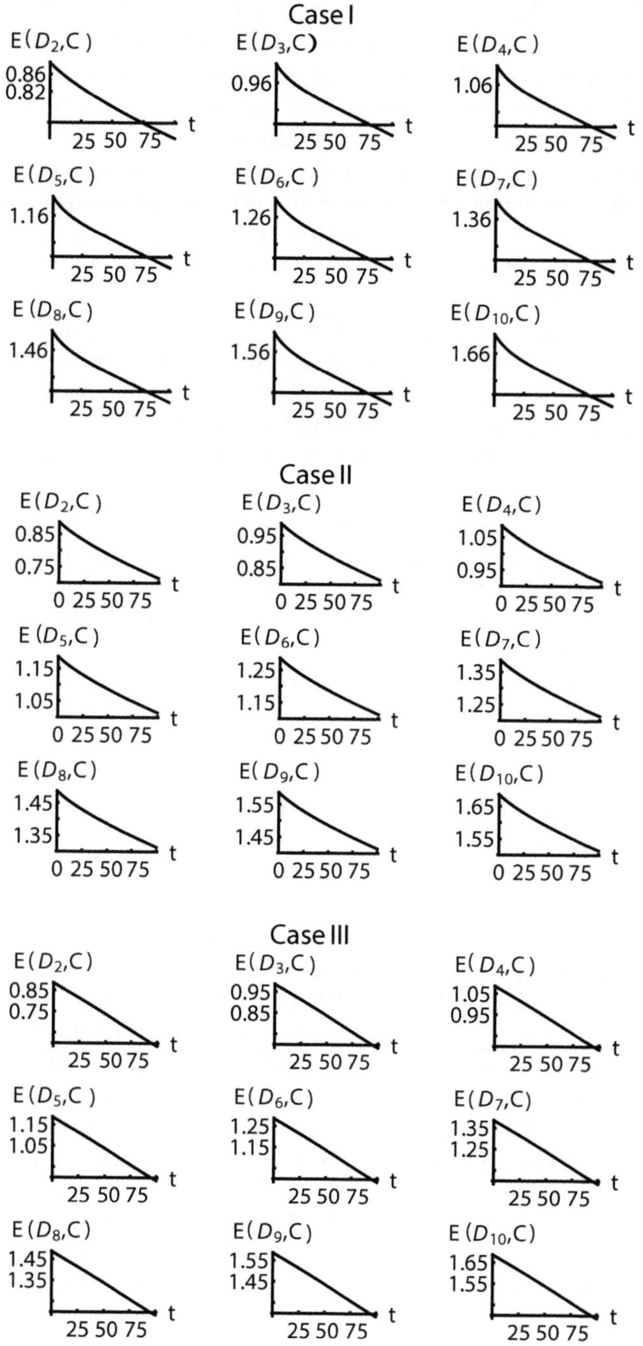


**Fig. 20.11** Income elasticities by (20.22), (20.27) and [ $\omega(t), k(t)$ ] as in Fig. 20.2

for $t > 50$. Thus in Table 20.1, Case I, the sectors 4, 7, 1 have high $\sigma_i$ (backed up with high $a_i$) corresponding to the vertical order in Case I, Fig. 20.4. For Case II, an analogous ranking and vertical order occurs with sectors 10, 1, 6, 2. In Case III, this order pattern is repeated with sectors 1, 2, 10, 9, 3. In short, sectors with *high* $\sigma_i$ (and high $a_i$) are *mechanized.*

This sectorial order of mechanization, as evident in Fig. 20.4, will also be reflected in the time paths of the factor *allocation fractions* of capital and labor in Fig. 20.7. But these sectoral evolutions of $\lambda_{K_i}(t)$, $\lambda_{L_i}(t)$, in Fig. 20.7 are partly modified by their respective *magnitudes* of—$\beta_i$, $\alpha_i$, (Table 20.1)—from the *demand side* of the multi-sector economy.

The demand-side composition of the economy exerts a particular influence on the time paths of the allocation fractions in *sector* 1, as shown for Cases I–III in Fig. 20.5 on a horizon up to $t = 600$. Below, we return to Fig. 20.5, and the sizes of the factor income shares exhibited in Fig. 20.6.

With *commodity* 2 as the *numeraire*, the time paths of our *nine relative prices*: $p_{i2}(t)$, $i = 1, 3, \ldots, 10$, are seen in Fig. 20.8, Cases I-III. As these relative general equilibrium prices play a fundamental allocative role in multi-sector economies, it is important that the numerical size and the overall profile for these relative prices (rising/falling) can be checked easily. Details about all the paths $p_{i2}(t)$ in Fig. 20.8 can be seen in Jensen and Lehmijoki (2011, p. 309); here p. 574 in Chap. 19.

Since the *numeraire* commodity 2 is produced by a technology with a relative *high* $\sigma_2$ (especially in Cases I and III), its costs (price) will, with increased $\omega(t)$ and mechanization, become *relatively cheap*, or equivalently, the other commodities become more expensive in terms of commodity 2. Accordingly, many time paths for the relative price $p_{i2}(t)$, $i > 2$, in Fig. 20.8 are eventually rising, especially in Case III.

The time paths of the *nine budget shares*, $e_i(t)$, (20.29–20.30)—as generated by (20.23), (20.27)—are shown in Fig. 20.9; at the bottom it is seen that the calculated paths of all the budget shares $e_i(t)$ do add up to one, any time. The evolution of $e_i(t)$ depends on the time paths of *income-* and *price elasticities*, and $E(D_i(t), C(t))$, $E(D_i, P_i)$ of CDES, (20.22), are shown in Figs. 20.10 and 20.11, conforming to the pattern mentioned in Sect. "CDES Indirect Utility and the Marshallian Demands (Budget System)" for increasing $C(t)$.

With our initial values, $K(0) = 1$, $L(0) = 1$, and every $\omega(0)$ approximately, $\omega(0) \approx 1.6$, our initial budget shares $e_i(0)$ are in all Cases I–III approximately: $e_i(0) \approx \alpha_i$, cf. Table 20.1 and Fig. 20.9. In fact, we have *selected* (calibrated) $\alpha_i$, Table 20.1 as the *lowest* budget *share* values in *Engel* 1857, cf. Table 20.2, which are always the *common initial* budget *shares* $e_i(0)$ in Fig. 20.9.

As Case I, Table 20.1, to indicate the technology regime (stage) around **1860–1870**. Then Fig. 20.9 may in Case I illustrate the evolution of budget shares $e_i(t)$ toward the *steady state*, cf. Fig. 20.2, in accordance with CDES consumer preference parameters ($\beta_i$), Table 20.1. Concomitant *factor reallocations* of growing labor L(t) and capital K(t) are seen in Fig. 20.7, *Case I.*

As the sectoral cost (technology) *parameters* of *Case* II and *Case* III indicate the technology regime (stage) reached at, respectively, **1890–1900**, and **1950–1960**. Then Figs. 20.9, 20.2, and 20.7 again show—with the *non-homothetic* CDES parameters ($\beta_i$)—the evolution of *budget shares* and *factor reallocations* toward the higher steady state or allowing for persistent growth. The long-run (asymptotic) factor allocations in Case I-III are shown on an extended time horizon for the capital good sector in Fig. 20.5.

Some *history patterns* of industrial and occupational transitions are recognized. Evidently the most drastic *reallocations* occur within our integrated food (agriculture) *industry* ($i = 2$). The sector, $i = 10$, in our Tables and Figures may as mentioned refer to *transport equipment* (automotive industry).

The Figs. 20.2, 20.3, 20.4, 20.5, 20.6, 20.7, 20.8, and 20.9 here with *non-homothetic* preferences can be directly compared with the corresponding Figs. 20.2, 20.3, 20.4, 20.5, 20.6, 20.7, 20.8, and 20.9 with *homothetic preferences* in Jensen and Lehmijoki (2011, p. 304–311); here p. 572–577 in Chap. 19. The differences between these two sets of Figs. 20.2, 20.3, 20.4, 20.5, 20.6, 20.7, 20.8, and 20.9 are mainly due to the *evolution* of the CDES *income elasticities* in Fig. 20.11, which evidently *all differ* from the *size* 1.00 that is implied by the *homothetic* CES income elasticities in Jensen and Lehmijoki (2011); here Chap. 19.

The CDES *price elasticities* in Fig. 20.10 evidently—in contrast to LES—include both price *inelastic* ($i = 2 - 4$), *elastic* ($i = 6 - 10$) demands and a *unit* elasticity by $\beta_5 = 0$, cf. (20.22) and Table 20.1. Similarly, the cross-price elasticities (not shown) have a much richer pattern (varying signs) with CDES than that of LES (same sign).

The *theoretical* and *empirical* importance of changes in *income* and *price* elasticities (budget shares) for *structural transformation* of economies can hardly be overstated. Such *quantitative* demonstration of the *transformation* was an objective of the *novel* dynamics of MSG models in Proposition 20.1.

## Conclusions

Once Lucas (1988, p. 5) "preferred to use the term 'theory' in a very narrow sense, to refer to an *explicit dynamic* system, something that can be put on a *computer* and run. This is what I mean by the '*mechanics*' of economic development". We have put the multi-sector growth model on a computer and *demonstrated* how the interacting *sectors* (industries) move on their **time paths**—as *solutions* of the dynamic system in Proposition 20.1, determined by the governing functions of parametric *non-homothetic CDES indirect utility* function and sectoral *CES cost functions*—**through** the **factor** (endowment) **space**. The *dimensions* of the state (*factor*) space with the explicit dynamics as in Proposition 20.1 can be increased to any *finite* number.

On this occasion we have followed up on the Walras-Pareto *legacy* of general equilibrium economics by *solving* the Walrasian general equilibrium dynamics for a ten-sector MSG model—which can be extended to any number ($N$) of sectors. The CDES demand system can easily accommodate any number of goods and services, $(N)$.

The challenge of further MSG extensions and future economic research is to *generalize* the CES cost function of two factors to a regular *multi-factor cost function* with *variable* elasticities of *factor substitution*, see Chap. 4 - which would, besides capital and labor, allow for intermediate inputs. We were confined to sectoral *value-added* elements of GDP. Other extensions of non-homothetic MSG models with CDES may include *imperfect competition* with monopolistic price "mark-ups", determined by *own-price* elasticities of consumer goods.

**Acknowledgments** For many discussions and comments, we are indebted to the late Arkady V. Kryazhimskiy, Steklov Institute of Mathematics, Russian Academy of Sciences, Moscow, Russia, and IIASA, Laxenburg, Austria.

## Bibliography

Barro RJ, Sala-i-Martin X (2004) Economic Growth Theory, 2nd edn. M.I.T. Press, Cambridge, Mass

Bonatti L, Felice G (2008) Endogenous growth and the changing sectoral composition in advanced economies. Structural Change and Economic Dynamics 19:109–131

Buera FJ, Kaboski JP (2009) Can Traditional Theories of Structural Change fit the Data. Journal of the European Economic Assoc 7:469–477

Buera FJ, Kaboski JP (2012) The Rise of the Service Economy. American Economic Review 102(6):2540–2569

Diewert WE (1974) Applications of Duality Theory. pp 106–171, In: Intriligator MD, Kendrick DA (eds) *Frontiers of Quantitative Economics*, Vol.2, North–Holland, Amsterdam

Echevarria C (1997) Changes in Sectoral Composition Associated with Economic Growth. International Economic Review 38:431–452

Echevarria C (2010) Non–homothetic preferences and growth. Journal of International Trade & Economic Development 9:2, 151–171

Engel E (1857) Die Productions– and Consumptionsverhaeltnisse des Koenigreichs Sachsen. Zeitschrift des Statistischen Bureaus des Koeniglich Saechsishen Ministerium des Inneren 8–9, reprint in: *Bulletin of the International Statistical Institute*, 9 (1895), 1–54

Herrendorf B, Valentinyi A (2012) Which Sectors Make Poor Countries So Unproductive. Journal of the European Econ Assoc 10:323–341

Herrendorf B, Rogerson R, Valentinyi A (2013) Two Perspectives on Preferences and Structural Transformation. AmerEcRev 103(7):2752–2789

Houthakker HS (1957) An International Comparison of Household Expenditure Patterns, Commemorating the Centenary of Engel's law. Econometrica 25:532–551

Houthakker HS (1960) Additive Preferences. Econometrica 28:244–257

Jensen BS, Larsen ME (2005) General Equilibrium Dynamics of Multi–Sector Growth Models. Journal of Economics 10:17–56

Jensen BS, Lehmijoki U (2011) Homothetic Multisector Growth Models. pp 289–318, in: Frontiers of Economics and Globalization, 11, La Grandville, O. de, (Ed.), Emerald, United Kingdom.

Jensen BS, de Boer P, van Daal J, Jensen PS (2011) Global Restrictions on the Parameters of the CDES Indirect Utility Function. Journal of Economics 102:217–235

Jensen BS, Lehmijoki U, Rovenskaya E (2015) Non–Homothetic Multisector Growth Models. Review of Development Economics 19(2):221–243

Kongsamut P, Rebelo S, Xie D (2001) Beyond Balanced Growth. Review of Economic Studies 68:869–882

Kuznets S (1966) Modern Economic Growth. Rate, Structure and Spread. Yale University Press, New Haven

Lehmijoki U (1984) Notes on Quasi–convexity of the Cost Function. Scandinavian Journal of Economics 86:385–389

Lucas RE (1988) On the Mechanics of Economic Development. Journal of Monetary Economics 22:3–42, Reprinted in Becker (1991)

Marshall A (1920) Principles of Economics, 8th edn. Macmillan, London

McFadden D (1978) Cost, Revenue, and Profit Functions. Chapter I.1, in: Fuss, M. and D. McFadden, D., (Eds), *Production Economics: A Dual Approach to Theory and Applications*, Vol.1, (Amsterdam: North–Holland,),

Meckl J (2002) Structural Change and Generalized Balanced Growth. Journal of Economics 77:241–266

Ngai LR, Pissarides CA (2007) Structural Change in a Multi–Sector Model of Growth. American Economic Review 97:429–443

Pareto V (1971) Manual of Political Economy. Trans. French Edition (1927) by A.S. Schwier; New York, A. M. Kelley Publishers.

Roy R (1947) La Distribution du Revenue entre les Divers Biens. Econometrica 15:205–225

Silberberg E, Suen W (2001) The Structure of Economics, A Mathematical Analysis, 3rd edn. McGraw–Hill, Singapore

Solow RM (2005) Reflections on Growth Theory. pp 3–10, Introduction, in: Aghion and Durlauf, (Eds).

Varian HR (1992) Microeconomic Analysis, 3rd edn. W.W. Norton & Company, New York

Walras L (1954) Elements of Pure Economics. George Allen and Unwin, London

Wold H, Jureen L (1953) Demand Analysis. John Wiley & Sons, New York

GPSR Compliance

*The European Union's (EU) General Product Safety Regulation (GPSR) is a set of rules that requires consumer products to be safe and our obligations to ensure this.*

*If you have any concerns about our products, you can contact us on ProductSafety@springernature.com*

In case Publisher is established outside the EU, the EU authorized representative is:

Springer Nature Customer Service Center GmbH
Europaplatz 3
69115 Heidelberg, Germany

**Batch number: 08998846**

Printed by Printforce, the Netherlands

The Elements and Dynamic Systems of Economic Growth and Trade Models

Bjarne S. Jensen

# The Elements and Dynamic Systems of Economic Growth and Trade Models

## Economic Theory and Axiomatic Analysis of Expanding Economies in Historical Perspective

Volume 2

Second Edition

palgrave
macmillan

Bjarne S. Jensen
The Faculty of Business and Social
Sciences
University of Southern Denmark (SDU)
Odense, Denmark

ISBN 978-3-031-52492-9 ISBN 978-3-031-52493-6 (eBook)
https://doi.org/10.1007/978-3-031-52493-6



This Palgrave Macmillan imprint is published by the registered company Springer Nature Switzerland AG
The registered company address is: Gewerbestrasse 11, 6330 Cham, Switzerland

# Chapters Brought with Permission

Jensen BS (2017) von Thünen: Capital, Production Functions, Marginal Productivity Wages and the Natural Wage. German Economic Review 18:51–80; here Chap. 3

Jensen BS, de Boer P, van Daal J, Jensen PS (2011) Global Restrictions on the Parameters of the CDES Indirect Utility Function. Journal of Economics 102:217–235; here Chap. 5

Jensen BS, Alsholm PK, Larsen ME, Jensen JM (2005) Dynamic Structure, Exogeneity, Phase Portraits, Growth Paths, and Scale and Substitution Elasticities. Review of International Economics 13:59–89; here Chap. 12

Jensen BS (2003) Walrasian General Equilibrium Allocations and Dynamics in Two–Sector Growth Models. German Economic Review 4:53–87; here Chap. 17

Jensen BS, Larsen ME (2005) General Equilibrium Dynamics of Multi–Sector Growth Models. Journal of Economics 10:17–56; here Chap. 18

Jensen BS, Lehmijoki U, Rovenskaya E (2015) Non–Homothetic Multisector Growth Models. Review of Development Economics 19(2):221–243; here Chap. 20

Jensen BS, Wang C (1997) General Equilibrium Dynamics of Basic Trade Models for Growing Economies. In Bjarne S. Jensen and Kar–Yiu Wong (eds.) *Dynamics, Economic Growth, and International Trade*, Ann Arbor: University of Michigan Press; here Chap. 21

Jensen BS, Richter M, Wang C, Alsholm PK (2001) Saving Rates, Trade, Technology, and Stochastic Dynamics. Review of Development Economics 5:182–204; here Chap. 22

Jensen BS, Palokangas T (2007) Stochastic Economic Dynamics. Copenhagen Business School Press, Denmark; here Chaps. 26, 32, and 33

Jensen BS, Wang C (1999) Basic Stochastic Dynamic Systems of Growth and Trade. Review of International Economics 7:378–402; here Chap. 27

# Preface to the First Edition

Two central problems in the pure theory of economic growth are analysed in this monograph: (1) the dynamic laws governing the economic growth processes, (2) the kinematic and geometric properties of the set of solutions to the dynamic systems.

With allegiance to rigor and the emphasis on the theoretical fundamentals of prototype mathematical growth models, the treatise is written in the theorem-proof style. To keep the exposition orderly and as smooth as possible, the economic analysis has been separated from the purely mathematical issues, and hence the monograph is organized in two books.

Regarding the scope and content of the two books, an "Introduction and Overview" has been prepared to offer both motivation and a brief account. The introduction is especially designed to give a recapitulation of the mathematical theory and results presented in Book II, which are used as the unifying mathematical framework in the analysis and exposition of the different economic growth models in Book I. Economists would probably prefer to go directly to Book I and proceed by consulting the mathematical theorems of Book II in confirming the economic theorems in Book I. Thereby, both the independence and interdependence of the economic and mathematical argumentations are respected.

In contrast to linear dynamics systems, which are unified by the powerful superposition principle, there is no dominant principle unifying all nonlinear dynamic systems. Hence, to analyse nonlinear dynamics successfully, it is at first necessary to specify a properly restricted class of dynamic systems. Thus, in short, the restricted class specified by the powerful homogeneity principle is the primary object for the global analyses in these two books. The homogeneity principle, encompassing the superposition principle, has indeed both mathematical and economic implications of major significance. Nevertheless, specific nonhomogeneous dynamic systems are also considered in the treatment of some basic economic growth models.

This monograph is intended for scholars in economics and applied mathematics. It can be used as a basic or supplementary curriculum text in economic and mathematical programmes.

The manuscript was, apart from the last chapter, completed by July 1992, which accordingly is reflected in the bibliographies. It was important also to include in this volume a systematic comparison of planar differential and difference equations.

Many individuals have contributed, each in an important way, to the completion of this treatise.

My interest in the problems of growth theory was inspired by Professor Ragnar Bentzel. Without his encouragement and advice at the early stage, this study would never have been undertaken. I must also acknowledge a great debt to the late Professor Herman Wold for his erudite guidance as teacher and advisor. He accentuated the need for and the importance of "hard theorems in soft sciences". His thoughts on axiomatization and empirical observation in economics remain in my memory. I am grateful to Professor Bertil Holmlund for his critique, suggestions, and helpful counsel on former versions of the text. Indeed, I am much obliged to the favourable academic environment at the University of Uppsala.

For many valuable discussions and comments through the years, I am much indebted to Mogens Esrom Larsen, University of Copenhagen. From Preben Alsholm at The Technical University of Denmark, I received constructive commentary. I am happy to express a deep-felt appreciation to my brother, Jens Martin Jensen, a physicist, who was always willing to discuss general mathematical issues and help with clarification of many intricate equations.

It is with great pleasure that I express my gratitude to Niels Henrik Börjesson, graduate student at the Copenhagen Business School, who did the final typing and endured many changes in the text. He formulated the layout, developed references, and carefully read the manuscript. Because of the technical character of the material and the size of the volume, these tasks involved great responsibility. Without his help, the text in its present form would not have been realized. Finally, I thank, Kathleen Gail Jensen for her linguistic improvements.

In closing, my sincere thanks are conveyed to the editor and staff at Kluwer Academic Publishers for their fine cooperation.

Of course, I am solely responsible for any remaining errors and omissions.

Copenhagen, Denmark
November, 1993

Bjarne S. Jensen

# Preface to the Second Edition

The additions to the 2. edition are very extensive : From two parts to six, and former two parts also include several new chapters.

To a large extent, the background for the additions of parts and topics has been the economic research program related to the international conference series with the same theme : Dynamics, Economic Growth, and International Trade, (DEGIT), held consecutively for 24 years at universities on five continents :

DEGIT I, Denmark (1996), DEGIT II, Hong Kong (1997), DEGIT III, Taiwan (1998), DEGIT IV, Tilburg (1999), DEGIT V, Rome (2000), DEGIT VI, Vienna (2001), DEGIT VII, Cologne (2002), DEGIT VIII, Helsinki (2003), DEGIT IX, Reykjavik (2004), DEGIT X, Mexico City (2005), DEGIT XI, Jerusalem (2006), DEGIT XII, Melbourne (2007), DEGIT XIII, Manila (2008), DEGIT XIV, Los Angeles (2009), DEGIT XV, Frankfurt (2010), DEGIT XVI, St. Petersburg (2011), DEGIT XVII, Milan (2012), DEGIT XVIII, Lima (2013), DEGIT XIX, Nashville (2014), DEGIT XX, Geneva (2015), DEGIT XXI, Nottingham (2016), DEGIT XXII, Paris (2017), DEGIT XXIII, Moscow (2018), DEGIT XXIV, Odense (2019).

Many individuals, colleagues, and friends have supported, each in an important way, to the completion of this volume.

It is with great pleasure that I express my gratitude to Victor Alexander Brandsen, graduate student at The Technical University of Denmark, who did the LaTeX version of the entire volume and endured many changes in the text. He formulated the layout, developed references, and carefully checked the manuscript. Because of the technical character of the material and the size of the volume, these tasks involved great responsibility. Finally, I thank my family for patience and support over the many years of writing.

In closing, my sincere thanks are conveyed to the editors and staff at Springer Nature and Palgrave Macmillan for the fine cooperation.

Of course, I am solely responsible for any remaining errors and omissions.

University of Southern Denmark (SDU) Bjarne S. Jensen
September, 2023

# Introduction and Overview

The *causes* of the *wealth* of nations and the long-term prospects of *economic evolution* have always been central topics in economics, from the writings of the classicists, neoclassicists, and into our modern epoch. Discussions on the propagation of population, capital accumulation, and income distribution were devoted to the understanding and description of the *process* (dynamics) of economic growth. In classical economics, increasing *wealth* (riches, progress of opulence, national income) originated from the *dynamic interaction* between *land*, *labor*, and *capital*, mostly with land (natural resources) supposed available in a fixed amount (severe restraint on states of the economy).

Macroeconomic theories of economic growth thus go far back to the beginning of the economic discipline, but the theoretical explanations and empirical results from particular growth models have, from the outset and later on, been the object of many controversies, due to the economic and *dynamic complexities* involved in any particular growth model of *continuous factor* (labor and capital) *accumulation*. Since *systems* of *nonlinear differential* equations are often the fundamentals of economic growth models, it is not surprising that the conjectured *behaviour* of *solutions* (evolutions) for the population, capital stock, wage and profit rates, income distribution have been controversial, without model solutions (conclusions) firmly and rigorously established.

On this background, the *Volume* has been divided into *six parts*. Each part treats particular elements, subjects, and growth models in separate chapters. We are now going to give a short outline of the content within the six parts and some main chapters.

*Part I : Elements of Economic Growth Models*

On some elements of economic growth models, it is instructive to compare economics with mechanics. Mechanics is divided in two parts: Statics, or the Theory of Equilibrium, and Dynamics, or the Theory of Motion.

Starting from the idea of forces as the cause of the mechanical movement of particles and bodies led to the mathematical definition of forces as a vector with components, direction and magnitude. Relating next the forces to a concept of motion as acceleration gives the *dynamic second-order* differential equation of motion to be solved for obtaining the path of the body movements. Relating the inverse square law of gravitational forces to body accelerations and solving the dynamic equations is the unique success story of body motion in celestial mechanics. Rather than using vector quantities of forces and accelerations to determine motion, *scalar quantities* as work, potential, energy, and action are used together with variational (extremal principles) methods to derive other particle and body equations of *state motions* as is now given by *dynamic first-order* differential equations to be solved.[1] Economic growth models are using economic *scalar* concepts as *state* variables that involve motion (*evolution*) obtained by the solutions of *dynamic first-order* differential equations.

The first *element* of economic growth models to consider in Part I, Chap. 1, are the first-order differential equations and the long-run properties of their solutions—stability and rapidity of growth. With the selection of *one-dimensional*, first-order, *non-linear autonomous* dynamic systems, this introductory chapter gives the possibility to illustrate the various stability properties and rapidity of growth with explicit solutions of the single dynamic (differential) equation. Readers may next go to *dynamics* in Chap. 28.

Other *elements* of economic growth models refer (as statics in mechanics) to the 'productive *forces*,' production *factors*, Labor and Capital, (L,K)—or the scalar *potentials*, production (output) *potential*, the production function, $Y = F(L, K)$, analytically representing technology and 'Division of Labor'. Mechanical equilibrium attained by balancing forces or max/min of potentials have resemblances in economic equilibrium, but economic equilibrium has a more complex structure, as elements of the economic systems are much more interrelated than those of mechanical systems. Verifying the existence or observing the equilibrium is certainly much more difficult in economics than in mechanics.

As basic *elements* of any economic growth model, Part I has chapters on *production* functions and cost functions, dealing with the historical *origin* in Chap. 3, and the merits of various functional forms and a new flexible extension of the CES function to *multi-factor* production functions with *variable* AUES (Allen-Uazwa) *substitution* elasticities in Chap. 4, which also considers the important *complementarity* elasticities of Hicks-Sato. Similarly *utility* functions are an important element of growth models, especially *optimal growth* models that will here be solved for the optimal saving rate in the Ramsey model. The flexible utility function, CDES (constant differences of elasticity of substitution), is discussed in detail, theoretically and empirically, in Chaps. 5 and 6.

With the Part I elements of *production functions*, we have also obtained and here given the analytic forms of the *factor rewards*, factor prices, factor (cost,

[1] Both Newton's and Lagrange's forms of the equations of motion may be derived from Hamilton's principle (stationary value (over path traversed) for time averages of the difference between kinetic and potential energies).

income) shares by marginal factor productivities of labor and capital, that enter all subsequent growth models. Similarly, the direct and indirect *utility functions* provide the *consumer* demand system and *budget shares* that subsequently enter as elements in growth models, especially multi-sector general equilibrium (MSG) growth models.[2]

*Part II : Basic One-Sector Growth Models*

The dynamics of economic growth models will seldom be described by either just one state variable or two independent state variables. Usually, to specify a *dynamic system* for a growing economy, we will be confronted with the necessity of using at least *two interdependent state variables.* As 'driving forces' behind the motion (output increases) of the body (economy), the *two* 'productive forces'*factors*, Labor and Capital, were considered above, together with the production (output) potential—function. The factor endowments of labor and capital, $[L(t), K(t)]$, will serve as dynamic *state variables*, i.e., their *initial values* and the *governing functions* of the *dynamic differential* equations will be able to determine all *future states* (factor endowments). But we cannot expect these two state variables to change independent of each other, i.e. the governing function of each state variable may generally have *both* state *variables* as arguments.

The crucial mathematical question is now whether we know of a *two-dimensional autonomous dynamic system* that is general enough to *encompass* essentially all the dynamic systems that usually appear in the various specifications of the basic economic growth models. In short, does there exist a *broad class* of differential equations that allows us subsequently to treat these growth models as simply special cases within such a *unifying class*? It turns out that the requirement of *homogeneous governing functions* will provide the fundamental class of differential equations—i.e., autonomous dynamic systems in normal form : $\dot{x} = F(x, y),\ \dot{y} = G(x, y),\ (x, y) \in R^2,\ F(0, 0) = 0,\ G(0, 0) = 0$, where the $C^1$-class functions, $F$ and $G$, are *homogeneous* of the same *degree*, $m \in R$.

This dynamic systems and its solution properties are established in Chap. 28—which provides an *axiomatic foundation* of many *basic economic growth models*—and it will be able to answer fundamental questions about the solutions, stability, and geometry of phase portraits raised by *classical* growth models and *neoclassical* growth models.

The main task is next to analytically describe and elucidate the properties of the actual *governing functions*, $F$ and $G$, with the specific *economic* assumptions.

[2] Our Parts I–IV correspond essentially to Book I–IV, Smith (1790, 1961), p.5, p.448, Smith (1999a), p.107, Smith (1999b), p.5, e.g., Part I as Book I : Of the Causes of Improvement in the productive Powers of Labour, and of the Order according to which its Produce is naturally distributed among different Ranks of the People.
Part II as Book II : Of the Nature, Accumulation, and the Employment of Stock.
Part III as Book III : Of the different Progress of Opulence in different Nations.
Part IV as Book IV : Of Systems of Political Economy—the Mercantile System, the Agricultural Systems.

Technology assumptions play a crucial role in economic growth models, where Chap. 2 serves as back-up. Since we will consider *homogeneous production functions* of degree $0 < m \leq 1$, all the standard descriptions of technology properties now involve intricate expressions. Generally, *scale* and *substitution* properties become intertwined, as the homogeneity parameter $m \neq 1$ also appears in every *derivative* of the production functions.

To Samuelson (1978), "A.Smith, Ricardo, Malthus, and Stuart Mill shared in common essentially one dynamic model of equilibrium, growth, and distribution—the same *canonical classical* model", which is the subject matter of Chaps. 7 and 8.

The *triple* laws of production (technology), population, and capital accumulation are the canonical elements, and they give the classical dynamic system :

$$\dot{L} = n \cdot L \cdot \frac{\partial F}{\partial L}(L, K)$$
$$\dot{K} = s_K \cdot K \cdot \frac{\partial F}{\partial L}(L, K)$$

where $s_K$ is the *saving parameter* of Total capital income—$K \cdot \frac{\partial F}{\partial K}(L, K)$— and $n$ is a *propagation parameter* to Total labor income—$L \cdot \frac{\partial F}{\partial L}(L, K)$. Economically, the methodology of homogeneous dynamics works out properly with the marginal rate of substitution, and the phase portraits are beautifully organized by the size of the substitution elasticity. The stability properties of the solutions $[L(t), K(t)]$ are described with the stability concepts, defined and demonstrated in Chap. 1. The obtained results for basic classical systems are stated in *Theorems 7.1–7.5* and *Propositions 7.1–7.4.*

The existence of positive *minimal* factor *rewards* for both factors, Labor and Capital, had the attention of the classicists, especially Ricardo and Malthus, and Chap. 8 gives the dynamic system with explicit parameters for the minimum (real) factor prices, $w_m, r_m$ :

$$\dot{L} = n \cdot L \cdot [\frac{\partial F}{\partial L}(L, K) - w_m] \quad = \quad P_1(L, K)$$
$$\dot{K} = s_K \cdot K \cdot [\frac{\partial F}{\partial L}(L, K) - r_m] \quad = \quad P_2(L, K)$$

This version of the canonical classical growth model is no longer a global homogeneous dynamic system, as there with *decreasing* returns to scale will now necessarily exist an *isolated interior* critical point, a *stationary state* solution, an attractor also called a *Malthusian* trap of stagnation.

By using Olech's theorem, the global asymptotic stability of the stationary state is proved, *Theorem 8.1*, and a phase portrait (*classical node*) of the Malthusian stagnation (trap) is shown. With *structural* parameter change such as *constant* returns to scale, the *stationary* state (equilibrium) can *bifurcate* here into [ not as Hopf into a closed curve (periodic solution) ] an always *expanding* economy converging in the long-run to steady state (balanced) growth, *Theorem 8.2.*

Replacing in the *governing functions* of the former wage- and capital incomes by *national income* in Chap. 9, the *aggregate* (macro) models have the dynamic system :

$$\dot{L} = n \cdot F(L, K)$$
$$\dot{K} = s \cdot F(L, K)$$

The results of Chaps. 7 and 8 carry over to the aggregate version. Chapter 9 ends with a *Synopsis* of the classical growth models.

The dynamic system of the seminal macro growth model, Solow (1956), was, Chap. 11:

$$\dot{L} = n \cdot L$$
$$\dot{K} = s \cdot F(L, K)$$

Labor (population) grows at an *exogenous* rate. The stability properties for the general model are discussed, complemented with explicit solutions to special cases, Cobb-Douglas and Leontief technology. It concludes with a clarification of the kinematic distinction between asymptotic ratio stability and the geometric (trajectory) convergence of the phase curves, which—together with important dynamic implications of *exogeneity* for per capita growth—are further studied with many explicit solutions in Chap. 12.

The last chapter in Part II of *one-sector* growth models studies the *optimal* growth solutions generated by the dynamics of the basic Ramsey *intertemporal* saving-consumption model. General sufficient conditions are derived for the existence of unique optimal persistent growth solutions within Ramsey models. In phase diagrams, the *optimal solution* (time paths, trajectory) is a *unique separator*. We give comprehensive quantitative applications—using CES-VES *production functions* and HARA (Hyperbolic Absolute Risk Aversion) *utility functions*, together with parametric sensitivity analyses—of these optimal time paths for observable saving and growth rates. The original Ramsey (1928) optimal saving model with *persistent growth* per capita is solved in closed form with *constant* (CEIS) and *variable* (VEIS) elasticity of *intertemporal substitution* with the *latter* to generate realistic *historically* observable evolutions of *saving rates* and economic *growth rates.* Chapter 13 is a main chapter with the old Ramsey model problems finally resolved.

*Part III : Two-Sector and Multi-Sector Growth Models*

The exposition proceeds by analyzing the economic/dynamic implications of shifting to various *two-sector* growth models that must give new focus and attention to the *output composition* and *factor allocation* issues involved in *general equilibrium* dynamics.

As to the *basic two-sector* growth models and *multi-sector* growth model Part III : *Chaps. 14–17* and *18–20*, the economy is producing a *capital good* $Y_1$ in *sector* 1 and *consumer goods* $Y_i$ in *sectors* $i > 1$. The *technologies* in each sector are described by *distinct production functions* exhibiting constant returns to scale $(m = 1)$, $Y_i = F_i(L_i, K_i) = L_i f_i(k_i) \equiv L_i y_i,\ i = 1, 2, , , , N$.

Regarding the *labor supply*, the traditional neoclassical assumption, $\dot{L} = nL$, is mainly used. The general equations of *factor* (labor and capital) *accumulation* for such *multi-sector* economies are :

$$\dot{L} = n\,L,$$
$$\dot{K} = Y_1 = F_1(L_1, K_1).$$

But these two *accumulation* equations themselves are *not* a *dynamic system* (deterministic process). The crucial question is then whether and how the accumulation equations can be transformed into *governing functions* of a homogeneous dynamic system in the *state variables*, L and K (*factor endowments*),

$$\dot{L} = Ln,$$
$$\dot{K} \equiv Y_1 = \mathrm{G}(L, K) = L\,\mathfrak{g}(k),$$

with $k = K/L$ and, $\mathfrak{g}(k) = Y_1/L \equiv (L_1/L)(Y_1/L_1) \equiv \lambda_{L_1} y_1 \equiv \lambda_{L_1}(k) y_1(k)$,

The standard director function, $h(k)$, becomes,

$$\dot{k} \;=\; h(k) \;=\; \mathfrak{g}(k) - n\,k,$$

Although the *one-dimensional* dynamics, $\dot{k} = h(k)$, look deceptively simple, the rather heavy task is now to *establish* the *existence* and to characterize mathematically and economically, the *global properties* of $g(k)$—in accordance with the *alternative assumptions* about sector technologies, factor allocation, saving behaviour, etc., that we adopt for the *two-sector* economy and the multi-sector economies.

In *Chap. 14*, the *sector technologies* are of *Leontief form*. Since we always want (require) that the total factor *endowments* $(L, K)$ to be *fully* and *efficiently utilized* (employed), this requirement together with Leontief ("fixed coefficients") technologies actually solves also the sectorial *factor allocation problem* $(L_1, L_2, K_1, K_2)$, and then gives the current *output composition* $(Y_1, Y_2)$ of the two-sector economy. Hence $g(k)$, is implicitly well determined.

Sorting out all the relations involved, the function $g(k)$, will here take the form,

$$g(k) = -\frac{y_1 k_2}{k_1 - k_2} + \left[\frac{y_1}{k_1 - k_2}\right] k, \quad k_1 \neq k_2.$$

where $k_1$ and $k_2$ are the *fixed* sectorial capital-labor ratios ("capital intensities") and $y_1$ is the *fixed* labor productivity of the capital good sector.

The dynamic analysis and solution methods can now follow the standard procedure of homogeneous dynamics. Since the dynamic system here is *linear*, it can of course be solved explicitly by the traditional algebraic methods, but the advantages of our calculus approach are used to give the *solutions* in more relevant economic forms in *Theorem 14.1*. The stability properties of capital-labor ratio and coordinates are given in *Corollary 14.1*. We have the global asymptotic ratio stability, if and only if,

$$\text{(i)}\ y_1 > nk_1, \quad \text{(ii)}\ k_2 > k_1 \quad \therefore \quad k_1 < \min\{y_1/n, k_2\}.$$

A unique directrix (ray, capital-labor ratio) may also exist with $k_2 > k_1$, but it will be repulsive, and the two-sector economy eventually disintegrates.

The *economic rationale* of the dynamic stability conditions called for a closer examination of the factor mobility and the implied *reallocation* of the growing factor supplies that—outside the trajectory of balanced growth—continually occur within this economy. The substance of the *sectorial capital intensity* condition is shown to be an implication of the *Rybczynski* theorem, extended to a growing two-sector economy with one of the outputs being a capital good—see *Corollary 14.3*.

For *two-sector* growth models with *flexible* sector technologies in Chaps. 15 and 16, the steps to get the function $g(k)$ is a much more complicated affair. This step cannot be accomplished just by invoking the assumptions of full employment and efficient allocation of the production factors. Demand side specifications have to be introduced, which here will be represented by either *proportional* or *classical saving* functions.

Flexible *prices* in the commodity and factor markets equilibrate supply and demand. Efficient factor allocation requires a common *wage-rental* ratio in both sectors. In short, general equilibrium values of every variable must be obtained for any given factor endowments, $(L, K)$. As to the details of our procedure for determining the *momentary general equilibrium solutions* of the two-sector economy with *proportional* and *classical* saving, we can only here refer to the relevant sections, *Chaps. The General Equilibrium Solutions* and *The General Equilibrium Model and Solutions*, where also the crucial *uniqueness* problems are considered in *Lemmas 15.1* and *16.1*.

Chapter 17 again reviews the two-sector economy, and solves the two-sector model as a miniature Walrasian general equilibrium system of momentary and moving equilibria. The Walrasian framework encompasses the fundamental neoclassical and classical two-sector growth models; the families of solutions of steady-state and persistent growth per capita in various competitive two-sector economies are parametrically characterized. The technology parameters of the capital good industry are decisive for obtaining long-run per capita growth in closed (global) economies. A review of the literature complements the theorems on the general equilibrium allocations, dynamic systems, and the time paths of Walrasian two-sector economies.

Chapter 18 analyses Walrasian general equilibrium systems and calculates the static and dynamic solutions for competitive market equilibria. The Walrasian framework encompasses the basic *multi-sector* growth (MSG) models with neoclassical production technologies in *N sectors* (industries). The endogenous behavior of all the relative prices is analyzed in detail, as are sectorial allocations of the primary factors, labor and capital. Dynamic systems of Walrasian multi-sector economies and the family of solutions (time paths) for steady-state and persistent growth per capita are parametrically characterized. The technology parameters of the capital good industry are decisive for obtaining long-run per capita growth in closed (global) economies.

Chapter 19 considers that Multisector growth (MSG) models and Computable general equilibrium (CGE) models, with their many sectors (industries and goods), are known as trying to convert Walrasian general equilibrium systems from an abstract economy representation into workable models with industrial structures changing as actually observed. Hence the main objective is to set out comparative static and dynamic systems for succinctly stating and explicitly solving MSG models. The Walrasian *general equilibrium* is completely stated by *one equation* and the *multisector dynamics* by *one differential equation*. Benchmark solutions are shown for three CES (Constant Elasticity of Substitution) parameter regimes of a *10-sector* general equilibrium model.

Chapter 20 extends the Multi-Sector Growth (MSG) models of Chap. 19, in which the CES homothetic utility functions are now replaced by *non-homothetic preferences* for the evolution of factor allocations and industrial structures in accordance with consumption expenditure patterns implied by the *non-unitary income elasticities* observed in all budget data since (Engel 1857). The comparative static general equilibrium solutions and particularly solving the dynamics of MSG models require explicit specifications of all demand and cost (price) functions. On the demand side, the CDES (constant differences of elasticity of substitution) *non-homothetic indirect utility* functions and Roy's identity provide the explicit Marshallian demand functions and budget shares. Sectorial CES cost functions and Shephard's lemma provide the explicit relative commodity price functions and the sectorial cost shares and capital-labor ratios. *Walrasian equilibria* are given by *one equation* and the *multisector dynamics* by *three differential equations.* Benchmark solutions are given for three cost regimes of a *10-sector* MSG model. History patterns of industrial/allocational evolutions are recognized.

*Part IV : International Trade and Economic Growth Models*

The reader undoubtedly feels that the transition from full-scale multi-sector growth models with non-homothetic preferences to two-sector trade models is a bit surprising. But trade models will often have to operate with *commodity prices fixed* externally, especially a *small open economy.* The fixed commodity prices imply that the two sectors are operating with fixed coefficient Leontief technologies, if they are producing both goods. Hence the growing small economy model resembles the two-sector model of Chap. 14. If specialized, we are back to the one-sector economy of Chap. 11. The *small open economies* will then be a *unified combination* of Chaps. 11 and 14.

Chapter 21 gives the Structure of Two-Sector Trade Models, and it provides a unified framework for analysing the General Equilibrium dynamics of growing two-factor—two-sector trading economies. A major distinction is international trade models for small open (fixed terms of trade) economies and large open economies (international general equilibrium prices). In terms of physical capital accumulation, savings are given by fixed saving rates of national income, or fixed proportions of capital income, or determined optimally by the Ramsey rule. There is exogenous and endogenous labor growth. The growth model for the small trading economy is explicitly solved. The main contribution of this chapter is a series of theorems, which lay down the necessary and sufficient conditions for the existence, uniqueness and asymptotic stability of the long-run capital-labor ratio in several parametric cases, with incomplete as well as complete specialization/diversification.

Chapter 22 develops a framework for analyzing the stochastic dynamics of *small growing trading* economies with CES sector technologies. The open neoclassical two-sector growth model with a *diffusion process* (uncertainty) for the aggregate saving/investment ratio is demonstrated with *sample paths* and long-run *probability distributions* of the overall factor endowment ratio. Stochastic endogenous growth and cycles require a combination of fundamental growth parameter values: saving rates, terms of trade, and sectorial substitution elasticities. It defines and demonstrates the conditions for full and partial specialization, under consideration of the factor *reversal* effects—two diversification cones—of the CES technology. With this theoretical background, it solves the same model under uncertainty, and it illustrates the regions within the parameter space that include parametric values generating non-stationary sample paths of stochastic endogenous growth and cycles. The chapter finally *compares* the results and the *expectations* of the *stochastic* model with those of its *deterministic counterpart* in Chap. 21, which serves indeed as the economic benchmark.

Production possibility curves (PPC) and five core theorems have played an important role in international trade theory. Despite the graphical appearance of PPC everywhere in the trade literature, no explicit expression has yet been obtained for *production possibility curves* (PPC).

Chapter 23 reviews Transformation Functions, Production Possibility Curves, and Factor Contract Curves, and presents *explicit formulas* of the *Transformation* Functions for *Pareto efficient* factor *allocations.* These *Production Possibility* Frontiers (Envelopes) are *explicitly* stated for any Cobb-Douglas (*CD*) sector *technology parameters* and any *factor endowments* of labor and capital. Exact *Variable Elasticity* of *Transformation* (*VET*) curves of non-joint productions are derived. *Core Theorems* of international trade are unified, extended, and economically stated explicitly with *structural parameter* formulas. Multiple output *Revenue* functions are obtained in *closed forms.*

The *output* formulas of the Transformation and Revenue functions are compared with the *autarky general equilibrium* expressions. Explicit *autarky formulas* of *comparative advantage* (price, cost) for prediction of *trade pattern* are derived and demonstrated for bilateral trading economies with *any* CD sector *technologies*, CD consumer *preferences*, and *any* country *endowment ratios* (proportions) of labor and capital.

With the background of the autarky general equilibria expressions of Chaps. 23, 24 now derives explicit *autarky formulas* of *comparative advantage* (price, cost) for prediction of trade patterns, which are demonstrated for bilateral trading economies with *any* CD sector *technologies*, CD consumer *preferences*, and *any* country *factor endowment ratios* (proportions) of labor and capital. For two trading economies, the chapter continues with the derivation and the demonstration of the *international general equilibrium* solutions, the *international terms of trade* (*world prices*) and *traded volumes.* These closed-form expressions provide a unified framework for all traditional standard trade models. They allow for international differences in country sizes, endowments, technologies and preferences, encompassing the major "pure trade theories" within a systematic analytic and historical perspective. In this unified framework, we derive the general existence conditions for the solutions under diversification and incipient country specialization.

The *agricultural sector* and agricultural cultivation systems are historically important for the populations, economic growth and international trade, especially in the eighteenth century. Chapter 25 examines the *Tellow Manor Farm* accounting records (1810–1819) for the Seven Field System of Land cultivation. The output and cost calculations with the Tellow Manor Accounts showed that the replacement of the *3-Field system* with *7-Field system* would increase *production* (output) by 83 pct. and increase *Land Rents* by 52 pct. The chapter shows the connection between cost calculations in Business Economics/Accounting and costs/prices in Macro-/Microeconomics. The Tellow quantitative agricultural model of 7-Field cultivation system serves as a benchmark for comparing/evaluating in *Denmark* and *England* the corresponding Agricultural output and Land rent increases. The agricultural cultivation *reforms*, 1760–1800, were very successful ("revolutions"), breaking economic Stagnation and the *Population* ('Malthusian') barrier.

*Part V : Stochastic Dynamic Systems*

Deterministic dynamics and stochastic dynamics *complement* each other. Basically, they contain the same theory. The governing functions of deterministic dynamics are essentially the *drift coefficients* of stochastic dynamics.

Chapter 26 extends the basic *deterministic* one-sector and two-sector growth models to a *stochastic* context in *continuous time*, using *Wiener processes* for the description of various sources of *uncertainties* in the growth rate of the *labor* force, the rate of capital *depreciation* and the *saving* rate. The *drift* and *diffusion coefficients* of the stochastic dynamic systems are *homogenous* of degree one in the two state variables, labor and capital—which allows a reduction into the stochastic dynamics of the capital-labor *ratio*. The crucial issue of hitting *absorbing boundaries* for the stochastic growth models is rigorously examined, and simple criteria (sufficient conditions) for *inaccessible* boundaries are established, a subject on which existing literature has been deficient. From the Kolmogorov forward equation is derived the *steady state probability* distribution of the capital-labor ratios. For both stochastic one- and two-sector growth models, the *sample paths*—of *transition* to *steady states* or for *persistent* endogenous growth—of particular state variables are simulated for many *parametric* specifications of the CD and CES *sector technologies* involved. Impacts of technology shocks are similarly demonstrated. All relevant sample paths are exhibited on both shorter and longer time horizons.

Uncertainties are intrinsic features of dynamic economic systems, and Chap. 27 considers the dynamic implications of factor endowment (labor, capital) uncertainties for a small growing trading economy. Our stochastic growth models extend the open neoclassical two-sector growth model of Chap. 21 to a stochastic environment in continuous time and extend the diffusion dynamics of one-sector growth models to a trading two-sector economy. We demonstrate that the basic propositions of deterministic steady-state growth and endogenous growth theory, under some specifications and certain parametric restrictions, are preserved within a stochastic framework.

*Part VI : Homogeneous Dynamic Systems*

Chapter 28 considers *autonomous dynamic* systems in the *normal* (explicit) form: $\dot{x} = F(x, y)$, $\dot{y} = G(x, y)$, $(x, y) \in R^2$, $F(0, 0) = 0, G(0, 0) = 0$, where the $C^1$-class functions, $F$ and $G$, are *homogeneous* of the same *degree*, $m \in R$. The $C^1$-class assumption about the *governing functions*, $F$, $G$, ensures everywhere the *existence* and *uniqueness* of the *coordinate solutions*: $[x, y] = [\varphi_1(t), \varphi_2(t)] = \varphi(t)$. By *homogeneity* property and by using the *ratio* variable, $r = y/x$, $x \neq 0$, we rewrite the *dynamic* system as: $\dot{x} = x|x|^{m-1} f(r)$, $\dot{y} = x|x|^{m-1} g(r)$, $x \neq 0$. The *ratio* of the individual coordinate solutions, $r = \rho(t) = \varphi_2(t)/\varphi_1(t)$, has the *time derivative* : $\dot{r} = dr/dt = |x|^{m-1} h(r)$, where, $h(r) = g(r) - rf(r)$, is called a *director function*, its roots, $h\,(\alpha) = 0$, are called *director roots*, and *rays*, $y = \alpha\, x$, are called *directrices*, and $f(\alpha)$, are called *directrix values*. A directrix reflects a *constant ratio solution*, i.e., $\rho\,(t) = \alpha$, $\varphi_2(t) = \alpha\, \varphi_1(t)$.

By $\dot{r}$ and $\dot{x}$ it is shown that *nonstationary ratio solution*, $\rho(t)$, must solve the *fundamental differential* equation : $\dot{r} = Q(r) = |k_0 \exp\{H(r)\}|^{m-1} h(r)$. Thus *dynamics* of any autonomous *system* of *two interdependent* homogeneous *differential* equations—having *same* degree of *homogeneity*—is essentially given succinctly through a *single* autonomous *differential* equation.

Having obtained, $\rho(t)$, corresponding *coordinate solutions*, $\varphi_1(t)$, $\varphi_2(t)$, are then given as : $\varphi_1(t) = k_0 \exp\{H[\rho(t)]\}$, $\varphi_2(t) = \rho(t)\varphi_1(t)$, and the *trajectories* as *loci* are given by the *equation* : $x - k_0 \exp\{H(y/x)\} = 0$.

Thus, we have obtained the *complete* set of *solutions* to the *homogeneous dynamic* system. Usually, the *non-stationary* ratio and coordinate *solutions cannot* be expressed in *closed form* (finite combination of elementary functions), but the fact that these *solutions* are obtained in terms of well-defined *primitives* [ integrands being determined by the *governing functions* : $f$, $g$ ], will allow us to deduce the *qualitative behaviour* of the family of solutions for *any specification* of the basic *governing functions* : $F$, $G$.

The global *asymptotic ratio stability* conditions follow from, $h(r)$, and are stated in *Theorem 28.4*, weaker *ratio* stabilities in *Theorem 28.5*. The *trajectory* geometry is given in *Theorem 28.8*. The *stability* properties of the *coordinate solutions* are summarized in *Theorems 28.9–28.12*.

Chapter 29 applies the results of the general theory of homogeneous dynamics, Chap. 28, to the special case, where $m = 1$, and the *governing functions* are *linear*. The linear system is of course well known, but our solution technique, based on calculus instead of linear algebra, is novel and helpful in obtaining relevant classification of *solutions* and the *phase portraits*. Rather than the traditional dichotomy, stable/unstable, we illustrate the use of the *kinematic* stability concepts for the *ratio* and *coordinate* solutions in *global* and *generic* versions. Bifurcation and *structural stability* are related to the regions in the parameter space, as are the kinematic stability properties. The solutions are obtained without coordinate transformations, and the main types of solutions for linear dynamics are classified directly with the *four parameters* $(a, b, c, d)$, the variation of which provides an *astoundingly* varied set of *solutions* and *phase portraits*. The parametric extension to *affine* dynamics supplements the linear dynamics.

Chapter 30 generalizes the theory of homogeneous dynamics to a wider class of differential equations. As homogeneous production functions gave the impetus to study the solutions to homogeneous dynamic systems, Chap. 28, it was also *Quasi* (also named, "Almost" or "Pseudo")—homogeneous *production* functions that lead us to study the qualitative properties of *Quasi-homogeneous dynamics*. While the *trajectories* for homogeneous dynamics are obtained from each other by a multiplication along the *rays* through the origin, the *trajectories* for quasi-homogeneous dynamics are obtained from each other by a multiplication along the family of *power curves* $y = (\alpha x)^\beta$, $x > 0$. With the *class* of quasihomogeneous *governing* functions, growth models, with the total *factor endowments* $(L, K)$ as state variables, will be able to *exhibit* also a *permanent increasing* capital-labor *ratio*. Many economic (allocational, distributional, etc.) implications of the quasihomogeneous technologies need to be further and fully explored, when such technologies are admitted to enter the dynamics of *economic growth* models.

Chapter 31 extends the results of linear continuous time dynamics, Chap. 29, to observations with their solutions from *discrete time* linear dynamical system. The linear *governing functions* may belong to $C^1$-class, but continuity fails with respect to solutions (time path) of discrete time processes (difference equations). The general coordinate solution and initial value problem of the *discrete linear* dynamic systems are presented in *Propositions 31.1–31.2*. The configurations of the phase portrait for the discrete time linear system are analysed in detail. The discrete time solutions are embedded in the continuous time solution of extended linear systems by *Theorem 31.1* to which correspond exact analogue discrete system matrices.

Chapter 32 considers *continuous* differential equation growth models with a *time delay* in the productive operation of installed capital. By a local nonlinear analysis, it is demonstrated that the *equilibrium* becomes *unstable* in a Hopf *bifurcation* for sufficiently *large delays*. Periodic solutions in the form of *limit cycles* are created in the bifurcation. In a specific example with a CD production function we show the bifurcation is *supercritical* such that the limit cycles are stable and exist for delays larger than the critical value. By numerical simulations with a CES production function, we show that the model may exhibit 'square wave' solutions and 'chaos' (*aperiodic oscillations*) for our single delay differential equation, if the delay is very large. The model phase portrait integrates the phenomena of *economic growth* and *cycles*.

Chapter 33 analyses two *basic stochastic models*: The *time homogeneous* Gaussian and the geometric Wiener diffusion of *two-dimensional vector processes*. Using the theory of stochastic processes and Ito lemma, the *probability* of *distributions* of the stochastic state vectors are described by the evolution of their *moments* (*expectation* and *covariance* as *functions* of time), as these moments satisfy certain systems of ordinary (deterministic) differential equations (ODE). By solving the latter ODE, the *explicit solutions* for the first-order and second-order *moment functions* are presented. The *forward Kolmogorov* equation is used partly to derive the results by *alternative* methods and partly to gain information on the probability distributions. The general *closed form* results on the *moment evolutions* (still unavailable) have many applications in the models of linear dynamics with uncertainty.

A common procedure may be discerned in Parts I–VI of our *axiomatic analysis* of *expanding economies*. The cooperation of *mathematics* and *economic theory* has to be properly organized. The two disciplines first advance with their own subject matter and methods, and only later combine efforts in a joint endeavor.

## Bibliography

Baumol WJ (1970) Economic Dynamics, 3rd edn. MacMillan, London

Cassel G (1925) Fundamental Thoughts in Economics. T. Fisher Unwin, London

Debreu G (1986) Theoretic Models: Mathematical Form and Economic Content. Econometrica 54:1259–1270

Domar ED (1946) Capital Expansion, Rate of Growth and Employment. Econometrica 14:137–47

Engel E (1857) Die Productions– and Consumptionsverhaeltnisse des Koenigreichs Sachsen. Zeitschrift des Statistischen Bureaus des Koeniglich Saechsishen Ministerium des Inneren 8–9, reprint in: *Bulletin of the International Statistical Institute*, 9 (1895), 1–54.

Harrod RF (1939) An Essay in Dynamic Theory. Economic J 49:14–33, or Stiglitz (1969)

Jones LE, Manuelli RE (1990) A Convex Model of Equilibrium Growth: Theory and Policy Implications. Journal of Political Economy 98:1008–1038

Lucas RE (1988) On the Mechanics of Economic Development. Journal of Monetary Economics 22:3–42, Reprinted in Becker (1991)

Lundberg E (1938) Studies in the Theory of Economic Expansion. P.S. King and Sons, London

Ramsey FP (1928) A Mathematical Theory of Saving. Economic Journal 38:543–559

Rebelo S (1991) Long–Run Policy Analysis and Long–Run Growth. Journal of Political Economy 99:500–521

Romer PM (1986) Increasing Returns and Long–Run Growth. Journal of Political Economy 94:1002–1037, Reprinted in Becker (1991)

Samuelson PA (1978) The Canonical Classical Model of Political Economy. Journal of Economic Literature 16:1415–1434

Smith A (1790, 1961) An Inquiry Into The Nature and Causes of The Wealth of Nations, vol 1–2, 5th edn. Methuen, London, (ed. E. Cannan)

Smith A (1999a) The Wealth of Nations, Books I-III. Penguin Classics, London, Skinner A (ed.)

Smith A (1999b) The Wealth of Nations, Books IV-V. Penguin Classics, London, Skinner A (ed.)

Solow RM (1956) A Contribution to the Theory of Economic Growth. Quarterly Journal of Economics 70:65–94, Reprinted in Stiglitz (1969), and in Becker (1991)

Stiglitz JE, Uzawa H (1969) Readings in the Modern Theory of Economic Growth. M.I.T. Press, Cambridge, Mass

Walras L (1954) Elements of Pure Economics. George Allen and Unwin, London

Yang X, Borland J (1991) A Microeconomic Mechanism for Economic Growth. J Political Economy 99:460–82

# CONTENTS

# List of Figures

# List of Tables

# List of Theorems

# List of Propositions

# List of Corollaries

# List of Lemmas

# PART IV

# International Trade and Economic Growth Models

CHAPTER 21

# General Equilibrium Dynamics of Basic Trade Models for Growing Economies

## INTRODUCTION

In the literature on the pure theory of trade, the two-factor, two-sector, two-country framework has provided a fundamental general equilibrium structure for static and comparative-static analyses of many issues related to factor allocation, output composition, relative prices, and trade patterns. Although the work on two-sector growth models has long ago been extended to trading economies, *stability* issues and *non-steady-state dynamics* have to be further analyzed. As is well known, many results and theorems of both static and dynamic trade theory rest on the *assumption* of *incomplete* specialization. A major purpose of this chapter is to study the *conditions* that will in the *long-run* preserve the *diversification* of a *small* trading economy and two *large* trading economies. However, when the parametric conditions of diversified steady-state growth are not satisfied, we give, for a small country, special attention to various forms of *endogenous* (persistent) growth per capita. Basic (prototype) dynamic trade models will be analyzed in detail.

A small trading economy, owing to the given terms of trade, can be conceived of as being restricted (by the outside world and competitive pricing) to operating with fixed-coefficient technologies. Nevertheless, the long-run stability of the *diversification* of a *small* trading country does *not* depend entirely, as in a closed economy, on the *ranking* of sectorial *factor* intensities. Alternative *trade patterns* give the growing two-sector economy some opportunities to remain diversified. However, besides *technology*, the *domestic demand* composition is of critical importance for preserving *domestic production* of both tradable

With co-author:
CHUNYAN WANG, Copenhagen Business School, Denmark



B. S. Jensen, *The Elements and Dynamic Systems of Economic Growth and Trade Models*, https://doi.org/10.1007/978-3-031-52493-6_21

goods. For two large trading countries, the long-run stability of incomplete specialization is likewise critically dependent on demand-side parameters.

Dynamic trade theory was initiated by Oniki and Uzawa (1965), who studied the effects of capital accumulation and labor growth on international equilibrium over time for two large countries. In this area, other studies were Bardhan (1966, 1970); Kemp (1969); Findlay (1970); Takayama (1972); Woodland (1982); Gandolfo (1994). Our work may especially be seen as extensions of the contributions of Stiglitz (1970); Deardorff (1971, 1973, 1974); Deardorff and Hanson (1978); Deardorff (1994); Smith (1976, 1977, 1984).

In Sect. "Structure of Two-Sector Trade Models", we present the general equilibrium structure of the trade models. Section "General Equilibrium Dynamics of a Small Trading Country" is devoted to dynamic two-sector models for *small* trading economies. As to capital accumulation, we consider *proportional*, *classical*, and *optimal* saving models. Section "General Equilibrium Dynamics of Large Trading Countries" presents a dynamic analysis of a two-sector growth model for two *large* countries with the *terms* of *trade* of international equilibrium *endogenously* determined. It may be called a two-factor Ricardian trade model, as we also allow for different sector technologies in the two countries. The *parametric conditions* of preserving *diversification* in both countries are obtained. Final comments are offered in Sect. "Final Comments".

## Structure of Two-Sector Trade Models

The structure of the two-sector trade models are formed by the *basic assumptions* of international immobile production factors, full employment, competitive prices, and trade balance equilibrium. The elements of a *competitive* two-sector economy with *homogenous* production functions will subsequently determine and impose important *restrictions* upon the character and *parameters* of the actual *homogenous dynamic* systems for a small or large economy trading in both goods.

### *Domestic Production and Factor Endowments*

Consider an economy consisting of a *capital* good industry (sector) and a *consumer* good industry (sector), labelled 1 and 2, respectively. The two-sector general equilibrium model is characterized by the following assumptions.

The *sector technologies* are described by production functions exhibiting *constant returns* to scale,

$$Y_i = F_i(L_i, K_i) = L_i f_i(k_i) = L_i y_i, \quad i = 1, 2, \tag{21.1}$$

where $f_i(k_i)$, $i = 1, 2$, have the properties

$$\forall k_i > 0 : \quad f_i'(k_i) = df_i(k_i)/dk_i > 0, \quad f_i''(k_i) = d^2 f_i(k_i)/dk_i^2 < 0, \tag{21.2}$$

$$\lim_{k_i \to 0} f_i'(k_i) = \overline{\beta} \leq \infty, \quad \lim_{k_i \to \infty} f_i'(k_i) = \underline{\beta} \geq 0, \quad f_i'(k_i) \in J = [\underline{\beta}, \overline{\beta}]. \tag{21.3}$$

Thus, the *intensive function* $f$ is a strictly concave monotonic increasing function on the nonnegative real line, with its slope decreasing from $\overline{\beta}$ at $k = 0$ to $\underline{\beta}$ at $k = +\infty$.

The *allocation ratios* (sector fractions) of *labor* are

$$L_1/L + L_2/L \equiv \lambda_1 + \lambda_2 \equiv 1. \quad \lambda_{L_1} = \lambda_1, \quad \lambda_2 = \lambda_{L_2}, \ \lambda_{L_i} = \lambda_i, \tag{21.4}$$

Then, the full employment condition may be rewritten as, cf. (21.4),

$$k \equiv \lambda_1 k_1 + \lambda_2 k_2 \equiv k_2 + (k_1 - k_2)\lambda_1. \tag{21.5}$$

Thus, the *overall* capital-labor ratio $k$ is the weighted average of the *sectorial* capital-labor ratios, $k_1$ and $k_2$, with the labor allocation ratios as weights. We note that, cf. (21.4)–(21.5)

$$\lambda_1 = \frac{k - k_2}{k_1 - k_2}, \qquad \lambda_2 = \frac{k_1 - k}{k_1 - k_2}. \tag{21.6}$$

The factor endowments belonging to the *diversification cone* $C_k \subset \Re^2_+$ are:

$$C_k = \{(L, K) \in \Re^2_+ \mid k_1 < K/L < k_2 \ \vee \ k_2 < K/L < k_1\}. \tag{21.7}$$

Total *domestic* (and per capita, $Y_i/L$) *production* of the two goods is, cf. (21.4),

$$Y_i = L_i y_i = L y_i \lambda_i, \quad i = 1, 2. \tag{21.8}$$

### *Prices, Incomes, Savings, and Trade Balance*

The **open** two-sector economy is assumed to operate under *perfect competition* ( *zero-profit* ) condition; absolute (money) *factor* prices $(w, r)$ are the same in both sectors, *output* prices $(P_1, P_2)$ represent *unit cost*, and *revenue* (total *cost* ) is *shared* $(\epsilon_{L_i}, \epsilon_{K_i})$ between the two factors.

Hence, we have the competitive *general equilibrium* relations, $i = 1, 2$ :

$$P_i Y_i = r K_i + w L_i, \quad \epsilon_{K_i} = \frac{r K_i}{P_i Y_i}, \quad \epsilon_{K_i} + \epsilon_{L_i} = 1, \tag{21.9}$$

$$\epsilon_{K_i} = \frac{k_i}{k_i + \omega} = \frac{k_i f_i'(k_i)}{y_i}, \quad \epsilon_{L_i} = \frac{\omega}{k_i + \omega}, \quad \omega = \frac{w}{r} = \frac{f_i(k_i)}{f_i'(k_i)} - k_i, \tag{21.10}$$

$$P_i = \frac{w}{y_i \epsilon_{L_i}} = \frac{rk_i}{y_i \epsilon_{K_i}}, \quad \frac{r}{P_i} = \frac{y_i}{k_i + \omega} = f_i'(k_i), \quad \frac{w}{P_i} = \frac{y_i \omega}{k_i + \omega}, \tag{21.11}$$

$$p = \frac{P_1}{P_2} = \frac{y_2}{y_1}\frac{\epsilon_{L_2}}{\epsilon_{L_1}} = \frac{y_2(k_1 + w/r)}{y_1(k_2 + w/r)} = \frac{f_2'(k_2)}{f_1'(k_1)}, \quad P_i \neq 0. \tag{21.12}$$

The *common* wage-rental *ratio*, $(\omega)$, becomes by (21.12),

$$\omega = \frac{w}{r} = \frac{k_1(y_2/y_1) - k_2(P_1/P_2)}{P_1/P_2 - y_2/y_1} = \frac{k_2(\epsilon_{K_1}/\epsilon_{K_2} - 1)}{1 - (y_2/y_1)(1/p)}. \tag{21.13}$$

An *open* competitive two-sector economy, trading at international prices determined in the world market, can only remain incompletely specialized (*diversified*, produce *both* goods, have a *common* positive, $\omega$), if the *range* of the *terms of trade*, $\mathbf{p} = \mathbf{P_1}/\mathbf{P_2}$, is confined to the zero-profit *price interval* with the *limits*, obtained from (21.13); cf. *Rybczynski lines*, Wong (1995),

$$k_1 > k_2: \quad \frac{y_2}{y_1} < p < \frac{y_2}{y_1}\frac{k_1}{k_2} = \frac{Y_2/K_2}{Y_1/K_1}, \tag{21.14}$$

$$k_2 > k_1: \quad \frac{y_2}{y_1}\frac{k_1}{k_2} < p < \frac{y_2}{y_1}. \tag{21.15}$$

When $(p)$ is given as a *fixed* number, we use—for factor endowments within the diversification *cone* $C_k$, (21.7)—the symbols: $\tilde{y}_i = f_i(\tilde{k}_i[\tilde{\omega}(p)])$, $i = 1, 2$, in (21.14)–(21.15), cf. Fig. 21.1.

*National income* (product), $Y$, is the monetary *value* of outputs from both sectors and represents aggregated factor incomes, cf. (21.8)–(21.9)

$$\begin{aligned} Y &= P_1 Y_1 + P_2 Y_2 = L(P_1 y_1 \lambda_1 + P_2 y_2 \lambda_2) \\ &= rK + wL = L(rk + w)\ v = L\, y(k). \end{aligned} \tag{21.16}$$

**Proposition 21.1 (Deardorff)** *With* ***given*** *prices* $(P_1, P_2)$ *and the monotonicity and concavity conditions (21.2)–(21.3), the per capita revenue (GNP) function,* $\mathbf{y(k)}$*, (21.16), is a concave* $C^1$*-class function on* $[0, \infty[$*, and* $y(k)$ *has a* ***linear segment*** *(flat) in the diversification* ***cone*** $C_k$ *(21.7), (21.14)–(21.15).*

***Proof*** The proposition is proved and geometrically illustrated as a *convex envelope* theorem in Deardorff (1971, p. 10) and Deardorff (1974, p. 297). □

The factor *income distribution* is defined by:

$$\delta_K = \frac{rK}{Y} = \frac{k}{\omega + k}, \quad \delta_L = \frac{wL}{Y} = \frac{\omega}{\omega + k}, \quad \delta_K + \delta_L = 1. \tag{21.17}$$

Let $\mathbf{Q_i}$, $i = 1, 2$, denote the quantitative size of the *domestic demand* (absorption level) for good 1 (investment) and good 2 (consumption), and they are respectively equal to domestic production, $\mathbf{Y_i}$, minus net exports, $\mathbf{X_i}$ i.e.,

$$Q_1 = Y_1 - X_1, \quad Q_2 = Y_2 - X_2. \tag{21.18}$$

The *trade balance* is assumed to satisfy the constraint:

$$P_1X_1 + P_2X_2 = 0, \quad \text{i.e.} \quad Y = P_1Q_1 + P_2Q_2, \tag{21.19}$$

i.e., trade *equilibrium* prevails with *no* foreign borrowing/lending allowed.

The *export* of goods by one *country A*, is *import* for another *country B* (the rest of world), i.e.,

$$X_{iA} = -X_{iB}, \qquad i = 1, 2. \tag{21.20}$$

Policy analyses based on open economy models, relaxing (21.19) with current account transmissions, have often just a single good, and in case of two goods, only one is traded, Obstfeld (1982), or nonspecialization in production is assumed, see Obstfeld (1989). A purely aggregative set-up in which every country produces the same, single good (and a rich country just producing more of it) can be useful in analyzing economies, interacting in a world of international trade, see Lucas (1993). Processes of factor accumulation, including growth of human capital, and international convergence issues are often in focus.

One of our main *objectives*, however, is to *merge* "old" and "new" *growth theory* with international *trade theory*. Accordingly, for our *dynamic analysis* below, with *diversification*, *specialization*, and *trade patterns* as *endogenous* issues, we need at least *two tradeable* goods. International trade in goods produced with labor or human capital as the sole factor of production is not considered, cf. Young (1991).

As to the division of *income* between *consumption* and *saving*, we shall first employ very simple aggregate *saving* functions, viz., *proportional* saving and *classical* saving that have been the standard polar opposites in much of both the growth and trade literature. Hence we alternatively use the *monetary saving* functions, cf. (21.16)–(21.17),

$$S = sY = P_1Q_1, \qquad 0 < s < 1, \tag{21.21}$$

$$S = s_K\delta_K Y = s_K rK = P_1Q_1, \qquad 0 < s_K \leq 1. \tag{21.22}$$

The *Ramsey* approach to consumer optimization over time (*optimal intertemporal saving*) has a prominent role in the literature on *two-sector optimal* growth models of *closed* economies, cf. Uzawa (1964), Srinivasan (1964), Cass (1965), Wan (1971), Drabicki and Takayama (1975), and in *open one-sector optimal* growth models with *financial* asset trading, see Becker and Foias (1987) and Obstfeld and Rogoff (1995). We shall employ *Ramsey saving* to a *small* two-sector economy *trading* in *both* goods.

*International trade* is the difference between domestic production and domestic demand. Combining (21.21), (21.19), and (21.16) gives the *export* monetary *value* of capital goods as:

$$P_1 X_1 = (1 - s)P_1 Y_1 - s P_2 Y_2. \tag{21.23}$$

Hence, *per capita export* ("excess supply") of *capital goods*, $\mathbf{X_1/L}$, positive or negative, may be written as, cf. (21.23), (21.8), and (21.6),

$$\begin{aligned} x_1 = X_1/L &= (1 - s)Y_1/L - s(P_2/P_1)Y_2/L \\ &= (1 - s)y_1\lambda_1 - (s/p)y_2\lambda_2 \\ &= \frac{1}{k_1 - k_2}\big[ - \{(s/p)y_2 k_1 + (1 - s)y_1 k_2\} \\ &\quad + \{(s/p)y_2 + (1 - s)y_1\}k\big], \end{aligned} \tag{21.24}$$

and per capita export of the *consumer good*, $\mathbf{x_2} = -\mathbf{p}\,\mathbf{x_1}$, positive or negative, cf. (21.19), (21.24).

Within the *diversification cone*, Fig. 21.1 summarizes diagrammatically the core of the *Heckscher-Ohlin model*, which "identifies a *mapping* from exogenously given factor supplies and exogenously given external product prices (determined in the international market place) into internal factor prices, output levels and consumption levels, the difference between the last two items being international trade", Leamer and Levinsohn (1995, p. 1345).

By using homogenous production functions of degree 1 and hence representing the factor supplies by the *capital-labor* ratio, **k**, this mapping and its various derivatives (theorems) are all represented by the shape of the respective curves *within* the diversification *cone* of Fig. 21.1. To obtain a coherent structural description of a small trading economy, *all* the *curves* in Fig. 21.1 are extended to *any* factor *endowments*, and they are shown for *two* values of, $\mathbf{p} = \mathbf{P_1/P_2}$.

Moreover, the curves. $\mathbf{Y_i/L}$, and, $\mathbf{x_i}$, $\mathbf{k} \in [0, \infty[$, in Fig. 21.1 will become *trajectories* related to the *state variable* **k(t)** of our *dynamic* systems of factor accumulation. It is evident that these trajectories are not closed curves. Accordingly, besides the determination of the *speed* (rapidity) of motion (growth), a dynamic analysis must address the issue of whether **k(t)** moves toward some *interior critical point* ("long-run equilibrium") within the *diversification* cone or towards the *endpoints* and then into regions with *complete specialization*. It is the possibilities of passing into or out of complete specialization that has always *complicated* the dynamic analysis of growing trading economies.

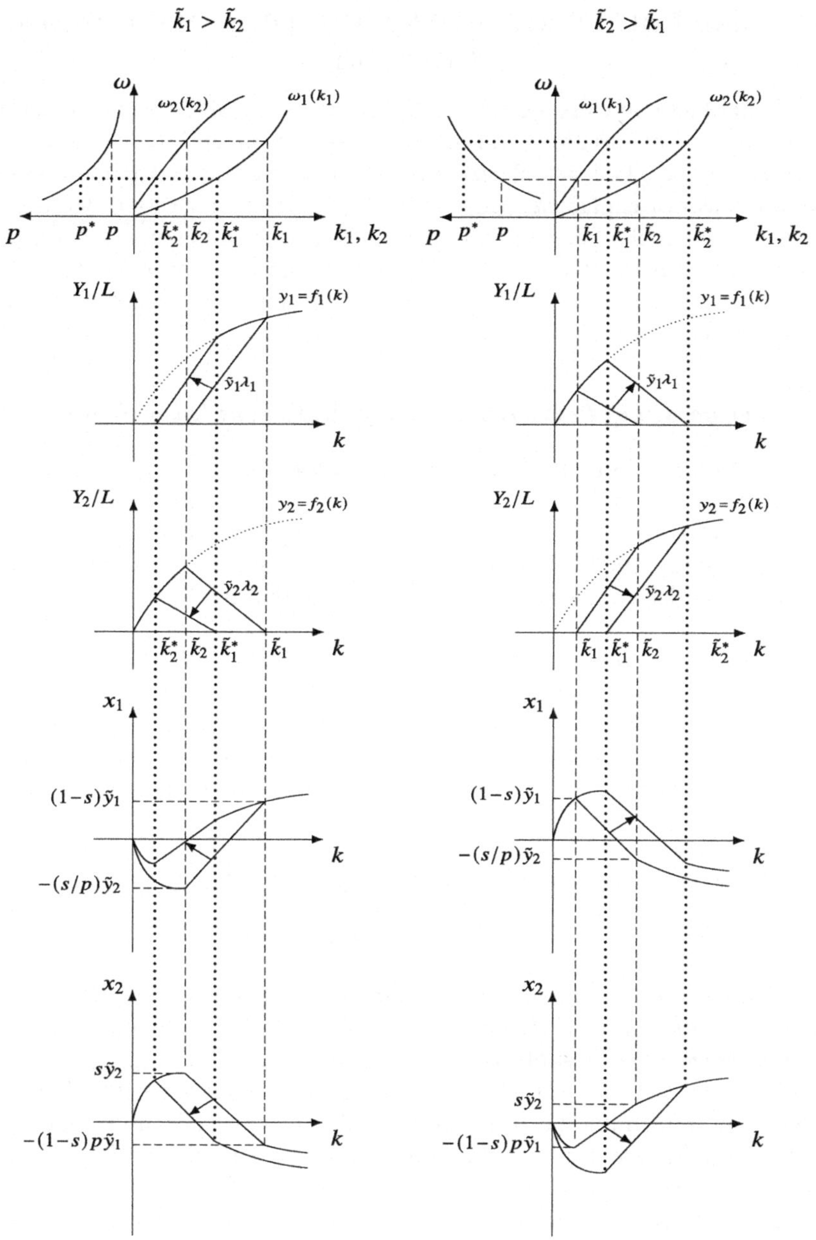


**Fig. 21.1** Wage-rental ratio, factor allocation, sector outputs, and trade patterns with proportional saving and given terms of trade

## General Equilibrium Dynamics of a Small Trading Country

The momentary (timeless) general equilibrium relationships between *exogenous* factor endowment variations and domestic production and trade patterns were described above. The actual size or evolution of the factor endowments, however, was not explained. Moreover, international trade itself will through time have feed-back effects upon the available factor endowments. For *endogenous* factor endowment variations, proper dynamic laws governing the process of factor accumulation are needed to supplement the momentary general equilibrium equations.

### *Dynamics by Proportional Saving, Exogenous Labor Growth*

*Dynamic Solutions, Stability, and Parameter Regions*

As to a dynamic model of a small trading economy, we must now perform a rigorous analysis of some specifications of factor accumulation. The domestic labor force of the small trading economy will by convention first be assumed to grow exponentially at an exogenous rate, $n > 0$, that is,

$$\dot{L} \equiv dL/dt = dL_1/dt + dL_2/dt = \dot{L}_1 + \dot{L}_2 = Ln \equiv L\,\mathfrak{f}(k). \qquad (21.25)$$

The domestic stock of capital goods increases by savings (investment demand). Depreciation of capital is ignored. Hence, with proportional *saving*, domestic *capital accumulation* (absorption) is described by the equation, cf. (21.21), (21.16):

$$\begin{aligned}\dot{K} \equiv dK/dt = Q_1 = s\,Y/P_1 = s\,[Y_1 + Y_2/p] = L\,(s/P_1)\,y \\ = L\,s\,[y_1\lambda_1 + (y_2/p)\lambda_2] \equiv L\,\mathfrak{g}(k). \qquad (21.26)\end{aligned}$$

Thus, with the *factor endowments*, $L$ and $K$, as *state variables*, the complete description of the *growth process* in the small *trading* economy is given by the *dynamic system*, (21.25)–(21.26).

This system (21.25)–(21.26) applies to growth processes with "fixed coefficient" sector technologies operating within the diversification cone (21.7) as well as to flexible sector technologies (21.1) operating with a domain of admissible endowment ratios, $k \in [0, \infty[$, cf. Fig. 21.1.

Within the *diversification* cone, we have, without loss of generality, that the dynamic system (21.25)–(21.26) of a small trading economy with proportional saving (and classical saving, cf. below) is always a *linear* system with *constant coefficients*: $\tilde{k}_1, \tilde{k}_2, \tilde{y}_1 = f_1(\tilde{k}_1), \tilde{y}_2 = f_2(\tilde{k}_2)$, cf. Fig. 21.1.

With complete *specialization*, the *nonlinear* system (21.25)–(21.26) with *flexible* neoclassical technology represents a simple *extension* of the standard nonlinear *Solow* model to a *small* trading economy.

The *differential equations* (21.25)–(21.26), linear or nonlinear, represent a *homogenous dynamic* system of *degree* 1. Such systems on $\mathbf{R}^2$ for any degree $m \in \mathbf{R}$ were studied in Jensen (1994); brought here in Chap. 28, upon which we shall draw below.

A seminal study of homogenous dynamics in $\mathbf{R}^n$ is Solow and Samuelson (1953).

Of course, the linearity of (21.25)–(21.26) within the diversification cone allows general closed form (quantitative) solutions. However, the main *economic issues* raised by (21.25)–(21.26) are *qualitative*, such as a partition of the *parameter space* (system parameters) into *regions* with roughly *similar* stability properties (structurally stable) of the family of solutions, cf. Gandolfo (1996, p. 338), Jensen (1994, p. 237); here Sect. "Structural Stability and Bifurcations".

A natural and useful tool in analyzing *homogenous* dynamics is a function, **h(k)**, called *director function* in Jensen (1994, p. 195); here Chap. 28. Sect. "Global Asymptotic Ratio Stability", pertaining to the *time derivative* of the *ratio* of the state variables.

In case of (21.25)–(21.26), it is easily seen that,

$$\begin{aligned} \dot{k} &= h(k) \equiv \mathfrak{g}(k) - k\,\mathfrak{f}(k) = (s/P_1)y - nk \\ &= s[y_1\lambda_1 + (y_2/p)\lambda_2] - nk, \qquad k \in [0, \infty[. \end{aligned} \tag{21.27}$$

**Lemma 21.1** *The director function, $h(k)$, (21.27), is of $C^1$-class on $[0, \infty[$, irrespective of $k_1 \gtrless k_2$ and diversification $(0 < \lambda_i < 1)$ or specialization $(\lambda_i = 0$ or $\lambda_i = 1)$; $h(k)$ is concave under the condition (21.2), and has a linear segment (flat) within $C_k$ (21.7), (21.14)–(21.15), as depicted in Fig. 21.2.*

***Proof*** The Lemma follows from Proposition 21.1. The $C^1$-class property and concavity of $y(k)$, $\mathfrak{g}(k)$, (21.27), and linearity of $nk$ establish the Lemma. □

As to the *parameter regions* of (21.27) and the long-term possibilities of diversification, we state:

**Theorem 21.1** *For a small, competitive, trading economy, facing given terms of trade p, within the limits of (21.14)–(21.15), with proportional saving and exogenous labor growth, the necessary and sufficient conditions for the existence of a long-run factor endowment ratio (capital-labor ratio),* **k** $= \kappa$, *with* ***incomplete*** *specialization (diversification), are given by the parameter conditions, see Fig. 21.2e and f:*

$$k_1 > k_2: \quad \frac{\tilde{Y}_1}{\tilde{K}_1} = \frac{\tilde{y}_1}{\tilde{k}_1} < \frac{n}{s} < \frac{\tilde{y}_2/p}{\tilde{k}_2} = \frac{\tilde{\epsilon}_{K_1}}{\tilde{\epsilon}_{K_2}}\frac{\tilde{Y}_1}{K_1}, \tag{21.28}$$

$$k_2 > k_1: \quad \frac{\tilde{y}_2/p}{\tilde{k}_2} < \frac{n}{s} < \frac{\tilde{y}_1}{\tilde{k}_1}. \tag{21.29}$$

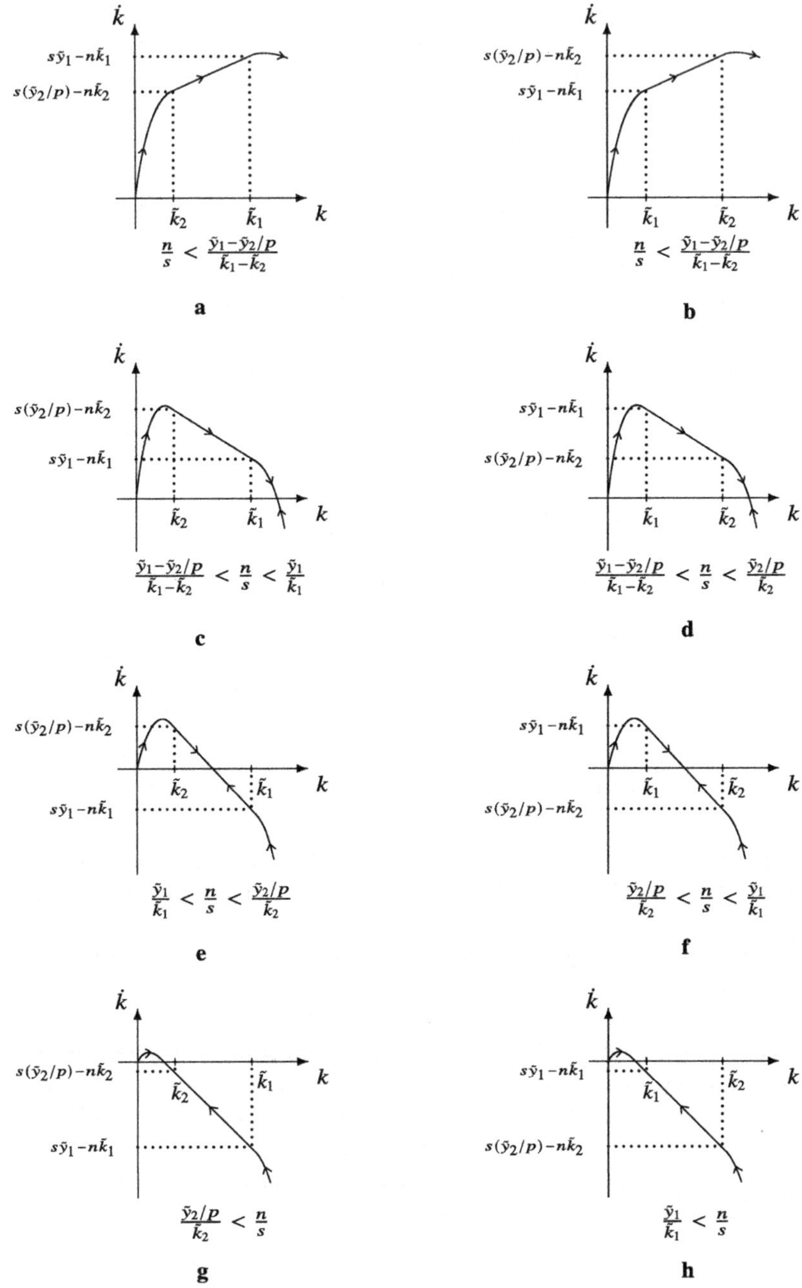


**Fig. 21.2** The director function, $\mathbf{h}(\mathbf{k})$, (21.27), with proportional saving and alternative parameter intervals for $\mathbf{n}/\mathbf{s}$. (**a**) $\tilde{k}_1 > \tilde{k}_2$. (**b**) $\tilde{k}_2 > \tilde{k}_1$. (**c**) $\tilde{k}_1 > \tilde{k}_2$. (**d**) $\tilde{k}_2 > \tilde{k}_1$. (**e**) $\tilde{k}_1 > \tilde{k}_2$. (**f**) $\tilde{k}_2 > \tilde{k}_1$. (**g**) $\tilde{k}_1 > \tilde{k}_2$. (**h**) $\tilde{k}_2 > \tilde{k}_1$

*When the **existence** conditions (21.28) and (21.29) are satisfied, then the family of solutions for $k(t)$ to (21.27) have **asymptotic** stability in the diversification cone, $C_k$ (21.7), (21.14)–(21.15), i.e.,*

$$\exists k_0 = \kappa \in C_k \quad : \quad k(t) = \kappa, \quad \forall t, \tag{21.30}$$

$$\forall k_0 \in C_k \setminus \{\kappa\} : \quad k(t) \to \kappa \ as\, t \to \infty. \tag{21.31}$$

*Hence, for a small trading economy with an **initial diversified** state, the unique diversified steady state, $\kappa$, is an **attractor** in $\mathbf{C_k}$, irrespective of the sector capital intensities: $k_1 \gtrless k_2$.*

*Furthermore, the unique steady state, $\mathbf{k} = \kappa$, obtained under diversification conditions (21.28)–(21.29) is a **global attractor** for any initial capital-labor ratio,*

$$\forall k_0 \in \mathbf{R} \setminus \{\kappa\} : \quad k(t) \to \kappa \ as\, t \to \infty. \tag{21.32}$$

*Thus, for any initial specialization, the small trading economy will, with the parameters (21.28)–(21.29) in the long run combine trade with competitive domestic production of both goods.*

*The long-run (steady-state) capital-labor ratio, $\mathbf{k} = \kappa$, of the diversified economy in Fig. 21.2e and f, is given by:*

$$\kappa = \frac{\tilde{k}_2\,(p - \frac{\tilde{y}_2}{\tilde{y}_1}\frac{\tilde{k}_1}{\tilde{k}_2})}{p - \tilde{y}_2/\tilde{y}_1 - (np/s)(\tilde{k}_1 - \tilde{k}_2)/\tilde{y}_1}$$
$$= \frac{\tilde{k}_2\,(1 - \tilde{\epsilon}_{\kappa_2}/\tilde{\epsilon}_{\kappa_1})}{1 - (\tilde{\epsilon}_{\kappa_2}\tilde{k}_2/\tilde{\epsilon}_{\kappa_1}\tilde{k}_1) - (n/s)(\tilde{k}_1 - \tilde{k}_2)/\tilde{y}_1}. \tag{21.33}$$

*A **specialized** steady state, $\mathbf{k} = \kappa$, is given by either, $f_1(\kappa)/\kappa = n/s$ or, $f_2(\kappa)/\kappa = np/s$. The steady state—diversified or specialized—proportional **growth rate** is: $\mathfrak{f}(\kappa) = \mathfrak{g}(\kappa)/\kappa = \mathbf{n}$.*

***Proof*** The procedure of proving (21.28)–(21.29) is the same, whence we only give case: $k_1 > k_2$.

With *diversification*, the director function $\mathbf{h}(\mathbf{k})$, (21.27), becomes, cf. (21.6), (21.14)

$$\dot{k} = h(k) = \frac{s}{\tilde{k}_1 - \tilde{k}_2}\left[(\tilde{y}_2/p)\tilde{k}_1 - \tilde{y}_1\tilde{k}_2\right] + s\left[\frac{(\tilde{y}_1 - \tilde{y}_2/p)}{\tilde{k}_1 - \tilde{k}_2} - \frac{n}{s}\right]k. \tag{21.34}$$

From the diversification restriction (21.14), we get two inequalities

$$(i) \quad \tilde{y}_1 - \tilde{y}_2/p > 0, \qquad (ii) \quad (\tilde{y}_2/p)\tilde{k}_1 - \tilde{y}_1\tilde{k}_2 > 0. \tag{21.35}$$

By $k_1 > k_2$ and $(ii)$, (21.35), it is immediately seen that the *intercept* of the line (21.34) is always *positive*. The *slope* of (21.34) is clearly *positive*, when the *parameters* satisfy the *inequality*, stated in Fig. 21.2a. When the latter inequality is not satisfied, the *slope* of (21.34) is *negative*.

With *negative* slope and *positive* intercept, the line (21.34) either *crosses* the $k$-axis *in* the diversification *interval* or cuts the $k$-axis *beyond* the diversification interval.

Incidently, note that the successive *parameter intervals* for **n/s** (top to down) in Fig. 21.2 are associated with *increasing* values of $n/s$, i.e., *larger* $n$ and/or *smaller* $s$.

To determine the *location* of the *line*, (21.34), we may calculate $h(k)$ at the specialization points

$$k = \tilde{k}_1 : \quad h(k) = s\tilde{y}_1 - n\tilde{k}_1, \tag{21.36}$$

$$k = \tilde{k}_2 : \quad h(k) = s(\tilde{y}_2/p) - n\tilde{k}_2. \tag{21.37}$$

The *value* of $h(k)$, (21.36), is *positive*, when $(n/s) < \tilde{y}_1/\tilde{k}_1$, which is depicted in Fig. 21.2c. The *value* of $h(k)$, (21.37), is *negative* when $(n/s) > (\tilde{y}_2/p)/\tilde{k}_2$, which is depicted in Fig. 21.2g.

By (21.35), it can be seen that $\frac{\tilde{y}_1 - \tilde{y}_2/p}{\tilde{k}_1 - \tilde{k}_2} < \frac{\tilde{y}_1}{\tilde{k}_1} < \frac{\tilde{y}_2/p}{\tilde{k}_2}$. Hence—with the value of $h(k)$, (21.36), *negative* and the value of $h(k)$, (21.37), *positive*—the line $h(k)$, (21.34), evidently passes through the diversification interval with the parameter restriction depicted in Fig. 21.2e. This establishes (21.28). Using (21.9), (21.11), we also have: $(Y_2\tilde{/}p)/\tilde{k}_2 = (Y_2\tilde{/}K_2)(P_2\tilde{/}P_1) = (Y_2P_2\tilde{/}rK_2)(r\tilde{/}P_1) = (Y_1\tilde{/}K_1)(\tilde{\epsilon}_{K_1}/\tilde{\epsilon}_{K_2})$.

The director function $h(k)$ on $k \in [0, \infty[$ and the respective parameter restrictions (belonging to the diversification interval) are shown in Fig. 21.2—with Fig. 21.2f, illustrating the *restriction*, (21.29).

The proof of (21.30)–(21.31) follows immediately from the *phase diagram*, Fig. 21.2e and f.

To prove (21.32), we first note that $h(k)$ with *specialization* and flexible technologies have the nonlinear forms, cf. (21.36)–(21.37)

$$h(k_1) = sf_1(k_1) - nk_1, \tag{21.38}$$

$$h(k_2) = (s/p)f_2(k_2) - nk_2. \tag{21.39}$$

With $n/s > f_1(k_1)/k_1$, it is seen that $\mathbf{h(k_1)}$, (21.38), is always negative for $k_1 > \tilde{k}_1$ as illustrated in Fig. 21.2e. This case is alternatively illustrated with solid lines in the traditional diagram, $k_1 > \kappa$, Fig. 21.3a below; see Wan (1971). Hence, an initial specialization in good 1 will eventually terminate, when the relative factor endowments attain the *upper endpoint* $\tilde{k}_1$ of the diversification interval in Fig. 21.2e.

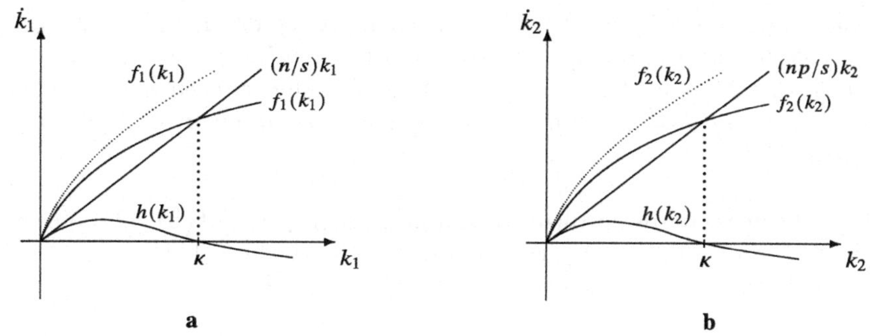


**Fig. 21.3** Phase diagrams and alternative shapes of $\mathbf{f_i(k_i)}$

With $n/s < (f_2(k_2)/p)/k_2$, it is seen that $\mathbf{h(k_2)}$, (21.39), is positive for small values of $k_2$, as illustrated in Fig. 21.2e. This case is alternatively illustrated with solid lines in Fig. 21.3b. As (21.39) coincides with (21.37) at the *lower endpoint* $\tilde{k}_2$ of the diversification interval, an initial specialization in good 2 eventually terminates as well.

The long-run diversified capital-labor *ratio*, $\kappa$, (21.33), is immediately obtained as the *root* of $h(k)$, (21.34), and a specialized $\kappa$ follows from (21.27) with either $\lambda_i = 0$.

The *expression* $\mathfrak{f}(\kappa) = \mathfrak{g}(\kappa)/\kappa$, $\kappa \neq 0$ for the proportional *growth rate* in steady state follows from (21.25) and $h(\kappa) = 0$, (21.27). □

**Remark 21.1** In a *closed* economy, the *Rybczynski theorem* and $k_2 > k_1$ imply that a high $k$—and hence a large production of the consumer good—will subsequently *reduce* the high momentary capital-labor *ratio*. This is *not* necessarily the case in a *trading economy*, as the large production of consumer goods implies a high export of consumer goods, which in turn, by the balance of trade equilibrium then implies a large import of capital goods—and hence the *high* momentary domestic capital-labor *ratio* may in fact further increase. Accordingly, in Fig. 21.2, $k_2 > k_1$ does **not** anywhere appear as a *sufficient stability* condition for a steady state. ▽

**Remark 21.2** Note, as stated in Theorem 21.1, that all the *inequalities* for $\mathbf{n/s}$ in Fig. 21.2 assume the *given prices* (terms of trade) to belong to the *zero-profit* price intervals (21.14)–(21.15). If $\mathbf{p}$ did it not belong to these intervals, we would *never* even temporarily and hence neither in the long-run (steady-state) experience *diversification*. Figure 21.2 would *neither* contain any *line segments*, and complete specialization will prevail for any factor endowment ratio, $k$. ▽

**Corollary 21.1** *When the parametric restrictions (21.28)–(21.29) of the dynamic system (21.25)–(21.26) are* **not** *satisfied, the small competitive trading* *economy will eventually be* specialized *in the* most capital intensive *good, except when both the saving rate, s, is very small, and the labor growth rate, n, is very high, cf. Fig. 21.2g and h. A* specialized steady state *will not always exist, in Fig. 21.2a–c and b–d. As to the cases of specialized non-steady-state growth, see Theorem 21.2.*

***Proof*** The proof of the corollary is analogous to the proof of (21.32) combined with the parameter regions given in Fig. 21.2a–c and b–d. The shape of $f_i(k_i)$ will decide the existence of a steady state, cf. Fig. 21.3. □

For given terms of trade, $p$ and labor growth $n$, it is evidently, besides *technology* conditions, the *domestic demand* composition, $s$, that is of decisive importance for the character of any steady state of the trading economy. Clearly, large domestic demand for capital goods relative to consumer goods will in the long run prevent competitive domestic production of both goods, cf. Corollary 21.1. *Only* if the domestic demand for capital goods (**s**), is properly restrained to the respective *intervals* (21.28)–(21.29), will *trade* be *compatible* with a *diversified steady state* of a small, growing, fully employed, *competitive* economy.

The possibilities for satisfying the diversification *criterion* (21.28)–(21.29) are directly *observable* in a small *currently diversified* competitive economy. Irrespective of the specification of the sectorial production functions, the average *productivity* of *capital* in the *capital good sector* ($Y_1/K_1$), (or capital-output ratio, $K_1/Y_1$, measured in the same units) and the *cost* shares, $\tilde{\epsilon}_{K_i}$, are *observable* in the *diversification interval* of Fig. 21.2, where, cf. Fig. 21.1, the *allocation ratios* ($\lambda_i$), output *mix* ($Y_1/Y_2$), income *distribution* ($\delta_K$), and *trade pattern* are continuously changing with $\mathbf{k(t)}$, but *sectoral* factor combinations ($\tilde{k}_i$) and cost shares ($\tilde{\epsilon}_{K_i}$) remain *time-invariant*.

Regarding the actual values of the *parameters* in (21.28), the country tables in Obstfeld and Rogoff (1995), Summers and Heston (1991), and Simon (1990) show the *range* of **s** (fraction of GNP) roughly as:

$$\begin{array}{ccc} 1885\text{-}1913 & 1921\text{-}1939 & 1973\text{-}1991 \\ 0.1 \le s \le 0.2 & 0.15 \le s \le 0.2 & 0.15 \le s \le 0.3 \end{array} \tag{21.40}$$

The parameter **n** ("natural rate of proliferation"), the capital-output ratio ($K_1/Y_1$) and cost shares, $\epsilon_{K_i}$, roughly, have the *range*:

$$0.005 \le n \le 0.3,\ 2 \le K_1/Y_1 \le 6,\ 0.25 \le \epsilon_{K_i} \le 0.8. \tag{21.41}$$

If we choose $K_1/Y_1 = 5$, then very *high* values of $n$ and *low* values of $s$ ($n/s = 0.02/0.1 = 0.2$) are needed to have $(n/s) > Y_1/K_1 = 0.2$. With a lower $K_1/Y_1 = 4$, it is evidently more *difficult* to satisfy $(n/s) > Y_1/K_1$, cf. (21.28). Although the latter may be met by, e.g., ($n = 0.028$, $s = 0.13$, $K_1/Y_1 = 5$), the actual parametric possibilities of **n/s** complying with the lower end point of the diversification *condition* (21.28) are very limited, especially in the later periods, cf. (21.40).

But when the *consumer* good sector is more *capital intensive*, it is evident that the *criterion* (21.29) is *easier* to satisfy within the range of the parameters in (21.40)–(21.41), especially in case of large differences between $\tilde{k}_1$ and $\tilde{k}_2$, hence between $\tilde{\epsilon}_{K_2}$ and $\tilde{\epsilon}_{K_1}$. If we still keep $K_1/Y_1 = 5$, then $n = 0.02, s = 0.12$ together with $\epsilon_{K_1} = 0.28$, $\epsilon_{K_2} = 0.35$ will satisfy (21.29). Furthermore, if modern agriculture with $\epsilon_K \geq 0.85$ is seen as the consumer good sector, then, e.g., the parameters: $K_1/Y_1 = 4$, $\epsilon_{K_1} = 0.3$, $\epsilon_{K_2} = 0.8$, and $n/s = 0.1 (= 0.02/0.2 = 0.015/0.15$, etc.) will comply with (21.29).

Thus, although not necessary, the *ranking* $\tilde{k}_2 > \tilde{k}_1$ is more *conducive* to *diversification*. Parametrically, the *scope* of Fig. 21.2f is *empirically* somewhat *larger* than Fig. 21.2e.

*Specialization and Rapidity of Endogenous Growth*

The *dynamic* implications of the *nonexistence* of a *steady-state* solution to the neoclassical *one-sector* growth model of a *closed* economy, which formally looks *similar* to the *specialized trading economy* with $\dot{k}_i = h(k_i)$, (21.38)–(21.39), were studied in Jensen and Larsen (1987); here Chap. 1. We will here briefly discuss the dynamics of a trading economy, *specialized* in the *consumer good* and hence *importing* all its *capital goods*, i.e., cf. (21.39)

$$\dot{k}_2 = h(k_2) = (s/p)f_2(k_2) - nk_2, \quad k_2 = k > \tilde{k}_2. \tag{21.42}$$

The character of the solutions to (21.42)—when no root (steady state) exists, cf. *Fig. 21.2b*—depends on the shape of $h(k_2)$ and essentially $f_2(k_2)$. We may summarize the *endogeneity* conditions and the *rapidity* of per *capita* income *growth* as follows.

**Theorem 21.2** *With constant returns to scale, (21.1), and exogenous labor growth, (21.25), a necessary condition for the endogenous growth of per capita income in a small* ***specialized*** *trading economy is that labor is inessential in production, i.e., cf. (21.1)*

$$\forall K_2 : \quad F_2(0, K_2) > 0. \tag{21.43}$$

*Under the condition (21.43) and the following alternative assumptions*

$$f_2(k_2) - (np/s)k_2 \ \rightarrow \ \varepsilon \geq 0 \ as \, k_2 \rightarrow \infty, \tag{21.44}$$

$$f_2'(k_2) \ \rightarrow \ \underline{\beta} = (np/s) \ as \, k_2 \rightarrow \infty, \tag{21.45}$$

$$f_2'(k_2) \ \rightarrow \ \underline{\beta} > (np/s) \ as \, k_2 \rightarrow \infty, \tag{21.46}$$

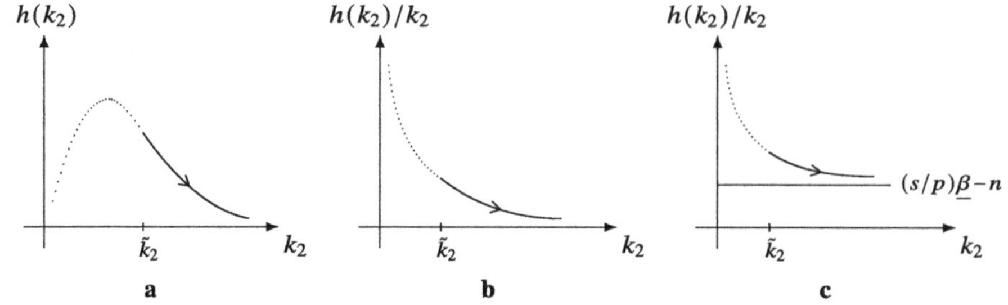


**Fig. 21.4** Rapidity of endogenous growth of per capita income. Bounded, polynomial, and exponential growth

*the capital-labor ratio* $k_2(t)$ *and per capita income,* $y_2(t)$ *will in the long run have time paths with the property of unbounded, linear, polynomial, exponential growth, respectively. With (21.44)–(21.46) as giving alternative shapes for* $f_2(k_2)$*, Fig. 21.3, corresponding properties of* $h(k_2)$*, (21.42), are shown in Fig. 21.4.*

***Proof*** The first part of the proof is given in Appendix A, section "Appendix A: Endogenous Growth and Inessential Labor". Using Fig. 21.3 above, we note that $f_2(k_2)$ by, respectively, (21.44)–(21.46), has the line $(np/s)k_2$ as asymptote, or eventually becomes "parallel" to, or always remains steeper than $(np/s)k_2$. The consequences of (21.44)–(21.46) for the rapidity of growth were proved in Jensen and Larsen (1987); here Chap. 1. It follows from $k_2(t)$ going to infinity and l'Hospital that *per capita income*, $y_2(t) = f_2[k_2(t)]$, grows, in the long-run, with the same rapidity as the *capital-labor ratio*, $k_2(t)$. □

The case of Fig. 21.4c with exponential growth is customarily referred to as *endogenous growth*, Barro and Sala-i-Martin (2004). See Romer (1986, 1994); Lucas (1988); Jones and Manuelli (1990); Rebelo (1991); Yang and Borland (1991). However, unbounded, linear or a polynomial increases of *per capita* income are relevant as growth prospects, too.

We want to emphasize that the production function, $F(L_2, K_2)$ must have the property: $\forall K_2: \quad F(0, K_2) > 0$, i.e., *labor* is *inessential.* Whether capital is inessential or not, $\forall L_2: \quad F(L_2, 0) \geq 0$, is immaterial for the endogenous growth properties in *Fig. 21.4.* When both capital and labor are inessential, the CES production function with substitution elasticity larger than 1 may give endogenous growth of per capita income, cf. Pitchford (1960) and Long and Wong (1997).

The general intensive form of the CES functions is, cf. (21.1)

$$y_i = f_i(k_i) = \gamma_i \left[(1 - a_i) + a_i k^{\frac{\sigma_i - 1}{\sigma_i}}\right]^{\frac{\sigma_i}{\sigma_i - 1}},$$

$$\gamma_i > 0, \qquad 0 < a_i < 1, \qquad 0 < \sigma_i < \infty. \tag{21.47}$$

**Corollary 21.2** *For a CES production function with a substitution elasticity,* $\sigma_2 \leq 1$*—or* $\sigma_2 > 1$ *and* $\gamma_2 a_i^{\frac{\sigma_2}{\sigma_2-1}} < np/s$*—the solutions,* $k_2(t)$ *to (21.42) cannot exhibit any endogenous (persistent) growth. The specialized steady-state capital-labor ratio is,*

$$\kappa = \left[ (1-a_2)^{-1} \left[ \left( \frac{\gamma_2\, s}{n\, p} \right)^{\frac{1-\sigma_2}{\sigma_2}} - a_2 \right] \right]^{\frac{\sigma_2}{1-\sigma_2}}. \tag{21.48}$$

*With* $\sigma_2 > 1$*, the solutions,* $k_2(t)$*, to (21.42) exhibit endogenous (persistent) per capita growth as follows,*

$$\textit{polynomial: } \gamma_2 a_2^{\frac{\sigma_2}{\sigma_2-1}} = np/s, \quad \textit{exponential: } \gamma_2 a_2^{\frac{\sigma_2}{\sigma_2-1}} > np/s. \tag{21.49}$$

***Proof*** From (21.47), we have

$$f_i'(k_i) = a_i \gamma_i \left[ a_i + (1-a_i) k_i^{\frac{1-\sigma_i}{\sigma_i}} \right]^{\frac{1}{\sigma_i-1}}. \tag{21.50}$$

Hence, by (21.47) and (21.50), we obtain the limits

$$\sigma_i < 1: \quad \lim_{k\to\infty} f_i(k) = \gamma_i \left[1-a_i\right]^{\frac{\sigma_i}{\sigma_i-1}}, \quad \lim_{k\to\infty} f_i'(k) = \underline{\beta} = 0, \tag{21.51}$$

$$\sigma_i > 1: \quad \lim_{k\to\infty} f_i(k) \approx \gamma_i a_i^{\frac{\sigma_i}{\sigma_i-1}} k, \quad \lim_{k\to\infty} f_i'(k) = \underline{\beta} = \gamma_i a_i^{\frac{\sigma_i}{\sigma_i-1}}. \tag{21.52}$$

With (21.51), or $\sigma_2 > 1$ and $\gamma_2 a_2^{\frac{\sigma_2}{\sigma_2-1}} < np/s$, a *root* (21.48) *exists* to (21.42), preventing endogenous (persistent) growth. The endogenous growth with rapidity (21.49) follows from (21.52), (21.45)–(21.46), Fig. 21.4, and $k = k_2$. □

With the CES function, the cases (21.44) are excluded, where linear growth is requiring $0 < \varepsilon \leq \lim_{k\to\infty} h(k) < \infty$. Either endogenous growth does not occur, or its *rapidity* will be at least polynomial.

*Polynomial* growth occurs with, e.g. $\gamma_2 = 1$, $a_2 = 0.3$, $\sigma_2 = 1.7$, $n = 0.01$, $p = 1$, $s = 0.186$, and hence *exponential* growth occurs with, e.g., $s = 0.2$. Accordingly, rather high substitution elasticities are generally required together with $0.2 < a_2 < 0.35$ and (21.40). The "total factor productivity" parameter, $\gamma_2$, and terms of trade ($\mathbf{p}$) may have ameliorating roles, cf. (21.49).

Regardless of the actual capital-intensive good of specialization and hence trade pattern, *persistent* growth of *per capita* national income of the trading economy occurs with a *high saving* rate $s$, *low* $n$, and a *low* $p = P_1/P_2$ (relatively *cheap capital* goods), which create the long-run opportunities for the necessary *specialization* and *rapid accumulation* of capital goods, cf. Fig. 21.2 and (21.26)–(21.27), and facilitate the *technology* (CES) to meet the *parametric conditions* (21.49).

Competitive factor pricing, (21.45)–(21.46), and $\mathbf{k(t)}$ approaching infinity imply that capital's (labor's) *share*, (21.9)–(21.10), converges to 1 (0):

$$\lim_{k_i\to\infty} \epsilon_{K_i} = \lim_{k_i\to\infty} \frac{k_i f_i'(k_i)}{f_i(k_i)} = \underline{\beta} \lim_{k_i\to\infty} \frac{k_i}{f_i(k_i)} = \underline{\beta}\,(1/\underline{\beta}) = 1. \tag{21.53}$$

Despite (21.53), the *real wage* exhibits *persistent* growth. With CES, (21.47), the wage-rental ratio, (21.10), is, $w/r = \omega = [(1 - a_i)/a_i]k_i^{1/\sigma_i}$. Hence, the latter, (21.42), (21.46), and (21.52) give, cf. Fig. 21.4c,

$$\lim_{t\to\infty} \frac{\dot{w}}{w(t)} = \frac{1}{\sigma_2} \lim_{t\to\infty} \frac{\dot{k}_2}{k_2(t)} = \frac{1}{\sigma_2}[\,(s/p)\,\underline{\beta} - n\,]. \tag{21.54}$$

The capital stock $\mathbf{K(t)}$ grows at the exponential rate $(s/p)\,\underline{\beta}$, which is *higher* than the combined exponential rates of the labor force $\mathbf{L(t)}$, and of the wage rate $\mathbf{w(t)}$. This explains the *limits* (21.53) of the factor shares.

### *Dynamics by Proportional Saving, Endogenous Labor Growth*

Any mathematical growth model is inevitably based on some fundamental set of assumptions, and the most critical ones should be fully elucidated. In this section, we therefore replace the assumption of *exogenous* labor growth by an *endogeneity* assumption. For economic growth, as observed over two centuries, the inclusion of increases in both population and per capita product is indispensable, Kuznets (1966, p. 20). As seen below, *persistent* per *capita* growth essentially *requires* that the *classical* (Malthusian) law of *population* (labor) growth is *terminated.*

For a small country with *fixed* terms of trade, and hence a fixed *real wage*, the latter cannot within the diversification cone endogenize the labor growth as in the *classical canonical* model of *closed* economies, cf. Niehans (1963), Samuelson (1978), Jensen (1994); here Chaps. 7–9 and 28. In this section, we modify our former analysis by allowing the *growth* rate of the *labor* force to depend in a "*semi-classical*" way on *living standards* [ consumption per capita, $c = Q_2/L$, cf. (21.18)–(21.19), (21.21), (21.16) ], i.e.[1]

$$\dot{L}/L = n\,c = n\,Q_2/L, \tag{21.55}$$

$$\begin{aligned}\dot{L} = n\,Q_2 &= n\,(1-s)\,Y/P_2 = L\,n\,[\,(1-s)/P_2\,]\,y \\ &= L\,n\,(1-s)\,(\,p\,y_1\,\lambda_1 + y_2\lambda_2\,) \equiv L\,\mathrm{f}(k).\end{aligned} \tag{21.56}$$

[1] The *parameter* $n$, (21.55), (21.56) is inherently and numerically *different* from the natural growth rate, $n$, (21.25), (21.41).

The *governing* function of capital accumulation remains the same as (21.26)

$$\dot{K} = s\,(Y/P_1) = L\,(s/P_1)\,y = L\,s\,(y_1\lambda_1 + (y_2/p)\lambda_2) \equiv L\,\mathfrak{g}(k). \qquad (21.57)$$

Hence, the *director* function $h(k)$ becomes

$$\begin{aligned}\dot{k} = h(k) &\equiv \mathfrak{g}(k) - k\,\mathfrak{f}(k) = (s/P_1)\,y - [n(1-s)/P_2]\,y\,k \\ &= [y_1\lambda_1 + (y_2/p)\lambda_2][s - np(1-s)k], \qquad k \in [0,\ \infty[. \qquad (21.58)\end{aligned}$$

**Theorem 21.3** *For a small, competitive, trading economy with proportional saving and endogenous ("semi-classical") labor growth, the necessary and sufficient conditions for the existence of a long-run capital-labor ratio,* $k = \kappa$, *with incomplete specialization are given by the parameter restrictions, see Fig. 21.5b:*

$$\tilde{k}_1 > \tilde{k}_2: \quad \frac{np\tilde{k}_1}{1+np\tilde{k}_1} < s < \frac{np\tilde{k}_2}{1+np\tilde{k}_2}, \qquad (21.59)$$

$$\tilde{k}_2 > \tilde{k}_1: \quad \frac{np\tilde{k}_2}{1+np\tilde{k}_2} < s < \frac{np\tilde{k}_1}{1+np\tilde{k}_1}. \qquad (21.60)$$

*When the existence conditions, (21.59)–(21.60), are satisfied, then the family of solutions for* $k(t)$ *to (21.58) have asymptotic stability in the diversification cone,* $C_k$ *(21.7), (21.14)–(21.15), i.e.,*

$$\exists k_0 = \kappa \in C_k \;:\; k(t) = \kappa,\ \forall t, \qquad (21.61)$$

$$\forall k_0 \in C_k \setminus \{\kappa\}: \; k(t) \to \kappa \text{ as } t \to \infty. \qquad (21.62)$$

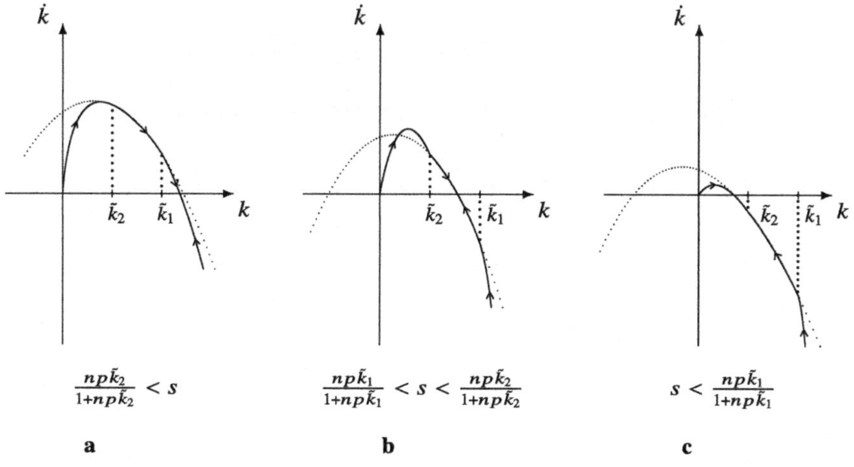


**Fig. 21.5** The director function, **h(k)**, (21.58), with parameter intervals for s

*Hence, for small trading economies with an initial diversified state, the unique diversified steady state, $\kappa$, is an attractor in $C_k$, irrespective of the sector capital intensities, $k_1 \gtrless k_2$.*

*Furthermore, the unique steady state, $\kappa$, obtained under the conditions (21.59)–(21.60) is a global attractor for any initial capital-labor ratio, i.e.*

$$\forall k_0 \in \mathbf{R} \setminus \{\kappa\} : \quad k(t) \rightarrow \kappa \text{ as } t \rightarrow \infty. \tag{21.63}$$

*Thus, for any initial specialization of the small trading economy, it will with the parameters (21.59)–(21.60), in the long run combine trade with competitive domestic production of both goods.*

*The long-run capital-labor ratio, $\mathbf{k} = \kappa$, of the diversified –, and specialized economy is,*

$$\kappa = \frac{s}{n\, p\, (1 - s)} \tag{21.64}$$

*The proportional growth rate in a diversified steady state is,*

$$\mathfrak{f}(\kappa) = \mathfrak{g}(\kappa)/\kappa = [\, n(1 - s)/P_2\,][\, \tilde{r}\kappa + \tilde{w}\,] = (s/P_1)(\tilde{r} + \tilde{w}/\kappa) \tag{21.65}$$

$$= n\,(1 - s)\, p\, \tilde{y}_1\, [\, \tilde{\epsilon}_{L_1} + \tilde{\epsilon}_{K_1}/\tilde{k}_1\,]$$

$$= \tilde{y}_2\, [\, n\,(1 - s)\, \tilde{\epsilon}_{L_2} + (s/p)(\tilde{\epsilon}_{K_2}/\tilde{k}_2)\,] \tag{21.66}$$

*The specialized steady-state growth rate is given by (21.66), without tilde, evaluated at $\kappa$, (21.64). The trajectories of the* ***phase portrait*** *of (21.56)–(21.57) are* ***straights lines*** *everywhere, parallel to the* ***ray*** *with the slope (21.64).*

***Proof*** The procedure of proving (21.59)–(21.60) is the same, whence we only give: Case $k_1 > k_2$, see Fig. 21.5.

Again, the diversification restrictions are, cf. (21.35)

$$(i) \quad \tilde{y}_1 - (\tilde{y}_2/p) > 0, \qquad (ii) \quad (\tilde{y}_2/p)\tilde{k}_1 - \tilde{y}_1\tilde{k}_2 > 0. \tag{21.67}$$

With *diversification*, the director function (21.58) becomes, cf. (21.6),

$$\begin{aligned} \dot{k} = h(k) \;=\; & \frac{1}{\tilde{k}_1 - \tilde{k}_2} \big\{ -np(1 - s)(\tilde{y}_1 - \tilde{y}_2/p)\, k^2 \\ & - \big[ s\,(\tilde{y}_2/p - \tilde{y}_1) + np(1 - s)((\tilde{y}_2/p)\tilde{k}_1 - \tilde{y}_1\tilde{k}_2) \big]\, k \\ & + s\,(\,(\tilde{y}_2/p\,)\, \tilde{k}_1 - \tilde{y}_1\tilde{k}_2)\,\big\} \end{aligned} \tag{21.68}$$

The *director function*, **h(k)**, (21.68), is a *parabola* with a positive discriminant

$$\Delta^2 = \frac{1}{4}\left[\frac{1}{\tilde{k}_1 - \tilde{k}_2}(s\{(\tilde{y}_2/p) - \tilde{y}_1\}\right.$$
$$\left. - np(1-s)\{(\tilde{y}_2/p)\tilde{k}_1 - \tilde{y}_1\tilde{k}_2\})\right]^2 > 0, \tag{21.69}$$

and hence has two real roots. The product of the roots, $\kappa_1$ and $\kappa_2$, is seen to be, cf. (21.68)

$$\kappa_1 \cdot \kappa_2 = -\frac{(\tilde{y}_2/p)\tilde{k}_1 - \tilde{y}_1\tilde{k}_2}{(n/s)p(1-s)(\tilde{y}_1 - \tilde{y}_2/p)} < 0, \tag{21.70}$$

which is always *negative* with diversification *conditions* (21.67). As the coefficient of the quadratic term of (21.68) is always negative with (21.67), the parabola has a shape with a maximum value. The parabolas are depicted in Fig. 21.5a–c, with solid lines in diversification interval and with dotted lines outside.

The director function, $h(k)$, (21.58), at the *specialization points* becomes

$$k = \tilde{k}_1 : \quad h(k) = \tilde{y}_1[s - n(1-s)p\tilde{k}_1], \tag{21.71}$$

$$k = \tilde{k}_2 : \quad h(k) = (\tilde{y}_2/p)[s - n(1-s)p\tilde{k}_2]. \tag{21.72}$$

The *value* of **h(k)**, (21.71) is *positive* when $s > n(1-s)p\tilde{k}_1$, which is equivalent to the condition stated in Fig. 21.5a. The value of $h(k)$, (21.72) is *negative* when $s < n(1-s)p\tilde{k}_2$, which is equivalent to the condition stated in Fig. 21.5c.

With a saving ratio (**s**) between these two limits, the director function $h(k)$, (21.58), passes through the diversification interval as depicted in Fig. 21.5b. This establishes (21.59). The proof of (21.60) is analogous. The proof of (21.61)–(21.62) follows directly from the *phase diagrams*, Fig. 21.5b.

The proof of (21.63) is straightforward, as the replacement of $\tilde{y}_1$ by $f_1(k_1)$ in (21.71) and $\tilde{y}_2$ by $f_2(k_2)$ in (21.72) does not affect the value of $h(k)$.

The long-run capital-labor ratio, $\kappa$, (21.64), can be obtained as the positive root of (21.58). However, it can be immediately verified, by noting that: $dK/dL \equiv \dot{K}/\dot{L} = s/[n\,p\,(1-s)]$, cf. (21.56)–(21.57)—which explains the *shape* of the *phase portrait*. The diversification conditions (21.59)–(21.60) also follow directly from (21.64) and the requirement that $\kappa$ is between $\tilde{k}_1$ and $\tilde{k}_2$.

The expression (21.66) follows from (21.56)–(21.57) and (21.10)–(21.11), (21.16). □

The *diversification possibilities* (21.59)–(21.60) may be *wide*, if $\tilde{k}_1$ and $\tilde{k}_2$ differ considerably; the crucial parameter (**n**), is *not* as (**s**), tied to the values (21.41).

**Corollary 21.3** *When the parametric restrictions (21.59)–(21.60) are not satisfied, the small competitive trading economy will be* specialized *in the* most capital intensive *good, except when the saving rate* (s) *is too small, cf. Fig. 21.5c. A specialized* ***steady state*** *in the capital intensive good will always* ***exist****. Hence, there is* ***no*** *possibility of endogenous (****persistent****) per capita growth with the* ***endogenous*** *labor growth (21.56).*

***Proof*** The proof of the corollary is analogous to the proof of (21.63). The necessary existence of a specialized steady-state growth follows again from (21.71)–(21.72), which for $k > \tilde{k}_1$ always have *roots*, irrespective of the shape of $y_1 = f_1(k_1)$ and $y_2 = f_2(k_2)$. □

**Remark 21.3** One might be inclined to see the absence of endogenous per capita growth in Corollary 21.3 as hinging on the particular specification of endogenous labor growth in (21.56). As to Corollary 21.3 being generally upheld, let us briefly examine the *classical* alternative to (21.56)–(21.57), viz.

$$\dot{L} = L\, n\,(w/P_2) \equiv L\, \mathfrak{f}(k). \tag{21.73}$$

Then by (21.73) and (21.57), we get, cf. (21.16)

$$\begin{aligned} \dot{k} = h(k) &\equiv \mathfrak{g}(k) - k\, \mathfrak{f}(k) = (s/P_1)y - n(w/P_2)k \\ &= n(r/P_2)[(s/np) - w/r]k + s(w/P_1). \end{aligned} \tag{21.74}$$

Imposing the diversification restrictions (21.14) upon (21.74), the *parameter conditions* for *diversification* become, after some calculations,

$$\frac{\tilde{y}_1}{\tilde{k}_1}\, \frac{\tilde{k}_1 - \tilde{k}_2}{\tilde{y}_2\tilde{k}_1 - \tilde{y}_1\tilde{k}_2 p} < \frac{n}{s} < \frac{\tilde{y}_2/p}{\tilde{k}_2}\, \frac{\tilde{k}_1 - \tilde{k}_2}{\tilde{y}_2\tilde{k}_1 - \tilde{y}_1\tilde{k}_2 p}. \tag{21.75}$$

Apart from a multiplicative factor, the *condition* (21.75) corresponds to (21.28). It is a bit more complicated than before, as (21.14) involves restriction on the fixed parameter $(w/P_2)$ in (21.74).

If the *condition* (21.75) is not met, and we get *specialization* in e.g., good 2, then (21.74) can be reduced to, cf. (21.10)–(21.11):

$$\dot{k} = h(k) = f_2(k_2)\,[\,(s/p) - (n + \epsilon_{K_2})\, k_2\,]. \tag{21.76}$$

Clearly, a steady state always *exists*, and hence *persistent* growth *per capita* is ***not*** possible with *classical* endogenous *labor* growth (21.73). ▽

### *Dynamics with Classical Saving*

In the literature on *open* economies and capital accumulation, the *classical saving* function has often been applied in the *dynamic* models, cf. Bardhan (1965a,b, 1966); Stiglitz (1970); Deardorff (1971); Smith (1984). For a small trading economy with classical saving, *domestic capital* accumulation is given by, cf. (21.22), (21.11), and (21.13),

$$\dot{K} = Q_1 = L\, s_K\, (r/P_1)\, k = L\, s_K\, [\tilde{y}_1/(\tilde{k}_1 + \tilde{\omega})]\, k$$
$$= \frac{L}{\tilde{k}_1 - \tilde{k}_2}[\, s_K\, (\tilde{y}_1 - \tilde{y}_2/p)\, k\,] \equiv L\, \mathfrak{g}(k). \tag{21.77}$$

Hence, (21.77) and *exogenous labor* growth, (21.25), give, cf. (21.11), (21.13),

$$\dot{k} = h(k) \equiv \mathfrak{g}(k) - k\, \mathfrak{f}(k) = [\, s_K (r/P_1) - n\,]\, k$$
$$= s_K \left[ \frac{\tilde{y}_1 - \tilde{y}_2/p}{\tilde{k}_1 - \tilde{k}_2} - \frac{n}{s_K} \right] k. \tag{21.78}$$

The last expression in both (21.77)–(21.78) applies to $k \in C_k$.

Except for the singular case, when the line segment of $h(k)$, (21.78) coincides with the $k$-axis, only *specialized* steady states exist with *classical saving*. With *specialization* in the capital intensive good, and $r/P_1 = f_1'(k_1) = (1/p) f_2'(k_2)$, cf. (21.77), (21.11), the *conditions* and *rapidity* of *persistent* growth of *per capita* income with *classical saving* are the *same* as stated in (21.43)–(21.46) of Theorem 21.2, and particularly, with CES in (21.49), (21.52), of Corollary 21.2.

The general conclusion that *classical* saving always leads to *complete specialization* in the long run would be *premature*, as the assumption of *exogenous labor* growth may again be critical in this specialization.

We shall again use the *endogeneity* of *labor* growth formulation (21.56) modified with classical consumption demand/supply of $Q_2$. We get, cf. (21.22), (21.19), and (21.16),

$$\dot{L} = n\, Q_2 = n/P_2\, [(1 - s_K) r K + w L]$$
$$= L\, n/P_2\, [\, (1 - s_K)\, r k + w\,] \equiv L\, \mathfrak{f}(k). \tag{21.79}$$

Then the *dynamic processes* (21.77), (21.79) give,

$$\dot{k} = h(k) \equiv \mathfrak{g}(k) - k\, \mathfrak{f}(k) = (s_K r/P_1)\, k - n/P_2[(1 - s_K)\, r k + w]\, k$$
$$= -n(1 - s_K)(r/P_2)\, k^2 + [\, s_K (r/P_1) - n(w/P_2)\,]\, k. \tag{21.80}$$

**Theorem 21.4** *For a small, competitive, trading economy with classical saving and endogenous labor growth, the necessary and sufficient conditions for the exis-*

*tence of a long-run capital-labor ratio, $k = \kappa$, with* **incomplete specialization** *are given by the parameter restrictions:*

$$\tilde{k}_1 > \tilde{k}_2 : \quad \frac{n\tilde{y}_2(\tilde{k}_1 - \tilde{k}_2)}{(\tilde{y}_1 - \tilde{y}_2/p)(1 + np\tilde{k}_2)} < s_K < \frac{np\tilde{y}_1(\tilde{k}_1 - \tilde{k}_2)}{(\tilde{y}_1 - \tilde{y}_2/p)(1 + np\tilde{k}_1)}, \tag{21.81}$$

$$\tilde{k}_2 > \tilde{k}_1 : \quad \frac{npy_1(\tilde{k}_1 - \tilde{k}_2)}{(\tilde{y}_1 - \tilde{y}_2/p)(1 + np\tilde{k}_1)} < s_K < \frac{n\tilde{y}_2(\tilde{k}_1 - \tilde{k}_2)}{(\tilde{y}_1 - \tilde{y}_2/p)(1 + np\tilde{k}_2)}. \tag{21.82}$$

*When the existence conditions, (21.81)–(21.82), are satisfied, then the family of solutions for $k(t)$ to (21.80) have asymptotic stability in the diversification cone, $C_k$ (21.7), and globally, irrespective of sector capital intensities: $k_1 \gtrless k_2$, i.e.*

$$\exists k_0 = \kappa \in C_k \; : \quad k(t) = \kappa, \quad \forall t, \tag{21.83}$$

$$\forall k_0 \in \mathbf{R} \setminus \{\kappa\} : \quad k(t) \to \kappa \; as \, t \to \infty. \tag{21.84}$$

*The* **diversified** *steady-state capital-labor ratio, $k = \kappa$, and its proportional balanced growth rate of $L(t)$ and $K(t)$ are given by:*

$$\kappa = \frac{(s_K/n)(\tilde{y}_1 - \tilde{y}_2/p) + p\,[\tilde{y}_1\tilde{k}_2 - (\tilde{y}_2/p)\tilde{k}_1]}{(1 - s_K)\,p\,(\tilde{y}_1 - \tilde{y}_2/p)}, \tag{21.85}$$

$$\begin{aligned} \mathfrak{f}(\kappa) &= \mathfrak{g}(\kappa)/\kappa = (n/P_2)\,[(1 - s_K)\,\tilde{r}\,\kappa + \tilde{w}] \\ &= (s_K/P_1)\,\tilde{r} \;=\; s_K\, f_1'(\tilde{k}_1). \end{aligned} \tag{21.86}$$

*Furthermore, the* **specialized** *steady-state capital-labor ratio, $k = \kappa$, and its proportional balanced growth rate are given by:*

$$\kappa = \frac{(s_K/n)\,\epsilon_K(\kappa)}{(1 - s_K)\,\epsilon_K(\kappa) + (1 - \epsilon_K(\kappa))\,p} \tag{21.87}$$

$$\mathfrak{f}(\kappa) = \mathfrak{g}(\kappa)/\kappa = s_K\, f_1'(\kappa). \tag{21.88}$$

***Proof*** The proof of (21.81) is analogous to that of (21.82). We give case $k_1 > k_2$.

With diversification, the function (21.80) becomes, cf. (21.16), (21.11), (21.13),

$$\begin{aligned} h(k) = \frac{n}{\tilde{k}_1 - \tilde{k}_2} \big\{ &- p(1 - s_K)(\tilde{y}_1 - \tilde{y}_2/p)\,k^2 \\ &+ \big[(s_K/n)(\tilde{y}_1 - \tilde{y}_2/p) - p(\tilde{y}_1\tilde{k}_2 - (\tilde{y}_2/p)\tilde{k}_1)\big]\,k \big\}. \end{aligned} \tag{21.89}$$

It is clear that the director function, $h(k)$, (21.89), has one zero root. As the coefficient of the quadratic term of (21.89) is always negative with $(\tilde{y}_1 -$

$\tilde{y}_2/p)/(\tilde{k}_1 - \tilde{k}_2) > 0$, (21.67), the shape of the *parabola* (21.89) is the same as in Figs. 21.5a–c.

The nonzero root of $h(k)$ can be calculated as given in (21.85). This root is also the attractive steady-state capital-labor ratio, if the root is positive and located between $\tilde{k}_1$ and $\tilde{k}_2$. As the denominator of (21.85) is always negative in case $\tilde{k}_1 > \tilde{k}_2$, a negative numerator requires that

$$1 > s_K > \frac{np[(\tilde{y}_2/p)\tilde{k}_1 - \tilde{y}_1\tilde{k}_2]}{\tilde{y}_1 - \tilde{y}_2/p}. \tag{21.90}$$

The condition that $\kappa$, (21.85) is located as $\tilde{k}_2 < \kappa < \tilde{k}_1$ is seen, after some manipulation, to further require that

$$\frac{n\tilde{y}_2(\tilde{k}_1 - \tilde{k}_2)}{(\tilde{y}_1 - \tilde{y}_2/p)(1 + np\tilde{k}_2)} < s_K < \frac{np\tilde{y}_1(\tilde{k}_1 - \tilde{k}_2)}{(\tilde{y}_1 - \tilde{y}_2/p)(1 + np\tilde{k}_1)}. \tag{21.91}$$

Comparing the left hand side of (21.91) with (21.90) and using $s_K \le 1$, it is seen that (21.90) is *always* satisfied by (21.91), which is (21.81).

The proof of (21.83)–(21.84) follows immediately from the shape of the *parabola*, $h(k)$, (21.89).

Finally, the long-run capital-labor ratio, (21.85), is a nonzero root of (21.89), and the balanced growth rate, (21.86), follows as usual from (21.79) and (21.77); (21.87)–(21.88) can be similarly obtained by replacing $r/P_i = f_i'(k)$, $w/P_i = f_i(k) - kf_i'(k)$ in (21.80), cf. (21.10). □

**Corollary 21.4** *There is no possibility of endogenous—***persistent***—per capita growth with classical saving, (21.77), and semiclassical labor growth, (21.79), or classical labor growth, (21.73), except for $\sigma_i$ infinite in (21.47).*

***Proof*** The function $h(k)$, (21.80) with specialization in, e.g., $k = k_1$, becomes, cf. (21.10)–(21.11),

$$h(k) = s_K f'(k)k - nk[(1 - s_K)f'(k)k + pf(k) - pkf'(k)]. \tag{21.92}$$

Taking the limit of $h(k)$ when $k \to \infty$, we have

$$\lim_{k\to\infty} h(k) = \lim_{k\to\infty} k^2[-n(1 - s_K)f'(k)] \to -\infty, \tag{21.93}$$

so there *must exist* a *root*, $h(\kappa) = 0$; hence, *no* persistent growth.

With classical labor growth (21.73) and classical saving (21.77), the function $h(k)$, (21.78), becomes, cf. (21.10), $p = P_1/P_2$,

$$\dot{k} = h(k) = s_K\,(r/P_1)\,k - n\,(w/P_2)\,k = k\,f'(k)\,[\,s_K - n\,p\,\omega(k)\,]. \tag{21.94}$$

For a CES function, (21.94) only gives $k(t) \to \infty$ in the *extreme* case of linear isoquants ($\sigma = \infty$), $\omega(k) =$ constant, cf. Jensen (1994, p. 45); here Sect. "Linear Isoquants" in Chap. 7. □

By comparing the endogenous *balanced growth* rates, (21.66) and (21.86), it is seen that, if the saving rates ($\mathbf{s}$) and ($\mathbf{s_K}$) have similar size, then *diversified* economies grow *faster* with *proportional* saving ($\mathbf{s}$) than with *classical* saving ($\mathbf{s_K}$). Evidently, savings from *wage income* contributes to maintaining a *larger* balanced growth rate. Another noteworthy aspect of (21.86) is that a *higher saving* rate, $s_K$ *unequivocally* [ irrespective of changes in $\kappa$, (21.85)] *increases* the it balanced *growth rate* of a *small*, diversified, *trading* country. A *higher* saving rate, $s_K$, in a classical **closed** two-sector growth model with endogenous labor growth will *not* necessarily increase the *balanced* growth rate, as *changes* in the *general equilibrium prices* and factor intensities may *offset* the effects of a larger $s_K$, Jensen (1994, p. 153); here page 476 in Chap. 16. Thus, with **trade** at ***fixed*** terms of *trade*, high *saving* rates **do** *increase* the *balanced growth rate* in also a classical setting of endogenous labor growth.

**Remark 21.4** With specialization as before, (21.42), let us compare savings from *capital income* (21.77) with savings from only *labor income*, cf. (21.10)–(21.11): $\dot{K} = Q_1 = Ls_w(w/P_1) = (s_w/p)[f_2(k_2) - k_2 f_2'(k_2)] \equiv L\,\mathfrak{g}(k)$, which, together with $\dot{L} = nL$, gives $\dot{k}_2 = h(k_2) \equiv (s_w/p)[f_2(k_2) - k_2 f_2'(k_2)] - nk_2$. Using l'Hospital, we get, $\lim_{k_2 \to \infty} h(k_2) \approx -nk_2$. Accordingly $h(k_2)$ has a *root*, preventing $k_2 \to \infty$. Thus, *despite* $f_2'(k_2)$ being properly *bounded below*, and also *exogenous labor* growth, *savings* from *only* **labor income** can **not**—in contrast to (21.26), (21.77)—generate **persistent** per *capita* growth. See hereto (21.53), (21.54), and OLG models with all savings from *wage income*, Galor and Lin (1997) and Bertola (1996). ▽

### *Dynamics of the Trading Economy with Optimal Saving*

Above, we analyzed the trading economy with the *saving rate* exogenous and constant, proportional and classical, respectively. In this section, the *saving rate* mostly *varies* over time, as it will be endogenously determined by infinitely lived consumers *maximizing* total lifetime *utility*.

The *representative consumer* is assumed to have a time additive intertemporal utility function

$$U = \int_0^\infty u[c(t)]e^{-\rho t}dt, \tag{21.95}$$

where the *decision* variable, $\mathbf{c}$, is per capita consumption, cf. (21.55), and $\rho$ is the constant subjective rate of *time preference* (discount rate). The *momentary* utility (felicity) function, **u(c)**, is assumed to be concave, increasing, and to satisfy the Inada derivative conditions:

$$\lim_{c \to 0} u'(c) = \infty, \qquad \lim_{c \to \infty} u'(c) = 0. \tag{21.96}$$

With $\rho > 0$, total lifetime utility **U** is bounded, if $u(c)$ is bounded over time.

**Remark 21.5** With exogenous labor growth, $L(t) = L_0 e^{nt}$, a social planner may maximize the objective function

$$U = \int_0^\infty u[c(t)]L(t)e^{-\rho t}dt = L_0 \int_0^\infty u[c(t)]e^{-(\rho-n)t}dt, \tag{21.97}$$

where (21.97) is *similar* to (21.95) with $\check{\rho} = \rho - n$. But with endogenous labor growth (21.56), the social planning objective analogous to (21.97) would be intractable. Hence, we stick here to (21.95); see Barro and Sala-i-Martin (2004), Deaton (1992). ▽

*Ramsey Saving and Exogenous Labor Growth*
For a *small*, two-sector *trading* economy, the domestic capital accumulation can be described by, cf. (21.19), (21.16), (21.12), and (21.55),

$$\begin{aligned} \dot{K} &= Q_1 = 1/P_1\,[Y - P_2\,Q_2] = L\,[\,y(k)/P_1 - (1/p)\,Q_2/L\,] \\ &= L\,[\,y(k)/P_1 - c/p\,] \equiv L\,\mathfrak{g}(k, c) \end{aligned} \tag{21.98}$$

With exogenous *Labor* growth (21.25), the function, **h(k, c)**, becomes, cf. (21.27), (21.98),

$$\dot{k} = h(k, c) \equiv \mathfrak{g}(k, c) - k\,\mathfrak{f}(k, c) = (1/P_1)\,y(k) - c/p - nk \tag{21.99}$$

**Proposition 21.2 (Stiglitz)** *For a small, competitive, trading economy with Ramsey saving and an exogenous labor growth, the necessary and sufficient condition for diversification is that the rate of time preference, $\rho$, has the particular value, $\tilde{\rho}$:*

$$\rho = \tilde{\rho} = y'(k)/P_1 - n = f_1'(k_1) - n = f_2'(k_2)/p - n \tag{21.100}$$

*There are multiple diversified steady states ($k$, $c = y(k)/P_2 - n\,p\,k$), but no transition dynamics. If $\rho$ is larger (less) than $\tilde{\rho}$, then the small trading economy will in the long run specialize in the labor (capital) intensive good. The transition dynamics (saddle paths) are shown in Fig. 21.6a.*

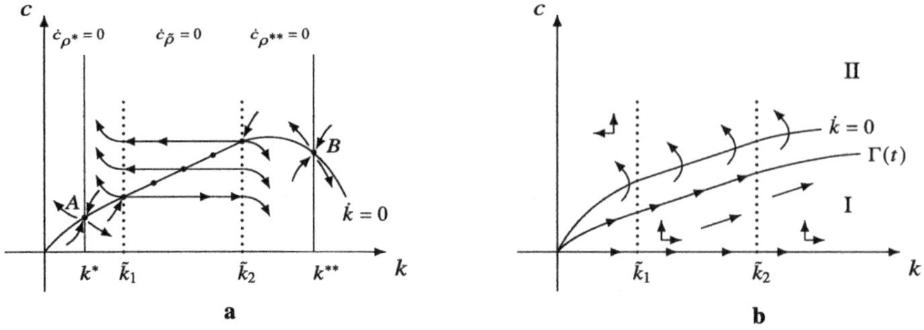


**Fig. 21.6** Dynamics of a small trading economy with optimal saving and exogenous labor growth. (**a**) Transitions to steady states. (**b**) Persistent growth

***Proof*** The Ramsey optimization problem is

$$\max U = \max_{c(t)} \int_0^\infty u[c(t)]\, e^{-\rho t} dt \tag{21.101}$$

$$\text{s.t.} \quad \dot{k} = h(k, c) = (1/P_1)\, y(k) - nk - c/p, \quad c \geq 0, \tag{21.102}$$

which is equivalent to maximizing the *current* value Hamiltonian function

$$\mathcal{H} = u[c(t)] + \pi(t)\,[\,(1/P_1)\, y(k) - nk - c/p\,], \tag{21.103}$$

with a *costate* variable, $\pi(t)$, and the transversality conditions:

$$k(0) = k_0, \quad \lim_{t\to\infty} \pi(t)\, e^{-\rho t}\, k(t) = 0. \tag{21.104}$$

The first order condition gives, cf. (21.103)

$$\frac{\partial \mathcal{H}}{\partial c} = u'(c) - (1/p)\,\pi(t) = 0, \tag{21.105}$$

and the maximum principle gives that

$$\dot{\pi}(t) = -\frac{\partial \mathcal{H}}{\partial k} + \rho\,\pi(t) = \pi(t)\left[\rho + n - y'(k)/P_1\right]. \tag{21.106}$$

By derivation and inserting the first order condition (21.105) into (21.106), we obtain the differential equation for per capita consumption, $c$, as

$$\dot{c} = -\frac{u'(c)}{u''(c)}\left[\frac{y'(k)}{P_1} - n - \rho\right] \equiv c\,\sigma(c)\left[\frac{y'(k)}{P_1} - n - \rho\right] \equiv \eta(k, c) \tag{21.107}$$

where $\sigma(c)$ is the *intertemporal* elasticity of *substitution*.

By (21.105) the *transversality* condition (21.104) becomes,

$$p\ u'(c)\, e^{-\rho t}\, k(t) \to 0 \text{ as } t \to \infty. \tag{21.108}$$

The equations (21.99), (21.102), and (21.107) define a *dynamic* system in $(\mathbf{k}, \mathbf{c})$. As concave GNP function, $y(k)$, has a *linear* segment in $C_k$, cf. Proposition 21.1, a *stationary* $\mathbf{c}$ occurs in $C_k$, iff $\rho$ has the *particular value* stated in (21.100), cf. (21.107), (21.16), (21.12), and (21.11). For every $\mathbf{k} \in C_k$, the optimal *control* variable $\mathbf{c}$ follows from $h(k, c) = 0$, (21.102). Outside the line $h(k, c) = 0$, $\dot{k}$ is either positive or negative and we will eventually be *specialized* as indicated in Fig. 21.6a.

When $\rho$ becomes *larger*, $\dot{\mathbf{c}}= \mathbf{0}$, (21.107), will therefore require $y'(k)$ to be larger, which gives a vertical line $k = k^* < \tilde{k}_1$, crossing the $\dot{\mathbf{k}}= \mathbf{0}$ curve, and giving a long-run *steady-state* **A** in Fig. 21.6a. Similarly, when $\rho$ becomes *smaller*, (21.107) will give a vertical line $k = k^{**} > \tilde{k}_2$, which crosses the $\dot{k} = 0$ curve after the diversification cone, implying *specialization* in the capital-intensive good, cf. point **B** in Fig. 21.6a. □

**Remark 21.6** The sufficiency of (21.101)–(21.106) can be proved simply. It is observed that the objective function $u[c(t)]e^{-\rho t}$ is a concave function in $(k, c)$-space, cf. (21.96). Furthermore, it can be shown, by using (21.105) and (21.96), that $\pi(t) = p\, u'(c) > 0$, and that the function, $h(k, c)$, in (21.102) is also concave in $c, k$. Therefore the necessary conditions provided by the maximum principle are also sufficient for optimal solutions. ▽

**Theorem 21.5** *With Ramsey saving and an exogenous labor growth,* ***persistent*** *(endogenous) per capita growth can be obtained,* ***if*** *the concave per capita GNP* ***function*** $\mathbf{y(k)}$ *and the intertemporal substitution* ***elasticity*** $\boldsymbol{\sigma}(\mathbf{c})$ *or the rate of* ***time preference*** $\boldsymbol{\rho}$ *satisfies, respectively:*

$$\lim_{k\to\infty} y'(k)/P_1 \equiv \beta/P_1 > n + \rho \tag{21.109}$$

$$\overline{\sigma} = \sup_{c>0} \sigma\,(c) < \frac{\beta/P_1 - n}{\beta/P_1 - (n+\rho)}, \quad i.e.\ \ \rho > \left[\frac{\beta}{P_1} - n\right]\left[\frac{\overline{\sigma} - 1}{\overline{\sigma}}\right] \tag{21.110}$$

*The* ***conditions*** *(21.109–21.110) ensure the* ***existence****—below the* ***isocline*** $\dot{k} = h(k, c) = 0$*—of a* ***separator****, the particular* ***orbit****,* $\boldsymbol{\Gamma}(t) \equiv [k^*(t), c^*(t)]$*, depicted in Fig. 21.6b. The existence of this* ***separator*** *is required for* ***persistent*** *(endogenous) per capita growth.*

***Proof*** See Appendix B, section "Appendix B: Proof of Theorem 21.5" □

With regard to Ramsey (optimal) saving, it has been incumbent on us to obtain *sufficient conditions*—applicable to a general GNP-*function*, $y(k)$ and a *general utility* function $u(c)$—that ensure *persistent* per *capita* growth. The condition (21.109) is analogous to (21.44)–(21.45) with a *low* $\rho$ taking over the role of a *large* $s$. But (21.109) is not always enough to ensure persistent growth, as (21.110) is also needed. However, if $u(c)$ *always* has $\sigma(c) \leq 1$, $\forall c > 0$, then (21.110) is *automatically* satisfied,[2] irrespective of the size of $\rho > 0$. If $\sigma(c) > 1$, then $\rho$ must be *large* enough to satisfy (21.110). Given now the existence of the *separator* $\Gamma(t)$ and hence *persistent* growth, see Fig. 21.6b, the actual selection of the *optimal* path in **region I** is discussed in Appendix B, section "Appendix B: Proof of Theorem 21.5".

For the class of *isoelastic*[3] utility functions $u(c)$, $\forall c$, $\sigma(c) = \sigma \gtrless 1$ and with the conditions (21.109)–(21.110), the *separator* in Fig. 21.6b is also the *unique optimal orbit* (solution) satisfying (21.101)–(21.104), see Appendix B, section "Appendix B: Proof of Theorem 21.5". For optimal saving and persistent growth, the factor shares behave as in (21.53), cf. (21.109).

*Ramsey Saving and Endogenous Labor Growth*

With the endogenous Labor growth, $\dot{L} = n\,Q_2 = L\,n\,c \equiv L\,\mathfrak{f}(k, c)$, (21.55), the function, $h(k, c)$, (21.99), accordingly becomes:

$$\dot{k} = h(k, c) = (1/P_1)\,y(k) - c/p - n\,c\,k \tag{21.111}$$

**Theorem 21.6** *With the Ramsey saving and an endogenous labor growth, a long-run* **steady state** *always* **exists,** *either in the diversification cone or in the specialization region, depending on the values of the parameters: $n$, $\rho$, $p$. Endogenous* **persistent** *per capita growth is therefore* **impossible,** *even with the property (21.109) of* $\mathbf{y(k)}$ *in (21.111).*

***Proof*** Using the maximum principle and first order conditions similar to those above, (21.105)–(21.106), we derive the differential equation for per capita consumption as

$$\dot{c} = -\frac{u'(c)}{u''(c)}\left[(1/P_1)\,y'(k) - \frac{n}{(1 + n\,p\,k)\,P_2}\,y(k) - \rho\right] = \eta(k, c). \tag{21.112}$$

Hence, (21.111)–(21.112) define a *dynamic system* in $k$ and $c$, and completely determine the behavior of the economic system. It is seen in (21.112) that $\dot{\boldsymbol{c}}$ is a *nonlinear* function in $k$, and

$$\lim_{k\to 0} \dot{c} = \infty, \quad \lim_{k\to\infty} \dot{c} = \frac{u'(c)}{u''(c)}\,\rho \equiv -c\,\sigma(c)\,\rho < 0. \tag{21.113}$$

[2] Hall (1988) estimated that $\sigma$ is much below unity, $0.1 < \sigma < 0.4$.

[3] A common practice is to use: $u(c) = \frac{c^{1-\theta}-1}{1-\theta}$, $\theta > 0$; $\sigma = 1/\theta$. See Barro and Sala-i-Martin (2004, p. 207).

Hence, the *curve*, $\dot{c} = 0$, (21.112), can *always* be *solved* for a $k = k^*$, giving a *vertical line* in the $(k, c)$-space, irrespective of the properties of $y(k)$.

For $\dot{k} = 0$, (21.111) we have, cf. (21.109)

$$c = \frac{y(k)}{(1 + n\,p\,k)\,P_2}, \qquad \lim_{k\to\infty} c = \frac{1}{n\,P_1} \lim_{k\to\infty} y'(k) > 0. \tag{21.114}$$

The *curves* for $\dot{\boldsymbol{k}} = \mathbf{0}$ and $\dot{\boldsymbol{c}} = \mathbf{0}$ will then always *cross* one another in the first quadrant, which establishes Theorem 21.6 □

**Remark 21.7** The sufficiency of the maximum principle can be proved by using the maximized Hamiltonian. It is known that if $(k^*, c^*, \pi^*)$ is a solution to (21.111)–(21.112), and the maximized Hamiltonian is strictly concave, then $(k^*, c^*, \pi^*)$ is the *unique* optimal solution; see Leonard and Long (1992). The Hamiltonian for (21.111) is now given as, cf. (21.103),

$$\mathcal{H} = u[c(t)] + \pi(t)\,[\,(1/P_1)\,y(k) - c/p - n\,c\,k\,]. \tag{21.115}$$

Then, the first order condition gives $\pi^* = u'(c^*)/(nk^* + 1/p)$, and $\dot{k} = 0$, (21.111), gives: $c^* = y(k^*)/[(1 + n\,p\,k^*)\,P_2]$. Inserting $\pi^*$ and $c^*$ into the Hamiltonian, (21.115), we get the *maximized* Hamiltonian as $\mathcal{H}^* = u\,[\,c^*(t)\,]$. To prove that the *maximized* Hamiltonian, $\mathcal{H}^*$, is a *concave* function, we need to calculate its first and second order derivatives. It gives

$$\frac{d\mathcal{H}^*}{dk^*} = u'(c^*)\frac{dc^*}{dk^*}, \qquad \frac{d^2\mathcal{H}^*}{dk^{*2}} = u''(c^*)\frac{dc^*}{dk^*} + u'(c^*)\frac{d^2c^*}{dk^{*2}} \tag{21.116}$$

Assume, $\dot{c} = 0$, (21.112), then we get:

$$\rho = \frac{y'(k^*)}{P_1} - \frac{n\,y(k^*)}{(1 + n\,p\,k^*)\,P_2} > 0. \tag{21.117}$$

Using the *positivity* property of $\rho$, (21.117), and $c^*$ to calculate, $\frac{dc^*}{dk^*}$ and $\frac{d^2c^*}{dk^{*2}}$, respectively, it is then seen that $\frac{dc^*}{dk^*} > 0$, $\frac{d^2c^*}{dk^{*2}} < 0$, therefore $\frac{d\mathcal{H}^*}{dk^*} > 0$, $\frac{d^2\mathcal{H}^*}{dk^{*2}} < 0$; hence, the concavity of the Hamiltonian is proved and the *sufficient* condition for the existence of the *unique optimal* solution is accordingly established. ▽

## General Equilibrium Dynamics of Large Trading Countries

In all the dynamic systems of a *small* trading economy above, the *terms of trade* were *exogenously* given by the world market conditions, and the actual size (parametric value) of the *price ratio* was important in forming various *parameter regions* related to the dynamic issues of diversification for a *small* country.

The exports (imports) of a **large** country, however, will affect the worldwide demand/supply conditions and the market clearing (equilibrium) *prices*. Hence, an *endogenous explanation* of the *terms of trade* requires supplementary determination of the *momentary international equilibrium* in the commodity markets. Moreover, the dynamic laws *governing* the *factor accumulation* of a *large* country, **A**, will also be affected by the momentary economic state in country **B**, representing the "rest of the world". Accordingly, the *dimensions* of the *dynamic system* have increased, but under some assumptions, the growth processes of *two interacting* countries are tractable, and their properties can be compared with those stated in Sect. "General Equilibrium Dynamics of a Small Trading Country".

### *Factor Accumulation and International Equilibrium Prices*

Flexible sector technology has been the standard assumption in dynamic two-factor, two-commodity, two-country trade models. From the very beginning, Oniki and Uzawa (1965) dealt with *neoclassical sector technologies*; see also Kemp (1969), Bardhan (1970), Woodland (1982), Gandolfo (1994). From this literature, it is well known that the *existence, uniqueness*, and global *stability* of the *international growth equilibrium* are ensured with proportional saving and the consumer good at all times being capital intensive in both countries. This global stability result applies, irrespective of long-run diversification or specialization in one or both countries. But our main object is again to obtain some *global stability conditions* that will *preserve diversification* in *both* countries. In this respect, the analysis in the literature has been inconclusive, in particular when their labor force (growing at the same rate) differ much in relative size, and their saving functions are either proportional or classical, see Takayama (1972, p. 406–409,433). The issue is hard to solve precisely with general production functions, which makes it difficult to delineate the *diversification region* for the state variables (factor endowment ratios).

To obtain some clues for a general understanding of the role of *country size* and *sectorial factor intensities* in the growth processes of large trading economies, we study the implications of *factor accumulation* with *fixed coefficient* technologies in *both* countries. As we allow for *internationally different Leontief technologies*, our approach accordingly examines the *dynamics* of an *extended* two-factor, two-sector *Ricardian* trade model. The consequences of internationally identical technologies appear as a special case.

The *terms of trade* and *international equilibrium* in the commodity markets will be determined from the *trade balance* equations of the two countries. By Walras' law, we need only consider market equilibrium for *one* good. Hence, *international equilibrium* requires that, cf. (21.18), (21.20), (subscripts $A$ and $B$ are used in the former single country symbols)

$$X_{1A} = Y_{1A} - Q_{1A} = -X_{1B} = -(Y_{1B} - Q_{1B}). \tag{21.118}$$

Let $\upsilon_A$, $\upsilon_B$ represent the country *shares* of world *labor* (population), i.e.,

$$\upsilon_A = L_A/(L_A + L_B), \qquad \upsilon_A + \upsilon_B = 1. \tag{21.119}$$

In terms of the factor endowments ratios, $k_A$, $k_B$, and the sectorial factor intensities, $k_{1A}, k_{2A}, k_{1B}, k_{2B}$, the *region* of *diversification*, $C_k^2 \subset \Re_+^2$, analogous to (21.7), is given by

$$C_k^2 = ]\min(k_{1A}, k_{2A}),\ \max(k_{1A}, k_{2A})[ \\ \times ]\min(k_{1B}, k_{2B}),\ \max(k_{1B}, k_{2B})[, \tag{21.120}$$

with the *boundaries* representing complete *specialization* in *one* of the countries. With *Leontief* sector technologies, $C_k^2$, (21.120), is a *diversification rectangle.*

Under the assumptions of competitive economies and proportional saving in Sect. "Structure of Two-Sector Trade Models", the *trade equilibrium condition* (21.118) will determine the international *price ratio*, $p = P_1/P_2$.

**Lemma 21.2** *For two large competitive trading economies, with proportional saving and Leontief sector technologies, the international equilibrium terms of trade,* $p = P_1/P_2$*, are given by:*

$$p = \frac{y_{2A}\, \upsilon_A\, s_A\, (k_{2B} - k_{1B})(k_A - k_{1A}) + y_{2B}\, \upsilon_B\, s_B\, (k_{2A} - k_{1A})(k_B - k_{1B})}{y_{1A}\, \upsilon_A\, (1 - s_A)(k_{2B} - k_{1B})(k_{2A} - k_A) + y_{1B}\, \upsilon_B (1 - s_B)(k_{2A} - k_{1A})(k_{2B} - k_B)} \tag{21.121}$$

*and, in the special case of internationally* ***identical*** *technologies,*

$$p = \frac{P_1}{P_2} = \frac{y_2}{y_1} \frac{\upsilon_A s_A \lambda_{2A} + \upsilon_B s_B \lambda_{2B}}{\upsilon_A (1 - s_A)\lambda_{1A} + \upsilon_B (1 - s_B)\lambda_{1B}} \\ = \frac{y_2}{y_1} \frac{(\upsilon_A\, s_A + \upsilon_B s_B)\, k_1 \ - \ \upsilon_A s_A\, k_A \ - \ \upsilon_B\, s_B\, k_B}{-[\, \upsilon_A (1 - s_A) + \upsilon_B (1 - s_B)\,]\, k_2 \ + \ \upsilon_A (1 - s_A)\, k_A \ + \ \upsilon_B (1 - s_B)\, k_B} \tag{21.122}$$

*The feasible* ***domain*** *of the terms of trade surface (TTS), (21.121)–(21.122),* $\boldsymbol{p = p(k_A, k_B)}$*, satisfying (21.14)–(21.15) is the entire diversification* ***rectangle****, (21.120).*

***Proof*** From (21.24) and (21.118) we have $\lambda_{L_{1A}} = \lambda_{1A}$, $\lambda_{L_{2A}} = \lambda_{2A}\ \lambda_{L_{1B}} = \lambda_{1B}$

$$X_{1A} = L_A[(1 - s_A) y_{1A} \lambda_{1A} - (s_A/p) y_{2A} \lambda_{2A}], \tag{21.123}$$

$$X_{1B} = L_B[(1 - s_B) y_{1B} \lambda_{1B} - (s_B/p) y_{2B} \lambda_{2B}], \tag{21.124}$$

where $\lambda_{1A}$ and $\lambda_{2A}$ are as (21.6) with $k = k_A$. Using (21.118) and solving, $X_{1A} = -X_{1B}$, (21.123)–(21.124), for the terms of trade, $p$, we get the expression (21.121). □

**Remark 21.8** The *terms* of *trade surfaces* (**TTS**), (21.121)–(21.122), have the equation form,

$$p = p(k_A, k_B) = \frac{a_0 + a_1 k_A + a_2 k_B}{b_0 + b_1 k_A + b_2 k_B}, \tag{21.125}$$

which belongs to the family of quadratics in three variables (*conic* surfaces). The *shape* of (21.125) is a *hyperbolic paraboloid*, upon which *hyperbolas* appear for fixed $k_A$ or fixed $k_B$. ▽

Traditionally, the *terms of trade* are determined by the *intersection* of reciprocal demand (*offer*) curves, Oniki and Uzawa (1965). In a growth context, the shifting offer curve technique is rather cumbersome. The same applies to the long-run offer curve methodology, Atsumi (1971).

**Remark 21.9** The *shape* of the terms of trade surface (TTS)—with flexible sector technologies (internationally *identical*) and no *inferior* goods of demand in either country—is similar to (21.122), i.e., having the monotone partial derivatives

$$k_2 > k_1 : \quad \partial p/\partial k_A > 0, \quad \partial p/\partial k_B > 0, \tag{21.126}$$

$$k_1 > k_2 : \quad \partial p/\partial k_A < 0, \quad \partial p/\partial k_B < 0. \tag{21.127}$$

A rigorous proof is given in Södersten (1964); cf. Rybczynski (1955), Findlay (1959), and Kemp (1969). ▽

### *Trade, Growth, and International Equilibrium Dynamics with Proportional Saving and Leontief Sector Technologies*

With *proportional saving* and the *same* exogenous labor growth, the *dynamics* of the *factor endowment ratios* of the two *large trading* economies, is described by, cf. (21.26)–(21.27) and (21.125),

$$\dot{k}_A = s_A\,[\,y_{1A}\,\lambda_{1A} + (y_{2A}/p(k_A, k_B))\,\lambda_{2A}\,] - n\,k_A = \mathcal{F}_A(k_A, k_B), \tag{21.128}$$

$$\dot{k}_B = s_B\,[\,y_{1B}\,\lambda_{1B} + (y_{2B}/p(k_A, k_B))\,\lambda_{2B}\,] - n\,k_B = \mathcal{F}_B(k_A, k_B), \tag{21.129}$$

where

$$\lambda_{1A} = \frac{k_A - k_{2A}}{k_{1A} - k_{2A}}, \qquad \lambda_{2A} = 1 - \lambda_{1A}, \tag{21.130}$$

$$\lambda_{1B} = \frac{k_B - k_{2B}}{k_{1B} - k_{2B}}, \qquad \lambda_{2B} = 1 - \lambda_{1B}, \tag{21.131}$$

$$p(k_A, k_B) = \frac{y_{2A}v_A s_A(k_{2B} - k_{1B})(k_A - k_{1A}) + y_{2B}v_B s_B(k_{2A} - k_{1A})(k_B - k_{1B})}{y_{1A}v_A(1 - s_A)(k_{2B} - k_{1B})(k_{2A} - k_A) + y_{1B}v_B(1 - s_B)(k_{2A} - k_{1A})(k_{2B} - k_B)} \tag{21.132}$$

$$k_A, k_B \in C_k^2. \tag{21.133}$$

Evidently, (21.128)–(21.129) represent a *nonlinear* and *non-homogenous dynamic* system in the *state* variables, $k_A$ and $k_B$. Moreover, many parameters are involved in a qualitative characterization of the *governing functions*, $(\mathcal{F}_A, \mathcal{F}_B)$. One important objective is to obtain the *parameter restrictions* upon $\mathcal{F}_A$ and $\mathcal{F}_B$ that ensure a unique *international* steady state, which is a global *attractor* located in the *interior* of $C_k^2$, (21.120). Economically, we get the global *stability conditions* that allow for long-run *diversification* in *both* countries.

The *intersection* of the two *curves* (nullclines), the $(\dot{k}_A = 0)$-curve and the $(\dot{k}_B = 0)$-curve, is the *international equilibrium* (*steady-state*) point, $(\boldsymbol{\kappa}_A, \boldsymbol{\kappa}_B)$. As it may be verified from the Eqs. (21.128)–(21.132), the *nullclines*, $\mathcal{F}_A(k_A, k_B) = 0$, $\mathcal{F}_B(k_A, k_B) = 0$ are both *quadratic* (conics) in the state variables. In general, $\mathcal{F}_A(k_A, k_B) = 0$, is a *hyperbola* (including degenerate ones) with a *vertical* asymptote and an *oblique* one, whereas $\mathcal{F}_B(k_A, k_B) = 0$ is a *hyperbola* (including degenerate ones) with a *horizontal* asymptote and an *oblique* one. These *nullclines* are shown in Fig. 21.7. Further analysis of the *vector field* $(\mathcal{F}_A, \mathcal{F}_B)$, (21.128)–(21.129), gives:

**Theorem 21.7** *For two large, competitive, trading economies, with the same exogenous labor growth, and with different proportional saving and different Leontief technologies, the necessary and sufficient conditions—for the existence, uniqueness, and the* ***global*** *stability of* ***diversified*** *steady-state growth in* ***both*** *countries—are given by the* ***joint*** *conditions:*

$$(i) \quad k_{2A} > k_{1A}, \quad k_{2B} > k_{1B}, \tag{21.134}$$

$$(ii) \quad \frac{s_A}{n} > \frac{k_{1A}}{y_{1A}}, \quad \frac{s_B}{n} > \frac{k_{1B}}{y_{1B}}, \tag{21.135}$$

$$(iii) \quad \frac{n\,k_{2B}}{y_{1A}\,(1 - s_A)} \geq \frac{v_A}{v_B}, \quad \frac{n\,k_{2A}}{y_{1B}\,(1 - s_B)} \geq \frac{v_B}{v_A}. \tag{21.136}$$

*If* ***only*** *(21.134) is* ***reversed****, and (21.135)–(21.136) are maintained, then the unique interior steady state is changed from a global attractor to a global* ***repeller****, and hence, at least* ***one*** *country will be completely* ***specialized****.*

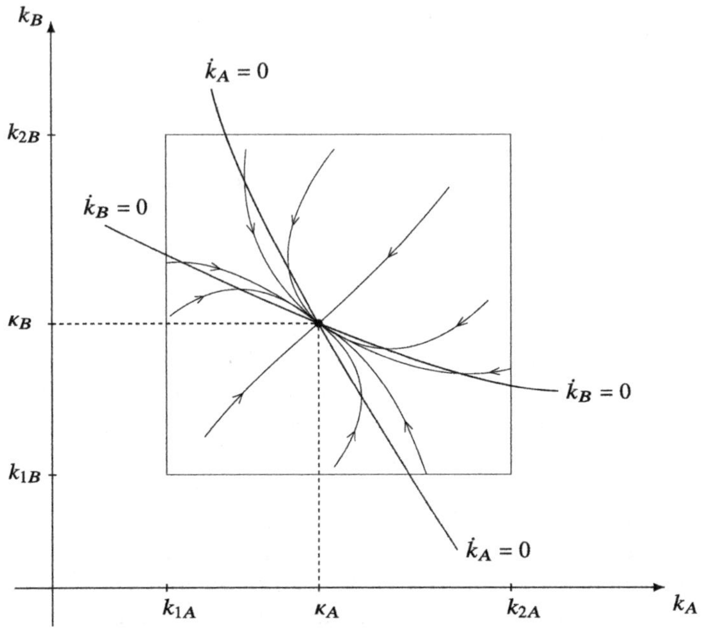


**Fig. 21.7** Phase portrait of (21.128)–(21.129) and the conditions (21.137)–(21.139)

*With internationally identical technologies, (21.134)–(21.136) become:*

$$(i) \quad k_2 > k_1, \tag{21.137}$$

$$(ii) \quad \frac{s_A}{n} > \frac{k_1}{y_1}, \quad \frac{s_B}{n} > \frac{k_1}{y_1}, \tag{21.138}$$

$$(iii) \quad \frac{n\,k_2}{y_1\,(1-s_A)} \geq \frac{v_A}{v_B}, \quad \frac{n\,k_2}{y_1\,(1-s_B)} \geq \frac{v_B}{v_A}. \tag{21.139}$$

***Proof*** The proof is based upon invariance properties of $C_k^2$. The *diversification rectangle*, $C_k^2$, is said to be *positively invariant*, if any *solution* $[k_A(t), k_B(t)]$ to the system (21.128)–(21.129) that starts in $C_k^2$ remains in $C_k^2$ forever. Likewise, $C_k^2$ is *negatively invariant* if any solution to (21.128)–(21.129), whenever observed in $C_k^2$, must have been there in the entire past. It can be shown that *positive* invariance of $C_k^2$ is *equivalent* to (21.134)–(21.136) including equalities in (21.135). Likewise, $C_k^2$ is *negatively* invariant iff (21.135)–(21.136) are satisfied, including equalities in (21.135), and both inequalities (21.134) are *reversed*. Furthermore, if $C_k^2$ is positively invariant and the inequalities (21.135) are *strict*, then there is only *one steady state* in $C_k^2$, and this steady state is a *global attractor*. If only (21.134) is reversed (negative invariance), then the interior steady state is a global *repeller*. The formal proof is given in Appendix C, section "Appendix C: Proof of Theorem 21.7". □

The necessary and sufficient *parameter conditions* (21.134)–(21.136) or (21.137)–(21.139) allow opportunities for *free trade* and *diversification* in *both countries* to coexist and be maintained during the *transition* dynamics towards a unique, *diversified*, *international* steady state. As is well known, the *one-factor* Ricardian trade model does *not* admit such long-run *diversification*.

It is observed from (21.134)–(21.136) that *larger saving* rates, $s_A$, $s_B$, and *larger capital* intensities in the *consumer good* industries, $k_{2A}$, $k_{2B}$, contribute to satisfying the **joint** conditions. Moreover, if e.g. the *share* $v_A$ is large, then a large $s_A$ helps to meet the **joint** conditions. However, the *range* of $(n/y_{1A})$ and $(n/y_{1B})$ has to be *restricted*. It is seen from parameter conditions (21.136) that the *relative size* of the *two* countries must *not* differ too much.

In comparing (21.135)–(21.136) with (21.138)–(21.139), the *former* conditions are evidently more *easily* met than the latter, because of greater *flexibility* in parameter variations. Thus, with accumulating factor endowments and free international trade, it is more *difficult* to sustain long-run *diversification* in both countries when the sector *technologies* are internationally *identical*. **Figure 21.7** is drawn for the *Heckscher-Ohlin-Samuelson* (HOS) case of *identical* technologies, and $C_k^2$ is a *square*.

When the inequalities (21.134) and (21.137) are *reversed*, it is generally not possible to indicate which country will be specialized and in which good, as any of the four boundaries in Fig. 21.7 can be attained, depending on the *initial values* (factor *endowment* ratios) of the *two* countries. The *stability* conditions (21.137)–(21.139) and the TTS *surface* (21.122) are closely linked to the *Rybczynski* theorem.

The *dynamic* international equilibrium model (21.128)–(21.133) of *two large* countries *trading* in two goods may be seen as an *extension* of the *closed economy* (autarky) growth models with *Leontief* technologies that *initiated* the *dynamic analysis* of *growing* two-sector economies, see Shinkai (1960); Jones (1965); Corden (1966); Stiglitz and Uzawa (1969); Ramanathan (1973, 1975); Jensen (1994); here Chap. 14, and Gandolfo (1996).

It may be observed that some *parameter* (sectoral factor intensity) *conditions*, (21.134), for an *attractor* in a simple dynamic general equilibrium *trade* model with two *large* countries—in contrast, cf. *Remark 21.1*, Fig. 21.2, to a *small* trading country (for which international trade is indispensable for growth)—are *similar* to *corresponding parameter conditions* of an *aggregated* (global, closed) *two-sector* economy.

The *relative size* of countries (21.136) are naturally involved in *maintaining* diversification within trading *subunits* of the world economy.

## Final Comments

We have analyzed *factor accumulation* processes for *small* and *large* two-sector economies that *trade freely* in both goods. As to *capital formation* in a *small* country, the implications of proportional, classical, and optimal saving were examined in combination with assumptions of exogenous or endogenous *labor growth*. Regarding the issues of long-run *diversification* and *persistent* (endogenous) *per capita growth*, a comparison of the theoretical economic results is presented in Table 21.1.

The *unifying* mathematical structure of the basic growth models for *small* and the international equilibrium of two *large trading* economies, diversified or specialized, was planar *homogenous dynamic systems* with labor and capital as the state variables. It encompasses the dynamics of classical, neoclassical, and some newer, endogenous per capita growth models. The regime of *exogenous population* (labor) growth and *high substitution* elasticities between labor and capital only occurs in later (*modern*) stages of economic development.

Of course, we have neglected many aspects of expanding factor endowments and factor reallocations that affect the growth of trading economies. Some extensions may introduce variable returns to scale, human capital, technical progress, presence of non-tradeable goods, disequilibrium dynamics, and uncertainty.

We hope, however, that the *theorems* and *propositions* on the general equilibrium *dynamics* of basic *two-dimensional trade* models contribute to building a theoretical framework and a *benchmark*—against which the results of extensions and *multi-dimensional* dynamic *trade models* can be appraised.

**Table 21.1** Dynamics of a small trading economy with constant returns to scale technologies

| Labor growth<br>Saving behavior | Exogenous labor growth | Endogenous labor growth |
|---|---|---|
| Proportional saving | Diversification: Limited range. Persistent growth: Possible. | Diversification: Limited range. Persistent growth: Not possible. |
| Classical saving | Diversification: Singularity. Persistent growth: Possible. | Diversification: Limited range. Persistent growth: Not possible. |
| Optimal saving | Diversification: Singularity. Persistent growth: Possible. | Diversification: Limited range. Persistent growth: Not possible. |

**Acknowledgments** Bjarne S. Jensen's research was supported by the Danish Social Sciences Research Council, grant no. 9500740.
We would like to thank Giancarlo Gandolfo, Alan V. Deardorff, and Kar-yiu Wong for their detailed comments and suggestions. Useful comments were received from Peter Skott, Harald Preissler, Niels Henrik Børjesson, Jimmie Thomsen.

## Appendix A: Endogenous Growth and Inessential Labor

Consider two *homogenous* $C^1$-class functions, $(\mathcal{F}, \mathcal{G})$, of *degree 1* as *governing functions* of dynamic systems in the plane

$$\dot{x} = \mathcal{F}(x, y) = x\,\mathcal{F}(1, y/x) = x\,\mathfrak{f}(r), \tag{21.140}$$

$$\dot{y} = \mathcal{G}(x, y) = x\,\mathcal{G}(1, y/x) = x\,\mathfrak{g}(r), \tag{21.141}$$

and

$$\dot{r} = h(r) = \mathfrak{g}(r) - r\mathfrak{f}(r). \tag{21.142}$$

**Definition 21.1** Endogenous (persistent) growth of any rapidity:

$$h(r) > 0, \quad \forall r > r_0. \tag{21.143}$$

From (21.142), we have, cf. (21.140)–(21.141)

$$\begin{aligned} \forall r \geq r_0, \quad h(r) > 0 &\Leftrightarrow \mathfrak{g}(r) > r\mathfrak{f}(r) \\ &\Leftrightarrow x\,\mathcal{G}(x, y) > y\,\mathcal{F}(x, y), \quad \forall y \geq r_0 x. \end{aligned} \tag{21.144}$$

**Lemma 21.3** *A necessary condition for persistent (endogenous) growth is:*

$$\mathcal{F}(0, y) \leq 0, \quad \forall y \geq 0. \tag{21.145}$$

Lemma 21.3 is implied by the last inequality of (21.144). If Lemma 21.3 is violated, there will be a *root* (steady state) in (21.142), which globally *prevents* $r(t) \to \infty$, i.e., persistent (endogenous) growth.

**Lemma 21.4** *With a homogenous dynamic system of degree 1 (21.140)–(21.141), and the first state variable growing exogenously* $\forall x \geq 0$: $\mathcal{F}(x, y) = x\,\mathfrak{f}(r) = x\,\mathcal{F}(1, 0) = x\,c_0$, $c_0 > 0$, *then a necessary condition for persistent endogenous growth is,* $\forall y > 0$: $\mathcal{G}(0, y) > 0$.

***Proof*** By (21.144) and exogeneity above, we get: $\mathcal{G}(x, y) > yc_0$, $\forall y \geq r_0 x$, which requires $\mathcal{G}(0, y) > 0$ for $y > 0$, as stated in Lemma 21.4. □

**Remark 21.10** With exogeneity and homogeneity of degree higher than 1, we can have persistent growth, without the condition, $\forall y > 0$: $\mathcal{G}(0, y) > 0$.

Example: $\mathcal{F}(x, y) = (1/2)x^2$, $\mathcal{G}(x, y) = xy$; $x \geq 0$, $y \geq 0$, we have, $h(r) = r - 1/2\,r = 1/2\,r$, which implies $r(t) \to \infty$, even with $\mathcal{G}(0, y) = 0$. But with a *higher* degree than *1*, the solutions $r(t)$ explode (infinite in finite time), cf. Jensen (1994, p. 190); here Theorem 28.3 in Sect. "On Solutions and Their Maximal Time Interval of Existence", and we have problems raised by Solow (1994). ▽

## Appendix B: Proof of Theorem 21.5

We consider the *dynamic system*, cf. (21.102) and (21.107),

$$\dot{k} = h(k, c) = y(k)/P_1 - n\,k - c/p \tag{21.146}$$

$$\dot{c} = \eta(k, c) = c\,\sigma(c)\,[\,y'(k)/P_1 - (n + \rho)\,] \tag{21.147}$$

in the *closed* first quadrant, $\overline{\mathbf{R}}^2_+$. The *constants*, $P_1$, $p$, $n$, and $\rho$, are assumed to be *positive*. The positive *intertemporal* elasticity of substitution $\sigma(c) = -u'(c)/[\,c\,u''(c)\,]$ depends on the utility function $u(c)$.

*Assumption 21.1* The per capita GNP-function $\mathbf{y(k)}$ has the continuity and differentiability properties as follows,

$$(i) \quad y(k) \in C^0([0, \infty[) \cap C^1(]0, \infty[), \qquad (ii) \quad y(0) \geq 0. \tag{21.148}$$

It is further assumed that

$$(iii) \quad \forall k > 0: \quad y'(k)/P_1 > n + \rho. \tag{21.149}$$

For a *concave* GNP-function with $y(k) \to \infty$ as $k \to \infty$, (21.149) becomes

$$(iv) \quad \lim_{k\to\infty} y'(k)/P_1 = \beta/P_1 > n + \rho. \tag{21.150}$$

It follows from (21.148)–(21.149) or (21.148) and (21.150) that the system (21.146)–(21.147) has *no stationary* solutions in $\overline{\mathbf{R}}^2_+$ [except possibly for (0, 0)], and that the positive $k$-axis ($c = 0$) is a trajectory (orbit).

**Lemma 21.5** *If there exists* $\delta > 0$ *and* $k_0 > 0$ *such that* $\forall k \geq k_0, \forall c > 0$*:*

$$\frac{y(k)/P_1}{k} - n - \sigma(c)\left[\frac{y'(k)}{P_1} - n - \rho\right] \geq \delta, \tag{21.151}$$

*then there exists to the system (21.146)–(21.147) an orbit*$-\Gamma(t) \equiv [k^*(t), c^*(t)]$, $t \in \mathbf{R}$, *such that* $k^*(t) \to \infty$, $c^*(t) \to \infty$, *as* $t \to \infty$*—which separates the first quadrant into two regions I and II in Fig. 21.6b. An orbit starting in the lower*

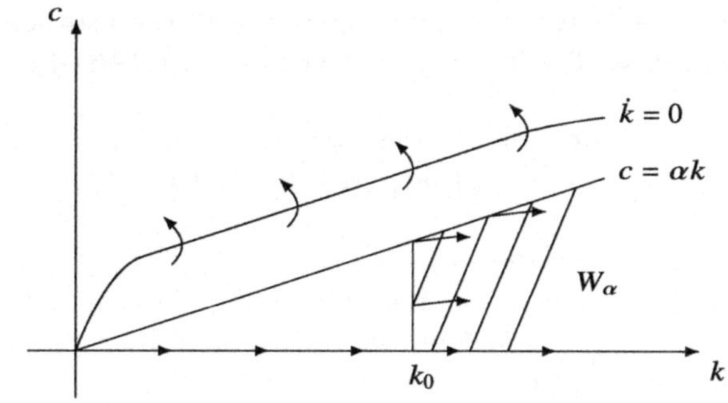


**Fig. 21.8** The positive invariant region, $\mathbf{W}_\alpha$, with endogenous (persistent) per capita growth

*region I has the same behavior as* $\Gamma$ *for* $t \to \infty$, *whereas an orbit starting in the upper region II eventually meets the* $c$*-axis,* $k = 0$.

***Proof*** Consider the *region* $W_\alpha = \{(k, c) \mid 0 \leq c \leq \alpha\, k \wedge k \geq k_0\}$, where $\boldsymbol{\alpha}$ is a *positive constant*, chosen such that $W_\alpha$ becomes *positively invariant*, cf. Fig. 21.8.

Since the *vector field* (21.146)–(21.147) is directed *inward* on the line $k = k_0$, and since the positive $k$-axis is a trajectory, the region $W_\alpha$ is *positive invariant*, iff the vector field points inward on the line $c = \alpha k$, $(k > k_0)$. Since the inward pointing *normal* to the line $c = \alpha k$ is $(\alpha, -1)$, we require,

$$\alpha\, h(k, \alpha k) \;-\; \eta\,(k, \alpha k) > 0, \qquad \text{for } \; k \geq k_0. \tag{21.152}$$

Inserting the expressions for $h\,(k, c)$, (21.146), and $\eta\,(k, c)$, (21.147), into (21.152), and simplifying, we find the requirement:

$$\frac{\alpha}{p} < \frac{y(k)/P_1}{k} - n - \sigma\,(\alpha\, k)\left[\, y'(k)/P_1 - (n + \rho)\,\right] \equiv R\,(k),\; k\; \geq\; k_0. \tag{21.153}$$

A positively *invariant* region $W_\alpha$ (with some $\alpha > 0$) *exists*, iff $\mathbf{R(k)}$ is *bounded* from *below* by a *positive constant*. By (21.151), we have for $k \geq k_0$

$$R\,(k)\; \geq\; \delta\; >\; 0. \tag{21.154}$$

Choose $(\alpha/p)$ to be any positive *constant less* than $\delta$. Then $W_\alpha$ is positively invariant. For any orbit in the *open* first quadrant, $\Re^2_+$, we have by (21.149) that $\dot{\mathbf{c}} > 0$, (21.147). Accordingly, it follows that any *orbit starting* in $W_\alpha$ must satisfy: $k(t) \to \infty$, $c(t) \to \infty$, as $t \to \infty$. Any orbit in $\Re^2_+$ must either behave as just characterized (class I), or *cross* the $\dot{\mathbf{k}} = 0$ nullcline (class II). In the *latter* case, the orbit will *meet* the $\mathbf{c}$ – **axis** eventually, since otherwise $c(t) \to \infty$ and,

$k(t) \to k_\varepsilon$ as $t \to \infty$, for some, $k_\varepsilon \geq 0$. For **t** sufficiently large, i.e., **k** sufficiently *small*, say $0 < k \leq k^*$, we have from (21.146)–(21.147):

$$-\frac{dc}{dk} = \frac{\sigma(c)\,[\,y'(k)/P_1 - n - \rho\,]}{-(1/c)\,[\,y(k)/P_1 - n\,k\,] + 1/p} \leq \frac{\bar{\sigma}\, y'(k)/P_1}{1/(2\,p)} \equiv a\, y'(k), \tag{21.155}$$

where $\bar{\sigma}$ is an *upper bound* for $\sigma(c)$. This immediately *rules out*, $k_\varepsilon > 0$, since then, $-\frac{\mathbf{dc}}{\mathbf{dk}}$, would be bounded above by a constant. If $k_\varepsilon = 0$, we find by integrating from $k$ to $k^*$, for $0 < k < k^*$:

$$c\,(k) \leq c\,(k^*) + a\, y(k^*), \quad 0 < k \leq k^*, \tag{21.156}$$

*contradicting*, $c\,(k) \to \infty$, as $k \to 0^+$.

To get the *separating orbit*, $\Gamma$, consider a *curve*, **C**, *connecting* $(k, c) = (1, 0)$ with $(k, c) = (0, 1)$, and *intersecting* the nullcline $\dot{k} = 0$ *once* (think of a circle). We can write, $\mathbf{C} = C_I \cup C_{II} \cup \{(1, 0), (0, 1)\}$, where $C_I$ and $C_{II}$ consists of the points through which pass orbits of class I and II, respectively. $C_{II}$ must be an *open* and *connected* part of $C$. Since $C_I$ and $C_{II}$ are both non-empty, $C_I \cup \{(1, 0)\}$ must be *closed*. The *separating* orbit $\Gamma$ goes through the *end point* of $C_I$. □

A powerful and useful extension of Lemma 21.5 is the *simpler* separator condition stated in:

**Corollary 21.5** *With the assumptions of (21.148) and (21.150), the* ***sufficient*** *conditions for existence of the separating orbit, $\Gamma(t)$, of Lemma 21.5, is given by the restriction:*

$$\overline{\sigma} = \sup_{c>0} \sigma(c) < \frac{(\beta/P_1) - n}{(\beta/P_1) - (n + \rho)}, \tag{21.157}$$

*where $\overline{\sigma}$ is the upper bound of the intertemporal substitution elasticity $\sigma(c)$ of $u(c)$ and where $\beta/P_1$ is given in (21.150).*

***Proof*** Since $\mathbf{y}\,(\mathbf{k}) \to \infty$ as $k \to \infty$, it follows from (21.150) and *l'Hospital* that $\mathbf{y}\,(\mathbf{k})/\mathbf{k} \to \beta$, as $k \to \infty$. Thus for any number $\varepsilon > 0$, there exists a number, $k_\varepsilon$, such that for $k > k_\varepsilon$, we have, cf. (21.151),

$$\begin{aligned} &\frac{y\,(k)/k}{P_1} - n - \sigma(c)\left[\frac{y'(k)}{P_1} - n - \rho\right] \\ &\geq \frac{\beta - \varepsilon}{P_1} - n - \sup_{c>0} \sigma(c)\left[\frac{\beta + \varepsilon}{P_1} - n - \rho\right] \\ &= \frac{\beta}{P_1} - n - \overline{\sigma}\left[\frac{\beta}{P_1} - n - \rho\right] - \frac{\varepsilon}{P_1}(1 + \overline{\sigma}) \equiv \delta \end{aligned} \tag{21.158}$$

By assumption (21.150) and (21.157), the *sum* of the first *three* terms of $\delta$ above is *positive*. Thus, by choosing $\varepsilon > 0$ sufficiently *small*, also $\delta$ is *positive*. Thus, the requirements of Lemma 21.5 are satisfied, and hence the *separating* orbit $\Gamma$ *exists*. □

**Lemma 21.6** *If any selected utility function $u(c)$ is assumed to satisfy:*

$$\forall c \geq c_0 \geq 0 : \quad 0 \leq u(c) \leq A\, c, \tag{21.159}$$

*where A is any positive constant, then* ***convergence*** *of the integral $U = \int_0^\infty u[\,c(t)\,]\, e^{-\rho t} dt$, for a solution $[k(t), c(t)]$ to system (21.146)–(21.147) is assured, if*

$$\overline{\sigma} = \sup_{c>0} \sigma(c) < \frac{\rho}{\beta / P_1 - (n + \rho)} \tag{21.160}$$

*where $\beta$ is given by (21.150).*

***Proof*** Let $\varepsilon > 0$. Choose $k_\varepsilon$ such that $y'(k) < \beta + \varepsilon$ for $k \geq k_\varepsilon$. Choose $t_\varepsilon$ such that $k(t) > k_\varepsilon$ for $t > t_\varepsilon$. Then from (21.147), we find

$$\forall t \geq t_\varepsilon : \quad \dot{c} < c \sup_{c>0} \sigma(c)\, [\,(\beta + \varepsilon)/P_1 - (n + \rho)\,] \equiv \alpha\, c \tag{21.161}$$

It follows from (21.161) that, $c(t) \leq c\,(t_\varepsilon)\, e^{\alpha\,(t - t_\varepsilon)}$, and hence, cf. (21.159),

$$u[\,c(t)\,]\, e^{-\rho t} \leq A\; c(t)\, e^{-\rho t} \leq A\; c\,(t_\varepsilon)\, e^{-\alpha\, t_\varepsilon}\, e^{-\,(\rho\, -\, \alpha)\, t} \tag{21.162}$$

Thus *convergence* of integral $U$ is assured, if, $\alpha < \rho$, which by (21.161) says

$$\overline{\sigma} = \sup_{c>0} \sigma(c) < \frac{\rho}{(\beta + \varepsilon)/P_1 - (n + \rho)} \tag{21.163}$$

With $\varepsilon > 0$, chosen sufficiently small, the *requirement* (21.163) can be satisfied by the *condition* (21.160). □

**Remark 21.11** The condition (21.160) is *stronger* that (21.157) of Corollary 21.5, since by assumption (21.150), we have:

$$\frac{\rho}{\beta / P_1 - (n + \rho)} < \frac{\beta / P_1 - n}{\beta / P_1 - (n + \rho)} \tag{21.164}$$

In short, the *existence* of *separating orbit* $\Gamma$ is *assured* by $\overline{\sigma} < 1$, but $\overline{\sigma} < 1$ does *not* itself ensure *convergence* of $\mathbf{U}$. However, for *isoelastic* $\mathbf{u(c)}$ with $\forall c$, $\sigma(c) = \sigma$ (constant), it can be verified that the *convergence* of $\mathbf{U}$ is in fact also *ensured* by the *existence* condition of the *separating orbit*, (21.157).

Indeed, with *constant* intertemporal elasticity of substitution, the separating orbit in Fig. 21.6b is the *optimal solution* $[k^*(t), c^*(t)]$, satisfying the *transversality* condition; see hereto Gandolfo (1996, p. 390).

It remains to be seen *how* (21.160) may be relaxed for general *non-isoelastic* $\mathbf{u}(\mathbf{c})$ in Ramsey problems. ▽

## APPENDIX C: PROOF OF THEOREM 21.7

The necessary and sufficient conditions for invariance of the diversification region, $C_k^2$, (21.133), (21.120), and global stability of (21.128)–(21.129) are obtained as follows.

### *Invariance of* $\mathbf{C}_\mathbf{k}^2$

To prove *positive invariance*, we first show that the *vector field* is directed inward on the boundary of $C_k^2$, (21.120), iff the inequalities (21.134)–(21.136) hold with strict inequalities.

The boundary of $C_k^2$, (21.120), cf. Fig. 21.7, consists of *four line* segments, leading to the following *four requirements* for positive invariance, with $\xi_A = \text{sign}(k_{2A} - k_{1A})$, and $\xi_B = \text{sign}(k_{2B} - k_{1B})$.

$$\xi_A \mathcal{F}_A(k_{1A}, k_B) > 0 \text{ for all } k_B \in I_B, \tag{21.165}$$

$$\xi_A \mathcal{F}_A(k_{2A}, k_B) < 0 \text{ for all } k_B \in \overline{I}_B, \tag{21.166}$$

$$\xi_B \mathcal{F}_B(k_A, k_{1B}) > 0 \text{ for all } k_A \in I_A, \tag{21.167}$$

$$\xi_B \mathcal{F}_B(k_A, k_{2B}) < 0 \text{ for all } k_A \in \overline{I}_A, \tag{21.168}$$

where $I_A$ is the *half-open interval between* $k_{1A}$ and $k_{2A}$, including $k_{2A}$, but not $k_{1A}$. $\overline{I}_A$ is its *closure*. $I_B$ and $\overline{I}_B$ are defined similarly.

Next, (21.165) and (21.167) are satisfied iff, cf. (21.128), (21.130), and (21.132)

$$\xi_A\,(y_{1A}\,s_A - n\,k_{1A}) > 0, \text{ and } \xi_B\,(y_{1B}\,s_B - n\,k_{1B}) > 0, \tag{21.169}$$

which gives (21.135) with $\xi_A > 0$, $\xi_B > 0$, cf. below.

It can be seen that, cf. (21.128) and (21.132),

$$\mathcal{F}_A(k_{2A}, k_B) = \frac{s_A\,y_{2A}\,v_B\,y_{1B}\,(1 - s_B)\,(k_{2B} - k_B) - n\,k_{2A}\,D}{D}, \tag{21.170}$$

where the *denominator*, $D$, is given by,

$$D = v_A\,s_A\,y_{2A}\,(k_{2B} - k_{1B}) + v_B\,s_B\,y_{2B}\,(k_B - k_{1B}). \tag{21.171}$$

Notice that $D$ has the *same sign* as, $k_{2B} - k_{1B}$.

The *numerator* is a polynomial of degree 1 in $k_B$, so it suffices that

$$\xi_A\,\xi_B\,[\,s_A\,y_{2A}\,v_B\,y_{1B}\,(1-s_B)\,(k_{2B}-k_B)\;-n\,k_{2A}\,D\,]\;<0, \tag{21.172}$$

for $k_B = k_{1B}$ and for $k_B = k_{2B}$. This gives the following two requirements

$$(i)\;\;\xi_A\,\xi_B\,[\,-n\,k_{2A}\,v_A\;+v_B\,y_{1B}\,(1-s_B)\,]\,s_A\,y_{2A}\,(k_{2B}-k_{1B})<0, \tag{21.173}$$

$$(ii)\;\;\xi_A\,\xi_B\,(\,-n\,k_{2A}\,)(v_A\,s_A\,y_{2A}\;+v_B\,s_B\,y_{2B})\,(k_{2B}-k_{1B})<0. \tag{21.174}$$

Using that $\xi_B\,(k_{2B}-k_{1B})>0$, we reduce (21.173) to:

$$\xi_A\,[\,-n\,k_{2A}\,v_A\;+v_B\,y_{1B}\,(1-s_B)\,]\;<0, \tag{21.175}$$

and (21.174) to the *simple* requirement, $\xi_A > 0$, i.e., $k_{2A} > k_{1A}$. Hence with $\xi_A > 0$, $\xi_B > 0$, i.e., (21.134), then (21.174)–(21.175) give (21.136).

*Requirement* (21.168) similarly leads to the two requirements:

$$\xi_B\;>0\,,\;\text{and}\;\;-\;n\,k_{2B}\,v_B\;+v_A\,y_{1A}\,(1-s_A\,)\;<0. \tag{21.176}$$

Finally, observe that when, $s_A/n = \frac{k_{1A}}{y_{1A}}$ (i.e., equality in one of the inequalities of (21.135) or (21.169)), then $\mathcal{F}_A(k_{1A}, k_B) = 0$ for all $k_B$. Thus the *line* $k_A = k_{1A}$ *consists of orbits*. When $s_B/n = \frac{k_{1B}}{y_{1B}}$, the *line* $k_B = k_{1B}$ consists of orbits.

When $\frac{n\,k_{2A}}{y_{1B}(1-s_B)} = \frac{v_B}{v_A}$—*equality* in one of (21.136) or (21.175)—then the *vector field* is directed *inward* on the *segment* $k_A = k_{2A}$ for $k_B \in\, ]k_{1B}, k_{2B}]$, and is *parallel* to the segment $k_B = k_{1B}$.

An analogous statement holds, when $\frac{n\,k_{2B}}{y_{1A}(1-s_A)} = \frac{v_A}{v_B}$.

We conclude that the *system* is *positively invariant*, also if one or several of the inequalities (21.135)–(21.136) are in fact equalities.

### *Global Stability*

We show that, *if* $C_k^2$ is *positively invariant*, and *if* the *inequalities* (21.135) are *strict*, then there is one *equilibrium* in $C_k^2$, and this equilibrium is a *global attractor*.

First notice that the nullcline, $\dot{\mathbf{k}}_A = 0$, i.e., $\mathcal{F}_A(k_A, k_B) = 0$, is a *hyperbola*, cf. Fig. 21.7, Fig. 21.9. It has the *vertical asymptote*:

$$\begin{aligned} k_A &= k_{1A} \\ &\quad+\frac{(k_{2A}-k_{1A})(s_A\,y_{1A}-n\,k_{1A})\,s_B\,y_{2B}}{n\,s_B\,y_{2B}\,(k_{2A}-k_{1A})+s_A\,(y_{2A}\,y_{1B}(1-s_B)+y_{1A}\,y_{2B}\,s_B)} \end{aligned} \tag{21.177}$$

which lies between, $k_A = k_{1A}$, and $k_A = k_{2A}$.

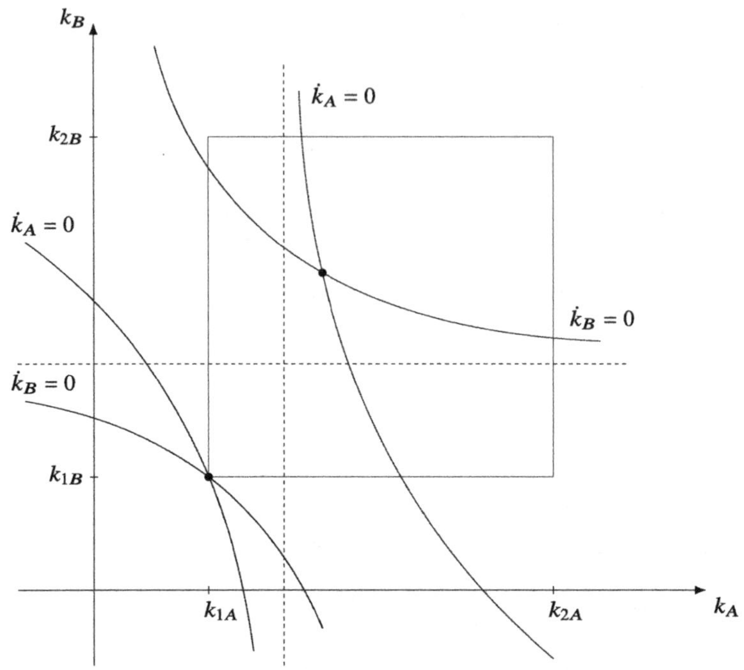


**Fig. 21.9** The shape and location of nullclines, $\dot{\mathbf{k}}_{\mathbf{A}}= \mathbf{0}$, $\dot{\mathbf{k}}_{\mathbf{B}}= \mathbf{0}$, for the dynamic system (21.128)–(21.129) of two large trading economies

Earlier, we found that $\mathcal{F}_A(k_{2A}, k_B) < 0$ for all $k_B > k_{1B}$. Let $\boldsymbol{k_{B0}}$ be the *root* of $D = 0$ (21.171). Then $k_{B0} < k_{1B}$, and we see that $\mathcal{F}_A(k_{2A}, k_B) > 0$ for $k_B$ close to $k_{B0}$ with $k_B > k_{B0}$. We conclude that one *branch* of the hyperbola $\mathcal{F}_A(k_A, k_B) = 0$ passes through the *line segment* $k_A = k_{2A}, k_B \leq k_{1B}$. This same branch has the upper *half-line* given by (21.177) as its *asymptote*. The other branch of that *hyperbola* goes through $(k_{1A}, k_{1B})$, and has the lower half-line given by (21.177) as its asymptote.

Since analogous statements can be made about the nullcline $\dot{\mathbf{k}}_B = 0$, the *nullclines* are located as shown in Fig. 21.9. We conclude that there is a *unique equilibrium* in $C_k^2$. This equilibrium is a *global attractor* (and a *node*).

When $\frac{k_{1A}}{y_{1A}}$ approaches $s_A/n$ from below, the *equilibrium* moves to the *boundary* $k_A = k_{1A}$. An analogous statement holds with $A$ replaced by $B$.

**Remark 21.12** Appendices A, B, and C are joint works with **Preben Kjeld Alsholm**, Technical University of Denmark. ▽

## Bibliography


Atsumi H (1971) The Long–Run Offer Function and a Dynamic Theory of International Trade. Journal of International Economics 1:267–299

Bardhan PK (1965a) Equilibrium Growth in the International Economy. Quarterly Journal of Economics 79:455–464

Bardhan PK (1965b) International Differences in Production Functions, Trade and Factor Prices. Economic Journal 75:81–87

Bardhan PK (1966) On Factor Accumulation and the Pattern of International Specialisation. Review of Economics Studies 33:39–44

Bardhan PK (1970) Economic Growth, Development, and Foreign Trade. Wiley–Interscience, New York

Barro RJ, Sala-i-Martin X (2004) Economic Growth Theory, 2nd edn. M.I.T. Press, Cambridge, Mass

Becker RA, Burmeister E (1991) Growth Theory, vol I–III. Edward Elgar, Aldershot

Becker RA, Foias C (1987) A Characterization of Ramsey Equilibrium. Journal of Economic Theory 41:173–184, Reprinted in Becker (1991)

Bertola G (1993) Factor Shares and Savings in Endogenous Growth. American Economic Review 83:1184–1190

Bertola G (1996) Factor Shares in OLG Models of Growth. European Economic Review 40:1541–1560

Bhagwati JN (1981) International Trade: Selected Readings, 2nd edn. MIT Press, Cambridge, MA

Cass D (1965) Optimum Growth in an Aggregative Model of Capital Accumulation. Review of Economic Studies 32:233–240, Reprinted in Becker (1991)

Corden WM (1966) The Two–Sector Growth Model with Fixed Coefficients. Review of Economic Studies 33:253–262

Deardorff AV (1971) Growth and Trade in a Two–Sector World. PhD thesis, Cornell University, unpublished Ph.D. dissertation

Deardorff AV (1973) The Gains from Trade in and out of Steady–State Growth. Oxford Economic Papers 25:173–191

Deardorff AV (1974) A Geometry of Growth and Trade. Canadian Journal of Economics 2:295–306

Deardorff AV (1994) Growth and International Investment with Diverging Populations. Oxford Economic Papers 46:477–491

Deardorff AV, Hanson JA (1978) Accumulation and a Long–Run Heckscher–Ohlin Theorem. Economic Inquiry 16:288–292

Deaton A (1992) Understanding Consumption. Clarendon Press, Oxford

Drabicki JZ, Takayama A (1975) On the Optimal Growth of the Two–Sector Economy. Keio Economic Studies 12:1–36

Ethier W, Ross SA (1971) International Capital Movements and Long Run Diversification. Journal of International Economics 1:301–314

Findlay R (1959) Factor Intensities, Technological Progress and the Terms of Trade. Oxford Economic Papers 11:111–121

Findlay R (1970) Factor Proportions and Comparative Advantage in the Long Run. Journal of Political Economy 78:27–34, Reprinted in Bhagwati (1981)

Findlay R (1984) Growth and Development in Trade Models. In Jones (1984)

Galor O, Lin S (1997) Dynamic Foundations for the Factor Endowment Model of International Trade

Gandolfo G (1994) International Economics I: The Pure Theory of International Trade, 2nd edn. Springer–Verlag, Berlin
Gandolfo G (1996) Economic Dynamics: Methods and Models, 3rd edn. Springer–Verlag, Berlin
Grossman GM, Rogoff K (1995) Handbook of International Economics, vol III. Elsevier, Amsterdam
Hall RE (1988) Intertemporal Substitution in Consumption. Journal of Political Economy 96:339–357
Hamada K (1974) An Economic Analysis of the Duty–Free Zone. Journal of International Economics 4:225–241
Jensen BS (1994) The Dynamic Systems of Basic Economic Growth Models. Kluwer Academic Publishers, Dordrecht
Jensen BS, Larsen ME (1987) Growth and Long–Run Stability. Acta Applicandae Mathematicae 9:219–237, Reprinted in Jensen (1994)
Johnson HG (1959) Economic Development and International Trade. Nationaløkonomisk Tidsskrift 97:253–272
Jones LE, Manuelli RE (1990) A Convex Model of Equilibrium Growth: Theory and Policy Implications. Journal of Political Economy 98:1008–1038
Jones RW (1965) The Structure of Simple General Equilibrium Models. J Political Economy 73:557–72, or Bhagwati (1981)
Jones RW, Kenen PB (1984) Handbook of International Economics, vol I. North–Holland, Amsterdam
Kemp MC (1969) The Pure Theory of International Trade and Investment. Prentice–Hall, New Jersey
Klundert Tvd, Smulders S (1992) Reconstructing Growth Theory: A Survey. De Economist 140:177–203
Kuznets S (1966) Modern Economic Growth. Rate, Structure and Spread. Yale University Press, New Haven
Leamer EE, Levinsohn J (1995) International Trade Theory: The Evidence. Ch. 26 in Grossman and Rogoff (1995).
Leonard D, Long NV (1992) Optimal Control Theory and Static Optimization in Economics. Cambridge University Press
Long NV, Wong KY (1997) Endogenous Growth and International Trade: A Survey
Lucas RE (1988) On the Mechanics of Economic Development. Journal of Monetary Economics 22:3–42, Reprinted in Becker (1991)
Lucas RE (1993) Making a Miracle. Econometrica 61:251–272
Niehans J (1963) Economic Growth with Two Endogenous Factors. Quarterly Journal of Economics 77:349–371
Obstfeld M (1982) Aggregate Spending and the Terms of Trade: Is There a Laursen–Metzler Effect? Quarterly Journal of Economics 97:251–270
Obstfeld M (1989) Fiscal Deficits and Relative Prices in a Growing World Economy. Journal of Monetary Economics 23:461–484
Obstfeld M, Rogoff K (1995) The Intertemporal Approach to the Current Account. Chapt. 34 in Grossman & Rogoff (1995).
Ohlin B (1933) Interregional and International Trade. Harvard University Press, Cambridge, MA
Oniki H, Uzawa H (1965) Patterns of Trade and Investment in a Dynamic Model of International Trade. Review of Economic Studies 32:15–38

Pitchford JD (1960) Growth and the Elasticity of Factor Substitution. Economic Record 36:491–504
Ramanathan R (1973) Adjustment Time in the Two–Sector Growth Model with Fixed Coefficients. Economic Journal 83:1236–1244
Ramanathan R (1975) The Elasticity of Substitution and the Speed of Convergence in Growth Models. Economic Journal 85:612–613
Rebelo S (1991) Long–Run Policy Analysis and Long–Run Growth. Journal of Political Economy 99:500–521
Romer PM (1986) Increasing Returns and Long–Run Growth. Journal of Political Economy 94:1002–1037, Reprinted in Becker (1991)
Romer PM (1994) The Origins of Endogenous Growth. Journal of Economic Perspectives 8:3–22
Rybczynski TM (1955) Factor Endowments and Relative Commodity Prices. Economica 22:336–341
Saint-Paul G (1992) Fiscal Policy in an Endogenous Growth Model. Quarterly Journal of Economies 107:1243–1259
Sala-i-Martin XX (1996) Regional Cohesion: Evidence and Theories of Regional Growth and Convergence. European Economic Review 40:1325–1352
Samuelson PA (1978) The Canonical Classical Model of Political Economy. Journal of Economic Literature 16:1415–1434
Shinkai Y (1960) On the Equilibrium Growth of Capital and Labor. International Economic Review 1:107–111
Simon JL (1990) Great and Almost–Great Magnitudes in Economics. Journal of Economic Perspectives 4:149–156
Smith MAM (1976) Trade, Growth and Consumption in Alternative Models of Capital Accumulation. Journal of International Economic 6:371–384
Smith MAM (1977) Capital Accumulation in the Open Two–Sector Economy. Economic Journal 87:273–282, Reprinted in Bhagwati (1981, chapter 25)
Smith MAM (1984) Capital Theory and Trade Theory, vol 6. Chapter 6 in Jones (1984)
Södersten B (1964) A Study of Economic Growth and International Trade. Almqvist and Wiksell, Stockholm
Solow RM (1956) A Contribution to the Theory of Economic Growth. Quarterly Journal of Economics 70:65–94, Reprinted in Stiglitz (1969), and in Becker (1991)
Solow RM (1994) Perspectives on Growth Theory. Journal of Economic Perspectives 8:45–54
Solow RM, Samuelson PA (1953) Balanced Growth under Constant Returns to Scale. Econometrica 21:412–424
Srinivasan TN (1964) Optimal Savings in a Two–Sector Model of Growth. Econometrica 32:358–373
Stiglitz JE (1970) Factor Price Equalization in a Dynamic Economy. Journal of Political Economy 78:456–488
Stiglitz JE, Uzawa H (1969) Readings in the Modern Theory of Economic Growth. M.I.T. Press, Cambridge, Mass
Summers R, Heston A (1991) The Penn World Table (Mark 5): An Expanded Set of International Comparisons, 1950–1988. Quarterly Journal of Economics 106:327–368
Swan TW (1956) Economic Growth and Capital Accumulation. Economic Record 32:334–361, Reprinted in Stiglitz (1969)
Takayama A (1972) International Trade. Holt, Rinehart, and Winston, New York

Uzawa H (1964) Optimal Growth in a Two–Sector Model of Capital Accumulation. Review of Economic Studies 31:1–25
Wan HY Jr (1971) Economic Growth. Harcourt Brace Jovanowich, New York
Wong KY (1995) International Trade in Goods and Factor Mobility. MIT Press, Cambridge, MA
Woodland AD (1982) International Trade and Resource Allocation. Amsterdam, North–Holland
Yang X, Borland J (1991) A Microeconomic Mechanism for Economic Growth. J Political Economy 99:460–82
Young A (1991) Learning by Doing and the Dynamic Effects of International Trade. Quarterly Journal of Economics 106:369–405

CHAPTER 22

# Saving Rates, Trade, Technology, and Stochastic Dynamics

## INTRODUCTION

Macroeconomic growth models have given main attention to the *real* (goods) *aspects* of economic development by mostly studying determinants of long-run growth, such as the laws of production (technology), population (demographics), and capital accumulation (saving/investment). These topics have in various forms always been the canonical elements of classical, Samuelson (1978), neoclassical, Solow (1956), and endogenous growth theory, Romer (1986), Lucas (1988), and Aghion and Howitt (1998).

As to the society as a whole, at least for closed or open economies with balanced trade, like any spending units with balanced budgets (expenditures equal to income), *real capital* constitutes the only form that *saving* can take. Moreover, since the financial net-position (financial assets vis-à-vis debts) does not change, macro (aggregate) growth modeling may abstract from and *ignore*, especially in a long-term perspective, the *financial aspects* of economic development. However, growing economies do involve a *financial sector* (asset markets, intermediaries, banks) in channeling savings toward investment. Financial intermediaries can affect the real growth rate by *altering* the *saving rate* (share of investment in GDP). The sign of this relationship is generally ambiguous, Levine (1991), Saint-Paul (1992), Pagano (1993), because the financial sector

With co-authors:
MARTIN RICHTER, Copenhagen Business School, Danske Research, Danske Bank, Copenhagen, Denmark
CHUNYAN WANG, Copenhagen Business School, Denmark
PREBEN K. ALSHOLM, Department of Mathematics and Computer Science, Technical University of Denmark, Denmark



B. S. Jensen, *The Elements and Dynamic Systems of Economic Growth and Trade Models*, https://doi.org/10.1007/978-3-031-52493-6_22

absorbs resources (reward for services supplied), but may also enhance saving incentives by offering risk-averse agents more efficient risk sharing via holding diversified portfolios. But as many types of increase in riskiness will apply to the yield on all assets, the actual possibility of hedging against risk by portfolio rearrangements is limited in many real-world situations, Sandmo (1969, 1970).

There is an extensive literature on the conditions and mechanisms by which financial intermediation may mobilize or cause shifts in savings and thereby accelerate/decelerate real economic growth, cf. Bencivenga (1991), Maddison (1992), King and Levine (1993), Berthelemy and Vardoudakis (1996), Greenwood and Smith (1997). But instead of modeling complex interactions between a financial sector and two real sectors (industries), we may allow for the exigency of the financial intermediaries and the existence of asset market effects on factor (real capital) accumulation by letting the aggregate saving/investment ratio be affected by a *diffusion process* (continuous-time uncertainties).

Openness to *trade* is another growth determinant, in particular for small trading economies. Our *open* stochastic *two-sector* growth model with balanced trade allows small economies—depending on the fixed terms of trade, saving rate, and technological parameters—to be *diversified* or *specialized* in producing only a consumer or capital good. Recent growth in emerging economies, like early *industrialization*, is often hefty driven by investments (*capital accumulation*). Exorbitant high saving ratios have indeed been observed in a number of Asian economies. But endogenous (persistent) growth per capita in small open economies also depends on key *technology* (intensity and substitution) *parameters* of the export (consumer or capital good) industry. *Endogenous* economic *growth* requires a *combination* of fundamental parameter values: saving rate, terms of trade, sectorial capital intensities, and substitution elasticities.

The *purpose* of this chapter is to develop a *framework* for *open, stochastic, two-sector dynamics* with *flexible* sector *technologies* of CES form, and contribute to identifying the *critical* numerical *values* of the *fundamental* growth *parameters.* We will illustrate the consequences of particular parameters by showing the *sample paths* and long-run *probability distributions* of the aggregate factor endowment ratio.

The foundation of our stochastic two-sector growth model was laid in Jensen and Wang (1999); here Chap. 27, upon which we draw heavily below. It resolved the critical issue of absorbing *boundaries* [lower (implosion) and upper (explosion)] by providing *sufficient* conditions for *inaccessible* boundaries in *finite* time. Having dispensed with boundary problems, it offered a few illustrative examples of stochastic dynamics using CD (Cobb-Douglas) sector technologies, which do not admit reversals of sectorial capital-labor ratios. Accordingly this small two-sector trading economy had only one diversification cone. In this chapter, we want to demonstrate (solve) stochastic dynamics with general CES technologies. But CES production functions and different substitution elasticities between industries (sectors) will, as is well-known, always imply the existence of sectorial *factor reversals* at some factor prices.

With regard to CES specifications, the empirical question of whether sectorial factor reversals have actually or frequently occurred within the observable range of factor price variation has in several studies been econometrically examined with mixed results, e.g., in tests of the Heckscher-Ohlin trade theorem and the factor-price equalization theorem, cf. Minhas (1962, 1963); Ethier (1979), Södersten and Reed (1994, p. 110), Fisher and Hillman (1984), and Gandolfo (1998, p. 90). By a suitable choice of initial values and with the prevalence of monotone solutions (trajectories), *deterministic* two-sector growth models may avoid the dynamic complications of factor reversals and of factor endowment domains with two diversification cones.

However, *stochastic* open two-sector dynamics with general CES technologies must (except occasionally for a narrow range of world market prices) cope with the factual mathematical-economic complication (existence) of two diversification cones, as the diffusion processes studied here imply a *nonzero probability* of observations anywhere in the domain of a nonnegative state variable (factor endowment ratio). Hence for CES sector technologies, a complete (global) characterization of the three-way relationship between commodity prices, factor prices, and sectorial factor proportions must, as our second objective, precede the enquiries into stochastic open two-sector dynamics.

The organization of the chapter is as follows. First, the general equilibrium structure of the small open economy is outlined. The commodity price-factor price correspondence is carefully stated and exhibited diagrammatically. Next, the steady-state growth, transition paths, and convergence to stationary distribution are demonstrated. Finally, stochastic endogenous growth paths with CES technologies are illustrated with a discussion of the critical parameter values involved.

## Structure of Open Two-Sector Growth Models

### *General Equilibrium of Small Trading Economies*

Consider an economy consisting of a *capital* good industry (sector) and a *consumer* good industry, labeled 1 and 2, respectively. The sector *technologies* are described by production functions exhibiting *constant returns* to scale,

$$Y_i = F_i(L_i, K_i) = L_i f_i(k_i) \equiv L_i y_i, \quad i = 1, 2 \tag{22.1}$$

where the function $f_i$ is a strictly concave monotonic increasing function on the nonnegative real line, i.e., $f_i(k_i) \equiv F_i(1, k_i)$, $k_i \equiv K_i/L_i$, $i = 1, 2$, have the properties

$$\forall k_i > 0: \quad f_i'(k_i) = df_i(k_i)/dk_i > 0, \quad f_i''(k_i) = d^2 f_i(k_i)/dk_i^2 < 0 \tag{22.2}$$

Full employment of labor and capital gives

$$L_1/L + L_2/L \equiv \lambda_1 + \lambda_2 = 1, \quad K/L \equiv k \equiv \lambda_1 k_1 + \lambda_2 k_2 \tag{22.3}$$

$$\lambda_1 = (k - k_2)/(k_1 - k_2), \quad \lambda_2 = (k_1 - k)/(k_1 - k_2), \quad Y_i = L_i y_i = L y_i \lambda_i \tag{22.4}$$

The open two-sector economy is assumed to operate under *perfect competition* (zero profit condition); absolute (money) *factor* prices $(w, r)$ are the same in both sectors; and *output* prices $(P_1, P_2)$ represent unit cost. Hence, we have the competitive *equilibrium* relations, $P_i Y_i = rK_i + wL_i$, $i = 1, 2$, and

$$\omega \equiv \frac{w}{r} = \omega_i = \frac{f_i(k_i)}{f_i'(k_i)} - k_i, \quad \frac{r}{P_i} = f_i'(k_i), \quad p \equiv \frac{P_1}{P_2} = \frac{f_2'(k_2)}{f_1'(k_1)} \tag{22.5}$$

A small, *open*, competitive two-sector economy can only remain *diversified* with common positive $\omega$, if the *range* of the *terms of trade*, $p \equiv P_1/P_2$, is confined to the zero profit price interval with the *limits*, cf. *Rybczynski lines*, Wong (1995),

$$\begin{aligned} &k_1 > k_2: \ \tilde{y}_2/\tilde{y}_1 < p < (\tilde{y}_2/\tilde{y}_1)(\tilde{k}_1/\tilde{k}_2); \\ &k_2 > k_1: \ (\tilde{y}_2/\tilde{y}_1)(\tilde{k}_1/\tilde{k}_2) < p < \tilde{y}_2/\tilde{y}_1 \end{aligned} \tag{22.6}$$

With $p$ as an exogenously fixed parameter, we use the symbols $\tilde{y}_i = f_i(\tilde{k}_i(\tilde{\omega}[p]))$, $i = 1, 2$, (22.6), where $\tilde{\boldsymbol{k}}_i$ are the *boundary values* of the *diversification cone* $C_k \subset \mathbb{R}_+^2$

$$C_k = \{(L, K) \in \mathbb{R}_+^2 \mid \tilde{k}_1 < K/L < \tilde{k}_2 \ \vee \ \tilde{k}_2 < K/L < \tilde{k}_1\} \tag{22.7}$$

Gross domestic product $Y$ is the monetary value of outputs from both sectors and represents aggregated gross factor incomes, cf. (22.1), (22.3), (22.4), and (22.5)

$$Y \equiv P_1 Y_1 + P_2 Y_2 = L(P_1 y_1 \lambda_1 + P_2 y_2 \lambda_2) = rK + wL = L(rk + w) \equiv Ly \tag{22.8}$$

Let $Q_i$, $i = 1, 2$, denote the quantitative size of the *domestic demand* (absorption level) for good 1 (gross investment) and good 2 (consumption), and $Q_i$ is equal to domestic production, $Y_i$, minus net exports, $X_i \lesseqgtr 0$, i.e.,

$$Q_i = Y_i - X_i, \tag{22.9}$$

The *trade balance* is assumed to satisfy the constraint

$$P_1 X_1 + P_2 X_2 = 0 \quad \therefore \quad Y = P_1 Q_1 + P_2 Q_2 \tag{22.10}$$

i.e., trade equilibrium prevails with no foreign borrowing/lending allowed.

For a *small* open country with commodity *prices* $(P_1, P_2)$, *exogenously* determined by the world market, we need to study in detail the *per-capita* GDP *function*, cf. (4), (6), (8), and convex hull (envelope), Deardorff (2001, Figure 1),

$$Y/L \equiv y = P_1 y_1 \lambda_1 + P_2 y_2 \lambda_2, \qquad k \in [0, \infty) \tag{22.11}$$

or, equivalently, with commodity (1) as numeraire $(P_1)$

$$y/P_1 = y_1\lambda_1 + (y_2/p)\lambda_2 = (y_2/p) + (y_1 - y_2/p)\lambda_1, \qquad k \in [0, \infty) \tag{22.12}$$

Depending on the overall factor *endowments ratio* (K/L), the small country may be specialized in good 1, nonspecialized (diversified), or specialized in good 2. According to the *pattern* of *specialization* and with only *one* diversification *cone*, cf. (5), and e.g., with $\tilde{k}_2 > \tilde{k}_1$, the common wage-rental ratio $\omega(k)$, (22.5), and the GDP function (22.12) become with, respectively: $\lambda_1 = 1, \lambda_2 = 0$; $\lambda_1 = (k - \tilde{k}_2)/(\tilde{k}_1 - \tilde{k}_2)$, $\lambda_2 = (\tilde{k}_1 - k)/(\tilde{k}_1 - \tilde{k}_2)$, cf. (4); and $\lambda_1 = 0, \lambda_2 = 1$:

$$\omega(k) = \begin{cases} \omega_1(k) \\ \omega_i(\tilde{k}_i) \\ \omega_2(k) \end{cases} \qquad y/P_1\,(k) = \begin{cases} f_1(k) & 0 \le k \le \tilde{k}_1 \\ \tilde{\theta}_2 + \tilde{\theta}_1 k & \tilde{k}_1 < k \le \tilde{k}_2 \\ f_2(k)/p & \tilde{k}_2 < k < \infty \end{cases} \tag{22.13}$$

where $\tilde{\theta}_1$ and $\tilde{\theta}_2$ are the *slope* and *intercept* of the *linear segment* of the *GDP function* $y/P_1$; explicitly, by collection they become,

$$\tilde{\theta}_1 \equiv [\tilde{y}_1 - (\tilde{y}_2/p)]/(\tilde{k}_1 - \tilde{k}_2) > 0,\ \tilde{\theta}_2 \equiv [(\tilde{y}_2/p)\tilde{k}_1 - \tilde{y}_1\tilde{k}_2]/(\tilde{k}_1 - \tilde{k}_2) > 0 \tag{22.14}$$

With *two* diversification *cones*, the wage-rental and GDP functions, with their horizontal and positively sloped, linear segments, become either

$$\omega(k) = \begin{cases} \omega_2(k) \\ \omega_i(\tilde{\tilde{k}}_i) \\ \omega_1(k) \\ \omega_i(\tilde{k}_i) \\ \omega_2(k) \end{cases} \qquad y/P_1\,(k) = \begin{cases} f_2(k)/p & 0 \le k \le \tilde{\tilde{k}}_2 \\ \tilde{\tilde{\theta}}_2 + \tilde{\tilde{\theta}}_1 k & \tilde{\tilde{k}}_2 < k \le \tilde{\tilde{k}}_1 \\ f_1(k) & \tilde{\tilde{k}}_1 < k \le \tilde{k}_1 \\ \tilde{\theta}_2 + \tilde{\theta}_1 k & \tilde{k}_1 < k \le \tilde{k}_2 \\ f_2(k)/p & \tilde{k}_2 < k < \infty \end{cases} \tag{22.15}$$

or

$$\omega(k) = \begin{cases} \omega_1(k) \\ \omega_i(\tilde{\tilde{k}}_i) \\ \omega_2(k) \\ \omega_i(\tilde{k}_i) \\ \omega_1(k) \end{cases} \qquad y/P_1\,(k) = \begin{cases} f_1(k) & 0 \le k \le \tilde{\tilde{k}}_1 \\ \tilde{\tilde{\theta}}_2 + \tilde{\tilde{\theta}}_1 k & \tilde{\tilde{k}}_1 < k \le \tilde{\tilde{k}}_2 \\ f_2(k)/p & \tilde{\tilde{k}}_2 < k \le \tilde{k}_2 \\ \tilde{\theta}_2 + \tilde{\theta}_1 k & \tilde{k}_2 < k \le \tilde{k}_1 \\ f_1(k) & \tilde{k}_1 < k < \infty \end{cases} \tag{22.16}$$

where $\tilde{\tilde{\theta}}_1$ and $\tilde{\tilde{\theta}}_2$ are similarly collected as

$$\tilde{\tilde{\theta}}_1 \equiv [\tilde{\tilde{y}}_1 - (\tilde{\tilde{y}}_2/p)]/(\tilde{\tilde{k}}_1 - \tilde{\tilde{k}}_2) > 0,\ \tilde{\tilde{\theta}}_2 \equiv [(\tilde{\tilde{y}}_2/p)\tilde{\tilde{k}}_1 - \tilde{\tilde{y}}_1\tilde{\tilde{k}}_2]/(\tilde{\tilde{k}}_1 - \tilde{\tilde{k}}_2) > 0 \tag{22.17}$$

and $\tilde{\tilde{y}}_i = f_i(\tilde{\tilde{k}}_i(\tilde{\tilde{\omega}}[p])), i = 1, 2$. In (22.15)–(22.16), we have $\tilde{\omega} > \tilde{\tilde{\omega}}$, and hence $\tilde{k}_i > \tilde{\tilde{k}}_i$.

**Remark 22.1** Within the diversification cones, economic expansion and structural change are connected, and there is no contradiction between the linearly increasing GDP function, $y/P_1\,(k)$, and constant absolute and relative factor rewards, [fixed wage-rental ratio $\tilde{\omega} = \omega(\tilde{k}_i)$]. The "*industrial structure*", $\lambda_1(k)$, is an *endogenous variable*, and the factors are continuously transferred to the industry yielding the highest labor productivity (revenue product) and hence produce a rising income per capita, cf. (22.12)–(22.14). Only when the possibilities of factor transfers are exhausted will real wages increase again. As to its practical substance, the diversification cone will not be experienced as a stage with social-economic tranquillity, and the labor force may somehow feel to bear the brunt of factor mobility (reallocation).

### *CES Technologies, Factor Reversals, Diversification Cones, and Relative Prices*

The general forms of the CES technologies are, for $\gamma_i > 0$, $0 < a_i < 1$, $\sigma_i > 0$, and $\varrho_i \equiv (\sigma_i - 1)/\sigma_i$, $-\infty < \varrho_i < 1$,

$$\sigma_i = 1, \quad f_i(k) = \gamma_i k^{a_i}, \quad i = 1, 2 \tag{22.18}$$

$$\sigma_i \neq 1, \quad f_i(k) = \gamma_i \left[(1 - a_i) + a_i k^{\varrho_i}\right]^{1/\varrho_i} \tag{22.19}$$

$$\sigma_i \neq 1, \quad f_i'(k) = a_i \gamma_i \left[a_i + (1 - a_i)k^{-\varrho_i}\right]^{(1-\varrho_i)/\varrho_i} \tag{22.20}$$

By evaluating (22.19)–(22.20), the limits or dominating ($\sim$) terms of $f_i(k)$ and $f_i'(k)$ become,

$$\sigma_i < 1: \begin{cases} \text{small } k: \; f_i(k) \sim \gamma_i a_i^{1/\varrho_i} k, & \lim_{k\to\infty} f_i(k) = \gamma_i (1-a_i)^{1/\varrho_i} \\ \lim_{k\to 0} f_i'(k) = \gamma_i a_i^{1/\varrho_i}, & \lim_{k\to\infty} f_i'(k) = 0 \end{cases} \tag{22.21}$$

$$\sigma_i > 1: \begin{cases} \lim_{k\to 0} f_i(k) = \gamma_i (1-a_i)^{1/\varrho_i}, & \text{large } k: \; f_i(k) \sim \gamma_i a_i^{1/\varrho_i} k \\ \lim_{k\to 0} f_i'(k) = \infty, & \lim_{k\to\infty} f_i'(k) = \gamma_i a_i^{1/\varrho_i} \end{cases} \tag{22.22}$$

For the CES sector technologies, (22.19) we have the well-known monotone relations between marginal rates of substitution $\omega_i$, (22.5), and capital-labor ratios $k_i$

$$\omega_i = \frac{1-a_i}{a_i} k_i^{1/\sigma_i}, \; k_i = \left[\frac{a_i}{1-a_i}\omega_i\right]^{\sigma_i}, \; \omega_i \in [0,\infty), \; k_i \in [0,\infty), \; i = 1, 2. \tag{22.23}$$

It is apparent from (22.23) that sectorial factor (capital-labor) ratio *reversals* (FRR) can only be avoided, if and only if $\sigma_1 = \sigma_2$ and $a_1 \neq a_2$. Some implications of FRR with CES-functions were first discussed by Minhas (1962), cf. Gandolfo (1998, p. 358).

Hence with CES and $\sigma_1 \neq \sigma_2$, there will exist one and *only one* intersection (reversal) *point* $(\bar{\boldsymbol{k}}, \bar{\boldsymbol{\omega}})$:

$$\bar{k} = \left[\frac{(1-a_2)/a_2}{(1-a_1)/a_1}\right]^{\frac{\sigma_1\sigma_2}{\sigma_2-\sigma_1}}, \quad \bar{\omega} = \left[\frac{[(1-a_2)/a_2]^{\sigma_2}}{[(1-a_1)/a_1]^{\sigma_1}}\right]^{\frac{1}{\sigma_2-\sigma_1}} \tag{22.24}$$

**Remark 22.2** The location of the intersection point, (22.24), is determined by the parameters $a_i$ and $\sigma_i$—such that

- $\bar{k}$ and $\bar{\omega}$ increase with $a_1$ and decrease with $a_2$.
- If $a_1 < a_2$, then $\bar{k}$ and $\bar{\omega}$ decrease with $\sigma_1$ and increase with $\sigma_2$.
- If $a_1 > a_2$, then $\bar{k}$ and $\bar{\omega}$ increase with $\sigma_1$ and decrease with $\sigma_2$.

Under *competitive* equilibrium conditions and *diversification*, the relation between relative factor prices and relative commodity prices follows from (22.5).

$$p = \frac{P_1}{P_2} = \frac{MP_{k_2}[k_2(\omega)]}{MP_{k_1}[k_1(\omega)]} = \frac{f_2'[k_2(\omega)]}{f_1'[k_1(\omega)]} \tag{22.25}$$

With CES marginal productivities, (22.20), the relative prices (22.25) become

$$p(\omega) = \frac{\gamma_2 a_2 \left[a_2 + (1-a_2)k_2(\omega)^{-\varrho_2}\right]^{(1-\varrho_2)/\varrho_2}}{\gamma_1 a_1 \left[a_1 + (1-a_1)k_1(\omega)^{-\varrho_1}\right]^{(1-\varrho_1)/\varrho_1}} \tag{22.26}$$

Using (22.23) together with (22.26) gives, after reductions and using $\sigma_i = 1/(1-\varrho_i)$,

$$p(\omega) = \frac{\gamma_2 a_2^{\sigma_2/(\sigma_2-1)} \left[1 + \left(\frac{1-a_2}{a_2}\right)^{\sigma_2} \omega^{1-\sigma_2}\right]^{1/(\sigma_2-1)}}{\gamma_1 a_1^{\sigma_1/(\sigma_1-1)} \left[1 + \left(\frac{1-a_1}{a_1}\right)^{\sigma_1} \omega^{1-\sigma_1}\right]^{1/(\sigma_1-1)}}, \quad \omega \in [0, \infty) \tag{22.27}$$

As clarified in Appendix, the CES marginal rate of substitution $\omega_i$ has always the limit values *zero* and *infinity*—irrespective of the numerical size of $\sigma_i$. Hence we should also evaluate the limit of relative prices $p$, (22.26), for $\omega$ at zero and infinity.

To this end, let

$$p^* \equiv \frac{\gamma_2\, a_2^{1/\varrho_2}}{\gamma_1\, a_1^{1/\varrho_1}}, \quad p^{**} \equiv \frac{\gamma_2\,(1-a_2)^{1/\varrho_2}}{\gamma_1\,(1-a_1)^{1/\varrho_1}}, \quad \frac{1}{\varrho_i} = \frac{\sigma_i}{\sigma_i - 1}; \quad \bar{p} \equiv p(\bar{\omega}) \tag{22.28}$$

**Remark 22.3** As to the influence of the parameters upon the values of $p^*$ and $p^{**}$, the following implications can be verified,

- If $\frac{1}{2} \le a_1 < a_2$ and $1 < \sigma_2 < \sigma_1$, then $p^* > p^{**}$.
- If $a_1 \ge \frac{1}{2}$, $a_2 < a_1$ and $\sigma_2 < \sigma_1 < 1$, then $p^* > p^{**}$.

**Theorem 22.1** *The graph of the function $p(\omega)$, (22.27)—the CES commodity price-factor price correspondence (CFC)—has finite and infinite limits, according to the following CES classification:*

$$\sigma_1 < 1, \quad \sigma_2 < 1: \qquad \lim_{\omega \to 0} p = p^* \qquad \lim_{\omega \to \infty} p = p^{**} \tag{22.29}$$

$$\sigma_1 > 1, \quad \sigma_2 > 1: \qquad \lim_{\omega \to 0} p = p^{**} \qquad \lim_{\omega \to \infty} p = p^* \tag{22.30}$$

$$\sigma_1 > 1, \quad \sigma_2 < 1: \qquad \lim_{\omega \to 0} p = 0 \qquad \lim_{\omega \to \infty} p = 0 \tag{22.31}$$

$$\sigma_1 < 1, \quad \sigma_2 > 1: \qquad \lim_{\omega \to 0} p = \infty \qquad \lim_{\omega \to \infty} p = \infty \tag{22.32}$$

*At the single reversal point* $(\bar{k}, \bar{\omega})$, *(22.24), diversification cones* $C_k$, *(22.7), degenerate to one point. The reversal price ratio,* $P_1/P_2 = \bar{p} \equiv p(\bar{\omega})$ *is always a maximum (iff* $\sigma_1 > \sigma_2$*) or a minimum (iff* $\sigma_2 > \sigma_1$*), cf. Fig. 22.1.*

*The substitution elasticities (22.29)–(22.30) give one or two diversification cones. There will be one cone, iff the relative prices* $p(\omega)$ *lie between* $p^*$ *and* $p^{**}$*. For* $p^* > p^{**}$, $(p^* < p^{**})$, *the single cone is located below (above) the reversal point* $(\bar{k}, \bar{\omega})$.

*The substitution elasticities (22.31)–(22.32) necessarily imply two diversification cones for any relative commodity price* $p$.

*For the substitution elasticities (22.29)–(22.31), the range of* $p(\omega)$, *(22.26)–(22.27) is bounded. With* $\gamma_1 = \gamma_2$, *and both substitutions elasticities small (22.29) or large (22.30), the range of* $p(\omega)$ *becomes a narrow interval, and there will be only small differences between the values of* $p^*$ *and* $p^{**}$ *(22.28)—especially so, when furthermore* $a_i, i = 1, 2$ *have similar size, cf. (22.27).*

***Proof*** Ad (22.29)–(22.30): With $\sigma_i < 1$ the brackets in (22.27) converge to one at $\omega = 0$, which establishes the limiting $p = p^*$. For large $\omega$, the numerator and denominator in (22.27) are approximately proportional to $\omega^{-1}$ with coefficients equal to the numerator and the denominator of $p^{**}$ (22.28). Similar arguments as above establish (22.30).

Ad (22.31)–(22.32): With $\sigma_1 > 1$ and $\sigma_2 < 1$ the numerator in (22.31) converges to a constant and the denominator converges to infinity at $\omega = 0$, which establish the limiting value of $p = 0$. For large $\omega$, the numerator of (22.31) converges to zero, whereas the denominator converges to a nonzero constant. Hence the limiting value of $p$ is zero. Arguments similar to those above establish (22.32). □

For competitive industries with CES technologies (22.19), the three-way relationship between relative commodity prices, relative factor prices, and sectorial factor proportions, (22.25)–(22.27), is exhibited in Fig. 22.1, applying here the familiar diagram, Samuelson (1949), where the right panels show (22.23) and the left panels show (22.27). The configuration of the graphs in the left panels is drawn in accordance with (22.29)–(22.32). These curves in the *left panels* are everywhere *inelastic* $[|(dp/p/dw/w)| < 1]$ in accordance with Stolper-Samuelson theorem, Deardorff and Stern (1994).

Incidentally, Theorem 22.1 and Fig. 22.1 highlight the extreme (bifurcation) position of CD in the CES family of sector technologies. With $\sigma_1 = \sigma_2 = 1$, there is of course no factor and price reversals and just monotone functions $p(\omega)$, cf. (22.18), (22.25) (rising/falling for $a_2 \gtrless a_1$). But also the finite limits $p^*$ and $p^{**}$, (22.28), disappear. The *range* of the *price* ratio $p(\omega)$ with CD is always the *entire* interval $[0, \infty[$. The reader may experience the dramatic effects of $\sigma_i$ upon the range of $p(\omega)$, (22.27), by calculating $p^*$ and $p^{**}$, (22.28). When $\sigma_1$ and $\sigma_2$ differ considerably from one, there is *little scope* for *relative* commodity *price variation*.

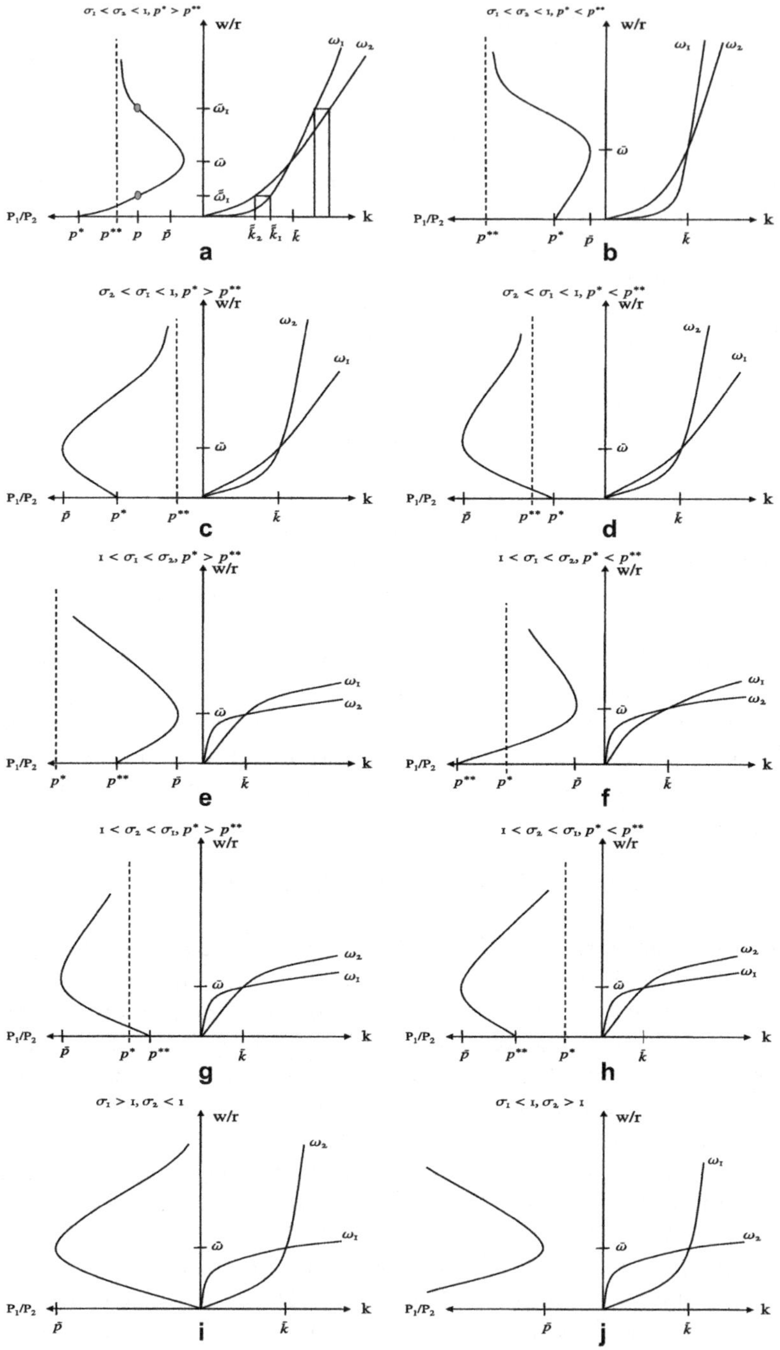


**Fig. 22.1** Diversification cones and price correspondence, (22.27). (**a**) $\sigma_1 < \sigma_2 < 1$, $p^* > p^{**}$. (**b**) $\sigma_1 < \sigma_2 < 1$, $p^* < p^{**}$. (**c**) $\sigma_2 < \sigma_1 < 1$, $p^* > p^{**}$. (**d**) $\sigma_2 < \sigma_1 < 1$, $p^* < p^{**}$. (**e**) $1 < \sigma_1 < \sigma_2$, $p^* > p^{**}$. (**f**) $1 < \sigma_1 < \sigma_2$, $p^* < p^{**}$. (**g**) $1 < \sigma_2 < \sigma_1$, $p^* > p^{**}$. (**h**) $1 < \sigma_2 < \sigma_1$, $p^* < p^{**}$. (**i**) $\sigma_1 > 1, \sigma_2 < 1$. (**j**) $\sigma_1 < 1, \sigma_2 > 1$

**Remark 22.4** The capital-labor ratio $k_i$ is often synonymous with "capital intensity" and the CD and CES parameter $a_i$ (22.18)–(22.19) is often referred to as a "distribution parameter". As a technological parameter, $a_i$ should not be interpreted and related especially to distributional issues. The effect of larger $a_i$ is seen from (22.23) to be a rightward *shift* in the $\omega_i$-curve (right panels, Fig. 22.1), i.e., a higher capital-labor ratio $k_i$ for all (any) factor prices. Hence $a_i$ is aptly characterized as a *capital-intensity* (rather than a distribution) *parameter*, Uzawa (1959, p. 459). A high capital-labor ratio can alternatively be due to a *movement* along the $\omega_i$-curve, the effect of which is determined by the *substitution* (flexibility) *parameter* $\sigma_i$. As to obtaining high capital-labor ratios, the effect of $\sigma_i$ will eventually dominate the effects of $a_i$, cf. Fig. 22.1. Technical *progress* has partly been accompanied by rising capital-labor ratios, which can be identified with and derived from larger values of the *intensity* ($a_i$) and/or *substitution* ($\sigma_i$) parameters.

## Stochastic Dynamic Systems for Small Trading Economies

### *Diffusion Process of the Capital-Labor Ratio*

The general dynamic neoclassical model of a small trading economy with *uncertainties* (stochastic elements $\epsilon_i$) in the growth rate of labor $n$, the gross saving rate $s$, and the capital depreciation rate $\delta$ is given by, Jensen and Wang (1999); here Chap. 27,

$$\dot{L} = L(n + \beta_1 \epsilon_1) \tag{22.33}$$

$$\dot{K} = L(s + \phi_3(k)\epsilon_3)(y/P_1) - (\delta + \beta_2 \epsilon_2)K \tag{22.34}$$

with $\beta_i \geq 0$, and $(\epsilon_1, \epsilon_2, \epsilon_3)$ is white noise related to a Wiener process $(w_1, w_2, w_3)$ with correlation structure

$$d\langle w_i, w_j\rangle = \rho_{ij}\, dt, \quad \rho_{ii} = 1, \quad i, j = 1, 2, 3 \tag{22.35}$$

where $\langle w_i, w_j\rangle$ is the quadratic variation process for the components of the Wiener process, Karatzas and Shreve (1991), Øksendal (1998). As to the formal connection between Wiener processes and white noise, see Holden et al. (1996, chapter 3). The function $\phi_3$ is conveniently chosen (to avoid boundary problems at zero) as

$$\phi_3(k) = \beta_3 \tanh(\lambda_3 k), \quad k \in [0, \infty), \quad \phi_3(0) = 0, \quad \phi_3(\infty) = \beta_3 \tag{22.36}$$

For the labor and capital stock, the associated *stochastic differential equations* to (22.33)–(22.34), are given by

$$dL = Ln\,dt + L\beta_1 dw_1 \tag{22.37}$$

$$dK = (sL(y/P_1) - \delta K)\,dt - \beta_2 K\,dw_2 + L(y/P_1)\phi_3(k)\,dw_3 \tag{22.38}$$

The *drift* and *diffusion* coefficients of the stochastic dynamic system (22.37)–(22.38) are *homogeneous* functions of *degree one* in the state variables $L$ and $K$, cf. the GDP function (22.13). The homogeneity of degree one allows us to reduce the two-dimensional stochastic system (22.37)–(22.38) to one-dimensional stochastic dynamics of the capital-labor ratio. If the process $k$ is positive and finite, then $b^2(k) > 0$ (non-degenerate), cf. (22.39) and hence the Wiener process, $(w_1, w_2, w_3)$, (22.37)–(22.38), can be reduced to a one-dimensional Wiener process $w$, (22.39), using Levy's characterization.

The stochastic dynamics for the *capital-labor ratio* is a *diffusion* (Ito) process on the interval $k \in (0, \infty)$, cf. Jensen and Wang (1999, Lemma 1 and (73)–(74)); here Lemma 27.1 and (27.76)–(27.77) in Chap. 27,

$$dk = a(k)\,dt + b(k)\,dw, \qquad k \in (0, \infty) \tag{22.39}$$

where the *drift* coefficient $\boldsymbol{a(k)}$ and *diffusion* coefficient $\boldsymbol{b(k)}$ are

$$\begin{aligned}
a(k) &= \bar{s}(k)(y/P_1) - \Theta k \\
\bar{s}(k) &= s - \rho_{13}\beta_1\phi_3(k) \\
\Theta &= n + \delta - (\beta_1^2 + \rho_{12}\beta_1\beta_2) \\
b^2(k) &= \beta^2 k^2 + \phi_3(k)^2(y/P_1)^2 - \rho\phi_3(k)(y/P_1)k \\
\beta^2 &= \beta_1^2 + \beta_2^2 + 2\rho_{12}\beta_1\beta_2 \\
\rho &= 2(\rho_{13}\beta_1 + \rho_{23}\beta_2)
\end{aligned} \tag{22.40}$$

With *one cone*, the stochastic differential equation (22.39) on *subintervals* (22.13) becomes

$$dk = \begin{cases} \{\bar{s}(k)f_1(k) - \Theta k\}dt + b_1(k)dw, & 0 < k \le \tilde{k}_1 \\ \{\bar{s}(k)\tilde{\theta}_2 + [\bar{s}(k)\tilde{\theta}_1 - \Theta]k\}dt + b_2(k)\,dw, & \tilde{k}_1 < k \le \tilde{k}_2 \\ \{\bar{s}(k)(f_2(k)/p) - \Theta k\}dt + b_3(k)\,dw, & \tilde{k}_2 < k < \infty \end{cases} \tag{22.41}$$

where the *components* $a_i(k)$ of $a(k)$ and $b_i^2(k)$ of $b(k)$, $i = 1, 2, 3$ are obtained by inserting the components of $y/P_1(k)$, as stated in (22.13); only the components of $a(k)$ are explicitly shown in (22.41).

In case of, e.g., $\sigma_2 > 1$, we incidentally note that for large $k$, the stochastic differential equation (22.40) is asymptotically given by the following geometric Wiener process, cf. (22.21), (22.36),

$$dk \sim \bar{a}_3 k\, dt + \bar{b}_3 k\, dw : \begin{array}{rcl} \bar{a}_3 &=& (s - \rho_{13}\, \beta_1\, \beta_3)\, (\gamma_2/p)\, a_2^{1/\rho_2} - \Theta, \\ \bar{b}_3^2 &=& \beta^2 + \beta_3\, (\gamma_2/p)\, a_2^{1/\rho_2}\, [\beta_3\, (\gamma_2/p)\, a_2^{1/\rho_2} - \rho] \end{array} \tag{22.42}$$

## *Inaccessible Boundaries*

*Sufficient* conditions for the general diffusion process (22.41)—with CES technologies and uncertainties in labor growth, capital depreciation, and saving rates—to have inaccessible lower ($k = 0$) and upper ($k = \infty$) boundaries are

$$k = 0\,; \quad \sigma_i < 1: \quad 2(n + \delta - s\gamma_1 a_1^{1/\varrho_1}) \leq \beta_1^2 - \beta_2^2 \tag{22.43}$$

$$k = 0\,; \quad \sigma_i \geq 1: \quad \text{Always inaccessible} \tag{22.44}$$

$$k = \infty; \quad \sigma_i \leq 1: \quad 2(n + \delta) \geq \beta_1^2 - \beta_2^2 \tag{22.45}$$

$$k = \infty; \quad \sigma_i > 1: \quad 2(n + \delta - s(\gamma_2/p)a_2^{1/\varrho_2}) \geq \beta_1^2 - \beta_2^2 - \Delta \tag{22.46}$$

where $\Delta \equiv [\beta_3(\gamma_2/p)a_2^{1/\varrho_2}]^2 - 2\rho_{23}\beta_2\beta_3(\gamma_2/p)a_2^{1/\varrho_2}$.

The derivation of (22.43)–(22.46) was given in Jensen and Wang (1999, Theorem (4)); here Theorem 27.4 in Chap. 27. The inaccessibility conditions ensure positivity and finiteness of $k$. These conditions (22.43)–(22.46) are mild restrictions and mostly satisfied for relevant economic parameter values.

## *Sample Paths and Stationary Distributions*

The sample path (trajectory) of the process $k(t)$, (22.39), is formally given by

$$k(t; \omega) = k(0) + \int_0^t a(k[u; \omega])\, du + \int_0^t b(k[u; \omega])\, dw_u(\omega) \tag{22.47}$$

where $k(0)$ is a fixed initial condition and $\omega$ symbolizes a particular realization of the Wiener process. The sample path (22.47) is in this chapter approximated by the Euler Scheme, Kloeden and Platen (1995).

The *scale density* function $\mathfrak{s}$ is defined by

$$\mathfrak{s}(k) = \begin{cases} \mathfrak{s}_1(k), & 0 < k \leq \tilde{k}_1 \\ \mathfrak{s}_2(k), & \tilde{k}_1 < k \leq \tilde{k}_2 \\ \mathfrak{s}_3(k), & \tilde{k}_2 < k < \infty \end{cases} \tag{22.48}$$

where, cf. (22.41)

$$
\begin{aligned}
\mathfrak{s}_1(k) &= \exp(-2 \int_{\tilde{k}_1}^{k} \tfrac{\bar{s}(u) f_1(u) - \Theta u}{b_1^2(u)}\, du) && 0 < k \leq \tilde{k}_1 \\
\mathfrak{s}_2(k) &= \exp(-2 \int_{\tilde{k}_1}^{k} \tfrac{\bar{s}(u)\tilde{\theta}_2 + [\bar{s}(u)\tilde{\theta}_1 - \Theta] u\}}{b_2^2(u)}\, du) && \tilde{k}_1 < k \leq \tilde{k}_2 \qquad (22.49) \\
\mathfrak{s}_3(k) &= \mathfrak{s}_2(\tilde{k}_2) \exp(-2 \int_{\tilde{k}_2}^{k} \tfrac{\bar{s}(u)(f_2(u)/p) - \Theta u}{b_3^2(u)}\, du) && \tilde{k}_2 < k < \infty
\end{aligned}
$$

The scale density is only uniquely determined up to a fixed, but arbitrary integration point in (22.49). For writing as in (22.49), a convenient choice is $\tilde{k}_1$, but for computational purposes, the integration point should be chosen with care. One way is to choose the deterministic steady state as the integration point.

The deterministic steady-state points are given by, cf. Jensen and Wang (1997, p. 93); here p. 633 in Chap. 21 and Jensen and Wang (1999, p. 395); here p. 988 in Chap. 27,

$$
\kappa = \left[ \frac{1 - a_1}{[(n+\delta)/(\gamma_1 s)]^{\rho_1} - a_1} \right]^{\frac{1}{\rho_1}} \quad \text{or} \quad \kappa = \left[ \frac{1 - a_2}{[p(n+\delta)/(\gamma_2 s)]^{\rho_2} - a_2} \right]^{\frac{1}{\rho_2}} \qquad (22.50)
$$

$$
\kappa = \tilde{\theta}_2 / [(n+\delta)/s] - \tilde{\theta}_1 \qquad (22.51)
$$

where (22.50) refers to the specialization intervals (22.13), and (22.51) refers to the diversification interval in (22.13). With two cones, the formulas (22.50) and (22.51) are easily adapted to either (22.15) or (22.16).

The *speed density* function $\mathfrak{m}$ is defined by, cf. (22.40), (22.49),

$$
\mathfrak{m}(k) = \frac{1}{b^2(k)\mathfrak{s}(k)}. \qquad (22.52)
$$

Accordingly the ***time-invariant probability density*** function $p$ (normalized speed density)—whenever it exits—is given by,

$$
p(k) = \mathfrak{m}(k)/m, \quad m = \int_0^{\infty} \mathfrak{m}(u)\, du < \infty, \quad P(k) = \int_0^{k} p(u)\, du \qquad (22.53)
$$

From the general diffusion process (22.41) with inaccessible boundaries, we can now consider particular cases. As we are mostly concerned with uncertainty in saving rate, we will first study the process (22.39) with $\beta_1 = \beta_2 = 0$ in (22.40), i.e.,

$$
dk = \{s[y/P_1\ (k)] - (n+\delta)k\}\, dt + \phi_3(k)[y/P_1\ (k)]k\, dw \qquad (22.54)
$$

or explicitly

$$dk = \begin{cases} \{sf_1(k) - (n+\delta)k\}\,dt - \phi_3(k) f_1(k) k\,dw, & 0 < k \le \tilde{k}_1 \\ \{s\tilde{\theta}_2 + [s\tilde{\theta}_1 - (n+\delta)]k\}\,dt - \phi_3(k)(\tilde{\theta}_2 + \tilde{\theta}_1 k) k\,dw, & \tilde{k}_1 < k \le \tilde{k}_2 \\ \{s(f_2(k)/p) - (n+\delta)k\}\,dt - \phi_3(k)(f_2(k)/p) k\,dw, & \tilde{k}_2 < k < \infty \end{cases} \tag{22.55}$$

## Stochastic Dynamics with CES Technologies

With *uncertainty* in the *saving* rate (22.55) and CES technologies, (22.19), we have the diffusion process

$$dk = \begin{cases} \{s\gamma_1[(1-a_1) + a_1 k^{\varrho_1}]^{1/\varrho_1} - (n+\delta)k\}dt \\ +\phi_3(k)\gamma_1[(1-a_1) + a_1 k^{\varrho_1}]^{1/\varrho_1} dw_3, & 0 < k \le \tilde{k}_1 \\ \{s\tilde{\theta}_2 + [s\tilde{\theta}_1 - (n+\delta)]k\}dt + \phi_3(k)[\tilde{\theta}_2 + \tilde{\theta}_1 k]dw_3, & \tilde{k}_1 < k \le \tilde{k}_2 \\ \{s(\gamma_2/p)[(1-a_2) + a_2 k^{\varrho_2}]^{1/\varrho_2} - (n+\delta)k\}dt \\ +\phi_3(k)(\gamma_2/p)[(1-a_2) + a_2 k^{\varrho_2}]^{1/\varrho_2} dw_3, & \tilde{k}_2 < k < \infty \end{cases} \tag{22.56}$$

We will study and demonstrate the properties of the stochastic solution to (22.56), when both sector technologies have substitution elasticities in the lower range. For the upper range, we will in Sect. "Stochastic Endogenous Growth" discuss and demonstrate the possibilities for stochastic endogenous (persistent) growth with (22.56).

### *Steady-State Growth and Convergence to Stationary Distributions*

Regarding the stochastic evolution of the capital labor ratio (22.56), some sample paths $k(t;\omega)$, (22.47), and the asymptotic (long-run) probability density $p(k)$, (22.53), together with the first- and second-order moments, will provide insights into various parametric versions of the diffusion process (22.56). Furthermore, we will provide the long-run probabilities, $p(\tilde{k}_i)$, and $p(\tilde{\tilde{k}}_i)$, if they are not negligible ($> 10^{-4}$) or irrelevant. Familiarity with stochastic open two-sector dynamics can be attained by illustrative applications.

**Example 22.1** $s = 0.2$, $n = 0.02$, $\delta = 0.05$, $\beta_1 = 0$, $\beta_2 = 0$, $\beta_3 = 0.1$, $\lambda_3 = 1$, $\rho_{ij} = 0\ (i \ne j)$, $\gamma_1 = \gamma_2 = 1$, $a_1 = 0.2$, $a_2 = 0.4$, $\sigma_1 = 0.4$, $\sigma_2 = 0.5$.

With the CES parameters of Example 22.1, the particular limiting values, (22.28), and reversal values (22.24) of the relative prices, wage-rental ratio and capital labor ratio are, cf. Fig. 22.1a

$$p^* = 0.85,\ p^{**} = 1.44,\ \bar{p} = 0.80,\ \bar{\omega} = 0.03, \bar{k} = 0.14. \tag{22.57}$$

Then *exogenous* relative commodity prices *between* $p^*$ and $p^{**}$, such as $p = 1$ or $p = 1.2$, give one diversification cone, whereas selecting exogenous relative prices between $\bar{p}$ and $p^*$, such as $p = 0.81$, give two diversification cones, i.e., we get, cf. (22.13)–(22.17), (22.23), and (22.27).

$$p = 1:\quad \tilde{\omega} = 2.32,\quad \tilde{k}_1 = 0.81, \tilde{k}_2 = 1.25,\quad \tilde{\theta}_1 = 0.30,\quad \tilde{\theta}_2 = 0.71, \tag{22.58}$$

$$p = 0.81:\quad \begin{array}{l} \tilde{\tilde{\omega}} = 0.007,\quad \tilde{\tilde{k}}_2 = 0.07, \tilde{\tilde{k}}_1 = 0.08,\quad \tilde{\tilde{\theta}}_1 = 2.53,\quad \tilde{\tilde{\theta}}_2 = 0.02, \\ \tilde{\omega} = 0.084,\quad \tilde{k}_1 = 0.21, \tilde{k}_2 = 0.24,\quad \tilde{\theta}_1 = 1.68,\quad \tilde{\theta}_2 = 0.14, \end{array} \tag{22.59}$$

$$p = 1.2:\quad \tilde{\omega} = 21.27,\quad \tilde{k}_1 = 1.95, \tilde{k}_2 = 3.77,\quad \tilde{\theta}_1 = 0.047, \tilde{\theta}_2 = 1.00. \tag{22.60}$$

Corresponding to the selected prices in (22.58)–(22.60), the values of $\tilde{\omega}$ and $\tilde{\tilde{\omega}}$, cannot be given by closed formulas, if $\sigma_1 \neq \sigma_2$, but are easily obtained numerically by solving (22.27). Next, the *endpoints* $\tilde{k}_i$ and $\tilde{\tilde{k}}_i$ of the respective *diversification cones* follow from (22.23). The slopes and the intercepts of the linear segments of the GDP function are also shown above, cf. (22.14), (22.17), and (22.19). The numerical values in (22.57)–(22.60) are not affected by any uncertainty and neither by the value of $s$, $n$, and $\delta$. Diversification *cones* only depend on *technology* and relative commodity *prices*.

For Example 22.1 with (22.58), the stochastic solution (*sample path*) of (22.56) from two initial values is shown in left panel of Fig. 22.2a, while the long-run *density* $\boldsymbol{p(k)}$ is exhibited in the right panel. The two sample paths of the capital-labor ratio eventually fluctuate around the *steady state*, $\boldsymbol{E(k)}$, which is very close to the *certainty equivalent* (deterministic) value $\boldsymbol{\kappa}$, (22.61), cf. (22.50). In the simulations of Examples 22.1 and 22.2, the same Wiener diffusion (realization) is employed for all initial values. Hence the two sample path will be close to each other in the long run. *Initial states* do *not* matter in the long run for stationary processes.

$$p = 1:\quad \kappa = 4.095;\quad \mathrm{E}(k) = 4.089,\ \sigma = 0.413,\ P(\tilde{k}_2) = 0.16\,10^{-12}. \tag{22.61}$$

Evidently, the probability of observing diversification is nearly zero, cf. $P(\tilde{k}_2)$. Even though the initial state, $k(0) = 1$, was diversified, the drift coefficient $a(k)$,

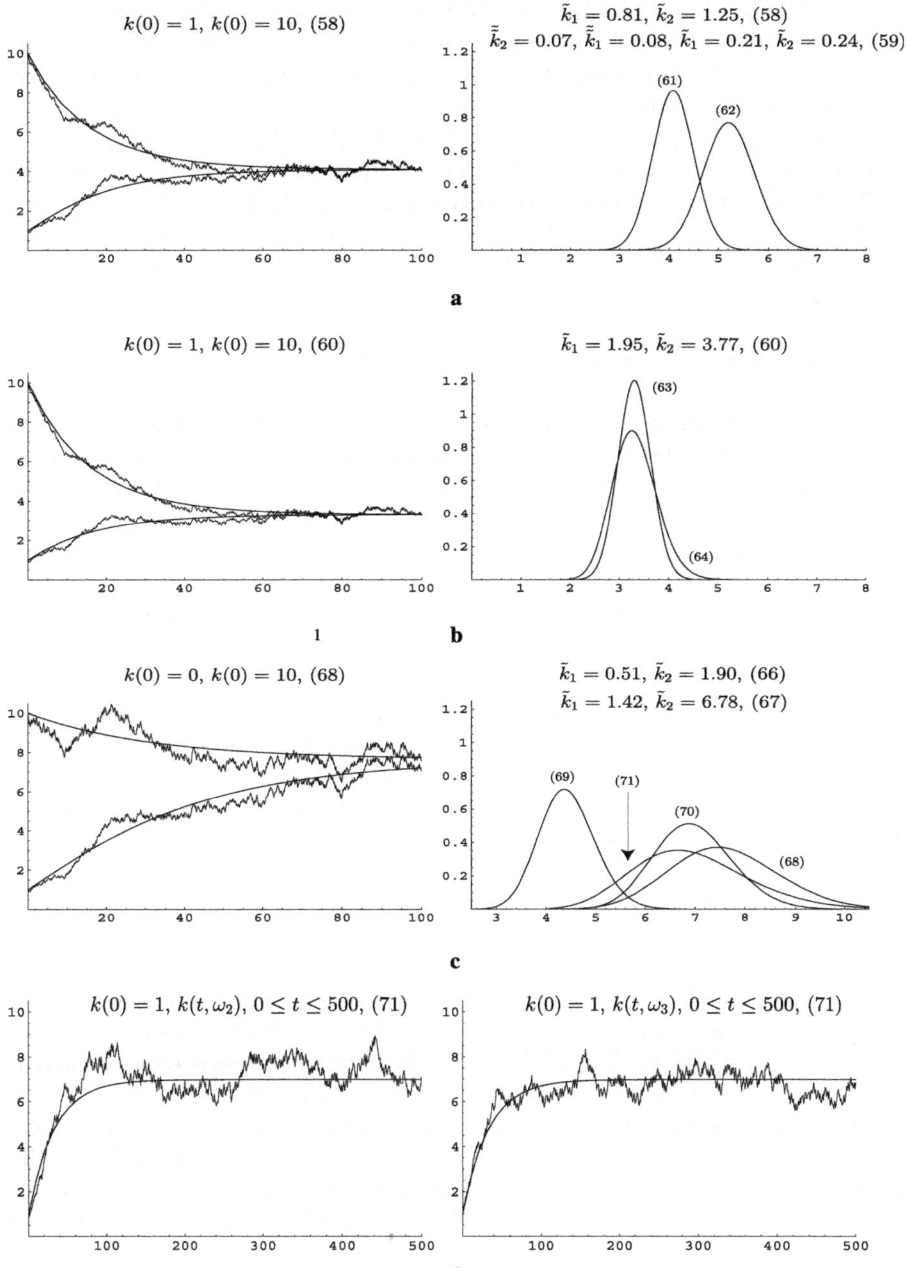


**Fig. 22.2** Solutions and densities of $k(t)$, (22.39)–(22.40). (**a**) Sample paths, $k(t, \omega_1)$, (22.56) and probability densities $p(k)$. (**b**) Sample paths, $k(t, \omega_1)$, (22.56) and probability densities $p(k)$. (**c**) Sample paths, $k(t, \omega_1)$, (22.56) and probability densities $p(k)$. (**d**) Sample paths, $k(t, \omega_2)$, $k(t, \omega_3)$, (22.41)

cf. (22.39)–(22.41), (22.54)–(22.56), will, with $p = 1$, soon and long before it settles into the steady state, move the economy of Example 22.1 to fully specializing in the consumer good industry and importing the capital good. The asymptotic density is shown in Fig. 22.2a.

If the exogenous term of trade is altered to $p = P_1/P_2 = 0.81$, then, of course, the relatively cheaper capital good offers more incentive to produce and specialize in the consumer good. Even though there are here in fact two diversification cones, cf. (22.59), they are very small and located close to the origin. Moreover, the economy will in the long run reach a higher steady state, cf. (22.62).

$$p = 0.81: \quad \kappa = 5.212; \quad \mathrm{E}(k) = 5.206, \ \sigma = 0.518. \tag{22.62}$$

If the term of trade is instead changed to $p = 1.2$, a major reconstruction in production and trade is necessary, as dictated by efficient factor endowment allocation. The location of the diversification cone is shown in (22.60), and the sample paths and asymptotic density function are illustrated in Fig. 22.2b. In the long run the small economy will most of the time be diversified, cf. (22.63),

$$p = 1.2: \quad \kappa = 3.31002; \quad \mathrm{E}(k) = 3.30990, \ \sigma = 0.332, \ P(\tilde{k}_2) = 0.914. \tag{22.63}$$

Besides *uncertainty* in the actual *saving* rate, $\beta_3 = 0.1$, we can briefly illustrate the implications of also uncertainty in the actual growth of the *labor* force and in the actual *depreciation* of the capital stock: (22.64) shows the effect of such additional uncertainty upon the first- and second-order moments, and the density is shown in Fig. 22.2b.

$$p = 1.2, \ \beta_1 = 0.01, \ \beta_2 = 0.03: \quad \mathrm{E}(k) = 3.315, \ \sigma = 0.449, \ P(\tilde{k}_2) = 0.843. \tag{22.64}$$

Comparing (22.63), (22.64), it is seen that $\mathrm{E}(k)$ has slightly increased due to the positive contribution of $\beta_1$ to the *drift* coefficient $a(k)$, whenever $\rho_{ij} = 0$, cf. (22.39)–(22.40). Both $\beta_1$ and $\beta_2$ contribute to a *larger diffusion* coefficient $b(k)$, and hence *larger dispersion*, $\sigma$, (22.64). However, overall it does not matter much to allow for *uncorrelated* disturbances, whenever some critical amount of uncertainty in the saving rate has already been admitted in the evolution of the process $k(t)$. However, if the uncertainty of saving was absent, then the dispersion is $(0.449^2 - 0.332^2)^{1/2} = 0.302$, because the underlining Wiener processes are uncorrelated.

**Example 22.2** $s = 0.2$, $n = 0.02$, $\delta = 0.05$, $\beta_1 = 0$, $\beta_2 = 0$, $\beta_3 = 0.1$, $\lambda_3 = 1$, $\rho_{ij} = 0$ $(i \neq j)$, $\gamma_1 = \gamma_2 = 1$, $a_1 = 0.2$, $a_2 = 0.4$, $\sigma_1 = 1.2$, $\sigma_2 = 1.5$.

With the *larger substitution* elasticities, the analogy of (22.57) is now, cf. Fig. 22.1e,

$$p^* = 1000.00,\ p^{**} = 0.82,\ \bar{p} = 0.63,\ \bar{\omega} = 0.03,\ \bar{k} = 0.00278. \tag{22.65}$$

With the numerical values in (22.65), we will very seldom see relative prices, $p \in (\bar{p}, p^{**})$, with two diversification cones.

Analogous to (22.58)–(22.60), we get the cones and GDP flats,

$$p = 1: \quad \tilde{\omega} = 2.30,\ \tilde{k}_1 = 0.51,\ \tilde{k}_2 = 1.90,\ \tilde{\theta}_1 = 0.31,\ \tilde{\theta}_2 = 0.72, \tag{22.66}$$

$$p = 1.3: \quad \tilde{\omega} = 5.37,\ \tilde{k}_1 = 1.42,\ \tilde{k}_2 = 6.78,\ \tilde{\theta}_1 = 0.16,\ \tilde{\theta}_2 = 0.85. \tag{22.67}$$

For Example 22.2 with (22.66), the sample path of the process $k(t)$, (22.56), from two initial values, is shown in *Fig. 22.2c*, which also includes the probability density $p(k)$ in the right panel. With a probability close to one, cf. (22.68), we again see a future steady state with specialization in the consumer good.

$$p = 1: \qquad \kappa = 7.633; \quad \mathrm{E}(k) = 7.604,\ \sigma = 1.085,\ P(\tilde{k}_2) = 4.91\,10^{-14}. \tag{22.68}$$

Comparing (22.61) and (22.68), the larger substitution elasticities have resulted in a higher level of per-capita income.

As in (22.63)–(22.64), a higher relative price $p = 1.3$ will give a rightward shift of the diversification cone, enlarge the cone, (22.67), and give a leftward shift of the density function, cf. *Fig. 22.2c*. Hence, the long-run prospect is now a ***diversified open economy***, cf. (22.67), (22.69). Although the evolution of GDP, $y/P_1\,(k)$ is stochastic on $k \in (0, \infty)$, we may note that the factor rewards are nonstochastic (stochastic within) (outside) diversification cones, cf. (22.13). The certainty of the factor remuneration (rate of return) is an ameliorating aspect of the diversification cone with its now stochastic factor reallocation, $\lambda_1(k)$, cf. Remark 22.1. Thus the volatility of the rates of return is completely eliminated by product (output) diversification of the small trading economy.

$$p = 1.3: \quad \kappa = 4.431; \quad \mathrm{E}(k) = 4.431,\ \sigma = 0.561,\ P(\tilde{k}_2) = 0.99988. \tag{22.69}$$

The effect of an increase in the saving rate, shifting $p(k)$ to the right, is shown in (22.70), where $\mathrm{E}(k)$ and the certainty equivalent $\kappa$ are now located just outside the cone, (22.67),

$$p = 1.3,\ s = 0.25: \ \kappa = 6.977; \quad \mathrm{E}(k) = 6.966,\ \sigma = 0.783,\ P(\tilde{k}_2) = 0.418. \tag{22.70}$$

Whereas deterministic dynamics always provide a definite answer to the question of long-run specialization, stochastic dynamics with concomitant uncertainty of future factor endowments will not, for the commodity price ratio and saving parameter in (22.70), allow this outcome to be predicted with much confidence, as the density function gives nearly equal chance to these two events in the long run, cf. $P(\tilde{k}_2)$, (22.70).

With additional and *correlated diffusion* processes involved, we get results such as,

$$\begin{aligned} &p = 1.3,\ s = 0.25,\ \beta_1 = 0.01,\ \beta_2 = 0.03,\ \rho_{13} = 0.4: \\ &\kappa = 6.977;\ \mathrm{E}(k) = 6.949,\ \sigma = 1.105,\ P(\tilde{k}_2) = 0.466. \end{aligned} \tag{22.71}$$

Comparing (22.70) and (22.71), the expectation $\mathrm{E}(k)$ has declined slightly in (22.71); by itself, the labor uncertainty $\beta_1$ will increase the drift coefficient $a(k)$, cf. (22.40), (22.64), but together with $\rho_{13} > 0$, the parameter $\beta_1$ will reduce the component $\bar{s}(k)$, (22.40), in the drift coefficient $a(k)$. With $\rho_{13} \neq 0$, a minor discrepancy between $\kappa$ and $\mathrm{E}(k)$ always occurs. The dispersion $\sigma$ increased in (22.71), despite that a $\rho_{13} > 0$ contributes to a smaller diffusion coefficient $b(k)$, (22.40); in this case, the dominant term in the diffusion coefficient $b(k)$ is $\beta^2 k^2$, and this explains the increased dispersion in (22.71).

### *Transition Paths*

The sample paths in Fig. 22.2 displayed the *transient* movements of the capital-labor ratio toward a *stationary* (steady-state) probability distribution under alternative parametrizations of the basic diffusion model, (22.39)–(22.40), by which both economic trends and fluctuations are just a manifestation of the process of stochastic growth.

As to the volatility and monotonicity properties of the transition paths for $k(t)$ in Fig. 22.2, we may incidentally note that during the *upward* phase, the recent historical (single) path looks deceptively more exact (regular, smooth) than the reality is; the inexactitude (volatility) is hidden by the fact that the occurrence of some negative random *shocks* has been *masked* (absorbed) by the temporary upwards contribution from the drift coefficient $a(k)$. Furthermore, the wildness (volatility) lies in wait, as the diffusion coefficient $b(k)$ increases with $k$, and hence the same absolute shocks have larger impacts upon the observed time path later on in the drive toward stationarity. To fully display the volatility aspects of transient motion, two sample paths (with different Wiener realizations, $\omega_1, \omega_2$) of the process (22.71) are shown on an extended *time* horizon in *Fig. 22.2d*. It offers some clues for understanding and properly interpreting the significance of fluctuating (ups/downs) empirical growth paths. The *smooth* and *monotone* curves in Figs. 22.2 and 22.3a and b show the trajectories derived from *deterministic* dynamics, $\beta_1 = \beta_2 = \beta_3 = 0$, of the small trading economy.

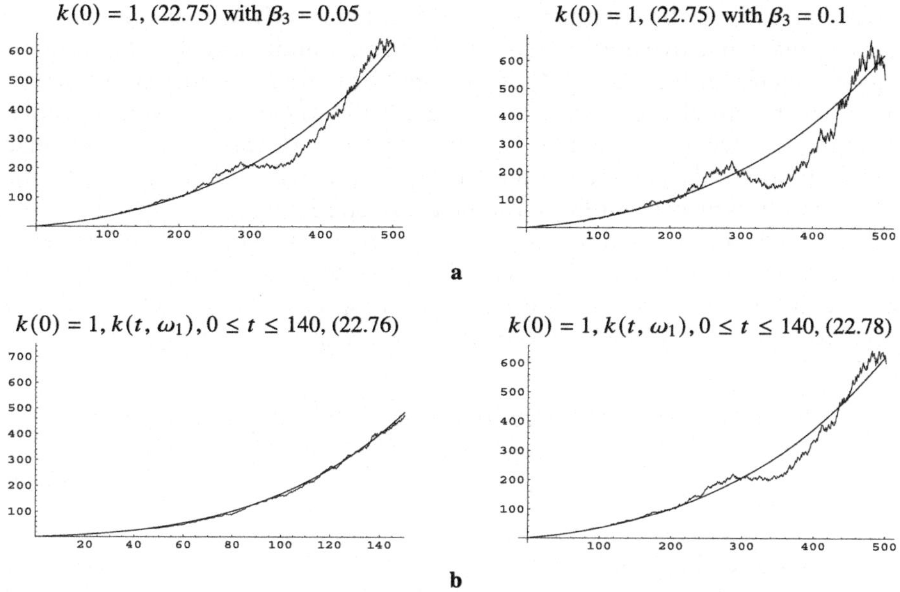


**Fig. 22.3** (**a**) Endogenous growth paths, $k(t, \omega_1)$, (22.75). (**b**) Endogenous growth paths, $k(t, \omega_1)$, (22.76), (22.78)

## STOCHASTIC ENDOGENOUS GROWTH

Parametric variation within the basic diffusion model (22.39)–(22.40) can also generate *nonstationary* stochastic processes with *persistent* (endogenous) *growth* paths for the capital-labor ratio, $k(t)$. Thus, a coherent treatment of *growth* and *cyclical* phenomena as *endogenous* events can be given within the general framework of the stochastic economic growth process (22.39)–(22.40). The real business cycle (RBC) research program, King et al. (1988), focuses on understanding and stochastically modeling the interaction of growth and cycles, e.g., by introducing temporary productivity (technology) shocks and optimal labor supply fluctuations. Although the diffusion model (22.39)–(22.40) like RBC models, only deals prima facie with the *real* fluctuations without any explicit role assigned to money, the interpretation and origin of the continuous uncertainty (diffusion) elements ($w_1$, $w_2$, $w_3$) need not be entirely restricted to the real sphere; some of these elements may also reflect ramifications from financial, money, and foreign exchange markets, as initially mentioned.

To incorporate *endogenous growth* in the stochastic process, (22.39)–(22.40), it is necessary that the *marginal product* of *capital accumulation* does not converge to zero, but does remain bounded below. To permit the long-run growth rate to be an endogenous outcome of time-invariant CES technologies, the sectorial substitution elasticity ($\sigma_i$) of the specialized industry must therefore be *larger* than one.

Parameters may be regarded as "constants that vary". As such constants are varied, qualitative dynamic behavior may change fundamentally. The technology parameters $\sigma_i$ and $a_i$, (22.19), should not be regarded historically invariant. Through technical progress, they will gradually undergo permanent secular changes, cf. Remark 22.4. It is beyond the scope of this essay to formalize the evolution of the parameter values, $\sigma_i$, $a_i$, but we will illustrate the stochastic dynamic consequences for $k(t)$ of some parameter regimes with $\sigma_i > 1$.

The deterministic condition for endogenous growth with $CES$ technologies was given in Jensen and Wang (1997, p. 91–93); here Chap. 21, and the analogous condition for *stochastic endogenous growth* was given (a.s., almost sure) in Jensen and Wang (1999, p. 391); here (27.83) in Chap. 27, as

$$\lim_{t\to\infty} k(t) = \infty \text{ a.s. } \Leftrightarrow \ s(\gamma_2/p)a_2^{1/\varrho_2} - (n+\delta) + \frac{1}{2}(\beta_1^2 - \beta_2^2 - \Delta)$$
$$= \bar{a}_3 - \frac{1}{2}\bar{b}_3^2 > 0 \tag{22.72}$$

where $\Delta$ is given in (22.46), and $\bar{a}_3$, $\bar{b}_3$ in (22.42). The asymptotic behavior for large values of $k(t)$ is described by (22.42), which has the solution, Dixit and Pindyck (1994, p. 71),

$$k(t) \sim k_0 \exp\left\{(\bar{a}_3 - \frac{1}{2}\bar{b}_3)t + \bar{b}_3 w(t)\right\} \tag{22.73}$$

with

$$\mathrm{E}[k(t)] = k_0 e^{\bar{a}_3 t}, \quad \sigma(t) = k_0 e^{\bar{a}_3 t}(e^{\bar{b}_3^2 t} - 1)^{1/2} \tag{22.74}$$

Observed that condition (22.72) implies condition (22.43) so the right hand side of (22.72) implies $S(0) = -\infty$ and $S(\infty) < \infty$. For big values of $k(t)$ the process behaves like a geometric Brownian motion since the drift and diffusion terms both convergence to two linear terms. This property restricts the process not to explode in finite time and we have $\lim_{t\to\infty} k(t) = \infty$ a.s.

We will briefly exhibit the stochastic solution to (22.56) under parametric regimes that satisfy the *necessary* and *sufficient* (with probability one) *condition* (22.72) for long-run per-capita growth.

**Example 22.3** $p = 1$, $s = 0.25$, $n = 0.02$, $\delta = 0.05$, $\beta_1 = 0$, $\beta_2 = 0$, $\lambda_3 = 1$, $\rho_{ij} = 0 \ (i \neq j)$, $\gamma_1 = \gamma_2 = 1$, $a_1 = 0.2$, $a_2 = 0.4$.

The exogenous price and parameter values of Example 22.3 must be supplemented with assumptions about $\sigma_i$. In the first case, (22.75), rather large values of $\sigma_i$ are chosen, and the corresponding price limits, reversal point, GDP flat, and the single diversification cone are

$$\begin{matrix}\sigma_1 = 3 \\ \sigma_2 = 4\end{matrix} : \begin{cases} p^* = 3.30,\ p^{**} = 0.70724,\ \bar{p} = 0.70723,\ \bar{\omega} = 0.079,\ \bar{k} = 7.7\,10^{-6} \\ \tilde{\omega} = 2.22,\ \tilde{k}_1 = 0.17,\ \tilde{k}_2 = 4.79,\ \tilde{\theta}_1 = 0.33,\ \tilde{\theta}_2 = 0.74 \end{cases} \tag{22.75}$$

The reversal point $(\bar{\omega}, \bar{k})$ is indeed very close to the origin, and evidently, the scope $p \in (\bar{p}, p^{**})$ for observing two cones here is extremely narrow, cf. Fig. 22.1e.

Condition (22.72) is satisfied by (22.75), and two stochastic endogenous growth paths, with respectively $\beta_3 = 0.05$ and $\beta_3 = 0.1$, are displayed in *Fig. 22.3*a and b. The timescale (unit: year, quarter, month) of economic growth models is seldom given much attention, and we cannot enter the details here. However, whatever unit is appropriate, the sample paths in Fig. 22.3a and b demonstrate the *endogenous* character of *growth* and *cycles* (with both shorter and longer periods) from the diffusion process (22.56). With a larger saving uncertainty, $\beta_3 = 0.1$, the intrinsic evolution of cycles around the long-term mean $E[k(t)]$, or as here the certainty equivalent, is more prevalent in the time path of Fig. 22.3a and b.

Another critical parameter in (22.72) is clearly the size of the *depreciation rate* $\delta$. In the next case, we have put $\delta = 0$ [which in terms of capital accumulation (22.38) is equivalent to the results from an alternative institutional setup, where the depreciation allowances $\delta P_1 K$ are fully reinvested by firms, and where the parameter $s$ is interpreted as the aggregate saving (household) rate of net disposable income]. Endogenous growth does not require the large substitution elasticities above. For illustrative purposes of Theorem 22.1, the $\sigma_i$ values below, (22.76), (22.78), are chosen in a way that two cones always occur, cf. (22.32); but the size of $\sigma_2$ has been selected such that the whole parameter constellation with (22.76) meets the growth condition (22.72). The latter of course prevents the economy from operating in any of the cones beyond a temporary epoch.

$$\begin{matrix}\delta = 0 \\ \sigma_1 = 0.9 \\ \sigma_2 = 1.8\end{matrix} : \begin{cases} \bar{p} = 0.84,\ \bar{\omega} = 0.56,\ \bar{k} = 0.17 \\ \tilde{\tilde{\omega}} = 0.11,\ \tilde{\tilde{k}}_2 = 0.040,\ \tilde{\tilde{k}}_1 = 0.58,\ \tilde{\tilde{\theta}}_1 = 3.14,\ \tilde{\tilde{\theta}}_2 = 0.35 \\ \tilde{\omega} = 2.18,\ \tilde{k}_1 = 1.96,\ \tilde{k}_2 = 2.18,\ \tilde{\theta}_1 = 0.32,\ \tilde{\theta}_2 = 0.71 \end{cases} \tag{22.76}$$

A sample path of (22.56), (22.76) is shown in Fig. 22.3b (top panel). The rapidity of growth is much faster in case (22.76) than in (22.75), as the state of the economy will already reach, $k(t, \omega) \approx 500$ around $t = 140$ rather than $t = 450$, cf. Fig. 22.3a and b. In contrast to (22.75), the sample path of (22.76) is not retarded by the downward phases of longer cycles. Clues to this distinct variety in the behavior of $k(t, \omega)$ can be obtained by examining the size of *drift* and *diffusion* coefficients of the *asymptotic* geometric Wiener process, i.e., $\bar{a}_3$, $\bar{b}_3$, (22.42), (22.72):

$$\begin{aligned}
(22.75):\quad & \beta_3 = 0.05, \quad \bar{a}_3 = 0.00368, \quad \bar{b}_3 = 0.0147, \quad \bar{a}_3/\bar{b}_3 = 0.250, \\
& \beta_3 = 0.10, \quad \bar{a}_3 = 0.00368, \quad \bar{b}_3 = 0.0295, \quad \bar{a}_3/\bar{b}_3 = 0.125, \\
(22.76):\quad & \beta_3 = 0.10, \quad \bar{a}_3 = 0.0118, \quad \bar{b}_3 = 0.0127, \quad \bar{a}_3/\bar{b}_3 = 0.928, \\
(22.78):\quad & \beta_3 = 0.10, \quad \bar{a}_3 = 0.0200, \quad \bar{b}_3 = 0.0360, \quad \bar{a}_3/\bar{b}_3 = 0.556
\end{aligned} \tag{22.77}$$

Thus, it appears from (22.77) that the drift coefficient is relatively much smaller in case (22.75) than in (22.76). The *weak drift* coefficient in (22.75) cannot strongly counteract a series of negative shocks (and hence the process $k(t)$ is vulnerable) and downswings cannot be avoided. However, a relative *strong drift* coefficient can, besides generating long-term growth, also absorb negative shocks along the sample path. Such a stochastic growth path will, like deterministic growth, exhibit a pronounced tendency for monotone evolution.

In our final case of case (22.78), *depreciation* ($\delta$) is restored, and to have an adequate substitution elasticity ($\sigma_2$) of empirical relevance, it has the size, $\sigma_2 = 2$. To satisfy (22.72), the *capital intensity* parameter ($a_2$) is increased. When $\sigma_2 > 1$, larger ($a_2$) effectively enhances the labor productivity $f_2(k)$ and the marginal product of capital $f_2'(k)$, cf. (22.21). Alternatively, the overall efficiency ("total productivity") parameter ($\gamma_2$) can be of critical importance in satisfying with (22.72).

$$\begin{array}{r} a_2 = 0.6 \\ \sigma_1 = 0.9 : \\ \sigma_2 = 2 \end{array} \left\{ \begin{array}{l} \bar{p} = 0.56, \quad \bar{\omega} = 0.15, \quad \bar{k} = 0.053 \\ \tilde{\tilde{\omega}} = 0.0080, \ \tilde{\tilde{k}}_2 = 0.00014, \ \tilde{\tilde{k}}_1 = 0.0037, \ \tilde{\tilde{\theta}}_1 = 20.47, \ \tilde{\tilde{\theta}}_2 = 0.16 \\ \tilde{\omega} = 1.31, \quad \tilde{k}_1 = 0.37, \quad \tilde{k}_2 = 3.90, \quad \tilde{\theta}_1 = 0.48, \ \tilde{\theta}_2 = 0.63 \end{array} \right. \tag{22.78}$$

A sample path of (22.56), (22.78), is shown in Fig. 22.3b (bottom panel). Compared to (22.75), the larger ($\sigma_2, a_2$) have each contributed to larger ($\bar{a}_3$, $\bar{b}_3$), cf. (22.77); the somewhat larger volatility in Fig. 22.3b, is due to the relatively stronger diffusion coefficient $\bar{b}_3$.

Regarding international comparisons of *elasticities of substitution*, Bairam (1989), offers support for elasticities above unity, rather early in Japan's development. For manufacturing in Taiwan, Wang (1995) finds substitution elasticities above two. Easterly and Fischer (1995) provide further evidence on substitution and growth experience related to economic fundamentals, preferences, technology, and factor endowment.

Generally, we should emphasize that the basic *endowment accumulation* parameters ($n, s, \delta$) only affect the *drift* coefficient, cf. (22.40), and hence their size—alongside *technology* parameters—is crucial for satisfying the endogenous growth criterion (22.72).

Finally, we may note that a *closed* economy could not have endogenous per-capita growth with the parameter regimes (22.76), (22.78). With *autarky*, the *capital good* industry must have $\sigma_1 > 1$ and moreover meet a condition similar to (22.72). The *small trading* economy has the option of endogenous growth by *specializing* in any industry satisfying (22.72) together with the *stochastic determinants* (parameters: $n, s, \delta, \beta_1, \beta_2, \beta_3, \rho_{ij}$) of endowment accumulation.

## Final Comments

Stochastic (probability) issues appear, according to Pierre-Simon Laplace, because we are partly knowing and partly ignorant. The dynamics of stochastic and deterministic growth models share a common element: the *drift coefficient*, which constitutes the kernel of our knowledge, based on economic theory and empirical (verified) data. The course of future events are admittedly uncertain, but the *diffusion coefficient*, similarly based on solid theoretical/empirical premises, governs the volatility of outcomes, and the mathematical *tool* of *continuous probability* of Norbert Wiener and Kiyoshi Ito allows probability calculations to be made about observable future events. In this essay, we developed a neoclassical stochastic dynamic general equilibrium model of a small open economy with balanced trade. We introduced a three-dimensional diffusion process into the factor endowment expansion of the trading economy. The dynamic implications of uncertainty in saving rates were of particular concern, as fluctuations in this critical parameter are prevalent in much cross-country evidence. The uncertainty in saving may interact with demographic and depreciation fluctuations. Furthermore, it was important for us to demonstrate stochastic dynamics in a setting of rather general assumptions about sector technologies. General CES functions were applied, despite the complication involved for price intervals and domains of specialization/diversification. The stochastic growth model was solved and illustrated for important regions within the parameter space, including parametric values generating nonstationary sample paths of stochastic endogenous growth and cycles. The stochastic outcomes and expectations were compared with their deterministic (certainty) equivalents that served as economic benchmarks. Stochastic dynamics properly employed, far from making economic growth models more abstract, actually serve as a powerful liberating framework enabling the analysis and integration of ever more realistic and complicated hypotheses. Stochastic and deterministic growth models contribute together to understanding significant aspects of the historical time series observed from growing trading economies.

## Appendix

*CES isoquants and the isoquant tangents*

The general CES function is

$$Y = F(L, K) = \gamma[(1-a)L^{\varrho} + aK^{\varrho}]^{1/\varrho}$$

and the level curve (isoquant) for $Y = \bar{Y}$ is

$$K = \left[(1/a)\left(\bar{Y}/\gamma\right)^{\varrho} - [(1-a)/a]\,L^{\varrho}\right]^{1/\varrho} \tag{22.79}$$

With $\varrho < 0$ ($\sigma < 1$), the level curves (22.79) have vertical and horizontal *asymptotes* given by, respectively,

$$\bar{L} = (\bar{Y}/\gamma)\,[1/(1-a)]^{1/\varrho}, \quad \bar{K} = (\bar{Y}/\gamma)\,(1/a)^{1/\varrho}. \tag{22.80}$$

With $\varrho > 0$, ($\sigma > 1$), the level curves (22.79) have the *axis intercepts*:

$$\bar{K} = (\bar{Y}/\gamma)\,(1/a)^{1/\varrho}, \quad \bar{L} = (\bar{Y}/\gamma)\,[1/(1-a)]^{1/\varrho} \tag{22.81}$$

**Lemma 22.1** *At the vertical, (horizontal), axis point* $(0, \bar{K})$, $(\bar{L}, 0)$, *(22.81), the isoquant tangents have, respectively, the slope:* $-\infty$ *and* $0$.

***Proof*** From (22.79), we have the tangent slope

$$\frac{dK}{dL} = -\frac{1-a}{a}L^{\varrho-1}\left[\frac{1}{a}\left(\bar{Y}/\gamma\right)^{\varrho} - \frac{1-a}{a}\,L^{\varrho}\right]^{1/\varrho-1} \tag{22.82}$$

which becomes infinite, as $L$ goes to 0. Next, by inserting the intercept $\bar{L}$, (22.81), into (22.82), this tangent slope becomes zero. □

Thus, we have by the asymptotes, (22.80), and Lemma 22.1 that, irrespective of the size of $\varrho$ ($\sigma$), the marginal rate of substitution $\omega = |dK/dL|$ ranges from zero to infinity.

Despite the different appearance and shape of the level curves, (22.79), $\sigma \lesseqgtr 1$, the formulas (22.23) apply, with no restrictions on $\sigma$.

## Bibliography


Aghion P, Howitt P (1998) Endogenous Growth Theory. The MIT Press, Cambridge, MA and London, England

Bairam E (1989) Learning–by–Doing: Variable Elasticity of Substitution and Economic Growth in Japan, 1878–1939. Journal of Development Studies 25:344–53

Bencivenga VR (1991) Financial Intermediation and Endogenous Growth. Review of Economic Studies 58:159–209

Berthelemy JC, Vardoudakis A (1996) Economic Growth, Convergence Clubs, and the Role of Financial Development. Oxford Economic Papers 48:300–28

Bourguignon F (1974) A Particular Class of Continuous–Time Stochastic Growth Models. Journal of Economic Theory 9:141–158

Chang FR, Malliaris AG (1987) Asymptotic Growth under Uncertainty—Existence and Uniqueness. Review of Economic Studies (54):169–174

Choi EK, Jensen BS (1999) Economic Growth and International Trade. Blackwell, Oxford

Deardorff AV (1971) Growth and Trade in a Two–Sector World. PhD thesis, Cornell University, unpublished Ph.D. dissertation

Deardorff AV (2001) Does Growth Encourage Factor Price Equalization? Review of Development Economics 5(2):169–181

Deardorff AV, Stern RN (1994) The Stolper–Samuelson Theorem: A Golden Jubilee. The University of Michigan Press, Ann Arbor

Dixit AK, Pindyck RS (1994) Investment under Uncertainty. Princeton University Press, New Jersey

Easterly W, Fischer S (1995) The Soviet Economic Decline. World Bank Economic Review 9:341–71

Ethier W (1979) The Theorems of International Trade in Time–Phased Economies. Journal of International Economics 9:225–77

Fisher FM, Hillman AL (1984) The Commodity Pattern of Trade and the Heckcher–Ohlin Theorem in the Presence of Aggregate and Commodity–Specific Factor–Intensity Reversals. Journal of International Economics 17:159–72

Galetovic A (1996) Specialization, intermediation, and growth. Journal of Monetary Economics 38:549–59

Gandolfo G (1998) International Trade Theory and Policy. Springer Verlag, Berlin

Greenwood J, Smith BD (1997) Financial markets in development, and the development of financial markets. Journal of Economic Dynamics and Control 21:145–81

Grinols EL (1987) Uncertainty and the Theory of International Trade. Harwood Academic Publishers, Chur, Switzerland

Helpman E, Razin A (1978) A Theory of International Trade under Uncertainty. Academic Press, N.Y.

Holden H, Øksendal B, Ubøe J, Zhang T (1996) Stochastic Partial Differential Equation. A Modeling White Noise Functional Approach. Birkäuser, Boston

Itô K, McKean HP Jr (1965) Diffusion Processes and Their Sample Paths. Springer–Verlag, Berlin

Jensen BS (1994) The Dynamic Systems of Basic Economic Growth Models. Kluwer Academic Publishers, Dordrecht

Jensen BS, Larsen ME (1987) Growth and Long–Run Stability. Acta Applicandae Mathematicae 9:219–237, Reprinted in Jensen (1994)

Jensen BS, Wang C (1997) General Equilibrium Dynamics of Basic Trade Models for Growing Economies. In Bjarne S. Jensen and Kar–Yiu Wong (eds.) *Dynamics, Economic Growth, and International Trade*, Ann Arbor: University of Michigan Press.

Jensen BS, Wang C (1999) Basic Stochastic Dynamic Systems of Growth and Trade. Review of International Economics 7:378–402, or in Choi & Jensen (1999)

Joshi S (1998) A framework to analyze comparative dynamics in a continuous time stochastic growth model. Economic Modelling 15:125–34

Karatzas I, Shreve SE (1991) Brownian Motion and Stochastic Calculus, 2nd edn. Springer Verlag, N.Y.

Karlin S, Taylor HM (1981) A Second Course in Stochastic Processes. Academic Press, N.Y.

Kemp MC (1976) Three Topics in the Theory of International Trade—Distribution, Welfare and Uncertainty. North–Holland/Elsevier, N.Y.

Kemp MC, Liviatan N (1973) Production and Trade Patterns under Uncertainty. Economic Record 49:215–27

King RG, Levine R (1993) Finance, entrepreneurship, and growth. Journal of Monetary Economics 32:513–42

King RG, Plosser CI, Rebelo ST (1988) Production, growth and business cycles: I., The basic neoclassical model, II., New directions. Journal of Monetary Economics 21:195–232, 309–41

Kloeden PE, Platen E (1995) Numerical Solutions to Stochastic Differential Equations, 2nd edn. Springer Verlag, Berlin

Klump R (1995) On the Institutional Determinants of Economic Development—Lessons from a Stochastic Neoclassical Growth Model. Jahrbuch für Wirtschaftswissenschaft 46:138–51

Lee JW (1995) Capital goods imports and long–run growth. Journal of Development Economics 48:91–110

Levine R (1991) Stock markets, growth, and tax policy. Journal of Finance 46:1445–65

Lucas RE (1988) On the Mechanics of Economic Development. Journal of Monetary Economics 22:3–42, Reprinted in Becker (1991)

Maddison A (1992) A Long–Run Perspective on Saving. Scandinavian Journal of Economics 94:181–196

Malliaris AG, Brock WA (1982) Stochastic Methods in Economics and Finance. North–Holland/Elsevier, Amsterdam

Merton RC (1975) An Asymptotic Theory of Growth under Uncertainty. Review of Economic Studies 42:375–393, Ch.17 in Merton (1990)

Minhas BS (1962) The Homohypallagic Production Function, Factor Intensity Reversals, and the Heckscher–Ohlin Theorem. The Journal of Political Economy 70:138–156

Minhas BS (1963) An International Comparison of Factor Costs and Factor Use. North–Holland, Amsterdam

Øksendal B (1998) Stochastic Differential Equations—An Introduction with Applications, 5th edn. Springer–Verlag, Berlin

Pagano M (1993) Financial markets and growth. European Economic Review 37:613–22

Pomery J (1984) Uncertainty in Trade Models. In Ronald W. Jones and Peter B. Kenen (eds.), *Handbook in International Economics*, Vol. I, N.Y.: North–Holland/–Elsevier.

Romer PM (1986) Increasing Returns and Long–Run Growth. Journal of Political Economy 94:1002–1037, Reprinted in Becker (1991)

Saint-Paul G (1992) Technological Choice, Financial Markets and Economic development. European Economic Review 36:763–81

Samuelson PA (1949) International Factor Price Equalisation Once Again. Economic Journal 59:181–197

Samuelson PA (1978) The Canonical Classical Model of Political Economy. Journal of Economic Literature 16:1415–1434

Sandmo A (1969) Capital Risk, Consumption, and Portfolio Choice. Econometrica 37:586–99

Sandmo A (1970) The Effect of Uncertainty on Saving Decisions. Review of Economic Studies 37:353–60

Södersten B, Reed G (1994) International Economics, 3rd edn. Macmillan Press, London

Solow RM (1956) A Contribution to the Theory of Economic Growth. Quarterly Journal of Economics 70:65–94, Reprinted in Stiglitz (1969), and in Becker (1991)

Uzawa H (1959) Prices of the Factors of Production in International Trade. Econometrica 27:448–68

Wang EC (1995) Factor Substitution Approach to Testing the Time Variation in Production: the Case of Taiwan's Manufacturing. Applied Economics 27:107–16

Wong KY (1995) International Trade in Goods and Factor Mobility. MIT Press, Cambridge, MA

CHAPTER 23

# Transformation Functions: Cost, Revenue Functions, Autarky General Equilibrium, Comparative Advantage

## INTRODUCTION

The *production possibility frontier* (**PPF**) curve is in a strange position. On the one hand, *production possibility curves* (**PPC**)—as summarizing the technology of two outputs and the factor endowments of the economy—are with numerous applications so firmly embedded in the consciousness of economists that there can hardly be any trade text or course that does not present PPC to demonstrate maximum outputs from any given endowments. Two-dimensional *diagrams* of concave PPF curves prevail in many other fields of economic analysis. On the other hand, the PPC as an explanatory geometric tool are paradoxically *never* seen *explicitly* stated by *analytic* expressions or *algebraic formulas*. One *purpose* of this chapter is to close this incredible long-standing gap in the literature by presenting particular **transformation functions** and their *graphs* (**PPC**) in *closed form*. Second *aim* is to use Pareto optimal allocations (PPC) to derive explicit *autarky general equilibria*.

The *explicit* PPC formulas—rigorously derived from *Pareto efficiency* conditions in *factor space* $(L, K)$ and *output space* $(Y_1, Y_2)$—will be an eye-opener for understanding the entire shape and slopes (tangents, marginal rate of transformations) of PPC (production efficient envelopes). Predominantly, PPC are graphically depicted like the positive orthants of ellipses and circles with *horizontal/vertical* tangents at *axis intercepts*. But this kind of PPC is both theoretically and quantitatively very *misleading* [cf. (23.74)], and they will *never* be obtained with *non-joint production* (distinct sectors, industries) of two

With co-author:
JACOPO ZOTTI, Department of Political and Social Sciences, University of Trieste, Italy





B. S. Jensen, *The Elements and Dynamic Systems of Economic Growth and Trade Models*, https://doi.org/10.1007/978-3-031-52493-6_23

outputs. As our explicit formulas will show, the *range* of PPC *slopes* is narrow, and the strictly concave shape of two-sector PPC envelopes will not in many cases differ much from straight lines.

By ***duality***, analytical expressions of **PPC** will alternatively provide *explicit* **Revenue** (GDP) *functions*. These quantitative (parametric) Revenue functions will enable us by their *explicit* first- and second-order *derivatives* to provide the *Core Theorems*[1] in precise *quantitative analytic* forms[2]—which is our third *objective*. We address all these five theorems and by analyzing them rigorously and quantitatively, we will obtain more proper (new) economic understandings and interpretations of these Core Theorems. Some theorems give clearly only *equilibria* of ***production sectors*** (supply), but nevertheless do contain *key relations* and results that are in fact **endowment invariant**, and such theorem is *robust* and carries over to ***general*** *equilibrium* formulas, where also *consumer preferences* (utility parameters) are involved. Rybczynski theorem relations are neither endowment invariant/nor robust.

The "*production indifference* (transformation) curve" was originated by Lerner (1932, p.346), when, in two-dimensional production diagrams, the assumption of "*constant opportunity cost*" (straight lines) was graphically *replaced* by curves "*concave* toward the axes", Leontief (1933, p.405).

[1] On "Five Theorems" and "Heckscher-Ohlin", cf. standard textbooks: Feenstra (2016, p.8), Caves et al. (2007, p.116), Ethier (1995, p.130), Gandolfo (1998, p.95), Wong (1995, p.30), Markusen et al. (1995, p.112), Kenen (2000, p.63), Krugman et al. (2018, p.124).

[2] As to their succinct verbal formulations, we cite (italics ours), Leamer (1984, p.3) :

> "The core of *general equilibrium trade theory* consist of *four* theorems that describe the *responsiveness* of *outputs* and *factor prices* to *changes* in *output prices* and *factor supplies*, and a fifth that identifies which commodity are exported and which are imported.
>
> 1. The Stolper-Samuelson theorem describes the relation between factor prices and output prices, *holding fixed factor supplies* [endowments].
> 2. The Rybczynski theorem links outputs to factor supplies, *given output prices*.
> 3. The Samuelson Duality theorem—*reciprocity relations*—describe the *correspondence* between the Stolper-Samuelson effects and the Rybczynski effects.
> 4. The Factor Price Equality theorem deals with the responsiveness of factor prices to factor supplies [ endowments ], *holding fixed output prices*.
>    The *fifth* theorem : The *Heckscher-Ohlin theorem* identifies the structure of *trade* as a function of either (a) the *difference* between autarky (pretrade) *prices* and posttrade prices or (b) the factor supplies [ *endowments* ].
>
> Since autarky prices are generally *unobservable*, this book will make use of only the quantitative [ endowments ] *version* of the Heckscher-Ohlin theorem."

Core Theorems 1–4 are succinctly restated on 1 line by proper partial derivatives in (23.173). See also Leamer and Levinsohn (1995, p.1345) and Meyer (1976, p.803).

However, the *concave* PPF curve was an *intricate* concept, representing the result of complicated economic processes and relations by which exogenous endowments were optimally allocated between sectors in accordance with marginal productivity conditions to ensure the maximum of one product for any preassigned amounts of the second product. Stolper and Samuelson (1941, p.68) established the connection between optimal factor allocations, *Factor Contract Curves* (**FCC**), and *maximal product curves* (**PPC**), cf. "contract curve, where utility indifference curves touch" Edgeworth (1881, 2003, p.36), Black (1957), Hsiao (1971, p.920). Computer programs have been set up to chart transformation curves for some equations with our **CD** parameters, Johnson (1966, p.693), but adopting a factor **endowment** ratio of *unity* implies, as we shall see, a serious *loss* of *generality* for *shapes* of PPC.

Our results are stated in Lemmas 23.1–23.2: *explicit* parametric factor contract curves (**FCC**) and Factor Allocation Curves (**FAC**) in Figs. 23.1, 23.2, and 23.3.

The most *important results* are in Theorems 23.1–23.4 and Theorem 23.5: *analytic* production possibility curves (**PPC**) and *parametric* **transformation functions** with *graphs* in Figs. 23.4, 23.5, 23.6, 23.7, and 23.8. Theorems 23.1–23.5 are restated and extended in Theorems 23.6–23.7 by giving **explicit** analytic **Revenue Functions** with their explicit partial derivatives (Hessian matrix) providing the exact comparative static elasticities involved in *"Core Theorems"*.

Especially important are proofs and exact demonstrations in Fig. 23.8 showing that the **transformation elasticity** along explicit PPC of Theorems 23.1–23.5 is **not** constant (isoelastic) but belong to the **VET** class (Variable Elasticities of Transformation).

The Pareto efficient **production sector** (production market and factor market) representations as derived in Theorems 23.6–23.7 are compared with their corresponding exact **general equilibrium** (GE) counterpart formulas.

Finally, the **GE** formulas give a *unified* analytic (parametric) treatment for a general **Standard Model** representation of **comparative advantage** in: Proposition 23.1, Corollaries 23.1–23.2, and Figs. 23.10 and 23.11.

With our Lemmas and Theorems, FCC and PPC can be generated for any **CD** *parameters* and *factor endowments* that may be used to study specific parameter impacts on autarky and international *general equilibria*.

All our contributions and basic conclusions can be extended to constant elasticity of substitution (**CES**) forms.

We proceed **axiomatically** in exposition and sections. Section "Endowments, Sector Allocations, Technologies, and Efficiency" gives the general framework of endowments and technology of autarky economies; Pareto efficiency conditions establish FCC and FAC in factor space. Section "Pareto Efficient Allocation and Production Possibility Curves" links FCC with PCC in analytic forms. This section contains the analytic groundwork and main theorems on Pareto Efficient Allocation and production possibility curves. Section "Explicit Transformation Functions and Transformation Curves" gives some explicit transformation functions and their production possibility curves. Section "Production Possibility Curves and Elasticity of Transformation" discusses PPC and their Elasticity of Transformation. Section "Leontief PPC Points, Autarky Outputs, Prices, Core Theorems" shows the singular two-sector PPC points for Leontief technologies with associated Core Theorem versions in Fig. 23.9a–b. Section "The Multiple Output Cost Function: $C = C(w, r, Y_1, Y_2)$" presents the Multiple Output Cost function. Section "Explicit PPC and Revenue Function: $Y = R(P_1, P_2, L, K)$" gives explicit Revenue function with Hessian matrices, generating Rybczynski Elasticities and transformation elasticities (VET). Section "General Equilibrium, Comparative Cost, and Trade Patterns" shows CD autarky general equilibrium and analytic comparative costs. Section "Conclusion and Final Comments" gives conclusions and final comments.

## Endowments, Sector Allocations, Technologies, and Efficiency

### *Two-Sector, Two-Factor, Two-Country Framework*

There are *two countries* in the world, *A* and *B*. These countries may produce *two* consumer goods (*sectors*), $i = 1, 2$, which are fully homogeneous throughout the world. In both sectors, they are using *two primary* production *factors*, labor and capital. Labor endowment in *country* $J = A, B$ is $L_J$, while capital endowment is $K_J$; its factor proportion (*endowment ratio*) is $k_J = K_J/L_J$. It is generally assumed that both factors are *fully employed*:

$$K_{1J} + K_{2J} = K_J\ ,\ \ L_{1J} + L_{2J} = L_J\ ;\ \ k_J = K_J/L_J\ ,\ \ k_{iJ} \equiv K_{iJ}/L_{iJ}\ ,\ \ i = 1, 2 \tag{23.1}$$

$$k_J = \lambda_{L_{1J}} k_{1J} + \lambda_{L_{2J}} k_{2J}\ ;\ \ k_{2J} = [k_J - \lambda_{L_{1J}} k_{1J}]/[1 - \lambda_{L_{1J}}]\ ,\ \ J = A, B \tag{23.2}$$

$$\lambda_{L_{1J}} \equiv L_{1J}/L_J = [k_J - k_{2J}]/[k_{1J} - k_{2J}]\ ,\ \ \lambda_{L_{2J}} = 1 - \lambda_{L_{1J}}\ ;\ \ i = 1, 2\ ,\ J = A, B \tag{23.3}$$

$$\lambda_{K_{1J}} \equiv K_{1J}/K_J = [k_{1J}/k_J]\,\lambda_{L_{1J}}\ ,\ \ \lambda_{K_{2J}} = 1 - \lambda_{K_{1J}}\ ;\ \ i = 1, 2\ ,\ J = A, B \tag{23.4}$$

where $\lambda_{L_{iJ}}, \lambda_{K_{iJ}}$ are shares—**fractions**—of labor (capital) **allocated** to sector $(i)$ in country $J$. $k_{iJ}$ is capital-labor *ratio* of sector $(i)$, country $J$. *Diversification*, production of *both goods*, is equivalent to the *inequalities*:

$$0 < \lambda_{L_{1J}} < 1 \Leftrightarrow 0 < \lambda_{K_{1J}} < 1\ :\ k_{1J} > k_J > k_{2J}\ ,\ k_{1J} < k_J < k_{2J}\ ;\ J = A, B \tag{23.5}$$

**Technologies** have *constant* returns to *scale* in *both* countries, $J = A, B$. For *sector*, $i = 1, 2$, and standard Cobb-Douglas (**CD**) *parameter* specifications,

$$Y_{i_J} = F_{i_J}(L_{i_J}, K_{i_J}) = \gamma_{i_J} L_{i_J}^{1-a_{i_J}} K_{i_J}^{a_{i_J}} = L_J \lambda_{L_{i_J}} y_{i_J} \ ; \quad y_{i_J} = \gamma_{i_J} k_{i_J}^{a_{i_J}},\ i = 1, 2 \tag{23.6}$$

$\boldsymbol{Y_{i_J}}$ : **non-joint** product of sector $(i)$ in country $J$, with sector average labor productivity, $y_{i_J} \equiv Y_{i_J}/L_{i_J}$, capital-labor ratio, $k_{i_J} \equiv K_{i_J}/L_{i_J}$, and *capital intensity parameter*: $a_{i_J}$, $0 < a_{i_J} < 1$, and $1 - a_{i_J}$ is the *labor intensity*.

Sector (industry) technologies for $Y_{i_J}$ with $\sigma_i = \infty$ , $i = 1, 2$, are:

$$Y_{i_J} = F_{i_J}(L_{i_J}, K_{i_J}) = \gamma_{i_J}[(1 - a_{i_J})L_{i_J} + a_{i_J}K_{i_J}] = L_J \lambda_{L_{i_J}} y_{i_J} \ ; \ i = 1, 2 \tag{23.7}$$

*Production Possibility Set*, (23.1), (23.6): Subset, $\boldsymbol{T_J}(\boldsymbol{Y_{1_J}}, \boldsymbol{Y_{2_J}} \ ; \ \boldsymbol{L_J}, \boldsymbol{K_J}) \subset \overline{\Re}^4_+$, technological opportunities [ input-output combinations, (23.6) ], and resource endowments (23.6) is a *closed convex cone*—within the *nonnegative* orthant.

The construction of the *production possibility frontier* (**PPF boundary**) from Production Possibility Set: $\boldsymbol{T_J}(\boldsymbol{Y_{1_J}}, \boldsymbol{Y_{2_J}} \ ; \ \boldsymbol{L_J}, \boldsymbol{K_J})$—offered by the two-sector production functions (23.6)—is one main objective. The *frontier* is obtained by using the *Pareto efficiency* principle (society unanimously prefers more of any good, if no amounts of other goods are diminished). The *existence* and *concavity* conditions for PPF boundary curves are well-known.

Basic problem: Can **PPC** of Pareto efficient values $(Y_{1_J}, Y_{2_J})$ be given by *algebraic* equations for *implicit-explicit* **transformation** functions.

### *Pareto Economic Efficiency of Factor Endowments in Production*

The production possibility frontier (PPF) for country $J$ is defined as the set of points in **output space** $(Y_{1_J}, Y_{2_J})$, which are *Pareto optimal*: For *any* $Y_{1_J}$, the *maximum* $Y_{2_J}$ obtained by any given endowments, $(L_J, K_J)$, vice versa. The *curve* (PPF) is typically described by *transformation* functions in *implicit*, $\widehat{\boldsymbol{T}}_J$, or *explicit* functional form $\boldsymbol{T}_J$, Samuelson (1947, 1983, p.230), Hicks (1946, p.319), Silberberg and Suen (2001, p.541), Mas-Colell et al. (1995, p.129), Lau (1972, p.281),

$$\widehat{T}_J(Y_{1_J}, Y_{2_J} \ ; \ L_J, K_J) = 0 \quad ; \quad Y_{2_J} = T_J(Y_{1_J} \ ; \ L_J, K_J) \tag{23.8}$$

Differentiable transformation functions (23.8) imply standard efficiency conditions. Discussion of transformation functions, $\widehat{T}_J$ or $T_J$, has been confined to essential marginal (derivative) properties in qualitative form. One *goal* is to get *quantitative* explicit (parametric) expressions of $T_J(Y_{1_J}; L_J, K_J)$, that is, *having* $L_J, K_J$ to see $\mathbf{T}_J$ (23.8) *specified* completely by *technology parameters*: $\gamma_{iJ}, a_{iJ}, i = 1, 2$, (23.6). Our **PPF** are *analytic* graphs of both: $\widehat{\mathbf{T}}_J$, $\mathbf{T}_J$ (23.8).

Apart from the **concavity** and **homogeneity** (degree one) properties of **transformation functions** (23.8), the actual shape of the PPF point set $(Y_{1J}, Y_{2J})$ were puzzling in many numerical simulations with graphics, Johnson (1966), Scarth and Warne (1973). **PPC** graphs of our *explicit* formulas of **CD**, $Y_{2J} = T_J(Y_{1J}; L_J, K_J)$, clarify the fundamental problems involved.

I : Pareto efficient factor allocation of labor and capital between *two sectors* imposes a *common marginal rate* of ***factor substitution***, **MRS**, $(\omega_J)$, of labor and capital (ratio of marginal productivities of labor/capital) by (23.6):

$$\frac{dK_J}{dL_J} = \frac{\frac{\partial \widehat{T_J}}{\partial L_J}}{\frac{\partial \widehat{T_J}}{\partial K_J}} = \frac{dK_{1J}}{dL_{1J}} = \frac{\frac{\partial F_{1J}}{\partial L_{1J}}}{\frac{\partial F_{1J}}{\partial K_{1J}}} = \frac{1 - a_{1J}}{a_{1J}} k_{1J} = \omega_J = \frac{1 - a_{2J}}{a_{2J}} k_{2J} = \frac{\frac{\partial F_{2J}}{\partial L_{2J}}}{\frac{\partial F_{2J}}{\partial K_{2J}}}$$

$$= \frac{dK_{2J}}{dL_{2J}} = \frac{\frac{\partial \widehat{T_J}}{\partial L_J}}{\frac{\partial \widehat{T_J}}{\partial K_J}} = \frac{\frac{\partial T_J}{\partial L_J}}{\frac{\partial T_J}{\partial K_J}} \tag{23.9}$$

II : An alternative to Pareto efficiency condition (23.9)—in finding maximum points (frontier) of outputs—is to impose a *common marginal rate* of *transformation* of *outputs*, **MRT**, $(\boldsymbol{p}_J)$, (ratio of marginal products of every factor):

$$\frac{dY_{2J}}{dY_{1J}} = \frac{\frac{\partial \widehat{T_J}}{\partial Y_{1J}}}{\frac{\partial \widehat{T_J}}{\partial Y_{2J}}} = \frac{\frac{\partial F_{2J}}{\partial K_{2J}}}{\frac{\partial F_{1J}}{\partial K_{1J}}} = \frac{\gamma_{2J}\, a_{2J}\, k_{2J}^{a_{2J}-1}}{\gamma_{1J}\, a_{1J}\, k_{1J}^{a_{1J}-1}} = p_J = \frac{\gamma_{2J}}{\gamma_{1J}} \frac{1 - a_{2J}}{1 - a_{1J}} \frac{k_{2J}^{a_{2J}}}{k_{1J}^{a_{1J}}} = \frac{\frac{\partial F_{2J}}{\partial L_{2J}}}{\frac{\partial F_{1J}}{\partial L_{1J}}}$$

$$= \frac{dY_{2J}}{dY_{1J}} = \frac{\frac{\partial \widehat{T_J}}{\partial Y_{1J}}}{\frac{\partial \widehat{T_J}}{\partial Y_{2J}}} = \frac{\partial T_J}{\partial Y_{1J}} \tag{23.10}$$

By (23.9), $0 < a_{iJ} < 1$, *Pareto efficient* $\boldsymbol{k}_{1J}, \boldsymbol{k}_{2J}$, can change, but *maintain* a

$$\frac{k_{1J}}{k_{2J}} = \frac{a_{1J}(1 - a_{2J})}{a_{2J}(1 - a_{1J})} = \boldsymbol{A}_J \ ; \quad a_{1J} \gtreqless a_{2J} \Leftrightarrow A_J \gtreqless 1 \Leftrightarrow k_{1J} \gtreqless k_{2J} \ ;$$

$$A_J - 1 = \frac{a_{1J} - a_{2J}}{a_{2J}(1 - a_{1J})} \tag{23.11}$$

*proportionality* (23.11) relation, $(\boldsymbol{A}_J > 0)$, hence both rise/fall together to keep proportionality. MRT requirement (23.10) gives the *same fundamental* Eq. (23.11), but **MRT** are *affected* by $\gamma_{iJ}$; later on *equivalence* relations.

### *Factor Contract Curves, Invariant Factor Allocation Curves*

The ratio condition, $k_{1J}/k_{2J} = A_J$, (23.11), gives all the *Pareto efficient sector allocations* of the total labor and capital *endowments* $(\boldsymbol{L_J}, \boldsymbol{K_J})$ in Country (J). Hence the *ratio*, $k_{1J}/k_{2J} = A_J$, (23.11), will geometrically—representing a *locus* of Pareto efficiency points—be exhibited by CD **Factor Contract Curves** (**FCC**) of *optimal* (efficient) factor allocations in the two-dimensional **factor space** $(L_J, K_J)$. By (23.11) and (23.1), we have,

$$\frac{k_{1J}}{k_{2J}} = \frac{K_{1J}/L_{1J}}{K_{2J}/L_{2J}} = \frac{K_{1J}/L_{1J}}{(K_J - K_{1J})/(L_J - L_{1J})} = A_J\ , \quad a_{1J} \neq a_{2J} \tag{23.12}$$

which is reduced to two equivalent expressions, stated either for $K_{1J}$ or $L_{1J}$:

$$K_{1J} = \frac{(A_J \cdot K_J)\, L_{1J}}{L_J + (A_J - 1)\, L_{1J}}\ ; \quad L_{1J} = \frac{L_J\, K_{1J}}{A_J\, K_J + (1 - A_J)\, K_{1J}}\ ; \quad J = A, B \tag{23.13}$$

The Eq. (23.13)—giving $(K_{1J})$ by a ratio in two linear expressions in $(L_{1J})$—represents, for *any size* of the *constants*, $(A_J \neq 1)$, $(K_J \neq 0)$, $(L_J \neq 0)$, *rectangular hyperbolas* with asymptotes parallel to the coordinate axes, see Allen (1938, p.74) on hyperbola details. By (23.13), we have geometric (qualitative) loci of (iso-tangency slopes) as **FCC curves**, here depicted in a standard Edgeworth factor box diagram by **explicit** ("parametric") expressions (analytical forms). We may state:

**Lemma 23.1** *With CD technologies (23.6) and* $A_J$, *(23.11),* **Pareto efficient** *sectoral allocations of labor and capital endowments,* $L_J, K_J$, *are represented in factor space by explicit* **factor contract curves, FCC,** *as graphs:*

$$K_{1J} = \Phi(L_{1J}) = \frac{(A_J \cdot K_J)\, L_{1J}}{L_J + (A_J - 1)\, L_{1J}}\ , \ A_J \neq 1;\ A_J = 1 : K_{1J} = \left[\frac{K_J}{L_J}\right] L_{1J} \tag{23.14}$$

**FCC** *(23.14) with fraction of labor* $\lambda_{L_{1J}}$ *as variable ("parameter") becomes,*

$$K_{1J} = \Phi\,(\lambda_{L_{1J}}) = \frac{L_J (A_J \cdot k_J)\ \lambda_{L_{1J}}}{1 + (A_J - 1)\, \lambda_{L_{1J}}}\ , \ A_J \neq 1;\ A_J = 1 : K_{1J} = L_J\, k_J \lambda_{L_{1J}} \tag{23.15}$$

*Eleven graphs* of $\Phi(L_{1J})$ (23.14) are—for *three* values of $\boldsymbol{a_{1J}}$: 0.3 , 0.5 , 0.7—seen in Figs. 23.1a–23.3a and 23.1b–23.3b, with the size of endowments: $L_J = 1$, $K_J = 2$. The eleven graphs of $\Phi(L_{1J})$ have *11* values of $\boldsymbol{a_{2J}}$ : 0.01, 0.1, 0.2, 0.3, 0.4, 0.5, 0.6, 0.7, 0.8, 0.9, 0.99. **FCC** and **FAC** are *not* affected by total factor productivity (TFP): $\gamma_{iJ}$.

**Lemma 23.2** *Endowment invariant* **Factor Allocation Curves, FAC,** *(23.16), are graphs of* $\varphi(\lambda_{L_{1J}})$*—with CD parameters,* $\mathbf{A}_J$ *(23.11)—in* Figs. 23.1c–23.3c. **FAC, FCC,** *are with,* $a_{1J} \gtrless a_{2J}$ *concave (convex) above (below) diagonal, Fig. 23.1, 23.2, and 23.3.*

$$\lambda_{K_{1J}} = \varphi(\lambda_{L_{1J}}) = \frac{A_J \cdot \lambda_{L_{1J}}}{1 + (A_J - 1)\,\lambda_{L_{1J}}}\ , \ A_J \neq 1\ ;\ A_J = 1 : \lambda_{K_{1J}} = \lambda_{L_{1J}} \tag{23.16}$$

The **fractions** of **labor, capital,** $\boldsymbol{\lambda}_{L_{iJ}}$, $\boldsymbol{\lambda}_{K_{iJ}}$, i = 1,2, (23.3–23.4), given by $\boldsymbol{\varphi}(\boldsymbol{\lambda}_{L_{1J}})$ in Figs. 23.1c–23.3c hold for *any* factor *endowments* $(L_J, K_J)$. For any *pair*, $(a_{1J}, a_{2J})$ is a **FAC**, (23.16), where *optimal* $\lambda_{L_{iJ}}$, $\lambda_{K_{iJ}}$ are located. In Figs. 23.1, 23.2, and 23.3, only FCC, FAC—with $\boldsymbol{a}_{1J} > \boldsymbol{a}_{2J}$, $\boldsymbol{a}_{2J} < 0.3, 0.5, 0.7$—are above the *diagonal*.

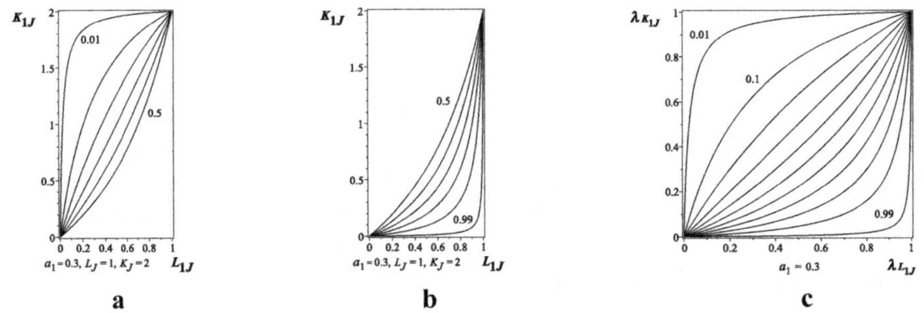


**Fig. 23.1** FCC, FAC: $K_{1J} = \Phi(L_{1J})$, (23.14), $\lambda_{K_{1J}} = \varphi(\lambda_{L_{1J}})$, (23.16)

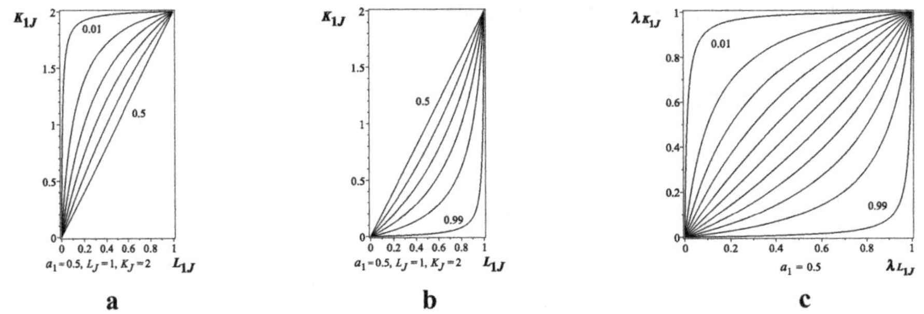


**Fig. 23.2** FCC, FAC: $K_{1J} = \Phi(L_{1J})$, (23.14), $\lambda_{K_{1J}} = \varphi(\lambda_{L_{1J}})$, (23.16)

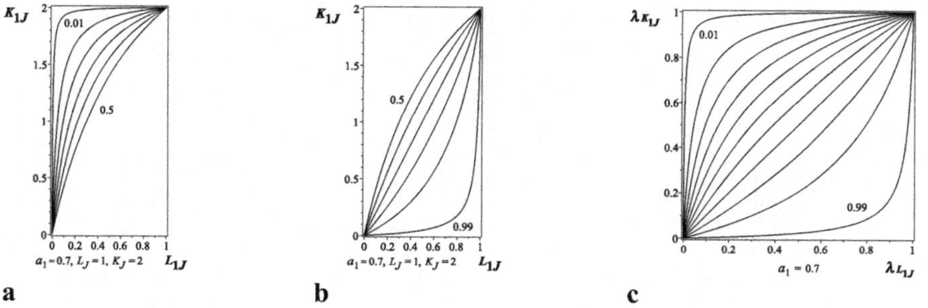


**Fig. 23.3** FCC, FAC: $K_{1J} = \Phi(L_{1J}), (23.14), \ \lambda_{K_{1J}} = \varphi(\lambda_{L_{1J}}), (23.16)$

## Pareto Efficient Allocation and Production Possibility Curves

Together with exogenous *endowments* $(L_J, K_J)$ and *technology parameters*, $\gamma_{iJ}, a_{iJ}, i = 1, 2$, (23.6), **labor allocation** variable—$\boldsymbol{\lambda}_{L_{1J}}$, $0 \leq \lambda_{L_{1J}} \leq 1$—is used (as "parameter") to ***determine*** **all** endogenous Pareto efficient variables.

**Theorem 23.1** *The Pareto efficient capital-labor ratios* $\boldsymbol{k}_{iJ}$ *are by (23.14):*

$$k_{1J} = \frac{A_J \cdot k_J}{1 + (A_J - 1)\,\lambda_{L_{1J}}} \ ; \ k_{2J} = \frac{k_J}{1 + (A_J - 1)\,\lambda_{L_{1J}}} \ ; \ A_J = 1 : k_{iJ} = k_J \tag{23.17}$$

*Along any FCC and FAC curve (23.15–23.17),* **Pareto efficient solutions** *of endogenous variables, (23.9–23.10), (23.6), are given as follows:* ***Eq.*** *(23.18) gives* **MRS** *of labor and capital—***slope** *at common* **tangency points** *of the sector isoquants—along the* **FCC** *(23.14) in* $(\boldsymbol{L}_J, \boldsymbol{K}_J)$*, Figs. 23.1, 23.2, and 23.3:*

$$\frac{dK_{iJ}}{dL_{iJ}} = \omega_J = -\frac{1 - a_{2J}}{a_{2J}} k_{2J} \equiv -\frac{1 - a_{2J}}{a_{2J}} \frac{k_J}{1 + (A_J - 1)\,\lambda_{L_{1J}}} \ ; \ i = 1, 2 \tag{23.18}$$

*In commodity space* $(\boldsymbol{Y}_{1J}, \boldsymbol{Y}_{2J})$*, the* **MRT**, $\boldsymbol{p}_J$ *of the outputs—all* **tangent slopes** *along production possibility curves,* **PPC** *of* $\hat{\mathbf{T}}_J, \mathbf{T}_J$ *(23.8), (23.6)—are given by*

$$\frac{dY_{2J}}{dY_{1J}} = p_J = -\frac{\gamma_{2J}}{\gamma_{1J}} \frac{a_{2J}}{a_{1J}} \frac{k_{2J}^{a_{2J}-1}}{k_{1J}^{a_{1J}-1}} \equiv -\frac{\gamma_{2J}}{\gamma_{1J}} \frac{a_{2J}}{a_{1J}} A_J^{1-a_{1J}} \left[\frac{k_J}{1 + (A_J - 1)\,\lambda_{L_{1J}}}\right]^{a_{2J}-a_{1J}} \tag{23.19}$$

$$\lambda_{L_{1J}} = 0 : \omega_J = \frac{1 - a_{2J}}{a_{2J}} k_J \ ; \ \underline{p}_J = \frac{\gamma_{2J}}{\gamma_{1J}} \frac{a_{2J}}{a_{1J}} A_J^{1-a_{1J}} k_J^{a_{2J}-a_{1J}} \tag{23.20}$$

$$\lambda_{L_{1J}} = 1 : \omega_J = \frac{1 - a_{1J}}{a_{1J}} k_J \ ; \ \overline{p}_J = \frac{\gamma_{2J}}{\gamma_{1J}} \frac{a_{2J}}{a_{1J}} A_J^{1-a_{2J}} k_J^{a_{2J}-a_{1J}} \tag{23.21}$$

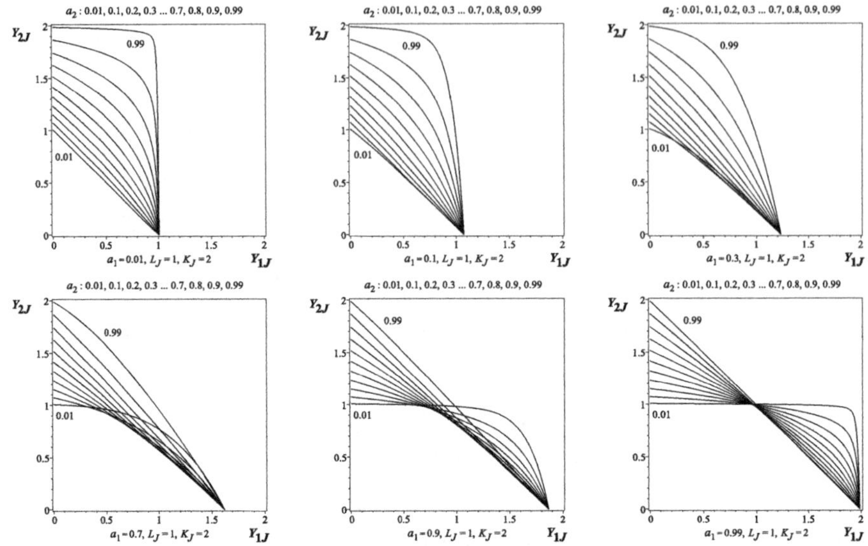


**Fig. 23.4** Production Possibility Curves of **Transformation Function**: $\widehat{T}_J(Y_{1J}, Y_{2J}\,; L_J, K_J) = 0$, (23.8), (23.22–23.23), $\gamma_{iJ} = 1$, for parameters of **FCC, FAC**, Figs. 23.1, 23.2, and 23.3—but also (23.8), (23.22–23.23), for: $a_{1J} = 0.01, 0.1, 0.9, 0.99$

**Graphs** *of* ***implicit*** *transformation functions,* $\widehat{\boldsymbol{T}}_J(\boldsymbol{Y}_{1J}, \boldsymbol{Y}_{2J}\,; \boldsymbol{L}_J, \boldsymbol{K}_J) = 0$, *(23.8), satisfying (23.9–23.11), (23.17), are the* **PPC**, *which—as oriented curves—are* **analytically** *expressed* ***by the two equations*****—or the** *vector function (23.24):*

$$Y_{1J} = L_J\,\gamma_{1J}\,\lambda_{L_{1J}}\left[\frac{A_J\,k_J}{1+(A_J-1)\,\lambda_{L_{1J}}}\right]^{a_{1J}} \equiv L_J\,h_1(\lambda_{L_{1J}}\,;\,k_J) \equiv H_1(\lambda_{L_{1J}}) \tag{23.22}$$

$$Y_{2J} = L_J\,\gamma_{2J}\,(1-\lambda_{L_{1J}})\left[\frac{k_J}{1+(A_J-1)\,\lambda_{L_{1J}}}\right]^{a_{2J}} \equiv L_J\,h_2(\lambda_{L_{1J}}\,;\,k_J) \equiv H_2(\lambda_{L_{1J}}) \tag{23.23}$$

***PPC*** *by the vector function* $H(\lambda_{L_{1J}})$*, (23.24), are exhibited* ***in*** Fig. 23.4,

$$PPC\;:\;[\,Y_{1J}\,,\,Y_{2J}\,] = [\,H_1(\lambda_{L_{1J}})\,,\,H_2(\lambda_{L_{1J}})\,] \equiv H(\lambda_{L_{1J}}),\quad 0 \le \lambda_{L_{1J}} \le 1 \tag{23.24}$$

$$\lambda_{L_{1J}} = 0\;:\;Y_{2J} = L_J\,\gamma_{2J}\,k_J^{a_{2J}}\;;\qquad \lambda_{L_{1J}} = 1\;:\;Y_{1J} = L_J\,\gamma_{1J}\,k_J^{a_{1J}} \tag{23.25}$$

$$E\,(Y_{2J}, Y_{1J}) \equiv \frac{dY_{2J}}{dY_{1J}}\frac{Y_{1J}}{Y_{2J}} = -\,\frac{a_{2J}}{a_{1J}}\,A_J\,\frac{\lambda_{L_{1J}}}{1-\lambda_{L_{1J}}} = -\,\frac{1-a_{2J}}{1-a_{1J}}\,\frac{\lambda_{L_{1J}}}{1-\lambda_{L_{1J}}} \tag{23.26}$$

Generally, (23.22–23.25) **link** by $\boldsymbol{\lambda}_{L_{1J}}$ via (23.17) all Pareto **efficient** factor *allocations* in **factor space** $(L_J, K_J)$—along any Factor Contract Curve, that is, any particular ***FCC*** curves, as well the parametrically shifting **FCC** in Figs. 23.1, 23.2, and 23.3—to their *corresponding* efficient **maximum points** (Frontier, **PPC**) in **output space** $(Y_{1J}, Y_{2J})$.

Hence, the set (locus) of ordered numbers $(Y_{1J}, Y_{2J})$, (23.22–23.25), $0 \leq \lambda_{L_{1J}} \leq 1$, is the production possibility curve (**PPC**) in output space, Fig. 23.4, that is, (23.22–23.25) give *graphs* of transformation function $\widehat{T}_J(Y_{1J}, Y_{2J}; L_J, K_J) = 0$, (23.8). The PPC (Cobb-Douglas's "envelopes") have elasticity property (23.26) that is changing along PPC—but MRT $(\frac{dY_{2J}}{dY_{1J}})$ are *constant* along *rays* $(\frac{Y_{2J}}{Y_{1J}})$.

Production possibility frontiers (transformation curves by endowment reallocations) are traced by (23.22–23.23) *without any recourse* to *numerical methods*. Such **explicit** "*one-parameter*" formula (23.24) of the **PPC** of $\widehat{\mathbf{T}}_J$ (23.8) has surprisingly **never** been obtained in the vast economic literature.

*Two* sets of PPF *graphs* in Fig. 23.4 have their FCC, FAC in Figs. 23.1, 23.2, and 23.3. *Four* additional sets of PPF graphs are exhibited in Fig. 23.4 to show cases of strong PPF *deviations* from linearity, due to *huge* differences of $a_{1J}$ and $a_{2J}$. It is large *differences* in sectoral *factor intensities* $\boldsymbol{a}_{1J}$ and $\boldsymbol{a}_{2J}$, and large *difference* of the factor *endowment ratio* $\boldsymbol{k}_J$ from *unity* that contribute to a **deviation** (bowing outward) of **PPF graphs** (23.8) from a **straight line**. Actual sizes of the PPF deviation also *measure* the *gains* in *outputs* by using *Pareto efficient* factor allocation *off* the diagonals (23.14), (23.16), in Figs. 23.1, 23.2, and 23.3.

In Theorem 23.1, all Pareto efficient endogenous variables and their *curves* in factor space and output space were given on *"parameter form"* with $\lambda_{L_{1J}}$: $0 \leq \lambda_{L_{1J}} \leq 1$ (labor allocation variable). If the *numbers* $\boldsymbol{\lambda}_{L_{1J}}$ can uniquely *relate* MRS to MRT—or later *points* in **price spaces**, factor prices $(\boldsymbol{\omega}_J)$, product prices $(\boldsymbol{p}_J)$—then we get by such $\boldsymbol{\lambda}_{L_{1J}}(\boldsymbol{\omega}_J)$ *functions* keys to answer important questions and to solve exactly many models in economic theory. By using our explicit *tangent coordinates* (MRS, MRT slopes), (23.18) and (23.19), we can also get a *function* for $\boldsymbol{\lambda}_{L_{1J}}(\boldsymbol{p}_J)$.

**Theorem 23.2** *Along any* **FCC**, *(23.15), we had by (23.9), (23.18),* **MRS=** $\omega_J$

$$k_{iJ} = k_{iJ}(\omega_J) = \frac{a_{iJ}}{1 - a_{iJ}}\, \omega_J\,, \quad i = 1, 2\,, \qquad J = A, B \tag{23.27}$$

$$MRS = \omega_J = \frac{1 - a_{2J}}{a_{2J}} \frac{k_J}{1 + (A_J - 1)\, \lambda_{L_{1J}}}\,, \qquad J = A, B \tag{23.28}$$

*By (23.28), (23.11), we get for* $\boldsymbol{\lambda}_{L_{1J}} = \boldsymbol{\lambda}_{L_{1J}}(\boldsymbol{\omega}_J; \boldsymbol{k}_J)$ **function** *expression:*

$$\lambda_{L_{1J}}(\omega_J; k_J) = \frac{(1-a_{2J})\, k_J}{a_{2J}\,(A_J-1)\,\omega_J} - \frac{1}{A_J-1} = \frac{[1-a_{1J}][1-a_{2J}]\, k_J}{(a_{1J}-a_{2J})\,\omega_J} - \frac{1}{A_J-1} \tag{23.29}$$

*For a given endowment ratio* ($\boldsymbol{k}_J$), *upper boundary* ($\overline{\boldsymbol{\omega}}_J$) *and lower boundary* ($\underline{\boldsymbol{\omega}}_J$) *of Domain* $\Omega_{\omega_J}$ *for the common* $\omega_J$ *to any* **FCC** *are evidently by (23.27):*

$$a_{1J} > a_{2J}: \ \underline{\omega}_J = \frac{1-a_{1J}}{a_{1J}}\, k_J \leqq \Omega_{\omega_J} \equiv (\omega_J; k_J) \leqq \frac{1-a_{2J}}{a_{2J}}\, k_J = \overline{\omega}_J \tag{23.30}$$

$$a_{1J} < a_{2J}: \ \underline{\omega}_J = \frac{1-a_{2J}}{a_{2J}}\, k_J \leqq \Omega_{\omega_J} \equiv (\omega_J; k_J) \leqq \frac{1-a_{1J}}{a_{1J}}\, k_J = \overline{\omega}_J \tag{23.31}$$

*For any* **PPC** *(23.22–23.23),* **MRT** *(23.19) is uniquely related to* **MRS** *(23.27–23.28):*

$$MRT = p_J = \frac{\gamma_{2J}\, a_{2J}\, k_{2J}^{a_{2J}-1}}{\gamma_{1J}\, a_{1J}\, k_{1J}^{a_{1J}-1}} = \frac{\gamma_{2J}}{\gamma_{1J}} \cdot \frac{a_{2J}^{a_{2J}}\,(1-a_{2J})^{1-a_{2J}}}{a_{1J}^{a_{1J}}\,(1-a_{1J})^{1-a_{1J}}} \cdot \omega_J^{a_{2J}-a_{1J}} \tag{23.32}$$

$$\equiv \frac{\gamma_{2J}}{\gamma_{1J}}\, \bar{A}_J\, \omega_J^{a_{2J}-a_{1J}} \equiv \Phi_J(\omega_J); \qquad E(p_J, \omega_J) = a_{2J} - a_{1J} \tag{23.33}$$

$$MRS = \omega_J = \Phi_J^{-1}(p_J) = \left[\frac{\gamma_{1J}\, p_J}{\gamma_{2J}\, \bar{A}_J}\right]^{\frac{1}{a_{2J}-a_{1J}}} \tag{23.34}$$

*Then, (23.34), (23.29) give* **labor allocation** *variable* $\lambda_{L_{1J}}$, *(23.17), as* $\boldsymbol{\lambda}_{L_{1J}}(\boldsymbol{p}_J; \boldsymbol{k}_J)$:

$$\lambda_{L_{1J}}(p_J; k_J) = \frac{[1-a_{1J}][1-a_{2J}]}{a_{1J}-a_{2J}} \left[\frac{\gamma_{1J}\, p_J}{\gamma_{2J}\, \bar{A}_J}\right]^{\frac{1}{a_{1J}-a_{2J}}} k_J - \frac{1}{A_J-1} \geq 0 \tag{23.35}$$

$$\equiv B(p_J)\, k_J - \frac{1}{A_J-1} = B(p_J)\, k_J - \frac{a_{2J}\,(1-a_{1J})}{a_{1J}-a_{2J}} \geq 0 \tag{23.36}$$

*Hence, the* **allocation function** $\boldsymbol{\lambda}_{L_{1J}}(\boldsymbol{p}_J; \boldsymbol{k}_J)$ *has by (23.36)* **elasticities***:*

$$E(\lambda_{L_{1J}}(p_J; k_J), k_J) = \frac{B(p_J)\, k_J}{\lambda_{L_{1J}}(p_J; k_J)} = 1 + \frac{1}{(A_J-1)\, \lambda_{L_{1J}}(p_J; k_J)} \tag{23.37}$$

$$E(\lambda_{L_{1J}}(p_J; k_J), p_J) = \frac{1}{a_{1J}-a_{2J}}\, \frac{B(p_J)\, k_J}{\lambda_{L_{1J}}(p_J; k_J)}; \ E(B, p_J) = \frac{1}{a_{1J}-a_{2J}} \tag{23.38}$$

*For given endowment ratio* ($\boldsymbol{k}_J$), *upper boundary* ($\overline{\boldsymbol{p}}_J$) *and lower boundary* ($\underline{\boldsymbol{p}}_J$) *of Ranges for* **MRT** = ($p_J$; $k_J$), *along any* **PPC**, *are derived by (23.30–23.33):*

$$\underline{p}_J = \frac{\gamma_{2J}}{\gamma_{1J}}\bar{A}_J\left[\frac{1-a_{2J}}{a_{2J}}k_J\right]^{a_{2J}-a_{1J}} \leqq (p_J\,;k_J) \leqq \frac{\gamma_{2J}}{\gamma_{1J}}\bar{A}_J\left[\frac{1-a_{1J}}{a_{1J}}k_J\right]^{a_{2J}-a_{1J}} = \overline{p}_J \tag{23.39}$$

$\underline{\boldsymbol{p}}_J$ *and* $\overline{\boldsymbol{p}}_J$ *are slopes of* ***PPC*** *at endpoints with output* $\boldsymbol{Y}_{1J} = 0$ *and* $\boldsymbol{Y}_{2J} = 0$.

Along the concave (convex) curves, FCC, FAC, Figs. 23.1, 23.2, and 23.3—$a_{1J} \gtrless a_{2J}$, with $k_{1J} \gtrless k_{2J}$, $\lambda_{K_{1J}} \gtrless \lambda_{K_{2J}}$, $\lambda_{L_{1J}} \lessgtr \lambda_{L_{2J}}$—*above* (below) the *diagonal*, the common **MRS** (23.28) is numerically *falling* (rising): declining (rising) from $[\frac{1-a_{2J}}{a_{2J}}]k_J$ to $[\frac{1-a_{1J}}{a_{1J}}]k_J$—cf.(23.30–23.31). But along any **FCC** and **FAC**, in Figs. 23.1, 23.2, and 23.3, **both** numbers $\lambda_{L_{1J}}$ and $\lambda_{K_{1J}}$ are always **increasing**. Along any **PPC**, Figs. 23.4, 23.6, 23.5c (F1), from $Y_{1J} = 0$ to $Y_{2J} = 0$, the **slope** (23.19) = MRT = $p_J = \Phi_J(\omega_J)$, (23.33), is always ($a_{1J} \gtrless a_{2J}$) *monotonic increasing*—for example, seen by Pareto efficient factor *reallocations* from A to B in Fig. 23.5a–b, where the *exact interval* (boundaries) of **MRS** (23.30–23.31) and **MRT** (23.39) are:

$$\textbf{Fig.23.5a}: k_{1J} = \omega_J\,, k_{2J} = \frac{1}{4}\omega_J;\; k_J = 2:$$
$$[\underline{\omega}_J, \overline{\omega}_J] = [2, 8],\ [\underline{p}_J, \overline{p}_J] = [0.65, 0.98] \tag{23.40}$$

$$\textbf{Fig.23.5b}: k_{1J} = \omega_J, k_{2J} = 4\omega_J;\; k_J = 2:$$
$$[\underline{\omega}_J, \overline{\omega}_J] = [0.5, 2.0], [\underline{p}_J, \overline{p}_J] = [0.98, 1.49] \tag{23.41}$$

In contrast to Fig. 23.5a–b, the *narrow Range* of **PPC** slopes, (23.39), (23.40–23.41), is seldom noticed in qualitative or quantitative (exact) **PPC** *diagrams*, seen further below in Figs. 23.5c (F1), 23.6–23.7.

Furthermore, Fig. 23.5a–b make clear that the **PPC** slope *Ranges* (23.39) are *changing* with the sizes of the *endowment ratio*, ($\boldsymbol{k}_J$). Note that the **MRT-MRS** function, $\boldsymbol{p}_J = \boldsymbol{\Phi}_J(\boldsymbol{\omega}_J)$, (23.33), is **convex** in Fig. 23.5a and **concave** in Fig. 23.5b. But MRT = $\boldsymbol{p}_J$ is always *increasing* with *downward* movements (i.e., from point A to point B) along any **concave** PPC, as $\boldsymbol{\omega}_J$ will then actually move in **opposite** directions in Figs. 23.5a–b.

The *equivalence* of the *two* $\boldsymbol{p}_J$*-boundary formulas* in (23.19–23.21) and (23.39) are simply checked by using the expressions for $A_J$ (23.11) and $\bar{A}_J$ (23.33). But note especially that the $p_J$*-representation* (PPC slope) on *parameter form* $\lambda_{L_{1J}}$ allows directly calculations of boundaries $[\underline{p}_J, \overline{p}_J]$, (23.19–23.21)—*without* requiring an *invertible function* $p_J = \Phi_J(\omega_J)$, (23.33), used in deriving the Range boundaries (23.39). It is *not* intuitively obvious that the two equations for MRS, MRT, (23.18), (23.19) imply an *endowment invariant*

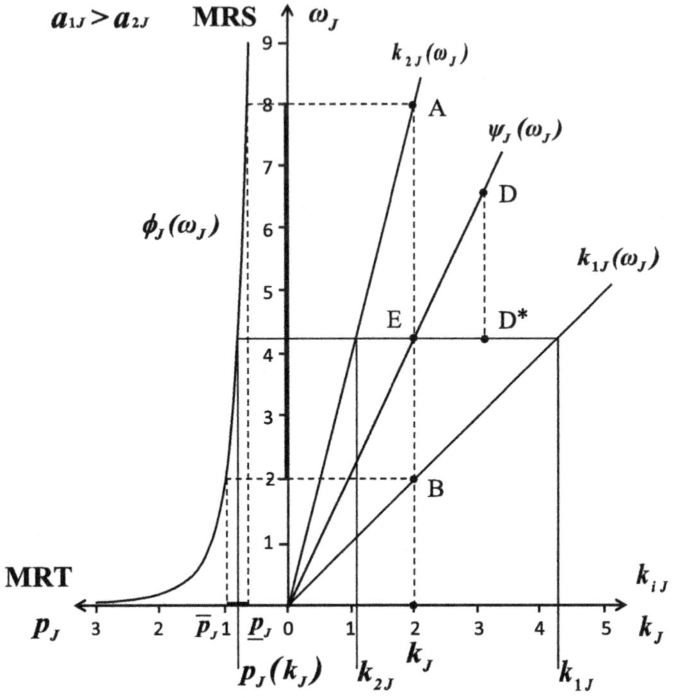


a

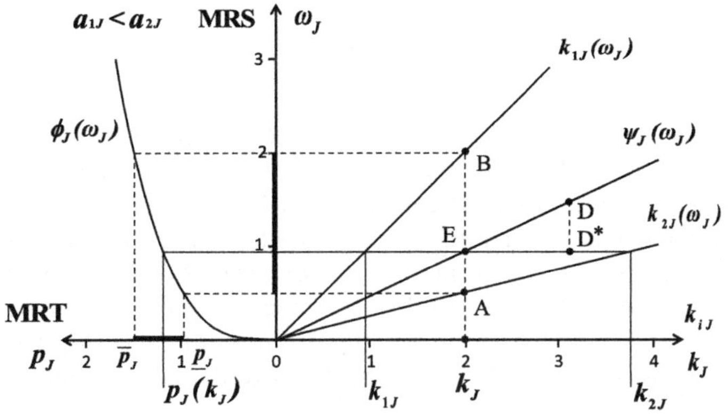


b

**Fig. 23.5** (**a**) $a_{1J} = 0.5$, $a_{2J} = 0.2$; $k_{iJ}(\omega_J)$, (23.27),(23.40); MRT $= p_J = \Phi_J(\omega_J)$, (23.33); $k_J = 2 : \Omega_{\omega J}$, (23.30–23.31), $[\underline{p}_J, \overline{p}_J]$, (23.39); $k_J = \Psi(\omega_J)$, (23.200); $\alpha_J = 0.4$. (**b**) Equations as 23.5a with $a_{1J} = 0.5$, $a_{2J} = 0.8$, $\alpha_J = 0.4$, $k_J = 2$, (23.41). (**c**) F1 : **PPC** (23.22–23.23), (23.63). F2–F3: **Output Ratio curves**.

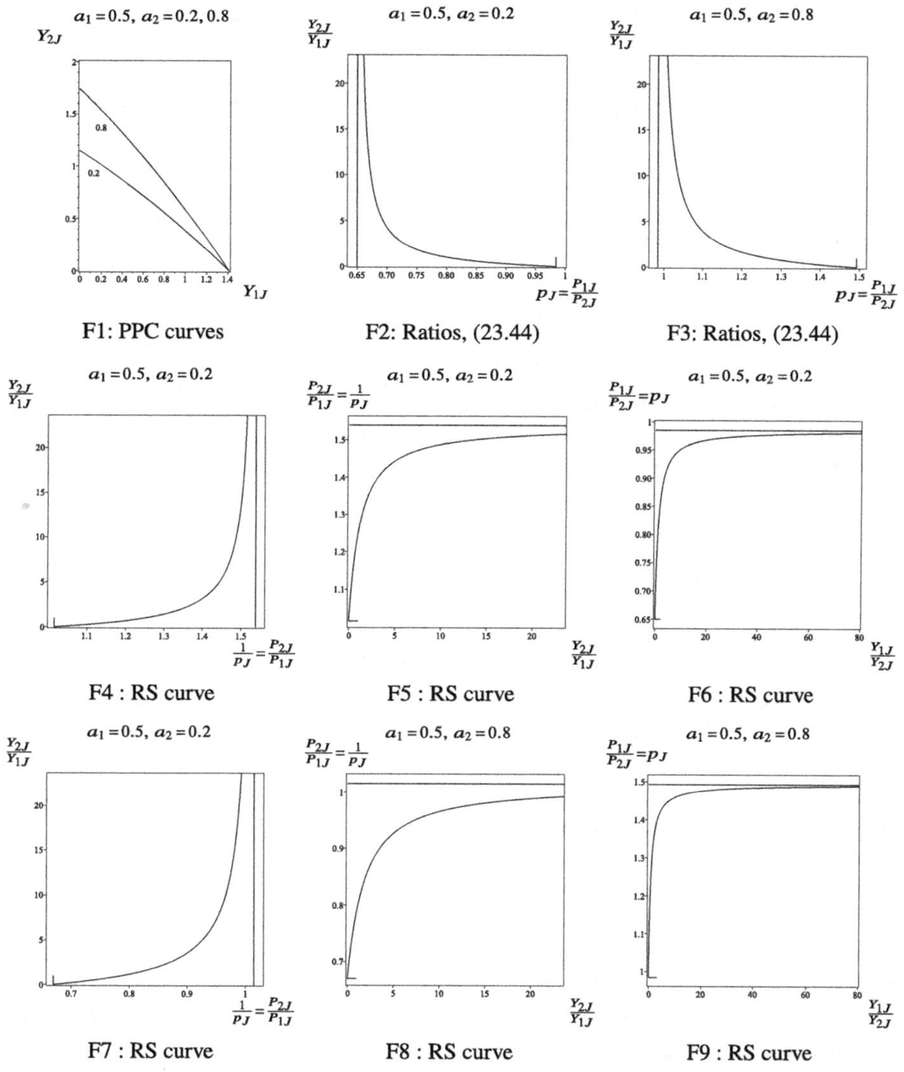


**c**

**Fig. 23.5** (continued) F4–F9: *Relative Supply—RS*[3]—curves : Relative Supply-Relative Price curves. (**d**) **Transformation Elasticities.** $\tau(p_J)$ *for* **PPC** *curves* of F1. NB. These two $\tau(p_J)$ curves coincide as $\tau(Y_{1J})$ curve on $Y_{1J}$ interval in Fig. 23.8a

*function* (23.33)—on *domain* (23.30–23.31), that are also directly obtained by (23.18), (23.28), with $\lambda_{L_{1J}} = 0$ and $\lambda_{L_{1J}} = 1$.

[3] As **RS**: F4–F5 and F8–F9 demonstrate, **RS curves** of the *Standard Model* in Krugman et al. (2018, p.154, 156–162) have *wrong shapes*—by missing proper vertical axis domains and the upper *horizontal asymptotes.* Similar *wrong-shaped* **RS**, Caves et al. (2007, p.26).

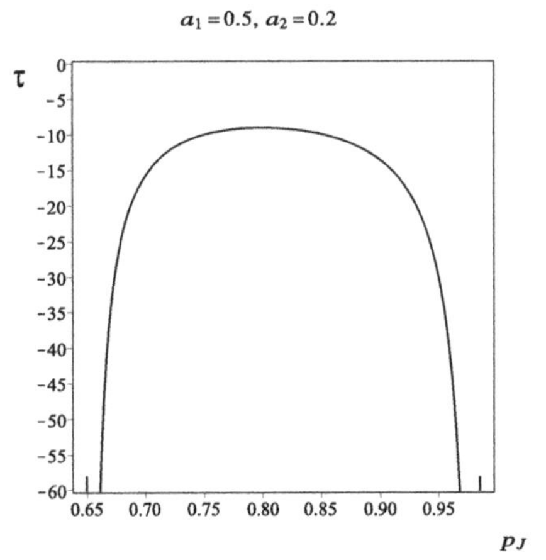


F2 : $\tau(p_J)$, (23.45-23.47) ; $k_J = 2$.

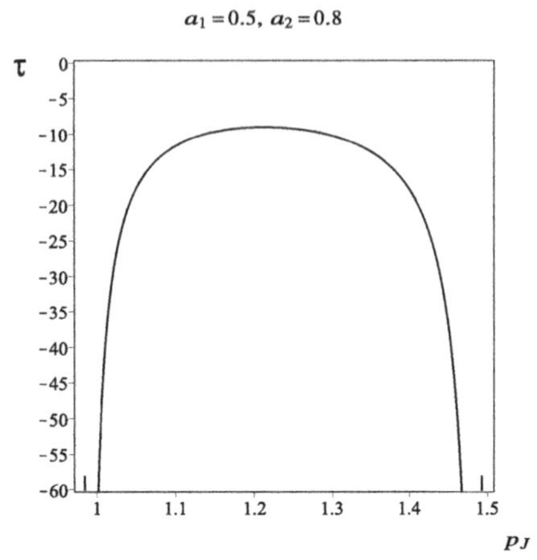


F3 : $\tau(p_J)$, (23.45-23.47) ; $k_J = 2$.

**d**

**Fig. 23.5** (continued)

The **MRT-MRS** function of Theorem 23.2, $p_J = \Phi_J(\omega_J)$, (23.33)—precisely exhibited in the *two* figures, Fig. 23.5a–b—links MRS along the parametrically selected concave (convex) FCC in Figs. 23.1, 23.2, and 23.3 with their corresponding MRT along their always concave PPC in Figs. 23.4, 23.6, and 23.7. This *endowment* **invariant** MRT-MRS **function** (23.33)—within their *endowment* **dependent domains** $\Omega_{\omega_J}$—applies to any **PPC** in Figs. 23.4, 23.6, and 23.7.

In Fig. 23.5a–b, the graphs of analytical function: $\boldsymbol{p_J = \Phi_J(\omega_J)}$, (23.33), are explicitly shown for $\mathbf{a}_{1J} \gtrless \mathbf{a}_{2J}$, together with the Pareto efficient sectoral capital-labor *ratios*, $\boldsymbol{k_{iJ} = k_{iJ}(\omega_J)}$, (23.27), (23.40–23.41). These diagrams will be used on many occasions below.[4]

[ In (23.40–23.41), for Figs. 23.6, 23.7, and 23.8, the **endowment ratio,** $k_J$ = **2**, is used as in Fig. 23.5a–d—and below in (23.202): $p_J(k_J) = p_J(2) = \mathbf{0.8}$, within the range (23.40), and $p_J(2) = \mathbf{1.2}$, within the range (23.41) ].

Along **PPC**, the explicit *relation* between **output ratios**, $Y_{2J}/Y_{1J}$ (ray slope), and **MRT**—PPC slopes, $\boldsymbol{p_J}$—is important, and it is needed to derive **explicit Relative Supply** (*RS*) **curves** of *Relative supply-Relative prices.*

[4] Samuelson (1949, p.188) first used curves (*qualitatively*), as in Fig. 23.5a–b, to summarize connections between relative prices ($p_J = \frac{P_{1J}}{P_{2J}}$), relative factor prices ($\frac{w_{iJ}}{r_{iJ}} = \omega_{iJ}$), and capital-labor ratios ($k_{iJ} = \frac{K_{iJ}}{L_{iJ}}$). But he used $\frac{L_i}{K_i} = \frac{1}{k_i}$, on the right horizontal axis, that is, in Fig. 23.5a–b, the *rays* would then be *two* rectangular *hyperbolas*: $\omega_i = [\frac{1-a_i}{a_i}]/k_i$, cf. (23.9). It is more convenient with *every curve* $\omega_i(k_i)$ in all cases to *originate* from: $(\mathbf{0}, \mathbf{0})$. It also applies to **GE locus**: $k_J = \Psi_J(\omega_J)$, (23.200) below, which Samuelson *never* showed.

We use Theorems 23.1–23.2 as follows: By (23.22–23.23), we get the **ratio**:

$$\frac{Y_{2J}}{Y_{1J}} = \frac{\gamma_{2J}}{\gamma_{1J}} \frac{(1-\lambda_{L_{1J}})}{\lambda_{L_{1J}}} \cdot \frac{[\,1+(A_J-1)\,\lambda_{L_{1J}}\,]^{a_{1J}-a_{2J}}\; k_J^{a_{2J}-a_{1J}}}{A_J^{a_{1J}}} \tag{23.42}$$

$$\frac{Y_{2J}}{Y_{1J}} = \frac{\gamma_{2J}}{\gamma_{1J}} \frac{(1-\lambda_{L_{1J}})}{\lambda_{L_{1J}}} \cdot \frac{[\,(A_J-1)\,B(p_J)\,]^{a_{1J}-a_{2J}}}{A_J^{a_{1J}}} \tag{23.43}$$

$\lambda_{L_{1J}}(p_J; k_J)$, (23.35–23.36), are used stepwise, (23.42–23.43) to give (23.44).

**Theorem 23.3** *Along any* **PPC**, *(23.22–23.23), (23.63), output ratio* $\frac{Y_{2J}}{Y_{1J}}$, *(23.43), is:*

$$\frac{Y_{2J}}{Y_{1J}} = \frac{\gamma_{2J}}{\gamma_{1J}} \frac{[\,\frac{A_J}{A_J-1} - B(p_J)\,k_J\,]}{B(p_J)\,k_J - \frac{1}{A_J-1}} \cdot \frac{[\,(A_J-1)\,B(p_J)\,]^{a_{1J}-a_{2J}}}{A_J^{a_{1J}}} \equiv q_J\,(p_J\,;\,k_J) \tag{23.44}$$

The **PPC** for Fig. 23.5a–b are seen in F1, Fig. 23.5c. The *output ratios* (23.44) are calculated and seen on *domains* $[\,\underline{p}_J, \overline{p}_J\,]$, (23.40–23.41), in F2, F3. For **F2**, the *Relative Supply curve*—**RS**—for $\frac{Y_{2J}}{Y_{1J}} = \boldsymbol{q_J\,(1/p_J\,;k_J)}$ with *domain* $[\,1/\overline{p}_J, 1/\underline{p}_J\,]$ *is shown* in F4—or equivalently with *axes reversed* in F5. **RS** $\frac{Y_{1J}}{Y_{2J}} = \frac{1}{q_J\,(p_J\,;\,k_J)}$, F6, has *similar* shape with *upper asymptote* as F5. For **F3**, the **RS** curves for $\frac{Y_{2J}}{Y_{1J}} = q_J\,(1/p_J\,;\,k_J)$ and $\frac{Y_{1J}}{Y_{2J}}$ are shown in F7–F9.

*Along Ratio curves*, (23.44), F2–F3, *their elasticity wrt.* $\boldsymbol{p_J}$ is $(\boldsymbol{\tau})$, cf. (23.69):

$$\tau \equiv E\left(\frac{Y_{2J}}{Y_{1J}}, \frac{dY_{2J}}{dY_{1J}}\right) = E\left(\frac{Y_{2J}}{Y_{1J}}, p_J\right) = \tau(p_J) \equiv \frac{dq_J\,(p_J\,;\,k_J)}{dp_J} \frac{p_J}{q_J\,(p_J\,;\,k_J)} < 0 \tag{23.45}$$

$$\tau(p_J) = 1 + \frac{1}{a_{1J}-a_{2J}} \left[ \frac{B(p_J)\,k_J}{[\,B(p_J)\,k_J - \frac{A_J}{A_J-1}\,][\,B(p_J)\,k_J - \frac{1}{A_J-1}\,]} \right] < 0 \tag{23.46}$$

$$\begin{aligned}\tau(p_J) &= 1 - \frac{1}{a_{1J}-a_{2J}} \left[ \frac{1 + \frac{1}{(A_J-1)\,\lambda_{L_{1J}}(p_J;k_J)}}{1-\lambda_{L_{1J}}(p_J;k_J)} \right] \\ &= 1 - \frac{E\,(\lambda_{L_{1J}}(p_J;k_J),\ p_J)}{1-\lambda_{L_{1J}}(p_J;k_J)} < 0 \end{aligned} \tag{23.47}$$

$\boldsymbol{\tau(p_J)}$, (23.45–23.47), *are seen* on F2–F3 domains $[\underline{p}_J, \overline{p}_J]$, (23.40–23.41), in Fig. 23.5d.

*By* (23.45) *and simple elasticity rules, we have* ***relative supply elasticities***:

$$0 < E\left[\frac{Y_{2J}}{Y_{1J}}, \frac{1}{p_J}\right] = E\left[\frac{Y_{2J}}{Y_{1J}}, \frac{P_{2J}}{P_{1J}}\right] = -\tau(p_J) = E\left[\frac{Y_{1J}}{Y_{2J}}, p_J\right]$$
$$= E\left[\frac{Y_{1J}}{Y_{2J}}, \frac{P_{1J}}{P_{2J}}\right] > 0 \qquad (23.48)$$

*The "mirror" of* ***transformation elasticities*** $\boldsymbol{\tau}(\boldsymbol{p}_J)$ in Fig. 23.5d *are the* ***relative supply elasticities*** along: **RS** curves F4–F6, **RS** curves F7–F9 in Fig. 23.5c.

***Proof*** The *elasticities* $\boldsymbol{\tau}(\boldsymbol{p}_J)$, (23.45), are easily calculated on computers, and the *numbers* (*curve*), for selected sizes of $a_{1J}$, $a_{2J}$, $k_J$, are seen in Fig. 23.5d.

From (23.44 to 23.45) and evaluating by using standard elasticity rules, for example, Allen (1938, p.252), we get the *explicit* expression for $\boldsymbol{\tau}(\boldsymbol{p}_J)$ in (23.46); the integer 1 originates as a unit elasticity number from the last term of (23.44), after using $E\,[B(p_J), p_J]$, (23.38). The last (composite) term of (23.46) is the elasticity result from the first term (quotient) of (23.44), after using again $E\,[B(p_J), p_J]$ and consolidating the elements on the form as stated in (23.46). The algebraic parametric formula (23.46) is illustrated in Fig. 23.5d.

The $\boldsymbol{\tau}(\boldsymbol{p}_J)$ result (23.46) can be *restated economically* in terms of the *allocation function* $\boldsymbol{\lambda}_{L_{1J}}(\boldsymbol{p}_J; \boldsymbol{k}_J)$ by directly inserting from (23.36) into (23.46)—giving:

$$\tau(p_J) = 1 - \frac{1}{a_{1J} - a_{2J}}\left[\frac{\lambda_{L_{1J}}(p_J; k_J) + 1/(A_J - 1)}{[1 - \lambda_{L_{1J}}(p_J; k_J)][\lambda_{L_{1J}}(p_J; k_J)]}\right] < 0 \qquad (23.49)$$

which is further simplified and now reduced to,

$$\tau(p_J) = 1 - \frac{1}{a_{1J} - a_{2J}}\left[\frac{1 + 1/\left[(A_J - 1)\,\lambda_{L_{1J}}(p_J; k_J)\right]}{1 - \lambda_{L_{1J}}(p_J; k_J)}\right] < 0 \qquad (23.50)$$

Inspecting (23.50) and noting *formulas* (23.37–23.38), the form (23.50) *gives* (23.47)—*confirmed* quantitatively to give the $\boldsymbol{\tau}(\boldsymbol{p}_J)$ *diagrams* in Fig. 23.5d. □

Although the **transformation elasticity** $\boldsymbol{\tau}(\boldsymbol{p}_J)$ is a *crucial* economic *property* and *measure* to *any* **PPC** (or **RS**), **explicit** *formulas* as (23.46–23.47) are so far *not* seen in the literature. The *simplicity* of (23.47) is striking indeed: $\boldsymbol{\tau}(\boldsymbol{p}_J)$ depends on just the *ratio* between $\boldsymbol{E}(\boldsymbol{\lambda}_{L_{1J}}(\boldsymbol{p}_J; \boldsymbol{k}_J), \boldsymbol{p}_J)$ and $\boldsymbol{\lambda}_{L_{1J}}(\boldsymbol{p}_J; \boldsymbol{k}_J)$—a *ratio* which then also explains the particular *shape* of curves in Fig. 23.5d that can now easily be explained, formally and economically.

Both $\lambda_{L_{1J}}(p_J; k_J)$ and $E(\lambda_{L_{1J}}(p_J; k_J), p_J)$ are always *positive*; $\boldsymbol{\lambda}_{L_{1J}}(\boldsymbol{p}_J; \boldsymbol{k}_J)$ is monotonic *increasing* in $p_J$ on *domain* $[\underline{p}_J, \overline{p}_J]$; hence, $1 - \lambda_{L_{1J}}(p_J; k_J)$ is monotonic *decreasing* from one to zero, which contributes to making

$\boldsymbol{\tau}(\boldsymbol{p}_J)$ very large ($\approx\ \infty$) close to $\overline{p}_J$. The *elasticity* $\boldsymbol{E}\,(\boldsymbol{\lambda}_{L_{1J}}(\boldsymbol{p}_J;\boldsymbol{k}_J),\ \boldsymbol{p}_J)$ is monotonic *decreasing* in $p_J$ on $[\underline{p}_J, \overline{p}_J]$, but very large ($\approx\ \infty$) close to $\underline{p}_J$, and is then declining rapidly and subsequently becoming nearly constant (horizontal asymptote), close to $\overline{p}_J$.[5] Evidently, the *transformation elasticity* $\boldsymbol{\tau}(\boldsymbol{p}_J)$ is *not* a *constant* in Fig. 23.5d; as for isoquants (indifference curves), numerical *large values* of $\boldsymbol{\tau}(\boldsymbol{p}_J)$ mean *little curvature* of **PPC**, while *small sizes* of $\tau(p_J)$ are associated with *sharply curved* **PPC**, cf. Fig. 23.4. We return to the fundamental technology issues involved with $\boldsymbol{\tau}(\boldsymbol{p}_J)$ and $\boldsymbol{\tau}(\boldsymbol{Y}_{1J})$ in Sect. "Production Possibility Curves and Elasticity of Transformation".

Here we obtain **Core** theorems in *explicit form* from Theorem 23.2:

**Theorem 23.4** *The* **MRT-MRS** *relation,* $p_J = \Phi_J(\omega_J)$*, (23.33), gives by the* **inverse,** $\omega_J = \Phi_J^{-1}(p_J)$*, (23.34), an explicit* **elasticity** *stated as, cf. (23.6), (23.9–23.10), (23.27), (23.32):*

$$E\,(\omega_J, p_J) = \frac{1}{a_{2J} - a_{1J}} = E\left[\frac{MP_{L_{iJ}}(k_{iJ}(\omega_J\,[\,p_J\,]))}{MP_{K_{iJ}}(k_{iJ}(\omega_J\,[\,p_J\,]))},\ p_J\right],\ p_J = \frac{dY_{2J}}{dY_{1J}} = \frac{P_{1J}}{P_{2J}};\ i = 1, 2 \tag{23.51}$$

$$= E\left[MP_{L_{iJ}}(k_{iJ}(\omega_J[\,p_J\,])),\ p_J\right] - E\left[MP_{K_{iJ}}(k_{iJ}(\omega_J[p_J])),\ p_J\right];\ i = 1, 2 \tag{23.52}$$

$$a_{1J} > a_{2J}\ :\ E\,[\,MP_{K_{iJ}}(k_{iJ}(\omega_J\,[\,p_J\,])),\ p_J\,] > 1, \quad E\,[\,MP_{L_{iJ}}(k_{iJ}(\omega_J\,[\,p_J\,])),\ p_J\,] < 0;\ i = 1, 2 \tag{23.53}$$

*which is,* **Stolper-Samuelson** *theorem, saying that* **marginal products** *(real factor reward) of* **one factor** *will rise (fall) in* **both** *sectors with changes in relative prices—*$p_J = \frac{P_{1J}}{P_{2J}}$*—according to production factor intensity parameters, (23.51–23.52):* $a_{1J} \gtrless a_{2J}$*; for example,* $a_{1J} > a_{2J}$*, (23.53), see* Fig. 23.5a–b. *Elasticities of* **outputs** *wrt.* **one-factor** *endowment change—fixed* $p_J = \frac{P_{1J}}{P_{2J}}$*— follow by elasticity,* $E\,(\lambda_{L_{1J}}(p_J; k_J),\ k_J)$*, (23.37), and,* $Y_{iJ} = L_J \lambda_{L_{iJ}} y_{iJ}$*, (23.6):*

$$E\,(Y_{1J}, K_J) = \frac{\partial Y_{1J}}{\partial K_J}\frac{K_J}{Y_{1J}} = E\,(\lambda_{L_{1J}}(p_J; k_J),\ k_J) = 1 + \frac{a_{2J}\,(1 - a_{1J})}{(a_{1J} - a_{2J})\,\lambda_{L_{1J}}(p_J; k_J)} \tag{23.54}$$

$$E\,(Y_{1J}, L_J) = \frac{\partial Y_{1J}}{\partial L_J}\frac{L_J}{Y_{1J}} = 1 - E\,(Y_{1J}, K_J) = \frac{-\,a_{2J}\,(1 - a_{1J})}{(a_{1J} - a_{2J})\,\lambda_{L_{1J}}(p_J; k_J)} \tag{23.55}$$

[5] This *shape* of transformation *elasticity* $\tau(p_J)$ *curves* in Fig. 23.5d—as explained by the behavior of last ratio in (23.47)—carries over to the *elasticity* $\tau(Y_{1J})$ *curves* in Fig. 23.8a–b.

$$E(Y_{2J}, K_J) = \frac{\partial Y_{2J}}{\partial K_J}\frac{K_J}{Y_{2J}} = E\left(1 - \lambda_{L_{1J}}(p_J; k_J),\, k_J\right)$$
$$= 1 - \frac{a_{1J}\,(1 - a_{2J})}{(a_{1J} - a_{2J})\,\lambda_{L_{1J}}(p_J; k_J)} \tag{23.56}$$

$$E\,(Y_{2J}, L_J) = \frac{\partial Y_{2J}}{\partial L_J}\frac{L_J}{Y_{2J}} = 1 - E\,(Y_{2J}, K_J) = \frac{a_{1J}\,(1 - a_{2J})}{(a_{1J} - a_{2J})\,\lambda_{L_{1J}}(p_J; k_J)} \tag{23.57}$$

*which is,* **Rybczynski** *theorem, saying that increases of one factor will expand output, which intensively uses that factor—*$a_{1J} \gtrless a_{2J}$*—and reduce the other sector output; for example,* $a_{1J} > a_{2J}$,

$$a_{1J} > a_{2J} \;:\Rightarrow\; E(Y_{1J}, K_J) > 1 \;\; and \;\; E(Y_{2J}, K_J) < 0 \tag{23.58}$$

$$a_{1J} > a_{2J} \;:\Rightarrow\; E(Y_{1J}, L_J) < 0 \;\; and \;\; E(Y_{2J}, L_J) > 1 \tag{23.59}$$

*For* $a_{1J} < a_{2J}$*, interchange of output subscripts in (23.58–23.59); cf.* Fig. 23.5b.

***Proof*** It is clearly a simple matter by Theorem 23.2 to get the physical marginal factor productivity elasticity formulas, as restated in (23.51–23.53).

Next constant product prices imply constant relative price ($p_J$), hence constant MRS: $\omega_J = \Phi_J^{-1}(p_J)$, constant capital-labor ratios, $k_{iJ}$, (23.27), and constant labor productivities: $y_{iJ}$ in, $Y_{iJ} = L_J \lambda_{L_{iJ}} y_{iJ}$, (23.6), that is, for given size of $L_J$, sector outputs $Y_{iJ}$ are proportional to $\lambda_{L_{iJ}}(p_J; k_J)$. Thus for *sector 1*, the elasticity, $E(Y_{1J}, K_J) = E\,(\lambda_{L_{1J}}(p_J; k_J), k_J)$, (23.37), which then gives (23.54). For sector technologies with constant returns to scale, (23.6), we immediately also have the sum: $E(Y_{1J}, K_J) + E(Y_{1J}, L_J) = 1$, which by (23.54) gives (23.55).

For *sector 2*, we have elasticities: $E(Y_{2J}, K_J) = E\,(\lambda_{L_{2J}}(p_J; k_J), k_J) = E\,[\,1 - \lambda_{L_{1J}}(p_J; k_J), k_J\,]$; evaluating the latter by again standard elasticity rules, Allen (1938, p.252), we get the *explicit* formula for $E(Y_{2J}, K_J)$ in (23.56)—which next by the sum condition establishes (23.57).

The *economic parametric* formula $E\,(\lambda_{L_{1J}}(p_J; k_J), k_J)$, (23.54), as is also *a common element* to formula $E(Y_{2J}, K_J)$, $E(Y_{2J}, L_J)$, is again used in (23.56–23.57)—hence, (23.58–23.59) follow immediately according to: $a_{1J} > a_{2J}$. □

The *Stolper-Samuelson* elasticities (comparative statics), (23.51–23.53) reflect *movements along* the **PPC** (23.22–23.23) of Theorem 23.1 in Figs. 23.4, 23.6, 23.7—but (23.51–23.53) geometrically also correspond to *vertical* movements (for *any* $k_J$) in Fig. 23.5a–b. The *marginal factor* productivity **elasticity** *formulas* (23.51–23.53) are *not* affected by changes in endowments ($\mathbf{L}_J, \mathbf{K}_J$)—that is, *endowment invariant.* Stolper-Samuelson marginal productivity *elasticities* (23.51–23.53)—as *technological* ($a_{1J}, a_{2J}$)

and *Pareto* factor allocation *efficient* (23.11) determined—numerically always *exceed* 1 (MRS changes more than MRT, "relative prices").

The *exact Rybczynski* elasticities (comparative statics), (23.54–23.57), reflect *shifting* of **PPC** (23.22–23.23) in Figs. 23.4, 23.6, 23.7—but (23.54–23.57) also correspond to *horizontal movements* (at *any* exogenous $p_J$) in Fig. 23.5a–b, where $\boldsymbol{\lambda}_{L_{1J}}(\boldsymbol{p}_J; \boldsymbol{k}_J)$ always changes *linearly* with $\boldsymbol{k}_J$, cf. (23.36). Rybczynski elasticities are *neither* endowment invariant *nor* price invariant, as (23.54–23.57) change with the *quantitative* magnitudes of $\lambda_{L_{1J}}(p_J; k_J)$, $E(\lambda_{L_{1J}}(p_J; k_J), k_J)$—but the *qualitative* (overall) simplicity, *larger* than 1 or *negative*, (23.58–23.59), is always satisfied.

So far **allocation function** $\lambda_{L_{1J}}(p_J; k_J)$, and its **elasticities**, wrt. $k_J$ and $p_J$, was helpful in our handling of the **general** *implicit* transformation function, exact **PPC** formulas, $\boldsymbol{\tau}(\boldsymbol{p}_J)$, and implications in Theorems 23.2–23.4. Next we get an **explicit** transformation function, $Y_{2J} = T_J(Y_{1J};\ L_J, K_J)$, (23.8).

## Explicit Transformation Functions and Transformation Curves

For an explicit transformation functions, $\mathbf{Y_{2J}} = \mathbf{T_J}(\mathbf{Y_{1J}}; \mathbf{L_J}, \mathbf{K_J})$, (23.8), the single *"parameter"*, $\boldsymbol{\lambda}_{L_{1J}}$ is *eliminated* from (23.22 to 23.23) of Theorem 23.1.

**Theorem 23.5** *Production Possibility Frontiers—***PPC***—in Commodity Space* $(Y_{1J}, Y_{2J})$ *are with* **CD** *technologies (23.6), (23.121) generated—in autarky economies of factor endowments,* $\mathbf{L_J}, \mathbf{K_J}$, *J=A,B—by explicit* **transformation functions** $\boldsymbol{Y_{2J} = T_J(Y_{1J}; L_J, K_J)}$*—with algebraic* $\boldsymbol{T_J(Y_{1J}; L_J, K_J)}$ *as:*

**Ex. 1.** $A_J = 1$, $a_{1J} = a_{2J} = \tilde{a}_J$, *CD equal factor intensity parameter case*[6]

$$Y_{2J} = T_J(Y_{1J}; L_J, K_J) = -\frac{\gamma_{2J}}{\gamma_{1J}} Y_{1J} + L_J\, \gamma_{2J}\, k_J^{\tilde{a}_J}\ ;\quad \frac{dY_{2J}}{dY_{1J}} = -\frac{\gamma_{2J}}{\gamma_{1J}}\ ;\ \lambda_{K_{1J}} = \lambda_{L_{1J}} \tag{23.60}$$

$$a_{1J} = 1/2 = a_{2J}\ :\ Y_{2J} = T_J(Y_{1J}; L_J, K_J) = -\frac{\gamma_{2J}}{\gamma_{1J}} Y_{1J} + \gamma_{2J}\,(L_J K_J)^{\frac{1}{2}} \tag{23.61}$$

**Linear** *PPC graphs (23.60),* $\boldsymbol{\tau} = -\infty$, *match diagonal FCC, Figs. 23.1, 23.2, and 23.3.*

[6] **Ex.1** is an extension of a *one-factor Ricardo* model, $Y_{iJ} = \gamma_{iJ} L_{iJ}$, $i = 1, 2$, to our *two-factor* two-sector CD model with *same* factor intensity parameters, cf. Samuelson (1947, 1983, p.234), resulting also in **linear PPC**, given by *explicit transformation function* (23.60). It has elasticity (23.26), $E(Y_{2J}, Y_{1J}) = -(\gamma_{2J}/\gamma_{1J})(Y_{1J}/Y_{2J})$, giving the relative "losses" of $Y_{2J}$ as *monotonic (hyperbolic)* increasing with $Y_{1J}$ along **linear** PPC (23.60). The linear PPC—with $a_{1J} = a_{2J}$—has a *constant* MRT and the $\tau(p_J) : -\infty$, (23.50).

If also $\gamma_{1J} = \gamma_{2J}$ in (23.60–23.61), then we would have the *same* CD technology (23.6), producing two different goods and linear PPC as: $Y_{2J} = T_J(Y_{1J}; L_J, K_J) = -Y_{1J} + L_J k_J^{\tilde{a}_J}$. However, we here still have *non-joint* production and *neither* a single factor (composite capital dose, capital aggregate), Samuelson (1947, 1983, p.234); more on this and (23.61), cf. (23.80), (23.92).

$$\textbf{Ex. 2.}\ a_{1J} = 1/2, \qquad A_J = \frac{1-a_{2J}}{a_{2J}}\ ; \qquad Y_{2J} = T_J(Y_{1J}\ ;\ L_J, K_J)\ : \tag{23.62}$$

$$Y_{2J} = \frac{L_J\,\gamma_{2J}\,k_J^{a_{2J}}\left[1 - \frac{a_{2J}\,(Y_{1J}/\gamma_{1J})^2}{2\,(1-a_{2J})\,L_J\,K_J}\left[\frac{1-2\,a_{2J}}{a_{2J}} + \left[\left[\frac{1-2a_{2J}}{a_{2J}}\right]^2 + \frac{4\,(1-a_{2J})\,L_J\,K_J}{a_{2J}\,(Y_{1J}/\gamma_{1J})^2}\right]^{\frac{1}{2}}\right]\right]}{\left[1 + \frac{(1-2\,a_{2J})\,(Y_{1J}/\gamma_{1J})^2}{2\,(1-a_{2J})\,L_J\,K_J}\left[\frac{1-2\,a_{2J}}{a_{2J}} + \left[\left[\frac{1-2\,a_{2J}}{a_{2J}}\right]^2 + \frac{4\,(1-a_{2J})\,L_J\,K_J}{a_{2J}\,(Y_{1J}/\gamma_{1J})^2}\right]^{\frac{1}{2}}\right]\right]^{a_{2J}}} \tag{23.63}$$

$$Y_{1J} = 0\ :\ Y_{2J} = L_J\,\gamma_{2J}\,k_J^{a_{2J}}\ ; \qquad Y_{2J} = 0\ :\ Y_{1J} = L_J\,\gamma_{1J}\,k_J^{a_{1J}} \tag{23.64}$$

*where (23.64) are endpoints—with specialization—of* **nonlinear** ***PPC***, *(23.63).* $\boldsymbol{T_J(Y_{1J}\ ;\ L_J, K_J)}$*; (23.62–23.63) are homogeneous of degree one in:* $(Y_{1J}, L_J, K_J)$.

*The concave* **PPC graphs** *(23.62–23.64) are, for selected* $\boldsymbol{a_{2J}}$ *parameter values, shown in* Fig. 23.6*—which in factor space* $(L_J, K_J)$ ***correspond*** *to the Factor Contract Curves,* **FCC**, Fig. 23.2, $\mathbf{a_{1J}} = \mathbf{1/2}$, *and endowments,* $L_J = 1, K_J = 2$.

***Proof*** **Ex.1**. $A_J = 1$, $a_{1J} = a_{2J} = \tilde{a}_J$. From (23.22) and inserting into (23.23) we get:

$$\lambda_{L_{1J}} = (Y_{1J}/\gamma_{1J})L_J^{-1}k_J{}^{-a_{1J}}\ ; \quad Y_{2J}/\gamma_{2J} = L_J\,[\,1 - (Y_{1J}/\gamma_{1J})L_J^{-1}k_J{}^{-a_{1J}}\,]\,k_J{}^{a_{1J}} \tag{23.65}$$

The last expression is equivalent to (23.60).

To see if there are other strictly explicit expressions, we rewrite (23.22) as:

$$(Y_{1J}/\gamma_{1J})/L_J\,(k_J\,A_J)^{a_{1J}} = \lambda_{L_{1J}}\,/\left[1 + (A_J - 1)\lambda_{L_{1J}}\right]^{a_{1J}} \tag{23.66}$$

The equation can only be solved explicitly for $\lambda_{L_{1J}}$ if $a_{1J}$ is equal to: 1/4, 1/3, 1/2, 2/3, or 3/4. Raising both sides to the power of 2, 3, 4 gives equations of second, third, fourth degree in $\lambda_{L_{1J}}$, cf. Nicholson and Snyder (2012, p.465).

**Ex.2.** $A_J \neq 1$. $a_{1J} = 1/2$; inserting $a_{1J} = 1/2$ into (23.66), squaring and rearrangement give the following quadratic equation:

$$A_J L_J^2 k_J \lambda_{L_{1J}}^2 - (Y_{1J}/\gamma_{1J})^2(A_J - 1)\lambda_{L_{1J}} - (Y_{1J}/\gamma_{1J})^2 = 0 \tag{23.67}$$

Solving (23.67) for the positive root gives:

$$\lambda_{L_{1J}} = \frac{(Y_{1J}/\gamma_{1J})}{2A_J L_J^2 k_J}\left[[Y_{1J}/\gamma_{1J}][A_J - 1] + \left[[Y_{1J}/\gamma_{1J}]^2[A_J - 1]^2 + 4A_J L_J^2 k_J\right]^{\frac{1}{2}}\right] \tag{23.68}$$

Insert root (23.68) into (23.23), rearrangement—and $A_J = \frac{1-a_{2J}}{a_{2J}}$— gives (23.63). □

*Intercepts* of the curves with the vertical axis are given by: $L_J \gamma_{2J} k_J^{a_{2J}}$ (23.6), hence increasing, decreasing as a function of $a_{2J}$, if $k_J \gtrless 1$—hence increasing in Fig. 23.6. It is seen from the figure that for fixed $Y_{1J} > 0$, $Y_{2J}$ is generally ***not*** a monotonic function of $a_{2J}$. Note that the intercept and also the slope given by (23.19) are proportional to TFP: $\gamma_{2J}$. When $k_J = 1$, all curves intercept the vertical axis at the same point: $L_J \gamma_{2J}$, (23.64).

Figure 23.7, $k_J = 1$: Distinct sector terms become $k_J^{a_{iJ}} = 1$; then (23.63)—and (23.22–23.23)—are formed by $A_J$ (23.11), which is *"symmetric"* in deviations of $a_{iJ}$ from 1/2. *Two* values of $a_{2J}$ give *same* $A_J$. Except for ***curve***, $a_{2J}$ = 0.01, 0.99 (*same* PPC-***not unique***), ***all*** other curves are very close to straight line for $a_{2J}$ = 0.5. The curve with $a_{2J}$ = 0.4, 0.6 (same **PPC**) is

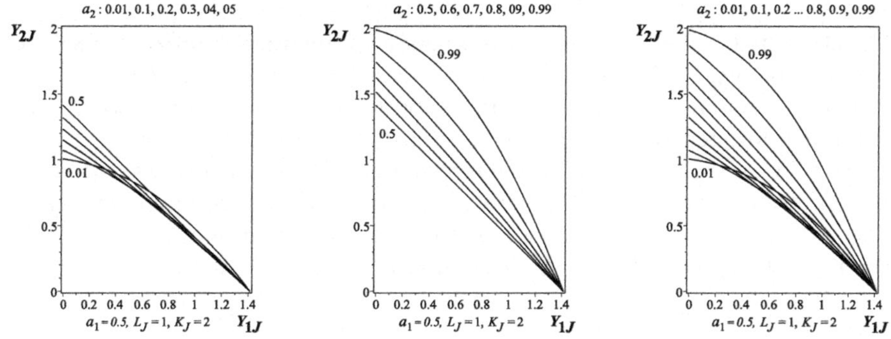


**Fig. 23.6** Production possibility curves of **transformation function**: $Y_{2J} = T_J(Y_{1J}; L_J, K_J)$, (23.62–23.64), $\gamma_{iJ} = 1$, $k_J = 2$, $L_J = 1$, for $a_{1J}$ = 0.5 and the $a_{2J}$ parameters of their **optimal FCC** and **FAC** in Fig. 23.2

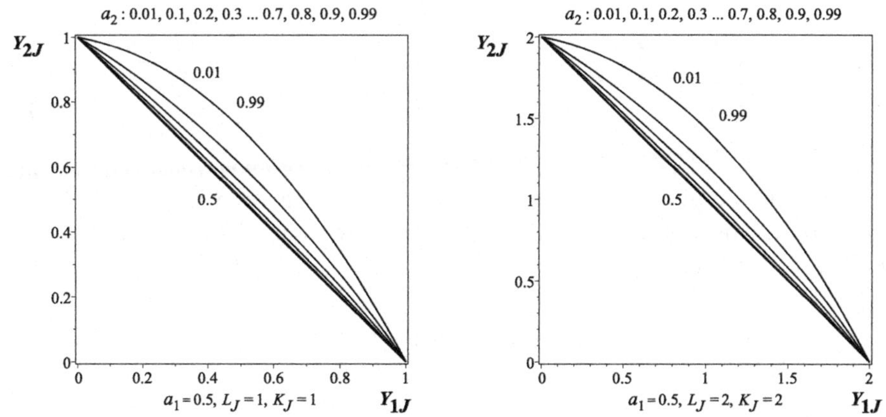


**Fig. 23.7** Production possibility curves of **transformation function**: $Y_{2J} = T_J(Y_{1J}; L_J, K_J)$ (23.63), in Fig. 23.6 for: $\gamma_{iJ} = 1$, $k_J = 1$, $L_J = 1$; $L_J = 2$

*indistinguishable* from the *straight line*. Thus, in *output space*, $(Y_{1J}, Y_{2J})$, **PPC** graphs, Figs. 23.6 and 23.7, do *not* deviate much from linearity,[7] despite the rather *large* (distinct) deviations of their corresponding **FCC** and **FAC** from the *diagonals* in Fig. 23.2.

## Production Possibility Curves and Elasticity of Transformation

Powell and Gruen (1968, p.315) proposed to *measure* intrinsic properties and the basic "*shape*" of the frontier of the production possibilities by an **elasticity** of **transformation** ($\boldsymbol{\tau}$) between the two **outputs** $Y_{1J}$ and $Y_{2J}$:

$$\tau = E(Y_{2J}/Y_{1J}, MRT) = E(Y_{2J}/Y_{1J}, dY_{2J}/dY_{1J}). \tag{23.69}$$

The elasticity ($\boldsymbol{\tau}$) *measures* the responsiveness of the **output ratio/"mix"** (*ray slope*) to changes in the **marginal** rate of *transformation* (**PPC** *slope*).

The general analytic-algebraic expression for the *substitution elasticity* $\sigma(k)$ of linear homogeneous *production* functions, $Y = F(L, K) = Lf(k)$, $Y/L = y = f(k)$, is the same as the *transformation elasticity* expression of *transformation* functions for **PPC**, that is, $\sigma(k)$ for concave monotonic increasing $y = f(k)$ has the *same* formula as $\boldsymbol{\tau(Y_{1J})}$ for concave monotonic decreasing $\boldsymbol{T_J}$: $Y_{2J} = T_J(Y_{1J}) \equiv T_J(Y_{1J}; L_J, K_J)$, $0 < Y_{1J} < T_J^{-1}(Y_{2J} = 0)$:

$$Y_{2J} = T_J(Y_{1J}) \ ; \ T_J' = dY_{2J}/dY_{1J} < 0 \ , \ T_J'' = d^2Y_{2J}/dY_{1J}^2 < 0 \ ; \ J = A, B \tag{23.70}$$

Like $\boldsymbol{\sigma(k)} > 0$, the *elasticity*, $\boldsymbol{\tau(Y_{1J})} < 0$, can be stated, see Hicks (1932, 1948, p.117–119, 242–245), cf. Arrow et al. (1961, p.230), Jensen (2017, p. 65), (here Chap. 3, p. 69), as

$$\tau(Y_{1J}) \equiv E\left(\frac{Y_{2J}}{Y_{1J}}, \frac{dY_{2J}}{dY_{1J}}\right) = E\left(\frac{T_J(Y_{1J})}{Y_{1J}}, T_J'\right) = -\frac{[T_J - T_J' \cdot Y_{1J}]\, T_J'}{T_J \cdot Y_{1J} \cdot T_J''} < 0 \tag{23.71}$$

The class of **CET** (*Constant Elasticity of Transformation*) curves are obtained by integrating the second-order differential equation, (23.71), and reparametrization of integration constants, Arrow et al. (1961), Jensen (2017, p. 76), (here Chap. 3, p. 81):

$$\tau(Y_{1J}) = \tau \ : \ Y_{2J} = T_J(Y_{1J}) = \gamma_J\Big[(1 - b_J) - b_J Y_{1J}^{\frac{\tau-1}{\tau}}\Big]^{\frac{\tau}{\tau-1}}, \ 0 < b_J < 1, \ \gamma_J > 0 \tag{23.72}$$

[7] On the shapes of **PPC** with **CES** sector technologies, see Scarth and Warne (1973, p.304), Jensen (2012, p.68).

or more "*symmetrically*"—$0 < B_J = \gamma_J^{\frac{\tau-1}{\tau}} b_J < \infty$ ; $C_J = \gamma_J^{\frac{\tau-1}{\tau}} (1 - b_J) > 0$:

$$Y_{2J}^{\frac{\tau-1}{\tau}} = C_J - B_J Y_{1J}^{\frac{\tau-1}{\tau}} \geq 0 ; \frac{dY_{2J}}{dY_{1J}} = -B_J \left[\frac{Y_{2J}}{Y_{1J}}\right]^{\frac{1}{\tau}} ; E\left(Y_{2J}, Y_{1J}\right) = -B_J \left[\frac{Y_{2J}}{Y_{1J}}\right]^{\frac{1+\tau}{\tau}} \tag{23.73}$$

$$Y_{2J}^2 + B_J Y_{1J}^2 = C_J, \; E\left(Y_{2J}, Y_{1J}\right) = -B_J \; ; \; Y_{2J}^2 + Y_{1J}^2 = C_J, \; Y_{2J} = [C_J - Y_{1J}^2]^{\frac{1}{2}} \tag{23.74}$$

*Unit elasticity*, $\tau = -1$, (23.74), gives positive orthants of *ellipses* and *circles*. **CET** curves (23.72–23.74): horizontal/vertical tangents at axis intercepts, (23.73).

The **PPC** (23.19–23.26) do *not* have horizontal/vertical tangents at *end* (axis) *points*, cf. (23.39)—and hence are *not* **CET** curves, but **VET** (*Variable Elasticity of Transformation*), (23.71), curves, for example, $\tau(Y_{1J})$ of $T_J(Y_{1J} ; L_J, K_J)$, (23.62), will *not* be constant but vary along PPC. Thus, **PPC** (frontier, *envelope*) derived with our *two* **CD** *non-joint output* technologies ($\sigma = 1$) are **VET** *transformation* curves—that will be discussed and shown in Fig. 23.8.

***Variable Transformation Elasticities: Non-Joint Production Technology***

The **VET** elasticities $\tau(Y_{1J})$ along graphs of *explicit* $T_J$, Theorem 23.5, (23.62–23.64), are shown in Fig. 23.8a—with the *same* parameter sets as Fig. 23.6. **PPC** with $a_{2J}$: 0.4 and 0.6, 0.01 and 0.99 have *same* $\tau(Y_{1J})$ numbers.

Even for the *explicit* $Y_{2J} = T_J(Y_{1J} ; L_J, K_J)$, (23.63), is the *calculations* of $\boldsymbol{\tau(Y_{1J})}$ by (23.71) a bit complicated; we need both the first-order and second-order derivatives of $Y_{2J} = T_J(Y_{1J})$ in (23.63), which is evidently cumbersome by hand, but is easily obtained by a computer that has been used together with (23.71) to generate all the selected VET *curves* of $\tau(Y_{1J})$, exhibited Fig. 23.8a.

By definition (23.69), transformation elasticity $\tau(Y_{1J})$ measures the sensitivity of the output ratio ("mix") at each PPC point to the changes in PPC tangent slopes. With linear PPC, (23.60), and $a_{2J} = 0.5$, Fig. 23.6, we have an extreme "output mix" *sensitivity* to the tangent slope, and $\tau(Y_{1J}) = -\infty$, cf. footnote 8. Only $a_{2J} \neq 0.5$ are used in Fig. 23.8a, where it is noted that *two* sizes of $a_{2J}$ give the **same** $\tau(Y_{1J})$ curve (cf. Fig. 23.5d, NB), which is not all clear from their different **PPC** *shape* in Fig. 23.6. For the pair $a_{2J} = 0.4, a_{2J} = 0.6$, the numbers $\tau(Y_{1J})$ are numerically very large, and hence, they cannot be observed in second (right) diagram of $\tau(Y_{1J})$.

**PPC** are in Fig. 23.6—and generally, cf. Fig. 23.4—more "linear" (flat, horizontal/vertical) close to their *end points*, which accordingly give numerically very large $\tau(Y_{1J})$ at also the end points in Fig. 23.8a and b.

At roughly the *middle* of the horizontal axis ($Y_{1J}$) in Fig. 23.8a, $\tau(Y_{1J})$ is numerically small, that is, where "curvature" of PPC is large and output ratio

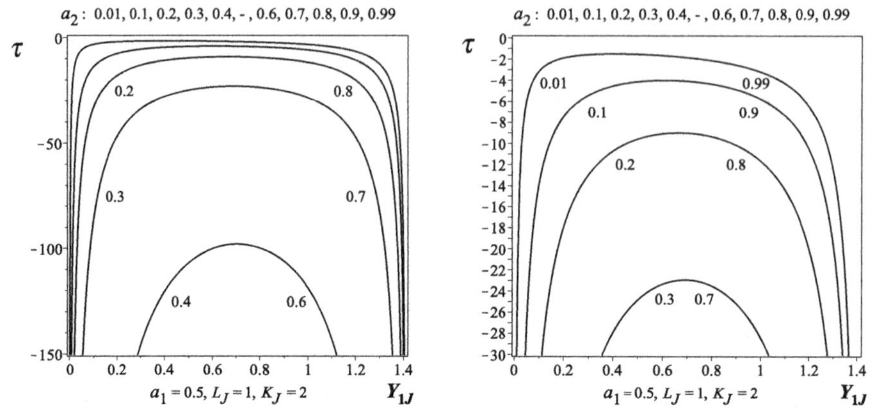


a

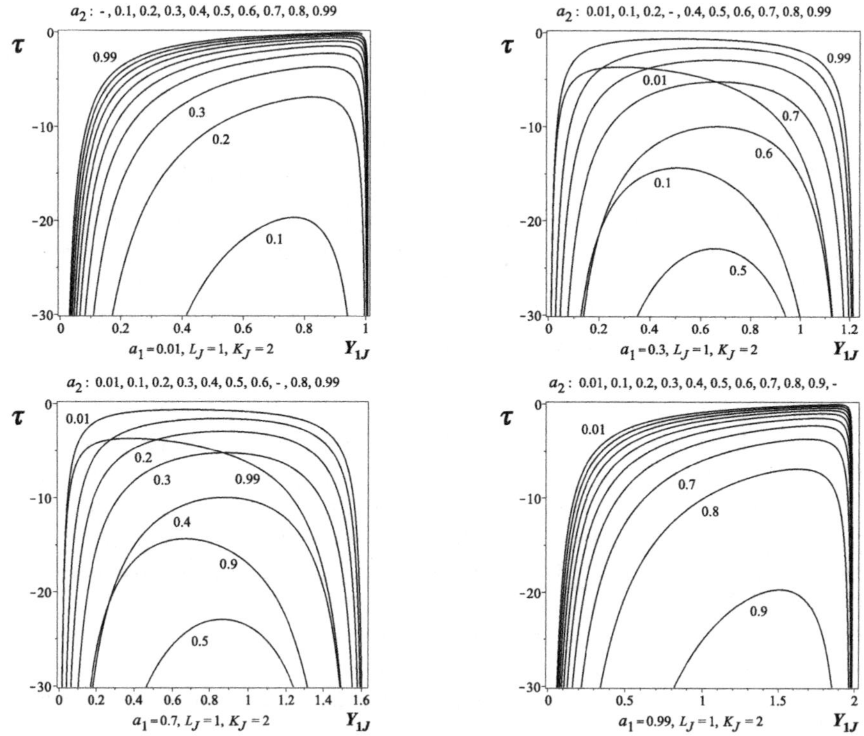


b

**Fig. 23.8** (a) **Transformation elasticities**. $\tau(Y_{1J})$, (23.71), for the production possibility curves (23.62–23.64) of the explicit, $Y_{2J} = T_J(Y_{1J}; L_J, K_J)$, in Fig. 23.6. The scaling units of the vertical axis differ in the two diagrams of Fig. 23.8a. (b) **Transformation elasticities**. $\tau(Y_{1J})$, (23.78), for the production possibility curves of the implicit, $\widehat{T}_J(Y_{1J}, Y_{2J}; L_J, K_J) = 0$, (23.8), (23.22–23.23), $\gamma_{iJ} = 1$, for selected parameters—$a_{1J}$ = 0.01, 0.3, 0.7, 0.99: Fig. 23.4

sensitivity to tangent slopes are small. Small $\tau(Y_{1J})$ values also identify sector factor allocations of the endowments that are most effective in the sense of maximizing the distance from the straight between the PPC end points.

For any ***implicit*** transformation function, $\widehat{\boldsymbol{T}}_J(\boldsymbol{Y}_{1J}, \boldsymbol{Y}_{2J}; \boldsymbol{L}_J, \boldsymbol{K}_J)=0$, with **PPC** in Fig. 23.4, we should also show their transformation elasticities $\tau(Y_{1J})$. Hereto, we use the ***representation*** of the **PPC** by (23.22–23.23) of Theorem 23.1:

$$Y_{iJ} = H_i(\lambda_{L_{1J}}) \; ; \quad \frac{dH_1(\lambda_{L_{1J}})}{d\lambda_{L_{1J}}} > 0\,, \; \lambda_{L_{1J}} = H_1^{-1}(Y_{1J}) \; ; \quad \frac{dH_2(\lambda_{L_{1J}})}{d\lambda_{L_{1J}}} < 0 \tag{23.75}$$

where signs of the derivatives follow from (23.22 to 23.23) and concavity of all PPC. Hence, *inverse* function $H_1^{-1}(Y_{1J})$ *exists globally*. We can express (23.71) as,

$$\tau(\lambda_{L_{1J}}) \equiv E\left(\frac{Y_{2J}}{Y_{1J}}, \frac{dY_{2J}}{dY_{1J}}\right) = -\frac{[\,Y_{2J} - \frac{dY_{2J}}{dY_{1J}} \cdot Y_{1J}\,]\,\frac{dY_{2J}}{dY_{1J}}}{Y_{2J} \cdot Y_{1J} \cdot \frac{d^2Y_{2J}}{dY_{1J}^2}} < 0 \tag{23.76}$$

By the chain rule, the first-order and second-order derivatives in (23.76) are:

$$\frac{dY_{2J}}{dY_{1J}} \equiv \frac{dY_{2J}}{d\lambda_{L_{1J}}}\cdot\frac{d\lambda_{L_{1J}}}{dY_{1J}} = \frac{dY_{2J}}{d\lambda_{L_{1J}}}\cdot\frac{1}{\frac{dY_{1J}}{d\lambda_{L_{1J}}}} \; ; \; \frac{d^2Y_{2J}}{dY_{1J}^2} \equiv \left(\frac{d}{d\lambda_{L_{1J}}}\frac{dY_{2J}}{dY_{1J}}\right)\cdot\frac{1}{\frac{dY_{1J}}{d\lambda_{L_{1J}}}} \tag{23.77}$$

Inserting (23.77) into (23.76) gives $\tau(\lambda_{L_{1J}})$; we next get $\tau(Y_{1J})$ by using (23.75):

$$\tau \equiv E\left(\frac{Y_{2J}}{Y_{1J}}, \frac{dY_{2J}}{dY_{1J}}\right) = \tau(\lambda_{L_{1J}}) \; ; \; \lambda_{L_{1J}} = H_1^{-1}(Y_{1J}) \; : \; \tau(Y_{1J}) = \tau\left[H_1^{-1}(Y_{1J})\right] \tag{23.78}$$

Clearly, in (23.78), $\tau(\lambda_{L_{1J}})$ and $\tau(Y_{1J})$ are long complicated expressions, but again they are easily handled on a computer[8] that was also used for $\tau(p_J)$, from (23.45) in Fig. 23.5d—but where $\tau(p_J)$ was given *explicitly* in (23.46–23.47).

The **VET** elasticities $\tau(Y_{1J})$ along PPC of Theorems 23.1–23.4, (23.22–23.25), are shown in Fig. 23.8b—with the **same** parameter sets as Fig. 23.4.

[8] The $\tau$-curves in Fig. 23.8b can either be drawn by using the "parameter representation" $[Y_{1J}(\lambda_{L_{1J}}), \tau(\lambda_{L_{1J}})]$; $0 \le \lambda_{L_{1J}} \le 1$—or by using $H_1^{-1}(Y_{1J})$ that can be generated by the MAPLE command Root Of $(f(x) = y, x)$, which for every used $Y_{1J}$ generates a corresponding $\lambda_{L_{1J}}$ by iteration. The $H_1^{-1}(Y_{1J})$ method is only preferable, if $a_1$ is close to 1 or $a_2$ is close to 0. In these cases the "parameter form" function $Y_{1J}(\lambda_{L_{1J}})$ will be very fast increasing close to $\lambda_{L_{1J}} = 0$.

First, in contrast to Fig. 23.8a, we note that in Fig. 23.8b (with $a_{1J} \neq 0.5$), there are no longer two parameter values of $a_{2J}$ with the same $\tau(Y_{1J})$ curves. Secondly, the minimum/small values of $\tau(Y_{1J})$ values no longer occur around the middle of the $Y_{1J}$ axis; extreme deviations of the two parameters from each other will move the minimum values of $\tau(Y_{1J})$ toward the axis ends of $Y_{1J}$. However, a *parameter symmetry* for the $\tau(Y_{1J})$ curves in the four diagrams of Fig. 23.8b should be noted—upper left and lower right, upper right and lower left. Some parameter combinations cannot be seen at all in Fig. 23.8b, as the entire $\tau(Y_{1J})$ curve is below the transformation elasticity, $\tau(Y_{1J}) = -30$. Comparing the four diagrams of Fig. 23.8b with their respective PPC in Fig. 23.4 will identify the PPC points with largest curvature [numerical minimum $\tau(Y_{1J})$]. Topics of maximum distances from linearity are left out here.

### *Technologies with CET Transformation Elasticities: Joint Production*

As a potential example of *explicit* transformation functions $T_J(Y_{1J}; L_J, K_J)$, (production possibility frontier), Samuelson (1966, p.34) examined the positive orthant *circle*, (23.74), $Y_{2J} = [L_J K_J - Y_{1J}^2]^{\frac{1}{2}}$, $C = L_J K_J$—which satisfies the *required* properties of *concavity* and *homogeneity* of first degree in the variables $(L_J, K_J, Y_{1J})$, and it had also twice continuously differentiability. He had verified that two countries, $J = A, B$, with just *common* (identical) *technology* behind linear *transformation* functions (**PPF**), (23.60), would *not* have **FPE** (equal factor prices by free trade). *Concave* **PPF** curves were *essential* elements in his famous **FPE** *theorem*, Samuelson (1948, 1949, p.172), where *two* production *functions* were *assumed* behind each country **PPF** curve, that is, *tacitly* assuming ***non-joint*** production in *both* countries.

So *could* (23.74) be obtained from any two *distinct* production functions? or is *joint* production indeed behind the concave homogeneous **PPF** (23.74)? There are several versions (characterizations) of the *restrictions* on a country's transformation function (PPF) which are *necessary conditions* to satisfy, if the underlying technology is one of *non-joint* production. The simplest conditions relate to the *rank* of a singular, negative semi-definite *Hessian matrix* of second-order partial derivatives of proposed (relevant) functions $T_J(Y_{1J}; L_J, K_J)$ to be: number of production factors minus one, that is, here *rank* : 1; cf. Samuelson (1966, p.39), Burmeister and Turnovsky (1971, p.104).

To test and *identify* uniquely two non-joint production functions *behind circle*, $Y_{2J} = T_J(Y_{1J}; L_J, K_J) = [L_J K_J - Y_{1J}^2]^{\frac{1}{2}}$, $C_J = L_J K_J$, (23.74), we are allowed to use the *same* functional form of such non-joint functions $F_{iJ}^*$ to test if they generate a transformation function $T_J^*$ of *same* functional form as $T_J$, (23.74)—that *evidently* here suggests trying **CD** functions, Samuelson (1966, p.38):

$$Y_{1J} = F_{1J}^* = L_{1J}^{\frac{1}{2}} K_{1J}^{\frac{1}{2}}, \ Y_{2J} = F_{2J}^* = L_{2J}^{\frac{1}{2}} K_{2J}^{\frac{1}{2}}, \ K_{1J} + K_{2J} = K_J, \ L_{1J} + L_{2J} = L_J \tag{23.79}$$

The maximal transformation function $T_J^*$ then came from solving the constrained *maximum output* problem (23.79)—this *solution* $T_J^*$ is (23.61) in **Ex.1**:

$$Y_{2J} = T_J^*(Y_{1J}; L_J, K_J) = -Y_{1J} + [L_J K_J]^{\frac{1}{2}}\,;\; T_J^*(Y_{1J}; L_J, K_J) < [L_J K_J - Y_{1J}^2]^{\frac{1}{2}} \tag{23.80}$$

The Hessian matrix of $T_J^*$ (23.80) has *rank* = 1 and is negative semi-definite, and hence (23.80) has *not* any *joint* production of its two outputs. The Hessian matrix of $T_J$ (23.74) is singular but has *rank* = 2 - so $T_J$ (23.74) *does* intrinsically involve ***joint*** production. *Circle* (23.74) is everywhere larger than linear $T_J^*$, (23.80), and Samuelson interprets here $\boldsymbol{T}_J$, (23.74), as involving *intermediate goods* so "cracked to make alternative amounts of good $\boldsymbol{Y}_{1J}$, $\boldsymbol{Y}_{2J}$ as *crude oil* is *cracked variable proportions* of gasoline/kerosene"; cf. Kohli (1983, p.211).

Thus, instead of the "Ricardo extension" of a *linear* **PPF**, (23.60–23.61), (23.79–23.80), Samuelson (1966, p.35) *wished* indeed that: "I could write down an *analytic expression* for $\mathrm{T_J}$ which comes definitely from a technology which involves *no* ***joint*** production. But also, even though modern and older economists spend most of their time in talking about the case where joint production is not permitted, I do *know* an analytic *expression* for *only one* non-trivial *case*, that in which *one good* uses but *one* the factors".

As far as we know the *literature*, there is still **not** anywhere given—apart from the *linear*, **Ex. 1**, (23.60–23.61)—for the beloved *two-factor two-good* case *analytic* formulas of a **PPF** with *non-joint* productions or given any **explicit transformation** function, $Y_{2J} = T_J(Y_{1J}\,; L_J, K_J)$. However, our reader *saw* above (**23.62–23.64**) such **explicit, algebraic** $\mathbf{T_J}$ in Theorem 23.5, **Ex. 2**, that certainly even with *underlying* **CD** sector technologies was an *intricate* and **nonlinear** *formula* to Fig. 23.6—with not CET but **VET** shown in Fig. 23.8a.

Incidentally, note that TFP parameters—$\gamma_{iJ}$—appear in many (all) terms together with the outputs in (23.63). Distinct $\gamma_{iJ}$ are crucially important for a *unique non-joint* production behind $T_J^*$; if the *intensity* parameters are the same, $a_{1J} = a_{2J}$, then, $\gamma_{iJ} = 1$ or $\gamma_{iJ} = \gamma_J$, are *not* admissible in (23.79–23.80), if *same* technology is to be *excluded*—as it was by our *distinct* $\gamma_{iJ}$ in (23.61). Burmeister and Turnovsky (1971, p.100) raise a non-joint problem with $T_J^*$ : $Y_{2J} = T_J^*(Y_{1J}; L_J, K_J) = -Y_{1J} + L_J^{1-\tilde{a}_J} K_J^{\tilde{a}_J}$ as **PPF** for an economy producing $Y_{1J}$ and $Y_{2J}$ *non-jointly*, which here also require *distinct* $\gamma_{iJ}$ as shown in (23.60).

The special *two-good case*, Samuelson (1966, p.35)—with *one sector* ($Y_{1J}$) using only **one factor** (Labor, $L_{1J}$), and with a two-factor CD technology of $Y_{2J}$—has an explicit *nonlinear* PPF $Y_{2J} = T_J(Y_{1J}\,; L_J, K_J)$ simply as:

$$Y_{1J} = \gamma_{1J} L_{1J}\,; \quad Y_{2J} = \gamma_{2J}(L_J - Y_{1J}/\gamma_{1J})^{1-a_{2J}} K_J^{a_{2J}} \equiv T_J(Y_{1J}\,; L_J, K_J) \tag{23.81}$$

If the two CD sector *outputs* (23.6) used **specific capital**, $\breve{K}_{1J}$, $\breve{K}_{2J}$, and *only labor* was a *common* (mobile) factor, then an explicit *nonlinear* **PPF** is derived by just inserting into a *single* labor (employment) *constraint*, $L_{2J} = L_J - L_{1J}$:

$$Y_{2J} = \gamma_{2J}\left[L_J - \left[\frac{Y_{1J}/\gamma_{1J}}{\breve{K}_{1J}^{a_{1J}}}\right]^{\frac{1}{1-a_{1J}}}\right]^{1-a_{2J}} \breve{K}_{2J}^{a_{2J}} \equiv T_J(Y_{1J}\,;\,L_J, \breve{K}_{1J}, \breve{K}_{2J}) \tag{23.82}$$

The *graphics* of (23.82) is seen in standard texts, for example, Caves et al. (2007, p.105), Södersten and Reed (1994, p.31). The procedure (23.82) to get an *explicit* **PPF** can be extended to *many goods* using ***one** common primary* factor. Moreover, as shown by Kemp and Long (1985, p.376), a similar procedure for a *smooth* **PPF** (23.82) can be extended to *N goods* and *M primary factors*, if **one** *good* ($Y_2$) is produced with a *smooth* production function (*using all M primary factors*), and if **all** *other* N-1 goods are produced with *fixed-coefficient* technologies. The extreme simplicity of this result and its proof was obtained by noting that **if** *all coefficients* of production are *fixed* for *all* goods (sectors) *but one*, **no *optimization***—as neither in (23.82)—is *needed* to get an *explicit* **PPF** function.

In the special **CET** class (23.72–23.74) of transformation functions, we had:

$$\widehat{T}_J(Y_{1J}, Y_{2J}\,;\,L_J, K_J) = G_J(Y_{1J}, Y_{2J}) - C_J = Y_{2J} + T_J(Y_{1J}) - C_J = 0 \tag{23.83}$$

where $C_J = (L_J, K_J)$ is only *one* (composite) endowment (input). As we saw for *circle* $\boldsymbol{T}_J$ in (23.80), **PPF** (23.83) assumes (has) **joint** production functions. The function $G_J(Y_{1J}, Y_{2J})$ can be extended to a *joint* production economy of *many* final *goods*, $G_J(Y_{1J}, Y_{2J}, \ldots, Y_{NJ})$; $G_J$ is called a **Factor Requirement Function**, Diewert (1974, p.119), which gives the *minimal* amount of **single** (composite, $\lambda_{K_{iJ}} = \lambda_{L_{iJ}}$) **input** $C_J$, needed to produce these *outputs.*

Thus *paradoxically*, we can **not** get any **CET** class transformation function by **non-joint** inputs: *Separate* industries, *Sector* production functions.

Henceforth, we will further study and elaborate on the actual **VET** properties of **explicit** two-factor *transformation functions* with *non-joint factors* $\boldsymbol{Y}_{2J} = \boldsymbol{T}_J(\boldsymbol{Y}_{1J}\,;\,\boldsymbol{L}_J, \boldsymbol{K}_J)$, *viz.* (23.62–23.64) that Samuelson (1966) *wished* to see, or *generally* as graphs (**PPC**) of **implicit**, $\widehat{\boldsymbol{T}}_J(\boldsymbol{Y}_{1J}, \boldsymbol{Y}_{2J}\,;\,\boldsymbol{L}_J, \boldsymbol{K}_J) = 0$, by (23.22–23.25).

## Leontief PPC Points, Autarky Outputs, Prices, Core Theorems

Before relating explicit *Revenue Functions* (23.165–23.167) to **PPC**, we ought here to *re-examine* the particular PPC implications that Pareto *efficient alloca-*

*tion* will *generate* with **Leontief** sector technologies ("fixed ratios", $\boldsymbol{k}_{iJ}, \boldsymbol{y}_{iJ}$). Leontief production functions are given by *constant* unit *output requirements* of *inputs* from labor, capital, $a_{L_{iJ}} = \frac{L_{iJ}}{Y_{iJ}} = \frac{1}{y_{iJ}}, a_{K_{iJ}} = \frac{K_{iJ}}{Y_{iJ}} = \frac{k_{iJ}}{y_{iJ}}$ ; i=1,2, as :

$$Y_{iJ} = min \left[ \frac{L_{iJ}}{a_{L_{iJ}}}, \frac{K_{iJ}}{a_{K_{iJ}}} \right] \; ; \; \frac{a_{K_{iJ}}}{a_{L_{iJ}}} = k_{iJ} \; ; \; \frac{a_{L_{1J}}}{a_{L_{2J}}} = \frac{y_{2J}}{y_{1J}} \; ; \; \frac{a_{K_{1J}}}{a_{K_{2J}}} = \frac{y_{2J}\, k_{1J}}{y_{1J}\, k_{2J}} \tag{23.84}$$

Parameters $(a_{L_{iJ}}, a_{K_{iJ}})$, *Full employment* of *Endowments* $(\mathbf{L}_J, \mathbf{K}_J)$ imply:[9]

$$a_{L_{1J}} Y_{1J} + a_{L_{2J}} Y_{2J} = L_J \quad ; \quad a_{K_{1J}} Y_{1J} + a_{K_{2J}} Y_{2J} = K_J \tag{23.85}$$

"*Fixed coefficients*" $(a_{L_{iJ}}, a_{K_{iJ}})$, instead of equivalent (*"re-parametrization"*) $(y_{iJ}, k_{iJ})$, can restate (23.86–23.89), (23.93–23.96)—but miss key *ratios* of economic theory. The **fixed** ratios, $\boldsymbol{k}_{iJ}$, reduce $\boldsymbol{\lambda}_{L_{1J}}(\boldsymbol{p}_J; \boldsymbol{k}_J)$, (23.35), to (23.3–23.5), and $\boldsymbol{E}(\boldsymbol{\lambda}_{L_{1J}}(\boldsymbol{k}_J), \boldsymbol{k}_J)$, (23.37) to, respectively :

$$\lambda_{L_{1J}}(p_J\,;\, k_J) \;=\; \lambda_{L_{1J}}(k_J) \;=\; \frac{k_J - k_{2J}}{k_{1J} - k_{2J}} \quad ; \quad E(\lambda_{L_{1J}}(k_J), k_J) \;=\; \frac{k_J}{k_J - k_{2J}} \tag{23.86}$$

Such $\boldsymbol{\lambda}_{L_{1J}}(\boldsymbol{k}_J)$ gives directly the *single efficient* (full employment, maximal) *diversified* **output point**, $(Y_{1J}, Y_{2J})$, by the expressions, cf.(23.6–23.7), (23.84):

$$\begin{aligned} k_{1J} \neq k_{2J} \;:\; Y_{1J} \;&=\; L_J\, \lambda_{L_{1J}}\, y_{1J} \;=\; L_J \frac{k_J - k_{2J}}{k_{1J} - k_{2J}}\, y_{1J} \\ &= -\frac{y_{1J}\, k_{2J}}{k_{1J} - k_{2J}} L_J + \frac{y_{1J}}{k_{1J} - k_{2J}} K_J \end{aligned} \tag{23.87}$$

$$\begin{aligned} k_{1J} \neq k_{2J} \;:\; Y_{2J} \;&=\; L_J [1 - \lambda_{L_{1J}}]\, y_{2J} \;=\; L_J \frac{k_{1J} - k_J}{k_{1J} - k_{2J}}\, y_{2J} \\ &= \frac{y_{2J}\, k_{1J}}{k_{1J} - k_{2J}} L_J - \frac{y_{2J}}{k_{1J} - k_{2J}} K_J \end{aligned} \tag{23.88}$$

As *ratios* $\boldsymbol{k}_{iJ}$ and $\boldsymbol{y}_{iJ}$ are all *constant* in (23.87–23.88), there is here—unlike Figs. 23.4, 23.6, and 23.7—only **one** diversified $(\boldsymbol{Y}_{1J}, \boldsymbol{Y}_{2J})$ for *given* factor endowments, $K_J, L_J$, that is, **PPC** of Theorems 23.1–23.5 collapse to *one point*, (23.87–23.88), and *ratio*,

$$\frac{Y_{2J}}{Y_{1J}}(k_J) = \frac{y_{2J}\,(k_{1J} - k_J)}{y_{1J}\,(k_J - k_{2J})};\; k_{1J} > k_J > k_{2J} : \frac{Y_{2J}}{Y_{1J}} \downarrow;\; k_{2J} > k_J > k_{1J} : \frac{Y_{2J}}{Y_{1J}} \uparrow \tag{23.89}$$

[9] Solving linear equations (23.85) for $(Y_{1J}, Y_{2J})$ give alternative expressions of $(Y_{1J}, Y_{2J})$ in (23.87–23.88). The I-O *matrices* (23.85), and *price* Eqs. (23.99–23.100), Jones (1965, p.558), are standard textbook *production/cost coefficient* matrices of technologies—or **zero profit** conditions, cf. note 16.

If we keep the *endowment ratio*, $k_J = K_J/L_J$, constant, the *output* (supply) *ratio* $Y_{2J}/Y_{1J}$ is constant too. With *varying* $\mathbf{k}_J$, the *output mix* (composition)—*ratio* $\frac{Y_{2J}}{Y_{1J}}(k_J)$, (23.89)—are rectangular *hyperbolas* in $(\mathbf{k}_J)$ that are either *falling* or *rising* curves under the $(k_{iJ})$ assumptions—stated in (23.89).

**Rybczynski** *lines* in output space $(Y_{1J}, Y_{2J})$ of *shifting* efficient PPC point, (23.87–23.88), caused by *single endowment* changes in $L_J$ or $K_J$, are by (23.87–23.88):

$$L_J : Y_{2J} = L_J [1 - \lambda_{L_{1J}}] y_{2J} = L_J \left[1 - \frac{Y_{1J}/y_{1J}}{L_J}\right] y_{2J} = -\frac{y_{2J}}{y_{1J}} Y_{1J} + y_{2J} L_J \tag{23.90}$$

By using $L_J = \frac{y_{1J}K_J - (k_{1J} - k_{2J})Y_{1J}}{y_{1J}k_{2J}}$ of (23.87), insert into (23.91), and rearranged:[10]

$$K_J : Y_{2J} = L_J \frac{k_{1J} - k_J}{k_{1J} - k_{2J}} y_{2J} = -\frac{y_{2J} k_{1J}}{y_{1J} k_{2J}} Y_{1J} + \frac{y_{2J}}{k_{2J}} K_J \tag{23.91}$$

If *sector* (output) *capital* intensities (*ratios*), $k_{iJ}$, (23.84), are **equal**, then (23.90–23.91) *merge* and become genuine **PPC** *lines* [ $\lambda_{L_{1J}}$ : free choice in (23.87–23.88) ]:

$$k_{1J} = k_{2J} = k_J : Y_{2J} = -\frac{y_{2J}}{y_{1J}} Y_{1J} + y_{2J} L_J \equiv T_J(Y_{1J}; L_J, K_J), \lambda_{K_{1J}} = \lambda_{L_{1J}} \tag{23.92}$$

with *specialized* endpoints, $Y_{1J} = 0 : Y^*_{2J} = L_J y_{2J}$, $Y_{2J} = 0 : Y^*_{1J} = L_J y_{1J}$.

Along Rybczynski *lines* (23.90–23.91), the *Rybczynski elasticities* of outputs wrt. capital and labor are given *directly* by (23.86), cf. Theorem 23.4, (23.54–23.57):[11]

$$\begin{aligned} E(Y_{1J}, K_J) &= E(\lambda_{L_{1J}}(k_J), k_J) = \frac{k_J}{k_J - k_{2J}}, \\ E(Y_{1J}, L_J) &= 1 - E(Y_{1J}, K_J) = \frac{-k_{2J}}{k_J - k_{2J}} \end{aligned} \tag{23.93}$$

$$\begin{aligned} E(Y_{2J}, K_J) &= \frac{-\lambda_{L_{1J}}(k_J)}{1 - \lambda_{L_{1J}}(k_J)} \frac{k_J}{k_J - k_{2J}} = \frac{k_J}{k_J - k_{1J}}, \\ E(Y_{2J}, L_J) &= 1 - E(Y_{2J}, K_J) = \frac{-k_{1J}}{k_J - k_{1J}} \end{aligned} \tag{23.94}$$

[10] Rybczynski lines (23.90–23.91) are *not* transformation functions, $Y_{2J} = T_J(Y_{1J}; L_J, K_J)$, as (23.60) in **Ex.1** of Theorem 23.5—but (23.90–23.91) are special one-factor *shifting* of PPC points.

[11] The elasticities, $E(Y_{iJ}, K_J)$, $E(Y_{iJ}, L_J)$, (23.93–23.94), follow, of course, also by (23.87–23.88).

Thus, *Rybczynski* output elasticities wrt. one-factor endowment changes give:

$$k_{1J} > k_J > k_{2J} \Rightarrow E(Y_{1J}, K_J) > 1 \; and \; E(Y_{2J}, K_J) < 0 \qquad (23.95)$$

$$k_{1J} > k_J > k_{2J} \Rightarrow E(Y_{1J}, L_J) < 0 \; and \; E(Y_{2J}, L_J) > 1 \qquad (23.96)$$

If $k_{1J} > k_J$, but $k_{1J}$ is close to $k_J$: $k_{1J} = 4, k_J = 3, k_{2J} = 2$, the negative elasticities, (23.95–23.96), are below one: $E(Y_{2J}, K_J) = -3, E(Y_{1J}, L_J) = -2$. The Rybczynski elasticities in (23.93–23.94) will be extended in Theorem 23.6.

Here we relate (23.93–23.94) to *Rybczynski elasticities* in another form,[12] viz.,

$$E(Y_{1J}, K_J) = \frac{-\lambda_{L_{2J}}}{\lambda_{K_{2J}} - \lambda_{L_{2J}}} = \frac{k_J}{k_J - k_{2J}}, \quad E(Y_{1J}, L_J) = \frac{\lambda_{K_{2J}}}{\lambda_{K_{2J}} - \lambda_{L_{2J}}} = \frac{-k_{2J}}{k_J - k_{2J}} \qquad (23.97)$$

$$E(Y_{2J}, K_J) = \frac{-\lambda_{L_{1J}}}{\lambda_{K_{1J}} - \lambda_{L_{1J}}} = \frac{k_J}{k_J - k_{1J}}, \quad E(Y_{2J}, L_J) = \frac{\lambda_{K_{1J}}}{\lambda_{K_{1J}} - \lambda_{L_{1J}}} = \frac{-k_{1J}}{k_J - k_{1J}} \qquad (23.98)$$

The *first* expressions in (23.97–23.98) are the *usual*[13] ones and helpful in a *qualitative* sense, but the *second* "clear *endowment-parameter*" formulas serve better our purposes[14] of comparing and *generalizing* "fixed-coefficient" cases to general technologies (*variable* capital-labor ratios) by *structural parameters.*

While the *Leontief* sector technologies and full employment (23.84–23.85) gave us well-defined quantitative *Rybczynski* elasticities (23.97–23.98), *analogous* to **CD** elasticities (23.54–23.57), the *Stolper-Samuelson* theorem elasticity (23.51–23.52) has here **no** *direct* **analogue** with *Leontief* technologies as, **MRS**, marginal factor productivities, and **MRT** do *not exist* at any *single* **PPC** (kink) point (23.87–23.88), along the lines (23.90–23.91). However, corresponding exactly to this *single* **PPC** point (23.87–23.88), there *exist* a **dual Leontief** two-output **cost** (money) *functions* that can be reparameterized as above (23.84).

[12] Endowment accounting and allocations (23.1–23.5)—in this notation—always give:

$$k_{1J} > k_J > k_{2J} \Leftrightarrow [\lambda_{K_{1J}} > \lambda_{L_{1J}}] \Leftrightarrow [\lambda_{K_{2J}} < \lambda_{L_{2J}}]$$

$$k_{1J} < k_J < k_{2J} \Leftrightarrow [\lambda_{K_{1J}} < \lambda_{L_{1J}}] \Leftrightarrow [\lambda_{K_{2J}} < \lambda_{L_{2J}}]$$

Of course, these *accounting identities* above for a two-sector economy hold, independent of any particular sector technology assumptions, but they do assume *full employment.* Note also that $\lambda_{K_{1J}} > \lambda_{L_{1J}}$ above does then *not* always imply: $\lambda_{K_{1J}} > \lambda_{K_{2J}}$, cf. Figs. 23.1a–23.3c.

[13] For example, Feenstra (2016, p.14), Gandolfo (2014, p.446), Wong (1995, p.33).

[14] On the role of (23.97–23.98) for the solutions in seminal two-sector growth models, cf. (14.47–14.48) in Sect. "The Economic Rationale of the Stability Conditions", and Figs. 14.2 and 14.3.

In *notation* of (23.122–23.123) below for **money** factor prices ($w_J$, $r_J$), money output prices ($P_{iJ}$), **Leontief** unit **cost** (price) functions become from (23.84):

$$P_{1J} = c_{1J}(w_J, r_J) = a_{L_{1J}} w_J + a_{K_{1J}} r_J = \frac{w_J + k_{1J} r_J}{y_{1J}} \; ; \; \omega_J = \frac{w_J}{r_J} \qquad (23.99)$$

$$P_{2J} = c_{2J}(w_J, r_J) = a_{L_{2J}} w_J + a_{K_{2J}} r_J = \frac{w_J + k_{2J} r_J}{y_{2J}} \; ; \; \omega_J = \frac{w_J}{r_J} \qquad (23.100)$$

and *output* (sector) *factor* **cost shares** of labor and capital expressed as,

$$\epsilon_{L_{iJ}} = \frac{w_J L_{iJ}}{P_{iJ} Y_{iJ}} = \frac{w_J}{P_{iJ} y_{iJ}} , \quad \epsilon_{K_{iJ}} = \frac{r_J K_{iJ}}{P_{iJ} Y_{iJ}} = \frac{r_J k_{iJ}}{P_{iJ} y_{iJ}} \; ; \; \frac{\epsilon_{L_{1J}}}{\epsilon_{L_{2J}}} = \frac{y_{2J}}{y_{1J}} \frac{1}{p_J} ,$$
$$\frac{\epsilon_{K_{1J}}}{\epsilon_{K_{2J}}} = \frac{y_{2J} k_{1J}}{y_{1J} k_{2J}} \frac{1}{p_J} \qquad (23.101)$$

Hence, *relative prices* ($p_J$) follow from (23.99 to 23.100) to be a function given by:

$$p_J = \frac{P_{1J}}{P_{2J}} = \frac{c_{1J}(w_J, r_J)}{c_{2J}[w_J, r_J]} = \Phi_J(w_J, r_J) = \frac{y_{2J}}{y_{1J}} \frac{(\omega_J + k_{1J})}{(\omega_J + k_{2J})} \equiv \Phi_J(\omega_J) \; ;$$
$$\omega_J, \; w_J, r_J \; : \in [0, \infty[ \qquad (23.102)$$

with an **inverse** ($k_{1J} \neq k_{2J}$) for the *relative factor prices* ($\omega_J$) of the form:

$$\omega_J = \Phi_J^{-1}(p_J) = k_{2J} \frac{\frac{y_{2J} k_{1J}}{y_{1J} k_{2J}} - p_J}{p_J - \frac{y_{2J}}{y_{1J}}} \; ; \; p_J \in [\underline{p}_J, \overline{p}_J] \; ; \; \omega_J, w_J, r_J \; : \in [0, \infty[ \qquad (23.103)$$

The relative prices, $p_J = \Phi_J(\omega_J)$, (23.102), and $\Phi_J^{-1}(p_J)$, are rectangular *hyperbolas*, falling/increasing, with lower and upper **price limits**, $[\underline{p}_J, \overline{p}_J]$, as:

$$k_{1J} > k_{2J} : \underline{p}_J = \frac{y_{2J}}{y_{1J}} < p_J(\omega_J) < \frac{y_{2J} k_{1J}}{y_{1J} k_{2J}} = \overline{p}_J, \; ;$$
$$k_{2J} > k_{1J} : \underline{p}_J = \frac{y_{2J} k_{1J}}{y_{1J} k_{2J}} < p_J(\omega_J) < \frac{y_{2J}}{y_{1J}} = \overline{p}_J \qquad (23.104)$$

**Endowment invariant** *curves* (23.102–23.103) with *Range* (23.104), see Fig. 23.9 [left]. Relative price *limits* $[\underline{p}_J, \overline{p}_J]$ (23.104) are *slopes* of Rybczynski lines, (23.90–23.91).

Solving (23.99–23.100) for $(w_J, r_J)$ in terms of the output prices $(P_{1J}, P_{2J})$ gives:

$$r_J = \frac{y_{1J} P_{1J} - y_{2J} P_{2J}}{k_{1J} - k_{2J}} \; ; \; w_J = \frac{y_{2J} k_{1J} P_{2J} - y_{1J} k_{2J} P_{1J}}{k_{1J} - k_{2J}} \tag{23.105}$$

*Stolper-Samuelson elasticities* of factor prices, $w_J$, $r_J$, wrt. output prices, $P_{1J}$, $P_{1J}$, come by simple elasticity rules directly from (23.105) and (23.101), (23.104):

$$E(w_J, P_{1J}) = \frac{-y_{1J} k_{2J} P_{1J}}{y_{2J} k_{1J} P_{2J} - y_{1J} k_{2J} P_{1J}} = \frac{-p_J}{\frac{y_{2J} k_{1J}}{y_{1J} k_{2J}} - p_J} = \frac{\epsilon_{K_{2J}}}{\epsilon_{K_{2J}} - \epsilon_{K_{1J}}} \tag{23.106}$$

$$E(w_J, P_{2J}) = \frac{y_{2J} k_{1J} P_{2J}}{y_{2J} k_{1J} P_{2J} - y_{1J} k_{2J} P_{1J}} = \frac{\frac{y_{2J} k_{1J}}{y_{1J} k_{2J}}}{\frac{y_{2J} k_{1J}}{y_{1J} k_{2J}} - p_J} = \frac{-\epsilon_{K_{1J}}}{\epsilon_{K_{2J}} - \epsilon_{K_{1J}}} \tag{23.107}$$

$$E(r_J, P_{1J}) = \frac{y_{1J} P_{1J}}{y_{1J} P_{1J} - y_{2J} P_{2J}} = \frac{p_J}{p_J - \frac{y_{2J}}{y_{1J}}} = \frac{-\epsilon_{L_{2J}}}{\epsilon_{L_{1J}} - \epsilon_{L_{2J}}} \tag{23.108}$$

$$E(r_J, P_{2J}) = \frac{-y_{2J} P_{2J}}{y_{1J} P_{1J} - y_{2J} P_{2J}} = \frac{-\frac{y_{2J}}{y_{1J}}}{p_J - \frac{y_{2J}}{y_{1J}}} = \frac{\epsilon_{L_{1J}}}{\epsilon_{L_{1J}} - \epsilon_{L_{2J}}} \tag{23.109}$$

with : $E(w_J, P_{1J}) + E(w_J, P_{2J}) = E(r_J, P_{1J}) + E(r_J, P_{2J}) = 1$; and for *"real"* factor prices: $E(\frac{w_J}{P_{1J}}, P_{1J}) + E(\frac{w_J}{P_{2J}}, P_{2J}) = E(\frac{r_J}{P_{1J}}, P_{1J}) + E(\frac{r_J}{P_{2J}}, P_{2J}) = -1$.

The sizes and pattern of **Stolper-Samuelson** *elasticities* (23.106–23.109) are **not** *isoelastic* (hyperbolic in $p_J$) but qualitatively always give with (23.104), (23.101):

$$k_{1J} > k_J > k_{2J} \Rightarrow E(r_J, P_{1J}) > 1 \; and \; E(r_J, P_{2J}) < 0 \tag{23.110}$$

$$k_{1J} > k_J > k_{2J} \Rightarrow E(w_J, P_{1J}) < 0 \; and \; E(w_J, P_{2J}) > 1 \tag{23.111}$$

Although elasticity (23.51–23.53) had **no** counterpart to (23.84), "concave" elasticities *properties* (23.110–23.111) *reappeared* from the *monetary* **dual** (23.99–23.100).

The *formulas*[15] (23.106–23.109) (especially last terms) and (23.110–23.111) are usually and here called *Stolper-Samuelson elasticities*, referring to *Leontief cost* (price) functions, **zero profit** conditions,[16] (23.99–

[15] Table with *all numerical elasticities,* (23.106–23.109), (23.93–23.94), selected years (1948,,1987) by a two-factor two-sector Leontief model on US GDP data, see Kohli (1991, p.150).

[16] *Zero profit* conditions (23.99–23.100) are standard "*equilibrium conditions*", Feenstra (2016, p.7)—and they come up again below with the **CD dual** and **cost shares** in (23.122–23.126).

23.100), but we should emphasize that the *economic* role/implications of $P_{1J}/P_{2J} = \Phi_J(w_J, r_J)$, (23.102), *differ* much from that played by the MRT-MRS function, $p_J = \Phi_J(\omega_J)$, (23.33).

Despite $\Phi_J(w_J, r_J)$ is assigned proper *intervals* (23.103–23.104), and the **graphs** (locus) of $\Phi_J$ and $\Phi_J^{-1}$ are exhibited by *curves* in Fig. 23.9a–b, [left panels] the *relative* factor (product) *prices*, $\frac{P_{1J}}{P_{2J}} = \Phi_J(\omega_J)$, (23.102), play *no factor allocation* role and hence do **not** affect output *composition* or *sizes* of the *outputs* (23.87–23.88), since (23.102) does not influence the allocation *variable* $\lambda_{L_{1J}}$ that is already fully "*technologically*" and "*endowment*" determined as $\lambda_{L_{1J}(k_J)}$, (23.86)—in contrast to (23.33), where "relative prices" did influence the factor *allocation variable*, $\lambda_{L_{1J}}(p_J\,;\,k_J)$, in (23.35–23.36), or as $\lambda_{L_{1J}}(\omega_J\,;\,k_J)$ in (23.29).

### *Leontief PPC Points and GE Prices of General Equilibrium Solutions*

With Leontief technologies in two-sector *general equilibrium* (**GE**) economics, there does exist a **unique** connection between the *relative* product (factor) *prices* and Pareto Efficient Allocation of the *factor endowments* ($k_J$).

The "*supply side*" of this Leontief "fixed-coefficient" economy above—with full and Pareto efficient factor allocation—is *summarized* by (23.102), (23.89):

$$\frac{P_{1J}\,Y_{1J}}{P_{2J}\,Y_{2J}} = \frac{y_{2J}\,(\omega_J + k_{1J})}{y_{1J}\,(\omega_J + k_{2J})} \cdot \frac{y_{1J}\,(k_J - k_{2J})}{y_{2J}\,(k_{1J} - k_J)} = \frac{\omega_J + k_{1J}}{\omega_J + k_{2J}} \cdot \frac{k_J - k_{2J}}{k_{1J} - k_J} \tag{23.112}$$

The "*demand side*" of the economy is described by consumption pattern of a representative consumer with *homothetic preferences*, maximizing—CD **utility** function of (23.196) with country-specific CD *parameter* ($\alpha_J$)—under income constraint. Thus, CD expenditure shares *summarize* demand side:

$$u_J = U_J\,(Y_{1J}\,, Y_{2J}) = Y_{1J}^{\alpha_J} Y_{2J}^{1-\alpha_J}\;;\quad Y_J = P_{1J}Y_{1J} + P_{2J}Y_{2J}\;;\quad \frac{P_{1J}\,Y_{1J}}{P_{2J}\,Y_{2J}} = \frac{\alpha_J}{1-\alpha_J} \tag{23.113}$$

Hence, Pareto efficiency, factor-, output market clearing prices will in *general equilibrium* (**GE**, Walrasian equilibria) *require* (23.112) to comply with (23.113):

$$\frac{\omega_J + k_{1J}}{\omega_J + k_{2J}} \cdot \frac{k_J - k_{2J}}{k_{1J} - k_J} = \frac{\alpha_J}{1-\alpha_J} \tag{23.114}$$

Solving (23.114) gives, by Leontief technologies and CD preferences, **autarky GE** expression, $\boldsymbol{k} = \boldsymbol{\Psi}_J(\boldsymbol{\omega}_J)$, for the **FEFP** (*Factor endowment-Factor price*) **locus** :

$$k_J = \frac{k_{1J}\,k_{2J} + [\,\alpha_J\,k_{1J} + (1-\alpha_J)\,k_{2J}\,]\,\omega_J}{\omega_J + (1-\alpha_J)\,k_{1J} + \alpha_J\,k_{2J}} \equiv \frac{k_{1J}\,k_{2J} + \breve{\beta}_J\,\omega_J}{\omega_J + \widetilde{\beta}_J} \equiv \Psi_J(\omega_J) \tag{23.115}$$

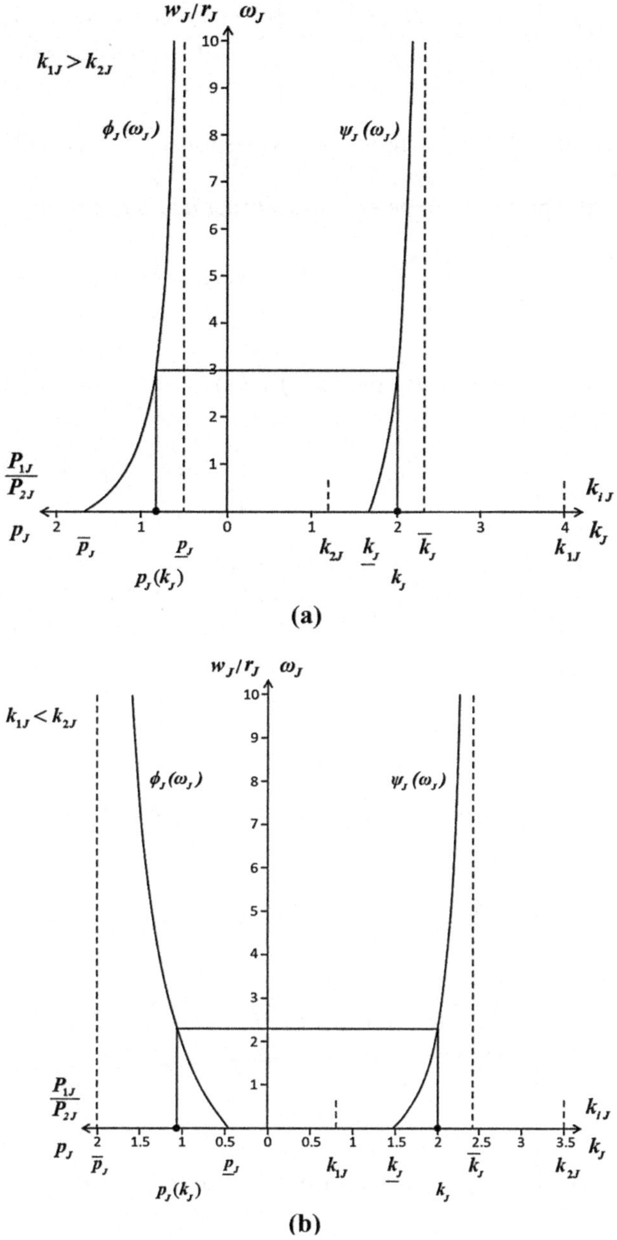


**Fig. 23.9** (**a**) $k_{1J} = 4$, $k_{2J} = 1.2$; $p_J = \Phi_J(\omega_J)$, (23.103), $[\underline{p}_J, \overline{p}_J]$, (23.104), (23.119); $\alpha_J = 0.4$; $k_J = 2$, $\omega_J = 3$; $k_J = \Psi(\omega_J)$, (23.116), $[\underline{k}_J, \overline{k}_J]$, (23.117); $p_J(k_J)$, (23.118). (**b**) Equations as Fig. 23.9a; $k_{1J} = 0.8$, $k_{2J} = 3.5$; $k_J = 2$, $\omega_J = 2.29$, (23.120)

$$\omega_J = \Psi_J^{-1}(k_J) = \frac{\widetilde{\beta}_J k_J - k_{1J} k_{2J}}{\breve{\beta}_J - k_J} = \frac{[(1-\alpha_J) k_{1J} + \alpha_J k_{2J}] k_J - k_{1J} k_{2J}}{\alpha_J k_{1J} + (1-\alpha_J) k_{2J} - k_J} \tag{23.116}$$

and seen in Fig. 23.9a–b [right panels]—similar to (23.200–23.201) in Fig. 23.5a–b.

Positive factor prices, $\omega_J = w_J/r_J$, and ***diversification*** impose *limits* on $k_J$:

$$\frac{k_{1J} k_{2J}}{(1-\alpha_J) k_{1J} + \alpha_J k_{2J}} = \frac{k_{1J} k_{2J}}{\widetilde{\beta}_J} = \underline{k}_J < k_J < \overline{k}_J = \breve{\beta}_J = \alpha_J k_{1J} + (1-\alpha_J) k_{2J} \tag{23.117}$$

The **GE** relative *commodity* prices, $\boldsymbol{p}_J(\boldsymbol{k}_J)$, are obtained by (23.102) and (23.116),

$$p_J(k_J) = \Phi_J[\omega_J = \Psi_J^{-1}(k_J)] = \frac{y_{2J}}{y_{1J}} \frac{[\Psi_J^{-1}(k_J) + k_{1J}]}{[\Psi_J^{-1}(k_J) + k_{2J}]} \tag{23.118}$$

To see *autarky* **GE** solutions of *two*-factor *two*-good models with **Leontief** technologies in Fig. 23.9a–b, we put *numbers* on the "fixed coefficients" (parameters), (23.84), $\alpha_J$ (23.113), price *range* $[\underline{p}_J, \overline{p}_J]$, (23.104), and the "cone" *limits*, $[\underline{k}_J, \overline{k}_J]$, (23.117):

**Fig. 23.9a** :$a_{L_{1J}} = 0.5\,,\ a_{K_{1J}} = 2\,,\ a_{L_{2J}} = 1\,,\ a_{K_{2J}} = 1.2\ :\ y_{1J} = 2\,,\ k_{1J} = 4\,,$

$y_{2J} = 1\,,\ k_{2J} = 1.2;\ k_J = 2\ ;\ \alpha_J = 0.4\ ;$

$[\underline{p}_J, \overline{p}_J] = [0.5\,,\ 1.66]\ ;\ \ [\underline{k}_J, \overline{k}_J] = [1.67\,,\ 2.32];\ \ p_J(k_J) = 0.83$ (23.119)

**Fig. 23.9b** :$a_{L_{1J}} = 2\,,\ a_{K_{1J}} = 1.6\,,\ a_{L_{2J}} = 1\,,\ a_{K_{2J}} = 3.5\ :\ y_{1J} = 0.5\,,\ k_{1J} = 0.8\,,$

$y_{2J} = 1\,,\ k_{2J} = 3.5;\ k_J = 2\ ;\ \alpha_J = 0.4\ ;$

$[\underline{p}_J\,,\ \overline{p}_J] = [0.45\,,\ 2.0]\ ;\ [\underline{k}_J\,,\ \overline{k}_J] = [1.49\,,\ 2.42];\ \ p_J(k_J) = 1.07$ (23.120)

## THE MULTIPLE OUTPUT COST FUNCTION: $C = C(w, r, Y_1, Y_2)$

Standard ***dual*** single output **money** *cost* functions $C_{iJ}$ and ***unit costs*** $c_{iJ}$ of $F_{iJ}$ (23.6) in sector ($\boldsymbol{i}$) are [$w_{iJ}$, $r_{iJ}$, are **money** factor *prices* of labor, capital ]:

$$C_{iJ}(w_{iJ}, r_{iJ}, Y_{iJ}) = \frac{1}{\gamma_{iJ}} \left[\frac{w_{iJ}}{1-a_{iJ}}\right]^{1-a_{iJ}} \left[\frac{r_{iJ}}{a_{iJ}}\right]^{a_{iJ}} Y_{iJ}\ ;\ i = 1, 2\,,\ J = A, B \tag{23.121}$$

$$c_{iJ}(w_{iJ}, r_{iJ}) = \frac{1}{\gamma_{iJ}} \left[\frac{w_{iJ}}{1-a_{iJ}}\right]^{1-a_{iJ}} \left[\frac{r_{iJ}}{a_{iJ}}\right]^{a_{iJ}} \; ; \; \epsilon_{L_{iJ}} = 1 - a_{iJ}, \; \epsilon_{K_{iJ}} = a_{iJ} \tag{23.122}$$

Pareto efficient factor allocations are due to **common** *money factor prices*,

$$\frac{dK_{iJ}}{dL_{iJ}} = MRS = \omega_J = \frac{w_J}{r_J} \equiv \frac{w_{iJ}}{r_{iJ}}, \; i = 1, 2; \; \frac{dY_{2J}}{dY_{1J}} = MRT = p_J \equiv \frac{P_{1J}}{P_{2J}} \tag{23.123}$$

The *prices* (unit *costs*) and *relative* commodity *prices* become by (23.122–23.123):

$$P_{1J} = c_{1J}(w_J, r_J) = \frac{r_J}{\gamma_{1J}\, a_{1J}^{a_{1J}}\, (1-a_{1J})^{1-a_{1J}}} \left[\frac{w_J}{r_J}\right]^{1-a_{1J}} = \beta_{1J}\, w_J^{1-a_{1J}}\, r_J^{a_{1J}} \tag{23.124}$$

$$P_{2J} = c_{2J}(w_J, r_J) = \frac{r_J}{\gamma_{2J}\, a_{2J}^{a_{2J}}\, (1-a_{2J})^{1-a_{2J}}} \left[\frac{w_J}{r_J}\right]^{1-a_{2J}} = \beta_{2J}\, w_J^{1-a_{2J}}\, r_J^{a_{2J}} \tag{23.125}$$

$$p_J = \frac{P_{1J}}{P_{2J}} = \frac{c_{1J}(w_J, r_J)}{c_{2J}(w_J, r_J)} = \frac{\gamma_{2J}\, a_{2J}^{a_{2J}}\, (1-a_{2J})^{1-a_{2J}}}{\gamma_{1J}\, a_{1J}^{a_{1J}}\, (1-a_{1J})^{1-a_{1J}}} \left[\frac{w_J}{r_J}\right]^{a_{2J}-a_{1J}} = \frac{\gamma_{2J}}{\gamma_{1J}} \bar{A}_J\, \omega_J^{a_{2J}-a_{1J}} \tag{23.126}$$

*Relative* ***Product*** *price*-***Factor*** *price* function, $\boldsymbol{p_J} =, \frac{\gamma_{2J}}{\gamma_{1J}} \bar{\boldsymbol{A}}_J\, \boldsymbol{\omega}_J^{a_{2J}-a_{1J}}$, (23.126), is the *endowment invariant* **MRT-MRS** function: $\boldsymbol{MRT} = \boldsymbol{p}_J = \boldsymbol{\Phi}_J(\boldsymbol{\omega}_J)$, (23.33), Theorem 23.2—as exhibited in the *left panels* of Fig. 23.5a–b.

Modern trade theory uses sector (product) unit cost functions extensively—at least formally. Generally, such sector functions, $P_{iJ} = c_{iJ}(w_J, r_J)$, are as (23.124–23.125) always nonnegative, concave, monotone increasing in $(w_J, r_J)$—and gradients, and Jacobian matrix, $\frac{\partial (c_{1J}, c_{2J})}{\partial (w_J, r_J)}$, have only *positive* elements:[17]

$$\frac{\partial c_{iJ}}{\partial w_J} = a_{L_{iJ}} = \frac{(w_J/r_J)^{-a_{iJ}}}{\gamma_{iJ}[\frac{a_{iJ}}{1-a_{iJ}}]^{a_{iJ}}} \; ; \; \frac{\partial c_{iJ}}{\partial r_J} = a_{K_{iJ}} = \frac{(w_J/r_J)^{1-a_{iJ}}}{\gamma_{iJ}[\frac{a_{iJ}}{1-a_{iJ}}]^{a_{iJ}-1}} \; ;$$

$$\frac{a_{K_{iJ}}}{a_{L_{iJ}}} = k_{iJ} = \frac{a_{iJ}}{1-a_{iJ}} \frac{w_J}{r_J} \tag{23.127}$$

[17] The question of *invertibility* and "univalence" of $P_{iJ} = c_{iJ}(w_J, r_J)$, $i = 1, 2$, gave a large controversial literature, cf. Dixit and Norman (1980, p.50). If the Jacobian matrix *determinant* of first-order derivatives (23.127) is *nonsingular* for all positive factor prices $(w_J, r_J)$, then continuity of the derivatives (23.127) ensures the Jacobian determinant to be everywhere either positive or negative—and thus an *inverse* of (23.124–23.125) will locally exist (unique) everywhere in the domain. But these local inverse functions will not always as the CD cost functions (23.124–23.126) be *univalent* (bijective) upon their global *domain* (23.128).

which evidently give elasticities, $E\,(c_{iJ}, w_J) = 1 - a_{iJ}$, $E\,(c_{iJ}, r_J) = a_{iJ}$, (23.122). Endowment invariance of the *product price-unit cost* functions (23.124–23.125)—also called *zero profit* conditions—and hence the *relative* price function, (23.126), $p_J = \Phi_J(\omega_J)$, are here simply coming from (23.122 to 23.123). The simplicity of the endowment *invariance* (23.124–23.126) *seem often* in the literature inadvertently to have *tacitly* but *wrongly supposed* that the **common** *factor price* ratio, $\omega_J = w_J/r_J$ in (23.123–23.126), (23.135–23.138) have the **domain,** $\Omega_{\omega_J}$ : *zero* to *infinity*—as the individual **sector** *factor price* ratios, $w_{iJ}/r_{iJ}$, **do** have in (23.122).

But for *two-sector* economies, producing *all* outputs *efficiently*, admissible **domains** for **common** relative factor prices, $\omega_J = MRS$, (23.123), are indeed tacitly **restricted**—as were $\omega_J$=*MRS*, (23.27–23.28), by the **endowment ratios** $(k_J)$ in Theorems 23.1–23.2, that is, **domains** $\Omega_{\omega_J}$, (23.18), (23.30–23.31):[18]

$$Y_{1J} = 0\,,\ \lambda_{L_{1J}} = 0:\ \underline{\omega}_J = \frac{1 - a_{2J}}{a_{2J}} k_J\ ;\ Y_{2J} = 0\,,\ \lambda_{L_{1J}} = 1:\ \overline{\omega}_J = \frac{1 - a_{1J}}{a_{1J}} k_J \tag{23.128}$$

Relative *prices* $\boldsymbol{p}_J(\boldsymbol{\omega}_J)$, (23.126), have the *endowment limited* **range**: (23.39).

The **inverse** of *unit cost* (price) functions (23.124–23.125) have **explicit** form:

$$w_J = \beta_{1J}^{\frac{-a_{2J}}{a_{2J}-a_{1J}}}\ \beta_{2J}^{\frac{a_{1J}}{a_{2J}-a_{1J}}}\ P_{1J}^{\frac{a_{2J}}{a_{2J}-a_{1J}}}\ P_{2J}^{\frac{-a_{1J}}{a_{2J}-a_{1J}}} \tag{23.129}$$

$$r_J = \beta_{1J}^{\frac{1-a_{2J}}{a_{2J}-a_{1J}}}\ \beta_{2J}^{\frac{a_{1J}-1}{a_{2J}-a_{1J}}}\ P_{1J}^{\frac{a_{2J}-1}{a_{2J}-a_{1J}}}\ P_{2J}^{\frac{1-a_{1J}}{a_{2J}-a_{1J}}} \tag{23.130}$$

***Proof*** The explicit inverse *formulas*, (23.129–23.130), are derived in the Appendix. □

**CD** *Stolper-Samuelson* elasticities for *monetary* factor prices, (23.131–23.132)—and next for "*real*", factor prices, (23.133–23.134)—come directly from (23.129 to 23.130).

$$E(w_J, P_{1J}) = \frac{\epsilon_{K_{2J}}}{\epsilon_{K_{2J}} - \epsilon_{K_{1J}}} = \frac{-a_{2J}}{a_{1J} - a_{2J}};\ E(w_J, P_{2J}) = \frac{-\,\epsilon_{K_{1J}}}{\epsilon_{K_{2J}} - \epsilon_{K_{1J}}} = \frac{a_{1J}}{a_{1J} - a_{2J}} \tag{23.131}$$

[18] Of course, noting, $\omega_J = w_J/r_J$, as the last term of (23.127), the lower $(\underline{\omega}_J)$ and upper $(\overline{\omega}_J)$ specialization limits for $\omega_J$ in (23.128) follow immediately from (23.127); and thus limits (Range) (23.39) of $p_J$, (23.126), are due to (23.128). But such global domain limits on functions as (23.124–23.126) and gradients (unit requirements), (23.127), (23.84), are routinely ignored or unspecified.

$$E(r_J, P_{1J}) = \frac{-\epsilon_{L_{2J}}}{\epsilon_{L_{1J}} - \epsilon_{L_{2J}}} = \frac{1 - a_{2J}}{a_{1J} - a_{2J}}; \; E(r_J, P_{2J}) = \frac{\epsilon_{L_{1J}}}{\epsilon_{L_{1J}} - \epsilon_{L_{2J}}} = \frac{-(1 - a_{1J})}{a_{1J} - a_{2J}} \tag{23.132}$$

$$E(\frac{w_J}{P_{1J}}, P_{1J}) = \frac{\epsilon_{K_{1J}}}{\epsilon_{K_{2J}} - \epsilon_{K_{1J}}} = \frac{-a_{1J}}{a_{1J} - a_{2J}}; \; E(\frac{w_J}{P_{2J}}, P_{2J}) = \frac{-\epsilon_{K_{2J}}}{\epsilon_{K_{2J}} - \epsilon_{K_{1J}}} = \frac{a_{2J}}{a_{1J} - a_{2J}} \tag{23.133}$$

$$E(\frac{r_J}{P_{1J}}, P_{1J}) = \frac{-\epsilon_{L_{1J}}}{\epsilon_{L_{1J}} - \epsilon_{L_{2J}}} = \frac{1 - a_{1J}}{a_{1J} - a_{2J}}; \; E(\frac{r_J}{P_{2J}}, P_{2J}) = \frac{\epsilon_{L_{2J}}}{\epsilon_{L_{1J}} - \epsilon_{L_{2J}}} = \frac{-(1 - a_{2J})}{a_{1J} - a_{2J}} \tag{23.134}$$

The ***isoelastic*** forms (23.131–23.134) for **CD** have for $a_{1J} > a_{2J}$, (23.122), the pattern[19] as (23.106–23.111). *Nominal* factor price elasticities (23.131–23.132), and "*real*", factor reward elasticities (23.133–23.134) add to *plus* one and *minus* one.

*Multiple output minimal factor cost* functions $\mathbf{C_J}\,(\mathbf{w_J}, \mathbf{r_J}, \mathbf{Y_{1J}}, \mathbf{Y_{2J}})$ for Pareto efficient production of *two outputs* must—with *non-joint inputs*, Hall (1973, p.884), Kohli (1983, p.212)—be the *sum* of the costs of producing *each separately*, that is, $C_J$ becomes by $c_{iJ}(w_J, r_J)$, $i = 1, 2$, (23.124–23.125), *explicitly*:

$$C_J = C_J\,(w_J, r_J, Y_{1J}, Y_{2J})\,, \qquad J = A, B \tag{23.135}$$

$$= \min_{L_J, K_J} \{w_J L_J + r_J K_J\}, \; s.t. \; \widehat{T}_J(Y_{1J}, Y_{2J}; L_J, K_J) = 0 \tag{23.136}$$

$$= C_{1J}\,(w_J, r_J, Y_{1J}) + C_{2J}\,(w_J, r_J, Y_{2J}) \tag{23.137}$$

$$= c_{1J}(w_J, r_J) Y_{1J} + c_{2J}(w_J, r_J) Y_{2J} = P_{1J}(w_J, r_J) Y_{1J} + P_{2J}(w_J, r_J) Y_{2J}$$

$$= \frac{w_J^{1-a_{1J}}\, r_J^{a_{1J}}}{\gamma_{1J}\, a_{1J}^{a_{1J}}\, (1 - a_{1J})^{1-a_{1J}}}\, Y_{1J} + \frac{w_J^{1-a_{2J}}\, r_J^{a_{2J}}}{\gamma_{2J}\, a_{2J}^{a_{2J}}\, (1 - a_{2J})^{1-a_{2J}}}\, Y_{2J} \tag{23.138}$$

$$= r_J \, [\frac{\omega_J^{1-a_{1J}}\; Y_{1J}}{\gamma_{1J}\, a_{1J}^{a_{1J}}\, (1 - a_{1J})^{1-a_{1J}}} + \frac{\omega_J^{1-a_{2J}}\; Y_{2J}}{\gamma_{2J}\, a_{2J}^{a_{2J}}\, (1 - a_{2J})^{1-a_{2J}}}] \tag{23.139}$$

In (23.139), *exogenous* factor prices $\omega_J = w_J / r_J$ must be in *domain* (23.128). The numbers, $\mathbf{Y_{1J}}, \mathbf{Y_{2J}}$, (23.137–23.139), are of course located on **PPC** of Figs. 23.4, and 23.6, given by (23.22–23.25), (23.29). The underlying endowments $(L_J, K_J)$ are given, respectively, by the sum of *derivatives* of (23.137) as in (23.127).

Another for trade theory important *duality* representation of the *transformation* function $\widehat{T}_J(Y_{1J}, Y_{2J}\,;\, L_J, K_J) = 0$ (and **PPC** in Theorems 23.1–23.2) is the **Revenue** (GNP) *function*, which in contrast to $C_J\,(w_J, r_J, Y_{1J}, Y_{2J})$, (23.135), consider the factor *endowments* $(L_J, K_J)$ and

[19] Cost share formulas, $\epsilon_{L_{iJ}}$, $\epsilon_{K_{iJ}}$, in (23.131–23.132) are standard, for example, Feenstra (2016, p.12).

the *output prices* $(P_{1J}, P_{2J})$ as **exogenous** variables—tacitly also in **price domain** (23.39).

## Appendix

The *unit cost* (price) functions in (23.124–23.125) were:

$$P_{1J} = \beta_{1J}\, w_J^{1-a_{1J}}\, r_J^{a_{1J}}$$
$$P_{2J} = \beta_{2J}\, w_J^{1-a_{2J}}\, r_J^{a_{2J}}$$

Hence, stepwise we get,

$$ln(P_{1J}) = ln(\beta_1) + (1 - a_{1J})\, ln(w_J) + a_{1J}\, ln(r_J)$$
$$ln(P_{2J}) = ln(\beta_2) + (1 - a_{2J})\, ln(w_J) + a_{2J}\, ln(r_J)$$

$$x_1 = ln\,(w_J) \qquad x_2 = ln\,(r_J) \tag{23.140}$$

$$(1 - a_{1J})\, x_1 + a_{1J}\, x_2 = ln\,(P_{1J}) - ln(\beta_1) = b_1$$
$$(1 - a_{2J})\, x_1 + a_{2J}\, x_2 = ln\,(P_{2J}) - ln(\beta_2) = b_2$$

Hence, in standard matrix notation,

$$a_{11}\, x_2 + a_{12}\, x_2 = b_1$$
$$a_{21}\, x_2 + a_{22}\, x_2 = b_2$$

$$x_1 = \frac{\begin{vmatrix} b_1 & a_{12} \\ b_2 & a_{22} \end{vmatrix}}{\begin{vmatrix} a_{11} & a_{12} \\ a_{21} & a_{22} \end{vmatrix}} \qquad x_2 = \frac{\begin{vmatrix} a_{11} & b_1 \\ a_{21} & b_2 \end{vmatrix}}{\begin{vmatrix} a_{11} & a_{12} \\ a_{21} & a_{22} \end{vmatrix}}$$

$$\begin{vmatrix} a_{11} & a_{12} \\ a_{21} & a_{22} \end{vmatrix} = (1 - a_{1J})\, a_{2J} - (1 - a_{2J})\, a_{1J} = a_{2J} - a_{1J}$$

$$x_1 = \frac{1}{a_{2J} - a_{1J}} \left[ ln\left(\frac{P_{1J}}{\beta_1}\right) a_{2J} - ln\,(\frac{P_{2J}}{\beta_2})\, a_{1J} \right]$$
$$x_2 = \frac{1}{a_{2J} - a_{1J}} \left[ ln\left(\frac{P_{2J}}{\beta_2}\right) (1 - a_{1J}) - ln\,(\frac{P_{1J}}{\beta_1})\, (1 - a_{2J}) \right]$$

which restated gives,

$$x_1 = ln\left[\left[\frac{P_{1J}}{\beta_1}\right]^{\frac{a_{2J}}{a_{2J}-a_{1J}}}\right] + ln\left[\left[\frac{P_{2J}}{\beta_2}\right]^{\frac{-a_{1J}}{a_{2J}-a_{1J}}}\right]$$

$$x_2 = ln\left[\left[\frac{P_{2J}}{\beta_2}\right]^{\frac{1-a_{1J}}{a_{2J}-a_{1J}}}\right] + ln\left[\left[\frac{P_{1J}}{\beta_1}\right]^{\frac{-(1-a_{2J})}{a_{2J}-a_{1J}}}\right]$$

which next by (23.140) gives,

$$w_J = e^{x_1} = \left[\frac{P_{1J}}{\beta_1}\right]^{\frac{a_{2J}}{a_{2J}-a_{1J}}} \left[\frac{P_{2J}}{\beta_2}\right]^{\frac{-a_{1J}}{a_{2J}-a_{1J}}}$$

$$r_J = e^{x_2} = \left[\frac{P_{2J}}{\beta_2}\right]^{\frac{1-a_{1J}}{a_{2J}-a_{1J}}} \left[\frac{P_{1J}}{\beta_1}\right]^{\frac{-(1-a_{2J})}{a_{2J}-a_{1J}}}$$

and restated as,

$$w_J = e^{x_1} = \beta_{1J}^{\frac{-a_{2J}}{a_{2J}-a_{1J}}} \beta_{2J}^{\frac{a_{1J}}{a_{2J}-a_{1J}}} P_{1J}^{\frac{a_{2J}}{a_{2J}-a_{1J}}} P_{2J}^{\frac{-a_{1J}}{a_{2J}-a_{1J}}}$$

$$r_J = e^{x_2} = \beta_{1J}^{\frac{1-a_{2J}}{a_{2J}-a_{1J}}} \beta_{2J}^{\frac{a_{1J}-1}{a_{2J}-a_{1J}}} P_{1J}^{\frac{a_{2J}-1}{a_{2J}-a_{1J}}} P_{2J}^{\frac{1-a_{1J}}{a_{2J}-a_{1J}}}$$

which is the *inverse* function (23.129–23.130).

### *Transformation Elasticity*

Jones (1965, p.41) and Jones (2002, p.585) gave an "*elasticity of substitution—$\boldsymbol{\sigma}_S$*—between commodities on the *supply* side (along the transformation schedule)", which can be written as (for sectoral substitution, $\sigma_1 = \sigma_2 = \sigma$):

$$\sigma_S = -1 + \frac{1}{|\lambda||\theta|}, \qquad \sigma = 1 \tag{23.141}$$

$$|\theta| = \epsilon_{L_{1J}} - \epsilon_{L_{2J}} = \epsilon_{K_{2J}} - \epsilon_{K_{1J}} = a_{2J} - a_{1J} \tag{23.142}$$

$$|\lambda| = \lambda_{L_1} - \lambda_{K_1} = \lambda_{K_2} - \lambda_{L_2} \tag{23.143}$$

Using (23.16) for CD ($\sigma = 1$) $\lambda_{K_1}$ gives,

$$|\lambda| = \lambda_{L_1} - \lambda_{K_1} = \lambda_{L_1} - \frac{A_J \cdot \lambda_{L_{1J}}}{1 + (A_J - 1)\,\lambda_{L_{1J}}} \tag{23.144}$$

$$|\lambda| = -\frac{\lambda_{L_1}(A_J - 1)(1 - \lambda_{L_{1J}})}{1 + (A_J - 1)\,\lambda_{L_{1J}}} \tag{23.145}$$

Then (23.145) and (23.142) give,

$$\sigma_S = -1 - \frac{1}{(a_{1J} - a_{2J}) \mid \lambda \mid} \tag{23.146}$$

$$\sigma_S = -1 + \frac{1}{a_{1J} - a_{2J}} \left[ \frac{1 + (A_J - 1)\lambda_{L_{1J}}}{\lambda_{L_{1J}}(1 - \lambda_{L_{1J}})(A_J - 1)} \right] \tag{23.147}$$

$$\sigma_S = -1 + \frac{1}{a_{1J} - a_{2J}} \left[ \frac{1 + 1/\left[ (A_J - 1)\, \lambda_{L_{1J}} \right]}{1 - \lambda_{L_{1J}}} \right] \tag{23.148}$$

The *transformation* elasticity ($\tau$) with CD technologies is seen, (23.47), as:

$$\tau = 1 - \frac{1}{a_{1J} - a_{2J}} \left[ \frac{1 + 1/\left[ (A_J - 1)\, \lambda_{L_{1J}} \right]}{1 - \lambda_{L_{1J}}} \right] \tag{23.149}$$

Thus, from these expressions follow the *equivalence*: $\boldsymbol{\sigma}_S = -\boldsymbol{\tau}$—such that $\boldsymbol{\sigma}_S$ is the *Relative Supply elasticity*, (23.48) of **RS** curves, as shown in Fig. 23.5c, F5–F7, F8–F9.

The *supply elasticity*—$\boldsymbol{\sigma}_S$—can be calculated as a "mirror", *reflection* of

$$\tau(p_J) = 1 - \frac{1}{a_{1J} - a_{2J}} \left[ \frac{1 + 1/\left[ (A_J - 1)\, \lambda_{L_{1J}}(p_J; k_J) \right]}{1 - \lambda_{L_{1J}}(p_J; k_J)} \right] < 0 \tag{23.150}$$

depicted in Fig. 23.5d.

## Explicit PPC and Revenue Function: $Y = R\,(P_1, P_2, L, K)$

### *Revenue Function: Pareto Efficient Allocations in Production*

The explicit transformation function or analytic production possibility frontier can give us an *explicit* **Revenue Function**: $Y_J = R_J\,(P_{1J}, P_{2J}, L_J, K_J)$—*Monetary National Product* = *Minimal Factor Incomes* = *Value Added*—cf. Feenstra (2016, p.6), Kohli (1991, p.36), Samuelson (1953–1954, p.3, 10):

$$Y_J = R_J\,(P_{1J}, P_{2J}, L_J, K_J) = C_J\,(w_J, r_J, Y_{1J}, Y_{2J}) = C_J, \quad J = A, B \tag{23.151}$$

$$= \max_{Y_{1J}, Y_{2J}} \{P_{1J} Y_{1J} + P_{2J} Y_{2J}\}, \; s.t. \; \widehat{T}_J(Y_{1J}, Y_{2J}; L_J, K_J) = 0 \tag{23.152}$$

$$= \min_{w_J, r_J} \{w_J L_J + r_J K_J\} = C_J, \; s.t. \; P_{iJ} = c_{iJ}(w_J, r_J) \; ; \quad i = 1, 2 \tag{23.153}$$

with $(\mathbf{Y_{1J}}, \mathbf{Y_{2J}})$ in (23.152) given by the *explicit*: $Y_{2J} = T_J(Y_{1J}; L_J, K_J)$, or by the *transformation* function $\widehat{T}_J(Y_{1J}, Y_{2J}; L_J, K_J) = 0$, (**PPC** in Theorems 23.1–23.5)—or in (23.153) by $(\mathbf{w_J}, \mathbf{r_J})$ satisfying the *minimal cost* Eqs. (23.121–23.123).

With *exogenous* prices $(\mathbf{P_{1J}}, \mathbf{P_{2J}})$, endowments $(\mathbf{L_J}, \mathbf{K_J})$, maximized *money value* of outputs $\mathbf{Y_J}$ (23.151) is a function *analytically* given by (23.22–23.23), (23.35):

$$Y_J \equiv P_{1J}Y_{1J} + P_{2J}Y_{2J} \;;\; Y_J = w_J(P_{1J}, P_{2J})L_J + r_J(P_{1J}, P_{2J})K_J \tag{23.154}$$

$$= P_{1J}\,H_1(\lambda_{L_{1J}}) + P_{2J}\,H_2(\lambda_{L_{1J}}) \tag{23.155}$$

$$= L_J\,[\, P_{1J}\,h_1\,(\lambda_{L_{1J}}(p_J\,;\,k_J)\,) + P_{2J}\,h_2\,(\lambda_{L_{1J}}(p_J\,;\,k_J))\,] \tag{23.156}$$

$$\equiv R_J\,(P_{1J}, P_{2J}, L_J, K_J) \equiv P_{2J}\,R_J\,(p_J, L_J, K_J) \equiv P_{2J}\,L_J\,\bar{R}_J\,(p_J, k_J) \tag{23.157}$$

$\mathbf{R_J}\,(\mathbf{P_{1J}}, \mathbf{P_{2J}}, \mathbf{L_J}, \mathbf{K_J})$ (23.157) is a nonnegative function of $(P_{1J}, P_{2J}, L_J, K_J)$ that is a *non-decreasing*, linearly homogeneous, *convex* function in $(P_{1J}, P_{2J})$, and a *non-decreasing*, linearly homogeneous, *concave* function in $(L_J, K_J)$.

Maximizing $\mathbf{Y_J}$ (23.152–23.153), a Pareto efficient economy (23.154–23.157) produces with *relative price*: $-p_J = -P_{1J}/P_{2J} = dY_{2J}/dY_{1J}$, (23.19). Hence, cf. (23.26):

$$E\,(Y_{2J}, Y_{1J}) \equiv \frac{dY_{2J}}{dY_{1J}}\frac{Y_{1J}}{Y_{2J}} = -\frac{P_{1J}Y_{1J}}{P_{2J}Y_{2J}} = -\frac{s_{1J}}{1 - s_{1J}} = -\frac{1 - a_{2J}}{1 - a_{1J}}\frac{\lambda_{L_{1J}}(p_J; k_J)}{1 - \lambda_{L_{1J}}(p_J; k_J)} \tag{23.158}$$

with $P_{1J}Y_{1J}/P_{2J}Y_{2J} = s_{1J}/s_{2J}$, where $\mathbf{s_{1J}} = \frac{P_{1J}Y_{1J}}{Y_J}$ is the *Revenue share* of good, $i = 1$, (23.152). Solving (23.158) for $\lambda_{L_{1J}}(p_J; k_J)$ gives,

$$s_{1J} = \frac{(1 - a_{2J})\,\lambda_{L_{1J}}(p_J; k_J)}{1 - a_{1J} + (a_{1J} - a_{2J})\lambda_{L_{1J}}(p_J; k_J)} \;;\quad \lambda_{L_{1J}}(p_J; k_J) = \frac{1 - a_{1J}}{\frac{1 - a_{2J}}{s_{1J}} + a_{2J} - a_{1J}} \tag{23.159}$$

Numerical **Revenue shares** $(s_{1J})$ follow with $\lambda_{L_{1J}}(p_J; k_J)$ from (23.35).

Anticipating here that $\lambda_{L_{1J}}(p_J; k_J)$, (23.159) corresponds to **GE** (23.203), if $\alpha_j$ is replaced by $\mathbf{s_{1J}}$. Similarly, by replacing $\alpha_j$ with $s_{1J}$ in (23.206), we get **macro factor shares** of *labor*, $\delta_{LJ} = \frac{w_J L_J}{Y_J}$, and *capital*, $\delta_{KJ} = \frac{r_J K_J}{Y_J}$, as :

$$\delta_{LJ} = 1 - a_{2J} + (a_{2J} - a_{1J})s_{1J}\,,\;\; \delta_{KJ} = a_{2J} - (a_{2J} - a_{1J})s_{1J}\,;\;\; J = A, B \tag{23.160}$$

From (23.159) and (23.160), we get,

$$\delta_{LJ}/s_{1J} = (1-a_{1J})/\lambda_{L_{1J}}(p_J;k_J) = (1-a_{2J})/s_{1J} + a_{2J} - a_{1J}\ ; \quad J = A, B \tag{23.161}$$

$$\delta_{KJ}/s_{1J} = \frac{a_{2J}(1-a_{1J}) + (a_{1J}-a_{2J})\lambda_{L_{1J}}(p_J;k_J)}{(1-a_{2J})\lambda_{L_{1J}}(p_J;k_J)} = a_{2J}/s_{1J} + a_{1J} - a_{2J} \tag{23.162}$$

Since an **explicit** Revenue function is seldom seen in the literature, we will give the **CD** *parametric* quantitative *form* of $\mathbf{R}_J\,(\mathbf{P}_{1J}, \mathbf{P}_{2J}, \mathbf{L}_J, \mathbf{K}_J)$, (23.157)—this explicit form of $\mathbf{R}_J$ is indeed behind the Hessian matrix (23.170) and the explicit elasticities below: (23.181–23.184).

We get $\mathbf{R}_J\,(\mathbf{P}_{1J}, \mathbf{P}_{2J}, \mathbf{L}_J, \mathbf{K}_J)$ by Theorems 23.1–23.2. Note from (23.35), (23.11):

$$(A_J - 1)\,\lambda_{L_{1J}}(p_J;k_J) = \frac{1-a_{2J}}{a_{2J}}\Big[\frac{\gamma_{1J}\,p_J}{\gamma_{2J}\,\bar{A}_J}\Big]^{\frac{1}{a_{1J}-a_{2J}}} k_J - 1 \tag{23.163}$$

By (23.163) and Theorem 23.1 with rewriting (23.22), we get **output** (supply),

$$Y_{1J} = L_J\gamma_{1J}\Big[\frac{A_J\,k_J}{1+(A_J-1)\lambda_{L_{1J}}}\Big]^{a_{1J}}\lambda_{L_{1J}} = L_J\gamma_{1J}\Big[\frac{a_{1J}}{1-a_{1J}}\Big]^{a_{1J}}\Big[\frac{\gamma_{1J}\,p_J}{\gamma_{2J}\,\bar{A}_J}\Big]^{\frac{-a_{1J}}{a_{1J}-a_{2J}}}\lambda_{L_{1J}} \tag{23.164}$$

that gives $Y_{1J}$—by inserting $\lambda_{L_{1J}}(p_J;k_J)$ from (23.35) of Theorem 23.2—as:

$$\begin{aligned} Y_{1J} &= \gamma_{1J}\frac{a_{1J}^{a_{1J}}(1-a_{1J})^{1-a_{1J}}}{a_{1J}-a_{2J}}\Big[\frac{\gamma_{1J}\,p_J}{\gamma_{2J}\,\bar{A}_J}\Big]^{\frac{-a_{1J}}{a_{1J}-a_{2J}}} \\ &\quad\times\Big[-a_{2J}L_J + (1-a_{2J})\Big[\frac{\gamma_{1J}\,p_J}{\gamma_{2J}\,\bar{A}_J}\Big]^{\frac{1}{a_{1J}-a_{2J}}} K_J\Big] \end{aligned} \tag{23.165}$$

Analogously from (23.23), (23.164), and inserting $\lambda_{L_{1J}}$ (23.35), we get **output**,

$$\begin{aligned} Y_{2J} &= \gamma_{2J}\frac{a_{2J}^{a_{2J}}(1-a_{2J})^{1-a_{2J}}}{a_{1J}-a_{2J}}\Big[\frac{\gamma_{1J}\,p_J}{\gamma_{2J}\,\bar{A}_J}\Big]^{\frac{-a_{2J}}{a_{1J}-a_{2J}}} \\ &\quad\times\Big[a_{1J}L_J - (1-a_{1J})\Big[\frac{\gamma_{1J}\,p_J}{\gamma_{2J}\,\bar{A}_J}\Big]^{\frac{1}{a_{1J}-a_{2J}}} K_J\Big] \end{aligned} \tag{23.166}$$

Thus, with $Y_{1J} = G_{1J}(p_J, L_J, K_J)$, $Y_{2J} = G_{2J}(p_J, L_J, K_J)$, in (23.165–23.166), the **Revenue** Function (23.157) is **explicitly** given by:

$$Y_J = R_J(P_{1J}, P_{2J}, L_J, K_J) = P_{1J}\, G_{1J}(p_J, L_J, K_J) + P_{2J}\, G_{2J}(p_J, L_J, K_J) \tag{23.167}$$

The **PPC** outputs, (23.165–23.166), are: **linearly** related to *Endowments*, $L_J$, $K_J$, **nonlinear** in *prices*, $P_{1J}$, $P_{2J}$, $p_J$ ; $\mathbf{Y_{1J}}$, $\mathbf{Y_{2J}}$, (23.165–23.166) are located on **PPC** of Figs. 23.4, 23.6, and 23.7. For $\tau(p_J)$ and $\tau(Y_{1J})$ along these PPC, see (23.194–23.195). In the special case of **fixed** *prices*, $(P_{1J}, P_{2J})$, **graphs** of **Revenue** function (23.167) are always **planes** in the positive octant of Space: $(Y_J, L_J, K_J)$.

### *Revenue Function: First-Order and Second-Order Derivatives*

The *monetary* function $\boldsymbol{Y_J}$ (23.154) of *Pareto efficient factor allocations* by the nonnegative, non-decreasing, convex-concave, explicit ***Revenue*** function, $\mathbf{R_J}$, (23.157), (23.167), has a **gradient** (vector) of the first-order derivatives,

$$\frac{\partial R_J(P_{1J}, P_{2J}, L_J, K_J)}{\partial (P_{1J}, P_{2J}, L_J, K_J)} = \left[\frac{\partial R_J}{\partial P_{1J}}, \frac{\partial R_J}{\partial P_{2J}}, \frac{\partial R_J}{\partial L_J}, \frac{\partial R_J}{\partial K_J}\right] = [\,Y_{1J}, Y_{2J}, w_J, r_J\,] \tag{23.168}$$

These *derivatives* $[\,Y_{1J}, Y_{2J}, w_J, r_J\,]$ are *solutions* of (23.152–23.153) by well-known **Shephard** *Duality Theorems*—and give by (23.168), (23.158), (23.160), *elasticities*:

$$E(R_J, P_{1J}) = s_{1J}\,,\;\; E(R_J, P_{2J}) = s_{2J}\,,\;\; E(R_J, L_J) = \delta_{LJ}\,,\;\; E(R_J, K_J) = \delta_{KJ} \tag{23.169}$$

The **Hessian matrix** of second-order derivatives of $\mathbf{R_J}$—containing *parametric information*, subsequently used in comparative static analyses—is:

$$\frac{\partial^2 R_J(P_{1J}, P_{2J}, L_J, K_J)}{\partial (P_{1J}, P_{2J}, L_J, K_J)^2} \equiv \begin{pmatrix} \frac{\partial^2 R_J}{\partial P_{1J}^2} & \frac{\partial^2 R_J}{\partial P_{1J}\partial P_{2J}} & \frac{\partial^2 R_J}{\partial P_{1J}\partial L_J} & \frac{\partial^2 R_J}{\partial P_{1J}\partial K_J} \\ \frac{\partial^2 R_J}{\partial P_{2J}\partial P_{1J}} & \frac{\partial^2 R_J}{\partial P_{2J}^2} & \frac{\partial^2 R_J}{\partial P_{2J}\partial L_J} & \frac{\partial^2 R_J}{\partial P_{2J}\partial K_J} \\ \frac{\partial^2 R_J}{\partial L_J\partial P_{1J}} & \frac{\partial^2 R_J}{\partial L_J\partial P_{2J}} & \frac{\partial^2 R_J}{\partial L_J^2} & \frac{\partial^2 R_J}{\partial L_J\partial K_J} \\ \frac{\partial^2 R_J}{\partial K_J\partial P_{1J}} & \frac{\partial^2 R_J}{\partial K_J\partial P_{2J}} & \frac{\partial^2 R_J}{\partial K_J\partial L_J} & \frac{\partial^2 R_J}{\partial K_J^2} \end{pmatrix} \tag{23.170}$$

$$= \begin{pmatrix} \frac{\partial Y_{1J}(P_{1J}, P_{2J}, L_J, K_J)}{\partial (P_{1J}, P_{2J}, L_J, K_J)} \\ \frac{\partial Y_{2J}(P_{1J}, P_{2J}, L_J, K_J)}{\partial (P_{1J}, P_{2J}, L_J, K_J)} \\ \frac{\partial w_J(P_{1J}, P_{2J}, L_J, K_J)}{\partial (P_{1J}, P_{2J}, L_J, K_J)} \\ \frac{\partial r_J(P_{1J}, P_{2J}, L_J, K_J)}{\partial (P_{1J}, P_{2J}, L_J, K_J)} \end{pmatrix} \equiv \begin{pmatrix} \frac{\partial Y_{1J}}{\partial P_{1J}} & \frac{\partial Y_{1J}}{\partial P_{2J}} & \frac{\partial Y_{1J}}{\partial L_J} & \frac{\partial Y_{1J}}{\partial K_J} \\ \frac{\partial Y_{2J}}{\partial P_{1J}} & \frac{\partial Y_{2J}}{\partial P_{2J}} & \frac{\partial Y_{2J}}{\partial L_J} & \frac{\partial Y_{2J}}{\partial K_J} \\ \frac{\partial w_J}{\partial P_{1J}} & \frac{\partial w_J}{\partial P_{2J}} & \frac{\partial w_J}{\partial L_J} & \frac{\partial w_J}{\partial K_J} \\ \frac{\partial r_J}{\partial P_{1J}} & \frac{\partial r_J}{\partial P_{2J}} & \frac{\partial r_J}{\partial L_J} & \frac{\partial r_J}{\partial K_J} \end{pmatrix} \tag{23.171}$$

$$\equiv \begin{pmatrix} \frac{\partial (Y_{1J}, Y_{2J})}{\partial (P_{1J}, P_{2J})} & \frac{\partial (Y_{1J}, Y_{2J})}{\partial (L_J, K_J)} \\ \frac{\partial (w_J, r_J)}{\partial (P_{1J}, P_{2J})} & \frac{\partial (w_J, r_J)}{\partial L_J, K_J)} \end{pmatrix} \tag{23.172}$$

$$\frac{\partial (Y_{1J}, Y_{2J})}{\partial (P_{1J}, P_{2J})} \neq 0 \; ; \; \frac{\partial (w_J, r_J)}{\partial (P_{1J}, P_{2J})} = \frac{\partial (Y_{1J}, Y_{2J})}{\partial (L_J, K_J)} \neq 0 \; ; \; \frac{\partial (w_J, r_J)}{\partial L_J, K_J)} = 0 \tag{23.173}$$

where (23.171) comes by (23.168), (23.170)—in (23.172–23.173) symbolized as Stolper-Samuelson *derivatives*, $\frac{\partial (w_J, r_J)}{\partial (P_{1J}, P_{2J})}$, Rybczynski *derivatives*, $\frac{\partial (Y_{1J}, Y_{2J})}{\partial (L_J, K_J)}$, terminology, Dixit and Norman (1980, p.54–55), Deardorff (2006, p.239, 257).

The **equality**: $\frac{\partial (w_J, r_J)}{\partial (P_{1J}, P_{2J})} = \frac{\partial (Y_{1J}, Y_{2J})}{\partial (L_J, K_J)}$, (23.173), is the ***reciprocity relations***, cf. (23.152–23.153), called "Samuelson *Duality* Theorem" in Leamer (1995, p.17). The derivatives, $\frac{\partial (w_J, r_J)}{\partial L_J, K_J)} = 0$, were called **FPE**, Factor Price Equality theorem (Core Theorem 4, cf. footnote 2). Here derivatives, $\frac{\partial (Y_{1J}, Y_{2J})}{\partial (P_{1J}, P_{2J})} \neq 0$, (23.173), will also be used below.

While the *first-order derivatives* (23.168) and hence (23.169) were always *positive*, the **second-order** *derivatives* (23.170–23.173) may be zero, and their signs may be *positive* or *negative*, cf. below (23.185) :

$$a_{1J} > a_{2J} \; : \; \frac{\partial Y_{1J}}{\partial L_J} = \frac{\partial w_J}{\partial P_{1J}} < 0 \; , \quad \frac{\partial Y_{2J}}{\partial L_J} = \frac{\partial w_J}{\partial P_{2J}} > 0 \tag{23.174}$$

$$a_{1J} > a_{2J} \; : \; \frac{\partial Y_{1J}}{\partial K_J} = \frac{\partial r_J}{\partial P_{1J}} > 0 \; , \quad \frac{\partial Y_{2J}}{\partial K_J} = \frac{\partial r_J}{\partial P_{2J}} < 0 \tag{23.175}$$

### ***Stolper-Samuelson Elasticities and Rybczynski Elasticities***

The *analytic Revenue* Function (23.167) will give quantitative expressions of the Stolper-Samuelson and Rybczynski **elasticities**—using *Reciprocity* (Symmetry) relations. The Stolper-Samuelson *derivatives* in (23.171–23.173) give the *nonzero impacts* of *product prices* $P_{iJ}$ upon factor prices, $w_J$ or $r_J$,

$$\frac{\partial w_J}{\partial P_{iJ}} \neq 0\,,\ \frac{\partial w_J}{\partial P_{iJ}}\frac{P_{iJ}}{w_J} \equiv E(w_J, P_{iJ})\ ;\ \frac{\partial r_J}{\partial P_{iJ}} \neq 0\,,\ \frac{\partial r_J}{\partial P_{iJ}}\frac{P_{iJ}}{r_J} \equiv E(r_J, P_{iJ}) \tag{23.176}$$

with corresponding Stolper-Samuelson *price elasticities* $E(\cdot)$ as stated, (23.176).

Rybczynski *derivatives* (23.171–23.173) give the nonzero *effect* of *endowment* changes $L_J$ or $K_J$ on outputs, $Y_{iJ}$:

$$\frac{\partial Y_{iJ}}{\partial L_J} \neq 0\,,\ \frac{\partial Y_{iJ}}{\partial L_J}\frac{L_J}{Y_{iJ}} \equiv E(Y_{iJ}, L_J)\ ;\ \frac{\partial Y_{iJ}}{\partial K_J} \neq 0\,,\ \frac{\partial Y_{iJ}}{\partial K_J}\frac{K_J}{Y_{iJ}} \equiv E(Y_{iJ}, K_J) \tag{23.177}$$

and formally corresponding Rybczynski *output elasticities* $E(\cdot)$ as in (23.177).

Thus, Stolper-Samuelson elasticities, (23.176), are obtained from the derivatives (23.168), (23.170–23.171) by using here the *Revenue* function (23.167)—giving the same result as the factor price elasticities known above (23.131–23.132):

$$E(w_J, P_{1J}) = \frac{\partial w_J}{\partial P_{1J}} \cdot \frac{P_{1J}}{w_J} = \frac{\partial^2 R_J}{\partial L_J\, \partial P_{1J}} \cdot \frac{P_{1J}}{\partial R_J/\partial L_J} = \frac{-\,a_{2J}}{a_{1J} - a_{2J}} \tag{23.178}$$

$$E(r_J, P_{1J}) = \frac{\partial r_J}{\partial P_{1J}} \cdot \frac{P_{1J}}{r_J} = \frac{\partial^2 R_J}{\partial K_J\, \partial P_{1J}} \cdot \frac{P_{1J}}{\partial R_J/\partial K_J} = \frac{1 - a_{2J}}{a_{1J} - a_{2J}} \tag{23.179}$$

The computer can verify (23.178–23.179) from derivations of (23.167), (23.165–23.166).

The Rybczynski elasticities, (23.177), are similarly obtained from the derivatives (23.168), (23.170–23.171) of *Revenue* function (23.167), for example,

$$E(Y_{1J}, L_J) = \frac{\partial Y_{1J}}{\partial L_J} \cdot \frac{L_J}{Y_{1J}} = \frac{\partial^2 R_J}{\partial P_{1J}\, \partial L_J} \cdot \frac{L_J}{\partial R_J/\partial P_{1J}} = \frac{-\,a_{2J}\,(1 - a_{2J})}{(a_{1J} - a_{2J})\, s_{1J}} + a_{2J} \tag{23.180}$$

where the last expression is seen in (23.181). In general, we can state:

**Theorem 23.6** *Rybczynski derivatives,* $\frac{\partial(Y_{1J}, Y_{2J})}{\partial(L_J, K_J)}$*, (23.171), become quantitative parametric Rybczynski output elasticities, using symmetric Hessian matrix, (23.170), (23.173), of the Revenue function,* $\mathbf{Y}_J = \mathbf{R}_J(\mathbf{P}_{1J}, \mathbf{P}_{2J}, \mathbf{L}_J, \mathbf{K}_J)$*, (23.157):*

$$E(Y_{1J}, L_J) \equiv \frac{-\,a_{2J}\,(1 - a_{1J})}{(a_{1J} - a_{2J})\,\lambda_{L_{1J}}(p_J; k_J)} \equiv \frac{-\,a_{2J}\,(1 - a_{2J})}{(a_{1J} - a_{2J})\, s_{1J}} + a_{2J} \tag{23.181}$$

$$E(Y_{2J}, L_J) \equiv \frac{a_{1J}(1 - a_{2J})}{(a_{1J} - a_{2J})[\lambda_{L_{1J}}(p_J; k_J)]} \equiv \frac{a_{1J}(1 - a_{1J})}{(a_{1J} - a_{2J})\, s_{2J}} + a_{1J} \tag{23.182}$$

$$E(Y_{1J}, K_J) \equiv 1 + \frac{a_{2J}(1 - a_{1J})}{(a_{1J} - a_{2J})\, \lambda_{L_{1J}}(p_J; k_J)} \equiv \frac{a_{2J}(1 - a_{2J})}{(a_{1J} - a_{2J})\, s_{1J}} + 1 - a_{2J} \tag{23.183}$$

$$E(Y_{2J}, K_J) \equiv 1 - \frac{a_{1J}(1 - a_{2J})}{(a_{1J} - a_{2J})[\lambda_{L_{1J}}(p_J; k_J)]} \equiv \frac{-a_{1J}(1 - a_{1J})}{(a_{1J} - a_{2J})\, s_{2J}} + 1 - a_{1J} \tag{23.184}$$

*Rybczynski elasticities, (23.181–23.184), in* $\boldsymbol{\lambda}_{L_{1J}}(\boldsymbol{p}_J; \boldsymbol{k}_J)$ *were derived in (23.54–23.57).*

*Elasticities (23.181–23.184) can be calculated by explicit formulas for outputs:* $Y_{1J} = G_{1J}(p_J, L_J, K_J)$, $Y_{2J} = G_{2J}(p_J, L_J, K_J)$, *in (23.165–23.167). Elasticities (23.181–23.184) come from Stolper-Samuelson Elasticities, (23.131–23.132), by using Revenue shares,* $s_{iJ}$, *(23.158), Macro factor shares,* $\delta_{LJ}$, $\delta_{KJ}$, *(23.161), (23.162):*

$$E(Y_{iJ}, L_J) = E(w_J, P_{iJ})\,\frac{\delta_{LJ}}{s_{iJ}}, \quad E(Y_{iJ}, K_J) = E(r_J, P_{iJ})\,\frac{\delta_{KJ}}{s_{iJ}};\ i = 1, 2 \tag{23.185}$$

***Proof*** The *correspondence* (23.185) follows as the consequences of the *equality* of the *derivatives* in (23.174–23.175):

$$\begin{aligned} &E(Y_{1J}, L_J) \\ &\equiv \frac{\partial Y_{1J}}{\partial L_J}\frac{L_J}{Y_{1J}} \Leftrightarrow \left[\frac{\partial Y_{1J}}{\partial L_J} = \frac{\partial w_J}{\partial P_{1J}}\right] \Leftrightarrow \frac{\partial w_J}{\partial P_{1J}}\frac{P_{1J}}{w_J}\frac{w_J}{P_{1J}}\frac{L_J}{Y_{1J}} \equiv E(w_J, P_{1J})\frac{\delta_{LJ}}{s_{1J}} \\ &\equiv \frac{-a_{2J}}{a_{1J} - a_{2J}}\left(\frac{1 - a_{2J}}{s_{1J}} + a_{2J} - a_{1J}\right) \equiv \frac{-a_{2J}(1 - a_{2J})}{(a_{1J} - a_{2J})s_{1J}} + a_{2J} \end{aligned} \tag{23.186}$$

that is, (23.186) comes by using $\frac{\delta_{LJ}}{s_{1J}}$ of (23.161); (23.186) is (23.181).

$$\begin{aligned} E(Y_{2J}, L_J) &\equiv \frac{\partial Y_{2J}}{\partial L_J}\frac{L_J}{Y_{2J}} \Leftrightarrow \left[\frac{\partial Y_{2J}}{\partial L_J} = \frac{\partial w_J}{\partial P_{2J}}\right] \Leftrightarrow \frac{\partial w_J}{\partial P_{2J}}\frac{P_{2J}}{w_J}\frac{w_J}{P_{2J}}\frac{L_J}{Y_{2J}} \\ &\equiv E(w_J, P_{2J})\frac{\delta_{LJ}}{s_{2J}} \\ &\equiv \frac{a_{1J}}{a_{1J} - a_{2J}}\left(\frac{1 - a_{1J}}{s_{2J}} + a_{1J} - a_{2J}\right) \equiv \frac{a_{1J}(1 - a_{1J})}{(a_{1J} - a_{2J})\, s_{2J}} + a_{1J} \end{aligned} \tag{23.187}$$

that is, (23.187) comes by using $\frac{\delta_{LJ}}{s_{2J}}$ from amending (23.161); (23.187) is (23.182).

$$E(Y_{1J}, K_J) \equiv \frac{\partial Y_{1J}}{\partial K_J}\frac{K_J}{Y_{1J}} \Leftrightarrow \left[\frac{\partial Y_{1J}}{\partial K_J} = \frac{\partial r_J}{\partial P_{1J}}\right] \Leftrightarrow \frac{\partial r_J}{\partial P_{1J}}\frac{P_{1J}}{r_J}\frac{r_J}{P_{1J}}\frac{K_J}{Y_{1J}} \equiv E(r_J, P_{1J})\frac{\delta_{KJ}}{s_{1J}}$$
$$\equiv \frac{1-a_{2J}}{a_{1J}-a_{2J}}\left(\frac{a_{2J}}{s_{1J}} + a_{1J} - a_{2J}\right) \equiv \frac{a_{2J}(1-a_{2J})}{(a_{1J}-a_{2J})s_{1J}} + 1 - a_{2J} \quad (23.188)$$

that is, (23.188) comes by using $\frac{\delta_{KJ}}{s_{1J}}$ of (23.162); (23.188) is (23.183).

$$E(Y_{2J}, K_J) \equiv \frac{\partial Y_{2J}}{\partial K_J}\frac{K_J}{Y_{2J}} \Leftrightarrow \left[\frac{\partial Y_{2J}}{\partial K_J} = \frac{\partial r_J}{\partial P_{2J}}\right] \Leftrightarrow \frac{\partial r_J}{\partial P_{2J}}\frac{P_{2J}}{r_J}\frac{r_J}{P_{2J}}\frac{K_J}{Y_{2J}}$$
$$\equiv E(r_J, P_{2J})\frac{\delta_{KJ}}{s_{2J}}$$
$$\equiv \frac{-(1-a_{1J})}{a_{1J}-a_{2J}}\left(\frac{a_{1J}}{s_{2J}} + a_{2J} - a_{1J}\right) \equiv \frac{-a_{1J}(1-a_{1J})}{(a_{1J}-a_{2J})s_{2J}} + 1 - a_{2J} \quad (23.189)$$

that is, (23.189) comes by using $\frac{\delta_{KJ}}{s_{2J}}$ from amending (23.162); (23.189) is (23.184). □

Rybczynski *comparative statics* ($L_J, K_J$), (23.181–23.184), reflect *shifting* of **PPC** (23.22–23.23), (23.63), in Figs. 23.4, 23.6, 23.7; and (23.181–23.184) correspond to *horizontal movements* in Fig. 23.5a–b (at *any* selected exogenous, $p_J, P_{1J}, P_{2J}$).

Standard texts, Dixit and Norman (1980, p.55), with usual qualitative **PPC** diagrams only give *inequalities* and *signs* for the *effects* of the factor endowment changes (23.181–23.184). Stolper-Samuelson and Rybczynski Elasticities[20] are **"Producer Equilibrium"** (Pareto efficient factor allocations)[21] results *without* consumer *demand* (utility-preference) functions being *involved* in the market clearing (*equilibrium*) of the *factor* and *commodity* markets.

Despite the expansions and contractions of *outputs* by (23.181–23.184), the *monetary Revenue amounts*, $\mathbf{Y}_J$ (23.154), always *increase* with *larger factor endowments*—evident by the last two *positive* elements, $\delta_{LJ}, \delta_{KJ}$, of (23.169).

[20] On *empirical* Stolper-Samuelson-, Rybczynski Elasticities with various *Revenue* (GDP) functions on US data, see Kohli (1991, p.133, p.137, p.169, p.173, p.183, p.206, p.222), and Harrigan (1997, p.478, 488). See Gundlach (2007), Gundlach and Becker (2007).

[21] Core Theorems 1–4 were in note 2 seen as being core of "general equilibrium trade theory". However, Core Theorems 1–4 do not provide, for example, General (Walrasian) Equilibrium (GE) output results of Endowment changes, see (8.12–8.13).

### *Second-Order Factor Partial Derivatives of $R_J$ ($P_{1J}$, $P_{2J}$, $L_J$, $K_J$)*

Partial derivatives, $\frac{\partial^2 R_J(P_{1J}, P_{2J}, L_J, K_J)}{\partial(L_J, K_J)^2} = \frac{\partial(w_J, r_J)}{\partial L_J, K_J)} = 0$, in (23.170–23.173) imply of course the zero elasticities: $E(w_J, L_J) = 0$, $E(w_J, K_J) = 0$, $E(r_J, L_J) = 0$, $E(r_J, K_J) = 0$. All these particular zero elasticities follow simply from always having *unchanged prices* of both *factors* and *outputs* along any **horizontal** *movements* [ by $\boldsymbol{\lambda}_{L_{1J}}(\boldsymbol{p}_J; \boldsymbol{k}_J)$, (23.35–23.36), with *endowment* $k_J = K_J/L_J$ *variations* ] **in** Fig. 23.5a–b.

When the *output price ratio*, $p_J = P_{1J}/P_{2J}$, is assumed *exogenously* fixed—for any Revenue functions, $R_J$ ($P_{1J}$, $P_{2J}$, $L_J$, $K_J$)—so is also thereby the *factor price ratio*, $\omega_J = w_J/r_J$, exogenously *fixed* by (23.33) or (23.126)—irrespective of whatever changes are made in $L_J$ or $K_J$, that is, $\frac{\partial(w_J, r_J)}{\partial L_J, K_J)} = 0$. ( *Leontief fixed* coefficients, *implicitly* imposed by *fixed*, $p_J = P_{1J}/P_{2J}$.)

That the *second-order* derivatives are always *zero*, $\frac{\partial^2 R_J(P_{1J}, P_{2J}, L_J, K_J)}{\partial(L_J, K_J)^2} = 0$, is clearly seen from our *explicit* (elaborate) $R_J$ ($P_{1J}$, $P_{2J}$, $L_J$, $K_J$) *plane* expression (23.165–23.167)—*linear* in the *endowments* of ($L_J$, $K_J$). These zero *derivative implications* of (23.167) that changes in factor supplies (endowments) have no effects on factor prices (*if* commodity prices are constant) has been called[22] "*factor price 'equalization'*" or "*factor price insensitivity*" theorem.

The result, $\frac{\partial^2 R_J(P_{1J}, P_{2J}, L_J, K_J)}{\partial(L_J, K_J)^2} = \frac{\partial(w_J, r_J)}{\partial L_J, K_J)} = 0$, (23.170), (23.173), follows economically from nothing but having Pareto efficient factor reallocation of *two mobile* factors with *homogeneous* (constant returns to scale) *production/cost* functions in *both* sectors. The *endowment invariance* of the **MRT-MRS** *relation* $\boldsymbol{p}_J = \boldsymbol{\Phi}_J(\boldsymbol{\omega}_J)$, (23.33), is again—via *reciprocity* relations [ *duality* interpretations of $\boldsymbol{Y}_J$, (23.151), (23.152–23.153), (23.154) ]—*showing* up in the *second-order* **factor** *partial* derivatives of the *Revenue* function[23] as ***being zero***. The details of the *output* effects and *price invariance* results of ($L_J$, $K_J$) variations were stated in Theorems 23.4 and 23.2—and the *relative* price (cost) functions (23.126) within the *domain*, (23.128).

### *Revenue Function, Output Prices, Transformation Elasticities*

The *price derivatives*, $\frac{\partial(Y_{1J}, Y_{2J})}{\partial(P_{1J}, P_{2J})} \neq 0$, (23.171–23.172), have received less attention (**not** included in *Core Theorems*, footnotes 2–4); here the *analytical use* of the *price elasticities* of *outputs* (supply) $E(Y_{iJ}, P_{jJ})$ *will* be demonstrated.

[22] Core Theorem 4 in footnote 2 was called "factor price insensitivity" or "derived factor demands are infinitely elastic" by Leamer (1995, p.17, 42). Feenstra (2016, p.8) has: Lemma ("factor price insensitivity").

[23] A general property of Revenue functions having: $\frac{\partial^2 R_J(P_{1J}, P_{2J}, L_J, K_J)}{\partial(L_J, K_J)^2} = 0$, is evidently important in choosing a proper functional form for $R_J(P_{1J}, P_{2J}, L_J, K_J)$, with the homogeneity restrictions; cf. Feenstra (2016, p.61–66), where *linearity* in $L_J$, $K_J$, often directly occur with "non-jointness in input quantities" (homogeneous distinct industry production functions), which applies to $\mathbf{R}_J$ (23.167) with the CD **PPC** outputs (23.165–23.166).

For *given* endowments $(L_J, K_J)$, partial *variations* of the *prices* correspond geometrically—like Stolper-Samuelson derivatives—to **vertical** movements in Fig. 23.5a–b and *movements along* **PPC** of Theorem 23.1. We give here an alternative *link-up* to **VET** *transformation elasticity* (23.45–23.48):

**Theorem 23.7** *From* Theorems 23.1–23.2, *we have from (23.22–23.23), (23.35):*

$$Y_{iJ} = H_i(\lambda_{L_{1J}}) = L_J h_i(\lambda_{L_{1J}}) = L_J h_i[\lambda_{L_{1J}}(p_J ; k_J)] \equiv G_i(p_J ; L_J, K_J) \tag{23.190}$$

$$Y_{1J} = G_{1J}(p_J ; L_J, K_J), \quad p_J = G_{1J}^{-1}(Y_{1J}) ; \quad Y_{2J} = G_{2J}(p_J ; L_J, K_J) \tag{23.191}$$

*with the explicit* $G_{1J}(p_J ; L_J, K_J)$ *and* $G_{2J}(p_J ; L_J, K_J)K_J)$ *in (23.165–23.166).*

*Hessian matrix elements* $\frac{\partial(Y_{1J}, Y_{2J})}{\partial(P_{1J}, P_{2J})}$, *(23.171–23.172), of* **Revenue Function,** $Y_J = R_J(P_{1J}, P_{2J}, L_J, K_J)$, *(23.167), are used to get* **transformation** *elasticity* $(\tau)$, *(23.69), between outputs* $Y_{1J}$ *and* $Y_{2J}$, *cf. Diewert (1974, p.144):*

$$\tau(p_J) = E\left(\frac{Y_{2J}}{Y_{1J}}, \frac{dY_{2J}}{dY_{1J}}\right) = \frac{Y_J \frac{\partial^2 R_J(P_{1J}, P_{2J}, L_J, K_J)}{\partial P_{1J}\,\partial P_{2J}}}{\frac{\partial R_J(P_{1J}, P_{2J}, L_J, K_J)}{\partial P_{1J}} \frac{\partial R_J(P_{1J}, P_{2J}, L_J, K_J)}{\partial P_{2J}}} \tag{23.192}$$

$$= \frac{Y_J \frac{\partial Y_{2J}}{\partial P_{1J}}}{Y_{1J}\,Y_{2J}} = \frac{Y_J \frac{\partial Y_{2J}}{\partial P_{1J}} \frac{P_{1J}}{Y_{2J}}}{P_{1J} Y_{1J}} \equiv \frac{E(Y_{2J}, P_{1J})}{s_{1J}} = \frac{E(Y_{2J}, p_J)}{s_{1J}} \tag{23.193}$$

$$= \frac{E\,(Y_{2J}(p_J ; L_J, K_J), \, p_J)}{s_{1J}(p_J ; L_J, K_J)} \equiv \frac{E\,(G_{2J}(p_J ; L_J, K_J), \, p_J)}{s_{1J}(p_J ; L_J, K_J)} \tag{23.194}$$

$s_{1J}(p_J ; L_J, K_J)$ *is in (23.159), (23.35).* $E\,(G_{2J}(p_J; L_J, K_J), p_J)$ *follows by (23.191).* $\tau(p_J)$, $s_{1J}(p_J ; L_J, K_J)$, *and* $E(Y_{2J}, p_J)$, *(23.194), have price domain: (23.39).*

$$\tau \equiv E\left(\frac{Y_{2J}}{Y_{1J}}, \frac{dY_{2J}}{dY_{1J}}\right) = \tau(p_J) ; \;\; p_J = G_{1J}^{-1}(Y_{1J}) \; : \; \tau(Y_{1J}) = \tau\left[G_{1J}^{-1}(Y_{1J})\right] \tag{23.195}$$

***$\tau(Y_{1J})$** is obtained from **$\tau(p_J)$**, (23.194), using the inverse function in (23.191).*

Although $\tau(p_J)$[24] and $\tau(Y_{1J})$ formulas (23.193–23.195) look a bit complex, *cross-price elasticity of output* (supply), $E(Y_{2J}, P_{1J}) = E(Y_{2J}, p_J)$, (23.194), (23.191) is easily calculated by a computer in relevant *price intervals* (23.39).

[24] $\tau(p_J) = E(\frac{Y_{2J}}{Y_{1J}}, \frac{dY_{2J}}{dY_{1J}}) = E(\frac{Y_{2J}}{Y_{1J}}, p_J) = E(Y_{2J}, p_J) - E(Y_{1J}, p_J)$ by (23.165–23.166), (23.191). On empirical supply price elasticities, see Kohli (1991, p.133, 137).

Hence, the reader can also verify (as we have done) that $\boldsymbol{\tau}(\boldsymbol{Y}_{1J})$, (23.195), *exactly reproduce* the **VET** elasticities $\tau(Y_{1J})$ as *shown* in Fig. 23.8a–b for **PPC**, Figs. 23.4, 23.6, and 23.7.

## General Equilibrium, Comparative Cost, and Trade Patterns

### *General Equilibrium of Autarky*

The production possibility curves (**PPC**) only represent *Pareto efficient production* (supply side) of an economy. General equilibrium (**GE**) includes *demand* by **utility** functions—here homothetic and with CD parameter ($\alpha_J$):

$$u_J = U_J(Y_{1J}, Y_{2J}) = Y_{1J}^{\alpha_J} Y_{2J}^{1-\alpha_J}\ ; \quad \frac{dY_{2J}}{dY_{1J}} = \frac{\partial U_J/\partial Y_{1J}}{\partial U_J/\partial Y_{2J}} = \frac{\alpha_J}{1-\alpha_J}\frac{Y_{2J}}{Y_{1J}} = \widetilde{MRS} \tag{23.196}$$

In **GE**: $MRT = \widetilde{MRS}$. In case of **Ex. 1**, (23.60), it means with (23.196) that: $\frac{Y_{2J}}{Y_{1J}} = \frac{\alpha_J}{1-\alpha_J}\frac{Y_{2J}}{Y_{1J}}$. Hence, inserting into PPF, (23.19), (23.26) and rearrangement yields in this case the **GE size** of $\lambda_{L_{1J}}$:

$$\textbf{Ex.1} \quad \textbf{GE}: \lambda_{L_{1J}} = \alpha_J\ ; \qquad J = A, B \tag{23.197}$$

Theorems 23.1 and 23.5, **Ex.2**, (23.63)—combined with (23.196)—restrict similarly by (23.19), (23.26), the **GE size** of $\lambda_{L_{1J}}$ as,

$$MRT = \frac{\lambda_{L_{1J}}}{1-\lambda_{L_{1J}}}\frac{1-a_{2J}}{1-a_{1J}}\frac{Y_{2J}}{Y_{1J}} = \frac{\alpha_J}{1-\alpha_J}\frac{Y_{2J}}{Y_{1J}} = \widetilde{MRS}\ ; \quad J = A, B \tag{23.198}$$

Solving **GE** condition (23.198) for $\lambda_{L_{1J}}$ gives generally explicit *sizes* of $\lambda_{L_{1J}}$:

$$\textbf{GE}: \lambda_{L_{1J}} = \frac{\alpha_J(1-a_{1J})}{1-\bar{\beta}_J}\ ; \qquad 0 < \bar{\beta}_J \equiv a_{2J} - \alpha_j(a_{2J} - a_{1J}) < 1 \tag{23.199}$$

$\boldsymbol{\lambda}_{L_{1J}}$ (23.199) locates the **GE points** on *any* curve in Figs. 23.1, 23.2, 23.3, 23.4, 23.5, and 23.6. Thus, the **GE** factor allocations (23.199) satisfy *factor market clearing* of (23.2), and we can always provide the key relations and curves of *production optimum* (Paretian efficient allocation), Theorem 23.2, with the proper **GE** *points* (**E**), $(\omega_J, k_J)$, in Fig. 23.5a–b—by proceeding as follows with (23.2), (23.11), (23.27), (23.199):

$$\begin{aligned} k_J &= \lambda_{L_{1J}} k_{1J}(\omega_J) + (1 - \lambda_{L_{1J}}) k_{2J}(\omega_J) = [1 + \lambda_{L_{1J}} (A_J - 1)] k_{2J}(\omega_J) \\ &= \left[1 + \frac{\alpha_J(1 - a_{1J})}{1 - \bar{\beta}_J}(A_J - 1)\right] \frac{a_{2J}}{1 - a_{2J}} \omega_J \ ; \quad J = A, B \\ &= \frac{a_{2J} - \alpha_j(a_{2J} - a_{1J})}{1 - a_{2J} + \alpha_j(a_{2J} - a_{1J})} \omega_J \equiv \frac{\bar{\beta}_J}{1 - \bar{\beta}_J} \omega_J \equiv \Psi_J(\omega_J) \end{aligned} \tag{23.200}$$

$$\omega_J = \Psi_J^{-1}(k_J) = \frac{1 - \bar{\beta}_J}{\bar{\beta}_J} k_J = \frac{1 - a_{2J} + \alpha_j(a_{2J} - a_{1J})}{a_{2J} - \alpha_j(a_{2J} - a_{1J})} k_J \ ; \ J = A, B \tag{23.201}$$

**GE** formula (23.200) could also be obtained by "Pareto" $\boldsymbol{\lambda}_{L_{1J}}$ (23.29) and (23.199).

The **GE** linear expressions, $k_J = \Psi_J(\omega_J)$, (23.200), and $\omega_J = \Psi_J^{-1}(k_J)$, (23.201) have elasticity, $E(\omega_J, k_J) = 1$, for *all parameters* and for *any endowment ratio* $k_J$ (23.2). Thus, (23.200–23.201)[25] represent all explicit CD **autarky** (closed economy) **GE loci**, $k_J = \Psi_J(\omega_J)$—and they are exhibited[26] in Fig. 23.5a–b for *two* particular important parameter classes.

The *autarky* **GE** solution (size) of relative commodity prices, $p_J = p_J(k_J)$, in country J, becomes—by $p_J = \Phi_J(\omega_J)$, (23.33), and $\omega_J = \Psi_J^{-1}(k_J)$, (23.201):

$$p_J(k_J) = \frac{\gamma_{2J}}{\gamma_{1J}} \bar{A}_J \left[\frac{1 - \bar{\beta}_J}{\bar{\beta}_J} k_J\right]^{a_{2J} - a_{1J}} = \frac{\gamma_{2J}}{\gamma_{1J}} \bar{A}_J \left[\frac{1 - a_{2J} + \alpha_j(a_{2J} - a_{1J})}{a_{2J} - \alpha_j(a_{2J} - a_{1J})} k_J\right]^{a_{2J} - a_{1J}} \tag{23.202}$$

Recalling $\bar{A}_J$, (23.32), (23.126), $p_J(k_J)$ is a large and comprehensive parametric formula—but (23.202) is the **foundation** of **comparative advantage** (cost).

The **GE** size of $\lambda_{L_{1J}}$ was given in (23.199)—restated here with $\lambda_{K_{1J}}$ (23.16) as,

$$\lambda_{L_{1J}} = \frac{1 - a_{1J}}{(1 - a_{2J})/\alpha_J + a_{2J} - a_{1J}} \ ; \ \lambda_{K_{1J}} = \frac{a_{1J}}{a_{2J}/\alpha_J + a_{1J} - a_{2J}} \ ; \ J = A, B \tag{23.203}$$

[25] The **Walrasian GE** *Factor endowment-Factor price* **locus**: $k = \Psi(\omega)$, has its background in economic growth theory, cf. Uzawa (1961–63, p.43), Jensen (2003, p.64, Chap. 17, p. 490).

Note here that $\omega_J = [(1 - \bar{\beta}_J)/\bar{\beta}_J] k_J$, (23.201), comes directly from (23.18) by GE $\lambda_{L_{1J}}$ (23.199).

[26] The **panels** of Fig. 23.5a–b summarize the **four-way connections** between goods prices, factor prices, sector factor ratios, and endowment ratios—a diagram, which *except* for the **GE locus**, was introduced by Samuelson (1949, p.188), and is now familiar in texts at all levels. But their displayed graphics of these curves are *only qualitative* and often incoherent (especially, the *left panel can never* have straight lines for the relative prices).

Figure 23.5a–b are rigorously extended to **CES** sector technologies in Jensen (2003, p.61, Chap. 17, p. 496, and Fig. 17.1).

which are both endowment ($k_J$) invariant. Moreover, we see that a larger consumer **preference** (23.196) for **good 1** ($\alpha_J$) will by (23.203) imply larger fractions of **both** $\lambda_{L_{1J}}$ and $\lambda_{K_{1J}}$—whatever the sizes of $a_{1J}$ and $a_{2J}$ might be.

*Factor shares* (relative remunerations, factor imputations) of labor and capital, $\delta_{LJ}, \delta_{KJ}$, in Pareto efficient production are obtained by (23.29) as:

$$\frac{\delta_{LJ}}{\delta_{KJ}} = \frac{\partial F_{iJ}/\partial L_{iJ}}{\partial F_{iJ}/\partial K_{iJ}} \cdot \frac{L_J}{K_J} = \frac{MRS}{K_J/L_J} = \frac{\omega_J}{k_J} = \frac{1-a_{2J}}{a_{2J}} \frac{1}{1+(A_J-1)\lambda_{L_{1J}}} \tag{23.204}$$

$$\delta_{LJ} = \frac{1-a_{2J}}{1+a_{2J}(A_J-1)\lambda_{L_{1J}}}, \quad \delta_{KJ} = 1-\delta_{LJ}\ ; \quad J = A, B \tag{23.205}$$

Factor shares $\delta_{LJ}$—for a given $k_J$—follow $\omega_J$ from A to B, Fig. 23.5a–b. But the **GE** sizes of $\delta_{LJ}, \delta_{KJ}$ are derived by (23.205), (23.203), (23.11), and become:

$$\delta_{LJ} = 1 - a_{2J} + \alpha_j(a_{2J} - a_{1J}) > 0\ ; \quad \delta_{KJ} = a_{2J} - \alpha_j(a_{2J} - a_{1J}) = \bar{\beta}_J \tag{23.206}$$

which are *endowment* ($k_J$) *invariant* in Cobb-Douglas **GE** economies.

The **GE sector outputs**, $Y_{iJ}(k_J)$, in *country* A and B are given by, (23.6), (23.27), (23.33), (23.199), (23.201), (23.206) :

$$\begin{aligned} Y_{1J} &= L_J \lambda_{L_{1J}} \gamma_{1J} \left[ k_{1J}[\omega_J(k_J)] \right]^{a_{1J}} \\ &= L_J \gamma_{1J} \frac{\alpha_J(1-a_{1J})}{1-\bar{\beta}_J} \left[ \frac{a_{1J}}{1-a_{1J}} \frac{1-\bar{\beta}_J}{\bar{\beta}_J} k_J \right]^{a_{1J}} \\ &= \gamma_{1J}\alpha_J \left[ \frac{a_{1J}^{a_{1J}}(1-a_{1J})^{1-a_{1J}}}{\bar{\beta}_J^{a_{1J}}(1-\bar{\beta}_J)^{1-a_{1J}}} \right] L_J^{1-a_{1J}} K_J^{a_{1J}} \equiv Y_{1J}(L_J K_J) \\ &\equiv L_J Y_{1J}(k_J) \end{aligned} \tag{23.207}$$

$$\begin{aligned} Y_{2J} &= L_J \lambda_{L_{2J}} \gamma_{2J} \left[ k_{2J}[\omega_J(k_J)] \right]^{a_{2J}} \\ &= L_J \gamma_{2J} \frac{[1-\alpha_J][1-a_{2J}]}{1-\bar{\beta}_J} \left[ \frac{a_{2J}}{1-a_{2J}} \frac{1-\bar{\beta}_J}{\bar{\beta}_J} k_J \right]^{a_{2J}} \\ &= \gamma_{2J}(1-\alpha_J) \left[ \frac{a_{2J}^{a_{2J}}(1-a_{2J})^{1-a_{2J}}}{\bar{\beta}_J^{a_{2J}}(1-\bar{\beta}_J)^{1-a_{2J}}} \right] L_J^{1-a_{2J}} K_J^{a_{2J}} \equiv L_J Y_{2J}(k_J) \end{aligned} \tag{23.208}$$

$$\frac{Y_{2J}}{Y_{1J}} = \frac{\gamma_{2J}}{\gamma_{1J}} \bar{A}_J \frac{1-\alpha_J}{\alpha_J} \left[ \frac{1-\bar{\beta}_J}{\bar{\beta}_J} k_J \right]^{a_{2J}-a_{1J}} \equiv Q_J(k_J) \tag{23.209}$$

$$Y_J = V_J(L_J, K_J) \equiv P_{2J} L_J [\, p_J(k_J) Y_{1J}(k_J) + Y_{2J}(k_J) \,] \equiv P_{2J} L_J \bar{V}_J(k_J) \tag{23.210}$$

$$Y_J = V_J(L_J, K_J) = P_{2J} L_J \bar{V}_J(k_J) = P_{2J} L_J \Theta_J k_J^{a_{2J}} \quad ; \quad \frac{y_J}{P_{2J}} = \Theta_J k_J^{a_{2J}} \tag{23.211}$$

$$\Theta_J = \frac{\gamma_{2J}}{\bar{\beta}_J^{a_{2J}}(1-\bar{\beta}_J)^{1-a_{2J}}}\left[\alpha_J a_{1J}^{a_{1J}}(1-a_{1J})^{1-a_{1J}} + (1-\alpha_J) a_{2J}^{a_{2J}}(1-a_{2J})^{1-a_{2J}}\right] \tag{23.212}$$

Both **GE outputs**, $Y_{iJ}$, (23.207–23.208)—through Endowment *shifting* **PPC** with factor allocation (23.199)—**increase nonlinearly** with larger $\mathbf{L_J}$ or $\mathbf{K_J}$ for **any size** of: $\gamma_{1J}, \gamma_{2J}, a_{1J}, a_{2J}, \alpha_j$. Thus, **GE** formulas (23.207–23.208) sharply **contrast PPC** outputs—**PPC** of $Y_{1J}(p_J, L_J, K_J), Y_{2J}(p_J, L_J, K_J)$, (23.165–23.166), and the *Rybczynski elasticities*, (23.181–23.184)—implied by the **Revenue** *function*, $\mathbf{R_J}(P_{1J}, P_{2J}, L_J, K_J)$, (23.151), (23.157), (23.167), and its *Hessian* matrix (23.170–23.173).

The **GE** elasticity, $E(p_J, k_J) = a_{2J} - a_{1J}$, (23.202), that is, **GE** *relative* output **prices**, $p_J(k_J)$, (23.202), always **changes** with *Endowments* $k_J$ along the GE *locus* (23.200–23.201)—in contrast to **horizontal** $k_J$ movements for the Rybczynski elasticities in Theorem 23.4. The *Rybczynski theorem* does **not** hold in **GE**.

The explicit **GE Value-Added** (money) function, $\mathbf{V_J}(\mathbf{L_J}, \mathbf{K_J})$, (23.210), is accordingly *much different* from **Revenue** functions, $R_J(P_{1J}, P_{2J}, L_J, K_J)$, (23.167), that were **linear** in Endowments, whereas **GE**, $Y_{iJ}$ (23.207–23.208) are *nonlinear* CD forms in Endowments—and so is **GE**, $Y_J$, (23.210), due to **GE** form of $p_J(k_J)$, (23.202). Moreover, collecting the elements of (23.210), we get **GE** formula (23.211)—with *composite* Cobb-Douglas **parameter** $\Theta_J$, (23.212).

Graphs of **GE** outputs/per capita $Y_{1J}(k_J), Y_{2J}(k_J)$, (23.207–23.208), and/or **GE** output *ratio*, $Q_J(k_J)$, (23.209), may be shown in a 4.*quadrant* to Fig. 23.5a–b.

### *Autarky GE Prices, Comparative Cost, Trade Patterns*

Economic theory governing trade between two countries dawned in Adam Smith's discussions of restraints upon the importation from foreign countries of goods that can be produced at home.[27] By scrutinizing the principle of *cheapness*

[27] Smith (1776, 1961, p.478):

> What is prudence in the conduct of every private family, can scarcely be folly in that of a great kingdom. If a *foreign* country can supply us with a commodity *cheaper* than we ourselves can make it, better *buy* [import] it from them *with* some *part* [export] of the produce of our *own industry*, employed [produced] in a way in which we have some *advantage*.

**Table 23.1** Structural parameters (23.6), (23.121), (23.196); Exogenous Variables

| Structural parameters | | | Exogenous variables |
|---|---|---|---|
| Technology | | Preference | Endowments |
| Parameters | | Parameters | |
| Total Factor Productivity | Factor Intensity | | |
| $\gamma_{iJ} > 0$ | $0 \leq a_{iJ} \leq 1$ | $0 \leq \alpha_J \leq 1$ | $K_J, L_J$ |
| $i = 1, 2$ | $i = 1, 2$ | | $k_J = K_J/L_J$ |
| $J = A, B$ | $J = A, B$ | $J = A, B$ | $J = A, B$ |

**Table 23.2** Determinants of Trade Patterns—Elements of Standard Model

| | Models | Technology | Endowments | Preferences |
|---|---|---|---|---|
| I | Ricardo | x | | |
| II | Mill | | | x |
| III | Marshall | x | | x |
| IV | Heckscher-Ohlin (HO) | x | x | |
| V | Heckscher-Ohlin-Linder (HOL) | | x | x |
| VI | Heckscher-Ohlin-Samuelson (HOS) | | x | |
| VII | Standard Model | x | x | x |

and advantage in more detail with some illustrations, Ricardo came up with the law of *comparative advantage*.[28] Anecdotes on the supreme status of the law of comparative advantage—mathematical, empirical, and counter factual (unobservable)—are famous and abound, see Costinot and Donaldson (2012, p.453).

For an overview and a comprehensive approach to examination of various models of international trade, we briefly summarize them by Tables 23.1 and 23.2. Latter table indicates by (x) *aspects*, which *differ across countries*, that is, international differences in technologies are seen in Ricardian models (Model I), and the table also indicates and gives information about parameters that are tacitly assumed *identical* internationally—for example, in Model VI (HOS), these are tacitly technology and preference parameters.

[28] Ricardo (1817, 1821, 1965, p.81, 175):

> The same rule which regulates the relative value of commodities in one country does not regulate the relative values of the commodities exchanged between two or more countries. Under a system of perfectly free commerce, *each country* naturally devotes its *capital* and *labor* to such *employments* [industries, goods, sectors] as are *most beneficial* to each. This pursuit of *individual advantages* is admirably connected with the *universal* good of the whole.

cf. Ruffin (2002, p.743).

The Ricardian term comparative advantage means the ability in *autarky* to produce a good at *lower* cost/price (*relative* to other goods), *compared* to another autarky country. Moreover, the law of *comparative advantage (cost)* says that a country *exports* (imports) the good with the *low* (high) *relative* ($p = P_1/P_2$) autarky price, and is given by an *inequality* in relative autarky prices (exports, $X_{1A} > 0$, imports, $X_{1A} < 0$) as:

$$P_{1A}/P_{2A} = p_A < P_{1B}/P_{2B} = p_B : \quad X_{1A} > 0 \tag{23.213}$$

The *prediction* of *bilateral trade patterns* in two open economies by the *autarky condition* (23.213), $X_{1A} > 0$: Export of good 1 by country A is (with precise assumptions) *not* violated in any *free trade model* with two goods [sectors]-two factors-two countries, $(2 \times 2 \times 2)$.

Thus, the Ricardian **Law** of **Comparative Costs** (23.213) is stated by the *inequality* in bilateral *autarky* **GE** *relative prices* (price ratios):

$$P_{1A}/P_{2A} = p_A(k_A) < P_{1B}/P_{2B} = p_B(k_B) : \quad X_{1A} > 0 \tag{23.214}$$

*World equilibrium terms of trade*[29] ($\boldsymbol{p}_w$) are usually assumed to fall strictly between the two countries relative prices (price ratios) under autarky:

$$p_A < p_W < p_B \tag{23.215}$$

excluding the case of one country (say A) being "small", hence $p_W = p_B$.

**Proposition 23.1** *General comparative cost principle (23.214) with full parameter generality by* **GE** ***autarky*** *commodity price ratio* $\boldsymbol{p}_J(\boldsymbol{k}_J)$*, (23.202) is:*

$$\frac{P_{1J}}{P_{2J}} = \frac{\gamma_{2J}}{\gamma_{1J}}\bar{A}_J\left[\frac{1 - a_{2J} + \alpha_j(a_{2J} - a_{1J})}{a_{2J} - \alpha_j(a_{2J} - a_{1J})}k_J\right]^{a_{2J}-a_{1J}} \equiv \frac{\gamma_{2J}}{\gamma_{1J}}\bar{A}_J\left[\frac{1 - \bar{\beta}_J}{\bar{\beta}_J}k_J\right]^{a_{2J}-a_{1J}} \tag{23.216}$$

*with* **GE** ***points*** *(23.216) of* $p_J(k_J)$*,* $J = A, B$*, on the* $\boldsymbol{p}_J$***-axis*** *in* Fig. 23.5a–b *and giving* ***trade patterns*** *(23.214) of the* **Standard Model** *in* Table 23.1.

*Parametrically* ***restricted*** *(23.216)-***Basic Model***—same factor intensity parameters in both A, B,* $\bar{A}_J = \bar{A}$ *(23.32–23.33)—has* ***autarky*** *price ratios* $p_J(k_J)$*:*

$$a_{iJ} = a_i\,;\ \beta_J \equiv a_2 - \alpha_j(a_2 - a_1)\,;\ \frac{P_{1J}}{P_{2J}} = \frac{\gamma_{2J}\,a_2^{a_2}\,(1 - a_2)^{1-a_2}}{\gamma_{1J}\,a_1^{a_1}\,(1 - a_1)^{1-a_1}}\left[\frac{1 - \beta_J}{\beta_J}k_J\right]^{a_2-a_1} \tag{23.217}$$

*giving* ***trade patterns*** *(23.214), seen in Fig. 23.8a–b for Fig. 23.11.*

[29] Marshall (1879, 1930, 1974) continued the study of Mill's examples [Mill (1848, 1875, 1909, p.361)] with an in-depth analysis of the *trade balance equilibrium* determination of "international values" (terms of trade) by "reciprocal demand" (offer, net-export) curves of two countries.

**Ricardo** *(I) implies dropping the subscript (J) from* $\beta_J$ *and* $k_J$ *in (23.216) or (23.217).* **Marshall** *(III) drops (J) from* $k_J$. **HO** *(IV) drops (J) from* $\beta_J$.

*Further* ***restricted*** *version of (23.217) is* **HOL**-***identical*** *technologies in A, B:*

$$a_{iJ} = a_i \ ; \ \gamma_{iJ} = \gamma_i \ ; \quad \frac{P_{1J}}{P_{2J}} = \frac{\gamma_2}{\gamma_1} \frac{a_2^{a_2} (1-a_2)^{1-a_2}}{a_1^{a_1} (1-a_1)^{1-a_1}} \left[ \frac{1-\beta_J}{\beta_J} k_J \right]^{a_2 - a_1} , \ J = A, B \tag{23.218}$$

*and is actually* **GE** ***illustrated*** *in* Fig. 23.10, *where* $a_2 > a_1$, *cf.* Fig. 23.5b.

*The* **Mill Model** *(II) just drops (J) from* $k_J$ *in (23.218).*

*If the two autarky CD economies have* ***identical*** *technologies,* ***the same preferences***—**HOS** *model with coinciding loci,* $\boldsymbol{\Psi}_A = \boldsymbol{\Psi}_B$, *in its* Fig. 23.10—*and hence only differ in factor endowments, the* **GE** *CD commodity* ***price ratio*** *formulas (23.218) are*—$\boldsymbol{\beta}_J = \boldsymbol{\beta} = \alpha a_1 + (1-\alpha) a_2$—***reduced*** *to:*

$$\frac{P_{1J}}{P_{2J}} = \frac{\gamma_2}{\gamma_1} \frac{a_2^{a_2} (1-a_2)^{1-a_2}}{a_1^{a_1} (1-a_1)^{1-a_1}} \left[ \frac{1-[\alpha a_1 + (1-\alpha) a_2]}{\alpha a_1 + (1-\alpha) a_2} k_J \right]^{a_2 - a_1} \tag{23.219}$$

The *trade patterns* (23.214) of Heckscher-Ohlin-Samuelson CD models—**HOS**—follow from **GE** (23.219), that is, from **exogenous** factor **endowment ratios** $\boldsymbol{k}_J$ and **technology exponents** in (23.219) (monotonicity directions in Fig. 23.5):

$$k_B > k_A \quad a_2 > a_1 \ ; \quad p_A(k_A) < p_B(k_B) \ : \ X_{1A} > 0 \quad (X_{2B} > 0 \ , \ X_{1B} < 0) \tag{23.220}$$

$$k_B > k_A \quad a_1 > a_2 \ ; \quad p_B(k_B) < p_A(k_A) \ : \ X_{1B} > 0 \quad (X_{2A} > 0 \ , \ X_{1A} < 0) \tag{23.221}$$

Pattern formulas (23.220–23.221) of **HOS** (23.219) *correspond* to HOS **Theorem**:

$$k_B > k_A \ ; \qquad k_{2B}(k_B) > k_{1B}(k_B) : \quad X_{2B} > 0 \ (X_{1A} > 0 \ , \ X_{1B} < 0) \tag{23.222}$$

$$k_B > k_A \ ; \qquad k_{2A}(k_A) < k_{1A}(k_A) : \quad X_{2A} > 0 \ (X_{1B} > 0 \ , \ X_{1A} < 0) \tag{23.223}$$

saying that: *Each* country will *export* the *good* that *uses* its *relative abundant factor most intensively* (relatively, with the larger sector factor input ratio)—called the:[30] **Heckscher-Ohlin Theorem.**

[30] See, for example, all graduate/undergraduate textbooks: Feenstra (2016, p.30), Caves et al. (2007, p.117), Gandolfo (1998, p.65), Wong (1995, p.91), Markusen et al. (1995, p.106), Södersten and Reed (1994, p.59), Ethier (1995, p.130), Kenen (2000, p.64). All this cited

Autarky **GE** *solutions* of the *sectoral* capital-labor ratios, $\mathbf{k}_{iJ}(\mathbf{k}_J)$, in the HOS/HOL/Basic Model are obtained from (23.9) and $\omega_J(k_J)$, (23.201)—with the parameter restrictions (23.219), (23.218), (23.217)—as:

$$HOS: k_{iJ} = \frac{a_i}{1-a_i}\frac{1-\beta}{\beta}k_J;\ HOL: k_{iJ} = \frac{a_i}{1-a_i}\frac{1-\beta_J}{\beta_J}k_J \quad (23.224)$$

$$Basic: k_{iJ} = \frac{a_i}{1-a_i}\frac{1-\beta_J}{\beta_J}k_J;\ Standard: k_{iJ} = \frac{a_{iJ}}{1-a_{iJ}}\frac{1-\bar{\beta}_J}{\bar{\beta}_J}k_J \quad (23.225)$$

where *Standard* model autarky solution (23.225) corresponds to (23.216).

Note that TFP *parameters*, $\gamma_i$, $\gamma_{iJ}$, always *appear* in $p_J(k_J)$, (23.219–23.216); but these TFP *parameters* cancelled out in (23.200–23.201) and hence have *vanished* from the **GE** autarky, $k_{iJ}(k_J)$ **formulas** (23.224–23.225), that is, (23.224–23.225) imply that HOS *statements* (formulas) (23.222–23.223) will *never*—theoretically or empirically—*correctly predict trade patterns*, except for the HOS parameter case (23.219).

The capital-labor ratio expressions $\boldsymbol{k}_{iJ}(\boldsymbol{k}_J)$, (23.224–23.225), are the endogenous *diversification cone boundaries—rays*, depicted in Figs. 23.10 and 23.11—that is *always* satisfied by the **GE** points, $\boldsymbol{k}_J = \boldsymbol{\Psi}_J(\boldsymbol{\omega}_J)$, (23.200), in *autarky*.

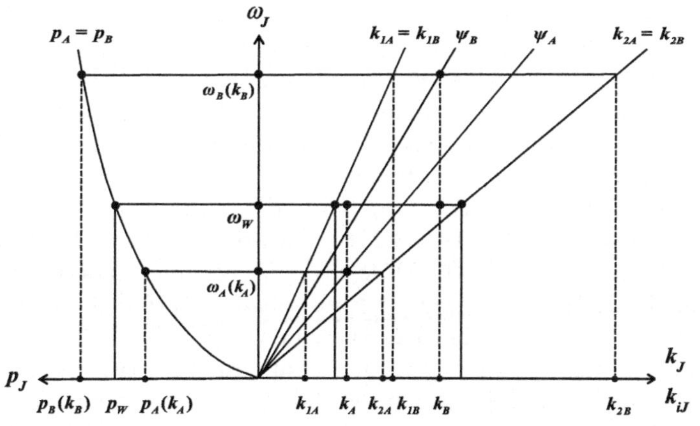


**Fig. 23.10** Relative prices $p_J(\omega_J)$, (23.126), with (23.218), $a_2 > a_1$—**HOL**—autarky **GE** locus, $k_J = \Psi_J(\omega_J)$, (23.200–23.201), autarky relative prices $p_J(k_J)$, (23.218), $p_W$, (23.215), and diversification cone boundaries in autarky (dashed lines), and world trade commodity (factor) prices, $(p_W, \omega_W)$, (solid lines)

literature also uses the term *Heckscher-Ohlin Model* as *synonymous* [ cf. Deardorff (2006, p.126)] with *HOS Model* ( *VI*, Table 23.1, where $HO \neq HOS$).

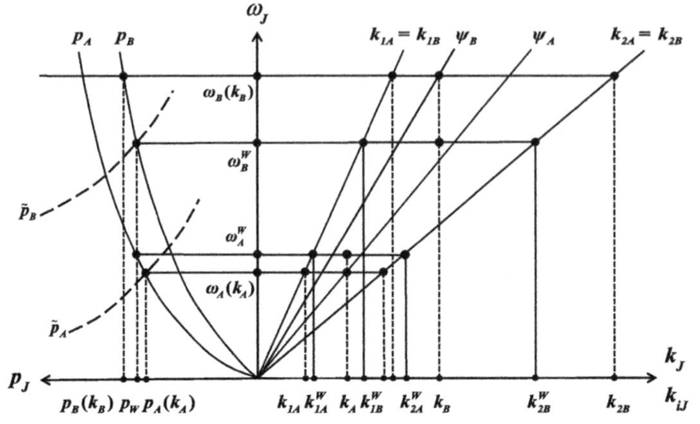


**Fig. 23.11** Relative prices, $p_J(\omega_J)$, (23.126), with (23.217), $a_2 > a_1$—**Basic Model**—autarky **GE** locus, $k_J = \Psi_J(\omega_J)$, (23.200–23.201), autarky relative prices $p_J(k_J)$, 23.217), $p_W$, (23.215), diversification cone boundaries, autarky (dashed lines), and world trade commodity (factor) prices, $(p_W, \omega_W)$, (solid lines)

By using the HOS expressions $k_{iJ}(k_J)$, (23.224), in (23.222–23.223), we get indeed the inequalities for the capital intensity parameters $(a_i)$ in (23.220–23.221). However, by using the HOL, Basic, or Standard Model expressions from (23.224 to 23.225) in (23.222–23.223), we just again get the same inequalities for the parameters $(a_i)$ as in (23.220–23.221), since the $\beta$, $\beta_J$, $\bar{\beta}_J$ elements drop out from the $k_{iJ}(k_J)$ inequalities in (23.222–23.223)—*single country* [ *not* cross-country (*comparative*) as (23.220–23.221) ].

But the country *preference* parameters within the $\beta_J$, $\bar{\beta}_J$ elements certainly did have influence on the two *autarky* price ratios $p_J(k_J)$, (23.217–23.218), J=A,B, that generate the relevant trade patterns.

As explained above, the *country-specific TFP parameters*, $\gamma_{iJ}$ [ affecting the *comparative inequality*, (23.214–23.216) ] are **missed** in (23.224–23.225) and hence **missed** and ignored by the **HOS** trade pattern rules (**Theorem**) as *stated* in (23.222–23.223). Thus, trade pattern *violating* **HOS** as being *converse* to (23.220–23.221), (23.222–23.223) are not surprising.

But the comprehensive (general) **comparative cost** (price) principle (23.214) with (23.216) will **never fail** for any of our parameters and endowments to give the proper export (import) pattern for all the (2 × 2 × 2) **Models** I-VII of Table 23.2. Let us briefly recapitulate further implications of the **Law** of the general Ricardo comparative cost principle (23.214).

**Corollary 23.1** *Country sizes are irrelevant for bilateral trade patterns—which are uniquely determined by technology parameters, preference parameters, and the exogenous factor endowment ratios of countries.*

*Countries with same technologies, preferences, and endowments do not trade. Countries with same technologies and GE factor price ratios do not trade.*[31]

***Proof*** The general *solution* for the *autarky* price ratios $p_J(k_J)$ in (23.216), depends only on technological parameters, consumer preferences, endowments ratios—but *not* on country sizes.

If $k_A = k_B$ in (23.219), then, $p_A(k_A) = p_B(k_B)$, implying: $X_{1A} = 0$, by (23.214).

If $\omega_A = \Psi_A^{-1}(k_A) = \frac{1-\beta_A}{\beta_A} k_A = \frac{1-\beta_B}{\beta_B} k_B = \omega_B$ in (23.201), then we have, $p_A(k_A) = p_B(k_B)$, cf. (23.218): preference differences and endowment differences cancel out in (23.214). On FPE before trade, Samuelson (1981, p.155). □

**Corollary 23.2** *If two countries differ in preferences and technologies (or endowments), then endowments (or technologies)* ***alone*** *cannot explain trade patterns-comparative advantage (comparative autarky GE price ratios).*

***Proof*** It comes by (23.214) and **GE** price expressions: (23.217), (23.216). □

## Conclusion and Final Comments

Let us summarize in overview fashion. The familiar historical starting point of production theory was a set of non-joint production (output, sector) functions with their marginal productivities of inputs describing the possibilities of substitution between factors to obtain a given output (isoquants)—as well as efficient allocation of given factor endowments to achieve maximum of outputs (production possibility curves, PPC), an output frontier referred to as a transformation function. The well-known Pareto optimal allocation conditions required that marginal rates of substitution (MRS) of two factors were equal in both sectors (outputs), or equivalently that the marginal rates of transformation (MRT) for the outputs were the same for both factors.

These common MRS or common MRT conditions certainly impose severe restrictions on actual (economic efficient) factor combinations (capital-labor ratios) used for both outputs. What these efficiency restrictions concretely imply for sector capital-labor ratios depend on the functional forms and

[31] Heckscher (1919, p.47) examined some: "fundamental assumptions concerning the *reasons for differences in comparative costs among countries*", that is, why are the autarky relative costs (prices) $p_A$ and $p_B$ different? cf. (23.213). As a keen economist, Heckscher correctly argued that countries with **same**—*technologies* and relative *factor prices*—do **not** trade, since then: "relative costs in one country cannot possibly differ from those in the other. Therefore trade between the countries will not arise", Heckscher (1919, p.47).

Hence behind the Ricardian inequality (23.213), he saw (emphasized) as a prerequisite an *inequality autarky relative factor prices*, $\omega_A$ and $\omega_B$: "different relative prices of the factors of production in the exchanging countries", Heckscher (1919, p.48).

parameter values of the actual production functions. With our **CD** forms and sector technology parameters, the *Pareto efficiency conditions* implied a strict *proportionality* between *sectoral capital-labor ratios* (23.11). Moreover, such sector capital-labor ratios will impose severe restrictions on the feasible sector allocation shares (fractions) of the total endowments. Indeed, the allocation fractions of capital and labor are then uniquely determined and here hyperbolic related (23.16). Thus, all the Pareto efficient factor combinations (capital-labor ratios) and *optimal factor allocations* (fractions) have only one "degree of freedom" (*free* variable), here *labor allocation variable*, $\lambda_{L_{1J}}$, $0 \leq \lambda_{L_{1J}} \leq 1$.

As well-known, there are mathematically various ways of representing *plane curves.* Cartesian equation forms, $\widehat{T}_J(Y_{1J}, Y_{2J}) = 0$ ; $Y_{2J} = T_J(Y_{1J})$, (23.8), are here seldom a convenient curve representation; instead, the *coordinates* $(Y_{1J}, Y_{2J})$ expressed independently as *functions* of the *single variable* $\lambda_{L_{1J}}$: $(Y_{1J}, Y_{2J}) = [H_1(\lambda_{L_{1J}}), H_2(\lambda_{L_{1J}})]$, (23.22–23.23), were much better for tracing out **PPC** of (23.8) in Figs. 23.4, 23.6, and 23.7. It is surprising that transformation curves (PPC) were not long ago explicitly given on the *analytic curve form* (23.22–23.23), which is particularly useful for calculating any *derivatives* and all PPC tangent slopes, MRT = $p_J(\lambda_{L_{1J}})$, even at the important end points (23.19–23.21).

Also the *"inverse"* of (23.19) was easily obtained: $\lambda_{L_{1J}} = \lambda_{L_{1J}}(p_J; k_J)$, as seen explicitly in (23.35–23.36); we did use this *variable* $\lambda_{L_{1J}}(p_J; k_J)$ on the *dual price* interval (23.39) for calculating *explicitly* basic *elasticity formulas* of **endowment** variations ($\mathbf{k_J}$) and **price** variations[32] ($\mathbf{p_J}$) in Theorems 23.2–23.4.

It is simple to adapt the factor *allocation variable* $\lambda_{L_{1J}}$ to include the *preference parameters* of consumer demand, (23.199), for an *autarky general equilibrium* (**GE**) model, (23.201), which is next the basis for calculating *comparative advantage*, (23.202), (23.216), to obtain *trade pattern* predictions from Proposition 23.1 of a fully fledged **Standard Model**, outlined in Tables 23.1 and 23.2.

Actual export-import patterns, trade volumes, and domestic factor allocations will depend on world market equilibrium prices, $\mathbf{p_W}$, (terms of trade), (23.215), indicated in Figs. 23.10 and 23.11. Model calculations of $\mathbf{p_W}$ still remain to be seen in the literature and will be among the topics of next chapter.

Throughout emphasis was put on rigor, proof, and quantitative analysis. By not only codifying the past of transformation and revenue functions but also extending them with explicit parametric form solutions and hopefully intuitive economic appeal, we look forward to see research generalizing our functional

[32] Figures 23.5a–b contain the **key** Pareto allocative relations (*functions, basic curves*) that are generalized with **CES** sector production and cost (price) functions—to analyze and solve *two-sector* and *multi-sector* **growth** models in Chaps. 17–20, cf. Figs. 17.1, 18.0, 19.1, 19.3, 20.1 and 20.3. The effects reflected by comparative statics of Stolper-Samuelson and Rybczynski elasticities—vertical and horizontal shifts in Fig. 23.5a–b—are replaced by *continuous* PPC shifts from factor accumulation along the general equilibrium (**GE**) *locus*—included in Fig. 23.5a–b.

forms to other parametric technologies (**CES**) with relevant applications in micro, general equilibrium, trade, growth, and welfare economics.

## Bibliography

Allen RGD (1938) Mathematical Analysis for Economists. MacMillan, London

Arrow KJ, Chenery HB, Minhas BS, Solow RM (1961) Capital–Labour Substitution and Economic Efficiency. Review of Economics and Statistics 43:225–250

Barone E (1908) Principi di Economia Politica. Tipografia Nazionale di G. Bertero, Rome

Black J (1957) A Formal Proof of the Concavity of the Production Possibility Function. Economic Journal 67:133–135

Blackorby C, Schworm W, Venables A (1993) Necessary and Sufficient Conditions for Factor Price Equalization. Review of Economic Studies 60:413–434

Blaug M, Lloyd P (eds) (2010) Famous Figures and Diagrams in Economics. Edward Elgar, Cheltenham UK

Burmeister E, Turnovsky SJ (1971) The Degree of Joint Production. International Economic Review 12:99–105

Caves RE, Frankel JA, Jones RW (2007) World Trade and Payments, 10th edn. Addison–Wesley, Boston

Chipman JS (1969) Factor Price Equalization and the Stolper–Samuelson Theorem. International Economic Review 10:399–406

Costinot A, Donaldson D (2012) Ricardo's Theory of Comparative Advantage: Old Ideas, New Evidence. American Economic Review 102:453–456

Deardorff AV (1980) The General Validity of the Law of Comparative Advantage. Journal of Political Economy 88:941–957

Deardorff AV (2006) Terms of Trade, Glossary of International Economics. World Scientific, Singapore

Deardorff AV, Stern RN (1994) The Stolper–Samuelson Theorem: A Golden Jubilee. The University of Michigan Press, Ann Arbor

Diewert WE (1974) Applications of Duality Theory. pp 106–171, In: Intriligator MD, Kendrick DA (eds) *Frontiers of Quantitative Economics*, Vol.2, North–Holland, Amsterdam

Dixit AK, Norman V (1980) Theory of International Trade: A Dual, General Equilibrium Approach. Cambridge University Press, U.K

Edgeworth FY (1881, 2003) Mathematical Psychics and Further Papers on Political Economy. Oxford University Press

Ethier WJ (1995) Modern International Economics, 3rd edn. W.W. Norton & Company, New York

Feenstra RC (2016) Advanced International Trade, 2nd edn. Princeton University Press

Flam H, Flanders MJ (1991) Heckscher–Ohlin Trade Theory. MIT Press, Cambridge, Mass

Gandolfo G (1998) International Economics I: The Pure Theory of International Trade, 3rd edn. Springer–Verlag, Berlin

Gandolfo G (2014) International Trade Theory and Policy. Springer–Verlag, Berlin Heidelberg

Grossman GM, Rogoff K (1995) Handbook of International Economics, vol III. Elsevier, Amsterdam

Gundlach E (2007) The Solow Model in the Empirrics of Growth and Trade. Oxford Review of Economic Policy 23:25–44

Gundlach E, Becker D (2007) Factor Price Equality and Biased Technical Change in a Two-Cone Trade Model. Review of Development Economics 11:685–698

Haberler G (1936) The Theory of International Trade. W. Hodge and Comp, London

Hall RE (1973) The Specification of Technology with Several Kinds of Output. Journal of Political Economy 81:868–892

Harrigan J (1997) Technology, Factor Supplies, and International Specialization: Estimating the Neoclassical Model. American Economic Review 87:475–494

Harwitz M (1972) A Note on Professor Chipman's Version of Mill's Law of International Values. Journal of International Economics 2:181–188

Heckscher EF (1919) The Effect of Foreign Trade on Distribution of Income. Ekonomisk Tidsskrift 21, Del II:1–32, translated (Svend Laursen) in Ellis, H.S., Metzler, L.A., eds. *Readings in the Theory of International Trade*, Blakiston, Philadelphia, (1949), 272–300; transl., in Flam. H & Flanders, M.J. (1991), (43–69).

Hicks JR (1932, 1948) The Theory of Wages. MacMillan, London

Hicks JR (1946) Value and Capital, 2nd edn. Clarendon Press, Oxford

Hsiao FST (1971) The Contract Curve and the Production Possibility Curve. Journal of Political Economy 79:919–923

Inada KI (1971) The production coefficient matrix and the Stolper–Samuelson connection. Econometrica 39:219–240

Inoue T, Wegge LL (1986) On the Geometry of the Production Possibility Frontier. International Economic Review 27:727–737

Jensen BS (2003) Walrasian General Equilibrium Allocations and Dynamics in Two–Sector Growth Models. German Economic Review 4:53–87

Jensen BS (2012) Comparative Cost and Factor Endowments: Ricardo and Ohlin. pp 55–83, Ch. 4 in Kemp et al., eds., (2012).

Jensen BS (2017) von Thünen: Capital, Production Functions, Marginal Productivity Wages and the Natural Wage. German Economic Review 18:51–80

Johnson HG (1966) Factor Market Distortions and the Shape of the Transformation Curve. Econometrica 34:686–698

Jones RW (1965) The Structure of Simple General Equilibrium Models. J Political Economy 73:557–72, or Bhagwati (1981)

Jones RW (1985) Relative Prices and Real Factor Rewards. Economics Letters 19

Jones RW (2002) Trade Theory and Factor Intensities: An Interpretive Essay. Review of International Economics 10:581–603

Jones RW (2010) Production Possibilities Frontiers. In *Famous Figures and Diagrams in Economics*, Blaug and Lloyd, (2010).

Jones RW, Easton ST (1982) Factor Intensities and Factor Substitution in General Equilibrium. Journal of International Economics 15:65–99

Kawano H, Ohta H, Jensen BS, Hwang AR (2017) Production, Distribution, and Trade: General Equilibrium with One Single Cobb–Douglas Parameter. Modern Economy 8:970–993

Kemp MC (1969) The Pure Theory of International Trade and Investment. Prentice–Hall, New Jersey

Kemp MC, Long NV (1985) Sharp Points in Production Surfaces. Oxford Economic Papers 37:375–381

Kemp MC, Wegge LLF (1969) On the Relation between Commodity Prices and Factor Rewards. International Economic Review 10:407–413

Kemp MC, Nakagawa H, Uchida T (2012) Positive and Normative Analysis in International Economics. Palgrave Macmillan, London

Kenen PB (2000) The International Economy, 4th edn. Prentice–Hall, New Jersey

Kohli U (1983) Non–Joint Technologies. Review of Economic Studies 50:209–219

Kohli U (1991) Technology, Duality, and Foreign Trade: The GNP Function Approach to Modelling Imports and Exports. UMP Press, Ann Arbor ; Harvester Wheatsheaf, London

Krugman PR, Obstfeld M, Melitz MJ (2018) International Economics–Theory and Policy, 11th edn. Pearson, UK

Kuga K (1972) The Factor Price Equalization Theorem. Econometrica 40:723–736

Lau L (1972) Profit Functions of Technologies with Multiple Inputs and Outputs. Review Econ Stat 54:281–289

Leamer E (2001) International Economics. Worth Publishers, New York

Leamer EE (1984) Sources of International Comparative Advantage – theory and evidence. MIT Press, Cambridge, Mass

Leamer EE (1995) The Heckscher–Ohlin Model in Theory and Practice, vol 77. Princeton Studies in International Finance, New Jersey

Leamer EE, Levinsohn J (1995) International Trade Theory: The Evidence. Ch. 26 in Grossman and Rogoff (1995).

Leontief WW (1933) The Use of Indifference Curves in the Analysis of Foreign Trade. Quarterly Journal of Economics 47:493–503

Lerner AP (1932) The Diagrammatical Representation of Cost Conditions in International Trade. Economica 37:319–334

Lerner AP (1933) Notes on Elasticity of Substitution – The Diagrammatical Representation. Review of Economic Studies 1:68–71

Linder SB (1961) An Essay on Trade and Transformation. John Wiley and Sons, New York

Lloyd P (2000) Generalizing the Stolper–Samuelson Theorem: A Tale of Two Matrices. Review of International Economics 8:597–613

Maneschi A, Thweatt W (1987) Barone's (1908) Representation of an Economy's Trade Equilibrium and the Gains from Trade. Journal of International Economics 22:375–382

Markusen JR, Melvin JR, Kaempfer WH, Maskus KE (1995) International Trade. McGraw–Hill, New York

Marshall A (1879, 1930, 1974) The Pure Theory of Foreign Trade, The Pure Theory of Domestic Values. Privately printed (1879); LSE, University of London (1930); Augustus M. Kelley Publishers (1974), New Jersey.

Mas-Colell A, Whinston MD, Green JR (1995) Microeconomic Theory. Oxford University Press, New York

Melvin JR (1969) Mill's Law of International Values. Southern Economic Journal 36:107–116

Meyer W (1976) The Rybczynski, Stolper–Samuelson, and Factor Price Equalization Theorems under Uncertainty. American Economic Review 66:797–808

Mill JS (1848, 1875, 1909) Principles of Political Economy, 7th edn. Longmans, Green and Co., London

Negishi T (1989) History of Economic Theory. Elsevier, Amsterdam, North–Holland

Negishi T (2014) Developments of International Trade Theory. Springer Japan, Tokyo, Advances in Japanese Business and Economics 2

Nicholson W, Snyder C (2012) Microeconomic Theory, 11th edn. South-Western, Mason, OH, USA

Ohlin B (1924) The Theory of Trade. AB Nordiska Bokhandelen, Stockholm, translated in Flam. H & Flanders, M.J. (1991), (76–214)

Ohlin B (1933, 1967) Interregional and International Trade. Harvard University Press, Cambridge, MA, *Revised Edition* (1967), Harvard University Press

Ohlin B (1970) The Business Cost Account Approach to International Trade Theory. The Swedish Journal of Economics 72:12–20

Oniki H, Uzawa H (1965) Patterns of Trade and Investment in a Dynamic Model of International Trade. Review of Economic Studies 32:15–38

Powell AA, Gruen FHG (1968) The Constant Elasticity of Transformation Production Frontier and the Linear Supply System. International Economic Review 9:315–328

Ricardo D (1817, 1821, 1965) The Principles of Political Economy and Taxation. J.M. Dent and Sons, London

Ruffin RJ (2002) David Ricardo's Discovery of Comparative Advantage. History of Political Economy 34:727–748

Rybczynski TM (1955) Factor Endowments and Relative Commodity Prices. Economica 22:336–341

Samuelson PA (1947, 1983) Foundations of Economic Analysis, Enlarged edn. Harvard University Press, Cambridge, Mass

Samuelson PA (1948, 1949) International Trade and The Equalisation of Factor Price. Economic Journal 58:163–184, International Factor Price Equalisation Once Again. *Economic Journal*, 59, 181–197

Samuelson PA (1949) International Factor Price Equalisation Once Again. Economic Journal 59:181–197

Samuelson PA (1953–1954) Prices of Factors and Goods in General Equilibrium. Review of Economic Studies 21:1–20

Samuelson PA (1966) The Fundamental Singularity Theorem for Non–Joint Production. International Economic Review 7:34–41

Samuelson PA (1972) Maximum Principles in Analytical Economics. American Economic Review 62:249–262

Samuelson PA (1981) Bertil Ohlin – (1899)–(1979). Journal of International Economics 62:147–163

Scarth WM, Warne RD (1973) The Elasticity of Substitution and the Shape of the Transformation Curve. Economica 40:299–304

Silberberg E, Suen W (2001) The Structure of Economics, A Mathematical Analysis, 3rd edn. McGraw–Hill, Singapore

Smith A (1776, 1961) The Wealth of Nations I–II. Methuen University Paperbacks, London

Södersten B, Reed G (1994) International Economics, 3rd edn. Macmillan Press, London

Stolper WF, Samuelson PA (1941) Protection and Real Wages. Review of Economic Studies 9:58–73

Uekawa Y (1971) Generalization of the Stolper–Samuelson theorem. Econometrica 39:197–218

Uekawa Y, Kemp MC, Wegge LLF (1972) P– and PN–Matrices, Minkowski– and Metzler Matrices, and Generalization of the Stolper–Samuelson and Samuelson–Rybczynski Theorems. Journal of International Economics 3:53–76

Uzawa H (1961–63) On a Two-Sector Model of Economic Growth: I–II. Rev Econ Stud 29:40–47, Rev. Econ. Stud. 30, 105–18

Wegge LLF, Kemp MC (1969) Generalization of the Stolper–Samuelson and Samuelson–Rybczynski Theorems in Terms of Conditional Input–Output Coefficients. International Economic Review 10:414–425

Wong KY (1995) International Trade in Goods and Factor Mobility. MIT Press, Cambridge, MA

Woodland AD (1982) International Trade and Resource Allocation. Amsterdam, North-Holland

CHAPTER 24

# Trade Balance, Terms of Trade, and World Equilibrium Prices

## Introduction

The pure theory of international trade has always been involved with the fundamental questions of what decides: (1) The *commodity pattern* (composition) of international *trade* between countries; (2) the "*international values*", i.e., the *prices* of both the *free traded commodities* and their *primary* production *factors*; (3) the *gains* from *foreign trade.*

Evidently the literature is overwhelming and hence many surveys have been made, Haberler (1936), Mundell (1960), Bhagwati (1964).

But (Chipman 1965, 1966) still surpasses all other historical accounts and expositions of theory evolution (together with many references to contemporary authors/discussions). His theory *chronology* has *three periods* of main/early contributors: I. *Classical* theory of comparative advantage, gains from trade (Smith, Ricardo, Mill); II. *Neo-classical* theory of international trade equilibrium and the equilibrium terms of trade (Marshall, Edgeworth, Haberler); III. *Modern* theory of factor endowments, factor price equalization, factor income distribution, two-sector growth models (Heckscher, Ohlin, Samuelson, Solow, Uzawa, Kemp).

Economic laws (theory) governing trade between two countries dawned in Adam Smith—Chap. 11 of restraints upon the importation from foreign countries of goods that can be produced at home, Smith (1776, 1961, p. 478): "What is prudence in the conduct of every private family, can scarcely be folly in that of a great kingdom. If a *foreign* country can supply us with a commodity

With co-author:
JACOPO ZOTTI, Department of Political and Social Sciences, University of Trieste, Italy



B. S. Jensen, *The Elements and Dynamic Systems of Economic Growth and Trade Models*, https://doi.org/10.1007/978-3-031-52493-6_24

*cheaper* than we ourselves can make it, better *buy* [import] it from them *with* some *part* [export] of the produce of our *own industry*, employed [produced] in a way in which we have some *advantage*".

By scrutinizing the principle of *cheapness* and advantage in more detail with some illustrations, Ricardo (1817, 1821, 1965, p. 81, p. 175), cf. Ruffin (2002, p. 743), came up with the law of *comparative advantage*: "Under a system of perfectly free commerce, *each country* naturally devotes its *capital* and *labour* to such *employments* [industries, goods, sectors] as are *most beneficial* to each. This pursuit of *individual advantages* is admirably connected with the *universal* good of the whole".

Precisely, the Ricardian term comparative advantage means the ability in *autarky* to produce a good at *lower* cost/price (*relative* to *other* goods), *compared* to another *autarky* country. Moreover, the *law* of *comparative advantage (cost)* says that a country *exports* (imports) the good with the *low* (high) *relative* ($\boldsymbol{p} = \boldsymbol{P}_1/\boldsymbol{P}_2$) *autarky* price, and it can be expressed an *inequality* in relative *autarky* prices:

$$P_{1A}/P_{2A} = p_A < P_{1B}/P_{2B} = p_B : \quad X_{1A} > 0 \tag{24.1}$$

The *prediction* of *trade patterns*—$\boldsymbol{X}_{1A} > 0$: *export* of good 1 by country A—in *open* economies by the *autarky condition*, (24.1), is (with precise assumptions) *not* violated in any *trade model* for: two countries, two goods [commodities, sectors], two factors (2 × 2 × 2).

The *world equilibrium terms of trade* ($\boldsymbol{p}_W$) are usually just taken (assumed, not proved) to fall strictly between the two countries relative prices (price ratios) under *autarky*, i.e.,

$$p_A < p_W < p_B \tag{24.2}$$

excluding the case of one country (say A) being '*small*', hence $p_W = p_B$.

The *bilateral* rule of comparing relative prices under autarky to determine trade patterns, (24.1), is *not* valid for a *multicommodity* (multisector, $\boldsymbol{i} \geq 3$) world, as demonstrated by Drabicki and Takayama (1979, p. 217). On these "higher dimensional" issues, see Deardorff (1980), Shimomura and Wong (1998). We focus on a *full story* of the (2 × 2 × 2) model, but in contrast to the available literature so far, *our objective* is to deduce and finally present *explicit* analytical *solutions* of the *world trade model* (2 × 2 × 2).

While comparative advantage *explains why* and *how* trade takes place, it does *not explain* (give) the *terms of trade: relative prices*, $\boldsymbol{p}_W$ in (24.2). Ricardo's numerical examples, cf. Chipman (1965, p. 482), offer no clear *size* of ($\boldsymbol{p}_W$) or hints to general answers. It was Stuart Mill, who first gave an analysis of the formation of "*international values*" [world market prices, determination of $\boldsymbol{p}_W$ in (24.2)], that offered a rigorous answer—discussed in detail by Chipman (1965, p. 485–86)—upon a pure trade theory example left by Ricardo.

Mill (1848, 1875, 1909, p. 352) stated: "When trade is established between two countries, the two commodities will exchange for each other at the *same rate* of interchange in *both* countries", i.e., the "law of one price" that will also be adhered to in our (2 × 2 × 2) model. Next Mill (1848, 1875, 1909, p. 359) says: "All trade, either between nations or individuals, is an *interchange* of commodities, in which the things that they respectively have to sell, constitute also their means of purchase: the supply brought by the one constitutes his demand for what is brought by the other. So that *supply* and *demand* are but another expression for *reciprocal demand*—or named the *Equation* of *International Demand*"—or today: the *trade balance* equation with a *zero* constraint—which is adopted here, too.

To handle the special trade case of Ricardo, Mill assumed that *consumers* in *both* countries had *identical* commodity demand functions of *simplest* functional form, Mill (1848, 1875, 1909, p. 361): "Let us therefore assume, that the influence of cheapness on demand conforms to some simple law, *common* to both countries and to both commodities. As the simplest possible and most convenient, let us suppose that in both countries any given increase of cheapness [fall in price] produces an proportional increase of consumption: or, in other words that value expended in the commodity, the cost incurred for the sake of obtaining it, is always the same, whether that cost [expenditure] affords a greater or smaller quantity of the commodity". In short, Mill used here *consumer demand* functions, generated today by Cobb-Douglas *utility* functions, as we will do for preferences below.

Marshall (1879, 1930, 1974) continued the study of Mill's examples with an in-depth analysis of the *trade balance equilibrium* determination of "international values" (terms of trade) by "reciprocal demand" (offer, net-export) curves of two countries. Let us hear, Marshall (1879, 1930, 1974, p. 1): "The function of pure theory and models is to *deduce definite conclusions* from *definite hypothetical premises.* The premises should approximate as closely as possible to the facts with which the corresponding applied theory has to deal. But the terms used in the pure theory must be cable of exact interpretation, and the hypotheses on which it is based must be simple and easily handled. The pure theory of foreign trade satisfies these conditions". Marshall supported his propositions/corollaries with 24 *offer-curve* diagrams; many now standard, cf. summary in Deardorff (2006, p. 322).

While *"classical"* trade theory (Smith, Ricardo) may have assumed, cf. Chipman (1966, p. 18), "*constant factor prices and different technologies*" among countries, Heckscher (1919, p. 47) examined some: "fundamental assumptions concerning the *reasons for differences in comparative costs among countries*", i.e. *why* are in (24.1) the *autarky* relative costs (prices) $\boldsymbol{p}_A$ and $\boldsymbol{p}_B$ different? As a keen economist, Heckscher correctly argued that countries with *same*—technologies and relative factor prices—do *not* trade; since then: "relative costs in one country cannot possibly differ from those in the other.

Therefore trade between the countries will not arise", Heckscher (1919, p. 47).

Hence behind the Ricardian inequality in (24.1), he saw (emphasized) as a prerequisite an *inequality* in *autarky relative factor prices*, $\omega_A$ and $\omega_B$: "different relative prices of the factors of production in the exchanging countries", Heckscher (1919, p. 48). But next opening *free trade* would itself affect the *relative* factor prices and maybe, even under some conditions, bring about not just partial, but full *factor price equalization* (FPE).

As to "modern factor endowment theory", Ohlin (1933, Appendix I) re-examined and *extends* the *general equilibrium* equation systems of Walras-Cassel for the *mutual interdependence pricing* of *commodities* and *factors* to *trading regions* (countries). He introduced and emphasized the role of different *factor endowments ratios*, $(k_A, k_B)$, among regions; but Ohlin (1933, p. 561–62) opted in most situations for *partial* factor price equalization.

Next Samuelson (1948, 1949, p. 169) enters the discussion: 'In attempting to devise a rigorous proof of the partial character of factor-price equalization, I made a surprising discovery: the proposition is false. It is not true that factor price equalization is impossible. It is not true that factor price equalization is highly improbable. On the contrary, not only is *factor-price equalization* possible and probable, but in a *wide variety* of circumstances it is *inevitable*". Samuelson (1949, p. 182) restated verbally *eight* conditions for **FPE**.

A major problem with Pareto efficient factor allocation in even two-sector economies with flexible sector technologies is that they in fact constitute "miniature Walrasian general equilibrium systems". Thus early work upon *two-sector growth models* in various *qualitative* versions addressed some of the major issues of this chapter, cf. Uzawa (1961–63), Oniki and Uzawa (1965), that were recently resolved *quantitatively* in Jensen (2003); here Chap. 17.

Our main result is finally for *internationally different* technologies and consumer preferences to have *solved explicitly* the *Basic Trade Model* ($2 \times 2 \times 2$) for the endogenous *terms of trade*, ($\boldsymbol{p}_W$), and presenting analytically the *international general equilibrium solutions* with *explicit existence conditions* upon *country endowments* for *preserving diversification* of the two trading economies. We proceed axiomatically in exposition and sections.

Sections "The Structure of the World Economy"–"PPC, Free Trade, and International Equilibrium Prices" solve analytically the international equilibrium allocations and terms of trade for two trading economies with Leontief two-sector technologies or classic linear PPC.

Section "The Structure of the World Economy" gives the general framework of autarky and open economies. Autarky general equilibrium serves as benchmark and gives expressions of comparative advantage. Section "PPC, Free Trade, and International Equilibrium Prices" solves the world trade balance equation and gives ($p_W$) in Propositions 24.1–24.2. Section "Linear PPC, General Equilibrium, and International Trade" exhibit results of basic trade models. Section "International Free Trade and World Market Prices" concludes and suggests further research.

## THE STRUCTURE OF THE WORLD ECONOMY

The world economy is composed by *two countries*, *A* and *B*, which have the same structure as the generic country *J* in Chap. 23. Both countries may produce *two consumer goods (sectors)*, $i = 1, 2$, *using* labor and capital. We make the standard assumption that the two goods are fully homogeneous throughout the world. International *migration* of the two primary factors is *excluded*, whereas intra-national factors' reallocation among sectors remains possible and frictionless, as in the autarky case of Chap. 23.

### *Framework: Factor Endowments, GDP Accounting*

Coherently with the notation of Chap. 23, the labor *endowment* in the two countries *A* and *B* is $\boldsymbol{L}_J$ with $J = A, B$, while the capital endowment is $\boldsymbol{K}_J$. For sake of exposition, we will address country *J* to identify country *A* as well as *B* altogether ($J = A, B$), unless it is necessary to distinguish among the two countries.

Since technology exhibits constant returns to scale (CRTS) in both countries and *factor markets* are perfectly competitive (zero profit), the Euler theorem ensures that revenues (the *monetary value* of *production*) in *each sector* equate the *factor income* of employed primary factors, which is also total *minimum production cost* ($C_{iJ}$),

$$P_{iJ}\, Y_{iJ} = w_J\, L_{iJ} + r_J\, K_{iJ} = C_{iJ}\,, \quad i = 1, 2 \tag{24.3}$$

The *sectoral cost shares* of labour and capital are easily defined as:

$$\epsilon_{L_{iJ}} = \frac{w_J\, L_{iJ}}{C_{iJ}}\,, \quad \epsilon_{K_{iJ}} = \frac{r_J\, K_{iJ}}{C_{iJ}}\ ; \quad \epsilon_{L_{iJ}} + \epsilon_{K_{iJ}} = 1\,, \quad i = 1, 2 \tag{24.4}$$

Total *national income* (Gross Domestic Product, GDP), ($Y_J$), is obtained as

$$Y_J = P_{1J}\, Y_{1J} + P_{2J}\, Y_{2J} = w_J\, L_J + r_J\, K_J \tag{24.5}$$

and the total (macro) factor income shares, $\delta_{LJ}$, $\delta_{KJ}$, in each country are

$$\delta_{LJ} = \frac{w_J\, L_J}{Y_J}\,, \quad \delta_{KJ} = \frac{r_J\, K_J}{Y_J}\ ; \quad \delta_{LJ} + \delta_{KJ} = 1 \tag{24.6}$$

By (24.6), the shares $\boldsymbol{\delta}_{LJ}$, $\boldsymbol{\delta}_{KJ}$, are *identically* linked to the country factor endowment ratio, $\boldsymbol{k}_J$, and to the relative factor price, $\boldsymbol{\omega}_J$, stated as

$$k_J = \frac{\delta_{KJ}}{\delta_{LJ}} \left[\frac{w_J}{r_J}\right] \equiv \frac{\delta_{KJ}}{\delta_{LJ}}\, \omega_J\,, \quad \omega_J \equiv \frac{w_J}{r_J} \tag{24.7}$$

Let $\boldsymbol{Q}_{iJ}$ denote the size of the *domestic final demand* (absorption level) for good $i = 1, 2$. Under trade openness, domestic final demand equalizes *domestic production*, $\boldsymbol{Y}_{iJ}$, minus *exports* $\boldsymbol{X}_{iJ}$, (with $X_{iJ} > 0$). When $X_{iJ} < 0$, country $J$ is *importing* good $i$:

$$Q_{iJ} = Y_{iJ} - X_{iJ} \tag{24.8}$$

The *trade balance* is assumed to satisfy the constraint

$$P_{1J}X_{1J} + P_{2J}X_{2J} = 0\,; \quad \text{i.e.} \quad Y_J = P_{1J}Q_{1J} + P_{2J}Q_{2J} \tag{24.9}$$

i.e., balanced trade prevails with no foreign borrowing/lending allowed. The *composition* of GDP, $Y_J$, (24.9), into "final demand" (expenditure shares), $s_{iJ}$, is

$$s_{iJ} \;\equiv\; P_{iJ}Q_{iJ}/Y_J\,; \quad \textstyle\sum_{i=1}^{2} s_{iJ} \;=\; 1 \tag{24.10}$$

The macro factor income shares $\delta_{LJ}$, $\delta_{KJ}$, (24.6), are GDP expenditure-weighted, (24.24), combinations of sectoral factor (cost) shares, $\epsilon_{L_iJ}$, $\epsilon_{K_iJ}$,

$$\delta_{LJ} \;=\; \textstyle\sum_{i=1}^{2} s_{iJ}\,\epsilon_{L_iJ}, \quad \delta_{KJ} \;=\; \sum_{i=1}^{2} s_{iJ}\,\epsilon_{K_iJ}, \quad \delta_{LJ} + \delta_{KJ} = 1 \tag{24.11}$$

The total factor *endowment ratio*, $\boldsymbol{k}_J$, satisfies the *identity*, cf. (24.7), (24.11):

$$k_J \;=\; \frac{\delta_{KJ}}{\delta_{LJ}}\,\omega_J \;=\; \left[\textstyle\sum_{i=1}^{2} s_{iJ}\,\epsilon_{K_iJ} \Big/ \sum_{i=1}^{2} s_{iJ}\,\epsilon_{L_iJ}\right]\omega_J \tag{24.12}$$

which is a convenient representation of full employment and factor endowment ratio, see (23.1).

The *factor allocation fractions* (23.3) and (23.4) can then be restated as

$$\lambda_{L_iJ} \;=\; s_{iJ}\,\epsilon_{L_iJ}/\delta_{LJ}\,, \qquad \lambda_{K_iJ} \;=\; s_{iJ}\,\epsilon_{K_iJ}/\delta_{KJ}\,, \quad i = 1, 2 \tag{24.13}$$

A diversified economy clearly requires that $\boldsymbol{\lambda}_{L_1J}$ (23.3) satisfies the *diversification condition*:

$$0 < \lambda_{L_1J}(p_J) < 1 \tag{24.14}$$

Solving this inequality with respect to $\boldsymbol{p}_J$ yields (after some manipulations) the following *relative price interval restriction*:

$$\bar{A}_J\,\frac{\gamma_{2J}}{\gamma_{1J}}\left[\frac{1 - a_{2J}}{a_{2J}}\,k_J\right]^{(a_{2J}-a_{1J})} < p_J < \bar{A}_J\,\frac{\gamma_{2J}}{\gamma_{1J}}\left[\frac{1 - a_{1J}}{a_{1J}}\,k_J\right]^{(a_{2J}-a_{1J})} \tag{24.15}$$

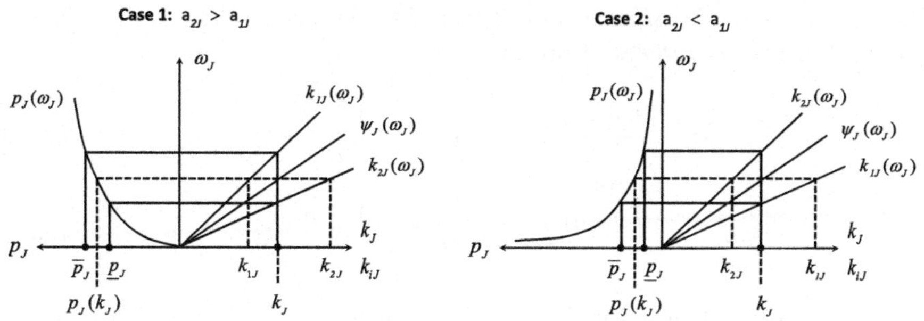


**Fig. 24.1** Relative factor prices, $\omega_J$, capital-labor ratios, $k_{iJ}$, relative commodity prices, $p_J(\omega_J)$, price interval of $p_J$, (24.15) and Walrasian autarky equilibria, $\Psi_J(\omega_J)$

For sake of exposition, we shall define

$$\underline{p}_J = \bar{A}_J \frac{\gamma_{2J}}{\gamma_{1J}} \left[ \frac{1 - a_{2J}}{a_{2J}} k_J \right]^{(a_{2J} - a_{1J})} \tag{24.16}$$

$$\overline{p}_J = \bar{A}_J \frac{\gamma_{2J}}{\gamma_{1J}} \left[ \frac{1 - a_{1J}}{a_{1J}} k_J \right]^{(a_{2J} - a_{1J})} \tag{24.17}$$

and prove that $\underline{p}_J < \overline{p}_J$ for any feasible parameter set, and observe that the relative price limits in condition (24.15) define the *closed interval* $\left[\underline{p}_J, \overline{p}_J\right]$ of the two-sector *geometry* in Fig. 24.1. Observe that this *interval* is solely determined by *technology* parameters. Since the relative price (the "opportunity cost") $\boldsymbol{p}_J$ is always the *slope* of the *production possibility frontier* (PPF), $\underline{p}_J$ ($\overline{p}_J$) in (24.15) is the *slope* of the *PPF*, when production of *sector* 1 (sector 2) is *zero*. Condition (24.15) in fact, is *equivalent* to the '*diversification cone*' (23.5). To see this, re-write (24.15) as

$$a_{2J} > a_{1J} : \frac{a_{1J}}{1 - a_{1J}} \left[ \frac{1}{\bar{A}_J} \frac{\gamma_{1J}}{\gamma_{2J}} p_J \right]^{\frac{1}{a_{2J} - a_{1J}}} < k_J < \frac{a_{2J}}{1 - a_{2J}} \left[ \frac{1}{\bar{A}_J} \frac{\gamma_{1J}}{\gamma_{2J}} p_J \right]^{\frac{1}{a_{2J} - a_{1J}}} \tag{24.18}$$

$$a_{1J} > a_{2J} : \frac{a_{2J}}{1 - a_{2J}} \left[ \frac{1}{\bar{A}_J} \frac{\gamma_{1J}}{\gamma_{2J}} p_J \right]^{\frac{1}{a_{2J} - a_{1J}}} < k_J < \frac{a_{1J}}{1 - a_{1J}} \left[ \frac{1}{\bar{A}_J} \frac{\gamma_{1J}}{\gamma_{2J}} p_J \right]^{\frac{1}{a_{2J} - a_{1J}}} \tag{24.19}$$

The relative *price diversification condition* (24.15) is equivalent to the following relative *factor price interval* restrictions:

$$a_{2J} > a_{1J} : \frac{1 - a_{2J}}{a_{2J}} k_J < \omega_J(p_J) < \frac{1 - a_{1J}}{a_{1J}} k_J \tag{24.20}$$

$$a_{1J} > a_{2J} : \frac{1 - a_{1J}}{a_{1J}} k_J < \omega_J(p_J) < \frac{1 - a_{2J}}{a_{2J}} k_J \tag{24.21}$$

As will be clear from Fig. 24.1 and further explained below, the conditions (24.15) and (24.18)–(24.21) are always satisfied by the *general equilibrium* solution in *autarky* (23.202). The *intervals* for the autarky general equilibrium solution $p_J(k_J)$ are given by closed intervals of (24.15).

### *Consumer Preferences and Demand Functions*

In each country $J$, there is a representative consumer with ***homothetic*** (preferences) of **CD** form:

$$u_J = U_J(Q_{1J}, Q_{2J}) = (Q_{1J})^{\alpha_J} (Q_{2J})^{1-\alpha_J} \tag{24.22}$$

where $Q_{iJ}$ is *consumption* of final good $\boldsymbol{i}$ in country $\boldsymbol{J}$.
Maximization of utility (24.22) under the budget constraint (24.5)

$$Y_J = P_{1J} \cdot Q_{1J} + P_{2J} \cdot Q_{2J}$$

yields the optimal *demanded* quantities $\boldsymbol{Q}_{iJ}$ and *expenditure* shares, $s_{iJ}$, (24.10),

$$Q_{1J} = \alpha_J \cdot (Y_J / P_{1J}) \; ; \quad Q_{2J} = (1 - \alpha_J) \cdot (Y_J / P_{2J}) \tag{24.23}$$

$$s_{1J} = P_{1J} Q_{1J} / Y_J = \alpha_J \; ; \; s_{2J} = P_{2J} Q_{2J} / Y_J = 1 - \alpha_J \tag{24.24}$$

### *Sector Technologies, Endowments and Global Diversification*

For later purposes, let us consider a parametrically *constrained* version of the *relative price interval restriction* (24.15) whereby $\boldsymbol{a}_{iA} = \boldsymbol{a}_{iB} = a_i$ and hence, $\bar{A}_A = \bar{A}_B = \bar{A}$:

$$\underline{p}_J = \bar{A} \frac{\gamma_{2J}}{\gamma_{1J}} \left[ \frac{1 - a_2}{a_2} k_J \right]^{(a_2 - a_1)} < p_J < \bar{A} \frac{\gamma_{2J}}{\gamma_{1J}} \left[ \frac{1 - a_1}{a_1} k_J \right]^{(a_2 - a_1)} = \overline{p}_J \tag{24.25}$$

In the *two-country* economy, condition (24.25) defines two *closed* price *intervals*: $\left[\underline{p}_A(k_A), \overline{p}_A(k_A)\right]$ and $\left[\underline{p}_B(k_B), \overline{p}_B(k_B)\right]$. It is excluded that any of these two closed price intervals fully contains the other.

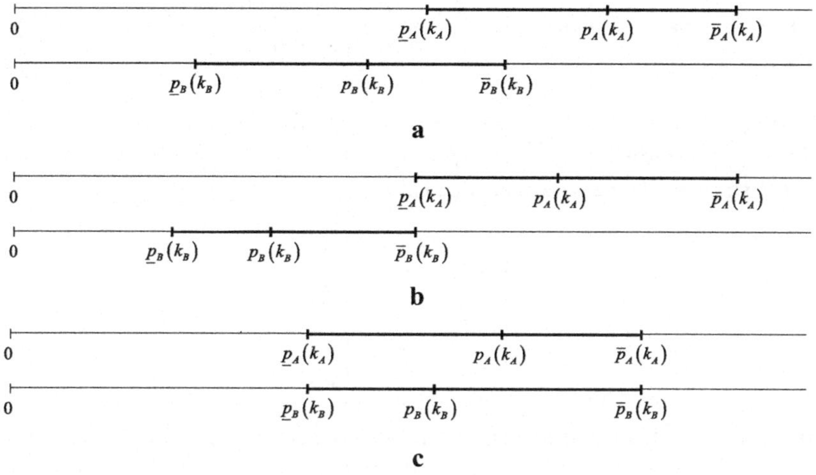


**Fig. 24.2** (**a**) Country price intervals partially overlap. In this case, *only* one of the two countries can specialize. This is either $A$ (Sector 2) or $B$ (Sector 1). (**b**) Country price intervals overlap at a *single* common *point* $\underline{p}_A = \overline{p}_B$. Both countries specialize with country $A$ ($B$) producing only good 2 (good 1). (**c**) Country price intervals coincide. In this case there is room for partial as well full specialization (one country will obviously specialize in one sector and the other in the other sector)

Without loss of *generality*, let $\underline{\boldsymbol{p}}_A \geq \underline{\boldsymbol{p}}_B$, as in Fig. 24.2a–c, and note that $\underline{p}_A \geq \underline{p}_B \Leftrightarrow \overline{p}_A \geq \overline{p}_B$ due to (24.25). Evidently, a ***necessary condition*** for the existence of a ***diversified*** international general equilibrium solution for the relative world ***price*** ($\boldsymbol{p}_W$) is that the ***intersection*** of the two ***price intervals*** $\left[\underline{p}_A, \overline{p}_A\right] \cap \left[\underline{p}_B, \overline{p}_B\right] \equiv \tilde{\boldsymbol{p}}$, is ***non-empty***: $\tilde{p} \neq \varnothing$.

By (24.25), we get the limits for the *ratio* of the *factor endowments* of the two countries, $(k_A/k_B)$, as:

$$\underline{p}_A \geq \underline{p}_B \Leftrightarrow \quad a_1 > a_2 : \frac{k_A}{k_B} \leq \left[\frac{\gamma_{1A}/\gamma_{2A}}{\gamma_{1B}/\gamma_{2B}}\right]^{\frac{1}{a_2-a_1}} \equiv \tilde{\gamma} \tag{24.26}$$

$$\underline{p}_A \geq \underline{p}_B \Leftrightarrow \quad a_1 < a_2 : \frac{k_A}{k_B} \geq \left[\frac{\gamma_{1A}/\gamma_{2A}}{\gamma_{1B}/\gamma_{2B}}\right]^{\frac{1}{a_2-a_1}} \equiv \tilde{\gamma} \tag{24.27}$$

With $\underline{p}_A \geq \underline{p}_B$ (see Fig. 24.2), $\tilde{p} \neq \varnothing$ requires: $\underline{p}_A \leq \overline{p}_B$, which stipulates that the factor *endowment ratio*, $(\boldsymbol{k}_A/\boldsymbol{k}_B)$ satisfies, cf. (24.25),

$$\underline{p}_A \leq \overline{p}_B \Leftrightarrow \quad a_1 > a_2 : \quad \frac{k_A}{k_B} \geq \frac{a_2/(1-a_2)}{a_1/(1-a_1)}\left[\frac{\gamma_{1A}/\gamma_{2A}}{\gamma_{1B}/\gamma_{2B}}\right]^{\frac{1}{a_2-a_1}} \equiv \tilde{a}\,\tilde{\gamma} \tag{24.28}$$

$$\underline{p}_A \leq \overline{p}_B \;\Leftrightarrow\; a_1 < a_2 : \quad \frac{k_A}{k_B} \leq \frac{a_2/(1-a_2)}{a_1/(1-a_1)} \left[ \frac{\gamma_{1A}/\gamma_{2A}}{\gamma_{1B}/\gamma_{2B}} \right]^{\frac{1}{a_2-a_1}} \equiv \widetilde{a}\,\widetilde{\gamma} \tag{24.29}$$

Note that, when $a_1 > a_2$ $[a_1 < a_2]$, then $\widetilde{a} < 1$ $[\widetilde{a} > 1]$.

Thus the condition, $\underline{p}_B \leq \underline{p}_A \leq \overline{p}_B \;\Leftrightarrow\; \widetilde{p} \neq \varnothing$, is met, *if* cf. (24.26), (24.28), (24.27), and (24.29):

$$a_1 > a_2 : \quad \widetilde{a}\,\widetilde{\gamma} \leq \frac{k_A}{k_B} \leq \widetilde{\gamma} \tag{24.30}$$

$$a_1 < a_2 : \quad \widetilde{\gamma} \leq \frac{k_A}{k_B} \leq \widetilde{a}\,\widetilde{\gamma} \tag{24.31}$$

If the *necessary* "factor endowment ratio" *conditions* (24.30–24.31) are satisfied, the *intersection* $[\,\widetilde{\boldsymbol{p}}\,]$ between the two *price (minimal cost)* intervals is *non-empty* (Fig. 24.2a). When the *equality* $(k_A/k_B) = \widetilde{a}\,\widetilde{\gamma}$ holds—endpoint of (24.30–24.31)—then $\underline{p}_A = \overline{p}_B$, and hence the intersection, $\widetilde{\boldsymbol{p}}$, between $[\,\underline{p}_A, \overline{p}_A]$ and $[\,\underline{p}_B, \overline{p}_B]$ is a *single* common *point*, (Fig. 24.2b).

When the other *equality* $(k_A/k_B) = \widetilde{\gamma}$ holds—endpoint of (24.30–24.31)—then two intervals, $[\,\underline{p}_A, \overline{p}_A]$ and $[\,\underline{p}_B, \overline{p}_B]$, *coincide* (and they are equal to $\widetilde{p}$), see Fig. 24.2c.

Thus, we see that the respective *endpoints* of (24.30), (24.31), (24.32), (24.33) determine the *largest potential interval* (range) for the factor *endowment ratio*, $(k_A/k_B)$, that are *compatible* with preserving the *production diversification* (two sectors) in *both* trading countries.

If the two countries have the *same* sector technologies (as in the HOS-HOL models, see below), $\widetilde{\gamma} = 1$, and the necessary *diversification* conditions (24.30–24.31) become:

$$a_1 > a_2 : \quad \widetilde{a} < \frac{k_A}{k_B} \leq 1 \tag{24.32}$$

$$a_1 < a_2 : \quad 1 \leq \frac{k_A}{k_B} < \widetilde{a} \tag{24.33}$$

Let us see two case examples, cf. Fig. 24.1, of the endowment ratio intervals (24.32), (24.33),

$$\textit{Case } 2 : a_1 = 0.5,\; a_2 = 0.25;\; a_1 > a_2 : \quad \widetilde{a} = 1/3 < \frac{k_A}{k_B} \leq 1 \tag{24.34}$$

$$\textit{Case } 1 : a_1 = 0.25,\; a_2 = 0.5;\; a_1 < a_2 : \quad 1 \leq \frac{k_A}{k_B} < 3 = \widetilde{a} \tag{24.35}$$

Although the assumption (hypothesis) of *diversification* was stressed as a *necessary* condition for *factor price equalization* (**FPE**), (see Samuelson (1948, 1949, p. 175, 178) and Samuelson (1949, p. 182, 193)), *no* explicit factor endowment *interval* like (24.32–24.33) for two countries was given then (later).

Moreover, consumer preferences and country sizes will *modify* these *intervals* (24.30–24.35)—*necessary*, but *not sufficient*—for the compatible endowment ratio, $(k_A/k_B)$, cf. Sect. "Existence of International General Equilibrium Solutions".

Incidentally, Fig. 24.2a and b reveal that the simple illustrative *assumption* $\underline{p}_A \geq \underline{p}_B$ plays a role in outlining the limiting cases of *"incipient specialization"* in the two countries [ "where nothing is being produced of one commodity, but where it is a matter of indifference, whether an infinitesimal amount is or is not being produced, so that price and marginal cost are equal", Samuelson (1949, p. 182) ].

When condition $\underline{p}_A \geq \underline{p}_B$ holds, cf. (24.26–24.27), there are three *possible specialization* cases:

(i) Country $A$ produces only good 2 (i.e. $p_W = \underline{p}_A$), and country $B$ does not specializes in any sector (because $\underline{p}_B < p_W < \overline{p}_B$); Fig. 24.2a.
(ii) Country $B$ produces only good 1 (i.e. $p_W = \overline{p}_B$), while country $A$ produces both goods (since $\underline{p}_A < p_W < \overline{p}_A$); Fig. 24.2a.
(iii) Both countries are specialized $(p_W = \underline{p}_A = \overline{p}_B)$, $A$ $(B)$ produces good 2 (1); Fig. 24.2b.

Clearly, these specialization patterns above just reverse with the assumption $\underline{p}_A < \underline{p}_B$.

## PPC, Free Trade, and International Equilibrium Prices

We assume now *free trade* between country $A$ and country $B$. Because of the total absence of frictions, national commodity markets are perfectly integrated into *one* world market, obeying the *law of one commodity price*, $\boldsymbol{P}_i$, and *one relative price*, $\boldsymbol{p}_W$:

$$P_{iA} = P_{iB} = P_{iW}\ , \quad i = 1, 2\ ; \quad p_A = p_B = p_W \tag{24.36}$$

Under trade openness, equilibrium on the goods markets requires (see 24.8)

$$Q_{iJ} = Y_{iJ} - X_{iJ}$$

Since the origin of the goods (home/import) is irrelevant in demand, the budget constraint (24.5) becomes

$$Y_J = P_{1W} Q_{1J} + P_{2W} Q_{2J} \tag{24.37}$$

Both countries are assumed to satisfy national *income*—factor income, final expenditure—*budget constraints* (*no* foreign *borrowing/lending* is allowed):

$$Y_J = P_{1W}Y_{1J} + P_{2W}Y_{2J} = w_J L_J + r_J K_J = P_{1W}Q_{1J} + P_{2W}Q_{2J} \tag{24.38}$$

Hence by (24.36–24.38), (24.23), we necessarily get the following relationships:

$$P_{1W}Q_{1J} = P_{1W}(Y_{1J} - X_{1J}) = \alpha_J(P_{1W}Y_{1J} + P_{2W}Y_{2J}) \ ;$$

$$P_{2W}Q_{2J} = P_{2W}(Y_{2J} - X_{2J}) = (1 - \alpha_J)(P_{1W}Y_{1J} + P_{2W}Y_{2J})$$

$$P_{1W}X_{1J} = (1-\alpha_J)\, P_{1W}Y_{1J} - \alpha_J \cdot P_{2W}Y_{2J} \ ; \quad P_{2W}X_{2J} = -\ (1-\alpha_J)\, P_{1W}Y_{1J} + \alpha_J \cdot P_{2W}Y_{2J} \tag{24.39}$$

Applying the notion of relative price $\boldsymbol{p}_W$ under the law of one price and the notion of sectoral *labor share*, $\boldsymbol{\lambda}_{L_{1J}}$, (23.3) gives by (24.39):

$$X_{1J} = L_J \left[ (1-\alpha_J)\,\lambda_{L_{1J}} \cdot y_{1J} - \frac{\alpha_J}{p_W}(1-\lambda_{L_{1J}}) \cdot y_{2J} \right] \tag{24.40}$$

$$X_{2J} = L_J \left[ -\ (1-\alpha_J)\ p_W\ \lambda_{L_{1J}} \cdot y_{1J} + \alpha_J\,(1-\lambda_{L_{1J}}) \cdot y_{2J} \right] \tag{24.41}$$

Let $\boldsymbol{v}_J$ represent the labor force (population) of country $J$ as a **share** of total *world* labor force $\boldsymbol{L}_W$ (with $L_W \equiv L_A + L_B$):

$$v_J = L_J / L_W\,, \qquad v_A + v_B = 1. \tag{24.42}$$

Use (24.42) into (24.40) and (24.41) to obtain *country exports* ($\gtrless 0$) of **good 1** and **good 2**:

$$X_{1J}\,(p_W; k_J) = L_W\, v_J \left[ (1-\alpha_J)\,\lambda_{L_{1J}} \cdot y_{1J} - \frac{\alpha_J}{p_W}(1-\lambda_{L_{1J}}) \cdot y_{2J} \right] \tag{24.43}$$

$$X_{2J}\,(p_W; k_J) = L_W\, v_J\, [-\ (1-\alpha_J)\ p_W\ \lambda_{L_{1J}} \cdot y_{1J} + \alpha_J\,(1-\lambda_{L_{1J}}) \cdot y_{2J}] \tag{24.44}$$

International *equilibrium* (market clearing) of *traded commodities* requires,

$$X_{1A} + X_{1B} = 0\ , \ \ X_{2A} + X_{2B} = 0\ ; \quad X_{iA} = -\,X_{iB} = M_{iB} \tag{24.45}$$

Recall that by Walras's law, $X_{2A}\,(p_W\,;k_A) = -X_{2B}\,(p_W\,;k_B)$, is satisfied by the international (*world*) equilibrium **terms of trade**, $p_W$, which are generally expressed by the following

**Proposition 24.1** *For two free - trading* **GE** *economies with the* **CD** *utility functions (24.22) and sector technologies,* $\mathbf{y}_{ij}$, *the international (world) equilibrium* **terms of trade,** $\mathbf{p}_W = \mathbf{P}_{1W}/\mathbf{P}_{2W}$, *are given by:*

$$p_W = \frac{\upsilon_A \alpha_A (1-\lambda_{L_{1A}}) \cdot y_{2A} + \upsilon_B \alpha_B (1-\lambda_{L_{1B}}) \cdot y_{2B}}{\upsilon_A (1-\alpha_A) \lambda_{L_{1A}} \cdot y_{1A} + \upsilon_B (1-\alpha_B) \lambda_{L_{1B}} \cdot y_{1B}} \tag{24.46}$$

$$= \frac{y_{2A}}{y_{1A}} \cdot \frac{\upsilon_A \alpha_A (1-\lambda_{L_{1A}}) + \upsilon_B \alpha_B (1-\lambda_{L_{1B}}) \cdot (y_{2B}/y_{2A})}{\upsilon_A (1-\alpha_A) \cdot \lambda_{L_{1A}} + \upsilon_B (1-\alpha_B) \lambda_{L_{1B}} \cdot (y_{1B}/y_{1A})} \tag{24.47}$$

*With* **same** *technologies in A, B,* $\mathbf{y}_{ij} = \mathbf{y}_i$, $\mathbf{k}_{ij} = \mathbf{k}_i$, *(24.46) gives:*

$$p_W = \frac{y_2}{y_1} \cdot \frac{\upsilon_A \alpha_A (1-\lambda_{L_{1A}}) + \upsilon_B \alpha_B (1-\lambda_{L_{1B}})}{\upsilon_A (1-\alpha_A) \cdot \lambda_{L_{1A}} + \upsilon_B (1-\alpha_B) \lambda_{L_{1B}}} \tag{24.48}$$

*Applying the* **Leontief,** $\boldsymbol{\lambda}_{L_{1A}}(\mathbf{k}_A)$, $\boldsymbol{\lambda}_{L_{1B}}(\mathbf{k}_B)$, *(23.86), to (24.46–24.48), gives:*

$$p_W = \frac{y_{2A}\, \upsilon_A\, \alpha_A\, (k_{2B} - k_{1B}) \cdot (k_A - k_{1A}) + y_{2B}\, \upsilon_B\, \alpha_B\, (k_{2A} - k_{1A}) \cdot (k_B - k_{1B})}{y_{1A}\, \upsilon_A\, (1-\alpha_A)(k_{2B} - k_{1B}) \cdot (k_{2A} - k_A) + y_{1B}\, \upsilon_B\, (1-\alpha_B)(k_{2A} - k_{1A}) \cdot (k_{2B} - k_B)} \tag{24.49}$$

$$p_W = \frac{y_2}{y_1} \cdot \frac{(\upsilon_A \alpha_A + \upsilon_B \alpha_B) k_1 - \upsilon_A \alpha_A \cdot k_A - \upsilon_B \alpha_B \cdot k_B}{-[\upsilon_A (1-\alpha_A) + \upsilon_B (1-\alpha_B)] k_2 + \upsilon_A (1-\alpha_A) \cdot k_A + \upsilon_B (1-\alpha_B) \cdot k_B} \tag{24.50}$$

***Proof*** Solving world market equilibrium condition (24.45) for *commodity* 1: $X_{1A}(p_W; k_A) = -X_{1B}(p_W; k_B)$, with the exports (24.43–24.44), gives the *international equilibrium* price ratio (terms of trade): $p_W$, (24.46). Cf. (21.112). □

The *terms of trade surfaces* (TTS) of (24.50), have the *algebraic* form,

$$p_W = \Phi(k_A, k_B) = \frac{a_0 + a_1 k_A + a_2 k_B}{b_0 + b_1 k_A + b_2 k_B}, \tag{24.51}$$

i.e., belongs to the family of quadratics in three variables (conic surfaces). Shape[1] of (24.51): *hyperbolic paraboloid* with hyperbolas for fixed $k_A$ or $k_B$.

Proposition 24.1 shows how the *world* relative *price ratio*, $p_W$, is *explicitly* determined by factor *endowments*, technology-, preference *parameters* of both countries, and next gives for *two countries* (A,B) their *trade patterns* (what commodity countries export or imports) that follow from the $p_W$, (24.49–24.50).

[1] Also the shapes of the terms of trade surfaces (TTS)—with *flexible* sector *technologies* (internationally *identical*) and *no inferior* goods of *demand* in either country—are similar to (24.51), i.e., having the monotone partial derivatives for the international *terms of trade*:

$$k_2 > k_1: \quad \partial p_W/\partial k_A > 0, \quad \partial p_W/\partial k_B > 0,$$

$$k_1 > k_2: \quad \partial p_W/\partial k_A < 0, \quad \partial p_W/\partial k_B < 0.$$

Rigorous proof is given in Södersten (1964); cf. Rybczynski (1955), and Kemp (1969).

Thus with Proposition 24.1, we get and can compare **trade** (international) **GE** (general equilibrium) **allocations** with the former **GE** solutions of **autarky** with the **CD** preferences and **Leontief** technologies (see Figs. 23.9a–b).

For later purposes, the use of Proposition 24.1 is illustrated in *simple* cases of *same* technologies, cf. (24.48), and *same* consumer preferences $\boldsymbol{\alpha}_J$ in *both* countries $A$ and $B$ that only *differ* in **endowments** $(k_A, k_B)$, and so specified as (see 23.120 and Fig. 23.9b)

$$\text{Fig. 23.9b: } a_{L_1} = 2,\ a_{K_1} = 1.6,\ a_{L_2} = 1,\ a_{K_2} = 3.5 :\ y_1 = 0.5, k_1 = 0.8,$$
$$y_2 = 1, k_2 = 3.5\ ;\ \alpha = 0.4\ [\underline{p}, \overline{p}] = [0.45, 2.0],\ [\underline{k}, \overline{k}] = [1.49, 2.42];$$
$$k_B = 2,\ p_B(k_B) = 1.07;\ k_A = 2.3,\ p_A(k_A) = 1.67 \qquad (24.52)$$

with $\mathbf{k_A} = \mathbf{2.3}$ chosen for country A and hence *autarky* $p_A(k_A) = 1.67$ (see 23.118). The factor *allocations* $\lambda_{L_{1A}}, \lambda_{L_{1B}}$, (23.86), $\lambda_{K_{1A}}, \lambda_{K_{1B}}$, (23.4), and **outputs** (23.87–23.88) are the **same** in both *autarky* and *trade*, and they become by (24.52):

$$\lambda_{L_{1A}} = 0.44,\ \lambda_{K_{1A}} = 0.16,\ Y_{1A} = 0.22,\ Y_{2A} = 0.56\ ;$$
$$\lambda_{L_{1B}} = 0.56,\ \lambda_{K_{1B}} = 0.22,\ Y_{1B} = 0.28,\ Y_{2B} = 0.44 \qquad (24.53)$$

With *same* $\alpha$, *same* country **size**, $v_A = v_B = 0.5$, we get by (24.50), (24.52):

$$p_W = \frac{y_2}{y_1} \cdot \frac{2\alpha k_1 - \alpha (k_A + k_B)}{-2(1-\alpha)k_2 + (1-\alpha_A)(k_A + k_B)}$$
$$= \frac{1}{0.5} \cdot \frac{2 \cdot 0.4 \cdot 0.8 - 0.4 \cdot 4.3}{-2 \cdot 0.6 \cdot 3.5 + 0.6 \cdot 4.3} = \frac{2.16}{1.62} = \frac{4}{3} = 1.33 \qquad (24.54)$$

This world market *equilibrium price* ratio, $p_W = P_1/P_2 \in [1.07, 1.67]$, and $p_W, p_B, p_A$, refer to Fig. 23.9b—with $\omega_B = 2.29$, and $\omega_A = 3$, $\omega_W = 4.58$, cf. (23.116). Although $p_W = 1.33$ is seen by expression (24.54), the *export* (import) *curves* (24.43–24.44), $(\boldsymbol{p})$, have with, (24.52–24.53), *explicit* quantitative forms, $\mathbf{L_W = 2}$:

$$X_{1A}(p) = 0.133 - \frac{0.222}{p},\quad X_{1B}(p) = 0.167 - \frac{0.178}{p}\ ;$$
$$X_{2A}(p) = 0.222 - 0.133\,p,\quad X_{2B}(p) = 0.178 - 0.167\,p \qquad (24.55)$$

By country outputs (24.53) (***PPC*** point) we get—world outputs: $Y_1 = Q_1 = 0.5$, $Y_2 = Q_2 = 1.0$, unchanged—and the *trade* volumes by (24.54–24.55), and country consumptions by (24.8) and (24.53):

$$X_{1A} = -0.033,\ Q_{1A} = 0.253,\ X_{2A} = 0.04,\ Q_{2A} = 0.52\ ;$$
$$X_{1B} = 0.033,\ Q_{1B} = 0.247,\ X_{2B} = -0.04,\ Q_{2B} = 0.48 \qquad (24.56)$$

*Optimal* consumptions with *trade* (24.56) compared to *autarky* (24.53) give representative consumer (community) *utility gains* in both A and B, cf. (24.37):

$$U_A(Q_{1A}, Q_{2A}) = 0.253^{0.4}\, 0.52^{0.6} = 0.390 >$$
$$U_A(Y_{1A}, Y_{2A}) = 0.22^{0.4}\, 0.56^{0.6} = 0.385 \tag{24.57}$$
$$U_B(Q_{1B}, Q_{2B}) = 0.247^{0.4}\, 0.48^{0.6} = 0.368 >$$
$$U_A(Y_{1B}, Y_{2B}) = 0.28^{0.4}\, 0.44^{0.6} = 0.367 \tag{24.58}$$

The *international* general *equilibrium solution* of the terms of trade (24.54) with *Leontief technologies* (24.52) can be related to diagrams of *Offer Curves.*

### *Export and Import Functions: Trade Balance, Offer Curves*

Proposition 24.1 was derived under the *assumption* that countries A, B, satisfied the *National Accounting* (income-expenditure) *Constraint*, (24.38). Hence their *International Trade Accounts* also satisfy the Trade Balance *Equation*, $P_1X_{1J} + P_2X_{2J} = 0$, $J = A, B$, i.e., for *any*, $p = P_1/P_2$:

$$P_1X_{1J} + P_2X_{2J} = 0,\ p\,X_{1J} + X_{2J} = 0:$$
$$X_{2A}(p) + p\,X_{1A}(p) = 0,$$
$$X_{2B}(p) + p\,X_{1B}(p) = 0 \tag{24.59}$$

Traditionally, international *equilibrium* terms of trade, $p_W$, is in texts/journal expositions shown as the *intersection* of two, so-called **Offer** Curves, which are nothing but the *Trade Balance Curve* (**TBC**) of country A and B, stated in (24.59). But despite the well-known *geometric constructions* of *Offer* curves from ***PPC*** curves and consumer *Utility* (Indifference) curves, surprisingly **no** *explicit* (analytic or algebraic) **expressions** of such two intersecting **TBC-Offer** *curves* seem given anywhere in the vast economic literature.

In Chap. 23, we saw *explicit one-parameter* formulas $[\, H_1(\lambda_{L_{1J}}),\ H_2(\lambda_{L_{1J}})\,]$ (see 23.22 and 23.23) of **PPC** curves, $\{Y_{1J}, Y_{2J}\}$. Similarly, *one-parameter* formulas in **(*p*)** can be obtained for the **TBC-Offer** (*export-import*) curves of country A, B, (24.59).

In fact, we have already obtained the actual formulas of the *explicit* export-import curves of (24.43) and (24.44) in $X_{iJ}\,(p)$, (24.55), and hence, $-X_{iJ}\,(p)$, cf. Fig. 24.3, to be used in the *trade balance* Eqs. (24.59). Thus, we can state, as follows:

*Country* B. Explicit *export, import* functions: $X_{1B}(p) > 0,\ -X_{2B}(p) > 0,$

$$X_{1B}\,(p) = L_W\, v_B \left[ (1-\alpha_B)\,\lambda_{L_{1B}}\, y_{1B} - \frac{\alpha_B}{p}\,(1-\lambda_{L_{1B}})\, y_{2B} \right]\ ;\ \lambda_{L_{1B}} = 0.56 \tag{24.60}$$

$$= 0.167\ -\ 0.178\,/\,p\ ,\quad p \in [\,1.07,\, 1.67\,] \tag{24.61}$$

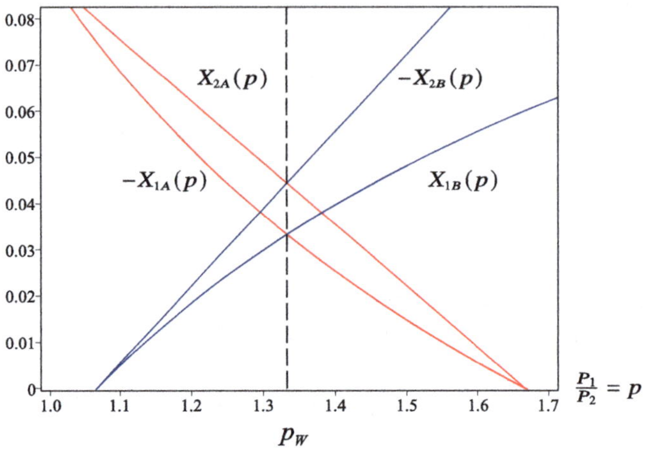


**Fig. 24.3** Export, $X_{1B}(p)$, (24.60–24.61), Import, $[-X_{2B}(p)]$, (24.62–24.63), and the Import, $-X_{1A}(p)$, (24.64–24.65), Export, $[X_{2A}(p)]$, (24.66–24.67)

$$-X_{2B}(p) = L_W v_B [(1-\alpha_B)\lambda_{L_{1B}} y_{1B}\, p - \alpha_B (1-\lambda_{L_{1B}}) y_{2B}];\ \lambda_{L_{1B}} = 0.56 \tag{24.62}$$

$$= -0.178 + 0.167\, p, \quad p \in [1.07, 1.67] \tag{24.63}$$

Explicit *Offer Curve*, $\mathbf{O}_B(p) = \{X_{1B}(p), -X_{2B}(p)\}$, (24.60–24.63), is in Fig. 24.4.

*Country* A. Explicit *import, export* functions: $-X_{1A}(p) > 0,\ X_{2A}(p) > 0$,

$$-X_{1A}(p) = L_W v_A \left[-(1-\alpha_A)\lambda_{L_{1A}} y_{1A} + \frac{\alpha_A}{p}(1-\lambda_{L_{1A}}) y_{2A}\right];\ \lambda_{L_{1A}} = 0.44 \tag{24.64}$$

$$= -0.133 + 0.222/p, \quad p \in [1.67, 1.07] \tag{24.65}$$

$$X_{2A}(p) = L_W v_A [-(1-\alpha_A)\lambda_{L_{1A}} y_{1A}\, p + \alpha_A (1-\lambda_{L_{1A}}) y_{2A}];\ \lambda_{L_{1A}} = 0.44 \tag{24.66}$$

$$= 0.222 - 0.133\, p, \quad p \in [1.67, 1.07] \tag{24.67}$$

Explicit *Offer Curve*, $\mathbf{O}_A(p) = \{-X_{1A}(p), X_{2A}(p)\}$, (24.64–24.67), is in Fig. 24.4.

Note that the "*parameter*" $(p)$—*ray slope* $(p)$—of $\mathbf{O}_A(p)$ has opposite orientation of $(p)$ in $\mathbf{O}_{o_B}(p)$; but at the *origin* of the Offer Curves, the "*parameter*"

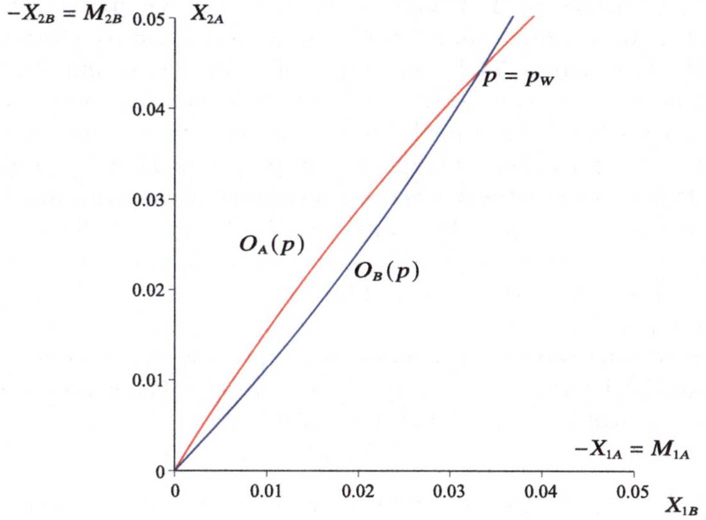


**Fig. 24.4** The *Offer Curve*: $O_B(p) = \{X_{1B}(p), -X_{2B}(p)\}$, (24.60–24.63), (24.68), and the *Offer Curve*: $O_A(p) = \{-X_{1A}(p), X_{2A}(p)\}$, (24.64–24.67), (24.69)

($\boldsymbol{p}$) begins at their respective autarky **GE** price, $p_J(k_J)$, in (23.118), cf. Fig. 23.9b.

The single *parameter* ($p$) is easily *eliminated* from the *Offer* curves, $\mathbf{O}_J(p)$, and the **algebraic** equation (function form) of *Offer Curves* in B and A are:

*Country* B. Explicit Offer—*export-import* curve: $\{X_{1B} > 0,\ -X_{2B} > 0\}$

$$-\ X_{2B} = \frac{0.178\ X_{1B}}{0.167 - X_{1B}} \equiv M_{2B}\,,\quad 0 \le X_{1B} < 0.167\ ;\quad E(M_{2B}, X_{1B}) = \frac{0.167}{0.167 - X_{1B}} \tag{24.68}$$

*Country* A. Explicit Offer—*import-export* curve: $\{-\ X_{1A} > 0,\ X_{2A} > 0\}$

$$X_{2A} = \frac{-\ 0.222\ X_{1A}}{0.133 - X_{1A}} \equiv \frac{0.222\ M_{1A}}{0.133 + M_{1A}}\ ,\ 0 \le M_{1A}\ ;\quad E(X_{2A}, M_{1A}) = \frac{0.133}{0.133 + M_{1A}} \tag{24.69}$$

$(X_{1B}, M_{2B}) = (0.033, 0.044) = (M_{1A}, X_{2A})$ - (24.56) as intersection, (24.68–24.69), and $\boldsymbol{p = p_W = 1.33}$, (24.54), is clearly *equivalent* to **TBC** intersection:

$$X_{2A}\,(p_W) +\ p_W\,X_{1A}\,(p_W)\ =\ X_{2B}\,(p_W) +\ p_W\,X_{1B}\,(p_W) \tag{24.70}$$

Offer Curves—$\mathbf{O}_A$ (24.69), $\mathbf{O}_B$, (24.68)—are rectangular hyperbolas, Fig. 24.4, and they are both **elastic**: $E(M_{2J}, X_{1J}) > 1$ .

With the analysis of TBC-Offer Curves above, we are in *classic* trade theory, where the country export-import curves were called *Reciprocal Demand* curves. By Proposition 24.1, the terms of trade ($p_W$), and the volumes of international trade flows (export-import) had their causes (determinants, parameters) on both the "supply" side (technology, endowment) and the "demand" side (consumer preferences), but here with *Leontief*—rigid sector, fixed coefficient—*technologies*, where each country (A, B) with their different *endowments* had only *one* **PPC** point (see 23.87 and 23.88), and accordingly exports-imports are essentially similar to trade between consumers of "*Exchange Economies*" (with no production and factor reallocation within countries implied).

Before we enter ordinary Reciprocal Demand analysis, we should also *apply* Proposition 24.1 with **CD** preferences to *terms of trade*, export-import and *Offer Curves* involved with *classical* linear **PPC**.

## Linear PPC, General Equilibrium, and International Trade

Whereas Leontief sector technologies above implied a PPC with zero *elasticity* of *transformation* ($\tau = 0$), the linear PPC had an infinite elasticity ($\tau = -\infty$), cf. Ex. 1 in Sect. "Explicit Transformation Functions and Transformation Curves".With the Consumer Demand of CD preferences (24.37), the *autarky* **GE** *tangency* output point on *linear* PPC in both countries requires evidently the *size* of **GE** labor *allocations* $\lambda_{L_{1J}}$ to be, cf. (23.197),

$$\mathbf{GE} \; : \lambda_{L_{1J}} = \alpha_J \; , \; \lambda_{L_{2J}} = 1 - \alpha_J \; ; \quad J = A, B \tag{24.71}$$

Here and for later purposes, the chosen *parameter set* for country A, B, are:

$$\frac{a_{L_{1J}}}{a_{L_{2J}}} = \frac{y_{2J}}{y_{1J}} = \frac{a_{K_{1J}}}{a_{K_{2J}}} \; ;$$

$$a_{L_{1B}} = 1.67 \, , \; a_{L_{2B}} = 1.11 ; \; y_{1B} = 0.6 \, , \; y_{2B} = 0.9 \; : \; p_B = 1.5 ; \; \alpha_B = 0.6 ;$$

$$a_{L_{1A}} = 2, \; a_{L_{2A}} = 1 ; \; y_{1A} = 0.5, \; y_{2A} = 1 \; : \; p_A = 2 \; ;$$

$$\alpha_A = 0.25 \; ; \; L_A = 2 \, , \; \mathbf{L_B} = \mathbf{4} \tag{24.72}$$

By (24.72), *maximal* PPC outputs, $Y^*_{1J} = L_J \, y_{1J} \, , Y^*_{2J} = L_J \, y_{2J}$ , J=A,B, are:

$$Y^*_{1A} = 1 \, , \; Y^*_{2A} = 2 \; ; \; Y^*_{1B} = 2.4, \; Y^*_{2B} = 3.6 \; ;$$

$$\lambda_{L_{1J}} = \alpha_J \; : \; Y_{1A} = 0.25 \, , \; Y_{2A} = 1.5 \; ; \; Y_{1B} = 1.44, \; Y_{2B} = 1.44 \tag{24.73}$$

The *autarky* **GE** outputs, consumptions ($Y_{iJ} = Q_{iJ}$, i= 1,2, J=A,B) are with (24.71–24.72) obtained as, $Y_{1J} = \alpha_J \, L_J \, , Y_{2J} = (1 - \alpha_J) \, L_J$ , and seen in (24.73), and the *total* (world) *output* of good 1 and 2, $(Y_1, Y_2)$, with autarky are:

$$Y_1 = Y_{1A}+Y_{1B} = 0.25 + 1.44 = 1.69 \; ; \; Y_2 = Y_{2A}+Y_{2B} = 1.5 + 1.44 = 1.94 \tag{24.74}$$

If autarky *labor allocation* $\lambda_{L_{1J}} = \alpha_J$ (24.71) are preserved in *both* countries after opening of *trade*, then the *terms of trade* $p_w$ becomes by (24.46), (24.72):

$$\begin{aligned} p_w &= \frac{L_A \alpha_A (1-\alpha_A) y_{2A} + L_B \alpha_B (1-\alpha_B) y_{2B}}{L_A (1-\alpha_A)\, \alpha_A y_{1A} + L_B (1-\alpha_B)\, \alpha_B y_{1B}} \\ &= \frac{2 \cdot 0.188 \cdot 1 + 4 \cdot 0.24 \cdot 0.9}{2 \cdot 0.188 \cdot 0.5 + 4 \cdot 0.24 \cdot 0.6} = 1.62 \end{aligned} \tag{24.75}$$

The *explicit* export-import curves, $X_{iJ}(p)$, (24.55), *trade balances* (24.59) are:

*Country* B. Explicit *export, import* functions: $X_{1B}(p) > 0, \; -X_{2B}(p) > 0$,

$$X_{1B}(p) = L_B[\,(1-\alpha_B)\,\lambda_{L_{1B}}\, y_{1B} - \frac{\alpha_B}{p}\,(1-\lambda_{L_{1B}})\, y_{2B}\,] \; ; \; \lambda_{L_{1B}} = \alpha_B = 0.6 \tag{24.76}$$

$$= 0.576 - 0.864\,/\,p\,, \quad p \in [\,1.5\,,\, 2.0\,] \tag{24.77}$$

$$-X_{2B}(p) = L_B[(1-\alpha_B)\,\lambda_{L_{1B}}\, y_{1B}\; p - \alpha_B\,(1-\lambda_{L_{1B}})\, y_{2B}] \; ; \; \lambda_{L_{1B}} = \alpha_B = 0.6 \tag{24.78}$$

$$= -\,0.864 + 0.576\; p\,, \quad p \in [\,1.5\,,\, 2.0\,] \tag{24.79}$$

*Offer Curve*, $\mathbf{O}_B(p) = \{X_{1B}(p), -X_{2B}(p)\}$, (24.76–24.79), looks as $\mathbf{O}_B(p)$, Fig. 24.4.

*Country* A. Explicit *import, export* functions: $-X_{1A}(p) > 0, \; X_{2A}(p) > 0$,

$$-X_{1A}(p) = L_A[-(1-\alpha_A)\lambda_{L_{1A}}\, y_{1A} + \frac{\alpha_A}{p}(1-\lambda_{L_{1A}})\, y_{2A}] ; \; \lambda_{L_{1A}} = \alpha_A = 0.25 \tag{24.80}$$

$$= -\,0.1875 + 0.375\,/\,p\,, \quad p \in [\,2.0\,,\, 1.5\,] \tag{24.81}$$

$$X_{2A}(p) = L_A[-\,(1-\alpha_A)\,\lambda_{L_{1A}}\, y_{1A}\; p + \alpha_A\,(1-\lambda_{L_{1A}}) y_{2A}] \; ; \; \lambda_{L_{1A}} = \alpha_A = 0.25 \tag{24.82}$$

$$= 0.375 - 0.1875\; p\,, \quad p \in [\,2.0\,,\, 1.5\,] \tag{24.83}$$

*Offer Curve*, $\mathbf{O}_A(p) = \{-X_{1A}(p), X_{2A}(p)\}$, (24.80–24.83), is as $\mathbf{O}_A(p)$, Fig. 24.4.

Trade with $p_W$ (24.75) gives similar *better* consumption [ higher indifference curve (utility level) ] in A and B—*Gains* by *Exchange*[2]—as seen, (24.56–24.58).

There can be many combinations of *trade* with *incomplete* specialization after opening of trade with other choices of $\lambda_{L_{1J}} \neq \alpha_J$, than in $p_W$, (24.75). In contrast to *Leontief* case with only one choice of $\lambda_{L_{1J}}$, the *linear* PPC allow *many* production (PPC) points, but they are not optimal as MRT of PPC differ from the CD marginal rate of substitution (24.22) in consumption.

The option of *complete specialization* seems **optimal** worldwide for *two* countries with *linear* PPC—representing *Pareto efficiency* of factor (Labor) allocation (maximum outputs, supply side), whenever $p_A \neq p_B$ in autarky, (24.72)—such that country A is specializing in good 2, ($\lambda_{L_{1A}} = 0$), country B, specializing in good 1, ($\lambda_{L_{1B}} = 1$).

The *export, import* functions, (24.118–24.44), for country B with $\lambda_{L_{1B}} = 1$, and for country A with $\lambda_{L_{1A}} = 0$, become explicitly in parameter values (24.72):

$$X_{1B}(p) = L_B(1-\alpha_B)y_{1B} = (1-\alpha_B)Y^*_{1B} = 0.96\,;$$
$$-X_{2B}(p) = (1-\alpha_B)Y^*_{1B}\,p = 0.96\,p \tag{24.84}$$

$$-X_{1A}(p) = L_A\frac{\alpha_A y_{2A}}{p} = \frac{\alpha_A Y^*_{2A}}{p} = \frac{0.5}{p}\;;\; X_{2A}(p) = L_A\alpha_A y_{2A} = \alpha_A Y^*_{2A} = 0.5 \tag{24.85}$$

*World market* equilibrium condition (24.45) for *good* 1: $-X_{1A}(p) = X_{1B}(p)$, or *good* 2: $X_{2A}(p) = -X_{2B}(p)$, gives with (24.84–24.85), the same *international equilibrium* terms of trade: $p_W = \frac{0.5}{0.96} = 0.52$. Here the *Offer Curves*, $\mathbf{O}_B(p)$ by (24.84), and, $\mathbf{O}_A(p)$ by (24.85), are *straight lines* (vertical/horizontal) with an intersection, also giving the ray *slope*: $p_W = 0.52$. The $p_W = 0.52$ is in contrast to (24.75) outside the *autarky* **GE** interval: $[\,p_A\,,\ p_B\,] = [\,1.5\,,\ 2.0\,]$. The economic content and implications of the dilemma of $p_W \notin [\,p_A\,,\ p_B\,]$ needs to be clarified and possibly rectified, as explained and illustrated below.

To this end, we restate the *international equilibrium* price ratio (24.46) in specialization case: $\lambda_{L_{1A}} = 0$, $\lambda_{L_{1B}} = 1$, and parameters (24.72), cf. (24.84–24.85):

$$p_W = \frac{\alpha_A\, y_{2A} L_A}{(1-\alpha_B)y_{1B}L_B} = \frac{\alpha_A\, Y^*_{2A}}{(1-\alpha_B)Y^*_{1B}} = \frac{0.25\cdot 2}{(1-0.6)\cdot 2.4} = 0.52 = \frac{X_{2A}}{X_{1B}} \tag{24.86}$$

With *specialization*, $\lambda_{L_{1A}} = 0$, $\lambda_{L_{1B}} = 1$, the *total* (world) *outputs* are given by (24.73) as, $(Y^*_1, Y^*_2) \equiv (Y^*_{1B}, Y^*_{2A})$—and equal to *total* country *consumptions*:

$$Y^*_1 = Y^*_{1B} = 2.4 = Q_{1A} + Q_{1B} = 0.96 + 1.44\;;$$
$$Y^*_2 = Y^*_{2A} = 2 = Q_{2A} + Q_{2B} = 1.5 + 0.5 \tag{24.87}$$

[2] Discussion/justification of this statement, see Grandmont and McFadden (1972, p. 109).

The country consumptions of good 1 and 2 follow from the exports/imports by (24.84–24.85) with $p = p_W = 0.52$, and specialized country outputs of (24.87):

$$Q_{1A} = X_{1B} = 0.96,\; Q_{2A} = Y^*_{2A} - X_{2A} = 2 - 0.5 = 1.5\,;$$
$$Q_{1B} = Y^*_{1B} - X_{1B} = 2.4 - 0.96 = 1.44,\; Q_{2B} = X_{2A} = 0.5 \qquad (24.88)$$

Evidently total *world outputs* with specialization, (24.87), $(Y_1^*, Y_2^*) = (2.4, 2.0)$ are *larger* than total world outputs from autarky, (24.74), $(Y_1, Y_2) = (1.69, 1.94)$. But only country A has clearly *gained* from the trade of specialized countries, as by (24.88), (24.73), $(Q_{1A}, Q_{2A}) = (0.96, 1.5) > (Y_{1A}, Y_{2A}) = (0.25, 1.5)$, and country B has *lost*, $(Q_{1B}, Q_{2B}) = (1.44, 0.5) < (Y_{1B}, Y_{2B}) = (1.44, 1.44)$.

Next, the numerical *size* of $p_W = 0.52$ in (24.86)—and its consequences seen above—can only be avoided by requiring our analytical-algebraic expression of a **unique** (free-trade) world *equilibrium terms of trade*, $p_W$ in (24.86)—with both counties *specialized* as—always to satisfy the condition of lying between the *slopes* of the **two linear PPC** of country A and B, that is, e.g., (24.72):

$$p_B = \frac{y_{2B}}{y_{1B}} \le p_W = \frac{\alpha_A\, y_{2A} L_A}{(1-\alpha_B)\, y_{1B} L_B} = \frac{\alpha_A\, Y^*_{2A}}{(1-\alpha_B) Y^*_{1B}} = \frac{X_{2A}}{X_{1B}} \le \frac{y_{2A}}{y_{1A}} = p_A \qquad (24.89)$$

To be brief—and expressed in our economic *notation*, (24.72), (24.86)—the **Proof** of *inequalities* (24.89) as the **necessary** and **sufficient** conditions for **both** countries to **specialize** is given by, Melvin (1969, p. 111), Harwitz (1972, p. 186), and Chipman (1979, p. 480)

To comply with the specialization conditions (24.89), some adjustments are needed in the parameter set numbers (24.72), which we will fully *rectify* to (24.89) by properly changing only *country* (labor) *size* $L_B$ in (24.72), viz.,

$$1.5 \le \frac{0.5}{0.4 \cdot 0.6\, L_B} \le 2 \;\Leftrightarrow\; 1.04 \le L_B \le 1.39\,;$$
$$\mathbf{L_B = 1.2} : \; Y^*_{1B} = 0.72\,,\; Y^*_{2B} = 1.08\,,\; Q_{1B} = 0.43\,,\; Q_{2B} = 0.43 \qquad (24.90)$$

i.e., **full** specialization confines $\mathbf{L_B}$ to the **open** (strict) *interval* ]1.04, 1.39[. Upon interval **boundaries** (weak inequality), only **one** country can be **specialized**, the *other* country must produce *both goods*.

Within the **open** interval, we choose $\mathbf{L_B} = 1.2$ to demonstrate trade (export, import) and the gains obtained by **two** specialized countries. First, the *maximum* possible PPC outputs of good 1 and 2 in *country* **B** must be changed with, $L_B = 1.2$, as done in (24.90), where the new *autarky* **GE** *outputs* (consumptions) in country B also replace those numbers shown in (24.73).

With **specialization**, the size of the *international equilibrium* price ratio $\mathbf{p}_W$ = **1.74** below follows immediately from (24.86), and so do the corresponding country exports/imports by (24.84–24.85) and (24.73):

$$p_W = \frac{0.5}{0.24 \cdot 1.2} = 1.74\,;\; X_{1B} = 0.29\,,\; -X_{2B} = 0.29 \cdot 1.74 = 0.5\,,$$

$$X_{2A} = 0.5\,,\; -X_{1A} = \frac{0.5}{1.74} = 0.29 \tag{24.91}$$

As each country now only produces their specialized commodity and imports the other, their **balanced trade** simply gives by (24.90–24.91) the **country consumption** levels of **both goods** as:

$$Q_{1A} = X_{1B} = 0.29,\; Q_{2A} = Y^*_{2B} - X_{2A} = 2 - 0.5 = 1.5\,;$$

$$Q_{1B} = Y^*_{1B} - X_{1B} = 0.72 - 0.29 = 0.43,\; Q_{2B} = X_{2A} = 0.5 \tag{24.92}$$

Comparing their respective **autarky** consumption levels, listed in (24.90) and (24.73), with their corresponding level with **trade** in (24.92), the result is that *both* countries have **larger** consumptions. More precisely, the outcome is here that *both* countries have maintained the **same** autarky consumption **level** in their specialized **export** good, and reached a **higher** consumption **level** of the **import** good.

This is a **general** trade theory *result* with **CD** utility[3] and linear **PCC** as further illustrated by *famous* classical-historical *trade* theory *examples* below.

### *Linear PPC, Reciprocal Demands, Terms of Trade—J.S. Mill*

Mill (1848, 1875, 1909, p. 593)—Equation of International Demand, (24.59), *'reciprocal demands'*—was the first ever to obtain numbers and a formula for the *terms of trade*, $p_W$. In Mill (1848, 1875, 1909, p. 598) and using Chipman (1979, p. 481)'s reconstruction of linear PPC and his CD utility parameters, we see (in our notation):

$$\frac{a_{L_{1J}}}{a_{L_{2J}}} = \frac{y_{2J}}{y_{1J}}\,;\; a_{L_{1B}} = 0.5\,,\; a_{L_{2B}} = 1 \,:\; y_{1B} = 2\,,\; y_{2B} = 1,\; p_B = 0.5\,;\; \alpha_B = 0.6\,;$$

$$a_{L_{1A}} = 1,\; a_{L_{2A}} = 1 \,:\; y_{1A} = 1,\; y_{2A} = 1,\; p_A = 1\,;\; \alpha_A = 0.25\,;\; L_B = 2,\; L_A = 4. \tag{24.93}$$

By (24.93), maximal PPC outputs, $Y^*_{1_J} = L_J\, y_{1J}\,, Y^*_{2_J} = L_J\, y_{2J}$ , J=A,B, are:

$$Y^*_{1A} = 4\,,\; Y^*_{2A} = 4\,,\; Y^*_{1B} = 4\,,\; Y^*_{2B} = 2\;;\; Y_{1A} = 1\,,\; Y_{2A} = 3\,,\; Y_{1B} = 2.4\,,\; Y_{2B} = 0.8 \tag{24.94}$$

[3] With CD, we could *not* have full specialization without *trade*, as CD does not permit consumption of only one good—such one good consumption could not be an *autarky* GE.

The *autarky* **GE** outputs, consumptions ($Y_{iJ} = Q_{iJ}$, i= 1,2, J=A,B) are with (24.93), (24.71), given as, $Y_{1J} = \alpha_J L_J$, $Y_{2J} = (1-\alpha_J) L_J$, and shown in (24.94).

If *autarky* labor allocation $\lambda_{L_{1J}} = \alpha_J$ (24.71) are preserved in *both* countries after opening of *trade*, then *terms of trade* $p_W$ becomes by (24.46), (24.93):

$$p_W = \frac{L_A\alpha_A(1-\alpha_A)y_{2A} + L_B\alpha_B(1-\alpha_B)y_{2B}}{L_A(1-\alpha_A)\alpha_A y_{1A} + L_B(1-\alpha_B)\alpha_B y_{1B}} = \frac{0.75+0.48}{0.75+0.96} = \frac{1.23}{1.71} = 0.72 \quad (24.95)$$

The export-import curves $X_{iJ}(p)$, and Offer Curves, cf. (24.76–24.83), become:

*Country* B. Explicit *export, import* functions: $X_{1B}(p) > 0$, $-X_{2B}(p) > 0$,

$$X_{1B}(p) = L_B[(1-\alpha_B)\lambda_{L_{1B}} y_{1B} - \frac{\alpha_B}{p}(1-\lambda_{L_{1B}}) y_{2B}]\,;\ \lambda_{L_{1B}} = \alpha_B = 0.6 \quad (24.96)$$

$$= 0.96 - 0.48/p\,, \quad p \in [0.5, 1.0] \quad (24.97)$$

$$-X_{2B}(p) = L_B[(1-\alpha_B)\lambda_{L_{1B}} y_{1B}\, p - \alpha_B(1-\lambda_{L_{1B}}) y_{2B}]\,;\ \lambda_{L_{1B}} = \alpha_B = 0.6 \quad (24.98)$$

$$= -0.48 + 0.96\,p\,, \quad p \in [0.5, 1.0] \quad (24.99)$$

Export-, Import-, and Offer Curve, $O_B(p)$, (24.96–24.99), look as in Figs. 24.3 and 24.4.

*Country* A. Explicit *import, export* functions: $-X_{1A}(p) > 0$, $X_{2A}(p) > 0$,

$$-X_{1A}(p) = L_A[-(1-\alpha_A)\lambda_{L_{1A}} y_{1A} + \frac{\alpha_A}{p}(1-\lambda_{L_{1A}}) y_{2A}]\,;\ \lambda_{L_{1A}} = \alpha_A = 0.25 \quad (24.100)$$

$$= -0.75 + 0.75/p\,, \quad p \in [0.5, 1.0] \quad (24.101)$$

$$X_{2A}(p) = L_A[-(1-\alpha_A)\lambda_{L_{1A}} y_{1A}\, p + \alpha_A(1-\lambda_{L_{1A}}) y_{2A}]\,;\ \lambda_{L_{1A}} = \alpha_A = 0.25 \quad (24.102)$$

$$= 0.75 - 0.75\,p\,, \quad p \in [0.5, 1.0] \quad (24.103)$$

Export-, Import-, and Offer Curve, $O_A(p)$, (24.100–24.103), look as in Figs. 24.3 and 24.4.

The *volumes* of country exports-imports (24.96–24.103) with $p_W = 0.72$, (24.95), are seen below—together with their new adjusted optimal consumptions:

$$-X_{1A} = 0.29,\ Q_{1A} = 1.29,\ X_{2A} = 0.21,\ Q_{2A} = 2.79\,;$$
$$X_{1B} = 0.61,\ Q_{1B} = 1.79,\ -X_{2B} = 0.85,\ Q_{2B} = 1.65 \quad (24.104)$$

*Optimal* consumptions with *trade* (24.104) compared to *autarky* (24.94) give representative consumer (community) *utilitygains* in both A and B, cf. (24.37):

$$U_A(Q_{1A}, Q_{2A}) = 1.29^{0.25}\, 2.79^{0.75} = 2.30 \; > \; U_A(Y_{1A}, Y_{2A}) = 1^{0.25}\, 3^{0.75} = 2.28 \tag{24.105}$$

$$U_B(Q_{1B}, Q_{2B}) = 1.79^{0.6}\, 1.65^{0.4} = 1.73 \; > \; U_B(Y_{1B}, Y_{2B}) = 2.4^{0.6}\, 0.8^{0.4} = 1.55 \tag{24.106}$$

But *both countries* with *linear* PPC can also do better than autarky, if they *trade* from *states* of Pareto efficient production, i.e., *complete* specialization.

The *terms of trade* $p_W$, (24.46)—with parameters (24.93) and *specialization* by comparative advantage, $p_B < p_A$, (24.93) as: $\lambda_{L_{1A}} = 0$, $\lambda_{L_{1B}} = 1$—becomes:

$$\lambda_{L_{1A}} = 0\,,\; \lambda_{L_{1B}} = 1 :\; p_W = \frac{L_A\, \alpha_A\, y_{2A}}{L_B\,(1-\alpha_B)\, y_{1B}} = \frac{1}{1.6} = \frac{5}{8} = 0.625 \tag{24.107}$$

Here *export-import* functions (24.118–24.41) for country B with $\lambda_{L_{1B}} = 1$, and country A with $\lambda_{L_{1A}} = 0$, then become in parameters (24.93), cf. (24.84–24.85):

$$\begin{aligned} X_{1B}(p) &= L_B\,(1-\alpha_B)\, y_{1B} = 1.6\;; \\ -X_{2B}(p) &= L_B\,(1-\alpha_B)\, y_{1B}\, p = 1.6\,p\;;\; p \in [0, \infty] \end{aligned} \tag{24.108}$$

$$-\,X_{1A}(p) = \frac{L_A \alpha_A y_{2A}}{p} = \frac{1}{p}\;;\; X_{2A}(p) = L_A\, \alpha_A\, y_{2A} = 1\;; \quad p \in [0, \infty] \tag{24.109}$$

Trade by $p_W$ (24.107), with export-imports (24.108–24.109), give consumptions after trade and specialization in country A and B, cf. max $Y^*_{iJ}$, (24.94), as follows,

$$\begin{aligned} &-\,X_{1A} = 1.6\,,\; Q_{1A} = 1.6,\; X_{2A} = 1,\; Q_{2A} = 3\;;\; X_{1B} = 1.6,\; Q_{1B} = 2.4, \\ &-X_{2B} = 1,\; Q_{2B} = 1 \end{aligned} \tag{24.110}$$

better than autarky consumptions (outputs), (24.94). *Utilities* of (24.110) are:

$$U_A(Q_{1A}, Q_{2A}) = 1.6^{0.25}\, 3^{0.75} = 2.56\;;\quad U_B(Q_{1B}, Q_{2B}) = 2.4^{0.6}\, 1^{0.4} = 1.69 \tag{24.111}$$

- *higher* than the autarky utility levels of country A and B in (24.105–24.106).

With *specialization*, the *Export-*, *Import-*, and *Offer* Curve, $O_B(p)$, and Export-, Import-, and Offer Curve, $O_A(p)$, (24.108–24.109)—with intersection $p_W = 0.625$, (24.107)—are shown in Figs. 24.5 and 24.6—diagrams that

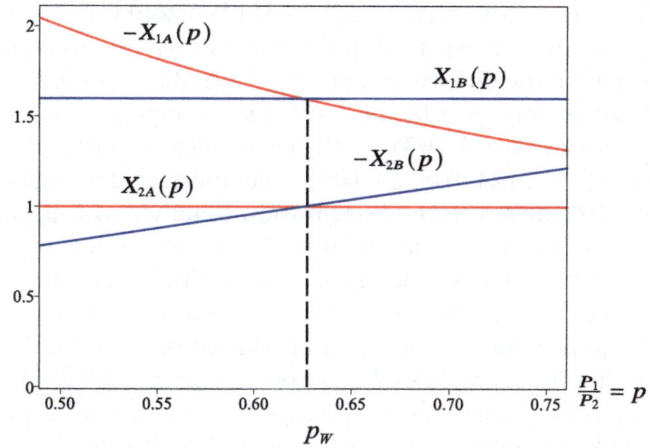


**Fig. 24.5** Specialization. Export, $X_{1B}(p)$, (24.108), Import, $[-X_{2B}(p)]$, (24.108), and Import, $-X_{1A}(p)$, (24.109), Export, $[X_{2A}(p)]$, (24.109) ; $p_W = 0.625$, (24.107)

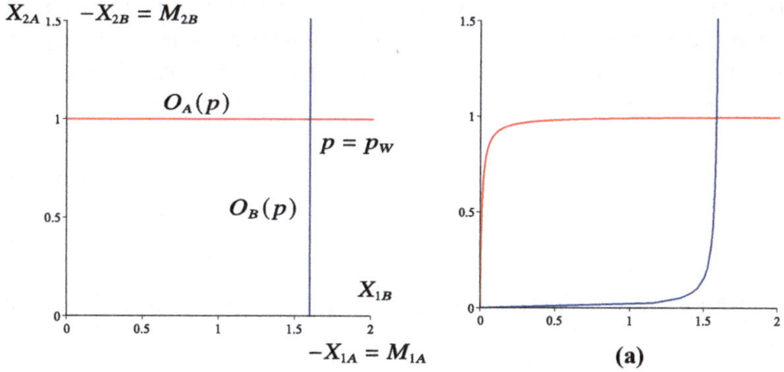


**Fig. 24.6** *Offer Curve*: $O_B(p) = \{X_{1B}(p), -X_{2B}(p)\}$, (24.108), and *Offer Curve*: $O_A(p) = \{-X_{1A}(p), X_{2A}(p)\}$, (24.109); Ray slope: $p_W = 0.625$, (24.107). (**a**) Fig. 24.4*. Offer Curve transition of $O_B(p)$ and $O_A(p)$ towards country specialization of B and A from, Figs. 24.4, 24.5, and 24.6a—converging to 24.6

also show how specialization curves (24.84–24.86) or (24.84–24.85), (24.91), would similarly be seen.

Note in Fig. 24.5 of trade from states of specialization that in contrast to *Import* demands, $[-X_{1A}(p)]$, $[-X_{2B}(p)]$, the supplies of *Exports* $X_{1B}(p)$, $X_{2A}(p)$ are **not** reacting to prices $(p)$, (*horizontal* curves). Such import (demand)-export (supply) *curves* hold *generally* in bilateral exchanges between participants with single endowments and CD utility functions, cf. Chipman

(1965, p. 686). Hence the vertical $O_B(p)$ and horizontal $O_A(p)$ *Offer Curves* in Fig. 24.6 hold *generally* with $CD$ preferences in *specialized* countries.[4]

At (0,0), *origin* of the Offer Curves in Fig. 24.6, the '*parameter*', $p = P_1/P_2$, begins for $O_B(p)$ as slope $p = 0$, and for $O_A(p)$ as slope $p = \infty$. A *convergence* of Offer Curves (24.96–24.103) to their specialized *limits* (straight lines—horizontal/vertical) of (24.108–24.109) is demonstrated in Fig. 24.6a.[5]

The *factor reallocations* from specialization together with *demand assumptions* saw Mill as keys to "terms of trade" and ranges for $p_W$. Mill (1848, 1875, 1909, p. 600): "The whole of the commodities which *two countries* can respectively make for *exportation* – with the labour and capital thrown *out of employment* by importation – will *exchange* against one another" (italics ours).

Let us examine his example of *labour* productivities (24.93) of country A, B, where A by comparative advantage exports good 2 and imports good 1. When A stops making good 1 ($n = Y_{1A} = 1$) and *reallocate* ($L_{1A} = 1$) to good 2, A can *beyond* ($Y_{2A} = 3$) make an *extra* output of *good* 2 to be exported: $n = X_{2A}$. Similarly, with B stopping good 2 ($m = Y_{2B} = 0.8$), B can beyond ($Y_{1B} = 2.4$) also make *more* of *good* 1 ($y_{1B} = 2$) to be exported: $X_{1B} = 1.6$. Quantity *ratio*, $X_{2A}/X_{1B} = 1/1.6$ is as a *price ratio*, the terms of trade, $\boldsymbol{p_w}$. Alternatively stated, *constant* (CD) country *budget shares* ($\alpha_A, \alpha_B$) for goods also after international trade, *requires* e.g., in country B for good 2: $n/m = p_W/p_B$, ("National Income" as $Y_B/p_B = Y_B/p_W$, same size). In short,

$$\frac{X_{2A}}{X_{1B}} = \frac{\alpha_A Y_{2A}^*}{(1-\alpha_B) Y_{1B}^*} = \frac{1}{1.6} = p_W \Leftrightarrow \frac{X_{2A}}{Y_{2B}} p_B = \frac{n}{m} p_B = \frac{1}{0.8} 0.5 = \frac{5}{8} \tag{24.112}$$

or just stated with the *algebraic symbols* of Mill (1848, 1875, 1909, p. 600), as follows:

$$0.5 = p_B \le \frac{P_{1W}}{P_{2W}} = p_W = \frac{n}{m} p_B \le p_A = 1 \Longleftrightarrow m \le n \le 2m \tag{24.113}$$

[4] Marshall (1879, 1930, 1974, p. 6); Marshall (1923, p. 331) introduced the diagrams of "International Demand" curves (now called Offer Curves, $O_B$, $O_A$ in Fig. 24.4) to obtain International Equilibrium Values (prices)—my acquaintance with economics commenced with reading Mill, while teaching mathematics and translating his doctrines into differential equations as far as they would go", Pigou and Marshall (1925, p. 412). Statics (science of equilibrium of forces) required an equilibrium (intersection of supply/demand—Offer Curves), but also stability conditions for attaining/preserving any market equilibrium. Existence and stability conditions of equilibria for classes of Offer Curves—extensions of Fig. 24.4—were proved in many Propositions. But the underlying curves shown in Fig. 24.3 are not seen in Marshall (1879, 1930, 1974), Marshall (1923).

[5] The Exceptional Specialization case of Mill, Fig. 24.6 is *noted* in Marshall (1879, 1930, 1974, p. 15, p. 29), Marshall (1923, p. 354)—but *without* the underlying curves, Fig. 24.5, Mill's $p_W$ (24.113) is missed.

If $n = m$, the whole advantage of this specialized trading goes to A (England)—if $n = 2m$, the whole advantage goes to B (Germany). For $n$ within interval (24.113), the two countries will **share** the ***advantage*** of their ***specialization*** and ***trading*** [ 'reciprocal demand'= balance, (24.59) ]—three *cases* of **Mill's law**, (24.113).

Mill's law, (24.113), has by (24.112) been parametrically ***extended*** to ***general*** CD utility (*consumer demand*) parameters (24.37), (24.111), and further by (24.107–24.110) been integrated into an analytic framework of *explicit* export-import, offer *curves* for *specialization*, Fig. 24.5 and 24.6, that came from the PPC *country data, parameters*, (24.93–24.94)—which we next use to a *linear* PPC of Ricardo.

## *Linear PPC, Comparative Advantage, Terms of Trade—D. Ricardo*

Classical arithmetic examples of comparative advantage by Ricardo[6] and modern standard illustrations of Ricardian linear PPC for two countries have endowments with *one factor* of production, Labor—like Mill's model (24.93). Above Mill (1848, 1875, 1909, p. 600) did refer to Labor and Capital, as does Ricardo.[7] The *two-factor* (composite *dose*) CD model with *same* factor intensity

[6] The numbers of Ricardo (1817, 1821, 1965, p. 82)'s productivity illustrations are in form of (24.93):

$$\frac{a_{L_{1J}}}{a_{L_{2J}}} = \frac{y_{2J}}{y_{1J}};\ a_{L_{1B}} = 80,\ a_{L_{2B}} = 90:$$

$$y_{1B} = 0.0125,\ y_{2B} = 0.0111,\ p_B = \frac{P_{1B}}{P_{2B}} = \frac{y_{2B}}{y_{1B}} = 0.88$$

$$a_{L_{1A}} = 120,\ a_{L_{2A}} = 100:$$

$$y_{1A} = 0.0833,\ y_{2A} = 0.0100,\ p_A = \frac{P_{1A}}{P_{2A}} = \frac{y_{2A}}{y_{1A}} = 1.20$$

Good 1 =Wine, Good 2= Cloth ; B= Portugal, A = England; $a_{L_{1J}}$, man-years. Portugal looks in every respect superior to England in productivity (50, 10, pct.); hereto Samuelson asks, Negishi (2014, p. 153): "Writing in the heyday of England's industrial revolution – Why this odd economic geography?" With Good 1 =Linen, Good 2= Cloth; B= Germany, A = England, the *four numbers* of $a_{L_{iJ}}$ (reciprocals $y_{iJ}$) in (24.93) also exhibit Germany superior to England in productivity. These four numbers in (24.93) is accounted for differently (another *technological-economic* explanation) in (24.114)—by introducing *capital* doses, $k_J^{\bar{a}_J}$, and $\gamma_{iJ}$ *parameters*. Similar explication can account for the *four numbers* of Portugal-England—but demonstration (24.114) needs no repeating for the *wine-cloth* data.

[7] Ricardo (1817, 1821, 1965, p. 81, 175): "The same rule which regulates the relative value of commodities in *one* country does *not* regulate the relative values of the commodities exchanged between *two* or more countries. Under a system of perfectly *free* commerce, *each country* naturally devotes its *capital* and *labour* to such *employments* [industries, goods, sectors] as are *most beneficial* to each [country]. This pursuit of *individual advantages* is admirably connected with the *universal* good of the whole". cf. Ruffin (2002, p. 743).

*parameters*, see (23.60), will *generalize* the 1-factor results already obtained with (24.93).

With $a_{1J} = a_{2J} = \tilde{a}_J$, we choose, $\tilde{a}_B = 0.2$, and $\tilde{a}_A = 0.25$; same *intensity parameters* imply same *capital-labor* ratios, as e.g., $k_{1B} = k_{2B} = k_B = 1.5$, and, $k_{1A} = k_{2A} = k_A = 2$. We adopt for convenience such $\gamma_{iJ}$ parameter sizes that **labor** productivities, $\boldsymbol{y}_{iJ}$, have *same* sizes[8] as in (24.93)—i.e., *two-factor* Ricardo-Mill *linear* **PPC**, (24.93–24.94), with $\boldsymbol{a}_{1J} = \boldsymbol{a}_{2J} = \tilde{\boldsymbol{a}}_J$, becomes:

$$\begin{aligned}
&\tilde{a}_B = 0.2,\ k_{iB} = k_B = 1.5\,;\ k_B^{\tilde{a}_B} = 1.5^{0.2} = 1.1;\\
&\gamma_{1B} = 1.8,\ \gamma_{2B} = 0.9;\ y_{1B} = \gamma_{1B}k_B^{\tilde{a}_B} = 2,\ y_{2B} = \gamma_{2B}k_B^{\tilde{a}_B} = 1\\
&\tilde{a}_A = 0.25,\ k_{iA} = k_A = 2\,;\ k_A^{\tilde{a}_A} = 2^{0.25} = 1.19;\\
&\gamma_{1A} = 0.84,\ \gamma_{2A} = 0.84;\ y_{1A} = \gamma_{1A}k_A^{\tilde{a}_A} = 1,\ y_{2A} = \gamma_{2A}k_A^{\tilde{a}_A} = 1\\
&p_B = \frac{y_{2B}}{y_{1B}} = \frac{\gamma_{2B}}{\gamma_{1B}} = 0.5 = -\frac{dY_{2B}}{dY_{1B}},\ p_A = \frac{y_{2A}}{y_{1A}} = \frac{\gamma_{2A}}{\gamma_{1A}} = 1 = -\frac{dY_{2A}}{dY_{1A}};\\
&\alpha_B = 0.6,\ \alpha_A = 0.25,\ L_B = 2,\ L_A = 4
\end{aligned} \tag{24.114}$$

The essence of Ricardo two-factor model and PPC slope in (24.114) is: Country *ratios* of sector *labor productivities* ($\boldsymbol{y}_{iJ}$) are decided *technologically* by the *ratios* of sector *efficiency* (total factor productivity) *parameters* ($\boldsymbol{\gamma}_{iJ}$).

The *countries* have different *endowment* ratios of labor and capital ($\boldsymbol{k}_J$)—England (A) is here (no odd geography) seen *better endowed* with *capital* than Germany (B), (Portugal[9])—and all *industries* (sectors)[10] can have different *average* (marginal) *productivities* of labor ($\boldsymbol{y}_{iJ}$), but *comparative advantage*

[8] With the $\gamma_{iJ}$ parameter sizes—and $y_{iJ}$–in (24.114), we get for *specialization* with (24.114) the same Eq. (24.107) and result $p_W = 0.625$—and export-import equations of specialization (24.108–24.109) apply without change to (24.114), i.e., *explicit* export-import and Offer *curves* for *specialization*, Figs. 24.5 and 24.6 hold exactly for *two-factor* Ricardo-Mill, (24.114).

[9] In all the numerical illustrations of formulas in Sects. "PPC, Free Trade, and International Equilibrium Prices"–"Linear PPC, General Equilibrium, and International Trade" from (24.52) and onwards, the geographic *Country* A is supposed—as in Mill, Marshall, Chipman above—to be England (B, Germany, Portugal, ect.) exporting always *cloth* (here good 2), $X_{2A} > 0$. All our formulas for PPC curves, Offer Curves, and MRT (relative price), $\frac{dY_{2J}}{dY_{1J}}$, $p_J = \frac{P_{1J}}{P_{2J}}$, require *good* 1 to be consistently selected as the *first* coordinate (horizontal) axis.

[10] Ricardian trade models for two countries with many (n - continuum) goods of constant unit labor requirements (24.93): $a_{L_{iJ}}$, i= 1,,n, J= A,B, were built by Dornbusch et al. (1977, p. 823). These are extended to many countries with technological efficiency varying across goods and countries ($\gamma_{iJ}$) by Eaton and Kortum (2002, p. 1745) and extended to production efficiency varying among any firms by Melitz (2003, p. 1700). Also the authors make assumptions about goods and firms with imperfect competition and geographic trade (transport) cost so that consumer demand affects domestic GE price ratios ($p_J$) and international GE price ratios ($p_W$), trade flows, and relevant market shares.

(trade patterns) of country $J$ (lower $\boldsymbol{p}_J$) depend on country *ratios* of *Hicks* (factor-neutral) technological *efficiency* parameters[11] (24.114):

$$p_B = \frac{P_{1B}}{P_{2B}} = \frac{\gamma_{2B}}{\gamma_{1B}} = 0.5 < \frac{\gamma_{2A}}{\gamma_{1A}} = 1 = \frac{P_{1A}}{P_{2A}} = p_A \ : \quad X_{1B} > 0 \ ; \ X_{2A} > 0 \tag{24.115}$$

Thus country export *patterns* by comparative advantage (24.115) and the *terms of trade* $p_W$, and export-import *volumes* with specialization from **Ricardian** trade *model* (24.114) are *those* of *Mill* in (24.107–24.110) and Figs. 24.5 and 24.6, cf.note 8.

The *linear* PPC-*two-factor* Ricardo-Mill trade model (24.114–24.115) is a sort of "*road-junction*" with model departures in many directions; with $k_{1J} = k_{2J} = k_J$ along *linear* PPC, *comparative advantage* (trade pattern) only depends on different *ratios* of $\gamma_{iJ}$ (efficiency) parameters, (24.115)—if the latter were the same, *no trade* (same $p_J$) *occurs*, as Findley et al. (2002, p. 147), Ohlin (1924, p. 98) *proved*. Hence *Ohlin* saw, $k_{1J} \neq k_{2J} \neq k_J$, as another basic *reason* for trade (*factor proportion* model), i.e., **nonlinear PPC** with MRT, Eqs. (23.10) and (23.19), that also allow *demand* to select **GE** points on **PPC**.

## International Free Trade and World Market Prices

### *Free Trade Balances and World Market Equilibrium*

Countries' international trade is always balanced. As commodity markets are fully integrated, world market equilibrium implies, cf. (24.8):

$$X_{iA} = Y_{iA} - Q_{iA} = -X_{iB} = -(Y_{iB} - Q_{iB}) \ ; \quad i = 1, 2 \tag{24.116}$$

In order to derive the equation of the world trade balance and its terms of trade, rewrite the optimal consumption demand for good 1 (24.23), using the definition of exports in (24.116), and using (24.5), (24.9), (24.10), (24.24), to give the *expenditure* expressions:

$$P_{1W}Q_{1J} = P_{1W} \cdot (Y_{1J} - X_{1J}) = \alpha_J \cdot (P_{1W}Y_{1J} + P_{2W}Y_{2J})$$

$$P_{1W}X_{1J} = (1 - \alpha_J)\, P_{1W}Y_{1J} - \alpha_J \cdot P_{2W}Y_{2J}. \tag{24.117}$$

In "*real* (goods) terms"—*exports per capita*, $x_{1J} = X_{1J}/L_J$—(24.117) becomes

$$x_{1J} = X_{1J}/L_J = (1 - \alpha_J)\, \lambda_{L_{1J}} \cdot y_{1J} - \frac{\alpha_J}{p} \lambda_{L_{2J}} \cdot y_{2J} \tag{24.118}$$

[11] For Ricardian technologies: $a_{1J} = a_{2J} = \tilde{a}_J$, *majestic* roles of $(\boldsymbol{\gamma}_{iJ})$ do *appear* in Table 24.1.

The *sectoral* **labor productivities** in country $J$, $y_{1_J}$, $y_{2_J}$, are determined along the Country **PPC** by the *functions*, cf. (23.22–23.23):

$$y_{1_J} = \gamma_{1_J} \left[ \frac{A_J k_J}{1 + (A_J - 1)\, \lambda_{L_{1J}}} \right]^{a_{1J}} \equiv H_{1_J}(\lambda_{L_{1J}}\,;\, k_J) \tag{24.119}$$

$$y_{2_J} = \gamma_{2_J} \left[ \frac{k_J}{1 + (A_J - 1)\, \lambda_{L_{1J}}} \right]^{a_{2J}} \equiv H_{2_J}(\lambda_{L_{1J}}\,;\, k_J) \tag{24.120}$$

In each country, the **labor allocation** function along its **PPC** (see 23.35 and 23.36), is:

$$\lambda_{L_{1J}}(p_J; k_J) = \frac{[1 - a_{1_J}][1 - a_{2_J}]}{a_{1_J} - a_{2_J}} \left[ \frac{\gamma_{1_J}\, p_J}{\gamma_{2_J}\, \bar{A}_J} \right]^{\frac{1}{a_{1J} - a_{2J}}} k_J \;-\; \frac{a_{2_J}\,(1 - a_{1_J})}{a_{1_J} - a_{2_J}} \tag{24.121}$$

Define now

$$\bar{B}_J \equiv \frac{[1 - a_{1_J}][1 - a_{2_J}]}{a_{1_J} - a_{2_J}} \left[ \frac{\gamma_{1_J}}{\gamma_{2_J}\, \bar{A}_J} \right]^{\frac{1}{a_{1J} - a_{2J}}}, \qquad J = A, B \tag{24.122}$$

and re-write $B(p_J)$ in (23.36) as

$$B(p_J) = \bar{B}_J \cdot p_J^{\frac{1}{a_{1J} - a_{2J}}}, \qquad J = A, B \tag{24.123}$$

Use finally (24.123) in (24.121) to re-write (23.35) as

$$\lambda_{L_{1J}} = \bar{B}_J \cdot p_J^{\frac{1}{a_{1J} - a_{2J}}} \cdot k_J - \frac{1}{A_J - 1}, \qquad J = A, B \tag{24.124}$$

### *Computation of the Endogenous Terms of Trade*

Consider Proposition 24.1 and observe that inserting (24.119), (24.120), and (24.121) into the $p_W$ - *trade equilibrium* Eq. (24.46), and using (24.124) yields the following $\mathbf{p}_W$ - *function*, $\boldsymbol{\Omega}\,(\cdot)$:

$$\Omega\,(p_W, k_A, k_B) = 0 \tag{24.125}$$

This is an *implicit* function for the terms of trade ($p_W$) in the factor endowments $k_A$ and $k_B$. In order to derive the explicit form for function $\Omega\,(\cdot)$, compute the *ratio* of the *sectoral labor productivities* in country $A$ as

$$\frac{y_{2A}}{y_{1A}} = \frac{1 - a_{1A}}{1 - a_{2A}}\, p_W \tag{24.126}$$

and then proceed with the two ratios of the sectoral labour productivities *between* countries, cf. (24.119–24.120), (24.124), $p_J = p_W$:

$$\frac{y_{1B}}{y_{1A}} = \frac{\gamma_{1B}}{\gamma_{1A}} \left[ \frac{A_B}{(A_A - 1)\bar{B}_B} \right]^{a_{1B}} \left[ \frac{(A_A - 1)\bar{B}_A}{A_A} \right]^{a_{1A}} p_W^{\frac{a_{1B}a_{2A} - a_{1A}a_{2B}}{(a_{2A} - a_{1A})(a_{2B} - a_{1B})}} \tag{24.127}$$

$$\frac{y_{2B}}{y_{2A}} = \frac{\gamma_{2B}}{\gamma_{2A}} \frac{\left[(A_A - 1)\bar{B}_A\right]^{a_{2A}}}{\left[(A_B - 1)\bar{B}_B\right]^{a_{2B}}} p_W^{\frac{a_{1B}a_{2A} - a_{1A}a_{2B}}{(a_{2A} - a_{1A})(a_{2B} - a_{1B})}} \tag{24.128}$$

Hence, we can give the expression for the *implicit function* $\Omega(p_W, k_A, k_B)$ in the following

**Theorem 24.1 Standard Model**—*for* $(2 \times 2 \times 2)$ *models of trading economies with CD sector technologies, (23.6), CD utility functions, (24.22), the international equilibrium terms of trade (relative price),* $p_W = P_{1W}/P_{2W}$, *(24.2), is an* ***implicit*** *function of the factor endowments,* $(\mathbf{k}_A, \mathbf{k}_B)$: $\Omega(p, k_A, k_B) = 0$*—with* ***solutions****, (roots* $p = p_W > 0$*), given by the equation (locus):*

$$\begin{aligned}
\Omega(p_W, k_A, k_B) &= \upsilon_A \left[ 1 - \alpha_A + \frac{1 - a_{1A}}{1 - a_{2A}} \alpha_A \right] \bar{B}_A \cdot k_A \cdot p_W^{\frac{1}{a_{1A} - a_{2A}}} \\
&+ \upsilon_B \left[ (1 - \alpha_B) \cdot D_1 + \alpha_B \cdot D_2 \right] \bar{B}_B \cdot k_B \cdot p_W^{\frac{a_{2A} - a_{1A} - a_{1B}a_{2A} + a_{1A}a_{2B}}{(a_{1B} - a_{2B})(a_{2A} - a_{1A})}} \\
&- \upsilon_B \left[ (1 - \alpha_B) \cdot D_1 + \alpha_B \cdot D_2 \cdot A_B \right] \cdot \frac{1}{A_B - 1} \cdot p_W^{\frac{a_{1B}a_{2A} - a_{1A}a_{2B}}{(a_{2B} - a_{1B})(a_{2A} - a_{1A})}} \\
&- \upsilon_A \frac{1}{A_A - 1} \left[ 1 - \alpha_A + \alpha_A \cdot \frac{a_{1A}}{a_{2A}} \right] = 0
\end{aligned} \tag{24.129}$$

*with:* $D_1 \equiv \frac{\gamma_{1B}}{\gamma_{1A}} \left[ \frac{A_B}{(A_B - 1)\bar{B}_B} \right]^{a_{1B}} \left[ \frac{(A_A - 1)\bar{B}_A}{A_A} \right]^{a_{1A}}$, $D_2 \equiv \frac{1 - a_{1A}}{1 - a_{2A}} \frac{\gamma_{2B}}{\gamma_{2A}} \frac{\left[(A_A - 1)\bar{B}_A\right]^{a_{2A}}}{\left[(A_B - 1)\bar{B}_B\right]^{a_{2B}}}$.

***Proof*** Insert (24.126), (24.127) and (24.128) into (24.46) and after several manipulations obtain (24.129). □

Observe that (24.129) is the formula for the *terms of trade* $(p_W)$ expressed in its fundamental determinants: *parameters* of *technology* and *preference* and the *exogenous factor endowments,* $(k_A, k_B)$.

**Proposition 24.2 Basic Model.** *The implicit function,* $\Omega(p_W, k_A, k_B) = 0$, *(24.129), becomes an* ***explicit*** *analytic terms of trade function (surface),* $\mathbf{p}_W = \mathbf{\Phi}(\mathbf{k}_A, \mathbf{k}_B)$, *if the CD sector technologies in both countries have* ***parameter*** *restrictions, cf. (24.25):*

$$a_{iA} = a_{iB} = a_i\ ,\ i = 1, 2\ :\ \bar{A}_A = \bar{A}_B = \bar{A} \tag{24.130}$$

$$\bar{A} \equiv \frac{a_2^{a_2}(1-a_2)^{1-a_2}}{a_1^{a_1}(1-a_1)^{1-a_1}} \qquad \bar{\gamma} \equiv \left[\left[\frac{\gamma_{2B}}{\gamma_{2A}}\right]^{a_1}\left[\frac{\gamma_{1A}}{\gamma_{1B}}\right]^{a_2}\right]^{\frac{1}{a_2-a_1}} \tag{24.131}$$

$$p_W = \Phi(k_A, k_B) = \bar{A}\left[\frac{\bar{\gamma}\, \upsilon_A \left[\frac{\gamma_{2A}}{\gamma_{1A}}\right]^{\frac{1}{a_2-a_1}}[1-\beta_A]k_A + \upsilon_B\left[\frac{\gamma_{2B}}{\gamma_{1B}}\right]^{\frac{1}{a_2-a_1}}[1-\beta_B]k_B}{\bar{\gamma}\,\upsilon_A\beta_A + \upsilon_B\beta_B}\right]^{a_2-a_1} \tag{24.132}$$

$$\beta_J \equiv \alpha_J a_1 + (1-\alpha_J)a_2\,, \quad J = A, B \tag{24.133}$$

*and the factor endowments,* $(k_A, k_B)$, *satisfy* ***diversification*** *conditions in Proposition 24.3 below that impose relevant restrictions (intervals) for the the factor endowment* ***ratios***, $(k_A/k_B)$.

***Proof*** With, $a_{iA} = a_{iB} = a_i$, see (24.130), (24.129) turns into an equation in $p_W^{\frac{1}{a_1-a_2}}$. Intuitive mathematical steps promptly lead to (24.132). Hence (24.130) implies a drastic simplification of (24.129), which with further compilations, cf. (24.131–24.133), become the *explicit* relative price function (24.132). The equilibrium value of the terms of trade (24.132) is positive, since $\bar{\beta}_J$, (24.133), is less than one for any $0 < a_i < 1$ and $0 < \alpha_J < 1$, which is sufficient for a positive $p_W$ in (24.132), (when feasible $p_W$ exist, cf. Proposition 24.3.) □

In comparison to the general *implicit* solution, $p_W$, (24.129), in Theorem 24.1, *solution*, $p_W$, (24.132) in Proposition 24.2 has the advantage to be in *closed form*, and yet *encompass* some degree of *"heterogeneity"* ($\bar{\gamma}$), (24.131), in the *sector technologies* across the trading countries.

The *international terms of trade* expression, $p_W$, (24.132)—illustrated geometrically as *surfaces (contours)* in Fig. 24.7a–b—depends as a **GE** *solution* on four sets of **Determinants**: (1) Factor endowment ratios (*exogenous variables*), (2) All sectoral technology *parameters*, (3) All consumer preference *parameters*, (4) Relative country sizes (*parameters*).

A direct *Corollary* of Proposition 24.2 gives a perspective on simple *submodels*.

**Corollary 24.1** *If CD sector technology parameters ('total factor productivity'),* $\gamma_{iJ}$, *are also the same in both countries,*

$$\gamma_{iA} = \gamma_{iB} = \gamma_i\,, \quad i = 1, 2 \;:\; \bar{\gamma} = 1 \tag{24.134}$$

*then (24.132) becomes:*

$$p_W = \Phi(k_A, k_B) = \bar{A}\,\frac{\gamma_2}{\gamma_1}\left[\frac{\upsilon_A(1-\beta_A)k_A + \upsilon_B(1-\beta_B)k_B}{\upsilon_A\cdot\beta_A + \upsilon_B\cdot\beta_B}\right]^{a_2-a_1} \tag{24.135}$$

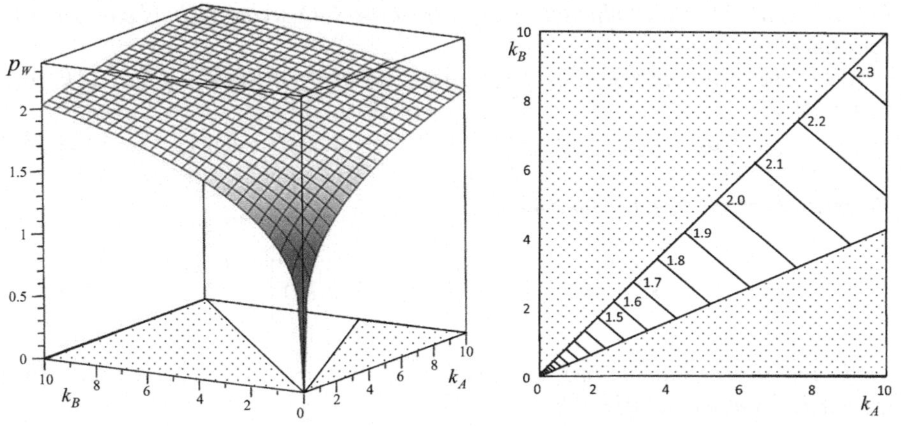


**(a)**

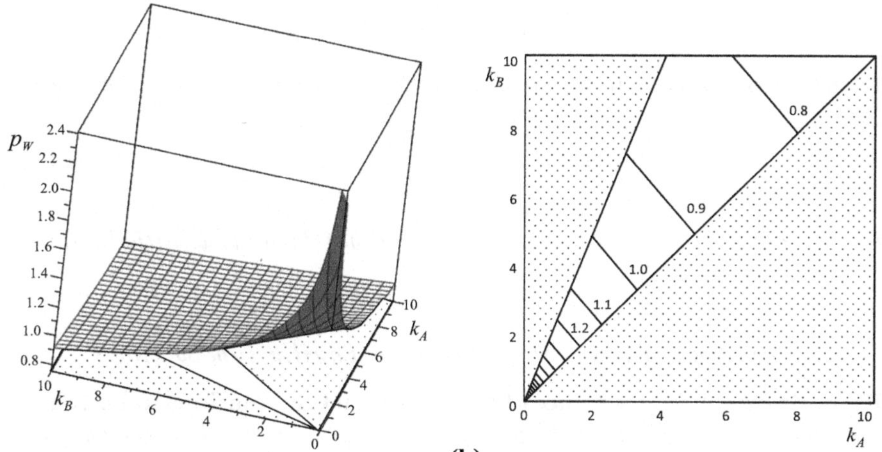


**(b)**

**Fig. 24.7** (**a**) *Terms of Trade Surface:* $p_W = \Phi(k_A, k_B)$, *(24.135), Case 1:* $a_1 = 0.25$, $a_2 = 0.5$, with: $\bar{A} = 0.8774$, $\gamma_1 = 2$, $\gamma_2 = 2.6$, $\alpha_A = 0.4$, $\alpha_B = 0.8$, $\upsilon_J = 0.5$, $\beta_A = 0.4$, $\beta_B = 0.3$, $p_W = \Phi(k_A, k_B) = \bar{A}\,\frac{\gamma_2}{\gamma_1}\left[\frac{\upsilon_A(1-\beta_A)k_A+\upsilon_B(1-\beta_B)k_B}{\upsilon_A\cdot\beta_A+\upsilon_B\cdot\beta_B}\right]^{a_2-a_1} = 1.1406\,[\,0.8571\,k_A + 1.0\,k_B\,]^{0.25}$. (**b**) *Terms of Trade Surface:* $p_W = \Phi(k_A, k_B)$, *(24.135), Case 2:* $a_1 = 0.50$, $a_2 = 0.25$, with: $\bar{A} = 1.1398$, $\gamma_1 = 2$, $\gamma_2 = 2.6$, $\alpha_A = 0.4$, $\alpha_B = 0.8$, $\upsilon_J = 0.5$, $\beta_A = 0.35$, $\beta_B = 0.45$, $p_W = \Phi(k_A, k_B) = \bar{A}\,\frac{\gamma_2}{\gamma_1}\left[\frac{\upsilon_A(1-\beta_A)k_A+\upsilon_B(1-\beta_B)k_B}{\upsilon_A\cdot\beta_A+\upsilon_B\cdot\beta_B}\right]^{a_2-a_1} = 1.4817\,/\,[\,0.8125\,k_A + 0.6875\,k_B\,]^{0.25}$

*i.e, the terms of trade solution ($p_W$) with same CD sector technologies in both countries.*

*With the same tastes, CD preferences, utility functions, cf. (24.22), and (24.133),*

$$\beta_A = \beta_B = \beta \equiv \alpha a_1 + (1-\alpha) a_2 \tag{24.136}$$

*the terms of trade (24.135) becomes:*

$$p_W = \Phi(k_A, k_B) = \bar{A}\frac{\gamma_2}{\gamma_1}\left[\frac{1-\beta}{\beta}\,(\upsilon_A k_A + \upsilon_B k_B)\right]^{a_2-a_1} \tag{24.137}$$

*With the same size of two countries,* $\upsilon_A = \upsilon_B = \frac{1}{2}$, *then (24.137) gives a HOS model solution:*

$$p_W = \Phi(k_A, k_B) = \bar{A}\frac{\gamma_2}{\gamma_1}\left[\frac{1-\beta}{2\beta}\,(k_A + k_B)\right]^{a_2-a_1} \tag{24.138}$$

*Finally, with the same factor endowments ratios,* $k_J = k_A = k_B$, *then (24.138) becomes:*

$$p_W = \Phi(k_J) = \bar{A}\frac{\gamma_2}{\gamma_1}\left[\frac{1-\beta}{\beta}\,k_J\right]^{a_2-a_1} \tag{24.139}$$

*i.e., the special Walrasian (general) equilibrium relative price ratio in autarky, see (23.202), (23.219).*

### *Existence of International General Equilibrium Solutions*

**Proposition 24.3 (Existence of International GE Solutions to Basic Trade Model)** *The solution $p_W$ (24.132) of the* $(2 \times 2 \times 2)$ *model exists economically as a feasible GE solution, when the factor endowments,* $(k_A, k_B)$, *satisfy the GE diversification cone conditions: (24.143–24.147)—expressed, cf. (24.30–24.31), in terms of the composite parameters:* ($\bar{\gamma}$), *(24.131);* ($\widetilde{\gamma}$), *(24.26);* ($\widetilde{a}$), *(24.28), together with the composite parameters,* ($\bar{\vartheta}$), ($\breve{\vartheta}$), ($\tilde{\vartheta}$), *defined by,*

$$\bar{\vartheta} = \frac{\upsilon_B}{\upsilon_A}\frac{1-\alpha_B}{\alpha_A}\frac{1-a_2}{1-a_1} \tag{24.140}$$

$$\breve{\vartheta} = \frac{\upsilon_B\,(1-\beta_B)\,a_2}{\bar{\gamma}\cdot\upsilon_A\alpha_A\,(a_1-a_2)+\upsilon_B\beta_B\,(1-a_2)} \tag{24.141}$$

$$\tilde{\vartheta} = \frac{\bar{\gamma}\cdot\upsilon_A\beta_A\,(1-a_1)-\upsilon_B\,(1-\alpha_B)\,(a_1-a_2)}{\bar{\gamma}\cdot\upsilon_A\,(1-\beta_A)\,a_1} \tag{24.142}$$

*When $a_1 > a_2$, the restrictions (intervals) upon the ratio, $(k_A/k_B)$ are given by:*

$$a_1 > a_2 : If \;\; \bar{\gamma} < \bar{\vartheta}\,, \quad then \quad \frac{k_A}{k_B} \in [\breve{\vartheta}\,\widetilde{\gamma}, \widetilde{\gamma}\,] \tag{24.143}$$

$$a_1 > a_2 : If \;\; \bar{\gamma} > \bar{\vartheta}\,, \quad then \quad \frac{k_A}{k_B} \in [\tilde{\vartheta}\,\widetilde{\gamma}, \widetilde{\gamma}\,] \tag{24.144}$$

$$a_1 > a_2 : If \;\; \bar{\gamma} = \bar{\vartheta}\,, \quad then \; \frac{k_A}{k_B} = \breve{\vartheta}\,\widetilde{\gamma} = \tilde{\vartheta}\,\widetilde{\gamma} = \widetilde{a}\,\widetilde{\gamma} \tag{24.145}$$

*When $a_1 < a_2$, the restrictions (intervals) upon the ratio, $(k_A/k_B)$ are given by:*

$$a_1 < a_2 : If \;\; \bar{\gamma} < \bar{\vartheta}\,, \quad then \quad \frac{k_A}{k_B} \in [\,\widetilde{\gamma}\,, \breve{\vartheta}\,\widetilde{\gamma}\,] \tag{24.146}$$

$$a_1 < a_2 : If \;\; \bar{\gamma} > \bar{\vartheta}\,, \quad then \quad \frac{k_A}{k_B} \in [\widetilde{\gamma}\,, \tilde{\vartheta}\,\widetilde{\gamma}] \tag{24.147}$$

$$a_1 < a_2 : If \;\; \bar{\gamma} = \bar{\vartheta}\,, \quad then \; \frac{k_A}{k_B} = \breve{\vartheta}\,\widetilde{\gamma} = \tilde{\vartheta}\,\widetilde{\gamma} = \widetilde{a}\,\widetilde{\gamma} \tag{24.148}$$

***Proof*** See **Appendix A**. □

Note that in contrast to conditions (24.30–24.31), *preference parameters* and *country sizes* appear in (24.140–24.142), and hence also appear in **GE** *diversification intervals* (24.143–24.147) for the endowment ratio $(k_A/k_B)$, (sufficient conditions, to ensure $p_W$—with diversification—exists).

**Corollary 24.2** *The* **GE** *diversification cone restrictions (intervals) for factor endowment ratios $(k_A/k_B)$ corresponding to Corollary 24.1, Assumption, (24.134), are given by, cf. (24.143–24.147):*

$$a_1 > a_2 : \;\; If \;\;\; 1 < \bar{\vartheta}\,, \quad then \; \frac{k_A}{k_B} \in [\breve{\kappa}\;, 1] \tag{24.149}$$

$$a_1 > a_2 : \;\; If \;\;\; 1 > \bar{\vartheta}\,, \quad then \; \frac{k_A}{k_B} \in [\tilde{\kappa}\;, 1] \tag{24.150}$$

$$a_1 < a_2 : \;\; If \;\;\; 1 < \bar{\vartheta}\,, \quad then \; \frac{k_A}{k_B} \in [\,1\,, \breve{\kappa}] \tag{24.151}$$

$$a_1 < a_2 : \;\; If \;\;\; 1 > \bar{\vartheta}\,, \quad then \; \frac{k_A}{k_B} \in [\,1\,, \tilde{\kappa}] \tag{24.152}$$

*with*

$$\breve{\kappa} \equiv \frac{\upsilon_B (1-\beta_B) a_2}{\upsilon_A (a_1 - a_2)\alpha_A + \upsilon_B \beta_B (1-a_2)} \qquad (24.153)$$

$$\tilde{\kappa} \equiv \frac{\upsilon_A \beta_A (1-a_1) - \upsilon_B (1-\alpha_B)(a_1 - a_2)}{\upsilon_A (1-\beta_A) a_1} \qquad (24.154)$$

The two cases in Fig. 24.7a–b have **GE** *endowment ratio intervals*, cf. (24.140–24.142), (24.152), (24.150),

$Case\ 1: a_1 = 0.25,\ a_2 = 0.5;\ \ a_1 < a_2:$

$$1 > \bar{\vartheta} = 1/3;\ \ 1 \leq \frac{k_A}{k_B} < 2.3333 = \tilde{\kappa} \qquad (24.155)$$

$Case\ 2: a_1 = 0.5,\ a_2 = 0.25;\ \ a_1 > a_2:$

$$1 > \bar{\vartheta} = 3/4;\ \tilde{\kappa} = 0.3846 \leq \frac{k_A}{k_B} < 1 \qquad (24.156)$$

which are *smaller* than the corresponding "*autarky*" endowment ratio intervals in (24.35–24.34).

The analysis of the effects on factor prices of free international trade in a few goods by Samuelson (1948, 1949) was supposedly extended to any number of goods and factors in general equilibrium, by "a succinct summary of the Walrasian statical model of general equilibrium in its competitive aspects", Samuelson (1953–1954, p. 1). However, it mostly deals with the interrelations between the factor prices and commodity prices of Pareto efficient (competitive) resource allocations mainly belonging to *production sector equilibria*. But interrelations between"localization" (countries) and "international trade" are only addressed by giving formal equation systems, Samuelson (1953–1954, p. 13). No *existence* proof of an *international general equilibrium* is provided—as in Propositions 24.2–24.3.

## International Free Trade Models and Results

The international trade models of Propositions 24.1–24.2 with the explicite *solution*: $\boldsymbol{p}_W = \boldsymbol{\Phi}(\boldsymbol{k}_A, \boldsymbol{k}_B)$, (24.132) allow for *countries differing* in sizes, endowments, technologies and preferences. They constitute a comprehensive framework for seeing how these elements affect the *existence* and the *quantitative aspects* of a *world trade equilibrium*. Moreover, if countries have the same size, $\upsilon_j = 0.5$, they may be considered as the *unified* model of *traditional* trade models with two production factors. All well-known models can be obtained as *special cases* of the *Basic Model* of Propositions 24.1–24.2—with *six submodels* reported in Table 24.1, cf. Table 23.1-2, where the Standard Model refers to Theorem 24.1.

**Table 24.1** Terms of trade $p_W = \Phi(k_A, k_B)$ (24.132) from Basic Model of trade theory in Proposition 24.2

| | | |
|---|---|---|
| I | Ricardo | $p_W = \bar{A}\left[\left[\frac{1-\beta}{\beta}\right]\cdot\frac{\bar{\gamma}\cdot v_A\left[\frac{\gamma_{2A}}{\gamma_{1A}}\right]^{\frac{1}{a_2-a_1}}+v_B\left[\frac{\gamma_{2B}}{\gamma_{1B}}\right]^{\frac{1}{a_2-a_1}}}{\bar{\gamma}\cdot v_A+v_B}\cdot k\right]^{a_2-a_1}$ |
| II | Mill | $p_W = \bar{A}\,\frac{\gamma_2}{\gamma_1}\left[\frac{v_A\left[1-\beta_A\right]+v_B\left[1-\beta_B\right]}{v_A\beta_A+v_B\beta_B}\cdot k\right]^{a_2-a_1}$ |
| III | Marshall | $p_W = \bar{A}\left[\frac{\bar{\gamma}\cdot v_A\left[\frac{\gamma_{2A}}{\gamma_{1A}}\right]^{\frac{1}{a_2-a_1}}\left[1-\beta_A\right]+v_B\left[\frac{\gamma_{2B}}{\gamma_{1B}}\right]^{\frac{1}{a_2-a_1}}\left[1-\beta_B\right]}{\bar{\gamma}\cdot v_A\beta_A+v_B\beta_B}\cdot k\right]^{a_2-a_1}$ |
| IV | HO | $p_W = \bar{A}\left[\left[\frac{1-\beta}{\beta}\right]\cdot\frac{\bar{\gamma}\cdot v_A\left[\frac{\gamma_{2A}}{\gamma_{1A}}\right]^{\frac{1}{a_2-a_1}}k_A+v_B\left[\frac{\gamma_{2B}}{\gamma_{1B}}\right]^{\frac{1}{a_2-a_1}}k_B}{\bar{\gamma}\cdot v_A+v_B}\right]^{a_2-a_1}$ |
| V | HOS | $p_W = \bar{A}\,\frac{\gamma_2}{\gamma_1}\left[\frac{1-\beta}{\beta}\cdot\left[v_Ak_A+v_Bk_B\right]\right]^{a_2-a_1}$ |
| VI | HOL | $p_W = \bar{A}\,\frac{\gamma_2}{\gamma_1}\left[\frac{v_A\left[1-\beta_A\right]k_A+v_B\left[1-\beta_B\right]k_B}{v_A\beta_A+v_B\beta_B}\right]^{a_2-a_1}$ |
| VII | Basic Model | $p_W = \bar{A}\left[\frac{\bar{\gamma}\,v_A\left[\frac{\gamma_{2A}}{\gamma_{1A}}\right]^{\frac{1}{a_2-a_1}}\left[1-\beta_A\right]k_A+v_B\left[\frac{\gamma_{2B}}{\gamma_{1B}}\right]^{\frac{1}{a_2-a_1}}\left[1-\beta_B\right]k_B}{\bar{\gamma}\,v_A\beta_A+v_B\beta_B}\right]^{a_2-a_1}$ |

HO=Heckscher-Ohlin, HOS=Heckscher-Ohlin-Samuelson, HOL=Heckscher-Ohlin-Linder

### *International Terms of Trade with Diversification*

For each model, the explicit expression of the international terms of trade can be easily obtained from (24.132). Table 24.1 presents the *explicit* analytic expressions of the *terms of trade* ($p_W$) for the six models under the *general* assumption that *countries* also *differ* in *size*, $v_J$. The simpler formulas for same country size follow immediately by using $v_J = 0.5$. Complying with (24.143–24.152), all terms of trade values ($\boldsymbol{p}_W$) from Table 24.1 lie between the relative *autarky general* equilibrium prices (see 23.216); see $\boldsymbol{p}_A$, $\boldsymbol{p}_B$, and $p_W$ in Tables 24.2, 24.3, 24.4, 24.5, 24.6, 24.7, and 24.8.

**Table 24.2** Selected GE solutions of the *extended Mill* trade model—Table 24.1

*Parameters and Endowments*: $\upsilon_J = 0.5$ ; $a_1 = 0.5$ ; $a_2 = 0.25$ ; $\gamma_1 = 2$ ; $\gamma_2 = 2.6$ ; $k_J = 2$

| | | PRICE INTERVAL (24.25) | | | | AUTARKY (23.201), (23.217) | | | | INTERNATIONAL EQUILIBRIUM (24.132), (23.34), (23.27), (23.35), (23.16), (24.118) | | | | | | | | | | | |
|---|---|---|---|---|---|---|---|---|---|---|---|---|---|---|---|---|---|---|---|---|---|
| $\alpha_A$ | $\alpha_B$ | $\underline{p}_A$ | $\overline{p}_A$ | $\underline{p}_B$ | $\overline{p}_B$ | $\omega_A$ | $\omega_B$ | $p_A$ | $p_B$ | $p_W$ | $\omega_A$ | $\omega_B$ | $k_{1A}$ | $k_{1B}$ | $k_{2A}$ | $k_{2B}$ | $\lambda_{L_{1A}}$ | $\lambda_{L_{1B}}$ | $\lambda_{K_{1A}}$ | $\lambda_{K_{1B}}$ | $x_{1A}$ |
| 0.2 | 0.5 | 0.95 | 1.25 | 0.95 | 1.25 | 4.67 | 3.33 | 1.01 | 1.10 | 1.05 | 3.93 | 3.93 | 3.93 | 3.93 | 1.31 | 1.31 | 0.26 | 0.26 | 0.52 | 0.52 | 0.45 |
| **0.5** | **0.5** | **0.95** | **1.25** | **0.95** | **1.25** | **3.33** | **3.33** | **1.10** | **1.10** | **1.10** | **3.33** | **3.33** | **3.33** | **3.33** | **1.11** | **1.11** | **0.40** | **0.40** | **0.67** | **0.67** | **0.00** |
| 0.8 | 0.5 | 0.95 | 1.25 | 0.95 | 1.25 | 2.44 | 3.33 | 1.18 | 1.10 | 1.14 | 2.85 | 2.85 | 2.85 | 2.85 | 0.95 | 0.95 | 0.55 | 0.55 | 0.79 | 0.79 | −0.43 |
| **0.2** | **0.2** | **0.95** | **1.25** | **0.95** | **1.25** | **4.67** | **4.67** | **1.01** | **1.01** | **1.01** | **4.67** | **4.67** | **4.67** | **4.67** | **1.56** | **1.56** | **0.14** | **0.14** | **0.33** | **0.33** | **0.00** |
| 0.5 | 0.2 | 0.95 | 1.25 | 0.95 | 1.25 | 3.33 | 4.67 | 1.10 | 1.01 | 1.05 | 3.93 | 3.93 | 3.93 | 3.93 | 1.31 | 1.31 | 0.26 | 0.26 | 0.52 | 0.52 | −0.45 |
| 0.8 | 0.2 | 0.95 | 1.25 | 0.95 | 1.25 | 2.44 | 4.67 | 1.18 | 1.01 | 1.10 | 3.33 | 3.33 | 3.33 | 3.33 | 1.11 | 1.11 | 0.40 | 0.40 | 0.67 | 0.67 | −0.88 |
| 0.2 | 0.8 | 0.95 | 1.25 | 0.95 | 1.25 | 4.67 | 2.44 | 1.01 | 1.18 | 1.10 | 3.33 | 3.33 | 3.33 | 3.33 | 1.11 | 1.11 | 0.40 | 0.40 | 0.67 | 0.67 | 0.88 |
| 0.5 | 0.8 | 0.95 | 1.25 | 0.95 | 1.25 | 3.33 | 2.44 | 1.10 | 1.18 | 1.14 | 2.85 | 2.85 | 2.85 | 2.85 | 0.95 | 0.95 | 0.55 | 0.55 | 0.79 | 0.79 | 0.43 |
| **0.8** | **0.8** | **0.95** | **1.25** | **0.95** | **1.25** | **2.44** | **2.44** | **1.18** | **1.18** | **1.18** | **2.44** | **2.44** | **2.44** | **2.44** | **0.81** | **0.81** | **0.73** | **0.73** | **0.89** | **0.89** | **0.00** |

**Table 24.3** Selected GE solutions of the *extended Marshall* trade model—Table 24.1

*Parameters and Endowments*: $\upsilon_J = 0.5$ ; $a_1 = 0.5$ ; $a_2 = 0.25$ ; $\gamma_{1A} = 2.4$ ; $\gamma_{1B} = 2.7$ ; $\gamma_{2A} = 2.6$ ; $\gamma_{2B} = 2.8$ ; $k_J = 2$

| | | PRICE INTERVAL (24.25) | | | | AUTARKY (23.201), (23.217) | | | | INTERNATIONAL EQUILIBRIUM (24.132), (23.34), (23.27), (23.35), (23.16), (24.118) | | | | | | | | | | | |
|---|---|---|---|---|---|---|---|---|---|---|---|---|---|---|---|---|---|---|---|---|---|
| $\alpha_A$ | $\alpha_B$ | $\underline{p}_A$ | $\overline{p}_A$ | $\underline{p}_B$ | $\overline{p}_B$ | $\omega_A$ | $\omega_B$ | $p_A$ | $p_B$ | $p_W$ | $\omega_A$ | $\omega_B$ | $k_{1A}$ | $k_{1B}$ | $k_{2A}$ | $k_{2B}$ | $\lambda_{L_{1A}}$ | $\lambda_{L_{1B}}$ | $\lambda_{K_{1A}}$ | $\lambda_{K_{1B}}$ | $x_{1A}$ |
| 0.2 | 0.5 | 0.79 | 1.04 | 0.76 | 0.99 | 4.67 | 3.33 | 0.84 | 0.87 | 0.86 | 4.27 | 3.59 | 4.27 | 3.59 | 1.42 | 1.20 | 0.20 | 0.34 | 0.43 | 0.60 | 0.27 |
| **0.5** | **0.5** | **0.79** | **1.04** | **0.76** | **0.99** | **3.33** | **3.33** | **0.91** | **0.87** | **0.89** | **3.66** | **3.07** | **3.66** | **3.07** | **1.22** | **1.02** | **0.32** | **0.48** | **0.59** | **0.73** | **-0.30** |
| 0.8 | 0.5 | 0.79 | 1.04 | 0.76 | 0.99 | 2.44 | 3.33 | 0.99 | 0.87 | 0.93 | 3.15 | 2.64 | 3.15 | 2.64 | 1.05 | 0.88 | 0.45 | 0.63 | 0.71 | 0.84 | −0.86 |
| **0.2** | **0.2** | **0.79** | **1.04** | **0.76** | **0.99** | **4.67** | **4.67** | **0.84** | **0.80** | **0.82** | **5.12** | **4.30** | **5.12** | **4.30** | **1.71** | **1.43** | **0.09** | **0.20** | **0.22** | **0.43** | **-0.29** |
| 0.5 | 0.2 | 0.79 | 1.04 | 0.76 | 0.99 | 3.33 | 4.67 | 0.91 | 0.80 | 0.86 | 4.34 | 3.64 | 4.34 | 3.64 | 1.45 | 1.21 | 0.19 | 0.32 | 0.42 | 0.59 | −0.87 |
| 0.8 | 0.2 | 0.79 | 1.04 | 0.76 | 0.99 | 2.44 | 4.67 | 0.99 | 0.80 | 0.89 | 3.71 | 3.12 | 3.71 | 3.12 | 1.24 | 1.04 | 0.31 | 0.46 | 0.57 | 0.72 | −1.42 |
| 0.2 | 0.8 | 0.79 | 1.04 | 0.76 | 0.99 | 4.67 | 2.44 | 0.84 | 0.95 | 0.90 | 3.60 | 3.02 | 3.60 | 3.02 | 1.20 | 1.01 | 0.33 | 0.49 | 0.60 | 0.74 | 0.81 |
| 0.5 | 0.8 | 0.79 | 1.04 | 0.76 | 0.99 | 3.33 | 2.44 | 0.91 | 0.95 | 0.93 | 3.10 | 2.60 | 3.10 | 2.60 | 1.03 | 0.87 | 0.47 | 0.65 | 0.73 | 0.85 | 0.24 |
| **0.8** | **0.8** | **0.79** | **1.04** | **0.76** | **0.99** | **2.44** | **2.44** | **0.99** | **0.95** | **0.96** | **2.68** | **2.25** | **2.68** | **2.25** | **0.89** | **0.75** | **0.62** | **0.83** | **0.83** | **0.94** | **−0.31** |

**Table 24.4** Selected GE solutions of the *extended HOS—HOL* trade models—Table 24.1

*Parameters and Endowments*: $\upsilon_J = 0.5$ ; $a_1 = 0.5$ ; $a_2 = 0.25$ ; $\gamma_1 = 2$ ; $\gamma_2 = 2.6$ ; $k_A = 1.8$; $k_B = 2.2$

| | | PRICE INTERVAL (24.25) | | | | AUTARKY (23.201), (23.217) | | | | INTERNATIONAL EQUILIBRIUM (24.132), (23.34), (23.27), (23.35), (23.16), (24.118) | | | | | | | | | | | |
|---|---|---|---|---|---|---|---|---|---|---|---|---|---|---|---|---|---|---|---|---|---|
| $\alpha_A$ | $\alpha_B$ | $\underline{p}_A$ | $\overline{p}_A$ | $\underline{p}_B$ | $\overline{p}_B$ | $\omega_A$ | $\omega_B$ | $p_A$ | $p_B$ | $p_W$ | $\omega_A$ | $\omega_B$ | $k_{1A}$ | $k_{1B}$ | $k_{2A}$ | $k_{2B}$ | $\lambda_{L_{1A}}$ | $\lambda_{L_{1B}}$ | $\lambda_{K_{1A}}$ | $\lambda_{K_{1B}}$ | $x_{1A}$ |
| 0.2 | 0.5 | 0.97 | 1.28 | 0.92 | 1.22 | 4.20 | 3.67 | 1.04 | 1.07 | 1.05 | 3.90 | 3.90 | 3.90 | 3.90 | 1.30 | 1.30 | 0.19 | 0.35 | 0.42 | 0.61 | 0.18 |
| **0.5** | **0.5** | **0.97** | **1.28** | **0.92** | **1.22** | **3.00** | **3.67** | **1.13** | **1.07** | **1.10** | **3.33** | **3.33** | **3.33** | **3.33** | **1.11** | **1.11** | **0.31** | **0.49** | **0.57** | **0.74** | **−0.27** |
| 0.8 | 0.5 | 0.97 | 1.28 | 0.92 | 1.22 | 2.20 | 3.67 | 1.22 | 1.07 | 1.14 | 2.87 | 2.87 | 2.87 | 2.87 | 0.96 | 0.96 | 0.44 | 0.65 | 0.70 | 0.85 | −0.71 |
| **0.2** | **0.2** | **0.97** | **1.28** | **0.92** | **1.22** | **4.20** | **5.13** | **1.04** | **0.98** | **1.01** | **4.67** | **4.67** | **4.67** | **4.67** | **1.56** | **1.56** | **0.08** | **0.21** | **0.20** | **0.44** | **−0.26** |
| 0.5 | 0.2 | 0.97 | 1.28 | 0.92 | 1.22 | 3.00 | 5.13 | 1.13 | 0.98 | 1.05 | 3.95 | 3.95 | 3.95 | 3.95 | 1.32 | 1.32 | 0.18 | 0.34 | 0.40 | 0.60 | −0.72 |
| 0.8 | 0.2 | 0.97 | 1.28 | 0.92 | 1.22 | 2.20 | 5.13 | 1.22 | 0.98 | 1.09 | 3.37 | 3.37 | 3.37 | 3.37 | 1.12 | 1.12 | 0.30 | 0.48 | 0.56 | 0.73 | −1.15 |
| 0.2 | 0.8 | 0.97 | 1.28 | 0.92 | 1.22 | 4.20 | 2.69 | 1.04 | 1.16 | 1.10 | 3.29 | 3.29 | 3.29 | 3.29 | 1.10 | 1.10 | 0.32 | 0.50 | 0.59 | 0.75 | 0.60 |
| 0.5 | 0.8 | 0.97 | 1.28 | 0.92 | 1.22 | 3.00 | 2.69 | 1.13 | 1.16 | 1.14 | 2.83 | 2.83 | 2.83 | 2.83 | 0.94 | 0.94 | 0.45 | 0.67 | 0.71 | 0.86 | 0.15 |
| **0.8** | **0.8** | **0.97** | **1.28** | **0.92** | **1.22** | **2.20** | **2.69** | **1.22** | **1.16** | **1.18** | **2.44** | **2.44** | **2.44** | **2.44** | **0.81** | **0.81** | **0.60** | **0.85** | **0.82** | **0.94** | **−0.28** |

**Table 24.5** Selected GE solutions of the *extended HO* trade models—Table 24.1

*Parameters and Endowments*: $\upsilon_J = 0.5$ ; $a_1 = 0.5$ ; $a_2 = 0.25$ ; $\gamma_{1A} = 2.4$ ; $\gamma_{2A} = 2.6$ ; $\alpha_J = 0.5$ ; $k_A = 1.8$ ; $k_B = 2.2$

| | | PRICE INTERVAL (24.25) | | | | AUTARKY (23.201), (23.217) | | | | INTERNATIONAL EQUILIBRIUM (24.132), (23.34), (23.27), (23.35), (23.16), (24.118) | | | | | | | | | | | |
|---|---|---|---|---|---|---|---|---|---|---|---|---|---|---|---|---|---|---|---|---|---|
| $\gamma_{1B}$ | $\gamma_{2B}$ | $\underline{p}_A$ | $\overline{p}_A$ | $\underline{p}_B$ | $\overline{p}_B$ | $\omega_A$ | $\omega_B$ | $p_A$ | $p_B$ | $p_W$ | $\omega_A$ | $\omega_B$ | $k_{1A}$ | $k_{1B}$ | $k_{2A}$ | $k_{2B}$ | $\lambda_{L_{1A}}$ | $\lambda_{L_{1B}}$ | $\lambda_{K_{1A}}$ | $\lambda_{K_{1B}}$ | $x_{1A}$ |
| 2.4 | 2.7 | 0.81 | 1.07 | 0.80 | 1.05 | 3.00 | 3.67 | 0.94 | 0.93 | 0.93 | 3.08 | 3.58 | 3.08 | 3.58 | 1.03 | 1.19 | 0.38 | 0.42 | 0.64 | 0.69 | −0.08 |
| 2.4 | 2.8 | 0.81 | 1.07 | 0.83 | 1.09 | 3.00 | 3.67 | 0.94 | 0.96 | 0.95 | 2.85 | 3.84 | 2.85 | 3.84 | 0.95 | 1.28 | 0.45 | 0.36 | 0.71 | 0.63 | 0.16 |
| 2.7 | 2.6 | 0.81 | 1.07 | 0.68 | 0.90 | 3.00 | 3.67 | 0.94 | 0.79 | 0.85 | 4.35 | 2.72 | 4.35 | 2.72 | 1.45 | 0.91 | 0.12 | 0.71 | 0.29 | 0.88 | −1.17 |
| 2.7 | 3.0 | 0.81 | 1.07 | 0.79 | 1.04 | 3.00 | 3.67 | 0.94 | 0.92 | 0.93 | 3.17 | 3.51 | 3.17 | 3.51 | 1.06 | 1.17 | 0.35 | 0.44 | 0.62 | 0.70 | −0.17 |
| 3.0 | 2.8 | 0.81 | 1.07 | 0.66 | 0.87 | 3.00 | 3.67 | 0.94 | 0.77 | 0.84 | 4.76 | 2.62 | 4.76 | 2.62 | 1.59 | 0.87 | 0.07 | 0.76 | 0.18 | 0.90 | −1.45 |
| 3.0 | 3.0 | 0.81 | 1.07 | 0.71 | 0.94 | 3.00 | 3.67 | 0.94 | 0.82 | 0.87 | 4.06 | 2.95 | 4.06 | 2.95 | 1.35 | 0.98 | 0.17 | 0.62 | 0.37 | 0.83 | −0.94 |

**Table 24.6** Selected GE solutions of **Basic Model**, *sizes, technologies, preferences*—Table 24.1

*Parameters and Endowments*: $\upsilon_J = 0.38$ ; $a_1 = 0.5$ ; $a_2 = 0.25$ ; $\gamma_{1A} = 2.4$ ; $\gamma_{2A} = 2.6$ ; $k_A = 1.8$ ; $k_B = 2.2$

| | | | | PRICE INTERVAL (24.25) | | | | AUTARKY (23.201), (23.217) | | | | INTERNATIONAL EQUILIBRIUM (24.132), (23.34), (23.27), (23.35), (23.16), (24.118) | | | | | | | | | | | |
|---|---|---|---|---|---|---|---|---|---|---|---|---|---|---|---|---|---|---|---|---|---|---|---|
| $\alpha_A$ | $\alpha_B$ | $\gamma_{1B}$ | $\gamma_{2B}$ | $\underline{p}_A$ | $\overline{p}_A$ | $\underline{p}_B$ | $\overline{p}_B$ | $\omega_A$ | $\omega_B$ | $p_A$ | $p_B$ | $p_W$ | $\omega_A$ | $\omega_B$ | $k_{1A}$ | $k_{1B}$ | $k_{2A}$ | $k_{2B}$ | $\lambda_{L_{1A}}$ | $\lambda_{L_{1B}}$ | $\lambda_{K_{1A}}$ | $\lambda_{K_{1B}}$ | $x_{1A}$ |
| 0.69 | 0.32 | 2.35 | 2.8 | 0.81 | 1.07 | 0.85 | 1.12 | 2.46 | 4.47 | 0.99 | 0.93 | 0.95 | 2.82 | 4.12 | 2.82 | 4.12 | 0.94 | 1.37 | 0.46 | 0.30 | 0.72 | 0.56 | −0.43 |
| 0.60 | 0.40 | 2.35 | 2.8 | 0.81 | 1.07 | 0.85 | 1.12 | 2.70 | 4.09 | 0.96 | 0.96 | 0.96 | 2.76 | 4.04 | 2.76 | 4.04 | 0.92 | 1.35 | 0.48 | 0.32 | 0.73 | 0.58 | −0.07 |
| 0.40 | 0.60 | 2.35 | 2.8 | 0.81 | 1.07 | 0.85 | 1.12 | 3.34 | 3.30 | 0.91 | 1.01 | 0.97 | 2.59 | 3.80 | 2.59 | 3.80 | 0.86 | 1.27 | 0.54 | 0.37 | 0.78 | 0.64 | 0.78 |
| 0.32 | 0.69 | 2.35 | 2.8 | 0.81 | 1.07 | 0.85 | 1.12 | 3.65 | 3.01 | 0.89 | 1.03 | 0.98 | 2.52 | 3.68 | 2.52 | 3.68 | 0.84 | 1.23 | 0.57 | 0.40 | 0.80 | 0.66 | 1.14 |
| 0.32 | 0.69 | 2.7 | 2.55 | 0.81 | 1.07 | 0.67 | 0.88 | 3.65 | 3.01 | 0.89 | 0.82 | 0.84 | 4.65 | 2.69 | 4.65 | 2.69 | 1.55 | 0.90 | 0.08 | 0.73 | 0.21 | 0.89 | −0.73 |
| 0.35 | 0.65 | 2.7 | 2.55 | 0.81 | 1.07 | 0.67 | 0.88 | 3.53 | 3.13 | 0.90 | 0.81 | 0.84 | 4.73 | 2.73 | 4.73 | 2.73 | 1.58 | 0.91 | 0.07 | 0.71 | 0.19 | 0.88 | −0.89 |
| 0.65 | 0.35 | 2.7 | 2.55 | 0.81 | 1.07 | 0.67 | 0.88 | 2.56 | 4.32 | 0.98 | 0.75 | 0.82 | 5.18 | 2.99 | 5.18 | 2.99 | 1.73 | 1.00 | 0.02 | 0.60 | 0.06 | 0.82 | −2.28 |
| 0.69 | 0.32 | 2.7 | 2.55 | 0.81 | 1.07 | 0.67 | 0.88 | 2.46 | 4.47 | 0.99 | 0.74 | 0.82 | 5.21 | 3.01 | 5.21 | 3.01 | 1.74 | 1.00 | 0.02 | 0.60 | 0.05 | 0.82 | −2.44 |

**Table 24.7** Selected GE solutions of *Basic Model*, country A *specialized* in good 2: $\boldsymbol{p_W = \underline{p}_A}$

*Parameters and Endowments*: $\upsilon_J = 0.38$ ; $a_1 = 0.5$ ; $a_2 = 0.25$ ; $\gamma_{1A} = 2.4$ ; $\gamma_{2A} = 2.6$ ; $k_A = 1.8$ ; $k_B = k_A / \left(\breve{\vartheta}\tilde{\gamma}\right)$, (24.144)

| | | | | | PRICE INTERVAL (24.25) | | | | AUTARKY (23.201), (23.217) | | | | INTERNATIONAL EQUILIBRIUM (24.132), (23.34), (23.27), (23.35), (23.16), (24.118) | | | | | | | | | | | |
|---|---|---|---|---|---|---|---|---|---|---|---|---|---|---|---|---|---|---|---|---|---|---|---|---|
| $\alpha_A$ | $\alpha_B$ | $\gamma_{1B}$ | $\gamma_{2B}$ | $k_B$ | $\underline{p}_A$ | $\overline{p}_A$ | $\underline{p}_B$ | $\overline{p}_B$ | $\omega_A$ | $\omega_B$ | $p_A$ | $p_B$ | $p_W$ | $\omega_A$ | $\omega_B$ | $k_{1A}$ | $k_{1B}$ | $k_{2A}$ | $k_{2B}$ | $\lambda_{L_{1A}}$ | $\lambda_{L_{1B}}$ | $\lambda_{K_{1A}}$ | $\lambda_{K_{1B}}$ | $x_{1A}$ |
| 0.69 | 0.32 | 2.35 | 2.80 | 5.30 | 0.81 | 1.07 | 0.68 | 0.90 | 2.46 | 10.7 | 0.99 | 0.75 | 0.81 | 5.40 | 7.90 | 0.00 | 7.90 | 1.80 | 2.63 | 0.00 | 0.51 | 0.00 | 0.75 | −2.57 |
| 0.60 | 0.40 | 2.35 | 2.80 | 5.51 | 0.81 | 1.07 | 0.67 | 0.89 | 2.70 | 10.2 | 0.96 | 0.76 | 0.81 | 5.40 | 7.90 | 0.00 | 7.90 | 1.80 | 2.63 | 0.00 | 0.55 | 0.00 | 0.78 | −2.23 |
| 0.40 | 0.60 | 2.35 | 2.80 | 6.18 | 0.81 | 1.07 | 0.65 | 0.86 | 3.34 | 9.26 | 0.91 | 0.78 | 0.81 | 5.40 | 7.90 | 0.00 | 7.90 | 1.80 | 2.63 | 0.00 | 0.67 | 0.00 | 0.86 | −1.49 |
| **0.32** | **0.69** | **2.40** | **2.60** | **4.56** | **0.81** | **1.07** | **0.64** | **0.84** | **3.65** | **6.24** | **0.89** | **0.78** | **0.81** | **5.40** | **5.40** | **0.00** | **5.40** | **1.80** | **1.80** | **0.00** | **0.77** | **0.00** | **0.91** | **−1.19** |
| 0.32 | 0.69 | 2.70 | 2.55 | 2.70 | 0.81 | 1.07 | 0.64 | 0.84 | 3.65 | 3.68 | 0.89 | 0.78 | 0.81 | 5.40 | 3.12 | 0.00 | 3.12 | 1.80 | 1.04 | 0.00 | 0.80 | 0.00 | 0.92 | −1.19 |
| 0.35 | 0.65 | 2.70 | 2.55 | 2.63 | 0.81 | 1.07 | 0.64 | 0.84 | 3.53 | 3.75 | 0.90 | 0.77 | 0.81 | 5.40 | 3.12 | 0.00 | 3.12 | 1.80 | 1.04 | 0.00 | 0.77 | 0.00 | 0.91 | −1.30 |
| 0.65 | 0.35 | 2.70 | 2.55 | 2.32 | 0.81 | 1.07 | 0.66 | 0.87 | 2.56 | 4.55 | 0.98 | 0.74 | 0.81 | 5.40 | 3.12 | 0.00 | 3.12 | 1.80 | 1.04 | 0.00 | 0.62 | 0.00 | 0.83 | −2.42 |
| 0.69 | 0.32 | 2.70 | 2.55 | 2.30 | 0.81 | 1.07 | 0.66 | 0.87 | 2.46 | 4.68 | 0.99 | 0.73 | 0.81 | 5.40 | 3.12 | 0.00 | 3.12 | 1.80 | 1.04 | 0.00 | 0.61 | 0.00 | 0.82 | −2.57 |

**Table 24.8** Selected GE solutions of **Basic Model**, *both* countries *specialized*: $\boldsymbol{p_w = \underline{p}_A = \overline{p}_B}$

*Parameters and Endowments*: $\upsilon_J = 0.38$ ; $a_1 = 0.5$ ; $a_2 = 0.25$ ; $\gamma_{1A} = \overline{\gamma}_{1A}$ ; $\gamma_{2A} = 2.6$ ; $k_A = 1.8$ ; $k_B = k_A/\left(\breve{\vartheta}\tilde{\gamma}\right)$, $\breve{\vartheta} = \tilde{\vartheta} = \tilde{a} = 1/3$, (24.147)

| | | | | | PRICE INTERVAL (24.25) | | | | AUTARKY (23.201), (23.217) | | | | INTERNATIONAL EQUILIBRIUM (24.132), (23.34), (23.27), (23.35), (23.16), (24.118) | | | | | | | | | | | |
|---|---|---|---|---|---|---|---|---|---|---|---|---|---|---|---|---|---|---|---|---|---|---|---|---|
| $\alpha_A$ | $\alpha_B$ | $\gamma_{1B}$ | $\gamma_{2B}$ | $k_B$ | $\underline{p}_A$ | $\overline{p}_A$ | $\underline{p}_B$ | $\overline{p}_B$ | $\omega_A$ | $\omega_B$ | $p_A$ | $p_B$ | $p_W$ | $\omega_A$ | $\omega_B$ | $k_{1A}$ | $k_{1B}$ | $k_{2A}$ | $k_{2B}$ | $\lambda_{L_{1A}}$ | $\lambda_{L_{1B}}$ | $\lambda_{K_{1A}}$ | $\lambda_{K_{1B}}$ | $x_{1A}$ |
| 0.69 | 0.32 | 2.35 | 2.80 | 0.12 | 2.31 | 3.05 | 1.76 | 2.31 | 2.46 | 0.24 | 2.82 | 1.94 | 2.31 | 5.40 | 0.12 | 0.00 | 0.12 | 1.80 | 0.00 | 0.00 | 1.00 | 0.00 | 1.00 | −0.90 |
| 0.60 | 0.40 | 2.35 | 2.80 | 0.11 | 2.35 | 3.09 | 1.78 | 2.35 | 2.70 | 0.21 | 2.79 | 2.01 | 2.35 | 5.40 | 0.11 | 0.00 | 0.11 | 1.80 | 0.00 | 0.00 | 1.00 | 0.00 | 1.00 | −0.77 |
| 0.40 | 0.60 | 2.35 | 2.80 | 0.11 | 2.35 | 3.09 | 1.78 | 2.35 | 3.34 | 0.17 | 2.65 | 2.12 | 2.35 | 5.40 | 0.11 | 0.00 | 0.11 | 1.80 | 0.00 | 0.00 | 1.00 | 0.00 | 1.00 | −0.51 |
| 0.76 | 0.69 | 2.40 | 2.60 | 5.40 | 0.81 | 1.07 | 0.62 | 0.81 | 2.29 | 7.38 | 1.00 | 0.75 | 0.81 | 5.40 | 5.40 | 0.00 | 5.40 | 1.80 | 0.00 | 0.00 | 1.00 | 0.00 | 1.00 | −2.82 |
| 0.32 | 0.69 | 2.70 | 2.55 | 0.18 | 1.64 | 2.16 | 1.25 | 1.64 | 3.65 | 0.25 | 1.81 | 1.52 | 1.64 | 5.40 | 0.18 | 0.00 | 0.18 | 1.80 | 0.00 | 0.00 | 1.00 | 0.00 | 1.00 | −0.59 |
| 0.35 | 0.65 | 2.70 | 2.55 | 0.16 | 1.69 | 2.23 | 1.29 | 1.69 | 3.53 | 0.23 | 1.88 | 1.55 | 1.69 | 5.40 | 0.16 | 0.00 | 0.16 | 1.80 | 0.00 | 0.00 | 1.00 | 0.00 | 1.00 | −0.62 |
| 0.65 | 0.35 | 2.70 | 2.55 | 0.16 | 1.69 | 2.23 | 1.29 | 1.69 | 2.56 | 0.32 | 2.04 | 1.43 | 1.69 | 5.40 | 0.16 | 0.00 | 0.16 | 1.80 | 0.00 | 0.00 | 1.00 | 0.00 | 1.00 | −1.15 |
| 0.69 | 0.32 | 2.70 | 2.55 | 0.17 | 1.67 | 2.20 | 1.27 | 1.67 | 2.46 | 0.35 | 2.03 | 1.40 | 1.67 | 5.40 | 0.17 | 0.00 | 0.17 | 1.80 | 0.00 | 0.00 | 1.00 | 0.00 | 1.00 | −1.24 |

### *Factor Price Equalization*

The *Basic Model (VII)* of international trade allows an exact analysis of the conditions under which factor price *equalization* (FPE) occurs. We distinguish between cases when *both* countries are *diversified*—their *exogenous* endowment ratios $(\boldsymbol{k}_A, \boldsymbol{k}_B)$ belong to the *intervals* (24.143–24.147) of Proposition 24.2—and some cases with *"incipient specialization"* in the two countries.

Without specialization, both countries produce two goods and equalization of free trade *commodity* prices (unit costs), gives their *factor* price ratio: $\boldsymbol{\omega}_J(\boldsymbol{p}_W)$ by (23.34).

**Corollary 24.3** *With* ***incomplete*** *specialization in both countries (24.143–24.147), factor price equalization occurs only and always, when CD technologies are internationally identical.*

*Hence* **FPE** *diversification intervals for the factor endowment ratios,* $(\boldsymbol{k}_A/\boldsymbol{k}_B)$*, must here be restricted to the closed* ***intervals*** *(24.149–24.152) of Corollary 24.2.* **FPE** *implies:* $\boldsymbol{k}_{iA}(\boldsymbol{p}_W) = \boldsymbol{k}_{iB}(\boldsymbol{p}_W)$.

***Proof*** Simply observe that relative factor prices (23.34) with $\boldsymbol{p}_J = \boldsymbol{p}_W$ solely depends on *technology* parameters—only if they are identical in the two countries are: $\boldsymbol{\omega}_A = \boldsymbol{\omega}_B$. □

Thus, the *wage-rental ratios* $(\boldsymbol{\omega}_A, \boldsymbol{\omega}_B)$ are *equal*—**FPE**—in the international general equilibrium solutions of the Mill, HOS, HOL, trade models, cf. Tables 24.2 and 24.4, *irrespective* of different consumer *preferences* and different *endowments* (but satisfying Corollary 24.2).

### *World General Equilibrium Allocations and Net Exports*

Using the analytical framework of both autarky and world trade models, we show—in Tables 24.2, 24.3, 24.4, and 24.5, [ for *autarky* and free international *trade* ]—the *general equilibrium* (**GE**) *solutions* of selected *endogenous* variables: (23.201), (23.217) [*autarky*], and: (24.132), (23.34), (23.27), (23.35), (23.16), (24.118) [*governed* by the *world* market *terms of trade*: $\boldsymbol{p}_J = \boldsymbol{p}_W = \boldsymbol{\Phi}(\boldsymbol{k}_A, \boldsymbol{k}_B)$, (24.132) ].

In Tables 24.2, 24.3, 24.4, and 24.5, we have always chosen: $a_1 = 0.50 > a_2 = 0.25$, cf. Case 2, Figs. 24.1, 24.7b, and Fig. 23.11. In Tables 24.2, 24.3, and 24.4, the relative *price intervals* (24.25) are the *same*, being unaffected by $(\boldsymbol{\alpha}_A, \boldsymbol{\alpha}_B)$.

First it is shown that *preferences* (the demand-side of the economy) are as important in affecting sectoral *factor allocations* and the *trade patterns*, (trade flows, net-export) as the supply-side is. Thus Table 24.2 gives numerical examples about the roles of *tastes* in shaping the *trade patterns* and the *size* of *net exports*. The two columns from left contain the size of the *preference parameters*, $\alpha_A$ and $\alpha_B$. Note that preferences *need* here to be *different* across *nations*, since there would be no trade otherwise (as seen in three rows).

In the first *two* rows, consumers in country $A$ relatively *dislike* good 1 in comparison to their counterparts in country $B$ ($\alpha_A < \alpha_B$), while in rows 4–5 they *prefer* good 1. For this reason, in rows 1–2, country $A$ is a net exporter of good 1, i.e. $X_{1A} > 0$ (last column), and a net importer in rows 4–5. Evidently, the *comparative cost* (advantage) principle for obtaining *trade patterns* by the general *autarky rule* (23.214) *changes* this *inequality* relation with (23.217) in rows 4–5. Moreover, as the international *gap* in preferences rises, the traded quantities increase.

As indicated by the *terms of trade* expression for the Mill's Model (Table 24.1, Model II), ($\boldsymbol{p}_W$) also depends on preference parameter $\boldsymbol{\alpha}_J$ via: $\boldsymbol{\beta}_J = \alpha_J a_1 + (1 - \alpha_J) a_2$, $J = A, B$, cf. (24.133). The higher $\boldsymbol{\alpha}_J$ ($J = A, B$) are, the higher is here $\boldsymbol{p}_W$, (24.132), as an increase in $\alpha_J$ is responsible for a larger demand of good 1 on the world level. Note that the *supply sides* of the two economies are *identical* ($\gamma_{1A} = \gamma_{1B} = \gamma_1$, $\gamma_{2A} = \gamma_{2B} = \gamma_2$) in the Mill's model. Thus *sectoral factor allocations* in the two economies are in fact the *same* after trade, i.e. $\lambda_{L_{1A}} = \lambda_{L_{1B}}$ and $\lambda_{K_{1A}} = \lambda_{K_{1B}}$, Table 24.2—demonstrating that international differences in consumers' *tastes* can *overwhelm* the effect due to *technology* or *endowments*. Similar results for trade patterns and factor allocations are illustrated in Tables 24.3, 24.4, and 24.5.

Table 24.3 considers countries with *differences* in *technologies* and *preferences*. In this *Marshall* model (combining Ricardo and Mill), we have: $\gamma_{2A}/\gamma_{1A} > \gamma_{2B}/\gamma_{1B}$, i.e., *country A* is *technologically* relatively more *efficient* in *good* (sector) 2. Preferences are only identical in the boldface cases. But once national consumers' tastes start to diverge, trade patterns are affected even to the point in which they are reversed. If consumers in country $A$ start preferring good 1, trade patterns remain unchanged with increasing imports of good 1. This is true, if preferences of country $B$'s consumers remain unchanged or dislike for good 1 increases in country B. However, if consumers in country $A$ ($B$) stop preferring (disliking) good 1, *trade* patterns may be *reversed*. *Country A* becomes a net *exporter* of *good* 1. But the *comparative* cost/price *principle* (23.214), never fails.

Let us briefly look into the logic behind the results of *HOS-HOL* models in Table 24.4. Here trade patterns and factor allocations are determined by endowments and preferences. Countries have different *factor endowments* (*country A* is more *labour-abundant* than country $B$), but are equipped with the same technologies ($\gamma_{iA} = \gamma_{iB}$). As *sector*/good 2 is more *labour intensive* than sector 1, country $A$ "should tend to" export commodity 2.

But such *trade pattern* can again be *reversed*, if the dislike (preference) for good 1 by consumers in country $A$ (country $B$) is sufficiently high. Note again that comparative cost (price) principle (23.214), never fails.

Table 24.5 provides some examples from *HO* trade models. In all cases, *country A* is relatively *labour abundant* ($k_A < k_B$), and *sector* (good) 1 is *capital intensive* ($a_1 > a_2$). Under these assumptions, country $A$ "should traditionally" be exporter of good 2 (the labour-intensive commodity) and *importer* of good 1—as seen in all rows, except one.

Note that the *interaction* between the *technological efficiency parameters* $(\gamma_{iA}, \gamma_{iB})$ of *sectors* in the two countries affects the size of net exports of country $A$ and thus all other variables. If the *relative technological efficiency*, $(\gamma_{2B}/\gamma_{1B})$, in country $B$ becomes very large (very favourable for good 2), as in *row 2*, Table 24.5, the comparative cost advantage of country B in good 1 vanishes totally, and *country A* will then be *exporter* of good 1.

In Table 24.6, the HO trade model cases of Table 24.5 are extended to also encompass *heterogeneity* in consumer preferences and in different *country sizes.*

In Tables 24.7 and 24.8, we give two cases with *"incipient specialization"* in the two countries, where Table 24.7 refers to Fig. 24.7a—Table 24.8 to Fig. 24.7b—discussed at the end of Sect. "Computation of the Endogenous Terms of Trade".

Note especially in Tables 24.7 and 24.8 that **FPE**, cf. Corollary 24.3, are preserved with countries "incipiently specialized"; we see: $k_{2A}(0.81) = k_{2B}(0.81) = 1.80$, and $k_A/k_B = 1.8/4.56 = 0.39$, as *endpoint* of the *interval*, (24.149), $\bar{\vartheta} = 2.37$—and: $k_A/k_B = 1.8/5.40 = 1/3$ at (24.145).

Propositions 24.1–24.2 and their consequences illustrated Tables 24.2, 24.3, 24.4, 24.5, 24.6, 24.7, and 24.8 *avoid*, "the *curse* of *general equilibrium models*, in which all that can be said is that everything depends on everything else", *Samuelson* (1983, p. 1481). We may elaborate a bit on this 'curse', as the mutual *interdependence* theory of *pricing* was stated, *Ohlin* (1933, p. 4) as: "The chain of causation does not proceed from costs to prices or from prices to costs, but is always characterized by *mutual interdependence*", and "The *law* of *supply* and *demand* is everywhere developed into a system of *general equilibrium*, in which the principle of mutual interdependence is fundamental". Accordingly *Ohlin* (1933, Appendix I) wanted to *extend* the closed general equilibrium *equation systems* of Walras-Cassel to a *general equilibrium price mechanism* for the commodities and factors of *trading* countries.[12]

Proposition 24.1 lifts the "curse" by giving *one complete equation*, (24.132), for $\boldsymbol{p}_W$ that decides *all* the other *international equilibrium variables* by their *equations*, listed in Tables 24.2, 24.3, 24.4, 24.5, 24.6, 24.7, and 24.8.

Two principles played a major role for the *calculation* of commodity prices: The *cost* approach and the total *interdependence* approach of supply and demand determination.

As we have seen, the *relative cost* functions, $\boldsymbol{p}_J = \boldsymbol{p}_J(\boldsymbol{\omega}_J)$, J=A,B, are not made superfluous by the *Walras equilibrium* relations, $\boldsymbol{k}_J = \boldsymbol{\Psi}_J(\boldsymbol{\omega}_J)$; the *"invisible" comparative costs*, $\boldsymbol{p}_J(\boldsymbol{\omega}_J)$, rule in *autarky* behind the **GE** loci (*curves*): $\boldsymbol{k}_J = \boldsymbol{\Psi}_J(\boldsymbol{\omega}_J)$, and rule in *free trading* economies behind the *surfaces* of the *international general equilibrium*: $\boldsymbol{p}_W = \boldsymbol{\Phi}(\boldsymbol{k}_A, \boldsymbol{k}_B)$.

[12] For an early version of our **general equilibrium model** see Laursen (1952).

## Conclusion

The problems with the *comparative cost* (price, advantage) principle in deriving *trade patterns* from autarky price ratios (24.1), and the problems with deriving *explicitly* the international general equilibrium *terms of trade* ($p_W$) of two countries, (24.2), have been with us for two hundred years (1817). We have seen that rigorous analytic (parametric) general equilibrium model solutions are not superfluous luxuries. They are indispensable for true understanding and for answering many long-open questions, as demonstrated by the Basic World Trade Model *solutions* and *existence conditions* in Propositions 24.1–24.3.

Methodologically (mathematically), it should be noted that our general equilibrium modelling was *designed* to generate relevant *comparative static solutions.* It is by aiming for comparative statics that *factor endowments* of the countries (as exogenous variables) got their crucial *analytic* trade model *significance* by giving an answer to (24.1) with the *autarky general equilibrium* formulas of *comparative advantage*: $\mathbf{p}_J(\mathbf{k}_J)$, (23.202), (23.214), and fixing *international general equilibrium* issues to get (24.2) on *parametric* form: $\mathbf{p}_W = \Phi(\mathbf{k}_A, \mathbf{k}_B)$, (24.132), which in Table 24.1 moreover could *unify* Ricardo (I), Mill (II) into Marshall (III), that then combined with Heckscher-Ohlin (IV) constitute the **Basic Model** (VII).

In this chapter, we have only dealt with the cases of "incipient specialization". The situations with the *factor endowment ratios* ($k_A/k_B$) beyond the *interval boundaries* of Proposition 24.3 have, for space reasons, not been included; but such specialization cases would only require revision (reductions) of the terms of trade expression (24.132) *intervals* for ($\boldsymbol{k_A/k_B}$) in Proposition 24.3.

We have mainly illustrated the $(2 \times 2 \times 2)$ *international general equilibrium allocations* of the **Basic Model** for *free trade* applications. But the level ($\gamma_{iJ}$) *parameters* (total factor productivity, TFP) may also play role as *tariffs*. Propositions 24.1–24.2 and Table 24.1, 24.2, 24.3, 24.4, 24.5, 24.6, 24.7, and 24.8 do indicate intricacies of tariff effects on international trade, as well as the complexity of trade policies.

Subject of further research would naturally be extensions to CES specified *autarky* and globally *trading* economies (regions), allowing for a larger parametric *heterogeneity* of their technologies and preferences.

## Appendix

**Remark 24.1** The assumption $\underline{p}_A \geq \underline{p}_B$ can be made without loss of generality.

In order to see this, verify with (24.25), that $\underline{p}_A \geq \underline{p}_B \Leftrightarrow \overline{p}_A \geq \overline{p}_B$. This means that it is excluded that any of the two intervals $[\underline{p}_J, \overline{p}_J]$, $J = A, B$ is a proper superset of the other. Hence, either the two intervals coincide (because $\underline{p}_A = \underline{p}_B \Leftrightarrow \overline{p}_A = \overline{p}_B$), or they do not. If they do not coincide, one of them will be located to the right side of the other. Note that only two cases are possible (because there are two countries in the model), i.e. either $\underline{p}_A \geq \underline{p}_B$ or

$\underline{p}_B \geq \underline{p}_A$. Since each case can be obtained from the other by simply switching the two country-specific indexes, it suffices to study only one of them.

### *Proof of Proposition 24.2*

Proposition 24.2 distinguishes the two cases $a_1 > a_2$ and $a_1 < a_2$. Since the proof is analogous ('symmetric') in the two cases, let us assume $a_1 > a_2$, and show how the conditions on the ratio $k_A/k_B$ are obtained with $a_1 > a_2$: *Conditions* (24.143), (24.144), and (24.145).

Observe first the condition $k_A/k_B \leq \widetilde{\gamma}$. It is easily seen that this condition equally holds in (24.143), (24.144), and (24.145), since $\widetilde{a}$ is less than one when $a_1 > a_2$. The condition $k_A/k_B \leq \widetilde{\gamma}$ corresponds to the assumption $\underline{p}_A \geq \underline{p}_B$. To see this, re-write $\underline{p}_A \geq \underline{p}_B$ as $(k_A/k_B)^{a_2-a_1} \leq (\gamma_{1A}/\gamma_{2A})/(\gamma_{1B}/\gamma_{2B})$ in virtue of (24.25) and use definition (24.27).

When $\underline{p}_A \geq \underline{p}_B$, an international general equilibrium solution exists only if the interval $[\underline{p}_A, \overline{p}_B]$ is non-empty, i.e. $\underline{p}_A \leq \overline{p}_B$. Verify that this condition is equivalent to $k_A/k_B \geq \widetilde{a} \cdot \widetilde{\gamma}$ because of the definitions of $\underline{p}_J$ and $\overline{p}_J$ given in (24.25). Note in particular that the interval collapses to to one single point (i.e., $\underline{p}_A = \overline{p}_B$) if $k_A/k_B = \widetilde{a} \cdot \widetilde{\gamma}$.

The condition $k_A/k_B \geq \widetilde{a} \cdot \widetilde{\gamma}$ is clearly verified in (24.145), where $k_A/k_B = \widetilde{a} \cdot \widetilde{\gamma}$. In (24.143), it follows from the fact that $k_A/k_B \geq \breve{\vartheta} \cdot \widetilde{\gamma}$ because $\breve{\vartheta}$ is larger than $\widetilde{a}$ for any $\bar{\gamma} < \bar{\vartheta}$. To see this, simply insert definition (24.141) for $\breve{\vartheta}$ and definition (24.28) for $\widetilde{a}$ into $\breve{\vartheta} > \widetilde{a}$, and prove that $\breve{\vartheta} > \widetilde{a} \Leftrightarrow \bar{\gamma} < \bar{\vartheta}$. With the same logic, the condition $k_A/k_B \geq \widetilde{\vartheta} \cdot \widetilde{\gamma}$ in (24.144) automatically implies $k_A/k_B \geq \widetilde{a} \cdot \widetilde{\gamma}$ because $\widetilde{\vartheta} > \widetilde{a}$ since $\bar{\gamma} > \bar{\vartheta}$.

Derive now conditions (24.143), (24.144), and (24.145), which all ensure that the international general equilibrium solution $p_W$ belongs to the closed interval $[\underline{p}_A, \overline{p}_B]$, which is non-empty because $\widetilde{a} \cdot \widetilde{\gamma} \leq k_A/k_B \leq \widetilde{\gamma}$. In (24.145), the interval coincides with one single point (i.e., $\underline{p}_A = \overline{p}_B$), as $k_A/k_B = \widetilde{a} \cdot \widetilde{\gamma}$. In this case, an international general equilibrium solution only exists if $p_W = \underline{p}_A = \overline{p}_B$. Prove that this requires $k_A/k_B = \breve{\vartheta}\,\widetilde{\gamma} = \widetilde{\vartheta}\,\widetilde{\gamma}$, which occurs when $\bar{\gamma} = \bar{\vartheta}$. To this aim, show that the condition $p_W = \underline{p}_A$ (which indicates that country *A* produces only good 2) may be written as $k_A/k_B = \breve{\vartheta} \cdot \widetilde{\gamma}$. To see this, insert the explicit expression for $p_W$ (24.132) and the definition of $\underline{p}_A$ (24.25) into $p_W = \underline{p}_A$, and obtain $k_A/k_B = \widetilde{\gamma}\,[\upsilon_B\,(1-\beta_B)\,a_2]/[\upsilon_B\beta_B\,(1-a_2) + \bar{\gamma} \cdot \upsilon_A\,(\beta_A - a_2)]$. Use definitions (24.133) and (24.141) to show that this condition is equivalent to $k_A/k_B = \breve{\vartheta} \cdot \widetilde{\gamma}$. Similarly, verify that the condition $p_W = \overline{p}_B$ (which indicates that country *B* produces only good 1) is equivalent to $k_A/k_B = \widetilde{\vartheta} \cdot \widetilde{\gamma}$. From above, we know that $\breve{\vartheta} = \widetilde{a} \Leftrightarrow \bar{\gamma} = \bar{\vartheta}$ and that $\widetilde{\vartheta} = \widetilde{a} \Leftrightarrow \bar{\gamma} = \bar{\vartheta}$. For transitivity it follows that $\breve{\vartheta} = \widetilde{\vartheta}$. We conclude that an international general equilibrium solution exists when $k_A/k_B = \widetilde{a} \cdot \widetilde{\gamma}$ if $\bar{\gamma} = \bar{\vartheta}$. Note that the condition $\bar{\gamma} = \bar{\vartheta}$ necessarily implies a positive $\widetilde{\vartheta}$, which is negative only if $\bar{\gamma} < (\upsilon_B/\upsilon_A) \cdot a_1/(1-a_1) \cdot \beta_B/\beta_A < \bar{\vartheta}$.

Observe now conditions $k_A/k_B \in [\breve{\vartheta}\tilde{\gamma}, \tilde{\gamma}]$ in (24.143) and $k_A/k_B \in [\tilde{\vartheta}\tilde{\gamma}, \tilde{\gamma}]$ in (24.144). Verify first that in (24.143), $\breve{\vartheta} \cdot \tilde{\gamma} < \tilde{\gamma}$ while in (24.144), $\tilde{\vartheta} \cdot \tilde{\gamma} < \tilde{\gamma}$. Prove in fact that $\breve{\vartheta} < 1$ and $\tilde{\vartheta} < 1$ for any $\bar{\gamma} > 0$. To this aim, use definition (24.141), and verify that $\breve{\vartheta} < 1$ is equivalent to $[\bar{\gamma} \cdot v_A\alpha_A + v_B(1+\alpha_B)](a_1 - a_2) > 0$, which is true per assumption ($a_1 > a_2$). Similarly, insert (24.141) in $\tilde{\vartheta} < 1$, and see that this yields $\bar{\gamma} \cdot v_A(\beta_A - a_1) - v_B(1-\alpha_B)(a_1 - a_2) < 0$, which holds true since $(\beta_A - a_1)$ is negative ($\alpha_A < 1$). Note that $\tilde{\vartheta}$ may be zero or negative (when $\bar{\gamma} \leq (v_B/v_A)\cdot a_1/(1-a_1)\cdot\beta_B/\beta_A$).

Derive now conditions $k_A/k_B \geq \breve{\vartheta} \cdot \tilde{\gamma}$ in (24.143) and $k_A/k_B \geq \tilde{\vartheta} \cdot \tilde{\gamma}$ in (24.144). Recall that in these two cases, $k_A/k_B > \tilde{a} \cdot \tilde{\gamma}$, which means that the interval $[\underline{p}_A, \overline{p}_B]$ is non-empty and discrete. In order to be feasible, the solution $p_W$ has to belong to this interval, i.e. $\underline{p}_A \leq p_W \leq \overline{p}_B$. Prove that this inequality is equivalent to the condition $k_A/k_B \geq \breve{\vartheta} \cdot \tilde{\gamma}$ when $\bar{\gamma} < \bar{\vartheta}$ and it is equivalent to $k_A/k_B \geq \tilde{\vartheta} \cdot \tilde{\gamma}$ in the opposite case ($\bar{\gamma} < \bar{\vartheta}$). To this aim, extend the result above ($p_W = \underline{p}_A \Leftrightarrow k_A/k_B = \breve{\vartheta}\cdot\tilde{\gamma}$) and obtain $p_W \geq \underline{p}_A \Leftrightarrow k_A/k_B \geq \breve{\vartheta}\cdot\tilde{\gamma}$. With the same logic, recover $p_W \leq \overline{p}_B \Leftrightarrow k_A/k_B \geq \tilde{\vartheta}\cdot\tilde{\gamma}$ (for $\tilde{\vartheta} > 0$) and $k_A/k_B > 0$ (for $\tilde{\vartheta} \leq 0$). It is thus proved that the condition $\underline{p}_A \leq p_W \leq \overline{p}_B$ is satisfied when a *pair* of conditions contemporaneously holds. These are $k_A/k_B \geq \breve{\vartheta}\cdot\tilde{\gamma}$ ***and*** $k_A/k_B \geq \tilde{\vartheta}\cdot\tilde{\gamma}$ (when $\tilde{\vartheta} > 0$) or $k_A/k_B \geq \breve{\vartheta} \cdot \tilde{\gamma}$ ***and*** $k_A/k_B > 0$ (when $\tilde{\vartheta} \leq 0$). From above we know that $\breve{\vartheta} > \tilde{a} \Leftrightarrow \bar{\gamma} < \bar{\vartheta}$ and $\tilde{\vartheta} < \tilde{a} \Leftrightarrow \bar{\gamma} < \bar{\vartheta}$. For transitivity it follows that $\breve{\vartheta} > \tilde{\vartheta} \Leftrightarrow \bar{\gamma} < \bar{\vartheta}$, which yields $k_A/k_B \geq \breve{\vartheta} \cdot \tilde{\gamma}$ in (24.143) and $k_A/k_B \geq \tilde{\vartheta} \cdot \tilde{\gamma}$ in (24.144). □

## BIBLIOGRAPHY

Allen RGD (1938) Mathematical Analysis for Economists. MacMillan, London

Arrow KJ, Chenery HB, Minhas BS, Solow RM (1961) Capital–Labour Substitution and Economic Efficiency. Review of Economics and Statistics 43:225–250

Baldwin RE (2008) The Development and Testing of Heckscher–Ohlin Trade Models: A Review. The MIT Press

Barone E (1908) Principi di Economia Politica. Tipografia Nazionale di G. Bertero, Rome

Bhagwati J (1964) The Pure Theory of International Trade: A Survey. Economic Journal 74:1–78, The Royal Economic Society, *Surveys of Economic Theory*, Volume 2, (1965), 156–239, London, Macmillan.

Black J (1957) A Formal Proof of the Concavity of the Production Possibility Function. Economic Journal 67:133–135

Blackorby C, Schworm W, Venables A (1993) Necessary and Sufficient Conditions for Factor Price Equalization. Review of Economic Studies 60:413–434

Blaug M, Lloyd P (eds) (2010) Famous Figures and Diagrams in Economics. Edward Elgar, Cheltenham UK

Burmeister E, Turnovsky SJ (1971) The Degree of Joint Production. International Economic Review 12:99–105

Caves RE, Frankel JA, Jones RW (2002) World Trade and Payments, 9th edn. Addison–Wesley, Boston

Chipman JS (1965) A Survey of the Theory of International, Part I. The Classical Theory. Econometrica 33:477–519, "Part II. The Neo–Classical Theory", 33, 685–760;

Chipman JS (1966) Part III. The Modern Theory. Econometrica 34:18–76

Chipman JS (1969) Factor Price Equalization and the Stolper–Samuelson Theorem. International Economic Review 10:399–406

Chipman JS (1979) Mill's 'Superstructure': How Well Does It Stand Up? History of Political Economy 11(4):477–500

Costinot A, Donaldson D (2012) Ricardo's Theory of Comparative Advantage: Old Ideas, New Evidence. American Economic Review 102:453–456

Deardorff AV (1980) The General Validity of the Law of Comparative Advantage. Journal of Political Economy 88:941–957

Deardorff AV (2006) Terms of Trade, Glossary of International Economics. World Scientific, Singapore

Deardorff AV, Stern RN (1994) The Stolper–Samuelson Theorem: A Golden Jubilee. The University of Michigan Press, Ann Arbor

Diewert WE (1974) Applications of Duality Theory. pp 106–171, In: Intriligator MD, Kendrick DA (eds) *Frontiers of Quantitative Economics*, Vol.2, North–Holland, Amsterdam

Dixit AK, Norman V (1980) Theory of International Trade: A Dual, General Equilibrium Approach. Cambridge University Press, U.K

Dornbusch R, Fischer S, Samuelson PA (1977) Comparative Advantage, Trade, and Payments in a Ricardian Model with a Continuum of Goods. American Economic Review 67:823–39

Drabicki J, Takayama A (1979) An Antinomy in the Theory of Comparative Advantage. Journal of International Economics 9:211–223

Eaton J, Kortum S (2002) Technology, Geography, and Trade. Econometrica 70:1741–80

Edgeworth FY (1881, 2003) Mathematical Psychics and Further Papers on Political Economy. Oxford University Press

Ethier WJ (1995) Modern International Economics, 3rd edn. W.W. Norton & Company, New York

Feenstra RC (2004) Advanced International Trade. Princeton University Press

Findley R, Jonung L, Lundahl M (2002) Bertil Ohlin – A Centennial Celebration (1899–1999). The MIT Press

Flam H, Flanders MJ (1991) Heckscher–Ohlin Trade Theory. MIT Press, Cambridge, Mass

Gandolfo G (1998) International Economics I: The Pure Theory of International Trade, 3rd edn. Springer–Verlag, Berlin

Gandolfo G (2014) International Trade Theory and Policy. Springer–Verlag, Berlin Heidelberg

Grandmont JM, McFadden D (1972) A Technical Note on Classical Gains From Trade. Journal of International Economics 2:109–125

Grossman GM, Rogoff K (1995) Handbook of International Economics, vol III. Elsevier, Amsterdam

Haberler G (1936) The Theory of International Trade. W. Hodge and Comp, London

Hall RE (1973) The Specification of Technology with Several Kinds of Output. Journal of Political Economy 81:868–892

Harwitz M (1972) A Note on Professor Chipman's Version of Mill's Law of International Values. Journal of International Economics 2:181–188

Heckscher EF (1919) The Effect of Foreign Trade on Distribution of Income. Ekonomisk Tidsskrift 21, Del II:1–32, translated (Svend Laursen) in Ellis, H.S., Metzler, L.A., eds. *Readings in the Theory of International Trade*, Blakiston, Philadelphia, (1949), 272–300; transl., in Flam. H & Flanders, M.J. (1991), (43–69).

Hicks JR (1932, 1948) The Theory of Wages. MacMillan, London

Hsiao FST (1971) The Contract Curve and the Production Possibility Curve. Journal of Political Economy 79:919–923

Inada KI (1971) The production coefficient matrix and the Stolper–Samuelson connection. Econometrica 39:219–240

Inoue T, Wegge LL (1986) On the Geometry of the Production Possibility Frontier. International Economic Review 27:727–737

Jensen BS (2003) Walrasian General Equilibrium Allocations and Dynamics in Two–Sector Growth Models. German Economic Review 4:53–87

Jensen BS (2017) von Thünen: Capital, Production Functions, Marginal Productivity Wages and the Natural Wage. German Economic Review 18:51–80

Johnson HG (1966) Factor Market Distortions and the Shape of the Transformation Curve. Econometrica 34:686–698

Jones RW (1965) The Structure of Simple General Equilibrium Models. J Political Economy 73:557–72, or Bhagwati (1981)

Jones RW (1985) Relative Prices and Real Factor Rewards. Economics Letters 19

Jones RW (2002) Trade Theory and Factor Intensities: An Interpretive Essay. Review of International Economics 10:581–603

Jones RW (2010) Production Possibilities Frontiers. In *Famous Figures and Diagrams in Economics*, Blaug and Lloyd, (2010).

Jones RW, Easton ST (1982) Factor Intensities and Factor Substitution in General Equilibrium. Journal of International Economics 15:65–99

Kawano H, Ohta H, Jensen BS, Hwang AR (2017) Production, Distribution, and Trade: General Equilibrium with One Single Cobb–Douglas Parameter. Modern Economy 8:970–993

Kemp MC (1969) The Pure Theory of International Trade and Investment. Prentice–Hall, New Jersey

Kemp MC, Wegge LLF (1969) On the Relation between Commodity Prices and Factor Rewards. International Economic Review 10:407–413

Kenen PB (2000) The International Economy, 4th edn. Prentice–Hall, New Jersey

Kohli U (1983) Non–Joint Technologies. Review of Economic Studies 50:209–219

Kohli U (1991) Technology, Duality, and Foreign Trade: The GNP Function Approach to Modelling Imports and Exports. UMP Press, Ann Arbor; Harvester Wheatsheaf, London

Krugman PR, Obstfeld M, Melitz MJ (2018) International Economics – Theory and Policy, 11th edn. Pearson, UK

Kuga K (1972) The Factor Price Equalization Theorem. Econometrica 40:723–736

Laursen S (1952) Production Functions and the Theory of International Trade. The American Economic Review 42(4):540–557

Leamer E (2001) International Economics. Worth Publishers, New York

Leamer EE (1984) Sources of International Comparative Advantage – theory and evidence. MIT Press, Cambridge, Mass

Leamer EE (1995) The Heckscher–Ohlin Model in Theory and Practice, vol 77. Princeton Studies in International Finance, New Jersey

Leamer EE, Levinsohn J (1995) International Trade Theory: The Evidence. Ch. 26 in Grossman and Rogoff (1995).

Leontief WW (1933) The Use of Indifference Curves in the Analysis of Foreign Trade. Quarterly Journal of Economics 47:493–503

Lerner AP (1932) The Diagrammatical Representation of Cost Conditions in International Trade. Economica 37:319–334

Lerner AP (1933) Notes on Elasticity of Substitution – The Diagrammatical Representation. Review of Economic Studies 1:68–71

Linder SB (1961) An Essay on Trade and Transformation. John Wiley and Sons, New York

Lloyd P (2000) Generalizing the Stolper–Samuelson Theorem: A Tale of Two Matrices. Review of International Economics 8:597–613

Maneschi A, Thweatt W (1987) Barone's (1908) Representation of an Economy's Trade Equilibrium and the Gains from Trade. Journal of International Economics 22:375–382

Markusen JR, Melvin JR, Kaempfer WH, Maskus KE (1995) International Trade. McGraw–Hill, New York

Marshall A (1879, 1930, 1974) The Pure Theory of Foreign Trade, The Pure Theory of Domestic Values. Privately printed (1879); LSE, University of London (1930); Augustus M. Kelley Publishers (1974), New Jersey.

Marshall A (1923) Money, Credit and Commerce. Macmillan

Mas-Colell A, Whinston MD, Green JR (1995) Microeconomic Theory. Oxford University Press, New York

Melitz MJ (2003) The Impact of Trade on Intra–Industry Relations and Aggregate Industry Productivity. Econometrica 71(6):1695–1725

Melvin JR (1969) Mill's Law of International Values. Southern Economic Journal 36:107–116

Meyer W (1976) The Rybczynski, Stolper–Samuelson, and Factor Price Equalization Theorems under Uncertainty. American Economic Review 66:797–808

Mill JS (1848, 1875, 1909) Principles of Political Economy, 7th edn. Longmans, Green and Co., London

Mundell RM (1960) The Pure Theory of international Trade. American Economic Review 50:67–110

Negishi T (1989) History of Economic Theory. Elsevier, Amsterdam, North–Holland

Negishi T (2014) Developments of International Trade Theory. Springer Japan, Tokyo, Advances in Japanese Business and Economics 2

Nicholson W, Snyder C (2012) Microeconomic Theory, 11th edn. South–Western, Mason, OH, USA

Ohlin B (1924) The Theory of Trade. AB Nordiska Bokhandelen, Stockholm, translated in Flam. H & Flanders, M.J. (1991), (76–214)

Ohlin B (1933) Interregional and International Trade. Harvard University Press, Cambridge, MA

Ohlin B (1933, 1967) Interregional and International Trade. Harvard University Press, Cambridge, MA, *Revised Edition* (1967), Harvard University Press

Ohlin B (1970) The Business Cost Account Approach to International Trade Theory. The Swedish Journal of Economics 72:12–20

Oniki H, Uzawa H (1965) Patterns of Trade and Investment in a Dynamic Model of International Trade. Review of Economic Studies 32:15–38

Pigou AC, Marshall A (1925) Memorials of Alfred Marshall. Macmillan

Powell AA, Gruen FHG (1968) The Constant Elasticity of Transformation Production Frontier and the Linear Supply System. International Economic Review 9:315–328

Ricardo D (1817, 1821, 1965) The Principles of Political Economy and Taxation. J.M. Dent and Sons, London

Ruffin RJ (2002) David Ricardo's Discovery of Comparative Advantage. History of Political Economy 34:727–748

Rybczynski TM (1955) Factor Endowments and Relative Commodity Prices. Economica 22:336–341

Samuelson PA (1947, 1983) Foundations of Economic Analysis, Enlarged edn. Harvard University Press, Cambridge, Mass

Samuelson PA (1948, 1949) International Trade and The Equalisation of Factor Price. Economic Journal 58:163–184, International Factor Price Equalisation Once Again. *Economic Journal*, 59, 181–197

Samuelson PA (1949) International Factor Price Equalisation Once Again. Economic Journal 59:181–197

Samuelson PA (1953–1954) Prices of Factors and Goods in General Equilibrium. Review of Economic Studies 21:1–20

Samuelson PA (1966) The Fundamental Singularity Theorem for Non–Joint Production. International Economic Review 7:34–41

Samuelson PA (1972) Maximum Principles in Analytical Economics. American Economic Review 62:249–262

Samuelson PA (1981) Bertil Ohlin – (1899)–(1979). Journal of International Economics 62:147–163

Samuelson PA (1983) Thünen at Two Hundred. Journal of Economic Lite–rature 21:1468–1488

Scarth WM, Warne RD (1973) The Elasticity of Substitution and the Shape of the Transformation Curve. Economica 40:299–304

Shimomura K, Wong KY (1998) The Law of Comparative Advantage without Social Utility Functions. Review of International Economics 6:401–406

Silberberg E, Suen W (2001) The Structure of Economics, A Mathematical Analysis, 3rd edn. McGraw–Hill, Singapore

Smith A (1776, 1961) The Wealth of Nations I–II. Methuen University Paperbacks, London

Södersten B (1964) A Study of Economic Growth and International Trade. Almqvist and Wiksell, Stockholm

Södersten B, Reed G (1994) International Economics, 3rd edn. Macmillan Press, London

Stolper WF, Samuelson PA (1941) Protection and Real Wages. Review of Economic Studies 9:58–73

Uekawa Y (1971) Generalization of the Stolper–Samuelson theorem. Econometrica 39:197–218

Uekawa Y, Kemp MC, Wegge LLF (1972) P– and PN–Matrices, Minkowski– and Metzler Matrices, and Generalization of the Stolper–Samuelson and Samuelson–Rybczynski Theorems. Journal of International Economics 3:53–76

Uzawa H (1961–63) On a Two–Sector Model of Economic Growth: I–II. Rev Econ Stud 29:40–47, Rev. Econ. Stud. 30, 105–18

Wegge LLF, Kemp MC (1969) Generalization of the Stolper–Samuelson and Samuelson–Rybczynski Theorems in Terms of Conditional Input–Output Coefficients. International Economic Review 10:414–425
Wong KY (1995) International Trade in Goods and Factor Mobility. MIT Press, Cambridge, MA
Woodland AD (1982) International Trade and Resource Allocation. Amsterdam, North–Holland

# Agricultural Economics, Land Rents, Cities, Transportation Costs, and Location Theory: von Thünen

## Introduction

As well known, the first quantitative calculations of the *marginal* productivities for *Labor* and *Capital*—with tables and algebraic formulas—were provided by von Thünen, as was discussed extensively and demonstrated with his *production functions* and *wage* formulas in Chap. 3. The objective here is to study and illustrate the quantitative calculations of **Average** and **Marginal** productivity [Marginal *Revenue* product, factor (*rental*) prices] of **Land** that are involved in von Thünen' calculations of Agricultural **Land rents** from the *Manorial Farm Accounts* of his Estate, *Tellow*. "The **effect** of *grain prices* and *land fertility* on **Agriculture**" was in the subtitle of his *Isolated State*[1] (Part 1).

We will briefly introduce and summarily state the content of the chapter sections. In Sect. "Agricultural Productions and Land Cultivation", von Thünen's system of *Rings* is presented and explained. Each ring has its distinct products and optimal cultivation methods/crop rotation. The *field* rotation of *Koppelwirtschaft* in Fig. 25.1a and 25.2, corresponds to the *Seven Field System* - **7 F** - of **Land cultivation** that von Thünen studied and analysed with *Manorial Farm Accounts* of *Tellow*.

Section "City Price, Transport Costs, Local Prices, and Land Rents" introduces the *transport costs* function, **t(x)**, over a *distance* (**x**), Talers per $Ton$ x $Km$, or Talers per $Bushel$ x $Mile$ in Fig. 25.3. Let the central city *market* price, **p(0)**, (distance zero) for *rye* be: $p(0) = \mathbf{1.5}$ Talers/Bushel. Then *transport costs*, **t(x)**, determines the **Local Farm** rye price: **p(x)** = **p(0)** - **t(x)**, falling with distance **(x)** from city as in Fig. 25.3.

[1] von Thünen (1990); Hall (1966). Hall (1966) is the English translation.



B. S. Jensen, *The Elements and Dynamic Systems of Economic Growth and Trade Models*, https://doi.org/10.1007/978-3-031-52493-6_25

From accounting data, the *local* total production **cost** of rye per *bushel*, **c(x)**, is known. The **difference** between the *local* farm **price**, **p(x)**, and the *Local* total production **cost** per *bushel*, **c(x)**, is the **Landrent margin** ('Surplus'—'Reinertrag des Bodens, oder die *Landrente*') *per bushel*: $\mathbf{m(x)} = \mathbf{p(x)} - \mathbf{c(x)}$.

The **land rent** *per hectare* is $\mathbf{r_A(x)} = \mathbf{m(x)\, q_A}$, where, $\mathbf{q_A} = \mathbf{Q/A}$, is *output* (bushels) per hectare (Average product of Land), **Acreage** = A hectare - $\mathbf{r_A(x)}$ is the *Marginal Revenue* product of Land (A).

The *curves* of, **m(x)**, $\mathbf{r_A(x)}$, for the **two** *farming/cultivation* systems, (7-*Field*, 3-*Field* ), are tabulated in Table 25.1 and seen in Figs. 25.5 and 25.6—showing their variation with the *distance* (**x**) from the city.

By the standard *marginal productivity* principle with local *variable* product price, **p(x)**, Fig. 25.3, and Table 25.1, the local *marginal revenue product* (MRP) is $\mathbf{r_A(x)} = MRP_A(x) = p(x)\,\mathbf{MP_A}\,(x)$. Thus, as $\frac{r_A(x)}{p(x)} = \mathbf{MP_A}\,\mathbf{(x)}$, we have a formula and *curve* for the local *Marginal product* of land, $\mathbf{MP_A}$ **(x)**—seen in Fig. 25.15—together with again, $\mathbf{r_A(x)}$, in Fig. 25.14.

In a subsection, the *hyperbolic transport cost* function, **t(x)**, Fig. 25.3, for driving a *wagon-load* of rye 5 *miles* from Tellow to Rostock, is *parametrically* described and obtained from *accounting data* (averages over years, 1815–1820), which in turn enters and gives the *parametric* local *Farm Price* function, **p(x)**, Tables 25.1, 25.3, and 25.4.

Section "Tellow Farm Accounts, Revenues, Costs, and Land Rents" presents the **Tellow—7-F, 3-F**—*Accounting Statements* ( Basic book-keeping period, 1810–1819 ) for *four* main *production* and *cost activities*: (1) Sowing Cost ('Aussaat'), (2) Cultivation Cost ('Bestellungskosten'), (3) Harvesting Cost ('Erntekosten'), (4) General Farming Cost ('Algemeine Kulturkosten') in the *money* unit (gold) **Talers**. So we have together for - **7-F, 3-F** - *Full Cost*, (**C**), *Revenue*, (**Y**), and *Land Rent*, ($\mathbf{R_A} = \mathbf{Y} - \mathbf{C}$) in **Talers**.

The **Local cost** activities (expenditures) were also *measured* (accounted) in *equivalence* units of **rye**. Such *equivalence* (common) of measurement helped to determine the quantitative *level* of *inputs* (activity) involved producing *output* and driving the output-related (variable) *unit costs* per bushel and per hectare, and account for the respective *cost shares* of the production (cultivation) *activities*. Moreover, on the **Revenue** side, *equivalence* units of **rye** was also applied to measure quantitatively the *total* (aggregate) of *output* (**Q**), associated with the, **7-F, 3-F,** *field* (cultivation, rotation) *systems*. A main element element of **7-F** was (besides reduced fallow) the expansion of Livestock and *Livestock outputs*, which accordingly is reflected in the Revenues, various Costs, and the Land Rents of Table 25.3 and 25.4, and Fig. 25.11.

These Tables 25.3, 25.4 and Figs. 25.11, 25.12, 25.13, 25.14, and 25.15 show the *connection* between cost calculations in Business Economics/Accounting (Betriebswirtschaft/Kostenrechnung) and costs/prices in Macro-/Microeconomics (Nationalökonomie). The *output* and *cost calculations* with **Tellow** *Manor Accounts* (1810–1819) showed that the *replacement* of **3 F** with **7 F** will *increase* production (*output*), **Q**, and per ha $\mathbf{q_A}$ with: **83** pct, $\varrho_q = \frac{q_{A7}}{q_{A3}} = \mathbf{1.83}$, and *increase* total *Land Rent*, $\mathbf{R_A}$, and per ha, $\mathbf{r_A}$, with: **52** pct, $\varrho_r = \frac{r_{A7}}{r_{A3}} = \mathbf{1.52}$.

In Sect. "Tellow—Output—Marginal Products of Land, Labor, Capital", the **Tellow** *Accounting* records of *Revenue* and *Activity costs* in **talers** and **rye** *equivalents* for **7 F/3 F** are used to obtain for **7 F/3 F** *measures* (in rye equivalents) of the **inputs** (factor services) of Land, Labor, Capital, (**A**, **L**, **K**), and their *cost shares* ($\epsilon_A$, $\epsilon_L$, $\epsilon_K$), and *factor ratios*: ***Land*** *intensities*, $\mathbf{l_A} = L/A$, $\mathbf{k_A} = K/A$: and, $\mathbf{k} = K/L$.

The *replacement* of **3 F** with **7 F** will still *increase output*, **Q**, and per ha, $\mathbf{q_A}$, with: **83** pct. and *increase* total *Land Rent*, $\mathbf{R_A}$, and per ha $\mathbf{r_A}$ with: **52** pct—but with **7 F** *field system*, the ***Land*** *intensities*, $\mathbf{l_A} = L/A$, $\mathbf{k_A} = K/A$ become much *larger* (especially $\mathbf{l_A}$) than for **3 F**.

In a subsection, the *cost shares* ($\epsilon_A$, $\epsilon_L$, $\epsilon_K$) and $\mathbf{k} = K/L$, calibrate **CES** production functions of **7 F/3 F**: $Q = F[A, L, K]$—with *intensive* form, $q_A = f(l_A, k_A)$—to the *Tellow Estate* in Figs. 25.16, 25.17, and 25.18.

Section "Six Rings, Grain Prices, Fertility, River Cities—Land Rents" gives *sensitivity* analysis of *Rings* (boundaries) to *grain price* changes **p(0)** and to *soil fertility*, Fig. 25.20a–b. Application of *Rings* are extended to *River Cities*, Fig. 25.1a–b, Hamburg and London.

Section "Agricultural Systems, History, Industries, Growth, and Trade" examines the **economic** results, **1760–1800**, of the *historical transitions* from **3 F**—to **7 F** and **11 F** on **Manor** Farms, Figs. 25.26 and 25.27—and to **7 F** and **6 F** for *consolidated* Village farms, Fig. 25.28.

The **Tellow** *quantitative agricultural model* and *accounting* experience with 7 **F**—*cultivation* system serves as *benchmark* for comparing/evaluating in Denmark and England the corresponding *Agricultural output* and *Land rent* **increases**—as well as the impact on the *Land intensities*, $l_A = L/A$, $k_A = K/A$. In our view, the agricultural *cultivation reforms* **1760–1800** were very successful ("*revolutions*"), breaking economic *Stagnation* and the *Population* ('Malthusian') barrier.

The literature references are included in each section. Section "Final Comments" has the final comments.

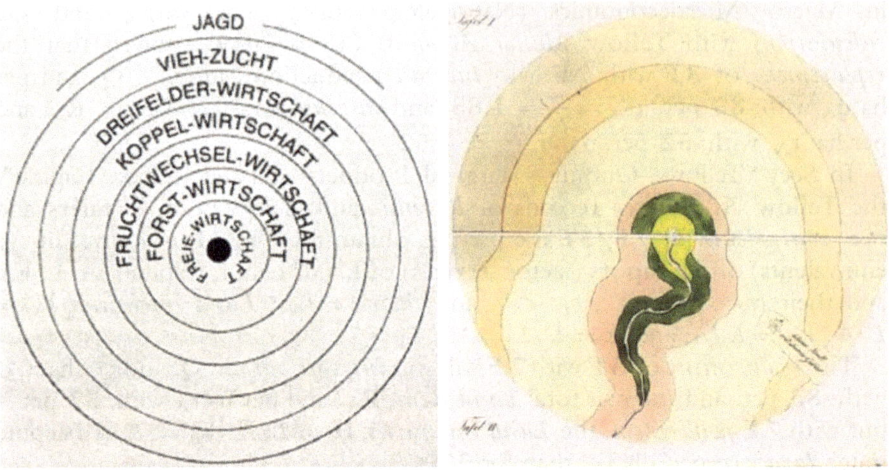


a

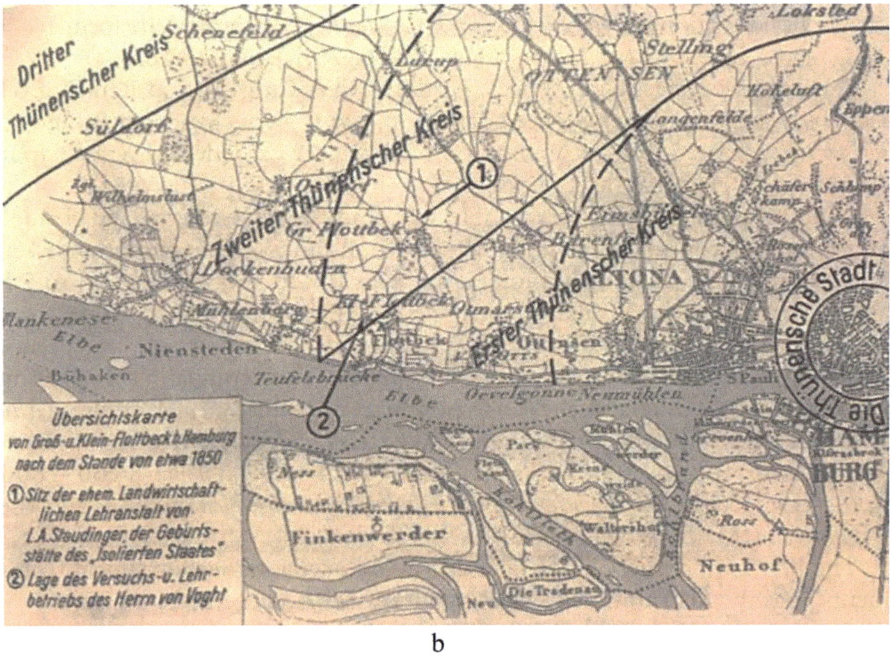


b

**Fig. 25.1** (**a**) von Thünen's Rings (Kreise) in Isolated State (Part 1, Agricultural Economics), 1.ed., 1826. *Source*: von Thünen (1990, p. 387). Johann Heinrich von Thünen (1783–1850).
(**b**) Hamburg area and River Elbe—1. Agricultural College, Gross-Flottbeck, 2. Klein-Flottbeck. *Source*: Bartz and Zühlsdorf (1994, p. 47), Ziegler and Schwarze (2014, p. 189)—1. "Birthplace" (1803) of *Isolated State* (Part 1) 2. Estate of Hamburger Merchant, Baron Casper Voght (1752–1839). 1. Agricultural College, Gross-Flottbeck, Holstein; Lucas Andreas Staudinger (1770–1842)

## Agricultural Productions and Land Cultivation

Regarding the basic agricultural economic questions—**product** (*commodities for sale*) **selections** and their **production** (*farming, cultivation*) **methods**—we quote von Thünen (1990, p. 12); Hall (1966, p. 8):

> It is on the whole obvious that *near* the *City* will be grown those **products** which are *heavy* or *bulky* in relation to their value and hence so expensive to transport that the *remoter* districts are *unable* to supply them. Here we shall also find the highly *perishable* products which must be used quickly.
> With *increasing distance* from the City, the *land* will progressively be given over to *products* cheap to *transport* in relation to their value.
> For this reason alone, fairly sharply differentiated *concentric rings* or *belts* will be formed around the *City*, each with its **own** particular staple **product** (*Haupterzeugnis*). From *ring* to *ring*, the staple **product**, and with it the entire **farming system** (*Wirtschaftssystem*) [production methods], will *change*; and in various *rings* we shall find *completely different farming* systems (italics, boldface ours).

His exactly drawn *six concentric rings* (in miles) are shown in Fig. 25.2, and *qualitatively* they are here described in some details, closely following, von Thünen (1990, pp. 13); Hall (1966, pp. 9) as:

**1.**

**Free Cash Cropping** [Free products and farming methods]—*'Freie Wirtschaft'*.

> Delicate *horticultural products* (cauliflower, strawberries, lettuce, etc.) cannot survive long journeys by wagon. They can moreover be sold only in small quantities, while still fresh. All these products will be grown near the city. Gardens will therefore occupy the land immediately around the city.
> Besides fruits and vegetables, *fresh milk* is a prime necessity for the city, and as this is a difficult, perishable, and costly product to transport, milk will be produced in the *first ring*. The price of milk will rise to point, where the *land* used for supporting milk production *cannot* obtain a higher *rental rate* (Land Rent, "Ackerpacht") from its use to any *other* product. Land is devoted to produce the *highest amount of feed* ('Viehfutter', fodder, e.g., clover, hay, straw, potatoes, roots) from the smallest area, and the animals are *stall-fed* (not on pasture, as the animals inevitably damage the growing plants).
> The distinctive feature of this *ring* is that it buys most of the *manure* it uses from the city—unlike the the remoter areas, which produce their own manure on the farms. In **Ring 1** land will **never** lie in bare **fallow** ('Reine Brache') for *two reasons*—first, the land rental rate is too high to allow any portion of the arable land to remain uncultivated, and secondly, the *fertility* of the *soil* may, by the purchase of city manure, be raised to the *point*, where the soil yields its *maximum output*—so that in contrast to the farther rings the need does not arise here to nurse (improve) the soil fertility by means of a bare fallow. Crops will be grown in such sequence that each prepares the soil for its successor; by no crops with low prices need to cultivated merely to allow and afford the soil a change.

**Fig. 25.2** Agricultural Productions and Cultivation: **The Six Rings** (concentric circles, "*Kreise*"). *Source*: von Thünen (1990, p. 387); Hall (1966, p. 216)

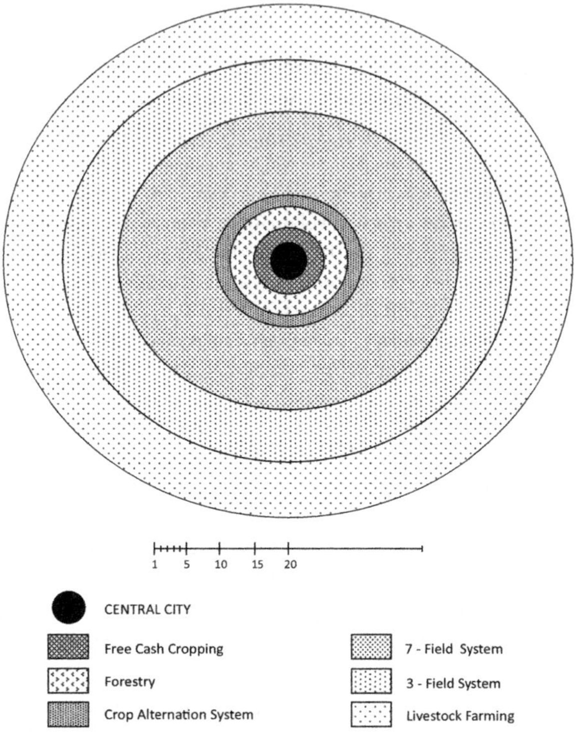


Then this is the system of **free cash cropping** ('freie Wirtschaft'), where the **crops** do **not** have to **rotate** according to a *fixed order* ('Fructfolge'). At a certain distance from the city, it becomes more advantageous to produce its own manure than buy this from the city. This point marks the **boundary** between the *first* and the beginning of the *second* ring (italics ours).

## 2.
## Forestry—'Forst-Wirtschaft'.

**Land** has to provide the *City* not only with *food* ('Lebensmitteln') —but also with all its needs in **fuel** ('Brennholz'), building timber ('Bauholz'), charcoal ('Kohlen'). The question arises, which section of the land will produce all these *varieties of wood*? cf. von Thünen (1990, p. 176; pp. 181, 187, 196, 198); Hall (1966, p. 106; 109, 114, 121, 123).
The primeval forests ('Urwälder') have vanished long ago, here each wood and forest is man-made. – Wood that is produced *near* the City becomes progressively *cheaper* to *transport*, but it will *occupy land* which yields *rent*. The *city price* of **wood** must therefore *cover* - besides the *production* cost (labor, capital) and its *transport* cost - in addition *land rent* [ a *rent* sufficient to *displace* the *best alternative* crop (e.g., grain) that may there be produced - a *general formula* for the price of every product and its area, where it is best cultivated ]. The invariable

*conclusion* to be drawn from all the cases we have examined is this: the *City* can be supplied with far **cheaper wood**, where this is *produced nearby* and not in the distant regions. Building **timber** will be grown within this *ring most distant* from the city. The *outer* fringe of the *forestry ring* will supply the *town* with **charcoal**. At the outer **edge** of the forestry *ring*, *wood* production yields the **same** *land rent* as does the adjacent *farming* land (italics ours).

**3.**
**Crop Alternation System** [Flexible cultivation methods ]—*'Fruchtwechsel-Wirtschaft'*.

All *arable* land is **cropped** (aller Acker trägt Früchte) and there is **no** bare **fallow**. All the manure it produces is used for *feed* (animal fodder) *crops*, which are grown on those *fields* (parcels, Schläge), *richest* in plant food (Pflanzenahrung, Reichtum, *fertility*). *Grain* and *feed* crops *alternate* all the time.

The *number* of fields vary, but typical is the: **6 - Field** alternation (*rotation*) system with crop *sequence*, 1.potatoes, 2.barley, 3.clover, 4.rye, 5.tares, 6.rye—von Thünen (1990, p. 169, p. 96); Hall (1966, p. 101, p. 53).
**4.**
**Seven Field System (7F)**[2] [ farming (cultivation, rotation) method ]—Holstein *'Koppel-Wirtschaft'*.

All *arable* land is *alternatively* in *grain* (Getreide) or *pasture* (Weide). Each *rotation* has **one** bare *fallow*. All the manure is taken to this fallow. The 7 - Field system has the the *crop sequence* (Fruchtfolge): 1.fallow, 2.rye (winter), 3.barley (spring), 4.oats (spring), 5.pasture, 6.pasture, 7.pasture, (italics ours), von Thünen (1990, p. 169, p. 34); Hall (1966, p. 101, p. 24).

**5.**
**Three Field System (3F)**[3] [ farming (cultivation, rotation) method ]—*'Dreifelder-Wirtschaft'*.

One [main] *part* of the *land* area is *permanently* in *pasture* (Weide). Each year *one field* (third of the tillage) is in bare **fallow**. All the manure is taken to this

[2] Hall (1966, p. 24) translates "Koppel-Wirtschaft" as the "Mecklenburg *improved seven coarse* **rotation**", and henceforth always just called the "*improved system*". For clear systematic reasons (rings, crop rotation systems, and crop cost calculations), it is here called (translated) as the "7 - ***Field*** **System**".

On history, evolutions, and spatial extensions of "Koppel-Wirtschaft", see Schmidt et al. (2018, p. 393).

[3] On *Manor Farms* (Estates) as *Tellow*, the permanent grass fields (*pasture*) of the "3 - Field System" can be a single land area of various sizes. For traditional **village communities**, the *permanent grass* area—*outside* (surrounding) their "3 - Field System" (fallow, rye, barley)—is essentially what is often called the "**Commons**" and "Woodlands" at the outskirts of the village. For history and problems of "3 - Field Systems", cf. Olsen (1962, p. 25), Timmer (1969, p. 377).

> fallow. The 3 - Field system has the the *crop sequence* (Fruchtfolge): 1.fallow, 2.rye (winter), 3.barley (spring), (italics ours), von Thünen (1990, p. 169, p. 115); Hall (1966, p. 101, p. 67).

**6.**
**Livestock Farming** [ Selective products and production methods ]—*'Vieh-Zucht'*.

> Farming depending on *cultivation* and the *sale* of *grain* (rye) has in **Figure 25.2** *ended* at 31.5 miles from the City. This, however, does *not* necessarily mark the absolute *limit* of farming; for if there a *product* which, in relation to value were *cheaper to transport* than *grain*, it might still be produced to advantage in this area. *Livestock farming* answers this description; and we will now try to determine the return ('Berechnung des Ertrags') of products, which *dairy farming* (*'Holländerei* oder *Kuherei'*) yields at this point. *Butter* is so cheap to transport relative its value, and in remoter areas it has lower cost of producing butter, meat, wool, etc (italics ours), von Thünen (1990, p. 231–232); Hall (1966, p. 149–150).

Thünen says the *role* and chief *advantages* of the **fallow** fields are: It prepares (*pulverize*) fallow land for the winter seed (rye) at the *lowest labor* cost, and it *activates* the *manure* and *humus* present in the *soil* far more than any green crop could. *Grass* is *indispensable* for any *livestock*. The *eating* and dung-producing capabilities of *livestock sizes* affect both *soil fertility* and *crop rotations* in **Rings 3–5**.

## City Price, Transport Costs, Local Prices, and Land Rents

As we shall see and demonstrate, Thünen did set up and **solved** a *quantitative economic* ***model*** with relevant tables to uniquely *determine* ***grain prices*** (*rye*) and derived the economic *optimal* ***form*** of *land cultivation* in **ring** *4 and 5* of the six rings (circles, Fig. 25.2 with their radius, distances from central city).

> Before we pass on to look at the *farming systems* of the second and the following *rings*, we must try to discover how *grain price* varies with *distances* from the **City**. We are making the **assumptions**:
>
> 1. The City is the only *market* for grain.
> 2. There is *no* navigable *river* or canal in the entire State, so that *all grain* has to be taken to the City by *horse* and *wagon*.
>
> In these conditions the *City* grain *price* will be the *norm* for the *entire* country. But grain cannot be as valuable in the rural areas as in the City, because, in order to obtain its market price, it must first be taken to the City. It follows that in the *country* districts, *grain* is *less valuable* than in the City by the *cost* of its *transport*. (italics ours), von Thünen (1990, p. 15); Hall (1966, p. 12).

The **City** *market* price (average price), **p(0)**, (distance zero) is supposed to be a given (exogenous) fixed number, here concretely for grain, **Rye**: $p(0) = \mathbf{1.5}$ gold Talers/Bushel. The empirical ('real world') Transportation Cost calculations were based on the *average cost* (from accounting data over *five years*) of transporting a *wagon load* of grain from his **Tellow** estate to the City, **Rostock**, a *distance* of 5 *miles*, see Fig. 25.4a–b.

The *transport cost (Talers)* of transporting *1 wagon load* over a *distance* (**x**) is *denoted*: **t(x)** Talers. Transport cost, **t(5)** = 5.33, Tellow-Rostock, is in Table 25.1, col. 3. The *arithmetic* (numerical) *expression* for **t(x)**, col. 3, is stated in (25.1,i), as derived by von Thünen (1990, p. 21); Hall (1966, p. 17).

1 *Load* = 2400 Lb (Hamburger Libra) = 28.5 *Bushels*. Hence, 199.5/28.5 = 7, gives **t(x)**: (25.1,ii), (25.2).

For *conversion* of (25.1,i) to transport *costs* **t(x)**, per *Ton* x *Km*, (25.1,iii), Table 25.1, column 5, cf. Sect. "Tellow Farm Accounts, Revenues, Costs, and Land Rents".

$$x \geq 0 \; : (i) \; t(x) \; = \; \frac{199.5\,x}{182 + x} \; ; \; (ii) \; t(x) \; = \; \frac{7\,x}{182 + x} \; ; \quad (iii) \; t(x) \; = \; \frac{172\,x}{1348 + x} \tag{25.1}$$

$$t(x) \; = \; \frac{7\,x}{182 + x} \quad ; \quad x \neq 0 \; : \; \tau(x) \; \equiv \; \frac{t(x)}{x} \; = \; \frac{7}{182 + x} \tag{25.2}$$

For **City** price **p(0)** = 1.5, ***Local*** *Farm Prices* (per bushel) of *Rye*, **p(x)**, are with **t(x)**, (25.2), given by:

$$p(x) = p(0) \; - \; t(x) \; = \; 1.5 \; - \; \frac{7\,x}{182 + x} \; = \; \frac{273 \; - \; 5.5\,x}{182 + x} \quad ; \qquad p(0) = t(x) \; + \; p(x) \tag{25.3}$$

see $t(x)$, $p(x)$, in Fig. 25.3—the last arithmetic $p(x)$ *formula* is in von Thünen (1990, p. 23); Hall (1966, p. 16).

The two **basic** $\boldsymbol{t(x)}$ and $\boldsymbol{p(x)}$ *expressions*, (25.2–25.3), are essentially underlying **all** other *economic formulas* and hence **all** their quantitative-economic *implications* in sections, tables, figures, and formulas below.

The *difference* between the Local Farm *price*, $\boldsymbol{p(x)}$, and the *Local* Total Production **cost** per *bushel*, **c(x)**, is Local **Land Rent** per **bushel**, **m(x)** = $R_A(x)/Q$, where $\mathbf{R_A(x)}$ is ***Total*** *Land Rents* ('Reinertrag des Bodens, oder die *Landrente*'), **Q** is Total production (*output*) on *Land area* (**A** ha), $\mathbf{Y} = p(x)\,Q$, i.e.,

$$p(0) \; = \; t(x) \; + \; p(x) \; ; \quad p(x) \; = \; c(x) \; + \; m(x) \; ; \qquad p(x) \; - \; c(x) \; \equiv \; m(x) \; \equiv \; R_A(x)/Q \; \Leftrightarrow \; \forall x \; R_A \; = \; Y - C \tag{25.4}$$

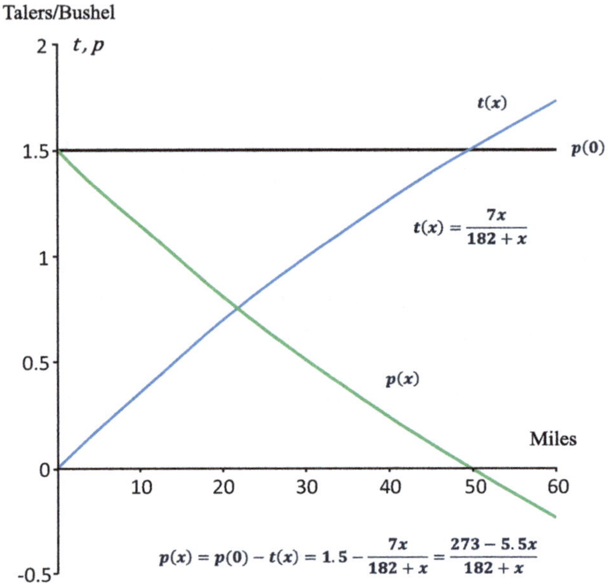


**Fig. 25.3** Transportation Costs, $t(x)$, City Rye Price, $p(0)$, and Local Farm Prices of Rye, $p(x)$

Arithmetic expression $\mathbf{R_A(x)}$, (25.5), is: von Thünen (1990, p. 52); Hall (1966, p. 36). $\mathbf{R_A(x)}$, (25.6), see Sect. "Tellow Farm Accounts, Revenues, Costs, and Land Rents".

$$7\,\text{F}.\;\; A = 220\; ha\,,\;\; Q = 3144\;:$$

$$R_A(x) = \frac{202202 - 7065\,x}{182 + x}\;;\;\; m(x) \equiv \frac{R_A(x)}{Q} = \frac{64.3 - 2.25\,x}{182 + x} \tag{25.5}$$

$$3\,\text{F}.\;\; A = 220\; ha\,,\;\; Q = 1720\;:$$

$$R_A(x) = \frac{130494 - 4155\,x}{182 + x}\;;\;\; m(x) \equiv \frac{R_A(x)}{Q} = \frac{75.9 - 2.42\,x}{182 + x} \tag{25.6}$$

$$7\,\text{F}.\;\; A = 220\; ha\,,\;\; Q = 3144\,,\;\; q_A = Q/A = \mathbf{14.3}\;:$$

$$r_A(x) \equiv m(x)\,q_A \equiv \frac{R_A(x)}{A} = \frac{919.1 - 32.1\,x}{182 + x} \tag{25.7}$$

$$3\,\text{F}.\;\; A = 220\; ha\,,\;\; Q = 1720\,,\;\; q_A = Q/A = \mathbf{7.82}\;:$$

$$r_A(x) \equiv m(x)\,q_A \equiv \frac{R_A(x)}{A} = \frac{593.2 - 18.9\,x}{182 + x} \tag{25.8}$$

**Table 25.1** Transportation Costs, City Rye Price, Local Farm Prices, and Local Land Rents—in Talers

| City distances | | Transport costs of Rye, Talers (Ta) | | | City price | Local prices | Local land rents, Talers (Ta) | | | |
|---|---|---|---|---|---|---|---|---|---|---|
| (x), Miles, Km. | | $t(x) = 7x / (182 + x)$ | | | $p(0)$ | $p(x) = p(0) - t(x)$ | $m(x) = R_A(x)/Q$ [ Ta/Bushel ]; $r_A(x) = R_A(x)/A$ [ Ta/ ha ] | | | |
| | | | | | | | 7 - *Field* System | | 3 - Field System | |
| Miles | Km. | Ta/ [Load x Mile ] | Ta / [Bushel x Mile ] | Ta / [ Ton x Km ] | Ta / Bushel | Ta/ Bushel | $m(x)$ | $r_A(x)$ | $m(x)$ | $r_A(x)$ |
| 1. | 2. | 3. | 4. | 5. | 6. | 7. | 8. | 9. | 10. | 11. |
| 0 | 0.0 | 0.00 | 0.000 | 0.00 | 1.5 | 1.500 | 0.353 | 5.05 | 0.417 | 3.26 |
| 1 | 7.4 | 1.09 | 0.038 | 0.94 | 1.5 | 1.462 | 0.339 | 4.84 | 0.402 | 3.14 |
| **5** | **37.1** | **5.33** | **0.187** | **4.61** | **1.5** | **1.313** | **0.284** | **4.06** | **0.341** | **2.67** |
| 10 | 74.2 | 10.4 | 0.364 | 8.97 | 1.5 | 1.136 | 0.218 | 3.12 | 0.270 | 2.11 |
| 15 | 111.3 | 15.2 | 0.532 | 13.12 | 1.5 | 0.968 | 0.156 | 2.23 | 0.202 | 1.58 |
| 20 | 148.4 | 19.8 | 0.693 | 17.06 | 1.5 | 0.807 | 0.096 | 1.38 | 0.137 | 1.07 |
| **24.7** | **183.3** | **23.8** | **0.836** | **20.59** | **1.5** | **0.664** | **0.043** | **0.62** | **0.079** | **0.62** |
| 25 | 185.5 | 24.1 | 0.845 | 20.81 | 1.5 | 0.655 | 0.039 | 0.57 | 0.075 | 0.59 |
| **28.6** | **212.2** | **27.1** | **0.951** | **23.39** | **1.5** | **0.549** | **0.000** | **0.00** | **0.032** | **0.25** |
| 30 | 222.6 | 28.2 | 0.990 | 24.38 | 1.5 | 0.510 | -0.015 | -0.20 | 0.016 | 0.13 |
| **31.4** | **233.0** | **29.4** | **1.030** | **25.35** | **1.5** | **0.470** | **-0.029** | **-0.42** | **0.000** | **0.00** |
| 40 | 296.8 | 35.9 | 1.261 | 31.04 | 1.5 | 0.239 | -0.115 | -1.64 | -0.093 | -0.73 |
| 45 | 333.9 | 39.5 | 1.388 | 34.15 | 1.5 | 0.112 | | | | |
| 49.6 | 368.0 | 42.7 | 1.500 | 36.89 | 1.5 | 0.000 | | | | |
| 50 | 371.0 | 43.0 | 1.509 | 37.12 | 1.5 | | | | | |

Source: von Thünen (1990, p.17–18, p.21, p.23, p.52, p.123–125); Hall (1966, p.14, p.16–17, p.36, p.66, p.71)
Columns (1,3,6,7,9,11) are his original numbers (1990)

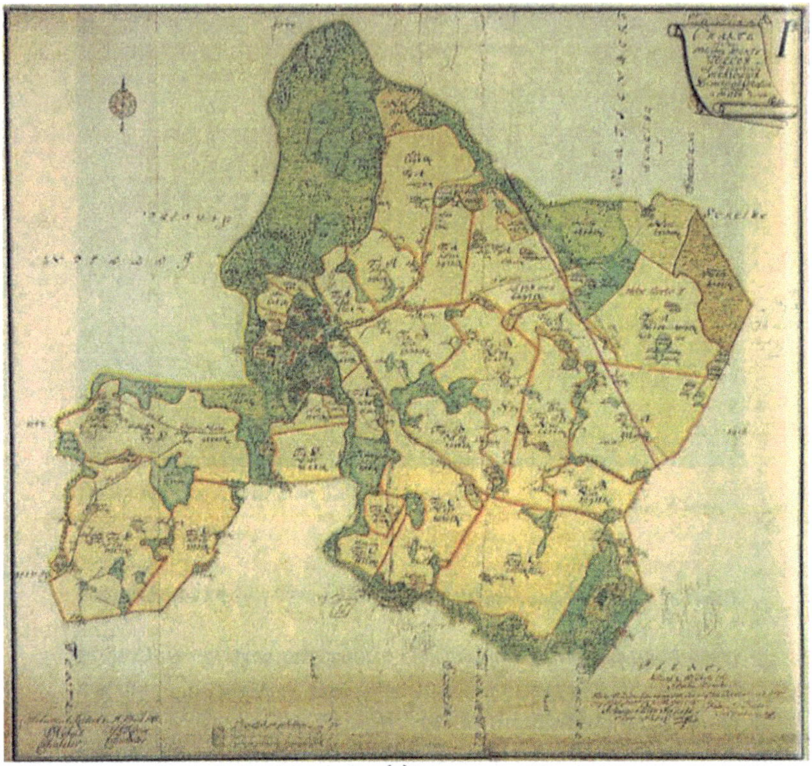

(a)

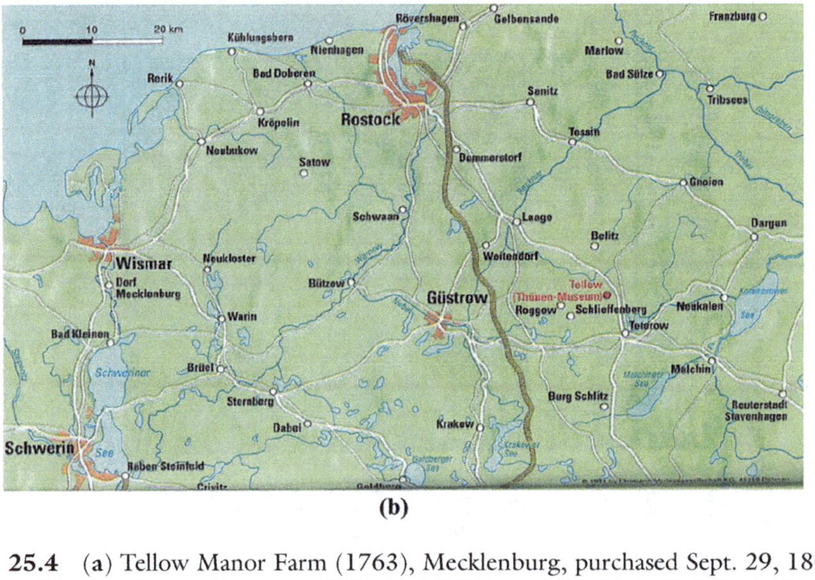


(b)

**Fig. 25.4** (**a**) Tellow Manor Farm (1763), Mecklenburg, purchased Sept. 29, 1809, by von Thünen *Source*: Bartz and Zühlsdorf (1994, p. 44)—Main Buildings, Forest, Fields, Roads. (**b**) Tellow Estate location and main road to Rostock City (37.1 km), Table 25.1. *Source*: Bartz and Zühlsdorf (1994, p. 60)—Duchy Mecklenburg (Region) and Main Cities

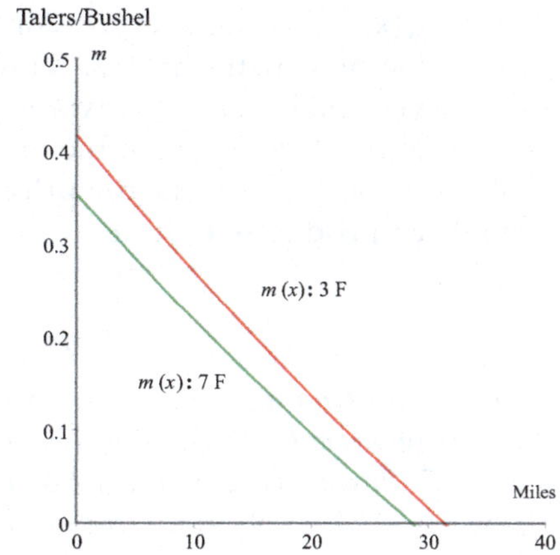


**Fig. 25.5** Local Land *rent Margins* per Bushel rye, $\boldsymbol{m(x)}$: 7 F, (25.5) ; $\boldsymbol{m(x)}$: 3 F, (25.6)

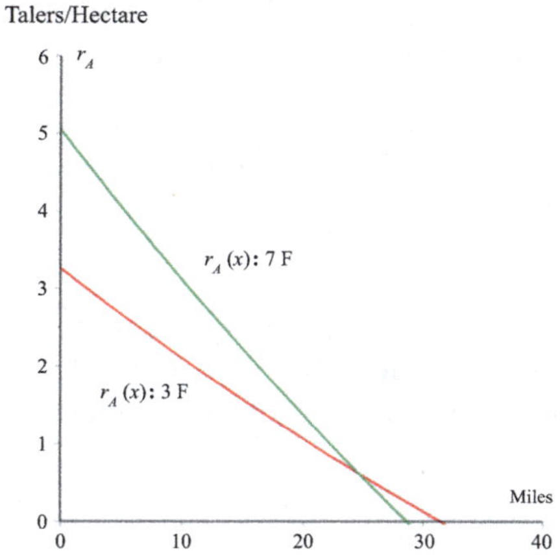


**Fig. 25.6** Local Land *Rents* per hectare, $\boldsymbol{r_A(x)}$: 7 F, (25.7) ; $\boldsymbol{r_A(x)}$: 3 F, (25.8)

With *Total* Land rent expressions $\mathbf{R_A(x)}$ of the **7** - ***Field*** *System* and **3** - ***Field*** *System*, (25.5–25.6), we get—by simple divisions with the respective Q (rye productions, outputs) and A (same size)—***unit*** (average) expressions of land rent as: **m(x)** and $\mathbf{r_A(x)}$ in (25.5–25.8), with their numbers in Table 25.1, columns 8–11, called Land **Rent Margin,** $\boldsymbol{m(x)}$ and Land **Rental Price,** $\boldsymbol{r_A(x)}$ of **1 ha** (100 $m^2$)—and shown in Figs. 25.5 and 25.6.

Although **m(x)**, (25.4–25.6), will be important for understanding and describing the cost relations involved in the two *farming systems* (**7-F**, **3-F**), and despite the fact that $m(x) = 0, r_A(x) = \mathbf{0}$ have the same **roots** in Figs. 25.5 and 25.6., cf. Table 25.1, columns 8–9, **x = 28.6** miles in the *7 - Field System*, and same roots, cf. columns 10–11, **x = 31.4** miles in the **3** - *Field System*, it is, however, *always* the *two* $\mathbf{r_A(x)}$ **curves** in Fig. 25.6 that *determine* the **selected** (rational, optimal) *farming system* at **any distance** (x)—they **cross** at, **x = 24.7** miles, cf. Table 25.1, column 9, 11. Thus, for $\boldsymbol{x} <$ **24.7**, the 7 - *Field System* is *selected*, and **Ring 5** with the **3** - *Field System* have the interval *boundaries*: **24.7** $\leq \boldsymbol{x} \leq$ **31.4**—in Fig. 25.6.

The $\mathbf{r_A(x)}$ curves and expressions (25.7–25.8)[4] reflect the most **critical** (scarce) **factor constraint**, viz., **land**, A = 220, and its **factor price** (rental rate) $\mathbf{r_A(x)}$—and hence the *maximum Land Rentals* (factor income), $\mathbf{R_A(x)} = \mathbf{r_A(x)\,A}$, at the *distance* (**x**) in the monetary unit (Taler).

We will come back to **factor prices** of land inputs (*land services* of 220 ha) and related **productivity** issues.

### *Transport Cost Function*

From *accounting data* (averages over years, 1815–1820), the costs of driving a *wagon-load* (28.57 bushels) of rye 5 *miles* from *Tellow* to Rostock, are: 2.57 *bushels* (rye), and 1.63 *Talers*, von Thünen (1990, p. 16); Hall (1966, p. 12). A wagon *cost* function $\boldsymbol{T(x)}$—Talers for *distance* ($\boldsymbol{x}$)—is calibrated/*parametrized* as:
$p_0 = p(0) = 1.5$ Taler/Bushel; Feed (Fuel) $\boldsymbol{\alpha_F}$: Bushel/Mile; Materials/repairs $\boldsymbol{\alpha_M}$: Taler/Mile,

$$p_0 = 1.5\,,\ \alpha_F = \frac{2.57}{5} = 0.514\,,\ \alpha_M = \frac{1.63}{5} = 0.326\ ;$$

$$T(x) = (\,p_0\,\alpha_F + \alpha_M)\,x\ ;\ T(x) = 1.097\,x \tag{25.9}$$

The *total transported* quantity, $\widetilde{\boldsymbol{Q}}\,(\boldsymbol{x})$—the wagon load itself (including wagon storage space allotments per mile), and the feed—to get *Load size* ($\widetilde{\boldsymbol{q}}$) to the City (market) by horses at *distances* ($x$) is given by:

$$\alpha_Q = \frac{30}{84} = 0.357;\quad \widetilde{Q}\,(x) = \widetilde{q} - \alpha_Q\,x + \alpha_F\,x = \widetilde{q} + (\alpha_F - \alpha_Q)\,x\ ;$$

$$\widetilde{Q}\,(x) = 28.57 + 0.157\,x \tag{25.10}$$

Storage $\boldsymbol{\alpha_Q}$: Bushel/Mile; 1 Bushel = 84 Lb; **1** Load = $\widetilde{\boldsymbol{q}}$ = 2400 Lb (Libra) = $\frac{2400}{84}$ = **28.57** Bushels.

Hence by (25.9–25.10), the **Transport Cost Function**, $t(1, x) \equiv \boldsymbol{t(x)}$, (25.1,ii), Talers per [1 Bushel x Miles] is:

$$t(x) = \frac{T(x)}{\widetilde{Q}\,(x)} = \frac{(\,p_0\,\alpha_F + \alpha_M)\,x}{\widetilde{q} + (\alpha_F - \alpha_Q)\,x}\ ;$$

$$t(x) = \frac{T(x)}{\widetilde{Q}\,(x)} = \frac{1.097\,x}{28.57 + 0.157\,x} = \frac{6.987\,x}{181.975 + x} \equiv \frac{7\,x}{182 + x} \tag{25.11}$$

[4] All functions $y = f(x)$, with $f(x)$ as a ratio of two linear expressions, $y = \frac{a+bx}{c+dx} \equiv \frac{A+Bx}{C+x}$, $d \neq 0$, are all *rectangular hyperbolas*, with asymptotes parallel to the co-ordinate axes, Allen (1938, p. 74). Some curves may look close to straight lines within the range shown in some diagrams, but they are all *non-linear*.

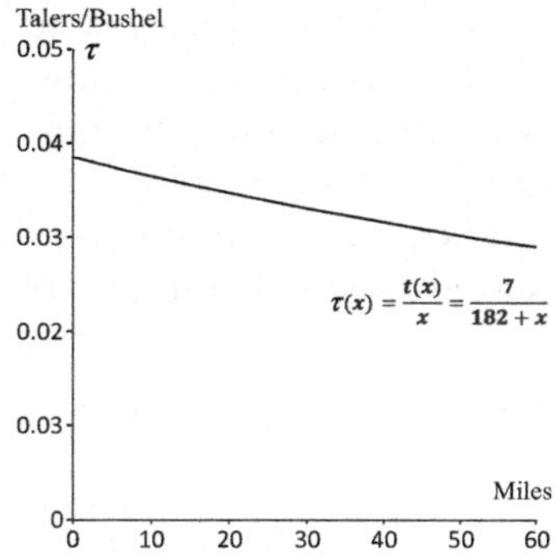


**Fig. 25.7** Average Transportation Cost—per Mile, $\tau(x) = t(x)/x$, (25.2), for distance (x)

**Table 25.2** Train Freight Rates - for distances ($x$), km.

| Distances km | Freight rates for wagon load classes: A-G A | B | C | D | E | F | G |
|---|---|---|---|---|---|---|---|
| 1. | 2. | 3. | 4. | 5. | 6. | 7. | 8. |
| 100 | 11.6 | 10.5 | 8.9 | 7.6 | 6.4 | 5.2 | 4.2 |
| 200 | 10.1 | 9.1 | 7.7 | 6.5 | 5.4 | 4.4 | 3.5 |
| 300 | 9.3 | 8.3 | 7.0 | 5.9 | 4.9 | 3.9 | 3.1 |
| 400 | 8.6 | 7.8 | 6.6 | 5.5 | 4.6 | 3.6 | 2.9 |
| 500 | 8.1 | 7.2 | 6.1 | 5.1 | 4.2 | 3.4 | 2.6 |
| 600 | 7.5 | 6.8 | 5.7 | 4.8 | 3.9 | 3.1 | 2.5 |
| 700 | 7.0 | 6.3 | 5.3 | 4.4 | 3.6 | 2.9 | 2.3 |
| 800 | 6.5 | 5.8 | 4.9 | 4.1 | 3.4 | 2.7 | 2.1 |
| 900 | 6.0 | 5.3 | 4.5 | 3.8 | 3.1 | 2.5 | 1.8 |
| 1000 | 5.5 | 4.9 | 4.1 | 3.5 | 2.9 | 2.3 | 1.5 |

*Source*: Petersen (1944, p.62).

Generally, (25.11) implies: $\boldsymbol{t(q,x)} = \boldsymbol{q\,t(x)}$. Hence for 1 load: $28.57 \cdot 6.987x = 199.6x$, rounded as, $28.5 \cdot 7x = 199.5x$, gives: $\boldsymbol{t(x)}$, (25.1,i), as Talers per [1 Load x Miles]. The *conversion* of transport costs $t(x)$, (25.1,i), in per Load x Miles to $\boldsymbol{t(x)}$, (25.1,iii), in per Ton x Km, follows as shown below.[5] On $\tau(x)$, see Fig. 25.7; Table 25.2.

The **Local Farm Prices**, $p(x)$, (25.3), of *rye* (per bushel) become with, $t(x)$, (25.11), and its *parameters*:

$$p(x) = p_0 - \frac{(p_0\,\alpha_F + \alpha_M)\,x}{\widetilde{q} + (\alpha_F - \alpha_Q)\,x} = \frac{p_0\,\widetilde{q} - (p_0\,\alpha_Q + \alpha_M)\,x}{\widetilde{q} + (\alpha_F - \alpha_Q)\,x}\;;$$

$$p(x) = \frac{42.855 - 0.862\,x}{28.57 + 0.157\,x} \equiv \frac{273 - 5.5\,x}{182 + x} \tag{25.12}$$

[5] 1000 Lb = 484.2 kg = 0.4842 ton; 1 Load = 2400 Lb = 2.4 · 0.4842 ton = 1.162 ton. 1 Bushel = 84 Lb = 40.67 kg. 1 ton = 1/1.162 Load = 0.861 Load, and 0.861 · 199.5 = 171.8 ≡ 172; thus, $t(x)$ per [Ton x Mile] is $t(x) = 172x/(182 + x)$. Next, 1 Mile = 7.42 Km, 1 Km = 0.135 Miles. Then $t(x)$ per [Ton x Km] is $t(x) = 172 \cdot 0.135x/(182 + 0.135x) = 172x/(1348 + x)$, i.e., (25.1,iii)—and Table 25.1, column 5 above. The volume measure of 1 Bushel is 54.4 Liters.

With the transport cost function **t(x)**, (25.11), and *local price* function **p(x)**, (25.12), of **rye**, we are now able to consider and *calculate* the *local production cost*, **c(x)**, per unit (bushel) of **rye** at various *distances* (**x**). The *arithmetic* expression of **c(x)**, however, follows immediately from the arithmetic equations of **p(x)**, (25.3), and **m (x)**, (25.5–25.6), together with *identity*, (25.4), i.e., we have the **c (x)** of ***seven/three*—Field System**:

**7 F.** $$Q = 3144 : c(x) = p(x) - m(x) = \frac{208.7 - 3.25\,x}{182 + x};$$

$$\pi(x) = \frac{m(x)}{p(x)} = 1 - \frac{c(x)}{p(x)}; \quad C(x) = c(x)\,Q \tag{25.13}$$

**3 F.** $$Q = 1720 : c(x) = p(x) - m(x) = \frac{197.1 - 3.08\,x}{182 + x};$$

$$\pi(x) = \frac{m(x)}{p(x)} = 1 - \frac{c(x)}{p(x)}; \quad C(x) = c(x)\,Q \tag{25.14}$$

with **c(x)** graphically shown in Fig. 25.8a. For the Price - Cost **ratio**, $\boldsymbol{\mu}(\boldsymbol{x}) = p(x)/c(x)$, see Fig. 25.12.

The 7 - *Field System* has everywhere *higher* production cost, $c(x)$, and so a *lower* land *rent margin/price* ratio, $\boldsymbol{\pi}(\boldsymbol{x}) = m(x)/p(x)$ in Fig. 25.8b—henceforth explained and accounted for in details.

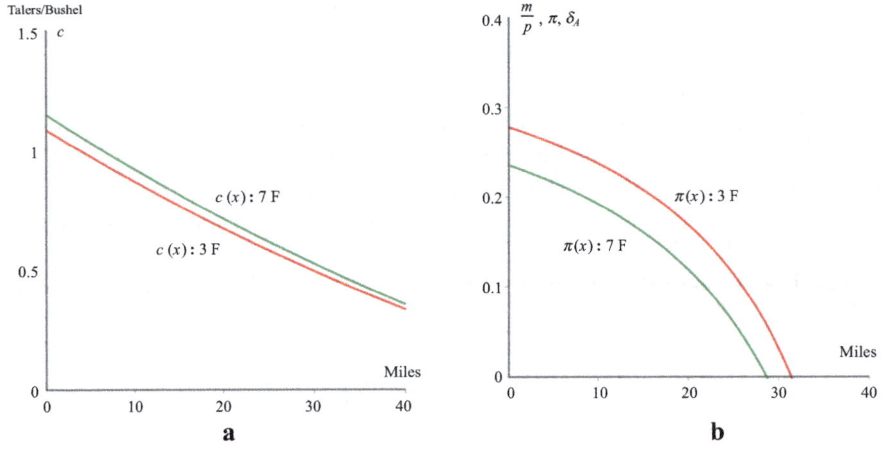


**Fig. 25.8** (**a**) Production Costs, Unit Costs, ***c*** **(*x*)**: **7 F**, (25.13) ; ***c*** **(*x*)**: **3 F**, (25.14). (**b**) $\frac{\textit{Land Rent Margin}}{\textit{Local Rye Price}}$ ratio, $\boldsymbol{\pi}(\boldsymbol{x}) = \frac{\boldsymbol{m(x)}}{\boldsymbol{p(x)}}$, $\pi(x)$: 7 F, (25.3), (25.5), (25.37); 3 F, (25.3), (25.6), (25.38)

But like the calibrated *parametric transport* cost function **t(x)**, (25.11), we must now study and obtain *empirically* calibrated *parametric cost* functions, **c(x)**, of the *two* cultivations systems, (25.13–25.14), Fig. 25.8a.

## Tellow Farm Accounts, Revenues, Costs, and Land Rents

There are *four* main *production cost activities*—extracted from the **Tellow** accounting systems:[6]

1. *Sowing* Cost ('Aussaat', the seed value of the three grain crops, related to *size* of grain *acreage*).
2. *Cultivation* Cost ('Bestellungskosten', the costs related the *size* of *arable acreage*, such as ploughing, harrowing, hoeing—which depend on the given land area and soil quality, but *not* on its *yield*).
3. *Harvesting* Cost ('Erntekosten', the costs related to the *size* of the *harvest*, such as manuring, bringing in the harvest, threshing, work to restore soil quality (fertility) by manure and so forth).
4. *General Farming* Cost ('Algemeine Kulturkosten', that can *not* be ascribed to a *single* product or activity, i.e., administation, farm buildings, livestock, bridges, ditches, interest on capital, tools).

From practical *experience* and *empirical data* of the **Tellow** Accounts are obtained—with corrections of *yield* and *cost* data to *uniform* soil *fertility* of **8-fold**[7] (Körner) —the **7-F** and **3-F** Accounting Statements.

**7-F.** Schematically, the *Farm Accounting Statement* of the **Seven Field System** can be given as:

**Revenue** - **Cost** Accounting Records in **Taler**: 7 - ***Field*** **System**, A = 220 ha, **Q** = 3144, p(5) = 1.29.[8]

[6] Tellow Manor Estate (size, **465 ha**) bought, 29. Sept 1809, Price **58103 Talers**. Basic bookkeeping period is, 1810–1819.

[7] 1 fold (bushel crop) is equal to 2.5 hl per hectare, i.e., 8 fold fertility represents a yield of 20 hl/ha, Hall (1966, xliix).

[8] We use here the Tellow *accounting* bushel price [ *local*, p(5) ] of rye (with two decimals), p(5) = 1.29 Talers, instead of p(5) = 1.291 Talers, von Thünen (1990, p. 34); Hall (1966, p. 26); the latter gives, Revenue: $Y = 1.291 \cdot 3144 = 4059$, and $C = 3191$, $R_A = 868$, von Thünen (1990, p. 36); Hall (1966, p. 27), instead of our: $Y = 4056$, $C = 310$, $R_A = 866$, seen above.

However, above our *rye* equivalents for 7 - *Field* System: $q_i$, $i = 1, , 4$, $q = 1976$, and *money* costs, $C_{im}$, $i = 2, , 4$, $C_m = 641$ Talers, are *exactly* as stated in von Thünen (1990, p. 42), Petersen (1944, p. 41). Hall (1966, p. 29–30) does *not* give $q_i$ *nor* $C_{ix}$.

With **7-F** accounts, von Thünen (1990, p. 49–52); Hall (1966, p. 33–36) gives: $R_A(x) = [(1 - a)\, p(x) - c_m\,]\, Q = (Q - q)\, p(x) - C_m = 1168\,[\,\frac{273 - 5.5x}{182 + x}\,] - 641 = \frac{202202 - 7065x}{182 + x}$, (in our notation), cf. (25.25), (25.27), and see Table 25.3, column 8, below.

| | | | | | | | | |
|---|---|---|---|---|---|---|---|---|
| A | **Revenue** | $Y$ = | **4056** | : $Y = p(5) \cdot Q$ | ; $Y = 1.29 \cdot$ **3144** | = **4056** | , $Q = Y/1.29$ | = **3144** |
| 1 | Sowing | $C_1$ = | 626 | : $C_1 = C_{1x}$ | | = 626 | | |
| 2 | Cultivation | $C_2$ = | 872 | : $C_2 = C_{2x} + C_{2m}$ | ; $C_{2x} = 0.75 \cdot C_2$ | = 654 | , $C_{2m} = 0.25 \cdot C_2$ | = 218 |
| 3 | Harvesting | $C_3$ = | 613 | : $C_3 = C_{3x} + C_{3m}$ | ; $C_{3x} = 0.75 \cdot C_3$ | = 459 | , $C_{3m} = 0.25 \cdot C_3$ | = 154 |
| 4 | General | $C_4$ = | 1079 | : $C_4 = C_{4x} + C_{4m}$ | ; $C_{4x} = 0.75 \cdot C_4$ | = 810 | , $C_{4m} = 0.25 \cdot C_4$ | = 269 |
| B | **Total Cost** | $C$ = | **3190** | : $C = C_x + C_m$ | ; $C_x$ | = **2549** | , $C_m$ | = **641** |
| C | **Land Rent** | $R_A$ = | **866** | : $R_A = Y - C$ | | | | |

**Local Cost** Accounting in *equivalence* units of **rye**. A= 220 ha, Q=3144, $q_A = \frac{Q}{A} = 14.3$, p(5) = 1.29.

| | | | | | |
|---|---|---|---|---|---|
| 1 | Sowing | $C_{1x}/p(5) = q_1$ | , $q_1 = 626/1.29 = 485$ | ; $a_1 = q_1/Q$ | , $a_1 = 485/3144 = 0.154$ |
| 2 | Cultivation | $C_{2x}/p(5) = q_2$ | , $q_2 = 654/1.29 = 507$ | ; $a_2 = q_2/Q$ | , $a_2 = 507/3144 = 0.161$ |
| 3 | Harvesting | $C_{3x}/p(5) = q_3$ | , $q_3 = 459/1.29 = 356$ | ; $a_3 = q_3/Q$ | , $a_3 = 356/3144 = 0.113$ |
| 4 | General | $C_{4x}/p(5) = q_4$ | , $q_4 = 810/1.29 = 628$ | ; $a_4 = q_4/Q$ | , $a_4 = 628/3144 = 0.200$ |
| D | **Local Cost** | $C_x/p(5) = q$ | , $q = 2549/1.29 =$ **1976** | ; **a** = $q/Q$ | , $a = 1976/3144 =$ **0.595** |

**Full Cost, Revenue, Land Rent** in **Taler**: 7 - *Field System*, A = 220 ha, Q = 3144, p(5) = 1.29.

**E Total Cost,** Unit costs : $C = \mathbf{3190} = C_x + C_m$ ; $c = \frac{3190}{3144} = 1.015$, $c_x = \frac{2549}{3144} = 0.811$, $c_m = \frac{641}{3144} = \mathbf{0.204}$ ; $Q - q = \mathbf{1168}$

**F Land Rent,** Unit rents : $Y = \mathbf{4056}$, $R_A = Y - C = \mathbf{866}$ ; $\rho = R_A / Q = \frac{866}{3144} = 0.275$, $c_{mA} = \frac{641}{220} = 2.9$, $r_A = R_A/A = \frac{866}{220} = \mathbf{3.936}$

*Source*: von Thünen (1990, p. 34, p. 42, p. 52, p. 124); Hall (1966, p. 26, p. 30, p. 73); Petersen (1944, p. 41, p. 63).
Notation is ours, and only some of **boldface** numbers above are seen in the pages of the reference list.

**3-F.** Schematically, the similar *Farm Accounting Statement* of the **Three Field System** becomes:
**Revenue - Cost** Accounting Records in **Taler: 3 - Field System**, A = 220 ha, **Q** = 1720, p(5) = 1.29.

| | | | | | | | | |
|---|---|---|---|---|---|---|---|---|
| A | **Revenue** | $Y$ = | **2219** | : $Y = p(5) \cdot Q$ | ; $Y = 1.29 \cdot$ **1720** | = **2219** | , $Q = Y/1.29$ | = **1720** |
| 1 | Sowing | $C_1$ = | 342 | : $C_1 = C_{1x}$ | | = 342 | | |
| 2 | Cultivation | $C_2$ = | 437 | : $C_2 = C_{2x} + C_{2m}$ | ; $C_{2x} = 0.75 \cdot C_2$ | = 328 | , $C_{2m} = 0.25 \cdot C_2$ | = 109 |
| 3 | Harvesting | $C_3$ = | 278 | : $C_3 = C_{3x} + C_{3m}$ | ; $C_{3x} = 0.75 \cdot C_3$ | = 209 | , $C_{3m} = 0.25 \cdot C_3$ | = 70 |
| 4 | General | $C_4$ = | 591 | : $C_4 = C_{4x} + C_{4m}$ | ; $C_{4x} = 0.75 \cdot C_4$ | = 442 | , $C_{4m} = 0.25 \cdot C_4$ | = 148 |
| B | **Total Cost** | $C$ = | **1648** | : $C = C_x + C_m$ | ; $C_x$ | = **1321** | , $C_m$ | = **327** |
| C | **Land Rent** | $R_A$ = | **571** | : $R_A = Y - C$ | | | | |

**Local Cost** Accounting in *equivalence* units of **rye**. A= 220 ha, Q=1720, $q_A = \frac{Q}{A} = 7.82$, p(5) = 1.29.

| | | | | | |
|---|---|---|---|---|---|
| 1 | Sowing | $C_{1x}/p(5) = q_1$ | , $q_1 = 342/1.29 = 265$ | ; $a_1 = q_1/Q$ | , $a_1 = 265/1720 = 0.154$ |
| 2 | Cultivation | $C_{2x}/p(5) = q_2$ | , $q_2 = 328/1.29 = 254$ | ; $a_2 = q_2/Q$ | , $a_2 = 254/1720 = 0.148$ |
| 3 | Harvesting | $C_{3x}/p(5) = q_3$ | , $q_3 = 209/1.29 = 162$ | ; $a_3 = q_3/Q$ | , $a_3 = 162/1720 = 0.094$ |
| 4 | General | $C_{4x}/p(5) = q_4$ | , $q_4 = 442/1.29 = 343$ | ; $a_4 = q_4/Q$ | , $a_4 = 343/1720 = 0.199$ |
| D | **Local Cost** | $C_x/p(5) = q$ | , $q = 1321/1.29 =$ **1024** | ; **a** = $q/Q$ | , $a = 1024/1720 =$ **0.595** |

**Full Cost, Revenue, Land Rent** in **Taler**: **3 - Field System**, A = 220 ha, Q = 1720, p(5) = 1.29.

| | | |
|---|---|---|
| E | **Total Cost,** Unit costs : | $C = \mathbf{1648} = C_x + C_m$ ; $c = \frac{1646}{1720} = 0.958$, $c_x = \frac{1321}{1720} = 0.768$, $c_m = \frac{327}{1720} = \mathbf{0.190}$ ; $Q - q = \mathbf{696}$ |
| F | **Land Rent,** Unit rents : | $Y = \mathbf{2219}$, $R_A = Y - C = \mathbf{571}$ ; $\rho = R_A / Q = \frac{571}{1720} = 0.332$ , $c_{mA} = \frac{327}{220} = 1.5$ , $r_A = R_A / A = \frac{571}{220} = \mathbf{2.595}$ |

*Source*: von Thünen (1990, p. 123–125); Hall (1966, p. 73); Petersen (1944, p. 51, p. 64); For **3-F**, cf. notes 11–12.

Notation is ours, and only some of **boldface** numbers above are seen in the pages of the reference list.

From money *Totals* (Talers) of the Accounting Statements, we immediately see the **share** of the *Land Rent* in **Revenue,**[9] $\boldsymbol{\delta}_{\mathbf{A}} = R_A/Y$, and the four *production* **Cost** shares, $\boldsymbol{\epsilon}_{\mathbf{i}} = C_i/C$, $i = 1, 2, 3, 4$, to be,

$$\textbf{7 F.} \qquad A = 220\ ha\,,\ Q = 3144\ :\ \delta_A = 0.214;$$
$$\epsilon_1 = 0.20,\ \epsilon_2 = 0.27,\ \epsilon_3 = 0.19,\ \epsilon_4 = 0.34;\ c_m = 0.204 \tag{25.15}$$

$$\textbf{3 F.} \qquad A = 220\ ha\,,\ Q = 1720\ :\ \delta_A = 0.257;$$
$$\epsilon_1 = 0.21,\ \epsilon_2 = 0.26,\ \epsilon_3 = 0.17,\ \epsilon_4 = 0.36;\ c_m = 0.187 \tag{25.16}$$

In total revenue-cost records for (7 F, 3 F) in Talers, the costs $\boldsymbol{C_i}$ , i= 2,3,4, are split into a **local** component $\boldsymbol{C_{ix}}$ and **external** (city) component $\boldsymbol{C_{im}}$ (*input prices* to costs $\boldsymbol{C_{im}}$ are *invariant* to location), and from recorded experience, the *same* weights, 0.75 and 0.25, are applied to *all* the activities, i= 2,3,4.

Although *external* Taler components $C_{im}$ enter the production cost $C_i$ of each *activity*, i= 2,3,4, we can (as invariant to location) add them for (7 F, 3 F) to the respective *Totals*, $C_m$: **641** and **327**, or as Talers per *unit of rye* production (output), $c_m = C_m/Q$: **0.204** and **0.190**, cf. accounting data above.

All the cost activity components in Talers, $C_{ix}$, i= 1,2,3,4, can of course be added to the (7 F, 3 F) accounting Totals, $C_x$: **1976** and **1321**, but each $C_{ix}$ and hence $C_x$ will change with the local activity *prices* of proper activity *input measures* (or amounts of production factors). Accordingly, von Thünen (1990, p. 36); Hall (1966, p. 28): "since *rye* has very *different prices* [Talers] in the different rings of the Isolated state we must to obtain a *general formula*

[9] The *Total Revenues* of a *seven field* farming system consist of revenues, *partly* from grain sales, and *partly* from animal products. By using their relative intrinsic nutritive values, oats and barley may be also given in rye terms, such that the *entire grain* harvest is expressed in *rye* (bushels rye). Between *rye* and *animal products* (butter, meat ) are assumed *fixed price-relations* [ constant everywhere, *x* ], such that it is possible to express the *total revenue* by a *rye harvest* (*production*) in bushels rye and its *rye price* (italics ours), von Thünen (1990, p. 37); Hall (1966, p. 28). These fixed-price relation assumptions are discussed later; but it is clearly said here by Thünen that the stated *rye production*, Q = 3144, on A = 220 ha above, does include such conversions of animal products (butter, wool, meat) to rye quantities [ bushel rye harvest (production) ].

[of activity costs, $C_x$ ], take *rye* as our *measure*, because *costs* and *revenue* are *related* to, and can be *measured* in, rye" (italics ours).

Thus, in other words, the variable Taler *rye price*, $p\,(x)$, (25.12), is chosen as an economic convenient alternative *numeraire* (accounting unit) for the *activity costs*, $C_{ix}$, i= 1,2,3,4, i.e., Tellow recorded Talers $C_{ix}$ may be converted to *size* measures (ray equivalence) in the *rye unit* (bushel) through the actual rye *accounting price* of $p\,(5) = 1.29$ at Tellow. The conversions of $C_{ix}$ to their ray *equivalents* $\boldsymbol{q_i}$—*quantitative* (physical) *activity measures*[10]—are seen in the accounting statements above—together with the activity variables, given as sizes of required *activity* per unit of *output*, $\boldsymbol{a_i} = q_i\,/\,Q$—collected for (7 F, 3 F)[11] as:

7 F. $$Q = 3144 \;:\; q = 1976\;;\; a_1 = 0.154,\; a_2 = 0.161,$$
$$a_3 = 0.113,\; a_4 = 0.200\;;\; a = q/Q = 0.628 \qquad (25.17)$$

3 F. $$Q = 1720 \;:\; q = 1024\;;\; a_1 = 0.154,\; a_2 = 0.148,$$
$$a_3 = 0.094,\; a_4 = 0.199\;;\; a = q/Q = 0.595 \qquad (25.18)$$

*Sizes* of $\boldsymbol{q_i}$ or *activity parameters*—$\boldsymbol{a_i}$, $\boldsymbol{a}$, (25.17–25.18)—are called ***cost-drivers*** in modern *Activity Based Costing* (ABC), Datar and Rajan (2018, p. 54, 180), *Prozesskostenrechnung*, Wöhe et al. (2016, p. 930), where cost drivers *quantitatively* describe proper *cause-and-effect* relationships between the activity measures and levels of total activity cost (or sizes of total activity cost per order or unit of output).

Thus the **local** costs, $C_x$ , local unit costs, $c_x = C_x/Q$, are obtained by summing the four activity costs, $C_{ix}$, unit costs, $c_{ix} = C_{ix}/Q$—with each $c_{ix}$ given by a *cost driver* $(a_i)$ and cost *driver price*, $p(x)$:

$$c_x(x) = (a_1 + a_2 + a_3 + a_4)\,p\,(x) \equiv a\,p\,(x)\;;$$
$$\mathbf{d\,(x)} = p\,(x) - c_x(x) = (1 - a)\,p\,(x)\;;\; \mathbf{a = q/Q} \qquad (25.19)$$

With $\boldsymbol{c_x(x)}$, the *local contribution margin* (Deckungsbeitrag/Stück) is $\mathbf{d\,(x)}$, (25.19)—and by $c_m$ and (25.12):

$$\mathbf{c(x)} = c_x(x) + c_m = a\,p\,(x) + c_m = a\,\frac{p_0\,\tilde{q} - (p_0\,\alpha_Q + \alpha_M)\,x}{\tilde{q} + (\alpha_F - \alpha_Q)\,x} + c_m\;;$$
$$C\,(x) = c(x)\,Q \qquad (25.20)$$

[10] The rye equivalent $q_1$ (rye seed size) is evidently a good measure of the sowing activity; rye equivalents, $q_i$, $i = 2, 3, 4$, are not literally sizes of rye inputs, but here useful quantities (indexes) as overall indicators for other activity (input) levels.

[11] For the 3 - Field farming system, the ray equivalents, $q_i$, and cost drivers, $a_i = q_i/Q$, cannot simply (as Tellow 7 - F) be derived directly from the *activity costs*, $C_{ix}$, i= 1,2,3,4„ as there is no such accounting data available for the 3 - F system. The 3 - F accounting data and cost drivers (25.17–25.18) are **reconstructions**—devised by a *two-step* procedure, see note 12.

**c(x)** is the **general** parametric cost function that was above *empirically calibrated* to (25.13–25.14), Fig. 25.8a.

The explicit *arithmetic* versions of (25.19) with $p(x)$, (25.12), and *Tellow accounting* cost driver parameters[12] (25.17–25.18) become for *7 - Field System*, A= 220 ha, $Q = 3144$, and *3 - Field System*, A= 220 ha, $Q = 1720$:

$$\textbf{7 F.}\quad c_x(x) = \frac{171.6 - 3.45\,x}{182 + x} = \frac{208.7 - 3.25\,x}{182 + x} - 0.204 = c(x) - c_m \; ;$$

$$C_x(x) = c_x(x)\,Q \tag{25.21}$$

$$\textbf{3 F.}\quad c_x(x) = \frac{162.5 - 3.27\,x}{182 + x} = \frac{197.1 - 3.08\,x}{182 + x} - 0.190 = c(x) - c_m \; ;$$

$$C_x(x) = c_x(x)\,Q \tag{25.22}$$

$$\textbf{7 F.}\quad d(x) = \frac{101.4 - 2.05\,x}{182 + x} = \frac{64.3 - 2.25\,x}{182 + x} + 0.204 = m(x) + c_m \; ;$$

$$D(x) = d(x)\,Q \tag{25.23}$$

$$\textbf{3 F.}\quad d(x) = \frac{110.5 - 2.23\,x}{182 + x} = \frac{75.9 - 2.42\,x}{182 + x} + 0.190 = m(x) + c_m \; ;$$

$$D(x) = d(x)\,Q \tag{25.24}$$

with $c_x(x)$ and $d(x)$ exhibited in Fig. 25.9 and 25.10—and hereto $c(x)$, $m(x)$ with $c_m$, shown above, Figs. 25.8a, and 25.5.

So (25.19), (25.12), give **Land rents** (25.25–25.27)—with the arithmetic versions seen in: (25.5–25.8), Table 25.1, Figs. 25.5 and 25.6.

$$\begin{aligned} \mathbf{m(x)} &= d(x) - c_m = (1 - a)\,p(x) - c_m \\ &= (1 - a)\,\frac{p_0\,\widetilde{q} - (p_0\,\alpha_Q + \alpha_M)\,x}{\widetilde{q} + (\alpha_F - \alpha_Q)\,x} - c_m \; ; \quad \mathbf{a = q/Q} \end{aligned} \tag{25.25}$$

[12] The *two-step* procedure for reconstruction of Data to the 3 F Accounting Statements consists of adjustments due to:
1. Different Field sizes and Production Activity reductions 2. Uniform Soil Fertility preservation and Yield reductions.
Ad.1 In 7 F system, 3/7 of 220 ha = 90 *ha* are *grain* fields, 90 ha pasture, 30 ha fallow; in 3 F system, 2/3 of tillage is *grain* fields, here 50 *ha*, 25 ha fallow, the rest of 220, 145 ha is permanent grass, i.e., in 3 F, *grain land* is nearly *halved*; these grain fields are *closer* to farmyard and buildings. Smaller distance (Entfernung) gives for 3 F some saving of labor time, reducing wage bills (Talers) and money cost accounts: $C_2$, $C_3$ of cultivation, harvesting activities with 10, 35 percent. Smaller corn fields reduce sowing cost $C_1$, other $C_i$, Q. All $C_i$ are split into $C_{ix}$, $C_m$ as 7 F. $C_{ix}/p(5)$ gives: $q_i$, i=1,2,3,4.
Ad.2 Uniform fertility amending of $q_3$, $q_4$, $C_m$, $Q$ above—with $\frac{6.72}{10}$—give the *local cost drivers*: $q_i$—and $a_i$ in **3-F** above.

**Fig. 25.9** Local Production Costs, $c_x(x)$: 7 F, (25.21) ; $c_x(x)$: 3 F, (25.22)

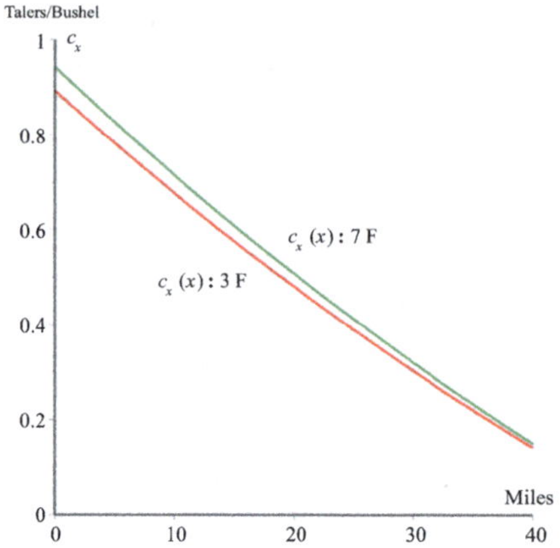


**Fig. 25.10** Contribution Margin, $\boldsymbol{d}\,(\boldsymbol{x})$. $d\,(x)$: 7 F, (25.23) ; $d\,(x)$: 3 F, (25.24)

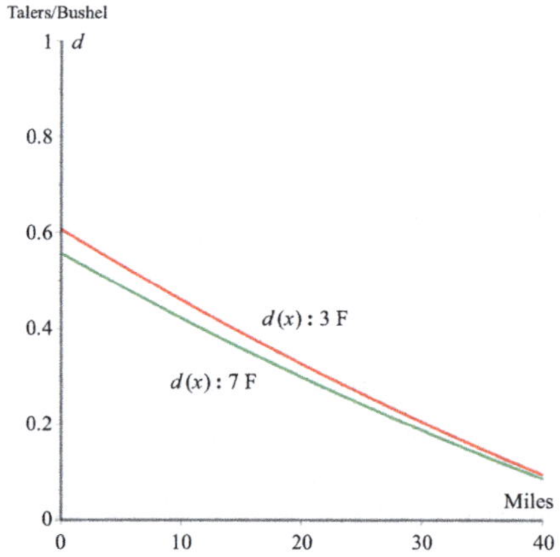


$$\mathbf{r_A(x)} = m(x)\,q_A = \left[ (1 - a)\,\frac{p_0\,\widetilde{q} - (\,p_0\,\alpha_Q + \alpha_M)\,x}{\widetilde{q} + (\alpha_F - \alpha_Q)\,x} - c_m \right] q_A \;;$$

$$\mathbf{R_A(x)} = r_A(x)\,A = m(x)\,q_A\,A \tag{25.26}$$

7 F. $Q = 3144$ : $\quad R_A(x) = m(x)\,q_A\,A = m(x)\,Q$

$$= 1168 \left[ \frac{273 - 5.5\,x}{182 + x} \right] - 641$$

$$= \frac{202202 - 7065\,x}{182 + x} \tag{25.27}$$

Local rye price $p(x)$, Total Local Revenues, Total Costs, Local Costs, Contribution Margins, External Costs, Land Rents, of *mobile Tellow*: $Y(x)$, $C(x)$, $C_x(x)$, $D(x)$, $C_m$, $R_A(x)$, (25.12–25.27), are in Tables 25.3 and 25.4.

**Table 25.3** **7 - Field System**. Land = **A = 220** ha; Production = **Q = 3144** Bushels Rye; $\boldsymbol{q_A = \frac{Q}{A} = 14.3}$

| Distances (x) - Miles | Local Rye prices, p(x) | Local Gross Revenue Y = p(x) Q = p(x) 3144 | Total Cost C(x) = $C_x(x) + C_m$ C(x) = c(x) Q = c(x) 3144 | Local Cost $C_x$ = p(x) q = p(x) 1976 | Contribution Margin D = p(x) (Q-q) = p(x) 1168 | External Cost $C_m$ | Land Rent $R_A$ (x) = D(x) – $C_m$ = p(x) 1168–641 | Land Rent $R_A(x) = r_A(x)$ A *3 - Field System* |
|---|---|---|---|---|---|---|---|---|
| 1. | 2. | 3. | 4. | 5. | 6. | 7. | 8. | 9. |
| 0 | 1.500 | 4716 | 3605 | 2964 | 1752 | 641 | **1111** | 717 |
| 5 | 1.313 | 4128 | 3235 | 2594 | 1534 | 641 | **893** | 587 |
| 10 | 1.136 | 3572 | 2886 | 2245 | 1327 | 641 | **686** | 464 |
| 15 | 0.968 | 3044 | 2554 | 1913 | 1131 | 641 | **490** | 347 |
| 20 | 0.809 | 2544 | 2240 | 1599 | 945 | 641 | **304** | 236 |
| **24.7** | **0.665** | 2091 | 1955 | 1314 | 777 | 641 | **136** | **136** |
| 25 | 0.656 | 2062 | 1937 | 1296 | 766 | 641 | 125 | **130** |
| **28.6** | **0.549** | 1726 | 1726 | 1085 | 641 | 641 | 0 | **55** |
| 30 | 0.512 | 1610 | 1653 | 1012 | 598 | 641 | –43 | **29** |
| **31.4** | **0.470** | 1477 | 1569 | 928 | 549 | 641 | –92 | 0 |
| 40 | 0.239 | | | | | | | |
| 45 | 0.112 | | | | | | | |
| 49.6 | 0.000 | | | | | | | |
| 50 | – | | | | | | | |

*Source*: von Thünen (1990, p. 42, p. 52, p. 123–125), Hall (1966, p. 36, p. 66, p. 71), Petersen (1944, p. 65).

**Table 25.4** **3 - Field System**. Land = **A = 220** ha; Production = **Q = 1720** Bushels Rye; $q_A = \frac{Q}{A} = 7.82$

| Distances (x) - Miles | Local Rye prices, p(x) | Local Gross Revenue Y = p(x) Q = p(x) 1720 | Total Cost C(x) = $C_x(x)+C_m$ C(x) = c(x) Q = c(x) 1720 | Local Cost $C_x$ = p(x) q = p(x) 1024 | Contribution Margin D = p(x) (Q-q) = p(x) 696 | External Cost $C_m$ | Land Rent R(x) = D(x) – $C_m$ = p(x) 696–327 | Land Rent R(x) = $r_A$ (x) A *7 - Field System* |
|---|---|---|---|---|---|---|---|---|
| 1. | 2. | 3. | 4. | 5. | 6. | 7. | 8. | 9. |
| 0 | 1.500 | 2580 | 1863 | 1536 | 1044 | 327 | 717 | **1111** |
| 5 | 1.313 | 2258 | 1671 | 1344 | 914 | 327 | 587 | **893** |
| 10 | 1.136 | 1954 | 1490 | 1163 | 791 | 327 | 464 | **686** |
| 15 | 0.968 | 1665 | 1318 | 991 | 674 | 327 | 347 | **490** |
| 20 | 0.809 | 1391 | 1155 | 828 | 563 | 327 | 236 | **304** |
| **24.7** | **0.665** | 1144 | 1008 | 681 | 463 | 327 | 136 | **136** |
| 25 | 0.656 | 1128 | 998 | 671 | 457 | 327 | **130** | 125 |
| **28.6** | **0.549** | 944 | 889 | 562 | 382 | 327 | **55** | 0 |
| 30 | 0.512 | 881 | 852 | 525 | 356 | 327 | **29** | –43 |
| **31.4** | **0.470** | 808 | 808 | 481 | 327 | 327 | 0 | –92 |
| 40 | 0.239 | | | | | | | |
| 45 | 0.112 | | | | | | | |
| 49.6 | 0.000 | | | | | | | |
| 50 | – | | | | | | | |

*Source*: von Thünen (1990, p. 119, p. 121–125); Hall (1966, p. 69, p. 71); Petersen (1944, p. 66)

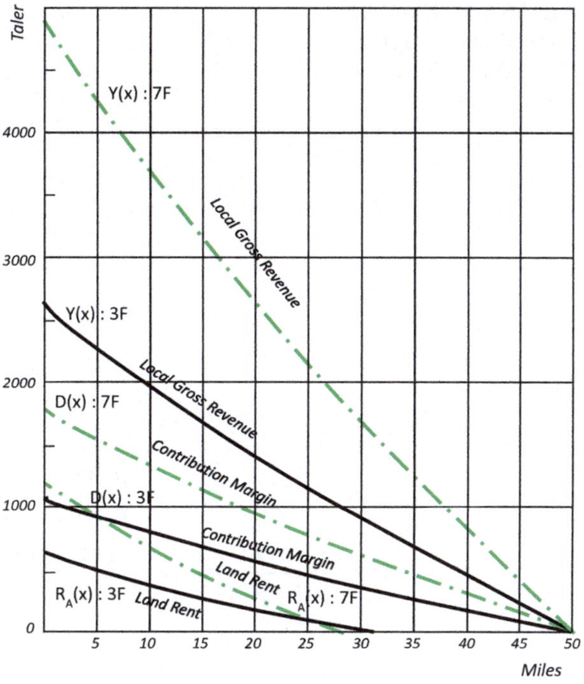


**Fig. 25.11** Total Revenue, $\boldsymbol{Y}(\boldsymbol{x})$, Contribution Margin, $\boldsymbol{D}(\boldsymbol{x})$, Land Rents, $\boldsymbol{R_A}(\boldsymbol{x})$ - of **7 F** and **3 F**. *Source*: Tables 25.3 and 25.4, and Petersen (1944, p. 65–67 - $\boldsymbol{D}(\boldsymbol{x})$, Deckungsbeitrag is his "*Marktleistung*")

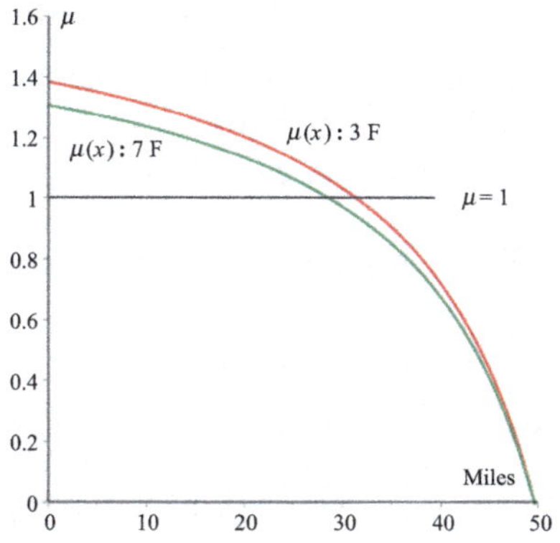


**Fig. 25.12** Price - Cost ratio (*mark-up*), $\boldsymbol{\mu}(\boldsymbol{x}) = \frac{p(x)}{c(x)}$. $\mu(x)$: 7 F, (25.28) ; $\boldsymbol{\mu}(\boldsymbol{x})$: 3 F, (25.29)

These *Revenues* $\boldsymbol{Y}(\boldsymbol{x})$, Contribution Margins $\boldsymbol{D}(\boldsymbol{x})$, and Land Rents $\boldsymbol{R_A}(\boldsymbol{x})$, of Tables 25.3 and 25.4 are *exhibited* in Fig. 25.11, where $D(x)$ and $R_A(x)$ have the *hyperbolic* shape of $\boldsymbol{d}(\boldsymbol{x})$ and $\boldsymbol{r_A}(\boldsymbol{x})$ in Figs. 25.10 and 25.6.

**7 F.** $$Q = 3144 \ : \ \mu(x) = \frac{p\,(x)}{c\,(x)} = \frac{273 \ - 5.5\,x}{208.7 - 3.25\,x} \ ;$$

$$\pi(x) = \frac{\mu(x) - 1}{\mu(x)} = \frac{r_A(x)/p(x)}{q_A} \tag{25.28}$$

**Fig. 25.13** Land Rent in Factor Income, $\delta_A^*(x)$
$\delta_A^*(x)$: 7 F, (25.41) ;
$\delta_A^*(x)$: 3 F, (25.42)

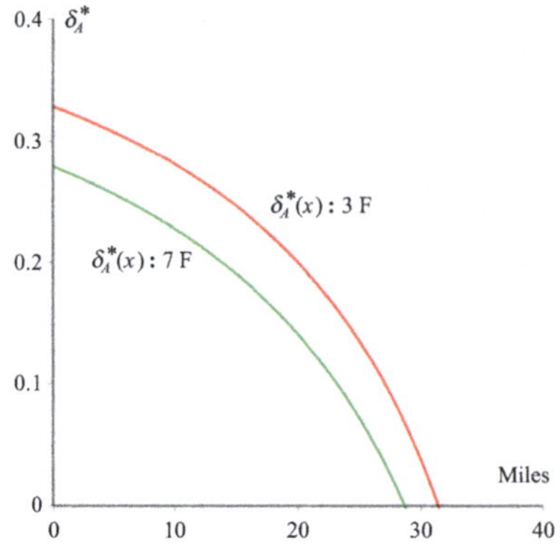


**3 F.**
$$Q = 1720 \; : \; \mu(x) = \frac{p\,(x)}{c\,(x)} = \frac{273 - 5.5\,x}{197.1 - 3.08\,x} \; ;$$
$$\pi(x) = \frac{\mu(x) - 1}{\mu(x)} = \frac{r_A(x)/p(x)}{q_A} \tag{25.29}$$

### *The Activity Costs, Land Intensities, and Land Productivity*

We supplement *cost* driver *activity parameters*, (per unit of *output*), $\boldsymbol{a_i = q_i / Q}$, (25.17–25.19), with per unit of *land (ha)*—**Land intensities** (*activity ratios*): $\mathbf{b_i} = \boldsymbol{q_i / A = a_i\, q_A}$, $i = 1, 2, 3, 4$—collected for (**7 F, 3 F**):

**7 F.** $A = 220\,ha \; : \; q = 1976 ; \; b_1 = 2.2, \; b_2 = 2.3, \; b_3 = 1.6, \; b_4 = 2.9 ;$
$$\mathbf{b} = \frac{\mathbf{q}}{\mathbf{A}} = 9.0 ; \; q_A = 14.3 \tag{25.30}$$

**3 F.** $A = 220\,ha \; : \; q = 1024 ; \; b_1 = 1.2, \; b_2 = 1.15, \; b_3 = 0.7, \; b_4 = 1.6 ;$
$$\mathbf{b} = \frac{\mathbf{q}}{\mathbf{A}} = 4.65 ; \; q_A = 7.82 \tag{25.31}$$

In contrast to $\boldsymbol{a_i}$ and *cost shares* $\boldsymbol{\epsilon_i}$ (25.15–25.16), in (25.30–25.31), ***land intensities*** $\boldsymbol{b_i}$ and ***land productivity*** $\mathbf{q_A}$ of the **7-F** *field system* are nearly the **double** of **3-F**. Land rents $\boldsymbol{r_A(x)}$, (25.26), become with (25.30–25.31):

$$r_A(x) = m(x)\, q_A = (1 - a)\, p\,(x)\, q_A - c_m\, q_A = (q_A - b)\, p(x) - c_{mA} \; ;$$
$$\frac{r_A(x)}{p(x)} = q_A - b - \frac{c_{mA}}{p(x)} \tag{25.32}$$

Local Land rents $\mathbf{r_A(x)}$, (25.32), are seen arithmetically for **7 F/3 F** in Figs. 25.6, and 25.14. The *parametric* ratio expression, $\frac{r_A(x)}{p(x)}$, (25.32), is in arithmetic form for 7 F/3 F, (25.33–25.34), directly obtained from (25.7–25.8), (25.3).

The **accounting** numbers of Tellow *land rental rates* at $\boldsymbol{x} = \mathbf{5}$, as well as $\mathbf{r_A(x)}$ for **any** distance **(x)**, can be seen as **factor price** of *using* the *production factor* **Land**, as defined by the standard *marginal productivity* principle, here with *variable* product price, $p(x)$, as the *marginal revenue product* (MRP), $r_A(x) = MRP_A\,(x) = p(x)\,MP_A\,(x)$. Thus, $\frac{r_A(x)}{p(x)}$, (25.33–25.34), is *confirmed* as $\mathbf{MP_A}$ **(x)** formula by (25.30–25.32):

**7 F.** $A = 220\ ha,\quad Q = 3144\ :$

$$\frac{r_A(x)}{p(x)} = \frac{919.1\ -\ 32.1\,x}{273\ -\ 5.5\,x} = MP_A\,(x) = 5.3 - 2.9\,\frac{182\,+\,x}{273\ -\ 5.5\,x} \tag{25.33}$$

**3 F.** $A = 220\ ha,\quad Q = 1720\ :$

$$\frac{r_A(x)}{p(x)} = \frac{593.2\ -\ 18.9\,x}{273 - 5.5\,x} = MP_A\,(x) = 3.17 - 1.5\,\frac{182\,+\,x}{273 - 5.5\,x} \tag{25.34}$$

$\mathbf{MP_A}\,(x)$[13] of **7 F/3 F** are seen: Fig. 25.15—*crossing* at **same point** $(x)$, as $\boldsymbol{r_A(x)}$, Fig. 25.14, $\boldsymbol{R_A(x)}$, Fig. 25.11.

The arithmetic form of the Land *rent margin/price* ratio, $\boldsymbol{\pi\,(x) = m(x)/p(x)}$, for 7 F/3 F, (25.13–25.14), (25.28–25.29), Fig. 25.8b, are obtained from (25.25), (25.15–25.18), to be:

**7 F.** $Q = 3144:$

$$\begin{aligned}\pi(x) &= \frac{m(x)}{p(x)} = 1 - a - \frac{c_m}{p\,(x)}\\ &= 0.372\ -\ \frac{0.204\,(182 + x)}{273\ -\ 5.5\,x} = \frac{64.3 - 2.25\,x}{273 - 5.5\,x}\\ &= \frac{\mu(x) - 1}{\mu(x)}\end{aligned} \tag{25.35}$$

[13] It is important to recall that production functions and marginal productivities always, e.g., $MP_A\,(x)$, involve and relate *quantities* (disregard money, Taler, amounts). Despite the many (non-monetary) *fixed* numbers: $q_A, q_i, a_i, b_i,\ i = 1, 2, 3, 4$, the Tellow production functions of rye *implicitly* involved in 7 F/3 F Accounting Statements are *not* necessarily Leontief functions, see below. Rye production functions require the *money amounts*, $c_m, c_{mA}$, converted to e.g. *rye equivalents* [ *increasing* with $(\boldsymbol{x})$ by smaller $p\,(x)$ ], i.e. *factor proportions* are changing, and so are, $MP_A\,(x)$, (25.32), (RHS), and (25.33–25.34). Note that in Fig. 25.15, 25.11, Tables 25.3 and 25.4, and everywhere, the *size* A = 320 ha is *not* changed at all; A (x), Tellow **A** (x), is moving.

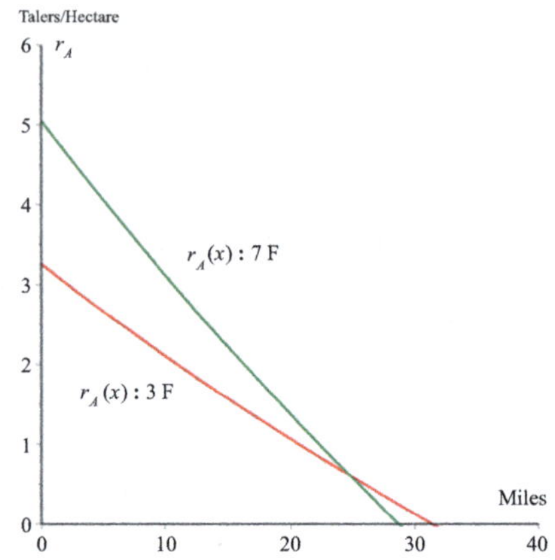


**Fig. 25.14** Local Land Rent per hectare, $r_A(x)$. $r_A(x)$: 7 F, (25.7) ; $r_A(x)$: 3 F, (25.8)

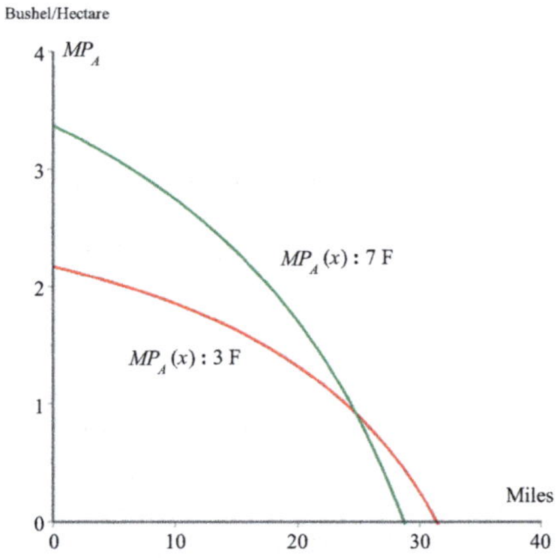


**Fig. 25.15** Local Marginal Product, $MP_A(x)$. $MP_A(x)$: 7 F, (25.33) ; $MP_A(x)$: 3 F, (25.34)

**3 F**. $Q = 1720$ :

$$\pi(x) = \frac{m(x)}{p(x)} = 1 - a - \frac{c_m}{p(x)}$$
$$= 0.405 - \frac{0.190\,(182 + x)}{273 - 5.5\,x} = \frac{75.9 - 2.42\,x}{273 - 5.5\,x}$$
$$= \frac{\mu(x) - 1}{\mu(x)} \tag{25.36}$$

Land Rent **share** of *Revenues*, $\boldsymbol{\delta_A(x)} = R_A(x)/Y(x)$, (25.15–25.16), are also given by formulas, (25.35–25.36), due to the basic *Accounting identity*: $\boldsymbol{\delta_A(x)} = r_A(x)\,A/p\,(x)\,Q = m(x)\,Q/p\,(x)\,Q = \boldsymbol{m(x)/p\,(x)}$.

But $\delta_A(x)$ expression, (25.37–25.38), RHS, follow alternatively directly from *dividing* (25.33–25.34) by, respectively, $\mathbf{q_A}$, (25.30–25.31):

**7 F.** $A = 220\ ha,\ Q = 3144:$

$$\delta_A(x) = \frac{R_A(x)}{Y(x)} = \frac{m(x)}{p(x)} = \pi(x) = \frac{64.3 - 2.25\,x}{273 - 5.5\,x} = \frac{MP_A(x)}{q_A} \equiv \epsilon_A(x) \tag{25.37}$$

**3 F.** $A = 220\ ha,\ Q = 1720:$

$$\delta_A(x) = \frac{R_A(x)}{Y(x)} = \frac{m(x)}{p(x)} = \pi(x) = \frac{75.9 - 2.42\,x}{273 - 5.5\,x} = \frac{MP_A(x)}{q_A} \equiv \epsilon_A(x) \tag{25.38}$$

The *comprehensive analytic* and *arithmetic information* in (25.37–25.38) has the ability to address, **unify**, and interpret issues (conceptual differences) between disparate *economic disciplines.* The **equality,** $\boldsymbol{\delta_A(x) = \epsilon_A(x)}$, (25.37–25.38)[14] shows a *connection* between *cost calculations* in *Business Economics/Accounting* (Betriebswirtschaft/Kostenrechnung) and costs/prices in *Macro-/Microeconomics* (Nationalökonomie).[15]

[14] $\epsilon_A = \frac{MP_A}{AP_A}$ = *cost share* of factor Land in the *Total Factor Cost* (C) of inputs from many primary (durable) factors = share of Revenue (Y) = Total factor income ($q_A = Q/A = AP_A$, Average Productivity of A, Land); $\boldsymbol{\epsilon_A}$ is like the shares of Labor, Capital, $\epsilon_L = \frac{MP_L}{AP_L}$, $\epsilon_K = \frac{MP_K}{AP_K}$—later in von Thünen (1990)'s marginal productivity analyses, cf. Jensen (2017, p. 61); here Chap. 3, p. 53.

[15] The *business* (Betrieb) total cost *accounting* item (term), $\boldsymbol{c(x)}$, is *recorded* cost object *assignments* only (Selbskosten) in the *fundamental* (firm accounting) equation: $\boldsymbol{m(x)} = p(x) - c(x)$, (25.4), i.e., $\boldsymbol{m(x)}$ is **not** included in any *accounted* costs, and $\boldsymbol{m(x)}$, Fig. 25.5, is in the accounting literature called *operating/profit margin* [ Earnings Before Interest, Taxes (EBIT), Land rent ], *Stückgewinn*—and $\boldsymbol{\pi(x)} = m(x)/p(x)$, is *operating/profit rate*, seen in Fig. 25.8b or "*Mark-up*", $\boldsymbol{\mu(x)}$, Fig. 25.12.

Macro-/Microeconomics describes a *representative* (industry) *Farm*'s production (cultivation) methods by a *Production* function, $Q = F(A, L, K, E)$—*intensive* (ratio) form, $q_A = \frac{Q}{A} = f(l_A, k_A, e_A)$—relating maximal output (Q) to relevant production factors, Land ($A$), Labor ($L$), $l_A = \frac{L}{A}$, Capital ($K$), $k_A = \frac{K}{A}$, Materials ($E$), $e_A = \frac{E}{A}$; $MP_A \equiv \frac{\partial F(A,L,K,E)}{\partial A}$. The *factor intensities* (Land ratios), $l_A, k_A, e_A$, may be compared to *activity* ratios (Land intensities): $b_i = q_i/A$, (25.30–25.31).

The corresponding (dual) minimal Total *Cost* function (Talers), $C_A = C_A(r_A, w, r_K, w_E, Q)$ - *unit* output *costs*, $c_A = \frac{C}{Q} = c_A(r_A, w, r_K, w_E)$ - with Taler *factor prices* $(r_A, w, r_K, w_E)$, output (Q), as arguments. The unit output (rye, Bushel) *factor cost* function (Talers), $c_A = c_A(r_A, w, r_K, w_E)$, is *different* from the *unit production* **cost driver**, (25.4), (25.20), function: $\mathbf{c(x)} = a\,p(x) + c_m$, Fig. 25.8a. The difference, $p(0) - t(x) = p(x)$, (25.4), locally observed rye (*same* as accounting rye) prices are equated to the unit *factor cost* function, i.e., $p(x) = c_A(r_A, w, r_K, w_E) \neq c(x)$; factor (rental) price of Land ($r_A$) in the $c_A$—function is assumed (constructed) to be numerically satisfy: $r_A(x) = p(x)\,MP_A(x) = p(x)\,\frac{\partial F(A,L,K,E)}{\partial A}$, and hence the total Land rent is, $R_A(x) = r_A(x)\,A$, i.e., with the Production function, $Q = F(A, L, K, E)$ or Factor cost function, $C_A(r_A, w, r_K, w_E, Q)$, together with the *local* rye prices $\mathbf{p(x)}$, we derive

We may note that **all** the 7 F/3 F - *curves*: $c(x)$, $d(x)$, $m(x)$, $\pi(x)$, $c_x(x)$, $\mu(x)$, and totals: $Y(x)$, $C(x)$, $C_x(x)$, $D(x)$—in Figs. 25.5, 25.8, 25.9, 25.10, 25.11, and 25.12, and Table 25.3 and 25.4 *never* **cross** each other.

Hence what matters for a given Land (Farm) size (220 ha) is **not** the: contribution margin, **d(x)**, profit margin, **m(x)**, **profit rate**, $\boldsymbol{\pi}$**(x)**, mark-up, $\boldsymbol{\mu}$**(x)**—but **instead Total** profit (Land rent), $\mathbf{R_A(x)}$, that *did* **cross**, Fig. 25.11, as did **local** rental rates, $\mathbf{r_A(x)}$, marginal products, $\mathbf{MP_A}$ **(x)**, in Figs. 25.14 and 25.15.

Thus, the **rental** rates, $\mathbf{r_A(x)}$, (Talers) are the **basic curves** making up an **envelope** in Fig. 25.14—that **locally** ($x$) decide the *optimal* **Land use**: The **cultivation method** and the **selection** of which **product** to **transport** and **sell** in the central *city* at the *market price*, **p(0)**.

The **7 F/3 F** *envelope* of the explicit **non-linear** Tellow *calibrated* $\mathbf{r_A(x)}$ *functions*, (25.7–25.8), (25.26), Fig. 25.14, *modify* the illustrative **linear** *Land Rent Profiles*, Beckmann and Puu (1990, p. 10), Fujita and Thisse (2002, p. 67), **linear** *Bid-Rent Curves*, Fujita et al. (2001, p. 16), of Spatial Economy and Urban Economics. Earlier contributions with *exact linear* $\mathbf{r_A(x)}$ functions—for constant $q_A = \frac{Q}{A}$, due to *exact linear* $\rho_A(x) = \frac{R_A}{Q}(x)$ in Dunn (1954, p. 173), Grotewold (1959, p. 349), and the result of assuming **invariant c(x)** $= c_m$ $[c_x(x) = 0]$, and assuming **proportional**: $\mathbf{t(x)} = \tau \cdot x$ $[p(x) = p(0) - \tau \cdot x]$, cf. (25.4), (25.20)—are *far from* von Thünen's original *assumptions* and completely *ignore* (as most Thünen references) his Tellow *accounting* based *activity cost* calculations of **7 F** and **3 F** *farming systems* that gave the **hyperbolic** *land rental* rates with *distance* (**x**): $\mathbf{r_A(x)}$ functions, (25.7–25.8), (25.26).

### *Manor Estate Accounting and National Income Accounting*

Let us briefly consider relationships between the Tellow *Manor Farm accounting statements* above[16] and National Income and Product Accounting (**NIPA**).

the same *local* Land rent size, $R_A(x) = \mathbf{m(x)}\, Q$, as were obtained by the *cost driver* function, $\mathbf{c(x)} = (q_A - b)\, p(x) - c_{mA}$, (25.32); the result, $\boldsymbol{\delta}_A(x) = \boldsymbol{\epsilon}_A(x)$, (25.37–25.38), confirms the logical (mathematical) coherence and the numerical accuracy of Land rent calculation by $\boldsymbol{c(x)}$ and $\boldsymbol{p(x)} = c_A(r_A, w, r_K, w_E)$. No black magic is involved, just dexterity ('Keine Hexerei, nur Behendigkeit'). Moreover, as mentioned in note 13, the *falling* Marginal Productivity curves of Land: $MP_A(x) = \frac{\partial F(A,L,K,E)}{\partial A}$, Fig. 25.15, are not reflecting the normal variation of the partial derivative $\frac{\partial F(A,L,K,E)}{\partial A}$, wrt. $A$ ($A = 220$ ha), cf. (25.32), but it is the *three factor intensities* (Land *ratios*), $l_A, k_A, e_A$, of **7 *F*/3 *F*** that are *different* in: $q_A = \frac{Q}{A} = f(l_A, k_A, e_A)$, for **7 *F*/3 *F*** with: $q_A = 14.3$, $q_A = 7.82$.

The representative **7 F/3 F** Tellow **Farms** ($A = 220$; $Q = 3144$, $Q = 1720$) are continuously *moving* (**x**) with *different* optimal *factor combinations*, $l_A, k_A, e_A$, at each *location* (**x**) in Figs. 25.14–25.15. On the different **7 F/3 F** sizes of $l_A, k_A$, see Sect. "CES Production Function Calibrated upon Tellow Accounts", (25.77–25.78).

[16] Let us here quote, von Thünen (1990, p. 29); Hall (1966, p. 23): "This problem [ *Farm Revenue - Land Rent* ] could be solved only by means of precise and *detailed calculations* on the *costs* of *every branch* of farming, based on *data* taken *from reality*"; and with this end in view, the author

National Accounting will determine total supplies of commodities available for satisfying Final Demand of *national consumption* and *investment* and measure *national incomes* distributed (*imputed*) to durable *production factors* in various industries.

Let us consider the possibility to estimate the **share**—$\delta_{\mathbf{A}}^{\mathbf{N}}$—of *Land Rent* in *National Income*—$\mathbf{Y_N}$—from the *Tellow* 7 **F**/3 **F** *accounting statements*[17] (representing Agriculture) and other historical records.

First, from the *stated* 7 **F**/3 **F** Total Revenues, $\boldsymbol{Y}$, must be deducted their *Sowing cost*, $C_1$, and similarly stated Total rye production (output), $\boldsymbol{Q}$, must reduced by *Rye Seed* quantities, $\boldsymbol{q_1}$, as they are not available for satisfying Final demand (Consumption). The *adjusted* 7 **F**/3 **F** numbers are:

7 **F**.

$$Y_A^* = Y - C_1 = 4056 - 626 = 3430,$$

$$Q^* = 3144 - 485 = 2659 ;$$

$$\delta_A^* = \frac{R_A}{Y_A^*} = \frac{866}{3430} = 0.25 \tag{25.39}$$

3 **F**.

$$Y_A^* = Y - C_1 = 2219 - 342 = 1877,$$

$$Q^* = 1720 - 265 = 1455 ;$$

$$\delta_A^* = \frac{R_A}{Y_A^*} = \frac{571}{1877} = 0.30 \tag{25.40}$$

kept (and is still keeping) extremely detailed accounts on his estate Tellow. Every single task which is undertaken at Tellow is noted in the work-book (Arbeitsjournal); and at the end *each year*, the *entries* are summarized (Übersicht) to show *how many* people were required for mowing or harrowing, how much work *one laborer* [Arbeitsquantum eines Arbeiter] or *one team* of horses [ Gespannne Pferde] could perform and so on.

In the same way, the Tellow finance [Geld]—and grain-books [ Kornrechnung ], when edited in association with the work-books [ Arbeitsrechnung ] supply the *data* for *calculating cost* of the *working forces* [Kosten der arbeitenden Kräfte], e.g., the *costs* of a day *laborer*'s family [ Tageslöhnerfamilie ], a team of *horses*, or a hoing *machine* [ Wechselhacken ], etc.

The *amount* [Quantität] and expense [Kosten] of the labor [der Arbeiten] taken to till a field [Bestellung eines Feldes] and harvest a crop [Einertung einer Frucht] gives us the *production costs* of this crop [Produktionskosten dieser Frucht]. Finally, *Revenue* ['Gross Product', Rohertrag ] minus *Production Costs* [Produktionskosten], gives the *Surplus, Land Rent* [ 'Net Product', reine Überschuss, Reinertrag], cf. $R_A = Y - C$, (25.4)—obtained from its cultivation [ den der Anbau der Frucht liefert ] (italics ours). It was necessary here to improve the economic terminology of the Hall (1966, p. 23) translation.

[17] Economic rationality and objective calculability as norm for planning and decisions in business firms presuppose the existence of well-organized accounting data and information, exemplified by the double-entry bookkeeping system that Baron Casper Voght demonstrated to Thünen in Hamburg 1803, Hippauf (2000, p. 27)—by its possibility to account for *differences* and for *comparing* firm results; cf. footnote 12 on adjusting (making) the cost drivers of four activity costs.

The numbers $\boldsymbol{\delta_A^*}$, (25.39–25.40), are 20 pct. larger than $\boldsymbol{\delta_A}$, (25.15–25.16). The *cultivation-* and *harvesting* costs, $C_2$, $C_3$, represent *factor costs* (recorded **expenses**) of *using* for a year *services* of *working forces*,[18] such as costs for services of all (annually employed day) *laborers*, and the costs of obtaining (maintaining) the services of *durable* physical *capital goods*, such as horses, cattle, hoeing machines, ploughs, equipments. The *general farming* costs, $C_4$, include *wages* of administrative employees and contracted **expenses** of using (leasing, renting) the services of durable *capital goods*, such as farm buildings, bridges, ditches. As expenses (rental rate) of farm buildings was used a 5 pct. interest rate on their book value (asset price).

General cost $C_4$ include expenses for some *non-durable goods* as utensils that cannot be ascribed product or activities and the expenses for external delivered materials (salt, metals). This part of $C_4$ (cost of non-durable external factor inputs) is to be deducted from $Y_A^*$, (25.39–25.40), to obtain *factor incomes*, distributed (imputed) to *Land, Labor*, and *Capital*—but $\boldsymbol{Y_A^*}$ are here taken as *Agricultural factor income*.

By the Accounting Identity and (25.39–25.40), the **7F/3F** *Land Rent shares* of *Tellow* Factor Income ($\boldsymbol{Y_A^*}$) is $\boldsymbol{\delta_A^*(x)} = R_A(x)/Y_A^*(x) = r_A(x)\,A/p\,(x)\,Q^*$—and with $q_A^* = Q^*/A$ and (25.33–25.34) as—$\delta_A^* = MP_A/q_A^*$:

**7F.** $A = 220\,ha\,,\ Q^* = 2659\,,\ q_A^* = 12.1\ :$

$$\delta_A^*(x) = \frac{MP_A}{q_A^*} = \frac{1}{12.1}\cdot\frac{919.1 - 32.1\,x}{273 - 5.5\,x} = \frac{76 - 2.65\,x}{273 - 5.5\,x} \qquad (25.41)$$

[18] See note 16; the annual accounting statement of year 1820 had an inventory list with, e.g.: 2 ploughs, 16 harrows, cf. Hippauf (2000, p. 164). A plough needed 2 men and 4 horses; the harrow was pulled by a team oxen, needing only 1 man.

After grain sales, *sheep* and *wool* was between 1810 and 1836 the *second* largest source of income at Tellow—the livestock increased from 618 to 1660 sheep, cf. Ahrend (2006, p. 63). Regarding the accounting calculations of Landrents in 1810–1815, an important remark is:

> von Thünen (1990, p. 30); Hall (1966, p. 23), "For the five years from 1810 to 1815, I worked out the *Land rents* of **each** crop (**product**) [ Reinertrag jeder einzelsen Frucht ] of *dairying, shep-farming* [der Holländerei, der Schäferei], and of every branch [jedes einzelnen Zweigs der Wirtschaft] of my estate Tellow, and, but 29.8 Talers annually, my findings *coincided* with the **Total Land Rent** [und diese *spezielle* Berechnung hat mit der **Summe des Reinertrags** eine Übereinstimmung bis auf 29.8 Taler jährlich gegeben]" (italics, boldface ours).

It was necessary again to improve Hall (1966, p. 23) translation. The crucial point here is not just the accounting accuracy, but that Costs and Land rents of *several products* (besides grain, rye) are included (summed) in the Tellow *Accounting Statements* above.

**3 F.** $A = 220\,ha\,,\ Q^* = 1455\,,\ q_A^* = 6.61\ :$

$$\delta_A^*(x) = \frac{MP_A}{q_A^*} = \frac{1}{6.61} \cdot \frac{593.2\ - 18.9\,x}{273\ -\ 5.5\,x} = \frac{90\ - 2.86\,x}{273\ -\ 5.5\,x} \tag{25.42}$$

which are depicted in Fig. 25.13 above. Rent shares $\boldsymbol{\delta_A^*(x)}$, (25.39–25.42), will be used in estimating, $\boldsymbol{\delta_A^N}$—the Land Rent *share* in National Income.

For *any* estate *size* **A** (ha), we have: $\varrho_r(x) \equiv R_{A7}(x)/R_{A3}(x) = r_{A7}(x)/r_{A3}(x) = MP_{A7}(x)/MP_{A3}(x)$, following from (25.33–25.34)—or by $r_A(x) = m(x)q_A$ (25.7–25.8) with, $\varrho_m(x) \equiv m_{A7}(x)/m_{A3}(x)$ and $\varrho_q \equiv q_{A7}/q_{A3}$:

$$\varrho_r(x) \equiv \frac{r_{A7}\,(x)}{r_{A3}\,(x)} = \frac{\frac{r_{A7}\,(x)}{p(x)}}{\frac{r_{A3}\,(x)}{p(x)}} = \frac{MP_{A7}(x)}{MP_{A3}(x)} = \frac{m_{A7}\,(x)\,q_{A7}}{m_{A3}\,(x)\,q_{A3}} = \varrho_m(x)\,\varrho_q\,;$$

$$\varrho_m(x) = \frac{m_{A7}(x)}{m_{A3}(x)}\,,\ \varrho_q = \frac{q_{A7}}{q_{A3}} \tag{25.43}$$

The equalities in (25.43) represent *general* economic (conceptional, definitional) *relations* and the numbers always satisfy accounting conditions (identities). Table 25.1 and *Accounting Statement* give $\boldsymbol{\varrho_r(5)}$ by (25.43):

$$\begin{aligned}\varrho_r(5) &= \frac{r_{A7}\,(5)}{r_{A3}\,(5)} = \frac{4.06}{2.67} = \frac{MP_{A7}(5)}{MP_{A3}(5)} = \frac{3.092}{2.034} = \mathbf{1.52}\\ &= \frac{r_{A7}\,(5)}{r_{A3}\,(5)} = \frac{3.936}{2.595} = \frac{MP_{A7}(5)}{MP_{A3}(5)} = \frac{3.051}{2.012}\end{aligned} \tag{25.44}$$

Thus at **Tellow** (1810–1819), *replacement* of **3 F** with **7 F** will *increase* **Land Rents** ($\mathbf{R_A}, \mathbf{r_A}$) with, $\boldsymbol{\varrho_r(5)}$ = 1.52, (**52** pct.). At *10 miles*, cf. Table 25.1, Land *rents* still increase with near *50* pct. [ $\varrho_r(10) = \frac{3.12}{2.11} = 1.48$ ] by going over to the **7 F** cultivation system. Let us next examine *economically* and *technologically* (productivities) what are behind and actually implied by this **Tellow** *rent increase*: $\boldsymbol{\varrho_r(5) = 1.52}$.

The *Accounting Statement* and (25.43), using $\varrho_m(x)$ and $\varrho_q$, give $\varrho_r(5)$ as—cf. (25.13–25.14), Figs. 25.5, 25.6, and 25.8,

$$\varrho_r(5) = \varrho_m(5)\,\varrho_q = 0.83 \cdot 1.83 = 1.52\,;$$

$$\varrho_m(5) = \frac{m_{A7}(5)}{m_{A3}(5)} = \frac{0.275}{0.332} = 0.83,\ \varrho_q = \frac{q_{A7}}{q_{A3}} = \frac{14.3}{7.82} = 1.83 \tag{25.45}$$

$$\varrho_r(5) = \varrho_\pi(5)\,\varrho_q = 0.83 \cdot 1.83 = 1.52\,;$$

$$\varrho_\pi(5) = \frac{\pi_{A7}(5)}{\pi_{A3}(5)} = \frac{\frac{m_{A7}(5)}{p(5)}}{\frac{m_{A3}(5)}{p(5)}} = \frac{0.275/1.29}{0.332/1.29} = \frac{0.213}{0.257} = 0.83^{19} \tag{25.46}$$

i.e., (25.45–25.46) show *Tellow* total *production* (**Q**)[20] and per ha ($\mathbf{q_A}$) **increased**:[21] **83** pct., $\varrho_q = \frac{q_{A7}}{q_{A3}} = \mathbf{1.83}$, and that the Tellow total *Land Rent* ($\mathbf{R_A}$) and per ha ($\mathbf{r_A}$) have **increased**: 52 pct., $\varrho_r(5) = \frac{r_{A7}(5)}{r_{A3}(5)} = \mathbf{1.52}$. The *Tellow* **profit margin** per rye *unit* (**m**), [ *Land Rent* per output unit ], and **profit rate** of rye *price*, $\pi$, [ *Land Rent* in farm selling price, **p (5)** ] would **decrease**: **17** pct., $\varrho_m(5) = \frac{m_{A7}(5)}{m_{A3}(5)} = 0.83 = \varrho_\pi(5) = \frac{\pi_{A7}(5)}{\pi_{A3}(5)}$—evidently **share** of ***Land Rent*** in *Farm* ***Revenue*** (**Y**) has **decreased** 17 pct., $\boldsymbol{\varrho_{\delta_A}}\mathbf{(5)}= 0.83$, which is illustrated by restating, (25.45–25.46), (25.44) RHS, using *Tellow* **7 F/3 F** *accounting* statements, $\boldsymbol{\delta_A}$, (25.15–25.16):

$$\begin{aligned}\varrho_{MP_A}(5) &= \frac{MP_{A7}(5)}{MP_{A3}(5)} = \mathbf{1.52} = \varrho_{\delta_A}(5)\,\varrho_{AP_A}(5) \\ &= \frac{\delta_{A7}(5)}{\delta_{A3}(5)}\frac{AP_{A7}(5)}{AP_{A3}(5)} = \frac{0.214}{0.257}\cdot\frac{14.3}{7.82} = \mathbf{0.83 \cdot 1.83}\end{aligned} \tag{25.47}$$

The *formula* (25.47) applies analogously with observable ***Revenue*** *shares* for **Labor,** $\boldsymbol{\delta_L}$, **Capital,** $\boldsymbol{\delta_K}$.

## Tellow—Output—Marginal Products of Land, Labor, Capital

The ***implications*** (25.44–25.47) of transition to the **7 F**- cultivation system can be regarded as *consequences* of sharp *increases* (upward **technology shift**) in *average productivity*, $\mathbf{AP_A} = Q/A = \mathbf{q_A}$, and *marginal productivity* $\mathbf{MP_A(x)}$, (25.43), of the production *factor* ***Land***, together with *using* in **7 F**-system

[19] $\varrho_\pi(5) = \varrho_\rho(5) = 0.83 \Leftrightarrow \varrho_\mu(5) = \frac{\mu_{A7}(5)}{\mu_{A3}(5)} = \frac{p(5)/c_{A7}(5)}{p(5)/c_{A3}(5)} = \frac{\frac{1.29}{1.015}}{\frac{1.29}{0.958}} = \frac{1.271}{1.347} = 0.94 = \frac{c_{A3}(5)}{c_{A7}(5)} = \frac{0.958}{1.015} = 0.94$, cf. (25.35–25.36).

[20] The grain production (harvest) of the new *Koppelwirtschaft* in Holstein, cf. note 25, Figs.25.21–25.22, increased a bit below *100 percent*, from the reduction of *fallow* and the new **7-field** rotations with grass and cattle, cf. Stamer (1998, p. 31). Regarding Norfolk Estate of landlord Thomas W. Coke, we may note as Parker (1955, p. 157): "In fact, in the *twenty* years, 1776–96, *rents* in Norfolk were *not* even *doubled*, being increased just over 1.5 times" (**50** *pct.*). One of the major instruments of agrarian change was the *long lease* (Coke gave 21-year leases as his usual practice). Tenant farmers were stipulated "not to sow 3 crops of grain successively - but endeavour to adhere to a **six-course** rotation", Parker (1955, p. 161).

[21] On further explanation of the *model* increases in production by the transition to 7 **F**: $\varrho_q = \frac{q_{A7}}{q_{A3}} = \mathbf{1.83}$, see (25.67–25.68).

**different amounts** of *factor services* (factor flows) from all **three** factors: *Land*, *Labor*, and *Capital*, $(A, L, K)$.

So far, we have accounted for the **7 F/3 F** ***land productivities***—$\mathbf{q_A} = Q/A$: 14.3, 7.82—by having the Land *cultivation intensities* calculated from their respective **activity** ratios: $b_i = q_i/A = a_i\, q_A,\ i = 1, 2, 3, 4$, cf. (25.30–25.31). With more data, *activity ratios* can give *measures* of **factor** *ratios*: $\mathbf{l_A} = L/A$, $\mathbf{k_A} = K/A$, for **7 F/3 F**—by using the **Tellow** accounting records in *Taler* and activity costs in *rye equivalents*.

To obtain *measures* of the *factor services* (**inputs**) of **A**, **L**, **K**, we will use their cost share estimates, as *factor cost* and *factor services* is here the same thing—and with here *Total Revenues* = *Total Costs*.

Total Revenues (***Y*** **=** ***p Q***) and various costs elements were given in *Tellow* Accounting Statements above.

In **7 F/3 F**, the costs/remuneration, $\widetilde{\mathbf{R}}_{\mathbf{A}}$, of **Land services** are assigned by summing *sowing* cost, $C_1$, and *land* (use) *rentals*, $R_A$, $[\,\widetilde{R}_A = R_A + C_1 = r_A\, A + p\, b_1\, A = (r_A + p\, b_1)\, A \equiv \widetilde{r}_A\, A\,]$. Total Costs are:

**7 F.**

$$\widetilde{R}_A = R_A + C_1 = 1492\,,\quad wL = C_{2x} + C_{3x} = 1113\,,$$
$$r_K\, K = C_4 + C_{2m} + C_{3m} = 1451 \tag{25.48}$$

**3 F.**

$$\widetilde{R}_A = R_A + C_1 = 913\,,\quad wL = C_{2x} + C_{3x} = 536\,,$$
$$r_K\, K = C_4 + C_{2m} + C_{3m} = 770 \tag{25.49}$$

As to the cost of **Labor services, w L**, in (25.48–25.49), they are estimated by regarding them as being essentially the **local** *components* of the *cultivation*, $C_{2x}$, and *harvesting*, $C_{3x}$, costs. The cost of **Capital services,** $\mathbf{r_K K}$, in (25.48–25.49), are estimated from seeing them as *consisting* of the *general* cost, $C_4$, and the cost of *equipment*, horses, and machinery involved in *cultivation*, $C_{2m}$, and *harvesting*, $C_{3m}$.

Having the actual Taler sizes of $\mathbf{Y} = \mathbf{p\,Q}$, we get from (25.48–25.49), the respective *factor cost* ***shares*** as:

**7 F.**

$$p\,Q = 4056 = \widetilde{r}_A A + wL + r_K K\,,\ \widetilde{\epsilon}_A = \frac{\widetilde{r}_A\, A}{p\,Q} = 0.368,$$
$$\epsilon_L = \frac{wL}{p\,Q} = 0.274,\ \epsilon_K = \frac{r_K K}{p\,Q} = 0.358 \tag{25.50}$$

**3 F.**

$$p\,Q = 2219 = \widetilde{r}_A A + wL + r_K K\,,\ \widetilde{\epsilon}_A = \frac{\widetilde{r}_A\, A}{p\,Q} = 0.411,$$
$$\epsilon_L = \frac{wL}{p\,Q} = 0.242,\ \epsilon_K = \frac{r_K K}{p\,Q} = 0.347 \tag{25.51}$$

With the *marginal revenue product* (MRP) of any factor as defined by its marginal productivity and the product price ($p$), cf. (25.33–25.34), the *cost shares* (25.50–25.51) are *ratios* of marginal and average productivities:

$$\textbf{7 F..} \quad \widetilde{\epsilon_A} = \frac{\widetilde{r_A}/p}{Q/A} = \frac{\widetilde{MP_A}}{AP_A} = 0.368, \quad \epsilon_L = \frac{w/p}{Q/L} = \frac{MP_L}{AP_L} = 0.274,$$

$$\epsilon_K = \frac{r_K/p}{Q/K} = \frac{MP_K}{AP_K} = 0.358 \tag{25.52}$$

$$\textbf{3 F.} \quad \widetilde{\epsilon_A} = \frac{\widetilde{r_A}/p}{Q/A} = \frac{\widetilde{MP_A}}{AP_A} = 0.411, \quad \epsilon_L = \frac{w/p}{Q/L} = \frac{MP_L}{AP_L} = 0.242,$$

$$\epsilon_K = \frac{r_K/p}{Q/K} = \frac{MP_K}{AP_K} = 0.347 \tag{25.53}$$

By known $\mathbf{AP_A}$ of land in 7 F/3 F, (25.30–25.31) and **Tellow**, $\mathbf{p\,(5) = p = 1.29}$, we get by (25.52–25.53), cf. (25.48–25.49),

$$\textbf{7 F.} \quad AP_A = 14.3\,; \ \widetilde{MP_A} = 0.368 \cdot 14.3 = 5.26\,;$$

$$\widetilde{r_A} = 1.29 \cdot 5.26 = 6.78\,; \ \widetilde{R_A} = 6.78 \cdot 220 = 1492 \tag{25.54}$$

$$\textbf{3 F.} \quad AP_A = 7.82\,; \ \widetilde{MP_A} = 0.411 \cdot 7.82 = 3.22\,;$$

$$\widetilde{r_A} = 1.29 \cdot 3.22 = 4.15\,; \ \widetilde{R_A} = 4.15 \cdot 220 = 913 \tag{25.55}$$

where for 7 F/3 F *gross rent*: $\boldsymbol{\widetilde{r_A} = r_A + p\,b_1}$, *gross* marginal product: $\widetilde{MP_A} = MP_A + b_1$, $\widetilde{\epsilon_A} = \epsilon_A + \frac{b_1}{q_A}$, relations and numbers can be checked by (25.54–25.55) and (25.44), (25.30–25.31). Whereas the Landrents, $\mathbf{R_A}$ and $\mathbf{r_A}$ by **7 F** *increased* at Tellow with **52** pct., the **Gross** rents, $\widetilde{\mathbf{R_A}}$ and $\widetilde{\mathbf{r_A}}$ *increased* **63** pct., cf. (25.44),

$$\varrho_{\,\widetilde{R}}(5) = \varrho_{\,\widetilde{r}}(5) = \frac{\widetilde{r_{A7}}\,(5)}{\widetilde{r_{A3}}\,(5)} = \frac{6.78}{4.15} = \frac{\widetilde{MP_{A7}}(5)}{\widetilde{MP_{A3}}(5)} = \frac{5.26}{3.22} = \mathbf{1.63}\,;$$

$$\varrho_{\,\widetilde{\epsilon_A}}(5) = \frac{\widetilde{\epsilon_{A7}}\,(5)}{\widetilde{\epsilon_{A3}}\,(5)} = \frac{0.368}{0.411} = \mathbf{0.90} \tag{25.56}$$

The **7 F/3 F** Marginal productivities: $\boldsymbol{\widetilde{MP_A}(x) = MP_A(x) + b_1}$ are *vertical shifts* of the curves in Fig. 25.15.

To explicitly derive average and marginal productivities of Land, Labor, and Capital in (25.52–25.53), it is useful to **restate** all *total factor cost/revenue* and their *shares* (25.50–25.51) in **ray equivalents,** $\boldsymbol{A_q}, \boldsymbol{L_q}, \boldsymbol{K_q}$:

**7 F.**
$$A_q = \frac{R_A}{p} + q_1 = 671 + 485 = 1156, \;\; L_q = q_2 + q_3 = 863,$$
$$K_q = q_4 + \frac{C_m}{p} = 1125\,; \;\; A_q + L_q + K_q = Q \qquad (25.57)$$

**3 F.**
$$A_q = \frac{R_A}{p} + q_1 = 443 + 265 = 708, \;\; L_q = q_2 + q_3 = 416,$$
$$K_q = q_4 + \frac{C_m}{p} = 596\,; \;\; A_q + L_q + K_q = Q \qquad (25.58)$$

We have already used $A_q$ in $\widetilde{R_A}$ (25.48–25.51) to get (25.57–25.58)—as could be done by *knowing size* of **A** = **220** ha. As to using the 7 F/3 F numbers of $L_q$ in (25.57–25.58), we *restate* $L_q$ in *equivalent monetary* (Taler) forms:

$$p\,L_q = C_{2x} + C_{3x} = w\,L = p\,MP_L\,L = p\,\epsilon_L AP_L\,L = p\,\epsilon_L\,Q = \epsilon_L\,Y \qquad (25.59)$$

Knowing only, $p\,L_q = p\,\epsilon_L\,Q = \epsilon_L\,Y$, in (25.59), we **cannot** proceed further without having *additional data measuring* either **L** or **w**. We found some proper *estimates* of *labor input* **L** in **3 F** to be **24** *man-years,*[22] i.e, labor services of **24** annual *full time* workers *per year.*

With **L** = **24,** $Q = 1720$, we get from (25.58–25.59):

$$L_q = MP_L\,L = 416\,; \; L = 24: \; MP_L = \frac{416}{24} = 17.33\,;$$
$$w = 1.29 \cdot 17.33 = 22.35\,; \; AP_L = \frac{1720}{24} = 71.7 \qquad (25.60)$$

**A** = 220 ha and (25.60) give the *factor* ratio: **L/A** = $l_A$ = **0.11**. Next, *capital input* (services) measured as *ray-equivalents,* $\mathbf{K_q}$ = **596,** (25.58), can alternatively here be *converted* into labor input units, *man-years.* Hence the

[22] von Thünen (1990, p. 610) gives various labor services of **11** *day laborers.* Hippauf (2000, p. 168) gives **13** *manor workers.*

*factor* ratios: $\mathbf{k} = K/L$ and $\mathbf{k_A} = K/A$ follow, (25.61), as do as well, $\mathbf{AP_K}$ and $\mathbf{MP_K}$ by (25.53):

$$\textbf{3 F.} \quad \frac{L}{A} = \frac{24}{220} = 0.11\,;\; L_q = 416,\; 1\,L = \frac{416}{24} = 17.33\,;$$

$$K_q = 596,\; K = \frac{596}{17.33} = 34.4,\; \frac{K}{L} = \frac{34.4}{24} = 1.4$$

$$\textbf{3 F.} \quad \frac{K}{A} = \frac{34.4}{220} = 0.16\,;\; AP_K = \frac{1720}{34.4} = 50\,;$$

$$MP_K = 0.347 \cdot 50 = 17.4\,;\; r_K = 1.29 \cdot 17.4 = 22.4 \tag{25.61}$$

Finally, note that *input procedures* (25.58–25.61) comply with *Tellow* revenue/cost (Taler) **accounting**, (25.51):

$$\begin{aligned} \textbf{3 F.} \quad Y = 2219 &= \tilde{r_A} A + wL + r_K K = 4.15 \cdot 220 \\ &+ 22.35 \cdot 24 + 22.4 \cdot 34.4 \\ &= 913 + 536 + 770 = 2219 \end{aligned} \tag{25.62}$$

Similarly, *measuring* Labor and Capital as in (25.60–25.61) can be applied to **7 F**, (25.57),—giving the **7 F** results:

$$\textbf{7 F.} \quad L_q = 863,\; L = \frac{863}{17.33} = 49.8\,;\; K_q = 1125,$$

$$K = \frac{1125}{17.33} = 64.9\,;\; \frac{K}{L} = \frac{64.9}{49.8} = 1.3 = \frac{K_q}{L_q} \tag{25.63}$$

$$\textbf{7 F.} \quad \frac{L}{A} = \frac{49.8}{220} = 0.23;\; AP_L = \frac{3144}{49.8} = 63.1;$$

$$MP_L = 0.274 \cdot 63.1 = 17.3\,;\; w = 1.29 \cdot 17.3 = 22.32 \tag{25.64}$$

$$\textbf{7 F.} \quad \frac{K}{A} = \frac{64.9}{220} = 0.30;\; AP_K = \frac{3144}{64.9} = 48.4;$$

$$MP_K = 0.358 \cdot 48.4 = 17.33;\; r_K = 1.29 \cdot 17.33 = 22.36 \tag{25.65}$$

satisfying *Tellow* revenue/cost (Taler) **accounting**, (25.50), with $p(5) = p = 1.29$:

$$\begin{aligned} \textbf{7 F.} \quad Y = 4056 &= \tilde{r_A} A + wL + r_K K = 6.78 \cdot 220 + 22.32 \cdot 49.8 \\ &+ 22.36 \cdot 64.9 \\ &= 1492 + 1113 + 1451 = 4056 \end{aligned} \tag{25.66}$$

How much *gross marginal products* (rents) of **Land**, $\varrho_{\tilde{r}}(5) = \frac{\widetilde{r_{A7}}(5)}{\widetilde{r_{A3}}(5)} = 1.63$— are *increased* by the **adoption** of the *cultivation* system **7 F** was *seen* in (25.56)- which will now be explained by factor ratios.

The labor/land, capital/land and capital/labor, **factor ratios**: $l_A = L/A$, $k_A = K/A$, $k = K/L$, **changed** from **7 F** to **3 F**, as seen in (25.67–25.68): $\varrho_{l_A}, \varrho_{k_A}, \varrho_k$—and the *implications* for the **changes** in **average** and **marginal** productivities of **Labor** and **Capital**, (25.70–25.71), follow from (25.60), (25.64) and (25.61), (25.65), as:[23]

$$\frac{Q_{A7}}{Q_{A3}} = \frac{3144}{1720} = \frac{b_{1A7}}{b_{1A3}} = \frac{2.2}{1.2} = \varrho_{b_1} = \varrho_q$$

$$= \frac{q_{A7}}{q_{A3}} = \frac{14.3}{7.82} = \mathbf{1.83} = \varrho_{q^*} = \frac{q^*_{A7}}{q^*_{A3}} = \frac{12.1}{6.61} \quad (25.67)$$

$$\varrho_{l_A} = \frac{l_{A7}}{l_{A3}} = \frac{0.23}{0.11} = \mathbf{2.09}\ ; \quad \varrho_{k_A} = \frac{k_{A7}}{k_{A3}} = \frac{0.30}{0.16} = \mathbf{1.88}\ ;$$

$$\varrho_k = \frac{k_7}{k_3} = \frac{1.3}{1.4} = \mathbf{0.93} \quad (25.68)$$

$$\varrho_{AP_A}(5) = \frac{AP_{A7}(5)}{AP_{A3}(5)} = \frac{14.3}{7.82} = 1.83\ ;$$

$$\varrho_{\widetilde{MP_A}}(5) = \frac{\widetilde{MP_{A7}}(5)}{\widetilde{MP_{A3}}(5)} = \frac{5.26}{3.22} = 1.63 = \frac{6.78}{4.15} = \varrho_{\tilde{r}_A}(5) \quad (25.69)$$

$$\varrho_{AP_L}(5) = \frac{AP_{L7}(5)}{AP_{L3}(5)} = \frac{63.1}{71.7} = 0.88\ ;$$

$$\varrho_{MP_L}(5) = \frac{MP_{L7}(5)}{MP_{L3}(5)} = \frac{17.33}{17.3} = 1.00 = \frac{22.32}{22.35} = \varrho_w(5) \quad (25.70)$$

[23] If the labor input estimate (25.60) of **3F** was changed to ***L* = 40 *man-years***, then 1 L = $L_q/40$ = 416/40 = 10.4 = $MP_L$, $AP_L$ = 1720/40= 4, and K= $K_q/10.4$ = 596/10.4= 57.3, $AP_K$ = 1720/57.3 = 30.0, $MP_K = \epsilon_K AP_K$ = 0.347 · 30 = 10.4, $l_A$ = 40/220 = 0.182, $k_A$ = 57.3/220 = 0.260. Similarly, *7F* (25.63–25.65) give: L = 863/10.4 = 83.0, K=1125/10.4 = 108.2, $AP_L$ = 3144/83 = 37.9, $MP_L$ = 10.38, $AP_K$ = 29.06, $MP_K$ = 10.4, $l_A$ = 0.377, $k_A$ = 0.492.

Thus, it can be verified that the alternative L, here by a proportion: 24/40 = 0.6, just changes the sizes of *all*: $l_A, k_A, AP_L, MP_L, AP_K, MP_K$—in both 3 F and 7 F with the *same* proportion: 0.6. Hence, all the **comparisons**: $\varrho_{l_A}, \varrho_{k_A}, \varrho_{AP_L}, \varrho_{MP_L}, \varrho_{AP_K}, \varrho_{MP_K}$, for **3 F** and **7 F** (25.67–25.71) still **hold**—they are *invariant* to specific numbers of L = 24 or L = 40. The invariances are due to (25.57–25.58).

$$\varrho_{AP_K}(5) = \frac{AP_{K7}(5)}{AP_{K3}(5)} = \frac{48.4}{50} = 0.97 \ ;$$

$$\varrho_{MP_K}(5) = \frac{MP_{K7}(5)}{MP_{K3}(5)} = \frac{17.33}{17.4} = 1.00 = \frac{22.36}{22.4} = \varrho_{r_K}(5) \qquad (25.71)$$

Here we note in (25.67) that, $\varrho_{b_1}$, and $\varrho_q$, $\varrho_{q^*}$ for *gross/net* outputs of **7 F** and **3 F** increased with the *same* rate: $\varrho_q = \varrho_{q^*} = \mathbf{1.83}$—due to equality of their *sowing activity parameter*—$a_1 = 0.154$, (25.17–25.18).

By (25.30–25.31), **Total** factor *input* per *hectare*, measured by *Land intensities* (activity ratio, b) rose **94 pct.**:

$$b_{A7} = \frac{q}{A} = \mathbf{9.0}, \quad b_{A3} = \frac{q}{A} = \mathbf{4.65} \ ; \quad \varrho_{b_A} = \frac{b_{A7}}{b_{A3}} = \frac{9.0}{4.65} = \mathbf{1.94} \qquad (25.72)$$

Transition from **3 F** to **7 F** reduces *Fallow* form 1/3 to 1/7, i.e. increase utilized (effective) land area by circa **30 pct.** [ (6/7)/(2/3) = 1.285 ]. Land *intensity* (factor *ratios*) nearly **doubled** (Labor more, 2.09), Land productivity (*Average* product, $q_A$) increased **80 pct.** (1.83) [ diminishing Marginal products, as e.g., (25.73–25.74)]. The Tellow Average product (output) increase, $\varrho_{AP_A} = \mathbf{1.83}$ does **not** represent only increased *grain* (rye) production, but includes *ray equivalent* sales (outputs) of *mutton, wool* (sheep farming), cf. note 18. Besides the picture of the Land intensity (factor) ratios, what also *stands out* in (25.67–25.72) is that the *Average* products of *Labor* and *Capital* has ***not*** increased (but declined) and that their *Marginal productivity* remain the same as before, **3 F**. The *capital-labor* ratio, (K/L), has only *declined* a bit, (25.68), and accordingly left their relative and absolute *factor prices* (25.70–25.71) unchanged. Clearly, the **agricultural system** change—**3 F-7 F**—have only increased *land productivity* and *land rents*—**not** *labor* productivity.

We return to (25.67–25.72) and comparisons of the **7F-3F** *farming systems* with *history* records in Sect. "Agricultural Systems, History, Industries, Growth, and Trade".

### *CES Production Function Calibrated upon Tellow Accounts*

*Tellow results* (25.67–25.71) are *not* tied to particular *production* functions. But we will use *linear homogeneous* functions, $Q = F[A, L, K] = A f(l_A, k_A)$—with *intensive* form, $q_A = f(l_A, k_A)$—of **CES** function:

$$Q = \gamma\,(\alpha_A A^{\rho} + \alpha_L L^{\rho} + \alpha_K K^{\rho})^{\frac{1}{\rho}} \ ;$$
$$\gamma > 0; \ \alpha_A + \alpha_L + \alpha_K = 1 \ ; \ -\infty \le \rho \le 1 \qquad (25.73)$$

$$q_A = \frac{Q}{A} = \gamma\,(\alpha_A + \alpha_L[l_A]^{\rho} + \alpha_K[k_A]^{\rho})^{\frac{1}{\rho}} \ ; \quad \sigma = \frac{1}{1-\rho} \qquad (25.74)$$

By (25.73), we have:

$$\frac{\partial Q}{\partial A} = \frac{\alpha_A \cdot Q \cdot A^{\rho-1}}{\alpha_A A^{\rho} + \alpha_L L^{\rho} + \alpha_K K^{\rho}} \,,$$
$$\frac{\partial Q}{\partial L} = \frac{\alpha_L \cdot Q \cdot L^{\rho-1}}{\alpha_A A^{\rho} + \alpha_L L^{\rho} + \alpha_K K^{\rho}} \,,$$
$$\frac{\partial Q}{\partial K} = \frac{\alpha_K \cdot Q \cdot K^{\rho-1}}{\alpha_A A^{\rho} + \alpha_L L^{\rho} + \alpha_K K^{\rho}} \tag{25.75}$$

$$\frac{\frac{\partial Q}{\partial A}}{\frac{Q}{A}} = \alpha_A \, \gamma \, [\alpha_A + \alpha_L \, l_A^{\rho} \, + \alpha_K \, k_A^{\rho} \,]^{\frac{1}{\rho}-1},$$
$$\frac{\frac{\partial Q}{\partial L}}{\frac{Q}{L}} = \alpha_L \, \gamma \, [\alpha_A + \alpha_L \, l_A^{\rho} \, + \alpha_K \, k_A^{\rho} \,]^{\frac{1}{\rho}-1},$$
$$\frac{\frac{\partial Q}{\partial K}}{\frac{Q}{K}} = \alpha_K \, \gamma \, [\alpha_A + \alpha_L \, l_A^{\rho} \, + \alpha_K \, k_A^{\rho} \,]^{\frac{1}{\rho}-1} \tag{25.76}$$

**CES** functions (25.73–25.74) can have the *parameters*, (rounded), cf. (25.52–25.53), and so have, $q_A, l_A, k_A$, (25.61–25.65):

**7 F.** $\alpha_A = 0.37 \,, \ \alpha_L = 0.27 \,, \ \alpha_K = 0.36 \;;$

$$\rho = -0.09 \,, \ \gamma = 33.4 \;; \ q_A = 14.3 \,, \ l_A = 0.23 \,, \ k_A = 0.30 \tag{25.77}$$

**3 F.** $\alpha_A = 0.41 \,, \ \alpha_L = 0.24 \,, \ \alpha_K = 0.35 \;;$

$$\rho = -0.11 \,, \ \gamma = 26.6 \;; \ q_A = 7.82 \,, \ l_A = 0.11 \,, \ k_A = 0.16 \tag{25.78}$$

From (25.75), we get:

$$MRS_{L\,K} = \frac{\frac{\partial Q}{\partial L}}{\frac{\partial Q}{\partial K}} = \frac{MP_L}{MP_K} = \frac{\alpha_L}{\alpha_K}\left[\frac{K}{L}\right]^{1-\rho} = \frac{w}{r_K} \;;$$
$$MRS_{A\,L} = \frac{MP_A}{MP_L} = \frac{\alpha_A}{\alpha_L}\left[\frac{A}{L}\right]^{1-\rho} = \frac{r_A}{w} \tag{25.79}$$

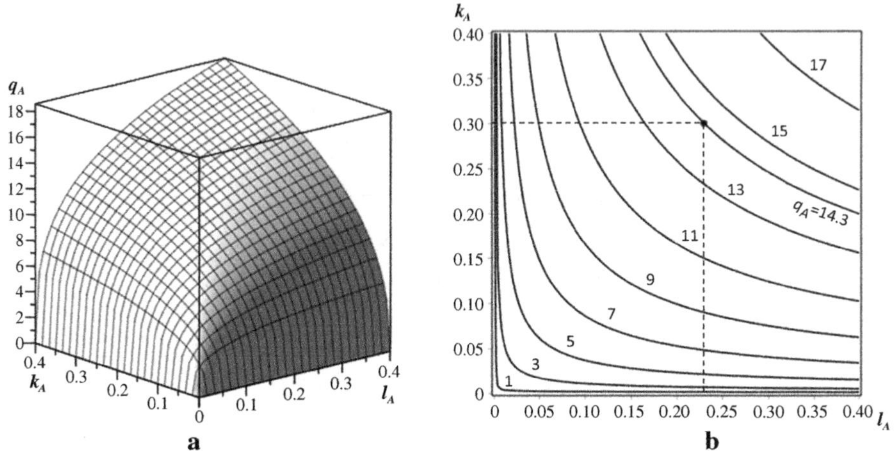


**Fig. 25.16** (**a**) CES function of **7 F**: $q_A = f\,(l_A, k_A)$, (25.74–25.77). (**b**) Isoquants of **7 F**: $q_A = f\,(l_A, k_A)$, (25.74–25.77)

and use the *ratio*, (25.79)—*Marginal* rate of *Factor Substitution*—to calibrate **CES**, (25.73), as follows:

$$\textbf{7 F.}\quad \frac{17.30}{17.33} = \frac{MP_L}{MP_K} = \frac{\alpha_L}{\alpha_K}\left[\frac{K}{L}\right]^{1-\rho} = \frac{0.27}{0.36}\,[\,1.3\,]^{1-\rho} \Leftrightarrow \rho = -0.09\,;$$

$$\sigma = \frac{1}{1-\rho} = \frac{1}{1.09} = 0.92 \tag{25.80}$$

$$\textbf{3 F.}\quad \frac{17.33}{17.40} = \frac{MP_L}{MP_K} = \frac{\alpha_L}{\alpha_K}\left[\frac{K}{L}\right]^{1-\rho} = \frac{0.24}{0.35}\,[\,1.4\,]^{1-\rho} \Leftrightarrow \rho = -0.11\,;$$

$$\sigma = \frac{1}{1-\rho} = \frac{1}{1.11} = 0.90 \tag{25.81}$$

where the **7 F** and **3 F** *estimates* of $\rho$ are *calibrated* from the expressions of *marginal* productivity ratios (25.80–25.81) - using the relevant **7 F** and **3 F** *numbers* in (25.77–25.78), (25.63–25.65), (25.60–25.61); the $\gamma$ *sizes* satisfy (25.74–25.78).

The **7 F** and **3 F** *calibrated* **CES** functions, (25.73–25.74), (25.77–25.78), are seen in *diagrams* of Figs. 25.16 and 25.17.

In Fig. 25.18 is shown for—$q_A = 14.3$, $l_A = 0.23$, $k_A = 0.30$—of **7 F**, (25.77), a CES function with the *assigned* substitution[24] of *lower* size: $\rho =$

[24] In Chap. 3 was later (1848) at Tellow for Labor and Capital, estimated, $\sigma = 1.4$, at K/L = 13.8.

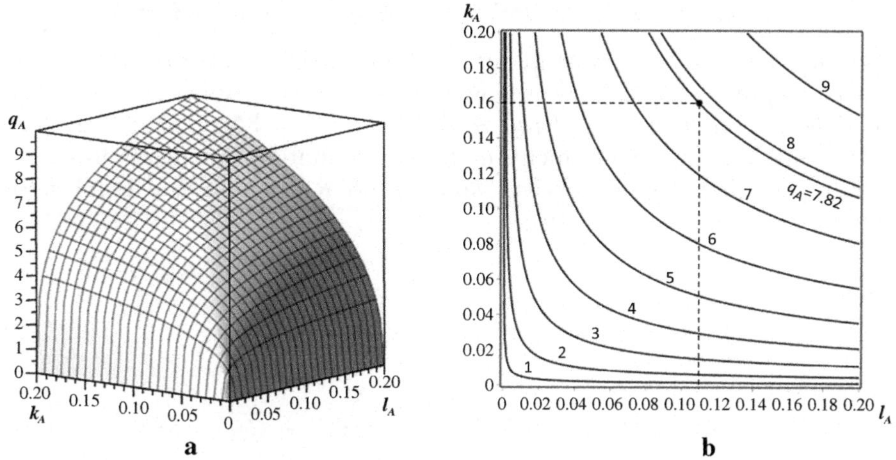


**Fig. 25.17** (**a**) *CES function* of **3 F**: $q_A = f(l_A, k_A)$, (25.74), (25.78). (**b**) *Isoquants* of **3 F**: $q_A = f(l_A, k_A)$, (25.74), (25.78)

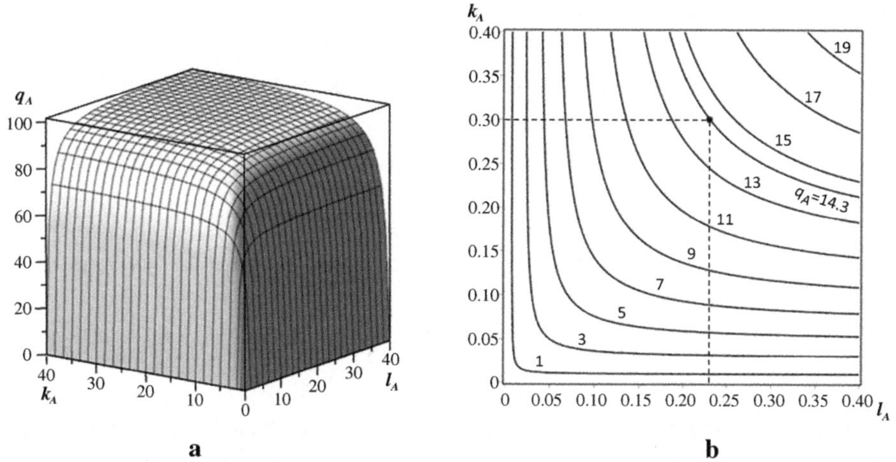


**Fig. 25.18** (**a**) *CES function* of **7 F**: $q_A = f(l_A, k_A)$, (25.77), $\rho = -1, \gamma = 39.2$. (**b**) *Isoquants* of **7 F**: $q_A = f(l_A, k_A)$, (25.77), $\rho = -1, \gamma = 39.2$

$-1$, $(\sigma = 1/2)$[25] that with *same*, $\alpha_A = 0.37$, $\alpha_L = 0.27$, $\alpha_K = 0.36$, implies a *higher* size of: $\gamma = 39.2$ (TFP, common/neutral Total Factor Productivity).

[25] In Chap. 3 was given the initial-value calibrated, (3.66–3.68), two-factor CES function with, $\sigma = 2$.

### *Factor Shares, Factor Prices, and Marginal Productivities*

To obtain here again appropriate marginal productivity *measures* of the *factor services* (**inputs**) of **A**, **L**, **K**, we will use their factor share estimates with Tellow Total *Factor Income* = Total *Value Added*, $= \boldsymbol{p\,Q^*} = \boldsymbol{Y^*}$, cf. (25.39–25.40), for various factor income elements in *Tellow* Accounting Statements above.

Remuneration of **Land services**, *land rentals*, $R_A$, $= r_A\,A$, and **Total** factor income were, cf. (25.48–25.49):

7 F.
$$A = 220;\ R_A = 866,\ wL = C_{2x} + C_{3x} = 1113,$$
$$r_K\,K = C_4 + C_{2m} + C_{3m} = 1451 \tag{25.82}$$

3 F.
$$A = 220;\ R_A = 571,\ wL = C_{2x} + C_{3x} = 536,$$
$$r_K\,K = C_4 + C_{2m} + C_{3m} = 770 \tag{25.83}$$

Having the actual Taler sizes of $\mathbf{Y}^*_{\mathbf{A}} = \mathbf{p}\,\mathbf{Q}^* = \mathbf{Y}^*$, we get from (25.82–25.83), the respective **factor shares** as:

7 F.
$$\mathbf{Y}^* = p\,Q^* = 3430 = r_A A + wL + r_K K,\ \epsilon_A^* = \frac{r_A\,A}{p\,Q^*} = 0.252,$$
$$\epsilon_L^* = \frac{wL}{p\,Q^*} = 0.324,\ \epsilon_K^* = \frac{r_K K}{p\,Q^*} = 0.424 \tag{25.84}$$

3 F.
$$\mathbf{Y}^* = p\,Q^* = 1877 = r_A A + wL + r_K K,\ \epsilon_A^* = \frac{r_A\,A}{p\,Q^*} = 0.304,$$
$$\epsilon_L^* = \frac{wL}{p\,Q^*} = 0.286,\ \epsilon_K^* = \frac{r_K K}{p\,Q^*} = 0.410 \tag{25.85}$$

With the *marginal revenue product* (MRP) of any factor as defined by its marginal productivity and the product price ($p$), cf. (25.33–25.34), the *factor shares* (25.84–25.85) are *ratios* of marginal and average productivities:

7 F.
$$\epsilon_A^* = \frac{r_A/p}{Q^*/A} = \frac{MP_A}{AP_A} = 0.252,\ \epsilon_L^* = \frac{w/p}{Q^*/L} = \frac{MP_L}{AP_L} = 0.324,$$
$$\epsilon_K^* = \frac{r_K/p}{Q^*/K} = \frac{MP_K}{AP_K} = 0.424 \tag{25.86}$$

3 F.
$$\epsilon_A^* = \frac{r_A/p}{Q^*/A} = \frac{MP_A}{AP_A} = 0.304,\ \epsilon_L^* = \frac{w/p}{Q^*/L} = \frac{MP_L}{AP_L} = 0.286,$$
$$\epsilon_K^* = \frac{r_K/p}{Q^*/K} = \frac{MP_K}{AP_K} = 0.410 \tag{25.87}$$

By (25.39–25.42), **7 F.**: $Q^* = 2659$, $q_A^* = 12.1$, **3 F.**: $Q^* = 1455$, $q_A^* = 6.61$, and with $q_A^* =$ **AP$_A$**, and **Tellow, p(5) = p = 1.29**, we get for the production factor **Land** (A) from (25.86–25.87):

$$\textbf{7 F.} \qquad AP_A = 12.1\,;\; MP_A = 0.252 \cdot 12.1 = 3.05\,;$$
$$r_A = 1.29 \cdot 3.05 = 3.94\,;\; R_A = 3.94 \cdot 220 = 866 \qquad (25.88)$$

$$\textbf{3 F.} \qquad AP_A = 6.61\,;\; MP_A = 0.304 \cdot 6.61 = 2.01\,;$$
$$r_A = 1.29 \cdot 2.01 = 2.593\,;\; R_A = 2.593 \cdot 220 = 571 \qquad (25.89)$$

To *explicitly* derive *average* and *marginal* productivities of **Land, Labor** and **Capital** in (25.86–25.87), it is useful here again to **restate** all *total factor income* and their *shares* (25.84–25.85) in **ray equivalents**, $A_q, L_q, K_q$:

$$\textbf{7 F.} \qquad A_q = \frac{R_A}{p} = 671,\; L_q = q_2 + q_3 = 863,\; K_q = q_4 + \frac{C_m}{p} = 1125\,;$$
$$A_q + L_q + K_q = 2659 = Q^* \qquad (25.90)$$

$$\textbf{3 F.} \qquad A_q = \frac{R_A}{p} = 443\,,\; L_q = q_2 + q_3 = 416,\; K_q = q_4 + \frac{C_m}{p} = 596\,;$$
$$A_q + L_q + K_q = 1455 = Q^* \qquad (25.91)$$

As to using the **7 F/3 F** numbers of $\mathbf{L_q}$ in (25.90–25.91), we *restate* $\mathbf{L_q}$ in *equivalent monetary* (Taler) forms:

$$p\,L_q = C_{2x} + C_{3x} = w\,L = p\,MP_L\,L = p\,\epsilon_L^*\,AP_L\,L = p\,\epsilon_L^*\,Q^* = \epsilon_L^*\,Y^* \qquad (25.92)$$

Knowing only, $\mathbf{p\,L_q} = p\,\epsilon_L^*\,Q^* = \epsilon_L^*\,Y^*$, in (25.92), we *cannot* as before proceed further without having *additional data measuring* either **L** or **w**. We use also here the earlier, cf. (25.60), proper *estimates* of *labor input* **L** in **3 F** to be **24** *man-years*, i.e, labor services of 24 annual *full time* workers *per year*. With **L = 24,** $Q^* =$ 1455, we get from (25.91–25.59):

$$L_q = MP_L\,L = 416\,;\; L = 24 : MP_L = \frac{416}{24} = 17.33\,;$$
$$w = 1.29 \cdot 17.33 = 22.35\,;\; AP_L = \frac{1455}{24} = 60.6 \qquad (25.93)$$

$A = 220$ ha and (25.93) give the *factor* ratio: $\mathbf{L/A = l_A} = 0.11$. *Capital input* (services) measured as *ray-equivalents*, $\mathbf{K_q}$ = **596**, (25.91), can alternatively here be *converted* into labor input units, *man-years.* Hence the *factor* ratios: $\mathbf{k} = K/L$ and $\mathbf{k_A} = K/A$ follow in (25.94), as do, $\mathbf{AP_K}$ and $\mathbf{MP_K}$ by (25.87):

$$\textbf{3 F.} \quad \frac{L}{A} = \frac{24}{220} = 0.11\,;\; L_q = 416,\; \frac{L_q}{L} = \frac{416}{24} = 17.33\;;$$
$$K_q = 596,\; K = \frac{596}{17.33} = 34.4,\; \frac{K}{L} = \frac{34.4}{24} = 1.4$$

$$\textbf{3 F.} \quad \frac{K}{A} = \frac{34.4}{220} = 0.16\;;\; AP_K = \frac{1455}{34.4} = 42.3\;;$$
$$MP_K = 0.410 \cdot 42.3 = 17.3\;;\; r_K = 1.29 \cdot 17.4 = 22.4 \qquad (25.94)$$

The *input procedures* (25.91–25.94) comply with *Tellow* revenue/cost (Taler) **accounting**, (25.85):

$$\textbf{3 F.} \quad Y^* = 1877 = r_A A + wL + r_K K = 2.593 \cdot 220 + 22.35 \cdot 24$$
$$+ 22.4 \cdot 34.4$$
$$= 571 + 536 + 770 = 1877 \qquad (25.95)$$

Similarly, *measuring* Labor and Capital as in (25.93–25.94) is applied to **7 F**, (25.90),—giving the **7 F** results:

$$\textbf{7 F.} \quad L_q = 863,\; L = \frac{863}{17.33} = 49.8\;;\; K_q = 1125,\; K = \frac{1125}{17.33} = 64.9\;;$$
$$\frac{K}{L} = \frac{64.9}{49.8} = 1.3 = \frac{K_q}{L_q} \qquad (25.96)$$

$$\textbf{7 F.} \quad \frac{L}{A} = \frac{49.8}{220} = 0.23\,;\; AP_L = \frac{2659}{49.8} = 53.4\,;$$
$$MP_L = 0.324, \cdot 53.4 = 17.3\;;\; w = 1.29 \cdot 17.3 = 22.32 \qquad (25.97)$$

$$\textbf{7 F.} \quad \frac{K}{A} = \frac{64.9}{220} = 0.30\,;\; AP_K = \frac{2659}{64.9} = 41.0\,;$$
$$MP_K = 0.424 \cdot 41.0 = 17.4\,;\; r_K = 1.29 \cdot 17.4 = 22.43 \qquad (25.98)$$

satisfying *Tellow* factor income (Taler) **accounting**, (25.84), with $p(5) = p = 1.29$:

$$\textbf{7 F.} \qquad Y^* = 3430 = r_A A + wL + r_K K = 3.94 \cdot 220 + 22.32 \cdot 49.8 + 22.43 \cdot 64.9 = 866 + 1113 + 1451 = 3430 \tag{25.99}$$

The labor/land, capital/land and capital/labor, **factor ratios**: $l_A = L/A$, $k_A = K/A$, $k = K/L$, **changed** from **7 F** to **3 F**, seen in (25.100–25.101): $\varrho_{l_A}, \varrho_{k_A}, \varrho_k$—and *implications* for **changes** in **average** and **marginal** productivities of **Land, Labor, Capital**, (25.102–25.104), follow from (25.88), (25.93), (25.97), (25.94), (25.98):

$$\frac{b_{1A7}}{b_{1A3}} = \frac{2.2}{1.2} = \varrho_{b_1} = \varrho_{q^*} = \frac{q^*_{A7}}{q^*_{A3}} = \frac{12.1}{6.61} = 1.83\ ;$$

$$\varrho_{\epsilon^*_A} = \frac{0.252}{0.304} = 0.83\ ;\ \varrho_{l_A} = \frac{l_{A7}}{l_{A3}} = \frac{0.23}{0.11} = 2.09 \tag{25.100}$$

$$\varrho_{k_A} = \frac{k_{A7}}{k_{A3}} = \frac{0.30}{0.16} = 1.88\ ;\ \varrho_k = \frac{k_7}{k_3} = \frac{1.3}{1.4} = 0.93\ ;$$

$$\varrho_{\epsilon^*_L} = \frac{0.324}{0.286} = 1.13\ ;\ \varrho_{\epsilon^*_K} = \frac{0.424}{0.410} = 1.03 \tag{25.101}$$

$$\varrho_{AP_A}(5) = \frac{AP_{A7}(5)}{AP_{A3}(5)} = \frac{12.1}{6.61} = 1.83\ ;$$

$$\varrho_{MP_A}(5) = \frac{MP_{A7}(5)}{MP_{A3}(5)} = \frac{3.05}{2.01} = 1.52 = \frac{3.94}{2.593} = \varrho_{r_A}(5) \tag{25.102}$$

$$\varrho_{AP_L}(5) = \frac{AP_{L7}(5)}{AP_{L3}(5)} = \frac{53.4}{60.6} = 0.88\ ;$$

$$\varrho_{MP_L}(5) = \frac{MP_{L7}(5)}{MP_{L3}(5)} = \frac{17.3}{17.33} = 1.00 = \frac{22.32}{22.35} = \varrho_w(5) \tag{25.103}$$

$$\varrho_{AP_K}(5) = \frac{AP_{K7}(5)}{AP_{K3}(5)} = \frac{41.0}{42.3} = 0.97\ ;$$

$$\varrho_{MP_K}(5) = \frac{MP_{K7}(5)}{MP_{K3}(5)} = \frac{17.4}{17.3} = 1.00 = \frac{22.43}{22.4} = \varrho_{r_K}(5) \tag{25.104}$$

$$7\,\mathbf{F}. \qquad \frac{r_A\,(5)}{w\,(5)} = \frac{MP_{A7}(5)}{MP_{L7}(5)} = \frac{3.05}{17.3} = 0.18 \ ; \qquad (25.105)$$

$$3\,\mathbf{F}. \qquad \frac{r_A\,(5)}{w\,(5)} = \frac{MP_{A3}(5)}{MP_{L3}(3)} = \frac{2.01}{17.33} = 0.12 \ ; \ 1.52 = \frac{0.176}{0.116} = \varrho_{\frac{r_A}{w}} \qquad (25.106)$$

$$\frac{r_A}{w} = MRS_{AL} = \frac{MP_A}{MP_L} = \frac{\epsilon_A^* \cdot AP_A}{\epsilon_L^* \cdot AP_L} = \frac{\epsilon_A^* \cdot L}{\epsilon_L^* \cdot A} = \frac{\epsilon_A^*}{\epsilon_L^*}\, l_A \ ;$$

$$\varrho_{\frac{r_A}{w}} = \frac{\varrho_{\epsilon_A^*}}{\varrho_{\epsilon_L^*}}\, \varrho_{l_A} = \frac{0.828}{1.132} \cdot 2.09 = 1.52 \qquad (25.107)$$

The results (25.100–25.101) are identical to (25.67–25.68), and (25.103–25.104) are nearly identical to (25.70–25.71), despite different sizes of average productivities. The marginal productivities (25.102–25.104) and (25.100–25.101), give the same substitutions elasticities, $\sigma = 0.92, \sigma = 0.90$ as in (25.80–25.81), and **CES** Figures similar to Figs. 25.16 and 25.17. With the **7 F** cultivation (rotation) system, the *rent-wage* ratio, $\frac{r_A}{w}$, is clearly seen to *rise*, 52 pct. in (25.106)–(25.107).

The **CES** restriction of *equal* pairwise substitution elasticity ($\sigma$) imposed on the *three classical* factors, **A**, **L**, **K**, should next, theoretically and empirically, be relaxed by using, e.g., **GCES**, N=3, Chap. 4, upon the *unique historical* economic data, provided by the quantitative **Tellow Estate** *factor income observations*—seen in this section.

## SIX RINGS, GRAIN PRICES, FERTILITY, RIVER CITIES—LAND RENTS

So far we have focused on and compared the *Land Rents*, $\mathbf{r_A(x)}$ and *Cultivation* system of *Rings* 4–5. The so-called *Crop Alternation* (Belgian, Mecklenburg farming) *System* ('Fruchtwechsel-Wirtschaft') of *Ring 3* are as **7F** Land *intensive* $(q_A, l_A, k_A)$ cultivations—without any fallow and grass field replaced by various feed (roots, clover, potatoes) crops. However, *soil* (fertility) differences prevent the data for land rents being directly comparable with **7F** Farming Accounting results (model) of Tellow, $\mathbf{r_A(x)}$ above.

The *second* ring, Forestry, was given particular attention by von Thünen (1990, Ch. 19). Despite high transport costs of heavy timber (compared to grain), long gestation periods, and *Land extensive* methods (small $l_A$, $k_A$), Land **rent-distance** curves, $\mathbf{r_A(x)}$, for firewood (fuel) and lumber were favourable to all other commodities (alternative land uses) rather close to the city (4–7 miles). In accordance with the rent calculations of, von Thünen (1990, p. 198); Hall (1966, p. 123), the $\mathbf{R_A(x)}$ *envelope* of 4 rings in Fig. 25.19, derived by Nellinger (2014, p. 70) includes a forestry part—and where the results in *Ring 1*, (Free

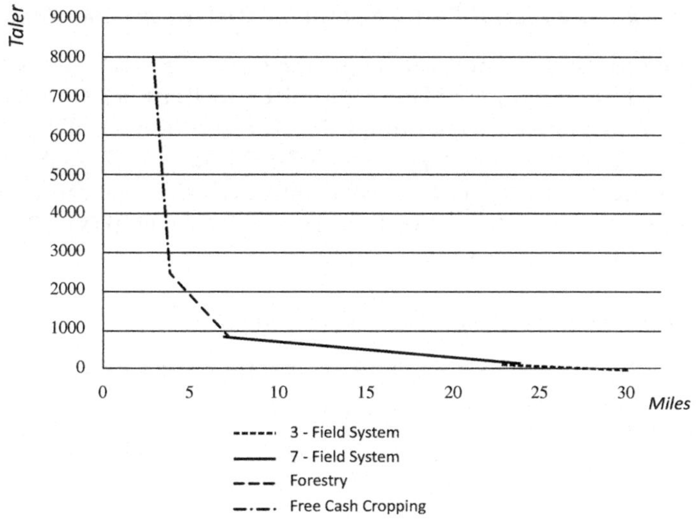


**Fig. 25.19** ***A* = 220 *ha*** - Land Rents, $R_A(x)$: *Envelope of 4 Rings* - linked to $R_A(x)$: **7 F, 3 F** - Fig. 25.11. *Source*: Nellinger (2014, p. 72). cf. Petersen (1944, p. 112)

Cash Cropping) reflect *vegetables* - potatoes (o. dung, m. dung), Nellinger (2014, p. 70) - and *horticultural* products. On early economic geography, see Dunn (1954, p. 178), Grotewold (1959, p. 350).

The **radius (x)** of Land rents $\mathbf{r_A(x)}$ for all six concentric circles around the *central city*, Fig. 25.2, are shown in *upper* half of Fig. 25.20a, with the *ring-boundaries* (**x-miles**) of Ring 6, 5, 4 seen in Table 25.1—Ring 5 ends (6 begins) at **x** = **40** miles, and Ring 4 (**7 F**) ends (5 begins, **3 F**) at, **x** = **24.7** miles. As may be noted in Fig. 25.19, Ring 1 ends (2 begins) at **x** = **4** miles, and Ring 2 (**Forestry**) ends (3 begins) at **x** = **7.3** miles.

In *lower* half of Fig. 25.20a, the plain of "Isolated State" is crossed by navigable river. Assuming that transport cost of *water freight* are one-tenth (**1/10**) of *land freight*, then the lower diagram shows how the *ring-boundaries* (**x-miles**) are changed. The *inner* rings *expand*, and ring 6 (uncultivated) has contracted and disappears entirely near the river. The effects of constructing inland highways would be similar (inner rings expands, if less marked).

The lower ring diagram suggests the regional economic role ('potent engine of growth') of the **River cities**, *Hamburg*, Fig. 25.1b, and *London*, cf. Wrigley (1967, p. 68). On the importance of London (Gregory King tables, 1688, 1696) as market for agricultural produce of the *six* agricultural counties (*wealthiest district*, 1640–1700) *north* of the Thames, see Ernle (1936, p. 146). Using the *Accounts* of King' Hall and King's College, University of Cambridge, von Thünen's Ring system is demonstrated as the zones that supplied *Cambridge* City & University with food during the period, 1450–1560, see Lee (2003, p. 261).

### *City Grain Prices, Land Fertility, and the Radius of Land Rent Rings*

The Local **Land Rent** per **hectare** Marginal *Revenue* Product (Rent)[26] of *Land* (factor *services*), $\mathbf{r_A(x)} = p(x)\,\mathbf{MP_A}$, is Local **Land Rent** per *output* (product) unit (bushel), $\mathbf{m(x)} = R_A(x)/Q$, times the *Average* Product of *Land*, $\mathbf{AP_A} = Q/A = q_A$, i.e.: $\mathbf{r_A(x)} = \mathbf{m(x)\,q_A}$, cf. (25.37–25.38), (25.7–25.8), (25.108). Thus to get the **radius** (outer limit of a cultivated ring), we can use the **root** of $\mathbf{r_A(x) = 0}$, or $\mathbf{m(x) = 0}$, cf. **Fig. 5–6**. Hence, by using, $\mathbf{p\,(x)}$, (25.12), and, $\mathbf{c\,(x)}$, (25.19–25.20), we have:

$$\mathbf{r_A(x)} = 0 \Leftrightarrow m(x) = 0 \Leftrightarrow p(x) - c(x) = 0$$

$$\Leftrightarrow p(x) - c_x(x) - c_m = 0 \Leftrightarrow p(x) - a\,p(x) - c_m = 0 \qquad (25.108)$$

$$\mathbf{r_A(x)} = 0 \Leftrightarrow p(x) = \frac{c_m}{1-a}\,, \; a = \frac{q}{Q}\,;$$

$$(i)\quad \mathbf{p(x)} = p(0) - \mathbf{t(x)} = p(0) - \frac{(p_0\,\alpha_F + \alpha_M)\,x}{\tilde{q} + (\alpha_F - \alpha_Q)\,x} \qquad (25.109)$$

$$\mathbf{r_A(x)} = 0 \Leftrightarrow \mathbf{p(x)} = \frac{c_m}{1-a} \Leftrightarrow \frac{p_0\,\tilde{q} - (p_0\,\alpha_Q + \alpha_M)\,x}{\tilde{q} + (\alpha_F - \alpha_Q)\,x} = \frac{c_m}{1-a} \qquad (25.110)$$

which with **parameters** of $\mathbf{t(x)}$, (25.9–25.10), and **7 F** and **3 F** *sizes* of, $\mathbf{a} = \frac{\mathbf{q}}{\mathbf{Q}}$, (25.17–25.18), $\mathbf{c_m}$, (25.15–25.16), give:

$$\mathbf{7\,F.}\quad \mathbf{p(x)} = \frac{p_0 \cdot 28.57 - (p_0 \cdot 0.357 + 0.326)\,x}{28.57 + 0.157\,x} = \frac{0.204}{1 - 0.628} \qquad (25.111)$$

$$\mathbf{3\,F.}\quad \mathbf{p(x)} = \frac{p_0 \cdot 28.57 - (p_0 \cdot 0.357 + 0.326)\,x}{28.57 + 0.157\,x} = \frac{0.190}{1 - 0.595} \qquad (25.112)$$

[26] Ricardo (1817, 1821, 1965, p. 35): " Rent is that portion of the produce of the earth which is paid (to the landlord) for the use of the original and indestructible powers of the soil. (It is often, however, confounded with interest and profit of capital)".

The Eqs. (25.111–25.112) give *radius* (**x**) of **zero** Land rents to **7 F** or **3 F** for alternative **City** prices: $\mathbf{p_0}$.

$$7\,\mathbf{F}.\quad p_0 = 1.5 : p(x) = \frac{273 - 5.5 \cdot x}{182 + x} = \frac{0.204}{0.382} \Leftrightarrow x = 28.6 \tag{25.113}$$

$$3\,\mathbf{F}.\quad p_0 = 1.5 : p(x) = \frac{273 - 5.5 \cdot x}{182 + x} = \frac{0.190}{0.405} \Leftrightarrow x = 31.4 \tag{25.114}$$

With $\mathbf{p_0} = \mathbf{1.5}$ in (25.111–25.112) give earlier expressions (25.113–25.114), and *radius* (**x**), Table 25.1, Figs. 25.6, 25.7, 25.8, 25.9, 25.10, 25.11, 25.12, 25.13, 25.14, 25.15, 25.16, 25.17, 25.18, 25.19, and 25.20a.

The effects of *lower* City price, e.g., $\mathbf{p_0} = \mathbf{1.5}$ for *radius* (**x**) of **zero** rents to **7 F** or **3 F** follow directly from Eqs. (25.111–25.112) as shown in (25.115–25.116)—giving also $r_A(x)$-*ring boundary*, (25.117), between them.

$$7\,\mathrm{F}.\quad p_0 = 1.2 : p(x) = \frac{218 - 4.8 \cdot x}{182 + x} = \frac{0.204}{0.382}$$
$$\Leftrightarrow 2.034\,x = 46.2 \Leftrightarrow x = 23.7 \tag{25.115}$$

$$3\,\mathbf{F}.\quad p_0 = 1.2 : p(x) = \frac{218 - 4.8 \cdot x}{182 + x} = \frac{0.190}{0.405}$$
$$\Leftrightarrow 2.13\,x = 53.71 \Leftrightarrow x = 26.2 \tag{25.116}$$

$$\mathbf{r_A(x)}\ 7\,\mathrm{F}. = \mathbf{3\,F}. : (2.034\,x - 46.2) \cdot \mathbf{14.3}$$
$$= (2.13\,x - 53.71) \cdot \mathbf{7.82} \Leftrightarrow x = 19.4 \tag{25.117}$$

Comparing (25.115–25.117), with (25.113–25.114) and Table 25.1, the *cultivated* area (*radius* of **3F**) *shrinks* **5.2** miles (31.4-26.2)—and **3F**-ring *width* has widened from before **6.7** miles (31.4-24.7) to **6.8** miles (26.2-19.4).

As to Ring **7 F**, it started before at x = 24.7 miles, Table 25.1, Fig. 25.19; with *lower* $p_0 = 1.2$, Ring **7 F** begins *closer* to City, x = 19.4 miles.

All these results of how much the concentric *Rings* of upper **Fig. 20a** and their *width* will change with lower *City prices* $p_0$ from 1.5 to 0.6 Taler are *depicted* by *radial length* from city—in left panel of Fig. 25.20b.

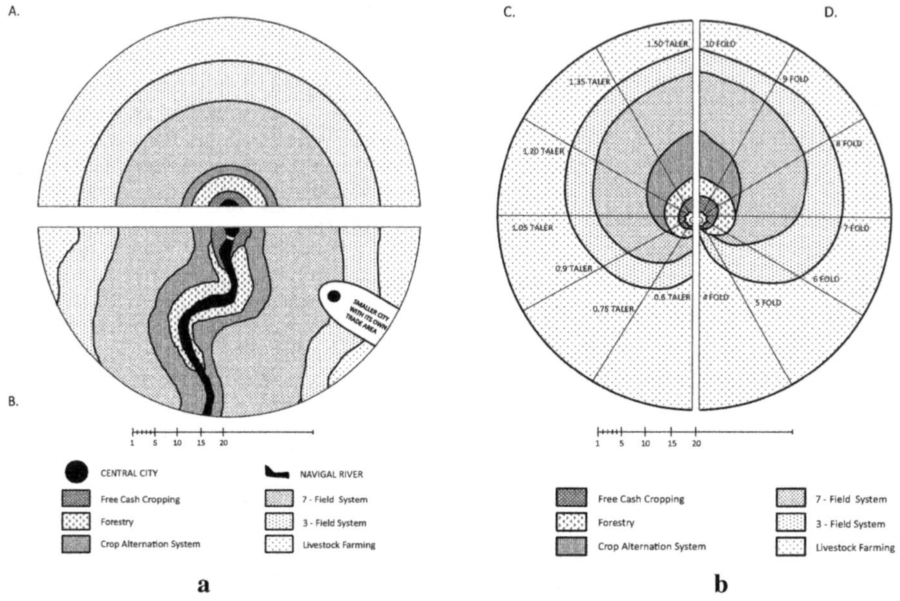


**Fig. 25.20** (**a**) *Land Rent Limits*, $r_A(x)$ - and *Rings*. (**b**) *Land Rent radius*, $r_A(x)$ - and $p_0$, $a = q/Q$. *Source*: von Thünen (1990, p. 387, p. 389); Hall (1966, p. 216, p. 217). See $r_A(x)$, Table 25.1, $R_A(x)$, Fig. 25.19

To demonstrate the implications of **Soil fertility** for *Land Rent* and the concentric *Ring System*, we compare the **8-fold** fertility (maintained assumption) with the **10-fold** alternative. Adjusting **7 F** [ **3 F** ] *outputs* (Q) in the *accounting statements* of Sect. "Tellow Farm Accounts, Revenues, Costs, and Land Rents" to a *higher* soil *fertility*—25 percent, 8- to 10-fold—change the *outputs*[27] to **Q**: 3144 · 1.25 = 3930 [ 1720 · 1.25 = 2150 ]. According to von Thünen (1990, p. 41–42); Hall (1966, p. 29–30), a soil fertility adjustment from 8-fold to 10-fold will change the cost *parameters*: $\mathbf{a} = \frac{\mathbf{q}}{\mathbf{Q}}$, (25.17–25.18), $\mathbf{c_m}$, (25.15–25.16), to become:

**7 F.**

$$Q = 3930;\; Q - q = 1710\,,\; q = 2220\,,\; \frac{Q}{A} = 17.86,$$

$$a = \frac{q}{Q} = 0.565\,,\; c_m = \frac{747}{3930} = 0.19 \tag{25.118}$$

[27] Arithmetically, *scaling up* with, $(1 + \frac{1}{n})$ is equivalent to *scaling down* with, $(1 - \frac{1}{n+1})$: 3144 $(1 + \frac{1}{4})$ = 3930 $(1 - \frac{1}{5})$ = 3144. It appears, von Thünen (1990, p. 39); Hall (1966, p. 26), that it was *original* (10-fold) accounting data that were converted to **8-fold** *Accounting Statements* (empirical data) for **7 F** and **3 F**, Sect. "Tellow Farm Accounts, Revenues, Costs, and Land Rents"—checked by Petersen (1944, p. 41).

**3 F.** $$Q = 2150; \; Q - q = 1000 \,, \; q = 1150 \,, \; \frac{Q}{A} = 9.77 \,,$$

$$a = \frac{q}{Q} = 0.535 \,, \; c_m = \frac{381}{2150} = 0.177 \qquad (25.119)$$

The effects of ***higher*** soil ***fertility*** from **8**- to **10**-fold, (25.118–25.119), for ***radius*** (**x**) of **zero** rents to **7 F** or **3 F** follow by using (25.111–25.112) as shown in (25.120–25.121)—giving also $r_A(x)$-***ring boundary***, (25.122), between them.

**7 F.** $$\frac{Q}{A} = 17.86, \; a = \frac{q}{Q} = 0.565 \;:$$

$$p(x) = \frac{273 - 5.5 \cdot x}{182 + x} = \frac{0.190}{0.435} \Leftrightarrow 2.58\,x = 84.18 \Leftrightarrow x = 32.6 \qquad (25.120)$$

**3 F.** $$\frac{Q}{A} = 9.77, \; a = \frac{q}{Q} = 0.535 \;:$$

$$p(x) = \frac{273 - 5.5 \cdot x}{182 + x} = \frac{0.177}{0.465} \Leftrightarrow 2.74\,x = 94.74 \Leftrightarrow x = 34.6 \qquad (25.121)$$

$$\mathbf{r_A(x)}\ \mathbf{7\,F.} = \mathbf{3\,F.} \;:\; (2.58\,x - 84.18) \cdot \mathbf{17.86} = (2.74\,x - 94.74) \cdot \mathbf{9.77}$$

$$\Leftrightarrow x = 29.9 \qquad (25.122)$$

Comparing (25.120–25.122), with (25.113–25.114) and Table 25.1, the ***cultivated*** area (***radius*** of **3F**) ***expands*** **3.2** miles (34.6-31.4)—and **3F**-ring ***width*** has narrowed from before **6.7** miles (31.4-24.7) to **4.7** miles (34.6-29.9).

As to Ring 7 **F**, it started before at x = 24.7 miles, Table 25.1, Fig. 25.19; with ***higher*** 10-fold, Ring **7 F** now begins at a ***longer distance*** from the City, **x** = **29.9** miles—von Thünen (1990, p. 124); Hall (1966, p. 118).

All these results of how much the concentric ***Rings*** of upper Fig. 25.20a and their ***width*** will change with higher soil ***fertility*** from **8**- to **10-fold** are ***depicted*** by ***radial length*** from city—in right panel of Fig. 25.20b.

Comparing the effects of higher City ***grain prices*** and higher ***soil fertility***, they have ***same*** effects on the cultivation systems:[28] both improve Land rent and promote the expansion of the more ***Land intensive*** **7 F** cultivation system—with fertility being (relatively) a stronger variable—in Fig. 25.20b, halving fertility has stronger agricultural cultivation & production (output) effects than halving central City grain prices.

[28] On further sensitivity analyses of the Land Rents for the systems **7F** and **3F** to a variation of ***grain price*** and ***soil fertility***, see Brauer (1950, p. 156–158).

The *results* from the *analytical-quantitative agricultural models* of the two cultivation systems, **7 F**, **3 F**, will be used as theoretical-empirical *benchmarks* for evaluating the agricultural cultivation reforms and the observable performance of countries (regions) in particular periods of economic history.

*Soil Fertility, Yield-Seed Ratios, Seed per Hectare, and Crop Yields per Hectare*
Agricultural *Land productivity* and *Soil fertility/output* concepts and their measurements have been difficult subjects in agricultural economics and related fields of agro-technology-chemistry-genetics. However, the soil fertility concept (8-, 10-fold) above will here briefly be related to particular important (standard) agronomic *yield* concepts. The *fold* (fertility) measure is called *Yield-Seed ratio*, ratio of *grain harvest* (bushel, hectoliter)/*grain sown* (bushel, hectoliter). The amount of *Seed* is measured: *hectoliter* (bushel) *per hectare* (acre). *Crop Yield* is measured: *hectoliter* (bushel) *per hectare (ha)* (acre)—with relationship:

$$x_A = Crop\ yield\ per\ ha \equiv Yield\ seed\ ratio\ (s_A) \cdot Seed\ per\ ha\ (b_A) \tag{25.123}$$

which for *8-fold, seed* per ha, $b_1 = 2.2$, (25.30), in **7 F**—and in **3 F**, $b_1 = 1.2$—give *Crop yields* per ha, $\mathbf{x_A}$:

$$\mathbf{7\,F} \qquad x_A = 8 \cdot b_1 = 8 \cdot 2.2 = \mathbf{17.6}\ ;\ \widetilde{q_A} = \widetilde{14.3}\ ; \tag{25.124}$$

$$\mathbf{3\,F} \qquad x_A = 8 \cdot b_1 = 8 \cdot 1.2 = \mathbf{9.6}\ ;\ \widetilde{q_A} = \widetilde{7.82} \tag{25.125}$$

The Crop *yields*, $\mathbf{x_A}$, (25.125), represent the potential (*maximum*) grain harvest (*output*) per ha that can be produced ('recovered') with best growing conditions and by using all other production factors most efficiently—from sowing until delivering (selling) grain output from the farm (Tellow). Actual (observed) Land productivities (Average products), $AP_A = \widetilde{q_A}$[29] are lower than $x_A$, but the *gap* (relatively) between them were seemingly the *same* for **7 F** and **3 F**: $x_A/\widetilde{q_A} = 14.3/17.6 = 7.82/9.6 = 0.81$, (25.124), (25.125).

Around year 1800, *sizes* of yield components (25.123) were in *North Sea* area: $x_A = 20, s_A = 10,\ b_A = 2$; *Baltic*: $x_A = 12, s_A = 4,\ b_A = 3$; *Russia*: $x_A = 9, s_A = 3,\ b_A = 3$.—see Van Zanden (1999, p. 361), Kjeldsen-Kragh (2007, p. 127). Further on Soil fertility, Crop yields and Chemical (Nitrogen), Legumes (Biological) fertilizers in Agricultural Revolution, 1750–1880, see Chorley (1981, p. 73), Brunt (2004, p. 194), Allen (2008, p. 202).

We may emphasize, however, that the *increased* Crop yields, ($\boldsymbol{x_A}$), Land productivity ($\boldsymbol{q_A}$), and Land rents ($\boldsymbol{r_A}$)—with **7 F**—were *not* due *soil* (fold)

[29] A tilde-symbol is here put on $\widetilde{q_A}$, (25.125), as our $q_A$ numbers—not directly comparable to single *arable crop yields*, $x_A$—are *ray-equivalents* of several outputs, cf. footnote 9, 18.

fertility improvements, but were *quantitatively accounted* for by *larger* Seed per ha, ($b_A$), (seed *intensity*, $b_1$), together with other *Land intensities*, $l_A, k_A$, (25.100–25.101), of **CES** production functions, (25.73–25.74), by the *factor input measurement* procedures, (25.91–25.99). We may note that adoption of **7 F** cultivation system certainly implied a higher *crop yield per acre*, (**17.6**), (due to larger input of seed per hectare, $b_A$) than **3 F**, (25.125), but the *ratio* of seed to "corn output" were the *same* for both **7F - 3F**, cf. $b_A / Q = q_1 / Q = a_1 = 0.154$, (25.17–25.18), (25.100), indicating that *same soil fertility* assumption of *8-fold* is maintained by *von Thünen*. The higher *crop yield* per hectare must naturally be followed up by more land intensive production method, such that actual *Land productivity, (Q/A)* is increased; on yield and land productivity measurements, see Overton (1996a, p. 72).

## Agricultural Systems, History, Industries, Growth, and Trade

> "The Isolated State presents, in its farming patterns, a picture of one and the same country viewed over several succeeding centuries. Only the *Three-Field* System existed in Mecklenburg a hundred *years ago*, and it alone suited the conditions of that time.—and in the *coming* century *Crop Alternation* may be as widespread as the *Seven-Field* System (*Koppelwirtschaft*) is *today*.
> As a country grows in Wealth and Population, more Intensive Cultivation becomes profitable [ vorteilhaft ]; and if the conditions have reached the stage, where a higher farming system is viable, the efforts of the farmer [ Landwirt] who first introduces it will prove permanent. The new system will prosper on his own land [ Gut], and slowly, but irresistibly, it will spread throughout the country to become the *ruling system*. This is what happened, when the **Seven-Field** System was first introduced in **Mecklenburg**; this is what has happened in **England**, where *Three-Field* System and *Seven-Field* System have given way to the **Crop Alternation** System", von Thünen (1990, p. 263); Hall (1966, p. 158).

### *Agricultural Cultivation Transition—Kingdom of Denmark, 1740–1805*

*Duchy of Holstein*

The German term **Koppelwirtschaft—7 Field System**, cf. Fig. 25.21a and b, originates from the *Duchy* **Holstein**, North of Hamburg, and its agricultural characteristics were *three* elements: 1. **Enclosure** of Land ('Einfriedigung'), Fig. 25.22,[30] by fencing and/or ditches, into several **distinct Fields** ('Kop-

[30] *Enclosure* ('Einfriedigung') of fields by *hedges, fences, walls* ('Wallhecken, Knicks) have conveniences for both use and access to farm buildings and advantages of *reducing labor* in *herding cattle*, preserving manured soil, and land fertility of the fields. For much of the year in the Spring and Summer Season, the cattle would be outside in suitable fenced *rotating private* fields. Smith (1776, 1961, p. 168) noted that cattle dislike dogs: "The advantage of *enclosure* is greater for pasture than for corn. It saves the labor of guarding the cattle, which feed better too when they are not liable to be disturbed by their keeper or his dog". In economic literature, the distinction

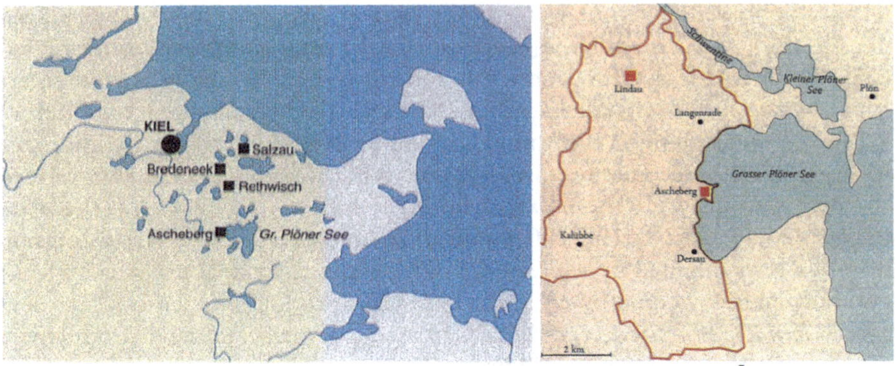


a b

**Fig. 25.21** (**a**) Koppelwirtschaft—East Holstein Estates *Source*: Skriver (2008, p. 62)—Estates: Saltau, Rethwisch, Bredeneek and Ascheberg (**b**) Ascheberg Estate—Manors, Villages *Source*: Lögstrup (2015, p. 104)—Ascheberg Manor Farm, Dairy Lindau, and 3 Villages

peln'), grains and grass (for *livestock* ('Viehhaltung'), along with using: 2. **Rotation** ('Fruchtfolge', *Alternating* cultivation of the *Fields*), combined with: 3. **Consolidation** ('Verkoppelung')[31] of the separate *Fields* into peasant **Farms** of *private* property (ownership or renting) or collective property (ownership).

The famous *Koppelwirtschaft—7 Field System* was used by the end of **1600** on *Manor farms* in the Eastern part of Holstein, Fig. 25.21a. As mentioned above, its merits compared to traditional **3F** was that it—besides the grain fields—had introduced and used grass fields much better than before. Three full years as continuous grass field allowed the grass to grow much stronger, and here having enclosed grass field allowed an early summer hay harvest (for winter food) in one grass field, while the cattle grassing in another one. Moreover the soils of the fields were less exhausted by having longer periods between being used for

between "open fields" and "enclosed fields" has been murky, as it involved much more than fields with hedges (fences), cf. "Enclosure Movement" below.

[31] The *'Enclosure Movement'* with *Koppelwirtschaft* of *village fields* [ *property strips* ('open field')], rearranged into *consolidated farms* ('closed' *property* boundaries) of different sizes with *field enclosures* (hedges, ditches) and *field* (crop) *rotations* ] began already 1739 with Count Hans Rantzau of Ascheberg Estate, Plön, East Holstein. He had been Danish Diplomat in London and learned about the new ideas, *systems* of Land *cultivation*—in particular, what was the proper *size* of *new farms* ('Siedlerstellen'), their *live-stocks* and *equipments*, and what *rental rate* to be expected from the tenant farmer ('Siedler'), cf. Stamer (1998, p. 30). Hans Rantzau obtained more "rent income" ("Pacht") from these peasants ('Siedlers') than before: i.e., partly *villeinage* at Manor and partly, as *rentals* (Landrent) from traditional lease of Village fields and Commons. He was earlier the first to replace *villeinage* of copyholders (Erbpächter) with a *fixed money land rent* (70 Talers) per farm (35 ha), and Christoph Rantzau was the first to abolish *serfdom* ('Leibeigenschaft') at his Estates before 1700, cf. Fridrich Aereboe (1865–1942) in Jannermann (2007, p. 169). More on this so-called Koppelwirtschaft in Schleswig-Holstein with individual farms and enclosure of the fields (in rotation), their regular size, and clearing of shrubs, see Rasmussen (2010b, p. 184).

**Fig. 25.22** Enclosure (Einfriedigung) of Individual Fields and Livestock in Holstein Koppelwirtschaft. *Source*: Stamer (1998, p. 32)

grain crops—and which, according to prevalent opinions and records, "resulted in nearly a *doubling* of the *grain* harvest", Stamer (1998, p. 30) [ cf. (25.67) ].

In Holstein, *villeinage*—the obligatory (unpaid) Labor services (ploughing, sowing, harvesting, spreading dung etc.) provided from peasant village farms (lease-copy holders, family, farmhands) in the fields and barns of the Manor Farms (Demesnes)—was high. Apart from domestic servants, the Manor Farm-Estate *owner* had *few* employees, (only management and supervisory staff). But a *Dairy* belonged to such Holstein Manor Farm-Estate, Fig. 25.21b, and it was run by a Tenant ('Holländer') employing paid workers (mostly milkmaids). As mentioned (note 30), the Ascheberg owner had in 1739 for some copyholders (Erbpächter) replaced the *villeinage* obligation with a *fixed money land rent* (70 Talers) per farm (35 ha)—e.g., a *consolidated* peasant *farm* (consisting of similar *enclosed* fields as known from the Manor Farm), with some *new* buildings (farmhouse and stable) outside the village—as seen in Fig. 25.22.

The experience in Holstein with the three elements—enclosure of fields, field rotation, consolidation of fields into separate farms—was observed with interest further north in Jutland[32] and Seeland, Fig. 25.23.

[32] Smith (1790, 1961, vol.2, p. 198) referred to trade with this region: "It is thus that Holland draws a great part of its subsistence from other countries; live cattle from Holstein and Jutland, and

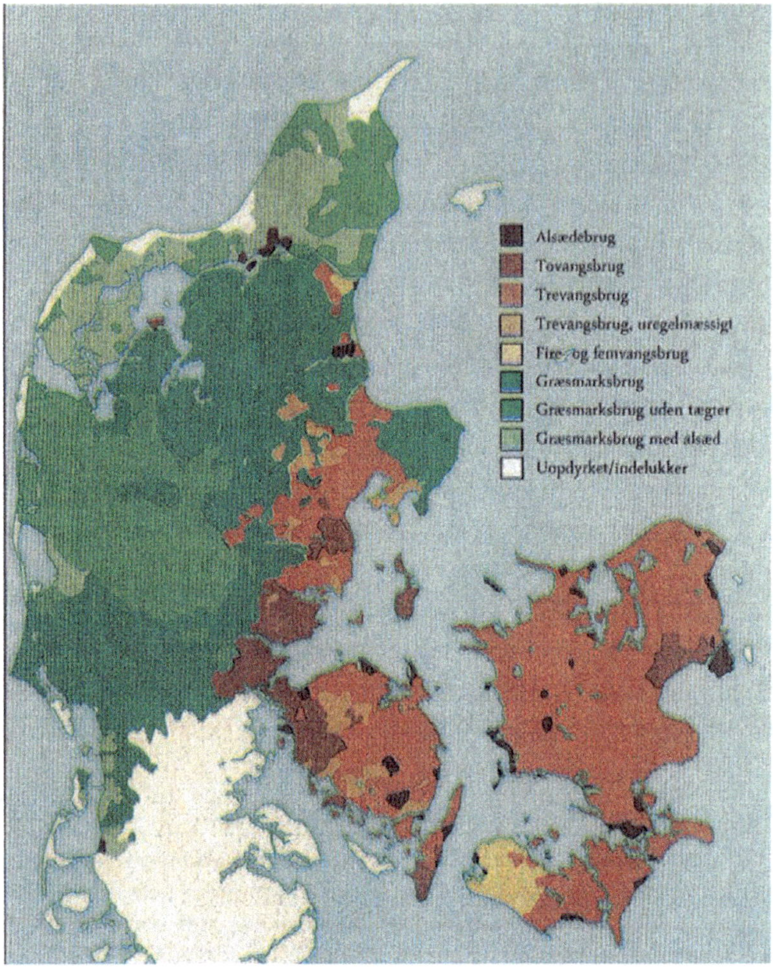


**Fig. 25.23** Land Cultivation Systems in Denmark, 1682–1683—Regions: Jutland, Fuen, Seeland. *Source*: Lögstrup (2015, p. 22)—Light brown: 2-Field, Brown: 3-Field, Yellow: 4-Field, Dark green: Grass-field system, Green: Grass with, Light green: Grass with seed, Black: All crops. White: Duchy Schleswig—politically ruled together (1460–1864) with the Duchy Holstein

corn from almost all the different countries of Europe". The herds of live cattle was driven down from Jutland, Fig. 25.23, along the "Oxen-Route" to Holstein and shipped to Holland (with ample grass fields). On ecological crises in Holland (inundation of arable land, areas with halving arable outputs between 1390–1440), other periods with sharply falling average and marginal products of land with contraction of agricultural outputs, and Dutch ships and merchants dominating Baltic trade, see Van Zanden (2002, p. 149–152).

*Jutland, Fuen, Seeland—Time Paths of Land Reforms and Results, 1750–1800*
Before presenting Land reforms,[33] Fig. 25.23, and discussing their economic results, we briefly state some political-economic facts about the period before (after[34]) 1750. Before 1740, there was *stagnation* and the agricultural prices were fluctuating and falling, whereas after **1750** *grain prices*[35] were fluctuating with a clear *rising* trend, cf. Fig. 25.31. The *Manor Farm* owners were encouraged by rising grain prices and now wanted to *increase supply* (grain production)—the Manor Farms started reforming their cultivation.

By adopting variants of the Holstein *Koppelwirtschaft*—7 **Field System**, which by higher *Land intensities* of Labor and Capital, $l_A = L/A$, $k_A = K/A$, required more *Labor services* used on *Manor* Farms that in Denmark was mainly obtained by the *'villeinage'* tenancy obligation that was imposed upon *Village* (Peasant) Farms.

Around **1710**, Denmark had, Hansen (1976, p. 40), about **660** *Manor* Farms (owned by Nobility, Crown, Institutions) to which also belonged/owned—as *copyholder* (leases transferred (inherited) to next generation) and *leaseholders* (life-long Leases)—about **60,000** *village* (peasant) farms, i.e., number of *Manor* Farms being *less* than **1** *percent* of the *total* number of farms.

In Denmark, ***Village Farm Land*** (Property, hartkorn) was normally, **9/10**, of the *Manor Estate* (Property, hartkorn), i.e., **Manor** Farms *cultivated* only about **10** *percent* of *Total* cultivated (arable) *Land.*

The *Land rents* per farm paid by Copyholders and Leaseholders could not be changed, as they were *fixed* (money or in kind) for lifetime. The Manor Farm *production* (cultivation) was the *main source* of income for Manor Estate owners. The only *flexible* contributions of the Village peasant farms to get larger Manor *Estate revenues* (outputs) were the **'villeinage'** tenancy (*boon works*—labor services) obligation[36] that was *not* regulated—but a discretionary *variable.*

[33] Before 1700, *Three-Field* (**3 F.**) systems (*brown*) dominated in the East (clay-soils); in Jutland (West, North), *Grass Field* systems (*green*), with permanent grass of 8–12 years, were prevalent.

[34] Politically, the period was characterized by the Seven Year War (1755–1762), Colonial War (1756–1763), US War of Independence (1776–1783). Economically, the years 1770–1805 were a booming ("flourishing") period in the Danish Kingdom.

[35] The contemporary Smith (1790, 1961, p. 232) notes: "The twenty years preceding **1750**, may well be set in opposition to the twenty years preceding **1770**". Marshall (1920, p. 189) noted: "Population increased nearly as much in 20 years following **1760** as in the preceding 60 years".

[36] In the *stagnation* period before 1740, *Adscription* ( peasant males, between 14–36 years, could not leave Manor Estates (Villages), where they were born) was enacted *Law* in Denmark 1733. The Law was regarded necessary to the national system for conscriptions of peasant males to Army units. In the countryside, taxation and conscription systems were administered by the private Manor Estate owners, cf. Lögstrup (1984, p. 287). For Village peasants it meant that the same person was their employer and public administrator. *Adscription* contributed to ensure supply of cheap dependent labor, and tenants and taxes of Village farms, Hansen (1976, p. 43); *villeinage* also increased—Law of 1733 was abolished 1788.

The Danish Land Reforms **1750–1800** are characterized by *three stages*:

I. *Enclosure* of Village *Commons*, Moors, *Wasteland*, 1750–1760;
II. *Manor Farm cultivation* (field, rotation) system reforms, 1760–1780;
III. *Village Farm* cultivations reform, field enclosure and *farm consolidations*, 1770–1800.

The three stages can succinctly be demonstrated by following the reforms and the results of one of Denmark's *largest* ***Estate*** owners, Count **Adam G. Molkte**, Chamberlain of the King, Prime Minister. August 6, **1746**, King **Frederic V** succeeded *Christian VI* and *reigned* (20 years) till January 24, **1766**. September 1746, the *King* gave a *Crown* Estate (free gift) to Molkte: *Manor Farm*, **Bregentved, 450** hectares, Haslev, **East Seeland**. The *Estate* also included more than 100 *Village* (Tenant) Farms. Before 1746, Molkte owned no Property (Land). During 1747–1751, he bought **4** *neighbouring Estates*, including, *Turebyholm* (1747), Juellinge, Tryggevaelde, cf. Fig. 25.24. These Seeland Manor and Estate acquisitions had reached more than **1500** hectares, making him enter higher nobility: **Count**, March 1750.

During 1754–1762, he had temporary possessions **Jutland** (e.g. Dronninglund, Lindenborg), and **Holstein** (e.g. Niendorf, (1760–1762), near Lübeck). In 1763–1765, Molkte bought **Funen** Estates and Manors, Glorup, and Rygaard, cf. Fig. 25.24, which he kept until his death, September **1792** (born 1710).

All these Manor Farms were cultivated by—*boon work*—from tenant farms and houses (cottages). In 1785 belonged to the **Manor** Farms: **361** Village farms and **320** houses—spread over **50** villages/parishes.

Molkte managed through *exchanges* with other *Estate* owners to become **single owner** in **34** *Villages* such that: 198 Village Tenant farms had *distances* less than 3 kilometer from the Manor farm, and 137 Village Tenant farms had between 3–5 km. to the Manor farm. A map of these arrangements for *efficiency* in the operation of **boon work** on **Seeland**, see Fig. 25.25.

I. **First stage**: *Enclosure* of Village *Commons*, Moors, *Wasteland*, 1750–1760 The *Commons* were not cultivated lands, but served together with the fallow for grazing of cattle from some village farms and houses. To extend the *arable land* area, the Estate owners were after 1750, with new regulations, allowed to let *Commons* become a part of the Manor farm, or partly shared with existing Village Tenant farms or else established (surveyed) as new Village Tenant farms. The uncultivated *Commons* covered large areas (often, up to around *20 percent* of Total Village land), and their arable use resulted, on Molkte Seeland Estates, Fig. 25.25, in more than 20 new Tenant Farm Villages. In 1759, the King gave to Molkte: Denmark's largest *Moor* (Lille Vildmose), **Jutland**, near Estate *Lindenborg* (1753–1762), with the object: make canals, drain lakes, and cultivate the land—a project not being a success. Other projects involved activities to reclaim heath, wastelands, cf. Rasmussen (2010a, p. 15).

II. **Second stage**: *Manor Farm cultivation* (field, rotation) system *reforms*, 1760–1780

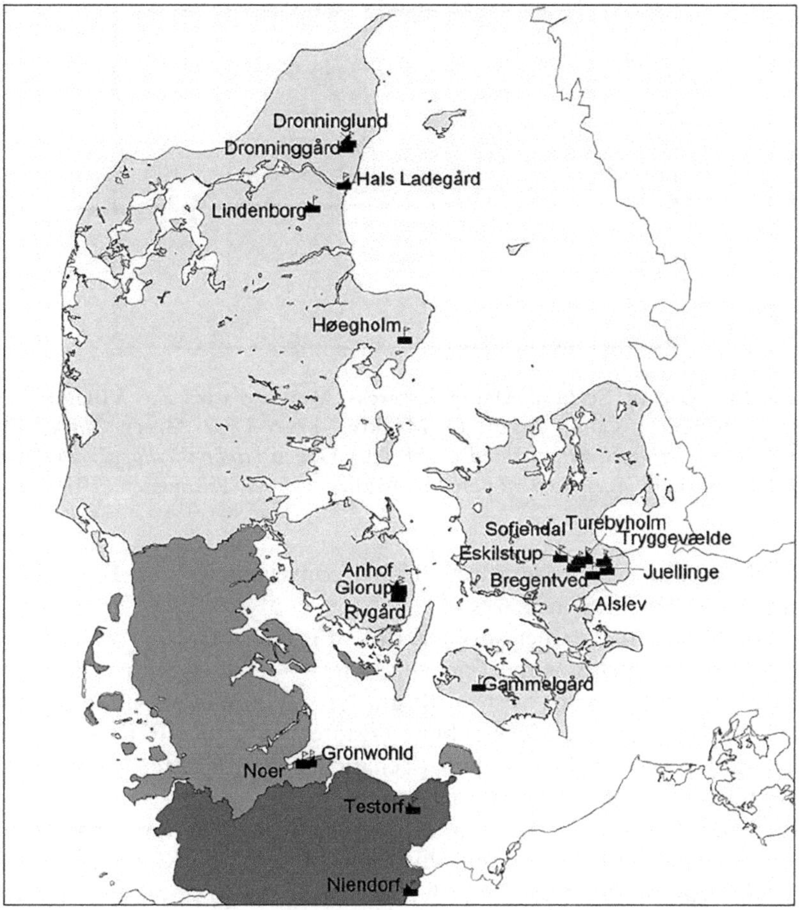


**Fig. 25.24** **1746–1792**: Map of all Manor Estates and Manor Farms, owned by Count **Adam G. Molkte**, in Regions: **Seeland** (e.g., Bregentved, Sofiendal, Turebyholm), **Jutland** (Lindenborg, Dronninglund), **Fuen** (Glorup, Rygaard), **Holstein** (Testorf, Niendorf). *Source*: Rasmussen (2010a, p. 14)

**Manor Farm**, *Turebyholm*, acquired (1747), was cultivated (**1749**) with **3** *large* fields: 1. *Häse* Marken (west), 2. *Kajhöys* Marken, 3. *Mölle* Marken (east); in (north) grass-brushwood area are: minor *enclosed fields* for cattle (cows, haifers). See Fig. 25.26.

To Molkte, a clear drawback of **3 F** *fields* was that they are *too large* for proper handling/cultivation. All the arable fields (1749) of *Turebyholm* consisted of about: *270* hectares—**3 F**: $\frac{270}{3}$ = **90** hectares. *Turebyholm* converted (1750–1751) to—7 **F** - 3 years grain/grass, 1 year fallow: $\frac{270}{7}$ = **40** (38.6) hectares. To the *enclosed fields* (1751) were made *hedges* for more than 5.5 kilometers.

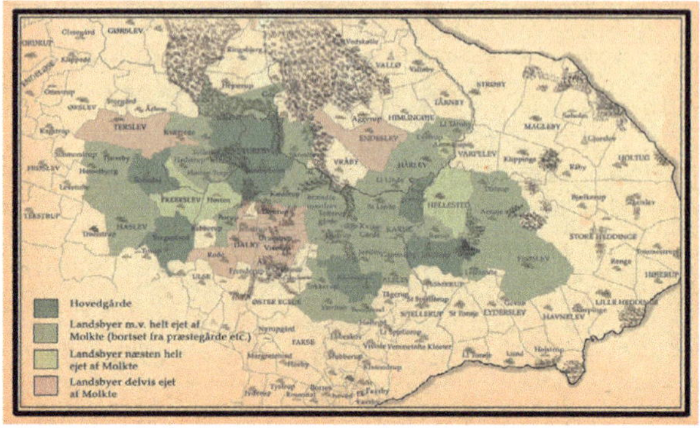


**Fig. 25.25** Map of **Seeland** Manor **Estates—Manor** Farms and **Villages** (Village Farms) —owned by Count **Adam G. Molkte**—1746–1792. **Green** (*dark*): **Manor** Farms. **Green**: *Villages*, *fully* owned by Molkte. **Green** (*light*): *Villages*, *mostly* owned by Molkte. **Red**: *Villages*, *partly* owned by Molkte. *Source*: Rasmussen (2010a, p. 12)

Finally, Manor *Turebyholm* was (1764) converted to—**11 F** - *cultivation* system: $\frac{270}{11}$ = **25** (24.5) hectares.

Count Molkte had earlier adopted the—**11 F**—*cultivation* system *enclosed* with *hedges* and *ditches* as the *'standard system'*—5 years with various grains, (rye, wheat, oats), 5 years "rest" with grasses, 1 year fallow—upon his **Manor Farms**. Molkte born in Mecklenburg (Estate Walkendorff) took (1761) his experienced *Niendorf* Leaseholder (Tenant Farmer, Pächter) to his **Seeland** Estates for reforming their cultivation.

North of *Bregentved* was completed (**1763**) new **Manor** Farm: *Sofiendal* (name, his wife)—**11 F**—(named, his 10 sons, and one King's field). The—**11 F—Manor** of *Bregentved* was finished (1765–1767), as shown with the *eleven fields* in Fig. 25.27. Further aspects of *Sofiendal*, see Boberg-Fazlic et al. (2023).

Here Fig. 25.27 looks similar to the Manor Farm of *Tellow* (1763) in Fig. 25.4a. Moreover, *von Thünen's* Manor of *Tellow* (1810), 465 hectares, cf. note 6, is about the same size as *Bregentved*, 450 hectares. We may note that *Tellow*—7 **F**—*field* size: $\frac{220}{7}$ = **30** (31.4) hectares—is close to—**11 F** - *field* size, **25** hectares.

III. **Third stage**: *Village* Farm *cultivations* reform, field *enclosure*, and Farm *consolidations*, 1770–1800.

Next, the traditional—**3 F**—*Village field system*, cf. Fig. 25.28a, had to be reformed on Molkte's **Seeland** Estates. The advantages and *Manor* Farm experience with the—**11 F**—11 field cultivation (*rotation*) system are transmitted to *Village Tenants* and implemented in a particular form: **Village—11 F—cultivation system**, which allowed *each* farmer to have **strips** (of different soil qualities and user rights) in all **11 Village fields**, as seen for **8 Farms** in Fig. 25.29.

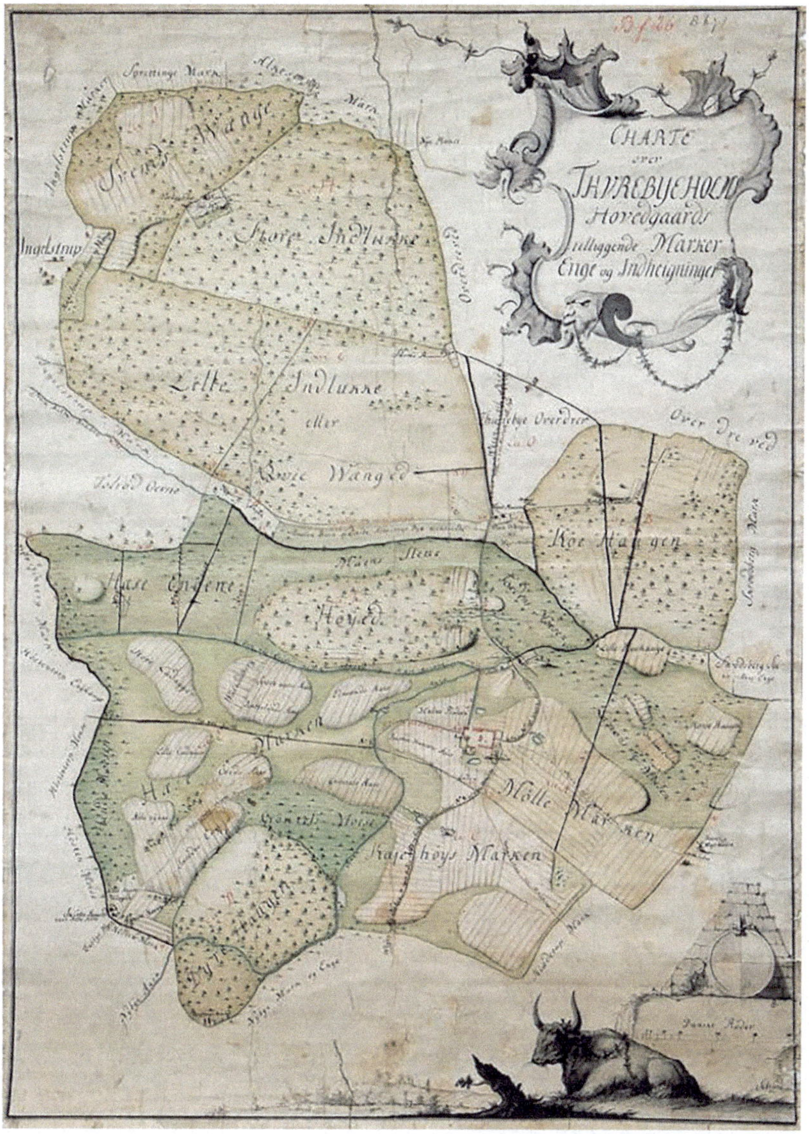

**Fig. 25.26** **Seeland**: *A.G. Molkte*, **Manor Farm**: **Turebyholm 1749**: **3 F - Field System**. One field—**West**—consists of parts, separated by low wet areas. **North**: Non-tilled grass-bush areas. **1750–1751**: **7 F - Field System**. **1764**: **11 F - Field System**, as *Bregentved Manor Farm*, in Fig. 25.27. *Source*: Rasmussen (2010a, p. 18)

We briefly discuss and illustrate the *Farm* and *Field* sizes involved in this **11 F** system for *Village Barup*. *Field size* of—**11 F**—is supposed to be: **15** hectares—hence total Village *acreage*: 11 · 15 = **165** ha.

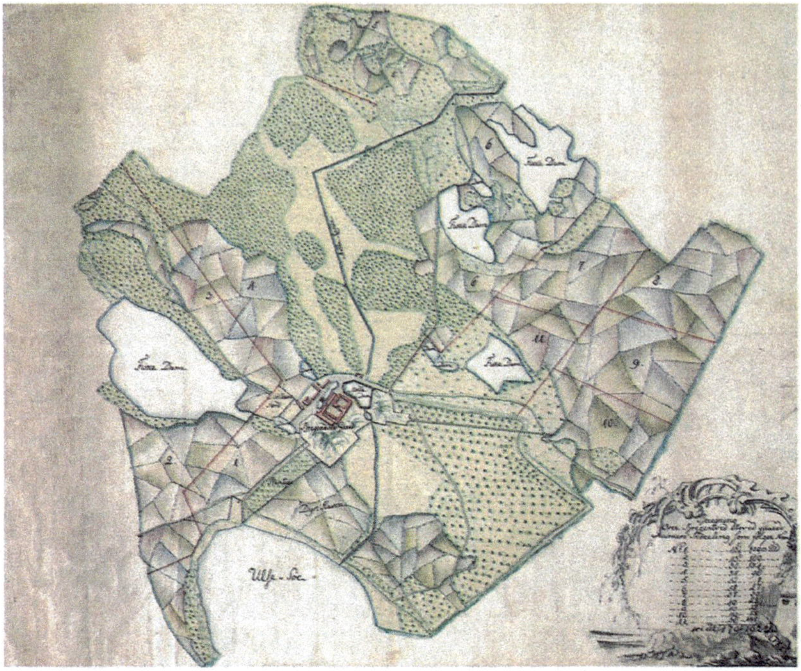

**Fig. 25.27** Bregentved Manor Farm of Count A.G. Molkte: 11- Field System (1760's). *Source*: Jespersen et al. (2010, p. 164)—C. Porskrog Rasmussen: Landlord and Reformer

a b

**Fig. 25.28** (**a**) Village Aarslev, 1768: 3 Fields with Strips *Source*: Feldbäk (1993, p. 14)—14 Farms, each: 108 Strips. (**b**) Village Aarslev, 1795: 14 Farms *Source*: Feldbäk (1993, p. 121)—7 Farms moved

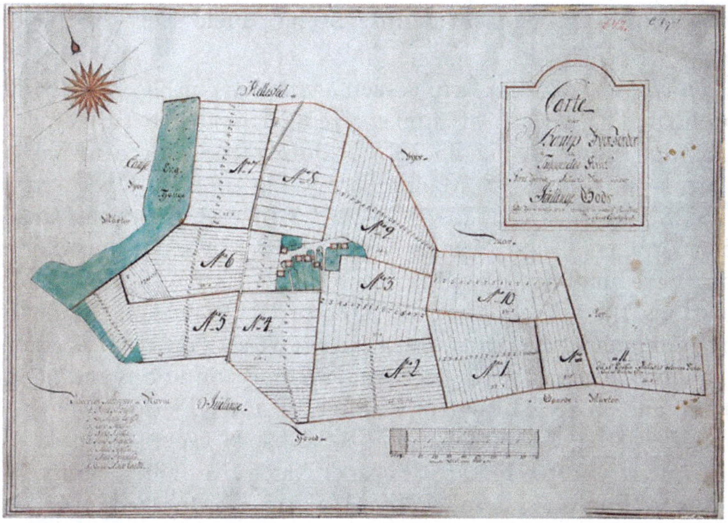

**Fig. 25.29** **Seeland** : *A.G. Molkte.* **1792**: **Village Barup**: *Village*— **11 F**—*Field System*—**8 Farms**—each **Farm** with 2–3 strips—in all **11 Fields**. *Source*: Rasmussen (2010a, p. 32)

Accordingly, the average *Farm size* of the **8** Farms is 165/8 = **20** (20.1) ha.

Only **1** strip of each *farm* in every field gives *strip size* = 15/8 = **1.8** ha

For **2** strips of each *farm* in every field implies *strip size* = **0.9** ha ; **3** strips: *strip size* = **0.6** ha.

In Fig. 25.29, it appears that most of the **11** *Fields* have: **16** strips: **2** strips to *each* Farm (8).

The Village Farmers are here with **Village 11 F** still (as **3 F**) working together in the fields, choosing same crop, etc., but they use/produce—by **11 F** rotation—the *same* Village *acreage* **165** ha much better/more. Several villages with 231 farms of Molkte had adopted the *Village* **11 F** by 1792. A clear advantage of this Fig. 25.29 system—for the *Estate owner*—is that the *costs* are much less in making the *hedges/ditches* for only 11 fields than the hedges/ditches for 11 fields on each of the 8 farms.

We briefly discuss Rotations, Field sizes, and *Farm Consolidation* for *Village Aarslev*—Fig. 25.28a and b.

Total Village *acreage* with **14 Farms** of (supposed) *average* size—**26 ha**—is $14 \cdot 26 =$ **364** ha.

With traditional—**3 F**—*cultivation* (rotation), the *Village fields* had the size: $\frac{364}{3} = \mathbf{120}$ ha

Village *acreage* was divided into about **100** *beams* (Äs) of different *quality*: **1** beam $= \frac{364}{100} = \mathbf{3.64}$ ha

*Each* farm had **108** *strips* (at least **1** in all beams): **1** *strip* $= \frac{26}{108} = \mathbf{0.24}$ ha; **108** strips, Fig. 25.28a; cf. Overton (1996a, p. 30).

*Cultivations* of *Consolidated* Farms, (26 ha), **Field** sizes, **7 F**: $\frac{26}{7}$ = **4**, (3.7) ha; **5 F**: $\frac{26}{5}$ = **5**, (5.2) ha.

One *consolidated* (26 ha) farm is seen (*scratched*) in Fig. 25.28b. The other 13 consolidated farms are of similar size (26 ha). The Farm *fields* of **7 F** or **5 F** are *not* shown in Fig. 25.28b (seldom seen/noticed for consolidated village farms—in contrast to Manor Farms, Fig. 25.27). Upon several farms in Fig. 25.28b are seen "squares" (sizes of 1.65 ha), indicating small parcels to *houses* (cottagers)—and 7 farms had in *Aarslev* to move outside the village and make new buildings upon the consolidated farm, cf. Fig. 25.22. Before consolidations, the *villages* consisted often of 10–20 peasant tenant farms.

All over Denmark, the *consolidated* ***Farms*** were of different *sizes*: 15–40 ha, 40–60 ha, above 60 ha, varying according to *soil* conditions and geographical location, cf. Fig. 25.23. The corresponding **7 F** and **5 F—Fields** have *sizes*, **7 F**: 2–5 ha; **5 F**: 3–8 ha; **7 F**: 5–8 ha; **5 F**: 8–12 ha. However, in many locations, especially **Fuen**, a six—**6 F**—*Field* (Mark) system (3 grain, 3 grass/1 clover), no fallow, cf. "English system", *Ring* 3, Fig. 25.2.—was adopted after Farm consolidation; see Hansen (1888, p. 75).

As *Land* cultivation with **crop rotation** seems now to have properly permitted operating with constant return to scale, $\mathbf{m} = \mathbf{1}$, in agricultural production (cf. below note 47), there is no optimal consolidated peasant farm size—and all are equally economic efficient for all product and factor prices.

Here—in short—nearly all peasant farmland (*acreage*) of Denmark's **5500** Villages was *reformed*, cf. Fig. 25.30, **1770–1808**, to be *cultivated* by *consolidated* farms—and **2/3** of peasant farms ( *size* > 15 ha ) operated/managed with *private ownership*, and the rest under various *tenant farmer* leasing forms. With private ownership of farms, the former *boon work* obligations was replaced by a money compensation. Freed from this boon work, the farmer (owner) could plan/cultivate much better his own *new fields*—with the results of larger farm *production* (output) and *revenues* to cover consolidated ownership costs.

We should note, as Hansen (1888, p. 84), that the timing in Fig. 25.30 of Farm *consolidation coincided* with adopting *new field systems* (cultivations, *rotations*)—it made little sense to *consolidate* the *Farm* and continue using the *old* **3 F** grain field-fallow system.

The *boon work* on Manor farms had *increased*—by about 25–30 percent, during 1770–1780, Hansen (1976, p. 63)—with the new more *labor intensive* **11 F** cultivation system, and new regulations and *personal liberty* reforms were politically necessary, governmentally supported, and enacted, especially from **1784**, onward; see Lögstrup (2015, Ch. 19–27). The Manor farms were subsequently operated with labor from more houses (cottagers) and full-time/part-time agricultural workers. In England, villeinage labor obligations (boon-work) were already abolished and substituted by *money rents* by year **1500**, cf. Allen (1992, p. 65), Ernle (1936, Ch.II).

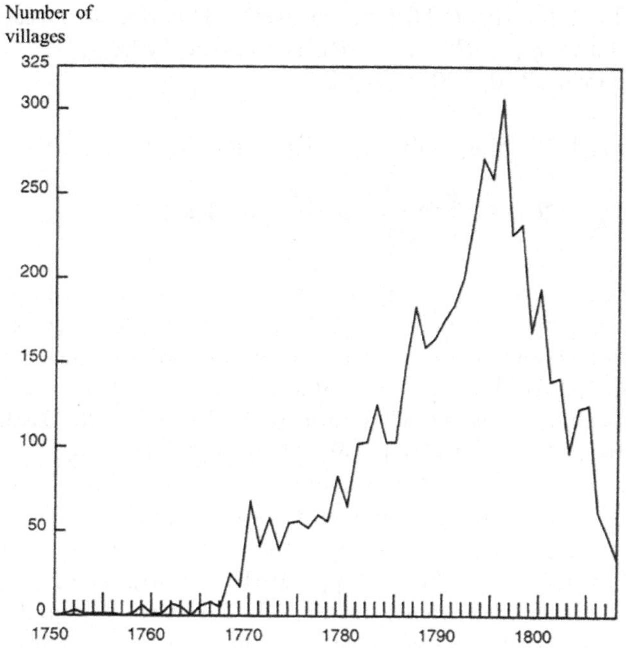


**Fig. 25.30** Village Enclosure Movement: Consolidation of Village Farms, Denmark, 1750–1808. *Source*: Feldbäk (1993, p. 119)—14 Villages, consolidated before 1750; 150 Villages, after 1808

*Agricultural Production, Population, and Consumption, 1760–1800*

To see the *expansion* of Agricultural production (outputs) during the period 1760–1800 of cultivation reforms on *Manor* farms and *consolidated* village (peasant) *Farms*, we first consider the empirical estimates of the total *Danish* grain production. The *grain harvest* after 1750 have been estimated between: 4–5 mill. barrels, and in years up to 1800 between: 8–9 mill. barrels, Feldbäk (1993, p. 123)—i.e., *lowest* estimate of *relative increase*: $\varrho_{Q_A} = \frac{Q_{AI}}{Q_{AII}} = \frac{8}{5} =$ **1.6**; *highest* estimate: $\varrho_{Q_A} = \frac{Q_{AI}}{Q_{AII}} = \frac{9}{4} =$ **2.3**. Hansen (1976, p. 69) has as best estimates of grain harvest, **c. 1770**: **4.5** mill. and **c. 1800**: **9** mill. barrels, that is $\varrho_{Q_A} = \frac{Q_{AI}}{Q_{AII}} = \frac{9}{4.5} =$ **2**, i.e., doubling of **Total** grain outputs in **30** years, restated as,

$$\varrho_{\mathbf{Q_A}}(30) = \frac{\mathbf{Q_A}(1800)}{\mathbf{Q_A}(1770)} = \mathbf{2}\ [\approx \frac{9}{4.5}]\ ;\quad \varrho_{\mathbf{A}}(30) = \frac{\mathbf{A}(1800)}{\mathbf{A}(1770)} = \mathbf{1.1} \tag{25.126}$$

The increase in total $\mathbf{Q_A}$, (25.126), includes the grain outputs that is due to **enlarging** the total *acreage*, (**A**) of *cultivation* (enclosure of commons, wastelands, mentioned above, potential up to 20 pct.) that in this period is assumed to have *increased*: **10** pct.—$\varrho_{\,\mathrm{A}}\,(30)$. The *Average product* of a unit (hectare) of Land, $q_A = Q_A/A = AP_A$, is accordingly from (25.126) obtained to have *increased*, 1770–1800, **82** pct.:

$$\varrho_{\mathrm{Q_A}}(30) = \varrho_{\mathrm{q_A}}(30) \cdot \varrho_{\,\mathrm{A}}(30) = \varrho_{\mathrm{AP_A}}(30) \cdot \varrho_{\,\mathrm{A}}\,(30) \quad ;$$

$$\varrho_{\mathrm{AP_A}}(30) = \frac{\varrho_{\mathrm{Q_A}}(30)}{\varrho_{\,\mathrm{A}}\,(30)} = \frac{2}{1.1} = \mathbf{1.82} \qquad (25.127)$$

The numbers above—$Q_{A\,I}$ and $Q_{A\,II}$—referred to estimates of total *grain harvests*; the grain output *deliveries* (sales) from agriculture to *markets*, transport (domestic and exports), are also seen doubling in this period. Export and shipping tonnage to Norway was doubled, Feldbäk (1993, p. 123). Similarly, there was about a *doubling* of livestocks, **1774**: 280,000, **1800**: 527,000, (horned) cattle, Hansen (1976, p. 69), Hansen (1888, p. 96).

Thus *relative increases* in the numbers, $\mathbf{Q_A}$, $\mathbf{q_A}$, $\varrho_{\mathrm{Q_A}}(30)$, (25.126–25.127), are regarded as the corresponding *relative increases* in *Agricultural* market **outputs** (grain equivalents)—similar to the *Tellow* Manor Farm outputs (*ray equivalents*) of sizes: $\mathbf{Q} = \mathbf{Q_A}$, and $\mathbf{q_A}$, (25.15–25.16). The Land *productivity effects* of the *Tellow transition* from **3 F** to **7 F** was calculated, see (25.67–25.68), (25.45), with the *Tellow* accounting data (information) and giving the result in *rye equivalents* : $\varrho_{\,q} = \frac{q_{A7}}{q_{A3}} = \mathbf{1.83}$, which is *not only* expressing larger grain outputs (sales), but also large increases in market deliveries of cattle (*livestock*) products.

For the period **1770–1800**, the *population* (thousands) increased, Johansen (1975, p. 22), **14** pct.:

$$\bar{\mathrm{N}}(1769) = 810 \;\; , \;\; \bar{\mathrm{N}}(1801) = 926 \;\; ;$$

$$\varrho_{\,\bar{\mathrm{N}}} = \frac{926}{810} = \mathbf{1.14} \;\; ; \quad \varrho_{\,\mathrm{N_A}} = \frac{735}{640} = \mathbf{1.15} \qquad (25.128)$$

Population increased with the same rate in the *countryside*, $\varrho_{\,\mathrm{N_A}}$, (25.128), Hansen (1888, II, p. 161).

*Grain prices* fluctuated over the years, but with a *rising* trend since 1760, see Fig. 25.31.

As to standard of living, the numbers, $\varrho_{\,\bar{\mathrm{N}}}$, and $\varrho_{\mathrm{AP_A}}(30)$, suggests no problem with *per capita food consumption*: $\varrho_{\mathrm{c}} \approx \frac{\varrho_{\mathrm{AP_A}}}{\varrho_{\bar{\mathrm{N}}}} = \frac{1.82}{1.14} = \mathbf{1.6}$; the per capita ***grain*** *consumption* increased from **1770**: 200 kg to **1800**: 300 kg, i.e., **50** pct., see here, Hansen (1976, p. 80).

The Danish reforms—**1760–1800**—of the *cultivation*—**field**—*system* on **Manor** Farms and **consolidated** peasant **Farms** raised **agricultural production** (outputs) to *unprecedented* levels—breaking the *Stagnation* and forever the *Population* ('Malthusian') barrier. On the Danish agricultural reforms, see Smout (1987, p. 93).

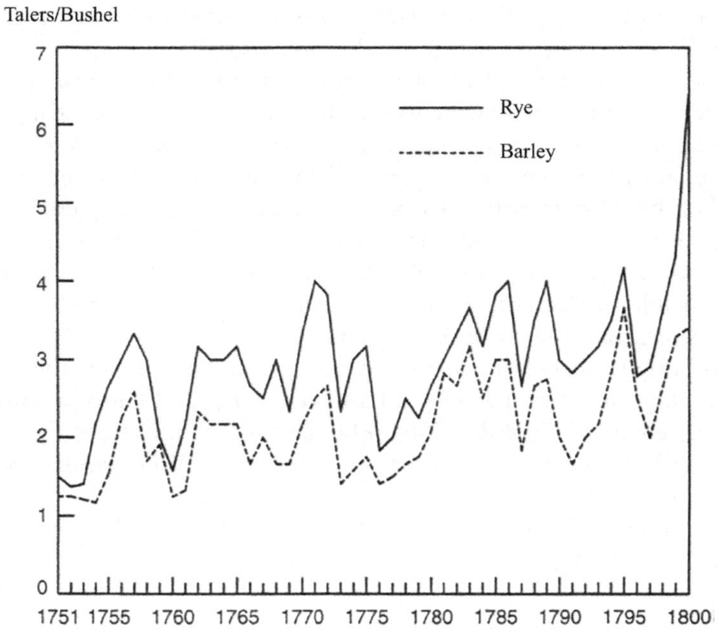


**Fig. 25.31** Prices (Church rates) of Rye, Barley, Talers/Bushel, Seeland Diocese 1751–1800. *Source*: Feldbäk (1993, p. 124)—Danish Booming Trade and Prosperity Period, 1750–1800

### *Agricultural Cultivation Transition—United Kingdom, 1730–1800*

About the *period*, **1750–1800**, Marshall (1920, p. 745) wrote:[37] "The improvement in agriculture moved very fast. **Implements** of all kinds were improved, ***draining*** was carried out on scientific principles, the ***breeding*** of ***farm animals*** was revolutionized by Bakewell's genius; ***turnips, clover***, rye grass, came into general use, and enabled the plan of ***refreshing land***—by letting it lie **fallow** to be **superseded** by that **alternating husbandry**" [ crop rotation ]. These and other changes constantly ***increased*** the **capital** required for the **cultivation** of *Land*; and thus in every way the modern ***commercial*** spirit spread into *Agriculture*' (boldface-italics ours).

During this **same** period (1750–1800), *husbandmen* (small farmers) disappeared, *freeholders* relatively reduced—and Hicks (1969, p. 119) said: "In the classical **Landlord-Tenant system** of England, the landlord finds a new function, entering with his tenants into a new kind of *partnership*—with *rent*

[37] English Agriculture as *leading reformer* beyond all others in the *period* 1750–1800 accords with Heckscher (1960, p. 61).

as regular return upon a *commercial investment*, but with a long-term interest to see and *keep* his able *tenants* through *uncertainty*".

For each farming unit—rent payments of English *Tenant farmers* (Pächter) to proprietors (landowners) were *fixed sums* (costs) of *money* or paying on *long-term loan* with a fixed money *interest* rate—*fixed* money *rents* were incentives to *maximize outputs* and *farm profits*. Whether the cultivation of *Land* is undertaken by **Manor Estate owners** (as *Tellow*) or by the **Tenant Farmer** system above, the Total **Landrent** [ Factor income (Value added) accounting for the Land acreage ] numbers $\mathbf{R_A(x)}$ and $\mathbf{r_A(x)}$ in our *Tables* and *formulas* are in principle *unchanged*. Rent data collection from *separate* Landlord and Tenant *registrations* may be more difficult.[38]

We will briefly deal with issues of some *bench-mark* numbers for evaluating the actual *increases* (higher levels) in **Land rents** ($r_A$) and **Land productivities** ($q_A$) obtained from *English* 1750–1800 farming (cultivation) *reforms* with *enclosure* and *alternating husbandry*—by using the **Tellow** *quantitative model* experience (7 **F.**) in an *analytical empirical* application.

Let elements of *National Income Accounting* be stated by components of **National** Income, $\mathbf{Y_N}$, as:

$$Y_N = wL + R_A + R \ , \ R_A = r_A A \ ;$$
$$\epsilon_L^N = \frac{W = wL}{Y_N} \ , \ \epsilon_A^N = \frac{R_A}{Y_N} \ , \ \epsilon_R^N = \frac{R}{Y_N} \ ; \ \epsilon_L^N = \epsilon_{L_A}^N \left[\frac{W_A}{Y_N}\right] + \epsilon_{L_M}^N \left[\frac{W_M}{Y_N}\right] \tag{25.129}$$

with *Labor* (**L**), and $\mathbf{l_N} = L/N$, **N** (population, or families) as *Labor participation* rate, **w** is wage per worker, $\mathbf{r_A}$ is *Land rent* per acre (ha), and **R** is a *Residual* income, accruing to *either* a factor Capital, **K** ($R = R_K = r_K K$), or some *other Residual* claimants [ as e.g. O'Rourke and Williamson (2002, p. 452), where *Residual R*, (25.129), *accrued* to: *Professionals* (church, military, bureaucracy), *Merchants*, Traders ] **Labor share**, $\boldsymbol{\epsilon_L^N}$, (25.129), includes **all** *Workers* in agriculture, manufactures, building, cottagers, paupers.

The **classic social tables** (estimates of income and population/families) of **England** and **Wales** by Gregory King and others have been *revised* by Lindert & Williamson for the *years*: 1688, 1759, 1802.

The **Absolute** *sizes* (million Sterling) of $\mathbf{Y_N}$, (25.130)—with Land rents $\mathbf{R_A^N}$ *calculated* from *data*—are given in Lindert and Williamson (1982, p. 393, p. 397, p. 401), and so the **Land** *rent* **shares**, $\boldsymbol{\epsilon_A^N}$, (25.129), become:

[38] The *timing* of the great *improvements* in *England* ('Agricultural Revolution') has lately been much debated by many economists and historians, contesting the view of Marshall above , cf. the extensive references to this chapter.

$$\mathbf{1688}: \ \epsilon_A^N = \frac{\mathbf{R_A^N}}{\mathbf{Y_N}} = \frac{12.209}{54.440} = \mathbf{0.22}\ ;$$

$$\mathbf{1759}: \ \epsilon_A^N = \frac{16.656}{71.366} = \mathbf{0.23}\ ;$$

$$\mathbf{1802}: \ \epsilon_A^N = \frac{38.0}{198.6} = \mathbf{0.19} \qquad (25.130)$$

A *size* $\boldsymbol{\epsilon}_{\mathbf{A}}^{\mathbf{N}} = \mathbf{0.23}$ in **1759** is *not* far off **Tellow 7 F** Land factor *share* $\boldsymbol{\delta}_{\mathbf{A}}^*$, (25.39), or $\boldsymbol{\delta}_{\mathbf{A}}^*(\mathbf{x})$, Fig. 25.13, $x < 10$. It will be noted (25.130) that ***nominal*** **Land rents,** $\mathbf{R_A^N}$, more than **doubled** from **1759** to **1802,** $\varrho_{\mathbf{R_A^N}} = \frac{38.0}{16.656} = \mathbf{2.28}$, and moreover that **National** Income, $\mathbf{Y_N}$, increased as: $\varrho_{Y_N} = \frac{198.6}{71.366} = 2.78$.

From (25.129), Lindert and Williamson (1982, p. 393, p. 397, p. 401), the **Labor** income **share,** $\boldsymbol{\epsilon}_{\mathbf{L}}^{\mathbf{N}}$, become:

$$1688: \ \epsilon_{L_M}^N = \frac{W_M}{Y_N} = \frac{4.27}{54.44} = 0.078\ , \ \epsilon_{L_A}^N = \frac{W_A}{Y_N} = \frac{2.08}{54.44} = \mathbf{0.038}\ ;$$

$$\epsilon_L^N = \mathbf{0.116} \qquad (25.131)$$

$$1759: \ \epsilon_{L_M}^N = \frac{3.80}{71.4} = 0.053\ , \ \epsilon_{L_A}^N = \frac{5.38}{71.4} = \mathbf{0.075}\ ; \ \epsilon_L^N = \mathbf{0.128} \qquad (25.132)$$

$$1802: \ \epsilon_{L_M}^N = \frac{2.60}{198.6} = 0.013\ , \ \epsilon_{L_A}^N = \frac{12.29}{198.6} = \mathbf{0.062}\ ; \ \epsilon_L^N = \mathbf{0.075} \qquad (25.133)$$

and so **residual** shares, $\epsilon_R^N$, (25.129), are— 1688: $\epsilon_R^N = \mathbf{0.66}$, 1759: $\epsilon_R^N = \mathbf{0.64}$, 1802: $\boldsymbol{\epsilon}_{\boldsymbol{R}}^{\boldsymbol{N}} = \mathbf{0.73}$. The *sizes* and social **trends** of $\boldsymbol{\epsilon}_{\mathbf{A}}^{\mathbf{N}}$ and $\boldsymbol{\epsilon}_{\mathbf{L}}^{\mathbf{N}}$ in (25.130–25.133) are seen in many *historical* references, e.g., Clark (2007a, p. 138, p. 199)—with $\boldsymbol{\epsilon}_{\boldsymbol{L}}^{\boldsymbol{N}}, \boldsymbol{\epsilon}_{\mathbf{R}}^{\mathbf{N}}$, (25.129), after 1800 *decomposed* into factor *shares* of Labor and Capital.

Lindert and Williamson (1982, op.cit) give *number* (million) of **All** families, **N** (25.134), and **Agriculture Farmer** families, $\mathbf{N_A}$ (*excluding* Laborers—and *excluding* all nobility Estate owners, "Landlords"), as:

$$1688: \ n_A^N \equiv \frac{N_A}{N} = \frac{0.23}{1.39} = 0.17\ ;$$

$$1759: \ n_A^N = \frac{0.38}{1.54} = 0.25\ ;$$

$$1802: \ n_A^N = \frac{0.32}{2.19} = 0.15 \qquad (25.134)$$

The *Composition* of the English **Farmer** *totals* $\mathbf{N_A}$ in (25.134) are of *agricultural-historical* interests:
*1688*: Freeholders (0.12), Farmers (0.11); *1759*: Freeholders (0.14), Farmers (**0.11**), Husbandmen (0.13); *1802*: Larger Freeholders (0.04), Lesser Freeholders (0.12), Farmers (**0.16**). Thus from **1759** to **1802**, the *absolute number* of **Tenant** Farmers (*families*) grew from **110,000** to **160,000**—increased **45** pct. However, a more detailed accounting—for both *Numbers* of *Freeholders* and *Farmers* and their respective *Average* family *income*—are necessary for *economically* describing and *distributional* explaining what happened in English Agriculture, as evident in the *Tables* for 1759–1802. In (25.135–25.137), are shown ***numbers*** (thousands), ***income*** (pounds) of larger/lesser Freeholders **F**, $\boldsymbol{n_A^{Fi}}, \boldsymbol{y_A^{Fi}}$, $i = 1, 2$,—Farmers, **f**, Husbandmen, **H**—and Cottagers,[39] **C**, Farm Workers, **W**:

$$\begin{aligned}
1759 : n_A^{F1} &= 20,\ \ y_A^{F1} = 152£ ;\ \ n_A^{F2} = 120,\ \ y_A^{F2} = 51£ ; \\
n_A^{C} &= 200\ ,\ \ y_A^{C} = 1 - 20£ \\
n_A^{f1} &= 10,\ \ y_A^{f1} = 117£ ;\ \ n_A^{f2} = 95,\ \ y_A^{f2} = 44£ ; \\
n_A^{H} &= 134,\ \ y_A^{H} = 16£ \qquad (25.135) \\
1802 : n_A^{F1} &= 40,\ \ y_A^{F1} = 200£ ;\ \ n_A^{F2} = 120,\ \ y_A^{F2} = 90£ \\
n_A^{f} &= 160,\ \ y_A^{f} = 120£ ;\ \ n_A^{W} = 340,\ \ y_A^{W} = 31£ \qquad (25.136)
\end{aligned}$$

$$\begin{aligned}
1759 - 1802 : \varrho_{y_A^{F1}} &= \frac{200}{152} = 1.32\ ;\ \ \varrho_{y_A^{F2}} = \frac{90}{51} = 1.76\ ; \\
\varrho_{y_A^{f1}} &= \frac{120}{117} = 1.03\ ;\ \ \varrho_{y_A^{f2}} = \frac{120}{44} = 2.73 \qquad (25.137)
\end{aligned}$$

As to **Laborers** (Cottagers) families, Lindert and Williamson (1982, op.cit) give *1688*: 314.000, *1759* $\boldsymbol{n_A^C}$ : **200.000**. *1802* $\boldsymbol{n_A^W}$ **340.000**. Thus from **1759** to **1802**, **Laborers** increased **70** pct. The increase of registered agricultural workers (Laborers) also come from the abandoned farming by Husbandmen. Average family (annual) income of Cottagers (1759), $\boldsymbol{y_A^C}$, is uncertain (includes paupers & seasonal farm workers with less half-year employment).

From (25.135–25.137), it is seen that the *numbers* of *Freeholders* remained intact and their family incomes increased. But *Tenant Farmers* became dominant with *leasing (renting)* only *larger farms* and hence with very large increases—$\boldsymbol{\varrho}_{y_A^{f2}}$—in Farmer family incomes, (25.137).

[39] On King's 1688 "Labouring families, out servants, cottagers, paupers ( 0.764 of 1.136 million)", see Overton (1996a, p. 41).

From **1759** to **1802**, *numbers* of *Esquire*[40] and *Gentlemen* families[41] [ High-Class families, Nobility ] increased from [ 800, 16,000 ] to [ 6,000, 20,000 ]—and their **Average** annual family *income* (pound Sterling) increased **50** pct.: (1078, 400) to (1500, 700), cf. Lindert and Williamson (1982, p. 396, p. 400).

*Land Rents per Acre and Agricultural Produce—England and Wales, 1760–1800*

By the National Factor Income identity $\mathbf{Y_N}$, (25.129), and Factor *shares*, (25.130–25.133), the *Absolute* **sizes** (million Sterling) of the components of $\mathbf{Y_N}$ are stated—together with their *relative increases*—as:

$$Y_N = R_A + wL + R \;;$$

$$1759: \; Y_N = 71.4 = 16.5 + 9.2 + 45.7 \;; \qquad \varrho_{wL} = \frac{14.9}{9.2} = 1.6 \tag{25.138}$$

$$\varrho_{Y_N} = \frac{198.6}{71.4} = 2.8\,, \; \varrho_{R_A} = \frac{38.0}{16.5} = 2.3 \;;$$

$$1801: \; Y_N = 198.6 = 38 + 14.9 + 145.7; \; \varrho_R = \frac{145.7}{45.7} = 3.2 \tag{25.139}$$

From *number* (millions) of *All* families, **N** (25.134), and *Average* family (household) sizes, the corresponding Total *Populations* $\bar{\mathbf{N}}$ are stated—together with official, census numbers, $\bar{\mathbf{N}}$ **(1750)**, $\bar{\mathbf{N}}$ **(1800)** —as:

$$\bar{\mathbf{N}}(1750) = 6.0 \; mill.\,, \; \bar{\mathbf{N}}(1759) = 1.54 \cdot 4 = \mathbf{6.16} \;;$$

$$\bar{\mathbf{N}}(1800) = 9.1 \;,; \; \bar{\mathbf{N}}(1802) = 2.2 \cdot 4.15 = \mathbf{9.13} \tag{25.140}$$

Thus in **period** 1750–1800, **Population** increased, $\varrho_{\bar{\mathbf{N}}} = \frac{9.1}{6.0} = 1.52$, and 1760–1802: $\varrho_{\bar{\mathbf{N}}} = \frac{9.13}{6.16} = 1.48$, i.e., **50** *percent*. To feed this growing population of England, and maintaining (at least preserving) food consumption, the Total agricultural *Produce/Output* has (without import) to expand ( similarly

[40] Ashton (1948, 1962, p. 59) gives number of *Enclosure Acts*, 1740–1750: 38; 1750–1760: 156; 1760–1770: 480, and higher figures in next decades. Ashton says: "The initiative usually came from the *Esquire* and the *Tithe-owner*—with Bills passed: ' For *dividing, allotting, and enclosing* the Open and Common *Fields, Meadows, Pastures*, and Common and *Waste* Lands '—of the particular Parish (Village) " (*italics ours*).

[41] The family incomes of Aristocracy with High titles: Gentleman, Esquire, Knight, Baronet, Lords (Viscount, Earl, Duke, Spiritual Lords) are *not* included in the *Land rents*, $\mathbf{R_A}$, (25.130–25.133), but are part of the *Residual*, **R**, in (25.138–25.139).

about **50** *percent* in this period, **1760–1800**. Did *English Agriculture*[42] succeed to accomplish *such task*? How could it be done within this *time span*? Let us analytically and quantitatively demonstrate how the ***agricultural production (cultivation) models*** in Sects. "Tellow Farm Accounts, Revenues, Costs, and Land Rents"–"Tellow—Output—Marginal Products of Land, Labor, Capital" can help to answer these questions.

By (25.130), (25.139), *nominal Total Land rents*, $\mathbf{R_A}$, more than *doubled* from **1759** to **1802**. But now we need facts and evidence to see how: $\mathbf{r_A} = \mathbf{R_A/A}$, $\mathbf{q_A} = \mathbf{Q/A}$, and **A**—evolved in England, **1760–1800**.

For selected *Estates* and *Farms*, Land **Rents** per **acre**, $\mathbf{r_A}$, (pound Sterling) *increased* about **50** *percent*: Lindert and Williamson (1982, p. 399)—Kingston *Estate*, 1790/1740, $\varrho_r(50)$, Hooton, Pagnall, Yorks *Estate*, 1793/1763, $\varrho_r(30)$, Norfolk *Farm* (225 acres), 1792/1757, $\varrho_r(35)$, 1799/1770, $\varrho_r(39)$—give,

$$\varrho_{r(50)} = \frac{r_A(1790)}{r_A(1740)} = \frac{0.567}{0.383} = 1.48 \ ; \ \varrho_{r(30)} = \frac{r_A(1793)}{r_A(1763)} = \frac{0.821}{0.467} = 1.76 \tag{25.141}$$

$$\varrho_{r(35)} = \frac{r_A(1792)}{r_A(1757)} = \frac{0.844}{0.533} = 1.58 \ ; \ \varrho_{r(1739)} = \frac{r_A(1799)}{r_A(1770)} = \frac{0.933}{0.577} = 1.62 \tag{25.142}$$

The English data of nominal $\mathbf{r_A}$ have a long history and published & discussed in a vast literature. Clark (2002, p. 297–298) gives estimated *average nominal rents* per *acre*, $\mathbf{r_A}$, (£ per acre) of farmland for England [ as a whole—*All England* Average, (25.143) ], *Regions* (25.144–25.145), by *Periods* from: 1480–1914; e.g., in (25.143): $\mathbf{r_A}(89) = r_A(1789) = r_A(1785-1789) = \mathbf{0.701}\,£$ ; $r_A(39) = r_A(1739) = r_A(1735-1739) = \mathbf{0.508}\,£$ ; $\boldsymbol{\varrho}_{\mathbf{r}}(50) = \varrho_r(1789-1739) = \mathbf{1.40}$, etc. - and similar to (25.141–25.142).

$$\varrho_r(50) = \frac{r_A(89)}{r_A(39)} = \frac{0.701}{0.508} = 1.40 \ ; \ \varrho_r(40) = \frac{r_A(89)}{r_A(49)} = \frac{0.701}{0.457} = 1.53 \ ;$$

$$\varrho_r(40) = \frac{r_A(94)}{r_A(54)} = \frac{0.817}{0.560} = 1.46$$

$$\varrho_r(40) = \frac{r_A(1795-99)}{r_A(1760-64)} = \frac{0.884}{0.590} = 1.50 \ ; \qquad \textit{All England Average} \tag{25.143}$$

[42] Overton (1996a, p. 206): "The transformation of *output* and *Land productivity* enabled the country to break out of a '**Malthusian trap**'—allowing the country to *exceed* the *barrier of 5.5 million* people for the first time".

$$\varrho_r(50) = \frac{r_A(89)}{r_A(39)} = \frac{0.690}{0.523} = 1.32 \ ; \ \varrho_r(40) = \frac{r_A(89)}{r_A(49)} = \frac{0.690}{0.499} = 1.38 \ ;$$

$$\varrho_r(40) = \frac{r_A(94)}{r_A(54)} = \frac{0.977}{0.561} = 1.74$$

$$\varrho_r(40) = \frac{r_A(1795-99)}{r_A(1760-64)} = \frac{0.936}{0.588} = 1.74 \ ; \qquad \textit{Midlands} \tag{25.144}$$

$$\varrho_r(50) = \frac{r_A(89)}{r_A(39)} = \frac{0.776}{0.548} = 1.42 \ ; \ \varrho_r(40) = \frac{r_A(89)}{r_A(49)} = \frac{0.776}{0.503} = 1.54 \ ;$$

$$\varrho_r(40) = \frac{r_A(94)}{r_A(54)} = \frac{0.795}{0.627} = 1.27$$

$$\varrho_r(40) = \frac{r_A(1795-99)}{r_A(1760-64)} = \frac{0.952}{0.635} = 1.50 \ ; \qquad \textit{South West} \tag{25.145}$$

Clearly, large countries as England have variations in *rents per acre* $\mathbf{r_A}$ and *rent increases* $\boldsymbol{\varrho_r}$ over time and regions, depending on the concentrations of Pasture, Light arable, Heavy arable clay soils. The south and east Midlands are highly arable with *high* $\mathbf{r_A}$ and $\boldsymbol{\varrho_r}$ after **1750–1760**. It appears from the Clark (2002) estimated current market (*'rack rental'*, full commercial ) $\mathbf{r_A}$- numbers in (25.143–25.145) that the *Nominal Land rents* (including *Tithe*) per acre **rose** in England *at least* **50** percent from **1760–1800**.

There are other sources for information about the sizes of $\mathbf{r_A}$ and $\varrho_r$, 1760–1800. Turner et al. (1997a, p. 310–11, p. 320–21) summarize—from a comprehensive *database* of **Estates** rather than Tenant Farms—the **Total rents** (without *Tithe*) annually *received* (actually *paid*), $\mathbf{R_A}$—and the Total acreage (**A**) involved—to obtain the rent, $\mathbf{r_A}$ (shillings per acre). For three years **1760–1762**, we see: 6.8 + 8.1 + 7.5)/3 = 7.5 shillings = *0.375 £* = $\mathbf{r_A}(1760-62)$. For the years **1798–1800**, we see: (11.8 + 11.9 + 12.4)/3 = 12.0 shillings = *0.600 £* = $\mathbf{r_A}(1798-1800)$. Hence $\boldsymbol{\varrho_r}\mathbf{(40)} = \frac{r_A(1798-1800)}{r_A(1760-1762)} = \frac{0.600}{0.375} = \frac{12}{7.5} = \mathbf{1.60}$.

For the sub-population of Estates, where Rent received coincide with Rents assessed, the same three years gives, **1760–1762**: (7.1 + 8.5 + 7.7)/3 = 7.8 shillings = *0.385 £* = $\mathbf{r_A}(1760-62)$; **1798–1800**: (12.2 + 13.7 + 14.5)/3 = 13.5 shillings = *0.673 £* = $\mathbf{r_A}(1798-1800)$. Hence $\boldsymbol{\varrho_r}\mathbf{(40)} = \frac{r_A(1798-1800)}{r_A(1760-1762)} = \frac{0.673}{0.385} = \frac{13.5}{7.8} = \mathbf{1.75}$.

*Land Rents, Factor Prices, Revenues, and Outputs—England and Wales, 1760–1800*

From the Clark data, (25.143–25.145), and the Estates database above, there is solid evidence confirming that **nominal** *Land rents* per *acre*, (including Tithe)

$\mathbf{r_A}$—in England **1760–1800**—*at least* **rose 50** percent, and **rose** at most *less* than **60** percent:

$$1.5 < \varrho_r(\mathbf{40}) = \frac{\mathbf{r_A(1800)}}{\mathbf{r_A(1760)}} < 1.6 \tag{25.146}$$

Clark (2002, p. 303) presents *Decennial averages* of English Agricultural (Farm) *nominal wages*, $\mathbf{w_A}$ (1480–1910), and $\mathbf{w_A}$ are for the decades in the same period as (25.146)—together with $\varrho_w(\mathbf{40})$ —given by,

$$\varrho_w(\mathbf{40}) = \frac{\mathbf{w_A(1800)}}{\mathbf{w_A(1760)}} = \frac{15.1\,d.\ per\ day}{11.4\,d.\ per\ day} = 1.32\ ;$$

$$\varrho_w(\mathbf{40}) = \frac{15.6\,d.}{11.7\,d.} = 1.33^{43} \tag{25.147}$$

Decennial *rent/wage* ratios, $\frac{\mathbf{r_A}}{\mathbf{w_A}}$, from (1480–1910) for England are also presented, and their indexes (1860 =100), *maximum* (1820 =105.6)—together with $\varrho_{\frac{r}{w}}(\mathbf{40})$—are for same period (25.147), given by:

$$\varrho_{\frac{r}{w}}(\mathbf{40}) = \frac{\frac{\mathbf{r_A}}{\mathbf{w_A}}\mathbf{(1800)}}{\frac{\mathbf{r_A}}{\mathbf{w_A}}\mathbf{(1760)}} = \frac{87.5}{80.5} = 1.09 \tag{25.148}$$

The *rent/wage* ratios, $\frac{\mathbf{r_A}}{\mathbf{w_A}}$, (1500–1910) are shown graphically, Clark (2002, p. 304), indicating that *factor income* distribution rises in favor of **Land** from 1750 and onward to a peak = 106 in 1820s. Lindert (2000, p. 19) finds: the "*ratio* of England's farmland *rents* to common-labor *wage* rates to have risen *most* in roughly: 1740–1810"—widening the usual measures of nominal income inequality.

Let us now examine the **rents** $\mathbf{r_A}$ per *acre* from a *productivity* and agricultural **output** point of view. The rise in rents measured in bushels of wheat per acre is a measure of the rise in *marginal productivity* of **Land**, viz. **p** = wheat price: $\mathbf{r_A/p} = \mathbf{MP_A}$, cf. (25.33–25.34), (25.43–25.44). For *wheat* prices, Annual Average Prices, **p(t)**, (shillings per Winchester quarter) at Eton & Winchester, Granger and Elliott (1967, p. 264–265), Ernle (1936, p. 488–489), give:

$$\varrho_p(\mathbf{34}) = \frac{\mathbf{p}\,(1798)}{\mathbf{p}\,(1764)} = \frac{51.8\,sh.}{41.5\,sh.} = 1.25\ ;$$

$$\varrho_p(\mathbf{32}) = \frac{\mathbf{p}\,(1798)}{\mathbf{p}\,(1766)} = \frac{51.8}{43.1} = 1.20^{44};\quad \frac{\mathbf{p}\,(1790)}{\mathbf{p}\,(1770)} = \frac{48}{45} = 1.07 \tag{25.149}$$

[43] Clark (2007b, p. 100).

[44] Clark (2002, p. 303) gives for *Agricultural prices*, **p(t)** [ Index, **p**(1870) =100 ]: $\varrho_p(\mathbf{30}) = \frac{\mathbf{p}\,(1789)}{\mathbf{p}\,(1760)} = \frac{68.4}{57.7} = 1.19$; $\varrho_p(\mathbf{30}) = \frac{\mathbf{p}\,(1799)}{\mathbf{p}\,(1770)} = \frac{84.5}{66.6} = 1.27$; $\varrho_p(\mathbf{40}) = \frac{\mathbf{p}\,(1799)}{\mathbf{p}\,(1760)} = \frac{84.5}{57.7} = 1.46$.

From rent increases, $\varrho_{\mathbf{r}}(\mathbf{40})$, and price increases $\varrho_{\mathbf{p}}(\mathbf{40})$, we have the increases in $\varrho_{\mathrm{MP_A}}(\mathbf{40})$:

$$\varrho_{\frac{r}{p}}(\mathbf{40}) \;=\; \frac{\frac{r_A}{p}(1800)}{\frac{r_A}{p}(1760)} \;=\; \frac{\varrho_{\mathbf{r}}(\mathbf{40})}{\varrho_{\mathbf{p}}(\mathbf{40})} \;=\; \varrho_{\mathrm{MP_A}}(\mathbf{40}) \qquad (25.150)$$

Using the numbers (25.146) and (25.149–25.150), we get with $\varrho_{\mathbf{p}}(\mathbf{34})$, $\varrho_{\mathbf{p}}(\mathbf{32})$, the inequalities for $\varrho_{\mathbf{p}}(\mathbf{40^*})$, (LHS):

$$1.20 \;=\; \frac{1.5}{1.25} \;<\; \varrho_{\frac{r}{p}}(\mathbf{40^*}) = \frac{\varrho_{\mathbf{r}}(\mathbf{40})}{\varrho_{\mathbf{p}}(\mathbf{40^*})} \;<\; \frac{1.6}{1.2} \;=\; 1.33\;;$$

$$1.027^{45} \;=\; \frac{1.5}{1.46} \;<\; \varrho_{\frac{r}{p}}(\mathbf{40}) \qquad (25.151)$$

Thus with (25.150–25.151), we have for $\varrho_{\mathrm{MP_A}}(\mathbf{40})$:

$$1.20 \;<\; \varrho_{\mathrm{MP_A}}(\mathbf{40}) = \frac{\mathbf{MP_A}(1800)}{\mathbf{MP_A}(1760)} \;<\; 1.33\;; \qquad \varrho_{\mathrm{MP_A}}(\mathbf{40}) \;>\; 1.027 \qquad (25.152)$$

Accordingly, the *marginal productivity* of *Land*, $\mathbf{MP_A}$, should—with wheat prices (25.149) as benchmark for output prices ($\mathbf{p}$), (25.150)—have increased *at least* **20** percent and *at most* **33** percent during the *period*, **1760–1800**, LHS (25.152); we return to the RHS case, $\varrho_{\mathrm{MP_A}}(\mathbf{40}) > 1.027$, below.

To get the *Agricultural Production* (Output) changes (**1760–1800**) corresponding to (25.152), we need the *sizes* of *Average* productivities of *Land*: $\mathbf{AP_A(1760)}$ and $\mathbf{AP_A(1800)}$, and the *increases*, $\varrho_{\mathrm{AP_A}}(\mathbf{40})$.

Having used *observed data* for nominal *rents* $r_A$, (25.143–25.146), and *observed* output *prices*, $p$, (25.149), the *implied* (calculated) "real rent" $\boldsymbol{r_A/p}$, (25.150–25.152), is equated to and seen as Marginal products of Land,

$$\frac{\mathbf{r_A}}{\mathbf{p}} = \mathbf{MP_A(A, L, K)} = \frac{\partial \mathbf{F(A, L, K)}}{\partial \mathbf{A}}\;;\; \mathbf{MP_A}(1800) = \frac{\partial F_I(A, L, K)}{\partial A}\;;$$

$$\mathbf{MP_A}(1760) = \frac{\partial F_{II}(A, L, K)}{\partial A} \qquad (25.153)$$

To maintain this equality requires changing **factor ratios** (Land *cultivation* intensities), $l_A = L/A$, $k_A = K/A$, $k = K/L$. For distinct *cultivation* systems **I/II**, (25.153), like **7 F/3 F**, *marginal* and *average* productivities (25.102–

[45] Here is used, $\varrho_{\mathbf{p}}(\mathbf{40}) = 1.46$, in the note 44 above.

25.104) can be *related* by using *Rent shares* in Revenue, $\boldsymbol{\delta_A} = \frac{R_A}{Y = p\,Q_A}$, (25.15–25.16), and the *Accounting* relations in (25.37–25.38). Thus, like (25.47), we have for year **1760** and year **1800**: $\varrho_{AP_A}(\mathbf{40}) = \frac{\varrho_{MP_A}(40)}{\varrho_{\delta_A}(40)}$—in the full version as,

$$\varrho_{AP_A}(40) = \frac{\mathbf{AP_A(1800)}}{\mathbf{AP_A(1760)}} = \frac{\mathbf{MP_A(1800)/MP_A(1760)}}{\boldsymbol{\delta_A}\mathbf{(1800)}/\boldsymbol{\delta_A}\mathbf{(1760)}} = \frac{\varrho_{MP_A}(40)}{\varrho_{\delta_A}(40)} \tag{25.154}$$

Exact farm accounting data for the *sizes* of $\boldsymbol{\delta_A}$**(1760)** and $\boldsymbol{\delta_A}$**(1800)** does not exist; but some evidence is available from *Young's national farm accounts* by **1771**—given in Allen (1992, p. 331: Table IV-1) as: **Revenue: 58.746** mill. pound = $\mathbf{p\,Q_A}$, Rent: 23.646 mill. pound = $\mathbf{R_A}$, i.e.,

$$\begin{aligned} \mathbf{1760}, 1770: \delta_A &= \frac{R_A}{p\,Q_A} = \frac{23.6}{58.7} = \mathbf{0.40}\ ; \\ \mathbf{1803}: \delta_A &= \frac{R_A}{p\,Q_A} = \frac{138}{478} = \mathbf{0.29}\ ; \quad \varrho_{\delta_A}(\mathbf{40}) = \frac{0.3}{0.4} = \mathbf{0.75} \end{aligned} \tag{25.155}$$

where $\boldsymbol{\delta_A}$ (1803) is from Young (1813, 1969, p. 431), showing **Rent** (including tithe, taxes) for the average expence (revenue) per *100 acres* in 1803. An *alternative*[46] to the estimate of $\varrho_{\delta_A}(\mathbf{40})$ in (25.155) is:

$$\begin{aligned} \mathbf{1760}, 1770: \delta_A &= \mathbf{0.35}\ ; \\ \mathbf{1790}: \delta_A &= \frac{R_A}{p\,Q_A} = \frac{127}{412} = 0.31\,; \\ \delta_A &= \frac{99}{360} = \mathbf{0.28}\ ; \quad \varrho_{\delta_A}(\mathbf{40}) = \frac{0.28}{0.35} = \mathbf{0.8} \end{aligned} \tag{25.156}$$

where, $\boldsymbol{\delta_A}(1790) = 0.31$, is from Chambers and Mingay (1966, p. 118), whereas, $\boldsymbol{\delta_A}(1790) = 0.28$, is again from Young (1813, 1969, p. 431). For the period (**1759–1802**), it is from (25.130) that Land rent *shares*, $\boldsymbol{\epsilon}_{\mathbf{A}}^{\mathbf{N}}$, of National income *declined* relatively by about 20 percent: $\frac{0.19}{0.23} = 0.83$—a bit less than $\varrho_{\delta_A}(\mathbf{40})$, (25.156).

With (25.155) and (25.152), we apply (25.154) and get the *increases* in Output—*Average Product* of Land:

$$\mathbf{1.6} = \frac{1.2}{0.75} < \varrho_{AP_A}(\mathbf{40}) = \frac{\mathbf{AP_A(1800)}}{\mathbf{AP_A(1760)}} = \frac{\varrho_{MP_A}(\mathbf{40})}{\varrho_{\delta_A}(\mathbf{40})} < \frac{1.33}{0.75} = \mathbf{1.8} \tag{25.157}$$

[46] The decrease in Landrent share, $\varrho_{\delta_A} = 0.80$, (25.156), is similar to, $\varrho_{\delta_A} = 0.83$, in (25.47), cf. note 19.

Thus, for a *given* Total Land acreage (**A**), an increase in the real *rent*, $\mathbf{r_A/p} = \mathbf{MP_A}$, of *20* percent, and a decline of the rent *share*, $\delta_A$, by *25* percent, the **output**, $\mathbf{Q_A}$, Land Productivity $\mathbf{AP_A}$, will have increased at *least* **60** percent during this 40 year period (**1760–1800**). If the rent **share**, $\delta_A$, only declined *20* percent, [with less inputs (intensive use) of the other factors ], then *Agricultural output*, $\mathbf{Q_A}$, from the given cultivated Land acreage will "*only*" have *increased* at *least* **50** percent during the same period.

$$\mathbf{1.5} = \frac{1.2}{0.8} < \varrho_{\,AP_A}(\mathbf{40}) = \frac{\varrho_{\,MP_A}(\mathbf{40})}{\varrho_{\,\delta_A}(\mathbf{40})} \quad ; \quad \varrho_{\,Q_A}(\mathbf{40}) = \varrho_{\,AP_A}(\mathbf{40}) \tag{25.158}$$

With (25.155) and the increase in real *rent*, $\mathbf{r_A/p} = \mathbf{MP_A}$, of only *2.7* percent, (25.151), RHS, we have at least *increases* in *Total Agricultural* **output**, $\mathbf{Q_A}$,—from constant *Land* acreage (A)—of **38** percent:

$$\mathbf{1.38} = \frac{1.027}{0.75} < \varrho_{\,AP_A}(\mathbf{40}) = \frac{\mathbf{AP_A(1800)}}{\mathbf{AP_A(1760)}} = \frac{\varrho_{\,MP_A}(\mathbf{40})}{\varrho_{\,\delta_A}(\mathbf{40})} \; ; \; \varrho_{\,Q_A(40)} = \varrho_{\,AP_A}(\mathbf{40}) \tag{25.159}$$

*Total Cultivated* Land acreage (**A**) was *not* constant in period (**1760–1800**). Expansion of (**A**) was at least **5** pct, $\varrho_A = \mathbf{1.05}$, i.e., *increases* Agricultural **output**, $\varrho_{\,Q_A(40)}$, beyond (25.159), to *at least* **45** pct.:

$$\varrho_{\,Q_A(40)} = \varrho_{\,AP_A(40)} \cdot \varrho_A \, , \; \varrho_A = \frac{A(1800)}{A(1760)} \quad ;$$

$$\varrho_{\,Q_A(40)} = \varrho_{\,AP_A(40)} \cdot \varrho_A = \mathbf{1.38 \cdot 1.05} = \mathbf{1.45} \tag{25.160}$$

For period **1760–1802**, *population* increased **48** pct, (25.140), $\varrho_{\bar{N}} = \frac{9.13}{6.16} = \mathbf{1.48}$.

So the *Agricultural output* increased at least, as $\varrho_{\,Q_A(40)} = \mathbf{1.45}$, (25.160), is/was *sufficient* to break the so-called **Malthusian trap**,[47] allowing the

[47] See Note 42. The *Malthusian trap* model (with population barriers) may be related to the Attractor ('Stagnation', stationary point) in the "*classical node*" of Fig. 8.1, Chap. 8, with decreasing return to scale ($\mathbf{m} < \mathbf{1}$), due to *Land* in *fixed* supply; see Galor and Weil (2000, p. 807), Galor (2011, p. 17). *Land* (acreage) cultivation with *crop rotation* now allows for macro (aggregate) models operating with $\mathbf{m} = \mathbf{1}$ in production (output), and the *node* Fig. 8.1 is replaced by phase portraits of *growing* Output, Population, Employment, Labor supplies in Fig. 8.3, LHS—which was assumed to include manufactured (Industry) output as well as the product of Agriculture; cf. Malthus (1803, 1958, II, p. 126).

*English population* of **18. century** to increase beyond any former historical[48] *ceiling*. Thus, the **Agricultural** sector of the English economy produced *unprecedented increases* in sizes of the *output* during the 1770s, 1780s, and 1790s—matching/maintaining the *per capita food consumption* of the *exorbitant increase* of *population* in the same period; cf. note 35.

The agricultural *output* increases $\varrho_{Q_A}(\mathbf{40})$ in (25.157–25.158) were expressed in *wheat equivalents*, cf. (25.149), whereas a *price index*, $\varrho_P(\mathbf{40}) = 1.46$, was used in (25.159–25.160), cf. note 44–45. Without getting involved in index-debates of standard of living, we may indicate some main components of agricultural *output* by showing the particular sales/revenues involved in the **1771** total **Revenue**: **58.746** mill. pound, (25.155).

These sales/revenues are, Allen (1992, p. 331: Table IV-1), Young (1771, p. 458–459):

1. Grain (wheat: 16.770 + barley: 10.496 + oats: 5.636) 32.902: **56** pct.
2. Peas/beans 4.050: 7 pct.
3. Dairy products 4.078: 7 pct.
4. Sheep (meat: 8.000 + wool: 4.944) 12.944: **22** pct.
5. Fatting beasts + young cattle 3.480: 6 pct.
6. Swine 1.283: 2 pct.

In Young (1771)'s national tables, the chief products of agriculture are *grain* and *livestock*. After 1771, wheat increased relatively more than barley, and livestock products became more important, especially dairy products and meat of cattle, although sheep mutton retained a significant part in revenue, cf. Ashton (1955, p. 245). Supplies of vegetables expanded, diets changed. Smith (1776, 1961, Ch.VII, p. 87) says: "Not only grain has become somewhat cheaper, but many other things, from which the industrious poor derive an agreeable and wholesome variety of food, have become a great deal cheaper. Potatoes, for example, do not at present, through the greater part of the kingdom, cost half the price which they used to do forty years ago. The same thing may be said of turnips, carrots, cabbages; things which were formerly never raised by the spade, but which are now commonly raised by the plough. All sort of garden stuff too has become cheaper"; cf. *Products*/market deliveries from all *six Rings* of Fig. 25.2.

Cottage industry (clothing,[49] candles, footwear) grew alongside the population, providing markets for farmers secondary products, wool, tallow and hides, contributing to higher demand for livestock products than for cereals.

The *new* English *farming* (cultivation, field) system—expressed by $\mathbf{F_I(A, L, K)}$, (25.153), analogous to **7F**—with crop rotation ['Norfolk

[48] See "Re-establishing" the English Agricultural revolution after 1750, Overton (1996b, p. 17); cf. Overton (1996a, p. 207). Divergent positions with many references are described in Allen (1999, p. 209), Clark (1998, p. 77).

[49] Smith (1776, 1961, p. 87): "The great improvements in the coarser manufactures of both linen and woollen cloth furnish the labourers with cheaper and better clothing". On the agricultural sector in Adam Smith, see Jeck (1994, p. 570).

four-course' (wheat, turnips, barley, clover), alternation], enclosure[50] (large consolidated Tenant farms) attained (as **7 F**) large *gains* in economic *efficiency* and *outputs*, which is achieved by *reallocation* (reducing fallow) and more intensive ( *expansion*) of existing *resources*[51] (labor and capital) rather than new inventions. The *new* system $\mathbf{F_I(A, L, K)}$ was *combined* with *more land* under cultivation (reducing waste-land) and *more employment* (agricultural labor, and artisans) in the *countryside*[52]—see Appendix. Thus, the ***improved English Agricultural*** system $\mathbf{F_I(A, L, K)}$ *provided* in the period (**1760–1800**)—as inferred from its *implications* (derivatives), indirect evidence, and *empirical data*, (25.153–25.160)—the **home grown food supplies** for its *fast growing* population.

## Final Comments

This chapter has dealt with a wide range of subjects: von Thünens *Ring* system of *Land cultivation* and their relation to transport costs and city grain prices, *analytical cost* and *production functions* related the the Tellow Estate Accounts, agricultural cultivation (field) systems, *empirical models*, and *agricultural history* for the second half of the 18th century in Denmark and England. Since the chapter does not lend itself to detailed summary, we only offer here a few remarks on our findings and main results. The three factor CES production of Land, Labor and Capital should be examined and evaluated empirically in relation to Manor Estate accounts in several countries. With Manorial data on production, land rents, and agricultural wages from the eighteenth century, several critical growth model issues of escaping stagnation and breaking population barriers could and ought to be finally resolved.

[50] Chambers and Mingay (1966, p. 88): "Enclosure was fatal to three classes: the small farmer, the cottager, and the squatter"—"Before enclosure, the cottager was a labourer with land, after enclosure he was a labourer without land" (p. 97). The small farmers (Husbandmen) was economically adversely affected by the abolition of "open fields" and the "commons", and the same were the cottagers. These two groups were combined as Agricultural workers in the updated Social Tables of Lindert and Williamson (1982, op.cit) for 1802, cf. (25.135–25.137). The squatters, often living in huts on wasteland, seemingly had often to leave the Parish (to avoid/reduce the "poor relief"), when new tenant farms was established by the Landlords on former Commons and Wastelands.

[51] As mentioned in note 47, *crop rotation* allowed macrodynamic models to operate with $\mathbf{m} = \mathbf{1}$ in production, and so generating solutions and phase portrait of *growing* Output, Population, Employment, Labor supplies in Fig. 8.3, LHS. With $\mathbf{m=1}$, and *canonical classical* growth models, large expansions *population* and *labor supplies* increases the rates (*rapidity*) of economic (output) growth, see. Chap. 7, (7.77), (7.79), and Chap. 9 ; cf. "Post-Malthusian Regime", Galor and Weil (2000, p. 807). "Demographic Transition" occurs at a later stage, but before "Modern Growth", see Galor and Weil (2000, p. 809), Galor (2011, p. 148), Hansen and Prescott (2002, p. 1208), Overton (1996a, p. 69), Clark and Cummins (2015).

[52] See Chambers (1953, p. 342–43) on the expansion of industry in the *rural* and *urban* centres, with *parallel* movement of prosperity and population, together with the conditions of an adequate labor supply at last fulfilled.

# Appendix: On English Land Rents, Outputs, and Costs

## *English Farm Accounts*

*Young's National Farm Accounts, 1771*

Above (25.155) was shown **revenue** and **rent** from *Young's national farm accounts*, **1771**, as seen in Allen (1992, p. 331: Table IV-1)—from which further **cost data** are given below:

Revenue: **58.746** mill. pounds = $\mathbf{p\,Q_A}$

Rent ('Surplus to Land'): 23.646 mill. pounds = $R_A$

1. Rent *share* of Revenue: 23.646/58.746 = **0.40** = $\boldsymbol{\delta}_\mathbf{A} = R_A/p\,Q_A$

Labor Costs: 15.989 mill. pounds = $w\,L$

2. Labor cost *share* of Revenue: 15.989/58.746 = **0.27** = $\boldsymbol{\delta}_\mathbf{L} = w\,L/p\,Q_A$

Capital Costs: 7.883 mill. pounds = $rK\;K$

3. Capital cost *share* of Revenue: 7.883/58.746 = **0.13** = $\boldsymbol{\delta}_\mathbf{K} = rK\;K/p\,Q_A$

Seed: 4.885 mill. pounds = $S_A$

4a. Seed cost *share* of Revenue: 4.885/58.746 = **0.09** = $\boldsymbol{\delta}_\mathbf{S} = S_A/p\,Q_A$

Other expenses of farming: 6.297 mill. pounds = $S_E$

4b. Other expense *share* of Revenue: 6.297/58.746 = **0.11** = $\boldsymbol{\delta}_\mathbf{E} = S_E/p\,Q_A$

4. Miscellaneous expense *share* of Revenue = 4a + 4b = $\boldsymbol{\delta}_\mathbf{S} + \boldsymbol{\delta}_\mathbf{E} = \boldsymbol{\delta}_\mathbf{M} = \mathbf{0.20}$

Total Cost: $C = 2+3+4 = 35.100$ mill. pounds ; $23.646 = R_A = p\,Q_A - C = 58.746 - 35.100$

We summarize the various *shares* of *Revenue*, $p\,Q_A$—satisfying the *Accounting identity*:

$$\delta_A + \delta_L + \delta_K + \delta_M = 0.40 + \mathbf{0.27} + 0.13 + 0.20 = 1 \tag{25.161}$$

The shares (25.161) are also seen/used in growth accounting calculations of Allen (1992, p. 228).

The Eq. (25.161) can be regarded as an overall *Accounting identity* of *Cost shares*, when *Rent* $R_A$ and $\delta_A$ represent the *factor* (user) *cost* of land in obtaining gross output and total revenue, $p\,Q_A$, cf. **A,B,C** in **7-F** and **3-F** accounting statements, Sect. "Tellow Farm Accounts, Revenues, Costs, and Land Rents".

The Revenue components of the **58.746** mill. pounds was shown above, and they are exactly as stated by Young (1771, p. 458–459). Similarly, Seed, Rents (*without* Tithe), and Labor cost are in (25.161) exactly as Young (1771, p. 458–459), but the low share, $\boldsymbol{\delta}_\mathbf{K} = 0.13$, *differs* somewhat from Young's.

Still more quantitative information may be extracted from Young (1771, p. 455–466), especially issues related to/depending on sizes of *Total* acreage (**A**), which his analyses *assume* are **32** mill. *acres* (14 mill. arable, 16 mill. grassland, 2 mill. wood) with Average *rent* per acre, $\mathbf{r_A} = \mathbf{0.7}$ pound/acre, $\mathbf{R_A} = 32 \cdot 0.7 =$ **22.400** mill. pound. *Labor* cost per acre, 1771, is, $\mathbf{w\,L/A} = \frac{16.000}{32.000} = \mathbf{0.5}$ pound per acre; $\boldsymbol{\delta_L = w L/p Q_A} = \frac{16.000}{58.746} = \mathbf{0.27}$. Finally, Young's *Revenue* per acre, $\mathbf{p Q_A/A}$, 1771, becomes: $\frac{58.746}{32.000} = \mathbf{1.84}$ pound per acre.

*South Midland Farming Estimations*

Allen (1992, p. 226: Table 11-9) estimates *Labor productivity* in South Midland farming—and give for years—circa 1700, circa 1800—expressions and numbers (stated in notation above, farm size, A acres):

| | | | |
|---|---|---|---|
| 1. Output per acre (pound per acre): | 3.51 | 3.42 | $p\,Q_A/A$ - Revenue, pound per acre |
| 2. Labor per acre (pound per acre): | 0.96 | 0.71 | $w\,L/A$ - Labor cost, pound per acre |
| 3. Output per worker (pound of output per pound of Labor cost): | 3.66 | 4.82 | $\frac{p\,Q_A}{w\,L} = \frac{Q_A/L}{w/p} = \frac{AP_L}{MP_L} = \frac{1}{\delta_L}$ |
| 4. Index for Row 3 [1600 : 2.27 = 100] | 1.61 | 2.12 | |

*Row 3* is Row 1 divided by Row 2, i.e., $3.66 = \frac{3.51}{0.96}$, $4.82 = \frac{3.42}{0.71}$.

The interpretation of the number **3.66** in Row 3 as "*Output per worker*" is misleading. With the notation in Row 3, $3.66 = \frac{p\,Q_A}{w\,L} = \frac{1}{\delta_L}$, is the *reciprocal* of Labor cost *share*: $\delta_L = 1/3.66 = \mathbf{0.27}$—as seen above in *Young's* national farm accounts and for 1771 with $\delta_L$ in (25.161).

Thus **Row 3–Row 4** (indexes) will *not* explain/show *changes* in the *Labor productivity* for Midlands, c.1700, c.1800—but rather reflect *changes* in *Labor* cost *shares* of *Revenue*, $\delta_L$ (via reciprocals).

According to Row 3 for circa 1800, $\delta_L = 1/4.82 = \mathbf{0.21}$, which compared to $\delta_L = 0.27$ for 1771, is a drastic *decline* in the *Labor* cost *share* during this period, $\varrho_{\delta_L}(\mathbf{30}) = \frac{0.21}{0.27} = \mathbf{0.78}$—in contrast to the $\varrho_{\epsilon_L^*}$ number in (25.101) for *new* Land intensive cultivations.

For the County of Suffolk, Young (1813, 1969, p. 431) gives *labor cost* share[53] for **1790**, $\delta_L = \frac{93}{330} = \mathbf{0.28}$, and for **1803**, $\delta_L = \frac{132}{431} = \mathbf{0.31}$, i.e, a **larger** $\delta_L$ than in **1771**, (25.161)—*conforming* to the factor (labor, capital) *intensity*[54] pattern, and the numbers of $\varrho_{\delta_L}$, $\varrho_{\epsilon_L^*}$ in (25.101); cf. note 52 on parallel expansion of employment (labor) in the *rural* centres/agriculture and *urban* centres before 1800.

[53] Young (1813, 1969, p. 431) gives *labor cost* share for 1790, $\delta_L = \frac{93}{360} = 0.26$, and 1803, $\delta_L = \frac{132}{478} = 0.28$; but the cost denominator includes tithes and rates, which were *not* included in the Land rents, 1771: $R_A = 23.646$. Hence the adjustments of $\delta_L$ for 1790, 1803, in text above—in order to be compared with, $\delta_L = 0.27$, 1771.

[54] Chambers and Mingay (1966, p. 18): "The farming methods employed: the hoeing of turnips as in the Norfolk system was heavy on manpower, while convertible husbandry in which grass and arable land alternated, required more labor than land permanently under grass"; cf. Timmer (1969, p. 392).

All these *South Midland* farming numbers above for circa 1800 are atypical for many (most) counties. The number, c.1800, **3.42** pounds per acre = $p\, Q_A/A = \mathbf{p\, AP_A}$, Revenue (output) per acre, is, ***paradoxically***, even *less* than c.1700: **3.51** pounds per acre = $p\, Q_A/A = \mathbf{p\, AP_A}$ - 3.51 *deviates*[55] much from, $p\, Q_A/A = \mathbf{1.84}$ pounds per acre, corresponding to, $\delta_L = 1/3.66 = \mathbf{0.27}$, (25.161), Young (1771).

No changes in the agricultural prices (**p**) support such "estimated decline" to **3.42** pounds per acre—and certainly does neither, $\varrho_{\mathbf{AP_A}}(\mathbf{40})$, (25.158–25.159).

## Bibliography


Aghion P, Durlauf S (eds) (2005) Handbook of Economic Growth, 1st edn. Elsevier, Amsterdam, North–Holland

Ahrend JC (2006) Die Korrespondenz Johann Heinrich von Thünens. Tellower Thünen Schriften 6, (Mecklenburg: Thünen–Museum–Tellow)

Allen RC (1982) The Effciency and Distributional Consequences of Eighteenth Century Enclosures. The Economic Journal 92:937–953

Allen RC (1988) The Price of Freehold Land and the Interest Rate in the Seventeenth and Eighteenth Centuries. The Economic History Review 41:33–50

Allen RC (1992) Enclosure and the Yeoman. Clarendon Press, Oxford

Allen RC (1999) Tracking the Agricultural Revolution in England. The Economic History Review 52:209–235

Allen RC (2000) Economic Structure and Agricultural Productivity in Europe, 1300–1500. The European Review of Economic History 4:1–26

Allen RC (2008) The Nitrogen Hypothesis and the English Agricultural Revolution: A Biological Analysis. The Journal of Economic History 68:182–210

Allen RC, O'Grada C (1988) On the Road again with Arthur Young: English, Irish, and French Agriculture during the Industrial Revolution. The Economic Journal 92:937–953

Allen RGD (1938) Mathematical Analysis for Economists. MacMillan, London

Andersen TB, Jensen PS, Skovsgaard CV (2016) The heavy plow and the agricultural revolution in Medieval Europe. Journal of Development Economics 118:133–149

Arrow KJ (1985) Maine and Texas—Economic History. American Economic Review 75:320–323

Ashley WJ (1913) Comparative Economic History and the English Landlord. Economic Journal 23:165–181

Ashton TS (1948, 1962) The Industrial Revolution. Oxford University Press, London

Ashton TS (1955) An Economic History of England: The 18th Century. Methuen & Co, London


[55] The South Midland Row 1 estimates: 3.51, 3.42, and Row 2 estimates: 0.96, 0.71, are also used in Allen (1992, p. 228: Table 11-10), which shows so-called Total Factor Productivity (TFP) calculations for c.1700, c.1800. But as these Row 1–2 estimates of "output per acre" and "labor productivity" are improper measures (as explained in text above), these TFP results are defective, too, and the results/conclusions—Allen (1992, p. 231)—about the agricultural employment (countryside) and labor productivity (before c.1800—'Landlords revolution') lack so far relevant justification and empirical support.

Bartz RP (2004) Die Thaer–Thünensche Tradition und die Entwicklung des ländliches Raumes. Tellower Thünen Schriften 4, (Mecklenburg: Thünen–Museum–Tellow)
Bartz RP, Zühlsdorf P (1994) Entdeckungen in Mecklenburg—Das Thünen–Museum–Tellow. Laumann Verlag, Dülmen
Beckett JV (1986) The Aristocracy in England 1660–1914. Basil Blackwell, Oxford
Beckett JV (1990) The Agricultural Revolution. Basil Blackwell, Oxford
Beckmann MJ, Puu T (1990) The Spatial Structures. Springer–Verlag, Berlin
Björn C (1987) The peasantry and agrarian reform in Denmark. Scandinavian Economic History Review 25:117–137
Blaug M (2002) Economic Theory In Retrospect, 3rd edn. Cambridge University Press, Cambridge
Boberg-Fazlic N, Jensen PS, Lampe M, Sharp P, Skovsgaard CV (2023) "Getting to Denmark": The Role of Agricultural Elites for Development. Journal of Economic Growth DOI 10.1007/s10887-023-09226-8
Brauer W (1950) Der Mathematiker–Ökonom. Kyklos 4:150–171
Brems H (1986) Pioneering Economic Theory 1630–1980. A Mathematical Restatement. The Johns Hopkins University Press, Baltimore
Brunt L (2003) Rehabilitating Arthur Young. The Economic History Review 56:265–299
Brunt L (2004) Nature or Nurture? Explaining English Wheat Yields in the Industrial Revolution, c.1770. The Journal of Economic History 64:193–225
Caselli F, Feyrer J (2007) The Marginal Product of Capital. Quarterly Journal of Economics 122:535–568
Chambers JD (1953) Enclosure and the Labor Supply in the Industrial Revolution. The Economic History Review 5:319–343
Chambers JD, Mingay GE (1966) The Agricultural Revolution, 1750–1880. Billing & Sons, Guildford, London
Chorley GPH (1981) The Agricultural Revolution in Northern Europe 1750–1880: Nitrogen, Legumes, and Crop Productivity. The Economic History Review 34:71–93
Christensen J, Christensen O, Jörgensen S, Nielsen M (2013) Omkostningsteori og Regnskab, 2nd edn. Syddansk Universitetsforlag, Odense
Clark C (1967) Von Thünen's Isolated State. Oxford Economic Papers 19:370–377
Clark G (1991) Yields Per Acre in English Agriculture, 1250–1860: Evidence from Labour Inputs. The Economic History Review 44:445–460
Clark G (1998) Commons Sense: Common Property Rights, Efficiency, and Institutional Change. The Journal of Economic History (58):73–102
Clark G (2002) Land rental values and the agrarian economy: England and Wales, 1500–1914. European Review of Economic History 6:281–308
Clark G (2004) The Price History of English Agriculture, 1209–1914. Research in Economic History 22:41–124
Clark G (2007a) A Farewell to Alms. Princeton University Press, Princeton
Clark G (2007b) The Long March of History: Farm Wages, Population, and Economic Growth, England 1209–1869. The Economic History Review 60:97–135
Clark G (2018) Growth or Stagnation? Farming in England 1200–1800. Economic History Review 71(1):55–81
Clark G, Cummins N (2015) Malthaus to modernity: wealth, status, and fertility in England, 1500–1879. Journal of Population Economics 28(1):3–24

Clark G, Huberman M, Lindert PH (1995) A British Food Puzzle, 1770–1850. The Economic History Review 48:315–237
Craft NFR (1985) British Economic Growth during the Industrial Revolution. Clarendon Press, Oxford
Datar SM, Rajan MV (2018) Horngren's Cost Accounting, 16th edn. Pearson Education, London
Dempsey BW (1960) The Frontier Wage, Thünen. Loyola University Press, Chicago, Teil 1 (parts), Teil 2
Dickinson HD (1969) Von Thünen's Economics. Economic Journal 79:894–902
Dunn ES (1954) The Equilibrium of Land-use Pattern in Agriculture. Southern Economic Journal (21):173–187
Ernle L (1936) English Farming: Past and Present, 5th edn. Longmans, Green and Co, London
Feldbäk O (1993) Danmarks Ökonomiske Historie 1500–1940. Systime Forlag, Herning
Fujita M, Thisse JF (2002) Economics of Agglomeration. Cambridge University Press, Cambridge
Fujita M, Krugman P, Venables AJ (2001) The Spatial Economy. MIT Press, Cambridge
Galor O (2005) From Stagnation To Growth: Unified Growth Theory. pp 172–293, in *Handbook 1A* Aghion & Durlauf, (eds.) (2005).
Galor O (2010) The 2008 Lawrence R. Klein Lecture—Comparative Economic Development: Insights From Unified Growth Theory. International Economic Review 51:1–44
Galor O (2011) Unified Growth Theory. Princeton University Press, Princeton and Oxford
Galor O, Weil DN (2000) Population, Technology, and Growth: From the Malthusian Regime to the Demographic Transition. American Econ Rev 90:806–828
Gilboy EW (1934) Wages in Eighteenth Century England. Russell & Russell, New York
Gilboy EW (1936) The Cost of Living and Real Wages in Eighteenth Century England. The Review of Economics and Statistics 18:134–143
Granger CWJ, Elliott CM (1967) A Fresh Look at Wheat Prices and Markets in the Eighteenth Century. The Economic History Review 20:257–265
Grotewold A (1959) von Thünen in Retrospect. Economic Geography 35:346–353
Hall P (ed) (1966) The Isolated State. Pergamon Press, Oxford, Wartenberg, C. M., Translation, Band 1, Band 2–3 (extracts)
Hansen GD, Prescott EC (2002) Malthus to Solow. American Economic Review 92:1205–1217
Hansen SA (1976) Ökonomisk Väkst i Danmark: 1720–1914. (Copenhagen: Akademisk Forlag)
Hansen VF (1888) Stavnsbaands-Lösningen og Landboreformerne, 1733–1807. G.E.C. Gads Boghandel, Copenhagen
Heckscher EF (1960) Industrialismen—Den Ekonomiska Utvecklingen Sedan 1750, 6th edn. Raben & Sjögren, Stockholm
Hicks JR (1969) A Theory of Economic History. Clarendon Press, Oxford
Hippauf R (2000) Johann Heinrich von Thünen—Ein Lebensbild. Hinstorff, Rostock
Jackson RV (1985) Growth and Deceleration in English Agriculture 1660–1790. The Economic History Review 38:333–351
Jacob W (1828) Tracts relating to the corn trade and corn laws: including the second report. London

Jannermann G (2007) Jugendlust, Arbeitsfreuden, und Arbeitskämpfe— Erinnerungen Friedrich Aereboe. Tellower Thünen Schriften 7, (Mecklenburg: Thünen–Museum–Tellow)

Jeck A (1994) The macrostucture of Adam Smiths's theoretical system: a reconstruction. European Journal of the History of Economic Thought 1:552–576

Jensen BS (2017) von Thünen: Capital, Production Functions, Marginal Productivity Wages and the Natural Wage. German Economic Review 18:51–80

Jensen P, Radu C, Sharp P (2022) To the Manor born: A new Microlevel Wage Database for Eighteenth-Century Denmark. European Review of Economic History (26):302–310

Jespersen KJV, Rasmussen CP, Raabyemagle H, Holstein P (2010) MOLTKE—Rigets Mägtigste Mand. Gads Forlag, Copenhagen

Johansen HC (1975) Befolkningsudvikling og Familiestruktur i det 18. Aarhundrede. Odense University Press, Odense

Kjeldsen-Kragh S (2007) The Role of Agriculture in Economic Development. CBS Press, Copenhagen

Klemm V (2004) Über agrarwissenshaftiche Lehren Thaers und Thünens—Unterschiede und Ursachen. pp 9–36, in Bartz (2004)

Köppen D (2002) Agrarökologishe Aspekte in der Lehre Thünens. pp 23–29, in *Berichte über Landwirtschaft*, Johann Heinrich von Thünen (1783–1850), Rauscher, Michael, Fritz Tack, ed., 215. Sonderheft, Landwirtschaftsverlag.

Krzymowski R, Minneman PG (1928) Graphical Presentaion of Thünen's Theory of Intensity. Journal of Farm Economics 10:461–482

Lampe M, Sharp PR (2018) A Land of Milk and Butter. University of Chicago Press, Chicago

Lee JS (2003) Feeding the Colleges: Cambridge's Food and Fuel Supplies, 1450–1560. The Economic History Review 56:243–264

Lindert PH (2000) When did Inequality rise in Britain and America? Journal of Income Distribution 9:11–25

Lindert PH, Williamson JG (1982) Revising England's Social Tables 1688–1812. Explorations in Economic History 19:385–408

Lindert PH, Williamson JG (1983) Reinterpreting Britain's Social Tables 1688–1913. Explorations in Economic History 20:94–109

Lloyd PJ (2001) The Origins of the von Thünen–Mill–Pareto–Wicksell–Cobb–Douglas Function. History of Political Economy 33:1–17

Lögstrup B (1984) The Landowner as Public Administrator: The Danish Model. Scandinavian Journal of History 9:283–312

Lögstrup B (2015) Bondens frisättelse—De danske Landboreformer 1750–1810. Gads Forlag, Copenhagen

Malthus TR (1803, 1958) An Essay on Population I–II, 2nd edn. J.M. Dent & Sons, London

Marshall A (1920) Principles of Economics, 8th edn. Macmillan, London

McCloskey DN (1972) The Enclosure of Open Fields: Preface to a Study of its Impacts on the Efficiency of English Agriculture in the Eighteen Century. The Journal of Economic History 32:15–35

Nellinger L (2014) Thünens umfassendes Raumwirtschaftsmodell, 57–126. Duncker & Humbolt, Berlin, pp 57–126, in *Studien zur Entwicklung der ökonomischen Theorie, XXIX*, Trautwein, Hans M. ed. Schriften des Vereins für Socialpolitik

Niehans J (1990) A History of Economic Theory, Classic Contributions 1720–1980. The Johns Hopkins University Press, Baltimore
Olsen E (1962) Danmarks Ökonomiske Historie siden 1750. Studier Nr 3 fra Köbenhavns Universitets Ökonomiske Institut (Copenhagen: G.E.C.Gads Forlag)
O'Rourke KH, Williamson JG (2002) Explaining Europe's Overseas Trade Boom, 1500–1800. The Journal of Economic History 62:417–456
Overton M (1984) Agricultural Productivity in Eighteenth–Century England: Some Further Speculations. The Economic History Review 37:244–251
Overton M (1996a) Agricultural Revolution in England. Cambridge University Press, Cambridge
Overton M (1996b) Re–Establishing the English Agricultural Revolution. The Agricultural History Review 44:1–20
Parker RAC (1955) Coke of Norfolk and the Agrarian Revolution. The Economic History Review 8:156–166
Persson KG, Sharp P (2015) An Economic History of Europe, 2nd edn. Cambridge University Press, Cambridge
Petersen A (1944) Thünen's Isolierte Staat. Verlag Paul Parey, Berlin
Rasmussen CP (2010a) A. G. Molkte og det holstenske kobbelbrug. Landbohistorisk Tidsskrift (2):9–48
Rasmussen CP (2010b) Innovative Feudalism. The development of dairy farming and "Koppelwirtschaft" on the Manors in Schleswig–Holstein in seventeenth and eighteenth centuries. The Agriculture History Review 58:172–190
Ricardo D (1817, 1821, 1965) The Principles of Political Economy and Taxation. J.M. Dent and Sons, London
Ricardo D (1965) The Principles of Political Economy and Taxation, 3rd edn. J. M. Dent & Sons, London
Samuelson PA (1954) The Transfer Problem and Transportation Cost. Economic Journal 64:264–289
Samuelson PA (1983) Thünen at Two Hundred. Journal of Economic Lite–rature 21:1468–1488
Schmidt TD, Jensen PS, Naz A (2018) Agricultural productivity and economic development: the contribution of clower to structural transformation in Denmark. Journal of Economic Growth 23:387–426
Schneider E (1934) Johann Heinrich von Thünen. Econometrica 2:1–12
Schneider E (1959) J. H. von Thünen und die Wirtschaftstheorie der Gegenwart. Duncker & Humbolt, Berlin, pp 14–28, in *Schriften des Vereins für Socialpolitik*, Hoffmann, W.G. ed., Neue Folge, 14
Schneider E (1964) Einführung in die Wirtschaftstheorie, II. Teil, 9th edn. J.C.B. Mohr/Paul Siebeck, Tübingen
Schneider E (1965) Einführung in die Wirtschaftstheorie, IV. Teil, 2nd edn. J.C.B. Mohr/Paul Siebeck, Tübingen
Schumpeter JA (1954) History of Economic Analysis. Oxford University Press, New York
Schwarze R (1995) Johann Heinrich von Thünens Jugendschrift "Beschreibung der Landwirtschaft in dem Dorfe Grossen–Flotbeck (1803). Duncker & Humbolt, Berlin, in *Studien zur Entwicklung der ökonomischen Theorie, XIV*, Rieter, H., ed. Schriften des Vereins für Socialpolitik
Schwarze R (2002) Klopstock und Voght im Leben des Lucas Andreas Staudinger. Tellower Thünen Schriften 3, (Mecklenburg: Thünen–Museum–Tellow)

Skriver JB (2008) MOESGAARD—Historien om en Herregaard. Moegaard Forlag, Höjbjerg

Smith A (1776, 1961) The Wealth of Nations I–II. Methuen University Paperbacks, London

Smith A (1790, 1961) An Inquiry Into The Nature and Causes of The Wealth of Nations, vol 1–2, 5th edn. Methuen, London, (ed. E. Cannan)

Smith A (1999a) The Wealth of Nations, Books I-III. Penguin Classics, London, Skinner A (ed.)

Smith A (1999b) The Wealth of Nations, Books IV-V. Penguin Classics, London, Skinner A (ed.)

Smout TC (1987) Landowners in Scotland, Ireland and Denmark in the age of improvement. Scandinavian Journal of History 12:79–97

Solow RM (1985) Economic History and Economics. American Economic Review 75:328–331

Stamer H (1998) Wohlstandspolitik. Verlag Walter G. Mühlau, Kiel

von Thünen JH (1990) Der Isolierte Staat. Verlag Gustav Fischer, 1. Auflage, (Jena 1910); 3. Auflage, (Jena 1930); 4. Auflage, (Stuttgart 1966); 5. Auflage, Verlag Scientia, (Aalen 1990).

von Thünen JH (1826) Der isolierte Staat in Beziehung auf Landwirtschaft und Nationalökonomie. Hamburg, Band 1 (Teil 1), 2.ed. (Rostock 1842); Band 2 (Teil 2.I), (Rostock 1850); Band 3 (Teil 2.II, Teil 3), (Rostock 1863)

von Thünen JH (1875) Der isolierte Staat in Beziehung auf Landwirtschaft und Nationalökonomie, 3rd edn. Band 1–3, (Gothic type)

Timmer PC (1969) The Turnip, The New Husbandry, and The English Agricultural Revolution. Quarterly Journal of Economics 83:375–395

Turgot ARJ (1769, 1977) Reflections on the Formation and the Distribution of Riches. The Hague, in The Economics of A.R.J. Turgot, Groenwegen, P.D. ed.

Turner M (1982) Agricultural Productivity in England in the Eighteenth Century: Evidence from Crop Yields. The Economic History Review 35:489–510

Turner ME, Beckett JV, Afton B (1997a) Agricultural Rent in England, 1690–1914. Cambridge University Press, Cambridge

Turner ME, Beckett JV, Afton B (1997b) Taking Stock: Farmers, Farm Records, and the Agricultural Output in England, 1700–1850. The Agriculture History Review 44:21–38

Turner ME, Beckett JV, Afton B (2001) Farm Production in England, 1700–1914. Oxford University Press, Oxford

Van Bavel BJP, Thoen E (1999) Land Productivity and Agro–systems in the North Sea Area. Brepols Publishers

Van Zanden JL (1999) The development of agricultural productivity in Europe 1500–1800. 357–375 in Van Bavel et al. (1999)

Van Zanden JL (2002) Taking the measure of the early modern economy: Historical national accounts for Holland in 1510/14. European Review of Economic History 6:131–163

Woermann E (1959) J. H. von Thünen und die Landwirtschaftliches Betriebslehre der Gegenwart. Duncker & Humbolt, Berlin, pp 28–45, in *Schriften des Vereins für Socialpolitik*, Hoffmann, W.G. ed., Neue Folge, 14

Wöhe G, Döring U, Brösel G (2016) Einführung in die Allgemeine Betriebswirtschaftslehre, 26th edn. Verlag Franz Vahlen, München

Wrigley EA (1967) A Simple Model of London's Importance in Changing English Society and Economy, 1650–1750. Past & Present 37:44–70
Young A (1771) The Farmer's Tour Through the East of England, vol IV. W. Strahan, London
Young A (1771, 1973) The Farmer's Kalendar—or Monthly Directory, vol IV. Robinson & Roberts, London, EP Publishing, 1973
Young A (1792) Travels in France and Italy during the years, 1787, 1788, 1789. W. Richardson, London
Young A (1808, 1971) General Report On Enclosures. B. McMillan, London, A.M. Kelley, New York
Young A (1813, 1969) General View of the Agriculture of the County of Suffolk, vol IV. C. Doble & Brendon, London, David & Charles Reprints, 1969
Ziegler A, Schwarze R (2014) Voght und Thünen—Von Brief zu Brief. Tellower Thünen Schriften 11, (Mecklenburg: Thünen–Museum–Tellow)
Ziegler A, Bartz RP, Krüger H (2013) Johann Heinrich von Thünen—Zitate. Tellower Thünen Schriften 10, (Mecklenburg: Thünen–Museum–Tellow), Laumann–Verlag, Dülmen

PART V

# Stochastic Dynamic Systems

CHAPTER 26

# Stochastic One-Sector and Two-Sector Models

## Introduction

To set the stage for the main content, exposition, and organization of our subject matter—stochastic neoclassical models of capital accumulation in continuous time with steady-state or persistent growth per capita—we will review some fundamental issues of "stochastic processes" (parameterized collections [sequences] of stochastic variables) that were first raised in the seminal papers of Mirman (1972), Mirman (1973), Brock and Mirman (1972), Brock and Mirman (1973), Merton (1975), Bourguignon (1974).

Since the concept of a steady-state equilibrium has played an important role in both positive and optimal theory of economic growth, Mirman asked whether the same questions can be posed in *random growth models* as in deterministic growth models:

> In what sense should one even discuss the *random evolution* of the system? How does one define a concept in the random case analogous to the deterministic steady state? Added to these questions are the usual questions of existence, uniqueness, and stability for the random analogue of the steady state. Mirman (1973, p. 220)

Then he redefined the concept of a steady state in a stochastic sense:

> This is done by using the distribution function of possible capital labor ratios generated by the stochastic growth process. Having *defined the steady state* in

With co-author:
MARTIN RICHTER, Copenhagen Business School, Danske Research, Danske Bank, Copenhagen, Denmar.



B. S. Jensen, *The Elements and Dynamic Systems of Economic Growth and Trade Models*, https://doi.org/10.1007/978-3-031-52493-6_26

> terms of a *distribution* function, we then show that, for each admissible policy, the corresponding stochastic system has a unique steady state distribution, which is a degenerate distribution in the deterministic theory.
> Moreover, it is shown that this unique steady state distribution is stable in the sense that the set of possible states of the system converges over time to a well-defined set, the analog of the deterministic steady state, which supports the unique steady state distribution.
> Finally, it is shown that the *sequence of distributions converges* to a *unique* steady state distribution. Mirman (1973, p. 220)

In implementing this research program and in the mathematical analysis, Mirman (1972, p. 224) first assumed that his *random variables* **A(t)**—"*technology shocks*"—were independent, identically distributed in *discrete time*, and at any time independent of the capital-labor ratios, **k(t)**; further, it was assumed that the *shocks* **A(t)** were always strictly *positive and finite* (bounded away from both zero and infinity). To further simplify the analysis and avoid the possibility of a steady state at either zero or infinity, the technology (production function) was assumed to satisfy the simple derivative conditions of Inada (satisfied by the CD technology). With these assumptions, Mirman used mathematical techniques similar to those in the theory of *Markov chains* to establish the stochastic generalization of the Solow growth model by showing the existence, uniqueness, and stability of stationary probability measures. With his assumptions, he proved that a stationary measure will always exist, and the stationary measure will be unique if the recurrent states all communicate and admit no cyclically moving subsets. Stability meant that iterates (sequences) of the *transition probability* tend to a unique asymptotic (time-invariant) probability measure (distribution). The tools of the Markov processes were used to demonstrate such stability (convergence) to the unique stationary *(steady-state) distribution* of the capital-labor ratio. In short, particular *neoclassical* assumptions and

> techniques from positive *deterministic* growth theory were combined with the tools of *Markov processes* to achieve a positive theory of *stochastic* economic growth. Mirman (1973, p. 230)

Mirman (1973) had assumed that his *random variables* A(t), (technology shocks), which influence the production process, are *strictly positive* and *finite*. "More precisely, for any capital stock, output can neither be arbitrarily large nor arbitrarily small (even with arbitrarily small probability)", but "it was not clear where the bounds of possible random effects should be set" (Mirman 1972, p. 271). Next, he addressed this problem with arbitrarily large/small outputs. Still, the existence of a stationary measure (steady-state distribution) was demonstrated with a fixed-point argument (Mirman 1972):

> However, it is possible that there *exists* a *positive probability* of *extinction* or *positive probability* of an *infinite capital stock* in the stochastically generalized notion of a steady state.

Mirman (1972, p. 271) studied *conditions* "for the existence of stationary measures having *zero probability* at *zero and infinity*", which is *analogous* to imposing the *Inada conditions* on the production process. For recent advances in the field of stochastic neoclassical growth models in discrete time, see Scenk-Hoppe (2002), Lau (2002).

The first and important *extension* of the stochastic study by Mirman and Brock of the *discrete-time*, neoclassical *one-sector growth* model to ***continuous-time*** *stochastic processes* was done by Merton (1975) and Bourguignon (1974). Besides existence and uniqueness, much more *specific* (parametric) structures of the steady-state (asymptotic, limit) *distributions* for the capital-labor ratio and other variables could now be examined. Thus, Merton (1975) and Merton (1990) derived *density* functions and *first and second moments* that would be obtained in a steady state, and a *comparison* of the results and biases (in expected value) between *deterministic* (certainty) and *stochastic* modeling was rigorously derived for a stochastic growth model with a CD production function. The source of *uncertainty* was not positive technology shocks, but the uncertainty element in Merton (1975) affected the *evolution* of the *labor* (population) stock, which he assumed followed a ***geometric Wiener process***. With the latter, the *boundary problems* at zero and infinity for the capital-labor ratio were essentially *absent* from the first *stochastic* Solow growth model in *continuous time*.

In the neoclassical one-sector growth model, the sources of *uncertainty* were extended by Bourguignon (1974) to *saving* and *depreciation rates*, and the more general CES technology was adopted. Hence, the *boundary problem* for the *capital-labor ratio* naturally came into focus, and the result was that

> *uncertainty can make the neoclassical model closer to the Harrod-Domar-type models of growth in introducing the possibility of a collapse of the economy.* Bourguignon (1974, p. 142)

In particular, *uncertainty* in the *saving rate* posed (without further parameter restrictions) a *serious* problem of the *lower boundary absorption* ($\mathbf{k}=0$). Since 1975, the consequences of such critical boundary problems have somehow been that this field of research in *continuous-time stochastic growth models* has not matured and in fact mostly *disappeared* from the economic literature.

A *new start* is needed and is here attempted, partly by first *resolving* the older methodological *problems* with ***absorbing boundaries*** and steady state and partly by *extending* the *stochastic neoclassical* framework to *one-sector and two-sector* models with parameters generating *endogenous* (persistent) *per capita growth*. Simulations of *sample paths* and asymptotic *density functions* will illustrate our theorems and the properties of the *parametric* stochastic processes.

The study of *deterministic general equilibrium dynamics* in two-sector and multi-sector growth models has been reviewed and extended in Jensen (2003); here Chap. 17, Jensen and Larsen (2005); here Chap. 18, with an emphasis on factor *allocation*, output *composition*, and the dualities for *commodity* and *factor prices*. Sample paths of the *stochastic two-sector analog* are here discussed and demonstrated.

For our purposes and as benchmarks, *production functions* of the Cobb-Douglas (CD) and constant elasticity of substitution (CES) forms are used in both the stochastic one-sector and two-sector growth models. These technologies must therefore first be introduced and adequately described.

## Neoclassical Technologies and CES Forms

The sector *technologies* are—in stochastic one-sector and two-sector dynamics—described by nonnegative, smooth, concave, homogeneous production functions, $F_i(L_i, K_i), i = 1, 2$, with *constant returns* to scale in labor and capital,

$$Y_i = F_i(L_i, K_i) = L_i F_i(1, k_i) \equiv L_i f_i(k_i) \equiv L_i y_i,\ L_i \neq 0;\ F_i(0, 0) = 0 \tag{26.1}$$

where the function $f_i(k_i)$ is strictly concave and monotonically increasing in the capital-labor ratio $k_i \in [0, \infty)$, i.e.,

$$\forall k_i > 0: \quad f_i'(k_i) = df_i(k_i)/dk_i > 0, \qquad f_i''(k_i) = d^2 f_i(k_i)/dk_i^2 < 0 \tag{26.2}$$

The *sectorial output elasticities*, $\epsilon_{L_i}, \epsilon_{K_i}, \epsilon_i$—with respect to marginal and proportional factor variation—are, cf. (26.1),

$$\epsilon_{L_i} \equiv E(Y_i, L_i) \equiv \frac{\partial Y_i}{\partial L_i}\frac{L_i}{Y_i} = \frac{MP_{L_i}}{AP_{L_i}} = 1 - \frac{k_i f_i'(k_i)}{f_i(k_i)} > 0,\ k_i \neq 0 \tag{26.3}$$

$$\epsilon_{K_i} \equiv E(Y_i, K_i) \equiv \frac{\partial Y_i}{\partial K_i}\frac{K_i}{Y_i} = \frac{MP_{K_i}}{AP_{K_i}} = \frac{k_i f_i'(k_i)}{f_i(k_i)} = E(y_i, k_i) > 0 \tag{26.4}$$

$$\epsilon_i \equiv \epsilon_{L_i} + \epsilon_{K_i} = 1. \tag{26.5}$$

At any point on the isoquants, the *marginal rates* of *technical substitution*, $\omega_i(k_i)$, are, by (26.2), positive *monotonic* functions,

$$\omega_i(k_i) = \frac{MP_{L_i}}{MP_{K_i}} = \frac{f_i(k_i)}{f_i'(k_i)} - k_i = \frac{\epsilon_{L_i}}{\epsilon_{K_i}} k_i > 0, \quad \forall k_i > 0. \tag{26.6}$$

*CES Production Functions*

General CES forms of $F_i(L_i, K_i)$, (26.1),$\gamma_i > 0, 0 < a_i < 1, \sigma_i > 0$ are

$$Y_i = F_i(L_i, K_i) = \gamma_i L_i^{1-a_i} K_i^{a_i} = L_i \gamma_i k_i^{a_i} \equiv L_i f_i(k_i) \tag{26.7}$$

$$Y_i = F_i(L_i, K_i) = \gamma_i \left[ (1 - a_i) L_i^{\frac{\sigma_i - 1}{\sigma_i}} + a_i K_i^{\frac{\sigma_i - 1}{\sigma_i}} \right]^{\frac{\sigma_i}{\sigma_i - 1}} \tag{26.8}$$

$$= L_i \gamma_i \left[ (1 - a_i) + a_i k_i^{(\sigma_i - 1)/\sigma_i} \right]^{\sigma_i/(\sigma_i - 1)} \equiv L_i f_i(k_i) \qquad (26.9)$$

$$f_i'(k_i) = \gamma_i a_i k_i^{a_i - 1}, \quad f_i'(k_i) = \gamma_i a_i \left[ a_i + (1 - a_i) k_i^{-(\sigma_i - 1)/\sigma_i} \right]^{1/(\sigma_i - 1)} \qquad (26.10)$$

The *limits* of $f_i(k_i)$ and $f_i'(k_i)$ become, $(\forall i : \sigma_i \gtrless 1 \Rightarrow a_i^{\sigma_i/(\sigma_i - 1)} \lessgtr 1)$,

$$\sigma_i < 1 : \begin{cases} \lim\limits_{k_i \to 0} f_i(k_i) = 0, & \lim\limits_{k_i \to \infty} f_i(k_i) = \gamma_i (1 - a_i)^{\frac{\sigma_i}{\sigma_i - 1}} \\ \lim\limits_{k_i \to 0} f_i'(k_i) = \gamma_i a_i^{\frac{\sigma_i}{\sigma_i - 1}}, & \lim\limits_{k_i \to \infty} f_i'(k_i) = 0 \end{cases} \qquad (26.11)$$

$$\sigma_i = 1 : \begin{cases} \lim\limits_{k_i \to 0} f_i(k_i) = 0, & \lim\limits_{k_i \to \infty} f_i(k_i) = \infty \\ \lim\limits_{k_i \to 0} f_i'(k_i) = \infty, & \lim\limits_{k_i \to \infty} f_i'(k_i) = 0 \end{cases} \qquad (26.12)$$

$$\sigma_i > 1 : \begin{cases} \lim\limits_{k_i \to 0} f_i(k_i) = \gamma_i (1 - a_i)^{\frac{\sigma_i}{\sigma_i - 1}}, & \lim\limits_{k_i \to \infty} f_i(k_i) = \infty \\ \lim\limits_{k_i \to 0} f_i'(k_i) = \infty, & \lim\limits_{k_i \to \infty} f_i'(k_i) = \gamma_i a_i^{\frac{\sigma_i}{\sigma_i - 1}} \end{cases} \qquad (26.13)$$

For the CES technologies, the *monotonic* relations between marginal rates of substitution, factor proportions, and output elasticities are, cf. (26.8–26.10),

$$\omega_i = \frac{1 - a_i}{a_i} k_i^{1/\sigma_i}, \qquad k_i = \frac{1}{c_i} [\omega_i]^{\sigma_i}, \quad c_i = \left[ \frac{1 - a_i}{a_i} \right]^{\sigma_i} \quad i = 1, 2. \qquad (26.14)$$

$$\epsilon_{K_i} = \left[ 1 + \frac{1 - a_i}{a_i} k_i^{\frac{1 - \sigma_i}{\sigma_i}} \right]^{-1} = \frac{1}{1 + c_i \omega_i^{1 - \sigma_i}}, \quad \epsilon_{L_i} = \frac{c_i \omega_i^{1 - \sigma_i}}{1 + c_i \omega_i^{1 - \sigma_i}} \qquad (26.15)$$

With two-sector models and CES technologies, it is apparent from (26.14) that sectorial *factor* ratio ("intensity") *reversals* can only be avoided if and only if $\sigma_1 = \sigma_2$ and $a_1 \neq a_2$. Hence, with $\sigma_1 \neq \sigma_2$, there will be a *reversal* point, $(k_i, \omega_i) = (\bar{k}, \bar{\omega})$:

$$\bar{k} = \left[ \frac{a_1(1 - a_2)}{a_2(1 - a_1)} \right]^{\frac{\sigma_1 \sigma_2}{\sigma_2 - \sigma_1}} = \left[ \frac{c_2^{\sigma_1}}{c_1^{\sigma_2}} \right]^{\frac{1}{\sigma_2 - \sigma_1}}, \quad \bar{\omega} = \left[ \frac{c_2}{c_1} \right]^{\frac{1}{\sigma_2 - \sigma_1}} \qquad (26.16)$$

# STOCHASTIC ONE-SECTOR GROWTH MODELS

### *Introduction of Stochastic Elements*

The standard deterministic neoclassical one-sector growth model is described by the *ordinary differential equations* (ODE), cf. (26.1),

$$dL/dt \equiv \dot{L} = Ln \tag{26.17}$$

$$dK/dt \equiv \dot{K} = Lsf(k) - \delta K \tag{26.18}$$

$$dk/dt \equiv \dot{k} = sf(k) - (n + \delta)k \tag{26.19}$$

This general model becomes, with *uncertainty* (stochastic elements $\epsilon_i$) in the growth rate of *labor* $n$, the gross *saving* rate $s$, and the capital *depreciation* rate $\delta$,

$$\dot{L} = L(n + \beta_1 \epsilon_1) \tag{26.20}$$

$$\dot{K} = L(s + \phi_3(k)\epsilon_3)f(k) - (\delta + \beta_2 \epsilon_2)K \tag{26.21}$$

where $\beta_i \geq 0$, and $(\epsilon_1, \epsilon_2, \epsilon_3)$ are "*white noise*" (stochastic process with a constant spectral density function), related to *Wiener processes* $(\boldsymbol{w}_1, \boldsymbol{w}_2, \boldsymbol{w}_3)$ with the correlation structure

$$d\langle w_i, w_j \rangle = \rho_{ij}\, dt, \quad \rho_{ii} = 1, \quad i, j = 1, 2, 3 \tag{26.22}$$

and $\langle w_i, w_j \rangle$ is the quadratic variation process for the components of the Wiener process, (Karatzas and Shreve 1991; Øksendal 2005). For the formal connection between Wiener processes and "white noise", see Holden et al. (1996, chap. 3).

The function $\boldsymbol{\phi}_3$ is, as later explained, here conveniently chosen (to *avoid* boundary problems at zero) as

$$\phi_3(k) = \beta_3 \tanh(\lambda_3 k), \quad k \in [0, \infty), \quad \phi_3(0) = 0, \quad \phi_3(\infty) = \beta_3 \tag{26.23}$$

For the labor and capital stock, the associated *stochastic differential equations* (**SDE**) to (26.20–26.21) are given by

$$dL = Ln\, dt + L\beta_1 dw_1 \tag{26.24}$$

$$dK = (sLf(k) - \delta K)\, dt - \beta_2 K\, dw_2 + Lf(k)\phi_3(k)\, dw_3 \tag{26.25}$$

The *drift* and *diffusion* coefficients of the stochastic dynamic system (26.24–26.25) are *homogeneous* functions of *degree 1* in the *state variables* $L$ and $K$. The homogeneity of degree 1 allows us to reduce the *two-dimensional stochastic* system (26.24–26.25) to *one-dimensional stochastic dynamics* of the *capital-labor ratio.*

As an alternative to the uncertainty in the saving rate, we also consider *uncertainty* (stochastic element $\epsilon_4$) in *technology*, more precisely, uncertainty ($\epsilon_4$) in the *total productivity* parameter ($\gamma$) of the production function $f(k)$, i.e.,

$$\dot{K} = Ls(\gamma + \phi_4(k)\,\epsilon_4)\,[f(k)/\gamma] - (\delta + \beta_2\,\epsilon_2)K \tag{26.26}$$

where $\boldsymbol{\phi_4}$ is similar to $\boldsymbol{\phi_3}$ defined in Eq. (26.23). Hence, with (26.26), the stochastic differential equation (26.25) is replaced by

$$dK = (sLf(k) - \delta K)\,dt - \beta_2 K\,dw_2 + Ls\,[f(k)/\gamma]\,\phi_4(k)\,dw_4. \tag{26.27}$$

The stochastic differential equations (26.24–26.25) or (26.24), (26.27) represent a *two-dimensional stochastic system*, driven by a *three-dimensional* Wiener process. For the purposes of simulations, i.e., computing the sample paths $L(t,\omega)$ and $K(t,\omega)$ or the ratio, $k(t,\omega) = K(t,\omega)/L(t,\omega)$, it is sufficient to use the Eqs. (26.24), (26.25) or (26.24),(26.27). In fact, the SDE (26.24) is the well-known geometric Wiener process. There is in general no closed-form expression for the solutions (sample paths) for $K(t,\omega)$ or $k(t,\omega)$.

However, to precisely examine the *absorbing boundary* conditions and *stationarity* conditions for the diffusion process, $\boldsymbol{k(t)}$, it is necessary to obtain an *analytical* expression for $\boldsymbol{k(t)}$ as given by a particular one-dimensional Wiener process. Fortunately, as both drift and diffusion coefficients are homogeneous functions of degree 1 in $K$ and $L$, it allows us to *analytically* describe $k(t)$ as a *one-dimensional* **SDE**, driven by a *one-dimensional* Wiener process, where the relevant drift coefficient and diffusion coefficient now need to be exactly determined, cf. Jensen and Wang (1999, Lemma 1); here Lemma 27.1 in Chap. 27.

### *The SDE of the Capital-Labor Ratio*

**Theorem 26.1** *The stochastic neoclassical dynamics for the capital-labor ratio $k(t)$ of (26.24–26.25) is a diffusion process given by the SDE,*

$$dk = -(K/L^2)\,dL + (1/L)\,dK + (K/L^3)\,dL^2 - (1/L^2)\,dLdK \tag{26.28}$$

$$= \left\{[s - \rho_{13}\beta_1\phi_3(k)]f(k) - \left[n + \delta - (\beta_1^2 + \rho_{12}\beta_1\beta_2)\right]k\right\}\,dt \qquad (26.29)$$
$$- \beta_1 k\,dw_1 - \beta_2 k\,dw_2 + \phi_3(k) f(k)\,dw_3$$

*The* **SDE** *(26.29) can in its domain be given in the compact form,*

$$dk = a(k)\,dt + b(k)\,dw, \qquad k(t) \in (0, \infty) \tag{26.30}$$

*with the **drift coefficient**,*

$$a(k) = \bar{s}(k) f(k) - \Theta k \tag{26.31}$$

$$\bar{s}(k) = s - \rho_{13}\beta_1\phi_3(k) \qquad \Theta = n + \delta - (\beta_1^2 + \rho_{12}\beta_1\beta_2) \tag{26.32}$$

*and the **diffusion coefficient**,*

$$b^2(k) = \beta^2 k^2 + \phi_3(k)^2 f(k)^2 - \rho\phi_3(k) f(k)k \tag{26.33}$$

$$\beta^2 = \beta_1^2 + \beta_2^2 + 2\rho_{12}\beta_1\beta_2 \qquad \rho = 2(\rho_{13}\beta_1 + \rho_{23}\beta_2). \tag{26.34}$$

***Proof*** Itô's Lemma: Let $\boldsymbol{X(t)} \in \mathbb{R}^n$ be a *general diffusion process*, and if $\boldsymbol{F(X)}$ is an arbitrary $C^2$ map from $\mathbb{R}^n \to \mathbb{R}$, then

$$dF(X) = F_x^T dX + 1/2 dX^T F_{xx} dX \tag{26.35}$$

i.e., $F(X)$, determined by diffusion process $X(t)$, is again a diffusion process, where $\boldsymbol{F_x}$ represents the partial derivatives with respect to $x$ of the function $F(x)$, and $\boldsymbol{F_{xx}}$ represents the Hessian matrix of the function $F(x)$, and where, $\boldsymbol{(dw_i)^2 = dt\ \forall i}$ ; $\boldsymbol{dw_i \cdot dw_j} = 0$ for $\boldsymbol{i \neq j}$ ;
$\boldsymbol{(dt)^2} = 0$ ; $\boldsymbol{dt \cdot dw_i} = 0$. Hence, with

$$X = (L, K)^T, \quad dX = (dL, dK)^T, \qquad F(X) = K/L \equiv k, \tag{26.36}$$

$$F_X = \begin{pmatrix} \frac{\partial F}{\partial L} \\ \frac{\partial F}{\partial K} \end{pmatrix} = \begin{pmatrix} -\frac{K}{L^2} \\ \frac{1}{L} \end{pmatrix}, \quad F_{XX} = \begin{pmatrix} \frac{\partial^2 F}{\partial L^2} & \frac{\partial^2 F}{\partial L \partial K} \\ \frac{\partial^2 F}{\partial K \partial L} & \frac{\partial^2 F}{\partial K^2} \end{pmatrix} = \begin{pmatrix} \frac{2K}{L^2} & \frac{-1}{L^2} \\ \frac{-1}{L^2} & 0 \end{pmatrix} \tag{26.37}$$

we get, cf. (26.35–26.37),

$$dk = -\frac{K}{L^2} dL + \frac{1}{L} dK + \frac{1}{2}\left(\frac{2K}{L} dL^2 - 2\frac{1}{L^2} dL dK + 0\, dK^2\right) \tag{26.38}$$

$$= -\frac{K}{L^2} dL + \frac{1}{L} dK + \frac{K}{L^3} dL^2 - \frac{1}{L^2} dL dK \tag{26.39}$$

which is (26.28).

Inserting (26.24) and (26.25) into (26.39) gives

$$dk = -\frac{K}{L^2} L(n\,dt + \beta_1\,dw_1) + \frac{1}{L} L[\{sf(k) - \delta k\}\,dt - \beta_2 k\,dw_2 + \phi_3(k) f(k)\,dw_3] + \frac{K}{L^3} L^2 (n\,dt + \beta_1\,dw_1)^2$$

$$
\begin{aligned}
& -\frac{1}{L^2} L(n\,dt + \beta_1\,dw_1) L[\{sf(k) - \delta k\}\,dt \\
& - \beta_2 k\,dw_2 + \phi_3(k) f(k)\,dw_3] \\
&= -k(n\,dt + \beta_1\,dw_1) + \{sf(k) - \delta k\}\,dt - \beta_2 k\,dw_2 \\
& + \phi_3(k) f(k)\,dw_3 + k(n\,dt + \beta_1\,dw_1)^2 - (n\,dt + \beta_1\,dw_1) \\
& \times [\{sf(k) - \delta k\}\,dt - \beta_2 k\,dw_2 + \phi_3(k) f(k)\,dw_3] \\
&= -nk\,dt - \beta_1 k\,dw_1 + sf(k)\,dt - \delta k\,dt - \beta_2 k\,dw_2 + \phi_3(k) f(k)\,dw_3 \\
& + k\beta_1^2\,dt - \beta_1\,dw_1\,[-\beta_2 k\,dw_2 + \phi_3(k) f(k)\,dw_3] \\
&= -nk\,dt - \beta_1 k\,dw_1 + sf(k)\,dt - \delta k\,dt - \beta_2 k\,dw_2 + \phi_3(k) f(k)\,dw_3 \\
& + k\beta_1^2\,dt + \rho_{12}\beta_1\beta_2 k\,dt - \rho_{13}\beta_1\phi_3(k) f(k)\,dt \\
&= \left\{sf(k) - \rho_{13}\beta_1\phi_3(k) f(k) - nk - \delta k + \beta_1^2 k + \rho_{12}\beta_1\beta_2)k\right\}\,dt \\
& - \beta_1 k\,dw_1 - \beta_2 k\,dw_2 + \phi_3(k) f(k)\,dw_3 \qquad (26.40)
\end{aligned}
$$

which *establishes* (26.29).

Finally, using Levy's characterization, the local martingale term, $-\beta_1 k\,dw_1 - \beta_2 k\,dw_2 + \phi_3(k) f(k)\,dw_3$, can be simplified to $\boldsymbol{b(k)\,dw}$, where $\boldsymbol{w}$ is a new one-dimensional *Wiener process*. The *diffusion coefficient* $\boldsymbol{b(k)}$ can be calculated by determining the *quadratic variation* of: $-\beta_1 k\,dw_1 - \beta_2 k\,dw_2 + \phi_3(k) f(k)\,dw_3$. Hence, we get

$$
\begin{aligned}
b(k)\,dw &\equiv -\beta_1 k\,dw_1 - \beta_2 k\,dw_2 + \phi_3(k) f(k)\,dw_3 \\
b^2(k)\,dt &\equiv [-\beta_1 k\,dw_1 - \beta_2 k\,dw_2 + \phi_3(k) f(k)\,dw_3]^2 \\
b^2(k)\,dt &= \beta_1^2 k^2\,dt + \beta_2^2 k^2\,dt + \phi_3(k)^2 f(k)^2\,dt + 2\beta_1\beta_2 k^2\,[dw_1, dw_2] \\
& \quad - 2\beta_1 k\phi_3(k) f(k)\,[dw_1, dw_3] - 2\beta_2 k\phi_3(k) f(k)\,[dw_2, dw_3] \\
b^2(k)\,dt &= \beta_1^2 k^2\,dt + \beta_2^2 k^2\,dt + \phi_3(k)^2 f(k)^2\,dt + 2\rho_{12}\beta_1\beta_2 k^2\,dt \\
& \quad - \rho_{13} 2\beta_1 k\phi_3(k) f(k)\,dt - 2\rho_{23}\beta_2 k\phi_3(k) f(k)\,dt \\
b^2(k) &= (\beta_1^2 + \beta_2^2 + 2\rho_{12}\beta_1\beta_2)k^2 + \phi_3(k)^2 f(k)^2 \qquad (26.41) \\
& \quad - 2(\rho_{13}\beta_1 + \rho_{23}\beta_2)\phi_3(k) f(k) k
\end{aligned}
$$

which is succinctly *summarized* in (26.33) together with (26.34). □

The *sample path* (trajectory) of the process $\boldsymbol{k(t)}$, (26.30–26.34), is formally given by

$$k(t;\omega) = k(0) + \int_0^t a(k[u;\omega])\,du + \int_0^t b(k[u;\omega])\,dw_u(\omega) \tag{26.42}$$

where $\boldsymbol{k(0)}$ is a fixed initial condition, and $\boldsymbol{\omega}$ symbolizes a particular *realization* of the Wiener process. The sample path (26.42) in this chapter is approximated by the Euler scheme, (Kloeden and Platen 1995).

**Remark 26.1** Note that correlation $\rho_{23}$ does *not* enter the drift coefficient in (26.31–26.32), because the *coefficient* of $dK^2$ is *zero*, cf. (26.37–26.38). Furthermore, note that our introduction of uncertainties (26.24–26.25) implies that the ***deterministic*** accumulation *parameters*, $\boldsymbol{s}$, $\boldsymbol{n}$, $\boldsymbol{\delta}$, only appear in the ***drift coefficient*** (26.31–26.32), but *not* in the ***diffusion*** coefficient (26.33–26.34). Some diffusion parameters $\beta_i$, $\rho_{ij}$, however, may appear in the drift coefficient (26.31–26.32).

From the ***derived diffusion process*** of the capital-labor ratio $\boldsymbol{k(t)}$ in Theorem 26.1, we can now analyze the *evolution* of the one-sector economy, with an emphasis on long-run behavior (asymptotic properties). The drift and diffusion coefficients, however, ***govern*** the evolution only at *interior* points of the state space. To fully define a diffusion process, the behavior at any *boundary* points *requires separate* specification. For our purposes of studying the long-run evolution of nontrivial states, we need to carefully examine the *conditions* that will make the *boundaries*, $k = 0$ or $k = \infty$, ***inaccessible*** for any *finite* time ($t < \infty$). If $a(0) = 0$ and $b(0) = 0$—as is often seen, cf. (26.30–26.34) and (26.11–26.13)— then $k(t) = 0$ is an ***absorbing*** boundary, i.e., the sample paths $k(t)$ remain at the zero position, once it is attained. Even if $a(0) \neq 0$, or $b(0) \neq 0$, and hence $k = 0$ is not an absorbing state, we cannot admit negative state values of $k(t)$, i.e., a ***viable*** (working) ***economic*** diffusion model must require that the ***inaccessibility*** of the boundary state $k = 0$ is ensured by imposing sufficient ***parameter restrictions*** on the actual drift and diffusion coefficients.

As the incremental Wiener processes $\boldsymbol{dw_i(t)} \in (-\infty, \infty)$ may occasionally take on very large negative values, the drift and diffusion coefficients must indeed be carefully studied to *prevent* the random variable $\boldsymbol{k(t)}$ from hitting the *lower boundary*, $k = 0$.

## BOUNDARIES, STEADY-STATE, AND CONVERGENCE

### *Terminology, Concepts, and Definitions*

Let the *transition probability* in the case of a *one-dimensional* stochastic process $X(t)$ be denoted

$$P(x,t;x_0,t_0) = \Pr[X(t) \le x \mid X(t_0) = x_0] \tag{26.43}$$

where $X(t)$ is the *state* of the process at instant $t$. The transition probability distribution $\boldsymbol{P}(\boldsymbol{x}, \boldsymbol{t}; \boldsymbol{x}_0, \boldsymbol{t}_0)$ is assumed to have a probability density function $\boldsymbol{p}(\boldsymbol{x}, \boldsymbol{t}; \boldsymbol{x}_0, \boldsymbol{t}_0)$, defined everywhere.

*Boundary Conditions* In terms of notation in (26.30), in the one-dimensional case, we define the following indefinite integrals (functions),

$$J(x) = \int_{x_0}^{x} \frac{a(u)}{b^2(u)} du; \quad \mathfrak{s}(x) = \exp\{-2J(x)\}, \ \mathcal{S}(x) = \int_{x_0}^{x} \mathfrak{s}(u) du \tag{26.44}$$

$$\mathfrak{m}(x) = \frac{\exp\{2J(x)\}}{b^2(x)} = \frac{1}{b^2(x)\mathfrak{s}(x)}, \ \mathcal{M}(x) = \int_{x_0}^{x} \mathfrak{m}(u) du \tag{26.45}$$

The functions $\boldsymbol{\mathfrak{s}(x)}$, $\mathcal{S}(\boldsymbol{x})$, $\boldsymbol{\mathfrak{m}(x)}$, and $\boldsymbol{\mathcal{M}(x)}$ are called, respectively, the *scale density* function, the *scale* function, the *speed density* function, and the *speed measure* of the stochastic processes $X(t)$; cf. Karlin and Taylor (1981, p. 194–196,229).

*Inaccessible Boundaries* Let the diffusion process $X(t)$ have two boundaries $r_1 < r_2$. *Sufficient* conditions: The boundaries $r_1$ and $r_2$ are inaccessible, if

$$\begin{array}{l} \forall x_0 \in [r_1, r_2], \mathcal{S}(r_1) = -\infty; \quad \mathcal{S}(r_2) = +\infty; \quad \text{equivalently,} \\ \mathfrak{s}(x) \text{ is not integrable on the closed interval } [r_i, x_0] \end{array} \tag{26.46}$$

or if

$$\mathcal{S}(r_i) = \lim_{x \to r_i} \mathcal{S}(x) = \lim_{x \to r_i} \int_{x_0}^{x} \mathfrak{s}(x) dx = \mp\infty; \quad i = 1, 2 \tag{26.47}$$

The *necessary* and *sufficient* condition is

$$\Sigma(r_i) \equiv \int_{x_0}^{r_i} [\mathcal{S}(r_i) - \mathcal{S}(x)]\mathfrak{m}(x) dx = +\infty; \quad i = 1, 2 \tag{26.48}$$

*Existence of Steady-State Distribution* A *time-invariant* distribution function $P(x)$ exists if and only if

$$\mathcal{S}(r_i) = \mp\infty \text{ and } \mathcal{M}(x) \text{ is finite at } r_i, \text{i.e., } |\mathcal{M}(r_i)| < \infty; \ i = 1, 2 \tag{26.49}$$

The existence of steady-state distribution $P(x)$—implying inaccessible boundaries—also implies the *c*onvergence of the nonstationary distribution functions $P(x, t)$ toward $P(x)$ as $t \to \infty$.

*Existence of Steady-State Density Function* A *time-invariant* probability density function $\boldsymbol{p}(\boldsymbol{x})$ exists if and only if the *speed* density $\mathfrak{m}(\boldsymbol{x})$ satisfies

$$\int_{r_1}^{r_2} \mathfrak{m}(x)dx < \infty, \quad p(x) = m\mathfrak{m}(x), \quad \int_{r_1}^{r_2} p(x)dx = 1 \tag{26.50}$$

where $\boldsymbol{m}$ is the *normalizing constant.*

The conditions and formulas above can be applied directly when we have the *same* stochastic differential equation (drift and diffusion coefficients) for the *whole interval* of $x$. For more details, see Karlin and Taylor (1981) and Mandl (1968).

**Remark 26.2** It is well known (Karlin and Taylor 1981, p. 359) that the solution (Itô-integral) to the stochastic differential equation (26.24) is the geometric Wiener process with the *continuous sample paths* (stochastic trajectories, realizations),

$$L(t) = L_0 \exp\{(n - \frac{1}{2}\beta_1^2)t + \beta_1 w_1(t)\}; \; 2n \gtrless \beta_1^2: \lim_{t\to\infty} L(t) = \begin{cases} \infty \\ 0 \end{cases} \tag{26.51}$$

Moreover, the *boundaries*, zero or infinity, are *inaccessible*, as the sample paths (26.51) cannot attain any of the two boundaries in *finite* time. It is instructive to prove the latter statement as a prelude to the general procedure of proving inaccessibility. From (26.24) and (26.44), the scale density $\mathfrak{s}(L)$ and the *scale function* $\mathcal{S}(L)$ become, cf. (26.44),

$$\mathfrak{s}(L) = \exp\left\{-2\int_{L_0}^{L} nL/(\beta_1^2 L^2)dL\right\} = (L/L_0)^{-2n/\beta_1^2} \tag{26.52}$$

$$\mathcal{S}(L) = \int_{L_0}^{L} \mathfrak{s}(L)dL = L_0/(1 - 2n/\beta_1^2)[(L/L_0)^{1-2n/\beta_1^2} - 1] \tag{26.53}$$

As $\mathcal{S}(0) = -\infty$ for $2n \geq \beta_1^2$, the latter is a *sufficient* parameter condition for the *inaccessibility* of the boundary: $k = 0$. But despite the finite $\mathcal{S}(0) = -L_0/(1 - 2n/\beta_1^2)$ for $2n < \beta_1^2$, the boundary $k = 0$ may not be still attainable.

The *speed density* $\mathfrak{m}(L)$ is, cf. (26.45),

$$\mathfrak{m}(L) = 2L^{2n/\beta_1^2}/(\beta_1^2 L^2) = (L_0^{2n/\beta_1^2}/\beta_1^2)L^{2n/\beta_1^2 - 2} \tag{26.54}$$

and we must now, with (26.53)–(26.54) and (26.48), evaluate

$$\Sigma(0) = \int_0^{L_0} [\mathcal{S}(L) - \mathcal{S}(0)]\mathfrak{m}(L)dL = \frac{L_0^{4n/\beta_1^2}}{\beta_1^2(1 - 2n/\beta_1^2)} \int_0^{L_0} \frac{dL}{L} = \infty \tag{26.55}$$

Thus, $\Sigma(0) = +\infty$ says that it takes *infinite* time to reach the zero boundary from any interior state, i.e., $L = 0$ is after all *inaccessible* for $2n < \beta_1^2$, as it *cannot* be attained in *finite* time. The same analysis can be applied to boundary $L = \infty$, which is neither attainable in finite time. From this examination of the *labor diffusion* process (26.24)—which has no steady-state distribution—it is clear that boundary problems for the capital-labor ratio diffusion are essentially due to boundary problems associated with the capital stock diffusion process.

### *Boundary Conditions: Neoclassical Growth Models*

*Labor growth and capital depreciation rates are uncertain*
From (26.30–26.34) with $\beta_3 = 0$, and the CES, $f = f_i$, (26.7–26.9), we have,

$$\sigma = 1, \quad dk = \{s\gamma k^a - \Theta k\}dt - \beta k dw, \tag{26.56}$$

$$\sigma \neq 1, \quad dk = \{s\gamma[(1-a) + ak^{(\sigma-1)/\sigma}]^{\sigma/(\sigma-1)} - \Theta k\}\, dt - \beta k\, dw. \tag{26.57}$$

**Theorem 26.2** *The sufficient conditions for the diffusion processes of one-sector neoclassical growth models to have inaccessible boundaries—with CES technologies (26.56–26.57) and uncertainties in both labor growth and capital depreciation—are:*

$$\sigma < 1: \begin{cases} k = 0 \ : \ 2(n + \delta - s\gamma a^{\sigma/(\sigma-1)}) \leq \beta_1^2 - \beta_2^2 \\ k = \infty: \ 2(n + \delta) \geq \beta_1^2 - \beta_2^2 \end{cases} \tag{26.58}$$

$$\sigma = 1: \begin{cases} k = 0 \ : \ \textit{always inaccessible} \\ k = \infty: \ 2\Theta + \beta^2 \geq 0 \Leftrightarrow 2(n + \delta) \geq \beta_1^2 - \beta_2^2 \end{cases} \tag{26.59}$$

$$\sigma > 1: \begin{cases} k = 0 \ : \ \textit{always inaccessible} \\ k = \infty: \ 2(n + \delta - s\gamma a^{\sigma/(\sigma-1)}) \geq \beta_1^2 - \beta_2^2 \end{cases} \tag{26.60}$$

*The parametric conditions, (26.58)–(26.60), with strict inequalities, ensure the existence and the long-run convergence of the stochastic capital-labor ratio $k(t)$ to a time-invariant (steady-state) probability distribution $P(k)$.*

***Proof*** $\sigma = 1$ : For an arbitrary $k_0 \in (0, \infty)$, the scale density function is given by, cf. (26.44), (26.56),

$$\mathfrak{s}(k) = \exp\left\{-2\int_{k_0}^{k} \frac{s\gamma k^a - \Theta k}{\beta^2 k^2} dk\right\}, \quad 0 < k \leq \infty \tag{26.61}$$

and, by simple integration, we get

$$\mathfrak{s}(k) = (k/k_0)^{2(\Theta/\beta^2)} \exp\left\{\frac{2s\gamma}{(1-a)\beta^2}(k^{-(1-a)} - k_0^{-(1-a)})\right\} \tag{26.62}$$

From (26.62), we have,

$$\mathcal{S}(0) = \int_{k_0}^{0} \mathfrak{s}(k)dk \equiv m_0 \int_{k_0}^{0} k^{2(\Theta/\beta^2)} \exp\left\{\frac{2s\gamma}{(1-a)\beta^2} k^{-(1-a)}\right\} dk \tag{26.63}$$

Since $1 - a > 0$ and $2s\gamma/[(1-a)\beta^2] > 0$, cf. (26.7), the exponential term in (26.63) will dominate and explode for $k \to 0$, and hence $\mathcal{S}(0)$ diverges, i.e., $\mathcal{S}(0) = -\infty$. Thus, the *lower boundary* $k = 0$ is always *inaccessible*, *irrespective* of the size of the drift and diffusion parameters.

$$\mathcal{S}(\infty) = \int_{k_0}^{\infty} \mathfrak{s}(k)dk \equiv m_0 \int_{k_0}^{\infty} k^{2(\Theta/\beta^2)} \exp\left\{\frac{2s\gamma}{(1-a)\beta^2} k^{-(1-a)}\right\} dk \tag{26.64}$$

Since $1 - a > 0$, cf. (26.7), the divergence of $\mathcal{S}(\infty)$ here only depends on the polynomial term in (26.64) with the exponent $2(\Theta/\beta^2)$. Hence, divergence of $\mathcal{S}(\infty)$ requires that $2(\Theta/\beta^2) \geq -1$, or, equivalently, $2(n+\delta) \geq \beta_1^2 - \beta_2^2$. Thus, the *upper* boundary $k = \infty$ is *inaccessible* by imposing the parameter restriction stated in (26.59).

$\sigma \neq 1$: From (26.57), we have the expressions, cf. (26.61),

$$\mathfrak{s}(k) = \exp\left\{-2 \int_{k_0}^{k} \frac{s\gamma[(1-a) + ak^{(\sigma-1)/\sigma}]^{\sigma/(\sigma-1)} - \Theta k}{\beta^2 k^2} dk\right\} \tag{26.65}$$

$\sigma < 1$ : From (26.65) and (26.11), we have,

$$\mathcal{S}(0) = \lim_{k \to 0} \int_{k_0}^{k} \mathfrak{s}(k)dk = \int_{k_0}^{0} (k/k_0)^{-2[s\gamma a^{\sigma/(\sigma-1)} - \Theta]/\beta^2} dk \tag{26.66}$$

Hence, it follows from (26.66) that the divergence of $\mathcal{S}(0)$ to $-\infty$ requires that the exponent must be less than or equal to $-1$, or equivalently, $2s\gamma a^{\sigma/(\sigma-1)} \geq 2\Theta + \beta^2$, which is the lower boundary condition in (26.58).

From (26.65) and (26.11), we have,

$$\mathcal{S}(\infty) = \lim_{k \to \infty} \int_{k_0}^{k} \mathfrak{s}(k)dk = \int_{k_0}^{\infty} (\frac{k}{k_0})^{\frac{2\Theta}{\beta^2}} \exp\{\frac{2s\gamma(1-a)^{\frac{\sigma}{\sigma-1}}}{\beta^2}(\frac{1}{k} - \frac{1}{k_0})\}\, dk \tag{26.67}$$

The polynomial term in (26.67) decides the divergence of $\mathcal{S}(\infty)$; it diverges to $+\infty$ if the exponent $2\Theta/\beta^2 \geq -1$, which gives the upper inaccessibility condition in (26.58).

$\sigma > 1$: From (26.65) and (26.13), we have,

$$\mathcal{S}(0) = \lim_{k\to 0}\int_{k_0}^{k} \mathfrak{s}(k)dk = \int_{k_0}^{0} (\frac{k}{k_0})^{\frac{2\Theta}{\beta^2}} \exp\left\{\frac{2s\gamma(1-a)^{\frac{\sigma}{\sigma-1}}}{\beta^2}\left(\frac{1}{k}-\frac{1}{k_0}\right)\right\} dk \tag{26.68}$$

The exponential term in (26.68) will always explode for $k \to 0$. Hence, $\mathcal{S}(0)$ is diverging, and accordingly, $k = 0$ is *inaccessible*, *irrespective* of parameter restrictions.

From (26.65) and (26.13), we have,

$$\mathcal{S}(\infty) = \lim_{k\to\infty}\int_{k_0}^{k} \mathfrak{s}(k)dk = \int_{k_0}^{\infty} (k/k_0)^{-2[s\gamma a^{\sigma/(\sigma-1)}-\Theta]/\beta^2} dk \tag{26.69}$$

$\mathcal{S}(\infty)$ is divergent, if and only if the *exponent* of the polynomial in (26.69) is larger than or equal to $-1$, which gives the *parametric inaccessibility restriction* as stated in (26.60). □

**Remark 26.3** Corresponding to the **CD** *case*, (26.59), *Bourguignon* (1974, p. 153-154), gave the upper-boundary *inaccessibility condition* as

$$2b/c \geq -1 \quad \Leftrightarrow \quad 2(n+\delta) \geq \beta_1^2 - \beta_2^2 - \beta_1\beta_2\rho_{12} \tag{26.70}$$

which *differs* from our *simpler expression* in (26.59). The *result* (26.70) is due a "misprint" in his *formula* for **dk** (p. 146), *equivalent* to *our* (26.38–26.39). Thus, we observe that, in *contrast* to his *result*, (26.70), the *correlation* $\rho_{12}$ has *no implication* for the *inaccessibility* of the upper-boundary. Incidentally, note that $\boldsymbol{\rho}_{12}$ does *not* enter the *boundary condition* for the **CES** *cases*, (26.58), (26.60).

By the way, LHS of the *boundary conditions* (26.58–26.60) represent, with $\beta_1 = \beta_2 = 0$, the *necessary* and *sufficient* conditions for the *existence* of a *nontrivial* (non-zero and finite) deterministic *steady state*. Evidently, $\beta_1 > 0$ makes it easier to *avoid* the trivial boundary $\boldsymbol{k} = \mathbf{0}$, but more likely to explode. Note that $\beta_2 > 0$ makes it easier to avoid explosion, but more likely to hit the boundary $k = 0$. The economic-mathematical intuition of such $\beta_i > 0$ effects is left to the reader.

### The Saving Rate Is Uncertain

It was seen in (26.30–26.34) that the *uncertainty* in *saving* behavior will always introduce *nonlinear* terms in the *diffusion* coefficient. Inaccessible boundaries here raise conditions that clash with common, deterministic, dynamic regularity properties. By (26.30–26.34) with $\beta_1 = \beta_2 = 0$, $\lambda_3 = \infty$, $\phi_3(k) = \beta_3$, cf. (26.23), we get

$$\sigma = 1, \quad dk = \{s\gamma k^a - (n+\delta)k\}dt + \beta_3\gamma k^a dw, \tag{26.71}$$

$$\sigma \neq 1, \quad dk = \{sf(k) - (n+\delta)k\}\,dt - \beta_3 f(k)\,dw, \; f(k) : (26.9) \tag{26.72}$$

**Theorem 26.3** *The diffusion process (26.30–26.34) with CD or CES functions, (26.7), (26.9), and uncertainty only in the saving rate -* $\beta_1 = \beta_2 = 0$, $\beta_3 \neq 0$ *- will have boundary properties and sufficient inaccessibility conditions as follows:*

$$\sigma < 1 \begin{cases} k = 0 \;\; : & 2[s\gamma a^{\sigma/(\sigma-1)} - (n+\delta)] \geq [\beta_3\gamma a^{\sigma/(\sigma-1)}]^2 \\ k = \infty : & \textit{always inaccessible} \end{cases} \tag{26.73}$$

$$\sigma = 1 \begin{cases} k = 0 \;\; : & \textit{inaccessible, if } a > \tfrac{1}{2}; \; \textit{poss.access. if } a < \tfrac{1}{2} \\ k = \infty : & \textit{always inaccessible} \end{cases} \tag{26.74}$$

$$\sigma > 1 \begin{cases} k = 0 \;\; : & \textit{possibly accessible} \\ k = \infty : & 2[s\gamma a^{\sigma/(\sigma-1)} - (n+\delta)] \leq [\beta_3\gamma a^{\sigma/(\sigma-1)}]^2 \end{cases} \tag{26.75}$$

***Proof*** **CD Case** Applying (26.44) to (26.71) gives,

$$\mathfrak{s}(k) = \exp\left\{\frac{(n+\delta)(k^{2(1-a)} + k_0^{2(1-a)}) - 2s\gamma(k^{1-a} - k_0^{1-a})}{\beta_3^2\gamma^2(1-a)}\right\} \tag{26.76}$$

From (26.44) and (26.76), we have,

$$\mathcal{S}(0) = \int_{k_0}^{0} \mathfrak{s}(k)dk \equiv m_0 \int_{k_0}^{0} \exp\left\{\frac{(n+\delta)k^{2(1-a)} - 2s\gamma k^{1-a}}{\beta_3^2\gamma^2(1-a)}\right\} dk \tag{26.77}$$

Since $1 - a > 0$, $\mathcal{S}(0)$ will *converge*, and, accordingly, $k = 0$ may possibly be accessible.

To decide whether $k = 0$ is in fact inaccessible, we must calculate $\Sigma(0)$. In the CD case, we have, for the lower boundary $k = 0$, cf. (26.48),

$$\Sigma(0) = \int_{k_0}^{0} [\mathcal{S}(0) - \mathcal{S}(k)]\mathfrak{m}(k)dk \tag{26.78}$$

The limit of the integrand $\mathcal{S}(k)\mathfrak{m}(k)$ in (26.78) is, cf. (26.44)–(26.45), (26.77),

$$\lim_{k\to 0} \mathcal{S}(k)\mathfrak{m}(k) =$$

$$\lim_{k\to 0} \frac{m_0 \int_{k_0}^{k} \exp\{[\beta_3^2\gamma^2(1-a)]^{-1}[(n+\delta)k^{2(1-a)}-2s\gamma k^{1-a}]\}dk}{\beta_3^2\gamma^2 k^{2a}\exp\{[\beta_3^2\gamma^2(1-a)]^{-1}[(n+\delta)k^{2(1-a)}-2s\gamma k^{1-a}]\}} \tag{26.79}$$

Since $[\beta_3^2\gamma^2(1-a)]^{-1} > 0$, the limit (26.79) *converges* iff $2(1-a) > 1$, i.e., $a < \frac{1}{2}$. Hence, with $a > \frac{1}{2}$, $\Sigma(0)$, (26.78) will be *divergent*, and thus the lower boundary is inaccessible.

From (26.44) and (26.76), we have,

$$\mathcal{S}(\infty) = \int_{k_0}^{\infty} \mathfrak{s}(k)dk \equiv m_0 \int_{k_0}^{\infty} \exp\left\{\frac{(n+\delta)k^{2(1-a)} - 2s\gamma k^{1-a}}{\beta_3^2\gamma^2(1-a)}\right\}dk \tag{26.80}$$

Since $1-a > 0$, and $k^{2(1-a)}$ is the dominating term, $\mathcal{S}(\infty)$ will always diverge, i.e., $k = \infty$ is *inaccessible.*

**CES Case** Applying (26.44)–(26.72) gives

$$\mathfrak{s}(k) = \exp\left\{-2\int_{k_0}^{k} \frac{s\gamma[(1-a)+ak^{(\sigma-1)/\sigma}]^{\sigma/(\sigma-1)} - (n+\delta)k}{\beta_3^2\gamma^2[(1-a)+ak^{(\sigma-1)/\sigma}]^{2\sigma/(\sigma-1)}}dk\right\} \tag{26.81}$$

$\sigma < 1$: From (26.81), we have, for small $k$, cf. (26.11),

$$\mathcal{S}(0) = \lim_{k\to 0}\int_{k_0}^{k} \mathfrak{s}(k)dk = \int_{k_0}^{0} \exp\left\{-2\int_{k_0}^{k} \frac{s\gamma a^{\sigma/(\sigma-1)} - (n+\delta)}{\beta_3^2\gamma^2 a^{2\sigma/(\sigma-1)}}k^{-1}dk\right\}dk$$

$$= \int_{k_0}^{0} (k/k_0)^{\frac{-2[s\gamma a^{\sigma/(\sigma-1)}-(n+\delta)]}{\beta_3^2\gamma^2 a^{2\sigma/(\sigma-1)}}} dk \tag{26.82}$$

$\mathcal{S}(0)$ diverges if the exponent of $k/k_0$ is less than or equal to $-1$, which immediately gives the condition (26.73).

From (26.81), we have, for large $k$, cf. (26.11),

$$\mathcal{S}(\infty) = \lim_{k\to\infty}\int_{k_0}^{k} \mathfrak{s}(k)dk = \int_{k_0}^{\infty} \exp\left\{-2\int_{k_0}^{k} \frac{s\gamma(1-a)^{\sigma/(\sigma-1)}-(n+\delta)k}{\beta_3^2\gamma^2(1-a)^{2\sigma/(\sigma-1)}}dk\right\}dk$$

$$= \int_{k_0}^{\infty} \exp\left\{\frac{(n+\delta)(k^2-k_0^2)-2[s\gamma(1-a)^{\sigma/(\sigma-1)}(k-k_0)]}{\beta_3^2\gamma^2(1-a)^{2\sigma/(\sigma-1)}}\right\}dk$$

$$\equiv m_0^3 \int_{k_0}^{\infty} \exp\left\{\frac{n+\delta}{\beta_3^2\gamma^2(1-a)^{2\sigma/(\sigma-1)}}k^2 - \frac{2s}{\beta_3^2\gamma(1-a)^{\sigma/(\sigma-1)}}k\right\}dk \tag{26.83}$$

As $1 - a > 0$, the constant denominators in (26.83) are positive, and since the $k^2$ term is the dominating term in the exponential expression, $\mathcal{S}(\infty)$ will always be divergent; hence, the upper boundary is always *in*accessible.

$\sigma > 1$: From (26.81), we have, for small $k$, cf. (26.13),

$$\mathcal{S}(0) = \lim_{k\to 0} \int_{k_0}^{k} \mathfrak{s}(k)dk = \int_{k_0}^{0} \exp\left\{-2\int_{k_0}^{k} \frac{s\gamma(1-a)^{\sigma/(\sigma-1)} - (n+\delta)k}{\beta_3^2\gamma^2(1-a)^{2\sigma/(\sigma-1)}} dk\right\} dk$$

$$\equiv m_1^0 \int_{k_0}^{0} \exp\left\{\frac{n+\delta}{\beta_3^2\gamma^2(1-a)^{2\sigma/(\sigma-1)}}k^2 - \frac{2s}{\beta_3^2\gamma(1-a)^{\sigma/(\sigma-1)}}k\right\} dk \tag{26.84}$$

Since $1 - a > 0$, $\mathcal{S}(0)$ will always converge, and hence $k = 0$ may possibly be accessible. Whether, in fact, $k = 0$ is attainable in finite time requires similar evaluations as shown above, cf. (26.78)–(26.79), (26.55).

From (26.81), we have, for large $k$, cf. (26.13),

$$\mathcal{S}(\infty) = \lim_{k\to\infty} \int_{k_0}^{k} \mathfrak{s}(k)dk = \int_{k_0}^{\infty} \exp\left\{-2\int_{k_0}^{k} \frac{s\gamma a^{\sigma/(\sigma-1)} - (n+\delta)}{\beta_3^2\gamma^2 a^{2\sigma/(\sigma-1)}} k^{-1} dk\right\}$$

$$= \int_{k_0}^{\infty} (k/k_0)^{\frac{-2[s\gamma a^{\sigma/(\sigma-1)} - (n+\delta)]}{\beta_3^2\gamma^2 a^{2\sigma/(\sigma-1)}}} dk \tag{26.85}$$

$\mathcal{S}(\infty)$ diverges if the exponent of $k/k_0$ is larger than or equal to $-1$, which is equivalent to the upper inaccessibility condition in (26.75). □

With uncertainty in the saving rate, the *drift* and *diffusion* coefficients in (26.20)–(26.21) now have *similar nonlinear elements*, that, if dominating, will prevent us from satisfying a sufficient lower inaccessibility condition, as the scale function $\mathcal{S}(k)$ at $k = 0$ is now finite, *whenever* $\sigma \geq 1$.

The factor accumulation process is likely to be much more severely affected (large volatility) by *uncertainty* about the *saving rate* than by uncertainties in labor growth and depreciation rates. The *lack* of any parametric *restrictions* preventing the *accessibility* of the *absorbing boundary* $k = 0$ (implosion,"economic collapse"), cf. (26.74), (26.75), represents a *critical* stochastic dynamic model complication for the system (26.30–26.34) and a mathematical issue to be adequately resolved below.

### *General Parameter Uncertainty and Inaccessible Boundaries*

To *dampen* the impact of the Wiener process $\boldsymbol{dw_3}$, near $k = 0$ in our (26.30–26.34), the *random element* $\boldsymbol{\epsilon_3}$ in the saving parameter must be *state dependent*, and to *preserve* (26.24)–(26.25) as a *homogeneous* stochastic *dynamic* system, the *function* $\boldsymbol{\phi_3(k)}$ was chosen, cf. (26.23).

From economic reasons, the actual *shape* of $\boldsymbol{\phi}_3(\boldsymbol{k})$ on the *domain* $k \in [0, \infty)$ is chosen as a monotonically *increasing* curve, but this curve should also—to avoid creating excessive saving parameter volatility—be *bounded* above by a *horizontal* asymptote. With these two stipulations upon relevant selections of $\phi_3(k)$, one choice might be the logistic (S-shaped) curve described by well-known exponential expression. But among the exponentials, a relevant and convenient *choice* of $\boldsymbol{\phi}_3(\boldsymbol{k})$, with proper domain and range for our purposes, is (26.23).

**Theorem 26.4** *The* ***sufficient*** *conditions for the general diffusion process (26.30–26.34)—with CES technologies and uncertainties in labor growth, capital depreciation, and saving rates—to have inaccessible lower and upper boundaries are:*

$$k = 0\,; \quad \sigma < 1: \quad 2(n + \delta - s\gamma a^{\sigma/(\sigma-1)}) \le \beta_1^2 - \beta_2^2 \tag{26.86}$$

$$k = 0\,; \quad \sigma \ge 1: \quad \textit{Always inaccessible} \tag{26.87}$$

$$k = \infty; \quad \sigma \le 1: \quad 2(n + \delta) \ge \beta_1^2 - \beta_2^2 \tag{26.88}$$

$$k = \infty; \quad \sigma > 1: \quad 2(n + \delta - s\gamma a^{\sigma/(\sigma-1)}) \ge \beta_1^2 - \beta_2^2 - \Delta \tag{26.89}$$

$$\Delta \equiv [\beta_3 \gamma a^{\sigma/(\sigma-1)}]^2 - 2\rho_{23}\beta_2\beta_3\gamma)a^{\sigma/(\sigma-1)}.$$

***Proof*** The *hyperbolic* function $\boldsymbol{\phi}_3(\boldsymbol{k}) = \boldsymbol{\beta}_3\mathbf{tanh}(\boldsymbol{\lambda}_3\boldsymbol{k})$, (26.23), is

$$\phi_3(k) = \beta_3 \tanh(\lambda_3 k) = \beta_3(e^{\lambda_3 k} - e^{-\lambda_3 k})/(e^{\lambda_3 k} + e^{-\lambda_3 k}), \quad k \ge 0 \tag{26.90}$$

It is well known and easily verified from (26.90) that for

$$\text{small } k : \phi_3(k) \sim \beta_3\lambda_3 k, \qquad \Leftrightarrow \qquad \phi_3(k)/\beta_3\lambda_3 k \to 1 \text{ as } k \to 0 \tag{26.91}$$

$$\text{large } k : \phi_3(k) \sim \beta_3, \qquad \Leftrightarrow \qquad \phi_3(k)/\beta_3 \to 1 \text{ as } k \to \infty \tag{26.92}$$

**Lower Boundary** $\sigma = 1$: With the CD production function (26.7), the scale density function $\mathfrak{s}(k)$ now becomes, cf. (26.44), (26.90),

$$\mathfrak{s}(k) = \exp\left\{-2\int_{k_0}^{k} \frac{[s - \rho_{13}\beta_1\phi_3(k)]\gamma k^a - \Theta k}{\beta^2 k^2 + \phi_3^2(k)\gamma^2 k^{2a} - \rho\phi_3(k)\gamma k^{(1+a)}}\, dk\right\} \tag{26.93}$$

Since $a < 1$, the *dominating* term in the numerator and the denominator of (26.93) becomes, for small $k$, cf. (26.91),

$$\mathfrak{s}(k) \sim \exp\left\{-2\int_{k_0}^{k} \frac{s\gamma k^a}{\beta^2 k^2} dk\right\} = \exp\{\frac{2s\gamma}{(1-a)\beta^2}(k^{-(1-a)} - k_0^{-(1-a)})\} \tag{26.94}$$

Since $1 - a > 0$, it is seen, from (26.94), that $\mathcal{S}(0) = \int_{k_0}^{0} \mathfrak{s}(k)dk$ is diverging at $k = 0$, cf. (26.63), and hence, the lower boundary is inaccessible.

$\sigma < 1$: With the CES function (26.9), the scale function with the dominating terms becomes, cf. (26.9), (26.11), (26.91), (26.94),

$$\mathcal{S}(0) = \lim_{k \to 0} \int_{k_0}^{k} \mathfrak{s}(k)dk = \int_{k_0}^{0} (k/k_0)^{2[\Theta - s\gamma a^{\sigma/(\sigma-1)}]/\beta^2} dk \tag{26.95}$$

Hence, it follows from (26.95) that the divergence of $\mathcal{S}_1(0)$ requires that the exponent $2[\Theta - s\gamma a^{\sigma/(\sigma-1)}]/\beta^2 \leq -1$, which is the lower boundary condition in (26.86), cf. (26.66).

$\sigma > 1$: With the CES function (26.7), the scale function with the dominating terms becomes, cf. (26.13),

$$\mathcal{S}(0) = \lim_{k \to 0} \int_{k_0}^{k} \mathfrak{s}(k)dk = \lim_{k \to 0} \int_{k_0}^{0} \exp\left\{ \frac{2s\gamma(1-a)^{\frac{\sigma}{\sigma-1}}}{\bar{b}^2}(k^{-1} - k_0^{-1}) \right\} dk \tag{26.96}$$

where $\bar{b}^2 \equiv \beta^2 + \beta_3^2\lambda_3^2\gamma^2(1-a)^{2\sigma/(\sigma-1)} - \rho\beta_3\lambda_3\gamma(1-a)^{\sigma/(\sigma-1)} > 0$.

Since the parameter $2s\gamma(1-a)^{\sigma/(\sigma-1)}/\bar{b}^2$ in the exponential term is always positive, it is seen by (26.96) that $\mathcal{S}(0)$ is always diverging; hence, $k = 0$ is inaccessible, irrespective of parameter restrictions, cf. (26.68).

**Upper Boundary** With the CD function (26.7), the scale density $\mathfrak{s}(k)$ becomes, cf. (26.44), (26.90),

$$\mathfrak{s}(k) = \exp\left\{ -2 \int_{k_0}^{k} \frac{[s - \rho_{13}\beta_1\phi_3(k)]\gamma k^a - \Theta k}{\beta^2k^2 + \phi_3^2(k)\gamma^2k^{2a} - \rho\phi_3(k)\gamma k^{(1+a)}} dk \right\} \tag{26.97}$$

Since $a < 1$, the ***dominating*** term in the numerator and denominator of (26.97) becomes, for large $k$, cf. (26.92),

$$\mathfrak{s}(k) \sim \exp\left\{ -2 \int_{k_0}^{k} \frac{-\Theta k}{\beta^2k^2} dk \right\} = (k/k_0)^{2\Theta/\beta^2} \tag{26.98}$$

The divergence of $\mathcal{S}(\infty)$ from (26.98) is analogous to the result in (26.64), (26.59); hence, we have (26.88) for $\sigma = 1$.

$\sigma < 1$: With the CES function (26.9), the scale density $\mathfrak{s}(k)$ becomes, keeping the dominant terms for large $k$, cf. (26.97), (26.92),

$$\mathfrak{s}(k) \sim \exp\left\{ -2 \int_{k_0}^{k} \frac{-\Theta k}{\beta^2k^2} dk \right\} = (k/k_0)^{2\Theta/\beta^2} \tag{26.99}$$

which is the same as (26.98), and the divergence of $\mathcal{S}(\infty)$ is analogous to (26.67), (26.58).

$\sigma > 1$: From (26.97), (26.9), (26.13), (26.92), we have, for large $k$,

$$\mathfrak{s}(k) \sim \exp\left\{-2\int_{k_0}^{k} \frac{(s-\rho_{13}\beta_1\beta_3)\gamma a^{\sigma/(\sigma-1)}k - \Theta k}{\beta^2k^2 + \beta_3^2\gamma^2 a^{2\sigma/(\sigma-1)}k^2 - \rho\beta_3\gamma a^{\sigma/(\sigma-1)}k^2}dk\right\}$$

$$= \exp\left\{-2\int_{k_0}^{k}(\bar{a}/\bar{b}^2)k^{-1}dk\right\} = (k/k_0)^{\bar{a}/\bar{b}^2} \tag{26.100}$$

$\bar{a} \equiv (s-\rho_{13}\beta_1\beta_3)\gamma a^{\frac{\sigma}{\sigma-1}} - \Theta$, $\bar{b}^2 \equiv \beta^2 + \beta_3^2\gamma^2 a^{\frac{\sigma}{\sigma-1}} - \rho\beta_3\gamma a^{\frac{\sigma}{\sigma-1}} > 0$.

Now $\mathcal{S}(\infty)$ from (26.100) *diverges*, cf. the analog (26.85) and (26.75), if the exponent is large: $\bar{a}/\bar{b}^2 \geq -1$. Rewriting the exponent, using (26.32), (26.34), gives our condition (26.89), where $\Delta \equiv \bar{b}^2 - \beta^2 + 2\rho_{13}\beta_1\beta_3\gamma a^{\sigma/(\sigma-1)} = [\beta_3\gamma a^{\sigma/(\sigma-1)}]^2 - 2\rho_{23}\beta_2\beta_3\gamma a^{\sigma/(\sigma-1)}$. □

The *assumptions* about $\boldsymbol{\phi}_3(\boldsymbol{k})$, (26.23), have *removed* the *uncertainty* in *saving rates* (26.21) entirely from the *lower boundary* problems with $\boldsymbol{\sigma \geq 1}$, cf. (26.74) and (26.75), because, with (26.23), we now have that (26.87) holds, irrespective of the size of *any drift* and *diffusion* parameters. With $\boldsymbol{\sigma < 1}$, proper parameter restrictions (26.86) can safeguard against attaining $k = 0$.

Thus, for *any substitution elasticity* of the CES technology, the *stochastic neoclassical growth model* of **Theorem 26.1**, (26.29–26.34), is made fully ***workable*** *without* ***any*** *boundary problems* (extinction, explosion).

### *Neoclassical SDE and Asymptotic Nonstationarity*

The relaxation of the *sufficient* inaccessibility condition $\mathcal{S}(\infty) = \infty$ does not itself in the long run imply an explosion. Still, to avoid any risk of implosion, we want to keep the sufficient *condition* $\mathcal{S}(0) = -\infty$. But, together with a *finite* $\mathcal{S}(\infty)$, we have the following well-known implications (with probability one),

$$[\mathcal{S}(0) = -\infty \wedge \mathcal{S}(\infty) < \infty] \Rightarrow \lim_{t\to\infty} k(t) = \infty \Rightarrow \lim_{t\to\infty} \mathrm{E}[k(t)] = \infty \tag{26.101}$$

Within our stochastic neoclassical growth model, a finite $\mathcal{S}(\infty)$ is simply equivalent to reversing the inequality in (26.88)–(26.89). For $\sigma \leq 1$, the reverse of (26.88) is $2(n+\delta) \leq \beta_1^2 - \beta_2^2$. The latter implies that $k(t) \to \infty$ as $t \to \infty$, but it is a pathological case, as the reversal of (26.88) also implies that $L(t) \to 0$ (although never reached in finite time). In short, no relevant stochastic endogenous growth is possible with $\sigma \leq 1$. Hence, as in the deterministic case, stochastic endogenous economic growth requires that the *marginal product* of *capital* is *bounded below*, i.e., $\sigma > 1$, cf. (26.13).

By reversing (26.89), the *sufficient condition* of persistent growth becomes, cf. (26.101), (26.87)

$$\sigma > 1: \mathcal{S}(\infty) < \infty \Leftrightarrow s\gamma a^{\frac{\sigma}{\sigma-1}} \geq n + \delta + 1/2(-\beta_1^2 + \beta_2^2 + \Delta) \tag{26.102}$$

which is the *stochastic analog* to the *deterministic* condition (with only $n+\delta$ on RHS) of endogenous (persistent) growth; see Jensen and Wang (1997, p. 93); here p. 633 in Chap. 21, Jensen and Larsen (1987); here Chap. 1.

We note from (26.102) that it is generally *more difficult* (higher *saving rates* are required) to *achieve persistent economic growth* per capita in the face of *uncertainty*—as $n - \frac{1}{2}\beta_1^2 > 0$ is now taken for granted in (26.102), and $\Delta$ is always positive when $\rho_{23} = 0$, cf. (26.89). Uncertainties in the *accumulation of capital*, (26.23), (26.25), ($\beta_2 \neq 0$, $\beta_3 \neq 0$) make the stochastic analog (26.102) harder to satisfy.

The *rapidity* of stochastic growth is not directly seen by (26.102). However, with $S(\infty) < \infty$, the stochastic differential equation (26.30) is, *asymptotically*,

$$dk \sim \bar{a}\,k\,dt + \bar{b}\,k\,dw \not\equiv (s - \rho_{13}\beta_1\beta_3)\gamma a^{\frac{\sigma}{\sigma-1}} - \Theta\}\,k\,dt + \left[\beta^2 + \beta_3^2\gamma^2 a^{\frac{2(\sigma-1)}{\sigma}} - \rho\beta_3\gamma a^{\frac{\sigma}{\sigma-1}}\right]^{\frac{1}{2}} k\,dw \tag{26.103}$$

i.e., *geometric* Wiener *processes* with sample paths:

$$k(t) \sim k_0 \exp\{(\bar{a} - \bar{b}^2/2)\,t + \bar{b}\,w(t)\};\quad 2\bar{a} > \bar{b}^2 \tag{26.104}$$

It is easily verified that the exponential growth condition, $\bar{a} - \frac{1}{2}\bar{b}^2 > 0$, in (26.104) is equivalent to (26.102). Thus, the *stochastic condition* (26.102) is indeed the *analog of deterministic* exponential per capita growth in the *neoclassical* growth model.

## Explicit Steady-State Distribution with CD Technologies

Having obtained the conditions for the *existence* of and convergence to a *steady-state* (time-invariant) *d*istribution, cf. (26.59), we also want to obtain as a *benchmark*—with CD sector technologies—a *closed-form* expression for the *time-invariant probability density* function $p(k)$ and the *distribution function* $P(k)$ of the diffusion process (26.56).

It turns out that the benchmark *distribution* function $P(k)$ for the CD economy can be expressed by *gamma* $\Gamma(\alpha)$ and *incomplete gamma* functions $\Gamma(\alpha, x_0)$, which are generally defined, respectively, by the improper integrals,

$$\Gamma(\alpha) \equiv \int_0^{\infty} x^{\alpha-1}e^{-x}dx, \quad \Gamma(\alpha, x_0) \equiv \int_{x_0}^{\infty} x^{\alpha-1}e^{-x}dx,\ \alpha > 0 \tag{26.105}$$

**Theorem 26.5** *The time-invariant (steady-state) distribution $P(k)$ for the stochastic process (26.56), cf.* Theorem 26.1, *will have a density function $p(k)$ if and only if:*

$$2\Theta + \beta^2 > 0 \quad \Leftrightarrow \quad 2(n+\delta) > \beta_1^2 - \beta_2^2 \tag{26.106}$$

*With (26.106), the time-invariant probability density function* $p(k)$ *is in closed form,*

$$p(k) = c_0 k^{-2[1+\Theta/\beta^2]} \exp\{-ck^{-(1-a)}\}, \qquad 0 < k < \infty \tag{26.107}$$

*where the constants* $c$ *and* $c_0$ *are given by,*

$$c = \frac{2s\gamma}{(1-a)\beta^2}, \quad c_0 = \frac{(1-a)c^\alpha}{\Gamma(\alpha)}, \quad \alpha = \frac{2\Theta + \beta^2}{(1-a)\beta^2} \tag{26.108}$$

*With the stationary density function* $p(k)$*, (26.107), the stationary distribution function*

$$P(k) = \int_0^k p(u)du \tag{26.109}$$

*can be given by the incomplete gamma functions as, cf. (26.105), (26.108)*

$$P(k) = \frac{1}{\Gamma(\alpha)} \Gamma(\alpha, ck^{-(1-a)}) \tag{26.110}$$

*The distribution* $P(k)$*, (26.110), will have finite first-order and second-order moments,* $\mathrm{E}(k)$ *and* $\mathrm{E}(k^2)$*, if and only if, respectively,*

$$\Theta > 0 \;\Leftrightarrow\; n + \delta > \beta_1^2 + \rho_{12}\beta_1\beta_2 \tag{26.111}$$

$$2\Theta - \beta^2 > 0 \;\Leftrightarrow\; 2(n+\delta) > 3\beta_1^2 + 4\rho_{12}\beta_1\beta_2 + \beta_2^2 \tag{26.112}$$

*With (26.111)–(26.112), the steady-state distribution* $P(k)$*, (26.110), will have first-order and second-order moments given by,*

$$\mathrm{E}(k) = \frac{\Gamma(\alpha^*)}{\Gamma(\alpha)} c^{(1-a)^{-1}}, \mathrm{E}(k^2) = \frac{\Gamma(\alpha^{**})}{\Gamma(\alpha)} c^{2(1-a)^{-1}}, \sigma^2 = \mathrm{E}(k^2) - [\mathrm{E}(k)]^2 \tag{26.113}$$

*where*

$$\alpha^* = \alpha - (1-a)^{-1} \qquad \textit{and} \qquad \alpha^{**} = \alpha - 2(1-a)^{-1} \tag{26.114}$$

*and* $\alpha$ *was given by (26.108).*

***Proof*** For the stochastic dynamic system (26.56), the *speed densities* are, cf. (26.44)–(26.45),

$$\mathrm{m}(k) = \frac{\exp\{-2\int_{\bar{k}}^{k} \frac{s\gamma\, u^a - \Theta u}{\beta^2\, u^2} du\}}{\beta^2\, k^2}, \qquad 0 < k < \infty \tag{26.115}$$

The *constant* $\tilde{k} > 0$ can be chosen arbitrarily, but for *numerical* purposes, it is convenient to let $\tilde{k}$ be close to the *mode* of the distribution.

After simple integration, we obtain,

$$\mathfrak{m}(k) = \frac{1}{\beta^2} k^{-2[1+\Theta/\beta^2]} \exp\left\{-\frac{2s\gamma}{(1-a)\beta^2} k^{-(1-a)}\right\}. \tag{26.116}$$

With the condition (26.106), the integral of the speed density, $\mathfrak{m}(k)$, (26.115–26.116) can be *normalized* to give the *probability density*, $p(k)$:

$$1 = \int_0^\infty c_0\, \mathfrak{m}(k) dk = \int_0^\infty p(k)\, dk \tag{26.117}$$

The normalizing constant $c_0$, (26.107–26.108), is here obtained by identifying $k^{a-1}$ of (26.116) with a transformed $\Gamma$-distribution, (26.110), with *position* parameter $c$ and *scala* parameter $1/\alpha$, both also given in (26.108).

The first-order and second-order moments are obtained from the density function $p(k)$ as,

$$\mathrm{E}(k) \equiv \int_0^\infty kp(k)dk, \qquad \mathrm{E}(k^2) \equiv \int_0^\infty k^2 p(k)dk. \tag{26.118}$$

By (26.118), (26.116), (26.107), and several substitutions of variables and lengthy rearrangements, we get the expression for $\mathrm{E}(k)$ and $\mathrm{E}(k^2)$ in (26.113).

Finally, we observe that

$$\alpha^* > 0 \quad \Leftrightarrow \quad \Theta > 0, \qquad \alpha^{**} > 0 \quad \Leftrightarrow \quad 2\Theta > \beta^2 \tag{26.119}$$

which gives the moment existence restrictions (26.111–26.112), and Theorem 26.5 is established. □

## Sample Paths and Asymptotic Densities with CD and CES Technologies

We include *simulations* of both sample paths and asymptotic (long-run stationary) densities of the stochastic growth models. For different sets of model parameters, we calculate the *steady-state* values (mean, mode, standard deviation) of the long-run stationary processes or, alternatively, simulate particular sample paths with *infinity* as *attractor* for parameters with stochastic *endogenous (persistent) growth*.

If they exist, *steady-state* values ($\kappa$) of the capital-labor ratio in *deterministic* one-sector growth models are the *critical points* of (26.19):

$$[\dot{k} = 0 \Leftrightarrow k(t) = \kappa] \Leftrightarrow \left[\frac{f(\kappa)}{\kappa} = \frac{n+\delta}{s}\right];\ AP_K(\kappa) = (n+\delta)/s \tag{26.120}$$

Closed-form expressions for the *root* values ($\kappa$)—LHS of (26.120) with CD and CES technologies, (26.122)—are given in **Table 26.1**, with explicit expressions for other *steady-state* properties, cf. (26.121–26.123), (26.4),

$$\omega(k) = \frac{1-a}{a} k^{1/\sigma} \tag{26.121}$$

$$f(k) = \gamma k^a \ ; \qquad f(k) = \gamma \left[(1-a) + a k^{\frac{\sigma-1}{\sigma}}\right]^{\frac{\sigma}{\sigma-1}} \tag{26.122}$$

$$f'(k) = \gamma a k^{a-1} ; \quad f'(k) = \gamma a \left[a + (1-a) k^{-(\sigma-1)/\sigma}\right]^{1/(\sigma-1)} \tag{26.123}$$

These formulas of Table 26.1 show *explicitly* how six *basic* (structural) parameters—*factor accumulation* parameters ($s, n, \delta$) and *technology* parameters ($\gamma$, $a$, $\sigma$)—determine various steady-state values (certainty equivalents). The tabulated CES formulas are rather elaborate parametric expressions, except $AP_K(\kappa)$ or its reciprocal ($K/Y$) at ($\kappa$).

The actual *invariance* of $AP_K(\kappa)$ to changes in *technology* parameters is a peculiarity that is solely tied to *one-sector* growth models [hence absent in Table 26.3] together with the *concept* of steady states (balanced growth: $\dot{L}/L = \dot{K}/K = \dot{Y}/Y$) and the *assumptions* of (i) $\dot{L}/L = n$ and (ii) constant gross saving rates, ($s$). By (26.19):

$$d \ln k(t)/dt \ = \ \dot{k}/k \ = \ \widehat{k} \ = \ s\,AP_K(k) - (n+\delta) \tag{26.124}$$

This growth equation (26.124) has played an important role in empirical convergence studies, cf. Sala-i-Martin (1996, p. 1342), Quah (1996), Barro and Sala-i-Martin (1992), Barro (1991). Here the invariance of $AP_K(\kappa)$, (26.120), (26.124), allows a simple numerical consistency check of all the calculations of $\boldsymbol{f}(\kappa)$ and ($\kappa$) in **Table 26.2**.

Although little commentary is allowed or necessary here, the extensive set of CD and CES parameter *cases* in Table 26.2—illustrating formulas of Table 26.1—deserve careful study and scrutiny, as such systematic steady-state numbers (*certainty equivalents*) are seldom shown; Table 26.2 is also important as a *benchmark* for corresponding *asymptotic expectations,* E($\boldsymbol{k}$), and the stochastic growth model simulations.

In addition to the *six* basic *accumulation* and *technology* parameters for ($\kappa$), E($k$) is also affected by the *uncertainty (volatility)* and *correlation* parameters: ($\beta_1, \beta_2, \beta_3, \beta_4, \lambda_3, \lambda_4, \rho_{ij}$), cf. (26.20–26.27), that are involved in the *drift* and *diffusion* coefficients, (26.31–26.34), of the stochastic capital-labor ratio, $k(t)$. As most cases in Table 26.2 show, despite their theoretical distinctions, the *actual values* of ($\kappa$) and E($\boldsymbol{k}$) nearly *coincide.* Moreover, as the CD cases (8–9) show, the additional impact of ($\beta_1 = 0.01, \beta_2 = 0.03$) on E($k$) needs five decimals to be seen.

In the CD cases (14–15) and CES case (10), the *starred* values of $(\beta_3, \lambda_3)$ indicate that they are both zero and instead *represent* $(\beta_4, \lambda_4)$. The CD cases (13–14) and CES cases (9–10) in Table 26.2 show that interchanging the level size and the uncertainty about $(s)$ and $(\gamma)$ are equivalent as to the impacts on $(\kappa)$, $E(k)$, $\sigma(k)$, *mode* $(k)$.

The *stationary densities* of $\boldsymbol{p(k)}$ are obtained, cf. (26.115–26.117), by numerically integrating and normalizing their respective *speed densities*, (26.44–26.45), with MATHEMATICA. Some $\boldsymbol{p(k)}$ are exhibited in Figs. 26.1, 26.2, 26.3, 26.4, 26.5, 26.6, 26.7, 26.8, 26.9 and 26.10. The *statistics* in Table 26.2—expectations, standard deviations, cf. (26.118)—for the stationary distribution are also calculated by using MATHEMATICA, but closed forms of $\sigma(k)$ are used as a control whenever they exist, cf. CD, (26.113). The modes are obtained by solving (26.125).

In Merton (1975), with a *one-sector* **CD** technology and *uncertainty* only in *labor growth*, it follows, Merton (1975, p. 383, footnote1), that the *deterministic* steady-state value, $(\boldsymbol{\kappa})$, has the *same* value as the *mode* of the *stationary* (steady-state) distribution and that $(\kappa)$ is *not* equal to the *expectation* $E(k)$ of the *stationary* distribution. But with uncertainty in both labor and depreciation rates, $\beta_2 \neq 0$, the mode and $(\kappa)$ do not necessarily coincide.

The *mode*$(k)$ (the most *probable long-run* value of $k$) can be obtained by differentiating the *density* $p(k)$ or *speed density* $\mathfrak{m}(k)$. By setting it equal to zero, we have, cf. (26.44)–(26.45),

$$p'(k) = 0 \;\Leftrightarrow\; \mathfrak{m}'(k) = 0 \;\Leftrightarrow\; b(k)b'(k) = a(k) \tag{26.125}$$

Solving (26.125), together with (26.30–26.34) and $\beta_3 = 0$, (26.56), gives

$$mode\,(k) = [\gamma s/(\Theta + \beta^2)]^{\frac{1}{1-\alpha}} = [\gamma s/(n + \delta + \beta_2^2 + \rho_{12}\beta_1\beta_2)]^{\frac{1}{1-\alpha}} \tag{26.126}$$

Since with **CD**, Table 26.1, we have $\boldsymbol{\kappa = [\gamma s/(n+\delta)]^{1/(1-\alpha)}}$, and

$$mode\,(k) \;=\; \kappa \;\;\Leftrightarrow\;\; \beta_2 \;=\; -\rho_{12}\beta_1\,; \;\; \beta_2 \neq 0 \tag{26.127}$$

This equality can only be satisfied if $\beta_1 \geq \beta_2$. With $\rho_{12} = 0$, $\beta_2 > 0$, and CD, cf. (26.126), we always find $mode(k) < \kappa$. See also Table 26.2.

Although the *mode* does not coincide with the *expectation*, the *stationary densities*, $\boldsymbol{p(k)}$—without being normal and frequently very *spiked density curves*—are often close to being *symmetric* (see the numbers in Table 26.2 and their shapes in Figs. 26.1, 26.2, 26.3, 26.4, 26.5, 26.6, 26.7, 26.8, 26.9 and 26.10). But for some stationary distributions with basic parameters close to the boundary of stationarity (endogenous growth), we find *heavy-tailed* distributions with an *expectation* significantly larger than the *mode*.

We have chosen in Figs. 26.1, 26.2, 26.3, 26.4, 26.5, 26.6, 26.7, 26.8, 26.9, 26.10 and 26.11 to *exhibit* the *sample paths* for $\boldsymbol{k(t)}$, $\boldsymbol{\omega(t)}$, and $\boldsymbol{y(t)}$.

**Table 26.1** Steady-state values (certainty equivalents) of one-sector growth models

| Variables | CD ($\sigma = 1$) | CES ($\sigma \neq 1$) |
|---|---|---|
| Capital-labor ratio: $K/L = \kappa$ | $\left(\frac{\gamma s}{n+\delta}\right)^{\frac{1}{1-a}}$ | $\left(\frac{1-a}{a}\right)^{\frac{\sigma}{\sigma-1}}\left[\frac{1}{a}\left(\frac{\gamma s}{n+\delta}\right)^{\frac{1-\sigma}{\sigma}}-1\right]^{\frac{\sigma}{1-\sigma}}$ |
| Average product of $L$: $AP_L = f(\kappa)$ | $\gamma^{\frac{1}{1-a}}\left(\frac{s}{n+\delta}\right)^{\frac{a}{1-a}}$ | $\gamma(1-a)^{\frac{\sigma}{\sigma-1}}\left[1-a\left(\frac{\gamma s}{n+\delta}\right)^{\frac{\sigma-1}{\sigma}}\right]^{\frac{\sigma}{1-\sigma}}$ |
| Marginal product of $L$: $MP_L(\kappa)$ | $(1-a)\gamma^{\frac{1}{1-a}}\left(\frac{s}{n+\delta}\right)^{\frac{a}{1-a}}$ | $\gamma(1-a)^{\frac{\sigma}{\sigma-1}}\left[1-a\left(\frac{\gamma s}{n+\delta}\right)^{\frac{\sigma-1}{\sigma}}\right]^{\frac{1}{1-\sigma}}$ |
| Average product of $K$: $AP_K(\kappa),\ f(\kappa)/\kappa$ | $\frac{n+\delta}{s}$ | $\frac{n+\delta}{s}$ |
| Capital-output ratio: $K/Y,\ \kappa/f(\kappa)$ | $\frac{s}{n+\delta}$ | $\frac{s}{n+\delta}$ |
| Marginal product of $K$: $MP_K(\kappa) = f'(\kappa)$ | $\frac{a(n+\delta)}{s}$ | $a\gamma^{\frac{\sigma-1}{\sigma}}\left(\frac{n+\delta}{s}\right)^{\frac{1}{\sigma}}$ |
| Wage-rental ratio: $\omega(\kappa)$ | $\frac{1-a}{a}\left(\frac{\gamma s}{n+\delta}\right)^{\frac{1}{1-a}}$ | $\left(\frac{1-a}{a}\right)^{\frac{\sigma}{1-\sigma}}\left[\frac{1}{a}\left(\frac{\gamma s}{n+\delta}\right)^{\frac{1-\sigma}{\sigma}}-1\right]^{\frac{1}{1-\sigma}}$ |
| Capital share: $\epsilon_K(\kappa) = 1-\epsilon_L(\kappa)$ | $a$ | $a\left(\frac{\gamma s}{n+\delta}\right)^{\frac{\sigma-1}{\sigma}}$ |
| Per capita consumption: $c_L(\kappa)$ | $(1-s)f(\kappa)$ | $(1-s)f(\kappa)$ |
| Per capita saving: $s_L(\kappa)$ | $sf(\kappa)$ | $sf(\kappa)$ |

**Table 26.2** Numerical cases for one-sector growth models: CD ($\sigma = 1$) and CES

| Parameter values—stationary models | | | | | | | | | | | | Model characteristics | | | | | | | | |
|---|---|---|---|---|---|---|---|---|---|---|---|---|---|---|---|---|---|---|---|---|
| Case | $s$ | $n$ | $\delta$ | $\gamma$ | $a$ | $\sigma$ | $\beta_1$ | $\beta_2$ | $\beta_3$ | $\lambda_3$ | $\kappa$ | $E(k)$ | Mode$(k)$ | $\sigma(k)$ | $\bar{\omega}$ | $f(\kappa)$ | $f(\kappa)/\kappa$ | $f'(\kappa)$ | $\epsilon_\kappa$ | $K/Y$ | $\frac{n+\delta}{s}$ |
| 1 | 0.20 | 0.02 | 0.05 | 1.0 | 0.20 | 1.0 | 0.01 | 0.03 | 0.00 | 0 | 3.715 | 3.718 | 3.656 | 0.353 | 14.858 | 1.323 | 0.356 | 0.070 | 0.20 | 2.857 | 0.350 |
| 2 | 0.20 | 0.02 | 0.05 | 1.0 | 0.25 | 1.0 | 0.01 | 0.03 | 0.00 | 0 | 4.054 | 4.057 | 3.986 | 0.398 | 12.163 | 1.388 | 0.342 | 0.088 | 0.25 | 2.857 | 0.350 |
| 3 | 0.20 | 0.02 | 0.05 | 1.0 | 0.40 | 1.0 | 0.01 | 0.03 | 0.00 | 0 | 5.753 | 5.753 | 5.632 | 0.631 | 8.629 | 2.014 | 0.350 | 0.140 | 0.40 | 2.857 | 0.350 |
| 4 | 0.20 | 0.02 | 0.05 | 3.0 | 0.40 | 1.0 | 0.01 | 0.03 | 0.00 | 0 | 35.900 | 35.900 | 35.143 | 3.936 | 53.849 | 12.565 | 0.350 | 0.140 | 0.40 | 2.857 | 0.350 |
| 5 | 0.20 | 0.02 | 0.05 | 1.0 | 0.40 | 1.0 | 0.00 | 0.00 | 0.10 | 1 | 5.753 | 5.736 | 5.685 | 0.694 | 8.629 | 2.014 | 0.350 | 0.140 | 0.40 | 1.000 | 1.000 |
| 6 | 0.25 | 0.02 | 0.05 | 1.0 | 0.40 | 1.0 | 0.00 | 0.00 | 0.05 | 1 | 8.345 | 8.341 | 8.329 | 0.403 | 12.517 | 2.336 | 0.280 | 0.112 | 0.40 | 3.571 | 0.280 |
| 7 | 0.25 | 0.02 | 0.05 | 1.0 | 0.40 | 1.0 | 0.00 | 0.00 | 0.10 | 1 | 8.345 | 8.329 | 8.282 | 0.806 | 12.517 | 2.336 | 0.280 | 0.112 | 0.40 | 3.571 | 0.280 |
| 8 | 0.30 | 0.02 | 0.08 | 1.0 | 0.40 | 1.0 | 0.00 | 0.00 | 0.10 | 1 | 6.240 | 6.22862 | 6.194 | 0.600 | 9.360 | 2.080 | 0.333 | 0.133 | 0.40 | 3.000 | 0.333 |
| 9 | 0.30 | 0.02 | 0.08 | 1.0 | 0.40 | 1.0 | 0.01 | 0.03 | 0.10 | 1 | 6.240 | 6.22858 | 6.102 | 0.830 | 9.360 | 2.080 | 0.333 | 0.133 | 0.40 | 3.000 | 0.333 |
| 10 | 0.20 | 0.02 | 0.08 | 1.0 | 0.40 | 1.0 | 0.01 | 0.03 | 0.10 | 1 | 3.175 | 3.162 | 3.072 | 0.541 | 4.762 | 1.587 | 0.500 | 0.200 | 0.40 | 2.000 | 0.500 |
| 11 | 0.20 | 0.01 | 0.08 | 1.0 | 0.40 | 1.0 | 0.00 | 0.00 | 0.10 | 1 | 3.784 | 3.770 | 3.726 | 0.517 | 5.676 | 1.703 | 0.450 | 0.180 | 0.40 | 2.222 | 0.450 |
| 12 | 0.20 | 0.01 | 0.08 | 2.0 | 0.40 | 1.0 | 0.00 | 0.00 | 0.10 | 1 | 12.014 | 11.969 | 11.833 | 1.644 | 18.021 | 5.406 | 0.450 | 0.180 | 0.40 | 2.222 | 0.450 |
| 13 | 0.20 | 0.01 | 0.08 | 0.3 | 0.40 | 1.0 | 0.00 | 0.00 | 0.10 | 1 | 0.509 | 0.508 | 0.504 | 0.033 | 0.763 | 0.229 | 0.450 | 0.180 | 0.40 | 2.222 | 0.450 |
| 14 | 0.30 | 0.01 | 0.08 | 0.2 | 0.40 | 1.0 | 0.00 | 0.00 | 0.10* | 1* | 0.509 | 0.509 | 0.504 | 0.033 | 0.763 | 0.153 | 0.300 | 0.120 | 0.40 | 3.333 | 0.300 |
| 15 | 0.33 | 0.01 | 0.08 | 1.0 | 0.40 | 1.0 | 0.00 | 0.00 | 0.10* | 1* | 8.719 | 2.375 | 8.719 | 0.079 | 13.078 | 2.378 | 0.273 | 0.109 | 0.40 | 3.667 | 0.273 |
| 16 | 0.25 | 0.02 | 0.05 | 1.0 | 0.60 | 1.0 | 0.01 | 0.03 | 0.10 | 1 | 24.105 | 23.960 | 22.949 | 4.312 | 16.070 | 6.749 | 0.280 | 0.168 | 0.60 | 3.571 | 0.280 |
| 1 | 0.20 | 0.02 | 0.05 | 1.0 | 0.25 | 0.5 | 0.01 | 0.03 | 0.0 | 0 | 3.476 | 3.479 | 3.428 | 0.309 | 36.252 | 1.217 | 0.350 | 0.031 | 0.088 | 2.857 | 0.350 |
| 2 | 0.20 | 0.02 | 0.05 | 1.0 | 0.40 | 0.5 | 0.01 | 0.03 | 0.0 | 0 | 4.095 | 4.097 | 4.035 | 0.375 | 25.157 | 1.433 | 0.350 | 0.049 | 0.140 | 2.857 | 0.350 |
| 3 | 0.20 | 0.02 | 0.05 | 1.0 | 0.60 | 0.5 | 0.01 | 0.03 | 0.0 | 0 | 5.643 | 5.642 | 5.552 | 0.539 | 21.228 | 1.975 | 0.350 | 0.074 | 0.210 | 2.857 | 0.350 |
| 4 | 0.20 | 0.02 | 0.05 | 3.0 | 0.60 | 0.5 | 0.01 | 0.03 | 0.0 | 0 | 19.929 | 19.949 | 19.657 | 1.756 | 264.766 | 6.975 | 0.350 | 0.024 | 0.070 | 2.857 | 0.350 |
| 5 | 0.20 | 0.02 | 0.05 | 1.0 | 0.40 | 1.5 | 0.01 | 0.03 | 0.0 | 0 | 7.633 | 7.635 | 7.412 | 0.988 | 5.815 | 2.672 | 0.350 | 0.199 | 0.568 | 2.857 | 0.350 |
| 6 | 0.25 | 0.02 | 0.05 | 1.0 | 0.40 | 1.5 | 0.01 | 0.03 | 0.0 | 0 | 13.148 | 13.147 | 12.724 | 1.795 | 8.356 | 3.681 | 0.280 | 0.171 | 0.611 | 3.571 | 0.280 |
| 7 | 0.25 | 0.02 | 0.05 | 1.0 | 0.60 | 1.5 | 0.01 | 0.03 | 0.0 | 0 | 401.664 | 398.071 | 345.493 | 120.230 | 36.293 | 112.466 | 0.280 | 0.257 | 0.917 | 3.571 | 0.280 |
| 8 | 0.20 | 0.02 | 0.05 | 1.0 | 0.60 | 1.5 | 0.01 | 0.03 | 0.0 | 0 | 55.715 | 55.493 | 51.178 | 12.365 | 9.725 | 19.500 | 0.350 | 0.298 | 0.851 | 2.857 | 0.350 |

(continued)

**Table 26.2** (continued)

| Parameter values—stationary models | | | | | | | | | | | | | Model characteristics | | | | | | | | |
|---|---|---|---|---|---|---|---|---|---|---|---|---|---|---|---|---|---|---|---|---|---|
| Case | $s$ | $n$ | $\delta$ | $\gamma$ | $a$ | $\sigma$ | $\beta_1$ | $\beta_2$ | $\beta_3$ | $\lambda_3$ | $\kappa$ | $E(k)$ | Mode($k$) | $\sigma(k)$ | $\bar{\omega}$ | $f(\kappa)$ | $f(\kappa)/\kappa$ | $f'(\kappa)$ | $\epsilon_\kappa$ | $K/Y$ | $\frac{n+\delta}{s}$ |
| 9 | 0.20 | 0.01 | 0.08 | 0.3 | 0.40 | 1.5 | 0.00 | 0.00 | 0.1 | 1 | 0.523 | 0.523 | 0.518 | 0.033 | 0.974 | 0.235 | 0.450 | 0.157 | 0.349 | 2.222 | 0.450 |
| 10 | 0.30 | 0.01 | 0.08 | 0.2 | 0.40 | 1.5 | 0.00 | 0.00 | 0.1* | 1* | 0.523 | 0.523 | 0.518 | 0.033 | 0.974 | 0.157 | 0.300 | 0.105 | 0.349 | 3.333 | 0.300 |
| 11 | 0.20 | 0.02 | 0.05 | 1.0 | 0.40 | 2.0 | 0.01 | 0.03 | 0.0 | 0 | 9.806 | 9.812 | 9.429 | 1.471 | 4.697 | 3.432 | 0.350 | 0.237 | 0.676 | 2.857 | 0.350 |
| 12 | 0.20 | 0.02 | 0.05 | 1.0 | 0.40 | 3.0 | 0.01 | 0.03 | 0.0 | 0 | 15.469 | 15.507 | 14.502 | 3.021 | 3.737 | 5.414 | 0.350 | 0.282 | 0.805 | 2.857 | 0.350 |
| 13 | 0.20 | 0.02 | 0.05 | 1.0 | 0.40 | 7.0 | 0.01 | 0.03 | 0.0 | 0 | 191.698 | 203.598 | 105.010 | 182.373 | 3.178 | 67.094 | 0.350 | 0.344 | 0.984 | 2.857 | 0.350 |
| 14 | 0.25 | 0.02 | 0.05 | 1.0 | 0.40 | 3.0 | 0.01 | 0.03 | 0.0 | 0 | 99.222 | 99.721 | 82.518 | 34.630 | 6.944 | 27.782 | 0.280 | 0.262 | 0.935 | 3.571 | 0.280 |
| Parameters—Endogenous growth models | | | | | | | | | | | | | | | | Limits for $k \to \infty$ | | | | | |
| 1 | 0.25 | 0.02 | 0.05 | 1.0 | 0.40 | 4.0 | 0.01 | 0.03 | 0 | 0 | | | | | | $\infty$ | 0.2947 | 0.2947 | | | |
| 2 | 0.20 | 0.02 | 0.05 | 1.0 | 0.60 | 2.0 | 0.01 | 0.03 | 0 | 0 | | | | | | $\infty$ | 0.3600 | 0.3600 | | | |
| 3 | 0.25 | 0.02 | 0.05 | 1.0 | 0.60 | 2.0 | 0.01 | 0.03 | 0 | 0 | | | | | | $\infty$ | 0.3600 | 0.3600 | | | |
| 4 | 0.30 | 0.02 | 0.05 | 1.0 | 0.60 | 2.0 | 0.01 | 0.03 | 0 | 0 | | | | | | $\infty$ | 0.3600 | 0.3600 | | | |

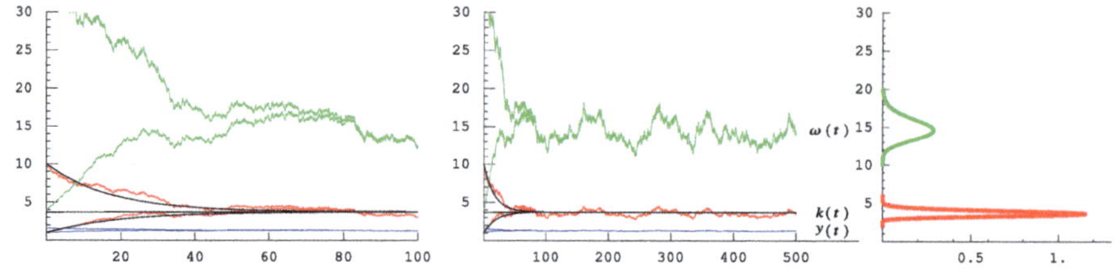


**Fig. 26.1** CD: case 1

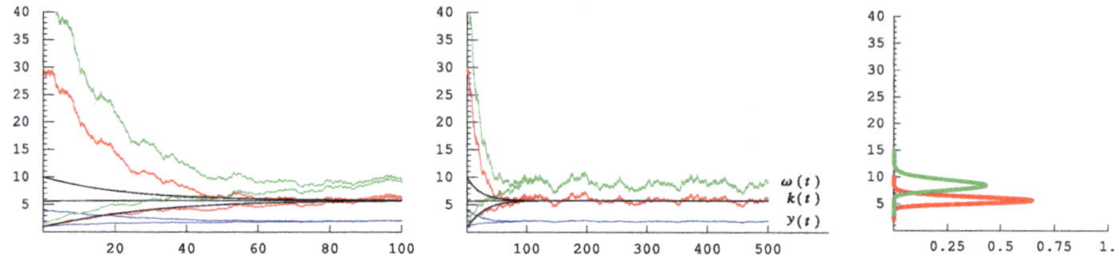


**Fig. 26.2** CD: case 3

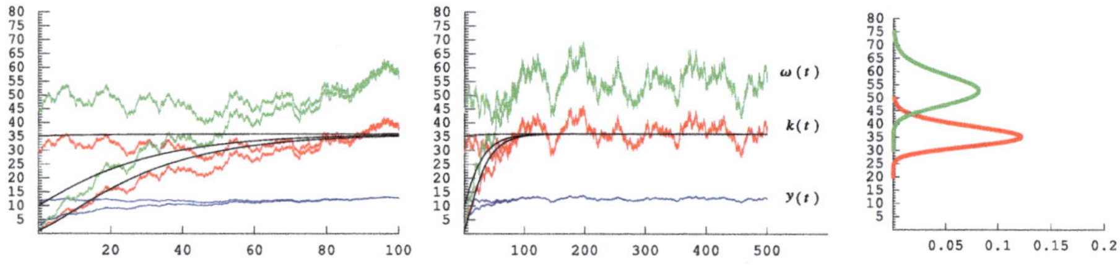


**Fig. 26.3** CD: case 4

All simulations are done using a simple *Euler scheme* of the underlying stochastic differential equations (SDE).

Hence, in *one-sector* models, we simulate the sample paths for the *capital-labor ratio*, $k(t)$, of the **SDE**, (26.30). The *sample path* (trajectory) of the stochastic process $k(t)$, (26.30), is *formally* given by

$$k(t) = k[t;\omega] = k(0) + \int_0^t a(k[u;\omega])\,du + \int_0^t b(k[u;\omega])\,dw_u[\omega] \qquad (26.128)$$

where $k(0)$ is a fixed *initial condition* and $[\omega]$ symbolizes a particular *realization* of the Wiener process. This sample path (26.128) is thus *approximated* by the Euler scheme, Kloeden and Platen (1995). The random numbers (realizations) used in the simulations are generated by the RAN2 GENERATOR from NUMERICAL RECIPES in C++ with the same initial seed. All processes are sampled with the same step size.

After having obtained the simulated sample path $k(t)$, by numerically solving the SDE, (26.128), the *sample paths* for the *wage-rental* ratio, $\boldsymbol{MRS = \omega(t)}$,

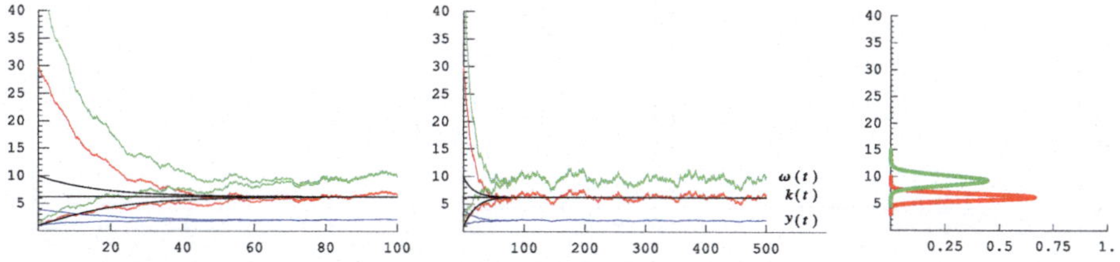


**Fig. 26.4** CD: case 8

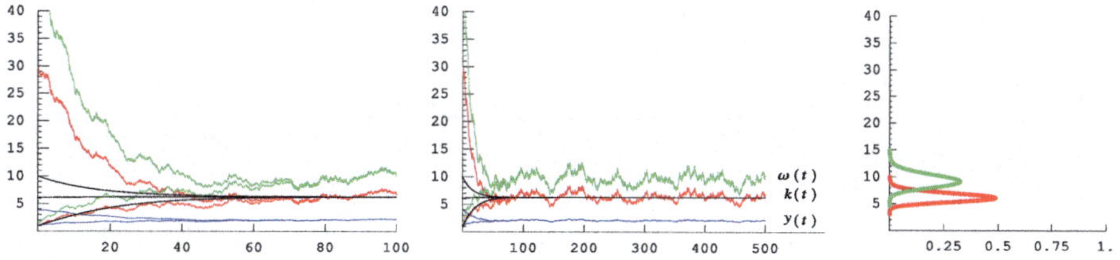


**Fig. 26.5** CD: case 9

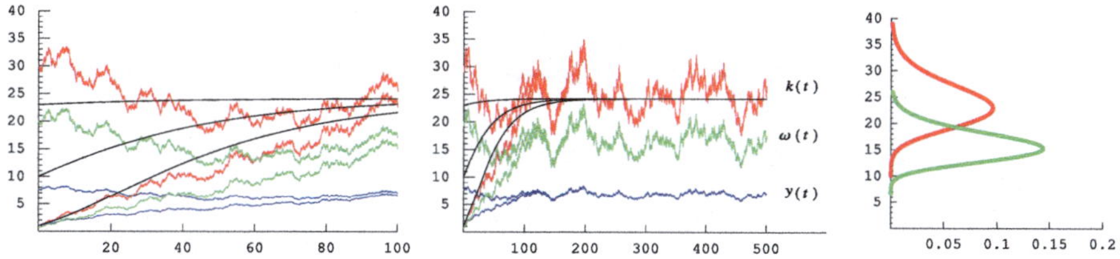


**Fig. 26.6** CD: case 16

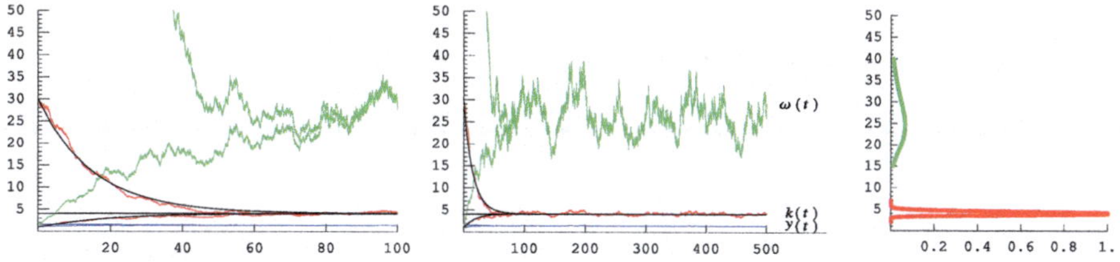


**Fig. 26.7** CES: case 2

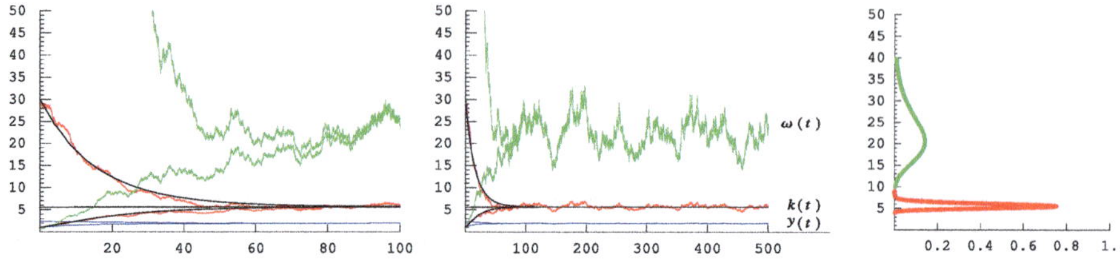


Fig. 26.8 CES: case 3

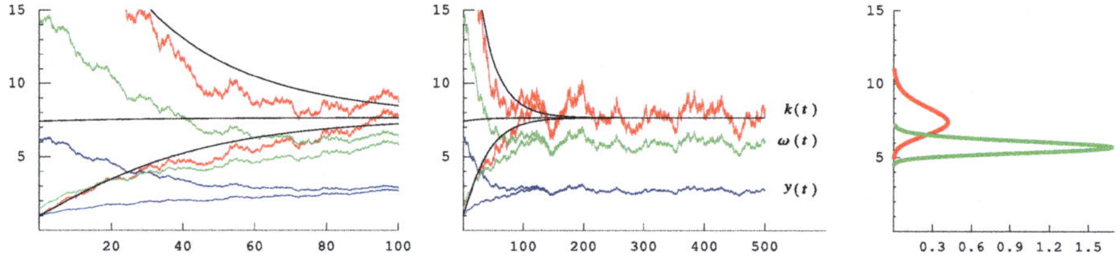


Fig. 26.9 CES: case 5

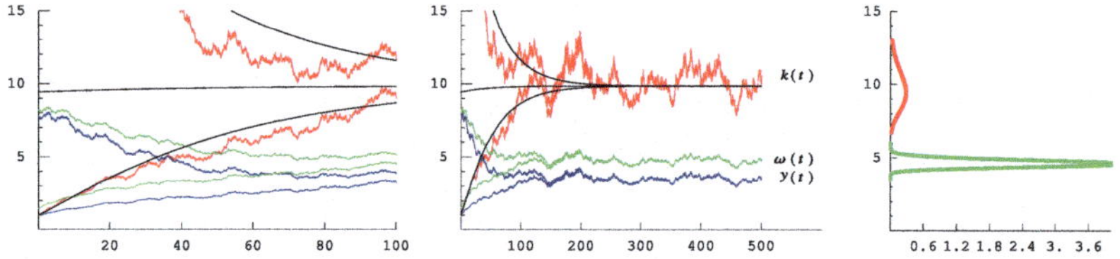


Fig. 26.10 CES: case 11

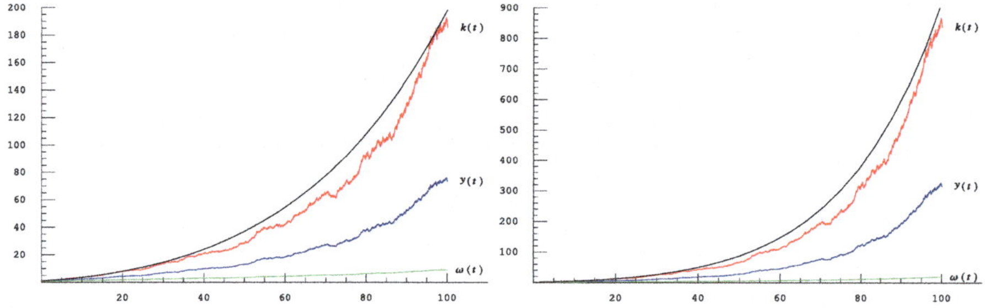


Fig. 26.11 CES: cases 3 and 4—endogenous growth

and *labor productivity*, $\boldsymbol{AP_L = y(t)}$—with the same realization of the Wiener process—are determined, for every simulated time point, by inserting the sample path $k(t)$, (26.128), into the **CD-CES** equations, (26.121–26.122):

$$\omega(t) = \frac{1-a}{a} k(t)^{1/\sigma} \tag{26.129}$$

$$y(t) = \gamma k(t)^a \; ; \qquad y(t) = \gamma \left[ (1-a) + ak(t)^{\frac{\sigma-1}{\sigma}} \right]^{\frac{\sigma}{\sigma-1}} \tag{26.130}$$

As observed in Table 26.2 and from (26.129), the numerical values of $k(t)$ in Figs. 26.1, 26.2, 26.3, 26.4, 26.5, 26.6, 26.7, 26.8, 26.9, 26.10 and 26.11 are *located* below (above) the values of $\omega(t)$, in CD cases, if $a < 1/2$ ($a > 1/2$), and if these conditions in CES cases are combined with $\sigma \leq 1$ ($\sigma \geq 1$). The values of $y(t)$, (26.130), are, with the selected size of ($\gamma$), located below the sample path of $k(t)$.

Among the alternative *initial values* $k(0)$ for sample paths (26.128) and deterministic trajectories (smooth curves) are: $[\boldsymbol{k(0)} = \mathbf{1, 10, 30}]$; corresponding values of $\boldsymbol{\omega(0)}$, $\boldsymbol{y(0)}$, follow from (26.129–26.130). With different parameter cases selected from Table 26.2, the relevant scaling of the vertical axis in Figs. 26.1, 26.2, 26.3, 26.4, 26.5, 26.6, 26.7, 26.8, 26.9, 26.10 and 26.11 is, for illustrative visual and comparative purposes, a delicate graphic problem (in particular without colors). However, the *salient features* of many *sample paths* arising from stationary and nonstationary stochastic dynamics are apparent in our Figs. 26.1, 26.2, 26.3, 26.4, 26.5, 26.6, 26.7, 26.8, 26.9, 26.10 and 26.11 for one-sector stochastic growth models.

In the CD case of Fig. 26.1, the *influence* of the respective *initial* values upon sample paths of $\omega(t)$ has mostly *disappeared* around ($t = 100$), cf. (LHS, *transient* movements), and the two curves have henceforth visually *merged* on the *long-run* time interval, ($t = 100 - 500$). The *asymptotic* (stationary) probability *density* of $\omega(t)$ is also depicted in Fig. 26.1, cf. (RHS, *light*). The sample paths of $k(t)$—and (transient/long-run) deterministic (*black*) trajectories and a horizontal line for ($\kappa$)—are similarly shown in Fig. 26.1, together with $p(k)$, (26.115–26.117), cf. (RHS, *dark* ). To avoid clutter, the sample paths of $y(t)$ are presented without a density curve on the RHS of Fig. 26.1.

The overall pattern of *transient motion* and *long-run evolution* for the *sample paths* of Fig. 26.1 is essentially repeated for their alternative CD and CES sample paths, as exhibited in Figs. 26.2, 26.3, 26.4, 26.5, 26.6, 26.7, 26.8, 26.9 and 26.10. But, evidently, the higher the long run (*steady-state level*) of the sample paths is located, the larger is the *volatility* of the process (and the standard deviation of its asymptotic density)—simply because the *diffusion coefficients*, $\boldsymbol{b(k)}$, (26.33–26.34), are *increasing* functions of ($k$).

It is noteworthy that in the short run (transient motion), the *upward (downward) parts* of sample paths look more regular (monotone) and deceptively less noisy than the underlying reality (process). The uncertainty (volatility) is hidden by the fact that the occurrence of some negative random shocks from the *diffusion term*, $\boldsymbol{b(k)\,dw}$, has been *masked* (absorbed) by the temporary upward contribution from the dominating *drift term*, $\boldsymbol{a(k)\,dt}$—which later loses its dominance and then leaves the scene free for the *volatility* effects of the diffusion term, $\boldsymbol{b(k)\,dw}$. Only with a low speed (drift) are bicycles susceptible to shocks and show erratic motions.

**Remark 26.4** For the stationary cases, the "*mean reverting effect*" for the *simulated sample paths*, $k(t)$, is ensured by strong mixing properties of the processes. This has the effect that, far from the equilibrium, the "mean reverting effect kills the volatility of the process". Closer to the mode of the distributions, we have more volatility, and the process behavior is more like a random walk. The mean reverting effect is also depicted in expectations, $\mathrm{E}\,[k(t)]$, since $\mathrm{E}\,[k(t)]$ converges exponentially fast toward the stationary mean value.

As mentioned at the beginning of this section, *parametric* variation within the basic stochastic growth model (26.30–26.34) can also generate *n*onstationary stochastic processes with *persistent* (endogenous) *growth solutions* (sample paths) for the capital-labor ratio, $k(t)$.

We will briefly exhibit the stochastic *solutions* to (26.57) under parametric CES regimes that satisfy the *fundamental sufficient* (with probability 1) *condition* (26.102) for long run per capita growth—which for (26.57) [with $\beta_3 = 0$] just corresponds to *reversing* the *condition*, (26.60).

Condition (26.102) with ($\beta_3 = 0$) is easily verified to be satisfied by the last *four* CES cases given in Table 26.2 [and, of course, by no other parameter cases listed in Table 26.2]; CES case 13 is close to, but not sufficient as $0.0687 < 0.0704$. The size of the *parameters* ($a$) and ($s$) are seen in Table 26.2 to be *c*ritical for reducing the actual size of the *substitution* elasticity ($\sigma$) that is required for satisfying (26.102).

The *endogenous stochastic* growth *paths* for $\boldsymbol{k(t)}$, $\boldsymbol{y(t)}$, and $\boldsymbol{\omega(t)}$, cf. (26.128–26.130), for the CES cases (3–4) are simulated and displayed in Fig. 26.11. The time scale (unit: year, quarter, month) of economic growth models is seldom given much attention. However, whatever unit is appropriate, the *sample paths* in Fig. 26.11 demonstrate the character of the possible *growth solutions* to the stochastic process (26.57). We see also that the growth effects of a *higher saving rate* are significant on an extended time horizon. Moreover, as mentioned above, for the transient *upward part* of sample paths, a *strong drift term* can now, besides generating long-term growth, also *absorb negative shocks* along sample paths; *fast motion (growth) is helpful.* Such a stochastic growth path will, like deterministic growth, exhibit a pronounced *tendency* for *monotone evolution.*

For large values of $k(t)$, the SDE (26.57) is approximated by an analogously parameterized *geometric Wiener* process, (26.103), with sample paths, (26.104), and their explicit expectation, standard deviation, given by cf. Dixit and Pindyck (1994, p. 71), de La Grandville (2001, p. 292):

$$\mathrm{E}[k(t)] \sim k_0 e^{\bar{a}\,t}\,, \quad \sigma(t) = k_0 e^{\bar{a}\,t}(e^{\bar{b}^2\,t} - 1)^{\frac{1}{2}} \tag{26.131}$$

Incidentally, we note that (26.131) is the one-dimensional version for the *expectation* vector and the *covariance* matrix of the GWD (Geometric Wiener Diffusion) model, cf. Jensen et al. (2007, Theorem 4, p. 88); here Theorem 33.4 in Chap. 33. Geometric Wiener processes have *no* asymptotic *stationary density* functions (curves) as shown in Figs. 26.1, 26.2, 26.3, 26.4, 26.5, 26.6, 26.7, 26.8, 26.9 and 26.10.

The uncertainty (volatility) expressed by $\sigma(t)$ in (26.131) seems overwhelming. However, the formula (26.131) describes the *potential* volatility associated with *all (infinite)* possible sample paths (realizations, stochastic simulations) for $k(t) = k[t;\omega]$, (26.128); hence (26.131) says nothing about an individual (single) sample path (realization, simulation), however erratic it may appear. Thus, the $\sigma(t)$ expression of volatility in (26.131) does not contradict the calm picture of the evolutions (sample paths) exhibited in Fig. 26.11.

Economic history (society and individual) is fortunately not repeated (replayed), and the unique growth histories (paths), although uncertain, look like the calm *(monotone) sample paths* exhibited in Fig. 26.11. Evidently, *stochastic growth* models contribute to our understanding of *historical time series* observed from growing economies.

## General Equilibria of Two-Sector Economies

Great emphasis was naturally first given to labor and capital accumulation in *aggregate* (one-sector) *g*rowth models. An extensive literature on two-sector growth models, however, began in the 1960s. The *seminal* work on *two-sector* growth models with flexible sector technologies was done by Uzawa (1961), Uzawa (1963), Solow (1961), Inada (1963), and Drandakis (1963). The main expositions and references to the early two-sector growth literature are Stiglitz and Uzawa (1969), Burmeister and Dobell (1970), Wan (1971), and Gandolfo (1980).

The study of *general equilibrium dynamics* in *two-sector* and *multi-sector growth* models has been reviewed and extended in Jensen (2003); here Chap. 17, Jensen and Larsen (2005); here Chap. 18—with an emphasis on factor *allocation*, output *c*omposition, and the dualities for *commodity* and *factor prices*.

### *Factor Endowment Allocation and Prices*

We now consider an economy consisting of a *capital* good industry (sector) and a *consumer* good industry, labeled, $i = 1, 2$, respectively. The *factor endowments,* total labor force ($L$) and the total capital stock ($K$), are inelastically supplied and are *fully employed* (utilized):

$$L = L_1 + L_2, \quad L_1/L + L_2/L \equiv \lambda_{L_1} + \lambda_{L_2} \equiv 1, \tag{26.132}$$

$$K = K_1 + K_2, \quad K_1/K + K_2/K \equiv \lambda_{K_1} + \lambda_{K_2} \equiv 1, \tag{26.133}$$

$$k \equiv K/L \equiv \lambda_{L_1} k_1 + \lambda_{L_2} k_2 \equiv k_2 + (k_1 - k_2)\lambda_{L_1}, \tag{26.134}$$

$$\lambda_{L_1} \equiv (k - k_2)\,/\,(k_1 - k_2), \quad \lambda_{K_i} \equiv (k_i/k)\,\lambda_{L_i}, \quad k_1 \neq k_2 \tag{26.135}$$

where the factor *allocation fractions* are denoted $\lambda_{L_i}, \lambda_{K_i}$ (26.132–26.133). Free *factor mobility* between the two industries and *efficient* factor *allocation* impose the *common* MRS condition, cf. (26.6),

$$\omega = \omega_1(k_1) = \omega_2(k_2), \tag{26.136}$$

For the variables $k_1$ and $k_2$ to satisfy (26.136), it is, beyond (26.2) and (26.6), further required that the *intersection* of the sectorial *range* for $\omega_1(k_1)$ and $\omega_2(k_2)$ is not empty,

$$\omega_i(k_i) \in \Omega_i = [\underline{\omega}_i, \overline{\omega}_i] \subseteq \mathbf{R}_+, \; \omega \in \Omega \equiv \Omega_1 \cap \Omega_2 = [\underline{\omega}, \overline{\omega}] \neq \emptyset, \tag{26.137}$$

The two industries are assumed to operate under *perfect competition* (zero excess profit); absolute (money) *input* (factor) *prices* $(w, r)$ are the same in both industries; and absolute (money) *output* (product, commodity) *prices* $(P_1, P_2)$ represent unit cost. Hence, we have the *competitive producer equilibrium* equations,

$$w = P_i \cdot MP_{L_i}, \quad r = P_i \cdot MP_{K_i}; \quad \omega = w/r, \qquad P_i \neq 0. \tag{26.138}$$

$$Y_i = Ly_i\lambda_{L_i}, \; P_iY_i = wL_i + rK_i, \; \epsilon_{L_i} = wL_i/P_iY_i, \; \epsilon_{K_i} + \epsilon_{L_i} = 1 \tag{26.139}$$

$$p \equiv \frac{P_1}{P_2} = \frac{MP_{K_2}}{MP_{K_1}} = \frac{f_2'(k_2)}{f_1'(k_1)} = \frac{f_2(k_2) - k_2 f_2'(k_2)}{f_1(k_1) - k_1 f_1'(k_1)} = \frac{MP_{L_2}}{MP_{L_1}} \tag{26.140}$$

*Gross domestic product*, $Y$, is the *monetary value* of sector outputs,

$$Y \equiv P_1Y_1 + P_2Y_2 = L(P_1y_1\lambda_{L_1} + P_2y_2\lambda_{L_2}) \equiv Ly \tag{26.141}$$

and is, with (26.138–26.140), equal to the total *factor incomes*:

$$Y = wL + rK = L(w + rk) = L(\omega + k)P_i f_i'(k_i) = Ly \tag{26.142}$$

Hence, the factor income *distribution shares,* $\delta_K + \delta_L = 1$, become,

$$\delta_K \equiv \frac{rK}{Y} \equiv \frac{rk}{y}, \; \delta_L \equiv \frac{wL}{Y}; \quad \delta_K \equiv \frac{k}{\omega + k}, \quad \frac{\delta_K}{\delta_L} \equiv \frac{k}{\omega} \tag{26.143}$$

The macro equivalence of total revenues and total expenditures gives the *decomposition* of GDP (26.141) into *expenditure shares,* $s_i$, as

$$s_i = P_i Y_i / Y, \quad \sum_{i=1}^{2} s_i \equiv \sum_{i=1}^{2} P_i Y_i / Y = 1 \tag{26.144}$$

**Lemma 26.1** *The macro factor income shares, $\delta_L$, $\delta_K$, (26.143), are expenditure-weighted combinations of the sectorial factor (cost) shares,*

$$\delta_L = \sum_{i=1}^{2} s_i \epsilon_{L_i}, \quad \delta_K = \sum_{i=1}^{2} s_i \epsilon_{K_i}, \quad \delta_K + \delta_L = 1 \tag{26.145}$$

*The factor allocation fractions, (26.132–26.133), are obtained by,*

$$L_i / L = \lambda_{L_i} = s_i \epsilon_{L_i} / \delta_L \qquad K_i / K = \lambda_{K_i} = s_i \epsilon_{K_i} / \delta_K \tag{26.146}$$

*The total factor endowment ratio, (26.134), satisfies the identity, cf. (26.143):*

$$K/L \equiv k \equiv \frac{\omega \delta_K}{\delta_L} \equiv \omega \sum_{i=1}^{2} s_i \epsilon_{K_i} \Bigg/ \sum_{i=1}^{2} s_i \epsilon_{L_i} \tag{26.147}$$

*which is a representation of Walras's law.*

***Proof*** By definition, we have,

$$\delta_L = wL/Y = [wL_1 + wL_2]/Y, \delta_K = rK/Y = [rK_1 + rK_2]/Y \tag{26.148}$$

From (26.139) and (26.144), we get

$$wL_i = \epsilon_{L_i} P_i Y_i = s_i \epsilon_{L_i} Y, \qquad rK_i = \epsilon_{K_i} P_i Y_i = s_i \epsilon_{K_i} Y \tag{26.149}$$

Hence, by (26.148) and (26.149) we obtain (26.145). Next, we obtain

$$\lambda_{L_i} = \frac{L_i}{L} = \frac{wL_i}{wL} = \frac{s_i \epsilon_{L_i} Y}{\delta_L Y} = \frac{s_i \epsilon_{L_i}}{\delta_L} \tag{26.150}$$

$$\lambda_{K_i} = \frac{K_i}{K} = \frac{rK_i}{rK} = \frac{s_i \epsilon_{K_i} Y}{\delta_K Y} = \frac{s_i \epsilon_{K_i}}{\delta_K} \tag{26.151}$$

as stated in (26.146). □

### *Commodity Prices and Factor Prices with CES*

The *connection* between relative *f*actor (service) prices and relative *commodity* prices follows from (26.6, 26.136, 26.138, 26.140),

$$p(\omega) = \frac{P_1}{P_2}(\omega) = \frac{MP_{K_2}[k_2(\omega)]}{MP_{K_1}[k_1(\omega)]} = \frac{f_2'[k_2(\omega)]}{f_1'[k_1(\omega)]}, \quad \omega = w/r. \tag{26.152}$$

The exact form of the function (26.152) needs particular attention. With (26.10) and (26.14), the *relative commodity* prices (comparative costs) (26.152) become, with $\sigma_i = 1$, $\sigma_i \neq 1$, and $\sigma_1 = \sigma_2 = \sigma$, respectively,

$$p(\omega) = \frac{f_2'[k_2(\omega)]}{f_1'[k_1(\omega)]} = \frac{\gamma_2 a_2 k_2(\omega)^{a_2-1}}{\gamma_1 a_1 k_1(\omega)^{a_1-1}} = \frac{\gamma_2 a_2^{a_2}(1-a_2)^{1-a_2}}{\gamma_1 a_1^{a_1}(1-a_1)^{1-a_1}}\omega^{(a_2-a_1)} \tag{26.153}$$

$$\begin{aligned} p(\omega) &= \frac{f_2'[k_2(\omega)]}{f_1'[k_1(\omega)]} = \frac{\gamma_2 a_2\left[a_2 + (1-a_2)k_2(\omega)^{-(\sigma_2-1)/\sigma_2}\right]^{1/(\sigma_2-1)}}{\gamma_1 a_1\left[a_1 + (1-a_1)k_1(\omega)^{-(\sigma_1-1)/\sigma_1}\right]^{1/(\sigma_1-1)}} \\ &= \frac{\gamma_2 a_2^{\sigma_2/(\sigma_2-1)}\left(1+c_2\omega^{1-\sigma_2}\right)^{1/(\sigma_2-1)}}{\gamma_1 a_1^{\sigma_1/(\sigma_1-1)}\left(1+c_1\omega^{1-\sigma_1}\right)^{1/(\sigma_1-1)}} \end{aligned} \tag{26.154}$$

$$p(\omega) = \frac{\gamma_2}{\gamma_1}\left[\left[\frac{a_2}{a_1}\right]^{\sigma}\frac{1+c_2\omega^{1-\sigma}}{1+c_1\omega^{1-\sigma}}\right]^{1/(\sigma-1)}_{,} \quad c_i = \left[\frac{1-a_i}{a_i}\right]^{\sigma} \tag{26.155}$$

### *Walrasian General Equilibrium and CES*

As to the demand (expenditure share) decomposition between consumption and investment (saving), we shall employ the "neoclassical" saving assumption, which has been standard in much of the growth literature. It is immaterial for our purposes whether investment is controlled by owners or managers.

Hence, we use the aggregate *monetary saving* function:

$$S = sY, \quad 0 < s < 1 \tag{26.156}$$

or alternatively stated by an expenditure condition for two commodities, (newly produced capital goods) and (consumer goods), cf. (26.141)

$$P_1 Y_1 = sY; \quad s = P_1 Y_1/Y; \quad 1 - s = P_2 Y_2/Y \tag{26.157}$$

The *competitive general equilibrium* (CGE) states (Walrasian equilibria), with market clearing prices on the commodity/factor markets and Pareto efficient endowments allocation, are obtained as follows.

From (26.157), (26.145), (26.146) we have,

$$\lambda_{L_1} = \frac{s\epsilon_{L_1}}{s\epsilon_{L_1} + (1-s)\epsilon_{L_2}}, \quad \lambda_{K_1} = \frac{s\epsilon_{K_1}}{s\epsilon_{K_1} + (1-s)\epsilon_{K_2}} \tag{26.158}$$

$$\delta_L = s\epsilon_{L_1} + (1-s)\epsilon_{L_2}, \quad \delta_K = s\epsilon_{K_1} + (1-s)\epsilon_{K_2}. \tag{26.159}$$

Finally, by (26.147) and (26.159), we obtain, $\forall k \in R_+, \forall \omega \in \Omega$, (26.137)

$$k \equiv \frac{\omega\delta_K}{\delta_L} \equiv \frac{\omega[s\epsilon_{K_1} + (1-s)\epsilon_{K_2}]}{s\epsilon_{L_1} + (1-s)\epsilon_{L_2}} \equiv \Psi(\omega). \tag{26.160}$$

The formula, $\Psi(\omega)$, (26.160), is a "reduced form" expression derived from the "structural equations" of the general equilibrium model, and it relates the endogenous two-sector *general equilibrium solutions* for the *wage-rental ratio*, $\omega = w/r$, to the exogenous *f*actor endowment ratios, $k = K/L$. Then, having obtained ($\omega$) from (26.160), we can go back through (26.158), (26.140) to get the associated general equilibrium solutions for *all* other endogenous variables: sector outputs, allocation fractions of inputs, income shares, and relative commodity prices.

The *competitive general equilibrium* (CGE) function, $\Psi(\omega)$, and its *graph*—as loci of timeless general equilibrium values and as trajectories of motion—are of paramount importance for inquiring into the statics, comparative statics, and dynamics of two-sector economies, and they will be called the *factor endowment-factor price* (FEFP) correspondence. Alternatively, a CGE function, $\Psi(\omega)$, may be dubbed the *Walrasian kernel*, since it selects in the Edgeworth box diagram the relevant *Walrasian equilibrium allocation* as a specific allocation (*point*) within the *core* of the *contract* curve, cf. Mas-Colell et al. (1995, p. 654). The locus of the Walrasian kernel, $k = \Psi(\omega)$, effectively *links* the *Pareto optimal allocations* [changing contract curves of expanding Edgeworth boxes] to the relevant *Walrasian equilibrium price vector*, $(p, \omega)$ [on the locus of the Factor Price-Commodity Price (FPCP) correspondence $p(\omega)$, (26.152–26.155)].

**CES Case** From (26.158–26.160), (26.15), we get

$$\lambda_{L_1} = \frac{1 + c_2\omega^{1-\sigma_2}}{1 + \frac{1-s}{s}\frac{c_2}{c_1}\omega^{\sigma_1-\sigma_2} + \frac{c_2}{s}\omega^{1-\sigma_2}}, \; \lambda_{K_1} = \frac{1 + c_2\omega^{1-\sigma_2}}{\frac{1}{s} + \frac{1-s}{s}c_1\omega^{1-\sigma_1} + c_2\omega^{1-\sigma_2}} \tag{26.161}$$

$$\delta_K = s\left(1 + c_1\omega^{1-\sigma_1}\right)^{-1} + (1-s)\left(1 + c_2\omega^{1-\sigma_2}\right)^{-1}$$
$$= \frac{1 + (1-s)c_1\omega^{1-\sigma_1} + sc_2\omega^{1-\sigma_2}}{1 + c_1\omega^{1-\sigma_1} + c_2\omega^{1-\sigma_2} + c_1c_2\omega^{2-\sigma_1-\sigma_2}}, \quad \delta_L = 1 - \delta_K \tag{26.162}$$

and hence finally by (26.162),

$$k = \Psi(\omega) = \frac{\omega\,\delta_K}{\delta_L} = \frac{\omega^{\sigma_1+\sigma_2} + sc_2\omega^{1+\sigma_1} + (1-s)c_1\omega^{1+\sigma_2}}{sc_1\omega^{\sigma_2} + (1-s)c_2\omega^{\sigma_1} + c_1c_2\omega} \tag{26.163}$$

The CGE function, $\boldsymbol{\Psi(\omega)}$, (26.163), is *monotonic*, cf. Jensen (2003, p. 65); here Lemma 17.2 in Chap. 17, and hence the *inverse*, $\omega = \Psi^{-1}(k)$, *exists* (not necessarily in closed form) for every $k \in [0, \infty)$.

## Dynamics of Two-Sector Economies

### *Deterministic Dynamics of Two-Sector Growth Models*

The equations of *factor accumulation* for neoclassical two-sector growth models with flexible sector technologies are formally given, Uzawa (1963, p. 106), by ($\delta$ is the depreciation rate of capital),

$$\dot{L} = nL \tag{26.164}$$

$$\dot{K} = Y_1 - \delta K = Ly_1\lambda_{L_1} - \delta K = L\left\{f_1(k_1)\lambda_{L_1} - \delta k\right\} \tag{26.165}$$

In the general equilibrium models of two-sector economies, the sector specific $k_1$ and $\lambda_{L_1}$, (26.165), are, through ($\omega$), (26.136), *uniquely* determined by the overall *factor* endowment *ratio* ($k$), cf. (26.160).

Hence, the accumulation equations (26.164–26.165) become genuine *autonomous* (time-invariant) *d*ifferential equations in the state variables $L$ and $K$ and represent a standard *homogeneous dynamic system*,

$$\dot{L} = Ln \equiv L\mathfrak{f}(k) \tag{26.166}$$

$$\dot{K} = L\left\{f_1\left(k_1[\Psi^{-1}(k)]\right)\lambda_{L_1}(\Psi^{-1}(k)) - \delta k\right\} \equiv L\mathfrak{g}(k) \tag{26.167}$$

As $\mathfrak{g}(k)$, (26.167), is an intricate function of ($k$), we rewrite $\mathfrak{g}(k)$ in an alternative form by (26.165), (26.142–26.143), cf. Burmeister and Dobell (1970, p. 111), Wan (1971, p. 119), Gandolfo (1980, p. 490),

$$\begin{aligned} \dot{K} &= s\,(Y/P_1) - \delta K = L\,(s\,(y/P_1) - \delta k) \\ &= L\,s\,(\omega + k) f_1'(k_1) - \delta K = L\,k\left\{\frac{s\,f_1'(k_1)}{\delta_K} - \delta\right\} = L\mathfrak{g}(k) \end{aligned} \tag{26.168}$$

From the *governing* function $\mathfrak{g}(k)$, (26.168), the *director* function that controls $\dot{k}$, $h(k) \equiv \mathfrak{g}(k) - k\mathfrak{f}(k)$, of (26.166–26.168), becomes,

$$\dot{k} = h(k) = k\left[\frac{sf_1'\left(k_1\left[\Psi^{-1}(k)\right]\right)}{\delta_K(\Psi^{-1}(k))} - (n+\delta)\right];\quad \omega = \Psi^{-1}(k) \tag{26.169}$$

The neoclassical demand side (savings) is *not* affected by factor *income distribution*, cf. (26.156). However, to succinctly express and decompose the governing functions of capital *a*ccumulation (26.168), the bounded share variable, $\delta_K(k)$, (26.142–26.143), is mainly a formal *auxiliary term* helpful in evaluating concrete cases.

If they exist, *steady-state* values $(\kappa)$ of the capital-labor ratio in *deterministic* two-sector growth models are the *critical points* of (26.169):

$$[\dot{k} = 0 \Leftrightarrow k(t) = \kappa\,] \Leftrightarrow \left[ \frac{f_1'\left(k_1\left[\Psi^{-1}(\kappa)\right]\right)}{\delta_K(\Psi^{-1}(\kappa))} = \frac{n+\delta}{s} \right] \tag{26.170}$$

Usually, only $\delta_K(\omega)$ and $k = \Psi(\omega)$ are explicitly available; thus, instead of solving (26.170) in $(k)$, it is convenient to solve (26.170) in $(\omega)$:

$$k(t) = \kappa \Leftrightarrow \left[ \frac{f_1'(k_1(\bar{\omega}))}{\delta_K(\bar{\omega})} = \frac{n+\delta}{s} \right]; \quad \kappa = \Psi(\bar{\omega}) \tag{26.171}$$

In the **CES case**, $\delta_K(\omega)$ and $\Psi(\omega)$ were given in (26.162–26.163), and $f_1'(k_1[\omega])$ becomes by, (26.10), (26.14), (26.136),

$$f_1'(k_1[\omega]) = \gamma_1\, a_1^{\frac{\sigma_1}{\sigma_1-1}} \left[ 1 + \left[ \frac{1-a_1}{a_1} \right]^{\sigma_1} \omega^{1-\sigma_1} \right]^{\frac{1}{\sigma_1-1}} \tag{26.172}$$

Closed-form expressions—as in Table 26.1 above—are *not* available for the *root* values $(\kappa, \bar{\omega})$, (26.170–26.171), with CD and CES technologies.

The *qualitative* properties of the family of *solutions* $k(t)$ to the *Walrasian general equilibrium* growth model (26.169) with CES sector technologies are summarized in:

**Proposition 26.1** *For the two-sector growth models (26.166–26.169) with CES sector technologies, the sufficient conditions for the existence of at least one positive steady-state solution [no positive, attractive, steady-state solution* $\kappa$ *exists with the RHS inequalities of (26.173–26.174) reversed] are:*

$$\sigma_1 < 1,\ \sigma_2 < 1: \quad \gamma_1\, a_1^{\frac{\sigma_1}{\sigma_1-1}} > (n+\delta)/s \tag{26.173}$$

$$\sigma_1 < 1,\ \sigma_2 > 1: \quad \gamma_1\, a_1^{\frac{\sigma_1}{\sigma_1-1}} > (n+\delta) \tag{26.174}$$

$\sigma_1 \le 1$ : *(Sufficient condition) Persistent growth of* $k(t)$ *is impossible.*
$\sigma_1 > 1$ : *Necessary and sufficient conditions for* $\lim_{t\to\infty} k(t) = \infty$ *are:*

$$\sigma_1 > 1,\ \sigma_2 < 1: \quad \gamma_1\, a_1^{\frac{\sigma_1}{\sigma_1-1}} > (n+\delta) \tag{26.175}$$

$$\sigma_1 > 1,\ \sigma_2 > 1: \quad \gamma_1\, a_1^{\frac{\sigma_1}{\sigma_1-1}} > (n+\delta)/s \tag{26.176}$$

*except that (26.175) is occasionally not sufficient for small initial values.*

***Proof*** See Jensen (2003); here Chap. 17. The proposition follows essentially from a straightforward examination of the sign of $h(k)$, (26.169), by a comparative evaluation of $f_1'(k_1[\omega])$, (26.172), and $\delta_K(\omega)$, (26.162).

The *difference* ($s$) in the RHS *constant* of the inequalities comes from $\delta_K(\omega)$, (26.162), taking values 1 or $s$—for $\omega \to 0$ or for $\omega \to \infty$—depending on the size of $\sigma_2$. The *boundary behavior* of the marginal product of capital, cf. (26.11–26.13), in the capital good sector, $f_1'(k_1[\omega])$, (26.172), is crucial for a steady-state or persistent growth. □

Proposition 26.1 shows explicitly that the *global existence issues* of any *steady-state* or *persistent* growth depend on the *size* of the key parameters: $\sigma_i$, $a_1$, $\gamma_1$, $s$, $n$, $\delta$. While the *accumulation* parameters ($s$, $n$, $\delta$) play some roles, the *fundamental* role of the *technology* parameters in the *capital* good sector ($\sigma_1$, $\gamma_1$, $a_1$) for deciding the types of the long-run *evolution* in the CGE growth models *complies* with observation and economic *intuition*, as well as confirms the strategic importance ascribed to capital good industries by economic historians and the general public, cf. Mahalanobis (1955), Rosenberg (1963).

The most important parameter in Proposition 26.1 is the *substitution elasticity* in the capital good sector, $\sigma_1$. The *total productivity* parameter $\gamma_1$ in the capital good sector matters in all the stated conditions (26.173–26.175). If we restrict $\gamma_1 = 1$ and if $\sigma_1 \simeq 2$, then (26.176) is usually satisfied for other relevant parameters, e.g., high saving rates. The critical role in Proposition 26.1 is played by $\sigma_1$ rather than $\sigma_2$.

The conclusions in Proposition 26.1 contrast sharply with earlier standard literature on two-sector growth models. Stiglitz and Uzawa (1969, p. 407) reported (with neoclassical saving) that a *sufficient* condition for uniqueness and stability of (convergence to) balanced (steady-state) growth paths is: "substitution elasticity in each sector greater than or equal to one". This condition is neither necessary nor sufficient for the long-run steady-state family. Indeed, a high value of $\sigma_1$ would *preclude* the existence of steady-state growth, cf. (26.175–26.176).

### *Neoclassical SDE of the Capital-Labor Ratio*

The deterministic model (26.164–26.165) becomes, with *uncertainties* (stochastic elements $\boldsymbol{\epsilon}_i$) in the growth rate of *labor*, ($\boldsymbol{n}$), the gross *saving* rate, ($\boldsymbol{s}$), and the capital *depreciation* rate ($\boldsymbol{\delta}$):

$$\dot{L} = L(n + \beta_1 \epsilon_1) \tag{26.177}$$

$$\dot{K} = L(s + \phi_3(k) \epsilon_3)Y/P_1 \; - \; (\delta + \beta_2 \epsilon_2)K \tag{26.178}$$

For the labor and capital stock, the associated *stochastic differential equations* (**SDE**) to (26.177–26.178) are given by

$$dL = Ln\,dt + L\beta_1 dw_1 \tag{26.179}$$

$$dK = (LsY/P_1) - \delta K)\,dt - \beta_2 K\,dw_2 + LY/P_1\phi_3(k)\,dw_3 \tag{26.180}$$

**Theorem 26.6** *The stochastic neoclassical dynamics for the capital-labor ratio of the two-sector model (26.179–26.180) is given by the SDE*

$$dk = a(k)\,dt + b(k)\,dw, \qquad k \in (0, \infty) \tag{26.181}$$

*where the drift coefficient* $a(k)$ *and diffusion coefficient* $b(k)$ *are,*

$$\begin{aligned} a(k) &= \bar{s}(k)(y/P_1) - \Theta k, \quad \bar{s}(k) = s - \rho_{13}\beta_1\phi_3(k) \\ \Theta &= n + \delta - (\beta_1^2 + \rho_{12}\beta_1\beta_2) \\ b^2(k) &= \beta^2 k^2 + \phi_3(k)^2(y/P_1)^2 - \rho\phi_3(k)(y/P_1)k \\ \beta^2 &= \beta_1^2 + \beta_2^2 + 2\rho_{12}\beta_1\beta_2, \quad \rho = 2(\rho_{13}\beta_1 + \rho_{23}\beta_2) \end{aligned} \tag{26.182}$$

*where* $y/P_1$ *is given by, cf. (26.142), (26.168),*

$$\frac{y}{P_1} = (\omega + k)\, f_1'\,(k_1(\omega)) = (\Psi^{-1}\,(k) + k) f_1'(k_1[\Psi^{-1}(k)]) \equiv \Upsilon(k) \tag{26.183}$$

***Proof*** The proof of Theorem 26.6 is a replication of the proof of Theorem 26.1 with $\boldsymbol{f(k)}$ in (26.31), (26.33) replaced by $\boldsymbol{\Upsilon(k)}$, (26.183). □

For the *one-sector* growth models, we obtained explicit conditions for the lower and upper boundaries—zero and ∞—to be *inaccessible* boundaries. These *explicit conditions*—stated in Theorems 26.2–26.4—were established after lengthy calculation, as their proofs showed.

With the examples considered here, the $\boldsymbol{\beta_i}$ *terms* only have a *second-order* effect, and the intuition from Proposition 26.1 will help to understand the stochastic system. We have not calculated the exact boundary conditions, which probably are not feasible due to the complex structure of $\boldsymbol{y/P_1}$, cf. (26.183).

## Sample Paths of Two-Sector Models and CES

We include a few *simulations* of stochastic two-sector growth models with some variation of the parameter to show the *critical parameter* values in long-run stationary processes and, alternatively, with infinity as the attractor in stochastic endogenous growth.

Numerical parameter cases illustrating **steady-state values** $(\kappa, \bar{\omega})$, (26.170–26.172), with CD/CES technologies are collected in Table 26.3.

**Table 26.3** Numerical cases for two sector growth models: CD and CES

| Parameters—stationary models | | | | | | | | | | | | Model characteristics | | | | | | | | | |
|---|---|---|---|---|---|---|---|---|---|---|---|---|---|---|---|---|---|---|---|---|---|
| Case | $s$ | $n$ | $\delta$ | $a_1$ | $a_2$ | $\sigma_1$ | $\sigma_2$ | $\beta_1$ | $\beta_2$ | $\beta_3$ | $\lambda_3$ | $\kappa$ | $E(k)$ | mode$(k)$ | $\sigma(k)$ | $\bar{\omega}$ | $f_1(\kappa_1(\bar{\omega}))$ | $\frac{f_1(\kappa_1(\bar{\omega}))}{\kappa_1(\bar{\omega})}$ | $f'(\kappa_1(\bar{\omega}))$ | $\epsilon_{\kappa_1}$ | $\delta_K(\bar{\omega})$ |
| 1 | 0.20 | 0.02 | 0.05 | 0.2 | 0.5 | 1.0 | 1.0 | 0.01 | 0.03 | 0.0 | 0 | 4.357 | 4.361 | 4.288 | 0.414 | 5.546 | 1.068 | 0.770 | 0.154 | 0.200 | 0.440 |
| 2 | 0.20 | 0.02 | 0.05 | 0.4 | 0.5 | 1.0 | 1.0 | 0.01 | 0.03 | 0.0 | 0 | 5.878 | 5.878 | 5.754 | 0.644 | 6.368 | 1.783 | 0.420 | 0.168 | 0.400 | 0.480 |
| 1 | 0.25 | 0.02 | 0.05 | 0.4 | 0.5 | 0.5 | 0.7 | 0.01 | 0.03 | 0.0 | 0 | 5.583 | 5.586 | 5.502 | 0.507 | 14.684 | 1.374 | 0.439 | 0.077 | 0.176 | 0.275 |
| 2 | 0.25 | 0.02 | 0.05 | 0.6 | 0.5 | 0.5 | 0.7 | 0.01 | 0.03 | 0.1 | 1 | 7.586 | 7.564 | 7.435 | 0.950 | 20.606 | 1.969 | 0.354 | 0.075 | 0.212 | 0.269 |
| 3 | 0.25 | 0.02 | 0.05 | 0.4 | 0.5 | 1.2 | 1.5 | 0.01 | 0.03 | 0.0 | 0 | 11.196 | 11.192 | 10.902 | 1.369 | 6.029 | 2.063 | 0.389 | 0.182 | 0.468 | 0.650 |
| 4 | 0.25 | 0.02 | 0.05 | 0.4 | 0.5 | 1.2 | 1.5 | 0.01 | 0.03 | 0.1 | 1 | 11.196 | 11.146 | 10.769 | 1.797 | 6.029 | 2.063 | 0.389 | 0.182 | 0.468 | 0.650 |
| 5 | 0.25 | 0.02 | 0.05 | 0.4 | 0.5 | 1.5 | 1.2 | 0.01 | 0.03 | 0.0 | 0 | 13.198 | 13.150 | 12.725 | 1.797 | 8.499 | 3.739 | 0.277 | 0.170 | 0.613 | 0.607 |
| 6 | 0.25 | 0.02 | 0.05 | 0.4 | 0.5 | 1.5 | 1.2 | 0.01 | 0.03 | 0.1 | 1 | 13.198 | 13.113 | 12.501 | 2.398 | 8.499 | 3.739 | 0.277 | 0.170 | 0.613 | 0.607 |
| Parameters—endogenous growth models | | | | | | | | | | | | | | | | | Limits for $k \to \infty$ | | | | |
| 1 | 0.25 | 0.02 | 0.05 | 0.6 | 0.5 | 2.0 | 1.5 | 0.01 | 0.03 | 0.0 | 0 | | | | | | $\infty$ | 0.360 | 0.360 | | |
| 2 | 0.25 | 0.02 | 0.05 | 0.6 | 0.5 | 2.0 | 1.5 | 0.01 | 0.03 | 0.1 | 1 | | | | | | $\infty$ | 0.360 | 0.360 | | |
| 3 | 0.30 | 0.02 | 0.05 | 0.6 | 0.5 | 2.0 | 1.5 | 0.01 | 0.03 | 0.1 | 1 | | | | | | $\infty$ | 0.360 | 0.360 | | |

The *sample path* of the stochastic process, $k(t)$, in *two-sector growth* models, (26.181), is *formally* given by:

$$k(t) = k[t; \omega] = k(0) + \int_0^t a(k[u; \omega])\, du + \int_0^t b(k[u; \omega])\, dw_u[\omega] \qquad (26.184)$$

where $k(0)$ is a fixed *initial condition*, and $[\omega]$ symbolizes a particular *realization* of the Wiener process. This sample path (26.184) is thus *approximated* by the Euler scheme, Kloeden and Platen (1995).

After having determined the simulated sample path, $k(t)$, the sample path for $\omega(t)$, $k_1(t)$, and $y/P_1\,(t)$ for the two-sector model (with the *same realization* of the Wiener process) is determined by using the respective equations, (26.169), (26.14), (26.163), (26.183), and (26.172),

$$\omega(t) \;=\; \Psi^{-1}\,[\,k(t)\,]\,; \quad k_i\,(t) \;=\; \left[\frac{a_i}{1-a_i}\,\Psi^{-1}\,[\,k(t)\,]\right]^{\sigma_i} \qquad (26.185)$$

$$y/P_1\,(t) \;=\; \Upsilon\,[\,k(t)\,] \;=\; [\,\Psi^{-1}\,[k(t)] \;+\; k(t)\,]\, f_1'\,(\,k_1\,[\Psi^{-1}\,[k(t)]\,) \qquad (26.186)$$

Some *sample paths,* (26.184–26.186), are exhibited in Figs. 26.12, 26.13 and 26.14.

From the **CGE** relationship, $\boldsymbol{\omega = \Psi^{-1}(k)}$, (26.169), (26.163), the stationary *density function* for $(\omega)$, called $\boldsymbol{\varphi\,(\omega)}$, is the stationary *density* function, $\boldsymbol{p(k)}$,

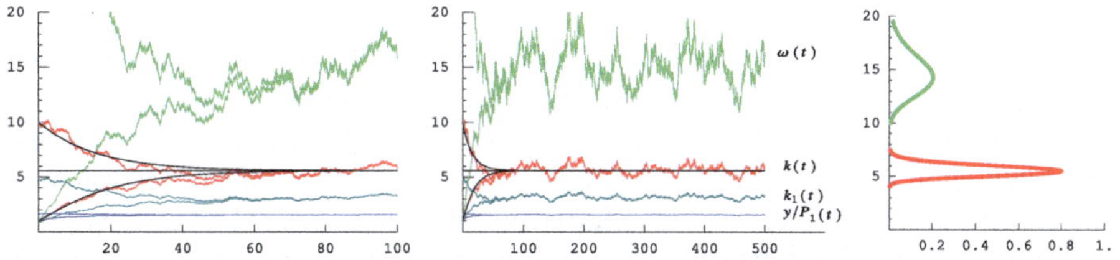


**Fig. 26.12** CES II: case 1

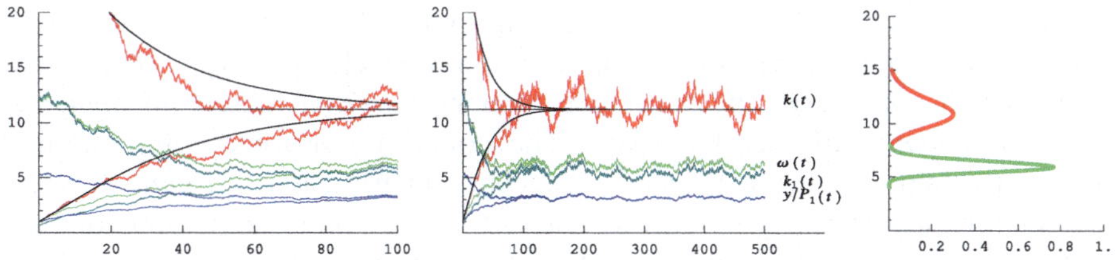


**Fig. 26.13** CES II: case 3

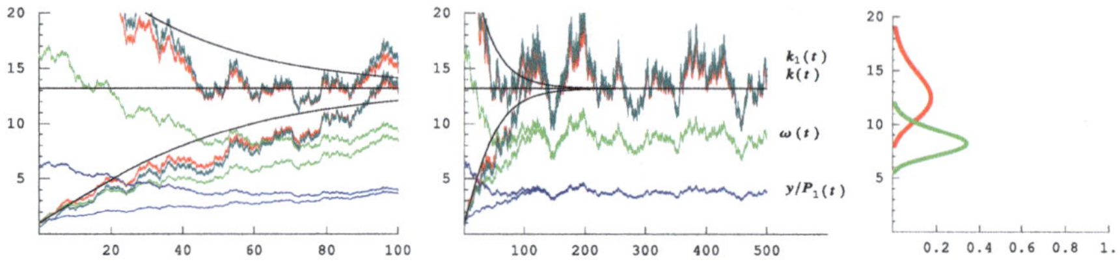


**Fig. 26.14** CES II: case 6

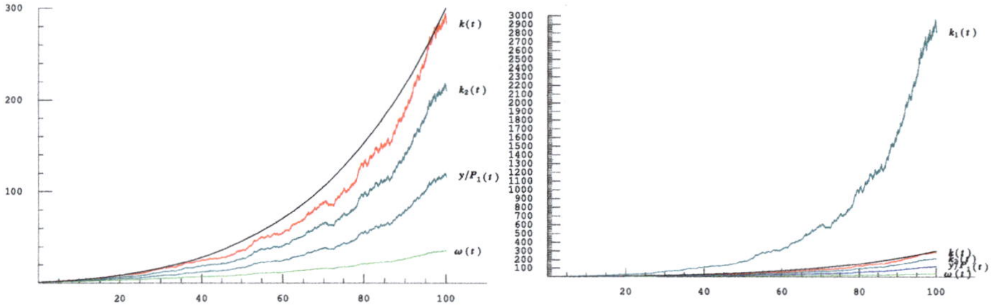


**Fig. 26.15** CES II: case 1—endogenous growth

*transformed* by the function $\mathbf{\Psi}^{-1}$. Hence, using the transformation theorem of densities, $\boldsymbol{\varphi}\,(\boldsymbol{\omega})$ in Figs. 26.12, 26.13 and 26.14 is,

$$\varphi\,(\omega) \;=\; p\,(\,\Psi(\omega))\,\Psi\,'(\omega) \tag{26.187}$$

where $\boldsymbol{p}$ is the *basic stationary density* function for $(\boldsymbol{k})$ as defined by the *drift* and *diffusion coefficients*: (26.44–26.45), (26.115–26.117).

The leading role of the *capital good* sector as an engine of *persistent growth* is exhibited by *sample paths* in Fig. 26.15. For proper scaling of the vertical axis, the *sample path* of $\boldsymbol{k_1(t)}$ is not included in the left panel, whereas it appears in the *right panel*. The *comments* given above to Fig. 26.11 apply similarly to Fig. 26.15.

*Stochastic (probability)* issues appear, according to *Pierre-Simon Laplace*, because we are partly knowing and partly ignorant. The *dynamics* of *stochastic* and *deterministic growth models* share a *common* element: the *drift coefficient*, which constitutes the substance of our *knowledge*, based on *economic theory* and *empirical* (verified) data. The course of future events is admittedly uncertain, but the *diffusion coefficient*, similarly based on *solid* theoretical/empirical *premises*, governs the *volatility* of outcomes. The mathematical *tool* of *continuous-time probability* of *Norbert Wiener* and *Kiyoshi Itô* allows probability *calculations* to be made about *observable* future *time paths.*

*Stochastic dynamics* properly employed, far from making economic growth models more abstract, actually serve as a *powerful* liberating *framework*, enabling the analysis and integration of ever more realistic and complicated hypotheses. *Stochastic* and *deterministic* growth models contribute together to a *genuine* understanding of historical time series in economics and other disciplines.

## Bibliography

Aghion P, Howitt P (1998) Endogenous Growth Theory. The MIT Press, Cambridge, MA and London, England

Arrow KJ, Chenery HB, Minhas BS, Solow RM (1961) Capital–Labour Substitution and Economic Efficiency. Review of Economics and Statistics 43:225–250

Barro RJ (1991) Economic Growth in a Cross–Section of Countries. Quarterly Journal of Economics 106:407–443

Barro RJ, Sala-i-Martin X (1992) Convergence. Journal of Political Economy 100:223–251

Bourguignon F (1974) A Particular Class of Continuous–Time Stochastic Growth Models. Journal of Economic Theory 9:141–158

Brock WA, Mirman L (1972) Optimal Economic Growth and Uncertainty: The Discounted Case. Journal of Economic Theory (4):479–513

Brock WA, Mirman L (1973) Optimal Economic Growth and Uncertainty: The No Discounting Case. International Economic Review (14):560–573

Burmeister E, Dobell AR (1970) Mathematical Theories of Economic Growth. Macmillan, London

Chang FR, Malliaris AG (1987) Asymptotic Growth under Uncertainty – Existence and Uniqueness. Review of Economic Studies (54):169–174

de La Grandville O (2001) Bond Pricing and Portfolio Analysis. MIT Press, Cambridge, Mass.

De Long JB, Summers LH (1991) Equipment Investment and Economic Growth. Quarterly Journal of Economics 106:445–502

Dixit AK, Pindyck RS (1994) Investment under Uncertainty. Princeton University Press, New Jersey

Drandakis EM (1963) Factor Substitution in the Two–Sector Growth Model. Rev Econ Stud 30:217–28

Gandolfo G (1980) Economic Dynamics: Methods and Models, 2nd edn. North–Holland, Amsterdam

Gandolfo G (1997) Economic Dynamics. Springer Verlag, Berlin/New York

Holden H, Øksendal B, Ubøe J, Zhang T (1996) Stochastic Partial Differential Equation. A Modeling White Noise Functional Approach. Birkäuser, Boston

Inada K (1963) On a Two–Sector Model of Economic Growth: Comments and a Generalization. Rev Econ Stud 30:119–27

Itô K, McKean HP Jr (1965) Diffusion Processes and Their Sample Paths. Springer–Verlag, Berlin

Jensen BS (1994) The Dynamic Systems of Basic Economic Growth Models. Kluwer Academic Publishers, Dordrecht

Jensen BS (2003) Walrasian General Equilibrium Allocations and Dynamics in Two–Sector Growth Models. German Economic Review 4:53–87; here Chap. 17

Jensen BS, Larsen ME (1987) Growth and Long–Run Stability. Acta Applicandae Mathematicae 9:219–237, Reprinted in Jensen (1994): here Chap. 1

Jensen BS, Larsen ME (2005) General Equilibrium Dynamics of Multi–Sector Growth Models. Journal of Economics 10:17–56; here Chap. 18
Jensen BS, Wang C (1997) General Equilibrium Dynamics of Basic Trade Models for Growing Economies. In Bjarne S. Jensen and Kar–Yiu Wong (eds.) *Dynamics, Economic Growth, and International Trade*, Ann Arbor: University of Michigan Press.
Jensen BS, Wang C (1999) Basic Stochastic Dynamic Systems of Growth and Trade. Review of International Economics 7:378–402, or in Choi & Jensen (1999)
Jensen BS, Richter M, Wang C, Alsholm PK (2001) Saving Rates, Trade, Technology, and Stochastic Dynamics. Review of Development Economics 5:182–204
Jensen BS, Wang C, Johnsen J (2007) Moment Evolution of Gaussian and Geometric Wiener Diffusions – derived by Itô's Lemma and Kolmogorov's Forward Equation
Jones RW (1965) The Structure of Simple General Equilibrium Models. J Political Economy 73:557–72, or Bhagwati (1981)
Karatzas I, Shreve SE (1991) Brownian Motion and Stochastic Calculus, 2nd edn. Springer Verlag, N.Y.
Karlin S, Taylor HM (1981) A Second Course in Stochastic Processes. Academic Press, N.Y.
Kemp MC (1969) The Pure Theory of International Trade and Investment. Prentice–Hall, New Jersey
Kloeden PE, Platen E (1995) Numerical Solutions to Stochastic Differential Equations, 2nd edn. Springer Verlag, Berlin
Klump R (1995) On the Institutional Determinants of Economic Development – Lessons from a Stochastic Neoclassical Growth Model. Jahrbuch für Wirtschaftswissenschaft 46:138–51
Lau SHP (2002) Further Inspection of the Stochastic Growth Model by an Analytical Approach. Macroeconomic Dynamics 6:748–757
Mahalanobis PC (1955) The approach of operational research to planning in India. Sankhya: Indian Journal of Statistics 16:3–62
Malliaris AG, Brock WA (1982) Stochastic Methods in Economics and Finance. North–Holland/Elsevier, Amsterdam
Mandl P (1968) Analytical Treatment of One–Dimensional Markov Processes. Springer–Verlag, Berlin, (Die Grundlehren der mathematischen Wissenschaften in Einzeldarstellungen, Band 151)
Mas-Colell A, Whinston MD, Green JR (1995) Microeconomic Theory. Oxford University Press, New York
Merton RC (1975) An Asymptotic Theory of Growth under Uncertainty. Review of Economic Studies 42:375–393, Ch.17 in Merton (1990)
Merton RC (1990) Continuous–Time Finance. Blackwell, Cambridge MA
Minhas BS (1962) The Homohypallagic Production Function, Factor Intensity Reversals, and the Heckscher–Ohlin Theorem. The Journal of Political Economy 70:138–156
Mirman LJ (1972) On the Existence of Steady State Measures for One Sector Growth Models with Uncertain Technology. International Economic Review 13(2):271–286
Mirman LJ (1973) The Steady State Behavior of a Class of One Sector Growth Models with Uncertain Technology. Journal of Political Economy 6(3):219–242
Øksendal B (2005) Stochastic Differential Equations, 6th edn. Universitext, Springer–Verlag, Berlin

Quah DT (1996) Empirics for Economic Growth and Convergence. European Economic Review 40:1353–1375
Rosenberg N (1963) Capital Goods, Technology, and Economic Growth. Oxford Economic Papers 15:217–27
Sala-i-Martin XX (1996) Regional Cohesion: Evidence and Theories of Regional Growth and Convergence. European Economic Review 40:1325–1352
Sandmo A (1970) The Effect of Uncertainty on Saving Decisions. Review of Economic Studies 37:353–60
Scenk-Hoppe KR (2002) Is there a Golden Rule for the Stochastic Solow Growth Model? Macroeconomic Dynamics 6:457–475
Solow RM (1961) Note on Uzawa's Two–Sector Model of Economic Growth. Rev Econ Stud 29:48–50, or Stiglitz (1969)
Stiglitz JE, Uzawa H (1969) Readings in the Modern Theory of Economic Growth. M.I.T. Press, Cambridge, Mass
Stigum BP (1972) Balanced Growth under Uncertainty. Journal of Economic Theory 5:42–68
Uzawa H (1961) On a Two–Sector Model of Economic Growth: I. Review of Economic Studies 29:40–47
Uzawa H (1963) On a Two–Sector Model of Economic Growth: II. Review of Economic Studies 30:105–18, Also in: Stiglitz and Uzawa (1969)
Wan HY Jr (1971) Economic Growth. Harcourt Brace Jovanovich, New York

CHAPTER 27

# Basic Stochastic Dynamic Systems of Growth and Trade

## Introduction

Stochastic elements will evidently appear in any economic growth process generated by factor endowment accumulation and technological change. It is not possible to know exactly how the labor force will grow. Neither will the actual evolution of capital stock be governed by a purely deterministic process. What happens then in *dynamic trade* models to the *steady-state* or *endogenous* (persistent) *growth* paths, when the traditional assumption of *certainty* is *relaxed*?

In the present chapter, we raise this question for neoclassical *two-sector growth* models of a *small* country that is *trading* in both commodities. Within the framework of Ito-Wiener *diffusion* processes for the factor endowment (capital/labor) ratio, particular attention is given to the long-run *probabilities* of *diversification* or complete *specialization*. As to the *existence* of a steady-state distribution, our central problem and objective are to obtain general *boundary inaccessibility* conditions. Another major goal is to derive the *steady-state* probability *distribution* of the capital-labor ratio in *closed form* for a trading economy. Parameters of stochastic trade models generating *persistent* (endogenous) *growth* per capital are analyzed. The *geometric* Wiener process appears to be the uncertainty analogue of deterministic endogenous growth paths. For our purposes and as benchmarks, sector production functions of the CD and CES form are used.

With co-author:
CHUNYAN WANG, Copenhagen Business School, Denmark





B. S. Jensen, *The Elements and Dynamic Systems of Economic Growth and Trade Models*, https://doi.org/10.1007/978-3-031-52493-6_27

In the literature on the pure theory of international trade, the implications of *uncertainty* for factor *allocation*, *production*, and *trade* patterns have long ago been studied by Kemp and Liviatan (1973), Batra (1974), Ruffin (1974b), Ruffin (1974a), Turnovsky (1974), Kemp (1976), Baron and Forsythe (1979), Kemp et al. (1981), Young (1984), and Pomery (1984). Instead of firms maximizing profit or expected profit and hence being indifferent toward risk, the main focus of these authors is upon *risk*-averse *producers* maximizing their *expected utility* from profits in a stochastic environment of random *prices*, *resource* uncertainty (randomness in factor endowments), or *technological* uncertainty (random parameters) in sector production functions. Recognition of these uncertainties and risk aversion tended to *invalidate* the fundamental theorems of *deterministic trade* theory. The latter, however, would carry over to a stochastic environment, if *uncertainty* can be *accommodated* by introducing *contingency* markets of the Arrow-Debreu type (Kemp et al. 1981; Kemp and Liviatan 1973) or allowing for trading risk in a *perfect* capital (security) market. For a systematic integration of the theory of international financial markets into international commodity trade theory, see Helpman and Razin (1978) and Grinols (1987).

So far, the analyses of various types of uncertainty and their implications have been conducted within essentially *static trade models* with *constant* expected aggregate *factor endowments*. Although the propositions about uncertainty in static or comparative static analyses (alternative capital stocks) are instructive, the process of capital *accumulation* with *uncertainty* is best represented by *stochastic* versions of economic *growth* models.

The *dynamic* implications of *resource* (labor, capital) *uncertainties* are particularly relevant, since a *small* growing trading country, as is usually assumed, faces *known*, constant world *prices* of traded goods.

Our basic *stochastic growth model* represents an extension of the open neoclassical two-sector growth model originated by Deardorff (1971, 1974), cf. Jensen and Wang (1997); here Chap. 21, to a stochastic environment in *continuous time*. Our diffusion dynamics extend the continuous-time stochastic one-sector growth model outlined by Merton (1975) and Bourguignon (1974) to a trading two-sector economy.

The structure of the chapter is as follows. First, we generalize the deterministic growth models to various stochastic dynamic systems and present the diffusion processes for the state variables: labor and capital. Next, by Ito's lemma, we derive diffusion processes for the capital-labor ratios. Moreover, the crucial boundary issues of the diffusion processes are examined, and actual *sufficient conditions* for *inaccessible* boundaries are obtained. From the Kolmogorov forward equation for a stationary probability density function, the *steady-state probability* distribution of the *capital-labor ratio* is derived in *closed form* for the trading economy.

## Structure of Two-Sector Trade Models

### *General Equilibrium and a Two-Sector Trading Economy*

Consider an economy consisting of a *capital* good industry (sector) and a *consumer* good industry (sector), labeled 1 and 2, respectively. The sector *technologies* are described by productions exhibiting *constant returns* to scale,

$$Y_i = F_i(L_i, K_i) = L_i f_i(k_i) \equiv L_i y_i, \quad i = 1, 2 \tag{27.1}$$

where the *intensive function* $f_i$ is a strictly concave monotonic increasing function on the nonnegative real line, i.e., $f_i(k_i)$, $k_i \equiv K_i/L_i$, $i = 1, 2$, have the properties

$$\forall k_i > 0: \quad f_i'(k_i) = df_i(k_i)/dk_i > 0, \quad f_i''(k_i) = d^2 f_i(k_i)/dk_i^2 < 0 \tag{27.2}$$

Full employment of labor and capital gives

$$L_1/L + L_2/L \equiv \lambda_{L_1} + \lambda_{L_2} = 1, \quad K/L \equiv k \equiv \lambda_{L_1} k_1 + \lambda_{L_2} k_2 \tag{27.3}$$

$$\lambda_{L_1} = (k - k_2)/(k_1 - k_2), \quad \lambda_{L_2} = (k_1 - k)/(k_1 - k_2), \quad Y_i = L_i y_i = L y_i \lambda_{L_i} \tag{27.4}$$

The factor endowments belonging to the *diversification cone* $C_k \subset \mathbb{R}_+^2$ are

$$C_k = \{(L, K) \in \mathbb{R}_+^2 \mid k_1 < K/L < k_2 \ \vee \ k_2 < K/L < k_1\} \tag{27.5}$$

The open two-sector economy is assumed to operate under *perfect competition* (zero profit condition); absolute (money) *factor* prices $(w, r)$ are the same in both sectors; and *output* prices $(P_1, P_2)$ represent unit cost. Hence, we have the competitive *general equilibrium* relations, $P_i Y_i = r K_i + w L_i$, $i = 1, 2$, and

$$\omega \equiv w/r = f_i(k_i)/f_i'(k_i) - k_i, \quad r/P_i = f_i'(k_i), \\ p \equiv P_1/P_2 = f_2'(k_2)/f_1'(k_1) \tag{27.6}$$

A small, *open*, competitive two-sector economy can only remain *diversified* with common positive $\omega$ if the *range* of the *terms of trade*, $p \equiv P_1/P_2$, is confined to the zero profit price interval with the limits (cf. Rybczynski lines in Wong (1995))

$$k_1 > k_2: \ \tilde{y}_2/\tilde{y}_1 < p < (\tilde{y}_2/\tilde{y}_1)(\tilde{k}_1/\tilde{k}_2); \tag{27.7}$$

$$k_2 > k_1: \ (\tilde{y}_2/\tilde{y}_1)(\tilde{k}_1/\tilde{k}_2) < p < \tilde{y}_2/\tilde{y}_1 \tag{27.8}$$

With $p$ as a fixed number, we use the symbols $\tilde{y}_i = f_i(\tilde{k}_i(\tilde{\omega}[p]))$, $i = 1, 2$, in (27.8) for factor endowments $k \in C_k$.

Gross domestic product $Y$ is the monetary value of outputs from both sectors and represents aggregated gross factor incomes, cf. (27.4), (27.6)

$$Y \equiv P_1 Y_1 + P_2 Y_2 = L(P_1 y_1 \lambda_{L_1} + P_2 y_2 \lambda_{L_2}) = rK + wL = L(rk + w) \equiv Ly \tag{27.9}$$

Let $Q_i$, $i = 1, 2$, denote the quantitative size of the *domestic demand* (absorption level) for good 1 (gross investment) and good 2 (consumption), and $Q_i$ is equal to domestic production, $Y_i$, minus net exports, $X_i \lesseqgtr 0$, i.e.,

$$Q_i = Y_i - X_i, \tag{27.10}$$

The *trade balance* is assumed to satisfy the constraint

$$P_1 X_1 + P_2 X_2 = 0 \quad \therefore \quad Y = P_1 Q_1 + P_2 Q_2 \tag{27.11}$$

i.e., trade equilibrium prevails with no foreign borrowing/lending allowed.

### *Deterministic Dynamics for a Small Two-Sector Trading Economy*

For the general deterministic dynamic neoclassical model of a small trading economy, a rigorous analysis can be performed by specification of the factor accumulation process. The domestic labor force grows exponentially at an exogenous rate, $n > 0$, and the domestic stock of capital goods increases by gross savings $S = sY$, $s > 0$, with the deduction of depreciation $\delta P_1 K$. Hence we have (27.9), $L \geq 0$, $K \geq 0$,

$$\dot{L} \equiv dL/dt = Ln \tag{27.12}$$

$$\begin{aligned} \dot{K} \equiv dK/dt &= Ls(y/P_1) - \delta K \\ &= L(s[y_1 \lambda_{L_1} + (y_2/p)\lambda_{L_2}] - \delta k) \\ &\equiv L\mathfrak{g}(k) \end{aligned} \tag{27.13}$$

Thus, with the *factor endowments* $L$ and $K$ as *state variables*, the complete description of the growth process in the small trading economy is given by the *dynamic system* (27.12)–(27.13). This system applies to growth processes with "fixed" sector technologies operating within the *diversification* cone (nonspecialization), as well as to *flexible* sector technologies operating outside the diversification cone.

From (27.12)–(27.13), we get for $k \in [0, \infty[$,

$$\begin{aligned}\dot{k} = h(k) \equiv g(k) - nk &= s(y/P_1) - (n+\delta)k \\ &= s[y_1\lambda_{L_1} + (y_2/p)\lambda_{L_2}] - (n+\delta)k \end{aligned} \tag{27.14}$$

The director function $h(k)$ is a $C^1$-function on $[0, \infty[$, and $h(k)$ is a concave function cf. (27.2) and has—like the per-capita real GDP-function $y/P_1$—a *linear segment* (flat) within the diversification cone (27.5); cf. Jensen and Wang (1997); here Chap. 21.

## Stochastic Dynamic Systems for Trading Economies

### *Introduction of Stochastic Elements*

Introducing *random* elements (uncertainty) of the growth rate of labor $n$, the saving rate $s$, and the capital depreciation rate $\delta$ into (27.12)–(27.13), we have

$$\dot{L} = L(n + \epsilon_1) \tag{27.15}$$

$$\dot{K} = L(s + \epsilon_3)(y/P_1) - (\delta + \epsilon_2)K \tag{27.16}$$

where the *random variables* $\boldsymbol{\epsilon}_i$, $i = 1, 2, 3$, are formally represented as

$$\epsilon_i = \Phi_i(L, K)dw_i/dt, \quad \text{or} \quad \epsilon_i = \beta_i dw_i/dt, \quad \beta_i \geq 0, \quad i = 1, 2, 3 \tag{27.17}$$

Here $\boldsymbol{w_i(t)}$ are standard *Wiener* processes (Karlin and Taylor 1981, p. 342); (Øksendal 1992, p. 14), and $\boldsymbol{\Phi_i(L, K)}$ is either a *nonnegative* function of $L(t)$ and $K(t)$ or, more simply, a *constant* $\beta_i \geq 0$. As first, we assume that the random variables $\boldsymbol{\epsilon_i}$ of the growth rate of labor, the saving rate, and the capital depreciation rate $\delta$ do *not* depend on the *state* variables $L$ and $K$. However, we will in Sect. "Final Comments" consider the general case of saving uncertainty.

Thus (27.15)–(27.17) become the *stochastic differential* equations,

$$dL = L(n + \beta_1 dw_1/dt)dt = L(ndt + \beta_1 dw_1) \tag{27.18}$$

$$\begin{aligned} dK &= L(s + \beta_3 dw_3/dt)(y/P_1)dt - (\delta + \beta_2 dw_2/dt)Kdt \\ &= L(\{s(y/P_1) - \delta k\}dt - \beta_2 k dw_2 + \beta_3(y/P_1)dw_3) \end{aligned} \tag{27.19}$$

They express formally that the *infinitesimal changes* $dL(t)$ and $dK(t)$ of the *state* variables $L$ and $K$ between instants $t$ and $t+dt$ are now *random* variables, *conditional* on the values of the random variables $L(t)$ and $K(t)$ at *time* $t$.

In differential symbols (27.18)–(27.19) have the common form

$$d\mathbf{X} = \mathbf{a}(\mathbf{X}, t)dt + \mathbf{b}(\mathbf{X}, t)d\mathbf{w} \tag{27.20}$$

where $\mathbf{a}(\mathbf{X}, t)$, $\mathbf{b}(\mathbf{X}, t)$ are respectively the *drift* and *diffusion* coefficients.

By comparing (27.12)–(27.13) with (27.18)–(27.19), it has accordingly been assumed that

(1) The stochastic process $w_i(t)$ is a standard Wiener process, and hence $dw_i(t)$ is a normal distribution with mean zero and variance proportional to $dt$.
(2) The *expectations* of (27.18)–(27.19) are assumed to be equal to the deterministic relations (27.12)–(27.13), which can be seen as a true representation of the dynamics of the expected values, $\mathrm{E}[L(t)]$ and $\mathrm{E}[K(t)]$. The values of the stochastic state variable $\mathbf{X}(t)$, (27.20), are determined completely when the Wiener process (path) $\mathbf{w}(t)$ is known up to time $t$ (Karlin and Taylor 1981, p. 346), and $\mathrm{E}[\int \mathbf{b}(\mathbf{X}, t)d\mathbf{w}(t)] = \mathbf{0}$.
(3) The *conditional* variance of $dL(t)$ and $dK(t)$ must necessarily be assumed to be of infinitesimal order $dt$ to avoid any *degeneracy* of the stochastic differential equation (27.18)–(27.19) into either the *deterministic* relationships (27.12)–(27.13) or into being dominated by the *pure* stochastic terms depending on $dw_i(t)$.
(4) The *drift* and *diffusion* coefficients in (27.18)–(27.19) are *autonomous*, i.e., independent of time $t$, hence the *governing functions* ("probabilistic laws") of the economic phenomena are *time invariant*.

The *stochastic dynamic system* (27.18)–(27.19), defined on the whole *nonnegative orthant* for $L$ and $K$, consists of *three subsystems*, allowing for, respectively, specialization in good 1, nonspecialization (diversification), and specialization in good 2. *Explicitly*, (27.18)–(27.19) become, with $\tilde{k}_2 > \tilde{k}_1$, cf. (27.9), (27.8), (27.1), (27.4),

$$\begin{aligned} dL &= L(ndt + \beta_1 dw_1), \qquad\qquad 0 < k \le \tilde{k}_1 \\ dK &= L(\{sf_1(k) - \delta k\}dt - \beta_2 k dw_2 + \beta_3 f_1(k) dw_3) \end{aligned} \tag{27.21}$$

$$\begin{aligned} dL &= L(ndt + \beta_1 dw_1), \qquad\qquad \tilde{k}_1 < k < \tilde{k}_2 \\ dK &= L(\{s[\tilde{y}_1\lambda_{L_1} + (\tilde{y}_2/p)\lambda_{L_2}] - \delta k\}dt - \beta_2 k dw_2 + \beta_3[\tilde{y}_1\lambda_{L_1} + (\tilde{y}_2/p)\lambda_{L_2}]dw_3) \end{aligned} \tag{27.22}$$

$$\begin{aligned} dL &= L(ndt + \beta_1 dw_1), \qquad\qquad k \ge \tilde{k}_2 \\ dK &= L(\{s(f_2(k)/p) - \delta k\}dt - \beta_2 k dw_2 + \beta_3 (f_2(k)/p) dw_3) \end{aligned} \tag{27.23}$$

The case with capital intensity (27.8) will give a system similar to (27.21)–(27.23). The *drift* and *diffusion* coefficients of the stochastic dynamic system (27.21)–(27.23) are *homogeneous functions* (in the Euler sense) of *degree one* in the state variables $L$ and $K$. The homogeneity property allows us to describe two-dimensional systems completely by the dynamics of the capital-labor ratio, cf. Jensen (1994); here Chaps. 2–16 and 28–31.

### *Stochastic Dynamics of the Capital-Labor Ratio*

**Lemma 27.1** *For the two-sector trading economy (27.18)–(27.19)—with uncertainties in labor growth rate, savings rate, and the capital depreciation rate—the stochastic dynamics for the capital-labor ratio is a diffusion process given by*

$$\begin{aligned} dk = &\{(s - \rho_{13}\beta_1\beta_3)(y/P_1) - [n + \delta - (\beta_1^2 + \rho_{12}\beta_1\beta_2)]k\}dt \\ &-\beta_1 k dw_1 - \beta_2 k dw_2 + \beta_3(y/P_1)dw_3, \qquad k \in [0, \infty[ \end{aligned} \tag{27.24}$$

*where $\rho_{ij}$ is the time-invariant correlation coefficient between the incremental Wiener processes $dw_i$ and $dw_j$.*

*Explicitly, (27.24) becomes for the three subintervals of $k$, cf. (27.21)–(27.23),*

$$dk = \{(s - \rho_{13}\beta_1\beta_3)f_1(k) - \Theta k\}dt + b_1(k)dw, \qquad 0 < k \le \tilde{k}_1 \tag{27.25}$$

$$dk = \{(s - \rho_{13}\beta_1\beta_3)\tilde{\theta}_2 + [(s - \rho_{13}\beta_1\beta_3)\tilde{\theta}_1 - \Theta]k\}dt + b_2(k)dw, \quad \tilde{k}_1 < k < \tilde{k}_2 \tag{27.26}$$

$$dk = \{(s - \rho_{13}\beta_1\beta_3)(f_2(k)/p) - \Theta k\}dt + b_3(k)dw, \qquad k \ge \tilde{k}_2 \tag{27.27}$$

*with*

$$\Theta \equiv n + \delta - (\beta_1^2 + \rho_{12}\beta_1\beta_2) \tag{27.28}$$

$$\beta^2 \equiv \beta_1^2 + \beta_2^2 + 2\rho_{12}\beta_1\beta_2 \tag{27.29}$$

$$\rho \equiv 2(\rho_{13}\beta_1 + \rho_{23}\beta_2) \tag{27.30}$$

$$\begin{aligned} b_1^2(k) &\equiv \beta^2 k^2 + \beta_3^2 f_1^2(k) - \rho\beta_3 f_1(k)k \\ b_2^2(k) &\equiv \beta^2 k^2 + \beta_3^2[\tilde{\theta}_2 + \tilde{\theta}_1 k]^2 - \rho\beta_3[\tilde{\theta}_2 + \tilde{\theta}_1 k]k \\ b_3^2(k) &\equiv \beta^2 k^2 + \beta_3^2[f_2(k)/p]^2 - \rho\beta_3[f_2(k)/p]k \end{aligned} \tag{27.31}$$

$$\tilde{\theta}_1 \equiv [\tilde{y}_1 - (\tilde{y}_2/p)]/(\tilde{k}_1 - \tilde{k}_2) > 0, \tag{27.32}$$

$$\tilde{\theta}_2 \equiv [(\tilde{y}_2/p)\tilde{k}_1 - \tilde{y}_1\tilde{k}_2]/(\tilde{k}_1 - \tilde{k}_2) > 0 \tag{27.33}$$

*and $\tilde{\theta}_1$ is the slope of the linear segment of the GDP-function $y/P_1$, while $\tilde{\theta}_2$ is the corresponding intercept, cf. (27.4), (27.8)–(27.9), (27.14).*

***Proof*** Ito's lemma: Let $\mathbf{X}(t) \in \mathbb{R}^n$ be a general diffusion process defined as in (27.20). Let $F(\mathbf{X}, t)$ be an arbitrary $C^2$-map from $\mathbb{R}^n \to \mathbb{R}$, then

$$dF(\mathbf{X}, t) = F_t dt + F_{\mathbf{x}}^T d\mathbf{X} + \frac{1}{2} d\mathbf{X}^T F_{\mathbf{xx}} d\mathbf{X} \tag{27.34}$$

i.e., $F(\mathbf{X}, t)$, determined by the diffusion process $\mathbf{X}(t)$, is again a diffusion process; $F_t$ and $F_{\mathbf{x}}$ represent the partial derivatives with respect to $t$ and $\mathbf{x}$ of the function $F(\mathbf{x}, t)$, $F_{\mathbf{xx}}$ represents the Hessian matrix of $F(\mathbf{x}, t)$, and the multiplication rules are: $(dw_i)^2 = dt$; $dw_i \cdot dw_j = \rho_{ij} dt$; $(dt)^2 = 0$; $dt \cdot dw_i = 0$.

The expression (27.24) is obtained after straightforward calculations from (27.18)–(27.19) by applying Ito's lemma (27.34) to the capital-labor ratio, $k = K/L$, i.e.,

$$dk = 0\,dt - (K/L^2)dL + (1/L)dK + (K/L^3)dL^2 - (1/L^2)dLdK + 0\,dK^2 \tag{27.35}$$

The expressions (27.25)–(27.27) are obtained from (27.24), using (27.1), (27.4), (27.9), together with $\lambda_{L_1} = 1$, $\lambda_{L_2} = 0$ for (27.25); with $\lambda_{L_1} = (k - \tilde{k}_2)/(\tilde{k}_1 - \tilde{k}_2)$, $\lambda_{L_2} = (\tilde{k}_1 - k)/(\tilde{k}_1 - \tilde{k}_2)$, and (27.8) for (27.26); and finally, $\lambda_{L_1} = 0$, $\lambda_{L_2} = 1$ for (27.27). See Karlin and Taylor (1981, p. 364), Malliaris and Brock (1982, p. 142), Klump (1995).

The expressions (27.31) of the squared diffusion coefficients are simply obtained by using the multiplication rules in combining the three diffusion terms of (27.24). □

**Corollary 27.1** *If only the labor growth rate and the capital depreciation rate are uncertain* ($\beta_3 = 0$), *the diffusion process of* $k(t)$ *is described by, cf. (27.24),*

$$dk = \{s(y/P_1) - \Theta k\}dt - \beta_1 k dw_1 - \beta_2 k dw_2 \tag{27.36}$$

*or explicitly*

$$dk = \begin{cases} \{sf_1(k) - \Theta k\}dt - \beta k dw & = & a_1(k)dt + b(k)dw, & 0 < k \le \tilde{k}_1 \\ \{s\tilde{\theta}_2 + [s\tilde{\theta}_1 - \Theta]k\}dt - \beta k dw & = & a_2(k)dt + b(k)dw, & \tilde{k}_1 < k < \tilde{k}_2 \\ \{s(f_2(k)/p) - \Theta k\}dt - \beta k dw & = & a_3(k)dt + b(k)dw, & k \ge \tilde{k}_2 \end{cases} \tag{27.37}$$

*where the diffusion coefficient of the combined incremental Wiener process* $dw(t)$ *in (27.37) is, cf. (27.29)–(27.31),*

$$b_i^2(k) = b^2(k) \equiv \beta^2 k^2 = (\beta_1^2 + \beta_2^2 + 2\rho_{12}\beta_1\beta_2)k^2 \tag{27.38}$$

Note that $\rho_{23}$ does not enter the drift coefficient in (27.24). Furthermore, note that our introduction of uncertainties (27.18)–(27.19) implies that the *deterministic* growth *parameters* $s$, $n$, $\delta$ only appear in the drift coefficients, cf. (27.25)–(27.27), but not in the diffusion coefficients (27.31). From (27.24), it is clear that *uncertainty* in the *saving* rate $s$ will always introduce *nonlinear* terms in the *diffusion* coefficient of the capital-labor ratio, creating as is well-known, difficulties in solving (27.24)–(27.33). Therefore, with respect to closed form probability distributions, we will later primarily investigate the situations in Corollary 27.1.

## Boundary Conditions, Steady State, and Convergence

From Lemma 27.1, with the derived diffusion processes of the capital-labor ratios on the state space $[0, \infty]$, we may now analyze the process evolution of the small competitive trading economy, with emphasis on long-run behavior (asymptotic properties). However, the drift and diffusion coefficients *govern* the process evolution only at *interior* points of the state space. To fully define a diffusion process, the behavior of any *boundary* points requires *separate* specification. For our purposes of studying the long-run evolution of nontrivial states, careful examination is needed of the *conditions* that will make the *boundaries*, $k = 0$ or $k = \infty$, *inaccessible* for any *finite* time ($t < \infty$). If $a_i(0) = 0$ and $b_i(0) = 0$—as is often seen cf. (27.25)–(27.27) and (27.37)—then $k(t) = 0$ is an *absorbing* boundary, i.e., the sample paths $k(t)$ remain at the zero position once it is attained. Even if $a_i(0) \neq 0$, or $b_i(0) \neq 0$, and hence $k = 0$ is not an absorbing state, we may not admit negative state values of $k(t)$, i.e., a *viable* (working) *economic* diffusion model must require that the *inaccessibility* of the boundary state $k = 0$ is ensured by imposing sufficient *parameter restrictions* on the actual drift and diffusion coefficients.

As the incremental Wiener processes $dw_i(t) \in ]-\infty, \infty[$ may occasionally take on very large negative values, the drift and diffusion coefficients must indeed be carefully chosen to prevent the random variable $k(t)$ from never hitting the lower boundary $k = 0$. The sort of "boxing match" between $a_i(k)$ and $b_i(k)$ must in the neighborhood of $k = 0$ be won by the drift coefficient $a_i(k)$, which evidently in this neighborhood must be positive and larger than $b_i(k)$. However, the exact inaccessibility *criteria* follows only from rigorous analysis related to the *divergence* of specific improper integrals of the drift and diffusion coefficients; see Appendix section "Appendix A: Boundary Conditions and Steady-State Distribution". Primarily the divergence of the so-called *scale function* $S(k)$ at $k = 0$ and $k = \infty$ is used to establish the *sufficient* parametric *conditions* for inaccessibility of the respective boundaries for various diffusion processes below.

**Remark 27.1** It is well-known, Karlin and Taylor (1981, p. 359), that the solution (Ito-integral) to the stochastic differential equation (27.18) is the geometric Wiener process with the *continuous sample paths* (stochastic trajectories, realizations),

$$L(t) = L_0 \exp\left\{\left(n - \frac{1}{2}\beta_1^2\right)t + \beta_1 w_1(t)\right\}; \quad 2n \gtrless \beta_1^2: \lim_{t\to\infty} L(t) = \begin{cases}\infty \\ 0\end{cases} \tag{27.39}$$

Furthermore, the *boundaries* zero or infinity are *inaccessible*, as the sample paths (27.39) *cannot* attain any of the two boundaries in *finite* time. It will be instructive to prove the latter statement as a prelude to the general procedure of proving inaccessibility below. From (27.18) and Appendix section "Appendix A: Boundary Conditions and Steady-State Distribution", the *scale density* $\mathfrak{s}(L)$ and the *scale function* $\mathcal{S}(L)$ become, cf. (27.111)

$$\mathfrak{s}(L) = \exp\{-2\int_{L_0}^{L} nL/(\beta_1^2 L^2)dL\} = (L/L_0)^{-2n/\beta_1^2} \tag{27.40}$$

$$\mathcal{S}(L) = \int_{L_0}^{L} \mathfrak{s}(L)dL = L_0/(1 - 2n/\beta_1^2)[(L/L_0)^{1-2n/\beta_1^2} - 1] \tag{27.41}$$

As $\mathcal{S}(0) = -\infty$ for $2n \geq \beta_1^2$, the latter is a *sufficient* parameter condition for the *inaccessibility* of the boundary $k = 0$. But despite the finite $\mathcal{S}(0) = -L_0/(1 - 2n/\beta_1^2)$ for $2n < \beta_1^2$, the boundary $k = 0$ may still not be attainable.

The *speed density* $\mathfrak{m}(L)$ is, cf. (27.112)

$$\mathfrak{m}(L) = 2L^{2n/\beta_1^2}/(\beta_1^2 L^2) = \left(L_0^{2n/\beta_1^2}/\beta_1^2\right) L^{2n/\beta_1^2 - 2} \tag{27.42}$$

and we must now with (27.41)–(27.42) and (27.115) evaluate

$$\begin{aligned}\Sigma(0) &= \int_0^{L_0} [\mathcal{S}(L) - \mathcal{S}(0)]\mathfrak{m}(L)dL \\ &= \frac{L_0^{4n/\beta_1^2}}{\beta_1^2(1 - 2n/\beta_1^2)} \int_0^{L_0} L^{-1}dL \\ &= +\infty\end{aligned} \tag{27.43}$$

Thus $\Sigma(0) = +\infty$ says that it takes *infinite* time to reach zero boundary from any interior state, i.e., $L = 0$ is after all also *inaccessible* for $2n < \beta_1^2$, as it *cannot* be attained in *finite* time. The same analysis can be applied to boundary $L = \infty$, which is neither attainable in finite time. From this examination of the *labor diffusion* process (27.18)—which have no steady-state distribution—it is also clear that boundary problems for the capital-labor ratio diffusion below are essentially due to boundary problems associated with the capital stock diffusion process. ∇

### *Labor Growth and Capital Depreciation Rates Are Uncertain*

*CD Case* The general intensive form of the CD (Cobb-Douglas) function is

$$f_i(k) = \gamma_i k^{a_i}, \quad \gamma_i > 0, \quad 0 < a_i < 1, \quad i = 1, 2 \tag{27.44}$$

with the following limits of $f_i(k)$ and $f_i'(k)$, ("Inada conditions"),

$$\lim_{k\to 0} f_i(k) = 0, \quad \lim_{k\to\infty} f_i(k) = \infty, \quad \lim_{k\to 0} f_i'(k) = \infty, \quad \lim_{k\to\infty} f_i'(k) = 0 \tag{27.45}$$

From (27.37)–(27.38) and the CD functions (27.44), we have,

$$dk = \begin{cases} \{s\gamma_1 k^{a_1} - \Theta k\}dt - \beta k dw & = & a_1(k)dt + b(k)dw, & 0 < k \leq \tilde{k}_1 \\ \{s\tilde{\theta}_2 + [s\tilde{\theta}_1 - \Theta]k\}dt - \beta k dw & = & a_2(k)dt + b(k)dw, & \tilde{k}_1 < k < \tilde{k}_2 \\ \{s(\gamma_2/p)k^{a_2} - \Theta k\}dt - \beta k dw & = & a_3(k)dt + b(k)dw, & k \geq \tilde{k}_2 \end{cases} \tag{27.46}$$

**Theorem 27.1** *The sufficient conditions for the diffusion process (27.46) of a small competitive trading economy—with CD technologies and uncertainties in both labor growth and capital depreciation—to have inaccessible boundaries are,*

$$k = 0 \ : \ \textit{Always inaccessible} \tag{27.47}$$

$$k = \infty: \ 2\Theta + \beta^2 \geq 0 \quad \Leftrightarrow \quad 2(n+\delta) \geq \beta_1^2 - \beta_2^2 \tag{27.48}$$

*The parametric condition (27.48) also ensures the existence and the long-run convergence of the stochastic capital-labor ratio $k(t)$ to a time-invariant (steady-state) probability distribution $P(k)$.*

***Proof*** Applying (27.111) of Appendix section "Appendix A: Boundary Conditions and Steady-State Distribution"

$$\mathfrak{s}_i(k) \equiv \exp\left\{-2\int_{k_0}^{k} \frac{a_i(u)}{b_i^2(u)} du\right\}, \quad i = 1, 2, 3 \tag{27.49}$$

to the system (27.46), we have

$$\mathfrak{s}_1(k) = \exp\left\{-2\int_{k_0}^{k} \frac{s\gamma_1 k^{a_1} - \Theta k}{\beta^2 k^2} dk\right\}, \quad 0 < k \leq \tilde{k}_1 \tag{27.50}$$

$$\mathfrak{s}_3(k) = \exp\left\{-2\int_{k_0}^{k} \frac{s(\gamma_2/p)k^{a_2} - \Theta k}{\beta^2 k^2} dk\right\}, \quad k \geq \tilde{k}_2 \tag{27.51}$$

From (27.50)–(27.51), we get by simple integration,

$$\mathfrak{s}_1(k) = (k/k_0)^{2(\Theta/\beta^2)} \exp\left\{\frac{2s\gamma_1}{(1-a_1)\beta^2}(k^{-(1-a_1)} - k_0^{-(1-a_1)})\right\} \tag{27.52}$$

$$\mathfrak{s}_3(k) = (k/k_0)^{2(\Theta/\beta^2)} \exp\left\{\frac{2s(\gamma_2/p)}{(1-a_2)\beta^2}(k^{-(1-a_2)} - k_0^{-(1-a_2)})\right\} \tag{27.53}$$

From (27.52), we have,

$$\mathcal{S}_1(0) = \int_{k_0}^{0} \mathfrak{s}_1(k)dk \equiv m_0^1 \int_{k_0}^{0} k^{2(\Theta/\beta^2)} \exp\left\{\frac{2s\gamma_1}{(1-a_1)\beta^2}k^{-(1-a_1)}\right\} dk \tag{27.54}$$

Since $1 - a_1 > 0$ and $2s\gamma_1/[(1-a_1)\beta^2] > 0$, cf. (27.44), the exponential term in (27.54) will dominate and explode for $k \to 0$, and hence $\mathcal{S}_1(0)$ diverges, i.e., $\mathcal{S}_1(0) = -\infty$. Thus, the *lower boundary* $k = 0$ is always *inaccessible*, *irrespective* of the size of the drift and diffusion parameters.

From (27.53), we have

$$\mathcal{S}_3(\infty) = \int_{k_0}^{\infty} \mathfrak{s}_3(k)dk \equiv m_0^3 \int_{k_0}^{\infty} k^{2(\Theta/\beta^2)} \exp\left\{\frac{2s(\gamma_2/p)}{(1-a_2)\beta^2}k^{-(1-a_2)}\right\} dk \tag{27.55}$$

Since $1 - a_2 > 0$, cf. (27.44), the divergence of $\mathcal{S}_3(\infty)$ here only depends on the polynomial term in (27.55) with the exponent $2(\Theta/\beta^2)$. Hence divergence of $\mathcal{S}_3(\infty)$ requires that $2(\Theta/\beta^2) \geq -1$, or equivalently $2(n+\delta) \geq \beta_1^2 - \beta_2^2$, cf. (27.28)–(27.29). Hence, the *upper* boundary $k = \infty$ is *inaccessible* by imposing the parameter restriction stated in (27.48).

The *existence* of $P(k)$ and the *convergence* of $P(k,t)$ toward $P(k)$ follow from (27.111)–(27.112), (27.46), and (27.116)

$$\begin{aligned} |\mathcal{M}_1(0)| &= \int_0^{\tilde{k}_1} \mathfrak{m}_1(k)dk = \int_0^{\tilde{k}_1} \frac{1}{\beta^2 k^2 \mathfrak{s}_1(k)} dk < \infty \\ \mathcal{M}_3(\infty) &= \int_{\tilde{k}_2}^{\infty} \mathfrak{m}_3(k)dk = \int_{\tilde{k}_2}^{\infty} \frac{1}{\beta^2 k^2 \mathfrak{s}_3(k)} dk < \infty \end{aligned} \tag{27.56}$$

The *finiteness* (convergence) of the *two* improper integrals in (27.56) is easily verified with a procedure similar to that above to require the *same* parameter conditions as obtained from (27.54)–(27.55), of which only (27.55) imposed effective restrictions as stated in (27.48). □

**Remark 27.2** Besides the proofs, we may offer some intuition for the results obtained. The general inaccessibility of the *lower* boundary (27.47) is essentially due to the CD property, $f_i'(k) \to \infty$ as $k \to 0$, (27.45), which enables the *nonlinear part* of the *drift* coefficient $a_1(k)$ in (27.46), in the neighborhood of $k = 0$ to *dominate* the linear drift ($\Theta k$) and diffusion ($\beta k$) elements. The sufficient inaccessibility condition of the *upper* boundary (27.48) prevents "explosion" (reaching $k = \infty$ in finite time) of the diffusion process (27.46). By (27.48), we see that large values of labor growth ($n$), large depreciation rate ($\delta$), and large uncertainty (high volatility) in depreciation ($\beta_2$) will naturally curb high values of $k(t)$, whereas a very high volatility in labor growth ($\beta_1$) spells trouble by giving chances for generating very high values of the ratio $k(t)$. Note that if $\beta_2 = 0$ and $\delta = 0$ (Merton 1975), then the sufficient condition (27.48) coincides with the condition for $L(t) \to \infty$, (27.39). Evidently, large values of $n$ and $\delta$ help in preventing $k(t)$ from attaining infinity.

The *divergence* conditions of $\mathcal{S}_1(0)$ and $\mathcal{S}_3(\infty)$, (27.47)–(27.48), are the same as the *convergence* conditions of $\mathcal{M}_1(0)$ and $\mathcal{M}_3(\infty)$, since the scale density functions $\mathfrak{s}_1(k)$ and $\mathfrak{s}_3(k)$ entered the respective improper integrals reciprocally. $\nabla$

*CES Case* The general intensive form of CES technology, $\gamma_i > 0, 0 < a_i < 1$, is,

$$f_i(k) = \gamma_i \left[(1 - a_i) + a_i k^{\varrho_i}\right]^{1/\varrho_i}, \quad 0 < \sigma_i < \infty, \tag{27.57}$$

$$\varrho_i \equiv (\sigma_i - 1)/\sigma_i, \quad -\infty < \varrho_i < 1 \tag{27.58}$$

By evaluating (27.57–27.58), the limits or *dominating* ($\sim$) terms of $f_i(k)$ and $f_i'(k)$ become,

$$\sigma_i < 1: \begin{cases} \text{small } k: \ f_i(k) \sim \gamma_i a_i^{1/\varrho_i} k, & \lim_{k\to\infty} f_i(k) = \gamma_i (1 - a_i)^{1/\varrho_i} \\ \lim_{k\to 0} f_i'(k) = \gamma_i a_i^{1/\varrho_i}, & \lim_{k\to\infty} f_i'(k) = 0 \end{cases} \tag{27.59}$$

$$\sigma_i > 1: \begin{cases} \lim_{k\to 0} f_i(k) = \gamma_i (1 - a_i)^{1/\varrho_i}, & \text{large } k: \ f_i(k) \sim \gamma_i a_i^{1/\varrho_i} k \\ \lim_{k\to 0} f_i'(k) = \infty, & \lim_{k\to\infty} f_i'(k) = \gamma_i a_i^{1/\varrho_i} \end{cases} \tag{27.60}$$

From (27.37)–(27.38) and the CES functions (27.57–27.58), we get the diffusion process,

$$dk = \begin{cases} \{s\gamma_1[(1 - a_1) + a_1 k^{\varrho_1}]^{1/\varrho_1} - \Theta k\}dt - \beta k dw, & 0 < k \le \tilde{k}_1 \\ \{s\tilde{\theta}_2 + [s\tilde{\theta}_1 - \Theta]k\}dt - \beta k dw, & \tilde{k}_1 < k < \tilde{k}_2 \\ \{s(\gamma_2/p)[(1 - a_2) + a_2 k^{\varrho_2}]^{1/\varrho_2} - \Theta k\}dt - \beta k dw, & k \ge \tilde{k}_2 \end{cases} \tag{27.61}$$

**Theorem 27.2** *The sufficient conditions for the diffusion process (27.61)—with CES technologies and uncertainties in both labor growth and capital depreciation—to have inaccessible boundaries are,*

$$\sigma_i < 1: \begin{cases} k = 0 \ : \ 2(n + \delta - s\gamma_1 a_1^{1/\varrho_1}) \leq \beta_1^2 - \beta_2^2 \\ k = \infty : \ 2(n + \delta) \geq \beta_1^2 - \beta_2^2 \end{cases} \tag{27.62}$$

$$\sigma_i > 1: \begin{cases} k = 0 \ : \ \textit{Always inaccessible} \\ k = \infty : \ 2(n + \delta - s(\gamma_2/p) a_2^{1/\varrho_2}) \geq \beta_1^2 - \beta_2^2 \end{cases} \tag{27.63}$$

***Proof*** From (27.61), we have the expressions, cf. (27.49),

$$\mathfrak{s}_1(k) = \exp\left\{-2\int_{k_0}^{k} \frac{s\gamma_1[(1-a_1) + a_1 k^{\varrho_1}]^{1/\varrho_1} - \Theta k}{\beta^2 k^2} dk\right\} \tag{27.64}$$

$$\mathfrak{s}_3(k) = \exp\left\{-2\int_{k_0}^{k} \frac{s(\gamma_2/p)[(1-a_2) + a_2 k^{\varrho_2}]^{1/\varrho_2} - \Theta k}{\beta^2 k^2} dk\right\} \tag{27.65}$$

$\sigma_i < 1$: From (27.64) and (27.59), we have, cf. (27.114),

$$\mathcal{S}_1(0) = \lim_{k \to 0} \int_{k_0}^{k} \mathfrak{s}_1(k) dk = \int_{k_0}^{0} (k/k_0)^{-2[s\gamma_1 a_1^{1/\varrho_1} - \Theta]/\beta^2} dk \tag{27.66}$$

Hence it follows from (27.66), that the divergence of $\mathcal{S}_1(0)$ to $-\infty$ requires that the exponent must be less than or equal to $-1$, or equivalently $2s\gamma_1 a_1^{1/\varrho_1} \geq 2\Theta + \beta^2$, which gives the lower boundary condition in (27.62).

From (27.65) and (27.59), we have, cf. (27.114),

$$\begin{aligned} \mathcal{S}_3(\infty) &= \lim_{k \to \infty} \int_{k_0}^{k} \mathfrak{s}_3(k) dk \\ &= \int_{k_0}^{\infty} (k/k_0)^{\frac{2\Theta}{\beta^2}} \exp\left\{\frac{2s(\gamma_2/p)(1-a_2)^{1/\varrho_2}}{\beta^2} (k^{-1} - k_0^{-1})\right\} dk \end{aligned} \tag{27.67}$$

The polynomial term in (27.67) decides the divergence of $\mathcal{S}_3(\infty)$; it diverges to $+\infty$ if the exponent $2\Theta/\beta^2 \geq -1$, which gives the inaccessibility condition in (27.62).

$\sigma_i > 1$: From (27.64) and (27.60), we have, cf. (27.114),

$$\begin{aligned} \mathcal{S}_1(0) &= \lim_{k \to 0} \int_{k_0}^{k} \mathfrak{s}_1(k) dk \\ &= \int_{k_0}^{0} (k/k_0)^{\frac{2\Theta}{\beta^2}} \exp\left\{\frac{2s\gamma_1(1-a_1)^{1/\varrho_1}}{\beta^2} (k^{-1} - k_0^{-1})\right\} dk \end{aligned} \tag{27.68}$$

The exponential term in (27.68) will always explode for $k \to 0$. Hence $\mathcal{S}_1(0)$ is diverging, and accordingly, $k = 0$ is *inaccessible*, *irrespective* of parameters restrictions.

From (27.65) and (27.60), we have, cf. (27.114),

$$\mathcal{S}_3(\infty) = \lim_{k\to\infty} \int_{k_0}^{k} \mathfrak{s}_3(k)dk$$
$$= \int_{k_0}^{\infty} (k/k_0)^{-2[s(\gamma_2/p)a_2^{1/\varrho_2}-\Theta]/\beta^2} dk \tag{27.69}$$

$\mathcal{S}_3(\infty)$ is divergent, if and only if the *exponent* of the polynomial in (27.69) is larger than or equal to $-1$, which gives the parametric *inaccessibility* restriction as stated in (27.63). □

**Remark 27.3** A comparison of the sufficient inaccessibility conditions in Theorems 27.1–27.2 reveals that the *crucial* strength (size) of *drift* coefficients near the boundaries depends on the savings *parameter* $s$ and the *derivative properties* of the CD and CES functions, (27.45), (27.59)–(27.60). With $\sigma_i < 1$, (27.62) says that the lower boundary is inaccessible, when $s$ and the derivative $f_i'(0)$, (27.59), dominate both the linear drift $2\Theta$ and linear diffusion ($\beta^2$) elements. The condition (27.62) for $k = \infty$ is the *same* as (27.48), cf. the upper limit of $f_i'(k_i)$, (27.45), (27.59). With $\sigma_i > 1$, the logic of (27.63) for $k = 0$ is the same as in (27.47), cf. the dominating infinity derivative of $f_i'(0)$ in both (27.45) and (27.60). Naturally, to avoid explosion of the capital-labor ratio, the saving rate and the upper bound of the derivative, (27.60), must not be too high, as expressed by (27.63) for $k = \infty$. ▽

**Remark 27.4** Any *one-dimensional* regular *diffusion* process is *completely* characterized by its *scale* function $\mathcal{S}(x)$ and its *speed* measure $\mathcal{M}(x)$, cf. (27.111)–(27.112). It holds with either reflecting or absorbing boundaries. If a regular diffusion on an open interval $]r_1, r_2[$ satisfies the inaccessible boundary conditions, cf. (27.113)–(27.115), and if the diffusion solves a stochastic differential equation, then this solution is unique even if the drift and diffusion coefficients do not satisfy the standard conditions of Lipschitz continuity and the linear growth conditions (see Itô and McKean 1965).

An unbounded slope of CD and CES functions with $\sigma_i > 1$ at $k = 0$ prevents Lipschitz continuity, but the solutions to (27.46) and (27.61) are still unique when inaccessibility of $k = 0$ is ensured by Theorems 27.1–27.2. Hence, with inaccessibility we need not be restricted to only the class of bounded slope (see the critique by Chang and Malliaris (1987)). ▽

### *The Saving Rate Is Uncertain*

It was seen in (27.24) that the *uncertainty* in *saving* behavior will always introduce *nonlinear* terms in the *diffusion* coefficient. Inaccessible boundaries here raise conditions that clash with common deterministic dynamic regularity properties.

*CD Case* From (27.25)–(27.33) with $\beta_1 = \beta_2 = 0$ and the CD functions (27.44), we have the diffusion process,

$$dk = \begin{cases} \{s\gamma_1 k^{a_1} - (n+\delta)k\}dt + \beta_3\gamma_1 k^{a_1} dw_3, & 0 < k \leq \tilde{k}_1 \\ \{s\tilde{\theta}_2 + [s\tilde{\theta}_1 - (n+\delta)]k\}dt + \beta_3[\tilde{\theta}_2 + \tilde{\theta}_1 k]dw_3, & \tilde{k}_1 < k < \tilde{k}_2 \\ \{s(\gamma_2/p)k^{a_2} - (n+\delta)k\}dt + \beta_3(\gamma_2/p)k^{a_2} dw_3, & k \geq \tilde{k}_2 \end{cases} \tag{27.70}$$

*CES Case* From (27.25)–(27.33) with $\beta_1 = \beta_2 = 0$ and the CES functions (27.57–27.58), we have the diffusion process,

$$dk = \begin{cases} \{s\gamma_1[(1-a_1) + a_1 k^{\varrho_1}]^{1/\varrho_1} - (n+\delta)k\}dt \\ +\beta_3\gamma_1[(1-a_1) + a_1 k^{\varrho_1}]^{1/\varrho_1} dw_3, & 0 < k \leq \tilde{k}_1 \\ \{s\tilde{\theta}_2 + [s\tilde{\theta}_1 - (n+\delta)]k\}dt + \beta_3[\tilde{\theta}_2 + \tilde{\theta}_1 k]dw_3, & \tilde{k}_1 < k < \tilde{k}_2 \\ \{s(\gamma_2/p)[(1-a_2) + a_2 k^{\varrho_2}]^{1/\varrho_2} - (n+\delta)k\}dt \\ +\beta_3(\gamma_2/p)[(1-a_2) + a_2 k^{\varrho_2}]^{1/\varrho_2} dw_3, & k \geq \tilde{k}_2 \end{cases} \tag{27.71}$$

**Theorem 27.3** *The diffusion process (27.70) or (27.71)—with CD or CES functions and uncertainty only in saving rate—will have boundary properties and sufficient inaccessibility conditions as follows*

$$\sigma_i = 1: \begin{cases} k = 0 \ : \ \textit{Inaccessible, if } a_1 > \frac{1}{2}; \ \textit{Possibly accessible, if } a_1 < \frac{1}{2} \\ k = \infty: \ \textit{Always inaccessible} \end{cases} \tag{27.72}$$

$$\sigma_i < 1: \begin{cases} k = 0 \ : \ 2[s\gamma_1 a_1^{1/\varrho_1} - (n+\delta)] \geq [\beta_3\gamma_1 a_1^{1/\varrho_1}]^2 \\ k = \infty: \ \textit{Always inaccessible} \end{cases} \tag{27.73}$$

$$\sigma_i > 1: \begin{cases} k = 0 \ : \ \textit{Possibly accessible} \\ k = \infty: \ 2[s(\gamma_2/p)a_2^{1/\varrho_2} - (n+\delta)] \leq [\beta_3(\gamma_2/p)a_2^{1/\varrho_2}]^2 \end{cases} \tag{27.74}$$

***Proof*** See Appendix section "Appendix B: Proof of Theorem 27.3". □

With uncertainty in the saving rate, the *drift* and *diffusion* coefficients in (27.70)–(27.71) now have *similar nonlinear elements*, that, if dominating, will prevent us from satisfying a sufficient inaccessibility condition, as the scale function $\mathcal{S}_1(k)$ at $k = 0$ is now finite, cf. (27.120) and (27.126), whenever $\sigma_i \geq 1$. It is the infinite derivatives ("Inada property") at $k = 0$, (27.45), (27.60), that instead of supporting inaccessibility as before, cf. (27.47) and (27.63), now create problems by also appearing in the diffusion coefficients (27.70)–(27.71). This derivative problem is not changed by using (27.25)–(27.27), which include all the types of uncertainty. We may note that with $a_1 < \frac{1}{2}$, (27.72), the zero boundary will in fact absorb certain sample paths of (27.70) in finite time. Thus, *uncertainty* about the *saving rate* was recognized by Bourguignon (1974, p. 151) as a serious *obstacle* to the economic *viability* of diffusion processes (27.70)–(27.71). The factor accumulation process is likely to be much more severely affected (large volatility) by *uncertainties* about the *saving* rate than by uncertainties in labor growth and depreciation rates. The *lack* of any parametric *restrictions* preventing the accessibility of the *absorbing boundary* $\boldsymbol{k = 0}$ (implosion, "*economic collapse*"), cf. (27.72) and (27.74), represents a *critical* stochastic dynamic model complication for the system (27.70)–(27.71) and a mathematical issue to be adequately resolved below.

### *General Parameter Uncertainties and Inaccessible Boundary Conditions*

To dampen the impact of the Wiener process $\boldsymbol{dw_3}$ near $k = 0$ in (27.16)–(27.17), the random element $\boldsymbol{\epsilon_3}$ in the saving parameter must be *state-dependent*, and to *preserve* (27.21)–(27.23) as a *homogeneous* stochastic *dynamic* system, the function $\Phi_3(L, K)$, (27.17), must be homogeneous of degree zero, i.e., $\boldsymbol{\Phi_3\ (L, K) = \phi_3(k)}$.

From economic reasons, the *shape* of $\phi_3(k)$ on the *domain* $k \in [0, \infty[$ should be chosen as a monotonically *increasing* curve, but this curve should also—to avoid creating excessive saving parameter volatility—be *bounded* above by a *horizontal* asymptote. With these two stipulations upon relevant selections of $\phi_3(k)$, one choice might be the logistic (S-shaped) curve described by well-known exponential expression. Among the exponentials, however, a relevant and convenient choice of $\boldsymbol{\phi_3(k)}$, with proper domain and range for our purposes, would be

$$\phi_3(k) = \beta_3 \tanh(\lambda_3 k), \quad k \in [0, \infty[, \quad \phi_3(0) = 0, \quad \phi_3(\infty) = \beta_3 \tag{27.75}$$

Thus, letting the *uncertainty* of the saving rate depend on the capital-labor ratio by (27.75), the stochastic differential equation of capital, (27.19), becomes, cf. (27.16)–(27.17)

$$\begin{aligned} dK &= L(s + \beta_3 \tanh(\lambda_3 k) dw_3/dt)(y/P_1)dt - (\delta + \beta_2 dw_2/dt)K dt \\ &= L(\{s(y/P_1) - \delta k\}dt - \beta_2 k dw_2 + \beta_3 \tanh(\lambda_3 k)(y/P_1) dw_3) \end{aligned} \tag{27.76}$$

With (27.76) and (27.18), we obtain as before, using (27.35) and Lemma 27.1, the stochastic differential equation for capital-labor ratio

$$dk = \{[s - \rho_{13}\beta_1\beta_3 \tanh(\lambda_3 k)](y/P_1) - [n + \delta - (\beta_1^2 + \rho_{12}\beta_1\beta_2)]k\}dt$$
$$- \beta_1 k dw_1 - \beta_2 k dw_2 + \beta_3 \tanh(\lambda_3 k)(y/P_1)dw_3 \quad (27.77)$$

The formulas (27.25)–(27.33) of Lemma 27.1 still apply after replacing $\beta_3$ with $\beta_3 \tanh(\lambda_3 k)$ everywhere.

**Theorem 27.4** *The sufficient conditions for the general diffusion process (27.77)—with CES technologies and uncertainties in labor growth, capital depreciation, and saving rates—to have inaccessible lower and upper boundary are,*

$$k = 0\,; \quad \sigma_i < 1: \quad 2(n + \delta - s\gamma_1 a_1^{1/\varrho_1}) \leq \beta_1^2 - \beta_2^2 \quad (27.78)$$
$$k = 0\,; \quad \sigma_i \geq 1: \quad \textit{Always inaccessible} \quad (27.79)$$
$$k = \infty; \quad \sigma_i \leq 1: \quad 2(n + \delta) \geq \beta_1^2 - \beta_2^2 \quad (27.80)$$
$$k = \infty; \quad \sigma_i > 1: \quad 2(n + \delta - s(\gamma_2/p)a_2^{1/\varrho_2}) \geq \beta_1^2 - \beta_2^2 - \Delta \quad (27.81)$$
$$\textit{where } \Delta \equiv [\beta_3(\gamma_2/p)a_2^{1/\varrho_2}]^2 - 2\rho_{23}\beta_2\beta_3(\gamma_2/p)a_2^{1/\varrho_2}.$$

***Proof*** See Appendix section "Appendix C: Proof of Theorem 27.4". □

The sufficient inaccessibility conditions (27.78)–(27.79) and (27.80)–(27.81) reflect, respectively, the requirements $S_1(0) = -\infty$ and $S_3(\infty) = \infty$. Note that (27.78)–(27.79) are the same as (27.62)–(27.63) and (27.47), i.e., Theorems 27.1–27.2 are confirmed as special cases of Theorem 27.4 with $\beta_3 = 0$. Furthermore, special cases of (27.81)—either $\beta_1 = \beta_2 = 0$ or $\beta_3 = 0$—give (27.74) of Theorem 27.3 and (27.63) of Theorem 27.2. But most important, the *assumption* (27.75) has *removed* the uncertainty of saving rate $\phi_3(k)$ in (27.76) entirely from the *lower* boundary problems, cf. (27.72) and (27.74), because with (27.75), we now have that (27.79) holds, irrespective of the size of *any drift* and *diffusion* parameters.

### *Stochastic Dynamics and Asymptotic Nonstationary Distributions*

Relaxing the sufficient inaccessibility condition $S_3(\infty) = \infty$ does not imply explosion, cf. (27.115) and Remark 27.1. But to avoid any risk of implosion, we want to keep the condition $S_1(0) = -\infty$. Moreover, together with a finite $S_3(\infty)$, we have the following well-known implications (with probability one),

$$[S_1(0) = -\infty \wedge S_3(\infty) < \infty] \Rightarrow \lim_{t\to\infty} k(t) = \infty \Rightarrow \lim_{t\to\infty} \mathrm{E}[k(t)] = \infty \quad (27.82)$$

A finite $\mathcal{S}_3(\infty)$ is simply equivalent to reversing the inequality in (27.80)–(27.81), cf. Appendix section "Appendix C: Proof of Theorem 27.4". For $\sigma_i \leq 1$, the reverse of (27.80) is $2(n+\delta) \leq \beta_1^2 - \beta_2^2$. The latter implies that $k(t) \to \infty$ as $t \to \infty$, but it is a pathological case as the reversal of (27.80) also implies that $L(t) \to 0$ (although never reached in finite time), cf. (27.39). In short, no relevant stochastic endogenous growth is possible with $\sigma_i \leq 1$. Hence as in the deterministic case, stochastic endogenous economic growth requires that the marginal product of capital is bounded below, i.e., $\sigma_i > 0$, $\rho_i > 0$, cf. (27.60).

By reversing (27.81), the sufficient condition of growth becomes, cf. (27.82), (27.79)

$$\sigma_i > 1: \ \mathcal{S}_3(\infty) < \infty \quad \Leftrightarrow \quad s(\gamma_2/p)a_2^{1/\varrho_2} \geq n + \delta + \frac{1}{2}(-\beta_1^2 + \beta_2^2 + \Delta) \tag{27.83}$$

which is the *stochastic analogue* to the *deterministic* condition—with only $n+\delta$ on the RHS—of endogenous (persistent) growth (see Jensen and Wang (1997, p. 93); here p. 633 in Chap. 21, Jensen and Larsen (1987)); here Chap. 1.

We see from (27.83) that it is generally more *difficult* (a higher average saving rate is required) to *achieve* persistent economic growth in the face of uncertainty—as $n - \frac{1}{2}\beta_1^2 > 0$ is now taken for granted in (27.83), cf. (27.39), and $\Delta$ is always positive when $\rho_{23} = 0$, cf. (27.81). Uncertainties in the accumulation of capital, (27.76), ($\beta_2 \neq 0$, $\beta_3 \neq 0$) make the stochastic analogue (27.83) harder to satisfy.

The *rapidity* of stochastic growth is not directly seen by (27.83). However, with $\mathcal{S}_3(\infty) < \infty$, the stochastic differential equation (27.77) is *asymptotically*, cf. (27.140)

$$\begin{aligned} dk \sim \bar{a}_3 k dt + \bar{b}_3 k dw_3 \equiv & \left\{(s - \rho_{13}\beta_1\beta_3)(\gamma_2/p)a_2^{1/\varrho_2} - \Theta\right\} kdt \\ & + \left[\beta^2 + \beta_3^2(\gamma_2/p)^2 a_2^{2/\varrho_2} - \rho\beta_3(\gamma_2/p)a_2^{1/\varrho_2}\right]^{1/2} kdw_3 \end{aligned} \tag{27.84}$$

which is the *geometric* Wiener *process* with the *sample paths* and *expectation*

$$k(t) \sim k_0 \exp\left\{\left(\bar{a}_3 - \frac{1}{2}\bar{b}_3^2\right)t + \bar{b}_3 w_3(t)\right\}, \quad 2\bar{a}_3 > \bar{b}_3^2 \tag{27.85}$$

$$\mathrm{E}[k(t)] \sim k_0 \exp\left\{\left(\bar{a}_3 - \frac{1}{2}\bar{b}_3^2\right)t\right\} \tag{27.86}$$

It is easily verified that the exponential growth condition $\bar{a}_3 - \frac{1}{2}\bar{b}_3^2 > 0$ in (27.85) is equivalent to (27.83). Thus, the stochastic condition (27.83) is indeed the analogue of deterministic exponential growth. The *small trading* economy that eventually *grows* as (27.83)–(27.86) is *finally specialized* in the *capital-intensive* good.

## THE CD CASE WITH CLOSED FORM STEADY-STATE DISTRIBUTION

Having obtained the conditions for the *existence* and convergence to a *steady-state* (time-invariant) *distribution*, cf. (27.48), we also want to obtain as a *benchmark*—with CD sector technologies of the small trading economy—a *closed form* expression for the *time-invariant probability density* function $p(k)$ and the *distribution function* $\boldsymbol{P}(\boldsymbol{k})$ of the diffusion process (27.46).

It turns out that the benchmark *distribution* function $P(k)$ for the trading economy can be expressed by *gamma* $\Gamma(\alpha)$ and *incomplete gamma* functions $\Gamma(\alpha, x_0)$, which are generally defined, respectively, by the improper integrals,

$$\Gamma(\alpha) \equiv \int_0^{\infty} x^{\alpha-1} e^{-x} dx, \quad \Gamma(\alpha, x_0) \equiv \int_{x_0}^{\infty} x^{\alpha-1} e^{-x} dx, \quad \alpha > 0 \qquad (27.87)$$

**Theorem 27.5** *The time-invariant (steady-state) distribution* $\boldsymbol{P}(\boldsymbol{k})$ *for the stochastic process (27.46), cf. Theorem 27.1, will have a density function* $\mathbf{p}(\boldsymbol{k})$*, if and only if*

$$2(\Theta - s\tilde{\theta}_1) + \beta^2 > 0 \quad \Leftrightarrow \quad 2(n + \delta - s\tilde{\theta}_1) > \beta_1^2 - \beta_2^2 \qquad (27.88)$$

*With (27.88), the time-invariant probability density function* $p(k)$ *is in closed form*

$$p(k) = \begin{cases} p_1(k) = \frac{m_1}{m} k^{-2[1+\Theta/\beta^2]} \exp\{-c_1 k^{-(1-a_1)}\}, & 0 < k \le \tilde{k}_1 \\ p_2(k) = \frac{m_2}{m} k^{-2[1+(\Theta-s\tilde{\theta}_1)/\beta^2]} \exp\{-c_2 k^{-1}\}, & \tilde{k}_1 < k < \tilde{k}_2 \\ p_3(k) = \frac{m_3}{m} k^{-2[1+\Theta/\beta^2]} \exp\{-c_3 k^{-(1-a_2)}\}, & k \ge \tilde{k}_2 \end{cases} \qquad (27.89)$$

*where the constants* $c_1, c_2, c_3, m_1, m_2, m_3$ *are given by,*

$$c_1 = 2s\gamma_1/[(1-a_1)\beta^2], \quad c_2 = 2s\tilde{\theta}_2/\beta^2, \quad c_3 = 2s(\gamma_2/p)/[(1-a_2)\beta^2]$$

$$m_1 = \tilde{k}_1^{\frac{2\Theta}{\beta^2}} e^{x_1}/\beta^2, \quad m_2 = \tilde{k}_1^{\frac{2[\Theta-s\tilde{\theta}_1]}{\beta^2}} e^{x_2}/\beta^2, \quad m_3 = \tilde{k}_1^{\frac{2[\Theta-s\tilde{\theta}_1]}{\beta^2}} \tilde{k}_2^{\frac{2s\tilde{\theta}_1}{\beta^2}} e^{x_2-x_3+x_4}/\beta^2$$

$$x_1 = c_1\tilde{k}_1^{-(1-a_1)}, \quad x_2 = c_2\tilde{k}_1^{-1}, \quad x_3 = c_2\tilde{k}_2^{-1}, \quad x_4 = c_3\tilde{k}_2^{-(1-a_2)}$$

*and with m involving gamma and incomplete gamma functions,*

$$m = C_1\Gamma(\alpha_1, x_1) + C_2[\Gamma(\alpha_2, x_3) - \Gamma(\alpha_2, x_2)] + C_3[\Gamma(\alpha_3) - \Gamma(\alpha_3, x_4)]$$

$$\alpha_1 = \frac{1 + 2\Theta/\beta^2}{1 - a_1}, \quad \alpha_2 = 1 + 2(\Theta - s\tilde{\theta}_1)/\beta^2, \quad \alpha_3 = \frac{1 + 2\Theta/\beta^2}{1 - a_2}$$

$$C_1 = [m_1/(1 - a_1)]c_1^{-\alpha_1}, \quad C_2 = m_2 c_2^{-\alpha_2}, \quad C_3 = [m_3/(1 - a_2)]c_3^{-\alpha_3}$$

*With the stationary density function $p(k)$, (27.89), the stationary distribution $P(k) = \int_0^k p(k)dk$ can be expressed by incomplete gamma functions as,*

$$P(k) = \begin{cases} P_1(k) = \frac{C_1}{m}\Gamma(\alpha_1, c_1 k^{-(1-a_1)}), & 0 < k \le \tilde{k}_1 \\ P_2(k) = P(\tilde{k}_1) + \frac{C_2}{m}[\Gamma(\alpha_2, c_2 k^{-1}) - \Gamma(\alpha_2, x_2)], & \tilde{k}_1 < k < \tilde{k}_2 \\ P_3(k) = P(\tilde{k}_2) + \frac{C_3}{m}[\Gamma(\alpha_3, c_3 k^{-(1-a_2)}) - \Gamma(\alpha_3, x_4)], & k \ge \tilde{k}_2 \end{cases} \tag{27.90}$$

*and the probability measures of the three-factor endowment regions are,*

$$P(k \le \tilde{k}_1) = P(\tilde{k}_1) = \frac{C_1}{m}\Gamma(\alpha_1, x_1) \tag{27.91}$$

$$P(\tilde{k}_1 \le k \le \tilde{k}_2) = P(\tilde{k}_2) - P(\tilde{k}_1) = \frac{C_2}{m}[\Gamma(\alpha_2, x_3) - \Gamma(\alpha_2, x_2)] \tag{27.92}$$

$$P(k > \tilde{k}_2) = 1 - P(\tilde{k}_2) = \frac{C_3}{m}[\Gamma(\alpha_3) - \Gamma(\alpha_3, x_4)] \tag{27.93}$$

*The distribution $P(k)$, (27.90), will have finite first- and second-order moments* $\mathrm{E}(k)$ *and* $\mathrm{E}(k^2)$, *if and only if, respectively,*

$$\Theta - s\tilde{\theta}_1 > 0 \;\Leftrightarrow\; n + \delta - s\tilde{\theta}_1 > \beta_1^2 + \rho_{12}\beta_1\beta_2 \tag{27.94}$$

$$2(\Theta - s\tilde{\theta}_1) - \beta^2 > 0 \;\Leftrightarrow\; 2(n + \delta - s\tilde{\theta}_1) > 3\beta_1^2 + 4\rho_{12}\beta_1\beta_2 + \beta_2^2 \tag{27.95}$$

*With (27.94)–(27.95), the steady-state distribution $P(k)$ will have first- and second-order* ***moments*** *given by*

$$\mathrm{E}(k) = \mu_1/m, \qquad \mathrm{E}(k^2) = \mu_2/m, \qquad \sigma^2 = \mathrm{E}(k^2) - [\mathrm{E}(k)]^2 \tag{27.96}$$

*where the constants $\mu_1$ and $\mu_2$ are given by the following expressions involving complete and incomplete gamma functions,*

$$\mu_1 = C_1^*\Gamma(\alpha_1^*, x_1) + C_2^*[\Gamma(\alpha_2^*, x_3) - \Gamma(\alpha_2^*, x_2)] + C_3^*[\Gamma(\alpha_3^*) - \Gamma(\alpha_3^*, x_4)]$$

$$\alpha_1^* = \alpha_1 - (1 - a_1)^{-1}, \quad \alpha_2^* = \alpha_2 - 1, \quad \alpha_3^* = \alpha_3 - (1 - a_2)^{-1}$$

$$C_1^* = [m_1/(1 - a_1)]c_1^{-\alpha_1^*}, \quad C_2^* = m_2 c_2^{-\alpha_2^*}, \quad C_3^* = [m_3/(1 - a_2)]c_3^{-\alpha_3^*}$$

$$\mu_2 = C_1^{**}\Gamma(\alpha_1^{**}, x_1) + C_2^{**}[\Gamma(\alpha_2^{**}, x_3) - \Gamma(\alpha_2^{**}, x_2)] + C_3^{**}[\Gamma(\alpha_3^{**}) - \Gamma(\alpha_3^{**}, x_4)]$$
$$\alpha_1^{**} = \alpha_1 - 2(1-a_1)^{-1}, \quad \alpha_2^{**} = \alpha_2 - 2, \quad \alpha_3^{**} = \alpha_3 - 2(1-a_2)^{-1}$$
$$C_1^{**} = [m_1/(1-a_1)]c_1^{-\alpha_1^{**}}, \quad C_2^{**} = m_2 c_2^{-\alpha_2^{**}}, \quad C_3^{**} = [m_3/(1-a_2)]c_3^{-\alpha_3^{**}}$$

***Proof*** For the stochastic system (27.46), the speed densities are, cf. (27.111)–(27.112)

$$\begin{aligned}
\mathfrak{m}_1(k) &= \tfrac{1}{\beta^2 k^2}\exp\{-2\textstyle\int_k^{\tilde{k}_1} \tfrac{s\gamma_1 k^{a_1} - \Theta k}{\beta^2 k^2} dk\}, && 0 < k \le \tilde{k}_1\\
\mathfrak{m}_2(k) &= \tfrac{1}{\beta^2 k^2}\exp\{2\textstyle\int_{\tilde{k}_1}^{k} \tfrac{s\tilde{\theta}_2 + [s\tilde{\theta}_1 - \Theta]k}{\beta^2 k^2} dk\}, && \tilde{k}_1 < k < \tilde{k}_2\\
\mathfrak{m}_3(k) &= \tfrac{1}{\beta^2 k^2}\exp\{2\textstyle\int_{\tilde{k}_1}^{\tilde{k}_2} \tfrac{s\tilde{\theta}_2 + [s\tilde{\theta}_1 - \Theta]k}{\beta^2 k^2} dk + 2\textstyle\int_{\tilde{k}_2}^{k} \tfrac{s(\gamma_2/p)k^{a_2} - \Theta k}{\beta^2 k^2} dk\}, && k \ge \tilde{k}_2
\end{aligned} \tag{27.97}$$

After simple integration, we obtain,

$$\begin{aligned}
\mathfrak{m}_1(k) &= m_1 k^{-2[1+\Theta/\beta^2]}\exp\{-\tfrac{2s\gamma_1}{(1-a_1)\beta^2}k^{-(1-a_1)}\}, && 0 < k \le \tilde{k}_1\\
\mathfrak{m}_2(k) &= m_2 k^{-2[1+\Theta/\beta^2 - s\tilde{\theta}_1/\beta^2]}\exp\{-\tfrac{2s\tilde{\theta}_2}{\beta^2}k^{-1}\}, && \tilde{k}_1 < k < \tilde{k}_2\\
\mathfrak{m}_3(k) &= m_3 k^{-2[1+\Theta/\beta^2]}\exp\{-\tfrac{2s(\gamma_2/p)}{(1-a_2)\beta^2}k^{-(1-a_2)}\}, && k \ge \tilde{k}_2
\end{aligned} \tag{27.98}$$

where the constants $m_1, m_2, m_3$ are given in Theorem 27.5.

By (27.98), we have, cf. (27.117)

$$m = \int_0^{\tilde{k}_1} \mathfrak{m}_1(k)dk + \int_{\tilde{k}_1}^{\tilde{k}_2} \mathfrak{m}_2(k)dk + \int_{\tilde{k}_2}^{\infty} \mathfrak{m}_3(k)dk \tag{27.99}$$

which gives—after changes of variables and limits of integrations together with rather lengthy calculations—the expression for $m$ as stated in Theorem 27.5. Thus by (27.98)–(27.99), the invariant density function $p(k)$, (27.89), is established.

Since the *parameter* $\alpha$ in the gamma and incomplete gamma functions has to be *positive*, it is seen from $\Gamma(\alpha_2, x_3)$ that,

$$\alpha_2 > 0 \quad \Leftrightarrow \quad 1 + 2(\Theta - s\tilde{\theta}_1)/\beta^2 > 0 \tag{27.100}$$

which gives the restriction for the existence of the density stated in (27.88) or rewritten using (27.28)–(27.29).

The first- and second-order moments are obtained from the density function as,

$$\mathrm{E}(k) \equiv \int_0^{\infty} kp(k)dk = \int_0^{\tilde{k}_1} kp_1(k)dk + \int_{\tilde{k}_1}^{\tilde{k}_2} kp_2(k)dk + \int_{\tilde{k}_2}^{\infty} kp_3(k)dk = \mu_1/m$$

$$\mathrm{E}(k^2) \equiv \int_0^{\infty} k^2 p(k)dk = \int_0^{\tilde{k}_1} k^2 p_1(k)dk + \int_{\tilde{k}_1}^{\tilde{k}_2} k^2 p_2(k)dk + \int_{\tilde{k}_2}^{\infty} k^2 p_3(k)dk = \mu_2/m$$

After several substitutions of variables and lengthy rearrangements, we get the expression for the parameters $\mu_1$ and $\mu_2$ as stated in Theorem 27.5.

Finally, from the incomplete gamma functions, $\Gamma(\alpha_2^*, x_2)$, $\Gamma(\alpha_2^{**}, x_2)$, we see that

$$\alpha_2^* > 0 \quad \Leftrightarrow \quad \Theta - s\tilde{\theta}_1 > 0, \qquad \alpha_2^{**} > 0 \quad \Leftrightarrow \quad 2(\Theta - s\tilde{\theta}_1) > \beta^2 \tag{27.101}$$

which gives the moment existence restrictions (27.94)–(27.95), and Theorem 27.5 is established. □

We may note that a steady-state distribution such as (27.90) with moments (27.96) does not imply that the expected growth rates of labor and capital are the same. *Stochastic steady-state* growth and *balanced* growth are *no longer equivalent* concepts (Stigum 1972).

***Applications*** Let us in the midst of abstract deductions give some *illustrative examples* of applying the formulas in this chapter and especially Theorem 27.5.

From (27.6) and (27.44), we have

$$p = \frac{\gamma_2 a_2 k_2^{a_2-1}}{\gamma_1 a_1 k_1^{a_1-1}}, \quad k_i = \frac{a_i}{1-a_i}\omega, \quad \omega = \left[ \frac{\gamma_1}{\gamma_2} \frac{a_1}{a_2} \frac{(\frac{1-a_1}{a_1})^{1-a_1}}{(\frac{1-a_2}{a_2})^{1-a_2}} p \right]^{\frac{1}{a_2-a_1}} \tag{27.102}$$

**Example 27.1** $p = 1$, $s = 0.2$, $n = 0.02$, $\delta = 0.05$, $\beta_1 = 0.01$, $\beta_2 = 0.03$, $\rho_{12} = 0$, $\gamma_1 = \gamma_2 = 1$, $a_1 = 0.2$, $a_2 = 0.25$.

First we must find the *three subintervals* of $\boldsymbol{k}$ as given by the *endpoints* $\tilde{k}_1$, $\tilde{k}_2$ of *diversification* cone, cf. (27.5), (27.8), and (27.102). Next, the price and

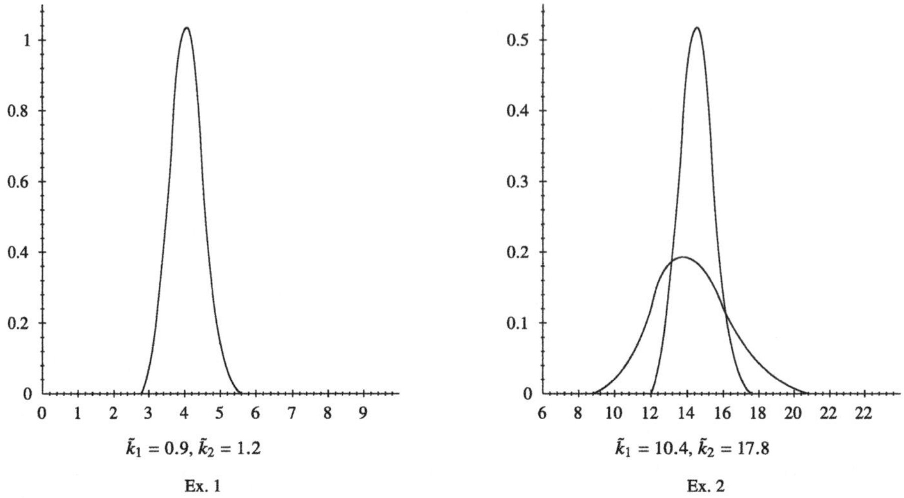


**Fig. 27.1** Probability density $p(k)$ (27.90)

parameter values of Example 27.1 give together with (27.44) and (27.33)

$$\omega = 3.5,\ \tilde{k}_1 = 0.9,\ \tilde{k}_2 = 1.2,\ \tilde{y}_1 = 0.97,\ \tilde{y}_2 = 1.04,\ \tilde{\theta}_1 = 0.23,\ \tilde{\theta}_2 = 0.78 \tag{27.103}$$

and $\Theta = 0.0699$, $\beta^2 = 0.001$, cf. (27.28)–(27.29). The expressions (27.96) and (27.91)–(27.93) give

$$\mathrm{E}(k) = 4.057,\ \sigma = 0.398,\ P(\tilde{k}_1) = 0.854 \cdot 10^{-85},\ P(\tilde{k}_2) = 0.686 \cdot 10^{-52} \tag{27.104}$$

and the *probability density* $\boldsymbol{p(k)}$, (27.89), is *shown* in Fig. 27.1.

On infinite time horizon, any diffusion process will in principle have a nonzero probability of observations anywhere in the state space, here $k \in [0, \infty[$. However, in Example 27.1, the *region* of *specialization* in the consumer good (all capital goods are imported) contains practically the *entire probability* distribution. The *expected* value $\mathrm{E}(k) = 4.057$, (27.104), is very close to the specialized *certainty (deterministic) steady-state* value of the capital-labor ratio,

$$\kappa = [s(\gamma_2/p)/(n+\delta)]^{1/(1-a_2)} = 4.054 \tag{27.105}$$

obtained from $\boldsymbol{f(\kappa)/\kappa} = (n+\delta)p/s$, cf. (27.14), (27.44), and $p, s, n, \delta, \gamma_2, a_2$ in Example 27.1.

In our second example, we want a *larger* diversification cone, which requires that the *sector technologies* (parameters $a_i$) differ more. Higher prices of the capital good also contribute to preserving some domestic production of $Y_1$.

**Example 27.2** $p = 1.3, s = 0.25, n = 0.01, \delta = 0.02, \beta_1 = 0.01, \beta_2 = 0.03, \rho_{12} = 0, \gamma_1 = \gamma_2 = 1, a_1 = 0.2, a_2 = 0.3.$

From Example 27.2 and (27.102), (27.44), (27.33), we get

$$\omega = 41.6,\ \tilde{k}_1 = 10.4,\ \tilde{k}_2 = 17.8,\ \tilde{y}_1 = 1.6,\ \tilde{y}_2 = 2.4,\ \tilde{\theta}_1 = 0.03,\ \tilde{\theta}_2 = 1.28 \tag{27.106}$$

and $\Theta = 0.0299$, $\beta^2 = 0.001$, cf. (27.28)–(27.29). The expressions (27.96) and (27.91)–(27.93) give

$$\mathrm{E}(k) = 14.38,\ \sigma = 2.18,\ P(\tilde{k}_1) = 0.014,\ P(\tilde{k}_2) = 0.932 \tag{27.107}$$

and the *probability density*, $p(k)$, (27.89), is shown in Fig. 27.1.

The probability measure of diversification region is nearly 0.92. The *expected* value $\mathrm{E}(k) = 14.38$, (27.107), is very close to the diversified certainty steady-state value of the capital-labor ratio (Jensen and Wang (1997, eq.(33)); here (21.33 in Chap. 21))

$$\kappa = \tilde{\theta}_2/[(n+\delta)/s - \tilde{\theta}_1] = 14.31 \tag{27.108}$$

obtained from (27.44) and $s, n, \delta, \tilde{\theta}_1, \tilde{\theta}_2$ in Example 27.2.

In Fig. 27.1, the density function with the same parameter values as Example 27.2 is also shown for smaller uncertainty parameters $\beta_1 = 0.005$, $\beta_2 = 0.01$. The latter does not change the values of (27.106) and (27.108), whereas the moments and the probabilities are now

$$\mathrm{E}(k) = 14.33, \quad \sigma = 1.57, \quad P(\tilde{k}_1) = 0.102 \cdot 10^{-9}, \quad P(\tilde{k}_2) = 0.99997 \tag{27.109}$$

i.e., the trading economy will always—despite omnipresent uncertainties about the growing factor supplies of labor and capital—have the *stochastic* factor endowment ratio $\boldsymbol{k(t)}$ between $\tilde{\boldsymbol{k}}_1$ and $\tilde{\boldsymbol{k}}_2$, and hence have *domestic production* of *both* goods. Probability statements (measures) about the *stochastic trade pattern* between $\tilde{k}_1$ and $\tilde{k}_2$ can be calculated from (27.10)–(27.11), (27.37), (27.90). As may be checked, the parametric values in Examples 27.1 and 27.2 *satisfy* the restrictions (27.88), (27.94)–(27.95).

The Ito rules of stochastic calculus suggest that the first-order moments are *upward* biased estimates of the certainty (deterministic) values (Merton (1975, p. 382)). However, $\mathrm{E}(\boldsymbol{k})$ and $\kappa$ in (27.104)–(27.105) and (27.107)–(27.109) agree remarkably well.

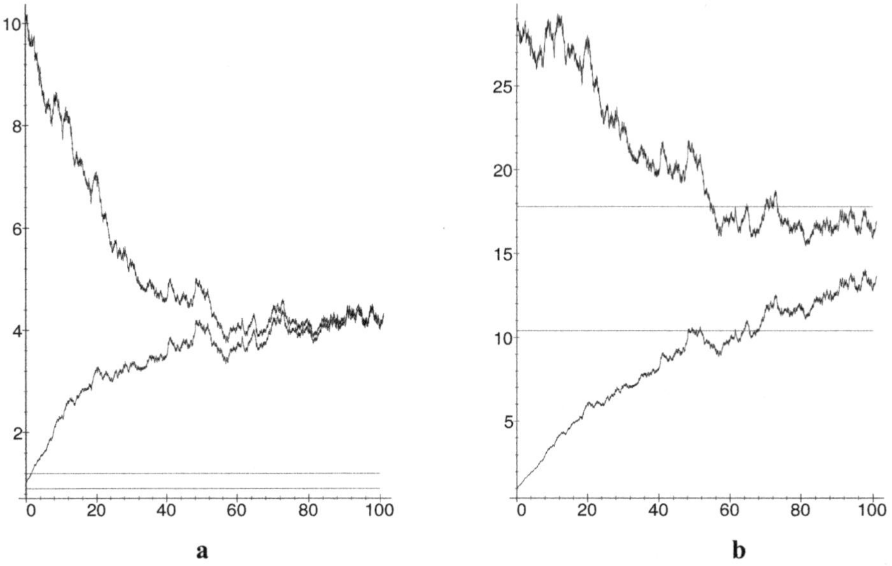


**Fig. 27.2** *Sample Paths* for $\boldsymbol{k(t)}$, ((27.46) (**a**) Example 27.1: $k(0) = 1, k(0) = 10$ (**b**) Example 27.2: $k(0) = 1, k(0) = 28$

For the parameters of Examples 27.1 and 27.2, Fig. 27.2 shows two simulated sample paths for $\boldsymbol{k(t)}$, (27.46), using *initial values* below and above $\mathrm{E}(\boldsymbol{k})$. The horizontal lines indicate the *diversification interval.* In the simulations, the same Wiener diffusion (realization) $\boldsymbol{w(t)}$ is employed for all initial values. Hence the two sample paths will *converge* in the *long run*. With the parameters of Examples 27.1 and 27.2 and the particular initial values chosen, it takes about *60–80 units of time* for the diffusion processes of $\boldsymbol{k(t)}$, (27.46), to *attain* their steady-state *distributions* in Fig. 27.1.

## Final Comments

In macroscopic and microscopic sciences, no rigid deterministic schemes (rigorously exact laws) are apparent in nature. We are compelled to appeal to stochastic models and probabilities. However, analytical stochastic dynamics of diffusion processes offer exact propositions as in deterministic dynamics. In economics, the study of deterministic models is often a prerequisite for extending dynamic analysis to the realm of uncertainty and probability calculations. If we find the economic universe capricious, the fault lies with our original model—not with the universe. For the basic stochastic models of a *small trading* economy, we may conclude that *uncertainties* in labor growth, depreciation, and saving rates still leave *fundamental results* of deterministic growth models *intact*, provided that the crucial issue of *inaccessible boundary conditions* is *resolved*. The closed form steady-state probability distribution in the CD case should be useful in comparative probability calculations. The formulas allow us to determine the probability of finding the state variables over the long run in any given region (specialized/diversified) of the state space. The parametric case of *stochastic endogenous (persistent)* growth establishes *asymptotically* the natural "uncertainty correspondence" between the sample paths of the *geometric Wiener process* and the exponential solutions of deterministic endogenous growth models.

## Appendix A: Boundary Conditions and Steady-State Distribution

Let the transition probability of the process (27.20)—in case of a *one-dimensional* stochastic process $X(t)$—be

$$P(x, t; x_0, t_0) = \Pr[X(t) \leq x \mid X(t_0) = x_0] \tag{27.110}$$

where $X(t)$ is the state of the process at instant $t$. The transition probability distribution $P(x, t; x_0, t_0)$ is assumed to have a probability density function $p(x, t; x_0, t_0)$, defined everywhere.

*Boundary Conditions* In terms of notation in (27.20), we define in the one-dimensional case the following indefinite integrals (functions),

$$J(x) = \int_{x_0}^{x} \frac{a(u)}{b^2(u)} du; \quad \mathfrak{s}(x) = \exp\{-2J(x)\}, \quad \mathcal{S}(x) = \int_{x_0}^{x} \mathfrak{s}(u) du \tag{27.111}$$

$$\mathfrak{m}(x) = \frac{\exp\{2J(x)\}}{b^2(x)} = \frac{1}{b^2(x)\mathfrak{s}(x)}, \quad \mathcal{M}(x) = \int_{x_0}^{x} \mathfrak{m}(u) du \tag{27.112}$$

The functions $\mathfrak{s}(x)$, $\mathcal{S}(x)$, $\mathfrak{m}(x)$, and $\mathcal{M}(x)$ are called, respectively, the *scale density* function, the *scale* function, the *speed density* function, and the *speed measure* of the stochastic processes $X(t)$; cf. Karlin and Taylor (1981, p. 194-196,229).

Let the diffusion process $X(t)$ have two boundaries $r_1 < r_2$.

*Inaccessible Boundaries Sufficient* conditions: The two boundaries $r_1$ and $r_2$ are inaccessible, if

$$\begin{aligned} &\forall x_0 \in [r_1, r_2],\ \mathcal{S}(r_1) = -\infty; \quad \mathcal{S}(r_2) = +\infty; \quad \text{equivalently,} \\ &\mathfrak{s}(x) \text{ is not integrable on the closed interval } [r_i, x_0] \end{aligned} \tag{27.113}$$

or else

$$\mathcal{S}(r_i) = \lim_{x \to r_i} \mathcal{S}(x) = \lim_{x \to r_i} \int_{x_0}^{x} \mathfrak{s}(x)dx = \mp\infty; \quad i = 1, 2 \tag{27.114}$$

The *necessary* and *sufficient* condition is

$$\Sigma(r_i) \equiv \int_{x_0}^{r_i} [\mathcal{S}(r_i) - \mathcal{S}(x)]\mathfrak{m}(x)dx = +\infty; \quad i = 1, 2 \tag{27.115}$$

*Existence of Steady-State Distribution* A *time-invariant* distribution function $P(x)$ exists, if and only if

$$\mathcal{S}(r_i) = \mp\infty \text{ and } \mathcal{M}(x) \text{ is finite at } r_i\text{, i.e., } |\mathcal{M}(r_i)| < \infty; \quad i = 1, 2 \tag{27.116}$$

The existence of steady-state distribution $P(x)$—implying inaccessible boundaries—also implies the *convergence* of the nonstationary distribution functions $P(x, t)$ toward $P(x)$ as $t \to \infty$.

*Existence of Steady-State Density Function* A *time-invariant* probability density function $p(x)$ exists, if and only if the *speed* density $\mathfrak{m}(x)$ satisfies

$$\int_{r_1}^{r_2} \mathfrak{m}(x)dx < \infty, \quad p(x) = m\mathfrak{m}(x), \quad \int_{r_1}^{r_2} p(x)dx = 1 \tag{27.117}$$

where $m$ is the normalizing constant.

The conditions and formulas above can be applied directly when we have the *same* stochastic differential equation (drift and diffusion coefficients) for the *whole interval* of $x$. For more details, see Karlin and Taylor (1981) and Mandl (1968).

## Appendix B: Proof of Theorem 27.3

*CD Case* Applying (27.111) to the system (27.70) gives, cf. (27.49),

$$\mathfrak{s}_1(k) = \exp\left\{\frac{(n+\delta)(k^{2(1-a_1)} + k_0^{2(1-a_1)}) - 2s\gamma_1(k^{1-a_1} - k_0^{1-a_1})}{\beta_3^2\gamma_1^2(1-a_1)}\right\} \tag{27.118}$$

$$\mathfrak{s}_3(k) = \exp\left\{\frac{(n+\delta)(k^{2(1-a_2)} + k_0^{2(1-a_2)}) - 2s(\gamma_2/p)(k^{1-a_2} - k_0^{1-a_2})}{\beta_3^2(\gamma_2/p)^2(1-a_2)}\right\} \tag{27.119}$$

From (27.111) and (27.118), we have,

$$\mathcal{S}_1(0) = \int_{k_0}^{0} \mathfrak{s}_1(k)dk \equiv m_0^1 \int_{k_0}^{0} \exp\left\{\frac{(n+\delta)k^{2(1-a_1)} - 2s\gamma_1 k^{1-a_1}}{\beta_3^2\gamma_1^2(1-a_1)}\right\} dk \tag{27.120}$$

Since $1 - a_1 > 0$, $\mathcal{S}_1(0)$ will *converge*, and accordingly $k = 0$ may possibly be accessible.

To decide whether $k = 0$ is in fact inaccessible, we need further to calculate $\Sigma(0)$. In this CD case, we have for the lower boundary $k = 0$, cf. (27.115),

$$\Sigma(0) = \int_{k_0}^{0} [\mathcal{S}_1(0) - \mathcal{S}_1(k)]\mathfrak{m}(k)dk \tag{27.121}$$

The limit of the integrand $\mathcal{S}_1(k)\mathfrak{m}(k)$ in (27.121) is, cf. (27.111)–(27.112), (27.120), (27.70)

$$\lim_{k\to 0} \mathcal{S}_1(k)\mathfrak{m}(k) =$$

$$\lim_{k\to 0} \frac{m_0^1 \int_{k_0}^{k} \exp\{[\beta_3^2\gamma_1^2(1-a_1)]^{-1}[(n+\delta)k^{2(1-a_1)} - 2s\gamma_1 k^{1-a_1}]\}dk}{\beta_3^2\gamma_1^2 k^{2a_1} \exp\{[\beta_3^2\gamma_1^2(1-a_1)]^{-1}[(n+\delta)k^{2(1-a_1)} - 2s\gamma_1 k^{1-a_1}]\}} \tag{27.122}$$

Since $[\beta_3^2\gamma_1^2(1-a_1)]^{-1} > 0$, the limit (27.122) *converges* iff $2(1-a_1) > 1$, i.e., $a_1 < \frac{1}{2}$. Hence with $a_1 > \frac{1}{2}$, $\Sigma(0)$, (27.121), will be ***divergent***, and thus the lower boundary is inaccessible.

From (27.111) and (27.119), we have,

$$\begin{aligned}\mathcal{S}_3(\infty) &= \int_{k_0}^{\infty} \mathfrak{s}_3(k)dk \\ &\equiv m_0^3 \int_{k_0}^{\infty} \exp\{\frac{(n+\delta)k^{2(1-a_2)} - 2s(\gamma_2/p)k^{1-a_2}}{\beta_3^2(\gamma_2/p)^2(1-a_2)}\}dk \end{aligned} \tag{27.123}$$

Since $1-a_2 > 0$, and $k^{2(1-a_2)}$ is the dominating term, $\mathcal{S}_3(\infty)$ will always diverge, i.e., $k = \infty$ is *inaccessible.*

*CES Case* Applying (27.111) to the system (27.71) gives, cf. (27.49)

$$\mathfrak{s}_1(k) = \exp\left\{-2\int_{k_0}^{k} \frac{s\gamma_1[(1-a_1) + a_1 k^{\varrho_1}]^{1/\varrho_1} - (n+\delta)k}{\beta_3^2\gamma_1^2[(1-a_1) + a_1 k^{\varrho_1}]^{2/\varrho_1}} dk\right\} \tag{27.124}$$

$$\mathfrak{s}_3(k) = \exp\left\{-2\int_{k_0}^{k} \frac{s(\gamma_2/p)[(1-a_2) + a_2 k^{\varrho_2}]^{1/\varrho_2} - (n+\delta)k}{\beta_3^2(\gamma_2/p)^2[(1-a_2) + a_2 k^{\varrho_2}]^{2/\varrho_2}} dk\right\} \tag{27.125}$$

$\sigma_i < 1$: From (27.124), we have for small $k$, cf. (27.59),

$$\mathcal{S}_1(0) = \lim_{k\to 0}\int_{k_0}^{k} \mathfrak{s}_1(k)dk = \int_{k_0}^{0} \exp\left\{-2\int_{k_0}^{k} \frac{s\gamma_1 a_1^{1/\varrho_1} - (n+\delta)}{\beta_3^2\gamma_1^2 a_1^{2/\varrho_1}} k^{-1}dk\right\} dk$$

$$= \int_{k_0}^{0} (k/k_0)^{\frac{-2[s\gamma_1 a_1^{1/\varrho_1} - (n+\delta)]}{\beta_3^2\gamma_1^2 a_1^{2/\varrho_1}}} dk \tag{27.126}$$

$\mathcal{S}_1(0)$ diverges if the exponent of $k/k_0$ is less than or equal to $-1$, which immediately gives the condition (27.73).

From (27.125), we have for large $k$, cf. (27.59),

$$\mathcal{S}_3(\infty) = \lim_{k\to\infty}\int_{k_0}^{k} \mathfrak{s}_3(k)dk$$

$$= \int_{k_0}^{\infty} \exp\left\{-2\int_{k_0}^{k} \frac{s(\gamma_2/p)(1-a_2)^{1/\varrho_2} - (n+\delta)k}{\beta_3^2(\gamma_2/p)^2(1-a_2)^{2/\varrho_2}} dk\right\} dk$$

$$= \int_{k_0}^{\infty} \exp\left\{\frac{(n+\delta)(k^2-k_0^2) - 2s(\gamma_2/p)(1-a_2)^{1/\varrho_2}(k-k_0)]}{\beta_3^2(\gamma_2/p)^2(1-a_2)^{2/\varrho_2}}\right\} dk$$

$$\equiv m_0^3 \int_{k_0}^{\infty} \exp\left\{\frac{n+\delta}{\beta_3^2(\gamma_2/p)^2(1-a_2)^{2/\varrho_2}}k^2 - \frac{2s}{\beta_3^2(\gamma_2/p)(1-a_2)^{1/\varrho_2}}k\right\} dk \tag{27.127}$$

As $1 - a_2 > 0$, the constant denominators in (27.127) are positive, and since the $k^2$ term is the dominating term in the exponential expression, $\mathcal{S}(\infty)$ will always be divergent, hence the upper boundary is always *inaccessible*.

$\sigma_i > 1$: From (27.124), we have for small $k$, cf. (27.60),

$$\mathcal{S}_1(0) = \lim_{k\to 0}\int_{k_0}^{k} \mathfrak{s}_1(k)dk = \int_{k_0}^{0} \exp\left\{-2\int_{k_0}^{k} \frac{s\gamma_1(1-a_1)^{1/\varrho_1} - (n+\delta)k}{\beta_3^2\gamma_1^2(1-a_1)^{2/\varrho_1}} dk\right\} dk$$

$$\equiv m_1^0 \int_{k_0}^{0} \exp\left\{\frac{n+\delta}{\beta_3^2\gamma_1^2(1-a_1)^{2/\varrho_1}}k^2 - \frac{2s}{\beta_3^2\gamma_1(1-a_1)^{1/\varrho_1}}k\right\} dk \tag{27.128}$$

Since $1 - a_1 > 0$, $\mathcal{S}_1(0)$ will always converge, and hence $k = 0$ may possibly be accessible. Whether in fact $k = 0$ is attainable in finite time requires similar evaluations as shown above, cf. (27.121)–(27.122), (27.43).

From (27.125), we have for large $k$, cf. (27.60),

$$\mathcal{S}_3(\infty) = \lim_{k\to\infty}\int_{k_0}^{k} \mathfrak{s}_3(k)dk = \int_{k_0}^{\infty} \exp\left\{-2\int_{k_0}^{k} \frac{s(\gamma_2/p)a_2^{1/\varrho_2} - (n+\delta)}{\beta_3^2(\gamma_2/p)^2 a_2^{2/\varrho_2}} k^{-1}dk\right\}$$

$$= \int_{k_0}^{\infty} (k/k_0)^{\frac{-2[s(\gamma_2/p)a_2^{1/\varrho_2}-(n+\delta)]}{\beta_3^2(\gamma_2/p)^2 a_2^{2/\varrho_2}}} dk \qquad (27.129)$$

$\mathcal{S}_3(\infty)$ diverges if the exponent of $k/k_0$ is larger than or equal to $-1$, which is equivalent to the condition in (27.74).

## Appendix C: Proof of Theorem 27.4

The *hyperbolic function* $\phi_3(k) = \beta_3 \tanh(\lambda_3 k)$, (27.75), is given by

$$\phi_3(k) = \beta_3 \tanh(\lambda_3 k) = \beta_3(e^{\lambda_3 k} - e^{-\lambda_3 k})/(e^{\lambda_3 k} + e^{-\lambda_3 k}), \quad k \geq 0 \qquad (27.130)$$

It is well-known and easily verified from (27.130) that for

$$\text{small } k:\ \phi_3(k) \sim \beta_3\lambda_3 k, \quad \Leftrightarrow \quad \phi_3(k)/\beta_3\lambda_3 k \to 1 \text{ as } k \to 0 \qquad (27.131)$$

$$\text{large } k:\ \phi_3(k) \sim \beta_3, \quad \Leftrightarrow \quad \phi_3(k)/\beta_3 \to 1 \text{ as } k \to \infty \qquad (27.132)$$

*Lower Boundary* $\sigma_i = 1$: With the CD production function (27.44), the scale density function $\mathfrak{s}_1(k)$ now becomes, cf. (27.49), (27.29)–(27.31), (27.75), (27.77),

$$\mathfrak{s}_1(k) = \exp\left\{-2\int_{k_0}^{k} \frac{[s - \rho_{13}\beta_1\phi_3(k)]\gamma_1 k^{a_1} - \Theta k}{\beta^2k^2 + \phi_3^2(k)\gamma_1^2 k^{2a_1} - \rho\phi_3(k)\gamma_1 k^{(1+a_1)}}dk\right\} \qquad (27.133)$$

Since $a_1 < 1$, the ***dominating*** term in the numerator and denominator of (27.133) becomes for small $k$, cf. (27.131),

$$\mathfrak{s}_1(k) \sim \exp\left\{-2\int_{k_0}^{k} \frac{s\gamma_1 k^{a_1}}{\beta^2 k^2}dk\right\} = \exp\{\frac{2s\gamma_1}{(1-a_1)\beta^2}(k^{-(1-a_1)} - k_0^{-(1-a_1)})\} \qquad (27.134)$$

Since $1-a_1 > 0$, it is seen from (27.134), that $\mathcal{S}_1(0) = \int_{k_0}^{0} \mathfrak{s}_1(k)dk$ is diverging at $k = 0$ cf. (27.54), and hence the lower boundary is inaccessible.

$\sigma_i < 1$: With the CES function (27.57–27.58), the scale function with the dominating terms becomes, cf. (27.77), (27.59), (27.131), (27.134)

$$\mathcal{S}_1(0) = \lim_{k\to 0}\int_{k_0}^{k} \mathfrak{s}_1(k)dk = \int_{k_0}^{0} (k/k_0)^{2[\Theta - s\gamma_1 a_1^{1/\varrho_1}]/\beta^2} dk \tag{27.135}$$

Hence it follows from (27.135), that the divergence of $\mathcal{S}_1(0)$ requires that the exponent $2[\Theta - s\gamma_1 a_1^{1/\varrho_1}]/\beta^2 \leq -1$, which is the lower boundary condition in (27.78), cf. (27.66).

$\sigma_i > 1$: With the CES function (27.57–27.58), the scale function with the dominating terms becomes, cf. (27.77), (27.60),

$$\begin{aligned}\mathcal{S}_1(0) &= \lim_{k\to 0}\int_{k_0}^{k} \mathfrak{s}_1(k)dk \\ &= \lim_{k\to 0}\int_{k_0}^{0} \exp\left\{\frac{2s\gamma_1(1-a_1)^{1/\varrho_1}}{\bar{b}_1^2}(k^{-1} - k_0^{-1})\right\} dk \end{aligned}\tag{27.136}$$

where $\bar{b}_1^2 \equiv \beta^2 + \beta_3^2\lambda_3^2\gamma_1^2(1-a_1)^{2/\varrho_1} - \rho\beta_3\lambda_3\gamma_1(1-a_1)^{1/\varrho_1} > 0$, cf. (27.31). Since the parameter $2s\gamma_1(1-a_1)^{1/\varrho_1}/\bar{b}_1^2$ in the exponential term is always positive, it follows from (27.136) that $\mathcal{S}_1(0)$ is always diverging, and hence $k = 0$ is inaccessible, irrespective of parameter restrictions, cf. (27.68).

*Upper Boundary* With the CD function (27.44), the scale density $\mathfrak{s}_3(k)$ becomes, cf. (27.49), (27.29)–(27.31), (27.75), (27.77),

$$\mathfrak{s}_3(k) = \exp\left\{-2\int_{k_0}^{k} \frac{[s - \rho_{13}\beta_1\phi_3(k)](\gamma_2/p)k^{a_2} - \Theta k}{\beta^2k^2 + \phi_3^2(k)(\gamma_2/p)^2k^{2a_2} - \rho\phi_3(k)(\gamma_2/p)k^{(1+a_2)}}dk\right\} \tag{27.137}$$

Since $a_2 < 1$, the ***dominating*** term in the numerator and denominator of (27.137) becomes for large $k$, cf. (27.132),

$$\mathfrak{s}_3(k) \sim \exp\left\{-2\int_{k_0}^{k} \frac{-\Theta k}{\beta^2k^2}dk\right\} = (k/k_0)^{2\Theta/\beta^2} \tag{27.138}$$

The divergence of $\mathcal{S}_3(\infty)$ from (27.138) is analogous to the result in (27.55), (27.48); hence we have (27.80) for $\sigma = 1$.

$\sigma < 1$: With the CES function (27.57–27.58), the scale density $\mathfrak{s}_3(k)$ becomes, keeping the dominant terms for large $k$, cf. (27.137), (27.132),

$$\mathfrak{s}_3(k) \sim \exp\left\{-2\int_{k_0}^{k} \frac{-\Theta k}{\beta^2k^2}dk\right\} = (k/k_0)^{2\Theta/\beta^2} \tag{27.139}$$

which is the same as (27.138), and the divergence of $S_3(\infty)$ is analogous to (27.67), (27.62).

$\sigma > 1$: From (27.137), (27.57–27.58), (27.60), (27.132), we have for large $k$,

$$\mathfrak{s}_3(k) \sim \exp\left\{-2\int_{k_0}^{k} \frac{(s-\rho_{13}\beta_1\beta_3)(\gamma_2/p)a_2^{1/\varrho_2}k - \Theta k}{\beta^2k^2+\beta_3^2(\gamma_2/p)^2a_2^{2/\varrho_2}k^2-\rho\beta_3(\gamma_2/p)a_2^{1/\varrho_2}k^2}dk\right\}$$

$$= \exp\left\{-2\int_{k_0}^{k}(\bar{a}_3/\bar{b}_3^2)k^{-1}dk\right\} = (k/k_0)^{\bar{a}_3/\bar{b}_3^2} \quad (27.140)$$

$\bar{a}_3 \equiv (s-\rho_{13}\beta_1\beta_3)(\gamma_2/p)a_2^{1/\varrho_2} - \Theta$, $\bar{b}_3^2 \equiv \beta^2 + \beta_3^2(\gamma_2/p)^2a_2^{2/\varrho_2} - \rho\beta_3(\gamma_2/p)$ $a_2^{1/\varrho_2} > 0$, cf. (27.31). $S_3(\infty)$ from (27.140) *diverges*, cf. the analogue (27.129) and (27.74), if the exponent $\bar{a}_3/\bar{b}_3^2 \geq -1$. Rewriting the latter, using (27.28)–(27.29), gives condition (27.81), where $\Delta \equiv \bar{b}_3^2 - \beta^2 + 2\rho_{13}\beta_1\beta_3(\gamma_2/p)a_2^{1/\varrho_2} = [\beta_3(\gamma_2/p)a_2^{1/\varrho_2}]^2 - 2\rho_{23}\beta_2\beta_3(\gamma_2/p)a_2^{1/\varrho_2}$, cf. (27.30).

## Bibliography


Baron DP, Forsythe R (1979) Models of the Firm and International Trade under Uncertainty. American Economic Review 69:565–74

Batra RN (1974) Resource Allocation in a General Equilibrium Model of Production under Uncertainty. Journal of Economic Theory 8:50–63

Bourguignon F (1974) A Particular Class of Continuous–Time Stochastic Growth Models. Journal of Economic Theory 9:141–158

Chang FR, Malliaris AG (1987) Asymptotic Growth under Uncertainty—Existence and Uniqueness. Review of Economic Studies (54):169–174

Deardorff AV (1971) Growth and Trade in a Two–Sector World. PhD thesis, Cornell University, unpublished Ph.D. dissertation

Deardorff AV (1974) A Geometry of Growth and Trade. Canadian Journal of Economics 2:295–306

Grinols EL (1987) Uncertainty and the Theory of International Trade. Harwood Academic Publishers, Chur, Switzerland

Helpman E, Razin A (1978) A Theory of International Trade under Uncertainty. Academic Press, N.Y.

Itô K, McKean HP Jr (1965) Diffusion Processes and Their Sample Paths. Springer–Verlag, Berlin

Jensen BS (1994) The Dynamic Systems of Basic Economic Growth Models. Kluwer Academic Publishers, Dordrecht

Jensen BS, Larsen ME (1987) Growth and Long–Run Stability. Acta Applicandae Mathematicae 9:219–237, here in Chap. 1.

Jensen BS, Wang C (1997) General Equilibrium Dynamics of Basic Trade Models for Growing Economies. In Bjarne S. Jensen and Kar–Yiu Wong (eds.) *Dynamics, Economic Growth, and International Trade*, Ann Arbor: University of Michigan Press; here Chap. 21.

Karlin S, Taylor HM (1981) A Second Course in Stochastic Processes. Academic Press, N.Y.

Kemp MC (1976) Three Topics in the Theory of International Trade—Distribution, Welfare and Uncertainty. North–Holland/Elsevier, N.Y.

Kemp MC, Liviatan N (1973) Production and Trade Patterns under Uncertainty. Economic Record 49:215–27

Kemp MC, Van Long N, Okuguchi K (1981) On the Possibility of Deriving Conclusions of Stolper–Samuelson Type When Commodity Prices Are Random. Economic Studies Quarterly 32:111–16

Klump R (1995) On the Institutional Determinants of Economic Development—Lessons from a Stochastic Neoclassical Growth Model. Jahrbuch für Wirtschaftswissenschaft 46:138–51

Malliaris AG, Brock WA (1982) Stochastic Methods in Economics and Finance. North–Holland/Elsevier, Amsterdam

Mandl P (1968) Analytical Treatment of One–Dimensional Markov Processes. Springer–Verlag, Berlin, (Die Grundlehren der mathematischen Wissenschaften in Einzeldarstellungen, Band 151)

Merton RC (1975) An Asymptotic Theory of Growth under Uncertainty. Review of Economic Studies 42:375–393, Ch.17 in Merton (1990)

Øksendal B (1992) Stochastic Differential Equations—An Introduction with Applications, 3rd edn. Springer–Verlag, Berlin

Pomery J (1984) Uncertainty in Trade Models. In Ronald W. Jones and Peter B. Kenen (eds.), *Handbook in International Economics*, Vol. I, N.Y.: North–Holland/–Elsevier.

Ruffin RJ (1974a) Comparative Advantage under Uncertainty. Journal of International Economics 4:261–73

Ruffin RJ (1974b) International Trade under Uncertainty. Journal of International Economics 4:243–59

Stigum BP (1972) Balanced Growth under Uncertainty. Journal of Economic Theory 5:42–68

Turnovsky SJ (1974) Technological and Price Uncertainty in a Ricardian Model of International Trade. Review of Economic Studies 41:201–17

Wong KY (1995) International Trade in Goods and Factor Mobility. MIT Press, Cambridge, MA

Young L (1984) Uncertainty and the Theory of International Trade in Long–Run Equilibrium. Journal of Economic Theory 32:67–92

PART VI

# Homogeneous Dynamic Systems

CHAPTER 28

# Homogeneous Dynamics in the Plane

## Introduction

The fundamental problem in the theory of ordinary differential equations is that of deducing the local or global properties of the *solutions* from the properties of the *governing functions* (given vector fields). The subject matter of ordinary differential equations has played a prominent role in both pure and applied mathematics. Evidently, some of the most important ideas in differential and integral calculus, analytical geometry, curve theory, group theory, and topology were developed in attempts to resolve particular dynamic or geometric problems involving differential equations. Like any branch of mathematics with a long history behind it, the study of ordinary differential equations has undergone profound changes. As is well known, the main endeavor was in the beginning and for a long time devoted to *quantitative* methods and appropriate techniques for actually solving (integrating) many special differential equations. The solutions were expressed either by finite formulas or by expansions in terms of infinite series. By the late nineteenth century (Lipschitz, Peano, Picard), the necessary and sufficient conditions for both the existence and the uniqueness of the solutions, from any initial values, were finally obtained. Moreover, with the existence conditions taken for granted, the main efforts had shifted to the study of the *qualitative* behavior of solutions, Poincaré (1928), Liapounoff (1947a). This new approach ("qualitative integration") utilized the topological properties of the phase space and the analytical properties of the governing functions in order to describe the local and global behavior of the solutions. From the number of fixed points (singularities) and the behavior of trajectories in their neighborhoods, crucial information about the *geometric* (topological) *configuration* of the *phase portrait* was obtained. Within recent years, interest in nonlinear differential



B. S. Jensen, *The Elements and Dynamic Systems of Economic Growth and Trade Models*, https://doi.org/10.1007/978-3-031-52493-6_28

equations has grown enormously; although many of these are not new, the systematic study of them is somehow a rather new phenomenon.

The subject of this chapter, *nonlinear homogeneous* differential equations (the *governing functions* are in the arguments homogeneous of the *same degree*, $\boldsymbol{m}$), has a genesis with contributions of repute over centuries—reaching back to *Leibniz*, who first used the method of separation of variables to integrate the *homogeneous differential* equation of the *first order*, see Ince (1956, pp. 18, p. 530). *Euler's theorems* on homogeneous functions and his concept of integrating factors and *exact differentials* further advanced the study of homogeneous differential equations and their *primitives*. Regarding the integral curves as a family of plane curves, the notorious significance of *homogeneity* was the *geometrical similarity* of integral curves. The problems of domain, singularities, uniqueness of integral curves, restrictions upon the degree of homogeneity, and so on, were left to the late nineteenth century.

The groundwork on *singularity descriptions* of first-order differential equations and planar autonomous dynamic systems was laid by Poincaré (1928) and extended by Bendixson (1901). In their real *analytical* systems, *homogeneous polynomials* of degree $m \geq 1$ were the dominant parts of the system—compared to the perturbation terms (power series of higher degree), cf. Sansone and Conti (1964, pp. 66, pp. 84), Nemytskii and Stepanov (1989, p. 81). Much later, when real *homogeneous functions* were considered as *governing* functions of two-dimensional *dynamic* systems, the *degree* of homogeneity was still restricted to *integers*, $m \geq 1$; see Sansone and Conti (1964, p. 49). The latter restriction upon $m$ is unsatisfactory for many application purposes, especially in *economics* and the *social sciences*, where $\boldsymbol{0 < m \leq 1}$ occurs more often. In fact, the value of $\boldsymbol{m}$ has not been given much attention in the mathematical literature, partly because the degree of homogeneity plays only a subordinate role in singularity classifications and in trajectory geometry. However, when due attention is also given to the *velocity of motion* as a function of the coordinates, then the value of $\boldsymbol{m}$ takes on great importance for the *kinematic* properties of the coordinate *solutions*.

The purpose of this chapter is to examine the $C^1$-class of *planar homogeneous dynamic systems* with *any degree* of homogeneity, $\boldsymbol{m} \in \mathbf{R}$. In particular, the long-run *stability* properties of the families of solutions will be analyzed here by drawing upon the *stability criteria* in Chap. 1.

The exposition will be self-contained and attempts to provide a unified framework for a discussion of the many aspects of homogeneous differential equations.

## Basic Framework, Assumptions, and Definitions

Consider the autonomous *dynamic* system (deterministic *process*) in the normal (explicit) form

$$\dot{x} = dx/dt = F(x, y), \quad (x, y) \in \mathbf{R}^2, \tag{28.1.1}$$

$$\dot{y} = dy/dt = G(x, y), \quad (x, y) \in \mathbf{R}^2. \tag{28.1.2}$$

The ordered pair of real numbers $(\boldsymbol{x}, \boldsymbol{y})$ is regarded as Cartesian coordinates of a point in the Euclidean plane. We shall throughout make use of:

*Assumption 28.1*

$$F \text{ and } G \text{ are real and of the } \mathbf{C}^1 - \text{class on } \mathbf{R}^2 \setminus \{(0, 0)\}, \tag{28.2.1}$$

$$F(0, 0) = 0, \ G(0, 0) = 0. \tag{28.2.2}$$

*Assumption 28.2*

$$F \text{ and } G \text{ are homogeneous (projective) functions of the same degree, } m \in \mathbf{R}. \tag{28.3}$$

Assumption 28.1 about the *governing* functions $\boldsymbol{F}$ and $\boldsymbol{G}$ ensures, for the system (28.1.1–2), the *existence* everywhere of a ***solution*** $\boldsymbol{\varphi}$ (coordinate (vector) function, mapping), defined on an interval $T$ of the real $t$-axis,

$$\varphi = (\varphi_1, \varphi_2), \quad \varphi : T \to \mathbf{R}^2, \quad T \subseteq \mathbf{R}. \tag{28.4}$$

The ***solution*** (28.4) has a representation as a ***history surface/curve*** (graph, time path, ***evolution***) in $\mathbf{R}^3$, called the history space,

$$\Gamma = \{[t, \varphi(t)] \mid t \in T\} \subset \mathbf{R}^3 \tag{28.5}$$

or, a representation as a ***phase curve*** (image points, phase path, ***motion***) in $\mathbf{R}^2$,

$$\varphi(t) = [x = \varphi_1(t), \ y = \varphi_2(t)], \quad t \in T \subseteq \mathbf{R}. \tag{28.6}$$

The ***phase curve*** (28.6) in the state (phase) space $\mathbf{R}^2$ will also be referred to as the (Cartesian) coordinate ***solution $\boldsymbol{\varphi(t)}$*** of the dynamic system (28.1.1–28.2.2).

By (28.2.2) the ***origin*** is a ***critical*** (singular) ***point*** of (28.1.1–28.2.2), implying the *existence* of a ***stationary*** coordinate solution, $\boldsymbol{\varphi(t) = (0, 0), \ \forall t}$.

The *uniqueness* everywhere—on the *punctured plane* $\mathbf{R}^2 \setminus \{(0,0)\}$—of the solutions (28.4) and history curves (28.5) is ensured by $\boldsymbol{F}, \boldsymbol{G} \in C^1$-class, (28.2.1). Clearly, $\boldsymbol{\varphi} \in C^2$-class.

The phase curve (28.6), tracing successive states of the process (28.1.1–2), is the *kinematic* representation (*time* parameterization) of the *trajectory* (image set, range of $\boldsymbol{\varphi}$, *orbit*)

$$\Phi = \{\varphi(t) \mid t \in T\} \subset \mathbf{R}^2. \tag{28.7}$$

Geometrically, the *trajectory* $\Phi$ (28.7) is the *projection* of the *history curve* $\Gamma$ (28.5) into the *state* space $\mathbf{R}^2$. As a *locus* (subset of $\mathbf{R}^2$), the trajectory could as well be represented by an *arc* (oriented curve) with an arbitrary *parameterization* or as a *curve* represented by an *equation*,

$$\Phi = \{(x, y) \mid \ell(x, y) = 0\} \subset \mathbf{R}^2, \tag{28.8}$$

where $\boldsymbol{\ell(x, y)}$ is a function of the *coordinates* (state variables).

Since (28.1.1–2) is ***autonomous***, the latter and uniqueness (28.2.1–2) further imply that the phase curves and hence the trajectories do not intersect each other.

By Assumption 28.2, $F$ and $G$ satisfy the identities

$$F(\lambda x, \lambda y) \equiv \lambda|\lambda|^{m-1} F(x, y); \ \forall\lambda \neq 0, \quad \forall(x, y) \in \mathbf{R}^2, \tag{28.9.1}$$

$$G(\lambda x, \lambda y) \equiv \lambda|\lambda|^{m-1} G(x, y); \ \forall\lambda \neq 0, \quad \forall(x, y) \in \mathbf{R}^2. \tag{28.9.2}$$

**Remark 28.1** As we are interested in exploring the general dynamic implications of $m \in \mathbf{R}$—not just the traditional cases of $m \in \mathbf{N}$ or $m \in \mathbf{Z}$—we here replace the usual Euler identities with the *generalized identities* (28.9.1–2). Our general approach to homogeneous dynamics also applies if the functions $F$ and $G$ in specific cases are restricted to a *domain,* $D \subset \mathbf{R}^2$.

But, as the identities (28.9.1–2) imply, the ***domain D*** of *any* homogeneous function of any number of variables is always a ***cone,*** since the domain must inherently include the ***ray*** through any point of the given domain, $\boldsymbol{D}$. The kinematic and geometric significance of the amendment (28.9.1–2) is further discussed in section "The Geometry of History Curves, Phase Curves, and Trajectories". ▽

Now, introducing the *ratio* variable, ($\boldsymbol{r}$)

$$r = y/x, \quad x \neq 0, \tag{28.10}$$

we have from, (28.1.1–2), (28.9.1–2), (28.10), Remark 28.1,

$$\dot{x} = x|x|^{m-1}F(1,r), \quad x \neq 0, \tag{28.11.1}$$

$$\dot{y} = x|x|^{m-1}G(1,r), \quad x \neq 0, \tag{28.11.2}$$

or, in simplified notation,

$$\dot{x} = x|x|^{m-1}f(r); \quad m \in \mathbf{R}, \quad x \neq 0, \tag{28.12.1}$$

$$\dot{y} = x|x|^{m-1}g(r); \quad m \in \mathbf{R}, \quad x \neq 0, \tag{28.12.2}$$

where

$$f(r) = F(1,r), \quad g(r) = G(1,r); \quad r \in \mathbf{R}. \tag{28.12.3}$$

Then the *ratio* of the *individual coordinate solutions* (28.6)

$$r = \rho(t) = \varphi_2(t)/\varphi_1(t) \tag{28.13}$$

has the *time derivative,* cf. (28.10), (28.12.1–3),

$$\begin{aligned} \dot{r} &= dr/dt = d(y/x)/dt = (x\dot{y} - y\dot{x})/x^2 \\ &= |x|^{m-1}g(r) - |x|^{m-1}rf(r) \\ &= |x|^{m-1}h(r), \end{aligned} \tag{28.14}$$

where

$$h(r) = g(r) - rf(r), \quad h \in C^1\text{-class}, \quad r \in \mathbf{R}. \tag{28.15}$$

Although the *ratio* $\boldsymbol{\rho(t)}$ satisfies the *non-autonomous* differential equation

$$\dot{r} = |\varphi_1(t)|^{m-1}h(r), \tag{28.16}$$

we shall subsequently be able to present an *autonomous* differential equation for the *ratio* solutions $\boldsymbol{\rho(t)}$, which will also provide the individual *coordinate* solutions, $\boldsymbol{\varphi_1(t)}$ and $\boldsymbol{\varphi_2(t)}$.

**Remark 28.2** A subset $\boldsymbol{P}$ of $\mathbf{R}^2$ is a *cone,* with vertex at the origin, if any point (vector) $\boldsymbol{p \in P}$ implies $\lambda p \in P$ for every nonnegative real scalar $\lambda$. The particular cones, consisting of a nonzero vector $p$ and all its multiples, $\boldsymbol{R_p} = \{\lambda p \mid \lambda > 0\}$, are ***rays*** (half-lines). A cone may be considered as the union of the rays it contains. A ray $R_p$ is called an *interior ray* of a cone $P$, if $P$ contains $R_q$ for $q$ in an $\epsilon$*-neighborhood* of $p$ for some $\epsilon > 0$. A *boundary ray* of a cone $P$ is a ray that is neither an *interior* ray of $P$ nor an *interior* ray of the *complement,*

$\complement P$. The *interior* of a cone $P$ is an *open* set that consists of *all* rays (points) of $P$ *except* for the boundary rays (points). A cone $C$ is *convex*, if the cone $(R_p + R_q)$ is contained in $C$, whenever $R_p$ and $R_q$ are rays of $C$. ▽

The *domain*, $D = \{(x, y) \in \mathbf{R}^2 \mid x \neq 0\}$, of the dynamic system (28.12.1–3) is *decomposed* by the function $\boldsymbol{h(y/x)}$, (28.15), into two *disjunct* sets $M_R$ and $M_C$, completely filling the domain, namely,

$$M_R = \{(x, y) \in D \mid h(y/x) = 0\}; \quad M_C = \{(x, y) \in D \mid h(y/x) \neq 0\}. \tag{28.17}$$

The *root set* $\mathcal{A}$ of $h(r) = 0$, (28.15), gives a *partition* of $\mathbf{R} = \mathcal{A} \cup \complement\mathcal{A}$, i.e.,

$$\mathcal{A} = \{\alpha \in \mathbf{R} \mid h(\alpha) = 0\}; \quad \overline{\mathcal{A}} = \mathcal{A} \cup \{\pm\infty\}; \quad \complement\mathcal{A} = \{r \in \mathbf{R} \mid h(r) \neq 0\}, \tag{28.18}$$

where $\overline{\mathcal{A}}$ is its closure (on the *extended* real line $\mathbf{R}^* = \mathbf{R} \cup \{\pm\infty\}$) and $\complement\mathcal{A}$ its complement. The complement is *open;* hence $\complement\mathcal{A}$ is the *disjoint union* of an at most countable set of *open intervals* of $\mathbf{R}$, and each interval may be characterized as a *maximal interval* of $\complement\mathcal{A}$, or, equivalently, an *open interval,* $]\underline{\alpha}, \overline{\alpha}[ \subseteq \complement\mathcal{A}$, which has *endpoints,* $\underline{\alpha}, \overline{\alpha} \in \overline{\mathcal{A}}$.

Corresponding to these *maximal* intervals of $\complement\mathcal{A}$, we shall consider, in the domain $D = \{(x, y) \in \mathbf{R}^2 \mid x \neq 0\}$, the *open convex cones*

$$C = \{(x, y) \in D \mid \underline{\alpha} < y/x < \overline{\alpha}\}, \quad ]\underline{\alpha}, \overline{\alpha}[ \subseteq \complement\mathcal{A}, \quad \underline{\alpha}, \overline{\alpha} \in \overline{\mathcal{A}}. \tag{28.19}$$

Note that the rays $R_p$, for $p = (1, \underline{\alpha}),\ (1, \overline{\alpha})$, are the *boundary rays* for the cone $C$ (28.19); the $x$-axis and the $y$-axis may be the right boundary ray or the left boundary ray of $C$.

Finally, we get from (28.17–28.19), cf. Remark 28.2,

$$D = \{(x, y) \in \mathbf{R}^2 \mid x \neq 0\} = M_R \cup M_C = \bigcup\{R_\alpha \mid \alpha \in \mathcal{A}\} \cup \bigcup\{R_r \mid r \in \complement\mathcal{A}\}, \tag{28.20}$$

where $\boldsymbol{R_r}$ is the *ray*

$$R_r = \{(x, y) \in D \mid y = r \cdot x\}, \quad r \in \mathbf{R}. \tag{28.21}$$

Thus, the *function* $\boldsymbol{h(r)}$, (28.15), gives a *decomposition* of the domain $D$ into a *union* of *disjoint* convex cones: the *rays* $R_\alpha$, for $\alpha \in \mathcal{A}$, and the *open convex cones* $C$ (28.19). As we shall presently see, the *phase curves* (28.6) of the solutions of (28.12.1–3) *cannot* leave these rays or cones, cf. Remark 28.7.

Motivated by the decomposition and partition analyses above, we are ready to adopt and to use henceforth the following terminology.

**Definition 28.1** The function $\boldsymbol{h(r)}$, (28.15), will be called a ***director function,*** and the *roots* of $\boldsymbol{h(r)}$, i.e., $\mathcal{A}$ (28.18) are called ***director roots.*** The latter are the *slopes* of the rays in $M_R$.

**Definition 28.2** A ray $\boldsymbol{R_\alpha} \subset D$ with $\boldsymbol{\alpha} \in \mathcal{A}$ will be called a ***directrix,*** i.e.,

$$\text{directrix: } y = \alpha x; \quad h(\alpha) = 0 \Leftrightarrow g(\alpha) = \alpha f(\alpha), \tag{28.22}$$

$$\text{stationary directrix: } y = \alpha x; \quad h(\alpha) = f(\alpha) = g(\alpha) = 0. \tag{28.23}$$

The special circumstances of (28.23) imply that the domain $D = \{(x, y) \in \mathbf{R}^2 \mid x \neq 0\}$ contains multiple resting points (stationary coordinate solutions), cf. (28.12.1–28.14). Consequently, the *origin* (0, 0) is not an isolated critical point of (28.1.1–28.2.2), if stationary directrices (28.23) exist in $D$.

**Definition 28.3** A *directrix* is *isolated* if it is a *boundary ray* for two open cones in $M_C$. The corresponding director root, $\alpha \in \mathcal{A}$, is isolated in $\mathcal{A}$.

**Remark 28.3** If the *governing* functions $\boldsymbol{F}$ and $\boldsymbol{G}$ of (28.1.1–2) are *analytic* (allow locally a power series expansion) in each variable in a domain including the axes, then the *director* function $\boldsymbol{h(r)}$ (28.15) will be *analytic* (even at $\pm\infty$), implying that the set of *director roots* $\mathcal{A}$ (28.18) will be *finite,* hence discrete. If $\mathcal{A}$ is *discrete,* then the corresponding directrices (28.22) are *isolated.* Usually, all directrices will be isolated. ▽

**Remark 28.4** By using the ratio variable (28.9.1–2), we were formally obliged to exclude the $y$-axis ($x = 0$) from the *domain* $D$ of (28.12.1–3) and its decomposition (28.20). Similarly, the $y$-axis ($\alpha = \pm\infty$) is formally excluded as a directrix, (28.22). But, as in (28.10–28.23), the whole treatment of the system (28.1.1–28.3) could be restated in the *reciprocal* ratio, $\tilde{r} = x/y, \ y \neq 0$, with now the exclusion of the $x$-axis. Indeed, our methodology allows an analysis of *homogeneous* dynamic systems in the *whole plane* $\mathbf{R}^2$. ▽

**Definition 28.4** The *value* of the *governing function* $\boldsymbol{f(r)}$ at $\boldsymbol{r = \alpha}$, $\alpha \in \mathcal{A}$ (28.18), will be called a directrix value, i.e., for a directrix (28.22–28.23), we define

$$\textit{directrix value}: \quad \boldsymbol{f(\alpha)}, \quad \alpha \in \mathcal{A}. \tag{28.24}$$

Incidentally, it is clear that there is no need to label $g(\alpha)$ after (28.24), since given $\alpha \neq 0$, the value of $f(\alpha)$ uniquely determines $g(\alpha)$ and vice versa, cf. (28.22).

**Definition 28.5** On a *maximal* interval, $]\underline{\alpha}, \overline{\alpha}[ \subseteq \complement\mathcal{A}$, we define a function, $H \in C^2$-class, by $\boldsymbol{H(r) = \int H'(r)dr}$, where

$$dH/dr = H'(r) = f(r)/h(r), \quad r \in ]\underline{\alpha}, \overline{\alpha}[ \subseteq \complement\mathcal{A}, \quad H' \in C^1\text{-class.} \tag{28.25}$$

Since the *integrand* $\boldsymbol{H'}$ belongs to the $C^1$-class on $]\underline{\alpha}, \overline{\alpha}[$, cf. (28.2.1–28.3), (28.12.1–3), (28.15), (28.18), its *primitive* (indefinite integral, quadrature) $\boldsymbol{H(r)} \in C^2$-class is well defined (exists) on this *interval,* $]\underline{\alpha}, \overline{\alpha}[$, and *unique* up to an *additive constant.*

The definition (28.25) of $\boldsymbol{H(r)}$ on *each* maximal interval of $\complement\mathcal{A}$ allows the extension of the *interval of definition* for the function $H(r)$ to all of $\complement\mathcal{A}$. But $H(r)$ cannot be extended continuously to points of $\mathcal{A}$, as it becomes unbounded. Precisely, for *nonstationary* directrices, cf. (28.22–28.23), we have

**Lemma 28.1** *Let* $\boldsymbol{H(r)}$ *be defined on the interval* $]\underline{\alpha}, \overline{\alpha}[$ *by (28.25). If* $f(\overline{\alpha}) \neq 0$, $[f(\underline{\alpha}) \neq 0]$, *then* $H(r)$ *is* ***unbounded*** *in the neighborhood of* $\overline{\alpha}$, $[\underline{\alpha}]$.

*Precisely, if* $h(r)$ *and* $f(\overline{\alpha})$, $[f(\underline{\alpha})]$, *have the same sign, then* $H(r) \to \infty$ *as* $r \to \overline{\alpha}$, *and* $H(r) \to -\infty$ *as* $r \to \underline{\alpha}$. *If* $h(r)$ *and* $f(\overline{\alpha})$, $[f(\underline{\alpha})]$, *have opposite signs, then* $H(r) \to -\infty$ *as* $r \to \overline{\alpha}$, *and* $H(r) \to \infty$ *as* $r \to \underline{\alpha}$.

***Proof*** Given that $f(\underline{\alpha}) \neq 0$, $f(\overline{\alpha}) \neq 0$, and assuming that $f(\overline{\alpha}) > 0$, there exists by continuity a small interval, $[r_0, \overline{\alpha}]$, $|r_0 - \overline{\alpha}| \leq \varepsilon$, where

$$f(r) > 0, \quad r \in [r_0, \overline{\alpha}], \tag{28.26.1}$$

$$h(r) > 0, \quad r \in ]\underline{\alpha}, \overline{\alpha}[. \tag{28.26.2}$$

From, (28.15) and (28.26.1–2), we have

$$1/H'(r) = (h/f) \in C^1\text{-class}, \quad r \in [r_0, \overline{\alpha}]. \tag{28.27}$$

By the $C^1$-property of $h/f$, (28.27), there exists an upper bound $B$, such that

$$|(h/f)'| < B, \quad r \in [r_0, \overline{\alpha}]. \tag{28.28}$$

Hence (28.26.1–2), (28.28) and $h(\overline{\alpha}) = 0$ give

$$h(r)/f(r) \leq B(\overline{\alpha} - r), \quad r \in [r_0, \overline{\alpha}], \tag{28.29}$$

which implies that

$$f(r)/h(r) \geq 1/B(\overline{\alpha} - r), \quad r \in [r_0, \overline{\alpha}[. \tag{28.30}$$

By (28.30) and (28.25), we get

$$\begin{aligned} H(r) &= H(r_0) + \int_{r_0}^{r} \frac{f(r)}{h(r)} dr \\ &\geq H(r_0) + \frac{1}{B} \int_{r_0}^{r} \frac{1}{\overline{\alpha} - r} dr = H(r_0) - \frac{1}{B} [\ln(\overline{\alpha} - r)]_{r_0}^{r} \\ &= H(r_0) + \frac{1}{B} \ln(\overline{\alpha} - r_0) - \frac{1}{B} \ln(\overline{\alpha} - r). \end{aligned} \tag{28.31}$$

Since $\ln(\overline{\alpha} - r) \to -\infty$ as $r \to \overline{\alpha}$, we have by (28.31) that

$$H(r) \to \infty \quad \text{as} \quad r \to \overline{\alpha}. \tag{28.32}$$

For negative signs in (28.26.1–2), the same result (28.32) is obtained.
With opposite signs in (28.26.1–2), we then have, cf. (28.30)

$$-f(r)/h(r) \geq 1/B(\overline{\alpha} - r), \quad r \in [r_0, \overline{\alpha}[, \tag{28.33}$$

and hence $H(r) \to -\infty$ as $r \to \overline{\alpha}$, cf. (28.31).
The behavior of $H(r)$ for $r \to \underline{\alpha}$ is obtained by analogous procedures. □

By Lemma 28.1, we may also note that the choice of the *constant of integration* in the definition of the function $H(r)$, (28.25), in *one* maximal interval from $\mathbb{C}\mathcal{A}$ is *independent* of the choice of the constant of integration in any *other* maximal interval.

**Remark 28.5** Since the dynamic system, (28.1.1–2), does not involve time explicitly, the choice of the origin of time is entirely arbitrary, and one of the arbitrary integration constants in the solution of the system can always be taken as an *additive constant* $t_0$ in time. We have deliberately chosen to reflect this property of *isotropy* in the presentation of the solutions below. ▽

The basic framework of this chapter now allows a complete solution of the system of nonlinear differential equations (28.1.1–28.3).

## Ratio Solutions, Coordinate Solutions, and Trajectories

The general behavior of the *homogeneous dynamic system* (28.1.1–28.9.2)—apart from directrix behavior, described by Theorem 28.2 below—is given by

**Theorem 28.1** *For any solution,* $\varphi = (\varphi_1, \varphi_2)$, *(28.4), with initial values in a cone* $C$, $(x_0, y_0) \in C$, *(28.19), and* $\mathbf{h(r)}$, $\mathbf{H(r)}$ *given by (28.15), (28.25),* *every ratio solution, $\rho = \varphi_2/\varphi_1$, (28.13), must solve the fundamental autonomous differential equation, $Q \in C^1$-class,*

$$\dot{r} = Q(r) = |k_0 \exp\{H(r)\}|^{m-1} h(r), \quad r \in ]\underline{\alpha}, \overline{\alpha}[ \subseteq \complement\mathcal{A} \tag{28.34}$$

*with the constant $k_0$ depending on $(x_0, y_0)$, precisely,*

$$k_0 = x_0 \exp\{-H(r_0)\}, \quad r_0 = y_0/x_0 \in ]\underline{\alpha}, \overline{\alpha}[ \subseteq \complement\mathcal{A}. \tag{28.35}$$

*The general solution of (28.34) is given by the formula*

$$r = \rho(t) = I^{-1}(t + t_0), \quad t + t_0 \in T = I(]\underline{\alpha}, \overline{\alpha}[) = ]\underline{t}, \overline{t}[, \tag{28.36}$$

*where the invertible function $I \in C^2$-class is the primitive*

$$I(r) = \int \frac{dr}{Q(r)} = t + t_0, \quad t_0 = I(r_0), \quad r, r_0 \in ]\underline{\alpha}, \overline{\alpha}[ \subseteq \complement\mathcal{A}. \tag{28.37}$$

*The individual **coordinate** solutions, the **history** and **phase** curves, are given by [with $\rho(t)$, $k_0$ from, respectively, (28.36), (28.35)]*

$$x = \varphi_1(t) = k_0 \exp\{H[\rho(t)]\}, \tag{28.38.1}$$

$$y = \varphi_2(t) = \rho(t)\varphi_1(t). \tag{28.38.2}$$

*The trajectories as **loci** are given by the equation [with $k_0$ of (28.35)]*

$$\ell(x, y) = 0 \;\; \textit{with} \;\; \ell(x, y) = x \exp\{-H(y/x)\} - k_0. \tag{28.39}$$

***Proof*** By (28.12.1) and (28.19), we have

$$\dot{x}/x = |x|^{m-1} f(r), \quad r \in ]\underline{\alpha}, \overline{\alpha}[ \subseteq \complement\mathcal{A}. \tag{28.40}$$

Eliminating $|x|^{m-1}$ from (28.40) by (28.14), we get

$$\frac{\dot{x}}{x} = \frac{f(r)\dot{r}}{h(r)}. \tag{28.41}$$

Integration of (28.41) with respect to time gives

$$\int \frac{\dot{x} dt}{x} = \int \frac{f(r)\dot{r} dt}{h(r)} \tag{28.42}$$

or, equivalently, cf. (28.25)

$$\int \frac{dx}{x} = \int \frac{f(r)dr}{h(r)} = \int H'(r)dr, \tag{28.43}$$

$$\ln|x| = H(r) + k, \tag{28.44}$$

where the constant of integration $k$ has to satisfy the initial condition

$$k = \ln|x_0| - H(r_0) = \ln(|x_0|\exp\{-H(r_0)\}) = \ln|k_0|. \tag{28.45}$$

Thus, we can express $x$ as a function of $r$

$$x = k_0 \exp\{H(r)\}, \tag{28.46}$$

and further

$$|x|^{m-1} = |k_0 \exp\{H(r)\}|^{m-1}. \tag{28.47}$$

Substituting this expression for $|x|^{m-1}$ into (28.14) establishes (28.34) and (28.35).

Regarding $\rho(t)$ in terms of primitives, we have from (28.34) by separation of variables

$$I(r) = \int \frac{dr}{Q(r)} = \int dt = t + t_0, \quad t_0 = I(r_0), \quad r, r_0 \in ]\underline{\alpha}, \overline{\alpha}[ \subseteq \complement\mathcal{A}, \tag{28.48}$$

where $t_0$ (summarizing the two integration constants) is an *arbitrary constant*, dependent on initial values, $\boldsymbol{r_0 = y_0/x_0}$.

The primitive $I(r)$ is defined on the *maximal* interval, $]\underline{\alpha}, \overline{\alpha}[$, and its derivative cannot change sign on $]\underline{\alpha}, \overline{\alpha}[$, since $h(r)$ and hereby $Q(r)$ cannot change sign on this interval, as $h(r)$ vanishes nowhere on $]\underline{\alpha}, \overline{\alpha}[$, cf. (28.17–28.19).

Therefore, the *primitive* $\boldsymbol{I(r)}$ is *monotonic* and hence has an *inverse,* i.e., there exists a *function* $\rho(t)$ such that $\boldsymbol{I[\rho(t)] = t}$. Hence, the *general* ratio solution of (28.34) is established as stated in (28.36).

Inserting the ratio solution $\boldsymbol{\rho(t)}$, (28.36), into (28.46) establishes (28.38.1–2).

Equation (28.39) follows by substitution of (28.10), (28.13) into (28.38.1), cf. (28.43–28.46). □

The *ratio* solutions $\boldsymbol{\rho(t)}$ and *coordinate* solutions $\boldsymbol{\varphi(t)}$ in Theorem 28.1 solely involve well-defined *primitives*. It is noted from (28.34), (28.36–28.37) that $\boldsymbol{\rho}(\boldsymbol{t})$ involves *two* distinct *quadratures*, $\boldsymbol{H}(\boldsymbol{r})$ and $\boldsymbol{I}(\boldsymbol{r})$, where only the latter is necessarily invertible. The same *two primitives* are involved in the coordinate solutions $\boldsymbol{\varphi}(\boldsymbol{t})$, (28.38.1–2), but as the *composite function* $\boldsymbol{H}[\boldsymbol{I}^{-1}(\boldsymbol{t}+\boldsymbol{t}_0)]$.

The *time interval* $T$ for the *ratio* solutions $\rho(t)$, (28.36), may be *finite* ($\bar{t} < \infty$) in the sense that $\rho(t)$ reaches an endpoint of the maximal interval $]\underline{\alpha}, \overline{\alpha}[$ in finite time. The time interval, $T$, may be *infinite* ($\bar{t} = \infty$) in the sense that $\rho(t)$ tends toward the endpoint in infinite time.

On the *time interval* $T$—either finite or infinite—the *coordinate* solutions $\varphi(t)$, (28.38.1–2), may go to infinity or zero. The coordinate solutions may explode, i.e., reach infinity in finite time, $\bar{t} < \infty$, although at $t = \bar{t}$ the corresponding ratio solution, $\rho(t)$, reaches the endpoint of the interval, $\overline{\alpha}$ or $\underline{\alpha}$.

Thus, by giving the **formulas** (28.36), (28.38.1–2)—and Theorem 28.2—we can say that the *general nonlinear homogeneous dynamic* system (28.1.1–28.3) has been **solved** by *quadrature* (primitives).

For different initial values $(x_0, y_0)$ in $C$, (28.19), it is clear from (28.34–28.35) that the governing functions of the *ratio* solutions are the *same* function, except for the value of the constant $k_0$. To compare the different ratio solutions on $]\underline{\alpha}, \overline{\alpha}[$, we need Lemma 28.2, and to compare the different coordinate solutions, we give the following corollary.

**Lemma 28.2** *Consider two autonomous differential equations with a positive proportionality factor*

$$(i)\ \dot{u} = Q(u), \quad (ii)\ \dot{v} = \beta Q(v);\ \beta \in \mathbf{R},\ \ Q \in C^1,\ \ \forall x:\ Q(x) \neq 0. \tag{28.49}$$

*Let $u(t)$ and $v(t)$ be, respectively, a solution of (i) and (ii). Then there always exists a constant $\tau$ such that $\boldsymbol{u}(\boldsymbol{t})$ and $\boldsymbol{v}(\boldsymbol{t})$ are related by*

$$v(t) = u(\beta t + \tau). \tag{28.50}$$

***Proof*** The lemma is confirmed most easily by differentiation of the solutions (28.50), i.e.,

$$\dot{v} = \beta \dot{u}(\beta t + \tau) = \beta Q[u(\beta t + \tau)] = \beta Q(v). \tag{28.51}$$

□

**Corollary 28.1** *On a maximal interval, $]\underline{\alpha}, \overline{\alpha}[$, the pair of ratio solutions, $\rho(t) = \varphi_2(t)/\varphi_1(t)$, $\rho^*(t) = \psi_2(t)/\psi_1(t)$, and the pair of coordinate solutions, $\varphi(t)$, $\psi(t)$, with initial values at $t = 0$, respectively, $(x_0, y_0)$ and $(\hat{x}_0, \hat{y}_0)$, are related by the transformations*

$$\rho^*(t) = \rho(\beta t + \tau), \tag{28.52}$$

$$\psi(t) = (\hat{k}_0/k_0)\varphi(\beta t + \tau), \tag{28.53}$$

*with*

$$(i)\ \beta = |\hat{k}_0/k_0|^{m-1}, \qquad (ii)\ \tau = I(\hat{r}_0) - I(r_0), \tag{28.54}$$

*where* $k_0, \hat{k}_0$ *are defined by (28.35) and* $\tau$ *is given by* $\rho^*(0) = \rho^*(\tau) = \hat{r}_0$ *or (28.54), cf. (28.37).*

***Proof*** With the initial values $(x_0, y_0)$, $(\hat{x}_0, \hat{y}_0)$, Lemma 28.2 applied to (28.34–28.35) gives

$$\dot{r} = |k_0 + \exp\{H(r)\}|^{m-1} h(r) = Q(r), \tag{28.55.1}$$

$$\dot{r} = |\hat{k}_0 + \exp\{H(r)\}|^{m-1} h(r) = \beta\, Q(r), \tag{28.55.2}$$

which establish the relation (28.52), and the affine transformation of the argument with the multiplicative factor $\beta$ as given in (28.54), cf. (28.50).

From (28.38.1), we have

$$\varphi_1(\beta t + \tau) = k_0 \exp\{H[\rho(\beta t + \tau)]\}. \tag{28.56}$$

The definition of $\rho^*(t)$, (28.34–28.35), and (28.38.1) give

$$\psi_1(t) = \hat{k}_0 \exp\{H[\rho^*(t)]\}, \tag{28.57}$$

which with (28.52) becomes

$$\psi_1(t) = \hat{k}_0 \exp\{H[\rho(\beta t + \tau)]\}. \tag{28.58}$$

Then (28.56) and (28.58) imply that

$$\psi_1(t) = (\hat{k}_0/k_0)\varphi_1(\beta t + \tau). \tag{28.59}$$

Furthermore, cf. (28.57), (28.59),

$$\begin{aligned}\psi_2(t) &\equiv \rho^*(t)\psi_1(t) = \rho(\beta t + \tau)(\hat{k}_0/k_0)\varphi_1(\beta t + \tau)\\ &= (\hat{k}_0/k_0)\rho(\beta t + \tau)\varphi_1(\beta t + \tau) \equiv (\hat{k}_0/k_0)\varphi_2(\beta t + \tau).\end{aligned} \tag{28.60}$$

Hence (28.59–28.60) establish (28.53).

The value of $\tau$ is obtained from (28.52), (28.36), and $\rho^*(0) = \hat{r}_0 = \rho(\tau) = I^{-1}(\tau + t_0)$. Hence the latter and (28.37) give the formal expression for $\tau$ in (28.54). □

Finally, we reiterate that, like the *primitive* $\boldsymbol{I(r)}$, the *function* $\boldsymbol{\rho(t)}$ is *monotonic*—increasing/decreasing with positive/negative *sign* of $\boldsymbol{Q(r)}$, [equivalently, *sign* of $\boldsymbol{h(r)}$, cf. (28.34–28.35)]—and assumes *all* values belonging to the interval $]\underline{\alpha}, \overline{\alpha}[$.

We conclude this section by adopting some more terminology:

**Definition 28.6** When $\boldsymbol{\rho(t)}$ increases from $\underline{\alpha}$ to $\overline{\alpha}$, the directrix $R_{\overline{\alpha}}$ is called *right attractive* and the directrix $R_{\underline{\alpha}}$ *left repulsive*. Corresponding definitions of left attractive and right repulsive apply to decreasing $\boldsymbol{\rho(t)}$.

**Definition 28.7** A *nonstationary* directrix (28.22) is called *attractive (repulsive)*, if it is *both* right and left attractive (repulsive), cf. Definition 28.6 and Remark 28.6 below.

Clearly, *attractive/repulsive* **directrices** must be *isolated*, cf. Definition 28.3.

## The Ratio and Coordinate Solutions on Directrices

On *directrices*, the *solutions* of the homogeneous dynamic system (28.1.1–28.3) can always be expressed in *closed form* (finite combination of elementary functions).

**Theorem 28.2** *For any solution,* $\boldsymbol{\varphi} = (\varphi_1, \varphi_2)$*, (28.4), with initial values on a directrix* $\boldsymbol{R_\alpha}$*,* $(\boldsymbol{x_0}, \boldsymbol{y_0}) \in \boldsymbol{R_\alpha}$*, (28.22), with slope* $\boldsymbol{\alpha} \in \mathcal{A}$*, (28.18), every ratio solution,* $\rho = \varphi_2/\varphi_1$*, (28.13), is the constant (stationary) solution*

$$\rho(t) = \alpha = y_0/x_0 = r_0, \quad \forall t, \quad \alpha \in \mathcal{A}. \tag{28.61}$$

*The phase curve of any coordinate solution,* $\varphi(t)$*, stays on the directrix* $R_\alpha$

$$y = \varphi_2(t) = \alpha\varphi_1(t) = \alpha x, \quad \alpha \in \mathcal{A}, \tag{28.62}$$

*where the first coordinate solutions* $\boldsymbol{\varphi_1(t)}$ *have the forms*

$$\textit{Case 1.}\quad \textit{Stationary},\ m \in \mathbf{R},\quad f(\alpha) = 0;\quad x = \varphi_1(t) = x_0, \tag{28.63}$$

$$\textit{Case 2.}\quad \textit{Increasing, decreasing}\ f(\alpha) > 0,\quad f(\alpha) < 0, \tag{28.64}$$

$$\textit{(i)}\ m = 1.\ x = \varphi_1(t) = x_0 \exp\{f(\alpha)t\}, \tag{28.65.1}$$

$$\textit{(ii)}\ m < 1.\ x = \varphi_1(t) = \pm[|x_0|^{1-m} + (1-m)f(\alpha)t]^{\frac{1}{1-m}}, \tag{28.65.2}$$

$$\textit{(iii)}\ m > 1.\ x = \varphi_1(t) = \pm 1/[|x_0|^{1-m} - (m-1)f(\alpha)t]^{\frac{1}{m-1}}. \tag{28.65.3}$$

***Proof*** By $h(\alpha) = 0$, $\alpha \in \mathcal{A}$, Eq. (28.14) becomes $\dot{r} = 0$, hence $\rho(t) =$ constant $= \varphi_2(t)/\varphi_1(t)$ that, with the initial condition, $r_0 = y_0/x_0 = \alpha$, establishes (28.61–28.62).

Next, we get from (28.12.1) that

$$\dot{x} = x|x|^{m-1} f(\alpha). \tag{28.66}$$

Case 1: $f(\alpha) = 0$ gives $\dot{x} = 0$, hence (28.63).
Case 2: $f(\alpha) \neq 0$ implies that (28.66) can be solved by separation of variables

$$\int |x|^{-m} d|x| = \int f(\alpha) dt. \tag{28.67}$$

(i), $m = 1$: (28.67) gives

$$\ln|x| = f(\alpha)t + k, \quad k = \ln|x_0|; \quad \therefore \quad (28.65.1).$$

(ii)–(iii), $m \neq 1$: (28.67) gives

$$|x|^{1-m}/(1-m) = f(\alpha)t + k, \quad k = |x_0|^{1-m}/(1-m). \tag{28.68}$$

Thus, (28.68) *establishes* (28.65.2–3) for, respectively, $m < 1$ and $m > 1$. □

By Theorem 28.2, the *directrix values* (28.24) are distinct *parameters* of directrix solutions, (28.62–28.65.3), and these coordinate solutions either evolve *exponentially* ($m = 1$), *polynomially* ($m < 1$), or *explosively* ($m > 1$). An explosive solution means that the coordinates become infinite in finite time (the escape time, $\bar{t}$).

**Remark 28.6** The *sign* of the directrix value, $f(\alpha)$, cf. (28.64), determines the *orientation* of the phase curve upon this *nonstationary* directrix. Since the sign of $f(r)$, for $r$ belonging to a neighborhood of $\alpha$, is the same as that of $f(\alpha)$, it is seen that the *orientation* of the *adjacent* phase curves on *both* sides of a nonstationary directrix is the *same* as the orientation on the directrix itself. Hence, the signs of the directrix values (28.24) also convey crucial information about the *family* of solutions *outside* the directrices. This motivated the Definition 28.7 above. ▽

**Remark 28.7** Phase curves (28.38.1–2) with initial values in a cone $C$ (28.19) cannot leave its closure $\overline{C}$. This is in general simply due to the fact that its *boundary rays,* cf. (28.19), are *directrices* (28.62) and hence *trajectories,* which cannot be crossed by other trajectories of the *autonomous* system (28.1.1–2). ▽

It is *noteworthy* from (28.14–28.15), (28.18), (28.61–28.62),

$$f(\alpha) \neq 0: \ h(\alpha) = 0 \Leftrightarrow \alpha = g(\alpha)/f(\alpha) = q(\alpha). \tag{28.69}$$

Thus, the ***director roots*** of ***nonstationary directrices,*** cf. Definitions 28.1–28.2, may be interpreted (or alternatively defined) as *fixed points* of a ***continuous mapping*** $\boldsymbol{q}$, given by the ***governing functions*** $\boldsymbol{f}$ and $\boldsymbol{g}$, (28.12.1–3). Conversely, the rays corresponding to these fixed points are nonstationary directrices—characterized by the property of ***maintaining*** a *constant ratio* of the individual coordinate solutions.

A simple criterion for the *coordinate axes* being directrices will be useful.

**Lemma 28.3** *A necessary and sufficient condition for the x-axis and the y-axis to be a directrix is, respectively,* $G(x, 0) = 0$ *and* $F(0, y) = 0$, *i.e.,*

$$x\text{-axis directrix} \Leftrightarrow G(x,0) = 0, \qquad \forall x \tag{28.70.1}$$

$$y\text{-axis directrix} \Leftrightarrow F(0, y) = 0. \qquad \forall y \tag{28.70.2}$$

***Proof*** For $r = \alpha = 0$, we have from (28.15) that $h(0) = 0$ is equivalent to $g(0) = G(1, 0) = G(x, 0) = 0$, cf. (28.11.1–28.12.3), hence 28.70.1. As to the reciprocal ratio $\tilde{r} = 1/r$, cf. Remark 28.4, we find, analogously to (28.14), that

$$\dot{\tilde{r}} = (1\dot{/}r) = |y|^{m-1}\tilde{h}(\tilde{r}), \quad \tilde{h} \in C^1\text{-class}, \tag{28.71}$$

where

$$\tilde{h}(\tilde{r}) = \tilde{f}(\tilde{r}) - \tilde{r}\tilde{g}(\tilde{r}) = F(\tilde{r}, 1) - \tilde{r}G(\tilde{r}, 1). \tag{28.72}$$

For $\tilde{r} = \tilde{\alpha} = 0$, it is seen from (28.72) that $\tilde{h}(\tilde{\alpha}) = 0$ is equivalent to $\tilde{f}(0) = F(0, 1) = F(0, y) = 0$, hence (28.70.2). □

**Remark 28.8** By comparison of (28.12.1–3), (28.14–28.15), and (28.71–28.72), it is observed that

$$\tilde{h}(\tilde{r}) = -h(r)/r^{m+1}. \tag{28.73}$$

Since $h, \tilde{h} \in C^1$-class, (28.73) implies

$$\tilde{h}(\tilde{r}) \to 0 \text{ as } \tilde{r} \to 0 \quad \Leftrightarrow \quad h(r)/r^{m+1} \to 0 \text{ as } r \to \infty \tag{28.74}$$

and in particular

$$\tilde{h}(0) = 0 \quad \not\Leftrightarrow \quad h(r) \to 0 \text{ as } r \to \infty. \tag{28.75}$$

The second coordinate solutions $\varphi_2(t)$ of a directrix solution along the $y$-axis follow from

$$\dot{y} = y|y|^{m-1}G(0, 1) = y|y|^{m-1}\tilde{g}(0). \tag{28.76}$$

They have the forms (28.63), (28.65.1–3). ▽

## The Geometry of History Curves, Phase Curves, and Trajectories

The first three sections of our inquiry have primarily been devoted to the questions of *existence*, *uniqueness*, and *construction* (establishment of primitives) of the *family* (complete set) of *solutions*, (28.4), (28.13), (28.34–28.38.2), (28.61–28.65.3), to the homogeneous dynamic system, (28.1.1–28.3). This section will mainly be concerned with the *geometry* of *solutions*, (28.5–28.6), and the *geometry* of *trajectories*, (28.7–28.8). We shall also discuss some technicalities and methodological issues that will be helpful in clarifying both the proofs and the scope of Theorems 28.1–28.2.

### *Vector and Tangent Fields*

Complementary to the basic framework of homogeneous dynamics above, we shall comment upon some *general* properties of the associated *vector fields*—a geometric *interpretation* of the *governing* functions, $\boldsymbol{F}$ and $\boldsymbol{G}$—which, in turn, will offer additional insight into the *geometry* of the *curve systems* (complete sets) of history curves, phase curves, and trajectories.

As is well known, to *illustrate* vector fields, it is sometimes convenient to represent not the vectors themselves at each point, but rather the *space curves (isoclines)* through the *points* with *parallel* field vectors. Obviously, an isocline is also the *locus* of points where, respectively, the set of history curves, phase curves, or trajectories—fitting the vector fields, solving the differential equations—have the *same slope*. These isoclines have traditionally been employed as *auxiliaries* in constructing *graphic solutions* (graphical integration) of differential equations; see the Euler-Cauchy approximation procedure (Bieberbach 1923, p. 41; Birkhoff and Rota 1989, p. 21; Collatz 1966, p. 14; Kamke 1960, p. 37).

The *history vector field*, $W(t, x, y)$, associated with the system (28.1.1–2), is given as,

$$W(t, x, y) = (1, F, G), \quad (t, x, y) \in \mathbf{R}^3. \tag{28.77}$$

The field vectors of $W(t, x, y)$ are, of course, at any point in the history space $\mathbf{R}^3$, *tangent vectors* to the system of *history curves* $\Gamma$, (28.5). Evidently, isoclines of the history space describe the set of points where the tangent vectors of the passing history curves are parallel. These isoclines (curves), however, will have *no* simple geometric shape imposed by just the *homogeneity* property of $F$ and $G$. Consequently, a simple geometrical structure of the system of history curves is neither implied nor supplied by the isoclines in $\mathbf{R}^3$.

But, of course, the *autonomy* of the vector field $W(t, x, y)$, cf. (28.1.1–2), implies that all the *history curves* are simply *translations* of each other along the time axis. The history curves of the solutions on a *directrix* all lie in a *plane* of the *history space*, cf. (28.62), (28.5).

The *phase vector (velocity) field*, $V(x, y)$, associated with (28.1.1–2), is given as

$$V(x, y) = (F, G), \quad (x, y) \in \mathbf{R}^2, \tag{28.78}$$

where the phase field vectors may also be given, cf. (28.11.1–28.12.3), as

$$[F, G] = F \cdot [1, G/F] = x|x|^{m-1} f(r) \cdot [1, g(r)/f(r)]; \quad f(r) \neq 0. \tag{28.79}$$

Evidently, at the point $(x, y)$, the *vectors* of $V(x, y)$ have a horizontal component $F(x, y)$ and a vertical component $G(x, y)$, and so we may interpret the *differential equations* (28.1.1–2) *kinematically* as defining the *motion* of a *point* $(x, y)$ in the plane by the condition that its *velocity* at every point is equal to the prescribed vector of $V(x, y)$. The field vectors of $V(x, y)$ are, of course, at any point in $\mathbf{R}^2$, *tangent vectors* to the system of *phase curves* (28.6) or trajectories $\Phi$ (28.7–28.8).

It is immediately apparent from (28.79) that the *homogeneity* of $\boldsymbol{F}$ and $\boldsymbol{G}$ implies that the ***isoclines*** in the *phase space* $\mathbf{R}^2$ are all *straight* lines through the *origin*. In terms of the geometry of the phase space, if the vector field $V(x, y)$ is *homogeneous*, then it defines a *ray-to-ray* mapping of the set of rays into itself. Consequently, the *homogeneity* of $F$ and $G$ of any degree, $m \in \mathbf{R}$, also gives a very *simple geometric structure* for the system of phase curves or trajectories. In every cone $C$ (28.19), all the phase curves or trajectories may be visualized as a radial blow-up (geometrically *similar*, with the origin as the center of similitude) of a single *representative* phase curve or trajectory from the respective cones.

The ***directrices***, (28.22), enjoy a special status of being, *simultaneously*, *isoclines* and *trajectories*, i.e., the *slope* of such *isoclines* coincides with the particular *direction* of the *phase field* vectors upon such isoclines. This coincidence naturally explains, cf. Theorem 28.2, why also the phase curves of the particular solutions with *initial values* hereupon will *never leave* but stay upon these directrices.

**Remark 28.9** Generally, for *directrices*, we have from (28.79) and (28.22) that

$$\begin{aligned}[F(x,y),G(x,y)] &= [F(x,\alpha x),G(x,\alpha x)] = x|x|^{m-1}[f(\alpha),g(\alpha)]\\ &= x|x|^{m-1}f(\alpha)[1,\alpha] = |x|^{m-1}f(\alpha)[x,\alpha x]\\ &= |x|^{m-1}f(\alpha)[x,y], \end{aligned} \tag{28.80}$$

which, in the special case of $m = 1$, becomes

$$\lambda = f(\alpha), \tag{28.81.1}$$

$$[F(x,y),G(x,y)] = [F(x,\alpha x),G(x,\alpha x)] = \lambda[x,\alpha x] = \lambda[x,y]. \tag{28.81.2}$$

Equation (28.81.1–2) is recognized as defining the *directrix value,* (28.24), as an *eigenvalue* of the governing vector function $[F, G]$ with the *directrix vector,* $[x, \alpha x]$, $x \neq 0$, as the associated *eigenvector.* Thus, finding a nonstationary solution $\varphi$ to the differential equations (28.1.1–28.3) with some constant ratio $\alpha \in \mathbf{R}$ of the components, $\varphi_2/\varphi_1 = \alpha$, $\forall t$, can for $\boldsymbol{m} = 1$ be reduced to solving the *nonlinear eigenvalue* problem (28.81.1–2).

The *eigenvalue concept,* however, *cannot* be extended to the general case, $\boldsymbol{m} \neq 1$, because the factor $|x|^{m-1}f(\alpha)$ in (28.80) actually *depends* on the *size* of the *vector*, $[x, \alpha x]$. Nevertheless, as was seen in Theorem 28.2, our concepts, the *directrix*, $[x, \alpha x]$, (28.22–28.23), and the corresponding *directrix value,* $f(\alpha)$, (28.24), allowed us to find solutions with constant ratio of the components for *any* $m \in \mathbf{R}$, cf. (28.63–28.65.3). ▽

Two *traditional* isoclines in $\mathbf{R}^2$ for autonomous plane systems (28.1.1–2) are

$$n_\infty = \{(x,y) \in D \mid F(x,y) = 0\}, \quad n_0 = \{(x,y) \in D \mid G(x,y) = 0\} \tag{28.82}$$

representing points with *vertical* and *horizontal* slopes of phase field vectors. For these two isoclines, we shall adopt the name *nil-lines* (nil-line bundles).

A cone $C$ (28.19) may include nil-lines from *both* $n_\infty$ and $n_0$, just *one*, or *none* of them, depending on the location of the roots of $f(r)$ and $g(r)$, cf. (28.12.1–3). The coincidence of the two types of nil-lines gives indeed a stationary directrix (28.23). In sketching the *phase portrait* (system of trajectories) of a homogeneous system, the directrices are much more helpful than the nil-lines (28.82).

A so-called *direction (tangent) field*, $d(x, y)$, is sometimes introduced as

$$d(x,y) = (1, G/F), \quad (x,y) \in \mathbf{R}^2; \quad F(x,y) \neq 0, \tag{28.83}$$

i.e., one regards $\boldsymbol{F}$ and $\boldsymbol{G}$ of the system (28.1.1–2) as *just* giving the *direction* at each point $(x, y)$ by the *direction cosines* (with respect to the $x$- and $y$-

axes) or, else, giving the *direction* by the *slopes*, $G/F$ (ignoring the two orientations of the tangent line segment or, better, encompassing both the positive and the negative orientation of tangents), cf. (28.79). By (28.2.1–2), $d(x, y)$ is continuous and completely determines—in the phase space—*curves* (loci, trajectories), e.g., (28.8), with continuously turning tangents whose slope at any point coincides with the slope (direction) prescribed by the tangent (direction) field (28.83). But, evidently, the *tangent field* $d(x, y)$ *neglects* a crucial aspect of the phase *vector field* (28.78), namely, apart from *orientations*, also the *length* of the phase *field (velocity)* vectors.

This negligence of the orientation and the *length* of the phase field vectors therefore also occurs by reducing the system, (28.1.1–28.12.3), to the *single* differential equation

$$\frac{dy}{dx} = \frac{\dot{y}}{\dot{x}} = \frac{G(x, y)}{F(x, y)} = \frac{g(y/x)}{f(y/x)} = q(y/x) = q(r), \qquad f(y/x) \neq 0. \quad (28.84)$$

Of course, it is not necessary to find a *coordinate solution* $\boldsymbol{\varphi(t)}$, (28.6), to the system (28.1.1–2) in order to compute its *trajectories;* we need only to solve the *first-order, scalar* differential equation (28.84). Then, if we can integrate (28.84), we will obtain the equation of the trajectories, $\boldsymbol{\ell(x, y) = 0}$, (28.8), in *closed form*. But (28.84), $d(x, y)$, or $\ell(x, y)$ reflect only the *set* ***(loci)*** properties of the original phase curves, $\boldsymbol{\varphi(t)}$, $\boldsymbol{t \in T}$, (28.6), i.e., attention is given only to deriving the curve representation (28.8) of the trajectories. The *kinematics*, and e.g., the *speed of the motion* along these trajectories is *irretrievably lost*, i.e., the phase and *history* curves are entirely *missed* by (28.84).

**Remark 28.10** As is well known from any modern textbook on ordinary differential equations today (but was troublesome in the past) the *assumption* $\boldsymbol{q \in C^1}$-class (which is stronger than the standard Lipschitzian uniqueness condition) implies that through any point of the *punctured plane*, $\mathbf{R}^2 \setminus \{(0, 0)\}$, there passes a *unique* integral curve (solution) of (28.84).

Therefore, $\boldsymbol{q \in C^1}$-class ensures that *any two solutions* (integral curves) of (28.84)—e.g., as given by the loci equations of the trajectories, (28.39)—that *pass* a *common* point, will *coincide* wherever *both* are defined. Then, those solutions of (28.84) having common points can be consolidated into a single maximal solution (integral curve), defined on a maximal (union) domain. Henceforth, a *particular* solution of (28.84) will always refer to the *maximal* solution (integral curve) passing the given point(s). The uniqueness of the consolidated integral curves will also apply if $q(y/x)$ itself was given by an expression consisting of some other $C^1$-functions, e.g., $f$ and $g$ in (28.84).

However, if $f(y/x) = 0$, but $g(y/x) \neq 0$ at some point of the punctured plane, we can at this point equivalently take $dx/dy = f(y/x)/g(y/x)$ and conclude from $dx/dy = 0$ that here the curve tangent is vertical; such a point will always be consolidated into a unique *maximal* solution (integral curve) of (28.84).

But a point at which *both* $f$ and $g$ are zero—hence the phase field vectors are zero vectors and the direction field is indeterminate, cf. (28.78), (28.83)—is a *critical* (singular) *point*. Such critical points do *not* belong to *any* integral curve of (28.84); cf. (28.23). ▽

We should now discuss the dynamic and geometric implications of the *generalized Euler identities,* (28.9.1–2), which imply that for *any* $m \in \mathbf{R}$

$$F(-x, -y) = -F(x, y), \quad G(-x, -y) = -G(x, y), \tag{28.85}$$

i.e., together with *any* solution $\varphi$, (28.4), $-\varphi$ is *also* a solution of (28.1.1–28.3). Notice that the *tangent field* has the property, cf. (28.83), (28.85),

$$d(-x, -y) = d(x, y). \tag{28.86}$$

Geometrically, (28.85–28.86) signifies that in the phase plane $\mathbf{R}^2$, a *reflection* (at the *origin*) of any phase curve $\boldsymbol{\varphi}(t)$ (trajectory $\Phi$) of *homogeneous dynamics,* (28.1.1–28.3), (28.9.1–2), is also a phase curve (trajectory); in short, the *phase portrait* of homogeneous dynamics is by (28.3), (28.9.1–2), ***symmetrical*** about the *origin*.

**Remark 28.11** The class of homogeneous functions is usually defined by the requirement that the Euler identities hold for some $m \in \mathbf{Z}$ and every value of a scalar $\lambda \in \mathbf{R}$, i.e.,

$$F(\lambda x_1, \lambda x_2, \ldots, \lambda x_n) \equiv \lambda^m F(x_1, x_2, \ldots, x_n), \; m \in \mathbf{Z}, \; \lambda \in \mathbf{R}. \tag{28.87}$$

However, in order for the identity to make sense, the *degree m* must clearly be restricted to *integer values,* $\mathbf{Z}$. Although the planar tangent fields implied by the Definitions (28.9.1–2) and (28.87) are always the same, cf. (28.86), the *orientation* of the trajectories will for $x < 0$ be *different* with (28.9.1–2) and (28.87), if $m$ is an *even* number. Thus, with $m$ even, one may just retain the orientation given by (28.87) rather than (28.9.1–2).

If we further want to allow for the degree $m$ to attain *any* real value, then the identity (28.87) may be generalized *either* as in (28.9.1–2) *or* as

$$F(\lambda x_1, \lambda x_2, \ldots, \lambda x_n) = \lambda^m F(x_1, x_2, \ldots, x_n), \; m \in \mathbf{R}, \; \lambda \geq 0. \tag{28.88}$$

In contrast to (28.9.1–2), cf. (28.85–28.86), the homogeneity *property* (28.88) does *not* necessarily impose a *symmetry* around the origin upon the phase portraits of planar homogeneous systems.

Our approach to planar homogeneous dynamics in sections "Basic Framework, Assumptions, and Definitions–The Ratio and Coordinate Solutions on Directrices" can with simple modifications also be used to treat planar dynamic systems with the governing functions satisfying only (28.88); and accordingly, the domains are then naturally restricted to half planes, $x > 0$, $x < 0$; cf. Remark 28.1. ▽

### *Heuristic Comments on Geometry, Dynamics, and Kinematics*

The theory of nonlinear differential equations presupposes a familiarity with a variety of ideas and methods laid out in several branches of mathematics. Aiming at supporting heuristic skills and acquiring a coherent conceptual framework for our general treatment of homogeneous dynamics and its geometric aspects, we here offer a few heuristic comments on the disciplines of geometry, dynamics, and kinematics.

Geometry per se studies the *spatial* (shape and size) properties of *geometric objects* (curves, surfaces, bodies). The objects are investigated by a variety of methods and mathematical tools, which accordingly form the two subdisciplines, *analytical geometry* and *differential geometry,* where the former mainly uses *algebraic methods,* whereas the latter primarily applies the *techniques* of differential and integral *calculus* in the investigations of the geometric objects. Of course, as is natural, many concepts, methods, and results of analytical geometry are extensively used in differential geometry. Both subdisciplines always conduct their investigations by introducing a *coordinate system,* but they traditionally emphasize that a coordinate system is a useful tool but no more, i.e., a *property* of a geometric object is called *geometric* only if it is *independent* (*invariant*) of the *special choice* of the *coordinates* (frame of reference). This geometric view of a particular coordinate system as just an *expedient tool* is often well taken also outside the discipline of geometry, e.g., in the study and the mathematical formulations of classical mechanics. However, we may ask for the indulgence to dwell a bit on the *coordinate issue* and related topics in *curve theory,* as these issues may inadvertently impart vagueness and improperly disparage the mathematical significance of the *Cartesian coordinate solutions,* stated in Theorems 28.1–28.2.

The study of *continuum mechanics* [the theory of *solid* (particle, rigid body)/*fluid* (liquid, gas) *motion*] is based on the mathematical apparatus of two subdisciplines, dynamics and kinematics. *Dynamics*—a part of physics or other sciences—is primarily concerned with *specification* of the fundamental *governing functions* and subsequent *solving* of differential equations underlying the motion, whereas *kinematics* is mainly devoted to the *mathematical description* of *motion* through the various methods of *curve theory,* supplied by analytical and differential geometry. Ideally, there would be no distinction between the curves of the solutions derived from the governing functions and the curves investigated in kinematics. But, unfortunately, the difficulties of obtaining the (*history, phase*) curve system belonging to the general solution of nonlinear dynamic systems creates the opportunity and need for some *exploratory* kinematic studies of the properties of many conceivable curve systems. In fact, the governing functions have, in many cases, been suggested by *tentative* kinematic investigations rather than being first established from factual, fundamental principles (laws).

Furthermore, factual research in dynamics will often desist from finding the most general solution of the basic dynamic differential equations. Rather, forsaking kinematics altogether, attention is restricted to only deriving—as in (28.84)—and then studying the *configurations* (portrait, picture) of the *trajectories* (loci) *consistent* with these *basic dynamic* differential *equations of motions.* The latter, interpreted *geometrically* as *vector fields,* cf. (28.78), is obviously not tied to adopting particular coordinate systems.

Now, as any representation of curves always requires the choice of some *coordinate* system—rectangular, polar, or whatever coordinates that are appropriate in the specific context—we may elaborate a bit on the concept of *curve* in space, the *mode* of its mathematical *representation,* and the mathematical *information* conveyed by typical curve representations.

The *simplest* notion of a curve is given by the *graph* for a *function* (vector function) of a *scalar* variable. Such a curve is always *represented* by an *explicit equation* between the dependent coordinate variable(s) and the independent variable (scalar). A curve so represented must not be intersected at more than one point by any line perpendicular to the axis of the independent variable. For such simple curve representation—when units of the axes are fixed—its intrinsic information content is fully conveyed by the elementary notion of geometric *shape.*

Therefore, the *geometric shape* of the *history curves* (28.5) aptly contains *all* the mathematical *information* about the *evolution* of dynamic $C^1$-class systems. The actual value of the *degree* of *homogeneity,* $m \in \mathbf{R}$, evidently affects the *shape* of the history curve $\Gamma$, (28.5), (28.38.1–2), cf. (28.34–28.37). Mathematically, motion or evolution is nothing but a *correspondence* between the *time scale* and *coordinates* (positions, states). This correspondence is expressed by a graph of an explicit function (however complicated), and so the *history curve* demands only the simplest possible representation of a curve. It is indeed grievous that the system of *history curves*—despite their existence and uniqueness—has been so difficult to derive from the corresponding dynamic differential equations. But without the history curves (describing the past, present, and future time path of the coordinates), one can only give some partial information about the motion (behavior) of the underlying dynamic system. As already mentioned, such *partial* information is conveyed by the *geometry* of the system of trajectories.

Generally, the *trajectories* cannot be described as graphs of functions; usually, their graph must be represented *implicitly* by an equation in the coordinate variables, e.g., for plane curves in rectangular coordinates as $\ell(x, y) = 0$, which now involves a function $\ell$ of two independent variables. Although more *flexibility* (a larger class of curves) is admitted by an implicit representation, it has a disadvantage that to acquire the points $(x, y)$ of the curve, one must actually solve the equation $\ell(x, y) = 0$ by some cumbersome calculations. However, as a *locus* (point set), the equation $\ell(x, y) = 0$ itself expresses some *global, geometric* property, i.e., a property true of the curve at every point on it. Also, the equation contains implicitly every property of the curve, and any particular property can be deduced from it by ordinary *algebra* (analytic geometry), without troubling about the possible complicated geometry of the actual curve form (unnamed picture). Therefore, the *trajectory equations,* (28.8), (28.39), certainly have merits of their own, especially, in studies of the *structural stability* of the phase portrait or *bifurcation* theory, see Arnold (1986, 1988), Casti (1979), Hirsch and Smale (1974), Shub (1987), Thom (1989) and Wiggins (1988).

As is well known from the theory of plane curves, an important kind of such a curve system arises when the curves do *not intersect* each other; then one and only one curve of the system passes through each point of the relevant part of the plane. Therefore, the function $\ell(x, y)$ can be written in the form:

$$\ell(x, y) = \ell^*(x, y) - k_0, \tag{28.89}$$

where $\ell^*$ has a stipulated form. The curve $\ell(x, y) = 0$, passing through $(x_0, y_0)$, is defined by $k_0 = \ell^*(x_0, y_0)$. Thus, each *point* $(x_0, y_0)$ or, equivalently, each *curve,* $\ell(x, y) = 0$, is associated with *one* and *only one* value of the *additive parameter* $k_0$. The system of *trajectories* for the autonomous differential equations (28.1.1–2) is of this type, (28.89), cf. (28.8), (28.39).

The geometric *similarity* of the *trajectories* of *homogeneous* dynamics, (28.1.1–28.3)—or equivalently, the *integral* curves of (28.84), cf. Remark 28.10—is easily verified, since there is clearly a choice of a constant $K$ such that the substitution $x \to Kx,\ y \to Ky$, carries the curve, $\ln x = H(y/x)$, into any given curve of the system (28.44), (28.39). In fact, multiplication along a ray corresponds to the addition of $\ln K$ to the parameter $k_0$. Incidentally, we may note that the *shape* of the *trajectories,* (28.39), (28.44), will normally be affected by the actual value $m \in \mathbf{R}$, since usually $m$ is involved in $H(r)$, cf. (28.25), (28.15). However, for some specifications of $f$ and $g$ (28.12.1–3), it may happen that (28.25) is independent of $m$, and accordingly, the *trajectories* (plane loci) are *invariant* to changes of $m \in \mathbf{R}$; then the value of $m$ only affects the *speed* of *motion* along the trajectories.

In curve theory, the most handy computational description of a curve is traditionally considered to be the *parametric representation.* For plane curves and a given coordinate system, both coordinates of the curve points are now functions of a third *independent* (auxiliary) variable $t$, a so-called *parameter, traversing* an *interval.* In the geometric investigation of such a curve with a parametric representation—called an arc (oriented curve)—it is sometimes convenient to emphasize only the *ordering* of the points. Thus, another parameterization by replacing $t$ with a *homeomorphism* (bijective, bicontinuous mapping), $t = \chi(u)$, is said to determine the same arc; the latter is accordingly the image of the *topological* mapping of an interval. For such a mapping into the plane, the individual coordinates of the arc points are always arranged in the same order as on a real straight line.

It has been apparent throughout our exposition and indeed from the very beginning, cf. (28.6–28.8), that geometrically, a trajectory may formally be represented in many ways, equationally and parametrically, in accordance with the chosen geometric tools from either *analytic* or *differential* geometry. The latter discipline often employs concepts and tools (curvature, torsion, rectification) that are *invariant* to the choice of admissible parameters. However, for any curve of *kinematics*, there is evidently no question of preferring and choosing among alternative parametric representations, since the parameter $t$ must denote the *time* variable, and the curve itself (outlining the *motion* of a point) is nothing else than the *phase curve* (28.6). Clearly, the phase curves have the exclusive privilege—among the topological equivalent (homeomorphic) parametric representations of the trajectories—of representing *solutions* of the dynamic system, i.e., no *phase curves* without the *history curves* and vice versa, cf. (28.5–28.6). Instead of history and phase curves, the term *paths*, respectively, time paths and phase paths, are occasionally used in kinematics to emphasize that *time* is definitely involved in the determination of the *curve points*, either as the independent variable or as the auxiliary variable (parameter).

It now behooves us to offer—on the background of our approach to homogeneous dynamics above—a new perspective on *prior* methodological developments and *precedents* in the literature, so that the *rationale* behind the new results—stated in Theorems 28.1–28.2, with corollaries—may be better recognized. Besides, familiarity with the essentials of Theorems 28.1–28.2 is needed for our *second stage*: the stability analysis in sections "The Stability Properties of Ratio Solutions and The Stability Properties of Coordinate Solutions".

## Miscellanea on Homogeneous Differential Equations

The literature comments below primarily intend to offer a *systematic* briefing of earlier contributions to our subject matter; we also take the opportunity to unify these diverse older elements into an alternative proof of Theorems 28.1–28.2. The counterpart of the latter in polar coordinates will be given as well. Finally, the connection between the degree of homogeneity and the time interval for the solutions is rigorously demonstrated.

### *Literature Comment 1*

In a retrospective review, we first look at the "classical" approach of devising solution methods by quadratures (primitives) for the ordinary first-order differential equation, $dy/dx = q(y/x)$, cf. (28.84), which is traditionally called a *homogeneous differential equation*, when the right-hand side is homogeneous of degree *zero* in the variables $x$ and $y$. This equation is often written in the *differential form*,

$$X(x, y)dx + Y(x, y)dy = 0, \tag{28.90}$$

with $X = G$ , $Y = -F$, satisfying (28.1.1–28.3). In this more symmetric form, the equation is homogeneous of degree $m$, but the degree of (28.90) can be changed arbitrarily, e.g., to degree zero, by an *integrating factor.* See references Bieberbach (1923, p. 8), Boole (1959, p. 75), Collatz (1966, p. 18), Ince (1956, p. 18), Kaplan (1967, p. 39–40), Kneschke (1956, p. 74), Murphy (1960, p. 34–35), Petrovski (1966, p. 17).

Suppose that the *real function* $q$ is defined and only *continuous* on a **domain** (strip, angular section) $\boldsymbol{E}$ in the *punctured* plane, i.e.,

$$dy/dx = q(y/x), \qquad q \in C^0\text{-class on } E, \tag{28.91.1}$$

$$E = \{(x, y) \in \mathbf{R}^2 \setminus \{(0, 0)\} \mid b_1 < y/x < b_2\}. \tag{28.91.2}$$

As to obtaining the solutions (integral curves) of (28.91.1–2), it was natural to make the *substitution* (change of variables)—sometimes called the Briot-Bouquet transformation (Nemytskii and Stepanov 1989, p. 101).

$$y(x)/x = r(x) \quad \therefore \quad y = rx, \quad dy/dx = r + xdr/dx. \tag{28.92}$$

Really, this device in solving (28.91.1–2) was used already in 1691 by *Leibniz*, cf. Ince (1956, p. 18, p. 530). Note that hereby the *ratio,* (28.10), is introduced as a new variable. By (28.92), (28.91.1), we have the new differential equation

$$r + x\,dr/dx = q(r); \quad dr/dx = x^{-1}[q(r) - r], \quad r \in\, ]b_1, b_2[. \tag{28.93}$$

Now it is immediately seen that a *separation* of the variables—also performed by Leibniz, Bernoulli, see Ince (1956, p. 531)—leads to the goal

$$\ln x = \int dx/x = \int \frac{dr}{q(r) - r} = L(r) + k, \quad r \in\, ]b_1, b_2[, \tag{28.94}$$

where $L(r)$ by (28.91.1) clearly *exists* as a *primitive* of the function: $1/[q(r) - r]$.

However, if the denominator in (28.94), $q(r) - r$, *vanishes* only at *finitely* many values, $r = \alpha_i$, $i = 1, \ldots, n$, in the open interval, $]b_1, b_2[$, then as easily seen by (28.93), the solutions (integral curves),

$$r = \alpha_i, \quad \therefore \quad y = \alpha_i x, \quad \alpha_i, \quad i = 1, \ldots, n, \quad r \in\, ]b_1, b_2[ \tag{28.95}$$

must be added to those from (28.94).

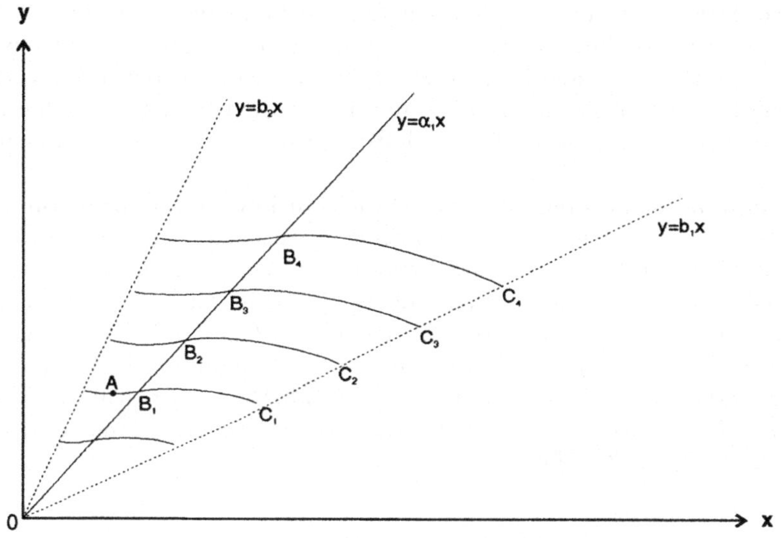


**Fig. 28.1** Integral curves (trajectories) to (28.91.1–28.91.2), $q \in C^0$-class

When it is only assumed that $q \in C^0$-class, then *several* solutions (integral curves) may pass through the *same* point $(x_0, y_0) \in E$, if the last integral expression of (28.94) *converges* as $r$ approaches one of the numbers $\alpha_i \in \mathcal{A}$, say $\alpha_j$. In this case, the behavior of the system of integral curves is shown schematically in Fig. 28.1. Here the curves $AB_1C_1$, $AB_1B_2C_2$, $AB_1B_3C_3$, etc., pass through the same point $A = (x_0, y_0)$, and they are all tangent to the ray $y = \alpha_1 x$, i.e., $B_1, B_2, B_3, B_4$ are inflection points of the respective integral curves.

In Fig. 28.1, however, if $q \in C^1$-class, then it is clear, as mentioned above in Remark 28.10, that the *particular* ray solution (integral curve), $y = \alpha_i x$, solving (28.90), *cannot* coincide anywhere with maximal solutions (consolidated integral curves) *emanating* on *either* side of this ray, as such points, e.g., $A$, obviously do not belong to the domain of the maximal ray solution. Thus, trajectories such as $AB_1C_1$ and $AB_1B_2C_2$ are ruled out by the assumption: $q \in C^1$-class; cf. Lemma 28.1, which showed that $L(r) = H(r)$, (28.96), had no limit as $r \to \alpha_i$.

Having now disposed of the *uniqueness* problem for maximal solutions, we turn to another historically troublesome *complication* for a rigorous treatment of (28.90), namely, the actual *extension* of the natural ***domain E*** for the *governing* function, $q(y/x)$, as well as the relevant *interval of definition* for the *primitive* $L(r)$, (28.94). Both problems are obviously important for an adequate investigation of the complete set (family) of solutions (system of integral curves).

The *strip* (domain), as traditionally and preliminarily stated in (28.91.2), is of no particular interest. However, the issue of the extension of a natural domain for the governing function $q(y/x)$ is now easily resolved. Since $q(y/x)$ is homogeneous of *degree zero,* it follows from Remark 28.1 that the entire punctured Euclidean plane, $\mathbf{R}^2 \setminus \{(0, 0)\}$, constitutes the natural domain for $q(y/x)$.

Regarding the possible extension of the actual interval of definition for the primitive $L(r)$, (28.94), it will be immediately realized from our exposition in section "" that a decomposition/partition analysis of the punctured plane by the roots of $q(r) - r$ would correspond exactly to the analysis conducted by the roots of the *director function* $\boldsymbol{h}(\boldsymbol{r})$, (28.15), cf. (28.69). Thus, depending on the location of the initial values, the relevant interval of definition for $L(r)$, (28.94), is a *maximal open* interval belonging to $\complement\mathcal{A}$ (28.18), rather than the arbitrary *interval* $]b_1, b_2[$; the latter may have the *nuisance* property of including a root value, $\alpha_i \in \mathcal{A}$, cf. (28.94).

### *The Quintessence of Theorems 28.1–28.2*

The discussion of the *classical homogeneous non-dynamic* differential equation, cf. (28.91.1–2), will now—together with the heuristics on geometry above—be linked up with Theorems 28.1–28.2 on *homogeneous dynamics.* The linkage consists essentially of two steps or rather is implemented by a *two-stage procedure.*

*First*—although the proof of Theorem 28.1 proceeded differently—we might have started "geometrically" by deducing the *trajectories* (loci), (28.39), outright from the "*classical*" equation (28.91.1–2), when $q$ is further *sharpened* with a *modern uniqueness* condition (here $C^1$-class) and when $q$ is also properly *supplemented,* as in our Basic framework above, with a rigorous *decomposition/partition* analysis (28.17–28.21) of the entire *domain/interval* of the *family* of solutions. Such an *alternative* procedure would have established (28.44), which is the same as (28.94), since, cf. (28.25), (28.84)

$$L(r) = H(r)\,, \text{ with } q = g/f. \tag{28.96}$$

Also, the additional ray trajectories, (28.62), (28.95), follow in the analytic case immediately, cf. Remark 28.3, as integral curves (straight lines) from (28.93–28.94).

The *primitive* (quadrature expression) for the *trajectories,* (28.39) or (28.44), is *almost available* in the literature, although in somewhat disguised form as an integration of a parametric representation but without emphasizing the relevant limits of integration (see, e.g., Sansone and Conti 1964, p. 49).

But surprisingly, the *autonomous homogeneous dynamic* system, (28.1.1–28.3), and its *solutions* by a *quadrature expression* have—as far as we are aware of the literature—*not* been *obtained* and seemingly have eluded all endeavors, despite serious and numerous attempts in the last century.

*Secondly*—and considered as the *fundamental* step—our procedure of obtaining the *solutions* $\boldsymbol{\varphi}(\boldsymbol{t})$, (28.38.1–2), (28.62), may be construed as simply using the *time derivative* of the basic *ratio* variable $\boldsymbol{r}$ (28.10) in *combination* with the classical quadrature expression for the *trajectories* in terms of the *same* "*parameter*" $r$, cf. (28.94–28.96). This combination gives for $\boldsymbol{r}$ the *autonomous* differential equation, (28.34), which now holds the *key* to unlocking homogeneous plane *dynamics*; the *ratio solution* $\boldsymbol{\rho}(\boldsymbol{t})$ is obtained by an additional, invertible quadrature, (28.36–28.37). Next, a *reparameterization* of the trajectories (28.94–28.95) in the *kinematic parameter* $\boldsymbol{t}$ (dynamic, independent variable, time)—through $\boldsymbol{\rho}(\boldsymbol{t})$—gives the *phase curves* $\varphi(t)$, (28.38.1–2), (28.62–28.65.3), which also then constitute the final *quadrature* expression for the *coordinate solution* $\boldsymbol{\varphi}(\boldsymbol{t})$, (28.4), (28.6), of the original *dynamic* system, (28.1.1–28.3).

Hence, *recapitulating* and retracing the steps, we have

$$\begin{aligned}(x, y) &= (x, rx) = k_0[\exp\{H(r)\}, r\exp\{H(r)\}]\\ &= k_0[\exp\{H[\rho(t)]\}, \rho(t)\exp\{H[\rho(t)]\}]\\ &= k_0[\exp\{H[I^{-1}(t+t_0)]\}, I^{-1}(t+t_0)\exp\{H[I^{-1}(t+t_0)]\}]\\ &= [\varphi_1(t), \varphi_2(t)].\end{aligned} \tag{28.97}$$

## *Literature Comment 2*

The literature, dealing with general aspects as well as numerous case studies of the *autonomous* dynamic system, (28.1.1–28.2.2), does occasionally show partial treatment of the *homogeneous* system, (28.1.1–28.3). This material is now included in standard textbooks. We briefly review also this work as a complement to our earlier sections–and the literature comment above.

The *homogeneity* properties (28.3) played a subsidiary role—*mostly*, $m \in \mathbf{N}$—in the research memoirs of Poincaré (Poincaré 1928, p. 19) and Bendixson (Bendixson 1901, p. 31), but their works initiated subsequent investigations (see Forster 1938; Mises 1939) on *homogeneous* plane systems that actually appeared as the *truncated* part (in perturbation studies) of holomorphic differential equations. In particular, we shall here follow and examine a long tradition of introducing *polar coordinates* for the variables of homogeneous differential equations.

Let $(\boldsymbol{\eta}, \boldsymbol{\vartheta})$ be plane *polar* coordinates with the pole at the *origin* of $(\boldsymbol{x}, \boldsymbol{y})$, i.e.,

$$x = \eta\cos\vartheta,\ \ y = \eta\sin\vartheta;\ \ r = y/x = \tan\vartheta,\ \ \sqrt{x^2+y^2} = \eta. \tag{28.98}$$

Then, changing the system (28.1.1–28.3) into polar form, we have for the *elongation* and *angular* velocities, cf. Sansone and Conti (1964, pp. 50), Nemytskii and Stepanov (1989, pp. 82),

$$\dot{\eta} = \dot{x}\cos\vartheta + \dot{y}\sin\vartheta \qquad = \eta^m Z(\vartheta), \tag{28.99.1}$$

$$\dot{\vartheta} = [-\dot{x}\sin\vartheta + \dot{y}\cos\vartheta]/\eta = \eta^{m-1}N(\vartheta), \tag{28.99.2}$$

where $Z$ and $N$ are the periodic functions,

$$Z(\vartheta) = F(\cos\vartheta, \sin\vartheta)\cos\vartheta + G(\cos\vartheta, \sin\vartheta)\sin\vartheta, \tag{28.99.3}$$

$$N(\vartheta) = -F(\cos\vartheta, \sin\vartheta)\sin\vartheta + G(\cos\vartheta, \sin\vartheta)\cos\vartheta. \tag{28.99.4}$$

For the system (28.99.1–4), assumption (28.2.1–2) again ensures the existence and the uniqueness everywhere of a *solution* $\boldsymbol{\zeta}$ (vector polar function), defined on an interval $T$

$$\zeta(t) = [\eta = \zeta_1(t),\ \vartheta = \zeta_2(t)], \quad t \in T. \tag{28.100}$$

By (28.100), we have an *alternative* coordinate representation of the *same history* curve $\Gamma$, (28.5), and *trajectory,* $\Phi$, (28.7–28.8), as provided by the Cartesian coordinate solution $\boldsymbol{\varphi}(\boldsymbol{t})$, (28.6). But as was the case for $\varphi(t)$, *no* quadrature expression has *yet* been offered for the dynamic *polar solution* (28.100). We shall now derive the complete set of solutions to the polar differential equations, (28.99.1–4). In doing so, we basically follow the *two-stage* procedure explained above.

Every *trajectory* from (28.99.1–4) will be given as a solution (integral curve) of the differential equation, cf. (28.83–28.84).

$$\frac{d\eta}{d\vartheta} = \frac{\dot{\eta}}{\dot{\vartheta}} = \eta \cdot \frac{Z(\vartheta)}{N(\vartheta)}, \quad N(\vartheta) \neq 0. \tag{28.101}$$

Hence we get, by *separation* of variables,

$$\ln\eta = \int \frac{d\eta}{\eta} = \int \frac{Z(\vartheta)}{N(\vartheta)} d\vartheta = \mathcal{H}(\vartheta) + \mathcal{K} \tag{28.102}$$

or

$$\eta = \mathcal{L}(\vartheta) = \mathcal{K}_0 \exp\{\mathcal{H}(\vartheta)\} \ \text{with}\ \mathcal{K}_0 = \eta_0 \exp\{-\mathcal{H}(\vartheta_0)\}, \tag{28.103}$$

where the primitive $\mathcal{H}(\vartheta)$ *exists* by the fundamental theorem of calculus and is *unique* as $N, Z \in C^1$-class. Also, from (28.101), it is easily seen that if $N(\vartheta)$ *vanishes* at angular values in the interval $[0, 2\pi]$, then *straight line* trajectories must be added to those of (28.103) to establish the complete set of trajectories, cf. (28.94–28.96) and (28.106).

Evidently, the *function* $N(\vartheta)$ and the *real* roots of the equation, $N(\vartheta) = 0$, are cast for similar roles as our *director function* $h(r)$ and the director roots, cf. Definition 28.1. Hence an analogous *decomposition/partition* analysis, cf. (28.18), can be performed with the *root set* $\Theta$:

$$\Theta = \{\theta \in \mathbf{R} \mid N(\theta) = 0\}, \quad \complement\Theta = \{\theta \in \mathbf{R} \mid N(\theta) \neq 0\}. \tag{28.104}$$

The companion of the *cones* (28.19) is given by *open* rectangular *half-strips*

$$C = \left\{(\eta, \vartheta) \in \mathbf{R}^2 \mid \eta > 0,\ \underline{\theta} < \vartheta < \bar{\theta}\right\}, \quad ]\underline{\theta}, \bar{\theta}[ \subseteq \complement\Theta, \quad \underline{\theta}, \bar{\theta} \in \Theta. \tag{28.105}$$

Analogously, for the *directrices* (28.22) one gets the *lines* (horizontals)

$$\mathcal{R}_\theta = \left\{(\eta, \vartheta) \in \mathbf{R}^2 \mid \eta > 0,\ \vartheta = \theta\right\}, \quad \theta \in \Theta. \tag{28.106}$$

Next, it is now easy—recalling the *quintessence* of Theorems 28.1–28.2 and here the second step—to establish the *quadrature* expression for the dynamic polar *solution*, (28.100). By (28.99.2), (28.102–28.103), we obtain in every strip, $C$, (28.105), the *autonomous* differential equation, $Q \in C^1$-class,

$$\dot{\vartheta} = Q(\vartheta) = [\mathcal{K}_0 \exp\{\mathcal{H}(\vartheta)\}]^{m-1} N(\vartheta), \quad \vartheta \in ]\underline{\theta}, \bar{\theta}[ \subseteq \complement\Theta, \ (\eta_0, \vartheta_0) \in C, \tag{28.107}$$

which must be solved by every *angular* coordinate *solution* $\boldsymbol{\zeta}_2(\boldsymbol{t})$.

The *general* solution of (28.107) becomes, cf. (28.36–28.37),

$$\begin{aligned} &\zeta_2(t) = \mathcal{I}^{-1}(t + t_0^*), \quad \zeta_2(t) \in ]\underline{\theta}, \bar{\theta}[ \subseteq \complement\Theta, \\ &t + t_0^* \in T = \mathcal{I}(]\underline{\theta}, \bar{\theta}[) = ]\underline{t}, \bar{t}[, \end{aligned} \tag{28.108}$$

where the invertible primitive function $\mathcal{I} \in C^2$-class is given as

$$\begin{aligned} \mathcal{I}(\vartheta) = \int d\vartheta / Q(\vartheta), \quad &\vartheta \in ]\underline{\theta}, \bar{\theta}[ \subseteq \complement\Theta, \\ &t + t_0^* \in T = \mathcal{I}(]\underline{\theta}, \bar{\theta}[) = ]\underline{t}, \bar{t}[. \end{aligned} \tag{28.109}$$

The *invertibility* of $\mathcal{I}(\vartheta)$ and hence the *monotonicity* of $\boldsymbol{\zeta}_2(\boldsymbol{t})$, (28.108), are due to $N(\vartheta)$ and $Q(\vartheta)$ *preserving* their *signs* on each *maximal* interval, $]\underline{\theta}, \bar{\theta}[ \subseteq \complement\Theta$.

The *elongation* (distance) *coordinate* solution $\zeta_1(t)$ is immediately obtained from the *kinematic reparameterization*—through (28.108)—of the trajectories, (28.103). Hence, together we have the *polar solutions*

$$\eta = \zeta_1(t) = \mathcal{K}_0 \exp\{\mathcal{H}[\zeta_2(t)]\}, \tag{28.110.1}$$

$$\vartheta = \zeta_2(t) = \mathcal{I}^{-1}(t + t_0^*). \tag{28.110.2}$$

Thus, in the strips (28.105), we have established by (28.110.1–2) the *polar counterpart,* $\zeta(t)$, to the Cartesian coordinate *solutions,* $\varphi(t)$, given in Theorem 28.1.

As to the *directrix solutions* of Theorem 28.2, the *polar counterpart* is easily—using (28.106) and then by (28.99.1), solving $\dot{\eta} = \eta^m Z(\theta)$—seen to be, cf. (28.66),

$$\text{Case 1. Stationary, } m \in \mathbf{R}, \quad Z(\theta) = 0; \quad \eta = \zeta_1(t) = \eta_0, \tag{28.111}$$

$$\text{Case 2. Increasing, decreasing } Z(\theta) > 0, \quad Z(\theta) < 0, \tag{28.112}$$

$$\text{(i)} \quad m = 1. \quad \eta = \zeta_1(t) = \mathcal{K}_0 \exp\{Z(\theta)t\}, \tag{28.113.1}$$

$$\text{(ii)} \quad m < 1. \quad \eta = \zeta_1(t) = [\mathcal{K}_0^{1-m} + (1-m)Z(\theta)t]^{\frac{1}{1-m}}, \tag{28.113.2}$$

$$\text{(iii)} \quad m > 1. \quad \eta = \zeta_1(t) = 1/[\mathcal{K}_0^{1-m} - (m-1)Z(\theta)t]^{\frac{1}{m-1}}, \tag{28.113.3}$$

$$\text{(1–2):} \quad m \in \mathbf{R} \quad \vartheta = \zeta_2(t) = \theta, \quad \forall t, \quad \theta \in \Theta. \tag{28.114}$$

**Definition 28.8** In the same capacity as $\boldsymbol{f(\alpha)}$, (28.24), (28.63–28.64), we employ, cf. (28.111–28.113.3)

$$\textit{directrix value}: \quad Z(\theta), \quad \theta \in \Theta. \tag{28.115}$$

The literature often adduces the introduction of *polar* coordinates as an expedient *tool* for obtaining the solutions of particular planar autonomous (especially homogeneous) dynamic systems. As to the special circumstances for having *closed-form* coordinate solutions, it is not possible to advance a priori judgment about the expediency of either coordinate system. For example, the question of which *invertible primitive*—$I$, (28.37), or $\mathcal{I}$, (28.109)—is most amenable to allow closed-form expressions [for certain specifications of the governing functions $F$ and $G$, cf. (28.1.1–2), (28.99.1–4)] has no general answer. Sometimes, integration operations leading to a closed-form primitive for $I$ are easier than the integration techniques for $\mathcal{I}$ and vice versa. In short, the *polar* coordinate version of homogeneous dynamics should *not, in general,* be deemed the most convenient approach for either solving the system (28.1.1–28.3) in closed form or generally solving it in terms of well-defined primitives. At any rate, the *polar solutions* (28.110.1–28.115) for the system (28.99.1–4) seem to have not been given and, to our knowledge, are *not available* in the literature.

The literature on *dynamic nonlinear homogeneous* differential equations has in various ways essentially been devoted to studying the *geometry* of the resultant *trajectories,* i.e., attention is confined to describing the behavior of the trajectories, (28.103), and the "ray trajectories", (28.106). The latter, our *directrices,* are noted as *invariant rays, integral rays, invariant radii,* see Sansone and Conti (1964, p. 51), Nemytskii and Stepanov (1989, p. 83), Birkhoff and Rota (1989, p. 19). Furthermore, much effort was expended on describing the geometric properties near the *origin* or in the *neighborhood* (strips, angular sections) of the invariant trajectories. For an elaborate configuration analysis of the trajectories in this way, see Sansone and Conti (1964, p. 53–63), Nemytskii and Stepanov (1989, p. 82–88). As to some simple (but often helpful) criteria for outlining the main disposition of the trajectories, see section "Asymptotic Ratio Stability and Trajectory Geometry".

In looking back, a fundamental deficiency and paradox must be noted: *geometric analysis* (often by topological methods) of *trajectories* is pursued partly as a substitute for a genuine *stability investigation* (*sensitivity* analyses with respect to the initial conditions) of the *dynamic systems.* Of course, the paradox is resolved—but not the deficiency—by recognizing the difficulties and the stalemate experienced in the many attempts to obtain the general solution in *nonlinear* dynamics.

### *On Solutions and Their Maximal Time Interval of Existence*

Regarding the time interval of definition $T$, (28.4), for the solutions of planar homogeneous dynamics, it was seen in Theorem 28.2 that the degree of homogeneity $\boldsymbol{m} \gtreqless 1$ was crucial for the extent of $T \subseteq \mathbf{R}$. For the non-directrix solutions of Theorem 28.1, it was also mentioned that $T$ could be either finite of infinite. However, for the general solution of (28.1.1–28.3), the linkage between the *maximal time interval* $T$ and the degree of homogeneity needs here to be rigorously established.

**Theorem 28.3** *Any maximal phase curve,* $\varphi(t)$ *(28.6), with corresponding trajectory* $\Phi$ *(28.7) tending toward infinity, satisfies:*

*(i) If* $m \leq 1$*, then* $\Phi$ *reaches infinity in infinite time.*
*(ii) If* $m > 1$*, then* $\Phi$ *reaches infinity in finite time.*

**Corollary 28.2** *Any maximal phase curve,* $\varphi(t)$ *(28.6), with corresponding trajectory* $\Phi$*, (28.7), tending toward* $(0, 0)$*, satisfies:*

*(i) If* $m \geq 1$*, then* $\Phi$ *reaches* $(0, 0)$ *in infinite time.*
*(ii) If* $m < 1$*, then* $\Phi$ *reaches* $(0, 0)$ *in finite time.*

***Proof*** The *polar* coordinate form (28.99.1–4) will be *convenient* in providing the proofs of Theorem 28.3 and Corollary 28.2.

ad (i), $m < 1$. From (28.99.1), we get

$$\eta^{-m}\frac{d\eta}{dt} = Z(\vartheta) \quad \Leftrightarrow \quad \frac{d(\eta^{1-m})}{dt} = (1-m)Z(\vartheta). \tag{28.116}$$

The continuous and periodic function $Z(\vartheta)$ is bounded above, i.e.,

$$Z(\vartheta) \leq B > 0, \quad \forall \vartheta \in \mathbf{R}. \tag{28.117}$$

Next, consider the solution (28.100) with the *initial* values, $(t, \eta, \vartheta) = (0, \eta_0, \vartheta_0)$, and assume that the corresponding trajectory $\Phi$, (28.7), cf. (28.98), tends to infinity.

Then for $t > 0$, we get from (28.116–28.117)

$$\frac{d(\eta^{1-m})}{dt} \leq (1-m)B \quad \Leftrightarrow \quad \eta^{1-m} - \eta_0^{1-m} \leq (1-m)Bt,$$

i.e.,

$$\eta(t) \leq \left[\eta_0^{1-m} + (1-m)Bt\right]^{\frac{1}{1-m}}. \tag{28.118}$$

Thus by (28.118) the elongation $\eta(t)$ is bounded along the trajectory $\Phi$ for any finite, positive $t$; hence $\Phi$ cannot reach infinity in finite time, which proves (i) for $m < 1$.

ad (i), $m = 1$. From (28.99.1) and (28.117), we get

$$\frac{d\eta}{dt} = \eta Z(\vartheta) \leq B\eta \quad \Leftrightarrow \quad \ln\frac{\eta(t)}{\eta_0} \leq Bt \quad \Leftrightarrow \quad \eta(t) \leq \eta_0 e^{Bt}. \tag{28.119}$$

Thus, by (28.119) the elongation $\eta(t)$ is again bounded along the trajectory $\Phi$ for any *finite*, positive $t$. Hence this implies/proves (i) for $m = 1$.

ad (ii), $m > 1$. For all $\vartheta$ with $N(\vartheta) \neq 0$, every trajectory $\Phi$ from (28.99.1–4) passing through the point $(\eta, \vartheta) = (\eta_0, \vartheta_0)$ satisfies, cf. (28.101–28.103),

$$\eta = \eta_0 \exp\left\{\int_{\vartheta_0}^{\vartheta} \frac{Z(\xi)}{N(\xi)} d\xi\right\}. \tag{28.120}$$

We divide the rest of the discussion in two cases:

Case I: The root set $\Theta$, (28.104), is empty.

Then (28.120) holds for all $\vartheta \in \mathbf{R}$, and for the polar solution (28.100) with initial values $(t, \eta, \vartheta) = (0, \eta_0, \vartheta_0)$, we have by inserting (28.120) into (28.99.2), cf. (28.107)

$$\frac{d\vartheta}{dt} = \eta_0^{m-1} \exp\left\{(m-1)\int_{\vartheta_0}^{\vartheta} \frac{Z(\xi)}{N(\xi)} d\xi \, N(\vartheta)\right\}. \tag{28.121}$$

Assume that the corresponding trajectory $\Phi$ tends to infinity. Then $\int_0^{2\pi} \frac{Z(\xi)}{N(\xi)} d\xi \neq 0$; otherwise $\Phi$ would be a closed curve and the phase portrait a center.

If $\int_0^{2\pi} \frac{Z(\xi)}{N(\xi)} d\xi > 0$, then by (28.120) the *elongation* $\eta \to \infty$ as $\vartheta \to \infty$. The latter and (28.121) then imply $N(\vartheta) > 0$. On the other hand, if $\int_0^{2\pi} \frac{Z(\xi)}{N(\xi)} d\xi < 0$, then $\eta \to \infty$ as $\vartheta \to -\infty$. The latter and (28.121) then imply $N(\vartheta) < 0$.

Henceforth, without loss of generality, we may assume

$$A = \int_0^{2\pi} \frac{Z(\xi)}{N(\xi)} d\xi > 0 \quad \text{and} \quad N(\vartheta) > 0. \tag{28.122}$$

By separation of variables in (28.121), we get

$$t(\vartheta) = \eta_0^{1-m} \int_{\vartheta_0}^{\vartheta} \exp\{(1-m)\int_{\vartheta_0}^{\chi} \frac{Z(\xi)}{N(\xi)} d\xi\} \frac{1}{N(\chi)} d\chi. \tag{28.123}$$

Since $A > 0$, we have

$$\exp\left\{(1-m)\int_{\vartheta_0}^{\chi} \frac{Z(\xi)}{N(\xi)} d\xi\right\} \leq \exp\left\{(1-m)A\left\lfloor \frac{\chi - \vartheta_0}{2\pi} \right\rfloor\right\} C, \tag{28.124.1}$$

where $\lfloor \frac{\chi-\vartheta_0}{2\pi} \rfloor$ denotes the integer part of $\frac{\chi-\vartheta_0}{2\pi}$ and

$$C = \max\left[\exp\{(1-m)\int_0^{v} \frac{Z(\xi)}{N(\xi)} d\xi\} \mid v \in [0, 2\pi]\right] \tag{28.124.2}$$

Let $\delta > 0$ be the minimal value of $N(\xi)$. Then from (28.123–28.124.1) and $1/N(\chi) < 1/\delta$, we have

$$t(\vartheta) \leq \frac{C\eta_0^{1-m}}{\delta} \int_{\vartheta_0}^{\vartheta} \exp\left\{(1-m)A\left\lfloor \frac{\chi - \vartheta_0}{2\pi} \right\rfloor\right\} d\chi. \tag{28.125}$$

With $1 - m < 0$, this integral converges as $\vartheta \to \infty$. Hence $\vartheta(t)$ reaches *infinity* in *finite time*, and so do $\eta(t)$, (28.120), and $\Phi$.

Case II: The root set $\Theta$, (28.104), contains one or several roots.

As before, let $(\eta_0, \vartheta_0)$ be the initial values of the polar solution (28.100) at $t = 0$.

If $\vartheta_0 \in \Theta$, (28.104), then $\vartheta(t) = \vartheta_0 = \Theta$ along the entire trajectory, cf. (28.99.2), (28.114). Furthermore, if the trajectory $\Phi$ tends to infinity, we must have $Z(\vartheta_0) > 0$, cf. (28.112), (28.115), and with $m > 1$ it follows from (28.113.3) that the *elongation* $\eta(t)$ becomes *infinite* in *finite* time. The latter proves (ii) for $\vartheta_0 \in \Theta$.

If $\vartheta_0 \in \complement\Theta$, (28.104), there exists an interval $]\underline{\theta}, \overline{\theta}[$ such that $\vartheta_0 \in ]\underline{\theta}, \overline{\theta}[$, $N(\underline{\theta}) = N(\overline{\theta}) = 0$, and $N(\vartheta)$ has constant sign for all $\vartheta \in ]\underline{\theta}, \overline{\theta}[$. Say positive. For all $\vartheta \in ]\underline{\theta}, \overline{\theta}[$, Eq. (28.120) holds.

Assume again that $\Phi$ tends to infinity. In any closed subinterval $J \in ]\underline{\theta}, \overline{\theta}[$, the function $\frac{Z(\vartheta)}{N(\vartheta)}$ is continuous, and hence the r.h.s. in (28.120) is bounded. Thus $\Phi$ is not maximal for $\vartheta \in J$, and hence $\Phi$ is defined for all $\vartheta \in ]\underline{\theta}, \overline{\theta}[$.

Since $N(\overline{\theta}) = 0$, we have $Z(\overline{\theta}) \neq 0$. From (28.120) and the fact that $\Phi$ tends to infinity, it follows that $Z(\overline{\theta}) > 0$. Choose $\varepsilon > 0$, such that

$$Z(\vartheta) \geq \frac{1}{2} Z(\overline{\theta}) \qquad \forall \vartheta \in [\overline{\theta} - \varepsilon, \overline{\theta}[. \tag{28.126}$$

There exists a point $(\eta_*, \overline{\theta} - \varepsilon)$ on $\Phi$, and when this point corresponds to $t = 0$, we have from (28.99.1) for $t > 0$

$$\frac{d\eta}{dt} = \eta^m Z(\vartheta) \geq \frac{1}{2} Z(\overline{\theta})\eta^m. \tag{28.127}$$

By separation of variable, we get

$$\eta^{-m}\frac{d\eta}{dt} \geq \frac{1}{2} Z(\overline{\theta}) \Leftrightarrow \frac{\eta^{1-m} - \eta_*^{1-m}}{1-m} \geq \frac{1}{2} Z(\overline{\theta})t \tag{28.128}$$

$$\Leftrightarrow \eta^{1-m} \leq \eta_*^{1-m} + \frac{1}{2}(1-m)Z(\overline{\theta})t, \tag{28.129}$$

i.e.,

$$\eta(t) \geq \left[\eta_*^{1-m} + \frac{1}{2}(1-m)Z(\overline{\theta})t\right]^{\frac{1}{1-m}}. \tag{28.130}$$

With $m > 1$, the *elongation* $\eta(t)$ in (28.130) becomes infinite in *finite* time. The latter *proves* (ii) for $\vartheta_0 \in \complement\Theta$, and Theorem 28.3 is *established*.

With the change of variables $u = 1/x$, $v = 1/y$, the Corollary 28.2 follows from Theorem 28.3, cf. the proof of Theorem 28.12. □

*Acknowledgments* Theorem 28.3 is a joint work in association with Peter Gross, University of Aalborg. ▽

Evidently, this *theorem* and the *corollary* show that *only* with $\boldsymbol{m} = 1$ can the solutions $\boldsymbol{\varphi}$ (28.4) be *extended* to both plus and minus infinity, i.e., $T = \mathbf{R}$.

Having erected a conceptual framework for obtaining the *family* (complete set) of *solutions* to (28.1.1–28.3) in terms of *primitives*, we are now ready to organize the discussion of stability properties in a new and rigorous way.

## The Stability Properties of Ratio Solutions

### *Dynamic Stability Concepts*

Although the term *stability* seems to convey a simple idea, it has been used in the literature with so many connotations that its content and scope needs to be scrutinized carefully before any precise meaning can be attached to "stability" properties of *dynamic* systems. Naturally, stability was a concept suggested by physics, where it meant, roughly speaking, that *small changes* in the *state* (initial conditions) of a physical system at some instant cause only *minimal changes* in the *behavior* (solutions) of the physical (dynamic) system at *all* later times. However, stability analysis has not always been restricted to the analysis of small changes in the initial values (*local* stability) but has been extended to *any* initial values (*global* stability) within the domain of the dynamic system. Furthermore, the immediate future states (*transient* aspects)—from whatever initial state—of some dynamic system may, for theoretical (and/or practical) purposes, be of less interest than the system behavior on large (infinite) time intervals ( *long-term* prospects). The benefit of abstracting from the details of transitional motions, which are heavily influenced by the initial conditions, is increased understanding of the fundamental *interactions* among the state variables of an unfolding dynamic process, hereby gaining insight into the consequences of such interaction for the *evolution* of the state variables after the elapse of a *long* period of time. Of course, the governing functions inherently outline the design of the interaction within the dynamic models and determine the long-run properties of the whole family of solutions as well. Typically, the governing functions, emanating from the factual field of research, will indicate forces and modes of operation that will often, if the attractive interaction is strong enough, establish over time some "stable patterns" among the coordinate solutions.

The *stability theory* of dynamic differential equations has mainly been devoted to studies of stability problems associated with *admissible stationary states* (stationary equilibria) of the dynamic systems. The central issue of such stability problems is whether all nonstationary solutions of the differential equations converge, as time goes to infinity, to the particular—globally or locally unique—stationary (constant) solution. Such a *stability* property of the *family* (complete set) of solutions converging to the *stationary* solution is traditionally called *asymptotic stability*.

It ought to be stressed that dynamic *stability* theory is not concerned with any special property of particular solutions but rather inquires into the overall ("qualitative") properties of the *general solution*, i.e., stability concepts have always reference to some property shared by a family of solutions. But, as emphasized in Chap. 1, the standard asymptotic stability concept, Lyapunov stability concept, and other traditional stability concepts—as employed in the literature in the *qualitative theory* of differential equations, see Arrowsmith and Place (1990), Bellman (1953), Birkhoff and Rota (1989), Casti (1979), Cesari (1963), Hirsch and Smale (1974), Liapounoff (1947a,b), Malkin (1959), Olech (1963), Rosen (1970), Sanchez (1968), Shub (1987), Šiljak (1969)—are often *inadequate* for the purpose of *classifying* the *families* of solutions that originate from dynamic models outside the disciplines of physics and classical mechanics, cf. Arnold (1978), Birkhoff (1927), Landau and Lifshitz (1989). In economic and social sciences, concepts and pertinent theories of dynamic processes often hinge on some *key ratios* between the *state variables*.

Now, the question of *ratio stability* in *homogeneous dynamic* systems will, in our approach, be a natural subject to discuss even before the issue of the *stability* of the *family* of the *coordinate solutions*, $\varphi(t)$, (28.6), is raised (section "The Stability Properties of Coordinate Solutions").

We shall reduce the discussion of ratio stability to *three* important cases. Recalling the fact that the *set* of *director roots* $\mathcal{A}$, (28.18), will correspond to *stationary* ratio solutions $\boldsymbol{\rho(t)}$, we then consider—apart from (28.70.2)— the possibilities of the root set $\mathcal{A}$ containing:

$$(1)\text{ one and only one root}\quad (2)\text{ several roots}\quad (3)\text{ null roots.} \tag{28.131}$$

### *Global Asymptotic Ratio Stability*

With regard to *global* asymptotic ratio stability, it is *necessary* to have one and only one root, $\alpha$, and *sufficient* that *all* the nonstationary ratios $\rho(t) = \varphi_2(t)/\varphi_1(t)$, (28.13), converge, as $t \to \bar{t} \le \infty$, to this particular constant ratio, $\rho(t) = \alpha$.

**Theorem 28.4** *The family of ratio solutions $\rho(t)$, (28.13), to Eqs. (28.1.1–28.3), (28.9.1–2) has global asymptotic stability if and only if the* ***director function*** *$h$, (28.15), satisfies:*

$$(i)\ h(\alpha) = 0, \quad (ii)\ h(r) > 0 \text{ for } r < \alpha, \quad (iii)\ h(r) < 0 \text{ for } r > \alpha. \tag{28.132}$$

***Proof*** If the function $\boldsymbol{h(r)}$, (28.15), has a unique root, $\alpha$, it follows from Theorem 28.2 that there exists a constant ratio solution, $\rho(t) = \alpha$, cf. (28.61).

It is well known that the necessary and sufficient conditions for the nonstationary solutions $\rho(t)$ of the first-order equation $\dot{\boldsymbol{r}} = \boldsymbol{Q(r)}$, (28.34), to satisfy $\rho(t) - \alpha \to 0$ as $t \to \bar{t} \le \infty$ are given by $Q(r) > 0$, for $r < \alpha$, and $Q(r) < 0$, for $r > \alpha$. The latter are equivalent to the inequalities (ii) and (iii), since the term $|k_0 \cdot \exp\{H(r)\}|^{m-1}$ is positive for all $r \ne \alpha$. □

**Corollary 28.3** *The family of ratio solutions $\rho(t)$, (28.13), to Eqs. (28.1.1–28.3), (28.9.1–2) has global asymptotic stability if the* ***director*** *function $h$, (28.15), for some neighborhood $N(\alpha)$ of $\alpha$ satisfies:*

$$(i)\ h(\alpha) = 0, \quad (ii)\ h'(\alpha) \le 0, \quad (iii)\ h'(r) < 0 \text{ for } r \in N(\alpha). \qquad (28.133)$$

***Proof*** The conditions (28.133) imply (28.132). □

Global asymptotic ratio stability is equivalent to the existence of a *unique attractive directrix*, cf. Definition 28.7. A unique *repulsive* directrix occurs with a change of signs in (ii) and (iii) of (28.132) or (28.133). Note from (28.133, ii) that a unique attractive or repulsive directrix permits an *inflection point* of the director function $h$ at $r = \alpha$.

With only one director root $\alpha$, we may also see a right or left attractive directrix, cf. Definition 28.6; the ratio solutions $\rho(t)$ have here only *one-sided asymptotic stability*.

**Corollary 28.4** *The family of ratio solutions $\rho(t)$, (28.13), to Eqs. (28.1.1–28.3), (28.9.1–2) has one-sided asymptotic stability if and only if the function $h$, (28.15), at $r = \alpha$ has either a maximum or a minimum,*

$$(i)\ h(\alpha) = 0, \quad (ii)\ h(r) < 0 \text{ for } r \neq \alpha \text{ or } h(r) > 0 \text{ for } r \neq \alpha. \qquad (28.134)$$

***Proof*** The conditions (28.134) follow immediately from the proof of Theorem 28.4, applied separately to the two intervals, $]-\infty, \alpha[$ and $]\alpha, \infty[$. □

Evidently, (28.134) implies $h'(\alpha) = 0$.

*Weaker Global Ratio Stabilities*

A special case with only a single directrix occurs with the $y$-axis directrix (28.70.2) and $\mathcal{A}$ empty. Rather than establish global *asymptotic* stability of the reciprocal ratio $\tilde{r} = 1/r$ around $\tilde{\rho}(t) = \tilde{\alpha} = 0$ by using Theorem 28.4 and (28.72), we may still prefer to keep the ratio variable $r$ and then try to establish some *weaker* global stabilities of the family of $\rho(t)$ solutions.

With $\mathcal{A}$ empty, the director function $h$ cannot change sign at all. When $h(r)$—and hence $Q(r)$, (28.34)—is positive/negative for all $r \in \mathbf{R}$, then the family of ratio solutions, $\rho(t)$, of (28.1.1–28.3) must increase/decrease toward $\pm\infty$ as time goes to infinity.

The governing function of the latter *family* is now with $\mathcal{A} = \emptyset$, given entirely by, cf. (28.34–28.35)

$$\dot{r} = Q(r) = |k_0 \exp\{H(r)\}|^{m-1} h(r); \quad r \in \mathbf{R}, \qquad (28.135.1)$$

$$k_0 = x_0 \exp\{-H(r_0)\}, \quad r_0 = y_0/x_0, \quad r_0 \in \mathbf{R}. \qquad (28.135.2)$$

To *classify* families of monotonic *increasing solutions* arising from differential equations

$$\dot{r} = P(r) \equiv \exp\{(m-1)H(r)\}h(r), \quad r \in [0, \infty[ \tag{28.135.3}$$

with $\boldsymbol{P(r) > 0}$ everywhere, we proposed, in Chap. 1, six new *criteria* for characterizing the respective *long-run stability* properties of the solutions to (28.135.3). These six criteria are designed in hierarchical order such that each one contains the predecessors and is contained in the successors, i.e., the stability criteria represent a succession from *higher* to *lower degrees* of stability. In Chap. 1, we also gave theorems that stated *stability conditions*—in terms of specific *properties* of the *governing function*—that are *sufficient* for the family of solutions to satisfy these six stability criteria.

**Theorem 28.5** *The set of ratio solutions to the Eqs. (28.1.1–28.3), represented by an arbitrary* ***pair***, $\boldsymbol{\rho}, \boldsymbol{\hat{\rho}}$, *has—with* $x \geq 0$, $F(0, y) = 0$, *(28.70.2), and* $P(r) > 0$ *everywhere (28.135.3)—respectively, strong/weak absolute stability, strong/weak relative stability, and strong/weak logarithmic stability,* ***if*** $\boldsymbol{P}$, *(28.135.3), in turn satisfies the conditions:*

$$P(r) \to 0 \text{ as } r \to \infty \quad \Rightarrow \quad \hat{\rho}(t) - \rho(t) \to 0 \text{ as } t \to \bar{t} \leq \infty, \tag{28.136.1}$$

$$P(r) < K \text{ everywhere} \quad \Rightarrow \quad |\hat{\rho}(t) - \rho(t)| < k < \infty, \ \forall t, \tag{28.136.2}$$

$$P(r)/r \to 0 \text{ as } r \to \infty \quad \Rightarrow \quad \hat{\rho}(t)/\rho(t) \to 1 \text{ as } t \to \bar{t} \leq \infty, \tag{28.136.3}$$

$$P(r)/r < K \text{ for } r > 0 \quad \Rightarrow \quad |\hat{\rho}(t)/\rho(t)| < k < \infty, \ \forall t, \tag{28.136.4}$$

$$P(r)/(r \ln r) \to 0 \text{ as } r \to \infty \quad \Rightarrow \quad \ln \hat{\rho}(t)/\ln \rho(t) \to 1 \text{ as } t \to \bar{t} \leq \infty, \tag{28.136.5}$$

$$P(r)/(r \ln r) < K \text{ for } r > 1 \quad \Rightarrow \quad |\ln \hat{\rho}(t)/\ln \rho(t)| < k < \infty, \ \forall t. \tag{28.136.6}$$

***Proof*** Given initial values $(x_0, y_0)$ and $(\hat{x}_0, \hat{y}_0)$ for (28.1.1–28.3) in $\mathbf{R}^2_+$, the corresponding ratio solutions to (28.1.1–28.3),

$$r = \rho(t), \quad r = \hat{\rho}(t) \tag{28.136.7}$$

satisfy, cf. (28.135.1–28.135.3),

$$\dot{\rho}(t) = \beta P[\rho(t)], \quad \dot{\hat{\rho}}(t) = \hat{\beta} P[\hat{\rho}(t)], \tag{28.136.8}$$

where $\beta = k_0^{m-1} > 0$, $\hat{\beta} = \hat{k}_0^{m-1} > 0$.

According to Lemma 28.2, cf. (28.50), there exist solutions to (28.135.3),

$$r = \rho_1(t), \quad r = \rho_2(t), \tag{28.136.9}$$

such that, cf. (28.136.7–28.136.8),

$$\rho(t) = \rho_1(\beta t + \tau_1), \quad \hat{\rho}(t) = \rho_2(\hat{\beta} t + \tau_2). \tag{28.136.10}$$

By Theorem 1.2 in Chap. 1, we have that, cf. (28.135.3), (28.136.9),

$$P(r) \to 0 \text{ as } r \to \infty \;\Rightarrow\; \rho_2(t) - \rho_1(t) \to 0 \text{ as } t \to \bar{t} \le \infty. \tag{28.136.11}$$

Hence with $\beta > 0$, $\hat{\beta} > 0$, (28.136.10–28.136.11) establish (28.136.1).

Similarly, Theorems 1.3–1.7 in Chap. 1 and (28.135.3), (28.136.7–28.136.10) establish (28.136.2–28.136.6). □

### *Local Asymptotic Ratio Stability*

More than one root in the set $\mathcal{A}$ preclude global asymptotic stability of the ratio solutions to (28.1.1–28.3). But we may still have *local* asymptotic ratio stability at *isolated* roots, $\alpha \in \mathcal{A}$—$\mathcal{A}$ being finite or infinite.

**Theorem 28.6** *The family of ratio solutions $\rho$, (28.13), to equations (28.1.1–28.3) has local asymptotic stability at $\alpha \in \mathcal{A}$ if and only if the director function $h$, (28.15), for some neighborhood $\mathcal{N}(\alpha)$ of $\alpha$, satisfies:*

$$(i)\ h(\alpha) = 0, \quad (ii)\ h(r) > 0 \text{ for } r < \alpha, \quad (iii)\ h(r) < 0 \text{ for } r > \alpha,\ r \in \mathcal{N}(\alpha). \tag{28.137}$$

***Proof*** The proof of this theorem is similar to that of Theorem 28.4. □

As mentioned before, local asymptotic ratio stability is equivalent to the existence of an attractive directrix. Similarly, Theorem 28.6 gives analogs to Corollaries 28.3–28.4. If a root $\alpha \in \mathcal{A}$ is not *isolated*, there exist constant ratio solutions arbitrarily close to $\alpha$, preventing local asymptotic stability. Nevertheless, we have—at least from one side—*weak absolute ratio stability.*

**Remark 28.12** If the director function $h$ successively changes sign at *consecutive* roots, $\alpha \in \mathcal{A}$, then the corresponding *directrices* are *successively attractive* and *repulsive*. This follows from Theorem 28.6 and its analog—change of signs in (ii) and (iii)—for repulsive directrices. ▽

**Remark 28.13** When the set $\mathcal{A}$, (28.18), contains only *two* roots, $\mathcal{A} = \{\alpha_1, \alpha_2\}$, and if $h(r)$ changes sign at both roots, then there exists *one attractive* and *one repulsive* directrix, cf. Remark 28.12. The director root for the repulsive directrix represents eo ipso a fluke as an initial ratio value, and we may therefore with such *two* director roots be said to have *generic asymptotic* ratio stability. A generic stability property is one which "almost all" solutions must share. ▽

The interface between *global* and *local* stability concepts may be pinpointed by expounding the notion: *genericity*.

**Definition 28.9** A *generic* property refers to a common characteristic (trait) shared by elements (individuals) of a wide class (genus). Thus the term generic case refers to all cases bar some exceptional ones (see, Arnold 1986, p. 3; Arnold 1988, p. 223).

Formally, a generic property often refer to *open* and *dense* sets, cf. Hirsch and Smale (1974, p. 154), Arrowsmith and Place (1990, p. 119). Nongeneric cases are usually identified with singularities of one kind or the other.

### *Absence of Any Ratio Stability*

In situations with $F(0, y) \neq 0$, cf. (28.70.2), and $\mathcal{A}$ empty, no directrices exist and hence no ratio stabilities. The solution $\rho(t)$ of (28.135.1–2) will either increase from $-\infty$ to $\infty$ or decrease from $\infty$ to $-\infty$. The corresponding trajectory will run from and to the $y$-axis. Consolidating these trajectories with the relevant $y$-axis points gives the *maximal* trajectories, cf. Chap., which are either *spiraling* or *closed* trajectories around the origin.

As to closed trajectories (periodic solutions), it is known, cf. Frommer (1934, p. 408), that if $F$ and $G$, (28.1.1–28.3), are homogeneous polynomials of *odd* degree, then a *necessary* and *sufficient* condition for *closed* trajectories is, cf. (28.25),

$$\int_{-\infty}^{\infty} H'(r)dr = 0. \tag{28.138}$$

Incidentally, we may note that "*limit cycles*" never occur in planar homogeneous dynamic systems, since the geometric similarity of the trajectories, cf. sections "Vector and Tangent Fields–Heuristic Comments on Geometry, Dynamics, and Kinematics", evidently precludes the existence of a limit cycle in the phase plane.

### *Asymptotic Ratio Stability and Trajectory Geometry*

The global asymptotic ratio stability property given by Theorem 28.4 does *not* necessarily imply that the *attractive* directrix is geometrically an *asymptote* of the phase curves/trajectories, (28.38.1–28.39). Of course, if the *directrix value* $f(\alpha)$, (28.64), is *negative*, then the attractive directrix must be an asymptote of all the phase curves (28.38.1–2), tending to $(0, 0)$. But with a *positive* directrix value, (28.64), the phase curves/trajectories (28.38.1–28.39) of all the growing solutions $\varphi(t)$ will—with (28.132)—*either* have the attractive directrix (28.62) as *asymptote* [possibly, just approaching (28.62)] *or* at infinity be *parallel* to the attractive directrix.

Therefore, we need *criteria* that can tell us which of the latter two configurations applies in concrete cases. We provide a criterion that is easy and helpful in many situations.

Since the direction field and the trajectories of homogeneous dynamics can be parameterized in terms of the ratio variable $r$, cf. (28.83–28.84), (28.97), we can give some *simple sufficient* conditions for the attractive directrix being (or not being) an *asymptote* of the trajectories.

**Theorem 28.7** *With the domain* $\mathbf{R}_+^2$, *the trajectory system (28.38.1–28.39) will—given (28.132),* $f(\alpha) > 0,\ \alpha > 0$*—approach the directrix (28.62) and normally have (28.62) as an* ***asymptote****, if* $q(r)$, *(28.84), satisfies*

$$(i)\ \exists r < \alpha : q(r) > \alpha, \quad (ii)\ \exists r > \alpha : q(r) < \alpha, \tag{28.139}$$

*or, at infinity be* ***parallel*** *to the directrix (28.62), if* $q(r)$ *satisfies*

$$(i)\ \forall r < \alpha : q(r) < \alpha, \quad (ii)\ \forall r > \alpha : q(r) > \alpha. \tag{28.140}$$

***Proof*** Within $\mathbf{R}_+^2$, choose two lines $\ell_+, \ell_-$ parallel to the directrix (28.62): $\ell_+$ above, $\ell_-$ below. They define a rectangular region $B$. If (28.139) is satisfied, the direction field vector $q(r)$, (28.83–28.84), points *into* B at the *intersection* of $\ell_+$ ($\ell_-$) with the respective ray, $y = rx$. Then asymptotic ratio stability (28.132), $f(\alpha) > 0$, and the monotonicity of $\rho(t)$ ensure that these trajectories remain in $B$ and approach the directrix (normally, also an asymptote). The geometric similarity of the phase portraits ensures that, as $t \to \infty$, all trajectories will approach the directrix.

The global property of the direction field (28.140), asymptotic ratio stability (28.132), and $f(\alpha) > 0$ together clearly prevent the phase curves/trajectories (28.38.1–28.39) from approaching the directrix (28.62). Instead, the phase curves move everywhere away from the directrix, but as $t \to \infty$, the slopes $q[\rho(t)]$ approach $\alpha$. □

With monotonicity of $\boldsymbol{q(r)}$, (28.84), the trajectories have no wriggles, and so we see ***phase portraits*** according to

**Theorem 28.8** *With the domain* $\mathbf{R}_+^2$, *the trajectory system (28.38.1–28.39) will—given (28.132),* $f(\alpha) > 0,\ \alpha > 0$*—be* ***hyperbolic*** *with the directrix (28.62)*

*as the asymptote, if $q(r)$, (28.84), satisfies*

$$\forall r \in \mathbf{R}_+ \setminus \{\alpha, r_0 \mid q(r_0) = \infty\} : \quad q'(r) < 0 \tag{28.141}$$

*or be **parabolic** with the directrix (28.62) as the axis, if $q(r)$ satisfies*

$$\forall r \in \mathbf{R}_+ \setminus \{\alpha\} : \quad q'(r) > 0 \tag{28.142}$$

*and be **straight lines** parallel to the directrix (28.62), if $q(r)$ satisfies*

$$\forall r \in \mathbf{R}_+ : \quad q'(r) = 0 \quad \Leftrightarrow \quad q(r) = \alpha. \tag{28.143}$$

***Proof*** Since (28.132), $f(\alpha) > 0$, and (28.141) imply (28.139), the hyperbolic shape of (28.38.1–28.39) on $\mathbf{R}_+^2$ follows with (28.141).

As (28.132), $f(\alpha) > 0$, and (28.142) imply (28.140), the parabolic shape of (28.38.1–28.39) on $\mathbf{R}_+^2$ follows with (28.142).

The linearity with (28.143) is obvious. □

**Remark 28.14** It should be noted that the domain of (28.1.1–28.3) in Theorems 28.7–28.8 was restricted to $\mathbf{R}_+^2$. Depending on the specifications of $F$ and $G$ and hence the character of the direction field, (28.83–28.84), we saw, with asymptotic ratio stability (28.132) and $f(\alpha) > 0$, several possible configurations (hyperbolic, parabolic, linear) of the phase portrait upon $\mathbf{R}_+^2$. However, if the domain of (28.1.1–28.3) is the entire plane $\mathbf{R}^2$, and the symmetry of the phase portrait around the origin $(0, 0)$ is either intrinsic by $F$ and $G$ themselves or imposed by (28.9.1–2), cf. (28.85) and Remark 28.11, then global *asymptotic ratio stability,* (28.132), and a *positive* directrix value, $f(\alpha) > 0$, (28.62), will only admit a *parabolic* configuration of the phase portrait or *straight* lines parallel to the directrix.

This fact can be recognized by noting the necessity of all the non-parallel trajectories to emanate from the origin (in order to preserve symmetry and geometrical similarity) with only one directrix in the plane. ▽

## The Stability Properties of Coordinate Solutions

The stability conditions (28.132), (28.136.1–28.136.6) for the family of *ratio solutions* imply an intrinsic coherence between the sets of *individual* coordinate solutions (state variables), $\boldsymbol{\varphi}_1(\boldsymbol{t})$ and $\boldsymbol{\varphi}_2(\boldsymbol{t})$. Despite such cohesive powers embedded in the working of the dynamic model, the *family* of *coordinate solutions* $\boldsymbol{\varphi}(\boldsymbol{t})$ to (28.1.1–28.3) might nevertheless include solutions with history/phase curves, displaying very different *rapidity/speed* of evolution/motion and thereby intuitively also very different coordinate *stabilities.*

### *Global Asymptotic Ratio Stability and Global Stabilities of Coordinate Solutions*

In this section, we discuss the different types of stability of the coordinate solutions associated with the global asymptotic ratio stability conditions (28.132). As to the *stability criteria* used below, we again refer to Chap. 1.

To start with, we observe a simple fact, as stated in Lemma 28.4.

**Lemma 28.4** *The sets of the individual coordinate solutions $\varphi_1(t)$ and $\varphi_2(t)$ to (28.1.1–28.3), (28.9.1–2) will—under the conditions of global asymptotic ratio stability, (28.132), and with a director root $\alpha \neq 0$—always have the* ***same*** *stability properties.*

***Proof*** By Theorem 28.4, we have for all the solutions of (28.34) that $\rho(t) \to \alpha$ as $t \to \infty$. Hence, as $t \to \infty$, $\varphi_1(t)$ and $\varphi_2(t)$ evolve proportionally by (28.38.2), and the lemma follows. □

Consider *any pair* of coordinate solutions to (28.1.1–28.3), (28.9.1–2),

$$\varphi(t) = [\varphi_1(t), \varphi_2(t)], \quad \psi(t) = [\psi_1(t), \psi_2(t)]. \tag{28.144}$$

We explained in section "Heuristic Comments on Geometry, Dynamics, and Kinematics" that the *degree* of homogeneity clearly affected the *shape* of the *history* curves from homogeneous dynamic systems. The actual *value* of the degree of homogeneity will play a crucial role in various *stability conditions* that refer to the *classification* of families of coordinate *solutions* that ultimately *increase* toward *infinity* on an *infinite* time interval.

Incidentally, we note that there *cannot* exist any coordinate stability for $\boldsymbol{m} > 1$ and a *positive directrix value*, since the solutions explode, i.e., become infinite in finite time, cf. (28.65.3) and section "On Solutions and Their Maximal Time Interval of Existence".

**Theorem 28.9** *The family of nonstationary coordinate solutions to (28.1.1–28.3) has—with Lemma 28.4 and a positive directrix value (28.24) and either $m = 1$ or $m < 1$—respectively, strong logarithmic and strong relative stability, i.e.,*

$$f(\alpha) > 0, \ m = 1 : \ln|\psi_i(t)|/\ln|\varphi_i(t)| \to 1 \quad \textit{as}\, t \to \infty, \quad i = 1, 2, \tag{28.145}$$

$$f(\alpha) > 0, \ m < 1 : |\psi_i(t)|/|\varphi_i(t)| \to 1 \quad \textit{as}\, t \to \infty, \quad i = 1, 2. \tag{28.146}$$

***Proof*** To prove (28.145–28.146), it suffices to examine two solutions, referred to in (28.144), a directrix solution $\varphi(t)$ of the form (28.65.2) or (28.65.1) and a non-directrix solution $\psi(t)$ of the form (28.38.1–2). Furthermore, by Lemma 28.4, it is enough to compare their first coordinate solutions.

*ad* $m = 1$. From (28.65.1) and (28.38.1), we have

$$\frac{\ln \psi_1(t)}{\ln \varphi_1(t)} = \frac{\ln(k_0 \exp\{H[\rho(t)]\})}{\ln(\hat{x}_0 \exp\{f(\alpha)t\})} = \frac{\ln|k_0| + H[\rho(t)]}{\ln|\hat{x}_0| + f(\alpha)t} . \tag{28.147}$$

By Lemma 28.1 and Theorem 28.4, the rule of l'Hospital can be used to evaluate the limit of (28.147), i.e.,

$$\lim_{t\to\infty} \frac{\ln \psi_1(t)}{\ln \varphi_1(t)} = \lim_{t\to\infty} \frac{d \ln \psi_1(t)/dt}{d \ln \varphi_1(t)/dt} = \lim_{t\to\infty} \frac{H'[\rho(t)]\dot{\rho}(t)}{f(\alpha)} =$$
$$\lim_{t\to\infty} \frac{(f[\rho(t)]/h[\rho(t)])h[\rho(t)]}{f(\alpha)} = \lim_{t\to\infty} \frac{f[\rho(t)]}{f(\alpha)} = \frac{f(\alpha)}{f(\alpha)} = 1 \tag{28.148}$$

using (28.25), (28.34) and $m = 1$. Thus, (28.148) establishes the *strong logarithmic* stability property of the family of coordinate solutions $\varphi(t)$, (28.145).

*ad* $m < 1$. From (28.65.2) and (28.38.1), we have

$$\frac{\psi_1(t)}{\varphi_1(t)} = \frac{k_0 \exp\{H[\rho(t)]\}}{[\hat{x}_0^{1-m} + (1-m)f(\alpha)t]^{\frac{1}{1-m}}} = \frac{k_0 \exp\{H[\rho(t)]\}}{[(1-m)f(\alpha)(t+t_0)]^{\frac{1}{1-m}}} . \tag{28.149}$$

By Lemma 28.1, we may also use the rule of l'Hospital to evaluate the limit of (28.149). Thus, one gets, cf. (28.25), (28.34)

$$\lim_{t\to\infty} \frac{\psi_1(t)}{\varphi_1(t)} = \lim_{t\to\infty} \frac{\dot{\psi}_1(t)}{\dot{\varphi}_1(t)} = \lim_{t\to\infty} \frac{k_0 \exp\{H[\rho(t)]\}H'[\rho(t)]\dot{\rho}(t)}{[(1-m)f(\alpha)(t+t_0)]^{\frac{m}{1-m}} f(\alpha)} =$$
$$\lim_{t\to\infty} \frac{k_0 \exp\{H[\rho(t)]\}\,(f[\rho(t)]/h[\rho(t)])\,|k_0 \exp\{H[\rho(t)]\}|^{m-1} h[\rho(t)]}{[(1-m)f(\alpha)(t+t_0)]^{\frac{m}{1-m}} f(\alpha)} =$$
$$\lim_{t\to\infty} \left[\frac{|k_0 \exp\{H[\rho(t)]\}|^m}{[(1-m)f(\alpha)(t+t_0)]^{\frac{m}{1-m}}}\right]\left[\frac{f[\rho(t)]}{f(\alpha)}\right] =$$
$$\lim_{t\to\infty} \left[\frac{|k_0|^m}{[(1-m)f(\alpha)]^{\frac{m}{1-m}}}\right]\left[\frac{\exp\{(1-m)H[\rho(t)]\}}{t+t_0}\right]^{\frac{m}{1-m}}\left[\frac{f[\rho(t)]}{f(\alpha)}\right]. \tag{28.150}$$

In (28.150), both the numerator (cf. Lemma 28.1 and Theorem 28.4) and the denominator of the middle fraction go to infinity as $t \to \infty$, so we apply the l'Hospital rule once more. Thus, using again (28.25), (28.34), we obtain

$$\lim_{t\to\infty}\frac{\exp\{(1-m)H[\rho(t)]\}}{t+t_0}=\lim_{t\to\infty}\exp\{(1-m)H[\rho(t)]\}[(1-m)H'[\rho(t)]\dot{\rho}(t)=$$

$$\lim_{t\to\infty}\exp\{(1-m)H[\rho(t)]\}(1-m)(f[\rho(t)]/h[\rho(t)])|k_0\exp\{H[\rho(t)]\}|^{m-1}h[\rho(t)]=$$

$$\lim_{t\to\infty}(1-m)|k_0|^{m-1}f[\rho(t)]=(1-m)|k_0|^{m-1}f(\alpha) \tag{28.151}$$

as the last result follows from the assumption, $\rho(t)\to\alpha$ for $t\to\infty$. Finally, the standard theorem on *composite* limits is applied to (28.150–28.151), i.e.,

$$\lim_{t\to\infty}\frac{|\psi_1(t)|}{|\varphi_1(t)|}=\left[\frac{|k_0|^m}{[(1-m)f(\alpha)]^{\frac{m}{1-m}}}\right][(1-m)|k_0|^{m-1}f(\alpha)]^{\frac{m}{1-m}}\left[\frac{f(\alpha)}{f(\alpha)}\right]=1, \tag{28.152}$$

which establishes the *strong relative* stability property of the family of coordinate solutions, (28.146). □

Theorem 28.9 is the most general and powerful stability result, bringing—with regard to the *values* of $\boldsymbol{m}$—the stability properties for families of *increasing* (but non-explosive) solutions to the general homogeneous dynamic system (28.1.1–28.3), under a simple, all-embracing rule.

However, it is possible—for $\boldsymbol{m}=1$, $\boldsymbol{m}=0$ and $\boldsymbol{m}<0$—to sharpen Theorem 28.9 by *adding* a very mild assumption to the conditions in (28.145–28.146).

**Theorem 28.10** *The family of nonstationary coordinate solutions to (28.1.1–28.3) has—with* Lemma 28.4, *a positive directrix value (28.24),* $\boldsymbol{m}=1$, *and a director function without an* ***inflection*** *point at* $r=\alpha$, *(28.133, ii)—weak relative stability, i.e.,*

$$f(\alpha)>0,\ m=1,\ h'(\alpha)<0:\ |\psi_i(t)|/|\varphi_i(t)|<k\ <\infty,\ \ \forall t,\quad i=1,2. \tag{28.153}$$

***Proof*** From (28.65.1), (28.38.1), and Lemma 28.4, we have

$$\frac{\psi_1(t)}{\varphi_1(t)}=\frac{k_0\exp\{H[\rho(t)]\}}{\hat{x}_0\exp\{f(\alpha)t\}}=\frac{k_0}{\hat{x}_0}\exp\{H[\rho(t)]-f(\alpha)t\}. \tag{28.154}$$

We consider the difference

$$\chi(t)=H[\rho(t)]-f(\alpha)t \tag{28.155}$$

and next, by (28.25), (28.34), $m = 1$ and the mean value theorem on $f$

$$|\dot{\chi}(t)| = |H'[\rho(t)]\dot{\rho}(t) - f(\alpha)| = |f[\rho(t)] - f(\alpha)| = |f'(\xi)||\rho(t) - \alpha| \\ < B_1|\rho(t) - \alpha|, \tag{28.156}$$

where the constant $B_1$ is an *upper* bound for $|f'(r)|$, i.e., $B_1 > |f'(\xi)|$, $\forall\xi$.

By $h'(\alpha) < 0$, and the mean value theorem on $h$, there exists a constant $B_2 > 0$, being a *lower* bound for $-h'(r)$ in a *neighborhood* $N(\alpha)$ of $\alpha$, such that for $r, \xi \in N(\alpha)$,

$$|h(r)| = |h'(\xi)(r - \alpha)| \geq B_2|r - \alpha|. \tag{28.157}$$

Hence, by (28.34), $m = 1$, $r = \rho(t)$, and (28.157), we get

$$|\dot{\rho}(t)| = |h[\rho(t)]| \geq B_2|\rho(t) - \alpha|. \tag{28.158}$$

Integrating (28.158) by separation of variables yields

$$\ln|r_0 - \alpha| - \ln|\rho(t) - \alpha| \geq B_2 t \Leftrightarrow |\rho(t) - \alpha| \leq |r_0 - \alpha|e^{-B_2 t}. \tag{28.159}$$

Substituting (28.159) in (28.156) and integrating gives, cf. (28.155)

$$\begin{aligned} |\chi(t)| &\leq |\chi(0)| + \int_0^t |\dot{\chi}(t)|dt \leq H(r_0) + B_1 \int_0^t |r_0 - \alpha|e^{-B_2 t}dt \\ &= H(r_0) + B_1|r_0 - \alpha|\left[\frac{1 - e^{-B_2 t}}{B_2}\right] \\ &\leq H(r_0) + B_1|r_0 - \alpha|/B_2. \end{aligned} \tag{28.160}$$

Finally, by (28.154–28.155) and (28.160), we obtain

$$\begin{aligned} \frac{|\psi_1(t)|}{|\varphi_1(t)|} &= \frac{|k_0|}{|\hat{x}_0|}\exp\{H[\rho(t)] - f(\alpha)t\} \leq \frac{|k_0|}{|\hat{x}_0|}\exp\{H(r_0) + B_1|r_0 - \alpha|/B_2\} \\ &= |x_0|/|\hat{x_0}|\exp\{(B_1/B_2)|r_0 - \alpha|\} = k < \infty, \quad \forall t, \end{aligned} \tag{28.161}$$

which establishes the *weak relative* stability property (28.153). □

**Remark 28.15** The weak relative stability property, (28.153), of the coordinate solutions does not require that (28.154) has a limit as $t \to \infty$; to have weak relative stability, only the boundedness of (28.154) must be satisfied, cf. (28.161). However, a limit of (28.154) as $t \to \infty$ may exist if stronger assumptions are imposed upon the governing functions (28.2.1–2), (28.12.1–3).

From (28.155–28.156), we have,

$$\dot{\chi}(t) = f'(\xi)[\rho(t) - \alpha]. \tag{28.162}$$

If $f(r)$ is known to be *strictly monotone,* then the *sign* of $f'(\xi)$ is *fixed* for any $\xi\ \in]\rho(t), \alpha[$. Moreover, as $\rho(t)$ is strictly monotone, we altogether see from (28.162) that $\chi(t)$, (28.155), is strictly *monotone.* Then the monotonicity of $\chi(t)$ and its boundedness (28.160) ensure a limit for $\chi(t)$, (28.155), as $t \to \infty$, and hence also a *limit* (depending on the *initial* values) for (28.154), as $t \to \infty$. But a *global* stability statement about the coordinate solutions will not become any stronger than (28.153), which allows for any initial values of the coordinate solutions. ▽

**Theorem 28.11** *The family of nonstationary coordinate solutions to (28.1.1–28.3) has—with* Lemma 28.4, *a positive directrix value (28.24), for* $\mathbf{m} = 0$ *or* $\mathbf{m} < 0$, *and a director function without an* ***inflection*** *point at* $r = \alpha$, *(28.133, ii)—respectively, weak and strong absolute stability, i.e.,*

$$f(\alpha) > 0,\ m = 0,\ h'(\alpha) < 0 : |\psi_i(t) - \phi_i(t)| < k\ < \infty,\ \forall t,\ \ i = 1, 2, \tag{28.163}$$

$$f(\alpha) > 0,\ m < 0,\ h'(\alpha) < 0 :\ \ \psi_i(t) - \phi_i(t) \to 0 \ as\, t \to \infty,\ i = 1, 2. \tag{28.164}$$

***Proof*** From (28.38.1), (28.65.2), and Lemma 28.4, we have

$$\psi_1(t) - \varphi_1(t) = x_0 e^{H(\rho) - H(r_0)} - [\hat{x}_0^{1-m} + (1-m) f(\alpha) t]^{\frac{1}{1-m}}. \tag{28.165}$$

And from (28.25), we approximate

$$H'(r) = \frac{f(r)}{h(r)} \doteq \frac{f(\alpha)}{h'(\alpha)(r - \alpha)}. \tag{28.166}$$

Integrating (28.166) yields

$$H(\rho) - H(r_0) \doteq \int_{r_0}^{\rho} \frac{f(\alpha)}{h'(\alpha)} \cdot \frac{1}{|\rho - \alpha|} d\rho = \frac{f(\alpha)}{h'(\alpha)} \ln \left| \frac{\rho - \alpha}{r_0 - \alpha} \right|. \tag{28.167}$$

By (28.34) and (28.167), we have

$$\begin{aligned} \dot{\rho} &= x_0^{m-1} e^{(m-1)[H(\rho) - H(r_0)]} h(\rho) \\ &\doteq x_0^{m-1} \left| \frac{\rho - \alpha}{r_0 - \alpha} \right|^{(m-1)\frac{f(\alpha)}{h'(\alpha)}} h'(\alpha)(\rho - \alpha). \end{aligned} \tag{28.168}$$

Since the ratio solutions $\rho(t)$ have asymptotic stability, our approximation, (28.168), is useful only for $h'(\alpha) < 0$, cf. (28.133).

Integration by separation of variables yields

$$\left[ \frac{|\rho - \alpha|^{(1-m)\frac{f(\alpha)}{h'(\alpha)}}}{(1-m)\frac{f(\alpha)}{h'(\alpha)}} \right]_{r_0}^{\rho} = x_0^{m-1} |r_0 - \alpha|^{(1-m)\frac{f(\alpha)}{h'(\alpha)}} h'(\alpha) t \tag{28.169}$$

or, equivalently,

$$\left| \frac{\rho - \alpha}{r_0 - \alpha} \right|^{\frac{f(\alpha)}{h'(\alpha)}} = x_0^{-1} \left[ x_0^{1-m} + (1-m) f(\alpha) t \right]^{\frac{1}{1-m}}. \tag{28.170}$$

By (28.165), (28.167), and (28.170), we obtain

$$\psi_1(t) = x_0 \exp\{H(\rho) - H(r_0)\} \doteq \left[ x_0^{1-m} + (1-m) f(\alpha) t \right]^{\frac{1}{1-m}}. \tag{28.171}$$

*ad* $m = 0$. We have by (28.165), (28.171), and $m = 0$ that

$$\lim_{t \to \infty} [\psi_1(t) - \varphi_1(t)] = x_0 - \hat{x}_0, \tag{28.172}$$

which establishes the ***weak absolute*** stability property of the coordinate solutions, (28.163).

*ad* $m < 0$. We have by (28.165), (28.171), and $m < 0$ that

$$\lim_{t \to \infty} [\psi_1(t) - \varphi_1(t)] = \lim_{t \to \infty} \left\{ \left[ x_0^{1-m} + (1-m) f(\alpha) t \right]^{\frac{1}{1-m}} - \left[ \hat{x}_0^{1-m} + (1-m) f(\alpha) t \right]^{\frac{1}{1-m}} \right\} = 0, \tag{28.173}$$

which establishes the ***strong absolute*** stability property of the coordinate solutions, (28.164). □

*Acknowledgments* Theorems 28.10–28.11 are a joint work in association with Mogens Esrom Larsen, University of Copenhagen. ∇

**Theorem 28.12** *The family of coordinate solutions to (28.1.1–28.3) has—with Lemma 28.4 and a negative directrix value, (28.24)—asymptotic stability*

$$f(\alpha) < 0: \ \varphi_i(t) = 0, \quad \psi_i(t) \to 0 \ \ as \ t \to \bar{t} \leq \infty, \quad i = 1, 2. \tag{28.174}$$

***Proof*** The origin is a singular point of (28.1.1–28.3). With $f(\alpha) < 0$, the unique attractive directrix exhibits always declining solutions, cf. (28.64–

28.65.3), which here reach the origin in finite time (implosion) with $m \leq 1$ and in infinite time with $m \geq 1$.

By a change of variables ($u = 1/x,\ v = 1/y$), we have, cf. (28.1.1–28.3),

$$\dot{u} = -x^{-2}\dot{x} = -x^{-2}F(x, y) = -u^2 F(1/u, 1/v), \qquad (28.175.1)$$

$$\dot{v} = -y^{-2}\dot{y} = -y^{-2}G(x, y) = -v^2 G(1/u, 1/v), \qquad (28.175.2)$$

which are homogeneous of degree $n = 2 - m$ in $(u, v)$. Hence the global properties (28.174) follow from the fact that with $f(\alpha) < 0$, the corresponding reciprocals, $[u(t), v(t)] = [1/\varphi_1(t), 1/\varphi_2(t)]$, (28.175.1–2), will then always be increasing and unbounded as $t \to \bar{t} \leq \infty$ for any value of $n = 2 - m$, cf. Theorems 28.9–28.11. □

### *Local Asymptotic Ratio Stability and the Stabilities of Coordinate Solutions*

In the case of $\mathcal{A}$ containing *several* director roots, cf. (28.131), the subject of coordinate stability has to be analyzed by distinguishing between two fundamentally different situations, viz, either the *directrix values* (28.24) all have the *same sign* (positive or negative) or the directrix values occur with *different signs.*

**Theorem 28.13** *The family of nonstationary coordinate solutions to (28.1.1–28.3), (28.9.1–2) has—for $\mathcal{A} = \{\alpha_1, \alpha_2, \ldots, \alpha_n\}$ with (28.137), positive directrix values (28.24) and either $m = 1$ or $m \leq 1$—respectively, weak logarithmic and weak relative stability, i.e.,*

$$\forall f(\alpha) > 0,\ m = 1 : |\ln \psi_i(t)/\ln \varphi_i(t)| < k,\ \forall t,\ i = 1, 2, \qquad (28.176)$$

$$\forall f(\alpha) > 0,\ m < 1 : |\psi_i(t)/\varphi_i(t)| < k,\ \forall t,\ i = 1, 2. \qquad (28.177)$$

***Proof*** Let $\alpha_i \in \mathcal{A}$ be a director root of any repulsive directrix, and $\alpha_j \in \mathcal{A}$ be a director root of any attractive directrix. Now, let $\varphi_1$ be the first coordinate solution along the repulsive directrix, $y = \alpha_i x$, and $\psi_1$ an arbitrary first coordinate solution.

For $m = 1$ we immediately obtain from (28.148)

$$\lim_{t\to\infty} \frac{|\ln \psi_1(t)|}{|\ln \varphi_1(t)|} = \lim_{t\to\infty} \frac{|f[\rho(t)]|}{|f(\alpha_i)|} = \frac{|f(\alpha_j)|}{|f(\alpha_i)|} = k < \infty, \qquad (28.178)$$

i.e., (28.178) and Lemma 28.4 establish the weak logarithmic stability property of the family of coordinate solutions, (28.176).

For $m \leq 1$, we get from (28.150)

$$\lim_{t\to\infty} \frac{\psi_1(t)}{\varphi_1(t)} =$$

$$\lim_{t\to\infty} \left[\frac{|k_0|^m}{[(1-m)f(\alpha_i)]^{\frac{m}{1-m}}}\right] \left[\frac{\exp\{(1-m)H[\rho(t)]\}}{t+t_0}\right]^{\frac{m}{1-m}} \left[\frac{f[\rho(t)]}{f(\alpha_i)}\right] \qquad (28.179)$$

and next, by (28.151)

$$\lim_{t\to\infty} \frac{\exp\{(1-m)H[\rho(t)]\}}{t+t_0} =$$

$$\lim_{t\to\infty} (1-m)|k_0|^{m-1} f[\rho(t)] = (1-m)|k_0|^{m-1} f(\alpha_j). \qquad (28.180)$$

Hence, (28.179–28.180) give, cf. (28.152),

$$\lim_{t\to\infty} \frac{|\psi_1(t)|}{|\varphi_1(t)|} = \left[\frac{|k_0|^m}{[(1-m)f(\alpha_i)]^{\frac{m}{1-m}}}\right] [(1-m)|k_0|^{m-1} f(\alpha_j)]^{\frac{m}{1-m}} \left[\frac{f(\alpha_j)}{f(\alpha_i)}\right]$$

$$= \left[\frac{|f(\alpha_j)|}{|f(\alpha_i)|}\right]^{\frac{1}{1-m}} = k < \infty, \qquad (28.181)$$

i.e., (28.181) and Lemma 28.4 establish the weak relative stability of the family of coordinate solutions, (28.177). □

**Remark 28.16** Theorem 28.13 gave *global* stability properties for the family (all solutions with initial values $(x_0, y_0) \in \mathbf{R}^2/\{0, 0\})$ of nonstationary coordinate solutions. The stronger stability properties of Theorems 28.10–28.11 still hold locally for the adjacent cones $C$ (28.19) of attractive directrices, cf. Definition 28.7.

In case of only *two* positive directrix values, $f(\alpha_1) > 0$, $f(\alpha_2) > 0$, the stabilities of Theorems 28.10–28.11 represent not just local but become *generic* stability properties of the coordinate solutions (with only the exceptional repulsive directrix solutions preventing global stability statements), cf. Remark 28.13. ▽

**Theorem 28.14** *The family of coordinate solutions to (28.1.1–28.3), (28.9.1–2) has—for $\mathcal{A} = \{\alpha_1, \alpha_2, \ldots, \alpha_n\}$ with (28.137) and negative* ***directrix*** *values (28.24)—asymptotic stability, i.e.,*

$$\forall f(\alpha) < 0: \ \varphi_i(t) = 0, \quad \psi_i(t) \to 0 \ \text{as} \ t \to \infty, \quad i = 1, 2. \qquad (28.182)$$

***Proof*** The stationary solution $\varphi = (0, 0), \forall t$ is the global attractor; the proof is similar to that of Theorem 28.12. □

When *both* positive and negative directrix values (28.24) occur, we have numerically ***increasing*** as well as numerically ***decreasing*** directrix solutions, cf. (28.64). Then it is impossible for the family of nonstationary coordinate solutions to (28.1.1–28.3) to possess some ***uniform*** global stability properties as in Theorems 28.13–28.14. However, if the attractive directrix values still have the same sign, it is only the coordinate solutions along some repulsive directrices that prevent global stability statements about the whole family of nonstationary coordinate solutions. The exceptional solutions allow us only to offer generic stability statements.

**Remark 28.17** If there is *one attractive* directrix and *one repulsive* directrix, but with *different signs* of their directrix values (28.24), then the families of coordinate solutions of (28.1.1–28.3)—depending on the *sign* of the attractive directrix value—have *generically* the stability properties demonstrated in Theorems 28.9–28.12, 28.14.

When there are several attractive directrices with different signs of their directrix values, then, of course, generic stability statements will be further narrowed in scope. Locally, however, Theorems 28.9–28.12 can always be applied around the attractive directrices, cf. Remark 28.16. ▽

## SYNOPSIS

As we have now completed the exposition of the qualitative behavior of the homogeneous dynamic system (28.1.1–28.3), (28.9.1–2), we should at this final stage recapitulate the various results and theorems, emphasizing the *fundamentals.* Stripped of the finer and complicating details, we may reduce planar homogeneous dynamics to a *few essentials.* We do this by offering three general propositions about autonomous homogeneous systems of ordinary normal differential equations.

**Proposition 28.1** *The dynamics of any autonomous system of two interdependent differential equations—having the same* ***degree*** *of homogeneity—can succinctly be described by a "****single****" autonomous differential equation.*

***Proof*** This proposition follows primarily from Theorem 28.1, which essentially replaced the autonomous system (28.1.1–28.3) by the autonomous equation (28.34), except for the singularities (28.61). Although (28.34) will be different for alternative initial values in (28.1.1–28.3), cf. (28.35), we still have that (28.34)—together with singularities (28.61) and associated solutions (28.63–28.65.3)—fully described the dynamic properties of the system (28.1.1–28.3), as (28.34) eventuates in the whole *family* of *solutions* (28.38.1–2), (28.52–28.54), to (28.1.1–28.3), (28.9.1–2). □

The qualitative theory of differential equations is often restricted to the study of the geometric (topological) properties of the trajectories. The geometry and disposition of the trajectories (28.39), (28.62), is an old subject, cf. (28.90–28.96), which only needed some amendments such as the decomposition analysis of the entire domain (28.19) and a closer examination of the relevant integrals, cf. Lemma 28.1. However, Eq. (28.34) was not confined to the description of only the trajectories; it was harnessed to deal with the genuine *dynamics* of (28.1.1–28.3), i.e., the description of the actual motion (*solutions*) along the trajectories, cf. (28.36–28.38.2), (28.97).

Naturally, the stability properties of this family had next to be analyzed.

**Proposition 28.2** *The prevalence of global or local asymptotic* ***ratio*** *stability within a planar homogeneous system is solely determined by the shape of the* ***graph*** *of the director function, (28.15), given by the governing functions, (28.12.1–3).*

***Proof*** The proposition follows from Theorems 28.4 and 28.6, which stated, respectively, the global and local conditions for the solutions of (28.34) to approach the singularities (28.61). The latter can be seen as employing the concept of an attractor to also dynamic systems with attractive rays (directrices). □

**Proposition 28.3** *The global stability properties of the* ***coordinate*** *solutions—from a homogeneous system with a unique attractive directrix and a positive directrix value, (28.24)—are almost unaffected by the various specifications of the governing functions. They primarily depend upon the actual* ***degree*** *of homogeneity.*

***Proof*** This proposition follows from Theorems 28.9–28.11. Although the existence of a directrix and the positivity of $f(\alpha)$ evidently depend on the actual specification of the governing functions, $f$ and $g$, other restrictions imposed upon $f$ and $g$ (apart from occasionally, $h'(\alpha) < 0$) did not matter—in contrast to the degree, $m$—for obtaining the stability properties of Theorems 28.9–28.11. □

Generally, the solutions, (28.36), (28.38.1–2), could not be expressed in closed forms. But the fact that these solutions, $\boldsymbol{\rho(t)}$, $\boldsymbol{\varphi(t)}$, were expressed in terms of well-defined *primitives,* (28.37), (28.25) —with integrands being determined by the basic *governing functions*, $\boldsymbol{f}$ and $\boldsymbol{g}$—allowed us to deduce the *qualitative* (stability) properties of the family of coordinate solutions to (28.1.1–28.3) for any specification of the governing functions, as evidenced in the proofs of Theorems 28.9–28.11.

## Concluding Comments

We have analyzed a wide class of planar dynamic systems sharing one fundamental property: the homogeneity of the governing functions. This class, (28.1.1–28.3), encompasses both nonlinear and linear differential equations. Besides dealing with the traditional topics of trajectory geometry and asymptotic stability, we have focused especially upon the kinematics of the families of growing solutions and demonstrated the inherent connection between the degrees of homogeneity of the governing functions and generalized stability properties of the respective families of solutions.

Beyond the mathematical discipline, the primary purpose of ***differential equations*** has always been to serve as a tool for the ***study*** of ***change***, first in the physical sciences, cf. Arnold (1978), Simmons (1972), and later also within the realms of biology and social sciences. As to the latter and perhaps especially ***economics***, the ***class*** of ***homogeneous*** functions (Euler) has a natural setting in many applications by its ability to take in and represent, conveniently and often adequately, the factual implications of varying the *scale* (levels) of every variable.

Likewise, in studies of the economic evolution for societies with similar institutions: if some proper state variables and the fundamental laws of economic dynamics are maintained as being applicable for both ***large*** and ***small*** countries, then the governing functions are likely to possess some overall properties akin to ***homogeneity***. Indeed, prototype ***economic growth*** models have, albeit tacitly, reflected such homogeneity properties and allowed for various degrees of homogeneity. Accordingly, our analysis and theorems on ***homogeneous dynamics*** provide a mathematical framework and an ***axiomatic foundation*** of basic economic growth models. The theorems may also find applications in other areas of social and biological process analysis.

## Bibliography

Arnold VI (1978) Mathematical Methods of Classical Mechanics. In: Springer–Verlag, New York

Arnold VI (1986) Catastrophe Theory, 2nd edn. Springer–Verlag, Berlin

Arnold VI (1988) Geometrical Methods in the Theory of Ordinary Differential Equations, 2nd edn. Springer–Verlag, New York

Arrowsmith DK, Place CM (1990) An Introduction to Dynamical Systems. Cambridge University Press, Cambridge

Bellman R (1953) Stability Theory of Differential Equations. McGraw–Hill, New York

Bendixson I (1901) Sur les courbes définies par des equations différentielles. Acta Mathematica 24:1–88

Bieberbach L (1923) Theorie der Differential–Gleichungen. Verlag von Julius Springer, Berlin

Birkhoff GD (1927) Dynamical Systems. American Mathematical Society Colloquium Publications IX 1927, Rev. ed. 1966, Providence, Rhode Island

Birkhoff G, Rota G (1989) Ordinary Differential Equations, 4th edn. John Wiley & Sons, New York

Boole G (1959) A Treatise on Differential Equations, 5th edn. Chelsea Publishing Company, New York, (MacMillan, London, 1859)
Casti J (1979) Connectivity, Complexity and Catastrophe in Large–Scale Systems. John Wiley & Sons, New York, Interscience Publication
Cesari L (1963) Asymptotic Behavior and Stability Problems in Ordinary Differential Equations, 2nd edn. Academic Press, New York, Springer–Verlag, Berlin, 1959
Collatz L (1966) Differentialgleichungen. B.G. Teubner, Stuttgart
Forster H (1938) Über das verhalten der Integralkurven einer gevönlichen Differentialgleichung erster Ordnung in der Umgebung eines singulären Punktes. Math Zeitsch 43:271–320
Frommer M (1934) Über das Auftreten von Wirbeln und Strudeln (geschlossener und spiraliger Integralkurven) in der Umgebung rationaler Un-be-stimmt-heits-stel-len. Math Annalen 109:395–424
Gauss KF (1963) Theory of the motion of the heavenly bodies moving about the sun in conic sections: A translation of Theoria motus. Dover Publications, New York
Goodman LE, Warner WH (2001a) Dynamics. Dover Publications, New York
Goodman LE, Warner WH (2001b) Statics. Dover Publications, New York
Hirsch MW, Smale S (1974) Differential Equations, Dynamical Systems and Linear Algebra. Academic Press, New York
Ince EL (1956) Ordinary Differential Equations. Dover Publications, New York
Kamke E (1960) Differentialgleichungen und Randwertprobleme;. Band 1: *Ge-vöhn-liche Differentialgleichungen,* 2. Auflage, VEB Verlag Technik, Berlin.
Kaplan W (1967) Ordinary Differential Equations. Addison–Wesley Pub. Comp, Mass
Kneschke A (1956) Differentialgleichungen, Lösungsmethoden und Lösungen;. Band 1: *Gevöhnliche Differentialgleichungen,* 5. Auflage, Akademische Verlagsgesellschaft, Leipzig.
Knudsen JM, Hjorth PG (1996) Elements of Newtonian Mechanics. Including Nonlinear Dynamics, second and enlarged edn. Springer-Verlag
Landau LD, Lifshitz EM (1989) Mechanics, 3rd edn. Pergamon Press, Oxford
Liapounoff AM (1947a) Probléme Général de la Stabilité du Mouvement. Annales de la Faculté des Sciences de Toulouse 2. Series, **9** (1907); *Annals of Mathe-matics Studies, no. 17,* Princeton University Press, New Jersey.
Liapounoff AM (1947b) Stability of Motion. Academic Press, New Jersey
Malkin IG (1959) Theorie der Stabilität einer Bewegung. R. Oldenburg, München
Mises Rv (1939) Über den Verlauf der Integralkurven einer Differentialgleichung erster Ordnung. Compositio Math 6:203–220
Murphy GM (1960) Ordinary Differential Equations and Their Solutions. D. Van Nostrand, Princeton, New Jersey
Nemytskii VV, Stepanov VV (1989) Qualitative Theory of Differential Equations. Dover Publications, New York
Olech C (1963) On the Global Stability of an Autonomous System on the Plane. pp 389–400, in *Contributions to Differential Equations,* Lasalle, J.P. and Diaz, J.B. (ed.), **1** (1963), Interscience, John Wiley and Sons, New York.
Petrovski IG (1966) Ordinary Differential Equations. Dover Publications, New York
Poincaré H (1928) Memoire sur les courbes définies par une equation differentielle. Journal de Mathematiques 3. serie, 7 (1881), 375–422; **8** (1882), 251–96; Oeuvres, Tome 1, 3–86, Gauthier–Villars, Paris.
Rosen R (1970) Dynamical System Theory in Biology, Volume 1: Stability Theory and Its Applications. Wiley–Interscience, New York

Sanchez DA (1968) Ordinary Differential Equations and Stability Theory: An Introduction. Dover Publications, New York

Sansone G, Conti R (1964) Non–Linear Differential Equation. Pergamon Press, London

Shub M (1987) Global Stability of Dynamical Systems. Springer–Verlag, New York

Simmons GF (1972) Differential Equations – with applications and historical notes. McGraw–Hill, New York

Thom R (1989) Structural Stability and Morphogenesis. An Outline of a General Theory of Models. Addison–Wesley, New York, W.A. Benjamin Inc., Reading, Mass., 1975

Šiljak D (1969) Nonlinear Systems. The Parameter Analysis and Design. John Wiley & Sons, New York

Wiggins S (1988) Global Bifurcations and Chaos. Springer–Verlag, New York

CHAPTER 29

# Linear and Affine Dynamics in the Plane

## Introduction

A definite theory exists for solving linear systems of ordinary differential equations with constant coefficients. "This theory is essentially a branch of linear algebra, and allows us to solve all autonomous linear equations" (Arnold 1973, p. 95). Furthermore, "In view of the fact that the solution of these equations does not, in principle, present any great difficulties, they are often considered to be of no great interest for theory, and in textbooks they are usually relegated to the position of simple exercises appended to the general theory of linear equations" (Pontryagin 1962, p. 41). Modern textbooks (Arrowsmith and Place 1982; Birkhoff and Rota 1989; Braun 1983; Hirsch and Smale 1974; Hochstadt 1964; Hurewitz 1958; Jordan and Smith 1977; Simmons 1972) give a detailed and rigorous treatment of the standard methods available for linear problems, supplemented with numerous mechanical, electrical, and engineering applications. The voluminous literature accumulated on the general properties of the solutions of linear differential equations must, therefore, no doubt leave the impression that no further contribution could be made to the standard normal linear dynamic system with real and constant coefficients. This impression, however, will fade rather quickly as we go on. Paradoxically, some fundamental aspects of this simple dynamic system are still unnoticed.

A characteristic feature of ordinary linear differential equations is, of course, the *linearity* (additivity and first-degree) property of the *governing* functions, as well as *homogeneity* property of the *governing* functions. The *term* homogeneity is often used in "*two*" ways, namely, *algebraic* (equational) sense and *functional* (projective, Euler) sense. Algebraically, an *affine* system consists of either "homogeneous linear" or "nonhomogeneous linear" equations, where the latter, besides the *coefficient matrix* of the *variables*, will include *separate* parametric *elements* (constant, external, exogenous, forcing, driving, or input



B. S. Jensen, *The Elements and Dynamic Systems of Economic Growth and Trade Models*, https://doi.org/10.1007/978-3-031-52493-6_29

terms) see (Pontryagin 1962, p. 39). Functionally, mappings are homogeneous in accordance with a well-known criterion, (28.9.1–2). Although the algebraic notion of homogeneous ("*free*") systems is seldom related to the class of homogeneous functions, the algebraic definition of the term homogeneity agrees, as a special case, cf. Murphy (1960, p. 82), with the functional criterion.

The mathematical methods of *solving* autonomous homogeneous linear differential equations are usually based on purely *algebraic methods,* namely the *reduction* of the *coefficient matrix* to the *Jordan form*. This is a straightforward procedure when *all eigenvalues* are *real* and *distinct,* but *not* so in the *general* case.

Our *solution technique*, based on *calculus,* will cover the *general* case, and it will avoid the algebra of eigenvalues as well as complex algebra. Furthermore, our *solutions* will be expressed in the *original coefficients* of the linear *governing functions*, which is a decisive *advantage* for the *factual* interpretation and understanding of the *dynamic system* under investigation in any *applied* field of research. Finally, as it is on basic elements of our subject that fresh illustration is most usefully bestowed, the *linear forms* offer the very opportunity of a thorough mastery of the fundamental ideas and methods underlying our approach to *planar homogeneous dynamics.*

Furthermore, an important object of this chapter is also to examine the *kinematic stability* properties of *ratio* and *coordinate* solutions to linear dynamics in the plane. The *geometrical* (topological) classification by Poincaré (1928, p. 13–18) of a *singularity* (critical point) as a *node* (noeud), *saddle* (col), *focus* (foyer), or *center* (centre) is, evidently, together with its uniqueness, of decisive importance for the global *asymptotic* stability/instability of the coordinate solutions. However, this now standard geometrical classification of the origin will be of much *less* significance (and especially so, the distinction between a node and a saddle) for classifying the *kinematics* of the nonsingular linear system by our *generalized* stability criteria.

## The Linear System, Director Function, and Directrices

Consider the dynamic system of two *linear forms*, with *real* coefficients in two real variables, $(x, y) \in \mathbf{R}^2$, cf. (28.11.1–28.12.3), and Remark 28.1 in section "Basic Framework, Assumptions, and Definitions", Remark 28.4,

$$\dot{x} = F(x, y) = ax + by = x(a + br) = xf(r), \tag{29.1.1}$$

$$\dot{y} = G(x, y) = cx + dy = x(c + dr) = xg(r), \tag{29.1.2}$$

or, in *vector-matrix* notation,

$$\dot{\mathbf{x}} = \begin{bmatrix} \dot{x}_1 \\ \dot{x}_2 \end{bmatrix} = \begin{bmatrix} a & b \\ c & d \end{bmatrix} \begin{bmatrix} x_1 \\ x_2 \end{bmatrix} = \mathbf{A}\mathbf{x}, \quad \mathbf{x} \in \mathbf{R}^2, \tag{29.2.1}$$

where the real coefficient matrix $\boldsymbol{A}$ has

$$\text{trace} = 2\mu = a + d, \text{ alternating trace} = 2\nu = a - d,$$
$$\text{determinant} = |A| = ad - bc. \tag{29.2.2}$$

The *director function* $\boldsymbol{h(r)}$, cf. Chap. 28 section "Basic Framework, Assumptions, and Definitions", of the linear system (29.1.1–2) is given by

$$h(r) = g(r) - rf(r) = c + (d - a)r - br^2, \quad b \neq 0. \tag{29.3}$$

This second-order polynomial (*parabola*) for $\boldsymbol{h(r)}$ has a *discriminant*, conveniently designated by $4\Delta^2$, and so

$$\Delta^2 = \tfrac{1}{4}(d - a)^2 + bc = \tfrac{1}{4}(d + a)^2 - (ad - bc) = \tfrac{1}{4}(d + a)^2 - |A|. \tag{29.4}$$

Since the *sign* of the *discriminant* (29.4) will be *instrumental* in systematizing the *qualitative* behavior of the *solutions*, as well as the *loci* forms of *trajectories*, and since its *numerical size* (the positive square root of either $\Delta^2$ or $|\Delta^2|$) will also *quantitatively* appear as a *parameter* of the *solutions*, we introduce the notation

$$\Delta^2 > 0 \ : \ \Delta \equiv +\sqrt{\Delta^2}\ ; \quad \Delta^2 < 0 \ : \ |\Delta| \equiv +\sqrt{|\Delta^2|}. \tag{29.5}$$

The sets of *director roots* $\mathcal{A} = \{\alpha \in \mathbf{R} \mid h(\alpha) = 0\} \subset \mathbf{R}$, cf. (29.3–29.4), are

$$\Delta^2 > 0 : \mathcal{A} = \{\alpha_1, \alpha_2\}; \ \alpha_1 = \frac{d - a}{2b} + \frac{\Delta}{b}, \ \alpha_2 = \frac{d - a}{2b} - \frac{\Delta}{b}, \tag{29.6.1}$$

$$\alpha_1 + \alpha_2 = (d - a)/b, \ \alpha_1 - \alpha_2 = 2\Delta/b, \ \alpha_1\alpha_2 = -c/b, \tag{29.6.2}$$

$$\Delta^2 = 0 : \mathcal{A} = \{\alpha\}; \ \alpha = (d - a)/2b = 2c/(a - d); \ \alpha^2 = -c/b, \tag{29.7}$$

$$\Delta^2 < 0 : \mathcal{A} = \emptyset. \tag{29.8}$$

The number and the *slopes* of *directrix*, $\boldsymbol{y = \alpha x}$, $\boldsymbol{\alpha \in \mathcal{A}}$, follow immediately from (29.6.1–29.8), and the respective set of director roots give a *decomposition* of the *domain*, $D = \mathbf{R}^2/\{0, 0\}$, into the *open cones*

$$\Delta^2 > 0 : C_1 = \{(x, y) \in D \mid (y/x) \in ]\alpha_1, \alpha_2[\},$$

$$C_2 = \{(x, y) \in D \mid (y/x) \notin [\alpha_1, \alpha_2]\}, \quad (29.9)$$

$$\Delta^2 = 0 : C_3 = \{(x, y) \in D \mid (y/x) > \alpha\},$$

$$C_4 = \{(x, y) \in D \mid (y/x) < \alpha\}, \quad (29.10)$$

$$\Delta^2 < 0 : C_5 = D, \quad (29.11)$$

where $C_1, C_2$ have two sheets, $C_3, C_4$ are open half-planes, and $C_5$ is the entire punctured plane.

As to the *directrix values*, $\boldsymbol{f(\alpha)}$, $\boldsymbol{\alpha \in \mathcal{A}}$, we get, cf. (29.1.1–2), (29.6.1–29.7),

$$\Delta^2 > 0 : f(\alpha_1) = a + b\alpha_1 = \tfrac{1}{2}(a + d) + \Delta = d - b\alpha_2, \quad (29.12.1)$$

$$f(\alpha_2) = a + b\alpha_2 = \tfrac{1}{2}(a + d) - \Delta = d - b\alpha_1, \quad (29.12.2)$$

$$\Delta^2 = 0 : f(\alpha) \;\; = a + b\alpha \;\; = \tfrac{1}{2}(a + d). \quad (29.13)$$

For the special case of *triangular* systems, i.e., with $\boldsymbol{bc = 0}$ in (29.1.1–29.2.2), a *negative* discriminant (29.4) *cannot* occur. For reference, we state the *director roots* and the *directrix values* of the *triangular cases*, cf. (29.6.1–2), (29.12.1–2)

$$c = 0,\ b \neq 0 : \alpha_1 = (d - a)/b,\ \alpha_2 = 0; \quad f(\alpha_1) = d,\ f(\alpha_2) = a, \quad (29.14.1)$$

$$b = 0,\ c \neq 0 : \alpha_1 = c/(a - d),\ \alpha_2 = \infty; \ f(\alpha_1) = a,\ f(\alpha_2) = d. \quad (29.14.2)$$

Triangularity and $a = d$ imply, $\Delta^2 = 0$, and hence only *one* director root $\alpha$ exists, which is either 0 or $\infty$, cf. (29.7), (29.14.1–2).

The *diagonal system* is a subordinate case of (29.14.1–2), i.e.,

$$b = 0,\ c = 0 \ : \ \alpha_1 = 0,\ \alpha_2 = \infty; \ f(\alpha_1) = a,\ f(\alpha_2) = d. \quad (29.15)$$

**Remark 29.1** The *existence* of *axis directrices* is equivalent to triangular/diagonal systems ($\boldsymbol{bc = 0}$), cf. Lemma 28.3 in section "The Ratio and Coordinate Solutions on Directrices", (28.70.1–2). Hence, with $\boldsymbol{bc \neq 0}$, the director roots (29.6.1) attain *finite nonzero* values. ▽

We observe from (29.4) that

$$bc \geq 0 \Rightarrow \Delta^2 \geq 0, \quad \Delta^2 \leq 0 \Rightarrow bc \leq 0, \tag{29.16.1}$$

$$\Delta^2 < 0 \Rightarrow |A| > 0, \quad |A| \leq 0 \Rightarrow \Delta^2 \geq 0. \tag{29.16.2}$$

A simple classification of the *signs* of the ***director roots*** (29.6.1–2) and the ***directrix values*** (29.12.1–2) will be useful —besides, $b > 0 : \alpha_1 > \alpha_2$, $b < 0 : \alpha_1 < \alpha_2$, and always $f(\alpha_1) > f(\alpha_2)$—viz.,

$bc > 0 \Rightarrow \alpha_1, \alpha_2$ have opposite signs,

$$\alpha_1 > 0, \ \alpha_2 < 0 \quad \text{for} \quad b > 0, \ c > 0, \tag{29.17.1}$$

$$\alpha_1 < 0, \ \alpha_2 > 0 \quad \text{for} \quad b < 0, \ c < 0, \tag{29.17.2}$$

$bc < 0 \Rightarrow \alpha_1, \alpha_2$ have same signs,

$$\alpha_1 > 0, \ \alpha_2 > 0 \quad \text{for} \quad b > 0, \ d > a \ \text{or} \ b < 0, \ d < a, \tag{29.18.1}$$

$$\alpha_1 < 0, \ \alpha_2 < 0 \quad \text{for} \quad b > 0, \ d < a \ \text{or} \ b < 0, \ d > a, \tag{29.18.2}$$

$bc > ad \Rightarrow f(\alpha_1), \ f(\alpha_2)$ have opposite signs,

$$f(\alpha_1) > 0, \ f(\alpha_2) < 0 \quad \text{for any} \quad a, b, c, d, \tag{29.19.1}$$

$bc < ad \Rightarrow f(\alpha_1), \ f(\alpha_2)$ have same signs,

$$f(\alpha_1) > 0, \ f(\alpha_2) > 0 \quad \text{for} \quad a + d > 0, \tag{29.20.1}$$

$$f(\alpha_1) < 0, \ f(\alpha_2) < 0 \quad \text{for} \quad a + d < 0. \tag{29.20.2}$$

**Remark 29.2** It follows from (29.12.1–2), (29.14.1–29.15), and (29.4) that the ***directrix values*** satisfy

$$f(\alpha_1)f(\alpha_2) = \tfrac{1}{4}(a+d)^2 - \Delta^2 = ad - bc = |A|. \tag{29.21}$$

▽

## The General Ratio Solution

The *family* (complete set) of *ratio* solutions $\boldsymbol{\rho}(t)$ to the linear system (29.1.1–2) will include both *stationary* and *nonstationary* ratio solutions.

Within the system (29.1.1–2), however, ***stationary ratio*** solutions will only exist when the discriminant (29.4) is nonnegative, and then they are immediately obtained from the director roots, see Theorem 28.2 in section "The Ratio and Coordinate Solutions on Directrices", (28.61),

$$\Delta^2 \geq 0 \; : \; \rho(t) = \alpha = r_0 = y_0/x_0, \; \forall t; \; \alpha \in \mathcal{A}, \tag{29.22}$$

where $\mathcal{A}$ is given by (29.6.1–29.7).

The *governing* function $\boldsymbol{Q(r)}$ of the *general nonstationary* ratio solution $\boldsymbol{\rho(t)}$ is, with $\boldsymbol{m = 1}$, always the *same* as the *director function* $\boldsymbol{h(r)}$, restricted to the appropriate intervals of $\complement\mathcal{A}$; see (29.6.1–29.8) and Theorem 28.1 in section "Ratio Solutions, Coordinate Solutions, and Trajectories", (28.34). Hence for the linear system (29.1.1–2), we have, cf. (29.3)

$$\dot{r} = Q(r) = h(r) = c + (d-a)r - br^2, \; r \in \complement\mathcal{A} \subseteq \mathbf{R}. \tag{29.23}$$

Deriving the nonstationary ratio solutions $\boldsymbol{\rho(t)}$ in terms of *primitives* requires solving the integral equation

$$I(r) = \int \frac{dr}{Q(r)} = \int \frac{dr}{h(r)} = \int \frac{dr}{c + (d-a)r - br^2} = t + t_0, \; r \in \complement\mathcal{A}. \tag{29.24}$$

This is a standard integral with *well-known closed-form* expressions, depending on the *sign* of the *discriminant,* (29.4). Thus, still assuming $b \neq 0$ in (29.24), we have, see Selby (1973, p. 419–420),

$$\Delta^2 > 0 : I(r) = \begin{cases} \frac{1}{\Delta}\text{artanh}\left(\frac{a-d+2br}{2\Delta}\right), & r \in ]\alpha_1, \alpha_2[, \\ \frac{1}{\Delta}\text{arcoth}\left(\frac{a-d+2br}{2\Delta}\right), & r \notin [\alpha_1, \alpha_2], \end{cases} \tag{29.25}$$

$$\Delta^2 = 0 : I(r) = \frac{2}{a-d+2br}, \quad r \in \mathbf{R}/\{\alpha\}, \tag{29.26}$$

$$\Delta^2 < 0 : I(r) = \frac{-1}{|\Delta|}\arctan\left(\frac{a-d+2br}{2|\Delta|}\right), \quad r \in \mathbf{R}. \tag{29.27}$$

The *general nonstationary ratio* solution is given as $\boldsymbol{\rho(t) = I^{-1}(t + t_0)}$, cf. (28.36). We obtain from this and (29.24–29.27)

$$\Delta^2 > 0 : \rho(t) = \begin{cases} \frac{d-a}{2b} + \frac{\Delta}{b}\tanh[\Delta(t+t_0)], & t_0 = I(r_0); \; r_0 \in ]\alpha_1, \alpha_2[, \\ \frac{d-a}{2b} + \frac{\Delta}{b}\coth[\Delta(t+t_0)], & t_0 = I(r_0); \; r_0 \notin [\alpha_1, \alpha_2], \end{cases} \tag{29.28}$$

$$\Delta^2 = 0 : \; \rho(t) = \frac{d-a}{2b} + \frac{1}{b}(t+t_0)^{-1}, \qquad t_0 = I(r_0); \; r_0 \in \mathbf{R}/\{\alpha\}, \tag{29.29}$$

$$\Delta^2 < 0 : \; \rho(t) = \frac{d-a}{2b} - \frac{|\Delta|}{b}\tan[|\Delta|(t+t_0)], \quad t_0 = I(r_0); \; r_0 \in \mathbf{R}, \tag{29.30}$$

where, respectively, $\boldsymbol{I}(\boldsymbol{r}_0)$ values are obtained by (29.25–29.27) for $r = r_0 = y_0/x_0$. Thus, (29.28–29.30) is the ***general nonstationary ratio solution*** of the *linear* system (29.1.1–2), $\boldsymbol{b} \neq 0$. The general nonstationary ratio solution for $b = 0$ is given below, cf. (29.66), (29.76).

In the case of a *nonnegative* discriminant ($\boldsymbol{\Delta}^2 \geq 0$), the formulas (29.28–29.29) may be restated in terms of *director roots* and *directrix values,* i.e., using (29.6.1–29.7), (29.12.1–29.13), we have

$$\Delta^2 > 0 : \rho(t) = \begin{cases} \frac{1}{2}(\alpha_1 + \alpha_2) + \frac{1}{2}(\alpha_1 - \alpha_2)\tanh[\frac{1}{2}b(\alpha_1 - \alpha_2)(t + t_0)], \\ \frac{1}{2}(\alpha_1 + \alpha_2) + \frac{1}{2}(\alpha_1 - \alpha_2)\coth[\frac{1}{2}b(\alpha_1 - \alpha_2)(t + t_0)], \end{cases} \tag{29.31}$$

$$\Delta^2 = 0 : \rho(t) = \alpha + 1/b(t + t_0), \tag{29.32}$$

where $\boldsymbol{b}(\boldsymbol{\alpha}_1 - \boldsymbol{\alpha}_2) = \boldsymbol{f}(\boldsymbol{\alpha}_1) - \boldsymbol{f}(\boldsymbol{\alpha}_2)$ is seen, cf. (29.6.2), to be always *positive.*

The *hyperbolic* functions may also be written in well-known exponential forms (with *real* arguments), $e^x = \cosh x + \sinh x$

$$\sinh x = \tfrac{1}{2}(e^x - e^{-x}), \qquad \cosh x = \tfrac{1}{2}(e^x + e^{-x}), \qquad x \in \mathbf{R}, \tag{29.33.1}$$

$$\tanh x = (e^x - e^{-x})/(e^x + e^{-x}), \qquad \coth x = 1/\tanh x, \qquad x \in \mathbf{R}. \tag{29.33.2}$$

Using (29.33.2), the *ratio solution* (29.31) becomes

$$\Delta^2 > 0 : \rho(t) = \begin{cases} \alpha_1 - \frac{\alpha_1 - \alpha_2}{\exp\{b(\alpha_1 - \alpha_2)(t + t_0)\} - 1}, & \rho(t) \in ]\alpha_1, \alpha_2[, \\ \alpha_1 + \frac{\alpha_1 - \alpha_2}{\exp\{b(\alpha_1 - \alpha_2)(t + t_0)\} - 1}, & \rho(t) \notin [\alpha_1, \alpha_2]. \end{cases} \tag{29.34}$$

## The General Coordinate Solution

The *family* of the (Cartesian) *coordinate solutions* $\boldsymbol{\varphi}(\boldsymbol{t}) = [\varphi_1(\boldsymbol{t}), \varphi_2(\boldsymbol{t})] = [\boldsymbol{x}(\boldsymbol{t}), \boldsymbol{y}(\boldsymbol{t})]$ to the linear system (29.1.1–2) consists—apart from the stationary solution, $\varphi(t) = [0, 0]$—of the *directrix* and the *non-directrix* solutions.

Along the *directrices* $R_\alpha$, the solutions $\boldsymbol{\varphi}(\boldsymbol{t})$ are given by Theorem 28.2 in section "The Ratio and Coordinate Solutions on Directrices" and $\boldsymbol{m} = 1$, in (28.61–28.62), (28.65.1), as

$$\Delta^2 > 0 : \varphi(t) = \begin{cases} x_0 \exp\{f(\alpha_1)t\}, \ \alpha_1 x_0 \exp\{f(\alpha_1)t\}, \\ x_0 \exp\{f(\alpha_2)t\}, \ \alpha_2 x_0 \exp\{f(\alpha_2)t\}, \end{cases} \tag{29.35}$$

$$\Delta^2 = 0 : \varphi(t) = x_0 \exp\{f(\alpha)t\}, \ \alpha x_0 \exp\{f(\alpha)t\}, \tag{29.36}$$

or, using (29.2.1–29.3), as

$$\Delta^2 > 0 : \varphi(t) = \begin{cases} e^{\frac{1}{2}(a+d)t} \exp\{\Delta t\}[x_0, y_0], & (x_0, y_0) \in R_{\alpha_1}, \\ e^{\frac{1}{2}(a+d)t} \exp\{-\Delta t\}[x_0, y_0], & (x_0, y_0) \in R_{\alpha_2}, \end{cases} \tag{29.37}$$

$$\Delta^2 = 0 : \varphi(t) = \quad e^{\frac{1}{2}(a+d)t}[x_0, y_0], \qquad (x_0, y_0) \in R_{\alpha}. \tag{29.38}$$

To present the *non-directrix* coordinate solutions $\boldsymbol{\varphi(t)}$ upon the respective *cones* (29.9–29.11) in closed form, the relevant expressions for $\exp\{H[\rho(t)]\}$ are needed in explicit terms, see Theorem 28.1 in section "Ratio Solutions, Coordinate Solutions, and Trajectories", (28.36). To this end, we first look for the functions $\boldsymbol{H(r)}$ with the derivative, cf. (28.25), (29.1.1), (29.3), as

$$H'(r) \equiv \frac{f(r)}{h(r)} = \frac{a+br}{c+(d-a)r-br^2}, \quad b \neq 0, \quad r \in \mathbb{C}\mathcal{A} \subseteq \mathbf{R}. \tag{29.39}$$

Since the integrand $\boldsymbol{H'(r)}$ is a rational function, it can be integrated in terms of *elementary* functions. Noting that $a + br = -\frac{1}{2}h'(r) + \frac{1}{2}(a+d)$, the *primitives* $\boldsymbol{H(r)}$ are easily found; we have

$$\begin{aligned} H(r) &= -\tfrac{1}{2}\log h(r) + \tfrac{1}{2}(a+d)\int \frac{dr}{h(r)} \\ &= -\tfrac{1}{2}\log h(r) + \tfrac{1}{2}(a+d)I(r), \; r \in \mathbb{C}\mathcal{A}, \end{aligned} \tag{29.40}$$

where $\boldsymbol{I(r)}$ is given respectively by (29.25–29.27). Then from (29.40)

$$\exp\{H(r)\} = \frac{\exp\{\frac{1}{2}(a+d)I(r)\}}{\sqrt{h(r)}}, \; r \in \mathbb{C}\mathcal{A}. \tag{29.41}$$

Since by definition, $I[\rho(t)] = t + t_0$, cf. (28.36) and so by (29.41)

$$\exp\{H[\rho(t)]\} = \exp\{\tfrac{1}{2}(a+d)(t+t_0)\}|h[\rho(t)]|^{-\frac{1}{2}}, \; \rho(t) \in \mathbb{C}\mathcal{A}. \tag{29.42}$$

Next, we must evaluate the expression, cf. (29.23),

$$h[\rho(t)] = c + (d-a)\rho(t) - b\rho^2(t), \quad \rho(t) \in \mathbb{C}\mathcal{A}. \tag{29.43}$$

*Inserting* the ratio solutions (29.28–29.30) into (29.43), we get after some manipulations and collections, using (29.4–29.6.2),

$$\Delta^2 > 0 : h[\rho(t)] = \begin{cases} \frac{\Delta^2}{b}\left[1 - \tanh^2[\Delta(t+t_0)]\right] = \frac{\Delta^2}{b}\cosh^{-2}[\Delta(t+t_0)], \\ -\frac{\Delta^2}{b}\left[\coth^2[\Delta(t+t_0)] - 1\right] = -\frac{\Delta^2}{b}\sinh^{-2}[\Delta(t+t_0)], \end{cases} \tag{29.44}$$

$$\Delta^2 = 0 : h[\rho(t)] = \quad (1/b)(t+t_0)^{-2}, \tag{29.45}$$

$$\Delta^2{<}0: h[\rho(t)] = \frac{\Delta^2}{b}\left[1+\tan^2[|\Delta|(t+t_0)]\right] = \frac{\Delta^2}{b}\cos^{-2}[|\Delta|(t+t_0)], \tag{29.46}$$

where the *last expressions* in (29.44) and (29.46) are due to standard formulas of *plane trigonometry* (hyperbolic and circular).

With $\varphi_1(t) = k_0 \exp\{H[\rho(t)]\}$, cf. (28.38.1), and (29.41–29.42) with $I(r_0) = t_0$, we have then the *first coordinate* solutions

$$\begin{aligned}\varphi_1(t) &= k_0 \exp\{H[\rho(t)]\} = x_0 \exp\{-H(r_0)\}\exp\{H[\rho(t)]\}\\ &= \frac{x_0|h(r_0)|^{1/2}}{\exp\left\{\frac{1}{2}(a+d)t_0\right\}}\cdot\frac{\exp\{\frac{1}{2}(a+d)(t+t_0)\}}{|h[\rho(t)]|^{1/2}}\\ &= x_0\,|h(r_0)|^{1/2}\exp\{\tfrac{1}{2}(a+d)t\}\,|h[\rho(t)]|^{-1/2}.\end{aligned} \tag{29.47}$$

Then by $h[\rho(0)] = h(r_0)$ and (29.44–29.47), the ***non-directrix first coordinate*** solutions become

$$\Delta^2{>}0 \quad : \varphi_1(t) = \begin{cases} x_0\,\mathrm{sech}[\Delta t_0]e^{\frac{1}{2}(a+d)t}\cosh[\Delta(t+t_0)], & x_0 \in C_1,\\ x_0\,\mathrm{cosech}[\Delta t_0]e^{\frac{1}{2}(a+d)t}\sinh[\Delta(t+t_0)], & x_0 \in C_2,\end{cases} \tag{29.48}$$

$$\Delta^2{=}0: \varphi_1(t) = \quad x_0 e^{\frac{1}{2}(a+d)t}[(t/t_0)+1], \qquad x_0 \in C_3 \vee C_4, \tag{29.49}$$

$$\Delta^2{<}0 \quad : \varphi_1(t) = \quad x_0 \sec[|\Delta| t_0]e^{\frac{1}{2}(a+d)t}\cos[|\Delta|(t+t_0)], \qquad x_0 \in C_5, \tag{29.50}$$

where $t_0$ is given by, respectively, (29.28–29.30) and

$$\mathrm{sech} = 1/\cosh,\;\; \mathrm{cosech} = 1/\sinh,\;\; \sec = 1/\cos. \tag{29.51}$$

The ***non-directrix second coordinate** solutions* $\boldsymbol{\varphi_2(t)}$ corresponding to (29.47–29.50) are simply obtained from the identity: $\boldsymbol{\varphi_2(t) \equiv \varphi_1(t)\rho(t)}$, see (28.38.2).

Hence by (29.47–29.50), (29.28–29.30), they are of the respective forms

$$\Delta^2{>}0: \varphi_2(t) = \begin{cases} \frac{x_0}{\cosh(\Delta t_0)}e^{\frac{1}{2}(a+d)t}\cosh[\Delta(t+t_0)]\left[\frac{d-a}{2b}+\frac{\Delta}{b}\tanh[\Delta(t+t_0)]\right],\\ \frac{x_0}{\sinh(\Delta t_0)}e^{\frac{1}{2}(a+d)t}\sinh[\Delta(t+t_0)]\left[\frac{d-a}{2b}+\frac{\Delta}{b}\coth[\Delta(t+t_0)]\right],\end{cases} \tag{29.52}$$

$$\Delta^2{=}0: \varphi_2(t) = \; x_0 e^{\frac{1}{2}(a+d)t}[(t/t_0)+1]\left[\frac{d-a}{2b}+\frac{1}{b(t+t_0)}\right], \tag{29.53}$$

$$\Delta^2{<}0: \varphi_2(t) = \; \frac{x_0}{\cos(|\Delta| t_0)}e^{\frac{1}{2}(a+d)t}\cos[|\Delta|(t+t_0)]\left[\frac{d-a}{2b}-\frac{|\Delta|}{b}\tan[|\Delta|(t+t_0)]\right]. \tag{29.54}$$

Thus, (29.37–29.38), (29.48–29.50), (29.52–29.54) represent the ***general coordinate solution*** of the *linear system* (29.1.1–2), $b \neq 0$. The general formulas for $b = 0$ are treated below, cf. (29.67–29.68), (29.77–29.78).

## Ratio and Coordinate Solutions of Triangular Systems

Up to now, we have first and foremost given the attention to linear dynamics with *nonzero* values of *all* the *system parameters:* $\boldsymbol{a, b, c, d}$. The treatment of the general system allows us to present briefly the special cases of *triangular* and *diagonal coefficient* matrices in (29.2.1), i.e., *with*: $\boldsymbol{bc = 0}$.

First of all, it must be noted that ***triangular*** systems *preclude* the existence of *circular* trigonometric *ratio* and *coordinate* solutions, (29.30), (29.50), and (29.54), since the *discriminant* (29.4) is always *nonnegative*

$$bc = 0 \;:\; \Delta^2 = \tfrac{1}{4}(d-a)^2 \geq 0. \tag{29.55}$$

Secondly, triangular systems with $d \neq a$ imply the existence of *two directrices*, one of which is either the $x$- or the $y$-axis as stated in (29.14.1–2), cf. Remark 29.1. But triangular systems with $d = a$, hence $\Delta^2 = 0$, have only *one* directrix, the $x$- or the $y$-axis, cf. (29.7)

For easy reference, we present here the relevant formulas for the *general ratio* solutions and the *general coordinate* solutions of *triangular* systems.

The case $\boldsymbol{c = 0}$, $\boldsymbol{b \neq 0}$, $\boldsymbol{d \neq a}$ is already covered by our formulas above. Hence, by (29.14.1), (29.22), (29.25), (29.28), (29.33.1), (29.37), (29.48), (29.52), and (29.55), we get

$$\rho(t) = \alpha = y_0/x_0 = r_0, \ \forall t; \quad \alpha \in \mathcal{A} = \{\alpha_1, \alpha_2\} = \{\tfrac{d-a}{b},\ 0\}, \tag{29.56}$$

$$\varphi(t) = \begin{cases} e^{dt}[x_0, y_0], & r_0 \in R_{\alpha_1}, \\ e^{at}[x_0, 0], & r_0 \in R_{\alpha_2}, \end{cases} \tag{29.57}$$

$$\rho(t) = \begin{cases} \frac{d-a}{2b}[1 + \tanh[(\frac{d-a}{2})(t+t_0)]], & r_0 \in ]\frac{d-a}{b}, 0[\,, \quad t_0 = I(r_0), \\ \frac{d-a}{2b}[1 + \coth[(\frac{d-a}{2})(t+t_0)]], & r_0 \notin ]\frac{d-a}{b}, 0[\,, \quad t_0 = I(r_0), \\ 1/[\frac{b}{d-a} + (\frac{1}{r_0} - \frac{b}{d-a})e^{(a-d)t}], & r_0 \neq (\frac{d-a}{b}) \wedge 0, \end{cases} \tag{29.58}$$

$$\varphi_1(t) = x_0 e^{at} + \tfrac{by_0}{d-a}(e^{dt} - e^{at}), \qquad x_0, y_0 \in C_1 \vee C_2, \tag{29.59}$$

$$\varphi_2(t) = \varphi_1(t)\rho(t) = y_0 e^{dt}, \qquad x_0, y_0 \in C_1 \vee C_2. \tag{29.60}$$

In the case of $\boldsymbol{b = 0}$, $\boldsymbol{c \neq 0}$, $\boldsymbol{d \neq a}$, the *director function* (29.3) collapses to a first-order polynomial

$$b = 0 \;:\; h(r) = c + (d-a)r. \tag{29.61}$$

The governing function of the ratio solutions, $\dot{r} = Q(r) = h(r)$, is here given by (29.61); hence, cf. (29.24)

$$I(r) = \int \frac{1}{Q(r)} = \int \frac{dr}{c + (d - a)r} = \frac{1}{d - a} \ln |c+(d-a)r| = t+t_0. \qquad (29.62)$$

With $b = 0$, $f(r) = a + br = a$, we have cf. (29.39–29.40), (29.62)

$$b = 0 : \; H(r) = \int \frac{f(r)}{h(r)} dr = aI(r) = \frac{a}{d - a} \ln |c + (d - a)r|. \qquad (29.63)$$

The formulas for the *directrix* and the *non-directrix* **ratio solutions** and **coordinate solutions** become, cf. (29.14.2), (29.61–29.63), (29.47).

$$\rho(t) = \alpha = y_0/x_0 = r_0, \; \forall t; \quad \alpha \in \mathcal{A} = \{\alpha_1, \alpha_2\} = \{\tfrac{c}{a-d}, \infty\}, \qquad (29.64)$$

$$\varphi(t) = \begin{cases} e^{at}[x_0, y_0], & f(\alpha_1) = a \\ e^{dt}[0, y_0], & f(\alpha_1) = d \end{cases} \qquad (29.65)$$

$$\begin{aligned} \rho(t) &= \tfrac{1}{d-a}[-c + e^{(d-a)(t+t_0)}] \\ &= \tfrac{c}{a-d} + (r_0 - \tfrac{c}{a-d})e^{(d-a)t}, \quad r_0 \neq \tfrac{c}{a-d}, \end{aligned} \qquad (29.66)$$

$$\varphi_1(t) = x_0 e^{at}, \quad x_0 \in C_1 \vee C_2, \qquad (29.67)$$

$$\begin{aligned} \varphi_2(t) &= \varphi_1(t)\rho(t) = y_0 e^{dt} - \tfrac{cx_0}{a-d}(e^{dt} - e^{at}) \\ &= x_0[(r_0 - \alpha_1)e^{dt} + \alpha_1 e^{at}]. \end{aligned} \qquad (29.68)$$

The special *degenerate* triangular systems with $a = d$, hence $\Delta^2 = 0$, cf. (29.55), appear in two versions, depending on the axis directrix.

For $\boldsymbol{c = 0, b \neq 0, a = d}$, we have, cf. (29.7), (29.14.1), (29.29), (29.38), (29.49), (29.53).

$$\rho(t) = \alpha = y_0/x_0 = r_0, \; \forall t; \quad \alpha \in \mathcal{A} = \{0\}, \qquad (29.69)$$

$$\varphi(t) = e^{at}[x_0, 0], \quad r_0 \in R_0, \qquad (29.70)$$

$$\rho(t) = \tfrac{1}{b(t+t_0)} = \tfrac{1}{bt+1/r_0}, \quad r_0 \notin R_0, \qquad (29.71)$$

$$\varphi_1(t) = x_0 e^{at}(t/t_0 + 1) = (x_0 + y_0 bt)e^{at}, \quad y_0 \neq 0, \qquad (29.72)$$

$$\varphi_2(t) = \varphi_1(t)\rho(t) = y_0 e^{at}, \quad y_0 \neq 0. \qquad (29.73)$$

For $\boldsymbol{b = 0, c \neq 0, a = d}$, we get, cf. (29.7), (29.14.2), (29.61–29.62), (29.67)

$$\rho(t) = \alpha = y_0/x_0 = r_0, \; \forall t; \quad \alpha \in \mathcal{A} = \{\infty\}, \qquad (29.74)$$

$$\varphi(t) = e^{at}[0, y_0], \quad r_0 \in R_\infty, \qquad (29.75)$$

$$\rho(t) = c(t + t_0) = ct + r_0, \quad r_0 \neq \infty, \tag{29.76}$$

$$\varphi_1(t) = x_0 e^{at}, \quad x_0 \neq \infty, \quad x_0 \neq 0 \tag{29.77}$$

$$\varphi_2(t) = \varphi_1(t)\rho(t) = x_0 e^{at}(ct + r_0) = (y_0 + x_0 ct)e^{at}, \quad x_0 \neq 0. \tag{29.78}$$

The *diagonal* systems, $b = 0,\ c = 0, d \neq a$, are covered as subordinate cases of the formulas, (29.64–29.68). The diagonal case with $d = a$, however, implies that the director function (29.61) becomes the null-polynomial, $h(r) = 0$; the set of director roots is then infinite, $\overline{\mathcal{A}} = R \cup \pm\infty$, and $\rho(t) = y_0/x_0,\ \forall t$; the *phase curves* of the *solutions* represent a "*star*": $\varphi(t) = e^{at}[x_0, y_0]$, $(x_0, y_0) \in \mathbf{R}^2 \setminus \{0, 0\}$.

## The Calculus Approach and Techniques of Integration

The general ratio and coordinate solutions in sections "The General Ratio Solution"–"Ratio and Coordinate Solutions of Triangular Systems" were obtained by *regular methods* of differential and integral *calculus*—*not* by methods from linear *algebra*. A calculus approach to solving systems of differential equations is likely, of course, to encounter the old "quadrature problem", which in the narrow sense meant a search for the relevant *primitives* expressed in *closed form* (finite combinations of elementary functions).

Such a request for closed forms is not insuperable to our fundamental "ratio integrals", $\boldsymbol{I}(\boldsymbol{r})$, (29.24–29.27), and $\boldsymbol{H}(\boldsymbol{r})$, (29.39–29.40). Throughout, the steps in calculus were performed deliberately with reference to rigorous, but well-known standard procedures.

Since laws that regulate physical or other processes are expressed mathematically by differential equations, we may here well appreciate the importance of *integration* for any mathematical *process* analysis. Indeed, the researcher in his attempts to draw definite conclusions from his premises is utterly dependent upon his ability to integrate differential equations—often requiring that he can rigorously perform several integrations. The following re-examination of our integration problems will further clarify the situation.

Now, from hindsight, we may observe that (29.23–29.30) suggest the convenience—for just the technical purpose of integration—of a provisional *substitution* of the *ratio variable* $r$ by a *variable* $s$, defined by

$$\Delta^2 \neq 0 : \ r = (d - a)/2b + (\Delta/b)s, \tag{29.79.1}$$

$$\Delta^2 = 0 : \ r = (d - a)/2b + (1/b)s. \tag{29.79.2}$$

Inserting (29.79.1–2) into (29.23) gives three simple differential equations:

$$\Delta^2 > 0 \ : \quad \dot{s} \ = \ \Delta(1 - s^2), \quad s \neq \pm 1, \tag{29.80.1}$$

$$\Delta^2 = 0 \ : \ \dot{s} \ = \ -s^2, \qquad s \neq 0, \tag{29.80.2}$$

$$\Delta^2 < 0 \ : \ \dot{s} \ = -|\Delta|(1+s^2), \ s \in \mathbf{R}. \tag{29.80.3}$$

As is well known, the principal solution of $\dot{u} = 1 - u^2$ is either $\tanh(t)$ or $\coth(t)$; further, the principal solution of $\dot{u} = 1 + u^2$ is $\tan(t)$. Hence (29.80.1–3) gives, respectively,

$$\Delta^2 > 0 : \ s(t) = \begin{cases} \tanh[\Delta(t+t_0)]; & s \in ]-1,1[, \quad t+t_0 \in \mathbf{R}, \\ \coth[\Delta(t+t_0)]; & s \notin ]-1,1[, \quad t+t_0 \in \mathbf{R}/\{0\}, \end{cases} \tag{29.81}$$

$$\Delta^2 = 0 : \ s(t) = \ 1/(t+t_0); \qquad s \notin 0, \qquad t+t_0 \in \mathbf{R}/\{0\}, \tag{29.82}$$

$$\Delta^2 < 0 : \ s(t) = -\tan[|\Delta|(t+t_0)]; \qquad s \in \mathbf{R}, \ t+t_0 \in \mathbf{R}/\{(\pi/2 + p\pi \mid p \in \mathbf{Z})\}. \tag{29.83}$$

Thus, (29.81–29.83) and the provisional substitution expressions (29.79.1–2) immediately offer the *general* formulas for our fundamental *ratio solutions* $\rho(t)$ presented in (29.28–29.30).

We may also extract the *coordinate solutions* $\varphi(t)$ from (29.81–29.83) and (29.79.1–2). The latter and (29.1.1) give

$$\Delta^2 \neq 0 : \dot{x}/x = a + br = \tfrac{1}{2}(a+d) + \Delta s, \tag{29.84.1}$$

$$\Delta^2 = 0 : \dot{x}/x = a + br = \tfrac{1}{2}(a+d) + s, \tag{29.84.2}$$

and integration over time yields

$$\Delta^2 \neq 0 : \ln|x| \equiv \ln \varphi_1(t) = k + \tfrac{1}{2}(a+d)t + \Delta \int s(t)dt, \tag{29.85.1}$$

$$\Delta^2 = 0 : \ln|x| \equiv \ln \varphi_1(t) = k + \tfrac{1}{2}(a+d)t + \int s(t)dt. \tag{29.85.2}$$

The latter *primitives* are easily derived from (29.81–29.83) as, cf. Selby (1973, p. 435,457))

$$\Delta^2 > 0 : \int s(t)dt = \begin{cases} (1/\Delta)\ln\cosh[\Delta(t+t_0)], \\ (1/\Delta)\ln\sinh[\Delta(t+t_0)], \end{cases} \tag{29.86}$$

$$\Delta^2 = 0 : \int s(t)dt = \ \ln(t+t_0), \tag{29.87}$$

$$\Delta^2 < 0 : \int s(t)dt = (1/|\Delta|)\ln\cos[|\Delta|\,(t+t_0)]. \tag{29.88}$$

Thus, the *general formulas* for the *first coordinate* solutions $\varphi_1(t)$, (29.48–29.50), follow immediately from (29.85.1–29.88), and the second coordinate solutions follow from the identity: $\varphi_2(t) = \varphi_1(t)\rho(t)$, cf. (29.52–29.54).

## General Coordinate Solutions and Initial Value Problems

One of the important applications of the theory of differential equations is that of determining the *future state* of a dynamic (physical, economic, etc.) system, given the *present state* or some other *initial state* (initial conditions)—specifying a ***unique particular solution.*** Thus, we may be more concerned with a particular behavior of a factual system than with all possible behaviors (solutions) of such a system.

As is well known, the standard procedure of solving *initial value problems* for the system (29.1.1–2) is to establish a proper *general solution,* containing *arbitrary, independent* constants. The latter are then assigned definite values from the equations of the general solution together with the prescribed initial state values—a separate calculation from simultaneous equations that is rather cumbersome and often leads to obscure expressions for these constants in terms of the initial values $(x_0, y_0)$. However, by our calculus approach, the *two* arbitrary constants $(\boldsymbol{r_0}, \boldsymbol{t_0})$ appearing in the *general solution formulas* of the *second-order* system (29.1.1–2) were actually assigned specific values already in (29.28–29.30). Despite the succinctness, inherent logic, and amenable character of our general solution formulas in sections "The General Coordinate Solution"–"Ratio and Coordinate Solutions of Triangular Systems", we may choose to *eliminate* the constants $(\boldsymbol{r_0}, \boldsymbol{t_0})$ by rewriting our general coordinate solution formulas *explicitly* in the terms of the *initial values,* $(\boldsymbol{x_0}, \boldsymbol{y_0})$. Hereby, the *general* and the *particular* solutions of the linear system (29.1.1–2) can simply be given by the ***same*** formulas.

Let the *initial values* for $\boldsymbol{t = 0}$ be $(\boldsymbol{x_0}, \boldsymbol{y_0})$, i.e.,

$$t = 0 \; : \; [\varphi_1(0), \varphi_2(0)] = [x_0, y_0]; \; \rho(0) = r_0 = y_0/x_0. \tag{29.89}$$

The procedures of restating (29.48–29.50), (29.52–29.54) are tedious, but straightforward, using well-known *argument addition* formulas of the *circular* and *hyperbolic* functions together with the *respective* expressions for $\boldsymbol{t_0}$ in (29.28–29.30).

Thus, the ***general*** **solution** of the linear system (29.1.1–2) becomes in ***closed form***—with a juxtaposition of the *pair* of individual *coordinate* solutions:

$$\Delta^2 > 0 : \begin{cases} \varphi_1(t) = e^{\frac{1}{2}(a+d)t} \left\{ x_0 \left[ \cosh(\Delta t) - \frac{d-a}{2\Delta} \sinh(\Delta t) \right] + y_0 \left[ \frac{b}{\Delta} \sinh(\Delta t) \right] \right\}, \\ \varphi_2(t) = e^{\frac{1}{2}(a+d)t} \left\{ y_0 \left[ \cosh(\Delta t) + \frac{d-a}{2\Delta} \sinh(\Delta t) \right] + x_0 \left[ \frac{c}{\Delta} \sinh(\Delta t) \right] \right\}, \end{cases} \tag{29.90}$$

$$\Delta^2{=}0:\begin{cases}\varphi_1(t) = e^{\frac{1}{2}(a+d)t}\left\{x_0\left[1-\frac{1}{2}(d-a)t\right]+y_0bt\right\},\\ \varphi_2(t) = e^{\frac{1}{2}(a+d)t}\left\{y_0\left[1+\frac{1}{2}(d-a)t\right]+x_0ct\right\},\end{cases} \tag{29.91}$$

$$\Delta^2{<}0:\begin{cases}\varphi_1(t) = e^{\frac{1}{2}(a+d)t}\left\{x_0\left[\cos(|\Delta|t)-\frac{d-a}{2|\Delta|}\sin(|\Delta|t)\right]+y_0\left[\frac{b}{|\Delta|}\sin(|\Delta|t)\right]\right\},\\ \varphi_2(t) = e^{\frac{1}{2}(a+d)t}\left\{y_0\left[\cos(|\Delta|t)+\frac{d-a}{2|\Delta|}\sin(|\Delta|t)\right]+x_0\left[\frac{c}{|\Delta|}\sin(|\Delta|t)\right]\right\}.\end{cases} \tag{29.92}$$

These versions of the coordinate solutions possess a distinct "*symmetry*" in the initial values $(\boldsymbol{x}_0, \boldsymbol{y}_0)$ and are strikingly *analogous* for $\boldsymbol{\Delta}^2 > 0$, resp. $\boldsymbol{\Delta}^2 < 0$.

It should also be noted in the case of $\Delta^2 \geq 0$ that the **formulas** (29.90–29.91) now cover *both* the *directrix* solutions (29.35–29.38) and the *non-directrix* solutions (29.48–29.49), (29.52–29.53). The non-degenerate ($a \neq d$) *triangular/diagonal* cases (29.59–29.60), (29.67–29.68) are covered by (29.90), and the degenerate ($a = d$) triangular/diagonal cases (29.72–29.73), (29.77–29.78) are covered by (29.91). Also, the *stationary* solution $\varphi(t) = (0, 0)$ is incorporated in (29.90–29.92), which indeed are applicable for *any* initial values $(\boldsymbol{x}_0, \boldsymbol{y}_0)$ throughout the whole *domain*, $D = \mathbf{R}^2$, of the *entire* system (29.1.1–2).

Manifestly, the *explicit* formulas (29.90–29.92) of the whole *family* of *coordinate solutions* (any *initial value* problem) are very convenient for *practical computational* purposes. As far as we know, they are *not* even today available anywhere in the literature on the linear dynamic system (29.1.1–2). Probably, these clear-cut expressions (29.90–29.92) in the initial values $(x_0, y_0)$ would not easily be forthcoming without the *calculus* approach and a *proper* handling of its *integration constants.*

We may put the *parametric formulas* (29.90–29.92) in ***vector*** and ***matrix*** forms, i.e.,

$$\Delta^2{>}0:\varphi(t) = e^{\frac{1}{2}(a+d)t}\begin{bmatrix}\cosh(\Delta t)-\frac{d-a}{2\Delta}\sinh(\Delta t) & \frac{b}{\Delta}\sinh(\Delta t)\\ \frac{c}{\Delta}\sinh(\Delta t) & \cosh(\Delta t)+\frac{d-a}{2\Delta}\sinh(\Delta t)\end{bmatrix}\begin{bmatrix}x_0\\ y_0\end{bmatrix}, \tag{29.93}$$

$$\Delta^2{=}0:\varphi(t) = e^{\frac{1}{2}(a+d)t}\begin{bmatrix}1-\frac{1}{2}(d-a)t & bt\\ ct & 1+\frac{1}{2}(d-a)t\end{bmatrix}\begin{bmatrix}x_0\\ y_0\end{bmatrix}, \tag{29.94}$$

$$\Delta^2{<}0:\varphi(t) = e^{\frac{1}{2}(a+d)t}\begin{bmatrix}\cos(|\Delta|t)-\frac{d-a}{2|\Delta|}\sin(|\Delta|t) & \frac{b}{|\Delta|}\sin(|\Delta|t)\\ \frac{c}{|\Delta|}\sin(|\Delta|t) & \cos(|\Delta|t)+\frac{d-a}{2|\Delta|}\sin(|\Delta|t)\end{bmatrix}\begin{bmatrix}x_0\\ y_0\end{bmatrix}. \tag{29.95}$$

As a matter of fact, the *solutions* (29.93–29.95) can be stated in a transparent and very compact form. Let us define

$$\zeta(t) = \begin{Bmatrix} \frac{1}{\Delta}\sinh(\Delta t) \\ t \\ \frac{1}{|\Delta|}\sin(|\Delta|t) \end{Bmatrix}, \quad \dot{\zeta}(t) = \begin{Bmatrix} \cosh(\Delta t) \\ 1 \\ \cos(|\Delta|t) \end{Bmatrix} \text{ for } \begin{Bmatrix} \Delta^2 > 0 \\ \Delta^2 = 0 \\ \Delta^2 < 0 \end{Bmatrix}. \tag{29.96}$$

Using (29.96) and the *parameters* $\boldsymbol{\mu}, \boldsymbol{\nu}$, cf. (29.2.2), the *solutions* (29.93–29.95) may be given in the *consolidated* form

$$\varphi(t) = e^{\mu t}\begin{bmatrix} \dot{\zeta}(t) + \nu\,\zeta(t) & b\,\zeta(t) \\ c\,\zeta(t) & \dot{\zeta}(t) - \nu\,\zeta(t) \end{bmatrix}\begin{bmatrix} x_0 \\ y_0 \end{bmatrix} = \Phi(t)\begin{bmatrix} x_0 \\ y_0 \end{bmatrix}. \tag{29.97}$$

From standard formulas, the functions $\boldsymbol{\zeta(t)}$ and $\boldsymbol{\dot{\zeta}(t)}$ of (29.96) satisfy

$$\zeta(t_1 + t_2) = \dot{\zeta}(t_1)\zeta(t_2) + \zeta(t_1)\dot{\zeta}(t_2), \tag{29.98.1}$$

$$\dot{\zeta}(t_1 + t_2) = \dot{\zeta}(t_1)\dot{\zeta}(t_2) + \Delta^2\zeta(t_1)\zeta(t_2). \tag{29.98.2}$$

Then by (29.97–29.98.2), it is easily verified that the *transition matrices* $\boldsymbol{\Phi(t)}$, $t \in \mathbf{R}$, $\Phi(0) = \boldsymbol{E}$ (identity matrix) satisfy the *commutative* law of matrix multiplication, i.e.,

$$\Phi(t_1 + t_2) = \Phi(t_1) \cdot \Phi(t_2) = \Phi(t_2) \cdot \Phi(t_1). \tag{29.99}$$

Evidently, the two columns of $\Phi(t)$, (29.97), considered as vectors, constitute a fundamental system of (29.2.1–2). Indeed, $\Phi(t)$ is a *principal fundamental matrix* since $\Phi(0) = \boldsymbol{E}$. Moreover, the one-parameter *group* of linear transformations—formed by the transition matrices $\boldsymbol{\Phi(t)}$, $t \in \mathbf{R}$, acting on the phase space—is the *phase flow* associated with (29.2.1–2), cf. Arnold (1973, p. 4). The *Lie-group* property of the *phase flow* follows immediately from (29.97), (29.99).

An alternative way of presenting the phase flow of the linear system (29.2.1–2) is given by the *flow map* (operator) $\boldsymbol{e^{At}} : \mathbf{R}^2 \to \mathbf{R}^2$, $t \in \mathbf{R}$, where $\boldsymbol{e^{At}}$ is a $2 \times 2$ matrix function defined by its uniformly convergent Taylor (exponential) series cf. Arnold (1973, p. 8), Braun (1983, p. 354), Grimshaw (1990, p. 42), Guckenheimer and Holmes (1986, p. 8), Perko (1993, p. 16).

Lengthy calculations are usually required to find the matrix (in an appropriate basis) of the operator $e^{At}$. In the *original coordinates* (basis), the most general, informative, succinct, closed-form expression for the matrix of $\boldsymbol{e^{At}}$ appears to be that of $\boldsymbol{\Phi(t)}$, (29.97), (29.93–29.95) i.e.,

$$\Delta^2 > 0 : e^{At} = \Phi(t) = \Phi_+(t) \equiv e^{\frac{1}{2}(a+d)t}\,\Phi_+^*(t), \tag{29.100}$$

$$\Delta^2 = 0 : e^{At} = \Phi(t) = \Phi_0(t) \equiv e^{\frac{1}{2}(a+d)t}\Phi_0^*(t), \tag{29.101}$$

$$\Delta^2 < 0 : e^{At} = \Phi(t) = \Phi_-(t) \equiv e^{\frac{1}{2}(a+d)t}\Phi_-^*(t), \tag{29.102}$$

where the **matrices** $\Phi_+^*(t)$, $\Phi_0^*(t)$, $\Phi_-^*$—for, *respectively*, positive, zero, and negative values of the *discriminant*—are those **stated** in (29.93–29.95).

Regarding the *determinant* of the operator $\boldsymbol{e^{At}}$, we have immediately from, (29.100–29.102),

$$|e^{At}| = |\Phi(t)| = |\Phi_+(t)| = |\Phi_0(t)| = |\Phi_-(t)| = e^{(a+d)t}, \tag{29.103}$$

since

$$|\Phi_+^*(t)| = |\Phi_0^*(t)| = |\Phi_-^*(t)| = 1, \tag{29.104}$$

as is easily verified directly from (29.93–29.95) and (29.4); see Arnold (1973, p. 113–114).

The *trace* of the operator $\boldsymbol{e^{At}}$ is obtained directly from (29.93–29.95) as,

$$\Delta^2 > 0 : \mathrm{Tr}\, e^{At} = \mathrm{Tr}\,\Phi_+(t) = 2e^{\frac{1}{2}(a+d)t}\cosh(\Delta t) > 0 \quad \forall t, \tag{29.105}$$

$$\Delta^2 = 0 : \mathrm{Tr}\, e^{At} = \mathrm{Tr}\,\Phi_0(t) = 2e^{\frac{1}{2}(a+d)t} > 0 \quad \forall t, \tag{29.106}$$

$$\Delta^2 < 0 : \mathrm{Tr}\, e^{At} = \mathrm{Tr}\,\Phi_-(t) = 2e^{\frac{1}{2}(a+d)t}\cos(|\Delta| t) \gtreqless 0. \tag{29.107}$$

The *discriminants* $\Delta_e^2$ of $e^{At}$ are, respectively, $\Delta^2 > 0 : \Delta_e^2 = e^{(a+d)t}\sinh^2(\Delta t)$; $\Delta^2 = 0 : \Delta_e^2 = 0$; $\Delta^2 < 0 : \Delta_e^2 = -e^{(a+d)t}\sin^2(|\Delta| t)$, cf. (29.4), (29.100–29.107).

## Initial Value Problems and Coordinate Transformations

This section is intended to supplement the basic material of our calculus approach with some complementary results in the area of linear algebra, which may be used in establishing the *general* coordinate *solutions* of (29.1.1–29.1.2).

The actual form of our *calculus* results, especially the *common* term in (29.90–29.92), $\exp\{\frac{1}{2}(a + d)t\}$, has inspired us to search for *new algebraic* procedures and transformations that will, in fact, reproduce the formulas (29.90–29.92) algebraically by matrix methods, even by matrix algebra working exclusively with the real domain operations.

Equations (29.2.1–2) may be considered as a linear mapping from $\mathbf{R}^2$ to $\mathbf{R}^2$ with matrix $A$. Although square matrices may allow the possibility of linear system description in diagonal form (eigenvalues, eigenvectors), the diagonalization technique does not work when eigenvectors of $A$ span only a one-dimensional subspace of $\mathbf{R}^2$. Thus, the action of $A$ cannot always be analyzed by looking only at what it does to eigenvectors. We are looking for an adequate algebraic procedure, with no exceptions. The hint to such a general algebraic procedure is the following lemma.

**Lemma 29.1** *The second power of the two by two matrix A, (29.2.1–2), can always be decomposed as (E, the unit matrix)*

$$A^2 = A \cdot A = (Tr\,A)A - |A|E = (a+d)A - (ad - bc)E. \quad (29.108)$$

***Proof*** The *characteristic polynomial* $P_A(\lambda)$ of the square matrix $A$ (29.2.1–2) is defined by the determinant of the matrix $A - \lambda E$, i.e.,

$$P_A(\lambda) = |A - \lambda \cdot E| = \lambda^2 - (\mathrm{Tr}\,A)\lambda + |A|. \quad (29.109)$$

The *Hamilton-Cayley theorem* says that every square matrix is a root of its characteristic polynomial. Hence, by (29.109), $A$ satisfies its own characteristic polynomial, i.e., $|A - \lambda E|$ reduces to the zero matrix if $\lambda$ is replaced by the matrix $A$,

$$P_A(A) = A^2 - (\mathrm{Tr}\,A)A + |A|E = A^2 - (a+d)A + (ad - bc)E = 0. \quad (29.110)$$

Thus, (29.110) establishes (29.108). □

Now, if the *trace* of $A$ is *zero,* we see from (29.108) that $A^2$ is not only diagonal, it is even a *scalar* matrix. Since solving the normal linear system $\dot{\mathbf{x}} = A\mathbf{x}$ (29.2.1–2) is equivalent to solving the normal second-order linear system $\ddot{\mathbf{x}} = A^2\mathbf{x}$, Lemma 29.1 also suggests a very simple way of obtaining the solutions of $\ddot{\mathbf{x}} = A^2\mathbf{x}$ when the trace of $A$ is zero. Furthermore, when trace $A$ is *not* zero, we should look for a *coordinate transformation* that gives a new normal linear system having a coefficient matrix with trace zero and then proceed by Lemma 29.1 to a second-order scalar system. Generally, such coordinate transformation is easily found. Such an *alternative* algebraic method of solving (29.2.1–2) seems *new* (Larsen and Jensen 1989), and we may summarize the general algebraic procedure in the following theorem.

**Theorem 29.1** *The coordinate solutions* $\mathbf{x}(t)$ *of the linear dynamic system, (29.2.1–2)*

$$\dot{\mathbf{x}} = A\mathbf{x}; \quad \mathbf{x}(0) = \mathbf{x}^0 \in \mathbf{R}^2 \quad (29.111)$$

*with initial values,* $\mathbf{x}^0 = (x_1^0, x_2^0) \in \mathbf{R}^2$, *are given by*

$$\mathbf{x}(t) = \upsilon(t)[\dot{z}(t)E + z(t)B]\mathbf{x}^0, \quad (29.112)$$

*where the matrix $\boldsymbol{B}$ is*

$$B = A - \mu E = \begin{pmatrix} \frac{a-d}{2} & b \\ c & \frac{d-a}{2} \end{pmatrix}, \tag{29.113}$$

*and where the scalar functions, $\boldsymbol{v(t)}, \boldsymbol{z(t)}$, solve, respectively, the initial value problems [with $\mu$, $\Delta^2$ as in (29.2.2), (29.4)]*

$$\dot{v} = \mu v; \qquad v(0) = 1, \tag{29.114}$$

$$\ddot{z} = \Delta^2 z; \qquad \dot{z}(0) = 1, \qquad z(0) = 0, \tag{29.115}$$

*with the solution of (29.114) as $\boldsymbol{v(t) = e^{\mu t}} = \exp\{\frac{1}{2}(\boldsymbol{a}+\boldsymbol{d})\boldsymbol{t}\}$ and the solution $\boldsymbol{z(t)}$ of (29.115) as given by the respective components of the zeta function $\boldsymbol{\zeta(t)}$, (29.96), for $\Delta^2 > 0$, $\Delta^2 = 0$, $\Delta^2 < 0$. The solutions (29.112) are written explicitly by the expression $\mathbf{x}(t) = \Phi(t)\mathbf{x}^0$, (29.97), or the formulas (29.93–29.95).*

**Corollary 29.1** *The general solution $\mathbf{x}(t)$ and the flow maps $e^{At}$ of the linear system (29.2.1–2) are given by the matrix expressions:*

$$\Delta^2 > 0 : \Phi_+(t) = e^{\frac{1}{2}(a+d)t}[\cosh(\Delta t)E + \frac{\sinh(\Delta t)}{\Delta}(A - \frac{a+d}{2}E)], \tag{29.116}$$

$$\Delta^2 = 0 : \Phi_0(t) = e^{\frac{1}{2}(a+d)t}[E + t(A - \frac{a+d}{2}E)], \tag{29.117}$$

$$\Delta^2 < 0 : \Phi_-(t) = e^{\frac{1}{2}(a+d)t}[\cos(|\Delta|t)E + \frac{\sin(|\Delta|t)}{|\Delta|}(A - \frac{a+d}{2}E)]. \tag{29.118}$$

***Proof*** Let $\boldsymbol{\mu} \in \mathbf{R}$ be a constant and $\boldsymbol{v(t)}$ the solution of the initial value problem

$$\dot{v} = \mu v, \quad v \neq 0, \quad v(0) = 1, \tag{29.119}$$

i.e., $v(t) = e^{\mu t}$. Then consider the coordinate transformation [substitution, dilation, stretching with the scalar variable $\boldsymbol{v}$ of (29.119)]

$$\mathbf{x} = v\mathbf{u}, \quad v \neq 0. \tag{29.120}$$

Next, (29.119–29.120), (29.111), together imply

$$\dot{\mathbf{x}} = v\dot{\mathbf{u}} + \dot{v}\mathbf{u} = A\mathbf{x} = vA\mathbf{u}. \tag{29.121}$$

Using (29.119) and (29.121), we get

$$v\dot{\mathbf{u}} + \mu v\mathbf{u} = vA\mathbf{u}. \tag{29.122}$$

Since $v \neq 0$, it cancels from (29.122); hence

$$\dot{\mathbf{u}} = (A - \mu E)\mathbf{u}. \tag{29.123}$$

As to the initial values $\mathbf{u}(0)$, we have from (29.111), (29.119–29.120) that

$$\mathbf{x}^0 = \mathbf{x}(0) = v(0)\mathbf{u}(0) = \mathbf{u}(0). \tag{29.124}$$

Now, if we choose $\mu$ of (29.119) correctly, namely

$$\mu = \tfrac{1}{2}(a + d), \tag{29.125}$$

then the new matrix in (29.123) is given as $\boldsymbol{B}$, (29.113), which has the trace zero. By (29.123–29.125), (29.113), we are left with the initial value problem

$$\dot{\mathbf{u}} = B\mathbf{u}, \ \mathbf{u}(0) = \mathbf{x}^0. \tag{29.126}$$

From Lemma 29.1, (29.113) and (29.4), we have

$$B^2 = (\mathrm{Tr}\, B)B - |B|E = 0 \cdot B - [-\tfrac{1}{4}(d - a)^2 - bc]E = \Delta^2 E, \tag{29.127}$$

and so (29.126–29.127) gives

$$\ddot{\mathbf{u}} = B^2\mathbf{u} = \Delta^2 E\mathbf{u}. \tag{29.128}$$

Let the (scalar) function $\boldsymbol{z(t)}$ be the *solution* of the initial value problem

$$\ddot{z} = \Delta^2 z, \tag{29.129.1}$$

$$\dot{z}(0) = 1, \quad z(0) = 0. \tag{29.129.2}$$

Note that $\dot{z}(t)$ also solves (29.129.1), but not (29.129.2). Thus, $\dot{z}(t)$ is not proportional to $z(t)$. Hence, the *pair* of *particular* solutions, $[\boldsymbol{z(t)}, \dot{\boldsymbol{z}}\boldsymbol{(t)}]$, constitutes a *basis* for the *general* solution of (29.129.1). Since $\mathbf{u}(t)$ solves (29.128), it can be obtained as a linear combination

$$\mathbf{u}(t) = \dot{z}(t)\mathbf{v} + z(t)\mathbf{w}, \tag{29.130}$$

where $\mathbf{v}$ and $\mathbf{w}$ are vectors in $\mathbf{R}^2$. As $\mathbf{u}(t)$, (29.130), also satisfies (29.126), we have

$$\dot{\mathbf{u}}(t) = \ddot{z}(t)\mathbf{v} + \dot{z}(t)\mathbf{w} = B\mathbf{u}(t) = \dot{z}(t)B\mathbf{v} + z(t)B\mathbf{w}. \tag{29.131}$$

Using (29.129.1) and (29.131), we get

$$\Delta^2 z(t)\mathbf{v} + \dot{z}(t)\mathbf{w} = \dot{z}(t)B\mathbf{v} + z(t)B\mathbf{w}. \tag{29.132}$$

Inserting the initial values (29.129.2) into (29.132) yields

$$\mathbf{w} = B\mathbf{v}. \tag{29.133}$$

Substitution of (29.133) into (29.130) gives

$$\mathbf{u}(t) = [\dot{z}(t)E + z(t)B]\mathbf{v}. \tag{29.134}$$

As $\mathbf{u}(0) = \mathbf{x}^0$, cf. (29.124), we get from (29.134), (29.129.2)

$$\mathbf{x}^0 = \mathbf{u}(0) = (1 \cdot E + 0 \cdot B)\mathbf{v} = \mathbf{v}. \tag{29.135}$$

Hence, (29.134–29.135) gives the solution of (29.126) in the form

$$\mathbf{u}(t) = [\dot{z}(t)E + z(t)B]\mathbf{x}^0. \tag{29.136}$$

Finally, (29.119–29.120), (29.125), (29.136) establish the *coordinate solution* $\mathbf{x}(t)$ as stated in (29.112–29.115). The explicit solutions of (29.129.1–2) for positive, zero, and negative values of $\Delta^2$ are well known, viz. $z(t) = \zeta(t)$, (29.96), which completes the proof of the theorem.

The formulas (29.116–29.118) follow directly from (29.112–29.113) and (29.96). □

## Stability of the Ratio and Coordinate Solutions

Generally, the issue of global, generic, or local asymptotic stability of the family of *ratio solutions* $\rho(t)$ is determined by the *number of director roots* and the *shape of the graph* of the *director function* $h(r)$, cf. Chap. 28, section "The Stability Properties of Ratio Solutions".

$$\dot{r} = h(r) = c + (d - a)r - br^2, \quad r \in \complement\mathcal{A} \subseteq \mathbf{R}, \tag{29.137}$$

For the linear system (29.1.1–2), we saw that, cf. (29.3), (29.23), where the existence of directrices (director roots), i.e., $\mathcal{A} \neq \emptyset$ required $\Delta^2 \geq 0$, (29.6.1–29.7).

For $bc \neq 0$, the *parabolas* (29.137) take the *alternative forms*, depicted in Fig. 29.1, cf. (29.17.1–29.18.2). For $bc = 0,\ a \neq d$, the director function (29.137) gives either parabolas or straight lines as depicted in Fig. 29.2, cf. (29.14.1–2); with $b = 0,\ c = 0,\ a \neq d$, the lines pass through the origin.

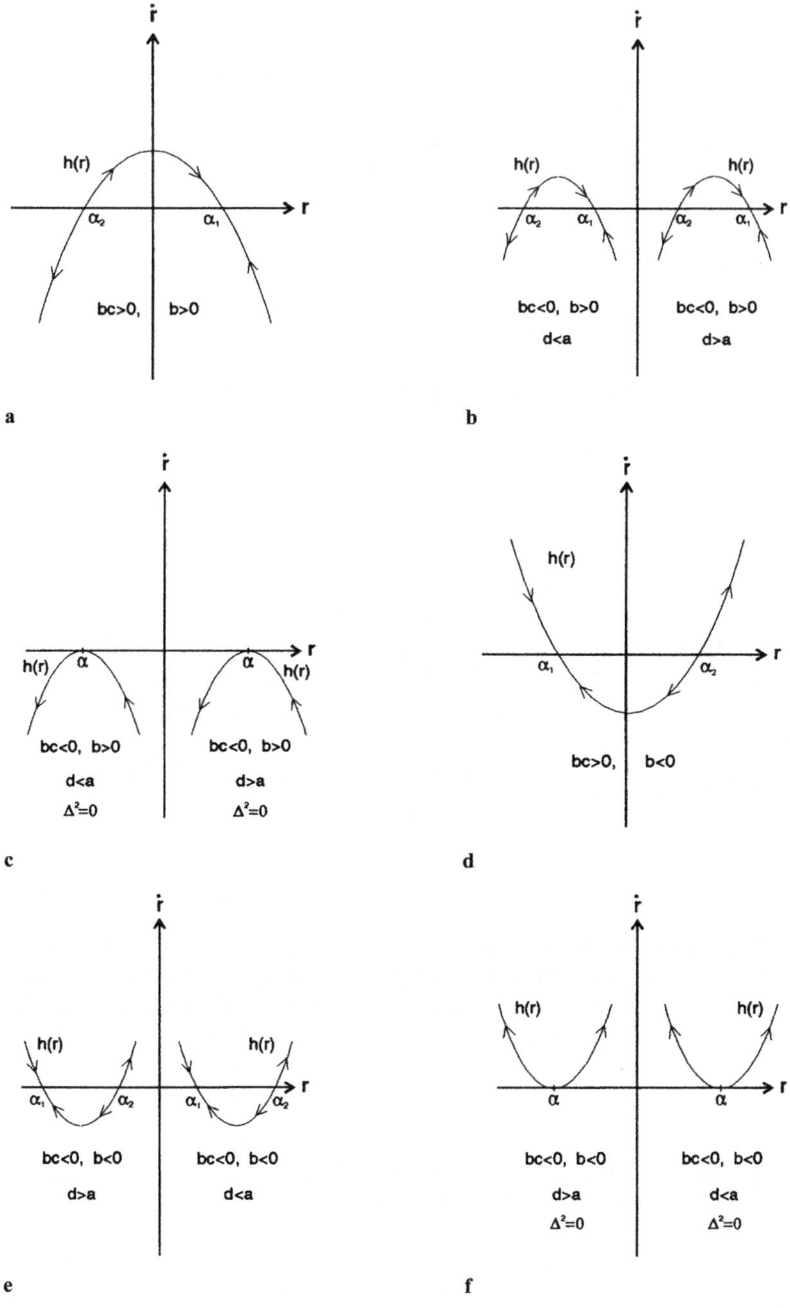


**Fig. 29.1** The director function $h(r)$, (29.137); $bc \neq 0$

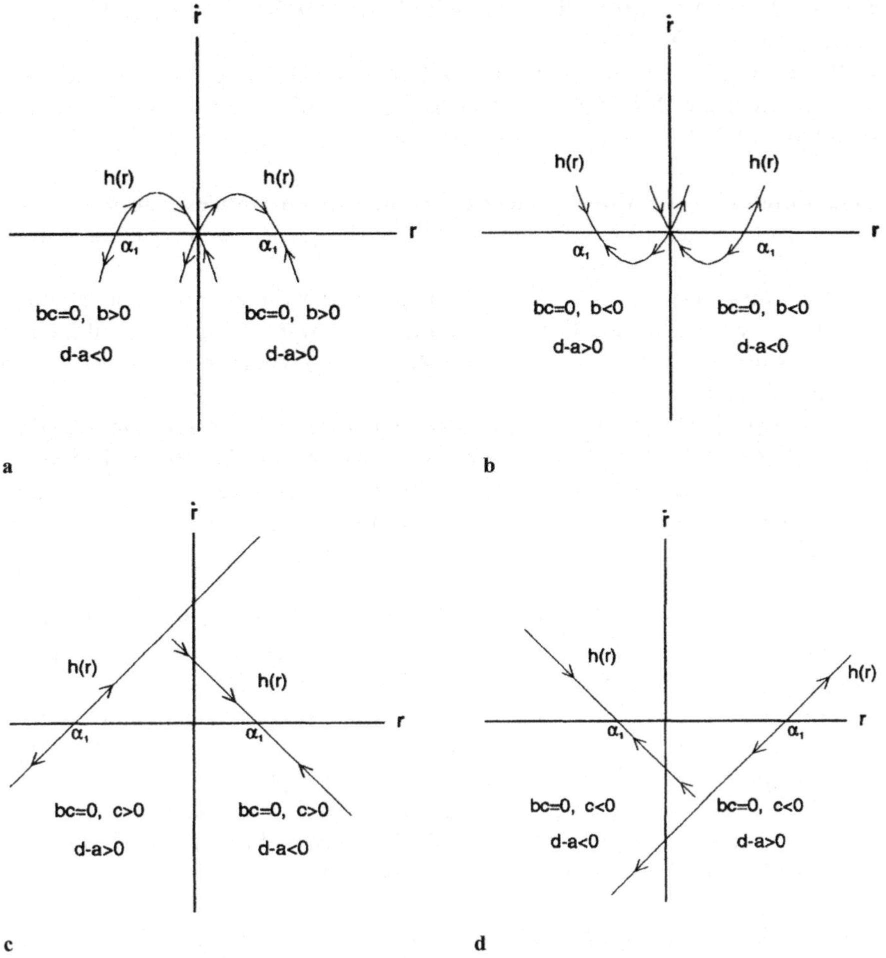


**Fig. 29.2** The director function $h(r)$, (29.137); $bc = 0,\ d \neq a$; triangular system

**Stability Proposition 29.1** *The family of* ***ratios*** *of solutions to the linear system (29.1.1–2) has—for* $\Delta^2 \geq 0$*, (29.4)—the stability properties:*

$$\Delta^2 > 0 : \textit{generic asymptotic ratio stability,} \tag{29.138}$$

$$\Delta^2 = 0 : \textit{asymptotic ratio stability,} \tag{29.139}$$

$$\Delta^2 = 0,\ b = c = 0,\ a = d : \textit{weak absolute ratio stability.} \tag{29.140}$$

***Proof*** Property (29.138) follows from (29.137), Theorem 28.6 in section "Local Asymptotic Ratio Stability" (28.137), Remark 28.13 in section "Local Asymptotic Ratio Stability", and (29.6.1–2); see also Fig. 29.1a–b, d–e, and (29.28), (29.34).

Property (29.139) follows from (29.137) and (29.7), together with consolidating Corollary 28.4 in section "Global Asymptotic Ratio Stability", (28.134) to $\mathbf{R}\backslash\{\alpha\}$; cf. Fig. 29.1c, f, and (29.29), (29.32). □

Regarding (29.140), this degenerate diagonal system implies that $\mathcal{A}$ is infinite, as $\dot{r} = h(r) = 0$, cf. (29.137) and the end of the section on triangular systems.

**Remark 29.3** For $\Delta^2 > 0,\ bc \neq 0$, the particular director root, labeled $\boldsymbol{\alpha}_1$—with positive contribution from $\Delta$, (29.6.1)—is always the *attractor* of the ratio solutions $\rho(t)$, cf. Fig. 29.1. Hence, the $\boldsymbol{R}_{\alpha_1}$-ray is always the *attractive* directrix in the phase plane.

Note that this "$\alpha_1$-attractor-rule" does *not* apply to the *triangular/diagonal* system, (29.14.1–29.15). When $\alpha_1$ is a *repeller* in Fig. 29.2a–d, then $\alpha_2$ (29.14.1–2) is the attractor, i.e., the $x$- or the $y$-axis is the attractive directrix. Still, (29.138) holds for non-degenerate triangular/diagonal systems. Degenerate $(a = d)$ triangular systems are subsumed by (29.139). ▽

Since we have already obtained the *general* formulas for the family of *ratio* solutions $\rho(t)$, *stability* properties, (29.138–29.140), may also be verified *directly* from (29.28–29.29) or better (29.31–29.32), (29.34).

As $\Delta^2 < 0$ implies $\mathcal{A} = \emptyset$ and excludes a $y$-axis directrix, cf. (29.16.1), there is here no question for any stability of the family of ratio solutions (29.30).

Corresponding to (29.138–29.140), the *stability* properties of the families of *coordinate solutions* $\boldsymbol{\varphi}(t) = [\varphi_1(t), \varphi_2(t)]$ are determined by $\boldsymbol{m} = 1$ and the *signs* of directrix values, cf. Chap. 28, section "The Stability Properties of Coordinate Solutions", (29.12.1–29.15), (29.19.1–29.20.2).

**Stability Proposition 29.2** *The family of nonstationary Cartesian coordinate solutions to the linear system (29.1.1–2) has—for $\Delta^2 \geq 0$, (29.4), and $bc \neq 0$, (29.6.1–29.7)—the stability properties:*

$$f(\alpha_1) < 0,\ f(\alpha_2) < 0 : \textit{global strong absolute stability,} \tag{29.141}$$

$$f(\alpha_1) = 0,\ f(\alpha_2) < 0 : \textit{global weak absolute stability,} \tag{29.142}$$

$$f(\alpha_1) > 0,\ f(\alpha_2) < 0 : \textit{generic weak relative stability,} \tag{29.143}$$

$$f(\alpha_1) > 0,\ f(\alpha_2) = 0 : \textit{generic weak relative stability,} \tag{29.144}$$

$$f(\alpha_1) > 0,\ f(\alpha_2) > 0 : \textit{generic weak relative stability,} \tag{29.145}$$

$$f(\alpha)\ < 0 : \textit{global strong absolute stability,} \tag{29.146}$$

$$f(\alpha)\ \geq 0 : \textit{generic weak relative stability.} \tag{29.147}$$

*The family of nonstationary Cartesian coordinate solutions to (29.1.1–2) has—for $\Delta^2 < 0$, (29.4)—the stability properties:*

$$a + d < 0 : \textit{global strong absolute stability,} \tag{29.148}$$

$$a + d = 0 : \textit{global weak absolute stability,} \tag{29.149}$$

$$a + d > 0 : \textit{no stability.} \tag{29.150}$$

***Proof*** Property (29.141) follows from Theorem 28.14 in section "Local Asymptotic Ratio Stability and the Stabilities of Coordinate Solutions", (28.182). As we have excluded the stationary solution $\varphi = (0, 0)$ from the family here considered, Theorem 28.14 then establishes strong absolute stability rather than the traditional asymptotic stability.

Property (29.142) can be verified from the formulas (29.35), (29.37), and (29.48); the $\alpha_1$-ray is the attractive stationary directrix, cf. Remark 29.3 and Fig. 29.7b, d in section "Parameter Space and the Hyperconic Phase Portrait".

Properties (29.143–29.145) follow from Theorem 28.10 in section "Global Asymptotic Ratio Stability and Global Stabilities of Coordinate Solutions", (28.153) when the global property of Theorem 28.10 is modified to a generic one that results from excluding the exceptional directrix solutions along the repulsive $\alpha_2$-directrix [solutions being either declining (29.143), stationary (29.144), or increasing (29.145)]; cf. Remark 28.16–28.17 in section "Local Asymptotic Ratio Stability and the Stabilities of Coordinate Solutions".

Property (29.146) follows from Theorem 28.12 in section "Global Asymptotic Ratio Stability and Global Stabilities of Coordinate Solutions", (28.174), with the member $\varphi = (0, 0)$ excluded.

Regarding (29.147), it may be verified from our general formulas of the coordinate solutions (29.91) together with $y_0 \neq \alpha x_0$ and the single director root $\alpha$, (29.7). Only the directrix solutions with $f(\alpha) > 0$ prevent a global weak relative stability property of the family, hence the generic property (29.147).

Regarding (29.148–29.150), when $\Delta^2 < 0$, the coordinate solutions (29.92) are easily verified to have—with $\varphi = (0, 0)$ excluded from the family—strong (weak) absolute stability for $a+d \leq 0$. For $a+d > 0$, we have no stability criteria for characterizing such a family of Cartesian coordinate solutions, where each coordinate solution, as $t \to \infty$, recurrently becomes zero and infinite. □

**Remark 29.4** A peculiarity of the linear dynamic system (29.1.1–2) is to be noted from (29.141–29.145). The combination, $f(\alpha_1) < 0$ and $f(\alpha_2) > 0$, does not appear in Stability Proposition II, as this combination cannot occur. The *directrix value* $f(\alpha_1) = \frac{1}{2}(a + d) + \Delta$, (29.12.1), of the attractive $\alpha_1$-directrix is *always positive,* if $f(\alpha_1)f(\alpha_2) < 0$, cf. (29.19.1), (29.21). This aspect of *attractive directrices* also holds for triangular and diagonal systems, as may easily be verified. In short, an *attractive* directrix of the linear system (29.1.1–2) must have a *positive* directrix value whenever the *two* directrix values have *opposite* signs. Consequently, generic weak relative stability of the coordinate solutions is much more prevalent than global strong absolute stability. ▽

**Stability Proposition 29.3** *The family of nonstationary Cartesian coordinate solutions to non-degenerate* ($d \neq a$) ***triangular*** *system of (29.1.1–2) has the stability properties:*

$$bc = 0, \quad a < 0, \; d < 0: \; \textit{global strong absolute stability,} \tag{29.151}$$

$$c = 0, \; b \neq 0, a < 0, \; d > 0: \; \textit{generic weak relative stability,} \tag{29.152}$$

$$c = 0, \; b \neq 0, d > a > 0: \; \textit{generic weak relative stability,} \tag{29.153}$$

$$c = 0, \; b \neq 0, a > 0, \; d < 0: \; \textit{generic weak relative stability,} \tag{29.154}$$

$$b = 0, \; c \neq 0, a > 0, \; d < 0: \; \textit{generic weak relative stability,} \tag{29.155}$$

$$b = 0, \; c \neq 0, a > d > 0: \; \textit{generic weak relative stability,} \tag{29.156}$$

$$b = 0, \; c \neq 0, a < 0, \; d > 0: \; \textit{generic weak relative stability.} \tag{29.157}$$

***Proof*** The proofs (29.151–29.157) are similar to those of (29.141), (29.143), (29.145) with $\boldsymbol{f}(\boldsymbol{\alpha}_i)$, $i = 1, 2$, given by (29.14.1–2). In (29.152–29.153) and (29.155–29.156), we have an attractive non-axis directrix. In (29.154) and (29.157), we have, respectively, an attractive $x$-axis ($y$-axis) directrix; (29.152) and (29.155) can be verified from the expressions (29.59–29.60) and (29.67–29.68). □

**Remark 29.5** The degenerate triangular systems ($a = d \neq 0$) have stability properties (29.146–29.153) for a negative/positive directrix value. The degenerate diagonal systems ($a = d \neq 0$) have the stability property (29.141) for $a < 0$ and global weak logarithmic stability for $a > 0$, cf. Theorem 28.13 in section "Local Asymptotic Ratio Stability and the Stabilities of Coordinate Solutions", (28.176). ▽

## The Geometry of the Phase Portrait

In this section, we present a complete description of the *global phase portrait*—the system of trajectory configurations in the phase plane. The geometric structure of the phase portrait will be analyzed primarily through the *loci forms*, $\boldsymbol{\ell}(\boldsymbol{x}, \boldsymbol{y}) = 0$, rather than the parameterized (kinematic) forms, $\boldsymbol{\varphi}(\boldsymbol{t})$, already shown in (29.90–29.92); cf. (28.6–28.8) and Chap. 28, section "Heuristic Comments on Geometry, Dynamics, and Kinematics".

The *general trajectory equation* for the linear system (29.1.1–2)—in the open cones (29.9–29.11)—can be written as, see Theorem 28.1 in section "Ratio Solutions, Coordinate Solutions, and Trajectories",

$$x = k_0 \exp\{H(y/x)\}\,; \quad k_0 = x_0 \exp\{-H(y_0/x_0)\}\,, \tag{29.158}$$

where the relevant, explicit forms of $\boldsymbol{H}$ are given by (29.40), (29.25–29.27). The geometric shapes of the loci (29.158), of course, depend solely on the specific values of the four *system* parameters: $\boldsymbol{a, b, c, d}$. We want to elucidate the role of their sign and size in outlining the phase portrait. The geometry of plane curves is available to illuminate the discussion.

It follows from (29.158), (29.41), and (29.3) that

$$x^2|h(r)| = k_0^2 \exp\{(a+d)I(r)\}\,, \quad r \in \mathbb{C}\mathcal{A}, \tag{29.159}$$

with

$$x^2|h(r)| = |cx^2 + (d-a)xy - by^2|. \tag{29.160}$$

### *Conic Trajectories*

In the case, trace $= a + d = 0$, we immediately note from (29.159–29.160)

$$a + d = 0 \;:\quad x^2|h(r)| = |cx^2 - 2axy - by^2| = k_0^2. \tag{29.161}$$

Hence, dependent on the *sign* of the discriminant (29.4), the *trajectories* (29.161) are the classical *conic sections* (with center at the origin):

$$a + d = 0 : \begin{cases} \Delta^2 > 0 \;:\; \text{hyperbolas,} \\ \Delta^2 = 0 \;:\; \text{parallel straight lines,} \\ \Delta^2 < 0 \;:\; \text{ellipses (circles: } a = d = 0,\; b = -c\text{).} \end{cases} \tag{29.162}$$

By standard formulas, the *slopes* of the orthogonal *symmetry* axes (transverse/conjugate axis, major/minor axis) are

$$\begin{aligned} \beta_i &= \frac{b+c}{a-d} \pm \sqrt{\left(\frac{b+c}{a-d}\right)^2 + 1} \\ &= \frac{b+c}{2a} \pm \sqrt{\left(\frac{b+c}{2a}\right)^2 + 1}, \quad i = 1, 2; \quad \beta_1 \cdot \beta_2 = -1. \end{aligned} \tag{29.163}$$

The *asymptotes* of the hyperbolas, (29.162), are the *directrices,* with their slopes given by the director roots (29.6.1), (29.14.1–29.15). The case of proper parabolas as trajectories is stated below.

### *Hyperconic Trajectories*

For, trace $= \boldsymbol{a} + \boldsymbol{d} \neq 0$, we get from (29.159–29.160) and (29.25–29.27) that the trajectories are represented by the equations

$$\Delta^2 > 0: \begin{cases} \dfrac{|cx^2+(d-a)xy-by^2|}{\exp\left\{\frac{a+d}{\Delta} artanh\left(\frac{(a-d)x+2by}{\Delta x}\right)\right\}} = k_0^2, \\ \dfrac{|cx^2+(d-a)xy-by^2|}{\exp\left\{\frac{a+d}{\Delta} arcoth\left(\frac{(a-d)x+2by}{\Delta x}\right)\right\}} = k_0^2, \end{cases} \tag{29.164}$$

$$\Delta^2 = 0: \quad \frac{|cx^2+(d-a)xy-by^2|}{\exp\left\{\frac{2(a-d)x}{(a-d)x+2by}\right\}} = k_0^2, \tag{29.165}$$

$$\Delta^2 < 0: \quad \frac{|cx^2+(d-a)xy-by^2|}{\exp\left\{-\frac{a+d}{|\Delta|} arctan\left(\frac{(a-d)x+2by}{|\Delta| x}\right)\right\}} = k_0^2. \tag{29.166}$$

The *trajectory configurations* implied by (29.164–29.166) will, as explained below, turn out to be well-defined *generalizations* of the *classical* conics.

When $\Delta^2 \geq 0$, the geometric analysis of (29.164–29.165) will be aided by alternative expressions in terms of director roots and the directrix values, helping to determine the location and shape of the trajectories. The director function $h(r)$ becomes, cf. (29.6.1–29.7),

$$\Delta^2 > 0 \ : \ h(r) = -b(r-\alpha_1)(r-\alpha_2); \quad \Delta^2 = 0 \ : \ h(r) = -b(r-\alpha)^2. \tag{29.167}$$

Using $\text{artanh}(u) = \frac{1}{2}\ln[(1+u)/(1-u)]$, $u^2 < 1$, and $\text{arcoth}(u) = \frac{1}{2}\ln[(u+1)/(u-1)]$, $u^2 > 1$, we see from (29.25–29.26), (29.6.1–29.7) that the integrals $\boldsymbol{I(r)}$ can be written as, cf. Selby (1973, p. 413-415)

$$\Delta^2 > 0 : I(r) = \int \frac{dr}{-b(r-\alpha_1)(r-\alpha_2)} = \frac{1}{2\Delta}\ln\left|\frac{r-\alpha_2}{r-\alpha_1}\right|, \tag{29.168}$$

$$\Delta^2 = 0 : I(r) = \int \frac{dr}{-b(r-\alpha)^2} = \frac{1}{b(r-\alpha)}. \tag{29.169}$$

Hence, by (29.167–29.169), (29.159–29.160), and (29.12.1–29.13)

$$\Delta^2 > 0 : |y-\alpha_1 x|^{f(\alpha_1)}|y-\alpha_2 x|^{-f(\alpha_2)} = \kappa_0, \tag{29.170}$$

$$\Delta^2 = 0 : |y-\alpha x| \exp\left\{\frac{f(\alpha)x}{-b(y-\alpha x)}\right\} = \kappa_0, \tag{29.171}$$

where $\kappa_0$ is an *arbitrary,* positive constant, depending on initial values.

Again, we want to state the relevant formulas of *triangular* systems.

For $c = 0,\ b \neq 0,\ d \neq a$, we have from (29.170) and (29.14.1)

$$|y-\alpha_1 x|^d \ |y|^{-a} = \kappa_0. \tag{29.172}$$

For $b = 0,\ c \neq 0,\ d \neq a$, we get from (29.158) and (29.63)

$$|y - \alpha_1 x|^a\ |x|^{-d} = \kappa_0. \tag{29.173}$$

Furthermore, if $c = 0,\ b \neq 0,\ d = a$, then (29.171) becomes

$$|y| \exp\left\{\frac{ax}{-by}\right\} = \kappa_0. \tag{29.174}$$

If $b = 0,\ c \neq 0,\ d = a$, then (29.61–29.62) and (29.159) yield

$$|x| \exp\left\{\frac{ay}{-cx}\right\} = \kappa_0. \tag{29.175}$$

Thus, the *loci* (29.166), (29.170–29.175) give another *complete description* of the *phase portrait*—in the original Cartesian coordinates $(\boldsymbol{x}, \boldsymbol{y})$—with (29.161–29.162) as special cases.

The case of *classical parabolas* as genuine trajectories in $(x, y)$ coordinates is now seen from (29.170) and (29.12.1–2) to require the *conditions*

$$\frac{f(\alpha_1)}{f(\alpha_2)} = \frac{\frac{1}{2}(a+d)+\Delta}{\frac{1}{2}(a+d)-\Delta} = 2; \quad \frac{f(\alpha_1)}{f(\alpha_2)} = \frac{\frac{1}{2}(a+d)+\Delta}{\frac{1}{2}(a+d)-\Delta} = \frac{1}{2}, \tag{29.176}$$

which together are equivalent to

$$a + d = \pm 6\Delta, \quad (a+d)^2 = 36\Delta^2. \tag{29.177}$$

Hence, by (29.177), (29.4), the *parabolic trajectories* [with vertex (0, 0) deleted]

$$(y - \alpha_1 x)^2 (y - \alpha_2 x)^{-1} = \kappa_0; \quad (y - \alpha_1 x)(y - \alpha_2 x)^{-2} = \kappa_0 \tag{29.178}$$

occur with the *system* parameter *restriction*

$$2(d+a)^2 - 9(ad - bc) = 0 \Leftrightarrow (d - 2a)(d - a/2) = -9bc/2. \tag{29.179}$$

In contrast to the hyperbolas, (29.162), the *symmetry* axis of *parabolas* (29.178) is a *directrix*. The branches of (29.178) become *parallel* at infinity to one directrix and *tangent* to the other directrix at the origin.

As the family members of (29.166), (29.170–29.175) will readily link up with the *classical conics* (29.162), (29.178), the whole family of well-defined loci in $\mathbf{R}^2$, as generated by the *linear fractional equation* (Birkhoff and Rota 1989, p. 17)

$$\frac{\dot{y}}{\dot{x}} = \frac{dy}{dx} = \frac{cx + dy}{ax + by}, \tag{29.180.1}$$

seems of sufficient importance to introduce the concept and terminology of *hyperconics* —encompassing the *subfamilies*: hyperparabolas, hyperhyperbolas, hyperellipses.

Whereas hyperparabolas and hyperhyperbolas only consist of *open* trajectories, the *hyperellipses* will also include closed trajectories (cycles); hyperellipses consist of circles, ellipses, circular (logarithmic) spirals, and elliptic spirals, as explained below.

The *direction (tangent) field* associated with (29.1.1–29.1.2) is given by, cf. (28.83–28.84), (29.180.1),

$$\frac{dy}{dx} = q(r) = \frac{g(r)}{f(r)} = \frac{c + dr}{a + br}. \tag{29.180.2}$$

Hence the tangent field $\boldsymbol{q(r)}$, (29.180.2), is entirely determined by *rectangular hyperbolas* with center $(-a/b, d/b)$; constant $-(ad - bc)/b^2 = -|A|/b^2$. Obviously, $r = -a/b$ corresponds to the ray (isocline ) with vertical slope of the tangent vectors, and $q(r) = d/b$ is the tangent slope at the crossing of the $y$-axis ($r = \pm\infty$). The *monotonicity* of the tangent field $q(r)$ is succinctly seen by, cf. (28.141–28.143),

$$q'(r) = \frac{ad - bc}{(a + br)^2} = \frac{|A|}{(a + br)^2}, \tag{29.181}$$

i.e., the *sign* of $\boldsymbol{q'(r)}$ is everywhere in the phase plane *exclusively* fixed by the *sign* of the *determinant*, $|A| \neq 0$.

Since (29.180.1–29.181) apply to *every* configuration of the hyperconic phase portrait, (29.162), (29.164–29.166), one cannot help being impressed by the multitude (richness) and thereby the *sensitivity* here of *plane curves* (trajectories) to *four parameters* of a simple tangent field.

## Parameter Space and the Hyperconic Phase Portrait

To describe and analyze the hyperconic phase portrait for any real value of the *system parameters,* we need to introduce the notion of a *parameter space* (Andronov et al. 1971, p. (xii)) and in particular to search for the *partition* of the parameter space into *regions*—each corresponding to a specific geometrical structure of the phase portrait—and then to determine the *change* in its geometrical structure when the *system parameters* move across the *boundary* of two such regions in the parameter space.

As an aid to clarification by *visualization*, we may give a pictorial description of important *regions* in our *four*-dimensional system parameter space by a *combination* of some *critical boundary curves* in the $(\boldsymbol{a}, \boldsymbol{d})$ *parameter plane*, viz.,

$$(i)\ \{(a,d) \mid a+d=0\}, \qquad (ii)\ \{(a,d) \mid (a+d)^2 = 36\Delta^2\}, \qquad (29.182)$$

$$(iii)\ \{(a,d) \mid \Delta^2 = 0\}, \qquad (iv)\ \{(a,d) \mid |A| = 0\}. \qquad (29.183)$$

$(i)$ is a bisector; the curves $(ii)$ are either two branches of hyperbolas, $(bc \neq 0)$ with the asymptotes $d = 2a, d = \frac{1}{2}a$, or just the latter straight lines $(bc = 0)$, cf. (29.179); $(iii)$ is either two straight lines $d = a \pm 2\sqrt{|bc|}$, $(bc < 0)$, a bisector $(bc = 0)$, or a void $(bc > 0)$, cf. (29.4), (29.16.1–2); the curves $(iv)$ are either two branches of rectangular hyperbolas $(bc \neq 0)$ or the axes $(bc = 0)$, cf. (29.2.2).

The *boundary curves* $(i)$–$(iv)$ are *depicted* in Fig. 29.3a–e for $\boldsymbol{bc \neq 0}$. Together, they determine the crucial *parameter regions*, shown in Figs. 29.4 and 29.5; the relevant *subfamilies* of the *hyperconic phase portrait* belonging to these *regions* are *indicated* in Fig. 29.5. Note how nicely the classical conics (29.177) fit into the respective regions. On curves (regions), (i)–(iv), see Fig. 33.1, too.

### *Parameter Regions and Trajectory Configurations*

As the system parameter space may visually be completely represented by points in the parameter regions of Fig. 29.4, we may now relate the *parameter regions* to the trajectory *configurations* in the *phase plane*. By drawing upon information of former sections, we briefly enumerate all possible configurations. The results are displayed in Fig. 29.6a, b, c, and d. Only a few comments are needed.

The geometric *shape* of the trajectories follows directly from the relevant hyperconic subfamily. The *location* of the *directrices* follows from (29.17.1–29.18.2), (29.14.1–29.15). The *orientation* (direction of motion for increasing $t$) of directrices is given by the directrix values, (29.19.1–29.20.2, 29.14.1–29.15). The orientation of the trajectories in the open cones (29.9–29.10) follows from the orientation of the attractive directrix, cf. Remark 29.3–29.4.

Since $y = 0$ gives $\dot{y} = cx$, the *orientation* of the cycling or spiraling trajectories in the *punctured plane* (29.11) is simply obtained from the *sign* of $\boldsymbol{c}$ (counterclockwise rotation being considered positive). The *outward/inward* direction (with reference to the origin) of the spiraling trajectories is determined by a positive/negative *sign* of $\boldsymbol{a + d}$, cf. (29.92).

### *Boundary Curves and Trajectory Configurations*

It is instructive to study carefully the special trajectory *configurations* that correspond to the boundary curves (29.182–29.183). Naturally, the boundary curves will show some *limiting trajectory configurations* marking the transition either the hyperconic subfamilies or classical conics and hyperconics, cf. Fig. 29.5. We briefly discuss the consequences of (29.182–29.183) for the disposition of the trajectories.

A *zero* value of the *determinant* $|A|$ and hence $\Delta^2 = \frac{1}{4}(d+a)^2$, cf. (29.4), imply that the *director roots* and the *directrix values* become, cf. (29.6.1–2), (29.12.1–2)

$$a+d>0: \alpha_1{=}d/b,\ \alpha_2{=}-a/b;\ f(\alpha_1){=}a+d,\ f(\alpha_2){=}0, \qquad (29.184.1)$$

$$a+d<0: \alpha_1{=}-a/b,\ \alpha_2{=}d/b;\ f(\alpha_1){=}0,\ f(\alpha_2){=}a+d. \qquad (29.184.2)$$

Thus $|\boldsymbol{A}| = 0$ always implies that one of directrices is a *stationary directrix*, with a director root tallying with the slope, $-\boldsymbol{a}/\boldsymbol{b} = -\boldsymbol{c}/\boldsymbol{d}$, of coinciding nil-lines ($\dot{x} = \dot{y} = 0$), cf. (29.180.1–2). Since either $f(\alpha_1) = 0$ or $f(\alpha_2) = 0$, it follows immediately from (29.170) that all the trajectories are straight lines and that they—except for the stationary directrix—must be parallel. Such simple loci properties are not obvious from the coordinate solutions (29.90), together with here $\boldsymbol{\Delta} = \frac{1}{2}|\boldsymbol{a}+\boldsymbol{d}|$. The trajectory configurations of the *boundary curves* $|\boldsymbol{A}| = 0$ in Fig. 29.4 are shown for $\boldsymbol{b} > 0$ in Figs. 29.7 and 29.8. The latter fit nicely into Fig. 29.6a, b, c, and d.

For a *zero value* of the *discriminant* $\boldsymbol{\Delta}^2$, it is seen from (29.7) that the director root $\alpha$ is *constant* along each boundary curve, $\boldsymbol{\Delta}^2 = 0$, in Fig. 29.4(a). The trajectory configurations are given in Fig. 29.9; their shape is a *limiting* form of hyperparabolas, just *before spirals* appear. Thus, the trajectories (29.171) are still, like hyperparabolas, *tangent* to the *single* directrix at the *origin* and *parallel* to this directrix at *infinity*.

As to the *boundary curves* (29.182 *ii*), the *director roots* and the *directrix values* are, cf (29.6.1–2), (29.12.1–2).

$$\alpha_1 = \frac{2d-a}{3b}, \quad \alpha_2 = \frac{d-2a}{3b}; \quad f(\alpha_1) = \frac{2}{3}(a+d), \quad f(\alpha_2) = \frac{1}{3}(a+d), \qquad (29.185)$$

where $\boldsymbol{\alpha}_1$ ($\boldsymbol{\alpha}_2$) refers to the *symmetry axis* of the *parabolas* for positive (negative) directrix values.

For the *hyperbolas* along the *boundary curve* (29.182 *i*), cf. the hyperbolas in (29.162), (29.163), the *directrices* are *asymptotes* with, cf. (29.6.1–2), (29.12.1–2),

$$\alpha_1 = -a/b + \sqrt{(a/b)^2 + c/b}, \quad \alpha_2 = -a/b - \sqrt{(a/b)^2 + c/b}, \qquad (29.186.1)$$

$$f(\alpha_1) = -f(\alpha_2) = \Delta = \sqrt{-|A|}. \qquad (29.186.2)$$

For the *ellipses* along (29.182 *i*), cf. the ellipses in (29.162), (29.163), their disposition—along **AB** without the endpoints, cf. Fig. 29.4a—are illustrated in Fig. 29.10. At the *point* **0**, we have *circles,* if $\boldsymbol{b} = -\boldsymbol{c}$.

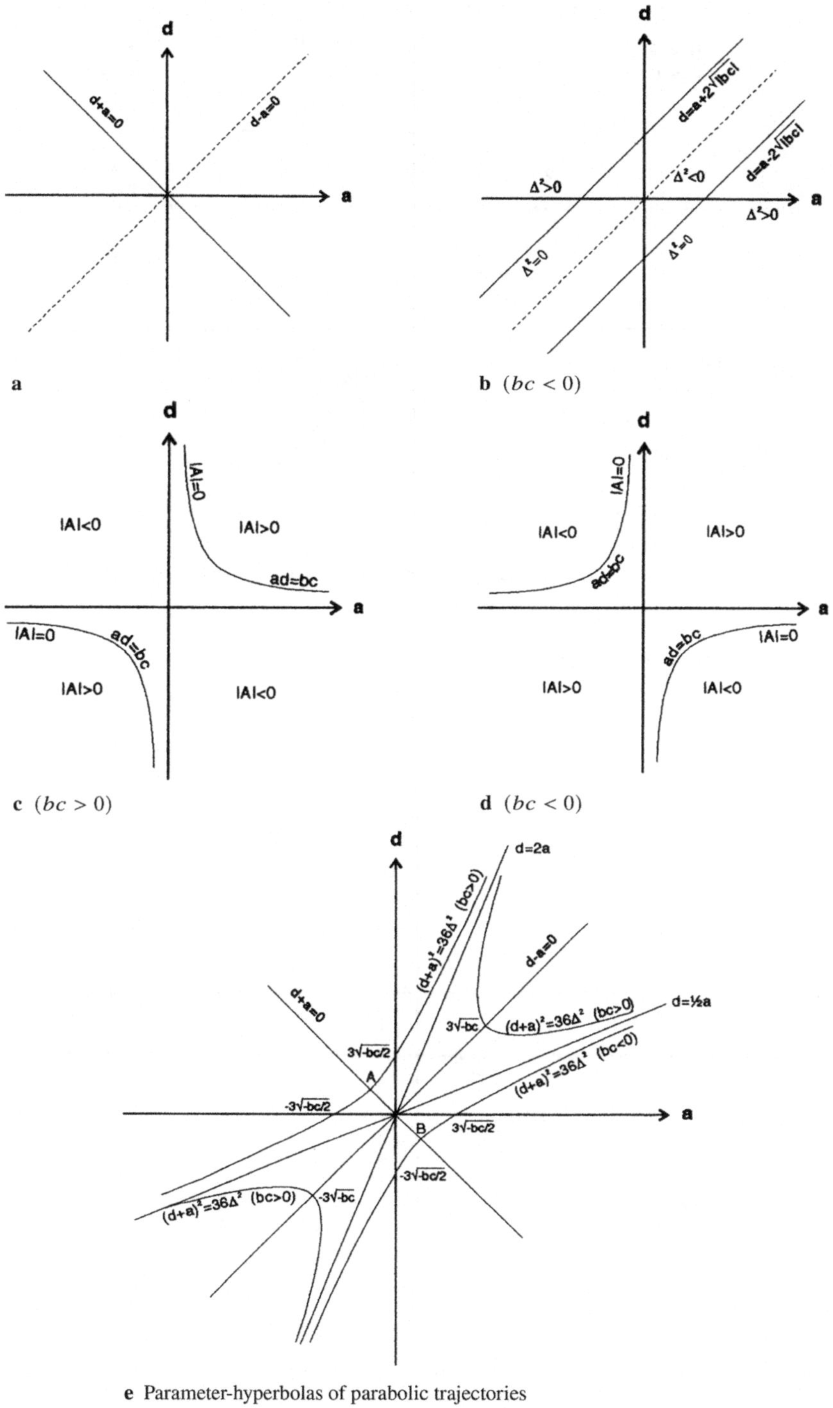


**Fig. 29.3** The parameter space and boundary curves (**a**) (bisectors). (**b**) ($bc < 0$). (**c**) ($bc > 0$). (**d**) ($bc < 0$). (**e**) Parameter-hyperbolas of parabolic trajectories

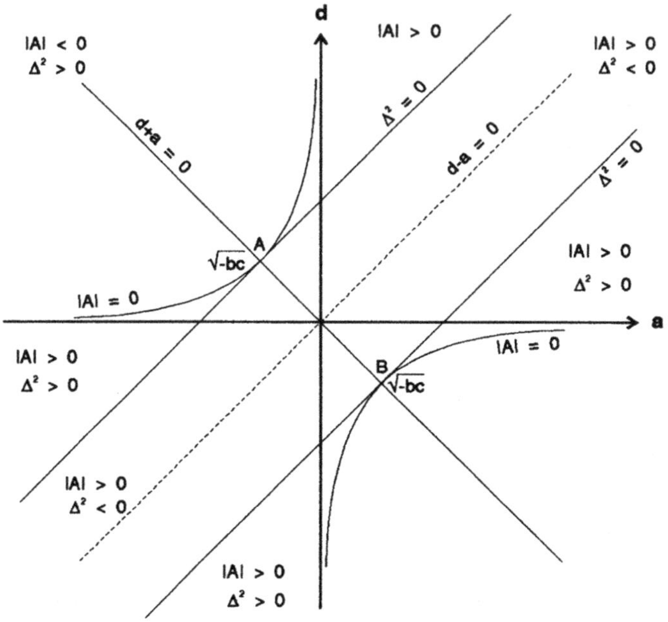


**a** Parameter regions ($bc < 0$)

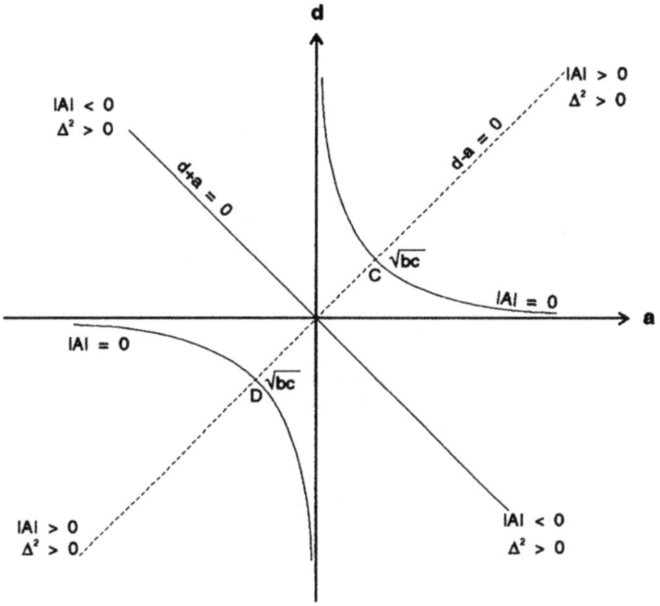


**b** Parameter regions ($bc > 0$)

**Fig. 29.4** Parameter regions. (**a**) Parameter regions ($bc < 0$). (**b**) Parameter regions ($bc > 0$)

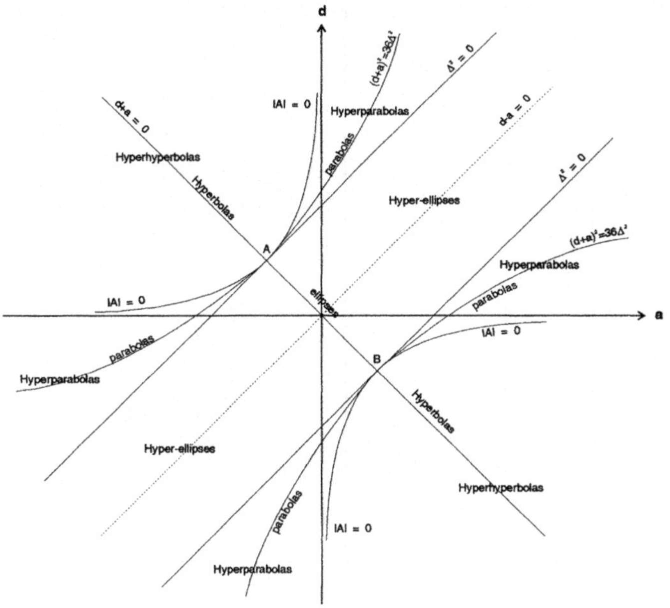


**a** Parameter regions ($bc < 0$) and hyperconics

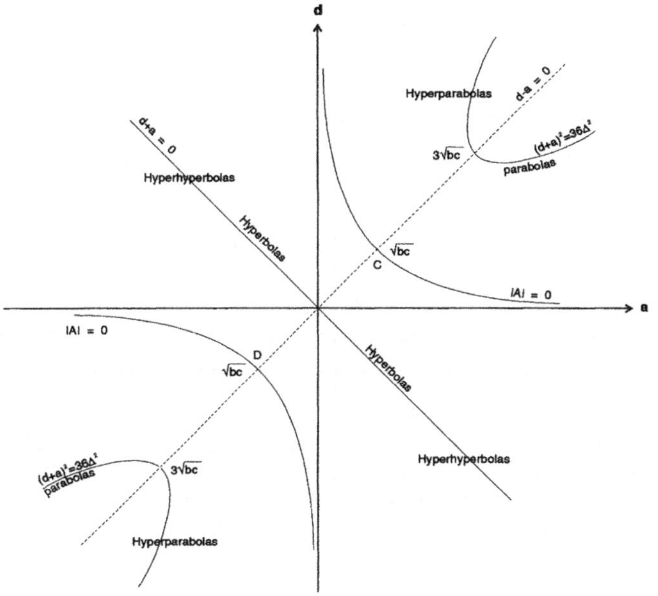


**b** Parameter regions ($bc > 0$) and hyperconics

**Fig. 29.5** The hyperconic phase portrait. (**a**) Parameter regions ($bc < 0$) and hyperconics. (**b**) Parameter regions ($bc > 0$) and hyperconics

a

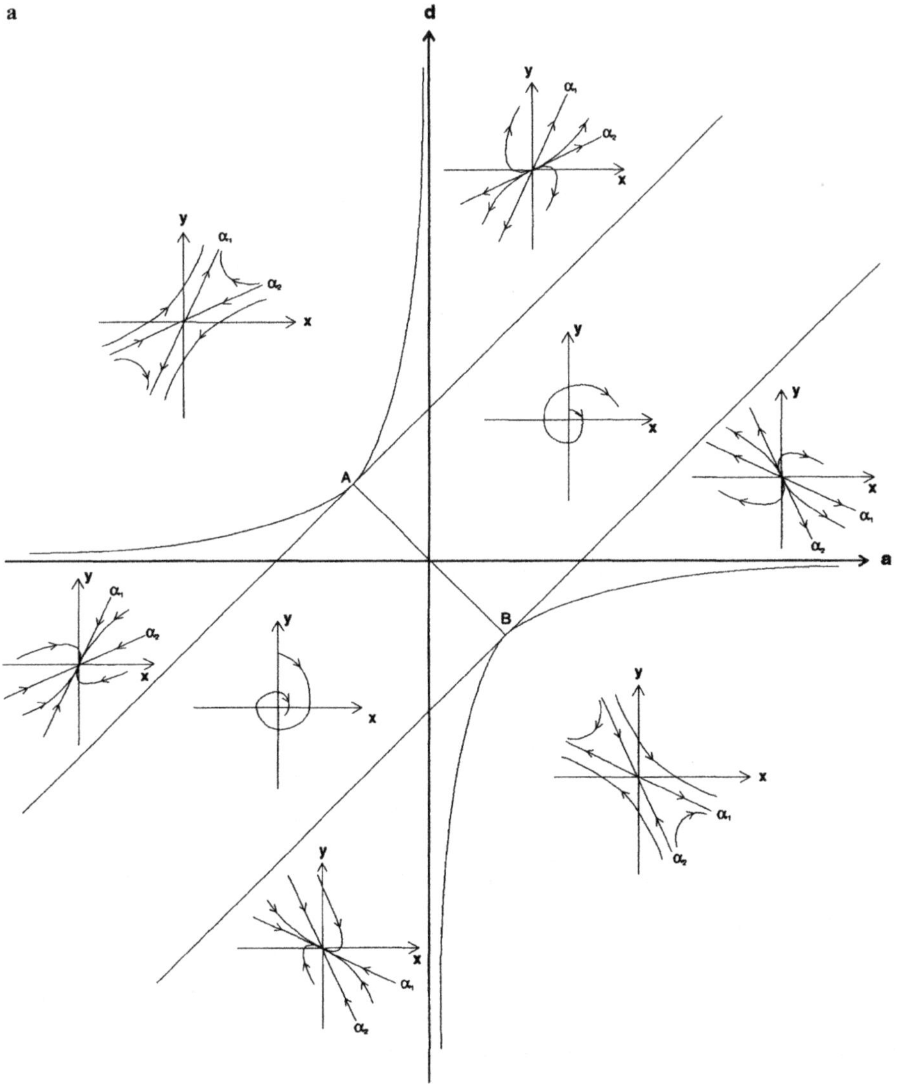


**Fig. 29.6** Trajectory configurations of parameter regions. (**a**) Trajectory configurations ($bc < 0, b > 0$). (**b**) Trajectory configurations ($bc < 0, b < 0$). (**c**) Trajectory configurations ($bc > 0, b > 0$). (**d**) Trajectory configurations ($bc > 0, b < 0$)

b

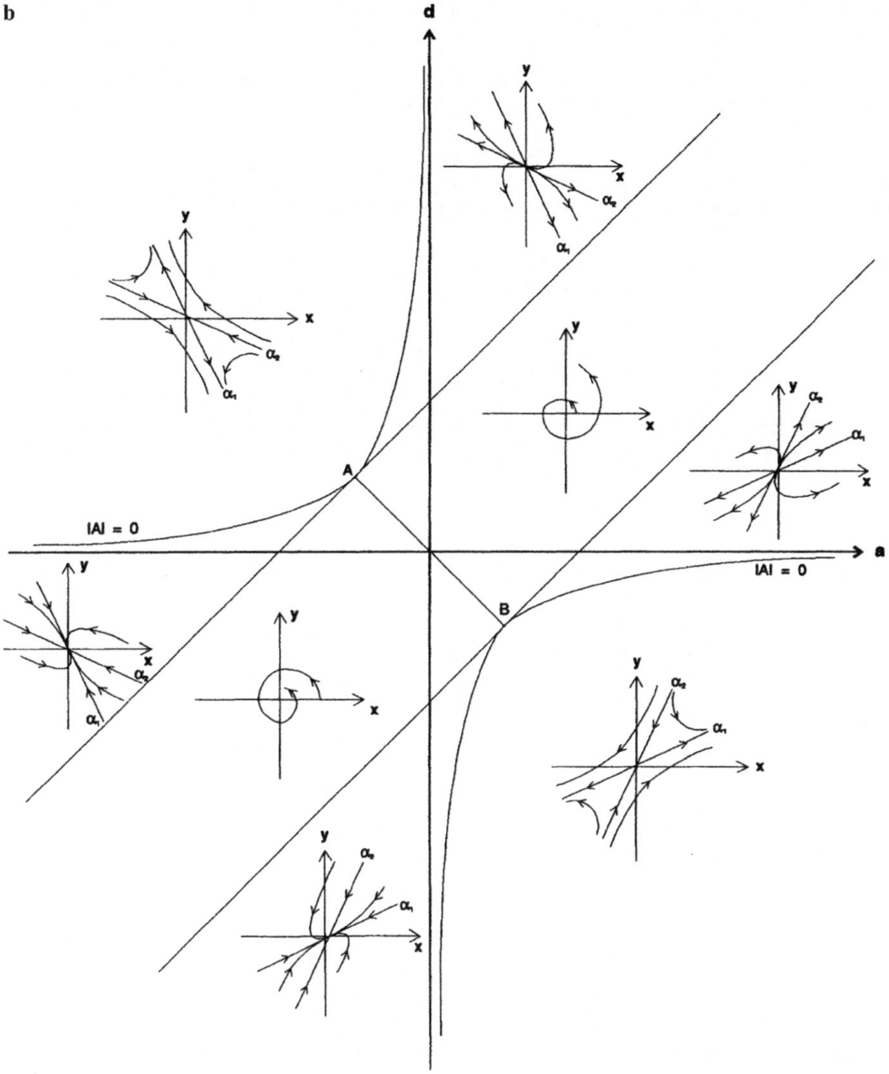


**Fig. 29.6** (continued)

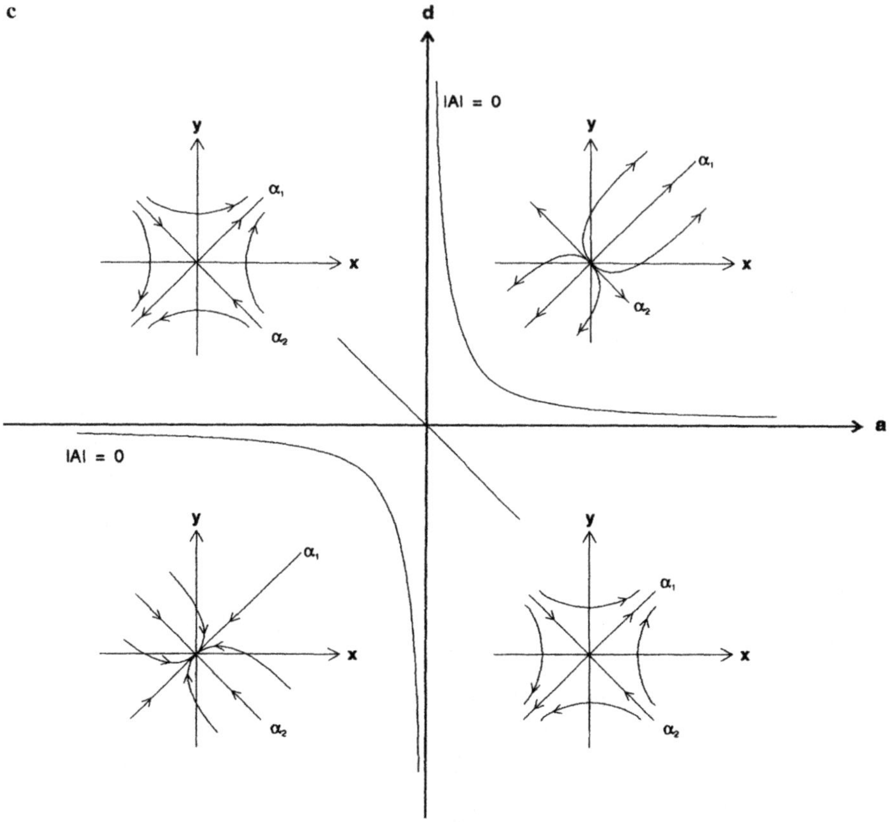


**Fig. 29.6** (continued)

**d**

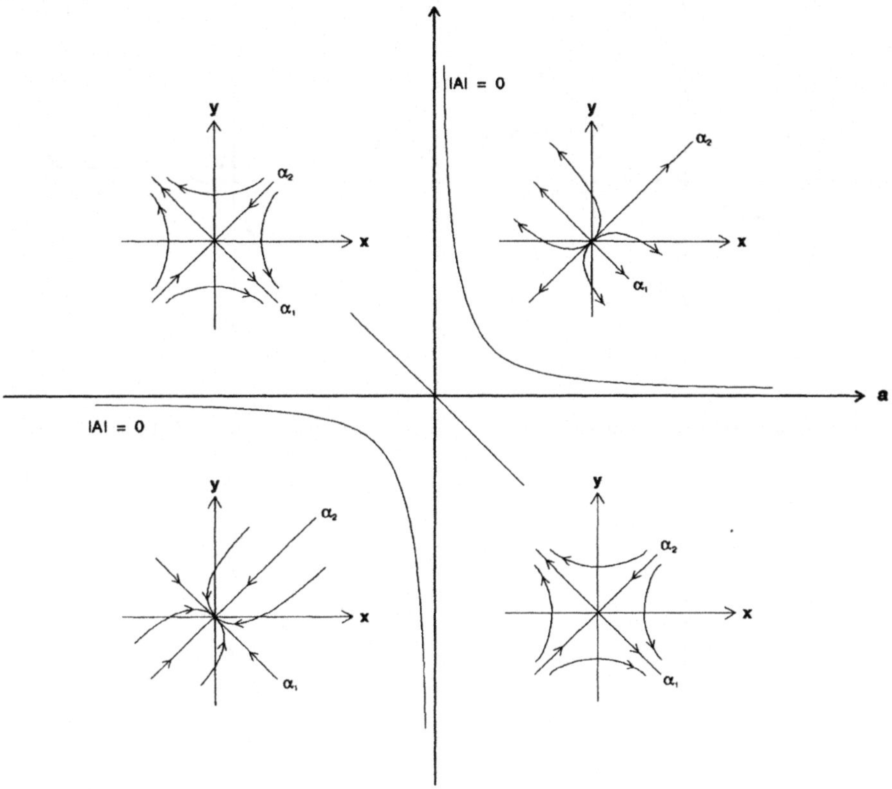


**Fig. 29.6** (continued)

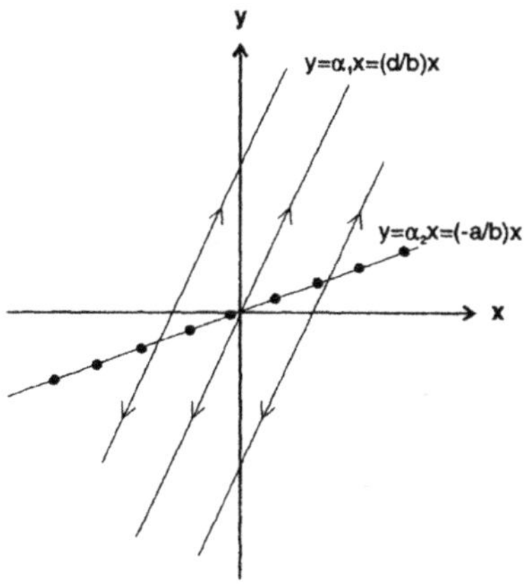


**a** Upper line: $|A| = 0$ (above $A$)

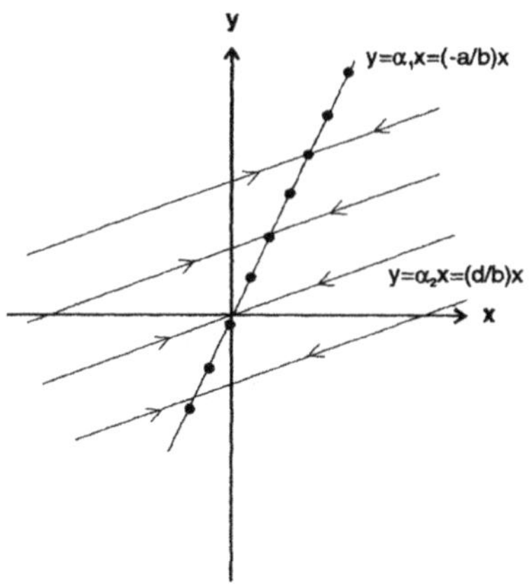


**b** Upper line: $|A| = 0$ (below $A$)

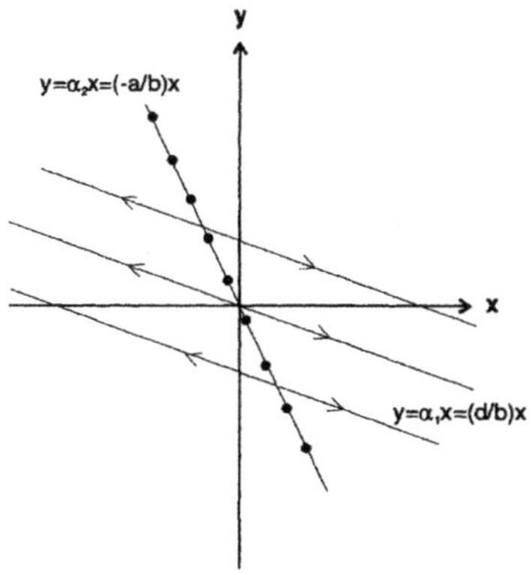


**c** Lower line: $|A| = 0$ (above $B$)

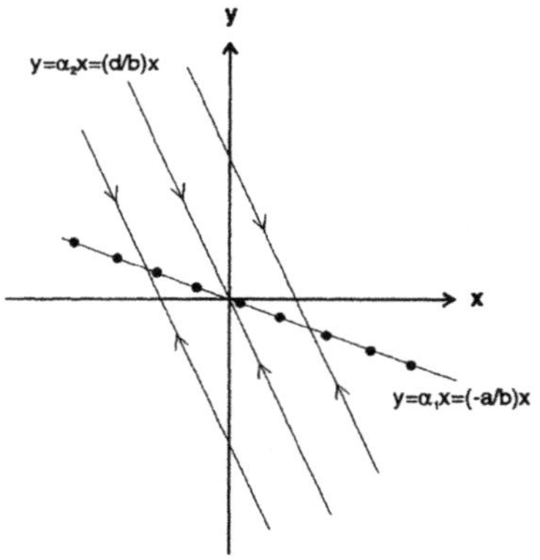


**d** Lower line: $|A| = 0$ (below $B$)

**Fig. 29.7** Trajectory configurations of boundary curves: $|A| = 0$, $(bc < 0,\ b > 0)$ (**a**) Upper line: $|A| = 0$ (above $A$) (**b**) Upper line: $|A| = 0$ (below $A$) (**c**) Lower line: $|A| = 0$ (above $B$) (**d**) Lower line: $|A| = 0$ (below $B$)

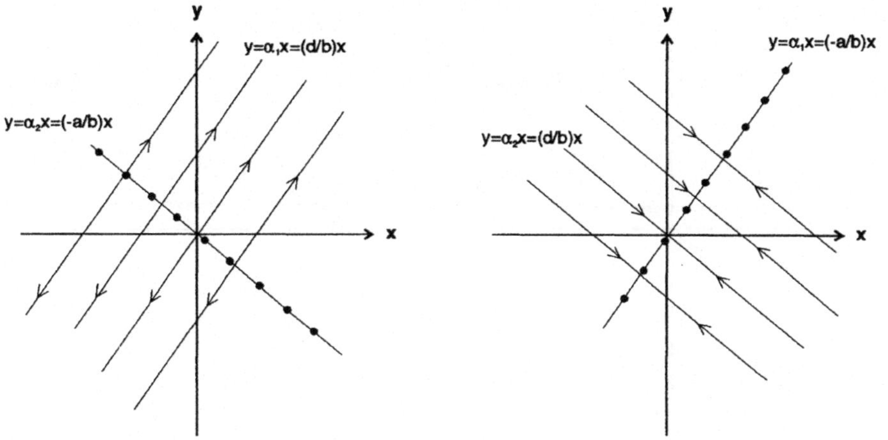


**a** Upper line: $|A| = 0$ **b** Lower line: $|A| = 0$

**Fig. 29.8** Trajectory configurations of boundary curves: $|A| = 0$, $(bc > 0, \ b > 0)$ (**a**) Upper line: $|A| = 0$ (**b**) Lower line: $|A| = 0$

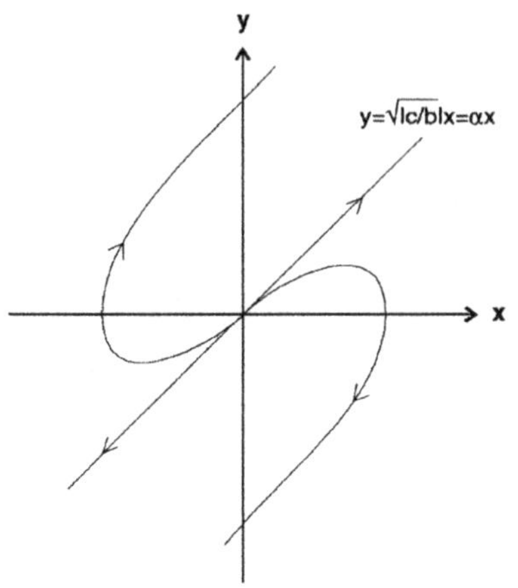


**a** Upper line: $\Delta^2 = 0$ (above $A$)

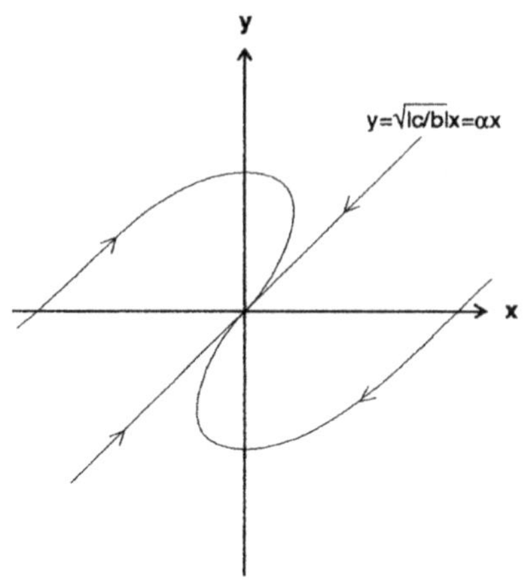


**b** Upper line: $\Delta^2 = 0$ (below $A$)

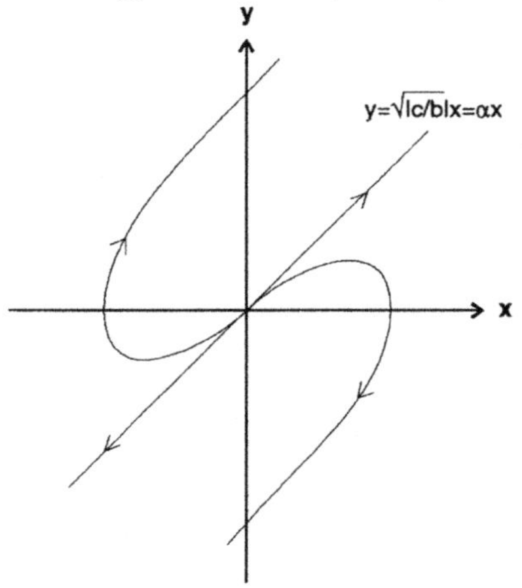


**c** Lower line: $\Delta^2 = 0$ (above $B$)

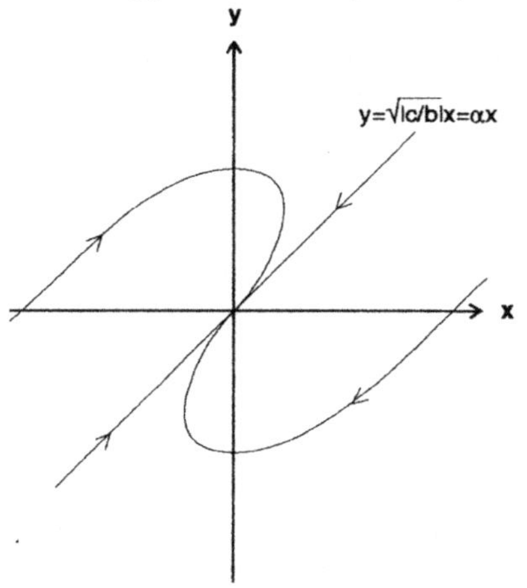


**d** Lower line: $\Delta^2 = 0$ (below $B$)

**Fig. 29.9** Trajectory configurations of boundary curves: $\Delta^2 = 0$ (**a**) Upper line: $\Delta^2 = 0$ (above $A$) (**b**) Upper line: $\Delta^2 = 0$ (below $A$) (**c**) Lower line: $\Delta^2 = 0$ (above $B$) (**d**) Lower line: $\Delta^2 = 0$ (below $B$)

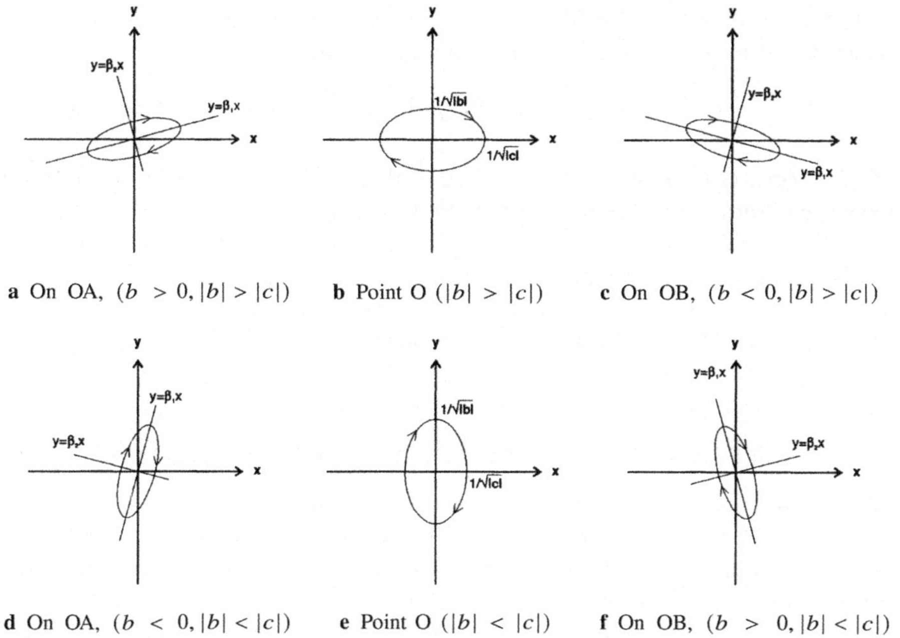


**a** On OA, $(b > 0, |b| > |c|)$ **b** Point O $(|b| > |c|)$ **c** On OB, $(b < 0, |b| > |c|)$

**d** On OA, $(b < 0, |b| < |c|)$ **e** Point O $(|b| < |c|)$ **f** On OB, $(b > 0, |b| < |c|)$

**Fig. 29.10** Trajectory configurations along curve: $AB$ (**a**) On OA, $(b > 0, |b| > |c|)$ (**b**) Point O $(|b| > |c|)$ (**c**) On OB, $(b < 0, |b| > |c|)$ (**d**) On OA, $(b < 0, |b| < |c|)$ (**e**) Point O $(|b| < |c|)$ (**f**) On OB, $(b > 0, |b| < |c|)$

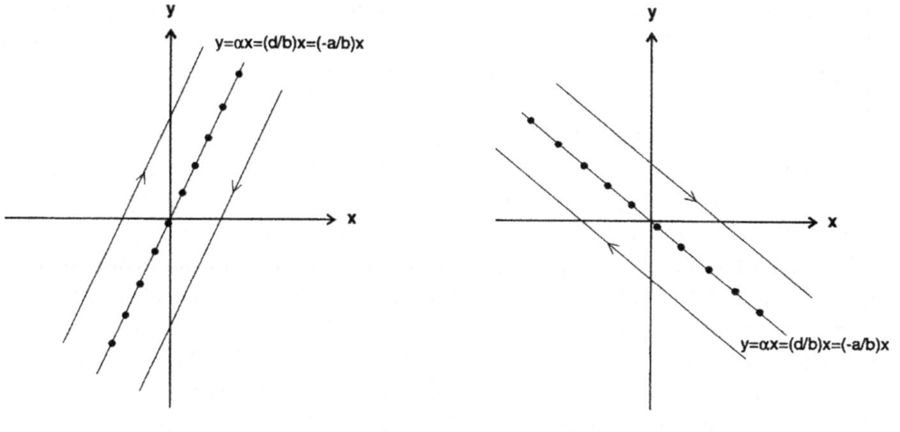


**a** $(bc < 0, b > 0)$ **b** $(bc < 0, b > 0)$

**Fig. 29.11** Trajectory configurations of $\Delta^2 = 0,\ |A| = 0,\ a + d = 0$; Point $A$ and $B$ (**a**) $(bc < 0, b > 0)$ (**b**) $(bc < 0, b > 0)$

On the *bisector*, $\boldsymbol{a} - \boldsymbol{d} = \mathbf{0}$, within the *parameter region* $\boldsymbol{\Delta}^2 < \mathbf{0}$ of Fig. 29.4a, we find, if $\boldsymbol{b} = -\boldsymbol{c}$, the *logarithmic* ("circular") *spirals:*

$$x^2 + y^2 = k_0 \exp\{(2a/b)\arctan(y/x)\}, \tag{29.187}$$

cf. (29.166). *Outside* the *bisectors*, $a + d = 0$, $a - d = 0$, in *region* $\boldsymbol{\Delta}^2 < \mathbf{0}$, we have the *elliptic spirals*. Note that the slopes, $\boldsymbol{\beta}_1, \boldsymbol{\beta}_2$, (29.163), of the *symmetry* axis of the *ellipses* upon $a + d = 0$ are helpful in determining the "vertices" of the elliptic spirals that are placed upon straight lines *parallel* to $a - d = 0$.

At the *points* **A** and **B** in Fig. 29.4a, the *four* boundary curves of (29.182–29.183) *coincide*. Then all the *trajectories* are now *straight* lines, *parallel* to the single *directrix* see Fig. 29.11.

## Structural Stability and Bifurcations

With a *complete* description of conceivable *trajectory configurations* and their relation to *parameter space*—any constellation of $\boldsymbol{a}, \boldsymbol{b}, \boldsymbol{c}, \boldsymbol{d}$—we will easily be able to answer the question: *what* happens to the *phase portrait* when the two *governing functions* of the system (29.1.1–2) *change*? Such an issue is obviously of independent mathematical significance. The question is also highly important for various *applications,* since whatever is considered factually significant must remain unchanged, when the parameters of the dynamic system vary slightly, i.e., the mathematical model—as an abstract idealization—must be *robust* if the *variation* of its coefficients does *not exceed* in absolute value a certain *positive* $\boldsymbol{\varepsilon}$. A dynamic system is defined to be *structurally stable* if an arbitrary small change (*perturbation*) of the system *parameters* does not change *topologically* the *phase portrait*. See (Andronov and Chaikin 1949, p. 55; Peixoto 1962, p. 101; Thom 1989, p. 25).

Usually, the concept of *topological equivalence* of phase portraits is defined as including the preservation of the *direction* of motion along the trajectories. But, sometimes, the orientation is ignored, and *only* the *loci configurations* of the portrait are considered.

Then, if structural stability is only concerned with the topological nature of *loci,* we see that the *linear dynamic* system (29.1.1–2) is a *structurally stable* system *everywhere* in the parameter space, *except* for such parameter constellations that are located on the *closed* line *segment* **AB** in Fig. 29.4a. Indeed, all *trajectories* along **AB**, apart from the critical point, are *closed,* whereas *outside* **AB** there exist no closed trajectories. Hence, there exist no homeomorphism transforming the trajectories along AB into the trajectories outside AB. This establishes the *structural instability* of system (29.1.1–2) for the specific parameter constellations *belonging* to **AB**. However, if structural stability is concerned not only with the configurations of the trajectories but also with their *orientations,* then the system (29.1.1–2) is *structurally stable* everywhere in the parameter space, *except* the parameter values associated with line *segment*

AB *and* the *boundary curves* (29.183, ***iv***), in Fig. 29.4. As is well known, the structural instability of (29.1.1–2) along the *latter* boundary *curve(zero determinant)* follows from the *impossibility* of establishing a *homeomorphic* transformation of the phase portrait of a *node* onto the phase portrait of a *saddle* point.

As a rule, structurally stable dynamic systems are predominant, and they form an *open,* everywhere-*dense* set in the *parameter* space. The *complement* of this open set is often called the set of *bifurcation points.* Accordingly, the *boundary curves* (29.183 ***iv***) and the *closed* line *segment* AB represent the *bifurcation points* of the linear system (29.1.1–2). The points A and B are *double* bifurcation points, whereby a perturbation of parameters, the structural instability (topological change of phase portrait), is clearly dramatized, cf. Fig. 29.5a.

*Topological equivalence* and structural stability of *phase portraits* have been the main subjects of the modern *qualitative* theory of ordinary differential equations. Such qualitative studies of (29.1.1–2) do *not* attach any significance to the *boundary curves* (29.183, ***iii***) between *parabolic* and *spiraling* trajectories, as they are qualitatively (topologically) the same. But neglecting the distinction between *monotonic* and *oscillatory solutions* is beset with grave dangers. Furthermore, within the *parameter region* $\Delta^2 < 0$, one cannot with impunity ignore the *common analytical* form (29.166) of spirals and ellipses.

In short, *topological* classification of trajectory configurations *discard* and obscure salient geometric properties that fruitfully may have been studied by the traditional methods and concepts in *analytical geometry*. The *hyperconic classification* of the trajectory configurations is the natural *extension* of the familiar *geometry* of *conic sections*.

## Parameter Space and Kinematic Stability Properties

The *topological* approach to ordinary differential equations has been *anathema* to the development of more refined *kinematic* stability concepts. Traditionally, studies of stability inquire into the temporal evolution of the state variables only to see whether they in time approach an *equilibrium state* or a *limit cycle.* The latter is *ruled out* for any *homogeneous dynamic* system, see Chap. 28, section "Heuristic Comments on Geometry, Dynamics, and Kinematics". As to the character of an equilibrium state of a dynamic system, depending on several parameters, it is usually found that the *parameter space splits* into *two* parts, viz, a *stability sector* (consisting of those parameter values for which the equilibrium is stable) and an *instability sector.* Separating them is the *stability boundary.* We now relate these two sectors to our discussion of ratio and coordinate stability properties in section "Stability of the Ratio and Coordinate Solutions" and the parameter regions of the hyperconic phase portrait displayed in section "Parameter Space and the Hyperconic Phase Portrait".

For the Cartesian *coordinate solutions* of (29.1.1–2), the *stability sector* (*global strong absolute* stability or *global asymptotic* stability, with $\varphi = (0, 0)$ included in the family), cf. (29.141), (29.146), (29.149), consists of the *lower* part of the hyperparabolic and hyperelliptic parameter regions in Fig. 29.5a (**bc** < **0**) or the *lower* (south-west) part of hyperparabolic parameter region in Fig. 29.5b (**bc** > **0**). The stability sector of *triangular system* (**bc** = **0**) is simply the *interior* of the third quadrant in the $(a, d)$-plane, cf. (29.151).

Along the *boundary* (with points A and B excluded) of the *stability sector* in Fig. 29.5, we have *global weak absolute* stability, cf. (29.142), (29.149).

Traditionally, the *instability sector* of (29.1.1–2) is the remaining part of the $(a, d)$-plane in Fig. 29.5. However, by introducing more refined kinematic stability concepts, we showed, cf. (29.143–29.145), (29.147), (29.152–29.157), that the family of nonstationary Cartesian coordinate solutions has *generic weak relative* stability in the hyperhyperbolic and the upper hyperparabolic parameter regions in Fig. 29.5. Only within the *upper* hyperelliptic parameter region of Fig. 29.5a was it *impossible* to attach any degree of stability to Cartesian coordinate solutions, cf. (29.150).

It is well known (Simmons 1972, p. 314; Jordan and Smith 1977, p. 51,294) and also appears from Fig. 29.5 that the *asymptotic* (strong absolute) *stability sector* constitutes *only* a *"quarter"* of the *parameter space* belonging to (29.1.1–2). For the *increasing*, non-oscillatory *solutions* of (29.1.1–2), it is surprising that their generic kinematic property—*weak relative stability*—has not gained attention anywhere in the literature; see any textbook among the references.

*Stability* theory has mostly paid attention to varied *geometric* rather than varied *kinematic* properties of *phase curve* families, cf. (28.6). Hence, the traditional emphasis upon the *critical point* of (29.1.1–2) as, e.g., a *node* or *saddle* point. In case the node is an *attractor*, there is of course a crucial difference between stability properties of the family coordinate solution associated with the node and the saddle point. But if the node is *not* an *attractor*, then the geometry of a node (hyperparabolic phase curves) and the geometry of a saddle point (hyperhyperbolic phase curves) have no bearing on the question of coordinate stability in generic situations, i.e., for *both* types of critical points, we have *weak relative* stability of the family of *nonstationary* solutions, cf. (29.145), (29.143), where the proviso *generic*—rather than a *global* property—is due in both cases to the exemption of the *repulsive directrix solutions*. For the saddle point, the *repulsive directrix* is often called the *stable* arm—with solutions flowing directly and consistently toward the equilibrium. But this stable arm, which kinematically is a fluke, has gained undue prominence in the literature at the expense of the prevalent generic stability property (29.143).

Generally, the *degree* of *homogeneity* of the linear system (29.1.1–2), $m = 1$, has traditionally *not* been adequately *utilized* in *unifying* the kinematic stability properties of the families of *increasing* coordinate solutions.

As was seen in section "Stability of the Ratio and Coordinate Solutions", cf. Stability Proposition 29.1, we always—irrespective of decreasing or increasing coordinate solutions—have *ratio* stability outside the hyperelliptic parameter region ($\Delta^2 < 0$). The latter region is rather "small" in a linear system, cf. Fig. 29.5. Hence *ratio stability* is—to a large extent and *regardless* of a node or a saddle point—another *unifying* qualitative property of the *kinematic* behavior of the linear system (29.1.1–2).

## Classification of Linear Dynamic Systems

An important task in investigating and understanding the behavior of a dynamic system ought to be a careful study of the *governing functions*—the fundamental laws upon which any solution depend. But the well-known difficulties encountered in solving simultaneous differential equations have probably discouraged many attempts to gain valuable insight into solutions from a penetrating, overall inspection of the basic governing functions.

"*Coordinate transformations*" have been resorted to in the endeavor to replace the *interacting system* by a formal system without or with less interaction. However, on the background of earlier sections, we may now offer a classification of linear plane dynamics that utilizes the information immediately conveyed by the governing functions (29.1.1–2). Our dynamic classification will then be compared with traditional equivalence classes and canonical forms based on standard coordinate transformations. The *dynamic model*—as specified by *governing functions*—will indicate *self/own-couplings* and *cross-couplings* among the state variables, see (Haken 1983b, p. 311; Haken 1983a, p. 56; Rosen 1970, p. 154). In terms of *cross-couplings*, there exist three classes for the linear system (29.1.1–2), viz.,

$$(i)\ \text{bilateral coupling} \Leftrightarrow \quad bc \neq 0, \tag{29.188}$$

$$(ii)\ \text{unilateral coupling} \Leftrightarrow \quad b = 0 \ \vee \ c = 0, \tag{29.189}$$

$$(iii)\ \text{no coupling} \Leftrightarrow \quad b = 0 \ \wedge \ c = 0. \tag{29.190}$$

The couplings (29.188–29.190) are obviously significant for a clear understanding of the subject matter of a factual dynamic process. But they are also important from a purely mathematical point of view, e.g., we have seen that (29.189–29.190) immediately *rule out oscillating* solutions (hyperelliptic phase curves); (29.190) is *trivial* dynamics from a practical point of view, and its plane representations by node or saddle point configurations only obscure the basic uncoupled system.

Self-couplings $(\boldsymbol{a}, \boldsymbol{d})$ and cross-couplings $(\boldsymbol{b}, \boldsymbol{c})$ may serve as *activators* or *inhibitors* of the individual state variables—according to the *positive* or *negative sign* of the coupling parameters—generally, the *signs* of the *partial derivatives* from the Jacobian matrix of the governing vector function.

The class of *bilateral* couplings (29.188) contain *two* important *subclasses*, which we may call

$$(1i) \quad \text{cooperative coupling} \quad \Leftrightarrow \quad bc > 0, \tag{29.191}$$

$$(2i) \quad \text{non-cooperative coupling} \Leftrightarrow \quad bc < 0. \tag{29.192}$$

Hence, *cooperative* coupling occurs with linkages of either *mutual* activators ($b > 0$, $c > 0$) or *mutual* inhibitors ($b < 0$, $c < 0$); at a point in the state space, the dynamic implication of (29.191) is that both variables *together* move *away* from the origin or *together* move toward the origin. Like (29.189), the *cooperative* coupling (29.191) is a *sufficient* condition for the absence of oscillating solutions (hyperelliptic phase curves), cf. Fig. 29.5b.

Although the cross-coupling (29.192) inclines one variable to increase and the other to decrease and is a *necessary* condition for hyperelliptic phase curves, a *non-cooperative* coupling (29.192) may be *dominated* by the *self-couplings*—especially if the latter are also of opposite nature and one self-coupling is preponderant, cf. (29.4). Thus, hyperelliptic phase curves (spirals) only occur if and only if the *non-cooperative* coupling (29.192) is *strong* enough to predominate over the preponderant self-coupling, cf. (29.4) and Fig. 29.3. Note that if self-couplings *neutralize* each other ($a + d = 0$) and a non-cooperative cross-coupling (29.192) *operates*, then the result will be *pure cycles*, cf. Figs. 29.5a, 29.10.

In factual studies, dynamic models are meant to generate intuition and to build understanding, i.e., besides describing (predicting) *what* happens (from any initial state), we also want to know *why* things happen. It requires us to recognize what leads to what and to stress which assumptions drive the conclusions (solutions). Of course, the larger and the more complex a dynamic model is, the harder it is to achieve that sort of understanding. However, linear dynamic models and, in particular, (29.1.1–2) should be expected to allow intuition and a factual grip on the subject matter to provide relevant *equivalence classes*, taking cognizance of crucial dynamic linkages among the state variables. We propose, and evidently have used throughout, the *classifications* (29.188–29.192) as the *natural* framework for systematizing and understanding the behavior of the solutions from the model (29.1.1–2).

The *dynamic* classification (29.188–29.192) may now briefly be compared with traditional classifications of (29.1.1–2) based on *algebraic* (linear) and *topological equivalence* relations, cf. Arnold (1973, p. 141). Thus, linear dynamic systems are said to be algebraically (linearly) equivalent if and only if their *eigenvalues* are *distinct* and *coincide*. Then linear dynamic systems, having the following matrices, are algebraically equivalent ($\sim$) when the parameters $\boldsymbol{a}, \boldsymbol{b}, \boldsymbol{c}, \boldsymbol{d}$ are all nonzero and distinct:

$$\begin{pmatrix} a & 0 \\ 0 & d \end{pmatrix} \sim \begin{pmatrix} d & 0 \\ 0 & a \end{pmatrix} \sim \begin{pmatrix} a & b \\ 0 & d \end{pmatrix} \sim \begin{pmatrix} a & 0 \\ c & d \end{pmatrix} \sim \begin{pmatrix} b+d & \frac{(b+d-a)b}{a-d} \\ d-a & a-b \end{pmatrix} \tag{29.193}$$

The matrices in (29.193) have the trace, $a + d$; the determinant, $ad$; and the same *eigenvalues*: $\lambda_1 = a$, $\lambda_2 = d$. Evidently, algebraic equivalence does not distinguish between diagonal, triangular, and square matrices and hence *violates* the classifications (29.188–29.190).

Linear dynamic systems are said to be topologically equivalent if and only if the number of eigenvalues with negative (and positive) real parts are the same. Clearly, topological equivalence violates (29.188–29.190) as well as (29.191–29.192). As is well known, traditional *eigenvalue criteria* mainly serve to classify *geometrically* the *local* phase portrait around the *critical point* (0, 0)—although inadequately compared to the hyperconic trajectory classification, cf. sections "Parameter Space and the Hyperconic Phase Portrait"–"Parameter Space and Kinematic Stability Properties". Neither do the *eigenvalues* properly address the *global* or *generic kinematic stability* properties of *ratios* and *coordinate solutions,* as discussed in section "Stability of the Ratio and Coordinate Solutions", and certainly they do reflect much information about the *intrinsic* nature of the underlying *dynamics,* as described by the *governing functions*, e.g., (29.188–29.192).

## Affine Dynamics in the Plane

In applied dynamics, e.g., in biology and economics, we will often immediately repudiate a dynamic model if it has a stationary (equilibrium) solution only at the origin—and more so, if the origin is a global attractor. Thus, to be meaningful, a stationary solution often has to be represented by some nonzero state values. The latter are even often required to be positive. From this viewpoint, the linear system (29.1.1–29.2.2) is unsatisfactory. Let us, therefore, in $\mathbf{R}^2$ consider the general *affine* system with real *nonzero constants* $(\boldsymbol{\delta}_1, \boldsymbol{\delta}_2)$,

$$\dot{\mathbf{x}} = \delta_1 + ax + by, \tag{29.194.1}$$

$$\dot{\mathbf{y}} = \delta_2 + cx + dy, \tag{29.194.2}$$

or in vector-matrix notation

$$\dot{\mathbf{x}} = \delta + A\mathbf{x}; \quad \mathbf{x} \in \mathbf{R}^2, \quad \boldsymbol{\delta} \in \mathbf{R}^2/\{0, 0\}. \tag{29.195}$$

### *Nonsingular Affine Dynamics*

As is well known, the affine system (29.194.1–2) has *one* or *no stationary* solution when the coefficient *matrix* $A$ is, respectively, *nonsingular* or *singular.* In the nonsingular case, the critical point is, $-\boldsymbol{A}^{-1}\boldsymbol{\delta}$, i.e., the *state value*

$$\bar{x} = (b\delta_2 - d\delta_1)/(ad - bc), \tag{29.196.1}$$

$$\bar{y} = (c\delta_1 - a\delta_2)/(ad - bc). \tag{29.196.2}$$

Accordingly, the *general coordinate solution* of the *nonsingular* affine system Equation (29.194.1–2) is

$$x(t) = \bar{x} + \varphi_1(t), \tag{29.197.1}$$

$$y(t) = \bar{y} + \varphi_2(t), \tag{29.197.2}$$

where $\boldsymbol{\varphi_1(t)}$, $\boldsymbol{\varphi_2(t)}$ are given by (29.90–29.92) with now the *initial conditions*, $[\boldsymbol{x_0^* = x_0 - \bar{x}},\ \boldsymbol{y_0^* = y_0 - \bar{y}}]$.

As is easily verified, the *stability* properties of the family of *coordinate* solutions $[x(t), y(t)]$, (29.197.1–2) are the same as stated in Stability Proposition 29.2–29.3, cf. section "Stability of the Ratio and Coordinate Solutions", except that (29.142) and (29.144) drop out in the nonsingular case under discussion here.

Regarding *ratio* stability, we see—when the *critical point* is the global attractor, cf. (29.141), (29.151)—that, cf (29.196.1–29.197.2),

$$\lim_{t\to\infty} \frac{y(t)}{x(t)} = \frac{\bar{y}}{\bar{x}} = \frac{c\delta_1 - a\delta_2}{b\delta_2 - d\delta_1}, \quad \bar{x} \neq 0, \tag{29.198}$$

i.e., the *limiting* ratio of $\boldsymbol{y(t)/x(t)}$ is *not* the *director root* of the attractive directrix, as in the linear system.

However, when the *critical point* is *repulsive* and the individual coordinate *solutions* go to plus or minus *infinity* as $t \to \infty$, then we see from (29.197.1–2) that

$$\begin{aligned} \lim_{t\to\infty} \frac{y(t)}{x(t)} &= \lim_{t\to\infty} \frac{y(t) - \bar{y} + \bar{y}}{x(t) - \bar{x} + \bar{x}} \\ &= \lim_{t\to\infty} \left(\frac{y(t) - \bar{y}}{x(t) - \bar{x}}\right) \cdot \lim_{t\to\infty} \left(\frac{1 + \frac{\bar{y}}{y(t)-\bar{y}}}{1 + \frac{\bar{x}}{x(t)-\bar{x}}}\right) = \lim_{t\to\infty} \frac{\varphi_2(t)}{\varphi_1(t)}. \end{aligned} \tag{29.199}$$

Hence, the *ratio stabilities* of nonsingular *affine* dynamics are the *same* as for the homogeneous system, i.e., we may also apply Stability Proposition 29.1, cf. section "Stability of the Ratio and Coordinate Solutions", to the system (29.194.1–2) whenever (29.196.1–2) is *repulsive*. If $\Delta^2 > 0$, the *limit* (29.199) will be the *director root* of the *attractive* directrix, cf. Remark 29.3.

### *Singular Affine Dynamics*

To obtain the *general* solution of the *singular* affine system, we have to now look for a *particular solution* that replaces (29.196.1–2) in (29.197.1–2). To find it, we transform (29.194.1–2) into *one second-order* differential equation, and hence with, $\boldsymbol{ad - bc = 0}$, we get

$$\ddot{x} - (a + d)\dot{x} = b\delta_2 - d\delta_1, \tag{29.200}$$

which has the *particular solution*

$$\check{x}(t) = \gamma t; \quad \gamma = (d\delta_1 - b\delta_2)/(a+d); \quad a + d \neq 0. \tag{29.201.1}$$

Next, (29.201.1) and $by = \dot{x} - ax - \delta_1$, cf. (29.194.1), give

$$\check{y}(t) = (\gamma/b)(1 - at) - \delta_1/b, \quad b \neq 0. \tag{29.201.2}$$

Thus, with $a + d \neq 0,\ b \neq 0$ the *general solution* of the *singular* affine system (29.194.1–2) is

$$x(t) = \check{x}(t) + \varphi_1(t), \tag{29.202.1}$$

$$y(t) = \check{y}(t) + \varphi_2(t), \tag{29.202.2}$$

where $\varphi_1(t),\ \varphi_2(t)$ are given by (29.90) with $\Delta = \frac{1}{2}(a+d)$ and the initial conditions, $[x_0^* = x_0,\ y_0^* = y_0 - (\gamma - \delta_1)/b]$.

In the special case of $a + d = 0$, we obtain from (29.200) and (29.194.1) the *particular* solution

$$\check{\check{x}}(t) = \tfrac{1}{2}(b\delta_2 - d\delta_1)t^2, \tag{29.203.1}$$

$$\check{\check{y}}(t) = [(b\delta_2 - d\delta_1)/b][t - \tfrac{1}{2}at^2] - \delta_1/b, \quad b \neq 0, \tag{29.203.2}$$

and hence with $a + d = 0,\ b \neq 0$ the *general solution* is

$$x(t) = \check{\check{x}}(t) + \varphi_1(t), \tag{29.204.1}$$

$$y(t) = \check{\check{y}}(t) + \varphi_2(t), \tag{29.204.2}$$

where $\varphi_1(t),\ \varphi_2(t)$ are given by (29.91) with $a+d = 0$ and the initial conditions, $[x_0^* = x_0,\ y_0^* = y_0 + \delta_1/b]$.

The *family* of coordinate solutions (29.203.1–2) has either global *weak absolute* stability or generic *weak relative* stability, depending on whether $a+d$ is negative or positive, cf. (29.142), (29.144). The *family* of coordinate solutions (29.204.1–2) has generic *weak relative* stability, cf. (29.147).

Regarding the behavior of *ratio solutions* from (29.202.1–2), it can be verified by (29.201.1–2) and (29.90) that for any initial values $(x_0, y_0)$ outside the trajectory of (29.201.1–2), we get

$$a + d > 0: \lim_{t\to\infty} \frac{y(t)}{x(t)} = \lim_{t\to\infty} \frac{\check{y}(t) + \varphi_2(t)}{\check{x}(t) + \varphi_1(t)} = \lim_{t\to\infty} \frac{\varphi_2(t)}{\varphi_1(t)} = \frac{d}{b}, \tag{29.205.1}$$

$$a + d < 0: \lim_{t\to\infty} \frac{y(t)}{x(t)} = \lim_{t\to\infty} \frac{\check{y}(t) + \varphi_2(t)}{\check{x}(t) + \varphi_1(t)} = \lim_{t\to\infty} \frac{\varphi_2(t)}{\varphi_1(t)} = -\frac{a}{b}. \tag{29.205.2}$$

Thus, the *ratio limits* (29.205.1–2) correspond to those of the *singular* linear system, cf. (29.184.1–2), although the trajectory configurations implied by (29.202.1–2) are very different from Figs. 29.7 and 29.8, as discussed below.

From (29.203.1–2), (29.204.1–2), (29.91) it can be verified that

$$a+d=0: \lim_{t\to\infty}\frac{y(t)}{x(t)}=\lim_{t\to\infty}\frac{\check{\check{y}}(t)+\varphi_2(t)}{\check{\check{x}}(t)+\varphi_1(t)}=\lim_{t\to\infty}\frac{\varphi_2(t)}{\varphi_1(t)}=-\frac{a}{b}=\frac{d}{b}, \tag{29.206}$$

which correspond to (29.7) with $a+d=0$.

**Remark 29.6** The singular affine system with $c=0$ is covered by (29.201.1–2) and (29.203.1–2), supplemented with $a=0 \ \vee \ d=0$.

In the case of $b=0$, the particular solutions are the solutions obtained from a similar equation (29.200) in the second coordinate. Accordingly, we get

$$\check{y}(t)=\varepsilon t,\ \varepsilon=(a\delta_2-c\delta_1)/(a+d), \tag{29.207.1}$$

$$\check{x}(t)=(\varepsilon/c)(1-dt)-\delta_2/c,\ c\neq 0, \tag{29.207.2}$$

$$\check{\check{y}}(t)=\tfrac{1}{2}(c\delta_1-a\delta_2)t^2, \tag{29.208.1}$$

$$\check{\check{x}}(t)=[(c\delta_1-a\delta_2)/c][t-\tfrac{1}{2}dt^2]-\delta/c,\ c\neq 0, \tag{29.208.2}$$

which again are to be supplemented with, $a=0 \ \vee \ d=0$. ▽

### *The Geometry of the Affine Phase Portrait*

Obviously, the complete system of *trajectory configurations* of the *nonsingular* affine system (29.194.1–2) is given by just a *translation,* cf. (29.197.1–2), of the *hyperconic phase portrait* of the linear system, as presented in sections "The Geometry of the Phase Portrait"–"Parameter Space and the Hyperconic Phase Portrait". However, the *phase portrait* of the *singular affine* system is radically different from the *singular* linear system. For the sake of completeness, the *loci forms,* $\boldsymbol{\ell}(\boldsymbol{x},\boldsymbol{y})=\mathbf{0}$, of (29.202.1–2) and (29.204.1–2) will be presented; see (Bieberbach 1923, p. 9).

The phase curves of (29.202.1–2) contain *one* and *only one* straight line trajectory, namely (29.201.1–2), which upon elimination of $t$ gives

$$y=(\gamma-\delta_1)/b-(a/b)x,\quad b\neq 0. \tag{29.209}$$

The other loci forms, contained in (29.202.1–2), are tedious to derive. But by (29.194.1–2)

$$\frac{dy}{dx} = \frac{cx + dy + \delta_2}{ax + by + \delta_1}. \tag{29.210}$$

Using the substitution

$$\nu = ax + by + \delta_1; \; d\nu/dx = a + b \cdot dy/dx, \quad b \neq 0, \tag{29.211}$$

and the singularity condition, $ad - bc = 0$, we get from (29.210–29.211), after some manipulations,

$$d\nu/dx = a + d + (b\delta_2 - d\delta_1)/\nu, \quad \nu \neq 0. \tag{29.212}$$

By separation of variables, integration, and (29.211), we arrive at the *loci equations*

$$a + d \neq 0 \quad : \quad -dx + by + \gamma \ln \mid ax + by + \delta_1 - \gamma \mid \; = \; \kappa_1, \tag{29.213}$$

$$a + d = 0 \quad : d^2x^2 - 2dbxy + b^2y^2 - 2b\delta_2 x + 2d\delta_1 y = \; \kappa_2, \tag{29.214}$$

where $\boldsymbol{\gamma}$ is given by (29.201.1) and $\boldsymbol{\kappa_1}, \boldsymbol{\kappa_2}$ are *arbitrary constants.*

Thus, the loci of the coordinate solutions (29.202.1–2) are given by (29.209) and (29.213); further, the loci of the coordinate solutions (29.204.1–2) are given by (29.214). Note that the symmetry axis of the parabolas (29.214) has the slope $\beta_1 = d/b$, cf. (29.163), (29.206)

Although the family of solutions (29.202.1–2) and (29.204.1–2) had the same *coordinate* and *ratio stabilities* as the singular linear system, the *geometry* of *trajectory* configurations (29.213–29.214) is very different from the singular linear case, as shown in Figs. 29.7 and 29.8. Clearly, only with, $a/c = b/d = \delta_1/\delta_2$, and $a + d = 0$, cf. (29.210), (29.214), the parallel straight lines in (29.162), will the picture of Fig. 29.8 reappear from *singular affine* dynamics.

## Concluding Comments

To be worthy of serious attention, ruminations on an old subject should embody a definite and reasonable point of view which is not already represented in print. Our treatment of linear and affine dynamics in the plane is apparently and embodies a point of view different from the algebraic and topological methodology prevalent today.

*Analysis* has been the dominant branch of mathematics for 300 years, and differential equations are the core of analysis. In any factual process, the state variables involved and their rates of change are coupled with one another by the basic scientific principles that govern the process. Always bringing into focus the original state variables and utilizing the fundamental *governing functions,* we have obtained and discussed the *general solution* of linear and affine dynamics and described the plane geometry of their trajectories. The outcome was the family of hyperbolic and circular trigonometric solutions and the *hyperconic phase portrait*. The *kinematic* stability properties of the families of ratio and coordinate solutions were described by our *generalized*, (weaker) *stability criteria*. Throughout, the tools have been the "modern" methods of analysis (calculus) and the concepts from the "ancient" theories of proportions (*ratios*) and *conic* sections.

## BIBLIOGRAPHY

Andronov AA, Chaikin CE (1949) Theory of Oscillations. Princeton University Press, New Jersey

Andronov AA, Leontovich EA, Gordon II, Maier AG (1971) Theory of Bifurcations of Dynamic Systems on a Plane. NASA and National Science Foundation, Washington, D.C

Arnold VI (1973) Ordinary Differential Equations. MIT Press, Mass

Arrowsmith DK, Place CM (1982) Ordinary Differential Equations. Chapman & Hall, London

Bieberbach L (1923) Theorie der Differential–Gleichungen. Verlag von Julius Springer, Berlin

Birkhoff G, Rota G (1989) Ordinary Differential Equations, 4th edn. John Wiley & Sons, New York

Braun M (1983) Differential Equations and Their Applications, 3rd edn. Springer–Verlag, New York

Grimshaw R (1990) Nonlinear Ordinary Differential Equations. Blackwell Scientific Publications, Oxford

Guckenheimer J, Holmes P (1986) Nonlinear Oscillations, Dynamical Systems, and Bifurcations of Vector Fields. Springer–Verlag, New York

Haken H (1983a) Advanced Synergetics. Springer–Verlag, Berlin

Haken H (1983b) Synergetics. An Introduction. Springer–Verlag, Berlin

Hirsch MW, Smale S (1974) Differential Equations, Dynamical Systems and Linear Algebra. Academic Press, New York

Hochstadt H (1964) Differential Equations, A Modern Approach. Holt, Rinehart, and Winston, New York

Hurewitz W (1958) Lectures on Ordinary Differential Equations. John Wiley & Sons, New York

Jordan DW, Smith P (1977) Non–linear Ordinary Differential Equations. Oxford University Press

Larsen ME, Jensen BS (1989) Coupled Linear Differential Equations with Real Coefficients. American Math Month 96:727–731

Murphy GM (1960) Ordinary Differential Equations and Their Solutions. D. Van Nostrand, Princeton, New Jersey

Peixoto MM (1962) Structural Stability on Two–Dimensional Manifolds. Topology 1:101–120

Perko L (1993) Differential Equations and Dynamical Systems. Springer–Verlag, New York

Poincaré H (1928) Memoire sur les courbes définies par une equation differentielle. Journal de Mathematiques 3. serie, 7 (1881), 375–422; **8** (1882), 251–96; Oeuvres, Tome 1, 3–86, Gauthier–Villars, Paris.

Pontryagin LS (1962) Ordinary Differential Equations. Addison–Wesley, Reading, Mass
Rosen R (1970) Dynamical System Theory in Biology, Volume 1: Stability Theory and Its Applications. Wiley–Interscience, New York
Selby SM (1973) Standard Mathematical Tables, 21st edn. The Chemical Rubber Co, Cleveland, Ohio
Simmons GF (1972) Differential Equations – with applications and historical notes. McGraw–Hill, New York
Thom R (1989) Structural Stability and Morphogenesis. An Outline of a General Theory of Models. Addison–Wesley, New York, W.A. Benjamin Inc., Reading, Mass., 1975

CHAPTER 30

# Quasihomogeneous Dynamics in the Plane

The principal aim of this chapter is to generalize the theory in Chap. 28 to a wider class of differential equations, which are called *quasihomogeneous*, (Arnold 1988). In Sect. "The Class of Quasihomogeneous Functions", we characterize the class of real quasihomogeneous functions on $\mathbf{R}^2$. Then we consider quasihomogeneous differential equations and examine some general aspects of the solutions. Section "Quasihomogeneous Autonomous Dynamic Systems" discusses the stability properties of quasihomogeneous dynamics within the framework presented in Chap. 1. Concluding comments are offered in Sect. "Concluding Comments".

## The Class of Quasihomogeneous Functions

In accordance with the concept presented in Arnold (1988, p. 5), we introduce:

**Definition 30.1** A nonvanishing $C^0$-function $f = f(x, y) : \mathbf{R}^2 \to \mathbf{R}$ is *quasihomogeneous* if there exist real numbers $\beta_1, \beta_2, \tilde{m};\ \beta_1, \beta_2 \neq 0$, such that

$$\forall (x, y) \in \mathbf{R}^2\ \forall \mu \in \mathbf{R}_+ :\ f(\mu^{\beta_1} x, \mu^{\beta_2} y) = \mu^{\tilde{m}} f(x, y). \tag{30.1}$$

The pair $(\beta_1, \beta_2)$ are called the *weights (exponents)* of $f$, and $\tilde{m}$ the *associated degree* of *quasihomogeneity*. Clearly, if $(\beta_1, \beta_2)$ are weights for $f$ with associated degree $\tilde{m}$, then $(A\beta_1, A\beta_2)$ are weights for $f$ with associated degree $A\tilde{m}$, $A \in \mathbf{R} \setminus \{0\}$.

With co-author:
PETER GROSS, Department of Mathematics and Computer Science, Technical University of Denmark, Denmark



B. S. Jensen, *The Elements and Dynamic Systems of Economic Growth and Trade Models*, https://doi.org/10.1007/978-3-031-52493-6_30

To remove such redundancy, we state

**Lemma 30.1** *Given a quasihomogeneous $C^0$-function $f : \mathbf{R}^2 \to \mathbf{R}$. Then there exist a $\beta \neq 0$ and an $m \in \mathbf{R}$, such that $(1, \beta)$ are the weights and $m$ the degree of $f$.*

***Proof*** Let $(\beta_1, \beta_2)$ be arbitrary weights for $f$, and $\tilde{m}$ the associated degree. Putting $\lambda = \mu^{\beta_1}$, $\beta = \frac{\beta_2}{\beta_1}$, $m = \frac{\tilde{m}}{\beta_1}$, we have for all $\lambda > 0$, cf. (30.1)

$$f(\lambda x, \lambda^{\beta} y) = f(\mu^{\beta_1} x, \mu^{\beta_2} y) = \mu^{\tilde{m}} f(x, y) = \lambda^{\frac{\tilde{m}}{\beta_1}} f(x, y) = \lambda^m f(x, y), \tag{30.2}$$

which proves that $(1, \beta)$ and $m$ are weights and associated degree of $f$. □

Henceforth, by the *weight* $\beta$ and the *degree* $m$ of a quasihomogeneous function $f$, we always mean the unique values chosen in Lemma 30.1.

Observe that any ***homogeneous*** $C^0$-function is ***quasihomogeneous*** with weight $\beta = 1$ and degree $m$ equal to the degree of homogeneity, i.e., the class of quasihomogeneous functions contains the class of homogeneous functions.

**Remark 30.1** It follows immediately from Definition 30.1, Lemma 30.1 and (30.2) with $\lambda = 1/x$ that a nonvanishing $C^0$-function $f : \mathbf{R}^2 \to \mathbf{R}$ is quasihomogeneous with weight $\beta$ and degree $m$ if and only if it can be written as

$$f(x, y) = x^m f(1, y/x^{\beta}) = x^m f(1, r^{\beta}), \quad r = y^{1/\beta}/x, \quad x \neq 0. \tag{30.3}$$

∇

With *differentiability,* a very useful characterization of the quasihomogeneous functions is given by the following generalization of Euler's relation:

**Theorem 30.1** *Assume $f \in C^1(\mathbf{R}^2)$. Then $f$ is quasihomogeneous of weight $\beta \neq 0$ and degree $m$ if and only if $f$ satisfies the relation*

$$x \frac{\partial f}{\partial x}(x, y) + \beta y \frac{\partial f}{\partial y}(x, y) = m \cdot f(x, y), \quad (x, y) \in \mathbf{R}^2. \tag{30.4}$$

***Proof*** If $f$ is quasihomogeneous, then by (30.2)

$$f(\lambda x, \lambda^{\beta} y) = \lambda^m f(x, y), \ \lambda > 0, \ (x, y) \in \mathbf{R}^2. \tag{30.5}$$

By the chain rule, (30.5) is differentiable in $\lambda$, and differentiation yields

$$x\frac{\partial f}{\partial x}(\lambda x, \lambda^\beta y) + \beta\lambda^{\beta-1}y\frac{\partial f}{\partial y}(\lambda x, \lambda^\beta y) = m\lambda^{m-1}f(x, y), \tag{30.6}$$

and putting $\lambda = 1$, we get (30.4).

Conversely, assume $f$ satisfies (30.4) and consider an arbitrary point $(x_0, y_0) \in \mathbf{R}^2$. Define the $C^1$-function $j : \mathbf{R}^2 \to \mathbf{R}$ by

$$j(\lambda) = f(\lambda x_0, \lambda^\beta y_0),\ \lambda \in \mathbf{R}_+. \tag{30.7}$$

Applying (30.4), we have

$$\begin{aligned} j'(\lambda) &= 1/\lambda\left[(\lambda x_0)\frac{\partial f}{\partial x}(\lambda x_0, \lambda^\beta y_0) + \beta(\lambda^\beta y_0)\frac{\partial f}{\partial y}(\lambda x_0, \lambda^\beta y_0)\right] \\ &= [m/\lambda]f(\lambda x_0, \lambda^\beta y_0) = [m/\lambda]j(\lambda),\ \lambda \in \mathbf{R}_+, \end{aligned} \tag{30.8}$$

such that $z = j(\lambda)$ is a solution to the simple *ODE*

$$dz/d\lambda - (m/\lambda)z = 0. \tag{30.9}$$

Integration yields

$$j(\lambda) = C \cdot \lambda^m,\ \lambda > 0; \quad j(1) = f(x_0, y_0), \tag{30.10}$$

$$\therefore \quad j(\lambda) = \lambda^m f(x_0, y_0). \tag{30.11}$$

□

**Remark 30.2** To avoid trivial technical problems, we henceforth only consider the *domain*

$$D = \mathbf{R}_+ \times \mathbf{R}_+. \tag{30.12}$$

Analysis in the other quadrants can be performed analogously by means of a suitable change of sign for the variables. Obviously, Definition 30.1 can be formulated for functions $f : D \to \mathbf{R}$ as well, cf. (30.1–2). Also, Theorem 30.1 can be proved analogously for functions $f : D \to \mathbf{R}$. ▽

Some important examples are contained in the following propositions:

**Proposition 30.1** *Let* $c_i \in \mathbf{R} \setminus \{0\}$, $a_i, b_i \in \mathbf{R}$, $i \in \{1, 2\}$, *and* $a_1 \neq a_2$, $b_1 \neq b_2$. *Then the function*

$$f(x, y) = c_1x^{a_1}y^{b_1} + c_2x^{a_2}y^{b_2}, \quad (x, y) \in D, \tag{30.13.1}$$

*is quasihomogeneous with weight β and degree m given by*

$$\beta = \frac{a_1 - a_2}{b_2 - b_1}, \qquad m = \frac{a_1 b_2 - a_2 b_1}{b_2 - b_1}. \tag{30.13.2}$$

***Proof*** Since $f \in C^1(D)$, (30.4) yields the condition

$$(a_1 + \beta b_1)c_1 x^{a_1} y^{b_1} + (a_2 + \beta b_2)c_2 x^{a_2} y^{b_2} = mf(x, y). \tag{30.14}$$

By the identity theorem of polynomials, (30.14) is satisfied if and only if

$$a_1 + \beta b_1 = a_2 + \beta b_2 = m. \tag{30.15}$$

Hence, (30.15) implies

$$a_1 - a_2 = \beta(b_2 - b_1). \tag{30.16}$$

Thus, (30.14–30.16) prove the proposition. □

**Remark 30.3** Note that if either $a_1 = a_2$ or $b_1 = b_2$, then $f$ is *not* quasihomogeneous—except for the trivial case with $a_1 = a_2$ and $b_1 = b_2$, where $f(x, y) = (c_1 + c_2)x^{a_1} y^{b_1}$. ▽

In the mathematical literature, special quasihomogeneous functions naturally appear as *particular* solutions to variant types of the partial differential equation (30.4), (see Aczel 1966; Ince 1956, p. 109; Smirnov 1964).

**Proposition 30.2** *Let* $a, b \in \mathbf{R} \setminus \{0\}$, $c \in \mathbf{R} \setminus \{0, 1\}$ *and* $d, \gamma \in \mathbf{R}$.
*Then the function*

$$f(x, y) = \gamma[(1 - c)x^{-a} + cy^{-b}]^{-\frac{d}{a}}, \quad (x, y) \in D \tag{30.17.1}$$

*is quasihomogeneous with weight β and degree m given by*

$$\beta = a/b, \quad m = d. \tag{30.17.2}$$

***Proof*** Since $f \in C^1(D)$, we have from (30.17.1)

$$x\partial f/\partial x = \gamma(1 - c)d[(1 - c)x^{-a} + cy^{-b}]^{-\frac{d}{a}-1}x^{-a}, \tag{30.18.1}$$

$$\beta y\partial f/\partial y = \beta\gamma c(db/a)[(1 - c)x^{-a} + cy^{-b}]^{-\frac{d}{a}-1}y^{-b}, \tag{30.18.2}$$

$$mf(x, y) = m\gamma[(1 - c)x^{-a} + cy^{-b}]^{-\frac{d}{a}-1}[(1 - c)x^{-a} + cy^{-b}]. \tag{30.18.3}$$

From (30.4) and (30.18.1–3), we get

$$(1 - c)dx^{-a} + c\beta(db/a)y^{-b} = (1 - c)mx^{-a} + cmy^{-b}. \tag{30.19}$$

By the identity theorem, (30.19) is satisfied if and only if

$$d = m \quad \text{and} \quad \beta(db/a) = m, \tag{30.20}$$

which establishes (30.17.1–2). □

Interesting applications of quasihomogeneous functions in general and of (30.17.1–2) in particular are found in economics (see Kolm 1976; Lau 1972, 1978; Panas 1985; Sato 1977), where "almost" (or "pseudo"-) homogeneity is used synonymously with quasihomogeneity.

## Quasihomogeneous Differential Equations

### *The Class of Quasihomogeneous Differential Equations*

**Definition 30.2** A differential equation on the domain $D$, (30.12),

$$-Q(x, y)dx + P(x, y)dy = 0, \quad (x, y) \in D, \tag{30.21}$$

where $P, Q$ are quasihomogeneous $C^1$-functions with *common weight* $\beta \neq 0$, is called a *quasihomogeneous differential equation* if the mapping $\Lambda$

$$\Lambda(x, y) = (\lambda x, \lambda^{\beta} y), \quad (x, y) \in D \tag{30.22}$$

maps the integral curves of (30.21) onto the integral curves of (30.21) for any fixed $\lambda > 0$; $\beta$ is then called the *weight* of (30.21).

**Remark 30.4** A quasihomogeneous differential equation with weight $\beta = 1$ has an integral curve picture (trajectory system), which is invariant under any multiplication with center (0, 0). But these are exactly the homogeneous differential equations, such that these are quasihomogeneous too. ▽

**Remark 30.5** Definition 30.2 is equivalent to the definition in Arnold (1988, p. 5). Hence, by the theorem in Arnold (1988, p. 5), the integral curves for (30.21) are obtained from each other by the transformation $\Lambda$, (30.22). So while the trajectories for a *homogeneous* differential equation are obtained from each other by a multiplication along the *rays* through the origin, the trajectories for a *quasihomogeneous* differential equation are obtained from each other by a multiplication along the family of *power curves* $y = A \cdot x^{\beta}$, $x > 0$. ▽

**Remark 30.6** If a quasihomogeneous differential equation (30.21) has a singular point, it follows that an entire curve of singular points exists. Since this usually implies existence of a common factor in $P$ and $Q$, we henceforth assume that (30.21) has *no singular* points. ▽

The following theorem relates quasihomogeneous functions to quasihomogeneous differential equations:

**Theorem 30.2** *Consider the differential equation (30.21), with $P$, $Q$ quasihomogeneous functions of* common *weight $\beta \neq 0$ and degrees $m_1, m_2$.*

*Then (30.21) is a quasihomogeneous differential equation if and only if*

$$m_2 - m_1 = \beta - 1. \tag{30.23}$$

***Proof*** Let $\Phi : (x, y) = [\varphi_1(s), \varphi_2(s)],\ s \in I$, be an arbitrary maximal solution to (30.21) and consider the curves $\tilde{\Phi}_\lambda : (x, y) = [\lambda\varphi_1(s), \lambda^\beta\varphi_2(s)],\ s \in I$, $\lambda \in \mathbf{R}_+$. For any fixed $\lambda$, $\tilde{\Phi}_\lambda$ is a maximal solution to (30.21), iff

$$-Q\left[\lambda\varphi_1(s), \lambda^\beta\varphi_2(s)\right]\lambda\varphi_1'(s) + P\left[\lambda\varphi_1(s), \lambda^\beta\varphi_2(s)\right]\lambda^\beta\varphi_2'(s) = 0 \tag{30.24.1}$$

or equivalently,

$$-\lambda^{m_2+1}Q\left[\varphi_1(s), \varphi_2(s)\right]\varphi_1'(s) + \lambda^{m_1+\beta}P\left[\varphi_1(s), \varphi_2(s)\right]\varphi_2'(s) = 0. \tag{30.24.2}$$

If $m_2 + 1 \neq m_1 + \beta$, (30.24.2) is satisfied if and only if

$$P[\varphi_1(s), \varphi_2(s)]\varphi_1'(s) \equiv 0 \quad \wedge \quad Q[\varphi_1(s), \varphi_2(s)]\varphi_2'(s) \equiv 0,\ s \in I. \tag{30.25}$$

As (30.21) is assumed to have no singular points, cf. Remark 30.6, it follows from (30.25) that either $\varphi_1'(s) \equiv 0,\ \varphi_2'(s) \neq 0$ or $\varphi_1'(s) \neq 0,\ \varphi_2'(s) \equiv 0$ for all $s \in I$, such that the integral curves are vertical or horizontal lines. Say vertical. Then $P(x, y)$ vanishes, and this is a contradiction. Hence it is *necessary*, for (30.21) to be quasihomogeneous that $m_2 + 1 = m_1 + \beta$, and it follows immediately from (30.24.1–2) that this condition is *sufficient* too. □

Expanding on Proposition 30.1, we give

**Proposition 30.3** *Let $c_i \in \mathbf{R} \setminus \{0\}$, $a_i, b_i \in \mathbf{R}$, $i \in \{1, 2, 3, 4\}$, and $a_1 \neq a_2$, $a_3 \neq a_4$, $b_1 \neq b_2$, $b_3 \neq b_4$.*

*Then the differential equation (30.21) with*

$$P(x, y) = c_1x^{a_1}y^{b_1} + c_2x^{a_2}y^{b_2}, \quad Q(x, y) = c_3x^{a_3}y^{b_3} + c_4x^{a_4}y^{b_4} \tag{30.26}$$

*is quasihomogeneous if and only if*

$$\Delta_1 = \begin{vmatrix} a_1 - a_2 & a_3 - a_4 \\ b_1 - b_2 & b_3 - b_4 \end{vmatrix} = 0, \quad \Delta_2 = \begin{vmatrix} a_1 - a_2 & a_3 - a_1 + 1 \\ b_1 - b_2 & b_3 - b_1 - 1 \end{vmatrix} = 0. \tag{30.27}$$

***Proof*** Since $a_1 \neq a_2$, $a_3 \neq a_4$, $b_1 \neq b_2$, and $b_3 \neq b_4$, it follows from Proposition 30.1 that $P$ and $Q$ are quasihomogeneous functions.

The equations determining the common weight $\beta$ are, cf. (30.16)

$$a_1 - a_2 = \beta(b_2 - b_1), \quad a_3 - a_4 = \beta(b_4 - b_3), \tag{30.28}$$

i.e., $\beta$ exists if and only if

$$\beta = \frac{a_1 - a_2}{b_2 - b_1} = \frac{a_3 - a_4}{b_4 - b_3} \quad \Leftrightarrow \quad \Delta_1 = 0. \tag{30.29}$$

With $\Delta_1 = 0$, (30.21) is quasihomogeneous iff $m_2 - m_1 = \beta - 1$, cf. (30.23), and by (30.15)

$$m_1 = a_1 + b_1\beta, \quad m_2 = a_3 + b_3\beta. \tag{30.30}$$

From (30.23) and (30.30), we obtain

$$[a_3 + b_3\beta - a_1 - b_1\beta = \beta - 1] \Leftrightarrow [a_3 - a_1 + 1 = \beta(b_1 - b_3 + 1)]. \tag{30.31}$$

By (30.28), $a_1 - a_2 = \beta(b_2 - b_1)$, and combining this with (30.31), we get

$$\beta = \frac{a_3 - a_1 + 1}{a_1 - a_2} = \frac{b_3 - b_1 - 1}{b_1 - b_2} \Leftrightarrow \Delta_2 = 0. \tag{30.32}$$

Thus, (30.29) and (30.32) establish (30.27). □

**Remark 30.7** Proposition 30.3 shows that *quasihomogeneity* of (30.21) with $P$ and $Q$ as (30.26) requires a loss of *two* degrees of freedom in the exponents, cf. (30.27), while *homogeneity* of (30.21) requires a loss of *three* degrees of freedom:

$$a_1 + b_1 = a_2 + b_2 = a_3 + b_3 = a_4 + b_4.$$

▽

**Remark 30.8** If one of the functions or both in (30.26) are not quasihomogeneous, then (30.21) is usually a cumbersome equation. ▽

It is usual to consider the differential equation

$$\frac{dy}{dx} = f(x, y), \quad (x, y) \in D. \tag{30.33}$$

Assume that $f$ is chosen in accordance with Definition 30.2 and Lemma 30.1. The associated Eq. (30.21) is

$$-f(x, y)dx + dy = 0, \tag{30.34}$$

and since the function 1 is quasihomogeneous of *any* weight (especially $\beta$) and of degree 0, it follows from Theorem 30.2 that (30.34) is quasihomogeneous if and only if $m = 1 - \beta$. This motivates

**Definition 30.3** If $f : D \to \mathbf{R}$ is a quasihomogeneous function of weight $\beta$ and degree $m$, the differential equation (30.34) is called *quasihomogeneous* of *weight* $\beta$, iff

$$m = \beta - 1. \tag{30.35}$$

When $f$ also satisfies the conditions of Proposition 30.1, it follows from (30.13.1–2) that (30.34) is quasihomogeneous if and only if

$$\frac{a_1 b_2 - a_2 b_1}{b_2 - b_1} = \frac{a_1 - a_2}{b_2 - b_1} - 1, \tag{30.36}$$

or, equivalently,

$$(a_1 + b_1) - (a_2 + b_2) = \begin{vmatrix} a_1 & b_1 \\ a_2 & b_2 \end{vmatrix}. \tag{30.37}$$

### *The Solutions to Quasihomogeneous Differential Equations*

We now derive some general properties of the solutions to (30.21–30.23). The main idea is that a suitable change of variables transforms (30.21) into a homogeneous differential equation.

**Lemma 30.2** *Consider the quasihomogeneous differential equation*

$$-Q(x, y)dx + P(x, y)dy = 0, \quad (x, y) \in D, \tag{30.38}$$

*where $P$ and $Q$ are quasihomogeneous $C^1$-functions of common weight $\beta \neq 0$ and degrees $m_1, m_2$, such that $m_2 - m_1 = \beta - 1$.*

*The coordinate transformation* $\Upsilon$ *given by*

$$(u, v) = \Upsilon(x, y) = (x, y^{1/\beta}), \quad (x, y) = \Upsilon^{-1}(u, v) = (u, v^{\beta}) \tag{30.39}$$

*transforms (30.38) into the homogeneous differential equation*

$$-G(u, v)du + F(u, v)dv = 0, \quad (u, v) \in D, \tag{30.40}$$

*where* $F$ *and* $G$ *are homogeneous functions of degree* $m = m_1 = m_2 + 1 - \beta$, *given by*

$$F(u, v) = P(u, v^{\beta}), \tag{30.41.1}$$

$$G(u, v) = \tfrac{1}{\beta} v^{1-\beta} Q(u, v^{\beta}). \tag{30.41.2}$$

***Proof*** Substituting $x = u,\ dx = du,\ y = v^{\beta},\ dy = \beta v^{\beta-1} dv$ into (30.38) yields immediately (30.40–30.41.2). The homogeneity of the functions $F$ and $G$ is verified by calculating $F(\lambda u, \lambda v)$ and $G(\lambda u, \lambda v)$, cf. (30.2),

$$F(\lambda u, \lambda v) = P(\lambda u, \lambda^{\beta} v^{\beta}) = \lambda^{m_1} P(u, v^{\beta}) = \lambda^{m_1} F(u, v), \tag{30.42}$$

$$\begin{aligned} G(\lambda u, \lambda v) &= \tfrac{1}{\beta}(\lambda v)^{1-\beta} Q(\lambda u, \lambda^{\beta} v^{\beta}) = \tfrac{1}{\beta}\lambda^{1-\beta} v^{1-\beta} \cdot \lambda^{m_2} Q(u, v^{\beta}) \\ &= \tfrac{1}{\beta}\lambda^{m_2+1-\beta} v^{1-\beta} Q(u, v^{\beta}) = \lambda^{m_2+1-\beta} G(u, v). \end{aligned} \tag{30.43}$$

□

It follows from Lemma 30.2 that the quasihomogeneous differential equations inherit a lot of properties from the homogeneous differential equations.

We therefore define the *director function* $h : \mathbf{R}_+ \to \mathbf{R}$ for (30.38) as the **director function** for the homogeneous differential equation (30.40), cf. Chap. 28, Sect. "Basic Framework, Assumptions, and Definitions", given by

$$h(r) = G(1, r) - rF(1, r) = \tfrac{1}{\beta} r^{1-\beta} Q(1, r^{\beta}) - rP(1, r^{\beta}), \quad r > 0. \tag{30.44}$$

In the homogeneous case, the *roots* of $h(r)$ define *directrices* as invariant *rays*. Here the *roots* of (30.44) define the **directrices** of (30.38) as invariant *power curves*. They are given by

**Theorem 30.3** *Let* $\alpha \in \mathbf{R}_+$. *The power curve* $y = \alpha^{\beta} x^{\beta}$, $x \in \mathbf{R}_+$, *is a maximal integral curve for (30.38) if and only if* $h(\alpha) = 0$.

***Proof*** The image of the curve $(x, \alpha^{\beta} x^{\beta})$ by $\Upsilon$, (30.39), is the curve $(u, v) = (x, \alpha x)$, which (cf. Aczel (1966, section 1)) is a maximal trajectory to (30.40) if and only if $h(\alpha) = 0$. □

Theorem 30.3 shows that the intrinsic *ratio* to consider is, cf. (30.3)

$$r = v/u = y^{1/\beta}/x, \quad r \in \mathbf{R}_+. \tag{30.45}$$

As in the homogeneous case, the geometry of the trajectory (phase) portrait can be described by introducing $r$ as an independent variable.

The main result is

**Theorem 30.4** *Assume $h(\alpha) = 0$ for an $\alpha \in \mathbf{R}_+$. Choose $a, b \in \mathbf{R}_+$ arbitrarily, such that $a \leq \alpha \leq b$.*

*If $h(r) \neq 0$ for $r \in [a, b] \setminus \{\alpha\}$, then $r \to \alpha$ along any maximal integral curve for (30.38) containing a point of the set*

$$D_\alpha = \{ (x, y) \in D : \ a \leq y^{1/\beta}/x \leq b \}. \tag{30.46}$$

*Along any such integral curve, we have either $r > \alpha$ or $r < \alpha$, and moreover*

$$\text{for } r > \alpha : \quad \frac{P(1, r^\beta)}{h(r)} \begin{cases} > 0 \\ < 0 \end{cases} \Rightarrow \quad x \to \begin{cases} 0 \\ +\infty \end{cases} \text{as } r \to \alpha^+, \tag{30.47}$$

$$\text{for } r < \alpha : \quad \frac{P(1, r^\beta)}{h(r)} \begin{cases} > 0 \\ < 0 \end{cases} \Rightarrow \quad x \to \begin{cases} +\infty \\ 0 \end{cases} \text{as } r \to \alpha^-. \tag{30.48}$$

***Proof*** First, we consider the homogeneous differential equation, (30.40).

Since $u > 0$, the classical substitution $r = v/u, \ v = ru$, into (30.40) gives, cf. (30.41.1–2), (30.44)

$$-h(r)du + uP(1, r^\beta)dr = 0. \tag{30.49}$$

Hence all integral curves, except the directrices, satisfy

$$\frac{du}{u} = \frac{P(1, r^\beta)}{h(r)}dr = \frac{F(1, r)}{h(r)}dr, \quad h(r) \neq 0, \tag{30.50}$$

which implies that $r$ can be used as a parameter along all these curves.

Integration of (30.50) yields, for the integral curve through $(u_0, r_0 u_0)$

$$\log u = \log u_0 + \int_{r_0}^{r} \frac{F(1, s)}{h(s)} ds. \tag{30.51}$$

Clearly, if $h(r) \neq 0$ for $r \in [a, b] \setminus \{\alpha\}$, we must have $\alpha$ as an endpoint of the definition interval for any maximal solution to (30.50). Since (30.40) has no singular points, $h(\alpha) = 0$ implies $F(1, \alpha) \neq 0$.

Using the latter and Taylor's formula, it is easily seen that the improper integral

$$\int_{r_0}^{\alpha} \frac{F(1,s)}{h(s)} ds \quad \text{diverges,}$$

whence we get from (30.51) that $|\log u| \to +\infty$ as $r \to \alpha$ along the integral curves.

Therefore, $u \to 0$, or $u \to +\infty$, along any integral curve, depending on the sign of the integrand, (30.50).

Since $u = x$, the sign criteria (30.47–30.48) follow immediately. □

We have the following corollaries:

**Corollary 30.1** *Assume $h(\alpha) = 0,\ h'(\alpha) \neq 0$ for an $\alpha \in \mathbf{R}_+$.*

*Then there exists an $\epsilon > 0$, such that along any maximal integral curve to (30.38) containing a point of the set*

$$D_\alpha = \{\ (x, y) \in D :\ \alpha - \epsilon\ \leq\ y^{1/\beta}/x\ \leq\ \alpha + \epsilon\ \}, \tag{30.52}$$

*we have $r \to \alpha$, and moreover*

$$\frac{P(1,\alpha^\beta)}{h'(\alpha)} \quad \begin{cases} > 0 \\ < 0 \end{cases} \quad \Rightarrow \quad x \to \begin{cases} 0 \\ +\infty \end{cases} \quad \text{as } r \to \alpha. \tag{30.53}$$

***Proof*** By Taylor's formula,

$$\frac{P(1,r^\beta)}{h(r)} = \frac{P(1,\alpha^\beta) + o(1)}{h'(\alpha)(r-\alpha) + o(r-\alpha)}\,, \tag{30.54}$$

which has the same sign as $\frac{P(1,\alpha^\beta)}{h'(\alpha)(r-\alpha)}$ for $|r - \alpha|$ sufficiently small. □

**Corollary 30.2** *If $h(\alpha) = 0$ and $h(r) \neq 0$ for $r \neq \alpha$, then $r \to \alpha$ along any maximal integral curve for (30.38), and the behavior of $x$ as $r \to \alpha$ is easily determined by Theorem 30.4.*

***Proof*** This corollary is obvious. □

Observe that *multiple* roots of $h$, (30.44), can be treated in the same way as in Corollary 30.1.

If there are *no directrices*, cf. Theorem 30.3, then either $h(r) < 0$ or $h(r) > 0$, and hence the ratio (30.45) tends to either infinity or 0. Since these two situations are, in principle, identical, we examine only the case of ratios tending to infinity.

Trajectories to (30.38), with ratio (30.45) tending to infinity, are geometrically classified into four types:

| | | |
|---|---|---|
| Type I | : | The trajectory tends to infinity. |
| Type II | : | The trajectory tends to (0, 0). |
| Type III | : | The trajectory tends to a point on one of the axes. |
| Type IV | : | Other behavior. |

**Proposition 30.4** *All trajectories to (30.38) with ratio (30.45) tending to* $+\infty$ *are topologically of the same type.*

***Proof*** If $\beta > 0$, the four classes above are invariant to the transformation (30.39), and hence it is sufficient to verify the proposition for a homogeneous system. But this follows immediately from the multiplication invariance.

If $\beta < 0$, class III is invariant, and class II becomes a part of class I under the transformation (30.39). If $\varphi = [\varphi_1(s), \varphi_2(s)]$ is a maximal solution in class I, it can only leave class I if $\varphi_1$ is bounded. But $\varphi_2(s) \to +\infty$, and hence $\varphi_1(s) \to 0$ in order to make the ratio diverge. Thus, if $\varphi$ leaves class I under the transformation (30.39), it enters class II. Now, for a homogeneous system, either class I or class II is empty (by multiplication invariance), so if *one* trajectory of type I becomes of type II, they all do.

This proves that two trajectories topologically of the same type still are of the same type after the transformation (30.39), and again, we are back in the homogeneous case, where the proposition is obvious. □

## Quasihomogeneous Autonomous Dynamic Systems

Consider the planar autonomous dynamic system given by

$$\dot{x} = dx/dt = P(x, y), \quad \dot{y} = dy/dt = Q(x, y), \quad (x, y) \in D, \tag{30.55}$$

where $P, Q \in C^1(D)$-class are given as in (30.38).

As the *geometry* of the phase portrait for (30.55) is determined by the differential equation

$$-Q(x, y)dx + P(x, y)dy = 0, \quad (x, y) \in D, \tag{30.56}$$

we adopt:

**Definition 30.4** System (30.55) is called a *quasihomogeneous dynamic system* if the associated differential equation (30.56) is quasihomogeneous.

With Definition 30.4, the main tool in deriving the properties of the solutions to (30.55) is to use Lemma 30.2 to transform quasihomogeneous dynamic systems (30.55) into homogeneous dynamic systems.

**Lemma 30.3** *Let $P, Q$ of (30.55) be given as in (30.38). Then (30.39) transforms the autonomous system (30.55) into a homogeneous system*

$$\dot{u} = F(u, v) = P(u, v^{\beta}), \tag{30.57.1}$$

$$\dot{v} = G(u, v) = \tfrac{1}{\beta} v^{1-\beta} Q(u, v) \tag{30.57.2}$$

*of degree*

$$m = m_1 = m_2 + 1 - \beta. \tag{30.57.3}$$

***Proof*** Substituting $x = u,\ \dot{x} = \dot{u},\ y = v^{\beta},\ \dot{y} = \beta v^{\beta-1}\dot{v}$ into (30.55) gives the homogeneous system (30.57.1–3), cf. (30.41.1–2). □

Of course, the trajectories of (30.55) consist of the integral curves of (30.56), supplied with the correct orientation. The *solutions* of (30.55) will now be related to the solutions of (30.57.1–3), which were investigated in Chap. 28.

### *Stability Properties of Coordinate Solutions*

We shall consider the stability of coordinate and ratio solutions to (30.55), using the stability concepts in Chaps. 28 and 1. These concepts become interesting when the coordinate solutions tend to infinity as time tends to infinity.

We need the following elementary lemma:

**Lemma 30.4** *Given a constant $a \in \mathbf{R}$, an interval $I$ of the type $]K, +\infty[$, $K \in \mathbf{R}$ and two functions $p_1, p_2 \in C^1(I)$, such that $p_1(t) \to +\infty$ and $p_2(t) \to +\infty$ as $t \to \infty$. Then*

$$\frac{\ln p_2(t)}{\ln p_1(t)} \to 1 \text{ as } t \to +\infty \quad \Rightarrow \quad \frac{\ln p_2(t)^a}{\ln p_1(t)^a} \to 1 \text{ as } t \to +\infty, \tag{30.58}$$

$$\frac{p_2(t)}{p_1(t)} \text{ bounded}, \ a \geq 0 \quad \Rightarrow \quad \frac{p_2(t)^a}{p_1(t)^a} \text{ bounded as } t \to +\infty, \tag{30.59}$$

$$\frac{p_2(t)}{p_1(t)} \to 1 \text{ as } t \to +\infty \quad \Rightarrow \quad \frac{p_2(t)^a}{p_1(t)^a} \to 1 \text{ as } t \to +\infty, \tag{30.60}$$

$$p_2(t) - p_1(t) \text{ bounded}, \ a > 1 \Rightarrow \frac{p_2(t)^a}{p_1(t)^a} \to 1 \text{ as } t \to +\infty, \tag{30.61}$$

$$p_2(t) - p_1(t) \text{ bounded}, \ a < 1 \ \Rightarrow \ p_2(t)^a - p_1(t)^a \to 0 \text{ as } t \to +\infty. \tag{30.62}$$

***Proof*** The only nontriviality is (30.62). In this case, we put $p_3(t) = p_2(t) - p_1(t)$; then $p_3 \in C^1(I)$ and is bounded on $I$. Then $p_2(t) = p_1(t) + p_3(t)$, such that

$$p_2(t)^a - p_1(t)^a = p_1(t)^a\{[1 + p_3(t)/p_1(t)]^a - 1\}. \tag{30.63}$$

Now $\frac{p_3(t)}{p_1(t)} \to 0$ as $t \to +\infty$, so by means of the binomial series, we have

$$\begin{aligned} p_2(t)^a - p_1(t)^a &= p_1(t)^a\left\{1 + a\frac{p_3(t)}{p_1(t)} + o\left[\frac{p_3(t)}{p_1(t)}\right] - 1\right\} \\ &= ap_1(t)^{a-1}p_3(t) + p_1(t)^{a-1}p_3(t)o(1) \to 0 \text{ as } t \to +\infty, \end{aligned} \tag{30.64}$$

provided that $a - 1 < 0$. □

In the stability discussion, we shall first of all consider the case where the coordinate solutions tend to infinity, and the ratio $r = \rho(t)$, (30.38), has a positive limit. Here we have

**Theorem 30.5** *Given* $\alpha \in \mathbf{R}_+$ *such that* $h(\alpha) = 0$. *Consider two maximal solutions* $[\varphi_1(t), \varphi_2(t)]$, $[\psi_1(t), \psi_2(t)]$ *to (30.55), such that* $\varphi_1(t)$ *and* $\psi_1(t)$ *tend to infinity and the ratios* $\rho_1(t) = \varphi_2(t)^{1/\beta}/\varphi_1(t)$, $\rho_2(t) = \psi_2(t)^{1/\beta}/\psi_1(t)$ *tend to* $\alpha$ *along the trajectories. Let* $m$ *denote the degree in (30.57.3).*

*Then for* $\beta > 0$, *the system (30.55) has the coordinate stabilities:*

$m > 1$ : $\psi_i(t)$ *and* $\varphi_i(t)$ *are only defined in a finite future,* $i \in \{1, 2\}$, (30.65)

$m \leq 1$ : $\dfrac{\ln \psi_i(t)}{\ln \varphi_i(t)} \to 1$ *as* $t \to +\infty$, $i \in \{1, 2\}$, (30.66)

$m \leq 1,\ h'(\alpha) < 0$ : $\dfrac{\psi_i(t)}{\varphi_i(t)}$ *bounded as* $t \to +\infty$, $i \in \{1, 2\}$, (30.67)

$m < 1$ : $\dfrac{\psi_i(t)}{\varphi_i(t)} \to 1$ *as* $t \to +\infty$, $i \in \{1, 2\}$, (30.68)

$m \leq 0,\ h'(\alpha) < 0,\ \beta > 1$ : $\psi_1(t) - \varphi_1(t)$ *bounded as* $t \to +\infty$, (30.69)

$\dfrac{\psi_2(t)}{\varphi_2(t)} \to 1$ *as* $t \to +\infty$, (30.70)

$m \leq 0,\ h'(\alpha) < 0,\ \beta < 1$ : $\psi_1(t) - \varphi_1(t)$ *bounded as* $t \to +\infty$, (30.71)

$\psi_2(t) - \varphi_2(t) \to 0$ *as* $t \to +\infty$, (30.72)

$$m < 0,\ h'(\alpha) < 0,\ \beta > 1:\ \psi_1(t) - \varphi_1(t) \to 0\ as\, t \to +\infty, \tag{30.73}$$

$$\frac{\psi_2(t)}{\varphi_2(t)} \to 1\ as\, t \to +\infty, \tag{30.74}$$

$$m < 0,\ h'(\alpha) < 0,\ \beta < 1:\ \psi_i(t) - \varphi_i(t) \to 0\ as\, t \to +\infty,\ i \in \{1, 2\}. \tag{30.75}$$

*If $\beta < 0$, then $\varphi_2(t)$ and $\psi_2(t)$ tend to zero as $\varphi_1(t)$ and $\psi_1(t)$ tend to infinity, and (30.66–30.75) apply for the first coordinates.*

***Proof*** The first assertion follows from (30.57.1–3) and the fact that the solutions to a homogeneous dynamic system of degree $m > 1$ "explode" as they tend to infinity, i.e., reach infinity in finite time if and only if $m > 1$.

The last seven assertions are proved analogously.

First, we note that $[\varphi_1(t), \varphi_2(t)^{1/\beta}]$ and $[\psi_1(t), \psi_2(t)^{1/\beta}]$ are solutions to the homogeneous system (30.57.3), then we apply one of the Theorems 28.9–28.12 in Chap. 28, and finally we apply Lemma 30.4 to the second coordinates.

Let us show (30.71–30.72):

Since $m \leq 0$ and $h'(\alpha) < 0$, Theorem 28.11 in Chap. 28 shows that $[\psi_1(t) - \varphi_1(t)]$ and $[\psi_2(t)^{1/\beta} - \varphi_2(t)^{1/\beta}]$ are bounded as $t \to +\infty$.

Applying (30.62) in Lemma 30.4 with $a = \beta < 1$, and $p_2 = \psi_2^{1/\beta}$, and $p_1 = \varphi_2^{1/\beta}$ we conclude that $\psi_2(t) - \varphi_2(t) = p_2(t)^\beta - p_1(t)^\beta \to 0$ as $t \to +\infty$.

The other cases are left to the reader. □

If $\beta > 0$ and the ratio converges, a trajectory to (30.55) can only tend to infinity in the way discussed in Theorem 30.4.

However, if $\beta < 0$, a solution $[\varphi_1(t), \varphi_2(t)]$ to (30.55) such that $\varphi_1(t) \to 0$ and $\varphi_2(t) \to +\infty$ corresponds to a solution to (30.57.1–3) tending to (0, 0) in the $(u, v)$-plane. Introducing new state variables $\xi, \eta \in \mathbf{R}_+$ in (30.57.1–3) by

$$\xi = 1/u,\ \eta = 1/v; \quad u = 1/\xi,\ v = 1/\eta, \tag{30.76}$$

the system (30.57.1–3) is transformed into the system

$$\dot{\xi} = R(\xi, \eta) = -\xi^2 F(1/\xi, 1/\eta), \tag{30.77.1}$$

$$\dot{\eta} = S(\xi, \eta) = -\eta^2 G(1/\xi, 1/\eta), \tag{30.77.2}$$

which obviously is homogeneous of degree $n = 2 - m$ in $(\xi, \eta)$, where $m$ denotes the degree in (30.57.1–3).

Using the system (30.77.1–2), we can show the following theorem.

**Theorem 30.6** *Given $\alpha \in \mathbf{R}_+$ such that $h(\alpha) = 0$. Consider (30.55) with weight $\beta < 0$, and let $[\varphi_1(t), \varphi_2(t)]$, $[\psi_1(t), \psi_2(t)]$ denote maximal solutions to (30.55), such that $\varphi_1(t)$ and $\psi_1(t)$ tend to zero and the ratios, $\rho_1(t) = \varphi_2(t)^{1/\beta}/\varphi_1(t)$,*

$\rho_2(t) = \psi_2(t)^{1/\beta}/\psi_1(t)$, *tend to* $\alpha$ *along the trajectories. Let* $m$ *denote the degree in (30.57.3).*

*Then for* $\beta < 0$, *the system (30.55) has the second coordinate stabilities:*

$$m < 1 \quad : \varphi_2(t) \text{ and } \psi_2(t) \text{ are only defined in a finite future,} \tag{30.78}$$

$$m = 1 \quad : \frac{\ln \psi_2(t)}{\ln \varphi_2(t)} \to 1 \text{ as } t \to +\infty, \tag{30.79}$$

$$m = 1,\ h'(\alpha) < 0 \quad : \frac{\psi_2(t)}{\varphi_2(t)} \text{ bounded as } t \to \infty, \tag{30.80}$$

$$m > 1 \quad : \frac{\psi_2(t)}{\varphi_2(t)} \to 1 \text{ as } t \to +\infty, \tag{30.81}$$

$$m \geq 2,\ h'(\alpha) < 0,\ \beta > -1 : \psi_2(t) - \varphi_2(t) \to 0 \text{ as } t \to \infty. \tag{30.82}$$

***Proof*** First, we notice that $[\varphi_1(t), \varphi_2(t)]$ is a solution to (30.55) if and only if $\varphi_1(t)^{-1}$, $\varphi_2(t)^{-1/\beta}$ is a solution to (30.77.1–2), and their definition intervals are identical.

To prove (30.78), we note that if $m < 1$, (30.77.1–2) is homogeneous of degree $n > 1$, and (30.78) now follows as (30.65). Furthermore, (30.66) tells us that if $m \geq 1$, $\varphi_i$ and $\psi_i$ are defined in an infinite future.

The assertions (30.79–30.82) are proved similar to Theorem 30.5.

We will show (30.82): since $m \geq 2$, we have $n \leq 0$ in (30.77.1–2), and Theorem 28.11 in Chap. 28 tells us that $\psi_2(t)^{-1/\beta} - \varphi_2(t)^{-1/\beta}$ is bounded as $t \to +\infty$. Now (30.62) with $a = -\beta < 1$, $p_2 = \psi_2^{-1/\beta}$, and $p_1 = \varphi_2^{-1/\beta}$ completes the proof. □

### *Stability Properties of Ratio and Quotient*

The only situation not yet treated is the case of no directrices in $\mathbf{R}^2_+$. In this case, we offer a statement about some weaker *ratio* stability properties.

As mentioned earlier, the intrinsic ratio to consider in the discussion of a quasihomogeneous system (30.55) depends on the weight $\beta$. However, from an application point of view, the *quotient* $z = y/x$ may be of some interest. We therefore also discuss quotient stability.

The ratio stability theorem in the case of no directrices is almost identical to Theorem 28.5 in Chap. 28, since the intrinsic ratio in our context is the same as the ratio of the homogeneous system (30.57.1–3), and so there is nothing new to prove. Hence, we may state

**Theorem 30.7** *Given two solutions* $[\varphi_1(t), \varphi_2(t)]$, $[\psi_1(t), \psi_2(t)]$ *to (30.57.1) such that the ratios* $\rho_1(t) = \varphi_2(t)^{1/\beta}/\varphi_1(t)$, $\rho_2(t) = \psi_2(t)^{1/\beta}/\psi_1(t)$ *tend to infinity along the trajectories.*

*Let $q(r)$ be defined by, cf. (30.57.1–3), (30.44–30.45)*

$$q(r) = \exp\{(m-1)\int \frac{P(1, r^{\beta})}{h(r)} dr\} h(r). \tag{30.83}$$

*Then the system (30.55) has the ratio stabilities:*

$$q(r) \to 0 \text{ as } r \to +\infty \quad : \rho_1(t) - \rho_2(t) \to 0 \text{ as } t \to \bar{t} \le \infty, \tag{30.84}$$

$$q(r) \text{ bounded as } r \to +\infty \quad : \rho_1(t) - \rho_2(t) \text{ bounded as } t \to \bar{t} \le \infty, \tag{30.85}$$

$$q(r)/r \to 0 \text{ as } r \to +\infty \quad : \rho_2(t)/\rho_1(t) \to 1 \text{ as } t \to \bar{t} \le \infty, \tag{30.86}$$

$$q(r)/r \text{ bounded as } r \to +\infty : \rho_2(t)/\rho_1(t) \text{ bounded as } t \to \bar{t} \le \infty, \tag{30.87}$$

$$q(r)/r \ln r \to 0 \text{ as } r \to +\infty : \frac{\ln \rho_2(t)}{\ln \rho_1(t)} \to 1 \text{ as } t \to \bar{t} \le \infty, \tag{30.88}$$

$$\frac{q(r)}{r \ln r} \text{ bounded as } r \to +\infty \quad : \frac{\ln \rho_2(t)}{\ln \rho_1(t)} \text{ bounded as } t \to \bar{t} \le \infty. \tag{30.89}$$

**Remark 30.9** Above, $\bar{t}$ denotes the endpoint of the time interval of existence for the solutions. ▽

The issue of *quotient stability* is interesting if there exists a directrix in $\mathbf{R}^2_+$ and both the state variables tend to infinity. This implies $\beta > 0$.

If $\beta < 1$, the quotient $y/x$ tends to zero and hence obviously possesses strong absolute stability. To obtain more information on this convergence, the quotient $x/y$ should be considered, and this corresponds to substituting $\beta$ by $1/\beta$.

Hence, we only consider the situation $\beta > 1$, in which case the quotient tends to infinity along the trajectories. Here the following theorem holds:

**Theorem 30.8** *Given $\alpha \in \mathbf{R}_+$ such that $h(\alpha) = 0$. Consider the system (30.55) with $\beta > 1$ and $m \le 1$. Let $[\varphi_1(t), \varphi_2(t)]$, $[\psi_1(t), \psi_2(t)]$ denote two maximal solutions to (30.55), such that $\varphi_1(t)$ and $\psi_1(t)$ tend to infinity and the ratios $\rho_1(t) = \varphi_2(t)^{1/\beta}/\varphi_1(t)$, $\rho_2(t) = \psi_2(t)^{1/\beta}/\psi_1(t)$ tend to $\alpha$ along the trajectories.*

*Let $z_1 = \varphi_2/\varphi_1$, $z_2 = \psi_2/\psi_1$ be quotients of the solutions.*

*Then the system (30.55) has the quotient stabilities:*

$$m \le 1 \quad : \frac{\ln z_2(t)}{\ln z_1(t)} \to 1 \text{ as } t \to +\infty, \tag{30.90}$$

$$m \le 1,\ h'(\alpha) < 0 : \frac{z_2(t)}{z_1(t)} \text{ bounded as } t \to +\infty, \tag{30.91}$$

$$m < 1 \qquad : \frac{z_2(t)}{z_1(t)} \to 1 \; as\, t \to +\infty, \tag{30.92}$$

$$m < 0 \; and \; \beta \leq 2 : \; z_2(t) - z_1(t) \to 0 \; as\, t \to +\infty. \tag{30.93}$$

***Proof*** ad. (30.90). Applying the relations

$$z_1(t) = \frac{\varphi_2(t)}{\varphi_1(t)} = \rho_1(t)\varphi_2(t)^{1-1/\beta}, \quad z_2(t) = \frac{\psi_2(t)}{\psi_1(t)} = \rho_2(t)\psi_2(t)^{1-1/\beta} \tag{30.94}$$

we have

$$\frac{\ln z_2(t)}{\ln z_1(t)} = \frac{\ln \rho_2(t) + (1 - \frac{1}{\beta}) \ln \psi_2(t)}{\ln \rho_1(t) + (1 - \frac{1}{\beta}) \ln \varphi_2(t)} = \frac{1 - 1/\beta + \frac{\ln \rho_2(t)}{\ln \psi_2(t)}}{(1 - 1/\beta)\frac{\ln \varphi_2(t)}{\ln \psi_2(t)} + \frac{\ln \rho_1(t)}{\ln \psi_2(t)}}. \tag{30.95}$$

Since $\rho_2(t) \to \alpha$ and $\psi_2(t) \to +\infty$, the numerator tends to $1 - 1/\beta$ as $t \to +\infty$. If $m \leq 1$, (30.66) shows that the denominator tends to $1 - 1/\beta$ as well; hence (30.90).

ad. (30.91–30.92). This is very easy. Writing

$$\frac{z_2(t)}{z_1(t)} = \frac{\rho_2(t)}{\rho_1(t)} \cdot \left[\frac{\psi_2(t)}{\varphi_2(t)}\right]^{1-1/\beta} \tag{30.96}$$

and applying (30.67–30.68), (30.59–30.60), and $\frac{\rho_2(t)}{\rho_1(t)} \to \frac{\alpha}{\alpha} = 1$, the results (30.91–30.92) follow.

ad. (30.93). Here the assumptions and the proof of (30.69–30.70) ensure the existence of functions $\epsilon_1(t), \epsilon_2(t), \epsilon_3(t)$, all tending to zero as $t \to +\infty$, such that $\psi_1(t) = \varphi_1(t) + \epsilon_1(t)$, $\psi_2(t)^{1/\beta} = \varphi_2(t)^{1/\beta} + \epsilon_2(t)$, and $\varphi_2(t) = [\alpha + \epsilon_3(t)]^\beta \varphi_1(t)^\beta$. Then the following calculation holds:

$$\begin{aligned} z_2(t) - z_1(t) &= \frac{\psi_2(t)}{\psi_1(t)} - \frac{\varphi_2(t)}{\varphi_1(t)} \\ &= \frac{[\varphi_2(t)^{1/\beta} + \epsilon_2(t)]^\beta}{\varphi_1(t) + \epsilon_1(t)} - [\alpha + \epsilon_3(t)]^\beta \varphi_1(t)^{\beta-1} \\ &= \frac{[\varphi_1(t)(\alpha + \epsilon_3(t)) + \epsilon_2(t)]^\beta}{\varphi_1(t) + \epsilon_1(t)} - [\alpha + \epsilon_3(t)]^\beta \varphi_1(t)^{\beta-1} \\ &= [\alpha + \epsilon_3(t)]^\beta \varphi_1(t)^{\beta-1} \left[\frac{[1 + \frac{\epsilon_2(t)}{\varphi_1(t)(\alpha+\epsilon_3(t))}]^\beta}{1 + \frac{\epsilon_1(t)}{\varphi_1(t)}} - 1\right]. \end{aligned} \tag{30.97}$$

Since $\frac{\epsilon_2(t)}{\varphi_1(t)(\alpha+\epsilon_3(t))} \to 0$ as $t \to +\infty$, this fraction can be expanded in its Maclaurin series, which yields

$$z_2(t) - z_1(t) = [\alpha + \epsilon_3(t)]^\beta \varphi_1(t)^{\beta-2} \cdot \left[ \frac{-\epsilon_1(t) + \frac{\beta\epsilon_2(t)}{\alpha+\epsilon_3(t)} + o(\frac{1}{\varphi_1(t)})}{1 + \frac{\epsilon_1(t)}{\varphi_1(t)}} \right]. \tag{30.98}$$

If $\beta \leq 2$, (30.98) clearly converges to zero as $t \to +\infty$, and this proves (30.93). □

**Remark 30.10** The stability properties (30.66)–(30.68) are independent of $\beta$. This is due to the fact that the stability properties in these cases are too weak to be affected by the coordinate transformation (30.39). For the same reason, the stability properties (30.79)–(30.81) and (30.90)–(30.92) are independent of $\beta$. ▽

## Concluding Comments

We have discussed several issues in the theory of quasihomogeneous functions, quasihomogeneous differential equations and quasihomogeneous dynamics. We may briefly summarize the main results in this way.

Given a planar autonomous dynamic system, one first has to consider whether it is quasihomogeneous or not. This is checked most easily by means of Theorems 30.1 and 30.2. Particular examples of calculating the weight $\beta$ and the degree $m$ were given in Propositions 30.1, 30.2, and 30.3.

Having a quasihomogeneous dynamic system, the geometry of the phase portrait can be described by using the director function and the directrices. This, together with the asymptotic behavior of the intrinsic ratio (parameterizing the integral curves), outlines the disposition of the trajectory system in the phase plane—as shown in Theorems 30.3, 30.4 (with corollaries) and Proposition 30.4.

To characterize the evolution (time paths) of the autonomous quasihomogeneous system, we classified the family of solutions by the qualitative (stability) properties demonstrated in Theorems 30.5 and 30.6. Special issues were treated in Theorems 30.7 and 30.8.

The class of quasihomogeneous functions is theoretically and empirically of particular interest in economics, where the traditional application of homogeneous functions invites the extension to weights $\beta \neq 1$.

A subject of further mathematical research would be to apply the theory of autonomous quasihomogeneous systems to the field of economic dynamics—especially to economic growth models, designed to allow for a more diversified set of time paths than admitted by autonomous homogeneous dynamics.

## BIBLIOGRAPHY

Aczel J (1966) Lectures on Functional Equations and their Applications. Academic Press, New York

Arnold VI (1988) Geometrical Methods in the Theory of Ordinary Differential Equations, 2nd edn. Springer–Verlag, New York

Ince EL (1956) Ordinary Differential Equations. Dover Publications, New York

Kolm S (1976) Structures Meta–Homogénes des Productions et Préférences. Canadian Journal of Economics 9:1–44

Lau L (1972) Profit Functions of Technologies with Multiple Inputs and Outputs. Review Econ Stat 54:281–289

Lau L (1978) Applications of Profit Functions. In Fuss, U. and McFadden, D. (1978) *Production Economics: A Dual Approach to Theory and Applications,* Vol. 1.

Panas EE (1985) Almost Homogeneous Functions: A Theoretical and Empirical Analysis with Special Emphasis on Labour Input: The Case of Swedish Ma-nu-fac-tu-ring Industries. Department of Economics, University of Uppsala, Uppsala

Sato R (1977) Homothetic and Non–Homothetic CES Production Functions. American Econ Rev 67:559–569

Smirnov VI (1964) A Course of Higher Mathematics, vol II, IV. Pergamon Press, New York

CHAPTER 31

# Discrete Linear Dynamics in the Plane

## Introduction

In describing many phenomena, we are naturally inclined to order our observations by their occurrence in time. As a scalar variable $t$, *time* is often treated as affording an instance of the abstract concept of a *continuum* (infinite divisibility), which accordingly is represented by the set of real numbers, $t \in \mathbf{R}$. Where the relevant *state* variables may also take values on a *continuous* domain, and when their *rates* of *change,* at any time, only depend on their *present* (current) state (i.e., the past only affects the future through the *present* state, irrespective of how the present state has been attained), then the theory of ordinary differential equations and the powerful tools of infinitesimal calculus are available for determining the subsequent history (*solutions*) of the state variables in *continuous* time.

In modeling certain phenomena, however, it is necessary to make allowance for the fact that the *rate* of *change* of the state variables depends not only on their *present* state, but also on their *past* history. Such situations may lead to formulations of differential equations with time delays (lags), e.g., *mixed differential-difference* equations, see Bellman and Cooke (1963, p. 42); Gandolfo (1980, p. 519). We emphasize that in such mixed dynamic systems, the requested *solutions* are yet to be differentiable and hence *continuous* functions, i.e., despite delayed reactions, a continuous-time variable still prevails.

However, if the *transition* from state to state *only* occurs at *discrete* (intermittent) values of the *time* variable—which is the characteristic feature of *difference equations*—then the time *paths* of the state variables obviously cannot

With co-author:
MOGENS ESROM LARSEN, Department of Mathematics, University of Copenhagen

 
B. S. Jensen, *The Elements and Dynamic Systems of Economic Growth and Trade Models*, https://doi.org/10.1007/978-3-031-52493-6_31

be represented by continuous functions, i.e., apart from a stationary state, the state variables will in discrete time necessarily exhibit *discontinuities* ("jumps").

But these jumps should certainly not be juxtaposed with the indivisibility of the state variables themselves. The latter will still be assumed to belong to a continuum, the field of real numbers. Likewise, the governing functions of the state transitions may belong to the $C^1$-class. Thus, the principle of *continuity* only necessarily *fails* with regard to the *solutions* (time path) of *discrete*-time processes (difference equations).

The finite *interval* of time (period, delay, lag) elapsing between changes in state may conveniently, and without loss of generality, be chosen as a *time unit,* and so the *domain* of the time variable becomes the set of *integers,* $t \in \mathbf{Z}$, or nonnegative integers, $t \in \mathbf{N}_0$.

The theory of difference equations has a long history with a vast literature, cf. Baumol (1958); Batchelder (1967); Boole (1958); Cogan and Norman (1963); Fort (1948); Goldberg (1986); Jordan (1965); Markoff (1896); Wold (1959); Miller (1968); Nörlund (1910, 1954, 1929). Recently, the facility of computer experiments has contributed greatly to a resurgence in the study of difference equations and dynamic systems as iterated maps. Yet to acquire a full understanding of even simple processes in discrete time is surprisingly troublesome.

On the backdrop above, this chapter is intended as a contribution to *comparative* studies, quantitative and qualitative, of *continuum* dynamics and *discrete* dynamics. The comparison here is confined to *planar linear* dynamics and hence draws extensively upon Chap. 29. For the linear systems, continuous and discrete, the elementary *solutions* are of the *exponential* type, respectively, $e^{\lambda t}$ and $\lambda^t$. Then a unified symbolic treatment of the exponentials will be helpful and instructive. Of course, $\boldsymbol{\lambda > 0 : \lambda^t \equiv e^{\ln \lambda t},\ t \in \mathbf{R};\ \lambda < 0 : \lambda^t \equiv (-1)^t |\lambda|^t \equiv (-1)^t e^{\ln|\lambda| t},\ t \in \mathbf{Z}}$. Evidently, there is no loss of generality in the domain, $\mathbf{Z}$, of discrete-time processes. Clearly, besides monotone exponential paths, the discrete solutions may also be located and alternate between two exponential curves. As to asymptotic stability in the discrete case, the eigenvalue criterion $|\lambda| \gtrless 1$ *is the analog to ln* $|\lambda| \gtrless 0$ in the continuous case. By adopting a common exponential form, the general solution of the difference equations may be compared with the analogous formulas in Chap. 29, Sect. "General Coordinate Solutions and Initial Value Problems".

The *geometry* of *phase portrait* for the *discrete* linear system will be a main object of our exposition. We shall give a *complete* description of the *solutions* in terms of the *governing* system (structural) *parameters.* Bifurcation points and structural stability *regions* of the *parameter space* are amply illustrated. A *comparison* with the corresponding *parameter regions* in Chap. 29, Sect. "Parameter Space and the Hyperconic Phase Portrait" will *highlight*—in the context of two well-known standard models—the *disparity* between *continuum* and *discrete dynamics.*

To bring out some *affinity* of the two types of dynamics as well, we examine the possibility of *embedding* the *solutions* of the *difference* equations into the solutions of some *correlate differential* equations, i.e., *merging sequences* of *points* from the *discrete* system exactly into *curves* generated by the *correlate continuous* system. To obtain the latter, it turns out that a properly defined *logarithmic matrix*, **log A**—rather than the *exponential matrix*, $e^A$—plays a *prominent* role as being the relevant *governing matrix* of the *correlate differential* equation system. A purely *algebraic* treatment of the *logarithmic matrix*, entirely independent of differential (difference) equations, is offered in the Appendix.

As an aid to clarification by visualization, *extensive illustrations* are provided for the *discrete linear systems*, nonsingular and singular. By observing in the phase plane the *solutions* of difference equations as *jumps* in the *state variables* (sequences of points) *located* on the *correlate curves*, it becomes apparent that the *jump patterns* arising from the *discrete-time* process (difference equations, iterated maps) are indeed *elaborate* in comparison with those of *continuous changes* of states in time along *phase curves*.

## BASIC FRAMEWORK OF THE DISCRETE LINEAR SYSTEM

Consider the discrete dynamic system of two linear forms, with real coefficients in two *real state* variables, $(\boldsymbol{x}, \boldsymbol{y}) \in \mathbf{R}^2,\ \boldsymbol{t} \in \mathbf{Z}$:

$$x_{t+1} = F(x_t, y_t) = ax_t + by_t, \tag{31.1a}$$

$$y_{t+1} = G(x_t, y_t) = cx_t + dy_t, \tag{31.1b}$$

or, in vector-matrix notation,

$$\mathbf{x}_{t+1} = \begin{bmatrix} x_{1_{t+1}} \\ x_{2_{t+1}} \end{bmatrix} = \begin{bmatrix} a & b \\ c & d \end{bmatrix} \begin{bmatrix} x_{1_t} \\ x_{2_t} \end{bmatrix} = A\mathbf{x}_t, \quad \mathbf{x} \in \mathbf{R}^2, \tag{31.2a}$$

where the *real coefficient* matrix $\boldsymbol{A}$ has

$$\text{trace} = 2\mu = a + d, \quad \text{determinant} = |A| = ad - bc. \tag{31.2b}$$

With a *discrete process* given on the *standard normal form* (31.1a–31.2b), the state vector $\mathbf{x}_t$ is determined over the set integers $t \in \mathbf{Z}$ by linear *recurrence relations* or a linear *mapping* on the *phase* (state) *space* $\mathbf{R}^2$.

**Remark 31.1** An *equivalent* form of the dynamic system (31.1b–31.2b) is provided by the *difference equations*,

$$\Delta x_t = x_{t+1} - x_t = (a-1)x_t + by_t, \tag{31.3a}$$

$$\Delta y_t = y_{t+1} - y_t = cx_t + (d-1)y_t, \tag{31.3b}$$

or in vector-matrix notation

$$\Delta \mathbf{x}_t = (A - E)x_t = A^* \mathbf{x}_t, \tag{31.4a}$$

where the real matrix $\boldsymbol{A}^*$ has

$$\begin{aligned} &\text{trace} &&= a + d - 2 \\ &\text{determinant} &&= |A^*| = (a-1)(d-1) - bc = |A| + 1 - (d+a) \end{aligned} \tag{31.4b}$$

The discrete linear forms (31.3a–31.4b) rather than (31.1a–31.2b) are a somewhat closer approximation and *analog* to the continuous linear forms in Chap. 29, Sect. "The Linear System, Director Function, and Directrices". As mentioned above, we shall later derive the *exact* correlate matrix of a continuous linear system that *encompasses* the behavior of discrete nonsingular systems (31.3a–31.4b). ▽

By a *solution* of the discrete dynamic systems (31.1a–31.4b) is meant a *function* $\boldsymbol{\varphi}$, defined on a subset $T$ of integer numbers and satisfying (31.1a–31.4b)

$$\varphi = (\varphi_1, \varphi_2), \quad \varphi : T \to \mathbf{R}^2, \quad T \subseteq \mathbf{Z}. \tag{31.5}$$

As the domain of the mapping $\varphi$ is a set of *consecutive* integers, $\boldsymbol{\varphi}$ is then a sequence with a *representation* as a *phase* (point) *sequence* in $\mathbf{R}^2$

$$\varphi(t) = [x = \varphi_1(t),\ y = \varphi_2(t)], \quad t \in T \subseteq \mathbf{Z}. \tag{31.6}$$

The *trajectory* (orbit) generated by (31.1a–31.4b) and obtained from $\boldsymbol{\varphi}$ is the *sequentially ordered* point set

$$\zeta = \{\varphi(t) \mid t \in T\} \subset \mathbf{R}^2. \tag{31.7}$$

In solving *initial value problems* of discrete dynamics, the main concern is usually the behavior of solutions in the immediate and distant future ($t \to \infty$) rather than in the past ($t \to -\infty$). Henceforth, the domain $T$ of the time variable can with impunity be restricted to the set $\mathbf{N}_0$ of nonnegative integers,

$$T = \mathbf{N}_0 = \{0\} \cup \mathbf{N} = \{0, 1, 2, 3, \ldots\} \tag{31.8}$$

For *any* initial value (point) $x_0 \in \mathbf{R}^2$, the unique *solution* $\varphi(t)$, (31.6), of (31.1a–31.4b) may be formally given as the *iterated mapping*

$$\varphi(t) = (A^t x_0), \quad t \in \mathbf{N}_0, \tag{31.9}$$

in which $\boldsymbol{A}$, (31.2a–2), is assumed *nonsingular* and where the $t$-iterate of $\boldsymbol{x}_0$, $\boldsymbol{A}^t\boldsymbol{x}_0$, is obtained by the $t$-fold *composition* $A^t = A \circ A^{t-1}$. Although the symbolic form (31.9) is valuable for some theoretical purposes and plainly shows the *computational procedure* of taking one point to another, it does not offer much insight into the actual location of subsequent iterates. Evidently, some more *transparent solution formulas* must be provided to plot a particular solution (trajectory) and to outline appropriately the *geometry* of the *phase portrait* of the discrete linear systems.

## Phase Plane Decomposition and Ratios

In describing the behavior of the solutions and the trajectory geometry of *continuous* homogeneous dynamic systems in the plane, nonlinear and linear, cf. Chap. 28, Sects. "Basic Framework, Assumptions, and Definitions" and Chap. 29, Sect. "The Linear System, Director Function, and Directrices", the *ratio* variable,

$$r_t = y_t/x_t, \quad x_t \neq 0, \tag{31.10}$$

played a significant role. An analogous role may be surmised for (31.10) in discrete homogeneous systems. Here this *ratio* will first be used to determine *invariant subspaces* in the phase plane. To this end, we get from (31.1a–2) and (31.10)

$$x_{t+1} = x_t(a + br_t) = x_t f(r_t), \tag{31.11a}$$

$$y_{t+1} = x_t(c + dr_t) = x_t g(r_t), \tag{31.11b}$$

and next the linear *fractional recurrence* equation of the *ratio variable*

$$r_{t+1} = \frac{c + dr_t}{a + br_t} = \frac{g(r_t)}{f(r_t)} = q(r_t), \quad f(r_t) \neq 0. \tag{31.12}$$

The *graph* of the function $\boldsymbol{q(r_t)}$ consists of rectangular *hyperbolas* with center $(-a/b, d/b)$, constant: $-(ad - bc)/b^2 = -|A|/b^2$. We may note that (31.12) is the *discrete* analog to the *continuous direction* (tangent) *field*, see (29.180.2).

Thus, a *fixed point* of the mapping (31.12) or, equivalently, a *stationary ratio* solution of the difference equation,

$$\Delta r_t = r_{t+1} - r_t = q(r_t) - r_t, \tag{31.13}$$

is then determined by the real *roots* of the polynomial

$$c + (d - a)r - b^2 = 0. \tag{31.14}$$

This expression corresponds exactly to the so-called director function, $h(r)$, of the continuous linear system, see (29.3). For ease of reference, the *director roots* $(\boldsymbol{\alpha_i})$ of (31.14) and *directrix values* $\boldsymbol{f(\alpha_i)}$, (31.11a–2) are here repeated—

for the case, $bc \neq 0$—in the notation of Chap. 29, Sect. "The Linear System, Director Function, and Directrices":

$$\Delta^2 = \tfrac{1}{4}(d-a)^2 + bc = \tfrac{1}{4}(d+a)^2 - (ad-bc) = \tfrac{1}{4}(d+a)^2 - |A|, \quad (31.15)$$

$$\Delta^2 > 0 : \Delta = +\sqrt{\Delta^2}, \qquad \Delta^2 < 0 : |\Delta| = +\sqrt{|\Delta^2|}, \quad (31.16)$$

$$\Delta^2 > 0 : \alpha_1 = \frac{d-a}{2b} + \frac{\Delta}{b}, \quad \alpha_2 = \frac{d-a}{2b} - \frac{\Delta}{b}, \quad (31.17)$$

$$\alpha_1 + \alpha_2 = \frac{d-a}{b}, \quad \alpha_1 - \alpha_2 = \frac{2\Delta}{b}, \quad \alpha_1 \cdot \alpha_2 = -\frac{c}{b}, \quad (31.18)$$

$$\Delta^2 = 0 : \alpha = \frac{d-a}{2b} = \frac{2c}{a-d}, \quad \alpha^2 = |\frac{c}{b}|, \quad (31.19)$$

$$\Delta^2 > 0 : \lambda_1 \equiv f(\alpha_1) = a + b\alpha_1 = \tfrac{1}{2}(a+d) + \Delta, \quad (31.20)$$

$$\lambda_2 \equiv f(\alpha_2) = a + b\alpha_2 = \tfrac{1}{2}(a+d) - \Delta, \quad (31.21)$$

$$\lambda_1 \cdot \lambda_2 = |A|, \quad (31.22)$$

$$\Delta^2 = 0 : \lambda \equiv f(\alpha) = a + b\alpha = \tfrac{1}{2}(a+d). \quad (31.23)$$

There is no need to repeat the expressions for the special case of triangular systems, $bc = 0$ in (31.1a–31.2b) and (31.11a–31.12), see (29.14.1–29.14.2)

Evidently, the *director roots*, $\alpha_i$, and the *directrix values* $f(\alpha_i)$ are the ***same*** for *continuous* and *discrete* linear dynamics; obviously, the real eigenvector/eigenvalues carry over from a common system matrix, $A$.

**Remark 31.2** It may be noted that the matrix, $(A - E) = A^*$ of the equivalent system (31.3a–31.4b), implies the *same* values for the *discriminant* (31.15) and the *director roots* (31.17–31.19), whereas the *directrix* (eigen) *values* (31.20–31.23) will each be *diminished* by one. ▽

### *Stationary Ratios and Directrix Solutions*

Corresponding to the stationary ratio solutions,

$$r = \rho(t) = \varphi_2(t)/\varphi_1(t) = \alpha_i, \quad \forall t \in \mathbf{N}_0, \quad (31.24)$$

with $\alpha_i$ from (31.17–31.19), the *lines*, $y = \alpha_i x$, contain the *trajectories* (31.7) of the *directrix solutions*,

$$\Delta^2 > 0 : \varphi(t) = \begin{cases} \lambda_1^t(x_0, \alpha_1 x_0) = \lambda_1^t(x_0, y_0), & t \in \mathbf{N}_0, \\ \lambda_2^t(x_0, \alpha_2 x_0) = \lambda_2^t(x_0, y_0), & t \in \mathbf{N}_0, \end{cases} \quad (31.25a)$$

$$\Delta^2 = 0 : \varphi(t) = \lambda^t(x_0, \alpha x_0) = \lambda^t(x_0, y_0), \quad t \in \mathbf{N}_0. \quad (31.25b)$$

***Proof*** The sequence $\varphi_1(t)$ is immediately obtained as the general solution to recurrence equation, cf. (31.11a), (31.17–31.23),

$$x_{t+1} = x_t(a + b\alpha_i) = \lambda_i x_t. \tag{31.26}$$

and hence (31.25a–2) follow immediately. □

In contrast to the continuous directrix solutions in Chap. 29, Sect. "The General Coordinate Solution", the *sequences* from the *discrete exponential* (with base $\lambda_i$) functions (31.25a–31.25b) are not always *monotone* (increasing or decreasing) sequences, nor are they geometrically confined to rays (half-lines). Clearly, if a directrix value, $\boldsymbol{\lambda}_i = \boldsymbol{f}\ (\boldsymbol{\alpha}_i)$, is *negative,* then $\boldsymbol{\lambda}_i^t$ have ***opposite*** signs for ***odd*** and ***even integers*** of $\boldsymbol{t}$, and so the corresponding point *sequence* from (31.25a–31.25b) *alternates* from one side of the *origin* to the other, upon the line $\boldsymbol{y}_i = \boldsymbol{\alpha}_i \boldsymbol{x}_i$.

Such alternations may occur on both directrices, (31.25a). If a directrix value is equal to minus one ($\boldsymbol{\lambda}_i = -\mathbf{1}$), then directrix solutions are *alternating sequences*, which now become *periodic* sequences with *period 2.* Generally, it is applying the *superposition* principle to *alternating sequences*—which are entirely different from *discrete* (aperiodic or periodic) *oscillations* (circular trigonometric functions)—that adds *more variety* to solutions and trajectories of *discrete* linear dynamics, compared to continuous-time processes. However, we shall nevertheless, as (31.25a–31.25b), look for some *continuous curves* in which the *general* discrete-time *sequence* $\varphi(t)$ of (31.1a–31.2b) may be *embedded.*

### *Nonstationary Ratio Solutions*

Before discussing the behavior of the coordinate solutions $\boldsymbol{\varphi(t)}$, we briefly examine the possibility of solving the *nonlinear* recurrence (difference) equations (31.12–31.13). The theory of "*sum calculus*" analogous to integral calculus is not helpful here. Even though nonlinear difference equations seldom can be solved in closed form, the *Eq. (31.12)* can, in fact, be *solved explicitly.*

To this end, we make the substitution, cf. Brand (1955, p. 489),

$$a + br_t = \frac{s_{t+1}}{s_t} \quad \Leftrightarrow \quad r_t = \frac{1}{b}\left(\frac{s_{t+1}}{s_t} - a\right), \tag{31.27}$$

which simply reduces (31.12) to the linear difference equation

$$s_{t+2} - (a + d)s_{t+1} + (ad - bc)s_t = 0. \tag{31.28}$$

The general nonstationary *ratio solution* $\boldsymbol{\rho(t)}$ can be obtained explicitly from (31.27–31.28). But a systematic treatment of (31.28) leads directly to the analysis of *general coordinate* solutions to (31.1a–31.2b).

## The General Solution and Initial Value Problems

There are several standard methods to solve planar linear difference equations with constant coefficients. Here we shall use simple and well-known procedures for obtaining the general solution of (31.1a–31.2b), although the objective is—similar to the phase flow in Chap. 29, Sect. "General Coordinate Solutions and Initial Value Problems"—to finally obtain *solution expressions explicitly* in terms of arbitrary *initial values*, $(\boldsymbol{x}_0, \boldsymbol{y}_0)$. Thus the *general* and *particular* solutions of (31.1a–31.2b) are given by the *same* formulas.

The linear system (31.1a–2) may be reduced to a simple *second-order* difference equation. By straightforward substitutions in (31.1a–2), we have

$$\begin{aligned} x_{t+2} &= ax_{t+1} + by_{t+1} = ax_{t+1} + b(cx_t + dy_t) \\ &= ax_{t+1} + bcx_t + d(x_{t+1} - ax_t) \\ &= (a+d)x_{t+1} + (bc - ad)x_t, \end{aligned} \tag{31.29}$$

and, rearranging more conveniently,

$$x_{t+2} - (a+d)x_{t+1} + (ad - bc)x_t = 0. \tag{31.30}$$

Also from (31.1a), we have, provided that $b \neq 0$,

$$y_t = (1/b)(x_{t+1} - ax_t). \tag{31.31}$$

Hence, with the general solution $\boldsymbol{x} = \boldsymbol{\varphi}_1(\boldsymbol{t})$ of (31.30), we next get the corresponding general solution $\boldsymbol{y} = \boldsymbol{\varphi}_2(\boldsymbol{t})$ by inserting $\boldsymbol{\varphi}_1$ into (31.31).

As is well known, the characteristic equation of (31.30) is, cf. (31.2b),

$$\lambda^2 - (a+d)\lambda + |A| = 0. \tag{31.32}$$

Evidently, the real and complex conjugate roots of (31.32) are, cf. (31.15–31.16), (31.20–31.23)

$$\Delta^2 > 0 \quad : \lambda_1 = \frac{1}{2}(a+d) + \Delta, \quad \lambda_2 = \frac{1}{2}(a+d) - \Delta, \tag{31.33}$$

$$\Delta^2 = 0 \quad : \lambda = \frac{1}{2}(a+d), \tag{31.34}$$

$$\Delta^2 < 0 \quad : \lambda_1 = \frac{1}{2}(a+d) + i|\Delta|, \quad \lambda_2 = \overline{\lambda}_1 = \frac{1}{2}(a+d) - i|\Delta|. \tag{31.35}$$

To *avoid complex* constants associated with (31.35), the latter is here given in equivalent *circular trigonometric form*, $|\boldsymbol{\lambda}|(\cos\boldsymbol{\theta} \pm \boldsymbol{i}\sin\boldsymbol{\theta})$, with *modulus*

$$|\lambda|^2 = |\lambda_1|^2 = |\lambda_2|^2 = \tfrac{1}{4}(a+d)^2 + \Delta^2 = |A| > 0, \tag{31.36}$$

and the ***unique angle θ*** (positive for counterclockwise rotations) such that

$$|\lambda| \cos\theta = |A|^{\frac{1}{2}} \cos\theta = \tfrac{1}{2}(a+d); \qquad 0 < \theta < \pi, \tag{31.37a}$$

$$|\lambda| \sin\theta = |A|^{\frac{1}{2}} \sin\theta = |\Delta|; \qquad 0 < \theta < \pi, \tag{31.37b}$$

$$\theta = \arccos\left(\frac{(a+d)/2}{|A|^{\frac{1}{2}}}\right) > 0. \tag{31.38}$$

After these preliminaries (31.29–31.38), we can state

**Proposition 31.1** *The general solution, $\boldsymbol{\varphi}(t) = [\boldsymbol{\varphi}_1(t), \boldsymbol{\varphi}_2(t)]$, $t \in \mathbf{N}_0$, of the discrete linear dynamic system (31.1a–2) is, for, respectively, $\Delta^2 > 0$, $\Delta^2 = 0$, $\Delta^2 < 0$, cf. (31.15–31.16), given by, cf. (31.17–31.23), (31.33–31.38),*

$$\Delta^2{>}0: \begin{cases} \varphi_1(t) = C_1\lambda_1^t + C_2\lambda_2^t, \\ \varphi_2(t) = C_1\alpha_1\lambda_1^t + C_2\alpha_2\lambda_2^t, \end{cases} \tag{31.39}$$

$$\Delta^2{=}0: \begin{cases} \varphi_1(t) = (C_1 + C_2 t)\lambda^t, \\ \varphi_2(t) = (C_1 + \frac{d+a}{d-a}C_2 + C_2 t)\alpha\lambda^t, \end{cases} \tag{31.40}$$

$$\Delta^2{<}0: \begin{cases} \varphi_1(t) = |\lambda|^t \left\{C_1 \cos(\theta t) + C_2 \sin(\theta t)\right\}, \\ \varphi_2(t) = \frac{|\lambda|^t}{b} \left\{\left[C_1 \frac{d-a}{2} + C_2|\Delta|\right] \cos(\theta t) + \left[C_2 \frac{d-a}{2} - C_1|\Delta|\right] \sin(\theta t)\right\}, \end{cases} \tag{31.41}$$

*where $\mathbf{C}_1$ and $\mathbf{C}_2$ in (31.39–31.41) are real arbitrary constants.*

***Proof*** For all three cases (31.33–31.35), the *general* solutions of the linear second-order equation (31.30) and hence the stated *first coordinate* solutions $\varphi_1(t)$ are standard results, see, e.g., Goldberg (1986, p. 134–142); Wold (1959, p. 152–155); Chiang (1984, p. 577–581); Gandolfo (1980, p. 53–57).

The three general *second coordinate* solutions $\varphi_2(t)$ are obtained by inserting the corresponding $\varphi_1(t)$-expression, for $t$ and $t+1$, into (31.31) and thereupon collecting terms.

In particular, $(\lambda_1 - a)/b = \alpha_1$, $(\lambda_2 - a)/b = \alpha_2$, cf. (31.20–31.22), is employed to attain (31.39). Similarly, $(\lambda - a)/b = \alpha$, cf. (31.23) is used to get (31.40).

Finally, cf. (31.31), (31.41)

$$\varphi_2(t) = \tfrac{1}{b}\left\{|\lambda|^{t+1}\left[C_1 \cos(\theta(t+1)) C_2 \sin(\theta(t+1))\right] - a|\lambda|^t \left[C_1 \cos(\theta t) + C_2 \sin(\theta t)\right]\right\} \tag{31.42}$$

is—by standard trigonometric argument addition formulas and by using $|\lambda|\cos\theta = \frac{1}{2}(a+d)$, $|\lambda|\sin\theta = |\Delta|$, cf. (31.37a–2)—reduced to (31.41), see Gandolfo (1980, p. 126–129). □

Solutions of *initial value problems* require the *elimination* of the arbitrary constants, $C_1$ and $C_2$, from (31.39–31.41). We shall perform the elimination procedure in a systematic way that will give important additional information about the nature of the family of functions (sequences), which satisfy the difference equations, (31.2a–2). To this end, we introduce the following *notation* and expressions for the case $\mathbf{\Delta^2 > 0}$, cf. (31.20–31.22), (31.15)

$$\delta \equiv \frac{1}{2}\ln\left|\frac{\lambda_1}{\lambda_2}\right| = \frac{1}{2}\ln\left|\frac{\frac{1}{2}(a+d)+\Delta}{\frac{1}{2}(a+d)-\Delta}\right|; \quad \lambda_1 \neq 0,\ \lambda_2 \neq 0; \quad \|A\| \equiv |\lambda_1 \cdot \lambda_2| > 0, \tag{31.43}$$

$$e^{\delta} = |\lambda_1/\lambda_2|^{1/2}, \quad e^{-\delta} = |\lambda_2/\lambda_1|^{1/2}, \tag{31.44a}$$

$$\cosh(\delta) = \tfrac{1}{2}(e^{\delta}+e^{-\delta}), \quad \sinh(\delta) = \tfrac{1}{2}(e^{\delta}-e^{-\delta}). \tag{31.44b}$$

**Proposition 31.2** *The entire family of solutions,* $\boldsymbol{\varphi(t) = [\varphi_1(t), \varphi_2(t)]}$, $t \in \mathbf{N}_0$, *solving the discrete linear dynamic system (31.1a–2)—with initial values* $(\boldsymbol{x_0, y_0}) \in \mathbf{R}^2$ *at* $t = 0$*—is given by*

$$\Delta^2 > 0 : \varphi(t) = \frac{1}{2}\begin{bmatrix} \lambda_1^t+\lambda_2^t-\frac{d-a}{2\Delta}(\lambda_1^t-\lambda_2^t) & \frac{b}{\Delta}(\lambda_1^t-\lambda_2^t) \\ \frac{c}{\Delta}(\lambda_1^t-\lambda_2^t) & \lambda_1^t+\lambda_2^t+\frac{d-a}{2\Delta}(\lambda_1^t-\lambda_2^t) \end{bmatrix}\begin{bmatrix} x_0 \\ y_0 \end{bmatrix} \tag{31.45}$$

$$\Delta^2 = 0 : \varphi(t) = \lambda^t\begin{bmatrix} 1+\frac{(a-d)/2}{\lambda}t & \frac{b}{\lambda}t \\ \frac{c}{\lambda}t & 1-\frac{(d-a)/2}{\lambda}t \end{bmatrix}\begin{bmatrix} x_0 \\ y_0 \end{bmatrix} \tag{31.46}$$

$$\Delta^2 < 0 : \varphi(t) = |\lambda|^t\begin{bmatrix} \cos(\theta t)-\frac{d-a}{2|\Delta|}\sin(\theta t) & \frac{b}{|\Delta|}\sin(\theta t) \\ \frac{c}{|\Delta|}\sin(\theta t) & \cos(\theta t)+\frac{d-a}{2|\Delta|}\sin(\theta t) \end{bmatrix}\begin{bmatrix} x_0 \\ y_0 \end{bmatrix} \tag{31.47}$$

*where* $\boldsymbol{\lambda_1, \lambda_2, \lambda}$, *and* $|\lambda|$ *are given by (31.33–31.36);* $\boldsymbol{\Delta}$, $\boldsymbol{|\Delta|}$, *and* $\boldsymbol{\theta}$ *are given by (31.15–31.16), (31.38).*

*The subfamily of the solutions* $\boldsymbol{\varphi(t)}$, *(31.45–31.47)—solving the discrete nonsingular system (31.1a–2) for any initial* $(\boldsymbol{x_0, y_0}) \in \mathbf{R}^2$ *at* $t = 0$*—can be restated as*

$$\Delta^2 > 0 \ : \varphi(t) = |A|^{\frac{t}{2}}\begin{bmatrix} \cosh(\delta t)-\frac{d-a}{2\Delta}\sinh(\delta t) & \frac{b}{\Delta}\sinh(\delta t) \\ \frac{c}{\Delta}\sinh(\delta t) & \cosh(\delta t)+\frac{d-a}{2\Delta}\sinh(\delta t) \end{bmatrix}\begin{bmatrix} x_0 \\ y_0 \end{bmatrix} \tag{31.48a}$$

*with* $\boldsymbol{|A| > 0}$, $\boldsymbol{a+d > 0}$, *and* $\boldsymbol{\delta > 0}$, *cf. (31.43);* $\boldsymbol{t \in \mathbf{N}_0}$.

$$\varphi(t) = (-1)^t \cdot |A|^{\frac{t}{2}} \begin{bmatrix} \cosh(\delta t) - \frac{d-a}{2\Delta}\sinh(\delta t) & \frac{b}{\Delta}\sinh(\delta t) \\ \frac{c}{\Delta}\sinh(\delta t) & \cosh(\delta t) + \frac{d-a}{2\Delta}\sinh(\delta t) \end{bmatrix} \begin{bmatrix} x_0 \\ y_0 \end{bmatrix} \tag{31.48b}$$

*with* $|A| > 0$, $a + d < 0$, *and* $\delta < 0$, *cf. (31.43);* $t \in \mathbf{N}_0$.

$$\varphi(t) = ||A||^{\frac{t}{2}} \begin{bmatrix} \cosh(\delta t) - \frac{d-a}{2\Delta}\sinh(\delta t) & \frac{b}{\Delta}\sinh(\delta t) \\ \frac{c}{\Delta}\sinh(\delta t) & \cosh(\delta t) + \frac{d-a}{2\Delta}\sinh(\delta t) \end{bmatrix} \begin{bmatrix} x_0 \\ y_0 \end{bmatrix} \tag{31.48c}$$

*with* $|A| < 0$, *and* $\delta \gtrless 0$, *if* $a + d \gtrless 0$, *cf. (31.43);* $t = 2n$, $n \in \mathbf{N}_0$.

$$\varphi(t) = ||A||^{\frac{t}{2}} \begin{bmatrix} \sinh(\delta t) - \frac{d-a}{2\Delta}\cosh(\delta t) & \frac{b}{\Delta}\cosh(\delta t) \\ \frac{c}{\Delta}\cosh(\delta t) & \sinh(\delta t) + \frac{d-a}{2\Delta}\cosh(\delta t) \end{bmatrix} \begin{bmatrix} x_0 \\ y_0 \end{bmatrix} \tag{31.48d}$$

*with* $|A| < 0$, *and* $\delta \gtrless 0$, *if* $a+d \gtrless 0$, *cf. (31.43);* $t = 2n+1$, $n \in \mathbf{N}_0$.

$$\Delta^2 = 0 \;:\; \varphi(t) = |A|^{\frac{t}{2}} \begin{bmatrix} 1 + \frac{(a-d)/2}{(a+d)/2}\,t & \frac{b}{(a+d)/2}\,t \\ \frac{c}{(a+d)/2}\,t & 1 - \frac{(d-a)/2}{(d+a)/2}\,t \end{bmatrix} \begin{bmatrix} x_0 \\ y_0 \end{bmatrix} \tag{31.49a}$$

*with* $|A| > 0$, $a + d > 0$; $t \in \mathbf{N}_0$.

$$\varphi(t) = (-1)^t \cdot |A|^{\frac{t}{2}} \begin{bmatrix} 1 + \frac{(a-d)/2}{(a+d)/2}\,t & \frac{b}{(a+d)/2}\,t \\ \frac{c}{(a+d)/2}\,t & 1 - \frac{(d-a)/2}{(d+a)/2}\,t \end{bmatrix} \begin{bmatrix} x_0 \\ y_0 \end{bmatrix} \tag{31.49b}$$

*with* $|A| > 0$, $a + d < 0$; $t \in \mathbf{N}_0$.

$$\Delta^2 < 0 \;:\; \varphi(t) = |A|^{\frac{t}{2}} \begin{bmatrix} \cos(\theta t) - \frac{d-a}{2|\Delta|}\sin(\theta t) & \frac{b}{|\Delta|}\sin(\theta t) \\ \frac{c}{|\Delta|}\sin(\theta t) & \cos(\theta t) + \frac{d-a}{2|\Delta|}\sin(\theta t) \end{bmatrix} \begin{bmatrix} x_0 \\ y_0 \end{bmatrix} \tag{31.50a}$$

*with* $|A| > 0$; $t \in \mathbf{N}_0$.

**Corollary 31.1** *The set of solutions (31.48d) may alternatively be written as*

$$\varphi(t) = ||A||^{\frac{t-1}{2}} \begin{bmatrix} \cosh[\delta(t-1)] - \frac{d-a}{2\Delta}\sinh[\delta(t-1)] & \frac{b}{\Delta}\sinh[\delta(t-1)] \\ \frac{c}{\Delta}\sinh[\delta(t-1)] & \cosh[\delta(t-1)] + \frac{d-a}{2\Delta}\sinh[\delta(t-1)] \end{bmatrix} \begin{bmatrix} x_1 \\ y_1 \end{bmatrix} \tag{31.51a}$$

*with* $|A| < 0$; $t = 2n + 1$, $n \in \mathbf{N}_0$, *and*

$$\begin{bmatrix} x_1 \\ y_1 \end{bmatrix} = A \begin{bmatrix} x_0 \\ y_0 \end{bmatrix}. \tag{31.51b}$$

*The set of solutions (31.46) and (31.49a–b) may be restated as*

$$\varphi(t) = \left(\frac{d+a}{2}\right)^{t-1} \begin{bmatrix} \frac{1}{2}(d+a)-\frac{1}{2}(d-a)t & bt \\ ct & \frac{1}{2}(d+a)+\frac{1}{2}(d-a)t \end{bmatrix} \begin{bmatrix} x_0 \\ y_0 \end{bmatrix}. \quad (31.52)$$

▽

**Corollary 31.2** *The general solution formulas of the families (31.45–31.47) are equivalent to the matrix expressions*

$$\Delta^2 > 0 : \varphi(t) = \frac{1}{2}\left[(\lambda_1^t + \lambda_2^t)E + \frac{1}{\Delta}(\lambda_1^t - \lambda_2^t)B\right]\varphi(0), \quad (31.53)$$

$$\Delta^2 = 0 : \varphi(t) = \lambda^t\left[E + \frac{t}{\lambda}B\right]\varphi(0), \quad (31.54)$$

$$\Delta^2 < 0 : \varphi(t) = |\lambda|^t\left[\cos(\theta t)E + \frac{\sin(\theta t)}{|\Delta|}B\right]\varphi(0), \quad (31.55)$$

*where* $(x_0, y_0) = \varphi(0)$, $t \in \mathbf{N}_0$, *and, cf. Chap. 29, Sect. "Initial Value Problems and Coordinate Transformations": (29.113), (29.108), (29.127),*

$$B = A - \mu E = \begin{pmatrix} \frac{a-d}{2} & b \\ c & \frac{d-a}{2} \end{pmatrix}, \quad (31.56)$$

$$B^2 = \Delta^2 E. \quad (31.57)$$

*Regarding the subfamilies (31.48a–31.50a), the solution formulas (31.48a), (31.49a), and (31.50a) are, respectively, equivalent to the matrix expressions,* $t \in \mathbf{N}_0$,

$$\Delta^2 > 0\ \varphi(t) = e^{\frac{\log|A|}{2}t}\left[\cosh(\delta t)E + \frac{\sinh(\delta t)}{\Delta}B\right]\varphi(0), \quad (31.58)$$

$$\Delta^2 = 0\ \varphi(t) = e^{\frac{\log|A|}{2}t}\left[E + \frac{t}{(a+d)/2}B\right]\varphi(0), \quad (31.59)$$

$$\Delta^2 < 0\ \varphi(t) = e^{\frac{\log|A|}{2}t}\left[\cos(\theta t)E + \frac{\sin(\theta t)}{|\Delta|}B\right]\varphi(0). \quad (31.60)$$

*Apart from the time domain, the formulas (31.48c–31.48d), cf. (31.51a), take the same principal form as (31.58), except that* $\log|\mathbf{A}|$ *is replaced by* $\log||\mathbf{A}||$, *and the factor* $(-\mathbf{1})^t$ *is also used in (31.58–31.59) to represent the solutions, (31.48b), (31.49b).*

***Proof*** The initial values at $t = 0$ are,

$$\varphi(0) = [\varphi_1(0), \varphi_2(0)] = [x_0, y_0]. \tag{31.61}$$

Then we get from (31.61) and (31.39)

$$x_0 = C_1 + C_2, \quad y_0 = C_1\alpha_1 + C_2\alpha_2. \tag{31.62}$$

By solving for the arbitrary constants, (31.62) gives

$$C_1 = \frac{y_0 - \alpha_2 x_0}{\alpha_1 - \alpha_2}, \quad C_2 = \frac{\alpha_1 x_0 - y_0}{\alpha_1 - \alpha_2}, \tag{31.63}$$

which, using (31.17–31.18), reduces to

$$C_1 = \frac{1}{2}\left[\left(1 - \frac{d-a}{2\Delta}\right)x_0 + \frac{b}{\Delta}y_0\right], \quad C_2 = \frac{1}{2}\left[\left(1 + \frac{d-a}{2\Delta}\right)x_0 - \frac{b}{\Delta}y_0\right]. \tag{31.64}$$

Furthermore, we also note from (31.63) and again (31.17–31.18) that

$$C_1\alpha_1 = \frac{1}{2}\left[-\frac{c}{\Delta}x_0 + \left(1 + \frac{d-a}{2\Delta}\right)y_0\right], \quad C_2\alpha_2 = \frac{1}{2}\left[-\frac{c}{\Delta}x_0 + \left(1 - \frac{d-a}{2\Delta}\right)y_0\right]. \tag{31.65}$$

Hence, (31.64–31.65) and (31.39) give

$$\varphi_1(t) = \frac{1}{2}\left\{\left[\left(1 - \frac{d-a}{2\Delta}\right)x_0 + \frac{b}{\Delta}y_0\right]\lambda_1^t + \left[\left(1 + \frac{d-a}{2\Delta}\right)x_0 - \frac{b}{\Delta}y_0\right]\lambda_2^t\right\}, \tag{31.66a}$$

$$\varphi_2(t) = \frac{1}{2}\left\{\left[\frac{c}{\Delta}x_0 + \left(1 + \frac{d-a}{2\Delta}\right)y_0\right]\lambda_1^t + \left[-\frac{c}{\Delta}x_0 + \left(1 - \frac{d-a}{2\Delta}\right)y_0\right]\lambda_2^t\right\}. \tag{31.66b}$$

After collecting terms and using matrix form, (31.66a–2) becomes

$$\begin{bmatrix}\varphi_1(t)\\ \varphi_2(t)\end{bmatrix} = \frac{1}{2}\begin{bmatrix} \lambda_1^t+\lambda_2^t - \frac{d-a}{2\Delta}(\lambda_1^t-\lambda_2^t) & \frac{b}{\Delta}(\lambda_1^t-\lambda_2^t) \\ \frac{c}{\Delta}(\lambda_1^t-\lambda_2^t) & \lambda_1^t+\lambda_2^t+\frac{d-a}{2\Delta}(\lambda_1^t-\lambda_2^t)\end{bmatrix}\begin{bmatrix}x_0\\ y_0\end{bmatrix}. \tag{31.67}$$

which is (31.45).

First, in the case—$|\boldsymbol{A}| > 0$ and $(\boldsymbol{a} + \boldsymbol{d}) > 0$—the directrix values $(\boldsymbol{\lambda}_1, \boldsymbol{\lambda}_2)$ are *both positive*, cf. (31.20–31.22), (31.33).

Next, by *dividing* the matrix elements with $(\boldsymbol{\lambda_1 \cdot \lambda_2})^{t/2}$, (31.67) becomes

$$\begin{bmatrix} \varphi_1(t) \\ \varphi_2(t) \end{bmatrix} = \frac{1}{2}(\lambda_1 \cdot \lambda_2)^{\frac{t}{2}} \cdot$$

$$\begin{bmatrix} \left(\frac{\lambda_1}{\lambda_2}\right)^{\frac{t}{2}} + \left(\frac{\lambda_2}{\lambda_1}\right)^{\frac{t}{2}} - \frac{d-a}{2\Delta}\left[\left(\frac{\lambda_1}{\lambda_2}\right)^{\frac{t}{2}} - \left(\frac{\lambda_2}{\lambda_1}\right)^{\frac{t}{2}}\right] & \frac{b}{\Delta}\left[\left(\frac{\lambda_1}{\lambda_2}\right)^{\frac{t}{2}} - \left(\frac{\lambda_2}{\lambda_1}\right)^{\frac{t}{2}}\right] \\ \frac{c}{\Delta}\left[\left(\frac{\lambda_1}{\lambda_2}\right)^{\frac{t}{2}} - \left(\frac{\lambda_2}{\lambda_1}\right)^{\frac{t}{2}}\right] & \left(\frac{\lambda_1}{\lambda_2}\right)^{\frac{t}{2}} + \left(\frac{\lambda_2}{\lambda_1}\right)^{\frac{t}{2}} + \frac{d-a}{2\Delta}\left[\left(\frac{\lambda_1}{\lambda_2}\right)^{\frac{t}{2}} - \left(\frac{\lambda_2}{\lambda_1}\right)^{\frac{t}{2}}\right] \end{bmatrix} \begin{bmatrix} x_0 \\ y_0 \end{bmatrix}. \tag{31.68}$$

Then, by substituting (31.44a–2) and $\boldsymbol{\lambda_1 \cdot \lambda_2 = |A|}$ into (31.68), we *obtain* (31.48a).

Second, in the case $\boldsymbol{|A| > 0}$ and $\boldsymbol{(a+d) < 0}$, the directrix values $(\boldsymbol{\lambda_1, \lambda_2})$ are *both negative,* cf. (31.20–31.22), (31.33). Then, by inserting $\lambda_1^t = (-1)^t|\lambda_1|^t$ and $\lambda_2^t = (-1)^t|\lambda_2|^t$ into (31.67), we see that the same matrix as before is now $|\lambda_1|$ and $|\lambda_2|$, except for the scalar $(-1)^t$ in front of (31.67). Proceeding as in (31.68) and using (31.44a–2), we obtain (31.48b) with $\boldsymbol{\delta < 0}$, cf. (31.43).

Finally, in the case of $\boldsymbol{|A| < 0}$, the directrix values have opposite signs, i.e., $\lambda_1 > 0$, $\lambda_2 < 0$, cf. (31.20–31.22). Here, inserting $\lambda_1^t$ and $\lambda_2^t = (-1)^t|\lambda_2|^t$ into (31.67) and dividing by $(\lambda_1 \cdot |\lambda_2|)^{t/2} = ||A||^{t/2}$—where $\boldsymbol{||A||}$ denotes the *numerical value* of the determinant, $\boldsymbol{|A|}$, cf. (31.43)—give no further difficulties whenever $\boldsymbol{t}$ is an *even* number. Hence, with $\boldsymbol{t = 2n}$, $n \in \mathbf{N}_0$, we get the same symbolic form as in (31.48a), and so we have established (31.48c).

For *odd* numbers of $t$, we will here see, e.g., the terms $(\lambda_2/\lambda_1)^{t/2}$ in (31.68) replaced by $(-1)^t(|\lambda_2|/\lambda_1)^{t/2}$. Hence for $\boldsymbol{t = 2n+1}$, $n \in \mathbf{N}_0$, a change of *sign* occurs in front of terms $(|\lambda_2|/\lambda_1)^{t/2}$ in (31.68), which accordingly simply *changes* cosh to sinh and analogously sinh to cosh. Hence we get (31.48d).

Alternatively, (31.48d) can just—with a step length of two—be started from $(x_1, y_1)$, and thereby written as given in the Corollary, (31.51a–2).

With a *zero* discriminant, $\boldsymbol{\Delta^2 = 0}$, we get, cf. (31.61) and (31.40),

$$x_0 = C_1, \quad y_0 = \left(C_1 + \frac{d+a}{d-a}C_2\right)\alpha, \tag{31.69}$$

which then gives, cf. (31.19)

$$C_1 = x_0, \quad C_2 = \frac{2b}{d+a}y_0 - \frac{d-a}{d+a}x_0. \tag{31.70}$$

Furthermore, from (31.70) and (31.19), we note that

$$C_2\alpha = \frac{d-a}{d+a}y_0 - \frac{(d-a)^2}{2b(d+a)}x_0 = \frac{d-a}{d+a}y_0 + \frac{2c}{d+a}x_0. \tag{31.71}$$

Next, inserting (31.70) into (31.40), and using (31.69), (31.71), and (31.23), we have

$$\varphi_1(t) = \lambda^t \left[ x_0 + \left( \frac{2b}{d+a}\, y_0 - \frac{d-a}{d+a}\, x_0 \right) t \right], \tag{31.72a}$$

$$\varphi_2(t) = \lambda^t \left[ y_0 + \left( \frac{d-a}{d+a}\, y_0 + \frac{2c}{d+a}\, x_0 \right) t \right]. \tag{31.72b}$$

Hence, collecting terms and using matrix form, (31.72a–b) and $\lambda = \frac{1}{2}(a+d)$, (31.34), immediately establish (31.46) and (31.52).

The form in (31.49a–2) follows from $|A| = (\frac{d+a}{2})^2 \neq 0$ and (31.46).

With a *negative* discriminant, $\mathbf{\Delta^2 < 0}$, we get, from (31.61) and (31.41),

$$x_0 = C_1, \quad y_0 = \frac{1}{b}\left( C_1 \frac{d-a}{2} + C_2 |\Delta| \right), \tag{31.73}$$

which gives

$$C_1 = x_0, \quad C_2 = \frac{b}{|\Delta|}\, y_0 - \frac{d-a}{2|\Delta|}\, x_0. \tag{31.74}$$

Furthermore, from (31.74) and (31.15), it is seen that

$$C_2 \frac{d-a}{2} - C_1 |\Delta| = b \left( \frac{d-a}{2|\Delta|}\, y_0 + \frac{c}{|\Delta|}\, x_0 \right). \tag{31.75}$$

Next, inserting (31.74) into (31.41), and using (31.73) and (31.75), we obtain

$$\varphi_1(t) = |\lambda|^t \left[ x_0 \cos(\theta t) + \left( \frac{b}{|\Delta|}\, y_0 - \frac{d-a}{2|\Delta|}\, x_0 \right) \sin(\theta t) \right], \tag{31.76a}$$

$$\varphi_2(t) = |\lambda|^t \left[ y_0 \cos(\theta t) + \left( \frac{d-a}{2|\Delta|}\, y_0 + \frac{c}{|\Delta|}\, x_0 \right) \sin(\theta t) \right]. \tag{31.76b}$$

Thus, collecting terms and using matrix form, (31.76a–2) establishes (31.47). The latter and (31.36) give (31.50a).

The *expressions* (31.53–31.55) and (31.58–31.60) follow immediately from Proposition 31.2, (31.56), and $\mathbf{|A|^{\frac{1}{2}} \equiv e^{\frac{\log|A|}{2}}}$. □

## DISCRETE- AND CONTINUOUS-TIME SOLUTIONS

A methodical comparison between the complete sets of solutions to the linear *difference* equations above and the linear *differential* equations in Chap. 30 may now be offered. As is well known, Guckenheimer and Holmes (1986, p. 16), the *continuous* planar system $\dot{x} = Ax$ has an exact *discrete* analog, viz.,

$$\dot{x} = Ax \quad \sim \quad x_{t+1} = e^{A}x_t, \quad t \in \mathbf{N}_0 \tag{31.77}$$

with the *exponential matrix* $\boldsymbol{e}^{\boldsymbol{A}}$, as stated as, e.g., $\boldsymbol{\Phi}(\mathbf{1})$ in (29.100–29.102).

However, as the *determinant* of $\boldsymbol{e}^{\boldsymbol{A}}$ is always *positive*, cf. (29.103), the family of solutions to (31.77) is clearly only a *subset* of the family of solutions to the discrete dynamic system (31.1a–31.2b), where, e.g., $|\boldsymbol{A}|$ is not restricted to be positive.

To achieve an *analogy* more *general* than (31.77), we must look for a certain coefficient matrix of *differential* equations that *corresponds* to the *general* coefficient *matrix* of the *difference* equations (31.2a), viz.,

$$\dot{x} = Lx = \log Ax \quad \sim \quad x_{t+1} = e^{L}x_t \equiv e^{\log A}x_t \equiv Ax_t, \quad t \in \mathbf{N}_0, \tag{31.78}$$

where $\boldsymbol{L} = \mathbf{log}\,\boldsymbol{A}$ symbolizes the so-called *logarithmic matrix* of $\boldsymbol{A}$.

The latter is seldom seen in the literature but is discussed in Brauer and Nohel (1969, p. 290) and Cesari (1963, p. 18), where it is shown that every *nonsingular* matrix has a *logarithm*. In the Appendix, we present and *explicitly* derive the expression for $\mathbf{log}\,\boldsymbol{A}$ of a regular (nonsingular) $2 \times 2$ real matrix $\boldsymbol{A}$.

Since the *general solution* of the *discrete* nonsingular linear system (31.2a) has already been derived in Proposition 31.2, we shall obtain the $\mathbf{log}\,\boldsymbol{A}$ matrix of the corresponding *continuous* linear system, cf. (31.78), by properly *extending* the *time domain* of the solutions (31.58–31.60) to $\mathbf{R}$ and then computing the *derivative* of these solutions. This procedure will easily and rigorously establish the $\mathbf{log}\,\boldsymbol{A}$ matrix of the corresponding linear *differential* equations, which accordingly have *solutions* that continuously *interpolate* (*embed*) the *discrete* solutions (31.48a–31.50a) of Proposition 31.2.

The principal solutions (31.58–31.60) (including the extension with $\mathbf{log}\,||\boldsymbol{A}||$), are well defined for $t \in \mathbf{R}$. The vector functions (31.48b) and (31.49b) allow only $t \in \mathbf{N}_0$, but the term $(-1)^t$ does not affect the *continuous curves* embedding subsets of the *point sequences* (31.48b), (31.49b).

Generally, we have

**Theorem 31.1** *The governing matrix,* $\boldsymbol{L} \equiv \boldsymbol{log}\,\boldsymbol{A}$, *of the* ***correlate*** *continuous linear dynamic system—which interpolates the principal solutions (31.58–31.60)* *and which **embeds** the solutions (31.48a–31.50a) into **phase curves** to the discrete nonsingular linear dynamic system (31.2a–31.2b)—is given, cf. (31.56) as*

$$\Delta^2 > 0: \qquad \log A = \frac{1}{2}\log||A||\,E + \frac{\delta}{\Delta}B \equiv$$

$$\begin{bmatrix} a_L\ b_L \\ c_L\ d_L \end{bmatrix} \equiv \begin{bmatrix} \frac{1}{2}\log||A|| - \frac{\delta}{\Delta}\frac{d-a}{2} & \frac{\delta}{\Delta}b \\ \frac{\delta}{\Delta}c & \frac{1}{2}\log||A|| + \frac{\delta}{\Delta}\frac{d-a}{2} \end{bmatrix}, \tag{31.79}$$

$$\Delta^2 = 0: \qquad \log A = \frac{1}{2}\log|A|E + \frac{1}{(a+d)/2}B \equiv$$

$$\begin{bmatrix} a_L\ b_L \\ c_L\ d_L \end{bmatrix} \equiv \begin{bmatrix} \frac{1}{2}\log|A| - \frac{(d-a)/2}{(a+d)/2} & \frac{b}{(a+d)/2} \\ \frac{c}{(a+d)/2} & \frac{1}{2}\log|A| + \frac{(d-a)/2}{(a+d)/2} \end{bmatrix}, \tag{31.80}$$

$$\Delta^2 < 0: \qquad \log A = \frac{1}{2}\log|A|E + \frac{\theta}{|\Delta|}B \equiv$$

$$\begin{bmatrix} a_L\ b_L \\ c_L\ d_L \end{bmatrix} \equiv \begin{bmatrix} \frac{1}{2}\log|A| - \frac{\theta}{|\Delta|}\frac{d-a}{2} & \frac{\theta}{|\Delta|}b \\ \frac{\theta}{|\Delta|}c & \frac{1}{2}\log|A| + \frac{\theta}{|\Delta|}\frac{d-a}{2} \end{bmatrix}. \tag{31.81}$$

**Corollary 31.3** *The logarithmic matrix* $\boldsymbol{L} \equiv \log \boldsymbol{A}$ *has trace:* $Tr\,\boldsymbol{L} \equiv Tr\log\boldsymbol{A}$, *discriminant:* $\boldsymbol{\Delta}_L^2 \equiv \boldsymbol{\Delta}_{\log A}^2$, *and determinant:* $|\boldsymbol{L}| \equiv |\log \boldsymbol{A}|$, *given by*

$$Tr\,L \equiv a_L + d_L = \begin{Bmatrix} \log||A|| = \log|\lambda_1| + \log|\lambda_2| \\ \log|A| \quad = 2\log|\lambda| \\ \log|A| \quad = 2\log|\lambda| \end{Bmatrix} \; for \begin{Bmatrix} \Delta^2 > 0 \\ \Delta^2 = 0 \\ \Delta^2 < 0 \end{Bmatrix}, \tag{31.82}$$

$$\Delta_L^2 \equiv \frac{1}{4}(d_L - a_L)^2 + b_L c_L = \begin{Bmatrix} \delta^2 \\ 0 \\ -\theta^2 \end{Bmatrix} \; for \begin{Bmatrix} \Delta^2 > 0 \\ \Delta^2 = 0 \\ \Delta^2 < 0 \end{Bmatrix}, \tag{31.83}$$

$$|L| \equiv a_L d_L - b_L c_L = \begin{Bmatrix} \frac{1}{4}(\log||A||)^2 - \delta^2 = \log|\lambda_1|\log|\lambda_2| \\ \frac{1}{4}(\log|A|)^2 \qquad = (\log|\lambda|)^2 \\ \frac{1}{4}(\log|A|)^2 + \theta^2 \;= (\log|\lambda|)^2 + \theta^2 \end{Bmatrix} \; for \begin{Bmatrix} \Delta^2 > 0 \\ \Delta^2 = 0 \\ \Delta^2 < 0 \end{Bmatrix}, \tag{31.84}$$

*with* $\boldsymbol{\lambda}$*'s,* $\boldsymbol{\theta}$, $\boldsymbol{\delta}$, *and* $||\boldsymbol{A}||$ *as stated in (31.20–31.23), (31.38), and (31.43).*

***Proof*** We get by *differentiating* (31.58),

$$\varphi'(t) = \frac{1}{2}\log|A|e^{\frac{\log|A|}{2}t}\left[\cosh(\delta t)E + \frac{\sinh(\delta t)}{\Delta}B\right]\varphi(0)$$
$$+e^{\frac{\log|A|}{2}t}\left[\delta\sinh(\delta t)E + \frac{\delta\cosh(\delta t)}{\Delta}B\right]\varphi(0),$$

and hence by using (31.58) and (31.57)

$$\begin{aligned}\varphi'(t) &= \frac{1}{2}\log|A|\varphi(t) + e^{\frac{\log|A|}{2}t}\left[\delta\sinh(\delta t)\frac{1}{\Delta^2}B^2 + \frac{\delta\cosh(\delta t)}{\Delta}B\right]\varphi(0)\\ &= \frac{1}{2}\log|A|\varphi(t) + \frac{\delta}{\Delta}Be^{\frac{\log|A|}{2}t}\left[\cosh(\delta t)E + \frac{\sinh(\delta t)}{\Delta}B\right]\varphi(0)\\ &= \left[\frac{1}{2}\log|A|E + \frac{\delta}{\Delta}B\right]\varphi(t) \qquad (31.85a)\\ &\equiv \log A\,\varphi(t), \qquad (31.85b)\end{aligned}$$

which establishes (31.79) in the generalized form when $\log|A|$ is replaced by $\log||A||$.

Next, we get, by *differentiating* (31.59),

$$\varphi'(t) = \frac{1}{2}\log|A|e^{\frac{\log|A|}{2}t}\left[E + \frac{t}{(a+d)/2}B\right]\varphi(0) + e^{\frac{\log|A|}{2}t}\left[\frac{1}{(a+d)^2}B\right]\varphi(0), \qquad (31.86a)$$

and hence by using (31.59) and $\frac{t}{[(a+d)/2]^2}B^2 \equiv 0$, cf. (31.57), with $\Delta^2 = 0$,

$$\begin{aligned}\varphi'(t) &= \frac{1}{2}\log|A|\varphi(t) + e^{\frac{\log|A|}{2}t}\left[\frac{t}{[(a+d)/2]^2}B^2 + \frac{1}{(a+d)/2}B\right]\varphi(0)\\ &= \frac{1}{2}\log|A|\varphi(t) + \frac{1}{(a+d)/2}Be^{\frac{\log|A|}{2}t}\left[E + \frac{t}{(a+d)/2}B\right]\varphi(0)\\ &= \left[\frac{1}{2}\log|A|E + \frac{1}{(a+d)/2}B\right]\varphi(t) \qquad (31.86b)\\ &\equiv \log A\,\varphi(t), \qquad (31.86c)\end{aligned}$$

which establishes (31.80).

Finally, we get by ***differentiating*** (31.60),

$$\varphi'(t) = \frac{1}{2}\log|A|e^{\frac{\log|A|}{2}t}\left[\cos(\theta t)E + \frac{\sin(\theta t)}{|\Delta|}B\right]\varphi(0)$$

$$+e^{\frac{\log|A|}{2}t}\left[-\theta\sin(\theta t)E + \frac{\theta\cos(\theta t)}{|\Delta|}B\right]\varphi(0), \qquad (31.87a)$$

and hence by using (31.60) and (31.57) with (31.16),

$$\varphi'(t) = \frac{1}{2}\log|A|\varphi(t) + e^{\frac{\log|A|}{2}t}\left[-\theta\sin(\theta t)\frac{1}{\Delta^2}B^2 + \frac{\theta\cos(\theta t)}{|\Delta|}B\right]\varphi(0)$$

$$= \frac{1}{2}\log|A|\varphi(t) + \frac{\theta}{|\Delta|}Be^{\frac{\log|A|}{2}t}\left[\cos(\theta t)E + \frac{\sin(\theta t)}{|\Delta|}B\right]\varphi(0)$$

$$= \left[\frac{1}{2}\log|A|E + \frac{\theta}{|\Delta|}B\right]\varphi(t) \qquad (31.87b)$$

$$\equiv \log A\ \varphi(t), \qquad (31.87c)$$

which establishes (31.81).

The expressions (31.82–31.84) follow directly from the respective matrix elements in (31.79–31.81) and by using hereto (31.15–31.16).

The last column in (31.84) is obtained as, cf. (31.43), (31.36), (31.34),

$$\frac{1}{4}(\log||A||)^2 - \delta^2 = \frac{1}{4}(\log|\lambda_1\cdot\lambda_2|)^2 - \frac{1}{4}(\log|\lambda_1/\lambda_2|)^2$$

$$= \frac{1}{4}(\log|\lambda_1| + \log|\lambda_2|)^2 - \frac{1}{4}(\log|\lambda_1| - \log|\lambda_2|)^2$$

$$= \log|\lambda_1|\cdot\log|\lambda_2|. \qquad (31.88a)$$

$$\frac{1}{4}(\log|A|)^2 = \frac{1}{4}(\log|\lambda|^2)^2 = (\log|\lambda|)^2, \qquad (31.88b)$$

$$\frac{1}{4}(\log|A|)^2 + \theta^2 = \frac{1}{4}(\log|\lambda|^2)^2 + \theta^2 = (\log|\lambda|)^2 + \theta^2. \qquad (31.88c)$$

□

## The Phase Portrait of Discrete Linear Dynamics

The system of trajectories obtained from the *solutions* $\boldsymbol{\varphi(t)}$, (31.48a–31.50a), describes the ***global phase portrait*** of the ***discrete*** nonsingular linear system, (31.1a–31.2a). The trajectory configurations of (31.48a–31.50a) and their continuous embedding loci can be analyzed by utilizing Theorem 31.1 and the trajectory configurations of linear differential equations given in Chap. 29.

The *traditional* necessary and sufficient conditions—the characteristic roots (31.33–31.35) being less than **1** in absolute value—for the *solutions* (31.48a–31.50a) to *converge* to **0** from *any* initial values can be restated as

**Lemma 31.1** *The subfamily of solutions (31.48a–31.50a) has global asymptotic stability, if and only if*

$$(i)\ Tr \log A < 0, \quad (ii)\ |\log A| > 0, \tag{31.89}$$

*which are equivalent to*

$$(i)\ |A| < 1, \quad (ii)\ |A| > -1 + Tr A, \quad (iii)\ |A| > -1 - Tr A. \tag{31.90}$$

***Proof*** A negative trace and a positive determinant are the conditions for the asymptotic stability of the solutions to linear differential equations. Hence, these two conditions are now applied to the $\log A$ matrix of Theorem 31.1.

From (31.82), we always have that

$$\text{Tr} \log A < 0 \Leftrightarrow ||A|| < 1 \Leftrightarrow -1 < |A| < 1. \tag{31.91}$$

When $\Delta^2 > 0$, we get, from (31.84) and (31.33),

$$|\log A| = \log|\lambda_1| \log|\lambda_2| = \log|\frac{1}{2}(a+d) + \Delta| \log|\frac{1}{2}(a+d) - \Delta| > 0. \tag{31.92}$$

To satisfy (31.92) together with (31.91), we only need to consider, $|\lambda_1| < 1$, $|\lambda_2| < 1$, i.e.,

$$-1 < \frac{1}{2}(a+d) + \Delta < 1 \Leftrightarrow -1 - \frac{1}{2}(a+d) < \Delta < 1 - \frac{1}{2}(a+d), \tag{31.93}$$

$$-1 < \frac{1}{2}(a+d) - \Delta < 1 \Leftrightarrow -1 - \frac{1}{2}(a+d) < -\Delta < 1 - \frac{1}{2}(a+d) \tag{31.94}$$

As $\Delta > 0$, and since by (31.93–31.94) the boundaries of $\Delta$ and $-\Delta$ are the same, it is clear that the first inequality in (31.93) and the second one in (31.94) are superfluous. Hence, the effective restrictions may be written as

$$\Delta^2 < \left[1 - \frac{1}{2}(a+d)\right]^2 \Leftrightarrow -1 + a + d < \frac{1}{4}(d+a)^2 - \Delta^2, \tag{31.95}$$

$$\Delta^2 < \left[-1 - \frac{1}{2}(a+d)\right]^2 \Leftrightarrow -1 - (a+d) < \frac{1}{4}(d+a)^2 - \Delta^2. \tag{31.96}$$

Thus (31.95–31.96) and (31.15) establish the second and third parts of (31.90); accordingly, only the last inequality in (31.91) remains an effective restriction.

When $\Delta^2 \leq 0$, $|\log A|$ is always positive, cf. (31.84). Hence, the requirement $|A| < 1$ is the restrictive part in (31.90).

Thus, the *interior* of the *triangular boundary* (31.90), cf. Fig. 31.1, represents the *asymptotic stability region* of the solutions (31.48a–31.50a). □

The *expressions* (31.90) are well-known stability (convergence) criteria for the phase sequences of the linear second-order difference equation, (31.30), cf. Goldberg (1986, p. 172), but they were here derived and confirmed by imposing standard convergence *conditions* (31.89) upon the correlate **log *A*** matrix of the *continuous*-time solutions.

The *signs* of *five magnitudes*—**Tr log *A*, |log *A*|, $\boldsymbol{\Delta^2}$, Tr *A*, |*A*|**—give *crucial qualitative* information about the ***log A*** matrices in Theorem 31.1 and hence also about qualitative behavior of the *solutions* to (31.1a–31.2b). As we have just seen, (31.90), the *signs* of first two determine the important issue of *convergence/divergence*. Since the *sign* of $\Delta_L^2$ and $\Delta^2$ are the same, cf. (31.83), we may still use the sign of $\Delta^2$ to distinguish between *oscillatory/non-oscillatory* behavior. Generally, the *family of solutions* to *difference equations* is ***larger*** than that of *solutions* to *differential equations*. This *aspect* is reflected in the ***log A*** *matrices* of Theorem 31.1, where the *sign* of **Tr *A***, cf. $\boldsymbol{\delta}$, (31.43), also affects the *sign* of the *off-diagonal* elements of the **log *A*** matrices for the non-oscillating families, cf. (31.79–31.80). Finally, the *sign* of $|A|$ is, as usual, also important for the phase portrait of non-oscillating solutions.

Thus, the different types of behavior of the *solutions* to the *discrete nonsingular* linear system depend on the *sign* of these *five magnitudes*. Because of some interdependence of signs, the possible 32 types (*excluding* 0, degenerate cases) reduce altogether to *16 types* of *qualitative distinct* solution families. *These 16 types*, organized after the *5 signs*, are *summarized* in Table 31.1.

As the *classification* of Table 31.1 is fundamentally based on the *critical numerical* values of the *two principal magnitudes*, **Tr *A*** and **|*A*|**, we can relate the *16 types* of Table 31.1 to *particular regions* in the *bifurcation* diagram, shown in Fig. 31.1. The 16 regions of Fig. 31.1 is a subdivision (italics) of the regions (with phase portraits) exhibited in Fig. 31.1.

The *boundary lines* of **Tr log *A* = 0** and **|log *A*| = 0** are seen from, respectively, (31.91) and (31.90). The *boundary curve* of $\boldsymbol{\Delta^2 = 0}$ is the *parabola* given by (31.15). The *region* of *convergence* is shown in Fig. 31.1 by a ***shaded triangle***, cf. Theorem 31.1. See here standard Fig. 31.1.

The solution formulas of *types* 1–3 were shown in (31.48a); *types* 4–9 correspond to (31.48c–31.48d), (31.51a); types 10–12 relate to (31.48b), and types *13–16* refer to (31.50a).

For the sake of completeness, the *trajectory configurations* of the *16 types* are illustrated in Figs. 31.2, 31.3, 31.4, 31.5, and 31.6, which may be compared

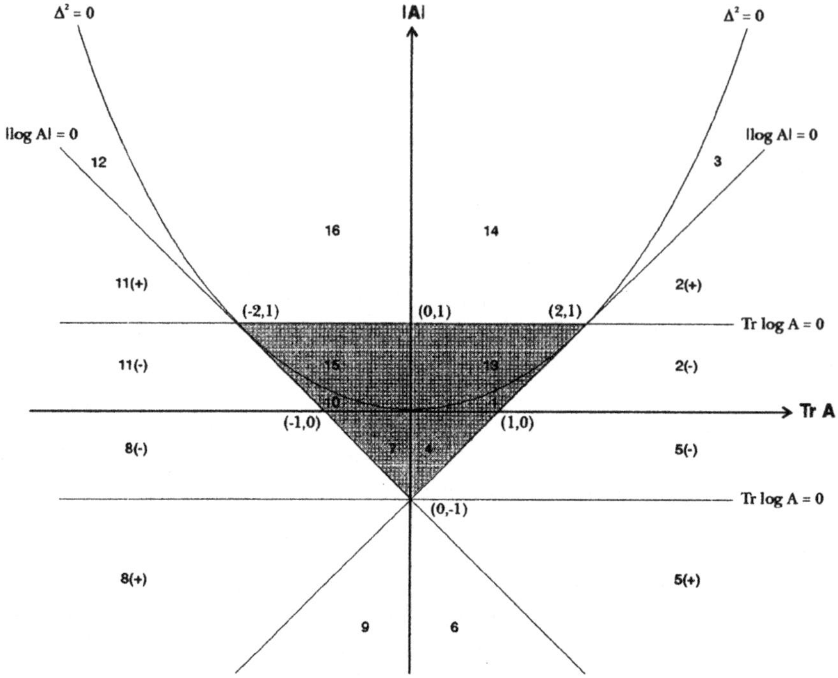


**Fig. 31.1** Parameter regions and the types of Table 31.1

**Table 31.1** Classification of the discrete nonsingular linear system (31.1a–31.2b)

| Type | $\Delta^2$ | Tr $A$ | $\|A\|$ | $\|\log A\|$ | Tr log $A$ | Behavior of solutions, (31.48a–4), (31.50a) |
|---|---|---|---|---|---|---|
| 1 | + | + | + | + | − | Monotone, parabolic, converging |
| 2 | + | + | + | − | ± | Monotone, hyperbolic, diverging |
| 3 | + | + | + | + | + | Monotone, parabolic, diverging |
| 4 | + | + | − | + | − | Reflecting in $\alpha_1$-directrix, parabolic, converging |
| 5 | + | + | − | − | ± | Reflecting in $\alpha_1$-directrix, hyperbolic, diverging |
| 6 | + | + | − | + | + | Reflecting in $\alpha_1$-directrix, parabolic, diverging |
| 7 | + | − | − | + | − | Reflecting in $\alpha_1$-directrix, parabolic, converging |
| 8 | + | − | − | − | ± | Reflecting in $\alpha_1$-directrix, hyperbolic, diverging |
| 9 | + | − | − | + | + | Reflecting in $\alpha_1$-directrix, parabolic, diverging |
| 10 | + | − | + | + | − | Reflecting in origo, parabolic, converging |
| 11 | + | − | + | − | ± | Reflecting in origo, hyperbolic, diverging |
| 12 | + | − | + | + | + | Reflecting in origo, parabolic, diverging |
| 13 | − | + | + | + | − | Elliptic, clockwise converging |
| 14 | − | + | + | + | + | Elliptic, clockwise diverging |
| 15 | − | − | + | + | − | Elliptic, counterclockwise converging |
| 16 | − | − | + | + | + | Elliptic, counterclockwise diverging |

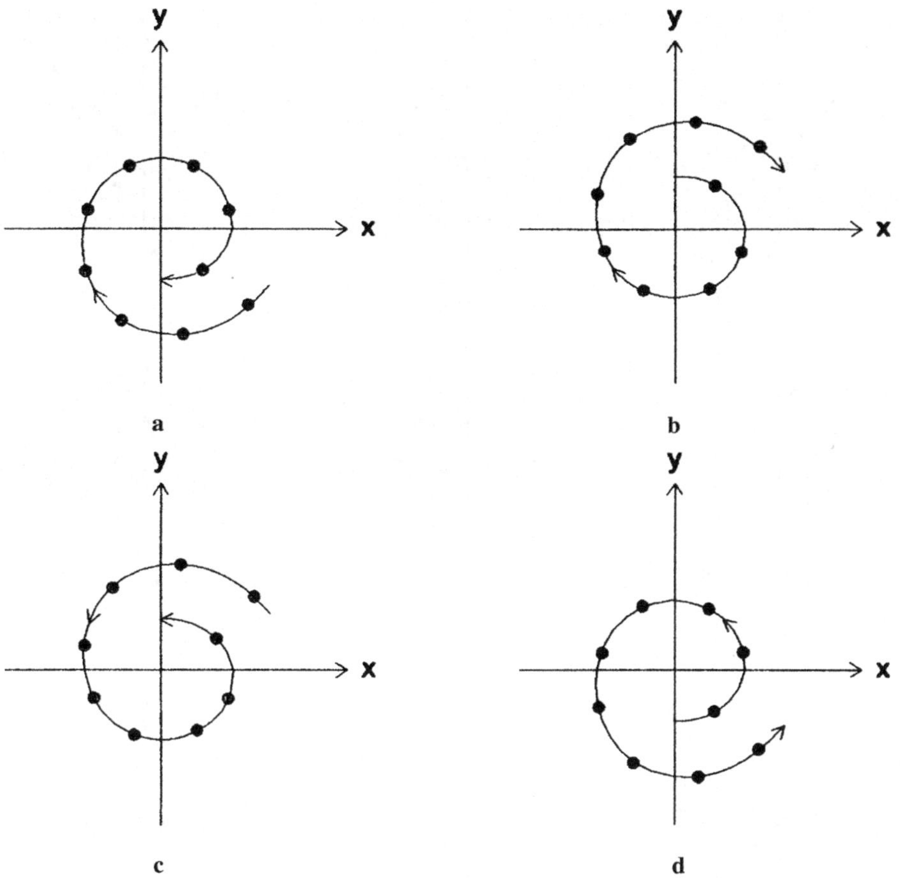


**Fig. 31.2** Trajectory configurations, ($bc < 0,\ \Delta^2 < 0$) (**a**) Oscillating, converging (**b**) Oscillating, diverging (**c**) Oscillating, converging (**d**) Oscillating, diverging

with the *trajectorial illustrations* shown within the *regions* of Fig. 29.6a–d in Chap. 29. The alphabetic *numbering* of the 12 pictures in each of the Figs. 31.3, 31.4, 31.5, and 31.6 corresponds to their type *numbers* in Table 31.1 and Fig. 31.1.

A selection of *degenerate* cases—with *trajectories* corresponding to the triangular points and boundary lines in Fig. 31.1—is *illustrated* in Fig. 31.7, which partly *corresponds* to Figs. 29.7, 29.8, 29.9, 29.10, and 29.11 in Chap. 29.

A comparison of these phase portraits for continuous and discrete linear dynamics clearly indicates that only *types* 1–3 and 13–16 are "*common*" to *both* dynamic systems, whereas the *types* **4–12** are the *new additional* families of *alternating* solutions that are *admissible only* in the *discrete* dynamic system.

Regarding the geometric *shape* of the *trajectory* configurations in Figs. 31.2, 31.3, 31.4, 31.5, and 31.6, some comments will be appropriate.

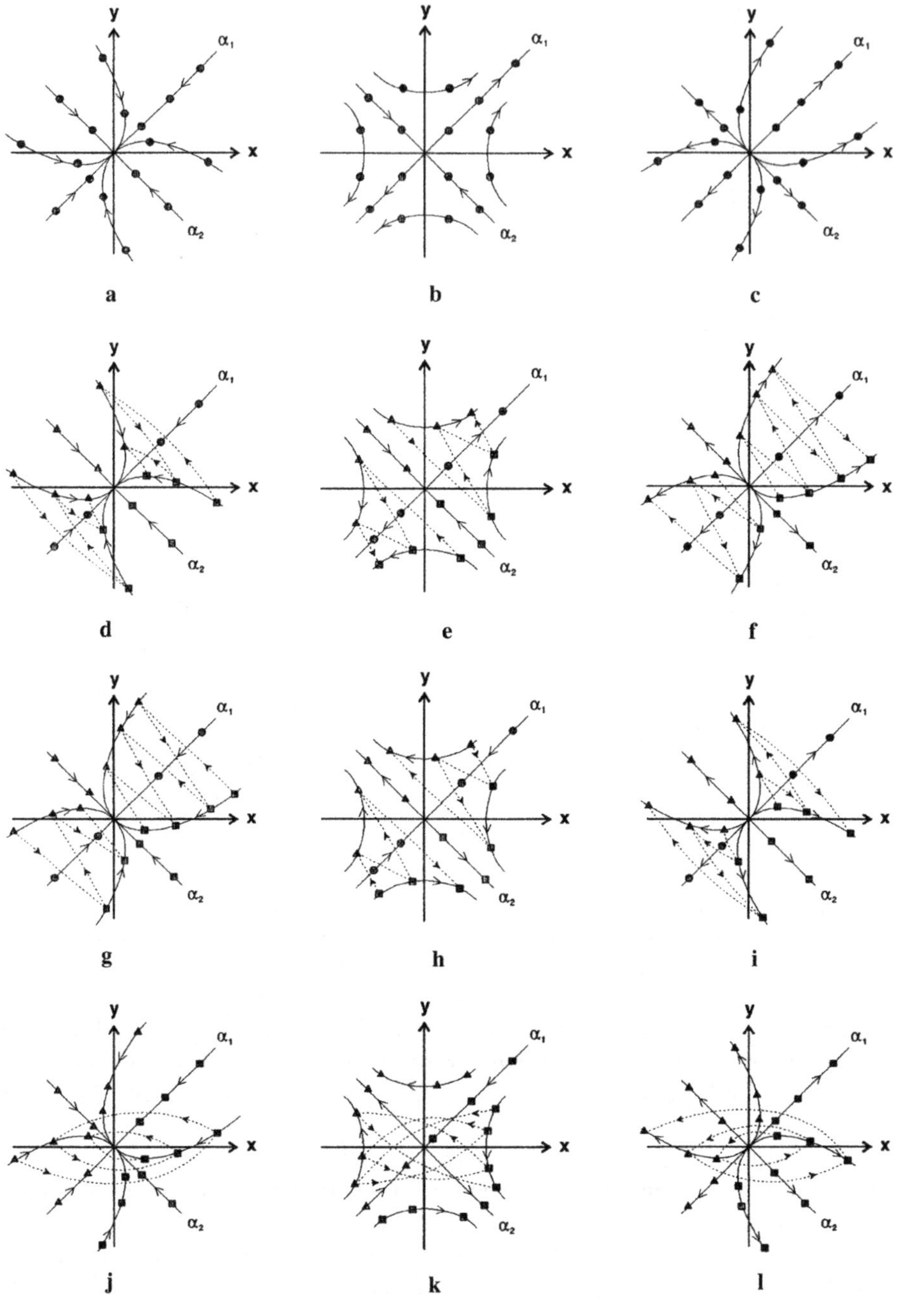


**Fig. 31.3** Trajectory configurations, ($bc > 0$, $b > 0$) (**a**) Monotone, converging (**b**) Monotone, diverging (**c**) Monotone, diverging (**d**) Alternating, converging (**e**) Alternating, diverging (**f**) Alternating, diverging (**g**) Alternating, converging (**h**) Alternating, diverging (**i**) Alternating, diverging (**j**) Alternating, converging (**k**) Alternating, diverging (**l**) Alternating, diverging

**Fig. 31.4** Trajectory configurations, ($bc > 0, \ b < 0$) (**a**) Monotone, converging (**b**) Monotone, diverging (**c**) Monotone, diverging (**d**) Alternating, converging (**e**) Alternating, diverging (**f**) Alternating, diverging (**g**) Alternating, converging (**h**) Alternating, diverging (**i**) Alternating, diverging (**j**) Alternating, converging (**k**) Alternating, diverging (**l**) Alternating, diverging

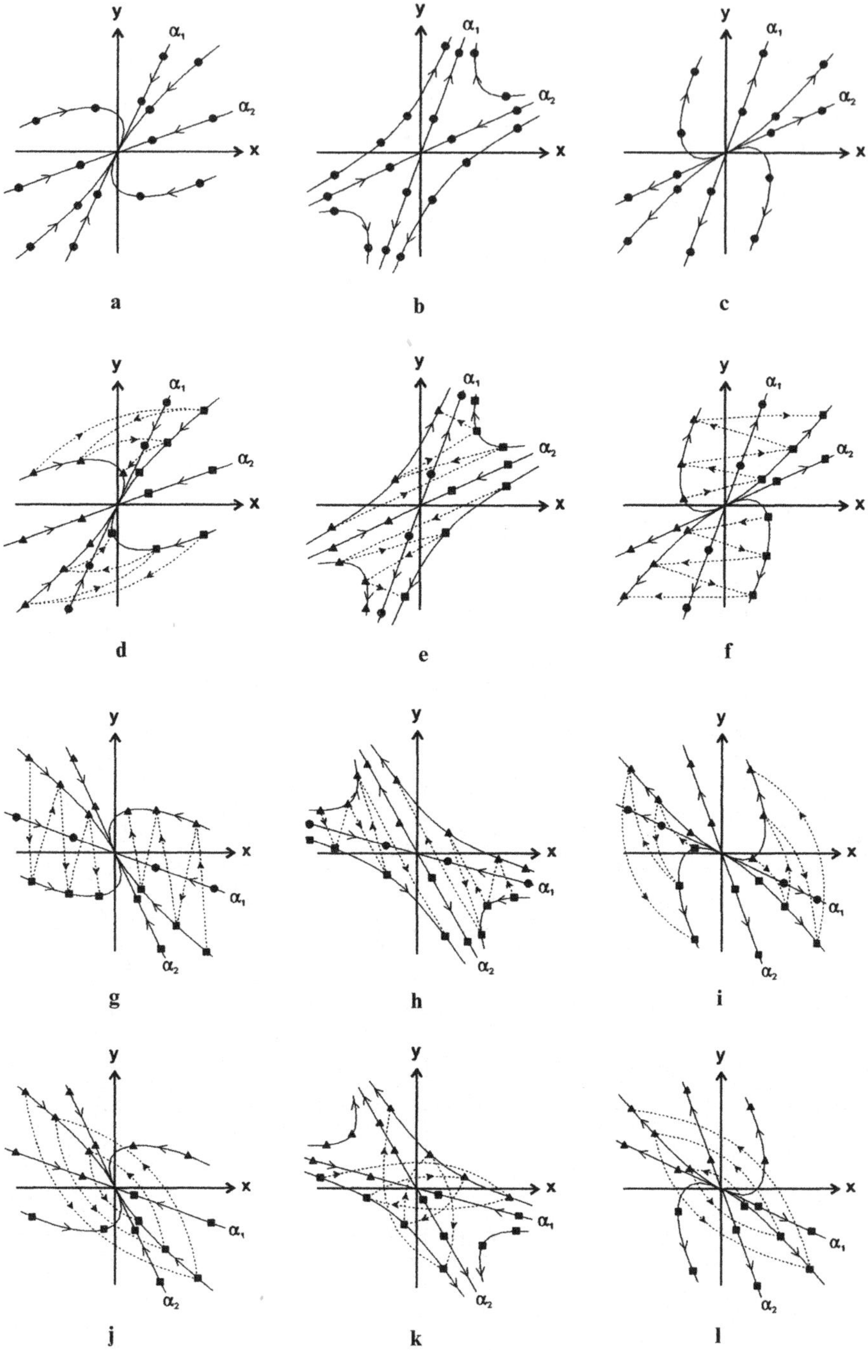


**Fig. 31.5** Trajectory configurations, ($bc > 0$, $b > 0$ $\Delta^2 > 0$) (**a**) Monotone, converging (**b**) Monotone, diverging (**c**) Monotone, diverging (**d**) Alternating, converging (**e**) Alternating, diverging (**f**) Alternating, diverging (**g**) Alternating, converging (**h**) Alternating, diverging (**i**) Alternating, diverging (**j**) Alternating, converging (**k**) Alternating, diverging (**l**) Alternating, diverging

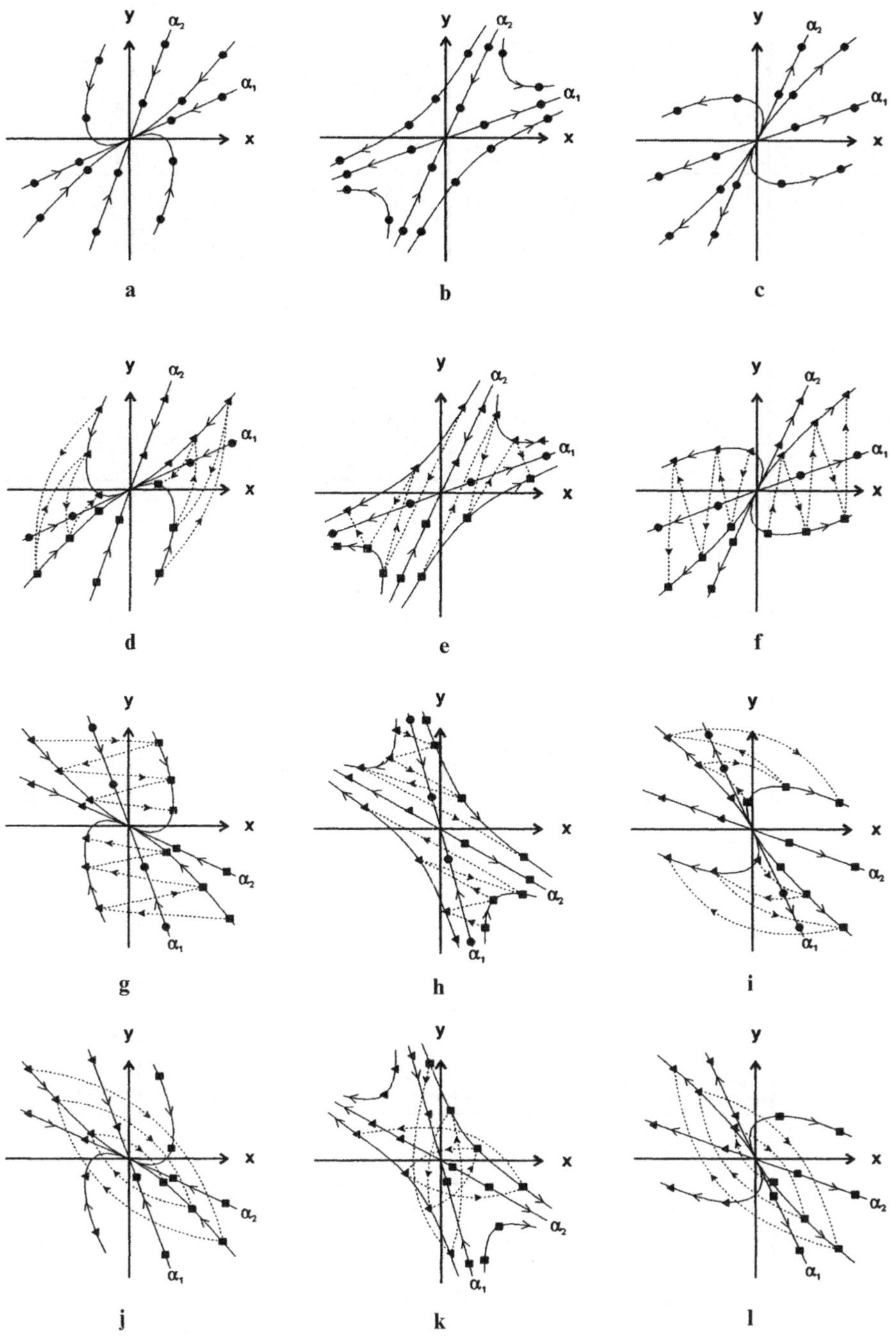


**Fig. 31.6** Trajectory configurations, ($bc > 0,\ b < 0\ \Delta^2 > 0$) (**a**) Monotone, converging (**b**) Monotone, diverging (**c**) Monotone, diverging (**d**) Alternating, converging (**e**) Alternating, diverging (**f**) Alternating, diverging (**g**) Alternating, converging (**h**) Alternating, diverging (**i**) Alternating, diverging (**j**) Alternating, converging (**k**) Alternating, diverging (**l**) Alternating, diverging

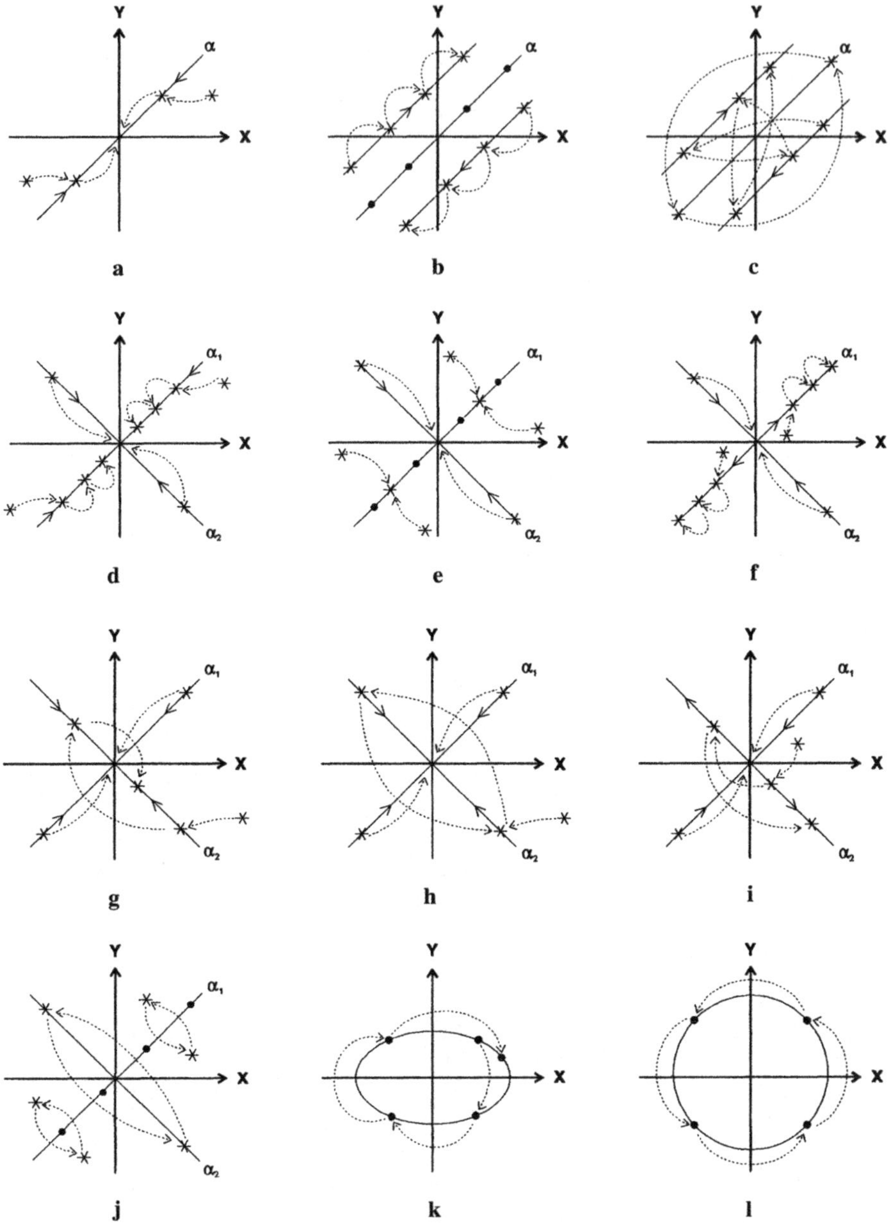


**Fig. 31.7** Trajectory configurations 31.7a–31.7c: ($b > 0$); 31.7d-31.7j: ($bc > 0$, $b > 0$); 31.7k-31.7l: ($\Delta^2 < 0$), cf. Fig. 31.1 (**a**) Point (0,0) $\begin{matrix} \Delta^2 & TrA & |A| & |\log A & Tr \log A \\ 0 & 0 & 0 & & \end{matrix}$ (**b**) Point (2,1) $\begin{matrix} \Delta^2 & TrA & |A| & |\log A & Tr \log A \\ 0 & 2 & 1 & 0 & 0 \end{matrix}$ (**c**) Point (-2,1) $\begin{matrix} \Delta^2 & TrA & |A| & |\log A & Tr \log A \\ 0 & -2 & 1 & 0 & 0 \end{matrix}$

With $\boldsymbol{\Delta}^2 < \mathbf{0}$, we have in Fig. 31.2 *always* oscillating point sequences located on the *spiral* curves of the correlate continuous-time solutions.

With $\boldsymbol{\Delta}^2 > \mathbf{0}$, the *locations* of the ***directrices*** follow from (31.17–31.18), cf. (29.17.1–29.18.2) in Chap. 29, Sect. "The Linear System, Director Function, and Directrices". Alternatively it is instructive here to obtain the *directrices* from the governing $\log A$ matrix, stated in (31.79), which give the ***director roots*** $(\boldsymbol{\alpha}_1^L, \boldsymbol{\alpha}_2^L)$ as, cf. (31.17), (31.79), (31.83)

$$\alpha_1^L = \frac{d_L - a_L}{2b_L} + \frac{\Delta_L}{b_L} = \frac{(\delta/\Delta)(d-a)}{2(\delta/\Delta)b} + \frac{\delta}{(\delta/\Delta)b} = \frac{d-a}{2b} + \frac{\Delta}{b} = \alpha_1. \tag{31.97}$$

Similarly, we get $\boldsymbol{\alpha}_2^L = \boldsymbol{\alpha}_2$; evidently, the *matrices* $\boldsymbol{A}$, (31.2a); $\boldsymbol{A} - \boldsymbol{E}$, (31.4a); $\boldsymbol{e}^{\boldsymbol{A}}$, (31.77); and $\mathbf{log}\,\boldsymbol{A}$, (31.79–31.81), have the *same* eigenvectors, see Hirsch and Smale (1974, p. 86–87)).

In short, the *number* and *location* of ***directrices*** in Figs. 31.3, 31.4, 31.5, and 31.6 are exactly the *same* as in the trajectory configurations of their relevant counterparts (***bc*-cases**) in Fig. 29.6a–d of Chap. 29.

As to the ***directrix values*** (eigenvalues) $(\boldsymbol{\lambda}_1^L, \boldsymbol{\lambda}_2^L)$ of the $\mathbf{log}\,\boldsymbol{A}$ matrix, they are, cf. (31.20–31.21), (31.79), (31.82–31.84),

$$\lambda_1^L = \frac{1}{2}(a_L + d_L) + \Delta_L = \frac{1}{2}\log ||A|| + \delta, \tag{31.98}$$

$$\lambda_2^L = \frac{1}{2}(a_L + d_L) - \Delta_L = \frac{1}{2}\log ||A|| - \delta, \tag{31.99}$$

$$\lambda_1^L \cdot \lambda_2^L = |L| = \log|\lambda_1|\,\log|\lambda_2|. \tag{31.100}$$

**Fig. 31.7** (continued) (**d**) On line $|A| = 0$, between (0,0) - (1,0) $\Delta^2\ TrA\ |A|\ |\log A\ Tr\log A$: $+\ +\ 0$ (**e**) Point (1,0) $\Delta^2\ TrA\ |A|\ |\log A\ Tr\log A$: $1/4\ \ 1\ \ 0$ (**f**) On line $|A| = 0$, beyond (1,0) $\Delta^2\ TrA\ |A|\ |\log A\ Tr\log A$: $+\ +\ 0$ (**g**) On line $|A| = 0$, between (0,0) - (-1,0) $\Delta^2\ TrA\ |A|\ |\log A\ Tr\log A$: $+\ -\ 0$ (**h**) Point (-1,0) $\Delta^2\ TrA\ |A|\ |\log A\ Tr\log A$: $1/4\ -1\ \ 0$ (**i**) On line $|A| = 0$, beyond (-1,0) $\Delta^2\ TrA\ |A|\ |\log A\ Tr\log A$: $+\ +\ 0$ (**j**) Point (0,-1) $\Delta^2\ TrA\ |A|\ |\log A\ Tr\log A$: $1\ \ 0\ -1\ \ 0\ \ 0$ (**k**) On line Tr $\log A = 0$, between (-2,1) - (2,1) $\Delta^2\ TrA\ |A|\ |\log A\ Tr\log A$: $-\ +-\ 1\ +\ 0$ (**l**) Point (0,1) $\Delta^2\ TrA\ |A|\ |\log A\ Tr\log A$: $-1\ \ 0\ \ 1\ +\ 0$

Whereas **Δ**, (31.16), was always positive, the sign of **δ** changes with the sign of **Tr** ***A***, cf. (31.43). Therefore, the *eigenvalues* (31.98–31.99) may ***interchange***, and as *elaborate* combinations of the structural *parameters* **(*a*, *b*, *c*, *d*)**, they have a more *intricate* pattern of variation than the *eigenvalues*, (31.20–31.21). As opposed to the *common* directrices (eigenvectors), (31.97), the *larger* family of solutions *admitted* by the *discrete* system essentially *originates* and is transmitted through more *diversity* in the *eigenvalues*, (31.98–31.99).

Let us take the parameter case (***bc*** **> 0, *b* > 0**) as an example. The *full-drawn curves* in Fig. 31.3a–c and in Fig. 31.3d–f are the *same*, and they were *also seen* in Fig. 29.6c of Chap. 29. With a negative **Tr** ***A***, we now get the same full-drawn curves in Figs. 31.3g–l, and 29.6d of Chap. 29 (with $\alpha_1$ and $\alpha_2$ reversed). Changing the *sign* of **Tr** ***A*** creates a change similar to changing the **sign** of ***b*** and ***c***, cf. (31.79). Thus, Fig. 31.3 displays features of *both* Fig. 29.6c and d from Chap. 29. Similarly, as seen in Figs. 31.4, 31.5, and 31.6, *each one* of them displays features of *two* figures (with the same sign of ***bc***) from Figs. 29.6a–d of Chap. 29. Hence, it should be observed that the elements (pictures) of Fig. 31.4 can be obtained from the corresponding elements of Fig. 31.3 by a *reflection* in the line $\boldsymbol{y} = \boldsymbol{x}$ and *interchanging* $\alpha_1$ and $\alpha_2$. Similarly, Figs. 31.6 can be obtained by *reflecting* Fig. 31.5 in the line $\boldsymbol{y} = \boldsymbol{x}$ and reversing $\alpha_1$ and $\alpha_2$.

As to the discrete forms (jumping, hopping) of the *sequence*, $\boldsymbol{\varphi}(t) \in \mathbf{R}^2$, $t \in \mathbf{N}_0$, *embedded* in the relevant *full-drawn curves* in Figs. 31.3, 31.4, 31.5, and 31.6, we shall relate the *salient features* of the *directrix values*, (31.20–31.21), and the *directrix solutions* in discrete time, (31.25a–2), to the *trajectory types* 1–12, Table 31.1, depicted in Fig. 31.3, 31.4, 31.5, and 31.6 for alternative bilateral *couplings* (***bc***), cf. Chap. 29, Sect. "Parameter Space and the Hyperconic Phase Portrait".

In Figs. 31.3, 31.4, 31.5, and 31.6, we have types, Table 31.1, for their *rows*:

| | |
|---|---|
| 1. row (type 1 3): | $\lambda_1 > 0,\ \lambda_2 > 0,$ |
| 2. row (type 4 6): | $\lambda_1 > 0,\ \lambda_2 < 0,\ \lambda_1 + \lambda_2 > 0,$ |
| 3. row (type 7 9): | $\lambda_1 > 0,\ \lambda_2 < 0,\ \lambda_1 + \lambda_2 < 0,$ |
| 4. row (type 10 12): | $\lambda_1 < 0,\ \lambda_2 < 0,$ |

and for *the columns*

| | |
|---|---|
| 1. column (type 1, 4, 7, 10): | $\lvert\lambda_1\rvert < 1,\ \lvert\lambda_2\rvert < 1,$ |
| 2. column (type 2, 5, 8, 11): | $\lvert\lambda_1\rvert > 1,\ \lvert\lambda_2\rvert < 1,$ or $\lvert\lambda_1\rvert < 1,\ \lvert\lambda_2\rvert > 1,$ |
| 3. column (type 3, 6, 9, 12): | $\lvert\lambda_1\rvert > 1,\ \lvert\lambda_2\rvert > 1.$ |

When *both* directrix values are *positive*, both *directrix solutions* (31.25a) always *remain* on their initial rays. The consecutive points of corresponding *non-directrix* solutions (31.48a), cf. (31.39), also *remain* on their initial full-drawn curves, as indicated by the ***dots*** (**∀*t***) on the *first row* figures.

With directrix values of *different* signs, our labeling, (31.20–31.21), always implies that $\lambda_1$ is positive and hence $\lambda_2$ negative. Again the $\alpha_1$-*directrix* solutions always *remain* on their initial *rays*, but the consecutive points of the $\alpha_2$-directrix solutions (31.25a) now *hop* across the origin—*alternate*—from one ray to its opposite, as indicated by the ***squares*** (***t even***) and ***triangles*** (***t odd***) on the second and third row figures. Of course, it is immaterial which attribute (even/odd) is attached to an $\alpha_2$-ray. The consecutive points of the corresponding *non-directrix* solutions (31.48c–4), (31.39)), now *hop across*—reflect in—the $\alpha_1$-directrix, as indicated by the *dashed* line in the alternating *type* 4–9 figures.

When *both* directrix values are *negative*, both *directrix* solutions (31.25a) then *hop* across the origin from one ray to its opposite as indicated by even/odd symbols in the figures in the fourth row. Successive points of the corresponding non-directrix solutions (31.48b) now hop across—reflect in—the origo (0, 0), as indicated by the *dashed* lines, *type* 9–12 figures. To avoid clutter, only one trajectory around the origin is shown.

The first (third) *column* with both directrix values numerically *less* (larger) than 1 evidently represents converging (diverging) *parabolic* phase portraits, and the second *column*, with either directrix value *larger* (less) than 1 gives the *hyperbolic* trajectories, as shown in Fig. 31.3, 31.4, 31.5, and 31.6.

Regarding the trajectory configurations of some *degenerate* cases, shown in Fig. 31.7, only a few comments are needed. All these trajectories refer in Fig. 31.1 to *bifurcation lines* and *points*, where certain *limiting* trajectory configurations occur—making the transition between some of the 14 types. Fig. 31.7a–j link up with Figs. 31.3, and 31.7k–l complement Fig. 31.2.

In Fig. 31.7a–c, there is, with $\mathbf{\Delta^2 = 0}$, only one directrix. The respective directrix values are 0, 1, −1. The respective directrix solutions map any of their initial values into the origin, itself, and a *period-two* alternation, cf. (31.25b).

Outside the directrix in Fig. 31.7a, every solution will for $\boldsymbol{t = 2}$ enter and remain at the *origin*. This follows from $|A| = 0$, $\operatorname{Tr} A = 0$, and $\Delta^2 = 0$, $A^2 = B^2 = 0$, (31.56–31.57), (31.9). Evidently, from any initial value, the route to the origin must always in Fig. 31.7a go through the directrix which also represents the *kernel* of the mapping (matrix) $A$.

The configurations in Fig. 31.7b–c appear from (31.40), (31.49a–2). The continuous analog to this case, ($\Delta_L^2 = 0$, $|L| = |\log A|$, $\operatorname{Tr} L = \operatorname{Tr} \log A{=}0$), cf. (31.82–31.84), is the differential equations with ($\Delta^2 = 0$, $|A| = 0$, $\operatorname{Tr} A = 0$), i.e., *either point* ($A$ and $B$) in Figs. 29.4 and 29.5 of Chap. 29. Hence, the *full-drawn lines* in Fig. 31.7b–c correspond to the *configuration* in Fig. 29.11a of Chap. 29.

With $\Delta^2 = 0$, the *non-degenerate* versions of the trajectories (not shown) from (31.49a–2) would (as in Fig. 31.7b–c) represent configurations (either monotone or reflecting in origo, cf. 1. row and 4. row figures above) similar to those shown in Fig. 29.9 of Chap. 29.

In Fig. 31.7d–i, there is with $\mathbf{\Delta^2 > 0}$ and $\mathbf{|A| = 0}$ always *one directrix (kernel)* with solution behavior as in Fig. 31.7a. The solutions on the other directrix follow immediately from the sign and size of the respective directrix values. In contrast to Fig. 31.7a, the *kernels* in Fig. 31.7d–i cannot eo ipso contain solution points starting from any initial values outside. Furthermore, in Fig. 31.7d–i, with one *zero* and one *nonzero* directrix value, it is seen from (31.39), (31.45), that *every solution,* starting outside the kernel will—from *time*, $t = 1$, and onward—be located on the other *directrix,* where they may converge, diverge, or alternate, or even alternate with period 2. The configurations in Fig. 31.7d–i and Fig. 31.7a of a *singular* system, ($|A| = 0$), of difference equations have *no analog* to the differential equations of Chap. 29. With $|\mathbf{A}| = \mathbf{0}$, the *logarithmic matrix* of Theorem 31.1 does *not exist,* and accordingly, the *solutions* are *not* among those with continuous analogs stated in Proposition 31.2. Hence, in Fig. 31.7a and d–i, there are, of course, no indications for the $\log \mathbf{A}$ matrix. But as far as the *difference equations* are concerned, it may be noted, for example, that Fig. 31.7d represents a limiting configuration, cf. Fig. 31.1, between Fig. 31.3a and d.

The situation with *two nonzero* directrix values, and at least one of them numerically equal to *one*, gives $|\log \mathbf{A}| = \mathbf{0}$, (31.84). So the straight *lines* with $|\log \mathbf{A}| = \mathbf{0}$ in Chap. 29 are *analogous* to the *hyperbolas* with $|\mathbf{A}| = \mathbf{0}$ in Figs. 29.3, 29.4, and 29.5 of Chap. 29, Sect. "Parameter Space and the Hyperconic Phase Portrait". Hence the trajectory configurations (not shown) of $|\log A| = 0$ in Fig. 31.1 correspond to the configurations exhibited in Figs. 29.7 and 29.8 of Chap. 29, Sect. "Parameter Space and the Hyperconic Phase Portrait". But, depending on the signs of the two directrix values and the actual size of the non-unit value we will see the solutions (31.39), (31.45), (31.48a–31.48d)—display monotone, either reflection in the $\alpha_1$-direction or reflection in origo—along the appropriate *parallel* straight line trajectories. An *extreme* version with directrix values $\lambda_1 = 1$, $\lambda_2 = -1$ is shown in Fig. 31.7j, where upon parallel straight lines, we have everywhere *period-2 alternations* around the stationary directrix. As to $|\log A| = 0$, see also Fig. 31.7b–c.

The *oscillations* from (31.50a) in Fig. 31.7k–l are, respectively, *nonperiodic* and of *period 4.* The trajectories on the line $\mathbf{Tr} \log \mathbf{A} = \mathbf{0}$ in Fig. 31.1 and 31.7k–l correspond to those with $\mathbf{Tr}\ \mathbf{A} = \mathbf{0}$ on the line segment $\boldsymbol{AB}$ in Figs. 31.4, 31.5, and 29.10 of Chap. 29. It is noteworthy that *closed trajectories* from difference equations are *not* tantamount to *periodic solutions,* cf. Fig. 31.7k.

Degenerate cases, as in Fig. 31.7a–j, could similarly be constructed to link up with the 12 types exhibited in Figs. 31.4, 31.5, and 31.6.

## Final Comments

The general solution and the corresponding trajectory configurations of the planar *difference* equation system (31.1a–31.1b) are rather seldom systematically presented in the literature. To obtain to a full understanding and a clear perspective on the overall implications of the *iterated* linear mapping of *phase points,* we have *embedded* the sequences and the geometry of the *phase portraits* of *discrete* linear dynamics into the *phase curves* and the relevant *hyperconic* phase portraits of well-defined *continuous* (interpolating) linear dynamic systems. The exposition of the *continuous* case in Chap. 29 always served as a standard reference to bring out fargoing parallels to the discrete case.

It may be emphasized that the interpolation of discrete linear dynamics by a continuous analog system has *no* connection with *numerical mathematics* (approximations, algorithms, discretization errors, etc.). The *embedding* referred to in this chapter is done by an *exact analog* (companion) *system*.

The merits and the factual choice between discrete- and continuous-time modeling, however, are topics beyond the scope of our discussion, which are to be the subject of further research in pure and applied mathematics.

## Appendix: The Exponential and Logarithmic Matrices of Regular Two-by-two Matrices

The exponential function is well defined for all real numbers, $y = e^x$, $x \in \mathbf{R}$, as a function with positive function values. The inverse, $x = \log y$, the logarithm, is only well defined for $y > 0$. Nevertheless, it is convenient to consider, besides the usual exponential function, also the function, $y = -e^x$, which has negative values and has the inverse $x = \log(|y|)$. In a sense, the logarithm is defined for all values, $y \in \mathbf{R} \setminus \{0\}$.

The exponential function may be expanded in a series as

$$e^x = \sum_{n=0}^{\infty} \frac{x^n}{n!}. \tag{31.101}$$

This may be used as a definition for the exponential function of a *matrix*,

$$A = \begin{bmatrix} a & b \\ c & d \end{bmatrix} \tag{31.102}$$

as

$$e^A = \sum_{n=0}^{\infty} \frac{A^n}{n!}. \tag{31.103}$$

Then, given a matrix $A$, it is natural to ask whether we could define and actually find another matrix $\boldsymbol{L} \equiv \mathbf{log}\, \boldsymbol{A}$, called the logarithm of $A$, such that

$$A = e^L \equiv e^{\log A}. \tag{31.104}$$

Even in simplest case with a diagonal matrix $A$, the existence of $L$ is not obvious. If one of the diagonal elements is zero, we might not find $L$, and if some of diagonal elements are negative, we have a problem to be resolved.

Now, if $\boldsymbol{S}$ is any complex regular matrix, then it follows from (31.103)

$$e^{S^{-1}AS} = \sum_{n=0}^{\infty} \frac{(S^{-1}AS)^n}{n!} = S^{-1} \sum_{n=0}^{\infty} \frac{A^n}{n!} S = S^{-1} e^A S. \tag{31.105}$$

Hence, by using any regular equivalent matrix $S$, we may compute $\boldsymbol{e}^{A}$ by the formula

$$e^A = S e^{S^{-1}AS} S^{-1}. \tag{31.106}$$

Thus, we should look for an appropriate choice of the transformation matrix $S$ that is convenient for the computation of $e^A$, (31.106).

Regarding the matrix (31.103), we have, cf. (31.2b), (31.15),

$$\mu = \frac{1}{2}(a+d), \qquad |A| = ad - bc, \qquad \Delta^2 = \mu^2 - |A|. \tag{31.107}$$

As usual, we shall proceed differently in the three situations: $\boldsymbol{\Delta^2 > 0}$, $\boldsymbol{\Delta^2 = 0}$, $\boldsymbol{\Delta^2 < 0}$.

*Case* $\Delta^2 > 0$. In this case, we choose the regular matrix, $b \neq 0$,

$$S = \begin{bmatrix} b & b \\ \mu - a + \Delta & \mu - a - \Delta \end{bmatrix}. \tag{31.108}$$

Then, we obtain the transformation

$$S^{-1}AS = \begin{bmatrix} \lambda_1 & 0 \\ 0 & \lambda_2 \end{bmatrix} \equiv \Lambda, \tag{31.109}$$

where, cf. (31.20–31.22), (31.33),

$$\lambda_1 = \mu + \Delta, \qquad \lambda_2 = \mu - \Delta. \tag{31.110}$$

Next, by (31.109), we simply have, for the powers

$$\Lambda^n = \begin{bmatrix} \lambda_1^n & 0 \\ 0 & \lambda_2^n \end{bmatrix}, \tag{31.111}$$

and hence by (31.103) and (31.111)

$$e^{\Lambda} = \sum_{n=0}^{\infty} \frac{1}{n!} \begin{bmatrix} \lambda_1^n & 0 \\ 0 & \lambda_2^n \end{bmatrix} = \begin{bmatrix} e^{\lambda_1} & 0 \\ 0 & e^{\lambda_2} \end{bmatrix}. \tag{31.112}$$

The diagonal elements of $\boldsymbol{e}^{\Lambda}$ are the eigenvalues of $\boldsymbol{e}^{A}$, and they are clearly positive. The eigenvectors of $e^{A}$ and $e^{\Lambda}$ are the same.

*Case* $\Delta^2 = 0$. In this case, there is a problem with the matrix (31.108), which is no longer regular. But we may replace it with the following regular matrix, $\varepsilon \neq 0$

$$S = \begin{bmatrix} b & b \\ \mu - a & \mu - a + \varepsilon \end{bmatrix}. \tag{31.113}$$

The transformation then becomes

$$S^{-1}AS = \begin{bmatrix} \mu & \varepsilon \\ 0 & \mu \end{bmatrix} \equiv \Lambda. \tag{31.114}$$

This matrix $\boldsymbol{\Lambda}$ may also be written as

$$\Lambda = \mu E + \varepsilon J, \tag{31.115}$$

where $\boldsymbol{E}$ is the unit matrix and

$$J = \begin{bmatrix} 0 & 1 \\ 0 & 0 \end{bmatrix}, \qquad J^2 = 0. \tag{31.116}$$

**Remark 31.3** Consider a matrix expression

$$C = k_1 E + k_2 M, \tag{31.117}$$

where $k_1, k_2$ are scalars, $E$ is the unit matrix, and $\boldsymbol{M}$ is any matrix. Since $\boldsymbol{k_1 E}$ commutes with every matrix, the powers of $\boldsymbol{C}$ can be calculated by the binomial theorem, i.e.,

$$C^n = (k_1 E + k_2 M)^n = \sum_{k=0}^{n} \binom{n}{k} (k_1 E)^{n-k} (k_2 M)^k = \sum_{k=0}^{n} \binom{n}{k} k_1^{n-k} k_2^k M^k. \tag{31.118}$$

With the commutative matrices in (31.117), it is well known that (31.118) and (31.103) give, cf. Perko (1993, p. 13); Hirsch and Smale (1974, p. 82)

$$\begin{aligned} e^C = \sum_{n=0}^{\infty} \frac{C^n}{n!} &= \sum_{n=0}^{\infty} \left[ \frac{1}{n!} \sum_{k=0}^{n} \frac{n!}{(n-k)!k!} (k_1 E)^{n-k} (k_2 M)^k \right] \\ = \sum_{k=0}^{\infty} \frac{(k_2 M)^k}{k!} \sum_{n=k}^{\infty} \frac{(k_1 E)^{n-k}}{(n-k)!} &= e^{k_2 M} e^{k_1 E} = e^{k_2 M} e^{k_1} = e^{k_1} e^{k_2 M}. \end{aligned} \tag{31.119}$$

▽

Using (31.118) with $M \equiv J$, (31.116), we get, for the powers of (31.115),

$$\Lambda^n = \sum_{k=0}^{n} \binom{n}{k} \mu^{n-k} \varepsilon^k J^k. \tag{31.120}$$

As $J^0 \equiv E,\ J^k = 0$ for $k \geq 2$, cf. (31.116), we get from (31.120),

$$\Lambda^n = \mu^n\ E + n\mu^{n-1}\varepsilon\ J, \tag{31.121}$$

and hence by (31.103) and (31.121)

$$\begin{aligned} e^{\Lambda} &= \sum_{n=0}^{\infty} \frac{\Lambda^n}{n!} = \sum_{n=0}^{\infty} \frac{\mu^N\ E + n\mu^{n-1}\varepsilon\ J}{n!} \\ &= e^{\mu}\ E + \varepsilon\ J \sum_{n=1}^{\infty} \frac{\mu^{n-1}}{(n-1)!} = e^{\mu}(\ E + \varepsilon\ J\ ). \end{aligned} \tag{31.122}$$

Thus, we get a matrix with only one eigenvalue, and it is again positive.

*Case* $\boldsymbol{\Delta^2 < 0}$. In this case, we may proceed as for $\Delta^2 > 0$, but here both $S$ and $\Lambda$ are complex matrices. However, we may keep the computation in *real numbers* by choosing

$$S = \begin{bmatrix} b & b \\ \mu - a + |\Delta| & \mu - a - |\Delta| \end{bmatrix}, \tag{31.123}$$

where $|\Delta| \equiv +\sqrt{|\Delta^2|} = \sqrt{-\Delta^2}$, cf. (31.16), (31.35).

Then the transformation becomes

$$S^{-1}AS = \begin{bmatrix} \mu & -|\Delta| \\ |\Delta| & \mu \end{bmatrix} \equiv \Lambda. \tag{31.124}$$

This matrix $\Lambda$ may also be written as

$$\Lambda = \mu E + |\Delta| I, \tag{31.125}$$

where

$$I = \begin{bmatrix} 0 & -1 \\ 1 & 0 \end{bmatrix}, \qquad I^2 = -E. \tag{31.126}$$

Using (31.118) with $M = I$, (31.126), we get for the powers of (31.125)

$$\Lambda^n = (\mu E + |\Delta| I)^n = \sum_{k=0}^{n} \binom{n}{k} \mu^{n-k} |\Delta|^k I^k$$
$$= \sum_{k=0}^{n} \binom{n}{2k} \mu^{n-2k} |\Delta|^{2k} (-1)^k E + \sum_{k=0}^{n} \binom{n}{2k+1} \mu^{n-2k-1} |\Delta|^{2k+1} (-1)^k I. \tag{31.127}$$

From (31.103) and (31.127), we compute the exponential matrix as

$$e^{\Lambda} = \sum_{n=0}^{\infty} \frac{\Lambda^n}{n!} = \sum_{n=0}^{\infty} \frac{1}{n!} \left[ \sum_k \binom{n}{2k} \mu^{n-2k} (-1)^k |\Delta|^{2k} E \right.$$
$$\left. + \sum_k \binom{n}{2k+1} \mu^{n-2k-1} (-1)^k |\Delta|^{2k+1} I \right]$$
$$= \sum_{k=0}^{\infty} \frac{(-1)^k |\Delta|^{2k}}{(2k)!} \sum_{n=2k}^{\infty} \frac{1}{(n-2k)!} \mu^{n-2k} E$$
$$+ \sum_{k=0}^{\infty} \frac{(-1)^k |\Delta|^{2k+1}}{(2k+1)!} \sum_{n=2k+1}^{\infty} \frac{1}{(n-2k-1)!} \mu^{n-2k-1} I$$
$$= e^{\mu} \left[ \sum_{k=0}^{\infty} \frac{(-1)^k |\Delta|^{2k}}{(2k)!} E + \sum_{k=0}^{\infty} \frac{(-1)^k |\Delta|^{2k+1}}{(2k+1)!} I \right]$$
$$= e^{\mu} \left[ \cos(|\Delta|) E + \sin(|\Delta|) I \right]. \tag{31.128}$$

The *general* series formula for the exponential matrix $e^A$, (31.103), may now in all the three cases, $\mathbf{\Delta^2 > 0}$, $\mathbf{\Delta^2 = 0}$, $\mathbf{\Delta^2 < 0}$, be replaced by a *closed-form* expression, cf. (31.106),

$$e^A = S e^{\Lambda} S^{-1}, \tag{31.129}$$

where $\boldsymbol{S}$ and $\boldsymbol{e^{\Lambda}}$ are given, respectively, by (31.108), (31.112); (31.113), (31.122); (31.123), (31.128).

The actual computation of $\boldsymbol{e^A}$ by (31.129) need not be performed here, since these *three* cases of $\boldsymbol{e^A}$ have already been *succinctly* offered in the nice *closed forms* that were presented in Chap. 29, Sect. "General Coordinate Solutions and Initial Value Problems" as $\boldsymbol{e^A = \Phi(1)}$, cf. (29.100–29.102), (29.93–29.95).

**Remark 31.4** The exponential matrix (31.129) is easily calculated by an alternative procedure (using the *Hamilton-Cayley theorem*). It follows from (31.56), (31.117), and (31.119) that

$$e^A = e^{\mu} e^B, \tag{31.130}$$

where, cf. (31.57)

$$B^{2n} = (\Delta^2)^n E, \quad B^{2n+1} = (\Delta^2)^n B, \quad n \in \mathbf{N}_0, \tag{31.131}$$

which then gives

$$e^B = \sum_{n=0}^{\infty} \frac{B^n}{n!} = \sum_{n=0}^{\infty} \frac{B^{2n}}{2n!} + \sum_{n=0}^{\infty} \frac{B^{2n+1}}{(2n+1)!} = \sum_{n=0}^{\infty} \frac{(\Delta^2)^n}{2n!} E + \sum_{n=0}^{\infty} \frac{(\Delta^2)^n}{(2n+1)!} B. \tag{31.132}$$

Then we get from (31.15–31.16), (31.132), and Selby (1973, p. 342, 472)

$$\begin{aligned} \Delta^2 > 0 : e^B &= \sum_{n=0}^{\infty} \frac{\Delta^{2n}}{2n!} E + \frac{1}{\Delta} \sum_{n=0}^{\infty} \frac{\Delta^{2n+1}}{(2n+1)!} B \\ &\equiv \cosh(\Delta) E + \frac{1}{\Delta} \sinh(\Delta) B, \end{aligned} \tag{31.133}$$

$$\begin{aligned} \Delta^2 < 0 : e^B &= \sum_{n=0}^{\infty} \frac{(-1)^n |\Delta|^{2n}}{2n!} E + \frac{1}{|\Delta|} \sum_{n=0}^{\infty} \frac{(-1)^n |\Delta|^{2n+1}}{(2n+1)!} B \\ &\equiv \cos(|\Delta|) E + \frac{1}{|\Delta|} \sin(|\Delta|) B. \end{aligned} \tag{31.134}$$

With $\Delta^2 = 0$, we immediately obtain from (31.56–31.57) and (31.103)

$$\Delta^2 = 0 : e^B = E + B. \tag{31.135}$$

Thus, by (31.130) and (31.133–31.135), the expression of $\Phi(1)$, (29.116–29.118), reappears. ▽

Regarding the *inverse problem* (31.104), the analog to (31.129)—for the required **log *A*** matrix—will presently be seen to become

$$\log A = S \log \Lambda S^{-1}, \tag{31.136}$$

where the matrix log Λ must satisfy

$$e^{\log \Lambda} \equiv \sum_{n=0}^{\infty} \frac{(\log \Lambda)^n}{n!} \equiv \Lambda \tag{31.137}$$

with Λ given, respectively, as (31.109), (31.115), and (31.125).

The formal logic of the logarithmic matrices in (31.136–31.137) is justified because it conforms with the result of the following "reverse procedure", cf. (31.129), (31.105), (31.106)

$$S\Lambda S^{-1} \equiv Se^{\log \Lambda}S^{-1} = e^{S \log \Lambda S^{-1}} \equiv e^{\log A} \equiv A. \tag{31.138}$$

Since the logarithmic matrix is seldom encountered in the literature, we shall calculate the **log *A*** matrix, (31.136), in the three cases above.

*Case* $\Delta^2 > 0$. In this case, it is easily seen from (31.109) and (31.137) that the log Λ matrix becomes

$$\log \Lambda = \begin{bmatrix} \log \lambda_1 & 0 \\ 0 & \log \lambda_2 \end{bmatrix}, \tag{31.139}$$

which is well defined if $\lambda_1$ and $\lambda_2$ are both positive. The latter then requires that the trace and the determinant of the *A* matrix are also both positive, which is here assumed, but later properly modified.

In order to facilitate subsequent calculations, we rewrite Λ, (31.109), and log Λ, (31.139), as, cf. (31.110), (31.107),

$$\Lambda = \mu E + \Delta D, \tag{31.140}$$

$$\log \Lambda = \log |A|^{1/2} E + \log \left( \frac{\mu + \Delta}{|A|^{1/2}} \right) D, \tag{31.141}$$

where the matrix *D* is

$$D = \begin{bmatrix} 1 & 0 \\ 0 & -1 \end{bmatrix}. \tag{31.142}$$

Hence from (31.136) and (31.141), we get

$$\log A = S \log \Lambda S^{-1} = \log |A|^{1/2} E + \log \left( \frac{\mu + \Delta}{|A|^{1/2}} \right) SDS^{-1}. \tag{31.143}$$

From (31.114) and (31.140), it is seen that

$$A = S\Lambda S^{-1} = \mu E + \Delta SDS^{-1}. \tag{31.144}$$

Thus, by (31.143) and (31.144), we obtain the logarithmic matrix of $A$ to be

$$\log A = \log|A|^{1/2}E + \log\left(\frac{\mu+\Delta}{|A|^{1/2}}\right)\frac{1}{\Delta}(A-\mu E). \tag{31.145}$$

*Case* $\Delta^2 = 0$. With a simple, positive eigenvalue of $A$, we get from (31.114), (31.115), and (31.137) that the log $\Lambda$ matrix must be, cf. (31.122)

$$\log\Lambda = \log(\mu E + \varepsilon J) = \begin{bmatrix} \log\mu & \frac{\varepsilon}{\mu} \\ 0 & \log\mu \end{bmatrix} = \log|\mu|E + \left(\frac{\varepsilon}{\mu}\right)J. \tag{31.146}$$

Then, from (31.136) and (31.146), it follows that

$$\log A = S\log\Lambda S^{-1} = \log\mu E + \left(\frac{\varepsilon}{\mu}\right)SJS^{-1}, \tag{31.147}$$

and, cf. (31.114–31.115)

$$A = S\Lambda S^{-1} = \mu E + \varepsilon SJS^{-1}. \tag{31.148}$$

Using here $\mu = |A|^{1/2}$, cf. (31.107), we obtain from (31.147–31.148),

$$\log A = \log|A|^{1/2}E + \frac{1}{\mu}(A-\mu E). \tag{31.149}$$

*Case* $\Delta^2 < 0$. To solve the inverse problem (31.136) in this case, we have to find the relevant log $\Lambda$ matrix, which requires only a bit more work here. With $\Lambda$ having the form (31.124–31.125), we should now look for a matrix of similar form

$$\log\Lambda = \nu E + \theta I, \tag{31.150}$$

such that, cf. (31.137), (31.128), and (31.125),

$$e^{\log\Lambda} = e^{\nu}[\cos(\theta)E + \sin(\theta)I] = \mu E + |\Delta|I = \Lambda. \tag{31.151}$$

Thus by (31.151), $\nu$ and $\theta$ must solve the equations

$$(i)\quad e^{\nu}\cos\theta = \mu, \qquad (ii)\quad e^{\nu}\sin\theta = |\Delta|, \tag{31.152}$$

which have the solutions, cf. (31.107), (31.38),

$$(i)\quad \nu = \log(\mu^2 + |\Delta|^2)^{1/2} = \log|A|^{1/2}, \qquad (ii)\quad \theta = \arccos\left(\frac{\mu}{|A|^{1/2}}\right). \tag{31.153}$$

The logarithmic matrix then becomes, cf. (31.136), (31.150), and (31.153),

$$\log A = S \log \Lambda S^{-1} = \nu E + \theta S I S^{-1}. \tag{31.154}$$

Furthermore, (31.124–31.125) imply that

$$A = S \Lambda S^{-1} = \mu E + |\Delta| S I S^{-1}. \tag{31.155}$$

Hence, we finally obtain from (31.154), (31.155), and (31.153) that

$$\log A = \log |A|^{1/2} E + \left( \frac{\arccos\left(\frac{\mu}{|A|^{1/2}}\right)}{|\Delta|} \right) (A - \mu E). \tag{31.156}$$

For $\Delta^2 \geq 0$, as mentioned above, we had in both cases, (31.139) and (31.146), a problem with possible *negative* eigenvalues. However, we may then define the $\log A$ matrix on the basis of the *absolute* eigenvalues or the *absolute* value of the *determinant* of $A$, $||A||$, cf. (31.107).

Another way to argue for such generalized definition of $\log A$ would be to consider the matrices, $A^2$ and $\Delta^2$, with squared and hence positive eigenvalues. It would then *not* be a problem to obtain $\log A^2$, and so get $\log A$ from the half of $\log A^2$, i.e., in short, cf. (31.136),

$$S^{-1} A^2 S = \Lambda^2, \quad \log A^2 = S \log \Lambda^2 S^{-1}, \quad \log A \equiv \frac{1}{2} \log A^2. \tag{31.157}$$

We will now use the *generalization* based on the *trace* and the *absolute* value of the *determinant*. Introducing the *symbol*

$$\beta = \left\{ \begin{matrix} \log \left| \frac{\mu+\Delta}{|A|^{1/2}} \right| \\ \arccos\left(\frac{\mu}{|A|^{1/2}}\right) \end{matrix} \right\} \quad \text{for} \quad \left\{ \begin{matrix} \Delta^2 > 0 \\ \Delta^2 < 0 \end{matrix} \right\}, \tag{31.158}$$

the *generalized definition* of the logarithm of the matrix (31.102) is tantamount to the computation of $\mathbf{\log A}$ as given by, cf. (31.145), (31.149), (31.156), $(\boldsymbol{\Delta} \sim |\boldsymbol{\Delta}|)$,

$$\log A = \begin{cases} \log ||A||^{\frac{1}{2}} \, E + \frac{\beta}{\Delta}(A - \mu E) \text{ for } \Delta^2 \neq 0, \\ \log |A|^{\frac{1}{2}} \, E + \frac{1}{\mu} (A - \mu E) \quad \text{for } \Delta^2 = 0. \end{cases} \tag{31.159}$$

As $\boldsymbol{\beta = \delta}$ **for** $\boldsymbol{\Delta^2 > 0}$, cf. (31.158), (31.43) and $\boldsymbol{\beta = \theta}$ **for** $\boldsymbol{\Delta^2 < 0}$, cf. (31.158), (31.38), it is evident that the *matrix* (31.159) is in *agreement* with $\mathbf{\log A}$, as stated in (31.79–31.81) of Theorem 31.1.

# BIBLIOGRAPHY

Batchelder PM (1967) An Introduction to Linear Difference Equations. Dover Publications, New York, Harvard University Press, 1927

Baumol WJ (1958) Topology of Second Order Linear Difference Equations with Contant Coefficients. Econometrica 26:258–285

Bellman R, Cooke KL (1963) Differential–Difference Equations. Academic Press, New York

Boole G (1958) Calculus of Finite Differences, 4th edn. Chelsea Publishing Company, New York, (MacMillan, London, 1860)

Brand L (1955) A Sequence Defined by a Difference Equation. American Math Month 62:489–92

Brauer F, Nohel JA (1969) The Qualitative Theory of Ordinary Differential Equations. Dover Publications, New York

Cesari L (1963) Asymptotic Behavior and Stability Problems in Ordinary Differential Equations, 2nd edn. Academic Press, New York, Springer–Verlag, Berlin, 1959

Chiang AC (1984) Fundamental Methods of Mathematical Economics, 3rd edn. McGraw–Hill, New York

Cogan EJ, Norman RZ (1963) Handbook of Calculus, Difference and Differential Equations, 2nd edn. Prentice–Hall, New Jersey

Fort T (1948) Finite Differences and Difference Equations in the Real Domain. Clarendon Press, Oxford

Gandolfo G (1980) Economic Dynamics: Methods and Models, 2nd edn. North–Holland, Amsterdam

Goldberg S (1986) Introduction to Difference Equations. Dover Publications, New York, John Wiley and Sons, 1958

Guckenheimer J, Holmes P (1986) Nonlinear Oscillations, Dynamical Systems, and Bifurcations of Vector Fields. Springer–Verlag, New York

Hirsch MW, Smale S (1974) Differential Equations, Dynamical Systems and Linear Algebra. Academic Press, New York

Jordan C (1965) Calculus of Finite Differences, 3rd edn. Chelsea Publishing Company, New York

Markoff AA (1896) Differenzenrechnung. B.G. Teubner, Leipzig

Miller KS (1960) An Introduction to the Calculus of Finite Differences and Difference Equations. Henry Holt and Company, New York

Miller KS (1968) Linear Difference Equations. W.A. Benjamin Inc., New York

Nörlund NE (1910) Bidrag til de Lineære Differensligningers Theori, V. Thanning & Appel, København

Nörlund NE (1929) Leçons sur les Équations Linéaires aux Différences Finies. Gauthier–Villars, Paris

Nörlund NE (1954) Vorlesungen Über Differenzenrechnung. Chelsea Publishing Company, New York, Verlag von Julius Springer, Berlin, 1924

Perko L (1993) Differential Equations and Dynamical Systems. Springer–Verlag, New York

Selby SM (1973) Standard Mathematical Tables, 21st edn. The Chemical Rubber Co, Cleveland, Ohio

Wold H (1959) Ends and Means in Econometric Model Building. pp 355–434, in *Probability and Statistics: The Harold Cramér Volume,* Grenander, U. (ed.), John Wiley and Sons, New York.

CHAPTER 32

# Hopf Bifurcation, Trends, Cycles, Square Waves, and Chaos

## INTRODUCTION

Time delays (time lags) in production/capital utilization and accumulation dynamics were introduced into basic aggregate growth models by Zhu and Huang (2003). Using a CD production function (Inada conditions), they performed a *global analysis* of the delay differential ("mixed difference-differential") equation. They showed that for sufficiently *small delays*, the *steady-state* solution (equilibrium) is *globally stable*; but the steady-state solution of the capital-labor ratio loses this global stability property, when the *delay (time lag)* is above a certain *critical value (length)*. Furthermore, they show that for *certain values* of the time delay, *all* solutions persistently *oscillate* (but not necessarily strictly periodic).

The *purpose* of the present chapter is—with CD and for particular CES technologies—to complement this global dynamic analysis by performing a *nonlinear, local analysis* of the dynamics of the delay (time lag) model, when the size of the time delay (lag) is close to the critical value. We show that for this *critical delay* value, a *Hopf bifurcation* (of a fixed point into a closed orbit in a neighborhood of the equilibrium) occurs, i.e., *periodic solutions* ("limit cycles") are created, when the steady-state solution (equilibrium) of the capital-labor ratio loses its local stability. We also derive an analytical expression, which determines the *stability* type (*supercritical* or *subcritical*) of the periodic solutions ("limit cycles"). Finally, we show that the delay model with CES

With co-author:
MORTEN BRØNS, Department of Mathematics and Computer Science, Technical University of Denmark, Denmark

 
B. S. Jensen, *The Elements and Dynamic Systems of Economic Growth and Trade Models*, https://doi.org/10.1007/978-3-031-52493-6_32

can exhibit dynamics with *solutions*, which have previously been observed in other (electrodynamic,engineering), delay differential equations, namely: *square waves* and *chaos* (aperiodic waves/cycles).

Economic models of business cycles [as recurrent fluctuations (upswing/downswing) in economic activity] have a long tradition as a specialized branch of economic theory with many hypotheses or paradigms exhibited. However, regarding their dynamic properties, it is worth emphasizing as done by Gabisch and Lorenz (1987, p. 3) that: "Whether or not a dynamic model of an economy is a business cycle model, i.e. a model which allows for fluctuations of major economic variables for a considerable amount of time, does not depend on the general motivated and paradigmatic features of a model, but rather on its mathematical structure. While, e.g. the introduction of a certain *lag-structure* in the *production function* can certainly not be a distinctive mark from an economic point of view, this structure may be the essential dynamic structure which allows for oscillatory motions of an economy. Therefore, this text will concentrate on those features of dynamic economic models which constitute the *essential fluctuation-generating forces*". It is the nature and *consequences* of these *delays (time lags)* that our theorem and solutions will demonstrate. The relevance and proper interpretation of all economic time lags (duration of delays) will depend on the time units (period) of measurement (year, quarter, month, day) for the economic variables. The delays/lags are not necessarily equal to integers of any time units. Treating economic variables as *continuous-time processes*, the actual occurring *delays* in such dynamic models can be studied for *any length* (real number). Often an analytical dilemma arises in economic dynamics, as noted by Goodwin (1990, p. 1): "There are two broad types of dynamical equation systems: continuous time and discrete time; both have frequently been in economics. The latter arises because there are significant *time-lags* in an economy. The trouble is that these occur in the context of *economic activity* which is substantially *continuous*, so that one should formulate *mixed difference-differential* systems, a procedure the complications of which place it beyond the scope of this book". We will face the complications, but also see the advantages of a rigorous approach to delay issues allowed by using the mixed dynamic system in continuous time.

## Dynamics of Growth and Cycles

Let us briefly review the derivation of the dynamics for the capital-labor ratio in growth models with time delays. The starting point is the neoclassical economic growth model,

$$\dot{L} = nL, \quad \dot{K} = sY(t) = sF(L, K) = sLF(1, k) \equiv Ls\gamma f(k);$$
$$k(t) = K(t)/L(t). \tag{32.1}$$

where $K$ is capital, $L$ is labor, and $n$ and $s$ are standard parameters ($n > 0$, $0 < s < 1$).

The production function $F$ is homogeneous of degree one; the *TPF* ("total factor productivity") *parameter* ($\gamma$) of $F$ is here *explicitly* specified together with the saving (investment) parameter ($s$), as this is a practical procedure in numerical simulations below, cf. (32.7).

The growth model is then modified to include a delay (time lag) $\tau$ in the productive operation (utilization) of installed (acquired) capital (machinery),

$$\dot{L} = nL, \quad \dot{K} = sY(t) = sF(L, K_\tau); \quad K_\tau = K(t-\tau) \tag{32.2}$$

with the standard notation $K_\tau = K(t-\tau)$.

From (32.2), we obtain the time derivative of $k(t) = K(t)/L(t)$ as,

$$\begin{aligned} \dot{k} &= \frac{L\dot{K} - K\dot{L}}{L^2} = \frac{sF(L, K_\tau)}{L} - n\frac{K}{L} = sF\left(1, \frac{K_\tau}{L}\right) - nk \\ &= s\gamma f\left(\frac{K_\tau}{L_\tau}\frac{L_\tau}{L}\right) - nk = s\gamma f\left(k_\tau \frac{L_0 e^{n(t-\tau)}}{L_0 e^{nt}}\right) - nk \\ &= s\gamma f(e^{-n\tau}k_\tau) - nk; \quad k_\tau \equiv K_\tau/L_\tau = K(t-\tau)/L(t-\tau) \end{aligned} \tag{32.3}$$

i.e.,

$$\dot{k} = s\gamma f(e^{-n\tau}k_\tau) - nk. \tag{32.4}$$

The delay model (32.4) may be combined with *depreciation* of the productively operating capital stock (same time lag, delay, $\tau$) to obtain the basic delay model, cf. Zhu and Huang (2003),

$$\dot{k} = s\gamma f(e^{-n\tau}k_\tau) - \delta k_\tau - nk. \tag{32.5}$$

For the mathematical analysis, it is convenient to introduce a new variable

$$q = e^{-n\tau}k = K_\tau/L; \qquad q_\tau = q(t-\tau) = e^{-n\tau}k_\tau = e^{-n\tau}(K_\tau/L_\tau) \tag{32.6}$$

which implies that the *standard* economic growth *model* with *delay* (32.5) becomes

$$\dot{q} = e^{-n\tau}\dot{k} = \beta f(q_\tau) - \delta q_\tau - nq \equiv h(q, q_\tau); \qquad \beta = s\gamma e^{-n\tau}. \tag{32.7}$$

The family of solutions $q(t)$ to (32.7) will generally display more oscillatory time path rather than the monotonicity usually seen with $\tau = 0$.

## Hopf Bifurcation Analysis

We will first assume that there exists an equilibrium (steady-state) solution, $q^*$, to (32.7):

$$\forall t \;\; q(t) = q^* = q^*_\tau = q^*(t-\tau) = e^{-n\tau}k^* = e^{-n\tau}k^*_\tau = e^{-n\tau}k^*(t-\tau) \qquad (32.8)$$

satisfying

$$\dot{q} = h(q^*, q^*) = \beta f(q^*) - (\delta + n)q^* = 0. \qquad (32.9)$$

It will be convenient to introduce the variable $z$ (*deviation* of $q$ from the equilibrium),

$$z = q - q^*; \qquad z_\tau = z(t-\tau) = q_\tau - q^* = q(t-\tau) - q^*; \qquad z = 0 \Leftrightarrow z_\tau = 0 \qquad (32.10)$$

We next assume that $f$, (32.7), is *analytic* (can be expanded as Taylor series), and as our dynamic analysis will be local, we will make up to a cubic/third-order Taylor expansion of $h$, (32.7), at the equilibrium ($z = 0$), to explicitly obtain the *parametrized dynamics*:

$$\dot{z} = h(q^* + z, q^* + z_\tau) = A_0 z + A_1 z_\tau + \frac{A_2}{2} z_\tau^2 + \frac{A_3}{6} z_\tau^3 + O\left(z_\tau^4\right) \qquad (32.11)$$

where the Taylor coefficients are,

$$A_0 = \frac{\partial h}{\partial q}(q^*, q^*) = -n, \qquad A_1 = \frac{\partial h}{\partial q_\tau}(q^*, q^*) = \beta f'(q^*) - \delta,$$

$$(32.12)$$

$$A_2 = \frac{\partial^2 h}{\partial q_\tau^2}(q^*, q^*) = \beta f''(q^*), \qquad A_3 = \frac{\partial^3 h}{\partial q_\tau^3}(q^*, q^*) = \beta f'''(q^*).$$

The basic properties and results are summarized in:

**Theorem 32.1** *Assume that $f$, (32.7), is analytic, and assume the existence of a steady-state (equilibrium) solution $q^*$, (32.9), i.e.*

$$h(q^*, q^*) \;\; = \;\; \beta f(q^*) - (\delta + n)q^* = 0. \qquad (32.13)$$

*If the ratio ($R$) of the first-order Taylor coefficients satisfies the condition,*

$$|R| = |A_0/A_1| = \left| \frac{-n}{\beta f'(q^*) - \delta} \right| < 1 \qquad (32.14)$$

*then there exists a critical delay (time lag), $\tau_0$, given by,*

$$\tau_0 = \frac{\arccos(R)}{\omega_0} = \frac{\arccos(-A_0/A_1)}{|A_1|\,[1-(A_0/A_1)^2]^{\frac{1}{2}}} = \frac{\arccos(-A_0/A_1)}{[A_1^2 - A_0^2]^{\frac{1}{2}}} = \frac{\arccos\left(\frac{n}{\beta f'(q^*)-\delta}\right)}{[(\beta f'(q^*)-\delta)^2 - n^2]^{\frac{1}{2}}} \tag{32.15}$$

*such that steady-state $q^*$, (32.13), is asymptotically stable for $\tau < \tau_0$, and unstable for $\tau > \tau_0$. Corresponding to $\tau_0$, (32.15), and the periodic solution of linearization of (32.11), its angular velocity, $\omega_0$, and period, $T_0$, are given by,*

$$\omega_0 = \left[A_1^2 - A_0^2\right]^{\frac{1}{2}}\ ; \qquad T_0 = 2\pi/\omega_0 = 1/\nu_0 \quad (\nu_0 : frequency) \tag{32.16}$$

*Furthermore, a family of small-amplitude periodic solutions bifurcates from the steady state, $q^*$, (32.13). The periodic solutions (limit cycles) exist for delays $\tau$ in an interval, either to the left or to the right of $\tau_0$.*

*The important qualitative properties of the periodic solutions (limit cycles) are determined by the sign and the numerical value of a number (cubic expansion parameter), $\tau_2$, given by*

$$\tau_2 = \frac{1}{8\,\omega_0^2}\left[\frac{2 - A_1\tau_0\,[2\,R^2 + 6\,R - 11] + R\,[4\,R\,(1+R) - 13]}{A_1\,(1+R)\,(5-4\,R)}A_2^2 - (A_1\tau_0 - R)A_3\right]$$

$$= \frac{1}{8}\,\frac{2 - A_1\tau_0\,[2(A_0/A_1)^2 + 6(A_0/A_1) - 11] + (A_0/A_1)\,[4(A_0/A_1)(1+(A_0/A_1)) - 13]}{A_1^3\,[1-(A_0/A_1)^2][1+(A_0/A_1)]\,[5-4(A_0/A_1)]}A_2^2 - \frac{1}{8}\,\frac{A_1\tau_0 - (A_0/A_1)}{A_1^2\,[1-(A_0/A_1)^2]}A_3. \tag{32.17}$$

*If $\tau_2 > 0$, the limit cycles existing for $\tau > \tau_0$ (supercritical) are stable/attractive;*
*if $\tau_2 < 0$, the limit cycles existing for $\tau < \tau_0$ (subcritical) are unstable/repulsive.*

*The period $T_2$ of the limit cycles is given by*

$$T_2 = \frac{2\pi}{\omega_0}\left(1 + \frac{\omega_2}{\omega_0\tau_2}[\tau - \tau_0]\right)O([\tau-\tau_0]^2) \tag{32.18}$$

*where*

$$\omega_2 = \frac{-1}{8\,\omega_0}\left[\frac{2\,R^2+6\,R-11}{(1+R)(5-4\,R)}A_2^2 + A_1A_3\right] \tag{32.19}$$

*The absolute/numerical value of $\tau_2$ tells how fast the amplitude $\epsilon$ of the limit cycles grows with the size of the delay deviation : $\tau - \tau_0$; amplitude $\epsilon$ of the limit cycle is given by,*

$$\epsilon = \sqrt{\frac{\tau - \tau_0}{\tau_2}} + O(\tau - \tau_0). \tag{32.20}$$

*The smaller $\tau_2$, the quicker the amplitude grows according to (32.20). In the untypical case $\tau_2 = 0$, the computations must be continued to higher order than three in (32.11)*

***Proof*** The stability of the equilibrium $z = 0$ of (32.11) can be determined by the linearization

$$\dot{z} = A_0 z + A_1 z_\tau \tag{32.21}$$

Solutions of this *linear* delay differential equation (32.21) have the complex form

$$z = Ce^{(\alpha+i\omega)t} = Ce^{\alpha t}(\cos\omega t + i\sin\omega t). \tag{32.22}$$

If all solutions have $\alpha < 0$, then the equilibrium $z = 0$ is stable, while it is unstable if there are solutions with $\alpha > 0$. Hence, a change of stability occurs at a value $\tau_0$ of the delay when there are solutions $z = Ce^{i\omega_0 t}$. Inserting such a solution, and taking real and imaginary parts yields

$$0 = A_0 + A_1\cos\omega_0\tau_0, \qquad \omega_0 = -A_1\sin\omega_0\tau_0. \tag{32.23}$$

which gives,

$$\cos\omega_0\tau_0 = -A_0/A_1, \qquad \sin\omega_0\tau_0 = -\frac{\omega_0}{A_1}. \tag{32.24}$$

Then squaring and adding yields a *critical angular velocity* (angular frequency), $\omega_0$, as

$$\omega_0 = \sqrt{A_1^2 - A_0^2} = |A_1|\,[1-(A_0/A_1)^2]^{\frac{1}{2}}, \tag{32.25}$$

Hence a *critical delay* (time lag) $\tau_0$ exists, cf. (32.24), (32.25),

$$\tau_0 = \frac{1}{\omega_0} \arccos(-A_0/A_1) = \frac{\arccos(-A_0/A_1)}{|A_1| \, [1 - (A_0/A_1)^2]^{\frac{1}{2}}} \tag{32.26}$$

*if*

$$|A_0/A_1| < 1. \tag{32.27}$$

Inserting the Taylor coefficient expressions (32.12) in (32.27) and (32.26) establishes (32.14) and (32.15).

At $\tau = \tau_0$, where the *local dynamics* changes—from exponential decay toward the equilibrium to the existence of exponentially growing solutions—the *linearized* delay differential equation (32.21) had periodic solutions with the *period*:

$$T_0 = \frac{2\pi}{\omega_0} = 1/\nu_0 \qquad (\nu_0 : \mathit{frequency}). \tag{32.28}$$

This indicates the *existence* of periodic solutions (*limit cycles*) for the *full nonlinear* delay differential equation (32.11) for delays $\tau$, close to $\tau_0$. In fact, the Hopf bifurcation theorem states that small amplitude periodic solutions do indeed exist (Diekmann et al. 1995; Guckenheimer and Holmes 1983). We proceed to look for these period solutions (limit cycles) following Morris (1976). Since the period cannot be expected to be exactly given by (32.28) for all $\tau$, the exact determination/computation of the period ($T$), (or angular velocity, $\omega$), is an important part of our task.

We now introduce a *scaled time* variable

$$\theta \quad = \quad \omega t \tag{32.29}$$

where $\omega$ is a parameter/constant close to the *critical* angular velocity, $\omega_0$. This transforms (32.11) into

$$\omega \, z' \quad = \quad A_0 z + A_1 z_{\omega\tau} + \frac{A_2}{2} z_{\omega\tau}^2 + \frac{A_3}{6} z_{\omega\tau}^3 + O\left(z_{\omega\tau}^4\right), \tag{32.30}$$

where $z' = \partial z/\partial\theta$. The coefficients $A_i$, $1 = 0, ..3$, are here the same as in (32.12). In (32.30) we will look for $2\pi$*-periodic solutions*, and determine the parameter $\omega = \omega(\tau)$ as we go along such that they have period $2\pi$.

Let $\epsilon$ be some *measure* of the *amplitude* of a *periodic* solution

$$z \quad = \quad z(\theta, \epsilon) \tag{32.31}$$

We expand the periodic solution in a Taylor series of the amplitude $\epsilon$,

$$z(\theta, \epsilon) = z^{(1)}(\theta)\epsilon + z^{(2)}(\theta)\epsilon^2 + z^{(3)}(\theta)\epsilon^3 + \ldots, \quad (32.32)$$

where

$$z^{(n)}(\theta) = \frac{1}{n!}\frac{\partial^n z}{\partial \epsilon^n}(\theta, 0) \quad (32.33)$$

and correspondingly expand $\omega$ and the delay $\tau$ at $\omega_0$, $\tau_0$, where the oscillation is initiated

$$\omega = \omega_0 + \omega_1\epsilon + \omega_2\epsilon^2 + \ldots, \quad (32.34)$$

$$\tau = \tau_0 + \tau_1\epsilon + \tau_2\epsilon^2 + \ldots. \quad (32.35)$$

Inserting these expansions in (32.30), we collect terms of the *same order* in $\epsilon$, and set each of the terms in the resulting power series equal to zero.

To *order* $\epsilon^1$, we get, ( $z^{(1)'} = \partial^2 z(\theta, 0)/\partial\epsilon\partial\theta$; $z^{(1)}_{\omega_0\tau_0} = z^{(1)}(\theta - \omega_0\tau_0)$ )

$$\omega_0 z^{(1)'} - A_0 z^{(1)} - A_1 z^{(1)}_{\omega_0\tau_0} = 0. \quad (32.36)$$

When ($\omega_0$, $\tau_0$) fulfill (32.24), the *complete solution* of (32.36) is,

$$z^{(1)}(\theta) = a\cos\theta + b\sin\theta. \quad (32.37)$$

We can fix the measure $\epsilon$ of the amplitude by picking the *initial conditions*: $z(0) = \epsilon$, $z'(0) = 0$, which gives

$$z^{(1)}(0) = 0, \quad z^{(1)'}(0) = 1, \quad z^{(j)}(0) = 0, \quad z^{(j)}(0) = 0 \text{ for } j \geq 2. \quad (32.38)$$

With this, we get

$$z^{(1)}(\theta) = \sin\theta. \quad (32.39)$$

Proceeding to *order* $\epsilon^2$, we get the equation

$$\omega_0 z^{(2)'} - A_0 z^{(2)} - A_1 z^{(2)}_{\omega_0\tau_0} = \omega_1 z^{(1)'} - A_1(\omega_0\tau_1 + \omega_1\tau_0) z^{(1)'}_{\omega_0\tau_0} + \frac{A_2}{2}\left(z^{(1)'}_{\omega_0\tau_0}\right)^2. \quad (32.40)$$

With the solution for $z^{(1)}$ from (32.39), then (32.40) can be rewritten as

$$\begin{aligned}&\omega_0 z^{(2)\prime} - A_0 z^{(2)} - A_1 z^{(2)}_{\omega_0\tau_0}\\&= \frac{1}{4}A_2\omega_0^2 + [-\omega_1 + A_0(\omega_1\tau_0 + \omega_0\tau_1)]\cos\theta + \omega_0(\omega_1\tau_0 + \omega_0\tau_1)\sin\theta\\&+ \frac{1}{4}\frac{A_2}{A_1^2}\left[(\omega_0^2 - A_0^2)\cos 2\theta + 2A_0\omega_0\sin 2\theta\right].\end{aligned} \tag{32.41}$$

The homogeneous part of this inhomogeneous linear equation is identical to the equation for $z^{(1)}$. Hence, the solution to the homogeneous equation is resonant with the $\sin\theta$ and $\cos\theta$ terms on the right hand side, and will give rise to *nonperiodic* solutions.

To obtain periodic solutions of *period* $2\pi$, we must require that the *resonant terms vanish*, i.e.

$$(-\omega_1 + A_0(\omega_1\tau_0 + \omega_0\tau_1)) = 0, \qquad \omega_0(\omega_1\tau_0 + \omega_0\tau_1) = 0. \tag{32.42}$$

These are linear equations in $\tau_1, \omega_1$, with solution

$$\tau_1 = 0, \qquad \omega_1 = 0. \tag{32.43}$$

With (32.43), we can find a *periodic solution* of (32.41) of the form

$$z^{(2)}(\theta) = a_0 + a_1\cos\theta + b_1\sin\theta + a_2\cos 2\theta + b_2\sin 2\theta. \tag{32.44}$$

By insertion in (32.41) and the initial conditions (32.38). The result is

$$a_0 = \frac{A_2}{4(A_0 + A_1)}, \tag{32.45}$$

$$a_1 = \frac{A_2(2A_1 - A_0)(A_1 - A_0)}{2A_1(A_1 + A_0)(5A_1 - 4A_0)}, \tag{32.46}$$

$$b_1 = \frac{A_2\omega_0(A_1 - A_0)}{2A_1(A_1 + A_0)(5A_1 - 4A_0)}, \tag{32.47}$$

$$a_2 = \frac{A_2(A_1^2 - 2A_0^2 + 2A_1A_0)}{2A_1(A_1 + A_0)(5A_1 - 4A_0)}, \tag{32.48}$$

$$b_2 = \frac{A_2\omega_0(A_1 - A_0)}{2A_1(A_1 + A_0)(5A_1 - 4A_0)}, \tag{32.49}$$

Finally turning to *order* $\epsilon^3$, we obtain

$$\omega_0 z^{(3)'} - A_0 z^{(3)} - A_1 z^{(3)}_{\omega_0\tau_0} = -\omega_2 z^{(1)'} - A_1(\omega_0\tau_2 + \omega_2\tau_0) z^{(1)'}_{\omega_0\tau_0} + A_2 z^{(1)}_{\omega_0\tau_0} z^{(2)}_{\omega_0\tau_0} + \tfrac{A_3}{6}\left(z^{(1)'}_{\omega_0\tau_0}\right)^3. \quad (32.50)$$

From the previous calculations, the right hand side is known. It has the form of a trigonometric polynomial,

$$u_0 + u_1 \cos\theta + v_1 \sin\theta + u_2 \cos 2\theta + v_2 \sin 2\theta + u_3 \cos 3\theta + v_3 \sin 3\theta. \quad (32.51)$$

The expressions for the coefficients are long and complicated. We are only interested in $u_1$ and $v_1$, as they multiply the resonant terms, which must be zero to allow periodic solutions. Thus one obtains,

$$u_1 = A_0\omega_0\tau_2 + (\tau_0 A_0 - 1)\omega_2 + \frac{\omega_0(-11A_1^2A_2^2 + 4A_1A_0A_2^2 - 4A_1A_0^2A_3 + A_1^2A_0A_3 + 5A_1^3A_3 + 4A_0^2A_2^2)}{8A_1^2(A_1 + A_0)(5A_1 - 4A_0)}, \quad (32.52)$$

$$v_1 = \omega_0^2\tau_2 + \omega_0\tau_0\omega_2 + \frac{4A_1A_0^2A_2^2 + 4A_0^3A_2^2 - 4A_1A_0^3A_3 + A_1^2A_0^2A_3 + 5A_1^3A_0A_3 + 2A_1^3A_2^2 - 13A_1^2A_0A_2^2}{8A_1^2(A_1 + A_0)(5A_1 - 4A_0)}. \quad (32.53)$$

Solving the equations $u_1 = 0$, $v_1 = 0$, one obtains $\tau_2$, (32.17) and $\omega_2$, (32.19), after simplifications using (32.14), (32.15), and (32.16).

Solving (32.35) for $\epsilon$ yields (32.20). The amplitude is only defined, when $\tau - \tau_0$ has the same sign as $\tau_2$; hence the periodic solutions exist only on one side of $\tau_0$, as described in the Theorem 32.1.

Inserting (32.20) in (32.34) yields

$$\omega = \omega_0 + \frac{\omega_2}{\tau_2}[\tau - \tau_0] + O([\tau - \tau_0]^2). \quad (32.54)$$

In the original time variable the period is $T = 2\pi/\omega$. Inserting (32.54) in the latter expression for $T$ and making a Taylor expansion in $\tau - \tau_0$ finally gives (32.18).

We omit the proof of the final statement of the theorem, concerning stability of the periodic solutions. The result is a standard property of the Hopf bifurcation, see e.g. Diekmann et al. (1995); Guckenheimer and Holmes (1983). □

The sign of $\tau_2$ gives important qualitative information about the periodic solution. Furthermore, the absolute value of $\tau_2$ tells how fast the amplitude of the periodic solutions grows with $\tau - \tau_0$. The smaller $\tau_2$, the quicker the amplitude grows according to (32.20). In the untypical case $\tau_2 = 0$, the computations must be continued to higher order.

The expression (32.17) for $\tau_2$ is complicated, and no direct interpretation in economic terms seems to be possible. In particular, it depends on both second and third derivatives of $f$, so convexity properties alone are not sufficient to determine $\tau_2$. Hence, one must turn to concrete computations as we do now for specific illustrative examples.

## The CD Technology and Time Delays

We apply Theorem 32.1 to the Eq. (32.7) with a Cobb-Douglas (CD) production function

$$F(L, K) = \gamma L^{1-a} K^a = L\gamma f(k) \equiv L\gamma k^a;\ 0 < a < 1 \tag{32.55}$$

$$\begin{aligned} f(q) &= q^a = (e^{-n\tau}k)^a\ ; \\ f'(q) &= aq^{a-1}, \\ f''(q) &= a(a-1)q^{a-2}, \\ f'''(q) &= a(a-1)(a-2)q^{a-3} \end{aligned} \tag{32.56}$$

The Eq. (32.13) has a unique steady-state (equilibrium), cf. (32.56), (32.8), (32.7),

$$q^* = \left[\frac{\beta}{n+\delta}\right]^{\frac{1}{1-a}} = \left[\frac{s\gamma}{n+\delta}\right]^{\frac{1}{1-a}} e^{\frac{-n\tau}{1-a}} = \kappa\, e^{\frac{-n\tau}{1-a}};\ k^* = q^* e^{n\tau} = \kappa\, e^{\frac{-an\tau}{1-a}};$$
$$\kappa = q^* e^{\frac{n\tau}{1-a}} \tag{32.57}$$

From the simple exact CD expressions, (32.57), we should note the *general inequalities*:

$$q^* < k^* < \kappa \tag{32.58}$$

Next we find with (32.12), (32.56), (32.57),

$$A_0 = -n, \tag{32.59}$$

$$A_1 = a(n+\delta) - \delta, \tag{32.60}$$

$$A_2 = \beta \left[\frac{\beta}{n+\delta}\right]^{\frac{a-2}{1-a}} a(a-1), \tag{32.61}$$

$$A_3 = \lambda_\beta \left[\frac{\beta}{n+\delta}\right]^{\frac{a-3}{1-a}} a(a-1)(a-2) \tag{32.62}$$

The bifurcation condition (32.14) becomes

$$|A_0/A_1| = \left|\frac{-n}{a(n+\delta)-\delta}\right| < 1 \Leftrightarrow n/\delta < \frac{1-a}{1+a} < 1 \tag{32.63}$$

Hence a *Hopf bifurcation* to periodic solutions can occur only, when the *depreciation* parameter $\delta$ is sufficiently large. In particular, when delay of the depreciation of the capital is omitted, corresponding to $\delta = 0$, the bifurcation condition is not fulfilled.

Thus, with $\delta = 0$, the steady-state is asymptotically *stable* for *all delays* $\tau$. This is in agreement with the results from Zhu and Huang (2003), where it is even shown that the steady-state/equilibrium is *globally* attracting.

Returning to situations where (32.63) is fulfilled, the bifurcation analysis can be applied. We find—according to Theorem 32.1—the *exact* critical delay $\tau_0$ as,

$$\tau_0 = \frac{\arccos(-A_0/A_1)}{|A_1|\,[1-(A_0/A_1)^2]^{\frac{1}{2}}} = \frac{\arccos\left(\frac{n}{a(n+\delta)-\delta}\right)}{|a(n+\delta)-\delta|\,[1-(\frac{n}{a(n+\delta)-\delta})^2]^{\frac{1}{2}}} \tag{32.64}$$

and the *exact* cubic expansion parameter as,

$$\tau_2 = \frac{1}{8\,\omega_0^2}\left[\frac{2 - A_1\tau_0\,[2\,R^2+6\,R-11] + R\,[4\,R\,(1+R)-13]}{A_1\,(1+R)\,(5-4\,R)}\,A_2^2\right.$$
$$\left. - (A_1\tau_0 - R)A_3\right] = \frac{1}{8[(a(n+\delta)-\delta)^2-n^2]}$$
$$\times\left[\left[2-(a(n+\delta)-\delta)\tau_0\left[2\left(\frac{-n}{a(n+\delta)-\delta}\right)^2+6\left(\frac{-n}{a(n+\delta)-\delta}\right)-11\right]\right.\right.$$
$$\left.\left. + \left(\frac{-n}{a(n+\delta)-\delta}\right)\left[4\left(\frac{-n}{a(n+\delta)-\delta}\right)\left(1+\frac{-n}{a(n+\delta)-\delta}\right)-13\right]\right]\right.$$

$$\times \frac{\left(\beta \left[\frac{\beta}{n+\delta}\right]^{\frac{a-2}{1-a}} a(a-1)\right)^2}{[a(n+\delta)-\delta][1+\frac{-n}{a(n+\delta)-\delta}][5-4(\frac{-n}{a(n+\delta)-\delta})]}$$
$$-\left[(a(n+\delta)-\delta)\,\tau_0 - \frac{-n}{a(n+\delta)-\delta}\right]\left[\beta\left[\frac{\beta}{n+\delta}\right]^{\frac{a-3}{1-a}} a(a-1)(a-2)\right]\Bigg]. \tag{32.65}$$

A general determination of the sign of $\tau_2$ as a function of the parameters is a huge task, and for specific applications a numerical computation is needed. However, special cases may be analyzed in full. As an example, we now consider the limit of small $a$. Using Taylor's theorem, the critical length of the delay becomes,

$$\tau_0 = \frac{\arccos(-A_0/A_1)}{|A_1|\,[1-(A_0/A_1)^2]^{\frac{1}{2}}} = \frac{\arccos(-n/\delta)}{|\delta|\,[(1-(n/\delta)^2]^{\frac{1}{2}}} + O(a) \tag{32.66}$$

The *cubic* expansion parameter similarly becomes,

$$\tau_2 = \frac{[(1/\beta)(1+n/\delta)]^2(n+\tau_0\delta^2)}{4(1-n/\delta)}\,a + O(a^2). \tag{32.67}$$

We note that $\tau_2 \to 0$ for $a \to 0$. As $n/\delta < 1$ follows from (32.63), each of the terms in the coefficient of $a$, (32.67) is positive, i.e. $\tau_2$ is *positive*. Hence the *Hopf bifurcation* is *supercritical.*

## THE CES TECHNOLOGY AND TIME DELAYS

Next we study the Hopf bifurcation of (32.7) with,

$$F(L,K) = \gamma\left[(1-a)L^{(\sigma-1)/\sigma} + aK^{(\sigma-1)/\sigma}\right]^{\sigma/(\sigma-1)};\ 0<a<1, \sigma>0, \sigma\neq 1 \tag{32.68}$$

$$f(k) \quad = \quad \left[(1-a) + ak^{(\sigma-1)/\sigma}\right]^{\sigma/(\sigma-1)}. \tag{32.69}$$

Solving (32.13) with (32.69), one obtains the unique steady-state, cf. (32.57), (32.58),

$$q^* = \left[\frac{1}{1-a}\left(\left[\frac{\beta}{n+\delta}\right]^{\frac{1-\sigma}{\sigma}} - a\right)\right]^{\frac{\sigma}{1-\sigma}};\ q^* < k^* < \kappa\ (\tau = 0) \tag{32.70}$$

which *economically* exists when the parameters satisfy,

$$\frac{1}{a}\left(\frac{\beta}{n+\delta}\right)^{(1-\sigma)/\sigma} > 1. \tag{32.71}$$

The bifurcation condition (32.14) is

$$|A_0/A_1| = \left|\frac{-n}{\beta^{(\sigma-1)/\sigma}(n+\delta)^{1/\sigma}a-\delta}\right| < 1. \tag{32.72}$$

Also for the CES production function, a *delay* in the capital stock *depreciation* is needed to obtain a critical/bifurcation time delay.

For $\delta = 0$ the economic condition for existence of a steady state (32.71) is

$$\frac{1}{a}\left(\frac{\beta}{n}\right)^{(1-\sigma)/\sigma} > 1. \tag{32.73}$$

But for $\delta = 0$ the bifurcation condition (32.72) is

$$\frac{1}{a}\left(\frac{\beta}{n}\right)^{(1-\sigma)/\sigma} < 1 \tag{32.74}$$

Evidently, both cannot be satisfied simultaneously. The general expressions for $\tau_2$ and $\omega_2$ are formidable, and we omit them here. Rather, as before, we turn as an example to the limiting case of small $a$. Again as an example, we consider the limit of small $a$. The critical delay from (32.15) is

$$\tau_0 = \frac{\arccos\left(-A_0/A_1\right)}{[A_1^2-A_0^2]^{\frac{1}{2}}} = \frac{\arccos\left(-n/\delta\right)}{|\delta|\,[(1-(n/\delta)^2]^{\frac{1}{2}}} + O(a) \tag{32.75}$$

so $n/\delta < 1$ is again needed for the existence of a critical delay. Next, we get

$$\tau_2 = \frac{[(1/\beta)(1+n/\delta)]^{\frac{\sigma+1}{\sigma}}(n+\tau_0\delta^2)\,\delta^{\frac{1-\sigma}{\sigma}}}{[8\sigma^2/(\sigma+1)](1-n/\delta)}\,a + O(a^2). \tag{32.76}$$

Here we also see that $\tau_2 \to 0$ for $a \to 0$, and, again, as each of the factors in the term linear in $a$ is positive, i.e. $\tau_2$ is positive, and the *Hopf bifurcation* is *supercritical.*

## CES and Delays with Cycles, Square Waves, and Chaos

Next we turn to numerical simulations to demonstrate that a number of typical features of delay differential equations appear in the present model (32.7) with the CES production function (32.69). The simulations are performed with a simple Euler method, using a time step, $\Delta t = \tau/200$. Tests with smaller time steps resulted in the same solutions with high accuracy. Two sets of basic economic parameters as shown in Table 32.1, together with variation of the delay time $\tau$.

Consider a *general* delay-differential equation

$$\dot{x} = h(x_\tau, x), \tag{32.77}$$

and consider $x_0 \neq y_0$ such that

$$h(x_0, y_0) = h(y_0, x_0) = 0. \tag{32.78}$$

It is well-known (Chow et al. 1992; Ivanov and Sharkovsky 1992) that under certain conditions, the general (32.77) allows a *periodic* solution with *period approximately*, $2\tau$, which is of the *square-wave* type. The periodic solution spends approximately time $\tau$ at each of $x_0, y_0$, with rapid transitions between these *almost constant states*. Without going into details, we demonstrate below the possibility of this feature with parameters of CES delay model, cf. Case 1.

**Parameter Case 1** Figure 32.1a shows the periodic solution for a slightly *supercritical* value of $\tau$. As expected from the Hopf theory, the solution is close to harmonic. As $\tau$ is increased, the periodic solution gradually turns into a

**Table 32.1** Parameter values for numerical simulations, together with computed quantities from Theorem 32.1: Critical point $q^*$, critical delay $\tau_0$, cubic expansion coefficient $\tau_2$, angular frequency of linearized system $\omega_0$, expansion coefficient for angular frequency $\omega_2$, and approximate period $T_2$ of limit cycles as a function of the deviation of the delay from the critical value

| | Case 1 | Case 2 |
|---|---|---|
| Basic parameters | | |
| $\sigma$ | 0.5 | 0.5 |
| $a$ | 0.6 | 0.3 |
| $n$ | 0.07 | 0.01 |
| $\delta$ | 0.12 | 0.02 |
| Hopf parameters | | |
| $\beta$ | 0.7 | 0.1 |
| $q^*$ | 7.710 | 4.333 |
| $\tau_0$ | 44.96 | 154.9 |
| $\tau_2$ | 0.5837 | 1.700 |
| $\omega_0$ | $5.506 \times 10^{-2}$ | $1.412 \times 10^{-2}$ |
| $T_0$ | 114.1 | 445.0 |
| $\omega_2$ | $5.986 \times 10^{-4}$ | $1.278 \times 10^{-4}$ |
| $T_2$ | $114.1 + 2.125(\tau - \tau_0)$ | $445.0 + 5.729(\tau - \tau_0)$ |

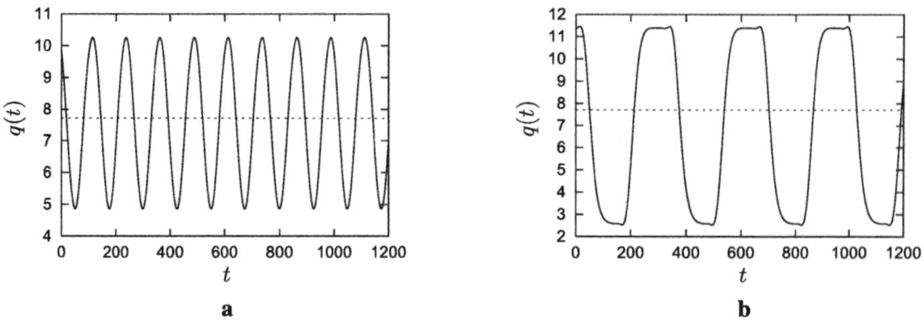


**Fig. 32.1** Numerical simulations for Case 1. The dashed line represents the equilibrium $q^*$. (**a**) $\tau = 50$ (**b**) $\tau = 150$

**Table 32.2** Parameter Case 1 and Fig. 32.1: Steady-state capital-labor ratios, with delays and no delay

| $\beta$ | $\tau$ | $s\gamma$ | $q^*$ | $k^*$ | $\kappa$ |
|---|---|---|---|---|---|
| 0.7 | 50 | 23.2 | 7.71 | 255.3 | 303.5 |
| 0.7 | 150 | 25420.9 | 7.71 | 279993.5 | 334483.4 |

*square wave* as shown in Fig. 32.1b. Solving Eq. (32.78) yields $x_0 = 2.57$, $y_0 = 11.4$, which agrees with the numerically obtained levels in the square wave.

In Table 32.2, we see a dramatic *difference* between $q^*$ and $k^*$; this *steady-state* discrepancy measures the *excess capital* (installed compared to operating) *per worker*—the long-run accumulation of idle (nonoperating) capital stocks, due to a time delay of the particular/critical size, $\tau_0$. Case (b) with *square waves* is extreme (generated by large values of TPF and delay), but it looks a bit like the so-called "ceiling/floor" models—patterns that have been associated with, e.g. the housing industry. Also rather large values of the basic parameter for the capital intensity and labor growth in Case 1 may support alternating time paths of "ceiling/floor" type for this and similar industries.

**Parameter Case 2** We shall demonstrate *transition to chaos.* As $\tau_2$ is smaller than for set 1, the amplitude of the periodic solution grows slower with $\tau$. An almost harmonic periodic solution quite far from the critical value $\tau_2$ is shown in Fig. 32.2a. However, increasing $\tau$ slightly as in Fig. 32.2b a *period doubling bifurcation* has occurred, as the solution now consists of *repeated pairs of different peaks.* This is even clearly demonstrated, when the *solution* is plotted as a *parameterized curve* $(\boldsymbol{q(t), q(t-\tau)})$, as in the right panels. It is well-known, see e.g. Guckenheimer and Holmes (1983), that a period doubling is typically the first step in a route to chaos. Indeed, a further increase of $\tau$, Fig. 32.2c, shows a solution with a complicated pattern of different peaks.

In Table 32.3, the *difference* between $q^*$ and $k^*$ is less pronounced than in Table 32.2. Still the steady-state (long-run) discrepancy is of tenfold size. The

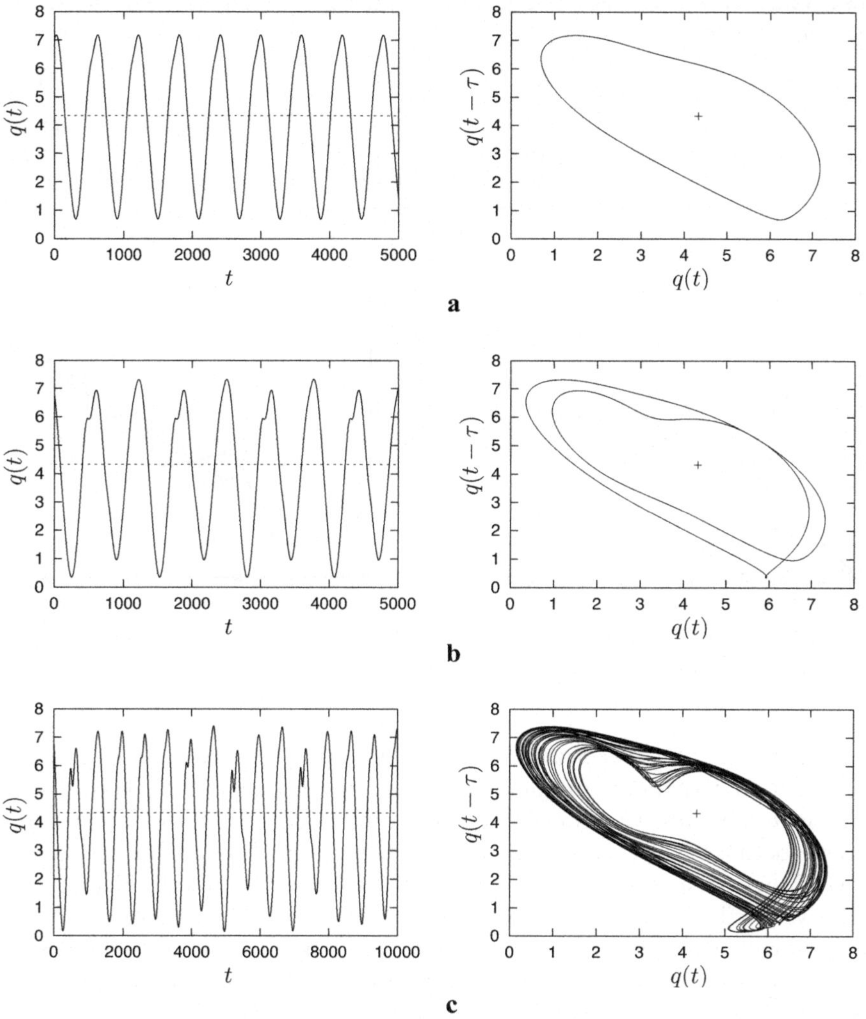


**Fig. 32.2** Numerical simulations for parameter Case 2. Left panels show time paths, $q(t)$, and the dashed lines represent the steady-state (equilibrium), $q^*$. Right panels show the pair $(q, q_\tau)$ in a phase plane; the marker represents the equilibrium, $(q, q_\tau) = (q^*, q^*)$. (**a**) $\tau = 220$ (**b**) $\tau = 240$ (**c**) $\tau = 255$

importance and gain from eliminating any delays (slack) in capital utilization is again demonstrated, cf.($\kappa$); the delay model provides some evidence for the increased economic-financial attention to "turn-key delivery/contracting" and "just in time" supply-chain management efforts.

Regarding the occurrence of chaotic motion, it is well-known that, cf. Lorenz (1989, p. 139): "While chaotic dynamics in *discrete-time* systems

**Table 32.3** Parameter Case 2 and Fig. 32.2: Steady-state capital-labor ratios, with delays and no delay

| $\beta$ | $\tau$ | $s\gamma$ | $q^*$ | $k^*$ | $\kappa$ |
|---|---|---|---|---|---|
| 0.01 | 220 | 0.90 | 4.33 | 39.08 | 42.40 |
| 0.01 | 240 | 1.10 | 4.33 | 47.73 | 51.95 |
| 0.01 | 255 | 1.28 | 4.33 | 55.45 | 60.52 |

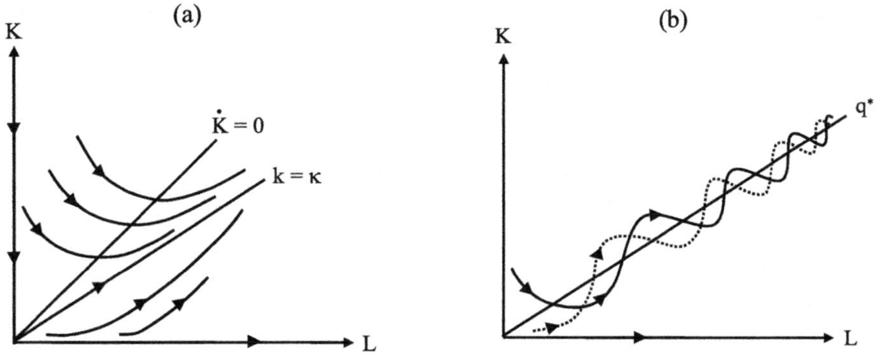


**Fig. 32.3** Phase portraits of $\{L(t), K(t) = L(t)k(t)\}$ from CES without delay (**a**), cf. Fig. 12.5, and with delay (**b**), Table 32.1

can already occur in *one-dimensional* systems like the logistic equation, the equivalent phenomenon in *continuous time* is restricted to at least *three-dimensional systems.* Canonically, chaos cannot occur in a two-dimensional system, because a trajectory cannot intersect itself. The cyclical motion in a two-dimensional system is thus restricted to a monotonically damped, or explosive oscillations, and closed orbits. The fact that chaos can occur in three-dimensional continuous-time systems the Lorenz attractor or the Rössler attractor can be illustrated with the help of so-called Poincare sections and maps".

As to *dimensional* aspects of any continuous-time model with its delays, it is essentially "*infinite dimensional*". Hence we can see chaotic time path of our single delay differential equation in the panels of Fig. 32.2. When the chaotic time paths from the delay model of Fig. 32.2 are exhibited as phase portraits in Fig. 32.3, the *fundamental* difference between dynamic systems with delays (b), and systems with no delays (a), is highlighted. Moreover, the portrait (b) observationally *integrates* the phenomena of *economic growth* and *cycles.*

## Final Comments

The search for various cycles in historical economic data has a long tradition—in Western economies essentially back until the take-off of industrialization with its rapid population and economic growth per capita. Two distinct "causes" (explanations, paradigms)) of recurrent industrial fluctuations can be found in the mainstream economic literature. One category of models relies heavily on exogenous forces (stochastic shocks) to start as well as to maintain cycles. Another type of models generated cycles endogenously by their own formal (mathematical) structure. We have only been concerned with the latter. However, in pure forms, both types of cyclical models have mostly ignored that industrial fluctuations (shorter or longer "waves") occur on the backdrop of, more or less, steady economic growth.

Despite many devices of "detrending" observed economic series, the dynamics of business cycle theory has been divorced from the dynamic systems of the basic (mainstream) growth models, which methodologically entered late in formal/quantitative economic theory that naturally, like mathematical physics/mechanics, began with equilibrium analysis and next to analyzing periodic motions (harmonic oscillators).

It seems instructive now to recall a perspective on model building from, Poincaré (1952, p. 181–182): " Long ago it was said: If Tycho had had instruments ten times as precise, we would never have had a Kepler, or a Newton, or astronomy. It is *misfortune* for a science to be born too late, when the means of observation have become too perfect. That is what is happening at this moment with respect to physical chemistry; the founders are *hampered* in their general grasp by third and *fourth decimal* places; happily they are men of robust faith.

As we get to know the properties of matter better, we see that *continuity reigns*. From the work of Andrews and Van der Waals, we see how the transition from the liquid to the gaseous state is made, and that is not abrupt. Similarly, there is no gap between the liquid and solid states. With this tendency there is no doubt a *loss* of *simplicity*. Such and such an effect was represented by *straight lines*; it is now necessary to connect these lines by more and more *complicated curves*. On the other hand, *unity* is gained. Separate categories quieted but did not satisfy the mind".

Hence beginning with aspirations and mathematical tools and data for cyclical "fine tuning" (epi-cycles) can hamper progress in overall economic understanding and successful application of dynamic models for secular growing economies. Thus, if we look at the numerical size (length) of the critical delays ($\tau_0$) above for Hopf bifurcations, and the necessary delays ($\tau$) for the limit cycles or "chaos", it is clear that the relevant time unit cannot be decades or years, and hardly quarters. But if these delays/lags refer to months or days, their proper interpretations and the economic impacts of such delays become more relevant for useful insights into the dynamics behind such observed data series.

Aperiodic oscillations ("chaos") on a small time scale is not "strange economics"; but their mathematical model is fairly complicated. However, the conclusion from our extension of the standard aggregate growth model is that ***delay differential equations*** offer a ***powerful*** mathematical ***instrument*** for a *coherent treatment* (integration)—as exhibited in Fig. 32.3—of economic *growth* and *cycle* models.

## Bibliography

Chow SN, Hale JK, Huang W (1992) From sine waves to square waves in delay equations. Proceedings of the Royal Society of Edinburgh 120A:223–229

Diekmann O, van Gils SA, Verduyn Lunel SM, Walther HO (1995) Delay Equations: Functional-, Complex-, and Nonlinear Analysis. Springer–Verlag, New York

Gabisch G, Lorenz HW (1987) Business Cycle Theory. Springer

Goodwin RM (1990) Chaotic Economic Dynamics. Oxford U. P.

Guckenheimer J, Holmes P (1983) Nonlinear Oscillations, Dynamical Systems, and Bifurcations of Vector Fields. Springer Verlag, New York

Ivanov AF, Sharkovsky AN (1992) Oscillations in singularly perturbed delay equations. Dynamics Reported (New Series) 1:164–224

Jensen BS (1994) The Dynamic Systems of Basic Economic Growth Models. Kluwer Academic Publishers, Dordrecht

Jensen BS, Alsholm PK, Larsen ME, Jensen JM (2005) Dynamic Structure, Exogeneity, Phase Portraits, Growth Paths, and Scale and Substitution Elasticities. Review of International Economics 13:59–89

Lorenz HW (1989) Business Cycle Theory. Springer

Morris HC (1976) A perturbative approach to periodic solutions of delay–differential equations. Journal of the Institute of Mathematics and its Applications 18:15–24

Poincaré H (1952) Science and Hypothesis. Dover Publ. N.Y

Puu T (2003) Attractors, Bifurcations, and Chaos. Springer

Zhu H, Huang W (2003) The economic growth models with time delays. In Jensen, B. S. and Palokangas, T., (eds), *Stochastic Economic Dynamics*, CUP, 2005.

CHAPTER 33

# Moment Evolution of Gaussian and Geometric Wiener Diffusions: Derived by Itô's Lemma and Kolmogorov̂'s Forward Equation

## INTRODUCTION

*Summary* The purpose of this chapter is to analyze two basic stochastic models in the plane: the time-homogeneous Gaussian and Geometric Wiener diffusions. Using the theory of stochastic processes and the Ito lemma, the probability distributions of the stochastic state vectors are described by the evolution of their moments (expectation and covariance as functions of time). These moments satisfy certain systems of (deterministic) ordinary differential equations (ODE). We solve these ODE and present explicit solutions (time paths) for the first- and second-order moments.

The forward Kolmogorov equation is used to derive the same moment functions by alternative solution methods and hereto gain further information on the probability distributions.

*Motivation* Uncertainty or incompleteness evidently prevails in the process descriptions of many scientific disciplines. Hence, stochastic models must often be used for an adequate mathematical representation of the dynamic systems. For any *stochastic process* $X(t)$, an ideal but unattainable situation is to get an explicit formula for the *probability distribution* $P(t, x)$ of $X(t)$ at any future instant $t$. We deal with the situations, where we want to obtain a collection of distributions $P(t, x)$—corresponding to various *drift* and *diffusion* coefficients, $a(x, t)$ and $B(x, t)$, that for $X(t)$ enter respectively, the system of *stochastic differential equations* (SDE) in the Ito form, or enter the *forward Kolmogorov partial differential equation* (PDE).

With co-authors:
CHUNYAN WANG, Copenhagen Business School, Denmark
JON JOHNSEN, Department of Mathematical Sciences, Aalborg University, Denmark



B. S. Jensen, *The Elements and Dynamic Systems of Economic Growth and Trade Models*, https://doi.org/10.1007/978-3-031-52493-6_33

Thus our intention is to elucidate to what extent the usual methods of the stochastic literature can provide *explicit* (closed form) expression of $P(t, x)$. It turns out that the use of both Ito's lemma and the forward Kolmogorov equation, can only give explicit formulas in the very simplest cases: the Gaussian diffusion (**GD**) and geometric Wiener diffusion (**GWD**), in which $a(X, t)$ and $B(X, t)$ are suitable first-order polynomials in the state variables $X$ alone.

For these two time-homogeneous diffusion processes, it is possible in the *two-dimensional* case to write up the complete expressions for the evolution of the *mean vector* and *covariance matrix*, and also for their probability distributions.

To our knowledge, these *moment solution formulas* have not been derived before, although their explicit evolution facilitates the understanding and modeling of stochastic processes in physical, biological, social (economics, finance), and technological sciences. Given the increasing usage of stochastic differential equations, the results are likely to be of general interest.

*Overview of Results* In Sect. "The Expectation Vector Functions", the *evolution* of the **mean vector** $m(t)$, for the **GD** and **GWD** models, is given in Theorem 33.1, with asymptotics in Corollary 33.1.

In Sect. "The Covariance Matrix Functions", the *evolution* of the **covariance matrix** $\Sigma(t)$, **covariance vector** $\sigma(t) = [\sigma_{xx}(t)\ \sigma_{xy}(t)\ \sigma_{yy}(t)]$, for the **GD** and **GWD** models, are given in Theorem 33.2, with asymptotics for covariances and correlation coefficients of the **GD** model in Corollary 33.2.

In Sect. "Probability Density Functions"—using the Kolmogorov partial differential equation—the *evolution* of the *density functions*, and the time paths for the mean vector $m(t)$ and the covariance matrix $\Sigma(t)$, of the **GD** and **GWD** models are corroborated in Theorems 33.3 and 33.4. However, a GWD density function for transition probability distribution does not exist, but the probability measure is given.

*The Limitations of the Methods* Regarding the difficulties of deriving the *explicit* moment formulas, it is easy to understand our restriction to diffusion processes in the *plane*. Indeed, the time dependence often emanates from an exponential matrix $e^{tA}$, and in higher dimensions, it is in general impossible to write the eigenvalues of $A$ as functions of its entries (in contrast to cases where the characteristic polynomial has the degree two). In three dimensions, there are six distinct second-order moments, and hence six linear differential equations to be solved explicitly. But according to Abel's theorem, even the general quintic polynomial is unsolvable algebraically. For planar diffusion processes, however, the *roots* of our *cubic* characteristic polynomial became *simple* expressions of at most eight *fundamental* drift- and diffusion parameters.

By the *Ito Lemma*, the *ordinary differential* equations for the first- and second-order *moments* are *uncoupled*, when drift- and diffusion coefficients depend *linearly* on state variables, $x$. In all other cases, knowledge of the *full* distribution $P(t, x)$ is required just to write down the moment differential equations. Alternatively, one could get an *infinite* number of *coupled* differential equations in moments of arbitrarily high order. We therefore only consider the **GD** and **GWD** models.

When applying the *Kolmogorov equation*, it is necessary to *know beforehand* that $P(t, x)$ has a *density* function. For our **GWD** model, this condition is not fulfilled (as we require the drift $Ax$ coefficient to have an arbitrary matrix $A$, we must as explained below use the Wiener process of dimension one). Moreover, the uniqueness of the obtained solution needs to be proved.

Needless to say, heavy calculations are involved in obtaining the final formulas for the second-order moment evolutions. The complications arise more from the intricate interconnections of the steps than from the difficulty of any step in particular. While computers cannot collect the intermediate elements into compact formulas, *computer* programs, (here Maple IV), can check and *confirm* the final *explicit* solutions that we obtain.

## Structure of Basic Diffusion Processes

### *Stochastic Preliminaries*

Consider the *stochastic differential equations* (**SDE**) in the Ito form,

$$dX = a(X,t)dt + B(X,t)dw \tag{33.1}$$

$$X(t) \in \mathbf{R}^n,\ a \in \mathbf{R}^n,\ B \in \mathbf{R}^{n\times r},\ w(t) \in \mathbf{R}^r \tag{33.2}$$

where $\boldsymbol{a(X,t)}$ is an $n$-dimensional *vector* function called the *drift coefficient*, and $\boldsymbol{B(X,t)}$ is an $n \times r$ *matrix* function, called the *diffusion coefficient*. The elements of $\boldsymbol{a}$ and $\boldsymbol{B}$ are Borel-measurable functions from $[0, \infty) \times \mathbf{R}^n$ into $\mathbf{R}$. The *stochastic state* vector is $\boldsymbol{X(t)} \in \mathbf{R}^n$, while $x \in \mathbf{R}^n$ denotes the state variable. The *random* (stochastic) vector, $\boldsymbol{dw} \in \mathbf{R}^r$, represents the *noise* in the stochastic dynamic system (33.1). As a stochastic process, $w(t)$ is assumed to be an $r$-dimensional standard *Wiener process* with $t \in \mathbf{R}$, and hence $w(t)$ has continuous (but nowhere differentiable) *sample paths* (phase paths, trajectories). The drift coefficient $a(X, t)$ determines the *local drift* (change, increment) of the *expected value* (mean, average trend of evolution) of the stochastic process $X(t)$ in a *short* interval of time from $t$ to $t+dt$ under the condition that $X(t) = x$. The *matrix product* $BB^T$ ($T$=transpose) of the diffusion coefficient $B(X, t)$ determines the *local dispersion* (the size of the central second-order moments, the mean square deviation of the stochastic process $X(t)$ from the original position $x$) during a *short* period of time from $t$ to $t+dt$. See Prohorov and Rozanov (1969, p. 258, 282).

From the probability theory, it is well-known that, if the multi-dimensional functions $a(x, t)$ and $B(x, t)$ satisfy both the Lipschitz and the linear growth conditions, and are continuous with respect to $t$, then the stochastic process $\boldsymbol{X(t)}$, *solving* (33.1), is a *continuous Markov process* with *transition* distribution (density) functions that are, under certain regularity assumptions, uniquely determined by only their first- and second-order moments. These *moments* are then completely described by, respectively, the *drift*- and *diffusion coefficients* in (33.1). Such *continuous Markov processes* are called *diffusion (Ito) processes.* In addition, when the *transition density* function, $\boldsymbol{p(x, t)}$, of a diffusion process exists, it *satisfies* the (forward) Kolmogorov equation (**PDE**),

$$\begin{aligned} \frac{\partial p(x,t)}{\partial t} &= \frac{1}{2}\sum_{j,k=1}^{n}\left[B(x,t)B^T(x,t)\right]_{j,k}\frac{\partial^2 p(x,t)}{\partial x_j \partial_{x_k}} \\ &\quad -\sum_{j=1}^{n} a_j(x,t)\frac{\partial p(x,t)}{\partial x_j}, \end{aligned} \tag{33.3}$$

where the *elements* of $a(x, t)$ and $B(x, t)B^T(x, t)$ enter, respectively, as the *coefficients* of the first- and second-order partial *derivatives.* See Prohorov and Rozanov (1969, p. 282). More generally, the *distribution* itself, $\boldsymbol{P(t, x)}$, solves (33.3). See also Appendix D.

Moreover, for any function of a diffusion process, $X(t)$, Itô's Lemma gives, cf. Karatzas and Shreve (1988); Øksendal (2005, pp. 48):

**Lemma 33.1 (Ito)** *Let $X(t) \in \mathbf{R}^n$ be a general diffusion process defined as in (33.1). Let $\boldsymbol{F(x, t)}$ be an arbitrary $C^2$ map from $\mathbf{R}^{n+1} \to \mathbf{R}$, then*

$$dF(X,t) = F_t dt + F_x^T dX + 1/2 dX^T F_{xx} dX \tag{33.4}$$

*i.e., $F(X, t)$, determined by diffusion process $X(t)$, is again a diffusion process, where $F_t$ and $F_x$ represent respectively the partial derivatives with respect to $t$ and $x$ of the function $F(x, t)$, and $F_{xx}$ represents the Hessian matrix of the function $F(x, t)$, and,* $\boldsymbol{(dw_i)^2 = dt\ \forall i;\ dw_i \cdot dw_j} = 0$, *for* $\boldsymbol{i \neq j;\ (dt)^2} = 0;\ \boldsymbol{dt \cdot dw_i} = 0$.

Using this Lemma, one can study many properties of the diffusion process $X(t)$ governed by (33.1). A well-known decisive property of a *diffusion process* is that its *conditional transition probability*, under certain regularity assumptions, is *uniquely* determined by only the first- or second-order moments, which again are *completely* determined by the *drift* and *diffusion* coefficients. Therefore it is *sufficient* to study the functions for the first- and the second-order moments of diffusion processes.

By Lemma 33.1, the following lemma for the *moment statistics* of the Ito *diffusion process* (33.1) can be *derived*, see Pugachev and Sinitsyn (1987, p. 302),

**Lemma 33.2** *The mean vector* $\boldsymbol{m}(\boldsymbol{t})$ *and variance-covariance matrix* $\boldsymbol{\Sigma}(\boldsymbol{t})$ *of the transition probability distribution for the family of solutions to the stochastic differential equation, (33.1), satisfy the deterministic ordinary differential equations (ODE),*

$$\dot{m} = \frac{dm(t)}{dt} = E\{a(X,t)\} \tag{33.5}$$

$$\dot{\Sigma}(t) = \frac{d\Sigma(t)}{dt} = E\left\{a(X,t)\left[X^T - m^T(t)\right]\right. \tag{33.6}$$

$$\left. + [X - m(t)]\, a^T(X,t) + B(X,t)B^T(X,t)\right\} \tag{33.7}$$

*where*

$$m(t) = [m_1\, m_2 \ldots m_n]^T = [E(X_1)\, E(X_2) \ldots E(X_n)]^T \tag{33.8}$$

$$\Sigma(t) = (\sigma_{ij})_{n\times n}, \quad \textit{and} \quad \sigma_{ij} = E[(X_i - m_i)(X_j - m_j)], \tag{33.9}$$

$$\textit{for } i, j = 1, 2, \ldots, n.$$

Therefore, $\boldsymbol{m}(\boldsymbol{t})$ and $\boldsymbol{\Sigma}(\boldsymbol{t})$ of the dynamic stochastic system (33.1) can be studied by solving the differential equations (33.5)–(33.7), and the *future* probabilistic behavior of the diffusion process $\boldsymbol{X}(\boldsymbol{t})$ is described by the *time paths* of these first- and second-order moments.

**Remark 33.1** The differential equations for the moments usually constitute an infinite coupled system, because the right hand sides of (33.5)–(33.7), and of the equations for the other moments, all contain moments of arbitrarily high order. Because knowledge about the full probability distribution, (probability density function), is necessary to solve (33.5) and (33.6–7), numerical methods are much more used in practice. For more details, see Soong (1973). ▽

But when the *drift*- and *diffusion* coefficients are *linear functions* in the state variables $\boldsymbol{x}$, the solution of (33.5) may be inserted in (33.6–7). However, although we specialize to dimension $n = 2$—and for the **GWD** model to a one-dimensional Wiener process—the resulting *system* for variances-covariance, $\boldsymbol{\sigma_{xx}(t)}$, $\boldsymbol{\sigma_{xy}(t)}$, $\boldsymbol{\sigma_{yy}(t)}$, is only barely solvable. The difficulty is to determine $\boldsymbol{e^{tA}}$, cf. Appendices section "Appendix B: Exponential Matrices in Two Dimensions" and "Appendix C: Exponentials in Three Dimensions". ▽

### *Linear Diffusion Processes in the Plane*

Henceforth we make *three* assumptions [occasionally the state vector $x$ is written as $(x, y)$, and similarly for $X(t)$]:

*Assumption 33.1* The stochastic dynamic system (33.1) is a *time-homogeneous* (independent of time) system in the Euclidean plane, i.e.

$$a(x,t) = a(x), \qquad B(x,t) = B(x); \qquad x \in \mathbf{R}^2. \tag{33.10}$$

*Assumption 33.2* The *drift* coefficients are *linear functions* of the state variables

$$a(x) = \begin{bmatrix} a_1(x) \\ a_2(x) \end{bmatrix} = Ax = \begin{bmatrix} a & b \\ c & d \end{bmatrix} \begin{bmatrix} x \\ y \end{bmatrix}; \qquad x = \begin{bmatrix} x \\ y \end{bmatrix}. \tag{33.11}$$

*Assumption 33.3* The *diffusion* coefficients and the vector $\boldsymbol{dw}$ may, respectively, take two forms, either

$$B(x)dw(t) = \begin{bmatrix} \beta_{11} & \beta_{12} \\ \beta_{21} & \beta_{22} \end{bmatrix} \begin{bmatrix} dw_1 \\ dw_2 \end{bmatrix}, \tag{33.12}$$

i.e., the noise vector has *two* different independent random elements, and the diffusion coefficients are given by a *constant matrix*—or

$$B(x)dw(t) = \begin{bmatrix} \beta x \\ \beta y \end{bmatrix} dw, \tag{33.13}$$

i.e., the noise vector has only *one* random element, but the components of the diffusion coefficient depend on the *state* of the system—(33.13) is often called a *geometric* Wiener diffusion (**GWD**) process.

Combining Assumption 33.1–33.3, we can get *two* basic time-homogeneous diffusion *models* in the Euclidean plane:

*GD Model: General Bivariate Gaussian Diffusion*
Using (33.10), (33.11), and (33.12), we have in compact notation,

$$dX = AXdt + Bdw \tag{33.14}$$

or explicitly,

$$\begin{aligned} dX &= (aX + bY)dt + \beta_{11}dw_1 + \beta_{12}dw_2, \\ dY &= (cX + dY)dt + \beta_{21}dw_1 + \beta_{22}dw_2. \end{aligned} \tag{33.15}$$

*GWD Model: Bivariate Geometric Wiener Diffusion*
With assumption (33.10), (33.11), and (33.13) we have,

$$dX = AXdt + \beta Xdw \tag{33.16}$$

or in explicit form,

$$\begin{aligned} dX &= (aX + bY)dt + \beta X dw \\ dY &= (cX + dY)dt + \beta Y dw \end{aligned} \tag{33.17}$$

**Remark 33.2** In practice, it is reasonable to think that the factors influencing the states of the system do interact, and to assume that the *uncertainties* attributable to the interacting factors are *correlated*. Therefore, it is necessary to include dependent *Wiener* processes that are correlated with *covariance* matrix $\Sigma$. The stochastic model takes the form

$$\begin{aligned} dX &= (aX + bY)dt + \beta_{11} dW_1 + \beta_{12} dW_2, \\ dY &= (cX + dY)dt + \beta_{21} dW_1 + \beta_{22} dW_2. \end{aligned} \tag{33.18}$$

In this case, $W_1$ and $W_2$ are *not* independent Wiener processes, but by using the linear transformation method to replace the correlated Wiener processes with the independent Wiener processes, the diffusion model (33.15) can be obtained:

Rewriting (33.18) in the vector-matrix form,

$$dX = AXdt + BdW \qquad W \sim N(0, \Sigma) \tag{33.19}$$

and letting $w = DW$ with $D = \Sigma^{-\frac{1}{2}}$, then $w \sim N(0, 1)$ are the *independent* Wiener processes. By *replacing* $W$ with $D^{-1}w$, then (33.19) can be transformed into the stochastic differential equations (33.15). In the following, we will therefore focus only on the analysis of the probability properties of the diffusion process with *independent* Wiener processes. ▽

## Dynamics of First- and Second-Order Moments

Applying Lemma 33.2 to (33.15) and (33.17 ), we get *ordinary differential equations* (**ODE**) for the *moments* of both the *Gaussian* and *geometric Wiener* processes.

**Proposition 33.1** *The components of the* ***mean vector*** *function,* $m = [m_x \; m_y]^T$, *satisfy the differential equations,*

$$\dot{m} = \begin{bmatrix} \dot{m}_x \\ \dot{m}_y \end{bmatrix} = Am = \begin{bmatrix} a & b \\ c & d \end{bmatrix} \begin{bmatrix} m_x \\ m_y \end{bmatrix} \tag{33.20}$$

*for both of the* ***GD*** *and* ***GWD models*** *(33.15) and (33.17), respectively.*

***Proof*** By applying (33.5) to (33.15) or (33.17),

$$\dot{m} = \begin{bmatrix} \dot{m}_x \\ \dot{m}_y \end{bmatrix} = E\{AX\} = E\begin{Bmatrix} ax + by \\ cx + dy \end{Bmatrix} = \begin{bmatrix} am_x + bm_y \\ cm_x + dm_y \end{bmatrix}$$

which is (33.20). □

**Proposition 33.2** *The* ***covariance vector*** *function,* $\sigma = [\sigma_{xx}\ \sigma_{xy}\ \sigma_{yy}]^T$*—equivalent to covariance matrix* $\Sigma$*—satisfies the differential equations,*

***GD Model***

$$\dot{\sigma} = C\sigma + \delta, \tag{33.21}$$

or

$$\begin{bmatrix} \dot{\sigma}_{xx} \\ \dot{\sigma}_{xy} \\ \dot{\sigma}_{yy} \end{bmatrix} = \begin{bmatrix} 2a & 2b & 0 \\ c & a+d & b \\ 0 & 2c & 2d \end{bmatrix} \begin{bmatrix} \sigma_{xx} \\ \sigma_{xy} \\ \sigma_{yy} \end{bmatrix} + \begin{bmatrix} \beta_{11}^2 + \beta_{12}^2 \\ \beta_{11}\beta_{21} + \beta_{12}\beta_{22} \\ \beta_{21}^2 + \beta_{22}^2 \end{bmatrix} \tag{33.22}$$

***GWD Model***

$$\dot{\sigma} = \tilde{C}\sigma + \tilde{\delta}(t) = (C + \beta^2 I)\sigma + \tilde{\delta}(t), \tag{33.23}$$

or

$$\begin{bmatrix} \dot{\sigma}_{xx} \\ \dot{\sigma}_{xy} \\ \dot{\sigma}_{yy} \end{bmatrix} = \begin{bmatrix} 2a + \beta^2 & 2b & 0 \\ c & a+d+\beta^2 & b \\ 0 & 2c & 2d + \beta^2 \end{bmatrix} \begin{bmatrix} \sigma_{xx} \\ \sigma_{xy} \\ \sigma_{yy} \end{bmatrix} + \begin{bmatrix} \beta^2 m_x^2 \\ \beta^2 m_x m_y \\ \beta^2 m_y^2 \end{bmatrix} \tag{33.24}$$

***Proof*** Applying (33.6–7)-(33.15) to get the differential equation for the covariance functions of the two diffusion processes, we get, cf. (33.12),

$$\begin{aligned} \frac{d\sum(t)}{dt} &= \begin{bmatrix} \dot{\sigma}_{xx}\ \dot{\sigma}_{xy} \\ \dot{\sigma}_{xy}\ \dot{\sigma}_{yy} \end{bmatrix} = E\left\{\begin{bmatrix} ax + by \\ cx + dy \end{bmatrix}\begin{bmatrix} x - m_x\ y - m_y \end{bmatrix}\right\} \\ &+ E\left\{\begin{bmatrix} x - m_x \\ y - m_y \end{bmatrix}\begin{bmatrix} ax + by\ cx + dy \end{bmatrix}\right\} \\ &+ E\left\{\begin{bmatrix} \beta_{11}\ \beta_{12} \\ \beta_{21}\ \beta_{22} \end{bmatrix}\begin{bmatrix} \beta_{11}\ \beta_{21} \\ \beta_{12}\ \beta_{22} \end{bmatrix}\right\} \end{aligned} \tag{33.25}$$

Since $E[x(x-m_x)] = E\left[(x-m_x)^2\right] = \sigma_{xx}$, etc., the right hand side of (33.25) becomes

$$\begin{bmatrix} 2a\sigma_{xx} + 2b\sigma_{xy} & c\sigma_{xx} + (a+d)\,\sigma_{xy} + b\sigma_{yy} \\ c\sigma_{xx} + (a+d)\,\sigma_{xy} + b\sigma_{yy} & 2c\sigma_{xy} + 2d\sigma_{yy} \end{bmatrix} + BB^T. \qquad (33.26)$$

By letting $\sigma = [\sigma_{xx}\ \sigma_{xy}\ \sigma_{yy}]^T$ and using (33.25) and (33.26), we get (33.22).

To obtain (33.24), applying (33.7)–(33.17), the first two terms in (33.7) are the same as those in (33.25), while the third term is, cf. (33.13),

$$E(BB^T) \quad = \quad E\left\{\begin{pmatrix} \beta x \\ \beta y \end{pmatrix}(\beta x\ \beta y)\right\} \quad = \quad E\left\{\begin{matrix} \beta^2 x^2 & \beta^2 xy \\ \beta^2 xy & \beta^2 y^2 \end{matrix}\right\}.$$

As $E(x^2) = \sigma_{xx} + m_x^2$, etc., the combination of terms as before yields (33.24).

□

**Remark 33.3** Since the homogeneous diffusion process is a *time-homogeneous* Gaussian diffusion, the ***differential equations*** (33.22) can also be derived directly from the following expression

$$\dot{\Sigma} \quad = \quad A\Sigma + \Sigma A^T + BB^T \qquad (33.27)$$

where $\Sigma = (\sigma_{ij})$, is the $2 \times 2$ covariance matrix, while $B$ and $A$ is given as in (33.15). The expression (33.27) is obtained in, e.g., Jacobsen (1991, 1970, pp. 12). ▽

Now, the differential equations for the moments of both the Gaussian and geometric Wiener diffusion processes have been obtained; clearly, the *mean functions* for the Gaussian diffusion process and for the geometric Wiener diffusion process *satisfy* the *same* differential equation.

Contrary to this, the differential equation for the *covariance function* of the Gaussian diffusion process is obviously ***different*** from that of the geometric diffusion process. For the geometric Wiener diffusion processes, it can be seen in (33.24), that the geometric parameter $\boldsymbol{\beta}$ appears not only in the non-homogeneous but also in the homogeneous parts of the differential equations.

In addition, the mean functions $m_x(t)$ and $m_y(t)$ now appear as components in the nonhomogeneous part of (33.24). Obviously they are functions of time $t$, satisfying (33.20). It is easily recognized that if one has $\boldsymbol{\beta}_1$ and $\boldsymbol{\beta}_2$ (instead of having just $\boldsymbol{\beta}$ for both state variables), or moreover two different Wiener processes $\boldsymbol{dw}_1$ and $\boldsymbol{dw}_2$ instead of just $\boldsymbol{dw}$, then the equation for the *covariance function in* (33.24) will be much more complex and probably impossible to solve.

It is worthwhile to try to *solve* (33.22)–(33.24) explicitly in *closed* form, in order to study the probability distribution, nonsingularity, stability, etc., of the diffusion processes.

## *Eigenvalues of A, C, and $\tilde{C}$*

As a preparation, we make a few observations on the *drift coefficient matrix* **A** in (33.20). It has a *trace, determinant*, and characteristic polynomial given by,

$$\mathrm{tr}A = a + d, \qquad |A| = ad - bc \tag{33.28}$$

$$|A - \lambda I| = \lambda^2 - (\mathrm{tr}A)\lambda + |A|; \tag{33.29}$$

The latter (33.29) has *discriminant* $4\Delta^2$ with,

$$\Delta^2 = \frac{1}{4}(a + d)^2 - (ad - bc) = \frac{1}{4}(d - a)^2 + bc. \tag{33.30}$$

Henceforth, we use the notation,

$$\Delta^2 > 0 : \Delta \equiv +\sqrt{\Delta^2}, \qquad \Delta^2 < 0 : \Delta \equiv +\sqrt{|\Delta^2|} \tag{33.31}$$

Generally, the *eigenvalues* of **A** may then be written, cf. (33.29)–(33.31), as

$$\Delta^2 > 0 \quad : \quad \lambda_1 = \frac{1}{2}(a + d) + \Delta, \qquad \lambda_2 = \frac{1}{2}(a + d) - \Delta \tag{33.32}$$

$$\Delta^2 = 0 \quad : \quad \lambda = \frac{1}{2}(a + d) \tag{33.33}$$

$$\Delta^2 < 0 \quad : \quad \lambda_1 = \frac{1}{2}(a + d) + i\Delta, \qquad \lambda_2 = \frac{1}{2}(a + d) - i\Delta \tag{33.34}$$

If the real *eigenvectors* corresponding to (33.32)–(33.33) are *normalized* to the form $(1, \boldsymbol{\alpha})$,(except for the vertical axis), their "*slopes*" $\boldsymbol{\alpha}$ can be calculated to be:

$$\Delta^2 > 0 \quad : \quad \alpha_1 = (d - a)/2b + \Delta/b\,, \quad \alpha_2 = (d - a)/2b - \Delta/b\,, \quad b \neq 0 \tag{33.35}$$

$$\Delta^2 = 0 \quad : \quad \alpha = (d - a)/2b = 2c/(a - d) \tag{33.36}$$

When $bc = 0$, $d \neq a$, one of the axes contains an eigenvector, whereas the other eigenvector has a slope given as $(d - a)/b$ or $c/(a - d)$.

With reference to the fundamental parameter elements of $\boldsymbol{A}$, (33.20), we can now analyze the *Ito coefficient matrix* $\boldsymbol{C}$, (33.21–33.22), defined in Proposition 33.2. Obviously $\boldsymbol{C}$ is real; it has a trace and determinant,

$$\text{tr } C = 3\,(a+d) = 3 \text{ tr } A, \tag{33.37}$$

$$|C| = 4\,(a+d)\,(ad-bc) = 4\text{tr } A\,|A| \tag{33.38}$$

and its *characteristic polynomial* is,

$$\begin{aligned} |C - \lambda I| &= \lambda^3 - 3\,(\text{ tr } A)\,\lambda^2 \\ &\quad + 2\left[(\text{ tr } A)^2 + 2\,|A|\right]\lambda - 4\,(\text{ tr } A)\,|A|\,. \end{aligned} \tag{33.39}$$

When *comparing* with the *eigenvalues* of $\boldsymbol{A}$, $\lambda_1$, and $\lambda_2$, or $\lambda$, (33.32–33.34), we get

**Lemma 33.3** *The* ***eigenvalues*** *of the Ito matrix* $\boldsymbol{C}$*, (33.21–33.22), associated with the Gaussian diffusion process, are in the nonsingular case,* $|C| \neq 0$*, given by*

$$\Delta^2 > 0 \quad : \quad \lambda_1^C = tr\,A, \quad \lambda_2^C = tr\,A + 2\Delta = 2\lambda_1, \quad \lambda_3^C = tr\,A - 2\Delta = 2\lambda_2 \tag{33.40}$$

$$\Delta^2 = 0 \quad : \quad \lambda_1^C = \lambda_2^C = \lambda_3^C = tr\,A = 2\lambda \tag{33.41}$$

$$\Delta^2 < 0 \quad : \quad \lambda_1^C = tr\,A, \quad \lambda_2^C = tr\,A + 2i\Delta = 2\lambda_1, \quad \lambda_3^C = tr\,A - 2i\Delta = 2\lambda_2 \tag{33.42}$$

*and are in the singular case,* $|C| = 4\,|A|\;tr\,A = 0$*, given as either special cases of (33.40–33.42) with* $tr\,A = 0$*, or of (33.40) with* $|A| = 0$ *[*$2\Delta = tr\,A$*, (33.30)].*

*The* ***eigenvalues*** *of the Ito matrix* $\tilde{\boldsymbol{C}}$*, (33.23–33.24), associated with the geometric Wiener diffusion process, are always given as,*

$$\lambda_i^{\tilde{C}} = \lambda_i^C + \beta^2, \qquad i = 1, 2, 3 \tag{33.43}$$

*with the* $\boldsymbol{\lambda}_i^C$ *given in (33.40)–(33.42).*

***Proof*** The *roots* of the *cubic* Eq. (33.39) can be calculated from the standard *Tartaglia-Cardano* formula, Selby (1973, p. 103), which after many reductions gives the simple *expressions* (33.40)–(33.42).

However, $\boldsymbol{\lambda}_1^C$ may also be obtained simply by noting that **tr** $\boldsymbol{A}$ is always a real root of (33.39). Hence, we get

$$|C - \lambda I| = (\lambda - \text{tr } A)(\lambda^2 - 2 \text{ tr } A\lambda + 4|A|), \tag{33.44}$$

from which it is seen immediately that the other roots of (33.44) are the *double* of those in (33.32)–(33.34), cf. (33.29)–(33.30).

As noted in (33.23), we have: $\tilde{\boldsymbol{C}} = \boldsymbol{C} + \boldsymbol{\beta}^2 \boldsymbol{I}$; hence (33.43) follows. □

## The Expectation Vector Functions

### *Solutions to the Differential Equations*

Obviously the *solution* to (33.20) may be written *abstractly* as,

$$m(t) = [\; m_x(t) \;\; m_y(t)\; ]^T = e^{tA} m^0 \tag{33.45}$$

but, as a *main result*, we state it *explicitly* in the *two-dimensional* case:

**Theorem 33.1** *The complete set of solutions to (33.20) for the expectation functions, $m(t) = e^{tA}m^0$, of the* **GD** *and* **GWD** *models, is—with the parameters of (33.30–33.31)—given by,*

$\Delta^2 > 0:$

$$m(t) = e^{\frac{1}{2}(a+d)t} \begin{bmatrix} \cosh(\Delta t) - \frac{d-a}{2\Delta}\sinh(\Delta t) & \frac{b}{\Delta}\sinh(\Delta t) \\ \frac{c}{\Delta}\sinh(\Delta t) & \cosh(\Delta t) + \frac{d-a}{2\Delta}\sinh(\Delta t) \end{bmatrix} m^0 \tag{33.46}$$

$\Delta^2 = 0:$

$$m(t) = e^{\frac{1}{2}(a+d)t} \begin{bmatrix} 1 - \frac{1}{2}(d-a)\,t & bt \\ ct & 1 + \frac{1}{2}(d-a)\,t \end{bmatrix} m^0 \tag{33.47}$$

$\Delta^2 < 0:$

$$m(t) = e^{\frac{1}{2}(a+d)t} \begin{bmatrix} \cos(\Delta t) - \frac{d-a}{2\Delta}\sin(\Delta t) & \frac{b}{\Delta}\sin(\Delta t) \\ \frac{c}{\Delta}\sin(\Delta t) & \cos(\Delta t) + \frac{d-a}{2\Delta}\sin(\Delta t) \end{bmatrix} m^0 \tag{33.48}$$

*where, $m^0 = \left[m_x(0)\, m_y(0)\right]^T$, is the initial value of the expectation function at time $t = 0$.*

***Proof*** Although the infinite series $\boldsymbol{e}^{tA}$ converges for all $t$ and all square matrices $A$, it seems impossible in general to express $\boldsymbol{e}^{tA}$ in closed form. But in the *two-dimensional* case the *series* may be summed in terms of *elementary functions* by an application of the Hamilton-Cayley Theorem; cf. Appendix section "Appendix B: Exponential Matrices in Two Dimensions", Jensen (1994, p. 307); here p. 1172 in Chap. 31. *Alternatively*, as to the *mean solutions*, $\boldsymbol{m}(t)$, (33.46–33.48), of (33.20), see hereto the *explicit expressions*, (29.93–29.95). □

### *Asymptotics of the Mean Functions*

For convenience we shall write $f \sim g$ whenever the functions $f(t)$ and $g(t)$ are such that the *ratio* $f(t)/g(t)$ tends to 1 for $t \to \infty$. Moreover, for two *vector* functions $u$ and $v$, the relation $u \sim v$ means that $u_j \sim v_j$ for each $j$.

**Corollary 33.1** *The asymptotic (long-run) behavior for $t \to \infty$ of the expectation functions $m(t)$ in Theorem 33.1 is given by*
$\Delta^2 > 0$ :

$$\lambda_1 < 0, \lambda_2 < 0: \qquad \lim_{t\to\infty} m(t) = 0 \tag{33.49}$$

$$\lambda_1 > 0, \lambda_2 \neq 0, \frac{m_x^0}{m_y^0} \neq \alpha_2: \quad m(t) \sim \frac{1}{2} e^{(\frac{1}{2}(a+d)+\Delta)t} \begin{bmatrix} 1 - \frac{d-a}{2\Delta} & \frac{b}{\Delta} \\ \frac{c}{\Delta} & 1 + \frac{d-a}{2\Delta} \end{bmatrix} m^0 \tag{33.50}$$

$$\lambda_1 > 0, \lambda_2 < 0, \frac{m_x^0}{m_y^0} = \alpha_2: \quad \lim_{t\to\infty} m(t) = 0 \tag{33.51}$$

$$\lambda_1 > 0, \lambda_2 > 0, \frac{m_x^0}{m_y^0} = \alpha_2: \quad m(t) \sim \frac{1}{2} e^{(\frac{1}{2}(a+d)+\Delta)t} \begin{bmatrix} 1 + \frac{d-a}{2\Delta} & -\frac{b}{\Delta} \\ -\frac{c}{\Delta} & 1 - \frac{d-a}{2\Delta} \end{bmatrix} m^0 \tag{33.52}$$

$$\Delta^2 \leq 0: \qquad tr\, A < 0 \qquad \lim_{t\to\infty} m(t) = 0 \tag{33.53}$$

***Proof*** Writing the components of $m(t)$, (33.46), in *alternative explicit* form gives

$$\begin{aligned} m_x(t) &= \frac{1}{2} e^{1/2(a+d+2\Delta)t} \left[ (1 - \frac{d-a}{2\Delta}) m_x(0) + \frac{b}{\Delta} m_y(0) \right] \\ &+ \frac{1}{2} e^{1/2(a+d-2\Delta)t} \left[ (1 + \frac{d-a}{2\Delta}) m_x(0) - \frac{b}{\Delta} m_y(0) \right] \end{aligned} \tag{33.54}$$

$$\begin{aligned} m_y(t) &= \frac{1}{2} e^{1/2(a+d+2\Delta)t} \left[ \frac{c}{\Delta} m_x(0) + (1 + \frac{d-a}{2\Delta}) m_y(0) \right] \\ &+ \frac{1}{2} e^{1/2(a+d-2\Delta)t} \left[ -\frac{c}{\Delta} m_x(0) + (1 - \frac{d-a}{2\Delta}) m_y(0) \right] \end{aligned} \tag{33.55}$$

When $\lambda_1 < 0$ and $\lambda_2 < 0$, the coefficients of $t$ in the expressions above are negative, and hence $\lim_{t\to\infty} m_x(t) = 0$, and $\lim_{t\to\infty} m_y(t) = 0$.

In the other cases, it is seen that the terms with $e^{1/2(a+d+2\Delta)t}$ are dominating; the terms $e^{1/2(a+d-2\Delta)t}$ become the dominating ones, only for special initial values, $r_0 = \frac{m_y(0)}{m_x(0)} = \alpha_2$. In this way, the Corollary will be verified. □

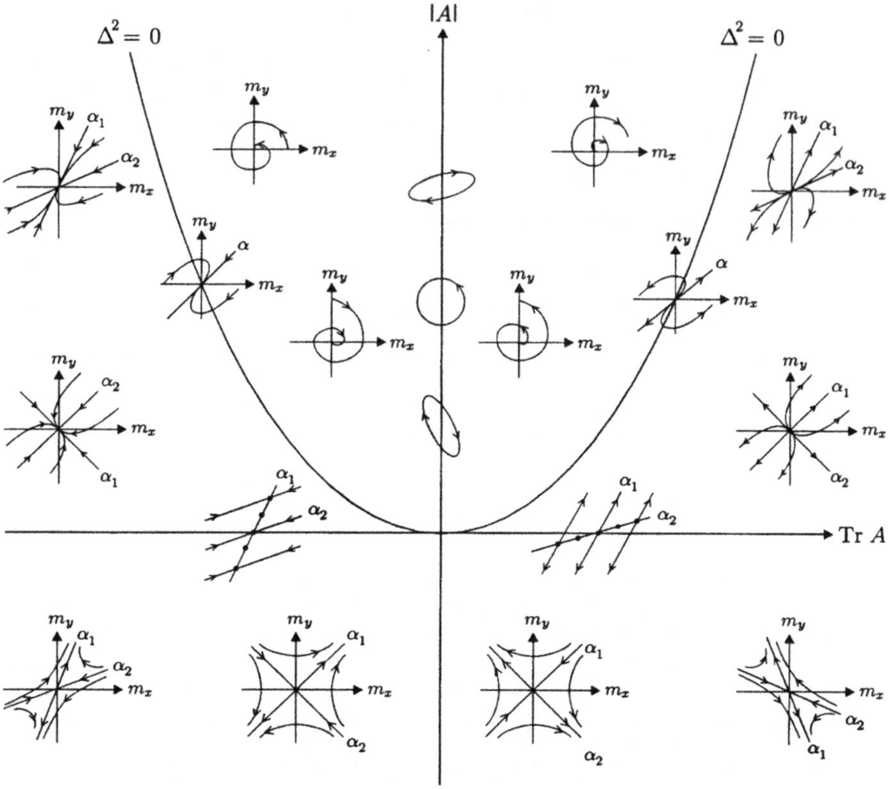


**Fig. 33.1** The drift parameter regions and mean functions (33.46)–(33.48)

**Remark 33.4** For *parameter regions* of the drift coefficients—as depicted on the plane (tr$A$, $|A|$), cf. (33.28)–(33.30)—the *geometry* of the global phase portraits and the *evolution* (exact time paths) of the *mean functions* (33.46)–(33.48) are shown in Fig. 33.1. As seen further below, the parameter regions for classifying the global behavior of the *covariance functions* will also correspond to the regions depicted in Fig. 33.1.

Those **GD** and **GWD** processes—with *asymptotic stationary* probability distributions—are located in the *interior* of the second (upper-left, shaded) quadrant in Fig. 33.1. For full dynamic description of the trajectory configurations in Fig. 33.1, see Jensen (1994, p. 235); here Sect. "Parameter Space and the Hyperconic Phase Portrait" in Chap. 29. ▽

Whereas the *sample paths* of the diffusion processes are always continuous but *nondifferentiable*, the *evolution* of their *moments* is *smoothly* changing (described by $C^{-1}$ -curves), as illustrated by the *mean functions* in Fig. 33.1.

# The Covariance Matrix Functions

### *Solutions to the Differential Equations*

From (33.21)–(33.24), the *covariance function* $\sigma = [\sigma_{xx}\ \sigma_{xy}\ \sigma_{yy}]^T$—which contains the three independent elements of the covariance matrix $\Sigma(t)$ for both the Gaussian and geometric Wiener processes—satisfies a *three-dimensional* ordinary differential equation in general of the form:

$$\dot{\sigma}(t) = C\sigma(t) + \delta(t). \tag{33.56}$$

The *complete solution* of (33.56) may be written

$$\sigma(t) = e^{tC}\left[\sigma(0) + \int_0^t e^{-C\tau}\delta(\tau)d\tau\right] \tag{33.57}$$

where the parameter $\sigma(0) \in \mathbf{R}^n$ plays the role of initial value of the solution. For a given particular solution $\bar{\sigma}$, the solution $\sigma(t)$ passing through $\sigma_0$ at $t = 0$, $\boldsymbol{\sigma}(\mathbf{0}) = \boldsymbol{\sigma}_0$, **is**

$$\sigma(t) = e^{tC}\sigma^*(0) + \bar{\sigma}(t) \tag{33.58}$$

$$\sigma^*(0) = \sigma_0 - \bar{\sigma}(0); \tag{33.59}$$

here $\boldsymbol{\sigma}^*(\mathbf{0})$ denotes the initial value of the solution to the corresponding homogeneous system. This notation is used below.

*Exponential Matrices $e^{tC}$ and $e^{t\tilde{C}}$*

As a first step in determining the solution in (33.57), we use the *eigenvalues* of $\boldsymbol{C}$ and $\tilde{\boldsymbol{C}}$, cf. Lemma 33.3, to calculate the exponential matrices, $\boldsymbol{e}^{tC}$ and $\boldsymbol{e}^{t\tilde{C}}$.

**Proposition 33.3** *The exponential matrix $e^{tC}$ of the* **CD** *model with* $\boldsymbol{C}$*, (33.21–33.22), is given by,*

$$e^{tC} = e^{(a+d)t}M(t) \tag{33.60}$$

*where the matrix $M(t)$ is presented in Tables 33.1, 33.2, and 33.3 as follows:*

*Table 33.1: The nonsingular case, $|C| \neq 0$, with matrix $M$ as $M_+$, $M_0$, $M_-$ for respectively: $\Delta^2 > 0$, $\Delta^2 = 0$ and $\Delta^2 < 0$*

*Table 33.2: The singular case, $|C| = 0$, and $tr\,A = 0$, with $M$ as $M_+$, $M_0$, $M_-$ for respectively: $\Delta^2 > 0$, $\Delta^2 = 0$ and $\Delta^2 < 0$*

*Table 33.3: The singular case, $|C| = 0$, and $|A| = 0$, with a single $M$ matrix.*

*The exponential matrix $e^{t\tilde{C}}$ of the* **CWD** *model with* $\tilde{\boldsymbol{C}}$*, (33.23–33.24), is given by*

$$e^{t\tilde{C}} = e^{\beta^2 t}e^{tC} = e^{(a+d+\beta^2)t}M(t) \tag{33.61}$$

*where the matrix* $\boldsymbol{M}(t)$ *is presented in the Tables 33.1, 33.2, and 33.3.*

**Table 33.1** The matrices $M_+$, $M_0$, $M_-$ for the **nonsingular** case: $|C| \neq 0$

$$M_+ = \begin{bmatrix} (1-\frac{bc}{2\Delta^2})\cosh(2\Delta t) - \frac{d-a}{2\Delta}\sinh(2\Delta t) + \frac{bc}{2\Delta^2} & -\frac{b(d-a)}{2\Delta^2}(\cosh(2\Delta t)-1) + \frac{b}{\Delta}\sinh(2\Delta t) & \frac{b^2}{2\Delta^2}(\cosh(2\Delta t)-1) \\ -\frac{c(d-a)}{4\Delta^2}(\cosh(2\Delta t)-1) + \frac{c}{2\Delta}\sinh(2\Delta t) & \frac{bc}{\Delta^2}(\cosh(2\Delta t)-1)+1 & \frac{b(d-a)}{4\Delta^2}(\cosh(2\Delta t)-1) + \frac{b}{2\Delta}\sinh(2\Delta t) \\ \frac{c^2}{2\Delta^2}\cosh(2\Delta t) & \frac{c(d-a)}{2\Delta^2}(\cosh(2\Delta t)-1) + \frac{c}{\Delta}\sinh(2\Delta t) & (1-\frac{bc}{2\Delta^2})\cosh(2\Delta t) - \frac{d-a}{2\Delta}\sinh(2\Delta t) + \frac{bc}{2\Delta^2} \end{bmatrix} \tag{33.61}$$

$$M_0 = \begin{bmatrix} (1-\frac{1}{2}(d-a)t)^2 & 2bt - b(d-a)t^2 & b^2t^2 \\ ct - \frac{1}{2}c(d-a)t^2 & 1-\frac{1}{2}(d-a)t^2 & bt + \frac{1}{2}b(d-a)t^2 \\ c^2t^2 & 2ct + c(d-a)t^2 & (1+\frac{1}{2}(d-a)t)^2 \end{bmatrix} \tag{33.62}$$

$$M_- = \begin{bmatrix} (1-\frac{bc}{2\Delta^2})\cos(2\Delta t) - \frac{d-a}{2\Delta}\sin(2\Delta t) + \frac{bc}{2\Delta^2} & -\frac{b(d-a)}{2\Delta^2}(\cos(2\Delta t)-1) + \frac{b}{\Delta}\sin(2\Delta t) & \frac{b^2}{2\Delta^2}(\cos(2\Delta t)-1) \\ -\frac{c(d-a)}{4\Delta^2}(\cos(2\Delta t)-1) + \frac{c}{2\Delta}\sin(2\Delta t) & \frac{bc}{\Delta^2}(\cos(2\Delta t)-1)+1 & \frac{b(d-a)}{4\Delta^2}(\cos(2\Delta t)-1) + \frac{b}{2\Delta}\sin(2\Delta t) \\ \frac{c^2}{2\Delta^2}\cos(2\Delta t) & \frac{c(d-a)}{2\Delta^2}(\cos(2\Delta t)-1) + \frac{c}{\Delta}\sin(2\Delta t) & (1-\frac{bc}{2\Delta^2})\cos(2\Delta t) - \frac{d-a}{2\Delta}\sin(2\Delta t) + \frac{bc}{2\Delta^2} \end{bmatrix} \tag{33.63}$$

**Table 33.2** The matrices $M_+$, $M_0$, $M_-$ for the **singularity**: $|C| = 0$, with $\mathrm{tr}A = 0$

$$M_+ = \frac{1}{2\Delta^2}\begin{bmatrix} (a^2+\Delta^2)\cosh(2\Delta t) + 2a\Delta\sinh(2\Delta t) + bc & 2ab\left[\cosh(2\Delta t) - 1\right] + 2b\Delta\sinh(2\Delta t) & b^2\left[\cosh(2\Delta t) - 1\right] \\ ac\left[\cosh(2\Delta t) - 1\right] + c\Delta\sinh(2\Delta t) & 2bc\left[\cosh(2\Delta t) - 1\right] + 2\Delta^2 & bd\left[\cosh(2\Delta t) - 1\right] + b\Delta\sinh(2\Delta t) \\ c^2\left[\cosh(2\Delta t) - 1\right] & 2cd\left[\cosh(2\Delta t) - 1\right] + 2c\Delta\sinh(2\Delta t) & (d^2+\Delta^2)\cosh(2\Delta t) + 2d\Delta\sinh(2\Delta t) + bc \end{bmatrix} \tag{33.64}$$

$$M_0 = \begin{bmatrix} (at+1)^2 & 2bt(at+1) & b^2t^2 \\ ct(at+1) & 2bct^2+1 & bt(dt+1) \\ c^2t^2 & 2ct(dt+1) & (dt+1)^2 \end{bmatrix} \tag{33.65}$$

$$M_- = \frac{1}{2\Delta^2}\begin{bmatrix} (a^2+\Delta^2)\cos(2\Delta t) + 2a\Delta\sin(2\Delta t) + bc & 2ab\left[\cos(2\Delta t) - 1\right] + 2b\Delta\sin(2\Delta t) & b^2\left[\cos(2\Delta t) - 1\right] \\ ac\left[\cos(2\Delta t) - 1\right] + c\Delta\sin(2\Delta t) & 2bc\left[\cos(2\Delta t) - 1\right] + 2\Delta^2 & bd\left[\cos(2\Delta t) - 1\right] + b\Delta\sin(2\Delta t) \\ c^2\left[\cos(2\Delta t) - 1\right] & 2cd\left[\cos(2\Delta t) - 1\right] + 2c\Delta\sin(2\Delta t) & (d^2+\Delta^2)\cos(2\Delta t) + 2d\Delta\sin(2\Delta t) + bc \end{bmatrix} \tag{33.66}$$

**Table 33.3** The matrix $M$ for the **singularity**: $|C| = 0$, with $|A| = 0$

$$M = \frac{1}{(a+d)^2}\begin{bmatrix} (ae^{\frac{1}{2}(a+d)t} + de^{-\frac{1}{2}(a+d)t})^2 & 2abe^{(a+d)t} + 2b(d-a) - 2bde^{-(a+d)t} & 2b^2\left[\cosh((a+d)t) - 1\right] \\ ace^{(a+d)t} + c(d-a) - dce^{-(a+d)t} & 2bc\left[\cosh((a+d)t) - 1\right] & bde^{(a+d)t} - b(d-a) - abe^{-(a+d)t} \\ 2c^2\left[\cosh((a+d)t) - 1\right] & 2cde^{(a+d)t} - 2c(d-a) - 2ace^{-(a+d)t} & (de^{\frac{1}{2}(a+d)t} + ae^{-\frac{1}{2}(a+d)t})^2 \end{bmatrix}$$

***Proof*** For $\Delta^2 > 0$, the eigenvalues of $C$ are distinct, cf. Appendix section "Appendix C: Exponentials in Three Dimensions",

$$e^{tC} = e^{\lambda_1^t C}\frac{(C-\lambda_2^C I)(C-\lambda_3^C I)}{(\lambda_1^C-\lambda_2^C)(\lambda_1^C-\lambda_3^C)} + e^{\lambda_2^t C}\frac{(C-\lambda_1^C I)(C-\lambda_3^C I)}{(\lambda_2^C-\lambda_1^C)(\lambda_2^C-\lambda_3^C)} + e^{\lambda_3^t C}\frac{(C-\lambda_1^C I)(C-\lambda_2^C I)}{(\lambda_3^C-\lambda_1^C)(\lambda_3^C-\lambda_2^C)}.$$

By inserting the eigenvalues of $C$ for $\Delta^2 > 0$, cf. (33.40), we get

$$\begin{aligned}
e^{tC} &= \frac{1}{8\Delta^2}e^{(\operatorname{tr} A+2\Delta)t}\left[C^2 - 2(\operatorname{tr} A-\Delta)C + \operatorname{tr} A(\operatorname{tr} A-2\Delta)I\right] \\
&+ \frac{1}{8\Delta^2}e^{(\operatorname{tr} A-2\Delta)t}\left[C^2 - 2(\operatorname{tr} A-\Delta)C + \operatorname{tr} A(\operatorname{tr} A+2\Delta)I\right] \\
&- \frac{1}{4\Delta^2}e^{(\operatorname{tr} A)t}\left[C^2 - 2(\operatorname{tr} A)C + (\operatorname{tr} A-2\Delta)(\operatorname{tr} A+2\Delta)I\right] \\
&= \frac{e^{(\operatorname{tr} A)t}}{4\Delta^2}\left[(\cosh(2\Delta t)-1)\,C^2 + 2(\operatorname{tr} A - \operatorname{tr} A\cosh(2\Delta t) + \Delta\sinh(2\Delta t))C\right] \\
&+ \frac{e^{(\operatorname{tr} A)t}}{4\Delta^2}\left[(\operatorname{tr} A)^2\cosh(2\Delta t) - 2\Delta\operatorname{tr} A\sinh(2\Delta t) - 4|A|\right] I.
\end{aligned} \tag{33.67}$$

Using that,

$$C^2 = \begin{bmatrix} 4a^2+2bc & 6ab+2bd & 2b^2 \\ 3ac+dc & (a+d)^2+4bc & 3bd+ab \\ 2c^2 & 6cd+2ac & 4d^2+2bc \end{bmatrix}, \tag{33.68}$$

a regrouping of the terms in (33.67) leads to $\boldsymbol{M}_+$, (33.61), in Table 33.1.

Similarly, when $\Delta^2 < 0$, there are also three distinct eigenvalues, and following the same procedures with (33.42), we get $\boldsymbol{M}_-$, (33.63), in Table 33.1.

For the case $\Delta^2 = 0$, it is seen from (33.41) that $C$ has *three identical* eigenvalues, $\lambda_1^C = \lambda_2^C = \lambda_3^C = \lambda^C = \operatorname{tr} A$. Hence, by Appendix section "Appendix C: Exponentials in Three Dimensions",

$$\begin{aligned}
e^{tC} &= e^{\lambda^C t}\left[I + t\left(C-\lambda^C I\right) + \frac{1}{2}t^2\left(C-\lambda^C I\right)^2\right] \\
&= e^{(\operatorname{tr} A)t}\left[I + (C-\operatorname{tr} A)t + \frac{1}{2}(C-\operatorname{tr} A)^2 t^2\right].
\end{aligned} \tag{33.69}$$

By inserting the matrices, cf. (33.22),

$$C - \operatorname{tr} A = \begin{bmatrix} a-d & 2b & 0 \\ c & 0 & b \\ 0 & 2c & d-a \end{bmatrix}, \tag{33.70}$$

$$(C - \operatorname{tr} A)^2 = \begin{bmatrix} (d-a)^2 + 2bc & -2b(d-a) & 2b^2 \\ -c(d-a) & 4bc & b(d-a) \\ 2c^2 & 2c(d-a) & (d-a)^2 + 2bc \end{bmatrix} \tag{33.71}$$

into (33.69), then $\boldsymbol{M}_0$, (33.62), in Table 33.1 is obtained.

The *singular* cases, (33.64), (33.65), (33.66), in Tables 33.2 and 33.3 are the relevant simplifications of $M_+$, $M_0$, and $M_-$ in Table 33.1.

From (33.24), we have $\tilde{\boldsymbol{C}} = C + \beta^2 I$, where $C$ and $\beta^2 I$ commute so that $e^{t\tilde{C}} = e^{\beta^2 tI} \cdot e^{tC} = e^{\beta^2 t} \cdot e^{tC}$. □

Having obtained *explicit* expressions for the exponential matrices $\boldsymbol{e}^{tC}$ and $\boldsymbol{e}^{t\tilde{C}}$, the problem is now by (33.58) and (33.57) to calculate the *particular solutions* of the two differential equations (33.22) and (33.24).

*Particular Solutions*

**Proposition 33.4** *For the GD, (33.21–33.22), particular solutions* $\bar{\boldsymbol{\sigma}}$ *are provided by the following expressions: In the nonsingular case,* $|C| = 4\,|A|\, tr\, A \neq 0$, *then* $\bar{\sigma}$ *can be taken as a constant vector:*

$$\bar{\sigma} = \frac{1}{2\,|A|\; tr\, A} \begin{bmatrix} -|A|\,(\beta_{11}^2 + \beta_{12}^2) - (d\beta_{11} - b\beta_{21})^2 - (b\beta_{22} - d\beta_{12})^2 \\ cd\beta_{11}^2 - 2ad\beta_{11}\beta_{21} + ab\beta_{21}^2 + cd\beta_{12}^2 - 2ad\beta_{12}\beta_{22} + ab\beta_{22}^2 \\ -|A|\,(\beta_{21}^2 + \beta_{22}^2) - (c\beta_{11} - a\beta_{21})^2 - (c\beta_{12} - a\beta_{22})^2 \end{bmatrix}$$

$$= \begin{bmatrix} \bar{\sigma}_{xx} \\ \bar{\sigma}_{xy} \\ \bar{\sigma}_{yy} \end{bmatrix} \tag{33.72}$$

*In the singular case,* $|C| = 4\,|A|\; tr\, A = 0$, *we may as a particular solution* $\bar{\sigma}$ *take, if,*

$$trA = 0 \quad : \quad \bar{\sigma}(t) = \begin{bmatrix} \gamma t \\ \frac{1}{2b}\left[\gamma - (\beta_{11}^2 + \beta_{12}^2)\right] - \frac{a}{b}\gamma t \\ -\frac{c}{b}\gamma t - \frac{a}{b^2}\gamma - \frac{\beta_{11}\beta_{21} + \beta_{12}\beta_{22}}{b} \end{bmatrix} \tag{33.73}$$

*where* $\gamma = \frac{1}{2|A|}\left[(d\beta_{11} - b\beta_{21})^2 + (d\beta_{12} - b\beta_{22})^2\right] + \frac{1}{2}(\beta_{11}^2 + \beta_{12}^2)$, *or if*

$$|A| = 0 \quad : \quad \bar{\sigma}(t) = \begin{bmatrix} \gamma t \\ \frac{1}{2b}\left[\gamma - (\beta_{11}^2 + \beta_{12}^2)\right] - \frac{a}{b}\gamma t \\ \frac{a^2}{b^2}\gamma t + \frac{a+d}{2b^2}(\beta_{11}^2 + \beta_{12}^2 - \gamma) - \frac{a}{b^2}\gamma - \frac{\beta_{12}\beta_{21}+\beta_{12}\beta_{22}}{b} \end{bmatrix} \tag{33.74}$$

*where* $\gamma$ *now denotes:* $(tr\ A)^{-2}\left[(d\beta_{11} - b\beta_{21})^2 + (d\beta_{12} - b\beta_{22})^2\right]$.

*For the* **GWD** *with* $\left|\tilde{C}\right| \neq 0$, *(33.23–33.24), a particular solution* $\tilde{\sigma}$ *is*

$$\hat{\sigma}(t) = e^{t\tilde{C}}\tilde{\sigma}(t);\ \tilde{\sigma}(t) = \int_0^t e^{-\tilde{C}\tau}\tilde{\delta}(\tau)d\tau = e^{t\tilde{C}}\left(1 - e^{-\beta^2 t}\right)\begin{bmatrix} m_x^2(0) \\ m_x(0)m_y(0) \\ m_y^2(0) \end{bmatrix} \tag{33.75}$$

*where* $m^0 = \left[m_x(0)\ m_y(0)\right]^T$ *is the initial value of the mean function, cf. Theorem 33.1.*

***Proof*** Concerning (33.72)–(33.74) for the **GD** model, see Appendix section "Appendix A: Particular Solutions for the GD Model". For the **GWD** model, (33.24) shows that the nonhomogeneous part depends on the mean function, which is a function of time $t$. Insertion of $\tilde{\boldsymbol{\delta}}(\boldsymbol{t})$, (33.23–33.24), into (33.57) gives (33.75) after lengthy reductions. □

**Remark 33.5** The RHS of **Formula** (33.75) for the **GWD** model is a *main result* of this study. It is noteworthy how the initial mean values of, $m_x$ and $m_y$, enter there in precisely the same manner as they themselves enter in $\tilde{\boldsymbol{\delta}}(\boldsymbol{t})$, cf. (33.23–33.24).

However, the reductions leading to the RHS of **Formula** (33.75) are really lengthy; it is decisive, first to have Theorem 33.1 on the *means* (33.46)–(33.48) available, and, secondly that there is an extensive cancellation of terms in the integrand of (33.75). The details are left out to save space, but a technical report may be obtained from the authors. Alternatively one could also make a computer-aided calculation of the integral, using Maple or similar software.

The full formula for $\boldsymbol{\Sigma}(\boldsymbol{t})$ in Theorem 33.2 below could in principle also be deduced by other methods. In fact, when $\boldsymbol{\Sigma}(\boldsymbol{0}) = \boldsymbol{0}$ in (33.85)–(33.87), Table 33.7, then we also arrive at the ensuing *moment formulae* from a *solution* of the **Kolmogorov equation**, cf. (33.3), and see Theorem 33.4 below. Although the argument is not without ambiguity, cf. Remark 33.10, it does give independent evidence of the *correctness* of (33.85)–(33.87), and hence of the **RHS** of (33.75). ▽

**Table 33.4** The **GD** covariance function $\sigma(t)$, for $\Delta^2 > 0, |C| \neq 0$

$$\sigma_{xx}(t) = e^{(a+d+2\Delta)t}k_1^* + e^{(a+d-2\Delta)t}k_2^* + e^{(a+d)t}k_3^* + \bar{\sigma}_{xx} \tag{33.76}$$

$$\begin{aligned}
k_1^* &= \tfrac{1}{4}\left(1 - \tfrac{d-a}{2\Delta}\right)^2 \sigma_{xx}^*(0) + \tfrac{b}{2\Delta}\left(1 - \tfrac{d-a}{2\Delta}\right)\sigma_{xy}^*(0) + \tfrac{b^2}{4\Delta^2}\sigma_{yy}^*(0)\\
k_2^* &= \tfrac{1}{4}\left(1 + \tfrac{d-a}{2\Delta}\right)\sigma_{xx}^*(0) - \tfrac{b}{\Delta}\left(\tfrac{1}{2} + \tfrac{d-a}{4\Delta}\right)\sigma_{xy}^*(0) + \tfrac{b^2}{4\Delta^2}\sigma_{yy}^*(0)\\
k_3^* &= \tfrac{b}{2\Delta^2}\left(c\sigma_{xx}^*(0) + (d-a)\sigma_{xy}^*(0) - b\sigma_{yy}^*(0)\right)\\
k_1^* &+ k_2^* + k_3^* = \sigma_{xx}^*(0)
\end{aligned}$$

$$\sigma_{xy}(t) = e^{(a+d+2\Delta)t}k_4^* + e^{(a+d-2\Delta)t}k_5^* + e^{(a+d)t}k_6^* + \bar{\sigma}_{xy} \tag{33.77}$$

$$\begin{aligned}
k_4^* &= \tfrac{c}{4\Delta}\left(1 - \tfrac{d-a}{2\Delta}\right)\sigma_{xx}^*(0) + \tfrac{bc}{2\Delta^2}\sigma_{xy}^*(0) + \tfrac{b}{4\Delta}\left(1 + \tfrac{d-a}{2\Delta}\right)\sigma_{yy}^*(0)\\
k_5^* &= -\tfrac{c}{4\Delta}\left(1 + \tfrac{d-a}{2\Delta}\right)\sigma_{xx}^*(0) + \tfrac{bc}{2\Delta^2}\sigma_{xy}^*(0) - \tfrac{b}{4\Delta}\left(1 - \tfrac{d-a}{2\Delta}\right)\sigma_{yy}^*(0)\\
k_6^* &= \tfrac{d-a}{4\Delta^2}\left(c\sigma_{xx}^*(0) + (d-a)\sigma_{xy}^*(0) - b\sigma_{yy}^*(0)\right)\\
k_4^* &+ k_5^* + k_6^* = \sigma_{xy}^*(0)
\end{aligned}$$

$$\sigma_{yy}(t) = e^{(a+d+2\Delta)t}k_7^* + e^{(a+d-2\Delta)t}k_8^* + e^{(a+d)t}k_9^* + \bar{\sigma}_{yy} \tag{33.78}$$

$$\begin{aligned}
k_7^* &= \tfrac{c^2}{4\Delta^2}\sigma_{xx}^*(0) + \tfrac{c}{2\Delta}\left(1 + \tfrac{d-a}{2\Delta}\right)\sigma_{xy}^*(0) + \tfrac{1}{4}\left(1 + \tfrac{d-a}{2\Delta}\right)^2\sigma_{yy}^*(0)\\
k_8^* &= \tfrac{c^2}{4\Delta^2}\sigma_{xx}^*(0) - \tfrac{c}{2\Delta}\left(1 - \tfrac{d-a}{2\Delta}\right)\sigma_{xy}^*(0) + \tfrac{1}{4}\left(1 - \tfrac{d-a}{2\Delta}\right)^2\sigma_{yy}^*(0)\\
k_9^* &= \tfrac{c}{2\Delta^2}\left(-c\sigma_{xx}^*(0) - (d-a)\sigma_{xy}^*(0) + b\sigma_{yy}^*(0)\right)\\
k_7^* &+ k_8^* + k_9^* = \sigma_{yy}^*(0)
\end{aligned}$$

*General Covariance Solutions*

Finally, by (33.58–33.59), (33.60–33.61), and Propositions 33.3–33.4, we get;

**Theorem 33.2** *The explicit covariance,* $\sigma(t) = [\sigma_{xx}(t)\ \sigma_{xy}(t)\ \sigma_{yy}(t)]^T$ *functions—solving (33.21–33.22) for the* **GD** *model with the nonsingular Ito coefficient matrix* $|C| \neq 0$*—are given by Tables 33.4, 33.5, 33.6 for the cases* $\Delta^2 > 0$, $\Delta^2 = 0$ *and* $\Delta^2 < 0$*, respectively.*

*The explicit covariance,* $\sigma(t) = [\sigma_{xx}(t)\ \sigma_{xy}(t)\ \sigma_{yy}(t)]^T$ *functions—solving (33.23–33.24) for the* **GWD** *model—are collected in Tables 33.7, 33.8, and 33.9 for the cases* $\Delta^2 > 0$, $\Delta^2 = 0$ *and* $\Delta^2 < 0$*, respectively.*

**Remark 33.6** It should be noted that the moments formulas (33.76–33.84) for the GD model with $|C| \neq 0$ have—independent of the sign $\Delta^2$—constant terms, $\bar{\sigma}_{xx}$, $\bar{\sigma}_{xy}$, $\bar{\sigma}_{yy}$, (33.72), depending on the drift ($A$), and diffusion ($B$)

**Table 33.5** The **GD** covariance function $\sigma(t)$, for $\Delta^2 = 0, |C| \neq 0$

$$\sigma_{xx}(t) = e^{(a+d)t}\left[\left(1 - \frac{1}{2}(d-a)t\right)^2 \sigma^*_{xx}(0) + 2bt\left(1 - \frac{1}{2}(d-a)t\right)\sigma^*_{xy}(0) + b^2t^2\sigma^*_{yy}(0)\right] + \bar{\sigma}_{xx} \quad (33.79)$$

$$\sigma_{xy}(t) = e^{(a+d)t}\left[\left(ct - \frac{1}{2}c(d-a)t^2\right)\sigma^*_{xx}(0) + \left(1 - \frac{1}{2}(d-a)^2t^2\right)\sigma^*_{xy}(0) + \left(bt + \frac{1}{2}b(d-a)t^2\right)\sigma^*_{yy}(0)\right] + \bar{\sigma}_{xy} \quad (33.80)$$

$$\sigma_{yy}(t) = e^{(a+d)t}\left[c^2t^2\sigma^*_{xx}(0) + 2ct\left(1 + \frac{1}{2}(d-a)t\right)\sigma^*_{xy}(0) + \left(1 + \frac{1}{2}(d-a)t\right)^2\sigma^*_{yy}(0)\right] + \bar{\sigma}_{yy} \quad (33.81)$$

**Table 33.6** The **GD** covariance function $\sigma(t)$, for $\Delta^2 < 0, |C| \neq 0$

$$\sigma_{xx}(t) = e^{(a+d)t}\left\{k_{10}^* \cos(2\Delta t) + k_{11}^* \sin(2\Delta t) + k_{12}^*\right\} + \bar{\sigma}_{xx} \tag{33.82}$$

$$k_{10}^* = \left(1 - \tfrac{bc}{2\Delta^2}\right)\sigma_{xx}^*(0) - \tfrac{b(d-a)}{2\Delta^2}\sigma_{xy}^*(0) + \tfrac{b^2}{2\Delta^2}\sigma_{yy}^*(0)$$
$$k_{11}^* = \tfrac{1}{\Delta}\left(-\tfrac{d-a}{2}\sigma_{xx}^*(0) + b\sigma_{xy}^*(0)\right)$$
$$k_{12}^* = \tfrac{b}{2\Delta^2}\left(c\sigma_{xx}^*(0) + (d-a)\,\sigma_{xy}^*(0) - b\sigma_{yy}^*(0)\right)$$
$$k_{10}^* + k_{12}^* = \sigma_{xx}^*(0)$$

$$\sigma_{xy}(t) = e^{(a+d)t}\left\{k_{13}^* \cos(2\Delta t) + k_{14}^* \sin(2\Delta t) + k_{15}^*\right\} + \bar{\sigma}_{xy} \tag{33.83}$$

$$k_{13}^* = \tfrac{1}{\Delta^2}\left(-\tfrac{c(d-a)}{4}\sigma_{xx}^*(0) + b\sigma_{xy}^*(0) + \tfrac{b(d-a)}{4}\sigma_{yy}^*(0)\right)$$
$$k_{14}^* = \tfrac{1}{2\Delta}\left(c\sigma_{xx}^*(0) + b\sigma_{yy}^*(0)\right)$$
$$k_{15}^* = \tfrac{d-a}{4\Delta^2}\left(c\sigma_{xx}^*(0) + (d-a)\,\sigma_{xy}^*(0) - b\sigma_{yy}^*(0)\right)$$
$$k_{13}^* + k_{15}^* = \sigma_{xy}^*(0)$$

$$\sigma_{yy}(t) = e^{(a+d)t}\left\{k_{16}^* \cos(2\Delta t) + k_{17}^* \sin(2\Delta t) + k_{18}^*\right\} + \bar{\sigma}_{yy} \tag{33.84}$$

$$k_{16}^* = \tfrac{c^2}{2\Delta^2}\sigma_{xx}^*(0) + \tfrac{c(d-a)}{2\Delta^2}\sigma_{xy}^*(0) + \left(1 - \tfrac{bc}{2\Delta^2}\right)\sigma_{yy}^*(0)$$
$$k_{17}^* = \tfrac{1}{\Delta}\left(c\sigma_{xy}^*(0) + \tfrac{d-a}{2}\sigma_{yy}^*(0)\right)$$
$$k_{18}^* = \tfrac{(-c)}{2\Delta^2}\left(c\sigma_{xx}^*(0) + (d-a)\,\sigma_{xy}^*(0) - b\sigma_{yy}^*(0)\right)$$
$$k_{16}^* + k_{18}^* = \sigma_{yy}^*(0)$$

elements. The terms $\mathbf{k}_i^*$ are independent of the *diffusion elements* (**B**). For the **moments** (33.85–33.87) of the **GWD** model, however, the *diffusion parameter* $\boldsymbol{\beta}$ is always involved in the *long-run solutions*, except for the trivial long-run *stationary* solution "0", see (33.96–33.97). ▽

**Remark 33.7** In both models the initial value $\boldsymbol{\sigma}(\mathbf{0})$ may be thought of as an *uncertainty* in the measurement of the *initial state vector*, $X(0)$. Then the explicit formulae allow a discussion of whether this *initial uncertainty* $\sigma(0)$ or the *diffusion coefficient* **B** plays the *dominating* role for $\boldsymbol{\sigma}(t)$, and hence for the future *deviations* of $\boldsymbol{X}(t)$ from the *mean value* $\boldsymbol{m}(t)$. ▽

**Table 33.7** The **GWD** covariance function $\sigma(t)$, for $\Delta^2 > 0$

$$\begin{aligned}\sigma_{xx}(t) =& e^{\left(a+d+2\Delta+\beta^2\right)t}\left\{k_1 + \left(1 - e^{-\beta^2 t}\right)\frac{1}{4}\left[\left(1 - \frac{d-a}{2\Delta}\right)m_x(0) + \frac{b}{\Delta}m_y(0)\right]^2\right\} + \\ & e^{\left(a+d-2\Delta+\beta^2\right)t}\left\{k_2 + \left(1 - e^{-\beta^2 t}\right)\frac{1}{4}\left[\left(1 + \frac{d-a}{2\Delta}\right)m_x(0) - \frac{b}{\Delta}m_y(0)\right]^2\right\} + \\ & e^{\left(a+d+\beta^2\right)t}\left\{k_3 + \left(1 - e^{-\beta^2 t}\right)\frac{b}{2\Delta^2}\left[cm_x^2(0) + (d-a)\,m_x(0)\,m_y(0) - bm_y^2(0)\right]\right\}\end{aligned} \tag{33.85}$$

where $k_1$, $k_2$, and $k_3$ are given in Table 33.4 with $\sigma_{xx}^*(0), \sigma_{xy}^*(0), \sigma_{yy}^*(0)$ replaced by $\sigma_{xx}(0), \sigma_{xy}(0), \sigma_{yy}(0)$

$$\begin{aligned}\sigma_{xy}(t) =& e^{\left(a+d+2\Delta+\beta^2\right)t}\left\{k_4 + \left(1 - e^{-\beta^2 t}\right)\left[\frac{c}{4\Delta}\left(1 - \frac{d-a}{2\Delta}\right)m_x^2(0) + \frac{bc}{2\Delta^2}m_x(0)\,m_y(0) + \frac{b}{4\Delta}\left(1 + \frac{d-a}{2\Delta}\right)m_y^2(0)\right]\right\} + \\ & e^{\left(a+d-2\Delta+\beta^2\right)t}\left\{k_5 + \left(1 - e^{-\beta^2 t}\right)\left[-\frac{c}{4\Delta}\left(1 + \frac{d-a}{2\Delta}\right)m_x^2(0) + \frac{bc}{2\Delta^2}m_x(0)\,m_y(0) - \frac{b}{4\Delta}\left(1 - \frac{d-a}{2\Delta}\right)m_y^2(0)\right]\right\} + \\ & e^{\left(a+d+\beta^2\right)t}\left\{k_6 + \left(1 - e^{-\beta^2 t}\right)\frac{d-a}{4\Delta^2}\left[cm_x^2(0) + (d-a)\,m_x(0)\,m_y(0) - bm_y^2(0)\right]\right\}\end{aligned} \tag{33.86}$$

where $k_4$, $k_5$, and $k_6$ are given in Table 33.4 with $\sigma_{xx}^*(0), \sigma_{xy}^*(0), \sigma_{yy}^*(0)$ replaced by $\sigma_{xx}(0), \sigma_{xy}(0), \sigma_{yy}(0)$

$$\begin{aligned}\sigma_{yy}(t) =& e^{\left(a+d+2\Delta+\beta^2\right)t}\left\{k_7 + \left(1 - e^{-\beta^2 t}\right)\frac{1}{4}\left[\frac{c}{\Delta}m_x(0) + \left(1 + \frac{d-a}{2\Delta}\right)m_y(0)\right]^2\right\} + \\ & e^{\left(a+d-2\Delta+\beta^2\right)t}\left\{k_8 + \left(1 - e^{-\beta^2 t}\right)\frac{1}{4}\left[\frac{c}{\Delta}m_x(0) + \left(1 - \frac{d-a}{2\Delta}\right)m_y(0)\right]^2\right\} + \\ & e^{\left(a+d+\beta^2\right)t}\left\{k_9 + \left(1 - e^{-\beta^2 t}\right)\frac{c}{2\Delta^2}\left[-cm_x^2(0) - (d-a)\,m_x(0)\,m_y(0) + bm_y^2(0)\right]\right\}\end{aligned} \tag{33.87}$$

where $k_7$, $k_8$, and $k_9$ are given in Table 33.4 with $\sigma_{xx}^*(0), \sigma_{xy}^*(0), \sigma_{yy}^*(0)$ replaced by $\sigma_{xx}(0), \sigma_{xy}(0), \sigma_{yy}(0)$

**Table 33.8** The **GWD** covariance function $\sigma(t)$, for $\Delta^2 = 0$

$$\sigma_{xx}(t) = e^{\left(a+d+\beta^2\right)t}\left[\left(\left(1-\frac{1}{2}(d-a)t\right)^2\sigma_{xx}(0)+2bt\left(1-\frac{1}{2}(d-a)t\right)\sigma_{xy}(0)+b^2t^2\sigma_{yy}(0)\right)\right.$$
$$\left.+\left(1-e^{-\beta^2 t}\right)\left[\left(1-\frac{1}{2}(d-a)t\right)m_x(0)-btm_y(0)\right]^2\right] \quad (33.88)$$

$$\sigma_{xy}(t) = e^{\left(a+d+\beta^2\right)t}\left[ct\left(1-\frac{1}{2}(d-a)t\right)\sigma_{xx}(0)+\left(1-\frac{1}{2}(d-a)^2t^2\right)\sigma_{xy}(0)+bt\left(1+\frac{1}{2}(d-a)t\right)\sigma_{yy}(0)\right.$$
$$\left.+\left(1-e^{-\beta^2 t}\right)\left(ct\left(1-\frac{1}{2}(d-a)t\right)m_x^2(0)+\left(1-\frac{1}{2}(d-a)^2t^2\right)m_x(0)m_y(0)+bt\left(1+\frac{1}{2}(d-a)t\right)m_y^2(0)\right)\right] \quad (33.89)$$

$$\sigma_{yy}(t) = e^{\left(a+d+\beta^2\right)t}\left[\left(c^2t^2\sigma_{xx}(0)+2ct\left(1+\frac{1}{2}(d-a)t\right)\sigma_{xy}(0)+\left(1+\frac{1}{2}(d-a)t\right)^2\sigma_{yy}(0)\right)\right.$$
$$\left.+\left(1-e^{-\beta^2 t}\right)\left(ctm_x(0)+\left(1+\frac{1}{2}(d-a)t\right)m_y(0)\right)^2\right] \quad (33.90)$$

**Table 33.9** The **GWD** covariance function $\sigma(t)$, for $\Delta^2 < 0$

$$\begin{aligned}\sigma_{xx}(t) = {} & e^{\left(a+d+\beta^2\right)t}\Bigg\{\Bigg(k_{10} + \left(1 - e^{-\beta^2 t}\right)\left[\left(1 - \frac{bc}{2\Delta^2}\right)m_x^2(0) - \frac{b(d-a)}{2\Delta^2}m_x(0)\,m_y(0) + \frac{b^2}{2\Delta^2}m_y^2(0)\right]\Bigg)\cos(2\Delta t) \\ & + \left\{k_{11} + \left(1 - e^{-\beta^2 t}\right)\left[-\frac{d-a}{2\Delta}m_x^2(0) + \frac{b}{\Delta}m_x(0)\,m_y(0)\right]\right\}\sin(2\Delta t) \\ & + k_{12} + \left(1 - e^{-\beta^2 t}\right)\frac{bc}{2\Delta^2}\left[cm_x^2(0) + (d-a)\,m_x(0)\,m_y(0) - bm_y^2(0)\right]\Bigg\}\end{aligned} \quad (33.91)$$

where $k_{10}$, $k_{11}$, and $k_{12}$ are given in Table 33.6 with $\sigma_{xx}^*(0), \sigma_{xy}^*(0), \sigma_{yy}^*(0)$ replaced by $\sigma_{xx}(0), \sigma_{xy}(0), \sigma_{yy}(0)$

$$\begin{aligned}\sigma_{xy}(t) = {} & e^{\left(a+d+\beta^2\right)t}\Bigg\{\Bigg(k_{13} + \left(1 - e^{-\beta^2 t}\right)\left[-\frac{c(d-a)}{4\Delta^2}m_x^2(0) + \frac{bc}{\Delta^2}m_x(0)\,m_y(0) + \frac{b(d-a)}{4\Delta^2}m_y^2(0)\right]\Bigg)\cos(2\Delta t) \\ & + \left\{k_{14} + \left(1 - e^{-\beta^2 t}\right)\left[\frac{c}{2\Delta}m_x^2(0) + \frac{b}{2\Delta}m_y^2(0)\right]\right\}\sin(2\Delta t) \\ & + k_{15} + \left(1 - e^{-\beta^2 t}\right)\frac{d-a}{4\Delta^2}\left[cm_x^2(0) + (d-a)\,m_x(0)\,m_y(0) - bm_y^2(0)\right]\Bigg\}\end{aligned} \quad (33.92)$$

where $k_{13}$, $k_{14}$, and $k_{15}$ are given in Table 33.6 with $\sigma_{xx}^*(0), \sigma_{xy}^*(0), \sigma_{yy}^*(0)$ replaced by $\sigma_{xx}(0), \sigma_{xy}(0), \sigma_{yy}(0)$

$$\begin{aligned}\sigma_{yy}(t) = {} & e^{\left(a+d+\beta^2\right)t}\Bigg\{\Bigg(k_{16} + \left(1 - e^{-\beta^2 t}\right)\left[\frac{c^2}{2\Delta^2}m_x^2(0) + \frac{c(d-a)}{2\Delta^2}m_x(0)\,m_y(0) + \left(1 - \frac{bc}{2\Delta^2}\right)m_y^2(0)\right]\Bigg)\cos(2\Delta t) \\ & + \left\{k_{17} + \left(1 - e^{-\beta^2 t}\right)\left[\frac{c}{\Delta}m_x(0)\,m_y(0) + \frac{d-a}{2\Delta}m_y^2(0)\right]\right\}\sin(2\Delta t) \\ & + k_{18} + \left(1 - e^{-\beta^2 t}\right)\frac{(-c)}{2\Delta^2}\left[cm_x^2(0) + (d-a)\,m_x(0)\,m_y(0) - bm_y^2(0)\right]\Bigg\}\end{aligned} \quad (33.93)$$

where $k_{16}$, $k_{17}$, and $k_{18}$ are given in Table 33.6 with $\sigma_{xx}^*(0), \sigma_{xy}^*(0), \sigma_{yy}^*(0)$ replaced by $\sigma_{xx}(0), \sigma_{xy}(0), \sigma_{yy}(0)$

*Compact versions* of the formulas for $\boldsymbol{\sigma}(t)$, $\boldsymbol{\Sigma}(t)$, may for the **GD** and **GWD** *models*—in the case of, $\boldsymbol{\sigma}(0) = \mathbf{0}$—be found in Theorems 33.3 and 33.4.

### *Asymptotics of the Covariance Functions*

From (33.76–33.93), the next result follows immediately,

**Corollary 33.2** *The asymptotic or long-run behavior, as* $t \to \infty$, *for the covariance function* $\sigma(t)$ *of the nonsingular* **GD** *modelwith* $|C| \neq 0$ *is given by*

$$\Delta^2 > 0 \quad : \quad \begin{cases} \lambda_1 < 0,\ \lambda_2 < 0 : & \lim\limits_{t\to\infty} \sigma(t) = \bar{\sigma} \\ \lambda_1 > 0 : & \sigma(t) \sim e^{\{a+d+2\Delta\}t} \begin{bmatrix} k_1^* \\ k_4^* \\ k_7^* \end{bmatrix} \end{cases} \tag{33.94}$$

$$\Delta^2 \leq 0 \quad : \quad trA < 0 : \quad \lim_{t\to\infty} \sigma(t) = \bar{\sigma} \tag{33.95}$$

*where* $\bar{\sigma}$ *isgiven in (33.72) and* $k_1^*, k_4^*, k_7^*$ *aregiven in (33.76–33.78).*

*The asymptotic behavior, as* $t \to \infty$, *for the covariance function* $\sigma(t)$ *of the* **GWD** *model, isgiven by*

$$\Delta^2 > 0 \quad : \quad \begin{cases} \lambda_1^{\tilde{C}} < 0,\ \lambda_2^{\tilde{C}} < 0 : & \lim\limits_{t\to\infty} \sigma(t) = 0 \\ \lambda_1^{\tilde{C}} > 0 : & \sigma(t) \sim e^{\{a+d+2\Delta+\beta^2\}t} \begin{bmatrix} k_1 + \kappa_1 \\ k_4 + \kappa_4 \\ k_7 + \kappa_7 \end{bmatrix} \end{cases} \tag{33.96}$$

$$\Delta^2 \leq 0 \quad : \quad a + d + \beta^2 < 0 : \quad \lim_{t\to\infty} \sigma(t) \equiv 0 \tag{33.97}$$

*where* $k_1, k_4, k_7$ *aregiven in (33.85–33.87), and*

$$\kappa_1 = \left[\frac{1}{4}\left(1 - \frac{d-a}{2\Delta}\right) m_x(0) + \frac{b}{\Delta} m_y(0)\right]^2 \tag{33.98}$$

$$\kappa_4 = \frac{c}{4\Delta}\left(1 - \frac{d-a}{2\Delta}\right) m_x^2(0) + \frac{bc}{2\Delta^2} m_x(0) m_y(0) + \frac{b}{4\Delta}\left(1 + \frac{d-a}{2\Delta}\right) m_y^2(0) \tag{33.99}$$

$$\kappa_7 = \frac{1}{4}\left[\frac{c}{\Delta} m_x(0) + \left(1 + \frac{d-a}{2\Delta}\right) m_y(0)\right]^2 \tag{33.100}$$

**Corollary 33.3** *The correlation coefficient of the* **GD** *model with* $|C| \neq 0$ *has the following asymptotics (in the notations of, 33.72, 33.76–33.78, 33.85–33.87, 33.96):*

$$\Delta^2 > 0 \quad : \quad \begin{cases} \lambda_1 < 0,\ \lambda_2 < 0: & \lim_{t\to\infty} \rho^2 = \frac{\bar{\sigma}_{xy}^2}{\bar{\sigma}_{xx}\bar{\sigma}_{yy}} \\ \lambda_1 > 0: & \lim_{t\to\infty} \rho^2 = \frac{[k_4^*]^2}{k_1^* k_7^*} = 1 \end{cases} \tag{33.101}$$

$$\Delta^2 = 0 \quad : \quad \begin{cases} trA < 0: & \lim_{t\to\infty} \rho^2 = \frac{\bar{\sigma}_{xy}^2}{\bar{\sigma}_{xx}\bar{\sigma}_{yy}} \\ trA > 0: & \lim_{t\to\infty} \rho^2 = 1 \end{cases} \tag{33.102}$$

$$\Delta^2 < 0 \quad : \quad trA < 0: \quad \lim_{t\to\infty} \rho^2 = \frac{\bar{\sigma}_{xy}^2}{\bar{\sigma}_{xx}\bar{\sigma}_{yy}} \tag{33.103}$$

*For the* **GWD** *model,*

$$\begin{array}{lll} \Delta^2 > 0 & : & \lim_{t\to\infty} \rho^2 = \frac{[k_4+\kappa_4]^2}{[k_1+\kappa_1][k_7+\kappa_7]} \\ \Delta^2 = 0 & : & \lim_{t\to\infty} \rho^2 = constant \end{array} \tag{33.104}$$

***Proof*** By the definition, $\boldsymbol{\rho^2(t)} = \frac{\sigma_{xy}^2(t)}{\sigma_{xx}^2(t)\sigma_{yy}^2(t)}$, and by using the asymptotics for the covariance function in the first part above, the asymptotics for the correlation function in the second part is obtained. □

**Remark 33.8** In Corollary 33.2, we have only given the asymptotics for the correlation coefficients of the **GD** model with $|\boldsymbol{C}| \neq \mathbf{0}$. It is interesting to note that, the **GD** model with the *singular* Ito coefficient matrix: $|\boldsymbol{C}| = \mathbf{0}$, e.g. in Table 33.2 with $\boldsymbol{\Delta^2 < 0}$, $\mathbf{tr}\boldsymbol{A} = \mathbf{0}$ and (33.73), the *asymptotics* [dominated by the *particular solutions* (33.73)] of the *correlation* coefficient gives a *constant*: $\lim_{t\to\infty} \boldsymbol{\rho^2} = -\frac{a^2}{bc} > \mathbf{0}$ ; see the related *ellipses, circles* of the *mean* functions in **Fig. 33.1**. ▽

*Stationarity* A *nonsingular diffusion* process is said to be *stationary*, or to have a stationary version, if it admits an *time-invariant probability* distribution. It is well known that a necessary and sufficient condition for the **GD** processes (33.14), with $|\Sigma(t)| \neq 0$, to be *stationary*, cf. (33.94–33.95), is that all eigenvalues of the *drift coefficient* **A**, cf. (33.32–33.34),—or equivalently the *Ito* coefficient matrix **C**, cf. (33.40–33.42)—have negative real parts.

Similarly, we see from (33.96) and (33.97) that the necessary and sufficient condition for the **GWD** processes (33.16) to be *stationary* is that all eigenvalues of the *Ito* coefficient matrix $\tilde{\mathbf{C}}$, cf. (33.43), have negative real parts.

Moreover, we note that the asymptotically stable *deterministic* system *remains stochastically* asymptotically stable upon *addition* of arbitrary strong disturbances ("*arithmetic noise*"), e.g. **GD** model. Such a stability property, determined entirely by the drift coefficient matrix $A$ disappears with higher (three-dimensional) diffusion processes. Furthermore, we note that with the addition of *geometric noise*, e.g. the **GWD** model, this *stability* property *cannot* be determined entirely by the drift matrix $\mathbf{A}$. With the **GWD** model, it can *only* be *stable* when $\boldsymbol{\lambda}_1^c < -\boldsymbol{\beta}^2$. Hence the *stability region* for the **GWD** model is *smaller* than for the **GD** model, see **Fig. 33.1**.

### *Singularity of the Covariance Matrix*

A diffusion process is said to be *nonsingular*, if its covariance matrix $\Sigma(t)$ is nonsingular for all $t > 0$, and *singular*, if $\Sigma(t)$ is singular for all $t > 0$.

For the **GD** model, (33.14–33.15), $\boldsymbol{\Sigma}(t), n = 2$, is *nonsingular*, if and only if

$$rank\ (B\ AB\ A^2B\ \cdots\ A^{n-1}B) = n \tag{33.105}$$

This *rank condition* is equivalent to *hypoellipticity* of the forward *Kolmogorov equation*, cf. Theorem 33.3 below. We state,

**Lemma 33.4** *Let $X(t)$ be described by the* **GD** *model, (33.14–33.15):*

*When $|B| \neq 0$, then $X(t)$ it is always nonsingular;*

*When $|B| = 0$, $X(t)$ is nonsingular, if and only if the columns of $B$ in (33.12) are not proportional to any eigenvector of $A$.*

*The eigenvectors are proportional to $(1, \alpha_1)$, $(1, \alpha_2)$ and $(1, \alpha)$, where $\alpha_1$, $\alpha_2$ and $\alpha$ are given in (33.35–33.36), i.e. $\frac{\beta_{11}}{\beta_{21}}$ or $\frac{\beta_{22}}{\beta_{12}} \neq \frac{d-a}{2b} \pm \frac{\Delta}{b} = \alpha_2$.*

***Proof*** When $|B| \neq 0$, (33.105) clearly holds.

But if $|B| = 0$, i.e. $\beta_{11}\beta_{22} - \beta_{12}\beta_{21} = 0$, then rank$(B) \neq 2$; next consider

$$(B\ \ AB) \quad = \quad \begin{bmatrix} \beta_{11}\ \beta_{12}\ a\beta_{11} + b\beta_{21}\ a\ \beta_{12} + b\beta_{22} \\ \beta_{21}\ \beta_{22}\ c\beta_{11} + d\beta_{21}\ \ c\beta_{12} + d\beta_{22} \end{bmatrix}. \tag{33.106}$$

Calculating all the determinants of the $2 \times 2$ submatrices, we get the same criteria, for the singularity of the submatrices, namely that

$$\frac{\beta_{11}}{\beta_{21}} \cdot \frac{\beta_{22}}{\beta_{12}} = 1 \qquad \text{and} \qquad \frac{\beta_{22}}{\beta_{12}} = \frac{d-a}{2b} \pm \frac{\Delta}{b} = \alpha_{i,} \quad i = 1, 2 \tag{33.107}$$

Given $|B| = 0$, the first equality is of course satisfied. Hence, the only way to avoid the singularity is that the second equality is *not* satisfied. Evidently, $\frac{\beta_{22}}{\beta_{12}}$ is the *slope* of the *column vector* of the diffusion matrix $\mathbf{B}$, (33.12). Therefore, the necessary and sufficient condition for $X(t)$ of the **GD** model to be *nonsingular* is that *none* of the *column* vectors of $\mathbf{B}$ coincide with any *eigenvector* of $\mathbf{A}$, (33.35), (33.36); see also **Fig. 33.1** □

## Probability Density Functions

### *Kolmogorov's Forward Equation*

In this section, we take an alternative approach to the treatment of the problems with the diffusion models in (33.14–33.15) and (33.16–33.17). For simplicity, the ***initial conditions*** are taken as ***deterministic***, i.e. $\boldsymbol{x}^0(\boldsymbol{\omega})$ is independent of $\omega \in \Omega$. Our models are written compactly as

$$dX = a(X)dt + B(X)dw, \quad X(0) = x^0, \tag{33.108}$$

and the *transition probability distribution* , $P(s, y, t, A)$, is given by

$$P(s, y, t, A) \quad = \quad P(X(t) \in A \mid X(s) = y) \tag{33.109}$$

for every $t > s > 0$, $y \in \mathbf{R}^n$ and each Borel set $A \subset \mathbf{R}^n$.

Moreover, provided that $P(s, y, t, \cdot)$—which is a probability measure on $\mathbf{R}^n$—is *known* to have a *transition probability density* function, $p(s, y, t, x)$, then $\boldsymbol{p(0, x^0, t, x)}$ *solves* the following system of equations (written with $\boldsymbol{u(t, x)}$ as the unknown), cf. (33.3):

$$\frac{\partial u}{\partial t} = \frac{1}{2} \sum_{j,k=1}^{n} b_{j,k}(x) \frac{\partial^2 u}{\partial x_j \partial_{x_k}} - \sum_{j=1}^{n} a_j(x) \frac{\partial u}{\partial x_j} \quad \text{for} \quad t > 0, \tag{33.110}$$

$$1 = \int_{\mathbf{R}^n} u(t, x)\, dx \quad \text{for each} \quad t > 0, \tag{33.111}$$

$$\delta_{x^0}(x) = \lim_{t \to 0_+} u(t, x); \tag{33.112}$$

where $\boldsymbol{b_{j,k}(x)}$ is a short hand for the $jk$th entry of $B(x)B(x)^T$; and $\boldsymbol{\delta_z}$ denotes the point mass (Dirac delta function) at $\boldsymbol{z}$ in $\mathbf{R}^n$. See Remark 33.10 below for assumptions and references.

The probability density $\boldsymbol{p(s, y, t, x)}$ is a *fundamental solution* to the *partial differential equation* (**PDE**) in (33.110), which is known as *Kolmogorov's forward equation* or the *Fokker-Planck equation.* See also Appendix D.

Our results in the previous sections may be found by solving (33.110)–(33.112) for the **GD** and **GWD** models. In addition, by doing so (or by the mere attempt to do so), further information may be derived; ultimately one finds the *probability distribution* for stochastic process $\boldsymbol{X(t)}$ at each fixed $t > 0$—and not just the first- and second-order *moments* for the diffusion $X(t)$.

*The GD Model*

For the Gaussian diffusion model it has been known how to attack (33.110)–(33.112) for a long time. A rather complete analysis was given in Hörmander (1967), and hence we only need here to give a brief account.

The main tool is the *Fourier transformation*, $\mathcal{F}$. Recall that $\mathcal{S}(\mathbf{R}^n)$ denotes the Fréchet space of rapidly decreasing $C^\infty$ functions, that is, those smooth $\boldsymbol{\varphi}(\boldsymbol{x})$ that for all multiindices $\alpha$ and $\beta$ in $\mathbf{N}_0^n$ satisfy

$$\sup\left\{ |x^\alpha \partial^\beta \varphi(x)| \;\middle|\; x \in \mathbf{R}^n \right\} < \infty; \tag{33.113}$$

where, $x^\alpha = x_1^{\alpha_1} \ldots x_n^{\alpha_n}$, and, $\partial^\beta = \partial_x^\beta = (\partial/\partial x_1)^{\beta_1} \ldots (\partial/\partial x_n)^{\beta_n}$.

Then $\mathcal{F}\boldsymbol{\varphi}$ defined by

$$\mathcal{F}\varphi(\xi) = \int_{\mathbf{R}^n} e^{-i\xi\cdot x}\varphi(x)\,dx \tag{33.114}$$

is a linear continuous bijection $\mathcal{F}$: $\mathcal{S}(\mathbf{R}^n) \to \mathcal{S}(\mathbf{R}^n)$, the *inverse* of which is given as $\mathcal{F}^{-1}\psi(x) = (2\pi)^{-n}\mathcal{F}\psi(-x)$. Moreover, the formulae

$$\mathcal{F}(\partial_x^\alpha \varphi) = i^{|\alpha|}\xi^\alpha \cdot \mathcal{F}\varphi, \quad \mathcal{F}(x^\alpha\varphi) = i^{|\alpha|}\partial_\xi^\alpha \mathcal{F}\varphi, \tag{33.115}$$

are valid for all multiindices $\alpha \in \mathbf{N}_0^n$ and all $\varphi \in \mathcal{S}(\mathbf{R}^n)$.

Furthermore, $\mathcal{F}$ extends to a linear continuous bijection $\mathcal{S}'(\mathbf{R}^n) \to \mathcal{S}'(\mathbf{R}^n)$, where $\mathcal{S}'(\mathbf{R}^n)$ denotes the dual space of tempered distributions. More precisely, any element $v$ of $\mathcal{S}'(\mathbf{R}^n)$ is a continuous linear map

$\mathcal{S}(\mathbf{R}^n) \to \mathbf{C}$, and, with the value at a given $\varphi \in \mathcal{S}(\mathbf{R}^n)$ denoted by $\langle v, \varphi \rangle$, then $\mathcal{F}v$ is the element of $\mathcal{S}'(\mathbf{R}^n)$ for which

$$\langle \mathcal{F}v, \varphi \rangle = \langle v, \mathcal{F}\varphi \rangle \quad \text{for every} \quad \varphi \in S(\mathbf{R}^n). \tag{33.116}$$

The space $\mathcal{S}'(\mathbf{R}^n)$ contains $L_p(\mathbf{R}^n)$ for every $p \in [1, \infty]$ and $M(\mathbf{R}^n)$—the Radon measures of finite total variation. In fact, the inclusion $M(\mathbf{R}^n) \subset \mathcal{S}'(\mathbf{R}^n)$ is given by $\langle \mu, \varphi \rangle = \int_{\mathbf{R}^n} \varphi\, d\mu$.

Moreover, $\mathcal{F}\mu(\xi) = \int e^{-i\xi\cdot x}\,d\mu$, since by (33.116),

$$\langle \mathcal{F}\mu, \varphi \rangle = \int_{\mathbf{R}^n} \mathcal{F}\varphi(x)\,d\mu(x) = \langle \int e^{-i\xi\cdot x}\,d\mu(x), \varphi \rangle. \tag{33.117}$$

In particular, if $\mu$ on $\mathbf{R}^n$ is given as the *probability distribution* of a stochastic variable $X$, this means that $\mathcal{F}\mu(-\xi) = E(e^{i\xi\cdot X})$, i.e. the *characteristic function* of $X$. As an example, $\mathcal{F}\delta_z = e^{-i\xi\cdot z}$.

Recall also that $\partial^\alpha u$ is a well-defined element of $\mathcal{S}'(\mathbf{R}^n)$ for each $u$ therein and each multi-index $\alpha$, namely $\langle \partial^\alpha u, \varphi \rangle = \langle u, (-1)^{|\alpha|}\partial^\alpha \varphi \rangle$. Using this definition, the identities in (33.115) carry over to all $u \in \mathcal{S}'(\mathbf{R}^n)$. Further details about these standard techniques are found in Rudin (1973).

Concerning the solution $\boldsymbol{u(t,x)}$ in (33.110), one can now for each $t \geq 0$ compute the *Fourier transform* in the $x$-variable and denote this by $\mathcal{F}u(t,\xi)$ or by $\hat{\boldsymbol{u}}(\boldsymbol{t},\boldsymbol{\xi})$. Because of formula (33.115), and since the *diffusion* coefficient $\boldsymbol{b}_{j,k}(\boldsymbol{x})$ in the **GD** model is *independent* of $x$, the *transformed* system

$$\frac{\partial \hat{u}}{\partial t} = -\frac{1}{2}\sum_{j,k=1}^{n} b_{j,k}\xi_j\xi_k\hat{u} + \sum_{j,k=1}^{n} a_{j,k}\xi_j\frac{\partial \hat{u}}{\partial \xi_k}, \tag{33.118}$$

$$1 = \hat{u}(t,0) \quad \text{for each } t > 0, \tag{33.119}$$

$$e^{-i\xi\cdot x^0} = \lim_{t\to 0_+} \hat{u}(t,\xi). \tag{33.120}$$

is *equivalent* to (33.110)–(33.112).

As noted in Hörmander (1967), when the *drift* coefficient $\boldsymbol{A} = (\boldsymbol{a}_{j,k})$, as in the **GD** model, is a *constant matrix*, then the Fourier transformed system, (33.118)–(33.120), is solved *uniquely* by,

$$\hat{u}(t,\xi) = \exp\left(-ix^0\cdot e^{tA^T}\xi - \frac{1}{2}\int_0^t (e^{sA^T}\xi)^T BB^T(e^{sA^T}\xi)\,ds\right) \tag{33.121}$$

for $t > 0$. By *comparison* with the *characteristic function* for Gaussian random variables, one gets the well-known result, (33.122)–(33.123):

**Theorem 33.3** *The GD model, (33.14–33.15), has a unique solution* $\boldsymbol{X}(\boldsymbol{t})$*, which for each* $t > 0$ *has a Gaussian distribution with the mean vector and covariance matrix, formally given by:*

$$m(t) = e^{tA}x^0 \tag{33.122}$$

$$\Sigma(t) = \int_0^t e^{sA}BB^Te^{sA^T}\,ds \tag{33.123}$$

*In particular,* $\boldsymbol{m}(\boldsymbol{t})$ *is given explicitly in (33.46–33.48), Theorem 33.1, and* $\boldsymbol{\Sigma}(\boldsymbol{t})$ *is given explicitly by the expressions in Theorem 33.2 (Tables 33.4, 33.5, and 33.6, with initial values,* $\boldsymbol{\Sigma}(0) = 0$*), and it is positive definite, i.e.* $\boldsymbol{\Sigma}(\boldsymbol{t}) > \boldsymbol{0}$*, if and only if Kolmogorov's equation (33.110) is* ***hypoelliptic*** *with the values of* $\boldsymbol{a}_{j,k}$ *and* $\boldsymbol{b}_{j,k}$ *used in the GD model; i.e., if and only if the* ***rank*** *condition (33.105) is fulfilled.*

***Proof*** See Theorem 8.2.10 in Arnold (1973) for the Gaussian distribution and the expressions for the mean and covariance (even between different times $s \neq t$). The equivalence with the *hypoellipticity* was observed in Hörmander (1967). □

Observe that since the rank condition (33.105) involves only $A$ and $B$, and not $t$, one has $\Sigma(t) > 0$ for every $t > 0$, if and only if $\Sigma(t) > 0$ holds at a single time $t$.

The formula for $\hat{\boldsymbol{u}}(\boldsymbol{t}, \boldsymbol{\xi})$ in (33.121) has another merit: suppose that $A$ and $B$ in (33.108) are such that $\Sigma(t)$ in (33.123) is only positive semi-definite. Then there is a subspace $N \subset \mathbf{R}^n$ such that the integral in (33.121) vanishes for every $\xi \in N$; consequently $|\hat{u}(t, \xi)| = 1$ for all $\xi \in N$. Therefore the transition probability $P(0, x^0, t, A)$ in (33.109) *cannot* have a density function $p$, for on the one hand, such a density would necessarily belong to $L_1$ with respect to the Lebesgue measure on $\mathbf{R}^n$, so $\hat{p}(0, x^0, t, \xi)$ would go to 0 for $|\xi| \to \infty$, and on the other hand, $p$ would solve (33.110)–(33.112) and therefore have $|\hat{p}(0, x^0, t, \xi)| = 1$ for $\xi \in N$, as we have just seen. This contradiction immediately leads to

**Proposition 33.5** *When* $\mathbf{x}^0$ *is independent of* $\omega$ *in* $\Omega$, *the properties:*

*(i) the* **GD** *model has a transition probability density* $\boldsymbol{p}(\mathbf{0}, \boldsymbol{x}^0, \boldsymbol{t}, \boldsymbol{x})$,
*(ii) the covariance function* $\Sigma(t)$ *is invertible for every* $t > 0$,
*(iii) the covariance function* $\Sigma(t)$ *is invertible for some* $t > 0$,

*are equivalent.*

**Remark 33.9** The formula in (33.123) is useful as a point of departure for an alternative determination of $\boldsymbol{\Sigma}(\boldsymbol{t})$. In fact, in *two* dimensions where $\boldsymbol{e}^{tA}$ can be written down explicitly, we have made a computer-aided calculation using Maple, and the result coincides with the formulae of Theorem 33.2, when the initial value $\Sigma(0)$ equals zero.

Specifically, this means that the *density function* $u(t, x) = p(0, x^0, t, x)$ becomes

$$p(0, x^0, t, x) = \frac{1}{\sqrt{(2\pi)^n |\Sigma(t)|}} e^{-\frac{1}{2}(x-m(t))^T \Sigma(t)^{-1}(x-m(t))} \tag{33.124}$$

with $\boldsymbol{m}(\boldsymbol{t})$, $\boldsymbol{\Sigma}(\boldsymbol{t})$ as in Theorems 33.1–33.2, respectively, *provided* $\Sigma(t) > 0$. ▽

**Remark 33.10** That the **GD** density function (33.124) *solves* (33.110)–(33.112) is known under the assumption that, first of all, $\boldsymbol{p}(\boldsymbol{s}, \boldsymbol{y}, \boldsymbol{t}, \boldsymbol{x})$ exists; secondly, the necessary derivatives

$$\frac{\partial p}{\partial t}, \quad a_j(x)\frac{\partial p}{\partial x_j}, \quad b_{j,k}(x)\frac{\partial^2 p}{\partial x_j x_k}, \quad j, k = 1, \ldots, n \tag{33.125}$$

exist as continuous functions; and, thirdly, the *transition function* of a diffusion process, $\boldsymbol{P}(\boldsymbol{s}, \boldsymbol{y}, \boldsymbol{t}, \boldsymbol{A})$ should have $\boldsymbol{a}(\boldsymbol{x})$ and $(\boldsymbol{b}_{j,k}(\boldsymbol{x}))_{j,k=1,\ldots,n}$ as the drift and diffusion coefficients with $y$-uniform convergence, cf. the definition of diffusion processes in Gikman and Skorokhod (1965, p. 375), [as observed in their

Remark 33.1, the existence of the derivatives in (33.125) is unnecessary because these always exist in the distribution sense in $\mathcal{S}'(\mathbf{R}^n)$].

However, the natural questions are not settled hereby: once a function solving (33.110)–(33.112) is obtained, it still has to be verified that it *coincides* with the density, $p(0, x^0, t, x)$, even when the latter is known to *exist* [in the **GD** case this is clear, however, since the adopted method shows the *uniqueness* of the solution]. Moreover, since $P(0, x^0, t, \cdot)$ is a probability measure for each $t > 0$, it is in $\mathcal{S}'(\mathbf{R}^n)$, cf. (33.116–33.117), so it is reasonable to ask whether it solves (33.110) in the distribution sense. Furthermore, it is a question whether any solution $u(t, x)$ of (33.110–33.112) coincides with $P(0, x^0, t, x)$ in general. ▽

*Geometric Wiener Diffusion*
The **GWD** model (33.16–33.17) turns out *not* to *have* probability densities.

**Proposition 33.6** *For the* **GWD** *model, (33.16–33.17), the solution of Kolmogorov's forward equation with side conditions, (33.110)–(33.112), is supported by a half-line in* $\mathbf{R}^n$.

*Hence a probability density function,* $p(0, x^0, t, x)$*, does not exist.*

***Proof*** The forward Kolmogorov equation (33.110) is here,

$$\frac{\partial u}{\partial t} = \frac{1}{2} \sum_{j,k=1}^{n} \beta^2 x_j x_k \frac{\partial^2 u}{\partial x_j \partial x_k} - \sum_{j,k=1}^{n} a_{j,k} x_k \frac{\partial u}{\partial x_j}, \tag{33.126}$$

since $\boldsymbol{b_{j,k}(x) = \beta^2 x_j x_k}$ for $j, k = 1,\ldots,n$.

The solution to (33.126), satisfying (33.111)–(33.112), is the *probability measure* $u(t, dx)$ on $\mathbf{R}^n$, defined for each $t > 0$ by the fulfillment of,

$$\int_{\mathbf{R}^n} \varphi(x) u(t, dx) \quad = \quad \int_{-\infty}^{\infty} \varphi(e^{t(A-\frac{\beta^2}{2} I)+r\beta I} x^0) e^{-\frac{r^2}{2t}} \frac{dr}{\sqrt{2\pi t}} \tag{33.127}$$

for every continuous bounded function $\varphi(x)$ on $\mathbf{R}^n$.

Clearly, $u(t, dx) = 0$ outside of the set:

$$\left\{ x \in \mathbf{R}^n \;\middle|\; \exists r \in \mathbf{R} \colon x = e^{t(A-\frac{1}{2}\beta^2 I)+r\beta I} x^0 \right\}, \tag{33.128}$$

which is a ($t$-dependent) *half-line*, since

$$e^{t(A-\frac{1}{2}\beta^2 I)+r\beta I} x^0 = e^{r\beta} e^{t(A-\frac{1}{2}\beta^2 I)} x^0 \tag{33.129}$$

As $\boldsymbol{u(t, dx)}$ is supported by *the Lebesgue null-set* (33.128), the *transition probability*, $\boldsymbol{P(0, x^0, t, dx)}$, cannot have a probability *density* function. □

That the $u(t, dx)$ stated in (33.127) actually is a *fundamental solution* of *Kolmogorov's equation* associated with the **GWD** model, (33.16–33.17), will not be proved here; the verification is quite lengthy and requires full use of the various techniques for partial differential equations. In fact, our "proof" here is based on determination of the solution to a corresponding **GD** model (for the "log" of $X$) followed by a transformation as a distribution density; cf. Hörmander (1985, ch.6) (a technical report may be obtained from the authors).

Moreover, in view of Remark 33.10, we are not able to definitely conclude that the solution (33.127) equals the transition probability $P(0, x^0, t, dx)$.

**Theorem 33.4** *Assuming that the probability measure $u(t, dx)$ in (33.127) is the probability distribution $P(0, x^0, t, dx)$ of $X(t)$ described by the **GWD** model, (33.16–33.17), then by insertion of $\varphi(x) = x$ in (33.127), we get*

$$E[X(t)] = \int_{\mathbf{R}^n} x u(t, dx) = \int_{-\infty}^{\infty} e^{-\frac{r^2}{2t}} e^{t(A - \frac{1}{2}\beta^2 I)} \cdot x^0 \frac{dr}{\sqrt{2\pi t}}$$

$$= e^{tA} \cdot x^0 \int_{-\infty}^{\infty} e^{-\frac{(r - t\beta)^2}{2t}} \frac{dr}{\sqrt{2\pi t}}$$

$$= e^{tA} \cdot x^0 \qquad (33.130)$$

*and by insertion of $\varphi(x) = x \cdot x^T$ in (33.127), we get*

$$E[X(t)X(t)^T] = \int_{\mathbf{R}^n} x \cdot x^T u(t, dx) = \qquad (33.131)$$

$$e^{\beta^2 t}(e^{tA}x^0)(e^{tA}x^0)^T \int_{-\infty}^{\infty} e^{-\frac{(r - 2t\beta)^2}{2t}} \frac{dr}{\sqrt{2\pi t}} = e^{\beta^2 t}(e^{tA}x^0)(e^{tA}x^0)^T.$$

*Hence by (33.130) and (33.131), we obtain the formal expression*

$$\Sigma(t) = E(XX^T) - E(X)E(X)^T = (e^{\beta^2 t} - 1)(e^{tA}x^0)(e^{tA}x^0)^T. \qquad (33.132)$$

*Expanding (33.132) by the explicit formulae (33.46), Theorem 33.1 for the mean values, $m(t) = e^{tA}x^0$, we find precisely: (33.85–33.87), (Table 33.7, Theorem 33.2), when the initial values $\Sigma(0)$ is: $\Sigma(0) = 0$.*

*Accordingly, under the assumption that **$u(t, dx)$** (33.127) is the probability **distribution**, we have not only the convenient expression in (33.132), but also independent evidence that parts of (33.85–33.87) are correct.*

*Formula (33.132) also shows that $\Sigma(t)$ is singular for every $t > 0$, when $\Sigma(0) = 0$, since, $y = e^{tA}x^0$ gives, $y \cdot y^T = (y_j y_k)$, which has rank 1.*

***Formulae from Stochastic Integration***

The conclusion in *Proposition 33.6* above that a *density* function does not exist can also be reached in the following way. The stochastic differential equation

$$dX = AX\,dt + BX\,dw \tag{33.133}$$

with $X(0) = x^0$, is known from the stochastic integrals to have the solution

$$X(t) = \exp\left[t\left(A - \frac{1}{2}B^2\right) + (w(t) - w(0))B\right] \cdot x^0, \quad t > 0, \tag{33.134}$$

when $A$ and $B$ commute. In particular, this holds when $B = \beta I$ and $A$ is arbitrary, as in our GWD model. See Arnold (1973, Thm. 8.5.2, Rem. 8.5.9) for a more general formula for $m$ independent Wiener processes. Since $[A, B] = 0$, (33.134) becomes,

$$\begin{aligned} X(t) &= e^{t(A-\frac{1}{2}\beta^2 I)} e^{(w(t)-w(0))\beta I} \cdot x^0 \\ &= e^{t(A-\frac{1}{2}\beta^2 I)} (e^{(w(t)-w(0))\beta} \cdot x^0). \end{aligned} \tag{33.135}$$

The vector $e^{(w(t)-w(0))\beta} \cdot x^0$ is in span$(x^0)$ for each $t > 0$ and $\omega \in \Omega$, and the linear mapping span$(x^0) \to \mathbf{R}^n$ given by $e^{t(A-\frac{1}{2}\beta^2 I)}$, has at most one-dimensional range; hence by (33.135), the vector $X(t)$ lies in a ($t$-dependent) subspace of $\mathbf{R}^n$.

Hence $P(0, x^0, t, \cdot)$ must vanish outside $e^{t(A-\frac{1}{2}\beta^2 I)}(\text{span}(x^0))$, and for this reason, the measure $\boldsymbol{P(0, x^0, t, \cdot)}$ does not have a density function.

## Final Comments

The *evolution* of the expectation and the covariance matrix of planar time-homogeneous diffusion processes is seldom systematically presented in the literature. We have obtained the *complete* set of *solutions* for the *moments* of the general bivariate Gaussian diffusion process and a broad class of planar geometric Wiener diffusion processes. They were derived from the ordinary differential equations generated by *Ito's Lemma*. These *closed-form* moment solutions—exposed in terms of the *basic* drift and diffusion coefficients—may offer useful insights and should find applications in factual studies of the diffusion dynamics within many areas of economic, social, and biological process analysis.

We have also related the moment solutions explicitly to the corresponding evolution of the transition *probability density* (or distribution), generated by Kolmogorov's forward equation, which may play a large role in the future research on stochastic differential equations.

**Acknowledgments** We wish to thank P. Alsholm (Technical University of Denmark) and J.M.S. Jensen (Vinci Computers) for kind assistance in computer calculations, and M. Jacobsen (University of Copenhagen), H. Spliid and H. Holst (Technical University of Denmark) for valuable comments and discussions. For discussions about the Kolmogorov equation, thanks are also due to Y. V. Prohorov (Steklov-Institute for Mathematics, Moscow).

## Appendix A: Particular Solutions for the GD Model

Based on the theory of ordinary differential equations, the particular solution of the affine differential equation

$$\dot{\sigma} = C\sigma + \delta \tag{33.136}$$

can be obtained as follows:

1. When coefficient matrix $C$ is nonsingular, i.e. $|C| \neq 0$, the critical point

$$\bar{\sigma} = -C^{-1}\delta. \tag{33.137}$$

In Proposition 33.2,

$$C = \begin{bmatrix} 2a & 2b & 0 \\ c & a+d & b \\ 0 & 2c & 2d \end{bmatrix}, \qquad \delta = \begin{bmatrix} \beta_{11}^2 + \beta_{12}^2 \\ \beta_{11}\beta_{21} + \beta_{12}\beta_{22} \\ \beta_{21}^2 + \beta_{22}^2 \end{bmatrix}, \tag{33.138}$$

hence

$$C^{-1} = \frac{1}{4\,\mathrm{tr}\,A\,|A|} \begin{bmatrix} -2d^2 - 2\,|A| & 4bd & -2b^2 \\ 2cd & -4ad & 2ab \\ -2c^2 & 4ac & -2a^2 - 2\,|A| \end{bmatrix}. \tag{33.139}$$

By inserting (33.138) and (33.139) into (33.137), then (33.72) follows.

2. When $C$ is singular, i.e. $|C| = 0$, then (33.22) implies

$$\begin{aligned} &\dddot{\sigma}_{xx} - 3\,(\mathrm{tr}\,A)\,\ddot{\sigma}_{xx} + 2\left[(\mathrm{tr}\,A)^2 + 2\,|A|\right]\dot{\sigma}_{xx} - 4\,(\mathrm{tr}\,A)\,|A|\,\sigma_{xx} \\ &= 2\,|A|\,(\beta_{11}^2 + \beta_{12}^2) + 2(d\beta_{11} - b\beta_{21})^2 + 2(d\beta_{12} - b\beta_{22})^2. \end{aligned} \tag{33.140}$$

When $\mathrm{tr}\,A = a + d = 0$, (33.140) becomes

$$\dddot{\sigma}_{xx} + 4\,|A|\,\dot{\sigma}_{xx} = 2\,|A|\,(\beta_{11}^2 + \beta_{12}^2) + 2(d\beta_{11} - b\beta_{21})^2 + 2(d\beta_{12} - b\beta_{22})^2. \tag{33.141}$$

Assuming that $\sigma_{xx} = \gamma t$, then by (33.141),

$$\gamma = \frac{\beta_{11}^2 + \beta_{12}^2}{2} + \frac{(d\beta_{11} - b\beta_{21})^2 + (d\beta_{12} - b\beta_{22})^2}{2\,|A|} \tag{33.142}$$

Based on (33.22), we get the relationship between $\sigma_{xx}$ and $\sigma_{xy}$ as

$$\sigma_{xy} = \frac{1}{2b}\left(\dot{\sigma}_{xx} - 2a\sigma_{xx} - \beta_{11}^2 - \beta_{12}^2\right), \tag{33.143}$$

the relationship between $\sigma_{yy}$ and $\sigma_{xx}$ as

$$\begin{aligned}\sigma_{yy} &= \tfrac{1}{2b^2}[\ddot{\sigma}_{xx} - (3a+d)\dot{\sigma}_{xx} + (2a^2 + 2ad - 2bc)\sigma_x^2 \\ &\quad +(a+d)(\beta_{11}^2 + \beta_{12}^2) - 2b(\beta_{11}\beta_{21} + \beta_{12}\beta_{22})]\end{aligned} \tag{33.144}$$

By inserting (33.142) and $\sigma_{xx} = \gamma t$ into (33.143) and (33.144), the particular solution of (33.73) is obtained.

When $|A| = ad - bc = 0$, (33.140) becomes

$$\dddot{\sigma}_{xx} - 3\,(\mathrm{tr}\,A)\,\ddot{\sigma}_{xx} + 2\,(\mathrm{tr}\,A)^2\,\dot{\sigma}_{xx} = 2(d\beta_{11} - b\beta_{21})^2 + 2(d\beta_{12} - b\beta_{22})^2 \tag{33.145}$$

Assuming that $\sigma_{xx} = \gamma t$, we get from (33.145)

$$\gamma = (trA)^{-2}\left[(d\beta_{11} - b\beta_{21})^2 + (d\beta_{12} - b\beta_{22})^2\right] \tag{33.146}$$

By inserting (33.146) and $\sigma_{xx} = \gamma t$ into (33.143) and (33.144), then the particular solution of (33.74) is obtained.

## Appendix B: Exponential Matrices in Two Dimensions

To calculate $e^{tA}$ for a matrix $A$ with entries $a$, $b$, $c$, and $d$, decompose it as

$$A = \frac{1}{2}(a+d)I + B, \qquad B = A - \frac{1}{2}(a+d)I = \begin{bmatrix} \frac{a-d}{2} & b \\ c & \frac{d-a}{2} \end{bmatrix}. \tag{33.147}$$

Since the matrices in (33.147) commute,

$$e^{tA} = e^{\frac{1}{2}(a+d)t} e^{Bt} \tag{33.148}$$

From the Hamilton-Cayley theorem, (33.29), tr$B = 0$ and (33.30) we get

$$B^2 = (\mathrm{tr}\,B)B - |B|I = \Delta^2 I, \tag{33.149}$$

and from this it is inferred that

$$B^{2n} = (\Delta^2)^n I, \qquad B^{2n+1} = (\Delta^2)^n B, \qquad n \in N_0 = \{0\} \cup N \tag{33.150}$$

Using (33.150) and the definition in (33.147), we have

$$\begin{aligned} e^{Bt} &= \sum_{n=0}^{\infty} \frac{t^n B^n}{n!} = \sum_{n=0}^{\infty} \frac{t^{2n} B^{2n}}{2n!} + \sum_{n=0}^{\infty} \frac{t^{2n+1} B^{2n+1}}{(2n+1)!} \\ &= \sum_{n=0}^{\infty} \frac{t^{2n} (\Delta^2)^n}{2n!} I + \sum_{n=0}^{\infty} \frac{t^{2n+1} (\Delta^2)^n}{(2n+1)!} B \end{aligned} \tag{33.151}$$

In case $\Delta^2 = 0$, and with $0^0 = 1,\ 0! = 1$, we immediately obtain from (33.151)

$$\Delta^2 = 0: \qquad e^{Bt} = I + tB \tag{33.152}$$

Thus, (33.152), (33.148), and (33.147) establish (33.47).

In case $\Delta^2 > 0$, (33.151) gives, cf. (33.31),

$$\begin{aligned} \Delta^2 > 0 \quad : e^{Bt} &= \sum_{n=0}^{\infty} \frac{(\Delta t)^{2n}}{2n!} I + \frac{1}{\Delta} \sum_{n=0}^{\infty} \frac{(\Delta t)^{2n+1}}{(2n+1)!} B \\ &= \cosh(\Delta t) I + \frac{1}{\Delta} \sinh(\Delta t) B \end{aligned} \tag{33.153}$$

In case $\Delta^2 < 0$, (33.151) gives analogously, cf. (33.31),

$$\begin{aligned} \Delta^2 < 0 \quad : e^{Bt} &= \sum_{n=0}^{\infty} \frac{(-1)^n (\Delta t)^{2n}}{2n!} I + \frac{1}{\Delta} \sum_{n=0}^{\infty} \frac{(-1)^n (\Delta t)^{2n+1}}{(2n+1)!} \\ &= \cos(\Delta t) I + \frac{1}{\Delta} \sin(\Delta t) B \end{aligned} \tag{33.154}$$

Thus, (33.153), (33.154), (33.148), and (33.147) establish (33.46), (33.48) respectively.

## Appendix C: Exponentials in Three Dimensions

To calculate the exponential matrix $e^{tC}$, we need the following

**Lemma 33.5** *If a* $3 \times 3$ *matrix A has three equal eigenvalues* $\lambda$*, then*

$$e^{tA} = e^{\lambda t} \left\{ I + t\,(A - \lambda I) + \frac{1}{2} t^2 \,(A - \lambda I)^2 \right\}, \tag{33.155}$$

*and if it has three distinct eigenvalues* $\lambda_1$, $\lambda_2$ *and* $\lambda_3$, *then*

$$e^{tA} = e^{\lambda_1 t}\frac{(A-\lambda_2 I)(A-\lambda_3 I)}{(\lambda_1-\lambda_2)(\lambda_1-\lambda_3)} + e^{\lambda_2 t}\frac{(A-\lambda_1 I)(A-\lambda_3 I)}{(\lambda_2-\lambda_1)(\lambda_2-\lambda_3)} + e^{\lambda_3 t}\frac{(A-\lambda_1 I)(A-\lambda_2 I)}{(\lambda_3-\lambda_1)(\lambda_3-\lambda_2)}. \tag{33.156}$$

***Proof*** See Apostol (1969). □

## Appendix D: The Basic Wiener Process and the Evolution of Transition Probability Densities

The fundamental stochastic process in continuous time is the *Wiener process (Brownian motion)*. The transition probability from any initial state (interval) to any other state (interval) is a fixed probability (unaffected by the past history of the stochastic process/states). A brief review of the methodology in Einstein (1905) is instructive and useful for an *exact derivation* of the *partial differential equation* (PDE) that generates the dynamics (evolution) of the probability densities from a Wiener process. The general solution of this PDE clarifies the origin and how the *conditional (transition) probability density function* of the Wiener process is calculated. Our demonstrations also provide a background for stochastic differential equations (SDE) and their solutions (sample paths), which are driven by the standard Wiener process.

### *Transition Probability Density and the Diffusion Equation*

Suppose we have a stochastic process described by the *conditional density* function, $p(x, t \mid x_0)$—with $x$ as the *state variable* (position, point) and $t$ as the *continuous-time* variable—describing for each value of $t$ the distribution of the states, e.g., the position of particles.

For a *small time step* (interval), $\tau$, the conditional distribution of states at time $t+\tau$ depends on its neighboring distribution. The *probability density* of the *increments* during the *period* $\tau$, is: $f(\Delta; \tau)$, with $\Delta$ as changes (distance) in the state (position) variable $x$ from any initial state (position), $x_0$.

The *probability* distribution of *increments* is assumed to have the *mean* zero:

$$\int_{-\infty}^{\infty} f(\Delta;\tau)d\Delta = 1\,; \quad E(\Delta) = \int_{-\infty}^{\infty} \Delta f(\Delta;\tau)d\Delta = 0 \tag{33.157}$$

With co-authors:
MOGENS ESROM LARSEN, Department of Mathematics, University of Copenhagen

and a *variance* proportional to the size of $\tau$:

$$\sigma_\Delta^2 = \int_{-\infty}^{\infty} \Delta^2 f(\Delta;\tau)d\Delta = b^2\tau \,; \quad b > 0 \quad (b^2 = D) \tag{33.158}$$

The conditional probability density function $p(x, t + \tau \mid x_0)$ at $t + \tau$ can then be obtained as a weighted average of the neighboring conditional probability density functions [a convolution of $p(x, t \mid x_0)$ and $f(\Delta; \tau)$, cf. (33.170) below],

$$p(x, t + \tau \mid x_0) = \int_{-\infty}^{\infty} p(x + \Delta, t \mid x_0) f(\Delta;\tau)d\Delta \tag{33.159}$$

The Taylor series of $p(x, t \mid x_0)$, developed from $(x, t)$ in both directions, yields

$$p(x, t + \tau \mid x_0) = p(x, t \mid x_0) + \frac{\partial p(x, t \mid x_0)}{\partial t}\tau + \cdots \tag{33.160}$$

and

$$p(x + \Delta, t \mid x_0) = p(x, t \mid x_0) + \frac{\partial p(x, t \mid x_0)}{\partial x}\Delta + \frac{1}{2}\frac{\partial^2 p(x, t \mid x_0)}{\partial x^2}\Delta^2 + \cdots \tag{33.161}$$

With substitution of (33.160) and (33.161) into the left and right side of (33.159), we obtain

$$p(x, t \mid x_0) + \frac{\partial p(x, t \mid x_0)}{\partial t}\tau \simeq p(x, t \mid x_0)\int_{-\infty}^{\infty} f(\Delta;\tau)d\Delta + \frac{\partial p(x, t \mid x_0)}{\partial x}\int_{-\infty}^{\infty} \Delta f(\Delta;\tau)d\Delta + \frac{1}{2}\frac{\partial^2 p(x, t \mid x_0)}{\partial x^2}\int_{-\infty}^{\infty} \Delta^2 f(\Delta;\tau)d\Delta \tag{33.162}$$

Reduction of (33.162) yields, using (33.157) and (33.158),

$$\frac{\partial p(x, t \mid x_0)}{\partial t}\tau \simeq \frac{1}{2}b^2\frac{\partial^2 p(x, t \mid x_0)}{\partial x^2}\tau \tag{33.163}$$

which shows that—*approximately* and independently of $\tau$—the *conditional density* function $p(x, t \mid x_0)$ satisfies the *diffusion* ("heat") equation:

$$\frac{\partial p(x, t \mid x_0)}{\partial t} = \frac{1}{2}b^2\frac{\partial^2 p(x, t \mid x_0)}{\partial x^2} \tag{33.164}$$

Thus, by making the *simple general descriptive assumptions* (33.157–33.159), and then the *first-order* (33.160) and the *second-order expansions* (33.161), Einstein (1905, 2005, p. 94) gave a clear-cut procedure for a *rigorous derivation* of the diffusion equation (33.164)—which of course physicists knew had a well-known ($b^2 = D$) solution.

To solve the *partial* differential equation (33.164), we use here the Fourier transformation ($\mathcal{F}$)

$$\mathcal{F}\, p(x,t\,|\,x_0) = \hat{p}(\xi,t\,|\,x_0) = \int_{-\infty}^{\infty} p(x,t\,|\,x_0)e^{-i\xi(x-x_0)}dx \tag{33.165}$$

to obtain the *ordinary* differential equation in $t$:

$$\frac{\partial \hat{p}}{\partial t}(\xi,t\,|\,x_0) = \frac{d\hat{p}}{dt}(\xi,t\,|\,x_0) = \frac{1}{2}\,b^2(-i\xi)^2\hat{p}(\xi,t\,|\,x_0) = -\frac{1}{2}\,b^2\xi^2\hat{p}(\xi,t\,|\,x_0) \tag{33.166}$$

Hence the solution of (33.166) is

$$\hat{p}(\xi,t\,|\,x_0) \;=\; \hat{\upsilon}(\xi)\, e^{-\frac{1}{2}b^2\xi^2 t} \tag{33.167}$$

Using the inverse Fourier transformation, we get the solution of (33.164) as the convolution (33.170) of the inverse of (33.167); we obtain, $\upsilon(x-x_0)$, cf. (33.167), as

$$\upsilon(x-x_0) \;=\; \mathcal{F}^{-1}\,\hat{\upsilon}(\xi) \;=\; \frac{1}{2\pi}\int_{-\infty}^{\infty}\hat{\upsilon}(\xi)e^{i\xi(x-x_0)}d\xi \tag{33.168}$$

and the Gauß kernel, $p_N(x,t\,|\,x_0)$, as

$$p_N(x,t\,|\,x_0) = \mathcal{F}^{-1}\,e^{-\frac{1}{2}b^2\xi^2 t} = \frac{1}{2\pi}\int_{-\infty}^{\infty} e^{-\frac{1}{2}b^2\xi^2 t}e^{i\xi(x-x_0)}d\xi = \frac{1}{\sqrt{2\pi b^2 t}}\,e^{-\frac{1}{2}\frac{(x-x_0)^2}{b^2 t}} \tag{33.169}$$

As the inverse Fourier transform takes a product into a convolution, we get, cf. (33.167–33.169),

$$\begin{aligned} p(x,t\,|\,x_0) \;&=\; \mathcal{F}^{-1}\,\hat{p}(\xi,t\,|\,x_0) \;=\; \frac{1}{2\pi}\int_{-\infty}^{\infty}\hat{p}(\xi,t\,|\,x_0)\,e^{i\xi(x-x_0)}d\xi \;= \\ \upsilon(x-x_0) * p_N(x,t\,|\,x_0) \;&=\; \int_{-\infty}^{\infty}\upsilon(x-x_0-s)\,p_N(s,t\,|\,x_0)ds \end{aligned} \tag{33.170}$$

Now, in the sense of "distribution" (generalized functions), the Gauß kernel (33.169) converges to the Dirac $\delta(\boldsymbol{x} - \boldsymbol{x}_0)$ function, for $t \to 0$. Hence (33.170) gives

$$p(x, 0 \mid x_0) = \lim_{t \to 0} p(x, t \mid x_0) = \upsilon(x - x_0) * \delta(x - x_0) = \upsilon(x - x_0) \qquad (33.171)$$

If we originally had chosen the boundary condition as

$$\upsilon(x - x_0) = \delta(x - x_0) \qquad (33.172)$$

then we would have the *conditional probability density* function as

$$p(x, t \mid x_0) = \delta(x - x_0) * p_N(x, t \mid x_0) = p_N(x, t \mid x_0) \qquad (33.173)$$

Thus, we may interpret the Gauß kernel (33.169, 33.173) as the solution (33.170) to the *diffusion* equation (33.164) with the *boundary condition*, (33.172). See also, Bachelier (1900, p. 46 ; 1964, p. 38).

## BIBLIOGRAPHY


Apostol TM (1969) Some Explicit Formulas for the Exponential Matrix $e^{tA}$. American Mathematical Monthly 76:289–292

Arnold L (1973) Stochastic Differential Equations: Theory and Applications. German original published by R. Oldenbourg Verlag, Munich

Bachelier L (1900) Theorie de la spéculation. Annales scientifiques de l'Ecole normmale supérieure, 3e série 17(1018), English translation in: Cootner, P. H. (ed.) *The Random Character of Stock Market Prices.* MIT Press, Cambridge Mass., 1964: 17–78

Chang FR, Malliaris AG (1987) Asymptotic Growth under Uncertainty—Existence and Uniqueness. Review of Economic Studies (54):169–174

Einstein A (1905) Über die von der molekularkinetischen Theorie der Wärme gefordete Bewegung von in ruhenden Flüssigkeiten suspendierten Teilschen. Annalen der Physik (17):549–560, Translated as "On the Motion of Small particles in Liquids at Rest required by the Molecular-Kinetic Theorey of Heat" in the following volumes: (i) Fürth, R. (ed.) *Albert Einstein: Investigations on the Theory of Brownian Movement* Dover Publ., New York. (ii) Stachel, J. (ed.) *Einsteins Miraculous Year. Five Papers that Changed the Face of Physics.* Princeton University Press, Princeton, 2005

Gikman II, Skorokhod AV (1965) Introduction to the Theory of Random Processes. W. B. Saunders Company, Philadelphia, London, Toronto, 1969, Russian original published by Nauka, Moscow

Hörmander L (1967) Hypoelliptic Second Order Differential Equations. Acta Math 119:147–171

Hörmander L (1985) The analysis of linear partial differential operators. Grundlehren der mathematischen Wissenschaften 256, 257, 274, 275

Ito K, McKean HP Jr (1974) Diffusion Processes and Their Sample Paths. Springer–Verlag, New York, Second printing

Jacobsen M (1991) Homogeneous Gaussian Diffusions in Finite Dimensions. Preprint 3, Institute of Mathematical Statistics, University of Copenhagen

Jensen BS (1994) The Dynamic Systems of Basic Economic Growth Models. Kluwer Academic Publishers, Dordrecht

Karatzas I, Shreve S (1988) Brownian Motions and Stochastic Calculus. Springer–Verlag, New York

Merton RC (1975) An Asymptotic Theory of Growth under Uncertainty. Review of Economic Studies 42:375–393, Ch.17 in Merton (1990)

Øksendal B (2005) Stochastic Differential Equations, 6th edn. Universitext, Springer–Verlag, Berlin

Prohorov YV, Rozanov YA (1969) Probability Theory. Springer

Pugachev VS, Sinitsyn IN (1987) Stochastic Differential Systems. John Wiley and Sons, New York

Rudin W (1973) Functional Analysis. McGraw–Hill

Selby SM (1973) Standard Mathematical Tables, 21st edn. The Chemical Rubber Co, Cleveland, Ohio

Soong TT (1973) Random Differential Equations in Science and Engineering. Academic Press, New York

# Bibliography


Acemoglu D, Restrepo P (2018) The Race between Man and Machine: Implications of Technology for Growth, Factor Shares, and Employment. American Economic Review 108(6):1488–1542

Aczel J (1966) Lectures on Functional Equations and their Applications. Academic Press, New York

Afonso O, Sequeira T, Almelda D (2023) Technological Knowledge and Wages: From Skill Premium to Wage Polarization. Journal of Economics 2023:1–17. https://doi.org/10.1007/s00712-023-00833-y

Aghion P, Durlauf S (eds) (2005) Handbook of Economic Growth, 1st edn. Elsevier, Amsterdam, North–Holland

Aghion P, Howitt P (1992) A Model of Growth through Creative Destruction. Econometrica 60:323–351

Aghion P, Howitt P (1998) Endogenous Growth Theory. The MIT Press, Cambridge, MA and London, England

Ahrend JC (2006) Die Korrespondenz Johann Heinrich von Thünens. Tellower Thünen Schriften 6, (Mecklenburg: Thünen–Museum–Tellow)

Akerlof G, Nordhaus WD (1967) Balanced Growth – A Razor's Edge. International Economic Review 8:343–348

Akin JS, Stewart JF (1979) Theoretical Restrictions on the Parameters of Indirect Addilog Demand Equations. Econometrica 47:779–780

Alexander SS (1949) The accelerator as a generator of steady growth. Quart J Economics 63:174–197

Alexander SS (1950) Mr. Harrod's dynamic model. Economic J 60:724–739

Allen RC (1982) The Effciency and Distributional Consequences of Eighteenth Century Enclosures. The Economic Journal 92:937–953

Allen RC (1988) The Price of Freehold Land and the Interest Rate in the Seventeenth and Eighteenth Centuries. The Economic History Review 41:33–50

Allen RC (1992) Enclosure and the Yeoman. Clarendon Press, Oxford

Allen RC (1999) Tracking the Agricultural Revolution in England. The Economic History Review 52:209–235





B. S. Jensen, *The Elements and Dynamic Systems of Economic Growth and Trade Models*, https://doi.org/10.1007/978-3-031-52493-6

Allen RC (2000) Economic Structure and Agricultural Productivity in Europe, 1300–1500. The European Review of Economic History 4:1–26
Allen RC (2008) The Nitrogen Hypothesis and the English Agricultural Revolution: A Biological Analysis. The Journal of Economic History 68:182–210
Allen RC, O'Grada C (1988) On the Road again with Arthur Young : English, Irish, and French Agriculture during the Industrial Revolution. The Economic Journal 92:937–953
Allen RGD (1932) The Foundations of a Mathematical Theory of Exchange. Economica 36:197–226
Allen RGD (1938) Mathematical Analysis for Economists. MacMillan, London
Amano A (1964) A further note on Professor Uzawa's Two–Sector Model of Economic Growth. Rev Econ Stud 31:97–101
Andersen S, Harrison GW, Lau MI, Rutstrom EE (2008) Eliciting Risk and Time Preferences. Econometrica 76:583–618
Andersen S, Harrison GW, Lau MI, Rutstrom EE (2018) Multiattribute Utility Theory, Intertemporal Utility, and Correlation Aversion. International Economic Review 59:537–555
Andersen TB, Jensen PS, Skovsgaard CV (2016) The heavy plow and the agricultural revolution in Medieval Europe. Journal of Development Economics 118:133–149
Andronov AA, Chaikin CE (1949) Theory of Oscillations. Princeton University Press, New Jersey
Andronov AA, Leontovich EA, Gordon II, Maier AG (1971) Theory of Bifurcations of Dynamic Systems on a Plane. NASA and National Science Foundation, Washington, D.C
Antony A (2010) A Class of Changing Elasticity of Substitution Production Functions. Journal of Economics 100:165–183
Apostol TM (1969) Some Explicit Formulas for the Exponential Matrix $e^{tA}$. American Mathematical Monthly 76:289–292
Arnold L (1973a) Stochastic Differential Equations: Theory and Applications. German original published by R. Oldenbourg Verlag, Munich
Arnold VI (1973b) Ordinary Differential Equations. MIT Press, Mass
Arnold VI (1978) Mathematical Methods of Classical Mechanics. In: Springer–Verlag, New York
Arnold VI (1986) Catastrophe Theory, 2nd edn. Springer–Verlag, Berlin
Arnold VI (1988) Geometrical Methods in the Theory of Ordinary Differential Equations, 2nd edn. Springer–Verlag, New York
Arrow KJ (1961) Additive Logarithmic Demand Functions and the Slutsky Relations. Review of Economic Studies 28:176–181
Arrow KJ (1971) Essays in The Theory of Risk–Bearing. North–Holland
Arrow KJ (1974) General Economic Equilibrium: Purpose, Analytic Techniques, Collective Choice. American Economic Review 64:253–272
Arrow KJ (1985) Maine and Texas – Economic History. American Economic Review 75:320–323
Arrow KJ, Debreu G (1954) Existence of an Equilibrium for an Competitive Economy. Econometrica 22:265–90
Arrow KJ, Kurz M (1970) Public Investment, The Rate of Return, and Optimal Fiscal Policy. The Johns Hopkins Press, Baltimore
Arrow KJ, Chenery HB, Minhas BS, Solow RM (1961) Capital–Labour Substitution and Economic Efficiency. Review of Economics and Statistics 43:225–250

Arrowsmith DK, Place CM (1982) Ordinary Differential Equations. Chapman & Hall, London

Arrowsmith DK, Place CM (1990) An Introduction to Dynamical Systems. Cambridge University Press, Cambridge

Ashenfelter OC, Card D (eds) (1999) Handbook of Labor Economics, vol 3A–3C. Amsterdam, Elsevier

Ashley WJ (1913) Comparative Economic History and the English Landlord. Economic Journal 23:165–181

Ashraf Q, Galor O (2011) Dynamics and Stagnation in the Malthusian Epoch. American Economic Review 101:2003–2041

Ashraf Q, Galor O (2013) The "Out of Africa" Hypothesis, Human Genetic Diversity, and Comparative Economic Developmnet. American Economic Review 103:1–46

Ashton TS (1948, 1962) The Industrial Revolution. Oxford University Press, London

Ashton TS (1955) An Economic History of England : The 18th Century. Methuen & Co, London

Atkeson A, Ogaki M (1996) Wealth–varying Intertemporal Elasticities of Substitution: Evidence from Panel and Aggregate Data. Journal of Monetary Economics 38:507–534

Atsumi H (1971) The Long–Run Offer Function and a Dynamic Theory of International Trade. Journal of International Economics 1:267–299

Attanasio OP, Weber G (1989) Intertemporal Substitution, Risk Aversion, and the Euler Equation for Consumption. Economic Journal 99:59–73

Attanasio OP, Weber G (1995) Is Consumption Growth Consistent with Intertemporal Optimization ? Evidence from the Consumer Expenditure Survey. Journal of Political Economy 103:1121–1157

Bachelier L (1900) Theorie de la spéculation. Annales scientifiques de l'Ecole normmale supérieure, 3e série 17(1018), English translation in: Cootner, P. H. (ed.) *The Random Character of Stock Market Prices.* MIT Press, Cambridge Mass., 1964: 17–78

Back K, Liu R, Teguia A (2019) Increasing Risk Aversion and Life Cycle Investing. Mathematics and Financial Economics 13:287–302

Bairam E (1989) Learning–by–Doing: Variable Elasticity of Substitution and Economic Growth in Japan, 1878–1939. Journal of Development Studies 25:344–53

Balasko Y (1988) Foundations of the Theory of General Equilibrium. Academic Press Inc., New York

Baldwin R (1992) The Growth Effects of 1992. Economic Policy 4(9):247–281

Baldwin RE (2008) The Development and Testing of Heckscher–Ohlin Trade Models: A Review. The MIT Press

Bardhan PK (1965a) Equilibrium Growth in the International Economy. Quarterly Journal of Economics 79:455–464

Bardhan PK (1965b) International Differences in Production Functions, Trade and Factor Prices. Economic Journal 75:81–87

Bardhan PK (1966) On Factor Accumulation and the Pattern of International Specialisation. Review of Economics Studies 33:39–44

Bardhan PK (1970) Economic Growth, Development, and Foreign Trade. Wiley–Interscience, New York

Barnett WA, Lee YW (1985) The Global Properties of the Miniflex Laurent, Generalized Leontief, and Translog Flexible Functional Forms. Econometrica 53:1421–1437

Baron DP, Forsythe R (1979) Models of the Firm and International Trade under Uncertainty. American Economic Review 69:565–74

Barone E (1908) Principi di Economia Politica. Tipografia Nazionale di G. Bertero, Rome

Barro RJ (ed) (1989) Modern Business Cycle Theory. Basil Blackwell, Oxford

Barro RJ (1991) Economic Growth in a Cross–Section of Countries. Quarterly Journal of Economics 106:407–443

Barro RJ (1999) Ramsey Meets Laibson in the Neoclassical Growth Model. Quarterly Journal of Economics 114:1125–1152

Barro RJ, Sala-i-Martin X (1992) Convergence. Journal of Political Economy 100:223–251

Barro RJ, Sala-i-Martin X (2004) Economic Growth Theory, 2nd edn. M.I.T. Press, Cambridge, Mass

Barten AP, Boehm V (1982) Consumer theory. pp 381–429, In: Arrow, K. J. and Intriligator, M. D. (eds), *Handbook of mathematical economics*, vol 2. North–Holland, Amsterdam.

Bartz RP (2004) Die Thaer–Thünensche Tradition und die Entwicklung des ländliches Raumes. Tellower Thünen Schriften 4, (Mecklenburg: Thünen–Museum–Tellow)

Bartz RP, Zühlsdorf P (1994) Entdeckungen in Mecklenburg – Das Thünen–Museum–Tellow. Laumann Verlag, Dülmen

Batchelder PM (1967) An Introduction to Linear Difference Equations. Dover Publications, New York, Harvard University Press, 1927

Batra RN (1974) Resource Allocation in a General Equilibrium Model of Production under Uncertainty. Journal of Economic Theory 8:50–63

Baumol WJ (1958) Topology of Second Order Linear Difference Equations with Contant Coefficients. Econometrica 26:258–285

Baumol WJ (1970) Economic Dynamics, 3rd edn. MacMillan, London

Becker RA, Burmeister E (1991) Growth Theory, vol I–III. Edward Elgar, Aldershot

Becker RA, Foias C (1987) A Characterization of Ramsey Equilibrium. Journal of Economic Theory 41:173–184, Reprinted in Becker (1991)

Becker RA, Boyd JH, Sung BY (1989) Recursive Utility and Optimal Capital Accumulation. I. Existence. Journal of Economic Theory 47:76–100

Beckett JV (1986) The Aristocracy in England 1660–1914. Basil Blackwell, Oxford

Beckett JV (1990) The Agricultural Revolution. Basil Blackwell, Oxford

Beckmann MJ, Puu T (1990) The Spatial Structures. Springer–Verlag, Berlin

Bellman R (1953) Stability Theory of Differential Equations. McGraw–Hill, New York

Bellman R, Cooke KL (1963) Differential–Difference Equations. Academic Press, New York

Bencivenga VR (1991) Financial Intermediation and Endogenous Growth. Review of Economic Studies 58:159–209

Bendixson I (1901) Sur les courbes définies par des equations différentielles. Acta Mathematica 24:1–88

Bentzel R (1953) Inkomstfördelingen i Sverige. Almqvist and Wiksell, Uppsala

Bentzel R, Hansen B (1954) On Recursiveness and Interdependency in Economic Models. Rev Econ Stud 22:153–168

Bentzel R, Johansson O (1959) Om Homogenitet i Produktionsfunktioner. Ekonomisk Tidsskrift 61:146–179

Bernoulli D (1738, 1954) Exposition of a New Theory on the Measurement of Risk. Econometrica 22:23–36

Berthelemy JC, Vardoudakis A (1996) Economic Growth, Convergence Clubs, and the Role of Financial Development. Oxford Economic Papers 48:300–28

Bertola G (1993) Factor Shares and Savings in Endogenous Growth. American Economic Review 83:1184–1190

Bertola G (1996) Factor Shares in OLG Models of Growth. European Economic Review 40:1541–1560

Bhagwati J (1964) The Pure Theory of International Trade: A Survey. Economic Journal 74:1–78, The Royal Economic Society, *Surveys of Economic Theory*, Volume 2, (1965), 156–239, London, Macmillan.

Bhagwati JN (1981) International Trade: Selected Readings, 2nd edn. MIT Press, Cambridge, MA

Bieberbach L (1923) Theorie der Differential–Gleichungen. Verlag von Julius Springer, Berlin

Birkhoff G, Rota G (1989) Ordinary Differential Equations, 4th edn. John Wiley & Sons, New York

Birkhoff GD (1927) Dynamical Systems. American Mathematical Society Colloquium Publications IX 1927, Rev. ed. 1966, Providence, Rhode Island

Björn C (1987) The peasantry and agrarian reform in Denmark. Scandinavian Economic History Review 25:117–137

Black J (1957) A Formal Proof of the Concavity of the Production Possibility Function. Economic Journal 67:133–135

Blackorby C, Schworm W, Venables A (1993) Necessary and Sufficient Conditions for Factor Price Equalization. Review of Economic Studies 60:413–434

Blanchard OJ, Fischer S (1992) Lectures on Macroeconomics. MIT Press

Blaug M (1985) Economic Theory in Retrospect, 4th edn. Cambridge University Press, Cambridge

Blaug M (2002) Economic Theory In Retrospect, 3rd edn. Cambridge University Press, Cambridge

Blaug M, Lloyd P (eds) (2010) Famous Figures and Diagrams in Economics. Edward Elgar, Cheltenham UK

Bliss C (1975) Capital Theory and the Distribution of Income. North–Holland, Amsterdam

Boberg-Fazlic N, Jensen PS, Lampe M, Sharp P, Skovsgaard CV (2023) 'Getting to Denmark': The Role of Agricultural Elites for Development. Journal of Economic Growth. https://doi.org/10.1007/s10887-023-09226-8

de Boer P, van Daal J, Rodrigues JFD (2023) Consumer preferences in CGE models, when data are scarce: Comparing the linear expenditure and the indirect addilog systems. Economic Systems Research 35:1–29

de Boer PMC, Paap R (2009) Testing non–nested demand relations: linear expenditure systems versus indirect addilog. Stat Neerlandica 63:368–384

Böhm-Bawerk Ev (1921) Positive Theorie des Kapitales. Vierte Auflage, Gustav Fischer Verlag, Jena ; transl. W. Smart, (1923) *Positive Theory of Capital*, Books for Libraries Press, New York.

Bonatti L, Felice G (2008) Endogenous growth and the changing sectoral composition in advanced economies. Structural Change and Economic Dynamics 19:109–131

Boole G (1958) Calculus of Finite Differences, 4th edn. Chelsea Publishing Company, New York, (MacMillan, London, 1860)

Boole G (1959) A Treatisve on Differential Equations, 5th edn. Chelsea Publishing Company, New York, (MacMillan, London, 1859)

Borts GH, Mishan EJ (1961–62) Exploring the 'Uneconomic Region' of the Production Function. Rev Econ Stud 29:300–312

Bourguignon F (1974) A Particular Class of Continuous–Time Stochastic Growth Models. Journal of Economic Theory 9:141–158

Brand L (1955) A Sequence Defined by a Difference Equation. American Math Month 62:489–92

Brauer F, Nohel JA (1969) The Qualitative Theory of Ordinary Differential Equations. Dover Publications, New York

Brauer W (1950) Der Mathematiker–Ökonom. Kyklos 4:150–171

Braun M (1983) Differential Equations and Their Applications, 3rd edn. Springer–Verlag, New York

Brems H (1970) Ricardo's Long–Run Equilibrium. History of Political Economy 2:225–245

Brems H (1986) Pioneering Economic Theory 1630–1980. A Mathematical Restatement. The Johns Hopkins University Press, Baltimore

Brock WA, Mirman L (1972) Optimal Economic Growth and Uncertainty: The Discounted Case. Journal of Economic Theory (4):479–513

Brock WA, Mirman L (1973) Optimal Economic Growth and Uncertainty: The No Discounting Case. International Economic Review (14):560–573

Browning M, Crossley TF (2000) Luxuries are Easier to Postpone: A Proof. Journal of Political Economy 108:1022–1026

Browning M, Hansen LP, Heckman JJ (1999) Micro Data and General Equilibrium Models. In: Taylor & Woodford (ed) Handbook of Macroecon.1, Elsevier, pp 543–633

Brunt L (2003) Rehabilitating Arthur Young. The Economic History Review 56:265–299

Brunt L (2004) Nature or Nurture ? Explaining English Wheat Yields in the Industrial Revolution, c.1770. The Journal of Economic History 64:193–225

Buera FJ, Kaboski JP (2009) Can Traditional Theories of Structural Change fit the Data. Journal of the European Economic Assoc 7:469–477

Buera FJ, Kaboski JP (2012) The Rise of the Service Economy. American Economic Review 102(6):2540–2569

Burk A (1936) Real Income, Expenditure Proportionality, and Frisch's "New Methods of Measuring Marginal Utility". Review of Economic Studies 4:33–52

Burmeister E (1967) The Existence of Golden Ages and Stability in the Two–Sector Model. Quart J Economics 81:146–154

Burmeister E (1968) The Role of the Jacobian Determinant in the Two–Sector Model. Internt Econ Rev 9:195–203

Burmeister E, Dobell AR (1970) Mathematical Theories of Economic Growth. Macmillan, London

Burmeister E, Turnovsky SJ (1971) The Degree of Joint Production. International Economic Review 12:99–105

Caballé J, Santos MS (1993) On Endogenous Growth with Physical and Human Capital. J Political Economy 101:1042–67

Calvet LE, Paoli S (2014) Twin Picks: Disentangling the Determinants of Risk–Taking in Household Portfolios. Journal of Finance 69:867–906

Carlson S (1953) A Study on the Pure Theory of Production. In: King PS, Sons (eds) 2, London

Carstensen K, Gundlach E, Hartman S (2009) The Augmented Solow Model with Mincerian Schooling and Externalities. German Economic Review 10:448–463

Caselli F, Feyrer J (2007) The Marginal Product of Capital. Quarterly Journal of Economics 122:535–568

Cass D (1965) Optimum Growth in an Aggregative Model of Capital Accumulation. Review of Economic Studies 32:233–240, Reprinted in Becker (1991)

Cassel G (1925) Fundamental Thoughts in Economics. T. Fisher Unwin, London

Cassel G (1934) Teoretisk Socialekonomi. Kooperative Förbundets Bokförlag, Stockholm

Casti J (1979) Connectivity, Complexity and Catastrophe in Large–Scale Systems. John Wiley & Sons, New York, Interscience Publication

Caves DW, Christensen LR (1980) Global Properties of Flexible Functional Forms. American Economic Review 70:422–432

Caves RE, Frankel JA, Jones RW (2002) World Trade and Payments, 9th edn. Addison–Wesley, Boston

Caves RE, Frankel JA, Jones RW (2007) World Trade and Payments, 10th edn. Addison–Wesley, Boston

Cesari L (1963) Assymptotic Behavior and Stability Problems in Ordinary Differential Equations, 2nd edn. Academic Press, New York, Springer–Verlag, Berlin, 1959

Chai A, Moneta A (2010) Retrospectives: Engel Curves. Journal of Economic Perspectives 24:225–240

Chambers JD (1953) Enclosure and the Labor Supply in the Industrial Revolution. The Economic History Review 5:319–343

Chambers JD, Mingay GE (1966) The Agricultural Revolution, 1750–1880. Billing & Sons, Guildford, London

Chang FR, Malliaris AG (1987) Asymptotic Growth under Uncertainty – Existence and Uniqueness. Review of Economic Studies (54):169–174

Chenery HB (1960) Patterns of Industrial Growth. American Economic Review 50:624–654

Chiang AC (1984) Fundamental Methods of Mathematical Economics, 3rd edn. McGraw–Hill, New York

Chipman JS (1965) A Survey of the Theory of International, Part I. The Classical Theory. Econometrica 33:477–519, "Part II. The Neo–Classical Theory.", 33, 685–760;

Chipman JS (1966) Part III. The Modern Theory. Econometrica 34:18–76

Chipman JS (1969) Factor Price Equalization and the Stolper–Samuelson Theorem. International Economic Review 10:399–406

Chipman JS (1979) Mill's 'Superstructure': How Well Does It Stand Up? History of Political Economy 11(4):477–500

Choi EK, Jensen BS (1999) Economic Growth and International Trade. Blackwell, Oxford

Chorley GPH (1981) The Agricultural Revolution in Northern Europe 1750–1880: Nitrogen, Legumes, and Crop Productivity. The Economic History Review 34:71–93

Chow SN, Hale JK, Huang W (1992) From sine waves to square waves in delay equations. Proceedings of the Royal Society of Edinburgh 120A:223–229

Christensen J, Christensen O, Jörgensen S, Nielsen M (2013) Omkostningsteori og Regnskab, 2nd edn. Syddansk Universitetsforlag, Odense

Christensen LR, Jorgensen DW, Lau LJ (1971) Conjugate Duality and the Transcendental Logarithmic Production Function. Econometrica 39:255–256
Christensen LR, Jorgenson DW, Lau LJ (1975) Transcendental Logarithmic Utility Functions. American Economic Review 65:367–383
Chung JW (1987) On the Estimation of Factor Substitution in the Translog Model. Review of Economics and Statistics 69:409–417
Chung JW (1994) Utility and Production Functions. Blackwell, Oxford
Clark C (1951) The Conditions of Economic Progress, 2nd edn. MacMillan, London
Clark C (1957) The Conditions of Economic Progress, 3rd edn. MacMillan, London
Clark C (1967) Von Thünen's Isolated State. Oxford Economic Papers 19:370–377
Clark C (1973) The Marginal Utility of Income. Oxford Economic Papers 25:145–159
Clark G (1991) Yields Per Acre in English Agriculture, 1250–1860: Evidence from Labour Inputs. The Economic History Review 44:445–460
Clark G (1998) Commons Sense : Common Property Rights, Efficiency, and Institutional Change. The Journal of Economic History (58):73–102
Clark G (2002) Land rental values and the agrarian economy: England and Wales, 1500–1914. European Review of Economic History 6:281–308
Clark G (2004) The Price History of English Agriculture, 1209–1914. Research in Economic History 22:41–124
Clark G (2007a) A Farewell to Alms. Princeton University Press, Princeton
Clark G (2007b) The Long March of History: Farm Wages, Population, and Economic Growth, England 1209–1869. The Economic History Review 60:97–135
Clark G (2018) Growth or Stagnation? Farming in England 1200–1800. Economic History Review 71(1):55–81
Clark G, Cummins N (2015) Malthaus to modernity: wealth, status, and fertility in England, 1500–1879. Journal of Population Economics 28(1):3–24
Clark G, Huberman M, Lindert PH (1995) A British Food Puzzle, 1770–1850. The Economic History Review 48:315–237
Clemhout S (1968) The Class of Homothetic Isoquant Production Functions. The Review of Economic Studies 35(1):91–104
Cobb CW, Douglas PH (1928) A Theory of Production. American Econ Rev, Suppl Papers and Proceedings 18:139–65
Coddington EA, Levinson N (1955) Theory of Ordinary Differential Equation. McGraw–Hill, New York
Cogan EJ, Norman RZ (1963) Handbook of Calculus, Difference and Differential Equations, 2nd edn. Prentice–Hall, New Jersey
Collatz L (1966) Differentialgleichungen. B.G. Teubner, Stuttgart
Corden WM (1966) The Two–Sector Growth Model with Fixed Coefficients. Review of Economic Studies 33:253–262
Cornwall J (1970) The Role of Demand and Investment in Long–Term Growth. Quart J Economics 84:48–69
Costinot A, Donaldson D (2012) Ricardo's Theory of Comparative Advantage: Old Ideas, New Evidence. American Economic Review 102:453–456
Craft NFR (1985) British Economic Growth during the Industrial Revolution. Clarendon Press, Oxford
Creedy J, Guest R (2008) Discounting and the Rate of Time Preference Rate. The Economic Record 84:109–127
Dalgaard CJ, Strulik H (2015) The Physiological Foundations of the Wealth of Nations. Journal of Economic Growth 20:37–73

Datar SM, Rajan MV (2018) Horngren's Cost Accounting, 16th edn. Pearson Education, London

David P (1992) The Marshallian Dynamics of Industrialization: Chicago, 1850–1890. Unpublished

David PA, Scadding JL (1974) Private Savings: Ultrarationality, Aggregation, and 'Denison's Law'. Journal of Political Economy 82:225–249

De Long JB, Summers LH (1991) Equipment Investment and Economic Growth. Quarterly Journal of Economics 106:445–502

Deardorff AV (1970) Growth Paths in the Solow Neoclassical Growth Model. Quarterly J of Economics 85:134–139

Deardorff AV (1971) Growth and Trade in a Two–Sector World. PhD thesis, Cornell University, unpublished Ph.D. dissertation

Deardorff AV (1973) The Gains from Trade in and out of Steady–State Growth. Oxford Economic Papers 25:173–191

Deardorff AV (1974) A Geometry of Growth and Trade. Canadian Journal of Economics 2:295–306

Deardorff AV (1980) The General Validity of the Law of Comparative Advantage. Journal of Political Economy 88:941–957

Deardorff AV (1994) Growth and International Investment with Diverging Populations. Oxford Economic Papers 46:477–491

Deardorff AV (2001) Does Growth Encourage Factor Price Equalization? Review of Development Economics 5(2):169–181

Deardorff AV (2006) Terms of Trade, Glossary of International Economics. World Scientific, Singapore

Deardorff AV, Hanson JA (1978) Accumulation and a Long–Run Heckscher–Ohlin Theorem. Economic Inquiry 16:288–292

Deardorff AV, Stern RN (1994) The Stolper–Samuelson Theorem: A Golden Jubilee. The University of Michigan Press, Ann Arbor

Deaton A (1992) Understanding Consumption. Clarendon Press, Oxford

Deaton A, Muelbauer J (1992) Economics and Consumer Behavior. Cambridge University Press, Cambridge

Deaton A, Muellbauer J (1985) Economics and Consumer Behavior. Cambridge University Press, Cambridge

Deaton AS (1986) Demand Theory. pp 1768–1839, in Griliches, Z. and M.D. Intriligator, (eds), *Handbook of Econometrics*, Vol. 3, Amsterdam, North–Holland.

Deaton AS, Muellbauer J (1980a) An Almost Ideal Demand System. American Economic Review 70:312–326

Deaton AS, Muellbauer J (1980b) Economics and Consumer Behavior. Cambridge University Press, Cambridge

Debreu G (1959) Theory of Value – An Axiomatic Analysis Of Economic Equilibrium. John Wiley and Sons, New York, Cowles Foundation Monograph No. 17, Yale University Press, New Haven

Debreu G (1976) Regular Differentiable Economies. Am Econ Rev 66:280–87, or chapter 19 in Debreu (1983)

Debreu G (1983) Mathematical Economics: Twenty papers of Gerard Debreu. Econometric Society Monographs No. 4, Cambridge University Press, Cambridge

Debreu G (1986) Theoretic Models: Mathematical Form and Economic Content. Econometrica 54:1259–1270

Dempsey BW (1960) The Frontier Wage, Thünen. Loyola University Press, Chicago, Teil 1 (parts), Teil 2
Denison EF (1958) A Note on Private Saving. Review of Economics and Statistics 40:261–267
Deschamps R (1973) Risk Aversion and Demand Functions. Econometrica 41:455–465
Dhrymes PJ (1962) A Multisectoral Model of Growth. Quarterly Journal of Economics 76:264–278
Dickinson HD (1954–55) A Note on Dynamic Economics. Rev Econ Stud 22:169–79
Dickinson HD (1969) Von Thünen's Economics. Economic Journal 79:894–902
Diekmann O, van Gils SA, Verduyn Lunel SM, Walther HO (1995) Delay Equations: Functional-, Complex-, and Nonlinear Analysis. Springer–Verlag, New York
Diewert WE (1974) Applications of Duality Theory. pp 106–171, In: Intriligator MD, Kendrick DA (eds) *Frontiers of Quantitative Economics*, Vol.2, North–Holland, Amsterdam
Diewert WE (1982) Duality Approaches to Microeconomic Theory. In: Arrow KJ, Intriligator MD (eds) *Handbook of Mathematical Economics*, Vol.2, North–Holland, Amsterdam
Diewert WE, Wales TJ (1987a) Flexible Functional Forms and Global Curvature Conditions. Econometrica 37:43–68
Diewert WE, Wales TJ (1987b) Flexible Functional Forms and Global Curvature Conditions. Econometrica 37:43–68
Diewert WE, Avriel M, Zang I (1981a) Nine Kinds of Quasiconcavity and Concavity. Journal of Economic Theory 25:397–420
Diewert WE, Avriel M, Zang I (1981b) Nine Kinds of Quasiconcavity and Concavity. Journal of Economic Theory 25:397–420
Dixit AK (1976) The Theory of Equilibrium Growth. Oxford University Press, Oxford
Dixit AK, Norman V (1980) Theory of International Trade: A Dual, General Equilibrium Approach. Cambridge University Press, U.K
Dixit AK, Pindyck RS (1994) Investment under Uncertainty. Princeton University Press, New Jersey
Dixit AK, Stiglitz JE (1977) Monopolistic Competition and Optimum Product Diversity. American Economic Review 67:297–308
Domar ED (1946) Capital Expansion, Rate of Growth and Employment. Econometrica 14:137–47
Dorfman R (1986) 'Comment: P. A. Samuelson, Thünen at Two Hundred,". Journal of Economic Literature 24:1773–1776
Dornbusch R, Fischer S, Samuelson PA (1977) Comparative Advantage, Trade, and Payments in a Ricardian Model with a Continuum of Goods. American Economic Review 67:823–39
Douglas PH (1934, 1957) The Theory of Wages. Macmillan, New York
Drabicki J, Takayama A (1979) An Antinomy in the Theory of Comparative Advantage. Journal of International Economics 9:211–223
Drabicki JZ, Takayama A (1975) On the Optimal Growth of the Two–Sector Economy. Keio Economic Studies 12:1–36
Drandakis EM (1963) Factor Substitution in the Two–Sector Growth Model. Rev Econ Stud 30:217–28
Duncan GJ, Holmlund B (1983) Was Adam Smith Right After All ? Another Test of the Theory of Compensating Wage Differentials. Journal of Labor Economics 1:366–379

Dunn ES (1954) The Equilibrium of Land-use Pattern in Agriculture. Southern Economic Journal (21):173–187

Durlauf SN (1996) On the and Divergence of Growth Rates. Economic Journal 106:1016–1018

Dybvig P (1981) Recovering Cardinal Utility. Review of Economic Studies 48:159–166

Easterly W (1994) Economic Stagnation, Fixed Factors, and Policy Thresholds. Journal of Monetary Economics 33:525–557

Easterly W, Fischer S (1995) The Soviet Economic Decline. World Bank Economic Review 9:341–71

Eaton J, Kortum S (2002) Technology, Geography, and Trade. Econometrica 70:1741–80

Echevarria C (1997) Changes in Sectoral Composition Associated with Economic Growth. International Economic Review 38:431–452

Echevarria C (2010) Non–homothetic preferences and growth. Journal of International Trade & Economic Development 9:2, 151–171

Edgeworth FY (1881, 2003) Mathematical Psychics and Further Papers on Political Economy. Oxford University Press

Einstein A (1905) Über die von der molekularkinetischen Theorie der Wärme gefordete Bewegung von in ruhenden Flüssigkeiten suspendierten Teilschen. Annalen der Physik (17):549–560, Translated as "On the Motion of Small particles in Liquids at Rest required by the Molecular-Kinetic Theorey of Heat" in the following volumes: (i) Fürth, R. (ed.) *Albert Einstein: Investigations on the Theory of Brownian Movement* Dover Publ., New York. (ii) Stachel, J. (ed.) *Einsteins Miraculous Year. Five Papers that Changed the Face of Physics.* Princeton University Press, Princeton, 2005

Eisner R (1958) On Growth Models and the Neoclassical Resurgence. Economic J 68:707–21

Eltis V (1984) The Classical Theory of Economic Growth. MacMillan, London

Engel E (1857) Die Productions– and Consumptionsverhaeltnisse des Koenigreichs Sachsen. Zeitschrift des Statistischen Bureaus des Koeniglich Saechsishen Ministerium des Inneren 8–9, reprint in: *Bulletin of the International Statistical Institute*, 9 (1895), 1–54.

Engel E (1895a) Die Lebenshaltung belgischer Arbeiterfamilien frueher und jetzt. Bulletin of the International Statistical Institute 9:1–124, with an Appendix, 1–54

Engel E (1895b) Die Productions– und Consumptionsverhaeltnisse des Koenigreichs Sachsen. Zeitschrift des Statistischen Bureaus des Koeniglich Saechsishen Ministerium des Inneren 8–9(22), reprint in, *Bulletin of the International Statistical Institute*, 9 (1895), 1–54

Epstein L (1975) A Disaggregated Analysis of Consumer Choice Under Uncertainty. Econometrica 45:877–892

Ernle L (1936) English Farming: Past and Present, 5th edn. Longmans, Green and Co, London

Ethier W (1979) The Theorems of International Trade in Time–Phased Economies. Journal of International Economics 9:225–77

Ethier W, Ross SA (1971) International Capital Movements and Long Run Diversification. Journal of International Economics 1:301–314

Ethier WJ (1995) Modern International Economics, 3rd edn. W.W. Norton & Company, New York

Evans DJ (2005) The Elasticity of Marginal Utility of Consumption: Estimates for 20 OECD Countries. Fiscal Studies 26:197–224

Färe R (1975) A Note On Ray–Homogeneous and Ray–Homothetic Production Functions. Swed Econ 77:366–72
Färe R (1984) The Existence of Plant Capacity. Int Econ Rev 25:209–213
Feenstra RC (2004) Advanced International Trade. Princeton University Press
Feenstra RC (2016) Advanced International Trade, 2nd edn. Princeton University Press
Feldbäk O (1993) Danmarks Ökonomiske Historie 1500–1940. Systime Forlag, Herning
Findlay R (1959) Factor Intensities, Technological Progress and the Terms of Trade. Oxford Economic Papers 11:111–121
Findlay R (1967) Neutral Technical Progress and the Relative Stability of Two–Sector Growth Models. Int Econ Rev 8:109–15
Findlay R (1970) Factor Proportions and Comparative Advantage in the Long Run. Journal of Political Economy 78:27–34, Reprinted in Bhagwati (1981)
Findlay R (1984) Growth and Development in Trade Models. In Jones (1984)
Findley R, Jonung L, Lundahl M (2002) Bertil Ohlin – A Centennial Celebration (1899–1999). The MIT Press
Fiori S (2012) Adam Smith on Method: Newtonianism, History, Institutions, and the 'Invisble Hand'. Journal of History of Economic Thought 34:411–435
Fisher D, Fleissig AR, Serletis A (2001) An Empirical Comparison of Flexible Demand System Functional Forms. Journal of Applied Econometrics 16:59–80
Fisher FM (1972) Gross Substitutes and The Utility Function. Journal of Economic Theory 4:82–87
Fisher FM, Hillman AL (1984) The Commodity Pattern of Trade and the Heckcher–Ohlin Theorem in the Presence of Aggregate and Commodity–Specific Factor–Intensity Reversals. Journal of International Economics 17:159–72
Flam H, Flanders MJ (1991) Heckscher–Ohlin Trade Theory. MIT Press, Cambridge, Mass
Forster H (1938) Über das verhalten der Integralkurven einer gevönlichen Differentialgleichung erster Ordnung in der Umgebung eines singulären Punktes. Math Zeitsch 43:271–320
Försund F (1971) A Note on Technically Optimal Scale in Inhomogeneous Production Functions. Swed J Econ 73:225–240
Försund F (1975) The Homothetic Production Function. Swed J Econ 77:234–244
Fort T (1948) Finite Differences and Difference Equations in the Real Domain. Clarendon Press, Oxford
Frisch R (1959) A Complete Scheme for Computing All Direct and Cross Demand Elasticities in a Model with Many Sectors. Econometrica 27:177–196
Frisch R (1964) Dynamic Utility. Econometrica 32:418–424
Frisch R (1965) Theory of Production. O. Reidel Publishing Company, Dordrecht, Holland
Frommer M (1934) Über das Auftreten von Wirbeln und Strudeln (geschlossener und spiraliger Integralkurven) in der Umgebung rationaler Un-be-stimmt-heits-stel-len. Math Annalen 109:395–424
Fujita M, Thisse JF (2002) Economics of Agglomeration. Cambridge University Press, Cambridge
Fujita M, Krugman P, Venables AJ (2001) The Spatial Economy. MIT Press, Cambridge
Furuno Y (1965) The Period of Production in Two–Sector Models of Economic Growth. Int Econ Rev 6:240–44
Gabisch G, Lorenz HW (1987) Business Cycle Theory. Springer

Galetovic A (1996) Specialization, intermediation, and growth. Journal of Monetary Economics 38:549–59
Galor O (1992) A Two–Sector Overlapping–Generations Model: A Global Characterization of the Dynamic System. Econometrica 60:351–386
Galor O (1996) Convergence ? Inferences from Theoretical Models. Economic Journal 106:1036–1069
Galor O (2005) From Stagnation To Growth: Unified Growth Theory. pp 172–293, in *Handbook 1A* Aghion & Durlauf, (eds.) (2005).
Galor O (2010) The 2008 Lawrence R. Klein Lecture – Comparative Economic Development: Insights From Unified Growth Theory. International Economic Review 51:1–44
Galor O (2011) Unified Growth Theory. Princeton University Press, Princeton and Oxford
Galor O (2016) The Agricultural Origin of Time Preference. American Economic Review 106:3064–3103
Galor O, Lin S (1997) Dynamic Foundations for the Factor Endowment Model of International Trade
Galor O, Weil DN (2000) Population, Technology, and Growth: From the Malthusian Regime to the Demographic Transition. American Econ Rev 90:806–828
Gamaletsos T (1973) Further Analysis of Cross–country Comparison of Consumer Expenditure Patterns. European Economic Review 4:1–20
Gamaletsos T (1974) Reply – Further analysis of cross–country comparison of consumer expenditure patterns. European Economic Review 5:307
Gandolfo G (1980) Economic Dynamics: Methods and Models, 2nd edn. North–Holland, Amsterdam
Gandolfo G (1994) International Economics I: The Pure Theory of International Trade, 2nd edn. Springer–Verlag, Berlin
Gandolfo G (1996) Economic Dynamics: Methods and Models, 3rd edn. Springer–Verlag, Berlin
Gandolfo G (1997) Economic Dynamics. Springer Verlag, Berlin/New York
Gandolfo G (1998a) International Economics I: The Pure Theory of International Trade, 3rd edn. Springer–Verlag, Berlin
Gandolfo G (1998b) International Trade Theory and Policy. Springer Verlag, Berlin
Gandolfo G (2010) Economic Dynamics: Methods and Models, 4th edn. Springer–Verlag, Berlin
Gandolfo G (2014) International Trade Theory and Policy. Springer–Verlag, Berlin Heidelberg
Garcia-Penalosa C, Turnovsky SJ (2005) Production Risk of the Functional Distribution of Income in a Developing Economy: Tradeoffs and Policy Responses. Journal of Development Economics 76:175–208
Gauss KF (1963) Theory of the motion of the heavenly bodies moving about the sun in conic sections: A translation of Theoria motus. Dover Publications, New York
Geary RC (1950–1951) A Note on "A Constant–Utility Index of the Cost of Living". Review of Economic Studies 18:65–66
Gikman II, Skorokhod AV (1965) Introduction to the Theory of Random Processes. W. B. Saunders Company, Philadelphia, London, Toronto, 1969, Russian original published by Nauka, Moscow
Gilboy EW (1934) Wages in Eighteenth Century England. Russell & Russell, New York

Gilboy EW (1936) The Cost of Living and Real Wages in Eighteenth Century England. The Review of Economics and Statistics 18:134–143

Ginsberg W (1973) Concavity and Quasiconcavity in Economics. Journal of Economic Theory 6:596–605

Goldberg S (1986) Introduction to Difference Equations. Dover Publications, New York, John Wiley and Sons, 1958

Goldin C, Katz LF (1998) The Origins of Technology–Skill Complementarity. Quarterly Journal of Economics 113:693–732

Goodman LE, Warner WH (2001a) Dynamics. Dover Publications, New York

Goodman LE, Warner WH (2001b) Statics. Dover Publications, New York

Goodwin RM (1961) The Optimal Growth Path for an Underdeveloped Economy. The Economic Journal 71:756–774

Goodwin RM (1990) Chaotic Economic Dynamics. Oxford U. P.

Grandmont JM, McFadden D (1972) A Technical Note on Classical Gains From Trade. Journal of International Economics 2:109–125

Granger CWJ, Elliott CM (1967) A Fresh Look at Wheat Prices and Markets in the Eighteenth Century. The Economic History Review 20:257–265

Gravelle H, Rees R (2004) Microeconomics, 3rd edn. Prentice Hall, Harlow

Greenwood J, Smith BD (1997) Financial markets in development, and the development of financial markets. Journal of Economic Dynamics and Control 21:145–81

Greenwood J, Hercowitz Z, Krusell P (1997) Long–Run Implications of Investment–Specific Technological Change. American Economic Review 87:342–362

Grimshaw R (1990) Nonlinear Ordinary Differential Equations. Blackwell Scientific Publications, Oxford

Grinols EL (1987) Uncertainty and the Theory of International Trade. Harwood Academic Publishers, Chur, Switzerland

Grossman GM, Rogoff K (1995) Handbook of International Economics, vol III. Elsevier, Amsterdam

Grossmann V (2005) White–Collar Employment, Inequality, and Technological Change. Journal of Economics 10:119–142

Grossmann V, Steger T, Trimborn T (2013) Dynamically optimal R/D subsidization. Journal of Economic Dynamics and Control 37:516–534

Grotewold A (1959) von Thünen in Retrospect. Economic Geography 35:346–353

Guckenheimer J, Holmes P (1983) Nonlinear Oscillations, Dynamical Systems, and Bifurcations of Vector Fields. Springer Verlag, New York

Guckenheimer J, Holmes P (1986) Nonlinear Oscillations, Dynamical Systems, and Birfurcations of Vector Fields. Springer–Verlag, New York

Guilkey DK, Knox Lovell CA (1980) On the Flexibility of the Translog Approximation. International Economic Review 21:137–147

Guilkey DK, Knox Lovell C, Sickles R (1983) A Comparison of the Performance of Three Flexible Functional Forms. International Economic Review 24:591–616

Gundlach E (2007) The Solow Model in the Empirrics of Growth and Trade. Oxford Review of Economic Policy 23:25–44

Gundlach E, Becker D (2007) Factor Price Equality and Biased Technical Change in a Two-Cone Trade Model. Review of Development Economics 11:685–698

Haberler G (1936) The Theory of International Trade. W. Hodge and Comp, London

Hacche G (1985) The Theory of Economic Growth, An Introduction. MacMillan, London

Hadley G, Kemp MC (1971) Variational Methods In Economics. Amsterdam, North–Holland Publ

Hahn FH (1965) On Two–Sector Growth Models. Rev Econ Stud 32:339–46, or Sen (1970)

Hahn FH, Matthews RCO (1964) The Theory of Economic Growth: A Survey. Economic Journal 74:779–902

Hahn FH, Matthews RCO (1965) The theory of economic growth: a survey. Economic J 74:779–902, or in *Survey of Economic Theory,* **2**, (American Economic Association/Royal Economic Society), Macmillan, London

Haken H (1983a) Advanced Synergetics. Springer–Verlag, Berlin

Haken H (1983b) Synergetics. An Introduction. Springer–Verlag, Berlin

Hall P (ed) (1966) The Isolated State. Pergamon Press, Oxford, Wartenberg, C. M., Translation, Band 1, Band 2–3 (extracts)

Hall RE (1973) The Specification of Technology with Several Kinds of Output. Journal of Political Economy 81:868–892

Hall RE (1988) Intertemporal Substitution in Consumption. Journal of Political Economy 96:339–357

Hamada K (1974) An Economic Analysis of the Duty–Free Zone. Journal of International Economics 4:225–241

Hamberg D (1956) Economic Growth and Instability. W.W. Norton, New York

Hanoch G (1975) Production and Demand Models with Direct and Indirect Implicit Additivity. Econometrica 43:395–419

Hanoch G (1977) Risk Aversion and Consumer Preferences. Econometrica 45:413–426

Hansen GD, Prescott EC (2002) Malthus to Solow. American Economic Review 92:1205–1217

Hansen SA (1976) Økonomisk Väkst i Danmark : 1720–1914. (Copenhagen: Akademisk Forlag)

Hansen VF (1888) Stavnsbaands–Lösningen og Landboreformerne, 1733–1807. G.E.C. Gads Boghandel, Copenhagen

Harberger AC (1962) The Incidence of the Corporation Income Tax. Jour Pol Econ 70:215–240

Harrigan J (1997) Technology, Factor Supplies, and International Specialization: Estimating the Neoclassical Model. American Economic Review 87:475–494

Harrod RF (1939) An Essay in Dynamic Theory. Economic J 49:14–33, or Stiglitz (1969)

Harrod RF (1973) Economic Dynamics. MacMillan, London

Harwitz M (1972) A Note on Professor Chipman's Version of Mill's Law of International Values. Journal of International Economics 2:181–188

Heckscher EF (1919) The Effect of Foreign Trade on Distribution of Income. Ekonomisk Tidsskrift 21, Del II:1–32, translated (Svend Laursen) in Ellis, H.S., Metzler, L.A., eds. *Readings in the Theory of International Trade*, Blakiston, Philadelphia, (1949), 272–300; transl., in Flam. H & Flanders, M.J. (1991), (43–69).

Heckscher EF (1960) Industrialismen – Den Ekonomiska Utvecklingen Sedan 1750, 6th edn. Raben & Sjögren, Stockholm

Heer B, Maussner A (2009) Dynamic General Equilibrium Modeling, 2nd edn. Springer, Dordrecht Heidelberg

Heij C, de Boer PMC, Franses PH, Kloek T, van Dijk HK (2004) Econometric Methods with Applications in Business and Economics. Oxford University Press, Oxford

Heijdra BJ (2017) Foundations of Modern Macroeconomics, 3rd edn. Oxford University Press, Oxford
Helmstädter E (1995) Wie künstlich ist von Thünens natürlicher Lohn. Schriften des Vereins für Socialpolitik Ed. H. Rieter, Duncker & Humbolt, Berlin
Helpman E, Razin A (1978) A Theory of International Trade under Uncertainty. Academic Press, N.Y.
Herrendorf B, Valentinyi A (2012) Which Sectors Make Poor Countries So Unproductive. Journal of the European Econ Assoc 10:323–341
Herrendorf B, Rogerson R, Valentinyi A (2013) Two Perspectives on Preferences and Structural Transformation. AmerEcRev 103(7):2752–2789
Hertel TW, Tsigas ME (1997) Structure of GTAP, In Hertel, TW. pp 13–73, In Hertel, TW *Global Trade Analysis: Modelling and Applications*, Cambridge University Press, Cambridge
Hertel TW, Preckel PV, Tsigas ME, Peterson EB, Surry Y (1991) Implicit Additivity as a Strategy for Restricting the Parameter Space in Computable General Equilibrium Models. Economic and Financial Computing 1:265–289
Hicks JR (1932, 1948) The Theory of Wages. MacMillan, London
Hicks JR (1937) Theorie Mathematique de la Valeur en Regime de la Libre Concurrence. Hermann, Editeurs, Paris
Hicks JR (1946) Value and Capital, 2nd edn. Clarendon Press, Oxford
Hicks JR (1969a) A Theory of Economic History. Clarendon Press, Oxford
Hicks JR (1969b) Direct and Indirect Additivity. Econometrica 37:353–354
Hicks JR (1970) Elasticities of Substitution Again: Substitutes and Complements. Oxford Economic Papers 22:289–296
Hillinger C (1969) The Measurement of Utility. Review of Economic Studies 36:111–116
Hippauf R (2000) Johann Heinrich von Thünen – Ein Lebensbild. Hinstorff, Rostock
Hirsch MW, Smale S (1974) Differential Equations, Dynamical Systems and Linear Algebra. Academic Press, New York
Hochstadt H (1964) Differential Equations, A Modern Approach. Holt, Rinehart, and Winston, New York
Holden H, Øksendal B, Ubøe J, Zhang T (1996) Stochastic Partial Differential Equation. A Modeling White Noise Functional Approach. Birkäuser, Boston
Hollander S (1980) On Professor Samuelson's Canonical Classical Model of Political Economy. J Econ Lit 18:559–74
Hollander S (1987) Classical Economics. Basil Blackwell, Oxford
Hörmander L (1967) Hypoelliptic Second Order Differential Equations. Acta Math 119:147–171
Hörmander L (1985) The analysis of linear partial differential operators. Grundlehren der mathematischen Wissenschaften 256, 257, 274, 275
Hotelling H (1932) Edgeworth's Taxation Paradox and the Nature of Demand and Supply Functions. Journal of Political Economy 40:577–616
Houthakker HS (1952) Compensated Changes in Quantities and Qualities Consumed. Review of Economic Studies 19:155–64
Houthakker HS (1957) An International Comparison of Household Expenditure Patterns, Commemorating the Centenary of Engel's law. Econometrica 25:532–551
Houthakker HS (1960a) Additive Preferences. Econometrica 28:244–257
Houthakker HS (1960b) The Influence of Prices and Income on Household Expenditures. Bulletin of the International Institute of Statistics 37:9–22

Houthakker HS (1961) The Present State of Consumption Theory. Econometrica 29:704–740

Houthakker HS (1965) A Note on Self-Dual Preferences. Econometrica 33:797–801

Hsiao FST (1971) The Contract Curve and the Production Possibility Curve. Journal of Political Economy 79:919–923

Hurewitz W (1958) Lectures on Ordinary Differential Equations. John Wiley & Sons, New York

Inada K (1963) On a Two–Sector Model of Economic Growth: Comments and a Generalization. Rev Econ Stud 30:119–27

Inada K (1964) On the Stability of Growth Equilibria in Two–Sector Models. Rev Econ Stud 31:127–42

Inada KI (1971) The production coefficient matrix and the Stolper–Samuelson connection. Econometrica 39:219–240

Ince EL (1956) Ordinary Differential Equations. Dover Publications, New York

Inoue T, Wegge LL (1986) On the Geometry of the Production Possibility Frontier. International Economic Review 27:727–737

Intriligator MD (1971) Mathematical Optimization and Economic Theory. Prentice-Hall, New Jersey

Irmen A (2020) Tasks, Technology in the Neoclassical Production Sector. Journal of Economics 131:101–121

Islam N (1995) Growth Empirics: A Panel Data Approach. Quarterly Journal of Economics 110:1127–1170

Itô K, McKean HP Jr (1965) Diffusion Processes and Their Sample Paths. Springer–Verlag, Berlin

Ito K, McKean HP Jr (1974) Diffusion Processes and Their Sample Paths. Springer–Verlag, New York, Second printing

Ito T (1978) A Note on the Positivity Constraint in Olech's Theorem. J Economic Theory 17:312–18

Ivanov AF, Sharkovsky AN (1992) Oscillations in singularly perturbed delay equations. Dynamics Reported (New Series) 1:164–224

Jackson RV (1985) Growth and Deceleration in English Agriculture 1660–1790. The Economic History Review 38:333–351

Jacob W (1828) Tracts relating to the corn trade and corn laws: including the second report. London

Jacobsen M (1991) Homogeneous Gaussian Diffusions in Finite Dimensions. Preprint 3, Institute of Mathematical Statistics, University of Copenhagen

Jannermann G (2007) Jugendlust, Arbeitsfreuden, und Arbeitskämpfe – Erinnerungen Friedrich Aereboe. Tellower Thünen Schriften 7, (Mecklenburg: Thünen–Museum–Tellow)

Jeck A (1994) The macrostucture of Adam Smiths's theoretical system: a reconstruction. European Journal of the History of Economic Thought 1:552–576

Jensen BS (1980) Expenditure System for the Danish Household Sector. In *Symposium i Anvendt Statistik*, (Lyngby: NEUCC, Denmark)

Jensen BS (1994) The Dynamic Systems of Basic Economic Growth Models. Kluwer Academic Publishers, Dordrecht

Jensen BS (2003) Walrasian General Equilibrium Allocations and Dynamics in Two–Sector Growth Models. German Economic Review 4:53–87

Jensen BS (2009) Dynamic Extensions of the Solow Growth Model (1956), Editorial. German Economic Review 10:378–383

Jensen BS (2012) Comparative Cost and Factor Endowments: Ricardo and Ohlin. pp 55–83, Ch. 4 in Kemp et al., eds., (2012).

Jensen BS (2017) von Thünen: Capital, Production Functions, Marginal Productivity Wages and the Natural Wage. German Economic Review 18:51–80

Jensen BS, Larsen ME (1986) Growth and Long–Run Stability. Tech. rep., Department of Mathematics, University of Copenhagen, Preprint series, No. 3

Jensen BS, Larsen ME (1987) Growth and Long–Run Stability. Acta Applicandae Mathematicae 9:219–237, Reprinted in Jensen (1994)

Jensen BS, Larsen ME (2005) General Equilibrium Dynamics of Multi–Sector Growth Models. Journal of Economics 10:17–56

Jensen BS, Lehmijoki U (2011) Homothetic Multisector Growth Models. pp 289–318, in: Frontiers of Economics and Globalization, 11, La Grandville, O. de, (Ed.), Emerald, United Kingdom.

Jensen BS, Palokangas T (2007) Stochastic Economic Dynamics. Copenhagen Business School Press, Denmark

Jensen BS, Richter M (2007) Stochastic one–sector and two–sector growth models in continuous time. In: Jensen BS, Palokangas T (eds) Stochastic Economic Dynamics, CBS Press, Copenhagen, pp 167–216

Jensen BS, Wang C (1997) General Equilibrium Dynamics of Basic Trade Models for Growing Economies. In Bjarne S. Jensen and Kar–Yiu Wong (eds.) *Dynamics, Economic Growth, and International Trade*, Ann Arbor: University of Michigan Press.

Jensen BS, Wang C (1999) Basic Stochastic Dynamic Systems of Growth and Trade. Review of International Economics 7:378–402, or in Choi & Jensen (1999)

Jensen BS, Richter M, Wang C, Alsholm PK (2001) Saving Rates, Trade, Technology, and Stochastic Dynamics. Review of Development Economics 5:182–204

Jensen BS, Alsholm PK, Larsen ME, Jensen JM (2005) Dynamic Structure, Exogeneity, Phase Portraits, Growth Paths, and Scale and Substitution Elasticities. Review of International Economics 13:59–89

Jensen BS, Wang C, Johnsen J (2007) Moment Evolution of Gaussian and Geometric Wiener Diffusions – derived by Itô's Lemma and Kolmogorov's Forward Equation

Jensen BS, de Boer P, van Daal J, Jensen PS (2011) Global Restrictions on the Parameters of the CDES Indirect Utility Function. Journal of Economics 102:217–235

Jensen BS, Lehmijoki U, Rovenskaya E (2015) Non–Homothetic Multisector Growth Models. Review of Development Economics 19(2):221–243

Jensen P, Radu C, Sharp P (2022) To the Manor born : A new Microlevel Wage Database for Eighteenth-Century Denmark. European Review of Economic History (26):302–310

Jespersen KJV, Rasmussen CP, Raabyemagle H, Holstein P (2010) MOLTKE – Rigets Mägtigste Mand. Gads Forlag, Copenhagen

Johansen HC (1975) Befolkningsudvikling og Familiestruktur i det 18. Aarhundrede. Odense University Press, Odense

Johansen L (1969) A Classical Model of Economic Growth. In *Socialism, Capitalism and Economic Growth, Essays in Honour of M. Dobb*, Feinstein, C.H. (ed.), Cambridge University Press, Cambridge.

Johansen L (1972) Production Functions. North–Holland, Amsterdam

Johansen L (1974) A Multi–Sectorial Study of Economic Growth, 2nd edn. North–Holland, Amsterdam

Johnson HG (1959) Economic Development and International Trade. Nationaløkonomisk Tidsskrift 97:253–272
Johnson HG (1966) Factor Market Distortions and the Shape of the Transformation Curve. Econometrica 34:686–698
Johnson HG (1971) The Two–Sector Model of General Equilibrium. George Allen and Unwin, London
Johnson WE (1913) The Pure Theory of Utility Curves. Economic J 23:483–513
Jones CI (1994) Economic growth and the relative price of capital. J Monetary Economics 34:359–82
Jones HG (1975) An Introduction to Modern Theories of Economic Growth. Nelson, London
Jones LE, Manuelli RE (1990) A Convex Model of Equilibrium Growth: Theory and Policy Implications. Journal of Political Economy 98:1008–1038
Jones LE, Manuelli RE (1997) The Sources of Growth. Journal of Economic Dynamics and Control 98:75–114
Jones RW (1956) Factor Proportions and the Heckscher–Ohlin Theorem. Review of Economic Studies 24:1–10
Jones RW (1965) The Structure of Simple General Equilibrium Models. J Political Economy 73:557–72, or Bhagwati (1981)
Jones RW (1985) Relative Prices and Real Factor Rewards. Economics Letters 19
Jones RW (1995) R & D–Based Models of Economic Growth. J Political Economy 103:759–784
Jones RW (2002) Trade Theory and Factor Intensities: An Interpretive Essay. Review of International Economics 10:581–603
Jones RW (2010) Production Possibilities Frontiers. In *Famous Figures and Diagrams in Economics*, Blaug and Lloyd, (2010).
Jones RW, Easton ST (1982) Factor Intensities and Factor Substitution in General Equilibrium. Journal of International Economics 15:65–99
Jones RW, Kenen PB (1984) Handbook of International Economics, vol I. North–Holland, Amsterdam
Jordan C (1965) Calculus of Finite Differences, 3rd edn. Chelsea Publishing Company, New York
Jordan DW, Smith P (1977) Non–linear Ordinary Differential Equations. Oxford University Press
Jörgensen E (1965) Income–Expenditure Relations of Danish Wage and Salary Earners. (Copenhagen: Statistical Inquires No. 14, Statistical Department)
Jorgenson DW (1960) On stability in the sense of Harrod. Economica 27:243–248
Jorgenson DW (1961) The Structure of Multi–Sector Dynamic Models. International Economic Review 2:276–293
Joshi S (1995) Recursive Utility and Optimal Growth under Uncertainty. Journal of Mathematical Economics 24:601–617
Joshi S (1998) A framework to analyze comparative dynamics in a continuous time stochastic growth model. Economic Modelling 15:125–34
Judd KL (1998) Numerical Methods in Economics. MIT Press, Mass
Kalman RE, Bertram JE (1960) Control system analysis and design via the 'second method' of Lyapunov, ASME. J Basic Eng pp 371–393
Kamke E (1960) Differentialgleichungen und Randwertprobleme;. Band 1: *Ge-vöhn-liche Differentialgleichungen,* 2. Auflage, VEB Verlag Technik, Berlin.
Kaplan W (1967) Ordinary Differential Equations. Addison–Wesley Pub. Comp, Mass

Karatzas I, Shreve S (1988) Brownian Motions and Stochastic Calculus. Springer–Verlag, New York

Karatzas I, Shreve SE (1991) Brownian Motion and Stochastic Calculus, 2nd edn. Springer Verlag, N.Y.

Karlin S (1959) Mathematical Methods and Theory in Games, Programming and Economics. Addison–Wesley Publishing Co, Boston, Mass

Karlin S, Taylor HM (1981) A Second Course in Stochastic Processes. Academic Press, N.Y.

Katayama S, Long NV (2010) A Dynamic Game of Status–seeking with Public Capital and an Exhaustible Resource. Optimal Control, Applications and Methods 31:43–53

Katz LF, Autor DH (1999) Changes in the Wage Structure and Earnings Inequality. pp 1463–1555, in: Ashenfelter, O.C. and Card, D., Ed., (1999), Vol. 3A.

Katzner DW (1968) A Note on the Differentiability of Consumer Demand Equations. Econometrica 36:415–418

Kawano H, Ohta H, Jensen BS, Hwang AR (2017) Production, Distribution, and Trade: General Equilibrium with One Single Cobb–Douglas Parameter. Modern Economy 8:970–993

Kemp MC (1969) The Pure Theory of International Trade and Investment. Prentice–Hall, New Jersey

Kemp MC (1976) Three Topics in the Theory of International Trade – Distribution, Welfare and Uncertainty. North–Holland/Elsevier, N.Y.

Kemp MC, Liviatan N (1973) Production and Trade Patterns under Uncertainty. Economic Record 49:215–27

Kemp MC, Long NV (1985) Sharp Points in Production Surfaces. Oxford Economic Papers 37:375–381

Kemp MC, Wegge LLF (1969) On the Relation between Commodity Prices and Factor Rewards. International Economic Review 10:407–413

Kemp MC, Van Long N, Okuguchi K (1981) On the Possibility of Deriving Conclusions of Stolper–Samuelson Type When Commodity Prices Are Random. Economic Studies Quarterly 32:111–16

Kemp MC, Nakagawa H, Uchida T (2012) Positive and Normative Analysis in International Economics. Palgrave Macmillan, London

Kenen PB (2000) The International Economy, 4th edn. Prentice–Hall, New Jersey

Keynes JM (1933, 1963) Essays in Biography. Norton & Company, N.Y

Keynes JM (1936) The General Theory of Employment, Interest and Money. MacMillan, London

Kim K (2012) Adam Smith's 'History of Astronomy' and View of Science. Cambridge Journal of Economics 36:799–820

King RG, Levine R (1993) Finance, entrepreneurship, and growth. Journal of Monetary Economics 32:513–42

King RG, Rebelo ST (1993) Transitional Dynamics and Economic Growth in the Neoclassical Model. American Economic Review 83:908–931

King RG, Plosser CI, Rebelo ST (1988) Production, growth and business cycles: I., The basic neoclassical model, II., New directions. Journal of Monetary Economics 21:195–232, 309–41

Kjeldsen-Kragh S (2007) The Role of Agriculture in Economic Development. CBS Press, Copenhagen

Klein LR, Rubin H (1947–1948) A Constant–Utility Index of the Cost of Living. Review of Economic Studies 15:84–87

Klemm V (2004) Über agrarwissenshaftiche Lehren Thaers und Thünens – Unterschiede und Ursachen. pp 9–36, in Bartz (2004)

Kloeden PE, Platen E (1995) Numerical Solutions to Stochastic Differential Equations, 2nd edn. Springer Verlag, Berlin

Klump R (1995) On the Institutional Determinants of Economic Development – Lessons from a Stochastic Neoclassical Growth Model. Jahrbuch für Wirtschaftswissenschaft 46:138–51

Klump R, de La Grandville O (2000) Economic Growth and the Elasticity of Substitution: Two Theorems and Some Suggestions. American Economic Review 90:282–291

Klump R, Preissler H (2000) CES Production Functions and Economic Growth. Scandinavian Journal of Economics 102:41–56

van de Klundert TC (2001) Growth Theory in Historical Perspective. No. 2357 in Books, Edward Elgar Publishing

Klundert Tvd, Smulders S (1992) Reconstructing Growth Theory: A Survey. De Economist 140:177–203

Kneschke A (1956) Differentialgleichungen, Lösungsmethoden und Lösungen;. Band 1: *Gevöhnliche Differentialgleichungen*, 5. Auflage, Akademische Verlagsgesellschaft, Leipzig.

Knudsen JM, Hjorth PG (1996) Elements of Newtonian Mechanics. Including Nonlinear Dynamics, second and enlarged edn. Springer-Verlag

Kohli U (1983) Non–Joint Technologies. Review of Economic Studies 50:209–219

Kohli U (1991) Technology, Duality, and Foreign Trade: The GNP Function Approach to Modelling Imports and Exports. UMP Press, Ann Arbor ; Harvester Wheatsheaf, London

Kolm S (1976) Structures Meta–Homogénes des Productions et Préférences. Canadian Journal of Economics 9:1–44

Kongsamut P, Rebelo S, Xie D (2001) Beyond Balanced Growth. Review of Economic Studies 68:869–882

Koopmans TC (1960) Stationary Ordinal Utility and Impatience. Econometrica 28:287–309

Koopmans TC, Diamond PA, Williamson RE (1960) Stationary Utility and Time Perspective. Econometrica 32:82–100

Köppen D (2002) Agrarökologishe Aspekte in der Lehre Thünens. pp 23–29, in *Berichte über Landwirtschaft*, Johann Heinrich von Thünen (1783–1850), Rauscher, Michael, Fritz Tack, ed., 215. Sonderheft, Landwirtschaftsverlag.

Krelle W (1987) von Thünen–Vorlesung. Zeitschrift f Wirtscafts– u Sozialwiss 107:5–28

Krugman P (1991) Increasing Returns and Geography. Jour of Pol Econ 99:483–499

Krugman PR, Obstfeld M, Melitz MJ (2018) International Economics – Theory and Policy, 11th edn. Pearson, UK

Krzymowski R, Minneman PG (1928) Graphical Presentaion of Thünen´s Theory of Intensity. Journal of Farm Economics 10:461–482

Kuga K (1972) The Factor Price Equalization Theorem. Econometrica 40:723–736

Kuznets S (1966) Modern Economic Growth. Rate, Structure and Spread. Yale University Press, New Haven

de La Grandville O (1989) In Quest of the Slutsky Diamond. American Economic Review 79:468–481 de La Grandville O (1997) Curvature and the Elasticity of Substitution: Straightening It Out. Journal of Economics 66:23–34

de La Grandville O (2001) Bond Pricing and Portfolio Analysis. MIT Press, Cambridge, Mass.

de La Grandville O (2009) Economic Growth – a Unified Approach. Cambridge University Press, Cambridge

de La Grandville O (2017) Economic Growth – A Unified Approach, 2nd edn. Cambridge University Press, Cambridge

de La Grandville O (2018) Why is Optimal Growth Theory Mute ? Restoring its Rightful Voice. Macroeconomic Dynamics 22:77–100

Ladrón-de-Guevara A, Ortigueira S, Santos MS (1999) A Two–Sector Model of Endogenous Growth with Leisure. Review of Economic Studies 66:609–31

Lagerlöf NP (2006) The Galor–Weil model revisited: A quantitative exercise. Review of Economic Dynamics 9:116–142

Lagrange JL (1811, 1997) Analytical Mechanics – Mecanique Analytique, vol 1–2. Translated by A. Boissonnade and V.N. Vagliente, Springer–Science+Business Media, B.V., Dordrecht

Laibson D (1997) Golden Eggs and Hyperbolic Discounting. Quarterly Journal of Economics 112:443–477

Laitner J (2000) Structural Change and Economic Growth. Review of Economic Studies 67:545–561

Lampe M, Sharp PR (2018) A Land of Milk and Butter. University of Chicago Press, Chicago

Landau LD, Lifshitz EM (1989) Mechanics, 3rd edn. Pergamon Press, Oxford

Larsen ME, Jensen BS (1989) Coupled Linear Differential Equations with Real Coefficients. American Math Month 96:727–731

Lau L (1972) Profit Functions of Technologies with Multiple Inputs and Outputs. Review Econ Stat 54:281–289

Lau L (1978a) Applications of Profit Functions. In Fuss, U. and McFadden, D. (1978) *Production Economics: A Dual Approach to Theory and Applications,* Vol. 1.

Lau LJ (1978b) Testing and Imposing Monotonicity, Convexity and Quasi–Convexity Constraints. pp 409–453, In: Fuss M, McFadden D (eds) *Production Economics: A Dual Approach to Theory and Applications*, Vol.1, North–Holland, Amsterdam

Lau SHP (2002) Further Inspection of the Stochastic Growth Model by an Analytical Approach. Macroeconomic Dynamics 6:748–757

Laursen S (1952) Production Functions and the Theory of International Trade. The American Economic Review 42(4):540–557

Lawrance EC (1991) Poverty and the Rate of Time Preference: Evidence from Panel Data. Journal of Political Economy 99:54–77

Leamer E (2001) International Economics. Worth Publishers, New York

Leamer EE (1984) Sources of International Comparative Advantage – theory and evidence. MIT Press, Cambridge, Mass

Leamer EE (1995) The Heckscher–Ohlin Model in Theory and Practice, vol 77. Princeton Studies in International Finance, New Jersey

Leamer EE, Levinsohn J (1995) International Trade Theory: The Evidence. Ch. 26 in Grossman and Rogoff (1995).

Lee JS (2003) Feeding the Colleges : Cambridge's Food and Fuel Supplies, 1450–1560. The Economic History Review 56:243–264

Lee JW (1995) Capital goods imports and long-run growth. Journal of Development Economics 48:91–110
Lee LF, Pitt MM (1986) Microeconometric Demand System with Binding Nonnegativity Constraints: The Dual Approach. Econometrica 54:1237–1242
Lehmijoki U (1984) Notes on Quasi-convexity of the Cost Function. Scandinavian Journal of Economics 86:385–389
Leigh AH (1946) Von Thünen's Theory of Distribution and the Advent of Marginal Analysis. Journal of Political Economy 54:481–502
Leonard D, Long NV (1992) Optimal Control Theory and Static Optimization in Economics. Cambridge University Press
Leontief WW (1933) The Use of Indifference Curves in the Analysis of Foreign Trade. Quarterly Journal of Economics 47:493–503
Lerner AP (1932) The Diagrammatical Representation of Cost Conditions in International Trade. Economica 37:319–334
Lerner AP (1933) Notes on Elasticity of Substitution – The Diagrammatical Representation. Review of Economic Studies 1:68–71
Leser CEV (1941) Family Budget Data and Price Elasticities of Demand. Review of Economic Studies 9:40–57
Levine R (1991) Stock markets, growth, and tax policy. Journal of Finance 46:1445–65
Lewis FD (1983) Fertility and Savings in the United States: 1830–1900. Journal of Political Economy 91:825–839
Liapounoff AM (1947a) Probléme Général de la Stabilité du Mouvement. Annales de la Faculté des Sciences de Toulouse 2. Series, **9** (1907); *Annals of Mathe-matics Studies, no. 17,* Princeton University Press, New Jersey.
Liapounoff AM (1947b) Stability of Motion. Academic Press, New Jersey
Linder SB (1961) An Essay on Trade and Transformation. John Wiley and Sons, New York
Lindert PH (2000) When did Inequality rise in Britain and America ? Journal of Income Distribution 9:11–25
Lindert PH, Williamson JG (1982) Revising England's Social Tables 1688–1812. Explorations in Economic History 19:385–408
Lindert PH, Williamson JG (1983) Reinterpreting Britain's Social Tables 1688–1913. Explorations in Economic History 20:94–109
Lloyd P (2000) Generalizing the Stolper–Samuelson Theorem: A Tale of Two Matrices. Review of International Economics 8:597–613
Lloyd PJ (1969) Elementary Geometric/Arithmetic Series and Early Production Theory. J Political Economy 77:21–34
Lloyd PJ (2001) The Origins of the von Thünen–Mill–Pareto–Wicksell–Cobb–Douglas Function. History of Political Economy 33:1–17
Lloyd PJ (2012) The Discovery of the Isoquant. History of Political Eco-nomy 44:619–641
Lögstrup B (1984) The Landowner as Public Administrator : The Danish Model. Scandinavian Journal of History 9:283–312
Lögstrup B (2015) Bondens frisättelse – De danske Landboreformer 1750–1810. Gads Forlag, Copenhagen
Long NV, Wong KY (1997) Endogenous Growth and International Trade: A Survey
Lorenz HW (1989) Business Cycle Theory. Springer
Lucas RE (1988) On the Mechanics of Economic Development. Journal of Monetary Economics 22:3–42, Reprinted in Becker (1991)

Lucas RE (1993) Making a Miracle. Econometrica 61:251–272

Lucas Jr RE (1998) On the Mechanics of Economic Development. Journal of Monetary Economics 22:3–42

Lucas Jr RE (2002) Lectures on Economic Growth. Harvard University Press, Cambridge, Mass

Lundberg E (1938) Studies in the Theory of Economic Expansion. P.S. King and Sons, London

Maddison A (1992) A Long–Run Perspective on Saving. Scandinavian Journal of Economics 94:181–196

Mahalanobis PC (1955) The approach of operational research to planning in India. Sankhya: Indian Journal of Statistics 16:3–62

Malkin IG (1959) Theorie der Stabilität einer Bewegung. R. Oldenburg, München

Malliaris AG, Brock WA (1982) Stochastic Methods in Economics and Finance. North–Holland/Elsevier, Amsterdam

Malthus TR (1803, 1958) An Essay on Population I–II, 2nd edn. J.M. Dent & Sons, London

Mandl P (1968) Analytical Treatment of One–Dimensional Markov Processes. Springer–Verlag, Berlin, (Die Grundlehren der mathematischen Wissenschaften in Einzeldarstellungen, Band 151)

Maneschi A, Thweatt W (1987) Barone's (1908) Representation of an Economy's Trade Equilibrium and the Gains from Trade. Journal of International Economics 22:375–382

Mankiw NG, Romer D, Weil DN (1992) A Contribution to the Empirics of Economic Growth. Quarterly Journal of Economics 107:407–437

Markoff AA (1896) Differenzenrechnung. B.G. Teubner, Leipzig

Markusen JR, Melvin JR, Kaempfer WH, Maskus KE (1995) International Trade. McGraw–Hill, New York

Marshall A (1879, 1930, 1974) The Pure Theory of Foreign Trade, The Pure Theory of Domestic Values. Privately printed (1879); LSE, University of London (1930); Augustus M. Kelley Publishers (1974), New Jersey.

Marshall A (1920) Principles of Economics, 8th edn. Macmillan, London

Marshall A (1923) Money, Credit and Commerce. Macmillan

Marshall A (1947) Principles of Economics, 8th edn. MacMillan, London

Mas-Colell A, Whinston MD, Green JR (1995) Microeconomic Theory. Oxford University Press, New York

Matsuyama K (2023) Non-CES Aggregators: A Guided Tour. Annual Review of Economics 15(1):235–265

Maussner A, Klump R (1996) Wachstumstheorie. Springer, Berlin

McCloskey DN (1972) The Enclosure of Open Fields : Preface to a Study of its Impacts on the Efficiency of English Agriculture in the Eighteen Century. The Journal of Economic History 32:15–35

McFadden D (1978) Cost, Revenue, and Profit Functions. Chapter I.1, in: Fuss, M. and D. McFadden, D., (Eds), *Production Economics: A Dual Approach to Theory and Applications*, Vol.1, (Amsterdam: North–Holland,),

McKenzie L (1954) On Equilibrium in Grahamic Model of World Trade and Other Competitive Sytems. Econometrica 22:147–161

Meade JE (1962) A Neo–Classical Theory of Economic Growth, 2nd edn. Allan and Unwin, London

Meckl J (2002) Structural Change and Generalized Balanced Growth. Journal of Economics 77:241–266
Mehra R, Prescott EC (1985) The Equity Premium, a Puzzle. Journal of Monetary Economics 15:145–161
Mehra R, Prescott EC (1988) The Equity Premium, A Solution ? Journal of Monetary Economics 15:145–161
Melitz MJ (2003) The Impact of Trade on Intra–Industry Relations and Aggregate Industry Productivity. Econometrica 71(6):1695–1725
Melvin JR (1969) Mill's Law of International Values. Southern Economic Journal 36:107–116
Merton RC (1971) Optimum Consumption and Portfolio Rules in a Continuous–Time Model. Journal of Econ Theory 3:373–413, Ch.5, Merton (1990)
Merton RC (1975) An Asymptotic Theory of Growth under Uncertainty. Review of Economic Studies 42:375–393, Ch.17 in Merton (1990)
Merton RC (1990) Continuous–Time Finance. Blackwell, Cambridge MA
Merton RC (1992) Continuous–Time Finance. Blackwell, Cambridge MA
Meyer W (1976) The Rybczynski, Stolper–Samuelson, and Factor Price Equalization Theorems under Uncertainty. American Economic Review 66:797–808
Mill JS (1848, 1875, 1909) Principles of Political Economy, 7th edn. Longmans, Green and Co., London
Mill JS (1973) Principles of Political Economy. A.M. Kelley Publishers, New Jersey
Miller KS (1960) An Introduction to the Calculus of Finite Differences and Difference Equations. Henry Holt and Company, New York
Miller KS (1968) Linear Difference Equations. W.A. Benjamin Inc., New York
Minhas BS (1962) The Homohypallagic Production Function, Factor Intensity Reversals, and the Heckscher–Ohlin Theorem. The Journal of Political Economy 70:138–156
Minhas BS (1963) An International Comparison of Factor Costs and Factor Use. North–Holland, Amsterdam
Mirman LJ (1972) On the Existence of Steady State Measures for One Sector Growth Models with Uncertain Technology. International Economic Review 13(2):271–286
Mirman LJ (1973) The Steady State Behavior of a Class of One Sector Growth Models with Uncertain Technology. Journal of Political Economy 6(3):219–242
Mises Rv (1939) Über den Verlauf der Integralkurven einer Differentialgleichung erster Ordnung. Compositio Math 6:203–220
Mitra T, Sorger G (2013) On Ramsey's Conjecture. Journal of Economic Theory 148:1953–1976
Mokyr J (1990) The Lever of Riches: Technological Creativity and Economic Progress. Oxford University Press, New York
Montes L (2008) Newton's real Influence on Adam Smith and its Context. Cambridge Journal of Economics 32:555–576
Morris HC (1976) A perturbative approach to periodic solutions of delay–differential equations. Journal of the Institute of Mathematics and its Applications 18:15–24
Moschini G (1999) Imposing Local Curvature Conditions in Flexible Demand Systems. Journal of Business and Economics 17:487–490
Mulligan C, Sala-i-Martin X (1993) A Note on the Time–Elimination Method For Solving Recursive Dynamic Economic Models. NBER WP (0116)
Mundell RM (1960) The Pure Theory of international Trade. American Economic Review 50:67–110

Murphy GM (1960) Ordinary Differential Equations and Their Solutions. D. Van Nostrand, Princeton, New Jersey

Murphy KM, Shleifer A, Vishny R (1989a) Income Distribution, Market Size, and Industrialization. Quarterly Journal of Economics 104:537–564

Murphy KM, Shleifer A, Vishny RW (1989b) Industrialization and the Big Push. The Journal of Political Economy 97:1003–1026

Murty KN (1982) Theoretical Restrictions on the Parameters of Indirect Addilog Demand Equations – A Comment. Econometrica 50:225–227

Muth JF (1954) A Note on Balanced Growth. Econometrica 22:493–495

Myrdal G (1973) Against the Stream. Critical Essays on Economics. Pantheon Books, N.Y

Nairay A (1984) Asymptotic Behavior and Optimal Propensities of a Consumption–Investment Model with Variable Time Preference. Journal of Economic Dynamics and Control 7:283–313

Negishi T (1989) History of Economic Theory. Elsevier, Amsterdam, North–Holland

Negishi T (2014) Developments of International Trade Theory. Springer Japan, Tokyo, Advances in Japanese Business and Economics 2

Neisser H (1962) On Equilibrium Growth of Capital and Labor. Int Econ Rev 3:136–37

Nellinger L (2014) Thünens umfassendes Raumwirtschaftsmodell, 57–126. Duncker & Humbolt, Berlin, pp 57–126, in *Studien zur Entwicklung der ökonomischen Theorie, XXIX*, Trautwein, Hans M. ed. Schriften des Vereins für Socialpolitik

Nelson RR (1956) A Theory of the Low-Level Equilibrium Trap in Underdeveloped Economies. The American Economic Review 46(5):894–908

Nemytskii VV, Stepanov VV (1989) Qualitative Theory of Differential Equations. Dover Publications, New York

von Neumann J (1945–46) A Model of General Economic Equilibrium. Rev Econ Stud 13:1–9

Neumann Jv, Morgenstern O (1953, 2007) Theory of Games and Economic Behavior, 3rd edn. Princeton University Press, Princeton and Oxford

Newbery D (1972) The Importance of Malleable Capital in Optimal Growth Models. Journal of Economic Theory 5:21–41

Newbery D (2008) The Ramsey Model. The New Palgrave. McMillan, London

Newman P (1962) Some Properties of Concave Funtions. J of Econ Theory 1:291–314

Ngai LR, Pissarides CA (2007) Structural Change in a Multi–Sector Model of Growth. American Economic Review 97:429–443

Nicholson W, Snyder C (2012) Microeconomic Theory, 11th edn. South–Western, Mason, OH, USA

Niehans J (1963) Economic Growth with Two Endogenous Factors. Quarterly Journal of Economics 77:349–371

Niehans J (1990) A History of Economic Theory, Classic Contributions 1720–1980. The Johns Hopkins University Press, Baltimore

Nikaido H (1964) Balanced Growth in Multi–sectoral Income Progagation under Autonomous Expenditure Schemes. Review of Econ Stud 31:25–42

Nonneman W, Vanhoudt P (1996) A further Augmentation of the Solow model and the Empirics of Economic Growth for OECD countries. Quarterly Journal of Economics 111:943–953

Nörlund NE (1910) Bidrag til de Lineære Differensligningers Theori, V. Thanning & Appel, København

Nörlund NE (1929) Leçons sur les Équations Linéaires aux Différences Finies. Gauthier–Villars, Paris

Nörlund NE (1954) Vorlesungen Über Differenzenrechnung. Chelsea Publishing Company, New York, Verlag von Julius Springer, Berlin, 1924

Obstfeld M (1982) Aggregate Spending and the Terms of Trade: Is There a Laursen–Metzler Effect? Quarterly Journal of Economics 97:251–270

Obstfeld M (1989) Fiscal Deficits and Relative Prices in a Growing World Economy. Journal of Monetary Economics 23:461–484

Obstfeld M, Rogoff K (1995) The Intertemporal Approach to the Current Account. Chapt. 34 in Grossman & Rogoff (1995).

Ogaki M (1992) Engel's Law and Cointegration. Journal of Political Economy 100:1027–1046

Ogaki M, Atkeson A (1997) Rate of Time Preference, Intertemporal Elasticity of Substitution, and Level of Wealth. Review of Economics and Statistics 79:564–572

Ogaki M, Qiang Z (2001) Decreasing Relative Risk Aversion and Tests of Risk Sharing. Econometrica 69:515–626

Ohlin B (1924) The Theory of Trade. AB Nordiska Bokhandelen, Stockholm, translated in Flam. H & Flanders, M.J. (1991), (76–214)

Ohlin B (1933) Interregional and International Trade. Harvard University Press, Cambridge, MA

Ohlin B (1933, 1967) Interregional and International Trade. Harvard University Press, Cambridge, MA, *Revised Edition* (1967), Harvard University Press

Ohlin B (1970) The Business Cost Account Approach to International Trade Theory. The Swedish Journal of Economics 72:12–20

Øksendal B (1992) Stochastic Differential Equations – An Introduction with Applications, 3rd edn. Springer–Verlag, Berlin

Øksendal B (1998) Stochastic Differential Equations – An Introduction with Applications, 5th edn. Springer–Verlag, Berlin

Øksendal B (2005) Stochastic Differential Equations, 6th edn. Universitext, Springer–Verlag, Berlin

Olech C (1963) On the Global Stability of an Autonomous System on the Plane. pp 389–400, in *Contributions to Differential Equations*, Lasalle, J.P. and Diaz, J.B. (ed.), **1** (1963), Interscience, John Wiley and Sons, New York.

Olsen E (1962) Danmarks Ökonomiske Historie siden 1750. Studier Nr 3 fra Köbenhavns Universitets Ökonomiske Institut (Copenhagen: G.E.C.Gads Forlag)

Olsen M, Bailey MJ (1981) Positive Time Preference. Journal of Political Economy 89:1–25

Oniki H, Uzawa H (1965) Patterns of Trade and Investment in a Dynamic Model of International Trade. Review of Economic Studies 32:15–38

O'Rourke KH, Williamson JG (2000) Globalization and History. MIT Press, Cambridge, Mass

O'Rourke KH, Williamson JG (2002) Explaining Europe's Overseas Trade Boom, 1500–1800. The Journal of Economic History 62:417–456

Ostroy JM (1984) A reformulation of the marginal productivity theory of distribution. Econometrica 52:599–630

Overton M (1984) Agricultural Productivity in Eighteenth–Century England: Some Further Speculations. The Economic History Review 37:244–251

Overton M (1996a) Agricultural Revolution in England. Cambridge University Press, Cambridge

Overton M (1996b) Re–Establishing the English Agricultural Revolution. The Agricultural History Review 44:1–20

Pagano M (1993) Financial markets and growth. European Economic Review 37:613–22

Pais A (1986) Inward Bound. Of Matter and Forces in the Physical World. Oxford University Press

Pampel T (2009) On the Dynamics of Basic Growth Models: Ratio Stability vs. Convergence and Divergence in State Space. German Economic Review 10:384–400

Panas EE (1985) Almost Homogeneous Functions: A Theoretical and Empirical Analysis with Special Emphasis on Labour Input: The Case of Swedish Ma-nu-fac-tu-ring Industries. Department of Economics, University of Uppsala, Uppsala

Parente SL, Prescott EC (1994) Barriers to Technology Adoption and Development. The Journal of Political Economy 102(2):298–321

Pareto V (1971) Manual of Political Economy. Trans. French Edition (1927) by A.S. Schwier ; New York, A. M. Kelley Publishers.

Parker RAC (1955) Coke of Norfolk and the Agrarian Revolution. The Economic History Review 8:156–166

Paroush J (1964) A Note on the CES Production Function. Econometrica 32(1/2):213–214

Pasinetti L (1962) Rate of Profit and Income Distribution in Relation to the Rate of Economic Growth. Rev Econ Stud 29:267–79, or Sen (1970)

Pasinetti LL (1981) Structural change and Economic Growth. Cambridge University Press

Peart S (1990) The Population Mechanism in W. S. Jevon's Applied Economics. The Manchester School of Economic and Social Studies 58:32–53

Peixoto MM (1962) Structural Stability on Two–Dimensional Manifolds. Topology 1:101–120

Perko L (1993) Differential Equations and Dynamical Systems. Springer–Verlag, New York

Persson KG, Sharp P (2015) An Economic History of Europe, 2nd edn. Cambridge University Press, Cambridge

Petersen A (1944) Thünen's Isolierte Staat. Verlag Paul Parey, Berlin

Petrovski IG (1966) Ordinary Differential Equations. Dover Publications, New York

Phelps ES (1966) Models of Technical Progress and the Golden Rule of Research. Review of Economic Studies 33:133–146

Pignalosa D (2019) On the role of the utility function in the estimation of preference parameters. Metroeconomica pp 1–28

Pigou AC, Marshall A (1925) Memorials of Alfred Marshall. Macmillan

Piketty T (2014) Capital in The Twenty–First Century. The Bellknap Press of Harvard University Press, London

Pitchford JD (1960) Growth and the Elasticity of Factor Substitution. Economic Record 36:491–504

Poincaré H (1928) Memoire sur les courbes définies par une equation differentielle. Journal de Mathematiques 3. serie, 7 (1881), 375–422; **8** (1882), 251–96; Oeuvres, Tome 1, 3–86, Gauthier–Villars, Paris.

Poincaré H (1952) Science and Hypothesis. Dover Publ. N.Y

Pollak RA (1969) Conditional Demand Functions and Consumption Theory. Quarterly Journal of Economics 83:60–78
Pomery J (1984) Uncertainty in Trade Models. In Ronald W. Jones and Peter B. Kenen (eds.), *Handbook in International Economics*, Vol. I, N.Y.: North–Holland/–Elsevier.
Pontryagin LS (1962) Ordinary Differential Equations. Addison–Wesley, Reading, Mass
Pontryagin LS, Boltyanskii VG, Gamkrelidze RV, Mishchenko EF (1962) The Mathematical Theory of Optimal Processes. Pergamon Press, Wiley, New York
Powell AA, Gruen FHG (1968) The Constant Elasticity of Transformation Production Frontier and the Linear Supply System. International Economic Review 9:315–328
Prais JS, Houthakker HS (1971) Analysis of Family Budgets, 2nd edn. Cambridge University Press, London
Pratt JW (1964) Risk Aversion in the Small and in the Large. Econometrica 32:122–136
Prescott EC (1998) Lawrence R. Klein Lecture 1997, Needed: A Theory of Total Factor Productivity. International Economic Review 39:525–551
Prohorov YV, Rozanov YA (1969) Probability Theory. Springer
Pugachev VS, Sinitsyn IN (1987) Stochastic Differential Systems. John Wiley and Sons, New York
Puu T (1971) Some Comments on "Inferior" (Regressive) Inputs. Swed J Economics 73:241–251
Puu T (2003) Attractors, Bifurcations, and Chaos. Springer
Quah DT (1996) Empirics for Economic Growth and Convergence. European Economic Review 40:1353–1375
Rader T (1981) Utility over Time: The Homothetic Case. Journal of Economic Theory 25:219–236
Ramanathan R (1973) Adjustment Time in the Two–Sector Growth Model with Fixed Coefficients. Economic Journal 83:1236–1244
Ramanathan R (1975) The Elasticity of Substitution and the Speed of Convergence in Growth Models. Economic Journal 85:612–613
Ramsey FP (1928) A Mathematical Theory of Saving. Economic Journal 38:543–559
Rasmussen CP (2010a) A. G. Molkte og det holstenske kobbelbrug. Landbohistorisk Tidsskrift (2):9–48
Rasmussen CP (2010b) Innovative Feudalism. The development of dairy farming and 'Koppelwirtschaft' on the Manors in Schleswig–Holstein in seventeenth and eighteenth centuries. The Agriculture History Review 58:172–190
Rebelo S (1991) Long–Run Policy Analysis and Long–Run Growth. Journal of Political Economy 99:500–521
Ricardo D (1817, 1821, 1965) The Principles of Political Economy and Taxation. J.M. Dent and Sons, London
Ricardo D (1965) The Principles of Political Economy and Taxation, 3rd edn. J. M. Dent & Sons, London
Rimmer MT, Powell AA (1996) An Implicitly Additive Demand System. Applied Economics 28:1613–1622
Robinson J (1965) The Economics of Imperfect Competition. Macmillan, London
Rockefellar RT (1970) Convex Analysis. Princeton University Press, New Jersey
Romer D (2001) Advanced Macroeconomics, 2nd edn. McGraw–Hill, Boston
Romer D (2019) Advanced Macroeconomics, 5th edn. McGraw–Hill, N.Y
Romer P (1986a) Cake Eating, Chattering, and Jumps: Existence Results for Variational Problems. Econometrica 54:897–908

Romer PM (1986b) Increasing Returns and Long-Run Growth. Journal of Political Economy 94:1002–1037, Reprinted in Becker (1991)

Romer PM (1989) Capital Accumulation in the Theory of Long-Run Growth. Ch. 2 in Barro, Robert J., ed. (1989).

Romer PM (1990) Endogenous Technological Change. Journal of Political Economy 98:S71–S102

Romer PM (1994) The Origins of Endogenous Growth. Journal of Economic Perspectives 8:3–22

Rosen R (1970) Dynamical System Theory in Biology, Volume 1: Stability Theory and Its Applications. Wiley–Interscience, New York

Rosenberg N (1963a) Capital Goods, Technology, and Economic Growth. Oxford Economic Papers 15:217–27

Rosenberg N (1963b) Technological Change in the Machine Tool Industry, 1840–1910. The J Economic History 23:414–443

Roy R (1942) De l'Utilite, Contribution a la Theorie des Choix. Hermann, Paris

Roy R (1947) La Distribution du Revenue entre les Divers Biens. Econometrica 15:205–225

Rudin W (1973) Functional Analysis. McGraw–Hill

Ruffin RJ (1974a) Comparative Advantage under Uncertainty. Journal of International Economics 4:261–73

Ruffin RJ (1974b) International Trade under Uncertainty. Journal of International Economics 4:243–59

Ruffin RJ (2002) David Ricardo's Discovery of Comparative Advantage. History of Political Economy 34:727–748

Ryan DL, Wales TJ (1998) A Simple Method for Imposing Local Curvature in Some Flexible Demand Systems. Journal of Business and Economics 16:331–338

Rybczynski TM (1955) Factor Endowments and Relative Commodity Prices. Economica 22:336–341

Saint-Paul G (1992a) Fiscal Policy in an Endogenous Growth Model. Quarterly Journal of Economies 107:1243–1259

Saint-Paul G (1992b) Technological Choice, Financial Markets and Economic development. European Economic Review 36:763–81

Sala-i-Martin XX (1996) Regional Cohesion: Evidence and Theories of Regional Growth and Convergence. European Economic Review 40:1325–1352

Salle L (1961) J. and Lefschetz, S. Stability by Lyapunov's Direct Method, Academic Press, New York

Samuelson PA (1937) A Note on Measurement of Utility. Review of Economic Studies 4:135–161, *The Collected Scientific Papers*, Vol. 1, p.212–216.

Samuelson PA (1942) Constancy of the Marginal Utility of Income. Chicago University Press. The Collected Scientific Papers 1:37–53

Samuelson PA (1947–1948) Some Implications of Linearity. Review of Economic Studies 15:88–90

Samuelson PA (1947, 1983) Foundations of Economic Analysis, Enlarged edn. Harvard University Press, Cambridge, Mass

Samuelson PA (1948, 1949) International Trade and The Equalisation of Factor Price. Economic Journal 58:163–184, International Factor Price Equalisation Once Again. *Economic Journal*, 59, 181–197

Samuelson PA (1949) International Factor Price Equalisation Once Again. Economic Journal 59:181–197

Samuelson PA (1950) The Problem of Integrability in Utility Theory. Economica 17:355–385
Samuelson PA (1953) Prices of Factors and Goods in General Equilibrium. Review of Economic Studies 21:1–20
Samuelson PA (1953–1954) Prices of Factors and Goods in General Equilibrium. Review of Economic Studies 21:1–20
Samuelson PA (1954) The Transfer Problem and Transportation Cost. Economic Journal 64:264–289
Samuelson PA (1965) Using Full Duality to Show that Simultaneously Additive Direct and Indirect Utilities implies Unitary Price Elasticity of Demand. Econometrica 33:781–796
Samuelson PA (1966a) The Collected Scientific Papers of Paul A. Samuelson. MIT Press, Mass
Samuelson PA (1966b) The Fundamental Singularity Theorem for Non–Joint Production. International Economic Review 7:34–41
Samuelson PA (1968) Two Generalizations of the Elasticity of Substitution. In: Wolfe J (ed) Value, Capital and Growth, Edinburgh University Press, Edinburgh, pp 467–81
Samuelson PA (1969a) Corrected Formulation of Direct and Indirect Additivity. Econometrica 37:355–359
Samuelson PA (1969b) Lifetime Portfolio Selection by Dynamic Stochastic Programming. Review of Economics and Statistics 51:239–246
Samuelson PA (1972a) Maximum Principles in Analytical Economics. American Economic Review 62:249–262
Samuelson PA (1972b) The General Saddlepoint Property of Optimal Control–Motions. Journal of Economic Theory 50:102–120
Samuelson PA (1974) Complementarity: An Essay on The 40th Anniversary of The Hicks–Allen Revolution in Demand Theory. Journal of Economic Literature 12:1255–1289
Samuelson PA (1978) The Canonical Classical Model of Political Economy. Journal of Economic Literature 16:1415–1434
Samuelson PA (1981) Bertil Ohlin – (1899)–(1979). Journal of International Economics 62:147–163
Samuelson PA (1983a) Foundations of Economic Analysis, enlarged edn. Harvard University Press, Cambridge
Samuelson PA (1983b) Thünen at Two Hundred. Journal of Economic Lite–rature 21:1468–1488
Samuelson PA (1986) Yes to Robert Dorfman´s Vindication of Thünen's Natural–Wage Derivation. Journal of Economic Literature 24:1777–1785
Sanchez DA (1968) Ordinary Differential Equations and Stability Theory: An Introduction. Dover Publications, New York
Sandelin B (1976) On the Origin of the Cobb–Douglas Production Function. Economy and History 19:117–23
Sandmo A (1969) Capital Risk, Consumption, and Portfolio Choice. Econometrica 37:586–99
Sandmo A (1970) The Effect of Uncertainty on Saving Decisions. Review of Economic Studies 37:353–60
Sansone G, Conti R (1964) Non–Linear Differential Equation. Pergamon Press, London

Sato R (1977) Homothetic and Non-Homothetic CES Production Functions. American Econ Rev 67:559–569

Scarf HE (1967) The Approximation of Fixed Points of a Continnuous Mapping. SIAM Jour Appl Math 15:1328–43

Scarf HE, Hansen T (1973) The Computation of Economic Equilibria. Yale University Press

Scarth WM, Warne RD (1973) The Elasticity of Substitution and the Shape of the Transformation Curve. Economica 40:299–304

Scenk-Hoppe KR (2002) Is there a Golden Rule for the Stochastic Solow Growth Model? Macroeconomic Dynamics 6:457–475

Schmidt TD, Jensen PS, Naz A (2018) Agricultural productivity and economic development: the contribution of clower to structural transformation in Denmark. Journal of Economic Growth 23:387–426

Schneider E (1934a) Johann Heinrich von Thünen. Econometrica 2:1–12

Schneider E (1934b) Theorie der Produktion. Springer–Verlag, Wien

Schneider E (1959) J. H. von Thünen und die Wirtschaftstheorie der Gegenwart. Duncker & Humbolt, Berlin, pp 14–28, in *Schriften des Vereins für Socialpolitik*, Hoffmann, W.G. ed., Neue Folge, 14

Schneider E (1964) Einführung in die Wirtschaftstheorie, II. Teil, 9th edn. J.C.B. Mohr/Paul Siebeck, Tübingen

Schneider E (1965) Einführung in die Wirtschaftstheorie, IV. Teil, 2nd edn. J.C.B. Mohr/Paul Siebeck, Tübingen

Schumpeter JA (1949) Vilfredo Pareto (1848–1923). The Quarterly Journal of Economics 63(2):147–173

Schumpeter JA (1954) History of Economic Analysis. Oxford University Press, New York

Schwarze R (1995) Johann Heinrich von Thünens Jugendschrift "Beschreibung der Landwirtschaft in dem Dorfe Grossen–Flotbeck (1803). Duncker & Humbolt, Berlin, in *Studien zur Entwicklung der ökonomischen Theorie, XIV*, Rieter, H., ed. Schriften des Vereins für Socialpolitik

Schwarze R (2002) Klopstock und Voght im Leben des Lucas Andreas Staudinger. Tellower Thünen Schriften 3, (Mecklenburg: Thünen–Museum–Tellow)

Selby SM (1973) Standard Mathematical Tables, 21st edn. The Chemical Rubber Co, Cleveland, Ohio

Sen A (1970) Growth Economics, Selected Readings. Penguin Books, London

Shane F, Loewenstein G, O'Donoghue T (2002) Time Discounting and Time Preference: A Critical Review. Journal of Economic Literature 40:351–401

Shepard RW (1967) The Notion of a Production Function. Unternehmensforschung 11:209–232

Shepard RW (1970) Theory of Cost and Production Functions. Princeton University Press, New Jersey

Shepard RW, Färe R (1974) The Law of Diminishing Returns. Zeitschrift für Nationalökonomi 34:69–90

Shimomura K, Wong KY (1998) The Law of Comparative Advantage without Social Utility Functions. Review of International Economics 6:401–406

Shinkai Y (1960) On the Equilibrium Growth of Capital and Labor. International Economic Review 1:107–111

Shinkai Y (1962) Balanced Growth and a Constant Degree of Employment of Labor: Reply to Professor Neisser. Int Econ Rev 3:138–44

Shoven JB, Whalley J (1984) Applied General–Equilibrium Models of Taxation and International Trade: An Introduction and Survey. Journal of Economic Literature 22:1007–1051
Shoven JB, Whalley J (1992) Applying General Equilibrium. Cambridge University Press, Cambridge, UK
Shub M (1987) Global Stability of Dynamical Systems. Springer–Verlag, New York
Silberberg E (1990) The Structure of Economics, 2nd edn. McGraw–Hill, New York
Silberberg E, Suen W (2001) The Structure of Economics, A Mathematical Analysis, 3rd edn. McGraw–Hill, Singapore
Simmons GF (1972) Differential Equations – with applications and historical notes. McGraw–Hill, New York
Simon JL (1990) Great and Almost–Great Magnitudes in Economics. Journal of Economic Perspectives 4:149–156
Skriver JB (2008) MOESGAARD – Historien om en Herregaard. Moegaard Forlag, Höjbjerg
Slutsky EE (1915) Sulla teoria del bilancio del consumatore. Giornale degli Economisti 51:1–26, translation: "on the theory of the budget of the consumer", In: *AEA series, readings in price theory*, 1953, George Allen and Unwin, London, pp 27–56
Smetters K (2003) The (interesting) Dynamic Properties of the Neoclassical Growth Model with CES Production. Review of Economic Dynamics 6:697–707
Smirnov VI (1964) A Course of Higher Mathematics, vol II, IV. Pergamon Press, New York
Smith A (1755, 1795) The Early Writings of Adam Smith,. In: Ralph Lindgren J (ed) The Adam Smith Library, Reprints of Economic Classics, Augustus M. Kelley Publ, New York
Smith A (1776, 1961) The Wealth of Nations I–II. Methuen University Paperbacks, London
Smith A (1790, 1961) An Inquiry Into The Nature and Causes of The Wealth of Nations, vol 1–2, 5th edn. Methuen, London, (ed. E. Cannan)
Smith A (1980) The History of Astronomy. In W.P.D.Wightman and J. C. Bryce, eds. Essays on Philosophical Subjects, pp.33–105, Clarendon Press, Oxford.
Smith A (1999a) The Wealth of Nations, Books I-III. Penguin Classics, London, Skinner A (ed.)
Smith A (1999b) The Wealth of Nations, Books IV-V. Penguin Classics, London, Skinner A (ed.)
Smith MAM (1976) Trade, Growth and Consumption in Alternative Models of Capital Accumulation. Journal of International Economic 6:371–384
Smith MAM (1977) Capital Accumulation in the Open Two–Sector Economy. Economic Journal 87:273–282, Reprinted in Bhagwati (1981, chapter 25)
Smith MAM (1984) Capital Theory and Trade Theory, vol 6. Chapter 6 in Jones (1984)
Smout TC (1987) Landowners in Scotland, Ireland and Denmark in the age of improvement. Scandinavian Journal of History 12:79–97
Södersten B (1964) A Study of Economic Growth and International Trade. Almqvist and Wiksell, Stockholm
Södersten B, Reed G (1994) International Economics, 3rd edn. Macmillan Press, London
Solow RM (2000a) Growth Theory, 2nd edn. Oxford
Solow RM (1956) A Contribution to the Theory of Economic Growth. Quarterly Journal of Economics 70:65–94, Reprinted in Stiglitz (1969), and in Becker (1991)

Solow RM (1961) Note on Uzawa's Two–Sector Model of Economic Growth. Rev Econ Stud 29:48–50, or Stiglitz (1969)

Solow RM (1985) Economic History and Economics. American Economic Review 75:328–331

Solow RM (1994) Perspectives on Growth Theory. Journal of Economic Perspectives 8:45–54

Solow RM (1999) Neoclassical Growth Theory. Chapter 9 in Taylor (1999), *Handbook of Macroeconomics,* 1, North–Holland: Elsevier, Amsterdam.

Solow RM (2000b) Growth Theory: An Exposition, 2nd edn. Oxford University Press, Oxford

Solow RM (2005) Reflections on Growth Theory. pp 3–10, Introduction, in: Aghion and Durlauf, (Eds).

Solow RM, Samuelson PA (1953) Balanced Growth under Constant Returns to Scale. Econometrica 21:412–424

Somermeyer WH (1974) Further analysis of cross–country comparison of consumer expenditure patterns–comment. European Economic Review 5:303–306

Somermeyer WH, Langhout A (1972) Shapes of Engel Curves and Demand Curves: Implications of the Expenditure Allocation Model, Applied to Dutch Data. European Economic Review 3:351–386

Soong TT (1973) Random Differential Equations in Science and Engineering. Academic Press, New York

Sorger G (1989) On the Optimality and Stability of Competitive Paths in Continuous Time Growth Models. Journal of Economic Theory 48:526–547

Sorger G (2002) On the Long–Run Distribution of Capital in the Ramsey Model. Journal of Economic Theory 105:226–243

Srinivasan TN (1964) Optimal Savings in a Two–Sector Model of Growth. Econometrica 32:358–373

Stamer H (1998) Wohlstandspolitik. Verlag Walter G. Mühlau, Kiel

Steger TM (2000) Economic Growth with Subsistence Consumption. Journal of Development Economics 62:343–361

Stigler GJ (1954) The Early History of Empirical Studies of Consumer Behaviour. Journal of Political Economy 69:95–113

Stiglitz JE (1969a) Allocation of Heterogeneous Capital Goods in a Two–Sector Economy. International Economic Review 10:379–390

Stiglitz JE (1969b) Behavior Towards Risk with Many Commodities. Econometrica 37:660–667

Stiglitz JE (1970) Factor Price Equalization in a Dynamic Economy. Journal of Political Economy 78:456–488

Stiglitz JE, Uzawa H (1969) Readings in the Modern Theory of Economic Growth. M.I.T. Press, Cambridge, Mass

Stigum BP (1972) Balanced Growth under Uncertainty. Journal of Economic Theory 5:42–68

Stolper WF, Samuelson PA (1941) Protection and Real Wages. Review of Economic Studies 9:58–73

Streissler EW (1995) Die Grenzproduktivitätstheorie der deutschen Protoklassik unter besonderer Berücksichtigung von J. H. v. Thünen. In: Rieter H (ed) Schriften des Vereins für Socialpolitik, Duncker & Humbolt, Berlin

Strulik H (2005) The Role of Human Capital and Population Growth in R/D–based Models of Economic Growth. Review of International Economics 13:129–145

Strulik H (2010) A Note On Economic Growth With Subsistence Consumption. Macroeconomic Dynamics 14:763–771

SU Nr 34 (1977) Økonomiske Forhold i Lønmodtagerhusstande: Forbrugsundersøgelsen 1971. Danmarks Statistik, København

Suits DB (1954) Dynamic Growth under Diminishing Returns to Scale. Econometrica 22:496–503

Summers R, Heston A (1991) The Penn World Table (Mark 5): An Expanded Set of International Comparisons, 1950–1988. Quarterly Journal of Economics 106:327–368

van Suntum U (1988) Vindicating Thünen's Tombstone Formula $\sqrt{ap}$. Jahrb f Nationalöku Stat 204:393–405

Swan TW (1956) Economic Growth and Capital Accumulation. Economic Record 32:334–361, Reprinted in Stiglitz (1969)

Sydsæter K (1981) Matematisk Analyse,I–II. SUB, Oslo

Takayama A (1963) On a Two–Sector Model of Economic Growth: A Comparative Static Analysis. Rev Econ Stud 30:95–104

Takayama A (1972) International Trade. Holt, Rinehart, and Winston, New York

Takayama A (1985) Mathematical Economics, 2nd edn. Cambridge University Press, Cambridge

Taylor JB, Woodford M (1999) Handbook of Macroeconomics. Elsevier, Amsterdam, 1, North–Holland

Thom R (1989) Structural Stability and Morphogenesis. An Outline of a General Theory of Models. Addison–Wesley, New York, W.A. Benjamin Inc., Reading, Mass., 1975

von Thünen JH (1990) Der Isolierte Staat. Verlag Gustav Fischer, 1. Auflage, (Jena 1910); 3. Auflage, (Jena 1930); 4. Auflage, (Stuttgart 1966); 5. Auflage, Verlag Scientia, (Aalen 1990).

von Thünen JH (1826) Der isolierte Staat in Beziehung auf Landwirtschaft und Nationalökonomie. Hamburg, Band 1 (Teil 1), 2.ed. (Rostock 1842); Band 2 (Teil 2.I), (Rostock 1850); Band 3 (Teil 2.II, Teil 3), (Rostock 1863)

von Thünen JH (1850) Der isolierte Staat in Beziehung auf Landwirtschaft und Nationalökonomie, 2nd edn. Hamburg, Band 1: Rostock, 1842, Band 2: Rostock, 1850. *Der isolierte Staat* (Band 1–2): Sammlung sozialwissenschaftlicher Meister, Waentig, H., ed. Verlag Gustav Fischer, Jena, 1930. Trans. Wartenberg, C. M.: *Von Thünen's Isolated State*, Oxford, 1966. Dempsey, B. W.: *The Frontier Wage, Jesuit Studies*, Chicago, 1960.

von Thünen JH (1875) Der isolierte Staat in Beziehung auf Landwirtschaft und Nationalökonomie, 3rd edn. Band 1–3, (Gothic type)

Timmer PC (1969) The Turnip, The New Husbandry, and The English Agricultural Revolution. Quarterly Journal of Economics 83:375–395

Tinbergen J (1960) Optimum Savings and Utility Maximization Over Time. Econometrica 28:481–489

Tobin J (1980) Asset Accumulation and Economic Activity. Basil Blackwell Publishers, Oxford, Yrjö Jahnsson Lectures

Tobin J, Houthakker HS (1950–51) The Effects of Rationing on Demand Elasticities. Review of Economic Studies 18:140–153

Turgot ARJ (1767) Observations sur le Mémoire de M. de Saint–Péravy. In: Daire E (ed) Oeuvres de Turgot, Paris, pp 418–433, translated as "Observations on a Paper by Saint-Péravy on the Subject of Indirect Taxation," in P. D. Groenewegen, *The Economics of A. R. J. Turgot*, The Hague, 1977, 109–122

Turgot ARJ (1769) Réflexions sur la formation et la distribution des richess. In: Ephémérides du citoyen, Paris, pp 1–71, Nov. 1769–Jan. 1770. reprinted in E. Daire (ed.), *Oeuvres de Turgot*, Paris, 1844, 1–71, translated as "Reflections on the Formation and the Distribution of Riches," New York, 1922.

Turgot ARJ (1769, 1977) Reflections on the Formation and the Distribution of Riches. The Hague, in The Economics of A.R.J. Turgot, Groenwegen, P.D. ed.

Turner M (1982) Agricultural Productivity in England in the Eighteenth Century: Evidence from Crop Yields. The Economic History Review 35:489–510

Turner ME, Beckett JV, Afton B (1997a) Agricultural Rent in England, 1690–1914. Cambridge University Press, Cambridge

Turner ME, Beckett JV, Afton B (1997b) Taking Stock : Farmers, Farm Records, and the Agricultural Output in England, 1700–1850. The Agriculture History Review 44:21–38

Turner ME, Beckett JV, Afton B (2001) Farm Production in England, 1700–1914. Oxford University Press, Oxford

Turnovsky SJ (1974) Technological and Price Uncertainty in a Ricardian Model of International Trade. Review of Economic Studies 41:201–17

Turnovsky SJ (2002) Intertemporal and Intratemporal Substitution, and the Speed of Convergence in the Neoclassical Growth Model. Journal of Economic Dynamics and Control 26:1765–1785

Turnovsky SJ, Garcia-Penalosa C (2008) Distributional Dynamics in a Neoclassical Growth Model: The Role of Elastic Labor Supply. Journal of Economic Dynamics and Control 32:1399–1431

Uekawa Y (1971) Generalization of the Stolper–Samuelson theorem. Econometrica 39:197–218

Uekawa Y, Kemp MC, Wegge LLF (1972) P– and PN–Matrices, Minkowski– and Metzler Matrices, and Generalization of the Stolper–Samuelson and Samuelson–Rybczynski Theorems. Journal of International Economics 3:53–76

Usher AP (1954) A History of Mechanical Inventions, Revised edn. Dover Pub, New York

Uzawa H (1959) Prices of the Factors of Production in International Trade. Econometrica 27:448–68

Uzawa H (1961) On a Two–Sector Model of Economic Growth: I. Review of Economic Studies 29:40–47

Uzawa H (1961–63) On a Two–Sector Model of Economic Growth: I–II. Rev Econ Stud 29:40–47, Rev. Econ. Stud. 30, 105–18

Uzawa H (1962) Production Functions with Constant Elasticities of Substitution. Review of Economic Studies 29:291–299

Uzawa H (1963) On a Two–Sector Model of Economic Growth: II. Review of Economic Studies 30:105–18, Also in: Stiglitz and Uzawa (1969)

Uzawa H (1964) Optimal Growth in a Two–Sector Model of Capital Accumulation. Review of Economic Studies 31:1–25

Uzawa H (1968) Time Preference, the Consumption Function, and Optimum Asset Holdings. pp 485–504, in Wolfe, J. N.: *Papers in Honour of Sir John Hicks: Value, Capital, and Growth*, University Press, Edinburgh.

Uzawa H (1969) Time Preference and the Penrose Effect in a Two–Class Model of Economic Growth. Journal of Political Economy 77:628–652

Uzawa H (1973) Towards a Keynesian Model of Monetary Growth. pp 53–74, in Mirrlees, J. A. & Stern, N. H.: *Models of Economic Growth*, Macmillan, London.
Van Bavel BJP, Thoen E (1999) Land Productivity and Agro–systems in the North Sea Area. Brepols Publishers
Van Zanden JL (1999) The development of agricultural productivity in Europe 1500–1800. 357–375 in Van Bavel et al. (1999)
Van Zanden JL (2002) Taking the measure of the early modern economy: Historical national accounts for Holland in 1510/14. European Review of Economic History 6:131–163
Varian HR (1988) Estimating Risk Aversion from Arrow–Debreu Portfolio Choice. Econometrica 56:973–979
Varian HR (1992) Microeconomic Analysis, 3rd edn. W.W. Norton & Company, New York
Vissing-Jorgensen A (2002) Limited Asset Market Participation and the Elasticity of Intertemporal Substitution. Journal of Political Economy 110:825–853
Šiljak D (1969) Nonlinear Systems. The Parameter Analysis and Design. John Wiley & Sons, New York
Walras L (1954) Elements of Pure Economics. George Allen and Unwin, London
Wan HY Jr (1971) Economic Growth. Harcourt Brace Jovanowich, New York
Wang EC (1995) Factor Substitution Approach to Testing the Time Variation in Production: the Case of Taiwan's Manufacturing. Applied Economics 27:107–16
Wegge LLF, Kemp MC (1969) Generalization of the Stolper–Samuelson and Samuelson–Rybczynski Theorems in Terms of Conditional Input–Output Coefficients. International Economic Review 10:414–425
Whitaker JK (1964) A note on the CES Production Function. Rev Econ Stud 31:166–67
Wicksell K (1934–35) Lectures on Political Economy I–II. George Routledge and Sons, London, Classen, E., (trans.), and Robbins, L., (ed.)
Wiggins S (1988) Global Bifurcations and Chaos. Springer–Verlag, New York
Woermann E (1959) J. H. von Thünen und die Landwirtschaftliches Betriebslehre der Gegenwart. Duncker & Humbolt, Berlin, pp 28–45, in *Schriften des Vereins für Socialpolitik*, Hoffmann, W.G. ed., Neue Folge, 14
Wöhe G, Döring U, Brösel G (2016) Einführung in die Allgemeine Betriebswirtschaftslehre, 26th edn. Verlag Franz Vahlen, München
Wold H (1952) Demand Analysis. Almquist & Wiksell, Uppsala, or J. Wiley and Sons, N.Y., 1953
Wold H (1959) Ends and Means in Econometric Model Building. pp 355–434, in *Probability and Statistics: The Harold Cramér Volume*, Grenander, U. (ed.), John Wiley and Sons, New York.
Wold H, Jureen L (1953) Demand Analysis. John Wiley & Sons, New York
Wong KY (1995) International Trade in Goods and Factor Mobility. MIT Press, Cambridge, MA
Woodland AD (1982) International Trade and Resource Allocation. Amsterdam, North–Holland
Wrigley EA (1967) A Simple Model of London's Importance in Changing English Society and Economy, 1650–1750. Past & Present 37:44–70
Yaari ME (1964) On the Existence of an Optimal Plan in a Continuous–Time Allocation Process. Econometrica 32:576–590

Yaari ME (1965) Convexity in the Theory of Choice Under Risk. Quarterly Journal of Economics 79:278–290

Yaari ME (1973) A Note on Separability and Quasiconcavity. Econometrica 45:1183–1186

Yang X, Borland J (1991) A Microeconomic Mechanism for Economic Growth. J Political Economy 99:460–82

Yoshihara K (1969) Demand Functions: An Application to the Japanese Expenditure Pattern. Econometrica 37:257–274

Young A (1771) The Farmer's Tour Through the East of England, vol IV. W. Strahan, London

Young A (1771, 1973) The Farmer's Kalendar – or Monthly Directory, vol IV. Robinson & Roberts, London, EP Publishing, 1973

Young A (1792) Travels in France and Italy during the years, 1787, 1788, 1789. W. Richardson, London

Young A (1808, 1971) General Report On Enclosures. B. McMillan, London, A.M. Kelley, New York

Young A (1813, 1969) General View of the Agriculture of the County of Suffolk, vol IV. C. Doble & Brendon, London, David & Charles Reprints, 1969

Young A (1991) Learning by Doing and the Dynamic Effects of International Trade. Quarterly Journal of Economics 106:369–405

Young AA (1928) Increasing Returns and Economic Progress. Economic Journal 38:527–542

Young L (1984) Uncertainty and the Theory of International Trade in Long–Run Equilibrium. Journal of Economic Theory 32:67–92

Yu W, Hertel TW, Preckel PV, Eales JS (2003) Projecting world food demand using alternative demand systems. Economic Modelling 21:99–129

Zeira J (2006) Machines as Engines of Growth. Dynamics, Economic Growth, and International Trade Conference (2006) Paper 011059

Zeuthen F (1937) On the Determinateness of the Utility Function. Review of Economic Studies 4:236–239

Zeuthen F (1955) Economic Theory and Method. Longmans, London

Zhu H, Huang W (2003) The economic growth models with time delays. In Jensen, B. S. and Palokangas, T., (eds), *Stochastic Economic Dynamics*, CUP, 2005.

Ziegler A, Schwarze R (2014) Voght und Thünen – Von Brief zu Brief. Tellower Thünen Schriften 11, (Mecklenburg: Thünen–Museum–Tellow)

Ziegler A, Bartz RP, Krüger H (2013) Johann Heinrich von Thünen – Zitate. Tellower Thünen Schriften 10, (Mecklenburg: Thünen–Museum–Tellow), Laumann–Verlag, Dülmen

# Author Index

Page numbers followed by 'n' refer to notes.





B. S. Jensen, *The Elements and Dynamic Systems of Economic Growth and Trade Models*, https://doi.org/10.1007/978-3-031-52493-6

# Subject Index

Page numbers followed by 'n' refer to notes.





B. S. Jensen, *The Elements and Dynamic Systems of Economic Growth and Trade Models*, https://doi.org/10.1007/978-3-031-52493-6

**B**



**C**

## D

## G

**M**



**N**

## Q



## R

S

## T

## Z

**Batch number: 09012984**

Printed by Printforce, the Netherlands